THIRD CANADIAN EDITION

Abnormal Psychology:

AN INTEGRATIVE APPROACH

David H. Barlow
Boston University

V. Mark Durand
University of South Florida–St. Petersburg

Sherry H. Stewart
Dalhousie University

NELSON / E D U C A T I O N

NELSON / EDUCATION

Abnormal Psychology, Third Canadian Edition

by David H. Barlow, V. Mark Durand, and Sherry H. Stewart

Vice President, Editorial Higher Education:
Anne Williams

Senior Acquisitions Editor:
Lenore Taylor-Atkins

Marketing Manager:
Ann Byford

Senior Developmental Editor:
Sandy Matos

Photo Researcher/Permissions Coordinator:
Kristiina Paul

Senior Content Production Manager:
Imoinda Romain

Production Service:
Integra Software Services Pvt. Ltd.

Copy Editor:
Joan Bondar

Proofreader:
Integra Software Services Pvt. Ltd.

Indexer:
Integra Software Services Pvt. Ltd.

Manufacturing Manager:
Joanne McNeil

Design Director:
Ken Phipps

Managing Designer:
Franca Amore

Interior Design:
Ellen Pettengell

Interior Design Modifications:
Dianna Little

Cover Design:
Martyn Schmoll

Cover Image:
Yulia.M/Getty Images

Compositor:
Integra Software Services Pvt. Ltd.

Printer:
R.R. Donnelley

Library and Archives Canada Cataloguing in Publication

Barlow, David H.

Abnormal psychology : an integrative approach / David H. Barlow, V. Mark Durand, Sherry H. Stewart. —3rd Canadian ed.

Includes bibliographical references and index
ISBN-13: 978-0-17-650219-5

1. Psychology, Pathological—Textbooks. I. Durand, Vincent Mark II. Stewart, Sherry H. (Sherry Heather), 1965- III. Title.

RC454.B36 2011   616.89
C2011-905709-3

ISBN-13: 978-0-17-650219-5
ISBN-10: 0-17-650219-X

About the Authors

David H. Barlow

David H. Barlow is an internationally recognized pioneer and leader in clinical psychology. A professor of psychology and psychiatry at Boston University, Dr. Barlow is Founder and Director Emeritus of the Center for Anxiety and Related Disorders, one of the largest research clinics of its kind in the world, and from 1996 to 2004 directed the clinical psychology programs. From 1979 to 1996, he was distinguished professor at the University at Albany–State University of New York. From 1975 to 1979 he was professor of psychiatry and psychology at Brown University, where he also founded the clinical psychology internship program. From 1969 to 1975 he was professor of psychiatry at the University of Mississippi, where he founded the Medical School psychology residency program. Dr. Barlow received his B.A. from the University of Notre Dame, his M.A. from Boston College, and his Ph.D. from the University of Vermont.

A fellow of every major psychological association, Dr. Barlow has received many awards in honour of his excellence in scholarship, including the National Institute of Mental Health Merit Award for long-term contributions to the clinical research effort; the 2000 Distinguished Scientist Award for applications of psychology from the American Psychological Association; the Distinguished Scientist Award from the Society of Clinical Psychology of the American Psychological Association; and a certificate of appreciation from the APA section on the clinical psychology of women for "outstanding commitment to the advancement of women in psychology." In 2004, he received the C. Charles Burlingame Award from the Institute of Living and was awarded an Honorary Doctorate of Humane Letters degree from the Massachusetts School of Professional Psychology. He also received career contribution awards from the Massachusetts, Connecticut, and California Psychological Associations, and, in 2000, was named Honorary Visiting Professor at the Chinese People's Liberation Army General Hospital and Postgraduate Medical School. In addition, the annual Grand Rounds in Clinical Psychology at Brown University was named in his honour, and he was awarded the first graduate alumni scholar award at the University of Vermont. During the 1997–1998 academic year, he was Fritz Redlich Fellow at the Center for Advanced Study in the Behavioral Sciences in Menlo Park, California.

Dr. Barlow has edited three journals, has served on the editorial boards of 19 different journals, and is currently Editor in Chief of the "Treatments that Work" series for Oxford University Press.

He has published more than 500 scholarly articles and written over 65 books and clinical manuals, including *Anxiety and Its Disorders*, 2nd edition, Guilford Press; *Clinical Handbook of Psychological Disorders: A Step-by-Step Treatment Manual*, 4th edition, Guilford Press; *Single-Case Experimental Designs: Strategies for Studying Behavior Change*, 3rd edition, Allyn & Bacon (with Matthew Nock and Michael Hersen); *The Scientist-Practitioner: Research and Accountability in the Age of Managed Care*, 2nd edition, Allyn & Bacon (with Steve Hayes and Rosemery Nelson); and *Mastery of Your Anxiety and Panic*, Oxford University Press (with Michelle Craske). The book and manuals have been translated in over 20 languages, including Arabic, Chinese, and Russian.

Dr. Barlow was one of three psychologists on the task force that was responsible for reviewing the work of more than 1,000 mental health professionals who participated in the creation of *DSM-IV*. He also chaired the APA Task Force on Psychological Intervention Guidelines. His current research program focuses on the nature and treatment of anxiety and related emotional disorders.

At leisure he plays golf, skis, and retreats to his home in Nantucket, where he loves to write, walk on the beach, and visit with his island friends.

V. Mark Durand

V. Mark Durand is known worldwide as an authority in the area of autism spectrum disorders. He is a professor of psychology at the University of South Florida–St. Petersburg, where he was the founding Dean of Arts and Sciences and Vice Chancellor for Academic Affairs. Dr. Durand is a fellow of the American Psychological Association. He has received over $4 million in continuous federal funding since the beginning of his career to study the nature, assessment, and treatment of behaviour problems in children with disabilities. Before moving to Florida, he served in a variety of leadership positions at the University at Albany, including associate director for clinical training for the doctoral psychology program from 1987 to 1990, chair of the psychology department from 1995 to 1998, and interim dean of Arts and Sciences from 2001 to 2002. There he established the Center for Autism and Related Disabilities at the University at Albany, SUNY. He received his B.A., M.A., and Ph.D.—all in psychology—at the State University of New York–Stony Brook.

Dr. Durand was awarded the University Award for Excellence in Teaching at SUNY–Albany in 1991 and in 1989 was named Distinguished Reviewer of the Year for the *Journal of the Association for Persons with Severe Handicaps*. Dr. Durand is currently a member of the Professional Advisory Board for the Autism Society of America and is on the board of directors of the International Association of Positive Behavioral Support. He serves on a number of editorial boards, reviews for dozens of journals, and has over 100 publications of functional communication, educational programming, and behaviour therapy. His books include *Severe Behavior Problems: A Functional Communication Training Approach, Sleep Better! A Guide to Improving Sleep for Children with Special Needs*, and most recently, *When Children Don't Sleep Well: Interventions for Pediatric Sleep Disorders*.

Dr. Durand developed a unique treatment for severe behaviour problems that is currently mandated by several states across the United States and is used worldwide. He has also developed an assessment tool that is used internationally and has been translated into more than 15 languages. In 1993 he was the keynote speaker for the Australian National Conference on Behaviour Modification; he has also lectured throughout Norway. He has been consulted by the departments of education in numerous U.S. states and by the U.S. Departments of Justice and Education. His current research program includes the study of prevention models and treatments for such serious problems as self-injurious behaviour.

In his leisure time he enjoys long-distance marathon running and has just completed his second marathon.

Sherry H. Stewart

Sherry H. Stewart has an international reputation for her work in the areas of addictions, anxiety disorders, and mental health–substance use disorder comorbidity. She is a professor of psychiatry and psychology at Dalhousie University. She served as the coordinator of the Dalhousie doctoral training program in clinical psychology from 2004 to 2006. Dr. Stewart has a cross-appointment as a professor in community health and epidemiology at Dalhousie, and holds research appointments at local teaching hospitals in the Halifax region. She received her B.Sc. (honours) in psychology from Dalhousie University in 1987 and her Ph.D. in clinical psychology from McGill University in 1993. She completed her clinical internship at the Toronto Hospital in 1992–1993. Dr. Stewart has been registered as a clinical psychologist in Nova Scotia since 1995. She ran a part-time private practice in Halifax until 2003, when she left her practice to become a mother.

Dr. Stewart is currently the associate editor of the international journals *Cognitive Behaviour Therapy* and *Current Drug Abuse Reviews* and serves on the editorial boards of the *Canadian Journal of Behavioural Science* and *Cognitive and Behavioral Practice*. She has provided reviews for numerous scientific journals and granting agencies. Dr. Stewart has published over 150 scientific journal articles, 20 book chapters, and four books. She has served as guest editor for several special issues of scholarly journals covering such topics as the comorbidity of alcohol abuse and pathological gambling, side effects of benzodiazepine medications, state-of-the-art cognitive-behavioural treatments for substance use disorders, the role of anxiety sensitivity in pain conditions, the relationship of anxiety sensitivity to substance misuse, and the psychological impact of the events of September 11, 2001.

Her research has been funded by a variety of local, national, and international granting agencies. Currently, Dr. Stewart heads projects funded by agencies such as the Canadian Institutes of Health Research, the Nova Scotia Department of Health Promotion and Protection, the Social Sciences and Humanities Research Council of Canada, the Canadian Tobacco Control Research Initiative, the Nova Scotia Gaming Foundation, and the Ontario Problem Gambling Research Centre. She holds a prestigious Investigator Award from the Canadian Institutes of Health Research for her research on the prevention of alcohol abuse in adolescents. She also holds a Killam Research Professorship from the Dalhousie Faculty of Science for her innovations in addictions research. The quality of her research has also been recognized through numerous other awards, including the Young Investigator Award from the Anxiety Disorders Association of America in 1999, the New Investigator Award from the Association for Advancement of Behavior Therapy Women's Special Interest Group in 1998, the President's New Researcher Award from the Canadian Psychological Association in 1998, and the Killam Prize in Science in 1997. In 2007, Dr. Stewart was elected to the Canadian Academy of Health Sciences, and she was appointed by the prime minister's office to the Board of Directors of the Canadian Centre on Substance Abuse.

In her leisure, Dr. Stewart enjoys international cuisine and travel, and spending time at her family cottage on the Bay of Fundy.

Brief Contents

Contents

3 | Clinical Assessment and Diagnosis 72

4 | Research Methods 104

8 | Eating and Sleep Disorders

9 | Physical Disorders and Health Psychology

10 | Sexual Disorders and Gender Identity Disorder 348

11 | Substance-Related Disorders and Impulse Control Disorders 392

12 | Personality Disorders 438

13 | Schizophrenia and Other Psychotic Disorders 476

14 | Developmental Disorders 512

15 | Cognitive Disorders 546

16 | Mental Health Services: Legal and Ethical Issues 572

Preface

Every once in a while, something dramatic happens in science. For example, evolutionary biologists, who long assumed that the process of evolution was gradual, suddenly had to adjust to evidence that it happens in fits and starts in response to such cataclysmic environmental events as meteor strikes. Similarly, geology was revolutionized by the discovery of plate tectonics.

Until recently, the science of psychopathology has been compartmentalized, with psychopathologists examining the separate effects of psychological, biological, and social influences. This approach is still reflected in popular media accounts that describe, for example, a newly discovered gene, a biological dysfunction, or early childhood experiences as a "cause" of a psychological disorder. This way of thinking still dominates discussions of causality and treatment in most psychology textbooks: "The psychoanalytic views of this disorder are … the biological views are …," and, often in a separate chapter, "psychoanalytic treatment approaches for this disorder are … cognitive-behavioural treatment approaches are … biological treatment approaches are…."

The success of previous editions of this book confirms our belief that this approach is no longer useful. Recent explosive advances in knowledge demonstrate that genetic and neuroscientific research depends on our understanding that psychological and social factors directly affect neurotransmitter function and even genetic expression. Similarly, we cannot study behavioural, cognitive, or emotional processes without appreciating the contribution of biological and social factors to psychological and psychopathological expression. Thus, we have abandoned the traditional compartmentalized approach to psychopathology, which, in any case, usually confused our students. Instead, we use a more accessible approach that accurately reflects the current state of our clinical science.

As colleagues, you are aware that we understand some disorders better than others. But we hope that you will share our excitement in conveying to the student both what we currently know about the causes and treatment of psychopathology and how far we have yet to go in understanding these complex interactions.

Our Approach

This is clearly the first of a new generation of abnormal psychology textbooks that offers an integrative and multidimensional perspective. (We acknowledge such one-dimensional approaches as biological, psychosocial, and supernatural as historic trends.) We include substantial current evidence of the reciprocal influences of biology and behaviour and of psychological and social influences on biology. Our examples hold students' attention; for example, we discuss genetic contributions to trauma exposure, the effects of early social and behavioural experience on later brain function and structure, new information on the relation of social networks to the common cold, and new data on psychosocial treatments for cancer such as mindfulness. We emphasize the fact that in the phenomenon of implicit memory and blind sight, which may have parallels in dissociative experiences, psychological science verifies the existence of the unconscious (although it does not much resemble the seething cauldron of conflicts envisioned by Freud). We acknowledge the often-neglected area of emotion theory for its rich contributions to psychopathology. We weave scientific findings from the study of emotions together with behavioural, biological, cognitive, and social discoveries to create an integrated tapestry of psychopathology.

Life-Span Developmental Influences

No modern view of abnormal psychology can ignore the importance of life-span developmental factors to the manifestation and treatment of psychopathology. Accordingly, although we include a developmental disorders chapter (Chapter 14), we consider the importance of development throughout the text; we discuss childhood anxiety, for example, in the context of the other anxiety disorders. This organization, which is for the most part consistent with *DSM-IV-TR,* helps students appreciate the need to study each disorder from childhood through adulthood. We note findings on developmental considerations in separate sections of each disorder chapter and, as appropriate, discuss how specific developmental factors affect causation and treatment.

Scientist-Practitioner Approach

We go to some length to explain why the scientist-practitioner approach to psychopathology is both practical and ideal. Like most of our colleagues, we view this as something more than simple awareness of how scientific findings apply to psychopathology. We show how every clinician contributes to general scientific knowledge through astute and systematic clinical observations, functional analyses of individual case studies, and systematic observations of series of cases in clinical settings. For example, we explain how information on dissociative phenomena provided by early psychoanalytic theorists remains relevant today. We also describe the formal methods used by scientist-practitioners, showing how abstract research designs are applied to research programs.

Clinical Cases

We have enriched the book with authentic clinical histories to illustrate scientific findings on the causes and treatment of psychopathology. We have all run active clinics for years, so most of the cases are from our own files, with supplements from case reports published by several noted Canadian practitioners. These clinical cases provide a fascinating frame of reference for the findings we describe. Most chapters begin with a case description, and most discussion of the latest theory and research is related to these very human cases.

Disorders in Detail

We cover the major psychological disorders in eleven chapters, focusing on three broad categories: clinical description, causal factors, and treatment and outcomes. We pay considerable attention to case studies and *DSM-IV-TR* criteria, and we include statistical data, such as prevalence and incidence rates, sex ratio, age of onset, and the general course or pattern for the disorder as a whole. In this edition, we have updated coverage of this statistical data and we continue to include information from the latest edition of the *DSM*—the text revision of *DSM-IV*, labelled as *DSM-IV-TR*. Throughout, we explore how biological, psychological, and social dimensions may interact to cause a particular disorder. Finally, by covering treatment and outcomes within the context of specific disorders, we provide a realistic sense of clinical practice.

Treatment

One of the best-received innovations in the earlier U.S. and Canadian editions of this text was our discussion of treatment in the context of the disorders that are its target instead of in a separate chapter, an approach that is supported by the development of specific psychosocial and pharmacological treatment procedures for specific disorders. We have retained this integrative format and improved on it, and we include treatment procedures in the key terms and glossary.

Legal and Ethical Issues

In our closing chapter, we integrate many of the approaches and themes that have been discussed throughout the text. We include case studies of people who have been involved directly with many legal and ethical issues and with the delivery of mental health services in Canada. We also provide a historical context for current perspectives so students will understand the effects of social and cultural influences on legal and ethical issues.

Special Photo Feature

We have included photos of actual clients who were diagnosed with psychological disorders. In every case, we have the individual's permission to use the photo; for cases in which we felt a person might not truly understand our purpose, we have not used the image. By showing these faces, which represent both genders and a variety of races, cultures, and stages of development, we hope to convey the hardship imposed by psychological disorders and help reduce the stigma, anxiety, and isolation that add to the burden of people who struggle with those disorders.

Diversity

Issues of culture and gender are integral to the study of psychopathology. Throughout the text, we describe current thinking about which aspects of the disorders are culturally specific and which are universal, and about the strong and sometimes puzzling effects of gender roles. Clearly, our field will grow in depth and detail as these subjects become standard research topics. For example, why do some disorders overwhelmingly affect females and others appear predominantly in males? And why does this apportionment sometimes change from one culture to another? In answering questions like these, we adhere closely to science, emphasizing that gender and culture are each one dimension among several that constitute psychopathology.

| New to the Third Canadian Edition

This exciting field moves at a rapid pace, and we take particular pride in how our book reflects the most recent developments. Therefore, once again, every chapter has been carefully revised to reflect the latest research studies on psychological disorders. Hundreds of new references appear in this edition, and some of the information they contain stuns the imagination. Nonessential material has been eliminated, some new headings have been added, and *DSM-IV* criteria are included in their entirety as tables in the appropriate disorder chapters.

The chapters on Anxiety Disorders (Chapter 5), Mood Disorders and Suicide (Chapter 7), Eating and Sleep Disorders (Chapter 8), Physical Disorders and Health Psychology (Chapter 9), Substance-Related and Impulse-Control Disorders (Chapter 11), Schizophrenia and Other Psychotic Disorders (Chapter 13), and Developmental Disorders (Chapter 14) have been the most heavily revised to reflect new research, but all chapters have been significantly updated and freshened. Some highlights of the changes include:

- In Chapter 2, An Integrative Approach to Psychopathology, the entire section on genetics has been rewritten to highlight the new emphasis on gene–environment interaction. The emerging field of epigenetics is integrated throughout the chapter. Also included are new studies on the relative contribution of genetic factors and environmental factors to both variability and stability in important human traits, as well as new evidence on the ability of early childhood experiences to override genetic influences in the development of behaviour.

- Chapter 3, Clinical Assessment and Diagnosis, now presents updated research findings on labelling and stigma and their relation to potential changes in the *DSM-5*, as well as examples of more fully developed, conceptually satisfying dimensional approaches to diagnosis, and reasons why these will probably not make an appearance until the *DSM-6*.

- In Chapter 4, Research Methods, a new concept that is now the focus of intense study—endophenotypes—is introduced. Another new section describes clinical trials and defines the differences among clinical trials, randomized clinical trials, and randomized control trials. The section "Studying Behaviour over Time" is completely rewritten, with a new example of prospective longitudinal research on the development of autism, as is the section "The Power of a Program of Research," using all-new examples to illustrate different research strategies and describing how these are used to answer complex questions in abnormal psychology.

- Chapter 5, Anxiety Disorders, now includes the conceptual basis of description of how a future diagnostic system using dimensional approaches for emotional disorders might work, as well as data supporting a possible new category of separation anxiety disorder in adults.

- Chapter 5 also describes consideration of the likely new name for generalized anxiety disorder in *DSM-5*, as well as likely changes to definitions of somatic symptoms in this diagnostic category.

- Descriptions of new major clinical trials for both adults and children with GAD evaluating the effects of psychological treatments and drugs are also presented in Chapter 5.

- Finally, Chapter 5 provides a description of a new disorder under consideration for inclusion in *DSM-5* called "olfactory reference syndrome."

- Chapter 6, Somatoform and Dissociative Disorders, describes a potential new *DSM-5* reorganization where the disorders of hypochondriasis, somatization disorder, and (somatoform) pain disorders are grouped together as varying examples of medically unexplained physical symptoms (MUPS) with a potential label of complex somatic symptom disorder. Chapter 6 also includes an updated review of the latest evidence on the induction of false memories and the role that false memory may play in various presentations of dissociation and psychopathology.

- Chapter 7, Mood Disorders and Suicide, is thoroughly rewritten and reorganized, with approximately 40 percent new material and 149 new references. Existing material has been streamlined and reorganized to facilitate reading and comprehension, resulting in a chapter that is shorter and more succinct than previous editions. Chapter 7 also includes data underscoring the combination of depression with impulse control problems as causal factors in suicide, as well as new data on the ability to detect implicit or out-of-awareness suicidal ideation as a possible powerful risk factor for depression.

- Chapter 8, Eating and Sleep Disorders, includes an update on the status of binge-eating disorder and the reasons why it will almost certainly be included as a disorder in the *DSM-5*, as well as new data on the disappointing follow-up of anti-obesity drugs for binge-eating disorder. Chapter 8 also presents recent results from a transdiagnostic psychological approach to the treatment of eating disorders, illustrating the importance of conceptualizing eating disorders on a dimension or spectrum.

■ Also presented in Chapter 8 is research that suggests that the effects of jet lag on circadian rhythms can be quite serious—at least among older adults.

■ In Chapter 9, Physical Disorders and Health Psychology, updated information is presented on the worldwide epidemic of AIDS, as well as new information on the effectiveness of psychological treatments for AIDS on immune functioning and survival time. Chapter 9 also includes updated information on the role of psychological factors on the progression and treatment of cancer, including new randomized controlled trials demonstrating increases in survival time from psychological treatments, as well as new hypotheses on the causes and maintaining factors of chronic fatigue syndrome.

■ Chapter 10, Sexual and Gender Identity Disorders, includes prevalence, social and psychological determinants, treatments, and likely changes to *DSM-5* for sexual dysfunction. Also presented is new information on the malleability of sexual identities relative to sexual arousal patterns, particularly in women, and new information on the very loose connections between gender nonconforming behaviour in children and sexual orientation and gender identity as an adult.

■ Chapter 11, Substance-Related and Impulse-Control Disorders, includes a discussion of a new longitudinal study that shows that hard drug use in high school predicts poorer job outcomes in young adults (under 29 years of age). The section on medical marijuana use is also completely revised and now describes its application in routine medical care in Canada. Chapter 11 also provides a revised section on fetal alcohol syndrome and updated data on cultural variations in binge drinking.

■ In addition to updated coverage of changes being discussed for *DSM-5*, Chapter 12, Personality Disorders, describes a large and important longitudinal study that finds impaired fear conditioning at age 3 predicts criminal status at age 23, which suggests a gene–environment interaction in the development of antisocial personality disorder. Chapter 12 also discusses a new prospective study, which shows that a history of abuse and neglect does predict later development of borderline personality disorder; updated research on the medical treatment of borderline personality disorder is also provided.

■ Chapter 13, Schizophrenia and Other Psychotic Disorders, now includes coverage of the outcomes from two large drug studies conducted in the United States (called the Clinical Antipsychotic Trials of Intervention Effectiveness or CATIE) and in the United Kingdom (called the Cost Utility of the Latest Antipsychotic Drugs in Schizophrenia Study or CUtLASS). These studies find that newer, second-generation drugs are no more effective or better tolerated than the older drugs.

■ In Chapter 14, Developmental Disorders, a great deal of new information on ADHD is presented, including a new section on ADHD comorbidity; new information on ADHD prevalence globally; significantly expanded coverage of genetics, including the only gene–environment interaction study; updated material on brain structural differences in children with ADHD; and a new discussion of the overlap among ADHD and opposition defiant disorder (ODD), conduct disorder, and bipolar disorder. Also, the section previously titled "Mental Retardation" is completely revised to recognize the use of the more acceptable term *intellectual disability*.

■ Chapter 15, Cognitive Disorders, includes a new section on Spectra and Dimensions, which describes the changes proposed for *DSM-5* to use two types of "Neurocognitive Disorders" (Major and Minor) to indicate their dimensional quality. Chapter 15 also provides updated information on the progress being made in the early identification of Alzheimer's disease (the Alzheimer's Disease Neuroimaging Initiative or ADNI), as well as an added discussion of the controversial nature of vascular dementia as different from dementia of the Alzheimer's type. New data are also presented on sex differences in dementia across developed and developing countries.

New Features

In addition to the changes highlighted earlier, we have added three new features to the third Canadian edition:

■ New *Student Learning Outcomes* at the start of each chapter assist instructors in accurately assessing and mapping questions throughout the chapter. The outcomes are mapped to the core APA goals and are integrated throughout the instructor resources and testing program.

■ In each disorder chapter is a new feature called *Innovative Approaches,* which discusses forward-thinking concepts such as proposed radical changes to simplify the diagnosis of depression, junk food taxes to prevent obesity, drugs that actually complement psychological treatments (but are not effective alone), the use of virtual reality to better assess and diagnose schizophrenia, and the development of designer drugs based on genetic profiles for attention deficit/hyperactivity disorder.

■ At the end of every disorder chapter is another new feature called *On the Spectrum*, which examines cutting-edge developments in the gradual but inexorable movement toward a more dimensional approach to studying psychopathology. Examples include new transdiagnostic assessment schemes and treatment for emotional disorders; previews of disorders in the *DSM-5*, where more dimensional approaches will be adopted; and the adoption of cross-cutting dimensional measures of, for example, anxiety or features of distorted reality for every patient to provide a richer description of psychopathology.

DSM-IV, DSM-IV-TR, *AND* DSM-5

Much has been said about the mix of political and scientific considerations that resulted in *DSM-IV*, and naturally, we have our own opinions (David H. Barlow had the interesting experience of sitting on the task force). Psychologists are often concerned about turf issues in what has become, for better or worse, the nosological standard in our field, and with good reason: in previous *DSM* editions, scientific findings sometimes gave way to personal opinions. However, this time most professional biases were left at the door while the task force almost endlessly debated the data. This process produced enough new information to fill every psychopathology journal for a year with integrative reviews, reanalysis of existing databases, and new data from field trials. From a scholarly point of view, the process was both stimulating and exhausting.

This book contains highlights of various debates that created the nomenclature, as well as recent updates. For example, we summarize and update the data and discussion of premenstrual dysphoric disorder and mixed anxiety depression, two disorders that did not make it into the final criteria. Students can thus see the process of making diagnoses, as well as the mix of data and inferences that are part of it.

In 2000, the American Psychiatric Association published a revision of the text accompanying the *DSM-IV* diagnostic criteria which updated the scientific literature and changed some of the criteria themselves, mostly in minor ways. Several senior clinical investigators from one of our research centres (DHB) participated in the text revision and much of this information has found its way into the current edition of this textbook. For example, the text revision (*DSM-IV-TR*) discusses the intense continuing debate on categorical and dimensional approaches to classification. We discuss this ongoing debate in Chapter 12 as it applies to the optimal classification of personality disorders.

Now DSM-5 is nearing completion with a publication date of May 2013, and one of us (DHB) is an appointed advisor to the DSM-5 task force. The first phase of this massive project involved a joint effort by the (United States) National Institute of Mental Health and the American Psychiatric Association in focusing on delineating needed research efforts to provide crucial information for the DSM-5 process. Research planning workgroups were formed in areas, such as neuroscience, problems/gaps in the current system, cross-cultural issues, and developmental issues with the charge of producing "white papers" outlining the required research agenda. The white papers, along with an article summarizing important recommendations, were published in 2002, with an update in 2008. The planning committee then organized a series of conferences to further these efforts. Eleven conferences were held from 2004 to 2007, chaired by members of the American and international research communities on topics such as externalizing disorders of childhood, personality disorders, and stress-induced and fear circuitry disorders. In 2007, the DSM-5 task force and the major committees covering large classes of disorders (anxiety, mood, schizophrenia, and so on) were appointed. Field trials testing proposed changes to the criteria continued into early 2012. It is already clear that DSM-5 will incorporate a more dimensional approach to classification. Likely, changes along these lines are presented in Chapter 4 and in the disorder chapters. For this reason, as noted above, we now end each disorder chapter with a special feature entitled On the Spectrum, highlighting new scientific findings illustrating and supporting a more dimensional approach to psychopathology.

Prevention

Looking to the future of abnormal psychology as a field, the prospect of helping the greatest number of people who display psychological disorders may lie in our ability to prevent these difficulties. Although this has long been a goal of many, we are now at the beginning of what appears to be a new age in prevention research. Numerous scientists from all over the globe are developing the methodologies and techniques that may finally provide us with the means to interrupt the debilitating toll of emotional distress caused by the disorders chronicled in this book. We therefore highlight these cutting-edge prevention efforts—such as preventing eating disorders, suicide, substance abuse, and health problems like HIV infection—in appropriate chapters as a means of celebrating these important events as well as to encourage the field to continue this important work.

Retained Features

From the Inside

The popularity of the case studies indicates that students appreciate the humanization of data that might otherwise appear dry and lifeless. To emphasize that psychological disorders affect real people who respond in a variety of ways, all 11 chapters on specific disorders conclude with a compassionate review of a first-person memoir by someone who survived or is living with a challenging psychological condition. Many of these are first-person accounts by Canadian writers, and several are new to this edition. These stories were chosen for the value of their deeply personal points of view; they complement the research-based text without pretending to be scientific.

Video Concept Reviews

VMD's *Video Concept Reviews* are video clips that review challenging topics that typically need more than one explanation. A list of these clips appears in every chapter, and the actual videos can be found within Abnormal Psychology CourseMate at www.abnormalpsych3CE.nelson.com. (For more details about CourseMate, see the description below under Learning Aids for the Student.)

Visual Summaries

At the end of each chapter on disorders is a colourful two-page chart that succinctly summarizes the causes, development, symptoms, and treatment of each disorder covered in the chapter. Our integrative approach is instantly evident in these diagrams, which show the interaction of biological, psychological, and social factors in the etiology and treatment of disorders. The visual summaries will help the instructor wrap up discussions, and students will appreciate them as study aids. There is a new visual summary after Chapter 1 outlining the historical timeline of significant events.

Pedagogy

Each chapter contains several Concept Checks that let students verify their comprehension at regular intervals. Answers are at the end of each chapter, along with a more detailed Summary; the Key Terms are listed in alphabetical order. Finally, each chapter concludes with two elements: a link to *Psychology CourseMate*, which includes chapter-specific interactive learning tools including the *Abnormal Psychology Videos,* and V. Mark Durand's *Video Concept Reviews* on challenging topics.

Learning Aids for the Student

Abnormal Psychology Videos

The *Abnormal Psychology Videos*, which include video clips of actual clients discussing their disorders, are available online through *CourseMate* (www.abnormalpsych3ce.nelson.com). Each video clip has specific questions written around it, and students can write their responses on-screen, as well as print them out. By chapter, the videos include:

- **Chapter 2, An Integrative Approach to Psychopathology:** Integrative Approach
- **Chapter 3, Clinical Assessment and Diagnosis:** Arriving at a Diagnosis; Psychological Assessment
- **Chapter 4, Research Methods:** Research Methods
- **Chapter 5, Anxiety Disorders: Panic Disorder:** Steve; Virtual Reality: A New Technique on the Treatment of Anxiety Disorders; Rapid Behavioural Treatment of a Specific Phobia (Snakes); Obsessive-Compulsive Disorder: Chuck
- **Chapter 6, Somatoform and Dissociative Disorders:** Dissociative Identity Disorder: Rachel; Body Dysmorphic Disorder: Doug
- **Chapter 7, Mood Disorders and Suicide:** Depressive Disorder: Barbara; Depressive Disorder: Evelyn; Bipolar Disorder: Mary
- **Chapter 8, Eating and Sleep Disorders:** Anorexia Nervosa: Susan; Twins with Anorexia Nervosa/Bulimia; Weight Control; Sleep Cycle
- **Chapter 9, Physical Disorders and Health Psychology:** Social Support and HIV: Orel; Studying the Effects of Emotion on Physical Health; Breast Cancer Support and Education
- **Chapter 10, Sexual and Gender Identity Disorders:** Erectile Dysfunction: Clark; Changing Over: Jessica
- **Chapter 11, Substance-Related and Impulse-Control Disorders:** Substance Use Disorder: Tim; Nicotine Dependence
- **Chapter 12, Personality Disorders:** Antisocial Personality Disorder: George; Borderline Personality Disorders; Dialectical Behaviour Therapy
- **Chapter 13, Schizophrenia and Other Psychotic Disorders:** Schizophrenia: Etta; Positive versus Negative Symptoms; Common Symptoms of Schizophrenia
- **Chapter 14, Developmental Disorders:** ADHD: Sean; Edward: ADHD in a Gifted Student; Life Skills Training; Bullying Prevention; Autism: The Nature of the Disorder; Autism: Christina; Rebecca: A First-Grader with Autistic Disorder; Lauren: A Kindergartner with Down Syndrome
- **Chapter 15, Cognitive Disorders:** Alzheimer's Disease: Tom; Amnestic Disorder: Mike; Amnestic Patient Interview: Endel Tulving; Neural Networks: Cognition and Dementia
- **Chapter 16, Mental Health Services:** Legal and Ethical Issues: False Memory Research

Abnormal Psychology CourseMate

Abnormal Psychology: An Integrative Approach, Third Canadian Edition includes CourseMate, which helps you make the grade.

Abnormal Psychology CourseMate includes:

- an interactive eBook, with highlighting, note-taking and search capabilities

- interactive learning tools including:
  - quizzes
  - flashcards
  - videos
  - power visuals
  - and more!

Within the chapters, any figure that includes the icon 🌐 indicates that the visual is available on the CourseMate site as an interactive PowerVisual. PowerVisuals test your skills and your memory. Go to www.abnormalpsych3ce.nelson.com to access these resources.

Teaching Aids for the Instructor

Videos

- *Abnormal Psychology: Inside/Out, Volume I: ISBN 978-0-534-20359-7*
- *Abnormal Psychology: Inside/Out, Volume II: ISBN 978-0-534-36480-9*
- *Abnormal Psychology: Inside/Out, Volume III: ISBN 978-0-534-50759-6*
- *Abnormal Psychology: Inside/Out, Volume IV: ISBN 978-0-534-63369-1*

Ancillaries

About NETA

The **Nelson Education Teaching Advantage (NETA)** program delivers research-based instructor resources that promote student engagement and higher-order thinking to enable the success of Canadian students and educators.

Instructors today face many challenges. Resources are limited, time is scarce, and a new kind of student has emerged: one who is juggling school with work, has gaps in his or her basic knowledge, and is immersed in technology in a way that has led to a completely new style of learning. In response, Nelson Education has gathered a group of dedicated instructors to advise us on the creation of richer and more flexible ancillaries that respond to the needs of today's teaching environments.

The members of our editorial advisory board have experience across a variety of disciplines and are recognized for their commitment to teaching. They include:

Norman Althouse, Haskayne School of Business, University of Calgary

Brenda Chant-Smith, Department of Psychology, Trent University

Scott Follows, Manning School of Business Administration, Acadia University

Jon Houseman, Department of Biology, University of Ottawa

Glen Loppnow, Department of Chemistry, University of Alberta

Tanya Noel, Department of Biology, York University

Gary Poole, Director, Centre for Teaching and Academic Growth and School of Population and Public Health, University of British Columbia

Dan Pratt, Department of Educational Studies, University of British Columbia

Mercedes Rowinsky-Geurts, Department of Languages and Literatures, Wilfrid Laurier University

David DiBattista, Department of Psychology, Brock University

Roger Fisher, PhD

In consultation with the editorial advisory board, Nelson Education has completely rethought the structure, approaches, and formats of our key textbook ancillaries. We've also increased our investment in editorial support for our ancillary authors. The result is the Nelson Education Teaching Advantage and its key components: *NETA Engagement, NETA Assessment,* and *NETA Presentation.* Each component includes one or more ancillaries prepared according to our best practices, and a document explaining the theory behind the practices.

NETA Engagement presents materials that help instructors deliver engaging content and activities to their classes. Instead of Instructor's Manuals that regurgitate chapter outlines and key terms from the text, NETA Enriched Instructor's Manuals (EIMs) provide genuine assistance to teachers. The EIMs answer questions like *What should students learn?, Why should students care?,* and *What are some common student misconceptions and stumbling blocks?* EIMs not only identify the topics that cause students the most difficulty, but also describe techniques and resources to help students master these concepts. Dr. Roger Fisher's *Instructor's Guide to Classroom Engagement (IGCE)* accompanies every Enriched Instructor's Manual.

NETA Assessment relates to testing materials: not just Nelson's Test Banks and Computerized Test Banks, but also in web quizzes, such as the quizzes available on CourseMate. Under *NETA Assessment,* Nelson's authors create multiple-choice questions that reflect research-based best practices for constructing effective questions and testing not just recall but also higher-order thinking. Our guidelines were developed by David DiBattista, a 3M National Teaching Fellow whose recent research as a professor of psychology at Brock University has focused on multiple-choice testing. All Test Bank authors receive training at workshops conducted by Prof. DiBattista, as do the copyeditors assigned to each Test Bank. A copy of *Multiple Choice Tests: Getting Beyond Remembering,* Professor DiBattista's guide to writing effective tests, is included with every Nelson Test Bank/Computerized Test Bank package.

NETA Presentation has been developed to help instructors make the best use of PowerPoint® in their classrooms. With a clean and uncluttered design developed by Maureen Stone of Stone-Soup Consulting, NETA Presentation features slides with improved readability, more multimedia and graphic materials, activities to use in class, and tips for instructors on the Notes page. A copy of *NETA Guidelines for Classroom Presentations* by Maureen Stone is included with each set of PowerPoint slides.

Instructor Ancillaries

Key instructor ancillaries for *Abnormal Psychology*, Third Canadian Edition, are provided on the *Instructor's Resource CD* (ISBN 978-0-17-661589-5), giving instructors the ultimate tool for customizing lectures and presentations. The IRCD includes:

NETA Engagement: The Enriched Instructor's Manual was written by Arielle Giordano. It is organized according to the textbook chapters and addresses key educational concerns, such as typical stumbling blocks student face and how to address them.

NETA Assessment: The Test Bank was written by Anastasia Bake, St. Clair College. It includes over 1500 multiple-choice questions written according to NETA guidelines for effective construction and development of higher-order questions. Also included are about 150 essay questions. Test Bank files are provided in Word format for easy editing and in PDF format for convenient printing, whatever your system.

The Computerized Test Bank by ExamView® includes all the questions from the Test Bank. The easy-to-use ExamView software is compatible with Microsoft Windows and Mac. Create tests by selecting questions from the question bank, modifying these questions as desired, and adding new questions you write yourself. You can administer quizzes online and export tests to WebCT, Blackboard, and other formats.

NETA Presentation: In the Microsoft® PowerPoint® lecture slides there is an average of 30 slides per chapter, many featuring key figures, tables, and photographs from *Abnormal Psychology: An Integrative Approach, Third Canadian Edition*. NETA principles of clear design and engaging content have been incorporated throughout.

Image Library: This resource consists of digital copies of figures, short tables, and some photographs used in the book. Instructors may use these jpegs to create their own PowerPoint® presentations.

DayOne: Day One—Prof InClass is a PowerPoint® presentation that you can customize to orient your students to the class and their text at the beginning of the course.

Additional Resources

- *Web Resources:* Through a password-protected website, professors have access to Teaching Activities, the Psychology Resource Centre, Teaching Techniques, and Downloadable Supplements. Go to **http://www.abnormalpsych3ce.nelson.com/instructor**

Titles of Interest

- *Looking into Abnormal Psychology: Contemporary Readings* by Scott O. Lilienfeld (ISBN 978-0-534-35416-9) is a fascinating 234-page reader comprising 40 articles from popular magazines and journals. Each article explores ongoing controversies regarding mental illness and its treatment.

- *Casebook in Abnormal Psychology* by Timothy A. Brown and David H. Barlow (ISBN 978-0-534-60586-5) is a comprehensive casebook that reflects the integrative approach, which considers the multiple influences of genetics, biology, familial, and environment factors into a unified model of causality as well as maintenance and treatment of the disorder. The casebook describes treatment methods that are the most effective interventions developed for a particular disorder. It also presents two undiagnosed cases in order to give students an appreciation for the complexity of disorders. The cases are strictly teaching and learning exercises similar to what many instructors use on their examinations.

Reviewers

Creating this third Canadian edition would not have been possible without the superb feedback of the reviewers. To them we express our deepest gratitude. The reviewers read the second Canadian edition and provided extraordinarily perceptive critical comments, pointed to relevant information, and offered new insights. Readers who take the time to communicate their thoughts offer the greatest rewards to writers and scholars.

For their assistance and their feedback, we thank the following reviewers:

Michael Ellery, Ph.D., *University of Manitoba*
Amanda Maranzan, *Lakehead University*
Peter G. Mezo, Ph.D., R.Psych., *Memorial University of Newfoundland*
David A. Moscovitch, Ph.D., *University of Waterloo*
Dr. Uzma Rehman, *University of Waterloo*
Alan Scoboria, Ph.D., C.Psych., *University of Windsor*

1 | Abnormal Behaviour in Historical Context

Bert Hardy/Hulton Archive/Getty Images

> *A clear and complete insight into the nature of madness, a correct and distinct conception of what constitutes the difference between the sane and the insane has, as far as I know, not been found.*
> —Schopenhauer, *The World as Will and Idea*

Characterize the nature of psychology as a discipline.	› Explain why psychology is a science (APA SLO 1.1.a) *(see textbook pages 6–9)*
Demonstrate knowledge and understanding representing appropriate breadth and depth in selected content areas of psychology.	› The history of psychology, including the evolution of methods of psychology, its theoretical conflicts, and its sociocultural contexts (APA SLO 1.2.b) *(see textbook pages 9–29)*
Use the concepts, language, and major theories of the discipline to account for psychological phenomena.	› Use theories to explain and predict behaviour and mental processes (APA SLO 1.3.d) *(see textbook pages 15–29)* › Integrate theoretical perspectives to produce comprehensive and multifaceted explanations (APA SLO 1.3.e) *(see textbook page 27)*
Explain major perspectives of psychology (e.g., behavioural, biological, cognitive, evolutionary, humanistic, psychodynamic, and sociocultural).	› Explain major perspectives in psychology (APA SLO 1.4a) *(see textbook pages 12–29)*

* Portions of this chapter cover learning outcomes suggested by the American Psychological Association (2007) in their guidelines for the undergraduate psychology major. Chapter coverage of these outcomes is identified above by APA Goal and APA Suggested Learning Outcome (SLO).

Today you may have gotten out of bed, had breakfast, gone to class, studied, and at the end of the day, enjoyed the company of your friends before falling asleep. It probably did not occur to you that many physically healthy people are unable to do some or any of these things. What they have in common is a **psychological disorder**, a psychological dysfunction within an individual that is associated with distress or impairment in functioning and a response that is not typical or culturally expected. Before examining exactly what this means, let's look at one individual's situation.

JODY | *The Boy Who Fainted at the Sight of Blood*

Jody, a 16-year-old boy, was referred to our anxiety disorders clinic after increasing episodes of fainting. Jody reported that he had always been somewhat queasy at the sight of blood. About two years before coming to our clinic, in his first biology class, the teacher showed a movie of a frog dissection to illustrate various points about anatomy. The film was particularly graphic, with vivid images of blood, tissue, and muscle. About halfway through, Jody felt a bit lightheaded and left the room, but the images did not leave him. He continued to be bothered by them and occasionally felt slightly queasy. He began to avoid situations in which he might see blood or an injury. He stopped looking at magazines that might have gory pictures. He found it difficult to look at raw meat, or even Band-Aids, because they brought the feared images to mind. Eventually, anything his friends or parents said that evoked an image of blood or injury caused Jody to feel lightheaded. It became so bad that if one of his friends exclaimed, "Cut it out!" he felt faint. Beginning about six months before his visit to the clinic, Jody actually fainted when he unavoidably encountered something bloody. His family physician could find nothing wrong with him, nor could several other physicians. By the time he was referred to our clinic, he was fainting five to ten times a week, often in class. Clearly, these epi-

sodes were problematic for him and disruptive in school; each time he fainted, the other students flocked around him, trying to help, and class was interrupted. Because no one could find anything wrong with Jody, the principal finally concluded that he was being manipulative and suspended him from school, even though he was an honour student.

Jody had what we now call blood-injury-injection phobia. His reaction was quite severe, thereby meeting the criteria for **phobia**, a psychological disorder characterized by marked and persistent fear of an object or situation. But many people have similar reactions that are not as severe when they receive an injection or see someone who is injured, whether or not blood is visible. For people who react as severely as Jody, this phobia can be very disabling. They may avoid certain careers, such as medicine or nursing. If they are so afraid of needles and injections that they avoid them even when they are necessary, they put their health at risk.

What Is a Psychological Disorder?

Keeping in mind the real-life problems faced by Jody, let's look more closely at the definition of a psychological disorder, or abnormal behaviour: It is a *psychological dysfunction within an individual associated with distress or impairment in functioning and a response that is not typical or culturally expected* (■ Figure 1.1). On the surface, these three criteria may seem obvious, but they were not easily arrived at, and it is worth exploring what they mean. You will see that no one criterion has yet been developed that fully defines abnormality.

Psychological Dysfunction

Psychological dysfunction refers to a breakdown in cognitive, emotional, or behavioural functioning. For example, if you are out on a date, it should be fun. If you experience severe fear all evening and just want to go home, even though you have nothing to be afraid of, and if the severe fear happens on every date, your

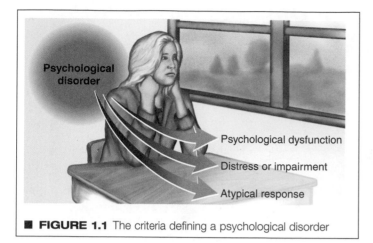

■ **FIGURE 1.1** The criteria defining a psychological disorder

emotions are not functioning properly. However, if all your friends agree that the person who asked you out is dangerous, then it would not be "dysfunctional" for you to be fearful and avoid the date.

A dysfunction was present for Jody: he fainted at the sight of blood. But many people experience a mild version of this reaction (feeling queasy at the sight of blood) without meeting the criteria for the disorder; knowing where to draw the line between normal and abnormal dysfunction is often difficult. For this reason, these problems are often considered to exist on a continuum or as a dimension, rather than as categories that are either present or absent. This is one reason that just having a dysfunction is not enough to meet the criteria for a psychological disorder.

Personal Distress

That the disorder or behaviour must be associated with distress adds an important component and seems clear: the criterion is satisfied if the individual is extremely upset. We can certainly say that Jody was very distressed and even suffered with his phobia. But remember, by itself this criterion does not define abnormal behaviour. It is often quite normal to be distressed—for example, if someone close to you dies. The human condition is such that suffering and distress are very much part of life—and that is not likely to change. Furthermore, for some disorders, by definition, suffering and distress are absent. Consider the person who feels extremely elated and acts impulsively as part of a manic episode. As we see in Chapter 7, one major difficulty with this problem is that people enjoy the manic state so much they are reluctant to begin treatment or stay in treatment very long. Thus, defining psychological disorder by distress alone doesn't work, although the concept of distress contributes to a good definition. The concept of impairment is useful, though it is not entirely satisfactory. For example, many people consider themselves shy or lazy, but this doesn't mean that they're abnormal. But if you are so shy that you find it impossible to date or even interact with people, and if you make every attempt to avoid interactions even though you would like to have friends, then your social functioning is impaired. Jody was clearly impaired by his phobia, but many people with similar, less severe reactions are not impaired. This difference again illustrates the important point that most psychological disorders are simply extreme expressions of otherwise normal emotions, behaviours, and cognitive processes.

CP PHOTO/AP/Charles Rex Arbogast

▲ Distress and suffering are a natural part of life and do not in themselves constitute a psychological disorder.

Atypical or Not Culturally Expected

Finally, the criterion that the response be atypical or *not culturally expected* is important but also insufficient to determine abnormality. At times, something is considered abnormal because it occurs infrequently; it deviates from the average. The greater the deviation, the more abnormal it is. You might say that someone is abnormally short or abnormally tall, meaning that the person's height deviates substantially from average, but this obviously isn't a definition of disorder. Many people are far from the average in their behaviour, but few would be considered disordered. We might call them talented or eccentric. Many artists, movie stars, and athletes fall into this category. For example, it's not normal to plan to have blood spurt from your clothes, but when Lady Gaga did this while performing it only enhanced her celebrity. The late novelist J. D. Salinger, who wrote *The Catcher in the Rye*, retreated to a small town in New Hampshire and refused to see any outsiders for years, but he

▲ Some religious behaviours may seem unusual to us but are culturally or individually appropriate.

▲ We accept extreme behaviours by entertainers, such as Lady Gaga, that would not be tolerated in other members of our society.

continued to write. Some male rock singers wear heavy makeup on stage. These people are well paid and seem to enjoy their careers. In most cases, the more productive you are in the eyes of society, the more eccentricities society will tolerate. Therefore, "deviating from the average" doesn't work very well as a definition.

Another view is that your behaviour is abnormal if you are violating social norms, even if some people are sympathetic to your point of view. This definition is very useful in considering important cultural differences in psychological disorders. For example, to enter a trance state and believe you are possessed would point to a psychological disorder in most Western cultures, but in many other societies the behaviour is accepted and expected (see Chapter 6). (A cultural perspective is an important point of reference throughout this book.)

An informative example of this view is provided by the prominent neuroscientist Sapolsky (2002), who worked closely with the Masai tribe in East Africa. One day Sapolsky's Masai friend Rhoda asked him to bring his jeep as quickly as possible to the Masai village, where a woman had been acting very aggressively and had been hearing voices. The woman had actually killed a goat with her own hands. Sapolsky and several Masai were able to subdue her and transport her to a local health centre. Realizing that this was an opportunity to learn more of the Masai's view of psychological disorders, Sapolsky had the following discussion:

"So Rhoda," I began laconically, "what do you suppose was wrong with that woman?"

She looked at me as if I was mad.

"She is crazy."

"But how can you tell?"

"She's crazy. Can't you just see from how she acts?"

"But how do you decide that she is crazy? What did she do?"

"She killed that goat."

"Oh," I said with anthropological detachment, "but Masai kill goats all the time."

She looked at me as if I were an idiot. "Only the men kill goats," she said.

"Well, how else do you know that she is crazy?"

"She hears voices."

Again, I made a pain of myself. "Oh, but the Masai hear voices sometimes." (At ceremonies before long cattle drives, the Masai trace-dance and claim to hear voices.) And in one sentence, Rhoda summed up half of what anyone needs to know about cross-cultural psychiatry. "But she hears voices at the wrong time." (2002, p. 138)

However, a social standard of *normal* has been misused. Consider, for example, the practice of committing political dissidents to mental institutions, which was common in the former Soviet Union before the fall of Communism. Although such dissident behaviour clearly violates social norms, it should not alone be cause for commitment.

Concept Check | 1.1

Check your understanding of the definitions of abnormal behaviour. Write the letter for any, all, or none of the following definitions in the blanks: (a) societal norm violation, (b) impairment in functioning, (c) dysfunction, and (d) distress.

1. Jan's neighbour collects aluminum cans and attaches them to the inside walls of her house for decoration. She has two rooms completely wallpapered with cans and has started on a third. Jan knows of no one else who engages in similar behaviour and, therefore, believes her neighbour to be abnormal. Jan could be using one of two definitions of abnormality. Which, if any, are they?

_____

(continued)

What Is a Psychological Disorder? **5**

2. Miguel recently began feeling sad and lonely. Although still able to function at work and fulfill his other responsibilities, he finds himself feeling down much of the time, and he worries about what is happening to him. Which of the definitions of abnormality apply to Miguel's situation? _____

3. Three weeks ago, Tony, a 35-year-old business executive, stopped showering, refused to leave his apartment, and started watching television talk shows. Threats of being fired have failed to bring Tony back to reality, and he continues to spend his days staring blankly at the television screen. Which of the definitions seem to describe Tony's situation? _____

4. Jane is afraid to leave her home. She used to force herself to go out to maintain contact with friends and relatives; however, recently she refuses to go anywhere. Which definitions apply to this situation? _____

In a very thoughtful analysis of the matter, Wakefield (1992, 1999) uses the shorthand definition "harmful dysfunction." A related concept that is also useful is to determine whether the behaviour is beyond the individual's control (something he or she doesn't want to do; Widiger & Sankis, 2000). Variants of these approaches are most often used in current diagnostic practice, as outlined in the fourth edition, text revision, of the *Diagnostic and Statistical Manual* (*DSM-IV-TR*, American Psychiatric Association, 2000a), which contains the current listing of criteria for psychological disorders. These approaches, which are largely unchanged in the fifth edition (*DSM-5*) based on recent drafts, guide our thinking in this book.

In conclusion, it is difficult to define "normal" and "abnormal" (Lilienfeld & Marino, 1995, 1999)—and the debate continues (Clark, 1999; Klein, 1999; Spitzer, 1999). The most widely accepted definition used in the *DSM-IV-TR* (and drafts of the *DSM-5*) describes behavioural, psychological, or biological dysfunctions that are unexpected in their cultural context and associated with present distress and impairment in functioning, or increased risk of suffering, death, pain, or impairment. This definition can be useful across cultures and subcultures if we pay careful attention to what is functional or dysfunctional (or out of control) in a given society. But it is never easy to decide what represents dysfunction, and some scholars have argued persuasively that the health professions will never be able to satisfactorily define *disease* or *disorder* (see, for example, Lilienfeld & Marino, 1995, 1999). Perhaps the best we can do is consider how the apparent disease or disorder matches a "typical" profile of a disorder—for example, major depression or schizophrenia—when most or all symptoms that experts agree are part of the disorder are present. We call this typical profile a *prototype*, and, as described in Chapter 3, the diagnostic criteria from *DSM-IV-TR* as well as the emerging criteria for *DSM-5* found throughout this book are all prototypes. This means that the patient may have only some features or symptoms of the disorder (a minimum number) and still meet criteria for the disorder because his or her set of symptoms is close to the prototype. This concept is described more fully in Chapter 3, where the diagnosis of psychological disorder is discussed.

Some controversial figures such as Thomas Szasz and George Albee are highly critical of medical diagnoses being used in the case of psychological disorders. In 1960, Szasz advanced his position that mental illness is a myth and that the practice of labelling mental illnesses should be abolished. For example, Szasz (1960) argued that a fundamental difference exists between the use of diagnoses for physical diseases and their use in mental illnesses. The former uses objective criteria (e.g., results of blood tests), but for mental illness, subjective judgments are required. Albee (1998, 2000) has argued that the biggest mistake made by the clinical psychology profession was uncritically accepting the concept of "mental disease" and using the medical model and associated diagnoses (e.g., the *DSM* system) in conceptualizing abnormal behaviour. Even among the many proponents of the *DSM* system, disagreement continues about how to define the concept of "disorder."

As noted earlier, creation of the *DSM-5* is in progress (Brown & Barlow, 2005; Krueger, Watson, & Barlow, 2005; Regier, Narrow, Kuhl, & Kupfer 2009), with publication due in May 2013. But the basic definition of psychological disorder will be largely unchanged.

As a challenge, take the problem of defining abnormal behaviour a step further and consider this: What if Jody passed out repeatedly but regained consciousness so quickly that neither his classmates nor his teachers even noticed? Furthermore, what if Jody continued to get good grades? Would fainting all the time at the mere thought of blood be a disorder? Would it be impairing? Dysfunctional? Distressing? What do you think?

The Science of Psychopathology

Psychopathology is the scientific study of psychological disorders. Within this field are specially trained professionals, including clinical and counselling psychologists, psychiatrists, psychiatric social workers, psychiatric nurses, marriage and family therapists, and mental health counsellors. Clinical psychologists typically receive a Ph.D. (Doctor of Philosophy) following a course of graduate-level study that lasts approximately five years. This education prepares them to conduct research into the causes and treatment of psychological disorders and to diagnose, assess, and treat these disorders. Instead of a Ph.D., clinical psychologists sometimes receive a Psy.D. (Doctor of Psychology) degree for which the training is similar to the Ph.D. but with more emphasis on clinical practice and less on research training. No Psy.D. programs currently exist in Canada; however, programs are currently in development in Québec (Dobson, 2003; Hunsley & Johnston, 2000). In Canada, regulation of the psychology profession is under the jurisdiction of the provinces and territories. Depending on the jurisdiction, a psychologist may have either a doctoral or a master's degree (Hunsley & Johnston, 2000). For example, within the province of Ontario, professional psychologists are regulated by the College of Psychologists of Ontario, as outlined in the Regulated Health Professions Act (1991). Largely to protect the public, but also in the interest of the profession (Goodman, 2000), only those who are licensed or registered with their provincial board or college are permitted to call themselves "psychologists" (e.g., in advertising). Note that the labels "psychotherapist" and "therapist" are not regulated by the provincial and territorial psychology boards or colleges. Thus, in Canada, the label of "psychologist" conveys information about the training and qualifications of the professional, whereas the label of "psychotherapist" does not. In addition, the terms "therapist" and "psychotherapist" are not specific to a particular profession. For example, a social worker, a psychologist, and a psychiatrist can all refer to themselves as "psychotherapists" if they provide therapy services to members of the public around psychological issues.

Psychologists with other specialty training, such as experimental and social psychologists, concentrate on investigating the basic determinants of behaviour but do not assess or treat psychological disorders. Although a great deal of overlap exists, *counselling psychologists* (who can receive a Ph.D., Psy.D., or Ed.D.—Doctor of Education) tend to study and treat adjustment and vocational issues encountered by relatively healthy individuals, whereas clinical psychologists usually concentrate on more severe psychological disorders.

Psychiatrists first earn an M.D. in medical school and then specialize in psychiatry during a three-year to four-year residency training program. Psychiatrists also investigate the nature and causes of psychological disorders, often from a biological point of view, make diagnoses, and offer treatments. Many psychiatrists emphasize drugs or other biological treatments, although most use psychosocial treatments as well.

Psychiatric social workers typically earn a master's degree in social work as they develop expertise in collecting information relevant to the social and family situation of the individual with a psychological disorder. Social workers also treat disorders, often concentrating on family problems associated with them. *Psychiatric nurses* have advanced degrees, such as a master's or a Ph.D., and specialize in the care and treatment of patients with psychological disorders, usually in hospitals as part of a treatment team. Finally, *marriage and family therapists and mental health counsellors* typically spend one to two years earning a master's degree and provide clinical services in hospitals or clinics, usually under the supervision of a doctoral-level clinician. Table 1.1 shows the number of each major category of mental health professionals currently practising in Canada.

The Scientist-Practitioner

The most important recent development in the history of psychopathology is the adoption of scientific methods to learn more about the nature of psychological disorders, their causes, and

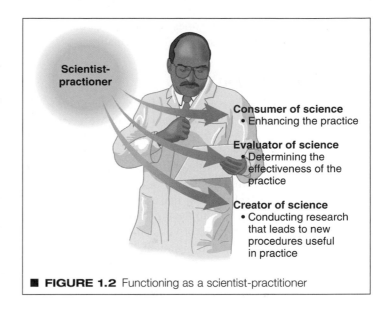

■ **FIGURE 1.2** Functioning as a scientist-practitioner

their treatment. Many mental health professionals take a scientific approach to their clinical work and are therefore referred to as **scientist-practitioners** (Barlow, Hayes, & Nelson, 1984; Hayes, Barlow, & Nelson-Gray, 1999). Mental health practitioners may function as scientist-practitioners at least one of three ways (see ■ Figure 1.2). First, they may keep up with the latest scientific developments in their field and therefore use the most current diagnostic and treatment procedures. In this sense, they are consumers of the science of psychopathology to the advantage of their patients. Second, scientist-practitioners evaluate their own assessments or treatment procedures to see whether they work. They are accountable not only to their patients but also to the government agencies and insurance companies that pay for the treatments, so they must demonstrate clearly that their treatments work. Third, scientist-practitioners might conduct research, often in clinics or hospitals, that produces new information about disorders or their treatment, thus becoming immune to the fads that plague our field often at the expense of patients and their families. For example, new "miracle cures" for psychological disorders that are reported several times a year in the popular media would not be used by a scientist-practitioner who did not have sound scientific data showing that they work. Such data flow from research that attempts three basic things: to describe psychological disorders, to determine their causes, and to treat them (see ■ Figure 1.3). These three categories compose an organizational structure that recurs throughout this book and is formally evident in the discussions of specific disorders beginning in Chapter 5.

TABLE 1.1 Mental Health Professionals Currently Practising in Canada

Profession	Number Currently Practising
Psychiatrists	3 600
Psychologists, master's level, and psychological associates	13 000
Psychiatric nurses	11 000
Psychiatric social workers	thousands

Source: Adapted from Goering, Wasylenki, & Durbin, 2000.

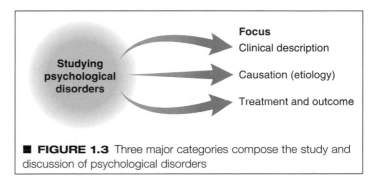

■ **FIGURE 1.3** Three major categories compose the study and discussion of psychological disorders

The Science of Psychopathology **7**

A general overview of the categories now will give you a clearer perspective on our efforts to understand abnormality.

Clinical Description

In hospitals and clinics we often say that a patient "presents" with a specific problem or set of problems, or we discuss the **presenting problem**. *Presents* is a traditional shorthand way of indicating why the person came to the clinic. Describing Jody's presenting problem is the first step in determining his **clinical description**, which represents the unique combination of behaviours, thoughts, and feelings that make up a specific disorder. The word *clinical* refers both to the types of problems or disorders you would find in a clinic or hospital and to the activities connected with assessment and treatment. Throughout this text are excerpts from many individual cases, most of them from our personal files.

Clearly, one important function of the clinical description is to specify what makes the disorder different from normal behaviour or from other disorders. Statistical data may also be relevant. For example, how many people in the population as a whole have the disorder? This figure is called the **prevalence** of the disorder. Statistics on how many new cases occur during a given period, such as a year, represent the **incidence** of the disorder. Other statistics include the *sex ratio*—that is, what percentage of males and females have the disorder—and the typical *age of onset*, which often differs from one disorder to another.

In addition to having different symptoms, a different age of onset, and possibly a different sex ratio and prevalence, most disorders follow a somewhat individual pattern, or **course**. For example, some disorders, such as schizophrenia (see Chapter 13), follow a *chronic course*, meaning that they tend to last a long time, sometimes a whole lifetime. Other disorders, like mood disorders (see Chapter 7), follow an *episodic course* in which the individual is likely to recover within a few months, only to have a recurrence of the disorder later. This pattern may repeat throughout a person's life. Still other disorders may have a *time-limited course*, meaning the disorder will improve without treatment in a relatively short period.

Closely related to differences in the course of disorders are differences in onset. Some disorders have an *acute onset*, meaning that they begin suddenly; others develop gradually over an extended time, which is sometimes called an *insidious onset*. It is important to know the typical course of a disorder so that we know what to expect and how best to deal with the problem. The anticipated course is an important part of the clinical description. For example, if someone has a mild disorder with acute onset that we know is time limited, we might advise the individual to forgo expensive treatment, because the problem will resolve soon enough, like a common cold. However, if the disorder is likely to last a long time (become chronic), the individual might want to seek treatment and take other appropriate steps. The anticipated course of a disorder is called the **prognosis**. So we might say, "the prognosis is good," meaning the individual will probably recover, or "the prognosis is guarded," meaning the probable outcome doesn't look good.

© Lawrence Manning/Corbis

▲ Children experience panic and anxiety differently from adults, so their reactions may be mistaken for symptoms of physical illness.

The patient's age may be a very important part of the clinical description. A specific psychological disorder occurring in childhood may present very differently from the same disorder in adulthood or old age. Children experiencing severe anxiety and panic often assume that they are physically ill because they have difficulty understanding there is nothing physically wrong. Because their thoughts and feelings are different from those experienced by adults with anxiety and panic, children are often misdiagnosed and treated for a medical disorder.

Causation, Treatment, and Outcomes

Etiology, or the study of origins, has to do with why a disorder begins (what causes it) and includes biological, psychological, and social dimensions. Because the etiology of psychological disorders is so important to this field, we devote an entire chapter to it (Chapter 2). Treatment is often important to the study of psychological disorders. If a new drug or psychosocial treatment is successful in treating a disorder, it may give us some hints about the nature of the disorder and its causes. For example, if a drug with a specific known effect within the nervous system alleviates a certain psychological disorder, we know that something in that part of the nervous system might be either causing the disorder or helping maintain it. Similarly, if a psychosocial treatment designed to help clients regain a sense of control over their lives is effective with a certain disorder, a diminished sense of control may be an important psychological component of the disorder itself.

As we see in the next chapter, psychology is never that simple. This is because the effect does not necessarily imply the cause. To use a common example, you might take an aspirin to relieve a tension headache that you developed during a gruelling day of taking exams. If you then feel better, it does not mean the headache was caused by a lack of aspirin in the first place. Nevertheless, many people seek treatment for psychological disorders, and treatment can provide interesting hints about the nature of the disorder.

In the past, textbooks emphasized treatment approaches in a very general sense, with little attention to the disorder being treated. For example, a mental health professional might be thoroughly trained in a single theoretical approach, such as psychoanalysis or behaviour therapy (both described later in the chapter), and then use that approach on every disorder. More recently, as our science has advanced, we have developed specific effective treatments that do not always adhere neatly to one theoretical approach but that have grown out of a deeper understanding of the disorder in question. For this reason, this book does not have separate chapters on such types of treatment approaches as psychodynamic, cognitive behavioural, or humanistic. Rather, the latest and most effective drug and psychosocial treatments are described in the context of specific disorders, in keeping with our integrative multidimensional perspective.

We now survey many early attempts to *describe* and *treat* abnormal behaviour, and more still to comprehend its *causes*, which will give you a better perspective on current approaches. In Chapter 2, we examine contemporary views of causation and treatment. In Chapter 3, we discuss efforts to describe, or classify, abnormal behaviour. In Chapter 4, we review research methods—our systematic efforts to discover the truths underlying description, cause, and treatment that allow us to function as scientist-practitioners. In Chapters 5 through 15, we examine specific disorders; our discussion is organized in each case in the now familiar triad of description, cause, and treatment. Finally, in Chapter 16 we examine legal, professional, and ethical issues that are relevant to psychological disorders and their treatment in Canada today. With that interview in mind, let us turn to the past.

The Past: Historical Conceptions of Abnormal Behaviour

For thousands of years, humans have tried to explain and control problematic behaviour. But our efforts always derive from the theories or models of behaviour that are popular at the time. The purpose of these models is to explain why someone is "acting like that." Three major models that have guided us date back to the beginnings of civilization.

Humans have always supposed that certain agents outside our bodies and environment influence our behaviour, thinking, and emotions. These agents, which might be divinities, demons, spirits, or other phenomena such as magnetic fields or the moon or the stars, are the driving forces behind the *supernatural model*. In addition, since ancient Greece, the mind has often been called the *soul* or the *psyche* and considered separate from the body. Although many have thought that the mind can influence the body and, in turn, the body can influence the mind, most philosophers looked for causes of abnormal behaviour in one or the other. This split gave rise to two traditions of thought about abnormal behaviour, summarized as the *biological model* and the *psychological model*.

These three models—the supernatural, the biological, and the psychological—are very old but still in use today.

The Supernatural Tradition

For much of our recorded history, deviant behaviour has been considered a reflection of the battle between good and evil. When confronted with unexplainable, irrational behaviour and by suffering and upheaval, people perceived evil. A noted historian chronicled the second half of the 14th century, a particularly difficult time for humanity, in *A Distant Mirror* (Tuchman, 1978). She very ably captures the conflicting tides of opinion on the origins and treatment of insanity during that bleak and tumultuous period.

Demons and Witches

One strong current of opinion put the causes and treatment of psychological disorders squarely in the realm of the supernatural. During the last quarter of the 14th century, religious and lay authorities supported these popular superstitions, and society as a whole began to believe in the reality and power of demons and witches. The Catholic Church had split, and a second centre, complete with a pope, emerged in the south of France to compete with Rome. In reaction to this schism, the Roman church fought back against the evil in the world that must have been behind this heresy.

Mary Evans Picture Library

▲ During the Middle Ages, individuals with psychological disorders were sometimes thought to be possessed by evil spirits that had to be exorcised through rituals.

People turned increasingly to magic and sorcery to solve their problems. During these turbulent times, the bizarre behaviour of people afflicted with psychological disorders was seen as the work of the devil and witches. It followed that individuals possessed by evil spirits were probably responsible for any misfortune experienced by the townspeople, which inspired drastic action against the possessed. Treatments included *exorcism*, in which various religious rituals were performed to rid the victim of evil spirits. Other approaches included shaving the pattern of a cross in the victims' hair and securing them to a wall near the front of a church so that they might benefit from hearing mass.

The conviction that sorcery and witches were causes of madness and other evils continued into the 15th century. Evil continued to be blamed for unexplainable behaviour, even after the European founding of the New World, as evidenced by the 1692 Salem witch trials. This event involved an outbreak of accusations of witchcraft alleged toward women in a Massachusetts village community (Boyer & Nissenbaum, 1974).

Stress and Melancholy

An equally strong opinion, even during this period, reflected the enlightened view that insanity was a natural phenomenon, caused by mental or emotional stress, and that it was curable (Alexander & Selesnick, 1966; Maher & Maher, 1985a). Mental depression and anxiety were recognized as illnesses (Kemp, 1990; Schoeneman, 1977), although symptoms such as despair and lethargy were often identified by the church with the sin of *acedia*, or sloth (Tuchman, 1978). Common treatments were rest, sleep, and a healthy and happy environment. Other treatments included baths, ointments, and various potions. Indeed,

during the 14th and 15th centuries, people with mental illnesses, along with people who had physical deformities or disabilities, were often moved from house to house in medieval villages, as neighbours took turns caring for them. We now know that this medieval practice of keeping people who have psychological disturbances in their own community is beneficial (see Chapter 13). (We return to this subject when we discuss biological and psychological models later in this chapter.)

One of the chief advisers to the king of France, a bishop and philosopher named Nicholas Oresme, also suggested that the disease of melancholy (depression), rather than demons, was the source of some bizarre behaviour. Oresme pointed out that much of the evidence for the existence of sorcery and witchcraft, particularly among people with psychological disorders, was obtained from people who were tortured and who, quite understandably, confessed to anything.

These conflicting crosscurrents of natural and supernatural explanations for mental disorders are represented more or less strongly in various historical works, depending on the sources consulted by historians. Some assume that demonic influences were the predominant explanations of abnormal behaviour during the Middle Ages (e.g., Zilboorg & Henry, 1941); others believe the supernatural had little or no influence. As we see in the handling of the severe psychological disorder experienced by King Charles VI of France in the late 14th century, both influences were strong, sometimes alternating in the treatment of the same case.

CHARLES VI | *The Mad King*

In the summer of 1392, King Charles VI of France was under a great deal of stress, in part because of the division of the Catholic Church. As he rode with his army to the province of Brittany, a nearby aide dropped his lance with a loud clatter and the king, thinking he was under attack, turned on his own army, killing several prominent knights before being subdued from behind. The army immediately marched back to Paris. The king's lieutenants and advisers concluded that he was mad.

During the following years, at his worst the king hid in a corner of his castle, believing he was made of glass, or roamed the corridors howling like a wolf. At other times he couldn't remember who or what he was. He became fearful and enraged whenever he saw his own royal coat of arms and would try to destroy it if it were brought near him.

The people of Paris were devastated by their leader's apparent madness. Some thought it reflected God's anger, because the king had failed to take up arms to end the schism in the Catholic Church; others thought it was God's

warning against taking up arms; still others thought it was divine punishment for heavy taxes (a conclusion some people might make today). But most thought the king's madness was caused by sorcery, a belief strengthened by a great drought that dried up the ponds and rivers, causing cattle to die of thirst. Merchants claimed their worst losses in 20 years.

Naturally, the king was given the best care available. The most famous healer in the land was a 92-year-old physician whose treatment program included moving the king to one of his residences in the country where the air was thought to be the cleanest in the land. The physician prescribed rest, relaxation, and recreation. After some time, the king seemed to recover. The physician recommended that the king not be burdened with the responsibilities of running the kingdom, claiming that if he had few worries or irritations, his mind would gradually strengthen and further improve.

Unfortunately, the physician died and the insanity of King Charles VI returned more seriously than before. This time, however, he came under the influence of the conflicting crosscurrent of supernatural causation. "An unkempt evil-eyed charlatan and pseudo-mystic named Arnaut Guilhem was allowed to treat Charles on his claim of possessing a book given by God to Adam by means of which man could overcome all affliction resulting from original sin" (Tuchman, 1978, p. 514). Guilhem insisted that the king's malady was caused by sorcery, but his treatments failed to effect a cure.

A variety of remedies and rituals of all kinds were tried but none worked. High-ranking officials and doctors of the university called for the "sorcerers" to be discovered and punished. "On one occasion, two Augustinian friars, after getting no results from magic incantations and a liquid made from powdered pearls, proposed to cut incisions in the king's head. When this was not allowed by the king's council, the friars accused those who opposed their recommendation of sorcery" (Tuchman, 1978, p. 514). Even the king himself, during his lucid moments, came to believe the source of madness was evil and sorcery. "In the name of Jesus Christ," he cried weeping in his agony, "if there is any one of you who is an accomplice in this evil I suffer, I beg him to torture me no longer but let me die!" (Tuchman, 1978, p. 515).

Treatments for Possession

With a perceived connection between evil deeds and sin on the one hand, and psychological disorders on the other, it is logical to conclude that the person is largely responsible for his or her own disorder, which might well be a punishment for evil deeds. Does this sound familiar? The acquired immune deficiency syndrome (AIDS) epidemic reflects a very similar belief among some people. Because the human immunodeficiency virus (HIV) is, in Western societies, most prevalent among practising homosexuals, some people believe it is a divine punishment for what they consider abhorrent behaviour. This view is slowly dissipating as the AIDS virus spreads to other "less sinful" segments of the population, but it still persists. Possession, however, is not always connected with sin and may be seen as involuntary and the possessed individual as blameless. Furthermore, exorcisms at least have the virtue of being relatively painless. Interestingly, they sometimes work, as do other forms of faith healing, for reasons we explore in subsequent chapters. But what if they did not? In the Middle Ages, if exorcism failed, some authorities thought that steps were necessary to make the body uninhabitable by evil spirits, and many people were subjected to confinement, beatings, and other forms of torture (Kemp, 1990).

Somewhere along the way, a creative "therapist" decided that hanging people over a pit full of poisonous snakes might scare the evil spirits right out of their bodies (to say nothing of terrifying the people themselves). Strangely, this approach sometimes worked; that is, the most disturbed, oddly behaving individuals would suddenly come to their senses and experience relief from their symptoms, if only temporarily. Naturally, this was reinforcing to the therapist, and, so, snake pits were built in many institutions. Many other treatments based on the hypothesized therapeutic element of shock were developed, including dunkings in ice-cold water.

The Moon and the Stars

Paracelsus, a Swiss physician who lived from 1493 to 1541, rejected notions of possession by the devil, suggesting instead that the movements of the moon and stars had profound effects on people's psychological functioning. This influential theory inspired the word *lunatic*, which is derived from the Latin word for moon, *luna*. You might hear some of your friends explain something crazy they did last night by saying, "It must have been the full moon." The belief that heavenly bodies affect human behaviour still exists, although no scientific evidence supports it. Despite much ridicule, millions of people around the world are convinced that their behaviour is influenced by the stages of the moon or the position of the stars. This belief is most noticeable today in followers of astrology, who hold that their behaviour and the major events in their lives can be predicted by their day-to-day relationship to the position of the planets. However, no serious evidence has ever confirmed such a connection.

Comments

The supernatural tradition in psychopathology is alive and well, although it is relegated, for the most part, to some cultures outside North America and to small religious sects within North America. Members of organized religions in most parts of the world look to psychology and medical science for help with major psychological disorders; in fact, the Roman Catholic Church requires that all health care resources be exhausted before spiritual solutions such as exorcism can be considered. Nonetheless, miraculous cures are sometimes achieved by exorcism, magic potions, rituals, and other

▲ In hydrotherapy, patients were shocked back to their senses by being submerged in ice-cold water.

methods that seem to have little connection with modern science. It is fascinating to explore them when they do occur, and we return to this topic in subsequent chapters. But such cases are relatively rare, and almost no one would advocate supernatural treatment for severe psychological disorders except, perhaps, as a last resort.

The Biological Tradition

Physical causes of mental disorders have been sought since early in history. Important to the biological tradition are a man, Hippocrates; a disease, syphilis; and the early consequences of believing that psychological disorders are biologically caused.

Hippocrates and Galen

The Greek physician Hippocrates (460–377 B.C.E.) is considered the father of modern medicine. He and his associates left a body of work called the *Hippocratic Corpus*, written between 450 B.C.E. and 350 B.C.E. (Maher & Maher, 1985a), in which they suggested that psychological disorders could be treated like any other disease. They did not limit their search for the causes of psychopathology to the general area of "disease," because they believed that psychological disorders might also be caused by brain pathology or head trauma and could be influenced by heredity (genetics). These were remarkably astute deductions for the time, and they have been supported in recent years. Hippocrates considered the brain to be the seat of wisdom, consciousness, intelligence, and emotion. Therefore, disorders involving these functions would logically be located in the brain. Hippocrates also recognized the importance of psychological and interpersonal contributions to psychopathology, such as the sometimes negative effects of family stress; on some occasions, he removed patients from their families.

The Roman physician Galen (ca. 129–198 C.E.) later adopted the ideas of Hippocrates and his associates and developed them further, creating a powerful and influential school of thought

within the biological tradition that extended well into the 19th century. One of the more interesting and influential legacies of the Hippocratic-Galenic approach is the *humoral theory* of disorders. Hippocrates assumed that normal brain functioning was related to four bodily fluids, or *humors:* blood, black bile, yellow bile, and phlegm. Blood came from the heart, black bile from the spleen, phlegm from the brain, and choler or yellow bile from the liver. Physicians believed that disease resulted from too much or too little of one of the humors; for example, too much black bile was thought to cause melancholia (depression). In fact, the term *melancholer*, which means black bile, is still used today in its derivative form *melancholy* to refer to aspects of depression. The humoral theory was, perhaps, the first example of associating psychological disorders with chemical imbalance, an approach that is widespread today.

The four humors were related to the Greeks' conception of the four basic qualities: heat, dryness, moisture, and cold. Each humor was associated with one of these qualities. Terms derived from the four humors are still sometimes applied to personality traits. For example, *sanguine* (red, like blood) describes someone who is ruddy in complexion—presumably from copious blood flowing through the body—and cheerful and optimistic, though insomnia and delirium were thought to be caused by excessive blood in the brain. *Melancholic*, of course, refers to a depressive personality (depression was thought to be caused by black bile flooding the brain). A *phlegmatic personality* (from the humor phlegm) indicates apathy and sluggishness but can also mean being calm under stress. A *choleric* person (from yellow bile or choler) is hot tempered (Maher & Maher, 1985a).

Excesses of one or more humors were treated by regulating the environment to increase or decrease heat, dryness, moisture, or cold, depending on which humor was out of balance. One reason King Charles VI's physician moved him to the less stressful countryside was to restore the balance in his humors (Kemp, 1990). In addition to rest, good nutrition, and exercise, two treatments were developed. In *bleeding* or *bloodletting*, a carefully measured amount of blood was removed from the body, often with leeches. In the other, vomiting was induced; indeed, in a well-known treatise on depression published in 1621, *Anatomy of Melancholy*, Burton recommended eating tobacco and a half-boiled cabbage to induce vomiting (Burton, 1621/1977). Three hundred years ago, under the influence of early biological traditions, Jody might have been diagnosed with an illness, a brain disorder, or some other physical problem and given the proper medical treatments of the day, including bed rest, a healthful diet, exercise, and other ministrations as indicated.

Hippocrates also coined the word *hysteria* to describe a concept he learned about from the Egyptians, who had identified what we now call the *somatoform disorders* (see Chapter 6). In these disorders, the physical symptoms appear to be the result of an organic pathology for which no organic cause can be found, such as

▲ Bloodletting, the extraction of blood from patients, was intended to restore the balance of humors in the body.

paralysis and some kinds of blindness. Because these disorders occurred primarily in women, the Egyptians (and Hippocrates) mistakenly assumed that they were restricted to women. They also presumed a cause: The empty uterus wandered to various parts of the body in search of conception (the Greek for "uterus" is *hysteron*). Numerous physical symptoms reflected the location of the wandering uterus. The prescribed cure might be marriage or, occasionally, fumigation of the vagina to lure the uterus back to its natural location (Alexander & Selesnick, 1966). Knowledge of physiology eventually disproved the wandering uterus theory; however, the tendency to stigmatize dramatic women as "hysterical" continued unabated well into the 1970s, when mental health professionals became sensitive to the prejudicial stereotype the term implied.

The 19th Century

The biological tradition waxed and waned during the centuries after Hippocrates and Galen, but was reinvigorated in the 19th century by two factors: the discovery of the nature and cause of syphilis, and strong support from the well-respected American psychiatrist John P. Grey.

Syphilis

Behavioural and cognitive symptoms of what we now know as advanced syphilis include believing that everyone is plotting against you (delusion of persecution) or that you are God (delusion of grandeur), as well as other bizarre behaviours. Although these symptoms are very similar to those of psychosis, researchers recognized that a subgroup of apparently psychotic patients deteriorated steadily, becoming paralyzed and dying within five years of onset. This course of events contrasted with that of most psychotic patients, who remained fairly stable. In 1825, the condition was designated a disease, *general paresis*, because it had consistent symptoms (presentation) and a consistent course that resulted in death. The relationship between general paresis and syphilis was only gradually established. Louis Pasteur's germ theory of disease, around 1870, facilitated the identification of the specific bacterial micro-organism that caused syphilis. Pasteur stated that all the symptoms of a disease were caused by a germ (bacterium) that had invaded the body.

Of equal importance was the discovery of a cure for general paresis. Physicians observed a surprising recovery in patients who had contracted malaria and deliberately injected others with blood from a soldier who was ill with malaria. Many recovered, because the high fever "burned out" the syphilis bacteria. Obviously, this type of experiment would not be ethically possible today. Ultimately, clinical investigators discovered that penicillin cures syphilis, but the malaria cure convinced many for the first time that "madness" and associated behavioural and cognitive symptoms could be traced directly to a curable infection. Many mental health professionals then assumed that comparable causes and cures might be discovered for all psychological disorders.

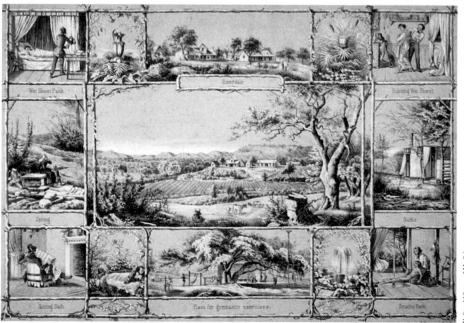

▲ In the 19th century, psychological disorders were attributed to mental or emotional stress, so patients were often treated sympathetically in a restful and hygienic environment.

The Biological Tradition　**13**

John P. Grey

The champion of the biological tradition in North America was a very influential psychiatrist named John P. Grey, who was appointed superintendent of a large hospital in New York in 1854 (Bockoven, 1963). Grey also became editor of the *American Journal of Insanity*, the precursor of the current *American Journal of Psychiatry*, and the flagship publication of the American Psychiatric Association. Grey's position was that insanity always has physical causes. Therefore, the mentally ill patient should be treated as physically ill. The emphasis was once again on rest, diet, and proper room temperature and ventilation, approaches used for centuries by previous therapists in the biological tradition. Grey even invented the rotary fan in order to ventilate his large hospital.

Under Grey's leadership, the conditions in hospitals greatly improved, and they became more humane, livable institutions. But in subsequent years they also became so large and impersonal that individual attention was not possible.

In fact, leaders in psychiatry at the end of the 19th century were alarmed at the increasing size and impersonality of mental hospitals and recommended that they be downsized. It was almost 100 years before the community mental health movement was successful in reducing the population of mental hospitals with the very controversial policy of deinstitutionalization, in which patients were released into their communities. Unfortunately, this practice had as many negative consequences as positive ones, including a large increase in the number of patients with chronic disabilities left homeless on the streets of our cities.

The Development of Biological Treatments

On the positive side, renewed interest in the biological origin of psychological disorders led, ultimately, to an increased understanding of the biological contributions to psychopathology and to the development of new treatments. In the 1930s, the physical interventions of electric shock and brain surgery were often used. Their effects, and the effects of new drugs, were discovered quite by accident. For example, insulin was occasionally given to stimulate appetite in psychotic patients who were not eating, but it also seemed to calm them down. In 1927, a Viennese physician, Manfred Sakel, began using higher and higher dosages until, finally, patients convulsed and became temporarily comatose (Sakel, 1958). Some actually recovered their mental health, much to the surprise of everybody, and their recovery was attributed to the convulsions. The procedure became known as *insulin shock therapy*, but it was abandoned because it was too dangerous, often resulting in prolonged coma or even death. Other methods of producing convulsions had to be found.

In the 1920s, Joseph von Meduna observed that schizophrenia was very rarely found in epileptics (which ultimately did not prove to be true). Some of his followers concluded that induced brain seizures might cure schizophrenia. Following suggestions on the possible benefits of applying electric shock directly to the brain—notably, by two Italian physicians, Cerletti and Bini, in 1938—a surgeon in London treated a depressed patient by sending six small shocks directly through his brain, producing convulsions (Hunt, 1980). The patient recovered. Though greatly modified, shock treatment is still with us today. The controversial modern uses of *electroconvulsive therapy* (ECT) are described in Chapter 7. It is interesting that even now we have very little knowledge of how ECT works.

During the 1950s, the first effective drugs for severe psychotic disorders were developed in a systematic way, and they were introduced to Canada by psychiatrist Heinz Lehman. Before that time, a number of medicinal substances, including opium (derived from poppies), had been used as sedatives, along with countless herbs and folk remedies (Alexander & Selesnick, 1966). With the discovery of *Rauwolfia serpentina* (later renamed *reserpine*) and another class of drugs called neuroleptics (major tranquilizers), for the first time hallucinatory and delusional thought processes could be diminished; these drugs also controlled agitation and aggressiveness. Other discoveries included *benzodiazepines* (minor tranquilizers), which seemed to reduce anxiety. By the 1970s, the benzodiazepines (known by such brand names as Valium and Librium) were among the most widely prescribed drugs in the world. As drawbacks and side effects of tranquilizers became apparent, along with their limited effectiveness, the number of prescriptions decreased somewhat (we discuss the benzodiazepines in more detail in Chapters 5 and 11).

Throughout the centuries, as Alexander and Selesnick (1966, p. 287) point out, "The general pattern of drug therapy for mental illness has been one of initial enthusiasm followed by disappointment." For example, bromides, a class of sedating drugs, were used at the end of the 19th and the beginning of the 20th centuries to treat anxiety and other psychological disorders. By the 1920s they were reported as being effective for many serious psychological and emotional symptoms. By 1928, one of every five prescriptions in the United States was for bromides. When their side effects, including various undesirable physical symptoms, became widely known, and experience began to show that their overall effectiveness was relatively modest, bromides largely disappeared from the scene.

Neuroleptics were also used less when attention focused on their many side effects, such as tremors and shaking. However, the positive effects of these drugs on some patients' psychotic symptoms of hallucinations, delusions, and agitation revitalized both the search for biological contributions to psychological disorders and the search for new and more powerful drugs, a search that has paid many dividends, as documented in later chapters.

Consequences of the Biological Tradition

In the late 19th century, John P. Grey and his colleagues, ironically, reduced or eliminated interest in treating patients with mental illnesses because they thought mental disorders were due to some as yet undiscovered brain pathology and were therefore incurable. The only available course of action was to hospitalize these patients. In fact, around the turn of the 20th century, some nurses documented clinical success in treating mental patients with psychological methods but were prevented from treating others for fear of raising hopes of a cure among family members. In place of treatment, interest centred on diagnosis, legal questions concerning the responsibility of patients for their actions during periods of insanity, and the study of brain pathology itself.

Emil Kraepelin (1856–1926) was the dominant figure during this period and one of the founding fathers of modern psychiatry. He was extremely influential in advocating the major ideas of the biological tradition, but he was little involved in treatment, reflecting the belief that disorders were due to brain pathology. His lasting contribution was in the area of diagnosis and classification, which we discuss in detail in Chapter 3. Kraepelin (1913) was one of the first to distinguish among various psychological disorders, seeing that each may have a different age of onset and course, with somewhat different clusters of presenting symptoms and probably a different cause. Many of his descriptions of schizophrenic disorders are still useful today.

By the end of the 19th century, a scientific approach to psychological disorders and their classification had begun with the search for biological causes. Furthermore, treatment was based on humane principles. However, there were many drawbacks, the most unfortunate being that active intervention and treatment were all but eliminated in some settings, despite the fact that some very effective approaches were available. It is to these that we now turn.

Concept Check | 1.3

For thousands of years, humans have tried to understand and control abnormal behaviour. Check your understanding of these historical theories and match them to the treatments used to "cure" abnormal behaviour: (a) marriage; fumigation of the vagina; (b) hypnosis; (c) bloodletting; induced vomiting; (d) patient placed in socially facilitative environments; and (e) exorcism; burning at the stake.

1. Supernatural causes; evil demons took over the victims' bodies and controlled their behaviours. _____

2. The humoral theory reflected the belief that normal functioning of the brain required a balance of four bodily fluids, or humors. _____

3. Maladaptive behaviour was caused by poor social and cultural influences within the environment. _____

The Psychological Tradition

It is a long leap from evil spirits to brain pathology as causes of psychological disorders. In the intervening centuries, where was the body of thought that put psychological development, both normal and abnormal, in an interpersonal and social context? In fact, this approach has a long and distinguished tradition. Plato, for example, thought that the two causes of maladaptive behaviour were the social and cultural influences in a person's life and the learning that took place in that environment. If something was wrong in the environment, such as abusive parents, a person's impulses and emotions would overcome reason. The best treatment was to reeducate the individual through rational discussion so that the power of reason would predominate (Maher & Maher, 1985a). This approach was very much a precursor to modern **psychosocial** approaches, which focus not only on

psychological factors but also on social and cultural ones. Other well-known early philosophers, including Aristotle, also emphasized the influence of the social environment and early learning on later psychopathology. These philosophers wrote about the importance of fantasies, dreams, and cognitions and thus anticipated, to some extent, later developments in psychoanalytic thought and cognitive science. They also advocated humane and responsible care for people with psychological disturbances.

Moral Therapy

During the first half of the 18th century, a strong psychosocial approach to mental disorders called **moral therapy** became influential (Taubes, 1998). The term *moral* really meant "emotional" or "psychological" rather than a code of conduct. Its basic tenets included treating institutionalized patients as normally as possible in a setting that encouraged and reinforced normal social interaction (Bockoven, 1963; Taubes, 1998), thus providing them with many opportunities for appropriate social and interpersonal contact. Relationships were carefully nurtured. Individual attention clearly emphasized positive consequences for appropriate interactions and behaviour; the staff made a point of modelling this behaviour. Lectures on various interesting subjects were provided, and restraint and seclusion were eliminated.

Once again, these are old ideas. The principles of moral therapy date back to Plato and beyond. But moral therapy as a system originated with the well-known French psychiatrist Philippe Pinel (1745–1826; Zilboorg & Henry, 1941). A former patient, Pussin, long since recovered, was working in the Parisian hospital La Bicêtre when Pinel took over. Pussin had already instituted remarkable reforms, remembering, perhaps, being shackled as a patient himself. Pussin persuaded Pinel to go along with the

▲ Patients with psychological disorders were freed from chains and shackles as a result of the influence of Philippe Pinel (1745–1826), a pioneer in making mental institutions more humane.

changes. Much to Pinel's credit, he did, first at La Bicêtre and then at the women's hospital Salpétrière (Maher & Maher, 1985b; Weiner, 1979), where a humane, socially facilitative atmosphere produced "miraculous" results.

After William Tuke (1732–1822) followed Pinel's lead in England, Benjamin Rush (1745–1813), often considered the founder of North American psychiatry, introduced moral therapy to the New World. It then became the treatment of choice in the leading hospitals. Asylums had appeared in the 16th century in Europe, with the intent of providing places of refuge for the confinement and care of people with mental illnesses. However, these early asylums were more like prisons than hospitals. Many housed beggars as well as people with a variety of mental illnesses, conditions were often deplorable, and little was provided to patients in the way of treatment regimens. It was the rise of moral therapy in Europe and North America that made institutions habitable and even therapeutic.

Sussman (1998) provides a description of the history of the development of asylums in Canada in the 19th century. He notes that institutionalizing people with mental illnesses in Canada began with humane intentions, to relieve the suffering and neglect of these individuals who had previously been placed in jails or poorhouses, or left to care for themselves in the community. The provinces proceeded relatively independently to develop separate and more adequate provisions for people with mental illness in the form of mental hospitals or "asylums" (see Table 1.2 for a summary). Asylum development in most provinces was influenced to a great extent by systems and movements in Great Britain and to a lesser extent by those in the United States. The involvement of religious orders in the care of people with mental illnesses in Québec was influenced by practices occurring in France. According to Sussman (1998), the development of asylums through the moral therapy movement did bring some relief to many people with mental illnesses.

Asylum Reform and the Decline of Moral Therapy

Unfortunately, after the mid-19th century, humane treatment declined because of a convergence of factors. First, it was widely recognized that moral therapy worked best when the number of patients in an institution was 200 or fewer, allowing for a great deal of individual attention. However, patient loads in existing hospitals increased to 1000, 2000, and more with the enormous waves of immigrants arriving in North America at the time.

A second reason for the decline of moral therapy has an unlikely source. The great crusader Dorothea Dix (1802–1887) campaigned endlessly for reform in the treatment of the insane throughout Canada and the United States. A schoolteacher who had worked in various institutions, she had firsthand knowledge of the deplorable conditions imposed on people with mental disorders, and she made it her life's work to inform the public and their leaders of these abuses. Her work became known as the **mental hygiene movement**.

According to Hurd, Drewry, Dewey, Pilgrim, Blumer, and Burgess (1916), Dix visited Canada in 1843 and 1844 and discovered appalling conditions involving the incarceration of "lunatics" at Beauport in Québec and in the Toronto Jail. She was involved in the construction of the asylum in St. John's, Newfoundland, in 1854. Probably most notable of her contributions to the mental hygiene movement in Canada was her appeal to the Nova Scotia Legislature in January 1850, when she described the deplorable conditions for people with mental illnesses at the time and argued for the development of an asylum in Nova Scotia:

> In imagination, for a short time, place yourselves in their stead:
> enter the horrid, noisome cell, invest yourselves with the foul,
> tattered garments which scantily serve the purposes of decent
> protection; cast yourselves upon the loathsome pile of filthy straw;
> find companionship in your own cries and groans, or in the
> wailings and gibberings of wretches miserable like yourselves; call

▲ Dorothea Dix (1802–1887) began the mental hygiene movement and spent much of her life campaigning in the United States and Canada for reform in the treatment of people with mental illnesses.

TABLE 1.2 Development of the First Asylums in Canada

Province	Date	Notes
Québec	1845	Beauport, or the Québec Lunatic Asylum, was opened.
New Brunswick	1847	The Provincial Lunatic Asylum was erected.
Ontario	1850	The Provincial Lunatic Asylum in Toronto admitted patients.
Newfoundland	1854	An asylum was erected and admitted its first patients.
Nova Scotia	1857	The first patients were admitted to the Provincial Hospital for the Insane.
Prince Edward Island	1877	The Prince Edward Island Hospital for the Insane was built.
Manitoba	1886	The Selkirk Lunatic Asylum admitted patients.
Saskatchewan	1911	The Saskatchewan Provincial Hospital admitted its first patients.
Alberta	1914	The Insane Asylum in Ponoka was opened.

Source: Adapted from Table 1 of: Sussman, S. "The First Asylums in Canada: A Response to Neglectful Community Care and Current Trends." *Canadian Journal of Psychiatry* 1998; 43(3):260-264.

for help and release, for blessed words or soothing and kind offices of care, till the dull walls are weary in sending back the echo of your moans; then, if self-possession is not overwhelmed under the imaginary miseries of what are the actual distresses of the insane, return to the consciousness of your sound intellectual health, and answer if you will longer refuse or delay to make adequate appropriations for the establishment of a provincial hospital for those who are deprived of reason, and thereby of all that gladdens life or makes existence a blessing. (Hurd et al., 1916, p. 493)

In addition to improving the standards of care, Dix worked hard to make sure that everyone who needed care received it, including homeless people. Through her efforts, humane treatment became more widely available in North American institutions. As her career drew to a close, she was rightly acknowledged as a hero of the 19th century.

Unfortunately, an unforeseen consequence of Dix's heroic efforts was a substantial increase in the number of mental patients. This influx led to a rapid transition from moral therapy to custodial care because hospitals were inadequately staffed. Dix reformed asylums and single-handedly inspired the construction of numerous new institutions. But even her tireless efforts and advocacy could not ensure sufficient staffing to allow the individual attention necessary for effective moral therapy. Unfortunately, institutionalization in Canada eventually "became a synonym for an inhumane response to mentally ill people" (Sussman, 1998, p. 262), often because resources were insufficient to provide adequate care.

An important mental health reformer and crusader who followed Dix's example was Clarence Hincks, a University of Toronto medical school graduate who cofounded the Canadian Committee for Mental Hygiene in 1918. Early in his career, he toured mental institutions throughout Manitoba. In his unpublished autobiography and his report to the Manitoba government, Hincks documented continued appalling conditions for the people with mental illnesses in these institutions (Griffin, 1989; Roland, 1990). Hincks often found that those working in institutions—including the superintendents—had no special psychiatric training. In one case there was only one doctor in charge of 700 patients, and he also acted as the superintendent. In one institution in Portage La Prairie, Hincks encountered a woman who had been left in a closet for two years, and had only been allowed out once, and then within the confines of a cage. Hincks noted that some of the institutions were not even meant for those with mental illness, but had come to house them anyway despite having no methods for caring for them. At another Manitoban institution, he discovered that mentally ill patients were locked into coffin-like boxes at night to sleep, and in another, "mentally defective" children were rolled in long strips of cotton at night, with their arms and legs bound, and then placed on shelves to sleep. Hincks had himself experienced and recovered from a bout of major depression while in university. His personal experience in recovering from depression led him to advocate for the idea that mental illness was treatable. Hincks's position stood in contrast to the prevailing view at the time that mental illness was incurable. In fact, one Manitoba institution that Hincks visited in 1918 in Portage La Prairie was named the "Home for Incurables" (Roland 1990).

A final blow to the practice of moral therapy, mentioned earlier, was the decision, in the middle of the 19th century, that mental illness was caused by brain pathology and, therefore, was incurable.

The psychological tradition lay dormant for a time, only to reemerge in several very different schools of thought in the 20th century. The first major approach was **psychoanalysis**, based on Sigmund Freud's (1856–1939) elaborate theory of the structure of the mind and the role of unconscious processes in determining behaviour. The second was **behaviourism**, associated with John B. Watson, Ivan Pavlov, and B. F. Skinner, which focuses on how learning and adaptation affect the development of psychopathology.

From *In Search of Sanity: A Chronicle of the Canadian Mental Health Association 1918-1988* by John D. Griffin MD, MA, DPM(E), FRCP(C). Reprinted with permission of the Canadian Mental Health Association

▲ Clarence Hincks (1885–1964) was an early crusader for the mental hygiene movement in Canada. He cofounded the Canadian National Committee for Mental Hygiene in 1918—a precursor to today's Canadian Mental Health Association.

Psychoanalytic Theory

Have you ever felt as if someone had cast a spell on you? Have you ever been mesmerized by a look across a room from an attractive woman or man, or a stare from a rock musician as you sat in front at a concert? If so, you have something in common with the patients of Austrian physician Anton Mesmer (1734–1815) and with millions of people since his time who have been hypnotized. Mesmer suggested to his patients that their problem was due to an undetectable fluid found in all living organisms called "animal magnetism" that could become blocked. Mesmer had his patients sit in a dark room around a large vat of chemicals with rods extending from it and touching the patients. Dressed in flowing robes, he might then identify and tap various areas of their bodies where their animal magnetism was blocked while suggesting strongly that they were being cured. Because of his rather unusual techniques, Mesmer was considered an oddity and maybe a charlatan and was strongly opposed by the medical establishment (Winter, 1998).

Benjamin Franklin put animal magnetism to the test by conducting a brilliant experiment in which patients received either magnetized water or nonmagnetized water with strong suggestions that they would get better. Neither the patient nor the therapist knew which water was which, making it a "double-blind" experiment (see Chapter 4). When both groups got better, Franklin concluded that animal magnetism, or mesmerism, was nothing more than strong suggestion (Gould, 1990; McNally, 1999). Nevertheless, Mesmer is widely regarded as the father of hypnosis, a state in which suggestible subjects sometimes appear to be in a trance.

Many distinguished scientists and physicians were very interested in Mesmer's powerful methods of suggestion. One of the best known, Jean Charcot (1825–1893), was head of the

The Psychological Tradition   **17**

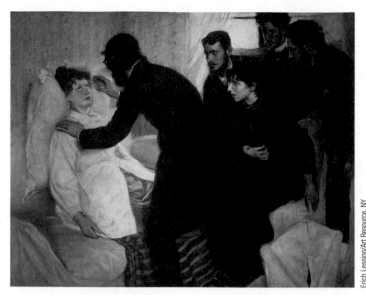

▲ Anton Mesmer (1734–1815) and other early therapists used strong suggestions to cure their patients, who were often hypnotized.

▲ Josef Breuer (1842–1925) worked on the celebrated case of Anna O. and, with Freud, developed the theory of psychoanalysis.

Salpétrière Hospital in Paris, where Philippe Pinel had introduced psychological treatments several generations earlier. A distinguished neurologist, Charcot demonstrated that some of the techniques of mesmerism were effective with several psychological disorders, and he did much to legitimize the fledgling practice of hypnosis while doing away with the flowing robes and chemicals. Significantly, in 1885 a young man named Sigmund Freud came from Vienna to study with Charcot.

After returning from France, Freud teamed up with Josef Breuer (1842–1925), who had experimented with a somewhat different hypnotic procedure. While his patients were in the highly suggestible state of hypnosis, Breuer asked them to describe their problems, conflicts, and fears in as much detail as they could. Breuer observed two extremely important phenomena during this process. First, patients often became extremely emotional as they talked and felt quite relieved and improved after emerging from the hypnotic state. Second, seldom would patients have gained an understanding of the relationship between their emotional problems and their psychological disorder. In fact, it was difficult or impossible for them to recall some of the details they had described under hypnosis. In other words, the material seemed to be beyond the awareness of the patient. With this observation, Breuer and Freud had "discovered" the **unconscious** mind and its apparent influence on the production of psychological disorders. This discovery is one of the most important developments in the history of psychology as a whole.

A close second was their discovery that recalling and reliving emotional trauma that has been made unconscious and releasing the accompanying tension is therapeutic—a process that became known as **catharsis**. A fuller understanding of the relationship between current emotions and earlier events is called *insight*. As we see throughout this book, particularly in Chapters 5 and 6 on anxiety and somatoform disorders, the existence of unconscious memories and feelings and the importance of processing emotion-laden information have been verified and reaffirmed.

Freud and Breuer's theories were based on systematic case observations. An excellent example is Breuer's classic description of his treatment of "hysterical" symptoms in Anna O. in 1895 (Breuer & Freud, 1957). Anna O. was a young woman who was perfectly healthy until she turned 21. Shortly before her problems began, her father developed a serious chronic illness that led to his death. Throughout his illness, Anna O. had cared for him, spending hours at his bedside. Five months after her father became ill, Anna noticed that during the day her vision blurred and periodically she had difficulty moving her right arm and both legs. Soon, she began to experience some difficulty speaking, and her behaviour became very erratic. Shortly thereafter, she consulted Breuer.

In a series of treatment sessions, Breuer dealt with one symptom at a time through hypnosis and subsequent "talking through," tracing each symptom to its hypothetical

▲ Jean Charcot (1825–1893) studied hypnosis and influenced Sigmund Freud to consider psychosocial approaches to psychological disorders.

▲ Bertha Pappenheim (1859–1936), famous as Anna O., was described as "hysterical" by Breuer.

causation in circumstances surrounding the death of Anna's father. One at a time her "hysterical" ailments disappeared, but only after treatment was administered to each respective behaviour. This process of treating one behaviour at a time fulfills a basic requirement for drawing scientific conclusions about the effects of treatment in an individual case study, as we see in Chapter 4.

Freud took these basic observations and expanded them into the **psychoanalytic model**, the most comprehensive theory yet constructed on the development and structure of our personalities. He also speculated on where this development could go wrong and produce psychological disorders.

Although most of it remains unproven, psychoanalytic theory has had a strong influence, and it is important to be familiar with its basic ideas; what follows is a brief outline of the theory. We focus on its three major facets: (1) *the structure of the mind* and the distinct functions of personality that sometimes clash with one another; (2) *the defence mechanisms* with which the mind defends itself from these clashes or conflicts; and (3) the *stages of early psychosexual development* that provide grist for the mill of our inner conflicts.

The Structure of the Mind

The mind, according to Freud, has three major parts or functions: the id, ego, and superego (see ■ Figure 1.4). These terms, like many from psychoanalysis, have found their way into our common vocabulary, and although you may have heard them, you may not be fully aware of their meaning. The **id** is the source of our strong sexual and aggressive energies or our instinctual drives—the "animal" within us. The positive energy or drive within the id is the libido. Even today some people explain low sex drive as an absence of *libido*. A less important source of energy is the death instinct, or *thanatos*. Much like matter and antimatter, these two basic drives toward life and dominance and fulfillment on the one hand, and death and destruction on the other, are continually in opposition.

▲ Sigmund Freud (1856–1939) is considered the founder of psychoanalysis.

The id operates according to the *pleasure principle*, with an overriding goal of maximizing pleasure and eliminating any associated tension or conflicts. The goal of pleasure, which is particularly prominent in childhood, often conflicts with social rules and regulations, as we see later. The id has its own characteristic way of processing information; referred to as primary process, this type of thinking is very emotional, irrational, illogical, led with fantasies, and preoccupied with sex, aggression, selfishness, and envy.

Fortunately for all of us, in Freud's view, the id's selfish and sometimes dangerous drives do not go unchecked. In fact, only a few months into life, we know we must adapt our basic demands to the real world; we must find ways to meet our basic needs without offending everyone around us. The part of our mind that ensures we act realistically is called the **ego**, and it operates according to the *reality principle* instead of the pleasure principle. The cognitive operations or thinking styles of the ego, characterized by logic and reason, are referred to as the *secondary process*, as opposed to the illogical and irrational primary process of the id.

The third important structure within the mind, the **superego**, or what we might call the *conscience*, represents the *moral principles* instilled in us by our parents and our culture. It is the voice within us that nags at us when we know we're doing something wrong. Because the purpose of the superego is to counteract the aggressive and sexual drives of the id that are potentially dangerous, the basis for conflict is readily apparent.

The role of the ego is to mediate conflict between the id and the superego, juggling their demands with the realities of the world. The ego is often called the executive or manager of our minds. If it mediates successfully, we can go on to the higher intellectual and creative pursuits of life. If it is unsuccessful, and the id or the superego becomes too strong, conflict will overtake us and psychological disorders will develop. Because these conflicts are all within the mind, they are called **intrapsychic conflicts**. Finally, Freud believed the id and the superego are almost

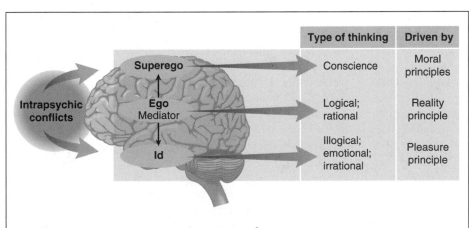

	Type of thinking	Driven by
Superego	Conscience	Moral principles
Ego Mediator	Logical; rational	Reality principle
Id	Illogical; emotional; irrational	Pleasure principle

Intrapsychic conflicts

■ **FIGURE 1.4** Freud's structure of the mind

Go to www.abnormalpsych3e.nelson.com to access an interactive version of this figure.

The Psychological Tradition **19**

entirely unconscious. We are fully aware only of the secondary processes of the ego, which is a relatively small part of the mind.

Defence Mechanisms

The ego fights a continual battle to stay on top of the warring id and superego. Occasionally, their conflicts produce anxiety that threatens to overwhelm the ego. The anxiety is a signal that alerts the ego to marshal **defence mechanisms**, unconscious protective processes that keep primitive emotions associated with conflicts in check so the ego can continue its coordinating function. Although Freud first conceptualized defence mechanisms, it was his daughter, Anna Freud, who developed the ideas more fully.

We all use defence mechanisms at times—sometimes they are adaptive and sometimes they are maladaptive. For example, have you ever done poorly on a test because the professor was unfair in the grading? And then when you got home, you yelled at your brother or perhaps at your dog? This is an example of the defence mechanism of displacement. The ego adaptively "decides" that expressing primitive anger at your professor might not be in your best interest. Because your brother and your dog don't have the authority to affect you in an adverse way, your anger is displaced to one of them. Indeed, the *DSM-IV-TR* includes an axis of defence mechanisms in the appendix. Here are some examples of defence mechanisms (adapted from the *DSM-IV-TR*, American Psychiatric Association, 2000a):

- *Denial*: Refuses to acknowledge some aspect of objective reality or subjective experience that is apparent to others (e.g., a person not facing the fact that a romantic relationship is over).
- *Displacement*: Transfers a feeling about, or a response to, an object that causes discomfort onto another, usually less threatening, object or person (e.g., kicking the dog when actually angry with a teacher).
- *Projection*: Falsely attributes own unacceptable feelings, impulses, or thoughts to another individual or object (e.g., a man with sexual feelings toward a certain woman thinks that woman is "coming on" to him).
- *Rationalization*: Conceals the true motivations for actions, thoughts, or feelings through elaborate reassuring or self-serving but incorrect explanations (e.g., after not getting into a certain graduate school, an aspiring graduate student decides that school was not really where she wanted to study after all).
- *Reaction formation*: Substitutes behaviour, thoughts, or feelings that are the direct opposite of unacceptable ones (e.g., a man with sexual feelings toward children crusades against child pornography).
- *Repression*: Blocks disturbing wishes, thoughts, or experiences from conscious awareness (e.g., a person "forgets" about an embarrassing experience).
- *Sublimation*: Directs potentially maladaptive feelings or impulses into socially acceptable behaviour (e.g., redirecting energy from underlying conflict into artistic expression and achievement).

Defence mechanisms have actually been subjected to scientific study, and some evidence indicates they may be of potential importance in the study of psychopathology and health (MacGregor, Davidson, Rowan, Barksdale, & MacLean, 2003; McGregor, Zanna, Holmes, & Spencer, 2001; Vaillant, Bond, &

Vaillant, 1986). For example, different psychological disorders seem to be associated with different defence mechanisms (Pollack & Andrews, 1989), which might be important in planning treatment. Vaillant (1976) noted that healthy defence mechanisms, such as humour and sublimation, were correlated with psychological health. Thus, the concept of defence mechanisms— "coping styles," in contemporary terminology—continues to be important to the study of psychopathology.

Psychosexual Stages of Development

Freud also theorized that during infancy and early childhood, we pass through several **psychosexual stages of development** that have a profound and lasting impact, thus providing the first developmental perspective on abnormal behaviour. The stages—oral, anal, phallic, latency, and genital—represent distinctive patterns of gratifying our basic needs and satisfying our drive for physical pleasure. For example, the oral stage, typically extending for approximately two years from birth, is characterized by a central focus on the need for food. In the act of sucking, necessary for feeding, the lips, tongue, and mouth become the focus of libidinal drives and, therefore, the principal source of pleasure. Freud hypothesized that, if we did not receive appropriate gratification during a specific stage or if a specific stage left a particularly strong impression (which he termed *fixation*), an individual's personality would reflect the stage throughout adult life. For example, fixation at the oral stage might result in excessive thumb sucking and emphasis on oral stimulation through eating, chewing pencils, or biting fingernails. Adult personality characteristics theoretically associated with oral fixation include dependency and passivity or, in reaction to these tendencies, rebelliousness and cynicism.

One of the more controversial and frequently mentioned psychosexual conflicts occurs during the phallic stage (from age three to age five or six), which is characterized by early genital self-stimulation. This conflict is the subject of the Greek tragedy *Oedipus Rex*, in which Oedipus is fated to kill his father and, unknowingly, to marry his mother. Freud asserted that all young boys relive this fantasy when genital self-stimulation is accompanied by images of sexual interactions with their mothers. These fantasies, in turn, are accompanied by strong feelings of envy and perhaps anger toward their fathers, with whom they identify but whose place they want to take. Furthermore, strong fears develop that the father may punish that lust by removing the son's penis—thus, the phenomenon of castration anxiety. This fear helps the boy keep his lustful impulses toward his mother in check. The battle of the lustful impulses on the one hand and castration anxiety on the other creates a conflict that is internal, or intrapsychic, called the *Oedipus complex*. The phallic stage passes uneventfully only if several things happen. First, the child must resolve his ambivalent relationship with his parents and reconcile the simultaneous anger and love he has for his father. If this happens, he may go on to channel his libidinal impulses into heterosexual relationships while retaining harmless affection for his mother. Development of the superego is another consequence of successfully resolving this conflict.

The counterpart conflict in girls, called the *Electra complex*, is even more controversial. Freud viewed the young girl as wanting to replace her mother and possess her father. Central to this possession is the girl's desire for a penis, so as to be more like her father and brothers—hence the term *penis envy*. According to Freud, the conflict is partially resolved when females develop healthy heterosexual relationships and look forward to having a baby, which he viewed as a healthy substitute for having a penis. It is the partial resolution of the Electra complex, resulting in a less highly developed superego, that makes females (in Freud's theory) less highly developed psychologically than are males. Needless to say, this particular theory has provoked marked consternation over the years as being sexist and demeaning. It is important to remember that it is theory, not fact; no systematic research exists to support it.

In Freud's view, all nonpsychotic psychological disorders resulted from underlying unconscious conflicts, the anxiety that resulted from those conflicts, and the implementation of ego defence mechanisms. Freud called such disorders **neuroses**, or *neurotic disorders*, from an old term referring to disorders of the nervous system.

Later Developments in Psychoanalytic Thought

Freud's original psychoanalytic theories have been greatly modified and developed in many different directions, mostly by his students or followers.

Anna Freud (1895–1982), Freud's daughter, concentrated on the way in which the defensive reactions of the ego determine our behaviour. In so doing, she was the first proponent of the modern field of **ego psychology** or self-psychology. Her book *Ego and the Mechanisms of Defense* (1946) is still influential. According to Anna Freud, the individual slowly accumulates adaptational capacities, skill in reality testing, and defences. Abnormal behaviour develops when the ego is deficient in regulating such functions as delaying and controlling impulses, or in marshalling appropriate normal defences to strong internal conflicts.

A related area that is quite popular today is referred to as object relations. In this school of thought are theorists Melanie Klein and Otto Kernberg. Kernberg's work on borderline personality disorder, in which some behaviour borders on being out of touch with reality and thus psychotic, has been widely applied (see Chapter 12). **Object relations** is the study of how children incorporate the images, memories, and sometimes the values of a person who was very important to them and to whom they were (or are) emotionally attached. *Object* in this sense refers to these important people, and the process of incorporation is called *introjection*. Introjected objects can become an integrated part of the ego or may assume conflicting roles in determining the identity, or self. For example, your parents may have conflicting views on relationships or careers, which, in turn, may be different from your own partly developed point of view. To the extent that these varying positions have been incorporated, the potential for conflict arises. One day you may feel one way about your career direction, and the next day you may feel quite differently. According to object relations theory, you tend to see the world through the eyes of the person incorporated into your self. Object relations theorists focus on how these disparate images come together to make up a person's identity, and on the conflicts that may emerge.

Carl Jung (1875–1961) and Alfred Adler (1870–1937) were students of Freud who came to reject his ideas and form their own schools of thought. Unlike Freud, both Jung and Adler believed that the basic quality of human nature is positive and that people have a strong drive toward self-actualization. Jung and Adler believed by removing barriers to both internal and external growth, the individual would naturally improve and flourish.

Others took psychoanalytical theorizing in different directions, emphasizing development over the life span and the influence of culture and society on personality. Karen Horney (1885–1952), Erich Fromm (1900–1980), and Erik Erikson (1902–1994) are associated with these ideas. For example, Horney reanalyzed Freud's male-oriented views of women's psychological development, and developed her own feminine psychology in which she recognized the influences of societal factors (e.g., Horney, 1967). Erikson's greatest contribution was his theory of development across the life span, in which he described in some detail the crises and conflicts that accompany eight specific psychosocial stages. For example, in the last of these stages, the *mature age*, beginning at about age 65, individuals review their lives and attempt to make sense of them, experiencing both the satisfaction of having completed some lifelong goals and despair at having failed at others. Scientific developments have borne out the wisdom of considering psychopathology from a developmental point of view.

Psychoanalytic Psychotherapy

Many techniques of psychoanalytic psychotherapy, or psychoanalysis, are designed to reveal the nature of unconscious mental

▲ Anna Freud (1895–1982), here with her father, contributed the concept of defence mechanisms to the field of psychoanalysis.

Hulton–Deutsch Collection/Corbis Canada

The Psychological Tradition

processes and conflicts through catharsis and insight. Freud developed techniques of **free association**, in which patients are instructed to say whatever comes to mind without the usual socially mandated censoring. Free association is intended to reveal emotionally charged material that may be repressed because it is too painful or threatening to bring into consciousness. Freud's patients lay on a couch, and he sat behind them so they would not be distracted. This method is how the couch became the symbol of psychotherapy. Other techniques include **dream analysis** (still quite popular today), in which the content of dreams, supposedly reflecting the primary process thinking of the id, is systematically related to symbolic aspects of unconscious conflicts. The therapist interprets the patient's thoughts and feelings from free association and the content of dreams and relates them to various unconscious conflicts. This procedure is often difficult because the patient may resist the efforts of the therapist to uncover repressed and sensitive conflicts and *may deny* the interpretations. The goal of this stage of therapy is to help the patient gain insight into the nature of the conflicts.

The relationship between the therapist, called the **psychoanalyst**, and the patient is very important. In the context of this relationship as it evolves, the therapist may discover the nature of the patient's intrapsychic conflict: In a phenomenon called **transference**, patients come to relate to the therapist very much as they did toward important figures in their childhood, particularly their parents. Patients who resent the therapist but can verbalize no good reason for it may be reenacting childhood resentment toward a parent. More often, the patient falls deeply in love with the therapist, which reflects strong positive feelings that existed earlier for a parent. In the phenomenon of *countertransference*, therapists project some of their own personal issues and feelings, often positive, onto the patient. Therapists are trained to deal with their own feelings as well as their patients', whatever the mode of therapy, and it is strictly against all ethical canons of the mental health professions to accept overtures from patients that might lead to relationships outside therapy.

Classical psychoanalysis requires therapy four to five times a week for two to five years to analyze unconscious conflicts, resolve them, and restructure the personality to put the ego back in charge. A recent study by Norman Doidge at the Canadian Institute of Psychoanalysis in Toronto showed that the mean length of treatment for patients undergoing psychoanalysis in Canada is 4.8 years, compared to 5.7 years in the United States and 6.6 years in Australia (Doidge et al., 2002). In psychoanalysis, reduction of symptoms (overt manifestations of psychological disorders) is seen as relatively inconsequential, because they are only expressions of underlying intrapsychic conflicts that arise from psychosexual developmental stages. Thus, eliminating a phobia or depressive episode would be of little use unless the underlying conflict was dealt with adequately, because another set of symptoms would almost certainly emerge (*symptom substitution*). Because of the extraordinary expense of psychoanalysis, and the lack of evidence that it is effective in alleviating psychological disorders, this approach is seldom used today.

Classical psychoanalysis is still practised, particularly in some large cities, but many psychotherapists employ a loosely related set of approaches referred to as **psychodynamic psychotherapy**. Although conflicts and unconscious processes are still emphasized,

and efforts are made to identify trauma and active defence mechanisms, therapists use an eclectic mixture of tactics, with a social and interpersonal focus. Seven tactics that characterize psychodynamic psychotherapy include (1) a focus on affect and the expression of patients' emotions, (2) an exploration of patients' attempts to avoid topics or engage in activities that hinder the progress of therapy, (3) the identification of patterns in patients' actions, thoughts, feelings, experiences, and relationships, (4) an emphasis on past experiences, (5) a focus on patients' interpersonal experiences, (6) an emphasis on the therapeutic relationship, and (7) an exploration of patients' wishes, dreams, or fantasies (Blagys & Hilsenroth, 2000). Two additional features characterize psychodynamic psychotherapy. First, it is significantly briefer than classical psychoanalysis. Second, psychodynamic therapists de-emphasize the goal of personality reconstruction, focusing instead on relieving the suffering associated with psychological disorders. Some forms of psychodynamic psychotherapy have strong scientific evidence for their effectiveness, such as interpersonal therapy (IPT) in the treatment of depression (see Chapter 7).

Comments

Pure psychoanalysis is of historical more than current interest, and classical psychoanalysis as a treatment has been diminishing in popularity for years (Robins, Gosling, & Craik, 1999). In 1980, the term *neurosis*, which specifically implied a psychoanalytic view of the causes of psychological disorders, was dropped from the *DSM*, the official diagnostic system of the American Psychiatric Association.

A major criticism of psychoanalysis is that it is basically unscientific, relying on reports by the patient of events that happened years ago. These events have been filtered through the experience of the observer and then interpreted by the psychoanalyst in ways that certainly could be questioned and might differ from one analyst to the next. Finally, there has been no careful measurement of any of these psychological phenomena and no obvious way to prove or disprove the basic hypotheses of psychoanalysis. This fact is important, because measurement and the ability to prove or disprove a theory are the foundations of the scientific approach.

Nevertheless, psychoanalytic concepts and observations have been very valuable, not only to the study of psychopathology and psychodynamic psychotherapy but also to the history of ideas in Western civilization. Careful scientific studies of psychopathology have supported the observation of unconscious mental processes, that is, the notion that basic emotional responses are often triggered by hidden or symbolic cues and the understanding that memories of events in our lives can be repressed and otherwise avoided in a variety of ingenious ways. The relationship of the therapist and the patient, called the *therapeutic alliance*, is an important area of study across most therapeutic strategies. These concepts, along with the importance of various coping styles or defence mechanisms, appear repeatedly throughout this book.

Freud's revolutionary idea that pathological anxiety emerges in connection with some of our deepest and darkest instincts brought us a long way from witch trials and incurable brain pathology. Before Freud, the source of good and evil and of urges and prohibitions was conceived as external and spiritual, usually in the guise of demons confronting the forces of good. Since Freud, we ourselves have become the battleground for these forces, and we are inexorably caught up in the battle, sometimes for better and sometimes for worse.

Humanistic Theory

We have already seen that Jung and Adler broke sharply with Freud. Their fundamental disagreement concerned the very nature of humanity. Freud portrayed life as a battleground where we are continually in danger of being overwhelmed by our darkest forces. Jung and Adler, by contrast, emphasized the positive, optimistic side of human nature. Jung talked about setting goals, looking toward the future, and realizing our fullest potential. Adler believed that human nature reaches its fullest potential when we contribute to other individuals and to society as a whole. He believed we all strive to reach superior levels of intellectual and moral development. Nevertheless, both Jung and Adler retained many of the principles of psychodynamic thought. Their general philosophies were adopted in the middle of the 20th century by personality theorists and became known as *humanistic psychology*.

Self-actualizing was the watchword for this movement. The underlying assumption is that all of us can reach our highest potential, in all areas of functioning, if only we have the freedom to grow. Inevitably, a variety of conditions may block our actualization. Because every person is basically good and whole, most blocks originate outside the individual. Difficult living conditions or stressful life or interpersonal experiences may move you away from your true self. Abraham Maslow (1908–1970) was most systematic in describing the structure of personality. He postulated a *hierarchy of needs*, beginning with our most basic physical needs for food and sex and ranging upward to our needs for self-actualization, love, and self-esteem. Social needs such as friendship fall somewhere in between. Maslow hypothesized that we cannot progress up the hierarchy until we have satisfied the needs at lower levels.

Carl Rogers (1902–1987) is, from the point of view of therapy, the most influential humanist. Rogers originated client-centred therapy, later known as **person-centred therapy** (Rogers, 1961). In this approach, the therapist takes a passive role, making as few interpretations as possible. The point is to give the individual a chance to develop during the course of therapy, unfettered by threats to the self. Humanist theorists have great faith in the ability of human relations to foster this growth. **Unconditional positive regard**, the complete and almost unqualified acceptance of most of the client's feelings and actions, is critical to the humanistic approach. *Empathy* is the sympathetic understanding of the individual's particular view of the world. The hoped-for result of person-centred therapy is that clients will be more straightforward and honest with themselves and will access their innate tendencies toward growth.

Like psychoanalysis, the humanistic approach has had a substantial effect on theories of interpersonal relationships. For example, the human potential movements so popular in the 1960s and 1970s were a direct result of humanistic theorizing. This approach also emphasized the importance of the therapeutic relationship in a way quite different from Freud's. Rather than seeing the relationship as a means to an end (transference), humanistic therapists believed relationships, including the therapeutic relationship, were the single most positive influence in facilitating human growth. In fact, Rogers made substantial contributions to the scientific study of therapist–client relationships. And research by W. H. Coons and colleagues at the Ontario Hospital in Hamilton (Coons, 1957, 1967; Coons & Peacock, 1970) provided evidence for the importance of the humanistic concept of empathy or "the opportunity for interpersonal interaction in a consistently warm and accepting social environment" (Coons, 1957, p. 1) in explaining the success of psychotherapy. Proponents of the humanistic model stress the unique, nonquantifiable experiences of the individual, emphasizing that people are more different than alike. Thus, it does not come as a surprise that many humanistic model proponents have not been much interested in doing research that would discover or create new knowledge. A major exception is Carl Rogers himself, who conducted important work on understanding how psychotherapy works, an area known today as "psychotherapy process" research.

Frederich (Fritz) Perls developed a therapy known as Gestalt therapy that has humanistic elements (Levitsky & Perls, 1970; Perls, 1969). Like the person-centred therapy approach, Gestalt therapy focuses on people's positive and creative potentials. Gestalt therapy helps clients to develop an awareness of their desires and needs, and to understand how they might be blocking themselves from reaching their potential. Unlike psychoanalytic therapy, Gestalt therapy does not involve delving into past experiences—instead, it is very focused on the present. Relative to person-centred therapy, which does not emphasize technique, Gestalt therapists are trained in the use of specific techniques. These include "I language," in which the therapist encourages the client to refer to "I" rather than to "it" to take more responsibility for emotions and behaviour, and the use of metaphor, in which the therapist uses stories or scenarios to illustrate and make a problem clearer to a client.

Where is the humanistic movement today? As Maslow noted, traditional person-centred therapy found its greatest application among individuals without psychological disorders. The application of person-centred therapy to more severe psychological disorders has decreased substantially over the decades, although certain variations have periodically arisen in some areas of psychopathology. For example, Les Greenberg and his colleagues at York University in Toronto have developed experiential and emotion-focused therapies that have their roots in both person-centred and Gestalt approaches (Goldman, Greenberg, & Angus, 2006; Greenberg, 2004; Greenberg, Elliott, & Lietaer, 2003; Greenberg & Watson, 2005). These variations of traditional humanistic therapy are well researched and have demonstrated effectiveness in treating certain forms of psychopathology, such as certain mood and anxiety disorders (see Chapters 5 and 7).

The Behavioural Model

As psychoanalysis swept the world at the beginning of the 20th century, events in Russia and North America eventually provided an alternative psychological model that was just as powerful. The **behavioural model** brought the systematic development of a more scientific approach to psychological aspects of psychopathology.

The behavioural model is more commonly referred to today as the cognitive-behavioural (e.g., Meichenbaum, 1995) or social learning model (e.g., Bandura, 1973, 1986), given the greater emphasis today on cognitive and social factors involved in learning. These more recent developments to the traditional behavioural model are described in Chapter 2.

Pavlov and Classical Conditioning

In his classic study of the salivation response in dogs, physiologist Ivan Petrovich Pavlov (1849–1936) of St. Petersburg, Russia, learned why dogs salivate before the presentation of food. This classic experiment initiated the study of **classical conditioning**, a type of learning in which a neutral stimulus is paired with a response until it elicits that response. The word *conditioning* (or *conditioned response*) resulted from an accident in translation from the original Russian. Pavlov was really talking about a response that occurred only on the "condition" of the presence of a particular event or situation (stimulus)—in this case, the footsteps of the laboratory assistant at feeding time. Thus, "conditional response" would have been more accurate. Conditioning is one way we acquire new information, particularly information that is somewhat emotional in nature. This process is not as simple as it first seems, and we continue to uncover many more facts about its complexity (Bouton, Mineka, & Barlow, 2001; Rescorla, 1988). But it can be quite automatic. Let's look at a powerful contemporary example.

Psychologists working in oncology units have studied a phenomenon well known to many cancer patients, their nurses and physicians, and their families. Chemotherapy, a common treatment for some forms of cancer, has side effects that include severe nausea and vomiting. But as documented in the research of Patricia Dobkin at the University of Montréal and others, these patients often experience severe nausea and, occasionally, vomiting, when they merely see the medical personnel who administer the chemotherapy or any equipment associated with the treatment itself, even on days when their treatment is not delivered (Morrow & Dobkin, 1988). For some patients, this reaction becomes associated with a wide variety of stimuli that evoke people or things present during chemotherapy—anybody in a nurse's uniform or even the sight of the hospital itself. The strength of the response to similar objects or people is usually a function of how similar these objects or people are. This phenomenon is called stimulus generalization because the response "generalizes" to similar stimuli. In any case, this particular reaction, obviously, is very distressing and uncomfortable, particularly if it is associated with a wide variety of objects or situations. Psychologists have had to develop specific treatments to overcome this response (Redd & Andrykowski, 1982); they are described more fully in Chapter 9.

▲ Ivan Pavlov (1849–1936) identified the process of classical conditioning, which is important to many emotional disorders.

Bettmann/Corbis Canada

Whether the stimulus is food, as in Pavlov's laboratory, or chemotherapy, the classical conditioning process begins with a stimulus that elicits a response in almost anyone and requires no learning; no conditions must be present for the response to occur. For these reasons, the food or chemotherapy is called the *unconditioned stimulus (UCS)*. The natural or unlearned response to this stimulus—in these cases, salivation or nausea—is called the *unconditioned response (UCR)*. Now the learning comes in. As we have already seen, any person or object associated with the unconditioned stimulus (food or chemotherapy) acquires the power to elicit the same response, but now the response, because it was elicited by the conditional or *conditioned stimuli (CS)*, is termed a *conditioned response (CR)*. Thus, the nurse associated with the chemotherapy becomes a conditioned stimulus. The nausea, which is almost the same as that experienced during chemotherapy, becomes the conditioned response.

With unconditioned stimuli as powerful as chemotherapy, a conditioned response can be learned in one trial. However, most learning of this type requires repeated pairing of the unconditioned stimulus (e.g., chemotherapy) and the conditioned stimulus (e.g., nurses' uniforms or hospital equipment). When Pavlov began to investigate this phenomenon, he substituted a metronome for the footsteps of his laboratory assistants so he could quantify the stimulus more accurately and, therefore, study the approach more precisely. What he also learned is that presentation of the CS (e.g., the metronome) without the food for a long enough period would eventually eliminate the conditioned response to the food. In other words, the dog learned that the metronome no longer meant that a meal might be on the way. This process was called **extinction**.

Because Pavlov was a physiologist, it was quite natural for him to study these processes in a laboratory and to be quite scientific about it. This method required precision in measuring and observing relationships and in ruling out alternative explanations. Although this approach is common in biology, it was not at all common in psychology at that time. For example, it was impossible for psychoanalysts to measure unconscious conflicts precisely, or even to observe them. Early experimental psychologists such as Edward Titchener (1867–1927) emphasized the study of **introspection**. Subjects simply reported on their inner thoughts and feelings after experiencing certain stimuli, but the results of this armchair psychology were inconsistent and discouraging to many experimental psychologists.

Watson and the Rise of Behaviourism

An early American psychologist, John B. Watson (1878–1958), is considered the founder of behaviourism. Strongly influenced by the work of Pavlov, Watson decided that to base psychology on introspection was to head in the wrong direction, that psychology could be made as scientific as physiology, and that psychology no more needed introspection or other nonquantifiable methods than did chemistry and physics (Watson, 1913). This point of view is reflected in a famous quotation from a seminal article published by Watson in 1913: "Psychology, as the behaviorist views it, is a purely objective experimental branch of natural science. Its theoretical goal is the prediction and control of behavior. Introspection forms no essential part of its methods" (p. 158). This, then, was the beginning of behaviourism and, like most revolutionaries,

Watson took his cause to extremes. For example, he wrote that "thinking," for purposes of science, could be equated with subvocal talking and that one need only measure movements around the larynx to study this process objectively.

Most of Watson's time was spent developing behavioural psychology as a radical empirical science, but he did dabble briefly in the study of psychopathology. In 1920, he and a student, Rosalie Rayner, presented an 11-month-old boy named Albert with a harmless fluffy white rat to play with. Albert was not afraid of the small animal and enjoyed playing with it. However, every time Albert reached for the rat, the experimenters made a loud noise behind him. After only five trials, Albert showed the first signs of fear if the white rat came near. The experimenters then determined that Albert displayed mild fear of any similar white furry object, even a Santa Claus mask with a white fuzzy beard. You may not think this is surprising, but keep in mind that this was one of the first examples ever recorded in a laboratory of actually producing fear of an object not previously feared. Of course, this experiment would be considered unethical by today's standards. For example, Watson and Rayner's failure to remove (or "recondition") Albert's fear before the end of the experiment, and their insufficient follow-up of the child's fears after the experiment, would be criticized on ethical grounds today (Harris, 1979).

Another student of Watson's, Mary Cover Jones, thought that if fear could be learned or classically conditioned in this way, perhaps it could also be unlearned or extinguished. She worked with a boy named Peter, who at two years, ten months old was already quite afraid of furry objects. Jones decided to bring a white rabbit into the room where Peter was playing for a short time each day. She also arranged for other children, whom she knew did not fear rabbits, to be in the same room. She noted that Peter's fear gradually diminished. Each time it diminished, she brought the rabbit closer. Eventually Peter was touching and even playing with the rabbit (Jones, 1924a, 1924b), and years later the fear had not returned.

▲ Mary Cover Jones (1896–1987) was one of the first psychologists to use behavioural techniques to free a patient from a phobia.

Archives of the History of American Psychology

The Beginnings of Behaviour Therapy

The implications of Jones's research were largely ignored for two decades, given the fervour associated with more psychoanalytic conceptions of the development of fear. But in the late 1940s and early 1950s, Joseph Wolpe (1915–1997), a pioneering psychiatrist from South Africa, became dissatisfied with prevailing psychoanalytic interpretations of psychopathology and began looking for something else. He turned to the work of Pavlov and became familiar with the wider field of behavioural psychology. He developed a variety of behavioural procedures for treating his patients, many of whom have phobias. His best-known technique was termed **systematic desensitization**. In principle, it was really very similar to Jones's treatment of little Peter. Individuals were gradually introduced to the objects or situations they feared so their fear could extinguish; that is, they could test reality and see that nothing bad really happened in the presence of the phobic object or scene. Wolpe added another element by having his patients do something that was *incompatible with fear* while they were in the presence of the dreaded object or situation. Because he could not always reproduce the phobic object in his office, Wolpe had his patients carefully and systematically *imagine* the phobic scene, and the response he chose was relaxation, because it was convenient. For example, Wolpe treated a young man with a phobia of dogs by training him first to relax deeply and then imagine he was looking at a dog across the park. Gradually, he could imagine the dog across the park and remain relaxed, experiencing little or no fear, and Wolpe then had him imagine he was closer to the dog. Eventually the young man imagined he was actually touching the dog while maintaining a very relaxed, almost trance-like state.

Wolpe reported success with systematic desensitization, one of the first wide-scale applications of the new science of behaviourism to psychopathology. Wolpe, working with fellow pioneers Hans Eysenck and Stanley J. Rachman in London, called this approach **behaviour therapy**. Wolpe eventually moved to the United States and Rachman to Canada, while Eysenck remained in the United Kingdom, which contributed to the dissemination of behaviour therapy knowledge and techniques throughout North America and Europe.

B. F. Skinner and Operant Conditioning

Sigmund Freud's influence extended far beyond psychopathology into many aspects of our cultural and intellectual history. Only one other behavioural scientist has made a similar impact, Burrhus Frederic (B. F.) Skinner (1904–1990). In 1938, he published *The Behavior of Organisms*, in which he laid out, in a comprehensive manner, the principles of operant conditioning, a type of learning in

Courtesy of Jack Rachman

▲ Stanley J. Rachman, recently retired from the University of British Columbia, is one of the original founders of the behaviour therapy approach.

▲ B. F. Skinner (1904–1990) studied operant conditioning, a form of learning that is central to psychopathology.

which behaviour changes as a function of what follows the behaviour. Skinner observed early on that a large part of our behaviour is not automatically elicited by an unconditioned stimulus (UCS) and we must account for this. In the ensuing years, Skinner did not confine his ideas to the laboratories of experimental psychology. He ranged broadly in his writings, describing, for example, the potential applications of a science of behaviour to our culture. Some of the best-known examples of his ideas are in the novel *Walden Two* (Skinner, 1948), in which he depicts a fictional society run on the principles of operant conditioning. In another well-known work, *Beyond Freedom and Dignity* (1971), Skinner lays out a broader statement of the problems facing our culture and suggests solutions based on his own view of a science of behaviour.

Skinner was strongly influenced by Watson's conviction that a science of human behaviour must be based on observable events and relationships among those events. The work of psychologist Edward L. Thorndike (1874–1949) also influenced Skinner. Thorndike is best known for the *law of effect*, which states that behaviour is either strengthened (likely to be repeated more frequently) or weakened (likely to occur less frequently) depending on the consequences of that behaviour. Skinner took the very simple notions that Thorndike had tested in the animal laboratories, using food as a reinforcer, and developed them in a variety of complex ways to apply to much of our behaviour. For example, if a five-year-old boy starts shouting at the top of his lungs in McDonald's, much to the annoyance of the people around him, it is unlikely his behaviour was automatically elicited by an unconditioned stimulus (UCS). Also, he will be less likely to do it in the future if his parents scold him, take him out to the car to sit for a bit, or consistently reinforce more appropriate behaviour. Then again, if the parents think his behaviour is cute and laugh, chances are he will do it again.

Skinner coined the term *operant conditioning* because behaviour "operates" on the environment and changes it in some way. For example, the boy's behaviour affects his parents' behaviour and probably the behaviour of other customers as well. Therefore, he changes his environment. Most things we do socially provide the context for other people to respond to us in one way or another, thereby providing consequences for our behaviour. The same is true of our physical environment, although the consequences may be long term (polluting the air eventually will poison us). Skinner preferred the term **reinforcement** to *reward* because it connotes the effect on the behaviour. Skinner once said that he found himself a bit embarrassed to be talking continually about reinforcement, much as Marxists used to see class struggle everywhere. But he pointed out that all of our behaviour is governed to some degree by reinforcement, which can be arranged in an endless variety of ways, in schedules of reinforcement. Skinner wrote a book on different schedules of reinforcement (Ferster & Skinner, 1957). He also believed that using punishment as a consequence is relatively ineffective in the long run and that the primary way to develop new behaviour is to positively reinforce desired behaviour. Much like Watson, Skinner did not see the need to go beyond the observable and quantifiable to establish a satisfactory science of behaviour. He did not deny the influence of biology or the existence of subjective states of emotion or cognition; he simply explained these phenomena as relatively inconsequential side effects of a particular history of reinforcement.

The subjects of Skinner's research were usually animals, mostly pigeons and rats. Using his new principles, Skinner and his disciples actually taught the animals a variety of tricks, including dancing, playing Ping-Pong, and playing a toy piano. To do this, he used a procedure called **shaping**, a process of reinforcing successive approximations to a final behaviour or set of behaviours. If you want a pigeon to play Ping-Pong, first you provide it with a pellet of food every time it moves its head slightly toward a Ping-Pong ball tossed in its direction. Gradually you require the pigeon to move its head ever closer to the Ping-Pong ball until it touches it. Finally, receiving the food pellet is contingent on the pigeon's actually hitting the ball back with its head. Pavlov, Watson, and Skinner contributed significantly to behaviour therapy (e.g., Wolpe, 1958), in which scientific principles of psychology are applied to clinical problems. Many psychologists and other mental health professionals quickly picked up on behaviour therapy techniques and began applying them with their patients in the 1950s and 1960s. For example, in an early application of these principles at the Lakeshore Psychiatric Hospital in Toronto, Richard Steffy and his colleagues describe how they used operant conditioning techniques to modify the behaviour of a ward of severely aggressive female patients. These researchers documented how reinforcements could be used by staff to decrease these patients' violent activity and to improve their self-care and social responsiveness (Steffy, Hart, Craw, Torney, & Marlett, 1969). Similar results were reported by Teodoro Ayllon and Jack Michael (1959) from a study conducted at the Saskatchewan Hospital in Weyburn, showing that the use of reinforcements by nursing staff could produce substantial reductions in psychiatric patients' undesirable behaviour and increases in patients' desirable behaviour. The ideas of Pavlov, Watson, and Skinner have continued to contribute substantially to current psychosocial treatments, and so we refer to them repeatedly in this book.

Comments

The behavioural model has contributed greatly to the understanding and treatment of psychopathology, as will be apparent in the chapters that follow. Nevertheless, this model is incomplete in itself and inadequate to account for what we now know about psychopathology. In the past, behaviourism had little or no room for biology, because disorders were considered, for the most part, environmentally determined reactions. The model also fails to account for development of psychopathology across the life span. Recent advances in our knowledge of how information is processed, both consciously and subconsciously, have added a layer of complexity. We also now know that learning can occur indirectly or vicariously through observing others in social interactions (Bandura, Jeffery, & Bachicha, 1974; Bandura & McDonald, 1963; Bandura, Ross, & Ross, 1963). Integrating all these dimensions requires a new model of psychopathology.

The Present: The Scientific Method and an Integrative Approach

As Shakespeare wrote, "What's past is prologue." We have just reviewed three different traditions or ways of thinking about causes of psychopathology: the supernatural, the biological, and the psychological (further subdivided into two major historical components: psychoanalytic and behavioural).

Supernatural explanations of psychopathology are still with us. Superstitions prevail, including beliefs in the effects of the moon and the stars on our behaviour. However, this tradition has little influence on scientists and other professionals. Biological, psychoanalytic, and behavioural models, by contrast, continue to further our knowledge of psychopathology, as we see in the next chapter. Even with the many advances in our understanding of mental disorders, no blood test exists for mental illness, and no specific known cure, as is often the case with physical illness. This fact helps explain why there are many, sometimes competing, models for mental disorders today.

Despite the fact that the biological, psychoanalytic, and behavioural models continue to improve our understanding of the various forms of psychopathology, each tradition has failed in at least one important way. First, scientific methods were not often applied to the theories and treatments within a tradition, mostly because methods that would have produced the evidence necessary to confirm or disconfirm the theories and treatments had not been developed. Lacking such evidence, various fads and superstitions were widely accepted that ultimately proved untrue or useless. New fads often superseded truly useful theories and treatment procedures. This trend was at work in the so-called discovery of the drug reserpine, which, in fact, had been around for thousands of years. King Charles VI was subjected to a variety of procedures, some of which have since been proved useful and others that were mere fads or even harmful. How we use scientific methods to confirm or disconfirm findings in psychopathology is described in Chapter 4. Second, health professionals tend to look at psychological disorders very narrowly, from their own point of view alone. John Grey assumed psychological disorders are the result of brain disease and that other factors have no influence whatsoever. John Watson assumed that all behaviours, including disordered behaviour, are the result of psychological and social influences and that the contribution of biological factors is inconsequential.

In the 1990s, two developments came together as never before to shed light on the nature of psychopathology: (1) the increasing sophistication of scientific tools and methodology (e.g., more sophisticated medical technology methods such as neuroimaging—see Chapter 3), and (2) the realization that no one influence—biological, behavioural, cognitive, emotional, or social—ever occurs in isolation. Every time we think, feel, or do something, the brain and the rest of the body are hard at work. Perhaps not as obvious, however, is the fact that our thoughts, feelings, and actions inevitably influence the function and even the structure of the brain, sometimes permanently. In other words, our behaviour, both normal and abnormal, is the product of the continual interaction of psychological, biological, and social influences.

The view that psychopathology is multiply determined had its early adherents. Perhaps the most notable was psychiatrist Adolf Meyer (1866–1950). Whereas most professionals during the first half of the 20th century held narrow views of the cause of psychopathology, Meyer steadfastly emphasized the equal contributions of biological, psychological, and sociocultural determinism. Although Meyer had some proponents, it was a century before the wisdom of his advice was fully recognized in the field.

By 2000, a veritable explosion of knowledge about psychopathology had occurred. The young fields of cognitive science and neuroscience began to grow exponentially as we learned more about the brain and about how we process, remember, and use information. At the same time, startling new findings from behavioural science revealed the importance of early experience in determining later development. It was clear that a new model was needed that would consider biological, psychological, and social influences on behaviour. This approach to psychopathology would combine findings from all areas with our rapidly growing understanding of how we experience life during different developmental periods, from infancy to old age. In 2010, the National Institute of Mental Health (NIMH) instituted a strategic plan to support further research and development on the interrelationship of these factors with the aim of translating research findings to front-line treatment settings (Insel, 2009). In the remainder of this book, we explore the reciprocal influences among neuroscience, cognitive science, behaviour science, and developmental science and demonstrate that the only currently valid model of psychopathology is multidimensional and integrative.

Concept Check | 1.4

Match the treatment with the corresponding psychological theory of behaviour: (a) behavioural model, (b) moral therapy, (c) psychoanalytic theory, and (d) humanistic theory.

1. Treating institutionalized patients as normally as possible and encouraging social interaction and relationship development. _____

2. Hypnosis, psychoanalysis-like free association and dream analysis, and balance of the id, ego, and superego. _____

3. Person-centred therapy with unconditional positive regard. _____

4. Classical conditioning, systematic desensitization, and operant conditioning. _____

SUMMARY

What Is a Psychological Disorder?

- A psychological disorder is (1) a psychological dysfunction or dyscontrol within an individual that is (2) associated with distress or impairment in functioning and (3) a response that is not typical or culturally expected. Although this definition is the most popular, no one description has yet been identified that defines the essence of abnormality.

The Science of Psychopathology

- The field of psychopathology is concerned with the scientific study of psychological disorders. Trained mental health professionals range from clinical and counselling psychologists to psychiatrists and psychiatric social workers and nurses. Each profession requires a specific type of training.
- Using scientific methods, mental health professionals can function as scientist-practitioners. They not only keep up with the latest findings but also use scientific data to evaluate their own work, and they often conduct research within their clinics or hospitals.
- Research about psychological disorders falls into three basic categories: description, causation, and treatment and outcomes.

The Supernatural, Biological, and Psychological Traditions

- Historically, three prominent approaches to abnormal behaviour have been used. In the supernatural tradition, abnormal behaviour is attributed to agents outside our bodies or social environment, such as demons or spirits, or the influence of the moon and stars; though still alive, this tradition has been largely replaced by biological and psychological perspectives. In the biological tradition, disorders are attributed to disease or biochemical imbalances; in the psychological tradition, abnormal behaviour is attributed to faulty psychological development and to social context.

- Each tradition has its own way of treating individuals who have psychological disorders. Supernatural treatments include exorcism to rid the body of the supernatural spirits. Biological treatments typically emphasize physical care and the search for medical cures, especially drugs. Psychological approaches use psychosocial treatments, beginning with moral therapy and including modern psychotherapy.
- Sigmund Freud, the founder of psychoanalytic therapy, offered an elaborate conception of the unconscious mind, much of which is still conjecture. In therapy, Freud focused on tapping into the mysteries of the unconscious through such techniques as catharsis, free association, and dream analysis. Though Freud's followers veered from his path in many ways, Freud's influence can still be felt today.
- One outgrowth of Freudian therapy is humanistic psychology, which focuses more on human potential and self-actualizing than on psychological disorders. Therapy that has evolved from this approach is known as person-centred therapy; the therapist shows almost unconditional positive regard for the client's feelings and thoughts.
- The behavioural model moved psychology into the realm of science, with an emphasis on findings from the laboratories of psychology as applied to human behaviour. Therapeutic techniques derived from this model include systematic desensitization, reinforcement, and shaping.

The Present: The Scientific Method and the Integrative Approach

- With the increasing sophistication of our scientific tools and new knowledge from cognitive science, behavioural science, and neuroscience, we now realize that no contribution to psychological disorders ever occurs in isolation. Our behaviour, both normal and abnormal, is a product of a continual interaction of psychological, biological, and social influences.

Key Terms

Answers to Concept Checks

1.1

1. a, c **2.** d **3.** b, c **4.** b

1.2

1. d **2.** c **3.** a **4.** f **5.** e **6.** b

1.3

1. e **2.** c **3.** d **4.** a

1.4

1. b **2.** c **3.** d **4.** a

Media Resources

Access an integrated eBook, Abnormal Psychology Videos (formerly Abnormal Psych Live CD-ROM), chapter-specific interactive learning tools (flashcards, quizzes, learning modules), and more in your Psychology CourseMate, available at **www.abnormalpsych3ce.nelson.com.**

Abnormal Psychology Video

Free Abnormal Psychology videos can be viewed on the website **www.abnormalpsych3ce .nelson.com**.

- *Roots of Behaviour Therapy:* This combined clip shows the historical progression of classical conditioning and the behavioural model from Pavlov through Watson and Skinner.

Video Concept Reviews

CourseMate also contains Mark Durand's *Video Concept Reviews* on these challenging topics:

- Concept Check—Abnormality
- Psychopathology
- Mental Health Professions
- The Scientist-Practitioner
- Presenting Problem
- Prevalence
- Incidence
- Course

- Prognosis
- Supernatural Views—Historical
- Supernatural Views—Current
- Emotion Contagion
- Hippocrates
- Moral Therapy
- Concept Check—Integrative Approach

Timeline of Significant Events

400 B.C.E.–1875

Mary Evans Picture Library

National Library of Medicine

Stock Montage

400 B.C.E.: Hippocrates suggests that psychological disorders have both biological and psychological causes.

1300s: Superstition runs rampant and mental disorders are blamed on demons and witches; exorcisms are performed to rid victims of evil spirits.

1400–1800: Bloodletting and leeches are used to rid the body of unhealthy fluids and restore chemical balance.

1793: Philippe Pinel introduces moral therapy and makes French mental institutions more humane.

400 B.C.E.	1300s	1500s	1825–1875

200 B.C.E.: Galen suggests that normal and abnormal behaviour are related to four bodily fluids, or humors.

1400s: Enlightened view that insanity is caused by mental or emotional stress gains momentum, and depression and anxiety are again regarded by some as disorders.

1500s: Paracelsus suggests that the moon and the stars affect people's psychological functioning, rather than possession by the devil.

1825–1875: Syphilis is differentiated from other types of psychosis in that it is caused by a specific bacterium; ultimately, penicillin is found to cure syphilis.

1930–1968

1930: Insulin shock therapy, electric shock treatments, and brain surgery begin to be used to treat psychopathology.

1943: The Minnesota Multiphasic Personality Inventory is published.

1950: The first effective drugs for severe psychotic disorders are developed. Humanistic psychology (based on ideas of Carl Jung, Alfred Adler, and Carl Rogers) gains some acceptance.

1958: Joseph Wolpe effectively treats patients with phobias using systematic desensitization based on principles of behavioural science.

1930	1943	1950	1968

1938: B. F. Skinner publishes *The Behavior of Organisms,* which describes the principles of operant conditioning.

1946: Anna Freud publishes *Ego and the Mechanisms of Defense.*

1952: The first edition of the *Diagnostic and Statistical Manual (DSM-I)* is published.

1968: *DSM-II* is published.

Bettmann/Corbis Canada

Imagno/Hulton Archive /Getty Images

1848–1920

1848: Dorothea Dix successfully campaigns for more humane treatment in American mental institutions.

1870: Louis Pasteur develops his germ theory of disease, which helps identify the bacterium that causes syphilis.

1900: Sigmund Freud publishes *The Interpretation of Dreams.*

1913: Emil Kraepelin classifies various psychological disorders from a biological point of view and publishes work on diagnosis.

1848	1870	1900	1920

1854: John P. Grey, head of New York's Utica Hospital, believes that insanity is the result of physical causes, thus de-emphasizing psychological treatments.

1895: Josef Breuer treats the "hysterical" Anna O., leading to Freud's development of psychoanalytic theory.

1904: Ivan Pavlov receives the Nobel Prize for his work on the physiology of digestion, which leads him to identify conditioned reflexes in dogs.

1920: John B. Watson experiments with conditioned fear in Little Albert using a white rat.

1980–2000

1990s: Increasingly sophisticated research methods are developed; no one influence—biological or environmental—is found to cause psychological disorders in isolation from the other.

1980: *DSM-III* is published.

2000: *DSM-IV-TR* is published.

1980	1990s	2000

1987: *DSM-III-R* is published.

1994: *DSM-IV* is published.

2 | An Integrative Approach to Psychopathology

PHOTOTAKE Inc./Alamy

The spirit within nourishes, and the mind, diffused through all the members, sways the mass and mingles with the whole frame.
—Virgil, *The Aeneid*

Demonstrate knowledge and understanding representing appropriate breadth and depth in selected content areas of psychology.	› Learning and cognition (APA SLO 1.2.a (1)) *(see textbook pages 55–60)*
	› Biological bases of behaviour and mental processes, including physiology, sensation, perception, comparative, motivation, and emotion (APA SLO 1.2.a (3)) *(see textbook pages 35–55, 60–63)*
	› Developmental changes in behaviour and mental processes across the life span (APA SLO 1.2.a (4)) *(see textbook pages 66–67)*
	› The interaction of heredity and environment (APA SLO 1.2.d (1)) *(see textbook pages 37–41)*
Use the concepts, language, and major theories of the discipline to account for psychological phenomena.	› Integrate theoretical perspectives to produce comprehensive and multifaceted explanations (APA SLO 1.3.e) *(see textbook pages 34–35, 66–67)*
Explain major perspectives of psychology (e.g., behavioural, biological, cognitive, evolutionary, humanistic, psychodynamic, and sociocultural).	› Explain major perspectives of psychology (APA SLO 1.4) *(see textbook pages 34, 55, 63)*

* Portions of this chapter cover learning outcomes suggested by the American Psychological Association (2007) in their guidelines for the undergraduate psychology major. Chapter coverage of these outcomes is identified above by APA Goal and APA Suggested Learning Outcome (SLO).

Remember Jody from Chapter 1? We knew he had a blood-injury-injection phobia, but we did not know why. Here we address the issue of causation. In this chapter we examine the specific components of a **multidimensional integrative approach** to psychopathology (see ■ Figure 2.1). *Biological* dimensions include causal factors from the fields of genetics and neuroscience. *Psychological* dimensions include causal factors from behavioural and cognitive processes, including learned helplessness, social learning, prepared learning, and even unconscious processes (in a different guise from Freud's days). Emotional influences contribute in a variety of ways to psychopathology, as do social and *interpersonal* influences. Finally, *developmental influences* figure in any discussion of causes of psychological disorders. You will become familiar with these areas as they relate to psychopathology and learn about some of the latest developments that are relevant to psychological disorders. But keep in mind what we confirmed

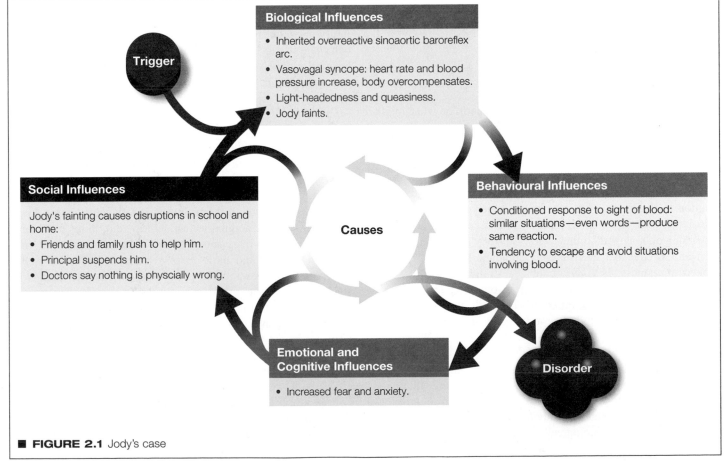

Biological Influences

- Inherited overreactive sinoaortic baroreflex arc.
- Vasovagal syncope: heart rate and blood pressure increase, body overcompensates.
- Light-headedness and queasiness.
- Jody faints.

Trigger

Social Influences

Jody's fainting causes disruptions in school and home:

- Friends and family rush to help him.
- Principal suspends him.
- Doctors say nothing is physcially wrong.

Causes

Behavioural Influences

- Conditioned response to sight of blood: similar situations—even words—produce same reaction.
- Tendency to escape and avoid situations involving blood.

Emotional and Cognitive Influences

- Increased fear and anxiety.

Disorder

■ **FIGURE 2.1** Jody's case

in the last chapter: No influence operates in isolation. Each dimension, biological or psychological, is strongly influenced by the others and by development, and they weave together in various complex and intricate ways to create a psychological disorder.

We explain briefly why we have adopted a multidimensional integrative model of psychopathology. Then we preview various causal influences and interactions, using Jody's case as background. After that, we look more deeply at specific causal influences in psychopathology, examining both the latest research and integrative ways of viewing what we know.

One-Dimensional or Multidimensional Models

To say that psychopathology is caused by a physical abnormality or by conditioning is to accept a linear or one-dimensional model which attempts to trace the origins of behaviour to a single cause. A linear causal model might hold that schizophrenia or a phobia is caused by a chemical imbalance or by growing up surrounded by overwhelming conflicts among family members. In psychology and psychopathology, we still encounter this type of thinking occasionally, but most scientists and clinicians believe abnormal behaviour results from multiple influences. A system, or feedback loop, may have independent inputs at many different points, but as each input becomes part of the whole, it can no longer be considered independent. This perspective on causality is systemic, which derives from the word system; it implies that any particular influence contributing to psychopathology cannot be considered out of context. Context, in this case, is the biology and behaviour of the individual, as well as the cognitive, emotional, social, and cultural environment, because any one component of the system inevitably affects the other components. This is a multidimensional model.

What Caused Jody's Phobia?

From a multidimensional perspective, let's look at what might have caused Jody's phobia (see Figure 2.1).

Behavioural Influences

The cause of Jody's phobia might at first seem obvious. He saw a movie with graphic scenes of blood and injury and had a bad reaction to it. His reaction, an unconditioned response, became associated with situations similar to the scenes in the movie, depending on how similar they were. But Jody's reaction reached such an extreme that even hearing someone say, "Cut it out!" evoked queasiness. Is Jody's phobia a straightforward case of classical conditioning? It might seem so, but one puzzling question arises: Why didn't the other kids in Jody's class develop the same phobia? As far as Jody knew, nobody else even felt queasy!

Biological Influences

We now know that much more is involved in blood-injury-injection phobia than a simple conditioning experience, although, clearly, conditioning and stimulus generalization contribute. In fact, we have learned a lot about this phobia (Marks, 1988; Page, 1994, 1996). Physiologically, Jody experienced a vasovagal

syncope, which is a common cause of fainting. When he saw the film he became mildly distressed, as many people would, and his heart rate and blood pressure increased accordingly, which he probably did not notice. Then his body took over, immediately compensating by decreasing his vascular resistance, lowering his heart rate and, eventually, lowering his blood pressure. The amount of blood reaching his brain diminished until he lost consciousness. Syncope means "sinking feeling" or "swoon" because of low blood pressure in the head. If Jody had quickly bent down and put his head between his knees, he might have avoided fainting, but it happened so quickly he had no time to use this strategy.

A possible cause of the vasovagal syncope is an overreaction of a mechanism that compensates for sudden increases in blood pressure by lowering it. Interestingly, the tendency to overcompensate seems to be inherited, which may account for the high rate of blood-injury-injection phobia in families (Öst, 1992). Do you ever feel queasy at the sight of blood? If so, chances are your mother or father or someone else in your immediate family has the same reaction. But many people with rather severe syncope reaction tendencies do not develop phobias. They cope with their reaction in various ways, including tensing their muscles whenever they are confronted with blood. Tensing the muscles very quickly raises blood pressure and prevents the fainting response. Furthermore, some people with little or no syncope reaction develop the phobia anyway (Öst, 1992). Therefore, the cause of blood-injury-injection phobia is complicated. If we said that the phobia is caused by a biological dysfunction (an overactive vasovagal reaction) or a traumatic experience (seeing a gruesome film) and subsequent conditioning, we would be partly right on both counts, but in adopting a one-dimensional causal model, we would miss the most important point: To cause blood-injury-injection phobia, a complex *interaction* must occur between behavioural and biological factors. Inheriting a strong syncope reaction definitely puts a person at risk for developing this phobia, but other influences are at work as well.

Emotional Influences

Jody's case is a good example of biology influencing behaviour. But behaviour, thoughts, and feelings can also influence biology, sometimes dramatically. What role did Jody's fear and anxiety play in the development of his phobia, and where did they come from? Emotions can affect physiological responses such as blood pressure, heart rate, and respiration, particularly if we know rationally we have nothing to fear, as Jody did. In his case, rapid increases in heart rate, caused by his emotions, may have triggered a stronger and more intense baroreflex. The baroreflex increases or decreases blood pressure in an effort to maintain a stable blood pressure in the body. Emotions also changed the way he thought about situations involving blood and injury and motivated him to behave in ways he didn't want to—avoiding all situations connected with blood and injury, even if it was important not to avoid them. As we see throughout this book, emotions play a substantial role in the development of many disorders.

Social Influences

We are all social animals; by our very nature we tend to live in groups such as families. Social and cultural factors make direct contributions to biology and behaviour. Jody's friends and family rushed to his aid when he fainted. Did their support help or hurt? His principal rejected him and dismissed his problem. What effect did this behaviour have on his phobia? Rejection, particularly by authority figures, can make psychological disorders worse than they otherwise would be. Then again, being supportive only when somebody experiences symptoms is not always helpful because the strong effects of social attention may actually increase the frequency and intensity of the reaction.

Developmental Influences

One more influence affects us all—the passage of time. As time passes, many things about ourselves and our environments change in important ways, causing us to react differently at different ages. Thus, at certain times we may enter a *developmental critical period* when we are more or less reactive to a given situation or influence than at other times. To go back to Jody, it is possible that he was previously exposed to other situations involving blood. Important questions to ask are these: Why did this problem develop when he was 16 years old and not before? Is it possible that his susceptibility to having a vasovagal reaction was highest in his teenage years? It may be that the timing of his physiological reaction, along with viewing the disturbing biology film, provided just the right (but unfortunate) combination to initiate his severe phobic response.

Concept Check | 2.1

Theorists have abandoned the notion that any one factor can explain abnormal behaviour; they favour an integrative model. Match each of the following scenarios to its most likely influence or influences: (a) behavioural, (b) biological, (c) emotional, (d) social, and (e) developmental.

1. The fact that some phobias are more common than others (such as fear of heights and snakes) and may have contributed to the survival of the species in the past suggests that phobias may be genetically prewired. This is evidence for which influence? _____

2. Jan's husband, Jinx, was an unemployed jerk who spent his life chasing women other than his wife. Jan, happily divorced for years, cannot understand why the smell of Jinx's brand of aftershave causes her to become nauseated. Which influence best explains her response?

   _____

3. Nathan, age 16, finds it more difficult than his seven-year-old sister to adjust to his parents' recent separation. This may be explained by what influences?

   _____

4. A traumatic ride on a Ferris wheel at a young age was most likely to have been the initial cause of Juanita's fear of heights. Her strong emotional reaction to heights is likely to maintain or even increase her fear. The initial development of the phobia is likely a result of _____ influences; however, _____ influences are likely perpetuating the phobia.

Outcome and Comments

Fortunately for Jody, he responded very well to brief but intensive treatment at one of our clinics, and he was back in school within seven days. Jody was gradually exposed, with his full cooperation, to words, images, and situations describing or depicting blood and injury while a sudden drop in blood pressure was prevented using applied muscle tension. Applied muscle tension is a simple behavioural technique that reduces vasovagal reactions by maintaining blood pressure. It has been used successfully in the treatment of people with blood and injury phobias, like Jody (Ditto, Wilkins, France, Lavoie, & Adler, 2003). Blaine Ditto and his colleagues at McGill University have also successfully applied this technique in the context of blood donor clinics, where vasovagal reactions can significantly complicate the blood collection process and discourage people from returning to donate blood again (Ditto et al., 2003). For Jody's exposure treatment, we began with something mild, such as the phrase "cut it out." By the end of the week, Jody was witnessing surgical procedures at the local hospital while practising applied muscle tension. Jody required close therapeutic supervision during this program. At one point, while driving home with his parents from an evening session, he had the bad luck to pass a car crash, and he saw a bleeding accident victim. That night, he dreamed about bloody accident victims coming through the walls of his bedroom. This experience made him call the clinic and request emergency intervention to reduce his distress, but it did not slow his progress. (Programs for treating phobias and related anxiety disorders are described more fully in Chapter 5. It is the issue of etiology or causation that concerns us here.)

As you can see, finding the causes of abnormal behaviour is a complex and fascinating process. Focusing on biological or behavioural factors would not have given us a full picture of the causes of Jody's disorder; we had to consider a variety of other influences and how they might interact. A discussion in more depth follows, examining the research underlying the many biological, psychological, and social influences that must be considered as causes of any psychological disorder.

Genetic Contributions to Psychopathology

What causes you to look like one or both of your parents or, perhaps, your grandparents? Obviously, it is the genes that you inherit from your parents and from your ancestors before them. **Genes** are very long molecules of DNA (deoxyribonucleic acid) at various locations on chromosomes within the cell nucleus. Ever since Gregor Mendel's pioneering work in the 19th century, we have known that physical characteristics such as hair colour and eye colour and, to a certain extent, height and weight are determined—or at least strongly influenced—by our genetic endowment. However, other factors in the environment influence our physical appearance as well. To some extent, our weight and even our height are affected by nutritional, social, and cultural factors. Consequently, our genes seldom determine our physical development in any absolute way. They do provide some boundaries to our development. Exactly where we go within these boundaries depends on environmental influences.

Except for identical twins, every person has a unique set of genes unlike those of anyone else in the world. Because there is plenty of room for the environment to influence our development within the constraints set by our genes, many reasons exist for the development of individual differences.

What about our behaviour and traits, our likes and dislikes? Do genes influence personality and, by extension, abnormal behaviour? This question of nature (genes) versus nurture (upbringing and other environmental influences) is age-old in psychology, and the answers that are beginning to emerge are fascinating. Before discussing them, let's review briefly what we know.

The Nature of Genes

We have known for a long time that each normal human cell has 46 chromosomes arranged in 23 pairs. In each pair, one chromosome comes from father and one from mother. We can actually see these chromosomes through a microscope, and we can sometimes tell when one is faulty and predict what problems it will cause.

The first 22 pairs of chromosomes provide programs for the development of the body and brain, and the last pair, called the *sex chromosomes*, determines an individual's sex. In females, both chromosomes in the 23rd pair are called X *chromosomes*. In males, the mother contributes an X *chromosome* but the father contributes a Y chromosome. This one difference is responsible for the variance in biological sex. Abnormalities in the sex chromosomal pair can cause ambiguous sexual characteristics (see Chapter 10).

The DNA molecules that contain genes have a certain structure, a double helix, which was discovered only about 50 years ago. The shape of a helix is like a spiral staircase. A double helix is two spirals intertwined, turning in opposite directions. Located on this double spiral are simple pairs of molecules bound together and arranged in different orders. On the X chromosome are approximately 160 million base pairs. The ordering of these base pairs determines how the body develops and works.

If something is wrong in the ordering of these molecules on the double helix, we have a defective gene, which may or may not lead to problems. If it is a single dominant gene, such as the type that controls hair or eye colour, the effect can be quite noticeable. A *dominant gene* is one of a pair of genes that determines a particular trait. A *recessive gene*, by contrast, must be paired with another recessive gene to determine a trait. When we have a dominant gene, using Mendelian laws of genetics, we can predict fairly accurately how many offspring will develop a certain trait, characteristic, or disorder, depending on whether one or both of the parents carry that dominant gene.

Most of the time, predictions are not so simple. Much of our development and, interestingly, most of our behaviour, personality, and even intelligence quotient (IQ) score are probably *polygenic*—that is, influenced by many genes, each contributing only a tiny effect, all of which, in turn, may be influenced by the environment. And because the human *genome*, or an individual's complete set of genes, comprises more than 20 000 genes (U.S. Department of Energy Office of Science, 2009), polygenic interactions can be quite complex. For this reason, most genetic scientists now use sophisticated procedures such as quantitative genetics and molecular genetics that allow them to look for patterns of influence across many genes (Kendler, 2006; Plomin & Davis, 2009; Rutter, Moffitt, & Caspi, 2006; Thapar & McGuffin, 2009). *Quantitative genetics* basically sums up all the tiny effects across many genes without necessarily telling us which genes are responsible for which effects. *Molecular genetics* focuses on examining the actual structure of genes with increasingly advanced technologies such as *DNA microarrays*; these technologies allow scientists to analyze thousands of genes at once and identify broad networks of genes that may be contributing to a particular trait (Plomin & Davis, 2009). Such studies have indicated that hundreds of genes can contribute to the heritability of a single trait (Gottesman, 1997; Hariri et al., 2002; Plomin et al., 1995; Rutter et al., 2006). There also continues to be research to identify specific genes that contribute to individual differences in traits or temperament, such as shyness or impulsivity (e.g., Gershon, Kelsoe, Kendler, & Watson, 2001).

It is very important to understand how genes work. Genes exert their influences on our bodies and our behaviour through a series of steps that produce proteins. Although all cells contain our entire genetic structure, only a small proportion of the genes in any one cell are "turned on" or expressed. In this way, cells become specialized, with some influencing liver function and others affecting personality. What is interesting is that environmental factors, in the form of social and cultural influences, can determine whether genes are "turned on." To take one example, in studies with rat pups, researchers have found that the absence of normal maternal behaviour of "licking and grooming" prevents the genetic expression of a glucocorticoid receptor that modulates stress hormones. This means rats with inadequate maternal care have greater sensitivity to stress (Meaney & Szyf, 2005). There is evidence that a similar model may be relevant in humans (Hyman, 2009). We present more examples later in the chapter when we discuss the interaction of genes and the environment. The study of gene expression and gene–environment interaction is the current frontier in the study of genetics (Kendler, 2006; Plomin & Davis, 2009; Rutter, 2006; Rutter et al., 2006; Thapar & McGuffin, 2009). In Chapter 4, we look at the actual methods scientists use to study the influence of genes. Here, our interest is in what they are finding.

NORMAL FEMALE

© Bio-Photo Associates/Science Source/Photo Researchers

▲ A normal female has 23 pairs of chromosomes.

New Developments in the Study of Genes and Behaviour

Scientists have now identified, in a preliminary way, the genetic contribution to psychological disorders and related behavioural patterns. The best estimates attribute about half of our enduring personality traits and cognitive abilities to genetic influence (Rutter, 2006). For example, McClearn et al. (1997) compared 110 Swedish identical twin pairs, at least 80 years old, with 130 same-sex fraternal twin pairs of a similar age and found heritability estimates for specific cognitive abilities, such as memory or ability to perceive spatial relations, ranged from 32 percent to 62 percent. This work built on earlier important twin studies, with different age groups showing similar results (e.g., Bouchard, Lykken, McGue, Segal, & Tellegen, 1990). Furthermore, a recently published important study of more than 1200 twins spanning 35 years confirmed that during adulthood (from early adulthood to late middle age) genetic factors determined stability in cognitive abilities, whereas environmental factors were responsible for any changes (Lyons et al., 2009). In other studies, the same heritability calculation for personality traits such as shyness or activity levels ranges between 30 percent and 50 percent (Bouchard et al., 1990; Kendler, 2001; Lochlin, 1992; Rutter, 2006; Saudino & Plomin, 1996; Saudino, Plomin, & DeFries, 1996).

It has also become clear that adverse life events such as a "chaotic" childhood can overwhelm the influence of genes (Turkheimer, Haley, Waldron, D'Onofrio, & Gottesman, 2003). For example, one member of a set of twins in the Lyons et al. (2009) study showed marked variability or change in cognitive abilities if his or her environment changed dramatically from the other twin's because of some stressful event such as death of a loved one.

For psychological disorders, the evidence indicates that genetic factors make some contribution to all disorders but account for less than half of the explanation. If one of a pair of identical twins has schizophrenia, there is a less-than-50-percent likelihood that the other twin will also (Gottesman, 1991). Similar or lower rates exist for other psychological disorders (Kendler & Prescott, 2006; Plomin, DeFries, McClearn, & Rutter, 1997; Rutter, 2006).

Behavioural geneticists have reached general conclusions in the past several years on the role of genes and psychological disorders relevant to this chapter's discussion of integrative approaches to psychopathology. First, specific genes or small groups of genes may ultimately be found to be associated with certain psychological disorders, as suggested in several important studies described later. But as discussed earlier, much of the current evidence suggests that contributions to psychological disorders come from many genes, each having a relatively small effect (Flint, 2009; Rutter, 2006). It is extremely important that we recognize this probability and continue to make every attempt to track the group of genes implicated in various disorders. Advances in gene mapping, molecular genetics, and linkage studies help with this difficult research (e.g., Gershon et al., 2001; Hettema, Prescott, Myers, Neale, & Kendler, 2005; Plomin et al., 1997). In linkage studies, scientists study individuals who have the same disorder, such as bipolar disorder, and also share other features, such as eye colour; because the location of the gene for eye colour is known, this allows scientists to attempt to "link" known gene locations (for eye colour, in this example) with the possible location of a gene contributing to the disorder (Flint, 2009; see Chapter 4).

Second, as noted earlier, it has become increasingly clear that genetic contributions cannot be studied in the absence of interactions with events in the environment that trigger genetic vulnerability or "turn on" specific genes (Rutter, 2010). It is to this fascinating topic that we now turn.

The Interaction of Genetic and Environmental Effects

In 1983, Eric Kandel, a distinguished neuroscientist and Nobel Prize winner, speculated that the process of learning affects more than behaviour. He suggested that the very genetic structure of cells may actually change as a result of learning, if genes that were inactive or dormant interact with the environment in such a way that they become active. In other words, the environment may occasionally turn certain genes on. This type of mechanism may lead to changes in the number of receptors at the end of a neuron, which, in turn, would affect biochemical functioning in the brain.

Although Kandel was not the first to propose this idea, it had enormous effect. Most of us assume that the brain, like other parts of the body, may well be influenced by environmental changes during development. But we also assume that once maturity is reached, the structure and function of our internal organs and most of our physiology are set or, in the case of the brain, hardwired. The competing idea is that the brain and its functions are plastic, subject to continual change in response to the environment, even at the level of genetic structure. Now there is strong evidence supporting that view (Kolb, Gibb, & Robinson, 2003; Landis & Insel, 2008; Owens, Mulchahey, Stout, & Plotsky, 1997; Robinson, Fernald, & Clayton, 2008).

▲ Genetic contributions to behaviour are evident in twins who were raised apart. When these brothers were finally reunited, they were both firefighters, and they discovered many other shared characteristics and interests.

© Thomas Wanstall/The Image Works

Genetic Contributions to Psychopathology **37**

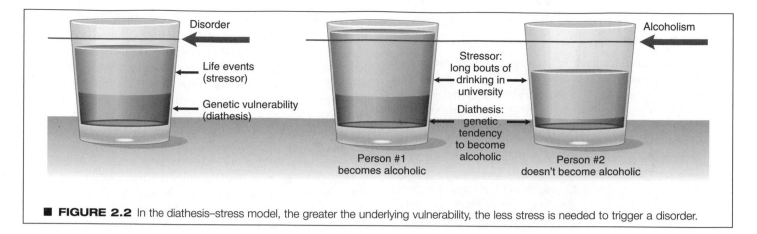

■ FIGURE 2.2 In the diathesis–stress model, the greater the underlying vulnerability, the less stress is needed to trigger a disorder.

With these new findings in mind, we can now explore gene–environment interactions as they relate to psychopathology. Two models have received the most attention: the diathesis–stress model and reciprocal gene–environment model (or gene–environment correlations).

The Diathesis–Stress Model

For years, scientists have assumed a specific method of interaction between genes and the environment. According to this **diathesis–stress model**, individuals inherit, from multiple genes, tendencies to express certain traits or behaviours, which may then be activated under conditions of stress (see **■** Figure 2.2). Each inherited tendency is a *diathesis*, which is a condition that makes a person susceptible to developing a disorder. When the right kind of life event, such as a certain type of stressor, comes along, the disorder develops. For example, according to the diathesis–stress model, Jody inherited a tendency to faint at the sight of blood. This tendency is the diathesis, or **vulnerability**. It would not become prominent until certain environmental events occurred. For Jody, this event was the sight of an animal being dissected when he was in a situation in which escape, or at least closing his eyes, was not acceptable. The stress of seeing the dissection under these conditions activated his genetic tendency to faint. Together, these factors led to him developing a disorder. If he had not taken biology, he might have gone through life without ever knowing he had the tendency, at least to such an extreme, although he might have felt queasy about minor cuts and bruises. You can see that the diathesis is genetically based and the stress is environmental, but they must interact to produce a disorder.

We might also take the case of someone who inherits a vulnerability to alcoholism, which would make that person substantially different from a close friend who does not have the same tendency. During university, both engage in extended drinking bouts, but only the individual with the so-called addictive genes begins the long downward spiral into alcoholism. The friend doesn't. Having a particular vulnerability doesn't mean you will develop the associated disorder. The smaller the vulnerability, the greater the life stress required to produce the disorder; conversely, with greater vulnerability, less life stress is required. This model of gene–environment interactions has been popular, although, in view of the relationship of the environment to the structure and function of the brain, it is greatly oversimplified.

This relationship has now been elegantly demonstrated in a landmark study by Caspi et al. (2003). These investigators are study-ing a group of 847 individuals in New Zealand who have undergone a variety of assessments for more than two decades, starting at the age of three. They noted whether the participants, at age 26, had been depressed during the past year. Overall, 17 percent of the study participants reported that they had experienced a major depressive episode during the prior year. The investigators also identified the genetic makeup of the individuals and, in particular, a gene that produces a substance called a chemical transporter that affects the transmission of serotonin in the brain. Serotonin, one of the four neurotransmitters we will talk about later in the chapter, is particularly implicated in depression. But the gene that Caspi et al. were studying comes in two common versions or alleles: the long allele (L) and the short allele (S). They had reason to believe, from prior work with animals, that individuals with at least two copies of the long allele (LL) were able to cope better with stress than individuals with two copies of the short allele (SS). Since the investigators had been recording all stressful life events for these individuals, they were able to test this relationship. In fact, in people with two S alleles, the risk for having a major depressive episode doubled if they had at least four stressful life events, compared with people experiencing four stressful events who had two L alleles.

The interesting finding occurs when we look at the childhood experience of these individuals. In people with the SS alleles, severe and stressful maltreatment during childhood more than doubled their risk of depression in adulthood compared with those individuals carrying the SS alleles who were not maltreated or abused (63 percent versus 30 percent). For individuals carrying the LL alleles, however, stressful childhood experiences did not affect the incidence of depression in adulthood, since 30 percent of this group became depressed whether or not they had experienced stressful childhood maltreatment. This relationship is shown in **■** Figure 2.3. Therefore, unlike the SS group, depression in the LL allele group seems related to stress in their recent past rather than childhood experiences. This study is by far the most important yet in demonstrating very clearly that neither genes nor life experiences (environmental events) can explain the onset of a disorder such as depression. It takes a complex interaction of the two factors.

Other studies have replicated or supported these findings (Binder et al., 2008; Kilpatrick et al., 2007; Rutter et al., 2006). For example, in the Kilpatrick et al. (2007) study on the development of post-traumatic stress disorder (PTSD), 589 adults who experienced the Florida hurricanes of 2004 were interviewed and DNA was collected to examine genetic structure. Individuals with the

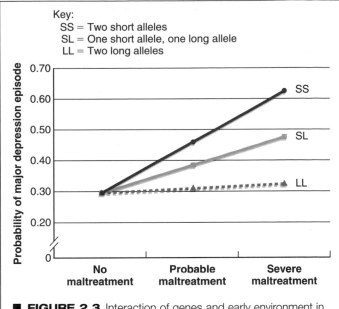

Key:
SS = Two short alleles
SL = One short allele, one long allele
LL = Two long alleles

■ FIGURE 2.3 Interaction of genes and early environment in producing adult major depression

Source: Reprinted with permission from A. Caspi, K. Sugden, T. E. Moffitt, A. Taylor, I. W. Craig, H. Harrington et al (2003). "Influence of Life Stress on Depression: Moderation by a Polymorphism in the 5-HIT Gene." *Science* 18 July 2003. Vol. 301 no. 5631 pp. 386–389. Reprinted with permission from AAAS.

same genetic makeup (SS) that signalled vulnerability in the Caspi et al. (2003) study were also more likely to develop PTSD after the hurricanes than those with the LL alleles. But another factor played a role as well. If individuals had a strong network of family and friends (strong social support), they were protected from developing PTSD even if they had the vulnerable genetic makeup and experienced a trauma (the hurricane). High-risk individuals (high hurricane exposure, SS alleles, and low social support) were at 4.5 times the risk of developing PTSD, as well as depression.

Also, in a study of the same group of New Zealand individuals by the investigators who carried out the study described earlier, Caspi et al. (2002) found that a different set of genes from those associated with depression seems to contribute to violent and antisocial behaviour in adults. But again, this genetic predisposition occurs only if the individuals were maltreated as children. That is, some children who were maltreated turned out to be violent and antisocial as adults, but they were four times more likely to do their

share of rape, robbery, and assault if they had a certain genetic makeup than were those who didn't have the genetic makeup. These studies require replication. In fact, subsequent research suggests that it is not just any one genetic variation that makes people susceptible to stress or other environmental influences (Goldman, Glei, Lin, & Weinstein, 2010; Risch et. al., 2009). A larger network of genes almost certainly plays a role in the development of depression and other disorders. However, these studies do provide powerful, if preliminary, support for the gene–environment interaction model that has had only indirect support until this time.

The Reciprocal Gene–Environment Model

With increased study, the web of interrelationships between genes and environment has been found to be even more complex. Some evidence now indicates that genetic endowment may *increase the probability* that an individual will experience stressful life events (e.g., Kendler, 2001, 2006; Rutter, 2006, 2010; Saudino, Pedersen, Lichtenstein, McClearn, & Plomin, 1997; Thapar & McGuffin, 2009). For example, people with a genetic vulnerability to develop a certain disorder, such as blood-injury-injection phobia, may also have a personality trait— let's say impulsiveness—that makes them more likely to be involved in minor accidents that would result in their seeing blood. In other words, they may be accident prone because they are continually rushing to complete things or to get to places without regard for their physical safety. These people, then, might have a genetically determined tendency to create the very environmental risk factors that trigger a genetic vulnerability to blood-injury-injection phobia.

This is the **reciprocal gene–environment model** or gene–environment correlation model (Kendler, 2001; Thapar & McGuffin, 2009) (see ■ Figure 2.4). Some evidence indicates that it applies to the development of depression, because some people may tend to seek out difficult relationships or other circumstances that lead to depression (Bebbington et al., 1988; Kendler et al., 1995; McGuffin, Katz, & Bebbington, 1988). (However, this did not seem to be the case in the New Zealand study described earlier [Caspi et al., 2003], because stressful episodes during adulthood occurred with about the same frequency in the SS and the LL groups.) McGue and Lykken (1992) have even applied the reciprocal gene–environment model to some fascinating data on the influence of genes on the divorce rate. For example, if you and your spouse each have an identical twin, and both identical twins have been divorced, the chance that you will also divorce increases greatly. Furthermore, if

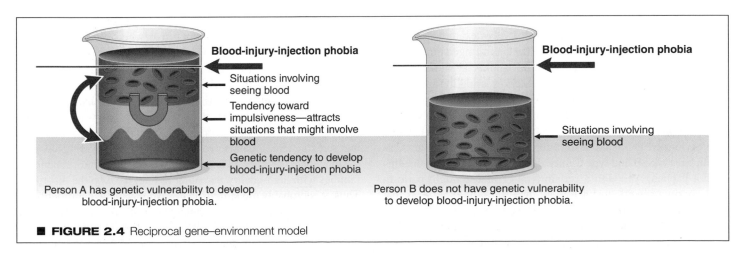

Blood-injury-injection phobia

Situations involving seeing blood

Tendency toward impulsiveness—attracts situations that might involve blood

Genetic tendency to develop blood-injury-injection phobia

Person A has genetic vulnerability to develop blood-injury-injection phobia.

Blood-injury-injection phobia

Situations involving seeing blood

Person B does not have genetic vulnerability to develop blood-injury-injection phobia.

■ FIGURE 2.4 Reciprocal gene–environment model

your identical twin and your parents and your spouse's parents have been divorced, the chance that you will divorce is 77.5 percent. Conversely, if none of your family members on either side has been divorced, the probability that you will divorce is only 5.3 percent.

This is the extreme example, but McGue and Lykken (1992) demonstrated that the probability of your divorcing doubles over the probability in the population at large if your fraternal twin is also divorced and increases sixfold if your identical twin is divorced. Why would this happen? Obviously, no one gene causes divorce. To the extent it is genetically determined, the tendency to divorce is almost certainly related to various inherited traits, such as being high-strung, impulsive, or short-tempered, that make someone hard to get along with (Jockin, McGue, & Lykken, 1996). Another possibility is that an inherited trait makes it more likely you will choose an incompatible spouse. To take a simple example, if you are passive and unassertive, you may well choose a strong, dominant mate who turns out to be impossible to live with. You get divorced but then find yourself attracted to another individual with the same personality traits, who is also impossible to live with. Some people would simply attribute this kind of pattern to poor judgment. Nevertheless, there's no doubt that social, interpersonal, psychological, and environmental factors play major roles in whether we stay married, and it's quite possible that our genes contribute to how we create our own environment.

Epigenetics and the Nongenomic "Inheritance" of Behaviour

To make things a bit more interesting but also more complicated, a number of recent reports suggest that studies to date have over-emphasized the extent of genetic influence on our personalities, our temperaments, and their contribution to the development of psychological disorders. This overemphasis may be partly the result of the manner in which these studies have been conducted (Moore, 2001; Turkheimer & Waldron, 2000). Several intriguing lines of evidence have come together in recent years to buttress this conclusion.

For example, in their animal laboratories, Crabbe, Wahlsten, and Dudek (1999) conducted a clever experiment in which three types of mice with different genetic makeups were raised in virtually identical environments at three sites, the home universities of the behavioural geneticists just named. Each mouse of a given type (e.g., type A) was genetically indistinguishable from all other mice of that type at each of the universities. The experimenters went out of their way to make sure the environments (e.g., laboratory, cage, and lighting conditions) were the same at each university. For example, each site had the same kind of sawdust bedding that was changed on the same day of the week. If the animals had to be handled, all of them were handled at the same time by experimenters wearing the same kind of glove. When their tails were marked for identification, the same type of pen was used. If genes determine the behaviour of the mice, then mice with virtually identical genetic makeup (type A) should have performed the same at all three sites on a series of tests, as should have type B and type C mice. But the results showed that this did not happen. Although a certain type of mouse might perform similarly on a specific test across all three sites, on other tests that type of mouse performed differently. Robert Sapolsky, a prominent neuroscientist, concluded, "genetic influences are often a lot less powerful than is commonly believed. The environment, even

working subtly, can still mold and hold its own in the biological interactions that shape who we are" (Sapolsky, 2000, p. 15).

In another fascinating program of research with rats (Cameron et al., 2005; Francis, Diorio, Liu, & Meaney, 1999; Weaver et al., 2004), the investigators studied stress reactivity and how it is passed through generations, using a powerful experimental procedure called *cross-fostering*, in which a rat pup born to one mother is assigned to another mother for rearing. They first demonstrated, as had many other investigators, that maternal behaviour affected how the young rats tolerated stress. If the mothers were calm and supportive, their rat pups were less fearful and better able to tolerate stress. But we don't know if this effect results from genetic influences or from being raised by calm mothers. This is where cross-fostering comes in. Francis et al. (1999) took some newly born rat pups of fearful and easily stressed mothers and placed them for rearing with calm mothers. Other young rats remained with their easily stressed mothers. With this interesting scientific twist, Francis et al. (1999) demonstrated that calm and supportive behaviour by the mothers could be passed down through generations of rats *independent of genetic influences*, because rats born to easily stressed mothers but reared by calm mothers grew up more calm and supportive. The authors concluded, "these findings suggest that individual differences in the expression of genes in brain regions that regulate stress reactivity can be transmitted from one generation to the next through behaviour. . . . The results . . . suggest that the mechanism for this pattern of inheritance involves differences in maternal care" (p. 1158).

In subsequent studies from this group (Cameron et al., 2005), the investigators demonstrated that the maternal behaviour had lastingly altered the endocrine response to stress by affecting gene expression. But this effect only occurred if the rat mother was calm and nurturing during the rat pups' first week of life. After that—it didn't matter. This highlights the importance of early experience on behaviour.

Other scientists have reported similar results (Anisman, Zaharia, Meaney, & Merali, 1998; Harper, 2005). For example, Suomi (1999), working with rhesus monkeys and using the cross-fostering strategies just described, showed that if genetically reactive and emotional young monkeys are reared by calm mothers for the first six months of their lives, the animals behaved in later life as if they were nonemotional and not reactive to stress at birth. In other words, the environmental effects of early parenting seem to override any genetic contribution to be anxious, emotional, or reactive to stress. Suomi (1999) also demonstrated that these emotionally reactive monkeys raised by "calm, supportive" parents were also calm and supportive when raising their own young, thereby influencing and even reversing the genetic contribution to the expression of personality traits or temperaments.

Strong effects of the environment have also been observed in humans. For example, Tienari et al. (1994) found that children of parents with schizophrenia who were adopted away as babies demonstrated a tendency to develop psychiatric disorders (including schizophrenia) themselves only if they were adopted into dysfunctional families. Those children adopted into functional families with high-quality parenting did not develop the disorders. Thus, it is probably too simplistic to say the genetic contribution to a personality trait or to a psychological disorder is approximately 50 percent. We can talk of a heritable (genetic) contribution only in the context of the individual's past and present environment.

In support of this conclusion, Suomi (2000) demonstrated that for young monkeys with a specific genetic pattern associated with a highly reactive temperament (emotional or susceptible to the effects of stress), early maternal deprivation (disruptions in mothering) will have a powerful effect on their neuroendocrine functioning and their later behavioural and emotional reactions. However, for animals not carrying this genetic characteristic, maternal deprivation will have little effect, just as was found in the New Zealand study in humans by Caspi et al. (2003), and it is likely this effect will be carried down through the generations. But, as noted in the example of genetic influences on cognitive abilities (Turkheimer et al., 2003), extremely chaotic early environments can override genetic factors and alter neuroendocrine function to increase the likelihood of later behavioural and emotional disorders (Ouellet-Morin et al., 2008).

How does this work? It seems that genes are turned on or off by cellular material that is located just outside of the genome ("epi," as in the word **epigenetics**, means on or around) and that stress, nutrition, or other factors can affect this epigenome, which is then immediately passed down to the next generation and maybe for several generations (Arai, Li, Hartley, & Feig, 2009). The genome itself isn't changed, so if the stressful or inadequate environment disappears, eventually the epigenome will fade. These new conceptualizations of the role of genetic contributions as only constraining environmental influences have implications for preventing unwanted personality traits or temperaments and even psychological disorders. That is, it seems that environmental manipulations, particularly early in life, may do much to override the genetically influenced tendency to develop undesirable behavioural and emotional reactions. Although current research suggests that environmental influences, such as peer groups and schools, affect this genetic expression, the strongest evidence exists for the effects of early parenting influences and other early experiences (Cameron et al., 2005; Collins et al., 2000; Ouellet-Morin et al., 2008).

Nowhere is the complexity of the interaction of genetic and environmental influences more apparent than in the famous cases of Chang and Eng, a pair of conjoined identical twins born to parents living in Thailand in 1810 (known as Siam at the time) who were joined at the chest. These individuals, who travelled around the world performing at exhibitions, were the source of the name Siamese twins. These twins were very entrepreneurial and successful with their entertaining and exhibitions, and they amassed a small fortune. In 1839 they settled down with their wives, a pair of sisters. These two marital pairs produced 12 children each. These identical twins obviously shared identical genes as well as nearly identical environments throughout their lives. Thus, we would certainly expect them to behave in very similar ways when it comes to personality features, temperaments, and psychological disorders. Instead, everybody who knew these twins noted that they had very distinct personalities. Chang was prone to moodiness and depression, and finally started drinking heavily. Eng, on the other hand, was much more cheerful, quiet, and thoughtful (Moore, 2001). It is interesting to speculate about the similarities and differences in personality and susceptibility to specific psychological disorders that we might expect in Krista and Tatiana Simms, conjoined twins born in Vernon, British Columbia, in October 2006. And how would we expect these similarities and differences in traits and behaviours to be impacted

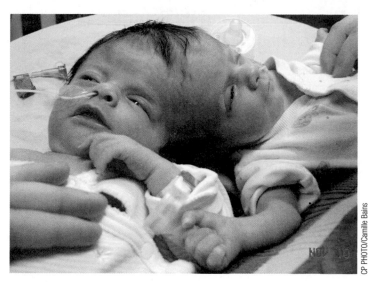

▲ Krista and Tatiana Simms, conjoined twins born in Vernon, British Columbia, in October 2006.

should the twins' parents and physicians decide to pursue surgical separation of these two girls, who are now joined at the head (CanWest News Service, 2006)?

In summary, a complex interaction between genes and the environment plays an important role in every psychological disorder (Kendler, 2001; Rutter, 2006, 2010; Turkheimer, 1998). Our genetic endowment does contribute to our behaviour, our emotions, and our cognitive processes and constrains the influence of environmental factors, such as upbringing, on our later behaviour, as is evident in the New Zealand study (Caspi et al., 2003) and its later replications. Environmental events, in turn, seem to affect our very genetic structure by determining whether certain genes are activated or not (Gottlieb, 1998; Landis & Insel, 2008). Furthermore, strong environmental influences alone may be sufficient to override genetic diatheses. Thus, neither nature (genes) nor nurture (environmental events) alone, but a complex interaction of the two, influences the development of our behaviour and personalities.

Concept Check | 2.2

Determine whether these statements relating to the genetic contributions of psychopathology are true (T) or false (F).

1. _____ The first 20 pairs of chromosomes program the development of the body and brain.

2. _____ No individual genes have been identified that cause any major psychological disorders.

3. _____ According to the diathesis–stress model, people inherit a vulnerability to express certain traits or behaviours that may be activated under certain stress conditions.

4. _____ The idea that individuals may have a genetic endowment to increase the probability that they will experience stressful life events and therefore trigger a vulnerability is in accordance with the diathesis–stress model.

5. _____ Environmental events alone influence the development of our behaviour and personalities.

Neuroscience and Its Contributions to Psychopathology

Knowing how the nervous system and, especially, the brain work is central to any understanding of our behaviour, emotions, and cognitive processes. This knowledge is the focus of **neuroscience**. To comprehend the newest research in this field, we first need an overview of how the brain and the nervous system function. The human nervous system includes the central nervous system, consisting of the brain and the spinal cord, and the peripheral nervous system, consisting of the somatic nervous system and the autonomic nervous system (see ■ Figure 2.5).

The Central Nervous System

The central nervous system (CNS) processes all information received from our sense organs and reacts as necessary. It sorts out what is relevant, such as a certain taste or a new sound, from what isn't, such as a familiar view or ticking clock; checks the memory banks to determine why the information is relevant; and implements the right reaction, whether it is to answer a question or to play a Chopin *étude*. The CNS performs a lot of exceedingly complex work. The spinal cord is part of the central nervous system, but its primary function is to facilitate the sending of messages to and from the brain, which is the other major component of the CNS and the most complex organ in the body. The brain uses an average of 140 billion nerve cells,

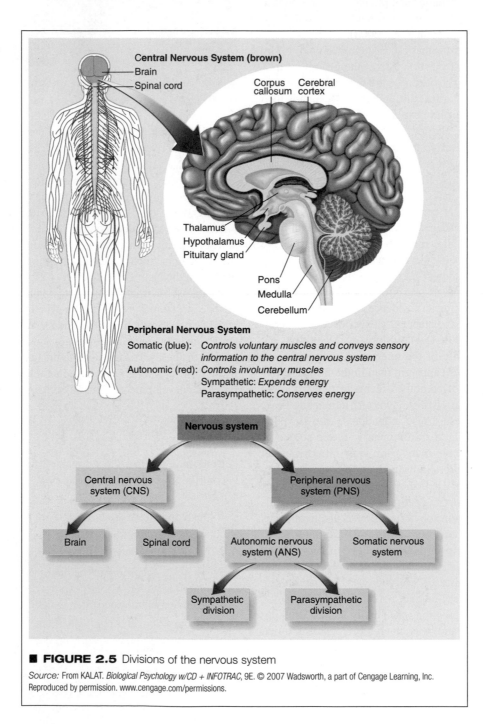

■ **FIGURE 2.5** Divisions of the nervous system

Source: From KALAT. *Biological Psychology w/CD + INFOTRAC*, 9E. © 2007 Wadsworth, a part of Cengage Learning, Inc. Reproduced by permission. www.cengage.com/permissions.

▲ The central nervous system screens out information that is irrelevant to the current situation. From moment to moment we notice what moves or changes more than what remains the same.

called **neurons**, to control our every thought and action. Neurons transmit information throughout the nervous system. Understanding how they work is important for our purposes, because current research has confirmed that neurons contribute to psychopathology.

The typical neuron contains a central cell body with two kinds of branches. One kind of branch is called a *dendrite*. Dendrites have numerous *receptors* that receive messages in the form of chemical impulses from other nerve cells, which are converted into electrical impulses. The other kind of branch, called an axon,

transmits these impulses to other neurons. Any one nerve cell may have multiple connections to other neurons. The brain has billions of nerve cells, so you can see how complicated the system becomes, far more complicated than the most powerful computer that has ever been built (or will be for some time).

Nerve cells are not actually connected. There is a small space through which the impulse must pass to get to the next neuron. The space between the axon of one neuron and the dendrite of another is called the **synaptic cleft** (see ■ Figure 2.6). What happens in

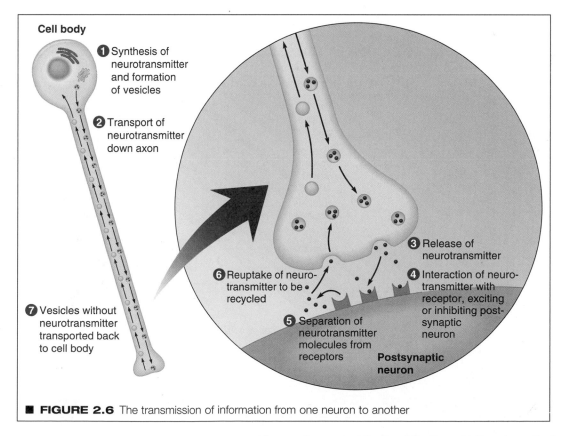

Cell body

① Synthesis of neurotransmitter and formation of vesicles

② Transport of neurotransmitter down axon

⑦ Vesicles without neurotransmitter transported back to cell body

⑥ Reuptake of neuro-transmitter to be recycled

⑤ Separation of neurotransmitter molecules from receptors

③ Release of neurotransmitter

④ Interaction of neuro-transmitter with receptor, exciting or inhibiting post-synaptic neuron

Postsynaptic neuron

■ **FIGURE 2.6** The transmission of information from one neuron to another this space is of great interest to psychopathologists. The chemicals that are released from the axon of one nerve cell and transmit the impulse to the receptors of another nerve cell are called **neurotransmitters**, which were mentioned briefly when we described the genetic contribution to depression in the New Zealand study by Caspi et al. (2003). Only in the past several decades have we begun to understand the complexity of neurotransmitters. Now, using increasingly sensitive equipment and techniques, scientists have identified many different types of neurotransmitters.

Major neurotransmitters relevant to psychopathology include *norepinephrine* (also known as noradrenaline), *serotonin, dopamine*, and *gamma aminobutyric acid (GABA)*. You will see these terms many times in this book. Excesses or insufficiencies of some neurotransmitters are associated with different groups of psychological disorders. For example, reduced levels of GABA were initially thought to be associated with excessive anxiety (Costa, 1985). Early research (Snyder, 1976, 1981) linked increases in dopamine activity to schizophrenia. Other early research found correlations between depression and high levels of norepinephrine (Schildkraut, 1965) and, possibly, low levels of serotonin (Siever, Davis, & Gorman, 1991). However, more recent research, described later in this chapter, indicates that these early interpretations were much too simplistic. Many types and subtypes of neurotransmitters are just being discovered, and they interact in very complex ways. In view of their importance, we will return to the subject of neurotransmitters shortly.

The Structure of the Brain

Having an overview of the brain is useful because many of the structures described here are later mentioned in the context of specific disorders. One way to view the brain (see ■ Figure 2.7) is to see it in two parts—the *brain stem* and the *forebrain*. The brain stem is the lower and more ancient part of the brain. Found in most animals, this structure handles most of the essential automatic functions such as breathing, sleeping, and moving around in a coordinated way. The forebrain is more advanced and has evolved more recently.

The lowest part of the brain stem, the *hindbrain*, contains the *medulla*, the *pons*, and the *cerebellum*. The hindbrain regulates many automatic activities, such as breathing, the pumping action of the heart (heartbeat), and digestion. The cerebellum controls motor coordination.

The *midbrain* coordinates movement with sensory input and contains parts of the *reticular activating system (RAS)*, which contributes to processes of arousal and tension such as whether we are awake or asleep.

At the very top of the brain stem are the *thalamus* and *hypothalamus*, which are involved very broadly with regulating behaviour and emotion. These structures function primarily as a relay between the forebrain and the remaining lower areas of the brain stem. Some anatomists even consider the thalamus and hypothalamus parts of the forebrain.

At the base of the forebrain, just above the *thalamus* and *hypothalamus*, is the *limbic system*. *Limbic* means "border." The limbic system, which figures prominently in much of psychopathology, includes such structures as the *hippocampus* (sea horse), *cingulate gyrus* (girdle), *septum* (partition), and *amygdala* (almond), all of

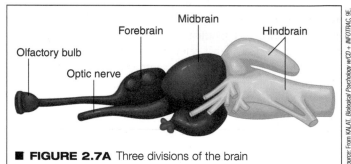

■ FIGURE 2.7A Three divisions of the brain

Source: From KALAT. *Biological Psychology w/CD + INFOTRAC*, 9E. © 2007 Wadsworth, a part of Cengage Learning, Inc. Reproduced by permission. www.cengage.com/permissions

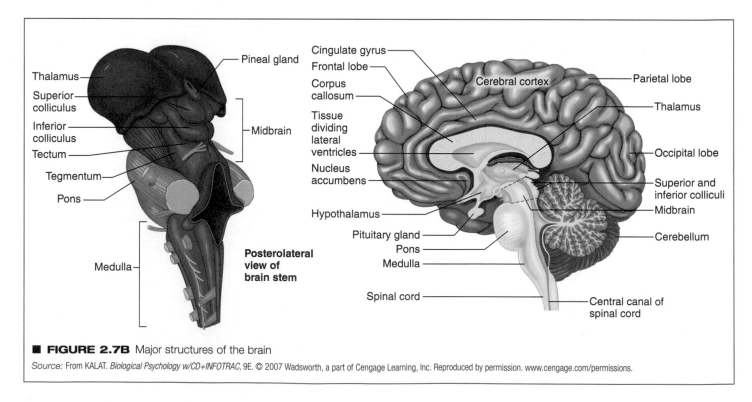

■ FIGURE 2.7B Major structures of the brain

Source: From KALAT. *Biological Psychology w/CD+INFOTRAC*, 9E. © 2007 Wadsworth, a part of Cengage Learning, Inc. Reproduced by permission. www.cengage.com/permissions.

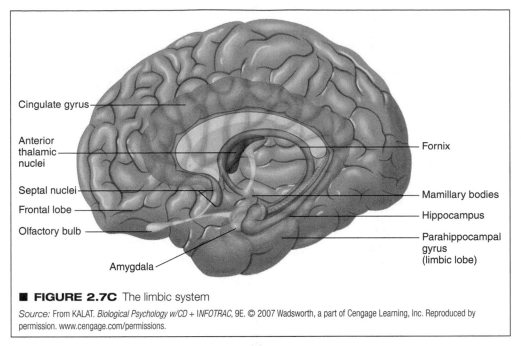

■ FIGURE 2.7C The limbic system

Source: From KALAT. *Biological Psychology w/CD + INFOTRAC*, 9E. © 2007 Wadsworth, a part of Cengage Learning, Inc. Reproduced by permission. www.cengage.com/permissions.

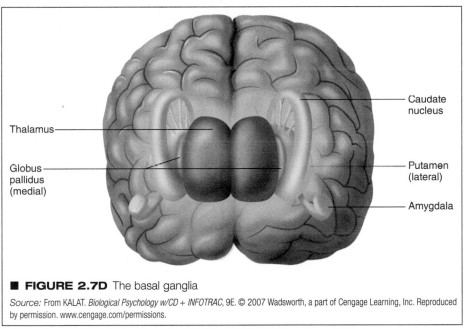

■ FIGURE 2.7D The basal ganglia

Source: From KALAT. *Biological Psychology w/CD + INFOTRAC*, 9E. © 2007 Wadsworth, a part of Cengage Learning, Inc. Reproduced by permission. www.cengage.com/permissions.

which are named for their approximate shapes. This system helps regulate our emotional experiences and expressions and, to some extent, our ability to learn and to control our impulses. It is also involved with the basic drives of sex, aggression, hunger, and thirst.

The *basal ganglia*, also at the base of the forebrain, include the *caudate* (tailed) *nucleus*. Because damage to these structures may make us change our posture or twitch or shake, they are believed to control motor activity. Later in this chapter we review some very interesting findings on the relationship of this area to obsessive-compulsive disorder.

The largest part of the forebrain is the *cerebral cortex*, which contains more than 80 percent of all the neurons in the central nervous system. This part of the brain provides us with our distinctly human qualities, allowing us to look to the future and plan, to reason, and to create. The cerebral cortex is divided into two hemispheres. Although the hemispheres look very much alike structurally and

operate relatively independently (both are capable of perceiving, thinking, and remembering), recent research indicates that each has different specialties. The left hemisphere seems to be chiefly responsible for verbal and other cognitive processes. The right hemisphere seems to be better at perceiving the world around us and creating images. The hemispheres may play differential roles in specific psychological disorders. For example, current theories about dyslexia (a learning disability involving reading) suggest it may be a result of the two hemispheres not specializing adequately or communicating properly with each other (Shaywitz, 2003). Each hemisphere consists of four separate areas or lobes: *temporal, parietal, occipital,* and *frontal* (see ■ Figure 2.8). Each is associated with different processes: the temporal lobe with recognizing various sights and sounds and with long-term memory storage; the parietal lobe with recognizing various sensations of touch; the occipital lobe with integrating and making sense of various visual inputs. These three lobes, located

Neuroscience and Its Contributions to Psychopathology

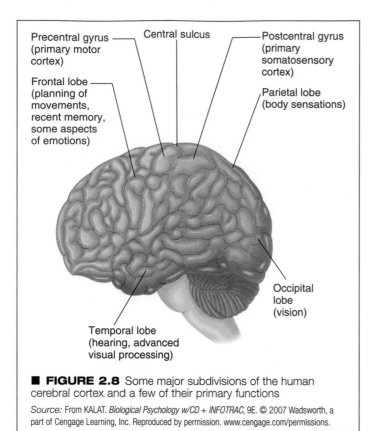

Precentral gyrus (primary motor cortex)

Central sulcus

Postcentral gyrus (primary somatosensory cortex)

Frontal lobe (planning of movements, recent memory, some aspects of emotions)

Parietal lobe (body sensations)

Occipital lobe (vision)

Temporal lobe (hearing, advanced visual processing)

■ **FIGURE 2.8** Some major subdivisions of the human cerebral cortex and a few of their primary functions

Source: From KALAT. *Biological Psychology w/CD + INFOTRAC*, 9E. © 2007 Wadsworth, a part of Cengage Learning, Inc. Reproduced by permission. www.cengage.com/permissions.

toward the back (posterior) of the brain, work together to process sight, touch, hearing, and other signals from our senses.

The frontal lobe is the most interesting from the point of view of psychopathology. It carries most of the weight of our thinking and reasoning abilities as well as our memory. It also enables us to relate to the world around us and to the people in it, to behave as social animals. When studying areas of the brain for clues to psychopathology, most researchers focus on the frontal lobe of the cerebral cortex, as well as on the limbic system and the basal ganglia.

Concept Check | 2.3

Check your understanding of the structures of the brain by listing which is being described in the sentences here:
(a) frontal lobe, (b) brain stem, (c) midbrain, or (d) cerebral cortex.

1. Movement, breathing, and sleeping depend on this ancient part of the brain, which is present in most animals. _____

2. This area contains parts of the reticular activating system and coordinates movement with sensory output. _____

3. More than 80 percent of the neurons in the human central nervous system are contained in this part of the brain, which gives us distinct qualities. _____

4. This area is responsible for most of our memory, thinking, and reasoning capabilities, and makes us social animals. _____

The Peripheral Nervous System

The peripheral nervous system coordinates with the brain stem to make sure the body is working properly. Its two major components are the *somatic nervous system* and the *autonomic nervous system* (*ANS*). The somatic nervous system controls the muscles, so damage in this area might make it difficult for us to engage in any voluntary movement, including talking. The autonomic nervous system includes the *sympathetic nervous system* (*SNS*) and *parasympathetic nervous system* (*PNS*). The primary duties of the ANS are to regulate the cardiovascular system (e.g., the heart and blood vessels) and the endocrine system (e.g., the pituitary, adrenal, thyroid, and gonadal glands) and to perform various other functions, including aiding digestion and regulating body temperature (see ■ Figure 2.9).

The *endocrine system* works a bit differently from other systems in the body. Each endocrine gland produces its own chemical messenger, called a **hormone**, and releases it directly into the bloodstream. The adrenal glands produce epinephrine (also called *adrenaline*) in response to stress, as well as salt-regulating hormones; the thyroid gland produces thyroxine, which facilitates energy, metabolism, and growth; the pituitary is a master gland that produces a variety of regulatory hormones; and the gonadal glands produce sex hormones such as estrogen and testosterone. The endocrine system is closely related to the immune system; it is also implicated in a variety of disorders, particularly the stress-related physical disorders discussed in Chapter 9.

The sympathetic and parasympathetic divisions of the ANS often operate in a complementary fashion. The SNS is primarily responsible for mobilizing the body during times of stress or danger, by rapidly activating the organs and glands under its control. When the sympathetic division goes on alert, the heart beats faster, thereby increasing the flow of blood to the muscles; respiration increases, allowing more oxygen to get into the blood and brain; and the adrenal glands are stimulated. All these changes help mobilize us for action. If we are threatened by some immediate danger, such as a mugger coming at us on the street, we are able to run faster or defend ourselves with greater strength than if the sympathetic nervous system had not innervated our internal organs. When you read in the newspaper that a woman lifted a heavy object to free a trapped child, you can be sure her sympathetic nervous system was working overtime. This system mediates a substantial part of our emergency or alarm reaction, discussed later in this chapter and in Chapter 5.

One of the functions of the parasympathetic system is to balance the sympathetic system. In other words, because we cannot operate in a state of hyperarousal and preparedness forever, the PNS takes over after the SNS has been active for a while, normalizing our arousal and facilitating the storage of energy by helping the digestive process.

One brain connection that is implicated in some psychological disorders involves the hypothalamus and the endocrine system. The hypothalamus connects to the adjacent pituitary gland, which is the master or coordinator of the endocrine system. The pituitary gland, in turn, may stimulate the cortical part of the adrenal glands on top of the kidneys. As we noted previously, surges of epinephrine tend to energize us, arouse us, and get our

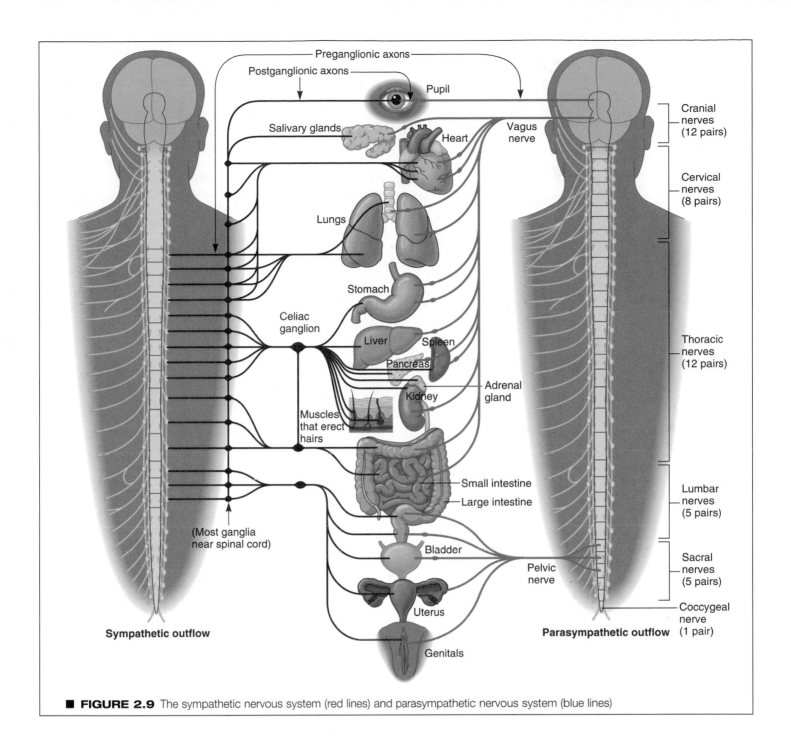

■ FIGURE 2.9 The sympathetic nervous system (red lines) and parasympathetic nervous system (blue lines)

bodies ready for threat or challenge. When athletes say their adrenaline was really flowing, they mean they were highly aroused and up for the game. The cortical part of the adrenal glands also produces the stress hormone *cortisol*. This system is called the *hypothalamic pituitary-adrenalcortical axis*, or *HPA axis* (see ■ Figure 2.10); it has been implicated in several psychological disorders.

This brief overview should give you a general sense of the structure and function of the brain and nervous system. New procedures for studying brain structure and function that involve photographing the working brain are discussed in Chapter 3. Here, we focus on what these studies reveal about the nature of psychopathology.

Neurotransmitters

The biochemical neurotransmitters in the brain and nervous system that carry messages from one neuron to another are receiving intense attention by psychopathologists (Bloom & Kupfer, 1995; Bloom, Nelson, & Lazerson, 2001; LeDoux, 2002; Iverson, 2006; Nestler, Hyman, & Malenka, 2008; Secko, 2005). These biochemicals were discovered only in the past several decades, and only in the past few years have we developed the extraordinarily sophisticated procedures necessary to study them. One way to think of neurotransmitters is as narrow currents flowing through the ocean of the brain. Sometimes they run parallel with other currents, only to separate again. Often they seem to meander aimlessly, looping back on themselves before moving on. Neurons

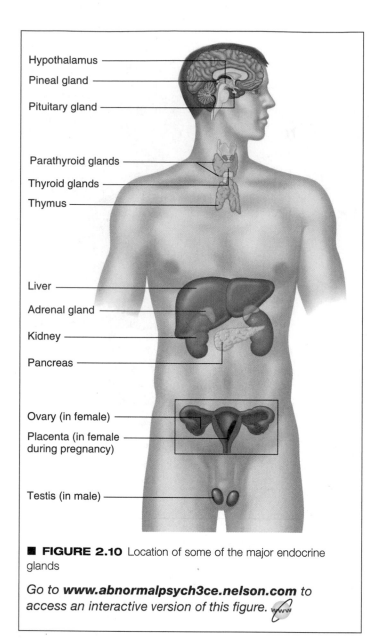

■ FIGURE 2.10 Location of some of the major endocrine glands

Go to **www.abnormalpsych3ce.nelson.com** *to access an interactive version of this figure.*

considerable flux, the neuroscience of psychopathology is an exciting area of study that may lead to new drug treatments among other advances. However, research findings that seem to apply to psychopathology today may no longer be relevant tomorrow. Many years of study will be required before it is all sorted out.

You may still read reports that certain psychological disorders are "caused" by biochemical imbalances, excesses, or deficiencies in certain neurotransmitter systems. For example, abnormal activity of the neurotransmitter serotonin is often described as causing depression, and abnormalities in the neurotransmitter dopamine have been implicated in schizophrenia. However, increasing evidence indicates that this is an enormous oversimplification. We are now learning that the effects of neurotransmitter activity are less specific. They often seem to be related to the way we process information (Bloom et al., 2001; Depue, Luciana, Arbisi, Collins, & Leon, 1994; Harmer et al., 2009; Kandel, Schwartz, & Jessell, 2000; LeDoux, 2002; Sullivan & LeDoux, 2004). Changes in neurotransmitter activity may make people more or less likely to exhibit certain kinds of behaviour in certain situations without causing the behaviour directly. In addition, broad-based disturbances in our functioning are almost always associated with interactions of the various neurotransmitters rather than with alterations in the activity of any one system (Depue & Spoont, 1986; Depue & Zald, 1993; Fineberg et al., 2010; LeDoux, 2002; Owens et al., 1997; Secko, 2005; Stahl, 2008; Xing, Zhang, Russell, & Post, 2006). In other words, the currents intersect so often that changes in one result in changes in the other, often in a way scientists have not yet been able to predict.

Research on neurotransmitter function focuses primarily on what happens when activity levels change. We can study this in several ways. We can introduce substances called **agonists** that effectively *increase* the activity of a neurotransmitter by mimicking its effects; substances called **antagonists** that *decrease*, or block, a neurotransmitter; or substances called **inverse agonists** that produce effects *opposite* to those produced by the neurotransmitter. By systematically manipulating the production of a neurotransmitter in different parts of the brain, scientists are able to learn more about its effects. Most drugs could be classified as either agonistic or antagonistic, although they may achieve these results in a variety of ways. That is, these drug therapies work by either increasing or decreasing the flow of specific neurotransmitters. Some drugs directly inhibit, or block, the production of a neurotransmitter. Other drugs increase the production of competing biochemical substances that may deactivate the neurotransmitter. Yet other drugs do not affect neurotransmitters directly but prevent the chemical from reaching the next neuron by closing down, or occupying, the receptors in that neuron. After a neurotransmitter is released, it is quickly drawn back from the synaptic cleft into the same neuron. This process is called **reuptake**. Some drugs work by blocking the reuptake process, thereby causing continued stimulation along the brain circuit.

Here we will focus on several classic neurotransmitters most relevant to psychopathology. Two types of neurotransmitters, *monoamines* and *amino acids*, have been most studied in regard to psychopathology. These are considered the "classic" neurotransmitters because they are synthesized in the nerve. Neurotransmitters in the monoamine class include norepinephrine (also known as noradrenaline), serotonin, and dopamine. Amino acid neurotransmitters include GABA and glutamate.

that are sensitive to one type of neurotransmitter cluster together and form paths from one part of the brain to the other.

Often these paths overlap with the paths of other neurotransmitters, but, as often as not, they end up going their separate ways (Bloom et al., 2001; Dean, Kelsey, Heller, & Ciaranello, 1993). There are thousands, perhaps tens of thousands, of these **brain circuits**, and we are just beginning to discover and map them (Arenkiel & Ehlers, 2009). Neuroscientists have identified several neural pathways that seem to play roles in various psychological disorders (Fineberg et al., 2010; LeDoux, 2002; Stahl, 2008; Tau & Peterson, 2010).

New neurotransmitters are frequently discovered, and existing neurotransmitter systems must be subdivided into separate classifications. Current estimates suggest that more than 100 different neurotransmitters, each with multiple receptors, are functioning in various parts of the nervous system (Borodinsky et al., 2004; Sharp, 2009). Also, scientists are increasingly discovering additional biochemicals and gases that have certain neurotransmitter properties. Because this dynamic field of research is in a state of

Glutamate and GABA

Two major neurotransmitters affect much of what we do. Each of these substances is in the amino acid category of neurotransmitters. The first, **glutamate**, is an excitatory transmitter that "turns on" many different neurons, leading to action. A second type of amino acid transmitter is **gamma aminobutyric acid**, or **GABA** for short, which is an inhibitory neurotransmitter. Thus, the job of GABA is to inhibit (or regulate) the transmission of information and action potentials. Because these two neurotransmitters work in concert to balance functioning in the brain, they have been referred to as the "chemical brothers" (LeDoux, 2002). Glutamate and GABA operate relatively independently at a molecular level, but the relative balance of each in a cell will determine whether the neuron is activated (fires) or not.

Another characteristic of these "chemical brothers" is that they are fast acting, as they would have to be for the brain to keep up with the many environmental influences that require action or restraint. Overactivity of the glutamate system could literally burn out sections of the nervous system in a worst-case scenario. Some people who like Chinese food and who are sensitive to glutamate may have experienced a few adverse reactions from a common additive in Chinese food referred to as MSG. MSG stands for monosodium glutamate; it can increase the amount of glutamate in the body, causing headaches, ringing in the ears, or other physical symptoms in some people. We return to some exciting new findings involving glutamate-specific receptors when we discuss new treatments for anxiety disorders in Chapter 5.

As noted earlier, GABA reduces postsynaptic activity, which, in turn, inhibits a variety of behaviours and emotions. GABA was discovered before glutamate and has been studied for a longer period; its best-known effect is to reduce anxiety (Charney & Drevets, 2002; Davis, 2002; Sullivan & LeDoux, 2004). Scientists have discovered that a particular class of drugs, the *benzodiazepines*, or minor tranquilizers, makes it easier for GABA molecules to attach themselves to the receptors of specialized neurons. Thus, the higher the level of benzodiazepine, the more GABA becomes attached to neuron receptors and the calmer we become (to a point). Because benzodiazepines have certain addictive properties, clinical scientists are working to identify other substances that may also modulate levels of GABA; these include certain natural steroids in the brain (Eser, Schule, Baghai, Romeo, & Rupprecht, 2006; Gordon, 2002; Rupprecht et al., 2009).

As with other neurotransmitter systems, we now know that GABA's effect is not specific to anxiety but has a broader influence. The GABA system rides on many circuits distributed widely throughout the brain. GABA seems to reduce overall arousal somewhat and to temper our emotional responses. For example, in addition to reducing anxiety, minor tranquilizers have an anticonvulsant effect, relaxing muscle groups that may be subject to spasms. Drug compounds that increase GABA are also under evaluation as treatments for insomnia (Sullivan & Guilleminault, 2009; Walsh et al., 2008). Furthermore, the GABA system seems to reduce levels of anger, hostility, aggression, and perhaps even positive emotional states such as eager anticipation and pleasure, making GABA a generalized inhibiting neurotransmitter, much as glutamate has a generalized excitatory function (Bond & Lader, 1979; Lader, 1975; Sharp, 2009). We are also learning that the GABA system is not just one system working in only one manner but

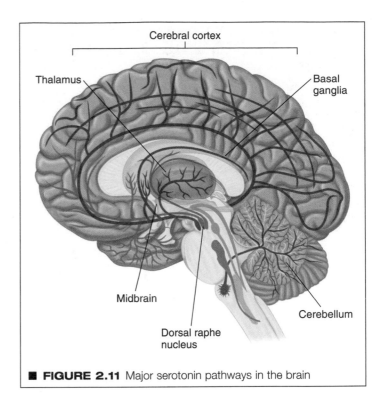

■ **FIGURE 2.11** Major serotonin pathways in the brain

is composed of a number of subsystems. Different types of GABA receptors seem to act in different ways, with perhaps only one of the subtypes having an affinity for the benzodiazepine component (D'Hulst, Atack, & Kooy, 2009; Gray, 1985; LeDoux, 2002; Pritchett, Lüddens, & Seeburg, 1989; Sharp, 2009). Therefore, the conclusion that this system is responsible for anxiety seems just as out of date as concluding that the serotonin system is responsible for depression (see the next section).

Serotonin

The technical name for **serotonin** is 5-hydroxytryptamine (5HT). It is in the monoamine category of neurotransmitters, along with norepinephrine and dopamine, discussed next. Approximately six major circuits of serotonin spread from the midbrain, looping around its various parts (Azmitia, 1978) (see ■ Figure 2.11). Because of the widespread nature of these circuits, many of them ending up in the cortex, serotonin is believed to influence a great deal of our behaviour, particularly the way we process information (Depue & Spoont, 1986; Harmer, 2008; Merens, Willem Van der Does, & Spinhoven, 2007; Spoont, 1992). It was genetically influenced dysregulation in this system that contributed to depression in the New Zealand study described earlier (Caspi et al., 2003).

The serotonin system regulates our behaviour, moods, and thought processes. Extremely low activity levels of serotonin are associated with less inhibition and with instability, impulsivity, and the tendency to overreact to situations. Low serotonin activity has been associated with aggression, suicide, impulsive

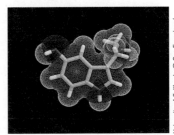

▲ Computer-generated model of serotonin

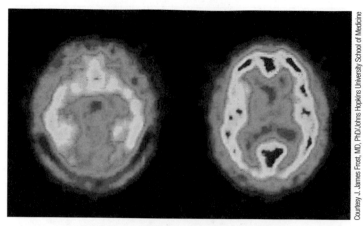

A PET scan shows the distribution of serotonergic neurons. This brain scanning method was recently used by researchers at the Toronto *PET* Centre to document increased serotonin receptor density in patients with schizophrenia (Tauscher et al., 2002).

overeating, and excessive sexual behaviour. However, these behaviours do not *necessarily* happen if serotonin activity is low. Other currents in the brain, or other psychological or social influences, may well compensate for low serotonin activity. Therefore, low serotonin activity may make us more vulnerable to certain

problematic behaviour without directly causing it (as mentioned earlier). On the other end, high levels of serotonin may interact with GABA to counteract glutamate (the same fact is emerging about other neurotransmitter systems).

To add to the complexity, serotonin has slightly different effects depending on the type or subtype of receptors involved, and we now know there are approximately 15 different receptors in the serotonin system (Owens et al., 1997; Sharp, 2009). Several classes of drugs primarily affect the serotonin system, including the tricyclic antidepressants such as imipramine (known by its brand name, Tofranil). However, the class of drugs called selective-serotonin reuptake inhibitors (SSRIs), including fluoxetine (Prozac) (see ■ Figure 2.12), affects serotonin more directly than other drugs, including the tricyclic antidepressants. SSRIs are used to treat a number of psychological disorders, particularly anxiety, mood, and eating disorders. The herbal medication St. John's wort, available in health food stores, also affects serotonin levels.

Norepinephrine

A third neurotransmitter system in the monoamine class important to psychopathology is **norepinephrine** (also known as **noradrenaline**) (see ■ Figure 2.13). We have already seen that norepinephrine, like epinephrine (referred to as a catecholamine), is part of the endocrine system.

How Neurotransmitters Work
Neurotransmitters are stored in tiny sacs at the end of the neuron Ⓐ. An electric jolt makes the sacs merge with the outer membrane, and the neurotransmitter is released into the synapse Ⓑ. The molecules diffuse across the gap and bind receptors, specialized proteins, on the adjacent neuron Ⓒ. When sufficient neurotransmitter has been absorbed, the receptors release the molecules, which are then broken down or reabsorbed by the first neuron and stored for later use Ⓓ.

How Serotonin Drugs Work
Prozac enhances serotonin's effects by preventing it from being absorbed Ⓔ. Redux and fenfluramine (antiobesity drugs) cause the release of extra serotonin into the synapse Ⓕ.

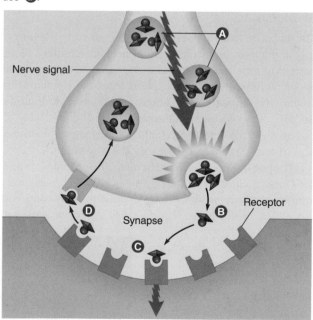

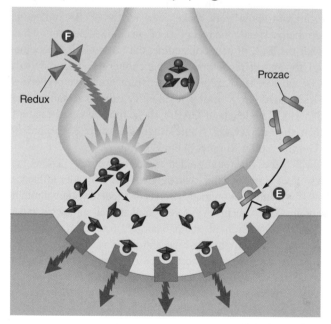

Receptor Variation
There are at least 15 different serotonin receptors, each associated with a different function.

■ **FIGURE 2.12** Manipulating serotonin in the brain

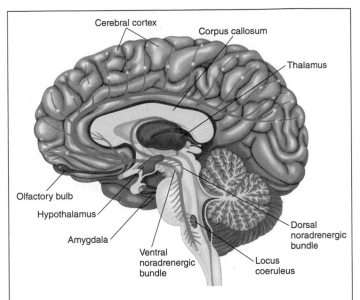

■ **FIGURE 2.13** Major norepinephrine pathways in the human brain

Source: From KALAT. *Biological Psychology w/CD + INFOTRAC*, 9E. © 2007 Wadsworth, a part of Cengage Learning, Inc. Reproduced by permission. www.cengage.com/permissions.

Go to **www.abnormalpsych3ce.nelson.com** *to access an interactive version of this figure.*

Norepinephrine seems to stimulate at least two groups (and probably several more) of receptors called *alpha-adrenergic* and *beta-adrenergic receptors*. Someone in your family may be taking a widely used class of drugs called *beta-blockers*, particularly if that person has hypertension or difficulties with regulating heart rate. As the name indicates, these drugs block the beta-receptors so that their response to a surge of norepinephrine is reduced, which keeps blood pressure and heart rate down. In the central nervous system, a number of norepinephrine circuits have been identified. One major circuit begins in the hindbrain, an area that controls basic bodily functions such as respiration. Another circuit appears to influence the emergency reactions or alarm responses (Charney & Drevets, 2002; Gray, 1987; Gray & McNaughton, 1996; Sullivan & LeDoux, 2004) that occur when we suddenly find ourselves in a dangerous situation, suggesting that norepinephrine may bear some relationship to states of panic (Charney et al., 1990; Gray & McNaughton, 1996). More likely, however, is that this system, with all its varying circuits coursing through the brain, acts in a more general way to regulate or modulate certain behavioural tendencies and is not directly involved in specific patterns of behaviour or in psychological disorders.

▲ Computer-generated model of GABA

Dopamine

Finally, **dopamine** is a major neurotransmitter in the monoamine class also termed a catecholamine because of the similarity of its chemical structure to epinephrine and norepinephrine. Dopamine has been implicated in the pathophysiology of schizophrenia (see ■ Figure 2.14) and disorders of addiction (LeFoll, Gallo, LeStrat, Lu, & Gorwood, 2009). New research also indicates it may play a significant role in depression (Dunlop & Nemeroff, 2007) and attention deficit hyperactivity disorder (Volkow et al., 2009). Remember the wonder drug reserpine mentioned in Chapter 1 that reduced psychotic behaviours associated with schizophrenia? This drug and more modern antipsychotic treatments affect a number of neurotransmitter systems, but their greatest impact may be that they block specific dopamine receptors, thus lowering dopamine activity (see, for example, Snyder, Burt, & Creese, 1976). Thus, it was long thought possible that in schizophrenia, dopamine circuits may be too active. The recent development of new antipsychotic drugs such as clozapine, which has only weak effects on certain dopamine receptors, suggests this idea may need revising. We explore the dopamine hypothesis in some detail in Chapter 13.

In its various circuits throughout specific regions of the brain, dopamine also seems to have a more general effect, best described as a switch that turns on various brain circuits possibly associated with certain types of behaviour. Once the switch is turned on, other neurotransmitters may then inhibit or facilitate emotions or behaviour

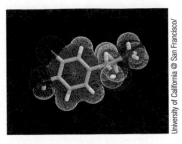

▲ Computer-generated model of norepinephrine

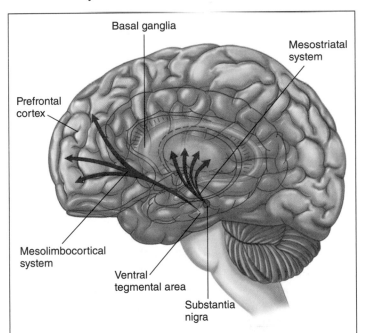

■ **FIGURE 2.14** Two major dopamine pathways: The mesolimbic system is apparently implicated in schizophrenia; the path to the basal ganglia contributes to problems in the locomotor system, such as tardive dyskinesia, which sometimes results from use of neuroleptic drugs

Source: From KALAT. *Biological Psychology w/CD + INFOTRAC*, 9E. © 2007 Wadsworth, a part of Cengage Learning, Inc. Reproduced by permission. www.cengage.com/permissions.

Go to **www.abnormalpsych3ce.nelson.com** *to access an interactive version of this figure.*

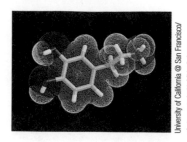

University of California @ San Francisco/ photo created with MidasSoftware

▲ Computer-generated model of dopamine

(Armbruster et al., 2009; Oades, 1985; Spoont, 1992; Stahl, 2008). Dopamine circuits merge and cross with serotonin circuits at many points and therefore influence many of the same behaviours. For example, dopamine activity is associated with exploratory, outgoing, pleasure-seeking behaviours (Elovainio, Kivimaki, Viikari, Ekelund, & Keltikangas-Jarvinen, 2005), and serotonin is associated with inhibition and constraint; thus, in a sense they balance each other (Depue et al., 1994).

Again, we see that the effects of a neurotransmitter—in this case, dopamine—are more complex than we originally thought. Researchers have thus far discovered at least five different receptor sites that are selectively sensitive to dopamine (Girault & Greengard, 2004; Owens et al., 1997). One of a class of drugs that affects the dopamine circuits specifically is L-dopa, which is a dopamine agonist (increases levels of dopamine). One of the systems that dopamine switches on is the locomotor system, which regulates ability to move in a coordinated way and, once turned on, is influenced by serotonin activity. Because of these connections, deficiencies in dopamine have been associated with disorders such as Parkinson's disease, in which a marked deterioration in motor behaviour includes tremors, rigidity of muscles, and difficulty with judgment. L-dopa has been successful in reducing some of these motor disabilities.

Concept Check | 2.4

Check your understanding of the major functions of four important neurotransmitters by matching them to the descriptions provided: (a) GABA, (b) serotonin, (c) dopamine, and (d) norepinephrine. _____

1. Which neurotransmitter binds to neuron receptor sites, inhibiting postsynaptic activity and reducing overall arousal? _____

2. Which neurotransmitter is a switch that turns on various brain circuits? _____

3. Which neurotransmitter seems to be involved in your emergency reactions or alarm responses? _____

4. Which neurotransmitter is believed to influence the way we process information, as well as to moderate or inhibit our behaviour? _____

Implications for Psychopathology

Psychological disorders typically mix emotional, behavioural, and cognitive symptoms, so identifiable lesions (or damage) localized in specific structures of the brain do not, for the most part, cause the disorders. Even widespread damage most often results in motor or sensory deficits, which are usually the province of the medical specialty of neurology; neurologists often work with neuropsychologists to identify specific lesions. But psychopathologists have been focusing lately on the more general role of brain function in the development of personality, with the goal of considering how different types of biologically driven personalities might be more vulnerable to developing certain types of psychological disorders. For example, genetic contributions might lead to patterns of neurotransmitter activity that influence personality. Thus, some impulsive risk takers may have low serotonergic activity and high dopaminergic activity.

Procedures for studying images of the functioning brain have recently been applied to *obsessive-compulsive disorder* (*OCD*). Individuals with this severe anxiety disorder suffer from intrusive, frightening thoughts—for example, that they might have become contaminated with poison and will poison their loved ones if they touch them. To prevent this drastic consequence, they engage in compulsive rituals such as frequent washing to try to scrub off the imagined poison. A number of investigators have found intriguing differences between the brains of patients with OCD and those of other people. Although the size and structure of the brain are the same, patients with OCD have increased activity in the part of the frontal lobe of the cerebral cortex called the *orbital surface* (Chamberlain et al., 2008). Increased activity is also present in the cingulate gyrus and, to a lesser extent, in the caudate nucleus, a circuit that extends from the orbital section of the frontal area of the cortex to parts of the thalamus. Activity in these areas seems to be correlated; that is, if one area is active, the other areas are also. These areas contain several pathways of neurotransmitters, and one of the most concentrated is serotonin.

Remember that one of the roles of serotonin seems to be to moderate our reactions. Eating behaviour, sexual behaviour, and aggression are under better control with adequate levels of serotonin. Research, mostly on animals, demonstrates that lesions (damage) that interrupt serotonin circuits seem to impair the ability to ignore irrelevant external cues, making the organism overactive. Thus, if we were to experience damage or interruption in this brain circuit, we might find ourselves acting on every thought or impulse that enters our heads.

Thomas Insel (1992) described a case originally reported by Eslinger and Damasio (1985) of a man who had been successful

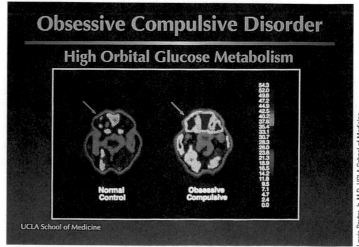

▲ Brain function is altered in people with OCD, but it normalizes after effective psychosocial treatment.

Lewis Baxter Jr. M.D. UCLA School of Medicine

as an accountant, husband, and father of two before undergoing surgery for a brain tumour. He made a good recovery from surgery and seemed to be fine, but in the following year his business failed and he separated from his family. Although his scores on IQ tests were as high as ever and all his mental functions were intact, he was unable to keep a job or even be on time for an appointment. What was causing all these problems? He was engaging in lengthy and uncontrollable compulsive rituals. Most of his days were consumed with washing, dressing, and rearranging things in the single room where he lived. In other words, he had classic obsessive-compulsive symptoms. The area of his brain damaged by removal of the tumour was a small area of his orbital frontal cortex.

This information seems to support a biological cause for psychopathology—in this case, OCD. You might think there is no need to consider social or psychological influences here. But Insel and other neuroscientists interpret these findings cautiously. First, this case involves only one individual. Other individuals with the *same* lesion might react differently. Also, brain-imaging studies are often inconsistent with one another on many important details. Sometimes pinpointing the increased or decreased activity is difficult because brains differ in their structure, just as bodies and faces do. Also, the orbital frontal cortex is implicated in other anxiety disorders and maybe other emotional disorders (Gansler et al., 2009; Goodwin, 2009; Sullivan & LeDoux, 2004), so the damage in this area of the brain may just increase negative affects more generally rather than OCD specifically. Therefore, more work has to be done, and perhaps technology has to improve further, before we can be confident about the relation of the orbital frontal cortex to OCD. It is possible that activity in this area may simply be a result of the repetitive thinking and ritualistic behaviour that characterizes OCD, rather than a cause. To take a simple analogy, if you were late for class and began running, massive changes would occur throughout your body and brain. If someone who did not know that you had just sprinted to class then examined you with brain scans, your brain functions would look different from those of the brain of a person who had walked to class. If you were doing well in the class, the scientist might conclude, wrongly, that your unusual brain function "caused" your intelligence.

Psychosocial Influences on Brain Structure and Function

At the same time that psychopathologists are exploring the causes of psychopathology, whether in the brain or in the environment, people are suffering and require the best treatments we have.

Sometimes the effects of treatment tell us something about the nature of psychopathology. For example, if a clinician thinks OCD is caused by a specific brain function or dysfunction or by learned anxiety to scary or repulsive thoughts, this view would determine choice of treatment, as we noted in Chapter 1. Directing a treatment at one or the other of these theoretical causes of the disorder and then observing whether the patient gets better will prove or disprove the accuracy of the theory. This common strategy has one overriding weakness. Successfully treating a patient's particular feverish state or toothache with aspirin does not mean the fever or toothache was caused by an aspirin deficiency,

because an effect does not imply a cause. Nevertheless, this line of evidence gives us some hints about causes of psychopathology, particularly when it is combined with other, more direct experimental evidence.

If you knew that someone with OCD might have a somewhat faulty brain circuit, what treatment would you choose? Maybe you would recommend brain surgery, or neurosurgery. Neurosurgery to correct severe psychopathology (called "psychosurgery") is an option still chosen today on occasion, particularly in the case of OCD when the suffering is severe and other treatments have failed (Aouizerate et al., 2006; Dougherty et al., 2002; Jenike et al., 1991; see also Chapter 5). For the accountant described previously, the removal of his brain tumour seems to have inadvertently eliminated an inhibitory part of the brain circuit implicated in OCD. Precise surgical lesions might dampen the runaway activity that seems to occur in or near this particular area of the brain triggering the OCD symptoms. This result would probably be welcome if all other treatments have failed, although psychosurgery is used seldom and has not been studied systematically.

Nobody wants to do surgery if less intrusive treatments are available. To use the analogy of a television set that has developed the "disorder" of going fuzzy, if you had to rearrange and reconnect wires on the circuit board every time the disorder occurred, the correction would be a major undertaking. Alternatively, if you could simply push some buttons on the remote and eliminate the fuzziness, the correction would be simpler and less risky. The development of drugs affecting neurotransmitter activity has given us one of those buttons. We now have drugs that, although not a cure or even an effective treatment in all cases, do seem to be beneficial in treating OCD. As you might suspect, most of them act by increasing serotonin activity in one way or another.

But is it possible to get at this brain circuit without either surgery or drugs? Could psychological treatment be powerful enough to affect the circuit directly? The answer now seems to be yes. To take one of the first examples, Lewis R. Baxter and his colleagues used brain imaging on patients who had not been treated and then took an additional, important scientific step (Baxter et al., 1992). They treated the patients with a cognitive-behavioural therapy known to be effective in OCD *called exposure and response prevention* (described more fully in Chapter 5) and then repeated the brain imaging. In a remarkable finding, widely noted in the world of psychopathology, Baxter and his colleagues discovered that the brain circuit had been changed (normalized) by a psychological intervention. The same team of investigators then replicated the experiment with a different group of patients and found the same changes in brain function (Schwartz, Stoessel, Baxter, Martin, & Phelps, 1996). In other examples, investigating teams noted changes in brain function after successful psychological treatment for depression (Brody et al., 2001; Martin, Martin, Rai, Richardson, & Royall, 2001), PTSD (Rabe, Zoellner, Beauducel, Maercker, & Karl, 2008), and specific phobia, which they termed "re-wiring the brain" (Paquette et al., 2003). In another intriguing study, Leuchter, Cook, Witte, Morgan, and Abrams (2002) treated patients with major depressive disorder with either antidepressant medications or placebo medications. (Remember that it is common for inactive placebo medications, which are just sugar pills, to result in behavioural and emotional changes in patients, presumably as a result of psychological factors such as increasing hope and expectations.) Measures of brain function showed that both antidepressant medications and placebos changed brain function but in somewhat different parts of the brain, suggesting different mechanisms of action for these two interventions. Placebos alone are not usually as effective as active medication, but every time clinicians prescribe pills, they are also treating the patient psychologically by inducing positive expectation for change, and this intervention changes brain function.

Petrovic, Kalso, Petersson, and Ingvar (2002), in an important study, looked more deeply into how placebo pills (in other words, psychological factors) can change brain function. Normal participants were given (with their consent) a harmless but painful condition in which their left hand was subjected to intense heat. These participants were informed that two potent analgesics (pain-reducing medications) would be used in the experiment. In fact, one of these drugs was an opioid, and the other was a placebo. Opioid-based drugs are used routinely in medical settings to relieve severe pain. Each participant experienced the painful stimulus under three conditions: (1) under the influence of an opioid drug, (2) under the influence of a placebo pill that the patient assumed was an opioid-based drug, and (3) with no drug (pain only). All participants experienced each condition multiple times, while brain-imaging procedures monitored their brain functioning (see Chapter 3) during administration of the painful stimulus. Whereas both the placebo drug and the opiate drug reduced pain to less than the level with no drug, the surprising results indicated that both treatments activated overlapping (although not identical) regions in the brain, primarily within the anterior cingulate cortex and the brain stem. These areas were not activated during the pain-only condition. Thus, it appears that the anterior cingulate cortex is responsible for control of the pain response in the brain stem and that cognitive expectations of pain relief created by the placebo condition cause these brain circuits to be turned on. It would seem that psychological treatments are another button on the remote with which we can directly change brain circuits.

A final intriguing area of research just beginning is exploring the specific ways in which drug or psychological treatments work in terms of changes in brain function. Are the changes similar or different? Kennedy et al. (2007) treated individuals with major depressive disorder with either a psychological treatment, cognitive-behavioural therapy (CBT), or the antidepressant drug venlafaxine. Although some brain changes were similar among the three treatment groups, complex differences were also noted, primarily in the way in which CBT facilitated changes in thinking patterns in the cortex that, in turn, affected the emotional brain. Sometimes this is called a "top down" change because it originates in the cortex and works its way down into the lower brain. Drugs, on the other hand, often seem to work more in a "bottom up" manner, reaching higher areas of the cortex (where thinking occurs) last. Many similar studies in this area are now in

progress. Because we know that some people respond better to psychological treatments, and others respond better to drugs, this research provides hope that we will one day be able to choose the best treatments or better combine treatments based on an analysis of the individual's brain function.

Interactions of Psychosocial Factors with Brain Structure and Function

Several experiments illustrate the interaction of psychosocial factors and brain function as reflected in neurotransmitter activity. Some even indicate that psychosocial factors directly affect levels of neurotransmitters. For example, Insel, Scanlan, Champoux, and Suomi (1988) raised two groups of rhesus monkeys identically except for their ability to control things in their cages. One group had free access to toys and food treats, but the second group got these toys and treats only when the first group did. In other words, the second group had the same number of toys and treats but they could not choose when they got them. Therefore, they had less control over their environment. In psychological experiments we say the second group was "yoked" with the first group, because their treatment depended entirely on what happened to the first group. The monkeys in the first group grew up with a sense of control over things in their lives and those in the second group didn't.

Later in their lives, all these monkeys were administered a benzodiazepine inverse agonist, a neurochemical that has the opposite effect of the neurotransmitter GABA; the effect is an extreme burst of anxiety. (The few times this neurochemical has been administered to people, usually scientists administering it to each other, the recipients have reported the experience—which lasts only a short time—to be one of the most horrible sensations they had ever endured.) When this substance was injected into the monkeys, the monkeys that had been raised with little control over their environment ran to a corner of their cage where they crouched and displayed signs of severe anxiety and panic. But the monkeys that had a sense of control behaved quite differently. They did not seem anxious at all. Rather, they seemed angry and aggressive, even attacking other monkeys near them. Thus, the very same level of a neurochemical substance, acting as a

▲ Rhesus monkeys injected with a specific neurotransmitter react with anger or fear, depending on their early psychological experiences.

neurotransmitter, had very different effects, depending on the psychological histories of the monkeys.

The Insel and colleagues (1988) experiment is an example of a significant interaction between neurotransmitters and psychosocial factors. Other experiments suggest that psychosocial influences directly affect the functioning and perhaps even the structure of the central nervous system. Scientists have observed that psychosocial factors routinely change the activity levels of many of our neurotransmitter systems, including norepinephrine and serotonin (Cacioppo et al., 2007; Coplan et al., 1996, 1998; Heim & Nemeroff, 1999; Ladd et al., 2000; Ouellet-Morin et al., 2008; Roma, Champoux, & Suomi, 2006; Sullivan, Kent, & Coplan, 2000). It also seems that the structure of neurons themselves, including the number of receptors on a cell, can be changed by learning and experience (Gottlieb, 1998; Kandel, 1983; Kandel, Jessell, & Schacter, 1991; Ladd et al., 2000; Owens et al., 1997) and that these effects on the central nervous system continue throughout our lives (Cameron et al., 2005; Spinelli et al., 2009; Suárez, Bennett, Goldstein, & Barlow, 2009).

We are now beginning to learn how psychosocial factors affect brain function and structure (Kolb, Gibb, & Robinson, 2003; Kolb & Whishaw, 1998). For example, William Greenough and his associates, in a series of classic experiments (Greenough, Withers, & Wallace, 1990), studied the cerebellum, which coordinates and controls motor behaviour. They discovered that the nervous systems of rats raised in a rich environment requiring a lot of learning and motor behaviour develop differently from those in rats that were couch potatoes. The active rats had many more connections between nerve cells in the cerebellum and grew many more dendrites. In a follow-up study, Wallace, Kilman, Withers, and Greenough (1992) reported that these structural changes in the brain began in as little as four days in rats, suggesting enormous plasticity in brain structure as a result of experience. Similarly, stress during early development can lead to substantial changes in the functioning of the HPA axis (described earlier in this chapter) that, in turn, make primates more or less susceptible to stress later in life (Barlow, 2002; Coplan et al.,

1998; Gillespie & Nemeroff, 2007; Spinelli et al., 2009; Suomi, 1999). It may be something similar to this mechanism that was responsible for the effects of early stress on the later development of depression in genetically susceptible individuals in the New Zealand study described earlier (Caspi et al., 2003). So, we can conclude that early psychological experience affects the development of the nervous system and thus determines vulnerability to psychological disorders later in life. It seems that the very structure of the nervous system is constantly changing as a result of learning and experience, even into old age, and that some of these changes become permanent (Kolb, Gibb, & Gorny, 2003; Suárez et al., 2009). This plasticity of the central nervous system helps us adapt more readily to our environment. These findings will be important when we discuss the causes of anxiety disorders and mood disorders in Chapters 5 and 7.

Comments

The specific brain circuits involved in psychological disorders are very complex systems identified by pathways of neurotransmitters traversing the brain. The existence of these circuits suggests that the structure and function of the nervous system play major roles in psychopathology. But other research suggests that the circuits are strongly influenced, perhaps even created, by psychological and social factors. Furthermore, both biological interventions, such as drugs, and psychological interventions or experience seem capable of altering the circuits. Therefore, we cannot consider the nature and cause of psychological disorders without examining both biological and psychological factors. We now turn to an examination of psychological factors.

Behavioural and Cognitive Science

Enormous progress has been made in understanding behavioural and cognitive influences in psychopathology. Some new information has come from the rapidly growing field of **cognitive science**, which is concerned with how we acquire and process information and how we store and ultimately retrieve it (one of the processes involved in memory). Scientists have also discovered that a great deal goes on inside our heads of which we are not necessarily aware. Because, technically, these cognitive processes are unconscious, some findings recall the unconscious mental processes that are so much a part of Freud's theory of psychoanalysis (although they do not look much like the ones he envisioned). A brief account of current thinking on what is happening during the process of classical conditioning will start us on our way.

Conditioning and Cognitive Processes

During the 1960s and 1970s, behavioural scientists in animal laboratories began to uncover the complexity of the basic processes of classical conditioning (Bouton, Mineka, & Barlow, 2001; Mineka & Zinbarg, 1996, 1998). Rescorla (1988) concluded that simply pairing two events closely in time (such as the food and the metronome in Pavlov's laboratories) is not really what's important in this type of learning; at the very least, it is a very simple summary. Rather, a variety of different judgments and

▲ William Greenough and his associates raised rats in a complex environment that required significant learning and motor behaviour, which affected the structure of the rats' brains. This research supports the role of psychological factors on biological development.

cognitive processes combine to determine the final outcome of this learning, even in lower animals such as rats.

To take just one simple example, Pavlov would have predicted that if the food and the metronome were paired, say, 50 times, then a certain amount of learning would take place. But Rescorla and others discovered that if one animal never saw the particular food at any time except for the 50 trials following the metronome sound, but the other animal saw the food many times *in between* the 50 times it was paired with the metronome, the two animals would learn very different things; that is, even though the metronome and the food were paired 50 times for each animal, the metronome *was much less meaningful* to the second animal (see ■ Figure 2.15). Put another way, the first animal learned that the sound of the metronome meant food came next; the second animal learned that the food sometimes came after the sound and sometimes without the sound. That two different conditions produce two different learning outcomes is really a commonsense notion, but it demonstrates, along with many far more complex scientific findings, that basic classical (and operant) conditioning paradigms really facilitate the learning of the *relationship* among events in the environment. This type of learning makes us able to develop working ideas about the world that allow us to make appropriate judgments. We can then respond in a way that will benefit or at least not hurt us. In other words, complex cognitive and emotional processing of information is involved when conditioning occurs, even in animals.

Learned Helplessness

Along similar lines, Martin Seligman, also working with animals, described the phenomenon of **learned helplessness**, which occurs when rats or other animals encounter conditions over which they have no control whatsoever. If rats are confronted with a situation in which they receive occasional foot shocks, they can function very well if they learn they can cope with these shocks by doing something to avoid them (say, pressing a lever). But if the animals learn their behaviour has no effect whatsoever on their environment— sometimes they get shocked and sometimes they don't, no matter what they do—they become very "helpless"; in other words, they give up attempting to cope and seem to develop the animal equivalent of depression.

Seligman drew some important conclusions from these observations. He theorized that the same phenomenon may happen with people who are faced with uncontrollable stress in their lives. Subsequent work revealed this to be true under one important condition: People become depressed if they decide or think they can do little about the stress in their lives, even if it seems to others that they could do something. People make an attribution that they have no control, and they become depressed (Abramson, Seligman, & Teasdale, 1978; Miller & Norman, 1979). We revisit this important psychological theory of depression in Chapter 7. It illustrates, once again, the necessity of recognizing that different people process information about events in the environment in

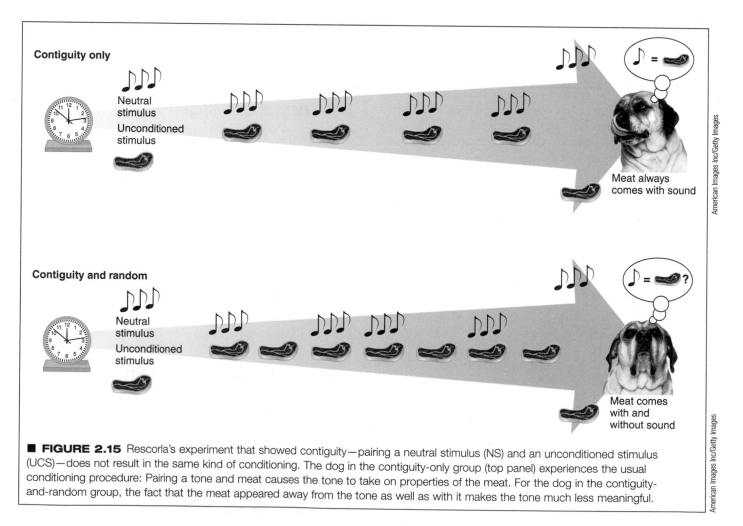

■ **FIGURE 2.15** Rescorla's experiment that showed contiguity—pairing a neutral stimulus (NS) and an unconditioned stimulus (UCS)—does not result in the same kind of conditioning. The dog in the contiguity-only group (top panel) experiences the usual conditioning procedure: Pairing a tone and meat causes the tone to take on properties of the meat. For the dog in the contiguity-and-random group, the fact that the meat appeared away from the tone as well as with it makes the tone much less meaningful.

different ways. These cognitive differences are an important component of psychopathology.

More recently, Seligman has turned his attention to the positive side of learned helplessness, which he terms "learned optimism" (Seligman, 1998, 2002). In other words, if people faced with considerable stress and difficulty in their lives nevertheless display an optimistic, upbeat attitude, they are likely to function better psychologically and physically. We will return to this theme repeatedly throughout this book but particularly in Chapter 9, when we talk about the effects of psychological factors on health. But consider this one example: In a study by Levy, Slade, Kunkel, and Kasl (2002), individuals between the ages of 50 and 94 who had positive views about themselves, and positive attitudes toward aging, lived 7.5 years longer than those without such positive optimistic attitudes. This prediction was still true after the investigators controlled for age, sex, income, loneliness, and physical capability to engage in household and social activities. This effect is extremely powerful, and exceeds the one to four years of added life associated with other factors such as low blood pressure, low cholesterol levels, and no history of obesity or cigarette smoking. Studies such as this have created interest in a new field of study called "positive psychology" where investigators explore factors that account for positive attitudes and happiness (Diener, 2000; Lyubomirsky, 2001). We will return to these themes in the chapters describing specific disorders.

Social Learning

Another influential psychologist was Canadian Albert Bandura. Bandura (1973, 1986) observed that organisms, including lower animals, do not have to actually experience certain events in their environment to learn effectively. Rather, they can learn just as much by observing what happens to someone else in a given situation. This fairly obvious discovery came to be known as **modelling** or **observational learning**. What is important is that, even in animals, this type of learning requires a symbolic integration of the experiences of others with judgments of what might happen to us. In other words, even an animal that is not very intelligent by human standards, such as a rat, must make a decision about the conditions under which its own experiences would be very similar to those of the animal it is observing. Bandura expanded his observations into a network of ideas in which behaviour, cognitive factors, and environmental influences converged to produce the complexity of behaviour that confronts us. He also specified in some detail the importance of the social context of our learning; that is, much of what we learn depends on our interactions with other people around us; thus, his approach became known as *social learning theory*.

Courtesy of Albert Bandura

▲ Albert Bandura developed social learning theory. His work expanded on traditional learning perspectives by highlighting the importance of social and cognitive factors in learning.

In the 1960s Bandura made very notable contributions to the understanding of children's aggressive behaviours. He and his students conducted a series of experiments using models interacting with a plastic Bobo doll (e.g., Bandura, Ross, & Ross, 1961, 1963). The results of these studies helped Bandura develop and refine his social learning theory. For example, Bandura and his colleagues (1963) conducted a study that was designed to examine the influence of consequences to the model on children's imitative learning of aggression. Nursery school children were randomly assigned to one of four groups. The first group observed a model who interacted aggressively with the Bobo doll and whose aggressive behaviour was rewarded. A second group of children observed a model who interacted aggressively with the Bobo doll but whose aggressive behaviour was punished. A third (control) group was exposed to highly expressive but nonaggressive models. A final additional control group had no exposure to models. All the children were then tested for the presence of aggressive responses. Children who had witnessed the aggressive model who was rewarded showed more imitative aggression. In contrast, children who had witnessed the aggressive model who was punished failed to reproduce the model's behaviour (Bandura et al., 1963). This important series of studies provided evidence consistent with Bandura's theory that the steps involved in vicarious learning are (1) noticing the model's behaviour (attention), (2) remembering the model's behaviour (retention), and (3) exhibiting the model's behaviour (reproduction). The findings also suggested an additional step in vicarious conditioning that involves motivation: Children are more likely to attend to, retain, and reproduce behaviours of models that have been rewarded for the behaviour, while they are less likely to emulate models who have been punished for their behaviour.

The basic idea in all Bandura's work is that a careful analysis of cognitive processes may well produce the most accurate scientific predictions of behaviour. Concepts of probability learning, information processing, and attention have become increasingly important in psychopathology (Barlow, 2002; Craighead, Ilardi, Greenberg, & Craighead, 1997; Mathews & MacLeod, 1994).

Prepared Learning

It is clear that biology and, probably, our genetic endowment influence what we learn. This conclusion is based on the fact that we learn to fear some objects much more easily than others, as is demonstrated in the important experiments of Swedish psychologist Arne Öhman. In other words, we learn fears and phobias selectively (Morris, Öhman, & Dolan, 1998; Öhman, Flykt, & Lundquist, 2000; Öhman & Mineka, 2001). Why might this be? According to the concept of **prepared learning**, we have become highly prepared for learning about certain types of objects or situations through evolution, because this knowledge contributes to the survival of the species (Mineka, 1985; Seligman, 1971). Even without any contact, we are more likely to learn to fear snakes or spiders than rocks or flowers, even if we know rationally that the snake or spider is harmless (e.g., Fredrikson, Annas, & Wik,1997; Pury & Mineka, 1997). In the absence of experience, however, we are less likely to fear guns or electrical outlets, even though they are potentially much more deadly.

Behavioural and Cognitive Science   **57**

Why do we so readily learn to fear snakes or spiders? One possibility is that when our ancestors lived in caves, those who avoided snakes and spiders eluded the deadly varieties and therefore survived in greater numbers to pass down their genes to us, thus contributing to the survival of the species (de Silva, Rachman, & Seligman, 1977). This idea is just a theory, of course, but at present it seems a likely explanation. Something within us recognizes the connection between a certain signal and a threatening event. In other words, certain UCSs (unconditioned stimuli) and CSs (conditioned stimuli) "belong" to each other. If you've ever gotten sick on cheap wine or bad food, chances are you won't make the same mistake again. This very quick or "one-trial" learning also occurs in animals that eat something that tastes bad or contains poison. It is easy to see that survival is associated with quickly learning to avoid poisonous food. When animals are shocked instead of poisoned when eating certain foods, however, they do not learn this association nearly as quickly, probably because in nature shock is not a consequence of eating, whereas being poisoned can be. Perhaps these selective associations are also facilitated by our genes (Barlow, 2002; Cook, Hodes, & Lang, 1986; Garcia, McGowan, & Green, 1972).

Cognitive Science and the Unconscious

Advances in cognitive science have revolutionized our conceptions of the unconscious. We are not aware of much of what goes on inside our heads, but our unconscious is not necessarily the seething cauldron of primitive emotional conflicts envisioned by Freud. Rather, we simply seem able to process and store information, and act on it, without having the slightest awareness of what the information is or why we are acting on it (Bargh & Chartrand, 1999). Is this fact surprising? Consider briefly these two examples.

Weiskrantz (1992) describes a phenomenon called *blind sight* or *unconscious vision*. He relates the case of a young man who, for medical reasons, had a small section of his visual cortex (the centre for the control of vision in the brain) surgically removed. Though the operation was considered a success, the young man became blind in both eyes. Later, during routine tests, a physician raised his hand to the left of the patient who, much to the shock of his doctors, reached out and touched it. Subsequently, scientists determined that he could not only reach accurately for objects but could also distinguish among objects and perform most of the functions usually associated with sight. Yet, when asked about his abilities, he would say, "I couldn't see anything, not a darn thing," and that all he was doing was guessing.

The phenomenon in this case, of course, is associated with real brain damage. Much more interesting, from the point of view of psychopathology, is that the same thing seems to occur in healthy individuals who have been hypnotized (Hilgard, 1992; Kihlstrom, 1992); that is, normal individuals, provided with hypnotic suggestions they are blind, are able to function visually but have no awareness or memory of their visual abilities. This condition, which illustrates a process of dissociation between behaviour and consciousness, is the basis of the dissociative disorders discussed in Chapter 6.

A second example, more relevant to psychopathology, is called **implicit memory** (Craighead et al., 1997; Graf, Squire, & Mandler, 1984; Kihlstrom, Barnhardt, & Tataryn, 1992; McNally, 1999;

Schacter, Chiu, & Ochsner, 1993). As has been described by cognitive psychologist Peter Graf and his colleagues at the University of British Columbia, implicit memory is apparent when someone clearly acts on the basis of things that have happened in the past but can't remember the events (Graf et al., 1984). In contrast, a good memory for events is called *explicit memory*. Much research attests to the distinctiveness of implicit and explicit memory processes (see review by Ryan & Cohen, 2003), including evidence that they differ in their developmental patterns (e.g., Billingsley, Smith, & McAndrews, 2002), underlying brain structures (e.g., Billingsley, McAndrews, & Smith, 2002), and degree to which they are affected by certain drugs (e.g., Stewart, Buffett-Jerrott, Finley, Wright, & Gomez, 2006). Implicit memory can be very selective for only certain events or circumstances. Clinically, we have already seen in Chapter 1 an example of implicit memory at work in the story of Anna O., the classic case first described by Breuer and Freud (1895/1957) to demonstrate the existence of the unconscious. It was only after therapy that Anna O. remembered events surrounding her father's death and the connection of these events to her paralysis. Thus, Anna O.'s behaviour (occasional paralysis) was evidently connected to implicit memories of her father's death. Many scientists have concluded that Freud's speculations on the nature and structure of the unconscious went beyond the evidence, but the existence of unconscious processes has since been demonstrated, and we must take them into account as we study psychopathology.

Concept Check | 2.5

Check your understanding of behavioural and cognitive influences by identifying the descriptions. Choose your answers from (a) learned helplessness, (b) modelling, (c) prepared learning, and (d) implicit memory.

1. Karen noticed that every time Don behaved well at lunch, the teacher praised him. Karen decided to behave better to receive praise herself. _____

2. Jin stopped trying to please his father because he never knows whether his father will be proud or outraged. _____

3. Greg fell into a lake as a baby and almost drowned. Even though Greg has no recollection of the event, he hates to be around large bodies of water. _____

4. Céline was scared to death of the tarantula, even though she knew it wasn't likely to hurt her. _____

What methods do we have for studying the unconscious? The black box refers to unobservable feelings and cognitions inferred by an individual's self-report. In recent decades, psychologists, confident in an established science of behaviour, have returned to the black box with new methods, attempting to reveal the unobservable. Such unobservable unconscious processes are often referred to as implicit cognitive processes or implicit cognition. Several methods for studying **implicit cognition** have been made possible by advances in technology. One of them is the Stroop colour-naming paradigm (see ■ Figure 2.16).

1. RED	6. GREEN	11. BLUE
2. PURPLE	7. PURPLE	12. PURPLE
3. GREEN	8. BROWN	13. BROWN
4. BLUE	9. BLUE	14. RED
5. BROWN	10. RED	15. GREEN

■ **FIGURE 2.16** The Stroop paradigm. Have someone keep time as you name the colours of the words and not the words themselves, and again while you name the words and colours together.

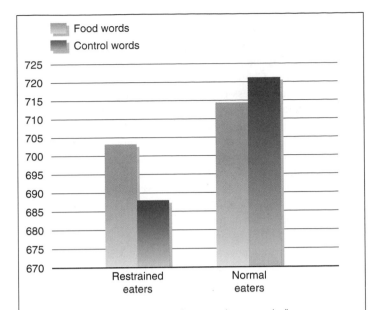

■ **FIGURE 2.17** Average colour-naming speeds (in milliseconds) for food and control words in restrained eaters and normal eaters. Only the restrained eaters show substantially slowed colour-naming for words pertaining to food as compared with their colour-naming speeds for words not pertaining to food.

Source: Adapted from J. A. Francis, S. H. Stewart and S. Hounsell, "Dietary Restraint and the Selective Processing of Forbidden and Nonforbidden Food Words," *Cognitive Therapy and Research, v. 21 (6)*, 1997, 633–646, reprinted with permission of Plenum Publishing Corporation.

In the Stroop paradigm, subjects are shown a variety of words, each printed in a different colour. They are shown these words very quickly and asked to name the colours in which the words are printed while ignoring their meaning. Colour naming is delayed when the meaning of the word attracts the subject's attention, despite his or her efforts to concentrate on the colour; that is, the meaning of the word interferes with the subject's ability to process colour information (see Kolb & Whishaw, 2003). For example, experimenters have determined that people with certain psychological disorders are much slower at naming the colours of words associated with their problem than the colours of words that have no relation to the disorder. Jody, for instance, would be much slower at naming the colour of words like *blood*, *injury*, and *dissect* than the colours of words that have no relation to his phobia. Francis, Stewart, and Hounsell (1997) used the Stroop task in a study with women who were chronic dieters or "restrained eaters" (Knight & Boland, 1989; Polivy & Herman, 1985). On the Stroop, these researchers compared participants' colour-naming speeds for words pertaining to food (e.g., *icing*, *chips*, *cookie*) versus words unrelated to food (e.g., animal words like *snakes*, *insect*, *elephants*). Women who were restrained eaters, but not women who were normal eaters, showed substantially slowed colour naming for words pertaining to food (i.e., for words pertaining to their eating problem; see ■ Figure 2.17). A review by Keith Dobson at the University of Calgary and David Dozois at the University of Western Ontario came to similar conclusions. Across 29 studies that examined Stroop effects in eating-disordered samples, they found that there was clear evidence of slowed colour-naming for food and body/weight words among those with bulimia, and of slowed colour-naming for body/weight words among those with anorexia (Dobson & Dozois, 2004). Thus, psychologists can now uncover particular patterns of emotional significance, even if the subject cannot verbalize them or is not even aware of them.

Cognitive-Behavioural Therapy

As scientists began to discover the important contributions of cognitive processes to behavioural development, psychologists began to integrate cognitive procedures and techniques directly into therapy. Among the originators of **cognitive-behavioural therapy (CBT)** was Aaron T. Beck (1976), who developed methods for dealing with faulty attributions and attitudes associated with learned helplessness and depression (see Chapter 7). CBT is a strong and growing therapy approach in Canada today, spearheaded by a number of internationally renowned scientist-practitioners, including Zindel Segal in Toronto, David A. Clark in Fredericton, David Zuroff in Montréal, and Martin Antony in Hamilton (see Chapters 5 and 7). Another therapy approach that emphasizes cognitive procedures and techniques, called *rational-emotive therapy*, was developed by Albert Ellis (1962). This approach also focuses directly on the irrational beliefs Ellis thought were at the root of maladaptive feelings and behaviour. And clinical psychologist Donald Meichenbaum combined techniques from psychodynamic and behaviour therapies to develop a novel approach he called *self-instructional training*; in this approach he worked on modifying what clients say to themselves about the consequences of their behaviour (Meichenbaum, 1977; Meichenbaum & Cameron, 1974). Meichenbaum and his colleagues applied this new cognitive-behavioural approach with success to a variety of populations including schizophrenics with attentional control problems (Meichenbaum & Cameron, 1973)

▲ Donald Meichenbaum, a clinical psychologist who recently retired from the University of Waterloo, is a key figure in the development of cognitive-behavioural therapy. His work integrated aspects of psychodynamic and behavioural therapies, resulting in techniques like self-instructional training.

Behavioural and Cognitive Science

and impulsive, hyperactive children (Meichenbaum, 1971; Meichenbaum & Goodman, 1971).

Cognitive-behavioural approaches to treatment are described in some detail in later chapters, particularly in Chapter 5 on anxiety disorders, Chapter 7 on mood disorders, and Chapter 9, in which we describe stress-reduction procedures. In general, cognitive-behavioural therapists examine in some detail the ongoing thinking processes of individuals who are anxious, depressed, or stressed. This examination is often accomplished by having patients monitor their thoughts during periods of distress. For example, a straight-A student who experiences depression might assume before taking a particular course in university that she almost certainly will do very poorly; she is then likely to become more depressed. Such negative thoughts are clearly unrealistic and irrational. Similarly, individuals with severe anxiety might continually focus on dangers that could arise in normal situations. Anxious individuals are said to have an attentional bias—their attention is focused on information related to threat, at the expense of other types of information (Owens, Asmundson, & Hadjistavropoulos, 2004; Stewart, Conrod, Gignac, & Pihl, 1998; Teachman & Woody, 2004). Individuals with these types of depression or anxiety are often not aware that their thinking is inappropriate or negative, because it is automatic or unconscious. Automatic thoughts are believed to arise from an underlying maladaptive schema, which is a cognitive belief system about some aspect of life. For example, the depressed student in the example just mentioned might have the automatic thought, "I'm going to fail that course," because she has an underlying negative self-evaluation schema, believing she can never do anything correctly (see Chapter 7). Beck thought that such a schema could be formed by negative experiences when the individual was growing up.

The point of cognitive-behavioural therapy is to work with the patient to uncover these automatic thoughts and develop a different set of attitudes and attributions. This process is called cognitive restructuring, because the goal is to restructure the maladaptive schema. Patients are also assigned specific behavioural tasks, such as entering fearful situations, in which they can work on their emotional and cognitive reactions. Procedures such as relaxation or exercise that change arousal or activity levels may also be a component of therapy.

Thus, the cognitive-behavioural approach continually targets both aspects of the problem: clarifying and modifying attributions and attitudes (cognitive), and avoiding situations that provoke unrealistic anxiety or depression, increasing activity, or improving social skills (behavioural). Such therapy is usually short term, requiring between 10 and 20 sessions. How specific cognitive-behavioural methods are used is described in more detail in the chapters on specific disorders.

Emotions

Emotions play an enormous role in our day-to-day lives and can contribute in major ways to the development of psychopathology (Gross, 2007; Kring & Sloan, 2010; Rottenberg & Johnson, 2007). Consider the emotion of fear. Have you ever found yourself in a really dangerous situation? Have you ever almost crashed your car and known for several seconds beforehand what was going to happen? Have you ever been swimming in the ocean and realized that you were out too far or caught in a current? Have you ever almost fallen from a height, such as a cliff or a roof? In any of these instances you would have felt an incredible surge of arousal. As the first great emotion theorist, Charles Darwin (1872), pointed out more than a century ago, this kind of

Charles Darwin, 1896

▲ Charles Darwin (1809–1882) drew this cat frightened by a dog to show the fight-or-flight reaction.

reaction seems to be programmed in all animals, including humans, which suggests that it serves a useful function. The alarm reaction that activates during potentially life-threatening emergencies is called the **flight-or-fight response**. If you are caught in ocean currents, your almost instinctual tendency is to struggle toward shore. You might realize rationally that you're best off just floating until the current runs its course and then, more calmly, swimming in later. Yet somewhere, deep within, ancient instincts for survival won't let you relax, even though struggling against the ocean will only wear you out and increase your chance of drowning. Still, this same kind of reaction might momentarily give you the strength to lift a car off your trapped brother or fight off an attacker. The whole purpose of the physical rush of adrenaline that we feel in extreme danger is to mobilize us to escape the danger (flight) or to withstand it (fight).

The Physiology and Purpose of Fear

How do physical reactions prepare us to respond this way? The great physiologist Walter Cannon (1929) speculated on the reasons. Fear activates your cardiovascular system. Your blood vessels constrict, thereby raising arterial pressure and decreasing the blood flow to your extremities (fingers and toes). Excess blood is redirected to the skeletal muscles, where it is available to the vital organs that may be needed in an emergency. Often people seem "white with fear"; that is, they turn pale as a result of decreased blood flow to the skin. "Trembling with fear," with your hair standing on end, may be the result of shivering and piloerection (in which body hairs stand erect), reactions that conserve heat when your blood vessels are constricted.

These defensive adjustments can also produce the hot and cold spells that often occur during extreme fear. Breathing becomes faster and, usually, deeper to provide necessary oxygen to rapidly circulating blood. Increased blood circulation carries oxygen to the brain, stimulating cognitive processes and sensory functions, which makes you more alert and able to think more quickly during emergencies. An increased amount of glucose (sugar) is released from the liver into the bloodstream, further energizing various crucial muscles and organs, including the brain. Pupils dilate, presumably to allow a better view of the situation. Hearing becomes more acute, and digestive activity is suspended, resulting in a reduced flow of saliva (the "dry mouth" of fear). In the short term, voiding the body of all waste material and eliminating digestive processes further prepare the organism for concentrated action and activity, so there is often pressure to urinate and defecate and, occasionally, to vomit. (This will also protect you if you have ingested poisonous substances during the emergency.)

It is easy to see why the flight-or-fight reaction is fundamentally important. Millennia ago, when our ancestors lived in very tenuous circumstances, those with strong emergency reactions were more likely to live through attacks and other dangers than those with weak emergency responses, and the survivors passed their genes down to us.

Emotional Phenomena

The **emotion** of fear is a subjective feeling of terror, a strong motivation for behaviour (escaping or fighting), and a complex physiological or arousal response. To define "emotion" is difficult, but most theorists agree that it is an action tendency (Lang, 1985, 1995; Lang, Bradley, & Cuthbert, 1998)—that is, a tendency to behave in a certain way (e.g., escape), elicited by an external event (a threat) and a feeling state (terror), accompanied by a (possibly) characteristic physiological response (Gross, 1999; Gross & Muñoz, 1995; Izard, 1992; Lazarus, 1991, 1995). One purpose of a feeling state is to motivate us to carry out a behaviour: If we escape, our terror, which is unpleasant, will be decreased, so decreasing unpleasant feelings motivates us to escape (Campbell-Sills & Barlow, 2007; Gross, 2007; Öhman, 1996). As Öhman (1996; Öhman, Flykt, & Lundquist, 2000) points out, the principal function of emotions can be understood as a clever means, guided by evolution, to get us to do what we have to do to pass on our genes successfully to coming generations. How do you think this works with anger or with love? What is the feeling state? What is the behaviour?

Emotions are usually short-lived, temporary states lasting from several minutes to several hours, occurring in response to an external event. **Mood** is a more persistent period of affect or emotionality. Thus, in Chapter 7 we describe enduring or recurring states of depression or excitement (mania) as mood disorders. But anxiety disorders, described in Chapter 5, are characterized by enduring or chronic anxiety and, therefore, could also be called mood disorders. Alternatively, both anxiety disorders and *mood disorders* could be called *emotional disorders*, a term not formally used in psychopathology. This is only one example of the occasional inconsistencies in the terminology of abnormal psychology. A related term you will see occasionally, particularly in Chapters 3 and 13, is **affect**, which usually refers to the momentary emotional tone that accompanies what we say or do. For example, if you just got an A+ on your test but you look sad, your friends might think your reaction strange because your affect is not appropriate to the event. The term *affect* can also be used more generally to summarize commonalities among emotional states that are characteristic of an individual. Thus, someone who tends to be fearful, anxious, and depressed is experiencing negative affect. Positive affect would subsume tendencies to be pleasant, joyful, excited, and so on.

The Components of Emotion

Emotion theorists now agree that emotion comprises three related components: *behaviour*, *physiology*, and *cognition*, but most emotion theorists tend to concentrate on one component or another (see ■ Figure 2.18). Emotion theorists who concentrate on behaviour think that basic patterns of emotion differ from one another in fundamental ways; for example, anger may differ from sadness not only in how it feels but also in how it manifests behaviourally and physiologically. These theorists also emphasize that emotion is a way of communicating between one member of the species and another. One function of fear is to motivate immediate and decisive action such as running away. But if you look scared, your facial expression will quickly communicate the possibility of danger to your friends, who may not have been aware that a threat is imminent. Your facial communication increases their chance for survival because they can now respond more quickly to the threat when it occurs.

Other scientists have concentrated on the physiology of emotions, most notably W. B. Cannon (1929), in some pioneering work, who viewed emotion as primarily a brain function. Research in this tradition suggests that areas of the brain associated with emotional expression are generally more ancient and primitive than areas associated with higher cognitive processes such as reasoning.

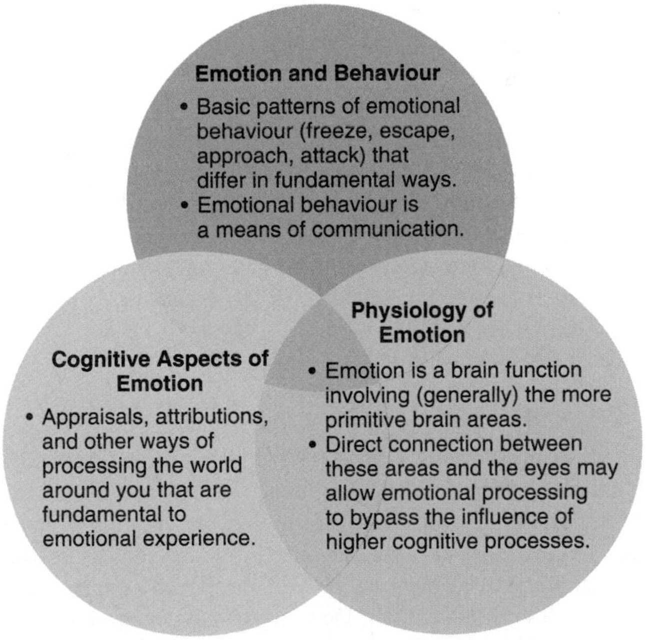

Emotion and Behaviour
- Basic patterns of emotional behaviour (freeze, escape, approach, attack) that differ in fundamental ways.
- Emotional behaviour is a means of communication.

Cognitive Aspects of Emotion
- Appraisals, attributions, and other ways of processing the world around you that are fundamental to emotional experience.

Physiology of Emotion
- Emotion is a brain function involving (generally) the more primitive brain areas.
- Direct connection between these areas and the eyes may allow emotional processing to bypass the influence of higher cognitive processes.

■ **FIGURE 2.18** Emotion has three important and overlapping components: behaviour, cognition, and physiology.

▲ Our emotional reaction depends on context. Fire, for example, can be threatening or comforting.

Other research demonstrates direct neurobiological connections between the emotional centres of the brain and parts of the eye (the retina) or ear that allow emotional activation without the influence of higher cognitive processes (LeDoux, 1996; Öhman, Flykt, & Lundquist, 2000; Zajonc, 1984, 1998); in other words, you may experience various emotions quickly and directly without necessarily thinking about them or being aware of why you feel the way you do.

Finally, a number of prominent theorists concentrate on studying the cognitive aspects of emotion. Notable among these theorists is Richard S. Lazarus (e.g., 1968, 1991, 1995), who proposes that changes in a person's environment are appraised in terms of their potential impact on that person. The type of appraisal you make determines the emotion you experience. For example, if you see somebody holding a gun in a dark alley, you will probably appraise the situation as dangerous and experience fear. You would make a very different appraisal if you saw a tour guide displaying an antique gun in a museum. Lazarus would suggest that thinking and feeling cannot be separated, but other cognitive scientists are concluding otherwise, by suggesting that, although cognitive and emotional systems interact and overlap, they are fundamentally separate (Teasdale, 1993). In fact, all components of emotion—behaviour, physiology, and cognition—are important, and theorists are adopting more integrative approaches by studying their interaction (Barrett, 2009; Gendron & Feldman Barrett, 2009; Gross, 2007).

Anger and Your Heart

When we discussed Jody's blood phobia, we observed that behaviour and emotion may strongly influence biology. Scientists have made important discoveries about the familiar emotion of anger. We have known for years that negative emotions such as hostility and anger increase a person's risk of developing heart disease (Chesney, 1986; MacDougall, Dembroski, Dimsdale, & Hackett, 1985). In fact, sustained hostility with angry outbursts contributes more strongly to death from heart disease than other well-known risk factors, including smoking, high blood pressure, and high cholesterol levels (Finney, Stoney, & Engebretson, 2002; Harburg,

Kaciroti, Gleiberman, Julius, & Schork, 2008; Suarez, Lewis, & Kuhn, 2002; Williams, Haney, Lee, Kong, & Blumenthal, 1980).

Why is this, exactly? Ironson and her colleagues (1992) asked a number of people with heart disease to recall something that made them very angry in the past. Sometimes these events had occurred many years earlier. In one case, an individual who had spent time in a Japanese prisoner-of-war camp during World War II became angry every time he thought about it. Ironson and her associates compared the experience of anger to stressful events that increased heart rate but were not associated with anger. For example, some participants imagined making a speech to defend themselves against a charge of shoplifting. Others tried to figure out difficult problems in arithmetic within a time limit. Heart rates during these angry situations and stressful ones were then compared to heart rates that increased as a result of exercise (riding a stationary bicycle).

The investigators found that the ability of the heart to pump blood efficiently through the body dropped significantly during anger but not during stress or exercise. In fact, remembering being angry was sufficient to cause the anger effect. If subjects were really angry, their heart-pumping efficiency dropped even more, putting them at risk for dangerous disturbances in heart rhythm (arrhythmias). This study was the first to prove that anger affects the heart through decreased pumping efficiency, at least in people who already have heart disease. Now Suarez et al. (2002) have demonstrated how anger may cause this effect. Inflammation produced by an overactive immune system in particularly hostile individuals may contribute to clogged arteries (and decreased heart pumping efficiency).

Emotions and Psychopathology

We now know that suppressing almost any kind of emotional response, such as anger or fear, increases sympathetic nervous system activity, which may contribute to psychopathology (Barlow, Allen, & Choate, 2004; Campbell-Sills & Barlow, 2007; Fairholme, Boisseau, Ellard, Ehrenreich, & Barlow, 2010). Other emotions seem to have a more direct effect. In Chapter 5, we study the phenomenon of *panic* and its relationship to anxiety disorders. One interesting possibility is that a panic attack is simply the normal emotion of fear occurring at the wrong time, when there is nothing to be afraid of (Barlow, 2002). Some patients with mood disorders become overly excited and joyful. They think they have the world on a string and they can do anything they want and spend as much money as they want because everything will turn out all right. Every little event is the most wonderful and exciting experience they have ever had. These individuals are suffering from *mania*, which is part of a serious mood disorder called *bipolar disorder*, discussed in Chapter 7. People who suffer from mania usually alternate periods of excitement with periods of extreme sadness and distress, when they feel that all is lost and the world is a gloomy and hopeless place. During extreme sadness or distress, people are unable to experience any pleasure in life and often find it difficult even to get out of bed and move around. If hopelessness becomes acute, they are at risk for suicide. This emotional state is *depression*, a defining feature of many mood disorders.

Thus, basic emotions of fear, anger, sadness or distress, and excitement may contribute to many psychological disorders and may even define them. Emotions and mood also affect our cognitive processes: If your mood is positive, then your associations, interpretations, and impressions also tend to be positive (Bower, 1981; Diener, Oishi, & Lucas, 2003). Your impression of people you first meet and even your memories of past events are coloured to a great extent by your current mood. If you are consistently negative or depressed, then your memories of past events are likely to be unpleasant. The pessimist or depressed person sees the bottle as half empty. In contrast, the cheerful optimist is said to see the world through rose-coloured glasses and to see the bottle as half full. This is a rich area of investigation for cognitive and emotion scientists (Eysenck, 1992; Rottenberg & Johnson, 2007; Teasdale, 1993), particularly those interested in the close interconnection of cognitive and emotional processes. Leading psychopathologists are beginning to outline the nature of emotion disruption (or dysregulation) and to understand how these disruptions interfere with thinking and behaviour in various psychological disorders (Barlow et al., 2004; Campbell-Sills & Barlow, 2007; Gross, 2007; Kring & Sloan, 2010).

Cultural, Social, and Interpersonal Factors

Given the welter of neurobiological and psychological variables impinging on our lives, is there any room for the influence of social, interpersonal, and cultural factors? Studies are beginning to demonstrate the substantial power and depth of such influences. In fact, researchers have now established that cultural and social influences can kill you. Consider the following example.

Voodoo, the Evil Eye, and Other Fears

In many cultures around the world, individuals may experience fright disorders, exaggerated startle responses, and other observable fear reactions. One example is the Latin American *susto*, characterized by various anxiety-based symptoms, including insomnia, irritability, phobias, and the marked somatic symptoms of sweating and increased heart rate (tachycardia). But *susto* has only one cause: The individual becomes the object of black magic, or witchcraft, and is suddenly badly frightened. In some cultures, the sinister influence is called the *evil eye* (Good & Kleinman, 1985; Tan, 1980), and the resulting fright disorder can be fatal. W. B. Cannon (1942), examining the Haitian phenomenon of voodoo death, suggested that the sentence of death by a medicine man may create an intolerable autonomic arousal in the subject, who has little ability to cope because absolutely no social support exists. Ultimately, the condition leads to damage to internal organs and death. Thus, from all accounts, an individual who is from a physical and psychological point of view functioning in a perfectly healthy and adaptive way suddenly dies because of marked changes in the social environment.

Fear and phobias are universal, occurring across all cultures. But what we fear is strongly influenced by our social environment and cultural context. As noted by cross-cultural psychologist John Berry of Queen's University, although all human societies exhibit commonalities and share basic psychological processes, such underlying commonalities are expressed by various groups in vastly different ways from one time and place to another (Berry, 2003).

Gender

Gender roles have a strong and sometimes puzzling effect on psychopathology. For example, everyone experiences anxiety and fear, and phobias are found all over the world. But phobias have a peculiar characteristic: The likelihood of your having a particular phobia is powerfully influenced by your gender! Someone who complains of an insect or small animal phobia severe enough to prohibit field trips or visits to friends in the country is almost certain to be female, as are 90 percent of the people with this phobia. As another example, dramatic gender differences exist in rates of mood disorders: About two-thirds of those with major depression are women (Hasin, Goodwin, Stinson, & Grant, 2005)—a gender difference that has been replicated in ten countries worldwide, including Canada (Andrade et al., 2003).

We think these substantial gender differences in rates of certain phobias and of depression have to do with cultural expectations of men and women, or our gender roles. For example, with respect to animal phobias, an equal number of men and women may have an experience that could lead to an insect or small animal phobia, such as being bitten by one, but in our society it isn't always acceptable for a man to show or even admit fear. So a man is more likely to hide or endure the fear until he gets over it. It is more acceptable for women to acknowledge fearfulness, and so a phobia develops. Similarly, gender roles may contribute to explain why depression is more common in women. When experiencing a negative life event, women tend to ruminate about it and to blame themselves, whereas men are more likely to engage in activity to take their minds off the negative event—a behaviour that may make men less likely to experience depression in response to stress (Goldstein, 2006; Nolen-Hoeksema, 2000b). This and other explanations for gender differences in depression will be reviewed more fully in Chapter 7.

Another important gender difference involves ways of coping with panic attacks. To avoid or survive a panic attack, an extreme experience of fear, some males drink alcohol instead of admitting they're afraid (see Chapter 5). In many cases this attempt to cope may lead to alcoholism (Stewart, Samoluk, & MacDonald, 1999), a disorder that affects many more males than females (see Chapter 11). One reason for this gender imbalance is that males are more likely than females to self-medicate their fear and panic with alcohol, and in so doing start down the slippery slope to addiction.

Bulimia nervosa, the severe eating disorder, occurs almost entirely in young females. Why? As we see in Chapter 8, a cultural emphasis on female thinness plagues our society and, increasingly, societies around the world. The pressures for males to be thin are less apparent, and of the few males who develop bulimia, a substantial percentage belong to the gay subculture where cultural imperatives to be thin are present.

Finally, in an exciting finding, Taylor (2002, 2006; Taylor et al., 2000) described a unique way in which females in many species respond to stress in their lives. This unique response to stress is called "tend and befriend" and refers to protecting themselves and their young through nurturing behaviour (tend) and forming alliances with larger social groups, particularly other females (befriend). Taylor et al. (2000) supposed that this response fits better with the way females respond to stress because it builds on the brain's attachment-caregiving system and leads to nurturing and affiliative behaviour. Furthermore, the response is characterized by identifiable neurobiological processes in the brain that are gender specific.

Gender doesn't cause psychopathology. But because gender role is a social and cultural factor that influences the form and content of a disorder, we attend closely to it in the chapters that follow.

Social Effects on Health and Behaviour

A large number of studies have demonstrated that the greater the number and frequency of social relationships and contacts, the longer you are likely to live. Conversely, the lower you score on a social index that measures the richness of your social life, the shorter your life expectancy. Studies documenting this finding have been reported in North America (Berkman & Syme, 1979; House, Robbins, & Metzner, 1982; Schoenbach, Kaplan, Fredman, & Kleinbaum, 1986) and in Sweden and Finland. The studies take into account existing physical health and other risk factors for dying young, such as high blood pressure, high cholesterol levels, and smoking habits, and still produce the same result. Studies also show that social relationships seem to protect individuals against many physical and psychological disorders, such as high blood pressure, depression, alcoholism, arthritis, the progression to AIDS, and low birth weight in newborns (Cobb, 1976; House, Landis, & Umberson, 1988; Leserman et al., 2000; Thurston & Kubzanksy, 2009).

Even whether or not we come down with a cold is strongly influenced by the quality and extent of our social network. Cohen and colleagues (Cohen, Doyle, Skoner, Rabin, & Gwaltney, 1997) used nasal drops to expose 276 healthy volunteers to one of two different rhinoviruses (cold viruses), and then they quarantined the subjects for a week. The authors measured the extent of participation in 12 different types of social relationships (e.g.,

spouse, parent, friend, colleague), as well as other factors, such as smoking and poor sleep quality, that are likely to increase susceptibility to colds. The surprising results were that the greater the extent of social ties, the smaller the chance of catching a cold, even after all other factors were taken into consideration (controlled for). In fact, those with the fewest social ties were more than four times more likely to catch a cold than those with the greatest number of ties. This effect also extends to pets! Compared to people without pets, those with pets evidenced lower resting heart rate and blood pressure, and responded with smaller increases in these variables during laboratory stressors (Allen, Blascovitch, & Mendes, 2002). What could account for this? Once again, social and interpersonal factors seem to influence psychological and neurobiological variables—for example, the immune system—sometimes to a substantial degree. Thus, we cannot really study psychological and biological aspects of psychological disorders (or physical disorders, for that matter), without taking into account the social and cultural context of the disorder.

How do social relationships have such a profound impact on our physical and psychological characteristics? We don't know for sure, but we have some intriguing hints. Some people think interpersonal relationships give meaning to life and that people who have something to live for can overcome physical deficiencies and even delay death. You may have known an elderly person who far outlived his or her expected time in order to witness a significant family event such as a grandchild's graduation from university. Once the event has passed, the person dies. Another common observation is that if one spouse in a long-standing marital relationship dies, particularly an elderly wife, the other often dies soon after, regardless of health status. It is also possible that social relationships facilitate health-promoting behaviours, such as restraint in the use of alcohol and drugs, getting proper sleep, and seeking appropriate health care (House, Landis, & Umberson, 1988; Leserman et al., 2000).

Sometimes social upheaval is an opportunity for studying the impact of social networks on individual functioning. When the Sinai Peninsula was dismantled and evacuated as part of peace negotiations with Egypt, Steinglass, Weisstub, and Kaplan De-Nour (1988) studied residents of an Israeli community threatened with dissolution. They found that believing that we are embedded firmly in a social context was just as important as actually having a social network. Poor long-term adjustment was best predicted in those who perceived that their social network was disintegrating, whether or not it actually did.

In another example, whether you live in a city or the country may be associated with your chances of developing schizophrenia, a very severe disorder. Lewis, David, Andreasson, and Allsbeck (1992) found that the incidence of schizophrenia was 38 percent greater in men who had been raised in cities than in those raised in rural areas. We have known for a long time that more schizophrenia exists in the city than in the country, but researchers thought that people with schizophrenia drifted to cities after developing schizophrenia or that other endemic urban factors such as drug use or unstable family relationships might be the real culprit. But Lewis and associates carefully controlled for such factors, and it now seems something about cities over and above those influences may contribute to the development of schizophrenia. We do not yet know what it is. This finding, if it is replicated and shown to be true, may be very important in view of the mass migration of individuals to overcrowded urban areas, particularly in less developed countries.

In summary, we cannot study psychopathology independently of social and interpersonal influences, and we still have much to learn. Heinrichs, Rapee, and Alden (2006), Kirmayer (2002), and Kirmayer and Groleau (2001) have nicely summarized our knowledge in concluding that many psychological disorders, such as social phobia and major depressive disorder, seem to occur in all cultures, but they may look different from one culture to another because individual symptoms are strongly influenced by social and interpersonal context. For example, as we see in Chapter 7, depression in Western culture is reflected in feelings of guilt and inadequacy, and in developing countries with physical distress such as fatigue or illness. In Canada, Asian migrants represent 36.5 percent of all Canadian immigrants (Statistics Canada, 2001). Laurence Kirmayer, a cross-cultural psychiatrist from McGill University, has described how affective expressions of depression are often perceived as self-centred and threatening to the social structure in many Asian cultures, such as in Chinese society. This cultural context results in affective and cognitive dimensions of depression being less readily endorsed by Chinese depressed patients (Kirmayer & Groleau, 2001). These types of cultural differences likely contribute to the consistent underutilization of mainstream mental health services by Asian Canadians (Li & Browne, 2000; Whitley, Kirmayer, & Groleau, 2006).

As another clear example of social influences on mental health, consider the high rates of various psychological disorders and problems among Aboriginal Canadians relative to other groups of Canadians. As we will discuss in more detail in the chapters to come, rates of suicide (see Chapter 7), substance abuse (see Chapter 11), and familial violence are all elevated among Aboriginal peoples (Bridges & Kunselman, 2005; Brownridge, 2003; Gotowiec & Beiser, 1993–1994). Poverty, an established risk factor for many psychological disorders (Richters, 1993), is higher among Aboriginal people (Lee, 2000), which very likely contributes substantially to their elevated rates of certain psychological disorders. However, the fact that more Aboriginal people live in poverty is not the only reason for the elevated rates of these psychological and social problems. Their unique experiences of a history of oppression by the majority culture also need to be considered as a contributing factor. These oppressive experiences include the maltreatment of Aboriginal children in the residential school system from the late 19th century to as recently as the 1980s (Grant, 1996; Haig-Brown, 1988) and the continued discrimination against, and reduced opportunities for, Aboriginal people (see review by Shepard, O'Neill, & Guenette, 2006).

Social and Interpersonal Influences on the Elderly

The effect of social and interpersonal factors on the expression of physical and psychological disorders may differ with age. Grant, Patterson, and Yager (1988) studied 118 men and women 65 years old or older who lived independently. Those with fewer meaningful contacts and less social support from relatives had consistently higher levels of depression and more reports of unsatisfactory quality of life. However, if these individuals became physically

▲ A long and productive life usually includes strong social relationships and interpersonal relations.

ill, they had more substantial support from their families than those who were not physically ill. This finding raises the unfortunate possibility that it may be advantageous for elderly people to become physically ill, because illness allows them to re-establish the social support that makes life worth living. If further research indicates that this is true, involving their families before they get ill might help maintain their physical health (and significantly reduce health care costs).

The study of older adults is growing at a rapid pace, in line with the increase in the proportion of our population that is elderly. Frank Denton and his colleagues at McMaster University made projections of the age distribution of the Canadian population for the 45-year period from 1996 to 2041. They conclude that substantial aging of the Canadian population appears virtually certain (Denton, Feaver, & Spencer, 1998). Some have suggested that with this growth will come a corresponding increase in the number of older adults with mental health problems, many of whom will not receive appropriate care (e.g., Gatz & Smyer, 1992). As you can see, understanding and treating the disorders experienced by older adults is necessary and important.

Social Stigma

Other factors make the consideration of social and cultural issues imperative to the study of psychopathology. Psychological disorders continue to carry a substantial stigma in our society. To be anxious or depressed is to be weak and cowardly. To be schizophrenic is to be unpredictable and crazy. For physical injuries in times of war, we award medals. For psychological injuries, the unfortunate soldiers earn scorn and derision, as has been highlighted by Roméo Dallaire, a high-ranking member of the Canadian military who led the peace-keeping mission in Rwanda (see Chapter 5). Often, a patient with psychological disorders does not seek health care for fear a co-worker might learn about the problem. With far less social support than for physical illness, people have less chance of full recovery. We discuss some of the consequences of social attitudes toward psychological disorders in Chapter 16.

Interpersonal Psychotherapy (IPT)

Much as drug treatments are based on biological dimensions of psychopathology, and cognitive-behavioural treatments emerged from the study of cognitive and behavioural aspects of psychopathology, a form of psychotherapy with proven effectiveness for some disorders (see Chapters 7 and 8) has been developed that emphasizes the resolution of interpersonal problems and stressors. As developed by Myrna Weissman and her late husband, Gerald Klerman (Gillies, 2001; Klerman, Weissman, Rounsaville, & Chevron, 1984; Weissman, 1995), **interpersonal psychotherapy (IPT)** grew from the work of psychiatrist Harry Stack Sullivan. Trained as a Freudian, Sullivan greatly emphasized current interpersonal relationships, in addition to interpersonal experiences during particular psychosexual stages of growth in childhood.

▲ In developing countries, personal upheaval due to political strife affects mental health.

In IPT, the patient and therapist work together on identifying life stresses that precipitated the psychological disorder and current interpersonal problems that are either the source of the life stress or intimately connected with it (Gillies, 2001). Typically, these include one or more of four kinds of interpersonal issues. One of the most common is an interpersonal role dispute, such as marital conflict. Experiencing the death of a loved one and making the necessary adjustments is a second common area of focus. Acquiring a new relationship through marriage or job change may be a third source of interpersonal stress. Finally, the fourth area is identifying and correcting deficits in social skills that make it difficult to form the relationships, particularly intimate relationships, that are so important to all of us. IPT, like cognitive-behavioural therapy, is brief, typically 10 to 15 sessions, and it has proven highly effective for problems such as depression (Gillies, 2001).

Global Incidence of Psychological Disorders

Although IPT is a form of psychotherapy that explicitly recognizes the important influence of interpersonal and social factors in psychological disorders, cultural influences must also be considered. In this section, we consider the impact of cultural influences by examining the incidence of psychological disorders in different cultures around the globe. Behavioural and mental health problems in developing countries are exacerbated by political strife, technological change, and massive movements from rural to urban areas. An important study from the Center for the Study of Culture and Medicine, headed by Arthur Kleinman, reveals that 10 to 20 percent of all primary medical services in poor countries are sought by patients with psychological disorders, principally anxiety and mood disorders (including suicide attempts), as well as alcoholism, drug abuse, and childhood developmental disorders. Record numbers of young men are committing suicide in Micronesia. Alcoholism levels among adults

in Latin America have risen to 20 percent. Treatments for disorders such as depression and addictive behaviours that are successful in North America can't be administered in countries where mental health care is limited. In China, more than a billion people are served by approximately 3000 mental health professionals. In contrast, Canada alone has more than 11 000 licensed psychologists (Bazana, 1999) to serve over 32 million people (Statistics Canada, 2006). And yet psychological services in Canada are very much underutilized, particularly by those Canadians with the greatest mental health needs (Hunsley, Lee, & Aubry, 1999). Using data collected during the 1994–1995 Population Health Survey, John Hunsley and his colleagues showed that only about 2 percent of those Canadians surveyed indicated that they had consulted a psychologist in the year before the survey (Hunsley et al., 1999). These shocking statistics suggest that in addition to their role in causation, social and cultural factors substantially maintain disorders, because most societies have not yet developed the social context for alleviating and ultimately preventing them. Changing society's attitude is just one of the challenges facing us.

Life-Span Development

Life-span developmental psychopathologists (e.g., Galambos & Leadbeater, 2002) point out that we tend to look at psychological disorders from a snapshot perspective: We focus on a particular point in a person's life and assume it represents the whole person. The inadequacy of this way of looking at people should be clear. Think back on your own life over the past few years. The person you were, say, three years ago, is very different from the person you are now, and the person you will be three years from now will have changed in important ways. To understand psychopathology, we must appreciate how experiences during different periods of development may influence our vulnerability to other types of stress or to psychological disorders (Charles & Carstensen, 2010; Rutter, 2002).

Important developmental changes occur at all points in life. For example, adulthood, far from being a relatively stable period, is highly dynamic, with important changes occurring into old age. Erik Erikson suggested that we go through eight major crises during our lives (Erikson, 1982), each determined by our biological maturation and the social demands made at particular times. Unlike Freud, who envisioned no developmental stages beyond adolescence, Erikson believed that we grow and change beyond the age of 65. During older adulthood, for example, we look back and view our lives either as rewarding or as disappointing.

Although aspects of Erikson's theory of psychosocial development have been criticized as being too vague (Shaffer, 1993), it demonstrates the comprehensive approach to human development advocated by life-span developmentalists. Basic research is beginning to confirm the importance of this approach. In one experiment at the University of Lethbridge by Bryan Kolb and his colleagues (Kolb, Gibb, & Gorny, 2003), animals were placed in complex environments either as juveniles, as adults, or in very old age, when cognitive abilities were beginning to decline (senescence). The researchers found that the environment had different effects on the brains of these animals depending on their developmental stage. Basically, the complex and challenging environments increased the size and complexity of neurons in the motor and sensory cortical regions in the adult and aged animals, but unlike the older groups, decreased the spine density of neurons in very young animals. Nevertheless, this decrease was associated with enhanced motor and cognitive skills when the animals became adults (Kolb, Gibb, & Gorny, 2003). In fact, even prenatal experience seems to affect brain structure, since the offspring of an animal housed in a rich and complex environment during the term of her pregnancy have the advantage of more complex cortical brain circuits after birth (Kolb, Gibb, & Robinson, 2003). Thus, we can infer that the influence of developmental stage and prior experience has a substantial impact on the development and presentation of psychological disorders, an inference that is receiving confirmation from sophisticated life-span developmental psychology research (e.g., Carstensen, Charles, Isaacowitz, & Kennedy, 2003; Isaacowitz, Smith, & Carstensen, 2003). For example, in depressive (mood) disorders, children and adolescents do not receive the same benefit from antidepressant drugs as do adults (Hazell, O'Connell, Heathcote, Robertson, & Henry, 1995; Santosh, 2009), and for many of them these drugs pose risks that are not present in adults (Santosh, 2009). Also, the gender distribution in depression is approximately equal until puberty, when it becomes more common in girls (Compas et al., 1997; Hankin, Wetter, & Cheely, 2007).

The Principle of Equifinality

When considering developmental influences on psychopathology, an important concept is the principle of **equifinality**. This principle is used in developmental psychopathology to indicate that we must consider many paths to a given outcome (Cicchetti, 1991). Like a fever, a particular behaviour or disorder may have several causes. Many examples of this equifinality principle exist; for example, a delusional syndrome may be an aspect of schizophrenia, but it can also arise from amphetamine abuse. Delirium, which involves difficulty focusing attention, often occurs in older adults after surgery, but it can also result from thiamine deficiency or renal (kidney) disease. Autism can sometimes occur in children whose mothers are exposed to rubella during pregnancy, but it can also occur in children whose mothers experience difficulties during labour.

Different paths can also result from the interaction of psychological and biological factors during various stages of development. How someone copes with impairment due to organic causes may have a profound effect on that person's overall functioning. For example, people with documented brain damage may have different levels of disorder. Those with healthy systems of social support, consisting of family and friends, as well as highly adaptive personality characteristics, such as marked confidence in their abilities to overcome challenges, may experience only mild behavioural and cognitive disturbance despite an organic pathology. Those without comparable support and personality may be incapacitated. This difference may be clearer if you think of people you know with physical disabilities. Some paralyzed from the waist down by accident or disease (paraplegics) have nevertheless become superb athletes or accomplished in business or the arts. Others with the same condition are depressed and hopeless; they have withdrawn from life or, even worse, ended their lives. Even the content of delusions and hallucinations that may accompany a disorder, and the degree to which they are frightening or difficult to cope with, is determined in part by psychological and social factors.

Researchers are exploring not only what makes people experience particular disorders but also what protects others from having the same difficulties. If you were interested in why someone would be depressed, for example, you would first look at people who display depression. But you could also study people in similar situations and from similar backgrounds who are not depressed. An excellent example of this approach is research on "resilient" children, which suggests that social factors may protect some children from being hurt by stressful experiences, such as one or both parents having a psychiatric disturbance (Cooper, Feder, Southwick & Charney, 2007; Garmezy & Rutter, 1983; Hetherington & Blechman, 1996; Weiner, 2000). The presence of a caring adult friend or relative can offset the negative stresses of this environment, as can the child's own ability to understand and cope with unpleasant situations. People brought up in violent or otherwise dysfunctional families who have successfully gone on to attend a postsecondary school might want to look back for the factors that protected them. Perhaps if we better understand why some people do not encounter the same problems as others in similar circumstances, we can better understand particular disorders, assist those who experience them, and even prevent some cases from occurring at all.

Conclusions

We have examined modern approaches to psychopathology and we have found the field to be complex indeed. In this brief overview (even though it may not seem brief), we have seen that contributions from (1) psychoanalytic theory, (2) behavioural and cognitive science, (3) emotional influences, (4) social and cultural influences, (5) genetics, (6) neuroscience, and (7) life-span developmental factors all must be considered when we think about psychopathology. Even though our knowledge is incomplete, you can see why we could never resume the one-dimensional thinking typical of the various historical traditions described in Chapter 1.

And yet, books about psychological disorders and news reports in the popular press often describe the causes of these disorders in one-dimensional terms without considering other influences. For example, how many times have you heard that a psychological disorder such as depression, or perhaps schizophrenia, is caused by a "chemical imbalance" without considering other possible causes? When you read that a disorder is caused by a chemical imbalance, it sounds like nothing else really matters, and all you have to do is correct the imbalance in neurotransmitter activity to "cure" the problem.

Based on research we will review when we talk about specific psychological disorders, there is no question whatsoever that psychological disorders are associated with altered neurotransmitter activity and other aspects of brain function (a chemical imbalance). But we have learned in this chapter that a chemical imbalance could, in turn, be caused by psychological or social factors such as stress, strong emotional reactions, difficult family interactions, changes caused by aging, or, most likely, some interaction of all these factors. Therefore, it is inaccurate and misleading to say that a psychological disorder is caused by a chemical imbalance, even though chemical imbalances almost certainly exist.

Similarly, how many times have you heard that alcoholism or other addictive behaviours were caused by lack of willpower, implying that if these individuals simply developed the right attitude, they could overcome their addiction? People with severe addictions may well have faulty cognitive processes, as indicated by their rationalizing their behaviour, their other faulty appraisals, or their attribution of their problems to stress in their lives or some other excuse. They may also misperceive the effects that alcohol has on them, and all these cognitions and attitudes contribute to someone developing an addiction. But considering only cognitive processes without considering other factors as causes of addictions would be as incorrect as saying that depression is caused by a chemical imbalance. In fact, our genes play a role in the development of addictive behaviours, as we learn in

Chapter 11. Evidence also exists that brain function in people with addictions may well be different from brain function in individuals who, say, ingest similar amounts of alcohol but do not develop addictive behaviour. Interpersonal, social, and cultural factors also contribute strongly to the development of addictive behaviours. To say, then, that addictive behaviours such as alcoholism are caused by lack of willpower or to certain faulty ways of thinking is also highly simplistic and just plain wrong.

If you learn one thing from this book it should be that psychological disorders do not have just one cause. They have many causes—these causes all interact with one another—and we must understand this interaction to appreciate fully the origins of psychological disorders. To do this requires a multidimensional integrative approach. In chapters covering specific psychological disorders, we return to cases very much like Jody's and consider them from this multidimensional integrative perspective. But first we must explore the processes of assessment and diagnosis used to measure and classify psychopathology.

Concept Check | 2.6

Fill in the blanks to complete these statements relating to the cultural, social, and developmental factors influencing psychopathology.

1. What we _____ is strongly influenced by our social environments.

2. The likelihood of your having a particular phobia is powerfully influenced by your _____.

3. A large number of studies have demonstrated that the greater the number and frequency of _____ relationships and _____, the longer you are likely to live.

4. The effect of social and interpersonal factors on the expression of physical and psychological disorders may differ with _____.

5. The principle of _____ is used in developmental psychopathology to indicate that we must consider a number of paths to a given outcome.

Summary

One-Dimensional or Multidimensional Models

- The causes of abnormal behaviour are complex and fascinating. You can say that psychological disorders are caused by nature (biology) and by nurture (psychosocial factors), and you would be right on both counts—but also wrong on both counts.
- To identify the causes of various psychological disorders, we must consider the interaction of all relevant dimensions: genetic contributions, the role of the nervous system, behavioural and cognitive processes, emotional influences, social and interpersonal influences, and developmental factors. Thus, we have arrived at a multidimensional integrative approach to the causes of psychological disorders.

Genetic Contributions to Psychopathology

- The genetic influence on much of our development and most of our behaviour, personality, and even IQ is polygenic—that is, influenced by many genes, each contributing only a tiny effect. This is assumed to be the case in abnormal behaviour as well, although individual genes have yet to be identified that relate to the major psychological disorders.
- In studying causal relationships in psychopathology, researchers look at the interactions of genetic and environmental effects. In the diathesis–stress model, individuals are assumed to inherit certain vulnerabilities that make them susceptible to a disorder when the right kind of stressor comes along. In the reciprocal gene–environment model, the individual's genetic vulnerability toward a certain disorder may make it more likely that he or she will experience the stressor that, in turn, triggers the genetic vulnerability and thus the disorder. In epigenetics, the immediate effects of the environment (such as early stressful experiences) influence cells that turn certain genes on or off. This effect may be passed down through several generations.

Neuroscience and Its Contributions to Psychopathology

- The field of neuroscience promises much as we try to unravel the mysteries of psychopathology. Within the nervous system, levels of neurotransmitter and neuroendocrine activity interact in very complex ways to modulate and regulate emotions and behaviour and contribute to psychological disorders.
- Critical to our understanding of psychopathology are the neurotransmitter currents called brain circuits. Of the neurotransmitters that may play a key role, we investigated five: serotonin, gamma aminobutyric acid (GABA), glutamate, norepinephrine, and dopamine.

Behavioural and Cognitive Science

- The relatively new field of cognitive science provides a valuable perspective on how behavioural and cognitive influences affect the learning and adaptation each of us experience throughout life. Clearly, such influences not only contribute to psychological disorders but also may directly modify brain functioning, brain structure, and even genetic expression. We examined some of the research in this field by looking at learned helplessness, modelling, prepared learning, implicit memory, and cognitive-behavioural therapy.

Emotions

- Emotions have a direct and dramatic impact on our functioning and play a central role in many disorders. Mood, a persistent period of emotionality, is often evident in psychological disorders.

Cultural, Social, and Interpersonal Factors

- Social and interpersonal influences profoundly affect both psychological disorders and biology. Interpersonal psychotherapy (IPT), a form of treatment that focuses on the resolution of social and interpersonal problems, has proven effectiveness for some disorders.

Life-Span Development

- In considering a multidimensional integrative approach to psychopathology, it is important to remember the principle of equifinality, which reminds us that we must consider the various paths to a particular outcome, not just the result.

Key Terms

affect, 61
agonist, 48
antagonist, 48
brain circuits, 48
cognitive science, 55
cognitive-behavioural therapy
    (CBT), 59
diathesis–stress model, 38
dopamine, 51
emotion, 61

epigenetics, 41
equifinality, 67
flight-or-fight response, 60
gamma aminobutyric acid
    (GABA), 49
genes, 35
glutamate, 49
hormone, 46
implicit cognition, 58
implicit memory, 58

interpersonal psychotherapy
    (IPT), 66
inverse agonist, 48
learned helplessness, 56
modelling, 57
mood, 61
multidimensional integrative
    approach, 33
neurons, 43
neuroscience, 42
neurotransmitters, 44

norepinephrine (also
    noradrenaline), 50
observational learning, 57
prepared learning, 57
reciprocal gene–environment
    model, 39
reuptake, 48
serotonin, 49
synaptic cleft, 43
vulnerability, 38

Answers to Concept Checks

2.1

1. b **2.** a (best answer) or c **3.** e
4. a (initial development of
phobia), c (maintenance of
phobia)

2.2

1. F (first 22 pairs)
2. T

3. T
4. F (reciprocal gene–
environment model)
5. F (complex interaction of
both nature and nurture)

2.3

1. b **2.** c **3.** d **4.** a

2.4

1. a **2.** c **3.** d **4.** c

2.5

1. b **2.** a **3.** d **4.** c

2.6

1. fear
2. gender
3. social, contacts
4. age
5. equifinality

Media Resources

CourseMate

Access an integrated eBook, Abnormal Psychology Videos (formerly Abnormal Psych Live CD-ROM), chapter-specific interactive learning tools (flashcards, quizzes, learning modules), and more in your Psychology CourseMate, available at **www.abnormalpsych3ce.nelson.com.**

Abnormal Psychology Video

Free Abnormal Psychology videos can be viewed on the website **www.abnormalpsych3ce .nelson.com**.

- *Integrative Approach*: This clip summarizes the integrative approach, showing how psychological factors affect our biology and our brain influences our behaviour.

Video Concept Reviews

CourseMate also contains Mark Durand's *Video Concept Reviews* on these challenging topics:

- Multidimensional Models
- Genetics: Phenotype and Genotype
- Genetics: Nature of Genes
- Genetics: Dominant versus Recessive Genes
- Genetics: Polygenic
- Diathesis–Stress Model
- Concept Check—Reciprocal Gene–Environment Model
- Neuroimaging
- Neurons
- Neurotransmitters/Reuptake
- Agonist/Antagonist
- Implicit Memory/Stroop Test
- Emotion

3 | Clinical Assessment and Diagnosis

© iStockphoto.com/Brad Killer

It is not the illness but the human being that needs help. As a doctor I am not concerned with the illness but with the human being.
—Georg Goddeck, *The Meaning of Illness*

Demonstrate knowledge and understanding representing appropriate breadth and depth in selected content areas of psychology:	› Biological bases of behaviour and mental processes, including physiology, sensation, perception, comparative, motivation, and emotion (APA SLO 1.2.a (3)) *(see textbook pages 86–89)*
	› The history of psychology, including the evolution of methods of psychology, its theoretical conflicts, and its socio-cultural contexts (APA SLO 1.2.b) *(see textbook pages 92–95)*
Identify appropriate applications of psychology in solving problems, such as:	› Psychological tests and measurements (APA SLO 4.2.c) *(see textbook pages 74–89)*

* Portions of this chapter cover learning outcomes suggested by the American Psychological Association (2007) in their guidelines for the undergraduate psychology major. Chapter coverage of these outcomes is identified above by APA Goal and APA Suggested Learning Outcome (SLO).

The processes of clinical assessment and diagnosis are central to the study of psychopathology and, ultimately, to the treatment of psychological disorders. **Clinical assessment** is the systematic evaluation and measurement of psychological, biological, and social factors in an individual presenting with a possible psychological disorder. **Diagnosis** is the process of determining whether the particular problem afflicting the individual meets all the criteria for a psychological disorder, as set 4th in the *Diagnostic and Statistical Manual of Mental Disorders*, 4th edition (text revision), or *DSM-IV-TR* (American Psychiatric Association, 2000a). In this chapter, after demonstrating assessment and diagnosis within the context of an actual case, we examine the development of the *DSM* into a widely used classification system for abnormal behaviour. Then we review the many assessment techniques available to the clinician. Finally, we turn to diagnostic issues and the related challenges of classification.

FRANK | *Young, Serious, and Anxious*

Frank, a 24-year-old mechanic, was referred to one of our clinics for evaluation and possible treatment of severe distress and anxiety centring on his marriage. He arrived neatly dressed in his work clothes. He reported that this was the first time he had ever seen a mental health professional. He wasn't sure that he really needed (or wanted) to be there, but he felt he was beginning to "come apart" due to his marital difficulties. What follows is a transcript of parts of this first interview.

THERAPIST: What sorts of problems have been troubling you during the past month?

FRANK: I'm beginning to have a lot of marital problems. I was married about nine months ago, but I've been really tense around the house and we've been having a lot of arguments.

THERAPIST: Is this something recent?

FRANK: Well, it wasn't too bad at first, but it's been worse lately. I've also been really uptight in my job, and I haven't been getting my work done.

We always begin by asking the patient to describe for us, in a relatively open-ended way, the major difficulties that have brought him or her to the office in the first place. When dealing with adults, or children old enough to tell us their story, this strategy tends to break the ice, and it reveals the central problems as seen through the patient's eyes.

After Frank described this major problem in some detail, the therapist then asked him about his marriage, his job, and other present life circumstances to get a better picture of his current situation. Frank seemed to be quite tense and anxious and would often look down at the floor while he talked, glancing up only occasionally to make eye contact. Sometimes his right leg would twitch. Although it was not easy to see at first because he was looking down, Frank was also closing his eyes very tightly for two to three seconds. It was during these periods when his eyes were closed that his right leg would twitch.

The interview proceeded for the next half hour, exploring marital and job issues. It became increasingly clear that Frank was feeling inadequate and anxious about handling situations in his life. By this time he was talking freely and looking up a little more at the therapist, but he was continuing to close his eyes and twitch his right leg slightly.

THERAPIST: Are you aware that once in a while you're closing your eyes while you're telling me this?

FRANK: I'm not aware all the time, but I know I do it.

THERAPIST: Do you know how long you've been doing that?

FRANK: Oh, I don't know, maybe a year or two.

THERAPIST: Are you thinking about anything when you close your eyes?

FRANK: Well, actually I'm trying not to think about something.

THERAPIST: What do you mean?

FRANK: Well, I have these really frightening and stupid thoughts, and ... it's hard to even talk about it.

THERAPIST: The thoughts are frightening?

FRANK: Yes, I keep thinking I'm going to take a fit, and I'm just trying to get that out of my mind.

THERAPIST: Could you tell me more about this fit?

FRANK: Well, you know, it's those terrible things where people fall down and they froth at the mouth, and their tongues come out, and they shake all over. You know, seizures. I think they call it epilepsy.

THERAPIST: And you're trying to get these thoughts out of your mind?

FRANK: Oh, I do everything possible to get those thoughts out of my mind as quickly as I can.

THERAPIST: I've noticed you moving your leg when you close your eyes. Is that part of it?

FRANK: Yes, I've noticed if I really jerk my leg and pray real hard for a little while, the thought will go away.

Source: Excerpt from "Behavioral Assessment: Basic Strategies and Initial Procedures" by R. O. Nelson and D. H. Barlow. In D. H. Barlow (Ed.), *Behavioral Assessment of Adult Disorders*, 1981. Copyright © 1981 by Guilford Press. Reprinted by permission.

of more pleasant things but had little success with this method. He vigorously resisted the images of harming... children, but despite this, they persisted.

...He concealed his thoughts from everyone else because he expected that others would find them unacceptable and conclude that there was something wrong with him.... [H]e was extremely worried that he might be going crazy and losing his mental stability. He was particularly worried that the intense anxiety might one day cause him to "lose control and snap."

Source: From *The Treatment of Obsessions* by Stanley Rachman. 2003. Oxford University Press.

What's wrong with Frank? The interview reveals an insecure young man experiencing substantial stress as he questions whether he is capable of handling marriage and a job. He reports that he loves his wife very much and wants the marriage to work and he is attempting to be as conscientious as possible on his job, a job from which he derives a lot of satisfaction and enjoyment. Also, for some reason, he is having troubling thoughts about seizures. Now let's consider one more case for purposes of illustration. This case (we'll call him Brian) was described by Stanley J. Rachman, a clinical psychologist at the University of British Columbia (Rachman 2003).

BRIAN | *Unwanted Thoughts of Harm*

A thirty-year-old self-employed bookkeeper referred himself for treatment...having failed to benefit from a variety of previous treatments, both psychiatric and psychological. He complained of...thoughts and images of harming himself, thoughts of hurting other people, and unwanted sexual thoughts and images. The [thought] of causing harm to children was the most distressing [to Brian] and generally focused on his five-year-old nephew. He described a recent example when he took his nephew out for a drive and had thoughts of "beating him up and dumping him in the side of the road." He also had thoughts of harming children who were unfamiliar to him, saying that these can be triggered by driving past a school or seeing children in a playground. He also had occasional thoughts of harming members of his family. His images of self-harm took two main forms. The first involved slashing his wrists, arms, and hands with a knife. The image usually lasted for fifteen to thirty seconds and was triggered by the sight of sharp objects. The second image/thought involved placing his hand on a hot element when cooking on the stove. He also reported unwanted sexual thoughts but said that the associated images were not as intense as those involving aggressive themes.

He reported having the harm images about three times a week and the thoughts of self-harm four to five times a day. The thoughts and images disturbed his concentration and ability to perform his work. He was depressed and slower than many times when he lost track of what he was doing. He tried to deal with the [thoughts] by deliberately thinking

So where do we go from here? How do we determine whether Frank has a psychological disorder or if he is simply one of many young men experiencing the normal stresses and strains of a new marriage who, perhaps, could benefit from some marital counselling? And what about Brian? Why is he having these troubling and persistent thoughts and mental images? The purpose of this chapter is to illustrate how mental health clinicians address these types of questions in a systematic way, assessing patients in order to study the basic nature of psychopathology as well as to make diagnoses and plan treatment.

Assessing Psychological Disorders

The process of clinical assessment in psychopathology has been likened to a funnel (Hawkins, 1979; Peterson, 1968). The clinician begins by collecting a lot of information across a broad range of the individual's functioning to determine where the source of the problem may lie. After getting a preliminary sense of the overall functioning of the person, the clinician narrows the focus by ruling out problems in some areas and concentrating on areas that seem most relevant.

To understand the different ways clinicians assess psychological problems, we need to understand three basic concepts that help determine the value of our assessments: reliability, validity, and standardization (see ■ Figure 3.1). Assessment techniques are subject to a number of strict requirements, not the least of which is some evidence (research) that they actually do what they are designed to do. One of the more important requirements of these assessments is that they be reliable. **Reliability** is the degree to which a measurement is consistent (Asmundson, Norton, & Stein, 2002). Imagine how irritated you would be if you had stomach pain and you went to four competent physicians and got four different diagnoses and four different treatments. The diagnoses would be said to be unreliable because two or more "raters" (the physicians) did not agree on the conclusion. We expect, in general, that presenting the same symptoms to different physicians will result in similar diagnoses. One way psychologists improve their reliability is by carefully designing their assessment devices and then conducting research on them to ensure that two or more raters will get the same answers (called *interrater reliability*). They also determine whether these techniques are stable across time. In other words, if you go to a clinician on Tuesday and are told you have an IQ of 110, you

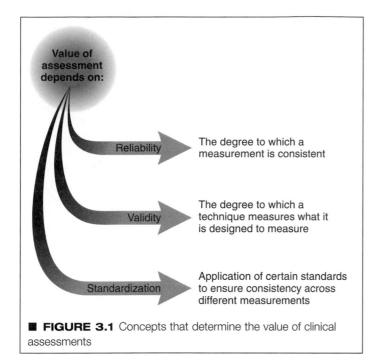

Value of assessment depends on:

Reliability → The degree to which a measurement is consistent

Validity → The degree to which a technique measures what it is designed to measure

Standardization → Application of certain standards to ensure consistency across different measurements

■ **FIGURE 3.1** Concepts that determine the value of clinical assessments

should expect a similar result if you take the same test again on Thursday. This is known as *test-retest reliability*. We return to the concept of reliability when we talk of diagnoses and classification.

Validity is whether something measures what it is designed to measure; in this case, whether a technique assesses what it is supposed to (Asmundson et al., 2002). Comparing the results of one assessment measure with the results of others that are better known allows you to begin to determine the validity of the first measure. This comparison is called *concurrent* or *descriptive validity*. For example, if the results from a standard, but very long, IQ test were essentially the same as the results from a new brief version, you could conclude that the brief version had concurrent validity. *Predictive validity* is how well your assessment tells you what will happen in the future. For example, does it predict who will succeed in school and who will not, which is one goal of an IQ test?

Standardization is the process by which a certain set of standards or norms is determined for a technique to make its use consistent across different measurements. The standards might apply to the procedures of testing, scoring, and evaluating data. To illustrate, the assessment might be given to large numbers of people who differ on important factors such as age, race, gender, socio-economic status, and diagnosis; their scores would then be used as a standard, or norm, for comparison purposes. For example, if you are a First Nations male, 19 years old, and from a working-class background, your score on a psychological test should be compared with the scores of others like you and not with the scores of very different people, such as a group of women of Asian descent in their 60s from middle-class backgrounds. Reliability, validity, and standardization are important to all forms of psychological assessment.

Clinical assessment consists of strategies and procedures that help clinicians acquire the information they need to understand their patients and assist them. These procedures include a *clinical interview* and, within the context of the interview, a *mental status exam* that can be administered either formally or informally, often a thorough *physical examination*, *behavioural observation and assessment*, and *psychological tests* (if needed).

The Clinical Interview

The clinical interview, the core of most clinical work, is used by psychologists, psychiatrists, and other mental health professionals. The interview gathers information on current and past behaviour, attitudes, and emotions, as well as a detailed history of the individual's life in general and of the presenting problem. Clinicians determine when the specific problem first started and identify other events (e.g., life stress, trauma, physical illness) that might have occurred about the same time. In addition, most clinicians gather at least some information on the patient's current and past interpersonal and social history, including family makeup (e.g., marital status, number of children, student currently living with parents), and on the individual's upbringing. Information on sexual development, religious attitudes (current and past), relevant cultural concerns (such as stress induced by discrimination), and educational history are also routinely collected. To organize information obtained during an interview, many clinicians use a **mental status exam**.

The Mental Status Exam

In essence, the mental status exam involves the systematic observation of somebody's behaviour. In the mental status exam, clinicians organize their observations of other people in a way that gives them sufficient information to determine whether a psychological disorder might be present (Nelson & Barlow, 1981). For the most part, the exams are performed relatively quickly by experienced clinicians in the course of interviewing or observing a patient. The exam covers five categories: appearance and behaviour, thought processes, mood and affect, intellectual functioning, and sensorium.

1. *Appearance and behaviour.* The clinician notes any overt physical behaviours such as Frank's leg twitch, as well as the individual's dress, general appearance, posture, and facial expression. For example, very slow and effortful motor behaviour, like Brian's slowed performance on tasks, is sometimes referred to as psychomotor retardation and may indicate severe depression.

2. *Thought processes.* When clinicians listen to a patient talk, they're getting a good idea of that person's thought processes. They might look for several things here. For example, does the

▲ During their first meeting, the mental health professional focuses on the problem that brought the person to treatment.

Assessing Psychological Disorders **75**

person talk really fast or really slowly? Does the patient make sense when he or she talks or are ideas presented with no apparent connection? In some patients with schizophrenia, a disjointed speech pattern, referred to as "looseness of association," is quite noticeable. In addition to rate or flow and continuity of speech, what about the content? For example, a clinician would note Brain's intense and distressing thoughts of harming children in this part of the mental status exam. Is there any evidence of delusions (distorted views of reality)? A typical delusion involves *delusions of persecution*, where someone thinks people are after him and out to get him all the time. The individual might also have *ideas of reference*, where everything everyone else does somehow relates back to him. *Hallucinations* are things a person sees or hears but that really aren't there. For example, the clinician might ask, "Do you ever see things or maybe hear things when you know there is nothing there?"

3. *Mood and affect*. Mood is the predominant feeling state of the individual, as we noted in Chapter 2. Does the person appear to be down in the dumps or continually elated? Does she or he talk in a depressed or hopeless fashion? Are there times when the depression seems to go away? For example, Brian's feelings of depression and his intense anxiety and worry about his thought patterns would be the clinician's focus in this part of the mental status exam. Affect, by contrast, refers to the feeling state that accompanies what we say at a given time. If a friend told you his or her mother has died and is laughing about it, or if your friend has just won the lottery and is crying, you would think it strange. A mental health clinician would note that your friend's affect is "inappropriate."

4. *Intellectual functioning*. Clinicians make a rough estimate of others' intellectual functioning just by talking to them. Do they seem to have a reasonable vocabulary? Can they talk in abstractions and metaphors (as most of us do much of the time)? How is the person's memory? We usually make some gross or rough estimate of intelligence that is noticeable only if it deviates from normal, such as concluding the person is above or below average intelligence. In Brian's mental status exam, for example, the clinician might look at Brian's answers to questions about his occupational achievement (i.e., he is successfully self-employed as a bookkeeper) and infer from Brian's use of language that this client is of average to above-average intelligence.

5. *Sensorium*. Sensorium is our general awareness of our surroundings. Do the individuals know what the date is, what time it is, where they are, who they are, and who you are? People with permanent brain damage or dysfunction—or temporary brain damage or dysfunction, often due to drugs or other toxic states—may not know the answer to these questions. If the patient knows who he or she is and who the clinician is and has a good idea of the time and place, the clinician would say that the patient's sensorium is "clear" and is "oriented times three" (to person, place, and time). In Brian's case, although his recurrent thoughts and images about harming himself and others were extremely distracting to him, he had no difficulties in terms of his awareness of his surroundings.

What can we conclude from these informal behavioural observations? Basically, they allow the clinician to make a preliminary determination of which areas of the patient's behaviour and condition should be assessed in more detail and perhaps more formally. If psychological disorders remain a possibility, the clinician may begin to hypothesize which disorders might be present. This process, in turn, provides more focus for the assessment and diagnostic activities to come.

We have already given examples of the type of information revealed by the mental status exam in the case of Brian. Let's now return to Frank's case. What have we learned from his mental status exam (see ■ Figure 3.2)? Observing Frank's persistent motor behaviour in the form of a twitch led to the discovery of a functional relationship with some troublesome thoughts regarding seizures. Beyond this, his appearance was appropriate, and the flow and content of his speech were reasonable; his intelligence was well within normal limits, and he was oriented times three. He did display an anxious mood; however, his affect was appropriate to what he was saying. Observations during the mental status exam suggested that we direct the remainder of the clinical interview and additional assessment and diagnostic activities to identifying the possible existence of a disorder characterized by intrusive, unwanted thoughts and the attempt to resist them—in other words, *obsessive-compulsive disorder*. Later we describe some of the specific assessment strategies, from among many choices, that we would use with Frank or Brian.

Patients usually have a good idea of their major concerns in a general sense ("I'm depressed"; "I'm phobic"); occasionally, the problem reported by the patient may not, after assessment, be the major issue in the eyes of the mental health clinician. The case of Frank illustrates this point well: He complained of distress relating to marital problems, but the clinician decided, on the basis of the initial interview, that the principal difficulties lay elsewhere. Frank wasn't attempting to hide anything from the clinician. Frank just didn't think his intrusive thoughts were the major problem; additionally, talking about them was very difficult for him because they were quite frightening, just as Brian's recurrent, unwanted thoughts were very distressing and anxiety provoking for him.

These examples illustrate the importance of conducting the clinical interview in a way that elicits the patient's trust and empathy. Psychologists and other mental health professionals are trained extensively in methods that put patients at ease and facilitate communication, including using non-threatening ways of seeking information and having appropriate listening skills. Information provided by patients to psychologists and psychiatrists is protected by laws of "privileged communication" or confidentiality; that is, even if authorities want the information the therapist has received from the patient, they cannot have access to it without the express consent of the patient. The only exception to this rule occurs when the clinician judges that, because of the patient's condition, some harm or danger to either the patient or someone else is imminent. At the outset of the initial interview, the therapist should inform the patient of the confidential nature of their conversation and the (quite rare) conditions under which that confidence would not hold.

Semistructured Clinical Interviews

Until relatively recently, most clinicians, after training, developed their own methods of collecting necessary information from patients. Different patients seeing different psychologists or other mental health professionals might encounter markedly different types and styles of interviews. *Unstructured interviews* follow no systematic

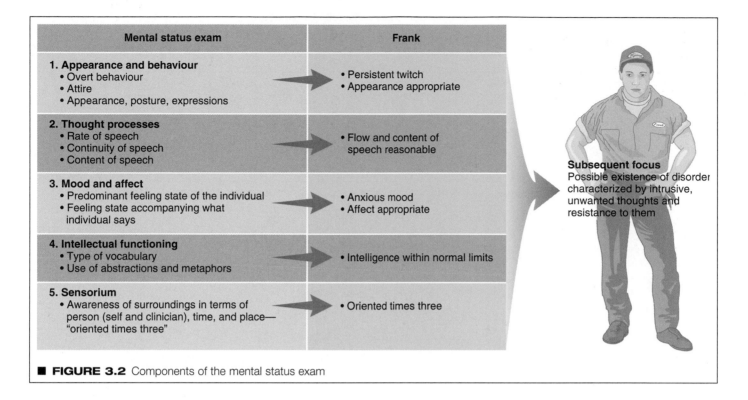

FIGURE 3.2 Components of the mental status exam

format. *Semistructured interviews* are made up of questions that have been carefully phrased and tested to elicit useful information in a consistent manner, so clinicians can be sure they have inquired about the most important aspects of particular disorders. Clinicians may also depart from set questions to follow up on specific issues—thus the label "semistructured." Because the wording and sequencing of questions has been carefully worked out over many years, the clinician can feel confident that a semistructured interview will accomplish its purpose. The disadvantage, of course, is that it robs the interview of some of the spontaneous quality of two people talking about a problem. Also, if applied too rigidly, this type of interview may inhibit the patient from volunteering useful information that is not directly relevant to the questions being asked. For these reasons, fully structured interviews administered wholly by a computer have not caught on, although they are used in some settings.

An increasing number of mental health professionals routinely use semistructured interviews. Some are quite specialized. For example, Frank's or Brian's clinician, in probing further into a possible obsessive-compulsive disorder, might use the *Anxiety Disorders Interview Schedule for DSM-IV (ADIS-IV)* (DiNardo, Brown, & Barlow, 1994)—developed specifically for diagnosing anxiety disorders—or the *Structured Clinical Interview for DSM-IV (SCID-IV)* (Spitzer, Williams, & Gibbon, 1994)—developed to assess a variety of the disorders discussed in the various chapters of this text. These two structured interviews were designed for use in making diagnoses according to the criteria contained in the *Diagnostic and Statistical Manual of Mental Disorders*, 4th edition (*DSM-IV*) and both are still applicable for making diagnoses according to the latest version of this diagnostic manual (i.e., the 4th edition, text revision [*DSM-IV-TR*]). According to the *ADIS-IV* interview schedule, shown in Table 3.1, the clinician first asks if the patient is bothered by thoughts, images, or impulses (obsessions) or currently feels driven to repeat some behaviour or thought over and over again (compulsions). Based on an eight-point rating scale that ranges from "never" to "occasionally" to "constantly," the clinician then asks the patient to rate each obsession on two measures:

TABLE 3.1 Sample Questions for Assessing Obsessive-Compulsive Disorder

1. Initial inquiry
　a. Currently, are you bothered by thoughts, images, or impulses that keep recurring to you and seem inappropriate or nonsensical but that you
　　can't stop from coming into your mind?　　　　　　　　　　　　　　　　　　　　　　　　　　　　　yes _____ no _____
　　If YES, specify: _____
　　_____

　b. Currently, do you feel driven to repeat some behaviour or to repeat something in your mind to try to feel less uncomfortable?
　　yes _____ no _____
　　If YES, specify: _____

Obsessions:
For each obsession, make separate ratings of persistence–distress and resistance using the scales and suggested queries that follow.
Persistence–distress:

(continued)

TABLE 3.1 Sample Questions for Assessing Obsessive-Compulsive Disorder (Continued)

How often does the obsession enter your mind? How distressing is it to you when _____ enters your mind? (What is the time frame?)

0	1	2	3	4	5	6	7	8

Never/ no distress	Rarely/ mild distress	Occasionally/ moderate distress	Frequently/ marked distress	Constantly/ extreme distress

Resistance:
How often do you attempt to get rid of the obsession by ignoring, suppressing, or trying to neutralize it with some thought or action?

0	1	2	3	4	5	6	7	8

Never	Rarely	Occasionally	Frequently	Constantly

	Persistence–distress	Resistance	Comments
a. Doubting (for example, locks, turning appliances off, and completion or accuracy of tasks)			
b. Contamination (for example, contracting germs from doorknobs, toilets, or money)	_____	_____	_____
c. Nonsensical impulses (for example, shouting or undressing in public)	_____	_____	_____
d. Aggressive impulses (for example, hurting self or others intentionally or destroying objects)	_____	_____	_____
e. Sexual (for example, obscene thoughts or images)	_____	_____	_____
f. Religious or satanic (for example, blasphemous thoughts or impulses)	_____	_____	_____
g. Accidental harm to others (for example, poisoning or hurting someone unknowingly)	_____	_____	_____
h. Horrific images (for example, mutilated bodies)	_____	_____	_____
i. Nonsensical thoughts or images (for example, numbers, letters, or songs)	_____	_____	_____
j. Other	_____	_____	_____
k. Other	_____	_____	_____

For each compulsion, make ratings of frequency using the scale and suggested queries that follow.
Frequency:
How often are you driven to perform such an action? (What is the time frame?)

0	1	2	3	4	5	6	7	8

Never	Rarely	Occasionally	Frequently	Constantly

Current compulsion

	Frequency	Comments
a. Counting (for example, certain letters or numbers or other objects in the environment)		
b. Checking (for example, locks, appliances, driving routes, important papers, or wastebaskets)	_____	_____
c. Washing	_____	_____
d. Hoarding (for example, newspapers, garbage, or trivial items)	_____	_____
e. Internal repetition (for example, phrases, words, or prayers)	_____	_____

(continued)

f. Adhering to certain rules or sequences (for example, ensuring symmetry, performing ritualistic acts, or adhering to a specific routine for daily activities)

_____

g. Other

_____

h. Other

_____

persistence-distress (how often it occurs and how much distress it causes) and *resistance* (types of attempts the patient makes to get rid of the obsession). For compulsions, the patient provides a rating of their *frequency*.

Concept Check | 3.1

Identify which part of the mental status exam is being performed in each of the following situations.

1. Dr. Swan listened carefully to Joyce's speech pattern, noting its speed, content, and continuity. She noticed no looseness of association but did hear indications of delusional thoughts and visual hallucinations.

    _____

2. Anwar arrived at the clinic accompanied by police, who had found him dressed only in shorts although the temperature was −5°C. He was reported to the police by someone who saw him walking very slowly down the street making strange faces and talking to himself.

    _____

3. When Lisa was brought to Dr. Miller's office, he asked if she knew the date and time, her identity, and where she was. _____

4. Dr. Jones viewed Tarik's laughter after discussing his near-fatal incident as inappropriate and noted that Tarik appeared to be elated. _____

5. Mark's vocabulary and memory seemed adequate, leading Dr. Epstein to estimate that Mark was of average intelligence. _____

Physical Examination

If the patient presenting with psychological problems has not had a physical exam in the past year, a clinician might recommend one, with particular attention to the medical conditions sometimes associated with the specific psychological problem. Many problems presenting as disorders of behaviour, cognition, or mood may, on careful physical examination, have a clear relationship to a temporary toxic state. This toxic state could be caused by bad food, the wrong amount or type of medicine, or the onset of a medical condition. For example, thyroid difficulties, particularly hyperthyroidism (overactive thyroid gland), may produce symptoms that mimic certain anxiety disorders, such as generalized anxiety disorder. Hypothyroidism (underactive thyroid gland) might produce symptoms consistent with depression. Certain psychotic symptoms, including delusions or hallucinations, might be associated with the development of a brain tumour. Withdrawal from cocaine often produces panic attacks, but many patients presenting with panic attacks are reluctant to volunteer information about their addiction, which may lead to an inappropriate diagnosis and improper treatment.

Usually, psychologists and other mental health professionals are well aware of the medical conditions and drug use and abuse that may contribute to the kinds of problems described by the patient. If a current medical condition or substance abuse situation exists, the clinician must ascertain whether it is merely co-existing or causal, usually by looking at the onset of the problem. If a patient has experienced severe bouts of depression for the past five years, but within the past year also developed hypothyroid problems or began taking a sedative drug, then we would not conclude the depression was caused by the medical or drug condition. If the depression developed simultaneously with the initiation of sedative drugs and diminished considerably when the drugs were discontinued, we would be likely to conclude the depression was part of a substance-induced mood disorder.

Behavioural Assessment

The mental status exam is one way to begin to sample how people think, feel, and behave and how these actions might contribute to or explain their problems. **Behavioural assessment** takes this process one step further by using direct observation to assess formally an individual's thoughts, feelings, and behaviour in specific situations or contexts; this information should explain why he or she is having difficulties at this time. Indeed, behavioural assessment may be

▲ In behavioural observation, clinicians or researchers directly observe behaviour in real-world or simulated situations.

much more appropriate than any interview in terms of assessing individuals who are not old enough or skilled enough to report their problems and experiences. Clinical interviews sometimes provide limited assessment information. Young children or individuals who are not verbal because of the nature of their disorder or because of cognitive deficits or impairments are not good candidates for clinical interviews. As we already mentioned, sometimes people deliberately withhold information because it is embarrassing or because they aren't aware that it is important. In addition to talking with a client in an office about a problem, some clinicians go to the person's home or workplace or even into the local community to observe the person and the reported problems directly. Others set up role-play simulations in a clinical setting to see how people might behave in similar situations in their daily lives. These techniques are all types of behavioural assessment.

In behavioural assessment, *target behaviours* are identified and observed with the goal of determining the factors that seem to influence those behaviours. It may seem easy to identify what is bothering a particular person (that is, the target behaviour), but even this aspect of assessment can be challenging. For example, when the mother of a seven-year-old child with a severe conduct disorder came to one of our clinics for assistance, she told the clinician, after much prodding, that her son "didn't listen to her" and he sometimes had an "attitude." The boy's schoolteacher, however, painted a very different picture. She spoke candidly of his verbal violence—of his threats toward other children and to her, threats she took very seriously. To get a clearer picture of the situation at home, the clinician visited one afternoon. Approximately 15 minutes after the visit began, the boy got up from the kitchen table without removing the drinking glass he was using. When his mother quite meekly asked him to put the glass in the sink, he picked it up and threw it across the room, sending broken glass throughout the kitchen. He giggled and went into his room to watch TV. "See," she said. "He doesn't listen to me!"

Obviously, this mother's description of her son's behaviour at home didn't give a good picture of what he was really like. It also didn't accurately portray her response to his violent outbursts. Without the home visit, the clinician's assessment of the problem and recommendations for treatment would have been very different. Clearly, this was more than simple disobedience. We developed strategies to teach the mother how to make requests of her son and how to follow up if he was violent.

Most clinicians assume that a complete picture of a person's problems requires direct observation in naturalistic environments. But going into a person's home, workplace, or school isn't always possible or practical, so clinicians sometimes set up analogue settings. For example, one of us studies children with autism (a disorder characterized

▲ Child clinical psychologist David Wolfe of the University of Western Ontario uses analogue behavioural observation techniques in his study of the interactions of abused children with their parents.

by social withdrawal and communication problems; see Chapter 14). The reasons for self-hitting (called *self-injurious*) behaviour are discovered by placing the children in simulated classroom situations, such as sitting alone at a desk, working in a group, or being asked to complete a difficult task (Durand & Crimmins, 1988). Observing how the children behave in these different situations helps us determine why they hit themselves, so we can design a successful treatment to eliminate the behaviour. David Wolfe (1991) uses contrived situations to assess the emotional reactions of parents with a history of abuse toward their children. By asking parents to have their children put away favourite toys, which usually results in problem behaviour by the child, the therapist can see how the parents respond. These observations are later used to develop treatments.

The ABCs of Observation

Observational assessment is usually focused on the here and now (Greene & Ollendick, 2000). Therefore, the clinician's attention is usually directed to the immediate behaviour, its antecedents (or what happened just before the behaviour), and its consequences (what happened afterward) (Baer, Wolf, & Risley, 1968). To use the example of the young boy, an observer would note that the sequence of events was (1) his mother asking him to put his glass in the sink (antecedent), (2) the boy throwing the glass (behaviour), and (3) his mother's lack of response (consequence). This antecedent-behaviour-consequence sequence (the ABCs) might suggest that the boy was being reinforced for his violent outburst by not having to clean up his mess. And because there was no negative consequence for his behaviour (his mother didn't scold or reprimand him), he will probably act violently the next time he doesn't want to do something (see ■ Figure 3.3).

This is an example of a relatively *informal observation*. During the home visit, the clinician took rough notes about what occurred. Later, in his office, he elaborated on the notes. A problem with this type of observation is that it relies on the observer's recollection as well as on his or her interpretation of the events. *Formal observation* involves identifying specific behaviours that are *observable* and *measurable* (called an *operational definition*). For example, it would be difficult for two people to agree on what "having an attitude" looks like. An operational definition, however, clarifies this behaviour by specifying that this is "any time the boy does not comply with his mother's reasonable requests." Once the target behaviour is selected and defined, an observer writes down each time it occurs, along with what happened just before (antecedent)

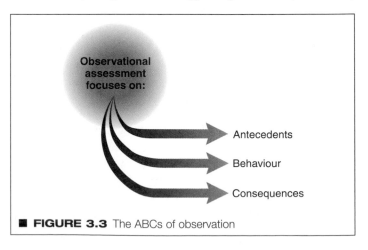

Observational assessment focuses on:

Antecedents

Behaviour

Consequences

■ **FIGURE 3.3** The ABCs of observation

and just after (consequence). The goal of collecting this information is to see whether there are any obvious patterns of behaviour and then to design a treatment based on these patterns.

Self-Monitoring

People can also observe their own behaviour to find patterns, a technique known as **self-monitoring** or *self-observation* (Haynes, Yoshioka, Kloezeman, & Bello, 2009). People trying to quit smoking may write down the number of cigarettes they smoke and the times when and places where they smoke. This observation can tell them exactly how big their problem is (e.g., they smoke two packs a day) and what situations lead them to smoke more (e.g., talking on the phone). The use of personal digital assistants (PDAs) is becoming common in these assessments. The goal here is to help clients monitor their behaviour more conveniently (Piasecki, Hufford, Solhan, & Trull, 2007). When behaviours occur only in private (such as purging by people with bulimia), self-monitoring is essential. Because the people with the problem are in the best position to observe their own behaviour throughout the day, clinicians often ask patients to self-monitor their behaviour to get more detailed information.

A more formal and structured way to observe behaviour is through checklists and *behaviour rating scales*, which are used as assessment tools before treatment and then periodically during treatment to assess changes in the person's behaviour (Blacker, 2005; Myers & Collett, 2006). Of the many such instruments for assessing a variety of behaviours, the *Brief Psychiatric Rating Scale* (Clarkin, Howieson, & McClough, 2008), assesses 18 general areas of concern. Each symptom is rated on a seven-point scale from 0 (not present) to 6 (extremely severe). The rating scale screens for moderate to severe psychotic disorders and includes such items as somatic concern (preoccupation with physical health, fear of physical illness, hypochondriasis), guilt feelings (self-blame, shame, remorse for past behaviour), and grandiosity (exaggerated self-opinion, arrogance, conviction of unusual power or abilities) (American Psychiatric Association, 2006).

A phenomenon known as *reactivity* can distort any observational data. Any time you observe how people behave, the mere fact of your presence may cause them to change their behaviour (Haynes et al., 2009). To test reactivity, you can tell a friend you are going to record every time she says the word *like*. Just before you reveal your intent, however, count the times your friend uses this word in a five-minute period. You will probably find that your friend uses the word less often when you are recording it. Your friend will react to the observation by changing the behaviour. The same phenomenon occurs if you observe your own behaviour, or self-monitor. Behaviours people want to increase, such as talking more in class, tend to increase, and behaviours people want to decrease, such as smoking, tend to decrease when they are self-monitored (e.g., Hufford, Shields, Shiffman, Paty, & Balabanis, 2002). Clinicians sometimes depend on the reactivity of self-monitoring to increase the effectiveness of their treatments.

Psychological Testing

We are confronted with so-called psychological tests in the popular press almost every week: "Twelve Questions to Test Your Relationship," "New Test to Help You Assess Your Lover's Passion," "Are You a Type Z Personality?" Although we may not want to admit it, many of us have probably purchased a magazine at some point to take one of these tests. Many are no more than entertainment, designed to make you think about the topic (and to make you buy the magazine). They are typically made up for the purposes of the article and include questions that, on the surface, seem to make sense. We are interested in these tests because we want to understand better why we and our friends behave the way we do. In reality, the tests usually tell us little.

In contrast, the tests used to assess psychological disorders must meet the strict standards we have noted. They must be reliable—so two or more people administering the same test to the same person will come to the same conclusion about the problem—and they must be valid—so they measure what they say they are measuring.

Psychological tests include specific tests to determine cognitive, emotional, or behavioural responses that might be associated with a specific disorder and more general tests that assess long-standing personality features. Specialized areas include *intelligence* testing to determine the structure and patterns of cognition. Neuropsychological testing determines the possible contribution of brain damage or dysfunction to the patient's condition. *Neurobiological procedures* use imaging to assess brain structure and function.

Projective Testing

We saw in Chapter 1 how Freud brought to our attention the presence and influence of unconscious processes in psychological disorders. At this point we should ask, "If people aren't aware of these thoughts and feelings, how do we assess them?" To address this intriguing problem, psychoanalytic workers developed several assessment measures known as **projective tests**. They include a variety of methods in which ambiguous stimuli, such as pictures of people or things, are presented to a person who is asked to describe what he or she sees. The theory here is that people project their own personality and unconscious fears onto other people and things—in this case, the ambiguous stimuli—and, without realizing it, reveal their unconscious thoughts to the therapist.

Because these tests are based in psychoanalytic theory, they have been, and remain, controversial. Even so, the use of projective tests is quite common, with a majority of clinicians administering them at least occasionally and most doctoral programs providing training in their use (Durand, Blanchard, & Mindell, 1988). Two of the more widely used projective tests are the Rorschach inkblot test and the Thematic Apperception Test.

More than 80 years ago, a Swiss psychiatrist named Hermann Rorschach developed a series of inkblots, initially to study perceptual processes, then to diagnose psychological disorders. The *Rorschach inkblot* test is one of the early projective tests. In its current form, the test includes ten inkblot pictures that serve as the ambiguous stimuli (see ■ Figure 3.4). The examiner presents the inkblots one by one to the person being assessed, who responds by telling what he or she sees (Rorschach, 1951).

Unfortunately, much of the early use of the Rorschach is extremely controversial because of the lack of data on reliability or validity, among other things. Until relatively recently, therapists administered the test any way they saw fit, although one of the most important tenets of assessment is that the same test be given in the same way each time—that is, according to standardized

■ **FIGURE 3.4** This inkblot resembles the ambiguous figures presented in the Rorschach test.

■ **FIGURE 3.5** Example of a picture resembling those in the Thematic Apperception Test

procedures. If you encourage someone to give more detailed answers during one testing session but not during a second session, you may get different responses as the result of your administering the test differently on the two occasions—not because of problems with the test or with administration by another person (interrater reliability).

To respond to the concerns about reliability and validity, John Exner developed a standardized version of the Rorschach inkblot test, called the *Comprehensive System* (Exner, 2003). Exner's system of administering and scoring the Rorschach specifies how the cards should be presented, what the examiner should say, and how the responses should be recorded (Clarkin et al., 2008). Varying these steps can lead to varying responses by the patient. Unfortunately, despite the attempts to bring standardization to the use of the Rorschach test, its use remains controversial. Critics of the Rorschach question whether research on the Comprehensive System supports its use as a valid assessment technique for people with psychological disorders (Garb, Wood, Lilienfeld, & Nezworski, 2005; Hunsley & Mash, in press).

The *Thematic Apperception Test* (TAT) is perhaps the best-known projective test, after the Rorschach. It was developed in 1935 by Morgan and Murray (Bellak, 1975). The TAT consists of a series of 31 cards: 30 with pictures on them and 1 blank card, although only 20 cards are typically used during each administration (see ■ Figure 3.5). Unlike the Rorschach, which involves asking for a straightforward description of what the test taker sees, the instructions for the TAT ask the person to tell a dramatic story about the picture. The tester presents the pictures and tells

the client, "This is a test of imagination, one form of intelligence." The person being assessed can "let your imagination have its way, as in a myth, fairy story, or allegory" (Stein, 1978, p. 186). Again like the Rorschach, the TAT is based on the notion that people will reveal their unconscious mental processes in their stories about the pictures (Dana, 1996).

Several variations of the TAT have been developed for different groups, including a Children's Apperception Test (CAT) and a Senior Apperception Technique (SAT). In addition, modifications of the test have evolved for use with a variety of racial and ethnic groups (Bellak, 1975; Dana, 1996). These modifications have included changes not only in the appearance of people in the pictures but also in the situations depicted.

Unfortunately, unlike recent trends in the use of the Rorschach, the TAT and its variants continue to be used inconsistently. How the stories people tell about these pictures are interpreted depends on the examiner's frame of reference as well as on what the patient may say. It is not surprising, therefore, that there is little reliability across raters using this system and questions remain about its use in psychopathology (Gieser & Stein, 1999).

Despite these problems, the TAT is still widely used, and some clinicians continue to report that they find it valuable in guiding their diagnostic and treatment decisions. Despite the popularity and increasing standardization of these tests, most clinicians who use projective tests have their own methods of administration and interpretation. When used as icebreakers, for getting people to open up and talk about how they feel about things going on in their lives, the ambiguous stimuli in these tests can be valuable tools. However, their relative lack of reliability and validity make them less useful as diagnostic tests (Anastasi, 1988). Concern over the inappropriate use of projective tests should remind you of the importance of the scientist-practitioner approach. Clinicians are not only responsible for knowing how to administer tests but also need to be aware of research that suggests the tests have limited usefulness as a means of diagnosing psychopathology.

Personality Inventories

Although many **personality inventories** are available, we look at the most widely used personality inventory in North America, the Minnesota Multiphasic Personality Inventory (MMPI; Hathaway & McKinley, 1943). In stark contrast to projective tests, which rely heavily on theory for an interpretation, the MMPI and similar inventories are based on an empirical approach, that is, the collection and evaluation of data. The administration of the MMPI is straightforward. The individual being assessed reads statements such as "I cry easily," or "I believe I am being followed," and answers either "true" or "false."

Obviously, clinicians have little room for interpretation of MMPI responses, unlike responses to projective tests such as the Rorschach and the TAT. A problem with administering the MMPI, however, is the time and tedium of responding to the 550 items on the original version and now the 567 items on the MMPI-2. A version of the MMPI is also now available that is appropriate for adolescents—MMPI-A (Nczami & Butcher, 2000). Individual responses on the MMPI are not examined; instead, the pattern of responses is reviewed to see if it resembles patterns from groups of people who have specific disorders (e.g., a pattern similar to a group with schizophrenia). Each group is represented on separate standard scales (Butcher, Graham, Williams, & Ben-Porath, 1990; see Table 3.2).

Fortunately, clinicians can have these responses scored by computer; the program also includes an interpretation of the results, thereby reducing problems of reliability. Given the potential for some people to answer in ways that would downplay their problems—faking answers to MMPI items such as "Someone has control over my mind"—the MMPI includes four

additional scales that determine the validity of each administration. For example, on the Lie scale (L), one statement is "I have never had a bad night's sleep." Answering "true" to this is an indication that the person may be falsifying answers to look good. The other scales are the F, or Infrequency scale, which measures false claims about psychological problems or determines whether the person is answering randomly; the K, or Defensiveness scale, which assesses whether the person sees himself or herself in unrealistically positive ways; and the ? or Cannot-Say scale, which simply measures the number of items the test taker did not answer.

■ Figure 3.6 is an MMPI profile or summary of scores from an individual being clinically assessed; we'll call him James S. First, let's see what this 27-year-old man's MMPI profile tells us about him (note that these scores were obtained on the previous version of the MMPI). The first three data points represent scores on the L, F, and K scales; the high scores on the L and K scales were interpreted to mean that James S. made a naïve attempt to look good for the evaluator and may have been trying to fake an appearance of having no problems. Another important part of his profile is the very high score on the Pd (psychopathic deviation) scale, which measures the tendency to behave in antisocial ways. The interpretation of this score is that James S. is "aggressive, unreliable, irresponsible; unable to learn from experience; may initially make a good impression but then psychopathic features will surface in longer interactions or under stress."

Why was James S. being evaluated? He is a young man with a criminal record that begins in his childhood. He was evaluated as part of his trial for kidnapping, raping, and murdering a middle-aged woman. Throughout his trial, he made up several contradictory stories to make himself look innocent (remember his high scores on the L and K scales), including blaming his brother. However, there was overwhelming evidence of his guilt, and he was sentenced to life in a correctional institution. His answers on the MMPI resembled those of others who act in violent and antisocial ways.

The MMPI is one of the most extensively researched assessment instruments in psychology (Cox, Weed, & Butcher, 2009). The

TABLE 3.2 Sample MMPI-2 Content Scales

Scale	Description of Content and Correlates
ANX (Anxiety)	General symptoms of anxiety and tension, sleep and concentration problems, somatic correlates of anxiety, excessive worrying, difficulty making decisions, and a willingness to admit to these problems
FRS (Fears)	Many specific fears and phobias including animals, high places, insects, blood, fire, storms, water, the dark, being indoors, dirt, and so on
OBS (Obsessiveness)	Excessive rumination, difficulty making decisions, compulsive behaviours, rigidity, feelings of being overwhelmed
DEP (Depression)	Depressive thoughts, anhedonia, feelings of hopelessness and uncertainty, possible suicidal thoughts
HEA (Health Concerns)	Many physical symptoms across several body systems: gastrointestinal, neurological, sensory, cardiovascular, dermatological, and respiratory; reports of pain and general worries about health
BIZ (Bizarre Mentation)	Psychotic thought processes, auditory, visual, or olfactory hallucinations, paranoid ideation, delusions
ANG (Anger)	Anger-control problems, irritability, impatience, loss of control, past or potential abusiveness
CYN (Cynicism)	Misanthropic beliefs, negative expectations about the motives of others, generalized distrust
ASP (Antisocial Practices)	Cynical attitudes, problem behaviours, trouble with the law, stealing, belief in getting around rules and laws for personal gain

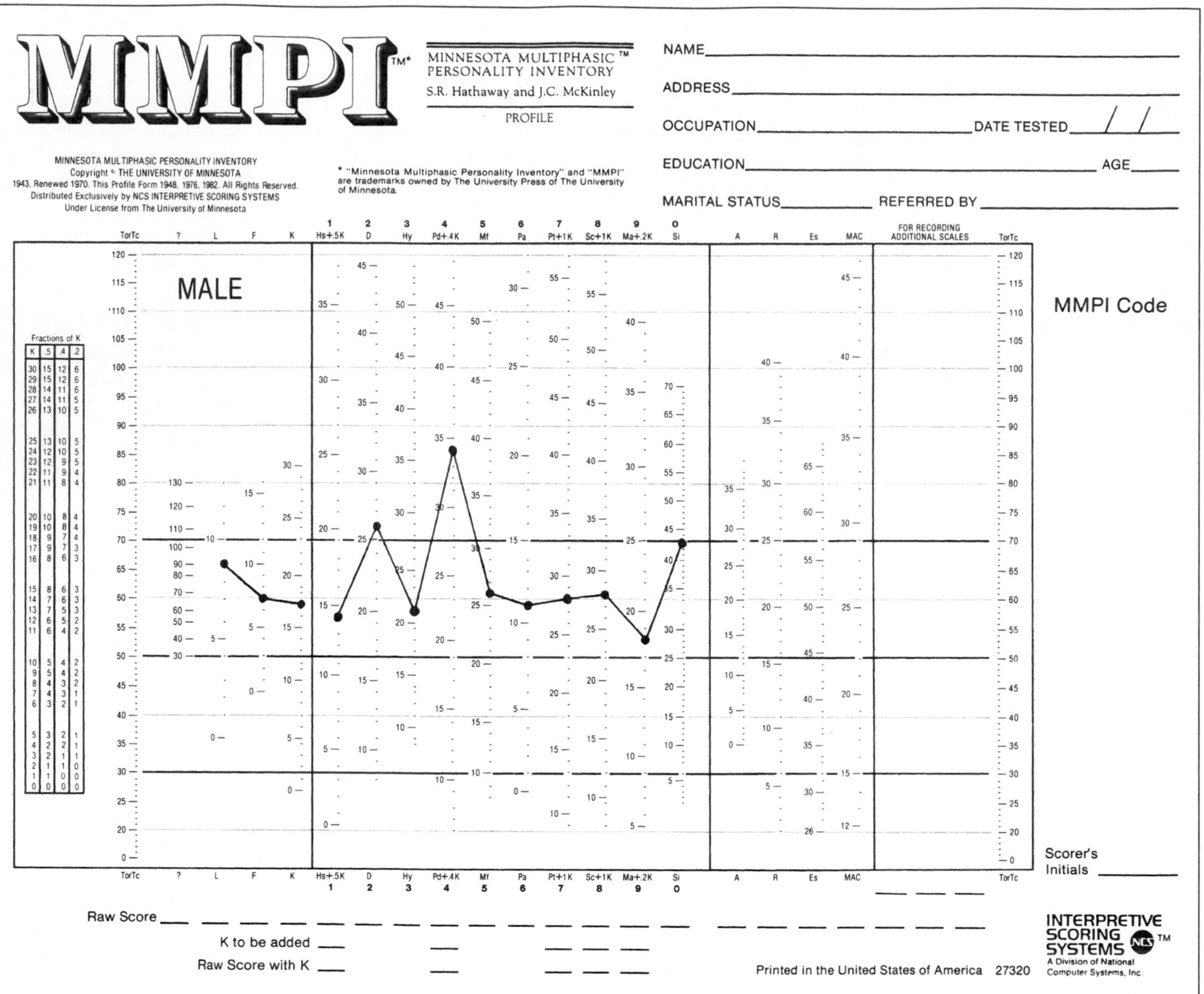

FIGURE 3.6 An MMPI profile

Source: Minnesota Multiphasic Personality Inventory profile form. Copyright © 1942, 1943, 1948, 1970, 1976, 1982 by the Regents of the University of Minnesota. All rights reserved. Reprinted by permission of the University of Minnesota Press.

original standardization sample—the people who first responded to the statements and set the standard for answers—included many people from Minnesota who had no psychological disorders and several groups of people who had particular disorders. The more recent versions of this test, the MMPI-2 and the MMPI-A, eliminate problems with the original version, problems partly resulting from the original selective sample of people and partly resulting from the wording of questions (Ranson, Nichols, Rouse, & Harrington, 2009). For example, some questions were sexist. One item on the original version asks the respondent to say whether she has ever been sorry she is a girl (Worell & Remer, 1992). Another item states, "Any man who is willing to work hard has a good chance of succeeding" (Hathaway & McKinley, 1943). Other items were criticized as insensitive to cultural diversity. Items dealing with religion, for example, referred almost exclusively to Christianity (Butcher et al., 1990). The MMPI-2 has also been standardized with a sample that adequately reflects the composition of the general population, including Black people and Aboriginal people

for the first time. In addition, new items have been added that deal with contemporary issues, such as type A personality, low self-esteem, and family problems.

Reliability of the MMPI is excellent when it is interpreted according to standardized procedures, and thousands of studies on the original MMPI attest to its validity with a range of psychological problems (Butcher, 2009). But a word of caution is necessary here. As they might with any other form of assessment, some clinicians look at an MMPI profile and interpret the scales on the basis of their own clinical experience and judgment only. By not relying on the standard means of interpretation, this practice compromises the instrument's reliability and validity.

In addition to the MMPI, another example of an instrument used to assess an important aspect of personality functioning is the Revised Psychopathy Checklist (PCL-R). The MMPI profile of antisocial criminal James S., discussed earlier, illustrates a constellation of behaviours and characteristics that some refer to as psychopathy (see Chapter 12). Psychopathy can be assessed directly using the PCL-R, which was developed by forensic psychologist Robert Hare and his colleagues at the University of British Columbia (Hare, 1991; Hare & Neumann, 2006; Harpur, Hart, & Hare, 2002). Since psychopaths are cunning and manipulative pathological liars (Hare & Neumann, 2006), it is difficult to use self-report measures to assess psychopathy (as a psychopath would likely lie and deny the existence of characteristics that would place him or her in a bad light!). Hare developed the PCL-R as an instrument to assess the characteristics of psychopathy using interviews with the client along with material from institutional files (e.g., records from correctional institutions) or significant others. The PCL-R consists of a checklist of 20 characteristics like pathological lying and superficial charm; this instrument is discussed in more detail in Chapter 12.

Intelligence Testing

"She must be very smart. I hear her IQ is 180!" What is IQ? What is intelligence? And how are they important in psychopathology? As many of you know from your introductory psychology course, intelligence tests were developed for one specific purpose: to predict who would do well in school. In 1904, a French psychologist, Alfred Binet, and his colleague, Théodore Simon, were commissioned by the government of France to develop a test that would identify "slow learners" who would benefit from remedial help. The two psychologists identified a series of tasks that presumably measured the skills children need to succeed in school, including tasks of attention, perception, memory, reasoning, and verbal comprehension. Binet and Simon gave their original series of tasks to a large number of children; they then eliminated those tasks that did not separate the slow learners from the children who did well in school. After several revisions and sample administrations, they had a test that was relatively easy to administer and that did what it was designed to do—predict academic success. In 1916, Lewis Terman of Stanford University translated a revised version of this test for use in North America; it became known as the *Stanford-Binet test*.

The test provided a score known as an **intelligence quotient**, or **IQ**. Initially, IQ scores were calculated by using the child's *mental age* (MA). For example, a child who passed all the questions on the seven-year-old level and none of the questions on the eight-year-old level received a mental age of seven. This mental age was then divided by the child's *chronological age* (CA) and multiplied by 100 to get the IQ score. However, there were problems with using this type of formula for calculating an IQ score. For example, a four-year-old needed to score only one year above his or her chronological age to be given an IQ score of 125, although an eight-year-old had to score two years above his or her chronological age to be given the same score (Bjorklund, 1989). Current tests use what is called a *deviation IQ*. A person's score is compared only with scores of others of the same age. The IQ score, then, is really an estimate of how much a child's performance in school will deviate from the average performance of others of the same age.

In addition to the revised version of the Stanford-Binet (*Stanford-Binet V*; Roid & Pomplun, 2005), another set of intelligence tests, developed by psychologist David Wechsler, is widely used. The Wechsler tests include versions for adults (*Wechsler Adult Intelligence Scale-III [WAIS-III]*), for children (*Wechsler Intelligence Scale for Children-Third Edition [WISC-III]*), and for young children (*Wechsler Preschool and Primary Scale of Intelligence-Revised [WPPSI-R]*). All these tests contain *verbal scales* (which measure vocabulary, knowledge of facts, short-term memory, and verbal reasoning skills) and *performance scales* (which assess psychomotor abilities, non-verbal reasoning, and ability to learn new relationships; Tulsky, Zhu, & Prifitera, 2000).

In both American and Canadian samples, the adult version of this intelligence test—the *WAIS-III*—has been shown to tap four distinct intellectual abilities: verbal comprehension, perceptual organization, processing speed, and working memory (Saklofske, Hildebrand, & Gorsuch, 2000; Wechsler, 1997). The fact that these same components have been supported in both Canadian and U.S. samples has been interpreted by some as evidence that the *WAIS-III* "is 'portable' across cultural boundaries" (Saklofske et al., 2000, p. 438). Others have been less optimistic about the "portability" of these intelligence tests to people from other countries and cultures, since these tests were developed and standardized largely with people from the majority culture in the United States. For example, several studies have documented lower than average scores on the verbal scales on the first two versions of the WISC in Canadian First Nations children (e.g., Beiser & Gotowiec, 2000; St. John, Krichev, & Bauman, 1976; Seyfort, Spreen, & Lahmer, 1980; see also review by Mushquash & Bova, 2007) and a large majority of a sample of Canadian Inuit children scored in the mentally retarded range when their scores on the second version of the WISC were compared with the usual norms (Wilgosh, Mulcahy, & Watters, 1986). These data suggest that children from these groups may have some difficulty understanding many of the test items or that many of the items may be tapping different abilities and skills in children from these cultural groups than in children from the majority population (Mushquash & Bova, 2007; Wilgosh et al., 1986). The findings caution against indiscriminate use of these tests with cultural groups outside those on whom the test was originally normed.

One of the biggest mistakes non-psychologists (and a distressing number of psychologists) make is to confuse IQ with intelligence. An IQ is a score on one of the intelligence tests we just described. An IQ score significantly higher than average means that the person has a significantly greater than average chance of doing well in our educational system. By contrast, a score significantly lower than average suggests the person will probably not do well in school. Does a lower than average IQ score mean a person is not intelligent? Not necessarily. First, numerous reasons exist for a low score. If the IQ test is administered in English and that is not the person's native language, the results will be affected.

Perhaps more important, however, is the lack of general agreement about what constitutes intelligence (Weinberg, 1989). Remember that the IQ tests measure abilities such as attention, perception, memory, reasoning, and verbal comprehension. But do these skills represent the totality of what we consider intelligence? Some recent theorists believe that what we think of as intelligence involves much more, including the ability to adapt to the environment, the ability to generate new ideas, and the ability to process information efficiently (Sternberg, 1988). We will discuss disorders that involve cognitive impairment, such as delirium and mental retardation, and IQ tests are typically used in assessing these disorders. Keep in mind, however, that we will be discussing IQ and not necessarily intelligence. In general, however, IQ tests tend to be reliable, and to the extent that they predict academic success, they are valid assessment tools.

Neuropsychological Testing

Sophisticated tests have been developed that can pinpoint the location of brain dysfunction (Goldstein, 2000). Fortunately, these techniques are generally available and relatively inexpensive. **Neuropsychological testing** measures abilities in areas such as receptive and expressive language, attention and concentration, memory, motor skills, perceptual abilities, and learning and abstraction in such a way that the clinician can make educated guesses about the person's performance and the possible existence of brain impairment. In other words, this method of testing assesses brain dysfunction by observing its effects on the person's ability to perform certain tasks. Although you do not see damage, you can see its effects.

A simple neuropsychological test often used with children is the Bender Visual-Motor Gestalt Test (Canter, 1996). A child is given a series of cards on which are drawn various lines and shapes. The task is for the child to copy what is drawn on the card. The errors on the test are compared with test results of other children of the same age; if the number of errors exceeds a certain amount, then brain dysfunction is suspected. This test is less sophisticated than other neuropsychological tests because the nature or location of the problem cannot be determined with this test. The Bender Visual-Motor Gestalt Test can be useful for psychologists, however, because it provides a simple screening instrument that is easy to administer and can detect possible problems. Two of the most popular advanced tests of organic damage that allow more precise determinations of the location of the problem are the Luria-Nebraska Neuropsychological Battery (Golden, Hammeke, & Purisch, 1980) and the Halstead-Reitan Neuropsychological Battery (Reitan & Davison, 1974). These offer an elaborate battery of tests to assess a variety of skills. For example, the Halstead-Reitan Neuropsychological Battery includes the Rhythm Test (which asks the person to compare rhythmic beats, to test sound recognition, attention, and concentration), the Strength of Grip Test (which compares the grip of the right and left hands), and the Tactile Performance Test (which requires the test taker to place wooden blocks in a form board while blindfolded, to test learning and memory skills) (Macciocchi & Barth, 1996).

Research on the validity of neuropsychological tests suggests they may be useful for detecting organic damage and cognitive

disorders (see Chapter 15). Canadian researchers have played a very important role in this crucial area of scientific endeavour (see review by Hayman-Abello, Hayman-Abello, & Rourke, 2003). More recent evidence suggests that performance on neuropsychological tests may even be useful in predicting the development of certain cognitive disorders. For example, one study by researchers at the University of Toronto found that a neuropsychological test battery was quite accurate in predicting the development of Alzheimer's disease in people who were part of the longitudinal Canadian Study of Health and Aging. Performance on tasks such as delayed verbal recall at the initial testing session with initially healthy participants accurately predicted whether or not the test-taker developed Alzheimer's disease five or ten years later (Tierney, Yao, Kiss, & McDowell, 2005). Most often, though, neuropsychological tests are used to help differentiate those who already have a given cognitive disorder from those people who do not. And neuropsychological tests are often quite accurate in doing so (e.g., Tierney, Snow, Szalai, Fisher, & Zorzitto, 1996). However, with this use of neuropsychological tests, we face the issue of **false positives** and **false negatives** (Boll, 1985). For any assessment strategy, the test will occasionally show a problem when none exists (false positives) and will not find a problem when indeed some difficulty is present (false negatives). The possibility of false results is particularly troublesome for tests of brain dysfunction; a clinician who fails to find damage that exists might miss an important medical problem that needs to be treated. Fortunately, neuropsychological tests are used primarily as screening devices and are routinely paired with other assessments to improve the likelihood that real problems will be found. The tests do well with regard to measures of reliability and validity, and they are often informed by recent developments in cognitive neuroscience (Stuss & Levine, 2002). On the downside, they can require hours to administer and are therefore not used routinely unless brain damage is suspected.

Neuroimaging: Pictures of the Brain

For more than a century we have known that many of the things that we do, think, and remember are partially controlled by specific areas of the brain. In recent years we have developed the ability to look inside the brain and take increasingly accurate pictures of its structure and function using a technique called **neuroimaging** (Kim, Schulz, Wilde, & Yudofsky, 2008). Neuroimaging can be divided into two categories. One category includes procedures that examine the structure of the brain, such as the size of various parts and whether they are damaged. In the second category are procedures that examine the actual *functioning* of the brain by mapping blood flow and other metabolic activity.

Images of Brain Structure

The first neuroimaging technique, developed in the early 1970s, uses multiple X-ray exposures of the brain from different angles; that is, X-rays are passed directly through the head. As with any X-ray, these are partially blocked or attenuated more by bone and less by brain tissue. The degree of blockage is picked up by detectors in the opposite side of the head. A computer then reconstructs pictures of various slices of the brain. This procedure, which takes about 15 minutes, is called a *computerized axial tomography (CAT) scan* or *CT scan*. It is relatively non-invasive

▲ This child is concentrating on a standard psychological assessment test.

and has proved useful in identifying and locating abnormalities in the structure or shape of the brain. CT scans are particularly useful in locating brain tumours, injuries, and other structural and anatomical abnormalities. One difficulty, however, is that these scans, like all X-rays, involve repeated X-radiation, which poses some risk of cell damage (Kim et al., 2008).

Several more recently developed procedures give greater resolution (specificity and accuracy) than a CT scan without the inherent risks of X-ray tests. A now commonly used scanning technique is called nuclear *magnetic resonance imaging (MRI)*. The patient's head is placed in a high-strength magnetic field through which radio frequency signals are transmitted. These signals "excite" the brain tissue, altering the protons in the hydrogen atoms. The alteration is measured, along with the time it takes the protons to "relax" or return to normal. Where there are lesions or damage, the signal is lighter or darker (Kim et al., 2008). Technology now exists that allows the computer to view the brain in layers, which enables precise examination of the structure. Although an MRI is more expensive than a CT scan and originally took as long as 45 minutes, this is changing as technology improves. Newer versions of MRI procedures take as little as 10 minutes; the time and cost are decreasing yearly. Another disadvantage of MRI at present is that someone undergoing the procedure is totally enclosed inside a narrow tube with a magnetic coil surrounding the head. People who are somewhat claustrophobic often cannot tolerate an MRI, as demonstrated in a study by a team at the University of British Columbia (McIsaac, Thordarson, Shafran, Rachman, & Poole, 1998).

Although neuroimaging procedures are useful for identifying damage to the brain, only recently have they been used to determine structural or anatomical abnormalities that might be associated with various psychological disorders. We review some tantalizing studies in subsequent chapters on specific disorders.

Images of Brain Functioning

Several widely used procedures are capable of measuring the actual functioning of the brain, as opposed to its structure. The first is called *positron emission tomography (PET)*. Subjects undergoing a PET scan are injected with a tracer substance attached to radioactive isotopes, groups of atoms that react distinctively. This substance interacts with blood, oxygen, or glucose. When parts of the brain become active, blood, oxygen, or glucose rushes to these areas of the brain, creating "hot spots" picked up by detectors that identify the location of the isotopes. Thus, we can learn what parts of the brain are working and what parts are not. To obtain clear images, the individual undergoing the procedure must remain motionless for 40 seconds or more. These images can be superimposed on MRI images to show the precise location of the active areas. The PET scans are also useful in supplementing MRI and CT scans in localizing the sites of trauma due to head injury or stroke as well as in localizing brain tumours (Cabeza & Nyberg, 2000).

More important, PET scans are used increasingly to look at varying patterns of metabolism that might be associated with different disorders. Recent PET scans have demonstrated that many patients with early Alzheimer's-type dementia (see Chapter 15) show reduced glucose metabolism in the parietal lobes. Other intriguing findings have been reported for obsessive-compulsive disorder and bipolar disorder (see Chapters 5 and 7). For example, as we will learn in more detail in Chapter 7, excess activity in the dopamine neurotransmitter system has been implicated in manic states among patients with bipolar mood disorder. Researchers at the University of British Columbia Mood Disorders Clinical Research Unit recently used PET to try to identify the brain regions involved in dopamine overactivity among a group of patients with bipolar disorder who were tested during the manic state (Yatham et al., 2002). In this same study, the researchers also used PET to examine the effects of drug therapy on dopamine activity in bipolar disorder by testing patients twice: before and after drug treatment. Despite the exciting uses of PET for increasing understanding of many forms of abnormal behaviour, PET scanning is very expensive: The cost is about $6 million to set up a PET facility and $500 000 a year to run it. Therefore, these facilities are available only in large medical centres.

A second procedure used to assess brain functioning is called *single photon emission computed tomography (SPECT)*. It works very much like PET, although a different tracer substance is used, and it is somewhat less accurate. It is also less expensive, however, and requires far less sophisticated equipment to pick up the signals. For this reason it is used more frequently. The most

▲ The patient is being positioned for a magnetic resonance imaging (MRI) scan.

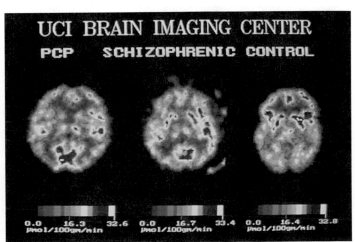

▲ The PET scans compare activity in the brain of a drug abuser (left), a person with schizophrenia (centre), and in a normal brain (right).

Assessing Psychological Disorders

exciting advances involve MRI procedures that have been developed to work much more quickly than the regular MRI (Barinaga, 1997; Cohen, Rosen, & Brady, 1992). Using sophisticated computer technology, these procedures take only milliseconds and, therefore, can actually take pictures of the brain at work, recording its changes from one second to the next (e.g., Stern et al., 2000). Because these procedures measure the functioning of the brain, they are called functional MRI, or fMRI (Cabeza & Nyberg, 2000). For example, fMRI was used by Kent Kiehl, Andra Smith, Robert Hare, and their colleagues at the University of British Columbia to explore how brain activity might be linked to the emotional abnormalities of psychopaths (Kiehl et al., 2001). Their findings suggested that the emotional deficits so often observed in psychopaths may be linked to a weakened input from limbic structures—the part of the brain responsible for regulating our emotional experiences (see Chapter 2). Today, fMRI has largely replaced PET scans in the leading brain-imaging centres (Cabeza & Nyberg, 2000), because it allows researchers to see the immediate response of the brain to a brief event, such as seeing a new face. This response is called an event-related fMRI. Even more powerful technology based on light sources is on the way (Barinaga, 1997). Shining infrared light through the head and picking up changes as the light is scattered by brain tissue at work may be a less expensive and more accurate way of learning how the brain works.

Brain imagery procedures hold enormous potential for illuminating the contribution of neurobiological factors to psychological disorders. A review by Ruth Lanius and her colleagues in London, Ontario, has illuminated the contributions of various brain-imaging techniques to our understanding of post-traumatic stress disorder (PTSD) (Lanius, Bluhm, Lanius, & Pain, 2006). For example, studies using fMRI have shown that PTSD participants who report primarily dissociative (numbing-type) responses to listening to scripts about their traumas showed very different patterns of brain activation than PTSD participants who experienced primarily hyperarousal patterns to trauma scripts. This finding suggests two distinct subtypes of patients with PTSD, with different neural mechanisms underlying their post-traumatic symptoms. As another example, in Chapter 5 on anxiety disorders, you will learn what fMRI procedures reveal about brain functioning in individuals such as Frank and Brian, who have obsessive-compulsive disorder.

Psychophysiological Assessment

Yet another method for assessing brain structure and function specifically and nervous system activity more generally is called **psychophysiological assessment**. As the term implies, *psychophysiology* refers to measurable changes in the nervous system that reflect emotional or psychological events. The measurements may be taken either directly from the brain or peripherally from other parts of the body.

Frank feared that he might have seizures. If we had any reason to suspect he might really have periods of memory loss or exhibit bizarre, trance-like behaviour, if only for a short period of time, it would be important for him to have an **electroencephalogram (EEG)**. Measuring electrical activity in the head related to the firing of a specific group of neurons reveals brain wave activity, the low-voltage electrical current ongoing in the brain, usually from the cortex. A person's brain waves can be assessed in both waking and sleeping states. In an EEG, electrodes are placed directly on various places on the scalp to record the different low-voltage currents.

We have learned much about EEG patterns in the past decades (Kim et al., 2008). Usually, we measure ongoing electrical activity in the brain. When brief periods of EEG patterns are recorded in response to specific events, such as hearing a psychologically meaningful stimulus, the response is called an *event-related potential (ERP)* or *evoked potential*. We have learned that EEG patterns are often affected by psychological or emotional factors and can be an index of these reactions, or a psychophysiological measure. In a normal, healthy, relaxed adult, waking activities are characterized by a very regular pattern of changes in voltage termed *alpha waves*.

Many types of stress-reduction treatments attempt to *increase* the frequency of the alpha waves, often by relaxing the patients in

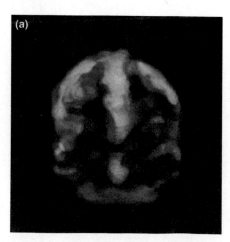 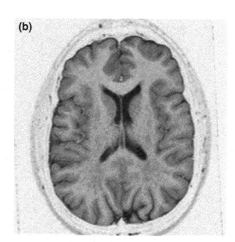 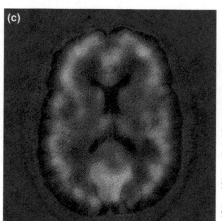

▲ A horizontal brain section (a) in a SPECT image clearly reveals parietal lobe damage in a person with schizophrenia. Images (b) and (c) are MRI photographs. SPECT images show metabolic activity and thus indicate the relationship between the brain and behaviour. The higher resolution MRI images show tissue variations.

some way. The alpha wave pattern is associated with relaxation and calmness. During sleep, we pass through several different stages of brain activity, at least partially identified by EEG patterns. During the deepest, most relaxed stage, typically occurring one to two hours after a person falls asleep, EEG recordings show a pattern of *delta* waves. These brain waves are slower and more irregular than the alpha waves, which is perfectly normal for this stage of sleep. We see in Chapter 5 that panic attacks occurring while a person is sound asleep come almost exclusively during the delta wave stage. If frequent delta wave activity occurred during the waking state, it might indicate dysfunction of localized areas of the brain.

Extremely rapid and irregular spikes on the EEG recordings of someone who is awake may reflect significant seizure disorders, depending on the pattern. The EEG recording is one of the primary diagnostic tools for identifying seizure disorders. Psychophysiological assessment of other bodily responses may also play a role in assessment. These responses include heart rate, respiration, and *electrodermal responding* (skin conductance), formerly called *galvanic skin response (GSR)*, which is a measure of sweat gland activity controlled by the peripheral nervous system. Remember from Chapter 2 that the peripheral nervous system and, in particular, the sympathetic division of the automatic nervous system (ANS) are very responsive to stress and emotional arousal.

Assessing psychophysiological responding to emotional stimuli is very important in many disorders, one being post-traumatic stress disorder. Stimuli such as sights and sounds associated with the trauma evoke strong psychophysiological responding, even if the patient is not fully aware of the nature of the trauma because memories of it are inaccessible.

Psychophysiological assessment is also used with many sexual dysfunctions and disorders. For example, sexual arousal can be assessed through direct measurement of penile circumference in males or vaginal blood flow in females in response to erotic stimuli, usually movies or slides (see Chapter 10). Sometimes the individual might be unaware of specific patterns of sexual arousal.

Physiological measures are also important in the assessment and treatment of conditions such as headaches and hypertension (Blanchard, 1992; Blanchard, Martin, & Dubbert, 1988); they form the basis for the treatment we call biofeedback. In biofeedback, as we see in Chapter 9, levels of physiological responding, such as blood pressure readings, are fed back to the patient (provided on a continuous basis) by meters or gauges so the patient can try to regulate these responses.

Nevertheless, physiological assessment is not without its limitations, for it requires a great deal of skill and some technical expertise. Even when administered properly, the measures sometimes produce inconsistent results because of procedural or technical difficulties or the nature of the response itself. For this reason, only clinicians specializing in certain disorders for which these measures are particularly important are likely to make extensive use of psychophysiological recording equipment, although more straightforward applications such as monitoring heart rate during relaxation exercises are more common. More sophisticated psychophysiological assessment is most often used in theoretical investigations of the nature of certain psychological disorders, particularly emotional disorders (Barlow, 2002; Heller, Nitschke, & Miller, 1998).

Concept Check | 3.2

In assessing psychological disorders, the reliability and validity of the techniques used to measure behaviour cannot be overlooked. Without these two factors, accurate assessment is impossible. Check your understanding of reliability and validity by marking each test R (reliable) or NR (not reliable) and V (valid) or NV (not valid).

1. EEG to show electrical activity in the brains of people who have seizures _____

2. Rorschach inkblots _____

3. Structured interviews with definite answers

    _____

Diagnosing Psychological Disorders

Thus far, we have looked at Frank's and Brian's functioning on a very individual basis; that is, we have closely observed their behaviour, cognitive processes, and mood, and we have conducted semistructured interviewing, behavioural assessment, and psychological tests. These operations tell us what is unique about Frank and about Brian, not what they may have in common with other individuals or even with each other.

Learning how Frank or Brian may resemble other people in terms of the problems each presents is also very important, for several reasons. If in the past people came in with similar problems or psychological profiles, we can go back and find a lot of information from their cases that might be applicable to Frank's case or to Brian's. We can see how the problems began for those other individuals, what factors seemed influential, and how long the problem or disorder lasted. Did the problem in the other cases just go away on its own? If not, what kept it going? Did it need treatment? Most important, what treatments seemed to relieve the problem for those other individuals? These general questions are very useful because they evoke a wealth of clinical and research information that enables the investigator to make certain inferences about what will happen next and what treatments may work. In other words, the clinician can establish a *prognosis*, a term we discussed in Chapter 1 that refers to the likely future course of a disorder under certain conditions.

Because classification is such an integral part of science and, indeed, of our human experience, we describe its various aspects individually (Millon, 1991). The term **classification** itself is very broad, referring simply to any effort to construct groups or categories and to assign objects or people to these categories on the basis of their shared attributes or relations—a nomothetic strategy. If the classification is in a scientific context, it is most often called **taxonomy**, which is the classification of entities for scientific purposes, such as insects or rocks or, if the subject is psychology, behaviours. If you apply a taxonomic system to psychological or medical phenomena or other clinical areas, you use the word **nosology**. The term **nomenclature** describes the names or labels of the disorders that make up the nosology (e.g., anxiety or mood disorders). Most mental health professionals use the classification system contained in the *Diagnostic and Statistical Manual of Mental Disorders*, 4th edition, text revision (*DSM-IV-TR*). This is the official system in North America and is used widely throughout the world. However, it is not the only recognized system. Another system used widely in Europe is the *International Classification of Diseases and Health Related Problems*, 10th edition (ICD-10) published by the World Health Organization (WHO, 1992). A clinician refers to the *DSM-IV-TR* or the *ICD-10* to identify a specific psychological disorder in the process of making a diagnosis.

During the past several years we have seen enormous changes in how we think about classifying psychopathology. Because these developments affect so much of what we do, we examine carefully the processes of classification and diagnosis as they are used in psychopathology. We look first at different approaches, examine the concepts of reliability and validity as they pertain to diagnosis, and then discuss our current system of classification in North America, the *DSM-IV-TR*.

Classification Issues

Classification is at the heart of any science, and much of what we have said about it is common sense. If we could not order and label objects or experiences, scientists could not communicate with one another and our knowledge would not advance. Everyone would have to develop a personal system, which, of course, would mean nothing to anyone else. In a biology or geology course, when studying insects or rocks, classification is fundamental. Knowing how one species of insects differs from another allows us to study its functioning and origins. When we are dealing with human behaviour or human behavioural disorders, however, the subject of classification becomes controversial. Some people have questioned whether it is proper or ethical to classify human behaviour. Even among those who recognize the necessity of classification, major controversies have arisen in several areas. Within psychopathology, for example, definitions of "normal" and "abnormal" are questioned, and so is the assumption that a behaviour or cognition is part of one category or disorder and not another. Some would prefer to talk about behaviour and feelings on a continuum from happy to sad or fearful to non-fearful, rather than to create such categories as mania, depression, and phobia. Of course, for better or worse, classifying behaviour and people is something we all do. Few of us talk about our own emotions or those of our friends by using a number on a scale (where 0 is totally unhappy and 100 is totally happy), although this approach might be more accurate. ("How do you feel about that?" "About 65.") Rather, we talk about being happy, sad, angry, depressed, fearful, and so on.

Categorical, Dimensional, and Prototypical Approaches

The **classical** (or pure) **categorical approach** to classification originates in the work of Emil Kraepelin (1856–1926) and the biological tradition in the study of psychopathology. Here we assume that every diagnosis has a clear underlying pathophysiological cause, such as a bacterial infection or a malfunctioning endocrine system, and that each disorder is unique. When diagnoses are thought of in this way, the causes could be psychological or cultural, instead of pathophysiological, but each disorder has only one set of

causative factors, which does not overlap at all with other disorders. Because each disorder is fundamentally different from every other, we need only one set of defining criteria, which everybody in the category has to meet. If the criteria for a major depressive episode are (1) the presence of depressed mood, (2) significant weight gain or weight loss when not dieting, and (3) diminished ability to think or concentrate, and seven additional specific symptoms, then, to be diagnosed with depression, an individual would have to meet all ten criteria. In that case, according to the classical categorical approach, the clinician would know the cause of the disorder.

▲ Emil Kraepelin (1856–1926) was one of the first psychiatrists to classify psychological disorders from a biological point of view.

Classical categorical approaches are quite useful in medicine. It is extremely important for a physician to make accurate diagnoses. If a patient has a fever accompanied by stomach pain, the doctor must determine quickly if the cause is stomach flu or an infected appendix. This distinction is not always easy to make, but physicians are trained to examine the signs and symptoms closely, and they usually reach the correct conclusion. To understand the cause of symptoms (infected appendix) is to know what treatment will be effective (surgery). But if someone is depressed or anxious, is there a similar type of underlying cause? As we saw in Chapter 2, probably not. Most psychopathologists believe psychological and social factors interact with biological factors to produce a disorder. Therefore, despite the beliefs of Kraepelin and other early biological investigators, the mental health field has not adopted a classical categorical model of psychopathology.

A second strategy is a **dimensional approach**, in which we note the variety of cognitions, moods, and behaviours with which the patient presents and quantify them on a scale. For example, on a scale of 1 to 10, a patient might be rated as severely anxious (10), moderately depressed (5), and mildly manic (2) to create a profile of emotional functioning (10, 5, 2). Although dimensional approaches have been applied to psychopathology, they are relatively unsatisfactory. Most theorists can't agree on how many dimensions are required; some say one dimension is enough; others have identified as many as 33 (Millon, 1991, 2004).

A third strategy for organizing and classifying behavioural disorders has found increasing support in recent years as an alternative to classical categorical or dimensional approaches. It is a categorical approach but with the twist that it basically combines some of the features of each of the former approaches. Called a **prototypical approach**, this alternative identifies certain essential characteristics of an entity so you (and others) can classify it, but it also allows for certain non-essential variations that do not necessarily change the classification. For example, if someone were to ask you to describe a dog, you could very easily give a general description (the essential, categorical characteristics), but you might not exactly describe a specific dog. Dogs come in different colours, sizes, and even species (the non-essential, dimensional variations), but they all share certain doggish characteristics that allow you to classify them separately from cats. Thus, requiring a certain number of prototypical criteria and only some of an additional number of criteria is adequate. Of course, this system is not perfect because greater blurring happens at the boundaries of categories, and some symptoms apply to more than one disorder. However, it has the advantage of fitting best with the current state of our knowledge of psychopathology, and it is relatively user friendly.

When this approach is used in classifying a psychological disorder, many of the different possible features or properties of the disorder are listed, and any candidate must meet enough (but not necessarily all) of them to fall into that category. Consider the *DSM-IV-TR* criteria defining a major depressive episode:

Criteria for Major Depressive Episode

A. Five (or more) of the following symptoms have been present during the same two-week period and represent a change from previous functioning; at least one of the symptoms is either (a) depressed mood or (b) loss of interest or pleasure.
Note: Symptoms that are clearly due to a general medical condition or mood-incongruent delusions or hallucinations should not be included.
1. Depressed mood most of the day
2. Markedly diminished interest or pleasure in all, or almost all, activities
3. Significant weight loss (when not dieting) or weight gain
4. Insomnia or hypersomnia nearly every day
5. Psychomotor agitation or retardation
6. Fatigue or loss of energy nearly every day
7. Feelings of worthlessness or excessive or inappropriate guilt
8. Diminished ability to think or concentrate or indecisiveness
9. Recurrent thoughts of death

▲ Despite their wide physical variation, all dogs belong to the same class of animals.

As you can see, the criteria include many non-essential symptoms, but if you have either depressed mood or marked loss of interest or pleasure in most activities and at least four of the remaining eight symptoms, you come close enough to the prototype to meet the criteria for a major depressive episode. One person might have depressed mood, significant weight loss, insomnia, psychomotor agitation, and loss of energy, whereas another person who also meets the criteria for major depressive episode might have markedly diminished interest or pleasure in activities, fatigue, feelings of worthlessness, difficulty thinking or concentrating, and suicidal ideation. Although both have the requisite five symptoms that bring them close to the prototype, they look very different because they share only one symptom. This is a good example of a prototypical category. The *DSM-IV-TR* is based on this approach.

Diagnosing forms of mental disorders is one very important activity engaged in by clinical psychologists and some other mental health professionals. The importance of establishing an accurate diagnosis cannot be stressed enough since errors in diagnosis can lead to inappropriate treatments being used with a given client. In part, accurate diagnoses are dependent on the strengths of the diagnostic system being used (e.g., *DSM-IV-TR*, *ICD-10*), but diagnostic accuracy is also dependent on the skills and training of the individual making the diagnosis. Therefore, only trained individuals are permitted to diagnose mental disorders, and the activity of diagnosis is often regulated to protect the public. For example, in Ontario, diagnosis is one activity that falls under the Regulated Health Professions Act (October 1999) that is relevant to psychologists. The *DSM-IV-TR* criteria for major depressive episode, as just illustrated, highlight the importance of the adequate training of the individual making the diagnosis. At first glance, many university students would meet criteria for major depressive episode since many experience depressed mood, weight gain, insomnia, fatigue, and indecisiveness. However, a well-trained professional would recognize that the *DSM-IV-TR* also specifies that each of these symptoms must be present all day, every day, for two full weeks in the past month (American Psychiatric Association, 2000a), resulting in a very much smaller proportion of students actually qualifying for the diagnosis.

Regardless of whether the classical categorical approach or the prototype approach to classification is used, diagnosis is involved. One limitation of the use of a medically derived concept such as diagnosis in psychology is that it relies on an acceptance of a disease model of mental illness drawn from medicine. Some continue to argue that this model is not suitable for the behavioural disorders for a variety of reasons (see reviews by Ausubel, 1971; Gorenstein, 1984; Horwitz, 2002). For example, some contend that psychiatric diagnoses play a very insignificant role in characterizing the kinds of difficulties faced by people seeking help for mental health issues (e.g., life problems such as social isolation, extramarital affairs, marital breakup, financial difficulties; see reviews in Horwitz, 2002; Gorenstein, 1984). On the other hand, some have argued that no inherent contradiction exists in viewing mental symptoms both as manifestations of illness and as expressions of problems in living (e.g., Ausubel, 1971). This debate has been ongoing for nearly five decades (Szasz, 1960).

Diagnosing Psychological Disorders **91**

Any classification system, whether it be a system involving the classical categorical approach, one involving the dimensional approach, or one involving the prototype approach, needs to be evaluated for two important characteristics: reliability and validity.

Reliability

Any system of classification should describe specific subgroups of symptoms that are clearly evident and can be readily identified by experienced clinicians. If two clinicians interview the patient at separate times on the same day (and assuming the patient's condition does not change during the day), the two clinicians should see, and perhaps measure, the same set of behaviours and emotions. The psychological disorder can thus be identified reliably. Obviously, if the disorder is not readily apparent to both clinicians, the resulting diagnoses might represent bias. For example, someone's clothes might provoke some comment. One of your friends might later say, "She looked kind of sloppy tonight." Another might comment, "No, that's just a real funky look; she's right in style." Perhaps a third friend would say, "Actually, I thought she was dressed kind of neatly." You might wonder if they had all seen the same person. In any case, there would be no reliability to their observations. Getting your friends to agree about someone's appearance would require a careful set of definitions that you all accept.

One of the most unreliable categories in current classification is the area of personality disorders—chronic, trait-like sets of inappropriate behaviours and emotional reactions that characterize a person's way of interacting with the world. Although great progress has been made, particularly with certain personality disorders, determining the presence or absence of this type of disorder during one interview is still very difficult. Morey and Ochoa (1989) asked 291 mental health professionals to describe an individual with a personality disorder they had recently seen, along with their diagnoses. Morey and Ochoa also collected from these clinicians detailed information on the actual signs and symptoms present in these patients. In this way, they were able to determine whether the actual diagnosis made by the clinicians matched the objective criteria for the diagnosis as determined by the symptoms. In other words, was the clinician's diagnosis accurate, based on the presence of symptoms that actually define the diagnosis?

Morey and Ochoa found substantial bias in making diagnoses. For example, for some reason, clinicians who were either less experienced or female, diagnosed borderline personality disorder more frequently than the criteria indicated. More experienced clinicians and male clinicians diagnosed the condition less frequently than the criteria indicated.

Patients who were white, female, or poor were diagnosed with borderline personality disorder more often than the criteria indicated. Although bias among clinicians is always a potential problem, the more reliable the nosology, or system of classification, the less likely it is to creep in during diagnosis.

Validity

In addition to being reliable, a system of nosology must be valid. Earlier we described validity as whether something measures what it is designed to measure. There are several different types of diagnostic validity. For one, the system should have construct validity. This means the signs and symptoms chosen as criteria for the presence of the diagnostic category are consistently associated or hang together, and what they identify differs from other categories. Someone meeting the criteria for depression should be discriminable from someone meeting criteria for social phobia. This discriminability might be evident not only in presenting symptoms but also in the course of the disorder and possibly in the choice of treatment. It may also predict familial aggregation, the extent to which the disorder would be found among the patient's relatives (Blashfield & Livesley, 1991; Cloninger, 1989).

In addition, a valid diagnosis tells the clinician what is likely to happen with the prototypical patient; it may predict the course of the disorder and the likely effect of one treatment or another. This type of validity is often called *predictive validity* and sometimes *criterion validity*, when the outcome is the criterion by which we judge the usefulness of the category. Finally, there is *content validity*, which simply means that if you create criteria for a diagnosis of, say, social phobia, it should reflect the way most experts in the field think of social phobia, as opposed to, say, depression. In other words, you need to get the label right.

Diagnosis before 1980

The classification of psychopathology, as the old adage goes, has a long past but a very recent history. Observations of depressed, phobic, or psychotic features stretch back to the earliest recorded observations of human behaviour. Many of these observations were so detailed and complete that we could make a diagnosis today of the individuals they described. Nevertheless, only recently have we attempted the very difficult task of creating a formal nosology that would be useful for scientists and clinicians around the world. As late as 1959, at least nine different systems of varying usefulness were used for classifying psychological disorders worldwide, but only three of the nine systems listed "phobic disorder" as a separate category (Marks, 1969). One reason for this confusion is that creating a useful nosology is easier said than done.

Early efforts to classify psychopathology arose out of the biological tradition, particularly the work of Emil Kraepelin, as described in Chapter 1 and mentioned earlier. Kraepelin first identified what we now know as the disorder of schizophrenia. His term for the disorder at the time was *dementia praecox*. Dementia praecox refers to deterioration of the brain that sometimes occurs with advancing age (dementia) and develops earlier than it is supposed to, or "prematurely" (praecox). This label (later changed to *schizophrenia*) reflected Kraepelin's belief that brain pathology is the cause of this particular disorder. Kraepelin's landmark 1913 book, *Textbook of Psychiatry*, described not only dementia praecox but also bipolar disorder, then called *manic depressive psychosis*. Kraepelin also described a variety of organic brain syndromes. Other well-known figures in their time, such as French psychiatrist Philippe Pinel, characterized psychological disorders, including depression (melancholia), as separate entities; but Kraepelin's theorizing that psychological disorders are basically biological disturbances had the greatest impact on the development of our nosology and led to an early emphasis on classical categorical strategies.

It was not until 1948 that the World Health Organization (WHO) added a section classifying mental disorders to the 6th edition of the *International Classification of Diseases and Health Related Problems (ICD)*. However, this early system did not have much influence. Nor did the first *Diagnostic and Statistical Manual (DSM-I)* published in 1952 by the American Psychiatric Association. Only in the late 1960s did systems of nosology begin to have some real influence on mental health professionals. In 1968, the American Psychiatric Association published a 2nd edition of its *Diagnostic and Statistical Manual (DSM-II)*. In 1969, the WHO published the 8th edition of the *ICD*. Nevertheless, these systems lacked precision, often differing substantially from each other and relying heavily on unproven theories of etiology not widely accepted by all mental health professionals. To make matters worse, the systems had very little reliability. Two mental health practitioners looking at the same patient often came to very different conclusions based on the nosology at that time. Even as late as the 1970s, many countries such as France and Russia had their own systems of nosology. In these countries, the same disorders would be labelled and interpreted very differently.

DSM-III and DSM-III-R

The year 1980 brought a landmark in the history of nosology: the 3rd edition of the *Diagnostic and Statistical Manual (DSM-III)* (American Psychiatric Association, 1980). Under the leadership of Robert Spitzer, the *DSM-III* departed radically from its predecessors. Three changes stood out. First, the *DSM-III* attempted to take an atheoretical approach to diagnosis, relying on precise descriptions of the disorders as they presented to clinicians rather than on psychoanalytic or biological theories of etiology. With this focus, the *DSM-III* became a tool for clinicians with a variety of points of view. For example, rather than classifying phobia under the broad category "neurosis," defined by intrapsychic conflicts and defence mechanisms, it was assigned its own category within a new broader group, "anxiety disorders."

The second major change in the *DSM-III* was that the specificity and detail with which the criteria for identifying a disorder were listed made it possible to study their reliability and validity. Although not all categories in the *DSM-III* (and its 1987 revision, *DSM-III-R*) achieved perfect reliability and validity, this system was a vast improvement over what was available before. Third, the *DSM-III* (and the *DSM-III-R*) allowed individuals with possible psychological disorders to be rated on five dimensions, or axes. The disorder itself, such as schizophrenia or mood disorder, was represented only on the first axis. More enduring (chronic) disorders of personality were listed on Axis II. Axis III consisted of any physical disorders and conditions that might be present. On Axis IV the clinician rated, in a dimensional fashion, the amount of psychosocial stress the person reported, and the current level of adaptive functioning was indicated on Axis V. This framework, called the *multiaxial system*, allowed the clinician to gather information about the individual's functioning in a number of areas rather than limiting information to the disorder itself.

Despite numerous shortcomings, such as low reliability in identifying some disorders and arbitrary decisions on criteria for many disorders, the *DSM-III* and *DSM-III-R* had a substantial impact. Maser, Kaelber, and Weise (1991) surveyed the international usage of various diagnostic systems and found that the *DSM-III* had become popular for a number of reasons. Primary among them were its precise descriptive format and its neutrality with regard to presuming a cause for diagnosis. The multiaxial format, which emphasizes a broad consideration of the whole individual rather than a narrow focus on the disorder alone, was also useful. Therefore, more clinicians around the world used the *DSM-III-R* at the beginning of the 1990s than the *ICD* system designed to be applicable internationally (Maser et al., 1991).

DSM-IV and DSM-IV-TR

By the late 1980s, clinicians and researchers realized the need for a consistent, worldwide system of nosology. The 10th edition of the *International Classification of Diseases (ICD-10)* was published in 1993. To make the *ICD-10* and the *DSM* as compatible as possible, work proceeded more or less simultaneously on both the *ICD-10* and the 4th edition of the *DSM (DSM-IV)* published in 1994. The *DSM-IV* task force decided to rely as little as possible on a consensus of experts. Any changes in the diagnostic system were to be based on sound scientific data. The revisers attempted to review the voluminous literature in all areas pertaining to the diagnostic system (Widiger et al., 1996, 1998) and to identify large sets of data that might have been collected for other reasons but that, with reanalysis, would be useful to the *DSM-IV*. Finally, 12 independent studies or field trials examined the reliability and validity of alternative sets of definitions or criteria and, in some cases, the possibility of creating a new diagnosis. (See Widiger et al., 1998. A description of one of these field trials appears on p. 93.)

Perhaps the most substantial change in the *DSM-IV* is that the distinction between organically based disorders and psychologically based disorders that was present in previous editions has been eliminated. As you saw in Chapter 2, we now know that even disorders associated with known brain pathology are substantially affected by psychological and social influences. Similarly, disorders previously described as psychological in origin certainly have biological components and, most likely, identifiable brain circuits.

The Multiaxial Format in the DSM-IV

The multiaxial system remained in the *DSM-IV*, with some changes in the five axes. Specifically, only personality disorders and mental retardation were now coded on Axis II. Pervasive developmental disorders, learning disorders, motor skills disorders, and communication disorders, previously coded on Axis II, were now all coded on Axis I. Axis IV, which rated the patient's amount of psychosocial stress, was not useful and was replaced. The new Axis IV is used for reporting psychosocial and environmental problems that might have an impact on the disorder. Axis V was essentially unchanged. In addition, optional axes were included for rating dimensions of behaviour or functioning that may be important in some cases. For example, there are axes for defence mechanisms or coping styles, social and occupational functioning, and relational functioning; clinicians might use them to describe the quality of relationships that provide the interpersonal context for the disorder.

In 2000, a committee updated the text that describes the research literature accompanying the *DSM-IV* diagnostic category and made minor changes to some of the criteria themselves to improve consistency (American Psychiatric Association, 2000 First & Pincus, 2002;). This text revision (*DSM-IV-TR*) helped clarify many issues related to the diagnosis of psychological disorders.

The use of dimensional axes for rating, for example, severity of the disorder in a uniform manner across all disorders will be greatly expanded in the *DSM-5* (Regier et al., 2009). A variety of proposals for creating these cross-cutting or superordinate dimensions are currently under evaluation. Another proposal, for example, is to rate the presence of anxiety in a global sense across disorders. Thus, one might diagnose bipolar disorder and provide a dimensional rating of the degree of anxiety also present because a greater degree of anxiety seems to predict a poorer response to treatment (Howland et al., 2009).

DSM-IV and Frank and Brian

In Frank's case, initial observations indicate an anxiety disorder on Axis I, specifically obsessive-compulsive disorder. However, he might also have long-standing personality traits that lead him systematically to avoid social contact. If so, there might be a diagnosis of schizoid personality disorder on Axis II. Unless Frank has an identifiable medical condition, there is nothing on Axis III. Job and marital difficulties would be coded on Axis IV, where clinicians note psychosocial or environmental problems that are not part of the disorder but might make it worse. Frank's difficulties with work would be noted by checking "occupational problems" and specifying "threat of job loss"; for "problems with primary support group," "marital difficulties" would be noted. On Axis V, the clinician would rate the highest overall level of Frank's current functioning on a 0-to-100 scale (100 indicates superior functioning in a variety of situations). At present, Frank's score is 55, which indicates moderate interference with functioning at home and at work.

It is important to emphasize that impairment is a crucial determination in making any diagnosis. For example, if someone, such as Frank, has all of the symptoms of obsessive-compulsive disorder but finds them only mildly annoying because the intrusive thoughts are not severe and don't occur that often, that person would not merit criteria for a psychological disorder. It is essential that the various behaviours and cognitions comprising the diagnosis interfere with functioning in some substantial manner. Thus, the criteria for disorders include the provision that the disorder must cause clinically significant distress or impairment in social, occupational, or other important areas of functioning. Individuals who have all the symptoms as noted earlier but do not cross this "threshold" of impairment could not be diagnosed with a disorder. As noted, one change in the *DSM-5* will be to make this judgment of severity and impairment more systematic by using a dimensional scale. In one of our own clinics, we have been doing something similar to this. That is, in addition to rating overall impairment on Axis V (e.g., Frank scored 55), impairment specifically associated with the Axis I disorder (if present) is also rated. A scale of 0 to 8 is used, where 0 is no impairment and 8 is severely disturbing or disabling (usually housebound and barely functional). The disorder must be rated at least a 4 in severity (definitely disturbing or disabling) to meet criteria for a psychological disorder. Many times, disorders such as obsessive-compulsive disorder would be rated a 2 or 3, meaning that all of the symptoms are there but in too mild a form to impair functioning; in this case, the disorder would be termed *subthreshold*. Subthreshold examples of emotional symptoms are mentioned again when we consider the diagnosis of mixed anxiety-depression later in this chapter. Using Frank as an example again, the severity of his obsessive-compulsive disorder would be rated 5. Whether the *DSM-5* will adopt a simple 0-to-8 scale such as this, or something somewhat more complex (e.g., Regier et al., 2009; Ro & Clark, 2009), will await further evaluation.

In diagnostic reports produced every day at one of our clinics, a summary of Frank's profile based on the multiaxial formulation of the *DSM-IV* would look like this:

Axis I	Obsessive-compulsive disorder
Axis II	Schizoid personality disorder
Axis III	None
Axis IV	Occupational problems: threat of job loss; problems with primary support group: marital difficulties
Axis V	55 (current)

Rachman's (2003) observations indicated that Brian had an Axis I anxiety disorder—namely, obsessive-compulsive disorder. However, Brian's case description includes indications that he may tend to avoid social contact due to social evaluative concerns, to the point of choosing a career that minimizes his social contact (i.e., self-employed bookkeeper). Thus, in Brian's case, the clinician would want to test further to determine whether Brian might also have a personality disorder on Axis II—namely, avoidant personality disorder.

Nothing in the information available on Brian's case indicates a medical disorder on Axis III. If Brian were married and his wife were pressuring him to start a family, the stress in this particular area might make his thoughts and images about harming children even more intense. Although this familial difficulty is not part of Brian's obsessive-compulsive disorder, it might be making his symptoms worse; thus, this stressor would be coded on Axis IV.

Finally, given the information available on the degree to which Brian's symptoms are interfering with his functioning in both his job (e.g., extreme difficulties concentrating at work) and his family interactions (e.g., he may be avoiding his extended family due to his particularly distressing thoughts about harming his young nephew), Brian would likely achieve a score of about 50 on the 0 to 100 functioning scale of Axis V.

Brian's summary based on the multiaxial formulation might look something like this:

Axis I	Obsessive-compulsive disorder
Axis II	Avoidant personality disorder
Axis III	None
Axis IV	Problems with primary support group: marital difficulties pertaining to wife's desire to start a family
Axis V	50 (current)

It is important to emphasize that impairment is a crucial determination in making any diagnosis. For example, if someone, such as Frank or Brian, has all of the symptoms of obsessive-compulsive disorder, but finds them only mildly annoying because the intrusive thoughts are not very severe and don't occur all that often, he would not merit criteria for a psychological disorder. It is essential that the various behaviours and cognitions composing the diagnoses interfere with functioning in some substantial manner. Thus, the criteria for disorders includes the provision that the disorder must cause clinically significant distress or impairment in social, occupational, or other important areas of functioning. Individuals who have all the symptoms as noted above but do not cross this threshold of impairment could not be diagnosed with a disorder. In one of the authors' clinics, in addition to rating overall impairment on Axis V, we also rate impairment specifically associated with the Axis I disorder (if present). We do this on a scale of 0 to 8, where 0 is no impairment whatsoever and 8 is very severely disturbing or disabling (usually housebound and barely functional). The disorder must be rated at least a 4 in severity (definitely disturbing/disabling) to meet criteria for a psychological disorder. Many times disorders such as obsessive-compulsive disorder would be rated a 2 or a 3 (e.g., 2 = slightly disturbing/disabling), meaning that all the symptoms are there but in too mild a form to impair functioning. In this case, the disorder would be termed subthreshold. Subthreshold examples of emotional symptoms are mentioned again when we consider the diagnosis of mixed anxiety-depression on page 97.

This multiaxial system organizes a range of important information that might be relevant to the likely course of the disorder and, perhaps, treatment. For example, two people might present with obsessive-compulsive disorder but look very different on Axes II through V; such differences would greatly affect the clinician's recommendations for the two cases.

Social and Cultural Considerations in the DSM-IV

By emphasizing levels of stress in the environment, the *DSM-III* and *DSM-IV* facilitate a more complete picture of the individual. Furthermore, the *DSM-IV* corrects a previous omission by including a plan for integrating important social and cultural influences on diagnosis. The plan allows the disorder to be described from the perspective of the patient's personal experience and in terms of the primary social and cultural group, such as Chinese or First Nations. The following are suggestions for accomplishing these goals (Mezzich et al., 1993, 1999):

1. What is the primary cultural reference group of the patient? For recent immigrants to the country as well as other ethnic minorities, how involved are they with their new culture versus their old culture? Have they mastered the language of their new country (e.g., English or French in Canada) or is language a continuing problem?
2. Does the patient use terms and descriptions from his or her old country or culture to describe the disorder? For example, as we will see in Chapter 5, *kayak-angst* in the Inuit culture is a type of anxiety disorder close to panic disorder with

▲ The *DSM-IV-TR* diagnostic guidelines take cultural considerations into account.

agoraphobia. Does the patient accept Western models of disease or disorder in which treatment is available in health care systems, or does the patient also have an alternative health care system in another culture (e.g., traditional herbal doctors in Chinese subcultures)?
3. What does it mean to have a disability? What kinds of disabilities are acceptable in a given culture, and which are not? For example, is it acceptable to be physically ill but not anxious or depressed? What are the typical family, social, and religious supports in the culture? Are they available to the patient? Does the clinician understand the first language of the patient as well as the cultural significance of the disorder?

These cultural considerations must not be overlooked in making diagnoses and planning treatment, and they are assumed throughout this book. But, as yet, there is no research supporting the use of these cultural formulation guidelines (Alarcon et al., 2002). The consensus is that we have a lot more work to do in this area to make our nosology truly culturally sensitive, and the *DSM-5* has commissioned a number of reviews addressing cultural variations (e.g., Lewis-Fernandez et al., 2009) and how these issues could be better integrated into the *DSM-5*.

Criticisms of the DSM-IV and DSM-IV-TR

Because the collaboration among groups creating the *ICD-10* and *DSM-IV* was largely successful, it is clear that the *DSM-IV* (and

▲ The kinds of disabilities that are accepted in a given culture are socially determined.

the closely related *ICD-10* mental disorder section) is the most advanced, scientifically based system of nosology ever developed. Nevertheless, any nosological system should be considered a work in progress (Brown & Barlow, 2005; Millon, 2004; Regier et al., 2009; Smith & Oltmanns, 2009).

We still have "fuzzy" categories that blur at the edges, making diagnostic decisions difficult at times. As a consequence, individuals are often diagnosed with more than one psychological disorder at the same time, which is called **comorbidity**. How can we conclude anything definite about the course of a disorder, the response to treatment, or the likelihood of associated problems if we are dealing with combinations of disorders (Brown & Barlow, 2009; Follette & Houts, 1996; Kupfer, First, & Regier, 2002)? Is there a way to identify essential features of comorbid disorders and, perhaps, rate them dimensionally (Brown & Barlow, 2009; Helzer et al., 2008)? Resolution of these tough problems simply awaits the long, slow process of science.

Criticisms centre on two other aspects of the *DSM-IV* and *ICD-10*. First, the systems strongly emphasize reliability, sometimes at the expense of validity. This is understandable, because reliability is so difficult to achieve unless you are willing to sacrifice validity. If the sole criterion for establishing depression were to hear the patient say at some point during an interview, "I feel depressed," the clinician could theoretically achieve perfect reliability. But this achievement would be at the expense of validity because many people with differing psychological disorders, or none, occasionally say they are depressed. Thus, clinicians could agree that the statement occurred, but it would

be of little use (Carson, 1991; Meehl, 1989). Second, as Carson (1996) points out, methods of constructing a nosology of mental disorders have a way of perpetuating definitions handed down to us from past decades, even if they might be fundamentally flawed. Carson (1991) makes a strong argument that it might be better to start fresh once in a while and create a new system of disorders based on emerging scientific knowledge rather than to simply fine-tune old definitions, but this is unlikely to happen because of the enormous effort and expense involved, and the necessity of discarding the accumulated wisdom of previous versions.

In addition to the daunting complexity of categorizing psychopathology, systems are subject to misuse, some of which can be dangerous and harmful. Diagnostic categories are just a convenient format for organizing observations that help professionals communicate, study, and plan. But if we reify a category, we literally make it a "thing," assuming it has a meaning that, in reality, does not exist. Categories may change occasionally with new knowledge, so none can be written in stone. If a case falls on the fuzzy borders between diagnostic categories, we should not expend all our energy attempting to force it into one category or another. It is a mistaken assumption that everything has to fit neatly somewhere.

A Caution about Labelling and Stigma

A related problem that occurs any time we categorize people is **labelling**. You may remember Kermit the Frog from *Sesame Street* sharing with us that "It's not easy being green." Something in human nature causes us to use a label, even one as superficial as skin colour, to characterize the totality of an individual ("He's green ... he's different from me"). We see the same phenomenon among psychological disorders ("He's a schizo"). Furthermore, if the disorder is associated with an impairment in cognitive or behavioural functioning, the label itself has negative connotations and contributes to stigma, which is a combination of stereotypic negative beliefs, prejudices, and attitudes resulting in reduced life opportunities for the devalued group in question, such as individuals with mental disorders (Hinshaw & Stier, 2008).

There have been many attempts over the years to categorize mental retardation. Most of the categories were based on the severity of the impairment or highest level of developmental ability that the individual could reach. But we have had to change the labels for these categories of cognitive impairment periodically as the stigma associated with them builds up. One early categorization described levels of severity as *moron, imbecile,* and *idiot*. When these terms were introduced they were rather neutral, simply describing the severity of a person's cognitive and developmental impairment. But as they began to be used in common language, they picked up negative connotations and were used as insults. As these terms gradually became pejorative, it was necessary to eliminate them as categories and come up with a new set of classifying labels that were less derogatory. One recent development is to categorize mental retardation functionally in terms of the levels of support needed by these individuals. In others words, a person's degree of

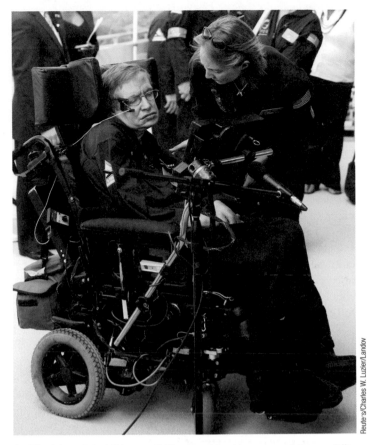

Reuters/Charles W. Luzier/Landov

▲ Would we label this man? Stephen Hawking, one of the world's leading physicists, is severely disabled by amyotrophic lateral sclerosis, a rare progressive degenerative disease of the spinal cord. Because he cannot activate his voice box or move his lips, Hawking types his words into an electronic voice synthesizer that "speaks" for him. He uses his thumbprint to autograph his books. "I have been lucky," he says. "I don't have anything to be angry about."

mental retardation is determined by how much assistance he or she requires (e.g., intermittent, limited, extensive, or pervasive) rather than by his or her IQ score (Lubinski, 2004; Luckasson et al., 1992). The current proposal for the *DSM-5* is to drop the term "mental retardation" and substitute "intellectual disability" as a more accurate term, which is consistent with recent changes by other organizations (American Psychiatric Association, 2010) (see Chapter 14).

In any case, once labelled, individuals with a disorder may identify with the negative connotations associated with the label (Hinshaw & Stier, 2008). This affects their self-esteem; although Ruscio (2004) indicates that the negative meanings associated with labelling are not a necessary consequence of making a diagnosis if it is relayed in a compassionate manner. Nevertheless, if you think of your own reactions to mental illness, you will probably recognize the tendency to generalize inappropriately from the label. In fact, for a variety of reasons Hinshaw and Stier (2008) note that stigmatization of individuals with mental disorders is increasing rather than decreasing. We have to remember that terms in psychopathology do not describe people but identify patterns of behaviour that may or may not occur in certain circumstances. Thus, whether the disorder is medical or psychological, we must resist the temptation to identify the person with the disorder: Note the different implications of "John is a diabetic" and "John is a person who has diabetes."

Creating a Diagnosis

During the extensive deliberations by thousands of people that led to the publication of the *DSM-IV*, several potentially new diagnostic categories were considered. Because one of us was a member of the task force, we can offer brief examples to illustrate how diagnostic categories are created.

Mixed Anxiety-Depression

Family physicians' offices, clinics, hospitals, and so on, are called *primary care settings* because they are where a person goes first with a problem. For years, people coming to these primary care clinics have complained of minor aches and pains that prove to have no physical basis. They also complain of feeling uptight, down in the dumps, and anxious. Health care professionals examining these individuals report that their symptoms of both anxiety and depression are classic but not frequent or severe enough to meet criteria for an existing anxiety or mood disorder.

The *DSM-IV* task force was concerned about issues like this one for several reasons. First, because many individuals present with some minor symptoms of a given disorder, it is important to set thresholds high enough that only people who clearly experience some impairment qualify for the category. (Thresholds are the minimum number of criteria required to meet the definition of a disorder.) The primary reason for this concern is that substantial legal and policy implications are contingent on a diagnosis. That is, someone who presents with a psychological disorder that clearly qualifies for a diagnosis becomes part of the loosely organized medico-legal system and is eligible to ask the government or private insurance companies for financial reimbursement or disability payments.

In Canada, the services provided by a psychologist are covered by provincial health insurance only if the psychologist is employed by a publicly funded institution like a hospital, community health clinic, school, social agency, or correctional facility. In contrast, services provided by a psychologist in private practice are not covered by provincial health care plans. These costs are either paid for by the patient or are covered partially or in full by health benefits through private insurance plans offered by employers. The services of psychiatrists are covered through provincial health insurance plans regardless of where the psychiatrist is employed (Canadian Psychological Association, 2004). Disability payments are covered by the Canada Pension Plan (CPP) based on contributions from workers and employers in Canada. The primary role of this plan is to replace a portion of income for contributors who cannot work because of a severe and prolonged disability such as a severe mental health disorder (Social Development

Canada, 2004). Some of the money to pay for the services of mental health professionals in Canada actually comes from taxpayers. And insurance companies and the CPP simply could not afford to pay for all the possible minor reasons a person might want to consult a psychologist or other mental health professional.

Clearly, if the diagnostic system includes people who have only minor symptoms, who are not particularly impaired and just feel down periodically, or who don't like their job and want disability (an all too common request in mental health clinics), the health care system would be even more strained and have fewer resources to treat the serious impairments. But if people are experiencing considerable problems and impairment in functioning, they should be covered in any health care system. For these reasons, minor complaints of dysphoric mood, characterized by vague complaints of anxiety and depression, were not considered sufficiently severe to constitute a formal diagnosis.

In 1989, Klerman and Weissman, reporting on a large study by Wells et al. (1989), found that patients who claimed to be anxious and mildly depressed *were* impaired in a number of areas when compared with normal controls and with patients with chronic medical conditions. Substantial impairment was present in the areas of physical and social functioning, not only causing patients to miss work but also interfering with their functioning in the home; it was worse than the impairment of many patients with chronic medical conditions. The evidence also suggested that these individuals were already imposing an enormous burden on the health care system by appearing in large numbers at community health clinics and the offices of family doctors. Barrett, Barrett, Oxman, and Gerber (1988), assessing patients from a rural primary care practice, found that as many as 14.4 percent of patients presented with principal complaints of anxiety and depression. Other studies also supported this finding (Katon & Roy-Byrne, 1991; Roy-Byrne & Katon, 2000). Finally, evidence suggested that such people were at greatly increased risk of developing more severe mood or anxiety disorders (Moras et al., 1996; Roy-Byrne & Katon, 2000).

Therefore, we concluded that it might be very valuable to identify these people and find out more about the etiology, course, and maintenance of the problem. The authors of the *ICD-10*, recognizing this phenomenon is prevalent throughout the world, had created a category of *mixed anxiety-depression*, but they had not defined it or created any criteria that would allow further examination of the potential disorder. Therefore, to explore the possibility of creating a new diagnostic category (Zinbarg & Barlow, 1996; Zinbarg et al., 1994, 1998), a study was undertaken that had three specific goals. First, if mental health professionals carefully administered semistructured interviews (the Anxiety Disorders Interview Schedule), would they find patients who fit the new category? Or would careful examination find the criteria for already existing disorders that had been overlooked by health professionals not well trained in identifying psychological disorders? Second, if mixed anxiety-depression did exist, was it really more prevalent in medical primary care settings than in outpatient mental health settings?

Third, what set of criteria (e.g., types and number of symptoms) would best identify the disorder?

The study to answer these questions was conducted simultaneously in seven different sites around the world (Zinbarg et al., 1994, 1998). Results indicated that people presenting with several symptoms of anxiety and depression, who did not meet criteria for an existing anxiety or mood disorder (because they did not have the right mix or severity of anxious or depressed symptoms), were common in primary care settings. Furthermore, they were substantially impaired in their occupational and social functioning and experienced a great deal of distress. Additional analysis revealed that such people could be distinguished from people with existing anxiety or mood disorders on the basis of their symptoms. Specifically, they presented with a set of emotional and behavioural symptoms that fall into the general category of negative affect, including behaviours such as difficulty sleeping and difficulty concentrating. These behaviours are often part of anxiety and mood disorders, but are not specific to either. (Negative affect and its symptoms are described more fully in Chapter 7.) In any case, because these people appeared both anxious and depressed, the potential new category possessed content validity.

This study also established some of the criteria important in determining *construct validity* for the new category of mixed anxiety-depression. However, because the category is so new, we do not have information on additional criteria important in establishing construct validity, such as course, response to treatment, and the extent to which the disorder aggregates in families, and we cannot yet verify the reliability of the diagnosis or anything about predictive validity. Therefore, the decision of the *DSM-IV* task force was to place this mixed anxiety-depression diagnosis in the appendix, which is reserved for new diagnoses under study. It is likely to become a full diagnostic category in future editions, but more research needs to be done first.

Premenstrual Dysphoric Disorder

Premenstrual dysphoric disorder (PMDD) evokes a very different issue that must be considered in the creation of any diagnostic category: bias and stigmatization. Evaluation of this extremely controversial category actually began well before the publication of *DSM-III-R* in 1987. Some clinicians had claimed to have identified a small group of women who presented with severe and sometimes incapacitating emotional reactions associated with the late luteal phase of their menstrual cycle (Rivera-Tovar, Pilkonis, & Frank, 1992). Subsequently, proposals were made to consider inclusion of this possible disorder in the *DSM-III-R*. In view of the difficulties and impairment associated with this condition, the proponents argued, women deserved the attention, care, and financial support that inclusion in a diagnostic category would provide. In addition, as with mixed anxiety-depression, proponents argued that the creation of this category would promote a substantial increase in research into the nature and treatment of the problem. Di Guilio and Reissing (2006) of the University of Ottawa, for example, argue that the accumulated research suggests that PMDD represents a distinct diagnostic entity that is separable from both normal premenstrual symptoms and major depression. They argue that recognition of this problem through formal diagnostic criteria would serve the important minority of women who suffer from this cyclical mood "disorder" (DiGuilio & Reissing, 2006).

Nevertheless, arguments against the category were marshalled along several fronts. First, opponents noted that relatively little scientific information existed in either the clinical or research literature on this topic. The available information was insufficient to warrant the creation of a new diagnostic category. More important were substantial objections that what could be a normal endocrinological stage experienced by all or most women would be stigmatized as a psychiatric disorder. Some pointed to research showing that women who complain of premenstrual emotional symptoms are significantly more likely than other women to be in distressing life situations (e.g., being battered); thus, to label them as having a mental disorder may mask the real, external (societal) sources of their difficulties (see review by Offman & Kleinplatz, 2004). In addition, the seeming similarities with the once widely accepted category of hysteria described in Chapter 1 were also noted. (Remember that this so-called disorder, characterized by a variety of incapacitating physical complaints without an identifiable medical basis, was thought to be caused by the wandering of the uterus.) Questions were raised about whether the disorder would best be described as endocrinological or gynecological rather than mental. Because premenstrual dysphoric disorder could occur only in women, should we include a comparable disorder associated with, for example, aggressiveness related to excessive male hormones? Feminist theorists Alia Offman and Peggy J. Kleinplatz of Carleton University and the University of Ottawa, respectively, have been highly critical of inclusion of this label in the DSM system for many of the reasons just noted (Offman & Kleinplatz, 2004).

The *DSM-III-R* task force decided to place this disorder in an appendix in the hope of promoting further study. The task force also wanted to clearly differentiate this syndrome from premenstrual syndrome (PMS), which has less severe and specific premenstrual symptomatology. One way of accomplishing this was by naming the condition *late luteal phase dysphoric disorder (LLPDD)*.

After the publication of *DSM-III-R*, LLPDD attracted a great deal of research attention. By 1991 Judith Gold, a psychiatrist from Halifax, Nova Scotia, who chaired the *DSM-IV* work group on this issue, estimated that one research article per month on LLPDD was published (Gold et al., 1996). A variety of scientific findings began to accrue that supported the inclusion of this disorder in the *DSM-IV*. For example, although the rather vague and less severe symptoms of PMS occur in 20 percent to 40 percent of women (Severino & Moline, 1989), only a very small proportion of them—about 4.6 percent—experience the more severe and incapacitating symptoms associated with LLPDD (Rivera-Tovar & Frank, 1990). In addition, abnormalities in several biological systems appear to be associated with clinically significant premenstrual dysphoria (see review by Gold et al., 1996), and several different types of treatment show some promise of being effective against LLPDD (e.g., Stone, Pearlstein, & Brown, 1991). Hurt and colleagues, in a reanalysis of data from 670

women, recommended a set of criteria for this disorder that were not very different from those proposed in the *DSM-III-R* (Hurt et al., 1992).

Nevertheless, arguments continue against including this label in the diagnostic system. Most opponents cite the issue of stigmatization, warning that recognition might confirm the cultural belief that menstruation and resulting disability make women unfit for positions of responsibility. (There have been several cases where accusations of the less severe condition of PMS have been used against a mother in an attempt to win child custody for the father; see Gold et al., 1996.) Also, classifying the condition as a disorder might sustain and strengthen religious and cultural taboos associated with the menstrual cycle that range from prohibition of sexual intercourse to actual banishment from regular living quarters. In Orthodox Judaism, for example, women are required to take a ritual communal bath called the *mikvah* after each period to cleanse themselves of menstrual impurities. Only then can they resume physical and sexual contact with their husbands (Reik, 1964). Those arguing against the disorder also point out that some of the symptoms outlined in the criteria for LLPDD involve anger, which would not be viewed as inappropriate in a male. Only in a female does society presume that anger signifies something is wrong.

What would you do? Would you call this condition a disorder to ensure that women experiencing it receive the attention and treatment they need? Or would you be more concerned with the potential for misuse of the diagnosis, particularly the social stigmatization? Interestingly, many women who have been given this label say they are quite comfortable with it. Some women presenting with other psychological disorders, such as depression, refuse to accept the suggestion that they have a psychiatric problem, insisting it is really premenstrual syndrome (Rapkin, Chang, & Reading, 1989). Early in 1994 the *DSM-IV* task force decided to retain the disorder in the appendix as needing further study. Among other problems, the committee wanted to see more epidemiological data using the new criteria and to examine more carefully the data on the relation of this problem to existing mood disorders.

Several additional research findings indicated that the name late luteal phase dysphoric disorder was not entirely accurate, because the symptoms may not be exclusively related to the endocrine state of the late luteal phase. Therefore, the name has been changed to *premenstrual dysphoric disorder (PMDD)*.

Since 1994, research has continued, and even accelerated, on the nature and treatment of PMDD, with thousands of papers published on this general topic (Gold, 1999; Grady-Weliky, 2003; Pearlstein, Yonkers, Fayyad, & Gillespie, 2005). Epidemiological studies from around the world now support the existence of disabling premenstrual symptoms in about 5 percent to 8 percent of women, with another 14 percent to 18 percent experiencing moderate symptoms (Angst, Sellaro, Stolar, Merikangas, & Endicott, 2001; Cunningham, Yonkers, O'Brien, & Eriksson, 2009; Gold, 1997a, 1997b; Ko, Lee, Chang, & Huang, 1996; Pearlstein & Steiner, 2008; Wittchen, Becker, Lieb, & Krause, 2002). And the American College of

Obstetricians and Gynecology has published systematic clinical practice guidelines recommending specific treatments (American College of Obstetricians and Gynecologists, 2002) and new information on effective treatment is published frequently (Freeman, Rickels, Sammel, Lin, & Sondheimer, 2009). One of the difficulties encountered has been distinguishing PMDD from premenstrual exacerbations of other disorders, such as binge eating disorder or mood disorders (Pearlstein et al., 2005). Hartlage and Gehlert (2001) proposed a method that carefully considers the nature and timing of the symptoms to make a valid distinction between PMDD and premenstrual exacerbations of other disorders. For example, the symptoms of PMDD must be absent or present only mildly postmenstrually. Also, to distinguish from a mood disorder, at least some symptoms must be different from those associated with a mood disorder, such as certain physical symptoms or anxiety. The accumulating evidence thus far seems to suggest that PMDD is best considered a disorder of mood rather than, for example, an endocrine disorder and that it should continue to be considered a mental disorder (Cunningham et al., 2009; Gold, 1999). Support for PMDD as a distinct psychological disorder in the *DSM-5* is more likely than in previous versions.

Beyond *DSM-IV*: Dimensions and Spectra

The process of changing the criteria for existing diagnoses and creating new ones will continue as our science advances. New findings on brain circuits, cognitive processes, and cultural factors that affect our behaviour could date diagnostic criteria relatively quickly.

Now the process to create the 5th edition of the *Diagnostic and Statistical Manual of Mental Disorders (DSM-5)* that began formally in 2006 is nearing completion, with publication scheduled for May 2013. The *DSM-5* task force has set clear criteria for reviewing diagnostic categories currently in the appendix in the *DSM-IV*. After each category is reviewed, one of the following actions is to be taken for each included disorder: (1) delete the disorder from the appendix, (2) "promote" it to the main manual, or (3) retain it in the appendix. The criteria for one decision or another would be based primarily on new research that would be either sufficient to establish the validity of the diagnosis or not (Kendler, Kupfer, Narrow, Phillips, & Fawcett, 2009). In addition, it is now clear to most professionals involved in this process that an exclusive reliance on discrete diagnostic categories has not achieved its objective in achieving a satisfactory system of nosology (Krueger, Watson, & Barlow, 2005). In addition to problems noted earlier with comorbidity and the fuzzy boundary between diagnostic categories, little evidence has emerged validating these categories, such as discovering specific underlying causes associated with each category (Regier et al., 2009). In fact, not one biological marker, such as a laboratory test, that would clearly distinguish one disorder from another has been discovered (Frances, 2009; Widiger & Samuel, 2005). It is also clear that the current categories lack treatment specificity. That is, certain treatments such as cognitive behavioural therapies or specific antidepressant drugs are effective for a large number of diagnostic categories that are not supposed to be all that similar. Therefore,

the *DSM-5* planners are beginning to assume that the limitations of the current diagnostic system are substantial enough that continued research on these diagnostic categories may never be successful in uncovering their underlying causes or helping us develop new treatments.

It may be time for a new approach. Most people agree that this approach will incorporate a dimensional strategy to a much greater extent than in the *DSM-IV* (Krueger et al., 2005; Kupfer et al., 2002; Widiger & Coker, 2003; Widiger & Sankis, 2000). The term "spectrum" is another way to describe groups of disorders that share certain basic biological or psychological qualities or dimensions. For example, in Chapter 14 you will read about the proposal in the *DSM-5* to eliminate the term "Asperger's syndrome" (a mild form of autism) and combine it with autistic disorder into a new category of "autism spectrum disorder." It is also clear at this point that research is not sufficiently advanced to attempt a wholesale switch to a dimensional or spectrum approach, so the proposed categories in the *DSM-5* that were posted on the *DSM-5* website in February 2010 (and removed in April 2010 for further study) look very much like the categories in the *DSM-IV* with some updated language and increased precision and clarity. One more substantial change may be the creation of the cross-cutting or superordinate dimensional ratings that we described earlier in the chapter. But, sparked by research and conceptual advances during the process of creating the *DSM-5*, more conceptually substantial and consistent dimensional approaches are in development, and may be ready for the 6th edition of the *DSM* in 10 to 20 years.

For example, in the area of personality disorders, Livesley, Jang, and Vernon (1998), in studying both clinical samples of patients with personality disorders and community samples, concluded that personality disorders were not qualitatively distinct from the personalities of normal-functioning individuals in community samples. Instead, personality disorders simply represent maladaptive, and perhaps extreme, variants of common personality traits (Widiger & Edmundson, in press; Widiger, Livesley, & Clark, 2009; Widiger & Samuel, 2005). Even the genetic structure of personality is not consistent with discrete categorical personality disorders. That is, personality dispositions more broadly defined, such as being shy and inhibited or outgoing, have a stronger genetic influence (higher genetic loading) than personality disorders as currently defined (First et al., 2002; Livesley & Jang, 2008; Livesley et al., 1998; Rutter, Moffitt, & Caspi, 2006; Widiger et al., 2009). For the anxiety and mood disorders, Brown & Barlow (2009) have proposed a new dimensional system of classification based on previous research (Brown, Chorpita, & Barlow, 1998) demonstrating that anxiety and depression have more in common than previously thought and may best be represented as points on a continuum of negative affect or a spectrum of emotional disorders (see Barlow, 2002; Brown & Barlow, 2005, 2009; Clark, 2005; Mineka, Watson, & Clark, 1998; Watson, 2005). Even for severe disorders with seemingly stronger genetic influences, such as schizophrenia, it appears that dimensional classification strategies or spectrum approaches might prove superior (Charney et al., 2002; Lenzenweger & Dworkin, 1996; Toomey, Faraone, Simpson, & Tsuang, 1998;

Widiger & Edmundson, in press; Widiger, 1997; Widiger & Samuel, 2005).

At the same time, exciting new developments from the area of neuroscience relating to brain structure and function will provide enormously important information on the nature of psychological disorders. This information could then be integrated with more psychological, social, and cultural information into a diagnostic system. But even neuroscientists are abandoning the notion that groups of genes or brain circuits will be found that are specifically associated with *DSM-IV* diagnostic categories, as noted in Chapter 2. Rather, it is now assumed that neurobiological processes will be discovered that are associated with specific cognitive, emotional, and behavioural patterns or traits (e.g., behavioural inhibition) that do not necessarily correspond closely with current diagnostic categories.

With this in mind, we can turn our attention to the current state of our knowledge about a variety of major psychological disorders. Beginning with Chapter 5, we attempt to predict the next major scientific breakthroughs affecting diagnostic criteria and definitions of disorders. Toward this end, we introduce a new section at the end of each disorder chapter entitled "On the Spectrum," detailing recent work that anticipates important changes in the years to come in how we think about psychological disorders. But first, we review the all-important area of research methods and strategies used to establish new knowledge of psychopathology.

Concept Check | 3.3

Identify each of the following statements related to diagnosing psychological disorders as either true (T) or false (F).

1. ___ The classical categorical approach to classification assumes there is only one set of causative factors per disorder with no overlap between disorders, and the prototypical approach uses essential, defining features, as well as a range of other characteristics.

2. ___ As in earlier versions, the *DSM-IV* retains a distinction between organically and psychologically based disorders.

3. ___ The *DSM-IV* eradicated the problem of comorbidity, the identification of two or more disorders in an individual at one time, which was previously caused by imprecise categories.

4. ___ If two or more clinicians agree on a patient's classification, the assessments are said to be valid.

5. ___ A danger in psychological classification is that a diagnostic label might be used to characterize personally the total individual.

Summary

Assessing Psychological Disorders

- Clinical assessment is the systematic evaluation and measurement of psychological, biological, and social factors in an individual with a possible psychological disorder; diagnosis is the process of determining that those factors meet all the criteria for a specific psychological disorder.
- Reliability, validity, and standardization are important components in determining the value of a psychological assessment.
- To assess various aspects of psychological disorders, clinicians may first interview and take an informal mental status exam of the patient. More systematic observations of behaviour are called behavioural assessment.
- A variety of psychological tests can be used during assessment, including projective tests, in which the patient responds to ambiguous stimuli by projecting unconscious thoughts; personality inventories, in which the patient takes a self-report questionnaire designed to assess personal traits; and intelligence testing that provides a score known as an intelligence quotient.
- Biological aspects of psychological disorders may be assessed through neuropsychological testing designed to identify possible areas of brain dysfunction. Neuroimaging can be used more directly to identify brain structure and function. Finally, psychophysiological assessment refers to measurable changes in the nervous system, reflecting emotional or psychological events that might be relevant to a psychological disorder.

Diagnosing Psychological Disorders

- The term *classification* refers to any effort to construct groups or categories and to assign objects or people to the categories on the basis of their shared attributes or relations. Methods of classification include classical categorical, dimensional, and prototypical approaches. Our current system of classification, the *Diagnostic and Statistical Manual*, 4th edition, text revision (*DSM-IV*), as well as in the forthcoming 5th edition (*DSM-5*), is based on a prototypical approach in which certain essential characteristics are identified but certain "non-essential" variations do not necessarily change the classification. The *DSM-IV-TR* categories are based on empirical findings to identify the criteria for each diagnosis. Although this system is the best to date in terms of scientific underpinnings, it is far from perfect, and research continues on the most useful way to classify psychological disorders.

Key Terms

behavioural assessment, 79	dimensional approach, 90	neuroimaging, 86	psychophysiological assessment, 88
classical categorical approach, 90	electroencephalogram (EEG), 88	neuropsychological testing, 86	reliability, 74
classification, 89	false negatives, 86	nomenclature, 89	self-monitoring, 80
clinical assessment, 73	false positives, 86	nosology, 89	standardization, 75
comorbidity, 96	intelligence quotient (IQ), 85	personality inventories, 83	taxonomy, 89
diagnosis, 73	labelling, 96	projective tests, 81	validity, 75
	mental status exam, 75	prototypical approach, 90	

Answers to Concept Checks

3.1

1. thought processes
2. appearance and behaviour 3. sensorium 4. mood and affect 5. intellectual functioning

3.2

1. R,V 2. NR, NV 3. R,V

3.3

1. T 2. F 3. F (still a problem) 4. F (reliable) 5. T

Media Resources

Access an integrated eBook, Abnormal Psychology Videos (formerly Abnormal Psych Live CD-ROM), chapter-specific interactive learning tools (flashcards, quizzes, learning modules), and more in your Psychology CourseMate, available at **www.abnormalpsych3ce.nelson.com.**

Abnormal Psychology Video

Free Abnormal Psychology videos can be viewed on the website **www.abnormalpsych3ce .nelson.com**.

- *Arriving at a Diagnosis:* A team discusses how it arrived at the conclusion that a patient has a panic disorder.
- *Looking at Contributing Factors:* The psychological team discusses factors in dysfunctional beliefs, family relationships, and behaviour patterns that might be contributing to a woman's major depressive disorder.

Video Concept Reviews

CourseMate also contains Mark Durand's *Video Concept Reviews* on these challenging topics:

- Clinical Assessment
- Reliability/Validity
- Standardization
- Mental Status Exam
- Behavioural Assessment
- Projective Tests
- Concept Check—Data-Based Approach
- Neuropsychological Testing
- False Positive/False Negative
- Psychophysiological Assessment
- Diagnosis/Classification
- Taxonomy/Nosology/Nomenclature
- Concept Check—Categorical versus Dimensional
- Classification Systems
- *DSM-IV*

4 | Research Methods

Stephen Coburn/Shutterstock

> *To a person uninstructed in natural history, his country or seaside stroll is a walk through a gallery filled with wonderful works of art, nine-tenths of which have their faces turned to the wall.*
> —Thomas Henry Huxley, *On the Educational Value of the Natural History Sciences*

Demonstrate knowledge and understanding representing appropriate breadth and depth in selected content areas of psychology:	› Relevant ethical issues, including a general understanding of the APA Ethics Code (APA SLO 2.1) *(see textbook pages 124–125)*
Describe the basic characteristics of the science of psychology	› (APA SLO 2.1) *(see textbook pages 105–108)*
Explain different research methods used by psychologists.	› Describe how various research designs address different types of questions and hypotheses (APA SLO 2.2.a) *(see textbook pages 108–115)* › Articulate strengths and limitations of various research designs, including distinguishing between qualitative and quantitative methods (APA SLO 2.2.b) *(see textbook pages 116–121)*
Design and conduct basic studies to address psychological questions using appropriate research methods.	› Recognize that theoretical and sociocultural contexts as well as personal biases may shape research questions, design, data collection, analysis, and interpretation (APA SLO 2.4.f) *(see textbook pages 122–123)*

* Portions of this chapter cover learning outcomes suggested by the American Psychological Association (2007) in their guidelines for the undergraduate psychology major. Chapter coverage of these outcomes is identified above by APA Goal and APA Suggested Learning Outcome (SLO).

Behavioural scientists explore human behaviour the same way other scientists study the path of a comet or the AIDS virus: They use the scientific method. As we've already seen, abnormal behaviour is a challenging subject because of the interaction of biological and psychological dimensions. Rarely are any simple answers available to such questions as "Why do some people have hallucinations?" or "How do you treat someone who is suicidal?"

In addition to the obvious complexity of human nature, another factor that makes an objective study of abnormal behaviour difficult is the inaccessibility of many important aspects of this phenomenon. The challenge is to get inside people's minds indirectly. Fortunately, as University of Regina psychologist Gordon Asmundson and his colleagues describe in their clinical research textbook, some very creative individuals have accepted this challenge (Asmundson et al., 2002). Many ingenious methods have been developed for studying scientifically what behaviours constitute problems, why people develop behavioural disorders, and how to treat these problems. Some of you will ultimately contribute to this important field by applying the methods described in this chapter. Many critical questions regarding abnormal behaviour have yet to be answered, and we hope that some of you will be inspired to take them on. However, understanding research methods is extremely important for all of you. You or someone close to you may need the services of a psychologist, psychiatrist, or other mental health provider. You may have questions such as these:

- Should childhood aggression be cause for concern, or is it a phase my child will grow out of?
- The *Canada AM* show reported that increased exposure to sunlight alleviates depression. Instead of seeing a therapist, should I buy a ticket to Hawaii?
- I read a story about the horrors of shock therapy. Should I advise my neighbour not to let her daughter have this treatment?
- My brother has been in therapy for three years but doesn't seem to be any better. Should I tell him to look elsewhere for help?

- My mother is still in her 50s but seems to be forgetting things. Friends tell me this is natural as you grow older. Should I be concerned?

To answer such questions, you need to be a good consumer of research. When you understand the correct ways of obtaining information—that is, research methodology—you will know when you are dealing with fact and not fiction. Knowing the difference between a fad and an established approach to a problem can be the difference between months of suffering and a quick resolution to a disturbing problem.

Important Concepts

As we said from the start, we examine several aspects of abnormal behaviour in this book. First, "What problems cause distress and impair functioning?" Second, "Why do people behave in unusual ways?" And third, "How do we help them behave in more adaptive ways?" The first question is about the nature of the problems people report; we explore research strategies that help us answer this question. The second question considers the causes, or *etiology*, of abnormal behaviour; we explore strategies for discovering why a disorder occurred. Finally, because we want to help people who have disorders, we describe how researchers evaluate treatments. Before we discuss specific strategies, however, we must consider several general ways of evaluating research.

Basic Components of a Research Study

The basic research process is very simple. You start with an educated guess, called a **hypothesis**, about what you expect to find. When you decide how you want to test this hypothesis, you have a **research design**. This includes the aspects you want to measure in the people you are studying (the **dependent variable**) and the influences on their behaviours (the **independent**

TABLE 4.1 The Basic Components of a Research Study

Component	Description
Hypothesis	An educated guess or statement to be supported by data
Research design	The plan for testing the hypothesis; affected by the question addressed, the hypothesis, and practical considerations
Dependent variable	Some aspect of the phenomenon that is measured and is expected to be changed or influenced by the independent variable
Independent variable	The aspect manipulated or thought to influence the change in the dependent variable
Internal validity	The extent to which the results of the study can be attributed to the independent variable
External validity	The extent to which the results of the study can be generalized or applied outside the immediate study

variable). For example, a researcher interested in understanding the strong relationship between panic attacks and alcohol abuse (see Chapter 2) might choose to study the effects of anxiety induction in the lab (the independent variable) on how much alcohol research participants choose to drink (the dependent variable). Finally, two forms of validity are specific to research studies: internal and external validity. **Internal validity** is the extent to which we can be confident that the independent variable is causing the dependent variable to change. **External validity** refers to how well the results relate to things outside your study; in other words, how well your findings describe similar individuals who were not among the study subjects. Although we discuss a variety of research strategies, they all have these basic elements (see Asmundson et al., 2002). Table 4.1 shows the essential components of a research study.

Hypothesis

Human beings look for order and purpose. We want to know why the world works as it does, and why people behave the way they do. Robert Kegan (cited in Lefrancois, 1990) describes us as "meaning-making" organisms, constantly striving to make sense of what is going on around us. In fact, fascinating research from social psychology tells us that we may have a heightened motivation to make sense of the world, especially if we experience situations that seem to threaten our sense of order and meaning (Proulx & Heine, 2009).

The familiar search for meaning and order also characterizes the field of abnormal behaviour. Almost by definition, abnormal behaviour defies the regularity and predictability we desire. It is this departure from the norm that makes the study of abnormal behaviour so intriguing. In an attempt to make sense of these phenomena, behavioural scientists construct hypotheses and then test them. Hypotheses are nothing more than educated guesses about the world. You may believe that watching violent television programs will cause children to be more aggressive. You may think that bulimia is influenced by media depictions of suppos-

edly ideal female body types. You may suspect that someone abused as a child is likely to abuse his or her significant other or child. These concerns are all testable hypotheses.

Once a scientist decides what to study, the next step is to put it in words that are unambiguous and in a form that is testable. Consider a study of how one's self-esteem (how you feel about yourself) affects depression. Ulrich Orth from the University of California–Davis and his colleagues from around the world gathered information from more than 4000 people over a number of years (Orth, Robins, Trzesniewski, Maes, & Schmitt, 2009). They knew from previous research that at least over a short period of time, having feelings of low self-esteem seems to put people at risk for later depression. In their study, these researchers posed the following hypothesis: "Prior low self-esteem will be a predictor of later depression across all age groups of participants." The way the hypothesis is stated suggests the researchers already know the answer to their question. They won't know what they will find until the study is completed, but phrasing the hypothesis in this way makes it testable. If, for example, people with high self-esteem are at equal risk for later depression, then other influences must be studied. This concept of **testability** (the ability to support the hypothesis) is important for science because it allows us to say that in this case, either (1) low self-esteem signals later depression, so maybe we can use this information for prevention efforts, or (2) there is no relationship between self-esteem and depression, so let's look for other early signs that might predict who will become depressed. The researchers did find a strong relationship between early self-esteem and depression for people in all age groups, which may prove useful for detecting people at risk for this debilitating disorder (Orth et al., 2009).

When they develop an experimental hypothesis, researchers also specify dependent and independent variables. A dependent variable is what is expected to change or be influenced by the study. Psychologists studying abnormal behaviour typically measure an aspect of the disorder, such as overt behaviours, thoughts, and feelings, or biological symptoms. In the study by Orth and colleagues, the main dependent variable (level of depression) was measured using the person's responses on a questionnaire about their depression (Center for Epidemiologic Studies Depression Scale). Independent variables are those factors thought to affect the dependent variables. The independent variable in the study was measured using responses on a questionnaire on self-esteem (the Rosenberg Self-Esteem Scale). In other words, changes in self-esteem over the years were thought to influence later levels of depression.

Internal and External Validity

The researchers in the study on self-esteem and depression used responses on the questionnaires collected from two very large studies conducted in the United States and Germany. Suppose they found that, unknown to them, most people who agree to participate in these types of studies have higher self-esteem than people who do not participate. This would have affected the data in a way that would limit what they could conclude about self-esteem and depression and would change the meaning of their results. This situation, which relates to internal validity, is called a **confound** (or **confounding variable**), defined as any factor occurring in a study that makes the results uninterpretable because a variable (in this instance, the type of population being studied) other than the independent variable (having high or low self-esteem) may also affect the dependent variable (depression).

Scientists use many strategies to ensure internal validity in their studies, three of which we discuss here: control groups, randomization, and analogue models. In a **control group**, people are similar to the experimental group in every way except that members of the experimental group are exposed to the independent variable and those in the control group are not. Because researchers can't prevent people from being exposed to many things around them that could affect the outcomes of the study, they try to compare people who receive the treatment with people who go through similar experiences except for the treatment (control group). Control groups help rule out alternative explanations for results, thereby strengthening internal validity.

Randomization is the process of assigning people to different research groups in such a way that each person has an equal chance of being placed in any group. Researchers can, for example, randomly place people in groups but still end up with more of certain people (e.g., people with more severe depression) in one group than another. Placing people in groups by flipping a coin or using a random number table helps improve internal validity by eliminating any systematic bias in assignment, but it does not necessarily eliminate bias in your group. You will see later that people sometimes "put themselves in groups," and this self-selection can affect study results. Perhaps a researcher treating people with depression offers them the choice of being either in the treatment group, which requires coming into the clinic twice a week for two months, or in a wait-list control group, which means waiting until some later time to be treated. The most severely depressed individuals may not be motivated to come to frequent treatment sessions and so will choose the wait-list group. If members of the treated group are less depressed after several months, it could be because of the treatment or because group members were less depressed to begin with. Groups assembled randomly avoid these problems.

Analogue models create in the controlled conditions of the laboratory aspects that are comparable (analogous) to the phenomenon under study. Bulimia researchers could ask volunteers to binge eat in the laboratory, questioning them before they ate, while they were eating, and after they finished to learn whether eating in this way made them feel more or less anxious, guilty, and so on. If they used volunteers of any age, gender, race, or background, the researchers could rule out influences on the participants' attitudes about eating that they might not be able to dismiss if the group contained only people with bulimia. In this way, such "artificial" studies help improve internal validity.

In a research study, internal and external validity often seem to be in opposition. On the one hand, we want to be able to control as many things as possible to conclude that the independent variable (the aspect of the study we manipulated) was responsible for the changes in the dependent variables (the aspects of the study we expected to change). On the other hand, we want the results to apply to people other than the participants of the study and in other settings; this is **generalizability**, the extent to which results apply to everyone with a particular disorder. If we control all aspects of a study so that only the independent variable changes, the result is not relevant to the real world. For example, if you reduce the influence of gender issues by only studying males, and if you reduce age variables by only selecting people from 25 to 30 years of age, and finally, if you limit your study to those with university degrees so that education level isn't an issue—then what you study (in this case, 25- to 30-year-old male university graduates) may not be relevant to many other populations. Internal and external validity are in this way often inversely related. Researchers constantly try to balance these two concerns and, as you will see later in this chapter, the best solution for achieving both internal and external validity may be to conduct several related studies.

Statistical versus Clinical Significance

The introduction of statistics is part of psychology's evolution from a prescientific to a scientific discipline. Statisticians gather, analyze, and interpret data from research. In psychological research, statistical significance typically means the probability of obtaining the observed effect by chance is small. As an example, consider a study evaluating whether a drug (naltrexone)—when added to a psychological intervention—helps those with alcohol addiction stay sober longer (Anton et al., 2006). The study found that the combination of medication and psychotherapy helped people stay abstinent 77 days on average and those receiving a placebo stayed abstinent 75 days on average. This difference was statistically significant. But is it an important difference? The difficulty is in the distinction between **statistical significance** (a mathematical calculation about the difference between groups) and **clinical significance** (whether or not the difference was meaningful for those affected) (Thirthalli & Rajkumar, 2009).

Closer examination of the results leads to concern about the size of the effect. Because this research studied a large group of people dependent on alcohol (1383 volunteers), even this small difference (75 days versus 77 days) was statistically different. However, few of us would say staying sober for two extra days was worth taking medication and participating in extensive therapy—in other words, the difference may not be clinically significant.

Fortunately, concern for the clinical significance of results has led researchers to develop statistical methods that address not just that groups are different but also how large these differences are, or **effect size**. Calculating the actual statistical measures involves fairly sophisticated procedures that take into account how much each treated and untreated person in a research study improves or worsens (Reichardt, 2006). In other words, instead of just looking at the results of the group as a whole, individual differences are considered as well. Some researchers have used more subjective ways of determining whether truly important change has resulted from treatment. The late behavioural scientist Montrose Wolf (1978) advocated the assessment of what he called *social validity*. This technique involves obtaining input from the person being treated, as well as from significant others, about the importance of the changes that have occurred. In the example here, we might ask the participants and family members if they thought the treatment led to truly important improvements in alcohol abstinence. If the effect of the treatment is large enough to impress those who are directly involved, the treatment effect is clinically significant. Statistical techniques of measuring effect size and assessing subjective judgments of change will let us better evaluate the results of our treatments.

The Average Client

Too often we look at results from studies and make generalizations about the group, ignoring individual differences. Kiesler (1966) labelled the tendency to see all participants as one homogeneous group the **patient uniformity myth**. Comparing groups according to their mean scores ("Group A improved by 50 percent over Group B") hides important differences in individual reactions to our interventions.

The patient uniformity myth leads researchers to make inaccurate generalizations about disorders and their treatments. To continue with our previous example, what if the researchers studying the treatment of alcoholism concluded that the experimental treatment was a good approach? And suppose we found that, although some participants improved with treatment, others worsened. Such differences would be averaged out in the analysis of the group as a whole, but for the person whose drinking increased with the experimental treatment, it would make little difference that "on the average" people improved. Because people differ in such ways as age, cognitive abilities, gender, and history of treatment, a simple group comparison may be misleading. Practitioners who deal with all types of disorders understand the heterogeneity of their clients and therefore do not know whether treatments that are statistically significant will be effective for a given individual. In our discussions of various disorders, we return to this issue.

▲ Studying people as part of a group sometimes masks individual differences.

In each of the statements provided, fill in the blanks with one of the following: hypothesis, dependent variable, independent variable, internal validity, external validity, or confound.

1. In a treatment study, the introduction of the treatment to the participants is referred to as the _____.

2. After the treatment study was completed, you found that many people in the control group received treatment outside of the study. This is called a _____.

3. A researcher's guess about what a study might find is labelled the _____.

4. Scores on a depression scale improved for a treatment group after therapy. The change in these scores would be referred to as a change in the _____.

5. A relative lack of confounds in a study would indicate good _____, whereas good generalizability of the results would be called good _____.

Studying Individual Cases

Consider the following scenario: A psychologist thinks she has discovered a new disorder. She has observed several men who seem to have similar characteristics. All complain of a specific sleep disorder: falling asleep at work. Each man has obvious cognitive impairments that were evident during the initial interviews, and all are similar physically, each with significant hair loss and a pear-shaped physique. Finally, their personality styles are extremely egocentric, or self-centred. On the basis of these preliminary observations, the psychologist has come up with a tentative name, the Homer Simpson disorder, and she has decided to investigate this condition and possible treatments. But what is the best way to begin exploring a relatively unknown disorder? One method is to use the **case study method**, investigating intensively one or more individuals who display the behavioural and physical patterns (Borckardt et al., 2008).

One way to describe the case study method is by noting what it is not. It does not use the scientific method. Few efforts are made to ensure internal validity and, typically, many confounding variables are present that can interfere with conclusions. Instead, the case study method relies on a clinician's observations of differences among one person or one group with a disorder, people with other disorders, and people with no psychological disorders. The clinician usually collects as much information as possible to obtain a detailed description of the person. Historically, interviewing the person

Hamamariah/Shutterstock

under study yields a great deal of information on personal and family background, education, health, and work history, as well as the person's opinions about the nature and causes of the problems being studied.

Case studies are important in the history of psychology. Sigmund Freud developed psychoanalytic theory and the methods of psychoanalysis on the basis of his observations of dozens of cases. Freud and Josef Breuer's description of Anna O. (see Chapter 1) led to development of the clinical technique known as free association. Sexuality researchers Virginia Johnson and William Masters based their work on many case studies and helped shed light on numerous myths regarding sexual behaviour (Masters & Johnson, 1966). Joseph Wolpe, author of the landmark book *Psychotherapy by Reciprocal Inhibition* (1958), based his work with systematic desensitization on more than 200 cases. As our knowledge of psychological disorders has grown, psychological researchers' reliance on the case study method has gradually decreased.

One difficulty with depending heavily on individual cases is that sometimes coincidences occur that are irrelevant to the condition under study. Unfortunately, coincidences in people's lives often lead to mistaken conclusions about what causes certain conditions and what treatment appears to be effective. Because a case study does not have the controls of an experimental study, the results may be unique to a particular person without the researcher realizing it or may derive from a special combination of factors that are not obvious. Complicating our efforts to understand abnormal behaviour is the portrayal of sensational cases in the media. Just before mass murderer Ted Bundy was executed, he proclaimed that pornography was to blame for his abhorrent behaviour. The case of Jeffrey Dahmer, who killed, mutilated, and cannibalized his victims, is known throughout the world. Attempts have been made to discover childhood experiences that could possibly explain both men's adult behaviour. What conclusions should we draw? Did Bundy have valuable insight into his own behaviour, or was he attempting to evade responsibility? Can acquaintances and friends of the Dahmer family shed accurate light on his development? We must be careful about concluding anything from such sensational portrayals.

Researchers in cognitive psychology point out that the public and researchers themselves are often, unfortunately, more highly influenced by dramatic accounts than by scientific evidence (Nisbett & Ross, 1980). Remembering our tendency to ignore this fact, we highlight research findings in this book. To advance our understanding of the nature, causes, and treatment of abnormal behaviour, we must guard against premature and inaccurate conclusions.

Research by Correlation

One of the fundamental questions posed by scientists is whether two variables relate to each other. A statistical relationship between two variables is called a **correlation**. For example, is schizophrenia related to the size of ventricles (spaces) in the brain? Are people with depression more likely to have negative attributions (negative explanations for their own and others' behaviour)? Is the frequency of hallucinations higher among older people? The answers depend on determining how one variable (e.g., number of hallucinations) is related to another (e.g., age). Unlike experimental designs, which involve manipulating or changing conditions, correlational designs are used to study phenomena just as they occur. The result of a correlational study—whether variables occur together—is important to the ongoing search for knowledge about abnormal behaviour.

One of the clichés of science is that correlation does not imply causation. In other words, two things occurring together does not necessarily mean that one caused the other. For example, the occurrence of marital problems in families is correlated with behaviour problems in children (Erath, Bierman, & Conduct Problems Prevention Research Group, 2006). If you conduct a correlational study in this area, you will find that in families with marital problems you tend to see children with behaviour problems; in families with fewer marital problems, you are likely to find children with fewer behaviour problems. The most obvious conclusion is that having marital problems will cause children to misbehave. If only it were as simple as that! The nature of the relationship between marital discord and childhood behaviour problems can be explained in a number of ways. It may be that problems in a marriage cause disruptive behaviour in the children. However, some evidence suggests the opposite may be true as well: The disruptive behaviour of children may cause marital problems (Rutter & Giller, 1984). In addition, evidence suggests genetic influences may play a role in conduct disorders and in marital discord (D'Onofrio et al., 2006; Lynch et al., 2006). So parents who are genetically more inclined to argue pass on those genes to children who then have an increased tendency to misbehave.

This example points out the problems in interpreting the results of a correlational study. We know that variable A (marital problems) is correlated with variable B (child behaviour problems). We do not know from these studies whether A causes B (marital problems cause child problems), whether B causes A (child problems cause marital problems), or whether some third variable, C, causes both (genes influence both marital problems and child problems).

The association between marital discord and child problems represents a **positive correlation**. This means that great strength or quantity in one variable (a great deal of marital distress) is associated with great strength or quantity in the other variable (more child disruptive behaviour). At the same time, lower strength or quantity in one variable (marital distress) is associated with lower strength or quantity in the other (disruptive behaviour). If you have trouble conceptualizing statistical concepts, you can think about this mathematical relationship in the same way you would a social relationship. Two people who are getting along well tend to go places together: "Where I go, you will go!" The correlation (or **correlation coefficient**) is represented as +1.00. The plus sign means there is a positive relationship, and the 1.00 means that it is a "perfect" relationship, in which the people are inseparable. Obviously, two people who like each other do not go everywhere together. The strength of their relationship ranges between 0.00 and +1.00 (0.00 means no relationship exists). The higher the number, the stronger the relationship, whether the number is positive or negative (e.g., a correlation of +0.80 is "stronger" than a correlation of +0.75). You would expect two

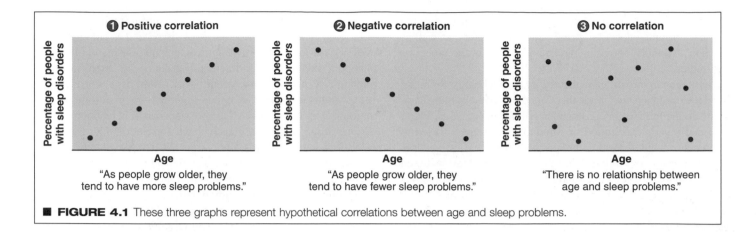

①Positive correlation

Percentage of people with sleep disorders

Age

"As people grow older, they tend to have more sleep problems."

②Negative correlation

Percentage of people with sleep disorders

Age

"As people grow older, they tend to have fewer sleep problems."

③No correlation

Percentage of people with sleep disorders

Age

"There is no relationship between age and sleep problems."

■ **FIGURE 4.1** These three graphs represent hypothetical correlations between age and sleep problems.

strangers, for example, to have a relationship of 0.00 because their behaviour is not related; they sometimes end up in the same place together, but this occurs rarely and randomly. Two people who know each other but do not like each other would be represented by a negative sign, with the strongest negative relationship being –1.00, which means, "Anywhere you go, I won't be there!"

Using this analogy, marital problems in families and behaviour problems in children have a relatively strong positive correlation represented by a number around +0.50. They tend to go together. On the other hand, other variables are strangers to each other. Schizophrenia and height are not related, so they don't go together and probably would be represented by a number close to 0.00. If A and B have no correlation, their correlation coefficient would approximate 0.00. Other factors have negative relationships: As one increases, the other decreases. (See ■ Figure 4.1 for an illustration of positive and negative correlations.) We used an example of **negative correlation** in Chapter 2, when we discussed social supports and illness. The more social supports that are present, the less likely it is that a person will become ill. The

negative relationship between social supports and illness could be represented by a number such as –0.40. The next time someone wants to break up with you, ask if the goal is to weaken the strength of your positive relationship to something like +0.25 (friends), to become complete strangers at 0.00, or to have an intense negative relationship approximating –1.00 (enemies).

A correlation allows us to see whether a relationship exists between two variables but not to draw conclusions about whether either variable causes the effects. This is a problem of **directionality**. In this case, it means that we do not know whether A causes B, B causes A, or a third variable, C, causes A and B. Therefore, even an extremely strong relationship between two variables (+0.90) shows nothing about the direction of causality.

Epidemiological Research

Scientists often think of themselves as detectives, searching for the truth by studying clues. One type of correlational research that is very much like the efforts of detectives is called **epidemiology**, the study of the incidence, distribution, and consequences of a particular problem or set of problems in one or more populations. Epidemiologists expect that by tracking a disorder among many people, they will find important clues to why the disorder exists. One strategy is to determine the **incidence** of a disorder, the estimated number of new cases during a specific period. For example, as we see in Chapter 11, the incidence of new cases of cocaine use has been decreasing over the past decade among most age groups in Canada. A related strategy involves determining **prevalence**, the number of people with a disorder at any one time. For example, the prevalence of alcohol dependence among Canadian adults is about 3 percent (Statistics Canada, 2002a). Epidemiologists study the incidence and prevalence of disorders among different groups of people. For instance, data from epidemiological research conducted by Statistics Canada

▲ The more social supports people have, the less likely it is that they will become ill.

indicate that the prevalence of alcohol dependence among women is substantially lower than among men (Statistics Canada, 2002a).

Although the primary goal of epidemiology is to determine the extent of medical problems, it is also useful in the study of psychological disorders. In the early 20th century, many people displayed symptoms of a strange mental disorder. Its symptoms were similar to those of organic psychosis, which is often caused by mind-altering drugs or great quantities of alcohol. Many patients appeared catatonic (immobile for long periods) or exhibited symptoms similar to those of paranoid schizophrenia. Victims were likely to be poor, which led to speculation about class inferiority. However, using the methods of epidemiological research, Goldberger found correlations between the disorder and diet, and he identified the cause of the disorder as a deficiency of the B vitamin niacin among people with poor diets. The symptoms were successfully eliminated by niacin therapy and improved diets. A long-term, widespread benefit of Goldberger's findings was the introduction of vitamin-enriched bread in the 1940s (Colp, 2009).

Researchers have used epidemiological techniques to study the effects of stress on psychological disorders. For example, researchers have examined the psychological effects of the September 11, 2001, terrorist attacks on the World Trade Center and the American Pentagon. Following those events, Blanchard et al. (2004) examined rates of two anxiety disorders—acute stress disorder and post-traumatic stress disorder (see Chapter 5)—in three samples of university students: those attending the University of Albany in New York state, those attending North Dakota State University in North Dakota, and those attending Augusta State University in Georgia. They found significantly greater rates of both acute stress disorder (28 percent versus 10 percent versus 19 percent, respectively) and post-traumatic stress disorder (11 percent versus 3 percent versus 7 percent, respectively) in the University of Albany students.

A similar study conducted in Saskatchewan by Gordon Asmundson and his colleagues showed rates of disorder comparable to those obtained by Blanchard and colleagues (2004) in the students from North Dakota and Georgia. More specifically, about 4 percent of the Canadian sample met the criteria for full or partial post-traumatic stress disorder following the events of September 11, 2001 (Asmundson, Carleton, Wright, & Taylor, 2004).

Taken together, these findings suggest a relationship between geographical proximity and impact of the trauma, with those living closer to the site of the terrorist attacks showing the greatest levels of distress. The studies by Blanchard et al. (2004) and Asmundson et al. (2004) are correlational studies because the investigators did not manipulate the independent variable. (They weren't involved in committing the terrorist acts!) Despite their correlational nature, these studies do show a relationship between stress and psychological problems.

Like other types of correlational research, epidemiological research can't tell us conclusively what causes a particular phenomenon. However, knowledge about the prevalence and course of psychological disorders is extremely valuable to our understanding, because it points researchers in the right direction.

Research by Experiment

An **experiment** involves the manipulation of an independent variable and the observation of its effects. We manipulate the independent variable to answer the question of causality. If we observe a correlation between social supports and psychological disorders, we can't conclude which of these factors influenced the other. We can, however, change the extent of social supports and see whether it triggers an accompanying change in the prevalence of psychological disorders—in other words, do an experiment.

What will this experiment tell us about the relationship between these two variables? If we increase the number of social supports and find no change in the frequency of psychological disorders, it may mean that the lack of such supports does not cause psychological problems. However, if we find that psychological disorders diminish with increased social support, we can be more confident that lack of support does contribute to disorders. However, because we are never 100 percent confident that our experiments are internally valid—that no other explanations are possible—we are cautious about interpreting our results. In the following section, we describe different ways researchers conduct experiments and consider how each one brings us closer to understanding abnormal behaviour.

Group Experimental Designs

With correlational designs, researchers observe groups to see how different variables are associated. In group experimental designs, researchers are more active. They actually change an independent variable to see how the behaviour of the people in the group is affected. Suppose researchers design an intervention to help reduce insomnia in older adults, who are particularly affected by the condition (Ancoli-Israel & Ayalon, 2009). They treat a number of individuals and follow them for ten years to learn whether their sleep patterns improve. The treatment is the independent variable; that is, it would not have occurred naturally. They then assess the treated group to learn whether their behaviour changed as a function of what the researchers did. Introducing or withdrawing a variable in a way that would not have occurred naturally is called *manipulating a variable*.

Unfortunately, a decade later the researchers find that the older adults treated for sleep problems still, as a group, sleep less than eight hours per night. Is the treatment a failure? Maybe not. The question that can't be answered in this study is what would have happened to group members if they hadn't been treated. Perhaps their sleep patterns would have been worse. Fortunately, researchers have devised ingenious methods to help sort out these complicated questions.

A special type of group experimental design is used more and more frequently in the treatment of psychological disorders and is referred to as a *clinical trial* (Durand & Wang, in press). A clinical trial is an experiment used to determine the effectiveness and safety of a treatment or treatments. The term clinical trial implies a level of formality with regard to how it is conducted. As a result, a clinical trial is not a design by itself but rather a method of evaluation that follows a number of generally accepted rules. For example, these rules cover how you should select the research participants, how many individuals should be included in the study, how they should be assigned to groups, and how the data should be analyzed—and this represents only a partial list. Also, treatments are usually applied using formal protocols to ensure that everyone is treated the same.

The terms used to describe these experiments can be confusing. "Clinical trials" is the overarching term used to describe the general category of studies that follow the standards described previously. Within the "clinical trial" category are "randomized clinical trials," which are experiments that employ randomization of participants into each experimental group. Another subset of clinical trials is "controlled clinical trials" which are used to describe experiments that rely on control conditions to be used for comparison purposes. Finally, the preferred method of conducting a clinical trial, which uses both randomization and one or more control conditions, is referred to as a "randomized controlled trial." We next describe the nature of control groups and randomization, and discuss their importance in **treatment outcome research**.

Control Groups

One answer to the what-if dilemma is to use a control group—people who are similar to the experimental group in every way except they are not exposed to the independent variable. In the previous study looking at sleep in older adults, suppose another group who didn't receive treatment was selected. Further suppose that the researchers also follow this group of people, assess them ten years later, and look at their sleep patterns over this time. They probably observe that, without intervention, people tend to sleep fewer hours as they get older (Cho et al., 2008). Members of the control group, then, might sleep significantly less than people in the treated group, who might themselves sleep somewhat less than they did ten years earlier. The control group allows the researchers to see that their treatment did help the treated participants keep their sleep time from decreasing further.

Ideally, a control group is nearly identical to the treatment group in such factors as age, gender, socioeconomic backgrounds, and the problems they are reporting. Furthermore, a researcher would do the same assessments before and after the independent variable manipulation (e.g., a treatment) to people in both groups. Any later differences between the groups after the change would, therefore, be attributable only to what was changed.

People in a treatment group often expect to get better. When behaviour changes as a result of a person's expectation of change rather than as a result of any manipulation by an experimenter, the phenomenon is known as a **placebo effect** (from the Latin, which means "I shall please"). Conversely, people in the control group may be disappointed that they are not receiving treatment (analogously, we could label this a *frustro effect*, from the Latin "to disappoint"). Depending on the type of disorder they experience (e.g., depression), disappointment may make them worse. This phenomenon would also make the treatment group look better by comparison.

One way researchers address the expectation concern is through **placebo control groups**. The word *placebo* typically refers to inactive medications such as sugar pills. The placebo is given to members of the control group to make them believe they are getting treatment (Wampold, Minami, Tierney, Baskin, & Bhati, 2005). A placebo control in a medication study can be carried out with relative ease because people in the untreated group receive something that looks like the medication administered to the treatment group. In psychological treatments, however, it is not always easy to devise something that people believe may help them but does not include the component the researcher believes is effective. Clients in these types of control groups are often given part of the actual therapy—for example, the same homework as the treated group—but not the portions the researchers believe are responsible for improvements.

Note that you can look at the placebo effect as one portion of any treatment (Kendall & Comer, in press). If someone you provide with a treatment improves, you would have to attribute the improvement to a combination of your treatment and the client's expectation of improving (placebo effect). Therapists want their clients to expect improvement; this helps strengthen the treatment. However, when researchers conduct an experiment to determine what portion of a particular treatment is responsible for the observed changes, the placebo effect is a confound that can dilute the validity of the research. Thus, researchers use a placebo control group to help distinguish the results of positive expectations from the results of actual treatment.

The **double-blind control** is a variant of the placebo control group procedure. As the name suggests, not only are the participants in the study "blind," or unaware of what group they are in or what treatment they are given (single blind), but so are the researchers or therapists providing treatment (double blind). This type of control eliminates the possibility that an investigator might bias the outcome. For example, a researcher comparing two treatments who expected one to be more effective than the other might "try harder" if the "preferred" treatment wasn't working as well as expected. On the other hand, if the treatment that wasn't expected to work seemed to be failing, the researcher might not push as hard to see it succeed. This reaction might not be deliberate, but it does happen. This phenomenon is referred to as an *allegiance effect* (Leykin & DeRubeis, 2009). If, however, both the participants and the researchers or therapists are "blind," there is less chance that bias will affect the results.

A double-blind placebo control does not work perfectly in all cases. If medication is part of the treatment, participants and researchers may be able to tell whether or not they have received it by the presence or absence of physical reactions (side effects). Even with purely psychological interventions, participants often know whether or not they are receiving a powerful treatment, and they may alter their expectations for improvement accordingly.

Comparative Treatment Research

As an alternative to using no-treatment control groups to help evaluate results, some researchers compare different treatments. In this design, the researcher gives different treatments to two or more comparable groups of people with a particular disorder and can then assess how or whether each treatment helped the people who received it. This is called **comparative treatment research**. In the sleep study we discussed, two groups of older adults could be selected, with one group given medication for insomnia, the other given a cognitive-behavioural intervention, and the results compared.

▲ In comparative treatment research, different treatments are administered to comparable groups of people.

The *process* and *outcome* of treatment are two important issues to be considered when different approaches are studied. *Process research* focuses on the mechanisms responsible for behaviour change, or "why does it work?" In an old joke, someone goes to a physician for a new miracle cold cure. The physician prescribes the new drug and tells the patient the cold will be gone in seven to ten days. As most of us know, colds typically improve in seven to ten days without so-called miracle drugs. The new drug probably does nothing to further the improvement of the patient's cold. The process aspect of testing medical interventions involves evaluating biological mechanisms responsible for change. Does the medication cause lower serotonin levels, for example, and does this account for the changes we observe? Similarly, in looking at psychological interventions, we determine what is "causing" the observed changes. This is important for several reasons. First, if we understand what the "active ingredients" of our treatment are, we can often eliminate aspects that are not important, thereby saving clients' time and money. For an example, one study of insomnia found that adding a relaxation training component to a treatment package provided no additional benefit— allowing clinicians to reduce the amount of training and focus on only those aspects that really improve sleep (e.g., cognitive-behavioural therapy) (Harvey, Inglis, & Espie, 2002). In addition, knowing what is important about our interventions can help us create more powerful, newer versions that may be more effective.

Outcome research focuses on the positive, negative, or both results of the treatment. In other words, does it work? Remember, *treatment process* involves finding out why or how your treatment works. In contrast, treatment outcome involves finding out what changes occur after treatment.

Single-Case Experimental Designs

B. F. Skinner's innovations in scientific methodology were among his most important contributions to psychopathology. Skinner formalized the concept of **single-case experimental**

designs. This method involves the systematic study of individuals under a variety of experimental conditions. Skinner thought it was much better to know a lot about the behaviour of one individual than to make only a few observations of a large group for the sake of presenting the "average" response. Psychopathology is concerned with the suffering of specific people, and this methodology has greatly helped us understand the factors involved in individual psychopathology (Barlow, Nock, & Hersen, 2009). Many applications throughout this book reflect Skinnerian methods.

Single-case experimental designs differ from case studies in their use of various strategies to improve internal validity, thereby reducing the number of confounding variables. As you will see, these strategies have strengths and weaknesses in comparison with traditional group designs. Although we use examples from treatment research to illustrate the single-case experimental designs, they, like other research strategies, can help explain why people engage in abnormal behaviour, as well as how to treat them.

Repeated Measurements

One of the more important strategies used in single-case experimental design is **repeated measurement**, in which a behaviour is measured several times instead of only once before you change the independent variable and once afterward. The researcher takes the same measurements repeatedly to learn how variable the behaviour is (How much does it change from day to day?) and whether it shows any obvious trends (Is it getting better or worse?). Suppose a young woman, Wendy, comes into the office complaining about feelings of anxiety. When asked to rate the level of her anxiety, she gives it a nine (ten is the worst). After several weeks of treatment, Wendy rates her anxiety at six. Can we say that the treatment reduced her anxiety? Not necessarily.

Suppose we had measured Wendy's anxiety each day during the weeks before her visit to the office (repeated measurement) and observed that it differed greatly. On particularly good days, she rated her anxiety from five to seven. On bad days, it was up between eight and ten. Suppose further that, even after treatment, her daily ratings continued to range from five to ten. The rating of nine before treatment and six after treatment may only have been part of the daily variations she experienced normally. Wendy could just as easily have had a good day and reported a six before treatment and then had a bad day and reported a nine after treatment, which would imply that the treatment made her worse!

Repeated measurement is part of each single-subject experimental design. It helps identify how a person is doing before and after intervention and whether the treatment accounted for any changes. ■ Figure 4.2 summarizes Wendy's anxiety and the added information obtained by repeated measurement. The top graph shows Wendy's original before-and-after ratings of her anxiety. The middle graph shows that with daily ratings her reports are variable and that just by chance the previous measurement was probably misleading. She had good and bad days

both before and after treatment and doesn't seem to have changed much.

The bottom graph shows a different possibility: Wendy's anxiety was on its way down before the treatment, which would also have been obscured with just before-and-after measurements. Maybe she was getting better on her own and the treatment didn't have much effect. Although the middle graph shows how the **variability** from day to day could be important in an interpretation of the effect of treatment, the bottom graph shows how the **trend** itself can also be important in determining the cause of any change. The three graphs illustrate important parts of repeated measurements: (1) the **level** or degree of behaviour change with different interventions (top); (2) the variability or degree of change over time (middle); and (3) the trend or direction of change (bottom). Again, before-and-after scores alone do not necessarily show what is responsible for behavioural changes.

Withdrawal Designs

One of the more common strategies used in single-subject research is a **withdrawal design**, in which a researcher tries to determine whether the independent variable is responsible for changes in behaviour. The effect of Wendy's treatment could be tested by stopping it for some time to see whether her anxiety increased. A simple withdrawal design has three parts. First, a person's condition is evaluated before treatment, to establish a **baseline**. Then comes the change in the independent variable—in Wendy's case, the beginning of treatment. Last, treatment is withdrawn ("return to baseline") and the researcher assesses whether Wendy's anxiety level changes again as a function of this last step. If with the treatment her anxiety lessens in comparison to baseline and then worsens after treatment is withdrawn, the researcher can conclude the treatment has reduced Wendy's anxiety.

How is this design different from a case study? An important difference is that the change in treatment is designed specifically to show whether treatment caused the changes in behaviour. Although case studies often involve treatment, they don't include any effort to learn whether the person would have improved without the treatment. A withdrawal design gives researchers a better sense of whether or not the treatment itself caused behaviour change.

Despite their advantages, withdrawal designs are not always appropriate. The

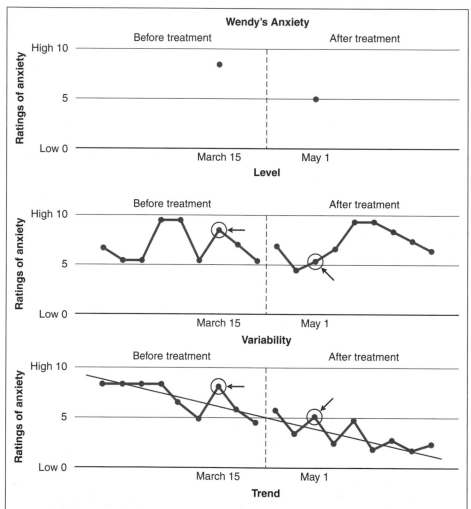

■ **FIGURE 4.2** The top graph seems to show Wendy's anxiety dropping significantly after treatment (measuring level). However, when you look at repeated measures before and after treatment, the middle graph reveals little change because her anxiety fluctuated a great deal (measuring variability). A different scenario is illustrated in the bottom graph (measuring trend), where her anxiety also varied. In general, there was a downward movement (improved anxiety) even before treatment, suggesting that she might have improved without help. Examining variability and trend can provide more information about the true nature of the change.

researcher is required to remove what might be an effective treatment, a decision that is sometimes difficult to justify for ethical reasons. In Wendy's case, a researcher would have to decide there was a sufficient reason to risk making her anxious again. A withdrawal design is also unsuitable when the treatment can't be removed. Suppose Wendy's treatment involved visualizing herself on a beach on a tropical island. It would be difficult—if not impossible—to stop her from imagining something. Similarly, some treatments involve teaching people skills, which might be impossible to unlearn. If Wendy learned how to be less anxious in social situations, how could she revert to being socially apprehensive?

Several counterarguments support the use of withdrawal designs (Barlow et al., 2009). Treatment is routinely withdrawn when medications are involved. *Drug holidays* are periods when the medication is withdrawn so that clinicians can determine whether it is responsible for the treatment effects. Any medication can have negative side effects, and unnecessary medication should be avoided. Sometimes treatment withdrawal happens naturally. Withdrawal does not have to be prolonged; a brief withdrawal may still clarify the role of the treatment.

Multiple Baselines

Another single-case experimental design strategy used often that doesn't have some of the drawbacks of a withdrawal design is the **multiple baseline**. Rather than stopping the intervention to see whether it is effective, the researcher starts treatment at different times across settings (home versus school), behaviours (yelling at spouse/partner or boss), or people. After waiting for a while and taking repeated measures of Wendy's anxiety both at home and at her office (the baseline), the clinician could treat her first at home. When the treatment begins to be effective, intervention could begin at work. If she improves only at home after beginning treatment but improves at work after treatment is used there also, we could conclude the treatment was effective. This is an example of using a multiple baseline across settings. Does internal validity improve with a multiple baseline? Yes. Any time other explanations for results can be ruled out, internal validity is improved. Wendy's anxiety improved only in the settings where it was treated, which rules out competing explanations for her anxiety reduction. However, if she had won the lottery at the same time treatment started and her anxiety decreased in all situations, we couldn't conclude her condition was affected by treatment.

Suppose a researcher wanted to assess the effectiveness of a treatment for a child's problem behaviours. Treatment could focus first on the child's crying then on a second problem, such as fighting with siblings. If the treatment was first effective only in reducing crying, and effective for reducing fighting only after the second intervention, the researcher could conclude that the treatment, not something else, accounted for the improvements. This is a multiple baseline conducted across behaviours.

Single-case experimental designs are sometimes criticized because they tend to involve only a small number of cases, leaving their external validity in doubt. In other words, we can't say the results we saw with a few people would be the same for everyone. However, although they are called *single-case* designs, researchers can and often do use them with several people at once, in part to address the issue of external validity. One of us studied the effectiveness of a treatment for the severe behaviour problems of children with autism (Durand, 1999) (see ■ Figure 4.3 on page 116). We taught the children to communicate instead of misbehave, using a procedure known as *functional communication training* (we discuss this in more detail in Chapter 14). Using a multiple baseline, we introduced this treatment to a group of five children. Our dependent variables were the incidence of the children's behaviour problems and their newly acquired communication skills. As Figure 4.3 shows, only when we began treatment did each child's behaviour problems improve and communication begin. This multiple baseline design let us rule out coincidence or some other change in the children's lives as explanations for the improvements.

Among the advantages of the multiple baseline design in evaluating treatments is that it does not require withdrawal of treatment and, as you've seen, withdrawing treatment is sometimes difficult or impossible. Furthermore, the multiple baseline typically resembles the way treatment would naturally be implemented. A clinician can't help a client with numerous problems simultaneously but can take repeated measures of the relevant behaviours and observe when they change. A clinician who sees predictable and orderly changes related to where and when the treatment is used can conclude the treatment is causing the change.

Concept Check | 4.2

Check your understanding of research methods by indicating which would be most appropriate in each of the following situations. Choose from (a) case study, (b) correlation, (c) randomized clinical trials, (d) epidemiology, (e) experiment, and (f) single-case experimental design.

1. A researcher changes the level of noise several times to see how it affects concentration in a group of people.

   _____

2. A group of researchers uses chance assignment to include participants in one of two treatment groups and uses published protocols to make sure treatment is applied uniformly. _____

3. A researcher wants to investigate the hypothesis that children listen to louder music as they go through adolescence. _____

4. A researcher is interested in studying a woman who had no contact with civilization and created her own language. _____

5. A researcher wants to know how different kinds of music will affect a five-year-old who has never spoken.

   _____

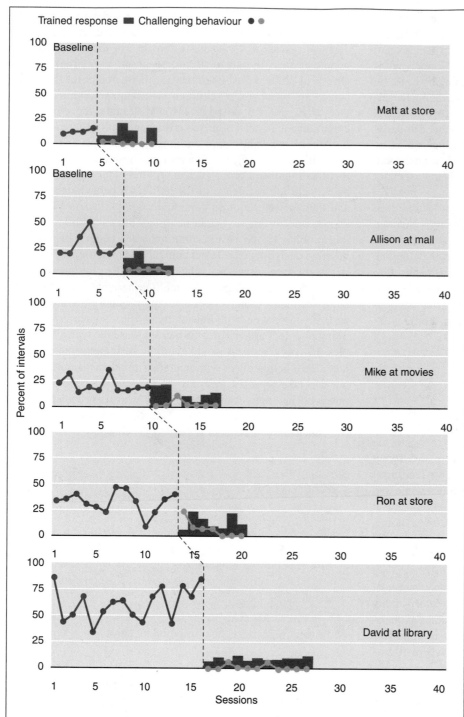

■ **FIGURE 4.3** This figure shows how a multiple baseline design was used to illustrate that the treatment—functional communication training—was responsible for improvements in the children's behaviours. The circles represent how often each child exhibited behaviour problems (called challenging behaviour), and the blue-shaded areas show how often they communicated without help from the teacher (referred to as unprompted communication).

Source: From "Functional Communication Training Using Assistive Devices: Recruiting Natural Communities of Reinforcement" by V. Mark Durand from *Journal of Applied Behavior Analysis, Vol. 32, No. 3,* Fall 1999, pp. 247–267. Reprinted by permission of the Society for the Experimental Analysis of Human Behavior.

Studying Genetics

We tend to think of genetics in terms of what we inherit from our parents: "He's got his mother's eyes." "She's thin just like her dad." "She's stubborn like her mother." This simple view of how we become the people we are suggests that how we look, think, feel, and behave is predetermined. Yet, as you saw in Chapter 2, we now know that the interaction between our genetic makeup and our experiences is what determines how we will develop. The goal of behavioural geneticists (people who study the genetics of behaviour) is to tease out the role of genetics in these interactions.

Genetic researchers examine **phenotypes**, the observable characteristics or behaviour of the individual, and **genotypes**, the unique genetic makeup of individual people. For example, a person with Down syndrome typically has some level of intellectual disability and a variety of other physical characteristics, such as slanted eyes and a thick tongue. These characteristics are the phenotype. The genotype is the extra 21st chromosome that causes Down syndrome.

Our knowledge of the phenotypes of different psychological disorders exceeds our knowledge of the genotypes, but that may soon change. Ever since the discovery of the double helix in 1953 by James Watson and Francis Crick, scientists have known we have to map the structure and location of every gene on all 46 chromosomes if we are to fully understand our genetic endowment. Beginning in 1990, scientists around the world, in a coordinated effort, began the **human genome project** (*genome* means all the genes of an organism). Using the latest advances in molecular biology, scientists working on this project completed a rough draft of the mapping of the approximately 25 000 human genes. This work identified hundreds of genes that contribute to inherited diseases. These exciting findings represent truly astounding progress in deciphering the nature of genetic endowment and its role in psychological disorders.

With the rapid advance of science, a third concept is now the focus of intense study—**endophenotypes**. Endophenotypes are the genetic mechanisms that ultimately contribute to the underlying problems causing the symptoms and difficulties experienced by people with psychological disorders (Grebb & Carlsson, 2009). In the case of schizophrenia (a disorder we discuss in Chapter 13), for example, researchers are not looking for a "schizophrenia gene" (genotype); instead, they are searching for the gene or genes responsible for the working memory problems characteristic of people with this disorder (endophenotype), as well as the genes responsible for other problems experienced by people with this disorder.

What follows is a brief review of the research strategies scientists use as they study the interaction between environment and genetics in psychological disorders. These complex approaches can be summarized into four categories: basic genetic epidemiology, advanced genetic epidemiology, gene finding, and molecular genetics (Kendler, 2005) (see Table 4.2). The table shows that these categories form a progression that starts by finding whether a disorder has a genetic component (basic genetic epidemiology). Once this is established, researchers explore the nature of the genetic influences by seeing how genetics affect aspects of the disorder (advanced genetic epidemiology). Going deeper still, scientists use sophisticated statistical methods (linkage and association studies), which we describe next, to find out just where the gene or genes are located in the genome (gene finding). Finally, switching to biological strategies, scientists are just at the genesis of examining what these genes do and how they interact with the environment to create the symptoms associated with psychological disorders (molecular genetics).

The specific research techniques used in the study of genetics—family studies, adoption studies, twin studies, genetic linkage analysis, and association studies—are described next.

▲ Although family members often resemble each other, genetics has to do with far more than what we inherit from our parents.

TABLE 4.2 The Basic Approaches Used to Assess Gene–Environment Influences in Psychological Disorders

Approach	Method	Question
Basic genetic epidemiology	Statistical analysis of family, twin, and adoption studies	Is the disorder inherited (heritability), and if so, how much of the disorder is attributable to genetics?
Advanced genetic epidemiology	Statistical analysis of family, twin, and adoption studies	If the disorder is found to be inherited, what are the factors that influence the disorder (e.g., is the change something that occurs early in development, is it different between males and females, and do the genetic influences affect environmental risk factors?)?
Gene finding	Statistical analysis of specific families or individuals (linkage and/or association studies)	Where is the gene (or genes) that influences the disorder?
Molecular genetics	Biological analysis of individual DNA samples	What biological processes do the genes affect to produce the symptoms of the disorder?

Source: Adapted from Kendler, K. S. (2005). Psychiatric genetics: A methodological critique. In N. C. Andreasen (Ed.), *Research advances in genetics and genomics: Implications for psychiatry* (Table I, p. 6). Washington, DC: American Psychiatric Publishing.

Family Studies

In **family studies**, scientists simply examine a behavioural pattern or emotional trait in the context of the family. The family member with the trait singled out for study is called the **proband**. If there is a genetic influence, presumably the trait should occur more often in first-degree relatives (parents, siblings, or offspring) than in second-degree or more distant relatives. The presence of the trait in distant relatives, in turn, should be somewhat greater than in the population as a whole. In Chapter 1 you met Jody, the adolescent with blood-injury-injection phobia who fainted at the sight of blood. The tendency of a trait to run in families, or familial aggregation, is as high as 60 percent for this disorder; that is, 60 percent of the first-degree relatives of someone with blood-injury-injection phobia have the same reaction to at least some degree. This is one of the highest rates of familial aggregation for any psychological disorder we have studied.

The problem with family studies is that family members tend to live together and there might be something in their shared environment that causes the high familial aggregation. For example, Mom might have developed a bad reaction to blood as a young girl after witnessing a serious accident. Every time she sees blood she has a strong emotional response. Because emotions are contagious, the young children watching Mom probably react similarly. In adulthood, they pass it on, in turn, to their own children.

Adoption Studies

How do we separate environmental from genetic influences in families? One way is through **adoption studies**. Scientists identify adoptees who have a particular behavioural pattern or psychological disorder and attempt to locate first-degree relatives who were raised in different family settings. Suppose a young man has a disorder and scientists discover his brother was adopted as a baby and brought up in a different home. The researchers would then examine the brother to see whether he also displays signs of the disorder. If they can identify enough sibling pairs (and they usually do after a lot of hard work), they can assess whether siblings brought up in different families display the disorder to the same extent as the original participant. If the siblings raised with different families have the disorder more often than would be expected by chance, the researchers can infer that genetic endowment is a contributor.

Twin Studies

Nature presents an elegant experiment that gives behavioural geneticists their closest possible look at the role of genes in development: identical (monozygotic) twins. These twins not only look alike but they have identical genes. Fraternal (dizygotic) twins, conversely, come from different eggs and have only about 50 percent of their genes in common, as do all first-degree relatives. In **twin studies**, the obvious scientific question is whether identical twins share the same trait—say, fainting at the sight of blood—more often than fraternal twins. Determining whether a trait is shared is easy with some physical traits, such as height. As Robert Plomin from the Institute of Psychiatry in London, England, points out, correlations in height for both first-degree relatives and fraternal twins are 0.45, and 0.90 for identical twins (Plomin, 1990). These findings show that heritability of height is about 90 percent, so approximately 10 percent of the variance is due to environmental factors. However, remember that this 90 percent heritability estimate is only the average contribution of genetic factors to height. An identical twin who was severely physically abused or selectively deprived of proper foods during development might be substantially different in height from the other twin, showing how environmental factors can have an impact on a given trait even among genetically identical individuals.

Behaviour genetics researchers Murray Stein, Kerry Jang, and John Livesley (2002) conducted a study on the heritability of social anxiety-related concerns. The variable of interest was *fear of negative evaluation*—a cognitive factor central to social phobia (see Chapter 5). The individuals in the

▲ University of British Columbia behaviour geneticists Kerry Jang and John Livesley have used the twin method to determine the heritable versus environmental contributions to a variety of forms of abnormal behaviour, including traits related to personality disorders and anxiety disorders.

Courtesy of UBC Department of Psychiatry

study were 437 twin pairs in the University of British Columbia's twin database. The investigators found that monozygotic twins had a greater degree of resemblance for fear of negative evaluation than did dizygotic twins, suggesting a significant heritable component. However, this way of studying genetics isn't perfect. You can assume monozygotic twins have the same genetic makeup and dizygotic twins do not. However, a complicating concern is whether monozygotic twins have the same experiences or environment as dizygotic twins. Some identical twins are dressed alike and are even given similar names. Yet the twins themselves influence each other's behaviour, and in some cases, monozygotic twins may affect each other more than dizygotic twins (Carey, 1992).

One way to address this problem is by combining the adoption study and twin study methods. If you can find identical twins, one of whom was adopted as an infant, you can estimate the relative roles of genes and the environment (nature versus nurture) in the development of behavioural patterns.

Genetic Linkage Analysis and Association Studies

The results of a series of family, twin, and adoption studies may suggest that a particular disorder has a genetic component, but they can't provide the location of the implicated gene or genes. To locate a defective gene, there are two general strategies: genetic linkage analysis and association studies (Fears, Mathews, & Freimer, 2009).

The basic principle of **genetic linkage analysis** is simple. When a family disorder is studied, other inherited characteristics are assessed at the same time. These other characteristics—called **genetic markers**—are selected because we know their exact location. If a match or link is discovered between the inheritance of the disorder and the inheritance of a genetic marker, the genes for the disorder and the genetic marker are probably close together on the same chromosome. For example, bipolar disorder (manic depression) was studied in a large Amish family (Egeland et al., 1987). Researchers found that two markers on chromosome 11—genes for insulin and a known cancer gene—were linked to the presence of mood disorder in this family, suggesting that a gene for bipolar disorder might be on chromosome 11. Unfortunately, although this is a genetic linkage study, it also illustrates the danger of drawing premature conclusions from research. This linkage study and a second study that purported to find a linkage between bipolar disorder and the X chromosome (Baron et al., 1987) have yet to be replicated; that is, different researchers have not been able to show similar linkages in other families (Craddock & Jones, 2001).

The inability to replicate findings in these studies is quite common (Fears et al., 2009). This type of failure casts doubt on conclusions that only one gene is responsible for such complex disorders. Be mindful of such limitations the next time you read in a newspaper or hear on television that a gene has been identified as causing some disorder.

The second strategy for locating specific genes, **association studies**, also uses genetic markers. Whereas linkage studies compare markers in a large group of people with a particular disorder, association studies compare such people to people without the disorder. If certain markers occur significantly more often in the people with the disorder, it is assumed the markers are close to the genes involved with the disorder. This type of comparison makes association studies better able to identify genes that may only be weakly associated with a disorder. Both strategies for locating specific genes shed new light on the origins of specific disorders and may inspire new approaches to treatment (Fears et al., 2009).

Studying Behaviour over Time

Sometimes we want to ask, "How will a disorder or behaviour pattern change (or remain the same) over time?" This question is important for several reasons. First, the answer helps us decide whether to treat a particular person. For example, should we begin an expensive and time-consuming program for a young adult who is depressed over the loss of a grandparent? You might not if you knew that with normal social supports the depression is likely to diminish over the next few months without treatment. On the other hand, if you have reason to believe a problem isn't likely to go away on its own, you might decide to begin treatment. For example, as you will see later, aggression among young children does not usually go away naturally and should be dealt with as early as possible.

It is also important to understand the developmental changes in abnormal behaviour because sometimes these can provide insight into how problems are created and how they become more serious. For example, you will see that some researchers identify newborns who are at risk for autism because they are siblings of a child with autism (see Chapter 14 for a discussion of autistic disorder) and then follow them through infancy until some develop the disorder themselves. This type of study is showing us that the pattern of the onset of this disorder is actually much different than parents report after the fact (they tend to remember drastic changes in the child's behaviour when, in fact, the changes occur gradually) (Rogers, 2009). Prospective studies (which record changes over time as they occur) sometimes reveal dramatic differences in the development of psychological disorders or their treatment compared to the information discovered through retrospective studies (which ask people to remember what happened in the past).

Prevention Research

An additional reason for studying clinical problems over time is that we may be able to design interventions and services to prevent these problems. Clearly, preventing mental health difficulties would save countless families significant emotional distress, and the financial savings could be substantial. Prevention research has expanded over the years to include a broad range of approaches. These different methods can be viewed in four broad categories: positive development strategies (health promotion), universal prevention strategies, selective prevention strategies, and indicated prevention strategies (Daniels, Adams, Carroll, & Beinecke, 2009). *Health promotion or positive development strategies* involve efforts to blanket entire populations of people—even those who may not be at risk—to prevent later problems and promote protective behaviours. The intervention is not designed to fix existing problems but, instead, focuses on skill building, for example, to keep problems from developing. For example, the Seattle Social Development Program targets young children in

public elementary schools in the Seattle school system that are in high-crime areas, providing intervention with teachers and parents to engage the children in learning and positive behaviours. Although this approach does not target one particular problem (e.g., drug use), long-term follow-up of these children suggests multiple positive effects in achievement and reductions in delinquency (Bailey, 2009; Lonczak, Abbott, Hawkins, Kosterman, & Catalano, 2002). *Universal prevention strategies* focus on entire populations and target certain specific risk factors (e.g., behaviour problems in inner-city classrooms) without focusing on specific individuals. The third approach to prevention intervention—*selective prevention*—specifically targets whole groups at risk (e.g., children who have parents who have died) and designs specific interventions aimed at helping them avoid future problems. Finally, *indicated prevention* is a strategy for those individuals who are beginning to show signs of problems (e.g., depressive symptoms) but do not yet have a psychological disorder.

To evaluate the effectiveness of each of these approaches, the research strategies used in prevention research for examining psychopathology across time combine individual and group research methods, including both correlational and experimental designs. We look next at two of the most often used designs: cross-sectional and longitudinal.

Cross-Sectional Designs

A variation of correlation research is to compare different people at different ages. For a **cross-sectional design**, researchers take a cross section of a population across the different age groups and compare them on some characteristic. For example, if they were trying to understand the development of alcohol abuse and dependence, they could take groups of adolescents at 12, 15, and 17 years of age and assess their beliefs about alcohol use. In an early comparison, Brown and Finn (1982) made some interesting discoveries. They found that 36 percent of the 12-year-olds thought the primary purpose of drinking was to get drunk. This percentage increased to 64 percent with 15-year-olds, but dropped again to 42 percent for the 17-year-old students. The researchers also found that 28 percent of the 12-year-olds reported drinking with their friends at least sometimes, a rate that increased to 80 percent for the 15-year-olds and to 88 percent for the 17-year-olds. Brown and Finn used this information to develop the hypothesis that the reason for excessive drinking among teens is a deliberate attempt to get drunk rather than a mistake in judgment once they are under the influence of alcohol. In other words, teenagers do not, as a group, appear to drink too much because once they've had a drink or two they show poor judgment and drink excessively. Instead, their attitudes before drinking seem to influence how much they drink later.

In cross-sectional designs, the participants in each age group are called **cohorts**; Brown and Finn studied three cohorts: 12-year-olds, 15-year-olds, and 17-year-olds. The members of each cohort are the same age at the same time and thus have all been exposed to similar experiences. Members of one cohort differ from members of other cohorts in age and in their exposure to cultural and historical experiences. You would expect a group of 12-year-olds in the early 1980s to have received a great deal of education about drug and alcohol use ("Just Say No"), whereas the 17-year-olds may not have. Differences among cohorts in their opinions about alcohol use may be related to their respective cognitive and emotional development at these different ages and to their dissimilar experiences. This **cohort effect**, the confounding of age and experience, is a limitation of the cross-sectional design.

Researchers prefer cross-sectional designs to study changes over time partly because they are easier to use than longitudinal designs (discussed next). In addition, some phenomena are less likely to be influenced by different cultural and historical experiences and therefore less susceptible to cohort effects. For example, the prevalence of Alzheimer's disease among people at ages 60 and 70—assumed to be strongly influenced by biology—is not likely to be greatly affected by different experiences among the study participants.

One question not answered by cross-sectional designs is how problems develop in individuals. For example, do children who refuse to go to school grow up to have anxiety disorders? Researchers cannot answer this question simply by comparing adults with anxiety problems and children who refuse to go to school. They could ask the adults whether they were anxious about school when they were children, but this **retrospective information** (looking back) is usually less than accurate. To get a better picture of how individuals develop over the years, researchers use longitudinal designs.

Longitudinal Designs

Rather than looking at different groups of people of differing ages, researchers may follow one group over time and assess change in its members directly. The advantage of **longitudinal designs** is that they do not suffer from cohort-effect problems and they allow the researchers to assess individual change. (■ Figure 4.4 illustrates both longitudinal and cross-sectional designs.

Daniel Nagin and Richard Tremblay (1999) have conducted a longitudinal study on physical aggression in boys. They followed more than 1000 boys from low-socioeconomic neighbourhoods in Montréal from age six in kindergarten to age 15 in high school, examining their levels of physical aggression over this period. Using this method, Nagin and Tremblay were able to identify four distinct groups of boys based on their levels and stability of aggression over this period. The first group was a *chronic physical aggression* group comprising boys who displayed persistently high levels of aggression over the nine years of the study. The second group was a *high but declining* group comprising boys who displayed a high level of aggression in kindergarten but showed a decrease thereafter. A third group was a *moderate but declining* group whose members showed moderate levels of aggression in kindergarten but showed a decrease thereafter. The final group was a *low* group whose members rarely displayed aggression during the study (Nagin & Tremblay, 1999).

In addition to measuring levels of physical aggression, the researchers also measured parental and early childhood variables that might help explain which boys would show persistently high aggression from childhood to adolescence. The researchers found that boys who displayed high hyperactivity or high oppositional behaviour in kindergarten were each about three times more likely than other boys to be a member of either the chronic physical

Longitudinal design

2015
25 years
old

2005
15 years
old

1995
5 years
old

1990

Same people followed across time

Cross-sectional design

5 yrs.

15 yrs

25 yrs.

People of different ages viewed at the same time

■ **FIGURE 4.4** Two research designs

aggression or the high but declining group. The researchers also found that boys with teenage mothers or the mothers with the least education were each about two times more likely than other boys to be a member of either the chronic or the high but declining group. Finally, the only characteristic that distinguished boys in the chronic physical aggression group from boys in the high but declining group was having a teenage mother or a mother with less education than other mothers (Nagin & Tremblay, 2001).

A more recent study with this same longitudinal sample of boys examined the longer-term impact of childhood aggression in terms of important outcomes in adolescence (Kokko, Tremblay, Lacourse, Nagin, & Vitaro, 2006). Aggression from ages 6 to 12 predicted physical violence

▲ University of Montréal child psychologist Richard Tremblay and his colleagues at the Research Unit on Children's Psychosocial Maladjustment have used a longitudinal design to examine the factors accounting for childhood physical aggression in boys as well as other childhood disruptive disorders.

and school dropout at age 17. In contrast to the researchers' expectations, however, childhood prosocial behaviour (e.g., helping, comforting, or sympathetic behaviours) did not exert a protective effect against either physical violence or school dropout at age 17 (Kokko et al., 2006). The longitudinal research of Tremblay and his colleagues is discussed further in Chapter 12.

Imagine conducting a major longitudinal study. Not only must the researcher persevere over months and years but so must the people who participate in the study. They must remain willing to continue in the project, and the researcher must hope they will not move away, or worse, die! Longitudinal research is costly and time consuming; it is also subject to the distinct possibility that the research question will have become irrelevant by the time the study is complete. Finally, longitudinal designs can suffer from a phenomenon similar to the cohort effect on cross-sectional designs. The **cross-generational effect** involves trying to generalize the findings to groups whose experiences are very different from those of the study participants. For example, the drug use histories of people who were young adults in the 1960s and early 1970s are vastly different from those of people born in the 1990s, as we will review in Chapter 11.

Sometimes psychopathologists combine longitudinal and cross-sectional designs in a strategy called the **sequential design**, which involves repeated study of different cohorts over time. Marvin Krank of the University of British Columbia, Okanagan, in Kelowna and his colleagues studied the development of alcohol and drug use among British Columbia youth (e.g., Krank & Wall, 2006; Krank, Wall, Wiers, Stewart, & Goldman, 2005). They used the sequential design to learn whether and how different forms of substance use and other risk behaviours changed over time among these youth. Their ambitious project, labelled the Project on Adolescent Trajectories and Health (PATH), involved collecting survey data from more than 1300 students in a large school district in western Canada. Briefly, students were recruited from all Grade 7 to 9 students in the school district. In the cross-

sectional part of the study, the researchers looked at rates of use of various substances among students in different grades (cohorts): Grade 7, Grade 8, and Grade 9. Krank and his colleagues then retested the students for the longitudinal part of the study once a year for the next two academic years. Both parts of the sequential design produced similar findings. For example, regarding the development of drinking behaviour, adolescents' use of alcohol increased across grades. While only 30 percent of Grade 7 students had one or more drinks in the past year, this rate rose to nearly 70 percent by the second year of testing among Grade 10 students (Krank et al., 2005).

The longitudinal portion of the study allowed for an examination of predictors of substance use initiation and escalation. Interestingly, measures of substance-related "implicit cognition" (i.e., cognitive processes about which people have no conscious awareness; see Chapter 2) at earlier waves predicted substance use at later testing waves. For example, implicit cognitions around alcohol were measured using two established tasks (Stacy, 1997). In the first, an ambiguous word task, the adolescents were asked to write down the first word that came to mind when they viewed each of a set of words. The word set included homographs like "draft" and "mug" with two possible meanings, only one of which is alcohol-related. In the second task, a behavioural associates task, the adolescents were asked to write down the first activity that came to mind in response to a set of outcomes such as "having fun" or "feeling relaxed." For both tasks, coders summed the number of alcohol-related responses each student generated. Scores on these alcohol-related implicit measures in the first year predicted a variety of drinking measures in the second year. The implicit alcohol measures in the first year even predicted initiation of drinking in the second year among those youth who did not drink in the first year (Krank et al., 2005). The PATH study results suggest that such implicit cognitive processes might be useful targets for alcohol abuse prevention in youth.

▲ Longitudinal studies can be complicated by the cross-generational effect; for example, young people in the 1960s shared experiences that were very different from those of young people today.

Studying Behaviour over Time **121**

Studying Behaviour across Cultures

Just as we can become narrowly focused when we study people only at a certain age, we can also miss important aspects by studying people from only one culture. Studying the differences in behaviour of people from different cultures can tell us a great deal about the origins and possible treatments of abnormal behaviours. Unfortunately, most research literature originates in Western cultures (Lambert et al., 1992), producing an ethnocentric view of psychopathology that can limit our understanding of disorders in general and can restrict the way we approach treatment (Gaw, 2008). Researchers in Malaysia—where psychological disorders are commonly believed to have supernatural origins—have described a disorder they call *sakit gila*, which has some features of schizophrenia but differs in important ways (Barrett et al., 2005). Could we learn more about schizophrenia (and *sakit gila*) by comparing the disorders themselves and the cultures in which they are found? Increasing awareness of the limited cultural scope of our research is creating a corresponding increase in cross-cultural research on psychopathology.

The designs we have described are adapted for studying abnormal behaviour across cultures. Some researchers view the effects of different cultures as though they were different treatments (Hobfoll, Canetti-Nisim, & Johnson, 2006). In other words, the independent variable is the effect of different cultures on behaviour, rather than, say, the effect of cognitive therapy versus simple exposure for the treatment of fears. The difference between looking at culture as a "treatment" and our typical design, however, is important. In cross-cultural research, we can't randomly assign infants to different cultures and observe how they develop. People from varying cultures can differ in any number of important ways—their genetic backgrounds, for one—that could explain variations in their behaviour for reasons other than culture.

The characteristics of different cultures can also complicate research efforts. Symptoms, or descriptions of symptoms, can be dissimilar in different societies (Gaw, 2008; Marsella & Kaplan, 2002). Nigerians who are depressed complain of heaviness or heat in the head, crawling sensations in the head or legs, burning sensations in the body, and a feeling that the belly is bloated with water (Ebigno, 1982). In contrast, people in North America report feeling worthless, being unable to start or finish anything, losing interest in usual activities, and thinking of suicide. Natives of China, on the other hand, are less likely to report feeling depressed or losing interest in favourite things but may have thoughts of suicide or worthlessness (Phillips, Francey, Edwards, & McMurray, 2007). These few examples illustrate that applying a standard definition of depression across different cultures will result in vastly different outcomes.

An additional complicating factor is varying tolerances, or thresholds, for abnormal behaviour. If people in different

▲ The same behaviours—for example, those of women in public—may be viewed very differently in different cultures.

cultures see the same behaviours very differently, researchers will have trouble comparing incidence and prevalence rates. Lambert and colleagues (1992) found that Jamaican parents and teachers report fewer incidents of abnormal child behaviour than do their North American counterparts. Does this represent a biological or environmental difference in the children themselves, the effects of different thresholds of tolerance in the societies, or a combination of all three? Understanding cultural attitudes and customs is essential to such research (Kohn, Wintrob, & Alarcón, 2009).

Finally, treatment research is also complicated by cross-cultural differences. Cultures develop treatment models that reflect their own values. In Japan, psychiatric hospitalization is organized in terms of a family model, with caregivers assuming parental roles. A family model was common in psychiatric institutions in 19th-century North America until it was replaced with the medical model common today (Colp, 2009). In Saudi Arabia, women are veiled when outside the home, which prevents them from uncovering their faces in the presence of therapists; custom thus complicates efforts to establish a trusting and intimate therapeutic client–therapist relationship (Dubovsky, 1983). Because in the Islamic view medicine and religion are inseparable, medical and religious treatments are combined (Baasher, 2001). As you can see, something as basic as comparing treatment outcomes is highly complex in a cross-cultural context.

The Power of a Program of Research

When we examine different research strategies independently, as we have done here, we often have the impression that some approaches are better than others. It is important to understand that this is not true. Depending on the type of question you are asking and the practical limitations inherent in the inquiry, any of the research techniques would be appropriate. Significant issues often are resolved not by one perfectly designed study but rather by a series of studies that examine different aspects of the problem—in a program of research. The research of one of this book's authors will be used to illustrate how complex research questions are answered with a variety of different research designs.

One of us (Durand) studies why children with autism spectrum disorders (see Chapter 14) display seemingly irrational behaviours such as self-injury (hitting or biting oneself) or aggression. The expectation is that the more we understand why these behaviours occur, the better the chances of designing an effective treatment. In an early study we used a single-subject design (withdrawal design) to test the influence of adult attention and escaping from unpleasant educational tasks on these problem behaviours (Carr & Durand, 1985). We found that some children hit themselves more when people ignore them, and others will hit themselves to get out of school assignments that are too difficult, showing that these disturbing behaviours can be understood by looking at them as primitive forms of communication (e.g., "Please come here" or "This is too hard"). This led us to consider what would happen if we taught these children to communicate with us more

appropriately (Durand, 1990). The next series of studies again used single-subject designs and demonstrated that teaching more acceptable ways of getting attention or help from others did significantly reduce these challenging behaviours (e.g., Durand & Carr, 1992). Several decades of research on this treatment (called functional communication training) demonstrates its value in significantly improving the lives of people with these once severe behaviour problems by reducing the severity of the misbehaviour through improving communication skills (Durand, in press).

One of the questions that face researchers in this area is why some children develop more severe forms of these behaviour problems, while others do not. To begin to answer this question, we conducted a three-year prospective longitudinal study on more than 100 children with autism to see what factors might cause more problems (Durand, 2001). We studied the children at age three and later at age six to determine what about the child or the family led to more severe problems. We found the following two factors to be the most important indicators of severe behaviour problems in the children: (1) if the parents were pessimistic about their ability to help their child or (2) if the parents were doubtful about their child's ability to change. These parents would "give up" and allow their child to dictate many of the routines around the house (e.g., eating dinner in the living room, or not going out to the movies because it would cause tantrums) (Durand, 2001).

This important finding then led to the next question: Could we make pessimistic parents more optimistic, and would this help prevent their children from developing more severe behaviour problems? To answer this question, we next relied on a randomized clinical trial to see if adding a cognitive behaviour intervention (described in more detail in the later chapters on the individual disorders) would help make pessimistic parents more optimistic. We wanted to teach these parents to examine their own pessimistic thoughts (e.g., "I have no control of my child" or "My child won't improve because of his/her autism") and replace them with more hopeful views of their world (e.g., "I can help my child" or "My child can improve his/her behaviour"). We hypothesized that this cognitive intervention would help them carry out the parenting strategies we offer them (including functional communication training) and in turn improve the outcomes of our behavioural interventions. We randomly assigned groups of pessimistic parents who also had a child with very severe behaviour problems to either a group that taught them how to work with their child or a group that used the same techniques but also helped them explore their pessimistic thinking and helped them view themselves and their child in a better light. The treatments were applied very formally, using written protocols to make sure that each group received the treatment as designed (Durand & Hieneman, 2008). What we found was that addition of the cognitive behavioural intervention had the expected effect—improving optimism and also improving child outcomes (Durand, Hieneman, Clarke, & Zona, 2009).

As this example indicates, research is conducted in stages, and a complete picture of any disorder and its treatment can be seen only after looking at it from many perspectives. An integrated program of research can help researchers explore various aspects of abnormal behaviour.

Replication

Scientists in general, and behavioural scientists in particular, are never really convinced something is true. People are very skeptical when it comes to claims about causes or treatment outcomes. Replicating findings is what makes researchers confident that what they are observing isn't a coincidence. We noted when we described the case study method that if we look at a disorder in only one person, no matter how carefully we describe and document what we observe, we cannot draw strong conclusions.

The strength of a research program is in its ability to replicate findings in different ways to build confidence in the results. If you look back at the research strategies we have described, you will find that replication is one of the most important aspects of each. The more times a researcher repeats a process (and the behaviour he or she is studying changes as expected) the more sure he or she is about what caused the changes.

Research Ethics

An important final issue involves the ethics of doing research in abnormal psychology. For example, the appropriateness of a clinician's delaying treatment to people who need it, just to satisfy the requirements of an experimental design, is often questioned. One single-case experimental design, the withdrawal design, can involve removing treatment for some time. Treatment is also withheld when placebo control groups are used in group experimental designs. Researchers across the world—in an evolving code of ethics referred to as the Declaration of Helsinki—are developing guidelines to determine just when it would be appropriate to use placebo-controlled trials (Roberts, Hoop, & Dunn, 2008). The fundamental question is this: When does a scientist's interest in preserving the internal validity of a study outweigh a client's right to treatment?

One answer to this question involves **informed consent**—a research participant's formal agreement to cooperate in a study following full disclosure of the nature of the research and the participant's role in it (Lubit, 2009). The concept of informed consent is actually derived from the war trials after World War II. Revelations that the Nazis had forced prisoners into so-called medical experiments helped establish the informed consent guidelines that are still used today. The ethical requirement of informed consent helps to prevent tragedies such as the psychic driving experiments conducted by Dr. Ewan Cameron on vulnerable psychiatric patients (without their consent) at the Allan Memorial Institute in Montréal from 1957 to 1964 (see Chapter 16 for more information). Informed consent procedures used today would also have prevented the unfortunate psychological consequences experienced by a Western Canadian boy who was, without his knowledge or consent about the situation, raised as a girl following a botched circumcision operation in 1966. This famous real-life experiment, conducted by sexologist Dr. John Money, is described in detail in Chapter 10. Today, because of ethical requirements of informed consent, in studies using some form of treatment delay or withdrawal, the participant is told about why it

will occur and the risks and benefits, and permission to proceed is then obtained. In placebo control studies, participants are told they may not receive an active treatment (all participants are blind to or unaware of which group they are placed in), but they are usually given the option of receiving treatment after the study ends.

True informed consent is at times elusive. The basic components are competence, voluntarism, full information, and comprehension on the part of the participant (Bankert & Amdur, 2006). In other words, research participants must be capable of consenting to participation in the research, they must volunteer or not be coerced into participating, they must have all the information they need to make the decision, and they must understand what their participation will involve. In some circumstances, all these conditions are difficult to attain. Children, for example, often do not fully appreciate what will occur during research. Similarly, individuals with cognitive impairments such as mental retardation or schizophrenia may not understand their role or their rights as participants. In institutional settings, participants should not feel coerced into taking part in research.

Certain general protections help ensure that these concerns are properly addressed. First, according to the Tri-Council Policy Statement for the Ethical Conduct for Research Involving Humans prepared by the former Medical Research Council of Canada (now replaced by the Canadian Institutes of Health Research), the Natural Sciences and Engineering Research Council of Canada, and the Social Sciences and Humanities Research Council of Canada, research in Canadian university and medical settings must be approved by a research ethics board (REB; Public Works and Government Services Canada, 2003). These are committees made up of university faculty and nonacademic people from the community. Each committee is made up of five members: Two members must have expertise in the methods or areas of research covered by the particular REB, one member must be an expert in ethics, a fourth member should be an expert in relevant law (this type of member is required for a biomedical REB and suggested for other REBs), and the final member is a layperson from outside of the institution. The purpose of the REB is to see that the rights of research participants are protected. The committee structure allows people other than the researcher to look at the research procedures to determine whether sufficient care is being taken to protect the welfare and dignity of the participants (O'Neill, 1998a; Truscott & Crook, 2004).

To safeguard those who participate in psychological research and to clarify the responsibilities of researchers, the Canadian Psychological Association (CPA) published *the Canadian Code of Ethics for Psychologists*, third edition, which includes general guidelines that apply to the various activities engaged in by psychologists, including conducting research (CPA, 2000; see also O'Neill, 1998b; Truscott & Crook, 2004). People in research experiments must be protected from both physical and psychological harm. In addition to the issue of informed consent, the CPA Code stresses that the welfare of the research participants is given priority over any other consideration, including experimental design. The CPA Code of Ethics is discussed in detail in Chapter 16.

Psychological harm is difficult to define, but its definition remains the responsibility of the investigator. Researchers must hold in confidence all information obtained from participants, who have the right to conceal their identity on all data, either written or informal. Whenever deception is considered essential to research, the investigator must satisfy a committee of peers that this judgment is correct. If deception is used, participants must be debriefed—that is, told in language they can understand the true purpose of the study and why it was necessary to deceive them.

The Society for Research in Child Development (2007) has endorsed ethical guidelines for research that address some issues unique to research on children. For example, these guidelines not only call for confidentiality, protection from harm, and debriefing but also require informed consent from children's caregivers and from the children themselves if they are age seven or older. These guidelines specify that the research must be explained to children in language they can understand so that they can decide whether they wish to participate. Many other ethical issues extend beyond protection of the participants, including how researchers deal with errors in their research, fraud in science, and the proper way to give credit to others. Doing a study involves more than selecting the appropriate design. Researchers must be aware of numerous concerns that involve the rights of the people in the experiment, as well as their own conduct.

A final and important development in the field that will help to "keep the face" on psychological disorders is the involvement of consumers in important aspects of this research—referred to as participatory action research (Kindon, Pain, & Kesby, 2007). The concern over not only how people are treated in research studies but also how the information is interpreted and used has resulted in many government agencies providing guidance on how the people who are the targets of the research (e.g., those with schizophrenia, depression, or anxiety disorders) should be involved in the process. The hope is that if people who experience these disorders are partners in designing, running, and interpreting this research, the relevance of the research, as well as the treatment of the participants in these studies, will be markedly improved.

Concept Check | 4.4

Indicate whether the following statements are true (T) or false (F).

1. ___ After the nature of the experiment and their roles in it are disclosed to the participants, they must be allowed to refuse or agree to sign an informed consent form.

2. ___ If the participant is in the control group or taking a placebo, informed consent is not needed.

3. ___ Research in universities or medical settings must be approved by the institution's research ethics board regarding whether or not the participants lack the cognitive skills to protect themselves from harm.

4. ___ Participants have a right to conceal their identities on all data collected and reported.

5. ___ When deception is essential to the research, participants do not have to be debriefed regarding the true purpose of the study.

Summary

- Research involves establishing a hypothesis that is then tested. In abnormal psychology, research focuses on hypotheses meant to explain the nature, the causes, or the treatment of a disorder.
- The individual case study is used to study one or more individuals in depth. Though case studies have an important role in the theoretical development of psychology, they are not subject to experimental control and must necessarily be suspect in terms of both internal and external validity.
- Research by correlation can tell us whether a relationship exists between two variables, but it does not tell us whether that relationship is a causal one. Epidemiological research is a type of correlational research that reveals the incidence, distribution, and consequences of a particular problem in one or more populations.
- Research by experiment can follow one of two designs: group or single case. In both designs, a variable (or variables) is manipulated and the effects are observed in order to determine the nature of a causal relationship.
- Genetic research focuses on the role of genetics in behaviour. These research strategies include family studies, adoption studies, twin studies, genetic linkage analyses, and association studies.
- Research strategies that examine psychopathology across time include cross-sectional and longitudinal designs. Both focus on differences in behaviour or attitudes at different ages, but the former does so by looking at different individuals at different ages, while the latter looks at the same individuals at different ages.
- The clinical picture, causal factors, and treatment process and outcome can all be influenced by cultural factors.
- The more the findings of a research program are replicated, the more they gain in credibility.
- Ethics are important to the research process, and ethical guidelines are spelled out by many professional organizations and research funding bodies in an effort to ensure the well-being of research subjects.

Key Terms

adoption studies, 117
analogue model, 107
association studies, 118
baseline, 114
case study method, 108
clinical significance, 107
cohort, 119
cohort effect, 120
comparative treatment research, 112
confound, 106
control group, 107
correlation, 109
correlation coefficient, 109
cross-generational effect, 121
cross-sectional design, 119

dependent variable, 105
directionality, 110
double-blind control, 112
effect size, 107
endophenotypes, 116
epidemiology, 110
experiment, 111
external validity, 106
family studies, 117
generalizability, 107
genetic linkage analysis, 118
genetic markers, 118
genotype, 116
human genome project, 116
hypothesis, 105
incidence, 110

independent variable, 105
informed consent, 124
internal validity, 106
level, 114
longitudinal design, 120
multiple baseline, 115
negative correlation, 110
patient uniformity myth, 108
phenotype, 116
placebo control group, 112
placebo effect, 112
positive correlation, 109
prevalence, 110
proband, 117
randomization, 107
repeated measurement, 113

research design, 105
retrospective information, 120
sequential design, 121
single-case experimental design, 113
statistical significance, 107
testability, 106
treatment outcome research, 112
trend, 114
twin studies, 118
variability, 114
withdrawal design, 114

Answers to Concept Checks

4.1

1. independent variable;
2. confound; 3. hypothesis;
4. dependent variable;
5. internal validity, external validity

4.2

1. e; 2. c; 3. b; 4. a; 5. f

4.3

1. L; 2. CS; 3. L; 4. CS;
5. L; 6. CS

4.4

1. T; 2. F; 3. T; 4. T; 5. F

Media Resources

CourseMate

Access an integrated eBook, Abnormal Psychology Videos (formerly Abnormal Psych Live CAccess an integrated eBook, Abnormal Psychology Videos (formerly Abnormal Psych Live CD-ROM), chapter-specific interactive learning tools (flashcards, quizzes, learning modules), and more in your Psychology CourseMate, available at **www.abnormalpsych3ce.nelson.com.**

Abnormal Psychology Video

Free Abnormal Psychology videos can be viewed on the website **www.abnormalpsych3ce .nelson.com**.

- *Research Methods:* David Barlow discusses the protocols and procedures in doing ethical research on clients with psychological problems. He explains the safeguards and the changes in the practices over time.

Video Concept Reviews

CourseMate also contains Mark Durand's *Video Concept Reviews* on these challenging topics:

- Hypothesis/Testability
- Independent/Dependent Variables
- Internal/External Validity
- Statistical versus Clinical Significance
- Case Study Method
- Correlational Research
- Correlation Coefficient
- Experiment
- Placebo Control Group
- Double-Blind Control
- Single-Case Experimental Design (Repeated Measures)
- Genetic Research (Family and Adoptee Studies)
- Longitudinal and Cross-Sectional Designs

5 | Anxiety Disorders

One thing is certain, that the problem of anxiety is a nodal point, linking up all kinds of the most important questions; a riddle, of which the solution must cast a flood of light upon our whole mental life.
—Sigmund Freud, *Introductory Lectures on Psychoanalysis*

© Erich Lessing/Art Resource, NY

Demonstrate knowledge and understanding representing appropriate breadth and depth in selected content areas of psychology:	› Biological bases of behaviour and mental processes, including physiology, sensation, perception, comparative, motivation, and emotion (APA SLO 1.2.a (3)) *(see textbook pages 131–134)*
Use the concepts, language, and major theories of the discipline to account for psychological phenomena.	› Describe behaviour and mental processes empirically, including operational definitions (APA SLO 1.3.a) *(see textbook pages 135–136, 141–142, 150–153, 156, 161–164, 168–171)*
Identify appropriate applications of psychology in solving problems, such as:	› Origin and treatment of abnormal behaviour (APA SLO 4.2.b) *(see textbook pages 137–140, 144–149, 154–156, 158–161, 165–168, 172–174)*

* Portions of this chapter cover learning outcomes suggested by the American Psychological Association (2007) in their guidelines for the undergraduate psychology major. Chapter coverage of these outcomes is identified above by APA Goal and APA Suggested Learning Outcome (SLO).

 Rapid Behavioural Treatment of a Specific Phobia (Snakes)
Obsessive-Compulsive Disorder: Chuck

The Complexity of Anxiety Disorders

Anxiety is complex and mysterious, as Freud realized many years ago. In some ways, the more we learn about it, the more baffling it seems. "Anxiety" is a specific type of disorder, but it is much more than that. It is an emotion implicated so heavily across the full range of psychopathology that we begin by exploring its general nature, both biological and psychological. Next, we consider fear, a somewhat different but clearly related emotion. We suggest that panic is fear that occurs, perhaps, at an inappropriate time. With these important ideas clearly in mind, we focus on specific anxiety disorders.

Anxiety, Fear, and Panic

Have you ever experienced anxiety? A silly question, you might say, because most of us feel some anxiety almost every day of our lives. Did you have a test in school today for which you weren't "perfectly" prepared? Did you have a date last weekend with somebody new? And how about that job interview coming up? Even thinking about that might make you nervous. But have you ever stopped to think about the nature of anxiety? What is it? What causes it?

Anxiety is a negative mood state characterized by bodily symptoms of physical tension, and apprehension about the future (American Psychiatric Association, 2000; Barlow, 2002). It is important to note that anxiety is very hard to study. In humans anxiety can be a subjective sense of unease, a set of behaviours (looking worried and anxious, fidgeting), or a physiological response originating in the brain and reflected in elevated heart rate and muscle tension. Because anxiety is difficult to study in humans, much of the research has been done with animals. For example, we might teach laboratory rats that a light signals an impending shock. The animals certainly look and act anxious when the light comes on. They may fidget, tremble, and perhaps cower in a corner. We might give them an anxiety-reducing drug and notice a reduction of anxiety in their reaction to the light. But is the rats' experience of anxiety the same as that of humans? It seems similar, but we don't know for sure; research with animals provides only general information about the nature of anxiety in humans. Thus, anxiety remains a mystery, and we are only beginning our journey of discovery. Because anxiety is also closely related to depression (Barlow, 2000, 2002; Brown & Barlow, 2005, 2009; Clark, 2005; Wilamowska et al., 2010), much of what we say here is relevant to Chapter 7.

Anxiety is not very pleasant, so why do we seem programmed to experience it almost every time we do something important? Surprisingly, anxiety is good for us, at least in moderate amounts. Psychologists have known for over a century that we perform better when we are a little anxious (Yerkes & Dodson, 1908). You would not have done as well on that test the other day if you had had no anxiety. You were a little more charming and lively on that date last weekend because you were anxious. And you will be better prepared for a job interview if you are anxious. In short, physical and intellectual performances are driven and enhanced by anxiety. Without it, very few of us would get much done.

But what happens when you have too much anxiety? You might actually fail the exam because you can't concentrate on the questions. All you can think about when you're too anxious is how terrible it will be if you fail. On that date with a new person, you might spend the evening with perspiration running off your face and a sick feeling in your stomach, unable to think of even one reasonably interesting thing to say. You might blow the interview for the same reason. Too much of a good thing can be harmful, and very few sensations are more harmful than severe anxiety that is out of control.

What makes the situation worse is that severe anxiety usually doesn't go away—that is, even if we "know" we really have nothing to be afraid of, we remain anxious. We constantly see examples of this kind of irrationality. Well-known singer and songwriter Alanis Morissette reportedly experiences severe anxiety. In one interview, she recounted an episode of anxiety that occurred shortly after she had moved to Los Angeles. Morissette was returning home to Canada for the holidays, and while writing cards on the plane, she suddenly began crying and shaking uncontrollably, and she felt as if she was going to faint. This experience scared her and she sought treatment ("The People's Courtney," 1995).

Morissette and countless other individuals who have anxiety-based disorders are well aware that they have little to fear in the situations they find so stressful. She should know, for example, that flying is the safest way to travel and that no objective danger existed in the situation when she experienced this anxiety attack. And yet Morissette, like others dealing with anxiety, cannot seem to shake her excessive fear. All the disorders discussed in this chapter are characterized by excessive anxiety, which takes many different forms.

▲ Even successful performers like Alanis Morissette can experience excessive anxiety.

In Chapter 2 we saw that **fear** is an immediate alarm reaction to danger. Like anxiety, fear can be good for us. It protects us by activating a massive response from the autonomic nervous system (increased heart rate and blood pressure, for example), which, along with our subjective sense of terror, motivates us to escape (flee) or, possibly, to attack (fight). As such, this emergency reaction is often called the flight-or-fight response.

Although not all emotion theorists agree, much evidence shows that fear and anxiety reactions differ psychologically and physiologically (Barlow, 2002; Bouton, 2005; Craske et al., 2010; Waddell, Morris, & Bouton, 2006). As noted earlier, anxiety is a future-oriented mood state, characterized by apprehension because we cannot predict or control upcoming events. In contrast, fear is an immediate emotional reaction to current danger characterized by strong escapist action tendencies and, often, a surge in the sympathetic branch of the autonomic nervous system (Barlow, Brown, & Craske, 1994; Craske et al., 2010). Someone experiencing fear might say, "I've got to get out of here right now or I may not make it."

ABNORMAL PSYCHOLOGY Videos

Steve, a Patient with Panic Disorder

The first time it happened to me, I was driving down the highway, and I had a kind of a knot in my chest. I felt like I had swallowed something and it got stuck, and it lasted pretty much overnight. . . . I felt like I was having a heart attack. . . . I assumed that's what was happening. I felt very panicky. A flushed feeling came over my whole body. I felt as though I was going to pass out.

Go to Psychology CourseMate at www. abnormalpsych3ce.nelson.com to watch this video.

What happens if you experience the alarm response of fear when you have nothing to be afraid of? Alanis Morissette's episode of unexpected crying, shaking, and feeling faint on the airplane is a good example of this kind of false alarm. Consider also the case of Gretchen, who appeared at one of our clinics.

GRETCHEN | *Attacked by Panic*

I was 25 when I had my first attack. It was a few weeks after I'd come home from the hospital. I had had my appendix out. The surgery had gone well, and I wasn't in any danger, which is why I don't understand what happened. But one night I went to sleep and I woke up a few hours later—I'm not sure how long—but I woke up with this vague feeling of apprehension. Mostly I remember how my heart started pounding. And my chest hurt; it felt like I was dying—that I was having a heart attack. And I felt kind of queer, as if I were detached from the experience. It seemed like my bedroom was covered with a haze. I ran to my sister's room, but I felt like I was a puppet or a robot who was under the control of somebody else while I was running. I think I scared her almost as much as I was frightened myself. She called an ambulance (Barlow, 2002).

This sudden overwhelming reaction came to be known as **panic**, after the Greek god Pan who terrified travellers with blood-curdling screams. In psychopathology, a **panic attack** is defined as an abrupt experience of intense fear or acute discomfort, accompanied by physical symptoms that usually include heart palpitations, chest pain, shortness of breath, and, possibly, dizziness (see DSM Table 5.1).

Three basic types of panic attacks are described in *DSM-IV*: situationally bound, unexpected, and situationally predisposed. If you know you are afraid of high places or of driving over long bridges, you might have a panic attack in these situations but not anywhere else; this is a *situationally bound (cued) panic attack*. By contrast, you might experience *unexpected (uncued) panic attacks* if you don't have a clue when or where the next attack will occur. The third type of panic attack, the *situationally predisposed panic attack*, is between these two types. You are more likely to, but will not inevitably, have an attack where you have had one before; for example, in a large mall. If you don't know whether it will happen today and it does, the attack is situationally predisposed (this type of panic attack may be dropped in *DSM-5* just to make differentiation simpler). We mention these types of attacks because they play a role in several anxiety disorders. Unexpected and situationally predisposed attacks are important in panic disorder. Situationally bound attacks are more common in specific phobias or social phobia (see ■ Figure 5.1). The famous painting by the Norwegian artist Edvard Munch that was depicted at the beginning of this chapter is thought to be the artist's own

DSM-IV-TR	**Table 5.1** Diagnostic Criteria for Panic Attack

The predominant complaint in a panic attack is a discrete period of intense fear or discomfort, in which at least four of the following symptoms developed abruptly and reached a peak within ten minutes:

1. Palpitations, pounding heart, or accelerated heart rate
2. Sweating
3. Trembling or shaking
4. Sensations of shortness of breath or smothering
5. Feeling of choking
6. Chest pain or discomfort
7. Nausea or abdominal distress
8. Feeling dizzy, unsteady, lightheaded, or faint
9. Derealization (feelings of unreality) or depersonalization (being detached from oneself)
10. Fear of losing control or going crazy
11. Fear of dying
12. Paresthesias (numbness or tingling sensations)
13. Chills or hot flushes

Source: Reprinted with permission from the *Diagnostic and Statistical Manual of Mental Disorders,* Fourth Edition, Text Revision, (Copyright © 2000). American Psychiatric Association.

depiction of a panic attack in progress. Munch was known to have panic attacks.

Remember that fear is an intense emotional alarm accompanied by a surge of energy in the autonomic nervous system that motivates us to flee from danger. Does Gretchen's panic attack sound like it could be the emotion of fear? A variety of evidence suggests it is (Barlow, 2002; Barlow, Chorpita, & Turovsky, 1996;

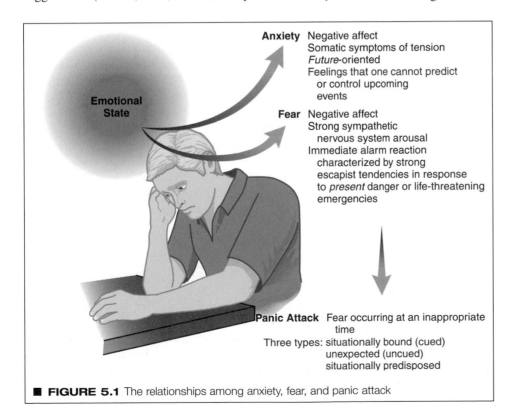

■ FIGURE 5.1 The relationships among anxiety, fear, and panic attack

Bouton, 2005), including similarities in reports of the experience of fear and panic, similar behavioural tendencies to escape, and similar underlying neurobiological processes.

Over the years we have recorded panic attacks during physiological assessments of patients (see, for example, Hofmann & Barlow, 1996). The physiological surge recorded in one patient is shown in ■ Figure 5.2. Notice the sudden dramatic increase in heart rate from minute 11 through minute 13, accompanied by increases in muscle tension (frontalis EMG) and finger temperature. This massive autonomic surge peaked and subsided within three minutes. The panic attack in the laboratory occurred quite unexpectedly from the patient's point of view and from ours. As the figure shows, fear and panic are experienced suddenly, which is necessary to mobilize us for instantaneous reaction to impending danger.

Causes of Anxiety Disorders

You learned in Chapters 1 and 2 that excessive emotional reactions have no simple one-dimensional cause but come from multiple sources. Next, we explore the biological, psychological, and social contributors and how they interact to produce anxiety disorders.

Biological Contributions

Increasing evidence shows that we inherit a tendency to be tense, uptight, and anxious (Clark, 2005; Eysenck, 1967; Gray & McNaughton, 1996). The tendency to panic also seems to run in families and probably has a genetic component which differs somewhat from genetic contributions to anxiety (Barlow, 2002; Craske, 1999; Craske & Barlow, 2008; Kendler et al., 1995). As with almost all emotional traits and psychological disorders, no single gene seems to cause anxiety or panic. Instead, contributions from collections of genes in several areas on chromosomes make us vulnerable when the right psychological and social factors are in place. Furthermore, a genetic vulnerability does not cause anxiety and/or panic directly. That is, stress or other factors in the environment can "turn on" these genes, as we reviewed in Chapter 2 (Gelernter & Stein, 2009; Kendler, 2006; Rutter, Moffitt, & Caspi, 2006; Schumacher et al., 2005; Smoller, Block, & Young, 2009).

Anxiety is also associated with specific brain circuits and neurotransmitter systems. For example, depleted levels of gamma aminobutyric acid (GABA), part of the GABA–benzodiazepine system, are associated with increased anxiety, although the relationship is not quite so direct. The noradrenergic system has also been implicated in anxiety, and evidence from basic animal studies, as well as studies of normal anxiety in humans, suggests the serotonergic neurotransmitter system is also involved (Lesch et al., 1996; Maier, 1997; Stein, Schork, & Gelernter, 2007). But increasing attention in the last several years is focusing on the

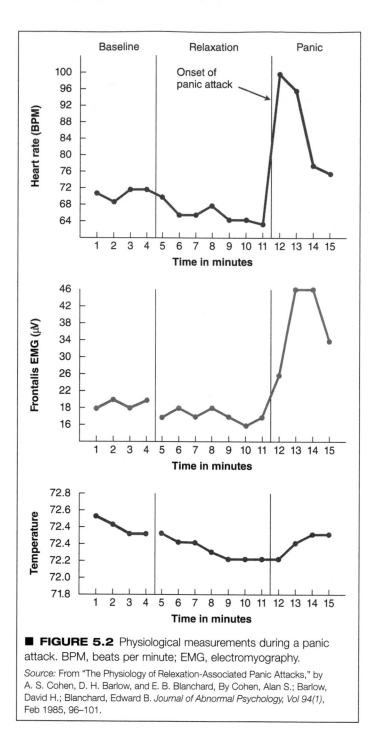

■ FIGURE 5.2 Physiological measurements during a panic attack. BPM, beats per minute; EMG, electromyography.

Source: From "The Physiology of Relaxation-Associated Panic Attacks," by A. S. Cohen, D. H. Barlow, and E. B. Blanchard, By Cohen, Alan S.; Barlow, David H.; Blanchard, Edward B. *Journal of Abnormal Psychology, Vol 94(1)*, Feb 1985, 96–101.

role of the corticotropin-releasing factor (CRF) system as central to the expression of anxiety (and depression) and the groups of genes that increase the likelihood that this system will be turned on (Heim & Nemeroff, 1999; Khan, King, Abelson, & Liberzon, 2009; Ladd et al., 2000; Smoller, Yamaki, & Fagerness, 2005; Sullivan, Kent, & Coplan, 2000). This is because CRF activates the hypothalamic–pituitary–adrenocortical (HPA) axis, described in Chapter 2, which is part of the CRF system, and this CRF system has wide-ranging effects on areas of the brain implicated in anxiety, including the emotional brain (the limbic system), particularly the hippocampus and the amygdala; the locus coeruleus in the brain stem; the prefrontal cortex; and the dopaminergic neurotransmitter system. The CRF system is also directly related to the GABA–benzodiazepine system and the serotonergic and noradrenergic neurotransmitter systems.

The area of the brain most often associated with anxiety is the limbic system (Britton & Rauch, 2009; Charney & Drevets, 2002; Gray & McNaughton, 1996; LeDoux, 1996, 2002; see Figure 2.7c on page 45), which acts as a mediator between the brain stem and the cortex. The more primitive brain stem monitors and senses changes in bodily functions and relays these potential danger signals to higher cortical processes through the limbic system. The late Jeffrey Gray, a prominent British neuropsychologist, identified a brain circuit in the limbic system of animals that seems heavily involved in anxiety (Gray, 1982, 1985; McNaughton & Gray, 2000) and may be relevant to humans. This circuit leads from the septal and hippocampal area in the limbic system to the frontal cortex. (The septal–hippocampal system is activated by CRF and serotonergic- and noradrenergic-mediated pathways originating in the brain stem.) The system that Gray calls the **behavioural inhibition system (BIS)** is activated by signals from the brain stem of unexpected events, such as major changes in body functioning that might signal danger. Danger signals in response to something we see that might be threatening descend from the cortex to the septal–hippocampal system. The BIS also receives a big boost from the amygdala (Davis, 1992; LeDoux, 1996, 2002). When the BIS is activated by signals that arise from the brain stem or descend from the cortex, our tendency is to freeze, experience anxiety, and apprehensively evaluate the situation to confirm that danger is present.

The BIS circuit is distinct from the circuit involved in panic. Gray (1982; Gray & McNaughton, 1996) and Graeff (1987, 1993; Deakin & Graeff, 1991) identified what Gray calls the **fight/flight system (FFS)**. This circuit originates in the brain stem and travels through several midbrain structures, including the amygdala, the ventromedial nucleus of the hypothalamus, and the central gray matter. When stimulated in animals, this circuit produces an immediate alarm-and-escape response that looks very much like panic in humans (Gray & McNaughton, 1996). Gray and McNaughton (1996) and Graeff (1993) think the FFS is activated partly by deficiencies in serotonin.

It is likely that factors in your environment can change the sensitivity of these brain circuits, making you more or less susceptible to developing anxiety and its disorders, a finding that has been demonstrated in several laboratories (Francis, Diorio, Plotsky, & Meaney, 2002; Stein et al., 2007). For example, one important study suggested that cigarette smoking as a teenager is associated with greatly increased risk for developing anxiety disorders as adults, particularly panic disorder and generalized anxiety disorder (Johnson et al., 2000). Nearly 700 adolescents were followed into adulthood. Teens who smoked 20 or more cigarettes daily were 15 times more likely to develop panic disorder and five times more likely to develop generalized anxiety disorder than teens who smoked less or didn't smoke. The complex interaction between smoking and panic disorder has been confirmed in more recent research (Feldner et al., 2009; Zvolensky & Bernstein, 2005). One possible explanation is that chronic exposure to nicotine, an addictive drug that increases somatic symptoms, as well as respiratory problems, triggers additional anxiety and panic, thereby increasing biological vulnerability to develop severe anxiety disorders.

Research into the neurobiology of anxiety and panic is still new, but we have made exciting progress by implicating two seemingly different brain systems and confirming the crucial role of the CRF system and the amygdala. Brain-imaging procedures will undoubtedly yield more information in the years to come, and this has already begun to happen (Britton & Rauch, 2009; Charney & Drevets, 2002). For example, there is now general agreement that in people with anxiety disorders the limbic system, including the amygdala, is overly responsive to stimulation or new information (abnormal bottom-up processing); at the same time, controlling functions of the cortex that would down-regulate the hyperexcitable amygdala are deficient (abnormal top-down processing), consistent with Gray's BIS model (Britton & Rauch, 2009; Ochsner et al., 2009).

Psychological Contributions

In Chapter 2, we reviewed some theories on the nature of psychological causes of anxiety. Remember that Freud thought anxiety was a psychic reaction to danger surrounding the reactivation of an infantile fearful situation. Behavioural theorists thought anxiety was the product of early classical conditioning, modelling, or other forms of learning (Bandura, 1986). But, evidence is accumulating (see, for example, Barlow, 2002; Suárez et al., 2009) that supports an integrated model of anxiety involving a variety of psychological factors. In childhood, we may acquire an awareness that events are not always in our control (Chorpita & Barlow, 1998). The continuum of this perception may range from total confidence in our control of all aspects of our lives to deep uncertainty about ourselves and our ability to deal with upcoming events. If you are anxious about schoolwork, you may worry you will do poorly on the next exam, even though all your grades have been A's and B's. A general "sense of uncontrollability" may develop early as a function of upbringing and other disruptive or traumatic environmental factors.

Interestingly, the actions of parents in early childhood seem to do a lot to foster this sense of control or a sense of uncontrollability (Chorpita & Barlow, 1998; Gunnar & Fisher, 2006). Generally, it seems that parents who interact in a positive and predictable way with their children by responding to their needs, particularly when the child communicates needs for attention, food, relief from pain, and so on, perform an important function. These parents teach their children that they have control over their environment and their responses have an effect on their parents and their environment. In addition, parents who provide a "secure home base" but allow their children to explore their world and develop the necessary skills to cope with unexpected occurrences enable their children to develop a healthy sense of control (Chorpita & Barlow, 1998). In contrast, parents who are overprotective and overintrusive and who "clear the way" for their children, never letting them experience any adversity, create a situation in which children never learn how to cope with adversity when it comes along. Therefore, these children don't learn that they can control their environment. A variety of evidence has accumulated supporting these ideas (Barlow, 2002; Chorpita & Barlow, 1998; Chorpita, Brown, & Barlow, 1998; Gunnar & Fisher, 2006; Lieb et al., 2000; Nolen-Hoeksema, Wolfson, Mumme, & Guskin, 1995; White, Brown, Somers, & Barlow, 2006). A sense of control (or lack of it) that develops from these early experiences is the psychological factor that makes us more or less vulnerable to anxiety in later life.

Most psychological accounts of panic (as opposed to anxiety) invoke conditioning and cognitive explanations that are difficult to separate (Bouton et al., 2001). Thus, a strong fear response initially occurs during extreme stress or perhaps as a result of a dangerous situation in the environment (a true alarm). This emotional response then becomes associated with a variety of external and internal cues. In other words, these cues, or conditioned stimuli, provoke the fear response and an assumption of danger, even if the danger is not actually present (Bouton, 2005; Bouton et al., 2001; Martin, 1983; Mineka & Zinbarg, 2006; Razran, 1961), so it is really a learned or false alarm. This is the conditioning process described in Chapter 2. External cues are places or situations similar to the one where the initial panic attack occurred. Internal cues are increases in heart rate or respiration that were associated with the initial panic attack, even if they are now the result of normal circumstances, such as exercise. Thus, when your heart is beating fast you are more likely to think of and, perhaps, experience a panic attack than when it is beating normally. Furthermore, you may not be aware of the cues or triggers of severe fear; that is, they are unconscious. This is most likely, as demonstrated in experimental work with animals, because these cues or triggers may travel from the eyes directly to the amygdala in the emotional brain without going through the cortex, the source of awareness (Bouton et al., 2001; LeDoux, 2002).

Social Contributions

Stressful life events trigger our biological and psychological vulnerabilities to anxiety. Most are social and interpersonal in nature—marriage, divorce, difficulties at work, death of a loved one, pressures to excel in school, and so on. Some might be physical, such as an injury or illness.

The same stressors can trigger physical reactions such as headaches or hypertension and emotional reactions such as panic attacks (Barlow, 2002). The particular way we react to stress seems to run in families. If you get headaches when under stress, chances are other people in your family also get headaches. If you have panic attacks, other members of your family probably do also. This finding suggests a possible genetic contribution, at least to initial panic attacks.

An Integrated Model

Putting the factors together in an integrated way, we have described a theory of the development of anxiety and related disorders called the *triple vulnerability theory* (Barlow, 2000, 2002; Suárez et al., 2009). The first vulnerability (or diathesis) is a *generalized biological vulnerability*. We can see that a tendency to be uptight or high-strung might be inherited. But a generalized biological vulnerability to develop anxiety is not sufficient to produce anxiety itself. The second vulnerability is a *generalized psychological vulnerability*. That is, you might also grow up believing the world is dangerous and out of control and you might not be able to cope when things go wrong based on your early experiences. If this perception is strong, you have a generalized psychological vulnerability to anxiety. The third vulnerability is a *specific psychological vulnerability* in which you learn from early experience, such as being taught by your parents, that some situations or objects are fraught with danger (even if they really aren't). Possible examples are dogs, if one of your parents is afraid of dogs, or being evaluated negatively by others, if this is something your parents worry about. These triple vulnerabilities are presented in ■ Figure 5.3 and revisited when we describe each anxiety disorder. If you are under a lot of pressure, particularly from interpersonal stressors, a given stressor could activate your biological tendencies to be anxious and your psychological tendencies to feel you might not be able to deal with the situation and control the stress. Once this cycle starts, it tends to feed on itself, so it might not stop even when the particular life stressor has long since passed. Anxiety can be general, evoked by many aspects of your life. But it is usually focused on one area, such as social evaluations or grades (Barlow, 2002).

As noted earlier, panic is also a characteristic response to stress that runs in families and may have a genetic component that is separate from anxiety. Furthermore, anxiety and panic are closely related (Barlow, 2002; Suárez et al., 2009) in that anxiety increases the likelihood of panic. This relationship makes sense from an evolutionary point of view, because sensing a possible future threat or danger (anxiety) should prepare us to react instantaneously with an alarm response if the danger becomes imminent (Bouton, 2005). Anxiety and panic need not occur together, but it makes sense that they often do.

Comorbidity of Anxiety Disorders

Before describing the specific anxiety disorders, it is important to note that they often co-occur. As we described in Chapter 3, the co-occurrence of two or more disorders in a single individual is referred to as *comorbidity*. The fact that rates of comorbidity among anxiety disorders (and depression) are high emphasizes the fact that all these disorders share the common features of anxiety and panic described here. They also share the same vulnerabilities, biological and psychological, for developing anxiety and panic. They differ only in the focus of anxiety (what they are anxious about) and, perhaps, the patterning of panic attacks. Of course, if each patient with an anxiety disorder also

had every other anxiety disorder, distinguishing among the specific disorders would make little sense. It would be enough to say, simply, that the patient had an anxiety disorder. But this is not the case, and, although rates of comorbidity are high, they vary somewhat from disorder to disorder (Allen et al., 2010; Bruce et al., 2005; Tsao, Mystkowski, Zucker, & Craske, 2002). A large-scale study completed at one of our centres examined the comorbidity of *Diagnostic and Statistical Manual of Mental Disorders*, fourth edition (*DSM-IV-TR*) anxiety and mood disorders (Brown & Barlow, 2002; Brown, Campbell, Lehman, Grisham, & Mancill, 2001). Data were collected from 1127 patients carefully diagnosed using a semistructured interview. If we examine just rates of comorbidity at the time of assessment, the results indicate that 55 percent of the patients who received a principal diagnosis of an anxiety or depressive disorder had at least one additional anxiety or depressive disorder at the time of the assessment. If we consider whether the patient met criteria for an additional diagnosis at any time in his or her life, rather than just at the time of the assessment, the rate increases to 76 percent.

By far, the most common additional diagnosis for all anxiety disorders was major depression, which occurred in 50 percent of the cases over the course of the patient's life. This becomes important when we discuss the relationship of anxiety and depression later in this chapter. Also important is the finding that additional diagnoses of depression or alcohol or drug abuse makes it less likely that you will recover from an anxiety disorder and more likely that you will relapse if you do recover (Bruce et al., 2005; Huppert, 2009).

Comorbidity with Physical Disorders

Anxiety disorders also co-occur with several physical conditions. A recent important study indicated that the presence of any anxiety disorder was uniquely and significantly associated with thyroid disease, respiratory disease, gastrointestinal disease, arthritis, migraine headaches, and allergic conditions (Sareen et al., 2006). Thus, people with these physical conditions are likely to have an anxiety disorder but are not any more likely to have another psychological disorder. Furthermore, the anxiety disorder most often begins before the physical disorder, suggesting (but not proving) that something about having an anxiety disorder might cause, or contribute to the cause of, the physical disorder. Finally, if someone has both an anxiety disorder and one of the physical disorders mentioned earlier, that person will suffer from greater disability and a poorer quality of life from both the physical problem and the anxiety problem than if that individual had just the physical disorder alone (Belik, Sareen & Stein, 2009; Sareen et al., 2006). Other studies have also found the same relationship between anxiety disorders, particularly panic disorders, and cardiovascular (heart)

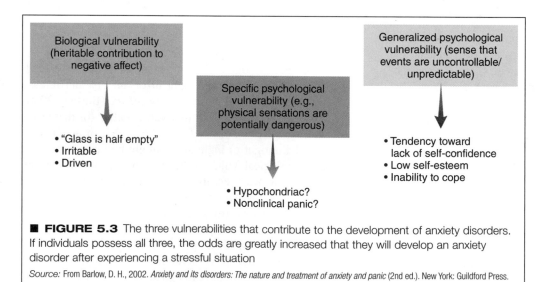

Biological vulnerability (heritable contribution to negative affect)

- "Glass is half empty"
- Irritable
- Driven

Specific psychological vulnerability (e.g., physical sensations are potentially dangerous)

- Hypochondriac?
- Nonclinical panic?

Generalized psychological vulnerability (sense that events are uncontrollable/ unpredictable)

- Tendency toward lack of self-confidence
- Low self-esteem
- Inability to cope

■ **FIGURE 5.3** The three vulnerabilities that contribute to the development of anxiety disorders. If individuals possess all three, the odds are greatly increased that they will develop an anxiety disorder after experiencing a stressful situation

Source: From Barlow, D. H., 2002. *Anxiety and its disorders: The nature and treatment of anxiety and panic* (2nd ed.). New York: Guildford Press.

disease (see, for example, Gomez-Caminero, Blumentals, Russo, Brown, & Castilla-Puentes, 2005).

Suicide

Based on epidemiological data, Weissman and colleagues found that 20 percent of patients with panic disorder had attempted suicide. They concluded that such attempts were associated with panic disorder. They also concluded that the risk of someone with panic disorder attempting suicide is comparable to that for individuals with major depression (Johnson, Weissman, & Klerman, 1990; Weissman, Klerman, Markowitz, & Ouellette, 1989). This finding was alarming, because panic disorder is quite prevalent and clinicians had generally not been on the lookout for possible suicide attempts in such patients. The investigators also found that even patients with panic disorder who did not have accompanying depression were at risk for suicide.

The Weissman study confirms that having any anxiety disorder, not just panic disorder, uniquely increases the chances of having thoughts about suicide (suicidal ideation) or making suicidal attempts (Sareen et al., 2006). Even if an individual has depression, which we know is a big risk for suicide attempts (see Chapter 7), anxiety disorders combined with depression will make the risk of suicide significantly greater than the risk for a person who has depression alone.

We now turn to descriptions of the individual anxiety disorders. But keep in mind that approximately 50 percent of individuals with these disorders will present with one or more additional anxiety or depressive disorders and, perhaps, some other disorders, particularly substance abuse disorders, as described later. For this reason, at the end of this chapter in the "On the Spectrum" feature, we consider new ideas for classifying and treating anxiety disorders that move beyond just looking at single disorders.

Concept Check 5.1

Complete the following statements about anxiety and its causes with the following terms: (a) comorbidity, (b) panic attack, (c) situationally bound, (d) neurotransmitter, (e) brain circuits, and (f) stressful.

1. A _____ is an abrupt experience of intense fear or acute discomfort accompanied by physical symptoms, such as chest pain and shortness of breath.

2. A _____ panic attack often occurs in certain situations but not anywhere else.

3. Anxiety is associated with specific _____ (e.g., behavioural inhibition system or fight/flight system) and _____ systems (e.g., noradrenergic).

4. The rates of _____ among anxiety disorders are high because they share the common features of anxiety and panic.

5. _____ life events can trigger biological and psychological vulnerabilities to anxiety.

Generalized Anxiety Disorder

Specific anxiety disorders are complicated by panic attacks or other features that are the focus of the anxiety. In generalized anxiety disorder, the focus is generalized to the events of everyday life. Therefore, we consider generalized anxiety disorder first.

Clinical Description

Is somebody in your family a worrywart? Is somebody in your family a perfectionist? Perhaps it is you! Most of us worry to some extent. As we have said, worry can be very useful. It helps us plan for the future, make sure that we're prepared for that test, or double-check that we've thought of everything before we head home for the holidays. The worry process itself is not pleasant, but without it nothing would go very smoothly. But what if you worry indiscriminately about everything? Furthermore, what if worrying is unproductive: No matter how much you worry, you can't seem to decide what to do about an upcoming problem or situation. And what if you can't stop worrying, even if you know it is doing you no good and probably making everyone else around you miserable? These features characterize **generalized anxiety disorder (GAD)**. Consider the case of Irene.

IRENE | *Ruled by Worry*

Irene was a 20-year-old university student with an engaging personality but not many friends. She came to the clinic complaining of excessive anxiety and general difficulties in controlling her life. Everything was a catastrophe for Irene. Although she carried a 3.7 grade-point average, she was convinced she would flunk every test she took. As a result, she repeatedly threatened to drop courses after only several weeks of classes because she feared that she would not understand the material.

Irene worried until she dropped out of the first university she attended after one month. She felt depressed for a while, and then decided to take a couple of courses at a local college, believing she could handle the work there better. After achieving straight A's at the college for two years, she enrolled once again in university as a third-year student. After a short time she began calling the clinic in a state of extreme agitation, saying she had to drop this or that course because she couldn't handle it. With great difficulty, her therapist and parents persuaded her to stay in the courses and to seek further help. In any course Irene completed, her grade was between an A and a B-minus, but she still worried about every test and every paper, afraid she would fall apart and be unable to understand and complete the work.

Irene did not worry only about school. She was also concerned about relationships with her friends, and whenever she was with her new boyfriend, she feared making a fool of herself and losing his interest. In fact, she reported that each date went extremely well, but she knew the next one would probably be a disaster. As the relationship progressed and some sexual contact seemed natural, Irene was worried

---

sick that her inexperience would make her boyfriend consider her naïve and stupid. Nevertheless, she reported enjoying the early sexual contact and admitted that he seemed to enjoy it also, but she was convinced the next time a catastrophe would happen.

Irene was also concerned about her health. She had minor hypertension, probably because she was somewhat overweight. She then approached every meal as if death itself might result if she ate the wrong types or amounts of food. She became reluctant to have her blood pressure checked for fear it would be very high, or to weigh herself for fear she was not losing weight. She severely restricted her eating and as a result had an occasional episode of binge eating, although not often enough to warrant concern.

In addition, Irene worried about her religious faith and about her relationships with her family, particularly her mother and sister. Although Irene had an occasional panic attack, this was not a major issue to her. As soon as the panic subsided she focused on the next possible catastrophe. In addition to high blood pressure, Irene had tension headaches and a "nervous stomach," with a lot of gas, occasional diarrhea, and some abdominal pain. Irene's life was a series of impending catastrophes. Her mother reported that she dreaded a phone call from Irene, let alone a visit, because she knew she would have to see her daughter through a crisis. For the same reason, Irene had very few friends. Even so, when she temporarily gave up her anxiety she was really fun to be with.

DSM-IV-TR	**Table 5.2** Diagnostic Criteria for Generalized Anxiety Disorder

A. Excessive anxiety and worry (apprehensive expectation), occurring more days than not for at least six months, about a number of events or activities (such as work or school performance).

B. The person finds it difficult to control the worry.

C. The anxiety and worry are associated with at least three (or more) of the following six symptoms (with at least some symptoms present for more days than not for the past six months. Note—only one item is required in children):

   1. Restlessness or feeling keyed up or on edge

   2. Being easily fatigued

   3. Difficulty concentrating or mind going blank

   4. Irritability

   5. Muscle tension

   6. Sleep disturbance (difficulty falling or staying asleep, or restless unsatisfying sleep)

D. The focus of the anxiety and worry is not confined to features of an Axis I disorder. That is, the anxiety or worry is not about having a panic attack (as in panic disorder), being embarrassed in public (as in social phobia), being contaminated (as in obsessive-compulsive disorder), being away from home or close relatives (as in separation anxiety disorder), gaining weight (as in anorexia nervosa), or having a serious illness (as in hypochondriasis), and is not part of post-traumatic stress disorder.

E. The anxiety, worry, or physical symptoms cause clinically significant distress or impairment in social, occupational, or other important areas of functioning.

F. Not due to the direct effects of a substance (e.g., drugs of abuse, medication) or a general medical condition (e.g., hyperthyroidism), and does not occur exclusively during a mood disorder, psychotic disorder, or a pervasive developmental disorder.

Source: Reprinted with permission from the *Diagnostic and Statistical Manual of Mental Disorders,* Fourth Edition, Text Revision, (Copyright © 2000). American Psychiatric Association.

Irene suffered from GAD, which is, in many ways, the basic syndrome that characterizes every anxiety disorder considered in this chapter (Brown, Barlow, & Liebowitz, 1994). The *DSM-IV-TR* criteria specify that at least six months of excessive anxiety and worry (apprehensive expectation) must be ongoing more days than not (see DSM Table 5.2). Furthermore, it must be difficult to turn off or control the worry process. This is what distinguishes pathological worrying from the normal kind we all experience occasionally as we prepare for an upcoming event or challenge. Most of us worry for a time but can set the problem aside and go on to another task. Even if the upcoming challenge is a big one, as soon as it is over the worrying stops. For Irene, it never stopped. She turned to the next crisis as soon as the current one was over.

The physical symptoms associated with generalized anxiety and GAD differ somewhat from those associated with panic attacks and panic disorder (covered next). Whereas panic is associated with autonomic arousal, presumably as a result of a sympathetic nervous system surge (for instance, increased heart rate, palpitations, perspiration, and trembling), GAD is characterized by muscle tension, mental agitation (Brown, Marten, & Barlow, 1995), susceptibility to fatigue (probably the result of chronic excessive muscle tension), some irritability, and difficulty sleeping. Focusing attention is difficult as the mind quickly switches from crisis to crisis. For children, only one physical symptom is required for a diagnosis of GAD, and research validates this strategy (Tracey, Chorpita, Douban, & Barlow, 1997). People with GAD mostly worry about minor, everyday life events, a characteristic that distinguishes GAD

from other anxiety disorders. When asked, "Do you worry excessively about minor things?" 100 percent of individuals with GAD respond "yes" compared to approximately 50 percent of individuals whose anxiety disorder falls within other categories (Barlow, 2002). Such a difference is statistically significant. Major events quickly become the focus of anxiety and worry, too. Adults typically focus on possible misfortune to their children, family health, job responsibilities, and more minor things such as household chores or being on time for appointments. Children with GAD most often worry about competence in academic, athletic, or social performance, as well as family issues (Albano & Hack, 2004; Furr, Tiwari, Suveg, & Kendall, 2009; Weems, Silverman, & La Greca, 2000). Older adults tend to focus, understandably, on health (Ayers, Thorp, & Wetherell, 2009; Beck & Averill, 2004; Person & Borkovec, 1995); they also have difficulty sleeping, which seems to make the anxiety worse (Beck & Stanley, 1997). Worry is such a prominent feature of GAD that one proposal for *DSM-5* is to change the name to "Generalized Worry Disorder" (Andrews et al., 2010).

Statistics

Although worry and physical tension are very common, the severe generalized anxiety experienced by Irene is quite rare. According to community surveys conducted in Edmonton and Ontario, approximately 1.1 percent of the Canadian population meet criteria for GAD during a given one-year period (Bland, Newman, & Orn, 1988; Offord et al., 1996; see also Health Canada, 2002). Similar rates are reported from around the world, for example, rural South Africa (Bhagwanjee, Parekh, Parvk, Petersen, & Sudebar, 1998) and the United States (Blazer, Hughes, George, Swartz, & Boyer, 1991; Kessler et al., 1994). Although GAD is one of the most common anxiety disorders, relatively few people with GAD come for treatment, compared with patients with panic disorder. Anxiety clinics report that only approximately 10 percent of their patients meet criteria for GAD, compared with 30 percent to 50 percent for panic disorder. This may be because most patients with GAD seek help from their primary care doctors, where they are found in large numbers (Roy-Byrne & Katon, 2000).

About two-thirds of individuals with GAD are female in both clinical samples (Woodman, Noyes, Black, Schlosser, & Yagla, 1999; Yonkers, Warshaw, Massion, & Keller, 1996) and epidemiological studies, which include people who do not necessarily seek out treatment (Blazer, George, & Hughes, 1991; Wittchen, Zhao, Kessler, & Eaton, 1994). But this sex ratio may be specific to developed countries. In the South African study mentioned here, GAD was more common in males.

Some people with GAD report onset in early adulthood. Stressful life events may play some role in the development of GAD. For example, Newman and Bland (1994) showed that a person with GAD is likely to have experienced an excess of life stressors compared with someone without this disorder. Nevertheless, most studies find that GAD is associated with an earlier and more gradual onset than most other anxiety disorders (Barlow, 2002; Brown et al., 1994; Woodman et al., 1999). Like Irene, many people have felt anxious and tense all their lives. Once it develops, GAD most often is chronic. One study found only an 8 percent probability of becoming symptom-free after two years of follow-up (Yonkers et al., 1996). Another found that patients with GAD retained their symptoms more consistently over five years than patients with panic disorder (Woodman et al., 1999).

GAD is prevalent among the elderly. In a large national comorbidity study, GAD was found to be most common in the group over 45 years of age, and least common in the youngest group, aged 15 to 24 (Wittchen et al., 1994). Flint (1994) reported prevalence rates of GAD in older adults to be as high as 7 percent. We also know that the use of minor tranquilizers in the elderly is very high, ranging from 17 percent to 50 percent in one study (Salzman, 1991). It is not entirely clear why drugs are prescribed with such frequency for the elderly. One possibility is that the drugs may not be entirely intended for anxiety. Prescribed drugs may be primarily for sleeping problems or other secondary effects of medical illnesses. In any case, benzodiazepines interfere with cognitive function (Buffett-Jerrott & Stewart, 2002) and put the elderly at greater risks for falling down and breaking bones, particularly their hips (Barlow, 2002). Major difficulties that hamper the investigation of anxiety in the elderly include the lack of good assessment instruments and treatment studies, largely because of insufficient research interest (Ayers et al., 2009; Beck & Stanley, 1997; Sheikh, 1992).

In a classic study, Rodin and Langer (1977) demonstrated that older adults may be particularly susceptible to anxiety about failing health or other life situations that begin to diminish whatever control they retain over events in their lives. This increasing lack of control, failing health, and gradual loss of meaningful functions may be a particularly unfortunate byproduct of the way the elderly are treated in Western culture. The result is substantial impairment in quality of life in older adults with GAD (Wetherell et al., 2004). If it were possible to change our attitudes and behaviour, we might well reduce the frequency of anxiety, depression, and early death among our elderly citizens.

Causes

What causes GAD? We have learned a great deal in the past several years. As with most anxiety disorders, there may be a genetic contribution. This conclusion is based on studies showing that GAD tends to run in families (Noyes, Clarkson, Crowe, Yates, & McChesney, 1987; Noyes et al., 1992). Twin studies strengthen this suggestion. Kendler, Neale, Kessler, Heath, and Eaves (1992a) found that the risk of GAD was somewhat greater for monozygotic (identical) female twins when one twin already had GAD than in dizygotic female twins. But in a later, more broadly focused study, Kendler et al. (1995) confirmed that what seems to be inherited is the tendency to become anxious rather than GAD itself.

For a long time, generalized anxiety disorder has posed a real puzzle to investigators. Although the definition of the disorder is relatively new, originating in 1980 with *DSM-III*, clinicians and psychopathologists were working with people with generalized anxiety long before diagnostic systems were developed. For years, clinicians thought that people who were generally anxious had simply not focused their anxiety on anything specific. Thus, such anxiety was described as free floating. But now scientists have looked more closely and have discovered some very interesting distinctions.

The first hints of difference of GAD from other anxiety disorders were found in the physiological responsivity of individuals with GAD. It is interesting that individuals with GAD do not respond as strongly as individuals with anxiety disorders in which panic is more prominent. In fact, several studies have found that individuals with GAD show less responsiveness on most physiological measures, such as heart rate, blood pressure, skin conductance, and respiration rate (Borkovec & Hu, 1990; Hoehn-Saric, McLeod, & Zimmerli, 1989; Roemer, Orsillo, & Barlow, 2002), than do individuals with other anxiety disorders.

When individuals with GAD are compared to nonanxious normal participants, the one physiological measure that consistently distinguishes the anxious group is muscle tension (Marten et al., 1993). People with GAD are chronically tense. For this reason, one proposal for *DSM-5* is to highlight muscle tension as the principal physical symptom in diagnosing GAD (Andrews et al., 2010). To understand this phenomenon of chronic muscle tension, we may have to know what's going on in the minds of people with GAD. With new methods from cognitive science, we are beginning to uncover the sometimes-unconscious mental processes ongoing in GAD (McNally, 1996).

Four distinct cognitive characteristics of people with GAD are outlined in a model developed by Québec researchers Michel Dugas and Robert Ladouceur and their colleagues (see Dugas, Gagnon, Ladouceur, & Freeston, 1998): (1) intolerance of uncertainty, (2) erroneous beliefs about worry, (3) poor problem

Courtesy of Dr. Robert Ladouceur/Laval University
Courtesy of Michel J. Dugas, Concordia University

▲ Robert Ladouceur, Michel Dugas, and their colleagues in Québec theorized about the role of intolerance of uncertainty and other cognitive factors in the etiology and maintenance of generalized anxiety disorder. They have also developed an effective psychosocial treatment for GAD.

orientation, and (4) cognitive avoidance. Although unpredictable events are known to produce anxiety in humans and animals (e.g., Seligman & Binik, 1977), people with GAD are less tolerant of situations involving uncertainty than people with other anxiety disorders or nonclinical controls (Ladouceur et al., 1999). People with GAD also hold stronger erroneous beliefs that worrying is effective in avoiding negative outcomes and promoting positive outcomes—beliefs that might maintain their worry. For example, they might believe that worrying about a family member's health is useful because if something should happen to the family member, then at least the worrier would not be taken by surprise (Ladouceur et al., 1999). People with GAD also have a poor orientation toward problems. For example, they tend to view problems as threats to be avoided rather than as challenges to be met (Dugas, Freeston, & Ladouceur, 1997).

The fourth cognitive characteristic of GAD in Ladouceur and Dugas's model pertains to the possibility that worry may serve an avoidance function. Borkovec and Inz (1990) have shown that people with GAD engage in frantic, intense thought processes or worry without accompanying images. This kind of worry may be exactly what causes these individuals to show less responsiveness on physiological measures (Borkovec, Shadick, & Hopkins, 1991; Roemer & Borkovec, 1993). They are thinking so hard about upcoming problems, they don't have the attentional capacity left for the all-important process of creating images of the potential threat, images that would elicit more substantial negative affect and autonomic activity. In other words, they avoid all the negative affect associated with the threat (Craske, 1999). Although people with GAD may avoid much of the unpleasantness and pain associated with the negative affect and imagery, the avoidance means that they are never able to work through their problems and arrive at solutions (Craske & Barlow, 1988). Therefore, they become chronic worriers, with accompanying autonomic inflexibility and quite severe muscle tension. Thus, intense worrying for an individual with GAD may serve the same maladaptive purpose as avoidance does for people with phobias. It prevents the person from facing the feared situation, and so adaptation never occurs.

Recent studies have tested various aspects of Ladouceur and Dugas's cognitive model of GAD. For example, University of Sherbrooke researcher Patrick Gosselin and his colleagues (Gosselin, Langlois, Freeston, Laberge, & Lemay, 2007) showed that, consist-

ent with model predictions, adolescents who are frequent worriers also hold more erroneous beliefs about worry and use more avoidance strategies. Another study by Dugas, Marchand, and Ladouceur (2005) showed that intolerance of uncertainty was related to GAD but not to panic disorder with agoraphobia, providing some support for the diagnostic specificity of this cognitive characteristic to GAD.

With new methods from cognitive science, we are beginning to uncover the sometimes unconscious mental processes ongoing in GAD (McNally, 1996). Evidence from this type of research, being conducted largely in Britain, indicates that individuals with GAD are highly sensitive to threat in general, particularly to a threat that has personal relevance. That is, they allocate their attention much more readily to sources of threat than people who are not anxious (Bradley, Mogg, White, Groom, & de Bono, 1999; Butler & Mathews, 1983; MacLeod, Mathews, & Tata, 1986; Mathews, 1997; Mogg, Mathews, & Weinman, 1989). Furthermore, this acute awareness of potential threat, particularly if it is personal, seems to be entirely automatic or unconscious (Eysenck, 1992; MacLeod & Mathews, 1991; Mathews, 1997; Mogg, Bradley, Millar, & White, 1995).

In summary, some people inherit a tendency to be tense, and they develop a sense early on that important events in their lives may be uncontrollable and potentially dangerous. Significant stress makes them apprehensive and vigilant. These emotions set off intense worry, which helps the individual avoid anxious images and physiological arousal in the short term, but eventually leads to the disorder of GAD (Roemer et al., 2002; Turovsky & Barlow, 1996). Cognitive factors such as intolerance of uncertainty, erroneous beliefs about worry, and poor problem orientation also seem to play contributing roles in causing and maintaining GAD (Ladouceur, Gosselin, & Dugas, 2000). This model is very current, as it combines findings from cognitive science with biological data from both the central and peripheral nervous systems. Time will tell whether the model is correct, although supporting data continue to come in (Borkovec, Alcaine, & Behar, 2004; Craske, 1999; DiBartolo, Brown, & Barlow, 1997; Mineka & Zinbarg, 2006). In any case, it is consistent with our view of anxiety as a future-oriented mood state focused on potential danger or threat, as opposed to an emergency or alarm reaction to actual present danger. A model of the development of GAD is presented in ■ Figure 5.4.

Treatment

GAD is quite common, and available treatments, both drug and psychological, are reasonably effective. Benzodiazepines are most often prescribed for generalized anxiety, and the evidence indicates that they give some relief, at least in the short term. Few studies have looked at the effects of these drugs for a period longer than eight weeks (Mathew & Hoffman, 2009). The therapeutic effect is relatively modest. Furthermore, benzodiazepines carry some risks. First, they seem to impair both cognitive and motor functioning (see, for example, Hindmarch, 1986, 1990; O'Hanlon, Haak, Blaauw, & Riemersma, 1982; van Laar, Volkerts, & Verbaten, 2001). Specifically, people don't seem to be as alert on the job or at school when they are taking benzodiazepines. The drugs may impair driving, and in older adults they seem to be associated with falls, resulting in hip fractures (Ray, Gurwitz, Decker, & Kennedy, 1992; Wang, Bohn, Glynn, Mogun, & Avorn, 2001). More important, benzodiazepines

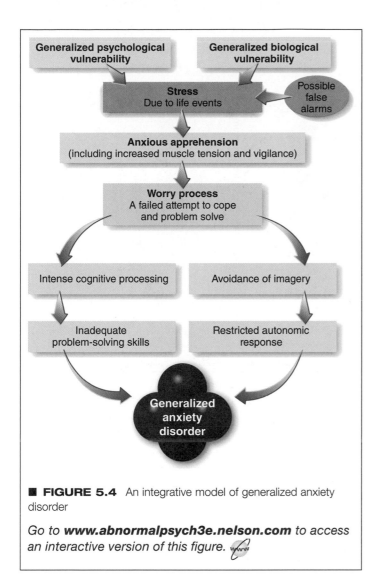

■ FIGURE 5.4 An integrative model of generalized anxiety disorder

*Go to **www.abnormalpsych3e.nelson.com** to access an interactive version of this figure.*

seem to produce both psychological and physical dependence, making it difficult for people to stop taking them (Mathew & Hoffman, 2009; Noyes, Garvey, Cook, & Suelzer, 1991; Rickels, Schweizer, Case, & Greenblatt, 1990). There is reasonably wide agreement that the optimal use of benzodiazepines is for the short-term relief of anxiety associated with a temporary crisis or stressful event, such as a family problem (Craske & Barlow, 2006). Under these circumstances, a physician may prescribe a benzodiazepine until the crisis is resolved but for no more than a week or two. There is stronger evidence for the usefulness of antidepressants in the treatment of GAD, such as paroxetine (Paxil) (Rickels, Rynn, Ivengar, & Duff, 2006) and venlafaxine (Effexor) (Schatzberg, 2000). These drugs may prove to be a better choice (Brawman-Mintzer, 2001; Mathew & Hoffman, 2009).

In the short term, psychological treatments seem to confer about the same benefit as drugs in the treatment of GAD, but psychological treatments are probably more effective in the long term (Barlow, Allen, & Basden, 2007; Barlow & Lehman, 1996; Borkovec, Newman, Pincus, & Lytle, 2002; Roemer et al., 2002). Recent reports of innovations in brief psychological treatments are encouraging. Because we now know that individuals with GAD seem to avoid "feelings" of anxiety and the negative affect associated with threatening images, clinicians have designed treatments

to help patients with GAD process the threatening information on an emotional level, using images, so that they will feel anxious (rather than avoid the anxious feeling). These treatments have other components, such as teaching patients how to relax deeply to combat tension. Borkovec and his colleagues found such a treatment to be significantly better than a placebo psychological treatment, not only at post-treatment but also at a one-year follow-up (Borkovec & Costello, 1993). In the early 1990s, we developed a cognitive-behavioural treatment (CBT) for GAD in which patients evoke the worry process during therapy sessions and confront anxiety-provoking images and thoughts head-on. The patient learns to use cognitive therapy and other coping techniques to counteract and control the worry process (Craske, Barlow, & O'Leary, 1992).

Ladouceur and his colleagues have also made important in-roads in the development of effective psychosocial interventions for GAD (see review by Dugas & Koerner, 2005). They developed and tested a GAD psychosocial treatment that targeted the four factors in their cognitive model of GAD described earlier (Ladouceur et al., 2000). For example, to combat erroneous beliefs about worry, the therapist used cognitive-behavioural strategies to help patients re-evaluate the actual usefulness of worry. Twenty-six GAD patients were randomly assigned to either a treatment condition or a delayed treatment control condition in which the patients received treatment after serving on the waiting list. Relative to those on the waiting list, those receiving the active treatment showed significant change in self-report, clinician, and significant-other ratings of GAD symptoms at post-treatment (see ■ Figure 5.5). Gains were found to be maintained at six-month and 12-month follow-ups. Moreover, 77 percent of the patients no longer met GAD diagnostic criteria following treatment. A more recent study by this research team showed that this intervention is also effective when delivered in a group format, thereby increasing its cost-effectiveness (Dugas et al., 2003).

Borkovec and Ruscio (2001) reviewed 13 controlled studies evaluating CBT treatments for GAD and found substantial gains compared with no treatment or alternative treatment such as psychodynamic therapy. Studies indicate that brief psychological treatments such as these alter the sometimes unconscious cognitive biases associated with GAD (Mathews, Mogg, Kentish, & Eysenck, 1995; Mogg, Bradley, Millar, & White, 1995). Recent studies also suggest that psychological interventions with GAD are effective to the extent that they focus on increasing the patient's ability to tolerate uncertainty (e.g., Ladouceur et al., 2000). Despite this success, it is clear we need more powerful treatments, both drug and psychological, for this chronic, treatment-resistant condition. Recently, a new psychological treatment for GAD has been developed that incorporates procedures focusing on acceptance rather than avoidance of distressing thoughts and feelings in addition to cognitive therapy. Meditational approaches help teach the patient to be more tolerant of these feelings (Orsillo, Roemer, & Barlow, 2003; Roemer & Orsillo, 2002; Roemer et al., 2002). Preliminary results are encouraging (Roemer & Orsillo, 2007).

Particularly encouraging is evidence that psychological treatments are effective with children who have generalized anxiety (Albano & Hack, 2004; Furr et al., 2009). Barrett, Dadds, and Rapee (1996) in Australia found significant benefit in children with severe GAD when cognitive behavioural procedures were combined with family therapy. After treatment, 95 percent of the children receiving this combination of therapies no longer met criteria for

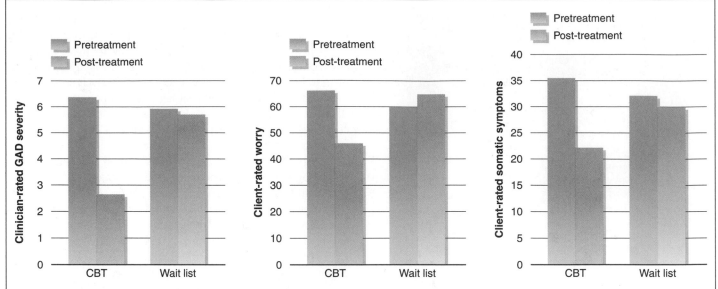

■ FIGURE 5.5 Pretreatment to post-treatment changes in clinician-rated GAD severity, client-rated worry, and client-rated somatic symptoms in patients receiving cognitive-behavioural therapy (CBT) versus wait-list controls

Source: Ladouceur, R. (1982). In vivo cognitive desensitization of flight phobia: A case study. *Psychological Reports, 50,* 459–462. Adapted with permission.

the diagnosis. Kendall et al. (1997) randomly assigned 94 children from 9 to 13 years of age to cognitive-behavioural therapy (CBT) or a wait-list control group. The majority of the children were diagnosed with GAD, but some had social phobia or separation anxiety. Based on teacher ratings, fully 70 percent of the treated children were functioning normally after treatment, and they maintained the gains for at least one year. Similarly, we are also making progress in adapting our treatments for the elderly, as important new studies show (Beck & Stanley, 1997; Stanley, Beck, & Glassco, 1997).

After trying several different drugs, Irene was treated with the CBT approach developed at our clinic and found herself much more able to cope with life. She completed college and graduate school, married, and is successful in her career as a counsellor in a nursing home. But even now, Irene finds it difficult to relax and stop worrying. She continues to experience mild to moderate anxiety, particularly when under stress; she takes minor tranquilizers on occasion to support her psychological coping skills.

Concept Check | 5.2

True (T) or false (F)?

1. ___ GAD is characterized by muscle tension, mental agitation, irritability, sleeping difficulties, and susceptibility to fatigue.

2. ___ Most studies show that in the majority of cases of GAD, onset is early in adulthood as an immediate response to a life stressor.

3. ___ GAD is prevalent in the elderly and in females in our society.

4. ___ GAD has no genetic basis.

5. ___ Cognitive-behavioural treatment and other psychological treatments for GAD are probably better than drug therapies in the long run.

Panic Disorder with and without Agoraphobia

Do you have a relative, maybe an eccentric aunt, for example, who never seems to leave the house? Family reunions or visits always have to be at her house. She never goes anywhere else. Most people attribute their old aunt's behaviour to her being a little odd or perhaps just not fond of travel. She is very warm and friendly when people come to visit, so she retains contact with the family.

In fact, your aunt may not be just odd or eccentric. She may have a very debilitating anxiety disorder **called panic disorder with agoraphobia (PDA)**, in which individuals experience severe unexpected panic attacks; they may think they're dying or otherwise losing control. Because they never know when an attack might occur, they develop **agoraphobia:** fear and avoidance of situations in which they would feel unsafe in the event of a panic attack or symptoms. These situations include those from which it would be hard or embarrassing to escape to get home or to a hospital. In severe cases, people with PDA are totally unable to leave the house, sometimes for years on end, as in the example of Mrs. M.

MRS. M. | *Self-Imprisoned*

Mrs. M. was 67 years old and lived in a second-floor walk-up apartment in a lower-middle-class section of the city. Her adult daughter, one of her few remaining contacts with the world, had requested an evaluation with Mrs. M.'s consent.

At her apartment building, I rang the front bell and entered a narrow hallway, Mrs. M. was nowhere in sight. Knowing that she lived on the second floor, I walked up the stairs and knocked on the door at the top. I opened the door when Mrs. M. asked me to come in. She was sitting in her living room, and I could quickly see the layout of the rest of the apartment. The living room was in the front; the kitchen was in the back, adjoining a porch. To the right of the stairs was the one bedroom, with a bathroom opening from it.

Mrs. M. was glad to see me and very friendly, offering me coffee and homemade cookies. I was the first person she had seen in three weeks. In fact, Mrs. M. had not left that apartment in 20 years, and she had suffered from panic disorder with agoraphobia for more than 30 years.

As she told her story, Mrs. M. conveyed vivid images of a wasted life. And yet she continued to struggle in the face of adversity and to make the best she could of her limited existence. Even areas in her apartment signalled the potential for terrifying panic attacks. She had not answered the door herself for the past 15 years because she was afraid to look into the hallway. She could enter her kitchen and go into the areas containing the stove and refrigerator, but for the past ten years she had not been to the part of the room that overlooked the backyard or out onto the back porch. Thus, her life for the past decade had been confined to her bedroom, her living room, and the front half of her kitchen. She relied on her adult daughter to bring groceries and visit once a week. Her only other visitor was the parish priest, who came to deliver communion every two to three weeks when he could. Her only other contact with the outside world was through the television and the radio. Her husband, who had abused both alcohol and Mrs. M., had died ten years earlier of alcohol-related causes. Early in her very stressful marriage she had her first terrifying panic attack and had gradually withdrawn from the world. As long as she stayed in her apartment, she was relatively free of panic. For this reason, and because in her mind there were few reasons left near the end of her life to venture out, she declined treatment.

Clinical Description

At the beginning of the chapter we talked about the related phenomena of anxiety and panic. In PDA, anxiety and panic are combined with *phobic avoidance* in an intricate relationship that can become as devastating as it was for Mrs. M. Many people who have panic attacks do not necessarily develop panic disorder. Similarly, many people experience anxiety and panic without developing agoraphobia. In those cases, the disorder is called **panic disorder without agoraphobia (PD)**.

To meet criteria for panic disorder (with or without agoraphobia) a person must experience an unexpected panic attack and develop substantial anxiety over the possibility of having another attack or about the implications of the attack or its consequences. In other words, he or she must think that each attack is a sign of impending death or incapacitation. A few individuals do not report concern about another attack but still change their behaviour in a way that indicates the distress the attacks cause them. They may avoid going to certain places or neglect their duties around the house for fear an attack might occur if they are too active.

The Development of Agoraphobia

Many people with panic disorder develop agoraphobia (see DSM Table 5.3). The term *agoraphobia* was coined in 1871 by Karl Westphal, a German physician, and, in the original Greek, refers to fear of the marketplace. This is a very appropriate term because the *agora*, the Greek marketplace, was a very busy, bustling area. One of the most stressful places for individuals with agoraphobia today is the shopping mall, the modern-day agora.

As noted by Stanley J. Rachman, "the consequences of panic can constitute a more serious problem than the panic itself" (Rachman, 1988, p. 259). Almost all agoraphobic avoidance behaviour is simply a complication of severe, unexpected panic attacks (Barlow, 2002; Craske & Barlow, 1988, 2008). Simply put, if you have had unexpected panic attacks and are afraid you may have another one, you want to be in a safe place or at least with a safe person who knows what you are experiencing if another attack occurs, so you can quickly get to a hospital or at least go into your bedroom and lie down (the home is usually a safe place). We know that anxiety is diminished for individuals with agoraphobia if they think a location or person is "safe" (Rachman, 1984), even if the person could do nothing effective if something bad did happen. If you are in a shopping mall or a crowded movie theatre or church, not only is it difficult to leave but you are also probably going to embarrass yourself if you try. You may think you will have to climb over everyone in church to get out, or get up in the middle of the movie and run out, or worse, faint in the movie theatre (in fact, individuals with agoraphobia

DSM-IV-TR	**Table 5.3** Diagnostic Criteria for Panic Disorder with Agoraphobia

A. Both 1 and 2:

  1. Recurrent unexpected panic attacks are present.

  2. At least one of the attacks has been followed by one month (or more) of one (or more) of the following: (a) persistent concern about having additional attacks, (b) worry about the implications of the attack or its consequences (e.g., losing control, having a heart attack, "going crazy"), or (c) a significant change in behaviour related to the attacks.

B. The presence of agoraphobia in which the predominant complaint is anxiety about being in places or situations from which escape might be difficult or embarrassing, or in which help may not be available in the event of an unexpected or situationally predisposed panic attack or panic-like symptoms. Agoraphobic fears typically involve characteristic clusters of situations that include being outside the home alone; being in a crowd or standing in a line; being on a bridge; and travelling in a bus, train, or automobile.

C. The panic attacks are not due to the direct physiological effects of a substance (e.g., drug of abuse, medication) or a general medical condition (e.g., hyperthyroidism).

D. The panic attacks are not better accounted for by another mental disorder, such as social phobia (e.g., occurring on exposure to feared social situations), specific phobia (e.g., on exposure to a specific social situation), obsessive-compulsive disorder (e.g., on exposure to dirt, in someone with an obsession about contamination), post-traumatic stress disorder (e.g., in response to stimuli associated with a severe stressor), or separation anxiety disorder (e.g., in response to being away from home or close relatives).

Source: Reprinted with permission from the *Diagnostic and Statistical Manual of Mental Disorders,* Fourth Edition, Text Revision, (Copyright © 2000). American Psychiatric Association.

TABLE 5.1 Typical Situations and Places Avoided by People with Agoraphobia

Being far from home	Staying at home alone
Buses	Stores
Cars (as driver or passenger)	Subways
Crowds	Supermarkets
Elevators	Theatres
Escalators	Trains
Planes	Tunnels
Restaurants	Waiting in line
Shopping malls	Wide streets

Source: From *Mastery of Your Anxiety and Panic II*, by D. H. Barlow and M. G. Craske, 1994. Albany, NY: Graywind Publications Incorporated. Reprinted by permission.

seldom if ever do any of these things). For these reasons, when they do go to church or to the movies, people with agoraphobia always plan for rapid escape (e.g., by sitting very near the door). A list of typical situations commonly avoided by someone with agoraphobia is found in Table 5.1.

Although agoraphobic behaviour initially is closely tied to the occasions of panic, it can become relatively independent of panic attacks (Craske & Barlow, 1988; Craske, Rapee, & Barlow, 1988). In other words, an individual who has not had a panic attack for years may still have strong agoraphobic avoidance, like Mrs. M. Agoraphobic avoidance seems to be determined by the extent to which you think or expect you might have another attack rather than by how many attacks you have actually had or how severe they have been. Thus, agoraphobic avoidance is simply one way of coping with unexpected panic attacks.

Other methods of coping with panic attacks include using (and eventually abusing) alcohol or drugs. Winnipeg psychiatrist Jitender Sareen and his colleagues have demonstrated that panic disorder is significantly associated with the use of cocaine, stimulants, and hallucinogens (Sareen et al., 2006). Similarly, a high comorbidity exists between panic disorder and alcohol abuse or dependence (see reviews by Cox, Norton, Swinson, & Endler, 1990, and Norton, Cox, & Belik, 2008). An experimental study by MacDonald, Baker, Stewart, and Skinner (2000) at Dalhousie University showed that panic-prone individuals may be more susceptible than others to the anxiety-reducing effects of alcohol when they are experiencing panic-like bodily sensations. This may explain why these individuals are more likely to develop alcohol abuse and dependence. In fact, recent treatment research has shown that intervening with panic-prone individuals' fear of anxiety leads to reductions in their problematic drinking (Watt, Stewart, Birch, & Bernier, 2006).

Some individuals do not actually avoid agoraphobic situations but endure them with "intense dread." For example, people who simply must go to work each day or, perhaps, travel as part of the job will endure untold agonies of anxiety and panic simply to achieve their goals. Thus, *DSM-IV-TR* notes that agoraphobia may be characterized either by avoiding the situations or by enduring them with marked distress.

Canadian hockey player Shayne Corson, a forward who has played 20 NHL seasons, won a Stanley cup, and served as a member of Canada's 1998 Olympic hockey team, experiences crippling panic attacks. His panic attacks would come on suddenly and unexpectedly. He experienced uncomfortable sensations in his chest that he worried might be signs of a heart attack. Corson would try to distract himself, but he found these attacks extremely distressing. When out at a restaurant or night-club, he reportedly wouldn't last more than four to five minutes before he would flee, fearful that he might experience a panic attack in public. Corson's panic attacks often occurred right on the Maple Leafs, bench in front of unsuspecting teammates and fans. Corson was prescribed anti-anxiety medication and saw a psychiatrist for treatment of his panic attacks (Hornby, 2001; Kennedy, 2001). Unfortunately, his symptoms reemerged and interfered so much with the effectiveness of his game that Corson decided to quit the Maple Leafs team during the 2003 playoffs (Hockey Hall of Fame and Museum, 2001). Corson eventually recovered sufficiently to return to his hockey career in 2004 (Foster, 2004).

Most patients with severe agoraphobic avoidance (and some with little avoidance) also display another cluster of avoidant behaviours that we call interoceptive avoidance or avoidance of internal physical sensations (Barlow & Craske, 2007; Brown, White, & Barlow, 2005; Craske & Barlow, 2008; Shear et al., 1997). These behaviours involve removing yourself from situations or activities that might produce the physiological arousal that somehow resembles the beginnings of a panic attack. Some patients might avoid exercise because it produces increased cardiovascular activity or faster respiration that reminds them of panic attacks. In fact, University of Regina researchers McWilliams and Asmundson (2001) showed that panic-prone university males reported engaging in exercise less frequently than other university males, consistent with the possibility that they might be avoiding exercise because of their fear of arousal sensations. Other patients might avoid sauna baths or any rooms in which they might perspire. Psychopathologists are beginning to recognize that this cluster of avoidance behaviours is every bit as important as more classical agoraphobic avoidance. A list of situations or activities typically avoided within the interoceptive cluster is found in Table 5.2.

Statistics

Panic disorder with or without agoraphobia is fairly common. Approximately 3.5 percent of the population meet the criteria for panic disorder at some point during their lives, two-thirds of them women (Eaton, Kessler, Wittchen, & Magee, 1994), and another 5.3 percent meet the criteria for agoraphobia (Kessler et al., 1994). The rates of agoraphobia may be somewhat overestimated as a result of methodological difficulties, but most people with panic disorder do have agoraphobic avoidance.

Onset of panic disorder usually occurs in early adult life—from mid-teens through about 40 years of age. The mean age of onset is between 25 and 29 (Craske & Barlow, 2001; Öst, 1987). Generally, panic disorder seems less pervasive among the elderly, but our estimates are not yet firm (e.g., Beck & Stanley, 1997).

Most initial unexpected panic attacks begin at or after puberty. In fact, puberty seems a better predictor of unexpected

TABLE 5.2 Interoceptive Daily Activities Typically Avoided by People with Agoraphobia

Running up flights of stairs	Getting involved in "heated" debates
Walking outside in intense heat	Hot, stuffy rooms
Having showers with the doors and windows closed	Hot, stuffy cars
Hot, stuffy stores or shopping malls	Having a sauna
Walking outside in very cold weather	Hiking
Aerobics	Sports
Lifting heavy objects	Drinking coffee or any caffeinated beverages
Dancing	Sexual relations
Eating chocolate	Watching horror movies
Standing quickly from a sitting position	Eating heavy meals
Watching exciting movies or sports events	Getting angry

Source: From *Mastery of Your Anxiety and Panic II*, by D. H. Barlow and M. G. Craske, 1994. Albany, NY: Graywind Publications Incorporated. Reprinted by permission.

panic attacks than age, because higher rates of panic attacks are found in girls after puberty compared with before puberty (Hayward et al., 1992). Furthermore, many prepubertal children who are seen by general medical practitioners have symptoms of hyperventilation that may well be panic attacks. However, these children do not report fear of dying or losing control—perhaps because they are not at a stage of their cognitive development where they can make these attributions (Nelles & Barlow, 1988).

As we have said, 75 percent or more of those who have agoraphobia are women (Barlow, 2002; Myers et al., 1984; Thorpe & Burns, 1983). In fact, the higher the severity of agoraphobic avoidance, the greater the proportion of women. For example, in our clinic, in a group of patients with panic disorder with mild agoraphobia, 72 percent were women; but if the agoraphobia was moderate, the percentage was 81 percent. Similarly, if agoraphobia was severe, the percentage was 89 percent. For a long time we didn't know why agoraphobia is more common in women, but now it seems the most logical explanation is cultural (Arrindell et al., 2003; Wolitzky-Taylor, Castriotta, Lenze, Stanley, & Craske, 2010). It is more accepted for women to report fear and to avoid numerous situations. Men, however, are expected to be stronger and braver—to "tough it out." Another possible reason pertains to gender differences in fear of anxiety. Research conducted at Dalhousie University and at the Royal Ottawa Hospital has shown that women are more fearful of anxiety symptoms than are men (Stewart, Taylor, & Baker, 1997), with women proving particularly fearful of the physical consequences of anxiety sensations (e.g., fearing an imminent heart attack; Foot & Koszycki, 2004). These gender differences are even observed in children (Walsh, Stewart, McLaughlin, & Comeau, 2004). A study by Schmidt and Koselka (2000) showed that women with panic-disorder have

greater agoraphobia because they believe panic attacks are more likely and because they are more afraid of the potential negative consequences of a panic attack.

What happens to men who have severe unexpected panic attacks? Is cultural disapproval of fear in men so strong that most of them simply endure panic? The answer seems to be "no." A large proportion of males with unexpected panic attacks cope in a culturally acceptable way: They consume large amounts of alcohol (see review by Cox et al., 1990). A study by clinical psychologist Brian Cox and his colleagues (Cox, Swinson, Shulman, Kuch, & Reichman, 1993), conducted at the Centre for Addiction and Mental Health in Toronto, compared 74 men and 162 women with panic disorder. Although the women reported higher levels of agoraphobic avoidance, the men reported higher levels of weekly alcohol intake and greater beliefs in alcohol as an effective way to cope with anxiety. In fact, a study conducted by researchers at the University of Québec at Montréal showed that the lower agoraphobic avoidance of men with panic disorder was associated with their alcohol use (Turgeon, Marchand, & Dupuis, 1998). The problem is that these men with panic disorder can become dependent on alcohol, and many begin the long downward spiral into serious addiction. Thus, males may end up with an even more severe problem than panic disorder with agoraphobia. Because these men are so impaired by alcohol abuse, clinicians may not realize they also have PDA. And even if they are successfully treated for their addiction, the anxiety disorder still requires treatment (Cox et al., 1993; Kushner, Abrams, & Borchardt, 2000; Kushner, Sher, & Beitman, 1990; Stewart & Conrod, 2008).

Cultural Influences

Panic disorder exists worldwide, although its expression may vary from place to place. In Lesotho, Africa, the prevalence of panic disorder (and generalized anxiety disorder) was found to be equal to or greater than in North America (Hollifield, Katon, Spain, & Pule, 1990). In a more comprehensive study, prevalence rates for panic disorder were remarkably similar in Canada, the United States, Puerto Rico, New Zealand, Italy, Korea, and Taiwan, with only Taiwan showing somewhat lower rates (Horwath & Weissman, 1997), perhaps because of a stigma about admitting to psychological problems in Taiwanese culture (Weissman et al., 1997). The most recent statistics from the Canadian Community Health Survey (Statistics Canada, 2002) suggest that the one-year prevalence of panic disorder is 1 percent in men, and 2 percent in women.

In another large-scale study, the Cross-National Collaborative Panic Study (1992), panic disorder patients from clinics in 14 countries were examined, including those from Europe, Latin America, and North America. Although panic disorder occurred in all the countries studied, some interesting differences in the prominent features of the disorder were observed cross-nationally. For example, phobic avoidance was more common in panic disorder patients in Canada and the United States relative to panic patients in Latin American clinics. In addition, fear of dying and choking or smothering sensations were more common in panic patients from southern countries relative to those in other countries.

Somatic symptoms of anxiety may be emphasized in developing cultures. Subjective feelings of dread or angst may not be part of the cultural idiom; that is, individuals do not attend to

Panic Disorder with and without Agoraphobia **143**

these feelings and do not report them, focusing only on bodily sensations. In Chapter 2 we described a fright disorder called *susto* in Latin America characterized by sweating, increased heart rate, and insomnia, but no reports of anxiety or fear, even though a severe fright is the cause. An anxiety-related, culturally defined syndrome prominent among Hispanic people, particularly those from the Caribbean, is called *ataques de nervios* (Liebowitz et al., 1994). The symptoms of an *ataque* seem quite similar to those of panic attacks, although such manifestations as shouting uncontrollably or bursting into tears may be associated more frequently with an *ataque* than with panic. Another culture-bound syndrome that bears some relation to panic disorder occurs among the Inuit of northern Canada and western Greenland. This syndrome is called *kayak-angst* and involves episodes of intense fear, worries about drowning, physical arousal sensations (rapid heartbeat and trembling), and intense disorientation that occur when a seal hunter or fisher is alone at sea (Amering & Katschnig, 1990; Katschnig, 1999). Like the relation of panic disorder to agoraphobic avoidance, *kayak-angst* can cause the hunter or fisher to avoid travel in the kayak, which can obviously lead to significant impairments in his or her livelihood (Katschnig & Amering, 1990; Katschnig, 1999).

Nocturnal Panic

Think back to the case of Gretchen, whose panic attack was described earlier in this chapter. Is there anything unusual about her report? Yes—she was sound asleep when it happened! Approximately 60 percent of the people with panic disorder have experienced such nocturnal attacks (Craske & Rowe, 1997; Uhde, 1994). In fact, panic attacks occur more frequently between 1:30 a.m. and 3:30 a.m. than at any other time (Taylor et al., 1986). In some cases, people are afraid to go to sleep at night. What is happening to them? Are they having nightmares? Research indicates they are not. Nocturnal attacks are studied in a sleep laboratory. Patients spend a few nights sleeping while attached to an electroencephalograph (EEG) machine that monitors their brain waves (see Chapter 3). We all go through various stages of sleep that are reflected by different patterns on the electro-encephalogram. (Stages of sleep are discussed fully in Chapter 8.) We have learned that nocturnal panics occur during delta wave or slow-wave sleep, which typically occurs several hours after we fall asleep and is the deepest stage of sleep. People with panic disorder often begin to panic when they start sinking into delta sleep, and then they awaken in the midst of an attack. Because there is no obvious reason for them to be anxious or panicky when they are sound asleep, most of these individuals think they are dying (Craske & Barlow, 1988; Craske & Rowe, 1997).

What causes nocturnal panic? Our best information at the current time is that the change in stages of sleep to slow-wave sleep produces physical sensations of "letting go" that are very frightening to an individual with panic disorder (Craske, Lang, Mystkowski, Zucker, & Bystritsky, 2002). This process is described more fully later when we discuss causes of panic disorder. Several other events also occur during sleep that resemble nocturnal

panic and are mistakenly thought to be the cause of nocturnal panic by some. Initially, we thought it might be nightmares, but nightmares and other dream-like activity occur only during a stage of sleep characterized by rapid eye movement (REM sleep), which typically occurs much later in the sleep cycle. Therefore, people are not dreaming when they have nocturnal panics, a conclusion consistent with patient reports. Some therapists are not aware of the stage of sleep associated with nocturnal panic attacks and so assume that patients are "repressing" their dream material, perhaps because it might relate to an early trauma too painful to be admitted to consciousness. As we've seen, this explanation is virtually impossible, because nocturnal panic attacks do not occur during REM sleep, so no well-developed dream or nightmare activity is going on when they happen. Thus, it is not possible for these patients to be dreaming anything.

A fascinating condition that at first glance appears similar to nocturnal panic is called *isolated sleep paralysis*. Have you ever found yourself awake at night, unable to move, your heart pounding as you stare at aspects of the room—maybe the clock, maybe the window—feeling that a presence is in the room with you? If you were from Newfoundland and Labrador, you would refer to this experience as being visited by the "Old Hag" (Hufford, 1982); if you were from an African or Caribbean culture, this experience would be captured by the expression "the witch is riding you" (Bell, Dixie-Bell, & Thompson, 1986); and if you were from China you would believe this experience is the result of being pressed down upon by a ghost (Yeung, Yong, & Chang, 2005). Isolated sleep paralysis occurs during the transitional state between sleep and waking. During this period the individual is unable to move and experiences a surge of terror that resembles a panic attack; occasionally, the person also has vivid hallucinations. One possible explanation is that REM sleep is spilling over into the waking cycle. This seems likely because one feature of REM sleep is lack of bodily movement. Another is vivid dreams, which could account for the experience of hallucination. The "Old Hag" is mentioned twice in E. Annie Proulx's novel *The Shipping News*, set in Newfoundland and Labrador.

Causes

It is not possible to understand panic disorder (with or without agoraphobia) without referring to the triad of contributing factors mentioned throughout this book: biological, psychological, and social. Strong evidence indicates that agoraphobia, for the most

▲ This drawing depicts a victim of isolated sleep paralysis being "ridden by the witch."

part, develops after a person has unexpected panic attacks (or panic-like sensations); but whether agoraphobia develops and how severe it becomes seem to be socially and culturally determined, as we noted earlier. Panic attacks and panic disorder, however, seem to be related most strongly to biological and psychological factors and their interaction.

At the beginning of the chapter, we discussed the triple vulnerability model of how biological, psychological, and social factors may contribute to the development and maintenance of anxiety and to an initial unexpected panic attack (Bouton et al., 2001; Bouton, 2005; Suárez et al., 2009; White & Barlow, 2002) (see Figure 5.3 on page 134). As noted earlier, we all inherit—some more than others—a vulnerability to stress, which is a tendency to be generally neurobiologically overreactive to the events of daily life (generalized biological vulnerability). But some people are also more likely than others to have an emergency alarm reaction (unexpected panic attack) when confronted with stress-producing events. These may include stress on the job or at school, death of a loved one, divorce, and positive events that are nevertheless stressful, such as graduating from school and starting a new career, getting married, or changing jobs. (Remember that other people might be more likely to have headaches or high blood pressure in response to the same kinds of stress.) Particular situations quickly become associated in an individual's mind with external and internal cues that were present during the panic attack (Bouton et al.,

2001). The next time the person's heart rate increases during exercise, she might assume she is having a panic attack (conditioning). Harmless exercise is an example of an internal cue or a conditioned stimulus for a panic attack. Being in a movie theatre when panic first occurred would be an external cue that might become a conditioned stimulus for future panics. Because these cues become associated with a number of different internal and external stimuli through a learning process, we call them *learned alarms*.

But none of this would make much difference without the next step. An individual must be susceptible to developing anxiety over the possibility of having another panic attack (a generalized psychological vulnerability). That is, he or she thinks the physical sensations associated with the panic attack mean something terrible is about to happen, perhaps death. This is what creates panic disorder. This tendency to believe that unexpected bodily sensations are dangerous reflects a specific psychological vulnerability to develop panic and related disorders. This causal sequence is depicted in ■ Figure 5.6.

Approximately 8 percent to 12 percent of the population has an occasional unexpected panic attack, often during a period of intense stress during the past year (Kessler et al., 2006; Mattis & Ollendick, 2002; Norton, Harrison, Hauch, & Rhodes, 1985; Suárez et al., 2009; Telch, Lucas, & Nelson, 1989). Most of these people do not develop anxiety (Telch et al., 1989). Only approximately 5 percent go on to develop anxiety over future panic

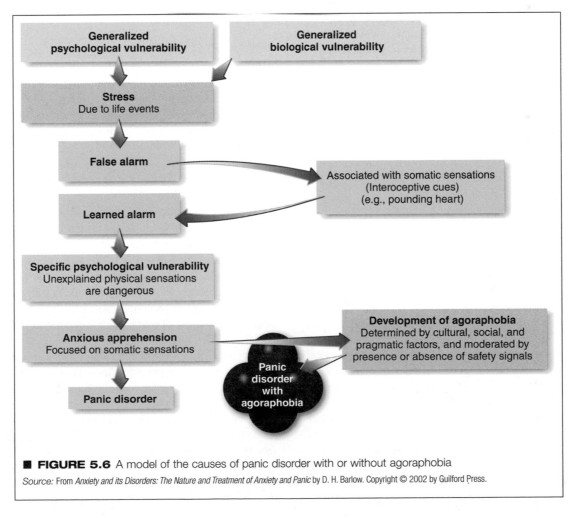

■ **FIGURE 5.6** A model of the causes of panic disorder with or without agoraphobia

Source: From *Anxiety and its Disorders: The Nature and Treatment of Anxiety and Panic* by D. H. Barlow. Copyright © 2002 by Guilford Press.

attacks and thereby meet the criteria for panic disorder, and these individuals are the ones who are susceptible to developing anxiety over the possibility of having another panic attack (a generalized psychological vulnerability). What happens to those individuals who don't develop anxiety? They seem to attribute the attack to events of the moment, such as an argument with a friend, something they ate, or a bad day, and go on with their lives, perhaps experiencing an occasional panic attack when they are under stress again. We can now measure one aspect of this psychological vulnerability, using an instrument known as the *anxiety sensitivity index* (Reiss, Peterson, Gursky, & McNally, 1986). One of the best tests of anxiety sensitivity as a vulnerability to experience panic attacks was demonstrated in an experiment conducted by Brad Schmidt and his colleagues (Schmidt, Lerew, & Jackson, 1997, 1999). Schmidt and colleagues (1997) administered the Anxiety Sensitivity Index to a large number of military recruits undergoing a stressful basic training regimen. High scores on the anxiety sensitivity index before basic training predicted the onset of unexpected panic attacks in the five weeks following basic training. In a different study, high scores on this index also predicted future panic attacks and anxiety in adolescents (Hayward, Killen, Kraemer, & Taylor, 2000). The experience of panic, in turn, elevated scores on the Anxiety Sensitivity Index at a later date, underscoring the cycle of panic and anxiety in those who are vulnerable (Schmidt et al., 1999; Weems, Hayward, Killen, & Taylor, 2002). The influential cognitive theories of David Clark (1986, 1996) explicate in more detail some cognitive processes that may be ongoing in panic disorder. Clark emphasizes the specific psychological vulnerability of people with this disorder to interpret normal physical sensations in a catastrophic way. In other words, although we all typically experience rapid heartbeat after exercise, if you have a psychological or cognitive vulnerability, you might interpret the response as dangerous and feel a surge of anxiety. This anxiety, in turn, produces more physical sensations because of the action of the sympathetic nervous system; you perceive these additional sensations as even more dangerous, and a vicious cycle begins that results in a panic attack. Thus, Clark emphasizes the cognitive process as most important in panic disorder.

But none of this would make much difference without the next step. Why would some people think something terrible is going to happen when they have an attack but others wouldn't? In a recent important study, young women at risk for developing anxiety disorders were followed prospectively for several years. Those women who had a history of having various physical disorders and were anxious about their health tended to develop panic disorder rather than another anxiety disorder such as social phobia (Rudaz, Craske, Becker, Ledermann, & Margraf, 2010). Thus, these women may have learned in childhood that unexpected bodily sensations may be dangerous—whereas other people experiencing panic attacks do not. This tendency to believe that unexpected bodily sensations are dangerous reflects a specific psychological vulnerability to develop panic and related disorders.

This specific psychological vulnerability is also reflected in the influential cognitive theories of David Clark (1986, 1996), who emphasizes the tendency of people with this disorder to interpret normal physical sensations in a catastrophic way. The

causal sequence for the development of panic disorder is depicted in Figure 5.6.

One hypothesis that panic disorder and agoraphobia evolve from psychodynamic causes suggested that early object loss and/or separation anxiety might predispose someone to develop the condition as an adult. Separation anxiety is what a child might feel at the threat of separation or upon actual separation from an important caregiver, such as the mother or father. Dependent personality tendencies often characterize a person with agoraphobia. These characteristics were hypothesized as a possible reaction to early separation. Nevertheless, despite some intriguing suggestions, little evidence indicates that patients who have PDA experienced separation anxiety during childhood more often than individuals with other psychological disorders or, for that matter, "normals" (Barlow, 2002; Thyer, 1993; van der Molen, van den Hout, van Dieren, & Griez, 1989). It is still possible, however, that the trauma of early separation might predispose someone to psychological disorders in general. (Separation anxiety disorder is discussed in the section on specific phobias.)

Treatment

As we noted in Chapter 1, research on the effectiveness of new treatments is important to psychopathology. Responses to certain specific treatments, whether drug or psychological, may indicate the causes of the disorder. We now discuss the benefits and some drawbacks of medication, psychological interventions, and a combination of these two treatments.

Medication

A large number of drugs affecting the noradrenergic, serotonergic, or GABA–benzodiazepine neurotransmitter systems or some combination seem effective in treating panic disorder, including high-potency benzodiazepines, the newer selective-serotonin reuptake inhibitors (SSRIs) such as Prozac and Paxil, and the closely related serotonin-norepinephrine reuptake inhibitors (SNRIs) such as venlafaxine (Barlow, 2002; Barlow & Craske, 2007; Pollack, 2005; Pollack & Simon, 2009; Spiegel, Wiegel, Baker, & Greene, 2000).

There are advantages and disadvantages to each class of drugs. SSRIs are currently the indicated drug for panic disorder based on all available evidence, although sexual dysfunction seems to occur in 75 percent or more of people taking these medications (Lecrubier, Bakker, et al., 1997; Lecrubier, Judge, et al., 1997). On the other hand, high-potency benzodiazepines such as alprazolam (Xanax), commonly used for panic disorder, work quickly but are hard to stop taking because of psychological and physical dependence and addiction. Therefore, they are not recommended as strongly as the SSRIs. Nevertheless, benzodiazepines remain the most widely used class of drugs in practice (Bruce et al., 2003). Also, all benzodiazepines adversely affect cognitive and motor functions to some degree. Therefore, people taking them in high doses often find their ability to drive a car or study somewhat reduced.

Approximately 60 percent of patients with panic disorder are free of panic as long as they stay on an effective drug (Lecrubier, Bakker, et al., 1997; Pollack & Simon, 2009), but 20 percent or more stop taking the drug before treatment is done (Otto, Behar, Smits, & Hofmann, 2009), and relapse rates are high (approximately 50 percent) once the medication is stopped (Hollon et al., 2005; Spiegel et al., 2000). The relapse rate is closer to 90 percent for those who stop taking benzodiazepines (see, for example, Fyer et al., 1987).

Psychological Intervention

Psychological treatments have proved quite effective for panic disorder. Originally, such treatments concentrated on reducing agoraphobic avoidance, using strategies based on exposure to feared situations. The strategy of exposure-based treatments is to arrange conditions in which the patient can gradually face the feared situations and learn there is nothing to fear. Most patients with phobias are well aware of this rationally, but they must be convinced on an emotional level as well by "reality testing" the situation and confirming that nothing dangerous happens. Sometimes the therapist accompanies the patients on their exposure exercises. At other times, the therapist simply helps patients structure their own exercises and provides them with a variety of psychological coping mechanisms to help them complete the exercises, which are typically arranged from least to most difficult. A sample of these is listed in Table 5.3.

Gradual exposure exercises, sometimes combined with anxiety-reducing coping mechanisms such as relaxation or breathing retraining, have proved effective in helping patients overcome agoraphobic behaviour. As many as 70 percent of patients undergoing these treatments substantially improve as their anxiety and panic are reduced and their agoraphobic avoidance is greatly diminished. Few, however, are cured, because many still experience some anxiety and panic attacks, although at a less severe level.

Effective psychological treatments have recently been developed that treat panic attacks directly (Barlow & Craske, 2007; Clark et al., 1994; Craske & Barlow, 2008; Klosko, Barlow, Tassinari, & Cerny, 1990). **Panic control treatment (PCT)** developed at one of our clinics concentrates on exposing patients with panic disorder to the cluster of interoceptive sensations that remind them of their panic attacks. The therapist attempts to create "mini" panic attacks in the office by having the patients exercise to elevate their heart rates or perhaps by spinning them in a chair to make them dizzy. A variety of exercises have been developed for this purpose (see Table 5.4). Patients also receive cognitive therapy. Basic attitudes and perceptions concerning the dangerousness of the feared but objectively harmless situations are identified and modified. As we learned earlier, many of these attitudes and perceptions are beyond the patient's awareness. Uncovering these unconscious cognitive processes requires a

TABLE 5.4 Exercising to Create the Sensation of Panic

1. Shake your head loosely from side to side for 30 seconds (to produce dizziness or disorientation).
2. Place your head between your legs for 30 seconds and then lift it quickly (to produce lightheadedness or blood rushing).
3. Take one step up, using stairs or a box or a footstool, and immediately step down. Do this repeatedly at a fast enough rate to notice your heart pumping quickly for one minute (to produce racing heart and shortness of breath).
4. Hold your breath for as long as you can or about 30 to 45 seconds (to produce chest tightness and smothering feelings).
5. Tense every part of your body for one minute without causing pain. Tense your arms, legs, stomach, back, shoulders, face—everything. Alternatively, try holding a pushup position for one minute or for as long as you can (to produce muscle tension, weakness, and trembling).
6. Spin in a chair for one minute. If you have a chair that spins, such as a desk chair, this is ideal. It's even better if someone is there to spin you around. Otherwise, stand up and turn around quickly to make yourself dizzy. Be near a soft chair or couch that you can sit on after one minute is up. This will produce dizziness and perhaps nausea as well.
7. Hyperventilate for one minute. Breathe deep and fast, using a lot of force. Sit down as you do this. This exercise might produce unreality, shortness of breath, tingling, cold or hot feelings, dizziness, or headache.
8. Breathe through a thin straw for one minute. Don't allow any air through your nose; hold your nostrils together (to produce feelings of restricted air flow or smothering).
9. Stare at a small spot on the wall or stare at yourself in the mirror for two minutes. Stare as hard as you can to produce feelings of unreality.

Source: From *Mastery of Your Anxiety and Panic II,* by D. H. Barlow and M. G. Craske, 1994. Albany, NY: Graywind Publications Incorporated. Reprinted by permission.

great deal of therapeutic skill. In addition to exposure to interoceptive sensations and cognitive therapy, patients are taught relaxation or breathing retraining to help them cope with increases in anxiety and to reduce excess arousal.

These psychological procedures are highly effective for panic disorder. Follow-up studies of patients who receive PCT indicate that most of them remain better after at least two years (Craske & Barlow, 2008; Craske, Brown, & Barlow, 1991). Remaining agoraphobic behaviour can then be treated with more standard exposure exercises. Although these treatments are quite effective, they are relatively new and not yet available to many individuals who suffer from panic disorder because administering them requires therapists to have advanced training (Barlow, Levitt, & Bufka, 1999; McHugh & Barlow, 2010).

Researchers have begun attempting to understand which aspects of PCT (i.e., exposure to interoceptive sensations, cognitive therapy, or relaxation and breathing retraining) are the most or least important components of the treatment. For example, as described by Hamilton researchers Martin Antony and Randi McCabe (2002), concerns have been raised about the breathing retraining component of PCT in that it does not seem to add to the effectiveness of PCT and may in fact lead to a poorer outcome for some patients by preventing them from learning that their catastrophic

TABLE 5.3 Situation-Exposure Tasks (From Least to Most Difficult)

Shopping in a crowded supermarket for 30 minutes alone
Walking five blocks away from home alone
Driving on a busy highway for 5 miles with spouse and alone
Eating in a restaurant, seated in the middle
Watching a movie while seated in the middle of the row

Source: From *Mastery of Your Anxiety and Panic II,* by D. H. Barlow and M. G. Craske, 1994. Albany, NY: Graywind Publications Incorporated. Reprinted by permission.

beliefs are unfounded. In a review of the literature, Steven Taylor (2001) recommends that therapists must exercise caution when using breathing retraining to ensure that it is not misused by panic patients as a means of escaping from or avoiding their feared bodily sensations. It should also be made clear that although psychological treatments like PCT are quite effective, they are relatively new and not yet available to many individuals who have panic disorder, because administering them requires therapists to have advanced training.

Combined Psychological and Drug Treatments

Partly because primary care physicians are usually the first clinicians to treat those suffering from panic disorder and psychological treatments are not available in those settings, when patients do get referred for psychological treatment, they are often already taking medications. So, important questions are as follows: How do these treatments compare to each other? And do they work together? One major study sponsored by the National Institute of Mental Health looked at the separate and combined effects of psychological and drug treatments (Barlow, Gorman, Shear, & Woods, 2000). In this double-blind study, 312 carefully screened patients with panic disorder were treated at four sites, two known for their expertise with medication treatments and two known for their expertise with psychological treatments. The purpose of this arrangement was to control for any bias that might affect the results because of the allegiance of investigators committed to one type of treatment or the other. Patients were randomized into five treatment conditions: psychological treatment alone (CBT); drug treatment alone (imipramine—IMI—a tricyclic antidepressant, was used because this study was begun before the SSRIs were available); a combined treatment condition (IMI + CBT); and two "control" conditions, one using placebo alone (PBO), and one using PBO + CBT (to determine the extent to which any advantage for combined treatment was caused by placebo contribution).

■ Figure 5.7 shows the results in terms of the percentage of patients who had responded to treatment by the end of three months of active treatment (termed the acute response), during which patients were seen weekly. Data were based on the judgment of an independent evaluator using the Panic Disorder Severity Scale, and included patients who dropped out along the way and were counted as failures. The data indicate that all treatment groups were significantly better than placebo, with some evidence that, among those who responded to treatment, people taking the drug alone did a little better than those receiving the CBT alone, but approximately the same number of patients responded to both treatments. Combined treatment was no better than individual treatments.

Figure 5.7 also presents the results after six additional months of maintenance treatment (nine months after treatment was initiated), during which patients were seen once per month. At this point, the results looked much as they did after initial treatment, except there was a slight advantage for combined treatment at

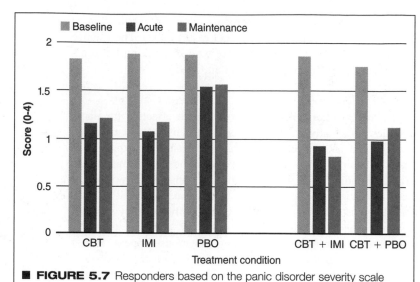

■ **FIGURE 5.7** Responders based on the panic disorder severity scale average item score after acute and after maintenance conditions

Source: From *Mastery of Your Anxiety and Panic II,* by D. H. Barlow and M. G. Craske, 1994. Albany, NY: Graywind Publications Incorporated. Reprinted by permission.

this point and the number of people responding to placebo had diminished. ■ Figure 5.8 shows the last set of results, six months after treatment was discontinued (15 months after it was initiated). At this point, patients on medication, whether combined with CBT or not, had deteriorated somewhat, and those receiving CBT without the drug had retained most of their gains. For example, 14 of 29 patients, or 48 percent of those who began the six-month follow-up phase, who were taking the drug combined with CBT (IMI + CBT) relapsed, with those who dropped out during this period counted as failures (intent to follow). Forty percent, or 10 of 25, of those patients who completed the follow-up phase relapsed. Notice the much lower relapse figure for the

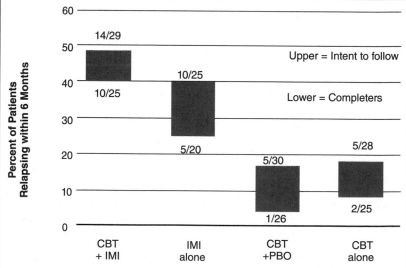

■ **FIGURE 5.8** Posttreatment relapse rates in patients with panic disorder

Source: Adapted from Barlow, D. H., Gorman, J. M., Shear, K. M., & Woods, S. W., 2000. Cognitive-behavioral therapy, imipramine, or their combination for panic disorder: A randomized controlled trial. *Journal of the American Medical Association, 283(19),* 2529–2536.

Virtual Reality: A New Technique on the Treatment of Anxiety Disorders

"I just feel really closed in, I feel like my heart is going to start beating really fast. . . . I won't be able to get enough air, I won't be able to breathe, and I'll pass out."

Go to Psychology CourseMate at www.abnormalpsych3ce.nelson. com to watch this video.

conditions containing CBT. Thus, treatments containing CBT without the drug tended to be superior at this point, because they had more enduring effects.

Most studies show that drugs, particularly benzodiazepines, may interfere with the effects of psychological treatments (Craske & Barlow, 2008). Because of this, our multisite collaborative team asked whether a sequential strategy where one treatment was delayed until later and only given to those patients who didn't do as well as hoped would work better than giving both treatments at the same time. In this study, currently in preparation for publication, 256 patients with PD or PDA completed three months of initial treatment with CBT. Fifty-eight of those patients did not reach an optimal level of functioning (high end-state functioning) and entered a trial where they either received continued CBT or paroxetine. The paroxetine was administered for up to one year, whereas the CBT was delivered for three

months. At the end of the one-year period, there was a strong suggestion, represented as a statistical trend, that more of the patients receiving paroxetine responded, compared to those receiving continued CBT. Specifically, 60 percent of the nonresponders receiving paroxetine became responders compared to 35 percent receiving continued CBT. Although this finding represented only a "trend" toward statistical significance ($p \leq 0.083$), further evaluation of effect sizes will help us evaluate the importance of this difference.

Looking at it the other way, another study (Craske et al., 2005) found that in the primary care setting, adding CBT to the treatment of patients already on medications resulted in significant further improvement compared to those patients on medication who did not have CBT added. Thus, a "stepped care" approach may be superior to combining treatments from the beginning.

Conclusions from this large and important study suggest no advantage to combining drugs and CBT because any incremental effect of combined treatment seems to be a placebo effect, not a true drug effect. Furthermore, the psychological treatments seemed to perform better in the long run (six months after treatment had stopped). This suggests the psychological treatment should be offered initially, followed by drug treatment for those patients who do not respond adequately or for whom psychological treatment is not available.

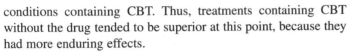

Innovative Approaches

Drugs That Make Psychological Treatments Work Better

Although recent research has shown that combining drug and psychological treatments for anxiety disorders may not produce any added benefit, investigation is beginning on a different drug that looks like it might enhance the effects of the best psychological interventions. This drug is called D-cycloserine (DCS), and it is an antibiotic that has been around awhile but used mostly to treat bacterial infections or tuberculosis. But neuroscientists working in the laboratory, such as Michael Davis at Emory University, made some interesting discoveries about this drug. Davis found that when rats who had learned a fear response, such as when a light was paired with a brief electric shock, were put into extinction trials in which the light that they had learned to fear was no longer paired with a frightening electric shock, an unexpected thing happened. Predictably, the animals gradually learned not to fear the light (their fear extinguished), but interestingly, providing them with the medication DCS during these extinction trials made extinction work faster and last longer (Walker, Ressler, Lu, & Davis, 2002). Further research indicated that this drug works in the amygdala, a structure in the brain involved in the learning and unlearning of fear and anxiety. DCS affects neurotransmitter

flow in a way that strengthens the extinction process (Hofmann, 2007).

Most recently, several investigators have used this drug with humans suffering from social anxiety disorder or panic disorder. DCS is given approximately an hour before the extinction or exposure trial, and the individual does not take the drug on an ongoing basis. For example, Michael Otto and his colleagues in one of our clinics (Otto et al., 2010) administered the most effective cognitive-behavioural intervention to patients with panic disorder either with or without the drug. (That is, one group got the drug and the other group got a placebo, and neither the patients nor the therapists knew which group was getting the drug and which was not, making it a double-blind experiment.) The people who got the drug improved significantly more during treatment than those who didn't get the drug. This is particularly noteworthy because the feared cues for people with panic disorder are physical sensations, and the drug DCS helped extinguish anxiety triggered by sensations such as increased heart rate or respiration. Stefan Hofmann and colleagues (2006) found a similar result with social anxiety disorder. If these results are replicated, we may have an important advance in treating anxiety disorders.

True (T) or false (F)?

1. ___ PD is a disorder in which an individual experiences anxiety and panic with phobic avoidance of what that person considers an "unsafe" situation.

2. ___ About 40 percent of the population meets the criteria for panic disorder at some point in their lives.

3. ___ Some individuals with panic disorder are suicidal, have nocturnal panic, and/or are agoraphobic.

4. ___ Psychological treatments like PCT or CBT are highly effective for treating panic disorder.

Specific Phobia

Remember Jody in Chapter 1? When he saw a film of the frog being dissected, Jody began feeling queasy. Eventually he reached the point of fainting if someone simply said, "Cut it out." Consider next the case of Bob, who has difficulties with flying. Bob's case and his treatment were described by Robert Ladouceur (1982). Jody and Bob have in common what we call a *specific phobia*.

BOB | *Too Scared to Fly*

Bob was a 29-year-old Caucasian man who worked as a translator. His main complaint was a fear of flying. Although his work as a translator did not necessitate air travel, the places he could travel for vacations were severely limited by his flying phobia. Bob had always been very interested in art and history and he had long dreamed of travelling in Europe. However, his intense fear of flying had prevented him from making the trip.

Bob had tried psychoanalytically oriented psychotherapy mainly to help with his phobia. However, despite being in therapy for six years, he reported that it had not been particularly helpful. Although his overall level of general anxiety was somewhat reduced, his flying phobia remained. He had ended this therapy a year earlier. He was not taking any medications for his anxiety.

Three years earlier, in an attempt to overcome his avoidance behaviour, he had purchased an airline ticket for a round trip from Québec to Paris. He purchased the ticket well in advance of his planned travel dates. However, Bob became increasingly anxious as the day of the trip approached. Eventually, he became so overwhelmed by his anxiety about the flight that he cancelled his trip and returned the ticket to the travel agent. He was even willing to pay a hefty financial penalty for his late cancellation— anything to avoid having to fly!

The therapist learned that Bob had never flown in his lifetime. This provided evidence that his fear of flying was not due to a direct traumatic experience during some previous flight (i.e., his phobia was not acquired through classical conditioning). Instead, it appeared that he had developed his flying phobia from various vicarious sources (e.g., seeing dangerous flights depicted in films or airplane crashes described in the news).

Source: Ladouceur, R. (1982). In vivo cognitive desensitization of flight phobia: A case study. *Psychological Reports, 50,* 459-462. Adapted with permission.

Clinical Description

A **specific phobia** is an irrational fear of a specific object or situation that markedly interferes with an individual's ability to function. Before *DSM-IV*, this category was called "simple" phobia to distinguish it from the more complex agoraphobia condition, but we now recognize there is nothing simple about it. Many of you might be afraid of something that is not dangerous, such as going to the dentist, or have a greatly exaggerated fear of something that is only mildly dangerous, such as driving a car or flying. For this reason, most people can identify to some extent with a phobia. Surveys indicate that specific fears of a variety of objects or situations occur in a majority of the population (Myers et al., 1984). But the very commonness of fears, even severe fears, often causes people to trivialize the psychological disorder known as a specific phobia. These phobias, in their severe form, can be extremely disabling, as we saw with Jody. DSM Table 5.4 lists some other examples of particularly impairing phobias seen at our clinics (Antony & Barlow, 2002).

In contrast to the devastating effects of phobias for some people, for others like Bob, phobias are simply a nuisance— sometimes an extremely inconvenient nuisance, but they can adapt to life with a phobia by simply working around it somehow. Where we live and work, some people are afraid to drive in the snow. We have had people come to our clinics who have been so severely phobic that during the winter they were ready to uproot, change their jobs and their lives, and move to a warmer climate. That is one way of dealing with a phobia. We discuss some other ways at the end of this chapter.

The major characteristic held in common by Jody and Bob, of course, is the *DSM-IV-TR* criterion of marked and persistent fear that is set off by a specific object or situation. Both also have recognized that their fear and anxiety are excessive or unreasonable. Finally, both went to considerable lengths to avoid situations where their phobic response might occur.

The similarities end there. In fact, there are as many phobias as there are objects and situations. The variety of Greek and Latin names contrived to describe phobias stuns the imagination. Table 5.5 gives only the phobias beginning with the letter A from a long list compiled from medical dictionaries and other diverse sources (Maser, 1985). Of course, this sort of list has little or no value for people studying psychopathology, but it does show the extent of the named phobias.

Before the publication of *DSM-IV* in 1994, no meaningful classification of specific phobias existed. However, we have now learned that the cases of Jody and of Bob represent types of specific phobia that differ in major ways. Four major subtypes of specific phobia have been identified: (1) animal type, (2) natural environment

Table 5.4 Diagnostic Criteria for Specific Phobia

A. Marked and persistent fear that is excessive or unreasonable, cued by the presence or anticipation of a specific object or situation (e.g., flying, heights, animals, receiving an injection, seeing blood).

B. Exposure to the phobic stimulus almost invariably provokes an immediate anxiety response, which may take the form of a situationally bound or situationally predisposed panic attack. Note: In children, the anxiety may be expressed by crying, tantrums, freezing, or clinging.

C. The person recognizes that the fear is excessive or unreasonable. Note: In children, this feature may be absent.

D. The phobic situation(s) is avoided or else is endured with intense anxiety or distress.

E. The avoidance, anxious anticipation, or distress in the feared situations interferes significantly with the person's normal routine, occupational (or academic) functioning, or social activities or relationships, or there is marked distress about having the phobia.

F. In individuals under age 18, the duration is at least six months.

G. The anxiety, panic attacks, or phobic avoidance associated with the specific object or situation are not better accounted for by another mental disorder, such as obsessive-compulsive disorder (e.g., fear of dirt, in someone with an obsession about contamination), post-traumatic stress disorder (e.g., avoidance of stimuli associated with a severe stressor), separation anxiety disorder (e.g., avoidance of school), social phobia (e.g., avoidance of social situations because of fear of embarrassment), panic disorder with agoraphobia, or agoraphobia without history of panic disorder.

Specify type:

1. Animal Type
2. Natural environment type (e.g., heights, storms, and water)
3. Blood-injection-injury type
4. Situational type (e.g., planes, elevators, or enclosed places)
5. Other type (e.g., phobic avoidance of situations that may lead to choking, vomiting, or contracting an illness; or in children, avoidance of loud sounds or costumed characters)

Source: Reprinted with permission from the *Diagnostic and Statistical Manual of Mental Disorders,* Fourth Edition, Text Revision, (Copyright © 2000). American Psychiatric Association.

TABLE 5.5 Phobias Beginning with "A"

Term	Fear of
Acarophobia	Insects, mites
Achluophobia	Darkness, night
Acousticophobia	Sounds
Acrophobia	Heights
Aerophobia	Air currents, drafts
Agoraphobia	Open spaces
Agyiophobia	Crossing the street
Aichmophobia	Sharp, pointed objects; knives; being touched by a finger
Ailurophobia	Cats
Algophobia	Pain
Amathophobia	Dust
Amychophobia	Laceration; being clawed, scratched
Androphobia	Men, (and sex with men)
Anemophobias	Air currents, wind, drafts
Anginophobia	Angina pectoris (brief attacks of chest pain)
Anthrophobia	Human society
Antlophobia	Floods
Apeirophobia	Infinity
Aphephobia	Physical contact, being touched
Apiphobia	Bees, bee stings
Astraphobia	Thunderstorms, lightning
Ataxiophobia	Disorder
Atephobia	Ruin
Auroraphobia	Northern lights
Autophobia	Being alone; solitude; oneself; being egotistical

Source: From "List of Phobias" by J. D. Maser, p. 805. In A. H. Tuma and J. D. Maser (Eds.), *Anxiety and the Anxiety Disorders, 1985.* Copyright © 1985 by Lawrence Erlbaum Associates. Reprinted by permission.

type (e.g., heights, storms, and water), (3) blood-injection-injury type, and (4) situational type (such as planes, elevators, or enclosed places). A fifth category, "other," includes phobias that do not fit any of the four major subtypes (e.g., situations that may lead to choking, vomiting, or contracting an illness; or, in children, avoidance of loud sounds or costumed characters). Although this subtyping strategy is useful, we also know that most people who suffer from phobia tend to have multiple phobias of several types (Hofmann, Lehman, & Barlow, 1997). This fact weakens the utility of subtyping, but subtyping remains useful enough to most likely be retained in *DSM-5* (LeBeau et al., 2010).

Blood-Injection-Injury Phobia

How do phobia subtypes differ from each other? We have already seen one major difference in the case of Jody. Rather than the usual surge of activity in the sympathetic nervous system and increased heart rate and blood pressure, Jody experienced a marked drop in heart rate and blood pressure and fainted as a consequence. Many people who have phobias and experience panic attacks in their feared situations report that they feel like they are going to faint but

they never do, because their heart rate and blood pressure are actually increasing. Therefore, those with **blood-injection-injury phobias** almost always differ in their physiological reaction from people with other types of phobia (Barlow & Liebowitz, 1995; Craske, Antony, & Barlow, 2006; Hofmann, Alpers, & Pauli, 2009; Öst, 1992). We also noted in Chapter 2 that blood-injection-injury phobia runs in families more strongly than any phobic disorder we know. This is probably because people with this phobia inherit a strong vasovagal response to blood, injury, or the possibility of an injection, all of which cause a drop in blood pressure and a tendency to faint (Grassick, 1990). The phobia develops over the possibility of having this response. The average age of onset for this phobia is approximately nine years (Antony, Brown, & Barlow, 1997a; LeBeau et al., 2010; Öst, 1989).

Situational Phobia

Phobias characterized by fear of public transportation or enclosed places are called **situational phobias**. Claustrophobia, a fear of small enclosed places (see Radomsky, Rachman, Thordarson, McIsaac, & Teachman, 2001), is situational, as is a phobia of planes (Ladouceur, 1982). Situational phobia tends to emerge around age 20 to 25 and has been shown to run in families (Craske et al., 2006; Curtis, Hill, & Lewis, 1990; LeBeau et al., 2010). The main difference between situational phobia and panic disorder with agoraphobia is that people with situational phobia never experience panic attacks outside the context of their phobic object or situation (Antony et al., 1997a; Antony, Brown, & Barlow, 1997). Therefore, they can relax when they don't have to confront their phobic situation. People with panic disorder, in contrast, might experience unexpected, uncued panic attacks at any time.

Natural Environment Phobia

Sometimes very young people develop fears of situations or events occurring in nature. These fears are called **natural environment phobias**. The major examples are heights, storms, and water. These fears also seem to cluster together (Antony & Barlow, 2002; Hofmann et al., 1997): If you fear one situation or event, such as deep water, you are likely to fear another, such as storms. Many of these situations have some danger associated with them and, therefore, mild to moderate fear can be very adaptive. For example, we should be careful in a high place or in deep water. It is entirely possible that we are somewhat prepared to be afraid of these situations; as we discussed in Chapter 2, something in our genes makes us very sensitive to these situations if any sign of danger is present. In any case, these phobias have a peak age of onset of about seven years. They are not phobias at all if they are only passing fears. They have to be persistent and to interfere substantially with the person's functioning, leading to avoidance of boat trips or summer vacations in the mountains where there might be a storm.

Animal Phobia

Fears of animals and insects are called **animal phobias**. Once again, these fears are common but become phobic only if severe interference with functioning occurs. For example, we have seen cases in our clinic where people with snake or mice phobias are unable to read magazines for fear of unexpectedly coming across a picture of one of these animals. There are many places that these people are unable to go, even if they want to very much, such as to the country to visit someone. The fear experienced by people with animal phobias is very different from an ordinary mild revulsion. The age of onset for these phobias, like that of natural environment phobias, peaks at around seven years (Antony et al., 1997a; LeBeau et al., 2010; Öst, 1987).

Other Phobias

Several additional types of phobias appear in considerable numbers and can cause substantial problems. For example, if you are afraid of contracting a disease and go to excessive and irrational lengths to avoid exposure to that disease, you may have an *illness phobia*. In these cases, the individuals do not believe they have the disease but are afraid they might acquire it in any number of ways (Barlow & Liebowitz, 1995; Craske et al., 1996). When this fear occurs in

▲ People who develop a natural environment phobia intensely fear such places as heights and events such as lightning.

severe form it can be very incapacitating, because individuals with illness phobia may avoid all contact with people or places where they might catch something (Asmundson & Taylor, 2005; Taylor & Asmundson, 2004). Illness phobia likely became more prevalent during the SARS epidemic, just as it became more prevalent during the AIDS epidemic (McCabe, 2003). During the SARS epidemic, some people who had no reason to believe they had contracted SARS avoided public gatherings, restaurants, and any contact whatsoever with strangers who displayed signs of a cold (or people who had recently travelled to China or Toronto) for fear of contracting the disease (Cheng & Tang, 2004; Lee-Baggley, DeLongis, Voorhoeave, & Greenglass, 2004; McCabe, 2003). Illness phobia can also resemble other disorders, such as obsessive-compulsive disorder (see p. 168) or hypochondriasis (see Chapter 6), but is sufficiently different to be classified as a type of specific phobia. We return to this issue when we discuss these two disorders.

Separation Anxiety Disorder

All the anxiety disorders described in this chapter may occur during childhood, and one additional anxiety disorder is unique to children. **Separation anxiety disorder** is characterized by a child's unrealistic and persistent worry that something will happen to his parents or other important people in his life, or that something will happen to the child himself that will separate him from his parents (e.g., he will be lost, or hurt in an accident). The child often refuses to go to school or to leave home, not because he is afraid of school but because he is afraid of separating from his loved ones. These fears can result in nightmares involving possible separation and by physical symptoms, distress, and anxiety (Barlow, Pincus, Heinrichs, & Choate, 2003).

Of course, all young children experience separation anxiety to some extent; this fear usually decreases as the child grows older. Therefore, a clinician must judge whether the separation anxiety is greater than would be expected at that particular age (Barlow et al., 2003; Ollendick & Huntzinger, 1990). It is also important to differentiate separation anxiety from school phobia. In school phobia, the fear is clearly focused on something specific to the school situation; the child can leave the parents or other attachment figures to go somewhere other than school. In separation anxiety, the act of separating from the parent or attachment figure provokes anxiety and fear. And there is now evidence that separation anxiety, if untreated, can extend into adulthood in approximately 35 percent of cases (Shear, Jin, Ruscio, Walters, & Kessler, 2006). Furthermore, very recent evidence suggests that we have overlooked this disorder in adults and that it occurs in approximately 6.6 percent of the adult population over the course of a lifetime (Shear et al., 2006). In some cases, the onset is in adulthood rather than carrying over from childhood. The focus of anxiety in adults is the same: that harm may befall loved ones during separation (Manicavasagar et al., 2010; Silove, Marnane, Wagner, Manicavasagar, & Rees, 2010).

Statistics

Specific fears occur in a majority of people. The ones most commonly found in the population at large, categorized by Agras, Sylvester, and Oliveau (1969), are presented in Table 5.6. Not

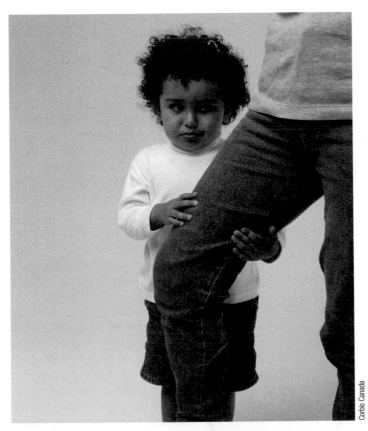

▲ A child with separation anxiety disorder persistently worries that parting with an important person drastically endangers either the loved one or the child.

TABLE 5.6 Prevalence of Intense Fears and Phobias

Intense Fear	Prevalence per 1,000 Population	Sex Distribution
Snakes	253	76% F
Heights	120	54% F
Flying	109	67% F
Enclosures	50	66% F
Illness	33	53% F
Death	33	31% F
Injury	23	48% F
Storms	31	84% F
Dentists	24	54% F
Journeys alone	16	100% F
Being alone	10	72% F

Phobia	Prevalence per 1,000 Population*	Sex Distribution
Illness/Injury	31(42%)	64% F
Storms	13(18%)	100% F
Animals	11(14%)	75% F
Agoraphobia	6(8%)	46% F
Death	5(7%)	60% F
Crowds	4(5%)	75% F
Heights	4(5%)	0% F

*Percentages of the total of those with phobias are in parentheses.

Source: Reprinted from *Comprehensive Psychiatry, 10 (2)*, S. Agras, D. Sylvester & D. Oliveau, "The Epidemiology of Common Fears and Phobia", 151–156. Copyright 1969, with permission from Elsevier.

surprisingly, fears of snakes and heights rank near the top. Notice also that the sex ratio among common fears is overwhelmingly female with a couple of exceptions. Among these exceptions is fear of heights, for which the sex ratio is approximately equal. Very few people who report specific fears qualify as having a phobia, but for approximately 6.4 percent of the Canadian population (9 percent of women; 4 percent of men), their fears are at some point severe enough to be classified as disorders and earn the label "phobia" (Offord et al., 1996). These numbers seem to be increasing in younger generations (Magee, Eaton, Wittchen, McGonagle, & Kessler, 1996). This percentage is very high, making specific phobia one of the most common psychological disorders.

As with common fears, the sex ratio for specific phobias is overwhelmingly female. In the Offord et al. (1996) survey of Ontarians aged 15 to 64, the lifetime prevalence rate was twice as high in women as in men (i.e., 8.9 percent for women and 4.1 percent for men). As noted by leading anxiety investigator Martin Antony, specific phobias represent an interesting paradox (Antony & Barlow, 2002). Despite the fact that specific phobia is a common, treatable, and well-understood condition, people with this condition present for treatment only rarely. For example, Antony and Barlow (2002) report that of a sample of 522 patients with anxiety disorders referred to a Canadian anxiety disorders clinic, only 6 percent received a principal diagnosis of specific phobia. Diagnoses of panic disorder, social phobia, and obsessive-compulsive disorder were much more common as primary diagnoses (Antony & Barlow, 2002).

Thus, even though phobias may interfere with an individual's functioning, only the most severe cases actually come for treatment, because affected people tend to work around their phobias; for example, someone with a fear of heights arranges her life so she never has to be in a tall building or other high place, just as Bob arranged his life so that he never had to fly. People with situational phobias of such things as driving, flying, or small enclosed places most frequently come for treatment. However, we have reason to believe that blood-injury-injection phobias are quite prevalent in the population (Agras et al., 1969; Myers et al., 1984); people with this phobia might seek help if they knew good treatments were available.

As noted by Antony, Brown, and Barlow (1997a), once a phobia develops, it tends to last a lifetime (run a chronic course; see also McCabe & Antony, 2002; Rowa, McCabe, & Antony, 2006). Thus, the issue of treatment, described shortly, becomes important.

Although most anxiety disorders look much the same in adults and children, clinicians must be very aware of the types of normal fears and anxieties experienced throughout childhood so they can distinguish them from specific phobias (Albano, Chorpita, & Barlow, 1996; King, 1993; Silverman & Rabian, 1993). Infants, for example, show marked fear of loud noises and strangers. At one to two years of age, children quite normally are very anxious about separating from parents, and fears of animals and the dark also develop and may persist into the fourth or fifth year of life. Fear of various monsters and other imaginary creatures may begin at about age three and last for several years. At age ten, children may fear evaluation by others and feel anxiety over their physical appearance. Generally, reports of fear decline with age, although performance-related fears of such activities as taking a test or talking in front of a large group may increase with age. Specific phobias seem to decline with old age (Ayers et al., 2009; Blazer, George, et al., 1991; Sheikh, 1992).

The prevalence of specific phobias varies from one culture to another. A variant of phobia in Chinese cultures is called *Pa-leng*, sometimes *frigo* phobia or "fear of the cold." *Pa-leng* can be understood only in the context of traditional ideas—in this case the Chinese concept of yin and yang (Tan, 1980). Chinese medicine holds that there must be a balance of yin and yang forces in the body for health to be maintained. Yin represents the cold, dark, windy, energy-sapping aspects of life; yang refers to the warm, bright, energy-producing aspects of life. Individuals with *Pa-leng* have a morbid fear of the cold. They ruminate over loss of body heat and may wear several layers of clothing even on a hot day. They may complain of belching and flatulence (passing gas), which indicate the presence of wind and therefore of too much yin in the body.

Causes

For a long time we thought that most specific phobias began with an unusual traumatic event. For example, if you were bitten by a dog, you developed a phobia of dogs. We now know this is not always

the case (Barlow, 2002; Craske et al., 2006; Öst, 1985; Rachman, 1977, 2002). This is not to say that traumatic conditioning experiences do not result in subsequent phobic behaviour. Almost every person with a choking phobia has had some kind of a choking experience. An individual with claustrophobia who recently came to our clinic reported being trapped in an elevator for an extraordinarily long time. These are examples of phobias acquired by direct experience, where real danger or pain results in an alarm response (a true alarm). As noted by Stanley J. Rachman, such direct conditioning is merely one way of developing a phobia. He notes that there are at least two other pathways: observing someone else experience severe fear (vicarious experience), or, under the right conditions, being told about danger. In fact, vicarious and informational transmission of fears can take place in the absence of any direct contact with the phobic object or situation (Rachman, 1977).

People develop phobias in at least one other way: by experiencing a false alarm (panic attack) in a specific situation. Remember our earlier discussion of unexpected panic attacks? Studies show that many people with phobias do not necessarily experience a true alarm resulting from real danger at the onset of their phobia. Many initially have an unexpected panic attack in a specific situation, related, perhaps, to current life stress. A phobia of that situation may then develop. Munjack (1984) studied people with specific phobias of driving. He noted that about 50 percent of the people who could remember when their phobia started experienced a true alarm due to a traumatic experience such as a car accident. The others had had nothing terrible happen to them while they were driving, but they had experienced an unexpected panic attack during which they felt they were going to lose control of the car and wipe out half the people on the highway. In fact, their driving was not impaired and their catastrophic thoughts were simply part of the panic attack.

We also learn fears vicariously (Rachman, 1977). Seeing someone else have a traumatic experience or endure intense fear may be enough to instill a phobia in the watcher. Remember, we noted earlier that emotions are very contagious. If someone you are with is either happy or fearful, you will probably feel a tinge of happiness or fear also. Öst (1985) describes how a severe dental fear developed in this way. An adolescent boy sat in the waiting room at the school dentist's office partly observing, but fully hearing, his friend who was being treated. Evidently, the boy's reaction to pain caused him to move suddenly, and the drill punctured his cheek. The boy in the waiting room who overheard the accident bolted from the room and developed a severe and long-lasting fear of dental situations. Nothing actually happened to the second person but you can certainly understand why he developed his phobia.

Sometimes just being warned repeatedly about a potential danger is sufficient for someone to develop a phobia. Öst (1985) describes the case of a woman with an extremely severe snake phobia who had never encountered a snake in her life. Rather, she had been told repeatedly while growing up about the dangers of snakes in the high grass. She was encouraged to wear high rubber boots to guard against this imminent threat—and she did so even when walking down the street. Rachman (1977) calls this mode of developing a phobia *information transmission*.

Terrifying experiences alone do not create phobias. As we have said, a true phobia also requires anxiety over the possibility of another extremely traumatic event or false alarm. Remember, when we are anxious, we persistently anticipate something terrible, and we are likely to avoid situations where that terrible thing might occur. If we don't develop anxiety, our reaction would presumably be in the category of normal fears experienced by more than half the population. Normal fear can cause mild distress, but it is usually ignored and forgotten. A diagram of the etiology of specific phobia is presented in ■ Figure 5.9.

In summary, several things have to occur for a person to develop a phobia. First, a traumatic conditioning experience often plays a role (even hearing about a frightening event is sufficient for some individuals). Second, fear is more likely to develop if we are "prepared"; that is, we seem to carry an inherited tendency to fear situations that have always been dangerous to the human race, such as being threatened by wild animals or trapped in small places (see Chapter 2).

We also have to be susceptible to developing anxiety by focusing on the possibility that the event will happen again. We have discussed the biological and psychological reasons for anxiety and have seen that at least one phobia, blood-injection-injury phobia, is highly heritable (Öst, 1989; Page & Martin, 1998). Patients with blood phobia probably also inherit a strong vasovagal response that makes them susceptible to fainting. This alone would not be sufficient to ensure their becoming phobic, but it combines with anxiety to produce strong vulnerability.

Several years ago, Fyer et al. (1990) demonstrated that approximately 31 percent of the first-degree relatives of people with specific phobias also had a phobia, compared with 11 percent of the first-degree relatives of normal controls. More interestingly, it seems that each subtype of phobia "bred true," in that relatives were likely to have identical types of phobia. Kendler, Karkowski, and Prescott (1999) and Page and Martin (1998) found relatively high estimates for heritability of individual specific phobias. We do not know for sure whether the tendency for phobias to run in families is caused by genes or by modelling, but the findings are at least suggestive of a unique genetic contribution to specific phobia (Antony & Barlow, 2002; Hettema et al., 2005; Smoller et al., 2005).

Finally, social and cultural factors are very strong determinants of who ultimately develops and reports a specific phobia. In most societies around the world, it is almost unacceptable for males to express fears and phobias. Thus, the overwhelming majority of reported specific phobias occur in women. What happens to the males? Very possibly they work hard to overcome their fears by repeatedly exposing themselves to their feared situations. Another more likely possibility is that they simply endure their fears without telling anyone about them and without seeking any treatment (Antony & Barlow, 2002). Pierce and Kirkpatrick (1992) asked male and female college students to report their fears on two occasions before watching a videotape of something frightening. Before the second evaluation, subjects were told their heart rate would be monitored to assess the "truthfulness" of their report. Reports from women were the same on both occasions, but men reported substantially more fear when it was important to be truthful. More recently, Ginsburg and Silverman (2000) reported that

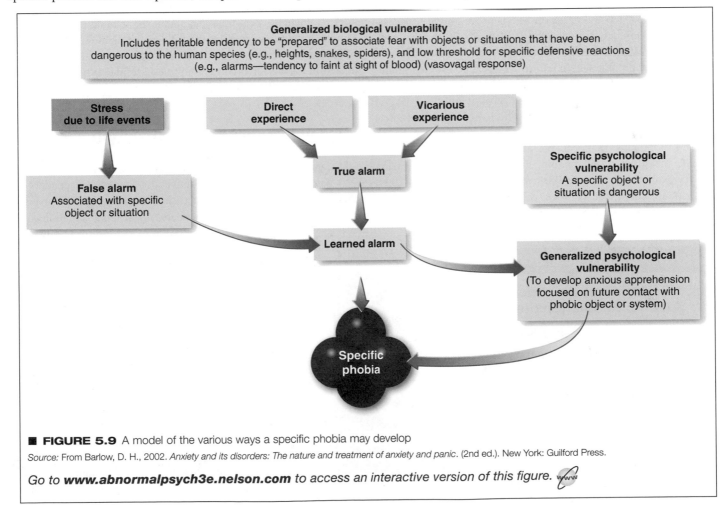

■ **FIGURE 5.9** A model of the various ways a specific phobia may develop

Source: From Barlow, D. H., 2002. *Anxiety and its disorders: The nature and treatment of anxiety and panic.* (2nd ed.). New York: Guilford Press.

Go to **www.abnormalpsych3e.nelson.com** *to access an interactive version of this figure.*

level of reported fear in children with anxiety disorders was a function of gender role but not biological sex. That is, a more masculine "tomboyish" girl would report less fear than a more feminine girl, illustrating the contribution of culture to the development of fear and phobia.

Treatment

Although the development of phobias is relatively complex, the treatment is fairly straightforward. Almost everyone agrees that specific phobias require structured and consistent exposure-based exercises. This approach was used successfully by Ladouceur (1982) in the treatment of Bob's flying phobia (described earlier). At a follow-up 14 months after his treatment had ended, Bob had made two overseas trips without any incapacitating anxiety. Nevertheless, most patients who expose themselves gradually to what they fear must be under therapeutic supervision. As was illustrated in Bob's case, individuals who attempt to carry out the exercises alone often attempt to do too much too soon and end up escaping the situation, which may strengthen the phobia. In addition, if a patient fears having another unexpected panic attack in this situation, it is helpful to direct therapy at panic attacks in the manner described for panic disorder (Antony, Craske, & Barlow, 2006; Craske et al., 2006). For separation anxiety, parents are often included to help structure the exercises and also to address parental reaction to childhood anxiety (Choate, Pincus, Eyberg, & Barlow, 2005). More recently, an intensive one-week program for girls ages 8 to 11 developed at one of our clinics in which the girls end up having a sleepover at the clinic has proven highly successful (Pincus, Santucci, Ehrenreich, & Ryberg, 2008; Santucci, Ehrenreich, Trosper, Bennett, & Pincus, 2009). In cases of blood-injury-injection phobia, where fainting is a real possibility, graduated exposure-based exercises must be done in specific ways. Individuals must tense various muscle groups during exposure exercises to keep their blood pressure sufficiently high to complete the practice (Ayala, Meuret, & Ritz, 2009; Öst & Sterner, 1987). New developments make it possible to treat many specific phobias, including blood phobia, in a single, daylong session (see, for example, Antony & Barlow, 2002; Antony et al., 2006; Craske et al., 2006; Öst, Ferebee, & Furmark, 1997; Öst, Svensson, Hellström, & Lindwall, 2001). Basically, the therapist spends most of the day with the individual, working through exposure exercises with the phobia object or situation. The patient then practises approaching the phobic situation at home, checking in occasionally with the therapist. It is interesting that in these cases not only does the phobia disappear but the tendency to experience the vasovagal response at the sight of blood also lessens considerably. It is also now clear based on brain-imaging work that these treatments change brain functioning by modifying neural circuitry. That is, these treatments "rewire" the brain (Paquette et al., 2003).

A new approach to the treatment of phobias is virtual reality exposure therapy. Virtual reality technology has recently gained interest as an effective medium for administering exposure therapy by putting phobic patients into an environment that simulates their real-world feared situation (Robillard, Bouchard, Fournie, & Renaud, 2003; Rothbaum, Hodges, & Kooper, 1997). Several studies have shown this new form of exposure therapy to be effective in the treatment of phobias of heights, spiders, flying, and small spaces (see review in Wald & Taylor, 2000). In vivo exposure therapy has some risks and limitations in the treatment of driving phobia (e.g., real-world driving situations are unpredictable and hard to control, presenting difficulties in allowing for graduated exposure to increasingly more anxiety-provoking driving situations). These risks and limitations make virtual reality a promising alternative modality for treating driving phobias. Researchers at the University of British Columbia reported on a driving phobia case who was successfully treated with virtual reality exposure therapy delivered in three sessions over ten days. Her ratings of driving anxiety and avoidance decreased from pretreatment to post-treatment, and she maintained her initial improvement at a seven-month follow-up (Wald & Taylor, 2000). These initial findings are promising and have recently been replicated in a study involving a multiple baseline across-participants design (Wald, 2002; see Chapter 4).

Social Phobia (Social Anxiety Disorder)

Are you shy? If so, you have something in common with 20 percent to 50 percent of university students, depending on which survey you read. In fact, the vast majority of university students experience symptoms of anxiety in social situations from time to time (Purdon, Antony, Monteiro, & Swinson, 2001). A much smaller number of people, who suffer severely around others, have **social phobia**, also called social anxiety disorder (SAD), which most likely will be the name adopted in the *DSM-5*. Consider the case of Billy, a 13-year-old boy.

BILLY | *Too Shy*

Billy was the model boy at home. He did his homework, stayed out of trouble, obeyed his parents, and was generally so quiet and reserved he didn't attract much attention. However, when he got to junior high school, something his parents had noticed earlier became painfully evident. Billy had no friends.

He was unwilling to attend social or sporting activities connected with school, even though most of the other kids in his class went to these events. When his parents decided to check with the guidance counsellor, they found that she had been about to call them. She reported that Billy did not socialize or speak up in class and was sick to his stomach all day if he knew he was going to be called on. His teachers had difficulty getting anything more than a yes or no answer from him. More troublesome was that he had been found hiding in a stall in the boys' washroom during lunch, which he said he had been doing for several months instead of eating. After Billy was referred to our clinic, we diagnosed a severe case of social phobia, an irrational and extreme fear of social situations. Billy's phobia took the form of extreme shyness. He was afraid of being embarrassed or humiliated in the presence of almost everyone except his parents.

Clinical Description

SAD is more than exaggerated shyness (Bögels et al., 2010; Hofmann et al., 2009; Schneier et al., 1996). The cases described here are typical of many that appear occasionally in the press over the years.

STEVE AND CHUCK | *Star Players?*

In the second inning of an All-Star game, Los Angeles Dodger second baseman Steve Sax fielded an easy grounder, straightened up for the lob to first, and bounced the ball past first baseman Al Oliver, who was less than 12 metres away. It was a startling error even in an All-Star game studded with bush-league mishaps. But hard-core baseball fans knew it was one more manifestation of a leading mystery of the 1983 season: Sax, 23, the National League Rookie of the Year, could not seem to make routine throws to first base. (Of his first 27 errors that season, 22 were bad throws.)

Chuck Knoblauch won the Golden Glove Award in 1997 but led the league in errors in 1999 with 26, most of them throwing errors. Announcers and reporters observed that his throws would be hard and on target to first base if he made a difficult play and had to quickly turn and throw the ball "without thinking about it." But if he fielded a routine ground ball and had time to think about the accuracy of his throw, he would throw awkwardly and slowly—and often off target. The announcers and reporters concluded that, because his arm seemed fine on the difficult plays, his problem must be "mental." For the 2001 season, he was moved to left field to avoid having to make that throw and by 2003 was out of baseball.

Football player Ricky Williams also interrupted his career partly because of severe social anxiety.

Whereas Knoblauch continued to struggle, Sax and Williams overcame their problems. Many other athletes are not so fortunate.

This problem is not limited to athletes but is also experienced by well-known lecturers and performers. Actress Scarlett Johansson avoided doing Broadway for many years due to intolerable performance anxiety. The inability of a skilled athlete to throw a baseball to first base or a seasoned performer to appear on stage certainly does not match the concept of "shyness" with which we are all familiar. Many of these performers may well be among our more gregarious citizens. And what if when you're with other people you continually worry about a physical reaction you have that is very noticeable to others, but difficult to control? For example, what if you blush to the extent that you're continually embarrassed? Or if your palms sweat so much that you're reluctant to shake hands?

What holds these seemingly different conditions together within the category of social anxiety disorder? Billy, Knoblauch, Sax, Williams, and Johansson (and anyone who worries about blushing or sweating excessively) all experienced marked and persistent anxiety focused on one or more social or performance situations. In Billy's case, these situations were any in which he might have to interact with people. For Knoblauch and Johansson, they were specific to performing some special behaviour in public. Individuals with performance anxiety usually have no difficulty with social interaction, but when they must do something specific in front of people, anxiety takes over and they focus on the possibility that they will embarrass themselves. The most common type of performance anxiety, to which most people can relate, is public speaking. Other situations that commonly provoke performance anxiety are eating in a restaurant or signing a paper in front of a clerk. Anxiety-provoking physical reactions include blushing, sweating, trembling, or, for males, urinating in a public restroom ("bashful bladder" or paruresis). Males with this problem must wait until a stall is available, a difficult task at times. What these examples have in common is that the individual is very anxious only while others are present and maybe watching and, to some extent, evaluating their behaviour. This is truly social anxiety disorder because the people have no difficulty eating, writing, or urinating in private. Only when others are watching does the behaviour deteriorate.

Individuals who are extremely and painfully shy in almost all social situations meet *DSM-IV-TR* criteria for the subtype *social phobia generalized type* (see DSM Table 5.5). It is particularly prominent in children. In the child program in one of our clinics, 100 percent of children and adolescents with social phobia met criteria for the generalized type (Albano, DiBartolo, Heimberg, & Barlow, 1995), as did Billy in the earlier example (Schneier et al., 1996). Because most people with SAD meet criteria for this subtype to at least some degree, it may be dropped in the *DSM-5* as being unnecessary (Bögels et al., 2010).

Statistics

According to the National Comorbidity Survey in the United States, as many as 13.3 percent of the general population experience social phobia at some point in their lives (Kessler et al., 1994). This makes social phobia the most prevalent psychological disorder in the United States. Similarly high rates of social phobia were revealed in a recent community survey by Stein, Torgrud, and Walker (2000). They interviewed about 2000 people in Winnipeg,

Table 5.5 Diagnostic Criteria for Social Phobia (Social Anxiety Disorder)

A. A marked and persistent fear of one or more social or performance situations in which the person is exposed to unfamiliar people or to possible scrutiny by others. The individual fears that he or she will act in a way (or show anxiety symptoms) that will be humiliating or embarrassing. *Note:* In children, there must be evidence of the capacity for age-appropriate social relationships with familiar people and the anxiety must occur in peer settings, not just in interactions with adults.

B. Exposure to the feared social situation almost invariably provokes anxiety, which may take the form of a situationally bound or situationally predisposed panic attack. *Note:* In children, the anxiety may be expressed by crying, tantrums, freezing, or shrinking from social situations with unfamiliar people.

C. The person recognizes that the fear is excessive or unreasonable. *Note:* In children, this feature may be absent.

D. The feared social or performance situations are avoided or are endured with intense anxiety or distress.

E. The avoidance, anxious anticipation, or distress in the feared social or performance situation(s) interferes significantly with the person's normal routine, occupational (academic) functioning, or social activities or relationships, or there is marked distress about having the phobia.

F. In individuals under age 18, duration is at least six months.

G. The fear or avoidance is not due to the direct physiological effects of a substance (e.g., a drug of abuse, medication) or a general medical condition, and is not better accounted for by another mental disorder (e.g., panic disorder with or without agoraphobia, separation anxiety disorder, body dysmorphic disorder, a pervasive developmental disorder, or schizoid personality disorder).

H. If a general medical condition or another mental disorder is present, the fear in criterion A is unrelated to it: e.g., the fear is not of stuttering, trembling in Parkinson's disease, or exhibiting abnormal eating behaviour in anorexia nervosa or bulimia nervosa.

Specify if:

Generalized: If the fears include most social situations (also consider the additional diagnosis of avoidant personality disorder).

Source: Reprinted with permission from the *Diagnostic and Statistical Manual of Mental Disorders,* Fourth Edition, Text Revision, (Copyright © 2000). American Psychiatric Association.

Calgary, Edmonton, and rural Alberta and found a one-year prevalence of 7.2 percent for social phobia. Of course, many more people are shy, but not severely enough to meet criteria for social phobia. The sex ratio favours females only somewhat (1.4 to 1.0), unlike other anxiety disorders where females predominate (Magee et al., 1996; see also Somers, Goldner, Waraich, & Hsu, 2006). This distribution differs a bit from the sex ratio of people with social phobias appearing at clinics, which is nearly 50-50 (Hofmann & Barlow, 2002; Marks, 1985), suggesting that males may seek help more frequently, perhaps because of career-related issues.

Social phobia usually begins during adolescence, with a peak age of onset at about 15 years. Social phobia also tends to be more prevalent in people who are young (18 to 29 years), undereducated, single, and of low socioeconomic class. Prevalence declines slightly among the elderly (Magee et al., 1996; Sheikh, 1992). Considering their difficulty meeting people, it is not surprising that a greater percentage of individuals with social phobia are single than in the population at large. The Ontario Mental Health

Survey further suggests that individuals with social phobia are more likely to drop out of school (Stein & Kean, 2000).

Social phobias distribute relatively equally among different ethnic groups (Magee et al., 1996). In a cross-national study of the rates of social phobia in Canada, the United States, Puerto Rico, and Korea, the authors found that the lifetime prevalence of the disorder was quite similar across the four countries surveyed. They did find, however, some different expressions of social phobia cross-culturally (Weissman et al., 1996). In Japan, the clinical presentation of anxiety disorders is best summarized under the label *shinkeishitsu*. One of the most common subcategories is referred to as *taijin kyōfushō* (Dinnel, Kleinknecht, & Tanaka-Matsumi, 2002; Kirmayer, 1991; Kleinknecht, Dinnel, Kleinknecht, Hiruma, & Hirada, 1997). Japanese people with this form of social phobia strongly fear looking people in the eye and are afraid that some aspect of their personal presentation (blushing, stuttering, body odour, and so on) will appear reprehensible. Thus, the focus of anxiety in this disorder is on offending or embarrassing others rather than embarrassing oneself as in social phobia. Japanese males with this disorder outnumber females by a three-to-two ratio (Takahasi, 1989). More recently it has been established that this syndrome is found in many cultures around the world, including North America. The key feature once again is preoccupation with a belief that one is embarrassing oneself and offending others with a foul body odour. This set of symptoms is now called "olfactory reference syndrome" and has been proposed as a possible new disorder pending further study to be published in the appendix of *DSM-5* (Feusner, Phillips, & Stein, 2010).

Although it makes intuitive sense that cross-cultural differences in social norms may relate to differences in the extent of social anxiety, cultural factors are rarely investigated in social phobia research. Heinrichs and her colleagues (2006) conducted a cross-cultural study that showed that collectivistic countries (e.g., Japan, Spain, and Korea) were more accepting toward socially reticent and withdrawn behaviours than were individualistic countries (e.g., Canada, Australia, the Netherlands, Germany, and the United States). Collectivistic countries also reported more social anxiety and greater fear of blushing. The more that attention-avoiding behaviours were accepted in a given culture, the greater were the levels of social anxiety. These fascinating results suggest that variations in social phobia rates across countries may be related to differences in cultural norms (Heinrichs et al., 2006).

Causes

We have noted that we seem to be prepared by evolution to fear certain wild animals and dangerous situations in the natural environment (see Chapter 2). Similarly, it seems we are also prepared to fear angry, critical, or rejecting people (Blair et al., 2008; Mineka & Zinbarg, 1996, 2006; Mogg, Philippot, & Bradley, 2004; Öhman, 1986). In a series of studies, Öhman and colleagues (e.g., Dimberg & Öhman, 1983; Öhman & Dimberg, 1978) noted that we learn more quickly to fear angry expressions than other facial expressions, and this fear diminishes much more slowly than other types of learning. Lundh and Öst (1996) demonstrated that people with social phobia who saw a number of pictures of faces were likely to remember critical expressions; Mogg and colleagues (2004) showed that socially anxious individuals more quickly recognized angry faces than "normals," whereas "normals" remembered the accepting expressions (Navarrete et al., 2009). Other studies show that individuals with generalized social phobia react to angry faces with greater activation of the amygdala and less cortical control or regulation than "normals" (Goldin, Manber, Hakimi, Canli, & Gross, 2009; Stein, Goldin, Sareen, Zorrilla, & Brown, 2002). Fox and Damjanovic (2006) demonstrated that the eye region specifically is the threatening area of the face.

Why should we inherit a tendency to fear angry faces? Our ancestors probably avoided hostile, angry, domineering people who might attack or kill them. In fact, in all species, dominant, aggressive individuals high in the social hierarchy tend to be avoided. Possibly, individuals who avoided people with angry faces were more likely to survive and pass their genes down to us. Of course, this is just a theory.

Jerome Kagan and his colleagues (see, for example, Kagan, 1994, 1997; Kagan, Reznick, & Snidman, 1988; Kagan & Snidman, 1991, 1999) have demonstrated that some infants are born with a temperamental profile or trait of inhibition or shyness that is evident as early as four months of age. Four-month-old infants with this trait become more agitated and cry more frequently when presented with toys or other age-appropriate stimuli than infants without the trait. There is now evidence that individuals with excessive behavioural inhibition are at increased risk for developing phobic behaviour (Biederman et al., 1990; Essex, Klein, Slattery, Goldsmith, & Kalin, 2010; Hirschfeld et al., 1992).

A model of the etiology of social phobia would look somewhat like models of panic disorder and specific phobia. Three pathways to social phobia are possible, as depicted in ■ Figure 5.10. First, someone could inherit a generalized biological vulnerability to develop anxiety, a biological tendency to be socially inhibited, or both. The existence of a generalized psychological vulnerability—such as the belief that events, particularly stressful events, are potentially uncontrollable—would increase an individual's vulnerability. When under stress, anxiety and self-focused attention could increase to the point of disrupting performance, even in the absence of a false alarm (panic attack). Second, when under stress, someone might have an unexpected panic attack in a social situation that would become associated (conditioned) to social cues. The individual would then become anxious about having additional panic attacks in the same or similar social situations. Third, someone might experience a real social trauma resulting in a true alarm. Anxiety would then develop (be conditioned) in the same or similar social situa-

tions. Traumatic social experiences may also extend back to difficult periods in childhood. Early adolescence—usually ages 12 through 15—is when children may be brutally taunted by peers who are attempting to assert their own dominance. This experience may produce anxiety and panic that are reproduced in future social situations. For example, McCabe, Anthony, Summerfeldt, Liss, and Swinson (2003) noted that 92 percent of adults with social phobia in their sample experienced severe teasing and bullying in childhood, compared to only 35 percent to 50 percent among people with other anxiety disorders. Such developmental experiences may produce anxiety and panic that are reproduced in future social situations and might also lead them to develop biased perceptions about the likelihood that others will treat them similarly in the future (Alden, 2001; Taylor & Alden, 2005).

University of British Columbia researcher Lynn Alden is a leading expert in interpersonal processes that contribute to social phobia. She has outlined an interpersonal transaction cycle whereby individuals with social phobia's interactions with people in their social environment contribute to and maintain the social anxieties. More specifically, people with social phobia have biased social perceptions and expectations that lead them to behave in certain maladaptive ways in social situations. The social behaviour of the socially anxious person in turn elicits negative reactions from others, which confirms the biased perceptions (see Alden & Taylor, 2004, for a review).

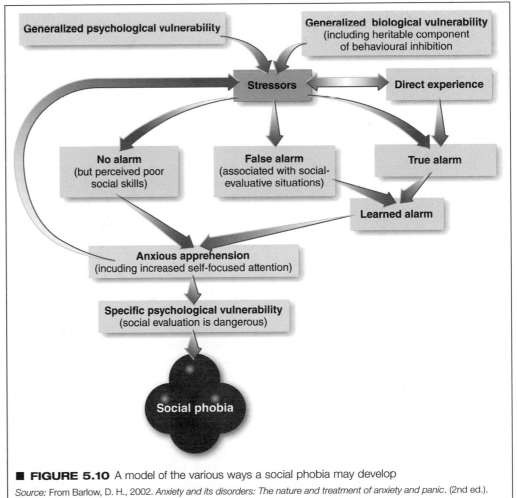

■ **FIGURE 5.10** A model of the various ways a social phobia may develop

Source: From Barlow, D. H., 2002. *Anxiety and its disorders: The nature and treatment of anxiety and panic.* (2nd ed.). New York: Guilford Press.

▲ University of British Columbia psychologist Lynn Alden has conducted important work on the interpersonal aspects of social phobia.

Alden and others have conducted considerable research on the various aspects of this hypothesized interpersonal cycle. For example, in some situations, people with social phobia incorrectly interpret others' behaviour as cold or unfriendly (Alden & Wallace, 1995) and they selectively attend to negative social information (Asmundson & Stein, 1994) and to anxiety-related symptoms that are noticeable to others, such as blushing (Spector, Pecknold, & Libman, 2003). Recent research has shown that people with social phobia also make more "upward comparisons" (i.e., assessments that someone else is superior to them) and fewer "downward comparisons" than controls, and that the upward comparisons that people with social phobia make cause them more anxiety and distress (Antony, Rowa, Liss, Swallow, & Swinson, 2005). Although people with social phobia do not always show maladaptive social behaviour, in certain situations they do. For example, when they are faced with a critical, controlling person, people who have social phobia avert their eyes, talk less, and engage in less personal disclosure (e.g., Alden, Bieling, & Meleshko, 1995; Meleshko & Alden, 1993). In turn, this behaviour evokes distinct negative reactions from other people. Socially anxious individuals are rated more negatively by others on a variety of measures (Ashbaugh, Antony, McCabe, Schmidt, & Swinson, 2005), including being rated as less intelligent by peers during social interactions (e.g., Paulhus & Morgan, 1997), and other people are less likely to desire future interactions with a socially anxious person after a first encounter (e.g., Meleshko & Alden, 1993; Papsdorf & Alden, 1998). These negative reactions from other people likely feed back to reinforce the biased social perceptions of people with social anxiety. And so the cycle continues.

But one more factor must fall into place to label it a social anxiety disorder. The individual with the vulnerabilities and experiences just described must also have learned growing up that social evaluation specifically can be dangerous. In fact, evidence indicates that some people with social phobia are predisposed to focusing their anxiety on events involving social evaluation. Some investigators (Bruch & Heimberg, 1994; Rapee & Melville, 1997) suggest that the parents of people with social phobia are significantly more socially fearful and concerned with the opinions of others than are the parents of patients with panic disorder and that they pass this concern on to their children. Fyer, Mannuzza, Chapman, Liebowitz, and Klein (1993) reported that the relatives of people with social phobia had a significantly greater risk of developing the disorder than the relatives of individuals without social phobia (16 percent versus 5 percent)—thus, the specific psychological vulnerability depicted in Figure 5.10. Interestingly, this psychological vulnerability factor may itself have a biological basis. A twin study by Stein, Jang, and Livesley (2002) showed that the tendency to fear being negatively evaluated by others is moderately heritable. Thus, as you can see,

a combination of biological, psychological, and interpersonal events seem to lead to the development of social phobia.

Treatment

Effective treatments have been developed for social phobia only in the past several years (Barlow & Lehman, 1996; Hofmann, 2004; Taylor, 1996; Turk, Heimberg, & Magee, 2008). Rick Heimberg and colleagues developed a cognitive-behavioural group therapy (CBGT) program in which groups of patients rehearse or role-play their socially phobic situations in front of one another (Heimberg et al., 1990; Turk et al., 2008). The group members participate in the role-playing, for example, acting as audience for someone who has extreme difficulty giving a speech. At the same time, the therapist conducts rather intensive cognitive therapy aimed at uncovering and changing the automatic or unconscious perceptions of danger that the socially phobic client assumes to exist. These treatments have proven to be more effective than comparison treatments involving education about anxiety and social phobia and social support for stressful life events. More important, a follow-up after five years indicates that the therapeutic gains are maintained (Heimberg, Salzman, Holt, & Blendell, 1993). Clark and colleagues (2006) evaluated a new and improved cognitive therapy program that emphasized more real-life experiences during therapy to disprove automatic perceptions of danger. This program substantially benefited 84 percent of individuals receiving treatment, and these results were maintained at a one-year follow-up. This outcome is the best yet for this difficult condition and significantly better than previous approaches to which it has been compared.

We have adapted these protocols for use with adolescents, directly involving parents in the group treatment process. Preliminary results suggest that severely socially phobic adolescents can attain relatively normal functioning in school and other social settings (Albano & Barlow, 1996) and that including the parents in the treatment process produces better outcomes than treating the adolescents alone (Albano, Pincus, Tracey, & Barlow, in preparation).

Effective drug treatments have been discovered as well (Van Ameringen, Mancini, Patterson, & Simpson, 2009). For a time, clinicians assumed that beta-blockers (drugs that lower heart rate and blood pressure, such as Inderal) worked well, particularly for performance anxiety, but the evidence does not seem to support that contention (Liebowitz et al., 1992; Turner, Beidel, & Jacob, 1994). Tricyclic antidepressants and, particularly, monoamine oxidase (MAO) inhibitors have been found to be more effective than placebo in the treatment of severe social anxiety (Liebowitz et al., 1992). Since 1999, the SSRIs Paxil, Zoloft, and Effexor have received approval for treatment of social anxiety disorder based on studies showing effectiveness compared to placebo (see, for example, Stein et al., 1998).

Several major studies have compared psychological and drug treatments. One large and important study compared MAO inhibitors to the psychological treatments described earlier. In this study (Heimberg et al., 1998; Liebowitz et al., 1999) 133 patients were randomly assigned to phenelzine (the MAO inhibitor), cognitive-behavioural group treatment (CBGT), drug placebo, or an educational-supportive group therapy that served as a placebo for the psychological treatment because it did not contain the cognitive-behavioural component. Results show that both active treatments are highly and equally effective compared to the two placebo conditions but that relapse tends to be more common after treatment stops among those taking medication. Another impressive study compared Clark's cognitive therapy described earlier to the SSRI drug Prozac, along with instructions to the patients with generalized social phobia to attempt to engage in more social situations (self-exposure). A third group received placebo plus instructions to attempt to engage in more social activities. Assessments were conducted before the 16-week treatment, at the midpoint of treatment, post-treatment, and then after three months of booster sessions. Finally, researchers followed up with patients in the two treatment groups 12 months later (Clark et al., 2003). Results are presented in ■ Figure 5.11. Both treatments did well, but the psychological treatment was substantially better at all times. This study is also notable because of the *extent* of change in treatment (most patients were cured or nearly cured with few remaining symptoms).

The evidence is mixed on the usefulness of combining SSRIs or related drugs with psychological treatments. Davidson, Foa, and Huppert (2004) found that a cognitive-behavioural treatment and an SSRI were comparable in efficacy but that the combination was no better than the two individual treatments; Blanco and colleagues (2010), however, did find an additive effect. As noted earlier, an exciting study suggests that adding the drug D-cycloserine (DCS) to cognitive-behavioural treatments significantly enhances the effects of treatment (Hofmann et al., 2006). Unlike SSRIs, this drug is known to facilitate the extinction of anxiety, an important part of cognitive behavioural treatments, by modifying neurotransmitter flow in the glutamate system as described in Chapter 2.

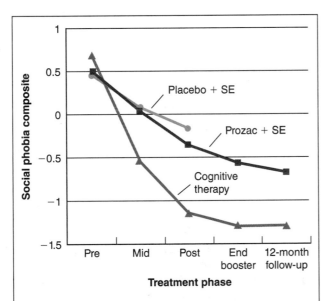

■ **FIGURE 5.11** Results from a comparison of Prozac and instructions to attempt more social interactions or "self-exposure" (Prozac + SE), placebo and the same instruction (placebo + SE), and cognitive therapy (CT) in the treatment of patients with generalized social phobia

Source: From "Cognitive Therapy versus Fluoxetine in Generalized Social Phobia: A Randomized Placebo-Controlled Trial," by D. M. Clark, A. Ehlers, F. McManus, A. Hackmann, M. Fennell, H. Campbell, T. Flower, C. Davenport, and B. Louis, in *Journal of Consulting and Clinical Psychology, 71,* p. 1058–1067. Copyright © 2003 by the American Psychological Association. Reprinted with permission.

Post-Traumatic Stress Disorder

Recently, we have heard a great deal about the severe and long-lasting emotional disorders that can occur after a variety of traumatic events. Perhaps the most impressive traumatic event is war, but emotional disorders also occur after physical assault (particularly rape), car accidents, natural catastrophes, or the sudden death of a loved one. The emotional disorder that follows a trauma is known as **post-traumatic stress disorder (PTSD)**.

Clinical Description

DSM-IV-TR describes the setting event for PTSD as exposure to a traumatic event during which a person feels fear, helplessness, or horror. Afterward, victims re-experience the event through memories and nightmares. When memories occur very suddenly and the victims find themselves reliving the event, they are having a *flashback*. Victims avoid anything that reminds them of the trauma. They display a characteristic restriction or numbing of emotional responsiveness, which may be very disruptive to interpersonal relationships. They are sometimes unable to remember certain aspects of the event. It is possible that victims unconsciously attempt to avoid the experience of emotion itself, like people with panic disorder, because intense emotions could bring back memories of the trauma. Finally, victims typically are chronically overaroused, easily startled, and quick to anger.

PTSD was first named in 1980 in *DSM-III* (American Psychiatric Association, 1980), but it has a long history. In 1666, the

British diarist Samuel Pepys witnessed the Great Fire of London that caused substantial loss of life and property and threw the city into chaos for a time. He captured the events in an account that is still read today. But Pepys did not escape the effects of the horrific event. Six months later, he wrote, "It is strange to think how to this very day I cannot sleep a night without great terrors of fire; and this very night could not sleep to almost 2 in the morning through thoughts of fire" (Daly, 1983, p. 66). The *DSM-IV* criteria show that difficulty sleeping and recurring intrusive dreams of the event are prominent features of PTSD. Pepys described his guilt at saving himself and his property while others died. He also experienced a sense of detachment and a numbing of his emotions concerning the fire, common experiences in PTSD.

One recent Canadian study on PTSD deals with the psychological impact of an airline disaster on community volunteers in a rural community (Mitchell, Stewart, Griffin, & Loba, 2004; Mitchell, Walters, & Stewart, 2006). Swissair Flight 111 crashed off the coast of Peggy's Cove in Nova Scotia on September 2, 1998. When local residents heard the crash, many went out in their boats and attempted to rescue survivors. Unfortunately, none of the 229 passengers and crew survived the crash, and these community volunteers unexpectedly were confronted with airplane debris, passenger's personal effects, and gruesome human remains. In some cases, they were faced with dismembered body parts, and the skin of crash victims had often separated from the rest of their bodies, a phenomenon called "degloving." Many volunteers continued assisting with the recovery work (e.g., volunteering for ground search and rescue) over the ensuing weeks and were continually exposed to these sights and smells. Well after their exposure to the disaster had ended, many volunteers reported psychological symptoms attributable to their trauma exposure. Many reported having intrusive memories of the horrors they had encountered in their volunteer work, avoiding reminders of the disaster, experiencing emotional numbing, and having difficulties sleep-

TABLE 5.7 Percentage of Swissair Disaster Volunteers Endorsing Each *DSM-IV-TR* PTSD Symptom on a Self-Report Scale

Symptom Domain Item	Percentage Endorsing (%)
Cognitive Re-experiencing	
Intrusive thoughts	69
Nightmares	39
Flashbacks	46
Emotional reactivity	77
Physiological reactivity	31
Avoidance	
Avoid thoughts of trauma	46
Avoid trauma reminders	39
Inability to recall trauma	31
Emotional Numbing	
Loss of interest	39
Detachment	53
Restricted affect	15
Foreshortened future	23
Somatic Hyperarousal	
Sleep disturbance	31
Increased irritability	23
Difficulty concentrating	46
Hypervigilance	46
Excessive startle	31

Source: Mitchell, T. L., Stewart, S. H., Griffin, K., & Loba, P. (2004). "We will never forget" The Swissair Flight 111 disaster and its impact on volunteers and communities. *Journal of Health Psychology, 9 (1)*, 237–253. Reprinted with permission.

ing. These are all common symptoms in PTSD. The percentage of volunteers reporting each of the 17 *DSM-IV-TR* PTSD symptoms is illustrated in Table 5.7.

Consider next the case of the Joneses from one of our clinics.

▲ Exposure to a traumatic event may create profound fear and helplessness. People who have post-traumatic stress disorder may re-experience such feelings in flashbacks, involuntarily reliving the horrifying event, such as these volunteers helping after the Swissair Flight 111 disaster in Nova Scotia.

THE JONESES | *One Victim, Many Traumas*

Mrs. Betty Jones and her four children arrived at a farm to visit a friend. (Mr. Jones was at work.) Jeff, the oldest child, was eight years old. Marcie, Cathy, and Susan were six, four, and two years of age. Mrs. Jones parked the car in the driveway, and they all started across the yard to the front door. Suddenly, Jeff heard growling somewhere near the house. Before he could warn the others, a large German shepherd charged and leapt at Marcie, the six-year-old, knocking her to the ground and tearing viciously at her face. The family, too stunned to move, watched the attack helplessly. After what seemed like an eternity, Jeff lunged at the dog and it moved away. The owner, in a state of panic, ran to a nearby house to get help. Mrs. Jones immediately put pressure on Marcie's facial wounds in an attempt to stop the bleeding. The owner had neglected to retrieve the dog, and it stood a short distance away, growling and barking at the frightened family. Eventually, the dog was restrained and Marcie was rushed to the hospital. Marcie, who was hysterical, had to be restrained on a padded board so emergency room physicians could stitch her wounds.

This case is unusual because not only did Marcie develop PTSD, but so did her eight-year-old brother. In addition, Cathy, four, and Susan, two, although quite young, also showed symptoms of the disorder, as did their mother. Jeff evidenced classic survivor guilt symptoms, reporting that he should have saved Marcie or at least put himself between Marcie and the dog. Both Jeff and Marcie regressed developmentally, wetting the bed (nocturnal enuresis) and experiencing nightmares and separation fears. In addition, Marcie, having been strapped down and given local anesthetic and stitches, became very frightened of any medical procedures and even of such routine daily events as having her nails trimmed or taking a bath. Furthermore, she refused to be tucked into bed, something she had enjoyed all her life, probably because it reminded her of the hospital board. Jeff started sucking his fingers, which he had not done for years. These behaviours, along with intense separation anxiety, are common, particularly in younger children (Eth, 1990; Silverman & La Greca, 2002). Cathy, the four-year-old, evidenced considerable fear and avoidance when tested, but denied having any problem when she was interviewed by a child psychologist. Susan, the two-year-old, also had some symptoms, but was too young to talk about them. However, for several months following the trauma she repeatedly said, without provocation, "Doggy bit sister."

Children's memories of traumatic events can become embellished over the years. For example, some children incorporate a superhero coming to the rescue. These intense memories are very malleable and subject to distortion (e.g., Garry & Wade, 2005; Porter, Spencer, & Birt, 2003; Porter, Yuille, & Lehman, 1999).

As indicated in the criteria (see DSM Table 5.6), PTSD is subdivided into acute and chronic. Acute PTSD can be diagnosed between one and three months after the event occurs. When PTSD continues longer than three months, it is considered chronic. Chronic PTSD is usually associated with more prominent avoidance behaviours (Davidson, Hughes, Blazer, & George, 1991), as well as with the more frequent co-occurrence of additional diagnoses such as social phobia. In delayed-onset PTSD, individuals show few if any symptoms immediately after a trauma, but later, perhaps years afterward, they develop full-blown PTSD. Why onset is delayed in some individuals is not yet clear.

As we noted, PTSD cannot be diagnosed until a month after the trauma. New to the *DSM-IV* is a disorder called **acute stress disorder**. This is really PTSD occurring within the first month after the trauma, but the different name emphasizes the very severe reaction that some people have immediately. PTSD-like symptoms are accompanied by severe dissociative symptoms, such as amnesia for all or part of the trauma, emotional numbing, and derealization, or feelings of unreality. According

---

DSM-IV-TR | **Table 5.6** Diagnostic Criteria for Post-Traumatic Stress Disorder

A. The person has been exposed to a traumatic event in which both of the following were present:

1. The person experienced, witnessed, or was confronted with an event or events that involve actual or threatened death or serious injury, or a threat to the physical integrity of himself or herself or others.

2. The person's response involved intense fear, helplessness, or horror. *Note:* In children, it may be expressed instead by disorganized or agitated behaviour.

B. The traumatic event is persistently re-experienced in one (or more) of the following ways:

1. Recurrent and intrusive distressing recollections of the event, including images, thoughts, or perceptions. *Note:* In young children, repetitive play may occur in which themes or aspects of the trauma are expressed.

2. Recurrent distressing dreams of the event. *Note:* In children, there may be frightening dreams without recognizable content.

3. Acting or feeling as if the traumatic event were recurring (includes a sense of reliving the experience, illusions, hallucinations, and dissociative flashback episodes, including those that occur on awakening or when intoxicated). *Note:* In young children, trauma-specific re-enactment may occur.

4. Intense psychological distress at exposure to internal or external cues that symbolize or resemble an aspect of the traumatic event.

5. Physiologic reactivity on exposure to internal or external cues that symbolize or resemble an aspect of the traumatic event.

C. Persistent avoidance of stimuli associated with the trauma and numbing of general responsiveness (not present before the trauma), as indicated by three (or more) of the following:

1. Efforts to avoid thoughts, feelings, or conversations associated with the trauma

2. Efforts to avoid activities, places, or people that arouse recollections of the trauma

3. Inability to recall an important aspect of the trauma

4. Markedly diminished interest or participation in significant activities

5. Feeling of detachment or estrangement from others

6. Restricted range of affect (e.g., unable to have loving feelings)

7. Sense of a foreshortened future (e.g., does not expect to have a career, marriage, children, or a normal life span)

D. Persistent symptoms of increased arousal (not present before the trauma), as indicated by two (or more) of the following:

1. Difficulty falling or staying asleep

2. Irritability or outbursts of anger

3. Difficulty concentrating

4. Hypervigilance

5. Exaggerated startle response

E. Duration of the disturbance (symptoms in B, C, and D) is more than one month.

F. The disturbance causes clinically significant distress or impairment in social, occupational, or other important areas of functioning.

Specify if:

1. Acute: if duration of symptoms is less than three months

2. Chronic: if duration of symptoms is three months or more

Specify if:

With delayed onset: if onset of symptoms at least six months after the stressor

Source: Reprinted with permission from the *Diagnostic and Statistical Manual of Mental Disorders,* Fourth Edition, Text Revision, (Copyright © 2000). American Psychiatric Association.

to one Australian study, 63 percent to 70 percent of individuals with acute stress disorder from motor vehicle accidents went on to develop PTSD up to two years after the trauma. In addition, 13 percent who did not meet criteria for acute stress disorder went on to develop PTSD. If the victim experienced very strong arousal and emotional numbing as part of his or her acute stress disorder, the likelihood of later developing PTSD was greater (Harvey & Bryant, 1998). Acute stress disorder was included in *DSM-IV* because many people with very severe early reactions to trauma could not otherwise be diagnosed and, therefore, could not receive insurance coverage for immediate treatment.

Statistics

Determining the prevalence rates for PTSD seems relatively straightforward: Simply observe victims of a trauma and see how many develop PTSD. But a number of studies have demonstrated the remarkably low prevalence of PTSD in populations of trauma victims. Stanley J. Rachman (1978) studied the British citizenry who endured numerous life-threatening air raids during Word War II. He concluded that "a great majority of people endured the air raids extraordinarily well, contrary to the universal expectation of mass panic. Exposure to repeated bombings did not produce a significant increase in psychiatric disorders. Although short-lived fear reactions were common, surprisingly few persistent phobic reactions emerged" (Rachman, 1991, p. 162). Similar results have been observed after disastrous fires, earthquakes, and floods (Green, Grace, Lindy, Titchener, & Lindy, 1983).

However, some studies have found a very high incidence of PTSD after trauma. Kilpatrick et al. (1985) sampled more than 2000 adult women who had personally experienced such trauma as rape, sexual molestation, robbery, and aggravated assault. Subjects were asked whether they had thought about suicide after the trauma, attempted suicide, or had a *nervous breakdown* (a lay term that has no meaning in psychopathology but is commonly used to refer to a severe psychological upset). The authors also analyzed the results based on whether the attack was completed or attempted, as shown in Table 5.8. Rape had the most significant emotional impact. Compared with 2.2 percent of nonvictims, 19.2 percent of rape victims had attempted suicide, and 44 percent reported suicidal ideation at some time following the rape. Similarly, Resnick, Kilpatrick, Dansky, Saunders, and Best (1993) found that 32 percent of rape victims met criteria for PTSD at some point in their lives. Looking at all types of trauma (e.g., physical assault, accidents) in a large sample of U.S. adult women, Resnick et al. (1993) found that 17.9 percent experienced PTSD. Taylor and Koch (1995) found that 15 percent to 20 percent of Canadian adults experiencing severe auto accidents developed PTSD. Other surveys indicate that among the population as a whole, 7.8 percent have experienced PTSD (Kessler, Sonnega, Bromet, Hughes, & Nelson, 1995), and combat and sexual assault are the most common traumas. The fact that a diagnosis of PTSD predicts suicidal attempts independently of any other problem, such as alcohol abuse, has recently been confirmed (Wilcox, Storr, & Breslau, 2009).

TABLE 5.8 Proportion of Victimization Groups Experiencing Major Mental Health Problems

| | \multicolumn{6}{c}{Problem} |
| Nervous Breakdown | \multicolumn{2}{c}{Suicidal Ideation} | | \multicolumn{2}{c}{Suicide Attempt} | |
Group	n	%	n	%	n	%
Attempted rape	7	9.0	23	29.5	7	8.9
Completed rape	16	16.3	44	44.0	19	19.2
Attempted molestation	2	5.4	12	32.4	3	8.1
Completed molestation	1	1.9	12	21.8	2	3.6
Attempted robbery	0	0.0	3	9.1	4	12.1
Completed robbery	5	7.8	7	10.8	2	3.1
Aggravated assault	1	2.1	7	14.9	2	4.4
Nonvictims	51	3.3	106	6.8	34	2.2

Source: Reprinted from *Journal of Consulting and Clinical Psychology Volume 53, Issue 6*, D. G. Kilpatrick, C. L. Best, L. J. Veronen, A. E. Amick, L. A. Villeponteaux and G. A. Ruff, "Mental Health Correlates of Criminal Victimization: A Random Community Survey," Pages No. 866-873, Copyright 1985, with permission from Elsevier.

What accounts for the discrepancies between the low rate of PTSD in citizens who endured bombing and shelling in London, England, and the relatively high rate in victims of crime? Investigators have now concluded that during air raids many people may not have directly experienced the horrors of dying, death, and direct attack. Close exposure to the trauma seems to be necessary to developing this disorder (Friedman, 2009; Keane & Barlow, 2002; King, King, Foy, & Gudanowski, 1996). But this is also evident among Vietnam veterans, where 18.7 percent developed PTSD, with prevalence rates directly related to amount of combat exposure (Dohrenwend, Turner, & Turse, 2006). Surveys of 76 victims of Hurricane Katrina also report a doubling of severe mental illness (Kessler, Galea, Jones, & Parker, 2006). The connection between proximity to the traumatic event and the development of PTSD was starkly evident following the terrorist attacks on the United States on September 11, 2001. Galea and colleagues (2002) contacted a representative sample of adults living south of 110th Street in Manhattan and found that 7.5 percent reported symptoms consistent with a diagnosis of acute stress disorder or PTSD. But among respondents who lived close to the World Trade Center (south of Canal Street), the prevalence of the disorder was 20 percent. Again, those who experienced the disaster most personally and directly seemed to be the ones most affected.

In addition, tens of thousands of public school children in New York City who lived close to the disaster experienced chronic nightmares, fear of public places, and other symptoms of PTSD. After the attack, a large study conducted with the help of U.S. government agencies estimated that 75 000 schoolchildren in New York City in Grades 4 through 12, or 10.5 percent of children in those grades, suffered PTSD after September 11 (Goodnough, 2002). In addition, 155 suffered from agoraphobia, or a fear of leaving a safe place such as home. Many of these children feared riding public transportation. Two-thirds of the children sampled lived near the World Trade Center or in other neighbourhoods directly affected by the tragedy, such as Staten Island, home to many who were killed, or Brooklyn, where smoke drifted over its neighbourhoods for days. We also know that once it appears, PTSD tends to last (i.e., it runs a chronic course) (Perkonigg et al., 2005).

But is this the whole story? It seems not. Some people experience the most horrifying traumas imaginable and emerge psychologically healthy. For others, even relatively mild stressful events are sufficient to produce a full-blown disorder. To understand how this can happen we must consider the etiology of PTSD.

Causes

PTSD is the one disorder for which we are sure of the etiology: Someone personally experiences a trauma and develops a disorder. However, whether or not someone develops PTSD is a surprisingly complex issue involving biological, psychological, and social factors. David Foy and his colleagues (Foy, Sipprelle, Rueger, & Carroll, 1984) concluded that the intensity of combat exposure contributed to the etiology of PTSD in a group of Vietnam War veterans, a finding recently confirmed, as noted earlier (Dohrenwend et al., 2006; Friedman, 2009), but did not account for all of it. For example, approximately 67 percent of prisoners of war developed PTSD (Foy, Resnick, Sipprelle, & Carroll, 1987). This means that 33 percent of the prisoners who endured long-term deprivation and torture *did not* develop the disorder. Similarly, Resnick, Kilpatrick, Dansky, Saunders, and Best (1993) demonstrated that the percentage of female crime victims who developed PTSD increased as a function of the severity of the trauma (see ■ Figure 5.12). In addition, children experiencing severe burns are likely to develop PTSD in proportion to the severity of the burns and the pain associated with them (Saxe et al., 2005). At lower levels of trauma, some people develop PTSD, but most do not. In our sample of the Swissair recovery volunteers, the longer the individual was involved in recovery work (presumably reflecting more severe exposure), the more severe and frequent were the PTSD symptoms; yet not all volunteers

developed PTSD, despite exposure to such an awful event (Mitchell et al., 2004). What accounts for these differences?

As with other disorders, we bring our own generalized biological and psychological vulnerabilities with us. The greater the vulnerability, the more likely we are to develop PTSD. If certain characteristics run in your family, you have a much greater chance of developing the disorder (Foy et al., 1987). A family history of anxiety suggests a generalized biological vulnerability for PTSD. True et al. (1993) reported that, given the same amount of combat exposure and one twin with PTSD, a monozygotic (identical) twin was more likely to develop PTSD than a dizygotic twin. This suggests some genetic influence in the development of PTSD. A twin study by Stein, Jang, Taylor, Vernon, and Livesley (2002) showed that PTSD symptoms after noncombat trauma are also moderately heritable. Interestingly, they further found that exposure to certain types of traumas (i.e., assaultive trauma like robbery but not nonassaultive trauma like car accidents) was also affected by genetics. In other words, genetic factors seem to influence the risk of being exposed to certain kinds of trauma, perhaps through inherited personality characteristics that affect what kinds of environments (e.g., risky versus safe) a person will choose. Nevertheless, as with other disorders, there is little or no evidence that genes directly cause PTSD (Norrholm & Ressler, 2009). Rather, genetic factors predispose individuals to be easily stressed and anxious, which then may make it more likely that a traumatic experience will result in PTSD.

Breslau, Davis, and Andreski (1995) demonstrated among a random sample of 1200 individuals that characteristics such as a tendency to be anxious, as well as factors such as minimal education, predict exposure to traumatic events in the first place and therefore an increased risk for PTSD. Breslau, Lucia, and Alvarado (2006) elaborated on this finding by showing that six-year-old children with externalizing (acting out) problems were more likely to encounter trauma (such as assaults), probably because of their acting out, and later develop PTSD. Higher intelligence predicted decreased exposure to these types of traumatic events. That is, personality and other characteristics, some of them at least partially heritable, may predispose people to the experience of trauma by making it likely that they will be in (risky) situations where trauma is likely to occur (Norrholm & Ressler, 2009). This is reminiscent of the studies on reciprocal gene–environment interactions we described in Chapter 2, in which existing vulnerabilities, some of them heritable, may help determine the kind of environment in which someone lives and, therefore, the type of psychological disorder that person may develop.

Also, there seems to be a generalized psychological vulnerability described in the context of other disorders based on early experiences with unpredictable or uncontrollable events. Foy et al. (1987) discovered that at very high levels of trauma, these vulnerabilities did not matter as much, because most prisoners of war (67 percent) developed PTSD. However, at low levels of stress or trauma, vulnerabilities matter a great deal in determining whether the disorder will develop. Family instability is one factor that may instill a sense the world is an uncontrollable, potentially dangerous place (Chorpita & Barlow, 1998; Suárez et al., 2009), so it is not surprising that individuals from unstable families are at risk for developing PTSD if they experience trauma. This factor was relevant in a study of more than 1600 male and female Vietnam veterans (King et al., 1996).

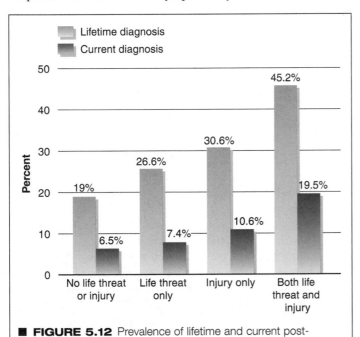

■ **FIGURE 5.12** Prevalence of lifetime and current post-traumatic stress disorder associated with assault characteristics

Source: Reprinted from *Journal of Consulting and Clinical Psychology Volume 61, Issue 6,* H. S. Resnick, D. G. Kilpatrick, B. S. Dansky, B. E. Saunders and C. L. Best, "Civilian Trauma and Posttraumatic Stress Disorder in a Representative National Sample of Women," Pages No. 984-991, Copyright 1993, with permission from Elsevier.

Basoglu and colleagues (1997) studied two groups of torture victims in Turkey. Thirty-four survivors had no history of political activity, commitment to a political cause or group, or expectations of arrest and torture. Compared with 55 tortured political activists, the nonactivists were subjected to less horrendous abuse but showed higher levels of psychopathology. It seemed that the political activists were more prepared psychologically for torture, which they generally experienced as predictable, thereby reducing later psychological symptoms. This study further demonstrates psychological factors that either protect against or increase the risk of developing PTSD.

Another psychological vulnerability factor is anxiety sensitivity, which we discussed previously in the context of panic disorder. A study by Fedoroff, Taylor, Asmundson, and Koch (2000) examined levels of anxiety sensitivity in 81 victims of car accidents who were receiving treatment for PTSD in Vancouver or Regina. Greater levels of anxiety sensitivity at pretreatment baseline predicted greater severity of PTSD. Moreover, the more a patient reduced his or her level of anxiety sensitivity over the course of treatment, the better the outcome in terms of his or her PTSD symptoms. In the study of the Swissair disaster volunteers, we similarly found that a greater fear of anxiety (specifically those who were most fearful of losing control when anxious) predicted greater levels of PTSD symptoms following exposure to the disaster work (Mitchell et al., 2004). These findings suggest that anxiety sensitivity is an important psychological vulnerability for PTSD.

Finally, social and cultural factors play a major role in the development of PTSD (e.g., Carroll, Rueger, Foy, & Donahoe,

1985). The results from several studies are very consistent in showing that, if you have a strong and supportive group of people around you, it is much less likely you will develop PTSD after a trauma. In a particularly interesting study, Vernberg, LaGreca, Silverman, and Prinstein (1996) studied 568 elementary-school children three months after Hurricane Andrew hit the coast of south Florida. More than 55 percent of these children reported moderate to very severe levels of PTSD symptoms. When the authors examined factors contributing to who developed PTSD symptoms and who didn't, social support from parents, close friends, classmates, and teachers was a very important protective factor. Similarly, positive coping strategies involving active problem solving seemed to be protective, whereas becoming angry and placing blame on others were associated with higher levels of PTSD. The broader and deeper the network of social support, the less chance of developing PTSD.

Why is this? We are all social animals and something about having a loving, caring group of people around us directly affects our biological and psychological responses to stress. In fact, several studies show that support from loved ones reduces cortisol secretion and HPA axis activity in children during stress (e.g., Nachmias, Gunnar, Mangelsdorf, Parritz, & Buss, 1996). It is likely that one reason for the very high prevalence of PTSD in Vietnam veterans is the tragic absence of social support when they returned from the war.

It seems clear that PTSD involves a number of neurobiological systems, particularly elevated corticotropin-releasing factor (CRF), which indicates heightened activity in the HPA axis, as described earlier in this chapter and in Chapter 2 (Amat et al., 2005; Charney, Deutch, Krystal, Southwick, & Davis, 1993; Gunnar & Fisher, 2006; Heim & Nemeroff, 1999; Ladd et al., 2000; Shin et al., 2004; Shin et al., 2009; Sullivan et al., 2000). You may remember that primates studied in the wild under extreme stress also have elevated levels of CRF and cortisol, the stress hormones. Chronic activation of stress hormones in these primates seems to result in permanent damage to the hippocampus, which regulates the stress hormones. Thus, chronic arousal and some other symptoms of PTSD may be directly related to changes in brain function and structure (Bremner, 1999; Bremner et al., 1997; McEwen & Magarinos, 2004). Evidence of damage to the hippocampus has appeared in groups of patients with war-related PTSD (Gurvits et al., 1996; Wang et al., 2010), adult survivors of childhood sexual abuse (Bremner et al., 1995), and firefighters exposed to extreme trauma (Shin et al., 2004). The hippocampus is a part of the brain that plays an important role in learning and memory. Thus, if there is damage to the hippocampus, we might expect some disruptions in learning and memory. Disruptions in memory functions, including short-term memory and recalling events, have been demonstrated in patients with PTSD (Sass et al., 1992). These memory deficits are also evident in veterans of the Gulf War (Vasterling, Brailey, Constans, & Sotker, 1998) and Holocaust survivors with PTSD, as compared to Holocaust survivors without PTSD or healthy Jewish adults (Golier et al., 2002). Bremner, Vermetten, Southwick, Krystal, and Charney (1998) suggest that the fragmentation of memory often seen in patients with PTSD may account for difficulties in recalling at least some aspects of their trauma.

Fortunately, as Bremner (1999) points out, some evidence indicates this damage to the hippocampus may be reversible. For

CP Photo/Jonathan Hayward

▲ Lieutenant-General (Retired) Roméo Dallaire, who is an activist promoting recognition of stress reactions in Canadian military personnel, has PTSD related to his experiences on a peacekeeping mission in Rwanda.

example, Starkman and colleagues (1999) reported results from patients who had some damage to their hippocampus because of Cushing's disease, which causes chronic activation of the HPA axis and increased flow of cortisol. They found increases of up to 10 percent in hippocampal volume following successful treatment for this disease. Further studies will confirm if the changes as a result of trauma can be reversed by treatment.

Earlier we described a panic attack as an adaptive fear response occurring at an inappropriate time. We have speculated that the "alarm reaction" that is a panic attack is similar in both panic disorder and PTSD but that in panic disorder the alarm is false. In PTSD, the initial alarm is true in that real danger is present (Jones & Barlow, 1990; Keane & Barlow, 2002). If the alarm is severe enough, we may develop a conditioned or learned alarm reaction to stimuli that remind us of the trauma (e.g., being tucked into bed reminded Marcie of the emergency room board). We may also develop anxiety about the possibility of additional uncontrollable emotional experiences (such as flashbacks, which are common in PTSD). Whether or not we develop anxiety partly depends on our vulnerabilities. This model of the etiology of PTSD is presented in ■ Figure 5.13.

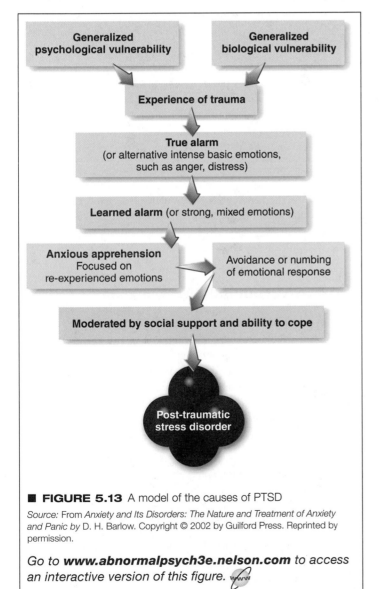

■ FIGURE 5.13 A model of the causes of PTSD

Source: From Anxiety and Its Disorders: The Nature and Treatment of Anxiety and Panic by D. H. Barlow. Copyright © 2002 by Guilford Press. Reprinted by permission.

Go to www.abnormalpsych3e.nelson.com to access an interactive version of this figure.

Treatment

From the psychological point of view, most clinicians agree that victims of PTSD should face the original trauma in order to develop effective coping procedures and thus overcome the debilitating effects of the disorder (Barlow & Lehman, 1996; Keane & Barlow, 2002; Najavits, 2007; Resick, Monson, & Rizvi, 2008). In psychoanalytic therapy, reliving emotional trauma to relieve emotional suffering is called catharsis. The trick, of course, is in arranging the re-exposure so it will be therapeutic rather than traumatic once again. Unlike the object of a specific phobia, a traumatic event is difficult to recreate, and very few therapists want to try. Therefore, *imaginal exposure*, in which the content of the trauma and the emotions associated with it are worked through systematically, has been used for decades under a variety of names. At present, the most common strategy to achieve this purpose with adolescents or adults is to work with the victim to develop a narrative of the traumatic experience that is then reviewed extensively in therapy. Cognitive therapy to correct negative assumptions about the trauma, such as blaming oneself in some way, feeling guilty, or both, is often part of treatment (Najavits, 2007; Resick et al., 2008).

Another complication is that trauma victims often repress the emotional side of their memories of the event and sometimes, it seems, the memory itself. This happens automatically and unconsciously. Occasionally, with treatment, the memories flood back and the patient dramatically relives the episode. Although this may be frightening to both patient and therapist, it can be therapeutic if handled appropriately. Evidence is now accumulating that early, structured interventions delivered as soon after the trauma as possible to those who require help are useful in preventing the development of PTSD (Bryant, Moulds, & Nixon, 2003; Ehlers et al., 2003; Litz, Gray, Bryant, & Adler, 2002). For example, in the study by Ehlers and colleagues (2003) of patients who had experienced a scary car accident and were clearly at risk for developing PTSD, only 11 percent developed PTSD after 12 sessions of cognitive therapy, compared with 61 percent of those receiving a detailed self-help booklet or 55 percent of those who were just assessed repeatedly over time but had no intervention. All patients who needed it were then treated with cognitive therapy. On the other hand, there is evidence that subjecting trauma victims to a single debriefing session, in which they are forced to express their feelings whether they are distressed or not, can be harmful (Ehlers & Clark, 2003).

Both Marcie, the young girl bitten by the dog, and her brother were treated simultaneously. The primary difficulty was Marcie's reluctance to be seen by a doctor or to undergo any physical examinations, so a series of experiences was arranged from least to most intense (see Table 5.9). Mildly anxiety-provoking procedures for Marcie included having her pulse taken, lying on an examination table, and taking a bath after accidentally cutting herself. The most intense challenge was being strapped on a restraining board. First Marcie watched her brother go through these exercises. He was not afraid of these particular procedures, although he was anxious about being strapped to a board because of Marcie's terror at the thought. After she watched her brother experience these situations with little or no fear, Marcie tried each one in turn. The therapist took instant photographs of her that she

TABLE 5.9 Fear and Avoidance Hierarchy for Marcie

	Pretreatment Fear Rating	Post-Treatment Fear Rating
Being strapped on a board	4	0
Having an electrocardiogram	4	0
Having a chest X-ray	4	0
Having M.D. listen to heart with stethoscope	3	0
Lying on examination table	3	0
Taking a bath after sustaining an accidentally inflicted cut	3	0
Allowing therapist to put bandage on a cut	2	0
Letting therapist listen to heart with stethoscope	1	0
Having pulse taken	1	0
Allowing therapist to examine throat with tongue depressor	1	0

Source: From Sibling Modeling in the Treatment of PTSD by P. P. Miller, A. M. Albano and D. H. Barlow, 1992. Paper presented at the annual meeting of the Association for the Advancement of Behavior Therapy, Boston, MA.

kept after completing the procedures. Marcie was also asked to draw pictures of the situations. The therapist and her family warmly congratulated her as she completed each exercise. Because of Marcie's age, she was not adept at imaginatively recreating memories of the traumatic medical procedures. Therefore, her treatment offered experiences designed to alter her current perceptions of the situations. Marcie's PTSD was successfully treated, and her brother's guilt was greatly reduced as a function of helping in her treatment.

A recent modification to traditional imaginal exposure therapy is Donald Meichenbaum's CBT treatment for PTSD. Meichenbaum (1994, 2006) uses a *constructivist-narrative* approach for treating individuals who have been traumatized (e.g., through rape). In this approach, the therapist assists the client in reconstructing his or her "story" about the traumatic event—changing the meaning that the client has attached to the traumatic event and helping the client develop adaptive coping strategies and a sense of survivorship (Meichenbaum, 1994, 2006).

Another newer psychological treatment for PTSD is known as *eye-movement desensitization and reprocessing* (EMDR; Shapiro, 1995, 1999). While thinking about their traumatic experience in therapy, the client is asked to follow the therapist's moving fingers with his or her eyes, all the while keeping the image of the trauma in mind. This unusual technique is said by proponents to facilitate rapid reprocessing of the traumatic event (Shapiro, 1999). Recently, a group of researchers at the University of British Columbia compared the efficacy of this newer approach to imaginal exposure and to relaxation training (S. Taylor et al., 2003). Sixty patients with PTSD were randomly assigned to one of the three treatment modalities. Treatments did not differ in their effects on PTSD symptoms of emotional numbing or physiological arousal. However, exposure therapy was superior to the other two treatments in that it led to larger reductions in avoidance and cognitive re-experiencing, achieved reductions in avoidance more quickly, and led to more patients who were PTSD-free after treatment. EMDR did not differ on any outcomes from relaxation training.

Drugs can also be effective for symptoms of PTSD (Dent & Bremner, 2009). Some of the drugs, such as SSRIs (e.g., Prozac and Paxil), that are effective for anxiety disorders in general have been shown to be helpful for PTSD, perhaps because they relieve the severe anxiety and panic attacks so prominent in this disorder.

Concept Check 5.5

Match the correct preliminary diagnosis with the cases below: (a) acute post-traumatic stress disorder, (b) acute stress disorder, and (c) delayed-onset post-traumatic stress disorder.

1. Judy witnessed a horrific tornado level her farm three weeks ago. Since then, she's had many flashbacks of the incident, trouble sleeping, and a fear of going outside in storms. _____

2. Jack was involved in a car accident six weeks ago in which the driver of the other car was killed. Since then, Jack has been unable to get into a car because it brings back the horrible scene he witnessed. Nightmares of the incident haunt him and interfere with his sleep. He is irritable and has lost interest in his work and hobbies. _____

3. Patricia was raped at the age of 17, 30 years ago. Just recently, she has been having flashbacks of the event, difficulty sleeping, and fear of sexual contact with her husband. _____

Obsessive-Compulsive Disorder

Obsessive-compulsive disorder (OCD) is the devastating culmination of the anxiety disorders. It is not uncommon for someone with OCD to experience severe generalized anxiety, recurrent panic attacks, debilitating avoidance, and major depression, all occurring simultaneously in conjunction with obsessive-compulsive symptoms. With OCD, establishing even a foothold of control and predictability over the dangerous events in life seems so utterly hopeless that victims resort to magic and rituals.

Clinical Description

In other anxiety disorders the danger is usually in an external object or situation, or at least the memory of one. In OCD the dangerous event is a thought, image, or impulse that the client attempts to avoid as completely as someone with a snake phobia avoids snakes (Clark & O'Connor, 2005). For example, has anyone ever told you not to think of pink elephants? If you really concentrate on not thinking of pink elephants, using every mental means possible, you will realize how difficult it is to suppress a suggested thought or image. Individuals with OCD fight this battle all day, every day, sometimes for most of their lives, and they usually fail miserably. In Chapter 3 we discussed the case of Frank, who experienced involuntary thoughts of epilepsy or seizures and prayed or shook his leg to try to distract himself. **Obsessions** are intrusive and mostly nonsensical thoughts, images, or urges that the individual tries to resist or eliminate. **Compulsions** are the thoughts or actions used to suppress the obsessions and provide relief. Frank had both obsessions and compulsions but his disorder was mild compared to the case of Richard.

RICHARD | *Enslaved by Ritual*

Richard, a 19-year-old first-year university student majoring in philosophy, withdrew from school because of incapacitating ritualistic behaviour. He abandoned personal hygiene because the compulsive rituals that he had to carry out during washing or cleaning were so time consuming that he could do nothing else. Almost continual showering gave way to no showering. He stopped cutting and washing his hair and beard, brushing his teeth, and changing his clothes. He left his room infrequently and, to avoid rituals associated with the toilet, defecated on paper towels, urinated in paper cups, and stored the waste in the closet. He ate only late at night when his family was asleep. To be able to eat he had to exhale completely, making a lot of hissing noises, coughs, and hacks, and then fill his mouth with as much food as he could while no air was in his lungs. He would eat only a mixture of peanut butter, sugar, cocoa, milk, and mayonnaise. All other foods he considered contaminants. When he walked he took very small steps on his toes while continually looking back, checking and rechecking. On occasion he ran quickly in place. He withdrew his left arm completely from his shirtsleeve as if he were injured and his shirt was a sling.

Like everyone with OCD, Richard experienced intrusive and persistent thoughts and impulses; in his case they were about sex, aggression, and religion. His various behaviours were efforts to suppress sexual and aggressive thoughts or to ward off the disastrous consequences he thought would ensue if he did not perform his rituals. Richard performed most of the repetitive behaviours and mental acts mentioned in the *DSM-IV-TR* criteria (see DSM Table 5.7). Compulsions can be either behavioural (handwashing, checking) or mental (thinking about certain words in a specific order, counting, praying, and so on; Foa et al., 1996; Purdon, 2009; Steketee & Barlow, 2002). The important thing is that they are believed to reduce stress or prevent a dreaded event. Compulsions are often "magical" in that they frequently bear no logical relation to the obsession.

Types of Obsessions and Compulsions

Based on statistically associated groupings, there are four major types of obsessions (Bloch, Landeros-Weisenberger, Rosario,

DSM-IV-TR | **Table 5.7** Diagnostic Criteria for Obsessive-Compulsive Disorder

A. Either obsessions or compulsions

Obsessions are defined by 1, 2, 3, and 4:

1. Recurrent and persistent thoughts, impulses, or images that are experienced, at some time during the disturbance, as intrusive and inappropriate, and cause marked anxiety or distress
2. The thoughts, impulses, or images are not simply excessive worries about real-life problems
3. The person attempts to ignore or suppress such thoughts, impulses, or images, or to neutralize them with some other thought or action
4. The person recognizes that the obsessional thoughts, impulses, or images are a product of his or her own mind (not imposed from without as in thought insertion)

Compulsions as defined by 1 and 2:

1. Repetitive behaviours (e.g., handwashing, ordering, checking) or mental acts (e.g., praying, counting, repeating words silently) that the person feels driven to perform in response to an obsession, or according to rules that must be applied rigidly
2. The behaviours or mental acts are aimed at preventing or reducing distress or preventing some dreaded event or situation; however, these behaviours or mental acts either are not connected in a realistic way with what they are designed to neutralize or prevent, or are clearly excessive

B. At some point during the course of the disorder, the person has recognized that the obsessions or compulsions are excessive or unreasonable. (*Note:* This does not apply to children.)

C. The obsessions or compulsions cause marked distress, are time-consuming (take more than one hour a day), or significantly interfere with the person's normal routine, occupational (or academic) functioning, or usual social activities or relationships.

D. If another Axis I disorder is present, the content of the obsessions or compulsions is not restricted to it (e.g., preoccupation with food in the presence of an eating disorder; hair pulling in the presence of trichotillomania; concern with appearance in the presence of body dysmorphic disorder; preoccupation with drugs in the presence of a substance use disorder; preoccupation with having a serious illness in the presence of hypochondriasis; preoccupation with sexual urges or fantasies in the presence of a paraphilia; or guilty ruminations in the presence of major depressive disorder).

E. The disturbance is not due to the direct effects of a substance (e.g., drugs of abuse, medication) or a general medical condition.

Specify if:

With poor insight: If, for most of the time during the current episode, the person does not recognize that the obsessions and compulsions are excessive or unreasonable.

Source: Reprinted with permission from the *Diagnostic and Statistical Manual of Mental Disorders,* Fourth Edition, Text Revision, (Copyright © 2000). American Psychiatric Association.

Pittenger, & Leckman, 2008; Mathews, 2009) and each is associated with a pattern of compulsive behaviour (see Table 5.10). Symmetry obsessions account for most obsessions (26.7 percent), followed by "forbidden thoughts or actions" (21 percent), cleaning and contamination (15.9 percent), and hoarding (15.4 percent) (Bloch et al., 2008). Symmetry refers to keeping things in perfect order or doing something in a specific way. As a child, were you careful not to step on cracks in the sidewalk? You and your friends might have kept this up for a few minutes before tiring of it. But what if you had to spend your whole life avoiding

TABLE 5.10 Types of Obsessions and Associated Compulsions

Symptom Subtype	Obsession	Compulsion
Symmetry/ exactness/"just right"	Needing things to be symmetrical/ aligned just so Urges to do things over and over until they feel "just right"	Putting things in a certain order Repeating rituals
Forbidden thoughts or actions (aggressive/sexual/ religious)	Fears, urges to harm self or others Fears of offending God	Checking Avoidance Repeated requests for reassurance
Cleaning/ contamination	Germs Fears of germs or contaminants	Repetitive or excessive washing Using gloves, masks to do daily tasks
Hoarding	Fears of throwing anything away	Collecting/saving objects with little or no actual or sentimental value such as food wrappings

Source: Adapted from Mathews (2009) and Bloch et al. (2008).

cracks, on foot or in a car, to prevent something bad from happening? You wouldn't have much fun. People with aggressive (forbidden) obsessive impulses may feel they are about to yell out a swear word in church. One patient of ours, a young and moral woman, was afraid to ride the bus for fear that if a man sat down beside her she would grab his crotch! In reality, this would be the last thing she would do, but the aggressive urge was so horrifying that she made every attempt possible to suppress it and to avoid riding the bus or similar situations where the impulse might occur.

Certain kinds of obsessions are strongly associated with certain kinds of rituals (Bloch et al., 2008; Calamari et al., 2004; Leckman et al., 1997a). For example, forbidden thoughts or actions, as

indicated in Table 5.11, seem to lead to checking rituals. Checking rituals serve to prevent an imagined disaster or catastrophe. Many are logical, such as repeatedly checking the stove to see whether you turned it off, but severe cases can be illogical. For example, Richard thought that if he did not eat in a certain way he might become possessed. If he didn't take small steps and look back, some disaster might happen to his family. A mental act, such as counting, can also be a compulsion. Obsessions with symmetry lead to ordering and arranging or repeating rituals; obsessions with contamination lead to washing rituals that may restore a sense of safety and control (Rachman, 2006). Like Richard, many patients have several kinds of obsessions and compulsions.

On rare occasions, patients, particularly children, will present with compulsions, but few or no identifiable obsessions. We saw an eight-year-old child who felt compelled to undress, put on his pajamas, and turn down the covers in a time-consuming fashion each night; he always repeated the ritual three times. He could give no particular reason for his behaviour; he simply had to do it.

Comedian Howie Mandel has OCD. Like the majority of people with OCD, his obsessions centre on themes of contamination. He is concerned he will be infected by germs from other people around him. Thus, Mandel carefully avoids shaking hands with other people, unless he is wearing latex gloves. Mandel has reported that his OCD symptoms cause him disruption when he stays in hotels. He reportedly orders two-dozen towels when he arrives at a hotel, and makes paths with them so that he does not have to step on the hotel carpets. He also avoids being around people if they have any sign of illness like a common cold. When his OCD symptoms are at their worst, his compulsions include retreating to a second "sterile" house he had built on his property where he isolates himself from the world. He even retreats there to avoid family members if he suspects any of them have something contagious like the flu (CBS News, 1999).

Tic Disorder and OCD

It is also common for tic disorder, characterized by involuntary movement (sudden jerking of limbs, for example), to co-occur in patients with OCD (particularly children) or in their families (Grados et al., 2001; Leckman et al., 2010). More complex tics with involuntary vocalizations are referred to as Tourette's disorder (Leckman et al., 2010; see Chapter 14). In some cases, these movements are not tics but may be compulsions, as they were in the case of Frank in Chapter 3 who kept jerking his leg if thoughts of seizures entered his head. Approximately 10 percent to 40 percent of children and adolescents with OCD also have had tic disorder at some point, leading to a suggestion that tic-related OCD be categorized as a subtype of OCD in *DSM-5* (Leckman et al., 2010). The obsessions in tic-related OCD are almost always related to symmetry.

Observations among one small group of children presenting with OCD and tics suggest that these problems occurred after a bout of strep throat. This syndrome has been referred

▲ Comedian Howie Mandel, host of the television game show *Deal or No Deal*, reportedly has OCD characterized by obsessions of becoming contaminated by germs.

to as pediatric autoimmune disorder associated with Streptococcal infection, or "Pandas." Confirmation of this association awaits further research (Leckman et al., 2010; Radomsky & Taylor, 2005; Swedo, 2002).

Hoarding

Recently, a group of patients have come to the attention of specialty clinics because they compulsively hoard things, fearing that if they throw something away, even a ten-year-old newspaper, they then might urgently need it (Frost, Steketee, & Williams, 2002; Grisham & Barlow, 2005; Samuels et al., 2002; Steketee & Frost, 2007a, 2007b). It is not uncommon for some patients' houses and yards to come to the attention of public health authorities. One patient's house and yard was condemned because junk was piled so high it was both unsightly and a fire hazard. Among her hoard was a 20-year collection of used sanitary napkins.

Basically, these individuals usually begin acquiring things during their teenage years and often experience great pleasure, even euphoria, from shopping or otherwise collecting various items. Shopping or collecting things may be a response to feeling down or depressed and is sometimes called, facetiously, "retail therapy." But unlike most people who like to shop or collect, these individuals then experience strong anxiety and distress about throwing anything away because everything has either some potential use or sentimental value in their minds, and their homes or apartments may become almost impossible to live in. Most of these individuals don't consider that they have a problem until family members or authorities insist that they receive help. The average age when these people come for treatment is approximately 50, after many years of hoarding (Grisham, Frost, Steketee, Kim, & Hood, 2006). Often they live alone. Recent careful analysis of the rapidly increasing knowledge of hoarding suggests that it has both similarities and differences with OCD as well as with impulse control disorders, and that, perhaps, it should be listed as a separate disorder in *DSM-5* (Mataix-Cols et al., 2010). This is unlikely, although it may be assigned to the appendix of *DSM-5* for further study. New treatments are in development at our clinic that teach people to assign different values to objects and to reduce anxiety about throwing away items that are somewhat less valued (Steketee & Frost, 2007a). Preliminary results are promising, but more information on long-term effects of these treatments is needed.

Statistics

A large epidemiological study put the lifetime prevalence of OCD at approximately 2.6 percent (Karno & Golding, 1991), although recent studies like that by Murray Stein and colleagues suggest that this may be a bit of an overestimate (Stein, Forde, Anderson, & Walker, 1997). A cross-national study of rates of OCD in Canada and six other countries found that rates were remarkably similar across cultures (Weissman et al., 1994). Of course, not all cases meeting criteria for OCD are as severe as Richard's. Obsessions and compulsions can be arranged along a continuum, like most clinical features of anxiety disorders. Between 10 percent and 15 percent of "normal" university students engaged in checking behaviour substantial enough to score within the range of patients with OCD (Frost, Sher, & Geen, 1986).

It would also be unusual not to have an occasional intrusive or strange thought. Many people have bizarre, sexual, or aggressive thoughts, particularly if they are bored—for example, when sitting in class. Gail Steketee and her colleagues collected examples of thoughts from ordinary people who do not have OCD. Some of these thoughts are listed in Table 5.11.

Have you had any of these thoughts? Most people do, but they let these thoughts go in one ear and out the other, so to speak. Certain individuals, however, are horrified by such thoughts, considering them signs of an alien, intrusive, evil force. The majority of individuals with OCD are female, but the ratio is not as large as for some other anxiety disorders. Rasmussen and Tsuang (1984, 1986) reported that 55 percent of 1630 patients were female. The Epidemiological Catchment Area (ECA) survey noted 60 percent females in their sample of OCD (Karno & Golding, 1991). Interestingly, in children the sex ratio is reversed, with more males than females (Hanna, 1995). This seems to be because boys tend to develop OCD earlier. By mid-adolescence the sex ratio is approximately equal, before becoming predominantly female in adulthood (Albano et al., 1996). Average age of onset ranges from early adolescence to the mid-20s but typically peaks earlier in males (at 13 to 15) than in females (at 20 to 24; Rasmussen & Eisen, 1990).

Obsessive-Compulsive Disorder

TABLE 5.11 Obsessions and Intrusive Thoughts Reported by Nonclinical Samples*

Harming
Impulse to jump out of high window
Idea of jumping in front of a car
Impulse to push someone in front of train
Wishing a person would die
While holding a baby, having a sudden urge to kick it
Thoughts of dropping a baby
The thought that if I forget to say goodbye to someone, they might die
Thought that thinking about horrible things happening to a child will cause it

Contamination or Disease
Thought of catching a disease from public pools or other public places
Thoughts I may have caught a disease from touching toilet seat
Idea that dirt is always on my hand

Inappropriate or Unacceptable Behaviour
Idea of swearing or yelling at my boss
Thought of doing something embarrassing in public, like forgetting to wear a top
Hoping someone doesn't succeed
Thought of blurting out something in church
Thought of "unnatural" sexual acts

Doubts about Safety, Memory, and So On
Thought that I haven't locked the house up properly
Idea of leaving my curling iron on the carpet and forgetting to pull out the plug
Thought that I've left the heater and stove on
Idea that I've left the car unlocked when I know I've locked it
Idea that objects are not arranged perfectly

*Examples were obtained from Rachman (1978) and from unpublished research by Dana Thordarson, Ph.D., and Michael Kyrios, Ph.D. (personal communication), at the University of British Columbia.

Source: From *Anxiety and its Disorders: The Nature and Treatment of Anxiety and Panic* by D. H. Barlow. Copyright © 2001 by Guilford Press. Reprinted by permission.

Once OCD develops, it tends to become chronic (Eisen & Steketee, 1998; Steketee & Barlow, 2002).

In Arabic countries, obsessive-compulsive disorder is easily recognizable, although as always cultural beliefs and concerns influence the content of the obsessions and the nature of the compulsions. In Saudi Arabia and Egypt, obsessions are primarily related to religious practices, specifically the Muslim emphasis on cleanliness. Contamination themes are also highly prevalent in India. Nevertheless, OCD looks remarkably similar across cultures. Insel (1984) reviewed studies from England, Hong Kong, India, Egypt, Japan, and Norway and found essentially similar types and proportions of obsessions and compulsions, as did Weissman et al. (1994) in reviewing studies from Canada, Finland, Taiwan, Africa, Puerto Rico, Korea, and New Zealand.

Causes

Many of us sometimes have intrusive, even horrific thoughts (Rachman & deSilva, 1978; Rachman, 2003) and occasionally engage in ritualistic behaviour, especially when we are under stress (Parkinson & Rachman, 1981a, 1981b; Rachman & deSilva, 2004). But very few of us develop obsessive-compulsive disorder. Once again, as with panic disorder and post-traumatic stress disorder, one must develop anxiety focused on the possibility of having additional intrusive thoughts.

The repetitive, intrusive, unacceptable thoughts of OCD may well be regulated by the brain circuit described in Chapter 2. However, the tendency to develop anxiety over having additional compulsive thoughts may have the same generalized biological and psychological precursors as anxiety in general (Suárez et al., 2009).

Why would people with OCD focus their anxiety on the occasional intrusive thought rather than on the possibility of a panic attack or some other external situation? One hypothesis is that early experiences taught them that some thoughts are dangerous and unacceptable because the terrible things they are thinking might actually happen and they would be responsible. The experiences would result in a specific psychological vulnerability to develop OCD. They learn this through the same process of misinformation that convinced the person with snake phobia that snakes were dangerous and could be everywhere. Clients with OCD equate thoughts with the specific actions or activity represented by the thoughts. Rachman and his colleagues call this "thought-action fusion" (Rachman, 1998; Rachman & Shafran, 1998; Shafran, Thordarson, & Rachman, 1996). Thought-action fusion may, in turn, be caused by attitudes of excessive responsibility and resulting guilt developed during childhood where even a bad thought is associated with evil intent (Clark & O'Connor, 2005; Salkovskis, Shafran, Rachman, & Freeston, 1999; Steketee & Barlow, 2002). One patient believed thinking about abortion was the moral equivalent of having an abortion.

Richard finally admitted to having strong homosexual impulses that were unacceptable to him and to his minister father, and he believed the impulses were as sinful as actual acts. Many people with OCD who believe in the tenets of fundamental religions, whether Christian, Jewish, or Islamic, present with similar attitudes of inflated responsibility and thought-action fusion. One study showed that the strength of religious belief, but not the type of belief, was associated with severity of OCD (Steketee, Quay, & White, 1991). Of course, the vast majority of people with fundamental beliefs do not develop OCD.

But what if the most frightening thing in your life was not a snake, or speaking in public, but a terrible thought that happened to pop into your head? You can't avoid it as you would a snake, so you resist this thought by attempting to suppress it or "neutralize" it using mental or behavioural strategies such as distraction, praying, or checking. These strategies become compulsions, but they are doomed to fail in the long term, because these strategies backfire and actually increase the frequency of the thought (Wegner, 1989). In fact, Christine

Purdon at the University of Waterloo and David A. Clark at the University of New Brunswick have conducted a large body of research in this area. On the basis of their work and reviews of the literature, they conclude that there is indeed an association between attempted thought suppression and obsessional thinking (Clark & Purdon, 1995; Purdon, 1999, 2004; Purdon & Clark, 2000). Moreover, if someone appraises a given negative thought as unacceptable, that person will be motivated to try to suppress the thought (Purdon, 2004). Once again, generalized biological and psychological vulnerabilities must be present for OCD to develop. Believing some thoughts are unacceptable and therefore must be suppressed (a specific psychological vulnerability) may put people at greater risk of OCD (Amir, Cashman, & Foa, 1997; Parkinson & Rachman, 1981b; Salkovskis & Campbell, 1994). A model of the etiology of obsessive-compulsive disorder that is somewhat similar to other models of anxiety disorders is presented in ■ Figure 5.14.

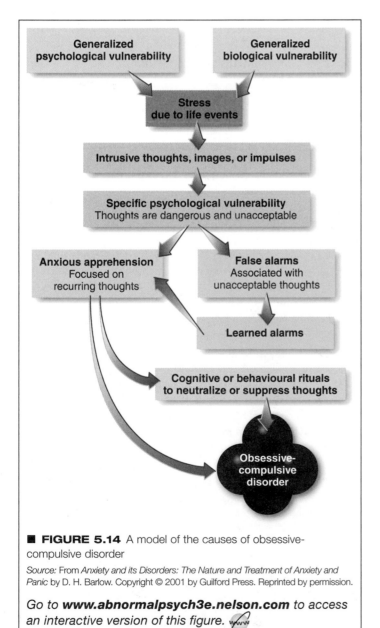

■ **FIGURE 5.14** A model of the causes of obsessive-compulsive disorder

Source: From Anxiety and its Disorders: The Nature and Treatment of Anxiety and Panic by D. H. Barlow. Copyright © 2001 by Guilford Press. Reprinted by permission.

Go to **www.abnormalpsych3e.nelson.com** *to access an interactive version of this figure.*

Treatment

Studies evaluating the effects of drugs on obsessive-compulsive disorder are showing some promise (Steketee & Barlow, 2002; Stewart, Jenike, & Jenike, 2009). The most effective seem to be those that specifically inhibit the reuptake of serotonin, such as clomipramine or the SSRIs, which benefit up to 60 percent of patients with OCD, with no particular advantage to one drug over another. However, the average treatment gain is moderate at best (Greist, 1990), and relapse frequently occurs when the drug is discontinued (Lydiard et al., 1996).

Highly structured psychological treatments work somewhat better than drugs, but they are not readily available. The most effective approach is exposure and ritual prevention (ERP), a process whereby the rituals are actively prevented and the patient is systematically and gradually exposed to the feared thoughts or situations (Barlow & Lehman, 1996; Foa & Franklin, 2001; Steketee & Barlow, 2002). Richard would be systematically exposed to harmless objects or situations that he thought were contaminated, including certain foods and household chemicals, and his washing and checking rituals would be prevented. Usually, this can be done by simply working closely with patients to see that they do not wash or check. In severe cases, patients may be hospitalized and the faucets removed from the bathroom sink for a time to discourage repeated washing. However the rituals are prevented, the procedures seem to facilitate "reality testing," because the client soon learns, at an emotional level, that no harm will result whether he carries out the rituals or not.

A treatment study led by Peter McLean at the University of British Columbia compared ERP to a CBT that targeted the dysfunctional cognitions characteristic of OCD such as thought-action fusion and inflated responsibility (McLean et al., 2001). Patients were randomized to either the ERP or CBT conditions and half in each group received their treatment immediately, while the other half served as a waiting list control (and received their assigned treatment later). Both treatments were delivered in a group context. Both types of treatment were better than the wait list control in terms of reducing symptoms of OCD. The ERP treatment was slightly more effective than CBT both immediately post-treatment and at a three-month follow-up. Inflated responsibility beliefs decreased with treatment improvement, but contrary to hypothesis, it decreased in both the CBT and the ERP conditions. Thus, preventing rituals does seem to allow for cognitive change in people with OCD, at least in terms of their inflated sense of responsibility. A more recent study by this same group (Whittal, Thordarson, & McLean, 2005) once again compared these two types of treatment, but this time when they were delivered in an individual (one-on-one) format. Although ERP and CBT were once again both highly effective in treating OCD symptoms, no differences were obtained in their overall efficacy when the treatments were delivered in an individual format (Whittal et al., 2005).

Studies are now available examining the combined effects of medication and psychological treatments. In one large study (Foa et al., 2005), ERP was compared to the drug clomipramine, as well as to a combined condition. ERP, with or without the drug, produced superior results to the drug alone, with 86 percent responding to ERP alone versus 48 percent to the drug alone. Combining the treatments did not produce any additional advantage. Also, relapse rates were high from the medication-only group when the drug was withdrawn.

Psychosurgery is one of the more radical treatments for obsessive-compulsive disorder. Psychosurgery is a misnomer that refers to neurosurgery for a psychological disorder. Jenike et al. (1991) reviewed the records of 33 patients with obsessive-compulsive disorder, most of them extremely severe cases who had failed to respond at all to either drug or psychological treatment. After a very specific surgical lesion to the cingulate bundle (cingulotomy), approximately 30 percent benefited substantially. Similarly, Rück et al. (2008) performed a related surgery (capsulotomy) on 25 patients who had not responded to five years of previous treatment; 35 percent (9 patients) benefited substantially, but six of those nine patients suffered from serious adverse side effects of the surgery. Considering that these patients seemed to have no hope whatsoever from other treatments, surgery deserves consideration as a last resort. Each year we understand more about the causes of OCD, and our treatments are improving. Before long, such radical treatments as psychosurgery will no longer be employed.

Concept Check | 5.6

Fill in the blanks to form facts about OCD.

1. _____ are intrusive and nonsensical thoughts, images, or urges an individual tries to eliminate or suppress.

2. The practices of washing, counting, and hoarding to suppress obsessions and provide relief are called _____.

3. _____ is a radical treatment for OCD involving a surgical lesion to the cingulate bundle.

From the Inside

Shake Hands with the Devil: The Failure of Humanity in Rwanda
by Lt.-Gen. Roméo Dallaire

One of the most widely publicized cases of PTSD in Canada's recent history occurred in a high-raking individual in the Canadian Armed Forces. Lieutenant-General Roméo Dallaire served for 35 years before retiring from the military.

In 1993, Dallaire was sent to Rwanda as commander of the United Nations peacekeeping mission. For this assignment, he was equipped with a small force to oversee a previously negotiated end to the civil war.

Violence erupted soon after the arrival of him and his troops; 800 000 people were killed in only a few short months (more than one-third of them children). Dallaire requested additional troops and arms from the UN, but his requests were rejected.

In this memoir, Dallaire recounts the horrific atrocities that he and his men witnessed. These horrors included ditches filled with thousand of bodies, people hacking others apart using machetes, and children being forced to kill other children.

Even after returning home to Canada, Dallaire could not escape the memories of what he had witnessed in Rwanda. He also felt extremely guilty and helpless about not having been able to stop the violence. He endured nightmares and became unable to function at work. He describes how, four years after his return home, he was required to return to Africa to testify at the International Criminal Tribunal for Rwanda and how this trip was a trigger for extreme intensification of his reliving symptoms. As he puts it, "The memories, the smells, and the sense of evil returned with a vengeance. . . . I was suffering, like so many of the soldiers who had served with me in Rwanda, from an injury called post-traumatic stress disorder" (p. xii). Dallaire began to abuse alcohol in an attempt to cope and was found unconscious and drunk in a park in Hull, Québec, in the summer of 2000. (Alcoholism is a common comorbid problem in people with PTSD; Stewart, 1996; Stewart, Pihl, Conrod, & Dongier, 1998.) Following this, he was given a medical discharge from the Canadian Forces, and received mental health services for his PTSD. Since this time, Dallaire has been advocating for better recognition and mental health services for those with PTSD in the military (Dallaire, 2003a).

In this memoir, Dallaire provides a detailed recounting of his painful experiences in Rwanda. He also courageously documents his own personal journey of experiencing post-traumatic stress disorder, through struggling to make sense of his experiences, to finding a measure of peace and hope. Dallaire's advocacy efforts have helped to change the attitude of the Canadian government toward post-traumatic stress disorder in the military. PTSD is now recognized as a disorder warranting a psychological disability pension (Thorne, 2000). Dallaire's powerful memoir has now been made into a feature-length film starring Québec actor Roy Dupuis.

Source: Shake Hands with the Devil: The Failure of Humanity in Rwanda by Lt.-Gen. Roméo Daillaire, 2003, Random House of Canada.

In Chapter 3, we introduced the idea that emerging conceptions of psychopathology move us away from an emphasis on categorical (individual) diagnoses to a consideration of larger dimensions, or spectra, in which similar and related diagnoses might be grouped. One such spectrum consists of what some call emotional disorders, including anxiety and depression (Leyfer & Brown, in press). But how would this dimensional approach to psychopathology change the way we make diagnoses? Recently, we speculated on how a future diagnostic system using dimensional approaches for emotional disorders might work (Brown & Barlow, 2009). To illustrate this approach, let's first consider a case from our clinic.

Mr. S was a high school teacher in his mid-50s who had been in a very serious car accident several months before coming in and was suffering from symptoms related to that accident. These included intrusive memories of the crash, "flashbacks" of the accident itself that were very intense emotionally, and images of the cuts and bruises on his wife's face. He also had a very strong startle reaction to any cues that reminded him of the accident and avoided driving in certain locations that were somewhat similar to where he had his accident. These symptoms intermingled with a similar set of symptoms emerging from a series of traumatic experiences that had occurred during his service in the Vietnam War. In addition to these trauma symptoms, he also spent a lot of his day worrying about various life events including his own health and that of his family. He also worried about his performance at work and whether he would be evaluated poorly by other staff members, despite the fact that he received consistently high evaluations for his teaching.

After considering everything he said and evaluating him clinically, it was clear that he met criteria for PTSD. He also met criteria for GAD, given his substantial worry that was occurring every day about life events unrelated to the trauma. In addition he had some mild depression, perhaps due in part to all of the anxiety he was experiencing. In summary, the patient could be diagnosed

with PTSD although he had substantial features of GAD as well as depression. But what would it look like if we attempted to describe his symptoms on a series of dimensions rather than on whether they meet criteria for one category or another?

■ Figure 5.15 displays a simplified version of one possible dimensional system (Brown & Barlow, 2009). In this dimensional scheme, "anxiety" (AN) is represented on the left because all individuals with anxiety or depressive disorders have some level of anxiety. Many individuals, but not all, are also depressed (DEP) (as was Mr. S). Mr. S would score fairly high on anxiety and somewhat lower on depression. Looking to the far right of the figure, Mr. S displayed a lot of behavioural avoidance as well as avoidance of physical sensations (interoceptive avoidance) (AV-BI). Mostly he was having difficulty driving and also would avoid cues connected with his earlier trauma by refusing if at all possible to engage in activities or conversations associated with the war. Another related type of

avoidance is when you avoid experiencing intense emotions or thoughts about emotional experiences. We call this cognitive and emotional avoidance (AV-CE) and Mr. S also scored relatively high on this aspect of avoidance.

But what was the focus of Mr. S's anxiety? Here we look at five characteristics that currently categorize anxiety disorder diagnoses. Looking first at trauma (TRM) focus, obviously, this earned the highest score on Mr. S's profile. He also was suffering from frequent flashbacks to his traumatic experiences, which as you may remember, are very similar to panic attacks and consist of strong autonomic surges, such as rapidly increasing heart rate. Thus, he scored high on panic and related autonomic surges (PAS). Other kinds of intrusive obsessive thoughts were not present and he scored low on this dimension (IC). His worry about his health and the health of his family caused him to score moderately high on somatic anxiety (SOM), but social anxiety (SOC) was not particularly high.

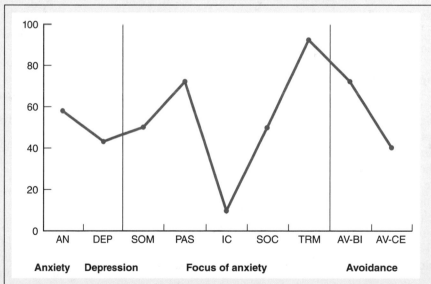

■ **FIGURE 5.15** Proposed *DSM-5* (or *6*) Dimensional Diagnosis of a Patient with PTSD. *AN*, anxiety; *DEP*, unipolar depression; *SOM*, somatic anxiety; *PAS*, panic and related autonomic surges; *IC*, intrusive cognitions; *SOC*, social evaluation; *TRM*, past trauma; *AV-BI*, behavioural and interoceptive avoidance; *AV-CE*, cognitive and emotional avoidance. Higher scores on the *y*-axis (0–100) indicate higher levels of the *x*-axis dimension, but otherwise the *y*-axis metric is arbitrary and is used for illustrative purposes.

Source: Reprinted from *Psychological Assessment, Volume 21, Issue 3*, T.A. Brown & D.H. Barlow, "A proposal for a dimensional classification system based on the shared features of the DSM-IV anxiety and mood disorders: Implications for assessment and treatment," Pages No. 256–271, Copyright 2009, with permission from Elsevier.

(Continued)

As you can see, this dimensional profile provides a more complete picture of Mr. S's clinical presentation than simply noting that he met criteria for PTSD. This is because the profile captures the relative severity of a number of key features of anxiety and mood disorders that are often present together in patients who might meet criteria for only a single diagnosis in the current categorical system. This profile also captures the fact that Mr. S had some depression that was below the severity threshold to meet criteria for mood disorder. Knowing all of this by glancing at Mr. S's profile in Figure 5.15 should help clinicians match therapy more closely to his presenting problems.

This is just one possible example, but it does provide some idea of what a diagnostic system might look like in the future. Although this system would not be ready for *DSM-5* (to be published in 2013) because we would need to do much more research on how best to make it work, a system like this might be ready for *DSM-6*.

Summary

The Complexity of Anxiety Disorders

- Anxiety is a future-oriented state characterized by negative affect in which a person focuses on the possibility of uncontrollable danger or misfortune; in contrast, fear is a present-oriented state characterized by strong escapist tendencies and a surge in the sympathetic branch of the autonomic nervous system in response to current danger.
- A panic attack represents the alarm response of real fear, but no actual danger exists.
- Panic attacks may be (1) unexpected (completely without warning), (2) situationally bound (always occurring in a specific situation), or (3) situationally predisposed (likely but unpredictable in a specific situation).
- Panic and anxiety combine to create different anxiety disorders.

Generalized Anxiety Disorder

- In generalized anxiety disorder (GAD), anxiety focuses on minor everyday events, not one major worry or concern.
- Both genetic and psychological vulnerabilities seem to contribute to the development of GAD.
- Though drug and psychological treatments may be effective in the short term, drug treatments are no more effective in the long term than placebo treatments. Successful treatment may help individuals with GAD focus on what is really threatening to them in their lives.

Panic Disorder with and without Agoraphobia

- In panic disorder with or without agoraphobia (a fear and avoidance of situations considered to be unsafe), anxiety is focused on the next panic attack.
- We all have some genetic vulnerability to stress, and many of us have had a neurobiological overreaction to some stressful event—that is, a panic attack. Individuals who develop panic disorder then develop anxiety over the possibility of having another panic attack.
- Both drug and psychological treatments have proven successful in the treatment of panic disorder. One psychological method, panic control treatment, concentrates on exposing patients to clusters of sensations that remind them of their panic attacks.

Specific Phobia

- In phobic disorders, the individual avoids situations that produce severe anxiety or panic. In specific phobia, the fear is focused on a particular object or situation.
- Phobias can be acquired by experiencing some traumatic event; they can also be learned vicariously or even taught.
- Treatment of phobias is rather straightforward, with a focus on structured and consistent exposure-based exercises.

Social Phobia

- Social phobia is a fear of being around others, particularly in situations that call for some kind of "performance" in front of other people.
- Though the causes of social phobia are similar to those of specific phobias, treatment has a different focus that includes rehearsing or role-playing socially phobic situations. In addition, drug treatments have been effective.

Post-Traumatic Stress Disorder

- Post-traumatic stress disorder (PTSD) focuses on avoiding thoughts or images of past traumatic experiences.
- The underlying cause of PTSD is obvious—a traumatic experience. But mere exposure is not enough. The intensity of the experience seems to be a factor in whether an individual develops PTSD; biological vulnerabilities, as well as social and cultural factors, appear to play a role as well.
- Treatment involves re-exposing the victim to the trauma in order to overcome the debilitating effects of PTSD.

Obsessive-Compulsive Disorder

- Obsessive-compulsive disorder (OCD) focuses on avoiding frightening or repulsive intrusive thoughts (obsessions) or neutralizing these thoughts through the use of ritualistic behaviour (compulsions).
- As with all the anxiety disorders, biological and psychological vulnerabilities seem to be involved in the development of OCD.
- Drug treatment seems to be only modestly successful in treating OCD. The most effective treatment approach is exposure and response prevention.

Key Terms

acute stress disorder, 163
agoraphobia, 140
animal phobia, 152
anxiety, 129
behavioural inhibition system (BIS), 132
blood-injection-injury phobia, 151

compulsions, 169
fear, 130
fight/flight system (FFS), 132
generalized anxiety disorder (GAD), 135
natural environment phobia, 152
obsessions, 169

obsessive-compulsive disorder (OCD), 168
panic, 130
panic attack, 130
panic control treatment (PCT), 147
panic disorder with agoraphobia (PDA), 140

panic disorder without agoraphobia (PD), 141
post-traumatic stress disorder (PTSD), 161
separation anxiety disorder, 152
situational phobia, 152
social phobia, 156
specific phobia, 150

Answers to Concept Checks

5.1

1. b 2. c 3. e d 4. a 5. f

5.2

1. T 2. F (more gradual)
3. T 4. F 5. T

5.3

1. F (with agoraphobia)
2. F (3.5%) 3. T 4. T

5.4

1. d 2. e 3. c 4. f 5. a 6. d 7. c

5.5

1. b 2. a 3. c

5.6

1. obsessions 2. compulsions
3. psychosurgery

Media Resources

CourseMate

Access an integrated eBook, Abnormal Psychology Videos (formerly Abnormal Psych Live CD-ROM), chapter-specific interactive learning tools (flashcards, quizzes, learning modules), and more in your Psychology CourseMate, available at **www.abnormalpsych3ce.nelson.com**.

Abnormal Psychology Videos

Free Abnormal Psychology videos can be viewed on the website **www.abnormalpsych3ce.nelson.com**.

- *Panic Disorder: Steve*: Steve discusses how panic attacks have disrupted his life.
- *Virtual Reality: A New Technique on the Treatment of Anxiety Disorders*: A virtual reality program helps one woman overcome her fear of riding the subway.
- *Rapid Behavioural Treatment of a Specific Phobia (Snakes)*: A demonstration of exposure therapy helps a person with snake phobia overcome her severe fear of snakes in just three hours.
- *Obsessive-Compulsive Disorder: Chuck*: Chuck discusses how his obsessions affect his everyday life, going to work, planning a vacation, and so on.

Video Concept Reviews

CourseMate also contains Mark Durand's *Video Concept Reviews* on these challenging topics.

- Anxiety
- Fear
- Characteristics of Anxiety Disorders
- Panic
- Panic Attacks
- Generalized Anxiety Disorder (GAD)—Description
- Panic Disorder

- Panic Control Treatment
- Concept Check: Medical versus Psychological Treatment
- Specific Phobia
- Phobia Subtypes
- Social Phobia
- Posttraumatic Stress Disorder (PTSD)
- Obsessive-Compulsive Disorder (OCD)

Exploring Anxiety Disorders

People with anxiety disorders:

> Feel overwhelming tension, apprehension, or fear when there is no actual danger
> May take extreme action to avoid the source of their anxiety

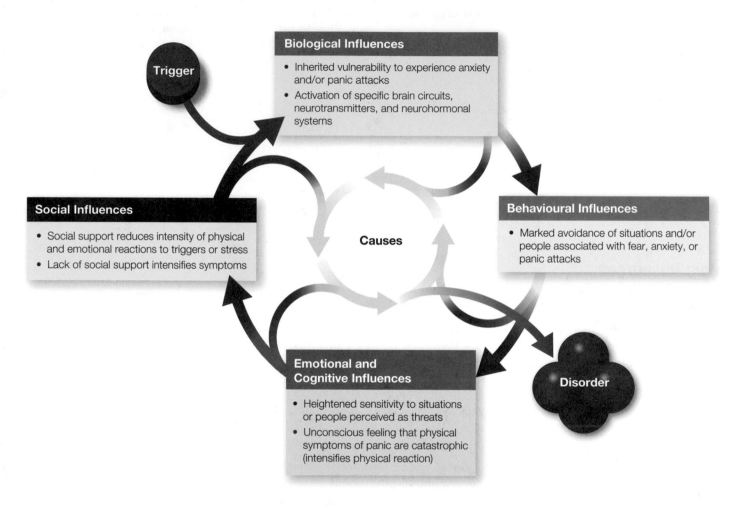

Trigger

Biological Influences

- Inherited vulnerability to experience anxiety and/or panic attacks
- Activation of specific brain circuits, neurotransmitters, and neurohormonal systems

Social Influences

- Social support reduces intensity of physical and emotional reactions to triggers or stress
- Lack of social support intensifies symptoms

Causes

Behavioural Influences

- Marked avoidance of situations and/or people associated with fear, anxiety, or panic attacks

Emotional and Cognitive Influences

- Heightened sensitivity to situations or people perceived as threats
- Unconscious feeling that physical symptoms of panic are catastrophic (intensifies physical reaction)

Disorder

TREATMENT FOR ANXIETY DISORDERS

Cognitive-Behavioural Therapy

- Systematic exposure to anxiety-provoking situations or thoughts
- Learning to substitute positive behaviours and thoughts for negative ones
- Learning new coping skills: relaxation exercises, controlled breathing, etc.

Drug Treatment

- Reduces the symptoms of anxiety disorders by influencing brain chemistry
  —antidepressants (Tofranil, Paxil, Effexor)
  —benzodiazepines (Xanax, Klonopin)

Other Treatments

- Managing stress through a healthy lifestyle: rest, exercise, nutrition, social support, and moderate alcohol or other drug intake

PhotoDisc/Getty Images

TYPES OF ANXIETY DISORDERS

Panic

People with panic disorders have had one or more panic attacks and are anxious and fearful about having future attacks.

© Photodisc/Getty Images

What is a panic attack?
A person having a panic attack feels:
- Apprehension leading to intense fear
- Sensation of "going crazy" or of losing control
- Physical signs of distress: racing heartbeat, rapid breathing, dizziness, nausea, or sensation of heart attack or imminent death

When/why do panic attacks occur?
Panic attacks can be:
- Situationally bound: Always occurring in the same situation, which may lead to extreme avoidance of triggering people, places, or events (see specific and social phobias)
- Unexpected: Can lead to extreme avoidance of any situation or place felt to be unsafe (agoraphobia)
- Situationally predisposed: Attacks may or may not occur in specific situations (between situationally bound and unexpected)

Phobias

People with phobias avoid situations that produce severe anxiety and/or panic. There are three main types:

Eyewire/Getty Images

Agoraphobia
- Fear and avoidance of situations, people, or places where it would be unsafe to have a panic attack: malls, grocery stores, buses, planes, tunnels, etc.
- In the extreme, inability to leave the house or even a specific room
- Begins after a panic attack but can continue for years even if no other attacks occur

Specific Phobia
- Fear of specific object or situation that triggers attack: heights, closed spaces, insects, snakes, or flying
- Develops from personal or vicarious experience of traumatic event with the triggering object or situation or from misinformation

Social Phobia
- Fear of being called for some kind of "performance" that may be judged: speaking in public, using a public restroom (for males), or generally interacting with people

Other Types

Eyewire/Getty Images

Generalized Anxiety
- Uncontrollable unproductive worrying about everyday events
- Feeling impending catastrophe even after successes
- Inability to stop the worry–anxiety cycle: e.g., Irene's fear of failure about school relationships and health even though everything seemed fine
- Physical symptoms of muscle tension

Post-Traumatic Stress
- Fear of re-experiencing a traumatic event: rape, war, life-threatening situation, etc.
- Nightmares or flashbacks (of the traumatic event)
- Avoidance of the intense feelings of the event through emotional numbing

Obsessive-Compulsive
- Fear of unwanted and intrusive thoughts (obsessions)
- Repeated ritualistic actions or thoughts (compulsions) designed to neutralize the unwanted thoughts: e.g., Richard's attempts to suppress "dangerous" thoughts about sex, aggression, and religion with compulsive washing and cleaning rituals

6 Somatoform and Dissociative Disorders

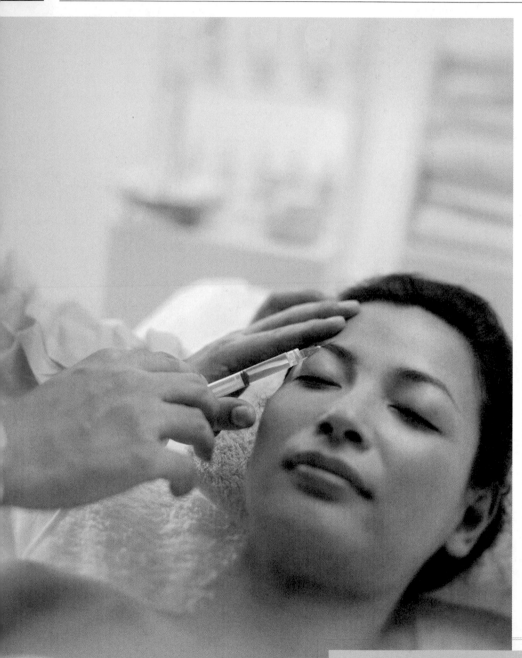

Floresco Productions/Getty Images

Why I became more afraid of living and of dying than others will forever remain an enigma.
—Carla Cantor, *Phantom Illness: Shattering the Myth of Hypochondria*

Use the concepts, language, and major theories of the discipline to account for psychological phenomena.	› Describe behaviour and mental processes empirically, including operational definitions (APA SLO 1.3.a (3)) *(see textbook pages 181–183, 185–186, 189–192, 195–196, 200–205)*
Identify appropriate applications of psychology in solving problems, such as:	› Origin and treatment of abnormal behaviour (APA SLO 4.2.b (3)) *(see textbook pages 184–185, 187–189, 192–195, 198–199, 207–211)*

* Portions of this chapter cover learning outcomes suggested by the American Psychological Association (2007) in their guidelines for the undergraduate psychology major. Chapter coverage of these outcomes is identified above by APA Goal and APA Suggested Learning Outcome (SLO).

Many people continually run to the doctor even though nothing is wrong with them. This is usually a harmless tendency that may even be worth some good-natured jokes. But for a few individuals, the preoccupation with their health or appearance becomes so great that it dominates their lives. Their problems fall under the general heading of **somatoform disorders**. *Soma* means body, and the problems preoccupying these people seem, initially, to be physical disorders. What the disorders have in common, however, is that there is usually no identifiable medical condition causing the physical complaints.

Have you ever felt "detached" from yourself or your surroundings? ("This isn't really me," or "That doesn't really look like my hand," or "There's something unreal about this place.") During these experiences some people feel as if they are dreaming. These mild sensations that most people experience periodically are slight alterations, or detachments, in consciousness or identity, and they are known as dissociative experiences or dissociation. For a few people, these experiences are so intense and extreme that they lose their identity entirely and assume a new one, or they lose their memory or sense of reality and are unable to function. We discuss several types of **dissociative disorders** in the second half of this chapter.

Somatoform and dissociative disorders are very strongly linked historically, and increasing evidence indicates that they share common features (Kihlstrom, 1994; Prelior, Yutzy, Dean, & Wetzel, 1993). They used to be categorized under one general heading: hysterical neurosis. You may remember (from Chapter 1) that the term *hysteria*, which dates back to the Greek Hippocrates, and the Egyptians before him, suggests that the cause of these disorders, which were thought to occur primarily in women, can be traced to a "wandering uterus." But the term *hysterical* came to refer more generally to physical symptoms without known organic cause, or to dramatic or histrionic behaviour thought to be characteristic of women. Freud (1894/1962) suggested that in a condition called *conversion hysteria* unexplained physical symptoms indicated the conversion of unconscious emotional conflicts into a more acceptable form. The historical term *conversion* remains with us (without the theoretical implications); however, the prejudicial and stigmatizing term *hysterical* is no longer used.

The term *neurosis*, as defined in psychoanalytic theory, suggested a specific cause for certain disorders. Specifically, neurotic disorders resulted from underlying unconscious conflicts, anxiety that resulted from those conflicts, and the implementation of ego defence mechanisms. *Neurosis* was eliminated from the diagnostic system in 1980, because it was too vague, applying to almost all non-psychotic disorders, and because it implied a specific but unproven cause for these disorders.

Somatoform and dissociative disorders are not well understood, but they have intrigued psychopathologists and the public for centuries. A fuller understanding provides a rich perspective on the extent to which normal, everyday traits found in all of us can evolve into distorted, strange, and incapacitating disorders.

Somatoform Disorders

The *DSM-IV-TR* lists five basic somatoform disorders: hypochondriasis, somatization disorder, conversion disorder, pain disorder, and body dysmorphic disorder. In each, individuals are pathologically concerned with the appearance or functioning of their bodies. The first three disorders covered in this section—hypochondriasis, somatization disorder, and pain disorder—overlap considerably, and the proposal for *DSM-5* is to combine these three disorders into a new category called *complex somatic symptom disorder* (American Psychiatric Association, 2010). Despite the overlap, subtle differences exist and the *DSM-5* proposal, if adopted, would continue to allow further specification of one of the three conditions within the new disorder.

Hypochondriasis

Clinical Description

Like many terms in psychopathology, **hypochondriasis** has ancient roots. To the Greeks, the *hypochondria* was the region below the ribs, and the organs in this region affected mental state. For example, ulcers and abdominal disorders were once considered part of the hypochondriacal syndrome. As the actual causes of such disorders were discovered, physical complaints without a clear cause continued to be labelled "hypochondriasis" (Barsky, Wyshak, & Klerman, 1986; Taylor & Asmundson, 2009; Woolfolk & Allen, in press). In hypochondriasis, severe anxiety is focused on the possibility of having a serious disease. The threat seems so real that reassurance from physicians does not seem to help. Consider the case of Kirsten, whose case is described in more detail by Stewart and Watt (2001).

KIRSTEN | *Invisibly Ill*

Kirsten was a 42-year-old married mother of three daughters. She also worked part time as a bank teller. She presented with a persistent fear of breast cancer and a preoccupation with the belief that she may have developed malignant tumours in her breasts.

Before the onset of Kirsten's illness, a female relative had developed breast cancer and had undergone a radical mastectomy. Kirsten herself had discovered small lumps in her breasts and had consulted her physician, fearing that she had developed breast cancer. Medical tests revealed that her physical symptoms were indicative of non-malignant fibroid masses and did not require intervention.

For several months before her psychological assessment, Kirsten had been visiting her family physician two times per month for breast examinations. These tests would temporarily allay her fears, but worries that she had developed breast cancer would return within days or even hours of her visits to the physician.

These concerns were exerting significant effects on her interpersonal and work life. Intrusive thoughts about breast cancer would interfere with her ability to concentrate at her bank job. She was so highly distressed by touching or looking at her own breasts that she had her husband assist her in putting on her brassiere and in applying creams or sunscreen in any area around her chest. Kirsten reported that she avoided the news and women's magazines for fear that she would come across an article or news item on breast cancer, which she found extremely distressing. She also avoided visiting her relative who had had the mastectomy because she found such contact to be upsetting.

Kirsten reported a strong fear of death, involving concerns that she would die from breast cancer and leave her three children motherless. Her husband was becoming exasperated with the demands she was placing on him. Her family physician was also becoming frustrated about Kirsten's constant need for reassurance and referred her for psychological assessment and possible cognitive-behavioural therapy.

Kirsten's problems are fairly typical of hypochondriasis. Research indicates that hypochondriasis shares many features with the anxiety and mood disorders, particularly panic disorder (Asmundson, Taylor, & Cox, 2001; Langlois, Pelletier, Ladouceur, & Boucher, 2005), including similar age of onset, personality characteristics, and patterns of familial aggregation (running in families). Indeed, research by Québec psychologist Guylaine Côté and her colleagues (1996) revealed that anxiety and mood disorders are frequently comorbid with hypochondriasis; that is, if individuals with a hypochondriacal disorder have additional diagnoses, these are most likely to be anxiety or mood disorders (see also Rief, Hiller, & Margraf, 1998). The *DSM-5* committee is even considering the possibility that many individuals with hypochondriasis might be better considered to have an anxiety disorder, a position that receives wide support (Taylor & Asmundson, 2009).

Hypochondriasis is characterized by anxiety or fear that one has a serious disease. Therefore, the essential problem is anxiety, but its expression is different from that of the other anxiety disorders. In hypochondriasis, the individual is preoccupied with bodily symptoms, misinterpreting them as indicative of illness or disease. Almost any physical sensation may become the basis for concern for individuals with hypochondriasis. Some may focus on normal bodily functions such as heart rate or perspiration, others on very minor physical abnormalities such as a cough. Some individuals complain of very vague symptoms, such as aches or fatigue. Because a key feature of this disorder is preoccupation with physical symptoms, individuals with hypochondriasis usually go initially to family physicians. They come to the attention of mental health professionals only after family physicians have ruled out realistic medical conditions as a cause (see DSM Table 6.1).

Another important feature of hypochondriasis is that reassurances from numerous doctors that the individual is healthy have, at best, only a short-term effect. It isn't long before patients like Kirsten are back in the office of another doctor on the assumption that the previous doctors have missed something. In studying this feature for purposes of modifying the diagnostic criteria in *DSM-IV*, Côté and her colleagues (1996) confirmed a subtle but interesting distinction (see also Craske et al., 1996; Kellner, Hernandez, & Pathak, 1992). Individuals who fear developing a disease, and therefore avoid situations they associate with contagion, are different from those who are anxious they actually have the disease like Kirsten. Individuals who have only marked fear of developing a disease are classified as having an *illness phobia*. Individuals who mistakenly believe they currently have a disease are diagnosed with hypochondriasis.

DSM-IV-TR	**Table 6.1** Diagnostic Criteria for Hypochondriasis

A. Preoccupation with fears of having, or the idea that a person has, a serious disease based on the person's misinterpretation of bodily symptoms.

B. The preoccupation persists despite appropriate medical evaluation and reassurance.

C. The belief in Criterion A is not of delusional intensity (as in delusional disorder, somatic type) and is not restricted to a circumscribed concern about appearance (as in body dysmorphic disorder).

D. The preoccupation causes clinically significant distress or impairment in social, occupational, or other important areas of functioning.

E. The duration of the disturbance is at least six months.

F. The preoccupation is not better accounted for by generalized anxiety disorder, obsessive-compulsive disorder, panic disorder, a major depressive episode, separation anxiety, or another somatoform disorder.

Specify if:

With poor insight: If, for most of the time during the current episode, the person does not recognize that the concern about having a serious illness is excessive or unreasonable.

Source: Reprinted with permission from the *Diagnostic and Statistical Manual of Mental Disorders,* Fourth Edition, Text Revision, (Copyright © 2000). American Psychiatric Association.

The work of Côté and her colleagues (1996) shows that these two groups differ further. Individuals with high disease conviction are more likely to misinterpret physical symptoms and display higher rates of checking behaviours and trait anxiety than individuals with illness phobia (see also Haenen, de Jong, Schmidt, Stevens, & Visser, 2000). Individuals with illness phobia have an earlier age or onset than those with disease conviction. Disease conviction has become the core feature of hypochondriasis. Of course, some people may have both a disease conviction and a fear of developing additional diseases (Kellner, 1986). In one study, 60 percent of a group of patients with illness phobia went on to develop hypochondriasis and panic disorder (Benedetti et al., 1997).

If you have just read Chapter 5, you may think that patients with panic disorder resemble patients with hypochondriasis. In fact, the two conditions co-occur quite commonly. For example, a study by a group of researchers in Winnipeg (Furer, Walker, Chartier, & Stein, 1997) found that nearly half of a group of patients with panic disorder also met diagnostic criteria for hypochondriasis and that hypochondriasis was more common in patients with panic disorder (48 percent) than in either a group of patients with social phobia (17 percent) or controls (14 percent).

Like those with hypochondriasis, patients with panic disorder also misinterpret physical symptoms as the beginning of the next panic attack, which they believe may kill them. However, panic disorder and hypochondriasis do have some important differences. Steven Taylor (1994, 1995) suggested that, although both disorders include characteristic concern with physical symptoms, patients with panic disorder typically fear immediate symptom-related catastrophes that may occur during the few minutes they are having a panic attack. Individuals with hypochondriacal concerns, on the other hand, focus on a long-term process of illness and disease (e.g., cancer or AIDS). In addition, the anxieties of individuals with panic disorder tend to focus on the specific set of 10 or 15 sympathetic nervous system symptoms associated with a panic attack. Hypochondriacal concerns range much wider.

▲ Steven Taylor (left) and Gordon Asmundson (right), psychologists at the University of British Columbia and the University of Regina, respectively, are well known for their work in the areas of anxiety and somatoform disorders. They have contributed substantially to the understanding of hypochondriasis.

Statistics

We know very little about the prevalence of hypochondriasis in the general population. Early estimates indicate that anywhere between 1 percent and 14 percent of medical patients are diagnosed with hypochondriasis (Barsky, Wyshak, Klerman, & Latham, 1990). A large study in which almost 1400 patients in primary care settings were carefully interviewed suggests that about 3 percent met criteria for hypochondriasis (Escobar, Waitzkin, Silver, Gara, & Holman, 1998). Although historically considered one of the "hysterical" disorders unique to women, the sex ratio is actually 50-50 (Asmundson, Taylor, Sevgur, & Cox, 2001; Kirmayer, Looper, & Taillefer, 2003; Kirmayer & Robbins, 1991). It was thought for a long time that hypochondriasis was more prevalent in elderly populations, but this does not seem to be true (Barsky, Frank, Cleary, Wyshak, & Klerman, 1991). In fact, hypochondriasis is spread fairly evenly across various phases of adulthood. Naturally, more elderly people go to see physicians, making the absolute number of patients with hypochondriasis in this age group somewhat higher than in the younger population, but among those people seeing a doctor, a similar proportion of elderly versus younger patients have hypochondriasis. Hypochondriasis may emerge at any time of life, with the peak age periods found in adolescence, middle age (40s and 50s), and after age 60 (Kellner, 1986). As with most anxiety and mood disorders, hypochondriasis is chronic (Taylor & Asmundson, 2009). In one study (Barsky, Fama, Bailey, & Ahern, 1998), a large group of more than 100 patients with hypochondriasis was followed for four to five years, as was a comparable non-hypochondriacal patient group from the same setting. Two-thirds of the patients still met criteria for the diagnosis of hypochondriasis, and these patients remained significantly more symptomatic than the comparison group. Other studies have found similar or somewhat lower percentages (Creed & Barsky, 2004; olde Hartman et al., 2009).

Culture-specific syndromes seem to fit comfortably with hypochondriasis (Kirmayer & Sartorius, 2007). Among these is the disorder of *koro*, in which there is the belief, accompanied by severe anxiety and sometimes panic, that the genitals are retracting into the abdomen. Most victims of this disorder are Chinese males, although it is also reported in females; there are very few reports of the problem in Western cultures. Rubin (1982) points to the central importance of sexual functioning among Chinese males. Typical sufferers are guilty about excessive masturbation, unsatisfactory intercourse, or promiscuity. These kinds of events may predispose men to focus their attention on their sexual organs, which could exacerbate anxiety and arousal, much as it does in the anxiety disorders, thereby setting off an "epidemic."

Another culture-specific disorder, prevalent in India, is an anxious concern about losing semen, something that obviously occurs during sexual activity. The disorder, called *dhat*, is associated with a vague mix of physical symptoms including dizziness, weakness, and fatigue that are not as specific as in *koro*. These low-grade depressive or anxious symptoms are simply attributed to a physical factor, semen loss. Other specific culture-bound somatic symptoms associated with emotional factors would include hot sensations in the head or a sensation of something crawling in the head, specific to African patients (Ebigno, 1986),

Somatoform Disorders **183**

and a sensation of burning in the hands and feet in Pakistani or Indian patients (Kirmayer & Weiss, 1993).

Somatic symptoms may be among the more challenging manifestations of psychopathology. First, a physician must rule out a physical cause for the somatic complaints before referring the patient to a mental health professional. Second, the mental health professional must determine the nature of the somatic complaints in order to know whether they are associated with a specific somatoform disorder or are part of some other psychopathological syndrome, such as a panic attack. Third, the clinician must be acutely aware of the specific culture or subculture of the patient, which often requires consultation with experts in cross-cultural presentations of psychopathology.

Causes

Investigators with generally differing points of view agree on psychopathological processes ongoing in hypochondriasis. Faulty interpretation of physical signs and sensations as evidence of physical illness is central, so almost everyone agrees that hypochondriasis is basically a disorder of cognition or perception with strong emotional contributions (Adler, Côté, Barlow, & Hillhouse, 1994; Barsky & Wyshak, 1990; Salkovskis & Clark, 1993; Taylor & Asmundson, 2004, 2009).

Individuals with hypochondriasis experience physical sensations common to all of us, but they quickly focus their attention on these sensations. Remember that the very act of focusing on yourself increases arousal and makes the physical sensations seem more intense than they actually are (see Chapter 5). If you also tend to misinterpret these as symptoms of illness, your anxiety will increase further. Increased anxiety produces additional physical symptoms, in a vicious cycle (Salkovskis & Warwick, 2001; Warwick & Salkovskis, 1990; see ■ Figure 6.1).

Using procedures from cognitive science such as the Stroop test (see Chapter 2), it has been confirmed that patients with hypochondriasis and those with high levels of health anxiety show enhanced perceptual sensitivity to illness cues (Hitchcock & Mathews, 1992; Owens, Asmundson, Hadjistavropoulos, & Owens, 2004; Pauli & Alpers, 2002). They also tend to interpret ambiguous stimuli as threatening (Haenen et al., 2000; Stewart & Watt, 2000). Thus, they quickly become aware (and frightened) of any sign of possible illness or disease. A minor headache, for example, might be interpreted as a sure sign of a brain tumour. Individuals with hypochondriasis, compared with those without, take a "better safe than sorry" approach to dealing with even minor physical symptoms, by getting it checked out as soon as possible (Smeets, de Jong, & Mayer, 2000). More fundamentally, they have a very restrictive concept of health as being totally symptom-free (Rief et al., 1998).

What causes individuals to develop this pattern of somatic sensitivity and distorted beliefs? Although it is not certain, the cause is unlikely to be found in isolated biological or psychological factors. There is every reason to believe the fundamental causes of hypochondriasis are similar to those implicated in the anxiety disorders (Barlow, 2002; Suárez et al., 2009). For example, evidence shows that hypochondriasis runs in families (Kellner, 1985), and that there is a modest genetic contribution (Taylor, Thordarson, Jang, & Asmundson, 2006). But this contribution may be non-specific, such as a tendency to overrespond to stress, and thus may be indistinguishable from the non-specific genetic contribution to anxiety disorders. Hyperresponsivity might combine with a tendency to view negative life events as unpredictable and uncontrollable and, therefore, to be guarded against at all times (Noyes et al., 2004; Suárez et al., 2009). As we noted in Chapter 5, these factors would constitute biological and psychological vulnerabilities to anxiety.

Why does this anxiety focus on physical sensations and illness? We know that children with hypochondriacal concerns often report the same kinds of symptoms that other family members may have reported at one time (Kellner, 1985; Kirmayer et al., 2003;

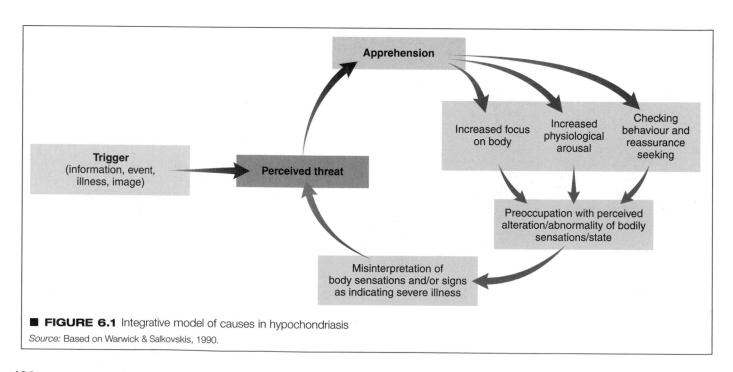

■ **FIGURE 6.1** Integrative model of causes in hypochondriasis
Source: Based on Warwick & Salkovskis, 1990.

Pilowsky, 1970). It is therefore quite possible, as in panic disorder, that individuals who develop hypochondriasis have *learned* from family members to focus their anxiety on specific physical conditions and illness. A study by Margo Watt found that adults with elevated hypochondriacal concerns reported more learning experiences in childhood around negative reactions to bodily symptoms than did adults with lower levels of hypochondriacal concerns (Watt & Stewart, 2000). These learning experiences involved being rewarded by parents (i.e., instrumental learning) when the child expressed bodily complaints (e.g., being allowed to miss school or receiving increased attention). These experiences also involved observing a parent or other family member expressing anxiety about bodily sensations (i.e., vicarious learning), or having a parent or family member verbally instruct the child that all bodily sensations are dangerous and signs of serious illness (Watt & Stewart, 2000).

Three other factors may contribute to this etiological process (Côté et al., 1996; Kellner, 1985). First, hypochondriasis seems to develop in the context of a stressful life event, as do many disorders, including anxiety disorders. Such events often involve death or illness. Recall that the beginning of Kirsten's disorder seemed to coincide with the serious illness (breast cancer) of a female relative. Second, people who develop hypochondriasis tend to have had a disproportionate incidence of disease in their family when they were children. Thus, even if they did not develop hypochondriasis until adulthood, they carry strong memories of illness that could easily become the focus of anxiety. Third, an important social and interpersonal influence may be operating (Noyes et al., 2003). Some people who come from families in which illness is a major issue seem to have learned that an ill person is often paid increased attention (Watt & Stewart, 2000). The "benefits" of being sick might contribute to the development of the disorder. A "sick person" who thus receives more attention and less responsibility is described as adopting a "sick role." These issues may be even more significant in somatization disorder.

Treatment

Recent years have seen substantial developments in our understanding of the effective treatment of hypochondriasis and health anxiety (Furer, Walker, & Stein, 2007; Taylor & Asmundson, 2004). Until relatively recently, it was common clinical practice to uncover unconscious conflicts through psychodynamic psychotherapy. However, results on the effectiveness of this kind of treatment have seldom been reported. In one study, only 4 out of 23 patients seemed to derive any benefit (Ladee, 1966). In contrast, for people with hypochondriasis who are willing to be referred to a mental health professional, emerging work suggests that cognitive-behavioural therapy can be very effective. Cognitive-behavioural therapy involves such techniques as exposure to health and illness information that the patient may be avoiding due to health anxiety (Furer & Walker, 2005), and learning to challenge illness-related misinterpretations of benign bodily sensations (e.g., learning to challenge thoughts that a simple rash is a sign of cancer) (e.g., Walker & Furer, 2006). Results from the work of psychologists Patricia Furer, John Walker, and Mark Freeston (2001) show that 83 percent of patients no longer meet diagnostic criteria for hypochondriasis after cognitive-behavioural therapy. In a scientifically controlled study, Warwick, Clark, Cobb, and Salkovskis (1996) randomly assigned 32 patients to either cognitive-behavioural therapy or a no-treatment wait-list control group. Like the treatment offered by Furer and colleagues, treatment in the Warwick et al. (1996) study focused on identifying and challenging illness-related misinterpretations of physical sensations and on showing patients how to create symptoms by focusing attention on certain body areas. Bringing on their own symptoms persuaded many patients that such events were under their control. Patients were also coached to seek less reassurance regarding their concerns. Patients in the treatment group improved an average of 76 percent, and those in the wait-list group only 5 percent; benefits were maintained for three months. Clark et al. (1998) replicated this result in a larger controlled study and showed that those treated with cognitive-behavioural therapy retained their gains at a one-year follow-up.

Another innovation in cognitive-behavioural treatment for hypochondriasis has been to adapt treatments that have been shown to be effective with related disorders. For example, given that worries about health are present in both generalized anxiety disorder (GAD) and hypochondriasis, Québec researchers Frederik Langlois and Robert Ladouceur (2004) adapted Ladouceur's cognitive-behavioural treatment for generalized anxiety disorder (see Chapter 5) to be suitable for those with hypochondriasis. Using a multiple baseline single case design across six individuals with hypochondriasis (see Chapter 4 for a review of this method), these authors showed that a therapy focusing on excessive worry was an effective treatment for health anxiety. Future controlled studies are needed to see if this promising treatment generalizes beyond the small number of cases examined in this preliminary study.

Finally, in a review of the scant available literature on the pharmacological treatment of hypochondriasis, Murray Enns and his colleagues concluded that some preliminary evidence exists of the effectiveness of antidepressant medications, especially the selective serotonin reuptake inhibitors (SSRIs; Enns, Kjernisted, & Lander, 2001; see also Kjernisted, Enns, & Lander, 2002).

Steven Taylor and his colleagues recently completed a meta-analysis of psychological and pharmacological treatments, in order to identify the most promising interventions for treating patients with hypochondriasis. They found that cognitive-behavioural therapy is the most effective treatment. They also found that fluoxetine (an SSRI) appears promising. Psychoeducation was sufficient only for mild cases of hypochondriasis. It is very likely we will see more research on the treatment of hypochondriasis in the future (Taylor, Asmundson, & Coons, 2003).

Somatization Disorder

Clinical Description

In 1859, Pierre Briquet, a French physician, described patients who came to see him with seemingly endless lists of somatic complaints for which he could find no medical basis (American Psychiatric Association, 1980). Despite his negative findings, patients returned shortly with either the same complaints or new lists containing slight variations. For more than a century this disorder was called *Briquet's syndrome*, before being changed in 1980 to **somatization disorder** (see review by Abbey, 2005). Consider the case of Linda.

LINDA | *Full-Time Patient*

Linda, an intelligent woman in her 30s, came to our clinic looking distressed and pained. As she sat down she noted that coming into the office was very difficult for her, as she had trouble breathing and considerable swelling in the joints of her legs and arms. She was also in some pain from chronic urinary tract infections and might have to leave at any moment to go to the washroom, but she was extremely happy she had kept the appointment. At least she was seeing someone who could help alleviate her considerable suffering. She said she knew we would have to go through a detailed initial interview, but she had something that might save time. At this point she pulled out several sheets of paper and handed them over. One section, some five pages long, described her contacts with the health care system for major difficulties only. Times, dates, potential diagnoses, and days hospitalized were noted. The second section, one and a half single-spaced pages, consisted of a list of all the medications she had taken for various complaints.

Linda felt she had any one of a number of chronic infections that nobody could properly diagnose. She had begun to have these problems in her teenage years. She often discussed her symptoms and fears with doctors and clergy. Drawn to hospitals and medical clinics, she had entered nursing school after high school. However, during hospital training, she noticed her physical condition deteriorating rapidly: She seemed to pick up the diseases she was learning about. A series of stressful emotional events resulted in her leaving nursing school.

After developing unexplained paralysis in her legs, Linda was admitted to a psychiatric hospital, and after a year she regained her ability to walk. On discharge she obtained disability status, which freed her from having to work full-time, and she volunteered at the local hospital. With her chronic but fluctuating incapacitation, on some days she could go in and on some days she could not. She was seeing a family practitioner and six specialists, who monitored various aspects of her physical condition. She was also seeing two ministers for pastoral counselling.

DSM-IV-TR | Table 6.2 Criteria for Somatization Disorder

A. A history of many physical complaints beginning before age 30 that occur over several years and result in treatment being sought or significant impairment in social, occupational, or other important areas of functioning.

B. Each of the following criteria must have been met, with individual symptoms occurring at any time during the course of disturbance.

1. Four pain symptoms: A history of pain related to at least four different sites or functions (such as head, abdomen, back, joints, extremities, chest, rectum, during sexual intercourse, during menstruation, or during urination).

2. Two gastrointestinal symptoms: A history of at least two gastro-intestinal symptoms other than pain (such as nausea, diarrhea, bloating, vomiting other than during pregnancy, or intolerance of several different foods).

3. One sexual symptom: A history of at least one sexual or reproductive symptom other than pain (such as sexual indifference, erectile or ejaculatory dysfunction, irregular menses, excessive menstrual bleeding, vomiting throughout pregnancy).

4. One pseudoneurologic symptom: A history of at least one symptom or deficit suggesting a neurological disorder not limited to pain (conversion symptoms such as blindness, double vision, deafness, loss of touch or pain sensation, hallucinations, aphonia, impaired coordination or balance, paralysis or localized weakness, difficulty swallowing, difficulty breathing, urinary retention, seizures; dissociative symptoms such as amnesia; or loss of consciousness other than fainting).

Source: Reprinted with permission from the *Diagnostic and Statistical Manual of Mental Disorders,* Fourth Edition, Text Revision, (Copyright © 2000). American Psychiatric Association.

Linda easily met and exceeded all the *DSM-IV-TR* diagnostic criteria for somatization disorder (see DSM Table 6.2). Do you notice any differences between Linda, who presented with somatization disorder, and Kirsten, who presented with hypochondriasis? Of course, Linda was more severely impaired and had in the past experienced symptoms of paralysis (which we now call conversion symptoms; see p. 189). But the more telling difference is that Linda was *not so afraid* as Kirsten that she had a disease. Linda was concerned with the symptoms themselves, not with what they might mean. Individuals with hypochondriasis most often take immediate action on noticing a symptom by calling the doctor or taking medication. People with somatization disorder, on the other hand, do not feel the urgency to take action but continually feel weak and ill, and they avoid exercising, thinking it will make them worse (Rief et al., 1998). Furthermore, Linda's entire

life revolved around her symptoms; she once said her symptoms were her identity: Without them she would not know who she was. By this she meant that she would not know how to relate to people except in the context of discussing her symptoms, much as other people might talk about their day at the office or their kids' accomplishments at school. Her few friends who were not health care professionals had the patience to relate to her sympathetically, through the veil of her symptoms, and she thought of them as friends because they "understood" her suffering.

Statistics

Somatization disorder is rare. *DSM-III-R* criteria required 13 or more symptoms from a list of 35, making diagnosis difficult. The criteria were greatly simplified for *DSM-IV* with only eight symptoms required (Cloninger, 1996). These criteria have been validated as easier to use and more accurate than alternative or past criteria (Yutzy et al., 1995). Katon and colleagues (1991) demonstrated that somatization disorder occurs on a continuum: People with only a few medically unexplained physical symptoms may experience sufficient distress and impairment of functioning to be considered to have a disorder that is called *undifferentiated somatoform disorder*. But this disorder is just somatization disorder with fewer than eight symptoms, and for that reason the label is likely to be eliminated in *DSM-5*. Using between four and six symptoms as criteria, Escobar and Canino (1989) found a prevalence of somatization disorder of 4.4 percent in one large city. The median prevalence in six samples of a large number of patients in

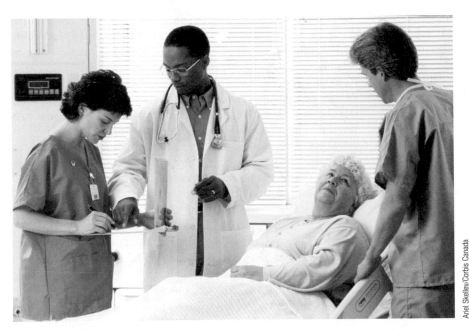

▲ In somatization disorder, primary relationships are often with medical caregivers; a person's symptoms are that person's identity.

Ariel Skelley/Corbis Canada

that individuals with somatization disorder tend to be women, unmarried, and from lower socio-economic groups (e.g., Swartz, Blazer, George, & Landerman, 1986). For instance, 68 percent of the patients in a large sample studied by Kirmayer and Robbins (1991) were female. In addition to a variety of somatic complaints, individuals may also have psychological complaints, usually anxiety or mood disorders (Kirmayer & Robbins, 1991; Lieb, Zimmerman, Friis, Hofler, Tholen, & Wittehen, 2002). Table 6.1 presents data from a large World Health Organization study on individuals presenting to primary care settings with either somatic complaints that would not be sufficient to meet criteria for disorder, or for somatization disorder. Notice that the rates are relatively uniform around the world for somatic complaints, as is the sex ratio (Gureje, Simon, Ustin, & Goldberg, 1997).

a primary care setting meeting these criteria was 16.6 percent (Creed & Barsky, 2004).

Linda's disorder developed during adolescence, apparently the typical age of onset. Several studies have demonstrated

Causes

Somatization disorder shares some features with hypochondriasis, including a history of family illness or injury during childhood. But this is a minor factor at best because countless

TABLE 6.1 Frequency of Two Forms of Somatization in a Cross-Cultural Study (N = 5438)*

Centre	ICD-10 Somatization Disorder (%)			Somatic Symptom Index (%)		
	Men	Women	Overall Prevalence	Men	Women	Overall Prevalence
Ankara, Turkey	1.3	2.2	1.9	22.3	26.7	25.2
Athens, Greece	0.4	1.8	1.3	7.7	13.5	11.5
Bangalore, India	1.3	2.4	1.8	19.1	20.0	19.6
Berlin, Germany	0.3	2.0	1.3	24.9	25.9	25.5
Groningen, the Netherlands	0.8	4.1	2.8	14.7	19.9	17.8
Ibadan, Nigeria	0.5	0.3	0.4	14.4	5.0	7.6
Mainz, Germany	1.0	4.4	3.0	24.9	17.3	20.6
Manchester, United Kingdom	0.0	0.5	0.4	21.4	20.0	20.5
Nagasaki, Japan	0.0	0.2	0.1	13.3	7.9	10.5
Paris, France	0.5	3.1	1.7	18.6	28.2	23.1
Rio de Janeiro, Brazil	1.5	11.2	8.5	35.6	30.6	32.0
Santiago, Chile	33.8	11.2	17.7	45.7	33.3	36.8
Seattle, United States	0.7	2.2	1.7	10.0	9.8	9.8
Shanghai, China	0.3	2.2	1.5	17.5	18.7	18.3
Verona, Italy	0.0	0.2	0.1	9.7	8.5	8.9
Total	1.9	3.3	2.8	19.8	19.7	19.7

Note: * Weighted to the first-stage (intake) sample.

Source: Adapted from Gureje et al., 1997. *The International Classification of Diseases,* 10th ed.

families experience chronic illness or injuries without passing on the sick role to children. Similar to etiological models of hypochondriasis, Laurence Kirmayer and his colleagues have theorized that patients with somatization disorder are more sensitive to physical sensations or overattend to them (Kirmayer, Robbins, & Paris, 1994; see also Duddu, Isaac, & Chaturvedi, 2006).

Given the past difficulty in making a diagnosis, few etiological studies of somatization disorder have been done. Early studies of possible genetic contributions had mixed results. For example, in a sophisticated twin study, Torgersen (1986) found no increased prevalence of somatization disorder in monozygotic pairs, but most studies find substantial evidence that the disorder runs in families and may have a heritable basis (Bell, 1994; Guze, Cloninger, Martin, & Clayton, 1986). A more startling finding emerged from these studies, however. Somatization disorder is strongly linked in family and genetic studies to *antisocial personality disorder* (ASPD; see Chapter 12), which is characterized by vandalism, persistent lying, theft, irresponsibility with finances and at work, and outright physical aggression. Individuals with antisocial personality disorder seem insensitive to signals of punishment and to the negative consequences of their often impulsive behaviour, and they apparently experience little anxiety or guilt.

ASPD occurs primarily in males and somatization disorder in females, but they share several features. Both begin early in life, typically run a chronic course, predominate among lower socioeconomic classes, are difficult to treat, and are associated with marital discord, drug and alcohol abuse, and suicide attempts, among other complications (Cloninger, 1978; Goodwin & Guze, 1984). Both family and adoption studies suggest that ASPD and somatization disorder tend to run in families and may well have a heritable component (e.g., Bohman, Cloninger, von Knorring, & Sigvardsson, 1984; Cadoret, 1978), although it is also possible that the behavioural patterns could be learned in a maladaptive family setting.

Yet the aggressiveness, impulsiveness, and lack of emotion characteristic of ASPD seem to be at the other end of the spectrum from somatization disorder. What could these two disorders possibly have in common? Although we don't yet have the answers, Lilienfeld (1992; Lilienfeld & Hess, 2001) reviews a number of hypotheses; we look at some of them here because they are a fascinating example of integrative biopsychosocial thinking about psychopathology.

One model with some support suggests that somatization disorder and ASPD share a neurobiologically based disinhibition syndrome characterized by impulsive behaviour (e.g., Cloninger, 1987; Gorenstein & Newman, 1980). Evidence indicates that impulsiveness is common in ASPD (e.g., Newman, Widom, & Nathan, 1985). Many of the behaviours and traits associated with somatization disorder also seem to reflect short-term gain at the expense of long-term problems. The continual development of new somatic symptoms gains immediate sympathy and attention (for a while) but eventually social isolation (Goodwin & Guze, 1984).

If individuals with ASPD and somatization disorder share the same underlying neurophysiological vulnerability, why do they behave so differently? The explanation is that social and cultural factors exert a strong effect. The major difference between the disorders is their degree of dependence (Cloninger, 1987; Widom, 1984). Aggression is strongly associated with males in most mammalian species, including rodents (Gray & Buffery, 1971). Gender roles are among the strongest components of identity. It is very possible that gender socialization accounts almost entirely for the profound differences in the expression of the same biological vulnerability among men and women.

These theoretical models are still preliminary and require a great deal more data before we can have confidence in their validity. But such ideas are at the forefront of our knowledge of psychopathology and reflect the kinds of integrative approach to psychopathology (described in Chapter 2) that will inevitably emerge as our knowledge increases.

Might these assumptions apply to Linda or her family? Linda's sister had been married briefly and had two children. She had been in therapy for most of her adult life. Occasionally, Linda's sister visited doctors with various somatic complaints, but her primary difficulty was unexplained periods of recurring amnesia that might last several days; these spells alternated with blackout periods during which she was rushed to the hospital.

Were there signs of impulsivity or ASPD in this family? The sister's older daughter, after a very stormy adolescence characterized by truancy and delinquency, was sentenced to jail for violations involving drugs and assault. In the midst of one session with us, Linda noted that she had kept a list of people with whom she had had sexual intercourse. The list numbered well over 20, suggesting substantial sexual impulsivity. Most of the sexual episodes occurred in the offices of mental health professionals or clergy!

This development in Linda's relationship with caregivers was very important because she saw it as the ultimate sign that the caregivers were concerned about her as a person and that she was important to them. But the relationships usually ended tragically. Several of the caregivers' marriages disintegrated and at least one mental health professional committed suicide. Linda herself was never satisfied or fulfilled by the relationships but was greatly hurt when they inevitably ended. The Canadian Psychological Association has decreed that it is *always* unethical to have *any* sexual contact with a patient at any time during treatment. Violations of this ethical canon have nearly always resulted in tragic consequences.

Treatment

Somatization disorder is exceedingly difficult to treat and no treatments exist with proven effectiveness to "cure" the syndrome. An additional complication noted by Laurence Kirmayer and his colleagues is that people with somatization disorder are very resistant to having a psychological cause applied to their physical symptoms, and this resistance makes them likely to avoid or discontinue psychological treatment (Kirmayer, Groleau, Looper, & Dao, 2004). In our clinics, we concentrate on providing reassurance, reducing stress, and, in particular, reducing the frequency of help-seeking behaviours. One of the most common patterns is the person's tendency to visit numerous medical specialists according to the symptom of the week. An extensive medical and physical workup occurs with every visit to a new physician (or to one who has not been seen for a while).

In treatment, to limit these visits, a gatekeeper physician is assigned to each patient to screen all physical complaints. Subsequent visits to specialists must be specifically authorized by this gatekeeper. In the context of a positive therapeutic relationship, most patients are amenable to this arrangement.

Additional therapeutic attention is directed at reducing the supportive consequences of relating to significant others on the basis of physical symptoms alone. More appropriate methods of interacting with others are encouraged. Because Linda, like many patients with this disorder, had managed to become eligible for disability payments, additional goals involved encouraging at least part-time employment with the ultimate goal of discontinuing disability.

In a recent review of behavioural medicine approaches to treatment, Karl Looper and Laurence Kirmayer (2002) of McGill University discuss the current state of research knowledge on the treatment of somatization disorder. Some interventions have been aimed at physicians working with these patients and others have been aimed at the patients themselves. Randomized controlled studies demonstrate that written consultation letters sent to referring physicians to educate them about somatization disorder are effective in reducing the excessive and costly help-seeking associated with this type of somatoform disorder. Unfortunately, this kind of intervention does not improve the psychological distress of patients with somatization disorder (Rost, Kashner, & Smith, 1994; Smith, Monson, & Ray, 1986). In terms of interventions aimed at the patients themselves, group cognitive-behavioural therapy has been shown to provide additional benefit not only in reducing health care costs, but also in improving somatization disorder patients' psychological well-being (Kashner, Rost, Cohen, Anderson, & Smith, 1995; Lidbeck, 1997).

Conversion Disorder

The term *conversion* has been used off and on since the Middle Ages (Mace, 1992) but was popularized by Freud, who believed the anxiety resulting from unconscious conflicts somehow was "converted" into physical symptoms to find expression. This conversion allowed the individual to discharge some anxiety without actually experiencing it. As in phobic disorders, the anxiety resulting from unconscious conflicts might be "displaced" onto another object.

Clinical Description

Conversion disorders generally have to do with physical malfunctioning, such as paralysis, blindness, or difficulty speaking (aphonia), without any physical or organic pathology to account for the malfunction (see DSM Table 6.3). Most conversion symptoms suggest that some kind of neurological disease is affecting sensory-motor systems, although conversion symptoms can mimic the full range of physical malfunctioning. For this reason, and because the term "conversion" implies a specific etiology for which there is limited evidence, the proposal for the *DSM-5* is to change the name to "functional neurological disorder" (with "functional" referring to a symptom without organic cause) (Stone, LaFrance, Levenson, & Sharpe, 2010).

Conversion disorders provide us with some of the most intriguing, sometimes astounding, examples of psychopathology.

DSM-IV-TR	**Table 6.3** Criteria for Conversion Disorder

A. One or more symptoms or deficits affecting voluntary motor or sensory function that suggest a neurological or general medical condition.

B. Psychological factors are judged to be associated with the symptom or deficit because the initiation or exacerbation of the symptom or deficit is preceded by conflicts or other stressors.

C. The symptom or deficit is not intentionally produced or feigned (as in factitious disorder or malingering).

D. The symptom or deficit cannot, after appropriate investigation, be fully explained by a general medical condition, or by the direct effects of a substance, or as a culturally sanctioned behaviour or experience.

E. The symptom or deficit causes clinically significant distress or impairment in social, occupational, or other important areas of functioning or warrants medical evaluation.

F. The symptom or deficit is not limited to pain or sexual dysfunction, does not occur exclusively during the course of somatization disorder, and is not better accounted for by another mental disorder.

Source: Reprinted with permission from the *Diagnostic and Statistical Manual of Mental Disorders,* Fourth Edition, Text Revision, (Copyright © 2000). American Psychiatric Association.

What could possibly account for somebody going blind when all visual processes are perfectly normal, or experiencing paralysis of the arms or legs when there is no neurological damage? Consider the case of Eloise.

ELOISE | *Unlearning Walking*

Eloise sat on a chair with her legs under her, refusing to put her feet on the floor. Her mother sat close by, ready to assist her if she needed to move or get up. Her mother had made the appointment and, with the help of a friend, had all but carried Eloise into the office. Eloise was a 20-year-old of borderline intelligence who was friendly and personable during the initial interview and who readily answered all questions with a big smile. She obviously enjoyed the social interaction.

Eloise's difficulty walking developed over five years. Her right leg had given way and she began falling. Gradually, the condition worsened to the point that six months before her admission to the hospital, Eloise could move around only by crawling on the floor.

Physical examinations revealed no physical problems. Eloise presented with a classic case of conversion disorder. Although she was not paralyzed, her specific symptoms included weakness in her legs and difficulty keeping her balance, with the result that she fell frequently. This particular type of conversion symptom is called *astasia-abasia*.

Eloise lived with her mother, who ran a gift shop in the front of her house in a very small rural town. Eloise had been schooled through exceptional education programs until she was about 15; after this, no further programs were available. When Eloise began staying home, her walking began to deteriorate.

In addition to blindness (see Fraser, 1994) and paralysis or weakness in the limbs, conversion symptoms may include the loss of the sense of touch. Some people have seizures, which may be psychological in origin, because no significant EEG changes can be documented. Another relatively common symptom is *globus hystericus*, the sensation of a lump in the throat that makes it difficult to swallow, eat, or sometimes talk. Conversion symptoms can also include aphonia or even total mutism. Consider the symptoms of Ms. A. described in the following case study (Wald, Taylor, & Scamvougeras, 2004).

MS. A. | *Loss of Voice*

Ms. A. was a retired emergency services worker whose work had exposed her to severe accidents and homicides. She presented with intermittent episodes of speech disruption that had been present for about a year. These periods of disruption in her speech usually lasted a few minutes and they were occurring several times per week. Between these episodes, her speech was completely normal. Although an extensive medical and neurological evaluation was performed, a physical basis for the speech problems could not be found.

During the episodes, Ms. A. was either unable to speak at all or she experienced difficulty speaking properly. Sometimes her speaking was markedly slowed down. At other times she was only able to say "mmm-mmm-mmm." These episodes began with a sensation of a "lump in the throat" (*globus hystericus*).

The condition was causing Ms. A. distress and it was interfering with her social life. She was very embarrassed about these episodes and consequently began to avoid social situations in case she might experience an episode of speech disruption in public.

Ms. A. was more likely to experience speech disruption when she was tired or stressed but the episodes could occur very unexpectedly as well. Remembering the traumatic events she had witnessed in her prior job in which she had been exposed to severely mutilated victims could also trigger speech disruption episodes, even though she reported that she had not been greatly upset at the time of witnessing the actual events.

Ms. A. had a history of medically unexplained somatic problems for more than a decade before she began to experience the episodes of speech disruption. For example, she had experienced periods of dizziness and tinnitus (ringing in the ears). These episodes had started when she was exposed to a reminder of a work-related traumatic event. The dizziness and tinnitus had not been responsive to traditional medical treatments. These symptoms had eventually completely resolved on their own, only to be replaced with the episodes of difficulty speaking.

Closely Related Disorders Distinguishing among conversion reactions, real physical disorders, and outright **malingering** (faking) is sometimes difficult. Several factors can help.

First, conversion reactions often have the same quality of indifference to the symptoms that is present in somatization disorder. This attitude, called *la belle indifférence*, is considered a hallmark of conversion reactions but, unfortunately, it is not a foolproof sign. A blasé attitude toward illness is sometimes displayed by people with actual physical disorders, and some people with conversion symptoms do become quite distressed.

Second, conversion symptoms are often precipitated by marked stress. C. V. Ford (1985) noted that the incidence of marked stress preceding a conversion symptom occurred in 52 percent to 93 percent of the studied patients. Often this stress takes the form of a physical injury. In one large survey, 324 out of 869 patients (37 percent) reported prior physical injury (Stone et al., 2009a). Thus, if the clinician cannot identify a stressful event preceding the onset of the conversion symptom, the clinician might more carefully consider the presence of a true physical condition. In addition, although people with conversion symptoms can usually function normally, they seem truly unaware either of this ability or of sensory input. For example, individuals with the conversion symptom of blindness can usually avoid objects in their visual field, but they will tell you they can't see the objects. Similarly, individuals with conversion symptoms of paralysis of the legs might suddenly get up and run in an emergency and then be astounded they were able to do this. It is possible that at least some people who experience miraculous cures during religious ceremonies may have been suffering from conversion reactions. These factors may help in distinguishing between conversion and organically based physical disorders, but clinicians sometimes make mistakes, although it is not common with modern diagnostic techniques. For example, Moene and colleagues (2000) carefully reassessed 85 patients diagnosed with conversion disorder and found 10 (11.8 percent) had developed some evidence of a neurological disorder approximately 2.5 years after the first exam. Stone and colleagues (2005), summarizing a number of studies, estimate the rate of misdiagnosis of conversion disorders that are really physical problems is approximately 4 percent, having improved considerably from earlier decades. In any case, ruling out medical causes for the symptoms is crucial to making a diagnosis of conversion and, given advances in medical screening procedures, will become the principal diagnostic criterion in the *DSM-5* (APA, 2010; Stone et al., 2010).

It can also be very difficult to distinguish between individuals who are truly experiencing conversion symptoms in a seemingly involuntary way and malingerers who are very good at faking symptoms. Once malingerers are exposed, their motivation is clear: They are either trying to get out of something, such as work or legal difficulties, or they are attempting to gain something, such as a financial settlement. Malingerers are fully aware of what they are doing and are clearly attempting to manipulate others to gain a desired end.

More puzzling is a set of conditions called **factitious disorders**, which fall somewhere between malingering and conversion disorders. The symptoms are under voluntary control, as with malingering, but the person has no obvious reason for voluntarily producing the symptoms except, possibly, to assume the sick role and receive increased attention. Tragically, this disorder may extend to producing symptoms in other members of the family. An adult, almost always a mother, may purposely make her child sick, evidently for the attention and pity then given to the mother who is causing the symptoms—a condition called *factitious disorder by proxy* or, sometimes, *Munchausen syndrome by proxy*

TABLE 6.2 Child Abuse Associated with Munchausen Syndrome by Proxy versus Typical Child Abuse

	Typical Child Abuse	Atypical Child Abuse (Munchausen Syndrome by Proxy)
Physical presentation of the child	Results from direct physical contact with the child; signs often detected on physical examination.	Misrepresentation of an acute or accidental medical or surgical illness not usually obvious on physical examination.
Obtaining the diagnosis	Perpetrator does not invite the discovery of the manifestation of the abuse.	Perpetrator usually presents the manifestations of the abuse to the health care system.
The victims	Children are either the objects of frustration and anger or are receiving undue or inappropriate punishment.	Children serve as the vector in gaining the attention the mother desires. Anger is not the primary causal factor.
Awareness of abuse	Usually present.	Not usually present.

Source: From "Munchausen syndrome by proxy: An atypical form of child abuse" by J.R. Check in *Journal of Practical Psychiatry and Behavioral Health,* 1998, Vol 4, No. 6. p. 341. © 1998. Reprinted by permission of Lippincott Williams & Wilkins.

(Check, 1998). Table 6.2 presents differences between typical child abuse and Munchausen syndrome by proxy. DSM Table 6.4 shows the diagnostic criteria for factitious disorders.

The offending parent may resort to very extreme tactics to create the appearance of illness in the child. For example, one mother stirred a vaginal tampon obtained during menstruation in her child's urine specimen. Another mother mixed feces into her child's vomit (Check, 1998). Because the mother typically establishes a positive relationship with a medical staff, the true nature of the illness is most often unsuspected and the staff perceives the parent as remarkably caring and totally involved in providing for her child's well-being. For this reason the mother is often very successful at eluding suspicion. Helpful procedures to assess the possibility of Munchausen syndrome by proxy include a trial separation of the mother and the child or video surveillance of the child while in the hospital. Now, an important study has appeared validating the utility of surveillance in hospital rooms of children with suspected Munchausen syndrome by proxy. In this study, video surveillance was the method used to establish the diagnosis in many cases. In one case a child was suffering from recurring *Escherichia coli* infections, and cameras caught the mother injecting her own urine into the child's intravenous line (Hall, Eubanks, Meyyazhagan, Kenney, & Johnson, 2000).

DSM-IV-TR	Table 6.4 Criteria for Factitious Disorders

A. Intentional production or feigning of physical or psychological signs or symptoms.

B. The motivation for the behaviour is to assume the sick role.

C. External incentives for the behaviour (such as economic gain, avoiding legal responsibility, or improving physical well-being, as in malingering) are absent.

Specify type:

- With predominantly psychological signs and symptoms if psychological signs and symptoms predominate in the clinical presentation
- With predominantly physical signs and symptoms if physical signs and symptoms predominate in the clinical presentation
- With combined psychological and physical signs and symptoms if neither psychological nor physical signs and symptoms predominate in the clinical presentation

Source: Reprinted with permission from the *Diagnostic and Statistical Manual of Mental Disorders,* Fourth Edition, Text Revision, (Copyright © 2000). American Psychiatric Association.

Not only can cases of Munchausen syndrome by proxy be missed by medical professionals and child welfare services, but errors in the opposite direction can also be made. A recent example is the case of a mother who was investigated by the Children's Aid Society of Ottawa for more than a year over allegations that she may have subjected her daughter to too many medical procedures. The agency had suspicions that the woman had Munchausen syndrome by proxy, but the case was closed without any finding of wrongdoing on this woman's part (Priest, 2003).

Unconscious Mental Processes in Conversion and Related Disorders Unconscious cognitive processes seem to play a role in much of psychopathology (although not necessarily as Freud envisioned them), but nowhere is this phenomenon more readily and dramatically apparent than when we attempt to distinguish between conversion disorders and related conditions. New information (reviewed in Chapter 2) on unconscious cognitive processes becomes important. We are all capable of receiving and processing information in a number of sensory channels (such as vision and hearing) without being aware of it. Remember the phenomenon of blind sight or unconscious vision? Weiskrantz (1980) and others discovered that people with small, localized damage to certain parts of their brains could identify objects in their field of vision, but they had no awareness whatsoever that they could see. Could this happen to people without brain damage? Consider the case of Celia.

CELIA | *Seeing through Blindness*

A 15-year-old girl named Celia was suddenly unable to see. Shortly thereafter she regained some of her sight, but her vision was so severely blurred that she could not read. When she was brought to a clinic for testing, psychologists arranged a series of sophisticated vision tests that did not require her to report when she could or could not see. One of the tasks required her to examine three triangles displayed on three separate screens and to press a button under the screen containing an upright triangle. Celia performed perfectly on this test without being aware that she could see anything (Grosz & Zimmerman, 1970). Was Celia faking? Evidently not, or she would have purposely made a mistake.

Sackeim, Nordlie, and Gur (1979) evaluated the potential difference between real unconscious process and faking by hypnotizing two subjects and giving each a suggestion of total blindness. One subject was also told it was extremely important that she appears to everyone to be blind. The second subject was not given further instructions. The first subject, evidently following instructions to appear blind at all costs, performed far below chance on a visual discrimination task similar to the upright triangle task. On almost every trial she chose the wrong answer. The second subject, with the hypnotic suggestion of blindness but no instructions to appear blind at all costs, performed perfectly on the visual discrimination tasks—although she reported she could not see anything.

How is this relevant to identifying malingering? In an earlier case, Grosz and Zimmerman (1965) evaluated a male who seemed to have conversion symptoms of blindness. They discovered that he performed much more poorly than chance on a visual discrimination task. Subsequent information from other sources confirmed that he was almost certainly malingering. To review these distinctions, someone who is truly blind would perform at a chance level on visual discrimination tasks. People with conversion symptoms, conversely, can see objects in their visual field and, therefore, would perform well on these tasks, but this experience is dissociated from their awareness of sight. Malingerers and, perhaps, individuals with factitious disorders simply do everything possible to pretend they can't see.

Statistics

We have already seen that conversion disorder may occur in conjunction with other disorders, particularly somatization disorder, as in the case of Linda. Linda's paralysis passed after several months and did not return, although on occasion she would report "feeling as if" it were returning. Conversion disorders are relatively rare in mental health settings, but remember that people who seek help for this condition are more likely to consult neurologists or other specialists. The prevalence estimate in neurological settings is high, averaging about 30 percent (Allin, Streeruwitz, & Curtis, 2005; Rowe, 2010; Stone et al., 2009). One study estimated that 10 percent to 20 percent of all patients referred to epilepsy centres have psychogenic, non-epileptic seizures (Benbadis & Allen-Hauser, 2000).

Like somatization disorder, conversion disorders are found primarily in women (Deveci et al., 2007; Folks, Ford, & Regan, 1984; Rosenbaum, 2000) and typically develop during adolescence or slightly thereafter. However, they occur relatively frequently in males at times of extreme stress (Chodoff, 1974). Conversion reactions are not uncommon in soldiers exposed to combat (Mucha & Reinhardt, 1970). The symptoms often disappear after a time, only to return later in the same or similar form when a new stressor occurs. Recall the case of Ms. A. whose original symptoms of dizziness and ringing in her ears resolved, only to return later in the form of the speech disruption episodes (Wald et al., 2004). A three-year longitudinal study of 88 patients by University of Toronto researchers suggests that, in the case of conversion disorders involving movement disturbances (like those seen in the case of Eloise), long-term prognosis is quite poor (Feinstein, Stergiopoulos, Fine, & Lang, 2001). The conversion disorder (i.e., the movement disturbance) had remitted or resolved in only 5 percent of the participants at the follow-up.

In some cultures, conversion symptoms are very common aspects of religious or healing rituals. Seizures, paralysis, and trances are common in some fundamentalist religious groups in North America (Griffith, English, & Mayfield, 1980), and they are often seen as evidence of contact with God. Individuals who exhibit such symptoms are thus held in high esteem by their peers. These symptoms do not meet criteria for a "disorder" unless they persist and interfere with an individual's functioning.

Causes

Freud described four basic processes in the development of conversion disorder. First, the individual experiences a traumatic event—in Freud's view, an unacceptable, unconscious conflict. Second, because the conflict and the resulting anxiety are unacceptable, the person represses the conflict, making it unconscious. Third, the anxiety continues to increase and threatens to emerge into consciousness, and the person "converts" it into physical symptoms, thereby relieving the pressure of having to deal directly with the conflict. This reduction of anxiety is considered to be the primary gain or reinforcing event that maintains the conversion symptom. Fourth, the individual receives greatly increased attention and sympathy from loved ones and may also be allowed to avoid a difficult situation or task. Freud considered such attention or avoidance to be the *secondary gain* or the secondarily reinforcing set of events.

We believe Freud was basically correct on at least three counts and possibly a fourth, although firm evidence supporting any of these ideas is sparse and Freud's views were far more complex than represented here. What seems to happen is that individuals with conversion disorder have experienced a traumatic event or events that must be escaped at all costs (Stone et al., 2009a). This might be combat, where death is imminent, or being exposed to an accident or homicide (as in the case of Ms. A.; Wald et al., 2004). Because simply running away is unacceptable in most

▲ The seizures and trances that may be symptomatic of conversion disorder are also common in some fundamentalist religious groups in North America.

cases, the socially acceptable alternative of getting sick is substituted; but getting sick on purpose is also unacceptable, so this motivation is detached from the person's consciousness. Finally, because the escape behaviour (the conversion symptoms) is successful to an extent in obliterating the traumatic situation, the behaviour continues until the underlying problem is resolved.

One study confirms these hypotheses, at least partially (Wyllie, Glazer, Benbadis, Kotagal, & Wolgamuth, 1999). In this study, 34 child and adolescent patients, 25 of them girls, were evaluated after receiving a diagnosis of psychologically based pseudoseizures (psychogenic non-epileptic seizures). Many of these children and adolescents presented with additional psychological disorders, including 32 percent with mood disorders and 24 percent with separation anxiety and school refusal. Other anxiety disorders were present in some additional patients.

When the extent of psychological stress in the lives of these children was examined, it was found that most of the patients had substantial stress, including a history of sexual abuse, recent parental divorce or death of a close family member, and physical abuse. The authors conclude that major mood disorders and severe environmental stress, especially sexual abuse, are common among children and adolescents with the conversion disorder of pseudoseizures, as have other studies (Roelofs, Keijsers, Hoogduin, Naring, & Moene, 2002).

The one step in Freud's progression of events about which some questions remain is the issue of primary gain. The notion of primary gain accounts for the feature of *la belle indifférence* (cited previously), where individuals seem not the least bit distressed about their symptoms. In other words, Freud thought that because symptoms reflected an unconscious attempt to resolve a conflict, the patient would not be upset by them. But as is illustrated in the case of Ms. A. (Wald et al., 2004), patients with conversion disorder are in fact often quite distressed by their symptoms. (Recall that Ms. A. was so embarrassed by her episodes of speech disruption that she began to avoid social gatherings.) Formal tests of this feature of indifference also provide little support for Freud's claim. For example, Lader and Sartorius (1968) compared patients with conversion disorder with control groups of anxious patients without conversion symptoms. The patients with conversion disorder showed equal or greater anxiety and physiological arousal than the control group. The impression of indifference may be more in the mind of the therapist than true of the patient.

Social and cultural influences also contribute to conversion disorder, which, like somatization disorder, tends to occur in less educated, lower socio-economic groups, in which knowledge about disease and medical illness is not well developed (Kirmayer et al., 2003; Swartz, Blazer, Woodbury, George, & Landerman, 1986). For example, Binzer, Andersen, and Kullgren (1997) noted that 13 percent of their series of 30 patients with motor disabilities due to conversion disorder had attended high school, compared with 67 percent in a control group with motor symptoms due to a physical cause. Prior experience with real physical problems, usually among other family members, tends to influence the later choice of specific conversion symptoms; that is, patients tend to adopt symptoms with which they are familiar (e.g., Brady & Lind, 1961). Furthermore, the incidence of these disorders has decreased over the decades (Kirmayer et al., 2003). The most likely explanation is that current knowledge of the real causes of physical problems by both patients and loved ones eliminates much of the possibility of secondary gain so important in these disorders.

Finally, many conversion symptoms seem to be part of a larger constellation of psychopathology. In some cases, individuals may have a marked biological vulnerability to develop the disorder when under stress, with biological processes like those discussed in the context of somatization disorder. In other cases, exposure to traumatic events may play a large contributing role, as in the case of Ms. A. (Wald et al., 2004). For countless other cases, however, biological contributory factors seem to be less important than the overriding influence of interpersonal factors, such as the actions of Eloise's mother, as we will see. We talk about Eloise's and Ms. A.'s treatments in the next section. There you will see that the extent of these patients' suffering and the successful resolution of their symptoms point primarily to a psychological and social etiology.

Treatment

Although few systematic controlled studies have evaluated the effectiveness of treatment for conversion disorders, we often treat these conditions in our clinics, as do others (e.g., Campo & Negrini, 2000; Rosebush & Mazurek, 2006), and our methods closely follow our thinking on etiology. Because conversion disorder has much in common with somatization disorder, many of the treatment principles are similar.

A principal strategy is to identify and attend to the traumatic or stressful life event, if it is still present (either in real life or in memory), and remove, if possible, sources of secondary gain. Therapeutic assistance in re-experiencing or reliving the event (catharsis) is a reasonable first step. In the case of Ms. A., Wald and colleagues (2004) employed cognitive-behavioural therapy involving imaginal exposure to trauma memories. The frequency of speech disturbance episodes decreased during the treatment until Ms. A. was virtually symptom-free (see Table 6.3). Her distress also declined during the therapy.

The therapist must also work very hard to reduce any reinforcing or supportive consequences of the conversion symptoms (secondary gain). For example, in the case of Eloise, it was quite clear that her mother found it convenient if Eloise stayed pretty much in one place most of the day while her mother attended to the store in the front of the house. Eloise's immobility was thus strongly reinforced by motherly attention and concern. Any unnecessary mobility was punished. The therapist must collaborate with both the patient and the family to eliminate such self-defeating behaviours.

Many times, removing the secondary gain is easier said than done. Eloise was successfully treated in the clinic. Through intensive daily work with the staff, she was able to walk again. To accomplish this she had to practise walking every day with considerable support, attention, and praise from the staff. When her mother visited, the staff noticed that she verbalized her pleasure with Eloise's progress, but her facial expressions or "affect" conveyed a different message. The mother lived a good distance from the clinic, so she could not attend sessions, but she promised to

TABLE 6.3 Session Content and Frequency of Speech Disturbance Outside of Treatment Sessions in Cognitive-Behavioural Treatment with Ms. A.

Session #	CBT Session Content	Homework? (yes/no)	Imaginal Exposure of Speech Episodes	Weekly Frequency Week #
1	1	Assessment	No	—
2	2	IE	No	3.0
3	3	IE + CR	No	2.0
4	4	IE + CR	Yes	2.0
5	5	IE + CR	Yes	4.0
6	6	IE + CR	Yes	6.0
7	7	IE + CR	Yes	3.0
17	8	CR	Yes	0.3
19	9	IE + CR	Yes	3.0
22	10	IE + CR	Yes	0.3
23	11	IE + CR	Yes	1.0
24	12	Check-in	Yes	0.0
25	13	Check-in	No	0.5
28	14	Check-in + brief CR	No	1.5
33	15	Check-in	No	0.6
43	16	Check-in + brief CR	No	0.3
51	17	Check-in	No	0.1
67	18	Check-in	No	0.0

Notes: — = not assessed quantitatively, but several episodes occurred; IE = imaginal exposure; CR = cognitive restructuring. All treatment sessions included a symptom review and (when appropriate), a homework review. Check-in consisted of symptom review and, if needed, homework planning.

Source: Wald, J., Taylor, S., & Scamvougeras, A. (2004). Cognitive-behavioral and neuropsychiatric treatment of a post-traumatic conversion disorder: A case study. *Cognitive Behaviour Therapy, 33,* 12–20, reprinted by permission of the publisher Taylor & Francis Group, http://www.informaworld.com.

Innovative Approaches

Conversion Symptoms and Brain Function: Cause or Effect?

Some conversion symptoms involve movements such as tremors that are perceived as involuntary. But what makes a movement either voluntary or involuntary? In one recent study, neuroscientists attempted to find out (Voon et al., 2010). These investigators assessed eight patients who presented with motor tremors without any neurological basis (conversion tremors). In a clever experiment, they used functional magnetic resonance imaging (fMRI) to compare brain activity during the conversion tremor, but also during a voluntary "mimicked" tremor in which patients were instructed to produce the tremor on purpose. The investigators found that the conversion tremor, as compared with the voluntary tremor, was associated with lower activity in the right inferior parietal cortex. Interestingly, this is an area of the brain that functions to compare internal predictions with actual events. In other words, if an individual wants to move his or her arm and then decides to go ahead and move it, this area of the brain determines if the desired action has occurred. Because we think about making a movement before we do it, the brain concludes (correctly in most cases) that we caused the movement to occur. But if this area of the brain is not functioning properly, then the brain might conclude that the movement is involuntary.

Of course, it is not clear whether this brain activity is a cause or a result of conversion symptoms, but these sophisticated brain-imaging technologies may eventually bring us closer to understanding at least one part of the puzzle of conversion symptoms in some people.

carry out the program at home after Eloise was discharged. She didn't, however. A follow-up contact six months after Eloise was discharged revealed that she had totally relapsed and was once again spending almost all her time in a room in the back of the house while her mother attended to business out front.

Cognitive-behavioural programs appear to hold promise in the treatment of conversion disorder. In one study, 65 percent of a group of 45 patients with mostly motor behaviour conversions (e.g., difficulty walking) responded well to such treatment. Interestingly, hypnosis, which was administered to approximately half of the patients, did not confer any additional benefit to the cognitive-behavioural treatment (Moene, Spinhoven, Hoogduin, & van Dyck, 2002).

Pain Disorder

A related somatoform disorder about which little is known is **pain disorder**. In pain disorder the person may have had clear physical reasons for pain, at least initially, but psychological factors play a major role in maintaining it, particularly anxiety focused on the experience of pain (Asmundson & Carleton, 2009). In the placement of this disorder in the *DSM-IV-TR*, serious consideration was given to removing it entirely from the somatoform disorders and putting it in a separate section, because a person rarely presents with localized pain without some physical basis, such as an accident or illness (see the diagnostic criteria in DSM Table 6.5). Therefore, it was very difficult to separate the cases where the causes were judged to be primarily psychological from the ones where the causes are primarily physical. Because pain disorder fits most closely within the somatoform cluster (an individual presents with physical symptoms judged to have strong psychological contributions), the decision was made to leave pain disorder in the somatoform section. In the *DSM-5*, the proposal is to make this condition part of a larger category called "complex somatic symptom disorder," as described in the beginning of the chapter. But the clinician could still specify complaints of chronic pain (and associated anxiety) as the principal focus. The three subtypes of pain disorder in the *DSM-IV-TR* run the gamut from pain judged to be due primarily to psychological factors to pain judged to be due primarily to a general medical condition. Several

studies suggest that this is a fairly common condition, with 5 percent to 12 percent of the population meeting criteria for pain disorder (Asmundson & Carleton, 2009; Frohlich, Jacobi, & Wittchen, 2006; Grabe et al., 2003).

An important feature of pain disorder is that the pain is real and it hurts, regardless of the causes (Aigner & Bach, 1999; King & Strain, 1991). According to the *DSM-IV-TR* criteria (see DSM Table 6.5), the pain disorder is considered "chronic" when it has persisted for six months or more. This length criterion is not completely arbitrary, as the chances of returning to work decrease substantially after six months' work absence due to back pain (Gervais et al., 1991). Consider the two cases described here.

THE MEDICAL STUDENT | *Temporary Pain*

During her first clinical rotation, a 25-year-old third-year medical student in excellent health was seen at her student health service for intermittent abdominal pain of several weeks' duration. The student claimed no past history of similar pain. Physical examination revealed no physical problems, but she told the physician that she had recently separated from her husband. The student was referred to the health service psychiatrist. No other psychiatric problems were found. She was taught relaxation techniques and given supportive therapy to help her cope with her current stressful situation. The student's pain subsequently disappeared, and she successfully completed medical school.

THE WOMAN WITH CANCER | *Managing Pain*

A 56-year-old woman with metastatic breast cancer who appeared to be coping appropriately with her disease had severe pain in her right thigh for a month. She initially obtained relief from a combination of drugs and subsequently received hypnotherapy and group therapy. These treatment modalities provided additional pain relief and enabled the patient to decrease her narcotic intake with no increase in pain.

The medical student's pain was seen as largely psychological. In the case of the second woman, the pain was probably related to cancer. But we now know that whatever its cause, pain has a strong psychological component (Gagliese & Katz, 2000; Melzack & Katz, 2004). Therefore, deciding whether a person experiencing pain qualifies for a somatoform pain disorder diagnosis can be quite difficult. Some research evidence suggests that looking at the way that the pain is described by the patient can be beneficial in making decisions about whether or not a somatoform pain disorder is present. A study by a Swiss research team showed that, when patients described their symptoms, those with predominantly physically based pain differed in several ways from those whose pain presumably stemmed from psychological factors. Those with predominantly physically based pain more often described a clear localization of the pain, used more sensory

DSM-IV-TR	**Table 6.5** Criteria for Pain Disorders

A. Pain in one or more anatomical sites is the predominant focus of the clinical presentation and is of sufficient severity to warrant clinical attention.

B. The pain causes clinically significant distress or impairment in social, occupational, or other important areas of functioning.

C. Psychological factors are judged to have an important role in the onset, severity, exacerbation, or maintenance of the pain.

D. The symptom or deficit is not intentionally produced or feigned (as in factitious disorder or malingering).

E. The pain is not better accounted for by a mood, anxiety, or psychotic disorder and does not meet criteria for dyspareunia.

Specify if:

Acute (duration of less than six months)

Chronic (duration of six months or more)

Source: Reprinted with permission from the *Diagnostic and Statistical Manual of Mental Disorders,* Fourth Edition, Text Revision, (Copyright © 2000). American Psychiatric Association.

words to describe the quality of their pain, and were better able to link their pain to situations that could increase or decrease it (Adler, Zamboni, Hofer, & Hemmeler, 1997).

If medical treatments for existing physical conditions are in place and pain remains, or if the pain seems clearly related to psychological factors, psychological interventions are appropriate. Because of the complexity of pain itself and the variety of narcotics and other medications prescribed for it, multidisciplinary pain clinics are part of most large hospitals (see Sullivan, 2003). (In Chapter 9, we discuss health psychology and the contribution of psychological factors to physical disorders, and we delve more deeply into types of pain disorders, their causes, and treatment.)

Body Dysmorphic Disorder

Have you ever wished you could change part of your appearance? Maybe the size of your nose or the way your ears stick out? Most people fantasize about improving something, but some relatively normal-looking people imagine they are so ugly they are unable to interact with others or otherwise function normally for fear that people will laugh at their ugliness. This curious affliction is called **body dysmorphic disorder (BDD)**, and at its centre is a preoccupation with some imagined defect in appearance by someone who actually looks reasonably normal, or even in someone whose appearance is judged by others as very attractive. In fact, actress Uma Thurman, who is well known for her striking Scandinavian features, has admitted that she has BDD (Kahn, 2001). Thus, this disorder has been referred to as "imagined ugliness" (Phillips, 1991). Consider the case of Jim.

JIM | Ashamed to Be Seen

In his mid-20s, Jim was diagnosed with suspected social phobia; he was referred to our clinic by another professional. Jim had just finished rabbinical school and had been offered a position at a synagogue in a nearby city. However, he found himself unable to accept because of marked social difficulties. Lately he had given up leaving his small apartment for fear of running into people he knew and being forced to stop and interact with them.

Jim was a good-looking young man of about average height, with dark hair and eyes. Although he was somewhat depressed, a mental status exam and a brief interview focusing on current functioning and past history did not reveal any remarkable problems. He had no sign of a psychotic process (he was not out of touch with reality). We then focused on Jim's social difficulties. We expected the usual kinds of anxiety about interacting with people or "doing something" (performing) in front of them. But this was not Jim's concern. Rather, he was convinced that everyone, even his good friends, were staring at a part of his body that he himself found absolutely grotesque. He reported that strangers would never mention his deformity and his friends felt too sorry for him to mention it. Jim thought his head was square! Like the Beast in Beauty and the Beast who could not

imagine people reacting to him with anything less than abhorrence, Jim could not imagine people getting past the fact that his head was square. Jim would frequently glance in the mirror or in windows to check this imagined defect in the shape of his head. To hide his condition as well as he could, Jim wore soft floppy hats and was most comfortable in winter, when he could all but completely cover his head with a large stocking cap. To us, Jim looked perfectly normal.

Clinical Description

To give you a better idea of the types of concerns people with body dysmorphic disorder present to health professionals, the locations of imagined defects in 30 patients are shown in Table 6.4. In another series of 23 adolescents with BDD, 61 percent focused on their skin and 55 percent on their hair (Albertini & Phillips, 1999). Many people with this disorder become fixated on mirrors (Veale & Riley, 2001). As illustrated in the case of Jim, they frequently check their presumed ugly feature to see if any change has taken place. Others avoid mirrors to an almost phobic extent. Quite understandably, suicidal ideation, suicide attempts, and suicide itself are frequent consequences of this disorder (Phillips, 1991; Zimmerman & Mattia, 1998). People with BDD also have "ideas of reference," which means they think everything that goes on in their world somehow is related to them—in this case, to their imagined defect. This disorder can cause considerable disruption in the patient's life. Many patients with severe cases become housebound for fear of showing themselves to other people.

If this disorder seems strange to you, you are not alone. For decades, this condition, previously known as *dysmorphophobia* (literally, fear of ugliness), was thought to represent a psychotic delusional state because the affected individuals were unable to realize, even for a fleeting moment, that their ideas were irrational. Whether this is true is still debated.

In the context of obsessive-compulsive disorder (OCD; see Chapter 5), a similar issue arose as to whether patients really *believe* in their obsessions or realize they are irrational. A minority (10 percent or less) of people with OCD believe their fears about contaminating others or need to prevent catastrophes with their rituals are perfectly realistic and reasonable. This brings up the very major issue of what is "delusional" and what isn't, which is even more important in BDD (see DSM Table 6.6).

For example, in the 30 cases examined by Phillips et al. (1993) and in 50 cases reported by Veale and colleagues (1996), about half the subjects were absolutely convinced their imagined bodily defect was real and a reasonable source of concern. Is this delusional? The *DSM-IV* task force wrestled long and hard with this issue and decided that individuals with BDD whose beliefs are so firmly held that they could be called delusional should receive a second diagnosis of delusional disorder, somatic type (see Chapter 13) in addition to BDD. Phillips, Menard, Pagano, Fay, and Stout (2006) looked closely at differences that may exist between delusional and nondelusional types and found nothing significant, beyond the fact that the delusional type was more severe and found in less

TABLE 6.4 Location of Imagined Defects in 30* Patients with Body Dysmorphic Disorder

Location	N	%
Hair†	19	63
Nose	15	50
Skin‡	15	50
Eyes	8	27
Head/face§	6	20
Overall body build/bone structure	6	20
Lips	5	17
Chin	5	17
Stomach/waist	5	17
Teeth	4	13
Legs/knees	4	13
Breasts/pectoral muscles	3	10
Ugly face (general)	3	10
Ears	2	7
Cheeks	2	7
Buttocks	2	7
Penis	2	7
Arms/wrists	2	7
Neck	1	3
Forehead	1	3
Facial muscles	1	3
Shoulders	1	3
Hips	1	3

Note: * Total is greater than 100 percent because most patients had "defects" in more than one location.

† Involved head hair in 15 cases, beard growth in two cases, and other body hair in three cases.

‡ Involved acne in seven cases, facial lines in three cases, and other skin concerns in seven cases.

§ Involved concerns with shape in five cases and size in one case.

Source: The American Journal of Psychiatry by American Psychiatric Association. Copyright 1993. Reproduced with permission of AMERICAN PSYCHIATRIC ASSOCIATION (JOURNALS) in the format Textbook via Copyright Clearance Center.

DSM-IV-TR	**Table 6.6** Criteria for Body Dysmorphic Disorder

A. Preoccupation with an imagined defect in appearance. If a slight physical anomaly is present, the person's concern is markedly excessive.

B. The preoccupation causes significant distress or impairment in social, occupational, or other important areas of functioning.

C. The preoccupation is not better accounted for by another mental disorder (e.g., dissatisfaction with body shape and size in anorexia nervosa).

Source: Reprinted with permission from the *Diagnostic and Statistical Manual of Mental Disorders,* Fourth Edition, Text Revision, (Copyright © 2000). American Psychiatric Association.

educated patients. Other studies have supported this lack of meaningful differences between these two groups (Mancuso, Knoesen, & Castle, in press; Phillips et al., 2010). It is also the case that these two groups both respond equally well to treatments for BDD and that the "delusional" group does not respond to drug treatments for psychotic disorders (Phillips et al., 2010). Thus, in the *DSM-5,* the proposal is that patients would receive just a BDD diagnosis, whether they are "delusional" or not, and the practice of giving them a second diagnosis of delusional disorder (a psychotic disorder) should be dropped (Phillips et al., 2010).

Statistics

The prevalence of BDD is hard to estimate because by its very nature it tends to be kept secret. However, the best estimates are that it is far more common than we had previously thought and that without some sort of treatment it tends to run a lifelong course (Phillips, 1991; Veale et al., 1996). One patient with BDD reported in Phillips et al. (1993) had endured her condition for 71 years, since the age of 9. If you think a university friend seems to have at least a mild version of BDD, you're probably correct. One study suggested that as many as 70 percent of university students report at least some dissatisfaction with their bodies; 28 percent of these appear to meet all the criteria for the disorder (Fitts, Gibson, Redding, & Deiter, 1989). However, this study was done by questionnaire and may well have reflected the large percentage of students who are concerned simply with weight.

Another study investigated the prevalence of BDD specifically in an ethnically diverse sample of 566 adolescents between the ages of 14 and 19. The overall prevalence of BDD in this group was 2.2 percent, with adolescent girls more dissatisfied than boys with their bodies, and blacks of both genders more satisfied with their bodies than Caucasians, Asians, and Hispanics (Mayville, Katz, Gipson, & Cabral, 1999).

BDD is not strongly associated with one sex or the other. According to published reports, slightly more females than males are affected in North America, but 62 percent of a large number of individuals with BDD in Japan were males. As you might suspect, very few people with this disorder get married. Age of onset ranges from early adolescence through the 20s, peaking at the age of 18 or 19 (Phillips et al., 1993; Veale et al., 1996; Zimmerman & Mattia, 1998). Individuals are somewhat reluctant to seek treatment. In many cases a relative will force the issue, demanding the individual get help; this insistence may reflect the disruptiveness of the disorder for family members. Severity is also reflected in the high percentage (24 percent) of past suicide attempts among the 50 cases described by Veale et al. (1996); 29 percent of the 30 cases described by Phillips et al. (1993); and 21 percent of a group of 33 adolescents (Albertini & Phillips, 1999).

One study of 62 outpatients with BDD found that the degree of psychological stress and impairment was generally worse than comparable indices in patients with depression, diabetes, or a recent myocardial infarction (heart attack), on several questionnaire measures (Phillips, 2000). Thus, BDD is among the more serious of psychological disorders. Further reflecting the intense suffering that accompanies this disorder, Veale (2000) collected information on

Doug, an Example of Body Dysmorphic Disorder

"I didn't want to talk to anybody. . . . I was afraid because what I saw on my face . . . they saw. . . . If I could see it, they could see it. And I thought there was like an arrow pointing at it. And I was very self-conscious. And I felt like the only time I felt comfortable was at night, because it was dark time."

Go to Psychology CourseMate at www.cengagebrain.nelson.com to watch this video.

25 patients with BDD who had sought cosmetic surgery in the past. Nine patients who could not afford surgery, or were turned down for other reasons, had attempted by their own hand to alter their appearance dramatically, often with tragic results. One example was a man preoccupied by his skin, which he believed was too "loose." He used a staple gun on both sides of his face to try to keep his skin taut. The staples fell out after ten minutes and he narrowly missed damaging his facial nerve. In a second example, a woman was preoccupied by her skin and the shape of her face. She filed down her teeth in order to alter the appearance of her jaw line. Yet another woman who was preoccupied by what she perceived as the ugliness of multiple areas of her body and desired liposuction, but could not afford it, used a knife to cut her thighs and attempted to squeeze out the fat. BDD is also stubbornly chronic. In a recent prospective study of 183 patients, only 21 percent were somewhat improved over the course of a year, and 15 percent of that group relapsed during that year (Phillips, Pagano, Menard, & Stout, 2006).

Individuals with BDD react to what they think is a horrible or grotesque feature. Thus, the psychopathology lies in their reacting to a deformity that others cannot perceive. Of course, social and cultural determinants of beauty and body image define, in large part, what is "deformed." Nowhere is this more evident than in the greatly varying cultural standards for body weight and shape, factors that play a major role in eating disorders, as we see in Chapter 8.

For example, in most cultures it is desirable for a woman's skin to be lighter and more perfectly smooth than a man's skin (Fallon, 1990; Liggett, 1974). Over the centuries freckles have not been popular, and in many cultures chemical solutions were used to remove them. Unfortunately, whole layers of skin disappeared and the underlying flesh was severely damaged (Liggett, 1974). Concerns with the width of the face, so common in BDD, can also be culturally determined. Until very recently, in some areas of France, Africa, Greenland, and Peru, the head of a newborn infant was reshaped, either by hand or by very tight caps secured by strings. Sometimes the face was elongated; other times it was widened. Similarly, attempts were made to flatten the noses of newborn infants, usually by hand (Fallon, 1990; Liggett, 1974). In Burma, women wear brass neck rings from an early age to lengthen the neck. One woman's neck was nearly 40 centimetres long (Morris, 1985).

Finally, many are aware of the old practice in China of binding girls' feet, often preventing the foot from growing to more than one-third of its normal size. Women's bound feet forced them to walk in

a way that was thought very seductive. As Brownmiller (1984) points out, the myth that an unnaturally small foot signifies extraordinary beauty and grace is still with us. Can you think of the fairy tale where a small foot becomes the identifying feature of the beautiful heroine?

What can we learn about BDD from such practices of mutilation around the world? The behaviour of individuals with BDD seems remarkably strange, because they go against current cultural practices that put less emphasis on altering facial features. In other words, people who simply conform to the expectations of their culture do not have a disorder (as noted in Chapter 1). Nevertheless, aesthetic plastic surgery, particularly for the nose and lips, is still widely accepted and, because it is most often undertaken by the wealthy, carries an aura of elevated status. In this light, BDD may not be so strange. As with most psychopathology, its characteristic attitudes and behaviour may simply be an exaggeration of normal culturally sanctioned behaviour.

Causes and Treatment

We know very little about either the etiology or the treatment of BDD. We have almost no information on whether it runs in families, and so we can't investigate a specific genetic contribution. Similarly, we do not have any meaningful information on biological

▲ In various cultures a child's head or face is manipulated to produce desirable features, as in the addition of rings to lengthen the neck of this Burmese girl.

or psychological predisposing factors or vulnerabilities. Of course, psychoanalytic speculations are numerous, but most centre on the defensive mechanism of displacement—that is, an underlying unconscious conflict would be too anxiety provoking to admit into consciousness, so the person displaces it onto a body part.

One interesting lead on causes of BDD comes from cross-cultural explorations of similar disorders. You may remember the Japanese variant of social phobia, *taijin kyofusho* (see Chapter 5), in which individuals may believe they have horrendous bad breath or body odour and thus avoid social interaction. But people with *taijin kyofusho* also have all the other characteristics of social phobia. In fact, patients who would be diagnosed with BDD in our culture might simply be considered to have severe social phobia in Japan and Korea. Possibly, then, social anxiety is fundamentally related to BDD, a connection that would give us further hints on the nature of the disorder.

Another approach to the study of etiology of BDD comes from studying the pattern of comorbidity of BDD with other disorders. BDD is a somatoform disorder because its central feature is a psychological preoccupation with somatic issues. For example, in hypochondriasis the focus is on physical sensations, and in BDD the focus is on physical appearance. We have already seen that many of the somatoform disorders tend to co-occur. Linda presented with somatization disorder but also had a history of conversion disorder. However, BDD does not tend to co-occur with the other somatoform disorders, nor does it occur in family members of patients with other somatoform disorders.

A disorder that does frequently co-occur with BDD and is also found among other family members is OCD (Chosak et al., 2008; Gustad & Phillips, 2003; Phillips et al., 2010; Phillips & Stout, 2006; Tynes, White, & Steketee, 1990; Zimmerman & Mattia, 1998). Is BDD a variant of OCD? They certainly have a lot of similarities (Yeh, Taylor, Thordarson, & Corcoran, 2003), and a major proposal for the *DSM-5* is to include BDD with the anxiety disorders, perhaps as a variant of OCD (Phillips et al., 2010). People with BDD complain of persistent, intrusive, and horrible thoughts about their appearance, and they engage in such compulsive behaviours as repeatedly looking in mirrors to check their physical features. BDD and OCD also have, approximately, the same age of onset and run the same course. One recent brain-imaging study demonstrated similar abnormal brain functioning between patients with BDD and patients with OCD. Perhaps most significantly, the two disorders appear to respond to similar treatments (Rauch et al., 2003).

First, drugs that block the reuptake of serotonin, such as clomipramine (Anafranil) and fluvoxamine (Luvox), provide relief to at least some people with BDD (Hadley, Kim, Priday, & Hollander, 2006). The first controlled study of the effects of drugs on BDD demonstrated that clomipramine was significantly more effective than desipramine, a drug that does not specifically block reuptake of serotonin, for the treatment of BDD, even BDD of the delusional type (Hollander et al., 1999). These are the same drugs that have the strongest effect in OCD. Second, exposure and response prevention, the type of behavioural therapy effective with OCD, has also been successful with BDD (McKay et al., 1997; Rosen, Reiter, & Orosan, 1995; Veale, Gourney, et al., 1996; Wilhelm, Otto, Lohr, & Deckersbach, 1999). In the Rosen et al. (1995) study, 82 percent of patients treated with this approach responded,

although these patients may have had somewhat less severe disorders than other series did (Wilhelm et al., 1999).

Jaime Williams, Thomas Hadjistavropoulos, and Donald Sharpe (2006), at the University of Regina, recently completed a meta-analysis on the relative effectiveness of psychological and pharmacological treatment approaches for BDD. They included studies that were either randomized controlled clinical trials (RCT; a design using both control groups and randomization as described in Chapter 4), cross-over designs (a design where each patient receives the medication and then is "crossed over" to placebo, or vice versa), or case series studies (single case experimental design repeated across a series of patients; see Chapter 4). Comparisons were between psychological (i.e., behavioural, cognitive-behavioural, or cognitive) and medication (i.e., antidepressant) therapies. Their findings supported the effectiveness of both types of therapy in reducing the severity of BDD symptoms. However, the effect sizes across studies suggest that cognitive-behavioural treatment (i.e., a combination of exposure and response prevention and cognitive restructuring) may be the most useful approach for treating BDD (see Table 6.5).

Plastic Surgery Because the concerns of people with BDD involve mostly the face or head, it is not surprising that the disorder is big business for the plastic surgery profession—but it's bad business. These patients do not benefit from surgery and may return for additional surgery or, on occasion, file malpractice lawsuits. Even worse, a study found that the preoccupation with imagined ugliness actually increased in people who had plastic surgery, dental work, or special skin treatments for their perceived problems (Phillips et al., 1993). Investigators estimate that as many as 8 percent to 25 percent of all patients who request plastic surgery may have BDD (Barnard, 2000; Crerand et al., 2004).

The most common procedures are rhinoplasties (nose jobs), facelifts, eyebrow elevations, liposuction, breast augmentation, and surgery to alter the jaw line. Surgeries of these types are increasing rapidly. Between 2000 and 2009, according to the American Society of Plastic Surgeons, the total number of cosmetic procedures increased 69 percent.

▲ Michael Jackson as a child and as an adult. Many people alter their features through surgery. However, people with body dysmorphic disorder are seldom satisfied with the results.

Somatoform Disorders **199**

TABLE 6.5 Meta-Analysis of Effectiveness of Various Treatment Approaches for Body Dysmorphic Disorder

Study	Design	N	Treatment Type	Effect Sizes*
Campisi (1995)	Case series	4	Behavioural	1.01–1.30
Geremia & Neziroglu (2001)	Case series	4	Cognitive	1.36–1.56
Gomez-Perez et al. (1994)	Case series	30	Behavioural	0.56–1.36
Khemlani-Patel (2001)	Case series	5	Cognitive-behavioural	1.18–1.69
Khemlani-Patel (2001)	Case series	5	Behavioural	0.99–1.29
Hollander et al. (1999)	Crossover trial	29	Medication**	0.56–0.92
McKay et al. (1997)	Case series	10	Behavioural	1.58
Neziroglu et al. (1996)	Case series	17	Cognitive-behavioural	1.48
Perugi et al. (1996)	Case series	15	Medication	0.66
Phillips et al. (1998/2001)	Case series	30	Medication	1.50
Phillips et al. (2002)	RCT***	67	Medication	0.53–0.98
Phillips & Najjar (2003)	Case series	15	Medication	1.76
Rosen et al. (1995)	RCT	54	Cognitive-behavioural	2.18
Veale et al. (1996)	RCT	19	Cognitive-behavioural	1.81–2.65
Wilhelm et al. (1999)	Case series	10	Cognitive-behavioural	1.13

Notes:

* Effect size refers to the magnitude of the treatment effect, with values greater than 0.80 representing a large effect of treatment, and values between 0.50 and 0.80 representing a moderate effect of treatment (Cohen, 1992).

** Medication refers to treatment with antidepressants (either a tricyclic antidepressant or a selective serotonin reuptake inhibitor).

*** RCT, randomized controlled trial.

Source: Williams, J., Hadjistavropoulos, T., & Sharpe, D. (2006). "A meta-analysis of psychological and pharmacological treatments for body dysmorphic disorder." *Behaviour Research and Therapy, 44*, 99–111.

The problem is that surgery for people with BDD seldom produces the desired results. These individuals return for additional surgery on the same defect or concentrate on some new defect. Hollander, Liebowitz, Winchel, Klumker, and Klein (1989) describe one patient who had four separate rhinoplasties and then became concerned about his thinning hair and sloped shoulders. Phillips et al. (1993) report that of 25 surgical or dental procedures, only two gave relief. In more than 20 cases, the severity of the disorder and accompanying distress actually increased after surgery. Clinical psychologists Randi McCabe and Martin Antony have recommended that assessments of body dysmorphic disorder symptoms routinely be made and that surgery outcomes, including quality of life assessments, be monitored in a standardized manner in the plastic surgery context (Ching, Thoma, McCabe, & Antony, 2003).

Dissociative Disorders

At the beginning of the chapter we said that when individuals feel detached from themselves or their surroundings, almost as if they are dreaming or living in slow motion, they are having dissociative experiences. Morton Prince, founder of the *Journal of Abnormal Psychology*, noted more than a century ago that many people experience something like dissociation occasionally (Prince, 1906–1907). It is most likely to happen after an extremely stressful event, such as an accident. It might also happen when you're very tired or under physical or mental pressure from, say, staying up all night cramming for an exam (Giesbrecht, Smeets, Leppink, Jelicic, & Merckelbach, 2007). Perhaps because you knew the cause, the dissociation may not have bothered you much (Dixon, 1963; Noyes, Hoenk, Kuperman, & Slymen, 1977). On the other hand, it may have been extremely frightening.

These kinds of experiences can be divided into two types. During an episode of depersonalization, your perception alters so that you temporarily lose the sense of your own reality. During an episode of **derealization**, your sense of the reality of the external world is lost. Things may seem to change shape or size; people may seem dead or mechanical. Symptoms of unreality are characteristic of the dissociative disorders because depersonalization is, in a sense, a psychological mechanism whereby one "dissociates" from reality. Depersonalization is often part of a serious set of conditions where reality, experience, and even our own identity seem to disintegrate. As we go about our daily lives, we ordinarily have an excellent sense of who we are and a general knowledge of the identity of other people. We are also aware of events around us, of where we are, and of why we are there. Finally, except for occasional small lapses, our memories remain intact so that events leading up to the current moment are clear in our minds.

But what happens if we can't remember why we are in a certain place or even who we are? What happens if we lose our sense that our surroundings are real? Finally, what happens if we not only forget who we are but also begin to think we are somebody else—somebody who has a different personality, different memories, and even different physical reactions, such as allergies, that we never had? These are examples of disintegrated experience (Cardeña & Gleaves, 2003; Putnam, 1991). In each case, there are alterations in our relationship to the self, to the world, or to our memory processes.

Although we have much to learn about these disorders, we briefly describe four of them—depersonalization disorder, dissociative amnesia, dissociative fugue, and dissociative trance disorder—before examining the fascinating condition of dissociative identity disorder. As you will see, the influence of social and cultural factors is strong in dissociative disorders. Even in severe cases, the expression of the pathology does not stray far from socially and culturally sanctioned forms (Giesbrecht, Lynn, Lilienfeld, & Merckelbach, 2008; Kihlstrom, 2005).

Depersonalization Disorder

When feelings of unreality are so severe and frightening that they dominate an individual's life and prevent normal functioning, clinicians may diagnose the very rare **depersonalization disorder**. In this disorder, the individual has repeated experiences of feeling detached from his or her own thoughts or body. The person may feel as if he or she is an outside observer of his or her own body or thoughts—for example, feeling as if he or she is dreaming. But unlike someone experiencing psychosis (see Chapter 13), the person experiencing episodes of depersonalization remains in good contact with reality—the person knows, for example, that he or she is not really an outside observer of his or her own body. As you can see, trying to describe the uncomfortable feeling of depersonalization can be very difficult to convey in words.

A 40-year-old woman with periods of depersonalization treated by Ottawa psychiatrist George Fraser described the experience as follows:

> Very often, I feel that I can't make contact with people, as if we are existing in different dimensions. I think they hear me speaking, but are puzzled about what I'm saying and, as I talk, I feel a gap between my intentions and my voice, as if my thoughts were a high slow-moving gear and way out the top of my consciousness is a little tiny gear going at top speed, which is my voice and I can't feel the connection. Sometimes I feel like I don't overlap with people. (Fraser, 1994, p. 142)

Consider next the case of Bonnie.

BONNIE | *Dancing away from Herself*

Bonnie, a dance teacher in her late 20s, was accompanied by her husband when she first visited the clinic and complained of "flipping out." When asked what she meant, she said,

> It's the most scary thing in the world. It often happens when I'm teaching my modern dance class. I'll be up in front and I will feel focused on. Then, as I'm demonstrating the steps, I just feel like it's not really me and that I don't really have

control of my legs. Sometimes I feel like I'm standing in back of myself just watching. Also I get tunnel vision. It seems like I can only see in a narrow space right in front of me and I just get totally separated from what's going on around me. Then I begin to panic and perspire and shake.

It turns out that Bonnie's problems began after she smoked marijuana for the first time about ten years before. She had the same feeling then and found it very scary, but with the help of friends she got through it. Lately the feeling recurred more frequently and more severely, particularly when she was teaching dance class.

You may remember from Chapter 5 that during an intense panic attack many people (approximately 50 percent) experience feelings of unreality. People undergoing intense stress or experiencing a traumatic event may also experience these symptoms, which, in fact, characterize the newly defined acute stress disorder. Feelings of depersonalization and derealization are part of several different disorders (Boon & Draijer, 1991). But when severe depersonalization and derealization are the primary problem, the individual meets the criteria for depersonalization disorder (Steinberg, 1991; see DSM Table 6.7).

Montréal researchers Jean Charbonneau and Kieron O'Connor (1999) interviewed 20 individuals who were self-referred from the general population as experiencing depersonalization. They found that in the majority of cases, onset occurred following a traumatic life event, after sexual abuse, or after giving birth. Simeon et al. (1997) described 30 cases of depersonalization disorder, 19 women and 11 men. Mean age of onset was 16.1 years and the course tended to be chronic, lasting an average of 15.7 years so far in those cases. All the patients were substantially impaired. Although none had any additional dissociative disorders, more than 50 percent had additional mood and anxiety disorders.

Guralnick, Schmeidler, and Simeon (2000) compared 15 patients with depersonalization disorder to 15 matched comparison subjects without the disorder on a comprehensive neuropsychological test battery that assessed cognitive function.

DSM-IV-TR	**Table 6.7** Criteria for Depersonalization Disorder

A. Persistent or recurrent experiences of feeling detached from, and as if an outside observer of, our own mental processes or body (e.g., feeling as if in a dream).

B. During the depersonalization experience, reality testing remains intact.

C. The depersonalization causes clinically significant distress or impairment in social, occupational, or other important areas of functioning.

D. The depersonalization experience does not occur exclusively during the course of another mental disorder, such as schizophrenia, panic disorder, acute stress disorder, or another dissociative disorder, and is not due to the direct physiological effects of a substance (e.g., a drug of abuse, a medication) or a general medical condition (e.g., temporal lobe epilepsy).

Source: Reprinted with permission from the *Diagnostic and Statistical Manual of Mental Disorders,* Fourth Edition, Text Revision, (Copyright © 2000). American Psychiatric Association.

Although both groups were of equal intelligence, the subjects with depersonalization disorder showed a distinct cognitive profile, reflecting some specific cognitive deficits on measures of attention, short-term memory, and spatial reasoning. Basically, these patients were easily distracted and had some trouble perceiving three-dimensional objects because they tended to "flatten" these objects into two dimensions. It is not clear how these cognitive and perceptual deficits develop, but they seem to correspond with reports of "tunnel vision" (perceptual distortions) and "mind emptiness" (difficulty absorbing new information) that characterize these patients.

Specific aspects of brain functioning are also associated with depersonalization (see e.g., Sierra & Berrios, 1998; Simeon, 2009; Simeon et al., 2000). Sierra and colleagues (2002) compared skin conductance responding, a psychophysiological measure of emotional responding, among 15 patients with depersonalization disorder, 11 patients with anxiety disorders, and 15 control participants without any disorder. Patients with depersonalization disorder showed greatly reduced emotional responding compared to other groups, reflecting a tendency to selectively inhibit emotional expression. Brain-imaging studies now confirm deficits in perception (Simeon, 2009; Simeon et al., 2000) and emotion regulation (Phillips et al., 2001). Other studies note dysregulation in the hypothalamic-pituitary-adrenocortical (HPA) axis among these patients, compared to normal controls (Simeon, Guralnik, Knutelska, Hollander, & Schmeidler, 2001), suggesting, again, deficits in emotional responding. Psychological treatments have not been systematically studied. A recent evaluation of the drug Prozac did not show any treatment effect compared to placebo (Simeon, Guralnik, Schneider, & Knutelska, 2004).

Dissociative Amnesia

Perhaps the easiest to understand of the severe dissociative disorders is one called **dissociative amnesia**, which includes several different patterns. People who are unable to remember anything, including who they are, are said to have **generalized amnesia**. Generalized amnesia may be lifelong or may extend from a period in the more recent past, such as six months or a year previously (see DSM Table 6.8 for the criteria for dissociative amnesia).

DSM-IV-TR	**Table 6.8** Criteria for Dissociative Amnesia

A. The predominant disturbance is one or more episodes of inability to recall important personal information, usually of a traumatic or stressful nature, that is too extensive to be explained by ordinary forgetfulness.

B. The disturbance does not occur exclusively during the course of dissociative identity disorder, dissociative fugue, post-traumatic stress disorder, acute stress disorder, or somatization disorder and is not due to the direct physiological effects of a substance (e.g., a drug of abuse, a medication) or a neurological or other general medical condition (e.g., amnesic disorder due to head trauma).

C. The symptoms cause clinically significant distress or impairment in social, occupational, or other important areas of functioning.

Source: Reprinted with permission from the *Diagnostic and Statistical Manual of Mental Disorders,* Fourth Edition, Text Revision, (Copyright © 2000). American Psychiatric Association.

THE WOMAN WHO LOST HER MEMORY

Several years ago a woman in her early 50s brought her daughter to one of our clinics because of the girl's refusal to attend school and other severely disruptive behaviour. The father, who refused to come to the session, was very quarrelsome, a heavy drinker, and, on occasion, abusive. The girl's brother, now in his mid-20s, lived at home and was a burden on the family. Several times a week a major battle erupted, complete with shouting, pushing, and shoving, as each member of the family blamed the others for all their problems. The mother, a very strong woman, was clearly the peacemaker responsible for holding the family together. Approximately every six months, usually after a family battle, the mother totally lost her memory and the family had her admitted to the hospital. After a few days away from the turmoil, the mother regained her memory and went home, only to repeat the cycle in the coming months. Although we did not treat this family (they lived too far away), the situation resolved itself when the children moved away and the stress decreased.

Far more common than general amnesia is **localized** or **selective amnesia**, a failure to recall specific events, usually traumatic, that occur during a specific period (Fraser, 1994). In fact, dissociative amnesia is very common during war (Cardena & Gleaves, 2003; Loewenstein, 1991). Sackeim and Devanand (1991) describe the interesting case of a woman whose father had deserted her when she was very young. She had also been forced to have an abortion at age 14. Years later, she came for treatment for frequent headaches. In therapy she reported early events (e.g., the abortion) rather matter-of-factly; but under hypnosis she would relive, with intense emotion, the early abortion and remember the fact that subsequently she was raped by the abortionist. She also had images of her father attending a funeral for her aunt, one of the few times she ever saw him. Upon awakening from the hypnotic state, she had no memory whatsoever of emotionally re-experiencing these events, and she wondered why she had been crying. In this case the woman did not have amnesia for the events themselves but rather for her intense emotional reactions to the events. In most cases of dissociative amnesia, the forgetting is very selective for traumatic events or memories rather than generalized.

A possible case of dissociative amnesia that has arisen in the Canadian legal system is the first-degree murder trial of Kenneth Mackay in Saskatoon (CBC Saskatchewan, 2003). Mackay was charged with killing Crystal Paskemin in 2000. Although Mackay admitted to having run over the victim with his truck, which he claims was an accident, he cannot explain why the victim's body was found burned. His defence lawyer claimed that Mackay had forgotten about burning the victim's body because of the trauma of the accident. In fact, a memory expert testified in court that Mackay may have had dissociative amnesia (CBC Saskatchewan, 2003). Despite the expert witness testimony, the jury rejected his defence, and Mackay was sentenced to life in prison with no possibility of parole for 25 years (O'Hara, 2004).

DSM-IV-TR	**Table 6.9** Criteria for Dissociative Fugue

A. The predominant disturbance is sudden, unexpected travel away from home or the customary place of work, with inability to recall the past.

B. Confusion about personal identity or assumption of new identity (partial or complete).

C. The disturbance does not occur exclusively during the course of dissociative identity disorder and is not due to the direct physiological effects of a substance (e.g., a drug of abuse, a medication) or a general medical condition (e.g., temporal lobe epilepsy).

D. The symptoms cause clinically significant distress or impairment in social, occupational, or other important areas of functioning.

Source: Reprinted with permission from the *Diagnostic and Statistical Manual of Mental Disorders,* Fourth Edition, Text Revision, (Copyright © 2000). American Psychiatric Association.

Dissociative Fugue

A closely related disorder that will almost certainly become a subtype of dissociative amnesia in *DSM-5* (APA, 2010; Ross, 2009) is referred to as **dissociative fugue**, with *fugue* literally meaning "flight" (*fugitive* is from the same root). In these curious cases, memory loss revolves around a specific incident—an unexpected trip (or trips). Mostly, individuals simply leave and later find themselves in a new place, unable to remember why or how they got there. Usually, they have left behind an intolerable situation (see DSM Table 6.9 for the diagnostic criteria for dissociative fugue).

In the 1920s, renowned British author Agatha Christie disappeared from her home one evening after she was to have gone out for a drive. Her car was found abandoned the next day. Mrs. Christie returned home several days later. Memory loss caused by the stresses of her mother's recent death and her husband's extramarital affair were said to have been the causes of her 11-day disappearance (Phillip, 2003).

During these trips a person sometimes assumes a new identity or at least becomes confused about the old identity. Like Agatha Christie, Alderwoman Darlene (Dar) Heatherington from Lethbridge, Alberta, vanished while on business in Great Falls, Montana, in May 2003. She went missing after renting a bicycle for a ride in the park, and Great Falls launched a large-scale search for her. Three days later she was found disoriented in a Las Vegas hotel parking lot (CTV.ca, 2003). Although the circumstances surrounding Dar Heatherington's trip to Las Vegas remain unclear, her story bears some striking similarities to

▲ Famous British mystery writer Agatha Christie once disappeared from her home for 11 days. Her memory loss and flight from home were reportedly triggered by the stresses of the recent death of her mother and knowledge of her husband's extramarital affair.

the disappearance of Agatha Christie (Philip, 2003). For example, before her disappearance, Ms. Heatherington was also stressed because of overwork and reportedly being stalked through letters and e-mail and by a prowler in her backyard (c-News, 2003; Harrington, 2003). She was mandated to receive psychotherapy by the Montana court. Might Agatha Christie or Dar Heatherington have experienced a dissociative fugue?

Later evidence emerged in the Heatherington case that made the possibility of a dissociative fugue appear unlikely. Specifically, although Ms. Heatherington initially claimed that she had been drugged, kidnapped, and sexually assaulted in explaining her sudden disappearance to Las Vegas, she later admitted to having made up this story. Taken together, these facts suggest that Dar Heatherington likely did not experience a dissociative fugue, although Agatha Christie may have. Consider next the clinical case of the misbehaving sheriff.

THE MISBEHAVING SHERIFF

Aktar and Brenner (1979) describe a 46-year-old sheriff who reported at least three episodes of dissociative fugue. On each occasion he found himself as far as 320 kilometres from his home. When he came to, he immediately called his wife, but he was never able to completely recall what he did while he was away, sometimes for several days. During treatment the sheriff remembered who he was during these trips. Despite his occupation, he became the outlaw type he had always secretly admired. He adopted an alias, drank heavily, mingled with a rough crowd, and went to brothels and wild parties.

Dissociative amnesia and fugue states usually do not appear before adolescence and usually occur in adulthood. It is rare for these states to appear for the first time after an individual reaches the age of 50 (Sackeim & Devanand, 1991). However, once they do appear, they may continue well into old age.

Fugue states usually end rather abruptly, like those of the misbehaving sheriff, and the individual returns home recalling most, if not all, of what happened. In this disorder, the disintegrated experience is more than memory loss, involving at least some disintegration of identity, if not the complete adoption of a new one.

An apparently distinct dissociative disorder not found in Western cultures is called *amok* (as in "running amok"). Most people with this disorder are males. Amok has attracted attention because individuals in this trance-like state often brutally assault and sometimes kill people or animals. If the person is not killed himself, he probably will not remember the episode. Running amok is only one of several "running" syndromes in which an individual enters a trance-like state and suddenly, imbued with a mysterious source of energy, runs or flees for a long time. Except for amok, the prevalence of running disorders is somewhat greater in women, as with most dissociative disorders. Among the Inuit, running disorder is termed *pivloktoq*. Among the Navajo tribe, it is called *frenzy witchcraft*. Despite their different culturally determined expression, running disorders seem to meet criteria for dissociative fugue, with the possible exception of amok.

Dissociative Trance Disorder

Dissociative disorders differ in very important ways across cultures. In many areas of the world, dissociative phenomena may occur as a trance or possession. The usual sorts of dissociative symptoms, such as sudden changes in personality, are attributed to possession by a spirit important in the particular culture. Often this spirit demands and receives presents or favours from the family and friends of the victim. Like other dissociative states, trance disorder seems to be most common in women and is often associated with stress or trauma, which, as in dissociative amnesia and fugue states, is current rather than in the past.

Trance and possession are a common part of some traditional religious and cultural practices and are not considered abnormal in that context. Dissociative trances commonly occur in India, Nigeria (where they are called *vinvusa*), Thailand (*phiipob*), and other Asian and African countries (Mezzich et al., 1992; Saxena & Prasad, 1989). In North America, culturally accepted dissociation commonly occurs during African-American prayer meetings (Griffith et al., 1980), First Nations sweat lodge ceremonies (Jilek, 1982), and Puerto Rican spiritist sessions (Comas-Diaz, 1981). Among Bahamians and blacks from the southern United States, trance syndromes are often referred to colloquially as "falling out."

Only when the state is undesirable and considered pathological by members of the culture is it defined as a **dissociative trance disorder** (DTD; see DSM Table 6.10). Although trance and possession are almost never seen in Western cultures, they are among the most common forms of dissociative disorders elsewhere. The proposal for the *DSM-5* is to diagnose DTD as a subtype of dissociative identity disorder (APA, 2010; Spiegel, in press).

Table 6.10 Research Criteria for Dissociative Trance Disorder

DSM-IV-TR

DSM-IV-TR APPENDIX

A. Either (1) or (2):

1. Trance (i.e., temporary marked alteration in the state of consciousness or loss of customary sense of personal identity without replacement by an alternate identity), associated with at least one of the following:

   (a) narrowing of awareness of immediate surroundings, or unusually narrow and selective focus on environmental stimuli

   (b) stereotyped behaviours or movements that are experienced as being beyond the person's control

2. Possession trance, a single or episodic alteration in the state of consciousness characterized by the replacement of customary sense of personal identity by a new identity. This is attributed to the influence of a spirit, power, deity, or other person, as evidenced by one (or more) of the following:

   (a) stereotyped and culturally determined behaviours or movements that are experienced as being controlled by the possessing agent

   (b) full or partial amnesia for the event

B. The trance or possession state is not accepted as a normal part of a collective cultural or religious practice.

C. The trance or possession state causes clinically significant distress or impairment in social, occupational, or other important areas of functioning.

D. The trance or possession trance state does not occur exclusively during the course of a psychotic disorder (including mood disorder with psychotic features and brief reactive psychosis) or dissociative identity disorder and is not due to the direct physiological effects of a substance or a general medical condition.

Source: Reprinted with permission from the *Diagnostic and Statistical Manual of Mental Disorders,* Fourth Edition, Text Revision, (Copyright © 2000). American Psychiatric Association.

Dissociative Identity Disorder

Clinical Description

People with **dissociative identity disorder (DID)** may adopt as many as 100 new identities, all simultaneously coexisting inside one body and mind. In some cases, the identities are complete, each with its own behaviour, tone of voice, and physical gestures. In other cases, only a few characteristics are distinct, because the identities are only partially independent. Consider the case of Jonah, originally reported by Ludwig, Brandsma, Wilbur, Bendfeldt, and Jameson (1972).

JONAH | *Bewildering Blackouts*

Jonah, a 27-year-old Black man, experienced severe headaches that were unbearably painful and lasted for increasingly longer periods. Furthermore, he couldn't remember things that happened while he had a headache, except that sometimes a great deal of time passed. Finally, after a particularly bad night, when he could stand it no longer, he arranged for admission to the local hospital. What really prompted Jonah to come to the hospital, however, was that other people told him what he did during his severe head-aches. For example, he was told that the night before he had a violent fight with another man and attempted to stab him. He fled the scene and was shot at during a high-speed chase by the police. His wife told him that during a previous headache he chased her and his three-year-old daughter out of the house, threatening them with a butcher knife. During his headaches, and while he was violent, he called himself "Usoffa Abdulla, son of Omega." Once he attempted to drown a man in a river. The man survived and Jonah escaped by swimming half a kilometre upstream. He woke up the next morning in his own bed, soaking wet, with no memory of the incident.

During Jonah's hospitalization, the staff was able to observe his behaviour directly, both when he had headaches and during other periods that he did not remember. He claimed other names at these times, acted differently, and generally seemed to be another person entirely. The staff distinguished three separate identities, or **alters**, in addition to Jonah. (Alters is the shorthand term for the different identities or personalities in DID.) The first alter was named Sammy. Sammy seemed rational, calm, and in control. The second alter, King Young, seemed to be in charge of all sexual activity and was particularly interested in having as many heterosexual interactions as possible. The third alter was the violent and dangerous Usoffa Abdulla. Characteristically, Jonah knew nothing of the three alters. Sammy was most aware of the other personalities. King Young and Usoffa Abdulla knew a little bit about the others but only indirectly.

In the hospital, psychologists determined that Sammy first appeared when Jonah was about six, immediately after Jonah saw his mother stab his father. Jonah's mother sometimes dressed him as a girl in private. On one of these occasions, shortly after Sammy emerged, King Young appeared. When Jonah was nine or ten he was brutally attacked by a group of white youths. At this point Usoffa Abdulla emerged, announcing that his sole reason for existence was to protect Jonah.

DSM-IV-TR criteria for dissociative identity disorder include amnesia, as in dissociative amnesia and dissociative fugue (see DSM Table 6.11). It is proposed that this symptom be given even more

DSM-IV-TR	**Table 6.11** Criteria for Dissociative Identity Disorder (Formerly Called Multiple Personality Disorder)

A. The person has two or more distinct identities or personality states (each with its own relatively enduring pattern of perceiving, relating to, and thinking about the environment and self).

B. At least two of these identities or personality states recurrently take control of the person's behaviour.

C. The person has an inability to recall important personal information that is too extensive to be explained by ordinary forgetfulness.

D. The disturbance is not due to the direct physiological effects of a substance (e.g., blackouts or chaotic behaviour during alcohol intoxication) or a general medical condition (e.g., complex partial seizures). Note: In children, the symptoms are not attributable to imaginary playmates or other fantasy play.

Source: Reprinted with permission from the *Diagnostic and Statistical Manual of Mental Disorders,* Fourth Edition, Text Revision, (Copyright © 2000). American Psychiatric Association.

prominence in the *DSM-5* (Spiegel, in press). In DID, however, identity has also fragmented. How many personalities live inside one body is relatively unimportant, whether there are three, four, or even 100 of them. Rather, the defining feature of this disorder is that certain aspects of the person's identity are dissociated. For this reason, the name was changed in the *DSM-IV-TR* from multiple personality disorder to dissociative identity disorder. This change also corrects the notion that multiple people somehow live inside one body.

Characteristics The person who becomes the patient and asks for treatment is usually a "host" identity. Host personalities usually attempt to hold various fragments of identity together but end up being overwhelmed. The first personality to seek treatment is seldom the original personality of the person. Usually, the host personality develops later (Putnam, 1992). Many patients have at least one impulsive alter who handles sexuality and generates income, sometimes by acting as a prostitute. In other cases, all alters may abstain from sex. Cross-gendered alters are not uncommon. For example, a small agile woman might have a strong powerful male alter who serves as a protector.

The transition from one personality to another is called a *switch* (Putnam, 1994). Usually, the switch is instantaneous (although in movies and television it is often drawn out for dramatic effect). Physical transformations may occur during switches. Posture, facial expressions, patterns of facial wrinkling, and even physical disabilities may emerge. In one study, changes in handedness occurred in 37 percent of the cases (Putnam, Guroff, Silberman, Barban, & Post, 1986).

Can DID Be Faked? Are the fragmented identities "real," or is the person faking them to avoid responsibility or stress? As with conversion disorders, it is very difficult to answer this question, for several reasons (Kluft, 1999). First, evidence indicates that individuals with DID are very suggestible (Bliss, 1984; Giesbrecht et al., 2008; Kihlstrom, 2005). It is possible that alters are created in response to leading questions from therapists, either during psychotherapy or while the person is in a hypnotic state.

THE HILLSIDE STRANGLER

During the late 1970s, Kenneth Bianchi brutally raped and murdered ten young women in the Los Angeles area and left their bodies naked and in full view on the sides of various hills. Despite overwhelming evidence that Bianchi was the "Hillside Strangler," he continued to assert his innocence, prompting some professionals to think he might have DID. His lawyer brought in a clinical psychologist, who hypnotized him and asked whether there were another part of Ken with whom he could speak. Guess what? Somebody called "Steve" answered and said that he had done all the killing. Steve also said that Ken knew nothing about the murders. With this evidence, the lawyer entered a plea of not guilty by reason of insanity.

The prosecution called on the late Martin Orne, one of the world's leading experts on hypnosis and dissociative disorders (Orne, Dinges, & Orne, 1984). Orne used procedures similar to those we described in the context of conversion blindness to determine whether Bianchi was simulating

Dissociative Disorders **205**

DID or had a true psychological disorder. For example, Orne suggested during an in-depth interview with Bianchi that a true multiple personality disorder included at least three personalities. Bianchi soon produced a third personality. By interviewing Bianchi's friends and relatives, Orne established that there was no independent corroboration of different personalities before Bianchi's arrest. Psychological tests also failed to show significant differences among the personalities; true fragmented identities often score differently on personality tests. Several textbooks on psychopathology were found in Bianchi's room; therefore, he presumably had studied the subject. Orne concluded that Bianchi responded like someone simulating hypnosis, not someone deeply hypnotized. On the basis of Orne's testimony, Bianchi was found guilty and sentenced to life in prison.

▲ The late Nicholas Spanos, a psychologist at Carleton University, was a leading expert worldwide on hypnosis, dissociative disorders, and false memories.

Some investigators have studied the ability of individuals to fake dissociative experiences. Carleton University psychologist Nicholas Spanos (now deceased) conducted important work on this issue. Spanos, Weeks, and Bertrand (1985) demonstrated in an experiment that a university student could simulate an alter if it was suggested that faking was plausible, as in the interview with Bianchi. All the students in the group were told to play the role of an accused murderer claiming his innocence. The subjects received exactly the same interview as Bianchi, word for word. More than 80 percent simulated an alternate personality in order to avoid conviction. Groups that were given more vague instructions, and no direct suggestion an alternate personality might exist, were much less likely to use one in their defence.

These findings on faking and the effect of hypnosis led Spanos (1994, 1996) to suggest that the symptoms of DID could, for the most part, be accounted for by therapists who inadvertently suggested the existence of alters to suggestible individuals, a model known as the "sociocognitive model" because the possibility of identity fragments and early trauma is socially reinforced by a therapist (Lilienfeld et al., 1999). A survey of American psychiatrists showed little consensus on the scientific validity of DID, with only one-third in the sample believing the diagnosis should be included without reservation in the *DSM-IV-TR* (Pope, Oliva, Hudson, Bodkin, & Gruber, 1999). A similar study of Canadian psychiatrists showed that fewer than one-third had no reservations about including DID in the *DSM-IV-TR* (Lalonde, Hudson, Gigante, & Pope, 2001). Canadian psychiatrists were significantly more skeptical about the legitimacy of the DID diagnosis than were the American psychiatrists. (We return to this point of view when we discuss false memories.)

However, objective tests suggest that many people with fragmented identities are not consciously and voluntarily simulating

(Kluft, 1991, 1999). For example, a study by University of British Columbia psychologist Eric Eich and his colleagues (Eich, Macaulay, Loewenstein, & Dihle, 1997a) compared the performance of real DID patients and simulators on objective memory tests. They found that "interpersonality amnesia" (i.e., in which events experienced by a particular personality state or identity are retrievable by the same identity but not by a different one; Eich, Macaulay, Loewenstein, & Pihle, 1997b) could not be explained by deliberate simulating. In another study, Condon, Ogston, and Pacoe (1969) examined a film about Chris Sizemore, the real-life subject of the book and movie *The Three Faces of Eve*. They determined that one of the personalities (Eve Black) showed *a transient micro-strabismus* (divergence in conjugant lateral eye movements) that was not observed in the other personalities. These optical differences have been confirmed by Miller (1989), who demonstrated that DID subjects had 4.5 times the average number of changes in optical functioning in their alter identities than control subjects who simulated alter personalities. Miller concludes that optical changes, including measures of visual acuity, manifest refraction, and eye muscle balance, would be difficult to fake. Ludwig et al. (1972) found that Jonah's various identities had different physiological responses to emotionally laden words, including galvanic skin response (GSR), a measure of otherwise imperceptible sweat gland activity, and electroencephalogram (EEG) brain waves. Using up-to-date functional magnetic

▲ Chris Sizemore's history of dissociative identity disorder was dramatized in *The Three Faces of Eve*.

resonance imaging (fMRI) procedures, changes in brain function were observed in one patient while switching from one personality to another. Specifically, this patient showed changes in hippocampal and medial temporal activity after the switch (Tsai, Condie, Wu, & Chang, 1999). A number of subsequent studies confirm that various alters have unique psychophysiological profiles (Putnam, 1997). Kluft (1999) suggests a number of additional clinical strategies to distinguish malingerers from patients with DID, including the observations that malingerers are usually eager to demonstrate their symptoms and do so in a very fluid fashion. Patients with DID, conversely, are more likely to attempt to hide symptoms.

Concept Check | 6.2

Check your understanding of the criteria for dissociative disorders and the different ways in which they may be presented. In each situation provided, write N if it does not fit the criteria for dissociative disorder. If it is a dissociative disorder, specify which type: (a) depersonalization disorder, (b) dissociative trance disorder, (c) generalized amnesia, and (d) dissociative identity disorder.

1. Ann was found wandering the streets, unable to recall any important personal information. After searching her purse and finding an address, doctors were able to contact her mother. They then found out that Ann had just been in a terrible accident and was the only survivor. Ann could not remember her mother or any details of the accident. She was very distressed. _____

2. Judith, who has metastatic breast cancer, complained of a pain in her head. She seemed to be coping appropriately with her disease. No cause for the pain in her head could be determined. _____

3. Karl was brought to a clinic by his mother. She was concerned because at times his behaviour was very strange. His speech and his way of relating to people and situations would change dramatically, almost as if he were a different person. What bothered her and Karl the most was that he could not recall anything he had done during these periods. _____

4. Freya complained about feeling out of control. She said that she felt sometimes as if she were floating under the ceiling and just watching things happen to her. She also experienced tunnel vision and felt uninvolved in the things that went on in the room around her. This always caused her to panic and perspire. _____

Statistics

Jonah had four identities, but the average number of alter personalities is reported by clinicians as closer to 15 (Ross, 1997; Sackeim & Devanand, 1991). Of people with DID, the ratio of females to males is as high as nine to one, although these data are based on accumulated case studies rather than survey research (Maldonado, Butler, & Spiegel, 1998). The onset is almost always in childhood,

often as young as four years of age, although it is usually approximately seven years after the appearance of symptoms before the disorder is identified (Maldonado et al., 1998; Putnam et al., 1986). Once established, the disorder tends to last a lifetime in the absence of treatment. The form it takes does not seem to vary substantially over the person's life span, although some evidence indicates that the frequency of switching decreases with age (Sackheim & Devanand, 1991). Different personalities may emerge in response to new life situations, as was the case with Jonah.

We don't have many good epidemiological studies on the prevalence of the disorder in the population at large, although investigators now think it is more common than previously estimated (Kluft, 1991; Ross, 1997). Some have argued that, in the past, dissociative disorders may have been overlooked or misdiagnosed by mental health professionals (Ross, Norton, & Wozney, 1989). Semistructured interviews of large numbers of inpatients with severe disturbances found prevalence rates of DID of between 3 percent and 6 percent in Canada and the United States (Horen, Leichner, & Lawson, 1995; Ross, 1997; Ross, Anderson, Fleisher, & Norton, 1991; Saxe et al., 1993), and approximately 2 percent in Holland (Friedl & Draijer, 2000). Additional studies in nonclinical samples, conducted in Winnipeg (Ross, 1991, 1997), suggest that between 0.5 percent and 1 percent of these large samples (more than 400 people in each) have DID.

A very large percentage of DID patients have simultaneous psychological disorders that may include substance abuse, depression, somatization disorder, borderline personality disorder, panic attacks, and eating disorders (Kluft, 1999; Ross et al., 1990). In one sample of over 100 patients, more than seven additional diagnoses were noted on the average (Ellason & Ross, 1997). Another study of 42 patients documented a pattern of severe comorbid personality disorders, including severe borderline pathology (Dell, 1998). It seems likely that different personalities will present with differing patterns of comorbidity, but the research has not yet been done. In some cases this high rate of comorbidity may reflect the fact that certain disorders, such as borderline personality disorder, share many features with DID—for example, self-destructive, sometimes suicidal behaviour and emotional instability.

For the most part, however, the high frequency of additional disorders accompanying DID simply reflects an intensely severe reaction to what seems to be in almost all cases horrible child abuse. Because auditory hallucinations are very common, DID is often misdiagnosed as a psychotic disorder. But the voices in DID are reported by patients as coming from inside their heads, not outside as in psychotic disorders. Because patients with DID are usually aware the voices are hallucinations, they don't report them and try to suppress them. These voices often encourage doing something against the person's will, so some individuals, particularly in other cultures, appear to be possessed by demons (Putnam, 1997). Although systematic studies are lacking, DID seems to occur in a variety of cultures throughout the world (Boon & Draijer, 1993; Coons, Bowman, Kluft, & Milstein, 1991; Ross, 1997). For example, Coons et al. (1994) found reports of DID in 21 different countries.

Causes

It is informative to examine current evidence on causes for all dissociative disorders, as we do later, but our emphasis here is on the etiology of DID. Life circumstances that encourage the development of DID seem quite clear in at least one respect. Almost every patient presenting with this disorder reports that he or she was horribly, often unspeakably, abused as a child.

SYBIL

You may have seen the movie *Sybil* that was based on the biography of the same name (Schreiber, 1973). Sybil's mother had schizophrenia and her father refused or was unable to intervene in the mother's brutality. Day after day throughout her childhood, Sybil was sexually tortured and occasionally nearly murdered. Before she was one year old, her mother began tying her up in various ways and, on occasion, suspending her from the ceiling. Many mornings her mother placed Sybil on the kitchen table and forcefully inserted various objects into her vagina. Sybil's mother reasoned, psychotically, that she was preparing her daughter for adult sex. In fact, she so brutally tore the child's vaginal canal that scars were evident during adult gynecological exams. Sybil was also given very strong laxatives but prohibited from using the bathroom. Because of her father's detachment and the normal appearance of the family, the abuse continued without interruption throughout Sybil's childhood.

Imagine you are a child in a situation like this. What can you do? You're too young to run away. You're too young to call the authorities. Although the pain may be unbearable, you have no way of knowing it is unusual or wrong. But you can do one thing! You can escape into a fantasy world; you can be somebody else. If the escape blunts the physical and emotional pain just for a minute or makes the next hour bearable, chances are you'll escape again. Your mind learns there is no limit to the identities that can be created as needed. Fifteen? Twenty-five? A hundred? Such numbers have been recorded in some cases. You do whatever it takes to get through life. Most surveys report a very high rate of childhood trauma in cases of DID (Gleaves, 1996; Ross, 1997). Putnam et al. (1986) examined 100 cases and found that 97 percent of the patients had experienced significant trauma, usually sexual or physical abuse. Sixty-eight percent reported incest. A four-site study by Colin Ross and colleagues (1990) was conducted on identified cases of DID from Winnipeg, Utah, California, and Ottawa. Ross et al. (1990) reported that, of 102 cases, 95 percent reported physical or sexual abuse, and the prevalence of abuse histories was found to be similar across sites. Unfortunately, the abuse is often as bizarre and sadistic as what Sybil suffered. Some children were buried alive. Some were tortured with matches, steam irons, razor blades, or glass. Now investigators have corroborated the existence of at least some early sexual abuse in 12 patients with DID, by examining early records, interviewing relatives and acquaintances, and so on (Lewis, Yeager, Swica, Pincus, & Lewis, 1997). However, Harold Merskey, a retired psychiatrist from the University of Western Ontario, exhaustively analyzed several studies claiming to corroborate abuse reports among DID patients (Piper & Merskey, 2004). Merskey noted several methodological deficiencies in the research in this area, causing them to question whether we yet have corroborative evidence of childhood abuse in DID. Similarly, Kluft (1995, 1999)

cautions that some reports of childhood abuse by DID patients are not true, but have been confabulated (made up).

In cases where childhood trauma does contribute to DID development, it is important to note that not all the trauma is caused by abuse. Putnam (1992) describes a young girl in a war zone who saw both her parents blown to bits in a minefield. In a heart-rending response, she tried to piece the bodies back together, bit by bit.

Such observations have led to wide-ranging agreement that DID is rooted in a natural tendency to escape or "dissociate" from the unremitting negative affect associated with severe childhood trauma (Kluft, 1984, 1991). A lack of social support during or after the trauma also seems implicated. A study of 428 adolescent twins by Waller and Ross (1997) demonstrated that a surprisingly high 33 percent to 50 percent of the variance in dissociative experience could be attributed to a chaotic, nonsupportive family environment. The remainder of the variance was associated with individual experience and personality factors.

The behaviour and emotions that make up disorders seem to be related to otherwise normal tendencies present in all of us to some extent. It is quite common for otherwise normal individuals to escape in some way from emotional or physical pain (Butler, Duran, Jasiukaitis, Koopman, & Spiegel, 1996; Spiegel & Cardena, 1991). Noyes and Kletti (1977) surveyed more than 100 survivors of various life-threatening situations and found that most had experienced some type of dissociation, such as feelings of unreality, a blunting of emotional and physical pain, and even separation from their bodies. Dissociative amnesia and fugue states are clearly reactions to severe life stress. But the life stress or trauma is in the present rather than the past, as in the case of the overwrought mother who had dissociative amnesia. Many patients are escaping from legal difficulties or severe stress at home or on the job (Sackheim & Devanand, 1991). But sophisticated statistical analyses indicate that ordinary dissociative reactions differ substantially from the pathological experiences we've described (Waller, Putnam, & Carlson, 1996; Waller & Ross, 1997), and that at least some people do not develop severe pathological dissociative experiences no matter how extreme the stress. These findings are consistent with our diathesis-stress model, in that only with the appropriate vulnerabilities (the diathesis) will a person react to stress with pathological dissociation.

You may have noticed that DID seems very similar in its etiology to post-traumatic stress disorder (PTSD). Both conditions feature strong emotional reactions to experiencing a severe trauma (Butler et al., 1996). But remember that not everyone goes on to experience PTSD after severe trauma. Only people who are biologically and psychologically vulnerable to anxiety are at risk for developing PTSD in response to moderate levels of trauma. However, as the severity of the trauma increases, a greater percentage of people develop PTSD as a consequence. But some people do not become victims of the disorder even after the most severe traumas, suggesting that individual psychological and biological factors interact with the trauma to produce PTSD.

There is a growing body of opinion that DID is a very extreme subtype of PTSD, with a much greater emphasis on the process of dissociation than on symptoms of anxiety, although both are present in each disorder (Butler et al., 1996). Some evidence also shows that the "developmental window" of vulnerability to the abuse that leads to DID closes at approximately nine years of age

(Putnam, 1997). After that, DID is unlikely to develop, although severe PTSD might. If true, this is a particularly good example of the role of development in the etiology of psychopathology.

We also must remember that we know relatively little about DID. Our conclusions are based on retrospective case studies or correlations rather than on the prospective examination of people who may have undergone the severe trauma that seems to lead to DID (Kihlstrom, Glisky, & Anguilo, 1994).Therefore, it is hard to say what psychological or biological factors might contribute, but there are hints concerning individual differences that might play a role.

Suggestibility Suggestibility is a personality trait distributed normally across the population, much like weight and height. Some people are much more suggestible than others; some are relatively immune to suggestibility; and the majority fall in the mid-range.

Did you ever have an imaginary childhood playmate? Many people did, and it is one sign of the ability to lead a rich fantasy life, which can be very helpful and adaptive. However, according to a literature review by Lise McLewin and Robert Muller (2006) at York University in Toronto, having had an imaginary childhood playmate is much more common among those with DID than among people in the general population. Having had an imaginary playmate in childhood also seems to correlate with being suggestible or easily hypnotized (some people equate the terms *suggestibility* and *hypnotizability*). A hypnotic trance is also very similar to dissociation (Bliss, 1986; Butler et al., 1996; Carlson & Putnam, 1989). People in a trance tend to be totally focused on one aspect of their world, and they become very vulnerable to suggestions by the hypnotist. There is also the phenomenon of self-hypnosis, in which individuals can dissociate from most of the world around them and "suggest" to themselves that, for example, they won't feel pain in one of their hands.

According to the *autohypnotic model*, people who are suggestible may be able to use dissociation as a defence against extreme trauma (Putnam, 1991). According to the work of Colin Ross and his colleagues, as many as 50 percent of DID patients clearly remember imaginary playmates in childhood (Ross et al., 1990); whether they were created before or after the trauma is not entirely clear. When the trauma becomes unbearable, the person's very identity splits into multiple dissociated identities. Children's ability

▲ A person in a hypnotic trance is very suggestible and may become very absorbed in a particular experience.

to distinguish clearly between reality and fantasy as they grow older may be what closes the developmental window for developing DID at approximately age nine. People who are less suggestible may develop a severe post-traumatic stress reaction but not a dissociative reaction. Once again, these explanations are all very speculative because no controlled studies of this phenomenon have been done (Giesbrecht et al., 2008; Kihlstrom et al., 1994).

Biological Contributions As in post-traumatic stress disorder, where the evidence is more solid, there is almost certainly a biological vulnerability to DID, but it is difficult to pinpoint. For example, in the large twin study mentioned earlier (Waller & Ross, 1997), none of the variance or identifiable causal factors were attributable to heredity: They were all environmental. In contrast, another twin study by Kerry Jang, John Livesley, and their colleagues found evidence for a strong genetic contribution to dissociative disorder symptoms. About half the variance in dissociative symptoms was attributable to genetic factors (Jang, Paris, Zweig-Frank, & Livesley, 1998). Given these inconsistent findings, more research is clearly needed on the role of genetic factors.

Some observations may provide some hints about brain activity during dissociation. Individuals with certain neurological disorders, particularly seizure disorders, experience many dissociative symptoms (Cardena, Lewis-Fernandez, Bear, Pakianathan, & Spiegel, 1996). Devinsky, Feldman, Burrowes, and Bromfield (1989) reported that approximately 6 percent of patients with temporal lobe epilepsy reported "out of body" experiences. About 50 percent of another series of patients with temporal lobe epilepsy displayed some kinds of dissociative symptoms (Schenk & Bear, 1981), including alternate identities or identity fragments.

Patients with dissociative experiences who have seizure disorders are clearly different from those who do not (Ross, 1997). The patients with seizures develop dissociative symptoms in adulthood that are not associated with trauma, in clear contrast to DID patients without seizure disorders. This is certainly an area for future study (Putnam, 1991).

Head injury and resulting brain damage may induce amnesia or other types of dissociative experience. But these conditions are usually easily diagnosed because they are generalized, irreversible, and associated with an identifiable head trauma (Butler et al., 1996). Finally, strong evidence exists that sleep deprivation produces dissociative symptoms such as marked hallucinatory activity (Giesbrecht et al., 2007). In fact, the symptoms of individuals with DID seem to worsen when they feel tired. Simeon and Abugal (2006) report that patients with DID ". . . often liken it to bad jet lag and feel much worse when they travel across time zones" (p. 210).

Real and False Memories One of the most controversial issues in the field of abnormal psychology today concerns the extent to which memories of early trauma, particularly sexual abuse, are accurate. Some suggest that many such memories are simply the result of strong suggestions by careless therapists. The stakes in this controversy are enormous, with considerable opportunity for harm to innocent people on each side of the controversy, as has been noted by Clare MacMartin and A. Daniel Yarmey (1999) at the University of Guelph.

On the one hand, if early sexual abuse did occur but was not remembered because of dissociative amnesia, it is crucially important to re-experience aspects of the trauma under the direction of a skilled therapist in order to relieve current suffering. Without therapy the patient is likely to experience PTSD or a dissociative disorder indefinitely. It is also important that perpetrators are held accountable for their actions, perhaps through the legal system, because abuse of this type is a crime, and prevention is an important goal. Connie Kristiansen and her colleagues at Carleton University have expressed concern that because the validity of recovered memories has been questioned, this may discourage those who have been abused from speaking out about their abuse, decreasing the chance that perpetrators of abuse will be punished for their crimes (e.g., Kristiansen, Gareau, Mittlehold, DeCourville, & Hovdestad, 1999).

On the other hand, if memories of early trauma are inadvertently created in response to a careless therapist, but the memories seem real to the patient, false accusations against loved ones could lead to irreversible family breakup and, perhaps, unjust prison sentences for the falsely accused perpetrators. In recent years, allegedly inaccurate accusations as a result of false memories have led to substantial lawsuits against therapists, resulting in awards of millions of dollars in damages. As with most issues that reach this level of contention and disagreement, it is clear that the final answer will not involve an all-or-none resolution; incontrovertible evidence exists that false memories can be created by reasonably well-understood psychological processes (Bernstein & Loftus, 2009; Geraerts et al., 2009; Lilienfeld et al., 1999; Schacter, 1995). But very good evidence also shows that early traumatic experiences can cause selective dissociative amnesia, with substantial implications for psychological functioning (Gleaves, 1996; Gleaves, Smith, Butler, & Spiegel, 2004; Kluft, 1999; Spiegel, 1995).

Victims of accusations deriving from allegedly false memories have formed a society called the False Memory Syndrome Foundation. One goal is to educate the legal profession and the public at large about false memories after psychotherapy, so that, in the absence of other objective evidence, such "memories" cannot be used to convict innocent people. In an official position statement on recovered memories, the Canadian Psychiatric Association warned that childhood memories later recovered in adulthood were of questionable reliability and should never be accepted without corroboration (Blackshaw, Chandarana, Garneau, Merskey, & Moscarello, 1996). Similarly, in 1998, the Canadian Psychological Association recommended to the federal justice minister that a full judicial inquiry should be undertaken in regards to all convictions in Canada that had stemmed from evidence involving recovered memories. Although the federal government rejected this recommendation, it illustrates the attempts of professional bodies to ensure that recovered memory evidence cannot be used to convict people innocent of the crime in question (see review by Porter, Campbell, Birt, & Woodworth, 2003).

Evidence supporting the existence of distorted or illusory memories comes from lab-based experiments conducted by cognitive psychologists. For example, Loftus, Coan, and Pickrell (1996) successfully convinced several individuals that they had been lost for an extended time when they were approximately five years old, which was not true. A trusted companion was recruited to plant the memory. In one case, a 14-year-old boy was told by his older brother that he had been lost in a nearby shopping mall when he was five years old, rescued by an older man, and ultimately reunited with his mother and brother. Several days after receiving this suggestion, the boy reported remembering the event and even that he felt very frightened when he was lost. As time went by, the boy remembered increasingly more details of the event, beyond those described in the plant, including an exact description of the older man. When he was finally told the incident never happened, the boy was very surprised, and he continued to describe details of the event as if they were true.

Another study by Stephen Porter at Dalhousie University and John Yuille and Darrin Lehman at the University of British Columbia (1999) further tested whether it is possible to "remember" a highly emotional event that never actually occurred. These researchers first contacted participants' parents to learn about which of a variety of stressful events (e.g., being seriously attacked by an animal) each participant had actually been exposed to as a child. Then, participants were brought into the laboratory and were encouraged by interviewers to "recover" a memory for a false event using guided imagery and repeated attempts to retrieve the memory. The false events were presented to the participants as actually having happened to them, according to their parents' reports. A shockingly large number of participants "recovered" a full (26 percent) or partial (another 30 percent) memory for the false experience.

But we also have plenty of evidence that therapists need to be very sensitive to signs of trauma that may not be fully remembered in patients presenting with symptoms of dissociative or post-traumatic stress disorders. Even if patients are unable to report or remember early trauma, it can sometimes be confirmed through corroborating evidence (Coons, 1994). In a compelling study, Williams (1994) interviewed 129 women with previously documented histories, such as hospital records, of having been sexually abused as children. Thirty-eight percent did not recall the incidents that had been reported to authorities at least 17 years earlier, even with extensive probing of their abuse histories. Dissociative amnesia was more extensive if the victim had been very young and knew the abuser. As noted earlier, Lewis et al. (1997) provided similar documentation of severe early abuse.

In one study, Elliot (1997) surveyed 364 individuals out of a larger group who had experienced substantial trauma such as a natural disaster, car accident, or physical abuse. Fully 32 percent reported delayed recall of the event, which suggested at least temporary dissociative amnesia. This phenomenon was most prevalent among combat veterans, people who had witnessed the murder or suicide of a family member, and those who had suffered sexual abuse. The severity of the trauma predicted the extent of the amnesia, and the most common trigger for recalling the trauma was a media presentation, such as a movie. As Brewin, Andrews, and Gotlib (1993) also point out, the available data from cognitive science do not necessarily support an extreme reconstructive model of (false) memory induced by careless therapists, because most individuals can recall important details of their childhood, particularly if they are unique and unexpected.

How will this controversy be resolved? Because false memories can be created through strong repeated suggestions by an authority figure, therapists must be fully aware of the conditions under which this is likely to occur, particularly when dealing with young children. This situation requires an extensive knowledge of the workings of memory and other aspects of psychological functioning and illustrates, once again, the dangers of dealing with inexperienced or inadequately trained psychotherapists. Elaborate tales of satanic abuse of children under the care of elderly women in daycare centres are most likely cases of memories implanted by aggressive and careless therapists or law enforcement officials (Lilienfeld et al., 1999). An extreme example is the case of Victoria, British Columbia, native Michelle Smith, who was treated by psychiatrist Dr. Lawrence Pazder (now deceased) in the late 1970s. During her therapy sessions, Ms. Smith came to "remember" instances of childhood satanic ritual abuse by her parents and other adults in Victoria. Although she originally sought therapy for depression related to a miscarriage, she was eventually diagnosed with DID by Dr. Pazder. With the help of her therapist, Ms. Smith wrote a book about her alleged childhood experiences that was entitled *Michelle Remembers* (Smith & Pazder, 1980). The book was later revealed as a fraud. It contains sections that strongly suggest that Ms. Smith's "memories" emerged as a consequence of hypnosis and therapist suggestion. The controversy around this book contributed to the recovered memory debate that began around this time and which continues to this day (Allen & Midwinter, 1990).

While there is evidence that some "memories" of abuse have been implanted by well-meaning therapists, many people with dissociative and post-traumatic stress disorders have truly suffered documented extreme abuse and trauma, which then becomes dissociated from awareness. It may be that future research will find that the severity of dissociative amnesia is directly related to the severity of the trauma in vulnerable individuals, and it is also likely to be proven as qualitatively different from ordinary dissociative experiences (e.g., Kluft, 1999; Waller et al., 1996). In other words, are there two kinds of memories: traumatic memories that can be dissociated and ordinary memories that cannot? At present, this is the scientific crux of the issue.

Advocates on both sides of this issue agree that clinical science must proceed as quickly as possible to specify the processes under which the implantation of false memories is likely and to define the presenting features that indicate a real but dissociated traumatic experience (Kihlstrom, 1997; Lilienfeld et al., 1999; Pope, 1996, 1997). Until then, mental health professionals must be extremely careful not to prolong unnecessary suffering, among both victims of actual abuse and victims falsely accused as abusers (Prout & Dobson, 1998).

Treatment

Individuals who experience dissociative amnesia or a fugue state usually get better on their own and remember what they have forgotten. The episodes are so clearly related to current life stress that prevention of future episodes usually involves therapeutic resolution of the distressing situations and increasing the strength of personal coping mechanisms. When necessary, therapy focuses on recalling what happened during the amnesic or fugue states, often with the help of friends or family who know what happened, so patients can confront the information and integrate it into their conscious experience. For more difficult cases, hypnosis or the use of benzodiazepines (minor tranquilizers) have been used, with suggestions from the therapist that it is okay to remember the events (Maldonado et al., 1998).

For DID, however, the process is not so easy. With the person's very identity shattered into many different elements, reintegrating the personality might seem hopeless. Fortunately, this is not always the case. Although no controlled research has been reported on the effects of treatment, many documented successes exist of attempts to reintegrate identities through long-term psychotherapy (Brand

et al., 2009; Ellason & Ross, 1997; Kluft, 2009; Putnam, 1989; Ross, 1997). Nevertheless, the prognosis for most people remains guarded. Coon (1986) found that only 5 out of 20 patients achieved a full integration of their identities. Ellason and Ross (1997) reported that 12 out of 54 (22.2 percent) patients in Canada and the United States had achieved integration two years after presenting for treatment, which in most cases had been continual. Of course, Russell Powell and his colleague have pointed out that these results could be attributed to factors other than therapy, because no experimental comparison was present (Powell & Howell, 1998).

The strategies that therapists use today in treating DID are based on accumulated clinical wisdom, as well as on procedures that have been successful PTSD (Gold & Seibel, 2009; Keane, Marx, & Sloan, in press; Maldonado et al., 1998; see Chapter 5). The fundamental goal is to identify cues or triggers that provoke memories of trauma or dissociation and to neutralize them. More importantly, the patient must confront and relive the early trauma and gain control over the horrible events, at least as they recur in the patient's mind (Kluft, 1996, 1999, 2009; Ross, 1997). To instill this sense of control, the therapist must skillfully, and very slowly, help the patient visualize and relive aspects of the trauma until it is simply a terrible memory instead of a current event. Because the memory is unconscious, aspects of the experience are often not known to either the patient or the therapist until they emerge during treatment. Hypnosis is often used to access unconscious memories and bring various alters into awareness. Because the process of dissociation may be very similar to the process of hypnosis, the latter may be a particularly efficient way to access traumatic memories (Maldonado et al., 1998). (Of course, as yet no evidence supports that hypnosis is a necessary part of treatment.) We know that DID seems to run a chronic course and very seldom improves spontaneously, which confirms that current treatments, primitive as they are, have some effectiveness.

It is possible that re-emerging memories of trauma may trigger further dissociation. The therapist must be on guard against this happening. Trust is important to any therapeutic relationship, but it is absolutely essential in the treatment of DID. Occasionally, medication is combined with therapy, but there is little indication that it helps much. What little clinical evidence there is indicates that antidepressant drugs might be appropriate in some cases (Coon, 1986; Kluft, 1996; Putnam & Loewenstein, 1993).

Concept Check | 6.3

Check your understanding of somatoform and dissociative disorders by identifying the type of disorder for each of these descriptions: (a) malingering, (b) factitious, (c) body dysmorphic, (d) pain disorder, and (e) dissociative amnesia.

1. Susan pretends to be sick so she can get supportive attention from her mother. _____

2. Mariko had considerable pain when she broke her arm. A year after it healed and with all medical tests indicating that her arm is fine, she still complains of the pain. It seems to intensify when she fights with her husband. _____

(continued)

3. William hated the way his ears stick out, so he had surgery to have them tacked down flat against his head. After the surgery, he still hated his ears. _____

4. Mikkel's car was rear-ended during a multiple-car accident. Even though extensive testing indicates that nothing is wrong with Mikkel's neck, he claims he is in pain. On weekends, the pain apparently disappears during softball games. The driver of the vehicle that hit him has $1 million insurance coverage for all accidents. _____

5. Carol cannot remember what happened last weekend. On Monday she was admitted to a hospital, suffering from cuts, bruises, and contusions. It also appeared that she had been sexually assaulted. _____

Phantom Illness: Shattering the Myth of Hypochondria
by Carla Cantor with Brian A. Fallon, M.D.

One warm June evening I found myself imprisoned, a patient on a psychiatric ward of a hospital a few miles from my New Jersey home. It was not at all what I had intended. I had come to the emergency room earlier that day in desperation: I had to talk to someone about the undiagnosed pain in my wrist, my thinning hair, and the unrelenting fear that I was morbidly ill. (p. 1)

Carla Cantor opens *Phantom Illness* with the story of a hospital stay that turned out to be the beginning of her road to recovery from lifelong hypochondria. Though not entirely a memoir, the book begins and ends with episodes and personal insights from Cantor's life as a hypochondriac. In between are straightforward chapters outlining current medical and psychiatric thinking on different types of somatic disorders, possible causes, and steps toward treatment. Throughout the book, Cantor weaves in strands of her personal experiences as well as revealing stories and insightful quotes from many people with different somatic disorders.

The hospital misadventure begins when an emergency-room physician misdiagnoses her condition as clinical depression. Cantor's reaction demonstrates the depths of her preoccupation with physical illness. "After the initial shock of hearing his words, I felt relief. . . . Finally, my illness would be diagnosed! Doctors would examine my inflamed wrist, psychiatrists would listen to me talk about the psychic pain of the past year, and they would all figure out whether I was really sick or just plain crazy" (p. 4).The hospital stay also seemed to promise relief from her stressful life. "Being in a hospital also seemed like a reasonable excuse for leaving behind the responsibilities and stresses that go with being a freelance writer and mother of two young children" (p. 4).

To her dismay, Cantor's overnight stay in the psychiatric ward was not the restful respite she had expected. "Suddenly, my undiagnosed illness didn't seem so terrible. I could live with it. In fact, maybe, just maybe, I thought, there really wasn't much wrong with me after all" (p. 5). She left the next morning, determined to overcome the problem on her own. "Perhaps the best thing to do was leave the pain alone. Accept the symptoms, ignore them" (p. 6). However, Cantor's lifelong problem resisted solution. "My existence was peppered with episodes of illness. When the going got tough, I'd get sick. Or just the opposite: when things seemed to be going well, I'd come down with a symptom, or at least what I interpreted as one" (p. 10). In addition, Cantor experienced the shame that is common to hypochondriacs. As one of the people she interviewed put it, "Unless you have it yourself, it's looked upon as a character flaw. . . . Hypochondria is not something you can admit to anyone. It's so embarrassing" (p. 51). She continued to suffer.

Help came to her by chance. Although Cantor had never before read anything about hypochondria, the moment she saw a newspaper article about the disorder, "suddenly something clicked for me. The myriad tests, the files of medical bills, the dozens of maladies for which doctors could never find a cause. There was something wrong with me, but not a deadly disease, which in my more rational moments, I believe I had always known" (p. 6). For Cantor, the realization that she was not alone was the catalyst to seek help.

After consulting with Brian Fallon, Cantor received treatment, including fluoxetine (Prozac), which helped her tremendously. She contacted Fallon with the idea of writing a book about hypochondria. Her rationale was that the book would spread information and hope to other hypochondriacs, whom she views as experiencing intense psychological pain.

If you're lucky, as I was, you finally wake up, not just intellectually but deep in your soul, to a simple paradox: if you are going to live out the rest of your life preparing for the day the tumor arrives, when you get the report of that terrible blood test, when you collapse in crushing pain, what's the point? Why would anyone want to live to 120 as a hypochondriac? (p. 290)

In the end, Cantor can rightfully claim that she and Fallon have achieved their goals of providing solid information and relieving the suffering of many people who have hypochondriacal worries about their health. "As I come to the close of my odyssey, I hope I have succeeded in accomplishing what I set out to do: erase a stigma, debunk some myths, lend some illumination to a puzzling, perpetually elusive malady" (p. 219).

As noted in the beginning of this chapter, somatoform and dissociative disorders are among the oldest recognized mental disorders. And yet, recent evidence indicates that we have much to learn about the nature of these disorders and that neither grouping of disorders may comprise a uniform category that reflects shared characteristics for purposes of classification (Mayou et al., 2005). For example, the grouping of somatoform disorders under the heading of "somatoform" is based largely on the assumption that "somatization" is a common process in which a mental disorder manifests itself in the form of physical symptoms. The specific disorders, then, simply reflect the different ways in which symptoms can be expressed physically. Recently, major questions have arisen concerning the classification of somatoform disorders, and a proposal now exists that would radically revise the classification of these disorders in the *DSM-5* (APA, 2010; Noyes, Stuart, & Watson, 2008; Voigt et al., 2010).

Specifically, and as noted at the beginning of the chapter, somatization disorder, hypochondriasis, undifferentiated somatoform disorder, and pain disorder all share presentations of somatic symptoms accompanied by cognitive distortions in the form of misattributions of or excessive preoccupation with symptoms. These cognitive distortions may include excessive anxiety about health or physical symptoms, a tendency to think the worst or "catastrophize" about these symptoms, and very strong beliefs that physical symptoms might be more serious than health-care professionals have recognized. Also, people presenting with these disorders often make health concerns a very central part of their lives; in other words, they adopt the "sick role." For this reason, the *DSM-5* may focus on the severity and number of physical symptoms, as well as the severity of anxiety focused on the symptoms, and group them into a new category entitled "Complex Somatic Symptom Disorder" (CSSD). Preliminary explorations of the validity and utility of this strategy indicate that this new dimensional approach, reflecting both physical and psychological symptom severity, would be very helpful to clinicians in predicting the course of the disorder as well as selecting among possible treatments (Noyes et al., 2008; Voigt et al., 2010).

Another advantage of this approach is that there would be less burden on physicians to make very tricky determinations on whether the symptoms have physical causes as is currently the case (see DSM Table 6.2 on page 186). Rather, the combination of chronic physical symptoms accompanied by the psychological factors of misattributing the meaning of the symptoms and excessive concern would be sufficient to make the diagnosis. The *DSM-5* proposal also suggests that the name of the larger category should be changed from "somatoform disorders" to "somatic symptom disorders"; the new category would include not only the *DSM-IV* somatoform disorders, but also psychological factors affecting medical conditions (see Chapter 9) and the factitious disorders because all involve the presentation of physical symptoms and/or concern about medical illness.

Summary

Somatoform Disorders

- Individuals with somatoform disorders are pathologically concerned with the appearance or functioning of their bodies and bring these concerns to the attention of health professionals, who usually find no identifiable medical basis for the physical complaints.

- There are several types of somatoform disorders. Hypochondriasis is a condition in which individuals believe they are seriously ill and become very anxious over this possibility. Somatization disorder is characterized by a seemingly unceasing and wide-ranging pattern of physical complaints that dominate the individual's life and interpersonal relationships. In conversion disorder, there is physical malfunctioning, such as paralysis, without any apparent physical problems. In pain disorder, psychological factors are judged to play a major role in maintaining physical suffering. In body dysmorphic disorder, a person who looks normal is obsessively preoccupied with some imagined defect in appearance (imagined ugliness).

- Distinguishing among conversion reactions, real physical disorders, and outright malingering, or faking, is sometimes difficult. Even more puzzling can be factitious disorder, in which the person's symptoms are feigned and under voluntary control, as with malingering, but for no apparent reason.

- The causes of somatoform disorders are not well understood, but some, including hypochondriasis and body dysmorphic disorder, seem very closely related to anxiety disorders.

- Treatment of somatoform disorders ranges from very basic techniques of reassurance and social support to those meant to reduce stress and remove any secondary gain for the behaviour. Recently, specifically tailored cognitive-behavioural therapy has proven successful with hypochondriasis. Patients with body dysmorphic disorder often turn to plastic surgery, which more often than not increases their preoccupation and distress.

Dissociative Disorders

- Dissociative disorders are characterized by alterations in perceptions: a sense of detachment from the self, from the world, or from memories.

- Dissociative disorders include depersonalization disorder, in which the individual's sense of personal reality is temporarily lost (depersonalization) and so is the reality of the external world (derealization). In dissociative amnesia, the individual may be unable to remember important personal information; in generalized amnesia the individual is unable to remember anything at all; more commonly, the individual is unable to recall particular events that occur during a specific time (localized or selective amnesia). In dissociative fugue, memory loss is combined with an unexpected trip (or trips). In the extreme, new identities, or alters, may be formed, as in dissociative identity disorder. Finally, the newly defined dissociative trance disorder is considered to cover dissociations that may be culturally determined.

- The causes of dissociative disorders are not well understood but often seem related to the tendency to escape psychologically from memories of traumatic events.

- Treatment of dissociative disorders involves helping the patient re-experience the traumatic events in a controlled therapeutic manner in order to develop better coping skills. In the case of dissociative identity disorder, therapy is often long term and may include antidepressant drugs. Particularly essential with this disorder is a sense of trust between therapist and patient.

Key Terms

alters, 205

body dysmorphic disorder
(BDD), 196

conversion disorder, 189

depersonalization disorder, 201

derealization, 200

dissociative amnesia, 202

dissociative disorders, 181

dissociative fugue, 203

dissociative identity disorder
(DID), 204

dissociative trance disorder
(DTD), 204

factitious disorders, 190

generalized amnesia, 202

hypochondriasis, 181

localized amnesia, 202

malingering, 190

pain disorder, 195

selective amnesia, 202

somatization disorder, 185

somatoform disorders, 181

Answers to Concept Checks

6.1

1. c **2.** D **3.** b

6.2

1. c **2.** N **3.** D **4.** a

6.3

1. b **2.** D **3.** C **4.** a **5.** e

Media Resources

Access an integrated eBook, Abnormal Psychology Videos (formerly Abnormal Psych Live CD-ROM), chapter-specific interactive learning tools (flashcards, quizzes, learning modules), and more in your Psychology CourseMate, available at **www.abnormalpsych3ce.nelson.com**.

Abnormal Psychology Videos

Free Abnormal Psychology videos can be viewed on the website **www.abnormalpsych3ce .nelson.com**.

- *Body Dysmorphic Disorder: Doug:* This interview by Katharine Phillips, an authority on this disorder, shows how it cripples this man's life until he seeks treatment for it.
- *Dissociative Identity Disorder: Rachel:* These three clips explore her multiple personalities, how she copes with them, and how they emerge in response to threats within the environment.

Video Concept Reviews

CourseMate also contains Mark Durand's *Video Concept Reviews* on these challenging topics.

- Somatoform Disorders
- Hypochondriasis
- Concept Check: Hypochondriasis Versus Other Disorders
- Conversion Disorder
- Body Dysmorphic Disorder
- Dissociative Disorders
- Depersonalization Disorder
- Dissociative Amnesia
- Dissociative Fugue
- Dissociative Trance Disorder
- Dissociative Identity Disorder
- False and Recovered Memories, Malingering

Exploring Somatoform and Dissociative Disorders

These two sets of disorders share some common features and are strongly linked historically as "hysterical neuroses." Both are relatively rare and not yet well understood.

SOMATOFORM DISORDERS
Characterized by a pathological concern with physical functioning or appearance

Hypochondriasis

Causes

Additional physical symptoms → Faulty interpretation of physical sensations → Intensified focus on symptoms → Increased anxiety → (cycle)

Characteristics

- Severe anxiety over physical problems that are medically undetectable
- Affects women and men equally
- May emerge at any age
- Evident in diverse cultures

Treatment

- Psychotherapy to challenge illness perceptions
- Counselling and/or support groups to provide reassurance

Somatization Disorder

Causes

Eventual social isolation → Continual development of new symptoms → Immediate sympathy and attention → (cycle)

Characteristics

- Reports of multiple physical symptoms without a medical basis
- Runs in families; probably heritable basis
- Rare—most prevalent among unmarried women in low socio-economic groups
- Onset usually in adolescence; often persists into old age

Treatment

- Hard to treat
- Cognitive-behavioural therapy (CBT) to provide reassurance, reduce stress, and minimize help-seeking behaviours
- Therapy to broaden basis for relating to others

Conversion Disorder

Causes

Social influences (symptoms learned from observing real illness or injury) → Life stresses or psychological conflict → Reduced by incapacitating symptoms → (cycle)

Characteristics

- Severe physical dysfunctioning (e.g., paralysis and blindness) without corresponding physical pathology
- Affected people are genuinely unaware that they can function normally
- May coincide with other problems, especially somatization disorder
- Most prevalent in low socio-economic groups, women, and men under extreme stress (e.g., soldiers)

Treatment

- Same as for somatization disorder, with emphasis on resolving life stress or conflict and reducing help-seeking behaviours

Body Dysmorphic Disorder (BDD)

Causes

Pathological attempts to "fix" the problem that prevents a more reality-based appraisal of the "defect" → Intrusive, anxiety-provoking idea that individual has a physical defect apparent to everyone → Intensified focus on imagined defects accompanied by extreme self-consciousness → Increased anxiety → (cycle)

Characteristics

- Socially disabling preoccupation with a normal physical feature that is believed to be hideous ("imagined ugliness")
- Prevalence is not known; affects men and women equally
- Associated with obsessive-compulsive disorder

Treatment

- CBT treatments seem most effective
- Drug treatments can provide relief for some sufferers
- Without treatment, BDD lasts a lifetime

DISSOCIATIVE DISORDERS

Characterized by detachment from the self (depersonalization) and objective reality (derealization)

Severe abuse during childhood
• Fantasy life is the only "escape"
• Practice becomes automatic and then involuntary

Similar etiology to post-traumatic stress disorder

Causes

Biological vulnerability likely

High suggestibility a possible trait

Controversy

The scientific community is divided over the question of whether multiple identities are a genuine experience or faked. Studies have shown that "false memories" can be created ("implanted") by therapists. Other tests confirm that various alters are physiologically distinct.

Disorder	Characteristics	Treatment
Dissociative Identity Disorder (DID)	• Affected person adopts new identities, or alters, that coexist simultaneously; the alters may be complete and distinct personalities or only partly independent • Average number of alters is 15 • Childhood onset; affects more women than men • Patients often suffer from other psychological disorders simultaneously • Rare outside of Western cultures	• Long-term psychotherapy may reintegrate separate personalities in 25 percent of patients • Treatment of associated trauma similar to post-traumatic stress disorder; lifelong condition without treatment
Depersonalization	• Severe and frightening feelings of detachment dominate the person's life • Affected person feels like an outside observer of his or her own mental or body processes • Causes significant distress or impairment in functioning, especially emotional expression and deficits in perception • Some symptoms are similar to those of panic disorder • Rare; onset usually in adolescence	• Psychological treatments similar to those for panic disorder may be helpful • Stresses associated with onset of disorder should be addressed • Tends to be lifelong
Dissociative Fugue	• Memory loss accompanies an unplanned journey • Person sometimes assumes a new identity or becomes confused about an old identity • Usually associated with an intolerable situation • Fugue states usually end abruptly • Typically adult onset	• Usually self-correcting when current life stress is resolved • If needed, therapy focuses on retrieving lost information
Dissociative Amnesia	• Generalized: Inability to remember anything, including identity; comparatively rare • Localized: Inability to remember specific events (usually traumatic); frequently occurs in war • More common than general amnesia • Usually adult onset for both types	• Usually self-correcting when current life stress is resolved • If needed, therapy focuses on retrieving lost information
Dissociative Trance	• Sudden changes in personality accompany a trance or "possession" • Causes significant distress and/or impairment in functioning • Often associated with stress or trauma • Prevalent worldwide, usually in a religious context; rarely seen in Western cultures • More common in women than in men	• Little is known

7 | Mood Disorders

Lawrence M Sawyer/Photodisc

My life is in ruins and . . . my body is uninhabitable. It is raging and weeping and full of destruction and wild energy gone amok. In the mirror I see a creature I don't know but must live and share my mind with.
—Kay Redfield Jamison, *An Unquiet Mind*

Demonstrate knowledge and understanding representing appropriate breadth and depth in selected content areas of psychology:	❯ Biological bases of behaviour and mental processes, including physiology, sensation, perception, comparative, motivation, and emotion (APA SLO 1.2.a (3)) *(see textbook pages 237–240)*
	❯ Variability and continuity of behaviour and mental processes within and across species (APA SLO 1.2.d (2)) *(see textbook pages 231–235, 257–259)*
Use the concepts, language, and major theories of the discipline to account for psychological phenomena.	❯ Describe behaviour and mental processes empirically, including operational definitions (APA SLO 1.3.a) *(see textbook pages 220–231, 257–258)*
	❯ Integrate theoretical perspectives to produce comprehensive and multifaceted explanations (APA SLO 1.3.e) *(see textbook pages 246–247, 259–260)*
Identify appropriate applications of psychology in solving problems, such as:	❯ Origin and treatment of abnormal behaviour (APA SLO 4.2.b) *(see textbook pages 247–256, 261)*

* Portions of this chapter cover learning outcomes suggested by the American Psychological Association (2007) in their guidelines for the undergraduate psychology major. Chapter coverage of these outcomes is identified above by APA Goal and APA Suggested Learning Outcome (SLO).

Think back over the last month of your life. It may seem normal in most respects; you studied during the week, socialized on the weekend, and thought about the future occasionally. Perhaps you were anticipating with some pleasure the next school break or seeing an old friend or a lover. But maybe sometime during the past month you also felt kind of down, maybe because you broke up with your boyfriend or girlfriend or, worse yet, somebody close to you died. Think about your feelings during this period. Were you sad? Perhaps you remember crying. Maybe you felt listless and you couldn't seem to get up the energy to go out with your friends. It may be that you feel this way occasionally for no good reason you can think of, and your friends think you're moody.

If you are like most people, you know your mood will pass. You will be back to your old self in a day or two. In fact, if you never felt down and always saw only what was good in a situation, it might be more remarkable than if you were depressed occasionally. Feelings of depression (and joy) are universal, which makes it all the more difficult to understand disorders of mood, disorders possibly so incapacitating that suicide may seem by far a better option than living. Consider the case of Katie.

KATIE | *Weathering Depression*

Katie was an attractive but very shy 16-year-old who came to our clinic with her parents. For several years, Katie had seldom interacted with anybody outside her family because of her considerable social anxiety. Going to school was very difficult, and as her social contacts decreased, her days became empty and dull. By the time she was 16, a deep, all-encompassing depression blocked the sun from her life. Here is how she described it later.

The experience of depression is like falling into a deep, dark hole that you cannot climb out of. You scream as you fall, but it seems like no one hears you. Some days you float upward without even trying; on other days, you wish that you would hit bottom so that you would never fall again. Depression affects the way you interpret events. It influences the way you see yourself and the way you see other people. I remember

looking in the mirror and thinking that I was the ugliest creature in the world. Later in life, when some of these ideas would come back, I learned to remind myself that I did not have those thoughts yesterday and chances were that I would not have them tomorrow or the next day. It is a little like waiting for a change in the weather.

But at 16, in the depths of her despair, Katie had no such perspective. She often cried for hours at the end of the day. She had begun drinking alcohol the year before, with the blessing of her parents, strangely enough, since the pills prescribed by her family doctor did no good. A glass of wine at dinner had a temporary soothing effect on Katie, and both she and her parents, in their desperation, were willing to try anything that might make her a more functional person. But one glass was not enough. She drank more and more often. She began drinking herself to sleep. It was a means of escaping what she felt: "I had very little hope of positive change. I do not think that anyone close to me was hopeful, either. I was angry, cynical, and in a great deal of emotional pain." Katie's life continued to spiral downward.

For several years, Katie had thought about suicide as a solution to her unhappiness. At 13, in the presence of her parents, she reported these thoughts to a psychologist. Her parents wept, and the sight of their tears deeply affected Katie. From that point on she never expressed her suicidal thoughts again, but they remained with her. By the time she was 16, her preoccupation with her own death had increased.

I think this was just exhaustion. I was tired of dealing with the anxiety and depression day in and day out. Soon I found myself trying to sever the few interpersonal connections that I did have, with my closest friends, with my mother, and my oldest brother. I was almost impossible to talk to. I was angry and frustrated all the time. One day I went over the edge. My mother and I had a disagreement about some unimportant little thing. I went to my bedroom where I kept a bottle of whiskey or vodka or whatever I was drinking at the time. I drank as much as I could until I could pinch myself as hard as I could and feel nothing. Then I got out a very sharp knife that I had been saving and slashed my wrist deeply. I did not feel anything but the warmth of the blood running from my wrist.

The blood poured out onto the floor next to the bed that I was lying on. The sudden thought hit me that I had failed, that this was not enough to cause my death. I got up from the bed and began to laugh. I tried to stop the bleeding with some tissues. I stayed calm and frighteningly pleasant. I walked to the kitchen and called my mother. I cannot imagine how she felt when she saw my shirt and pants covered in blood. She was amazingly calm. She asked to see the cut and said that it was not going to stop bleeding on its own and that I needed to go to the doctor immediately. I remember as the doctor shot Novocain into the cut he remarked that I must have used an anesthetic before cutting myself. I never felt the shot or the stitches.

After that, thoughts of suicide became more frequent and much more real. My father asked me to promise that I would never do it again and I said I would not, but that promise meant nothing to me. I knew it was to ease his pains and fears and not mine, and my preoccupation with death continued.

Think for a moment about your own experience of depression. What are the major differentiating factors between your feelings and Katie's? Clearly, Katie's depression was outside the boundaries of normal experience by virtue of its intensity and duration. In addition, her severe or "clinical" depression interfered substantially with her ability to function. Finally, she experienced several of the associated psychological and physical symptoms that accompany clinical depression.

Because of their sometimes tragic consequences, we need to develop as full an understanding as possible of mood disorders. In the following sections, we describe how various emotional experiences and symptoms interrelate to produce specific mood disorders. We offer detailed descriptions of different mood disorders and examine the many criteria that define them. We discuss the relationship between anxiety and depression, and the causes and treatment of mood disorders. We conclude with a discussion of suicide.

An Overview of Depression and Mania

The disorders described in this chapter used to be categorized under several different general labels, such as "depressive disorders," "affective disorders," or even "depressive neuroses." Beginning with the *DSM-III*, these problems have been grouped under the heading **mood disorders** because they are characterized by gross deviations in mood.

The fundamental experiences of depression and mania contribute, either singly or together, to all the mood disorders. We describe each state and discuss its contributions to the various mood disorders. Then we briefly describe the additional defining criteria, features, or symptoms that define the specific disorders.

The most commonly diagnosed and most severe depression is called a **major depressive episode.** The *DSM-IV-TR* criteria indicate an extremely depressed mood state that lasts at least two weeks and includes cognitive symptoms (such as feelings of worthlessness

and indecisiveness) and disturbed physical functions (such as altered sleeping patterns, significant changes in appetite and weight, or a very notable loss of energy) to the point that even the slightest activity or movement requires an overwhelming effort (see DSM Table 7.1). The episode is typically accompanied by a marked general loss of interest and of the ability to experience any pleasure from life, including interactions with family or friends and accomplishments at work or at school. (The inability to experience pleasure is termed *anhedonia*.) Although all symptoms are important, recent evidence suggests the physical changes (sometimes called *somatic* or *vegetative* symptoms) are central to this disorder (Bech, 2009; Buchwald & Rudick-Davis, 1993; Keller et al., 1995; Kessler & Wang, 2009), as they strongly indicate a full major depressive epi-

---

DSM-IV-TR | **Table 7.1** Criteria for Major Depressive Episode

A. Five (or more) of the following symptoms have been present during the same two-week period and represent a change from previous functioning; at least one of the symptoms is either (1) depressed mood or (2) loss of interest or pleasure.

Note: Do not include symptoms that are clearly due to a general medical condition, or mood-incongruent delusions or hallucinations.

1. Depressed mood most of the day, nearly every day, as indicated by either subjective report (e.g., feels sad or empty) or observation made by others (e.g., appears tearful). *Note:* In children and adolescents this can be an irritable mood.
2. Markedly diminished interest or pleasure in all, or almost all, activities most of the day, nearly every day (as indicated by either subjective account or observation made by others).
3. Significant weight loss when not dieting or weight gain (e.g., a change of more than 5 percent of body weight in a month), or decrease or increase in appetite nearly every day. *Note:* In children, consider failure to make expected weight gains.
4. Insomnia or hypersomnia nearly every day.
5. Psychomotor agitation or retardation nearly every day (observable by others, not merely subjective feelings of restlessness or being slowed down).
6. Fatigue or loss of energy nearly every day.
7. Feelings of worthlessness or excessive or inappropriate guilt (which may be delusional) nearly every day (not merely self-reproach or guilt about being sick).
8. Diminished ability to think or concentrate, or indecisiveness, nearly every day (either by subjective account or as observed by others).
9. Recurrent thoughts of death (not just fear of dying), recurrent suicidal ideation without a specific plan, or a suicide attempt or a specific plan for committing suicide.

B. The symptoms do not meet criteria for a mixed episode.

C. The symptoms cause clinically significant distress or impairment in social, occupational, or other important areas of functioning.

D. The symptoms are not due to the direct physiological effects of a substance (e.g., a drug of abuse, a medication) or a general medical condition (e.g., hypothyroidism).

E. The symptoms are not better accounted for by bereavement (i.e., after the loss of a loved one) and persist for longer than two months or are characterized by marked functional impairment, morbid preoccupation with worthlessness, suicidal ideation, psychotic symptoms, or psychomotor retardation.

Source: Reprinted with permission from the *Diagnostic and Statistical Manual of Mental Disorders*, Fourth Edition, Text Revision, (Copyright © 2000). American Psychiatric Association.

Major Depressive Disorder: Barbara

"I've been sad, depressed most of my life. . . . I had a headache in high school for a year and a half. . . . There have been different periods in my life when I wanted to end it all. . . . I hate me, I really hate me. I hate the way I look, I hate the way I feel. I hate the way I talk to people. . . . I do everything wrong. . . . I feel really hopeless."

Go to Psychology CourseMate at www.abnormalpsych3ce. nelson.com to watch this video.

sode. The average duration of such an episode if untreated is approximately nine months (Eaton et al., 1997; Tollefson, 1993).

The second fundamental state in mood disorders is abnormally exaggerated elation, joy, or euphoria. In **mania**, individuals find extreme pleasure in every activity; in fact, some patients compare their daily experience of mania to a continuous sexual orgasm. They become extraordinarily active (hyperactive), requiring very little sleep, and may develop grandiose plans, believing they can accomplish anything they desire. A proposal for the *DSM-5* is to highlight this feature by adding "persistently increased activity or

energy" to the "A" criteria (see DSM Table 7.2; American Psychiatric Association, 2010). Speech is typically very rapid and may become incoherent, because the individual is attempting to express so many exciting ideas at once; this feature is typically referred to as *flight of ideas*.

The *DSM-IV-TR* criteria for a manic episode require a duration of only one week, less if the episode is severe enough to require hospitalization. Hospitalization could occur, for example, if the individual was engaging in self-destructive buying sprees, charging thousands of dollars in the expectation of making a million dollars the next day. Irritability is often part of a manic episode, usually near the end. Paradoxically, being anxious or depressed is also commonly part of mania, as described later. The average duration of an untreated manic episode is two to six months (Angst & Sellaro, 2000; Angst, 2009; Solomon et al., 2010).

The *DSM-IV-TR* also defines a **hypomanic episode**, a less severe version of a manic episode that does not cause marked impairment in social or occupational functioning. (*Hypo* means "below"; thus, the episode is below the level of a manic episode.) A hypomanic episode is not in itself necessarily problematic, but it does contribute to the definition of several mood disorders.

The Structure of Mood Disorders

Individuals who experience either depression or mania are said to have a *unipolar mood disorder*, because their mood remains at one "pole" of the usual depression-mania continuum. Because mania by itself is extremely rare, almost everyone with a unipolar mood disorder has unipolar depression. Someone who alternates between depression and mania is said to have a *bipolar mood disorder*, travelling from one "pole" of the depression–elation continuum to the other and back again. However, this label is somewhat misleading, because depression and elation may not exactly be at opposite ends of the same mood state; in fact, though related, they are often relatively independent. An individual can experience manic symptoms but feel somewhat depressed or anxious at the same time. This combination is called **dysphoric manic** or a **mixed episode** (Angst, 2009; Angst & Sellaro, 2000; Cassidy, Forest, Murry, & Carroll, 1998; Hantouche, Akiskal, Azorin, Chatenet-Duchene, & Lancrenon, 2006). The patient usually experiences such symptoms of mania as being out of control or dangerous and becomes anxious or depressed about them. Research suggests that manic episodes are characterized by dysphoric (anxious or depressive) features more commonly than was thought, and dysphoria can be severe (Cassidy, Forest, Murry, & Carroll, 1998). In one study, 30 percent of 1090 patients hospitalized for acute mania had mixed episodes (Hantouche et al., 2006). In a more recent, carefully constructed study of over 4000 patients, as many as two-thirds of patients with bipolar depressed episodes also had manic symptoms, most often racing thoughts (flight of ideas), distractibility,

DSM-IV-TR	**Table 7.2** Criteria for Manic Episode

A. A distinct period of abnormally and persistently elevated, expansive, or irritable mood, lasting at least one week (or any duration if hospitalization is necessary).

B. During the period of mood disturbance, three (or more) of the following symptoms have persisted (four if the mood is only irritable) and have been present to a significant degree:

  1. inflated self-esteem or grandiosity

  2. decreased need for sleep (e.g., feels rested after only three hours of sleep)

  3. more talkative than usual or pressure to keep talking

  4. flight of ideas or subjective experience that thoughts are racing

  5. distractibility (i.e., attention too easily drawn to unimportant or irrelevant external stimuli)

  6. increase in goal-directed activity (either socially, at work or school, or sexually) or psychomotor agitation

  7. excessive involvement in pleasurable activities that have a high potential for painful consequences (e.g., engaging in unrestrained buying sprees, sexual indiscretions, or foolish business investments)

C. The symptoms do not meet criteria for a mixed episode.

D. The mood disturbance is sufficiently severe to cause marked impairment in occupational functioning or in usual social activities or relationships with others, or to necessitate hospitalization to prevent harm to self or others, or there are psychotic features.

E. The symptoms are not due to the direct physiological effects of a substance (e.g., a drug of abuse, a medication, or other treatment) or a general medical condition (e.g., hyperthyroidism).

Note: Manic-like episodes that are clearly caused by somatic antidepressant treatment (e.g., medication, electroconvulsive therapy, light therapy) should not count toward a diagnosis of bipolar I disorder.

Source: Reprinted with permission from the *Diagnostic and Statistical Manual of Mental Disorders*, Fourth Edition, Text Revision, (Copyright © 2000). American Psychiatric Association.

and agitation. These patients were also more severely impaired (Goldberg et al., 2009) than those without concurrent depression and manic symptoms. The rare individual who suffers from manic episodes alone also meets criteria for bipolar mood disorder because experience shows that most of these individuals can be expected to become depressed at a later time (Goodwin & Jamison, 2007; Miklowitz & Johnson, 2006). It is likely that in the *DSM-5* the term "mixed episode" will be eliminated in favour of specifying whether a predominantly manic or predominantly depressive episode is present, and then noting "with mixed features" to be more precise (American Psychiatric Association, 2010).

Depressive Disorders

Clinical Descriptions

The most easily recognized mood disorder is **major depressive disorder, single episode**, defined by the absence of manic or hypomanic episodes before or during the episode (see DSM Table 7.3). We now know that an occurrence of just one isolated depressive episode in a lifetime is rare (Angst, 2009; Eaton et al., 2008; Judd, 1997, 2000; Kessler & Wang, 2009).

If two or more major depressive episodes occurred and were separated by at least two months during which the individual was not depressed, **major depressive disorder, recurrent**, is diagnosed. Otherwise, the criteria are the same as for major depressive disorder, single episode. Recurrence is very important in predicting the future course of the disorder as well as in choosing appropriate treatments. Individuals with recurrent major depression usually have a family history of depression, unlike people who experience single episodes. As many as 85 percent of single-episode cases later experience a second episode and thus meet criteria for major depressive disorder, recurrent (Angst, 2009; Eaton et al., 2008; Judd, 1997, 2000), based on follow-ups as long as 23 years (Eaton et al., 2008). In the first year following an episode, the risk of recurrence is 20 percent, but rises as high as 40 percent in the second year (Boland & Keller, 2009). Because of this finding and others reviewed later, clinical scientists have recently concluded that unipolar depression is often a chronic

CP Photo/Aaron Harris

▲ Canadian singer and songwriter Sarah McLachlan has reportedly had bouts of depression. Her music provides her fans a window into her emotional pain. She has said of her early work that "it was almost as if I needed to be depressed to be creative" (Waliszewski & Smithouser, 1997).

condition that waxes and wanes over time but seldom disappears. The median lifetime number of major depressive episodes is four to seven; in one large sample, 25 percent experienced six or more episodes (Angst, 1988, 2009; Angst & Preizig, 1996; Kessler & Wang, 2009). The median duration of recurrent major depressive episodes is four to five months (Boland & Keller, 2009; Kessler et al., 2003), somewhat shorter than the average length of the first episode.

On the basis of these criteria, how would you diagnose Katie? Katie experienced severely depressed mood, feelings of worthlessness, difficulty concentrating, recurrent thoughts of death, sleep difficulties, and loss of energy. She clearly met the criteria for major depressive disorder, recurrent. Katie's depressive episodes were quite severe when they occurred, but she tended to cycle in and out of them.

Dysthymic disorder shares many of the symptoms of major depressive disorder but differs in its course. The symptoms are somewhat milder but remain relatively unchanged over long periods of time, sometimes 20 or 30 years or more (Angst, 2009; Klein, 2008; Klein, Schwartz, Rose, & Leader, 2000; Klein, Shankman, & Rose, 2006).

Dysthymic disorder is defined as a persistently depressed mood that continues for at least two years, during which the patient cannot be symptom-free for more than two months at a time (see DSM Table 7.4). Dysthymic disorder differs from a major depressive episode only in the severity, chronicity, and number of its symptoms, which are milder and fewer but last longer. In a ten-year prospective follow-up study described later, 22 percent of people suffering from dysthymia eventually experienced a major depressive episode (Klein et al., 2006).

DSM-IV-TR	**Table 7.3** Diagnostic Criteria for Major Depressive Disorder, Single Episode

A. There is the presence of a single major depressive episode.

B. The major depressive episode is not better accounted for by schizoaffective disorder and is not superimposed on schizophrenia, schizophreniform disorder, delusional disorder, or psychotic disorder not otherwise specified.

C. There has never been a manic episode, a mixed episode, or a hypomanic episode. *Note:* This exclusion does not apply if all of the manic-like, mixed-like, or hypomanic-like episodes are substance or treatment induced, or are due to the direct physiological effects of a general medical condition.

Specify (for current or most recent episode): With postpartum onset

Source: Reprinted with permission from the *Diagnostic and Statistical Manual of Mental Disorders*, Fourth Edition, Text Revision, (Copyright © 2000). American Psychiatric Association.

A. Depressed mood for most of the day, for more days than not, as indicated either by subjective account or observation by others, for at least two years. *Note:* In children and adolescents, mood can be irritable and duration must be at least one year.

B. Presence, while depressed, of two (or more) of the following:

 1. Poor appetite or overeating

 2. Insomnia or hypersomnia

 3. Low energy or fatigue

 4. Low self-esteem

 5. Poor concentration or difficulty making decisions

 6. Feelings of hopelessness

C. During the two-year period (one year for children or adolescents) of the disturbance, the person has never been without the symptoms in Criteria A and B for more than two months at a time.

D. No major depressive episode has been present during the first two years of the disturbance (one year for children and adolescents); that is, the disturbance is not better accounted for by chronic major depressive disorder, or major depressive disorder, in partial remission.

 Note: There may have been a previous major depressive episode provided there was a full remission (no significant signs or symptoms for two months) before development of the dysthymic disorder. In addition, after the initial two years (one year in children or adolescents) of dysthymic disorder, there may be superimposed episodes of major depressive disorder, in which case both diagnoses may be given when the criteria are met for a major depressive episode.

E. There has never been a manic episode, a mixed episode, or a hypomanic episode, and criteria have never been met for cyclothymic disorder.

F. The disturbance does not occur exclusively during the course of a chronic psychotic disorder, such as schizophrenia or delusional disorder.

G. The symptoms are not due to the direct physiological effects of a substance (e.g., a drug of abuse, a medication) or a general medical condition (e.g., hypothyroidism).

H. The symptoms cause clinically significant distress or impairment in social, occupational, or other important areas of functioning.

Specify if:

Early onset: If onset is before age 21 years

Late onset: If onset is age 21 years or older

Source: Reprinted with permission from the *Diagnostic and Statistical Manual of Mental Disorders*, Fourth Edition, Text Revision, (Copyright © 2000). American Psychiatric Association.

Double Depression

Recently, individuals have been studied who experience both major depression episodes and dysthymic disorder, and who are therefore said to have **double depression**. Typically, dysthymic disorder develops first, perhaps at an early age, and then one or more major depressive episodes occur later (Boland & Keller, 2009; Klein et al., 2006). Identifying this particular pattern is important because it is associated with severe psychopathology and a problematic future course (Boland & Keller, 2009; Klein et al., 2006). For example, Keller, Lavori, Endicott, Coryell, and Klerman (1983) found that 61 percent of patients with double depression had not recovered from the underlying dysthymic disorder two years after follow-up. The investigators also found that patients who had recovered from the superimposed major

JACK | *A Life Kept Down*

Jack was a 49-year-old divorced white man who lived at his mother's home with his ten-year-old son. He complained of chronic depression, saying he finally realized he needed help. Jack reported that he had been a pessimist and a worrier for much of his adult life. He consistently felt kind of down and depressed and did not have much fun. He had difficulty making decisions, was generally pessimistic about the future, and thought very little of himself. During the past 20 years, the longest period he could remember in which his mood was "normal" or less depressed lasted only four or five days.

Despite his difficulties, Jack had managed to finish college and obtain a master's degree in public administration. People told him his future was bright and he would be highly valued in state government. Jack did not think so. He took a job as a low-level clerk in a state agency, thinking he could always work his way up. He never did, remaining at the same desk for years.

Jack's wife, fed up with his continued pessimism, lack of self-confidence, and relative inability to enjoy day-to-day events, became discouraged and divorced him. Jack moved in with his mother so she could help care for his son and share expenses.

About five years before coming to the clinic, Jack had experienced a bout of depression worse than anything he had previously known. His self-esteem went from low to nonexistent. From indecisiveness, he became totally unable to decide anything. He was exhausted all the time and felt as if lead had filled his arms and legs, making it difficult even to move. He became unable to complete projects or to meet deadlines. Seeing no hope, he began to consider suicide. After tolerating a listless performance for years from someone they had expected to rise through the ranks, Jack's employers finally fired him.

After about six months, the major depressive episode resolved and Jack returned to his chronic but milder state of depression. He could get out of bed and accomplish some things, although he still doubted his own abilities. However, he was unable to obtain another job. After several years of waiting for something to turn up, he realized he was totally unable to solve his own problems and that without help his depression would certainly continue. After a thorough assessment, we determined that Jack had a classic case of double depression.

depressive episode experienced very high rates of relapse and recurrence. Consider the case of Jack.

Onset and Duration

The mean age of onset for major depressive disorder is 25 years in community samples of subjects who are not in treatment (Burke, Burke, Regier, & Rae, 1990) and 29 years for patients who are in treatment (Judd et al., 1998a), but the average age of onset seems to be decreasing (Kessler et al., 2003; Weissman, Bruce, Leaf, Florio, & Holzer, 1991). In fact, the prevalence of major depression increases dramatically during the adolescent

A diagnosis of a mood disorder requires many different qualifications known as specifiers. But it is quite likely that the number of specifiers will be dramatically reduced in the future. This is because increasing evidence indicates that the two factors that most importantly describe mood disorders are severity and chronicity and that these two factors can be represented along two dimensions. (This classification scheme is presented in Table 7.1.) Thus, depression could range from mild to severe and also could be characterized as time limited or "nonchronic" as opposed to chronic. Currently, as one can see in Table 7.1, moderate to severe depression would meet criteria for a major depressive disorder that could be described as either chronic or nonchronic, whereas more mild depression would meet criteria for a minor depressive disorder if nonchronic, or dysthymic disorder if chronic. But the labels of mild depression, dysthymia, and major depression, as well as some other specifiers such as melancholic, would no longer be necessary if we categorized depression only on the basis of severity and chronicity. It is very likely that this dimensional approach and other advances to characterizing mood disorders along dimensions will be increasingly used in future systems of classification.

TABLE 7.1 *DSM-IV* Depressive Disorders as a Function of Severity and Chronicity

Severity	Nonchronic	Chronic
Moderate-severe	Nonchronic major depressive disorder	Chronic major depressive disorder
Mild	Minor depressive disorder	Dysthymic disorder

Source: Adapted from Klein, D. N. (2010). *Chronic depression: Diagnosis and classification. Current Directions in Psychological Science, 19(2),* 96–100.

years (e.g., Offord et al., 1987), particularly in adolescent girls (Georgiades, Lewinsohn, Monroe, & Seeley, 2006; see also review in Santor & Kusumakar, 2001). A frightening finding is that the incidence of depression and consequent suicide seem to be steadily increasing (Kessler et al., 2003; Lewinsohn, Rohde, Seeley, & Fischer, 1993). In 1989, a survey of people in five different American cities (Klerman & Weissman, 1989; Wickramaratne, Weissman, Leaf, & Holford, 1989) revealed a greatly increased risk of developing depression in younger people. Among those born before 1905, only 1 percent had developed depression by age 75; of those born since 1955, 6 percent had become depressed by age 24. A later study based on very similar surveys conducted in Canada, Puerto Rico, Italy, Germany, France, Taiwan, Lebanon, and New Zealand suggests that this trend toward developing depression at increasingly earlier ages is occurring worldwide (Cross-National Collaborative Group, 1992). As we noted previously, the length of depressive episodes is variable, with some lasting as little as two weeks; in more severe cases, an episode might last for several years, with the average duration of the first episode being six to nine months if untreated (Angst, 2009; Boland & Keller, 2009; Hasin et al., 2005; Kessler et al., 2003). Although nine months is a long time to suffer with a severe depressive episode, evidence indicates that even in the most severe cases, the probability of remission of the episode within one year approaches 90 percent (Kessler & Wang, 2009). Even in those severe cases in which the episode lasts five years or longer, 38 percent can be expected to eventually recover

(Mueller et al., 1996). Occasionally, however, episodes may not entirely clear up, leaving some residual symptoms. In this case, the likelihood of a subsequent episode with another incomplete recovery is much higher (Boland & Keller, 2009). Knowing this is important to treatment planning, because treatment should be continued much longer in these cases.

Recent evidence also identifies important subtypes of dysthymic disorder. Although the typical age of onset has been estimated to be in the early 20s, adolescent onset of depression is associated with (1) greater chronicity (it lasts longer), (2) relatively poor prognosis (response to treatment), and (3) a stronger likelihood of the disorder running in the family of the affected individual (Gotlib, Lewinsohn, Seeley, Rohde, & Redner, 1993; Klein, Taylor, Dickstein, & Harding, 1988; Santor & Kusumakar, 2001). A greater prevalence of current personality disorders has been found in patients with early-onset dysthymia than in patients with major depressive disorder (Pepper et al., 1995). Adolescents who have recovered from dysthymic disorder still have a lower level of social support and higher levels of stress than adolescents with major depressive disorders or other nonmood disorders (Klein, Lewinsohn, & Seeley, 1997). These findings may further reflect the insidiousness of the psychopathology in early-onset dysthymia. Investigators have found a rather high prevalence of dysthymic disorder in children (Kovacs, Gatsonis, Paulauskas, & Richards, 1989), and Kovacs, Akiskal, Gatsonis, and Parrone (1994) found that 76 percent of a sample of dysthymic children later developed major depressive disorder.

Dysthymic disorder may last 20 to 30 years or more, although a preliminary study reported a median duration of approximately five years in adults (Rounsaville, Sholomskas, & Prusoff, 1988) and four years in children (Kovacs et al., 1994). Klein et al. (2000) conducted a five-year naturalistic follow-up of 86 adults with dysthymic disorder and found that 53 percent had recovered at some point, but 45 percent of those had relapsed. The whole sample of 86 patients spent approximately 70 percent of the five-year follow-up period meeting full criteria for a mood disorder. These findings demonstrate the chronicity of dysthymia. Even worse, patients with dysthymia were more likely to attempt suicide than a comparison group with episodes of major depressive disorder during the five-year period. Conversely, Kovacs et al. (1994) found that almost all children with dysthymia in their sample eventually recovered from it. It is relatively common for major depressive episodes and dysthymic disorder to co-occur (double depression; McCullough et al., 2000). Among those who have had dysthymia, as many as 79 percent have also had a major depressive episode at some point in their lives.

From Grief to Depression

At the beginning of the chapter, we asked if you had ever felt down or depressed. Almost everyone has. But if someone you love has died—particularly if the death was unexpected and the person was a member of your immediate family—you may, after your initial reaction to the trauma, have experienced most of the symptoms of a major depressive episode: anxiety, emotional numbness, and denial (Kendler, Myers, & Zisook, 2008). In fact, the frequency of severe depression following the death of a loved one is so high (approximately 62 percent) that mental health professionals do not consider it a disorder unless very severe symptoms appear, such as psychotic features or suicidal ideation, or the less alarming symptoms last longer than two months (Jacobs, 1993). Some grieving individuals require immediate treatment because they are so incapacitated by their symptoms (e.g., severe weight loss, no energy whatsoever) that they cannot function.

▲ Queen Victoria remained in such deep mourning for her husband, Prince Albert, that she was unable to perform as monarch for several years after his death.

We must confront death and process it emotionally. All religions and cultures have rituals, such as funerals and burial ceremonies, to help us work through our losses with the support and love of our relatives and friends (Bonanno & Kaltman, 1999; Shear, 2006). Usually the natural grieving process resolves within the first several months, although some people grieve for a year or longer (Clayton & Darvish, 1979; Currier, Neimeyer, & Berman, 2008; Maciejewski, Zhang, Block, & Prigerson, 2007). Grief often recurs at significant anniversaries, such as the birthday of the loved one, holidays, and other meaningful occasions, including the anniversary of the death. Mental health professionals are concerned when someone does not grieve after a death, because grieving is our natural way of confronting and handling loss.

When grief lasts beyond the normal time, mental health professionals become concerned (Neimeyer & Currier, 2009). After a year or so, the chance of recovering from severe grief without treatment is considerably reduced and, for approximately 10 percent to 20 percent of bereaved individuals (Bonanno, 2006; Jacobs, 1993; Middleton, Burnett, Raphael, & Martinek, 1996), a normal process becomes a disorder. At this stage, suicidal thoughts increase substantially (Stroebe, Stroebe, & Abakoumkin, 2005). Many of the psychological and social factors related to mood disorders in general, including a history of past depressive episodes (Horowitz et al., 1997; Jacobs, Hansen, Berkman, Kasl, & Ostfeld, 1989), also predict the development of a normal grief response into a **pathological grief reaction** or **impacted grief reaction**.

A longitudinal study by a group including researchers at the University of British Columbia (Bonanno et al., 2002) showed that pre-loss dependency was predictive of a pathological grief reaction following the loss of a spouse. Particularly prominent symptoms of a pathological grief reaction include intrusive memories and distressingly strong yearnings for the loved one, and avoiding people or places that are reminders of the loved one (Horowitz et al., 1997). In cases of long-lasting grief, the rituals intended to help us face and accept death were ineffective. As with victims who have post-traumatic stress, one therapeutic approach is to help grieving individuals re-experience the trauma under close supervision. Usually the grieving person is encouraged to talk about the loved one, the death, and the meaning of the loss while experiencing all the associated emotions, until he or she can come to terms with reality. This would include finding some meaning in the traumatic loss, incorporating positive emotions associated with memories of the relationship into the intense negative emotions connected with the loss, and arriving at the position that the person can cope with the pain and life will go on (Bonanno & Kaltman, 1999).

Some researchers have cautioned against treating pathological grief reaction and depression in the same manner. For example, at the University of British Columbia, John Ogrodniczuk and his colleagues (2003) showed that dimensions of pathological grief could be distinguished from dimensions of depression among close to 400 psychiatric out-patients who had experienced one or more significant losses. And it was the grief dimensions that showed the most improvement in group therapy specifically designed to treat pathological grief reaction (Ogrodniczuk et al., 2003). The authors warn that clinicians should not assume the absence of a pathological grief reaction in someone who has lost a loved one, even if the person is not displaying depressive symptoms.

Bipolar Disorders

The key identifying feature of bipolar disorders is the tendency of manic episodes to alternate with major depressive episodes in an unending roller coaster ride from the peaks of elation to the depths of despair. Beyond that, bipolar disorders are parallel in many ways to depressive disorders. For example, a manic episode might occur only once or repeatedly. Consider the case of Jane.

JANE | *Funny, Smart, and Desperate*

Jane was the wife of a well-known surgeon and the loving mother of three children. They lived in an old country house on the edge of town with plenty of room for the family and pets. Jane was nearly 50; the older children had moved out; the youngest son, 16-year-old Mike, was having substantial academic difficulties in school and seemed very anxious. Jane brought Mike to the clinic to find out why he was having problems.

As they entered the office, I observed that Jane was well dressed, neat, vivacious, and personable; she had a bounce to her step. She began talking about her wonderful and successful family before she and Mike even reached their seats. Mike, by contrast, was very quiet and reserved. He seemed resigned and perhaps relieved that he would have to say very little during the session. By the time Jane sat down, she had mentioned the personal virtues and material achievement of her husband, and the brilliance and beauty of one of her older children, and she was proceeding to describe the second child. But before she finished, she noticed a book on anxiety disorders and, having read voraciously on the subject, began a litany of various anxiety-related problems that might be troubling Mike.

In the meantime, Mike sat in the corner with a small smile on his lips that seemed to be masking considerable distress and uncertainty over what his mother might do next. It became clear as the interview progressed that Mike had obsessive-compulsive disorder, which disturbed his concentration both in and out of school. He was failing all his courses.

It also became clear that Jane herself was in the midst of a *hypomanic* episode, evident in her unbridled enthusiasm, grandiose perceptions, "uninterruptible" speech, and report that she needed very little sleep these days. She was also easily distracted, as when she quickly switched from describing her children to the book on the table. When asked about her own psychological state, Jane readily admitted that she was a "manic depressive" (the old name for *bipolar disorder*) and that she alternated rather rapidly between feeling on top of the world and feeling very depressed; she was taking medication for her condition. I immediately wondered if Mike's obsessions had anything to do with his mother's condition.

Mike was treated intensively for his obsessions and compulsions, but he made little progress. He said that life at home was very difficult when his mother was depressed.

She sometimes went to bed and stayed there for three weeks. During this time, she seemed be in a depressive stupor, essentially unable to move for days. It was up to the children to care for themselves and their mother, whom they fed by hand. Because the older children had now left home, much of the burden had fallen on Mike. Jane's profound depressive episodes would remit after about three weeks, and she would immediately enter a hypomanic episode that might last several months or more. During hypomania, Jane was, for the most part, funny and entertaining and a delight to be with—if you could get a word in edgewise. Consultation with her therapist, an expert in the area, revealed that he had prescribed a number of medications but was so far unable to bring her mood swings under control.

Jane had **bipolar II disorder**, in which major depressive episodes alternate with hypomanic episodes rather than full manic episodes (see DSM Table 7.5). As we noted earlier, hypomanic episodes are less severe. Although she was noticeably "up," Jane functioned pretty well while in this mood state. The criteria for **bipolar I disorder** are the same, except the individual experiences a full manic episode. As in the criteria set for depressive disorder, for the manic episodes to be considered separate, they must have a symptom-free period of at least two months between them. Otherwise, one episode is seen as a continuation of the last.

The case of Billy illustrates a full manic episode. This individual was first encountered when he was admitted to a hospital.

DSM-IV-TR	**Table 7.5** Diagnostic Criteria for Bipolar II Disorder

A. There is the presence (or history) of one or more major depressive episodes.

B. There is the presence (or history) of at least one hypomanic episode.

C. There has never been a manic episode or a mixed episode.

D. The mood symptoms in Criteria A and B are not better accounted for by schizoaffective disorder and are not superimposed on schizophrenia, schizophreniform disorder, delusional disorder, or psychotic disorder not otherwise specified.

E. The symptoms cause clinically significant distress or impairment in social, occupational, or other important areas of functioning.

Specify current or most recent episode:

Hypomanic: If currently (or most recently) in a hypomanic episode

Depressed: If currently (or most recently) in a major depressive episode

Specify:

With postpartum onset (for current or most recent depressive episode)

Longitudinal course specifiers (with and without interepisode recovery)

With seasonal pattern (applies only to the pattern of major depressive episodes)

With rapid cycling

Source: Reprinted with permission from the *Diagnostic and Statistical Manual of Mental Disorders*, Fourth Edition, Text Revision, (Copyright © 2000). American Psychiatric Association.

BILLY | *The World's Best at Everything*

Before Billy reached the ward you could hear him laughing and carrying on in a deep voice; it sounded as if he was having a wonderful time. As the nurse brought Billy down the hall to introduce him to the staff, he spied the Ping-Pong table. Loudly, he exclaimed, "Ping-Pong! I love Ping-Pong! I have only played twice but that is what I am going to do while I am here; I am going to become the world's greatest Ping-Pong player! And that table is gorgeous! I am going to start work on that table immediately and make it the finest Ping-Pong table in the world. I am going to sand it down, take it apart, and rebuild it until it gleams and every angle is perfect!" Billy soon went on to something else that totally absorbed his attention.

The previous week, Billy had emptied his bank account, taken his credit cards and those of his elderly parents with whom he was living, and bought every piece of fancy stereo equipment he could find. He thought that he would set up the best sound studio in the city and make millions of dollars by renting it to people who would come from far and wide. This episode had precipitated his admission to the hospital.

▲ Margaret Trudeau, former wife of the late Pierre Trudeau, recently revealed that she has struggled with bipolar disorder throughout her adult life. She was treated as an inpatient at the Royal Ottawa Hospital in 2001 and has gone public with her story in hopes of helping reduce the stigma associated with this mental health disorder (Berthiaume, 2006).

During manic or hypomanic phases, patients often deny they have a problem, which was characteristic of Billy. Even after spending inordinate amounts of money or making foolish business decisions, these individuals, particularly if they are in the midst of a full manic episode, are so wrapped up in their enthusiasm and expansiveness that their behaviour seems perfectly reasonable to them. The high during a manic state is so pleasurable, people may stop taking their medication during periods of distress or discouragement in an attempt to bring on a manic state once again; this is a serious challenge to professionals.

Returning to the case of Jane, we continued to treat Jane's son Mike for several months. We had made very little progress before the school year ended. Because Mike was doing so poorly, the school administrators informed his parents that he would not be accepted back the next year. Mike and his parents wisely decided it might be a good idea if he got away from the house and did something different for a while, and he began working and living at a ski and tennis resort. Several months later, his father called to tell us that Mike's obsessions and compulsions

had completely lifted since he'd been away from home. The father thought Mike should continue living at the resort, where he had entered school and was doing better academically. He now agreed with our previous assessment that Mike's condition might be related to his relationship with his mother. Several years later, we heard that Jane, in a depressive stupor, had killed herself, an all-too-tragic outcome in bipolar disorder.

Like dysthymic disorder, **cyclothymic disorder** is a chronic alternation of mood elevation and depression that

▲ Actress Catherine Zeta-Jones has recently announced that she struggles with bipolar II disorder.

does not reach the severity of manic or major depressive episodes (see DSM Table 7.6). Individuals with cyclothymic disorder tend to be in one mood state or the other for many years with relatively few periods of neutral (or euthymic) mood. This pattern must last for at least two years (one year for children and adolescents) to meet criteria for the disorder. Individuals with cyclothymic disorder alternate between the kinds of mild depressive symptoms Jack experienced during his dysthymic states and the sorts of hypomanic episodes Jane experienced. In neither case was the behaviour severe enough to require hospitalization or immediate intervention. Much of the time, such individuals are just considered moody.

DSM-IV-TR	**Table 7.6** Criteria for Cyclothymic Disorder

A. For at least two years, the presence of numerous periods with hypomanic symptoms and numerous periods with depressive symptoms that do not meet criteria for a major depressive episode. *Note:* In children and adolescents, the duration must be at least one year.

B. During the above two-year period (one year in children and adolescents), the person has not been without the symptoms in Criterion A for more than two months at a time.

C. No major depression episode, manic episode, or mixed episode has been present during the first years of the disturbance.

Note: After the initial two years (one year in children and adolescents) of cyclothymic disorder, there may be superimposed manic or mixed episodes (in which case both bipolar I disorder and cyclothymic disorder may be diagnosed) or major depressive episodes (in which case both bipolar II disorder and cyclothymic disorder may be diagnosed).

D. The symptoms in Criterion A are not better accounted for by schizoaffective disorder and are not superimposed on schizophrenia, schizophreniform disorder, delusional disorder, or psychotic disorder not otherwise specified.

E. The symptoms are not due to the direct physiological effects of a substance (e.g., a drug of abuse, a medication) or a general medical condition (e.g., hyperthyroidism).

F. The symptoms cause clinically significant distress or impairment in social, occupational, or other important areas of functioning.

Source: Reprinted with permission from the *Diagnostic and Statistical Manual of Mental Disorders*, Fourth Edition, Text Revision, (Copyright © 2000). American Psychiatric Association.

Bipolar Disorder: Mary

Whoo, whoo, whoo—on top of the world!. . . It's going to be one great day! . . . I'm incognito for the Lord God Almighty. I'm working for him. I have been for years. I'm a spy. My mission is to fight for the American way . . . the Statue of Liberty. . . . I can bring up the wind, I can bring the rain, I can bring the sunshine, I can do lots of things. . . . I love the outdoors. . . .

Go to Psychology CourseMate at www.abnormalpsych3ce. nelson.com to watch this video.

However, the chronically fluctuating mood states are, by definition, substantial enough to interfere with functioning. Furthermore, people with cyclothymia should be treated because of their increased risk to develop the more severe bipolar I or bipolar II disorder (Akiskal, 2009; Akiskal & Pinto, 1999; Alloy & Abramson, 2001; Goodwin & Jamison, 2007; Otto & Applebaum, in press).

Onset and Duration

The average age of onset for bipolar I disorder is 18, and for bipolar II disorder it is 22, although cases of both can begin in childhood (Angst, 2009; Judd et al., 2003; Merikangas & Pato, 2009). This is somewhat younger than the average age of onset for major depressive disorder, and bipolar disorders begin more acutely; that is, they develop more suddenly (Angst & Sellaro, 2000; Johnson, Turkheimer, Gottesman, & Bouchard, 2009). About one-third of the cases of bipolar disorder begin in adolescence (Taylor & Abrams, 1981), and the onset is often preceded by minor oscillations in mood or mild cyclothymic mood swings (Goodwin & Ghaemi, 1998; Goodwin & Jamison, 1990). Only 10 percent to 13 percent of bipolar II disorder cases progress to full bipolar I syndrome (Coryell et al., 1995; Depression Guideline Panel, 1993). The distinction between unipolar and bipolar mood disorder also seems well defined because only 5.2 percent of a large group of 381 patients with unipolar depression experienced a manic episode during a ten-year follow-up period (Coryell et al., 1995), although Angst and Sellaro (2000), in reviewing some older studies, estimated the rate of individuals with depression later experiencing mania at closer to 25 percent. In any case, if these disorders were more closely related, we would expect to see more individuals moving from one to the other.

It is relatively rare for someone to develop bipolar disorder after the age of 40. Once it does appear, the course is chronic; that is, mania and depression alternate indefinitely. Therapy usually involves managing the disorder with ongoing drug regimens that prevent recurrence of episodes. Suicide is an all-too-common consequence of bipolar disorder, usually occurring during depressive episodes, as it did in the case of Jane (Angst, 2009; Valtonen et al., 2007). Estimates of suicide attempts in bipolar disorder range from 12 percent to as high as 48 percent over a lifetime, and this rate is approximately 20 times higher than for individuals without bipolar disorder (Goodwin & Jamison, 2007). Rates of completed suicide are four times

higher in people with bipolar disorder than for people with recurrent major depression (Brown, Beck, Steer, & Grisham, 2000; Miklowitz & Johnson, 2006). Even with treatment, patients with bipolar disorder tend to do poorly, with one study showing 60 percent of a large group experiencing poor adjustment during the first five years after treatment (Goldberg, Harrow, & Grossman, 1995; Goodwin et al., 2003). A more comprehensive and longer follow-up of 219 patients reported that only 16 percent recovered; 52 percent suffered from recurrent episodes, 16 percent had become chronically disabled, and in one study 8 percent had committed suicide (Angst & Sellaro, 2000); in another study with a lengthy, 40-year follow-up, 11 percent had committed suicide (Angst, Angst, Gerber-Werder, & Gamma, 2005).

In typical cases, cyclothymia is chronic and lifelong. In about one third to one half of patients, cyclothymic mood swings develop into full-blown bipolar disorder (Kochman et al., 2005). In one sample of cyclothymic patients, 60 percent were female, and the age of onset was often during the teenage years or before, with some data suggesting the most common age of onset to be 12 to 14 years (Goodwin & Jamison, 2007). The disorder is often not recognized, and sufferers are thought to be high-strung, explosive, moody, or hyperactive (Akiskal, 2009; Biederman et al., 2000; Goodwin & Jamison, 2007). One subtype of cyclothymia is based on the predominance of mild depressive symptoms, one on the predominance of hypomanic symptoms, and another on an equal distribution of both.

Concept Check | 7.1

Match the word to its definition: (a) mania, (b) hypomanic episode, (c) anhedonia, (d) dysthymic episode, (e) major depressive episode, or (f) bipolar disorder.

1. A tendency for manic episodes to alternate with major depressive episodes. _____

2. A period of abnormally extreme elation, joy, or euphoria. _____

3. The inability to experience pleasure. _____

4. Similar to major depressive disorder but differs in course. Symptoms are somewhat milder but remain unchanged for long periods. _____

5. Similar to a manic episode except it is less severe. _____

Postpartum Depression

Diagnosing a mood disorder is not a straightforward task; great diversity of symptoms is possible within any of the diagnostic categories, as is illustrated in ■ Figure 7.1. Other symptoms, or

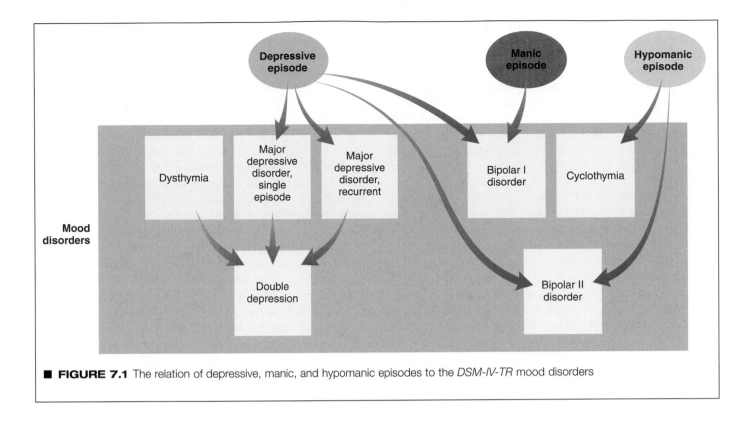

■ FIGURE 7.1 The relation of depressive, manic, and hypomanic episodes to the *DSM-IV-TR* mood disorders

specifiers, may or may not accompany a mood disorder; when they do, they are often helpful in determining the most effective treatment. For example, the *postpartum onset specifier* can apply to both major depressive and manic episodes. It is characterized by severe manic or depressive episodes that first occur during the postpartum period (the four weeks immediately following childbirth), typically two to three days after delivery. The postpartum incidence, however, is quite low, approximately one per 1000 deliveries (Meltzer & Kumar, 1985). If a new mother experiences one of these severe postpartum episodes, the chances are approximately 50 percent that she will experience another episode with subsequent births (Davidson & Robertson, 1985; Depression Guideline Panel, 1993).

Celebrities like singer and songwriter Sarah McLaughlin (see Jones, 2004) and politician Maureen McTeer (wife of former prime minister Joe Clark) have spoken publicly about their battles with postpartum depression. For example, in her autobiography, *In My Own Name*, McTeer describes her struggle in trying to juggle the multiple roles of new mother, prime minister's wife, feminist role model, and lawyer, all within the public spotlight of politics. In her book, she describes her postpartum depression symptoms: "After the initial euphoria following Catherine's birth, I felt alone and depressed. I cried a great deal and seemed unable to pull out of my funk" (McTeer, 2003, p. 84).

Postpartum depression expert Valerie Whiffen at the University of Ottawa concluded that the risks for developing mood disorders during the postpartum period might be overestimated (Whiffen, 1992). One study found no differences in the rates of minor and major depression in a group of childbearing women, either during pregnancy or after delivery, and in a well-matched control group (O'Hara, Zekoski, Philipps, & Wright, 1990). A close examination of women with postpartum depression by Whiffen and her colleagues revealed no essential differences

between the characteristics of this mood disorder and others (Whiffen, 2003, 2004; Whiffen & Gotlib, 1993). In other words, postpartum depression does not seem to require a separate category in the *DSM-IV-TR* (Purdy & Frank, 1993).

Some research is emerging on the risk factors for postpartum depression that may ultimately assist in early identification. For example, Whiffen's work suggests that having an infant with a difficult temperament is an important type of stressor that can contribute to postpartum depression (Whiffen & Gotlib, 1989a). Moreover, research by McGill University researchers Phyllis Zelkowitz and Tamara Milet (2001) indicates that low socioeconomic status and high levels of life stress are also related to the persistence of postpartum depression following birth of the child. Early recognition is very important (Steiner, 2002) because in a few tragic cases, a mother in the midst of an episode has killed her newborn child (Purdy & Frank, 1993). One well-known case is a murder-suicide that took place in Toronto in August of 2000. Suzanne Killinger-Johnson, a psychiatrist, jumped in front of a subway train with her six-month-old son. The baby died instantly and the mother died the next day. Killinger-Johnson was believed to have been suffering from postpartum depression.

Specifiers Describing Course of Mood Disorders

Three specifiers may accompany recurrent mania or depression: longitudinal course, rapid cycling, and seasonal pattern. Differences in course or temporal pattern may require different treatment strategies.

1. *Longitudinal course specifiers.* Whether the individual has had major episodes of depression or mania in the past is important, as is whether the individual fully recovered

between past episodes. Other important determinations are whether the patient with a major depressive episode had dysthymia before the episode (double depression) and whether the patient with bipolar disorder experienced a previous cyclothymic disorder. Antecedent dysthymia or cyclothymia predicts a decreasing chance of full interepisode recovery (Judd et al., 1998b). Most likely, the patient will require a long and intense course of treatment to maintain a normal mood state for as long as possible after recovering from the current episode (Mueller et al., 1999; Solomon et al., 2000).

2. *Rapid-cycling specifier.* This temporal specifier applies only to bipolar I and bipolar II disorders. Some people move very quickly in and out of depressive or manic episodes. An individual with bipolar disorder who experiences at least four manic or depressive episodes within a year is considered to have a rapid-cycling pattern, which is apparently a severe variety of bipolar disorder that does not respond well to standard treatments (Angst, 2009; Bauer et al., 1994; Kupka et al., 2005; Schneck et al., 2004, 2008) and which is associated with a higher probability of suicide attempts (Coryell et al., 2003). Some evidence indicates that alternative drug treatment such as anticonvulsants and mood stabilizers may be more effective with this group of patients (Kilzieh & Akiskal, 1999; Post et al., 1989).

   Approximately 20 percent of bipolar patients experience rapid cycling. As many as 90 percent are female, a higher rate than in other variations of bipolar disorder (e.g., Coryell et al., 2003; Wehr, Sack, Rosenthal, & Cowdry, 1988), and this finding is consistent across ten studies (Kilzieh & Akiskal, 1999). Unlike bipolar patients in general, most people with rapid cycling begin with a depressive episode rather than a manic episode (McElroy & Keck, 1993). In most cases, rapid cycling tends to increase in frequency over time and can reach very severe states in which patients cycle between mania and depression without any break. Fortunately, rapid cycling does not seem to be permanent, because fewer than 3 percent of patients continue with rapid cycling across a five-year period (Coryell, Endicott, & Keller, 1992), with 80 percent returning to a non–rapid-cycling pattern within two years (Coryell et al., 2003).

3. *Seasonal pattern specifier.* This temporal specifier applies both to bipolar disorders and to recurrent major depressive disorder. It accompanies episodes that occur during certain seasons (e.g., winter depression). Some mood disorders do seem tied to seasons of the year. The most usual pattern is a depressive episode that begins in the late fall and ends with the beginning of spring. In bipolar disorder, individuals may become depressed during the winter and manic during the summer. This condition is called **seasonal affective disorder (SAD)**.

Although some studies have reported seasonal cycling of manic episodes, the overwhelming majority of seasonal mood disorders involve winter depression (Lewy, 1993). A community-based telephone survey conducted in Toronto found that the prevalence of the seasonal subtype of major depression (i.e., winter depression SAD) was about 3 percent (Levitt, Boyle, Joffe, & Baumal, 2000). Unlike more severe melancholic types of depression, people with winter depressions tend toward excessive sleep (rather than decreased sleep), increased appetite (rather than decreased appetite), and weight gain (rather than weight loss), symptoms shared with atypical depressive episodes. As you may have noticed, SAD seems a bit different from other major depressive episodes. A study by Winnipeg psychiatrist Murray Enns and his colleagues (2006) showed that SAD patients are characterized by different personality profiles than those with nonseasonal depression. For example, the SAD patients scored higher on a personality factor called openness (see Chapter 12), relative both to norms in the general population and to a group of nonseasonally depressed patients. The authors suggest that the elevated openness scores in people with SAD may reflect a heightened sensitivity to their environments, which may be why these people are prone to experiencing amplified reactions to reduced light levels during the winter months (Enns et al., 2006). In contrast, family studies conducted by Raymond Lam and his colleagues at the University of British Columbia have not yet revealed any differential aggregation that would suggest winter depressions are really a separate type of depression (Allen, Lam, Remick, & Sadovnick, 1993).

A number of biological explanations for SAD are beginning to appear (see review by Sohn & Lam, 2005). For example, emerging evidence suggests that SAD may be related to daily and seasonal changes in the production of melatonin, a hormone secreted by the pineal gland. Because exposure to light suppresses melatonin production, it is produced only at night. Melatonin production also tends to increase in winter, when there is less sunlight. One theory is that increased production of melatonin might trigger depression in vulnerable people (Goodwin & Jamison, 1990; Lee et al., 1998). (We return to this topic when we discuss biological contributions to depression.) Another possibility is that circadian rhythms, which are thought to have some relationship to mood, are delayed in winter (Lewy & Sack, 1987; Wirz-Justice, 1998).

As you might expect, the prevalence of SAD is higher in extreme northern and southern latitudes because there is less winter sunlight. For example, a study conducted in Toronto showed that SAD occurred in 11 percent of those in the sample who were diagnosed with depression (Levitt et al., 2000). In contrast, a study conducted in the northern city of Thompson, Manitoba, showed that SAD occurred in about 20 percent of those with depression (Williams & Schmidt, 1993), and another study conducted in a small Canadian Arctic Inuit community showed markedly elevated rates of SAD compared to previous studies using similar methods (Haggarty et al., 2002). However, the causes of SAD are more complex than simply living in a northern climate. Magnusson and Axelsson (1993) studied rates of SAD in 252 descendants of Icelanders who had immigrated to northern Manitoba. They found very low rates of SAD in this group (i.e., a 1.2 percent prevalence rate, which is lower than rates observed on the east coast of the United States!). It is possible that this group has somehow genetically adapted to the reduced number of daylight hours in their environment, which provides some protection from the development of SAD (Magnusson & Axelsson, 1993).

▲ Most seasonal affective disorders involve depression in winter, when the light is low and the days are short.

2007 Jeff Schultz/AlaskaStock.com

SAD also seems quite stable. In one group of 59 patients, 86 percent experienced a depressive episode each winter during a nine-year period of observation, with only 14 percent recovering during that time. For 26 (44 percent) of these patients, whose symptoms were more severe to begin with, depressive episodes began to occur during other seasons as well (Schwartz, Brown, Wehr, & Rosenthal, 1996). Rates in children and adolescents are between 1.7 percent and 5.5 percent, according to one study, with higher rates in postpubertal girls (Swedo et al., 1995), but the study needs replication.

Prevalence of Mood Disorders

Several large epidemiological studies estimating the prevalence of mood disorder have been carried out in recent years (Kessler et al., 1994; Weissman et al., 1991). Prevalence rates in Canadian studies have been quite variable, ranging from 4.1 percent in the Ontario Health Survey, to 10.3 percent and 11 percent in surveys in Toronto and Calgary, respectively (De Marco, 2000; Offord et al., 1996; Patten, 2000). As Roger Bland, a leading psychiatric epidemiologist from the University of Alberta, has pointed out, different research methods may account for the differing rates of prevalence (Bland, 1997). Scott Patten at the University of Calgary provides another explanation for different prevalence rates. He argues that prevalence rates for depression in Canada appear to be decreasing, suggesting progress in public health efforts toward combating depression in our country (Patten, 2002).

Wittchen, Knauper, and Kessler (1994) compiled a summary of major prevalence studies from around the world. The figures for major depressive disorder of 16 percent lifetime and 6.5 percent in the preceding ten months have recently been confirmed in the most sophisticated study to date (Kessler et al., 2003). The studies agree that women are twice as likely to have mood disorders as men.

In Children and Adolescents

You might assume that depression requires some experience with life, that an accumulation of negative events or disappointments might create pessimism, which then leads to depression. Like many reasonable assumptions in psychopathology, this one is not uniformly correct. We now have evidence that three-month-old babies can become depressed (Field et al., 1988). Infants of depressed mothers display marked depressive behaviours (sad faces, slow movement, lack of responsiveness), even when interacting with a nondepressed adult (Field et al., 1988). Whether this behaviour or temperament is due to a genetic tendency inherited from the mother, the result of early interaction patterns with a depressed mother, or a combination is not yet clear.

Most investigators agree that mood disorders are fundamentally similar in children and in adults (Lewinsohn, Hops, Roberts, Seeley, & Andrews, 1993; Pataki & Carlson, 1990). Therefore, no "childhood" mood disorders in the *DSM-IV-TR* are specific to a developmental stage, unlike anxiety disorders. However, it also seems clear that the "look" of depression changes with age. For example, children under three years of age might manifest depression by their facial expressions as well as by their eating, sleeping, and play behaviour, quite differently from children between the ages of 9 and 12. The work of psychologist Ian Gotlib, formerly of the University of Western Ontario, and his colleagues has shown that adolescents who are forced to limit their activities because of illness or injury are at high risk for depression (Lewinsohn, Gotlib, & Seeley, 1997).

Estimates on the prevalence of mood disorders in children and adolescents vary widely, although more sophisticated studies are beginning to appear. The general conclusion is that depressive disorders occur less frequently in children than in adults but rise dramatically in adolescence, when, if anything, depression is more frequent than in adults (Kashani, Hoeper, Beck, & Corcoran, 1987; Lewinsohn et al., 1993; Petersen et al., 1993). For example, in a recent epidemiological survey of major depressive disorder in Canadians, using data from the Canadian Community Health Survey, Patten et al. (2006) found that the peak annual prevalence was in the group aged 15 to 25 years (i.e., 5 percent prevalence), with lower rates in the adult age ranges. Furthermore, some evidence indicates that, in young children, dysthymia is more prevalent than major depressive disorder, but this ratio reverses in adolescence. Like adults, adolescents experience major depressive disorder more frequently than dysthymia (Kashani et al., 1983; Kashani et al., 1987). Major depressive disorder in adolescents is also a largely female disorder (Santor & Kusumakar, 2001), as it is in adults, although this is not true for more mild depression. Only among the adolescents referred to treatment does the gender imbalance exist (Compas et al., 1997), though why more girls reach a more severe state requiring referral to treatment is not clear.

Looking at mania, children below the age of nine seem to present with more irritability and emotional swings rather than classic manic states, and they are often mistaken as being hyperactive. In addition, their symptoms are more chronic in that they are always present rather than episodic as in adults (Biederman et al., 2000). This presentation seems to continue through adolescence (Faraone et al., 1997), although adolescents may appear more typically manic. Bipolar disorder seems to be rare in childhood, although case studies of children as young as four years of age displaying bipolar symptoms have been reported (Poznanski, Israel, & Grossman, 1984), and the diagnosis may be mistaken for conduct disorder or attention deficit/hyperactivity disorder (ADHD). However, the prevalence of bipolar disorder rises substantially in adolescence, which is not surprising in that many adults with bipolar disorder report a first onset during the teen years (Keller & Wunder, 1990).

One developmental difference between children and adolescents on the one hand and adults on the other is that children, especially boys, tend to become aggressive and even destructive during depressive episodes. For this reason, childhood depression (and mania) is sometimes misdiagnosed as hyperactivity or, more often, conduct disorder in which aggression and even destructive behaviour are common. Often conduct disorder and depression co-occur (Lewinsohn et al., 1993; Petersen et al., 1993). Puig-Antich (1982) found that one-third of prepubertal depressed boys met full criteria for a conduct disorder, which developed at approximately the same time as the depressive disorder and remitted with the resolution of the depression. Biederman and colleagues (1987) found that 32 percent of children with ADHD also met criteria for major depression, and between 60 percent and 90 percent of children and adolescents with mania also have ADHD (Biederman et al., 2000). In any case, successful treat-

▲ Among adolescents, severe major depressive disorder occurs mostly in girls.

ment of the underlying depression (or spontaneous recovery) also resolves the associated problems in these specific cases. Adolescents with bipolar disorder may also become aggressive, impulsive, sexually provocative, and accident-prone (Carlson, 1990; Keller & Wunder, 1990).

Whatever the presentation, mood disorders in children and adolescents are very serious because of their likely consequences. In an important prospective study, conducted as part of the Ontario Child Health Study, Fleming, Boyle, and Offord (1993) followed 652 adolescents with either a major depressive disorder or a conduct disorder for four years. These adolescents largely continued to experience serious psychopathology and markedly impaired functioning. Lewinsohn, Rhode, Seeley, Klein, and Gotlib (2000) also followed 274 adolescents with major depressive disorder into adulthood and identified several risk factors for additional depressive episodes as adults. Prominent among these were conflicts with parents, being female, and a higher proportion of family members experiencing depressive episodes. Their more recent longitudinal work shows that young adults who had experienced an episode of major depressive disorder in adolescence exhibited a very pervasive pattern of psychosocial impairments in areas such as interpersonal functioning, quality of life, and occupational performance. Reduced life satisfaction in young adulthood was uniquely associated with a history of major depressive disorder, rather than with a history of other mental disorders, in adolescence (Lewinsohn, Rohde, Seeley, Klein, & Gotlib, 2003, 2006). These findings underline the seriousness of adolescent depression, in terms of negative consequences continuing into adulthood.

In the Elderly

Only recently have we seriously considered the problem of depression in the elderly. A Canadian study by Dalhousie University researcher Kenneth Rockwood and colleagues estimated that 18 percent to 20 percent of nursing home residents may experience major depressive episodes (Rockwood, Stolee, & Brahim, 1991; see also Katz, Leshen, Kleban, & Jethanandani, 1989), which are likely to be chronic if they appear first after the age of 60 (Rapp, Parisi, & Wallace, 1991). Late-onset depressions are associated with marked sleep difficulties, hypochondriasis, and agitation. It can be difficult to diagnose depression in the elderly because the presentation of mood disorders is often complicated by the presence of medical illnesses or symptoms of dementia (e.g., Blazer, 1989; Small, 1991). That is, elderly people who become physically ill or begin to show signs of dementia might become depressed about it, but the signs of depression would be attributed to the illness or dementia and thus missed. Nevertheless, the overall prevalence of major depressive disorder is the same or slightly lower in the elderly as in the general population (Patten et al., 2006; Weissman et al., 1991). perhaps because stressful life events that trigger major depressive episodes decrease with age. But, as noted by Ian Gotlib, milder symptoms that do not meet criteria for major depressive disorder may be more common among the elderly (Gotlib & Nolan, 2000), perhaps due to illness and infirmity (Roberts, Kaplan, Shema, & Strawbridge, 1997).

Anxiety disorders frequently accompany depression in the elderly (in about a third of cases), particularly generalized anxiety disorder and panic disorder (Lenze et al., 2000), and when they do, patients are more severely depressed. Depression can also contribute to physical disease in the elderly (Grant, Patterson, & Yager, 1988; House, Landis, & Umberson, 1988). In fact, being depressed doubles the risk of death in elderly patients who have suffered a heart attack or stroke (Schulz, Drayer, & Rollman, 2002). An even more tragic finding is that symptoms of depression are increasing substantially in our growing population of elderly people. Wallace and O'Hara (1992) in a longitudinal study found that elderly citizens became increasingly depressed over a three-year period. They suggest, with some evidence, that this trend is related to increasing illness and reduced social support; in other words, as we become frailer and more alone, the psychological result is depression, which, of course, increases the probability that we will become even frailer and have even less social support. This vicious cycle is deadly.

The earlier gender imbalance in depression disappears after the age of 65. In early childhood, boys are more likely to be depressed than girls, but an overwhelming surge of depression in adolescent girls produces an imbalance in the sex ratio (Santor & Kusumakar, 2001) that is maintained until old age, when just as many women are depressed, but increasing numbers of men are also affected (Wallace & O'Hara, 1992). From the perspective of the life span, this is the first time since early childhood that the sex ratio for depression is balanced.

▲ Depression among the elderly is a serious problem that can be difficult to diagnose because the symptoms are often similar to those of physical illness or dementia.

Across Cultures

We noted the strong tendency of anxiety to take very physical or somatic forms in some cultures; instead of talking about fear, panic, or general anxiety, many people describe stomachaches, chest pains or heart distress, and headaches. According to the research of Laurence Kirmayer (2001; Kirmayer & Jarvis, 2006), much the same tendency exists across cultures for mood disorders, which is not surprising given the close relationship of anxiety and depression. Feelings of weakness or tiredness particularly characterize depression that is accompanied by mental or physical slowing or retardation.

Although somatic symptoms that characterize mood disorders seem roughly equivalent across cultures, it is difficult to compare subjective feelings. The way people think of depression may be influenced by the cultural view of the individual and the role of the individual in society (Jenkins, Kleinman, & Good, 1990; Ryder et al., 2008). For example, in societies that focus on *the individual* instead of the *group*, it is common to hear statements such as "I feel blue," or "I am depressed." However, in cultures where the individual is tightly integrated into the larger group, someone might say, "Our life has lost its meaning," referring to the group in which the individual resides (Manson & Good, 1993). Despite these influences, it is generally agreed that the best way to study the nature and prevalence of mood disorders (or any other psychological disorder) in other cultures is first to determine their prevalence using standardized criteria (Neighbors, Jackson, Campbell, & Williams, 1989). The *DSM* criteria are increasingly used, along with semistructured interviews in which the same questions are asked, with some allowances for different words that might be specific to a culture or subculture.

One such study is the International Consortium of Psychiatric Epidemiology (ICPE) study, which used the same structured interview and diagnostic criteria in ten countries, including Canada (Andrade et al., 2003). The Canadian data were collected by a team led by David Offord of the Chedoke-McMaster Hospital in Hamilton, Ontario. As shown in ■ Figure 7.2, the highest rates of major depressive episode were observed in the U.S. sample (16.9 percent prevalence), and the lowest in the Japanese (3.0 percent prevalence). Compared with the prevalence rates in the other countries, the rates in the Canadian sample were moderate (8.3 percent prevalence).

Kinzie, Leung, Boehnlein, and Matsunaga (1992) used a structured interview to determine the percentage of adult members of a First Nations reserve who met criteria for mood disorders. The lifetime prevalence for any mood disorder was 19.4 percent in men, 36.7 percent in women, and 28 percent overall, approximately four times higher than in the general population. Examined by disorder, almost all the increase is accounted for by greatly elevated rates of major depression. A study of mental health services use among the Cree of James Bay, Québec, indicated that depression was the most common psychiatric illness, occurring in 16.5 percent of the 242 Cree people who were receiving treatment by nursing or other medical professionals in the region (Lavallee, Robinson, & Laverdure, 1991). Similar findings emerged in a more recent study conducted in a Canadian Arctic Inuit community of about 1100 people (Haggarty, Cernovsky, Kermeen, & Merskey, 2000). This study revealed an estimated rate of past-week depression

of 26.5 percent—a rate that is much higher than that seen in the general population. As noted by Laurence Kirmayer (Kirmayer, Boothroyd, Tanner, Adelson, & Robinson, 2000; Kirmayer, Simpson, & Cargo, 2003), the appalling social and economic conditions faced by many groups of Aboriginal peoples in North America, as well as their long history of cultural oppression and marginalization, fulfill all the requirements for chronic major life stress, which is so strongly related to the onset of mood disorders, particularly major depressive disorder.

Among the Creative

Is there truth in the enduring belief that genius is allied with madness? Several researchers have attempted to find out. The results are surprising. Handel wrote *The Messiah* in only three weeks, apparently during a manic episode, and Rossini composed *The Barber of Seville* in only 13 days during a likely period of hypomania (Endler, 1990). Table 7.2 lists a group of famous poets, many of whom won the coveted Pulitzer Prize. As you can see, all almost certainly had bipolar disorder. Many committed suicide. These eight poets are among the 36 born in the 20th century who are represented in *The New Oxford Book of American Verse*, a collection reserved for the most distinguished poets. It is certainly striking that about 20 percent of these 36 poets exhibited bipolar disorders, given the population prevalence of slightly less than 1 percent.

Many composers, artists, and writers, whether suspected of mood disorders or not, speak of periods of inspiration when thought processes quicken, moods lift, and new associations are generated (Jamison, 1989). Perhaps something inherent in manic states fosters creativity. But, as noted by the late Norman Endler, "it is one thing to have the high degree of energy that exists in a manic state; it is another thing to channel it in a direction that creates new works and accomplishes effective tasks" (Endler, 1990, p. 19). It is also possible that the genetic vulnerability to

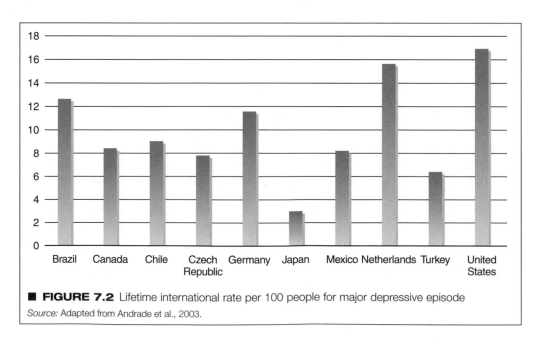

■ **FIGURE 7.2** Lifetime international rate per 100 people for major depressive episode

Source: Adapted from Andrade et al., 2003.

TABLE 7.2 Partial Listing of Major 20th-Century Poets, Born between 1895 and 1935, with Documented Histories of Manic-Depressive Illness

Poet	Pulitzer Prize in Poetry	Treated for Major Depressive Illness	Treated for Mania	Committed Suicide
Hart Crane (1899–1932)		X	X	X
Theodore Roethke (1908–1963)	X	X	X	
Delmore Schwartz (1913–1966)		X	X	
John Berryman (1914–1972)	X	X	X	X
Randall Jerrell (1914–1965)		X	X	X
Robert Lowell (1917–1977)	X	X	X	
Anne Sexton (1928–1974)	X	X	X	X
Sylvia Plath* (1932–1963)	X	X		X

Note: * Plath, although not treated for mania, was probably bipolar II.

Source: Goodwin & Jamison, 1990.

mood disorders is independently accompanied by a predisposition to creativity (Richards, Kinney, Lunde, Benet, & Merzel, 1988). In other words, the genetic patterns associated with bipolar disorder may also carry the spark of creativity. Yet another possibility is suggested by the work of Ghadirian, Gregoire, and Kosmidis (2001), Montréal researchers who conducted a scientific study into the relationship of bipolar disorder to creativity. They compared a group of 20 patients with bipolar disorder to a group of 24 patients with other mental health disorders on measures of creativity. While the bipolar patients were not any more creative than the patients with other disorders, the researchers did find that moderately ill patients were significantly more creative than severely ill patients. These findings suggest that creativity may peak at a stage of the illness where symptoms are moderate, but that creativity may actually decline as symptoms become progressively worse (Ghadirian et al., 2001). These various possibilities are little more than speculations at present, but the study of creativity and leadership, so highly valued in all cultures, may well be enhanced by a deeper understanding of "madness" (Endler, 1990; Goodwin & Jamison, 1990; Prien et al., 1984).

Anxiety and Depression

One of the mysteries faced by psychopathologists is the apparent overlap of anxiety and depression. Some of the latest theories on the causes of depression are based, in part, on this research. Several theorists have concluded that the two moods are more alike than different. This may seem strange, because you probably do not feel the same when you are anxious as when you are depressed. However, we now know that almost everyone who is depressed, particularly to the extent of having a disorder, is also anxious (Barlow, 2002; Brown, Campbell, Lehman, Grisham, & Mancill, 2001; DiNardo & Barlow, 1990; Sanderson, DiNardo, Rapee, & Barlow, 1990), but not everyone who is anxious is depressed.

Let's examine this fact for a moment: *Almost all depressed patients are anxious, but not all anxious patients are depressed.* This means that certain core symptoms of depression are not found in anxiety and, therefore, reflect what is "pure" about depression. These core symptoms are the inability to experience pleasure (anhedonia) and a depressive "slowing" of both motor and cognitive functions until they are extremely laboured and effortful (Moras et al., 1996; Rottenberg, Gross, Wilhelm, Najmi, & Gotlib, 2002). Cognitive content (what is thought about) is usually more negative in depressed individuals than in anxious ones (Clark, 2001; Greenberg & Beck, 1989).

Recently, ongoing research in one of the authors' clinics has identified symptoms that seem central to panic and anxiety. In panic, the symptoms reflect primarily autonomic activation (excessive physiological symptoms such as heart palpitations and dizziness); muscle tension and apprehension (excessive worrying about the future) seem to reflect the essence of anxiety (Brown et al., 1998; Zinbarg & Barlow, 1996; Zinbarg et al., 1994). Many people with depression also have symptoms of anxiety or panic. More important, a large number of symptoms help define *both* anxiety and depressive disorders. Because these symptoms are *not specific* to either kind of disorder, they are called symptoms of *negative affect* (Brown et al., 1998; Tellegen, 1985).

Several research groups have identified pure anxious or depressive symptoms as well as symptoms of negative affect that are common to both mood states (e.g., Brown et al., 1998; Endler, Macrodimitris, & Kocovski, 2003; Moras et al., 1996; Zinbarg et al., 1994). For example, a study by Ryan Hong (2007) at the University of Western Ontario has shown that while worry is broadly associated with both anxiety and depression, rumination is uniquely associated with depression in a sample of university students in Singapore. A summary of symptoms specific to anxiety, specific to depression, and common to both states is presented in Table 7.3. Ultimately, research in this area may cause us to rethink our diagnostic criteria and combine anxiety and mood disorders into one

TABLE 7.3 Symptoms Specific to Anxiety and to Depression as Well as Symptoms Shared by Both States

Pure Anxiety Symptoms
Apprehension
Tension
Edginess
Trembling
Excessive worry
Nightmares

Pure Depression Symptoms
Helplessness
Depressed mood
Loss of interest
Lack of pleasure
Suicidal ideation
Diminished libido

Mixed Anxiety and Depression Symptoms (Negative Affect)
Anticipating the worst
Worry
Poor concentration
Irritability
Hypervigilance
Unsatisfying sleep
Crying
Guilt
Fatigue
Poor memory
Middle/late insomnia
Sense of worthlessness
Hopelessness
Early insomnia

Source: Adapted from "The DSM-IV Field Trial for Mixed Anxiety Depression" by R. E. Zinbarg, D. H. Barlow, M. Liebowitz, L. Street, E. Broadhead, W. Katon, P. Roy-Byrne, J. P. Lepine, M. Teherani, J. Richards, P. J. Brantley, and H. Kraemer, 1994, *American Journal of Psychiatry 151(8)*, 1153–1162.

larger category. Symptoms of negative affect alone are often less severe than full-blown anxiety or mood disorders, but their presence increases the risk of more severe disorders, suggesting that these symptoms are on a continuum with major depression and anxiety disorders (Solomon, Haaga, & Arnow, 2001).

Now think back for a minute to the case of Katie. You remember she was severely depressed and clearly had experienced a major depressive episode along with serious suicidal ideation. A review of the list of depressive symptoms shows that Katie had all of them, thus meeting the criteria for major depressive disorder outlined in the *DSM-IV-TR*. However, remember that Katie's difficulty began with her dread of interacting with her classmates or teachers for fear of making a fool of herself. Finally, she became so anxious that she stopped going to school. After seeing a doctor who recommended she be "persuaded" to attend school, her parents became firmer. As Katie explained, however,

> I felt nauseated and sick each time that I went into the school building and so each day I was sent home. Uncomfortable physical experiences like sweaty palms, trembling, dizziness, and nausea accompanied my anxiety and fear. For me, being in a classroom, being in the school building, even the anticipation of being in school, triggered anxiety and illness. All of the sensations of anxiety draw your attention away from your surroundings and toward your own physical feelings. All of this would be bearable if it wasn't so extremely intense. I found myself battling the desire to escape and seek comfort. And, each escape brings with it a sense of failure and guilt. I understood that my physical sensations were inappropriate for the situation but I couldn't control them. I blamed myself for my lack of control.

Katie's case is rather typical in that severe anxiety eventually turned into depression. She never really lost the anxiety; she just became depressed too. Epidemiological studies have confirmed that major depression usually follows anxiety and may be a consequence of it (Andrade et al., 2003; Kessler et al., 1996). Katie's case also illustrates another common form of *comorbidity* or co-occurrence of two types of problems—namely, she also shows some symptoms suggestive of borderline personality disorder, like her self-harm behaviour (see Chapter 12). Recent research by John Abela and his colleagues at McGill University has shown that individuals with comorbid depression and borderline personality disorder report greater levels of depressive symptoms than people with depression alone (Abela, Payne, & Moussaly, 2003). They have also shown that this is at least partly due to comorbid individuals' greater cognitive vulnerability to depression. (We discuss cognitive vulnerability to depression later in this chapter.) Like co-occurring anxiety and depression, personality disorders (which are long-standing in nature; see Chapter 12) tend to develop before the depression in people with both disorders. The finding that depression often follows anxiety and personality disorders leads us to a consideration of the causes of depression and other mood disorders.

Causes of Mood Disorders

In Chapter 2 we described *equifinality* as the same end product resulting from possibly different causes. Just as a fever may have many causes, depression may also have a number of causes. For example, a depressive disorder that arises in winter has a different precipitant than a severe depression following a death, even though the episodes might look quite similar. Nevertheless, psychopathologists are identifying biological, psychological, and social factors that seem strongly implicated in the etiology of mood disorders, whatever the precipitating factor. An integrative theory of the etiology of mood disorders considers the interaction of biological, psychological, and social dimensions and also notes the very strong relationship between anxiety and depression. Before describing this, we review evidence pertaining to each contributing factor.

Biological Dimensions

Familial and Genetic Influences

Studies that would allow us to determine the genetic contribution to a particular disorder or class of disorders would be very difficult to do. Three types of strategies can help us estimate this contribution, however. In *family studies*, we look at the prevalence of a given disorder in the first-degree relatives of an individual known to have the disorder (the proband). As noted in a review by Randy Katz, family studies have shown that both unipolar depression and bipolar disorder run in families (R. Katz & McGuffin, 1993). Despite wide variability, the rate in relatives of probands with mood disorders is consistently about two to three times greater than in relatives of controls who don't have mood disorders (Gershon, 1990; Klein, Lewinsohn, Rohde, Seeley, & Durbin, 2002; Levinson, 2009). Klein et al. (2002) also demonstrated that increasing severity and recurrence of major depression in the proband was associated with higher rates of depression in relatives.

The difficulty with family studies, of course, is that we cannot separate from true genetic contributions the effects of a common psychosocial environment. This problem is solved with a second strategy, *adoption studies*, in which we look at the biological relatives of an individual with a given disorder who was adopted at an early age. If a genetic contribution exists, the adopted probands with the disorder should have more biological relatives *with* the same disorder than the adopted probands *without* the disorder. Unfortunately, the data here are mixed. For example, some studies report a greater risk of mood disorder among the biological relatives of adoptees with a mood disorder (Mendlewicz & Rainer, 1977; Wender et al., 1986). In another study, no greater risk of having a mood disorder was found in the biological relatives of the adopted probands (Von Knorring, Cloninger, Bohman, & Sigvardsson, 1983).

The best evidence that genes have something to do with mood disorders comes from *twin studies*, in which we examine the frequency with which identical twins (with identical genes) have the disorder, compared with fraternal twins, who share only 50 percent of their genes (as do all first-degree relatives). If a genetic contribution exists, the disorder should be present in identical twins to a much greater extent than in fraternal twins. A number of twin studies, including those by Randy Katz an colleagues suggest that the mood disorders are heritable (e.g., McGuffin & Katz, 1989; McGuffin et al., 2003). The strongest of the new studies is presented in ■ Figure 7.3 (McGuffin et al., 2003). As you can see, an identical twin is two to three times more likely than a fraternal twin to present with a mood disorder if the first twin has a mood disorder (66.7 percent of identical twins and 18.9 percent of fraternal twins if the first twin has bipolar disorder; 45.6 percent versus 20.2 percent if the first twin has unipolar disorder). But notice that if one twin has unipolar disorder, the chances of a co-twin having bipolar disorder are slim to none. Severity may

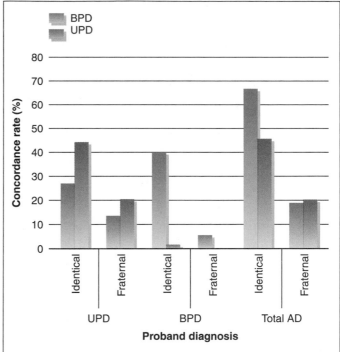

■ **FIGURE 7.3** Co-occurrence of types of mood disorders in twins for unipolar (UPD) and bipolar (BPD) affective disorder (AD)

Source: From "The Heritability of Bipolar Affective Disorder and the Genetic Relationship to Unipolar Depression" by P. McGuffin, F. Rijsdijk, M. Andrew, P. Sham, R. Katz, and A. Cardno, *Archives of General Psychiatry, 60,* 497–502. Copyright 2003 by the American Medical Association. Adapted with Permission.

also be related to amount of concordance (the degree to which something is shared). For example, if one twin had severe depression (defined as three or more major depressive episodes), then 59 percent of the identical twins and 30 percent of the fraternal twins also presented with a mood disorder. If the individual presented with fewer than three episodes, the concordance rate dropped to 33 percent in identical twins and 14 percent in fraternal twins. This means severe mood disorders may have a stronger genetic contribution than less severe disorders, a finding that holds true for most psychological disorders.

Kendler, Neale, Kessler, Heath, and Eaves (1993) estimated heritability of major depressive disorders in a large number of female twins to be from 41 percent to 46 percent, well within the range reported in Figure 7.3. Even in older adults, estimates of heritability remain in the moderate range of approximately 35 percent (McGue & Christensen, 1997).

Now, two recent reports have appeared suggesting sex differences in genetic vulnerability to depression. Bierut et al. (1999) studied 2662 twin pairs in the Australian twin registry and found the characteristically higher rate of depressive disorders in women. Estimates of heritability in women ranged from 36 percent to 44 percent, consistent with other studies. But estimates for men were lower and ranged from 18 percent to 24 percent. These results agree for the most part with an important study of men in North America by Lyons et al. (1998). The authors conclude that environmental events play a larger role in causing depression in men than in women.

Note that bipolar disorder confers an increased risk of developing *some* mood disorder but not necessarily bipolar disorder. This conclusion supports findings noted previously that bipolar disorder may simply be a more severe variant of mood disorders rather than a fundamentally different disorder. Then again, of identical twins concordant for a mood disorder, 80 percent are also concordant for polarity. In other words, if one identical twin is unipolar, the other twin has an 80 percent chance of being unipolar. This finding suggests that these disorders may be inherited separately and may therefore be separate disorders after all (Nurnberger & Gershon, 1992). A twin study by Randy Katz and colleagues drew similar conclusions and noted that most of the genetic variance in vulnerability to bipolar disorder is specific to the bipolar syndrome (McGuffin et al., 2003).

Although research continues to raise questions about the relative contributions of psychosocial and genetic factors to mood disorders, overwhelming evidence suggests that such disorders are familial and almost certainly reflect at least a small underlying genetic vulnerability, particularly for women. As with other psychological disorders, it seems unlikely that we will find any single dominant gene that is responsible (Nurnberger & Gershon, 1992), although occasional reports appear to the contrary.

In conclusion, the best estimates of genetic contributions to depression fall in the range of approximately 40 percent for women, but seem to be significantly less for men. Genetic contributions to bipolar disorder seem to be somewhat higher. This means that from 60 percent to 80 percent of the causes of depression can be attributed to environmental factors, as we noted in Chapter 4. Behavioural geneticists break down environmental factors into events shared by twins (experiencing the same upbringing in the same house, and perhaps, experiencing the same stressful events) and events that are not shared. What part of our experience causes depression? Wide agreement exists that it is the unique nonshared events, rather than what is shared, that interact with biological vulnerability to cause depression (Bierut et al., 1999; Plomin et al., 1997).

Joint Heritability of Anxiety and Depression

Although most studies have looked at specific disorders in isolation, a growing trend is to examine the heritability of related groups of disorders. Evidence supports the supposition of a close relationship among depression, anxiety, and panic. For example, data from family studies indicate that the more signs and symptoms of anxiety and depression a given patient has, the greater the rate of anxiety or depression or both in first-degree relatives and children (Hammen, Burge, Burney, & Adrian, 1990; Kovacs et al., 1989; Leckman, Weissman, Merikangas, Pauls, & Prusoff, 1983; Puig-Antich & Rabinovich, 1986; Weissman, 1985). In several important reports from a major set of data on more than 2000 female twins, Ken Kendler and his colleagues (Kendler, Heath, Martin, & Eaves, 1987; Kendler, Neale, Kessler, Heath, & Eaves, 1992b; Kendler et al., 1995) also found that the same genetic factors contribute to both anxiety and depression. Social and psychological explanations seemed to account for the factors that differentiate anxiety from depression. These findings suggest, once again, that the biological vulnerability for mood disorders may not be specific to that disorder but may reflect a more general predisposition to anxiety or mood disorders. The specific form of the disorder would be determined by unique psychological, social, or additional biological factors (Akiskal, 1997; Kilpatrick et al., 2007; Rutter, 2010).

Neurotransmitter Systems

Mood disorders have been the subject of more intense neurobiological study than almost any other area of psychopathology, with the possible exception of schizophrenia. New findings describing the relationship of specific neurotransmitters to mood disorders appear almost monthly and are punctuated by occasional reports of so-called breakthroughs. In this difficult area, most breakthroughs prove to be illusory, but false starts provide us with an ever-deeper understanding of the enormous complexity of the neurobiological underpinnings of mood disorders (Green, Mooney, Posener, & Schildkraut, 1995).

In Chapter 2, we observed that we now know that neurotransmitter systems have many subtypes and interact in many complex ways, with one another and with neuromodulators (products of the endocrine system). Research implicates low levels of serotonin in the etiology of mood disorders (Berney, Sookman, Leyton, Young, & Benkelfat, 2006; Rosa-Neto et al., 2004; Sokolov & Kutcher, 2001) but only in relation to other neurotransmitters, including norepinephrine and dopamine (e.g., Goodwin & Jamison, 1990; Spoont, 1992). Remember that the apparent primary function of serotonin is to regulate our emotional reactions. For example, we are more impulsive, and our moods swing more widely, when our levels of serotonin are low, possibly because one of the functions of serotonin is to regulate systems involving norepinephrine and dopamine (Mandell & Knapp, 1979). According to the "permissive" hypothesis, when serotonin levels are low, other neurotransmitters are permitted to range more widely, become dysregulated, and contribute to mood irregularities, including depression. A drop in norepinephrine would be one of the consequences. Mann and colleagues (1996) used sophisticated brain-imaging procedures (PET scans) to confirm impaired serotonergic transmission in patients with depression, but subsequent research suggested that this relationship holds only for more severe patients with suicidal tendencies (Mann, Brent, & Arango, 2001; Thase, 2009). Current thinking is that the balance of the various neurotransmitters and their subtypes is more important than the absolute level of any one neurotransmitter (Carver, Johnson, & Joormann, 2009).

In the context of this delicate balance, there is continued interest in the role of dopamine, particularly in relationship to manic episodes, atypical depression, or depression with psychotic features (Dunlop & Nemeroff, 2007; Garlow & Nemeroff, 2003; Thase, 2009). For example, the dopamine agonist L-dopa seems to produce hypomania in bipolar patients (see, for instance, Van Praag & Korf, 1975), along with other dopamine agonists (Silverstone, 1985). Chronic stress also reduces dopamine levels and produces depressive-like behaviour (Thase, 2009). But, as with other research in this area, it is quite difficult to pin down any relationships with certainty.

The Endocrine System

Investigators became interested in the endocrine system when they noticed that patients with diseases affecting this system sometimes became depressed. For example, hypothyroidism, or Cushing's disease, affects the adrenal cortex. This disease leads to excessive secretion of cortisol and, often, to depression (and anxiety).

In Chapter 2, and again in Chapter 5 on anxiety disorders, we discussed the brain circuit called the HPA axis. This axis begins in the hypothalamus and runs through the pituitary gland, which coordinates the endocrine system (see Figure 2.10 on page 48). One of the glands influenced by the pituitary is the cortical section of the adrenal gland. The adrenal gland produces the stress hormone cortisol, which is called a stress hormone because it is elevated during stressful life events. (We discuss this system in more detail in Chapter 9.) For now, it is enough to know that cortisol levels are elevated in depressed patients, a finding that makes sense considering the relationship between depression and severe life stress (Bradley et al., 2008; Thase, 2009).

This connection led to the development of what was thought to be a biological test for depression, the dexamethasone suppression test (DST). Dexamethasone suppresses cortisol secretion in normal subjects. However, when dexamethasone was given to depressed patients, much less suppression was noticed, and what did occur didn't last very long (Carroll, Martin, & Davies, 1968; Carroll et al., 1980). Approximately 50 percent of depressed patients show this reduced suppression, particularly if their depression is severe (Rush et al., 1997). The thinking was that in depressed patients, the adrenal cortex secreted too much cortisol. This oversecretion of cortisol was thought to overwhelm the suppressive effects of dexamethasone in depressed people. This theory was heralded as very important, because it promised the first biological laboratory test for a psychological disorder. However, later research demonstrated that individuals with other disorders, particularly anxiety disorders, also demonstrate this nonsuppression effect (Feinberg & Carroll, 1984; Goodwin & Jamison, 2007). This obviously cast doubt on the usefulness of a test to diagnose depression. Thus, as with early theories about single neurotransmitters, our understanding of the role of cortisol in producing depression has proven overly simplistic.

Researchers nevertheless remain very interested in the relationship of cortisol to depression. Recent research in this area has taken some exciting new turns. Investigators have discovered that neurotransmitter activity in the hypothalamus regulates the release of hormones that affect the HPA axis. **Neurohormones** are an increasingly important focus of study in psychopathology (e.g., Ladd, Owens, & Nemeroff, 1996). We have literally thousands of neurohormones. Determining their effects on the central nervous system and sorting out their relationship to the various neurotransmitter systems (see Chapter 2) is likely to be a very complex task indeed.

Sleep and Circadian Rhythms

Earlier we discussed the findings on seasonal affective disorder (SAD), noting that a characteristic symptom is an increase in sleeping. We have known for several years that sleep disturbances are a hallmark of most mood disorders. Most important, people who are depressed have a significantly shorter period after falling asleep before rapid eye movement (REM) sleep begins. Depressed individuals have diminished slow-wave sleep, which is the deepest, most restful part of sleep (Kupfer, 1995). (We discuss the process of sleep in more detail in Chapter 8.) In addition to entering REM sleep *much more quickly*, depressed patients experience REM activity that is much more intense, and the stages of deepest sleep don't occur until later and sometimes not at all. It is not yet clear whether sleep disturbances also characterize bipolar patients (Goodwin & Jamison, 1990), although preliminary evidence suggests patterns of *increased* rather than *decreased* sleep (Kupfer, 1995).

Another interesting finding is that depriving depressed patients of sleep, particularly during the second half of the night, causes temporary improvement in their condition (Wehr & Sack, 1988), although the depression returns when the patients start sleeping normally again (see review in Frecska, Perenyi, & Arato, 2003). A literature review by Peter and Trevor Silverstone (2004), psychiatrists in Edmonton and Toronto, respectively, notes that sleep deprivation appears helpful for some bipolar disorder patients during the depressed phase, with no accompanying switches into mania observed. In any case, because sleep patterns reflect a biological rhythm, a relationship may exist among seasonal affective disorder, sleep disturbances in depressed patients, and a more general disturbance in biological rhythms. This would not be surprising if it were true, because most mammals are exquisitely sensitive to day length at the latitudes at which they live, and this "biological clock" controls eating, sleeping, and weight changes. Thus, substantial disruption in circadian rhythm might be particularly problematic for some vulnerable individuals (Moore, 1999).

An additional interesting finding is that patients with bipolar disorder and their children (who are at risk for the disorder) show increased sensitivity to *light* (e.g., Nurnberger et al., 1988); that is, they show greater suppression of melatonin when they are exposed to light at night. Evidence also indicates that extended bouts of insomnia trigger manic episodes (Wehr, Goodwin, Wirz-Justice, Breitmeier, & Craig, 1982). These findings and others suggest that mood disorders may be related to disruptions in our circadian (daily) rhythms. For example, sleep deprivation may temporarily readjust the biological rhythms of depressed patients (Boivin, 2000). Light therapy for seasonal affective disorder (SAD) may have a similar effect (we'll discuss this later in this chapter). Goodwin and Jamison (1990) suggest that the specific genetic vulnerability to mood disorders may well be related to low levels of serotonin, which somehow affect the regulation of our daily biological rhythms (Kupfer, 1995). Of course, many of the results cited here are very preliminary, and this theory, although fascinating, is still only speculative.

A promising area of investigation focuses on characteristics of brain waves in depressed and anxious individuals. Measuring electrical activity in the brain with electroencephalogram (EEG) was described in Chapter 3, where we also described a type of brain wave activity, alpha waves, that indicate calm, positive feelings.

Davidson (1993) and Heller and Nitschke (1997) noted differential alpha activity in the two hemispheres of the brain in depressed individuals. These investigations demonstrated that depressed individuals exhibit greater right-side anterior activation of their cerebral hemispheres (and less left-side activation) than nondepressed individuals. Furthermore, the research of Ian Gotlib and his colleagues indicates that right-sided anterior activation is also found in patients who are no longer depressed (Gotlib, Ranganath, & Rosenfeld, 1998), suggesting this brain function might represent a vulnerability to depression. If these findings are confirmed (Gotlib & Abramson, 1999), this type of brain functioning could become an indicator of a biological vulnerability to depression.

Psychological Dimensions

Stressful Life Events

In reviewing genetic contribution to the causes of depression, we noted that fully 60 percent to 80 percent of the causes of depression could be attributed to psychological experiences. Furthermore, most of those experiences are unique to the individual. Stress and trauma are among the most striking unique contributions to the etiology of all psychological disorders. This is reflected throughout psychopathology and is evident in the wide adoption of the diathesis–stress model of psychopathology presented in Chapter 2 (and referred to throughout this book), which describes possible genetic and psychological vulnerabilities. But in seeking what activates this vulnerability (diathesis), we usually look for a stressful or traumatic life event.

You would think it would be sufficient to ask people whether anything major had happened in their lives before they developed depression or some other psychological disorder. Most people do report losing a job, getting divorced, having a child, or graduating from school and starting a career. But, as with most issues in the study of psychopathology, the significance of a major event is not easily discovered (Kessler, 1997), so most investigators have stopped simply asking patients whether something bad (or good) happened, and they have begun to look at the context of the event as well as the *meaning* it has for the individual.

For example, losing a job is stressful for most people, but it is far more difficult for some than others. A few people might even see it as a blessing. If you were laid off as a manager in a large corporation because of a restructuring, but your wife is the president of another corporation and makes more than enough money to support the family, it might not be so bad. Furthermore, if you are an aspiring writer or artist who has not had time to pursue your art, becoming jobless might be the opportunity you have been waiting for, particularly if your wife has been telling you for years to devote yourself to your creative pursuits.

Now consider losing your job if you are a single mother of two young children living from day to day and, because of a recent dentist's bill, you have to choose between paying the electric bill or buying food. The stressful life event is the same, but the context is very different and transforms the significance of the event substantially. To complicate the scenario further, think for a minute about how such a woman might react to losing her job.

One woman might well decide she is a total failure and thus becomes unable to carry on and provide for her children. Another woman might realize the job loss was not her fault at all and take advantage of a job-training program while scraping by somehow. Thus, both the context of the life event and its meaning are important. This approach to studying life events, developed by George W. Brown (1989) and associates in England, is represented in ■ Figure 7.4.

G. W. Brown's considerable advance in studying life events is difficult to carry out, and the methodology is still evolving; many psychologists are actively developing new methods (e.g., Dohrenwend & Dohrenwend, 1981; Hammen, 2005; Monroe, Slavich, & Georgiades, 2009; Monroe & Roberts, 1990; Monroe, Rohde, Seeley, & Lewinsohn, 1999). One crucial issue is the bias inherent in remembering events. If you ask people who are currently depressed what happened when they first became depressed more than five years ago, you will probably get different answers from those they would give if they were not currently depressed. Because current moods distort memories, many investigators have concluded that the only useful way to study stressful life events is to follow people prospectively, to determine more accurately the precise nature of events and their relation to subsequent psychopathology.

In any case, in summarizing a large amount of research, it is clear that stressful life events are strongly related to the onset of mood disorders (Grant, Compas, Thurm, McMahon, & Gipson, 2004; Hammen, 2005; Kendler, Karkowski, & Prescott, 1999b; Kessler, 1997; Mazure, 1998; Monroe et al., 2009; Monroe & Reid, 2009). Measuring the context of events and their impact in a random sample of the population, several studies have found a marked relationship between severe and, in some cases, traumatic life events and the onset of depression (Brown, 1989; Brown, Harris, & Hepworth, 1994, Kendler, Karkowski, & Prescott, 1999a; Mazure, 1998). Severe events precede nearly all types of depression (Brown et al., 1994). The work of Ian Gotlib and colleagues indicates that major life stress is a somewhat stronger predictor for initial episodes of depression compared with recurrent episodes (e.g., Lewinsohn, Allen, Seeley, & Gotlib, 1999). In addition, for people with recurrent depression, the clear occurrence of a severe life stress before or early in the latest episode predicts a much poorer response to treatment and a longer time before remission

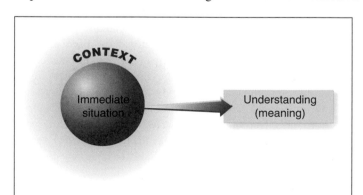

■ **FIGURE 7.4** Context and meaning in life stress situations

Source: From "Life Events and Measurement" by G. W. Brown, 1989. In G. W. Brown and T. O. Harris (Eds.), *Life Events and Illness*. Copyright © 1989 by The Guilford Press. Reprinted by permission.

(Monroe et al., 2009; Monroe, Kupfer, & Frank, 1992), as well as a greater likelihood of recurrence (Monroe et al., 2009; Monroe, Roberts, Kupfer, & Frank, 1996). Again, the context and meaning are probably more important than the exact nature of the event itself, although the breakup of a relationship is particularly likely to lead to depression in adolescents (Monroe, Rohde, Seeley, & Lewinsohn, 1999). The work of Williams, Connolly, and Segal (2001) similarly suggests that romantic relationships play a key role in vulnerability to depression in adolescent girls.

Despite this strong relationship, scientists are discovering that not all stressful events are totally independent of the depression. Remember in Chapter 2 where we noted that our genetic endowment might actually increase the probability that we will experience stressful life events? We referred to this as the reciprocal *gene–environment model* (Saudino et al., 1997). One example would be people who tend to seek out difficult relationships because of genetically based personality characteristics that then lead to depression. Another example would be people who display problematic social behaviours, such as complaining too often about personal difficulties to others, which may result in interpersonal rejection. Rejection in turn serves as a trigger for a depressive episode (Vaerum & McCabe, 2001; Wiebe & McCabe, 2002). Now, Kendler et al. (1999a) report that about one-third of the association between stressful life events and depression is not the usual arrangement of stress triggering depression, but rather individuals vulnerable to depression who are placing themselves in high-risk stressful environments. The relationship of stressful events to the onset of episodes in bipolar disorder is also strong (Ellicott, 1988; Goodwin & Jamison, 1990; Johnson & Roberts, 1995; Reilly-Harrington, Alloy, Fresco, & Whitehouse, 1999). However, several issues may be particularly relevant to the etiology of bipolar disorders (Goodwin & Ghaemi, 1998). First, stressful life events seem to trigger early mania and depression, but as the disorder progresses these episodes seem to develop lives of their own. In other words, once the cycle begins, a psychological or pathophysiological process takes over and ensures the disorder will continue (e.g., Post, 1992; Post et al., 1989). Second, some of the precipitants of manic episodes seem to be related to loss of sleep, as in the postpartum period (Goodwin & Jamison, 1990), or as a result of jet lag, that is, disturbed circadian rhythms. In most cases of bipolar disorder, nevertheless, stressful life events are substantially indicated not only in provoking relapse, but also in preventing recovery (Johnson & Miller, 1997).

Finally, although almost everyone who becomes depressed has experienced a significant stressful event, most people who experience such events do not become depressed. Although the data are not yet as precise as we would like, somewhere between 20 percent and 50 percent of individuals who experience severe events become depressed. Thus, between 50 percent and 80 percent of individuals do not develop depression or, presumably, any other psychological disorder. Once again, data strongly support the interaction of stressful life events with some kind of vulnerability, either genetic, psychological, or, more likely, a combination of the two influences.

Given a genetic vulnerability (diathesis) and a severe life event (stress), what happens then? Research has isolated a number of psychological and biological processes. To illustrate one, let's return to Katie. Her life event was attending a new school.

KATIE | *No Easy Transition*

I was a serious and sensitive 11-year-old at the edge of puberty and at the edge of an adventure that many teens and preteens embark on—the transition from elementary to junior high school. A new school, new people, new responsibilities, new pressures. Academically, I was a good student up to this point but I didn't feel good about myself and generally lacked self-confidence.

Katie began to experience severe anxiety reactions. Then she became quite ill with the flu. After recovering and attempting to return to school, Katie discovered that her anxieties were worse than ever. More important, she began to feel she was losing control.

As I look back I can identify events that precipitated my anxieties and fears, but then everything seemed to happen suddenly and without cause. I was reacting emotionally and physically in a way that I didn't understand. I felt out of control of my emotions and body. Day after day I wished, as a child does, that whatever was happening to me would magically end. I wished that I would awaken one day to find that I was the person I was several months before.

Katie's feeling of loss of control leads to another important psychological factor in depression: learned helplessness.

Learned Helplessness

To review our discussion in Chapter 2, Martin E. P. Seligman discovered that dogs and rats have an emotional reaction to events over which they have no control. If rats receive occasional shocks, they can function reasonably well, if they can cope with the shocks by doing something to avoid them, such as pressing a lever. But if they learn that nothing they do helps them avoid the shocks, they eventually become very helpless, give up, and manifest an animal equivalent of depression (Seligman, 1975).

Do humans react the same way? Seligman suggests we seem to, but only under one important condition: People become anxious and depressed when they make an attribution that they have no control over the stress in their lives (Abramson, Seligman, & Teasdale, 1978; Miller & Norman, 1979).These findings evolved into an important model called the **learned helplessness theory of depression**. Often overlooked is Seligman's point that anxiety is the first response to a stressful situation. Depression may follow marked hopelessness about coping with the difficult life events (Barlow, 1988, 2002; Mineka & Kelly, 1989). The depressive attributional style is (1) *internal*, in that the individual attributes negative events to personal failings ("It is all my fault"), (2) *stable*, in that, even after a particular negative event passes, the attribution that "additional bad things will always be my fault" remains, and (3) *global*, in that the attributions extend across a wide variety of issues. Research continues on this interesting concept, but you can see how it applies to Katie. Early in her difficulties with attending school, she began to believe events were totally out of her control and that she was unable even to begin to cope. More important, in her eyes the bad situation was all her fault: "I blamed myself for my lack of control." A downward spiral into a major depressive episode followed.

But a major question remains: Is learned helplessness a cause of depression or a correlated side effect of becoming depressed? If it were a cause, learned helplessness would have to exist before the depressive episode. Results from a five-year longitudinal study in children may shed some light on this issue. Nolen-Hoeksema, Girgus, and Seligman (1992) reported that negative attributional style did not predict later symptoms of depression in *young* children; rather, stressful life events seemed to be the major precipitant of symptoms. However, as they *grew older*, they tended to develop more negative cognitive styles, which *did* tend to predict symptoms of depression in reaction to additional negative events. Nolen-Hoeksema and colleagues speculate that meaningful negative events early in childhood may give rise to negative attributional styles in a developmental fashion, making these children more vulnerable to future depressive episodes when stressful events occur.

This thinking recalls the types of psychological vulnerabilities theorized to contribute to the development of anxiety disorders (Barlow, 1988, 2002; Suárez, Bennett, Goldstein, & Barlow, 2009). That is, in a person who has a nonspecific genetic vulnerability to either anxiety or depression, stressful life events activate a psychological sense that life events are uncontrollable (Barlow, 2002; Chorpita & Barlow, 1998). Evidence suggests that negative attributional styles are not specific to depression but characterize anxiety patients as well (Heimberg, Klosko, Dodge, & Shadick, 1989; Barlow, 2002; Suárez et al., 2009). This overlap may indicate that a psychological (cognitive) vulnerability is no more specific for mood disorders than is genetic vulnerability. Both types of vulnerabilities may underlie numerous disorders.

Abramson, Metalsky, and Alloy (1989) revised the learned helplessness theory to de-emphasize specific attributions and highlight the development of a *sense of hopelessness* as a crucial cause of many forms of depression. Attributions are important only to the extent that they contribute to a sense of hopelessness. This fits well with recent thinking on crucial differences between anxiety and depression. Both anxious and depressed individuals feel helpless and believe they lack control, but only in depression do they give up and become hopeless about ever regaining control (Alloy & Abramson, 2006; Barlow, 1991, 2002; Chorpita & Barlow, 1998).

Evidence from the work of Ian Gotlib and his colleagues indicates that a pessimistic style of attributing negative events to our own character flaws results in hopelessness (Gotlib & Abramson, 1999). This style may predate and therefore, in a sense, contribute to anxious or depressive episodes that follow negative or stressful events (Gotlib & Abramson, 1999). In fact, a recent longitudinal study by McGill University psychologists John Abela and Sabina Sarin (2002) followed children in grade 7 for ten weeks, obtaining information on their initial attributional styles, negative life events, and later symptoms of depression. This study obtained results supporting the hopelessness theory of depression, as has more recent work by this same research group (e.g., Abela, Aydin, & Auerbach, 2006).

Negative Cognitive Styles

In 1967, Aaron T. Beck (1967, 1976) suggested that depression may result from a tendency to interpret everyday events in a negative way. According to Beck, people with depression make the worst of everything; for them, the smallest setbacks are major catastrophes. In his extensive clinical work, Beck observed that all his depressed patients thought this way, and he began classifying the types of cognitive errors that characterized this style. From the long list he compiled, two representative examples are arbitrary inference and overgeneralization. Arbitrary inference is evident when a depressed individual emphasizes the negative rather than the positive aspects of a situation. A high school teacher may assume he is a terrible instructor because two students in his class fell asleep. He fails to consider other reasons they might be sleeping (up all night partying) and infers that his teaching style is at fault. As an example of overgeneralization, when your professor makes one critical remark on your paper, you then assume you will fail the class, despite a long string of very positive comments and good grades on other papers. You are overgeneralizing from one small remark. According to Beck, people who are depressed think like this all the time. They make cognitive errors in thinking negatively *about themselves*, their *immediate world*, and their *future*, three areas that together are called the **(depressive) cognitive triad** (see ■ Figure 7.5).

In addition, Beck theorized, after a series of negative events in childhood, individuals may develop a deep-seated negative schema, an enduring negative cognitive belief system about some aspect of life (Beck, Epstein, & Harrison, 1983; Dozois, Frewen, & Covin, 2006; Young, Rygh, Weinberger, & Beck, 2008). In a self-blame schema, individuals feel personally responsible for every bad thing that happens. With a negative self-evaluation schema, they believe they can never do anything

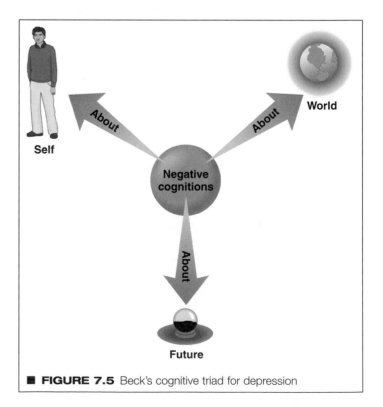

Self

About

About

World

Negative cognitions

About

Future

■ **FIGURE 7.5** Beck's cognitive triad for depression

correctly. In Beck's view, these cognitive errors and schemas are automatic, that is, not necessarily conscious. Indeed, an individual might not even be aware of thinking negatively and illogically. Thus, very minor negative events can lead to a major depressive episode.

A variety of evidence supports a cognitive theory of emotional disorders in general and depression in particular (Goodman & Gotlib, 1999; Ingram, Miranda, & Segal, 2006; Mazure, Bruce, Maciejewski, & Jacobs, 2000; Reilly-Harrington et al., 1999), and Canadian researchers have been at the forefront of developments in testing Beck's cognitive theory of depression (Rector, Segal, & Gemar, 1998). The thinking of depressed individuals is consistently more negative than that of nondepressed individuals (Dobson & Shaw, 1987; Gotlib & Abramson, 1999; Zuroff, Blatt, Sanislow, Bondi, & Pilkonis, 1999) in each dimension of the cognitive triad—the self, the world, and the future (e.g., Bradley & Mathews, 1988; Segal, Hood, Shaw, & Higgins, 1988).

Research by Nicholas Kuiper and his colleagues at the University of Western Ontario has focused on the self-component of Beck's cognitive triad. For example, Derry and Kuiper (1981) asked depressed and nondepressed individuals to complete a "self-referent encoding task" in which they rated a series of traits as to whether or not each described him or her. The depressed group viewed traits with depressive content (e.g., stupid, boring) as being significantly more applicable to themselves than did nondepressed participants. Conversely, the depressed group viewed traits with nondepressive content (e.g., nice, attractive) as being significantly less applicable to themselves. Keith Dobson and Brian Shaw (1987) replicated this finding and took it a step further by showing that when depressed patients were in remission (i.e., no longer actively depressed), their self-descriptiveness ratings of depressive content traits were no different from those made by a nondepressed comparison group. More recently, Brinker, Harris, Guyitt, and Dozois (2006) took this research yet another step further by having participants complete the self-referent encoding task and subsequently asking them to indicate how important it was for them to possess or fail to exhibit each trait. They found that the greater the importance of positive traits that an individual believed he or she lacks, the higher the person's level of depression. For example, if a person believed it was very important to be nice but also felt that she was not a nice person, then she was at higher risk for depressed mood. Conversely, the more important the negative traits a person believed he or she is free of, the lower the person's level of depression. For example, if a person believed it was very important not to be boring and also felt that he was not a boring person, then he was at lower risk for depressed mood (Brinker et al., 2006).

Findings from a variety of prominent Canadian research teams suggest that depressive cognitions seem to emerge from distorted and probably automatic methods of processing information. For example, people are more likely to recall negative events when they are depressed than when they are not depressed. And people who are depressed are also more likely to recall negative events than are nondepressed individuals (Gotlib, Roberts, & Gilboa, 1996; see also Derry & Kuiper, 1981). A study by Marlene Moretti at Simon Fraser University

and her colleagues used a cognitive task involving faces displaying different emotions to examine the processing of socially relevant information in depression. Participants were instructed to select the target expression that was most informative about how the person in the picture felt about the participant, or about another person. The nondepressed participants showed a bias toward selecting the faces with positive expressions as most informative about how the person in the picture felt about them, whereas the depressed participants selected both negative and positive faces. No such difference between depressed and nondepressed participants was seen in the condition in which choices were based on how the target was feeling about another person. These results suggest that depressed people have less access to positive social information about themselves and that this bias doesn't extend to their access to positive social information about other people (Moretti et al., 1996).

Much of the recent work in this area has focused on whether these cognitive biases are stable features of the individual or whether they instead shift with a depressed person's mood state. Some interesting work by David Dozois at the University of Western Ontario and Keith Dobson at the University of Calgary demonstrates that the answer to this question is complex. These authors followed 45 depressed patients over six months. Participants completed tests of information processing (e.g., the self-referent encoding task described earlier) as well as tests of cognitive organization, which allowed the researchers to determine how closely related certain topics were to one another in a given person. Each test was completed twice, once when all participants were depressed and again six months later, when half of the participants had recovered from their depression. Only those who had recovered from their depression showed less negative cognitive biases on the two information-processing tasks at the six-month follow-up than they had when they were actively depressed. In contrast, these same individuals showed a high level of interconnectedness of negative material at both testing times on the tests of cognitive organization. These results are consistent with Beck's theoretical predictions that underlying negative schemas are stable in individuals prone to depression and that these schemas become activated by negative events, in turn triggering negative information-processing biases (Dozois & Dobson, 2001). Dozois and Dobson have continued to use the above-mentioned tests of cognitive organization with clinically depressed research participants. Their more recent work has shown that higher levels of inter-connectedness of negative material and lower levels of inter-connectedness of positive material are associated with recurrent depression (Dozois & Dobson, 2003).

The implications of Beck's theory are very important. By recognizing cognitive errors and the underlying schemas, we can correct them and alleviate depression and related emotional disorders. In developing ways to do this, Beck became the father of cognitive therapy, one of the most important developments in psychotherapy in the past 50 years.

Cognitive Vulnerability for Depression: An Integration

Seligman and Abramson, on the one hand, and Beck, on the other, developed their theories independently, and good evidence indicates their models are independent, in that some people may have a negative outlook (dysfunctional attitudes), whereas others may explain things negatively (hopeless attributes; Joiner & Rudd, 1996; Spangler, Simons, Monroe, & Thase, 1997). Nevertheless, the basic premises overlap a great deal and considerable evidence suggests that depression is always associated with pessimistic explanatory style and negative cognitions. Evidence also exists that cognitive vulnerabilities predispose some people to view events in a very negative way, putting them at risk for depression (e.g., Ingram, Miranda, & Segal, 2006; Mazure, et al., 2000; Reilly-Harrington et al., 1999).

Social and Cultural Dimensions

Marital Relations

Marital dissatisfaction and depression are strongly related. Findings from several studies indicate that marital disruption often precedes depression (Davila, Stroud, & Starr, 2009). Bruce and Kim (1992) collected data on 695 women and 530 men and then reinterviewed them up to one year later. During this period some participants separated from or divorced their spouses, though the majority reported stable marriages. Approximately 21 percent of the women who reported a marital split during the study experienced severe depression, a rate three times higher than that for women who remained married. Nearly 17 percent of the men who reported a marital split developed severe depression, a rate nine times higher than that for men who remained married. However, when the researchers considered only those participants with no history of severe depression, 14 percent of the men who separated or divorced during the period experienced severe depression, as did approximately 5 percent of the women. In other words, *only the men* faced a heightened risk of developing a mood disorder for the first time immediately following a marital split. Is remaining married more important to men than to women? It would seem so.

Monroe, Bromet, Connell, and Steiner (1986), as well as O'Hara (1986), also implicated factors in the marital relationship as predicting the later onset of depression. Important findings from the Monroe et al. (1986) study emphasize the necessity of separating marital conflict from marital support. In other words, it is possible that high marital conflict and strong marital social support may both be present at the same time or may both be absent. The work of Ian Gotlib and his colleagues indicates that high conflict, low support, or both, are particularly important in generating depression (Barnett & Gotlib, 1988; Gotlib & Beach, 1995).

Another finding with considerable support is that depression, particularly if it continues, may lead to substantial deterioration in marital relationships (Beach, Jones, & Franklin, 2009; Beach, Sandeen, & O'Leary, 1990; Gotlib & Beach, 1995; Davila et al., 2009; Paykel & Weissman, 1973; Uebelacker & Whisman, 2006). It is not hard to figure out why. Being around someone who is continually negative, ill tempered, and pessimistic becomes tiring after a while. Because emotions are contagious, the spouse probably begins to feel bad also. These kinds of interactions precipitate arguments or, worse, make the nondepressed spouse want to leave (Joiner & Timmons, 2009; Whisman, Weinstock, & Tolejko, 2006).

But conflict within a marriage seems to have different effects on men and women. Depression seems to cause men to withdraw or otherwise disrupt the relationship. For women, in contrast, it is problems in the relationship that most often cause depression. Thus, for both men and women, depression and problems in marital relations are associated, but the causal direction is different (Fincham, Beach, Harold, & Osborne, 1997), a result also found by Spangler, Simons, Monroe, and Thase (1996). Given these factors, Beach, Jones, & Franklin (2009) suggest that therapists treat disturbed marital relationships at the same time as the mood disorder to ensure the highest level of success for the patient and the best chance of preventing future relapses. Individuals with bipolar disorder are less likely to be married at all, and more likely to get divorced if they do marry, although those who stay married have a somewhat better prognosis perhaps because their spouses are helpful in regulating their treatments and keeping them on medications (Davila et al., 2009).

Mood Disorders in Women

As noted by psychiatric epidemiologist Roger Bland and others, data on the prevalence of mood disorders indicate dramatic gender imbalances (Bland, 1997). Although bipolar disorder is evenly divided between men and women, almost 70 percent of the individuals with major depressive disorder and dysthymia are women (Bland, 1997; Nolen-Hoeksema, 1987; Kessler, 2006; Weissman et al., 1991). What is particularly striking is that, even though overall rates of disorder may vary from country to country, this gender imbalance is constant around the world (Andrade et al., 2003; Kessler, 2006; Weissman & Olfson, 1995). For example, data from the previously mentioned Canadian Community Health Survey study on the prevalence of depression indicated that the past-year prevalence of major depression was 5.0 percent for women but only 2.9 percent for men (Patten et al., 2006). Often overlooked is the similar ratio for most anxiety disorders, particularly panic disorder and generalized anxiety disorder. Women represent an even greater proportion of specific phobias, as we noted in Chapter 2. What could account for this?

It may be that gender differences in the development of emotional disorders are strongly influenced by perceptions of uncontrollability (Barlow, 1988, 2002). If you feel a sense of mastery over your life and the difficult events we all encounter, you might experience occasional stress but you will not feel the helplessness central to anxiety and mood disorders. The source of these differences is cultural, in the sex roles assigned to men and women in our society. Males are strongly encouraged to be independent, masterful, and assertive; females, by contrast, are expected to be more passive, to be sensitive to other people, and, perhaps, to rely on others more than males do. Although these stereotypes are slowly changing, they still describe current sex roles, to a large extent. But this culturally induced dependence and passivity may well put women at severe risk for emotional disorders by increasing their feelings of uncontrollability and helplessness. Evidence has accumulated that parenting styles encouraging stereotypic gender roles are implicated in the development of early psychological vulnerability to later depression or anxiety

(Chorpita & Barlow, 1998; Suárez et al., 2009), specifically, a smothering overprotective style that prevents the child from developing initiative.

The value women place on intimate relationships may also put them at risk (Hammen, Marks, Mayol, & DeMayo, 1985; Whiffen & Demidenko, 2006). Disruptions in such relationships, combined with an inability to cope with the disruptions, may be far more damaging to women than to men. Data from Fincham et al. (1997) and Spangler et al. (1996), described earlier, seem to support this view. However, data from Bruce and Kim (1992), reviewed earlier, suggest that if the disruption actually reaches the stage of divorce, men who had previously been functioning well are at greater risk for depression.

Another potentially important gender difference is that women tend to ruminate more than men about their situation and blame themselves for being depressed (Nolen-Hoeksema, 1990, 2000b; Nolan-Hoeksema, Larson, & Grayson, 1999; Nolen-Hoeksema, Wisco, & Lyubomirsky, 2008). Men tend to ignore their feelings, perhaps engaging in activity to take their minds off them (Addis, 2008). This male behaviour may be therapeutic because "activating" people (getting them busy doing something) is a common element of successful therapy for depression (Dimidjian, Martell, Addis, & Herman-Dunn, 2008; Jacobson, Martell, & Dimidjian, 2001).

As Janet Stoppard at the University of New Brunswick points out, women are at a disadvantage in our society (Stoppard, 1989, 1999, 2000; Stoppard & McMullen, 2003): They experience more discrimination, poverty, sexual harassment, and abuse than do men. They also earn less respect and accumulate less power. The majority of the people living in poverty in North America are women and children. Women, particularly single mothers, have a difficult time entering the workplace. Therefore, the meaning of conflict in a relationship is greater for women than for men, who are likely to respond more to problems at work. Data from the Canadian National Population Health Survey indicate that rates of depression are 2.5 times higher in single women with a child under five years old than among married mothers (Cairney, Thorpe, Rietschlin, & Avison, 1999). In fact, married women employed full-time outside the home report levels of depression no greater than those of employed married men. Single, divorced, and widowed women experience significantly more depression than men in the same categories (Weissman & Klerman, 1977). These results do not necessarily mean that people should get a job to avoid becoming depressed. Indeed, for a man or woman, feeling mastery, control, and value in the strongly socially supported role of homemaker and parent should be associated with low rates of depression. Moreover, recent findings from the Canadian National Population Health Survey show that work stress can be associated with depression in both men and women. It is just that gender may alter the type of work stress that is most strongly associated with depression (i.e., psychological demands predict depression in men whereas physical demands do so in women; Wang & Patten, 2001).

A further possible contributing factor to the higher rates of depression in women pertains to a particular type of stressor—specifically, abuse histories. A study by Robert Levitan and his colleagues at the University of Toronto indicated that a history of abuse in childhood was a risk factor for depression (Levitan et al., 1998). A later study by this same research group noted a particularly strong association between early sexual abuse and comorbid depression and anxiety (Levitan, Rector, Sheldon, & Goering, 2003). Another Toronto study by Sahay, Piran, and Maddocks (2000) examined the prevalence of sexual victimization in 60 female patients with depression. An alarming 65 percent reported sexual violation in childhood, adolescence, or adulthood. The work of Valerie Whiffen has established that female outpatients are more likely than male outpatients to experience depression and to report childhood and adult sexual abuse and victimization (e.g., Whiffen & Clark, 1997). These studies are certainly suggestive of the possibility that the higher rates of abuse experiences may help explain women's greater susceptibility to depression.

Finally, other disorders may reflect gender role stereotypes, but in the opposite direction. Disorders associated with aggressiveness, overactivity, and substance abuse occur far more frequently in men than in women (Barlow, 2002). Identifying the reasons for gender imbalances across the full range of psychopathological disorders may prove important in discovering causes of disorders.

Social Support

In Chapter 2, we examined the powerful effect of social influences on our psychological and biological functioning. We cited several examples of how social influences seem to contribute to early death, such as the evil eye or lack of social support in old age. In general, the greater the number and frequency of your social relationships and contacts, the longer

▲ Of the impoverished people in North America, the majority are women and children.

© David Urbina/PhotoEdit

you are likely to live (e.g., House, Landis, & Umberson, 1988). It is not surprising, then, that social factors influence whether we become depressed (Beach et al., 2009).

In an early landmark study, Brown and Harris (1978) first suggested the important role of social support in the onset of depression. In a study of a large number of women who had experienced a serious life stress, they discovered that only 10 percent of the women who had a friend in whom they could confide became depressed, compared with 37 percent of the women who did not have a close supportive relationship. Later prospective studies have also confirmed the importance of social support (or lack of it) in predicting the onset of depressive symptoms at a later time (e.g., Cutrona, 1984; Joiner, 1997; Lin & Ensel, 1984; Monroe, Imhoff, Wise, & Harris, 1983; Phifer & Murrell, 1986). Other studies have established the importance of social support in speeding recovery from depressive episodes (Johnson et al., 2008, 2009; Keitner et al., 1995; McLeod, Kessler, & Landis, 1992; Sherbourne, Hays, & Wells, 1995).

A Canadian randomized control study by Misri, Kostaras, Fox, and Kostaras (2000) examined the effects of partner support on the treatment of women with postpartum depression. Relative to control group patients, women who received the treatment involving partner support showed a significant decrease in their symptoms of depression, attesting to the importance of social support in recovery from postpartum depression. Johnson, Winett, Meyer, Greenhouse, and Miller (1999) examined the effects of social support in speeding recovery from both manic and depressive episodes in patients with bipolar disorder, and they came up with a surprising finding. A socially supportive network of friends and family helped speed recovery from depressive episodes, but not manic episodes. This finding highlights the uniquely different quality of manic episodes. In any case, these and related findings on the importance of social support have led to an exciting new psychosocial therapeutic approach for emotional disorders called interpersonal psychotherapy, which we discuss later in this chapter.

An Integrative Theory

How do we put all this together? Basically, depression and anxiety may often share a common, genetically determined biological vulnerability (Barlow, 2002; Barlow et al., 1996; Suárez et al., 2009) that can be described as an overactive neurobiological response to stressful life events. Once again, this vulnerability is simply a general tendency to develop depression (or anxiety) rather than a specific vulnerability for depression or anxiety itself. This biological vulnerability to develop depression seems stronger for women than for men (Bierut et al., 1999). But, only 20 percent to 40 percent of the causes of depression can be attributed to genes. For the remainder, we look at life experience.

People who develop mood disorders also possess a psychological vulnerability experienced as feelings of inadequacy for coping with the difficulties confronting them. As with anxiety, we may develop this sense of control in childhood (Barlow, 2002; Chorpita & Barlow, 1998). It may range on a continuum from total confidence to a complete inability to cope. When vulnerabilities

are triggered, the giving-up process seems crucial to the development of depression (Alloy et al., 1990; Alloy & Abramson, 2006). A variety of evidence indicates that these attitudes and attributions correlate rather strongly with such biochemical markers of stress and depression as byproducts of norepinephrine (e.g., Samson, Mirin, Hauser, Fenton, & Schildkraut, 1992) and with hemispheric lateral asymmetry (Davidson 1993; Heller & Nitschke, 1997).

The causes of this psychological vulnerability can be traced to early adverse experience in the form of childhood adversity or exposure to caregivers with psychopathology perhaps years before the onset of mood disorders. For example, Taylor and Ingram (1999) demonstrated that children of depressed mothers possess a less positive self-concept and more negative information processing if one probes for this vulnerability. This enduring psychological vulnerability intensifies the biochemical and cognitive response to stress later in life (Goodman & Gotlib, 1999, Nolen-Hoeksema, 2000a; Nolen-Hoeksema et al., 1992).

Good evidence suggests that stressful life events trigger the onset of depression in most cases, particularly initial episodes. How do these factors interact? The best current thinking is that stressful life events activate stress hormones, which, in turn, have wide-ranging effects on the neurotransmitter systems, particularly those involving serotonin, norepinephrine, and the CRF system. Evidence also indicates that activation of stress hormones over the long term may actually turn on certain genes, producing long-term structural and chemical changes in the brain. For example, processes triggered by long-term stress may lead to atrophy of neurons in the hippocampus that help regulate emotions. Such structural change might permanently affect the regulation of neurotransmitter activity. The extended effects of stress may also disrupt the circadian rhythms in certain individuals, who then become susceptible to the recurrent episodic cycling that seems so uniquely characteristic of the mood disorders (Moore, 1999; Post, 1992).

As noted earlier, triggering stressful life events also activate a dormant psychological vulnerability characterized by negative thinking and a sense of helplessness and hopelessness. What we have so far is a possible mechanism for the diathesis–stress model. Finally, it seems clear that factors such as interpersonal relationships or our gender may protect us from the effects of stress and therefore from developing mood disorders. Alternatively, these factors may at least determine whether we quickly recover from these disorders.

In summary, biological, psychological, and social factors all influence the development of mood disorders, as depicted in ■ Figure 7.6. This model does not account for the varied presentation of mood disorders—unipolar, bipolar, and so on. In other words, why would someone with an underlying genetic vulnerability who experiences a stressful life event develop a bipolar disorder rather than a unipolar disorder or, for that matter, an anxiety disorder? As with the anxiety disorders and other stress disorders, specific psychosocial circumstances, such as early learning experiences, may interact with specific genetic vulnerabilities and personality characteristics to produce the rich variety of emotional disorders. Only time will tell.

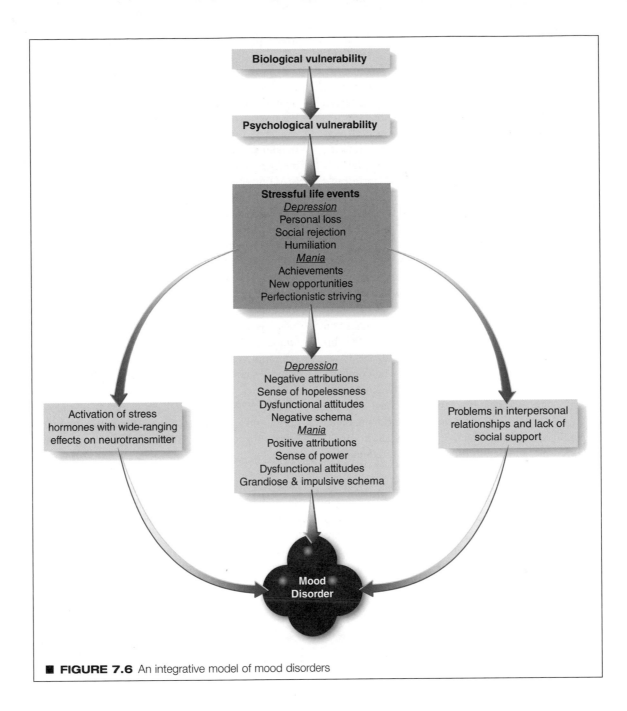

■ FIGURE 7.6 An integrative model of mood disorders

Treatment

We have learned a great deal about the neurobiology of mood disorders during the past several years. Findings on the complex interplay of neurochemicals are beginning to shed light on the nature of mood disorders. As we have noted, the principal effect of medications is to alter levels of these neurotransmitters and other related neurochemicals. Other biological treatments, such as electroconvulsive therapy (ECT), dramatically affect brain chemistry. A more interesting development, however, alluded to throughout this book, is that powerful psychological treatments also alter brain chemistry. Despite these advances, most cases of depression go untreated because neither health care professionals nor patients recognize and correctly identify or diagnose depression. Similarly, many professionals and patients are unaware of

the existence of successful treatments (Delano-Wood & Abeles, 2005; Hirschfeld et al., 1997). For this reason, it is very important to learn about treatments for depression.

Medications

Antidepressants

Three basic types of **antidepressant** medications are used to treat depressive disorders: tricyclic antidepressants, monoamine oxidase (MAO) inhibitors, and the newer selective serotonin reuptake inhibitors (SSRIs).

Tricyclic antidepressants are widely used treatments for depression. The best-known variants are probably imipramine (Tofranil) and amitriptyline (Elavil). It is not yet clear how these drugs work, but initially, at least, they block the reuptake of certain neurotransmitters, allowing them to pool in the synapse and, as the theory goes, desensitize or down-regulate the transmission of that particular neurotransmitter (so less of the neurochemical is transmitted). Tricyclic antidepressants seem to have their greatest effect by down-regulating norepinephrine, although other neurotransmitter systems, particularly serotonin, are also affected. This process then has a complex effect on both presynaptic and postsynaptic regulation of neurotransmitters activity, eventually restoring appropriate balance. This process takes a while to work, often between two and eight weeks. During this time, many patients feel a bit worse and develop side effects such as blurred vision, dry mouth, constipation, difficulty urinating, drowsiness, weight gain (at least 6 kilograms), and, perhaps, sexual dysfunction. For this reason, as many as 40 percent of these patients stop taking the drug, thinking that the cure is worse than the disease. Nevertheless, with careful management, many side effects disappear. Tricyclics alleviate depression in approximately 50 percent of patients, compared with approximately 25 percent to 30 percent of patients taking placebo pills, based on a summary analysis of more than 100 studies (American Psychiatric Association, 2000a; Depression Guideline Panel, 1993; see Table 7.4). If dropouts are excluded and only those who complete treatment are counted, success rates increase to between 65 percent and 70 percent. Another issue clinicians must consider is the potential cardiac side effect of the tricyclic antidepressants (Tingelstad, 1991). In fact, tricyclics are *lethal* if taken in excessive doses; therefore, they must be prescribed with great caution to patients with suicidal tendencies.

MAO inhibitors work very differently; as their name suggests, they block the enzyme monoamine oxidase that breaks down such neurotransmitters as norepinephrine and serotonin. The result is roughly equivalent to the effect of the tricyclics. Because they are not broken down, the neurotransmitters pool in the synapse, ultimately leading to a down-regulation or desensitization. The

MAO inhibitors seem to be as effective as, or slightly more effective than, the tricyclics (American Psychiatric Association, 2000b; Depression Guideline Panel, 1993), with somewhat fewer side effects. But MAO inhibitors are used far less often because of two potentially serious consequences: Consuming foods and beverages containing tyramine, such as cheese, red wine, or beer, can lead to severe hypertensive episodes and, occasionally, death. In addition, many other drugs that people take daily, such as cold medications, are dangerous and even fatal in interaction with an MAO inhibitor. For this reason, MAO inhibitors are usually prescribed only when tricyclics are not effective (see Endler, 1990).

Pharmaceutical companies have developed a new generation of more selective MAO inhibitors that are short acting and do not interact negatively with tyramine (Baldessarini, 1989). Testing is still continuing on these new drugs.

The class of drugs currently considered the first choice in drug treatment for depression seems to have a specific effect on the serotonin neurotransmitter system (although such drugs affect other systems to some extent). These *selective-serotonin reuptake inhibitors (SSRIs)* specifically block the presynaptic reuptake of serotonin. This temporarily increases levels of serotonin at the receptor site, but again the precise long-term mechanism of action is unknown, although levels of serotonin are eventually increased (Gitlin, 2009; Thase & Denko, 2008). Perhaps the best-known drug in this class is *fluoxetine* (Prozac). Like many other medications, Prozac was initially hailed as a breakthrough drug; it even made the cover of *Newsweek* (March 26, 1990). Then reports began to appear that it might lead to suicidal preoccupation, paranoid reactions, and, occasionally, violence (e.g., Mandalos & Szarek, 1990; Teicher, Glod, & Cole, 1990). Prozac went from being a wonder drug in the eyes of the press to a potential menace to modern society. Of course, neither conclusion was true. More recent findings indicate that the risks of suicide with this drug are no greater than with any other antidepressant, and the effectiveness

TABLE 7.4 Efficacy of Various Antidepressant Drugs for Major Depressive Disorder

Drug	Drug Efficacy		Drug Placebo	
	Inpatient	Outpatient	Inpatient	Outpatient
Tricyclics	50.0%	51.5%	25.1%	21.3%
SD	(6.5)	(5.2)	(11.5)	(3.9)
N	[33]	[102]	[8]	[46]
Monoamine oxidase inhibitors (MAOIs)	52.7%	57.4%	18.4%	30.9%
SD	(9.7)	(5.5)	(22.6)	(17.1)
N	[14]	[21]	[9]	[13]
Selective serotonin reuptake inhibitors (SSRIs)	54.0%	47.4%	25.5%	20.1%
SD	(10.1)	(12.5)	(21.7)	(7.8)
N	[8]	[39]	[2]	[23]

Notes: The percentage shown in the Drug Efficacy column is the anticipated percentage of patients provided the treatment shown who will respond. The Drug Placebo column shows the expected percentage difference in patients given a drug versus a placebo based on direct drug–placebo comparisons in trials that included at least these two cells. The numbers in parentheses are the standard deviations of the estimated percentage of responders. The bracketed numbers give the number of studies for which these estimates are calculated.

Source: Adapted from *Depression Guideline Panel*, April 1993.

is about the same (Fava & Rosenbaum, 1991). However, Prozac has its own set of side effects, the most prominent of which are physical agitation, sexual dysfunction, or low desire (which is very prevalent, occurring in 50 percent to 75 percent of cases), insomnia, and gastrointestinal upset. But these side effects, on the whole, seem to bother most patients less than the side effects associated with tricyclic antidepressants, with the possible exception of the sexual dysfunction. Studies suggest similar effectiveness of SSRIs and tricyclics with dysthymia (Lapierre, 1994).

Two new antidepressants seem to have somewhat different mechanisms of neurobiological action. Venlafaxine is related to tricyclic antidepressants but acts in a slightly different manner, reducing some of the associated side effects as well as the risk of damage to the cardiovascular system. Other typical side effects remain, including nausea and sexual dysfunction. Nefazodone is closely related to the SSRIs but seems to improve sleep efficiency instead of disrupting sleep. Both drugs are roughly comparable in effectiveness to older antidepressants (American Psychiatric Association, 2000b; Preskorn, 1995; Thase & Kupfer, 1996).

Finally, there has been a great deal of interest lately in the antidepressant properties of the natural herb St. John's wort (*Hypericum*). St. John's wort is very popular in Europe and it began catching on in Canada and the United States around 1995 (Canterbury Farms, 1997). While uncontrolled trials suggest benefits for those who complete treatment (e.g., Simeon, Nixon, & Milin, 2005), a large North American study showed no specific effectiveness for the herb compared with placebo treatments or other medications (Hypericum Depression Trial Study Group, 2002). The latter controlled trial has been criticized because it included only severely depressed patients, and St. John's wort might work better with people who are only mildly depressed. Furthermore, it is significant that even the active antidepressant drug did no better than placebo in this study, although this finding is not uncommon, since many studies on the effects of drugs on depression do not show differences between drug and placebo. In any case, St. John's wort is available primarily in health food stores and similar outlets, and there is no guarantee that any given brand of St. John's wort contains the appropriate ingredients, since this herb is not regulated by any government agency. Moreover, Health Canada issued a letter to Canadian physicians, pharmacists, and alternative medicine practitioners warning them about the possibility of negative drug interactions with St. John's wort (e.g., with drug treatments for HIV, immunosuppressant drugs taken by transplant patients, antidepressants, and oral contraceptives; Health Canada, 2000a). For example, there have been case reports of grogginess, weakness, and lethargy resulting from the combination of St. John's wort and prescribed antidepressants such as paroxetine (Vermani, Milosevic, Smith, & Katzman, 2005).

Current studies indicate that drug treatments effective with adults are not necessarily effective with children (American Psychiatric Association, 2000b; Boulos, Kutcher, Marton, Simeon, Ferguson, & Roberts, 1991; Geller et al., 1992; Ryan, 1992). Sudden deaths of children under 14 who were taking tricyclic antidepressants have been reported, particularly during exercise, as in routine school athletic competition (Tingelstad, 1991). The causes imply cardiac side effects. Traditional antidepressant drug treatments are usually effective with the elderly, but administering them takes considerable skill because older people may experience a variety of side effects not experienced by younger adults, including memory impairment and physical agitation (e.g., Deptula & Pomara, 1990; Marcopulos & Graves, 1990).

Clinicians and researchers have concluded that recovery from depression, although important, may not be the most important therapeutic outcome (Frank et al., 1990; Prien & Kupfer, 1986). The large majority of people eventually recover from a major depressive episode, some rather quickly. A more important goal is often to delay the next depressive episode or even prevent it entirely (Prien & Potter, 1993; Thase, 1990; Thase & Kupfer, 1996). This prevention is particularly important for patients who retain some symptoms of depression or have a past history of chronic depression or multiple depressive episodes. Because all these factors put people at risk for relapse, it is recommended that drug treatment go well beyond the termination of a depressive episode, continuing perhaps 6 to 12 months after the episode is over, or even longer (American Psychiatric Association, 2000b). The drug is then gradually withdrawn over a period of weeks or months. (We return later to strategies for *maintaining* therapeutic benefits.)

Antidepressant medications have relieved severe depression and undoubtedly prevented suicide in tens of thousands of patients around the world. Although these medications are readily available, many people refuse or are not eligible to take them. Some are wary of long-term side effects. Women of childbearing age must protect themselves against the possibility of conceiving while taking antidepressants, because they can damage the fetus. In addition, 40 percent to 50 percent of patients do not respond to these drugs, and a substantial number of the remainder are left with residual symptoms. A review of the literature by Michael Bagby and his colleagues at the University of Toronto indicates that response to antidepressant medications appears to be better in those with high social support and

▲ Of the synthetic drugs for depression, fluoxetine (Prozac, left), is the most widely used; the common groundcover Hypericum (St. John's wort, right) is popular as a natural treatment in Europe and in North America.

Treatment **249**

worse in those with co-occurring anxiety disorders (Bagby, Ryder, & Cristi, 2002).

An epidemiologic study by Cynthia Beck and colleagues at the University of Calgary made use of the Canadian Community Health Survey to examine rates of antidepressant drug use in relation to diagnoses of depression and other disorders (Beck, Williams, et al., 2005). They began their study with the premise that antidepressant utilization could be used as an indicator of appropriate treatment for major depression. After adjusting for probable successful outcomes of treatment, they found that more than 50 percent of those with major depression had been prescribed an antidepressant. While this rate might be seen as either "the cup half empty" or as "the cup half full," the authors note that the use of antidepressant medications in Canada has increased substantially since the early 1990s. Research by this group has also shown that the SSRIs are now the most commonly used type of antidepressant in Canada among those with major depressive episodes in the previous year (Beck, Patten, et al., 2005).

Lithium

Another type of antidepressant drug, *lithium carbonate,* is a common salt widely available in the natural environment (Nemeroff, 2006). It is found in our drinking water in amounts too small to have any effect. However, the side effects of therapeutic doses of lithium are potentially more serious than those of other antidepressants. Dosage has to be very carefully regulated to prevent toxicity (poisoning) and lowered thyroid functioning, which might intensify the lack of energy associated with depression. Substantial weight gain is also common. Lithium, however, has one major advantage that distinguishes it from other antidepressants: It is often effective in preventing and treating manic episodes. For this reason it is most often referred to as a mood-stabilizing drug. Because tricyclic antidepressants can induce manic episodes, even in individuals without pre-existing bipolar disorder (Goodwin & Ghaemi, 1998; Goodwin & Jamison, 2007; Prien et al., 1984), lithium is the treatment of choice for bipolar disorder, as outlined in the Canadian Network for Mood and Anxiety Treatment guidelines (Yatham et al., 2006).

We are not sure how lithium works (Endler, 1990). It may limit the availability of dopamine and norepinephrine, but it may have more important effects on some of the neurohormones in the endocrine system, particularly those that influence the production and availability of sodium and potassium, electrolytes found in body fluids (Goodwin & Jamison, 1990). Results indicate that 50 percent of bipolar patients respond well to lithium initially, meaning at least a 50 percent reduction in manic symptoms (Goodwin & Jamison, 2007). Thus, although effective, lithium provides many people with inadequate therapeutic benefit. Patients who don't respond to lithium can take other drugs with antimanic properties, including anticonvulsants such as carbamazepine and valproate (Divalproex), as well as calcium channel blockers such as verapamil (Keck & McElroy, 2002; Sachs & Rush, 2003; Thase & Denko, 2008). Valproate has recently overtaken lithium as the most commonly prescribed mood stabilizer for bipolar disorder (Goodwin et al., 2003; Keck & McElroy, 2002; Thase & Denko, 2008) and is equally effective, even for patients with rapid-cycling symptoms (Calabrese et al., 2005).

But newer studies show that these drugs have one distinct disadvantage: They are less effective than lithium in preventing suicide (Thase & Denko, 2008; Thies-Flechtner, Muller-Oerlinghausen, Seibert, Walther, & Greil, 1996; Tondo, Jamison, & Baldessarini, 1997). Goodwin and colleagues (2003) reviewed records of more than 20 000 patients taking either lithium or valproate and found the rate of completed suicides was 2.7 times higher in people taking valproate than in people taking lithium. Thus, lithium remains the preferred drug for bipolar disorder (Goodwin & Ghaemi, 1998; Goodwin & Jamison, 2007). This finding was confirmed in a large trial demonstrating no advantage to adding a traditional antidepressant drug such as an SSRI to a mood stabilizer such as lithium (Sachs et al., 2007).

For those patients who *do* respond to lithium, studies following patients for up to five years report that approximately 70 percent relapse, even if they continue to take the lithium (Frank et al., 1999; Gitlin, Swendsen, Heller, & Hammen, 1995; Peselow, Fieve, Difiglia, & Sanfilipo, 1994). Nevertheless, for almost anyone with recurrent manic episodes, maintenance on lithium or a related drug is recommended to prevent relapse (Yatham et al., 2006).

Another problem with drug treatment of bipolar disorder is that people usually like the euphoric or high feeling that mania produces and they often stop taking lithium to maintain or regain the state; that is, they do not comply with the medication regimen. Because the evidence now clearly indicates that individuals who stop their medication are at considerable risk for relapse, other treatment methods, usually psychological in nature, are used to increase compliance.

Electroconvulsive Therapy and Transcranial Magnetic Stimulation

When someone does not respond to medication (or in an extremely severe case), clinicians may consider a more dramatic treatment, **electroconvulsive therapy (ECT),** the most controversial treatment for psychological disorders after psychosurgery. In Chapter 1, we described how ECT was used in the early 20th century. Despite many unfortunate abuses along the way, ECT is considerably changed today. It is now a safe and reasonably effective treatment for severe depression that has not improved with other treatments (American Psychiatric Association, 2000; Gitlin, 2009; National Institute of Mental Health, 2003; Nemeroff, 2006).

In current administrations, patients are anaesthetized to reduce discomfort and given muscle-relaxing drugs to prevent bone breakage from convulsions during seizures. Electric shock is administered directly through the brain for less than a second, producing a seizure and a series of brief convulsions that usually lasts for several minutes. In current practice, treatments are administered once every other day for a total of six to ten treatments (fewer if the patient's mood returns to normal). Side effects are generally limited to short-term memory loss and confusion that disappear after a week or two, although some patients may have long-term memory problems. For severely depressed inpatients with psychotic features, controlled studies indicate that approximately 50 percent of those *not responding* to medication will benefit. Continued treatment with medication or psychotherapy is then necessary because the relapse rate approaches 60 percent (American Psychiatric Association Practice Guideline, 2000; Depression Guideline Panel, 1993; Fernandez, Levy, Lachar, & Small, 1995; Gitlin, 2009). For example, Sackeim and colleagues (2001) treated 84 patients with ECT and then randomly assigned them to follow-up placebo or one of several antidepressant drug treatments. All patients assigned to placebo relapsed within six months compared to 40 percent to 60 percent on medication. Thus, follow-up treatment with antidepressant drugs or psychological treatments is necessary, but relapse is still high. Nevertheless, it may not be in the best interest of psychotically depressed and acutely suicidal inpatients to wait three to six weeks to determine whether a drug or psychological treatment is working; in these cases, immediate ECT may be appropriate.

We do not really know why ECT works. Repeated seizures induce massive functional and perhaps structural changes in the brain, which seems to be therapeutic. There is some evidence that ECT increases levels of serotonin, blocks stress hormones, and promotes neurogenesis in the hippocampus. Because of the controversial nature of this treatment, its use declined considerably during the 1970s and 1980s (American Psychiatric Association, 2001).

Recently, another method for altering electrical activity in the brain by setting up a strong magnetic field has been introduced. This procedure is called *transcranial magnetic stimulation (TMS),* and it works by placing a magnetic coil over the individual's head to generate a precisely localized electromagnetic pulse. Anesthesia is not required, and side effects are usually limited to headaches. Initial reports, as with most new procedures, showed promise in treating depression (Fitzgerald et al., 2003, 2006; George, Lisanby, & Sackheim, 1999), and recent reviews have confirmed that TMS can be effective (Schutter, 2009). But results from several important clinical trials with severe or treatment-resistant psychotic depression reported ECT to be clearly more effective than TMS (Eranti et al., 2007). It may be that TMS is more comparable to antidepressant medication than to ECT (Gitlin, 2009).

Several other nondrug approaches for treatment-resistant depression are in development. Vagus nerve stimulation involves implanting a pacemaker-like device that generates pulses to the vagus nerve in the neck, which, in turn, is thought to influence neurotransmitter production in the brain stem and limbic system (Gitlin, 2009; Marangell et al., 2002). Sufficient evidence has accumulated, but results are generally weak and it has been little used. Deep brain stimulation has been used with a few severely depressed patients. In this procedure, electrodes are surgically implanted in the limbic system (the emotional brain). These electrodes are also connected to a pacemaker-like device (Mayberg et al., 2005). Time will tell if this is a useful treatment.

Phototherapy for Seasonal Affective Disorder

A specific therapy has been developed for the treatment of the seasonal subtype of depression (i.e., SAD). Recall from our earlier discussion of SAD the role of increased production of melatonin in this disorder. Some clinicians reasoned that exposure to bright light might slow melatonin production in

individuals with SAD (Blehar & Rosenthal, 1989; Lewy, Kern, Rosenthal, & Wehr, 1982). In **phototherapy**, the specific treatment developed for SAD, most patients are exposed to two hours of very bright light (2500 lux) immediately on awakening (Lam & Levitt, 1999). If the light exposure is effective, the patient begins to notice a lifting of mood within three to four days and a remission of winter depression in one to two weeks. Patients are also asked to avoid bright lights in the evening (from shopping malls and the like), so as not to interfere with the effects of the morning treatments. But this treatment is not without side effects, as illustrated by the work of Anthony Levitt and colleagues at the Sunnybrook Health Sciences Centre in Toronto. Approximately 19 percent of patients experience headaches, 17 percent have eyestrain, and 14 percent just feel "wired" (Levitt et al., 1993).

Phototherapy is relatively new, but recent studies strongly support its effectiveness (Eastman, Young, Fogg, Liu, & Meaden, 1998; Lewy et al., 1998; Terman, Terman, & Ross, 1998). In these studies, morning light was compared with evening light, which was predicted to be less effective. In two of these studies, a clever "negative ion generator" served as a placebo treatment in which patients sat in front of the box for the same amount of time as in the phototherapy and "expected" the treatment would work following instructions from the investigator but did not see the light. The results, presented in Table 7.5, showed a significantly better response for morning light, compared with evening light or placebo. Evening light was better than placebo. Moreover, the work of Raymond Lam and colleagues indicates that not only is phototherapy effective in treating depression in SAD patients, it is also effective in reducing suicidality (Lam, 1994; Lam, Tam, Shiah, Yatham, & Zis, 2000). Relatively longer exposure to light (e.g., 60 minutes per day as opposed to only 30 minutes per day) tends to be associated with a better outcome (Levitt, Lam, & Levitan, 2002). As we noted earlier, the most common form of light therapy uses medium exposure durations of two hours per day (Lam & Levitt, 1999).

Phototherapy's mechanism of action in treating SAD has not been fully established, but one study indicated that morning light

TABLE 7.5 Summary of Remission Rates

	Remission Rate (%) (Number of Patients)		
	Morning Light	Evening Light	Placebo (Negative-Ion Generator)
Terman et al. (1998)			
First treatment	54 (25 of 46)	33 (13 of 39)	11 (2 of 19)
	60 (28 of 47)	30 (14 of 47)	Not done
Eastman et al. (1998)			
First treatment	55 (18 of 33)	28 (9 of 32)	16 (5 of 31)
Lewy et al. (1998)			
First treatment	22 (6 of 27)	4 (1 of 24)	Not done
Crossover	27 (14 of 51)	4 (2 of 51)	Not done

is superior to evening light due to the fact that morning light produced phase advances of the melatonin rhythm, suggesting that advances in circadian rhythm are an important factor in treatment (Terman, Terman, Lo, & Cooper, 2001). In any case, it seems clear that light therapy is the treatment of choice for winter depression (Lam & Levitt, 1999) and it may even be effective for nonseasonal depression (Kripke, 1998).

Psychosocial Treatments

Of the effective psychosocial treatments now available for depressive disorders, two major approaches are most effective. The first is cognitive-behavioural; Aaron T. Beck, the founder of cognitive therapy, is most closely associated with this approach. The second approach, interpersonal psychotherapy, was developed by Myrna Weissman and Gerald Klerman.

Cognitive Therapy

Beck's **cognitive therapy** grew directly out of his observations of the role of deep-seated negative thinking in generating depression (Beck, 1967, 1976; Beck & Young, 1985; Clark, Beck, & Alford, 1999; Young et al., 2001). David A. Clark describes the approach as follows. First, clients are taught to examine carefully their thought processes while they are depressed and to recognize "depressive" errors in thinking. This task is not always easy, because many thoughts are automatic and beyond clients' awareness. Negative thinking seems natural to them. Clients are taught that errors in thinking can directly cause depression. Treatment involves correcting cognitive errors and substituting less depressing and (perhaps) more realistic thoughts and appraisals. Later in therapy, underlying negative cognitive schemas (characteristic ways of viewing the world) that trigger specific cognitive errors are targeted, not only in the office but also as part of the client's daily life. The therapist purposefully takes a Socratic approach, making it clear that therapist and client are working as a team to uncover faulty thinking patterns and the underlying schemas from which they are generated. Therapists must be skillful and highly trained (see Clark et al., 1999). What follows is an example of an actual interaction between Beck and a client named Irene.

BECK AND IRENE | *A Dialogue*

Because an intake interview had already been completed by another therapist, Beck did not spend time reviewing Irene's symptoms in detail or taking a history. Irene began by describing her "sad states." Beck almost immediately started to elicit her automatic thoughts during these periods.

THERAPIST: What kind of thoughts were you having during these four days when you said your thoughts kept coming over and over again?

PATIENT: Well, they were just—mostly, "Why is this happening again"—because, you know, this isn't the first time he's been out of work. You know, "What am I going to

do"—like I have all different thoughts. They are all in different things like being mad at him, being mad at myself for being in this position all the time. Like I want to leave him or if I could do anything to make him straighten out and not depend so much on him. There's a lot of thoughts in there.

THERAPIST: Now can we go back a little bit to the sad states that you have? Do you still have that sad state?

PATIENT: Yeah.

THERAPIST: You have it right now?

PATIENT: Yeah, sort of. They were sad thoughts about—I don't know—I get bad thoughts, like a lot of what I'm thinking is bad things. Like not—there is like, ah, it isn't going to get any better, it will stay that way. I don't know. Lots of things go wrong, you know, that's how I think.

THERAPIST: So one of the thoughts is that it's not going to get any better?

PATIENT: Yeah.

THERAPIST: And sometimes you believe that completely?

PATIENT: Yeah, I believe it, sometimes.

THERAPIST: Right now do you believe it?

PATIENT: I believe—yeah, yeah.

THERAPIST: Right now you believe that things are not going to get better?

PATIENT: Well, there is a glimmer of hope but it's mostly. . . .

THERAPIST: What do you kind of look forward to in terms of your own life from here on?

PATIENT: Well, what I look forward to—I can tell you but I don't want to tell you. (Giggles). Um, I don't see too much.

THERAPIST: You don't want to tell me?

PATIENT: No, I'll tell you but it's not sweet and great what I think. I just see me continuing on the way I am, the way I don't want to be, like not doing anything, just being there, like sort of with no use, that like my husband will still be there and he will, you know, he'll go in and out of drugs or whatever he is going to do, and I'll just still be there, just in the same place.

By inquiring about Irene's automatic thoughts, the therapist began to understand her perspective—that she would go on forever, trapped, with her husband in and out of drug centres. This hopelessness about the future is characteristic of most depressed patients. A second advantage to this line of inquiry is that the therapist introduced Irene to the idea of looking at her own thoughts, which is central to cognitive therapy.

Source: Young, J. E., Weinberger, A. D., & Beck, A. T. (2001). Cognitive therapy for depression. In D. H. Barlow (Ed.), *Clinical handbook of psychological disorders* (3rd ed., pp. 264–308). New York: Guilford Publications.

Between sessions, clients are instructed to *monitor* and *log* their thought processes carefully, particularly in situations in which they might feel depressed. They also attempt to change their behaviour by carrying out specific activities assigned as homework, such as tasks in which clients can test their faulty thinking. For example, a client who has to participate in an upcoming meeting might think, "If I go to that meeting, I'll just make a fool of myself and all my colleagues will think I'm stupid." The therapist might instruct the client to go to the meeting, predict ahead of time the reaction of her colleagues, and then see what really happens. This part of treatment is called *hypothesis testing* because the client makes a hypothesis about what's going to happen (usually a depressing outcome) and then, most often, discovers it is incorrect ("My colleagues congratulated me on my presentation"). The therapist typically schedules other activities to reactivate depressed patients who have given up most activities, helping them put some fun back into their lives.

Interpersonal Psychotherapy

We have seen that major disruptions in our interpersonal relationships are an important category of stresses that can trigger mood disorders (Joiner & Timmons, 2009; Kendler, Hettema, Butera, Gardner, & Prescott, 2003). In addition, people with few, if any, important social relationships seem at risk for developing and sustaining mood disorders (Beach et al., 2009; Sherbourne et al., 1995). **Interpersonal psychotherapy (IPT)** (Bleiberg & Markowitz, 2008; Gillies, 2001; Klerman, Weissman, Rounsaville, & Chevron, 1984; Weissman, 1995) focuses on resolving problems in existing relationships and learning to form important new interpersonal relationships.

Therapist Laurie Gillies of the Ontario Institute for Studies in Education and the University of Toronto has described the approach as follows (Gillies, 2001). Like cognitive-behavioural approaches, IPT is highly structured and seldom takes longer than 15 to 20 sessions, usually scheduled once a week. After identifying life stressors that seem to precipitate the depression, the therapist and patient work collaboratively on the patient's current interpersonal problems. Typically, these include one or more of four interpersonal issues: (1) dealing with interpersonal role disputes, such as marital conflict; (2) adjusting to the loss of a relationship, such as grief over the death of a loved one; (3) acquiring new relationships, such as getting married or establishing professional relationships; and (4) identifying and correcting deficits in social skills that prevent the person from initiating or maintaining important relationships (Gillies, 2001).

To take a common example, the therapist's first job is to identify and define an interpersonal dispute (Gillies, 2001; Weissman, 1995), perhaps with a wife who expects her spouse to support her but has had to take an outside job to help pay bills. The husband might expect the wife to share equally in generating income. If this dispute seems to be associated with the onset of depressive symptoms and to result in a continuing series of arguments and disagreements without resolution, it would become the focus for IPT.

After helping identify the dispute, the next step is to bring it to a resolution. First, the therapist helps the patient determine the stage of the dispute.

1. *Negotiation stage:* Both partners are aware it is a dispute, and they are trying to renegotiate it.
2. *Impasse stage:* The dispute smoulders beneath the surface and results in low-level resentment, but no attempts are made to resolve it.
3. *Resolution stage:* The partners are taking some action, such as divorce or separation.

The therapist works with the patient to define the dispute clearly for both parties and develop specific strategies for resolving it.

Studies comparing the results of cognitive therapy and IPT to those of tricyclic antidepressants and other control conditions have found that psychosocial approaches and medication are equally effective, and all treatments are more effective than placebo conditions, brief psychodynamic treatments, or other appropriate control conditions for both major depressive disorder and dysthymia (Beck, Hollon, Young, Bedrosian, & Budenz, 1985; Blackburn & Moore, 1997; Hollon et al., 1992; Hollon & Dimidjian, 2009; Miller, Norman, & Keitner, 1989; Paykel & Scott, 2009; Schulberg et al., 1996; Shapiro et al., 1995). Depending on how "success" is defined, approximately 50 percent to 70 percent or more of people benefit from treatment to a significant extent, compared with approximately 30 percent in placebo or control conditions.

One study, sponsored by the National Institutes of Mental Health (NIMH) and carried out in three different clinics in North America (Elkin et al., 1989), reported no essential differences in effectiveness among interpersonal psychotherapy, cognitive therapy, and tricyclic antidepressants, when all patients who were treated were included in the results, whether or not they had dropped out. At one clinic medication was more effective than cognitive therapy if the patients were severely depressed (Elkin et al., 1995), a finding that may indicate less skillful cognitive therapists administering the treatment at that site (Hollon, 1993; Jacobson & Hollon, 1996a, 1996b). Similar studies, such one conducted by clinical psychologist Peter McLean at the University of British Columbia (McLean & Taylor, 1992), have not found a difference in treatment effectiveness based on severity of depression. In fact, DeRubeis, Gelfand, Tang, and Simons (1999) carefully evaluated the effects of cognitive therapy versus medication in severely depressed patients only across four studies and found no advantage for one treatment or the other. In any case, when patients in the NIMH study who had recovered were followed up for 18 months, the results of this study were very disappointing (Shea et al., 1992). Of all patients entering treatment, only 30 percent of those who received cognitive therapy remained well, compared with 26 percent of those who received IPT, 19 percent in the tricyclic drug group, and 20 percent in the placebo group. Shea et al. (1992) concluded that treatments were just not delivered long enough (or well enough) to effect meaningful change. More recently, O'Hara, Stuart, Gorman, and Wenzel (2000) demonstrated more positive effects for IPT in a group of women with postpartum depression, demonstrating that this approach is a worthwhile strategy in patients with postpartum depression who are reluctant to go on medication because, for example, they are breast-feeding.

Research by Darcy Santor and Vivek Kusumakar at Dalhousie University evaluated the effectiveness of IPT in depressed adolescents. Twenty-five adolescents (mean age of 16 years) received 12 weeks of IPT. The majority of teens improved substantially on both self-ratings and clinician ratings of depression symptoms. Depending on the criteria used, 80 percent to 84 percent of the teens were no longer showing meaningful levels of depressive symptoms by therapy completion. The study suggests that IPT may be effective for treating moderate to severe depression in adolescents, although this needs to be demonstrated in a future randomized control study before we can be sure that the changes were actually due to the therapy (Santor & Kusumakar, 2001).

In view of the seriousness of mood disorders in children and adolescents, work has begun on preventing these disorders in these age groups (Muñoz, 1993). Most researchers focus on instilling in children social and problem-solving skills that are adequate to prevent the kinds of social stress so often associated with depression. In fact, Sanders and colleagues (1992) and Dadds, Sanders, Morrison, and Rebgetz (1992) determined that disordered communication and problem-solving skills, particularly within the family, are characteristic of depressed children and a natural target for treatment. Beardslee et al. (1997) have observed sustained effects from a preventive program directed at families with children between the ages of 8 and 15 in which one parent had experienced a recent episode of depression. Eighteen months after participating in six to ten family sessions, these families were doing substantially better on most measures than the control families.

In another preventive effort, Gilham, Reivich, Jaycox, and Seligman (1995) taught cognitive and social problem-solving techniques to 69 children in Grade 5 and Grade 6 who were at risk for depression. Compared with children in a matched no-treatment control group, the prevention group reported fewer depressive symptoms during the two years they were followed. More importantly, moderate to severe symptoms were reduced by half and the positive effects of this program increased during the period of follow-up. In a replication, Seligman, Schulman, DeRubeis, and Hollon (1999) conducted a similar course for university students who were at risk for depression based on a pessimistic cognitive style. After three years, students taking the eight-session program experienced less anxiety and depression than a control group receiving the assessments only. This suggests that it might be possible to "psychologically immunize" children and adolescents against depression by teaching appropriate cognitive and social skills before they enter puberty.

Combined Treatments

A few studies have tested the very important question of whether combining psychosocial treatments with medication is effective in treating depression (e.g., Beck et al., 1985; Blackburn & Moore, 1997; Hollon et al., 1992; Miller, Norman, Keitner, Bishop, & Down, 1989). With one exception, the results thus far do not strongly suggest any immediate advantage of combined treatment over separate drug or psychosocial treatment. The exception to this finding is a very large study recently reported by Keller et al. (2000) on the treatment of chronic major depression that was conducted at 12 different clinics. In this, the largest study ever conducted on the treatment of depression, 681 patients were assigned to receive either antidepressant medication (nefazodone), a cognitive-behavioural therapy constructed specifically for chronically depressed patients, or the combination of two treatments.

Forty-eight percent of patients receiving each of the individual treatments were either remitted or responded in a clinically satisfactory way, compared with 73 percent of the patients receiving combined treatment. Because this study was conducted with only a subset of depressed patients, those with chronic depression, the findings would need to be replicated before we could say combined treatment was useful for depression generally. In addition, because the study did not include a condition in which the cognitive-behavioural treatment was combined with placebo, we cannot rule out the fact that the enhanced effectiveness of the combined treatment was due to placebo factors. A review by Zindel Segal and his colleagues at the Centre for Addiction and Mental Health in Toronto suggests that combined treatment is generally just as effective as separate drug or psychosocial therapies in the treatment of depression. However, when the depression is severe, combined drug and psychosocial treatments appear to have some additional benefits over either treatment administered separately (Segal, Vincent, & Levitt, 2002).

In any case, drugs and cognitive behavioural treatments clearly operate in different ways. Medication, when it works, does so more quickly than psychosocial treatments, which in turn have the advantage of increasing the patient's long-range social functioning (particularly in the case of IPT) and also protecting against relapse or recurrence (particularly cognitive therapy). Combining treatments, therefore, might take advantage of the drugs' rapid action and the psychosocial protection against recurrence or relapse, thereby allowing eventual discontinuation of the medications. For example, Fava, Grandi, Zielezny, Rafanelli, and Canestrari (1996) assigned patients who had been successfully treated with antidepressant drugs to either cognitive-behavioural treatment of residual symptoms or standard clinical management. Four years later, patients treated with cognitive-behavioural procedures had a substantially lower relapse rate (35 percent) than patients in the clinical management position (70 percent). In a second study with patients with recurrent depressive episodes, the authors essentially replicated the results (Fava, Rafanelli, Grandi, Conti, & Belluardo, 1998).

Preventing Relapse

Given the high rate of recurrence in depression, it is not surprising that well over 50 percent of patients on antidepressant medication relapse if their medication is stopped within four months after their last depressive episode (Hollon, Shelton, & Loosen, 1991; Thase, 1990). Therefore, one important question has to do with **maintenance treatment** to *prevent* relapse or recurrence over the long term.

In several studies, cognitive therapy reduced rates of subsequent relapse in depressed patients by more than 50 percent over groups treated with antidepressant medication (e.g., Evans et al., 1992; Kovacs, Rush, Beck, & Hollon, 1981; Simons, Murphy, Levine, & Wetzel, 1986). Evans et al. (1992) found that cognitive therapy prevented subsequent relapse to the same extent as did continuing medication over a two-year period. Data on relapse presented in ■ Figure 7.7 show that 50 percent of a group whose medication was stopped relapsed during the same period, compared with 32 percent of a group whose medication was continued at least one year. Relapse rates were only 21 percent for the group receiving cognitive therapy alone and 15 percent for those receiving cognitive therapy combined with medication. It is

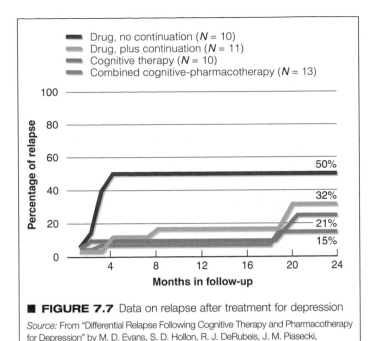

■ FIGURE 7.7 Data on relapse after treatment for depression

Source: From "Differential Relapse Following Cognitive Therapy and Pharmacotherapy for Depression" by M. D. Evans, S. D. Hollon, R. J. DeRubeis, J. M. Piasecki, W. M. Grove, M. J. Garvey and V. B. Tuason, 1992, *Archives of General Psychiatry, 49,* 802–808. © 1992 by the American Medical Association. Reprinted by permission.

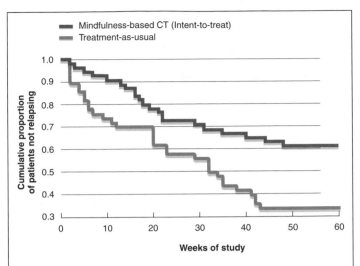

■ FIGURE 7.8 Survival (nonrelapse/nonrecurrence) curves comparing relapse/recurrence to major depression for treatment as usual and Segal's mindfulness-based cognitive therapy in patients with three or more previous episodes of major depression (CT, cognitive therapy)

Source: From "Prevention of relapse/recurrence in major depression by mindfulness-based cognitive therapy" by J. D. Teasdale, Z. V. Segal, J.M. Williams, V. A. Ridgeway, J. M. Soulsby, & M. A. Lau, 2000, *Journal of Consulting and Clinical Psychology, 4,* 615–623.

interesting that the cognitive therapy was not continued beyond the initial 12-week period. Some more recent data suggest that adding a supplemental phase to the end of a regular phase of cognitive therapy, that specifically focuses on teaching patients skills to prevent relapse significantly reduces relapse among the highest-risk patients with recurrent major depression (Jarrett et al., 2001).

Zindel Segal and his colleagues are currently collaborating with researchers in the United Kingdom on a variant of traditional cognitive therapy that is specifically designed to prevent depressive relapse. This new therapy is called mindfulness-based cognitive therapy (Segal, Williams, & Teasdale, 2002). It is a group therapy designed to teach recovered depressed patients to disengage from the kinds of negative thinking that can precipitate a relapse to depression. More specifically, they are trained in mindfulness meditation to help them become more aware of their thoughts and feelings and to view their thoughts as mental events rather than as accurate reflections of reality. In a recent randomized control study, 145 patients recovered from depression were assigned to receive either mindfulness-based cognitive therapy or treatment as usual, and relapse of major depression was assessed over a 60-week period. For patients with a history of recurrent depression, the mindfulness treatment significantly reduced their risk of another relapse (Teasdale et al., 2000). The proportion of patients not relapsing in both groups is presented in ■ Figure 7.8. A more recent study by this research team has shown that mindfulness-based cognitive therapy works in preventing depressive relapse by changing patients' relationships to their negative thoughts (e.g., by allowing them to distance themselves from their thoughts and feelings; Teasdale et al., 2002).

Because psychosocial treatments affect biological aspects of disorders, and drug treatments affect psychological components, the integrative model of mood disorders is helpful in studying the effects of treatment. Evidence suggests that psychological treatments alter neurochemical correlates of depression. McKnight, Nelson-Gray,

and Barnhill (1992) used either cognitive therapy or tricyclic medication to treat groups of patients with major depressive disorder. They found that an abnormal pretreatment response to the dexamethasone suppression test (DST) of cortisol secretion did *not* predict which treatment would be more effective, and both produced a normalization of post-treatment DST responses. Similarly, the work of Zindel Segal and his colleagues has shown that successful cognitive therapy and tricyclic medication both decrease thyroid hormone levels (Joffe, Segal, & Singer, 1996).

Psychosocial Treatments for Bipolar Disorder

Although medication, particularly lithium, is the preferred treatment for bipolar disorder, most clinicians emphasize the need for psychosocial intervention to manage interpersonal and practical problems such as marital and job difficulties that result from the disorder (Clarkin, Haas, & Glick, 1988). Until recently, the principal objective of psychosocial intervention was to increase compliance with medication regimens such as lithium (Cochran, 1984). We noted before that the "pleasures" of

▲ Zindel Segal is a clinical psychologist who heads the cognitive therapy unit at the Centre for Addiction and Mental Health. He has been heavily involved in the development of a new variant of cognitive therapy called mindfulness-based cognitive therapy that is designed to prevent relapses to depression in people with recurrent major depression.

a manic state make refusal to take lithium a major therapeutic obstacle. Giving up drugs between episodes or skipping dosages during an episode significantly undermines treatment. Therefore, a careful integration of psychosocial and lithium treatments is very important (Goodwin & Jamison, 2007; Scott, 1995).

In a small pilot study, family therapy was added to a drug regimen. A significant increase in the percentage of patients with bipolar disorder who fully recovered was seen in the combined treatment (56 percent) relative to those who had drug treatment alone (20 percent) (see ■ Figure 7.9). During a two-year follow-up, patients who received psychosocial treatment had less than half the recidivism of those who had drug treatment alone (Miller, Keitner, Epstein, Bishop, & Ryan, 1991). Family tension is associated with relapse in bipolar disorder and preliminary studies indicate that psychosocial treatment directed at helping families understand symptoms and develop new coping skills and communication styles (Simoneau, Miklowitz, Richards, Saleen, & George, 1999) and prevent relapse (Miklowitz, 2001; Miklowitz & Goldstein, 1997; Miklowitz, Simoneau, Sachs-Ericsson, Warner, & Suddath, 1996). More recently, Miklowitz et al. (2000) have demonstrated that their family-focused treatment combined with medication results in significantly less relapse one year following initiation of treatment than patients receiving crisis management and medication over the same period of time.

In another important study, Lam et al. (2003) showed that patients with bipolar disorders treated with cognitive therapy plus medication relapsed significantly less over one year than a control group receiving just medication. This finding replicates, in part, earlier results by Perry, Tarrier, Morriss, McCarthy, and Limb (1999).

Let us now return to Katie who, you will remember, had made a serious suicide attempt in the midst of a major depressive episode.

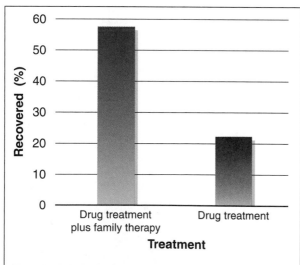

■ **FIGURE 7.9** Percentage of patients with bipolar disorder who recovered after standard drug treatment or drug treatment plus family therapy.

Source: Adapted from "Families of Bipolar Patients: Dysfunction, Course of Illness, and Pilot Treatment Study" by I. W. Miller, G. I. Keitner, N. B. Epstein, D. S. Bishop and C. E. Ryan, 1991. Paper presented at the annual meeting of the Association for the Advancement of Behavior Therapy, New York. Adapted by permission.

KATIE | *The Triumph of the Self*

Like the overwhelming majority of people with serious psychological disorders, Katie had never received an adequate course of treatment, although she was evaluated periodically by various mental health professionals. She lived in a rural area where competent professional help was not readily available. Her life ebbed and flowed with her struggle to subdue anxiety and depression. When she could manage her emotions sufficiently, she took an occasional course in the high school independent study program. Katie discovered that she was fascinated by learning. She enrolled in a local community college at the age of 19 and did extremely well, despite the fact that she had not progressed beyond Grade 9 in school. At the college she earned a high school equivalency degree. She went to work in a local factory. But she continued to drink heavily and to take Valium; on occasion, anxiety and depression would return and disrupt her life.

Finally, Katie left home, attended college full-time, and fell in love. But the romance was one-sided, and she was rejected.

> One night after a phone conversation with him, I nearly drank myself to death. I lived in a single room alone in the dorm. I drank as much vodka as quickly as I could. I fell asleep. When I awoke, I was covered in vomit and couldn't recall falling asleep or being sick. I was drunk for much of the next day. When I awoke the following morning, I realized I could have killed myself by choking on my own vomit. More importantly, I wasn't sure if I fully wanted to die. That was the last of my drinking.

Katie decided to make some changes. Taking advantage of what she had learned in the little treatment she had received, she began looking at life and herself differently. Instead of dwelling on how inadequate and evil she was, she began to pay attention to her strengths. "But I now realized that I needed to accept myself as is, and work with any stumbling blocks that I faced. I needed to get myself through the world as happily and as comfortably as I could. I had a right to that." Other lessons learned in treatment now became valuable, and Katie became more aware of her mood swings:

> I learned to objectify periods of depression as [simply] periods of "feeling." They are a part of who I am, but not the whole. I recognize when I feel that way, and I check my perceptions with someone that I trust when I feel uncertain of them. I try to hold on to the belief that these periods are only temporary.

Katie developed other strategies for coping successfully with life:

> I try to stay focused on my goals and what is important to me. I have learned that if one strategy to achieve some goal doesn't work there are other strategies that probably will. My endurance is one of my blessings. Patience, dedication, and

discipline are also important. None of the changes that I have been through occurred instantly or automatically. Most of what I have achieved has required time, effort, and persistence.

Katie dreamed that if she worked hard enough she could help other people who had problems similar to her own. Katie pursued that dream and earned her Ph.D. in psychology.

Suicide

Statistics

Most days we are confronted with news about the war on cancer or the frantic race to find a cure for AIDS. We also hear never-ending admonitions to improve our diet and to exercise more to prevent heart disease. But another cause of death ranks right up there with the most frightening and dangerous medical conditions—the decision to kill themselves made by more than a million people per year worldwide (World Health Organization, 2000). Most epidemiologists agree that the actual number of suicides may be even higher than official statistics suggest. Many of these unreported suicides occur when people purposefully drive off a bridge or a cliff (Blumenthal, 1990). According to the work of Isaac Sakinofsky, head of the high-risk consultation clinic at the Centre for Addiction and Mental Health in Toronto, suicide rates in Canada are highest in Alberta, Québec, and the Northwest Territories and lowest in Newfoundland and Labrador (Sakinofsky, 1998). A comparison of suicides in Canada and the United States pertains to rates of suicides by gunshot, given that the two countries have very different national policies on gun control. Suicides by gunshot continue to account for the majority of suicides in the United States. In Canada, we implemented restrictive gun-control legislation in the 1970s, which was associated with long-lasting reductions in suicide rates. There have not been corresponding increases in suicide by other means in Canada since we implemented this legislation (Carrington, 1999; Leenaars & Lester, 1996).

As you might expect from the incidence of depression in Aboriginal people, their suicide rate is extremely high, although great variability exists across specific groups of Indigenous peoples. Some groups have rates up to 800 times the national average (Chandler & Lalonde, 1998). Elevated suicide rates appear to be specific to Aboriginal people living on the reserves (Cooper, Corrado, Karlberg, & Adams, 1992), which is likely the result of stressful conditions associated with life on the reserve (e.g., low income, overcrowding). Other studies suggest that alcohol abuse is also a likely contributing factor (Malchy, Enns, Young, & Cox, 1997; Wilkie, Macdonald, & Hildahl, 1998).

The suicide rate among Canadian Inuit has been alarmingly high in recent years. Boothroyd, Kirmayer, Spreng, Malus, and Hodgins (2001) studied cases of completed suicides in Nunavik to identify risk factors. Most cases were young males aged 15 to 24

▲ James Bartleman, Lieutenant Governor of Ontario (2002–2007), is a member of the Mjnikaning First Nation. His early years were marked by discrimination and poverty. Despite his many successes, Bartleman struggles with depression. He is determined to decrease the high rates of suicide among young people in many Canadian Aboriginal communities, and he is an active advocate for reducing the stigma associated with mental illness.

who usually committed suicide by hanging or gunshot. Psychiatric problems such as depression, personality disorder, and drug abuse were very common in these cases.

Even more frightening is the dramatic increase in death by suicide in recent years, most evident among adolescents. Between 1960 and 1988 the suicide rate in adolescents rose from 3.6 to 11.3 per 100 000 population, an increase of 200 percent compared with a general population increase of 17 percent. For teenagers, suicide is the third-leading cause of death, behind motor vehicle accidents and homicide (Ventura, Peters, Martin, & Maurer, 1997). Suicide rates among the elderly have also increased dramatically. This rise has been connected to the growing incidence of medical illness in our oldest citizens and to their increasing loss of social support. As we have noted, a strong relationship exists between illness or infirmity and hopelessness or depression (Brown, Beck, Steer,

▲ Men often choose violent methods of committing suicide. Canadian musician Richard Manuel, best known for his membership in the highly influential 1960s and 1970s rock group The Band and for his musical collaborations with Bob Dylan, committed suicide by hanging himself.

& Grisham, 2000; Gallagher-Thompson & Osgood, 1997; National Center for Health Statistics, 1993). Suicide is not attempted only by adolescents and adults: Rosenthal and Rosenthal (1984) described 16 children aged two to five years who had attempted suicide at least once, many injuring themselves severely.

Regardless of age, in every country around the world except China, males are four times more likely to *commit* suicide than females (Centers for Disease Control [CDC], 2010; Nock et al., in press; World Health Organization, 2010). This startling fact seems to be related in part to gender differences in the types of suicide attempts. Males generally choose far more violent methods, such as guns and hanging; females tend to rely on less violent options, such as drug overdose (Buda & Tsuang, 1990; Gallagher-Thompson & Osgood, 1997). More men commit suicide during old age and more women during middle age, in part because most attempts by older women are unsuccessful (Berman, 2009; Kuo, Gallo, & Tien, 2001). The suicide rate for young men in the United States is now the highest in the world, even surpassing rates in Japan and Sweden, countries long known for high rates of suicide (Blumenthal, 1990). But, as we noted, older men (over 65) in all countries are most at risk for completing suicide worldwide (McIntosh, Santos, Hubbard, & Overholser, 1994).

In China, and uniquely in China, more women commit suicide than do men, particularly in rural settings (Murray, 1996; Murray & Lopez, 1996; Nock et al., 2008). What accounts for this culturally determined reversal? Chinese scientists agree that China's suicide rates, probably the highest in the world, are due to an absence of stigma. In fact, suicide, particularly among women, is often portrayed in classical Chinese literature as a reasonable solution to problems. A rural Chinese woman's family is her entire world, and suicide is an honourable solution if the family collapses. Furthermore, highly toxic farm pesticides are readily available and it is possible that many women who did not necessarily intend to kill themselves die after accidentally swallowing poison.

In addition to completed suicides, two other important indices of suicidal behaviour are **suicidal attempts** (the person survives) and **suicidal ideation** (thinking seriously about suicide). Although males *commit* suicide more often than females in most of the world, females attempt suicide at least three times as often (Berman & Jobes, 1991). This high incidence may reflect the fact that more women than men are depressed and that depression is strongly related to suicide attempts (Frances, Franklin, & Flavin, 1986). Some estimates place the ratio of attempted to completed suicides at 50 or more to one (Garfield & Zigler, 1993). In addition, results from another study (Kovacs, Goldston, & Gatsonis, 1993) suggest that among adolescents, the ratio of thoughts about suicide to attempts is between three to one and six to one. In other words, between 16 percent and 30 percent of adolescents in this study who had thought about killing themselves actually attempted it. "Thoughts" in this context does not refer to a fleeting philosophical type of consideration but rather to a serious contemplation of the act. The first step down the dangerous road to suicide is thinking about it (Mishara, 1999).

In a study of university students (whose rate of suicide is only about half that of the general population), approximately 10 percent to 25 percent had thoughts about suicide during the past 12 months (Brener, Hassan, & Barrios, 1999; Meehan, Lamb, Saltzman, & O'Carroll, 1992; Schwartz & Whitaker, 1990). Only a minority of these students with thoughts of suicide (perhaps around 15 percent) attempt to kill themselves, and only a few succeed (Kovacs et al., 1993). Nevertheless, given the enormity of the problem, suicidal thoughts are taken very seriously by mental health professionals.

Causes

Past Conceptions

The great sociologist Emile Durkheim (1951) defined several suicide types, based on the social or cultural conditions in which they occurred. One type is "formalized" suicides that were approved of, such as the ancient custom of *hara-kiri* in Japan, in which an individual who brought dishonour to himself or his family was expected to impale himself on a sword. Durkheim referred to this as *altruistic suicide*. Durkheim also recognized the loss of social supports as an important provocation for suicide; he called this *egoistic suicide*. (Elderly citizens who kill themselves after losing touch with their friends or family fit into this category.) Magne-Ingvar, Ojehagen, and Traskman-Bendz (1992) found that only 13 percent of 75 individuals who had seriously attempted suicide had an adequate social network of friends and relationships. *Anomic suicides* are the result of marked disruptions, such as the sudden loss of a high-prestige job. ("Anomie" is feeling lost and confused.) Finally, *fatalistic suicides* result from a loss of control over our own destiny. The mass suicide of 39 Heaven's Gate cult members is an example of this type, because the lives of those people were largely in the hands of Marshall Applewhite, a supreme and charismatic leader.

Durkheim's work was important in alerting us to the social contribution to suicide. Freud (1917, 1957) believed that suicide (and depression, to some extent) indicated unconscious hostility directed inward to the self rather than outward to the person or situation causing the anger. Indeed, suicide victims often seem to be psychologically "punishing" others who may have rejected them or caused some other personal hurt. Current thinking considers social and psychological factors but also highlights the potential importance of biological contributions.

Concept Check | 7.3

Check your understanding of types of suicides by matching the following summaries with the correct suicide type. Choose from (a) altruistic, (b) egoistic, (c) anomic, and (d) fatalistic.

1. Ralph's wife left him and took the children. He is a well-known television personality but, because of a conflict with the new station owners, he was recently fired. If Ralph kills himself, his suicide would be considered

   _____

2. Sam killed himself while a prisoner of war in Vietnam.

   _____

3. Sheiba lives in a remote village in Africa. She was recently caught in an adulterous affair with a man in a nearby village. Her husband wants to kill her but won't have to because of a tribal custom that requires her to kill herself. She leaps from the nearby "sinful woman's cliff." _____

4. Mabel lived in a nursing home for many years. At first, her family and friends visited her often; now they come only at Christmas. Her two closest friends in the nursing home died recently. She has no hobbies or other interests. Mabel's suicide would be identified as what type?

   _____

Risk Factors

Edward Shneidman pioneered the study of risk factors for suicide (Shneidman, 1989; Shneidman, Farberow, & Litman, 1970). Among the methods he and others have used to study those conditions and events that make a person vulnerable is **psychological autopsy**. The psychological profile of the person who committed suicide is reconstructed through extensive interviews with friends and family members who are likely to know what the individual was thinking and doing in the period before death. This and other methods have allowed researchers to identify a number of risk factors for suicide.

Family History

If a family member committed suicide, the risk increases that someone else in the family will also (Kety, 1990; Mann, Waternaux, Haas, & Malone, 1999; Mann et al., 2005). This may not be surprising, because so many people who kill themselves are depressed, and depression runs in families. Nevertheless, the question remains: Are people who kill themselves simply adopting a familiar solution or does an inherited trait, such as impulsivity, account for increased suicidal behaviour in families? The possibility that something is inherited is supported by several adoption studies. One found an increased rate of suicide in the biological relatives of adopted individuals who had committed suicide, compared with a control group of adoptees who had not committed suicide (Schulsinger, Kety, & Rosenthal, 1979; Wender et al., 1986). In a small study of people whose twins had committed suicide, ten out of 26 surviving monozygotic co-twins, and none of nine surviving dizygotic co-twins had themselves attempted suicide (Roy, Segal, & Sarchiapone, 1995). This finding suggests some biological (genetic) contribution to suicide, even if it is relatively small.

Neurobiology

A variety of evidence suggests that low levels of serotonin may be associated with suicide and with violent suicide attempts (Asberg, Nordstrom, & Traskman-Bendz, 1986; Cremniter et al., 1999; Winchel, Stanley, & Stanley, 1990). As we have noted, extremely low levels of serotonin are associated with impulsivity, instability, and the tendency to overreact to situations (Spoont, 1992). It is very possible then that low levels of serotonin may contribute to creating a vulnerability to act impulsively. This impulsiveness may include suicide, which is sometimes a very impulsive act. Studies by Brent and colleagues (2002) and Mann and colleagues (2005) suggest that transmission of vulnerabilities for a mood disorder, including the trait of impulsivity, may mediate family transmission of suicide attempts.

Existing Psychological Disorders

More than 90 percent of people who kill themselves have a psychological disorder (Conwell et al., 1996; Orbach, 1997). Suicide is often associated with mood disorders and for good reason. As many as 60 percent of suicides (75 percent of adolescent suicides) are associated with an existing mood disorder (Brent & Kolko, 1990; Frances et al., 1986). Lewinsohn, Rohde, and Seeley (1993) concluded that, in adolescents, suicidal behaviour is in large part an expression of severe depression. But many people with mood disorders do not attempt suicide, and, conversely, many people who attempt suicide do not have mood disorders. Therefore, depression and suicide, although very strongly related, are still independent. Looking more closely at the relationship of mood disorder and suicide, some investigators have isolated hopelessness, a specific component of depression, as strongly predictive of suicide (Beck, 1986; Beck, Steer, Kovacs, & Garrison, 1985; Kazdin, 1983), at least among Caucasians (Enns, Inayatulla, Cox, & Cheyne, 1997).

Alcohol use and abuse are associated with approximately 25 percent to 50 percent of suicides and are particularly evident in adolescent suicides (Berman, 2009; Brener et al., 1999; Conwell et al., 1996; Hawton, Houston, Haw, Townsend, & Harriss, 2003; Woods et al., 1997). Brent and colleagues (1988) found that about one-third of adolescents who commit suicide were intoxicated when they died and that many more might have been under the influence of drugs. Combinations of disorders, such as substance abuse and mood disorders in adults or mood disorders and conduct disorder in children and adolescents, seem to create a stronger vulnerability than any one disorder alone (Conwell et al., 1996; Nock, Hwang, Sampson, &

Kessler, 2009; Woods et al., 1997). In fact, Woods et al. (1997) found that substance abuse combined with other risk-taking behaviours such as getting into fights, carrying a gun, or smoking were predictive of teenage suicide, possibly reflecting impulsivity in these troubled adolescents. Esposito and Clum (2003) also noted that the presence of anxiety and mood (internalizing) disorders predicted suicide attempts in adolescents. Past suicide attempts are another strong risk factor and must be taken seriously (Berman, 2009). Cooper and colleagues (2005) followed almost 8000 individuals who were treated in the emergency room for deliberate self-harm for up to four years. Sixty of these people had killed themselves, which is 30 times the risk compared to population statistics.

A disorder characterized more by impulsivity than depression is borderline personality disorder (see Chapter 12). Frances and Blumenthal (1989) suggest that these individuals, known for making manipulative and impulsive suicidal gestures without necessarily wanting to destroy themselves, sometimes kill themselves by mistake in as many as 10 percent of the cases. The combination of borderline personality disorder and depression is particularly deadly (Soloff, Lynch, Kelly, Malone, & Mann, 2000).

The association of suicide with severe psychological disorders, especially depression, belies the myth that it is a response to disappointment in people who are otherwise healthy.

Stressful Life Events

Perhaps the most important risk factor for suicide is a severe, stressful event experienced as shameful or humiliating, such as a failure (real or imagined) in school or at work, an unexpected arrest, or rejection by a loved one (Blumenthal, 1990; Brent et al., 1988; Conwell, Duberstein, & Caine, 2002; Joiner & Rudd, 2000; Shaffer, Garland, Gould, Fisher, & Trautmen, 1988). Physical and sexual abuse are also important sources of stress (Kirmayer, Malus, & Boothroyd, 1996; Wagner, 1997). New evidence now confirms that the stress and disruption of natural disasters increase the likelihood of suicide (Krug et al., 1998). Based on data from 337 countries experiencing natural disasters in the 1980s, the authors

concluded that the rates of suicide increased 13.8 percent in the four years after severe floods, 31 percent in the two years after hurricanes, and 62.9 percent in the first year after an earthquake. Given pre-existing vulnerabilities—including psychological disorders, traits of impulsiveness, and lack of social support—a stressful event can often put a person over the edge. An integrated model of the causes of suicidal behaviour is presented in ■ Figure 7.10.

Is Suicide Contagious?

We hear all too often of the suicide of a teenager or celebrity. Most people react with sadness and curiosity. Some people react by attempting suicide themselves, often by the same method they have just heard about. Gould (1990) reported an increase in suicides during a nine-day period after wide-spread publicity about a suicide. Clusters of suicides (several people copying one person) seem to predominate among teenagers, with as many as 5 percent of all teenage suicides reflecting an imitation (Gould, 1990; Gould, Greenberg, Velting, & Shaffer, 2003).

Why would anyone want to copy a suicide? First, suicides are often romanticized in the media: An attractive young person under unbearable pressure commits suicide and becomes a martyr to friends and peers by getting even with the (adult) world for creating such a difficult situation. Also, media accounts often describe in detail the methods used in the suicide, thereby providing a guide to potential victims. Little is reported about the paralysis, brain damage, and other tragic consequences of the incomplete or failed suicide or about the fact that suicide is almost always associated with a severe psychological disorder. More important, even less is said about the futility of this method of solving problems (Gould, 1990; O'Carroll, 1990). To prevent these tragedies, the media should not inadvertently glorify suicides in any way, and mental health professionals must intervene immediately in schools and other locations with people who might be depressed or otherwise vulnerable to the contagion of suicide. But it isn't clear that suicide is really "contagious" in the

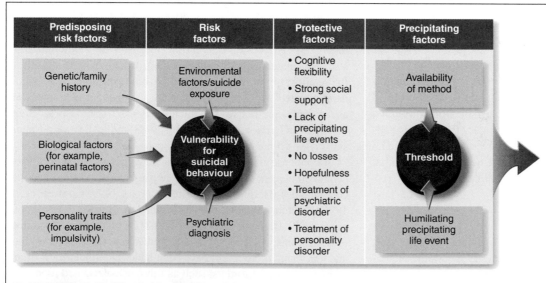

■ **FIGURE 7.10** Threshold model for suicidal behaviour.

Source: From "Clinical Assessment and Treatment of Youth Suicide" by S. J. Blumenthal and D. J. Kupfer, 1988, *Journal of Youth and Adolescence, 17,* 1–24.

infectious disease sense. Rather, the stress of a friend's suicide or some other major stress may affect several individuals who are vulnerable because of existing psychological disorders (Joiner, 1999). Nevertheless, effective intervention is essential.

Treatment

Despite the identification of important risk factors, predicting suicide is still an uncertain art. Individuals with very few precipitating factors unexpectedly kill themselves, and many who live with seemingly insurmountable stress and illness and have little social support or guidance somehow survive and overcome their difficulties.

Mental health professionals are very thoroughly trained in assessing for possible suicidal ideation (Joiner et al., 2007). Others might be reluctant to ask leading questions for fear of putting the idea in someone's head. However, we know it is far more important to check for these "secrets" than to do nothing, because the risk of inspiring suicidal thoughts is very small and the risk of leaving them undiscovered is enormous (Berman, 2009). Gould and colleagues (2005) found that more than 1000 high school students who were asked about suicidal thoughts or behaviours during a screening program showed no risk of increased suicidal thoughts compared to a second group of 1000 students who had the screening program without the questions about suicide. Therefore, if there is any indication whatsoever that someone is suicidal, the mental health professional will inquire, "Has there been any time recently when you've had some thoughts about hurting yourself or possibly killing yourself?"

The mental health professional will also check for possible humiliations and determine whether any of the factors are present that might indicate a high probability of suicide. For example, does a person who is thinking of suicide have a detailed plan or just a vague fantasy? If a plan is discovered that includes a specific time, place, and method, the risk is obviously high. Does the detailed plan include putting all personal affairs in order, giving away possessions, and other final acts? If so, the risk is higher still. What specific method is the person considering? Generally, the more violent the method (guns, hanging, poison, and so on), the greater the risk it will be used. Does the person really understand what might actually happen? Many people do not understand the effects of the pills on which they might overdose. Finally, has the person taken any precautions against being discovered? If so, the risk is extreme (American Psychiatric Association, 2003).

If a risk is present, clinicians attempt to get the individual to agree to or even sign a "no-suicide contract." Usually, this includes a promise not to do anything remotely connected with suicide without contacting the mental health professional first. If the person at risk refuses a contract (or the clinician has serious doubts about the patient's sincerity) and the suicidal risk is judged to be high, immediate hospitalization is indicated, even against the will of the patient. Whether the person is hospitalized or not, treatment aimed at resolving underlying life stressors and treating existing psychological disorders should be initiated immediately.

In view of the public health consequences of suicide, many programs have been implemented to reduce the rates of suicide both in Canada and in other parts of the world. They include curriculum-based programs in which teams of professionals go into schools or other organizations to educate people about suicide and provide information on handling life stress. The United Kingdom targeted reducing suicide rates by 15 percent, and policymakers and mental health professionals are determining the best methods for achieving this goal (Lewis, Hawton, & Jones, 1997). More than 200 suicide prevention and crisis centres across Canada provide 24-hour phone service to people in crisis, including those considering suicide (Dyck & White, 1998). Some findings are encouraging, such as a study showing that suicide rates declined in the years following the establishment of suicide prevention centres in several cities (Lester, 1991). Unfortunately, however, most research indicates that such educational and crisis phone line programs are not effective (Garfield & Zigler, 1993; Shaffer, Garland, Vieland, Underwood, & Busner, 1991). As Garfield and Zigler (1993) point out, hotline volunteers must be backed up by competent mental health professionals who can identify potentially serious risks.

More helpful are programs targeted to at-risk individuals, including adolescents in schools where a student has committed suicide. The Institute of Medicine (2002) recommends making services available immediately to friends and relatives of victims. In a study following a suicide in a high school, Brent and colleagues (1989) identified 16 students as strongly at risk and referred them for treatment. Another important step is limiting access to lethal weapons for anyone at risk for suicide.

Specific treatments for people at risk have also been developed. For example, British psychologist Paul Salkovskis and his colleagues (Salkovskis, Atha, & Storer, 1990) treated 20 patients at high risk for *repeated* suicide attempts with a cognitive-behavioural problem-solving approach. Results indicated that they were significantly less likely to attempt suicide in the six months following treatment. Marsha Linehan and her colleagues (e.g., Linehan & Kehrer, 1993) developed a noteworthy treatment for the type of impulsive suicidal behaviour associated with borderline personality disorder (see Chapter 12).

In an important study, David Rudd and colleagues developed a brief psychological treatment targeting young adults who were at risk for suicide due to the presence of suicidal ideation accompanied by previous suicidal attempts or mood or substance use disorders (Rudd et al., 1996). They randomly assigned 264 young people to either a new treatment or to treatment as usual in the community. Patients spent approximately nine hours each day for two weeks at a hospital treatment facility. Treatment consisted of problem solving, developing social competence, coping more adaptively with life's problems, and recognizing emotional and life experiences that may have precipitated the suicide attempt or ideation. Patients were assessed up to two years following treatment, and results indicated reductions in suicidal ideation and behaviour as well as marked improvement in problem-solving ability. Furthermore, the brief experimental treatment was significantly more effective at retaining the highest-risk young adults in the program. This program has now been expanded into the first psychological treatment for suicidal behaviour with empirical support for its efficacy (Rudd, Joiner, & Rajab, 2001). With the increased rate of suicide, particularly in adolescents, the tragic and paradoxical act is receiving increased scrutiny from public health authorities. The quest will go on to determine more effective and efficient ways of preventing the most serious consequences of any psychological disorder, suicide.

Holiday of Darkness
by Norman Endler

The late Norman Endler was an eminent clinical psychologist from York University. He not only conducted research on the nature and causes of emotional disorders, but he also experienced first-hand the terrifying turmoil of bipolar disorder. He provided a compelling account of his experiences with episodes of depression and mania in a book he entitled *Holiday of Darkness: A Psychologist's Personal Journey Out of His Depression* (Endler, 1990).

Endler was a high achiever. He had an international reputation for his interactional model of anxiety (see Chapter 5) and was chairman of the psychology department at York University when he experienced his first episode of depression. He attributes the triggering event to the professional humiliation he experienced when one spring he learned that his research grant that he had held for more than 12 years was not going to be renewed. Later that same month, Endler reports that he began

> having difficulty sleeping, my sex drive was completely gone, and my appetite was beginning to go. For the first time in my life, I felt overwhelmed by my job and remarked to a number of people how difficult it was being chairman. . . . At work I was sullen and rarely spoke to or listened to anyone. . . . I wandered in and out of my office—almost in a fog. I went home in the middle of the day. (Endler, 1990, p. 7)

By the end of May, he noted that "every little thing was becoming a monumental task. Everything was becoming a test of my personal competence" (Endler, 1990, p. 8). But he was too proud to seek help until his symptoms were so severe that he could no longer concentrate on giving lectures in summer school. Then he consulted with his family doctor, admitting he was experiencing a depressive episode.

In retrospect, Endler realized that he had experienced an episode of hypomania before plummeting into his first depression. Here is how he described that period:

> Most of the time I was busy, busy, busy; taping records, playing tennis, skiing, writing manuscripts, talking to Ann, reading, going to movies, staying up late at night, waking up early in the morning, always on the go—busy, busy, busy. Furthermore, I was boasting about all the energy I had that enabled me to keep up this fast pace. . . . [My wife] asked me to slow down and take it easy. . . . Instead of occasionally "idling" in neutral I was always in "overdrive". (Endler, 1990, pp. 5–6)

Endler's personal experiences convinced him of the importance of biological treatments for depression but also made him aware of their side effects. For example, he was administered monoamine oxidase inhibitors to treat his depression and suffered a severe hypertensive (i.e., high blood pressure) reaction. When he was correctly diagnosed with bipolar illness, lithium and ECT were both extremely helpful treatments for him. His book contains a section in which he attempts to dispel some myths about ECT. He also speaks about the continuing stigma attached to emotional disorders. Clearly, it would take a great deal of courage for a mental health professional to speak out about his own experiences with a mood disorder. In fact, many colleagues warned him that writing this book might be perceived as poor judgment on his part.

Norman Endler's dual role as both expert and patient provides a unique perspective on the disorder that has no doubt been extremely helpful to many individuals with bipolar illness.

Source: From *Holiday of Darkness: A Psychologist's Personal Journey Out of His Depression* by Norman Endler, 1982. Reprinted with permission of Wall & Emerson, Inc.

The mood disorders discussed in this chapter as well as the anxiety disorders discussed in Chapter 5 are often lumped together under the term "emotional disorders." This is because these disorders have many common features, including difficulty in managing intense emotional experiences. This difficulty is often referred to as "emotion dysregulation." It is also the case that these groups of disorders share common risk factors including the same set of genetic risk factors (described earlier). They are also highly comorbid. That is, many people with an anxiety disorder also have, or have had, depressive disorders, and most people with depression either have, or have had, an anxiety disorder. The presence of significant anxiety is associated with more severe forms of depression and bipolar disorders as well as a longer course and poorer outcomes from treatment (Coryell et al., 2009; Fava et al., 2008). Individuals suffering from anxiety and mood disorders both experience more frequent and intense negative moods than healthy individuals, and view these experiences as much more aversive. They also experience similar negative cognitive processes.

Psychological treatments for the mood and anxiety disorders differ from disorder to disorder, but all share common components. These include changing negative attitudes, cognitive styles, and attributions; preventing avoidance of situations or experiences that might provoke intense emotions such as anxiety or depression; and encouraging therapeutic activities and exposure to experiences that trigger strong emotions. Recognizing these advances, we have developed a new unified transdiagnostic psychological treatment in one of our clinics that is designed to be applicable to anyone suffering from emotional disorders even if they have more than one emotional disorder (comorbidity), unusual variations of an anxiety or mood disorder, or for some reason don't quite meet the criteria for one of the diagnostic categories of anxiety and mood disorders (Barlow et al., in press a, in press b). The term "unified" is used because it integrates principles that are relevant to all emotional disorders. The new treatment, called the unified protocol (UP) for *Transdiagnostic Treatment of Emotional Disorders* (Barlow et al., in press a), consists of five core modules: (1) increasing awareness of emotional experiences (because people with emotional disorders are uncomfortable with their emotions and often try to suppress or ignore them); (2) encouraging greater flexibility in appraisals and attributions concerning emotional situations (because people with anxiety and mood disorders usually just think the worst when they are experiencing intense emotions); (3) identifying and preventing tendencies to avoid certain situations and intense emotions (because patients are often unaware of many of their avoidant tendencies such as trying to distract themselves when they are feeling anxiety); (4) engaging patients in exercises designed to evoke physical sensations analogous to those typically associated with their anxiety and distress; and (5) encouraging patients to increase their tolerance of intense or uncomfortable emotions through exposure to both the situational cues or triggers as well as their own internal physical cues associated with intense emotions. Preliminary results show that this treatment is effective across a broad range of disorders (Ellard, Fairholme, Boisseau, Farchione, & Barlow, 2010). If these results hold up upon further testing, then the UP should eliminate the necessity for applying a different treatment to every single variation of an emotional disorder and, perhaps, be more effective across a broad range of emotional disorders.

Other recent research is making the idea of transdiagnostic treatment more interesting. Researchers have found that the most important function of antidepressant drugs may not be changes in neurotransmitter activity, although this obviously occurs, but rather changes in the neuropsychological process of regulating emotional reactions that seem to occur very soon after beginning antidepressant drugs, and before full therapeutic effect is noted (Harmer, 2010). If this is the case, the fundamental mechanism of action of transdiagnostic psychological treatments, as well as antidepressant drugs (which work equally well in anxiety disorders), may be more similar than different in that they both target emotion dysregulation.

Summary

An Overview of Depression and Mania

- Mood disorders are among the most common psychological disorders, and the risk of developing them is increasing worldwide, particularly in younger people.
- Two fundamental experiences can contribute either singly or in combination to all the specific mood disorders: a major depressive episode and mania. A less severe episode of mania that does not cause impairment in social or occupational functioning is known as a *hypomanic episode*. An episode of mania coupled with anxiety or depression at the same time is known as a *dysphoric* manic or *mixed episode*.

The Structure of Mood Disorders

- An individual who has episodes of depression only is said to have a *unipolar disorder*. An individual who alternates between depression and mania has a *bipolar disorder*.

Depressive Disorders

- Major depressive disorder may be a single episode or recurrent, but it is always time limited; in another form of depression, *dysthymic disorder*, the symptoms are somewhat milder but remain relatively unchanged over long periods. In cases of *double depression*, an individual experiences both depressive episodes and dysthymic disorder.
- Approximately 20 percent of bereaved individuals may experience pathological grief reaction, in which the normal grief response develops into a full-blown mood disorder.

Bipolar Disorders

- The key identifying feature of bipolar disorders is an alternation of manic episodes and major depressive episodes. *Cyclothymic disorder* is a milder but more chronic version of bipolar disorder.
- Patterns of additional features that sometimes accompany mood disorders, called specifiers, may predict the course or patient response to treatment, as does the temporal patterning or course of mood disorders. One pattern, seasonal affective disorder, often occurs in winter.

Prevalence of Mood Disorders

- Mood disorders in children are fundamentally similar to mood disorders in adults.
- Symptoms of depression are increasing dramatically in our elderly population.

- The experience of anxiety across cultures varies, and it can be difficult to make comparisons, especially, for example, when we attempt to compare subjective feelings of depression.

Anxiety and Depression

- Some of the latest theories on the causes of depression are based, in part, on research into the relationship between anxiety and depression. Anxiety almost always precedes depression, and everyone with depression is also anxious.

Causes of Mood Disorders

- The causes of mood disorders lie in a complex interaction of biological, psychological, and social factors. From a biological perspective, researchers are particularly interested in the role of neurohormones. Psychological theories of depression focus on learned helplessness and depressive cognitive schemas as well as interpersonal disruptions.

Treatment

- A variety of treatments, both biological and psychological, have proven effective for mood disorders, at least in the short term. For those individuals who do not respond to antidepressant drugs or psychosocial treatments, a more dramatic physical treatment, *electroconvulsive therapy (ECT)*, is sometimes used. Two psychosocial treatments—*cognitive therapy* and *interpersonal therapy (IPT)*—seem to be effective in treating depressive disorders.
- Relapse and recurrence of mood disorders are common in the long term, and treatment efforts must focus as well on maintenance treatment, that is, on preventing relapse or recurrence.

Suicide

- Suicide is often associated with mood disorders but can occur in their absence. In any case, the incidence of suicide has been increasing in recent years, particularly among adolescents, for whom it is the third-leading cause of death.
- In understanding suicidal behaviour, two indices are important: *suicidal attempts* (that are not successful) and *suicidal ideation* (serious thoughts about committing suicide). Important, too, in learning about risk factors for suicides is the psychological autopsy, in which the *psychological profile* of an individual who has committed suicide is reconstructed and examined for clues.

Key Terms

Answers to Concept Checks

7.1

1. f 2. A 3. C 4. d 5. b

7.2

1. b 2. c 3. A 4. D 5. e

7.3

1. c 2. D 3. a 4. b

Media Resources

 CourseMate

Access an integrated eBook, Abnormal Psychology Videos (formerly Abnormal Psych Live CD-ROM), chapter-specific interactive learning tools (flashcards, quizzes, learning modules), and more in your Psychology CourseMate, available at **www.abnormalpsych3ce.nelson.com**.

Abnormal Psychology Videos

Free Abnormal Psychology videos can be viewed on the website **www.abnormalpsych3ce .nelson.com**.

- *Depressive Disorder: Barbara:* Barbara suffers from a major depressive disorder that's rather severe and long-lasting.

- *Depressive Disorder: Evelyn:* Evelyn has a major depressive disorder that gives a more positive view of long-term prospects for change.

- *Bipolar Disorder: Mary:* Mary is shown in both a manic and depressive phase of her illness. You may notice the similarity of the delusions in both phases of her illness.

Video Concept Reviews

CourseMate also contains Mark Durand's *Video Concept Reviews* on these challenging topics.

- Overview of Moods
- Overview of Mood Disorders
- Major Depressive Disorder
- Major Depression: Single or Recurrent Episode
- Dysthymia
- Double Depression
- Bipolar I Disorder

- Bipolar II Disorder
- Cyclothymic Disorder
- Concept Check: Dysthymia Versus Major Depression
- Mood Disorders: Course Specifiers
- Learned Helplessness
- Electroconvulsive Therapy (ECT)
- Suicide

Exploring Mood Disorders

People with mood disorders experience one or both of the following:

> **Mania:** A frantic "high" with extreme overconfidence and energy, often leading to reckless behaviour

> **Depression:** A devastating "low" with extreme lack of energy, interest, confidence, and enjoyment of life

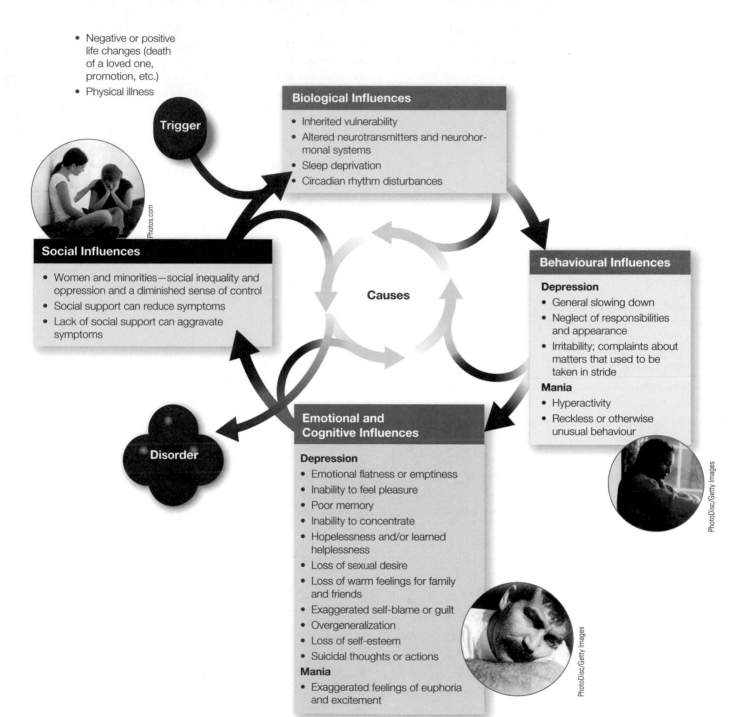

- Negative or positive life changes (death of a loved one, promotion, etc.)
- Physical illness

Trigger

Biological Influences
- Inherited vulnerability
- Altered neurotransmitters and neurohormonal systems
- Sleep deprivation
- Circadian rhythm disturbances

Causes

Social Influences
- Women and minorities—social inequality and oppression and a diminished sense of control
- Social support can reduce symptoms
- Lack of social support can aggravate symptoms

Behavioural Influences

Depression
- General slowing down
- Neglect of responsibilities and appearance
- Irritability; complaints about matters that used to be taken in stride

Mania
- Hyperactivity
- Reckless or otherwise unusual behaviour

Disorder

Emotional and Cognitive Influences

Depression
- Emotional flatness or emptiness
- Inability to feel pleasure
- Poor memory
- Inability to concentrate
- Hopelessness and/or learned helplessness
- Loss of sexual desire
- Loss of warm feelings for family and friends
- Exaggerated self-blame or guilt
- Overgeneralization
- Loss of self-esteem
- Suicidal thoughts or actions

Mania
- Exaggerated feelings of euphoria and excitement

Photos.com

PhotoDisc/Getty Images

PhotoDisc/Getty Images

TYPES OF MOOD DISORDERS

Depressive

Major Depressive Disorder
Symptoms of major depressive disorder:
- begin suddenly, often triggered by a crisis, change, or loss
- are extremely severe, interfering with normal functioning
- can be long term, lasting months or years if untreated

Some people have only one episode, but the pattern usually involves repeated episodes or lasting symptoms.

Dysthymia
Long-term unchanging symptoms of mild depression, sometimes lasting 20 to 30 years if untreated. Daily functioning not as severely affected, but over time impairment is cumulative.

Double Depression
Alternating periods of major depression and dysthymia

Brand X Pictures/Getty Images

Bipolar

People who have a bipolar disorder live on an unending emotional roller coaster.

Types of Bipolar Disorders
- **Bipolar I:** major depression and full mania
- **Bipolar II:** major depression and mild mania
- **Cyclothymia:** mild depression with mild mania, chronic and long term

During the **Depressive Phase**, the person may:
- lose all interest in pleasurable activities and friends
- feel worthless, helpless, and hopeless
- have trouble concentrating
- lose or gain weight without trying
- have trouble sleeping or sleep more than usual
- feel tired all the time
- feel physical aches and pains that have no medical cause
- think about death or attempt suicide

During the **Manic Phase**, the person may:
- feel extreme pleasure and joy from every activity
- be extraordinarily active, planning excessive daily activities
- sleep little without getting tired
- develop grandiose plans leading to reckless behaviour: unrestrained buying sprees, sexual indiscretions, foolish business investments, etc.
- have "racing thoughts" and talk on and on
- be easily irritated and distracted

TREATMENT OF MOOD DISORDERS
Treatment for mood disorders is most effective and easiest when it's started early. Most people are treated with a combination of these methods.

Treatment

Medication
Antidepressants can help to control symptoms and restore neurotransmitter functioning.
Common types of antidepressants:

- Tricyclics (Tofranil, Elavil)
- Monamine oxidase inhibitors (MAOIs): (Nardil, Parnate); MAOIs can have severe side effects, especially when combined with certain foods or over-the-counter medications
- Selective-serotonin reuptake inhibitors or SSRIs (Prozac, Zoloft) are newer and cause fewer side effects than tricyclics or MAOIs
- Lithium is the preferred drug for bipolar disorder; side effects can be serious; and dosage must be carefully regulated

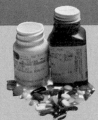

PhotoDisc/Getty Images

Cognitive-Behavioural Therapy
Helps depressed people:

- learn to replace negative depressive thoughts and attributions with more positive ones
- develop more effective coping behaviours and skills

Interpersonal Psychotherapy
Helps depressed people:

- focus on the social and interpersonal triggers for their depression (such as the loss of a loved one)
- develop skills to resolve interpersonal conflicts and build new relationships

Electroconvulsive Therapy (ECT)

- For severe depression, ECT is used when other treatments have been ineffective. It usually has temporary side effects, such as memory loss and lethargy. In some patients, certain intellectual and/or memory functions may be permanently lost.

Light Therapy

- For seasonal affective disorder

PhotoDisc/Getty Images

8 | Eating and Sleep Disorders

© Oote Boe/Alamy

I saw that I needed to work from the "inside out," from my feelings, my dreams, my angers, rather than from the "outside in," which began with my body.
—Geneen Roth, *Feeding the Hungry Heart: The Experience of Compulsive Eating*

Demonstrate knowledge and understanding representing appropriate breadth and depth in selected content areas of psychology:	› Biological bases of behaviour and mental processes, including physiology, sensation, perception, comparative, motivation, and emotion (APA SLO 1.2.a (3)) *(see textbook pages 272–275, 293–299)*
Use the concepts, language, and major theories of the discipline to account for psychological phenomena:	› Describe behaviour and mental processes empirically, including operational definitions (APA SLO 1.3.a) *(see textbook pages 269–276, 290–299)*
Identify appropriate applications of psychology in solving problems, such as:	› Origin and treatment of abnormal behaviour (APA SLO 4.2.b) *(see textbook pages 278–290, 274–295, 300–302)*

* Portions of this chapter cover learning outcomes suggested by the American Psychological Association (2007) in their guidelines for the undergraduate psychology major. Chapter coverage of these outcomes is identified above by APA Goal and APA Suggested Learning Outcome (SLO).

Most of us take our bodies for granted. We wake up in the morning assuming we will be alert enough to handle our required daily activities; we eat two or three meals a day and perhaps some snacks in between; we may engage in some vigorous exercise, and, on some days, in sexual activity. We don't focus on our functioning to any great degree unless it is disrupted by illness or disease. And yet, psychological and social factors can significantly disrupt these "activities of survival." In this chapter we talk about psychological disruptions of two of our relatively automatic behaviours, eating and sleeping, which have substantial impact on the rest of our behaviour.

Eating Disorders: An Overview

Although some of the disorders we discuss in this chapter can be deadly, many of us are not aware they are widespread. They began to increase during the 1950s or early 1960s and have spread insidiously over the ensuing decades. In **bulimia nervosa**, out-of-control eating episodes, or **binges**, are followed by self-induced vomiting, excessive use of laxatives, or other attempts to "purge" (get rid of) the food. In **anorexia nervosa**, the person eats nothing beyond minimal amounts of food, so body weight sometimes drops dangerously. The chief characteristic of these related disorders is an overwhelming, all-encompassing drive to be thin. In fact, in a study of 176 patients receiving treatment for an eating disorder in Pisa, Italy, and Toronto, a full 83 percent evidenced an extremely high drive for thinness (Ramacciotti et al., 2002). Work by Toronto-based researchers has shown that patients with bulimia nervosa do not differ from those with anorexia nervosa in terms of drive to be thin (Garner, Olmsted, & Polivy, 1983). Of the people with anorexia nervosa who are followed over an extended time, up to 20 percent die as a result of their disorder, with slightly more than 5 percent dying within ten years (e.g., Keel et al., 2003; Millar et al., 2005; Papadopoulos, Ekbom, Brandt, & Ekselius, 2009; Sullivan, 1995; Zipfel, Lowe, Deter, & Herzog, 2000). In fact, anorexia nervosa has the highest mortality rate of any psychological disorder reviewed in this book, including depression (Papadopoulos et al., 2009; Park, 2007). As many as 30 percent of anorexia-related deaths are suicides, which is 50 times higher than the risk of death from suicide in the general population (Agras, 2001; Chavez & Insel 2007; Keel et al., 2003; Thompson & Kinder, 2003).

A growing number of studies in different countries indicate that eating disorders are widespread and that they increased dramatically in Western countries from about 1960 to 1995, according to the most recent data we have (Hoek, 2002). In Switzerland, from 1956 to 1958 the number of new cases of anorexia nervosa under treatment among females between the ages of 12 and 25 was 3.98 per 100 000. There were 16.76 new cases per 100 000 from 1973 to 1975, a fourfold increase (Willi & Grossman, 1983). Similar results were found in Scotland by Eagles, Johnston, Hunter, Lobban, and Millar (1995) between 1965 and 1991; by Lucas, Beard, O'Fallon, and Kurlan (1991) in North America over a 50-year period; and by Moller-Madsen and Nystrup (1992) in Denmark between 1970 and 1989.

Even more dramatic are the data for bulimia nervosa. Garner and Fairburn (1988) reviewed rates of referral to a major eating disorder centre in Toronto. Between 1975 and 1986, the referral rates for anorexia rose slowly, but the rates for bulimia rose dramatically—from virtually none to more than 140 per year (see ■ Figure 8.1). Similar findings have been reported from other parts of the world (Hay & Hall, 1991; Lacey, 1992). The reason for this increase is not known. Toronto researchers Paul Garfinkel and Barbara Dorian (2001) have suggested that it may relate to the increased prevalence of dieting and preoccupation with the body among young women who are simultaneously being exposed to social pressures toward consumption and incredible food availability.

Other studies estimate a sixfold increase in death rates among those with eating disorders compared with the normal population (Crisp, Callender, Halek, & Hsu, 1992; Patton, 1988). The mortality rate from eating disorders, particularly anorexia, is the highest for any psychological disorder, even depression (Harris & Barraclough, 1998; Keel et al., 2003; Vitiello & Lederhendler, 2000).

Although reports of cases of eating disorders are documented throughout history, eating problems were not recognized as psychological disorders until relatively recently. In 1872, Sir William Withey Gull, a British physician, was the first to use the term *anorexia nervosa*. According to psychiatrists Sidney Kennedy and David Goldbloom (1996), the first Canadian description of anorexia nervosa appeared in the *Maritime Medical Journal* in 1895. The recognition of bulimia nervosa as a

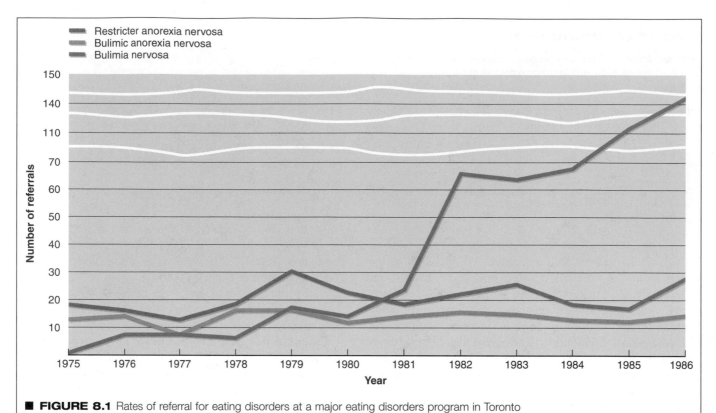

Key (top left of figure):
- Restricter anorexia nervosa
- Bulimic anorexia nervosa
- Bulimia nervosa

■ **FIGURE 8.1** Rates of referral for eating disorders at a major eating disorders program in Toronto

Source: From "Relationship Between Anorexia Nervosa and Bulimia Nervosa: Diagnostic Implications" by D. M. Garner and C. G. Fairburn, 1988, p. 60. In D. M. Garner and P. E. Garfinkel (Eds.), *Diagnostic Issues in Anorexia and Bulimia Nervosa.* © 1988 by Brunner/Mazel, Inc. Reprinted with permission.

separate entity did not occur until much later, when the condition was described in the 1970s (e.g., Russell, 1979). Eating disorders were included for the first time as a separate group of disorders in the *DSM-IV*; before then, they had been classified as one of the disorders usually first diagnosed in infancy, childhood, or adolescence (see Chapter 14) because of their typical onset in adolescence.

What makes this increase in eating disorders even more intriguing is that the increase tends to be culturally specific. Until recently, eating disorders were not found in developing countries, where access to sufficient food is so often a daily struggle; only in the West, where food is generally plentiful, have they been rampant. Now this is changing; evidence suggests that eating disorders are going global. Unsystematic interviews with health professionals in Asia (Efon, 1997), as well as more formal studies (Lee, 1993), show estimates of prevalence in those countries, particularly Japan and Hong Kong, are approaching those in Canada, the United States, and other Western countries. Not everyone in the world is at risk. Eating disorders tend to occur in a relatively small segment of the population. More than 90 percent of the severe cases are young females, mostly in families with upper-middle and upper-class socioeconomic status, who live in a socially competitive environment. Perhaps the most visible example is the late Diana, Princess of Wales, who recounted her seven-year battle with bulimia (Morton, 1992). She reported bingeing and vomiting four or more times a day during her honeymoon. Canadian singer/songwriter Alanis Morissette has also

revealed that she struggled with an eating disorder during her teenage years (McQueen, 2005).

The specificity of these disorders in terms of sex, age, and social class is unparalleled and makes the search for causes even more interesting. In these disorders, unlike almost any other, the strongest contributions to etiology seem to be socio-cultural rather than psychological or biological factors. We look in some detail at bulimia nervosa and anorexia nervosa. We then briefly consider a further category under consideration for inclusion in the *DSM* called **binge-eating disorder**.

▲ The late Princess of Wales spoke candidly about her battle against bulimia.

Bulimia Nervosa

You may be familiar with bulimia nervosa from your own experience or a friend's. It is one of the most common psychological disorders on university campuses. Consider the case of Phoebe.

PHOEBE | *Apparently Perfect*

Phoebe was a popular, attractive, intelligent, and talented teenager. By the time she was finishing high school, she had accomplished a great deal. She was on the student council throughout her high school years and she dated the captain of the football team. Phoebe had many talents, among them a beautiful singing voice and marked ability in ballet. Each year at Christmastime, her ballet company performed the *Nutcracker Suite*, and Phoebe attracted much attention with her poised performance in a lead role. She played on several of the school athletic teams. Phoebe maintained an A-minus average, was considered a model student, and was headed for a top-ranked university.

But Phoebe had a secret: She was haunted by her belief that she was fat and ugly. Every single bite of food that she put in her mouth was, in her mind, another step down the inexorable path that led to the end of her success and popularity. Phoebe had been concerned about her weight since she was 11. Ever the perfectionist, she began regulating her eating in junior high school. She would skip breakfast (over the protestations of her mother), eat a small bowl of pretzels at noon, and allow herself one half of whatever she was served for dinner.

This behaviour continued into high school, as Phoebe struggled to restrict her eating to occasional binges on junk food. Sometimes she stuck her fingers down her throat after a binge (she even tried a toothbrush once), but this tactic was unsuccessful. In Grade 10, Phoebe reached her full adult height of 1.57 metres and weighed 50 kilograms; she continued to fluctuate between 48 and 50 kilograms throughout high school. By the time she was in Grade 12, Phoebe was obsessed with what she would eat and when. She used every bit of her willpower to restrict her eating, but occasionally she failed.

One day during the fall of Grade 12, she came home after school, and alone in front of the TV, she ate two big boxes of candy. Depressed, guilty, and desperate, she went to the bathroom and stuck her fingers further down her throat than she had ever before dared. She vomited. And she kept vomiting. Although so physically exhausted that she had to lie down for half an hour, Phoebe had never in her life felt such an overwhelming sense of relief from the anxiety, guilt, and tension that always accompanied her binges. She realized that she had actually gotten to eat all that candy and now her stomach was empty. It was the perfect solution to her problems.

Phoebe learned very quickly what foods she could easily vomit. And she always drank lots of water. She began to restrict her eating even more. She ate almost nothing until after school, but then the results of her dreaming, scheming, and planning all morning would be realized. Although the food sometimes varied, the routine did not. She might pick up a dozen doughnuts and a box of cookies. When she got home, she might make a bowl of popcorn.

And then she ate and ate, forcing down the doughnuts, cookies, and popcorn until her stomach actually hurt. Finally, with a mixture of revulsion and relief, she purged, forcing herself to vomit. When she was done, she stepped on the scale to make sure she had not gained any weight and then collapsed into bed and slept for about half an hour.

This routine went on for about six months, until April of that same academic year. By this time Phoebe had lost much of her energy, and her schoolwork was deteriorating. Her teachers noticed this and saw that she looked ill. She was continually tired, her skin was broken out, and her face puffed up, particularly around her mouth. Her teachers and mother suspected that she might have an eating problem. When they confronted her, she was relieved her problem was finally out in the open.

In an effort to eliminate opportunities to binge and purge, her mother rearranged her schedule to be home in the afternoon when Phoebe got there; in general, her parents minimized the occasions when Phoebe was left alone, particularly after eating. This tactic worked for about a month. Mortally afraid of gaining weight and losing her popularity, Phoebe resumed her pattern, but she was now much better at hiding it. For six months, Phoebe binged and purged approximately 15 times a week.

When Phoebe went away to university that fall, things became more difficult. Now she had a roommate in residence to contend with, and she was more determined than ever to keep her problem a secret. Although the student health service offered workshops and seminars on eating disorders for first-year university students, Phoebe knew that she could not break her cycle without the risk of gaining weight. To avoid the communal bathroom in the residence, she went to a deserted place behind a nearby building to vomit. Social life at university often involved drinking beer and eating fattening foods, so she vomited more often. Nevertheless, she gained 5 kilograms and weighed 55 kilograms. Gaining weight is common among first-year university students, but her mother commented without thinking one day that Phoebe seemed to be putting on weight. This remark was devastating to Phoebe.

She kept her secret until the beginning of her second year in university, when her world fell apart. One night, after drinking a lot of beer at a party, Phoebe and her friends went to Kentucky Fried Chicken. Although Phoebe did not truly binge because she was with friends, she did eat a lot of fried chicken, the most forbidden food on her list. Her guilt, anxiety, and tension increased to new heights. Her stomach throbbed with pain, but when she tried to vomit, her gag reflex seemed to be gone. Breaking into hysterics, she called her boyfriend and told him she was ready to kill herself. Her loud sobbing and crying attracted the attention of her friends in her residence, who attempted to comfort her. She confessed her problem to them. She also called her parents. At this point, Phoebe realized that her life was totally out of control and that she needed professional help.

Clinical Description

The hallmark of bulimia nervosa is eating a larger amount of food—typically, more junk food than fruits and vegetables—than most people would eat under similar circumstances (Fairburn & Cooper, 1993; Fairburn, Cooper, Shafran, & Wilson, 2008; Wilson & Pike, 2001). Patients with bulimia readily identify with this description, even though the actual caloric intake for binges varies significantly from person to person (Franko, Wonderlich, Little, & Herzog, 2004). Just as important as the *amount* of food eaten is the fact that the eating is experienced as *out of control* (Fairburn, Cooper, & Cooper, 1986), a criterion that is an integral part of the definition of binge eating. Both criteria characterized Phoebe.

Another important criterion is that the individual attempts to *compensate* for the binge eating and potential weight gain, usually by **purging techniques**. Techniques include self-induced vomiting immediately after eating, as in the case of Phoebe, and using laxatives (drugs that relieve constipation) and diuretics (drugs that result in loss of fluids through greatly increased frequency of urination). Some people use both methods. Research by Howard Steiger and colleagues at McGill University has shown that women with bulimia who use laxatives are generally more impulsive than those who do not (Bruce, Koerner, Steiger, & Young, 2003). While some use laxatives and diuretics, others attempt to compensate in other ways. Some fast for long periods between binges. Others exercise excessively. However, rigorous exercising is usually more characteristic of anorexia nervosa. Caroline Davis and her colleagues at York University (Davis et al., 1997) found that fully 81 percent of a group of patients with anorexia nervosa exercised excessively, compared with 57 percent of a group of patients with bulimia nervosa. Interestingly, activity levels increase at least a year prior to the development of full-blown anorexia nervosa, suggesting that excessive exercise may be an early warning sign for anorexia nervosa development (Davis, Blackmore, Katzman, & Fox, 2005).

Bulimia nervosa is subtyped in the *DSM-IV-TR* into purging type and nonpurging type (exercise or fasting). But the nonpurging type has turned out to be rare, accounting for only 6 percent to 8 percent of patients with bulimia (Hay & Fairburn, 1998; Striegal-Moore, Cachelin, Dohm, Pike, Wifley, & Fairburn, 2001). A study by Paul Garfinkel and his colleagues compared purging versus nonpurging bulimics (Garfinkel et al., 1996). In comparison with nonpurging bulimics, those who purged developed their eating disorder at a younger age and had higher rates of comorbid depression, anxiety disorders, and alcohol abuse, as well as higher rates of earlier sexual abuse (Garfinkel et al., 1996). However, other studies have found little evidence of any differences between purging and nonpurging types of bulimia, leading some to question whether this manner of subtyping is useful (e.g., Franko et al., 2004).

Purging is not a particularly efficient method of reducing caloric intake. Vomiting reduces approximately 50 percent of the calories that were just consumed, less if it is delayed at all (Kaye, Weltzin, Hsu, McConaha, & Bolton, 1993); laxatives and related procedures have very little effect, acting, as they do, so long after the binge.

One of the more important additions to the *DSM-IV-TR* criteria is the specification of a psychological characteristic clearly present in Phoebe (see DSM Table 8.1). Despite her accomplishments and success, she felt her continuing popularity and self-esteem would be determined largely by the weight and shape of her body. Paul Garfinkel (1992) noted that, of 107 women seeking treatment for bulimia nervosa, only 3 percent did not share this attitude. Recent investigations confirm the construct validity of the diagnostic category of bulimia nervosa, suggesting that the major features of the disorder (bingeing, purging, overconcern with body shape, etc.) "cluster together" in someone with this problem (Bulik, Sullivan, & Kendler, 2000; Fairburn et al., 2003; Franko et al., 2004; Gleaves, Lowe, Snow, Green, & Murphy-Eberenz, 2000; Keel, Mitchell, Miller, Davis, & Crow, 2000). One problem with the *DSM-IV-TR* criteria is that the "nonpurging" subtype has proved difficult to define, and may not be necessary in the *DSM-5* (van Hoeken, Veling, Sinke, Mitchell, & Hoek, 2009).

Medical Consequences

Chronic bulimia with purging has a number of medical consequences (Pomeroy, 2004). One is salivary gland enlargement caused by repeated vomiting, which gives the face a chubby appearance. This was very noticeable with Phoebe. Repeated vomiting also may erode the dental enamel on the inner surface of the front teeth. More important, continued vomiting may upset the chemical balance of bodily fluids, including sodium and potassium levels. This condition, called an *electrolyte imbalance*,

---

DSM-IV-TR | **Table 8.1** Criteria for Bulimia Nervosa

A. Recurrent episodes of binge eating. An episode of binge eating is characterized by both of the following:

  1. Eating, in a discrete period of time (e.g., within any two-hour period), an amount of food that is definitely larger than most people would eat during a similar period of time and under similar circumstances

  2. A sense of lack of control over eating during the episode (e.g., a feeling that one cannot stop eating or control what or how much one is eating)

B. Recurrent inappropriate compensatory behaviour in order to prevent weight gain, such as self-induced vomiting; misuse of laxatives, diuretics or other medications; fasting; or excessive exercise.

C. The binge eating and inappropriate compensatory behaviours both occur, on average, at least twice a week for three months.

D. Self-evaluation is unduly influenced by body shape and weight.

E. The disturbance does not occur exclusively during episodes of anorexia nervosa.

Specify type:

Purging type: During the current episode of bulimia nervosa, the person has regularly engaged in self-induced vomiting or the misuse of laxatives, diuretics, or enemas.

Nonpurging type: During the current episode of bulimia nervosa, the person has used other inappropriate compensatory behaviours, such as fasting or exercise, but has not regularly engaged in self-induced vomiting or the misuse of laxatives, diuretics, or enemas.

Source: Reprinted with permission from the *Diagnostic and Statistical Manual of Mental Disorders,* Fourth Edition, Text Revision, (Copyright © 2000). American Psychiatric Association.

---

can result in serious medical complications if unattended, including cardiac arrhythmia (disrupted heartbeat) and renal (kidney) failure, both of which can be fatal. Surprisingly, young women with bulimia also develop more body fat than age- and weight-matched healthy controls (Ludescher et al., 2009), the very effect they are trying to avoid. Normalization of eating habits will quickly reverse the imbalance. Intestinal problems resulting from laxative abuse are also potentially serious; they can include severe constipation or permanent colon damage. Finally, some individuals with bulimia have marked calluses on their fingers or the backs of their hands caused by the friction of contact with the teeth and throat when repeatedly sticking their fingers down their throats to stimulate the gag reflex.

Associated Psychological Disorders

An individual with bulimia usually presents with additional psychological disorders, particularly anxiety and mood disorders (see review by O'Brien & Vincent, 2003). We compared 20 patients with bulimia nervosa to 20 individuals with panic disorder and another 20 with social phobia (Schwalberg, Barlow, Alger, & Howard, 1992). The most striking finding was that fully 75 percent of the patients with bulimia also presented with an anxiety disorder such as social phobia or generalized anxiety disorder; patients with anxiety disorders, in contrast, did not necessarily have an elevated rate of eating disorders. Mood disorders, particularly depression, also commonly co-occur with eating disorders (e.g., Dunkley & Grillo, 2007). For several years, one prominent theory suggested that eating disorders are simply a way of expressing depression. But almost all evidence indicates that depression follows bulimia and may be a reaction to it (Brownell & Fairburn, 1995; Hsu, 1990). Some research suggests a high prevalence of borderline personality disorder in patients with bulimia (e.g., Cassin & von Ranson, 2005; Kennedy, McVey, & Katz, 1990). Finally, substance abuse commonly accompanies bulimia nervosa and vice versa (see review by Stewart & Brown, 2007). For example, Stewart, Brown, Theakston, Devoulyte, and Larsen (2003) studied 58 women receiving treatment for alcoholism through Addiction Prevention and Treatment Services in the Capital District Health Authority in Nova Scotia. A full 71 percent of the women alcoholics reported binge eating, with 91 percent of those displaying binge-eating patterns that clinicians would consider severe. In a study by Kristin von Ranson at the University of Calgary and her colleagues, eating disorders were associated with nicotine dependence in adolescent girls and with alcohol abuse in adult women (von Ranson, Iacono, & McGue, 2002). Toronto psychiatrists Allan Kaplan and Blake Woodside have examined smoking across the eating disorders and have shown that those with binge-purge types of eating disorders smoke the most, and that smoking is related to impulsive personality traits (Anzengruber et al., 2006). Research by Elliot Goldner and colleagues in Vancouver suggests that bulimia may also be related to other behaviours suggesting poor impulse control, such as compulsive shoplifting (Goldner, Geller, Birmingham, & Remick, 2000). In sum, bulimia seems related to anxiety disorders, mood disorders, substance use disorders, borderline personality, and impulse control disorders.

Anorexia Nervosa

Like Phoebe, the overwhelming majority of individuals with bulimia are within 10 percent of their normal weight (Hsu, 1990). In contrast, individuals with anorexia nervosa (which literally means a "nervous loss of appetite," an incorrect definition because appetite often remains healthy) differ in one important way from individuals with bulimia. They are so successful at losing weight that they put their lives in considerable danger. Both anorexia and bulimia are characterized by a morbid fear of gaining weight and losing control over eating. The major difference seems to be whether the individual is successful at losing weight. People with anorexia are proud of both their diets and their extraordinary control, and they usually do not see themselves as having an illness. People with bulimia are ashamed of both the problem itself and their lack of control, and they tend to be secretive about their bulimic symptoms (Brownell & Fairburn, 1995). The denial of illness in anorexia and the shame and secrecy in bulimia mean that people with eating disorders do not seek treatment as early as they should (Couturier & Lock, 2006; Kaplan & Garfinkel, 1999). Consider the case of Julie.

JULIE | *The Thinner the Better*

Julie was 17 years old when she first came for help. If you looked hard enough past her sunken eyes and pasty skin, you could see that she had once been attractive. But at present, she looked emaciated and unwell. Eighteen months earlier she had been overweight, weighing almost 65 kilograms at 1.55 metres. Her mother, a well-meaning but overbearing and demanding woman, nagged Julie incessantly about her appearance. Her friends were kinder but no less relentless. Julie, who had never had a date, was told by a friend she was cute and would have no trouble at all getting dates if she lost some weight. So she did! After many previous unsuccessful attempts, she was determined to succeed this time.

After several weeks on a strict diet, Julie noticed she was losing weight. She felt a control and mastery that she had never known before. It wasn't long before she received positive comments, not only from her friends but also from her mother. Julie began to feel good about herself. The difficulty was that she was losing weight too fast. She stopped menstruating. But now nothing could stop her from dieting. By the time she reached our clinic, she weighed 35 kilograms, but she thought she looked fine and, perhaps, could even stand to lose a bit more weight. Her parents had just begun to worry about her. In fact, Julie did not initially seek treatment for her eating behaviour. Rather, she had developed a numbness in her left lower leg and a left foot drop that a neurologist determined was caused by peritoneal nerve paralysis believed to be related to inadequate nutrition. The neurologist referred her to our clinic.

Like most people with anorexia, Julie said she probably should put on a little weight, but she didn't mean it. She thought she looked fine but she had "lost all taste for food," a report that may not have been true, because most people with anorexia crave food at least some of the time but control their cravings. Nevertheless, she was participating in most of her usual activities and continued to do extremely well in school and in her extracurricular pursuits. Her parents were happy to buy her most of the workout videotapes available, and she began doing one every day, and then two. When her parents suggested she was really exercising enough, perhaps too much, she worked out when no one was around. After every meal, she exercised with a workout tape until, in her mind, she had burned up all the calories she had just taken in.

Responses to the current physical fitness and exercise craze can become extreme for female athletes (Davis & Strachan, 2001). Perhaps the best-known example was world-class gymnast Christy Henrich, who died of kidney failure at the age of 22. Christy weighed approximately 43 kilograms at the peak of her career. Later, during repeated hospitalizations for anorexia, Christy had to be physically restrained to prevent excessive exercise; like Julie, she exercised to the point of exhaustion if given half a chance. When she died in 1994, Christy weighed only 30 kilograms. Elaine Tanner, who represented Canada in swimming at the Commonwealth Games, the Pan-Am Games, and the Olympics in the 1960s (winning 15 medals and setting new records), also developed anorexia after competing in the Olympics at age 17 (Bornath, 2002). She was finally able to overcome her disorder, but it took 19 years! The tragic consequences of anorexia among young celebrities and within the modelling world have also been well publicized in the media. In November 2006, 21-year-old Brazilian model Ana Carolina Reston died, weighing just 40 kilograms.

Clinical Description

Bulimia nervosa is more common than anorexia, but they have a great deal of overlap. For example, many individuals with bulimia have a history of anorexia; that is, they once used fasting to reduce their body weight below desirable levels (Fairburn et al., 2008; Fairburn, Welch, Doll, Davies, & O'Connor, 1997; Mitchell & Pyle, 1988).

Although decreased body weight is the most notable feature of anorexia nervosa, it is not the core of the disorder. Many people lose weight because of a medical condition, but people with anorexia have an intense fear of obesity and relentlessly pursue thinness (Bruch, 1986; Fairburn et al., 2008; Garfinkel & Garner, 1982; Hsu, 1990; Schlundt & Johnson, 1990; Stice, Cameron, Killen, Hayward, & Taylor, 1999). As with Julie, the disorder most commonly begins in an adolescent who is actually overweight or who perceives herself to be. She then starts a diet that escalates into an obsessive preoccupation with being thin. She continues to see herself as overweight despite her weight loss. In fact, a study by Randi McCabe at McMaster University showed that patients with anorexia nervosa have a tendency to overreport their body weight (McCabe, McFarlane, Polivy, & Olmsted, 2001). As we noted earlier, the work of Caroline Davis and her colleagues (1997) indicates that severe, almost punishing

exercise is common in anorexia, as with Julie. Dramatic weight loss is achieved through severe caloric restriction or by combining caloric restriction and purging.

The *DSM-IV-TR* specifies two subtypes of anorexia nervosa (see DSM Table 8.2). In the *restricting type*, individuals diet to limit calorie intake; in the *binge-eating/purging type*, they rely on purging. Unlike individuals with bulimia, binge-eating/purging anorexics binge on relatively small amounts of food and purge more consistently, in some cases each time they eat. Approximately half the individuals who meet criteria for anorexia engage in binge eating and purging (Agras, 1987; Fairburn et al., 2008; Garfinkel, Moldofsky, & Garner, 1979). Prospective data collected over eight years on 136 individuals with anorexia reveal few differences between these two subtypes on severity of symptoms or personality (Eddy et al., 2002). At that time, fully 62 percent of the restricting subtype had begun bingeing or purging. Thus, subtyping may not be useful in predicting the future course of the disorder but rather may reflect a certain phase or stage of anorexia, a finding confirmed in a more recent study (Eddy et al., 2008). For this reason, a proposal likely to be adopted in the *DSM-5* specifies that subtyping refer only to the last three months (Peat, Mitchell, Hoek, & Wonderlich, 2009).

An individual with anorexia is never satisfied with his or her weight loss. Staying the same weight from one day to the next or gaining any weight is likely to cause intense panic, anxiety, and depression. Only continued weight loss every day for weeks on end is satisfactory. Although *DSM-IV-TR* criteria specify body weight 15 percent below that expected, the average is approximately 25 percent to 30 percent below normal by the time treatment is sought (Hsu, 1990). Another

---

DSM-IV-TR | **Table 8.2** Criteria for Anorexia Nervosa

A. Refusal to maintain body weight at or above a minimally normal weight for age and height (e.g., weight loss leading to maintenance of body weight less than 85 percent of that expected or failure to make expected weight gain during period of growth, leading to body weight less than 85 percent of that expected).

B. Intense fear of gaining weight or becoming fat, even though underweight.

C. Disturbance in the way in which body weight or shape is experienced; undue influence of body weight or shape on self-evaluation, or denial of the seriousness of the current low body weight.

D. In postmenarcheal females, amenorrhea—the absence of at least three consecutive menstrual cycles. (A woman is considered to have amenorrhea if her periods occur only following hormone, e.g., estrogen, administration.)

Specify type:

Restricting type: During the episode of anorexia nervosa, the person does not regularly engage in binge eating or purging behaviour (i.e., self-induced vomiting or the misuse of laxatives or diuretics).

Binge-eating/purging type: During the episode of anorexia nervosa, the person has regularly engaged in binge eating or purging behaviour (i.e., self-induced vomiting or the misuse of laxatives or diuretics).

Source: Reprinted with permission from the *Diagnostic and Statistical Manual of Mental Disorders,* Fourth Edition, Text Revision, (Copyright © 2000). American Psychiatric Association.

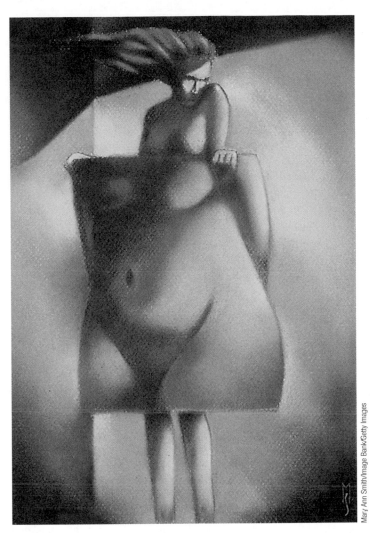

▲ Many women with anorexia are overweight or perceive themselves to be overweight when they develop an obsessive preoccupation with being thin.

rooms, looking at it periodically. We review research that seems to explain these curious behaviours.

Medical Consequences

One common medical complication of anorexia nervosa is cessation of menstruation (amenorrhea), which also occurs relatively often in bulimia (Crow, Thuras, Keel, & Mitchell, 2002). This feature can be an objective physical index of the degree of food restriction, but is inconsistent because it does not occur in all cases (Franko et al., 2004). Because of this inconsistency, amenorrhea is likely to be dropped as a diagnostic criterion in the *DSM-5* (Attia & Roberto, 2009; Fairburn et al., 2008; Mitchell, Cook-Myers, & Wonderlich, 2005). Other medical signs and symptoms of anorexia include dry skin, brittle hair or nails, and sensitivity to or intolerance of cold temperatures. Also, it is relatively common to see *lanugo,* downy hair on the limbs and cheeks. Cardiovascular problems, such as chronically low blood pressure and heart rate, can also result. If vomiting is part of the anorexia, electrolyte imbalance and resulting cardiac and kidney problems can result, as in bulimia (Mehler et al., 2010).

Associated Psychological Disorders

Like bulimia nervosa, anxiety disorders and mood disorders are often present in individuals with anorexia (Agras, 2001; Garfinkel et al., 1996; Kaye et al., 1993; O'Brien & Vincent, 2003; Vitiello & Lederhendler, 2000). Interestingly, one that seems to co-occur frequently is obsessive-compulsive disorder (OCD; see Chapter 5). In anorexia nervosa, unpleasant thoughts are focused on gaining weight and the individual engages in a variety of behaviours, some of them ritualistic, to rid herself of such thoughts. Future research will determine whether anorexia and OCD are truly similar or simply resemble each other. Substance abuse is also common in individuals with anorexia nervosa (Keel et al., 2003; Root et al., 2010; Stewart & Brown, 2007), and, in conjunction with anorexia, is a strong predictor of mortality, particularly by suicide.

key criterion of anorexia is a marked disturbance in body image—the way a person sees and feels about her body. When Julie looked at herself in the mirror, she saw something very different from what others saw. Others saw an emaciated, sickly, frail girl in the throes of semistarvation. Julie saw a girl who needed to lose at least a few kilograms from some parts of her body. For Julie, her face and buttocks were the problems. Other girls might focus on other parts, such as the arms or legs or stomach.

After seeing numerous doctors, people like Julie become good at mouthing what others expect to hear. They may agree they are underweight and need to gain a few kilograms—but they don't believe it. Question further and they will tell you that the person in the mirror is fat. For this reason, individuals with anorexia seldom seek treatment on their own. Usually, pressure from somebody in the family leads to the initial visit, as in Julie's case (Agras, 1987; Fairburn et al., 2008; Sibley & Blinder, 1988). Some anorexic individuals show increased interest in cooking and food. Some have become expert chefs, preparing all the food for the family. Others hoard food in their

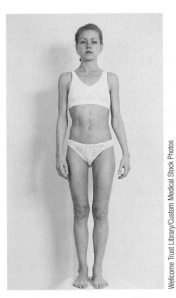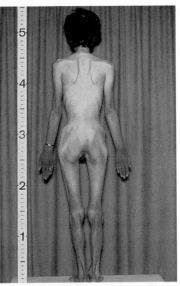

▲ These women are at different stages of anorexia.

Concept Check | 8.1

Decide whether the following are characteristics of
(a) anorexia nervosa or (b) bulimia nervosa.

1. The major component of this disorder is binge eating.
   _____

2. This often leads to electrolyte imbalance, resulting in
   serious medical problems._____

3. Individuals with this disorder are successful at losing
   weight. _____

4. In the *DSM-IV-TR* this disorder is divided into two subtypes,
   restricting and binge-eating/purging type. _____

5. Amenorrhea, the absence of at least three consecutive
   menstrual cycles, frequently occurs. _____

Binge-Eating Disorder

Recent research has focused on a group of individuals who experience marked distress due to binge eating but do not engage in extreme compensatory behaviours and therefore cannot be diagnosed with bulimia (Castonguay, Eldredge, & Agras, 1995; Fairburn et al., 1998; Spitzer et al., 1991). These individuals have binge-eating disorder (BED). Currently, BED is in the appendix of the *DSM-IV-TR* as a potential new disorder requiring further study, but it will almost certainly be included as a disorder in its own category in the *DSM-5* (Wonderlich, Gordon, Mitchell, Crosby, & Engel, 2009). Evidence that supports this distinction includes somewhat different patterns of heritability compared to other eating disorders (Bulik et al., 2000), as well as a greater likelihood of occurring in males and a later age of onset. There is also a greater likelihood of remission and a better response to treatment of BED compared to other eating disorders (Striegel-Moore & Franko, 2008; Wonderlich et al., 2009).

Individuals who meet preliminary criteria for BED are often found in weight-control programs. For example, Brody, Walsh, and Devlin (1994) studied mildly obese participants in a weight-control program and identified 18.8 percent who met criteria for BED. In other programs, with participants ranging in degree of obesity, close to 30 percent met criteria (e.g., Spitzer et al., 1993). But Hudson and colleagues (2006) concluded that BED is a disorder caused by a separate set of factors from obesity without BED and is associated with more severe obesity. The general consensus is that about 20 percent of obese individuals in weight-loss programs engage in binge eating, with the number rising to approximately 50 percent among candidates for bariatric surgery (surgery to correct severe or morbid obesity). Fairburn, Cooper, Doll, Norman, and O'Connor (2000) identified 48 individuals with BED and were able to prospectively follow 40 of them for five years. The prognosis was relatively good for this group, with only 18 percent retaining the full diagnostic criteria for BED at a five-year follow-up. The percentage of this group who were obese, however, increased from 21 percent to 39 percent at the five-year mark.

About half of individuals with BED try dieting before bingeing, and half start with bingeing and then attempt to diet (Abbott et al., 1998); those who begin bingeing first become more severely affected by BED and are more likely to have additional disorders (Spurrell, Wilfley, Tanofsky, & Brownell, 1997). It's also increasingly clear that individuals with BED have some of the same concerns about shape and weight as people with anorexia and bulimia, which distinguishes them from individuals who are obese without BED (Fairburn et al., 2008; Goldschmidt et al., 2010; Grilo, Masheb, & White, 2010; Hrabosky, Masheb, White, & Grilo, 2007). It seems that approximately 33 percent of those with BED binge to alleviate "bad moods" or negative affect (e.g., Grilo, Masheb, & Wilson, 2001; Stice, Akutagawa, Gaggar, & Agras, 2000; Stice et al., 2001). These individuals are more psychologically disturbed than the 67 percent who do not use bingeing to regulate mood (Grilo et al., 2001).

Statistics

Clear cases of bulimia have been described for thousands of years (Parry-Jones & Parry-Jones, 2002), but bulimia nervosa was recognized as a distinct psychological disorder only in the 1970s (Boskind-Lodahl, 1976; Russell, 1979). Therefore, information on prevalence has been acquired relatively recently.

We have already noted that the overwhelming majority (90 to 95 percent) of individuals with bulimia are women; most are white and middle to upper-middle class. The 5 percent to 10 percent of cases who are male have a slightly later age of onset, and a homosexual or bisexual orientation appears to be a specific risk factor for males, especially for those who develop bulimia nervosa (Carlat, Camargo, & Herzog, 1997; Rothblum, 2002). Research by D. Blake Woodside and colleagues in Toronto indicates that men with eating disorders are similar in most respects to women with eating disorders (Woodside, Garfinkel, Lin, Goering, & Kaplan, 2001). One place that men and women with eating disorders may differ, however, is in personality risk factors such as perfectionism (Woodside et al., 2004). Men's lower levels of these personality risk factors may help explain why bulimia is an overwhelmingly female disorder. In addition to men with a homosexual or bisexual orientation, male athletes in sports that require weight regulation, such as wrestling, are another large group of males with eating disorders. However, the gender imbalance in bulimia was not always present. Historians of psychopathology note that for hundreds of years, the vast majority of (unsystematically) recorded cases were male (Parry-Jones & Parry-Jones, 1994, 2002). Because women with bulimia are overwhelmingly preponderant today, most of our examples are women.

Age of onset is typically 16 to 19 years (Fairburn et al., 1997; Garfinkel et al., 1995; Mitchell & Pyle, 1988), although signs of impending bulimic behaviour can occur much earlier, as in Phoebe's case. Schlundt and Johnson (1990), summarizing a large number of surveys, suggest that between 6 percent and 8 percent of young women, especially on university campuses, meet the criteria for bulimia nervosa. Gross and Rosen (1988) reported that as many as 9 percent of high school girls would meet criteria, although only about 2 percent were purging at that age. Most people who seek treatment are in the purging subtype.

A somewhat different view of the prevalence of bulimia comes from studies of the population as a whole rather than of specific groups of adolescents. In one of the better studies, sampling more than 8000 individuals in Ontario, the lifetime prevalence was 1.1 percent for females and 0.1 percent for males (Garfinkel et al., 1995). Another 2.3 percent of females showed partial syndromes in which they displayed some of the symptoms of bulimia nervosa, but not enough to meet the full *DSM-IV-TR* diagnostic criteria (Garfinkel et al., 1995). The low prevalence rate observed for males is consistent with earlier reports (Carlat & Camargo, 1991). In a careful study in New Zealand (Bushnell, Wells, Hornblow, Oakley-Browne, & Joyce, 1990), the lifetime prevalence of bulimia nervosa among women aged 18 to 44 years was 1.6 percent. However, the rate was substantially higher among younger women. For instance, among women aged 18 to 24, the prevalence was 4.5 percent. Among women aged 25 to 44, the prevalence was 2 percent, but it was only 0.4 percent among women aged 45 to 64. Numbers seem to be highest in urban areas (Hoek et al., 1995).

In an important prevalence study by Kendler and colleagues (1991), 2163 twins (more than 1000 sets of twins) were interviewed, and the lifetime prevalence of bulimia nervosa was found to be 2.8 percent, increasing to 5.3 percent when marked bulimic symptoms that did not meet full criteria for the disorder were included. Once again, the prevalence was greatest in younger women. As is evident in ■ Figure 8.2, the risk was much higher for females born after 1960 than for females born before 1960. Nevertheless, as pointed out by Fairburn and his colleagues (Fairburn & Beglin, 1990; Fairburn, Hay, & Welch, 1993), estimates are probably low, because many individuals with eating disorders refuse to participate in studies. Therefore, the percentages represent only those individuals who consented to participate in the survey.

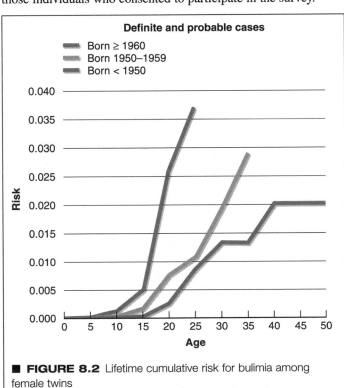

■ **FIGURE 8.2** Lifetime cumulative risk for bulimia among female twins

Source: The American Journal of Psychiatry by American Psychiatric Association. Copyright 1991. Reproduced with permission of AMERICAN PSYCHIATRIC ASSOCIATION (JOURNALS) in the format Textbook via Copyright Clearance Center.

Once bulimia develops, it tends to be chronic if untreated (Fairburn et al., 2000; Keel & Mitchell, 1997); one study by Todd Heatherton and colleagues shows the "drive for thinness" and accompanying symptoms were still present in a group of women ten years after diagnosis (Joiner, Heatherton, & Keel, 1997). In an important study of the course of bulimia, referred to earlier, Fairburn et al. (2000) identified a group of 102 females with bulimia nervosa and followed 92 of them prospectively for five years. About one-third improved to the point where they no longer met diagnostic criteria each year, but another third who had improved previously then relapsed. Between 50 percent and 67 percent evidenced serious eating disorder symptoms at the end of each year of the five-year study, indicating that this disorder has a relatively poor prognosis. In a follow-up study, Fairburn et al. (2003) reported that the strongest predictors of persistence were a history of childhood obesity and a continuing overemphasis on the importance of being thin. In addition, individuals tend to retain their bulimic symptoms, instead of shifting to other eating disorder symptomatology, providing further validation for bulimia nervosa as a diagnostic category (Keel et al., 2000).

The same high percentage (90 percent to 95 percent) of individuals with anorexia are female, with onset also in adolescence, usually around the age of 13 (Fairburn, Cooper, Doll, & Welch, 1999; Herzog, 1988). Studies cited in the beginning of this chapter noted the increase in rates of anorexia, particularly in the 1960s and 1970s. Walters and Kendler (1995) have now analyzed data from the same 2163 twins mentioned earlier to determine the prevalence of anorexia nervosa. The results indicate that 1.62 percent met criteria for lifetime prevalence and this figure increased to 3.70 percent with the inclusion of marked anorexic symptoms that did not meet full criteria for the disorder. These results are in agreement with data from the Toronto eating disorders program displayed in Figure 8.1 (page 270), suggesting that bulimia is somewhat more common than anorexia. Once anorexia develops, its course seems more chronic than even bulimia, and it is more resistant to treatment (Garfinkel, 2002; Herzog et al., 1999; Vitiello & Lederhendler, 2000).

Cross-Cultural Considerations

We have already discussed the very culturally specific nature of anorexia and bulimia. A particularly striking finding is that these disorders develop in immigrants who have recently moved to Western countries (Anderson-Fye, 2009; Nasser, 1988). One of the more interesting studies is Nasser's (1986) survey of 50 Egyptian women in London universities and 60 Egyptian women in Cairo universities. None of the women studied in Cairo had eating disorders, but 12 percent of the Egyptian women in England had developed eating disorders. Mumford, Whitehouse, and Platts (1991) found the same result with Asian women living in North America. The prevalence of eating disorders varies among most North American minority populations. The prevalence of eating disorders among black and Asian North American females is lower than among Caucasians, but they are more frequent among Aboriginal women (Crago, Shisslak, & Estes, 1997). Generally, surveys reveal that black adolescent girls have less body dissatisfaction, fewer weight concerns, and a more positive self-image, and perceive themselves to be thinner than they actually are, compared with Caucasian adolescent girls (Celio, Zabinski, & Wilfley,

2002). Major risk factors for eating disorders in all groups include being overweight, being in a higher social class, and acculturating to the Western majority (Crago et al., 1997; Raich et al., 1992; Smith & Krejci, 1991; Wilfley & Rodin, 1995).

One culturally determined difference in criteria for eating disorders has been reported by Lee, Leung, Wing, Chiu, and Chen (1991). In traditional Chinese cultures, it has been widely assumed that being slightly plump is highly valued, with ideals of beauty focused on the face rather than the body. Therefore, in this group, acne was more often reported as a precipitant for anorexia nervosa than was a fear of being fat, and body image disturbance was rare (Lee, Hsu, & Wing, 1992). Patients said they refused to eat because of feelings of fullness or pain, although it is possible they related food intake to their skin conditions. Beyond that, they met all criteria for anorexia. More recent studies, however, call into question this ideal (Kawamura, 2002). Leung, Lam, and Sze (2001) analyzed data from the Miss Hong Kong Beauty Pageant from 1975 to 1999 and found that winners were taller and thinner than the average Chinese woman, with a curvaceous narrow-waist-and-full-hip body shape. They note that this ideal matches depictions of beauty in classical Chinese literature, and it challenges the notion that plumpness is valued, at least in Hong Kong.

In Japan, the prevalence of anorexia nervosa among teenage girls is still lower than the rate in North America but, as mentioned previously, it seems to be increasing. The need to be thin or the fear of becoming overweight has not been as important in Japanese culture as it is in North America, although this may be changing as cultures around the world become more Westernized (Kawamura, 2002). Body image distortion and denial that a problem exists are clearly present in Japanese patients who have the disorder (Ritenbaugh, Shisstak, Teufel, Leonard-Green, & Prince, 1993).

An interesting study by Madhulika Gupta and her colleagues at the University of Western Ontario compared weight-related body image concerns in young women aged 18 to 24 years in Canada and in India (Gupta, Chaturvedi, Chandarana, & Johnson, 2001). This cross-cultural study found that women's overall levels of the core eating disorder features of drive for thinness and body dissatisfaction did not differ between the two cultures. However, body image concerns presented slightly differently in the two samples. In the Canadian women, body dissatisfaction was related to concerns about the weight of the abdomen, hips, thighs, and legs. In the Indian women, in contrast, body dissatisfaction was related to concerns about the weight of the face, neck, shoulders, and chest (i.e., upper torso).

In conclusion, anorexia and bulimia are relatively homogeneous and, until recently, overwhelmingly associated with Western cultures. In addition, the frequency and pattern of occurrence among minority Western cultures differs somewhat but is associated with closer identification with Caucasian middle-class values.

Developmental Considerations

Because the overwhelming majority of cases begin in adolescence, it is very clear that anorexia and bulimia are strongly related to development (McVey, Pepler, Davis, Flett, & Abdolell, 2002; Polivy, Herman, Mills, & Brock, 2003). As pointed out by Striegal-Moore, Silberstein, and Rodin (1986) and Attie and Brooks-Gunn (1995), differential patterns of physical development in girls and boys interact with cultural influences to create eating disorders. After puberty, girls gain weight primarily in fat tissue, whereas boys develop muscle and lean tissue. As the ideal look in Western countries is tall and muscular for men and thin and prepubertal for women, physical development brings boys closer to the ideal and takes girls farther away.

Causes

As with all the disorders discussed in this book, biological, psychological, and social factors contribute to the development of these serious eating disorders, but the evidence is increasingly clear that the most dramatic factors are social and cultural.

Social Dimensions

Remember that anorexia and bulimia are the most culturally specific psychological disorders yet diagnosed. What drives so many young people into a punishing and life-threatening routine of semistarvation or purging? For many young Western women, looking good is more important than being healthy. In fact, for young females in middle- to upper-class competitive environments, self-worth, happiness, and success are determined to a large extent by body measurements and percentage of body fat, factors that have little or no correlation with personal happiness and success in the long run. The cultural imperative for thinness directly results in dieting, the first dangerous step down the slippery slope to anorexia and bulimia (Polivy & Herman, 1993).

What makes the modern emphasis on thinness in women even more puzzling is that standards of desirable body sizes change much like fashion styles in clothes, if not as quickly (Cash & Pruzinsky, 2002). Several groups of investigators have documented this phenomenon in some interesting ways. Garner, Garfinkel, Schwartz, and Thompson (1980) collected data from *Playboy* magazine centrefolds and from contestants in major beauty pageants from 1959 to 1978. During this period, both *Playboy* centrefolds and the beauty pageant contestants became significantly thinner. Bust and hip measurements became smaller, although waists became somewhat larger, suggesting a change in what is considered desirable in the shape of the body in addition to weight. The preferred shape during the 1960s and 1970s was thinner and more tubular than before (Agras & Kirkley, 1986). Wiseman, Gray, Mosimann, and Ahrens (1992) updated the research, collecting data from 1979 to 1988, and reported that 69 percent of the *Playboy* centrefolds and 60 percent of the beauty pageant contestants weighed 15 percent or more below normal for their age and height, actually meeting one of the criteria for anorexia. Data from both studies are presented in ■ Figure 8.3. More recently, Rubinstein and Caballero (2000) compiled data on weight and height from beauty pageant winners from 1922 through 1999. They found that since the 1970s, most of these winners would be considered undernourished.

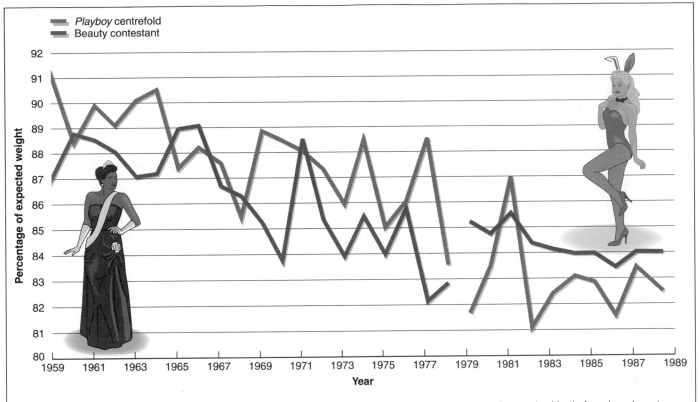

■ FIGURE 8.3 Average percentage of expected weight of *Playboy* centrefolds and contestants in a major North American beauty pageant, 1959–1988

Source: From "Cultural Expectations of Thinness in Women: An Update" by C. V. Wiseman and J. J. Gray, J. E. Mosimann and A. H. Ahrens, 1992, *International Journal of Eating Disorders, 11(1)*, 85–89. © 1992 by John Wiley & Sons, Inc.

Levine and Smolak (1996) refer to "the glorification of slenderness" in magazines and on television, where the vast majority of females are thinner than average North American women. Because overweight men are two to five times more common as television characters than overweight women, the message from the media to be thin is clearly aimed at women (Fouts & Burggraf, 2000). Grabe, Ward, and Hyde (2008), reviewing 77 studies, demonstrated a strong relationship between exposure to media images depicting the thin-ideal body and body image concerns in women. An analysis of prime-time situation comedies revealed that 12 percent of female characters were dieting and many were making disparaging comments about their body image (Tiggemann, 2002). Stice, Schupak-Neuberg, Shaw, and Stein (1994) established a strong relationship between amount of media exposure and eating disorder symptomatology in university women. In another study, girls who watched eight or more hours of TV per week reported significantly greater body dissatisfaction than girls who watched less TV (Gonzalez-Lavin & Smolak, 1995; Levine & Smolak, 1996). Finally, Thompson and Stice (2001) found that risk for developing eating disorders was directly related to the extent to which women internalize or "buy in" to the media messages and images glorifying thinness, a finding also confirmed by Cafri, Yamamiya, Brannick, and Thompson (2005).

During the 1920s, the ideal female body was similar in shape to the ideal today (Agras & Kirkley, 1986); however, this shape was achieved through fashion (e.g., through the use of girdles) rather than dieting. In fact, no diet articles appeared in the magazines of the period that were sampled, whereas today we see what Brownell and Rodin (1994) have called "the dieting maelstrom," in which health professionals, the media, and a powerful diet and food industry all have stakes.

The problem with today's standards is that they are increasingly difficult to achieve, because the size and weight of the average woman has increased over the years with improved nutrition; size has also generally increased throughout history (Brownell, 1991; Brownell & Rodin, 1994). Whatever the cause, the collision between our culture and our physiology (Brownell, 1991; Brownell & Fairburn, 1995) has had some very negative effects, one of which is that women are no longer satisfied with their bodies.

A second clear effect is the dramatic increase, especially among women, in dieting and exercise to achieve what may in fact be an impossible goal. Look at the increase in dieting since the 1950s. Dwyer, Feldman, Seltzer, and Mayer reported in 1969 that more than 80 percent of female high school students in Grade 12 wanted to lose weight and that 30 percent were dieting. Among their male counterparts, fewer than 20 percent wanted to lose weight and only 6 percent were dieting. More recently, Hunicutt and Newman (1993) surveyed a sample of 3632 students in Grade 8 and Grade 10 and found that 60.6 percent of females and 28.4 percent of males were dieting. Although these studies are not directly comparable, younger girls typically diet less than older girls, suggesting the increase in dieting is even more dramatic.

▲ Changing concepts of ideal weight are evident in a 17th-century painting by Peter Paul Rubens and in a recent photograph of a fashion model.

in men (see ■ Figure 8.4). Women, however, rated their current figures as much heavier than the most attractive, which, in turn, was rated as heavier than the ideal.

A study by Forestell, Humphrey, and Stewart (2004) at Dalhousie University using figures similar to those displayed in Figure 8.4 showed that undergraduate women are particularly critical of women's hip size when making evaluations of physical attractiveness. An additional interesting finding from the Fallon and Rozin (1985) study was that women's judgment of ideal female body weight was less than the weight that men thought was most attractive. This conflict between reality and fashion seems most closely related to the current epidemic of eating disorders. In fact, the efforts of some people to maintain thin, athletic shapes are almost superhuman. Contestants in major beauty pageants work out an average of 14 hours per week, with some exercising 35 hours per week (Trebbe, 1979).

Fallon and Rozin (1985), studying male and female undergraduates, found that men rated their current size, their ideal size, and the size they figured would be most attractive to the opposite sex as approximately equal; indeed, they rated their ideal body weight as *heavier* than the weight females thought most attractive

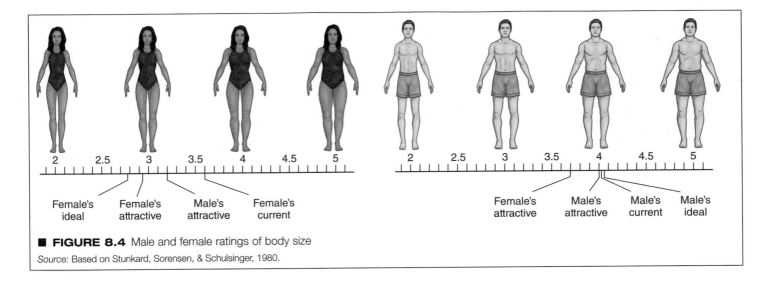

FIGURE 8.4 Male and female ratings of body size

Source: Based on Stunkard, Sorensen, & Schulsinger, 1980.

Now we have some more specific information on how these attitudes about body image are socially transmitted in adolescent girls. Paxton, Schutz, Wertheim, and Muir (1999) explored the influence of close friendship groups on attitudes concerning body image, dietary restraint, and extreme weight-loss behaviours. In a very clever experiment, the authors identified 79 different friendship cliques in a group of 523 adolescent girls. They found that these friendship cliques tended to share the same attitudes toward body image, dietary restraint, and the importance of attempts to lose weight. It was also clear from the study that these friendship cliques contributed significantly to the formation of individual body image concerns and eating behaviours. In other words, if your friends tend to use extreme dieting or other weight-loss techniques, there is a greater chance that you will too (Field et al., 2001; Vanderwal & Thelen, 2000).

Most people who diet don't develop eating disorders, but Patton, Johnson-Sabine, Wood, Mann, and Wakeling (1990) determined in a prospective study that adolescent girls who dieted were eight times more likely to develop an eating disorder one year later than those who weren't dieting. Telch and Agras (1993) noted marked increases in bingeing during and after rigorous dieting in 201 obese women. Stice, Cameron, Killen, Hayward, and Taylor (1999) demonstrated that one of the reasons that attempts to lose weight may lead to eating disorders is that weight reduction efforts in adolescent girls are more likely to result in weight gain than weight loss! To establish this finding, 692 girls, initially the same weight, were followed for four years. Girls who attempted dieting faced a more than 300 percent greater risk of obesity than those who did not diet. Results are presented in ■ Figure 8.5.

It is not yet entirely clear why dieting leads to bingeing in some people but not all (Polivy & Herman, 1993), but the relationship is strong (Davis et al., 1988). A daily diary study by Howard Steiger and his colleagues at the Douglas Hospital Eating Disorders Unit in Montreal showed that patients' attempts to limit and control their dietary intake contributed to binge cravings, but were not direct antecedents to binge-eating episodes (Engelberg, Gauvin, & Steiger, 2005). The researchers concluded that dietary restraint sets the stage for binge eating (Urbszat, Herman, & Polivy, 2002), but does not necessarily trigger its occurrence.

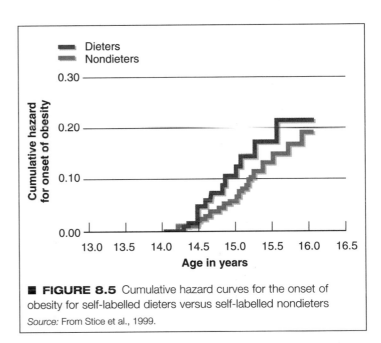

FIGURE 8.5 Cumulative hazard curves for the onset of obesity for self-labelled dieters versus self-labelled nondieters

Source: From Stice et al., 1999.

Instead, factors like negative affect may operate to trigger individual binge-eating episodes (as discussed earlier) among those who are currently restricting their dietary intake.

The work of Janet Polivy and C. Peter Herman at the University of Toronto has contributed much to our understanding of the negative consequences of chronic dieting. Their early lab-based work showed how a broken diet can readily lead to a binge in women who chronically restrict their diets (e.g., Polivy & Herman, 1985). Their recent work focuses on the more general negative psychological impacts of dieting, such as low self-esteem, food preoccupation, and negative mood—a phenomenon they have labelled the "false hope syndrome" (e.g., Polivy, 2001; Polivy & Herman, 2002; Trottier, Polivy, & Herman, 2005). In brief, this perspective asserts that people's false hopes about self-change attempts are initially strongly reinforced. Recall the praise that Julie received from her friends and her mother when she first started to lose weight. Unfortunately, the positive feelings and sense of control that people feel with their initial successes at self-change lead

Courtesy of the University of Toronto

▲ Janet Polivy is a clinical psychologist at the University of Toronto. Her work with C. Peter Herman has contributed significantly to the understanding of why chronic dieting is so closely linked with binge eating and eating disorders.

them to continue to pursue unrealistic or even impossible goals for weight loss that ultimately result in extreme disappointment and a decline in self-esteem.

The conflict over body image would be bad enough if size were infinitely malleable, but it is not. Increasing evidence indicates a strong genetic contribution to body size (e.g., Livesley, Jang, & Thordarson, 2005; Rutherford, McGuffin, Katz, & Murray, 1993); that is, some of us are born to be heavier than others, and we are all shaped differently. Although most of us can be physically fit, very few can achieve the levels of fitness and shape so highly valued today. It is biologically nearly impossible (Brownell, 1991; Brownell & Fairburn, 2002). Nevertheless, many young people in our society fight biology to the point of starvation. In adolescence, cultural standards are often experienced as peer pressure and are much more influential than reason and fact. The high number of males who are homosexual among the relatively small numbers of males with eating disorders has also been attributed to pressures in the gay culture to be physically trim (Carlat et al., 1997; Feldman & Meyer, 2007). Conversely, pressure to appear more fit and muscular are also very apparent for a substantial proportion of men (Pope et al., 2000).

Dietary Restraint

As mentioned previously, those with eating disorders tend to display a strong preoccupation with food. We have known since the 1950s that long-term dieting can cause preoccupation with food (e.g., hoarding food, collecting recipes; see Keys, Brozek, Henschel, Michelson, & Taylor, 1950). More recent studies using experimental cognitive tasks have confirmed this relationship of dieting to food preoccupations. Several studies have shown that chronic dieters pay more attention to information about food than to other types of information (e.g., Francis, Stewart, & Hounsell, 1997; Stewart & Samoluk, 1997). Chronic dieters also appear to remember information better when it pertains to food (Israeli & Stewart, 2001). These attentional and memory biases favouring information about food are consistent with the possibility that chronic dieting causes a preoccupation with food and eating, which in turn could contribute to binge eating.

If cultural pressures to be thin are as important as they seem to be in triggering eating disorders, then such disorders would be expected to occur where these pressures are particularly severe, which is the case with ballet dancers, who are under extraordinary pressures to be thin. In an important study, Garner, Garfinkel, Rockert, and Olmsted (1987) followed a group of 11- to 14-year-old female students in an internationally acclaimed ballet school in Toronto. Their conservative estimate was that at least 25 percent of these girls developed eating disorders during the two years of the study. In another study, Szmukler, Eisler, Gillis, and Haywood

(1985) examined 100 adolescent female ballet students in London, England. Fully 7 percent were diagnosed with anorexia nervosa, and an additional 3 percent were borderline cases. Another 20 percent had lost a significant amount of weight, and 30 percent were clearly afraid of becoming fat, although they were actually below normal weight (Garner & Garfinkel, 1985). All these figures are much higher than in the population as a whole.

Similar results are apparent among athletes, particularly females, such as gymnasts, figure skaters, and tennis players (Davis & Strachan, 2001). For example, in a study of 41 female Canadian competitive figure skaters, Gail Taylor and Diane Ste-Marie of the University of Ottawa found that all the figure skaters had used weight-control measures at some point in their lives. About 93 percent reported that they perceived weight-loss pressures to be associated with the sport of figure skating (Taylor & Ste-Marie, 2001). And in a study of female gymnasts, Gretchen Kerr and her colleagues at the University of Toronto found that disordered eating patterns were particularly common among those gymnasts who had received negative comments about their weight (Kerr, Berman, & de Souza, 2006).

The case of Canadian tennis player Carling Bassett illustrates how weight-loss pressures in competitive athletics can serve as triggers for an eating disorder. Bassett was Canada's leading female tennis player in the 1980s and was inducted into Canada's Sports Hall of Fame. She experienced a three-year bout of bulimia, which she developed as a teenager while she was competing professionally.

Photodisc

▲ Ballet dancers and female athletes face extreme pressures to be thin and appear to be at high risk for the development of eating disorders.

"At fifteen, I wasn't heavy by any means" she told a reporter, "but I gained a lot of weight; I went from 111 to 126 [pounds; 51 to 57 kilograms]. At fourteen, fifteen, sixteen . . . you want to look good all the time. You start feeling pressure" (Neill & Sider, 1992). Bassett was introduced to self-induced vomiting as a weight-control strategy at age 16 by an older female tennis player. She said about purging: "It's so easy to get into and so hard to get out of. I hated myself that I couldn't stop." Her mother recalls the negative impact the eating disorder had on Bassett and her family: "She became skeletal. You'd try to force food on her, and she'd just throw up. We screamed and yelled." Bassett kept her eating disorder hidden from other tennis players, even from her husband, tennis star Robert Seguso, until her symptoms became so disruptive that she attempted recovery with Seguso's help (Neill & Sider, 1992).

What goes on in ballet classes or in competitive sports that has such a devastating effect on girls? Consider the case of Phoebe again.

PHOEBE | *Dancing to Destruction*

Phoebe remembered very clearly that during her early years in ballet, the older girls talked incessantly about their weight. Phoebe performed very well and looked forward to the rare compliment. In fact, the ballet mistress seemed to comment more on weight than on dance technique, often remarking, "You'd dance better if you lost weight." If one little girl managed to lose a kilogram through heroic dieting, the instructor always pointed it out: "You've done well working on your weight; the rest of you had better follow this example." One day, without warning, the instructor said to Phoebe, "You need to lose three kilograms before the next class." At that time Phoebe was 1.57 metres and weighed 44 kilograms. The next class was in two days. After one of these admonitions and several days of restrictive eating, Phoebe experienced her first uncontrollable binge.

Early in high school, Phoebe gave up the rigours of ballet to pursue a variety of other interests. She did not forget the glory of her starring roles as a young dancer or how to perform the steps. She still danced by herself sometimes and retained the grace that serious dancers effortlessly display. But in university, as she stuck her head in the toilet bowl, vomiting for perhaps the third time that day, she realized that she had learned one lesson in ballet class more deeply and thoroughly than any other—the life-or-death importance of being thin at all costs.

Family Influences

Much has been made of the possible significance of family interaction patterns in cases of eating disorders. Several investigators (e.g., Attie & Brooks-Gunn, 1995; Bruch, 1985; Humphrey, 1986, 1988, 1989; Minuchin, Rosman, & Baker, 1978) have found that the "typical" anorexic's family is successful, hard driving, concerned about external appearances, and eager to maintain harmony. To accomplish these goals, family members often deny or ignore conflicts or negative feelings and tend to attribute their problems to other people at the expense of frank communication among themselves (Fairburn et al., 1990).

Pike and Rodin (1991) confirmed the differences in interactions within the families of girls with disordered eating in comparison with control families. Basically, mothers of girls with disordered eating seemed to act as "society's messengers" in wanting their daughters to be thin (Steinberg & Phares, 2001). They were very likely to be dieting themselves and, generally, were more perfectionistic than control mothers in that they were less satisfied with their families and family cohesion (Fairburn et al., 1997; Fairburn et al., 1999). A study by D. Blake Woodside and his colleagues reported similar findings from data collected in the international Price Foundation family study of eating disorders. Participants were recruited from London, Los Angeles, Munich, New York, Philadelphia, Pittsburgh, and Toronto. Mothers of those girls with eating disorders showed elevated levels of perfectionism and more concerns about weight and shape than did the controls (Woodside et al., 2002). Other family studies by Howard Steiger and colleagues demonstrated that a link exists between the abnormal eating attitudes of daughters and their mothers (Steiger, Stotland, Trottier, & Ghadirian, 1996) and that family preoccupation with appearance had a direct influence on body dissatisfaction and eating disorder symptoms (Leung, Schwartzman, & Steiger, 1996). More recently, Caroline Davis and colleagues have shown that family preoccupation with appearance exerts its greatest negative effects in influencing weight preoccupation in more anxiety-prone young women (Davis, Shuster, Blackmore, & Fox, 2004).

Lynn Carpenter is the mother of the late Sheena Carpenter—a young anorexic woman who died of starvation in Toronto at age 22. Lynn has candidly spoken about the role of parents' attitudes toward weight and shape in inadvertently triggering eating disorder behaviours in their children. Sheena had wanted to be a model or an actress. When she died, she weighed only 23 kilograms. In a candid interview, Lynn Carpenter talked about the role she believes she had in initiating her daughter's illness: "Sheena didn't stand a chance. I always had body issues, so she grew up with me always griping about my cellulite. Always negative." These messages about the importance of being thin reportedly had an effect on Sheena quite early in life. Lynn recalled an event that took place when Sheena was only six years old. On a hot summer day, Lynn found Sheena dressed in a snowsuit and doing jumping jacks. "Look Mom," Sheena said, "This way I won't put on any weight." But Lynn Carpenter was not the sole messenger in relaying society's message about the importance of low body weight to her daughter. Apparently, when Sheena was 14 years old, a modelling agency told her a thinner face would make her more photogenic. Sheena Carpenter's tragic story led to her mother establishing a refuge in Toronto called Sheena's Place, which offers support programs and group sessions to women with eating disorders. Canadian singer Anne Murray, whose daughter—Dawn Langstroth—has also struggled with anorexia, is the honorary chair of Sheena's Place (Strobel, 2002).

Whatever the pre-existing relationships, after the onset of an eating disorder, particularly anorexia, family relationships can deteriorate quickly. Nothing is more frustrating than watching your daughter starve herself at a dinner table where food is plentiful. Educated and knowledgeable parents, including psychologists and psychiatrists with full understanding of the disorder at hand, have reported resorting to physical violence (e.g., hitting or slapping) in moments of extreme frustration, in a vain attempt to get their daughters to put some food, however little, in their mouths. The parents' guilt and anguish, very evident in the interview with Lynn Carpenter (Strobel, 2002), often exceed the levels of anxiety and depression present in the children with the disorder.

Biological Dimensions

Like most psychological disorders, eating disorders run in families and thus seem to have a genetic component (Strober, 2002). Although completed studies are only preliminary, they suggest that relatives of patients with eating disorders are four to five times more likely than the general population to develop eating disorders themselves, with the risks for female relatives of patients with anorexia a bit higher (e.g., Hudson, Pope, Jonas, & Yurgelun-Todd, 1983; Strober, Freeman, Lampert, Diamond, & Kaye, 2000).

In important twin studies of bulimia by Kendler and colleagues (1991) and of anorexia by Walters and Kendler (1995), researchers used structured interviews to ascertain the prevalence of the disorders among 2163 female twins. In 23 percent of identical twin pairs, both twins had bulimia, as compared with 9 percent of fraternal twins. Because no adoption studies have yet been reported, strong sociocultural influences cannot be ruled out, and other studies have produced inconsistent results (Fairburn, Cowen, & Harrison, 1999). For anorexia, numbers were too small for precise estimates, but the disorder in one twin did seem to confer a significant risk for both anorexia and bulimia in the co-twin. However, once again, no clear agreement exists on just what (if anything) is inherited (Fairburn et al.,1999). Hsu (1990) speculates that nonspecific personality traits such as emotional instability and, perhaps, poor impulse control might be inherited. In other words, a person might inherit a tendency to be emotionally responsive to stressful life events and, as one consequence, might eat impulsively in an attempt to relieve stress and anxiety. Data from Kendler et al. (1995) support this interpretation. Klump, Kaye, and Strober (2001) mention perfectionist traits with negative affect. This biological vulnerability might then interact with social and psychological factors to produce an eating disorder.

A twin study by Vancouver-based researchers Livesley and colleagues (2005) suggests that some symptoms of eating disorders may themselves have a partially genetic basis. In a community-recruited sample of 221 twin pairs, they estimated that body mass index is 57 percent heritable, purging is 42 percent heritable, and concern for overeating is 20 percent heritable. The rest of the variance in these eating disorder domains is attributable to environmental influences.

Obviously, biological processes are quite active in the regulation of eating and thus of eating disorders, and substantial evidence points to the hypothalamus as playing an important role. Investigators have studied the hypothalamus and the major neurotransmitter systems—including norepinephrine, dopamine, and, particularly, serotonin—that pass through it to determine whether something is malfunctioning when eating disorders occur (Vitiello & Lederhendler, 2000). Low levels of serotonergic activity are associated with impulsivity in general and binge eating specifically (see Chapter 2). Thus, most drugs currently under study as bulimia treatments target the serotonin system (e.g., de Zwaan, Roerig, & Mitchell, 2004; Garfinkel, 2002; Kaye et al., 1998; Walsh et al., 1997).

Some interesting research also points to the role of exercise in causing or maintaining anorexia nervosa. Recall the case of Julie who also reported having "lost all taste for food." According to the work of John Pinel and his colleagues at the University of British Columbia, Julie and other anorexics differ from most people who are starving because food lacks "positive incentive value" for them in terms of their desire to actually eat it (Pinel, Assanand, & Lehman, 2000). According to W. Frank Epling and W. David Pierce, Julie's reported loss of positive incentive to eat can be explained by the fact that she was exercising excessively—completing a workout videotape after every meal. These researchers describe a phenomenon they refer to as "activity anorexia" (see Chapter 4) where excessive physical activity can paradoxically cause a loss of appetite (Belke, Pierce, & Duncan, 2006; Epling & Pierce, 1992; Pierce & Epling, 1996) for reasons that are not yet well understood.

If investigators do find a strong association between neurobiological functions and eating disorders, the question of cause or effect remains. At present, the consensus is that some neurobiological abnormalities do exist in people with eating disorders, but they are a result of semistarvation or a binge-purge cycle rather than a cause, although they may well contribute to the maintenance of the disorder once it is established.

Psychological Dimensions

Clinical observations indicate that many young women with eating disorders have a diminished sense of personal control and confidence in their own abilities and talents (Bruch, 1973, 1985; Striegal-Moore, Silberstein, & Rodin, 1993; Walters & Kendler, 1995). They also display more perfectionistic attitudes learned, perhaps, from their families, which may reflect attempts to exert control over important events in their lives (Fairburn et al., 1997; Fairburn, Shafran, & Cooper, 1999; Joiner, Heatherton, & Keel, 1997; Woodside et al., 2002). Canadian psychologist Todd Heatherton and his colleagues have noted that people with anorexia nervosa and bulimia nervosa share perfectionistic traits and those traits likely play a crucial role in their eating disorders (Heatherton & Baumeister, 1991; see also Davis, 1997; Goldner, Cockell, & Srikameswaran, 2002; Hewitt, Flett, & Ediger, 1995; Pliner & Haddock, 1996). However, perfectionism alone is only weakly associated with the development of an eating disorder, because individuals must first consider themselves overweight and also manifest low self-esteem before the trait of perfectionism makes a contribution, as indicated by the work of Kathleen Vohs at the University of British Columbia (Abramson, Bardone-Cone, & Vohs, 2006; Vohs, Bardone, Joiner, Abramson, & Heatherton, 1999; Vohs et al., 2001). Similarly, a study by McGee, Hewitt, Sherry, Parkin, and Flett (2005) showed that perfectionism predicted eating disorder symptoms, but only among women who were dissatisfied with their bodies.

Specific distortions in perception of body shape change frequently, depending on day-to-day experience. McKenzie, Williamson, and Cubic (1993) found that bulimic women judged their body size to be larger than, and their ideal weight to be less than, same-size controls did. Indeed women with bulimia judged that their bodies were larger after they ate a chocolate bar and soft drink, whereas the judgments of women in control groups were unaffected by snacks. Thus, rather minor events related to eating may activate fear of gaining weight, further distortions in body image, and corrective schemes such as purging.

Rosen and Leitenberg (1985) observed substantial anxiety before and during snacks, which they theorized is relieved by purging. They suggested the state of relief strongly reinforces the purging, in that we tend to repeat behaviour that gives us pleasure or relief from anxiety. This seemed to be true for Phoebe. One method of reducing the anxiety associated with eating that motivates purging is binge exposure with response prevention. In this treatment the client who has an eating disorder is repeatedly exposed to her preferred binge food (e.g., chips, ice cream) and each time she is prevented from engaging in binge eating and purging. This technique has been shown to be successful in reducing urges to binge, lack of control, feelings of guilt, and feelings of anxiety for women with bulimia nervosa and anorexia nervosa, binge-purge subtype (Kennedy, Katz, Neitzert, Ralevski, & Mendlowitz, 1995). However, other evidence suggests that in

treating bulimia, reducing the anxiety associated with eating is less important than countering the tendency to overly restrict food intake and the associated negative attitudes about body image that lead to bingeing and purging (e.g., Agras, Schneider, Arnow, Raeburn, & Telch, 1989; Fairburn, Agras, & Wilson, 1992; Fairburn et al., 2008; Wilson & Pike, 2001).

An Integrative Model

Although the three major eating disorders are identifiable based on their unique characteristics, and the specific diagnoses have some validity, it is becoming increasingly clear that all eating disorders have much in common in terms of causal factors (Fairburn et al., 2003, 2007). Thus, we have integrated a discussion of the causes of eating disorders.

In putting together what we know about eating disorders, it is important to remember, once again, that no one factor seems sufficient to cause them (see ■ Figure 8.6). Individuals with eating

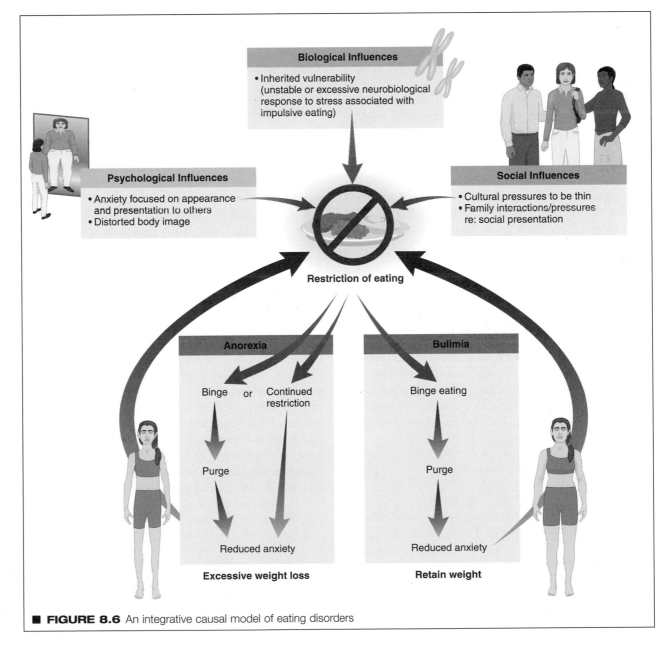

■ **FIGURE 8.6** An integrative causal model of eating disorders

disorders may have some of the same biological vulnerabilities (such as being highly responsive to stressful life events) as individuals with anxiety disorders (Kendler et al., 1995; Rojo, Conesa, Bermudez, & Livianos, 2006). Anxiety and mood disorders are also common in the families of individuals with eating disorders (Schwalberg et al., 1992), and negative emotions and "mood intolerance" seem to trigger binge eating in many patients (Davis et al., 1988; Polivy & Herman, 1993). In addition, as we will see, drug and psychosocial treatments with proven effectiveness for anxiety disorders are also the treatments of choice for eating disorders. Indeed, we could conceptualize eating disorders as anxiety disorders focused exclusively on becoming overweight.

In any case, it is clear that social and cultural pressures to be thin motivate significant restriction of eating, usually through severe dieting. However, many people go on strict diets, including adolescent females, but only a small minority develop eating disorders, so dieting alone does not explain eating disorders. An emphasis on looks and achievement, and perfectionistic tendencies, in higher-income, high-achieving families may also help establish very strong attitudes about the overriding importance of physical appearance to popularity and success. These attitudes result in an exaggerated focus on body shape and weight. Finally, there is the question of why a minority of individuals with eating disorders can successfully control their intake through dietary restraint, resulting in alarming weight loss, whereas the majority are unsuccessful at losing weight and compensate in a cycle of bingeing and purging. These differences may be determined by biology or physiology, such as a genetically determined disposition to be somewhat thinner to begin with. Then again, perhaps pre-existing personality characteristics, such as a tendency to be overcontrolling or a tendency to act impulsively, are important determinants of which disorder a girl develops—anorexia nervosa or bulimia nervosa, respectively (Goldner, Srikameswaran, Schroeder, Livesley, & Birmingham, 1999; Polivy & Herman, 2002).

Treatment of Eating Disorders

Only since the 1980s have there been treatments for bulimia; treatments for anorexia had been around much longer but were not well developed. Rapidly accumulating evidence indicates that at least one, possibly two, psychological treatments are effective, particularly for bulimia nervosa. Certain drugs may also help, although the evidence is not so strong.

Drug Treatments

At present, drug treatments have generally not been found to be effective in the treatment of anorexia nervosa (e.g., Attia, Haiman, Walsh, & Flater, 1998; Crow, Mitchell, Roerig, & Steffen, 2009; Garner & Needleman, 1996; Hsu, 1990; Kruger & Kennedy, 2000; Vitiello & Lederhendler, 2000). A case series by researchers at the Children's Hospital of Eastern Ontario in Ottawa suggests that the atypical antipsychotic medication olanzapine may be helpful in the treatment of anorexia nervosa in children, but controlled studies are still needed (Boachie, Goldfield, & Spettigue,

2003). Interestingly, although a side effect of olanzapine in the treatment of schizophrenia is weight gain (Chapter 13), this effect would be considered desirable when treating an emaciated patient with anorexia. The drugs generally considered the most effective for bulimia (e.g., Prozac) are the same antidepressant medications proven effective for mood disorders and anxiety disorders (Kaye, Strober, Stein, & Gendall, 1999; Walsh et al., 1997; Wilson et al., 1999; Wilson & Fairburn, 2002). Effectiveness is usually measured by reductions in the frequency of binge eating as well as by the percentage of patients who stop binge eating and purging (Flament, Furino, & Godart, 2005). In two studies, one of tricyclic antidepressant drugs and the other of fluoxetine (Prozac), researchers found the average reduction in binge eating and purging was, respectively, 47 percent and 65 percent (Walsh, 1991; Walsh, Hadigan, Devlin, Gladis, & Roose, 1991). However, although antidepressants are more effective than placebo in the short term, the available evidence suggests that, pending further evaluation, antidepressant drugs alone do not have substantial long-lasting effects on bulimia nervosa (Walsh, 1995; Wilson & Fairburn, 2002). Nonetheless, research by Maureen Whittal at the University of British Columbia and her colleagues suggests that antidepressants show promise in enhancing the effects of psychosocial treatment (Whittal, Agras, & Gould, 1999).

Psychosocial Treatments

Until recently, psychosocial treatments were directed at the patient's low self-esteem and difficulties in developing an individual identity. Disordered patterns of family interaction and communication were also targeted for treatment. However, these treatments alone have not had the effectiveness that clinicians had hoped they might (e.g., Minuchin et al., 1978; Russell, Szmukler, Dare, & Eisler, 1987). Short-term cognitive-behavioural treatments target problem eating behaviour and associated attitudes about the overriding importance and significance of body weight and shape, and these strategies have become the treatment of choice for bulimia (Pike, Devlin, & Loeb, 2004; Wilson & Fairburn, 2002; Wilson, Grilo, & Vitousek, 2007).

Bulimia Nervosa

In the cognitive-behavioural treatment approach pioneered by British psychologist Christopher Fairburn (1985), the first stage is teaching the patient the physical consequences of binge eating and purging, as well as the ineffectiveness of vomiting and laxative abuse for weight control. The adverse effects of dieting are also described. Patients are scheduled to eat small, manageable amounts of food five or six times per day with no more than a three-hour interval between any planned meals and snacks, which eliminates the alternating periods of overeating and dietary restriction that are hallmarks of bulimia. In later stages of treatment, cognitive therapy focuses on altering dysfunctional thoughts and attitudes about body shape, weight, and eating. Coping strategies for resisting the impulse to binge and purge are also developed, including arranging activities so the individual will not spend time alone after eating during the early stages of treatment (Fairburn et al., 2008; Fairburn, Marcus, & Wilson, 1993; Garner, Fairburn, & Davis, 1987; Wilson & Pike, 2001). Evaluations of short-term (approximately three months) cognitive-behavioural treatments for bulimia have been good, showing a mean reduction in purging of 79 percent; 57 percent of the patients eliminated bingeing and purging altogether (Craighead & Agras, 1991). Furthermore, these results seem to last (e.g., Pike, Walsh, Vitousek, Wilson, & Bauer, 2003; Whittal et al., 1999).

In a thorough, carefully conducted study, Fairburn et al. (1993) evaluated three different treatments. Cognitive-behavioural therapy (CBT) focused on changing eating habits and changing attitudes about weight and shape; behaviour therapy (BT) focused only on changing eating habits; and interpersonal psychotherapy (IPT) focused on improving interpersonal functioning. For patients receiving CBT, both binge eating and purging declined by more than 90 percent at a one-year follow-up. In addition, 36 percent of the patients had ceased all binge eating and purging; the others had occasional episodes. Attitudes toward body shape and weight also improved. These results were significantly better than the results from BT. Even more interesting was the finding that IPT did as well as CBT at the one-year follow-up, although CBT was more effective at the assessment immediately after treatment was completed. This result indicates that IPT caught up with CBT in terms of effectiveness by the end of the one-year follow-up. This is particularly interesting because IPT does not concentrate directly on disordered eating patterns or dysfunctional attitudes about eating but rather on improving interpersonal functioning, a focus that may, in turn, promote changes in eating habits and attitudes. Both treatments were more effective than BT. Patients in the two effective treatments had retained their gains at a six-year follow-up (Fairburn et al., 1995). Very similar results were found in a study by Agras, Walsh, Fairburn, Wilson, and Kraemer (2000), comparing the effectiveness of CBT and IPT in the treatment of bulimia nervosa.On the basis of these studies, we can conclude that CBT is the preferred psychological treatment for bulimia nervosa because it works significantly faster. Clearly, we need to understand much more about how to improve such treatments to deal more successfully with the growing number of patients with eating disorders.

Many programs for eating disorders in Canada (e.g., Toronto, Halifax) rely on both CBT and IPT techniques. In fact, not only is integration of these two treatment modalities quite commonplace, but data also support the effectiveness of combined CBT and IPT in the treatment of women with eating problems. For example, a study conducted in Australia in two clinical settings showed that women with eating disorders who completed a ten-week integrated CBT/IPT program were significantly improved on most measures of eating pathology and general psychopathology at the end of treatment and at follow-up, relative to those women on a waiting list (Crafti, 2002).

PHOEBE | Taking Control

During her second year in university, Phoebe entered a short-term cognitive-behaviour therapy program. She made good progress during the first several months and worked carefully to eat regularly and gain control over her eating.

She also made sure that she was with somebody during her high-risk times and planned alternative activities that would reduce her temptation to purge if she felt she had eaten too much at a restaurant or drunk too much beer at a party. During the first two months, Phoebe had three slips; she and her therapist discussed what led to her temporary lapses. Much to Phoebe's surprise, she did not gain weight on this program, even though she did not have time to increase her exercise. Nevertheless, she still was preoccupied with food, was concerned about her weight and appearance, and had strong urges to vomit if she thought she had overeaten the slightest amount.

During the nine months following treatment, Phoebe reported that her urges seemed to decrease somewhat, although she had one major slip after eating a big pizza and drinking a lot of beer. She reported that she was thoroughly disgusted with herself for purging and was quite careful to return to her program after this episode. Two years after finishing treatment, Phoebe reported that her urges to vomit had disappeared, a report confirmed by her parents. All that remained of her problem were some very bad but increasingly distant memories.

Another variant of CBT, developed by Ron Davis of Lakehead University and his colleagues in Toronto, is brief group psychoeducation for bulimia nervosa. The main goal of psychoeducation is to help bulimic individuals normalize their eating and reduce their body image disturbance. This goal is achieved through providing them with information relevant to bulimia nervosa and with useful strategies such as meal planning, problem solving, and self-monitoring. The main differences from CBT are that psychoeducation is briefer, is delivered in a lecture-type format, and is not tailored to the unique needs of individual patients (Davis & Olmsted, 1992). Research has shown this approach to be better than a wait list control in helping bulimic individuals reduce their symptoms (Davis, Olmsted, & Rockert, 1990). The intervention is particularly effective for those with less severe bulimia (Davis, Olmsted, & Rockert, 1992). Nonetheless, improvements in bulimia are even better when the psychoeducation approach is followed by 16 weeks of CBT than when patients receive the psychoeducation approach alone (Davis, McVey, Heinmaa, Rockert, & Kennedy, 1999).

Short-term treatments for eating disorders, although clearly effective for many, are no panacea. Indeed, some people do not benefit at all from either brief psychoeducation or short-term CBT. Evidence now suggests that combining drugs with psychosocial treatments might boost the overall outcome, at least in the short term (Whittal et al., 1999; Wilson et al., 1999). In one large study (Walsh et al., 1997), CBT was significantly superior to supportive psychotherapy in the treatment of bulimia nervosa; and, adding two antidepressant medications to CBT, including an SSRI, modestly increased the benefit of CBT. But CBT remains the preferred treatment for bulimia. Evidence also shows that people who do not respond to CBT might benefit from IPT methods (Fairburn, Jones, Peveler, Hope, & O'Connor,

1993; Klerman, Weissman, Rounsaville, & Chevron, 1984) or from antidepressant medication (Walsh et al., 2000).

Both private and public eating disorder treatment centres and clinics can be found across Canada (e.g., Halifax, Montreal, Toronto, and Vancouver). Programs at many of these centres and clinics are world renowned for the quality of services they provide as well as for the important research they contribute in terms of understanding, preventing, and treating eating disorders. Most of these centres and clinics provide combinations of psychoeducation, psychotherapy (e.g., CBT and IPT), and pharmacological treatments to their clients with eating disorders. Most programs are staffed by multidisciplinary teams involving psychologists, psychiatrists, nutritionists, nurses, occupational therapists, and social workers, each of whom has unique skills to provide in assisting the people with eating disorders in their recovery.

Binge-Eating Disorder

Smith, Marcus, and Kaye (1992) have adapted CBT treatments for bulimia to obese binge eaters, and the preliminary results look promising. In their study, the frequency of binge eating was reduced by an average of 81 percent, with 50 percent of the participants totally abstinent from bingeing by the end of treatment. Agras, Telch, Arnow, Eldredge, and Marnell (1997) followed 93 obese individuals with binge-eating disorder for one year and found that immediately after treatment 41 percent of the participants abstained from bingeing and 72 percent binged less frequently. After one year, binge eating was reduced by 64 percent, and 33 percent of the group remained abstinent. Importantly, those who had stopped binge eating during CBT maintained a weight loss of approximately four kilograms over the follow-up period; those who continued to binge gained almost three kilograms. Thus, stopping binge eating is critical to sustaining weight loss in obese patients, a finding consistent with other studies of weight-loss procedures (Marcus, Wing, & Hopkins, 1988; Marcus et al., 1990; Telch, Agras, & Rossiter, 1988). In contrast to results with bulimia, it appears that IPT is as effective as CBT for binge eating (Wilfley et al., 2002).

Fortunately, it appears that self-help procedures may also be useful in the treatment of BED (e.g., Loeb, Wilson, Gilbert, & Labouvie, 2000; Peterson et al., 1998). Jacqueline Carter of the Toronto Hospital teamed up with Christopher Fairburn to conduct one of the best studies of this approach (Carter & Fairburn, 1998). They randomly assigned 72 females with BED to a pure self-help group in which participants were simply mailed their manual, a guided self-help in which therapists would meet with the patients periodically as they read the manual, or a wait-list control group. Fifty percent of the guided self-help group and 43 percent of the pure self-help group eliminated binge eating versus 8 percent of the wait-list control group. These improvements were maintained at a six-month follow-up. If further studies confirm these findings, then a self-help approach should probably be the first treatment offered before engaging in more expensive and time-consuming therapist-led treatments.

Anorexia Nervosa

In anorexia, of course, the most important initial goal is to restore the patient's weight to a point that is at least within the low-normal range (American Psychiatric Association, 2010). If body weight is below 85 percent of the average healthy body weight for a given individual or if weight has been lost rapidly and the individual continues to refuse food, inpatient treatment is recommended (American Psychiatric Association, 2010; Casper, 1982) because severe medical complications, particularly acute cardiac failure, could occur if weight is not restored immediately. If the weight loss has been more gradual and seems to have stabilized, weight restoration can be accomplished on an outpatient basis.

Restoring weight is probably the easiest part of treatment. Clinicians who treat patients in different settings, as reported in a variety of studies, find that at least 85 percent will be able to gain weight. The gain is often as much as one quarter to a half a kilogram a day until weight is within the normal range. Typical strategies used with inpatients are outlined in Table 8.1. In fact, knowing they can leave the hospital when their weight gain is adequate is often sufficient to motivate individuals with anorexia (Agras, Barlow, Chapin, Abel, & Leitenberg, 1974). Julie gained about eight kilograms during her five-week hospital stay.

Then the difficult stage begins. As Hsu (1988) and others have demonstrated, initial weight gain is a poor predictor of long-term

TABLE 8.1 Strategies to Attain Weight Gain

1. Weight restoration occurs in conjunction with other treatments, such as individual and family therapy, so that the patient does not feel that eating and weight gain are the only goals of treatment.

2. The patient trusts the treatment team and believes that she will not be allowed to become overweight.

3. The patient's fear of loss of control is contained; this may be accomplished by having her eat frequent, smaller meals (e.g., four to six times per day, with 400 to 500 calories per meal) so as to produce a gradual but steady weight gain (e.g., an average of half a pound [one fifth a kilogram] per day).

4. A member of the nursing staff is present during mealtimes to encourage the patient to eat and to discuss her fears and anxiety about eating and weight gain.

5. Gradual weight gain rather than the amount of food eaten is regularly monitored, and the result is made known to the patient; thus, the patient should be weighed at regular intervals, and she should know whether she has gained or lost weight.

6. Some negative and positive reinforcements exist, such as the use of graduated levels of activity and bedrest, whether or not these reinforcements are formally conceptualized as behaviour modification techniques, so that the patient may thereby learn that she can control not only her behaviour but also the consequence of her behaviour.

7. The patient's self-defeating behaviour, such as surreptitious vomiting or purging, is confronted and controlled.

8. The dysfunctional conflict between the patient and the family about eating and food is not re-enacted in the hospital; or if the pattern is to be re-enacted in a therapeutic lunch session, the purpose is clearly defined.

outcome in anorexia. Without attention to the patient's underlying dysfunctional attitudes about body shape, she will almost always relapse. For restricting anorexics, the focus of treatment must shift to their marked anxiety over becoming obese and losing control of eating, as well as to their undue emphasis on thinness as a determinant of self-worth, happiness, and success. In this regard, effective treatments for restricting anorexics are similar to those for patients with bulimia nervosa (Fairburn et al., 2008; Pike, Loeb, & Vitousek, 1996; Vitousek, Watson, & Wilson, 1998). In one well-done study (Pike, Walsh, Vitousek, Wilson, & Bauer, 2003), extended (one-year) outpatient CBT was found to be significantly better than continued nutritional counselling in preventing relapse after weight restoration, with only 22 percent failing (relapsing or dropping out) with CBT versus 73 percent failing with nutritional counselling. More recently, Carter et al. (2009) reported similar findings and both studies demonstrate the ineffectiveness of nutritional counselling alone.

Other research highlights the importance of assessing clients with eating disorders' readiness for change, since patients with anorexia nervosa are often difficult to treat (Goldner, 1989). Interventions, derived from those used in the treatment of substance abuse disorders (see Chapter 11), are being developed that focus on enhancing the patient's motivation to change (see Kaplan & Garfinkel, 1999). For example, a study by Joanne Gusella and her colleagues at the IWK Health Centre in Halifax administered a motivational measure to 34 adolescents with eating disorders before the commencement of an eating disorder group. Those girls who reported being more ready to change at treatment outset showed greater improvements in their eating disorder symptoms over the course of the group. The group also assisted the girls in earlier stages to be more ready to change by the end of the group (Gusella, Butler, Nichols, & Bird, 2003). A similar study by Josie Geller at the St. Paul's Hospital Eating Disorders Program in Vancouver examined motivation to change in 56 adult women with anorexia. Like the findings in Gusella's study, Geller (2002) found that anorexic patients who were at a more advanced stage of readiness to change were more likely to complete assigned behavioural recovery activities (e.g., increasing caloric intake) and to accept intensive treatment for their anorexia. Given the clear importance of motivation to change in recovery from anorexia, new treatments that target motivational enhancement are promising innovations in eating disorders treatment (Dunn, Neighbors, & Larimer, 2006; Kaplan & Garfinkel, 1999).

In addition, every effort is made to include the family in order to accomplish two goals. First, the negative and dysfunctional communication regarding food and eating must be eliminated and meals made more structured and reinforcing. Second, attitudes toward body shape and image distortion are discussed at some length in family sessions. Unless the therapist attends to these attitudes, individuals with anorexia are likely to face a lifetime preoccupation with weight and body shape, struggle to maintain marginal weight and social adjustment, and be subject to repeated hospitalization. Family therapy seems effective, particularly with young girls with a short history of the disorder (Eisler et al., 1997). Recent research by a team at the Hospital for Sick Children in Toronto showed that a substantially less costly family group psychoeducation approach was just as effective as a more traditional family therapy approach in assisting hospitalized adolescents with anorexia and their families, at least in the short term (Geist, Heinmaa, Stephens, Davis, & Katzman, 2000). Nevertheless, the long-term results of treatment for anorexia are more discouraging than for bulimia, with substantially lower rates of full recovery than for bulimia over a 7.5-year period (Eddy et al., 2008; Herzog et al., 1999). A recent proposal to focus treatment more directly on the extreme anxiety over gaining weight using therapeutic principles successful in anxiety disorders is promising (Steinglass et al., 2010).

Probably one of the most talked-about stories of the treatment of anorexia nervosa in Canadian history involves the Montreux Clinic—an expensive and exclusive private clinic for women and adolescents with anorexia nervosa in Victoria, British Columbia. Montreux was directed by Peggy Claude-Pierre—a mother who had helped her own two teenage daughters overcome eating disorders. Claude-Pierre received a good deal of media attention, including interviews by Oprah Winfrey and Pamela Wallin, given her claims of a striking 90 percent recovery rate for clinic patients and the message of hope contained in her reported treatment philosophy of unconditional love. The clinic came under investigation when a former employee made allegations that the staff was inadequately trained and the clients not properly screened. More serious allegations were made that clients were being force-fed and held against their will. Although, as mentioned earlier, it is essential for very emaciated patients with anorexia to be hospitalized to prevent potentially severe medical complications, these clients were admitted to Montreux with no medical supervision. In fact, the director Claude-Pierre did not have a graduate degree in psychology or any medical training. In spite of strong protests from her supporters, the residential clinic was eventually closed in December 1999 on the order of the local health officer (Dineen, 2002; McLintock, 2002).

Preventing Eating Disorders

Attempts are being made to prevent the development of eating disorders (Stice, Shaw, & Marti, 2007). If successful methods are confirmed, they will be very important, because many cases of eating disorders are resistant to treatment and most individuals who do not receive treatment suffer for many years, in some cases all their lives (Eddy et al., 2008; Keel, Mitchell, Miller, Davis, & Crow, 1999; Killen, 1996; Herzog et al., 1999). Before implementing a prevention program, however, it is necessary to target specific behaviours to change. Killen et al. (1994) conducted a prospective analysis on a sample of 887 young adolescent girls. Over a three-year interval, 32 girls, or 3.6 percent of the sample, developed symptoms of eating disorders.

Early concern about being overweight was the most powerful predictive factor of later symptoms. The instrument used to measure weight concerns is presented in Table 8.2. Girls who scored high on this scale (an average score of 58) were at substantial risk for developing serious symptoms. Killen et al. (1996) then evaluated a prevention program on 967 girls from 11 to 13 years of age in Grade 6 and Grade 7. Half the girls were put on the intervention program and the other half were not. The program emphasized the normality of female weight gain after puberty and that excessive caloric restriction could actually cause increased gain. The interesting

TABLE 8.2 Weight Concerns

1. How much more or less do you feel you worry about your weight and body shape than other girls your age?
   a. I worry a lot less than other girls. (4)*
   b. I worry a little less than other girls. (8)
   c. I worry about the same as other girls. (12)
   d. I worry a little more than other girls. (16)
   e. I worry a lot more than other girls. (20)
2. How afraid are you of gaining three pounds [1.5 kilograms]?
   a. Not afraid of gaining (4)
   b. Slightly afraid of gaining (8)
   c. Moderately afraid of gaining (12)
   d. Very afraid of gaining (16)
   e. Terrified of gaining (20)
3. When was the last time you went on a diet?
   a. I've never been on a diet. (3)
   b. I was on a diet about one year ago. (6)
   c. I was on a diet about six months ago. (9)
   d. I was on a diet about three months ago. (12)
   e. I was on a diet about one month ago. (15)
   f. I was on a diet less than one month ago. (18)
   g. I'm now on a diet. (21)
4. How important is your weight to you?
   a. My weight is not important compared with other things in my life. (5)
   b. My weight is a little more important than some other things. (10)
   c. My weight is more important than most, but not all, things in my life. (15)
   d. My weight is the most important thing in my life. (20)
5. Do you ever feel fat?
   a. Never (4)
   b. Rarely (8)
   c. Sometimes (12)
   d. Often (16)
   e. Always (20)

Notes: * Value assigned to each answer is in parentheses. Thus, if you chose an answer worth 12 in questions 1, 2, 3, and 5, and an answer worth 10 in question 4, your score would be 58. Remember that the prediction from this scale worked for girls aged 11 to 13 but hasn't been evaluated in university students.

Source: Killen, 1996.

results were that the intervention had relatively little effect on the treatment group as a whole compared with the control group. But for those girls at high risk for developing eating disorders (as reflected by a high score on the scale in Table 8.2), the program significantly reduced weight concerns (Killen, 1996; Killen et al., 1994). The authors conclude from this preliminary study that the most cost-effective preventive approach would be to carefully screen 11- and 12-year-old girls who are at high risk for developing eating disorders and to apply the program selectively to them (Killen, 1996). Our best hope for dealing effectively with eating disorders may lie with preventive approaches such as this.

In Canada, Gail McVey and Ron Davis have examined the effectiveness of a program aimed at girls in Grade 6 that is designed to promote a healthy body image and ultimately prevent the development of eating disorders. The program was tested on 258 girls, who were assigned to either the intervention or to a control group. The intervention focused on countering the effects of the media portrayals of the desirability of being thin as well as training the girls in self-esteem enhancement, stress-management,

and peer relationship skills. Relative to the control group, the six-session intervention was successful in improving body image satisfaction and self-esteem and in reducing dieting attitudes immediately following the intervention. Unfortunately, these benefits were not maintained one year following the intervention (McVey, Davis, Tweed, & Shaw, 2004).

Niva Piran of the Ontario Institute for Studies in Education ran a prevention program for young women that emphasized changes in the school culture at a well-known ballet school in Toronto (Piran, 1998). In focus groups, students explored their experiences of body image dissatisfaction at the school and outside school. They each formed an action plan to implement changes in the school culture (Piran, 2001). Specific changes included moving away from a focus on a body shape and toward an increased focus on body conditioning and physical stamina, and not permitting teachers to make comments about students' body shape (recall the impact of Phoebe's experiences with her ballet instructor's comments about her body weight and shape). This prevention program has been very successful: Abnormal eating attitudes have decreased among girls in the school, as have rates of bingeing, vomiting, and laxative abuse (Piran, 1999). In view of the severity and chronicity of eating disorders, preventing these disorders through widespread educational and intervention efforts would be clearly preferable to waiting until the disorders develop (Piran, 1997, 2004).

Concept Check | 8.2

Check your understanding by identifying the eating disorder in the following scenarios. Choose your answers from (a) bulimia nervosa, (b) anorexia nervosa, and (c) binge-eating disorder.

1. Jason has been having episodes lately when he eats prodigious amounts of food. He's been putting on a lot of weight because of it. _____

2. I noticed Sally eating a whole pie, a cake, and two bags of potato chips the other day when she didn't know I was there. She ran to the bathroom when she was finished and it sounded as if she was vomiting. _____

3. Kirsten wants to lose some weight though she is already slim. She counts her calories carefully and keeps her daily intake at about 400 calories. She exercises for about four hours every day. _____

4. Pravin eats large quantities of food in a short time. She then takes laxatives and exercises for long periods to prevent weight gain. She has been doing this almost daily for several months and feels she will become worthless and ugly if she gains even a small amount. _____

5. Mari has lost several kilograms and now weighs less than 40 kilograms. She eats only a small portion of the food her mother serves her and fears that intake above her current 500 calories daily will make her fat. Since losing the weight, Mari has stopped having periods. She sees a fat person in the mirror. _____

Sleep Disorders: An Overview

We spend about one-third of our lives asleep. That means most of us sleep nearly 3000 hours per year. Many people think we need eight hours of sleep in a 24-hour period, but the ideal amount varies considerably from person to person: Five to six hours per night is enough for some people; others may need nine hours or more. Our sleep patterns change as we age. Infants sleep as much as 16 hours per day, and people in their early 20s average seven to eight hours per day. When people pass the age of 50, their total sleep per day can drop below six hours.

For many of us, sleep is energizing, both mentally and physically. However, you or someone you know may have a problem with sleeping. Most of us know what it's like to have a bad night's sleep. The next day we're a little groggy, and as the day wears on we may become irritable. Imagine, if you can, that it has been years since you've had a good night's sleep. Your relationships suffer, it is difficult to do your schoolwork, and your efficiency and productivity at work are diminished. Lack of sleep might also affect you physically. As noted by sleep researcher Charles Morin at Laval University, people who do not get enough sleep report more health problems and are more often hospitalized than people who sleep normally (Morin, 1993). According to the research of Harvey Moldofsky, director of the University of Toronto Centre for Sleep and Chronobiology, and his colleagues, some chronic physical health problems are linked to insomnia: circulatory problems, digestive and respiratory disease, migraines, allergies, and rheumatic disorders (Sutton, Moldofsky, & Badley, 2001). Why are health problems linked to sleep problems? Perhaps because immune system functioning is reduced with the loss of even a few hours of sleep (Irwin et al., 1994; Jaffe, 2000; Savard, Laroche, Simard, Ivers, & Morin, 2003). Sleep problems are a costly health problem resulting in substantial annual expenditures due to lost worker productivity, absenteeism, and related outcomes (Chilcott & Shapiro, 1996; Morin, Rodrigue, & Ivers, 2003; Walsh & Ustun, 1999).

Here you might ask yourself how sleep disorders fit into a textbook on abnormal psychology. Different variations of disturbed sleep clearly have physiological bases and therefore could be considered purely medical concerns. However, like other physical disorders, sleep problems interact in important ways with psychological factors.

Before moving on to consider the various sleep disorders that people can experience, we should first discuss the normal stages of sleep and how we cycle between these stages during a

▲ Charles Morin is the director of the Centre on Sleep Disorders at Laval University in Québec and is a past president of the Canadian Sleep Society. Dr. Morin's research has contributed substantially to the understanding of the relationships between sleep and cognitive and immunological functions, and he has made important contributions in developing empirically validated treatments for insomnia.

Courtesy of Charles Morin

typical sleep episode, to better understand how and when this cycle is interrupted in abnormal sleep. As clearly described by University of British Columbia psychologist Stanley Coren in his popular book *Sleep Thieves* (1996), sleep can be divided into two broad states: (1) the slow-wave state in which the person sleeps deeply, and (2) the **rapid eye movement (REM)** state in which the brain appears as if it is awake and in which the sleeper experiences dreams. Between these two broad states are some transition stages. Sleep researchers traditionally refer to four numbered stages of sleep that differ in the depth of sleep involved. In Stage 1, the person transitions through wakefulness into drowsiness and then sleep. During this stage, the person drifts in and out of awareness of his or her surroundings. In Stage 2, the person is truly sleeping, yet the sleep is light (i.e., the sleeper can easily be aroused). When awoken from this stage of sleep, 70 percent of people report that they didn't think they were asleep, but were just "dozing and thinking" (Coren, 1996). Stages 3 and 4 make up deep, slow-wave sleep. Stage 3 involves moderately deep sleep and Stage 4 very deep sleep. Not only are people hard to awaken when in Stage 4 sleep, but when awoken, they may appear disoriented for a few minutes (Coren, 1996).

Throughout the night, we show a 90-minute cycle of sleep, progressing from light sleep, to deeper sleep, then back to light sleep, and ending with REM sleep and dreaming. When we awaken in the morning, we typically awaken out of REM sleep during a dream. Normal sleepers spend about 20 percent of their sleep time in deep sleep, 30 percent dreaming, and 50 percent in light sleep (Coren, 1996).

Several disorders covered in this book are frequently associated with sleep complaints, including schizophrenia, major depression, bipolar disorder, and anxiety-related disorders. Individuals with a wide range of developmental disorders (see Chapter 14) are also at greater risk for having sleep disorders (Durand, 1998). For example, Penny Corkum of Dalhousie University and her colleagues note that reports of sleep problems in children with attention deficit/hyperactivity disorder (ADHD) are prevalent, although the exact nature of sleep problems in children with ADHD remains to be determined (Corkum, Tannock, & Moldofsky, 1998; see also Weiss, Wasdell, Bomben, Rea, & Freeman, 2006). You may think at first that a sleep problem is the result of a psychological disorder. For example, how often have you been anxious about a future event (an upcoming exam, perhaps) and not been able to fall asleep? However, the relationship between sleep disturbances and mental health is more complex. Sleep problems may cause the difficulties people experience in everyday life (Bonnet, 2000), or they may result from some disturbance common to a psychological disorder. For example, Mullane and Corkum (2006) examined the possibility that sleep problems contribute to ADHD symptoms in children. In a series of three cases, they implemented a behavioural treatment for children with sleep problems and ADHD. While the behavioural treatment was effective in treating the sleep problems, it had no impact on the ADHD symptoms. This study provides preliminary evidence that ADHD is not simply secondary to sleep problems in children suffering from both disorders.

In Chapter 5 we explained how a brain circuit in the limbic system may be involved with anxiety. We know that this region of the brain is also involved with our dream sleep, or REM sleep (Verrier, Harper, & Hobson, 2000). This mutual neurobiological connection suggests that anxiety and sleep may be interrelated in important ways. Similarly, REM sleep seems to be related to depression, as noted in Chapter 7 (Emslie, Rush, Weinberg, Rintelmann, & Roffwarg, 1994). In one study, researchers found that cognitive-behavioural therapy improved depression in men and also normalized their REM sleep patterns (Nofzinger et al., 1994). Furthermore, sleep deprivation has temporary antidepressant effects on some people (Hillman, Kripke, & Gillin, 1990), although in people who are not already depressed, sleep deprivation may bring on a depressed mood (Boivin et al., 1997).

In yet another example of the relation of sleep problems to psychological disorders, sleep difficulties are commonly reported by people with schizophrenia in the prodromal phase (i.e., just before the onset of the psychotic episode; see Chapter 13 and Herz, 1985). For example, in a study conducted at four sites in Canada and the United States, Miller et al. (2002) found that sleep disturbances were experienced by 37 percent of the patients with schizophrenia just before the onset of their psychotic episode. We do not fully understand how psychological disorders are related to sleep, yet accumulating research points to the importance of understanding sleep if we are to complete the broader picture of abnormal behaviour.

Sleep disorders are divided into two major categories: **dyssomnias** and **parasomnias**. Dyssomnias involve difficulties getting enough sleep—not being able to fall asleep until 2 a.m. when you have a 9 a.m. class—and complaints about the quality of sleep, such as not feeling refreshed even though you have slept the whole night. The parasomnias are characterized by abnormal events that occur during sleep, such as nightmares and sleepwalking.

The clearest and most comprehensive picture of your sleep habits can be determined only by a **polysomnographic (PSG) evaluation**. The patient spends one or more nights sleeping in a sleep laboratory, being monitored on measures that include respiration; leg movements; brain wave activity, measured by an *electroencephalograph* (EEG); eye movements, measured by an *electrooculograph* (EOG); muscle movements, measured by an *electromyograph* (EMG); and heart activity, measured by an *electrocardiogram* (ECG). Daytime behaviour and typical sleep patterns are also noted, for example, whether the person uses drugs or alcohol, is anxious about work or interpersonal problems, takes afternoon naps, or has a psychological disorder. A less time-consuming and less costly alternative to the comprehensive assessment of sleep involves using a wristwatch-size device called an *actigraph* that records the number of arm movements. The data can be downloaded onto a computer to determine the length and quality of sleep

▲ This subject is participating in a polysomnograph, an overnight electronic evaluation of sleep patterns.

(Monk, Buysse, & Rose, 1999). Actigraphs are useful aids in monitoring sleep in insomnia treatment outcome studies (Vallières & Morin, 2003).

In addition, clinicians and researchers find it helpful to know the average number of hours the individual sleeps each day, taking into account **sleep efficiency (SE)**, the percentage of time actually spent asleep, not just lying in bed trying to sleep. Sleep efficiency is calculated by dividing the amount of time sleeping by the amount of time in bed (Milner, Fogel, & Cote, 2006). An SE of 100 percent would mean you fall asleep as soon as your head hits the pillow and do not wake up at all during the night. In contrast, an SE of 50 percent would mean half your time in bed is spent trying to fall asleep. Such measurements help the clinician determine objectively how well you sleep.

One way to determine whether a person has a problem with sleep is to observe his or her *daytime sequelae*, or behaviour while awake. For example, if it takes you 90 minutes to fall asleep at night, but this doesn't bother you and you feel rested during the day, then you do not have a problem. A friend who also takes 90 minutes to fall asleep but finds this delay anxiety provoking and is fatigued the next day might be considered to have a sleep problem.

Dyssomnias

Primary Insomnia

Insomnia is one of the most common sleep disorders. You may picture someone with insomnia as being awake all the time. However, it isn't possible to go completely without sleep. For example, after being awake for about 40 hours, a person begins having **microsleeps** that last several seconds or longer (Roehrs, Carskadon, Dement, & Roth, 2000). In the very rare occurrences of *fatal familial insomnia* (a degenerative brain disorder), total lack of sleep eventually leads to death (Fiorino, 1996). Despite the common use of the term *insomnia* to mean "not sleeping," it actually applies to a number of complaints (Savard et al., 2003). People are considered to have insomnia if they have trouble falling asleep at night (difficulty initiating sleep), if they wake up frequently or too early and can't go back to sleep (difficulty maintaining sleep), or even if they sleep a reasonable number of hours but are still not rested the next day (nonrestorative sleep). Consider the case of Kathryn.

KATHRYN | *Tossing and Turning*

Kathryn, who was 73, reported having serious sleep problems ever since her husband died 19 years earlier. She could not fall asleep until she had lain in bed for several hours, and she awakened a number of times each night. She had an average of four to five hours of broken sleep per night. It is not surprising she was chronically tired throughout the day and complained that fatigue interfered with her friendships. She no longer enjoyed going out with her friends because she fell asleep in public, which was very embarrassing to her.

Kathryn used nonprescription sleeping pills on and off over the years, and sometimes she just lay in bed listening to the radio and nodding off occasionally. When her sleep problems started, Kathryn recognized that her distress over her husband's death was probably to blame. As the years passed, she assumed poor sleep was normal for a person her age and her fatigue was also part of the aging process. However, during the past months she began to realize she wasn't playing with her grandchildren or leaving her house because she was too tired. On the advice of a friend, she decided to get some help.

Clinical Description

Kathryn's symptoms meet the *DSM-IV-TR* criteria for **primary insomnia**, with primary indicating the complaint is not related to other medical or psychiatric problems (see DSM Table 8.3). Kathryn's is a typical case of insomnia. She had trouble both initiating and maintaining sleep. Other people sleep all night but still feel as if they've been awake for hours. Although most people can carry out necessary daily activities, their inability to concentrate can have serious consequences, such as debilitating accidents when they attempt to drive long distances (like bus drivers do). Kathryn wouldn't drive her car on the highway because she feared falling asleep at the wheel. Students with insomnia may do poorly in school because of difficulty concentrating.

Statistics

Almost a third of the population reports some symptoms of insomnia during any given year (National Sleep Foundation, 2009). For many of these individuals, sleep difficulties are a lifetime affliction (Mendelson, 2005). One study suggests that nearly one-quarter of Canadians report insomnia (Sutton et al., 2001). In another study, 31 percent of the people who expressed concern about sleep continued to experience difficulties a year later (Ford & Kamerow, 1989), a result showing that sleep problems may become chronic. Approximately 35 percent of elderly persons report excessive daytime sleepiness (Blazer, 1999; Whitney et al., 1998).

Several psychological disorders are associated with insomnia (Benca, Obermeyer, Thisted, & Gillin, 1992). Total sleep time often decreases with depression, substance use disorders, anxiety disorders, and dementia of the Alzheimer's type. The interrelationship between alcohol use and sleep disorders can be particularly troubling. Alcohol is often used to initiate sleep (Schuckit, 2009b). In small amounts it may work, but it also interrupts ongoing sleep. Interrupted sleep causes anxiety, which often leads to repeated alcohol use and an obviously vicious cycle (Stewart, 1996).

Women report insomnia twice as often as men (Sutton et al., 2001). Does this mean that men sleep better than women? Not necessarily. Remember, a sleep problem is considered a disorder *only if you experience discomfort* about it. Women may be more frequently diagnosed as having insomnia because they more often report the problem, not necessarily because their sleep is disrupted more. Women may be more aware of their sleep patterns than men or may be more comfortable acknowledging and seeking help for problems.

Just as normal sleep needs change over time, complaints of insomnia differ in frequency among people of different ages. Estimates of insomnia among young children range from 25 percent to more than 40 percent (Mindell, 1993). As children move into adolescence, their biologically determined sleep schedules shift toward a later bedtime (Mindell & Owens, 2009; Sadeh,

---

DSM-IV-TR   **Table 8.3** Criteria for Primary Insomnia

A. The predominant complaint is difficulty initiating or maintaining sleep, or nonrestorative sleep, for at least one month.

B. The sleep disturbance (or associated daytime fatigue) causes clinically significant distress or impairment in social, occupational, or other important areas of functioning.

C. The sleep disturbance does not occur exclusively during the course of narcolepsy, breathing-related sleep disorder, circadian rhythm sleep disorder, or a parasomnia.

D. The disturbance does not occur exclusively during the course of another mental disorder (e.g., major depressive disorder, generalized anxiety disorder, a delirium).

E. The disturbance is not due to the direct physiological effects of a substance (e.g., a drug of abuse, a medication) or a general medical condition.

Source: Reprinted with permission from the *Diagnostic and Statistical Manual of Mental Disorders*, Fourth Edition, Text Revision, (Copyright © 2000). American Psychiatric Association.

Raviv, & Gruber, 2000). However, at least in North America, children are still expected to rise early for school, causing chronic sleep deprivation. As people age, the percentage who complain of sleep problems rises to more than 25 percent for people over the age of 65 (Mellinger, Balter, & Uhlenhuth, 1985). This increase in reports of sleeping problems among older people makes sense when you remember that the number of hours we sleep decreases as we age.

Causes

Insomnia accompanies many medical and psychological disorders, including pain and physical discomfort, physical inactivity during the day, and respiratory problems. Sometimes insomnia is related to problems with the biological clock and its control of temperature. Light exposure causes an acute increase in human body temperature, which normally falls during the night (Song & Rusak, 2000). People who can't fall asleep at night may have a delayed temperature rhythm: Their body temperature doesn't drop and they don't become drowsy until later at night (Morris, Lack, & Dawson, 1990). As a group, people with insomnia seem to have higher body temperatures than good sleepers, and their body temperatures seem to vary less; this lack of fluctuation may interfere with sleep (Lack, Gradisar, Van Someren, Wright, & Lushington, 2008).

Among the other factors that can interfere with sleeping are drug use and a variety of environmental influences such as changes in light, noise, or temperature. People admitted to hospitals often have difficulty sleeping because the noises and routines differ from those at home. Other sleep disorders, such as *sleep apnea* (a disorder that involves obstructed nighttime breathing) or *periodic limb movement disorder* (excessive jerky leg movements), can cause interrupted sleep and may seem similar to insomnia.

Finally, various psychological stresses can also disrupt your sleep (Morin, 1993). Poll your friends around the time of final exams to see how many of them are having trouble falling asleep or are not sleeping through the night. The stress you experience during such times may interfere with your sleep, at least temporarily. A survey study by Sutton and colleagues (2001) found that having a very stressful life was one of the three strongest predictors of insomnia among Canadians. A study by Morin et al. (2003) compared 40 individuals with insomnia to 27 good sleepers. They found that those with insomnia reported a greater impact of daily minor stressors and a greater intensity of major negative life events than the good sleepers. Not only did the insomniac people perceive their lives to be more stressful, they also reported greater levels of arousal before sleep than did the good sleepers (Morin et al., 2003).

Research by Charles Morin and his colleagues also shows that people with insomnia may have unrealistic expectations about how much sleep they need ("I need a full eight hours") and about how disruptive disturbed sleep will be ("I won't be able to think or do my job if I sleep for only five hours") (Morin, Stone, Trinkle, Mercer, & Remsberg, 1993). These studies illuminate the role of cognition in insomnia, proving that our thoughts alone may disrupt our sleep.

Is poor sleeping a learned behaviour? It is generally accepted that people associate the bedroom and bed with the frustration and anxiety that go with insomnia. Eventually, the arrival of bedtime itself may cause anxiety (Ebben & Spielman, 2009). Interactions associated with sleep may contribute to children's sleep problems. For example, one study found that when a parent was present when the child fell asleep, the child was more likely to wake during the night (Adair, Bauchner, Philipp, Levenson, & Zuckerman, 1991). Researchers think

▲ In many cultures, all family members share the same bed (left). In North America, children usually sleep alone (right).

that some children learn to fall asleep only with a parent present; if they wake up at night, they are frightened at finding themselves alone and their sleep is disrupted. However, it is unlikely that learning alone accounts for children's sleep difficulties. Instead, biological and psychological factors are likely reciprocally related. For example, Adair and colleagues (1991) noted that a child's temperament (or personality) may play a role in explaining the relation between parental presence when a child is going to sleep, and sleep problems in the child. The children with sleep problems had comparatively more difficult temperaments, and their parents were presumably present to attend to sleep initiation difficulties. In other words, personality characteristics, sleep difficulties, and parental reaction interact in a reciprocal manner to produce and maintain sleep problems.

Cultural factors may also play a role. Cross-cultural sleep research has focused primarily on children. In the predominant culture in North America, infants are expected to sleep on their own, in a separate bed, and, if possible, in a separate room. However, in many other cultures as diverse as rural Guatemala and Korea and urban Japan, the child spends the first few years of life in the same room and sometimes the same bed as the mother (Mosko, Richard, & McKenna, 1997). In many cultures, mothers report that they do not ignore the cries of their children (Lee, 1992; Morelli, Rogoff, Oppenheim, & Goldsmith, 1992), in stark contrast to North America, where most pediatricians recommend that parents ignore the cries of their infants at night (Ferber, 1985). One conclusion from this research is that sleep can be negatively affected by cultural norms, as in North America. Unmet demands can result in stress that negatively affects the ultimate sleep outcome for children (Durand, 2008). In fact, research by Morin and colleagues shows that insomnia is most often precipitated by stressful events (in 65 percent of cases) in the domains of family, health, and work/school (Bastien, Vallières, & Morin, 2004).

People may be biologically vulnerable to disturbed sleep. This vulnerability differs from person to person and can range from mild to more severe disturbances. For example, a person may be a light sleeper (easily aroused at night) or have a family history of insomnia, narcolepsy, or obstructed breathing. All these factors can lead to eventual sleeping problems. Such influences have been referred to as predisposing conditions (Spielman & Glovinsky, 1991); they may not, by themselves, always cause problems, but they may combine with other factors to interfere with sleep (see ■ Figure 8.7).

An Integrative Model

Biological vulnerability may in turn interact with sleep stress (Durand, 2008), which includes a number of events that can negatively affect sleep. For example, poor bedtime habits (such as having too much alcohol or caffeine) can interfere with falling asleep (Stepanski, 2006). Note that biological vulnerability and sleep stress influence each other (see the double arrows in the integrative model of sleep disturbance in Figure 8.7). Although we may intuitively assume that biological factors come first,

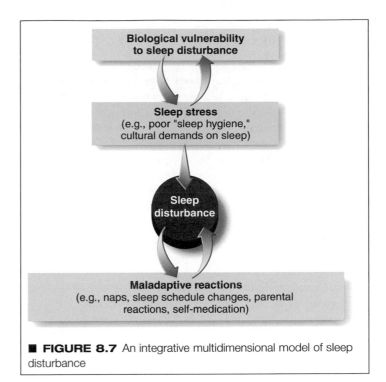

■ **FIGURE 8.7** An integrative multidimensional model of sleep disturbance

extrinsic influences such as poor sleep hygiene (the daily activities that affect how we sleep) can affect the physiological activity of sleep. One of the most striking examples of this phenomenon is jet lag, in which people's sleep patterns are disrupted, sometimes seriously, when they fly across several different time zones. Whether disturbances continue or become more severe may depend on how they are managed. For example, many people react to disrupted sleep by taking over-the-counter sleeping pills. Unfortunately, most people are not aware that **rebound insomnia** may occur when the medication is withdrawn. This rebound leads people to think they still have a sleep problem, re-administer the medicine, and go through the cycle repeatedly. In other words, taking sleep aids can perpetuate sleep problems (Westra & Stewart, 2002).

Other ways of reacting to poor sleep can also prolong problems. It seems reasonable that a person who hasn't had enough sleep can make up for this loss by napping during the day. Unfortunately, naps that alleviate fatigue during the day can also disrupt sleep the next night. Anxiety can also extend the problem, as demonstrated by the research of Charles Morin. Lying in bed worrying about school, family problems, or even about not being able to sleep will interfere with your sleep (Morin, 1993; Uhde, Cortese, & Vedeniapin, 2009).

Primary Hypersomnia

Insomnia involves not getting enough sleep (the prefix *in* means "lacking" or "without"), and **hypersomnia** is a problem of sleeping too much (*hyper* means "in great amount" or "abnormal excess"). Many people who sleep all night find themselves falling asleep several times the next day. Consider the case of Ann.

ANN | *Sleeping in Public*

Ann, a college student, came to my office to discuss her progress in class. We talked about several questions that she had gotten wrong on the last exam, and as she was about to leave she said that she never fell asleep during my class. This seemed like faint praise, but I thanked her for the feedback. "No," she said, "you don't understand. I usually fall asleep in all of my classes, but not in yours." Again, I didn't quite understand what she was trying to tell me and joked that she must pick her professors more carefully. She laughed. "That's probably true. But I also have this problem with sleeping too much."

As we talked more seriously, Ann told me that excessive sleeping had been a problem since her teenage years. In situations that were monotonous or boring, or when she couldn't be active, she fell asleep. This could happen several times a day, depending on what she was doing. Recently, large lecture classes had become a problem unless the lecturer was particularly interesting or animated. Watching television and driving long distances were also problematic.

Ann reported that her father had a similar problem. He had recently been diagnosed with *narcolepsy* (which we discuss next) and was now getting help at a clinic. Both she and her brother had been diagnosed with hypersomnia. Ann had been prescribed Ritalin (a stimulant medication) about four years ago and said that it was only somewhat effective in keeping her awake during the day. She said the drug helped reduce the sleep attacks but did not eliminate them altogether.

The *DSM-IV-TR* diagnostic criteria for hypersomnia include not only the excessive sleepiness that Ann described but also the subjective impression of this problem (American Psychiatric Association, 2000a; see DSM Table 8.4). Remember that whether insomnia is a problem depends on how it affects each person individually. Ann found her disorder very disruptive because it interfered with her driving and paying attention in class. Hypersomnia caused her to be less successful academically and also upset her personally, both of which are defining features of this disorder. She slept approximately eight hours each night, so her daytime sleepiness couldn't be attributed to insufficient sleep.

Several factors that can cause excessive sleepiness would not be considered hypersomnia. For example, people with insomnia (who get inadequate amounts of sleep) often report being tired during the day. In contrast, people with hypersomnia sleep through the night and appear rested upon awakening but still complain of being excessively tired throughout the day. Another sleep problem that can cause a similar excessive sleepiness is a breathing-related sleep disorder called **sleep apnea**. People with this problem have difficulty breathing at night. They often snore loudly, pause between breaths, and wake in the morning with a dry mouth and headache. In identifying hypersomnia, you need to rule out insomnia, sleep apnea,

DSM-IV-TR | Table 8.4 Criteria for Primary Hypersomnia

A. The predominant complaint is excessive sleepiness for at least one month (or less if recurrent) as evidenced by either prolonged sleep episodes or daytime sleep episodes that occur almost daily.

B. The excessive sleepiness causes clinically significant distress or impairment in social, occupational, or other important areas of functioning.

C. The excessive sleepiness is not better accounted for by insomnia and does not occur exclusively during the course of another sleep disorder (e.g., narcolepsy, breathing-related sleep disorder, circadian rhythm sleep disorder, or a parasomnia) and cannot be accounted for by an inadequate amount of sleep.

D. The disturbance does not occur exclusively during the course of another mental disorder.

E. The disturbance is not due to the direct physiological effects of a substance (e.g., a drug of abuse, a medication) or a general medical condition.

Specify if:

Recurrent: if there are periods of excessive sleepiness that last at least three days occurring several times a year for at least two years.

Source: Reprinted with permission from the *Diagnostic and Statistical Manual of Mental Disorders*, Fourth Edition, Text Revision, (Copyright © 2000). American Psychiatric Association.

or other reasons for sleepiness during the day (American Psychiatric Association, 2000a).

We are just beginning to understand the nature of hypersomnia, so relatively little research has been done on its causes. Genetic influences seem to be involved in a portion of cases, with individuals having an increased likelihood of having certain genetic factors (Buysse, Strollo, Black, Zee, & Winkelman, 2008). A significant subgroup of people diagnosed with hypersomnia previously were exposed to a viral infection such as mononucleosis, hepatitis, and viral pneumonia, which suggests there may be more than one cause (Hirshkowitz, Seplowitz, & Sharafkhaneh, 2009).

Narcolepsy

Ann described her father as having **narcolepsy**, a different form of the sleeping problem she and her brother shared (Bassetti & Aldrich, 1996). In addition to daytime sleepiness, people with narcolepsy experience *cataplexy*, a sudden loss of muscle tone (see DSM Table 8.5). Cataplexy occurs while the person is awake, and it can range from slight weakness in the facial muscles to complete physical collapse. Cataplexy lasts from several seconds to several minutes; it is usually preceded by strong emotion such as anger or happiness. Imagine that while cheering for your favourite team, you suddenly fall asleep, or while arguing with a friend, you collapse to the floor in a sound sleep!

Cataplexy appears to result from a sudden onset of REM sleep. Instead of falling asleep normally and going through the four non-rapid eye movement (NREM) sleep stages (i.e., Stages 1 to 4, discussed previously) that typically precede REM sleep, people with narcolepsy periodically progress right to this dream sleep stage almost directly from the state of being awake. One outcome of REM sleep is the inhibition of input to the muscles, and this seems to be the process that leads to cataplexy.

Two other characteristics distinguish people who have narcolepsy (American Sleep Disorders Association, 1990), both of which were discussed in Chapter 5 in the context of Newfoundlanders' experience of the "Old Hag" and African and Caribbean people's experience of being "ridden by the witch." Specifically, people with narcolepsy commonly report *sleep paralysis* and *hypnagogic hallucinations*. Sleep paralysis refers to a brief period after awakening when the person can't move or speak that is often frightening to those who go through it. Hypnagogic hallucinations are vivid experiences that begin at the start of sleep and are said to be unbelievably realistic because they include not only visual aspects but also touch, hearing, and even the sensation of body movement. Examples of hypnagogic hallucinations, which, like sleep paralysis, can be quite terrifying, include the vivid illusion of being caught in a fire or flying

through the air. Narcolepsy is relatively rare, occurring in 0.03 percent to 0.16 percent of the population, with the numbers approximately equal among males and females. The problems associated with narcolepsy usually are first seen during the teenage years. Fortunately, the cataplexy, hypnagogic hallucinations, and sleep paralysis often decrease in frequency over time, although sleepiness during the day does not seem to diminish with age.

Sleep paralysis and hypnagogic hallucinations may serve a role in explaining a most unusual phenomenon—UFO experiences. Each year numerous people report sighting unidentified flying objects—UFOs—and some even tell of visiting with inhabitants of other planets (Sheaffer, 1986). A group of scientists led by the late Nicholas Spanos, whose research was first discussed in Chapter 6, examined people who had had such experiences, separating them into those who had nonintense experiences (seeing only lights and shapes in the sky) and those with intense experiences (seeing and communicating with aliens; Spanos, Cross, Dickson, & DuBreuil, 1993). They found that a majority of the reported UFO incidents occurred at night, and that 60 percent of the intense UFO stories were associated with sleep episodes. Specifically, the reports of these intense accounts were often described in ways that resembled accounts of people experiencing a frightening episode of sleep paralysis and hypnagogic hallucination, as illustrated by the following account:

> I was lying in bed facing the wall, and suddenly my heart started to race. I could feel the presence of three entities standing beside me. I was unable to move my body but could move my eyes. One of the entities, a male, was laughing at me, not verbally but with his mind. He made me feel stupid. He told me telepathically, "Don't you know by now that you can't do anything unless we let you?" (Spanos et al., 1993, p. 627)

Specific genetic models of narcolepsy are now being developed (Tafti, 2009). Previous research with Doberman pinschers and Labrador retrievers, who also inherit this disorder, suggests that narcolepsy is associated with a cluster of genes on chromosome 6, and it may be an autosomal recessive trait. Advances in understanding the etiology and treatment of such disorders can be credited to the help of "man's best friend."

Breathing-Related Sleep Disorders

For some people, sleepiness during the day or disrupted sleep at night has a physical origin, namely, problems with breathing while asleep. In the *DSM-IV-TR* these problems are diagnosed as **breathing-related sleep disorder**s (see DSM Table 8.6). People whose breathing is interrupted during their sleep experience numerous brief arousals throughout the night and do not feel rested even after eight or nine hours asleep (Hirshkowitz et al., 2009). For all of us, the muscles in the upper airway relax during sleep, constricting the passageway somewhat and making breathing a little more difficult. For some, unfortunately, breathing is constricted a great deal and may be very laboured (*hypoventilation*) or, in the extreme, there may be short periods (10 to 30 seconds) when they stop breathing

▲ Excessive sleepiness can be very disruptive.

© Spencer Grant/Photo Edit

DSM-IV-TR	**Table 8.6** Criteria for Breathing-Related Sleep Disorder

A. Sleep disruption, leading to excessive sleepiness or insomnia, which is judged to be due to a sleep-related breathing condition (e.g., obstructive or central sleep apnea syndrome or central alveolar hypoventilation syndrome).

B. The disruption is not better accounted for by another mental disorder and is not due to the direct physiological effects of a substance (e.g., a drug of abuse, a medication) or another general medical condition (other than a breathing-related disorder).

Source: Reprinted with permission from the *Diagnostic and Statistical Manual of Mental Disorders,* Fourth Edition, Text Revision, (Copyright © 2000). American Psychiatric Association.

altogether, called *sleep apnea*. Often the affected person is only minimally aware of breathing difficulties and doesn't attribute the sleep problems to the breathing. However, a bed partner usually notices loud snoring (which is one sign of this problem) or will have noticed frightening episodes of interrupted breathing. Other signs that a person has breathing difficulties are heavy sweating during the night, morning headaches, and episodes of falling asleep during the day (*sleep attacks*) with no resulting feeling of being rested (Hauri, 1982). As noted by Charles George at the University of Western Ontario and his colleagues, sleep apnea is associated with an increased number of motor vehicle accidents (Hartenbaum et al., 2006), likely due to these associated sleep attacks.

There are three types of apnea, each with different causes, daytime complaints, and treatment: obstructive, central, and mixed sleep apnea. *Obstructive sleep apnea* occurs when airflow stops despite continued activity by the respiratory system (Abad & Guilleminault, 2009). In some people, the airway is too narrow; in others, some abnormality or damage interferes with the ongoing effort to breathe. Everyone in a group of people with obstructive sleep apnea reported snoring at night (Guilleminault, 1989). Obesity is sometimes associated with this problem, as is increasing age. Some work now suggests that the use of MDMA (ecstasy) can lead to obstructive apnea even in young and otherwise healthy adults (McCann, Sgambati, Schwartz, & Ricaurte, 2009). Obstructive sleep apnea is most common in males and is thought to occur in 10 percent to 20 percent of the population (Jennum & Riha, 2009).

The second type of apnea, *central sleep apnea,* involves the complete cessation of respiratory activity for brief periods and is often associated with certain central nervous system disorders, such as cerebral vascular disease, head trauma, and degenerative disorders (Buysse et al., 2008). Unlike people with obstructive sleep apnea, those with central sleep apnea wake up frequently during the night but they tend not to report excessive daytime sleepiness and often are not aware of having a serious breathing problem. Because of the lack of daytime symptoms, people tend not to seek treatment, so we know relatively little about this disorder's prevalence or course. The third breathing disorder, *mixed sleep apnea,* is a combination of both obstructive and central sleep apneas. All these breathing difficulties interrupt sleep and result in symptoms similar to those of insomnia.

Concept Check | 8.3

Check your understanding of sleep disorders. Match the following descriptions of sleeping problems with the correct term: (a) cataplexy, (b) hypersomnia, (c) insomnia, (d) sleep apnea, and (e) sleep paralysis.

1. Jing-Mei averages only three to four hours of sleep per night. She has trouble functioning at work and occasionally falls asleep while driving. _____

2. It seems as if all Fred ever does is sleep. He averages 12 hours per night and takes at least two naps every day. _____

3. Sometimes when Trudy awakens, she cannot move or speak. This is terrifying. _____

4. Torben sometimes experiences sudden loss of muscle tone in his arms when he is under extreme stress. It usually lasts only a couple of minutes. _____

5. Susan's husband is extremely overweight. He snores every night and often wakes up exhausted as though he never slept. Susan suspects that he may have _____ and makes an appointment at the local clinic.

Circadian Rhythm Sleep Disorders

"Spring forward; fall back": Many Canadians use this mnemonic device to remind themselves to turn the clocks ahead one hour in the spring and back again one hour in the fall. Most of us consider the shift to daylight savings time a minor inconvenience and are thus surprised to see how disruptive this time change can be. For at least a day or two, we may be sleepy during the day and have difficulty falling asleep at night, almost as if we had jet lag. The difficulty has to do with how our biological clocks adjust to this change in time. Convention says to go to sleep at this new time while our brains are saying something different. If the struggle continues for any length of time, you may have what is called a **circadian rhythm sleep disorder**. This disorder is characterized by disturbed sleep (either insomnia or excessive sleepiness during the day) brought on by the brain's inability to synchronize its sleep patterns with the current patterns of day and night.

In the 1960s, German and French scientists identified several bodily rhythms that seem to persist without cues from the environment—rhythms that are self-regulated (Aschoff & Wever, 1962; Siffre, 1964). Because these rhythms don't exactly match our 24-hour day, they are called "circadian" (from *circa* meaning "about" and *dian* meaning "day"). If our circadian rhythms don't match the 24-hour day, why isn't our sleep completely disrupted over time?

Fortunately, our brains have a mechanism that keeps us in sync with the outside world. As noted by Michael Antle at the University of Calgary, our biological clock is in the *suprachiasmatic nucleus* in the hypothalamus (Antle & Silver, 2005). Connected to the suprachiasmatic nucleus is a pathway that comes from our eyes. The light we see in the morning and the decreasing light at night signal the brain to reset the biological clock each day (see also Coren, 1996). Unfortunately, some people have trouble sleeping when they want to because of problems with their circadian rhythms, since sleep onset is closely related to circadian rhythms (Mistlberger & Rusak, 2005). The causes may be outside the person (e.g., crossing several time zones in a short amount of time) or internal.

Not being synchronized with the normal sleep-wake cycles causes people to be interrupted when they do try to sleep, and to be tired during the day. There are several different types of circadian rhythm sleep disorders. *Jet lag type* is, as its name implies, caused by rapidly crossing multiple time zones (Buysse et al., 2008). People with jet lag usually report difficulty going to sleep at the proper time and feeling fatigued during the day. Interestingly, older people, introverts (loners), and early risers (morning people) are most likely to be negatively affected by these time zone changes (Gillin, 1993). Research with mice suggests that the effects of jet lag can be quite serious—at least among older adults. When older mice were exposed to repeated artificial jet lag, a significant number of them lived shorter lives (Davidson et al., 2006). *Shift-work-type* sleep problems are associated with work schedules (Åkerstedt & Wright Jr., 2009). Many people, such as hospital employees, police, or emergency personnel, work at night or must work irregular hours; as a result, they may have problems sleeping or experience excessive sleepiness during waking hours. Unfortunately, the problems of working (and thus staying awake) at unusual times can go beyond sleep and may contribute to cardiovascular disease, ulcers, and breast cancer in women (Richardson, 2006). Research suggests that people with circadian rhythm disorders are at greater risk of having one or more personality disorders (Dagan, Dela, Omer, Hallis, & Dar, 1996). Almost two-thirds of all workers on rotating shifts complain of poor sleep (Neylan, Reynolds, & Kupfer, 2003).

In contrast with jet lag and shift-work sleep-related problems, which have external causes such as long-distance travel and job selection, several circadian rhythm sleep problems seem to arise from within the person experiencing the problems. Extreme night owls, people who stay up late and sleep late, may have a problem known as *delayed sleep phase type*. Sleep is delayed or later than normal bedtime. At the other end of the extreme, people with an advanced sleep phase type of circadian rhythm disorder are "early to bed and early to rise." Here, sleep is advanced or earlier than normal bedtime. In part because of our general lack of knowledge about the latter, the *DSM-IV-TR* does not include the advanced sleep phase type as a circadian rhythm sleep disorder (see DSM Table 8.7).

Research on why our sleep rhythms are disrupted is advancing quickly, and we are now beginning to understand the circadian rhythm process. Scientists believe the hormone *melatonin* contributes to the setting of our biological clocks that tell us when to sleep. This hormone is produced by the pineal gland, in the centre of the brain. Melatonin (don't confuse this with *melanin,* the chemical that determines skin colour) has been nicknamed the "Dracula hormone" because its production is

DSM-IV-TR	**Table 8.7** Criteria for Circadian Rhythm Sleep Disorder (Sleep-Wake Schedule Disorder)

A. A persistent or recurrent pattern of sleep disruption leading to excessive sleepiness or insomnia that is due to a mismatch between the sleep-wake schedule required by a person's environment and his or her circadian sleep-wake pattern.

B. The sleep disturbance causes clinically significant distress or impairment in social, occupational, or other important areas of functioning.

C. The disturbance does not occur exclusively during the course of another sleep disorder or other mental disorder.

D. The disturbance is not due to the direct physiological effects of a substance (e.g., a drug of abuse, a medication) or a general medical condition.

Specify type:

Delayed sleep phase type: A persistent pattern of late sleep onset and late awakening times, with an inability to fall asleep and awaken at a desired earlier time

Jet lag type: Sleepiness and alertness that occur at an inappropriate time of day relative to local time, occurring after repeated travel across more than one time zone

Shift work type: Insomnia during major sleep period or excessive sleepiness during major awake period associated with night shift work or frequently changing shift work

Unspecified Type

Source: Reprinted with permission from the *Diagnostic and Statistical Manual of Mental Disorders,* Fourth Edition, Text Revision, (Copyright © 2000). American Psychiatric Association.

stimulated by darkness and ceases in daylight. When our eyes see it is nighttime, this information is passed on to the pineal gland, which, in turn, begins producing melatonin. Researchers believe that both light and melatonin help set the biological clock. Thus, this hormone may help us treat some of the sleep problems people experience. For example, melatonin may be used as a treatment for people who experience severe jet lag and other sleep problems associated with circadian rhythm disruption (Sack & Lewy, 1993).

Concept Check 8.4

The term *dyssomnia* refers to conditions in which there are disturbances in the amount, quality, and timing of sleep. There are a number of different types of dyssomnia. Match the type with the situations given: (a) primary insomnia, (b) primary hypersomnia, (c) narcolepsy, (d) breathing-related sleep disorder, and (e) circadian rhythm sleep disorder.

1. Suzy can hardly make it through a full day of work if she doesn't take a nap during her lunch hour. No matter how early she goes to bed in the evening, she still sleeps as late as she possibly can in the morning.

(continued)

2. Jerod wakes up several times each evening because he feels he is about to hyperventilate. He can't seem to get enough air, and often his wife will wake him to tell him to quit snoring. _____

3. Charlie has had considerable trouble sleeping since he started a new job that requires him to change shifts every three weeks. Sometimes he works during the day and sleeps at night, and other times he works at night and sleeps during the day. _____

4. Rikke has problems staying awake throughout the day. Even while talking on the phone or riding the bus across town, she often loses muscle tone and falls asleep for a while. _____

5. Ruhan can rarely fall asleep at a decent hour anymore. Every evening he reads, or drinks warm milk, or watches television until he can sleep. When he does fall asleep, he wakes up two or three times during the night, and each time it takes him a while to fall into a deep sleep again. _____

Treatment of Dyssomnias

When we can't fall asleep or we awaken frequently, or when sleep does not restore our energy and vitality, we need help. Several biological and psychological interventions have been designed and evaluated to help people regain the benefits of normal sleep.

Medical Treatments

Perhaps the most common treatments for insomnia are medical. According to a Statistics Canada report, based on the 2002 Canadian Community Health Survey, 13.4 percent of Canadians (or 3.3 million people) suffer from insomnia. Of those people suffering from insomnia, 29 percent use sleep medications: 23 percent use prescribed sleep medications and 6 percent use over-the-counter sleep aids. Thus, an estimated 4 percent of Canadians in the general population use medications for insomnia (Tjepkema, 2005). People who complain of insomnia to a medical professional are likely prescribed one of several benzodiazepine medications, which include short-acting drugs such as triazolam (Halcion) and long-acting drugs such as flurazepam (Dalmane). Short-acting drugs (those that cause only brief drowsiness) are preferred because the long-acting drugs sometimes do not stop working by morning, and people report more daytime sleepiness. The long-acting benzodiazepines are sometimes preferred when negative effects such as daytime anxiety are observed in people taking the short-acting drugs (Neubauer, 2009). Newer medications, such as those that work directly with the melatonin system (e.g., ramelteon [Rozerem]), are also being developed to help people fall and stay asleep. People over the age of 65 are most likely to use medication to help them sleep. A study by Keith Brownlee and his colleagues at Lakehead University showed that older patients were significantly more likely than younger patients to be prescribed benzodiazepines for insomnia (Brownlee et al., 2003). Benzodiazepine prescriptions for insomnia are a

particularly important problem among elderly people in nursing homes (Voyer, Verreault, Mengue, & Morin, 2006).

There are several drawbacks to medical treatments for insomnia (Pagel, 2006). First, benzodiazepine medications can cause excessive sleepiness. Second, people can easily become dependent on them and rather easily misuse them, deliberately or not. Third, these medications are meant for short-term treatment and are not recommended for use longer than four weeks. Longer use can cause dependence and rebound insomnia. A newer concern for some medications (e.g., Ambien) is that they may increase the likelihood of sleepwalking-related problems, such as sleep-related eating disorder (Morgenthaler & Silber, 2002). Therefore, although medications may be helpful for sleep problems that will correct themselves in a short period (e.g., insomnia because of anxiety related to hospitalization), they are not intended for long-term chronic problems.

To help people with hypersomnia or narcolepsy, physicians usually prescribe a stimulant such as methylphenidate (Ritalin, the medication Ann was taking) or modafinil (Nevsimalova, 2009). Cataplexy, or loss of muscle tone, can be treated with antidepressant medication, not because people with narcolepsy are depressed but because antidepressants suppress REM (or dream) sleep. Also, gamma-hydroxybutyrate (GHB) is the first medication specifically approved to treat cataplexy. (This also is one of the "date rape" drugs that we discuss in Chapter 11.) Cataplexy seems to be related to the sudden onset of REM sleep; therefore, the antidepressant medication can be helpful in reducing these attacks.

Treatment of breathing-related sleep disorders focuses on helping the person breathe better during sleep. For some, this means recommending weight loss. In some people who are obese, the neck's soft tissue compresses the airways. Unfortunately, this treatment has not proven to be very successful for breathing-related sleep disorders (Guilleminault & Dement, 1988). For mild or moderate cases of obstructive sleep apnea, treatment can involve medications including those that help stimulate respiration (e.g., medroxyprogesterone) or the tricyclic antidepressants, which are thought to act on the locus coeruleus, which affects REM sleep such that the respiratory muscles do not relax as much (Kryger, 2000).

The gold standard for the treatment of obstructive sleep apnea involves the use of a mechanical device—called the continuous positive air pressure (CPAP) machine—that improves breathing. Patients wear a mask that provides slightly pressurized air during sleep and it helps them breathe more normally throughout the night. Unfortunately, many people have difficulty using the device because of issues of comfort and some even experience a form of claustrophobia. To assist these individuals, a variety of strategies are tried, including the use of psychological interventions including desensitization for claustrophobia, patient and partner education, and attendance of support groups (Abad & Guilleminault, 2009). Severe breathing problems may require surgery to help remove blockages in parts of the airways.

An interesting treatment for people with mild apnea is being explored by researchers in collaboration with a Swiss didgeridoo instructor. A didgeridoo is a long instrument constructed from tree limbs hollowed out by termites. The instructor observed that people who practised using this wind instrument had less daytime sleepiness. In one of a series of treatment studies, evidence points to the effectiveness of several months of daily practice using this instrument in improving the sleep of people with interrupted breathing (Puhan et al., 2006).

Environmental Treatments

Because medication as a primary treatment isn't usually recommended (Doghramji, 2000; Roehrs & Roth, 2000), other ways of getting people back in step with their sleep rhythms are usually tried. One general principle for treating circadian rhythm disorders is that *phase delays* (moving the bedtime later) are easier than *phase advances* (moving bedtime earlier). Scheduling shift changes in a clockwise direction (going from day to evening schedule) seems to help workers adjust better. People can best readjust their sleep patterns by going to bed several hours later each night, until bedtime is at the desired hour (Buysse et al., 2008). A drawback of this approach is that it requires the person to sleep during the day for several days, which is obviously difficult for people with regularly scheduled responsibilities.

Another recent effort to help people with sleep problems involves using *bright light* to trick the brain into readjusting the biological clock. (In Chapter 7 we described the pioneering work of Raymond Lam with light therapy for seasonal affective disorder.) Very bright light may help people with circadian rhythm problems readjust their sleep patterns (Bjorvatn & Pallesen, 2009). People typically sit in front of a bank of fluorescent lamps that generate light greater than 2500 lux, an amount significantly different from normal indoor light (250 lux). Several hours of exposure to this bright light have successfully reset the circadian rhythms of a number of individuals (Czeisler & Allan, 1989). Although this type of treatment is still new, it provides some hope for people with sleep problems.

Psychological Treatments

As you can imagine, the limitations of using drugs to help people sleep better has led to the development of psychological treatments. Table 8.3 lists and briefly describes some of the psychological approaches to insomnia.

▲ Bright light therapy can help people with circadian rhythm sleep disorders readjust their sleep patterns.

Pascal Goetgheluck/Science Photo Library

TABLE 8.3 Some Psychological Treatments for Insomnia

Sleep Treatment	Description
Cognitive	This approach focuses on changing the sleepers' unrealistic expectations and beliefs about sleep ("I must have eight hours of sleep each night"; "If I get less than eight hours of sleep it will make me ill"). The therapist attempts to alter beliefs and attitudes about sleeping by providing information on topics such as normal amounts of sleep and a person's ability to compensate for lost sleep.
Cognitive relaxation	Because some people become anxious when they have difficulty sleeping, this approach uses meditation or imagery to help with relaxation at bedtime or after a night of waking.
Graduated extinction	Used for children who have tantrums at bedtime or wake up crying at night, this treatment instructs the parent to check on the child after progressively longer periods of time, until the child falls asleep on his or her own.
Paradoxical intention	This technique involves instructing individuals in the opposite behaviour from the desired outcome. Telling poor sleepers to lie in bed and try to stay awake as long as they can is used to try to relieve the performance anxiety surrounding efforts to try to fall asleep.
Progressive relaxation	This technique involves relaxing the muscles of the body in an effort to introduce drowsiness.

Given the links of anxiety to insomnia, Viens, De Koninck, Mercier, St-Onge, and Lorrain (2003) from the University of Ottawa compared progressive relaxation with a treatment they referred to as anxiety management training (which basically combined progressive relaxation with cognitive relaxation techniques). Both groups were able to get to sleep more quickly following therapy, as shown in ■ Figure 8.8. The top panel shows declines in sleep onset latency according to patient self-report, and the bottom panel shows these same treatment-induced declines according to a hand-held clock device that more objectively assesses time to sleep onset. Furthermore, lab-based sleep evaluations showed that participants in both groups increased in slow-wave sleep and sleep satisfaction. Both groups also showed decreases in anxiety and depression. Finally, the treatments were equally effective (Viens et al., 2003).

Other research shows that some psychological treatments for insomnia may be more effective than others. For adult sleep problems, stimulus control may be recommended. People are instructed to use the bedroom only for sleeping and for sex and not for work or other anxiety-provoking activities (e.g., watching the news on television). The work of Charles Morin and colleagues suggests that *progressive relaxation or sleep hygiene* (changing daily habits that may interfere with sleep) alone may not be as effective as stimulus control alone for some people (Lacks & Morin, 1992).

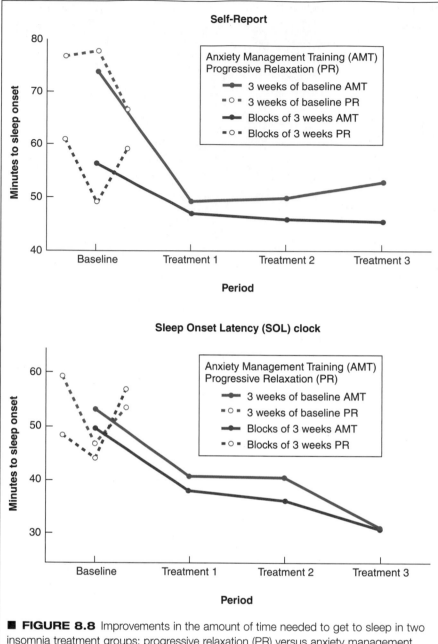

Self-Report

Sleep Onset Latency (SOL) clock

Legend (both panels):
Anxiety Management Training (AMT)
Progressive Relaxation (PR)
— ●— 3 weeks of baseline AMT
- ○ - 3 weeks of baseline PR
— ●— Blocks of 3 weeks AMT
- ○ - Blocks of 3 weeks PR

■ **FIGURE 8.8** Improvements in the amount of time needed to get to sleep in two insomnia treatment groups: progressive relaxation (PR) versus anxiety management training (AMT). The top panel shows self-report data and the bottom panel shows findings with a device that objectively monitors sleep onset latency.

Source: Viens, M., De Koninck, J., Mercier, P., St-Onge, M. & Lorrain, D. (2003). "Trait anxiety and sleep-onset insomnia: Evluation of treatment using anxiety management training." *Journal of Psychosomatic Research*, 54, 31–37.

Kathryn's sleep problems were addressed with several techniques. She was instructed to limit her time in bed to about four hours of sleep time (sleep restriction), about the amount of time she actually slept each night. The period was lengthened when she began to sleep through the night. Kathryn was also asked not to listen to the radio while in bed and to get out of bed if she couldn't fall asleep (stimulus control). Finally, therapy involved confronting her unrealistic expectations about how much sleep was enough for a person of her age (cognitive therapy; see Bélanger, Savard, & Morin, 2006). Within about three weeks of treatment, Kathryn was sleeping longer (six to seven hours per night as opposed to four to five hours previously) and had fewer

interruptions in her sleep. Also, she felt more refreshed in the morning and had more energy during the day.

Kathryn's results mirror those of studies by Charles Morin and his colleagues that find combined treatments to be effective in older adults with insomnia (e.g., Morin, Kowatch, Barry, & Walton, 1993). One such study, using a randomized placebo-control design, found that both medical and psychological approaches were effective in improving the sleep of older adults (Morin, Colecchi, Stone, Sood, & Brink, 1999). Over the long term, however, the psychological treatment was better able to maintain its effectiveness with this group (see also review by Morin & Wooten, 1996). Morin's more recent work has examined the effectiveness of sequential (CBT and medication) treatments for insomnia. Participants either received: (1) medication and then combined medication and CBT; (2) combined treatment and then CBT alone; or (3) CBT alone. For the first treatment group, significant improvements only appeared after the introduction of CBT, while in the other two groups improvement appeared near the beginning of treatment. The study also showed that the treatment involving combined treatment followed by CBT alone led to the best outcomes. These findings show that sleep improvement seems to be affected by the way in which medication and CBT are combined.

For young children, some of the cognitive treatments may not be possible. Instead, treatment often includes setting up bedtime routines such as a bath, followed by a parent reading a story, to help children go to sleep at night. Graduated extinction (described in Table 8.3) has been used with some success for bedtime problems as well as for waking up at night (Durand, 2008). Integrating both medical and behavioural treatments seems especially important for insomnia. Research suggests that short-term use of medication in combination with other types of interventions may prove to be a quick and lasting treatment for insomnia (Milby et al., 1993; Morin & Azrin, 1988).

Psychological treatment research for the other dyssomnias is virtually nonexistent. For the most part, counselling or support groups assist in managing the psychological and social effects of disturbed sleep, and they are especially helpful for people who experience feelings of low self-esteem and depression (Bootzin et al., 1993).

Preventing Sleep Disorders

Sleep professionals generally agree that a significant portion of the sleep problems people experience daily can be prevented by following a few steps during the day. Referred to as *sleep*

TABLE 8.4 Good Sleep Habits

Establish a set bedtime routine.
Develop a regular bedtime and a regular time to awaken.
Eliminate all foods and drinks that contain caffeine six hours before bedtime.
Limit any use of alcohol or tobacco.
Try drinking milk before bedtime.
Eat a balanced diet, limiting fat.
Go to bed only when sleepy and get out of bed if you are unable to fall asleep or back to sleep after 15 minutes.
Do not exercise or participate in vigorous activities in the hours before bedtime.
Do include a weekly program of exercise during the day.
Restrict activities in bed to those that help induce sleep.
Reduce noise and light in the bedroom.
Increase exposure to natural and bright light during the day.
Avoid extreme temperature changes in the bedroom (that is, too hot or too cold).

Source: From V. M. Durand (1998). *Sleep Better! A Guide to Improving Sleep for Children with Special Needs,* p. 60. Baltimore: Paul H. Brookes Publishing Co., adapted by permission.

DSM-IV-TR **Table 8.8** Criteria for Nightmare Disorder

A. Repeated awakenings from the major sleep period or naps with detailed recall of extended and extremely frightening dreams, usually involving threats to survival, security, or self-esteem. The awakenings generally occur during the second half of the sleep period.

B. On awakening from the frightening dreams, the person rapidly becomes oriented and alert (in contrast to the confusion and disorientation seen in sleep terror disorder and some forms of epilepsy).

C. The dream experience, or the sleep disturbance resulting from the awakening, causes significant distress or impairment in social, occupational, or other important areas of functioning.

D. The nightmares do not occur exclusively during the course of another mental disorder (e.g., a delirium, post-traumatic stress disorder) and are not due to the direct physiological effects of a substance (e.g., a drug of abuse, a medication) or a general medical condition.

Source: Reprinted with permission from the *Diagnostic and Statistical Manual of Mental Disorders,* Fourth Edition, Text Revision, (Copyright © 2000). American Psychiatric Association.

hygiene, these changes in lifestyle can be relatively simple to follow and can help avoid problems such as insomnia for some people (Gellis & Lichstein, 2009). Some sleep hygiene recommendations rely on allowing the brain's normal drive for sleep to take over, replacing the restrictions we place on our activities that interfere with sleep. For example, setting a regular time to go to sleep and awaken each day can help make falling asleep at night easier. Avoiding the use of caffeine and nicotine—which are both stimulants—can also help prevent problems such as nighttime awakening. Table 8.4 illustrates a number of the sleep hygiene steps recommended for preventing sleep problems. Although there is little controlled prospective research on preventing sleep disorders, practising good sleep hygiene appears to be among the most promising techniques available.

A few studies have investigated the value of educating parents about the sleep of their young children in an effort to prevent later difficulties. Adachi and colleagues (2009), for example, provided 10 minutes of group guidance and a simple educational booklet to the parents of four-month-old children. They followed up on these children three months later and found that, compared to a randomly selected control group of children, the ones whose parents received education about sleep experienced fewer sleep problems. Because so many children display disruptive sleep problems, this type of preventive effort could significantly improve the lives of many families.

Parasomnias

Have you ever been told that you walk in your sleep? Talk in your sleep? Have you ever had troublesome nightmares? Do you grind your teeth in your sleep? If you answered "yes" to one or more of these questions (and it's likely you did), you have experienced sleep problems in the category of parasomnia. Parasomnias are not problems with sleep itself but abnormal events that occur either during sleep or during that twilight time between sleeping and waking. Some of the events associated with parasomnia are not unusual if they happen while you are awake (walking to the kitchen to look into the refrigerator) but can be distressing if they take place while you are sleeping.

Parasomnias are of two types: those that occur during rapid eye movement (REM) sleep, and those that occur during non–rapid eye movement (NREM) sleep. As you might have guessed, **nightmares** occur during REM or dream sleep. The prevalence of nightmare disorder is unknown, but we do know that between 10 percent and 50 percent of children aged three to five years have nightmares that are severe enough to concern their parents. As many as 50 percent of adults experience occasional nightmares, while only 3 percent of young adults report frequent nightmares (*DSM-IV-TR*, American Psychiatric Association, 2000a). The research of Tore Nielsen, Philippe Stenstrom, and Ross Levin (2006) in Montréal indicates that women experience more frequent nightmares than men do. To qualify as a *DSM-IV-TR* nightmare disorder, these nightmares must be so distressful that they impair a person's ability to carry on normal activities (see DSM Table 8.8). Some researchers distinguish nightmares from *bad dreams* by whether or not you wake up as a result. Nightmares are defined as very disturbing dreams that awaken the sleeper; bad dreams are those that do not awaken the person experiencing them. According to Montréal researchers Antonio Zadra and Don Donderi (2000), university students report an average of 30 bad dreams and ten nightmares per year. Because nightmares are so common, you would expect that a great deal of research would have focused on their causes and treatment. Unfortunately, this is not so, and we still know little about why people have nightmares and how to treat them. Fortunately, they tend to decrease with age.

Sleep terrors, which most commonly afflict children, usually begin with a piercing scream. The child is extremely upset, often sweating, and frequently has a rapid heartbeat. On the surface, sleep terrors appear to resemble nightmares—the child cries and appears frightened—but they occur during NREM sleep and therefore are not caused by frightening dreams (see DSM Table 8.9). During sleep terrors children cannot be

▲ A nightmare is distressing for both child and parent.

easily awakened and comforted, as they can during a nightmare. Children do not remember sleep terrors, despite their often dramatic effect on the observer (Durand, 2008). Approximately 5 percent of children (more boys than girls) may experience sleep terrors; for adults, the prevalence rate is less than 1 percent (Buysse, Reynolds, & Kupfer, 1993). As with nightmares, we know relatively little about sleep terrors, although several theories have been proposed, including the possibility of a genetic component because the disorder tends to occur in families (Durand, 2008).

Treatment for sleep terrors usually begins with a recommendation to wait and see if they disappear on their own. If the problem is frequent or continues a long time, sometimes antidepressants (imipramine) or benzodiazepines are recommended, although their effectiveness has not yet been clearly demonstrated (Mindell, 1993). In an approach called *scheduled awakenings*, parents of children experiencing chronic sleep terrors are instructed to awaken their child briefly approximately 30 minutes before a typical episode. In a controlled study, this simple technique was shown to be successful in almost completely eliminating these disturbing events (Durand & Mindell, 1999).

It might surprise you to learn that **sleepwalking** (also called *somnambulism*) occurs during NREM sleep (Broughton, 2000). Thus, when people walk in their sleep they are probably not acting out a dream. This parasomnia typically occurs during the first few hours while a person is in the deep stages of sleep. The *DSM-IV-TR* criteria for sleepwalking require that the person leave the bed (see DSM Table 8.10). Because sleepwalking occurs during the deepest stages of sleep, waking someone during an episode is difficult; if the person is wakened, he or she typically will not remember what has happened. It is not true, however, that waking a sleepwalker is somehow dangerous.

Sleepwalking is primarily a childhood problem, although a small proportion of adults are affected. A relatively large number of children—from 15 percent to 30 percent—have at least one episode of sleepwalking, with about 2 percent reported to have multiple incidents (Thorpy & Glovinsky, 1987). For the most part, the course of sleepwalking is short, and few people over the age of 15 continue to exhibit this parasomnia. When sleepwalking occurs among adults, it is often associated with other psychological disorders (Kales, Soldatos, Caldwell, et al., 1980).

We do not yet clearly understand why some people sleepwalk, although factors such as extreme fatigue, previous sleep deprivation, the use of sedative or hypnotic drugs, and stress have been implicated (Shatkin & Ivanenko, 2009). On occasion,

DSM-IV-TR	**Table 8.9** Criteria for Sleep Terror Disorder

A. Recurrent episodes of abrupt awakening from sleep, usually occurring during the first third of the major sleep episode and beginning with a panicky scream.

B. Intense fear and signs of autonomic arousal, such as tachycardia, rapid breathing, and sweating, during each episode.

C. Relative unresponsiveness to efforts of others to comfort the person during the episode.

D. No detailed dream is recalled and there is amnesia for the episode.

E. The episodes cause clinically significant distress or impairment in social, occupational, or other important areas of functioning.

F. The disturbance is not due to the direct physiological effects of a substance (e.g., a drug of abuse, a medication) or a general medical condition.

DSM-IV-TR	**Table 8.10** Criteria for Sleepwalking Disorder

A. Repeated episodes of rising from bed during sleep and walking about, usually occurring during the first third of the major sleep episode.

B. While sleepwalking, the person has a blank, staring face, is relatively unresponsive to the efforts of others to communicate with him or her, and can be awakened only with great difficulty.

C. On awakening (either from the sleepwalking episode or the next morning), the person has amnesia for the episode.

D. Within several minutes after awakening from the sleepwalking episode, there is no impairment of mental activity or behaviour (although there may initially be a short period of confusion or disorientation).

E. The sleepwalking causes clinically significant distress or impairment in social, occupational, or other important areas of functioning.

F. The disturbance is not due to the direct physiological effects of a substance (e.g., a drug of abuse, a medication) or a general medical condition.

sleepwalking episodes have been associated with violent behaviour, including homicide and suicide (Cartwright, 2006). In one case in Toronto, a 23-year-old man, Kenneth Parks, drove to his in-laws' house, killed his mother-in-law, and attempted to kill his father-in-law. He was acquitted of the charges of murder, using sleepwalking as his legal defence (Broughton, Billings, & Cartwright, 1994). Such cases are controversial, although there is evidence for the legitimacy of some violent behaviour coinciding with sleepwalking episodes. There also seems to be a genetic component to sleepwalking, with a higher incidence observed among identical twins and within families (Broughton, 2000). A related disorder, *nocturnal eating syndrome,* is when individuals rise from their beds and eat although they are still asleep (Striegel-Moore et al., 2010). This problem may be more frequent than previously thought; it was found in almost 6 percent of individuals in one study who were referred because of insomnia complaints (Manni, Ratti, & Tartara, 1997; Winkelman, 2006).

Concept Check | 8.5

Diagnose the following sleep problems: (a) primary hypersomnia, (b) narcolepsy, (c) sleep terrors, and (d) primary insomnia.

1. Ashley wakes up screaming nearly every night. Her parents rush to comfort her, but she doesn't respond. Her heart rate is elevated during these episodes, and her pyjamas are soaked in sweat. The next day, Ashley has no memory of the experience. _____

2. Rick has been having difficulty falling asleep at night for a month. He also feels exhausted in the morning even after nights when he thought he had slept well. He is chronically tired at work, and his supervisors have reprimanded him for inattention. _____

3. Marco sleeps 10 to 12 hours per night yet still feels sleepy at work after dragging himself out of bed. He finds himself napping on his lunch hour. He has been sleeping excessively for two months. _____

Marya Hornbacher begins her memoir, "It was a landmark event: We were having lunch. We were playing normal."

Those who believe that eating lunch is "playing normal" will recognize Marya's story. At age five, contrary to all appearances, she believed that she was fat. At age nine, she was bingeing and purging while watching *Brady Bunch* reruns. Hornbacher recounts in (sometimes grisly) detail the journey from self-conscious little girl to full-grown woman bent on self-inflicted starvation. At her all-time low, she weighs 24 kilograms and is still not sure that she's thin enough.

How does she get to that point? Hornbacher traces the influence her parents had on her self-image. She also recognizes the pressures of her peers, of society, and the limitations of her own personality. She points out that "junior high is an unpleasant experience for many people" (p. 65)—and certainly most people can relate to that. In fact, many young women can probably relate to some of the feelings of self-loathing in this memoir. But most do not hate their bodies with such ferocity that they willingly commit to starve themselves. When a schoolmate tells the school counsellor that Hornbacher is throwing up, "As mad as I said I was at the time, I had never been so grateful for anything in my life. . . . I was worth giving a shit about" (p. 81).

She describes in wrenching detail the cult-like, lonely world of eating disorders in which nearly every waking thought centres on food, exercise, and weight loss. She views the prospect of attending boarding schools with questions like, "How will I throw up without offending? How will I do my callisthenics at night while reading a book?" (p. 101).

For Hornbacher, the underlying issue is one of self-control; she wants to limit her needs. "I distinctly did not want to be seen as bulimic. I wanted to be an anorectic. . . . a person whose passions were ascetic rather than hedonistic. . . . " (p. 107). She believes the issue of self-control resonates most with women: "We claim a loss of appetite, a most-sacred aphysicality" (p. 118) and "we turn skeletons into goddesses and look to them as if they might teach us how to not-need" (p. 119).

Hornbacher is very intelligent and has done a lot of research on anorexia and bulimia. Her narrative is peppered with facts about eating disorders and the people who experience them. She knows, for example, the telltale signs of bulimia. She has included a comprehensive bibliography at the end of this book. Yet she still has an eating disorder herself. In the final pages, to bring the reader up to speed on her present-day struggles, she tells of running on the treadmill for an hour and a half, "until my bad knee feels like it's exploding with every step, but I have lost weight!" (p. 288). Although she doesn't give us the happy ending we're hoping for, she does provide a realistic glimpse into the struggle with food that she still faces every day.

In the *DSM-IV-TR,* eating disorders for the most part are considered to be mutually exclusive. For example, according to *DSM-IV* guidelines, a person cannot meet criteria for both anorexia and bulimia. But investigators working in this area have discovered that features of the various eating disorders overlap considerably (Fairburn et al., 2008). Furthermore, a large portion of patients, perhaps as many as 50 percent or more, who meet criteria for a clinically severe eating disorder do not meet criteria for anorexia or bulimia and are diagnosed with "eating disorder not otherwise specified" (eating disorder NOS) (Fairburn & Bohn, 2005). As described earlier in the chapter, some of these patients would now meet criteria for "binge eating disorder," which is likely to be included as a full-fledged diagnostic category in the *DSM-5.* A schematic representation of the relationship of anorexia, bulimia, and eating disorder NOS is presented in ■ Figure 8.9. The figure's two inner circles, representing anorexia and bulimia, overlap; this overlapping area would include those people who would meet criteria for both disorders, if the *DSM-IV* allowed such overlap.

As noted in Figure 8.6 (p. 285), these eating disorders have very similar causal influences including similar inherited biological vulnerabilities, similar social influences (primarily cultural influences glorifying thinness), and a strong family influence toward perfectionism in all things. Finally, all eating disorders seem to share anxiety focused on one's appearance and presentation to others as well as distorted body image. Now, Christopher Fairburn and associates have proposed a transdiagnostic

treatment protocol designed to be applicable across several eating disorder diagnoses (Fairburn, 2008; Fairburn, Cooper, Doll, et al., 2009). In this treatment protocol, the essential components of cognitive-behavioural therapy (CBT) directed at causal factors common to all eating disorders are targeted in an integrated way. (Individuals with anorexia and a very low weight who would need inpatient treatment would be excluded until their weight was restored to an adequate level when they could then benefit from the program.) Thus, the principal focus of this protocol is on the distorted evaluation of body shape and weight, and maladaptive attempts to control weight in the form of strict dieting, possibly accompanied by binge eating, and methods to compensate for overeating such as purging, laxative misuse, and so on. Because additional psychological problems, including difficulty tolerating negative moods, tendencies to perfectionism, accompanying low self-esteem, and interpersonal difficulties commonly accompany eating disorders, Fairburn and colleagues developed what they called an "enhanced treatment" (CBT-E) that also addresses these factors (Fairburn, Cooper, Shafran, Bohn, et al., 2008). In a landmark study (Fairburn,

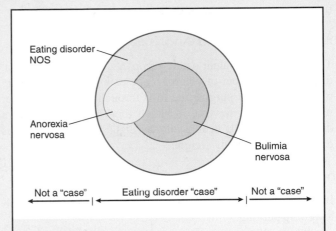

■ **FIGURE 8.9** Schematic representation of the relationship among common eating disorders.
Source: From Fairburn and Bahn (2005).

Cooper, Doll, et al., 2009), this CBT-E protocol was evaluated against a more focused transdiagnostic protocol dealing only with features specific to the eating disorders. Findings indicated that, indeed, the enhanced protocol was more effective than the focused protocol in treating eating disorders and accompanying complex psychopathology—including perfectionism and interpersonal difficulties—whereas the focused protocol was all that was required for any of the eating disorders without complex psychopathology. This transdiagnostic protocol has already been adopted widely in eating disorder clinics around the world and represents yet another example of the trend away from dealing with discrete, narrowly defined diagnostic categories in favour of more broad-based dimensions of psychopathology within a spectrum of related disorders.

Summary

- The prevalence of eating disorders has increased rapidly over the last half century. As a result, they are included for the first time as a separate group of disorders in the *DSM-IV-TR*.

Bulimia Nervosa and Anorexia Nervosa

- There are two prevalent eating disorders. In bulimia nervosa, dieting results in out-of-control binge-eating episodes that are often followed by purging the food through vomiting or other means. Anorexia nervosa, in which food intake is cut down dramatically, results in substantial weight loss and sometimes dangerously low body weight.

Binge-Eating Disorder

- In binge-eating disorder, a pattern of binge eating is *not* followed by purging.

Statistics and Course for Eating Disorders

- Bulimia nervosa and anorexia nervosa are largely confined to young, middle- to upper-class women in Western cultures who are pursuing a thin body shape that is culturally mandated and biologically inappropriate, making it extremely difficult to achieve.
- Without treatment, eating disorders become chronic and can, on occasion, result in death.

Causes

- In addition to sociocultural pressures, causal factors include possible biological and genetic vulnerabilities (the disorders tend to run in families), psychological factors (low self-esteem), social anxiety (fears of rejection), and distorted body image (relatively normal-weight individuals view themselves as fat and ugly).

Treatment

- Several psychosocial treatments are effective, including cognitive-behavioural approaches combined with family therapy and interpersonal psychotherapy. Drug treatments are less effective at the current time.

Sleep Disorders

- Sleep disorders are highly prevalent in the general population and are of two types: dyssomnias (disturbances of sleep) and parasomnias (abnormal events such as nightmares and sleep-walking that occur during sleep).
- Of the dyssomnias, the most common disorder, primary insomnia, involves the inability to initiate sleep, problems maintaining sleep, or failure to feel refreshed after a full night's sleep. Other dyssomnias include primary hypersomnia (excessive sleep), narcolepsy (sudden and irresistible sleep attacks), circadian rhythm sleep disorders (sleepiness or insomnia caused by the body's inability to synchronize its sleep patterns with day and night), and breathing-related sleep disorders (disruptions that have a physical origin, such as sleep apnea, that leads to excessive sleepiness or insomnia).
- The formal assessment of sleep disorders, a polysomnographic (PSG) evaluation, is typically done by monitoring the heart, muscles, respiration, brain waves, and other functions of a sleeping client in the lab. In addition to such monitoring, it is helpful to determine the individual's sleep efficiency (SE), a percentage based on the time the individual *actually* sleeps as opposed to time spent in bed trying to sleep.
- Benzodiazepine medications have been helpful for short-term treatment of many of the dyssomnias, but they must be used carefully, or they might cause rebound insomnia, a withdrawal experience that can cause worse sleep problems after the medication is stopped. Any long-term treatment of sleep problems should include psychological interventions such as stimulus control and sleep hygiene.
- Parasomnias such as nightmares occur during REM (or dream) sleep, and sleep terrors and sleepwalking occur during NREM sleep.

Key Terms

Answers to Concept Checks

8.1

1. b 2. b 3. a 4. a 5. a

8.2

1. c 2. a 3. b 4. a 5. b

8.3

1. c 2. b 3. e 4. a 5. d

8.4

1. b 2. d 3. e 4. c 5. a

8.5

1. c 2. d 3. a

Media Resources

 CourseMate

Access an integrated eBook, Abnormal Psychology Videos (formerly Abnormal Psych Live CD-ROM), chapter-specific interactive learning tools (flashcards, quizzes, learning modules), and more in your Psychology CourseMate, available at **www.abnormalpsych3ce.nelson.com.**

Abnormal Psychology Videos

Free Abnormal Psychology videos can be viewed on the website **www.abnormalpsych3ce .nelson.com**.

- *Anorexia Nervosa: Susan:* Susan talks about her fears of not being "skinny enough."
- *Twins with Anorexia Nervosa/Bulimia:* Two twins talk about their battle with food.
- *Weight Control:* Consider how researchers are helping people deal with the obesity epidemic.
- *Sleep Cycle:* This clip describes the normal cycle of REM and NREM sleep throughout the night—a cycle that may be altered in sleep disorders.

Video Concept Reviews

CourseMate also contains Mark Durand's *Video Concept Reviews* on these challenging topics.

- Bulimia Nervosa—Including Bingeing and Purging
- Anorexia Nervosa: An Overview
- Anorexia Nervosa: Subtypes and Associated Features
- Concept Check: Difference Between Anorexia and Bulimia
- Binge Eating Disorder
- Concept Check: Why Obesity Is Not in *DSM-IV*

- Dyssomnias and Parasomnias
- Polysomnographic (PSG) Evaluation
- Primary Insomnia
- Hypersomnia
- Narcolepsy
- Alien Abduction and Sleep
- Circadian Rhythm Disorders

Exploring Eating Disorders

Individuals with eating disorders:

> Feel a relentless, all-encompassing drive to be thin

> Are overwhelmingly young females from middle- to upper-class families, who live in socially competitive environments

> Lived only in Western countries until recently

Psychological—Diminished sense of personal control and self-confidence, causing low self-esteem. Distorted body image.

Social—Cultural and social emphasis on slender ideal, leading to body dissatisfaction and preoccupation with food and eating.

Causes

Biological—Possible genetic tendency to poor impulse control, emotional instability, and perfectionistic traits

EATING DISORDERS

Disorder	Characteristics	Treatment
Bulimia Nervosa	• Out-of-control consumption of excessive amounts of mostly non-nutritious food within a short time • Elimination of food through self-induced vomiting and/or abuse of laxatives or diuretics • To compensate for binges, some bulimics exercise excessively or fast between binges • Vomiting may enlarge salivary glands (causing a chubby face), erode dental enamel, and cause electrolyte imbalance resulting in cardiac failure or kidney problems • Weight usually within 10 percent of normal • Age of onset is typically 16 to 19 years of age	• Drug treatment, such as antidepressants • Short-term cognitive-behavioural therapy (CBT) to address behaviour and attitudes on eating and body shape • Interpersonal psychotherapy (IPT) to improve interpersonal functioning • Tends to be chronic if left untreated
Anorexia Nervosa	• Intense fear of obesity and persistent pursuit of thinness; perpetual dissatisfaction with weight loss • Severe caloric restriction, often with excessive exercise and sometimes with purging, to the point of semi-starvation • Severely limiting caloric intake may cause cessation of menstruation, downy hair on limbs and cheeks, dry skin, brittle hair or nails, sensitivity to cold, and danger of acute cardiac or kidney failure • Weight at least 15 percent below normal • Average age of onset is about 13 years of age	• Hospitalization (at 70 percent below normal weight) • Outpatient treatment to restore weight and correct dysfunctional attitudes on eating and body shape • Family therapy • Tends to be chronic if left untreated; more resistant to treatment than bulimia
Binge-Eating	• Similar to bulimia with out-of-control food binges, but no attempt to purge the food (vomiting, laxatives, diuretics) or compensate for excessive intake • Marked physical and emotional stress; some sufferers binge to alleviate bad moods • Binge eaters share some concerns about weight and body shape as individuals with anorexia and bulimia • Tends to affect more older people than either bulimia or anorexia	• Short-term CBT to address behaviour and attitudes on eating and body shape • IPT to improve interpersonal functioning • Drug treatments that reduce feelings of hunger • Self-help approaches

PhotoDisc/Getty Images

Exploring Sleep Disorders

Characterized by extreme disruption in the everyday lives of affected individuals, and are an important factor in many psychological disorders.

SLEEP DISORDERS

Diagnosing Sleep Disorders

A polysomnographic (PSG) evaluation assesses an individual's sleep habits with various electronic tests to measure airflow, brain activity, eye movements, muscle movements, and heart activity. Results are weighed with a measure of sleep efficiency (SE), the percentage of time spent asleep.

Dyssomnias
Disturbances in the timing, amount, or quality of sleep

Disorder	Characteristics	Causes	Treatment
Primary Insomnia	• Characteristics include difficulty initiating sleep, difficulty maintaining sleep, or nonrestorative sleep.	• Causes include pain, insufficient exercise, drug use, environmental influences, anxiety, respiratory problems, and biological vulnerability.	• Treatment may be medical (benzodiazepines) or psychological (anxiety reduction, improved sleep hygiene); combined approach is usually most effective.
Narcolepsy	• Characteristics include sudden daytime onset of REM sleep combined with cataplexy, a rapid loss of muscle tone that can be quite mild or result in complete collapse. Often accompanied by sleep paralysis and/or hypnagogic hallucinations.	• Causes are likely to be genetic.	• Treatment is medical (stimulant drugs).
Primary Hypersomnia	• Characteristics include abnormally excessive sleep and sleepiness, and involuntary daytime sleeping. Classified as a disorder only when it's subjectively perceived as disruptive.	• Causes may involve genetic link and/or excess serotonin.	• Treatment is usually medical (stimulant drugs).
Breathing-Related Sleep Disorder	• Characteristics include disturbed sleep and daytime fatigue resulting from hypoventilation (laboured breathing) or sleep apnea (suspended breathing).	• Causes may include narrow or obstructed airway, obesity, and increasing age.	• Treatments to improve breathing are medical or mechanical.
Circadian Rhythm Sleep Disorder	• Characteristics include sleepiness or insomnia.	• Caused by inability to synchronize sleep patterns with current pattern of day and night due to jet lag, shift work, delayed sleep, or advanced sleep (going to bed earlier than normal bedtime).	• Treatment includes phase delays to adjust bedtime and bright light to readjust biological clock.

Parasomnias
Abnormal behaviours that occur during sleep

Nightmares

Frightening REM dreams that awaken the sleeper. Nightmares qualify as nightmare disorder when they are stressful enough to impair normal functioning. Causes are unknown, but they tend to decrease with age.

Sleep Terrors

Occur during non-REM (nondreaming) sleep and most commonly afflict children. Sleeping child screams, cries, sweats, sometimes walks, has rapid heartbeat, and cannot easily be awakened or comforted. More common in boys than girls, and possible genetic link since tend to run in families. May subside with time.

Sleepwalking

Occurs at least once during non-REM sleep in 15 to 30 percent of children under age 15. Causes may include extreme fatigue, sleep deprivation, sedative or hypnotic drugs, and stress. Adult sleepwalking is usually associated with other psychological disorders. May have a genetic link.

9 Physical Disorders and Health Psychology

Phil Date/Shutterstock

As a surgeon treating cancer, it had fallen to me on hundreds of occasions to break bad news to patients and to give them ongoing support. . . . Strangely, observing the effects of that kind of news on many, many people did not prepare me at all for my personal disaster with AIDS.
—Orville Messenger, *Borrowed Time: A Surgeon's Struggle with Transfusion-Induced AIDS*

Demonstrate knowledge and understanding representing appropriate breadth and depth in selected content areas of psychology:	❯ Biological bases of behaviour and mental processes, including physiology, sensation, perception, comparative, motivation, and emotion (APA SLO 1.2.a (3)) *(see textbook pages 318–319)*
	❯ The interaction of mind and body (APA SLO 1.2.d (5)) *(see textbook pages 315–333)*
Use the concepts, language, and major theories of the discipline to account for psychological phenomena.	❯ Describe behaviour and mental processes empirically, including operational definitions (APA SLO 1.3.a) *(see textbook pages 315–333)*
	❯ Identify antecedents and consequences of behaviour and mental processes (APA SLO 1.3.b) *(see textbook pages 315–333)*
Identify appropriate applications of psychology in solving problems, such as:	❯ The pursuit and effect of healthy lifestyles (APA SLO 4.2.a) *(see textbook pages 333–341)*
	❯ Origin and treatment of abnormal behaviour (APA SLO 4.2.b) *(see textbook pages 320–341)*

* Portions of this chapter cover learning outcomes suggested by the American Psychological Association (2007) in their guidelines for the undergraduate psychology major. Chapter coverage of these outcomes is identified above by APA Goal and APA Suggested Learning Outcome (SLO).

At the beginning of the 20th century, the leading causes of death were influenza, pneumonia, diphtheria, tuberculosis, and gastrointestinal infections. Since then, the yearly death rate from these diseases has been greatly reduced (see Table 9.1). This reduction represents a revolution in public health that eliminated many infectious diseases and mastered many more. But the enormous success of our health care system in reducing mortality from disease has revealed a more complex and challenging problem: At present, some major contributing factors to illness and death in this country are psychological and behavioural. Consider for example, the relationship between genital herpes and stress.

In Chapter 2, we described the profound effects of psychological and social factors on brain structure and function. These factors seem to influence neurotransmitter activity, the secretion of neurohormones in the endocrine system, and, at a more fundamental level, gene expression. We have repeatedly looked at the complex interplay of biological, psychological, and social factors in the production and maintenance of psychological disorders. It will come as no surprise that psychological and social factors are very important to many additional disorders, including endocrinological disorders such as diabetes and disorders of the immune system such as acquired immune deficiency syndrome (AIDS). The difference between these and the other disorders discussed in this chapter is that they are clearly physical disorders. They have known (or strongly inferred) physical causes and, for the most part, observable physical pathology (e.g., genital herpes, damaged heart muscle, malignant tumours, measurable hypertension). Contrast this with the somatoform disorders discussed in Chapter 6: In conversion disorders, for example, clients complain of physical damage or disease but show no physical pathology. In the *DSM-IV-TR*, physical

TABLE 9.1 The Leading Causes of Death in Canada in 1921–1925 and 1997 (Rates per 100 000 Population)

1921–1925	Rate	1997	Rate
1. Cardiovascular and renal diseases	222	1. Diseases of the circulatory system	265
2. Influenza, bronchitis, and pneumonia	141	2. Cancer	196
3. Diseases of early infancy	111	3. Respiratory diseases	67
4. Tuberculosis	85	4. Unintentional injuries	28
5. Cancer	76	5. Diseases of the digestive system	25
6. Gastritis, duodenitis, enteritis, colitis	72	6. Endocrine diseases, etc.	24
7. Accidents	52	7. Diseases of the nervous system	22
8. Communicable diseases: Diphtheria, whooping cough, measles, scarlet fever, and typhoid fever.	47	8. Mental disorders	20
		9. Suicide	12
		10. Genito-urinary diseases	12

Source: Figures for 1921–25 from *Historical Statistics of Canada*, Section B. Vital Statistics and Health (B35-50) by Statistics Canada, 2002, Ottawa. Figures for "1997 Leading Causes of Death and Hospitalization in Canada" by Health Canada, Population and Public Health Branch, 2000, Ottawa.

disorders such as hypertension and diabetes are coded separately on Axis III. However, there is a provision for recognizing *psychological factors affecting medical condition*.

The study of how psychological and social factors affect physical disorders used to be distinct and somewhat separate from the remainder of psychopathology. Early on, the field was called psychosomatic medicine (Alexander, 1950), which meant that psychological factors affected somatic (physical) function. *Psychophysiological disorder* was a label used to communicate a similar idea. Such terms are less often used today because they are misleading. Describing as psychosomatic a disorder with an obvious physical component gave the impression that psychological ("mental") disorders of mood and anxiety did not have a strong biological component. As we now know, this assumption is not viable. Dividing the causes of mental disorders and physical disorders is not at all supported by current evidence. Biological, psychological, and social factors are implicated in the cause and maintenance of every disorder.

The contribution of psychosocial factors to the etiology and treatment of physical disorders is widely studied. Some of the discoveries are among the more exciting findings in all of psychology and biology. For example, in Chapter 2, we described briefly the specific harmful influences of anger on heart function. The tentative conclusion from that research was the pumping efficiency of an angry person's heart is reduced, risking dangerous disturbances of heart rhythms (Ironson et al., 1992; Robins & Novaco, 2000). We also discussed recent studies demonstrating that psychological factors, including psychological treatment, increase survival time in patients with cancer (Spiegel, Bloom, Kramer, & Gotheil, 1989). Remember, too, the physical and mental deterioration of elderly people who are removed from social networks of family and friends (Hawkley & Cacioppo, 2007). Also, long-term unemployment among men who previously held steady jobs is associated with a doubling of the risk of death over the following five years compared with men who continued working (Morris, Cook, & Shaper, 1994). In fact, researchers have isolated stress due to economic uncertainty as the principal cause of plummeting ages of life expectancy for Eastern Europe after the fall of communism (Stone, 2000).

The shift in focus from infectious disease to psychological factors has been called the second revolution in public health. Two closely related new fields of study have developed. In the first, **behavioural medicine** (Meyers, 1991; Rachman & Philips, 1980), knowledge derived from behavioural science is applied to the prevention, diagnosis, and treatment of medical problems. This is an interdisciplinary field in which psychologists, physicians, and other health professionals work closely together to develop new treatments and preventive strategies (Schwartz & Weiss, 1978). A second field, **health psychology**, is not interdisciplinary, and it is usually considered a subfield of behavioural medicine. Practitioners study psychological factors that are important to the promotion and maintenance of health; they also analyze and recommend improvements to health care systems and health policy formation within the discipline of psychology (Kazarian & Evans, 2001; Stone, 1987; Taylor, 2009).

Psychological and social factors influence health and physical problems in two distinct ways (see ■ Figure 9.1). First, they can affect the basic biological processes that lead to illness and

disease. Second, long-standing behaviour patterns may put people at risk of developing certain physical disorders. Sometimes both of these avenues contribute to the etiology or maintenance of disease (Kiecolt-Glaser & Newton, 2001; Williams, Barefoot, & Schneiderman, 2003). Consider the example of *AIDS*. AIDS is a disease of the immune system that is directly affected by stress (Cohen & Herbert, 1996; Kennedy, 2000), so stress may promote the deadly progression of AIDS (a conclusion pending confirmation from additional studies). This is an example of how psychological factors may directly influence biological processes. We also know that a variety of things we may choose to do put us at risk for AIDS, such as having unprotected sex or sharing needles. Because no medical cure for AIDS exists yet, our best weapon is large-scale behaviour modification to *prevent acquisition* of the disease.

Other behavioural patterns contribute to disease. Fully 50 percent of deaths from the 10 leading causes of death today can be traced to behaviours common to certain lifestyles (Centers for Disease Control [CDC], 2003; Taylor, 2009). Cigarette smoking is a major behavioural contributor to mortality (Brannon & Feist, 1997; McGinnis & Foege, 1993). Smoking is estimated to have caused more than 45 000 deaths in Canada in 2000 alone (Peto, Lopez, Boreham, & Thun, 2006). Behavioural patterns subsumed under unhealthy lifestyles also include poor eating habits, lack of

1 Psychosocial factors (such as negative emotions and stress) disrupt basic biological processes, which may lead to physical disorders and disease.

Stress

Lack of control

2 "Risky" behaviours cause or contribute to a variety of physical disorders and disease.

Smoking
Drinking
Poor eating habits
No exercise

■ **FIGURE 9.1** Psychosocial factors directly affect physical health.

exercise, and insufficient injury control (e.g., not wearing seat-belts). These behaviours are grouped under the label lifestyle because they are, for the most part, enduring habits that are an integral part of a person's daily living pattern (Faden, 1987; Oyama & Andrasik, 1992). We return to lifestyles in the closing pages of this chapter when we look at efforts to modify them and promote health.

Psychological and Social Factors That Influence Biology

We have much to learn about how psychological factors affect physical disorders and disease. Available evidence suggests that the same kinds of causal factors active in psychological disorders—social, psychological, and biological—play a role in some physical disorders (Mostofsky & Barlow, 2000; Taylor, Repetti, & Seeman, 1997; Uchino, 2009). But the factor attracting the most attention is stress, particularly the neurobiological components of the stress response.

The Nature of Stress

In 1936, a young scientist in Montréal named Hans Selye noticed that one group of rats he injected with a certain chemical extract developed ulcers and other physiological problems, including atrophy of immune system tissues. But a control group of rats that received a daily saline (salt water) injection that should not have had any effect developed the same physical problems. Selye pursued this unexpected finding and discovered that the daily injections them-selves seemed to be the culprit rather than the injected substance. Furthermore, many different types of environmental changes pro-duced the same results. Borrowing a term from engineering, he decided the cause of this non-specific reaction was *stress*. As so often happens in science, an accidental or serendipitous observation led to a new area of study, in this case, *stress physiology* (Selye, 1936).

Selye theorized that the body goes through several stages in response to *sustained* stress. The first phase is a type of *alarm* response to immediate danger or threat. With continuing stress, we seem to pass into a stage of *resistance*, in which we mobilize various coping mechanisms to respond to the stress. Finally, if the stress is too intense or lasts too long, we may enter a stage of *exhaustion*, in which our bodies suffer permanent damage or death (Selye, 1936, 1950). Selye called this sequence the **general adaptation syndrome** (GAS). Although Selye was not correct in all the details of his theory, the idea that chronic stress may inflict permanent bodily damage or contribute to disease has been confirmed and elaborated on in recent years (Kemeny, 2003; Robles, Glaser, & Kiecolt-Glaser, 2005; Sapolsky, 1990, 2000).

▲ Hans Selye, a scientist at McGill University, suggested in 1936 that stress contributes to certain physical problems.

The word *stress* means many things in modern life. In engin-eering, stress is the strain on a bridge when a heavy truck drives across it; stress is the *response* of the bridge to the truck's weight. But stress is also a *stimulus*. The truck is a "stressor" for the bridge, just as being fired from a job or facing a difficult final exam is a stimulus or stressor for a person. These varied meanings can create some confusion, but we concentrate on **stress** as the physiological response of the individual to a stressor.

The Physiology of Stress

In Chapter 2, we described the physiological effects of the early stages of stress, noting in particular its activating effect on the sympathetic nervous system, which mobilizes our resources during times of threat or danger by activating internal organs to prepare the body for immediate action, either fight or flight. These changes increase our strength and mental activity. We also noted in Chapter 2 that the activity of the endocrine system increases when we are stressed, primarily through activation of the HPA axis. Although a variety of neurotransmitters begin flowing in the nervous system, much attention has focused on the endocrine system's neuromodulators or neuropeptides, hormones affecting the nervous system that are secreted by the glands directly into the bloodstream (Chaouloff & Groc, 2010; Owens, Mulchahey, Stout, & Plotsky 1997; Taylor, Maloney, Dearborn, & Weiss, 2009). These neuromodulating hormones act very much like neurotransmitters in carrying the brain's messages to various parts of the body. One of the neurohormones, *corticotropin releasing factor* (CRF), is secreted by the hypothalamus and stimulates the pituitary gland. Farther down the chain of the HPA axis, the pituitary gland (along with the autonomic nervous system) activates the adrenal gland, which secretes, among other things, the hormone cortisol. Because of their very close relation-ship to the stress response, cortisol and other related hormones are known as the *stress hormones*.

Remember that the HPA axis is closely related to the limbic system. The hypothalamus, at the very top of the brain stem, is right next to the limbic system, which contains the hippocampus and seems to control our emotional memories. The hippocampus is very responsive to cortisol. When stimulated by this hormone during HPA axis activity, the hippocampus helps to *turn off* the stress response, completing a feedback loop between the limbic system and the various parts of the HPA axis.

This loop may be important for several reasons. Working with animals, Robert Sapolsky and his colleague Michael Meaney at McGill University (e.g., Sapolsky & Meaney, 1986) showed that increased levels of cortisol in response to chronic stress may kill nerve cells in the hippocampus. If hippocampal activity is thus compromised, excessive cortisol is secreted and, over time, the ability to turn off the stress response decreases, which leads to further aging of the hippocampus. These findings indicate that chronic stress leading to chronic secretion of cortisol may have long-lasting effects on physical function, including brain damage. Cell death may, in turn, lead to deficient problem-solving abilities among senior citizens and, ultimately, dementia. This physio-logical process may also affect our susceptibility to infectious disease and our recovery from it in other pathophysiological sys-tems. Sapolsky and Meaney's work is important because we now know that hippocampal cell death associated with chronic stress and anxiety occurs in humans with, for example, post-traumatic stress disorder (see Chapter 5). The long-term effects of this cell death are not yet known.

Contributions to the Stress Response

Stress physiology is profoundly influenced by psychological and social factors (Kemeny, 2003; Taylor et al., 2009). This link has been demonstrated by Sapolsky (1990, 2000, 2007). He studied baboons living freely in a national reserve in Kenya because their primary sources of stress, like those of humans, are psychological rather than physical. As with many species, baboons arrange themselves in a social hierarchy with dominant members at the top and submissive members at the bottom. And life is tough at the bottom! The lives of subordinate animals are made difficult (Sapolsky calls it "stressful") by continual bullying from the dominant animals, and they have less access to food, preferred resting places, and sexual partners. Particularly interesting are Sapolsky's findings on levels of cortisol in the baboons as a function of their social rank in a dominance hierarchy. Remember from our description of the HPA axis that the secretion of cortisol from the adrenal glands is the final step in a cascade of hormone secretion that originates in the limbic system in the brain during periods of stress. The secretion of cortisol contributes to our arousal and mobilization in the short run but, if produced chronically, it can damage the hippocampus. In addition, muscles atrophy, fertility is affected by declining testosterone, hypertension develops in the cardiovascular system, and the immune response is impaired. Sapolsky discovered that dominant males in the baboon hierarchy ordinarily had *lower* resting levels of cortisol than subordinate males. When an emergency occurred, however, cortisol levels rose more quickly in the dominant males than in the subordinate males.

Sapolsky and his colleagues sought the causes of these differences by working backward up the HPA axis. They found an excess secretion of CRF by the hypothalamus in subordinate animals, combined with a diminished sensitivity of the pituitary gland (which is stimulated by CRF). Therefore, subordinate animals, unlike dominant animals, continually secrete cortisol, probably because their lives are so stressful. In addition, their HPA system is less sensitive to the effects of cortisol and therefore less efficient in turning off the stress response.

Sapolsky also discovered that subordinate males have fewer circulating lymphocytes (white blood cells) than dominant males, a sign of immune system suppression. In addition, subordinate males evidence less circulating high-density lipoprotein cholesterol, which puts them at higher risk for atherosclerosis and coronary heart disease, a subject we discuss later in this chapter.

What is it about being on top that produces positive effects? Sapolsky concluded that it is primarily the psychological benefits of having *predictability* and *controllability* concerning events in one's life. Parts of his data were gathered during years in which a number of male baboons were at the top of the hierarchy, with no clear "winner." Although these males dominated the rest of the animals in the group, they constantly attacked one another. Under these conditions, they displayed hormonal profiles more like those of subordinate males. Thus, dominance combined with stability produced optimal stress hormone profiles. But the most important factor in regulating stress physiology seems to be a sense of control (Sapolsky & Ray, 1989), a finding strongly confirmed in subsequent research (Kemeny, 2003; Sapolsky, 2007). Control of social situations and the ability to cope with any tension that arises go a long way toward blunting the long-term effects of stress.

Stress, Anxiety, Depression, and Excitement

If you have read the chapters on anxiety, mood, and related psychological disorders, you might conclude, correctly, that stressful life events combined with psychological vulnerabilities such as an inadequate sense of control are a factor in psychological and physical disorders. Is there any relationship between emotional and physical disorders? A very strong one seems to exist. Vaillant (1979) studied more than 200 male university undergraduates between 1942 and 1944 who were mentally and physically healthy. He followed these men closely for more than 30 years. Those who developed psychological disorders or who were highly stressed became chronically ill or died at a significantly higher rate than men who remained

© Thomas Dobner 2006/Alamy

▲ Baboons at the top of the social hierarchy have a sense of predictability and control that allows them to cope with problems and maintain physical health; baboons at the bottom of the hierarchy show the symptoms of stress because they have little control over access to food, resting places, and mates.

well adjusted and free from psychological disorders, a finding that has been repeatedly confirmed (e.g., Katon, 2003). This suggests that the same types of stress-related psychological factors that contribute to psychological disorders may also contribute to the later development of physical disorders and that stress, anxiety, and depression are closely related. Can you tell the difference among feelings of stress, anxiety, depression, and excitement? You might say, "No problem," but these four states have a lot in common. Which one you experience may depend on your *sense of control* at the moment, or how well you think you can cope with the threat or challenge you are facing (Barlow, 2002; Barlow, Rapee, & Reisner, 2001; Suárez, Bennett, Goldstein, & Barlow, 2009). This continuum of feelings from excitement through stress and anxiety to depression is shown in ■ Figure 9.2.

Consider how you feel when you are excited. You might experience a rapid heartbeat, a sudden burst of energy, or a jumpy stomach. But if you're well prepared for the challenge—for example, if you're an athlete, really up for the game and confident in your abilities, or a musician, sure you are going to give an outstanding performance—these feelings of excitement can actually be pleasurable.

Sometimes when you face a challenging task, you feel you could handle it if you only had the time or help you need; but because you don't have these resources, you feel pressured. In response, you may work harder to do better and be perfect, even though you think you will be all right in the end. If you are under too much pressure, you may become tense and irritable or develop a headache or an upset stomach. This is what stress feels like. If something really is threatening and you believe that you can do little about it, you may feel anxiety. The threatening situation could be anything from a physical attack to making a fool of yourself in front of someone. As your body prepares for the challenge, you worry about it incessantly. Your sense of control is considerably less than if you were stressed. In some cases, there may not be any difficult situation out there at all. Sometimes we are anxious for no reason except that we feel certain aspects of our lives are out of control. Finally, individuals who always perceive life as threatening may lose hope about ever having control and slip into a state of *depression*, no longer trying to cope.

To sum up, the underlying physiology of these particular emotional states seems relatively similar. This is why we refer to the activation of specific neurotransmitters and neurohormones in discussing anxiety, depression, and stress-related physical disorders. But psychological factors—like a sense of control and confidence that we can cope with stress or challenges, called **self-efficacy** by Albert Bandura (1986; Benight & Bandura, 2004)—seem to differ and thus lead to different feelings (Taylor et al., 1997).

The Immune System and Physical Disorders

Have you had a cold recently? How did you pick it up? Did you spend the day with someone else who had a cold? Did someone sneeze nearby while you were sitting in class? Exposure to cold viruses is a necessary factor in developing a cold, but the level of stress you are experiencing at the time seems to play a major role in whether the exposure results in a cold. Sheldon Cohen and his associates (Cohen, 1996; Cohen, Doyle, & Skoner, 1999; Cohen, Tyrrell, & Smith, 1991, 1993) exposed volunteer participants to a specific dosage of a cold virus and followed them closely. They found that the chance a participant would get sick was directly related to how much stress the person had experienced during the past year. Cohen and colleagues (1995) also linked the intensity of stress and negative affect at the time of exposure to the later *severity* of the cold, as measured by mucus production. In an interesting twist, Cohen, Doyle, Turner, Alper, and Skoner (2003) have demonstrated that how sociable you are—that is, the quantity and quality of your social relationships—affects whether you come down with a cold when exposed to the virus, perhaps because socializing with friends relieves stress (Cohen & Janicki-Devarts, 2009). Finally, a positive and optimistic cognitive style protects against developing a cold (Cohen & Pressman, 2006). These are among the first

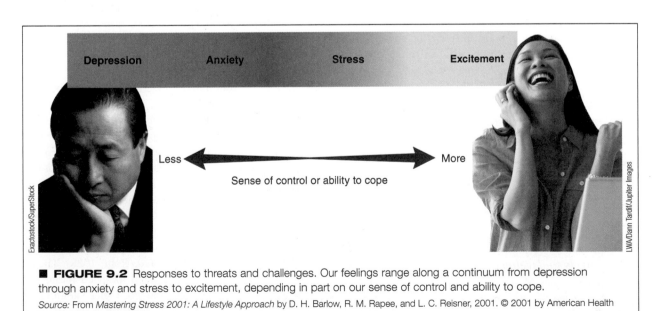

■ **FIGURE 9.2** Responses to threats and challenges. Our feelings range along a continuum from depression through anxiety and stress to excitement, depending in part on our sense of control and ability to cope.

Source: From *Mastering Stress 2001: A Lifestyle Approach* by D. H. Barlow, R. M. Rapee, and L. C. Reisner, 2001. © 2001 by American Health Publishing Co. Reprinted by permission.

well-controlled studies to demonstrate that stress and related factors increase the risk of infection.

Think back to your last exam. Did you (or your roommate) have a cold? Exam periods are stressors that have been shown to produce increased infections, particularly of the upper respiratory tract (Glaser et al., 1987, 1990). Therefore, if you are susceptible to colds, maybe you should skip final exams! A better solution is to learn how to control your stress before and during exams. Almost certainly, the effect of stress on susceptibility to infections is mediated through the **immune system**, which protects the body from any foreign materials that may enter it.

Research dating back to the original reports of Hans Selye (1936) demonstrates the detrimental effects of stress on immune system functioning. Humans under stress show clearly increased rates of infectious diseases, including colds, herpes, and mononucleosis (e.g., Cohen & Herbert, 1996; Taylor, 2009; Vander Plate, Aral, & Magder, 1988). Direct evidence links a number of stressful situations to lowered immune system functioning, including marital discord or relationship difficulties (Kiecolt-Glaser et al., 2005; Kiecolt-Glaser & Newton, 2001; Uchino, 2009), job loss, and the death of a loved one (Hawkley & Cacioppo, 2007; Morris et al., 1994; Pavalko, Elder, & Clipp, 1993). Furthermore, these stressful events affect the immune system rapidly. Studies in laboratories have demonstrated weakened immune system response within two hours of exposure to stress (Kiecolt-Glaser & Glaser, 1992; Weisse, Pato, McAllister, Littman, & Breier, 1990; Zakowski, McAllister, Deal, & Baum, 1992).

We have already noted that emotional disorders seem to make us more susceptible to developing physical disorders (Katon, 2003; Robles et al., 2005; Vaillant, 1979). In fact, direct evidence indicates that depression lowers immune system functioning (Herbert & Cohen, 1993; Miller & Blackwell, 2006; Stone, 2000; Weisse, 1992), particularly in older adults (Herbert & Cohen, 1993). It may be that the level of depression—and, more importantly, the underlying sense of uncontrollability that accompanies most depressions—is the crucial mechanism in lowering immune system functioning, a mechanism present during most negative stressful life events, such as job loss (Miller & Blackwell, 2006; Robles et al., 2005; Weisse, 1992). Depression can also lead to poor self-care and a tendency to engage in riskier behaviours. For humans, like Sapolsky's baboons, the ability to retain a sense of control over events in our lives may be one of the most important psychological contributions to good health.

Chronic stress may be more problematic for the immune system than acute or sudden stress because the effects are, by definition, longer lasting. In the 1970s, the nuclear power plant at Three Mile Island in Pennsylvania leaked. Many residents feared that any exposure to radiation they might have sustained would lead to cancer or other illnesses, and they lived with this fear for years. More than six years after the explosion, some individuals who had been in the area during the crisis still had lowered immune system functioning (McKinnon, Weisse, Reynolds, Bowles, & Baum, 1989). A similar finding has been reported for people who care for chronically ill family members, such as Alzheimer's disease patients (Kiecolt-Glaser & Glaser, 1987; Mills et al., 2004).

To understand how the immune system protects us, we must first understand how it works. We take a brief tour of the immune system next, using ■ Figure 9.3 as a visual guide, and then we examine psychological contributions to the biology of two diseases strongly related to immune system functioning: AIDS and cancer.

A Brief Overview

The immune system identifies and eliminates foreign materials, called **antigens**, in the body—usually bacteria, viruses, or parasites. But the immune system also targets the body's own cells that have become aberrant or damaged in some way, perhaps as part of a malignant tumour. Donated organs are foreign, and so the immune system attacks them after surgical transplant; consequently, it is necessary to suppress the immune system temporarily after surgery.

The immune system has two main parts: the *humoral* and the *cellular*. Specific types of cells function as agents of both. White blood cells (*macrophages*), called *leukocytes*, do most of the work. They surround identifiable antigens and destroy them. They also signal *lymphocytes*, which consist of B cells and T cells.

B cells operate within the humoral part of the immune system, releasing molecules that seek out antigens with the purpose of neutralizing them. The B cells produce *antibodies*, which combine with the antigens to neutralize them. After the antigens are neutralized, *memory B cells* are created so that the next time that antigen is encountered, the immune system response will be even faster. This action accounts for the success of inoculations you may have received for mumps or measles as a child. An inoculation actually contains small amounts of the targeted organism, but not enough to make you sick. Your immune system then "remembers" this antigen and prevents you from coming down with the full disease when you are exposed to it.

T cells operate in the cellular branch of the immune system. They don't produce antibodies. One subgroup, called *killer T cells*, was discovered in 1973 in Winnipeg by the late cancer researcher Arnold H. Greenberg (Bleackley, Green, Lockshin, Melino, & Zakeri, 2001; Greenberg, 1994). Killer T cells directly destroy viruses and cancerous processes (O'Leary, 1990; Roitt, 1988). Then *memory T cells* are created to speed future responses to the same antigen. Other subgroups of T cells help regulate the immune system. For example, *helper T cells* enhance the immune system

---

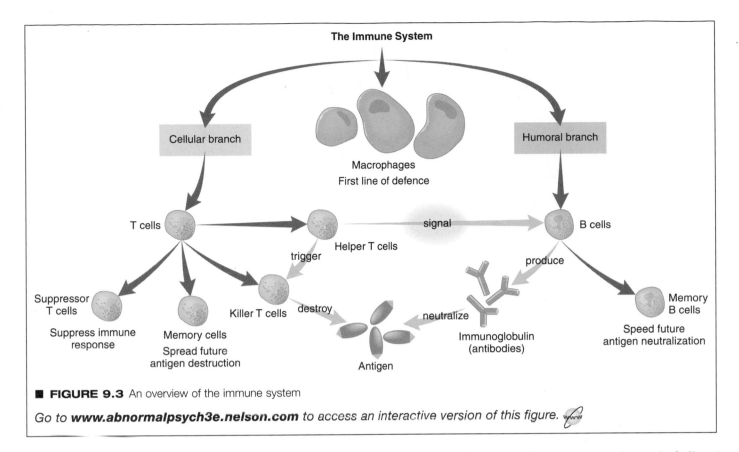

The Immune System

Cellular branch

Humoral branch

Macrophages
First line of defence

T cells

Helper T cells

signal

B cells

trigger

Suppressor
T cells

Suppress immune
response

Killer T cells

Memory cells

Spread future
antigen destruction

destroy

produce

neutralize

Antigen

Immunoglobulin
(antibodies)

Memory
B cells

Speed future
antigen neutralization

■ **FIGURE 9.3** An overview of the immune system

Go to **www.abnormalpsych3e.nelson.com** *to access an interactive version of this figure.*

response by signalling B cells to produce antibodies and telling killer T cells to destroy the antigen. *Suppressor T cells* suppress the production of antibodies by B cells when they are no longer needed.

We should have twice as many helper T cells as suppressor T cells. With too many helper T cells, the immune system may attack the body's normal cells rather than antigens. When this happens, we have what is called an **autoimmune disease**, such as **rheumatoid arthritis**. With too many suppressor T cells, the body is subject to invasion by a number of antigens. The human immunodeficiency virus (HIV) directly attacks the helper T cells, thereby severely weakening the immune system and causing AIDS.

Until the mid-1970s, most scientists believed the brain and the immune system operated independently of each other. However, in 1974, Ader and Cohen (1975, 1993) made a startling discovery. Working with a classical conditioning paradigm, they gave sugar-flavoured water to rats, together with a drug that suppresses the immune system. Ader and Cohen then demonstrated that giving the same rats only the sweet-tasting water produced similar changes in the immune system. In other words, the rats had "learned" (through classical conditioning) to respond to the water by suppressing their immune systems. We now know there are many connections between the nervous system and the immune system. For example,

Dr. Andrejs Liepins/Photo Researchers, Inc.

▲ This coloured scanning electron micrograph (SEM) shows a killer T cell (yellow) attacking a cancer cell (pink).

nerve endings exist in many immune system tissues, including the thymus, the lymph nodes, and the bone marrow. These findings have generated a new field known as **psychoneuroimmunology**, or **PNI** (Ader & Cohen, 1993; Brown, 1994), which simply means the object of study is *psycho*logical influences on the *neuro*logical responding implicated in our *immune* response.

Researchers have learned a great deal recently about pathways through which psychological and social factors may influence immune system functioning. Direct connections among the brain (central nervous system), the HPA axis (hormonal), and the immune system have already been described. Behavioural changes in response to stressful events, such as increased smoking or poor eating habits, may also suppress the immune system (Cohen & Herbert, 1996) (see ■ Figure 9.4). Now scientists have uncovered a chain of molecules that connects stress to the onset of disease by turning on certain genes (Cole et al., 2010). Basically, stress seems to activate certain molecules in cells that activate genes (called a transcription factor), in this case the GABA-1 transcription factor that activates the interleukin-6 gene. This gene makes a protein that turns on the inflammatory response, which brings infection-fighting cells of the immune system to the area. This is great if you've cut yourself, but very damaging if it occurs over a long period of time. It is this chronic inflammatory response that exacerbates cancer, heart disease, and diabetes, and shortens life. Of course, other genes, such as the serotonin transporter gene mentioned in Chapter 2, are also implicated in making one vulnerable to certain types of stressors (Way & Taylor, 2010). Undoubtedly, many more groups of genes and integrative psychobiological paths implicated in the effects of the stress response will be discovered (Segerstrom & Sephton, 2010).

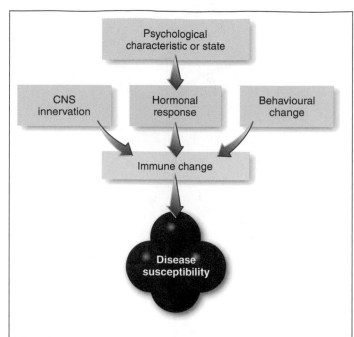

FIGURE 9.4 Pathways through which psychological factors might influence onset and progression of immune system-mediated disease. For simplicity, arrows are drawn in only one direction, from psychological characteristics to disease. No lack of alternative paths is implied.

Source: From Cohen & Herbert, 1996.

Concept Check | 9.1

The immune system protects the body from foreign bodies that may enter it. Sometimes stress has such an effect on the immune system that the body becomes susceptible to infections. Assess your knowledge of the immune system by matching components of the system with their function in the body: (a) B cells, (b) killer T cells, (c) suppressor T cells, and (d) memory cells.

1. This subgroup targets viral infections within the cells by directly destroying the antigens. _____

2. Lymphocytes that operate within the humoral part of the system. _____

3. These are created so that when a specific antigen is encountered in the future, the immune response will be faster. _____

4. These T cells stop the production of antibodies by B cells when they are no longer needed. _____

AIDS

The ravages of the AIDS epidemic have made this disease the highest priority of public health systems around the world. The number of people worldwide living with HIV continues to grow, reaching an estimated 33.4 million in 2008, which is 20 percent higher than in 2000 (UNAIDS, 2009). Only in 2004 did adult and child deaths begin to level off with aggressive treatment and prevention efforts in some parts of the world (Bongaarts &

Over, 2010). Despite this modest success, 2.7 million new HIV infections occurred worldwide in 2008, and 2 million people died of AIDS (Grabbe & Bunnell, 2010; UNAIDS, 2009). An estimated 430 000 new infections occurred among children under the age of 15 in 2008, with most new infections stemming from transmission in utero, during delivery, or as a result of breastfeeding (UNAIDS, 2009). In the hardest hit regions in southern Africa, between 20 percent and 40 percent of the adult population are believed to be HIV positive, comprising two-thirds of cases worldwide, with approximately 18 million children orphaned by the disease (Klimas, Koneru, & Fletcher, 2008). AIDS is also spreading rapidly to the densely populated regions of India and China (Normile, 2009), and in Latin America, rates are projected to rise from 2 million in 2006 to 3.5 million by 2015 (Cohen, 2006).

Although intravenous drug use and homosexual activity remain the primary modes of acquiring HIV in North America, in most of the world (and particularly the underdeveloped world) it is heterosexual activity that brings people in contact with HIV. Once a person is infected with HIV, the course of the disease is quite variable. After several months to several years with no symptoms, patients may develop minor health problems such as weight loss, fever, and night sweats, symptoms that make up the condition known as **AIDS-related complex (ARC)**. A diagnosis of AIDS itself is not made until one of several serious diseases appears, such as pneumocystis pneumonia, cancer, dementia, or a wasting syndrome in which the body literally withers away. The median time from initial infection to the development of full-blown AIDS has been estimated to range from 7.3 to 10 years or more (Pantaleo, Graziosi, & Fauci, 1993). Clinical scientists have developed powerful new combinations of drugs referred to as highly active antiretroviral therapy (HAART) that suppress the virus in those infected with HIV, even in advanced cases (Hammer et al., 2006; Thompson et al., 2010). This has been a very positive development that has slowed disease progression and decreased mortality. For example, most people with AIDS die within one year of diagnosis without treatment, as is the case in many developing countries (Zwahlen & Egger, 2006). But the proportion of people who receive treatment surviving with AIDS two years or longer increased to 85 percent by 2005, and the death rate from AIDS declined 80 percent since 1990 (Knoll, Lassmann, & Temesgen, 2007). Nevertheless, HAART does not seem to be a cure, because the most recent evidence suggests the virus is seldom eliminated but rather lies dormant in reduced numbers; thus, infected patients face a lifetime of taking multiple medications (Buscher & Giordano, 2010; Cohen, 2002; Hammer et al., 2006). Also, the percentage who drop out of HAART because of severe side effects, such as nausea and diarrhea, is high—61 percent in one study (O'Brien, Clark, Besch, Myers, & Kissinger, 2003). For this reason, earlier recommendations were to postpone treatment until those infected are in imminent danger of developing symptomatic disease (Cohen, 2002; Hammer et al., 2006), but in view of the success of this treatment regimen with cases of newly acquired HIV, current recommendations are to start as early as possible after detecting infection and to work closely with patients to increase adherence to the schedule for the medication (Thompson et al., 2010). Unfortunately, drug-resistant strains of HIV are now being transmitted.

Because AIDS is a relatively new disease, and takes at least several years to develop, we are still learning about the factors, including possible psychological factors, that extend survival (Klimas et al., 2008; Taylor, 2009). Investigators identified a group of people who have been exposed repeatedly to the AIDS virus but have not contracted the disease. A major distinction of these people is that their immune systems, particularly the cellular branch, are robust and strong (Ezzel, 1993), most likely because of genetic factors (Kaiser, 2006). Therefore, efforts to boost the immune system may contribute to the prevention of AIDS.

Because psychological factors impact immune system functioning, investigators have begun to examine whether these psychological factors influence the progression of HIV. For example, high levels of stress and depression and low levels of social support have been associated with a faster progression to disease (Leserman, 2008; Leserman et al., 2000). But an even more intriguing question is whether psychological interventions can slow the progression of the disease, even among those who are symptomatic (Cole, 2008; Gore-Felton & Koopman, 2008). In fact, several important studies suggest that cognitive-behavioural stress-management (CBSM) programs may have positive effects on the immune systems of individuals who are already symptomatic (Antoni et al., 2000; Carrico & Antoni, 2008; Lutgendorf et al., 1997). Specifically, Lutgendorf and colleagues (1997) used an intervention program that significantly decreased depression and anxiety compared to a control group that did not receive the treatment. More important, there was a significant reduction in antibodies to the herpes simplex virus II in the treatment group compared to the control group, which reflects the greater ability of the cellular component of the immune system to control the virus. In a study by Antoni and colleagues (2000), 73 gay or bisexual men already infected with HIV and symptomatic with the disease were assigned to a CBSM program or a control group receiving usual care without the program. As in previous studies, men receiving the stress-management treatment showed significantly lower posttreatment levels of anxiety, anger, and perceived stress than those in the control group, indicating the treatment was effective. More important, as long as a year after the intervention had ended, men who had received the treatment evidenced better immune system functioning as indicated by higher levels of T cells.

Learning that one has an incurable terminal illness is extremely stressful for anyone. This happens every day to individuals stricken with HIV. The stress of learning you are carrying the AIDS virus can be devastating as can be dealing with the emergence of HIV-related symptoms in those who are infected with the virus. In a study by Montréal researchers José Côté and Carolyn Pepler, 90 hospitalized HIV-positive men were randomly assigned to one of two psychosocial interventions intended to help regulate emotional response to an exacerbation of HIV symptoms, or to a control group. One intervention was skills-based in which the men learned cognitive coping skills for dealing with their illness and the other an emotion-focused intervention in which the men were encouraged to express their feelings about their illness. Before and after the intervention, all men were assessed for mood, distress, and anxiety levels. Both active interventions produced beneficial effects on overall negative mood (see ■ Figure 9.5) compared with the control group. The cognitive coping skills group showed some additional benefits, including overall decrease in distress and intrusive thoughts about their illness, as well as decreases in

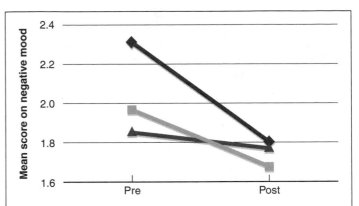

■ **FIGURE 9.5** Means for negative mood for the coping skills training intervention (diamond), the emotional expression intervention (square), and the control condition (triangle) at preintervention (Pre) and postintervention (Post)

Source: From "A randomized trial of a cognitive coping intervention for acutely ill HIV-positive men" by J. K. Côté & C. Pepler, 2002, *Nursing Research, 51(4)*, 237–244.

anxiety after each session. These findings point to the importance of psychological factors like cognitive coping in regulating emotional reactions to the emergence of symptoms among those infected with HIV (Côté & Pepler, 2002).

Another place that psychological factors can play a role in HIV/AIDS treatment is in the area of medication compliance. In order for medications like HAART to exert any positive effects in patients with HIV, patients have to be compliant with taking their medications. A group of researchers in Ottawa (Balfour et al., 2006) recently examined a four-session intervention that involved learning techniques to increase medication adherence. After the four sessions, intervention patients reported significantly higher readiness to start HAART medication, compared to controls.

But can such psychosocial interventions actually affect not only distress levels and readiness to initiate medications in HIV-positive patients, but also the course of the illness? Antoni et al. (1991) studied the effects of administering a psychosocial stress-reduction treatment to a group of individuals who believed they might have the HIV virus, during the weeks before they were tested for HIV. Half the group received the stress-reduction program; the other half received the usual medical and psychological care. Unfortunately, many individuals in this group turned out to be HIV positive. However, similar to the findings in the Côté and Pepler (2002) study, of those in the Antoni et al. (1991) study, only those who had undergone the psychosocial stress-reduction procedures did *not* show substantial increases in anxiety and depression. Furthermore—and more importantly—they actually demonstrated *increases* in their immune system functioning as measured by such indices as helper T and killer T cells. What was most encouraging about this study, however, was that a follow-up showed less disease progression in the stress-reduction group two years later (Ironson et al., 1994). A more recent study tracked a group of HIV-infected men without AIDS for 7.5 years (Leserman et al., 2000).

Remember, though, that the participants in the Antoni et al. (1991) study were in a very early asymptomatic stage of the disease, which stands in contrast to the subjects in the Côté and Pepler (2002) study, who were at an advanced stage of the illness and required hospitalization. Now, important new studies suggest the same cognitive-behavioural stress-management program may have positive effects on the immune systems of individuals who are already symptomatic (Antoni et al., 2000; Lutgendorf et al., 1997). Specifically, the intervention program used in the Lutgendorf et al. (1997) study significantly decreased depression and anxiety, compared with a control group that did not receive the treatment.

A review of the literature on the effects of group therapy for HIV positive individuals concludes that, although further study is warranted, changes in immune and endocrine activity seem to be associated with structured group interventions for patients with early-stage disease (Sherman et al., 2004). It is too early to tell whether these results will be strong or persistent enough to translate into increased survival time for AIDS patients, although results from Antoni and colleagues (2000, 2006) suggest they might. If stress and related variables *are* clinically significant to immune response, functioning, and disease progression in HIV-infected patients, as suggested by a number of studies (Cole, 2008; Leserman, 2008), then psychosocial interventions to bolster the immune system might increase survival rates and, in the most optimistic scenario, prevent the slow deterioration of the immune system (Carrico & Antoni, 2008; Kennedy, 2000). Of course, the most effective interventions focus on changing behaviour to prevent acquiring HIV in the first place, such as reducing risky behaviour and promoting safe sexual practices (Temoshok, Wald, Synowki, & Garzino-Demo, 2008). Few areas of study in behavioural medicine and health psychology are more urgent.

Cancer

Among the more far-reaching developments in the study of illness and disease is the discovery that the development and course of different varieties of **cancer** are also subject to psychosocial influences (Williams & Schneiderman, 2002). This has resulted in a new field of study called **psycho-oncology** (Anderson & Baum, 2001; Greer, 1999). *Oncology* is the study of cancer. Results from a landmark study by Spiegel et al. (1989) showing survival rates of patients with advanced breast cancer who received psychosocial treatment compared with those who did not are presented in ■ Figure 9.6.

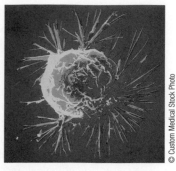

▲ Breast cancer cell

Those who received therapy lived twice as long on the average (approximately three years) as the control group (approximately 18 months). Four years after the study began, one-third of the therapy patients were still alive, and all the patients receiving the best medical care without therapy had died. Spiegel and colleagues (1996) later demonstrated that this brief psychosocial treatment can be implemented relatively easily in oncology clinics everywhere. Clinical trials involving large numbers of patients with cancer are in progress to evaluate more thoroughly the life-prolonging and life-enhancing effects of psychosocial treatments for cancer.

A notable example is the work of psychologist Linda Carlson at the University of Calgary and the Tom Baker Cancer Centre. She and her colleagues have been conducting research on the effectiveness of mindfulness-based stress reduction interventions

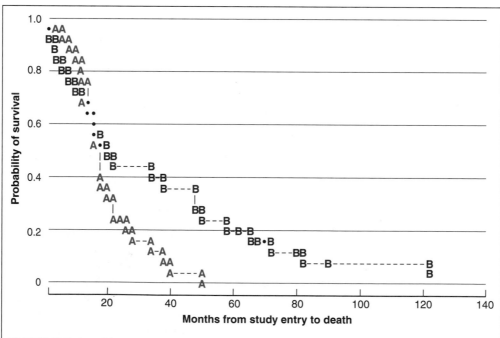

■ **FIGURE 9.6** Survival time for women with advanced breast cancer. In a study of women being treated for advanced breast cancer, researchers found that women in a treatment group (*N* = 50) who received psychosocial intervention survived significantly longer than did women who were in a control group (*N* = 36) with no psychosocial treatment. A = control, B = psychosocial intervention.

Source: Adapted from "Effect of Psychosocial Treatment on Survival of Patients with Metastatic Breast Cancer" by D. Spiegel, J. R. Bloom, H. C. Kramer and E. Gotheil, 1989, *Lancet, 14*, 888–891. © 1989 by The Lancet Ltd. Reprinted by permission.

Breast Cancer Support and Education

"Women who had low self-esteem, low body image, feelings of low control, low optimism, and a lack of support at home were even more likely to benefit from an education intervention."

Go to Psychology CourseMate at www.abnormalpsych3ce.nelson.com to watch this video.

for individuals diagnosed with cancer (see Chapter 7 for a description of mindfulness-based therapy). In one study, she examined the effects of an eight-week mindfulness-based therapy for cancer outpatients. She found pre- to post-treatment improvements in fatigue, stress, mood problems, and sleep problems (Carlson & Garland, 2005). In another study, Carlson and her colleagues showed that early-stage breast cancer and prostate cancer patients who participated in an eight-week mindfulness program evidenced decreases in stress, improvements in sleep, and increases in quality of life (Carlson, Speca, Patel, & Goodey, 2004). The mindfulness-based intervention also led to beneficial changes in biological indices of immune system function (i.e., measures of the functioning of the HPA axis).

The initial success of these treatments has generated a great deal of interest in exactly how they work. Possibilities include better health habits, closer adherence to medical treatment, and improved endocrine functioning and response to stress, all of which may improve immune function (Classen, Sephton, Diamond, & Spiegel, 1998). Andersen, Kiecolt-Glaser, and Glaser (1994) have suggested similar factors as important, but also stress the benefits of enhanced social adjustment and coping. Nezu et al. (1999) demonstrated that problem-solving skills reduced cancer-related distress substantially. Preliminary evidence even shows that psychological factors may contribute not only to the course but also to the development of cancer and other diseases (e.g., Stam & Steggles, 1987). Perceived lack of control, inadequate coping responses, overwhelmingly stressful life events, or the use of inappropriate coping responses (such as denial) may all contribute to the development of cancer (Schneiderman, Antoni, Ironson, LaPerriere, & Fletcher, 1992; Williams & Schneiderman, 2002). However, most studies on which these conclusions are based involve retrospective psychological tests of people who have cancer; much stronger evidence is required to demonstrate that psychological factors may contribute to the onset of cancer.

Psychological factors are also prominent in treatment and recovery from cancer in children (Koocher, 1996). Many different types of cancer

require invasive and painful medical procedures (Courneya et al., 2003); the suffering can be very difficult to bear, not only for the children but also for the parents and health care providers. Children usually struggle and cry hysterically, so to complete many of the procedures, they must be physically restrained. Not only does their behaviour interfere with successful completion, but the stress and anxiety associated with repeated painful procedures may also have their own detrimental effect on the disease process.

Research by pediatric psychologists has shown that when children are coping with the pain of surgery, some coping strategies are better than others (e.g., Bennett-Branson & Craig, 1993; Reid, Chambers, McGrath, & Finley, 1997). For example, a study conducted by Graeme Reid of the University of Western Ontario and his colleagues (1997) showed that children who reported that they used distraction as a way of coping experienced less pain and distress following surgery. In contrast, children who used emotion-focused avoidance (i.e., the free expression of emotion without efforts to regulate feelings when in pain) experienced more pain and distress following surgery (Reid et al., 1997). More recent research by Carl von Bayer at the University of Saskatchewan and his colleagues compared the efficacy of two different strategies in helping children manage pain (Piira, Hayes, Goodenough, & von Bayer, 2006). For younger children, a strategy that prompted children to distract themselves and focus their attention externally was more effective, whereas for older children, the distraction intervention was equally effective as an alternative strategy where children were prompted to direct their attention toward their internal sensations. Other psychological procedures designed to reduce pain and stress in children undergoing surgery and painful medical procedures include breathing exercises, watching films of exactly what happens to take the uncertainty out of the procedure, and rehearsal of

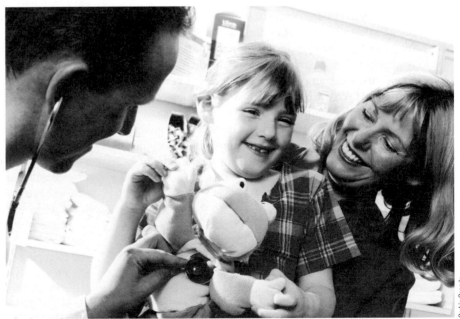

▲ Psychological preparation reduces suffering and facilitates recovery in children who undergo surgery.

▲ Patrick McGrath, a pediatric health psychologist at Dalhousie University and the IWK Health Centre in Halifax, has made many important contributions to the understanding of pain in children and adolescents. He currently holds a Canada Research Chair and received the Order of Canada for his important work on understanding and treating children's pain.

the procedure with dolls, all of which make the interventions much more tolerable and therefore more successful for young patients (Hubert, Jay, Saltoun, & Hayes, 1988; McGrath & DeVeber, 1986). These procedures are used more routinely today for children about to undergo surgery or painful medical procedures. Pediatric psychologist Patrick McGrath at Dalhousie University and his colleagues have also developed a handbook for parents outlining ways to help make cancer treatments less painful for children (e.g., McGrath, Finley, & Turner, 1992).

Some psychological procedures have also been demonstrated to be effective in reducing pain among adult cancer patients (see review by Sellick & Zaza, 1998). Unfortunately, although health care professionals are familiar with most nonpharmacological strategies for managing pain in cancer patients, they rarely recommend or use these strategies with patients, as shown by the work of Christine Zaza and her colleagues at the University of Waterloo (Zaza, Sellick, Willan, Reyno, & Browman, 1999). Thus, health psychologists need to focus efforts making effective therapies for pain control in cancer patients more available to patients in need of these services.

Cardiovascular Problems

The cardiovascular system comprises the heart, blood vessels, and complex control mechanisms for regulating their function. Many things can go wrong with this system and lead to **cardiovascular disease**. For example, many individuals, particularly older individuals, experience **strokes**, also called **cerebral vascular accidents (CVA)**, which are temporary blockages of blood vessels leading to the brain or a rupture of blood vessels in the brain that results in temporary or permanent brain damage and loss of functioning. The cardiovascular problems receiving the most attention these days are hypertension and coronary heart disease, and we look at both. First, let's consider the case of John.

JOHN | *The Human Volcano*

John is a 55-year-old business executive, married, with two teenage children. For most of his adult life, John has smoked about a pack of cigarettes each day. Although he maintains a busy and active schedule, John is mildly obese, partly from regular meals with business partners and colleagues. He has been taking several medications for high blood pressure since age 42. John's doctor has warned him

repeatedly to cut down on his smoking and to exercise more frequently, especially because John's father died of a heart attack. Although John has episodes of chest pain, he continues his busy and stressful lifestyle. It is difficult for John to slow down, as his business has been doing extremely well during the past ten years.

Moreover, John believes that life is too short, that he has no time to slow down. He sees relatively little of his family and works late most evenings. Even when he's at home, John typically works into the night. It is very difficult for him to relax; he feels a constant urgency to get as many things done as possible and prefers to work on several tasks simultaneously. For instance, John often proofreads a document, engages in a phone conversation, and eats lunch all at the same time. He attributes much of the success of his business to his working style. Despite his success, John is not well liked by his peers. His co-workers and employees often find him overbearing, easily frustrated, and, at times, even hostile. His subordinates in particular claim he is overly impatient and critical of their performance.

Do you think John has a problem? Today most people would recognize that John's behaviours and attitudes make his life unpleasant and also possibly lethal. Some of these behaviours and attitudes appear to operate directly on the cardiovascular system and may result in hypertension and coronary heart disease.

Hypertension

Hypertension (high blood pressure) is a major risk factor not only for stroke and heart disease but also for kidney disease, all of which make hypertension an extremely serious medical condition. Blood pressure increases when the blood vessels leading to organs and peripheral areas constrict (become narrower), forcing more and more blood to muscles in central parts of the body. Because so many blood vessels have constricted, the heart muscles must work much harder to force the blood to all parts of the body, which causes the increased pressure. These factors produce wear and tear on the ever-shrinking blood vessels and lead to cardiovascular disease.

A small percentage of cases of hypertension can be traced to specific physical abnormalities such as kidney disease or tumours on the adrenal glands (Papillo & Shapiro, 1990), but the overwhelming majority have no specific verifiable physical cause and are considered **essential hypertension**. In blood pressure readings, the first value is called the systolic blood pressure, the pressure when the heart is pumping blood. The second value is the diastolic blood pressure, the pressure between beats when the heart is at rest. Generally, elevations in diastolic pressure seem to be more worrisome in terms of risk of disease.

Previously, blood pressure was defined as high by the World Health Organization if it exceeded 160/95 (Papillo & Shapiro, 1990), although measures of 140/90 or above were considered "borderline" and cause for concern (Wolf-Maier et al., 2003). The new guidelines, released by the Joint National Committee on Prevention, Detection, Evaluation, and Treatment of High Blood

Pressure, are a bit different. The new guidelines change the former blood pressure definitions to the following:

- Normal: less than 120/less than 80
- Prehypertension: 120–139/80–89
- Stage 1 hypertension: 140–159/90–99
- Stage 2 hypertension: at or greater than 160/at or greater than 100.

So 140/90 is no longer considered "borderline"—it is hypertension and should be treated with lifestyle changes to avoid medication (Taylor, 2003).

According to the latest comprehensive survey, 26.7 percent of North Americans between age 35 and age 64 suffer from hypertension, with a corresponding and shocking figure of 44.2 percent in 6 European countries. These are extraordinary numbers when you consider that hypertension, contributing to as many fatal diseases as it does, has been called the "silent killer." Even more striking is the fact that in both Canada and the United States, Black people are much more likely to develop hypertension and to have hypertensive vascular diseases than white people (Brannon & Feist, 1997; Yan et al., 2003). This makes hypertension a principal disorder of concern among Black people (International Interdisciplinary Conference on Hypertension in Blacks, 1999). Saab and colleagues (1992) demonstrated that during laboratory stress tests, Black people without high blood pressure show greater vascular responsiveness, including heightened blood pressure. Thus, Black people in general may be at greater risk to develop hypertension.

You will not be surprised to learn there are biological, psychological, and social contributions to the development of this potentially deadly condition. As noted by Karina Davidson and her colleagues, it has been clear since the 1930s that an elevated cardiovascular response to stress is associated with hypertension (Gerin et al., 2000; Linden, Gerin, & Davidson, 2003). It has also long been clear that hypertension runs in families and very likely is subject to marked genetic influences (Papillo & Shapiro, 1990; Williams, Mar-

chuk, & Gadde, 2001). As established by the work of Blaine Ditto and his colleagues (e.g., Adler, Ditto, France, & France, 1994), when stressed in the laboratory, even individuals with normal blood pressure show greater reactivity in their blood pressure if their parents have high blood pressure than do individuals with normal blood pressure whose parents also had normal blood pressure (see also Clark, 2003; Fredrikson & Matthews, 1990). Thus, it doesn't take much to activate an inherited vulnerability to hypertension. In fact, the offspring of people with hypertension are at twice the risk of developing hypertension than children of parents with normal blood pressure (Brannon & Feist, 1997; Kaplan, 1980).

Dennis Turk, Donald Meichenbaum, and Myles Genest report that elevated blood pressure is evident even during the first few weeks of life in babies of hypertensive parents (Turk, Meichenbaum, & Genest, 1983). Studies examining neurobiological causes of hypertension have centred on two factors central to the regulation of blood pressure: autonomic nervous system activity and mechanisms regulating sodium in the kidneys. When the sympathetic branch of the autonomic nervous system becomes active, one consequence is the constriction of blood vessels, which produces greater resistance against circulation; that is, blood pressure is elevated (Guyton, 1981). Because the sympathetic nervous system is very responsive to stress, many investigators have long assumed that stress is a major contributor to essential hypertension. Sodium and water regulation, one of the functions of the kidneys, is also important in regulating blood pressure. Retaining too much salt increases blood volume and heightens blood pressure. This is one reason that people with hypertension are often told to restrict their intake of salt.

Psychological factors, such as personality, coping style, and, again, level of stress, have been used to explain individual differences in blood pressure (Leclerc, Rahn, & Linden, 2006; Taylor, 2009; Winters & Schneiderman, 2000). For example, in a review of 28 studies, Uchino et al. (1996) found a strong relationship between levels of social support and blood pressure. Loneliness, depression, and uncontrollability are psychological mechanisms that may contribute to the association between hypertension and social support. Also, both anger and hostility have been associated with increases in blood pressure in the laboratory setting (Jamner, Shapiro, Goldstein, & Hug, 1991; King, Taylor, Albright, & Haskell, 1990; Miller, Smith, Turner, Guijarro, & Hallet, 1996). The notion that hostility or repressed hostility predicts hypertension (and other cardiovascular problems) can be traced back to Alexander (1939), who suggested that an inability to express anger could result in hypertension and other cardiovascular problems. What may be more important is not whether anger is suppressed but rather how frequently anger and hostility are experienced (Brondolo et al., 2003; Winters & Schneiderman, 2000).

Let's return to the case of John for a moment. John clearly has hypertension. Do you detect any anger in John's case study? John's hypertension may well be related to his stressful lifestyle, frustration levels, and hostility. In fact, work conducted at Dalhousie University by Karina Davidson and her colleagues has shown that the ability to control anger by expressing these feelings constructively is associated with markedly lower blood pressure in the population (Davidson, MacGregor, Stuhr, Dixon, & MacLean, 2000), suggesting that it might help patients too. General stress management interventions also appear effective in helping control

Charles Thatcher/Stone/Getty Images

▲ In both Canada and the United States, Black people develop hypertension in disproportionately high numbers.

Cardiovascular Problems **325**

high blood pressure in hypertensive patients as identified in a comprehensive review of the literature by University of British Columbia health psychologist Wolfgang Linden and his colleagues (Spence, Barnett, Linden, Ramsden, & Taenzer, 1999). In particular, individualized cognitive-behavioural interventions using a variety of techniques appear to be more likely to be effective than single-component interventions such as relaxation or biofeedback alone (Linden & Moseley, 2006; Spence et al., 1999). Relaxation and biofeedback procedures are discussed in more detail later in this chapter.

Coronary Heart Disease

It may not surprise you that psychological and social factors contribute to high blood pressure, but can changes in behaviour and attitudes prevent heart attacks? The answers are still not entirely clear, but increasing evidence indicates that psychological and social factors are implicated in coronary heart disease (Winters & Schneiderman, 2000). Why is this important? Heart disease is the number one cause of death in Western countries, including Canada (see Table 9.1 on page 313).

Coronary heart disease (CHD), quite simply, is a blockage of the arteries supplying blood to the heart muscle (the *myocardium*). A number of terms describe heart disease. Chest pain resulting from partial obstruction of the arteries is called *angina pectoris* or, usually, just *angina*. *Atherosclerosis* occurs when a fatty substance or plaque builds up inside the arteries and causes an obstruction. *Ischemia* is the name for deficiency of blood to a body part caused by the narrowing of the arteries by too much plaque. And *myocardial infarction*, or *heart attack*, is the death of heart tissue when a specific artery becomes completely clogged with plaque. Arteries can constrict or become blocked for a variety of reasons other than plaque. For example, a blood clot might lodge in the artery.

It seems clear that we inherit a vulnerability to CHD (and to many other physical disorders), and other factors such as diet, exercise, and culture make very important contributions to our cardiovascular status (Thoresen & Powell, 1992). But what sort of psychological factors contribute to CHD?

A variety of studies suggest strongly that stress, anxiety, and anger, combined with poor coping skills and low social support, are implicated in CHD (Lett et al., 2005; Matthews, 2005; Suls & Bunde, 2005; Taylor, 2009; Winters & Schneiderman, 2000). Some studies indicate that even healthy men who experience stress are later more likely to experience CHD than low-stress groups (Rosengren, Tibblin, & Wilhelmsen, 1991). For such individuals, stress-reduction procedures may prove to be an important preventive technique. There is a great deal of evidence on the value of stress-reduction procedures in preventing future heart attacks (Williams & Schneiderman, 2002). One report from a group of researchers in the Netherlands summarized results from 37 studies, using analytic procedures that combine the results from these studies. The effects of stress-reduction programs on CHD were apparent. Specifically, these studies in the aggregate yielded a 34 percent reduction in death from heart attacks, a 29 percent reduction in the recurrence of heart attacks; and a significant positive effect on blood pressure, cholesterol levels, body weight, and other risk factors for CHD (Dusseldorp, van Elderen, Maes, Meulman, & Kraaij, 1999). A recent review by Wolfgang Linden

and his colleagues is a bit more conservative in its conclusions. These authors suggest that psychological interventions, when added to usual care, can be of benefit for people with CHD as long as they are provided by well-trained professionals, offered to individuals who are in demonstrated distress, and tailored to the patient's individual needs (Langosch, Budde, & Linden, 2007). They conclude that there is consistent evidence that existing psychological distress can be effectively reduced by such interventions, and that this may also have a positive additional effect in helping the patient adhere to modifying other risk factors for CHD (Langosch et al., 2007). Interestingly, a recent controlled trial by Simon Bacon at Concordia University and his colleagues suggests that an exercise intervention may be just as effective as a stress-reduction intervention, with both proving superior to medical care alone in reducing emotional distress and improving markers of cardiovascular risk in people with CHD (Blumenthal et al., 2005).

Can we identify, before an attack, people who are under a great deal of stress that might make them susceptible to a first heart attack? The answer seems to be "yes," but the answer is more complex than we first thought. Clinical investigators reported several decades ago that certain groups of people engage in a cluster of behaviours in stressful situations that seem to put them at considerable risk for CHD. These behaviours include excessive competitive drive, a sense of always being pressured for time, impatience, incredible amounts of energy that may show up in accelerated speech and motor activity, and angry outbursts. This set of behaviours, which came to be called the **type A behaviour pattern**, was first identified by two cardiologists (Friedman & Rosenman, 1959, 1974). The **type B behaviour pattern**, also described by these clinicians, applies to people who basically do not have type A attributes. In other words, the type B individual is more relaxed, less concerned about deadlines, and seldom feels the pressure or, perhaps, the excitement of challenges or overriding ambition.

The concept of the type A personality or behaviour pattern is widely accepted in our hard-driving, goal-oriented culture. Indeed, some early studies supported the concept of type A behaviour as putting people at risk for CHD (Friedman & Rosenman, 1974). But the most convincing evidence came from two large prospective studies that followed thousands of patients over a long period to determine the relationship of their behaviour to heart disease. The first study was the Western Collaborative Group Study (WCGS). In this project, 3154 healthy men, aged 39 to 59, were interviewed at the beginning of the study to determine their typical behavioural patterns. They were then followed for eight years. The basic finding was that the men who displayed a type A behaviour pattern at the beginning of the study were at least twice as likely to develop CHD as the men with a type B behaviour pattern. When the investigators analyzed the data for the younger men in the study (aged 39 to 49), the results were even more striking, with CHD developing approximately six times more frequently in the type A group than in the type B group (Rosenman et al., 1975).

A second major study is the Framingham Heart Study that has been ongoing for more than 40 years (Haynes, Feinleib, & Kannel, 1980) and has taught us much of what we know about the development and course of CHD. In this study, 1674 healthy men and women were categorized by type A or type B behaviour pattern and followed for eight years. Once again, both men and women with a type A pattern were more than twice as likely to develop

▲ Both type A behaviour and coronary heart disease (CHD) seem to be culturally determined.

three to five times greater incidence of CHD levels (Marmot & Syme, 1976; Matsumoto, 1996). Clearly, socio-cultural differences are important (Baker, Richter, & Anand, 2001).

Despite these results, at least in Western cultures, the type A concept has proven much more complex and elusive than scientists had hoped. First, it is very difficult to determine whether someone is type A from structured interviews, questionnaires, or other measures of this construct, because the measures often do not agree with one another. Many people have some of the characteristics of type A but not all of them, and others present with a mixture of types A and B. The notion that we can divide the world into two types of people—an assumption underlying the early work in this area—has long since been discarded. As a result, more recent studies have not necessarily supported the relationship of type A behaviour to CHD (Dembroski & Costa, 1987; Hollis, Connett, Stevens, & Greenlick, 1990).

Concept Check | 9.2

Heart disease is the primary cause of death in Western countries like Canada. Assess your knowledge of some of the major factors in heart disease by matching the following terms with the definitions provided: (a) coronary heart disease (CHD), (b) atherosclerosis, (c) angina, and (d) myocardial infarction.

1. The death of heart tissue when a specific artery becomes completely clogged with plaque. _____

2. The buildup of a fatty substance inside the arteries that causes an obstruction. _____

3. Chest pain resulting from partial obstruction of the arteries. _____

4. A blockage of the arteries supplying blood to the heart muscle. _____

CHD as were their type B counterparts (in men, the risk was nearly three times as great). But, in the male group, the results were evident only in those individuals in higher-status white-collar occupations, not in individuals with blue-collar socio-economic status and occupations. For women, the results were strongest for those with a low level of education (Eaker, Pinsky, & Castelli, 1992).

Population-based studies in Europe essentially replicated these results (DeBacker, Kittel, Kornitzer, & Dramaix, 1983; French-Belgian Collaborative Group, 1982). It is interesting that a large study of Japanese men conducted in Hawaii did not replicate these findings (Cohen & Reed, 1985). In fact, the prevalence of type A behaviour among Japanese men is much lower than among men in North America (18.7 percent versus approximately 50 percent). Similarly, the prevalence of CHD is equally low (Japanese men 4 percent, North American men 13 percent; Haynes & Matthews, 1988). In a study that illustrates the effects of culture more dramatically, 3809 North Americans of Japanese descent were classified into groups according to how "traditionally Japanese" they were (in other words, did they speak Japanese at home, retain traditional Japanese values and behaviours, and so on). Those who were the "most Japanese" had the lowest incidence of CHD, not significantly different from Japanese men in Japan. In contrast, the group that was the "least Japanese" had a

The Role of Chronic Negative Emotions

At this point, investigators decided that something might be wrong with the type A construct itself (Matthews, 1988; Rodin & Salovey, 1989). A consensus developed that some behaviours and emotions representative of the type A personality might be very important in the development of CHD, but not all of them. The primary factor that seems to be responsible for much of the relationship is anger (Miller et al., 1996). Ironson and colleagues (1992) found that anger impaired the pumping efficiency of the heart in individuals with heart disease, putting them at risk for dangerous disturbances in heart rhythm (*arrhythmias*). This study confirms earlier findings relating the frequent experience of anger to later CHD (Houston, Chesney, Black, Cates, & Hecker, 1992; Smith, 1992). Results from an important study strengthen this conclusion. Iribarren et al. (2000) evaluated 374 young, healthy North American adults, both Caucasian and Black, over 10 years. Those with high hostility and anger showed evidence of coronary artery calcification, an early sign of CHD.

Is type A irrelevant to the development of heart disease? Most investigators conclude that some components of the type A construct are important determinants of CHD, with a chronically high

© Chris Cheadle/Alamy

level of negative affect, such as anger, one of the prime candidates, and the time urgency/impatience factor another (Williams et al., 2003; Winters & Schneiderman, 2000). Recall again the case of John who had all the type A behaviours, including time urgency, but also had frequent angry outbursts. John was clearly high in a personality trait referred to as hostility. A recent study conducted at Dalhousie University by Karina Davidson and her colleagues suggests that an intervention focusing on reducing hostility may be very useful for men with CHD (Gidron, Davidson, & Bata, 1999). A group of men with CHD who were high in hostility were randomly assigned to a hostility intervention or to an information-control group. Immediately following the intervention and two months later, the men who had received the active intervention reported less hostility and were also observed to be less hostile. Moreover, the men who had received the active intervention showed lower diastolic blood pressure at follow-up. These results are very promising and support the important role of anger and hostility in CHD. Whether a hostility-reduction intervention can prevent future heart attacks in CHD men remains to be determined (Gidron et al., 1999).

But what about people who experience varieties of negative affect closely related to anger on a chronic basis? Look back to Figure 9.2 (p. 317) and notice the close relationship among stress, anxiety, and depression. Some evidence indicates that the physiological components of these emotions and their effects on the cardiovascular system may be similar. We also know that the emotion of anger, so commonly associated with stress, is closely related to the emotion of fear, as evidenced in the fight-flight syndrome. Fight is the typical behavioural action tendency associated with anger, and flight or escape is associated with fear. But our bodily alarm response, activated by an immediate danger or threat, is associated with both emotions.

Some investigators, after reviewing the literature, have concluded that anxiety and depression are as important as anger in the development of CHD (Albert, Chae, Rexrode, Manson, & Kawachi, 2005; Barlow, 1988; Frasure-Smith & Lesperance, 2005; Strike & Steptoe, 2005; Suls & Bunde, 2005), even anxious and depressive features noticeable at an early age (Grossardt, Bower, Geda, Colligan, & Rocca, 2009). In a study of 896 people who had had heart attacks, Frasure-Smith, Lesperance, Juneau, Talajic, and Bourassa (1999) found that patients who were depressed were three times more likely to die in the year following their heart attacks than those who were not depressed, regardless of how severe their initial heart disease was. And as noted by Québec clinical psychologist Kim Lavoie and her colleagues (2004), panic disorder and CHD often co-occur, and CHD patients with comorbid panic disorder suffer greater morbidity and mortality rates than do CHD patients without comorbid panic disorder. Thus, it may be that the chronic experience of the negative emotions of stress (anger), anxiety (fear or panic), and depression (ongoing) and the neurobiological activation that accompanies these emotions provide the most important psychosocial contributions to CHD and perhaps to other physical disorders. On the other hand, in the Ironson et al. (1992) study, subjects who were asked to imagine being in situations that produced performance anxiety (having to give a speech or take a difficult test) did not experience the same effect on their hearts as those who imagined anger—at least, not in those individuals with

existing CHD. As has been cautiously noted by Brian Baker of the University of Toronto, we still have much to learn about these relationships (Baker et al., 2001).

Chronic Pain

Pain is not in itself a disorder, yet for most of us it is the fundamental signal of injury, illness, or disease. The importance of pain in our lives cannot be underestimated. Without low levels of pain providing feedback on the functioning of the body and its various systems, we would incur substantially more injuries. For example, you might lie out in the hot sun a lot longer. You might not roll over while sleeping or shift your posture while sitting, thereby affecting your circulation in a way that might be harmful. Reactions to this kind of pain are mostly automatic; that is, we are not aware of the discomfort. When pain crosses the threshold of awareness, which varies a great deal from one person to another, we are forced to take action. If we can't relieve the pain ourselves or we are not sure of its cause, we usually seek medical help. The cost of chronic pain in Canada, including medical expenses, lost productivity, and lost income (but not including the social costs) is estimated to exceed $10 billion annually (Chronic Pain Association of Canada [CPAC], 2003). In fact, 80 percent of all visits to physicians are due to pain (Gatchel & Turk, 1996).

There are two kinds of clinical pain: acute and chronic. **Acute pain** typically follows an injury and disappears once the injury heals or is effectively treated, often within a month (Philips & Grant, 1991). **Chronic pain**, by contrast, may begin with an acute episode but does not decrease over time, even when the injury has healed or effective treatments have been administered. Typically, chronic pain is in the muscles, joints, or tendons, particularly in the lower back. Vascular pain due to enlarged blood vessels may be chronic, as may headaches and pain caused by the slow degeneration of tissue, as in some terminal diseases, and by the growth of cancerous tumours that impinge on pain receptors (Melzack & Wall, 1982; Taylor, 1999). Surveys indicate that more than 18 percent of Canadians endure severe chronic pain (CPAC, 2003). Thus, in Canada alone, millions of people experience chronic pain, yet most researchers now agree that the cause of chronic pain and the resulting enormous drain on our health care system are substantially psychological and social (Dersh, Polatin, & Gatchel, 2002; Turk & Monarch, 2002). Consider the case of Preepi, described by Christine Korol and Kenneth Craig (2001) of the University of British Columbia.

PREEPI | *Resigned to Pain*

Preepi was injured when she slipped on a wet floor while she was carrying a stack of dishes in the restaurant where she worked two years ago. She has been unable to work since her injury and complains of severe low back pain and numbness down her right leg. She was 52 at the time she was first assessed in a multidisciplinary pain program and presented as having a severe disability (e.g., she was only able to stand or sit for five minutes at a time, had severely decreased range of motion and little strength, and relied primarily on her family to help her with her activities of daily living). She reported through a Punjabi interpreter to the psychologist on the team that her mother-in-law and her two teenage children took care of household chores for her and that her husband was very helpful because he would rub her back and bring her pain medication.

Despite support from her family, Preepi felt guilty about not being able to care for her family, reported that it was God's will that she suffer, and was resigned to the fact that, after two years, she would probably always suffer. On careful assessment, Preepi was diagnosed as depressed with occasional suicidal ideation. She was admitted to the chronic pain management program in the clinic, and the treatment team noted that they would have to pay special attention to the many factors contributing to her continued disability (e.g., family solicitousness, resignation and help-lessness, depressed mood, and sedentary lifestyle).

Source: Reprinted from Korol, C. T., & Craig, K. D. (2001). "Pain from the perspectives of health psychology and culture." In Kazarian, S. S. & Evans, D. R. (Eds), *Handbook of cultural health psychology* (pp. 241–265).

To better understand the experience of pain, clinicians and researchers generally make a clear distinction between the subjective experience termed *pain*, reported by the patient, and the overt manifestations of this experience, termed *pain behaviours*. Pain behaviours include changing the way one sits or walks, continually complaining about pain to others, grimacing, and, most important, avoiding various activities, particularly those involving work or leisure. Finally, an emotional component of pain called *suffering* sometimes accompanies pain and sometimes does not (Fordyce, 1988; Liebeskind, 1991). Because they are so important, we first review psychological and social contributions to pain.

Psychological and Social Aspects

In mild forms, chronic pain can be an annoyance that eventually wears you down and takes the pleasure out of your life. Severe chronic pain may cause you to lose your job, withdraw from your family, give up the fun in your life, and focus your entire awareness on seeking relief. What is interesting for our purposes is that the *severity* of the pain does not seem to predict the reaction to it. Some individuals experience intense pain frequently and yet continue to work productively, rarely seek out medical services, and lead reasonably normal lives; others become invalids. These differences appear to be due primarily to psychological factors (Dersh et al., 2002; Gatchel, 2005; Sullivan, Bishop, & Pivik, 1995; Turk & Monarch, 2002). It will come as no surprise that these factors are the same as those implicated in the stress response and other negative emotional states, such as anxiety and depression (Ohayon & Schatzberg, 2003; see Chapters 5 and 7).

The determining factor seems to be the individual's general sense of control over the situation: whether or not he or she can deal with the pain and its consequences in an effective and meaningful way. Recall Preepi's feelings of hopelessness and resignation

toward her pain; these psychological factors likely contributed to her distress and pain-related disability as much as the original work-related injury itself. As observed by researchers Bandura, O'Leary, Taylor, Gauthier, and Gossard (1987), when a positive sense of control is combined with a generally optimistic outlook about the future, the person experiences substantially less distress and disability (see also Gatchel & Turk, 1999; Keefe & France, 1999; Otis & Pincus, 2008; Zautra, Johnson, & Davis, 2005). Positive psychological factors are also associated with active attempts to cope, such as exercise and other regimens, as opposed to suffering passively as Preepi did (Strahl, Kleinknecht, & Dinnel, 2000; Turk & Gatchel, 2002).

Canadian research groups have been at the forefront in research on the involvement of anxiety-related factors in explaining chronic pain. For example, the research of Gordon Asmundson and colleagues suggests that the fear of pain could predispose a person to the development of chronic pain following a physical injury. The idea is that people who fear pain will tend to avoid activity following an injury because of concerns that they may reinjure themselves or experience uncontrollable pain. This avoidance of activity reduces their anxiety in the short term but can contribute to maintaining pain in the long term, because their bodies become deconditioned due to the lack of exercise (Asmundson, Jacobson, Allerdings, & Norton, 1996; Stewart & Asmundson, 2006). Recall Preepi's sedentary lifestyle following her injury at work. In the short term, her avoidance of the movement involved in completing her household chores might have helped her avoid unpleasant pain sensations in her back, but in the longer term, her inactivity probably led to deconditioning, which may have maintained or even exacerbated her pain.

Another important psychological factor is pain catastrophizing. Canada Research Chair Michael Sullivan at McGill University defines **pain catastrophizing** as "an exaggerated negative response brought to bear during actual or anticipated painful experience" (Sullivan et al., 2001). A catastrophizer might think or feel the following things when experiencing pain: "I can't stop thinking of how much it hurts," (rumination), "I worry that something serious might happen," (magnification), and "There is nothing I can do to reduce the intensity of the pain," (helplessness; see Sullivan et al., 1995). For example, Preepi appeared to experience thoughts about her helplessness in controlling the pain, which led to her feeling resigned to suffer. Pain catastrophizing is associated with a number of pain-related outcomes (Sullivan, Tripp, Rodgers, & Stanish, 2000), suggesting that it may be a risk factor for chronic pain and disability (Sullivan et al., 2001). In fact, Sullivan, Lynch, and Clark (2005) recently showed that catastrophizing predicted pain-related disability over and above the contributions of pain severity in a sample of patients with chronic pain.

Further evidence for the role of catastrophizing in pain-related disability has been supplied by Sullivan and Stanish (2003), who developed and tested a novel early intervention for chronic pain called the Pain Disability Prevention (PDP) Program. It is a ten-week cognitive-behavioural program designed to increase involvement in goal-directed activity on a daily basis and to minimize psychological barriers to activity involvement after a worker has sustained an occupational injury. Patients making claims through the Workers' Compensation Board in Nova Scotia who had sustained soft-tissue injuries to their back, who were still off work six weeks after injury, and who showed at least one warning sign that their pain might become more chronic were eligible to participate in the program. Preepi would have been an eligible candidate for this intervention six weeks after she had sustained her injury at the restaurant. The authors described results from the first 104 patients who were offered the program. The success rate was 60 percent: 45 percent returned to work and another 15 percent were deemed ready to return to work. Psychological factors were quite important in predicting who would benefit from the program: Pretreatment scores on pain catastrophizing, fear of movement or reinjury, and depression could be used to accurately predict success in the program in 92 percent of the cases. These preliminary results are promising and suggest the importance of an early focus on pain catastrophizing to prevent acute pain from becoming chronic. However, this approach now needs to be investigated in a randomized, controlled design so we can be sure that the observed changes were actually due to the PDP intervention (Sullivan & Stanish, 2003).

That the experience of pain can be largely disconnected from disease or injury is perhaps best exemplified by *phantom limb pain*—a phenomenon that has been described and investigated extensively by Joel Katz and his colleagues (e.g., Katz & Gagliese, 1999; Wilkins, McGrath, Finley, & Katz, 2004). In this not uncommon condition, people who have lost an arm or leg feel excruciating pain in the limb that is no longer there. Furthermore, they can describe in exquisite detail the exact location of the pain and its type, such as a dull ache or a sharp cutting pain. The fact that they are fully aware that the limb is amputated does nothing to relieve the pain. Evidence suggests that changes in the sensory cortex of the brain may contribute to this phenomenon (Flor et al., 1995; Katz & Gagliese, 1999; Ramachandran, 1993). Generally, someone who thinks pain is disastrous, uncontrollable, or reflective of personal failure experiences more intense pain and greater psychological distress than someone who does not feel this way (Edwards et al., 2009; Gatchel et al., 2007; Gil, Williams, Keefe, & Beckham, 1990). Thus, treatment programs for chronic pain concentrate on psychological factors.

Other examples of psychological influences on the experience of pain are encountered every day. Athletes with significant tissue damage frequently continue to perform and report relatively little pain. In an important study, 65 percent of war veterans wounded in combat reported feeling no pain. Presumably, their attention was focused externally on what they had to do to survive rather than internally on the experience of pain (Melzack & Wall, 1982).

Social factors also influence how we experience pain. Fordyce (1976, 1988; see also Turk, 1996) has studied social forms of pain behaviour such as verbal complaints, facial expressions, and obvious limps or other symptoms that may reflect strong social contingencies. For example, family members who were formerly critical and demanding may become caring and sympathetic (Kerns et al., 1991; Otis & Pincus, 2008; Romano, Jensen, Turner, Good, & Hops, 2000). Recall the behaviour of Preepi's husband, her mother-in-law, and her two teenage children. Although her family members likely meant well, their sympathy and helpfulness may actually have helped maintain Preepi's chronic pain. This phenomenon is referred to as *operant* control

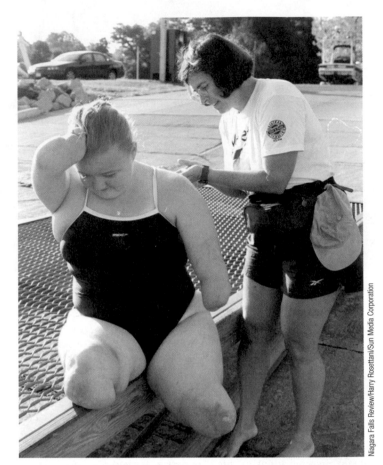

Niagara Falls Review/Harry Rosettani/Sun Media Corporation

▲ It is not uncommon for people to feel specific pain in limbs that are no longer part of them.

of pain behaviour, because the behaviour clearly seems to be under the control of social consequences. But these consequences have an uncertain relation to the amount of pain actually experienced.

By contrast, a strong network of social support may reduce pain. Jamison and Virts (1990) studied 521 chronic pain patients (with back, abdominal, and chest conditions) and discovered that those who lacked social support from their families reported more pain sites and showed more pain behaviour, such as staying in bed. These patients also exhibited more emotional distress *without* rating their pain as any more intense than subjects with strong socially supportive families. The subjects with strong support returned to work earlier, showed less reliance on medications, and increased their activity levels more quickly than the others. Even

Photo by Hugh Wesley, courtesy of Joel Katz

▲ Joel Katz is a Canada Research Chair in the study of pain at York University. His work has contributed to the understanding of the phenomenon of phantom limb pain, and he has recently contributed to revising and updating the original gate control theory of pain developed by his mentor, Ronald Melzack.

having just a photo of a loved one to look at reduces the experience of pain (Master et al., 2009).

Although these results may seem to contradict studies on the operant control of pain, different mechanisms may be at work. General social support may reduce the stress associated with pain and injury and promote more adaptive coping procedures and control. However, specifically reinforcing pain behaviours, particularly in the absence of social supports, may powerfully increase such behaviour. These very complex issues have not yet been entirely sorted out.

Biological Aspects

Gate Control Theory

No one thinks pain is entirely psychological, just as no one thinks it is entirely physical. The *gate control theory* developed by pain researcher Ronald Melzack at McGill University (Melzack & Katz, 2004; Melzack & Wall, 1965, 1982) accommodates both psychological and physical factors. According to this theory, nerve impulses from painful stimuli make their way to the spinal column and from there to the brain. An area called the *dorsal horns of the spinal column* acts as a "gate" and may open and transmit sensations of pain if the stimulation is sufficiently intense. Specific nerve fibres referred to as *small fibres* (A-delta and C fibres) and *large fibres* (A-beta fibres) determine the pattern as well as the intensity of the stimulation. Small fibres tend to open the gate, thereby increasing the transmission of painful stimuli, whereas large fibres tend to close the gate.

Most important for our purpose is that the brain sends signals back down the spinal cord that may affect the gating mechanism. For example, a person with negative emotions such as fear or anxiety may experience pain more intensely because the basic message from the brain is to be vigilant against possible danger or threat. Then again, in a person whose emotions are more positive or who is totally absorbed in an activity (such as a runner intent on finishing a long race), the brain sends down an inhibitory signal that closes the gate. Although many think that the gate control theory is overly simplistic (and it has recently been updated; see Melzack, 1999, 2005), research findings continue to support its basic elements, particularly as it describes the complex interaction of psychological and biological factors in the experience of pain (Edwards, Campbell, Jamison, & Wiech, 2009; Gatchel, Peng, Peters, Fuchs, & Turk, 2007; Gatchel & Turk, 1999; Otis & Pincus, in press; Turk & Monarch, 2002).

Endogenous Opioids

The neurochemical means by which the brain inhibits pain is a very important discovery (Taylor, 2009). Drugs such as heroin and morphine are manufactured from opioid substances. It now turns out that **endogenous** (natural) **opioids** exist within the body. Called *endorphins* or *enkephalins*, they act very much like neurotransmitters. The brain uses them to shut down pain, even in the presence of marked tissue damage or injury. Because endogenous opioids are distributed widely throughout the body, they may be implicated in a variety of psychopathological conditions, including eating disorders and, more commonly, the "runners' high" that accompanies the release of endogenous opioids after

intense (and sometimes painful) physical activity. Albert Bandura, Janel Gauthier, and their colleagues (1987) found that people with a greater sense of self-efficacy and control had a higher tolerance for pain than individuals with low self-efficacy, and they actually increased their production of endogenous opioids when they were confronted with a painful stimulus. Recently, Edwards et al. (2009) have articulated the neurobiological processes underlying the effectiveness of psychological coping procedures that successfully alter the experience of pain. Certain procedures, such as reappraising the significance of the pain instead of catastrophizing or thinking the worst about it, activate a variety of brain circuits that modulate or diminish pain experience and allow for more normal functioning.

Gender Differences in Pain

Most animal and human studies have been conducted on males to avoid the complications of hormonal variation. But men and women seem to experience different types of pain. On the one hand, in addition to menstrual cramps and labour pains, women experience migraine headaches, arthritis, carpal tunnel syndrome, and temporomandibular joint pain (TMJ) more frequently than men do (Miaskowski, 1999). Men, on the other hand, have more cardiac pain and backache. Men and women also seem to have somewhat different pain-regulating mechanisms. Although both males and females have endogenous opioid systems, this system may be more powerful in men. In contrast, the female neurochemistry may be based on an estrogen-dependent neuronal system that may have evolved to cope with the pain associated with reproductive activity (Mogil, Sternberg, Kest, Marek, & Liebeskind, 1993). It is an "extra" pain-regulating pathway in females that, if taken away by removing hormones, has no implications for the remaining pathways, which continue to work as well. One implication of these findings is that males and females may benefit from different kinds of drugs, different kinds of psychosocial interventions, or unique combinations of these treatments to best manage and control pain.

Chronic Fatigue Syndrome

In the mid-19th century, a rapidly growing number of patients showed a lack of energy, marked fatigue, a variety of aches and pains, and, on occasion, low-grade fever. No physical pathology could be discovered, and George Beard (1869) labelled the condition *neurasthenia*, literally, "lack of nerve strength" (Abbey & Garfinkel, 1991a; Costa e Silva & DeGirolamo, 1990; Morey & Kurtz, 1989). The disease was attributed to the demands of the time, including a preoccupation with material success, a strong emphasis on hard work, and the changing role of women. Neurasthenia disappeared in the early 20th century in Western cultures but remains the most prevalent form of psychopathology in China (Good & Kleinman, 1985; Kleinman, 1986). Now **chronic fatigue syndrome (CFS)** is spreading rapidly throughout the Western world (Jason, Fennell, & Taylor, 2006; Prins, van der Meer, & Bleijenberg, 2006). The symptoms of CFS, listed in Table 9.2, are almost identical to those of neurasthenia and, until recently, were attributed to viral

TABLE 9.2 Definition of Chronic Fatigue Syndrome

Inclusion Criteria
1. Clinically evaluated, medically unexplained fatigue of at least six months duration that is • of new onset (not lifelong) • not resulting from ongoing exertion • not substantially alleviated by rest • a substantial reduction in previous level of activities 2. The occurrence of four or more of the following symptoms: • subjective memory impairment • sore throat • tender lymph nodes • muscle pain • joint pain • headache • unrefreshing sleep • post-exertional malaise lasting more than 24 hours

Source: Adapted from Fukuda et al., 1994.

infection—specifically the Epstein-Barr virus (Straus et al., 1985) or, most recently, XMRV, a retrovirus with some similarities to HIV (Kean, 2010)—immune system dysfunction (Straus, 1988), exposure to toxins, or clinical depression (Chalder, Cleare, & Wessely, 2000; Costa e Silva & De Girolamo, 1990). Although promising leads appear on occasion, no evidence has yet to support any of these hypothetical physical causes (Chalder et al., 2000; Jason et al., 2003; Kean, 2010; Prins et al., 2006).

People with CFS suffer considerably and often must give up their careers. As leading CFS researcher Susan Abbey of the Centre for Addiction and Mental Health in Toronto has pointed out, both neurasthenia in the 19th century and CFS in the present have been attributed to an extremely stressful environment, the changing role of women, and the rapid dissemination of new technology and information (Abbey & Garfinkel, 1991a). Both disorders are most common in women. It is possible, of course, that a virus or a specific immune system dysfunction will be found to account for CFS. Another possibility suggested by Abbey and Garfinkel (1991a) is that the condition represents a rather non-specific response to stress. But it is not clear why certain individuals respond with chronic fatigue instead of some other psychological or physical disorder.

Psychological factors have been implicated. For example, a study by Katherine White at the University of Calgary, Darrin Lehman at the University of British Columbia, and their colleagues examined the role of two cognitive factors (i.e., causal attributions for the CFS and locus of control) in relation to psychological adjustment to the illness in individuals with CFS (White, Lehman, Hemphill, Mandel, & Lehman, 2006). Their results suggest that when an individual perceives the cause of the CFS as being internal (e.g., worrying too much) and believes that he or she has no control over the illness, feelings of helplessness and depression may result.

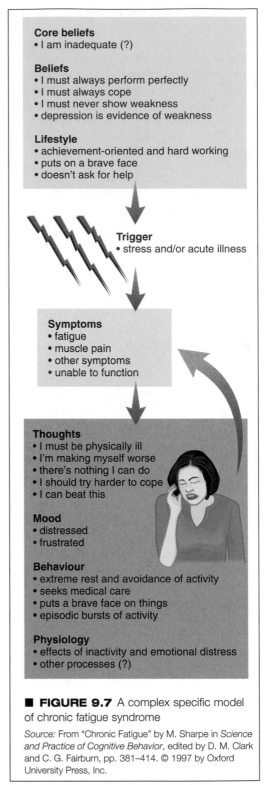

FIGURE 9.7 A complex specific model of chronic fatigue syndrome

Source: From "Chronic Fatigue" by M. Sharpe in *Science and Practice of Cognitive Behavior*, edited by D. M. Clark and C. G. Fairburn, pp. 381–414. © 1997 by Oxford University Press, Inc.

Michael Sharpe (1997) has developed one of the first models of the causes of CFS that accounts for all its features (see ■ Figure 9.7). Sharpe theorizes that individuals with particularly achievement-oriented lifestyles (driven, perhaps, by a basic sense of inadequacy) undergo a period of extreme stress or acute illness. They misinterpret the lingering symptoms of fatigue, pain, and inability to function at their usual very high levels as a continuing disease that is worsened by activity and improved by rest. This results in behavioural avoidance, helplessness, depression, and frustration. They think they should be able to conquer the problem and cope with its symptoms. Chronic inactivity, of course, leads to lack of stamina, weakness, and increased feelings of depression and helplessness that in turn result in episodic bursts of long activity followed by further fatigue. Sharpe's model thus focuses on individual-level cognitive and behavioural factors that cause and maintain the chronic fatigue and emotional symptoms. Recently, Myrtis Fossey and her colleagues (2004) in Montréal have pointed out that the psychological maladjustment (e.g., depression) seen in CFS patients may also be the result of living with a chronic illness that is poorly recognized and not well understood.

Pharmacological treatment has not proven effective for CFS (Chalder et al., 2000; Sharpe, 1992), but Sharpe in Oxford has developed a cognitive-behavioural program that includes procedures to increase activity, regulate periods of rest, and direct cognitive therapy at the cognitions specified in Figure 9.7 (see also White et al., 2006). This treatment also includes relaxation, breathing exercises, and general stress-reduction procedures, interventions we describe in the next section (Sharpe, 1992, 1993, 1997). Time will tell whether Sharpe's approach to CFS is correct in whole or in part, but it is the first comprehensive model and it does have treatment implications. In the first controlled trial evaluating this approach, 60 patients were assigned to the cognitive-behavioural treatment or to treatment as usual. Seventy-three percent of the patients in the treatment group improved on measures of fatigue, disability, and illness belief, a result far superior to the control group (Sharpe et al., 1996).

Now the results are in from a more sophisticated large-scale evaluation of a similar cognitive-behavioural approach to CFS (Deale, Chalder, Marks, & Wessely, 1997). In a clinical trial conducted in London, England, 60 patients with CFS were randomly assigned to cognitive-behavioural therapy or relaxation exercises alone. The results indicated that fatigue diminished and overall functioning improved significantly more in the group that received cognitive-behavioural therapy. As is evident in Table 9.3, 70 percent of individuals who completed cognitive-behavioural therapy achieved substantial improvement in physical functioning at a six-month follow-up, compared with only 19 percent of those in the relaxation-only group. These results are encouraging.

TABLE 9.3 Patients with Chronic Fatigue Syndrome Who Had Good Outcomes at Six-Month Follow-Up*

Study Group	N	%
Treatment completers		
Cognitive-behavioural therapy (N = 27)	19	70
Relaxation (N = 26)	5	19
Completers plus dropouts		
Cognitive-behavioural therapy (N = 30)	19	63
Relaxation (N = 30)	5	17

Note:* An increase of 50 percent or more, from pretreatment to six-month follow-up, or an end score of 83 or more on the physical functioning scale of the medical outcome study short-form general health survey.

Source: The American Journal of Psychiatry by American Psychiatric Association. Copyright 1997. Reproduced with permission of AMERICAN PSYCHIATRIC ASSOCIATION (JOURNALS) in the format Textbook via Copyright Clearance Center.

Psychosocial Treatment of Physical Disorders

Certain experiments suggest that pain is not only bad for you, but it may also kill you. It has been shown that postsurgical pain in rats doubles the rate at which a certain cancer metastasizes (spreads) to the lungs (Page, Ben-Eliyahu, Yirmiya, & Liebeskind, 1993). Rats undergoing abdominal surgery *without* morphine developed twice the number of lung metastases as rats who were given morphine for the same surgery. In fact, the rats undergoing surgery with the pain-killing drug had even lower rates of metastases than rats that did not have surgery.

This effect may result from the interaction of pain with the immune system. Pain may reduce the number of natural killer (NK) cells in the immune system, perhaps because of the general stress reaction to the pain. Thus, if a rat is in extreme pain, the associated stress may further enhance the pain, completing a vicious circle. If this finding is found to apply to humans, it is important because the general consensus is that we are very reluctant to use pain-killing medication in chronic diseases such as cancer. Some estimates suggest that fewer than half of all cancer patients receive sufficient pain relief. Now direct evidence is available on the benefits of early pain relief in patients undergoing surgery. Findings from Joel Katz, Anthony Vaccarino, Ron Melzack, and their colleagues, along with Chris France and his colleagues, have shown that patients receiving pain medication before surgery reported less pain after surgery and requested less pain medication (Coderre, Katz, Vaccarino, & Melzack, 1993; Keefe & France, 1999). Adequate pain-management procedures, either medical or psychological, are an essential part of the management of chronic disease.

A variety of psychosocial treatments have been developed for physical disorders and pain, including biofeedback, relaxation procedures, and hypnosis (Gatchel, 2005; Linden & Moseley, 2006; Otis & Pincus, 2008; Otis et al., in press; Turk & Monarch, 2002). But because of the overriding role of stress in the etiology and maintenance of many physical disorders, comprehensive stress-management programs are increasingly incorporated into medical centres in which such disorders are treated. We briefly review specific psychosocial approaches to physical disorders and describe a typical comprehensive stress-management program.

Biofeedback

Biofeedback is a process of making patients aware of specific physiological functions that, ordinarily, they would not notice consciously, such as heart rate, blood pressure, muscle tension in specific areas of the body, EEG rhythms (brain waves), and patterns of blood flow (Andrasik, 2000). This is the first step, but the second step is more remarkable. In the 1960s, Neal Miller reported that rats could *learn to directly control* many of these responses. He used a variation of operant conditioning procedures in which the animals were reinforced for increases or decreases in their physiological responses (Miller, 1969). Although it was subsequently difficult to replicate these findings with animals, clinicians applied the procedures with some success to humans who had various physical disorders or stress-related conditions, such as hypertension and headache.

Clinicians use physiological monitoring equipment to make the response, such as heart rate, visible or audible to the patient. The patient then works with the therapist to learn to control the response. A successful response produces some type of signal. For example, if the patient is successful in lowering his or her blood pressure by a certain amount, the pressure reading will be visible on a gauge and a tone will sound. It wasn't long before researchers discovered that humans could discriminate changes in autonomic nervous system activity with a high degree of accuracy (Blanchard & Epstein, 1977).

One goal of biofeedback has been to reduce tension in the muscles of the head and scalp, thereby relieving headaches. Pioneers in this field found that biofeedback was successful in this area (Holroyd, Andrasik, & Noble, 1980), although no more successful than deep muscle relaxation procedures (Andrasik, 2000; Blanchard & Andrasik, 1982; Blanchard, Andrasik, Ahles, Teders, & O'Keefe, 1980; Holroyd & Penzien, 1986). Because of these results, some have thought that biofeedback might achieve its effects with tension headaches by simply teaching people to relax. However, Holroyd and colleagues (1984) concluded instead that the success of biofeedback, at least for headaches, may depend not on reducing tension but on the extent to which the procedures instill a sense of control over the pain. (How do you think this relates to the study of stress in baboons described in the beginning of the chapter?)

Whatever the mechanism, biofeedback and relaxation are more effective treatments than, for example, placebo medication interventions, and the results of these two treatments are not altogether interchangeable, in that some people benefit more from biofeedback and others benefit from relaxation procedures. For this reason, applying both treatments is a safe strategy (Andrasik, 2000). Several reviews have found that 38 percent to 63 percent of patients undergoing relaxation or biofeedback achieve significant reductions in headaches compared with approximately 35 percent who receive placebo medication (Blanchard, 1992; Blanchard et al., 1980; Holroyd & Penzien, 1986). Furthermore, the effects of biofeedback and relaxation seem to be long lasting (Andrasik, 2000; Blanchard, 1987; Lisspers & Öst, 1990).

Relaxation and Meditation

Various types of relaxation and meditation procedures have also been used, either alone or in combination with other procedures, to treat patients with physical disorders and pain (e.g., Culos-Reed, Carlson, Daroux, & Hately-Aldous, 2006). In *progressive muscle relaxation*, devised by Edmund Jacobson in 1938, people become acutely aware of any tension in their bodies and counteract it by relaxing specific muscle groups. In Jacobson's original conception, learning the art of relaxation was a structured procedure that took months or even years to master. In most clinics today, however, the procedure is usually taught in a matter of weeks, and it is very seldom used as the sole treatment (Bernstein & Borkovec, 1973; Bernstein, Borkovec, & Hazlett-Stevens, 2000). Several procedures focus attention either on a specific part of the body or on a single thought or image. This attentional focus is often accompanied by regular slowed breathing. In *transcendental meditation* (TM), attention is focused solely on a repeated syllable, or the *mantra*.

Herbert Benson stripped transcendental meditation of what he considered its non-essentials and developed a brief procedure he calls the **relaxation response**, in which a person silently repeats a mantra to minimize distraction by closing the mind to intruding thoughts. Although Benson suggested focusing on the word *one*, any neutral word or phrase would do. Individuals who meditate for 10 or 20 minutes a day report feeling calmer or more relaxed throughout the day. These brief, simple procedures can be very powerful in actually reducing the flow of certain neurotransmitters and stress hormones, an effect that may be mediated by an increased sense of control and mastery (Benson, 1975, 1984). Benson's ideas are very popular and are now taught in many medical schools and offered by many major hospitals (Roush, 1997). Relaxation has generally positive effects on headaches, hypertension, and acute and chronic pain, although the results are sometimes relatively modest (Taylor, 2009). Nonetheless, relaxation and meditation are almost always part of a comprehensive pain-management program.

▲ In biofeedback, the patient learns to control physiological responses that are visible on a screen.

Rachel Epstein/PhotoEdit

A Comprehensive Stress-Reduction and Pain-Reduction Program

In our own stress-management program (Barlowet et al., 2001), individuals practise a variety of stress-management procedures presented to them in a workbook. First, they learn to monitor their stress very closely and to identify the stressful events in their daily lives. (Samples of a stressful events record and a daily stress record are in ■ Figure 9.8.) Note that clients are taught to be very specific about recording the times they experience stress, the intensity of the stress, and what seems to trigger the stress. They also note the somatic symptoms and thoughts that occur when they are stressed. All this monitoring becomes important in carrying through with the program, but it can be very helpful in itself, as it reveals precise patterns and causes of stress and helps clients learn what changes to make to better cope.

After learning to monitor stress, clients are taught deep muscle relaxation, which involves first tensing various muscles to identify the location of different muscle groups. (Instructions for tensing specific muscle groups are included in Table 9.4. on page 336) Clients are then systematically taught to relax the muscle groups beyond the point of inactivity, that is, to actively let go of the muscle so no tension remains in it.

Appraisals and attitudes are an important part of stress, and clients learn how they exaggerate the negative impact of events in their daily lives. In the program, therapist and client use cognitive therapy to develop more realistic appraisals and attitudes, as exemplified in the case of Sally.

SALLY | *Improving Her Perception*

Sally is a 40-year-old real estate agent.

SALLY: My mother is always calling just when I'm in the middle of doing something important and it makes me so angry, I find that I get short with her.

THERAPIST: Let's try and look at what you just said in another way. When you say that she always phones in the middle of something, it implies 100 percent of the time. Is that true? How likely is it, really, that she will call when you are doing something important?

SALLY: Well, I suppose that when I think back over the last ten times she's called, most of the times I was just watching TV or reading. There was once when I was making dinner and it burned because she interrupted me. Another time, I was busy with some work I had brought home from the office, and she called. I guess that makes it 20 percent of the time.

Daily Stress Record
(sample)

Week of

	8	Extreme stress
7	
6	Much stress
5	
4	Moderate stress
3	
2	Mild stress
1	
0	No stress

	(1)	(2)	(3)	(4)	(5)	(6)
Date	Starting time	Ending time	Highest stress (0–8)	Triggers	Symptoms	Thoughts
1-5	10:00am	11:00am	7	Sales meeting	Sweating, headache	my figures are bad
1-7	5:15pm	5:35pm	6	Traffic jam	Tension, impatience	I'll never get home
1-8	12:30pm	12:32pm	3	Lost keys	Tension	I can't find my keys
1-9	3:30pm	4:30pm	4	Waiting for guests	Sweating, nausea	Are they lost?

■ **FIGURE 9.8** Methods for monitoring stress

Source: From *Mastering Stress 2001: A Lifestyle Approach* by D. H. Barlow, R. M. Rapee, and and L. C. Reisner, 2001, p. 28. Copyright © 2001 by the American Health Publishing Co. Adapted with permission.

THERAPIST: OK, great; now let's go a bit further. So what if she calls at an inconvenient time?

SALLY: Well, I know that one of my first thoughts is that she doesn't think anything I do is important. But before you say anything, I know that is a major overestimation since she obviously doesn't know what I'm doing when she calls. However, I suppose I also think that it's a major interruption and inconvenience to have to stop at that point.

THERAPIST: Go on. What is the chance that it is a major inconvenience?

SALLY: When I was doing my work, I forgot what I was up to and it took me ten minutes to work it out again. I guess that's not so bad; it's only ten minutes. And when the dinner burned, it was really not too bad, just a little burned. Part of that was my fault anyway, because I could have turned the stove down before I went to the phone.

THERAPIST: So, it sounds like quite a small chance that it would be a major inconvenience, even if your mother does interrupt you.

SALLY: True. And I know what you are going to say next. Even if it is a major inconvenience, it's not the end of the world. I have handled plenty of bigger problems than this at work.

TABLE 9.4 Suggestions for Tensing Muscles

Large Muscle Groups	Suggestions for Tensing Muscles
Lower arm	Make fist, palm down, and pull wrist toward upper arm.
Upper arm	Tense biceps; with arms by side, pull upper arm toward side without touching. (Try not to tense the lower arm while doing this; let the lower arm hang loosely.)
Lower leg and foot	Point toes upward to knees.
Thighs	Push feet hard against the floor.
Abdomen	Pull in stomach toward back.
Chest and breathing	Take a deep breath and hold it about 10 seconds, then release.
Shoulders and lower neck	Shrug shoulders, bring shoulders up until they almost touch ears.
Back of neck	Put head back and press against back of chair.
Lips	Press lips together; don't clench teeth or jaw.
Eyes	Close eyes tightly but don't close too hard (be careful if you have contacts).
Lower forehead	Pull eyebrows down and in (try to get them to meet).
Upper forehead	Raise eyebrows and wrinkle your forehead.

Source: From Mastering Stress 2001: A Lifestyle Approach by D. H. Barlow, R. M. Rapee, and L. C. Reisner, 2001. © 2001 by American Health Publishing Co. Reprinted by permission.

In this program, individuals work hard to identify unrealistic negative thoughts and to develop new appraisals and attitudes almost instantaneously when negative thoughts occur. Such assessment is often the most difficult part of the program. After the session just related, Sally began using what she had learned in cognitive therapy to reappraise stressful situations. Finally, clients in stress-reduction programs develop new coping strategies, such as time management and assertiveness training. During time-management training, patients are taught to prioritize their activities and pay less attention to non-essential demands. During assertiveness training, they learn to stand up for themselves in an appropriate way. Clients also learn other procedures for managing everyday problems.

A number of studies have evaluated some version of this comprehensive program. The results suggest that it is generally more effective than individual components alone, such as relaxation or biofeedback, for chronic pain (Keefe, Dunsmore, & Burnett, 1992; Otis & Pincus, 2008; Turk & Monarch, 2002), CFS (Deale et al., 1997), tension headaches (Blanchard et al., 1990; Lipchik, Holroyd, & Nash, 2002), hypertension (Ward, Swan, & Chesney, 1987), temporomandibular joint (jaw) pain (Turner, Mancl, & Aaron, 2006), and cancer pain (Andersen et al., 2007; Crichton & Morey, 2003). A summary "meta-analysis" of 22 studies of treatments for chronic lower back pain also found comprehensive psychological treatments effective (Hoffman, Papas, Chatkoff, & Kerns, 2007).

Drugs and Stress-Reduction Programs

North Americans rely heavily on over-the-counter analgesic medication for pain, particularly headaches. Some evidence suggests that chronic reliance on these medications lessens the efficacy of comprehensive programs in the treatment of headaches. Michultka, Blanchard, Appelbaum, Jaccard, and Dentinger (1989) matched high analgesic users to low analgesic users in terms of age, duration of headache activity, and response to comprehensive treatment. Only 29 percent of high users versus 55 percent of low users achieved at least a 50 percent reduction in headache activity. In addition, Holroyd, Nash, Pingel, Cordingley, and Jerome (1991) compared a comprehensive cognitive-behavioural treatment to an antidepressant drug, amitriptyline, in the treatment of tension headaches. The psychological treatment produced at least a 50 percent reduction in headache activity in 56 percent of the patients, whereas the drug produced a comparable reduction in only 27 percent of users. It is important that psychological treatment also seems to reduce drug consumption fairly consistently (Radnitz, Appelbaum, Blanchard, Elliott, & Andrasik, 1988) not only for headaches but also for severe hypertension.

Concept Check | 9.4

Check your understanding by matching the treatments to the scenarios: (a) biofeedback, (b) meditation and relaxation response, and (c) cognitive coping procedure.

1. Mary is often upset by the stupid things other people are always doing. Her doctor wants her to realize her exaggeration of these events. _____

2. Karl can't seem to focus on anything at work. He feels too stressed. He needs a way of minimizing intruding thoughts that he can do at work in a short time.

_____

3. Kamal's blood pressure soars when he feels stressed. His doctor showed him how to become aware of his body processes in order to control them better.

_____

Denial as a Means of Coping

We have emphasized the importance of confronting and working through our feelings, particularly after stressful or traumatic events. Beginning with Freud, mental health professionals have recognized the importance of reliving or processing intense emotional experiences in order to put them behind us and to develop better coping responses. For example, individuals undergoing coronary artery bypass surgery who were optimistic recovered more quickly, returned to normal activities more rapidly, and reported a stronger quality of life six months after surgery than those who were not optimistic (Scheier et al., 1989). Scheier and colleagues also discovered that optimistic people are less likely to use denial as a means of coping with a severe stressor such as surgery. Bruce Compas and colleagues (2006) studied anxiety and pain complaints in 164 adolescents with recurrent abdominal pain. Adolescents who regularly used denial, avoidance, and wishful thinking had higher levels of anxiety and somatic complaints than those who attempted to cope more directly with the pain. Most mental health professionals work to eliminate denial because it has many negative effects. For example, people who deny the severe pain connected with disease may not notice meaningful variations in their symptoms, and they typically avoid treatment regimens or rehabilitation programs.

But is denial always harmful? Health psychologist Shelley Taylor (2009) points out that most individuals who are functioning well deny the implications of a potentially serious condition, at least initially. A common reaction is to assume that what they have is not serious or will go away quickly. Most people with serious diseases react this way, including those with cancer (Meyerowitz, 1983) and CHD (Krantz & Deckel, 1983). Several groups of investigators (see, e.g., Hackett & Cassem, 1973; Meyerowitz, 1983) have found that during that extremely stressful period when a person is first diagnosed, denial may help patients endure the shock more easily. They are then better able to develop coping responses later. The value of denial as a coping mechanism may depend more on timing than on anything else. In the long run, however, all evidence indicates that at some point we must face the situation, process our emotions, and come to terms with what is happening (Compas, Boyer, Stanger, Colletti, & Thomsen, 2006).

Modifying Behaviours to Promote Health

In the beginning of the chapter, we talked about psychological and social factors influencing health and physical problems in two distinct ways: by directly affecting biological processes and through unhealthy lifestyles. In this section, we consider the effects of an unhealthy lifestyle.

Research is teaching us that many common diseases can be prevented and others can be postponed or controlled simply by making positive lifestyle changes. Unhealthy eating habits, lack of exercise, and smoking are three of the most common behaviours that put us at risk in the long term for many physical disorders. High-risk behaviours and conditions are listed in Table 9.5. Many of these behaviours contribute to the diseases and physical disorders that are among the leading causes of death in Canada, including not only CHD and cancer, but also accidents of various kinds (related to consuming alcohol and not using safety restraints), cirrhosis of the liver (related to excessive consumption of alcohol), and a variety of respiratory diseases, including influenza and pneumonia (related to smoking and stress; Sexton, 1979).

Behavioural self-care is also very important in the management of diabetes: The patient must regularly administer and adjust insulin and medications, self-test blood glucose levels,

TABLE 9.5 Areas for Health-Risk Behaviour Modification

- Smoking
- Hyperlipidemia
- High blood pressure
- Dietary habits related to disease

  High sodium; low calcium, magnesium, potassium—high blood pressure

  High fat—cardiovascular disease and cancer of the prostate, breast, colon, and pancreas

  High simple carbohydrates—diabetes mellitus

  Low fibre—diabetes mellitus, digestive diseases, cardiovascular disease, colon cancer

  Low intake of Vitamins A and C—cancer
- Sedentary lifestyle
- Obesity
- Substance abuse (alcohol and drug)
- Nonuse of seat belts
- High-risk sexual behaviour
- Non-adherence to recommended immunization and screening procedures
- High stress levels and type A personality
- High-risk situations for childhood accidents, neglect, abuse
- Poor dental hygiene/infrequent care
- Sun exposure
- Poor-quality relationships/supports
- Occupational risks

Source: Reprinted from "Primary Care and Health Promotion: A Model for Preventive Medicine" by M. B. Johns et al, 1987, *American Journal of Preventive Medicine, 3 (6):* 351. © 1987.

and manage his or her diet and exercise levels (Vallis et al., 2003). Considerable work is ongoing to develop effective behaviour modification procedures to improve diet, increase adherence to drug and medical treatment programs, and develop optimal exercise programs. Often the health psychologist using these behaviour modification procedures with a client who has a stress-related physical disorder must begin by helping the patient enhance his or her motivation to change unhealthy behaviours (Vallis et al., 2003)—just as we discussed for the eating disorders (see Chapter 8), and as we will discuss for the substance use disorders (see Chapter 11). Here, we review briefly four areas of interest: injury control, the prevention of AIDS, efforts to reduce smoking in China, and a major community intervention designed to reduce the risk for coronary heart disease (CHD).

Injury Control

Injuries are the fourth leading cause of death in Canada across all age ranges (see Table 9.1 on page 313) and the top cause of death for people aged 1 to 45. Furthermore, the loss of productivity to the individual and to society from injuries is far greater than from other leading causes of death: heart disease, cancer, and stroke (Rice & MacKenzie, 1989). For this reason, methods for reducing injury have become a major focus within the areas of health psychology and behavioural medicine. Spielberger and Frank (1992) point out that psychological variables are crucial in mediating virtually all the factors that lead to injury. The psychological contributors have been understudied until recently, but they are now beginning to receive attention.

A good example is the work now being conducted on preventing accidents in children (e.g., Peterson & Roberts, 1992). Injuries kill more children than the next six causes of childhood death combined (Dershewitz & Williamson, 1977), and yet most people, including parents, don't think too much about prevention, even in their own children, because they usually consider injuries to be due to fate and, therefore, out of their hands (Peterson, Farmer, & Kashani, 1990; Peterson & Roberts, 1992). However, a variety of programs have been proven effective for preventing injuries in children. For example, children have been systematically and successfully taught to escape fires (Jones & Haney, 1984), identify and report emergencies (Jones & Kazdin, 1980), safely cross streets (Yeaton & Bailey, 1978), ride bicycles safely, and deal with injuries such as serious cuts (Peterson & Thiele, 1988). In many of these programs, the participating children maintained the safety skills they had learned for months after the intervention—as long as assessments were continued, in most cases. Because little evidence indicates that repeated warnings are effective in preventing injuries, programmatic efforts to change behaviour are very important, and yet such programs are non existent in most communities.

AIDS Prevention

Earlier we documented the spread of AIDS, particularly in developing countries. In developed countries like Canada and the United States, AIDS is most commonly accounted for by high-risk sexual contact among male homosexuals or bisexuals or those with a history of injection drug use (CDC, 1994). According to the Canadian Youth, Sexual Health, and AIDS study conducted at Queen's University, Acadia University, the University of Laval, and the University of Alberta (Boyle, Doherty, Fortin, & MacKinnon, 2002), Canadian youth are another population that is highly vulnerable to HIV infection. This increased vulnerability is due to the high prevalence of risky behaviours and attitudes in this group (e.g., risky sexual behaviour, substance use including injection drug use, and beliefs that HIV is not a threat to them).

Although existing data suggest that HIV prevalence is currently low among youth (Health Canada, 2002), the high levels of risky attitudes and behaviours in this group show that the potential for HIV spread certainly exists among young Canadians (Boyle et al., 2002). In developing countries, particularly in Africa, AIDS is almost exclusively linked to heterosexual intercourse with an infected partner (CDC, 1994). There is no vaccine for the disease. *Changing high-risk behaviour is the only effective prevention strategy* (Catania et al., 2000).

Comprehensive programs are particularly important because testing to learn whether a person is HIV positive or HIV negative does little to change behaviour (e.g., Landis, Earp, & Koch, 1992). Even educating at-risk individuals is generally ineffective in changing high-risk behaviour (Helweg-Larsen & Collins, 1997). A successful comprehensive behaviour change program focusing on high-risk youth was conducted by William Fisher of the University of Western Ontario and his colleagues (Fisher, Fisher, Bryan, & Misovich, 2002). This study assessed the effects of three school-based HIV prevention interventions on urban, minority high school students' levels of HIV prevention knowvledge, motivation, behavioural skills, and actual behaviour (i.e., condom use). These outcomes were assessed at one month, three months, and one year following the interventions. The three interventions were classroom-based, peer-based, and a combined treatment. Each was compared with a "standard-of-care" control condition (i.e., the school's standard HIV/AIDS curriculum, which consisted largely of brief HIV prevention education delivered in health classes).

▲ The prevalence of AIDS is high in Africa, where these women are taking part in a memorial ceremony for those who have died of the disease.

In the classroom-based intervention, teachers taught five classes focusing on (1) factual information about HIV transmission and prevention and dispelling myths (e.g., that there are "safe" partners); (2) changing students' attitudes and social norms about HIV risk and prevention; (3) enhancing students' motivation to engage in HIV prevention; (4) training in behavioural skills for abstinence from sex and for acquiring and using condoms; and (5) training in effectively communicating about safer sex. In the peer-based intervention, the same material was presented, but by popular peers through informal contacts with same-sex friends and acquaintances. The combined treatment involved both the classroom-based and the peer-based interventions described above.

Some of the results are displayed in Table 9.6 for sexually inexperienced students (top panel) and for sexually experienced students (bottom panel); these results show levels of knowledge, motivation, and behavioural skills in adolescents in the four conditions at pretreatment and again at one month following the treatment. The main results were as follows:

1. For sexually inexperienced students, participation in the classroom intervention and the combined intervention resulted in significantly greater increases in HIV prevention *knowledge* than did participation in the control intervention. For sexually experienced students, knowledge increased more for students in any of the three experimental interventions relative to students in the control group (see Table 9.6).

2. For sexually inexperienced students, HIV prevention *motivation* (i.e., attitudes about HIV prevention) increased for those in the classroom and combined interventions relative to those receiving the control intervention. For the sexually experienced students, HIV prevention motivation increased for those in the peer and combined interventions relative to those in the control group (see Table 9.6).

3. For both the sexually inexperienced and experienced youth, exposure to the combined intervention increased *behavioural skills* for remaining abstinent and for acquiring and using condoms relative to exposure to the control intervention (see Table 9.6).

4. The three experimental interventions increased actual HIV prevention *behaviour* (i.e., condom use) in at least one of the longer-term follow-ups (i.e., three-month or one-year) relative to the control intervention.

These findings are very promising indeed and point to the importance of adding psychological techniques (motivational enhancement, behavioural skills training) to educational efforts in preventing HIV in youth. Health Canada funded a study on the status of HIV prevention for youth in Canada (Health Canada, 1999). In this study, a consortium of researchers from across Canada described our nation's current HIV prevention activities within education and public health systems, from policymakers to teachers and public health nurses. The report noted that, although Canada was in the forefront of the initial response to HIV/AIDS, gaps now exist in our education and health systems with respect to HIV prevention in teenagers. The report recommended that Canadian schools' current focus on

TABLE 9.6 Results of the HIV Prevention Program for High-Risk Adolescents

Measure	Classroom	Peer	Combined	Control
Sexually Inexperienced Participants (n = 777)				
Knowledge				
Pretreatment	13.07	13.72	13.57	12.51
Post-treatment	15.61*	14.35	16.58*	13.01
Motivation				
Pretreatment	3.97	4.08	4.09	3.93
Post-treatment	4.17*	4.16	4.30*	3.95
Behavioural Skills				
Pretreatment	3.68	3.84	3.82	3.68
Post-treatment	3.85	3.82	4.04*	3.69
Sexually Experienced Participants (n = 755)				
Knowledge				
Pretreatment	12.91	13.50	13.95	13.00
Post-treatment	15.03*	14.94*	16.19*	13.38
Motivation				
Pretreatment	4.30	4.27	4.42	4.23
Post-treatment	4.20	4.37*	4.46*	4.10
Behavioural Skills				
Pretreatment	3.96	4.11	4.11	4.09
Post-treatment	3.98	4.10	4.19*	3.98

Notes: Significant pretreatment to post-treatment increase relative to standard-of-care control is indicated via an asterisk (*).

Source: From "Information-Motivation-Behavioral Skills Model–Based HIV Risk Behavior Change Intervention for Inner-City High School Youth" by J. D. Fisher, W. A. Fisher, A. D. Bryan, and S. J. Misovich, 2002, *Health Psychology, 21(2)*, 177–186. © 2002 by the American Psychological Association.

sexual diseases within the school curriculum be more broadly based. The authors also suggested increasing the availability of youth-friendly sexual health services, involving parents to a greater degree, and promoting better knowledge of sexual risk-taking behaviour among youth. It was emphasized that schools should be part of a broader, community-wide response to HIV/AIDS. The role of the schools was seen to be in teaching students about HIV risks and in helping students make responsible choices. Incorporating more effective HIV prevention programs (e.g., Fisher et al., 2002) into Canadian schools, could help bridge the current gaps in prevention identified in the 1999 Health Canada report.

Smoking in China

Despite efforts by the government to reduce smoking among its citizens, China has one of the most tobacco-addicted populations in the world. Approximately 250 million people in China are habitual smokers, 90 percent of them male. In an attempt to reach these individuals, health professionals took advantage of the strong family ties in China and decided to persuade the children of smokers to intervene with their fathers. In so doing, they conducted the largest study yet reported of attempted behaviour modification to promote health. In 1989, the Chinese government developed an antismoking campaign in 23 primary schools in Hangzhou, the capital of the Zhejiang province. Children took home antismoking literature and questionnaires to almost 10 000 fathers. They then wrote letters to their fathers asking them to quit smoking, and they submitted monthly reports on their fathers' smoking habits to the schools. Approximately nine months later, the results were assessed. Indeed, the children's intervention had some effect. Almost 12 percent of the fathers in the intervention group had quit smoking for at least six months. By contrast, in a control group of another 10 000 males, the quit rate was only 0.2 percent ("Somber News," 1993).

Since then, the Chinese government has become more involved in smoking prevention efforts. For example, Ma and colleagues (2008) identified several myths that characterize Chinese smokers. These include (1) the identification of smoking as a symbol of personal freedom, (2) a perception that tobacco is important in social and cultural interactions, (3) the perception that the health effects of smoking can be controlled through reasonable and measured use, and (4) the importance of tobacco to the economy. At present, the Chinese government is considering ways to counter these prevailing misconceptions as a prelude to developing more effective preventative programs.

Community Studies to Reduce Risk for Coronary Heart Disease

One of the best-known and most successful efforts to reduce risk factors for disease was a community study conducted by Meyer, Nash, McAlister, Maccoby, and Farquhar (1980). Rather than assemble three groups of people, these investigators studied three entire communities in central California that were reasonably alike in size and type of residents between 1972 and 1975. The target was reduction of risk factors for coronary heart disease (CHD). The positive behaviours that were introduced focused on smoking, high blood pressure, diet, and weight reduction.

In Tracy, the first community, no interventions were conducted, but detailed information was collected from a random sample of adults to assess any increases in their knowledge of risk factors as well as any changes in risk factors over time. In addition, participants in Tracy received a medical assessment of their cardiovascular factors. The residents of Gilroy and part of Watsonville were subjected to a media blitz on the dangers of behavioural risk factors for CHD, the importance of reducing these factors, and helpful hints for doing so. Most residents of Watsonville also had a face-to-face intervention in which behavioural counsellors worked with the townspeople judged to be at particularly high risk for CHD. Subjects in all three communities were surveyed once a year for three years following the

---

Innovative Approaches

Reducing Sexual Infections among Inner-City Black Females

HIV and other sexually transmitted infections are highly prevalent among adolescents, and particularly among Black adolescents (Weinstock, Berman, & Cates, 2004). To reduce the incidence of infection, a new focus is on tailoring programs to reduce risky sexual behaviour to specific groups, for example, inner-city Black adolescent females (DiClemente et al., 2004, 2008). In one successful program called SiHLE (Sistas Informing, Healing, Living, Empowering), HIV-related interpersonal and social processes that are more characteristic of inner-city Black adolescent females are targeted, such as having older male sex partners who are more demanding, having violent dating partners, being stereotyped by the media, perceiving society as having limited regard for Black teens, and a reluctance to negotiate about safer sex. Unlike many prevention programs that focus only on cognitive decision-making skills, SiHLE also focuses on developing relational skills; building motivation through instilling pride, self-efficacy, perceived value, and importance in the community; and modifying the usual and customary peer influences these girls experience. The purpose of this intervention is to create an environment that enhances adolescents' likelihood of reducing risky sexual behaviour and adopting and sustaining preventative behaviours. Five hundred and twenty-two sexually experienced Black girls aged 14 to 18 participated, with half randomized to SiHLE and half to a comparison condition. The program consisted of four one-hour group sessions emphasizing ethnic and gender pride, HIV knowledge, communication, condom use skills, and healthy relationships. A comparison condition also meeting in groups emphasized exercise and nutrition. Results from this program were very promising (DiClemente et al., 2004, 2008). Girls receiving the SiHLE intervention used condoms more often, had less unprotected sex, fewer sexual partners, and reduced sexually transmitted infections and unwanted pregnancies at a one-year follow-up than girls in the comparison groups. More recent initiatives under way focus on integrating the family as behavioural change agents by working together with counsellors to help delay adolescents' first experience with sexual intercourse, limit the number of sexual partners, and support health-promoting behaviours, such as protected sex.

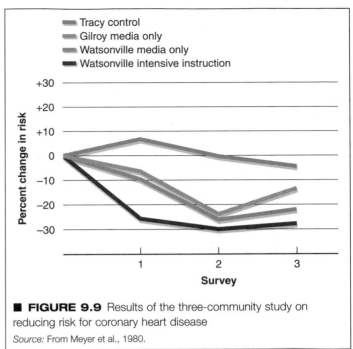

▲ Approximately 250 million people in China are habitual smokers, 90 percent of them male. Thus, Chinese men are at very high risk of smoking-related diseases such as cardiovascular disease and lung cancer.

■ **FIGURE 9.9** Results of the three-community study on reducing risk for coronary heart disease
Source: From Meyer et al., 1980.

intervention. Results indicate that the interventions were markedly successful at reducing risk factors for CHD in these communities (see ■ Figure 9.9). Furthermore, the residents of Watsonville who also received individual counselling had substantially higher knowledge of risk factors, and their risk factors were substantially lower than for people in Tracy, or even in Gilroy and people in the part of Watsonville that received only the media blitz.

Large-scale community interventions like this cost money, although in many communities the media are willing to donate time to such a worthy effort. Results show that mounting an effort like this is worthwhile to individuals, to the community, and to public health officials, because many lives will be saved, and disability leave will be decreased to an extent that will more than cover the original cost of the program.

A similar program was mounted in Québec—the Québec Heart Health Demonstration project (see Pelletier, Moisan, Roussel, & Gilbert, 1997), a heart health promotion and prevention program implemented by regional public health departments in 10 municipalities (rural, suburban, and urban) in the province.

The investigators attempted to develop and maintain a multi-factorial, community-based, health promotion/disease prevention heart health program over a five-year period. A group of matched municipalities not exposed to the program was also included in the study. Relative to previous American initiatives like the Meyer et al. (1980) study just described, the Québec program was more community-based (e.g., community volunteers controlled both the program objectives and activities) and thus was much less expensive to implement. Regarding behavioural change objectives, the program aimed for a 5 percent increase in the number of people who (1) know their blood pressure, (2) know their cholesterol level, (3) have adopted a low-fat diet, (4) are physically active (defined as 20 minutes at least three times per week), and (5) do not smoke.

Hout, Paradis, and Ledoux (2004) evaluated the effects of the Québec Heart Health Demonstration Project on adult dietary behaviours (i.e., adopting a low-fat diet). Nearly 5000 adults in experimental and control communities were administered a self-report food frequency questionnaire in 1993 before the program was implemented. A similar number were administered this measure after the program was implemented in 1997 (but not necessarily the same people who originally completed the measures). While diet quality improved over this interval (at least in the suburban and urban communities), unexpectedly, the degree of improvement was not greater in the communities exposed to the intervention than in control communities. The researchers suggest that current trends toward improved (heart-healthy) diets are strong enough that the program did not exert effects over and above these societal trends. They recommend that more intensive (and thus more expensive) community-based interventions are required (Huot et al., 2004). The data are still out as to whether the Québec Heart Health Demonstration Project exerted effects in its other behavioural target areas (e.g., smoking, physical activity).

Dr. Orville Messenger was a well-regarded surgeon at a hospital in Moncton, New Brunswick, when he underwent open-heart surgery for a cardiac condition in Halifax in 1985. Eight months later, he was just coming to terms with his cardiologist's recommendation that he find a less stressful career, when he received a devastating phone call telling him that he may have received AIDS-contaminated blood during a transfusion associated with his heart surgery, and that he would need to go to Halifax again to take a blood test. *Borrowed Time* is Dr. Messenger's memoir, co-authored with his wife Dorothy, a registered nurse, of his ten-year struggle as a surgeon living with AIDS.

The Messengers recount their devastation at learning the results of Dr. Messenger's blood test:

> I put down the telephone receiver in a state of complete shock, my mouth dry and my mind whirling. Friends arrived just then for dinner and we had to put on a good appearance while at the same time our thoughts were elsewhere. [We were] trying but unable to comprehend what we had just been told. I don't think I can ever describe just how devastated and let down we felt, especially after having overcome so many obstacles with respect to my heart disease and lost career. (pp. 14–15)

In the 1980s, most Canadian physicians knew very little about HIV. Dr. Messenger had to consult with an infectious-disease expert in San Francisco to learn more about the illness and what he and his family could expect in terms of his prognosis and life expectancy. In his memoir, Dr. Messenger recounts his relative relief in learning that he might have several healthy years left, and that he was unlikely to infect his children.

The family moved to Ottawa where Dr. Messenger took a position at the Canadian Medical Protective Association. Although he was no longer working as a physician with patients, he and his family kept his diagnosis quiet for many years. Since little was known about HIV/AIDS at that time, the Messengers feared possible negative effects of public reaction on their four children, and worried about the possible impact of stigma on Dr. Messenger's career. Remember that at this time, the climate was one of public fear and ignorance about HIV/AIDS. It was during his years in Ottawa that Dr. Messenger first began to experience the onset of early symptoms of the disease. It was also at this time that he privately struggled with associated depression and thoughts of suicide. He describes the incredible emotional toll of the knowledge of pending death, and notes frequently wondering if it would have been easier for him and his family to have learned of his diagnosis only when he began to get sick.

In 1990, the family moved to Halifax to be closer to Dr. Messenger's physicians. Two years later, he retired from his position with the Canadian Medical Protective Association because he was experiencing extreme fatigue and chronic headaches. His symptoms worsened and he struggled repeatedly with AIDS-related pneumonia. In addition, he became afflicted with bowel and sinus infections, partial paralysis in his hand and arm, and herpes infections.

After nearly a decade of struggling with the illness, the Messengers decided to make their private ordeal public by writing this memoir. They describe the difficult process of writing the memoir as follows: "To tell our personal story has required us to re-live events and recapture emotions. It was an experience far more difficult than we had ever imagined. Were it not for the encouragement of special friends, we would have stopped short of completion" (p. iii). They dedicated the book to people who were living with AIDS and coping alone. They wanted these people to know that there were others who had struggled with similar experiences. In the book, the Messengers discuss what life was like living with the disease, and how it was to raise a family in the shadow of this illness.

The Messengers candidly reveal their emotional and spiritual attempts to cope, and what strategies worked for them as well as those that failed. Their primary goal in writing the book was to raise money for research to find a cure for AIDS. *Borrowed Time* made the *Globe and Mail* bestseller list in June 1995, only a few short months before Dr. Messenger's death at only 52 years old. This inspiring memoir is sure to help many better understand both the physical and psychological impact of this devastating disease, and it provides an important message of hope to those similarly living on "borrowed time."

Source: Borrowed Time: A Surgeon's Struggle with Transfusion-Induced AIDS by Orville and Dorothy Messenger (Mosaic Press, 1995).

In this chapter and earlier chapters we have described the profound influence of psychological factors on brain function and structure, showing how, for example, psychological interventions may affect physical illnesses such as CHD and AIDS. The fascinating study of the placebo response adds another layer to the discussion. To take one example, do "phony" placebo pills really decrease pain—or is it just that individuals think or report that they are feeling less pain? This is one of the major controversies in the study of placebo responses, not only for pain but also for conditions such as depression.

With the help of the latest brain-imaging technology, several experiments have demonstrated that when pain is induced in some volunteers (e.g., by injecting salt water in their jaws) after they are given a placebo, their brains operate in such a way that they actually feel less pain as opposed to simply thinking they feel less pain or reporting that they feel less pain (Wager, 2005; Zubieta et al., 2005). Specifically, broad areas of the brain are affected, but the most important system that is activated may be the endogenous opioid system (or endorphins), which, among other functions, suppresses pain. Increased endorphin activity across broad areas of the brain was associated with lower ratings of pain intensity, as well as reductions in the sensations of pain and emotional reactions to it. Thus, the studies show that the placebo effect is certainly not "all in your head." "Phony" pills really do spur chemical changes in the brain that reduce pain.

But does it also work the other way? Do medical treatments, such as drugs, affect what are clearly psychological processes, and if they do, are drugs affecting different regions in the brain compared to purely psychological interventions to achieve the same end? For example, we know that drugs can relieve anxiety and depression, but the presumption is that these medications are having their effects in different areas of the brain compared to psychological treatments. Now, an interesting study has demonstrated that physical pain (such as that caused by physical injury) and social pain (such as hurt feelings caused by social rejection) may rely on some of the same behavioural and neural mechanisms (DeWall et al., 2010). In one experiment, participants took a drug commonly used for physical pain, acetaminophen (Tylenol), while another group took a placebo. They then recorded on a form their hurt feelings every day for three weeks. Subjects taking the acetaminophen reported substantially fewer hurt feelings than the placebo group. In a second experiment, the investigators found that the acetaminophen reduced neural responses to social rejection in brain regions known to be associated with both social pain as well as physical pain (the dorsal anterior cingulate cortex and the anterior insula). These findings indicate substantial overlap between social and physical pain (Wager, 2005). They also illustrate again the theme of this book: You cannot easily separate brain function induced biochemically from brain function induced by psychological factors, including expectancies and appraisals. The body and the mind are indeed inseparable, and only a multidimensional integrative approach focusing on the full spectrum of responding will produce a complete understanding of behaviour, either normal or pathological.

Summary

Psychological and Social Factors that Influence Biology

- Psychological and social factors play a major role in developing and maintaining many physical disorders.
- Two fields of study have emerged as a result of a growing interest in psychological factors contributing to illness. Behavioural medicine involves the application of behavioural science techniques to prevent, diagnose, and treat medical problems. Health psychology is a subfield that focuses on psychological factors involved in the promotion of health and well-being.
- Psychological and social factors may contribute directly to illness and disease through the psychological effects of stress on the immune system and other physical functioning. If the immune system is compromised, it may no longer be able to attack and eliminate antigens from the body effectively, or it may even begin to attack the body's normal tissue instead, a process known as autoimmune disease.
- Growing awareness of the many connections between the nervous system and the immune system has resulted in the new field of psychoneuroimmunology.
- Diseases that may be related in part to the effects of stress on the immune system include AIDS, rheumatoid arthritis, and cancer.
- Long-standing patterns of behaviour or lifestyle may put people at risk for developing certain physical disorders. For example, unhealthy sexual practices can lead to AIDS and other sexually transmitted diseases, and unhealthy behavioural patterns, such as poor eating habits, lack of exercise, or type A behaviour pattern, may contribute to cardiovascular diseases such as stroke, hypertension, and coronary heart disease.
- Of the leading causes of death in Canada, about half of these deaths can be traced to lifestyle behaviours.

- Psychological and social factors also contribute to chronic pain. The brain inhibits pain through naturally occurring endogenous opioids, which may also be implicated in a variety of psychological disorders.
- Chronic fatigue syndrome is a relatively new disorder attributed at least in part to stress but may also have a viral or immune system dysfunction component.

Psychosocial Treatment of Physical Disorders

- A variety of psychosocial treatments have been developed with the goal of either treating or preventing physical disorders. Among these are biofeedback and the relaxation response.

A Comprehensive Stress-Reduction and Pain-Reduction Program

- Comprehensive stress-reduction and pain-reduction programs include not only relaxation and related techniques, but also new methods to encourage effective coping, including stress-management, realistic appraisals, and improved attitudes through cognitive therapy.
- Comprehensive programs are generally more effective than individual components delivered singly.

Modifying Behaviours to Promote Health

- Other interventions aim to modify such behaviours as unsafe sexual practices, smoking, and unhealthy dietary habits. Such efforts have been made in a variety of areas, including injury control, AIDS prevention, smoking cessation campaigns in China, and a community study focused on reducing risk factors for coronary heart disease.

Key Terms

acute pain, 328
AIDS-related complex (ARC), 320
antigens, 318
autoimmune disease, 319
behavioural medicine, 314
biofeedback, 333
cancer, 322
cardiovascular disease, 324

cerebral vascular accident (CVA), 324
chronic fatigue syndrome (CFS), 331
chronic pain, 328
coronary heart disease (CHD), 326
endogenous opioids, 331
essential hypertension, 324

general adaptation syndrome (GAS), 315
health psychology, 314
hypertension, 324
immune system, 318
pain catastrophizing, 329
psychoneuroimmunology (PNI), 319
psycho-oncology, 322

relaxation response, 334
rheumatoid arthritis, 319
self-efficacy, 317
stress, 315
stroke, 324
type A behaviour pattern, 326
type B behaviour pattern, 326

Answers to Concept Checks

9.1

1. b **2.** a **3.** d **4.** c

9.2

1. d **2.** b **3.** c **4.** a

9.3

3

9.4

1. c **2.** b **3.** a

Media Resources

 CourseMate

Access an integrated eBook, Abnormal Psychology Videos (formerly Abnormal Psych Live CD-ROM), chapter-specific interactive learning tools (flashcards, quizzes, learning modules), and more in your Psychology CourseMate, available at **www.abnormalpsych3ce.nelson.com**.

Abnormal Psychology Videos

Free Abnormal Psychology videos can be viewed on the website **www.abnormalpsych3ce .nelson.com**.

- *Studying the Effects of Emotions on Physical Health:* This video illustrates recent findings on how emotional experiences—such as stress, loneliness, and sociability—affect physical health.

- *Social Support and HIV: Orel:* This African American client demonstrates the power of strong social support from family and friends, as well as pursuing personal interests such as art, to deal with the ongoing struggles of being an HIV/AIDS patient.

- *Breast Cancer Support and Education:* This clip investigates whether providing group support or group education is more helpful to women facing breast cancer.

Video Concept Reviews

CourseMate also contains Mark Durand's *Video Concept Reviews* on these challenging topics.

- Behavioural Medicine
- Health Psychology
- Stress
- General Adaptation Syndrome (GAS)
- HPA-Stress Response Cycle
- AIDS-Related Complex (ARC)
- Cancer and Psycho-oncology

- Hypertension
- Acute and Chronic Pain
- Concept Check: Integrative Process With Physical Disorders
- Chronic Fatigue Syndrome
- Biofeedback and Relaxation Techniques

Exploring Physical Disorders and Health Psychology

Psychological and behavioural factors are major contributors to illness and death.
> Behavioural medicine applies behavioural science to medical problems.
> Health psychology focuses on psychological influences on health and improving health care.

PSYCHOLOGICAL AND SOCIAL FACTORS INFLUENCE BIOLOGY

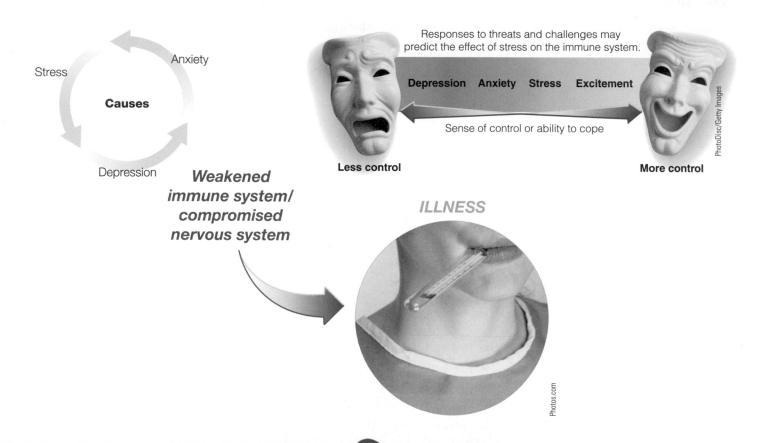

Stress

Anxiety

Causes

Depression

Weakened immune system/ compromised nervous system

Responses to threats and challenges may predict the effect of stress on the immune system.

Depression   Anxiety   Stress   Excitement

Sense of control or ability to cope

Less control

More control

PhotoDisc/Getty Images

ILLNESS

Photos.com

AIDS (Acquired Immune Deficiency Syndrome)

- The human immunodeficiency virus (HIV) attacks the immune system and opportunistic infections develop uncontrollably.
- Psychological treatments focus on strengthening the immune system and gaining a sense of control.
- Although drug therapy may control the virus, there is so far no biological means of prevention and the disease is still always fatal.

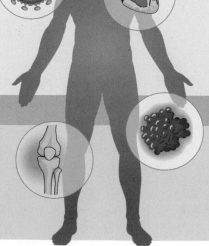

Chronic Pain

- May begin with an acute episode but does not diminish when injury heals.
- Typically involves joints, muscles, and tendons; may result from enlarged blood vessels, tissue degeneration, or cancerous tumours.
- Psychological and social influences may cause and maintain chronic pain to a significant degree.

Cardiovascular Problems

- The heart and blood vessels can be damaged by
  - *Stroke:* Blockage or rupture of blood vessels in the brain
  - *Hypertension:* Constriction of blood vessels at organs and extremities puts extra pressure on the heart, which eventually weakens
  - *Coronary heart disease:* Blockage of arteries supplying blood to the heart
- Biological, psychological, and social factors contribute to all these conditions and are addressed in treatment.

Cancer

- Abnormal cell growth produces malignant tumours
- Psychosocial treatments may prolong life, alleviate symptoms, and reduce depression and pain.
- Different cancers have different rates of recovery and mortality.
- Psychoncology is the study of psychosocial factors involved in the course and treatment of cancer.

PSYCHOSOCIAL TREATMENTS FOR PHYSICAL DISORDERS

The stress reaction associated with pain may reduce the number of natural killer cells in the immune system:

Disease or Injury;
Enhanced Disease
or Injury

Extreme
Pain

Causes

Stress

Biofeedback

- Electronic monitors make physiological responses such as heartbeat visible on a computer screen
- Patient learns to increase or decrease the response, thereby improving functioning (decreasing tension)
  – Developing a sense of control may be therapeutic

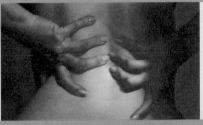

PhotoDisc/Getty Images

Relaxation and Meditation

- **Progressive muscle relaxation:** Person learns to locate physical tension and to counteract it by relaxing a specific muscle group
- **Meditation:** Focusing attention on a specific body part or process or on an affirming thought or image; in some forms, focusing on a single silently repeated syllable (mantra) "empties" the mind. Meditation is accompanied by slow, regular breathing
  – Meditating daily for at least 10 to 20 minutes imparts calm and relaxation by reducing certain neurotransmitters and stress hormones and increasing a sense of control

PhotoDisc/Getty Images

BEHAVIOUR MODIFICATION TO PROMOTE HEALTH

Many injuries and diseases can be prevented or controlled through lifestyle changes involving diet, substance use, exercise, and safety precautions.

Injury Control

- Injuries are the leading cause of death for people aged 1 to 45, especially children
- Most people consider injuries to be out of their control and therefore do not change high-risk behaviours
- In children, prevention focuses on
  – escaping fires
  – crossing streets
  – using car seats, seat belts, and bicycle helmets
  – first aid

PhotoDisc/Getty Images

AIDS Prevention

- Changing high-risk behaviour through individual and community education is the only effective strategy
  – Eliminate unsafe sexual practices through cognitive-behavioural self-management training and social support networks
  – Show drug abusers how to clean needles and make safe injections
- Target minorities and women, groups that do not perceive themselves to be at risk
  – Media coverage focuses on gay white males
  – More women are infected through heterosexual interactions than through intravenous drug use

PhotoDisc/Getty Images

10 | Sexual Disorders and Gender Identity Disorder

Man, dominated by drives, has no power over himself.... We are in bondage in proportion as we are dominated by drives.
—Benedict de Spinoza

Bob Thomas/Photographer's Choice/Getty Images

348

Demonstrate knowledge and understanding representing appropriate breadth and depth in selected content areas of psychology:	❯ Biological bases of behaviour and mental processes, including physiology, sensation, perception, comparative, motivation, and emotion (APA SLO 1.2.a (3)) *(see textbook pages 368–372)*
Use the concepts, language, and major theories of the discipline to account for psychological phenomena.	❯ Describe behaviour and mental processes empirically, including operational definitions (APA SLO 1.3.a) *(see textbook pages 354–366, 376–382)*
Identify appropriate applications of psychology in solving problems, such as:	❯ Origin and treatment of abnormal behaviour (APA SLO 4.2.b) *(see textbook pages 367–368)*
	❯ Psychological tests and measurements (APA SLO 4.2.c) *(see textbook pages 357–359, 372–376, 382–387)*

* Portions of this chapter cover learning outcomes suggested by the American Psychological Association (2007) in their guidelines for the undergraduate psychology major. Chapter coverage of these outcomes is identified above by APA Goal and APA Suggested Learning Outcome (SLO).

You have probably read magazine surveys reporting sensational information on sexual practices. According to one, men can reach orgasm 15 or more times a day (in reality, such ability is very rare) and women fantasize about being raped (this is even rarer). Surveys like this fail us on two counts: First, they claim to reveal sexual norms when they are really, for the most part, distorted half-truths. Second, the facts they present typically are not based on any scientific methodology that would make them reliable— although they do sell magazines.

What is normal sexual behaviour? As we will see, it depends. When does sexual behaviour that is somewhat different from the norm become a disorder? Again, it depends. Current views tend to be quite tolerant of a variety of sexual expressions, even if they are unusual, unless the behaviour is associated with a substantial impairment in functioning. Three kinds of sexual behaviour meet this definition of impairment. In *gender identity disorder*, a person experiences psychological dissatisfaction with his or her biological sex. The disorder is not specifically sexual, but rather is a disturbance in a person's sense of identity as a male or a female. But these disorders are often grouped with sexual disorders, as in the *DSM-IV-TR*. Individuals with *sexual dysfunction* find it difficult to function adequately while having sex. For example, they may not become aroused or achieve orgasm. *Paraphilia*, the relatively new term for sexual deviation, includes disorders in which sexual arousal occurs primarily in the context of inappropriate objects or individuals. *Philia* means a strong attraction or liking, and *para* indicates that the attraction is abnormal. Paraphilic arousal patterns tend to be focused rather narrowly, often precluding mutually consenting adult patterns, even if they are desired. Before describing these three types of disorders, we return to our initial question, "What is normal sexual behaviour?" to gain an important perspective.

What Is Normal?

Determining the prevalence of sexual practices accurately requires careful surveys that sample specific populations. For more than 50 years, sex researchers and public health officials have relied on the comprehensive survey of sexual behaviours and attitudes by a pioneer investigator into sexual behaviour, Alfred Kinsey (Kinsey, Pomeroy, & Martin, 1948; Kinsey, Pomeroy, Martin, & Gebhard,

1953). But more recent surveys are updating our knowledge on what is currently "normal" sexual behaviour in our culture. Some such studies have focused on rates of sexual risk taking and some on issues such as gender differences in different aspects of sexual behaviours.

As we discussed briefly in Chapter 9, the sexual risks taken by university students, other young adults, and adolescents remain alarmingly high despite the well-publicized AIDS epidemic and the high rates of other sexually transmitted diseases (STDs; Maticka-Tyndale, 2001). For example, a study by DeBuono, Zinner, Daamen, and McCormack (1990) showed that although condom use in university women increased from 12 percent in 1975 to 41 percent in 1989, more than half the sexually active university women still practised unprotected sex in the late 1980s!

According to Eleanor Maticka-Tyndale at the University of Windsor, other areas of concern from the perspective of AIDS and STD prevention are the number of sexual partners that young people have and the seeming casualness of these encounters (Maticka-Tyndale, 2001). Youth most commonly move through a pattern of serial monogamy—they are with one partner for a time and then move on to another exclusive partner when that relationship ends. But some youth engage in sex outside a primary relationship (e.g., when travelling or when away from a primary partner, or in a casual sexual encounter). Three Canadian surveys suggest that about one-third of adolescent males and about one-quarter of adolescent females report two or more sexual partners in a year (see Table 10.1). The cumulative number of sexual partners an adolescent has can thus add up over the years, increasing his or her risk for AIDS and other STDs (Maticka-Tyndale, 2001). Another recent national survey of Canadian students in Grades 7, 9, and 11 showed that among those who were sexually active, oral contraceptive use was more common (84 percent to 90 percent) than condom use (64 percent to 80 percent). This pattern has been used to explain the increases in adolescent STD rates at a time when teen pregnancy rates have been on the decline in Canada (Boyce et al., 2006).

Gender Differences

Although both men and women tend toward a monogamous (one partner) pattern of sexual relationships, gender differences in sexual behaviour do exist, and some of them are quite dramatic.

TABLE 10.1 Proportion of Male and Female Adolescents with Multiple Intercourse Partners in Past Year

	Males (%)	Females (%)
National Population Health Survey, 1996[a]		
15–17 years, 1 partner	31	24
18–19 years, 1 partner	38	24
Nova Scotia, 1996, Grades 10–12)[b]		
15–18 years, 2 partners	20	17
Québec, 1998[c]		
15–19 years, 1 partner	32	33

Notes:

[a] Maticka-Tyndale, McKay, & Barrett, 2001

[b] Langille, 2000

[c] Institut de la statistique du Québec, 2001

Source: From "Sexual Health and Canadian Youth: How Do We Measure Up?" by E. Maticka-Tyndale, 2001, *Canadian Journal of Human Sexuality*, 10(1-2), 1–17.

One common finding among sexual surveys is that a much higher percentage of men than women report that they masturbate (self-stimulate to orgasm; Fortier, Mottard, & Trudel, 2003; Oliver & Hyde, 1993). When Cindy Meston and her colleagues surveyed 702 students at the University of British Columbia, their findings supported this difference: 80 percent of men versus only 48 percent of women reported masturbating alone (Meston, Trapnell, & Gorzalka, 1996). The results of this survey are shown in Table 10.2. Among those who did masturbate, the frequency of masturbation was also greater for men than for women. Thus, gender differences in masturbation appear to persist today even when other long-standing gender differences in sexual behaviour, such as the probability of engaging in premarital intercourse, have virtually disappeared (Clement, 1990; Meston et al.,).

Meston and colleagues' study (1996) also revealed that endorsement of many types of sexual fantasy was significantly higher for men than women (e.g., intercourse, oral-genital sex, sadism, and promiscuity fantasies). The only fantasy endorsed more often by women involved dressing in erotic garments (see the right side of Table 10.2). Men also reported fantasizing more frequently than women (Meston et al., 1996).

Another continuing gender difference is reflected in attitudes toward casual premarital sex, with men expressing a far more permissive attitude than women do, although this gap is becoming much smaller. Meston et al. (1996) found in their study with undergraduates that, in comparison with females, males reported having experienced a greater number of one-night stands, predicted a greater number of sexual partners in the next five years, and reported more frequent fantasies about having sex with someone other than their steady dating partner. By contrast, no significant mean differences existed between males and females in self-reported number of sexual partners or number of sexual partners in the past year (Meston et al., 1996).

An impressive series of studies has assessed gender differences in basic or core beliefs about sexual aspects of ourselves. These core beliefs about sexuality are referred to as "sexual self-schemas," and the findings echo those of a study conducted a decade earlier (Hatfield et al., 1988). Specifically, in a series of studies (Andersen & Cyranowski, 1994; Andersen, Cyranowski, & Espindle, 1999; Cyranowski, Aarestad, & Andersen, 1999), Andersen and colleagues demonstrated that women tend to report the experience of passionate and romantic feelings as an integral part of their sexuality as well as an openness to sexual experience. However, a substantial number of women also hold an embarrassed, conservative, or self-conscious schema that sometimes conflicts with more positive aspects of their sexual attitudes. Conversely, men evidence feelings of power, independence, and aggression as part of their sexuality, in addition to being passionate, loving, and open to experience. Men do not generally possess negative core beliefs reflecting self-consciousness, embarrassment, or feeling behaviourally inhibited.

What happened to the sexual revolution? Where are the effects of the "anything goes" attitude toward sexual expression and fulfillment that supposedly began in the 1960s and 1970s? Clearly some change has occurred. The double standard has disappeared, in that women, for the most part, no longer feel constrained by a stricter and more conservative social standard of sexual conduct. The sexes are definitely drawing together in their attitudes and behaviour, although some differences in attitudes and core beliefs remain. Regardless, the overwhelming majority of individuals engage in heterosexual, vaginal intercourse in the context of a relationship with one partner. Based on these data, the sexual revolution may be largely a creation of the media, focusing as it does on extreme or sensational cases. In fact, what appeals to us sexually seems to have strong evolutionary roots that foster propagation of the species. For example, men with "attractive" (to women) faces have higher sperm quality. Women with "attractive" (to men) bodies are more fertile; and both men and women with "attractive" voices lose their virginity sooner (Gallup & Frederick, 2010). Thus sexual attraction (and behaviour) is closely tied to evolutionary mandates reflecting the importance of this behaviour for the species.

Cultural Differences

What is normal in 21st-century Western countries like Canada and the United States may not necessarily be normal in other parts of the world (McGoldrick, Loonan, & Wohlsifer, 2007). The Sambia in Papua New Guinea believe semen is an essential substance for growth and development in young boys of the tribe. They also believe semen is not produced naturally; that is, the body is incapable of producing it spontaneously. Therefore, all young boys in the tribe, beginning at approximately age seven, become semen recipients by engaging exclusively in homosexual oral sex with teenage boys. Only oral sexual practices are permitted; masturbation is forbidden and totally absent. Early in adolescence the boys switch roles and become semen providers to younger boys. Heterosexual relations and even contact with the opposite sex are prohibited until the boys become teenagers. Late in adolescence, the boys are expected to marry and begin exclusive heterosexual activity. And they do, with no exceptions (Herdt, 1987; Herdt & Stoller, 1989). By contrast, the Munda of

TABLE 10.2 Percentages of University Men and Women Who Participated in Various Interpersonal Sexual Activities

	Men (n = 275)	Women (n = 427)		Men (n = 275)	Women (n = 427)
Light Petting			**Oral Sex**		
Kissing on the lips	80	81	Mutual oral stimulation of genitals	44	46
Deep kissing	73	74	Oral stimulation of partner's genitals	51	53
Erotic embrace (clothed)	72	71	Having genitals orally stimulated	55	50
Breast petting (clothed)	68	72	**Intercourse**		
Male lying prone on female (clothed)	73	70	Male superior position	50	52
Kissing of sensitive (nongenital) areas	75	73	Female superior position	47	49
Heavy Petting			Vaginal entry from rear	36	40
Stroking and petting partner's genitals	67	65	Side by side	28	34
Having genitals caressed by partner	67	64	Sitting position	35	42
Breast petting (nude)	68	68	Anal	5	11
Mutual undressing of each other	63	62	Frequency of kissing and petting (0–8 scale)	5.40	5.37
Male kissing female's nude breasts	69	68	Nonvirgin status (percent of sample)	61	57
Having anal area caressed	25	32	Age of first intercourse (nonvirgins only) (yrs)	17.29	17.5
Caressing partner's anal area	29	26	Frequency of intercourse (nonvirgins only) (0–8)	2.65	3.01
Mutual masturbation to orgasm	41	41	**Promiscuity Fantasies**		
Fantasy Total	33	25*	Mate swapping fantasies	17	8*
Gender Orientation Fantasies			Forbidden lover in sexual adventures	44	36
Homosexual fantasies	11	18	Being a prostitute	9	16
Fantasizing you are of the opposite sex	14	11	Having ≥1 partner simultaneously	71	31*
Dressing in clothes of opposite sex	13	11			
Intercourse Fantasies			**Miscellaneous Fantasies**		
Having intercourse in unusual positions	84	53*	Sexual relations with animals	3	4
Anal intercourse	34	10*	Using artificial devices for stimulation	32	23
Sexual intercourse	93	81*	Dressing in erotic garments	34	51
Masochism Fantasies			Oral-genital sex	76	47*
Being tied up or bound during sex	40	35	Frequency of fantasies (0–8 scale)	4.63	2.92*
Being forced to submit to sex	29	35	Masturbating alone (percent of sample)	80	48*
Being sexually degraded	6	9	Masturbation frequency (masturbators only; 0–8)	3.81	2.46*
Sadism Fantasies			Age of first interest in sex (in years)	13.50	15.00*
Whipping or beating sexual partner	11	4	Ideal frequency of sexual intercourse	4.43	3.85*
Degrading sexual partner	9	3*			
Forcing partner to submit to sex	29	13*			

Note: Significant gender differences indicated via asterisks (*).

Source: From "Ethnic and Gender differences in sexuality: Variations in sexual behavior between Asian and Non-Asian university students" by C. M. Meston, P. D. Trapnell, and B. B. Gorzalka, 1996, *Archives of Sexual Behavior, 25(1)*, 44–49.

What Is Normal?

TABLE 10.3 Group Differences between North American and Swedish Female Undergraduates Regarding Premarital Sex

	North America	Sweden
Variable	**Mean/(SD)**	**Mean/(SD)**
Age at first coitus	16.97 (1.83)	16.80 (1.92)
Age of first coital partner	18.77 (2.88)	19.10 (2.96)
Perceived age of social acceptance for females to engage in premarital coitus	18.76 (2.57)	15.88 (1.43)
Perceived age of social acceptance for males to engage in premarital coitus	16.33 (2.13)	15.58 (1.20)

Source: From "Affective Reactions of American and Swedish Women to Their First Premarital Coitus: A Cross Comparison" by I. M. Schwartz, 1993, *Journal of Sex Research*, 30, 18–26. © by the Society for the Scientific Study of Sex. Reprinted by permission.

northeast India require adolescents and children to live together, but in this group both male and female children live in the same setting. The sexual activity, consisting mostly of petting and mutual masturbation, is all heterosexual (Bancroft, 1989).

Even in Western cultures, some variations exist. Schwartz (1993) surveyed attitudes surrounding the first premarital experience of sexual intercourse in nearly 200 North American female undergraduates and compared them with a similar sample in Sweden, where attitudes toward sexuality are somewhat more permissive. The average age at the time of first intercourse for the woman and the age of her partner are presented in Table 10.3, as well as the age the women thought it was socially acceptable in their culture for them to have sexual intercourse. Acceptable perceived ages for both men and women were significantly younger in Sweden, but few other differences existed, with one striking exception: 73.7 percent of Swedish women but only 56.7 percent of North American women used some form of contraception during their first sexual intercourse, a significant difference. Surveys since then show few changes (Herlitz & Forsberg, 2010; Weinberg, Lottes, & Shaver, 1995). In about half of more than 100 societies surveyed worldwide, premarital sexual behaviour is culturally accepted and encouraged; in the remaining half, premarital sex is unacceptable and discouraged (Bancroft, 1989; Broude & Greene, 1980). Thus, what is normal sexual behaviour in one culture is not necessarily normal in another, and the wide range of sexual expression must be considered in diagnosing the presence of a disorder.

The Development of Sexual Orientation

Reports suggest that homosexuality runs in families (Bailey & Benishay, 1993), and concordance for homosexuality is more common among monozygotic twins than among dizygotic twins or natural siblings (Bailey & Pillard, 1991; Bailey, Pillard, Neale, & Agyei, 1993; Whitnam, Diamond, & Martin, 1993). This finding is associated with differential exposure to hormones early in life, perhaps before birth (Ehrhardt et al., 1985; Gladue, Green, & Hellman, 1984), and the actual structure of the brain might be different in homosexuals and heterosexuals (Allen & Gorski, 1992; Byne et al., 2000; LeVay, 1991). Research by Martin Lalu-

mière at the University of Lethbridge and his colleagues, Ray Blanchard, and Kenneth Zucker at the Centre for Addiction and Mental Health in Toronto, also suggests possible biological contributions to sexual orientation. Using meta-analysis, defined earlier as a statistical technique for summarizing the results across studies, these researchers found that individuals with homosexual orientations have a 39 percent greater chance of being non-right-handed (left-handed or mixed-handed) than those with heterosexual orientations (Lalumière, Blanchard, & Zucker, 2000; see also Blanchard, Cantor, & Bogaert, 2006). Another report suggests a possible gene (or genes) for homosexuality on the X chromosome (Hamer, Hu, Magnuson, Hu, & Pattatucci, 1993). In two well-done twin studies (Bailey & Pillard, 1991; Bailey et al., 1993), homosexual orientation was found to be shared in approximately 50 percent of monozygotic twins, compared with 16 percent to 22 percent of dizygotic twins. Approximately the same, or a slightly lower, percentage of non-twin brothers or sisters were homosexual. According to a literature review by Toronto-based researcher Meredith Chivers and her colleagues, there is now strong evidence accumulated that genes do influence sexual orientation, although specifically which genes contribute to this remains unknown (Mustanski, Chivers, & Bailey, 2002).

The principal conclusion drawn in the media is that sexual orientation has a biological cause. Gay rights activists are decidedly split on the significance of these findings. Some are pleased with the biological interpretation, because people can no longer assume homosexuals have made a morally depraved choice of supposedly deviant arousal patterns. Others, however, note how quickly the public has pounced on the implication that something is biologically wrong with individuals with homosexual arousal patterns, assuming that someday the abnormality will be detected in the fetus and prevented, perhaps through genetic engineering.

Do such arguments over biological causes sound familiar? Think back to studies described in Chapter 2 that attempted to link complex behaviour to particular genes. In almost every case, these studies could not be replicated, and investigators fell back on a model in which genetic contributions to behavioural traits and psychological disorders come from many genes, each making a relatively small contribution to *vulnerability*. This generalized biological vulnerability then interacts in a complex way with various environmental conditions, personality traits, and other contributors to determine behavioural patterns. We also discussed reciprocal gene–environment interactions in which certain learning experiences and environmental events may affect brain structure and function and genetic expression.

The same thing is now happening with sexual orientation. For example, Bailey et al. (1999) could not, in a later study, *replicate* the report suggesting a specific gene for homosexuality (Hamer et al., 1993). Most theoretical models outlining these complex interactions for sexual orientation imply that many pathways to the development of heterosexuality or homosexuality may exist and that no single factor, biological or psychological, can predict the outcome (Bancroft, 1994; Byne & Parsons, 1993). It is likely, too, that different types of homosexuality (and, perhaps, heterosexuality), with different patterns of etiology, may be discovered (Diamond et al., in press; Savin-Williams, 2006) (see the Innovative Approaches box). Bem (1996) refers to his model as "exotic becomes erotic," a phrase that summarizes the principles of the

Have you heard the song "I Kissed a Girl" by Katy Perry? Could it be that sexual orientation is malleable, at least for some people? Dr. Lisa Diamond has studied women over time (longitudinal studies) and discovered that interpersonal and situational factors exerted a substantial influence on women's patterns of sexual behaviour and sexual identities, a finding much less true for men (Diamond, 2007; Diamond et al., in press). Among women who initially identified themselves as heterosexual, lesbian, bisexual, or "unlabelled," after 10 years more than two-thirds of women had changed their identity label a few times. When women changed their sexual identi-ties, they typically broadened rather than narrowed their potential range of attractions and relationships.

Why is this true for women, but not so much for men? Researchers don't know for certain, but these innovative longi-tudinal studies have already taught us a lot about the origins of sexual orientation. Almost certainly, in our view, scientists will pin down biological contributions to the formation of sexual orientation, both heterosexual and homosexual. And just as certainly, the environment and experience will be found to powerfully influence how these patterns of potential sexual arousal develop.

theory nicely. Bem proposes that we inherit a temperament to behave in certain ways that later interacts with environmental factors to produce sexual orientation. For example, if a boy prefers active and aggressive or "boy-typical" behaviours, he will feel very similar to his same-sex peers. A young boy who feels less aggressive may avoid rough-and-tumble play in favour of "girl-typical" activities. Their activities, whether typical or atypical, lead children to feel different from either their opposite or their same-sex peers. A young boy with boy-typical activities will feel more different from girls than he does from boys, making the opposite sex more "exotic." Sexual attraction in later years will be to the group of more exotic individuals. A young boy who engages in girl-typical activities is likely to feel more different from other boys than he does from girls (or other boys with atyp-ical activities). Therefore, what is exotic to this boy is other boys. Sexual attraction later follows.

Bem has some evidence that gay men and women feel more different from their same-sex peers than do heterosexual men and women, but little direct evidence indicates this feeling, in turn, determines sexual attraction. Some evidence from other sources, however, supports the attractiveness of novel or exotic stimuli. What is important for our purposes is that this theory combines biological and psychological or environmental variables, and suggests how they interact to form sexual orientation (see ■ Figure 10.1). Almost certainly, in our view, scientists will pin down biological contributions to the formation of sexual orienta-tion, both heterosexual and homosexual. And just as certainly, the environment and experience will be found to powerfully influence how these patterns of potential sexual arousal develop.

One of the more intriguing findings from the twin studies of Bailey and colleagues is that approximately 50 percent of the monozyotic twins with *exactly* the *same genetic structure* as well as the *same environment* (growing up in the same house) did *not* have the same sexual orientation (Bailey & Pillard, 1991). Also intriguing is the finding in a study of 302 homosexual men that males growing up with older brothers are more likely to be homo-sexual, whereas having older sisters, or younger brothers or sis-ters, is not correlated with later sexual orientation. In fact, each additional older brother increased the odds of homosexuality by

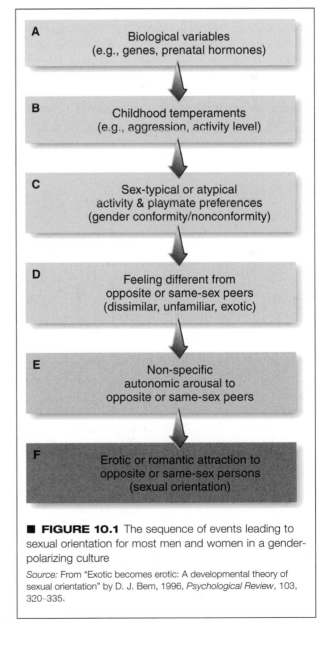

A Biological variables
(e.g., genes, prenatal hormones)

B Childhood temperaments
(e.g., aggression, activity level)

C Sex-typical or atypical
activity & playmate preferences
(gender conformity/nonconformity)

D Feeling different from
opposite or same-sex peers
(dissimilar, unfamiliar, exotic)

E Non-specific
autonomic arousal to
opposite or same-sex peers

F Erotic or romantic attraction to
opposite or same-sex persons
(sexual orientation)

■ **FIGURE 10.1** The sequence of events leading to sexual orientation for most men and women in a gender-polarizing culture

Source: From "Exotic becomes erotic: A developmental theory of sexual orientation" by D. J. Bem, 1996, *Psychological Review*, 103, 320–335.

one-third! This may suggest the importance of environmental influences, although the mechanism has not been identified (Blanchard, 2008; Blanchard & Bogaert, 1996, 1998; Jones & Blanchard, 1998).

In any case, the simple one-dimensional claims that homosexuality is caused by a gene or by early developmental experiences will continue to appeal to the general populace. Although we could be wrong, neither explanation is likely to be proven correct. Almost certainly, biology sets certain limits within which social and psychological factors affect development (Diamond, 1995; Diamond et al., in press; Långström, Rahman, Carlström, & Lichtenstein, 2010).

Gender Identity Disorder

What is it that makes you think you are a man? Or a woman? Clearly, it's more than your sexual arousal patterns or your anatomy. It's also more than the reactions and experiences of your family and society. The essence of your masculinity or femininity is a deep-seated personal sense called gender identity. This sense of the self as male or female is typically consolidated by age three or four (Bradley & Zucker, 1997; Zucker & Bradley, 2004). **Gender identity disorder** is present if a person's physical gender is inconsistent with that person's sense of identity. People with this disorder feel trapped in a body of the wrong sex (see DSM Table 10.1). Consider the case of Joe. We return to Joe in our discussion of treatment.

JOE | *Trapped in the Wrong Body*

Joe was a 17-year-old male and the last of five children. Although his mother had wanted a girl, he became her favourite child. His father worked long hours and had little contact with the boy. For as long as Joe could remember, he had thought of himself as a girl. He began dressing in girls' clothes totally of his own accord before he was five years old and continued cross-dressing into junior high. He developed interests in cooking, knitting, crocheting, and embroidering, skills he acquired by reading an encyclopedia. His older brother often scorned him for his distaste of such "masculine" activities as hunting.

Joe associated mostly with girls during this period, although he remembered being strongly attached to a boy in Grade 1. In his sexual fantasies, which developed at about 12 years of age, he pictured himself as a female having intercourse with a male. His extremely effeminate behaviour made him the object of scorn and ridicule when he entered high school at age 15. Usually passive and unassertive, he ran away from home and attempted suicide. Unable to continue in high school, he attended secretarial school, where he was the only male in his class. During his first interview with a therapist he reported, "I am a woman trapped in a man's body and I would like to have surgery to become a woman."

DSM-IV-TR | **Table 10.1** Criteria for Gender Identity Disorder

A. A strong and persistent cross-gender identification (not merely a desire for any perceived cultural advantages of being the other sex).

In children, the disturbance is manifested by four (or more) of the following:

1. Repeatedly stated desire to be, or insistence that he or she is, the other sex.
2. In boys, preference for cross-dressing or simulating female attire; in girls, insistence on wearing only stereotypical masculine clothing.
3. Strong and persistent preferences for cross-sex roles in make-believe play or persistent fantasies of being the other sex.
4. Intense desire to participate in the stereotypical games and pastimes of the other sex.
5. Strong preference for playmates of the other sex.

In adolescents and adults, the disturbance is manifested by symptoms, such as a stated desire to be the other sex, frequent passing as the other sex, desire to live or be treated as the other sex, or the conviction that he or she has the typical feelings and reactions of the other sex.

B. Persistent discomfort with his or her sex or sense of inappropriateness in the gender role of that sex.

In children, the disturbance is manifested by any of the following: in boys, the assertion that his penis or testes are disgusting or will disappear or the assertion that it would be better not to have a penis, or aversion toward rough-and-tumble play and rejection of male stereotypical toys, games, and activities; in girls, rejection of urinating in a sitting position, the assertion that she has or will grow a penis, or the assertion that she does not want to grow breasts or menstruate, or marked aversion toward normative feminine clothing.

In adolescents and adults, the disturbance is manifested by symptoms such as a preoccupation with getting rid of primary and secondary sex characteristics (e.g., request for hormones, surgery, or other procedures to physically alter sexual characteristics to simulate the other sex) or the belief that he or she was born the wrong sex.

C. The disturbance is not concurrent with a physical intersex condition.

D. The disturbance causes clinically significant distress or impairment in social, occupational, or other important areas of functioning.

Code based on current age:

302.60 Gender identity disorder in children

302.85 Gender identity disorder in adolescents or adults

Specify if (for sexually mature individuals):

Sexually attracted to males

Sexually attracted to females

Sexually attracted to both

Sexually attracted to neither

Source: Reprinted with permission from the *Diagnostic and Statistical Manual of Mental Disorders*, Fourth Edition, Text Revision, (Copyright © 2000). American Psychiatric Association.

Gender identity disorder (or *transsexualism*, as it used to be called) must be distinguished from *transvestic fetishism*, a paraphilic disorder (discussed later) in which individuals, usually males, are sexually aroused by wearing articles of clothing associated with the opposite sex. There is an occasional preference on the part of the male for the female role, but the primary purpose of cross-dressing is sexual gratification. In the case of gender identity disorder, the primary goal is not sexual but rather the desire to live life openly in a manner consistent with that of the other gender.

Gender identity disorder must also be distinguished from *intersex individuals* (*hermaphrodites*), who are actually born with ambiguous genitalia associated with documented hormonal or other physical abnormalities. Depending on their particular mix of characteristics, they are usually "assigned" to a specific sex at birth, sometimes undergoing surgery as well as hormonal treatments to alter their sexual anatomy. Individuals with gender identity disorder, by contrast, have no demonstrated physical abnormalities. We return to the issue of intersex individuals later.

Finally, gender identity disorder must be distinguished from the same-sex arousal patterns of a male who sometimes behaves effeminately, or a woman with same-sex arousal patterns and masculine mannerisms. Such an individual does not feel like a woman trapped in a man's body or have any desire to be a woman, or vice versa. Note also, as the *DSM-IV-TR* criteria do, that gender identity is independent of sexual arousal patterns (Savin-Williams, 2006). For example, a male-to-female transsexual (a biological male with a feminine gender identity) may be sexually attracted to females. Similarly, Eli Coleman and his associates (Coleman, Bockting, & Gooren, 1993) reported on nine female-to-male cases in which the individuals were sexually attracted to men. Thus, heterosexual women before surgery were gay men after surgery. Chivers and Bailey (2000) compared a group of female-to-male individuals who were attracted to men (a rare occurrence) to a group of female-to-male individuals who were attracted to women (the usual pattern) both before and after surgery. They found the groups did not differ in the strength of their gender identity (as males), although the latter group was more sexually assertive and, understandably, more interested in surgery to create an artificial penis. And Lawrence (2005) studied 232 male-to-female cases both before and after surgery and found that the majority (54 percent) were mostly heterosexual (attracted to women) before the surgery. This changed after surgery slightly for some and dramatically for a few, such that only 25 percent remained attracted to women after surgery, thus making them technically gay. This latter group may constitute a distinct subset of male-to-female cases with a different pattern of development called *autogynephilia*, in which gender identity disorder begins with a strong and specific sexual attraction to a fantasy of oneself (*auto*) as a female (*gyne*). This fantasy then progresses to a more comprehensive all-encompassing identity as a female. Individuals in this subgroup of biological males were not effeminate as boys, but became sexually aroused while cross-dressing and to fantasies of themselves as women. Over time, these fantasies progress to *becoming* a woman (Bailey, 2003; Carroll, 2007). This distinction is controversial, but is supported by research (Carroll, 2007).

Proposed changes regarding gender identity disorder for the *DSM-5* are not substantial, although research is beginning to support a more nuanced dimensional view of gender identity that may become viable for the future (American Psychological Association [APA], 2010; Cohen-Kettenis & Pfäfflin, 2010). Gender identity disorder is relatively rare. The estimated incidence based on studies in Sweden, Australia, and the Netherlands is 1 in 37 000 in Sweden, 1 in 24 000 in Australia, and 1 in 11 000 in the Netherlands for biological males, compared to 1 in 103 000 in Sweden, 1 in 150 000 in Australia, and 1 in 30 000 in the Netherlands for biological females (Baker, van Kesteren, Gooren, & Bezemer, 1993; Ross, Walinder, Lundstrom, & Thuwe, 1981; Sohn & Bosinski, 2007). These numbers reflect the fact that gender identity disorder occurs approximately three times more frequently in males than in females (APA, 2008). Many countries now require a series of legal steps to change gender identity. In Germany, between 2.1 and 2.4 per 100 000 in the population took at least the first legal step of changing their first names in the 1990s; in that country, the male:female ratio of people with gender identity disorder is 2.3:1 (Weitze & Osburg, 1996). Since 2006, in New York City people may choose to alter the sex listed on their birth certificates following surgery.

Probably the best-known case of male-to-female transsexualism in Canada is Enza Anderson. She gained international attention when she ran for mayor of Toronto in November 2000 and came in third. In the 2003 Toronto municipal election, she ran for a city council seat and placed second. Enza has always felt she was female and started dressing as a girl secretly as a teen, borrowing clothes from her mother. She was raised in a very traditional Italian Catholic family; she has managed to keep her transsexualism

▲ Enza Anderson is a columnist and transsexual activist living in Toronto. She gained international attention when she ran for mayor of Toronto in 2000.

Chatham Daily News/Diana Martin/Sun Media Corporation

Gender Identity Disorder **355**

a secret from her father to this day because he would not approve. Enza takes estrogen and has had electrolysis hair-removal treatments; she would like to receive breast implants and is considering gender reassignment surgery sometime in the future. Such treatments are not covered by health insurance in Ontario and are quite expensive. Enza trained and worked as a civil engineer but is not working in the engineering field because she cannot as easily dress as a woman and be herself. She is a columnist and a strong activist within the gay-lesbian-bisexual-transgendered community in Toronto (you can visit Enza Anderson's website at http://tgmedia.enacre.net/lorna_lynne/enza.html).

In some cultures, individuals with mistaken gender identity (i.e., those who would be considered to have gender identity disorder in Western culture) are accorded the status of shaman or seer and treated as wisdom figures (see Carmody & Carmody, 1993, for a discussion of the role of the shaman in Native religions). Stoller (1976) reported on two contemporary feminized Native-American men who were not only accepted but also esteemed by their tribes for their expertise in healing rituals. When the white settlers began to colonize North America, they labelled such individuals "berdache," leading to the unfortunate oppression of these people (Herdt, 1987). Jacobs, Thomas, and Lang (1997) have edited a fascinating book of readings on the subject of gender identity in various Native tribes in North America called *Two-Spirit People*. Based on the study of such individuals in certain Native cultures, Williams (1986) has argued that individuals with mistaken gender identity should be considered a third gender (i.e., an alternative or intermediate gender), since berdaches appear to be accepted by their societies as distinct from both men and women. Contrary to the respect accorded these individuals in some cultures, social tolerance for them is relatively low in Western cultures today, where they are the objects of curiosity at best and derision at worst.

Causes

Research has yet to uncover any specific biological contributions to gender identity disorder, although it seems likely that a biological predisposition will be discovered. Coolidge, Thede, and Young (2002) estimated that genetics contributed about 62 percent to creating a vulnerability to experience gender identity disorder in their twin sample. Thirty-eight percent of the vulnerability came from nonshared (unique) environmental events. A recent study from the Netherlands twin registry suggested that 70 percent of the vulnerability for cross-gender behaviour (behaving in a manner consistent with the opposite biological sex) was genetic as opposed to environmental, but this behaviour is not the same as gender identity, which was not measured (as explained later) (van Beijsterveldt, Hudziak, & Boomsma, 2006). Gomez-Gil et al. (2010) found a somewhat higher prevalence of gender-identity disorder than would be expected by chance in non-twin siblings of a larger group (995) of individuals with gender identity disorder. Segal (2006), on the other hand, found two monozygotic (identical) female twin pairs in which one twin had gender identity disorder and the other did not; no unusual medical or life history factors were identified to account for this difference. Nevertheless, genetic contributions are clearly part of the picture.

Early research suggested that, as with sexual orientation, slightly higher levels of testosterone or estrogen at certain critical periods of development might masculinize a female fetus or feminize a male fetus (e.g., Gladue et al., 1984; Keefe, 2002). Variations in hormonal levels could occur naturally or because of medication that a pregnant mother is taking. Scientists have studied girls aged 5 to 12 with an intersex condition known as *congenital adrenal hyperplasia* (CAH). In CAH, the brains of these chromosomal females are flooded with male hormones (androgens), which, among other results, produce mostly masculine external genitalia, although internal organs (ovaries and so on) remain female. Meyer-Bahlburg and colleagues (2004) studied 15 girls with CAH, who had been correctly identified as female at birth and raised as girls, and looked at their development. Compared to groups of girls and boys without CAH, the CAH girls were masculine in their behaviour, but there were no differences in gender identity. Thus, scientists have yet to establish a link between prenatal hormonal influence and later gender identity, although it is still possible that one exists. Structural differences in the area of the brain that controls male sex hormones have also been observed in individuals with male-to-female gender identity disorder (Zhou, Hofman, Gooren, & Swaab, 1995), with the result that the brains are comparatively more feminine. But it isn't clear whether this is a cause or an effect.

At least some evidence suggests that gender identity firms up between 18 months and 3 years of age (Ehrhardt & Meyer-Bahlburg, 1981; Money & Ehrhardt, 1972) and is relatively fixed after that. But newer studies suggest that possible pre-existing biological factors have already had their impact. One interesting case illustrating this phenomenon was originally reported by Green and Money (1969), who described the sequence of events that occurred in the case of David/Brenda.

DAVID/BRENDA

A set of male identical twins was born into a well-adjusted family in Winnipeg. Several weeks later, an unfortunate accident occurred. Although circumcision went routinely for one boy, the physician's hand slipped so that the electric current in the device burned off the penis of the second boy. The parents consulted specialists in children with intersexual problems and were faced with a choice. The specialists suggested that the easiest solution would be to reassign their son as a girl, and the parents agreed. At the age of several months, David became Brenda. The parents purchased a new wardrobe and treated the child in every way possible as a girl. These twins were followed through childhood and, on reaching puberty, the young girl was given hormonal replacement therapy.

After six years the doctors lost track of the case but assumed she had adjusted well. In fact, Brenda endured almost intolerable inner turmoil. We know this because two clinical scientists found the family and reported a long-term follow-up (Diamond & Sigmundson, 1997) and because this person, whose real name was David/Brenda Reimer, told the story from his own point of view as an adult in a book called *As Nature Made Him* (Colapinto, 2001) and on the *Oprah* television show. Brenda never adjusted to her assigned gender. As a child she preferred rough-and-tumble play and resisted wearing girls' clothes. In public bathrooms she often insisted on urinating while standing up, which usually made a mess. By early adolescence Brenda was pretty sure that she was a boy, but her doctors pressed her to act more feminine.

When she was 14, she confronted her parents, telling them that she was so miserable she was considering suicide. At that point they told her the true story and the muddy waters of her mind began to clear. Shortly thereafter, Brenda had additional surgery, changing her back to David. He was married in 1990 and became the father of three adopted children. However, he continued to struggle throughout his adult life with emotional difficulties, and died in May 2004, at age 38, from an apparent suicide (Canadian Press, 2004). His mother is reportedly of the opinion that her son's suicide is directly related to the emotional hardship he suffered as a consequence of the gender experiment (Canadian Press, 2004).

It certainly seems that biology expressed itself in David/ Brenda's case. However, other case studies of children whose gender was reassigned very early in life show that the children adapted successfully (e.g., Bradley, Oliver, Chernick, & Zucker, 1998; Gearhart, 1989). For example, Toronto-based researcher Susan Bradley and her colleagues (1998) reported on the outcome of another Canadian case similar in many respects to the case of David/Brenda. During a circumcision at two months of age, the patient sustained a burn of the penile shaft and the penis eventually sloughed off. The remainder of the male genitalia was removed at age seven months, and a decision was made by the parents to raise the child as a girl. The patient was interviewed by the authors at ages 16 and 26 to examine her long-term adjustment. At both times, the patient was living socially as a woman and denied any uncertainty about being a female, providing support for Green and Money's (1969) original position on the importance of environmental factors in determining gender identity. However, like David/Brenda, the patient recalled that she had self-identified as a "tomboy" as a child. As an adult, she described herself as bisexual in sexual orientation and reported having relationships with both men and women, although she was primarily attracted to women. She was also employed in a blue-collar job usually dominated by men. This case illustrates that it is possible for a female gender identity to emerge in a biologically "normal" genetic male, even in the presence of masculine tendencies (Bradley et al., 1998).

Kenneth Zucker and Susan Bradley have also studied boys who behave in feminine ways, investigating what makes them that way and following what happens to them (e.g., see review by Zucker, 2005a). Research from their clinic discovered that when most young boys spontaneously display "feminine" interests and behaviours, they are typically discouraged by most families and these behaviours usually cease. However, boys who consistently display these behaviours are not discouraged, and are sometimes encouraged, as seemed to be the case with Joe (Zucker & Bradley, 1995; see also

Green, 1987). It has also been suggested that a parent's preference for a girl or a boy might influence how a child is raised within the family with respect to encouragement or discouragement of gender-stereotypic behaviours in the child (see review by Bradley & Zucker, 1997). There is no evidence that mothers of boys referred for gender identity problems wanted a girl more than control mothers (Zucker et al., 1994). However, there is evidence that the maternal wish for a girl is greater when the older children are all male (Zucker & Bradley, 1995) and that gender dysphoria in feminine male adults is more common in men who grew up with several older brothers (Blanchard, Zucker, Cohen-Kettenis, Gooren, & Bailey, 1996). Moreover, evidence from the Gender Identity Clinic in Toronto does suggest that, at least for some mothers of boys with gender identity disorder, the mother's difficulty in dealing with her disappointment about not having a girl does indeed have an impact on the way in which she relates to her son (Zucker & Bradley, 1995; Zucker, Bradley, & Ipp, 1993). Girls with gender identity disorder have been less systematically studied with respect to the role of family factors (Bradley & Zucker, 1997; see review by Zucker, 2005b).

Other factors, such as excessive attention and physical contact on the part of the mother, may also play some role, as may a lack of male playmates during the early years of socialization (Green, 1987). These are just some of the factors identified as characteristic of effeminate boys. Remember that as-yet-undiscovered biological factors may also contribute to the spontaneous display of cross-gender behaviours and interests. However, when effeminate boys have been followed up over time, very few seem to develop the "wrong" gender identity (Green, 1987), although follow-ups are continuing to more precisely evaluate this issue. The most likely outcome of effeminate behaviour in a boy in childhood is the development of homosexual preferences, but even this particular sexual arousal pattern seems to occur exclusively in only approximately 40 percent of the feminine boys. Another 32 percent show some degree of bisexuality, sexual attraction to both their own and the opposite sex. Looking at it from the other side, 60 percent were functioning heterosexually (Green, 1987). We can safely say that the causes of gender identity disorder are still something of a mystery.

Treatment

Treatment is available for gender identity disorder in a few specialty clinics around the world, although much controversy surrounds treatment (Carroll, 2007). At present the most common decision is to use **sex reassignment surgery** to alter the anatomy physically to be consistent with the identity. Recently, psychosocial treatments to directly alter mistaken gender identity itself have been attempted in a few cases.

Sex Reassignment Surgery

To qualify for surgery at a reputable clinic, individuals must live in the opposite-sex role for one to two years so they can be sure they want to change sex. They also must be stable psychologically, financially, and socially (Blanchard & Steiner, 1990). In male-to-female candidates, hormones are administered to promote gynecomastia (the growth of breasts) and the development of other secondary sex characteristics. Facial hair is typically removed through electrolysis. If the individual is satisfied with the events of the trial period, the genitals are removed and a vagina is constructed.

For female-to-male transsexuals, an artificial penis is typically constructed through plastic surgery, using sections of skin and muscle from elsewhere in the body, such as the thigh. Breasts are surgically removed. Genital surgery is more difficult and complex in biological females. Estimates of transsexuals' satisfaction with surgery indicate predominantly successful adjustment (approximately 75 percent improved) among those who could be reached for follow-ups, with female-to-male conversions adjusting better than male-to-female (Bancroft, 1989; Blanchard & Steiner, 1990; Bodlund & Kullgren, 1996; Carroll, 2000; Green & Fleming, 1990; Kuiper & Cohen-Kettenis, 1988). However, many people were not available for follow-up. Approximately 7 percent of sex reassignment cases later regret surgery (Bancroft, 1989; Lundstrom, Pauly, & Walinder, 1984). This regret is unfortunate, because the surgery is irreversible. Also, as many as 2 percent attempt suicide after surgery, a rate much higher than for the general population. Nevertheless, surgery has made life worth living for some people who suffered the effects of existing in what they felt to be the wrong body.

A controversial issue in Canada has been whether sex reassignment surgery should be a publicly funded medical procedure. The treatment of this issue varies by province and territory. Several jurisdictions (e.g., Alberta, British Columbia, Saskatchewan) fund sex reassignment surgery, whereas others do not (see http://www.egale.ca/index.asp?lang=E&item=1086 for detailed information on the policies around this issue in each province and territory). The procedure was funded in Ontario from 1969 until 1998. In the 30 years that the procedure was publicly funded in Ontario, statistics show that there were, on average, six people approved for the surgery each year at an average cost of $28 000. The cost of the procedure, and efforts to cut costs in health care spending, led the Ontario government to delist this surgery as eligible for medicare coverage. However, advocacy groups such as Egale Canada argue that it is a human rights issue and that transgendered people's dignity is being harmed by the change in access to this surgery. In fact, four transsexual individuals took the Ontario government to task in September 2003, in an important human rights hearing (Egale Canada, 2003). In November 2005, the Human Rights Tribunal ruled that the province should pay for sex reassignment surgery for three of the four complainants. However, the tribunal stopped short of requiring the Ontario government to relist this procedure as an eligible expense under the province's public health insurance plan (CUPE, 2005).

Treatment of Intersexuality

As we noted, surgery and hormonal replacement therapy have been standard treatment for many intersex individuals (hermaphrodites) born with physical characteristics of both sexes. This group has been the subject of more careful evaluation, resulting in some new ideas and new approaches to treatment (Fausto-Sterling, 2000a, 2000b). Specifically, Anne Fausto-Sterling has suggested previously that there are actually five sexes: males; females; "herms," who are true hermaphrodites, or people born with both testes and ovaries; "merms," who are anatomically more male than female but possess some aspect of female genitalia; and "ferms," who have ovaries but possess some aspect of male genitalia. She estimates, based on the best evidence available, that for every 1000 children born, 17, or 1.7 percent, may be intersexual in some form. What Fausto-Sterling (2000b) and others have noted is that indi-

viduals in this group are often dissatisfied with surgery, much as David/Brenda was in the case we described. In some instances doctors, on observing anatomical sexual ambiguity after birth, treat it as an emergency and immediately perform surgery.

Fausto-Sterling suggests that an increasing number of pediatric endocrinologists, urologists, and psychologists are beginning to examine the wisdom of early genital surgery that results in an irreversible gender assignment. Instead, health professionals may want to examine very closely the precise nature of the intersex condition and consider surgery only as a last resort—and only when they are quite sure the particular condition will lead to a specific psychological gender identity. Otherwise, psychological treatments to help individuals adapt to their particular sexual anatomy, or their emerging gender identity, might be more appropriate.

Psychosocial Treatment

In some clinics, therapists, in cooperation with their clients, attempt to change gender identity itself before considering surgery. Most adult clients cannot conceive of changing their basic identity. However, some individuals request psychosocial treatment before embarking on a treatment course leading to surgery, usually because they are in great psychological distress or because surgery is immediately unavailable. The first successful effort to change gender identity was reported from our sexuality clinic (Barlow, Reynolds, & Agras, 1973). Joe, described earlier, was extremely depressed and suicidal; because surgery was not possible at his age without parental consent, which was not forthcoming, he agreed to a course of psychosocial treatment.

Joe's greatest difficulty was the ridicule and scorn heaped on him for his extremely effeminate gestures. We developed a behavioural rating scale for gender-specific motor behaviour (Barlow et al., 1979; Beck & Barlow, 1984) to help Joe identify the precise ways he sat, stood, and walked that were stereotypically masculine or feminine. Through behavioural rehearsal and modelling, we taught him to act in a more typically masculine manner when he so chose. Very soon he reported enormous satisfaction in avoiding ridicule by simply choosing to behave differently in some situations. What followed was more extensive role-playing and rehearsal for social skills as he learned to make better eye contact and converse more positively and confidently. After this phase of therapy, he was better adjusted, but he still felt he was really a woman and he was strongly sexually attracted to males.

During the next phase, a female therapist worked directly on Joe's fantasies in an intense, almost hypnotic way, encouraging him to imagine himself in sexual situations with a woman and to generate more characteristically masculine fantasies as he went about his daily business. After several months of intensive training, Joe's gender identity began to change, slowly at first and then more rapidly. At the end of this phase, much to his delight, he reported that he now felt like a 17-year-old boy in addition to behaving like one, although he was still sexually attracted to males. Because he expressed a strong desire to become sexually attracted to females, procedures were implemented to alter his patterns of sexual arousal, and at a five-year follow-up Joe had made a very successful adjustment.

Two additional cases were treated in a similar fashion (Barlow, Abel, & Blanchard, 1979) and also resulted in altered gender identity. These two individuals, who were somewhat older than

Joe, wanted to retain their homosexual arousal patterns, and they were assisted in adjusting to a standard homosexual lifestyle without the burden of mistaken gender identity. Similar efforts to treat gender identity disturbance in prepubescent boys have been successful in a large number of cases with follow-ups of four years or more (Rekers, Kilgus, & Rosen, 1990).

The issue of whether gender identity disorder in children should be treated has been hotly debated. On one side of the issue are researchers and theorists such as Nancy Bartlett of Mount Saint Vincent's University and her colleagues Paul Vasey and William Bukowski of the University of Lethbridge and Concordia University, respectively. They argue against the placement of gender identity disorder of childhood in the *DSM* system, on the basis of an extensive literature review. They believe that children who experience discomfort with the socially prescribed gender role behaviours of their sex, but who do not experience discomfort with their biological sex, should not be labelled with gender identity disorder and certainly should not be treated. They express concern that considering gender identity disorder in children a mental disorder may contribute to social stigmatization of these children (Bartlett, Vasey, & Bukowski, 2000).

On the other side of the argument are researchers such as Kenneth Zucker, who argue that psychosocial interventions should be initiated for those children evidencing symptoms of gender identity disorder (e.g., Stein, Zucker, & Dixon, 2001). He argues that without treatment, children with gender identity disorder are socially ostracized and that the condition is associated with considerable pain and suffering and should be taken seriously. He argues against the common conception among pediatricians that children "grow out of" this pattern of behaviour. Zucker also points out that there is some evidence that gender identity problems are easier to resolve if they are treated in childhood as opposed to in adolescence or adulthood (Stein et al., 2001). Zucker argues for an eclectic approach to treatment like that used at his Gender Identity Clinic in Toronto. Psychosocial treatment at this clinic combines the involvement of parents in treatment, the discouragement of the child's cross-gender behaviour, and the promotion of opportunities for the child to develop same-sex friendships and skills (Bradley & Zucker, 1997).

Sexual Dysfunctions: Clinical Descriptions

Before describing **sexual dysfunctions**, note that the problems that arise in the context of sexual interactions may occur in both heterosexual and homosexual relationships. Inability to become aroused or reach orgasm seem to be as common in homosexual as in heterosexual relationships, but we discuss them in the context of heterosexual relationships, which are the majority of cases we see in our clinic. The three stages of the sexual response cycle—desire, arousal, and orgasm (see ■ Figure 10.2)—are each

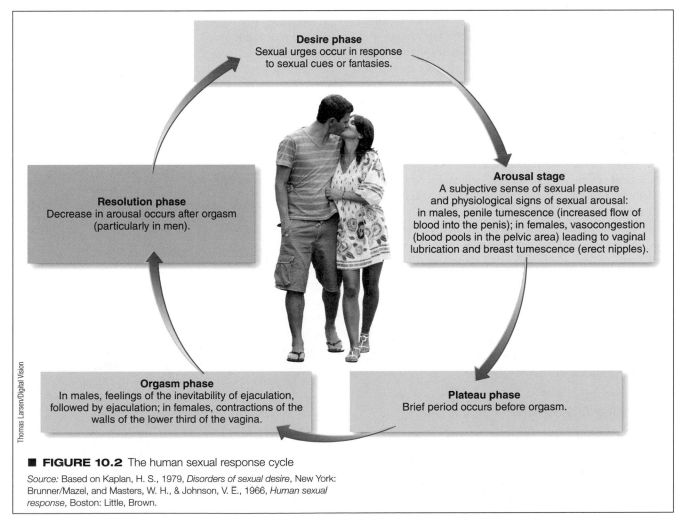

Desire phase
Sexual urges occur in response to sexual cues or fantasies.

Arousal stage
A subjective sense of sexual pleasure and physiological signs of sexual arousal: in males, penile tumescence (increased flow of blood into the penis); in females, vasocongestion (blood pools in the pelvic area) leading to vaginal lubrication and breast tumescence (erect nipples).

Plateau phase
Brief period occurs before orgasm.

Orgasm phase
In males, feelings of the inevitability of ejaculation, followed by ejaculation; in females, contractions of the walls of the lower third of the vagina.

Resolution phase
Decrease in arousal occurs after orgasm (particularly in men).

Thomas Larsen/Digital Vision

■ **FIGURE 10.2** The human sexual response cycle

Source: Based on Kaplan, H. S., 1979, *Disorders of sexual desire*, New York: Brunner/Mazel, and Masters, W. H., & Johnson, V. E., 1966, *Human sexual response*, Boston: Little, Brown.

TABLE 10.4 Categories of Sexual Dysfunction among Men and Women

	Sexual Dysfunction	
Type of Disorder	**Men**	**Women**
Desire	Hypoactive sexual desire disorder (little desire to have sex) Sexual aversion disorder (aversion to and avoidance of sex)	Hypoactive sexual desire (little or no desire to have sex) Sexual aversion disorder (aversion to and avoidance of sex)
Arousal	Male erectile disorder (difficulty attaining or maintaining erection)	Female sexual arousal disorder (difficulty attaining or maintaining lubrication or swelling response)
Orgasm	Inhibited male orgasm Premature ejaculation	Inhibited female orgasm
Pain	Dyspareunia (pain associated with sexual activity)	Dyspareunia (pain associated with sexual activity) Vaginismus (muscle spasms in the vagina that interfere with penetration)

Source: From *Sexual Dysfunction: A Guide for Assessment and Treatment* by J. P. Wincze and M. P. Carey, 1991. © 1991 by Guilford Press. Reprinted by Permission.

associated with specific sexual dysfunctions. In addition, pain can become associated with sexual functioning, which leads to additional dysfunctions.

An overview of the *DSM-IV-TR* categories of the sexual dysfunctions we examine is in Table 10.4. As you can see, both males and females can experience parallel versions of most disorders, which take on specific forms determined by anatomy and other gender-specific characteristics. However, two disorders are sex specific: Premature ejaculation obviously occurs only in males, and vaginismus, painful contractions of the vagina during attempted penetration, appears only in females. Sexual dysfunctions can be either *lifelong* or *acquired*. "Lifelong" refers to a chronic condition that is present during a person's entire sexual life; "acquired" refers to a disorder that begins after sexual activity has been relatively normal. In addition, disorders can either be generalized, occurring every time the individual attempts sex, or they can be situational, occurring only with some partners or at certain times, but not with other partners or at other times. Finally, sexual dysfunctions are further specified as (1) due to psychological factors or (2) due to psychological factors combined with a general medical condition. The latter specification occurs when there is a demonstrable vascular, hormonal, or associated physical condition known to contribute to the sexual dysfunction.

We have learned much about the prevalence of the various sexual dysfunctions around the world from a large survey called the *Global Study of Sexual Attitudes and Behaviors, 2001–2002* (Nicolosi et al., 2006). This survey focused on adults aged 40 to 80 years. The surprising estimates of prevalence of sexual dysfunctions are presented and discussed in the context of each disorder. But taken together, fully 28 percent of all Canadian women and 18 percent of all Canadian men experience sexual dysfunction, making this class of disorder one of the most prevalent of all psychological or physical disorders.

Sexual Desire Disorders

Hypoactive Sexual Desire Disorder

A person with **hypoactive sexual desire disorder** has little or no interest in any type of sexual activity (see DSM Table 10.2). It is very difficult to assess low sexual desire, and a great deal of clinical judgment is required (Bach, Wincze, & Barlow, 2001;

DSM-IV-TR | **Table 10.2** Criteria for Hypoactive Sexual Desire Disorder

A. Persistently or recurrently deficient (or absent) sexual fantasies and desire for sexual activity. The judgment of deficiency or absence is made by the clinician, taking into account factors that affect sexual functioning, such as age and the context of the person's life.

B. The disturbance causes marked distress or interpersonal difficulty.

C. The sexual dysfunction is not better accounted for by another Axis I disorder (except another sexual dysfunction) and is not due exclusively to the direct physiological effects of a substance (e.g., a drug of abuse, a medication) or a general medical condition.

Specify type:
  Lifelong type
  Acquired type
Specify type:
  Generalized type
  Situational type
Specify:
  Due to psychological factors
  Due to combined factors

Source: Reprinted with permission from the *Diagnostic and Statistical Manual of Mental Disorders*, Fourth Edition, Text Revision, (Copyright © 2000). American Psychiatric Association.

Pridal & LoPiccolo, 2000; Segraves & Woodard, 2006; Wincze, Bach, & Barlow, 2008; Wincze, 2009). You might gauge it by frequency of sexual activity—say, less than twice a month for a married couple. Or you might determine whether someone ever thinks about sex or has sexual fantasies. Then there is the person who has sex twice a week but really doesn't want to and thinks about it only because his wife wants to have sex more often. This individual might, in fact, have no desire whatsoever, despite having frequent sex. Consider the case of Mr. and Mrs. C.

MR. AND MRS. C. | *Getting Started*

Mrs. C., a 31-year-old very successful businesswoman, was married to a 32-year-old lawyer. They had two children, ages two and five, and had been married eight years when they entered therapy. The presenting problem was Mrs. C's lack of sexual desire. Mr. and Mrs. C. were interviewed separately during the initial assessment and both professed attraction to and love for their partner. Mrs. C. reported that she could enjoy sex once she got involved and usually was orgasmic. The problem was her total lack of desire to get involved in the first place. She avoided her husband's sexual advances and looked on his affection and romanticism with great skepticism and, usually, anger and tears. Mrs. C. was raised in an upper-middle-class family that was supportive and loving. However, from age 6 to 12 she had been repeatedly pressured into sexual activity by a male cousin who was five years her senior. This sexual activity was always initiated by the cousin, always against her will. She did not tell her parents because she felt guilty, as the boy did not use physical force to make her comply. It appeared that romantic advances by Mr. C. triggered memories of abuse by her cousin.

The treatment of Mr. and Mrs. C. is discussed later in this chapter.

Problems of hypoactive sexual desire disorder used to be presented as marital rather than sexual difficulties. Since the recognition in the late 1980s of hypoactive sexual desire as a distinct disorder, however, more and more couples present to sex therapy clinics with one of the partners reporting this problem (Hawton, 1995; Pridal & LoPiccolo, 2000). Best estimates suggest that more than 50 percent of patients who come to sexuality clinics for help complain of hypoactive sexual desire (Kaplan, 1979; Pridal & LoPiccolo, 2000). In many clinics it is the most frequent presenting complaint of women; men present more often with erectile dysfunction (Hawton, 1995). Earlier studies (e.g., Frank, Anderson, & Rubinstein, 1978) suggested that approximately 25 percent of individuals might have hypoactive sexual desire. The global survey mentioned earlier suggests that 11 percent of Canadian women and 5 percent of Canadian men report a sexual dysfunction involving a lack of interest in sex (Nicolosi et al., 2006). For men the prevalence increases with age; for women, it decreases with age (Laumann et al., 1999). Schreiner-Engel and Schiavi (1986) noted that patients with this disorder rarely have sexual fantasies, seldom masturbate (in their sample, 35 percent of the women and 52 percent of the men never masturbated and most of the rest masturbated no more than once a month), and attempt intercourse once a month or less. Suggested revisions for the *DSM-5* would recognize that one of the reasons for low desire is that these individuals experience little sexual arousal, leading to a new label of "sexual interest/arousal disorder" (Brotto, 2010a).

Sexual Aversion Disorder

On a continuum with hypoactive sexual desire disorder is **sexual aversion disorder**, in which even the thought of sex or a brief casual touch may evoke fear, panic, or disgust (Kaplan, 1987; see DSM Table 10.3). In some cases, the principal problem might actually be panic disorder (see Chapter 5), in which the fear or alarm response is associated with the physical sensations of sex.

DSM-IV-TR	**Table 10.3** Criteria for Sexual Aversion Disorder

A. It is the persistent or recurrent extreme aversion to, and avoidance of, all (or almost all) genital sexual contact with a sexual partner.

B. The disturbance causes marked distress or interpersonal difficulty.

C. The sexual dysfunction is not better accounted for by another Axis I disorder (except another sexual dysfunction).

Specify type:
   Lifelong type
   Acquired type

Specify type:
   Generalized type
   Situational type

Specify:
   Due to psychological factors
   Due to combined factors

Source: Reprinted with permission from the *Diagnostic and Statistical Manual of Mental Disorders,* Fourth Edition, Text Revision, (Copyright © 2000). American Psychiatric Association.

In other cases, sexual acts and fantasies may trigger traumatic images or memories similar to but perhaps not as severe as those experienced by people with post-traumatic stress disorder (see Chapter 5). There are few data on prevalence, but the majority of those presenting to clinics with sexual aversion disorder seem to be women (Brotto, 2010b; Wincze et al., 2008). Consider the case of Lisa from one of our clinics.

LISA | *The Terror of Sex*

Lisa was 36, had been married for three years, and was a full-time student. She had been married once before. Lisa reported that sexual problems had begun nine months earlier. She complained of poor lubrication during intercourse and of having "anxiety attacks" during sex. She had not attempted intercourse in two months and had tried only intermittently during the past nine months. Despite their sexual difficulties, Lisa had a loving and close relationship with her husband. She could not remember precisely what had happened nine months ago except that she had been under a great deal of stress and experienced an anxiety attack during sex. Even her husband's touch was becoming increasingly intolerable because she was afraid it might bring on the scary feelings again. Her primary fear was of having a heart attack and dying during sex.

Among male patients presenting for sexual aversion disorder, 10 percent experienced panic attacks during attempted sexual activity. Kaplan (1987) reports that 25 percent of 106 patients presenting with sexual aversion disorder also met criteria for panic disorder. In such cases, treating the panic may be a necessary first step. Because sexual aversion disorder is basically anxiety or panic focused on sexual activity, one proposal for the *DSM-5* is to move it to the anxiety disorder category (Brotto, 2010b).

Sexual Arousal Disorders

Disorders of arousal are called **male erectile disorder** and **female sexual arousal disorder** (see DSM Table 10.4). The problem here is not desire. Many individuals with arousal disorders have frequent sexual urges and fantasies and a strong desire to have sex. Their problem is in becoming aroused: A male has difficulty achieving or maintaining an erection, and a female cannot achieve or maintain adequate lubrication (Basson, 2007; Rosen, 2007; Segraves & Althof, 1998; Wincze, 2009; Wincze et al., 2008). Consider the case of Bill.

BILL | *Long Marriage, New Problem*

Bill, a 58-year-old white man, was referred to our clinic by his urologist. He was a retired accountant who had been married for 29 years to his 57-year-old wife, a retired nutritionist. They had no children. For the past several years, Bill had had difficulties obtaining and maintaining an erection. He reported a rather rigid routine he and his wife had developed to deal with the problem. They scheduled sex for Sunday mornings. However, Bill had to do chores first, including letting the dog out, washing the dishes, and shaving. The couple's current behaviour consisted of mutual hand stimulation. Bill was "not allowed" to attempt insertion until after his wife had climaxed. Bill's wife was adamant that she was not going to change her sexual behaviour and "become a whore," as she put it. This included refusing to try K-Y jelly as a lubricant appropriate to her postmenopausal decrease in lubrication. She described their behaviour as "lesbian sex."

Bill and his wife agreed that despite marital problems over the years, they had always maintained a good sexual relationship until the onset of the current problem and that sex had kept them together during their earlier difficulties. Useful information was obtained in separate interviews. Bill masturbated on Saturday night in an attempt to control his erection the following morning; his wife was unaware of this. In addition, he quickly and easily achieved a full erection when viewing erotica in the privacy of the sexuality clinic laboratory (surprising the assessor). Bill's wife privately acknowledged being very angry with her husband for an affair that he had had 20 years earlier.

At the final session, three specific recommendations were made: for Bill to cease masturbating the evening before sex, for the couple to use a lubricant, and for them to delay the morning routine until after they had had sexual relations. The couple called back one month later to report that their sexual activity was much improved.

The old and somewhat pejorative terms for male erectile disorder and female arousal disorder are *impotence* and *frigidity*, but these are imprecise labels that do not specify the specific phase of the sexual response in which the problems are localized. The man typically feels more impaired by his problem than the woman does by hers. Inability to achieve and maintain an erection makes intercourse difficult or impossible. Women who are unable to achieve

vaginal lubrication, however, may be able to compensate by using a commercial lubricant (Schover & Jensen, 1988; Wincze, 2009). In women, arousal and lubrication may decrease at any time but, as in men, such problems tend to accompany aging (Bartlik & Goldberg, 2000; Basson, 2007; DeLamater & Sill, 2005; Laumann et al., 1999; Morokoff, 1993; Rosen, 2000). In addition, until relatively recently, some women were not as concerned as men about experiencing intense pleasure during sex as long as they could consummate the act; this is generally no longer the case (Morokoff, 1993; Wincze & Carey, 2001). It is unusual for a man to be completely unable to achieve an erection. More typical is a situation like Bill's, where full erections are possible during masturbation and partial erections during attempted intercourse, but with insufficient rigidity to allow penetration.

Before we describe the prevalence of arousal disorders and other sexual dysfunctions, we need to note an important study in which 100 well-educated, happily married couples who were not seeking treatment were carefully interviewed (Frank et al., 1978). More than 80 percent of these couples reported that their marital and sexual relations were happy and satisfying. Surprisingly, 40 percent of the men reported occasional erectile and ejaculatory difficulties, and 63 percent of the women reported occasional dysfunctions of arousal or orgasm. But the crucial finding was that these dysfunctions did not detract from the respondents' overall sexual satisfaction. More recently, only 45 percent of women having trouble with orgasm in one study reported the issue as problematic (Fugl-Meyer & Sjogren Fugl-Meyer, 1999). These studies indicate that sexual satisfaction and occasional sexual dysfunction are not mutually exclusive categories (Bradford & Meston, in press; Graham, 2010). In the context of a healthy relationship, occasional or partial sexual dysfunctions are easily accommodated. But this does raise problems for diagnosing sexual dysfunctions. Should a sexual problem be identified as a diagnosis when dysfunction is clearly present but the person is not distressed about it? This is one debate that has occurred during discussions about possible revisions for the *DSM-5* (Balon, Segraves, & Clayton, 2007; Zucker, 2010).

The prevalence of erectile dysfunction is startlingly high and increases with age. Data from the global survey mentioned earlier indicate that 7 percent of Canadian men report sexual dysfunctions involving erection difficulties (Nicolosi et al., 2006). But this figure most certainly underestimates the prevalence because erectile dysfunction increases rapidly in men after age 60. Data from another study suggest that at least some impairment is present in approximately 40 percent of men in their 40s and 70 percent of men in their 70s (Feldman et al., 1994; Kim & Lipshultz, 1997). Male erectile disorder is easily the most common problem for which men seek help, accounting for 50 percent or more of the men referred to specialists for sexual problems (Hawton, 1995). The prevalence of female arousal disorders is somewhat more difficult to estimate because many women still do not consider absence of arousal to be a problem, let alone a disorder.

The Nicolosi et al. (2006) survey reports a prevalence of 12 percent of Canadian women experiencing a sexual dysfunction involving lubrication difficulties. Because disorders of desire, arousal, and orgasm often overlap, it is difficult to estimate precisely how many women with specific arousal disorders present to sex clinics (Segraves & Althof, 1998; Wincze & Carey, 2001). And some researchers, including Rosemary Basson and Lori Brotto in Vancouver, argue that the current definition of female arousal disorder focuses too much on "genital events" (e.g., lubrication difficulties), and instead should focus on women's subjective arousal. This is because studies have shown that women with arousal disorder often show normal vaginal responding to erotic movies while reporting low subjective excitement (see review in Basson et al., 2004).

Orgasm Disorders

Inhibited Orgasm

An inability to achieve an orgasm despite adequate sexual desire and arousal is commonly seen in women (Stock, 1993; Wincze, 2009) but **inhibited orgasm** is relatively rare in men. Consider the case of Greta and Will.

GRETA AND WILL | *Loving Disunion*

Greta, a teacher, and Will, an engineer, were a very attractive couple who came together to the first interview and entered the office clearly showing affection for each other. They had been married for 5 years and were in their late 20s. When asked about the problems that had brought them to the office, Greta quickly reported that she didn't think that she had ever had an orgasm—"didn't think" because she wasn't really sure what an orgasm was! She loved Will very much and on occasion would initiate lovemaking, although with decreased frequency over the past several years.

Will certainly didn't think Greta was reaching orgasm. In any case, he reported, they were clearly going in "different directions" sexually, in that Greta was less and less interested. She had progressed from initiating sex occasionally early in their marriage to almost never doing so, except for an occasional spurt every six months or so, when she would initiate two or three times in a week. But Greta noted that it was the physical closeness she wanted most during these times rather than sexual pleasure. Further inquiry revealed that she did, in fact, become sexually aroused on occasion but had never in her life reached orgasm, even during several attempts at masturbation mostly before her marriage. Both Greta and Will reported that the sexual problem was a concern to them because everything else about their marriage was very positive.

Greta had been brought up in a strict but loving and supportive Catholic family that more or less ignored sexuality. The parents were always very careful not to display their affections in front of Greta and when her mother caught Greta touching her genital area, she was cautioned rather severely to avoid that kind of activity.

We discuss Greta and Will's treatment later.

An inability to reach orgasm, or **female orgasmic disorder** (see DSM Table 10.5), is the most common complaint among women who seek therapy for sexual problems. One study suggests that approximately 25 percent of women report significant difficulty reaching orgasm (Heiman, 2000). The problem is equally present in different age groups, and unmarried women were 1.5 times more likely than married women to experience orgasm disorder. In the global survey mentioned earlier, 11 percent of Canadian women reported a sexual dysfunction involving an inability to achieve orgasm (Nicolosi et al., 2006). In diagnosing this problem, it is necessary to determine whether the women "never or almost never" reach orgasm (Wincze & Carey, 2001). This distinction is important because only approximately 50 percent of all women experience reasonably regular orgasms during sexual intercourse (LoPiccolo & Stock, 1987). Therefore, approximately 50 percent do not achieve orgasm with every sexual encounter, unlike most men, who tend to experience orgasm more consistently. Thus, the "never or almost never" inquiry is important, along with establishing the extent of the couple's distress, in diagnosing orgasmic dysfunction.

Female

A. It is a persistent or recurrent delay in, or absence of, orgasm following a normal sexual excitement phase. Women exhibit wide variability in the type of intensity of stimulation that triggers orgasm. The diagnosis of female orgasmic disorder should be based on the clinician's judgment that the woman's orgasmic capacity is less than would be reasonable for her age, sexual experience, and the adequacy of sexual stimulation she receives.

B. The disturbance causes marked distress or interpersonal difficulty.

C. The orgasmic dysfunction is not better accounted for by another Axis I disorder (except another sexual dysfunction) and is not due exclusively to the direct physiological effects of a substance (e.g., a drug of abuse, a medication) or a general medical condition.

Specify type:

Lifelong type

Acquired type

Specify type:

Generalized type

Situational type

Specify:

Due to psychological factors

Due to combined factors

Male

A. It is a persistent or recurrent delay in, or absence of, orgasm following a normal sexual excitement phase during sexual activity that the clinician, taking into account the person's age, judges to be adequate in focus, intensity, and duration.

B. The disturbance causes marked distress or interpersonal difficulty.

C. The orgasmic dysfunction is not better accounted for by another Axis I disorder (except another sexual dysfunction) and is not due exclusively to the direct physiological effects of a substance (e.g., a drug of abuse, a medication) or a general medical condition.

Specify type:

Lifelong type

Acquired type

Specify type:

Generalized type

Situational type

Specify:

Due to psychological factors

Due to combined factors

Source: Reprinted with permission from the *Diagnostic and Statistical Manual of Mental Disorders*, Fourth Edition, Text Revision, (Copyright © 2000). American Psychiatric Association.

In the global survey, approximately 5 percent of Canadian men report a sexual dysfunction involving inability to achieve orgasm (Nicolosi et al., 2006). Men seldom seek treatment for this condition. It is quite possible that in many cases some men reach climax through alternative forms of stimulation than sexual intercourse and that **male orgasmic disorder** is accommodated by the couple (Apfelbaum, 2000).

Some men who are unable to ejaculate with their partners can obtain an erection and ejaculate during masturbation. In the most usual pattern ejaculation is delayed; this is called *retarded ejaculation*. Occasionally men experience *retrograde ejaculation*, in which ejaculatory fluids travel backward into the bladder rather than forward. This phenomenon is usually due to the effects of certain drugs or a coexisting medical condition and should not be confused with male orgasmic disorder.

Premature Ejaculation

A far more common male orgasmic disorder is **premature ejaculation** (see DSM Table 10.6), ejaculation that occurs well before the man and his partner want it to (Althof, 2006; Polonsky, 2000; Wincze, 2009). Consider the rather typical case of Gary.

GARY | *Running Scared*

Gary, a 31-year-old salesman, engaged in sexual activity with his wife three or four times a month. He noted that he would like to have sex more often, but his very busy schedule kept him working about 80 hours a week. His primary difficulty was an inability to control the timing of his ejaculation. Approximately 70 percent to 80 percent of the time he ejaculated within seconds of penetration. This pattern had been constant since he met his wife approximately 13 years earlier. Previous experience with other women, although limited, was not characterized by premature ejaculation. In an attempt to delay his ejaculation, Gary distracted himself by thinking of nonsexual things (scores of ball games or work-related issues) and sometimes attempted sex soon after a previous attempt because he seemed not to climax as quickly under these circumstances. Gary reported masturbating very seldom (three or four times a year at most). When he did masturbate, he usually attempted to reach orgasm quickly, a habit he acquired during his teens to avoid being caught by a family member.

One of his greatest concerns was that he was not pleasing his wife, and under no circumstances did he want her told that he was seeking treatment. Further inquiry revealed that he made many extravagant purchases at his wife's request, even though it strained their finances, because he wanted to please her. He felt that if they had only met recently, his wife probably would not even have accepted a date with him because he had lost much of his hair and she had lost weight and was more attractive than she used to be. Treatment for Gary and his wife is described shortly.

The frequency of premature ejaculation seems to be quite high. In the Nicolosi et al. (2006) survey, 9 percent of all Canadian men reported a sexual dysfunction involving premature ejaculation, making it the most frequent male sexual dysfunction. A high rate was also reported in a survey conducted by Guy Grenier and Sandra Byers at the University of New Brunswick: 23 percent of a sample of male university alumni self-identified with premature ejaculation (Grenier & Byers, 2001). This difficulty is also a presenting complaint in as many as 60 percent of men who seek treatment (Malatesta & Adams, 1984; Polonsky, 2000). (Many men also present with erectile dysfunction as the major problem.) In one clinic, premature ejaculation was the principal complaint of 16 percent of men seeking treatment (Hawton, 1995).

DSM-IV-TR	**Table 10.6** Criteria for Premature Ejaculation

A. It is persistent or recurrent ejaculation with minimal sexual stimulation before, on, or shortly after penetration and before the person wants it. The clinician must take into account factors that affect duration of the excitement phase, such as age, novelty of the sexual partner or situation, and recent frequency of sexual activity.

B. The disturbance causes marked distress or interpersonal difficulty.

C. The premature ejaculation is not due exclusively to the direct effects of a substance (e.g., withdrawal from opioids).

Specify type:

    Lifelong type

    Acquired type

Specify type:

    Generalized type

    Situational type

Specify:

    Due to psychological factors

    Due to combined factors

Source: Reprinted with permission from the *Diagnostic and Statistical Manual of Mental Disorders*, Fourth Edition, Text Revision, (Copyright © 2000). American Psychiatric Association.

It is very difficult to define "premature." An adequate length of time before ejaculation varies from individual to individual. Some surveys indicate that men who complain of premature ejaculation typically climax no more than one or two minutes after penetration, compared with seven to ten minutes in individuals without this complaint (Strassberg, Kelly, Carroll, & Kircher, 1987). A perception of lack of control over orgasm, however, may be the more important psychological determinant of this complaint (Wincze et al., 2008). The work of Grenier and Byers (2001) suggests that men's self-identifying with premature ejaculation had three components: a behavioural component (i.e., the regularity of their rapid ejaculation experiences), an emotional component (i.e., worry or concern about ejaculating too early), and an efficiency component (i.e., perceiving that they have little control over the timing of their ejaculation).

Although occasional early ejaculation is perfectly normal, serious and consistent premature ejaculation appears to occur primarily in inexperienced men with less education (Laumann et al., 1999). Grenier and Byers (2001) found the only predictor of premature ejaculation in their sample was a lower frequency of intercourse. The contrast in ages between men with erectile disorder and those complaining of premature ejaculation is striking. Although premature ejaculation is typically seen in young men (American Psychiatric Association, 2000a), the majority of men consulting physicians about erectile disorder are between 40 and 64 years of age (IMS Health Canada, 2004a).

Sexual Pain Disorders

In the *sexual pain disorders*, intercourse is associated with marked pain (see DSM Table 10.7). For some men and women, sexual desire is present, and arousal and orgasm are easily attained, but the pain of intercourse is so severe that sexual behaviour is disrupted. This subtype is named **dyspareunia**, which, in

DSM-IV-TR	**Table 10.7** Criteria for Sexual Pain Disorders

Dyspareunia

A. It is recurrent or persistent genital pain associated with sexual intercourse in either a male or a female.

B. The disturbance causes marked distress or interpersonal difficulty.

C. The disturbance is not caused exclusively by vaginismus or lack of lubrication, is not better accounted for by another Axis I disorder (except another sexual dysfunction), and is not due exclusively to the direct physiological effects of a substance (e.g., a drug of abuse, a medication) or a general medical condition.

Specify type:

    Lifelong type

    Acquired type

Specify type:

    Generalized type

    Situational type

Specify:

    Due to psychological factors

    Due to combined factors

Vaginismus

A. It is recurrent or persistent involuntary spasm of the musculature of the outer third of the vagina that interferes with sexual intercourse.

B. The disturbance causes marked distress or interpersonal difficulty.

C. The disturbance is not better accounted for by another Axis I disorder (e.g., somatization disorder) and is not due exclusively to the direct physiological effects of a general medical condition.

Specify type:

    Lifelong type

    Acquired type

Specify type:

    Generalized type

    Situational type

Specify:

    Due to psychological factors

    Due to combined factors

Source: Reprinted with permission from the *Diagnostic and Statistical Manual of Mental Disorders*, Fourth Edition, Text Revision, (Copyright © 2000). American Psychiatric Association.

its original Greek, means "unhappily mated as bedfellows" (Wincze & Carey, 2001). Obviously this name is not very accurate or descriptive, but it has been used for decades and is accepted. As noted by clinical psychologist Irv Binik and his colleagues at McGill University, dyspareunia is diagnosed only if no medical reasons for pain can be found. It can be very tricky to make this assessment (Binik, 2010; Binik, Bergeron, & Khalifé, 2007, 2000; Payne et al., 2005).

Several years ago a patient of ours described having sharp pains in his head like a migraine headache that began during ejaculation and lasted for several minutes. This man, in his 50s at the time, had had a healthy sexual relationship with his wife until a severe fall approximately two years earlier that left him with a partial disability and with a severe limp. The pain during ejaculation developed shortly thereafter. Extensive medical examination by a number of specialists revealed no physical reason for the pain. Thus, he met the criteria for dyspareunia, and psychosocial interventions were administered—in this case, without benefit. He subsequently engaged in manual stimulation of his wife and, occasionally, intercourse, but he avoided ejaculation.

Marta Meana, Irv Binik, and their colleagues have conducted a good deal of research on dyspareunia in women. They have found that the degree of dyspareunic pain in women is associated with depressive and anxious symptoms. Their research also suggests that women's dyspareunia is associated with marital adjustment problems (Meana, Binik, Kahlife, & Cohen, 1998) and with hostility and psychotic symptoms (Schultz, Basson, & Binik, 2005).

Dyspareunia is rarely seen in clinics, but estimates range from 1 percent to 5 percent of men (Bancroft, 1989; Spector & Carey, 1990) and a more substantial 10 percent to 15 percent of women (Hawton, 1995; Rosen & Leiblum, 1995). In the global survey we have been discussing throughout this chapter, 7 percent of Canadian women reported a sexual dysfunction involving pain during intercourse (Nicolosi et al., 2006). Glatt, Zinner, and McCormack (1990) report that many women experience pain occasionally, but it either resolves or is not sufficient to motivate them to seek treatment.

When those with dyspareunia do seek treatment, Lori Brotto of the University of British Columbia recommends that such cases should be approached from a pain-management perspective. In particular, she recommends focusing on the patient's chronic pain, the impact of the dyspareunia on the couple's relationship, and any associated psychological effects (Graziottin & Brotto, 2004). Irv Binik and his colleagues (Binik, 2005; Binik, et al., 2007, 2000; Payne et al., 2005) agree that dyspareunia is better conceptualized as a pain disorder (see Chapter 9) rather than as a sexual dysfunction, as in the current conceptualization in the *DSM-IV-TR*.

In the commoner **vaginismus**, the pelvic muscles in the outer third of the vagina undergo involuntary spasms when intercourse is attempted (Bancroft, 1997; Binik et al., 2007). The spasm reaction of vaginismus may occur during any attempted penetration, including a gynecological exam or insertion of a tampon (Beck, 1993; Reissing et al., 1999). Many women report sensations of "ripping, burning, or tearing during attempted intercourse" (Beck, 1993, p. 384). Although vaginismus is considered a sexual pain disorder, the experience of pain is not necessary for the diagnosis in the *DSM-IV-TR* (Reissing et al., 1999), which has led to some criticism (e.g., Payne et al., 2005). In addition, the *DSM-IV-TR* criterion of vaginal spasm has been criticized as inadequate to make a diagnosis of vaginismus. According to Irv Binik and his colleagues, other markers, like pain, fear of pain, and behavioural avoidance, should be included in the definition of vaginismus in future editions of the *DSM* (Reissing, Binik, & Khalife, 2004). Consider the case of Jill.

JILL | *No Way In*

Jill was referred to our clinic by another therapist because she had not consummated her marriage of one year. At 23 years of age, she was an attractive and loving wife who managed a motel while her husband worked as an accountant. Despite numerous attempts in a variety of positions to engage in intercourse, Jill's severe vaginal spasms prevented penetration of any kind. Jill was also unable to use tampons. With great reluctance, she submitted to gynecological exams at infrequent intervals. Sexual behaviour with her husband consisted of mutual masturbation or, on occasion, Jill had him rub his penis against her breasts to the point of ejaculation. She refused to engage in oral sex. Jill, a very anxious young woman, came from a family in which sexual matters were seldom discussed and sexual contact between the parents had ceased some years before. Although she enjoyed petting, Jill's general attitude was that intercourse was disgusting. Furthermore, she expressed some fears of becoming pregnant despite taking adequate contraceptive measures. She also thought that she would perform poorly when she did engage in intercourse, therefore embarrassing herself with her new husband.

Although there is no data on the prevalence of vaginismus in community samples, best estimates are that it affects 6 percent of women (Bradford & Meston, in press). Crowley, Richardson, and Goldmeir (2006) found that 25 percent of women who report suffering from some sexual dysfunction experience vaginismus. The prevalence of this condition in cultures with very conservative views of sexuality, such as Ireland, may be much higher—as high as 42 percent to 55 percent in at least two clinic samples (Barnes, Bowman, & Cullen, 1984; O'Sullivan, 1979). (Of course, results from any one clinic may not be applicable even to other clinics, let alone to the population of Ireland.) Because vaginismus and dyspareunia both involve pain and overlap quite a bit in women, current proposals suggest combining these two problems in a single pain-related category (Binik, 2005; Binik, 2010; Payne et al., 2005). Results from one North American survey indicate that approximately 7 percent of women have one or the other types of sexual pain disorder, with higher proportions of younger and less educated women reporting this problem (Laumann et al., 1999).

Concept Check | 10.1

Diagnose the following gender identity and sexual disorders.

1. Gina has always dressed in masculine clothing and prefers male friends. She identifies with males and wants to be treated as one. She binds her breasts to hide them and feels trapped in the wrong body. She is considering surgery to become her "true" self. She is attracted only to women. Her situation indicates (a) gender identity disorder, (b) fetishism, (c) sexual aversion disorder, or (d) transvestism. _____

2. Kenisha is in a serious relationship and is quite content. Lately, though, the thought of her boyfriend's touch disgusts her. Kenisha has no idea what is causing this. She could be experiencing (a) panic disorder, (b) sexual arousal disorder, (c) sexual aversion disorder, or (d) both (a) and (b). _____

3. After Quan was injured playing football, he started having pain in his arm during sex. All medical reasons for the pain have been ruled out. Quan is probably displaying (a) dyspareunia, (b) vaginismus, or (c) male orgasmic disorder. _____

4. Kelly has no real desire for sex. She has sex only because she feels that otherwise her husband may leave her. Kelly has (a) sexual aversion disorder, (b) hypoactive sexual desire, (c) boredom, or (d) female sexual arousal disorder. _____

Assessing Sexual Behaviour

There are three major aspects to the assessment of sexual behaviour (Wiegel, Wincze, & Barlow, 2002):

1. *Interviews*, usually supported by numerous questionnaires because patients may provide more information on paper than in a verbal interview.
2. A *thorough medical evaluation*, to rule out the variety of medical conditions that can contribute to sexual problems.
3. *Psychophysiological assessment*, to measure directly the physiological aspects of sexual arousal.

Interviews

All clinicians who conduct interviews for sexual problems should be aware of several useful assumptions (Wiegel et al., 2002; Wincze, 2009). For example, they must demonstrate to the patient through their actions and interviewing style that they are comfortable talking about these issues. Because many patients do not know the various clinical terms professionals use to describe the sexual response cycle and various aspects of sexual behaviour, clinicians must always be prepared to use the vernacular (language) of the patient, realizing also that terms vary from person to person.

The following are examples of the questions asked in semistructured interviews in our sexuality clinic:

- How would you describe your current interest in sex?
- Do you avoid engaging in sexual behaviour with a partner?
- Do you have sexual fantasies?
- How often do you currently masturbate?
- How often do you engage in sexual intercourse?
- How often do you engage in mutual caressing or cuddling without intercourse?
- Have you ever been sexually abused or raped or had a negative experience associated with sex?
- Do you have problems attaining an erection? [or] Do you have problems achieving or maintaining vaginal lubrication?
- Do you ever have problems reaching orgasm?
- Do you ever experience pain associated with sexual activity?

A clinician must be careful to ask these questions in a manner that puts the patient at ease. During an interview lasting approximately two hours, the clinician also covers non-sexual relationship issues and physical health and screens for the presence of additional psychological disorders. When possible, the partner is interviewed concurrently.

Patients may volunteer in writing some information they are not ready to talk about, so they are usually given a variety of questionnaires that help reveal sexual activity and attitudes toward sexuality.

Medical Examination

Any human sexuality clinician routinely inquires about medical conditions that affect sexual functioning. A variety of drugs, including some commonly prescribed for hypertension, anxiety, and depression, often disrupt sexual arousal and functioning. Recent surgery or concurrent medical conditions must be evaluated for their impact on sexual functioning; often the surgeon or treating physician may not have described possible side effects, or the patient may not have told the physician that a medical procedure or drug has affected sexual functioning. Some males with specific sexual dysfunctions such as erectile disorder have already visited a urologist—a physician specializing in disorders of the genitals, bladder, and associated structures—before coming to a sexuality clinic, and many females already have visited a gynecologist. These specialists may check levels of sexual hormones necessary for adequate sexual functioning and, in the case of males, evaluate vascular functioning necessary for an erectile response.

Psychophysiological Assessment

Many clinicians assess the ability of individuals to become sexually aroused under a variety of conditions by taking psychophysiological measurements while the patient is either awake or asleep. In men, penile erection is measured directly, using, for example, a *penile strain gauge* developed in our clinic (Barlow, Becker, Leitenberg, & Agras, 1970; see also Kuban, Barbaree, & Blanchard, 1999). As the penis expands, the strain gauge picks up the changes and records them on a polygraph. Note that patients are often not aware of these more objective measures of their arousal; their awareness differs as a function of the type of problem they have. Penile rigidity is also important to measure in cases of erectile dysfunction, because large erections with insufficient rigidity will not be adequate for intercourse (Wiegel et al., 2002).

The comparable device for women is a *vaginal photoplethysmograph* (Everaerd, Laan, Roth, & van der Velde, 2000; Geer, Morokoff, & Greenwood, 1974; Prause & Janssen, 2006; Rosen & Beck, 1988). This device, which is smaller than a tampon, is inserted by the woman into her vagina. A light source at the tip of the instrument and two light-sensitive photoreceptors on the sides of the instrument measure the amount of light reflected back from the vaginal walls. Because blood flows to the vaginal walls during arousal, the amount of light passing through them decreases with increasing arousal. In their work at the University of British Columbia, Cindy Meston and Boris Gorzalka have used this device to study normal and abnormal sexual arousal in women (e.g., Meston & Gorzalka, 1996; Meston, 2000).

Typically in the clinic of one of the authors of this textbook, individuals undergoing physiological assessment view an erotic

Erectile Dysfunction: Clark

"In the process of becoming aroused, all of a sudden it would be over. And I didn't understand that at all. So then everything is coupled with a bunch of depressing thoughts, like fear of failure.

And so I begin to say, is this happening to me because I'm afraid I'm going to fail, and I don't want to be embarrassed by that?

It's really very difficult to deal with emotionally.... The worse I feel about myself, the slower I am sexually, and sometimes I describe it as the fear of losing masculinity."

Go to Psychology CourseMate at www.abnormalpsych3ce.nelson.com to watch this video.

time, a condition that had now progressed to approximately 80 percent of the time. In addition, he reported that he had no control over ejaculation, often ejaculating before penetration with only a semi-erect penis. Over the past five years, he had lost most interest in sex and was coming to treatment only at his wife's insistence. Thus, this man simultaneously experienced erectile dysfunction, premature ejaculation, and low sexual desire. Because of the frequency of such combinations, we discuss the causes of various sexual dysfunctions together, reviewing briefly the biological, psychological, and social contributions and specifying causal factors thought to be associated exclusively and specifically with one or another dysfunction.

videotape for two to five minutes or, on occasion, listen to an erotic audiotape (e.g., Bach, Brown, & Barlow, 1999; Weisburg, Brown, Wincze, & Barlow, 2001). The patient's sexual responsivity during this time is assessed psychophysiologically. Patients also report subjectively on the amount of sexual arousal they experience. This assessment allows the clinician to observe carefully the conditions under which arousal is possible for the patient. For example, many individuals with psychologically based sexual dysfunctions may achieve strong arousal in a laboratory but be unable to become aroused with a partner (Bancroft, 1997; Sakheim, Barlow, Abrahamson, & Beck, 1987).

Because erections most often occur during REM sleep in physically healthy men, psychophysiological measurement of *nocturnal penile tumescence* (NPT) was in the past used frequently to determine a man's ability to obtain normal erectile response. If he could attain normal erections while he was asleep, the reasoning went, then the causes of his dysfunction were psychological. An inexpensive way to monitor nocturnal erections is for the clinician to provide a simple "snap gauge" that the patient fastens around his penis each night before he goes to sleep. If the snap gauge has come undone, he has probably had a nocturnal erection. But this is a crude and often inaccurate screening device that should never supplant medical and psychological evaluation (Carey, Wincze, & Meisler, 1993; Mohr & Beutler, 1990; Wiegel et al., 2001). Finally, we now know that lack of NPT could also be due to psychological problems, such as depression, or to a variety of medical difficulties that have nothing to do with physiological problems preventing erections (Rosen, 2000; Wiegel et al., 2001).

Causes of Sexual Dysfunction

Individual sexual dysfunctions seldom present in isolation. Usually a patient referred to a sexuality clinic complains of a wide assortment of sexual problems, although one may be of most concern (Rosen, 2007; Wincze, 2009). A 45-year-old man recently referred to one of the authors' clinics had been free of problems until ten years earlier, when he was under a great deal of pressure at work and was preparing to take a major career-related licensing examination. He began experiencing erectile dysfunction about 50 percent of the

Biological Contributions

Many physical and medical conditions contribute to sexual dysfunction (Basson, 2007; Rosen, 2007; Wiegel et al., 2002; Wincze & Carey, 2001; Wincze et al., 2008). Although this is not surprising, most patients, and even many health professionals, are, unfortunately, unaware of the connection. Neurological diseases and other conditions that affect the nervous system, such as diabetes and kidney disease, may directly interfere with sexual functioning by reducing sensitivity in the genital area, and they are a common cause of erectile dysfunction in males (Rosen, 2007; Wincze, 2009). Feldman et al. (1994) reported that 28 percent of men with diabetes experienced complete erectile failure. Vascular disease is a major cause of erectile difficulties. The two relevant vascular problems are arterial insufficiency (constricted arteries), which makes it difficult for blood to reach the penis, and venous leakage (blood flows out too quickly for an erection to be maintained; Wincze & Carey, 2001).

Chronic illness can also indirectly affect sexual functioning. For example, it is not uncommon for individuals who have had heart attacks to be wary of the physical exercise involved in sexual activity to the point of preoccupation. They often become unable to achieve arousal despite being assured by their physicians that sexual activity is safe for them (Cooper, 1988). Also, coronary artery disease and sexual dysfunction commonly coexist, and it is now recommended that men presenting with erectile dysfunction should be screened for cardiovascular disease (Jackson, Rosen, Kloner, & Kostis, 2006).

A major physical cause of sexual dysfunction is prescription medication. Antihypertensive medications, in the class known as beta-blockers, including propranolol, may contribute to sexual dysfunction. Selective-serotonin reuptake inhibitor (SSRI) antidepressant medications and other antidepressant and antianxiety drugs may also interfere with sexual desire and arousal in both men and women (Balon, 2006; Segraves & Althof, 1998). A number of these drugs, particularly the psychoactive drugs, may dampen sexual desire and arousal by altering levels of certain subtypes of serotonin in the brain. Sexual dysfunction—specifically low sexual desire and arousal difficulties—is the most widespread side effect of the antidepressant SSRIs, such as Prozac (see Chapter 7), and as many as 80 percent of individuals who take these medications may experience some degree of sexual dysfunction, although estimates closer to 50 percent seem more reliable (Balon, 2006; Montejo-Gonzalez et al., 1997).

Some people are aware that alcohol suppresses sexual arousal, but they may not know that most *other drugs of abuse*, such as cocaine and heroin, also produce widespread sexual dysfunction in frequent users and abusers, both male and female. Cocores, Miller, Pottash, and Gold (1988) and Macdonald, Waldorf, Reinarman, and Murphy (1988) reported that more than 60 percent of a large number of cocaine users had a sexual dysfunction. In the Cocores group's study, some of the patients also abused alcohol.

There is also the misconception that alcohol facilitates sexual arousal and behaviour. As explained in a review article by Toronto-based researcher Alexander McKay (2005), what actually happens is that alcohol at low and moderate levels reduces social inhibitions so people feel more like having sex (and perhaps are more willing to request it; Crowe & George, 1989; Wiegel et al., 2001). In fact, people's expectation that arousal will increase when they drink alcohol may have more effect than any disinhibition that does occur because of the effects of the alcohol itself, at least at low doses (Roehrich & Kinder, 1991; Wilson, 1977). Physically, alcohol is a central nervous system *suppressant*, and for men to achieve erection and women to achieve lubrication is much more difficult when the central nervous system is suppressed (Schiavi, 1990). Chronic alcohol abuse may cause permanent neurological damage and may virtually eliminate the sexual response cycle. Such abuse may lead to liver and testicular damage, resulting in decreased testosterone levels and concomitant decreases in sexual desire and arousal. This dual effect of alcohol (social disinhibition and physical suppression) has been recognized since the time of Shakespeare:

> It provokes the desire, but it takes away the performance; therefore much drink may be said to be an equivocator with lechery: it makes him and it mars him; it sets him on and it takes him off; it persuades him and disheartens him; makes him stand to and not stand to; in conclusion, equivocates him in a sleep, and giving him the lie, leaves him. (*Macbeth*, II, iii, 29)

Chronic alcoholism can also cause fertility problems in both men and women. Fahrner (1987) examined the prevalence of sexual dysfunction among male alcoholics and found that 75 percent had erectile dysfunction, low sexual desire, and premature or delayed ejaculation.

Many people report that cocaine or marijuana enhances sexual pleasure. Although little is known about the effects of marijuana across the wide range of use, it is unlikely that chemical effects increase pleasure. Rather, in those individuals who report some enhancement of sexual pleasure (and many don't), the effect may be psychological in that their attention is focused more completely and fully on sensory stimulation (Buffum, 1982), a factor that seems to be an important part of healthy sexual functioning. If so, imagery and attentional focus can be enhanced with non-drug procedures such as meditation, in which a person practises concentrating on something with as few distractions as possible. Finally, a report from Mannino, Klevens, and Flanders (1994), studying more than 4000 veterans of the U.S. Armed Forces, suggests that cigarette smoking contributes to erectile dysfunction.

TABLE 10.5 Contributing Factors to Low Sexual Desire in a Clinic-Referred Sample of Women (*n* = 47)

Contributing Factor	Percent Cases Where Relevant
Psychological factors decreasing arousability	85
Minimal sexual stimuli or context	53
Emotional intimacy lacking	50
Depression	43
Androgen deficiency	25

Source: © 2001 from "Using a different model for a female sexual response to address women's problematic low sexual desire" by R. Basson. *Journal of Sex and Marital Therapy, 27(5)*, 395–403. Reproduced by permission of Taylor & Francis, Inc.

Psychological Contributions

The work of Rosemary Basson of the Vancouver Hospital Centre for Sexuality, Gender Identity, and Reproductive Health has contributed much to our understanding of psychological contributions to low sexual desire in women (e.g., Basson, 2001, 2006; Basson, Brotto, & Laan, 2005). For example, Basson (2001) studied 47 women referred to her clinic for low sexual desire. Identified contributing factors are summarized in Table 10.5. As shown in the table, psychological factors that decreased arousability were the most common contributing variable, being relevant in 85 percent of the cases. Environmental factors (e.g., insufficient sexual context), depression, and perceptions that emotional intimacy was lacking in the relationship were each relevant in approximately half of the cases. The one biological factor investigated—androgen deficiency as suggested by the referring doctor—was the contributing factor least commonly involved. It proved relevant in only one-quarter of the cases in this study.

But psychological contributing factors obviously compose a broad category of influences. How do we account for sexual dysfunction from a psychological perspective? One important psychological concept is that of performance anxiety, which can be further broken into several components. One component is arousal, another is cognitive processes, and third is *negative affect*.

When confronted with the possibility of having sexual relations, individuals who are dysfunctional tend to expect the worst and find the situation to be relatively negative and unpleasant. As far as possible, they avoid becoming aware of any sexual cues (and therefore are not aware of how aroused they are physically, thus underreporting their arousal). They also may distract themselves with negative thoughts, such as "I'm going to make a fool of myself; I'll never be able to get aroused; she [or he] will think I'm stupid" (Renaud & Byers, 2001). We know that as arousal increases, a person's attention focuses more intently and consistently. But the person who is focusing on negative thoughts will find it impossible to become sexually aroused. A recent study by Marta Meana's group has shown that there may be gender differences in the types of negative thoughts that distract attention away from sexual enjoyment. Specifically, women were shown to be more susceptible to "appearance-based" negative thoughts (e.g., "If the lights are on during sexual activity, I worry too much about how appealing my body is to my partner"), whereas men were more susceptible to "performance-based" negative thoughts (e.g., "During sexual activity, I think too much about whether my partner is happy with the way I am touching his/her body.") (Meana & Nunnink, 2005).

People with normal sexual functioning react to a sexual situation very positively. They focus their attention on the erotic cues and do not become distracted. When they become aroused, they focus even more strongly on the sexual and erotic cues, allowing themselves to become increasingly sexually aroused. The model presented in ■ Figure 10.3 illustrates both functional and dysfunctional sexual arousal (Barlow, 1986; Barlow, Chorpita, & Turovsky, 1996; Sbrocco & Barlow, 1996). These experiments demonstrate that sexual arousal is strongly determined by psychological factors, particularly cognitive and emotional factors, that are powerful enough to determine whether blood flows to the appropriate areas of the body, such as the genitals, confirming once again the strong interaction of psychological and biological factors in most of our functioning.

We know little about the psychological (or biological) factors associated with premature ejaculation (Althof, 2007; Bradford & Meston, in press; Ertekin, Colakoglu, & Altay, 1995; Weiner,

1996). We do know that the condition is most prevalent in young men and that excessive physiological arousal in the sympathetic nervous system may lead to rapid ejaculation. These observations suggest some men may have a naturally lower threshold for ejaculation; that is, they require less stimulation and arousal to ejaculate. Unfortunately, the psychological factor of anxiety also increases sympathetic arousal. Thus, when a man becomes anxiously aroused about ejaculating too quickly, his concern only makes the problem worse. We return to the role of anxiety in sexual dysfunctions later.

Social and Cultural Contributions

The model of sexual dysfunction displayed in Figure 10.3 helps explain why some individuals may be dysfunctional now, but not how they *became* that way in the first place. Although we do not know for sure why some people develop problems, many people learn early that sexuality can be negative and somewhat threatening, and the responses they develop reflect this belief. This negative cognitive set has been termed *erotophobia*, which is presumably learned early in childhood from families, religious

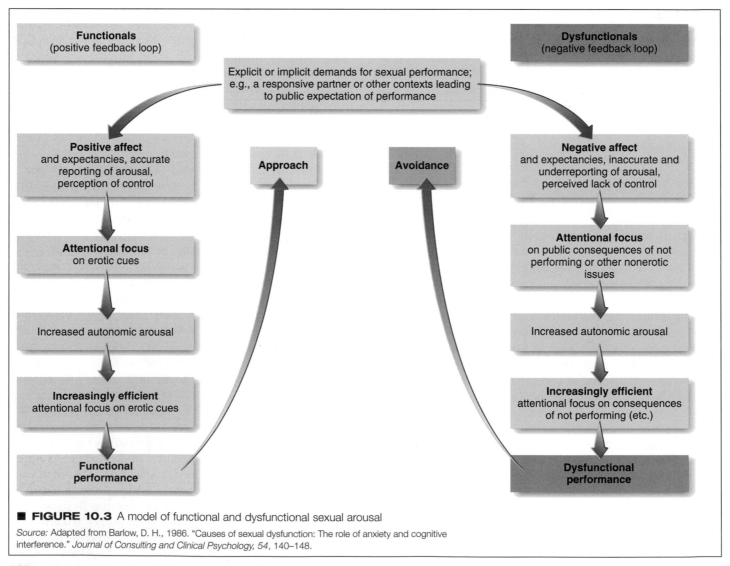

■ **FIGURE 10.3** A model of functional and dysfunctional sexual arousal

Source: Adapted from Barlow, D. H., 1986. "Causes of sexual dysfunction: The role of anxiety and cognitive interference." *Journal of Consulting and Clinical Psychology, 54,* 140–148.

authorities, or others (Byrne & Schulte, 1990). Erotophobia seems to predict sexual difficulties later in life (Byrne & Schulte, 1990). Thus, for some individuals, sexual cues become associated early with negative affect. In other cases, both men and women may experience specific negative or traumatic events after a period of relatively well-adjusted sexuality. These negative events might include sudden failure to become aroused or actual sexual trauma such as rape. Meston and her colleagues have shown that childhood sexual abuse may exert its negative effects on adult sexual functioning by way of its impact on the meanings that women attribute to many sexuality-relevant concepts (Meston & Heiman, 2000). For example, a woman who was sexually abused as a child may think of concepts pertaining to sex as bad or dirty, which in turn would have a negative impact on her ability to function sexually.

Laumann et al. (1999) found a substantial impact of early traumatic sexual events on later sexual functioning. For example, if women experienced sexual victimization through adult sexual contact before puberty, or were forced to have sexual contact of some kind, they were approximately twice as likely to have orgasmic dysfunction as women who had not been touched before puberty or forced to have sex at any time. For male victims of adult–child contact, the probability of experiencing erectile dysfunction is more than three times greater than if they had not had the contact. Thus, traumatic sexual acts of all kinds have long-lasting effects on subsequent sexual functioning, in both men and women, sometimes lasting decades beyond the original event. Such stressful events may initiate negative affect, in which individuals experience a loss of control over their sexual response cycle, throwing them into the kind of dysfunctional pattern depicted in Figure 10.3. It is common for people who experience erectile failure during a particularly stressful time to continue sexual dysfunction long after the stressful situation has ended (Hall, 2007).

In addition to generally negative attitudes or experiences associated with sexual interactions, several other factors may contribute to sexual dysfunction. Among these, the most common is a marked deterioration in close interpersonal relationships. It is difficult to have a satisfactory sexual relationship in the context of growing dislike for a partner. Occasionally, the partner may no longer seem physically attractive. Kelly, Strassberg, and Kircher (1990) found that anorgasmic women, in addition to displaying more negative attitudes toward masturbation, greater sex guilt, and greater endorsement of sex myths, reported discomfort in telling their partners what sexual activities might increase their arousal or lead to orgasm, such as direct clitoral stimulation. Poor sexual skills might also lead to frequent sexual failure and, ultimately, lack of desire.

Thus, social and cultural factors seem to affect later sexual functioning. Researchers studying this phenomenon have constructed an important concept called script theory of sexual functioning. According to this theory, we all operate according to "scripts" that reflect social and cultural expectations and guide our behaviour (Gagnon, 1990; Laumann, Gagnon, Michael, & Michaels, 1994). Discovering these scripts, both in individuals and across cultures, will tell us much about sexual functioning. For example, a person who learns that sexuality is potentially dangerous, dirty, or forbidden is more vulnerable to developing sexual dysfunction later in life. This pattern is most evident in cultures with very restrictive attitudes toward sex (McGoldrick, Loonan, & Wohlsifer, 2007; Meston, Trapnell, & Gorzalka, 1998). For example, vaginismus is relatively rare in North America but is the most common cause of unconsummated marriages in Ireland (Barnes, 1981; O'Sullivan, 1979).

Cultural scripts may also contribute to the type of sexual dysfunction reported. In India, for example, Verma, Khaitan, and Singh (1998) reported that 77 percent of a large number of male patients in a sexuality clinic in India reported difficulties with premature ejaculation. In addition, 71 percent of male patients complained of being extremely concerned about nocturnal emissions associated with erotic dreams. The authors note that this focus on problems with ejaculation is most likely due to a strongly culturally held belief in India that loss of semen causes depletion of physical and mental energy. It is also interesting that out of 1000 patients presenting to this clinic, only 36 were female, most likely reflecting the devaluation of sexual experiences for females due to religious and social reasons in India.

Cultural factors may also play a role in sexual attitudes, which in turn may contribute to sexual dysfunctions. A study by Lori Brotto and her colleagues, conducted with students at the University of British Columbia, compared Euro-Canadian women's sexual attitudes and functioning to those of Asian women (Brotto, Chik, Ryder, Gorzalka, & Seal, 2005). They found that Euro-Canadian women had significantly more sexual knowledge and experiences, more liberal attitudes, and higher rates of desire, arousal, sexual receptivity, and sexual pleasure than the Asian women. Anxiety from anticipated sexual activity was significantly higher in Asian women. Beyond these significant ethnic group comparisons, the degree of acculturation to Western culture was significantly related to sexual attitudes, even after accounting for how long the women had lived in Canada. The authors suggest that assessing the level of acculturation may be important in the treatment of Asian women's sexual dysfunctions.

Even in Canadian culture, certain socially communicated expectations and attitudes may stay with us despite our relatively enlightened and permissive attitude toward sex. Cyranowski and colleagues (1999) have demonstrated that a negative sexual self-schema (being emotional and self-conscious about sex) and a concept similar to Byrne's erotophobia and Gagnon's scripts may later lead to sexual difficulties under stressful situations. Zilbergeld (1992) has elaborated a number of myths about sex believed by many men, and Heiman and LoPiccolo (1988) have done the same for women. These myths are listed in Table 10.6. Baker and DeSilva (1988) converted an earlier version of Zilbergeld's male myths into a questionnaire and presented it to groups of sexually functional and dysfunctional men. They found that men with dysfunctions showed significantly greater belief in the myths than did men who were sexually functional. We explore such myths further in our discussion of treatment.

The Interaction of Psychological and Physical Factors

Having reviewed the various causes, we must now say that seldom is any sexual dysfunction associated exclusively with either psychological or physical factors (Bancroft, 1997; Rosen,

TABLE 10.6 Myths of Sexuality

Heiman and LoPiccolo's Myths of Female Sexuality (1988)	Zilbergeld's Myths of Male Sexuality (1992)
1. Sex is only for women under 30.	1. We're liberated folks who are very comfortable with sex.
2. Normal women have an orgasm every time they have sex.	2. A real man isn't into sissy stuff like feelings and communicating.
3. All women can have multiple orgasms.	3. All touching is sexual or should lead to sex.
4. Pregnancy and delivery reduce women's sexual responsiveness.	4. A man is always interested in and always ready for sex.
5. A woman's sex life ends with menopause.	5. A real man performs in sex.
6. There are different kinds of orgasm related to a woman's personality. Vaginal orgasms are more feminine and mature than clitoral orgasms.	6. Sex is centred on a hard penis and what's done with it.
7. A sexually responsive woman can always be turned on by her partner.	7. Sex equals intercourse.
8. Nice women aren't aroused by erotic books or films.	8. A man should be able to make the earth move for his partner, or at the very least knock her socks off.
9. You are frigid if you don't like the more exotic forms of sex.	9. Good sex requires orgasm.
10. If you can't have an orgasm quickly and easily, there's something wrong with you.	10. Men don't have to listen to women in sex.
11. Feminine women don't initiate sex or become wild and unrestrained during sex.	11. Good sex is spontaneous, with no planning and no talking.
12. Double jeopardy: You're frigid if you don't have sexual fantasies and wanton if you do.	12. Real men don't have sex problems.
13. Contraception is a woman's responsibility, and she's just making up excuses if she says contraceptive issues are inhibiting her sexuality.	

Source: Adapted from *Becoming Orgasmic: A Sexual and Personal Growth Program for Women, Revised & Expanded*, by Julia R. Heiman, Ph.D. and Josephe Lopiccolo, Ph.D. © 1976, 1988 by Prentice Hall Press, a Division of Simon & Schuster, and from *The New Male Sexuality* by B. Zilbergeld. © 1992 Bantam Books, New York.

2007; Wiegel et al., 2006). More often it's a subtle combination of factors. To take a typical example, a young man, vulnerable to developing anxiety and holding to a certain number of sexual myths (the social contribution), may experience erectile failure unexpectedly after using drugs or alcohol, as many men do (the biological contribution). He will anticipate the next sexual encounter with anxiety, wondering whether the failure might happen again. This combination of experience and apprehension activates the psychological sequence depicted in Figure 10.3 (page 370), regardless of whether he's had a few drinks.

In summary, socially transmitted negative attitudes about sex may interact with a person's relationship difficulties and predispositions to develop performance anxiety and, ultimately, lead to sexual dysfunction. From a psychological point of view, we don't know why some individuals develop one dysfunction and not another, although it is common for several dysfunctions to occur in the same patient. Very possibly, an individual's specific biological predispositions interact with psychological factors to produce a specific sexual dysfunction.

Treatment of Sexual Dysfunction

Unlike most other disorders discussed in this book, one surprisingly simple treatment is effective for a large number of individuals who experience sexual dysfunction: education. Ignorance of the most basic aspects of the sexual response cycle and

intercourse often leads to long-lasting dysfunctions (Bach et al., 2001; Wincze et al., 2008; Wincze & Carey, 2001). Consider the case of Carl, who recently came to our sexuality clinic.

CARL | *Never Too Late*

Carl, a 55-year-old white man, was referred to our clinic by his urologist because Carl had difficulty maintaining an erection. Although he had never been married, he was at present involved in an intimate relationship with a 50-year-old woman. This was only his second sexual relationship. He was reluctant to ask his partner to come to the clinic because of his embarrassment in discussing sexual issues. A careful interview revealed that Carl engaged in sex twice a week, but requests by the clinician for a step-by-step description of his sexual activities revealed a very unusual pattern: Carl skipped foreplay and immediately proceeded to intercourse! Unfortunately, because his partner was not aroused and lubricated, he was unable to penetrate her. His valiant efforts sometimes resulted in painful abrasions for both of them. Two sessions of extensive sex education, including very specific instructions for carrying out foreplay, provided Carl with a whole new outlook on sex. For the first time in his life he had successful, satisfying intercourse, much to his delight and his partner's.

In the case of hypoactive sexual desire disorder, one common presentation is a marked difference within a couple that leads to one partner being labelled as having low desire. For example, if one partner is quite happy with sexual relations once a week but the other partner desires sex every day, the latter partner may accuse the former of having low desire and, unfortunately, the former partner might agree. Facilitating better conditions often resolves these misunderstandings. Fortunately, for people with this and more complex sexual dysfunctions, treatments are now available, both psychosocial and biological (medical). Advances in medical treatments, particularly for erectile dysfunction, have been dramatic in just the past few years. We look first at psychosocial treatments; then we examine the latest medical procedures.

Psychosocial Treatments

Among the many advances in our knowledge of sexual behaviour, none was more dramatic than the publication in 1970 of *Human Sexual Inadequacy* by Masters and Johnson. The procedures outlined in this book literally revolutionized sex therapy by providing a brief, direct, and reasonably successful therapeutic program for sexual dysfunctions. Underscoring once again the common basis of most sexual dysfunctions, a very similar approach to therapy is taken with all patients, male and female, with slight variations depending on the specific sexual problem (e.g., premature ejaculation, orgasmic disorder). This intensive program involves a male and a female therapist to facilitate communication between the dysfunctional partners. (Masters and Johnson were the original male and female therapists.) Therapy is conducted daily for two weeks.

The actual program is quite straightforward. In addition to providing basic education about sexual functioning, altering deep-seated myths, and increasing communication, the clinicians' primary goal is to eliminate psychologically based performance anxiety (refer back to Figure 10.3 on page 370). To accomplish this, Masters and Johnson introduced *sensate focus* and *nondemand pleasuring*. In this exercise, couples are instructed to refrain from intercourse or genital caressing and simply to explore and enjoy each other's body through touching, kissing, hugging, massaging, or similar kinds of behaviour. In the first phase, nongenital pleasuring, breasts and genitals are excluded from the exercises. After successfully accomplishing this phase, the couple moves to genital pleasuring but with a ban on orgasm and intercourse and clear instructions to the man that achieving an erection is not the goal.

At this point, arousal should be re-established and the couple should be ready to attempt intercourse. So as not to proceed too quickly, this stage is also broken down into parts. For example, a couple might be instructed to attempt the beginnings of penetration; that is, the depth of penetration and the time it lasts are only very gradually built up, and both genital and nongenital pleasuring

continue. Eventually, full intercourse and thrusting are accomplished. After this two-week intensive program, recovery was reported by Masters and Johnson for the vast majority of more than 790 sexually dysfunctional patients, with some differences in the rate of recovery depending on the disorder. Close to 100 percent of individuals with premature ejaculation recovered, whereas the rate for more difficult cases of lifelong generalized erectile dysfunction was closer to 60 percent.

Specialty sexuality clinics based on the pioneering work of Masters and Johnson were established to administer these new treatment techniques. Subsequent research revealed that many of the structural aspects of the program did not seem necessary. For example, one therapist seems to be as effective as two (LoPiccolo, Heiman, Hogan, & Roberts, 1985), and seeing patients once a week seems to be as effective as seeing them every day (Heiman & LoPiccolo, 1983a, 1983b). It has also become clear in the succeeding decades that the results achieved by Masters and Johnson were much better than those achieved in clinics around the world using similar procedures. Reasons for this difference are not entirely clear. One possibility is that because patients had to take at least two weeks off and fly to St. Louis to meet with Masters and Johnson, they were very highly motivated to begin with.

Sex therapists have expanded on and modified these procedures over the years to take advantage of recent advances in knowledge (e.g., Bach et al., 2001; Bancroft, 1997; Leiblum & Rosen, 2000; Wincze, 2009; Wincze et al., 2008). Results with sex therapy for erectile dysfunction indicate that as many as 60 percent to 70 percent of the cases show a positive treatment outcome for at least several years, although there may be some slipping after that (Rosen, 2007; Sarwer & Durlak, 1997; Segraves & Althof, 1998). For better treatment of *specific* sexual dysfunctions, sex therapists integrate specific procedures into the context of general sex therapy. For example, to treat premature ejaculation, most sex therapists use a procedure developed by Semans

▲ A therapist usually treats a sexual dysfunction in one partner by seeing the couple together.

Treatment of Sexual Dysfunction   **373**

(1956), sometimes called the *squeeze* technique, in which the penis is stimulated, usually by the partner, to nearly full erection. At this point the partner firmly squeezes the penis near the top where the head of the penis joins the shaft, which quickly reduces arousal. These steps are repeated until (for heterosexual partners) eventually the penis is briefly inserted in the vagina without thrusting. If arousal occurs too quickly, the penis is withdrawn and the squeeze technique is employed again. In this way the man develops a sense of control over arousal and ejaculation. Reports of success with this approach over the past 20 years suggest that 60 percent to 90 percent of men benefit, but the success rates drop to about 25 percent after 3 years or more of follow-up (Althof, 2007; Polonsky, 2000; Segraves & Althof, 1998). Gary, the 31-year-old salesman, was treated with this method, and his wife was very cooperative during the procedures. Brief marital therapy also persuaded Gary that his insecurity over his perception that his wife no longer found him attractive was unfounded. After treatment, he reduced his work hours somewhat, and the couple's marital and sexual relations improved.

Lifelong female orgasmic disorder may be treated with explicit training in masturbatory procedures (Basson et al., 2004). For example, Greta was still unable to achieve orgasm with manual stimulation by her husband, even after proceeding through the basic steps of sex therapy. At this point, following certain standardized treatment programs for this problem (e.g., Heiman, 2000; Heiman & LoPiccolo, 1988), Greta and Will purchased a vibrator and Greta was taught to let go of her inhibitions by talking out loud about how she felt during sexual arousal, even shouting or screaming if she wanted to. In the context of appropriate genital pleasuring and disinhibition exercises, the vibrator brought on Greta's first orgasm. With practice and good communication, the couple eventually learned how to bring on Greta's orgasm without the vibrator. Although Will and Greta were both delighted with her progress, Will was concerned that Greta's screams during orgasm would attract the attention of the neighbours. When they planned a vacation at a lake, they were concerned about whether the cabin had electricity to power the vibrator in case they needed it! Summaries of results from several studies, including work by Meston and her colleagues, suggests 70 percent to 90 percent of women will benefit from treatment, and these gains are stable and even improve over time (Heiman, 2007; Heiman & Meston, 1997; Segraves & Althof, 1998).

To treat vaginismus, the woman and, eventually, the partner gradually insert larger and larger dilators at the woman's own pace (see Basson et al., 2004). After the woman (and then the partner) can insert the largest dilator, in a heterosexual couple the woman gradually inserts the man's penis. These exercises are carried out in the context of genital and nongenital pleasuring so as to retain arousal. Of course, close attention must be accorded to any increased fear and anxiety that may be associated with the process, which may trigger memories of early sexual abuse that may have contributed to the onset of the condition. These procedures are highly successful, with a large majority of women (80 percent to 100 percent) overcoming vaginismus in a relatively short time (Beck, 1993; Binik et al., 2007; Leiblum & Rosen, 2000; Segraves & Althof, 1998; ter Kuile et al., 2007). However, Elke Reissing, Irv Binik, and Samir Khalife (1999) in Montréal have been critical of this literature's focus on the achievement of penile–vaginal intercourse as the indicator of therapy "success." These researchers argue that additional relevant outcomes that should be (but rarely are) assessed are (1) whether the vaginal muscle spasm has in fact been resolved, (2) whether interference with intercourse has been decreased, (3) whether intercourse is less painful or more pleasurable, and (4) whether the couple is experiencing greater sexual satisfaction (Reissing et al., 1999). These authors have also suggested that there may be two subtypes of vaginismus requiring two different types of treatment. First, there may be a subtype involving a phobia of penetration for which cognitive-behavioural techniques developed for fear reduction (see Chapter 5) would be most appropriate. Second, there may be a separate subtype involving genital pain for which psychosocial techniques developed for the treatment of chronic pain (see Chapter 9) would be most appropriate. This intriguing speculation is certainly deserving of further investigation.

▲ Yitzchak (Irv) Binik is a clinical psychologist at McGill University and the Sex and Couple Therapy Service of the Royal Victoria Hospital. His research has contributed substantially to the understanding and effective treatment of a variety of sexual dysfunctions, including vaginismus and dyspareunia.

Photo by Guy L'Heureux/McGill University

A variety of treatment procedures have also been developed for low sexual desire (e.g., Basson et al., 2004; Pridal & LoPiccolo, 2000; Wincze, 2009; Wincze & Carey, 2001). At the heart of these treatments are the standard re-education and communication phases of traditional sex therapy, with, possibly, the addition of masturbatory training and exposure to erotic material. Of course, each case may require individual strategies. Remember Mrs. C., who was sexually abused by her cousin? Therapy involved helping the couple understand the impact of the repeated, unwanted sexual experiences in Mrs. C's past and to approach sex so that Mrs. C. was much more comfortable with foreplay. She gradually lost the idea that once sex was started she had no control. She and her husband worked on starting and stopping sexual encounters. Cognitive restructuring was used to help Mrs. C. interpret her husband's amorousness in a positive rather than a skeptical light. In general, the clinical literature suggests that approximately 50 percent to 70 percent of individuals with low sexual desire benefit from sex therapy, at least initially (Hawton, 1995; Segraves & Althof, 1998).

Gilles Trudel, André Marchand, and their colleagues at the University of Quebéc at Montréal recently conducted the first extensive controlled study on the treatment of hypoactive sexual desire disorder with a novel, short-term, cognitive-behavioural group treatment program. Seventy-four couples (aged 20 to 55 years) in which the woman had low sexual desire participated in the treatment. Results showed that the treatment protocol was effective: It decreased symptoms of the disorder and also improved overall cognitive, behavioural, and marital functioning in these couples (Trudel et al., 2001).

Medical Treatments

A variety of pharmacological and surgical techniques have been developed in recent years to treat sexual dysfunction, almost all focusing on male erectile disorder. But the drug Viagra, which was introduced in Canada in March 1999, and similar drugs such as Levitra and Cialis, introduced subsequently, are the best known. We look at the four most popular procedures: oral medication, injection of vasoactive substances directly into the penis, surgery, and vacuum device therapy. Please note that it is important to combine any medical treatment with a comprehensive educational and sex therapy program to ensure maximum benefit.

Several so-called wonder drugs for various disorders have been introduced with a flourish, including Prozac for depression and Redux for obesity. As noted in Chapter 2, the usual course is initial overwhelming enthusiasm that the drug is a cure-all, followed by a period of profound disappointment as people realize the drug is not what it was promised to be and may even be harmful in some cases. Finally, rationality sets in and the drug, if it has been proven effective in a number of studies, usually is found to be of moderate benefit to some people and becomes a useful part of a treatment plan. The wonder drug of 1999 was sildenafil (brand name Viagra) for erectile dysfunction. Guy Lafleur, a famous hockey player from the Montréal Canadiens, was the spokesman in the initial marketing campaign for Viagra in Canada. Results from several clinical trials suggest that between 50 percent and 80 percent of a large number of men benefit from this treatment (Conti, Pepine, & Sweeney, 1999; Goldstein et al., 1998) in that erections become sufficient for intercourse, compared to approximately 30 percent who benefit from placebo. Results are similar with Cialis and Levitra (Carrier et al., 2005). However, as many as 30 percent may experience severe headaches as a side effect, particularly at higher doses (Rosen, 2000, 2007; Virag, 1999), and reports of sexual satisfaction are not optimal. For example, Virag (1999) evaluated a large number of men and defined success as both ability to engage in intercourse and the patient's rating of sexual satisfaction on a scale of 0 to 10. By these criteria, 32 percent of the men were successful if success was defined as an erection sufficient to engage in intercourse, and satisfaction of at least 7 on the 0 to 10 scale. Results were categorized as fair for the 29 percent who reported adequate erection but satisfaction from 4 to 6, and unsatisfactory for 39 percent with inadequate erection and satisfaction rated as 0 to 3. Thus, erections were sufficiently firm for intercourse in 61 percent of the men, consistent with other studies, but only 32 percent rated the results as at least good, suggesting the need for, perhaps, additional drug or psychological treatment. Only time will tell how effective the treatment really is, but its reception is following the same course as other wonder drugs. For example, in 1999 (the year Viagra was introduced in this country), prescriptions dispensed in Canada for erectile dysfunction climbed to 655 000—almost quadrupling the previous market (IMS Health Canada, 2004a)! By 2003, Viagra had become the most common treatment for erectile disorder, representing 90 percent of the 1.3 million prescriptions dispensed for erectile disorder in Canada that year (IMS Health Canada, 2004a), despite a cost of between $12 and $13 a pill (IMS Health Canada, 2004b). There was also some hope that Viagra would be useful for dysfunction in postmenopausal women, but initial results have been very disappointing (Kaplan et al., 1999).

There are also concerns about whether men with erectile disorders are actually accessing this effective treatment from their physicians. A study by William Fischer of the University of Western Ontario and his colleagues was conducted with nearly 3000 men with erectile disorder worldwide (Fischer, Marchie, & Norris, 2004). These researchers found that relatively few men with erectile disorder talk with their physician about their sexual dysfunction (about 58 percent), fewer still discuss therapy with Viagra with their physician (about 42 percent), and fewer still currently use Viagra to treat their erectile disorder (about 16 percent; see ■ Figure 10.4). The authors refer to this pattern of sharp and sequential decline as the "cascade effect" of treatment-seeking behaviour in men with erectile disorder. The findings suggest the need for increased educational and motivational interventions to assist men with erectile disorder to seek appropriate treatment (Fischer et al., 2004).

For some time, yohimbine (Carey & Johnson, 1996) and testosterone (Schiavi, White, Mandeli, & Levine, 1997) have been used to treat erectile dysfunction. But although they are safe and have relatively few side effects, they have only negligible effects on erectile dysfunction (Mann et al., 1996). Cindy Meston and her colleagues have produced results suggesting that yohimbine—when combined with another drug, L-arginine glutamate—is superior to placebo in increasing vaginal responses to erotic stimuli among women with sexual arousal disorder (Meston & Worcel, 2002); future research still needs to establish the utility of this drug combination in treating symptoms of the disorder outside the laboratory. More recently, a group of researchers at the University of Western Ontario has reported preliminary evidence that testosterone may alleviate hypoactive sexual desire in women (Van Anders, Chernick, Chernick, Hampson, & Fischer, 2005).

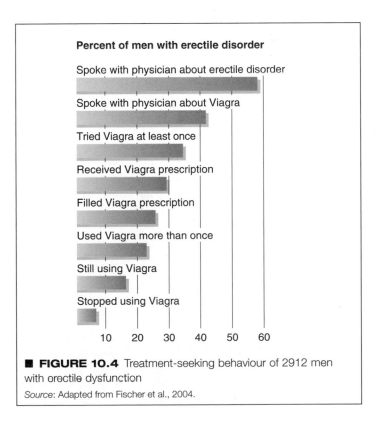

Percent of men with erectile disorder

Spoke with physician about erectile disorder

Spoke with physician about Viagra

Tried Viagra at least once

Received Viagra prescription

Filled Viagra prescription

Used Viagra more than once

Still using Viagra

Stopped using Viagra

10 20 30 40 50 60

■ **FIGURE 10.4** Treatment-seeking behaviour of 2912 men with erectile dysfunction

Source: Adapted from Fischer et al., 2004.

Some urologists teach patients to inject vasodilating drugs such as *papaverine* or *prostaglandin* directly into the penis when they want to have sexual intercourse. These drugs dilate the blood vessels, allowing blood to flow to the penis and thereby producing an erection within 15 minutes that can last from one to four hours (Kim & Lipshultz, 1997; Rosen, 2000; Segraves & Althof, 1998). Because this procedure is a bit painful (although not as much as you might think), a substantial number of men, usually 50 percent to 60 percent, stop using it after a short time. In one study, 50 to 100 patients discontinued papaverine for various reasons (Lakin, Montague, Vanderbrug Medendorp, Tesar, & Schover, 1990; Segraves & Althof, 1998). Side effects include bruising and, with repeated injections, the development of fibrous nodules in the penis (Gregoire, 1992; Rosen, 2000). Although some patients have found papaverine very helpful, it needs more study, and scientists are attempting to develop more palatable ways to deliver the drug. A soft capsule that contains the drug, called MUSE (Medical Urethral System for Erections), can be inserted directly into the urethra, but this is somewhat painful, less effective than injections, and remains awkward and artificial enough to most likely preclude wide acceptance (Delizonna, Wincze, Litz, Brown, & Barlow, 2001). On the other hand, Heiman and colleagues (2006) recently demonstrated that topical application of papaverine externally to women's genitalia produced vasocongestion and arousal in postmenopausal women, compared to placebo in the laboratory. Studies must now determine whether this drug treatment is effective outside of the laboratory.

Insertion of *penile prostheses* or implants has been a surgical option for almost 100 years; only recently are they good enough to approximate normal sexual functioning. One procedure involves implanting a semirigid silicone rod that can be bent by the male into correct position for intercourse and manoeuvred out of the way at other times. In a more popular procedure, the male squeezes a small pump that is surgically implanted into the scrotum, forcing fluid into an inflatable cylinder and thus producing an erection. The newest model of penile prosthetic device is an inflatable rod that contains the pumping device, which is more convenient than having the pump outside the rod. However, surgical implants fall short of restoring presurgical sexual functioning or ensuring satisfaction in most patients (Gregoire, 1992; Kim & Lipshultz, 1997) and are now generally used only if other approaches don't work. On the other hand, this procedure has proved useful for men who must have a cancerous prostate removed, because this surgery often causes erectile dysfunction, although newer "nerve-sparing" surgeries lessen the effect to some extent (Ramsawh, Morgentaler, Covino, Barlow, & DeWolf, 2005).

Another approach is *vacuum device therapy*, which works by creating a vacuum in a cylinder placed over the penis. The vacuum draws blood into the penis, which is then trapped by a specially designed ring placed around the base of the penis. Although using the vacuum device is rather awkward, between 70 percent and 100 percent of users report being able to achieve an erection with this device, particularly if psychosocial sex therapy is ineffective (Segraves & Althof, 1998; Witherington, 1988). The procedure is also less intrusive than surgery or injections, but remains awkward and artificial enough to, most likely, preclude wide acceptance (Delizonna et al., 2001).

Summary

Treatment programs, both psychosocial and medical, offer hope to most people who have sexual dysfunctions. Unfortunately, such programs are not readily available in many locations because few health and mental health professionals are trained to apply them, although the availability of Viagra for male erectile dysfunction is widespread. Psychosocial treatment of sexual arousal disorders requires improvement, and treatments for low sexual desire are largely untested. New medical developments appear yearly, but most are still intrusive and clumsy. New drugs such as Viagra (and, more recently, Cialis and Levitra) appear promising, and many more Viagra-like drugs are in development (Rosen, 2000).

Unfortunately, most health professionals tend to ignore the issue of sexuality in aging. Along with the usual emphasis on communication, education, and sensate focus, appropriate lubricants for women and a discussion of methods to maximize the erectile response in men should be a part of any sexual counselling for older couples. More important, even with reduced physical capabilities, continued sexual relations, not necessarily including intercourse, should be a very enjoyable and important part of an aging couple's relationship. Further research and development in the treatment of sexual dysfunction must address all these issues. Nevertheless, the overwhelming consensus is that a combination of psychological and drug treatment, when indicated, will continue to be the treatment strategy of choice.

Paraphilia: Clinical Descriptions

If you are like most people, your sexual interest is directed to other physically mature adults (or late adolescents), all of whom are capable of freely offering or withholding their consent. But what if you are sexually attracted to something or somebody other than another adult? What if you are attracted to a vacuum cleaner? (Yes, it does happen!) Or what if your only means of obtaining sexual satisfaction is to commit a brutal murder? Such patterns of sexual arousal and countless others exist in a large number of individuals, causing untold human suffering both for them and, if their behaviour involves other people, for their victims. As noted in the beginning of the chapter, these disorders of sexual arousal are called **paraphilias** (Fedoroff, 2003).

Over the years, we have assessed and treated a large number of these individuals, ranging from the slightly eccentric and sometimes pitiful case to some of the most dangerous killer-rapists encountered anywhere. We begin by describing briefly the major types of paraphilia, using in all instances cases from our own files. As with sexual dysfunctions, it is unusual for an individual to have just one paraphilic pattern of sexual arousal (Bradford & Meston, in press; Laws & O'Donohue, 2008; Langstrom & Seto, 2006). Many of our cases may present with two, three, or more patterns, although one is usually dominant (Abel et al., 1987; Abel, Becker, Cunningham-Rathner, Mittelman, & Rouleau, 1988; Brownell, Hayes, & Barlow, 1977). Furthermore, it is not uncommon for individuals with paraphilia to also have comorbid mood, anxiety, and substance abuse disorders (Raymond, Coleman, Ohlerking, Christenson, & Miner, 1999).

▲ A crowded bus or subway car is a typical setting for frotteuristic activity, in which a person takes advantage of forced physical contact with strangers to become aroused.

A police stakeout caught the perpetrator, who turned out to have a strong fetish for brassieres. As another example of fetishistic behaviour related to tactile stimulation, it is relatively common for a urologist to be called to the emergency room to remove surgically a long thin object, such as a pencil or the arm of an eyeglass frame, from a man's urethra. Men who insert such objects think that partially blocking the urethra in this way can increase the intensity of ejaculation during masturbation. However, if the entire object slips into the penis, major medical intervention is required.

Voyeurism and Exhibitionism

Voyeurism is the practice of observing an unsuspecting individual undressing or naked in order to become aroused. **Exhibitionism**, by contrast, is achieving sexual arousal and gratification by exposing one's genitals to unsuspecting strangers. See DSM Table 10.9 for the criteria for both disorders. Consider the case of Robert.

Although paraphilias are not widely prevalent and estimates of their frequency are hard to come by, some disorders, such as transvestic fetishism, seem relatively common (Bancroft, 1989; Mason, 1997). You may have been the victim of *frotteurism* in a large city, typically on a crowded subway or bus. (We mean really crowded, with people packed in like sardines.) In this situation women have been known to experience more than the usual jostling and pushing from behind. What they discover, much to their horror, is a male with a frotteuristic arousal pattern rubbing against them until he is stimulated to the point of ejaculation. Because the victims cannot escape easily, the frotteuristic act is usually successful (Lussier & Piché, 2008).

Fetishism

In **fetishism**, a person is sexually attracted to non-living objects (see DSM Table 10.8). There are almost as many different types of fetishes as there are objects, although women's undergarments and shoes are very popular. Fetishistic arousal is associated with two different classes of objects or activities: (1) an inanimate object or (2) a source of specific tactile stimulation, such as rubber, particularly clothing made out of rubber. Shiny black plastic is also used (Bancroft, 1989; Junginger, 1997). Most, if not all, of the person's sexual fantasies, urges, and desires focus on this object. A third source of attraction (sometimes called *partialism*) is a part of the body, such as the foot, buttocks, or hair, but this attraction is no longer technically classified as a fetish because distinguishing it from more normal patterns of arousal is often difficult.

In one city for several months, bras hung out on women's backyard clotheslines disappeared. The women in the neighbourhood soon began talking to each other and discovered that bras were missing from every clothesline for blocks around.

ROBERT | *Outside the Curtains*

Robert, a 31-year-old married blue-collar worker, reported that he first started "peeping" into windows when he was 14. He rode around the neighbourhood on his bike at night, and when he spotted a female through a window he stopped and watched. During one of these episodes, he felt the first pangs of sexual arousal. Eventually, he began masturbating while watching, thereby exposing his genitals, although out of sight. When he was older, he drove around until he spotted some prepubescent girls. He parked his car near them, unzipped his fly, called them over, and attempted to carry on a nonsexual conversation. Later he was sometimes able to talk a girl into mutual masturbation and fellatio. Although he was arrested several times, paradoxically the threat of arrest increased his arousal (Barlow & Wincze, 1980).

Source: Barlow & Wincze, 1980.

DSM-IV-TR Table 10.8 Criteria for Fetishism

A. Over a period of at least six months, the person experiences recurrent, intense sexually arousing fantasies, sexual urges, or behaviours involving the use of non-living objects (e.g., female undergarments).

B. The fantasies, sexual urges, or behaviours cause clinically significant distress or impairment in social, occupational, or other important areas of functioning.

C. The fetish objects are not limited to articles of female clothing used in cross-dressing (as in transvestic fetishism) or devices designed for the purpose of tactile genital stimulation (e.g., a vibrator).

Source: Reprinted with permission from the *Diagnostic and Statistical Manual of Mental Disorders*, Fourth Edition, Text Revision, (Copyright © 2000). American Psychiatric Association.

Remember that anxiety actually increases arousal under some circumstances. Many voyeurs just don't get the same satisfaction from attending readily available strip shows at a local bar. Although paraphilias may occur separately, it is not unusual to find them co-occurring.

Although prevalence is unknown (Murphy & Page, 2008), in a random sample of 2450 adults in Sweden, 31 percent reported at least one incident of being sexually aroused by exposing their genitals to a stranger and 7.7 percent reported at least one incident of being sexually aroused by spying on others having sex (Langstrom & Seto, 2006). To meet diagnosis for exhibitionism, the behaviour must occur repeatedly and be compulsive or out of control.

Transvestic Fetishism

In **transvestic fetishism**, sexual arousal is strongly associated with the act of dressing in clothes of the opposite sex, or cross-dressing (see DSM Table 10.10). Consider the case of Mr. M.

MR. M. | *Strong Man in a Dress*

Mr. M., a 31-year-old married police officer, came to our clinic seeking treatment for uncontrollable urges to dress in women's clothing and appear in public. He had been doing this for 16 years and had been discharged from the Armed Forces for cross-dressing. Since then, he had risked public disclosure on several occasions. Mr. M.'s wife had threatened to divorce him because of the cross-dressing, and yet she frequently purchased women's clothing for him and was "compassionate" while he wore them.

Note that Mr. M. was in the Armed Forces before he joined the police force. It is not unusual for males who are strongly inclined to dress in female clothes to compensate by associating with so-called macho organizations. Some of our cross-dressing patients have been associated with various paramilitary organizations. Nevertheless, most individuals with this disorder do not seem to display any compensatory behaviours. The same survey in Sweden mentioned earlier found 2.8 percent of men and 0.4 percent of women reported at least one episode of transvestic fetishism (Langstrom & Zucker, 2005).

Interestingly, the wives of many men who cross-dress have accepted their husbands' behaviour and can be quite supportive if it is a private matter between them. Docter and Prince (1997) reported that 60 percent of more than 1000 cases of transvestic fetishism were married at the time of the survey. Some people, both married and single, join cross-dressing clubs that meet periodically or subscribe to newsletters devoted to the topic. Research by Kurt Freund and his colleagues at the Centre for Addiction and Mental Health in Toronto suggests that transvestic fetishism is indistinguishable from other fetishes in most respects (Freund, Seto, & Kuban, 1996).

Concept Check | 10.2

People have a wide range of sexual preferences. Check your understanding of some sexual paraphilias: (a) exhibitionism, (b) voyeurism, or (c) fetishism.

This is a story about Peeping Tom.

1. Peeping Tom loves to look through Susie's bedroom window and watch her undress. He gets extremely excited as she slowly exposes her voluptuous body. He is practising _____.

2. What Peeping Tom does not realize is that Susie knows that he is watching. She is aroused by slowly undressing while Tom is watching, and fantasizes about what he is thinking. Susie enjoys _____.

3. Peeping Tom also loves to look at Susie's shoes while she is undressing, especially her ultra-high black stilettos. This is a form of _____.

4. What Peeping Tom would be shocked to find out is that Susie is really not "Susie"; she is actually Scott, who can become aroused only if he wears feminine clothing. Scott's problem is _____.

▲ Belts, chains, and handcuffs may increase sexual arousal in individuals with sadistic or masochistic tendencies.

can become dangerous and costly. It was not unusual that Mr. M. presented with three different patterns of deviant arousal, in his case sexual masochism, sexual sadism, and transvestic fetishism.

Sadistic Rape

After murder, rape is the most devastating assault one person can make on another. It is not classified as a paraphilia because most instances of rape are better characterized as an assault by a male (or, quite rarely, a female) whose patterns of sexual arousal are not paraphilic. Instead, many rapists meet criteria for antisocial personality disorder (see Chapter 12) and may engage in a variety of antisocial and aggressive acts (Bradford & Meston, in press; McCabe & Wauchope, 2005; Quinsey, 2010). In fact, many rapes could be described as opportunistic, in that an aggressive or antisocial individual with a marked lack of empathy and disregard for inflicting pain on others (Bernat, Calhoun, & Adams, 1999) spontaneously takes advantage of a vulnerable and unsuspecting woman. These unplanned assaults often occur during robberies or other criminal events. Rapes can also be motivated by anger and vindictiveness against specific women and may have been planned in advance (Hucker, 1997; Knight and Prentky, 1990; McCabe & Wauchope, 2005; Quinsey, 2010).

A number of years ago, we determined in our sexuality clinic that certain rapists do fit definitions of paraphilia closely and could probably better be described as sadists,

Sexual Sadism and Sexual Masochism

Both **sexual sadism** and **sexual masochism** are associated with either inflicting pain or humiliation (sadism; see Marshall & Hucker, 2006) or suffering pain or humiliation (masochism; see DSM Table 10.11). Although Mr. M. was extremely concerned about his cross-dressing, he was also disturbed by another problem. To maximize his sexual pleasure during intercourse with his wife, he had her wear a collar and leash, tied her to the bed, and handcuffed her. He sometimes tied himself with ropes, chains, handcuffs, and wires, all while he was cross-dressed. Mr. M. was concerned he might injure himself seriously. As a member of the police force, he had heard of cases—and even investigated one himself—in which an individual was found dead, very tightly and completely bound up in harnesses, handcuffs, and ropes. In many such cases something goes wrong and the individual accidentally hangs himself or herself, an event that should be distinguished from the closely related condition called *hypoxiphilia*, which involves self-strangulation to reduce the flow of oxygen to the brain and enhance the sensation of orgasm.

It may seem paradoxical that some people have to either inflict or receive pain to become sexually aroused, but these types of cases are not uncommon. On many occasions, the behaviours themselves are quite mild and harmless (Krueger, 2010), but they

DSM-IV-TR	**Table 10.11** Criteria for Sexual Sadism and Sexual Masochism

Sexual Sadism

A. Over a period of at least six months, the person experiences recurrent, intense sexually arousing fantasies, sexual urges, or behaviours involving acts (real, not simulated) in which the psychological or physical suffering (including humiliation) of the victim is sexually exciting to the person.

B. The fantasies, sexual urges, or behaviours cause clinically significant distress or impairment in social, occupational, or other important areas of functioning.

Sexual Masochism

A. Over a period of at least six months, the person experiences recurrent, intense sexually arousing fantasies, sexual urges, or behaviours involving the act (real, not simulated) of being humiliated, beaten, bound, or otherwise made to suffer.

B. The fantasies, sexual urges, or behaviours cause clinically significant distress or impairment in social, occupational, or other important areas of functioning.

Source: Reprinted with permission from the *Diagnostic and Statistical Manual of Mental Disorders*, Fourth Edition, Text Revision, (Copyright © 2000). American Psychiatric Association.

▲ Murderer Paul Bernardo obtained sexual gratification from inflicting pain and humiliation upon his victims (sadism).

a finding that has since been confirmed (McCabe & Wauchope, 2005; Qinsey, 2010). We constructed two audiotapes on which were described (1) mutually enjoyable sexual intercourse and (2) sexual intercourse involving force on the part of the male (rape). Each tape was played twice for selected listeners. The nonrapists became sexually aroused to descriptions of mutually consenting intercourse, but not to those involving force. Rapists, however, became aroused to both types of descriptions, suggesting that they are sexually aroused by the infliction of pain and suffering that occurs during rape (Abel, Barlow, Blanchard, & Guild, 1977). Paul Bernardo would be an example of this type of sadistic rapist. Bernardo and his wife, Karla Homolka, were involved in the rape and murder of two teenage girls in St. Catharines, Ontario, as well as in the rape and death of Karla's younger sister, Tammy. Bernardo also turned out to be the "Scarborough Rapist," who was alleged to be responsible for terrorizing and raping more than 20 women in the Toronto area.

Pedophilia and Incest

Perhaps the most tragic sexual deviance is a sexual attraction to children (or very young adolescents), called **pedophilia** (Blanchard, 2010; Seto, 2009; see DSM Table 10.12). Individuals with this pattern of arousal may be attracted to male children, female children, or both. If the children are the

DSM-IV-TR — Table 10.12 Criteria for Pedophilia

A. Over a period of at least six months, the person experiences recurrent, intense sexually arousing fantasies, sexual urges, or behaviours involving sexual activity with a prepubescent child or children (generally aged 13 years or younger).

B. The fantasies, sexual urges, or behaviours cause clinically significant distress or impairment in social, occupational, or other important areas of functioning.

C. The person is at least aged 16 years and at least five years older than the child or children in Criterion A.

Note: Do not include an individual in late adolescence involved in an ongoing sexual relationship with a 12- or 13-year-old.

Specify if:

    Sexually attracted to males

    Sexually attracted to females

    Sexually attracted to both

Specify if:

    Limited to incest

Specify type:

    Exclusive type (attracted only to children)

    Nonexclusive type

Source: Reprinted with permission from the *Diagnostic and Statistical Manual of Mental Disorders*, Fourth Edition, Text Revision, (Copyright © 2000). American Psychiatric Association.

person's relatives, the pedophilia takes the form of **incest.** Although pedophilia and incest have much in common, victims of pedophilia tend to be young children, and victims of incest tend to be girls who are beginning to mature physically. William Marshall at Queen's University demonstrated by using penile strain gauge measures that incestuous males are, in general, more aroused to adult women than are males with pedophilia, who tend to focus exclusively on children (Marshall, 1997; Marshall, Barbaree, & Christophe, 1986). Thus, incestuous relations may have more to do with availability and interpersonal issues in the family than pedophilia, as in the case of Tony.

TONY | *More and Less a Father*

Tony, a 52-year-old married television repairman, came in very depressed. About ten years earlier he had begun sexual activity with his 12-year-old daughter. Light kissing and some fondling gradually escalated to heavy petting and, finally, mutual masturbation. When his daughter was 16 years old, his wife discovered the ongoing incestuous relationship. She separated from her husband and eventually divorced him, taking their daughter with her. Soon, Tony remarried. Just before his initial visit to our clinic, Tony had visited his daughter, then 22 years old, who was living alone in a different city. They had not seen each other for five years. A second visit, shortly after the first, led to a recurrence of the incestuous behaviour. At this point, Tony became extremely depressed and told his new wife the whole story. She contacted our clinic with his full cooperation while his daughter sought treatment in her own city.

We return to the case of Tony later, but several features are worth noting. First, Tony loved his daughter very much and was bitterly disappointed and depressed over his behaviour. On occasion, a child molester is abusive and aggressive, sometimes killing the victims; in these cases, the disorder is often both sexual sadism and pedophilia. A study by Philip Firestone and colleagues of the University of Ottawa showed that child molesters who kill or attempt to kill their victims can be differentiated from child molesters who are not physically abusive and from controls in terms of their sexual arousal response to sexual vignettes (Firestone, Bradford, Greenberg, & Nunes, 2000). These researchers had these three groups of men listen to three types of vignettes describing three types of scenes (i.e., sex with a consenting adult, sex with a "consenting" child, and assault involving a child victim) and measured their arousal responses with phallometry. They measured the percentage of men in each group who showed stronger sexual arousal responses to the two types of vignettes involving children compared with their arousal responses to the vignettes involving the consenting adult. Study results are displayed in ■ Figure 10.5. It was found that a greater proportion of both types of child molesters showed enhanced arousal responses to the vignette describing sex with a "consenting" child relative to men in the control group (see Figure 10.5a). However, the homicidal child molesters showed increased sexual arousal to the vignette describing the assault on the child victim relative to the men in both other groups (see Figure 10.5b).

An example of a homicidal child molester is the case of 36-year-old Michael Briere. The Montréal native pled guilty to the murder of ten-year-old Holly Jones in Toronto. Jones was abducted while walking home from a friend's house in May 2003. Her dismembered body was found a day later. Briere was arrested a month later and charged with her murder. A statement of facts filed with the court revealed that Briere had abducted Jones off the street. Consistent with the established link between child pornography offences and pedophilia (Seto, Cantor, & Blanchard, 2006), the abduction occurred after Briere had viewed child pornography that he had downloaded off the Internet. He sexually assaulted the little girl, strangled her, and then dismembered her body to dispose of it. Briere pled guilty and was sentenced to life in prison in June 2004 (CBC News Online, 2003a, 2003b, 2004a; "Briere Pleads Guilty," 2004). The horrors of such cases appearing all too often in the media might make people think that most child molesters are physically violent toward their victims.

In fact, most child molesters are not physically abusive. Very rarely is a child actually physically forced or injured. This fact is illustrated by the relative numbers of men available for the two groups of child molesters in the Firestone et al. (2000) study: only 27 men qualified for the homicidal child molesters group, as compared with 189 men in the nonhomicidal child molesters group. For the more usual case of a nonhomicidal child molester, from the molester's perspective, no harm is

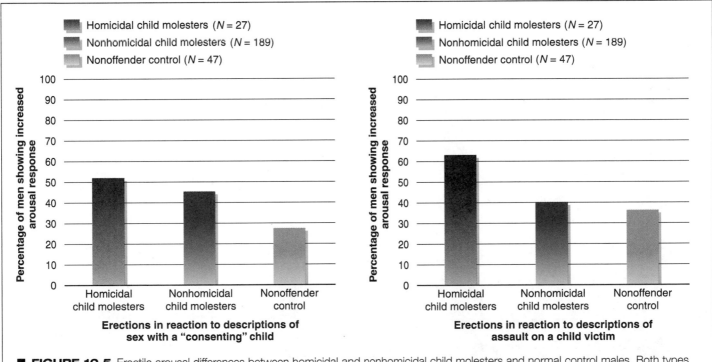

■ **FIGURE 10.5** Erectile arousal differences between homicidal and nonhomicidal child molesters and normal control males. Both types of child molesters became aroused to descriptions of sex with a "consenting" child (Figure 10.5a), while only the homicidal child molesters became aroused to descriptions of assault on a child (Figure 10.5b)

Note: Percentages reflect the proportion of men in each group who showed a larger arousal response to the vignette in question relative to their arousal response to descriptions of sex with a consenting adult.

Source: The American Journal of Psychiatry by American Psychiatric Association. Copyright 2000. Reproduced with permission of AMERICAN PSYCHIATRIC ASSOCIATION (JOURNALS) in the format Textbook via Copyright Clearance Center.

Paraphilia: Clinical Descriptions   **381**

done because there are no physical force or threats. In fact, child molesters often rationalize their behaviour as "loving" the child or teaching the child useful lessons about sexuality. The child molester almost never considers the psychological damage the victim suffers, and yet these interactions often destroy the child's trust and ability to share intimacy. For example, male victims of the molestations by Christian brothers at the Mount Cashel orphanage in Newfoundland in the 1970s reported long-term negative consequences of these interactions in their adult lives, including flashbacks of the abuse experiences, difficulties forming relationships with women, and a lack of trust ("Newfoundland Brother Gets 4 Years," 1992). Moreover, research has shown a connection between childhood sexual abuse by adults and increased risk for subsequent sexual victimization in adulthood in women (e.g., Stermac, Reist, Addison, & Millar, 2002). Child molesters rarely gauge their power over the children, who may participate in the molestation without protest, yet be very frightened and unwilling. Often children feel responsible for the abuse because no outward force or threat was used by the adult, and only after the abused children grow up are they able to understand they were powerless to protect themselves and not responsible for what was done to them.

Paraphilia in Women

Paraphilia is seldom seen in women and was thought to be totally absent in women for many years, with the possible exception of sadomasochistic practices. But in recent years, several reports have appeared describing individual cases or small series of cases (Seto, 2009). Now estimates suggest that approximately 5 percent

DSM-IV-TR	**Table 10.13** Criteria for Paraphilia Not Otherwise Specified

This category is included for coding paraphilias that do not meet the criteria for any of the specific categories. Examples include, but are not limited to, telephone scatologia (obscene phone calls), necrophilia (corpses), partialism (exclusive focus on part of body), zoophilia (animals), coprophilia (feces), klismaphilia (enemas), and urophilia (urine).

Source: Reprinted with permission from the *Diagnostic and Statistical Manual of Mental Disorders*, Fourth Edition, Text Revision, (Copyright © 2000). American Psychiatric Association.

to 10 percent of all sexual offenders are women (Logan, 2009; Wiegel, 2008). For example, J. Paul Fedoroff and his colleagues at the forensic service of the Centre for Addiction and Mental Health in Toronto have reported what seems to be the largest series of cases of women with paraphilia—12 cases seen in their clinic (Fedoroff, Fishell, & Fedoroff, 1999). Although some women had more than one paraphilia, five of them presented with pedophilia, four with exhibitionism, and three with sadomasochistic tendencies.

To take several examples, one heterosexual woman had been convicted of sexually molesting an unrelated nine-year-old boy while she was babysitting. It seems she had touched the boy's penis and asked him to masturbate in front of her while she watched religious programs on television. It is not unusual for individuals with paraphilia to rationalize their behaviour by engaging in some other practices that they consider to be morally correct or uplifting at the same time. Yet another woman came to treatment because of her "uncontrollable" rituals of undressing in front of her apartment window and masturbating approximately five times a month. In addition she would, on occasion, drive her truck through the neighbourhood, where she would attempt to befriend cats and dogs by offering them food. She would then place honey or other food substances on her genital area so the animals would lick her. As with most paraphilias, the woman herself was horrified by this activity and was seeking treatment to eliminate it, although she found it highly sexually arousing. (See DSM Table 10.13 for the criteria for paraphilia not otherwise specified.)

Causes of Paraphilia

Although no substitute for scientific inquiry, case histories often provide hypotheses that can then be tested by controlled scientific observations. Let's return to the cases of Robert and Tony to see if their histories contain any clues.

▲ The Mount Cashel Orphanage in Newfoundland was the site of a set of well-known cases of pedophilia in which many young male victims were molested by Christian Brothers at the orphanage in the 1970s. The victims suffered adverse psychological consequences of these molestation experiences into adulthood.

CP Photo/Andrew Vaughan

ROBERT | *Revenge on Repression*

Robert (who sought help for exhibitionism) was raised by a very stern authoritarian father and a passive mother in a small town in British Columbia. His father, who was a firm believer in Fundamentalist Christian religion, often preached the evils of sexual intercourse to his family. Robert learned little about sex from his father except that it was bad, so he suppressed any emerging heterosexual urges and fantasies, and as an adolescent felt very uneasy around girls his own age. By accident, he discovered a private source of sexual gratification: staring at attractive and unsuspecting females through the window. This led to his first masturbatory experience.

Robert reported in retrospect that being arrested was not so bad because it disgraced his father, which was his only way of getting back at him. In fact, the courts treated him lightly (which is not unusual), and his father was publicly humiliated, forcing the family to move away from their small town.

Source: Barlow & Wincze, 1980.

TONY | *Trained Too Young*

Tony, who sought help because of an incestuous relationship with his daughter, reported an early sexual history that contained a number of interesting events. Although he was brought up in a reasonably loving and outwardly normal Catholic family, he had an uncle who did not fit the family pattern. When he was nine or ten, Tony was encouraged by his uncle to observe a game of strip poker that the uncle was playing with a neighbour's wife. During this period, he also observed his uncle fondling a waitress at a drive-in restaurant and shortly thereafter was instructed by his uncle to fondle his young female cousin. Thus, he had an early model for mutual fondling and masturbation and obtained some pleasure from interacting in this way with young girls. Although the uncle never touched Tony, his behaviour was clearly abusive.

When Tony was about 13, he engaged in mutual manipulation with a sister and her girlfriend, which he remembers as pleasurable. Later, when Tony was 18, a brother-in-law took him to a prostitute and he first experienced sexual intercourse. He remembered this visit as unsatisfactory because, on that and subsequent visits to prostitutes, he ejaculated prematurely—a sharp contrast to his early experience with young girls. Other experiences with adult women were also unsatisfactory. When he joined the Armed Forces and was sent overseas, he sought out prostitutes who were often as young as 12.

These cases remind us that deviant patterns of sexual arousal often occur in the context of other sexual and social problems. Undesired kinds of arousal may be associated with deficiencies in levels of "desired" arousal with consensual adults; this was certainly true for both Tony and Robert, whose sexual relationships with adults were incomplete. As William Marshall has pointed out, in many cases, an inability to develop adequate social relations with the appropriate people for sexual relationships seems to be associated with developing inappropriate sexual outlets (Marshall, 1997; see also Barlow & Wincze, 1980). Indeed, integrated theories of the causes of paraphilias all note the presence of disordered relationships during childhood and adolescence with resulting deficits in healthy sexual development (Marshall & Barbaree, 1990; Ward & Beech, 2008). However, many people with deficient sexual and social skills do not develop deviant patterns of arousal.

Early experience seems to have an effect that may be quite accidental. Tony's early sexual experiences just happened to be of the type he later found sexually arousing. Robert's first erotic experience occurred while he was "peeping." But many of us do not find our early experiences reflected in our sexual patterns.

Another factor may be the nature of the person's early sexual fantasies. For example, in a famous study, Stanley J. Rachman demonstrated that sexual arousal could become associated with a neutral object—a boot, for example—if the boot was repeatedly presented while the individual was sexually aroused (Rachman & Hodgson, 1968; see also Bancroft, 1989). One of the most powerful engines for the development of unwanted arousal may be *early sexual fantasies that are repeatedly reinforced through the very strong sexual pleasure associated with masturbation.* Before a pedophile or sadist ever acts on his behaviour, he may fantasize about it thousands of times while masturbating. Expressed as a clinical or operant conditioning paradigm, this is another example of a learning process in which a behaviour (sexual arousal to a specific object or activity) is repeatedly reinforced through association with a pleasurable consequence (orgasm). This mechanism may explain why paraphilias are almost exclusively male disorders. The basic differences in frequency of masturbation between men and women that exist across cultures may contribute to the differential development of paraphilias. As we have seen, on rare occasions, cases of women with paraphilia do turn up (Fedoroff et al., 1999; Hunter & Mathews, 1997; Stoller, 1982).

However, if early experiences contribute strongly to later sexual arousal patterns, then what about the Sambia males who practise exclusive homosexual behaviour during childhood and early adolescence and yet are exclusively heterosexual as adults? Of course, in such cohesive societies, the social demands or "scripts" for sexual interactions are much stronger and more rigid than in our culture and thus may override the effects of early experiences (Baldwin & Baldwin, 1989).

In addition, therapists and sex researchers who work with paraphilics have observed what seems to be an incredibly strong sex drive. It is not uncommon for some paraphilics to masturbate three or four times a day. In one case seen in our clinic, a sadistic rapist masturbated approximately every half hour all day long, just as often as it was physiologically possible. We have speculated elsewhere that activity this consuming may be related to the obsessional processes of obsessive-compulsive disorder (Barlow, 2002). In both instances, the very act of trying to suppress unwanted emotionally charged thoughts and fantasies seems to have the paradoxical effect of increasing their frequency and intensity (see Chapter 5). This process is also ongoing in eating disorders and addictions, when attempts to restrict strong addictive cravings lead to uncontrollable increases in the undesired behaviours. (Recall Janet Polivy and Peter Herman's work on the causal role of dietary restraint in explaining binge eating, discussed in Chapter 8.) Psychopathologists are becoming interested in the phenomenon of weak inhibitory control across these disorders, which may indicate a weak biologically based behavioural inhibition system (BIS) in the brain (Fowles, 1993; Kafka, 1997) that might repress serotonergic functioning. (You may remember from Chapter 5 that the BIS is a brain circuit associated with anxiety and inhibition.)

The model shown in ■ Figure 10.6 incorporates the factors thought to contribute to the development of paraphilia. Nevertheless, all speculations, including the hypotheses we have described, have little scientific support at this time. For example, this model does not include the biological dimension. Excess arousal in paraphilics could be biologically based. Before we can make any steadfast conclusions here, more research is needed.

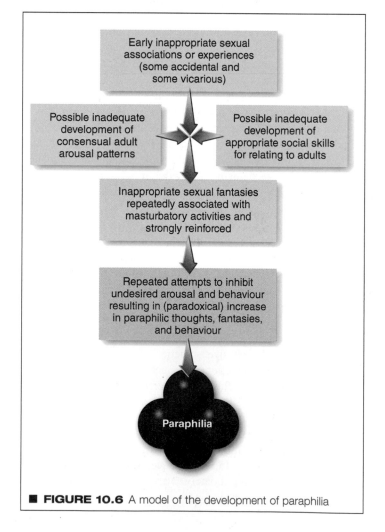

■ **FIGURE 10.6** A model of the development of paraphilia

Assessing and Treating Paraphilia

Assessment

In recent years, we have developed sophisticated methods for assessing specific patterns of sexual arousal (Looman & Marshall, 2001; Maletzky, 1998; Wincze, 2009). This is important in studying paraphilia because sometimes even the individual presenting with the problem is not fully aware of what caused the arousal. An individual once came in complaining of uncontrollable arousal to open-toed white sandals worn by women. He noted that he was irresistibly drawn to any woman wearing open-toed white sandals and would follow her for long distances. These urges occupied much of his summer. Subsequent assessment revealed that the sandal itself had no erotic value for this individual; rather, he had a strong sexual attraction to women's feet, particularly moving in a certain way.

Using the model of paraphilia described previously, we assess each patient not only for the presence of deviant arousal but also for levels of appropriate arousal to adults, for social skills, and for the ability to form relationships. Tony had no problems with social skills: He was 52 years old, reasonably happily married, and generally compatible with his second wife. His major difficulty was his continuing strong incestuous attraction to his daughter. Nevertheless, he loved his daughter very much and wanted strongly to interact in a normal fatherly way with her.

Psychosocial Treatment

Several treatment procedures are available for decreasing unwanted arousal. Most are behaviour therapy procedures directed at changing the associations and context from arousing and pleasurable to neutral. One procedure, carried out entirely in the imagination of the patient, called **covert desensitization**, was first described by Cautela (1967; see also Barlow, 1993). Sexually arousing images are associated with the very consequences of the behaviour that bring the patient to treatment in the first place. The notion here is that the patient's arousal patterns are undesirable because of their long-term consequences, but the immediate pleasure, and thus strong reinforcement, they provide more than overcomes any thoughts of possible harm or danger that might arise in the future. This model also applies to much unwanted addictive behaviour, as we will discuss in Chapter 11.

In imagination, harmful or dangerous consequences can be associated quite directly with the unwanted behaviour and arousal in a very powerful and emotionally meaningful way. One of the most powerful negative aspects of Tony's behaviour was his embarrassment over the thought of being discovered by his current wife, other family members, or, most important, the family priest. Therefore, he was guided through the fantasy described here.

TONY | *Imagining the Worst*

You are alone with your daughter in your trailer. You realize that you want to caress her breasts. So you put your arm around her, slip your hand inside her blouse, and begin to caress her breasts. Unexpectedly, the door to the trailer opens and in walks your wife with Father X. Your daughter immediately jumps up and runs out the door. Your wife follows her. You are left alone with Father X. He is looking at you as if waiting for an explanation of what he has just seen. Seconds pass, but they seem like hours. You know what Father X must be thinking as he stands there staring at you. You are very embarrassed and want to say something, but you can't seem to find the right words. You realize that Father X can no longer respect you as he once did. Father X finally says, "I don't understand this; this is not like you." You both begin to cry. You realize that you may have lost the love and respect of both Father X and your wife, who are very important to you. Father X asks, "Do you realize what this has done to your daughter?" You think about this and you hear your daughter crying; she is hysterical. You want to run, but you can't. You are miserable and disgusted with yourself. You don't know if you will ever regain the love and respect of your wife and Father X.

Source: Excerpt reproduced with permission of the authors and publisher from "Measurement and Modification of Incestuous Behavior: A Case Study" by T. L. Harbert, D. H. Barlow, M. Hersen, and J. B. Austin, 1974, *Psychological Reports, 34,* 79–86. © Psychological Reports, 1974.

During six or eight sessions, the therapist narrates such scenes dramatically, and the patient is then instructed to imagine them every day until all arousal disappears. The results of Tony's treatment are presented in ■ Figure 10.7. "Card-sort scores" are a measure of how much Tony wanted sexual interactions with his daughter in comparison with his desire for nonsexual fatherly interactions. His incestuous arousal was largely eliminated after three to four weeks, but the treatment did not affect his desire to interact with his daughter in a healthier manner. These results were confirmed by psychophysiological measurement of his arousal response. A return

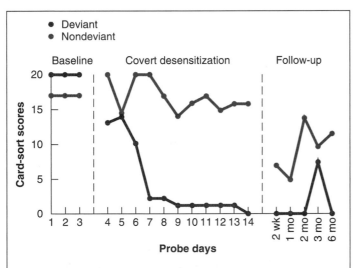

■ **FIGURE 10.7** Ratings of Tony's incestuous urges (deviant) and desire for normal interactions with daughter (nondeviant) during covert desensitization treatment

Source: Reproduced with permission of the authors and publisher from "Measurement and Modification of Incestuous Behavior: A Case Study" by T. L. Harbert, D. H. Barlow, M. Hersen, and J. B. Austin, 1974, *Psychological Reports, 34,* 79–86. © Psychological Reports, 1974.

of some arousal at a three-month follow-up prompted us to ask Tony whether anything unusual was happening in his life. He confessed that his marriage had taken a turn for the worse and sexual relations with his wife had all but ceased. A period of marital therapy restored the therapeutic gains (see Figure 10.7). Several years later, after his daughter's therapist decided she was ready, she and Tony resumed a nonsexual relationship, which they both wanted.

Two major areas in Tony's life needed treatment: deviant (incestuous) sexual arousal and marital problems. As noted by Howard Barbaree and Michael Seto at the Centre for Addiction and Mental Health in Toronto, most individuals with paraphilic arousal patterns need a great deal of attention to family functioning or other interpersonal systems in which they operate (Barbaree & Seto, 1997). In addition, many require intervention to help strengthen appropriate patterns of arousal. In **orgasmic reconditioning**, patients are instructed to masturbate to their usual fantasies but to substitute more desirable ones just before ejaculation. With repeated practice, subjects should be able to begin the desired fantasy earlier in the masturbatory process and still retain their arousal. This technique, first described by Davison (1968), has been used with some success in a variety of different settings (Brownell et al., 1977; Maletzky, 1998). Finally, as with most strongly pleasurable but undesirable behaviours (including addiction), care must be taken to provide the patient with coping skills to prevent slips or relapses (see Chapter 11). **Relapse prevention** treatment created for addictions (Laws, 1989; Laws & O'Donohue, 1997) does just that. Patients are taught to recognize the early signs of temptation and to institute a variety of self-control procedures before their urges become too strong.

The success of treatment with this rich array of procedures is surprisingly high when carried out by an experienced professional. Maletzky and his colleagues reported on the treatment over 17 years of some 7000 sexual offenders of numerous types. A variety of procedures were used in a program of three to four months in a clinic devoted exclusively to this type of treatment. The numbers of people successfully treated are presented by category in Table 10.7 (Maletzky, 1998). These are truly astounding numbers. What makes them even more impressive is that Maletzky collected objective physiological outcome measures on almost every case, in addition to patients' reports of progress. In many cases, he also obtained corroborating information from families and legal authorities.

In his follow-up of these patients, Maletzky defined a treatment as successful when someone had (1) completed all treatment sessions, (2) demonstrated no deviant sexual arousal on plethysmograph testing at any annual follow-up testing session, (3) reported no deviant arousal or behaviour at any time since treatment ended, and (4) had no legal record of any charges of deviant sexual activity, even if unsubstantiated. He defined as a treatment failure anyone who was not a success. Any offender who did not complete treatment for any reason was counted as a failure, even though some may well have benefited from the partial treatment and gone on to recover.

Although these results are extremely good overall, men who rape have the lowest success rate among all offenders with a single diagnosis, and individuals with multiple paraphilias have the lowest success rate of any group. Maletzky also examined factors associated with failure. Among the strongest predictors were a history of unstable social relationships, an unstable

TABLE 10.7 Treatment Outcome for Paraphilias (*n* = 7186)

Category	*N*	Percentage Meeting Criteria for Success[a]
Situational pedophilia, hetero-sexual	3012	95.6
Predatory pedophilia, heterosexual	864	88.3
Situational pedophilia, homosexual	717	91.8
Predatory pedophilia, homosexual	596	80.1
Exhibitionism	1130	95.4
Rape	543	75.5
Voyeurism	83	93.9
Public masturbation	77	94.8
Frotteurism	65	89.3
Fetishism	33	94.0
Transvestic fetishism	14	78.6
Telephone scatologia	29	93.1
Zoophilia	23	95.6

Notes:

[a] A treatment success was defined as an offender who:

1. Completed all treatment sessions.*

2. Reported no covert or overt deviant sexual behaviour at the end of treatment or at any follow-up session.†

3. Demonstrated no deviant sexual arousal, defined as greater than 20 percent on the penile plethysmograph, at the end of treatment or at any follow-up session.†

4. Had no repeat legal charges for any sexual crime at the end of treatment or at any follow-up session.†

* Any offender who dropped out of treatment, even if the offender met other criteria for success, was counted as a treatment failure.

† Follow-up sessions occurred at 6, 12, 24, 36, 48, and 60 months after the end of active treatment.

Source: From Maletzky, 1998.

employment history, strong denial that the problem exists, a history of multiple victims, and a situation in which the offender continues to live with a victim (as might be typical in cases of incest). Moreover, despite these very encouraging statistics, it remains clear that we must continue to incorporate effective treatments into our correctional system and to develop improved treatments that specifically focus on relapse prevention, given the high rates of sexual offenders (e.g., pedophiles) and the fact that so many who have been incarcerated show up in the correctional system again as reoffenders.

Other groups using similar treatment procedures have achieved comparable success rates (Abel, 1989; Becker, 1990; Fagan et al., 2002; Pithers, Martin, & Cumming, 1989). In general, results are less satisfactory when general summaries of the outcomes from all studies are evaluated, including programs that do not always incorporate these approaches (e.g., Hall, 1995; Quinsey, Khanna, & Malcolm, 1998). Thus, therapist knowledge and expertise seem to be important.

William Marshall and his colleagues have been studying empathy deficits in specific groups of sexual offenders and implications for treatment. Their research has shown that both child molesters and rapists display empathy deficits toward their victims. In other words, they suppress empathy toward their victims, failing to consider the psychological or physical damage the woman or child is experiencing (Fernandez & Marshall, 2003; Fernandez, Marshall, Lightbody, & O'Sullivan, 1999; Marshall, Hamilton, & Fernandez, 2001; Marshall & Moulden, 2001). Based on this research, many therapy programs for rapists and child molesters now include techniques designed to increase the perpetrators' empathy with their victims (Marshall, 1999).

▲ William Marshall is a clinical psychologist at Queen's University. He has conducted important work in a variety of areas pertaining to the understanding and treatment of paraphilias. Most recently, his research has focused on the empathy deficits that rapists and child molesters display for their victims and on techniques for correcting these deficits in treatment.

Drug Treatments

The most popular drug used to treat paraphilics is an antiandrogen called *cyproterone acetate* (Bradford, 1997; Seto, 2009). This "chemical castration" drug eliminates sexual desire and fantasy by reducing testosterone levels dramatically, but fantasies and arousal return as soon as the drug is removed. A second drug is *medroxyprogesterone* (Depo-Provera is the injectable form), a hormonal agent that reduces testosterone (Fagan et al., 2002). These drugs may be useful for dangerous sexual offenders who do not respond to alternative treatments or for suppressing temporarily the sexual arousal of patients who require it, but they are not always successful. In an earlier report (Maltezky, 1991) it was necessary to administer the drug to only 8 of approximately 5000 patients. More recently, Rösler and Witztum (1998) of Hadassah University Hospital in Jerusalem reported successful "chemical castration" of 30 men with severe long-standing paraphilia using triptoretin, which inhibits gonadotropin secretion in men. This drug appears to be somewhat more effective than the other drugs mentioned here, with fewer side effects. Rösler and Witztum (2000) argue that this drug has promise in providing an effective pharmacotherapy for paraphilias, but this conclusion is based on a single study thus far.

Summary

Based on evidence from a number of clinics, the psychosocial treatment of paraphilia is surprisingly effective. Success rates ranging from 70 percent to 100 percent with follow-ups for longer than ten years in some cases seem to make this one of the more treatable psychological disorders. However, most results are uncontrolled observations from a small number of clinical research centres, and it seems that results are not as good in other clinics and offices. In any case, like treatment for sexual dysfunctions, psychosocial approaches to paraphilia are not readily available outside of specialized treatment centres. In the meantime, the outlook for most individuals with this disorder is bleak because paraphilias run a very chronic course and recurrence is common.

Concept Check | 10.3

Check your understanding of paraphilias by matching the scenarios with the correct label: (a) fetishism, (b) voyeurism, (c) exhibitionism, or (d) sexual masochism.

1. Jane enjoys being slapped with leather whips during foreplay. _____
2. Bryan often watches through dorm windows with his binoculars in hopes of seeing women undress. _____
3. Miguel has a collection of women's panties that arouse him. _____
4. Angelo finds arousal in walking up to strangers in the park and showing them his genitals. _____

From the Inside

Gender Outlaw: On Men, Women, and the Rest of Us
by Kate Bornstein

In *Gender Outlaw*, Kate Bornstein aptly describes her identity as based on collage: She is a transsexual lesbian whose female lover is becoming a man. She sees identity, and especially gender, as being fluid and changeable. Her writing is playful and sometimes flippant but she has a serious underlying message: She wants people to set aside all preconceived notions of "gender" and just look at the real person inside.

True to her personality, Bornstein's book is arranged in a collage-like format. Quotations from other sources are displayed on the left side of the page and originate from such disparate sources as the *Tao Te Ching*, John F. Kennedy, the Beatles, and Holly Hughes's *Clit Notes*. She also includes snippets from her personal correspondence, appearances on talk shows, and other interviews. This book is mainly a collection of ideas on gender and identity but is interspersed with personal photos and tales of Bornstein's personal experiences. In Chapter 3, for example, she explains the "nuts and bolts" of her gender reassignment surgery. Toward the end of the book, she reprints the entire text of her play *Hidden: A Gender*.

Bornstein questions our most basic assumptions about gender: "Are you a woman because you can bear children? Are you a man because you can father children?" (pp. 56–57). She herself claims membership to neither camp. "I know I'm not a man—about that much I'm very clear, and I've come to the conclusion that I'm probably not a woman either, at least not according to a lot of people's rules on this sort of thing" (p. 8). She believes that we blindly accept the gender designation we're given at birth and as a result, we're limiting ourselves. Why must we choose between being either a man or a woman? She hasn't.

And yet she has had gender reassignment surgery and she does want to "pass" as a woman. She relates an incident in which an acquaintance referred to her as he: "The world

slowed down. The words echoed in my ears over and over and over. Attached to that simple pronoun was the word *failure*, quickly followed by the word *freak*" (emphasis in original, p. 126).

Some of the most interesting passages involve Bornstein's own experiences. For example, she points out the absurdities of living as a transgendered person. "When I first went through my gender change, I was working for an IBM subsidiary in Philadelphia. The biggest quandary there was *'which bathroom is it going to use?'*" (p. 84).

Bornstein also talks about the isolation of being a transsexual—even from other transsexuals. "See, when we walk into a restaurant and we see another transsexual person, we look the other way, we pretend we don't exist. There's no sly smile, no secret wink, signal, or handshake. Not yet. We still quake in solitude at the prospect of recognition, even if that solitude is in the company of our own kind" (p. 60). She provides other insider information, such as the "unspoken hierarchy" of male-to-female transgendered people that range from the postoperative transsexuals at the top to the "closet cases" (transvestites who hide their cross-dressing) at the bottom (pp. 67–68).

This book is categorized as "gender studies/memoir" and the study of gender does seem to be its main thrust. Bornstein briefly mentions three marriages and fatherhood (p. 143) but provides no details. But she infuses the personal into the general, with questions like "Do you think I'm a former man, and that now I'm a woman? Do you think I'm still a man?" (p. 104). (*Hint:* Are you still thinking in terms of only two genders?)

Source: © 1995 From *Gender Outlaw: On Men, Women, and the Rest of Us* by Kate Bornstein. Reprinted by permission of Routledge/Taylor & Francis Books, Inc.

Summary

What Is Normal?

- Patterns of sexual behaviour, both heterosexual and homosexual, vary around the world, in terms of both behaviour and risks. Approximately 20 percent of individuals who have been surveyed engage in sex with numerous partners, which puts them at risk for sexually transmitted diseases such as AIDS.
- Three different types of disorders are associated with sexual functioning and gender identity: *gender identity disorder, sexual dysfunctions, and paraphilias.*

Gender Identity Disorder

- Gender identity disorder is a dissatisfaction with one's biological sex and the sense that one is really the opposite gender (e.g., a woman trapped in a man's body). A person develops gender identity between 18 months and 3 years of age, and it seems that both appropriate gender identity and mistaken gender identity have biological roots influenced by learning.
- Treatment includes both psychosocial approaches, which have been attempted on only a few cases thus far, and sex reassignment surgery.

Sexual Dysfunctions: Clinical Descriptions

- Sexual dysfunction includes a variety of disorders in which people find it difficult to function adequately during sexual relations.
- Specific sexual dysfunctions include disorders of sexual desire—hypoactive sexual desire disorder and sexual aversion disorder—in which interest in sexual relations is extremely low or nonexistent; disorders of sexual arousal—male erectile disorder and female sexual arousal disorder—in which achieving or maintaining adequate penile erection or vaginal lubrication is problematic; and orgasmic disorders—female orgasmic disorder and male orgasmic disorder—in which orgasm occurs too quickly or not at all. The most common disorder in this category is premature ejaculation, which occurs in males; inhibited orgasm is commonly seen in females.
- Sexual pain disorders, in which unbearable pain is associated with sexual relations, include dyspareunia and vaginismus.

Assessing Sexual Behaviour

- The three components of assessment are interviewing, a complete medical evaluation, and psychophysiological assessment.

Causes of Sexual Dysfunction

- Sexual dysfunction is associated with socially transmitted negative attitudes about sex, interacting with current relationship difficulties and anxiety focused on sexual activity.

Treatment of Sexual Dysfunction

- Psychosocial treatment of sexual dysfunctions is generally successful but not readily available. In recent years, various medical approaches have become available, including the drug Viagra. These treatments focus mostly on male erectile dysfunction and are promising.

Paraphilia: Clinical Descriptions

- Paraphilia is sexual attraction to inappropriate people, such as children, or to inappropriate objects, such as articles of clothing.
- The paraphilias include fetishism, in which sexual arousal occurs almost exclusively in the context of inappropriate objects or individuals; exhibitionism, in which sexual gratification is attained by exposing the genitals to unsuspecting strangers; voyeurism, in which sexual arousal is derived from observing unsuspecting individuals undressing or naked; transvestic fetishism, in which individuals are sexually aroused by wearing clothing of the opposite sex; sexual sadism, in which sexual arousal is associated with inflicting pain or humiliation; sexual masochism, in which sexual arousal is associated with experiencing pain or humiliation; and pedophilia, in which there is a strong sexual attraction toward children. Incest is a type of pedophilia in which someone typically focuses on a child who is beginning to mature physically and to whom that person is related.

Causes of Paraphilia

- The development of paraphilia is associated with deficiencies in consensual adult sexual arousal, deficiencies in consensual adult social skills, deviant sexual fantasies that may develop before or during puberty, and attempts by the individual to suppress thoughts associated with these arousal patterns.

Assessing and Treating Paraphilia

- Psychosocial treatments of paraphilia, including covert sensitization, orgasmic reconditioning, and relapse prevention, seem highly successful but are available only in specialized clinics.

Key Terms

Answers to Concept Checks

10.1

1. a **2.** c **3.** a **4.** b

10.2

1. b **2.** a **3.** c **4.** c

10.3

1. d **2.** b **3.** a **4.** c

Media Resources

CourseMate

Access an integrated eBook, Abnormal Psychology Videos (formerly Abnormal Psych Live CD-ROM), chapter-specific interactive learning tools (flashcards, quizzes, learning modules), and more in your Psychology CourseMate, available at **www.abnormalpsych3ce.nelson.com**.

Abnormal Psychology Videos

Free Abnormal Psychology videos can be viewed on the website **www.abnormalpsych3ce .nelson.com**.

- *Erectile Dysfunction: Clark:* This illustrates a rather complicated case in which depression, physical symptoms, and cultural expectations all seem to play a role in Clark's problem.

- *Changing Over: Jessica:* Jessica discusses her life as a transsexual, both before and after her sex reassignment surgery.

Video Concept Reviews

CourseMate also contains Mark Durand's *Video Concept Reviews* on these challenging topics.

- Normal Versus Abnormal Sexual Behaviour
- Sexual Orientation
- Sexual and Gender Identity Disorders
- Gender Identity Disorders
- Concept Check: Gender Identity Disorder, Transvestic Fetishism, and Transgendered
- Sexual Reassignment Surgery
- Human Sexual Response Cycle

- Hypoactive Sexual Desire Disorder
- Sexual Aversion Disorder
- Male Erectile Disorder and Female Sexual Arousal Disorder
- Inhibited Orgasm
- Premature Ejaculation
- Sexual Pain Disorders (Dyspareunia)
- Vaginismus
- Photoplethysomograph
- Paraphilias

Exploring Sexual and Gender Identity Disorders

> Sexual behaviour is considered normal in our culture unless it is associated with one of three kinds of impaired functioning—gender identity disorder, sexual dysfunction, or paraphilia.

> Sexual orientation probably has a strong biological basis that is influenced by environmental and social factors.

GENDER IDENTITY DISORDERS

Present when a person feels trapped in a body that is the "wrong" sex, that does not match his or her innate sense of personal identity. (Gender identity is independent of sexual arousal patterns.) Relatively rare.

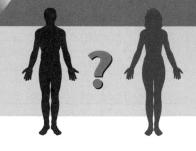
PhotoDisc/Getty Images

Causes

Biological Influences

- Not yet confirmed, although likely to involve prenatal exposure to hormones
  - Hormonal variations may be natural or result from medication

Psychological Influences

- Gender identity develops between 1 1/2 and 3 years of age
  - "Masculine" behaviours in girls and "feminine" behaviours in boys evoke different responses in different families

Treatment

- Sex reassignment surgery: removal of breasts or penis; genital reconstruction
  - Requires rigorous psychological preparation and financial and social stability
- Psychosocial intervention to change gender identity
  - Usually unsuccessful except as temporary relief until surgery

PARAPHILIAS

Sexual arousal occurs almost exclusively in the context of inappropriate objects or individuals.

Types

- ***Fetishism:*** Sexual attraction to non-living objects
- ***Voyeurism:*** Sexual arousal achieved by viewing unsuspecting person undressing or naked
- ***Exhibitionism:*** Sexual gratification from exposing one's genitals to unsuspecting strangers
- ***Transvestite fetishism:*** Sexual arousal from wearing opposite-sex clothing (cross-dressing)
- ***Sexual sadism:*** Sexual arousal associated with inflicting pain or humiliation
- ***Sexual masochism:*** Sexual arousal associated with experiencing pain or humiliation
- ***Pedophilia:*** Strong sexual attraction to children
- ***Incest:*** Sexual attraction to family member

Causes

- Pre-existing deficiencies
  - In levels of arousal with consensual adults
  - In consensual adult social skills
- Treatment received from adults during childhood
- Early sexual fantasies reinforced by masturbation
- Extremely strong sex drive combined with uncontrollable thought processes

Treatment

- ***Covert sensitization:*** Repeated mental reviewing of aversive consequences to establish negative associations with behaviour
- ***Relapse prevention:*** Therapeutic preparation for coping with future situations
- ***Orgasmic reconditioning:*** Pairing appropriate stimuli with masturbation to create positive arousal patterns
- ***Medical:*** Drugs that reduce testosterone to suppress sexual desire; fantasies and arousal return when drugs are stopped

PhotoDisc/Getty Images

Photos.com

©PhotoDisc/Getty Images

SEXUAL DYSFUNCTIONS

Sexual dysfunctions can be
- **Lifelong:** Present during entire sexual history
- **Acquired:** Interrupts normal sexual pattern
- **Generalized:** Present in every encounter
- **Situational:** Present only with certain partners or at certain times

The Human Sexual Response Cycle
A dysfunction is an impairment in one of the sexual response stages.

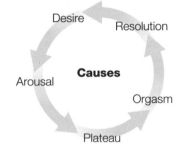

Types of Sexual Dysfunctions

Sexual Desire Disorders
- **Hypoactive sexual desire disorder:** Apparent lack of interest in sexual activity or fantasy
- **Sexual aversion disorder:** Extreme persistent dislike of sexual contact

Sexual Arousal Disorders
- **Male erectile disorder:** Recurring inability to achieve or maintain adequate erection
- **Female sexual arousal disorder:** Recurring inability to achieve or maintain adequate lubrication

Orgasm Disorders
- **Inhibited orgasm:** Inability to achieve orgasm despite adequate desire and arousal
- **Premature ejaculation:** Ejaculation before it is desired, with minimal stimulation

Sexual Pain Disorders
- **Dyspareunia:** Marked pain associated with intercourse for which there is no medical cause; occurs in males and females
- **Vaginismus:** Involuntary muscle spasms in the front of the vagina that prevent or interfere with intercourse

Psychological Contributions
- Distraction
- Underestimates of arousal
- Negative thought processes

Psychological and Physical Interactions
- A combination of influences is almost always present
  - Specific biological predisposition and psychological factors may produce a particular disorder

Causes

Socio-Cultural Contributions
- Erotophobia, caused by formative experiences of sexual cues as alarming
- Negative experiences, such as rape
- Deterioration of relationship

Biological Contributions
- Neurological or other nervous system problems
- Vascular disease
- Chronic illness
- Prescription medication
- Drugs of abuse, including alcohol

Treatment

- **Psychosocial:** Therapeutic program to facilitate communication, improve sexual education, and eliminate anxiety. Both partners participate fully.
- **Medical:** Almost all interventions focus on male erectile disorder, including drugs, prostheses, and surgery. Medical treatment is combined with sexual education and therapy to achieve maximum benefit.

Jupiter Images

11 | Substance-Related Disorders and Impulse Control Disorders

I've seen the needle and the damage done.
A little part of it in everyone.
But every junkie's like a settin' sun.
—Neil Young, "Needle and the Damage Done" (1972)

Mediolmages/Photodisc/Getty Images

Demonstrate knowledge and understanding representing appropriate breadth and depth in selected content areas of psychology:	❯ Biological bases of behaviour and mental processes, including physiology, sensation, perception, comparative, motivation, and emotion (APA SLO 1.2.a (3)) *(see textbook pages 398–400, 415–416, 423–425)*
Use the concepts, language, and major theories of the discipline to account for psychological phenomena.	❯ Describe behaviour and mental processes empirically, including operational definitions (APA SLO 1.3.a) *(see textbook pages 393–416, 429–431)*
Identify appropriate applications of psychology in solving problems, such as:	❯ Origin and treatment of abnormal behaviour (APA SLO 4.2.b) *(see textbook pages 416–429)*

Would you be surprised if we told you that a group of psychological disorders costs Canadian citizens nearly $20 billion each year, kills nearly 50 000 Canadians annually, and is implicated in street crime, homelessness, and interpersonal violence? Would you be even more surprised to learn that most of us have behaved in ways characteristic of these disorders at some point in our lives? You shouldn't. Smoking cigarettes, drinking alcohol, and using illegal drugs are all related to these disorders, and they are responsible for astronomical financial costs and the tragic waste of tens of thousands of human lives each year (Single, Robson, Rehm, & Xie, 1996). In this chapter we explore the **substance-related disorders**, which are associated with the abuse of drugs such as alcohol, cocaine, heroin, and a variety of other substances that people take to alter the way they think, feel, and behave. These disorders represent a problem that has cursed us for millennia and continues to affect how we live, work, and play.

Equally disruptive to the people affected, **impulse-control disorders** represent a number of related problems that involve the inability to resist acting on a drive or temptation. Included in this group are those who cannot resist aggressive impulses or the impulse to steal, to set fires, to gamble, or, for some, to pull out their own hair. Controversy surrounds both substance-related and impulse-control disorders because our society sometimes believes that these problems result simply from a lack of "will." If you wanted to stop drinking, using cocaine, or gambling, well, you would just stop. We first examine those individuals who are being harmed by their use of a variety of chemical substances (substance-related disorders) and then turn our attention to the puzzling array of disorders that are under the heading of impulse-control disorders.

Perspectives on Substance-Related Disorders

The cost in lives, money, and emotional turmoil has made the issue of alcohol and drug abuse a major concern worldwide. In 1992 the Roman Catholic Church issued a new universal catechism, officially declaring that drug abuse and drunk driving are sins (Riding, 1992). Yet from the well-known heavy drug use of music legend Neil Young in his early career and the death of two of his close friends from drug overdoses (McDonough, 2002) to the boozing and drug involvement of singer and songwriter

Leonard Cohen (Walsh, 2001), illicit drug use and heavy drinking occupy the lives of many. Consider the public controversies surrounding former Alberta premier Ralph Klein's intoxicated behaviour while visiting a homeless shelter in 2001 and former British Columbia premier Gordon Campbell's embarrassing driving-while-intoxicated charge in Hawaii in 2003. Both politicians have since quit drinking alcohol (O'Malley & Missio, 2003). Stories such as these are not only about the rich and famous, but are also retold in every corner of our society.

Consider the case of Danny, who has the disturbing but common habit of **polysubstance use,** using multiple substances. (We cover this issue in more detail later in the chapter.)

DANNY | *Multiple Dependencies*

At the age of 35, Danny was in jail, awaiting trial on charges that he broke into a gas station and stole money. Danny's story illustrates the lifelong pattern that characterizes the behaviour of many people who are affected by substance-related disorders.

Danny grew up in the suburbs. He was well liked in school and an average student. Like many of his friends, he smoked cigarettes in his early teens and drank beer with his friends at night behind his high school. Unlike most of his friends, however, Danny almost always drank until he was obviously drunk; he also experimented with many other drugs, including cocaine, heroin, speed (amphetamines), and downers (barbiturates).

After high school, Danny attended a local community college for one semester, but he dropped out after failing most of his courses. His dismal performance seemed to be related to his missing most classes. He had difficulty getting up for classes after partying most of the night. His moods were highly variable, and he was often unpleasant. Danny's family knew he occasionally drank too much, but they didn't know (or didn't want to know) about his other drug use. He had for years forbidden anyone to go into his room, after his mother found little packets of white powder (probably cocaine) in his sock drawer. He said he was keeping them for a friend and that he would return them immediately. Money was sometimes missing from the house, and once some stereo equipment "disappeared," but if anyone in his family suspected Danny, they never admitted it.

After high school, Danny held a series of low-paying jobs, and when he was working his family reassured themselves that he was back on track and things would be fine. Unfortunately, he rarely held a job for more than a few months. He was usually fired for poor job attendance and performance. Because he continued to live at home, Danny could survive despite frequent periods of unemployment. When he was in his late 20s, Danny announced that he needed help and planned to check into an alcohol rehabilitation centre; he still would not admit to using other drugs. His family's joy and relief were overwhelming, and no one questioned his request for several thousand dollars to help pay for the private program he said he wanted to attend. Danny disappeared for several weeks, presumably because he was in the rehabilitation program. However, a call from the local police station put an end to this fantasy: Danny had been found quite high, living in an abandoned building. Danny had spent his family's money on drugs and had had a three-week binge with some friends.

Danny's deceptiveness and financial irresponsibility greatly strained his relationship with his family. He was allowed to continue living at home, but his parents and siblings excluded him from their emotional lives. Danny seemed to straighten out, and he held a job at a gas station for almost two years. He became friendly with the station owner and his son. However, without any obvious warning, Danny resumed drinking and using drugs and was arrested for robbing the very place that had kept him employed for many months.

Why did Danny become dependent on drugs when many of his friends and siblings did not? Why did he steal from his family and friends? What ultimately became of him? We return to Danny's frustrating story later when we look at the causes and treatment of substance-related disorders.

Although each drug described in this chapter has unique effects, they have similarities in the ways they are used and how people who abuse them are treated. We first survey some concepts that apply to substance-related disorders in general, noting important terminology and addressing several diagnostic issues.

Can you use drugs and not abuse them? Can you abuse drugs and not become addicted to or dependent on them? To answer these important questions, we first need to outline what we mean by *substance use, substance intoxication, substance abuse,* and *dependence.* The term *substance* refers to chemical compounds that are ingested in order to alter mood or behaviour. Although you might first think of drugs such as cocaine and heroin, this definition also includes more commonplace legal drugs such as alcohol, the nicotine found in tobacco, and the caffeine in coffee and tea. As we will see, these so-called safe drugs also affect mood and behaviour, they can be addictive, and they account for more health problems and mortality than all the illegal drugs combined. You could make a good argument for directing drug abuse prevention efforts toward cigarette smoking (nicotine use) because of its addictive properties and negative health consequences.

Levels of Involvement

To understand substance-related disorders, we must first know what it means to ingest **psychoactive substances**—which alter mood or behaviour—to become intoxicated or high, to abuse these substances, and to become dependent on or addicted to them.

Use

Substance use is the ingestion of psychoactive substances in moderate amounts that do not significantly interfere with social, educational, or occupational functioning. Most of you reading this chapter probably use some sort of psychoactive substance on occasion. Drinking a cup of coffee in the morning to wake up or smoking a cigarette and having a drink with a friend to relax are examples of substance use, as is the occasional ingestion of illegal drugs such as marijuana, cocaine, amphetamines, or barbiturates.

Intoxication

Our physiological reaction to ingested substances—drunkenness or getting high—is referred to as **substance intoxication**. For a person to become intoxicated, it depends on which drug he or she takes, how much is ingested, and the person's individual biological reaction (see DSM Table 11.1). For many of the substances we discuss here, intoxication is experienced as impaired judgment, mood changes, and lowered motor ability (e.g., problems walking or talking).

Abuse

Defining **substance abuse** by how much of a substance is ingested is problematic. For example, is drinking two glasses of wine in an hour abuse? Three glasses? Six? Is taking one injection of heroin considered abuse? The *DSM-IV-TR* (American Psychiatric Association, 2000a) defines substance abuse in terms of how significantly it interferes with the user's life (see DSM Table 11.2). If substances disrupt your education, job, or relationships with others, and put you in physically dangerous situations (e.g., while driving), and if you have related legal problems, you would be considered a drug abuser. Some evidence suggests that high school drug use can predict later job outcomes. In one study, researchers controlled for factors such as educational interests and other problem behaviour, and still found that repeated hard drug use (using one or more of the following: amphetamines,

DSM-IV-TR	**Table 11.1** Criteria for Substance Intoxication

A. A person develops a reversible substance-specific syndrome due to recent ingestion of (or exposure to) a substance. *Note:* Different substances may produce similar or identical syndromes.

B. Clinically significant maladaptive behavioural or psychological changes due to the effect of the substance on the central nervous system (e.g., belligerence, mood liability, cognitive impairment, impaired judgment, impaired social or occupational functioning) develop during or shortly after use of the substance.

C. The symptoms are not due to a general medical condition and are not better accounted for by another mental disorder.

Source: Reprinted with permission from the *Diagnostic and Statistical Manual of Mental Disorders,* Fourth Edition, Text Revision, (Copyright © 2000). American Psychiatric Association.

barbiturates, crack, cocaine, PCP, LSD, other psychedelics, crystal meth, inhalants, heroin, or other narcotics) predicted poor job outcomes at age 29 (Ringel, Ellickson, & Collins, 2007).

Danny seems to fit this definition of abuse. His inability to complete a semester of community college was a direct result of drug use. Danny often drove while drunk or under the influence of other drugs, and he had already been arrested twice. In fact, Danny's use of multiple substances was so relentless and pervasive that he would be diagnosed as drug dependent, which indicates a severe form of the disorder.

▲ Intoxication

▲ Substance use

Substance Dependence

Drug dependence is usually described as addiction. Although we use the term *addiction* routinely when we describe people who seem to be enslaved by drugs, some disagreement exists about how to define addiction, or **substance dependence** (Strain, 2009). In one definition, the person is physiologically dependent on the drug or drugs, requires increasingly more of the drug to experience the same effect (**tolerance**), and will respond physically in a negative way when the substance is no longer ingested (**withdrawal**; American Psychiatric Association, 2007). Tolerance and withdrawal are physiological reactions to the chemicals being ingested. How many of you have experienced a headache when you didn't have your morning coffee? You were probably going through caffeine withdrawal. In a more extreme example, withdrawal from alcohol can cause *alcohol withdrawal delirium* (or *delirium tremens*—the DTs), in which a person can experience frightening

▲ Substance abuse

Barbara Peacock/Taxi/Getty Images

DSM-IV-TR **Table 11.3** Criteria for Substance Dependence

A. The person displays a maladaptive pattern of substance use, leading to clinically significant impairment or distress, as manifested by three (or more) of the following, occurring at any time in the same 12 months:

1. Tolerance, as defined by either of the following:
   a. a need for markedly increased amounts of the substance to achieve intoxication or desired effect
   b. markedly diminished effect with continued use of the same amount of the substance

2. Withdrawal, as manifested by either of the following:
   a. the characteristic withdrawal syndrome for the substance (refer to Criteria A and B of the criteria sets for Withdrawal from the specific substances)
   b. the same (or a closely related) substance is taken to relieve or avoid withdrawal symptoms

3. The substance is often taken in larger amounts or over a longer period than was intended.

4. There is a persistent desire or unsuccessful efforts to cut down or control substance use.

5. A great deal of time is spent in activities necessary to obtain the substance (e.g., visiting multiple doctors or driving long distances), use the substance (e.g., chain-smoking), or recover from its effects.

6. Important social, occupational, or recreational activities are given up or reduced because of substance use.

7. The substance use is continued despite knowledge of having a persistent or recurrent physical or psychological problem that is likely to have been caused or exacerbated by the substance (e.g., current cocaine use despite recognition of cocaine-induced depression, or continued drinking despite recognition that an ulcer was made worse by alcohol consumption).

Specify if:

With physiological dependence: Evidence of tolerance or withdrawal (i.e., either Item 1 or 2 is present)

Without physiological dependence: No evidence of tolerance or withdrawal (i.e., neither Item 1 nor 2 is present)

Source: Reprinted with permission from the *Diagnostic and Statistical Manual of Mental Disorders,* Fourth Edition, Text Revision, (Copyright © 2000). American Psychiatric Association.

hallucinations and body tremors. Withdrawal from many substances can bring on chills, fever, diarrhea, nausea and vomiting, and aches and pains. However, not all substances are physiologically addicting. For example, you do not go through severe physical withdrawal when you stop taking LSD. Cocaine withdrawal has a pattern that includes anxiety, lack of motivation, and boredom (Leamon, Wright, & Myrick, 2008), and withdrawal from marijuana includes such symptoms as nervousness, appetite change, and sleep disturbance (Ehlers et al., 2010). In fact, although previously believed not to be a problem, marijuana (cannabis) withdrawal is now being considered for inclusion in the *DSM-5* (Martin, Chung, & Langenbucher, 2008). We return to the ways drugs act on our bodies when we examine the causes of abuse and dependence.

Another view of substance dependence uses the drug-seeking behaviours themselves as a measure of dependence. The repeated use of a drug, a desperate need to ingest more of the substance (stealing money to buy drugs, standing outside in the cold to smoke), and the likelihood that use will resume after a period of abstinence are behaviours that define the extent of drug dependence. Such behavioural reactions are different from the physiological responses to drugs we described before and are sometimes referred to in terms of *psychological dependence.* The *DSM-IV-TR* definition of substance dependence combines the physiological aspects with the behavioural and psychological aspects (see DSM Table 11.3; American Psychiatric Association, 2000a).

This definition of dependence must be seen as a work in progress. By these criteria, many people can be considered dependent on such activities as sex, work, or even eating chocolate. ■ Figure 11.1 shows the results of applying the *DSM-IV-TR* definition of dependence to a variety of daily activities, including substance use (Franklin, 1990). Is your own behaviour on this list? Obviously, what most people consider

▲ Substance dependence

Photos.com

ACCORDING TO THE STANDARD psychiatric definition, any drug user who passes three of the nine tests below is hooked. Several researchers were asked to apply the tests not only to drugs but also to other substances and activities—chocolate, sex, shopping. Their responses show it's possible to become addicted to all sorts of things. For example, serious runners could pass three of the tests by spending more time running than originally intended, covering increasing distances, and experiencing withdrawal symptoms (a devoted runner forced to stop because of an injury, say, might become anxious and irritable). Of course, that sort of dependency isn't necessarily destructive. Conversely, a drug that fails the addictiveness test—LSD, for instance—may be harmful just the same. That so many things are potentially addictive suggests the addiction's cause is not confined to the substance or activity—our culture may play a large role too.

	Nicotine	Alcohol	Caffeine	Cocaine	Crack	Heroin	Ice*	LSD	Marijuana	PCP	Valium, Xanax, etc.†	Steroids	Chocolate	Running	Gambling	Shopping	Sex	Work	Driving	Television	Mountain climbing
TAKES substance or does activity more than originally intended	✓	✓	✓	✓	✓	✓	✓		✓	✓	✓	✓	✓	✓	✓	✓	✓	✓		✓	✓
WANTS to cut back or has tried to cut back but failed	✓	✓	✓	✓	✓	✓	✓		✓	✓	✓	✓	✓	✓	✓	✓	✓	✓		✓	✓
SPENDS lots of time trying to get substance or set up activity, taking substance or doing activity, or recovering	✓	✓		✓	✓	✓	✓	✓	✓	✓	✓			✓	✓	✓	✓	✓		✓	✓
IS OFTEN intoxicated or suffers withdrawal symptoms when expected to fulfill obligations at work, school, or home		✓		✓	✓	✓			✓	✓	✓				?						
CURTAILS or gives up important social, occupational, or recreational activities because of substance or activity		✓		✓	✓	✓			✓	✓	✓			✓	✓	✓	✓	✓		✓	✓
USES substance or does activity despite persistent social, psychological, or physical problems caused by substance or activity	✓	✓	✓	✓	✓	✓	✓	✓	✓	✓	✓	✓	✓	✓	✓	✓	✓	✓		✓	✓
NEEDS more and more of substance or activity to achieve the same effect (tolerance)	✓	✓	✓	✓	✓	✓	✓				✓				?						
SUFFERS characteristic withdrawal symptoms when activity or substance is discontinued (cravings, anxiety, depression, jitters)	✓	✓	✓	✓	✓	✓	✓				✓			✓	✓	✓	✓	✓		✓	✓
TAKES substance or does activity to relieve or avoid withdrawal symptoms	✓	✓	✓	✓	✓	✓	✓				✓										

*Methamphetamine
†Benzodiazepines

Research by Valerie Fahey

■ **FIGURE 11.1** Ice, LSD, chocolate, TV: is everything addictive?

Source: From the sidebar "Is Everything Addictive?" researched by Valerie Fahey, In Health, January/Feburary 1990. Reprinted from *In Health*, © 1990 by permission. For subscriptions, please call 1-800-274-2522.

serious addiction to drugs is qualitatively different from dependence on shopping or television. But some have argued that problematic forms of gambling behaviour (see Figure 11.1), now classified as "pathological gambling" in the "Impulse Control Disorders" section of the *DSM-IV-TR* (see Langewisch & Frisch, 1998), share much in common with substance dependence and should be recategorized as an "addiction without the drug" (Potenza, 2001).

Let's go back to the questions we started with: Can you use drugs and not abuse them? Can you abuse drugs and not become addicted to or dependent on them? The answer to the first question is yes. Obviously, some people drink wine or beer regularly without drinking to excess. Although it is not commonly believed, some people use drugs such as heroin, cocaine, or crack (a form of cocaine) on an occasional basis (for instance, several times a year) without abusing them (Goldman & Rather, 1993). What is disturbing is that we do not know ahead of time who is likely to become dependent with even a passing use of a substance.

It may seem counterintuitive, but dependence can be present without abuse. For example, cancer patients who take morphine for pain may become dependent on the drug—build up a tolerance and go through withdrawal if it is stopped—without abusing it (Portenoy & Mathur, 2009). Later in this chapter we discuss biological and psychosocial theories of the causes of substance-related disorders and of why we have individualized reactions to these substances.

Expert professionals in the substance use field were asked about the relative "addictiveness" of various drugs (Franklin, 1990). The survey results are shown in ■ Figure 11.2. You may be surprised to see nicotine placed just ahead of methamphetamine and crack cocaine as the most addictive of drugs. Although this is only a subjective rating by these experts, it shows that our society sanctions or proscribes drugs based on factors other than their addictiveness.

Diagnostic Issues

In early editions of the *DSM*, alcoholism and drug abuse weren't treated as disorders in and of themselves. Instead, they were categorized as *sociopathic personality disturbances* (a forerunner of the current *antisocial personality disorder*, which we discuss in Chapter 12), because substance use was seen as a symptom of other problems. It was considered a sign of moral weakness, and the influence of genetics and biology was hardly acknowledged. A separate category was created in the *DSM-III* in 1980, and since then we have acknowledged the complex biological and psychological nature of the problem.

The *DSM-IV-TR* term *substance-related disorders* indicates several subtypes of diagnoses for each substance, including dependence, abuse, intoxication, and/or withdrawal. These distinctions help clarify the problem and focus treatment on the appropriate aspect of the disorder. Danny received the diagnosis "cocaine dependence" because of the tolerance he showed for the drug, his use of larger amounts than he intended, his unsuccessful attempts to stop using it, and the activities he gave up in order to buy it. His pattern of use was more pervasive than simple abuse, and the diagnosis of dependence provided a clear picture of his need for help.

Symptoms of other disorders can complicate the substance abuse picture significantly. For example, do some people drink to excess because they are depressed, or do drinking and its consequences (e.g., loss of friends, job) create depression? Some researchers have estimated that more than half the people with alcohol disorders have an additional psychiatric disorder, such as major depression, antisocial personality disorder, or bipolar dis-

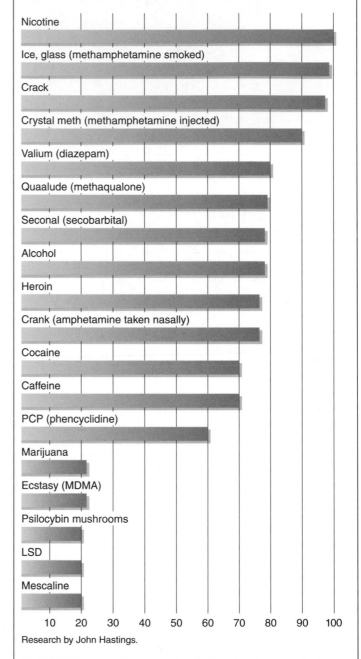

TO RANK today's commonly used drugs by their addictiveness, experts were asked to consider two questions: How easy is it to get hooked on these substances, and how hard is it to stop using them? Although a person's vulnerability to a drug also depends on individual traits—physiology, psychology, and social and economic pressures—these rankings reflect only the addictive potential inherent in the drug. The numbers are relative rankings, based on the experts' scores for each substance.

Research by John Hastings.

■ **FIGURE 11.2** Easy to get hooked on, hard to get off of.

Source: From the sidebar, "Easy to Get Hooked On, Hard to Get Off" researched by John Hastings, *In Health, November/December 1990*, p. 37. Reprinted from In Health, © 1990 by permission. For subscription, please call 1-800-274-2522.

order (Compton, Cottler, Jacobs, Ben-Abdallah, & Spitznagel, 2003; Conrod & Stewart, 2005; McGovern, Xie, Segal, Siembab, & Drake, 2006). For example, in an epidemiological study of six countries, including Canada, alcohol disorders were found to be highly comorbid with mood and anxiety disorders (Merikangas et al., 1998). As another example, in reviews of the literature by Canadian researchers (Crockford & el-Guebaly, 1998; Stewart & Kushner, 2003), alcohol disorders were shown to be highly comorbid with pathological gambling.

Concept Check | 11.1

To check your understanding of substance-related definitions, read the following case summaries and then state whether they describe (a) use, (b) intoxication, (c) abuse, or (d) dependence.

1. Jonas is a member of the high school football team and is out celebrating a big win. Jonas doesn't drink alcohol, but doesn't mind taking a puff of marijuana every now and then. Because Jonas had such a good game, he decides to smoke marijuana to celebrate. Despite his great performance in the game, Jonas is easily irritated, laughing one minute, and yelling the next. During a game of darts, at which he usually excels, Jonas barely hits the target. And the more Jonas boasts about his stats, the more difficult it is to understand him. _____

2. Jill routinely drinks diet cola. Instead of having coffee in the morning, she heads straight for the fridge. Another habit of Jill's is having a cigarette immediately after dinner. If for some reason Jill is unable to have her diet cola in the morning or her cigarette in the evening, she is not dependent on them and can still function normally. Jill also smokes marijuana with her friends every few weeks to escape the real world. _____

3. Steve is a 23-year-old university student who started drinking heavily when he was 16. Instead of getting drunk at weekend parties, Steve drinks a moderate amount every night. In high school Steve would become drunk after about six beers; now his tolerance has more than doubled. Steve claims alcohol relieves the pressures of university life. He once attempted to quit drinking, but he had chills, fever, diarrhea, nausea and vomiting, and body aches and pains. At one point, he even experienced scary hallucinations and tremors.

_____

4. Jamila is 32 and has just been fired from her third job in one year. She has been absent from work two days a week for the past three weeks. Not only did her boss telephone her and find her speech slurred, but she was also seen at a local pub in a drunken state during regular office hours. On one occasion as Jamila returned to work on her lunch hour, she was pulled over by police and found to be intoxicated. During her previous job, she came to work with alcohol on her breath and was unable to conduct herself in an orderly fashion. When confronted about her problem, Jamila went home and tried to forget the situation by drinking more.

_____

Substance use might occur concurrently with other disorders for several reasons (Grant & Dawson, 1999; Stewart, 1996; Strain, 2009). First, substance-related disorders and anxiety and mood disorders are highly prevalent in our society and may occur together frequently just by chance. Second, drug intoxication and withdrawal can cause symptoms of anxiety, depression, and psychosis, and can increase risk taking. For example, analyses of data collected in the Canadian National Population Health Survey have shown that those who have been drinking in the past year (particularly heavy drinkers) are at increased risk for clinical depression (Patten & Charney, 1998; Wang & Patten, 2002). Second, a laboratory-based study by Ellery, Stewart, and Loba (2005) showed that ingestion of alcohol led to increased risk-taking among regular gamblers when they were using a video lottery terminal (VLT) relative to gamblers ingesting a nonalcoholic control beverage. This finding suggests that alcohol's effects in increasing risk-taking may contribute to the high co-occurrence of alcohol and gambling disorders. A third explanation for the high comorbidity of substance use disorders with other mental health problems is that the mental health disorders cause the substance use disorder. For example, people with anxiety disorders like post-traumatic stress disorder or social phobia may self-medicate with substances for their anxiety symptoms, resulting in a substance use disorder (Stewart, 1996; Stewart, Morris, Mellings, & Komar, 2006).

Because substance-related disorders can be so complicated, the *DSM-IV-TR* tries to define when a symptom is a result of substance use and when it is not. Basically, if symptoms seen in schizophrenia or in extreme states of anxiety appear during intoxication or within six weeks after withdrawal from drugs, they aren't considered signs of a separate psychiatric disorder. So, for example, individuals who show signs of severe depression just after they have stopped taking heavy doses of stimulants would not be diagnosed with a major mood disorder. However, individuals who were severely depressed before they used stimulants and those whose symptoms persist for more than six weeks after they stop might have a separate disorder (Mack et al., 2003).

We now turn to the individual substances themselves, their effects on our brains and bodies, and how they are used in our society. We have grouped the substances into five general categories:

1. **Depressants:** These substances result in behavioural sedation and can induce relaxation. They include alcohol (ethyl alcohol) and the sedative, hypnotic, and anxiolytic drugs in the families of barbiturates (e.g., Seconal) and benzodiazepines (e.g., Valium, Halcion, Xanax).
2. **Stimulants:** These substances cause us to be more active and alert and can elevate mood. Included in this group are amphetamines, cocaine, nicotine, and caffeine.
3. **Opiates:** The major effect of these substances is to produce analgesia temporarily (reduce pain) and euphoria. Heroin, opium, codeine, morphine, and oxycodone are included in this group.
4. **Hallucinogens:** These substances alter sensory perception and can produce delusions, paranoia, and hallucinations. Marijuana and LSD are included in this category.

5. **Other drugs of abuse:** Other substances that are abused but do not fit neatly into one of the categories here include inhalants (e.g., airplane glue), anabolic steroids, and other over-the-counter and prescription medications (e.g., nitrous oxide). These substances produce a variety of psychoactive effects that are characteristic of the substances described in the previous categories.

Depressants

Depressants primarily decrease central nervous system activity. Their principal effect is to reduce our levels of physiological arousal and help us relax. Included in this group are alcohol and the sedative, hypnotic, and anxiolytic drugs such as those prescribed for insomnia (see Chapter 8).These substances are among those most likely to produce symptoms of physical dependence, tolerance, and withdrawal. We first look at the most commonly used of these substances—alcohol—and the **alcohol use disorders** that can result.

Alcohol Use Disorders

Danny's substance abuse began when he drank beer with friends, a rite of passage for many teenagers. Alcohol has been widely used throughout history. For example, scientists have found evidence of wine or beer in pottery jars at the site of a Sumerian trading post in western Iran and in Soviet Georgia that date back 7000 years (McGovern, 2007). For hundreds of years, Europeans drank large amounts of beer, wine, and hard liquor. When they came to North America in the early 1600s, they brought their considerable thirst for alcohol with them. Alcohol was not a problem for Native Canadians until the French introduced brandy and the British introduced rum (Smart, 1985; Stewart, 2002).

Reports of the early missionaries contain many descriptions of intoxication among Natives and early settlers (e.g., Dailey, 1968); government control activities and antidrinking movements quickly followed (Smart, 1985; Stewart, 2002). For example, the Temperance Movement allowed for the benefits of moderate drinking while morally condemning the heavy use of spirits (Stewart, 2002; Vallee, 1998). The Women's Christian Temperance Union tried to have alcohol education courses introduced into schools and was successful in several Canadian provinces (Smart, 1985; Stewart, 2002). The work of Temperance Movement proponents paved the way for the American Prohibition (1919–1933). Although prohibition did reduce overall levels of use in the United States, it had some unintended side effects, such as increases in organized crime and bootlegging, some of which originated in Canada (Stewart, 2002). These problems led to the repeal of Prohibition near the beginning of the Depression.

Clinical Description

Although alcohol is a depressant, its initial effect is as an apparent stimulant. We generally experience a feeling of well-being, our inhibitions are reduced, and we become more outgoing. These reactions are partly because what is initially depressed—or slowed—are the inhibitory centres in the brain. With continued drinking, however, alcohol depresses more areas of the brain, which impedes the ability to function properly. Motor coordination is impaired (staggering, slurred speech), reaction time is slowed, we become confused, our ability to make judgments is reduced, even vision and hearing can be negatively affected, all of which help to explain why driving while intoxicated is clearly very dangerous.

Effects

Alcohol affects many parts of the body (see ■ Figure 11.3). After it is ingested, it passes through the esophagus (1) and into the stomach (2), where small amounts are absorbed. From there, most of it travels to the small intestine (3), where it is easily absorbed into the bloodstream. The circulatory system distributes the alcohol throughout the body, where it contacts every major organ, including the heart (4). Some of the alcohol goes to the lungs, where it vaporizes and is exhaled, a phenomenon that is the basis for the breath analyzer test that measures levels of intoxication. As alcohol passes through the liver (5) it is broken down or metabolized into carbon dioxide and water by enzymes (Maher, 1997). An average-size person is able to metabolize about 7 to 10 grams of alcohol per hour, an amount comparable to about one glass of beer or one ounce of 90-proof spirits (Moak & Anton, 1999).

Most of the substances we describe in this chapter, including marijuana, the opiates, and tranquilizers, interact with specific

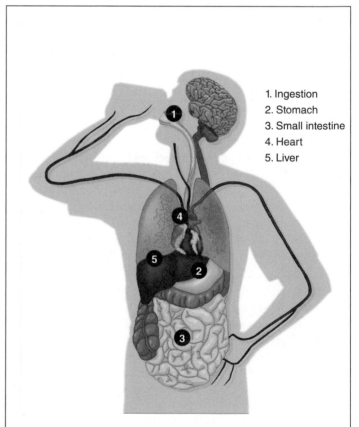

1. Ingestion
2. Stomach
3. Small intestine
4. Heart
5. Liver

■ **FIGURE 11.3** The path travelled by alcohol throughout the body (see text for complete description)

Go to **www.abnormalpsych3e.nelson.com** *to access an interactive version of this figure.*

Substance Use Disorder: Tim

"When I drink, I don't care about anything, as long as I'm drinking. Nothing bothers me. The world doesn't bother me. So when I'm not drinking, the problems come back, so you drink again. The problems will always be there. You just don't realize it when you're drinking. That's why people tend to drink a lot."

Go to Psychology CourseMate at www.abnormalpsych3ce.nelson.com to watch this video.

receptors in the brain cells. The effects of alcohol, however, are much more complex. Alcohol influences a number of different neuroreceptor systems, which makes it difficult to study. For example, the **gamma aminobutyric acid (GABA) system**, which we discussed in Chapter 2 and Chapter 5, seems to be particularly sensitive to alcohol. GABA, as you will recall, is an inhibitory neurotransmitter. Its major role is to interfere with the firing of the neuron it attaches to. When GABA attaches to its receptor, chloride ions enter the cell and make it less sensitive to the effects of other neurotransmitters. Alcohol seems to reinforce the movement of these chloride ions; as a result, the neurons have difficulty firing. In other words, although alcohol seems to loosen our tongues and makes us more sociable, it makes it difficult for neurons to communicate with each other (Oscar-Berman, Shagrin, Evert, & Epstein, 1997). Because the GABA system seems to act on our feelings of anxiety, alcohol's anti-anxiety properties may result from its interaction with the GABA system (Conrod, Pihl, Stewart, & Dongier, 2000).

Blackouts, the loss of memory for what happens during intoxication, may result from the interaction of alcohol with the *glutamate system*. The *serotonin system* also appears to be sensitive to alcohol. This neurotransmitter system affects mood, sleep, and eating behaviour and is thought to be responsible for alcoholic cravings (Oscar-Berman et al., 1997). Alcohol also exerts effects on the dopamine reward system, and these effects may be respon-

sible for the pleasurable feelings people experience when drinking alcohol (Conrod, Peterson, Pihl, & Mankowski, 1997). Finally, as noted by Christina Gianoulakis of McGill University, at certain doses, alcohol also results in release of endogenous opioids—our bodies' naturally occurring analgesics—which may explain why alcohol has pain-numbing effects (Gianoulakis, 2001; Peterson et al., 1996). Because alcohol affects so many neurotransmitter systems, we should not be surprised that it has such widespread and complex effects.

The long-term effects of heavy drinking are often severe. Withdrawal from chronic alcohol use typically includes hand tremors and, within several hours, nausea or vomiting, anxiety, transient hallucinations, agitation, insomnia, and, at its most extreme, **withdrawal delirium** (or **delirium tremens**—the **DTs**), a condition that can produce frightening hallucinations and body tremors. The devastating experience of DTs can be reduced with adequate medical treatment (Schuckit, 2009b).

Whether alcohol will cause organic damage depends on genetic vulnerability, frequency of use, the length of drinking binges, the blood alcohol levels attained during the drinking periods, and whether the body is given time to recover between binges (Mack et al., 2003). Consequences of long-term excessive drinking include liver disease, pancreatitis, cardiovascular disorders, and brain damage (see ■ Figures 11.4 and 11.5).

Part of the folklore concerning alcohol is that it permanently kills brain cells (neurons). As you will see later, this may not be true. Some evidence for brain damage comes from the experiences of people who are alcohol dependent and experience blackouts, seizures, and hallucinations. Memory and the ability to perform certain tasks may also be impaired. More seriously, two types of organic brain syndromes may result from long-term heavy alcohol use: dementia and Wernicke-Korsakoff syndrome. *Dementia*, which we discuss more fully in Chapter 15, involves

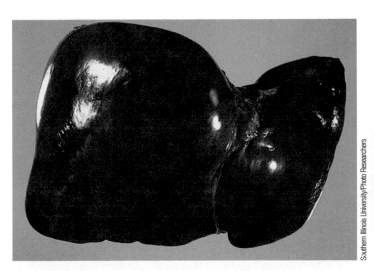
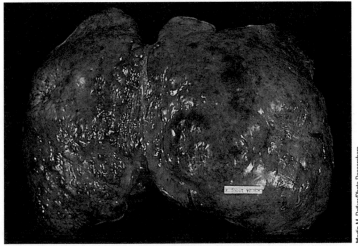

■ **FIGURE 11.4** A healthy liver (left) and a cirrhotic liver scarred by years of alcohol abuse (right)

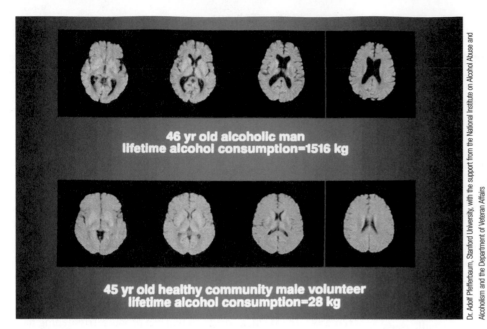

46 yr old alcoholic man
lifetime alcohol consumption=1516 kg

45 yr old healthy community male volunteer
lifetime alcohol consumption=28 kg

Dr. Adolf Pfefferbaum, Stanford University, with the support from the National Institute on Alcohol Abuse and Alcoholism and the Department of Veteran Affairs

■ **FIGURE 11.5** The dark areas in the top brain images show the extensive loss of brain tissue that result from heavy alcohol use.

the general loss of intellectual abilities and can be a direct result of neurotoxicity or "poisoning of the brain" by excessive amounts of alcohol (Leamon et al., 2008). *Wernicke-Korsakoff syndrome* results in confusion, loss of muscle coordination, and unintelligible speech (Schuckit, 2009b); it is believed to be caused by a deficiency of thiamine, a vitamin metabolized poorly by heavy drinkers. The dementia caused by this disease does not go away once the brain is damaged.

The effects of alcohol abuse extend beyond the health and well-being of the drinker. Although alcohol was suspected for years to negatively affect prenatal development, this connection has been studied in earnest for only a short time (Jones & Smith, 1973; Lemoine, Harousseau, Borteyru, & Menuet, 1968). **Fetal alcohol syndrome (FAS)** is now generally recognized as a com-

▲ Physical characteristics of fetal alcohol syndrome include skin folds at the corners of the eyes, a low nasal bridge, a short nose, a groove between nose and upper lip, small head circumference, small eye openings, a small midface, and a thin upper lip.

bination of problems that can occur in a child whose mother drank while she was pregnant. These problems include fetal growth retardation, cognitive deficits, behaviour problems, and learning difficulties (Barr & Streissguth, 2001; Hamilton, Kodituwakku, Sutherland, & Savage, 2003; Kerns, Don, Mateer, & Streissguth, 1997). In addition, children with fetal alcohol syndrome often have characteristic facial features (Caprara, Nash, Greenbaum, Rovet, & Koren, 2007).

Statistics on Use

Because alcohol consumption is legal in North America, we know more about it than most of the other psychoactive substances that we discuss in this chapter (with the possible exception of nicotine and caffeine, which are also legal here). Despite a national history of heavy alcohol use, most adults in Canada drink in moderation. For example, in the recent Canadian Addiction Survey (CAS), about 23 percent of Canadians were found to exceed low-risk guidelines for alcohol consumption, and about 17 percent were classified as high-risk drinkers (Canadian Centre for Substance Abuse [CCSA], 2004). Alcohol use in Canada diminished over the period from 1989 to 1994 (see CCSA, 1999); this decline was paralleled in many other major industrialized countries, including the United States (Horgan, Sparrow, & Brazeau, 1986; U.S. Department of Health and Human Services, 1990). ■ Figure 11.6 shows that change in alcohol consumption in 25 countries between 1979 and 1984. Reduced consumption over this time period may have reflected increased public awareness of the health risks associated with alcohol use and abuse. A change in demographics may also partly account for the decline, because the proportion of the population over age 60 had increased, and alcohol use among people in this age group is historically low (Stewart, 2002). However, statistics in Canada have recently reversed, and alcohol use has now risen to levels that exceed 1989 rates (CCSA, 2004).

Men are more likely than women to drink alcohol and are also more likely to drink heavily (Statistics Canada, 2003). For example, a 1998–1999 Canadian survey found that 16 percent of adult men were classified as heavy drinkers, compared with only 4 percent of adult women. Drinking practices also vary across societies, even in Westernized countries. For example, a comparison of the results of the 1998 Canadian Campus Survey conducted with the undergraduates at 16 universities across Canada, with the 1999 College Alcohol Study of 119 colleges and universities in the United States, revealed that a higher proportion of Canadian than American students drink alcohol, but that a higher proportion of American students are binge drinkers (episodic heavy drinkers; Kuo et al., 2002, 2003).

Statistics on Abuse and Dependence

Our everyday experience tells us that not everyone who drinks becomes dependent on alcohol or abuses it. However, researchers estimate that about 9 percent of Canadian drinkers experience

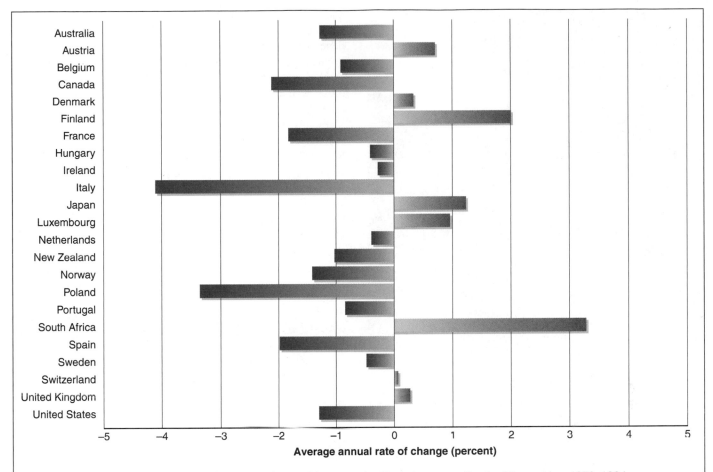

■ FIGURE 11.6 Average annual rate of change (percent) in per capita Alcohol consumption for 25 countries, 1979–1984.

Source: From *Alcoholic Beverage Taxation and Control Policies (8th ed.),* by Ron Brazeau and Nancy Burr, 1992. Copyright © Brewers Association of Canada. Reprinted by permission.

some level of problem with alcohol (CCSA, 2004), with about 3 percent of Canadian adults thought to be alcohol dependent in any given year (Statistics Canada, 2002a). For example, in the 2004 Canadian Addiction Survey, 5 percent of current drinkers admitted to experiencing physical health problems as a consequence of their drinking, 3 percent reported financial problems related to their alcohol use, and 3 percent reported problems in their social life or friendships due to their drinking (CCSA, 2004). Among the general population, young (18–29), single males are most likely to be heavy drinkers and to have alcohol use problems (Statistics Canada, 2002a).

Outside Canada, rates of alcohol use disorders vary widely. For example, in a comparison of lifetime rates of alcohol dependence diagnoses obtained in epidemiological studies around the world, researchers from Simon Fraser University found that the lowest reported rate was 1.2 percent in rural villages in Taiwan, whereas the highest reported rate was in the American National Comorbidity Survey at 14.1 percent (Somers, Goldner, Waraich, & Hsu, 2004). They observed a clustering of low prevalence rates among the Asian studies (Hong Kong and Taiwan) (Somers et al., 2004). Such cultural differences can be accounted for by different attitudes toward drinking, the availability of alcohol, physiological reactions, and family norms and patterns (Lee, 1992).

Progression

Remember that Danny went through periods of heavy alcohol and drug use, but also had times when he was relatively "straight" and did not use drugs. Similarly, many people who abuse alcohol or are dependent on it fluctuate between drinking heavily, drinking "socially" without negative effects, and being abstinent, not drinking at all (Schuckit, 2009a; Vaillant, 1983). It seems that about 20 percent of people with severe alcohol dependence have a spontaneous remission and do not re-experience problems with drinking (Ludwig, 1985; Vaillant, 1983).

Alcohol researchers Linda and Mark Sobell, who worked at the Addiction Research Foundation in Toronto in the 1980s and 1990s, noted that it was previously thought that once problems arose with drinking, they would become steadily worse, following a predictable downward pattern as long as the person kept drinking (Sobell & Sobell, 1993). In other words, like a disease that isn't treated properly, alcoholism will get progressively worse if left unchecked. First championed by Jellinek more than 60 years ago, this view continues to influence the way people view and treat the disorder (Jellinek, 1946, 1952, 1960). Unfortunately, Jellinek based his model of the progression of alcohol use on a now famous but faulty study (Jellinek, 1946).

▲ Males aged 18 to 29 are most vulnerable to drinking problems.

convulsions, and hepatitis or pancreatitis. This study suggests a common pattern among people with chronic alcohol abuse and dependence, one with increasingly severe consequences. This progressive pattern is not inevitable for everyone who abuses alcohol, although we do not yet understand what distinguishes those who are and those who are not susceptible (Schuckit, 2009a).

Finally, statistics frequently link alcohol with violent behaviour (Bye, 2007). A review of numerous studies conducted by Robert Pihl and his colleagues established that many people who commit such violent acts as murder, rape, and assault are often intoxicated at the time of the crime (Murdoch, Pihl, & Ross, 1990). We hope you are skeptical of this type of correlation. Just because drunkenness and violence overlap does not mean that alcohol will necessarily make you violent. Laboratory studies show that alcohol does make participants more aggressive (Bushman, 1993; see also review by Hoaken & Stewart, 2003). However, whether a person behaves aggressively outside the

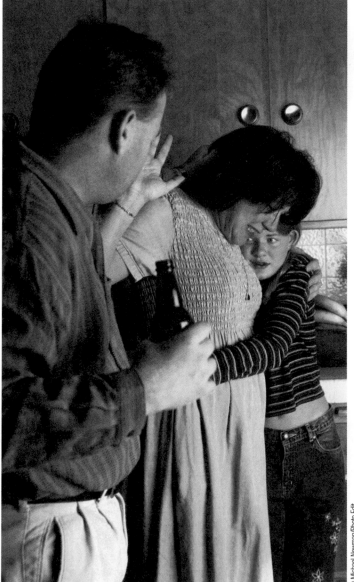

▲ Intoxication is often involved in cases of domestic violence.

It appears instead that the course of *alcohol dependence* may be progressive for most people, although the course of *alcohol abuse* may be more variable. For example, early use of alcohol may predict later abuse. A study of almost 6000 lifetime drinkers by David DeWit and his colleagues at the Centre for Addiction and Mental Health found that drinking at an early age—from age 11 to 14—was predictive of later alcohol use disorders (DeWit, Adlaf, Offord, & Ogborne, 2000). A second study followed 636 male inpatients in an alcohol rehabilitation centre (Schuckit et al., 1993). Among these chronically alcohol-dependent men, a general progression of alcohol-related life problems did emerge, although not in the specific pattern proposed by Jellinek. Three-quarters of the men reported moderate consequences of their drinking in their 20s, such as demotions at work. During their 30s, the men had more serious problems, such as regular blackouts and signs of alcohol withdrawal. By their late 30s and early 40s, these men demonstrated long-term serious consequences of their drinking, which included hallucinations, withdrawal

▲ Robert Pihl, a clinical psychologist at McGill University, has made many notable contributions to the understanding and treatment of alcohol abuse and dependence. In particular, his work has focused on understanding the relation between alcohol and aggression, and on identifying factors that mediate familial-genetic risk for alcoholism.

laboratory probably involves several interrelated factors, such as the quantity and timing of alcohol consumed, the person's history of violence, his or her expectations about drinking, and what happens to the individual while intoxicated. Alcohol does not cause aggression, but it may reduce the fear associated with being punished, and it may impair the ability to consider the consequences of acting impulsively (Nestor, 2002; Pihl, Peterson, & Lau, 1993). Robert Pihl's most recent work suggests that people with poorer executive cognitive function (planning, organizing abilities) are more likely than others to behave aggressively when intoxicated (Hoaken, Shaunessey, & Pihl, 2003; Pihl, Assad, & Hoaken, 2003). Toronto-based researchers Christine Wekerle and the late Anne-Marie Wall (2002) have further noted that alcohol intoxication can also increase the risk of being the victim of violence.

Sedative, Hypnotic, or Anxiolytic Substance Use Disorders

The general group of depressants also includes sedative (calming), *hypnotic* (sleep-inducing), and anxiolytic (anxiety-reducing) drugs (Ciraulo & Sarid-Segal, 2009). These drugs include the barbiturates and the benzodiazepines. **Barbiturates** (which include Amytal, Seconal, and Nembutal) are a family of sedative drugs first synthesized in Germany in 1882 (McKim, 1991). They were prescribed to help people sleep and replaced such drugs as alcohol and opium. Barbiturates were widely prescribed by physicians during the 1930s and 1940s, before their addictive properties were fully understood. By the 1950s they were among the drugs most abused by adults in North America (Franklin & Frances, 1999).

The **benzodiazepines** (which today include Valium, Xanax, Rohypnol, and Halcion) have been used since the 1960s, primarily to reduce anxiety. These drugs were originally touted as a miracle cure for the anxieties of living in our highly pressured technological society. Although it has been known since the 1980s that they are not appropriate for reducing the tension and anxiety resulting from everyday stresses and strains (Cooperstock & Hill, 1982), billions of doses of benzodiazepines are consumed by North Americans each year (Shabecoff, 1987). Sixteen million prescriptions of benzodiazepines were made to Canadians in 2000 alone (Gadsby, 2001). In general, benzodiazepines are considered much safer than barbiturates, with less risk of abuse and dependence (Warneke, 1991). Nonetheless, as noted by clinical psychologist Henny Westra of York University, the potential for developing dependence on benzodiazepines for those using them

in the treatment of anxiety or sleep disorders should not be minimized (e.g., Westra & Stewart, 1998). The potential for benzodiazepine dependence was recognized as early as the 1970s, as is illustrated in the following case study, published in the *Canadian Psychiatric Association Journal* in 1978.

SUSAN | *Taking a Harmless Muscle Relaxant or an Addictive Drug?*

Susan was a 30-year-old Caucasian woman with a small child. She had recently separated from her husband. Susan had originally been prescribed a low dose of Diazepam by her general practitioner as a muscle relaxant for a backache. Over three months, Susan increased her dose until she reached a level 12 times greater than the dose prescribed by her physician!

On her initial psychiatric evaluation, Susan stated that Diazepam helped her to be "fully awake," "to get energy," and "to get motivated." She would take a dose immediately upon awakening, and thereafter every two to three hours. Susan reported that when she failed to take the drug, she would experience dizziness, vomiting, headaches, and drowsiness.

Following her visit to a psychiatrist, she was admitted to hospital, where she displayed extreme restlessness, anxiety, trembling, irritability, and suspiciousness. She was put on a gradual dose reduction to withdraw her from the medication. During this process, Susan was administered other (nonaddictive) medications to minimize her experience of anxiety and agitation, and to prevent seizures, which can occur during benzodiazepine withdrawal.

Susan cooperated fully with the gradual tapering of her Diazepam for five days. Despite her intense craving for the medication, she was willing to remain at the lower dose. However, on the fifth day, Susan refused to go through gradual withdrawal any longer and demanded abrupt cessation of the medication. At this point her withdrawal symptoms became quite severe: insomnia, trembling, agitation, emotional lability, photophobia (aversion to light), blurred vision, pain behind the eyes, headaches, nausea, and muscle and stomach cramps. She became very paranoid, hostile, irritable, and tearful. Susan developed visual hallucinations (e.g., seeing insects) and illusions (e.g., seeing the sink faucet moving). These symptoms subsided over two weeks.

On a follow-up visit to her psychiatrist a week after her discharge, Susan reported that she had been free of all the withdrawal symptoms she experienced while in hospital. Her sleep had also returned to normal.

Source: Adapted from Agrawal, 1978.

Susan's case illustrates the features of benzodiazepine dependence. High tolerance developed in that Susan escalated her dose over time to achieve the original effect, to the point that she was able to take very large doses without drowsiness. She experienced a very severe set of benzodiazepine withdrawal symptoms during her hospitalization—some of which she had experienced previously in milder form when she missed a dose of her medication at home. The author of this case study published this report to warn other doctors about the potential for addiction to this type of medication and to argue against its indiscriminate prescription by physicians (Agrawal, 1978). We return to this theme in our From the Inside box at the end of this chapter in which we describe some of the experiences of Joan Gadsby in her struggle with benzodiazepine dependence (see page 432).

In addition to the potential for dependence with the anxiolytics, reports on the misuse of Rohypnol show how dangerous these drugs can be. Rohypnol (otherwise known as "roofies") gained a following among teenagers in the 1990s because it has the same effect as alcohol without the telltale odour. However, disturbing reports have emerged of men giving the drug to women without their knowledge, making it easier for them to engage in date rape; this led to Rohypnol being nicknamed the "date rape drug" (Ramsey, 2003; Smith & Wesson, 1999).

Clinical Description

At low doses, barbiturates relax the muscles and can produce a mild feeling of well-being. However, larger doses can have results similar to those of heavy drinking: slurred speech and problems walking, concentrating, and working. At extremely high doses the diaphragm muscles can relax so much as to cause death by suffocation. In fact, overdosing on barbiturates is a common means of suicide.

Like the barbiturates, benzodiazepines are used to calm an individual and induce sleep. In addition, drugs in this class are prescribed as muscle relaxants and anticonvulsants (antiseizure medications; Ciraulo & Sarid-Segal, 2009). People who use them for nonmedical reasons report first feeling a pleasant high and a reduction of inhibition, similar to the effects of drinking alcohol. However, with continued use, tolerance and dependence can develop. Users who try to stop taking the drug experience symptoms like those of alcohol withdrawal (anxiety, insomnia, tremors, and delirium; Westra & Stewart, 1998).

The *DSM-IV-TR* criteria for sedative, hypnotic, and anxiolytic drug use disorders do not differ substantially from those for alcohol disorders (see DSM Table 11.4). Both include maladaptive behavioural changes such as inappropriate sexual or aggressive behaviour, variable moods, impaired judgment, impaired social or occupational functioning, slurred speech, motor coordination problems, and unsteady gait.

Like alcohol, sedative, hypnotic, and anxiolytic drugs affect the brain by acting on the GABA neurotransmitter system (Ciraulo & Sarid-Segal, 2009); as a result, when people combine alcohol with any of these drugs, there can be synergistic effects (Fils-Aime, 1993). In other words, if you drink alcohol after taking a benzodiazepine or barbiturate, the total effects can reach dangerous levels. One theory about actress Marilyn Monroe's death in 1962 is that she combined alcohol with too many barbiturates and unintentionally killed herself. Actor Heath Ledger's death in 2008 was attributed to the combined effects of oxycodone and a variety of other barbiturates and benzodiazepines.

Statistics

Barbiturate use has declined and benzodiazepine use has increased since 1960 (Warneke, 1991). A study by Neutel (2005), which used

DSM-IV-TR	**Table 11.4** Criteria for Alcohol Intoxication

A. Recent ingestion of alcohol

B. Clinically significant maladaptive behavioural or psychological changes (e.g., inappropriate sexual or aggressive behaviour, mood lability, impaired judgment, impaired social or occupational functioning) that developed during, or shortly after, alcohol use

C. One or more of the following signs, developing during, or shortly after, alcohol use:
1. Slurred speech
2. Incoordination
3. Unsteady gait
4. Nystagmus (involuntary rapid and repetitive movement of the eyes)
5. Impairment in attention or memory
6. Stupor or coma

D. The symptoms are not due to a general medical condition and are not better accounted for by another mental disorder

Source: Reprinted with permission from the *Diagnostic and Statistical Manual of Mental Disorders,* Fourth Edition, Text Revision, (Copyright © 2000). American Psychiatric Association.

the National Population Health Survey data, showed that 4 percent of Canadians use benzodiazepines, with higher rates among women, the elderly, and smokers. A study by Ruiz, Offermanns, Lanctot, and Busto (1993) compared rates of benzodiazepine prescriptions in Canada (a developed country) and Chile (a developing country) over five years. Total benzodiazepine use was similar in the two countries, but the patterns of use of specific benzodiazepines differed substantially. For example, over the five years, a substantial increase in rapidly eliminated benzodiazepines (like Halcion) was observed in Canada, whereas a substantial increase in slowly eliminated benzodiazepines (like Valium) was observed in Chile. This difference is significant because the slowly eliminated benzodiazepines are associated with a greater risk of falls than the rapidly eliminated benzodiazepines (Ray, Thapa, & Gideon, 2000).

Stimulants

Of all the psychoactive drugs used in Canada, the most commonly consumed are the stimulants. Included in this group are caffeine (in coffee, chocolate, and many soft drinks), nicotine (in tobacco products such as cigarettes), amphetamines, and cocaine. You probably used caffeine when you got up this morning. In contrast to the depressant drugs, stimulants—as their name suggests—make you more alert and energetic. They have a long history of use. Chinese physicians, for example, have used an amphetamine compound called Ma-huang for more than 5000 years (King & Ellinwood, 1997). Ma-huang (or ephedra) was marketed in North America in health food stores as a dietary supplement and weight-loss aid. Ma-huang made the news when its manufacture and sale was banned, given its links to serious health problems (e.g., it can cause a serious rise in blood pressure) and even deaths (Canadian Press, 2003). The case of Ma-huang provides an important illustration of how natural compounds can be just as dangerous as manufactured drugs. We describe several stimulants and their effects on behaviour, mood, and cognition.

Amphetamine Use Disorders

At low doses, amphetamines can induce feelings of elation and vigour, and can reduce fatigue. You literally feel "up." However, after a period of elevation, you come back down and "crash," feeling depressed or tired. In sufficient quantities, stimulants can lead to **amphetamine use disorders**.

Amphetamines are manufactured in the laboratory; they were first synthesized in 1887 and later used as a treatment for asthma and as a nasal decongestant (McCann & Ricaurte, 2009). Because amphetamines also reduce appetite, some people take them to lose weight. Long-haul truck drivers, pilots, and some university students trying to "pull all-nighters" use amphetamines to get that extra energy boost and stay awake. In fact, the use of amphetamines by two U.S. pilots to stay awake has been implicated in the "friendly fire" death of four Canadian soldiers in Afghanistan in 2002. The case increased awareness of how common amphetamine use is among pilots and has raised consciousness of possible negative consequences of this practice such as impaired judgment (Campbell, 2003). Amphetamines are prescribed for people with narcolepsy, a sleep disorder characterized by excessive sleepiness (see Chapter 8). Some of these drugs (Ritalin) are even given to children with attention deficit/hyperactivity disorder (discussed in Chapter 14), although these too are being abused for their psycho-stimulant effects (Barrett, Darredeau, & Pihl, 2006a).

The *DSM-IV-TR* diagnostic criteria for amphetamine intoxication include significant behavioural symptoms, such as euphoria or affective blunting, changes in sociability, interpersonal sensitivity, anxiety, tension, anger, stereotyped behaviours, impaired judgment, and impaired social or occupational functioning. In addition, physiological symptoms occur during or shortly after amphetamine or related substances are ingested, including heart rate or blood pressure changes, perspiration or chills, nausea or vomiting, weight loss, muscular weakness, respiratory depression, chest pain, seizures, or coma. The danger in using amphetamines and the other stimulants is their negative effects, like those experienced by the pilots involved in the friendly fire incident in Afghanistan. Severe intoxication or overdose can cause hallucinations, panic, agitation, and paranoid delusions (Mack et al., 2003). Amphetamine tolerance builds quickly, making it doubly dangerous. Withdrawal often results in apathy, prolonged periods of sleep, irritability, and depression.

Periodically, certain "designer drugs" appear in local mini-epidemics (Morgan, 1997). An amphetamine called methylene-dioxymethamphetamine (MDMA), first synthesized in 1912 in Germany, was used as an appetite suppressant (McCann & Ricaurte, 2009). Recreational use of this drug, now commonly called Ecstasy, rose sharply in the late 1980s. Among Toronto students surveyed in 1999, past-year use of Ecstasy was 7 percent, the highest rate observed in a gradual upward trend since 1991 (Bernstein, Adlaf, & Paglia, 2002). Rates may be much higher in certain subcultures. For example, a study by Dalhousie clinical psychologist Sean Barrett and his colleagues examined drug use among rave attendees in Montréal. They found that 65 percent of rave-goers had used Ecstasy (Gross, Barrett, Shestowsky, & Pihl, 2002). The effects of this drug are best described by a user: "just like speed but without the comedown, and you feel warm and trippy like acid, but without the possibility of a major freak-out"

▲ Designer drugs, especially Ecstasy, are popular among young people.

(O'Hagan, 1992, p. 10). A purified crystallized form of amphetamine, called "ice," is ingested through smoking. This drug causes marked aggressive tendencies and stays in the system longer than cocaine, making it particularly dangerous (Stein & Ellinwood, 1993). However enjoyable these new amphetamines may be in the short term, the potential for users to become dependent on them is extremely high, with great risk for long-term difficulties. Moreover, death can result: in 1999, there were nine MDMA-related deaths in Ontario (Bernstein et al., 2002).

Amphetamines stimulate the central nervous system by enhancing the activity of norepinephrine and dopamine. Specifically, amphetamines help the release of these neurotransmitters and block their reuptake, thereby making more of them available throughout the system (McCann & Ricaurte, 2009). Too much amphetamine—and therefore too much dopamine and norepinephrine—can lead to hallucinations and delusions. As we see in Chapter 13, this effect has stimulated theories on the causes of schizophrenia, which can also include hallucinations and delusions.

Cocaine Use Disorders

The use and misuse of drugs, such as those leading to **cocaine use disorders**, wax and wane according to societal fashion, moods,

Chris Lisle/CORBIS Canada

▲ For centuries, Latin Americans have chewed coca leaves to get relief from hunger and fatigue.

and sanctions (Uddo, Malow, & Sutker, 1993). Cocaine replaced amphetamines as the stimulant of choice in the 1970s (Jaffe, Rawson, & Ling, 2005). Cocaine is derived from the leaves of the coca plant, a flowering bush indigenous to South America.

Latin Americans have chewed coca leaves for centuries to get relief from hunger and fatigue (Gootenberg, 2009). Cocaine was introduced into North America in the late 19th century and was widely used from then until the 1920s. In1885, Parke, Davis & Co. manufactured coca and cocaine in 15 different forms, including coca-leaf cigarettes and cigars, inhalants, and crystals. For people who couldn't afford these products, a cheaper alternative was in Coca-Cola, which up until 1903 contained 60 milligrams of cocaine per 240 millilitre serving (Weiss & Iannucci, 2009).

Clinical Description

Like the amphetamines, in small amounts cocaine increases alertness, produces euphoria, increases blood pressure and pulse, and causes insomnia and loss of appetite (see DSM Table 11.5). Remember that Danny snorted (inhaled) cocaine when he partied through the night with his friends. He later said the drug made

him feel powerful and invincible—the only way he really felt self-confident. The effects of cocaine are short lived; for Danny they lasted less than an hour, and he had to snort repeatedly to keep himself up. During these binges he often became paranoid, experiencing exaggerated fears that he would be caught or that someone would steal his cocaine. Such paranoia is common among cocaine abusers, occurring in two-thirds or more (Mack et al., 2003; Satel, 1992). Cocaine also makes the heart beat more rapidly and irregularly, and it can have fatal consequences, depending on a person's physical condition and the amount of the drug ingested.

We saw that alcohol can damage the developing fetus. It has also been suspected that the use of cocaine (especially crack) by pregnant women may adversely affect their babies. Susan Potter of Acadia University, Philip Zelazo of McGill University, and their colleagues (Potter, Zelazo, Stack, & Papageorgiou, 2000) conducted a carefully controlled study of the cognitive effects of cocaine exposure on the developing fetus. They found subtle deficits in auditory information processing in the cocaine-exposed infants that may help explain the growing evidence that fetal cocaine exposure is associated with subsequent language deficits among children exposed to this drug while still developing in the mother's uterus (Potter et al., 2000).

Statistics

Cocaine use across most age groups in Canada has decreased in recent years. Surveys continue to indicate low levels of past-year cocaine use in the general population in Canada. For example, a 1998–1999 Toronto survey found that about 1 percent of adults

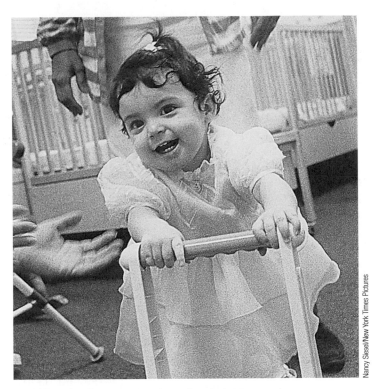

▲ This little girl's mother used cocaine during her pregnancy. Research continues into the effects of the drug on children of dependent mothers.

Nancy Siesel/New York Times Pictures

and about 6 percent of students used cocaine in the past year (Bernstein et al., 2002). Cocaine is most often snorted through the nose, but it may also be injected. In Vancouver, 80 percent of needle exchange clients inject cocaine (Strathdee et al., 1997). In Montréal, this figure is 70 percent (Hankins, 1997), and in Halifax it is 52 percent (Grandy, 1995). Crack cocaine is a crystallized form of cocaine that is smoked rather than snorted or injected (Closser, 1992). Surveys in Toronto indicate that use of crack cocaine is reported by fewer than 1 percent of adults and by about 2 percent of students (Bernstein et al., 2002).

Cocaine is in the same group of stimulants as amphetamines because it has similar effects on the brain. The "up" seems to come primarily from the effect of cocaine on the dopamine system. Cocaine enters the bloodstream and is carried to the brain. There, the cocaine molecules block the reuptake of dopamine. As you know, neurotransmitters released at the synapse stimulate the next neuron and then are recycled back to the original neuron. Cocaine seems to bind to places where dopamine neurotransmitters re-enter their home neuron, blocking their reuptake by the neuron. The dopamine that cannot be taken in by the neuron remains in the synapse, causing repeated stimulation of the next neuron. This stimulation of the dopamine neurons in the "pleasure pathway" (the site in the brain that seems to be involved in the experience of pleasure) causes the high associated with cocaine use.

As late as the 1980s, many felt cocaine was a wonder drug that produced feelings of euphoria without being addictive (Weiss & Iannucci, 2009). Such a conservative source as the *Comprehensive Textbook of Psychiatry* in 1980 indicated that "taken no more than two or three times per week, cocaine creates no serious prob-

lems" (Grinspoon & Bakalar, 1980). Just imagine—a drug that gives you extra energy, helps you think clearly and more creatively, and lets you accomplish more throughout the day, all without any negative side effects! In our highly competitive and complex technological society, this would be a dream come true. But, as you probably realize, such temporary benefits have a high cost. Cocaine fooled us. Dependence does not resemble that of many other drugs early on, and typically people only find that they have a growing inability to resist taking more (Weiss & Iannucci, 2009). Few negative effects are noted at first; however, with continued use, sleep is disrupted, increased tolerance causes a need for higher doses, paranoia and other negative symptoms set in, and the cocaine user gradually becomes socially isolated.

Again, Danny's case illustrates this pattern. He was a social user for a number of years, using cocaine only with friends and only occasionally. Eventually he had more frequent episodes of excessive use or binges, and he found himself increasingly craving the drug between binges. After the binges, Danny would crash and sleep. Cocaine withdrawal isn't like that of alcohol. Instead of rapid heartbeat, tremors, or nausea, withdrawal from cocaine produces pronounced feelings of apathy and boredom. Think for a minute about how dangerous this type of withdrawal is. First, you're bored with everything and find little pleasure in the everyday activities of work or relationships. The one thing that can "bring you back to life" is cocaine. As you can imagine, a particularly vicious cycle develops: Cocaine is abused, withdrawal causes apathy, cocaine abuse resumes. The atypical withdrawal pattern misled people into believing that cocaine was not addictive. We now know that cocaine abusers go through patterns of tolerance and withdrawal comparable to those experienced by abusers of other psychoactive drugs (Weiss & Iannucci, 2009).

Nicotine Use Disorders

When you think of addicts, what image comes to mind? Do you see dirty and dishevelled people huddled on an old mattress in an abandoned building, waiting for the next fix? Do you picture businesspeople huddled outside a city building on a rainy afternoon furtively smoking cigarettes? Both these images are accurate, because the nicotine in tobacco is a psychoactive substance that produces patterns of dependence, tolerance, and withdrawal—**nicotine use disorders**—comparable to the other drugs we have discussed so far (Hughes, 2009). In 1942, Scottish physician Lennox Johnson "shot up" nicotine extract and found after 80 injections that he liked it more than cigarettes and felt deprived without it (Kanigel, 1988). This colourless, oily liquid is what gives smoking its pleasurable qualities.

The tobacco plant is indigenous to North America, and First Nations people cultivated and smoked the leaves centuries ago. Today, about one-quarter of all Canadians smoke, which is down from the 49.5 percent who smoked in 1965 (Physicians for a Smoke-Free Canada, 2002).

The *DSM-IV-TR* does not describe an intoxication pattern for nicotine. Rather, it lists withdrawal symptoms, which include depressed mood, insomnia, irritability, anxiety, difficulty concentrating, restlessness, and increased appetite and weight gain. Nicotine in small doses stimulates the central nervous system; it can also relieve stress and improve mood. But it can also cause high

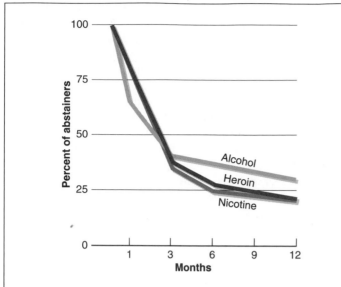

■ FIGURE 11.7 Relapse rates for nicotine compared with alcohol and heroin. Smokers trying to give up cigarettes backslide about as frequently as alcoholics and heroin addicts.

Source: Adapted from "Nicotine Becomes Addictive" by R. Kanigel, 1988, *Science Illustrated*, October/November, pp.12–14, 19–21. © 1988 *Science Illustrated*. Reprinted with permission.

blood pressure and increase the risk of heart disease and cancer (Stewart, Cutler, & Rosen, 2009). High doses can blur your vision, cause confusion, lead to convulsions, and sometimes even cause death. Once smokers are dependent on nicotine, going without it causes these withdrawal symptoms (Slade, 1999). If you doubt the addictive power of nicotine, consider that the rate of relapse among people trying to give up drugs is equivalent among those using alcohol, heroin, and cigarettes (see ■ Figure 11.7).

Nicotine is inhaled into the lungs, where it enters the bloodstream. Only 7 to 19 seconds after a person inhales the smoke, the nicotine reaches the brain (Benowitz, 1996). Nicotine appears to stimulate specific receptors—nicotinic acetylcholine receptors—in the midbrain reticular formation and the limbic system, the site of the "pleasure pathway" mentioned earlier (McGehee, Heath, Gelber, Devay, & Role, 1995). Some evidence also points to how nicotine may affect the fetal brain, possibly increasing the likelihood that children of mothers who smoke during pregnancy will smoke later in life (Kandel, Wu, & Davies, 1994). Smokers dose themselves throughout the day in an effort to keep nicotine at a steady level in the bloodstream (10 to 50 nanograms per millilitre; Dalack, Glassman, & Covey, 1993).

New research that may help explain why cigarette smoking and alcohol drinking are so commonly paired has recently emerged. A lab-based study by Sean Barrett and colleagues showed that nicotine administration (as delivered through tobacco smoke) leads to increases in alcohol consumption among a significant majority of smokers (Barrett, Tichauer, Leyton, & Pihl, 2006b). The authors suggest that one potential explanation for the finding that nicotine increases alcohol responding is that simultaneous smoking may make drinking alcohol more rewarding in terms of effects on the dopamine reward system (Barrett et al., 2006b).

Smoking has also been linked with signs of negative affect, such as depression, anxiety, and anger (Rasmusson, Anderson, Krishnan-Sarin, Wu, & Paliwal, 2006). For example, many people who quit smoking but later resume report that feelings of depression or anxiety were responsible for the relapse (Hughes, 2009). This finding suggests that nicotine may help improve mood.

Severe depression is found to occur significantly more often among people with nicotine dependence (Breslau, Kilbey, & Andreski, 1993). Does this mean that smoking causes depression or depression causes smoking? There is a complex and bi-directional relationship between cigarette smoking and negative affect (Leventhal, Kahler, Ray, & Zimmerman, 2009). In other words, being depressed increases your risk of becoming dependent on nicotine, and at the same time, being dependent on nicotine will increase your risk of becoming depressed. Genetic studies suggest that a genetic vulnerability combined with certain life stresses may combine to make you vulnerable to both nicotine dependence and depression (e.g., Kendler et al., 1993).

Caffeine Use Disorders

Caffeine is the most common of the psychoactive substances, used regularly by 90 percent of all North Americans (Juliano & Griffiths, 2009). Called the "gentle stimulant" because it is thought to be the least harmful of all the addictive drugs, caffeine can still lead to **caffeine use disorders**. This drug is found in tea, coffee, many cola drinks, and cocoa products. High levels of caffeine are added to the "energy drinks" that are widely consumed in North America today but are banned in some European countries (including France, Denmark, and Norway) due to health concerns.

As most of you have experienced firsthand, caffeine in small doses can elevate your mood and decrease fatigue. In larger doses, it can make you feel jittery and can cause insomnia. Because caffeine takes a relatively long time to leave our bodies (it has a blood half-life of about six hours), sleep can be disturbed if the caffeine is ingested in the hours close to bedtime. This effect is especially pronounced among those already suffering from insomnia (Saln-Pascual, Castao, Shiromani, Valencia-Flores, & Campos, 2006). As with the other psychoactive drugs, people react differently to caffeine; some are very sensitive to it and others can consume relatively large amounts with little effect (see DSM Table 11.6). Research suggests that moderate use of caffeine (a cup of coffee per day) by pregnant women does not harm the developing fetus (CARE Study Group, 2008).

ABNORMAL PSYCHOLOGY Video

Nicotine Dependence

"You simply can't focus on the nicotine itself. Many of the medications do that—they focus on replacing the nicotine, such as nicotine gum or the patch—and that's very valuable, but you really have to focus on all the triggers, the cues, and the environment."

Go to Psychology CourseMate at www.abnormalpsych3ce.nelson.com to watch this video.

DSM-IV-TR	**Table 11.6** Criteria for Caffeine Intoxication

A. Recent consumption of caffeine, usually in excess of 250 mg (e.g., more than two to three cups of brewed coffee)

B. Five (or more) of the following signs, developing during, or shortly after, caffeine use:

1. Restlessness
2. Nervousness
3. Excitement
4. Insomnia
5. Flushed face
6. Diuresis
7. Gastrointestinal disturbance
8. Muscle twitching
9. Rambling flow of thought and speech
10. Tachycardia or cardiac arrhythmia
11. Periods of inexhaustibility
12. Psychomotor agitation

C. The symptoms in Criterion B cause clinically significant distress or impairment in social, occupational, or other important areas of functioning

D. The symptoms are not due to a general medical condition and are not better accounted for by another mental disorder (e.g., anxiety disorder)

Source: Reprinted with permission from the *Diagnostic and Statistical Manual of Mental Disorders,* Fourth Edition, Text Revision, (Copyright © 2000). American Psychiatric Association.

As with other stimulants, regular caffeine use can result in tolerance and dependence on the drug. Those of you who have experienced headaches, drowsiness, and a generally unpleasant mood when denied your morning coffee have had the withdrawal symptoms characteristic of this drug (Juliano & Griffiths, 2009). Caffeine's effect on the brain seems to involve the neuro-modulator *adenosine* and, to a lesser extent, the neurotransmitter *dopamine* (Herrick, Shecterle, & St. Cyr, 2009). Caffeine seems to block adenosine reuptake. However, we do not yet know the role of adenosine in brain function or whether the interruption of the adenosine system is responsible for the elation and increased energy that come with caffeine use.

Opioids

The word *opiate* refers to the natural chemicals in the opium poppy that have a narcotic effect (they relieve pain and induce sleep; see DSM Table 11.7). In some circumstances, they can cause **opioid use disorders**. The broader term *opioids* refers to the family of substances that includes natural opiates, synthetic variations (methadone, pethidine), and the comparable substances that occur naturally in the brain (enkephalins, beta-endorphins, and dynorphins; Mack et al., 2003). In *The Wizard of Oz,* the Wicked Witch of the West puts Dorothy,

DSM-IV-TR	**Table 11.7** Criteria for Opioid Intoxication

A. Recent use of an opioid

B. Clinically significant maladaptive behavioural or psychological changes (e.g., initial euphoria followed by apathy, dysphoria, psychomotor agitation or retardation, impaired judgment, or impaired social or occupational functioning) that developed during, or shortly after, opioid use

C. Pupillary constriction (or pupillary dilation due to anoxia from severe overdose) and one (or more) of the following signs, developing during, or shortly after, opioid use:

1. Drowsiness or coma
2. Slurred speech
3. Impairment in attention or memory

D. The symptoms are not due to a general medical condition and are not better accounted for by another mental disorder

Specify if:
    With perceptual disturbances

Source: Reprinted with permission from the *Diagnostic and Statistical Manual of Mental Disorders,* Fourth Edition, Text Revision, (Copyright © 2000). American Psychiatric Association.

Toto, and their companions to sleep by making them walk through a field of poppies, an allusion to the opium poppies used to produce morphine, codeine, and heroin.

Just as the poppies lull the Tin Man, the Scarecrow, Dorothy, the Cowardly Lion, and Toto, opiates induce euphoria, drowsiness, and slowed breathing. High doses can lead to death if respiration is completely depressed. Opiates are also *analgesics*, substances that help relieve pain. People are sometimes given morphine before and after surgery to calm them and help block pain.

A newer prescription opiate drug used in the treatment of pain is oxycodone (OxyContin). This drug appears to be of increasing concern in terms of its potential for abuse and for lethal overdose. Oxycodone has featured prominently in the news on the east coast, particularly in Cape Breton, Nova Scotia, where it has become a popular street drug. Along with other prescription

▲ Opium poppies

HLPhoto/Shutterstock

narcotics, oxycodone was linked to the death of 12 residents in 2003–2004. Although controversy continues about the degree to which these statistics represent cause for particular concern, the Nova Scotia College of Physicians and Surgeons sent out a letter to its members, providing practice guidelines to minimize inappropriate prescribing of oxycodone and thus minimize its abuse potential (Moulton, 2004). More recently, the manufacturers of oxycodone have been fined $635 million for misleading the public about the addictive properties of the drug (Lindsey, 2007).

Withdrawal from opioids can be so unpleasant that people continue to use these drugs despite a sincere desire to stop. However, barbiturate and alcohol withdrawal can be even more distressing. The perception among many people that opioid withdrawal can be life threatening stems from the experiences of heroin addicts in the 1920s and 1930s. These users had access to cheaper and purer forms of the drug than are available today, and withdrawal had more serious side effects than withdrawal from the weaker versions currently in use (McKim, 1991). Even so, people who cease or reduce their opioid intake begin to experience symptoms within 6 to 12 hours; these include excessive yawning, nausea and vomiting, chills, muscle aches, diarrhea, and insomnia—temporarily disrupting work, school, and social relationships. The symptoms can persist for one to three days, and the process is completed in about a week.

Because opiate users tend to be secretive, estimates of the exact number of people who use, abuse, or are dependent on these drugs are difficult to come by. It is known that women are at particular risk of abusing and becoming dependent on prescription opioids (e.g., codeine; Conrod, Pihl, et al., 2000). Emergency room admissions over the period between 1995 and 2002 indicate a 34.5 percent increase resulting from the most commonly abused opiate—heroin (Substance Abuse and Mental Health Services Administration, 2003).

People who use opiates face risks beyond addiction and the threat of overdose. Because these drugs are usually injected intravenously, users are at increased risk for HIV infection and therefore AIDS. In fact, a survey conducted in the late 1990s (Strathdee et al., 1997) showed that HIV incidence among injection drug users in Vancouver was the highest ever documented among injection drug users in the developed world (Wood & Kerr, 2006). Estimates of the number of injection drug users in Canada vary widely from 50 000 to 100 000, with high numbers in Vancouver and in the other major urban centres of Montréal and Toronto (CCSA, 1999). A recent epidemiological study suggests that the prevalence of HIV infection among injection drug users in Vancouver is between 17 percent and 31 percent in different subgroups (Buxton, 2005). As shown in ■ Figure 11.8, HIV infection rates are much higher among injection drug users in unstable housing situations than among those in stable housing (Wood & Kerr, 2006). The Buxton (2005) study also showed that Aboriginal injection drug users are becoming HIV positive at twice the rate of non-Aboriginal injection drug users.

The life of an opiate addict is bleak. Results from a 24-year follow-up study of more than 500 opiate addicts paints a pessimistic picture of their lives (Hser, Anglin, & Powers, 1993). At the follow-up in 1985–1986, 27.7 percent of addicts had died, and the mean age at death was only about 40 years. Almost half the deaths

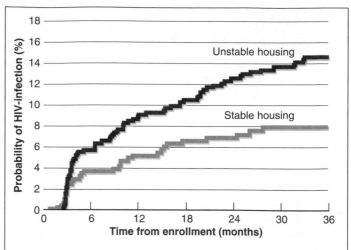

■ **FIGURE 11.8** HIV incidence rates among two groups of Vancouver injection drug users: those in stable living situations (e.g., living in a home or apartment) versus those in unstable housing situations (e.g., homeless, living in single room occupancy hotel in the downtown eastside).

Sources: "What do you do when you hit rock bottom? Responding to drugs in the City of Vancouver." Evan Wood and Thomas Kerr. *The International Journal of Drug Policy, 17* (2006).

were the results of homicide, suicide, or accident, and about a third were from drug overdose. Seven percent to 8 percent of the group had a fairly stable pattern of daily narcotic use.

The high or "rush" experienced by users comes from activation of the body's natural opioid system. In other words, the brain already has its own opioids—called enkephalins and endorphins—that provide narcotic effects (Simon, 1997). Heroin, opium, morphine, and other opiates activate this system (just as does alcohol at certain doses; Gianoulakis, 2001; Peterson et al., 1996). The discovery of the natural opioid system has allowed us to study the effects of addictive drugs on the brain and has led to important discoveries that may help us treat people dependent on these drugs.

Hallucinogens

Next we explore the substances that can lead to **hallucinogen use disorder**. They essentially change the way the user perceives the world. Sight, sound, feelings, taste, and even smell are distorted, sometimes in dramatic ways, when a person is under the influence of drugs such as marijuana and LSD.

Marijuana

Marijuana is the name given to the dried parts of the cannabis or hemp plant (its full scientific name is *Cannabis sativa*; Iversen, 2000). Cannabis grows wild throughout the tropical and temperate regions of the world, which accounts for one of its nicknames, "weed." Marijuana was the drug of choice in the 1960s and early 1970s. Although it has decreased in popularity, it is still the most routinely used illicit substance in Canada, with 10 percent of Toronto adults reporting marijuana use in a 1999 survey (Bernstein et al., 2002), and 24 percent of Vancouver adults reporting marijuana use in the more recent Canadian Community Epidemiology Network on Drug Use survey (Buxton, 2005). A cross-cultural study by ter Bogt, Schmid, and Gabhainn (2006) examined marijuana use among 15-year-olds in 31 different countries. The results showed that Canadian male adolescents had the highest prevalence of frequent cannabis use.

People who smoke marijuana often experience altered perceptions of the world (see DSM Table 11.8). Reactions to marijuana usually include mood swings. Otherwise normal experiences seem extremely funny, or the person might enter a dreamlike state where time seems to stand still. Users often report heightened sensory experiences, seeing vivid colours, or appreciating the subtleties of music. Perhaps more than any other drug, however, marijuana can produce very different reactions in people. It is not uncommon for someone to report having no reaction to the first use of the drug; it also appears that people can "turn off" the high if they are sufficiently motivated (Hall & Degenhardt, 2009). The feelings of well-being produced by small doses can change to paranoia, hallucinations, and dizziness when larger doses are taken. Research on frequent marijuana users suggests that impairments of memory, concentration, motivation, self-esteem, relationships with others, and employment are common negative outcomes of long-term use (Haas & Hendin, 1987; Roffman & Barnhart, 1987). The impairment in motivation—apathy, or unwillingness to carry out long-term plans—has sometimes been called *amotivational syndrome*, although how prevalent this problem is remains unclear (Iversen, 2000).

The evidence for marijuana tolerance is contradictory. Chronic and heavy users report tolerance, especially to the euphoric high (Mennes, Ben Abdallah, & Cottler, 2009); they are unable to reach the levels of pleasure they experienced earlier. However, evidence also indicates "reverse tolerance," when regular users experience more pleasure from the drug after repeated use. Major signs of withdrawal do not usually occur with marijuana. Chronic users who stop taking the drug report a period of irritability, restlessness, appetite loss, nausea, and difficulty sleeping

Photodisc

▲ Marijuana

(Johnson, 1991); but no evidence suggests they go through the craving and psychological dependence characteristic of other substances (Grinspoon & Bakalar, 1997).

The use of marijuana for medicinal purposes is controversial. In the United States, the media frequently describe individuals who illegally use marijuana to help ward off the nausea associated with chemotherapy or to ease the symptoms of other illnesses such as glaucoma, and the medical benefits of this drug may be promising (Grinspoon & Bakalar, 1997). Unfortunately, marijuana smoke may contain as many carcinogens as tobacco smoke, and long-term use may contribute to diseases such as lung cancer. Obviously, this potential health risk should be weighed against the benefits of using marijuana under certain medical circumstances. In 1999, Health Canada began giving exemptions on compassionate grounds to certain patients to allow them to legally use marijuana for medicinal purposes. Seriously ill people who have diseases such as multiple sclerosis, spinal cord injuries, HIV/AIDS, cancer, arthritis, and epilepsy, who are not benefiting from traditional medications, are eligible for this exemption (Pearson, 2002).

Controversy also surrounds proposals to decriminalize the use and possession of small amounts of marijuana. Back in 2004, Parliament was debating a bill that would have mandated handing out fines rather than court sentences to people found with 15 grams or less of marijuana. Although the Liberal government had put forward this bill to decriminalize possession of small quantities of marijuana before they lost power, the Conservative government has since killed that bill. At present, people gain a criminal record if they are found guilty of possession of even a small amount of marijuana (Carrigg & Luymes, 2007). Marijuana was first banned in Canada in 1923 under the Opium and Drug Act. Since 1997, marijuana has been covered by the Controlled Drugs and Substances Act. In 2000, more than 30 000 Canadians were charged with simple possession. Most of those convicted of possession did not go to jail but received a criminal record.

DSM-IV-TR	**Table 11.8** Criteria for Cannabis Intoxication

A. Recent use of cannabis

B. Clinically significant maladaptive behavioural or psychological changes (e.g., impaired motor coordination, euphoria, anxiety, sensation of slowed time, impaired judgment, social withdrawal) that developed during, or shortly after, cannabis use

C. Two (or more) of the following signs, developing within two hours of cannabis use:
  1. Conjunctival injection (i.e., bloodshot eyes)
  2. Increased appetite
  3. Dry mouth
  4. Tachycardia

D. The symptoms are not due to a general medical condition and are not better accounted for by another mental disorder

Specify if:

  With perceptual disturbances

Source: Reprinted with permission from the *Diagnostic and Statistical Manual of Mental Disorders,* Fourth Edition, Text Revision, (Copyright © 2000). American Psychiatric Association.

Those in favour of decriminalizing possession or use of small amounts of marijuana argue that the penalties have been too harsh and that people who received a criminal record for possession have had difficulties obtaining employment and travelling internationally as a consequence. Proponents also argue that government resources directed toward law enforcement could be more usefully spent on public health campaigns to educate the public about marijuana use and addiction. Those opposed to marijuana decriminalization note that when drugs are legalized, rates of use increase and that decriminalizing marijuana possession sends conflicting messages to Canadian youth. Opponents also express concern that marijuana is a "gateway drug" that can pave the way to use of harder drugs. They also cite statements made by the director of U.S. drug policy in 2002 that marijuana is the most heavily abused drug in the United States and that addiction rates have risen in recent years. Finally, critics note that since the United States is not taking similar steps, such a change in Canadian law might create difficulties for the Canada–U.S. border if smuggling marijuana from Canada to the United States were to increase as a consequence (Canada Online, 2003).

Most marijuana users inhale the drug by smoking the dried leaves in marijuana cigarettes; others use preparations such as hashish, which is the dried form of the resin in the leaves of the female plant. Marijuana contains more than 80 varieties of the chemicals called *cannabinoids*, which are believed to alter mood and behaviour. The most common of these chemicals includes the *tetrahydrocannabinols* (THC).

LSD and Other Hallucinogens

On a Monday afternoon in April 1943, Albert Hoffmann, a scientist at a large Swiss chemical company, prepared to test a newly synthesized compound. He had been studying derivatives of ergot, a fungus that grows on diseased kernels of grain, and sensed that he had missed something important in the 25th compound of the lysergic acid series. Ingesting what he thought was an infinitesimally small amount of this drug, which he referred to in his notes as LSD-25, he waited to see what subtle changes might come over him as a result. Thirty minutes later he reported no change; but some 40 minutes after taking the drug he began to feel dizzy and had a noticeable desire to laugh. Riding his bicycle home, he hallucinated that the buildings he passed were moving and melting. By the time he arrived home, he was terrified that he was losing his mind. Albert Hoffmann was experiencing the first recorded "trip" on LSD (Stevens, 1987).

LSD (*d*-lysergic acid diethylamide), sometimes referred to as "acid," is the most common hallucinogenic drug. It is produced synthetically in laboratories, although naturally occurring derivatives of this grain fungus (ergot) have been found historically. In Europe during the Middle Ages, an outbreak of illnesses occurred as a result of people's eating grain that was infected with the fungus. One version of this illness—later called *ergotism*—constricted the flow of blood to the arms or legs and eventually resulted in gangrene and the loss of limbs. Another type of illness resulted in convulsions, delirium, and hallucinations. Years later, scientists connected ergot with the illnesses and began studying

▲ Canadian Olympic snowboarding champion Ross Rebagliati was stripped of his gold medal in 1998 after testing positive for marijuana. He later had his medal reinstated, as there was no policy in place for the sport stating that marijuana is a banned substance. Neither is marijuana considered performance-enhancing (Kingsley, 1998).

versions of this fungus for possible benefits. This is the type of work Albert Hoffmann was engaged in when he discovered LSD's hallucinogenic properties.

LSD remained in the laboratory until the 1960s, when it was first produced illegally for recreational use. The mind-altering effects of the drug suited the social effort to reject established culture and enhanced the search for enlightenment that characterized the mood and behaviour of many people during the decade. The late Timothy Leary, at the time a Harvard research professor, first used LSD in 1961 and immediately began a movement to have every child and adult try the drug and "turn on, tune in, and drop out."

During this time, LSD was also being experimented with in the context of therapy. For example, based on the spirituality theory of sobriety (i.e., that spirituality can induce sobriety from alcohol among those with alcohol disorders), some reasoned that therapists could exploit the spiritual aspect of the LSD trip to assist in recovery from alcoholism. In the 1950s, Dr. Humphrey Osmond performed an experiment to test this theory on a sample of 1000 patients with a history of severe alcoholism receiving treatment at the Weyburn Hospital in Saskatchewan. Participants were administered a single high dose of LSD. Osmond reported that 50 percent did not drink alcohol again, leading him to argue strongly for the efficacy of this approach (Lee & Shlain, 1985). In fact, William (Bill) Wilson, co-founder of Alcoholics Anonymous (AA), is known to have experimented with and advocated this controversial approach to the treatment of alcoholism (Roberts & Hruby, 1984).

A number of other hallucinogens exist, some occurring naturally in a variety of plants: *psilocybin* (found in certain species of mushrooms), *lysergic acid amide* (found in the seeds of the morning glory plant), *dimethyltryptamine* (DMT; found in the bark of the Virola tree, which grows in South and Central America), *mescaline* (found in the peyote cactus plant), and *phenecyclidine* (PCP; processed synthetically).

The *DSM-IV-TR* diagnostic criteria for hallucinogen intoxication are similar to those for marijuana (see DSM Table 11.9 on page 413) and so they are not provided separately here. These criteria include perceptual changes such as the subjective intensification of perceptions, depersonalization, and hallucinations. Physical symptoms include pupillary dilation, rapid heartbeat, sweating, and blurred vision (American Psychiatric Association, 2000c). Many users have written about hallucinogens, and they describe a variety of experiences. The kinds of sensory distortions reported by Hoffmann are characteristic reactions. People tell of watching intently as a friend's ear grows and bends in beautiful spirals or of looking at the bark of a tree and seeing little civilizations living there. These people will tell you that they usually know what they are seeing isn't real, but that it looks as real as anything they have ever seen. But many also recount experiences that are more intense than hallucinations, with an emotional content that sometimes takes on religious proportions.

Tolerance develops quickly to many of the hallucinogens, including LSD, psilocybin, and mescaline (Jones, 2009). If taken repeatedly over several days, these drugs completely lose their effectiveness. However, sensitivity returns after about a week of abstinence. For most hallucinogens, no withdrawal symptoms are reported. Even so, a number of concerns have been expressed about their use. One is the possibility of psychotic reactions. Stories in the press about people jumping out of windows because they believed they could fly or stepping into moving traffic with the mistaken idea that they couldn't be hurt make for sensational reading, but little evidence suggests that using hallucinogens produces a greater risk than being drunk or under the influence of any other drug. People do report having "bad trips"; these are the sort of frightening episodes in which clouds turn into threatening monsters or deep feelings of paranoia take over. Usually someone on a bad trip can be "talked down" by supportive people who provide constant reassurance that the experience is the temporary effect of the drug and it will wear off in a few hours.

▲ The psychedelic art of the 1960s reflects the visual distortions that result from taking hallucinogens.

We still do not fully understand how LSD and the other hallucinogens affect the brain. Most of these drugs bear some resemblance to neurotransmitters; LSD, psilocybin, lysergic acid amide, and DMT are chemically similar to serotonin; mescaline resembles norepinephrine; and several other hallucinogens we have not discussed are similar to acetylcholine. However, the mechanisms responsible for the hallucinations and other perceptual changes that users experience remain unknown.

Other Drugs of Abuse

Other substances are used by individuals to alter sensory experiences. These drugs do not fit neatly into the classes of substances we just described but are nonetheless of great concern because they can be physically damaging to those who ingest them. We briefly describe *inhalants*, *steroids*, and a group of drugs commonly referred to as *designer drugs*.

Inhalants include a variety of substances found in volatile solvents—making them available to breathe into the lungs directly. Among the more common inhalants are spray paint, hair spray, paint thinner, gasoline, amyl nitrate, nitrous oxide ("laughing gas"), nail polish remover, felt-tipped markers, airplane glue, contact cement, dry-cleaning fluid, and spot remover (Sakai & Crowley, 2009). Inhalant use is most commonly observed among young males (aged 13 to 15) who are economically disadvantaged (Franklin & Frances, 1999). In Canada, inhalant use is a particular problem among Aboriginal youth (Coleman, Charles, & Collins, 2001). These drugs are rapidly absorbed into the bloodstream through the lungs by inhaling them from containers or on a cloth held up to the mouth and nose. The high associated with the use of inhalants resembles that of alcohol intoxication and usually includes dizziness, slurred speech, incoordination, euphoria, and lethargy (American Psychiatric Association, 2000c). Users build up a tolerance to the drugs, and withdrawal—which involves sleep disturbance, tremors, irritability, and nausea—can last from two to five days. Unfortunately, use can also increase aggressive and antisocial behaviour, and long-term use can damage bone marrow, the kidneys, the liver, and the brain (Sakai & Crowley, 2009).

Anabolic-androgenic steroids (more commonly referred to as steroids or "roids") are derived from or are a synthesized form of the hormone testosterone (Pandina & Hendren, 1999). The legitimate medical uses of these drugs focus on people with asthma, anemia, and breast cancer, and males with inadequate sexual development. However, the anabolic action of these drugs (that can produce increased body mass) has resulted in their illicit use by those wanting to bulk up and improve their physical abilities. Some estimates suggest that approximately 2 percent of males will use the drug illegally at some point in their lives (Kanayama, Brower, Wood, Hudson, & Pope Jr., in press; Pandina & Hendren, 1999). Users sometimes administer the drug on a schedule of several weeks or months followed by a break from its use—called "cycling"—or combine several types of steroids—called "stacking." Steroid use differs from other drug use because the substance does not produce a desirable high but instead is used to enhance performance and body size. One well-known Canadian example involves sprinter Ben Johnson who won the 100-metre dash at the 1988 Seoul Olympic Games. He was later stripped of his gold medal after officials found he had taken anabolic steroids to enhance his performance (BBC, 2004). Research on the long-term effects of steroid use suggests that mood disturbances are common (e.g., depression, anxiety, and panic attacks; Pope & Brower, 2009), and there is a concern that more serious physical consequences may result from its regular use.

The term *designer drugs* is applied to a growing group of drugs developed by pharmaceutical companies to target specific diseases and disorders. It was only a matter of time before some would use the developing technology to design "recreational drugs." We have already described one of the more common illicit designer drugs—methylene-dioxymethamphetamine (MDMA, or Ecstasy)—in the section on stimulants. This amphetamine is one of a small but feared growing list of related substances that includes 3,4-methelenedioxyeth-amphetamine (MDEA or Eve), and 2-(4-Bromo-2,5-dimethoxy-phenyl)-ethylamine (BDMPEA or Nexus). Their ability to heighten a person's auditory and visual perception, as well as the senses of taste and touch, have been incorporated into the activities of those who attend nightclubs, all-night dance parties (known as raves), or large social gatherings of primarily gay men (called circuit parties; McDowell, 1999).

Another drug associated with the "drug club" scene is ketamine (street names include K, Special K, and Cat Valium), a dissociative anesthetic that produces a sense of detachment along with a reduced awareness of pain (McDowell, 1999). Gamma hydroxy-butyrate (GHB, or liquid Ecstasy) is a central nervous system depressant that was marketed in health food stores in the 1980s as a means of stimulating muscle growth. Users report that, at low doses, it can produce a state of relaxation and increased tendency to verbalize, but at higher doses or in combination with alcohol or other drugs, it can result in seizures, severe respiratory depression, and coma. Use of all these drugs can result in tolerance and dependence, and their increasing popularity among adolescents and young adults raises significant public health concerns.

Concept Check | 11.2

Identify the terms relating to substance abuse from the following descriptions.

1. These drugs influence perception, distorting feelings, sights, sounds, and smells.
2. Greater and greater amounts of a substance are required to achieve the same effect.
3. These substances affect behaviour, cognition, and mood. Many accepted, commonly used substances are in this category.
4. An unpleasant physical response occurs when a dependent user stops taking a substance.
5. Substances that include alcohol, reduce arousal, and cause relaxation.

Causes

People continue to use psychoactive drugs for their effects on mood, perception, and behaviour despite the obvious negative consequences of abuse and dependence. We saw that. despite his clear potential as an individual, Danny continued to use drugs to his detriment. Various factors help explain why people like Danny persist in using drugs. Drug abuse and dependence, once thought to be the result of moral weakness, are now believed to be influenced by a combination of biological and psychosocial factors.

Why do some people use psychoactive drugs without abusing or becoming dependent on them? Why do some people stop using these drugs or use them in moderate amounts after being dependent on them, and others continue a lifelong pattern of dependence despite their efforts to stop? These questions continue to occupy the time and attention of researchers throughout the world.

Biological Dimensions

Familial and Genetic Influences

In 2007, when American model and television personality Anna Nicole Smith died from an apparently accidental overdose of at least nine prescription medications—including methadone,

Valium, and the sedative chloral hydrate—the unfortunate news created a media sensation. The tragedy was compounded by the fact that, just months before, her only son Daniel had died, also from an apparent drug overdose. Did the son inherit a vulnerability to addiction from his mother? Did he pick up Anna Nicole's habits from living with her over the years? Is it just a coincidence that both mother and son were so involved with drugs?

As you already have seen throughout this book, many of the psychological disorders are influenced in important ways by genetics. Mounting evidence indicates that drug abuse generally, and alcohol abuse specifically, follows this pattern. A great deal of animal research confirms the importance of genetic influences on substance abuse (Crabbe, Belknap, & Buck, 1994). Work with humans (twin, family, and adoption studies) indicates that certain people may be genetically vulnerable to drug abuse (Strain, 2009). Twin studies of smoking, for example, find a moderate genetic influence (Hardie, Moss, & Lynch, 2006; McCaffery, Papandonatos, Stanton, Lloyd-Richardson, & Niaura, 2008). However, most genetic data on substance abuse come from research on alcoholism, which is widely studied because alcohol use is legal and a great many people are dependent on it (Gordis, 2000b; Lerman et al., 1999). Among men, both twin and adoption studies suggest genetic factors play a role in alcoholism (McGue, 1999). The research on women, however, is sometimes contradictory. Several studies suggest that genetics has relatively little influence on alcoholism in women (e.g., McGue, Pickens, & Svikis, 1992), and others suggest the disorder may be inherited in some form (e.g., Pickens et al., 1991).

A group of researchers—the Collaborative Study on the Genetics of Alcoholism (COGA)—have worked together to search for the genes that may influence alcoholism. Two studies have pointed to genes that may influence alcoholism on chromosomes 1, 2, 7, and 11, and a gene on chromosome 4 that may serve to protect people from becoming dependent (Long et al., 1998; Reich et al., 1998). As the search for the genes responsible for alcoholism continues, the next obvious question is how these genes work to influence addiction—a field of research called functional genomics.

One genetic factor that appears to be involved in alcoholism involves the body's ability to metabolize alcohol. The liver produces an enzyme called **alcohol dehydrogenase (ADH)** that breaks down acetaldehyde, a byproduct of alcohol. If acetaldehyde is not broken down but builds up in the body, the person becomes very ill. The drug disulfiram (Antabuse) helps people stop drinking by chemically preventing the breakdown of acetaldehyde so that people feel sick when they drink. In some people of Asian descent, ADH seems to be absent naturally, so many Asians have difficulty metabolizing alcohol (Gordis, 2000b). The result is a physiological response, known as the skin-flushing response. It is characterized by reddening and warmth of the face, dizziness, and nausea, and is experienced by 30 percent to 50 percent of Asians. This response is thought to contribute to the relatively low rates of alcohol use disorders in Asians (Newlin, 1989).

Knowledge about the influence of genetics has increased rapidly. In 1990, a study suggested that alcoholism may be related to a particular gene, DRD2 (Blum et al., 1990). This gene appears to regulate the sensitivity of receptors to dopamine. As we see later in this chapter, the dopamine system affects the ability of drugs to provide pleasurable experiences, and the DRD2 gene was thought to influence alcoholism by increasing the positive quality of these experiences. However, more recent research disputes the role of this gene in alcoholism (Gordis, 2000b). Research is now examining whether certain genes affect the sedative-hypnotic effects of alcohol or how people experience withdrawal, and whether this influences who will ultimately become dependent (Prescott & Kendler, 1999). Genetic research to date tells us that substance abuse in general is affected by our genes, but no one gene causes substance abuse or dependence. Research suggests that genetic factors may affect how people experience certain drugs, which in turn may partly determine who will or will not become abusers.

Neurobiological Influences

For the most part, the pleasurable experiences caused by psychoactive substances partly explain why people continue to use them (Strain, 2009). In behavioural terms, people are positively reinforced for using drugs. Complex and fascinating studies indicate the brain appears to have a natural "pleasure pathway" that mediates our experience of reward. All abused substances seem to affect this internal reward centre. In other words, what psychoactive drugs may have in common is their ability to activate this reward centre and provide the user with a pleasurable experience, at least for a time.

The pleasure centre was discovered more than 50 years ago by James Olds and Peter Milner at McGill University, who studied the effects of electrical stimulation on rat brains (Olds, 1956; Olds & Milner, 1954). If certain areas were stimulated with very small amounts of electricity, the rats behaved as if they had received something very pleasant, such as food. The exact location of the area in the human brain is still subject to debate, although it is believed to include the *dopaminergic system* and its *opioid-releasing neurons*, which begin in the midbrain *ventral tegmental area* and then work their way forward through the *nucleus accumbens* and on to the frontal cortex (Korenman & Barchas, 1993).

How do different drugs that affect different neurotransmitter systems all converge to activate the pleasure pathway, which is primarily made up of dopamine-sensitive neurons? Researchers are only beginning to sort out the answers to this question, but some surprising findings have emerged in recent years. For example, we know that amphetamines and cocaine act directly on the dopamine system. Other drugs, however, appear to increase the availability of dopamine in more roundabout and intricate ways.

Another relevant issue in understanding the role of dopamine in drug rewards is the phenomenon of *sensitization*. This refers to the fact that, in animal studies, repeated exposure to stimulant drugs like amphetamines leads to an increased dopamine release when taking the drug. Isabelle Boileau, Alain Dagher, Marco Leyton, and their colleagues at the Montréal Neurological Institute have recently demonstrated this phenomenon in healthy humans. Ten participants were administered amphetamine in the laboratory on three occasions over five days. Their brain responses to amphetamine were examined using positron emission tomography

(PET; see Chapter 3) on three occasions: the first day of exposure, two weeks following the third exposure, and one year following the third exposure. Consistent with sensitization, the PET scans showed increased dopamine release to amphetamine at the two later testing times relative to the first day of amphetamine exposure. Interestingly, they also found that novelty-seekers and impulsive individuals were most prone to amphetamine sensitization (Boileau et al., 2006).

This complicated picture is far from complete. Other pleasure pathways may exist in the brain, as noted by McGill-trained drug abuse researcher Roy Wise (1988). The future should yield even more interesting insights into the interaction of drugs and the brain. One aspect that awaits explanation is how drugs not only provide pleasurable experiences (positive reinforcement) but also how they help remove unpleasant experiences such as pain, feelings of illness, or anxiety (negative reinforcement). Aspirin is a negative reinforcer: We take it not because it makes us feel good, but because it stops us from feeling bad. In much the same way, one property of the psychoactive drugs is that they stop people from feeling bad, an effect as powerful as making them feel good.

With several drugs, negative reinforcement is related to the anxiolytic effect, the ability to reduce anxiety (outlined briefly in our discussion on the sedative, hypnotic, and anxiolytic drugs). Alcohol has an anxiolytic effect. The neurobiology of how these drugs reduce anxiety seems to involve the septal–hippocampal system (Gray, 1987), which includes a large number of GABA-sensitive neurons. As noted by Robert Pihl and his colleagues (1993), certain drugs may reduce anxiety by enhancing the activity of GABA in this region, thereby inhibiting the brain's normal reaction (anxiety or fear) to anxiety-producing situations.

Researchers have identified individual differences in the way people respond to alcohol. Understanding these response differences is important because they may help explain why some people continue to use drugs until they acquire a dependence on them, whereas others stop before this happens. A number of studies have compared individuals with and without a family history of alcoholism. For example, research by Robert Pihl, Jordan Peterson, and their colleagues suggests that individuals at high familial genetic risk for alcoholism may experience more of a pleasurable response to alcohol ingestion than do others. This pleasurable response is indexed through heart rate increases to alcohol and degree of beta-endorphin release to alcohol ingestion (Peterson, Pihl, Seguin, Finn, & Stewart, 1993, Peterson et al., 1996; Stewart, Finn, & Pihl, 1992). Thus, this laboratory-based research on the effects of alcohol suggests that what may be inherited among those genetically vulnerable to alcoholism is a propensity to experience the pleasurable consequences of drinking to a greater extent than others.

Psychological Dimensions

Positive Reinforcement

We have shown that the substances people use to alter mood and behaviour have unique effects. The high from heroin differs substantially from the experience of smoking a cigarette, which in turn differs from the effects of amphetamines or LSD. Nevertheless, it is important to point out the similarities in the way people react to most of these substances. The feelings that result from using them are pleasurable in some way, and people will continue to take the drugs to recapture the pleasure. Research shows quite clearly that many of the drugs used and abused by humans also seem to be pleasurable to animals (Young & Herling, 1986). Laboratory animals will work to have injected into their bodies drugs such as cocaine, amphetamines, opiates, sedatives, and alcohol, which demonstrates that even without social and cultural influences, these drugs are pleasurable.

Human research also indicates that to some extent all the psychoactive drugs provide a pleasurable experience (Strain, 2009). People are often very inventive in how they administer these drugs in order to maximize their euphoric effects. For example, individuals who are dependent on heroin sometimes combine it with benzodiazepines (such as Valium) to intensify their pleasure (American Psychiatric Association, 2000c). Cocaine users may heat the drug and inhale the fumes in a process known as "freebasing," or use the highly concentrated form known as crack to obtain a more rapid and intense experience. Such activities tend to increase as tolerance increases and more of the substance is needed to produce the high that is the hallmark of drug use. An interesting study by Sean Barrett of Dalhousie University and his colleagues investigated patterns of polysubstance use among Canadian university students. For example, the authors found that tobacco use increases when an individual is also using alcohol, cannabis, psilocybin, MDMA, cocaine, amphetamine, LSD, or methylphenidate. They also found that alcohol, tobacco, and cannabis are frequently mixed with other substances. The authors suggest that these patterns can be explained by students' attempts to enhance the pleasurable experience with one drug, by simultaneously using another drug (Barrett et al., 2006a).

Negative Reinforcement

Most researchers have looked at how drugs help reduce unpleasant feelings through negative reinforcement. Many people are likely to initiate and continue drug use to escape from unpleasantness in their lives. In addition to the initial euphoria, many drugs provide escape from physical pain (opiates), from stress (alcohol), or from panic and anxiety (benzodiazepines). This phenomenon has been explored under a number of different names, including *tension reduction*, *negative affect*, and *self-medication*, each of which has a somewhat different focus (Strain, 2009).

Basic to many views of abuse and dependence is the premise that substance use becomes a way for users to cope with the unpleasant feelings that go along with life circumstances (Cooper, Russell, & George, 1988; Zack, Toneatto, & MacLeod, 1999). Drug use by soldiers in Vietnam is one tragic example of this phenomenon. Almost 42 percent of these mostly young men experimented with heroin, half of whom became dependent, because the drug was readily available and because of the extreme stress of the war (Jaffe et al., 1997). It is interesting that only 12 percent of these soldiers were still using heroin three years after their return home (Robins, Helzer, & Davis, 1975), which suggests that once the stressors were removed, the men no longer needed the drug to relieve their pain. People who experience trauma such as sexual abuse are more likely to abuse alcohol (Stewart, 1996). This observation emphasizes the important role played by each aspect of abuse and dependence—biological, psychological, social, and cultural—in determining who will and who will not have difficulties with these substances. Research showing that adolescents tend to use drugs as a way to cope with unpleasant feelings (Chassin, Pillow, Curran, Molina, & Barrera, 1993) suggests that to prevent people from using drugs, we may need to address influences such as stress and anxiety, a strategy we examine in our discussion on treatment.

Many people who use psychoactive substances experience an unpleasant crash after being high. So why don't they just stop taking drugs? One explanation involves an interesting integration of both the positive and negative reinforcement processes (Solomon, 1980; Solomon & Corbit, 1974). This *opponent-process theory* holds that an increase in positive feelings will be followed by an increase in negative feelings a short time later. Similarly, an increase in negative feelings will be followed by a period of positive feelings. Athletes often report feeling depressed after finally attaining a long-sought goal. The opponent-process theory claims that this mechanism is strengthened with use and weakened by disuse. So a person who has been using a drug for some time will need more of it to achieve the same results (tolerance). At the same time, the negative feelings that follow drug use tend to intensify. For many people, this is the point at which the motivation for drug taking shifts from desiring the euphoric high to alleviating the increasingly unpleasant crash. Unfortunately, the best remedy is more of the same drug—referred to as "the hair of the dog that bit you" in the case of alcohol. The sad irony here is that the very drug that can make you feel so bad is also the one thing that can take away your pain. People can become enslaved by this insidious cycle.

Researchers have also looked at substance abuse as a way of self-medicating for other problems (Conrod, Pihl, et al., 2000). If people have difficulties with anxiety, for example, they may be attracted to barbiturates, benzodiazepines, or alcohol because of their anxiety-reducing qualities. In one study, researchers were successful in treating a group of cocaine addicts who had ADHD with methylphenidate (Ritalin) (Levin, Evans, Brooks, & Garawi, 2007). They had hypothesized that these individuals used cocaine to help focus their attention. Once their ability to concentrate improved with the methylphenidate, the users reduced their use of cocaine. Research is just beginning to outline the complex interplay among stressors, negative feelings, other psychological disorders, and negative reactions to the drugs themselves as causative factors in psychoactive drug use.

Cognitive and Learning Factors

What people expect to experience when they use drugs influences how they react to them. A person who expects to be less inhibited when he or she drinks alcohol will act less inhibited whether that person actually drinks alcohol or a placebo he or she thinks is alcohol (Moss & Albery, 2009). This observation about the influence of how we think about drug use has been labelled an *expectancy effect* and has received considerable research attention.

Expectancies develop before people actually use drugs, perhaps as a result of parents' and peers' drug use, advertising, and media figures who model drug use (Moss & Albery, 2009). In one study, a large group of students in Grades 7 and 8 were given questionnaires that focused on their expectations about drinking. The researchers re-examined the students one year later to see how their expectancies predicted their later drinking (Christiansen, Smith, Roehling, & Goldman, 1989). One surprising finding was the marked increase in drinking among the students only one year later. When researchers first questioned them, about 10 percent of the students reported getting drunk two to four times per year. This number had risen to 25 percent by the next year. The students' expectations of drinking did predict who would later have drinking problems. Students who thought that drinking would improve their social behaviour and their cognitive and motor abilities (despite all evidence to the contrary) were more likely to have drinking problems one year later. These results suggest that children may begin drinking partly because they believe drinking will have positive effects.

Expectations appear to change as people have more experience with drugs, although their expectations are similar for alcohol, nicotine, marijuana, and cocaine (Simons, Dvorak, & Lau-Barraco, 2009). Some evidence from the laboratory of Peter Finn, a clinical psychologist from Montréal, points to positive expectancies—believing you will feel good if you take a drug—as an indirect influence on drug problems. In other words, what these beliefs may do is to increase the likelihood you will take certain drugs, which in turn will increase the likelihood that problems will arise (Finn, Sharkansky, Brandt, & Turcotte, 2000).

Once people stop taking drugs after prolonged or repeated use, powerful urges called "cravings" can interfere with efforts to remain off these drugs (Epstein, Marrone, Heishman, Schmittner, & Preston, 2010). If you've ever tried to give up ice cream and then found yourself compelled to have some, you have a limited idea of what it might be like to crave a drug. These urges seem to be triggered by factors such as the availability of the drug, contact with things associated with drug taking (e.g., sitting in a bar), specific moods (e.g., being depressed), or having a small dose of the drug. For example, one study used a virtual reality apparatus to simulate visual, auditory, and olfactory (an alcohol-dipped tissue) cues (Lee et al., 2009) for alcohol-dependent adults. The participants could choose among kinds of alcoholic beverages (e.g., beer, whiskey, or wine), snacks, and drinking environments (beer garden, restaurant, and pub). The researchers found significant increases in cravings for alcohol under these conditions (Lee et al., 2009). This type of technology may make it easier for clinicians to assess potential problem areas for clients, which can then be targeted to help keep them from relapsing. Research is under way to determine how cravings may work in the brain and if certain medications can be used to reduce these urges and help supplement treatment (Skinner & Aubin, 2010).

Important research by Shep Seigel, Marvin Krank, and Riley Hinson at McMaster University in the 1980s examined the role of conditioning in accounting for important aspects of addiction such as craving. If a particular stimulus (e.g., sitting in a bar, the presence of a needle in an injection drug user) is repeatedly paired with drug taking and consequent unconditioned drug effects, then that stimulus can become a conditioned stimulus signalling that the drug effect is coming (Siegel, 1982). Stimuli that can serve as such conditioned stimuli do not have to be external stimuli such as drug paraphernalia; internal stimuli can also serve as conditioned stimuli. For example, negative emotions could serve as a conditioned stimulus, if the drug user frequently takes the drug in response to an unpleasant emotional state such as anxiety (Westra & Stewart, 2002). According to the research of Shep Siegel and of many others since, with repeated learning opportunities involving pairing of the conditioned stimulus with drug taking, the drug taker will develop conditioned compensatory responses that are in the opposite direction to the drug's original (unconditioned) effect. For example, if decreased heart rate is the unconditioned drug effect, a conditioned compensatory response could involve increased heart rate. This conditioned compensatory response is initiated when the drug taker is exposed to the cues (conditioned stimulus) associated with drug taking.

This phenomenon can explain many aspects of addiction including tolerance, craving, and overdose. With respect to tolerance, as the conditioned compensatory response develops, it works against (in the opposite direction to) the unconditioned drug effect, reducing the subjective experience of the drug effect for the user. With respect to craving, when the user is exposed to cues normally associated with drug taking, this initiates the conditioned compensatory response, which is experienced subjectively as craving for the drug. Finally, with respect to overdose, it is commonly observed that heroin users, for example, are more likely to overdose when injecting in an unfamiliar environment, even when using their same dose. From the perspective of conditioning theory, this happens because the usual drug cues are not present to initiate the conditioned compensatory response and thus the user experiences the full unconditioned effect of the drug, resulting in an overdose (Siegel, Hinson, Krank, & McCully, 1982). Although much of this research was conducted with animals, it has had important implications for treatment of those with substance dependence.

Another factor studied so far only in people who drink alcohol is a cognitive phenomenon called alcohol myopia. This condition has been defined as "a state of shortsightedness in which superficially understood, immediate aspects of experience have a disproportionate influence on behaviour and emotion" (Steele & Josephs, 1990, p. 923). Picture someone who is drunk, carefully and methodically placing one foot in front of the other as he or she walks so as not to fall, walking straight into the path of an oncoming truck. Although alcohol myopia may not explain why people drink in the first place, it may help us understand why they continue to drink when they know excessive drinking can have severe negative consequences. People under the influence of alcohol may not be able to evaluate properly the risks involved in their continued drinking. Tara MacDonald and her colleagues at Queen's University in Kingston have conducted some fascinating work demonstrating that alcohol myopia explains why people are more likely to take health risks (e.g., engaging in unprotected sex) when they are intoxicated (MacDonald, Fong, Zanna, & Martineau, 2000; MacDonald, MacDonald, Zanna, & Fong, 2000; MacDonald, Zanna, & Fong, 1996, 1998).

Social Dimensions

We pointed out the importance of exposure to psychoactive substances as a necessary prerequisite to their use and possible abuse. You could probably list many ways in which people are exposed to these substances—through friends, through the media, and so on. For example, research on the consequences of cigarette advertising suggests the effects of media exposure may be more influential than peer pressure in determining whether teens smoke (Jackson, Brown, & L'Engle, 2007). Research such as this has led to increasing restrictions by the Canadian government on how and where cigarette companies can advertise their product (Canadian Council on Smoking & Health and Physicians for a Smoke Free Canada, 2003). Legislation that requires vendors to hide their "power wall" of cigarettes is implemented provincially rather than federally. In Nova Scotia, a law was put in place on March 2007 that required vendors to hide tobacco products in their stores and that did not allow in-store tobacco product advertising (Young, 2007). Manitoba, Saskatchewan, Alberta (Hall, 2007), and British Columbia (Blais, 2007) have all put similar legislation in place. Ontario has adopted legislation that bans all tobacco product displays and advertising ("Province-wide smoking ban adopted," 2005).

Research suggests that drug-addicted parents spend less time monitoring their children than do parents without drug problems (Dishion, Patterson, & Reid, 1988) and that this is an important contribution to early adolescent substance use (Barnes, Hoffman, Welte, Farrell, & Dintcheff, 2006). When parents do not provide

▲ Many young children are exposed to drug use.

appropriate supervision, their children develop friendships with peers who supported drug use. Children influenced by drug use at home may be exposed to peers who use drugs as well. A self-perpetuating pattern seems to be associated with drug use that extends beyond the genetic influences we discussed previously.

The work of Alberta psychologist Nancy Galambos and her colleagues further affirms that parents' behaviour does matter in determining the alcohol use and drug-taking patterns of their teenage offspring. For example, Galambos, Barker, and Almeida (2003) followed more than 100 Canadian families for 3.5 years to examine the influence of parenting behaviours and of peers on children's adjustment in early adolescence. The results showed that parents who used firm behavioural control were able to stop the upward spiral of externalizing behaviours (i.e., acting-out behaviours, including substance abuse) among those teens who were affiliating with deviant peers. Studies such as these suggest that parenting can exert an important influence on teenagers' use of alcohol and drugs and may do so even in the face of potentially negative peer influences.

How does our society view people who are dependent on drugs? This issue is of tremendous importance because it affects efforts to legislate the sale, manufacture, possession, and use of these substances. It also dictates how drug-dependent individuals are treated. Two views of substance abuse and dependence characterize contemporary thought: moral weakness and the disease model of dependence. According to the *moral weakness view*, drug use is seen as a failure of self-control in the face of temptation; this is a psychosocial perspective. Drug users lack the character or moral fibre to resist the lure of drugs. We saw earlier, for example, that the Catholic Church made drug abuse an official sin—an indication of its disdain. The *disease model*, in contrast, assumes that drug dependence is caused by an underlying physiological disorder; this is a biological perspective. Just as diabetes or asthma can't be blamed on the afflicted individuals, neither should drug dependence. As noted by Canadian clinical psychologist G. Alan Marlatt, Alcoholics Anonymous and similar organizations see drug dependence as an incurable disease over which the addict has no control (Marlatt, 1985).

Obviously, neither perspective does justice to the complex interrelationship between the psychosocial and biological influences that affect substance disorders. Viewing drug use as moral weakness leads to punishing those who have the disorder, whereas a disease model includes seeking treatment for a medical problem. Conversely, people certainly help determine the outcome of treatment for drug abuse and dependence, and messages that the disorder is out of their control can at times be counterproductive. A comprehensive view of substance-related disorders that includes both psychosocial and biological influences is needed for this important societal concern to be addressed adequately.

Cultural Dimensions

When we examine a behaviour as it appears in different cultures, it is necessary to re-examine what is considered abnormal (Kohn, Wintrob, & Alarcon, 2009). Each culture has its own preferences for psychoactive drugs as well as its own proscriptions for substances it finds unacceptable. Keep in mind that in addition to defining what is or is not acceptable, cultural norms affect the

rates of substance abuse and dependence in important ways. For example, in certain cultures, including Korea, members are expected to drink alcohol heavily on certain social occasions (Lee, 1992). As we have seen before, exposure to these substances, in addition to social pressure for heavy and frequent use, may facilitate their abuse, and this may explain the high abuse rates in countries like Korea. However, poor economic conditions in certain parts of the world limit the availability of drugs, which appears in part to account for the relatively low prevalence of substance abuse in Mexico and Brazil (de Almeidia-Filho, Santana, Pinto, & de Carvalho-Neto, 1991; Ortiz & Medicna-Mora, 1988).

As yet we do not know whether biological differences across cultures contribute to the varying use and abuse rates. Looking ahead to what we may find through future research, it is important for us to consider that biological factors may interact with cultural norms in a complex way. For example, it seems logical that cultural norms may develop over time as a consequence of biological differences. Certain cultures may adapt their drug use (e.g., condoning substance use only in "safe" social surroundings) to

▲ In many cultures, alcohol is used ceremonially.

ethnically idiosyncratic reactions (e.g., a tendency to react aggressively). However, we have seen in looking at other disorders that behaviour can also affect biology, and we may discover that the norms established by a society affect the biology of its people. Research on the cultural dimensions of substance abuse is in its infancy, but it holds great promise for helping unravel the mysteries of this disorder.

An Integrative Model

Any explanation of substance use, abuse, and dependence must account for the basic issue raised earlier in this chapter: Why do some people use drugs without abusing them or becoming dependent on them? ■ Figure 11.9 illustrates how the multiple influences we have discussed may interact to account for this process. Access to a drug is a necessary but obviously not sufficient condition for abuse or dependence. Exposure has many sources, including the media, parents, peers, and, indirectly, lack of supervision. Whether people use a drug depends also on social and cultural expectations, some encouraging and some discouraging, such as laws against possession or sale of the drug.

The path from drug use to abuse and dependence is more complicated (see Figure 11.9). As major stressors aggravate many of the disorders we have discussed, so too do they increase the risk of abuse and dependence on psychoactive substances. Genetic influences may be of several different types. Some individuals may inherit a greater sensitivity to the positively reinforcing effects of certain drugs and others to the negatively reinforcing effects (anxiolytic or analgesic) of certain drugs. Other psychiatric

conditions may indirectly put someone at risk for substance abuse. For example, antisocial personality disorder, characterized by the frequent violation of social norms (see Chapter 12), is thought to include a lowered rate of arousal, which may account for the increased prevalence of substance abuse in this group.

Equifinality, the concept that a particular disorder may arise from multiple and different paths, is particularly appropriate to substance disorders. It is clear that abuse and dependence cannot be predicted from one factor, be it genetic, neurobiological, psychological, or cultural. We saw, for example, that some people with the DRD2 gene common to many with substance abuse problems do not become abusers. Many people who experience the most crushing stressors, such as abject poverty or bigotry and violence, cope without resorting to drug use. There are different pathways to abuse, and we are only now beginning to identify their basic outlines.

Once a drug has been used repeatedly, biology and cognition conspire to create dependence. Continual use of most drugs causes tolerance, which requires the user to ingest more of the drug to produce the same effect. Conditioning is also a factor. If pleasurable drug experiences are associated with certain settings, a return to such a setting will later cause urges to develop, even if the drugs themselves are not available.

This obviously complex picture still does not convey the intricate lives of people who develop substance-related disorders (Wills, Vaccaro, McNamara, & Hirky, 1996). Each person has his or her own story and path to abuse and dependence. We have only begun to discover the commonalities of substance disorders; we need to understand a great deal more about how all the factors interact to produce them.

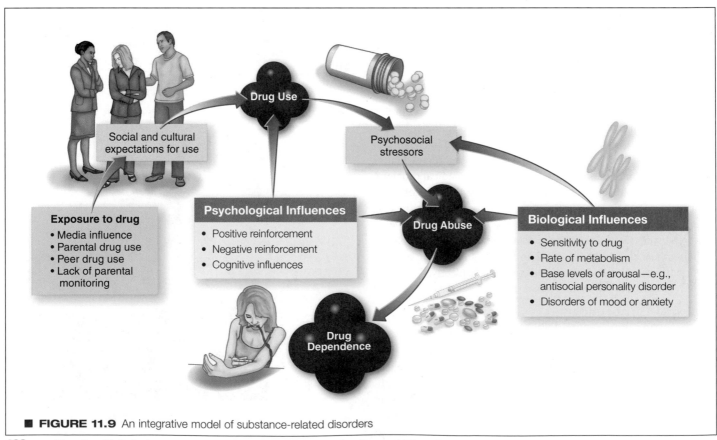

■ **FIGURE 11.9** An integrative model of substance-related disorders

Treatment

When we left Danny, he was in jail, awaiting the legal outcome of being arrested for robbery. At this point in his life, Danny needs more than legal help; he needs to free himself from his addiction to alcohol and cocaine. And the first step in his recovery has to come from him. Danny must admit he needs help, that he does indeed have a problem with drugs, and that he needs others to help him overcome his chronic dependence. The personal motivation to work on a drug problem appears to be essential in the treatment of substance abuse (Miller, 2009), and substance abusers arrive at treatment at different stages of readiness to change their substance use behaviour (Prochaska, DiClemente, & Norcross, 1997). A therapist cannot help someone change who doesn't want to change This can be a problem in treating substance abuse just as it is for people with psychological disorders such as anorexia nervosa (see Chapter 8) and antisocial personality disorder (see Chapter 12) and medical disorders like diabetes that require behavioural management (see Chapter 9). A specific psychological technique called *motivational interviewing* (Miller & Rollnick, 2002) has been developed to help individuals with substance use disorders increase their motivation to change and move toward a stage where they are ready to work on modifying their problematic substance use (see also Brown et al., 2007). Recently, this type of approach has been successfully extended to the treatment of pathological gambling by researchers in Calgary (Hodgins, Currie, & el-Guebaly, 2001; Hodgins, Currie, el-Guebaly, & Peden, 2004). Fortunately (and at last), Danny's arrest seemed to shock him into realizing how serious his problems had become, and he was now at a stage where he was ready to confront his substance dependence head on.

Treating people who have substance-related disorders is a difficult task. Perhaps because of the combination of influences that often work together to keep people hooked, the outlook for those who are dependent on drugs is often not very positive. We will see in the case of heroin dependence, for example, that a best-case scenario is often just trading one addiction (heroin) for another (methadone). And even people who successfully cease taking drugs may feel all their lives the urge to resume drug use.

Treatment for substance-related disorders focuses on several areas. Sometimes the first step is to help someone through the withdrawal process; and for some, the ultimate goal is abstinence. In other situations the goal is to get a person to maintain a less harmful, more moderate level of drug use without escalating its intake, and sometimes it is geared toward preventing exposure to drugs.

We discuss the treatment of substance-related disorders as a group because treatments have so much in common. For example, many programs that treat people for dependence on a variety of substances also teach skills for coping with life stressors. Biological treatments focus on how to mask the effects of the ingested substances. We discuss the obvious differences among substances as they arise.

Biological Treatments

Agonist Substitution

Increased knowledge about how psychoactive drugs work on the brain has led researchers to explore ways of changing how they are experienced by people who are dependent on them. One method, **agonist substitution**, involves providing the person with a safer drug that has a chemical makeup similar to the addictive drug (therefore the name agonist). Methadone is an opiate agonist that is often given as a heroin substitute (Kleber, 1999). Methadone is a synthetic narcotic developed in Germany during World War II when morphine was not available for pain control; it was originally called *adolphine* after Adolf Hitler (Bellis, 1981). Although it does not give the quick high of heroin, methadone initially provides the same analgesic (pain-reducing) and sedative effects. However, when users develop a tolerance for methadone, it loses its analgesic and sedative qualities. Because heroin and methadone are *cross-tolerant*, acting on the same neurotransmitter receptors, a heroin addict who takes methadone may become addicted to the methadone instead (O'Brien, 1996), trading a more harmful behavioural pattern for a much less harmful alternative (a notion referred to as **harm reduction**, as we will discuss in more detail later in this chapter; see, for example, Roberts & Marlatt, 1999). Methadone maintenance therapy is the most widely known and well-researched treatment for opioid dependency (Krambeer, von McKnelly, Gabrielli, & Penick, 2001).

Research suggests that when addicts combine methadone with counselling, many reduce their use of heroin (Ball & Ross, 1991). In fact, methadone maintenance programs have effectively reduced heroin dependence and are available in most countries affected by heroin addiction (Murray, 1998). Additional benefits of methadone maintenance (especially in conjunction with psychotherapy) are decreased criminality, because the addict is no longer engaging in illegal activities to get drugs, and decreased risk of HIV/AIDS and hepatitis (e.g., Millson et al., 2007), because the addict is no longer injecting heroin and thus is no longer exposed to unsafe injection practices (see review by Murray, 1998).

All the news is not good, however. A proportion of people under methadone treatment continue to abuse other substances such as cocaine (Condelli, Fairbank, Dennis, & Rachal, 1991) and benzodiazepines (Iguchi et al., 1990). Research suggests that some people who use methadone as a substitute for heroin benefit significantly, but they may be dependent on methadone for the rest of their lives (O'Brien, 1996). Although some practitioners argue that methadone may be used continually without harmful side effects (e.g., Murray, 1998), the current trend in methadone treatment is that the individual is gradually weaned off methadone in the final treatment phase (see Krambeer et al., 2001).

A newer substitution treatment for heroin dependence is with the drug *buprenorphine* (Jaffe & O'Keefe, 2003; Srivastava & Kahan, 2006). In France, high-dosage buprenorphine is currently the main substitution treatment for narcotic addiction (Poirier et al., 2004). According to Eder et al. (1998), buprenorphine may offer some advantages over methadone in the treatment of opioid dependence. For example, because buprenorphine is a partial opiate agonist (rather than a full agonist like methadone), it may involve less of a risk for dependence and produce fewer withdrawal symptoms on eventual discontinuation. In fact, some research suggests that buprenorphine treatment is as effective as, or more effective than, methadone maintenance in the treatment of opioid dependence. For example, an Austrian study by

Giacomuzzi et al. (2003) showed that buprenorphine-maintained participants showed significantly less consumption of opioids and cocaine compared with participants in the methadone group at the end of the study. They also found that buprenorphine showed a slight advantage over methadone in terms of certain withdrawal symptoms (e.g., fewer stomach cramps, less fatigue, fewer chills, and less heart pounding with buprenorphine). Such results suggest promise for this newer substitute, but more research is needed (Giacomuzzi et al., 2003; Srivastava & Kahan, 2006).

Addiction to cigarette smoking is also treated by a substitution process. The drug—nicotine—is provided to smokers in the form of gum, patch, inhaler, or nasal spray, which lack the carcinogens included in cigarette smoke; the dose is later tapered off to lessen withdrawal from the drug. In general, these replacement strategies successfully help people stop smoking, although they work best with supportive psychological therapy (Hughes, 2009). People must be taught how to use the gum properly, and a portion of the people who successfully quit smoking become dependent on the gum itself (Etter, 2009). The nicotine patch, which requires less effort and provides a steadier nicotine replacement, may be somewhat more effective in helping people quit smoking (Hughes, 2009). Another medical treatment for smoking—*bupropion (Zyban)*—is also commonly prescribed, under the trade name *Wellbutrin,* as an antidepressant. This drug curbs the cravings without being an agonist for nicotine (rather than helping smokers trying to quit by making them less depressed).

A recent controlled trial by researchers at the University of Western Ontario showed that combining physical exercise with nicotine replacement therapy not only facilitates smoking cessation, but also delays weight gain in women smokers, suggesting promise for this particular combination of behavioural and pharmacotherapies (Prappavessis et al., 2007).

Antagonist Treatments

We described how many of the psychoactive drugs produce euphoric effects through their interaction with the neurotransmitter systems in the brain. What would happen if the effects of these drugs were blocked, so that the drugs no longer produced the pleasant results? Would people stop using the drugs? **Antagonist drugs** block or counteract the effects of psychoactive drugs, and a variety of drugs that seem to cancel out the effects of opiates have been used with people dependent on a variety of substances (O'Brien & Cornish, 1999). The most often prescribed opiate-antagonist drug, *naltrexone*, has had only limited success with individuals who are not simultaneously participating in a structured treatment program (Goldstein, 1994). When it is given to a person who is dependent on opiates, it produces immediate withdrawal symptoms, an extremely unpleasant effect. A person must be withdrawn from the opiate completely before starting naltrexone, and because it removes the euphoric effects of the opiates, the user must be highly motivated to continue treatment.

Naltrexone has also been evaluated as a treatment for alcohol dependence because it prevents alcohol reinforcement by inhibiting dopamine release in the nucleus accumbens (O'Malley, 1996; Stewart, Collins, Blackburn, Ellery, & Klein, 2005). Recent research shows that naltrexone blocks alcohol-induced pleasurable stimulation in humans (Peterson, Conrod, Vassileva, Gianoulakis, & Pihl, 2006). Results suggest that naltrexone may enhance an overall treatment approach that includes therapy (O'Malley et al., 1992). University of Calgary psychiatrists David Crockford and Nady el-Guebaly have described the results of a case study of a 49-year-old man with comorbid alcohol dependence and pathological gambling who was effectively treated for both disorders with naltrexone. The naltrexone was particularly beneficial in helping reduce this patient's cravings (Crockford & el-Guebaly, 1998). Other drugs are now being studied to see if they can help improve the outcomes of people who want to reduce their drug use. For example, a relatively new drug—ondansetron—is being studied and may be particularly helpful for people who developed alcoholism at or before their early 20s (Johnson et al., 2000; Kranzler, 2000). Overall, naltrexone and the other drugs being explored are not magic bullets that shut off the addict's response to psychoactive drugs and put an end to dependence. They do appear to help some drug abusers handle withdrawal symptoms and the craving that accompanies attempts to abstain from drug use; antagonists may therefore be a useful addition to other therapeutic efforts.

Aversive Treatment

In addition to looking for ways to block the euphoric effects of psychoactive drugs, workers in this area may prescribe drugs that make ingesting the abused substances extremely unpleasant. The expectation is that a person who associates the drug with feelings of illness will avoid using the drug. The most commonly known aversive treatment uses *disulfiram* (Antabuse) with people who are alcohol dependent (Ivanov, 2009). Antabuse prevents the breakdown of acetaldehyde, a byproduct of alcohol, and the resulting building of acetaldehyde causes feelings of illness. People who drink alcohol after taking Antabuse experience nausea, vomiting, and elevated heart rate and respiration. Ideally, Antabuse is taken each morning, before the desire to drink wins out (Nathan, 1993). Unfortunately, noncompliance is a major concern, and a person who skips the Antabuse for a few days is able to resume drinking. In Canada, the supplier of brand-name disulfiram (i.e., Antabuse) discontinued this product in 2001 (Pharmacists.ca, 2003). However, this medication is still available in Canada in non–brand-name form (i.e., as disulfiram).

Efforts to make smoking aversive have included the use of silver nitrate in lozenges or gum. This chemical combines with the saliva of a smoker to produce a bad taste in the mouth. Research has not shown it to be particularly effective (Jensen, Schmidt, Pedersen, & Dahl, 1991). Both Antabuse for alcohol abuse and silver nitrate for cigarette smoking have generally been less than successful as treatment strategies on their own, primarily because they require that people be extremely motivated to continue taking them outside the supervision of a mental health professional (Leccese, 1991).

Other Biological Treatments

Medication is frequently prescribed to help people deal with the often very disturbing symptoms of withdrawal. *Clonidine*, developed to treat hypertension, has been given to people withdrawing from opiates. Because withdrawal from certain pre-scribed medications, such as the sedatives, can cause cardiac arrest or seizures, these drugs are gradually tapered off to minimize dangerous reactions. In addition, sedative drugs (benzodiazepines) are often prescribed to help minimize discomfort for people withdrawing from other drugs such as alcohol (McCreery & Walker, 1993).

One of the few controlled studies of the use of medication to treat cocaine abuse (Gawin et al., 1989) found that *desipramine*, one of the antidepressant drugs, was more effective in increasing abstinence rates among cocaine users than lithium or a placebo. However, 41 percent of those receiving the medication were unable to achieve even a month of continuous cocaine abstinence, suggesting it may not be helpful for a large subgroup of users. Other medications—such as *acamprostate* (which affects the glutamate and GABA neurotransmitter systems) and several SSRIs (selective serotonin reuptake inhibitors) including Zoloft and Prozac—are now being tested for their potential therapeutic properties, especially for alcohol dependence (Gordis, 2000d).

Psychosocial Treatments

Most of the biological treatments for substance abuse show some promise for people who are trying to eliminate their drug habit. However, none of these treatments alone is successful for most people (American Psychiatric Association, 2000c). Most research indicates a need for social support or therapeutic intervention. Because so many people need help to overcome their substance disorder, a number of models and programs have been developed. Unfortunately, in no other area of psychology have unvalidated and untested methods of treatment been so widely accepted. A reminder: Just because a program has not been subject to the scrutiny of research does not mean it doesn't work, but the sheer number of people receiving services of unknown value is cause for concern. We next review several therapeutic approaches that have been evaluated.

Concept Check | 11.3

Substance-related disorders are difficult to treat. See whether you understand how these treatments work. Read the examples and match them with the following terms: (a) dependent, (b) cross-tolerant, (c) agonist substitution, and (d) antagonist.

1. Methadone is used to help heroin addicts kick their habit in a method called _____.

2. Heroin and methadone are _____, which means they affect the same neurotransmitter receptors.

3. Unfortunately, the heroin addict may become permanently _____ on methadone.

4. _____ drugs block or counteract the effects of psychoactive drugs and are sometimes effective in treating addicts.

Inpatient Facilities

Inpatient treatment facilities are designed to help substance-dependent people get through the initial withdrawal period and to provide supportive therapy so they can go back to their communities (Morgan, 1981). Inpatient care can be extremely expensive (Miller & Hester, 1986). The question arises, then, as to how effective this type of care is compared with outpatient therapy that can cost 90 percent less. Research suggests there may be no difference between intensive residential-setting programs and quality outpatient care in the outcomes for alcoholic patients (Miller & Hester, 1986) or for drug treatment in general (Guydish, Sorensen, Chan, Werdegar, & Acampora, 1999; Smith, Kraemer, Miller, DeBusk, & Taylor, 1999). Although some people do improve as inpatients, they may not need this expensive care.

Alcoholics Anonymous and Its Variations

Without question, the most popular model for the treatment of substance abuse is a variation of the 12-step program first developed by Alcoholics Anonymous (AA). Established in 1935 by two alcoholic professionals, William "Bill W." Wilson and Robert "Dr. Bob" Holbrook Smith, the foundation of AA is the notion that alcoholism is a disease and alcoholics must acknowledge their addiction to alcohol and its destructive power over them. The addiction is seen as more powerful than any individual, and therefore they must look to a higher power to help them overcome their shortcomings. Central to the design of AA is its independence from the established medical community and the freedom it offers from the stigmatization of alcoholism (Denzin, 1987; Robertson, 1988). An important component is the social support it provides through group meetings.

Since 1935, AA has steadily expanded to include almost 106 000 groups in more than 100 countries (White & Kurtz, 2008). In one survey conducted by researcher Robin Room, formerly of the Addiction Research Foundation in Toronto, more than 3 percent of the adult population has at one time attended an AA meeting (Room, 1993). The 12 steps of AA are the basis of its philosophy (see Table 11.1). In them you can see the reliance on prayer and a belief in God.

Reaction is rarely neutral to AA and similar organizations, like Cocaine Anonymous and Narcotics Anonymous (Miller, Gold, & Pottash, 1989). Many people credit the approach with saving their lives, whereas others object that its reliance on spirituality and adoption of a disease model foster dependence. Because participants attend meetings anonymously and only when they feel the need to, conducting systematic research on its effectiveness has been unusually difficult (Miller & McCrady, 1993). There have been numerous attempts, however, to evaluate AA's effect on alcoholism (Emrick, Tonigan, Montgomery, & Little, 1993). Although there are not enough data to show what percentage of people abstain from using alcohol as a result of participating in AA, Emrick and his colleagues found that those people who regularly participate in AA activities and follow its guidelines carefully are more likely to have a positive outcome. Other studies suggest that persons who fully participate in AA do as well as those receiving cognitive-behavioural treatments (Ouimette, Finney, & Moos, 1997). Conversely, a very large number of

TABLE 11.1 Twelve Suggested Steps of Alcoholics Anonymous

1. We admitted we were powerless over alcohol—that our lives had become unmanageable.

2. Came to believe that a power greater than ourselves could restore us to sanity.

3. Made a decision to turn our will and our lives over to the care of God as we understood Him.

4. Made a searching and fearless moral inventory of ourselves.

5. Admitted to God, to ourselves, and to another human being the exact nature of our wrongs.

6. Were entirely ready to have God remove all these defects of character.

7. Humbly asked Him to remove our shortcomings.

8. Made a list of all persons we had harmed, and became willing to make amends to them all.

9. Made direct amends to such people wherever possible, except when to do so would injure them or others.

10. Continued to take personal inventory and, when we were wrong, promptly admitted it.

11. Sought through prayer and meditation to improve our conscious contact with God as we understood Him, praying only for knowledge of His will for us and the power to carry that out.

12. Having had a spiritual awakening as the result of these steps, we tried to carry this message to alcoholics and to practise these principles in all our affairs.

Source: The Twelve Steps are reprinted with permission of Alcoholics Anonymous World Services, Inc. (A.A.W.S.) Permission to reprint the Twelve Steps does not mean that A.A.W.S. has reviewed or approved the contents of this publication, or that A.A.W.S. necessarily agrees with the views expressed herein. A.A. is a program of recovery from alcoholism only—use of the Twelve Steps in connection with programs and activities which are patterned after A.A., but which address other problems, or in any other non-A.A. context, does not imply otherwise.

▲ Mary Walsh, the well-known comedian, has struggled with an alcohol use disorder and has publicly acknowledged being a member of Alcoholics Anonymous (AA).

people who initially contact AA for their drinking problems seem to drop out: 50 percent after four months and 75 percent after 12 months (Alcoholics Anonymous, 1990). AA is clearly an effective treatment for some people with alcohol dependence. We do not yet know, however, who is likely to succeed and who is likely to fail in AA. Other treatments are needed for the large numbers of people who do not respond to AA's approach.

Controlled Use

One of the tenets of AA is total abstinence; recovering alcoholics who have just one sip of alcohol are believed to have "slipped" until they again achieve abstinence. However, some researchers question this assumption and believe at least a portion of abusers of several substances (notably alcohol and nicotine) may be capable of becoming social users without resuming their abuse of these drugs. Some people who smoke only occasionally are thought to react differently to nicotine than heavy users (Goldstein, 1994).

In the alcoholism treatment field, the notion of teaching people **controlled drinking** is extremely controversial. Mark and Linda Sobell conducted an important study showing were assigned either to a program that taught them how to drink in moderation or to a group that was abstinence oriented. The Sobells followed the men for more than two years, maintaining contact with 98 percent of them. At the two-year follow-up, those who participated in the controlled drinking group were functioning well 85 percent of the time, whereas those in the abstinence group were doing well only 42 percent of the time—a significant difference. Nonetheless, some of the men in both groups had serious relapses and required rehospitalization, and some were incarcerated. Thus, controlled drinking may be a viable alternative to abstinence for some alcohol abusers, although it clearly isn't a cure.

The controversy over this study began with a paper published by Pendery, Maltzman, and West (1982). The authors had contacted the men in the Sobell study after ten years and found that only one of the 20 men in the experimental group maintained a pattern of controlled drinking. Although this re-evaluation made headlines, it had a number of flaws, as pointed out by Alan Marlatt and his colleagues (Marlatt, Larimer, Baer, & Quigley, 1993). Most serious was the lack of data on the abstinence group over the same ten-year follow-up period.

The controversy over the Sobell study still had a chilling effect on controlled drinking as a treatment of alcohol abuse in the United States. In contrast, controlled drinking is widely accepted as a treatment for alcoholism in the United Kingdom (Rosenberg, 1993; Rosenberg & Melville, 2005). This approach is more widely accepted in Canada than in the United States, but less so than in the United Kingdom. Research on this approach in the ensuing years (Marlatt et al., 1993) seems to show that controlled drinking is at least as effective as abstinence, but that neither treatment is successful for 70 percent to 80 percent of patients over the long term—a rather bleak outlook for people with alcohol dependence.

▲ Linda and Mark Sobell conducted important research on substance use disorders during their time at the Addiction Research Foundation in Toronto. One of the Sobells' more important contributions was their work on the effectiveness of controlled drinking approaches.

Component Treatment

Most comprehensive treatment programs aimed at helping people with substance abuse and dependence problems have several different components thought to boost the effectiveness of the "treatment package." We saw in our review of biological treatments that their effectiveness is increased when psychologically-based therapy is added. In aversion therapy, which uses a conditioning model, substance use is paired with something extremely unpleasant, such as a brief electric shock or feelings of nausea. For example, a person might be offered a drink of alcohol and receive a painful shock when the glass reaches his or her lips. The goal is to counteract the positive associations of substance use with negative associations. The negative associations can also be made by imagining unpleasant scenes in a technique called *covert sensitization* (Cautela, 1966); the person might picture himself or herself beginning to snort cocaine and be interrupted with visions of becoming violently ill (Kearney, 2006).

One component that seems to be a valuable part of therapy for substance use is *contingency management* (Higgins et al., 2008; Petry, Martin, Cooney, & Kranzler, 2000). Here, the clinician and client together select the behaviours that the client needs to change and decide on the reinforcers that will reward reaching certain goals, perhaps money or small retail items like CDs. In a study of cocaine abusers, clients received cash vouchers (up to almost $2000) for having cocaine-negative urine specimens (Higgins et al., 2006). This study found greater abstinence rates among cocaine-dependent users with the contingency management approach and other skills training than among users in a more traditional counselling program that included a 12-step approach to treatment.

Another package of treatments is the *community reinforcement approach* (Higgins, Sigmon, & Heil, 2008). Several different facets of the drug problem are addressed, to help identify and correct aspects of the person's life that might contribute to substance use, or interfere with efforts to abstain. First, a spouse, friend, or relative who is not a substance user is recruited to participate in relationship therapy in order to help the abuser improve his or her relationships with other important people. Second, clients are taught how to identify the antecedents and consequences that influence their drug taking. For example, if they are likely to use cocaine with certain friends, clients are taught to recognize the relationship and encouraged to avoid the associations. Third, clients are given assistance with employment, education, finances, or other social service areas that may help reduce their stress. Fourth, new recreational options help the person replace substance use with new activities. There is now strong empirical support for the effectiveness of this approach with alcohol and cocaine abusers (Higgins et al., 2008).

Attempts to match treatments to the particular needs of individual clients (treatment matching) has received increased attention from workers in the area of substance abuse. For example, the National Institute on Alcohol Abuse and Alcoholism initiated Project MATCH (Matching Alcoholism Treatment to Client Heterogeneity) to assess whether people with differing characteristics (having little hope for improvement versus searching for spiritual meaning) would respond better or worse to different treatments (Project MATCH Research Group, 1993). Initial reports suggest that well-run programs of various types can be effective with a range of people with substance use problems (Project MATCH Research Group, 1997). Although no exact matches are yet recommended, research is ongoing to help clinicians tailor their treatments to the particular needs of their substance-abusing clients (Jaffe et al., 1996; Project MATCH Research Group, 1998).

Research by Patricia Conrod and her colleagues in London, England, suggests that matching on the basis of a substance-abusing client's personality and motivations for substance use improves outcomes for substance-abusing women (Conrod, Stewart, et al., 2000). In Conrod's et al. study, female substance abusers recruited from the community were randomly assigned to receive one of three brief interventions: (1) a motivation-matched intervention involving personality-specific motivational and coping skills training; (2) a motivational control intervention involving a film about substance abuse and a supportive discussion with a therapist; or (3) a motivation-mismatched intervention targeting a theoretically different personality profile. The personality profiles targeted were (1) anxiety sensitivity (associated with benzodiazepine dependence and comorbid anxiety disorders), (2) hopelessness (associated with opioid analgesic dependence and comorbid depression), (3) impulsivity (associated with cocaine and alcohol dependence and comorbid antisocial personality disorder), and (4) sensation seeking (associated with exclusive alcohol dependence). Assessment at six months post-intervention indicated that only the matched intervention was superior to the motivational control intervention in reducing the severity and frequency of problematic substance abuse and in preventing the use of multiple medical services (see ■ Figure 11.10 for sample study result). These findings indicate promise for client-treatment matching approaches that match at the level of motivations for substance abuse.

Relapse Prevention

Another kind of treatment directly addresses the problem of relapse. The **relapse prevention** treatment model developed by Alan Marlatt looks at the learned aspects of dependence and sees relapse as a failure of cognitive and behavioural coping skills (Marlatt & Gordon, 1985). Therapy involves helping people

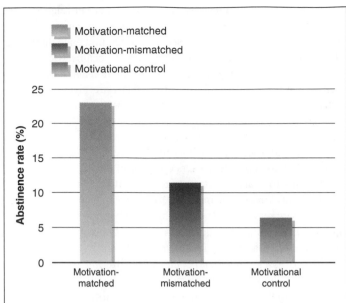

■ **FIGURE 11.10** Abstinence rates from alcohol following treatment in three groups: motivation-matched, motivation-mismatched, and motivational control intervention. Only the motivation-matched intervention resulted in an abstinence rate that was significantly higher than the motivational control intervention.

Source: Adapted from "Efficacy of brief coping skills interventions that match different personality profiles of female substance abusers" by P. J. Conrod, S. H. Stewart, R. O. Pihl, S. Cote, V. Fontaine, & M. Dongier, 2000, *Psychology of Addictive Behaviors, 14,* 231–242.

remove any ambivalence about stopping their drug use by examining their beliefs about the positive aspects of the drug ("There's nothing like a cocaine high") and confronting the negative consequences of its use ("I fight with my wife when I'm high"). High-risk situations are identified ("having extra money in my pocket") and strategies are developed to deal with potentially problematic situations as well as with the craving that arises from abstinence. Incidents of relapse are dealt with as occurrences from which the person can recover; instead of looking on these episodes as inevitably leading to more drug use, people in treatment are encouraged to see them as episodes brought on by temporary stress or a situation that can be changed. Research on this technique suggests that it may be particularly effective for alcohol problems (Irvin, Bowers, Dunn, & Wang, 1999), marijuana dependence (Stephens, Roffman, & Simpson, 1994), smoking (Gruder et al., 1993; Shiffman et al., 1996), and cocaine abuse (Carroll, 1992).

Harm Reduction

In direct contrast to the current zero tolerance, "Just say no to drugs" approach taken by the United States government to combat substance abuse and dependence, a very different approach is currently predominant in Europe and elsewhere around the world (Marlatt, 1998). This approach is known as *harm reduction*—an approach also championed by Alan Marlatt (e.g., Roberts & Marlatt, 1999). The harm reduction approach recognizes that substance use occurs in society and seeks to minimize the harm associated with substance use as its primary

goal. Abstinence can be the final goal of a substance-abusing client within a harm reduction approach, but it does not have to be. Thus, the controlled drinking interventions developed by the Sobells represent an example of the harm reduction approach.

Another example of the harm reduction approach is the establishment of safe injection sites (SISs) for injection drug users. In fact, Canada's first such facility opened in Vancouver in September 2003 (Follman, 2003). Injection drug use represents an increasing health problem in Canada—increasing the risk for overdose and HIV/AIDS and hepatitis C infections. At SISs, it is legal for drug users to inject their drug using clean equipment, under medical supervision. SISs minimize the risk of overdose, disease, and other negative health effects that can result from using unclean equipment and unsafe injecting practices. SISs also direct substance-dependent clients to treatment programs and operate as primary health care units (Elliott, Malkin, & Gold, 2002).

The establishment of the Vancouver SIS has been widely criticized by conservative politicians within Canada and by the American government (Follman, 2003). Opponents argue that SISs condone or encourage drug use and that a strict abstinence-oriented approach would better contain drug use (Elliott et al., 2002). Proponents argue that SISs offer a safer, hygienic place to inject, with access to medical intervention and other health and social services, providing a positive message of concern for the drug user's health and well-being. Proponents argue that SISs can benefit the broader community as well, by reducing the public nuisance associated with drug taking in the streets of the community (e.g., discarded needles).

Scientific evidence lends support to the use of SISs. The experiences of countries such as Switzerland, Germany, the Netherlands, and Australia suggest that including SISs as part of a broader government drug policy will benefit both drug users and communities (Elliott et al., 2002). Results of the Vancouver SIS thus far appear favourable (e.g., Wood et al., 2004, 2006). For example, studies have shown that the presence of the SIS has led to an increased uptake of clients into detoxification programs and addiction treatment, to a reduction in public drug injection, and to a decrease in the amount of injection-related litter in the Vancouver downtown eastside area (Wood et al., 2004, 2006). Moreover, the negative effects projected by critics do not appear to have materialized. The presence of the SIS in Vancouver has not led to an increase in drug-related crime, rates of arrest for drug trafficking, assaults, or robbery. In fact, rates of vehicle break-ins and theft have decreased in the area since the opening of the SIS (Wood et al., 2004).

Prevention

In education-based programs, harm reduction approaches to prevention and early intervention (e.g., Dimeff, Baer, Kivlahan, & Marlatt, 2002) appear more promising than programs encouraging a "no drug use" message (Pentz, 1999). And fortunately, more comprehensive programs that involve skills training to avoid or resist social pressures (such as peers) and environmental pressures (such as media portrayals of drug use) can be effective in preventing drug abuse among some.

Over the past several years, the strategies for preventing substance abuse and dependence have shifted from education-based approaches to more wide-ranging approaches including the use of

We see that the problem with drug abuse is not just use of the drug. A complicating factor in drug abuse includes the brain's desire to continue to use the drug, especially when in the presence of stimuli and situations usually associated with the drug. This "drug seeking" and relapse continue to interfere with successful treatment. Groundbreaking research is now exploring where in the brain these processes occur, which in turn may lead to new approaches to help people remain drug free (Kalivas, 2005).

Taking this one step further, new research with animals suggests the possibility of creating "vaccines" that would use the immune system to fight drugs such as heroin, just as your body attacks infectious bacteria (Anton & Leff, 2006). A vaccine that would take away the pleasurable aspects of smoking is now being tested with humans (Moreno et al., 2010). What this means is that—theoretically—children could be vaccinated early in their lives, and if they tried a drug, it would not have the pleasurable effects that would encourage repeated use. These "vice vaccines" could hold the answer to one of our most pressing social issues.

On the other end of the intervention spectrum, new and more comprehensive prevention approaches may help many individuals avoid trying dangerous drugs. One such approach is being used in

Montana—called the Montana Meth Project (Generations United, 2006). Initially funded by software billionaire Timothy Siegel, this initiative supports advertising and community action programs to inform youth across the state about the devastating effects of methamphetamine use. The project uses dramatic and sometimes shocking pictures and video ads, and its surveys suggest that the methods were successful in changing attitudes about meth use in many 12- to 17-year-olds. Although no controlled research yet exists, this may be an additional powerful tool for reducing drug dependence.

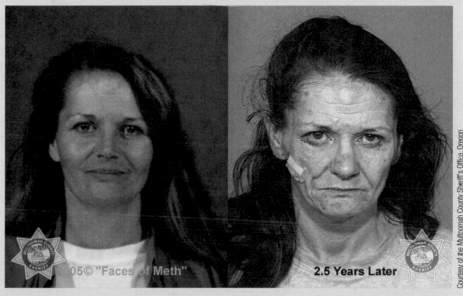

▲ The Montana Meth Project used photos like these from Faces of Meth, a project of the Multnomah County Sheriff's Office in Portland, Oregon.

community-based interventions (Gordis, 2000c). For example, community-based intervention strategies to reduce binge drinking and alcohol-related injuries (e.g., car crashes, assaults) can involve mobilizing communities to encourage responsible beverage service (i.e., not serving too much alcohol to bar patrons), limit alcohol access to underage drinkers, increase local enforcement of drinking and driving laws, and use zoning laws to limit access to alcohol (Holder et al., 2000). But implementing this sort of intervention is obviously beyond the scope of one research investigator or even a consortium of researchers collaborating across many sites. It requires the cooperation of governmental, educational, and even religious institutions. We may need to rethink our approach to preventing drug use and abuse.

Impulse-Control Disorders

A number of the disorders we describe in this book start with an irresistible impulse—usually one that will ultimately be harmful to the person affected. Typically, the person experiences increasing

tension leading up to the act and, sometimes, pleasurable anticipation of acting on the impulse. For example, paraphilias such as pedophilia (sexual attraction to children), eating disorders, and the substance-related disorders in this chapter often commence with temptations or desires that are destructive but difficult to resist. The *DSM-IV-TR* includes five additional impulse-control disorders (labelled "impulse-control disorders not elsewhere classified") that are not included under other categories—intermittent explosive disorder, kleptomania, pyromania, pathological gambling, and trichotillomania (Moeller, 2009; Nock, Cha, & Dour, in press).

Intermittent Explosive Disorder

People with **intermittent explosive disorder** have episodes in which they act on aggressive impulses that result in serious assaults or destruction of property (Coccaro & McCloskey, 2010). Although it is unfortunately common among the general population to observe aggressive outbursts, when you rule out the influence of other disorders (e.g., antisocial personality disorder, borderline personality disorder, a psychotic disorder, and

Alzheimer's disease) or substance use, this disorder is not often diagnosed. In a rare but important large study of more than 9000 people, researchers found that the lifetime prevalence of this disorder was 7.3 percent (Kessler et al., 2006).

This diagnosis is controversial and has been debated throughout the development of the *DSM*. One concern, among others, is that by validating a general category that covers aggressive behaviour it may be used as a legal defence—insanity—for all violent crimes (Coccaro & McCloskey, 2010).

Research is at the beginning stages for intermittent explosive disorder and focuses on the influence of neurotransmitters such as serotonin and norepinephrine and testosterone levels, along with their interaction with psychosocial influences (stress, disrupted family life, and parenting styles). These and other influences are being examined to explain the origins of this disorder (Moeller, 2009). Cognitive-behavioural interventions (e.g., helping the person identify and avoid "triggers" for aggressive outbursts) and approaches modeled after drug treatments appear the most effective for these individuals, although few controlled studies yet exist (McCloskey, Noblett, Deffenbacher, Gollan, & Coccaro, 2008).

Kleptomania

The story of wealthy actress Winona Ryder stealing $5500 worth of merchandise from Saks Fifth Avenue in Beverly Hills, California, in December 2001, was as puzzling as it was titillating. Why risk a multimillion-dollar career over some clothes that she could easily afford? Was hers a case of **kleptomania**—a recurrent failure to resist urges to steal things that are not needed for personal use or their monetary value? This disorder appears to be rare, but it is not well studied, partly because of the stigma associated with identifying oneself as acting out this illegal behaviour. The patterns described by those with this disorder are strikingly similar—the person begins to feel a sense of tension just before stealing, which is followed by feelings of pleasure or relief while the theft is committed (Nock et al., in press). People with kleptomania score high on assessments of impulsivity, reflecting their inability to judge the immediate gratification of stealing compared to the long-term negative consequences (e.g., arrest, embarrassment) (Grant & Kim, 2002). Patients with kleptomania often report having no memory (amnesia) about the act of shoplifting (Hollander, Berlin, & Stein, 2009). Brain-imaging research supports these observations, with one study finding damage in areas of the brain associated with poor decision making (inferior frontal regions) (Grant, Correia, & Brennan-Krohn, 2006).

There appears to be high comorbidity between kleptomania and mood disorders, and to a lesser extent with substance abuse and dependence (Baylé, Caci, Millet, Richa, & Olié, 2003). Some refer to kleptomania as an "antidepressant" behaviour, or a reaction on the part of some to relieve unpleasant feelings through stealing (Fishbain, 1987). To date, only case study reports of treatment exist, and these involve either behavioural interventions or use of antidepressant medication.

Pyromania

Just as we know that someone who steals does not necessarily have kleptomania, it is also true that not everyone who sets fires is considered to have **pyromania**—an impulse-control disorder that involves having an irresistible urge to set fires. Again, the pattern parallels that of kleptomania, where the person feels a tension or arousal before setting a fire and a sense of gratification or relief while the fire burns. These individuals will also be preoccupied with fires and the associated equipment involved in setting and putting out these fires (Lejoyeux, McLoughlin, & Ades, 2006). Also rare, pyromania is diagnosed in less than 4 percent of arsonists (Scott, Hilty, & Brook, 2003), because arsonists can include people who set fires for monetary gain or revenge rather than to satisfy a physical or psychological urge. Because so few people are diagnosed with this disorder, research on etiology and treatment is almost nonexistent. Research that has been conducted follows the general group of arsonists (of which only a small percentage have pyromania) and examines the role of a family history of fire setting along with comorbid impulse disorders (antisocial personality disorder and alcoholism). Treatment is generally cognitive-behavioural and involves helping the person identify the signals that initiate the urges and teaching coping strategies to resist the temptation to start fires (Bumpass, Fagelman, & Brix, 1983; McGrath, Marshall, & Prior, 1979).

Pathological Gambling

Gambling has a long history—for example, dice have been found in Egyptian tombs (Greenberg, 2005). It is growing in popularity in this country, and in many places it is a legal and acceptable form of entertainment. Perhaps as a result, and unlike the other impulse-control disorders, which are relatively rare, **pathological gambling** affects an increasing number of people (Greenberg, 2005). It is estimated that among pathological gamblers, 14 percent have lost at least one job, 19 percent have declared bankruptcy, 32 percent have been arrested, and 21 percent have been incarcerated (Gerstein et al., 1999). As opportunities for legal gambling have increased in recent years, pathological gambling has become a prevalent problem both in Canada and in the United States (Ladouceur, 1996, 2007). In fact, a recent national survey of approximately 35 000 Canadians found that the highest prevalence of gambling problems occurs in areas where gambling is most accessible (i.e., in provinces where there are high concentrations of video lottery terminals and permanent casinos) (Cox, Yu, Afifi, & Ladouceur, 2005). The *DSM-IV-TR* criteria for pathological gambling set forth the associated behaviours that characterize people who are problem gamblers (see DSM Table 11.9). These include the same pattern of urges we observe in the other impulse-control disorders. Note, too, the parallels with substance dependence, with the need to gamble increasing amounts of money over time and the "withdrawal symptoms" such as restlessness and irritability when attempting to stop. In fact, these parallels to substance abuse have led to discussions about recategorizing pathological gambling in the *DSM-5;* some believe that this disorder should be moved from the group of disorders called "impulse-control disorders not elsewhere classified" to the "substance-related disorders" category and that this "substance-related disorders" category should be renamed "addiction and related disorders" (Moeller, 2009).

There is a growing body of research on the nature and treatment of pathological gambling. For example, work is under way to explore the biological origins of the urge to gamble among

Table 11.9 Criteria for Pathological Gambling

A. The person displays persistent and recurrent maladaptive gambling behaviour as indicated by five (or more) of the following:

1. Is preoccupied with gambling (e.g., preoccupied with reliving past gambling experiences, handicapping or planning the next venture, or thinking of ways to get money with which to gamble)

2. Needs to gamble with increasing amounts of money to achieve the desired excitement

3. Has repeated unsuccessful efforts to control, cut back, or stop gambling

4. Is restless or irritable when attempting to cut down to stop gambling

5. Gambles as a way of escaping from problems or of relieving dysphoric mood (e.g., feelings of helplessness, guilt, anxiety, depression)

6. After losing money gambling, often returns another day to get even (chasing his or her losses)

7. Lies to family members, therapist, or others to conceal the extent of involvement with gambling

8. Has committed illegal acts such as forgery, fraud, theft, or embezzlement to finance gambling

9. Has jeopardized or lost a significant relationship, job, or educational or career opportunity because of gambling

10. Relies on others to provide money to relieve a desperate financial situation caused by gambling

B. The gambling behaviour is not better accounted for by a manic episode.

Source: Reprinted with permission from the *Diagnostic and Statistical Manual of Mental Disorders*, Fourth Edition, Text Revision, (Copyright © 2000). American Psychiatric Association.

pathological gamblers. In one study, brain-imaging technology (echoplanar functional magnetic resonance imaging) was used to observe brain function while gamblers observed videotapes of other people gambling (Potenza et al., 2003). A decreased level of activity was observed in those regions of the brain that are involved in impulse regulation when compared to controls, suggesting an interaction between the environmental cues to gamble and the brain's response (which may be to decrease the ability to resist these cues). Abnormalities in the dopamine system (which may account for the pleasurable consequences of gambling) and the serotonin system (involved in impulsive behaviour) have been found in some studies of pathological gamblers (Moeller, 2009).

Treatment of gambling problems is difficult. Those with pathological gambling exhibit a combination of characteristics—including denial of the problem, impulsivity, and continuing optimism ("One big win will cover my losses!")—that interfere with effective treatment. Pathological gamblers often experience cravings similar to those who are substance dependent (Wulfert, Franco, Williams, Roland, & Maxson, 2008; Wulfert, Maxson, & Jardin, 2009). Treatment is often similar to substance dependence treatment, and there is a parallel Gambler's Anonymous that incorporates the same 12-step program we discussed previously. However, the evidence of effectiveness for Gambler's Anonymous suggests that 70 percent to 90 percent drop out of these programs and that the desire to quit must be present before intervention (McElroy & Arnold, 2001). Cognitive-behavioural interventions are also being studied, with one study including a variety of components—setting financial limits, planning

alternative activities, preventing relapse, and imaginal desensitization. This preliminary research provides a more optimistic view of potential outcomes (Dowling, Smith, & Thomas, in press).

Trichotillomania

The urge to pull out one's own hair from anywhere on the body, including the scalp, eyebrows, and arms, is referred to as **trichotillomania**. This behaviour results in noticeable hair loss, distress, and significant social impairments. This disorder can often have severe social consequences, and, as a result, those affected can go to great lengths to conceal their behaviour. Compulsive hair pulling is more common than once believed and is observed in between 1 percent and 5 percent of college students, with females reporting the problem more than males (Scott et al., 2003). There may be some genetic influence on trichotillomania, with one study finding a unique genetic mutation in a small number of people (Zuchner et al., 2006). Stress also seems to be involved, and there is an increased overlap with post-traumatic stress disorder (Chamberlain, Menzies, Sahakian, & Fineberg, 2007). There is considerable controversy over just how this problem should be classified, and there is a proposal to reclassify it from "impulse control disorders not elsewhere classified" to "anxiety and obsessive-compulsive spectrum disorders" in the *DSM-5* (Nock et al., in press). Research using serotonin-specific reuptake inhibitors holds some promise for treatment, as do cognitive-behavioural interventions, although rigorous research trials have yet to be conducted (Chamberlain et al., 2007).

In addition to these five impulse-control disorders, other impulsive behaviours may occasionally rise to the level of these difficulties. Some individuals show the same irresistible urges to engage in compulsive buying or shopping (oniomania), self-mutilation, skin picking (psychogenic excoriation), severe nail biting (onychophagia), and excessive computer use ("Internet addiction") (McElroy & Arnold, 2001). There is a limited but growing literature that will help us understand and ultimately treat these impulse-control problems.

Concept Check | 11.4

Match the following disorders with their corresponding symptoms: (a) pathological gambling, (b) trichotillomania, (c) intermittent explosive disorder, (d) kleptomania, and (e) pyromania.

1. This rarely diagnosed disorder is characterized by episodes of aggressive impulses and can sometimes be treated with cognitive-behavioural interventions, drug treatments, or both. _____

2. This disorder begins with the person feeling a sense of tension that is released and followed with pleasure after they have committed a robbery. _____

3. This disorder refers to compulsive hair pulling and is more common in females than males.

_____

4. Individuals with this disorder are preoccupied with fires and the equipment involved in setting and putting out fires. _____

Addiction by Prescription: One Woman's Triumph and Fight for Change
by Joan E. Gadsby

In *Addiction by Prescription*, Joan E. Gadsby explains how she began taking tranquilizers and sleeping pills on prescription from her family physician, in 1966, following the death of her son to a brain tumour. Thus began her 23-year addiction to benzodiazepines. She describes in vivid detail how this addiction threatened her family relationships, her previously successful career in marketing and politics, and her physical health.

In 1970, Gadsby gave birth to a second child. Gadsby describes the effects of her benzodiazepine use on her labour (e.g., weak contractions) and on her new daughter's physical health (e.g., her daughter was placed under observation due to slow responses after birth). It was only years later that Gadsby realized that these events were very likely linked to her benzodiazepine use at the time of her pregnancy and delivery. Gadsby also experienced marked cognitive side effects of her benzodiazepine use, including attentional and memory impairments, and she survived several unintentional overdoses. The book very clearly highlights the dangers of long-term prescribing of benzodiazepines by family physicians to treat stress.

It was in 1990, after she almost died following one of her unintentional overdoses, that Gadsby made the decision to stop taking the drugs. Without medical support or supervision, and while living all alone, she began the gradual process of discontinuing her tranquilizers and sleeping pills, which she had been prescribed continuously for more than 20 years. She describes the horrific process of withdrawal as follows:

For months I was crippled by feelings of dread and slept for as little as an hour a night. Scarcely a day passed that I didn't think I was going to die. Simply getting dressed and leaving the house was a huge undertaking. ... [W]ithdrawal gave me no choice but to take indefinite leave from my job…. (pp. 15–16)

Providing a message of hope for others struggling with discontinuation of benzodiazepines, Gadsby also clearly describes the joys associated with her recovery from addiction:

As the weeks passed, and I slowly regained my senses, I was overwhelmed by the intricacy and beauty I saw in everyday things…. Driving down toward Vancouver from my home one day shortly after discontinuing the pills, I saw the beauty of the city's skyline with a sharpened perception I hadn't known in years…. I experienced intense feelings of regret and sadness for all the years I had lost, but I also felt reborn. (pp. 16–17)

Since writing this memoir, Gadsby has continued with great dedication and persistence with her advocacy efforts around the world. Her goal is to increase awareness and bring about much overdue systemic change around attitudes and practices surrounding the prescription of tranquilizers and sleeping pills, particularly to women. Gadsby has been free of her prescription drug addiction for two decades now. Her courage, strength, and determination will inspire hope for many individuals and families dealing with benzodiazepine addiction.

Source: From Addiction by Prescription: One Woman's Triumph and Fight for Change by Joan E. Gadsby. Key Porter Books, 2000.

Research on a spectrum of disorders that covers the substance-related disorders or the impulse-control disorders is in its infancy. One of the difficulties in researching these disorders is their complexity. The problems that fall under disorders of substance use or impulse control are multifaceted and overlap a great deal with other disorders (comorbidity). For example, people with disorders as wide-ranging as antisocial personality disorder (see Chapter 12) (Copeland, Shanahan, Costello, & Angold, 2009), anxiety disorders (see Chapter 5) (Hofmann, Richey, Kashdan, & McKnight, 2009), schizophrenia (see Chapter 13) (Horsfall, Cleary, Hunt, & Walter, 2009), bipolar disorder (see Chapter 7) (Joshi & Wilens, 2009), and depression (see Chapter 7) (Rao, Hammen, & Poland, 2009) all have an increased risk of also meeting criteria for a substance-related disorder. At the same time, there are other mental health concerns that resemble the pattern of use, dependence, and withdrawal of the substance-related disorders but do not involve the use of mood-altering substances. For example, as we have seen, discussion is under way to include pathological gambling as part of a new category of disorders, "addiction and related disorders," in the *DSM-5*—which would then expand the "addictions" beyond just mood-altering substances (Moeller, 2009). Other problems that cause real dysfunction among some people, including "Internet addiction" (Block, 2008) and even "tanning addiction" (Poorsattar & Hornung, 2010), are being taken seriously as similar types of problems.

One contender for a spectrum of disorders that is currently being researched is referred to as the *externalizing spectrum* (Krueger, Markon, Patrick, & Iacono, 2005; Sher, Martinez, & Littlefield, in press). This categorization includes the substance-related disorders along with antisocial behaviour (a personality disorder characterized by the violation of social norms with a disregard for the rights and feelings of others; see Chapter 12) and personality traits such as aggression and impulsivity, all of which often occur together (Krueger et al., 2005). If we return to the case of Danny, we can see that he displayed many if not all of the characteristics of this spectrum of disorders. Recall that, in addition to his substance abuse problems, he would steal from his family and his employers, he lied frequently to everyone, and yet he never expressed any true remorse for how his behaviour impacted others—all characteristics of antisocial personality disorder. In fact, even awaiting trial in jail for his DWI-related traffic fatality, he was talking to as many people as he could to try to blame the medication he was on at the time for his difficulty and never admitted any guilt or expressed any concern for the family of the woman he killed. This collection of difficulties, which have at their core a variety of characteristics including novelty seeking and sensation seeking, is now being explored in a variety of research paradigms (including genetic research) as a possible unifying spectrum that may lead to a deeper understanding of these troubling problems (e.g., Dick et al., 2008).

Summary

Perspectives on Substance-Related Disorders

- In the *DSM-IV-TR*, substance-related disorders are divided into the depressants (alcohol, barbiturates, and benzodiazepines), stimulants (amphetamine, cocaine, nicotine, and caffeine), opiates (heroin, codeine, and morphine), and hallucinogens (marijuana and LSD).
- Specific diagnoses are further categorized as substance dependence, substance abuse, substance intoxication, and substance withdrawal.
- Nonmedical drug use continues to cost Canadians billions of dollars and seriously impairs the lives of millions of Canadians each year.

Depressants, Stimulants, Opioids, and Hallucinogens

- Depressants are a group of drugs that decrease central nervous system activity. The primary effect is to reduce our levels of physiological arousal and help us relax. Included in this group are alcohol and the sedative, hypnotic, and anxiolytic drugs such as those prescribed for insomnia.
- Stimulants, the most commonly consumed psychoactive drugs, include caffeine (in coffee, chocolate, and many soft drinks), nicotine (in tobacco products such as cigarettes), amphetamines, and cocaine. In contrast to the depressant drugs, stimulants make us more alert and energetic.
- Opiates include opium, morphine, codeine, and heroin; they have a narcotic effect—relieving pain and inducing sleep. The broader-term opioids is used to refer to the family of substances that includes these opiates as well as synthetic variations created by chemists (methadone, pethidine) and the similarly acting substances that occur naturally in our brains (enkephalins, beta-endorphins, and dynorphins).
- Hallucinogens essentially change the way the user perceives the world. Sight, sound, feelings, and even smell are distorted, sometimes in dramatic ways, in a person under the influence of drugs such as marijuana and LSD.
- A number of other substances that do not readily fit into the drug classes of depressants, stimulants, opiates, or hallucinogens, are also used by individuals to alter sensory experiences. Examples of these other drugs of abuse are inhalants, steroids, and designer drugs like ketamine.

Causes and Treatments of Substance-Related Disorders

- Most psychotropic drugs seem to produce positive effects by acting directly or indirectly on the dopaminergic system (the "pleasure pathway"). In addition, psychosocial factors such as expectations, stress, and cultural practices interact with the biological influences to influence drug use.
- Substance dependence is treated successfully only with a minority of those affected, and the best results reflect the motivation of the drug user and a combination of biological and psychosocial treatments.
- Programs aimed at preventing drug use may have the greatest chance of significantly affecting the drug problem.

Impulse-Control Disorders

- In the *DSM-IV-TR,* impulse-control disorders include five separate disorders: intermittent explosive disorder, kleptomania, pyromania, pathological gambling, and trichotillomania.

Key Terms

agonist substitution, 423
alcohol dehydrogenase (ADH), 417
alcohol use disorders, 400
amphetamine use disorders, 407
antagonist drugs, 424
barbiturates, 405
benzodiazepines, 405
caffeine use disorders, 410
cocaine use disorders, 407
controlled drinking, 426
delirium tremens (DTs), 401

depressants, 399
fetal alcohol syndrome (FAS), 402
gamma aminobutyric acid (GABA) system, 401
hallucinogen use disorder, 412
hallucinogens, 399
harm reduction, 423
impulse-control disorders, 393
intermittent explosive disorder, 429
kleptomania, 430

LSD (*d*-lysergic acid diethylamide), 414
marijuana (cannabis), 412
nicotine use disorders, 409
opiates, 399
opioid use disorders, 411
other drugs of abuse, 400
pathological gambling, 430
polysubstance use, 393
psychoactive substances, 394
pyromania, 430
relapse prevention, 427

stimulants, 399
substance abuse, 394
substance dependence, 395
substance intoxication, 394
substance-related disorders, 393
tolerance, 395
trichotillomania, 431
withdrawal, 395
withdrawal delirium, 401

Answers to Concept Checks

11.1

1. b **2.** a **3.** d **4.** c

11.2

1. hallucinogens
2. tolerance
3. psychoactive
4. withdrawal
5. depressants

11.3

1. c **2.** b **3.** a **4.** d

11.4

1. c **2.** d **3.** b **4.** e

Media Resources

CourseMate

Access an integrated eBook, Abnormal Psychology Videos (formerly Abnormal Psych Live CD-ROM), chapter-specific interactive learning tools (flashcards, quizzes, learning modules), and more in your Psychology CourseMate, available at **www.abnormalpsych3ce.nelson.com**.

Abnormal Psychology Videos

Free Abnormal Psychology videos can be viewed on the website **www.abnormalpsych3ce .nelson.com**.

- *Substance Use Disorder: Tim:* Tim describes the key criteria and shows how the disorder has had an impact on his life.

- *Nicotine Dependence:* Learn how nicotine increases the power of cues associated with smoking and how this research might help in the design of more effective programs to help people quit tobacco.

Video Concept Reviews

CourseMate also contains Mark Durand's *Video Concept Reviews* on these challenging topics.

- Substance Intoxication, Abuse and Dependence
- Tolerance and Withdrawal
- Alcohol Use Disorders
- Sedative, Hypnotic, and Anxiolytic Substances
- Stimulants
- Amphetamine Use Disorders
- Cocaine Use Disorders
- Nicotine Use Disorders
- Caffeine Use Disorders

- Opioid Use Disorders
- Hallucinogen Use Disorders
- Marijuana
- LSD and Other Hallucinogens
- Inhalants
- Anabolic Steroids
- Designer Drugs
- Drug Use: Psychological Perspective
- Concept Check: Impulse Control Disorders versus Substance Use

Exploring Substance-Related Disorders

> Many kinds of problems can develop when people use and abuse substances that alter the way they think, feel, and behave.

> Once seen as due to personal weakness, drug abuse and dependence are now thought influenced by both biological and psychosocial factors.

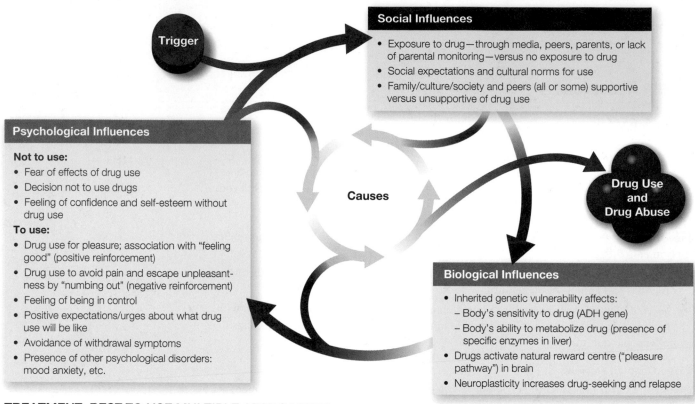

Social Influences

- Exposure to drug—through media, peers, parents, or lack of parental monitoring—versus no exposure to drug
- Social expectations and cultural norms for use
- Family/culture/society and peers (all or some) supportive versus unsupportive of drug use

Trigger

Causes

Drug Use and Drug Abuse

Psychological Influences

Not to use:
- Fear of effects of drug use
- Decision not to use drugs
- Feeling of confidence and self-esteem without drug use

To use:
- Drug use for pleasure; association with "feeling good" (positive reinforcement)
- Drug use to avoid pain and escape unpleasantness by "numbing out" (negative reinforcement)
- Feeling of being in control
- Positive expectations/urges about what drug use will be like
- Avoidance of withdrawal symptoms
- Presence of other psychological disorders: mood anxiety, etc.

Biological Influences

- Inherited genetic vulnerability affects:
  - Body's sensitivity to drug (ADH gene)
  - Body's ability to metabolize drug (presence of specific enzymes in liver)
- Drugs activate natural reward centre ("pleasure pathway") in brain
- Neuroplasticity increases drug-seeking and relapse

TREATMENT: BEST TO USE MULTIPLE APPROACHES

Psychosocial Treatments

- Aversion therapy—to create negative associations with drug use (shocks with drinking, imagining nausea with cocaine use)
- Contingency management to change behaviours by rewarding chosen behaviours
- Alcoholics Anonymous and its variations
- Inpatient hospital treatment (can be expensive)
- Controlled use
- Community reinforcement
- Relapse prevention

Biological Treatments

- Agonist substitution
  - Replacing one drug with a similar one (methadone for heroin, nicotine gum and patches for cigarettes)
- Antagonist substitution
  - Blocking one drug's effect with another drug (naltrexone for opiates and alcohol)
- Aversive treatments
  - Making taking drug very unpleasant (using Antabuse, which causes nausea and vomiting when mixed with alcohol, to treat alcoholism)
- Drugs to help recovering person deal with withdrawal symptoms (clonidine for opiate withdrawal, sedatives for alcohol, etc.)

TYPES OF DRUGS

	Examples	Effects
Depressants	Alcohol, barbiturates (sedatives: Amytal, Seconal, Nembutal), benzodiazepines (antianxiety: Valium, Xanax, Halcion)	• Decreased central nervous system activity • Reduced levels of body arousal • Relaxation
Stimulants	Amphetamines, cocaine, nicotine, caffeine	• Increased physical arousal • User feels more alert and energetic
Opiates	Heroin, morphine, codeine	• Narcotic—reduce pain and induce sleep and euphoria by mirroring opiates in the brain (endorphins, etc.)
Hallucinogens	Marijuana, LSD, Ecstasy	• Altered mental and emotional perception • Distortion (sometimes dramatic) of sensory perceptions

Exploring Impulse-Control Disorders

Characterized by inability to resist acting on a drive or temptation. Sufferers often perceived by society as having a problem simply due to a lack of "will."

TYPES OF IMPULSE-CONTROL DISORDERS

Disorder		Characteristics	Treatment
Intermittent Explosive		• Acting on aggressive impulses that result in assaults or destruction of property • Current research is focused on how neurotransmitters and testosterone levels interact with psychosocial influences (stress, parenting styles)	Cognitive-behavioural interventions (helping person identify and avoid triggers for aggressive outbursts) and approaches modelled after drug treatments appear most effective
Kleptomania		• Recurring failure to resist urges to steal unneeded items • Feeling tense just before stealing, followed by feelings of pleasure or relief when committing the theft • High comorbidity with mood disorders and, to a lesser degree, with substance abuse/dependence	Behavioural interventions or antidepressant medication
Pathological Gambling		• Preoccupation with gambling/with need to gamble increasing amounts of money to feel the same excitement • "Withdrawal symptoms" of restlessness and irritability when attempting to stop • May have a biological component involving brain activity (decreased activity in brain region controlling impulse regulation, abnormalities in dopamine and serotonin systems)	Gamblers Anonymous; similar to substance-dependence treatment
Trichotillomania		• Urge to pull out one's own hair from anywhere on the body • Sufferers go to great lengths to conceal behaviour • Relatively common (seen 1–5 percent of college students)	SSRIs may help; cognitive-behavioural interventions hold promise
Pyromania		• Irresistible urge to set fires • Feeling aroused prior to setting fire then a sense of gratification or relief while the fire burns • Rare; diagnosed in less than 4 percent of arsonists	Cognitive-behavioural interventions (helping person identify signals triggering urges, and teaching coping strategies to resist setting fires)

Tom Morrison/Getty Images

Mauro Speziale /Getty Images

Tom and Steve/Getty Images

Wedgworth/Custom Medical Stock Photo(CMSP)

Joel Sartore/Getty Images

12 | Personality Disorders

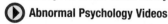
Photos.com

> *I experienced a strong urge to harm myself ... I wanted to electrocute myself by putting a metal knife into a light socket ... I wanted to feel something that would "jolt" me back into a sense of feeling.*
> —Jane Wanklin, *Let Me Make It Good: A Chronicle of My Life with Borderline Personality Disorder*

Demonstrate knowledge and understanding representing appropriate breadth and depth in selected content areas of psychology:	❭ Biological bases of behaviour and mental processes, including physiology, sensation, perception, comparative, motivation, and emotion (APA SLO 1.2.a (3)) *(see textbook pages 454–457)*
Use the concepts, language, and major theories of the discipline to account for psychological phenomena.	❭ Describe behaviour and mental processes empirically, including operational definitions (APA SLO 1.3.a) *(see textbook pages 439–470)*
Identify appropriate applications of psychology in solving problems, such as:	❭ Origin and treatment of abnormal behaviour (APA SLO 4.2.b) *(see textbook pages 446–450, 457–463, 464–470)*

* Portions of this chapter cover learning outcomes suggested by the American Psychological Association (2007) in their guidelines for the undergraduate psychology major. Chapter coverage of these outcomes is identified above by APA Goal and APA Suggested Learning Outcome (SLO).

According to the *DSM-IV-TR*, **personality disorders** are "enduring patterns of perceiving, relating to, and thinking about the environment and oneself that are exhibited in a wide range of social and personal contexts," and "are inflexible and maladaptive, and cause significant functional impairment or subjective distress" (American Psychiatric Association, 2000a, p. 686). Now that we have highlighted this definition of personality disorders, what do you think it means?

We all think we know what a "personality" is. It's all the characteristic ways a person behaves and thinks: "Michael tends to be shy"; "Mindy likes to be very dramatic"; "Juan is always suspicious of others"; "Annette is very outgoing"; "Bruce seems to be very sensitive and gets upset very easily over minor things"; "Sean has the personality of an eggplant!" We tend to type people as behaving in one way in many different situations. For example, like Michael, many of us are shy with people we don't know, but we aren't shy around our friends. A truly shy person is shy even among people he or she has known for some time. The shyness is part of the way the person behaves in most situations. We have all probably behaved in all the ways noted here ("dramatic," "suspicious," "outgoing," "easily upset"). However, we usually consider a way of behaving as part of a person's personality only if it occurs many times and in many places. In this chapter we look at characteristic ways of behaving in relation to personality disorders. First we examine in some detail how we conceptualize personality disorders and the issues related to them; then we describe the disorders themselves.

An Overview

What if a person's characteristic ways of thinking and behaving cause significant distress to the self or others? What if the person can't change this way of relating to the world and is unhappy? We might consider this person to have a "personality disorder." The *DSM-IV-TR* definition notes that these personality characteristics are "inflexible and maladaptive and cause significant functional impairment or subjective distress." Unlike many of the disorders we have already discussed, personality disorders are chronic; they do not come and go but originate in childhood and continue throughout adulthood. Because they affect personality, these chronic problems pervade every aspect of a person's life. If a man is overly suspicious, for example (a sign of a possible paranoid personality disorder), this trait will affect almost everything he does, including his employment (he may have to change jobs frequently if he believes co-workers conspire against him), his relationships (he may not be able to sustain a lasting relationship if he can't trust anyone), and even where he lives (he may have to move often if he suspects his landlord is out to get him).

The *DSM-IV-TR* notes that having this disorder may distress the affected person. However, individuals with personality disorders may not feel any subjective distress; indeed, it may be acutely felt by others because of the actions of the person with the disorder. As noted by forensic psychologist Robert Hare, professor emeritus at the University of British Columbia, this distress is particularly common with antisocial personality disorder, because the individual may show a blatant disregard for the rights of others yet exhibit no remorse (Hare, 1993). In certain cases, someone other than the person with the personality disorder must decide whether the disorder is causing significant functional impairment, because the affected person often cannot make such a judgment.

The *DSM-IV-TR* lists ten specific personality disorders and several others that are being studied for future considerations; we review them all. Unfortunately, as we see later, many people who have personality disorders in addition to other psychological problems tend to do poorly in treatment. Data from several studies show that people who are depressed have a worse outcome in treatment if they also have a personality disorder (Sanderson & Clarkin, 1994; Shea et al., 1990). Nonetheless, the prospects for treatment success for people who have personality disorders may be more optimistic than previously thought (Howes & Vallis, 1996; Ogrodniczuk & Piper, 2001; Perry, Banon, & Ianni, 1999). For example, Michael Vallis and Janice Howes have suggested that there are grounds to be cautiously optimistic about the potential uses of cognitive therapy in individuals with personality disorders (Vallis et al., 2000).

Most disorders we discuss in this book are on Axis I of the *DSM-IV-TR*, which includes the standard traditional disorders. The personality disorders are included in a separate axis, Axis II, because as a group they are distinct. The characteristic traits are more ingrained and inflexible in people who have personality disorders, and the disorders themselves are less likely to be successfully modified.

Having personality disorders on a separate axis requires the clinician to consider in each assessment whether the person has a personality disorder. In the axis system, a patient can receive a diagnosis on only Axis I, only Axis II, or on both axes. A diagnosis on both Axis I and Axis II indicates that a person has both a current disorder (Axis I) and a more chronic problem (e.g., personality disorder). As you will see, it is not unusual for one person to be diagnosed on both axes.

You may be surprised to learn that the category of personality disorders is controversial, because it involves several unresolved issues. Examining these issues can help us understand all the disorders described in this book.

Categorical and Dimensional Models

Most of us are sometimes suspicious of others and a little paranoid, or overly dramatic, or too self-involved, or reclusive. Fortunately, these characteristics don't last for too long or are not overly intense, and they don't significantly impair how we live and work. People with personality disorders, however, display problem characteristics over extended periods and in many situations, which can cause great emotional pain for themselves, others, or both (Ferguson, 2010b). Their difficulty, then, can be seen as one of *degree* rather than *kind*; in other words, the problems of people with personality disorders may just be extreme versions of the problems many of us experience on a temporary basis, such as being shy or suspicious.

The distinction between problems of *degree* and problems of *kind* is usually described in terms of *dimensions* instead of *categories*. The issue that continues to be debated in the field is whether personality disorders are extreme versions of otherwise normal personality variations (dimensions) or ways of relating that are different from psychologically healthy behaviour (categories; Widiger & Trull, 2007; Gunderson, 1992). For example, John Livesley and his colleagues have been strongly advocating for a change from the current categorical approach to personality disorders used in the *DSM-IV-TR* to a dimensional-based approach (e.g., Livesley, 2006, 2007; Livesley, Schroeder, Jackson, & Jang, 1994). We can see the difference between dimensions and categories in everyday life. For example, we tend to look at gender categorically. Our society views us as being in one category—female—or the other—male. Yet we could also look at gender in terms of dimensions. For example, we know that "maleness" and "femaleness" are partly determined by hormones. We could identify people along testosterone, estrogen, or both dimensions and rate them on a continuum of maleness and femaleness rather than in the absolute categories of male or female. We also often label people's size categorically, as tall, average, or short. But height can also be viewed dimensionally, in centimetres or inches.

Most people in the field see personality disorders as extremes on one or more personality dimensions. Yet because of the way people are diagnosed with the *DSM*, the personality disorders—like most of the other disorders—end up being viewed in categories. You have two choices—either you do ("yes") or you do not ("no") have a disorder. For example, either you have antisocial personality disorder or you don't. The *DSM* doesn't rate *how* obsessive or compulsive you are; if you meet the criteria, you are labelled as having obsessive-compulsive personality disorder. No in-between is possible when it comes to personality disorders. Using categorical models of behaviour has advantages, the most important being convenience. With simplification, however, come problems. One is that the mere act of using categories leads clinicians to reify the disorders, that is, to view disorders as real "things," comparable to the realness of an infection or a broken arm. Some argue that personality disorders are not things that exist but points at which society decides a particular way of relating to the world has become a problem. The important unresolved issue comes up again: Are personality disorders just an extreme variant of normal personality, or are they distinctly different disorders?

Many researchers believe that many or all personality disorders represent extremes on one or more personality dimensions. Consequently, some have proposed that the *DSM-IV-TR* personality disorders section be replaced or at least supplemented by a dimensional model in which individuals would not only be given categorical diagnoses but also would be rated on a series of personality dimensions (Livesley & Jang, 2000; Widiger, 1991). Widiger (1991) believes such a system would have at least three advantages over a purely categorical system: (1) It would retain more information about each individual, (2) it would be more flexible because it would permit both categorical and dimensional differentiations among individuals, and (3) it would avoid the often arbitrary decisions involved in assigning a person to a diagnostic category.

Although no general consensus exists about what the basic personality dimensions might be, there are several contenders (Eysenck & Eysenck, 1975; Tellegen, 1978; Watson, Clark, & Harkness, 1994). One of the more widely accepted is called the "Big Five" or the *five-factor model* of personality, and is taken from work on normal personality (Goldberg, 1993; Jang, Livesley, Angleitner, Riemann, & Vernon, 2002; McCrae & Costa Jr., 2008; Stewart & Devine, 2000). In this model, people can be rated on a series of personality dimensions, and the combination of five components describes why people are so different. The five factors or dimensions are *extraversion* (talkative, assertive, and active versus silent, passive, and reserved); *agreeableness* (kind, trusting, and warm versus hostile, selfish, and mistrustful); *conscientiousness* (organized, thorough, and reliable versus careless, negligent, and unreliable); *neuroticism* (nervous, moody, and temperamental versus even-tempered); and *openness to experience* (imaginative, curious, and creative versus shallow and imperceptive; McCrae & Costa Jr., 2008). On each dimension, people are rated high, low, or somewhere in between.

Cross-cultural research establishes the universal nature of the five dimensions. In German, Portuguese, Hebrew, Chinese, Korean, and Japanese samples, individuals have personality trait structures similar to North American samples (McCrae & Costa, 1997). A number of researchers, including John Livesley and his colleagues, are trying to determine whether people with personality disorders can also be rated in a meaningful way along the dimensions identified in the five-factor model and whether the system will help us better understand these disorders (Clark, 1993; Krueger, Caspi, Moffit, Silva, & McGee, 1996; Schroeder, Wormworth, & Livesley, 1993; Skodol et al., 2005).

Some researchers (e.g., Bagby, Marshall, & Georgiades, 2005; Widiger, 1993) have attempted to map the *DSM-IV-TR* personality disorders onto the characteristics of the five-factor model, as outlined in DSM Table 12.1. For example, we can see how the five-factor model helps us distinguish between people with avoidant personality disorder versus schizoid personality disorder—two personality disorders described more fully later in the chapter. According to their *DSM-IV-TR* definitions, both disorders are characterized by low levels of social involvement, but for very different reasons. When we view these two personality disorders from within the framework of the five-factor model of personality, although both are characterized by low extraversion, only avoidant personality disorder is additionally characterized by high neuroticism (see DSM Table 12.1).

An alternative model that derives from clinical work with people who have personality disorders is proposed by Westen and Shedler (2004). Their model identifies 12 personality dimensions (as opposed to the five in the five-factor model) that not only overlap with *DSM* criteria but also introduce new aspects of personality not previously tapped in the *DSM* (see Table 12.1). In addition to Westen and Shedler's model, there are over a dozen other dimensional systems of classifying personality disorders having varying levels of support but, as yet, no one approach dominates the field (South, Oltmanns, & Krueger, in press).

DSM-IV-TR

Table 12.1 Relationship between Each Personality Disorder and Characteristics of the Five-Factor Model of Personality

	Five-Factor Model Personality Trait				
Disorder	**N**	**E**	**O**	**A**	**C**
Cluster A					
Paranoid		low	low	low*	
Schizoid		low*			
Schizotypal	high*	low*	high*		
Cluster B					
Borderline	high*	high		low	low
Narcissistic	high	high		low*	high
Histrionic	high*	high*	high*		low
Antisocial				low*	low*
Cluster C					
Dependent	high*			high*	
Avoidant	high*	low*			
Obsessive-compulsive	high	low	low		high*

Notes: N = neuroticism, E = extraversion, O = openness to experience, A = agreeableness, C = conscientiousness. Asterisks indicate defining features of a given *DSM-IV-TR* personality disorder; otherwise features can be considered associated features. Blank spaces indicate that a given trait is not relevant to the personality disorder in question.

Source: Adapted from Widiger, Trull, Clarkin, Sanderson, and Costa (1994).

TABLE 12.1 Two Dimensional Models of Personality

Dimension	Description
Five-Factor Model	
Neuroticism	Proneness to psychological distress and impulsive behaviour
Extraversion	Tendency to join in social situations and feel joy and optimism
Openness to experience	Curiosity, receptivity to new ideas, and emotional expressiveness
Agreeableness	Extent to which someone shows both compassion and hostility toward others
Conscientiousness	Degree of organization and commitment to personal goals
Westen and Shedler Model	
Psychological health	Ability to love others, find meaning in life, and gain personal insights
Psychopathy	Lack of remorse, presence of impulsiveness, and tendency to abuse drugs
Hostility	Deep-seated ill will
Narcissism	Self-importance, grandiose assumptions about oneself, and tendency to treat others as an audience to provide admiration
Emotional dysregulation	Intense and uncontrolled emotional reactions
Dysphoria	Depression, shame, humiliation, and lack of any pleasurable experiences
Schizoid orientation	Constricted emotions, inability to understand abstract concepts such as metaphors, and few or no friends
Obsessionality	Absorption in details, stinginess, and fear of dirt and contamination
Thought disorder	Such as believing one has magical powers over others or can directly read their minds
Oedipal conflict	Adult pursuit of romantic partners who are already involved with others, inappropriate seductiveness, and intense sexual jealousy
Dissociated consciousness	Fragmenting of thought and perception often related to past sexual abuse
Sexual conflict	Anxieties and fears regarding sexual intimacy

Source: Bower, B. (1999). Personality conflicts: A clinical upstart elbows its way into the personality-assessment fray. *Science News, 156,* 88–90.

Again, an obstacle to the adoption of a dimensional approach to personality disorders is the lack of consensus regarding the most appropriate framework. However, there is a growing consensus that the next version of the *Diagnostic and Statistical Manual*—the *DSM-5*—should incorporate aspects of a dimensional approach to personality disorders (South et al., in press).

Personality Disorder Clusters

The *DSM-IV-TR* divides the personality disorders into three groups, or "clusters"; this will probably continue until a strong scientific basis is established for viewing them differently (American Psychiatric Association, 2000a). The cluster division is based on resemblance. Cluster A is called the "odd" or "eccentric" cluster; it includes paranoid, schizoid, and schizotypal personality disorders. Cluster B is the "dramatic," "emotional," or "erratic" cluster; it consists of antisocial, borderline, histrionic, and narcissistic personality disorders. Montréal researchers Karl Looper and Joel Paris have found that all four disorders in this cluster are characterized by elevated impulsivity (Looper & Paris, 2000). Cluster C is the "anxious" or "fearful" cluster; it includes avoidant, dependent, and obsessive-compulsive personality disorders. Michael Bagby and his colleagues at the Centre for Addiction and Mental Health in Toronto have obtained some research support for the existence of these three clusters (Bagby, Joffe,

Parker, & Schuller, 1993), as have Birendra Sinha and David Watson (2004) of Edmonton. However, more recent work shows that the proposed three-cluster structure only holds when the personality disorders are assessed by clinicians, and not when they are assessed via patient self-reports (Yang, Bagby, Costa, Ryder, & Herbst, 2002). We follow this three-cluster order in our review.

Statistics and Development

Canadian data on the prevalence of personality disorders are generally lacking, save in the case of antisocial personality disorder (Health Canada, 2002). However, American studies indicate that personality disorders are found in 0.5 percent to 2.5 percent of the general population, 10 percent to 30 percent of those served in inpatient settings, and in 2 percent to 10 percent of those individuals in outpatient settings (American Psychiatric Association, 2000a), which makes them relatively common. As you can see from Table 12.2, schizoid, narcissistic, and avoidant personality disorders are relatively rare, occurring in less than 1 percent of the general population. Paranoid, schizotypal, histrionic, dependent, and obsessive-compulsive personality disorders are found in 1 percent to 4 percent of the general population.

Personality disorders are thought to originate in childhood or adolescence and continue into the adult years (Cloninger & Svakic, 2009) and to be so ingrained it is difficult to pinpoint an

TABLE 12.2 Statistics and Development of Personality Disorders

Disorder	Prevalence	Gender Differences	Course
Paranoid personality disorder	0.5 percent to 2.5 percent (Bernstein, Useda, & Siever, 1993)	More common in males (O'Brien, Trestman, & Siever, 1993)	Insufficient information
Schizoid personality disorder	Less than 1 percent in Canada, United States, New Zealand, Taiwan (Weissman, 1993)	More common in males (O'Brien et al., 1993)	Insufficient information
Schizotypal personality disorder	3 percent to 5 percent (Weissman, 1993)	More common in males (Kotsattis & Neale, 1993)	Chronic: some go on to develop schizophrenia
Antisocial personality disorder	3 percent in males; less than 1 percent in females (Sutker, Bugg, & West, 1993)	More common in males (Dulit, Marin, & Franes, 1993)	Dissipates after age 40 (Hare, McPherson & Forth, 1988)
Borderline personality disorder	1 percent to 3 percent (Widiger & Weissman, 1991)	Females make up 75 percent of cases (Dulit, et al, 1993)	Symptoms gradually improve if individuals survive into their 30s (Dulit et al., 1993); approximately 6 percent die by suicide (Perry, 1993)
Histrionic personality disorder	2 percent (Nestadt et al., 1990)	Equal numbers of males and females (Nestadt et al., 1990)	Chronic
Narcissistic personality disorder	Less than 1 percent (Zimmerman & Coryell, 1990)	More prevalent among men	May improve over time (Cooper & Ronningstam, 1992; Gunderson, Ronningstam, & Smith, 1991)
Avoidant personality disorder	Less than 1 percent (Reich, Yates, & Nduaguba, 1989; Zimmerman & Coryell, 1990)	Equal numbers of males and females (Millon, 1986)	Insufficient information
Dependent personality disorder	2 percent (Zimmerman & Coryell, 1989)	May be equal numbers of males and females (Reich, 1987)	Insufficient information
Obsessive-compulsive personality disorder	4 percent (Weissman, 1993)	More common in males (Stone, 1993)	Insufficient information

onset. Maladaptive personality characteristics develop over time into the maladaptive behaviour patterns that create distress for the affected person and draw the attention of others. Our relative lack of information about such important features of personality disorders as their developmental course is a repeating theme. The gaps in our knowledge of the course of about half these disorders are visible in Table 12.2. One reason for this dearth of research is that many individuals do not seek treatment in the early developmental phases of their disorder, but only after years of distress. This delay makes it difficult to study people with personality disorders from the beginning, although a few research studies have helped us understand the development of several disorders.

People with borderline personality disorder are characterized by their volatile and unstable relationships; they tend to have persistent problems in early adulthood, with frequent hospitalizations, unstable personal relationships, severe depression, and suicidal gestures. Almost 10 percent attempt suicide, and approximately 6 percent succeed in their attempts (Skodol & Gunderson, 2008). On the bright side, their symptoms gradually improve if they survive into their 30s (Zanarini, Frankenburg, Hennen, Reich, & Silk, 2006), although elderly individuals may have difficulty making plans and may be disruptive in nursing homes

▲ Personality disorders tend to begin in childhood.

maureen rigdon/Shutterstock

(Hunt, 2007). People with antisocial personality disorder display a characteristic disregard for the rights and feelings of others; they tend to continue their destructive behaviours of lying and manipulation through adulthood. Fortunately, as indicated by the research of Robert Hare, Leslie McPherson, and Adelle Forth (1988), some tend to burn out after the age of about 40 and engage in fewer criminal activities. As a group, however, the problems of people with personality disorders continue, as shown when researchers follow their progress over the years (Ferguson, 2010b).

Gender Differences

Borderline personality disorder is diagnosed much more frequently in females, who make up about 75 percent of the identified cases (Cloninger & Svakic, 2009; Dulit et al., 1993; see Table 12.2). Historically, histrionic and dependent personality disorders were identified by clinicians more often in women (Dulit et al., 1993; Stone, 1993), but according to more recent studies of their prevalence in the general population, equal numbers of males and females may have histrionic and dependent personality disorders (Lilienfeld, VanValkenburg, Larntz, & Akiskal, 1986; Nestadt et al., 1990; Reich, 1987). If this observation holds up in future studies, why have these disorders been predominantly diagnosed among females in general clinical practice and in other studies (Dulit et al., 1993)?

Do the disparities indicate differences between men and women in certain basic genetic or sociocultural experience, or do they represent biases on the part of the clinicians who make the diagnoses? Take, for example, a study by Ford and Widiger (1989), who sent fictitious case histories to clinical psychologists for diagnosis. One case described a person with *antisocial personality disorder*, which is characterized by irresponsible and reckless behaviour and usually diagnosed in males; the other case described a person with *histrionic personality disorder*, which is characterized by excessive emotionality and attention seeking and more often diagnosed in females. The patient was identified as male in some versions of each case and as female in others, although everything else was identical. As the graph in ■ Figure 12.1 shows, when the antisocial personality disorder case was labelled male, most psychologists gave the correct diagnosis. However, when the same case was labelled female, most psychologists diagnosed it as histrionic personality disorder rather than antisocial personality disorder. This finding of an underdiagnosis of antisocial personality disorder in female clients was replicated in a similar study conducted in Toronto with psychiatry residents (Belitsky et al., 1996). In the original Ford and Widiger (1989) study, being labelled a woman increased the likelihood of a diagnosis of histrionic personality disorder. The authors concluded that the psychologists incorrectly diagnosed more women as having histrionic personality disorder (Ford & Widiger, 1989).

Such gender differences in diagnoses have been criticized by several authors. For example, some have argued that histrionic personality disorder, like several of the other personality disorders, is biased against females. Many of the features of histrionic personality disorder, such as overdramatization, vanity, seductiveness, and overconcern with physical appearance, are characteristic of the Western "stereotypical female" (Kaplan, 1983). This disorder may

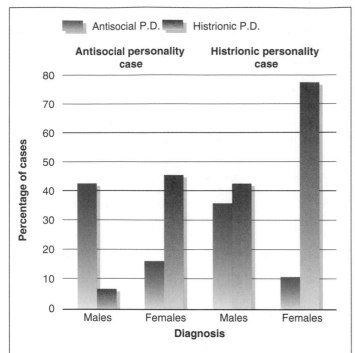

■ FIGURE 12.1 Gender bias in diagnosing personality disorders. Data are shown for the percentage of cases clinicians rated as antisocial personality disorder or histrionic personality disorder, depending on whether the case was described as a male or a female.

Source: Adapted from "A Description of the DSM-III-R and DSM-IV Personality Disorders with the Five-Factor Model of Personality" by Widiger, Trull, Clarkin, Sanderson, and Costa, 90, *Personality Disorders and the Five-Factor Model of Personality, 2nd edition* by Paul T. Costa and Thomas A. Widiger (Eds). © 2002 by the American Psychological Association. Reprinted with permission from *Diagnostic and Statistical Manual of Mental Disorders*, Fourth Edition, Text Revision. Copyright © 2000 American Psychiatric Association.

simply be the embodiment of extremely "feminine" traits (Chodoff, 1982); branding such an individual mentally ill, according to Kaplan, reflects society's inherent bias against females. Interestingly, the "macho" personality (Mosher & Sirkin, 1984; Pantony & Caplan, 1991), in which the individual possesses stereotypically masculine traits, is nowhere to be found in the *DSM*. What do you think the sex ratio would be for people diagnosed with this "personality disorder"?

Remember, however, that just because certain disorders are observed more in men or in women doesn't necessarily indicate bias (Lilienfeld et al., 1986). And when it is present, bias can occur at different stages of the diagnostic process. The criteria for the disorder may themselves be biased (*criterion gender bias*), or the assessment measures and the way they are used may be biased (*assessment gender bias*; Widiger & Spitzer, 1991). In general, the criteria themselves do not appear to have strong gender bias (Jane, Oltmanns, South, & Turkheimer, 2007), although there may be some tendency for clinicians to use their own bias when using the criteria and therefore diagnose males and females differently (Morey, Alexander, & Boggs, 2005). As studies continue, researchers will try to make the diagnosis of personality disorders more accurate with respect to gender and more useful to clinicians.

Comorbidity

Looking at Table 12.2 (page 443) and adding up the prevalence rates across the personality disorders, you might conclude that between 20 percent and 30 percent of all people are affected. In fact, the percentage of people in the general population with a personality disorder is estimated to be between 0.5 percent and 2.5 percent (American Psychiatric Association, 2000a). What accounts for this discrepancy? A major concern with the personality disorders is that people tend to be diagnosed with more than one. The term *comorbidity* historically describes the condition in which a person has multiple diseases (Caron & Rutter, 1991). A fair amount of disagreement exists about whether the term should be used with psychological disorders because of the frequent overlap of different disorders (e.g., Nurnberg et al., 1991). In just one example, Morey (1988) conducted a study of 291 persons who were diagnosed with personality disorder and found considerable overlap (see Table 12.3). In the far left column of Table 12.3 is the primary diagnosis, and across the table are the percentages of people who also meet the criteria for other disorders. For example, a person identified with borderline personality disorder also has a 32 percent likelihood (i.e., almost a one in three chance) of fitting the definition of another supposedly different personality disorder—paranoid personality disorder (Grove & Tellegen, 1991).

Do people really tend to have more than one personality disorder? Are the ways we define these disorders inaccurate, and do we need to improve our definitions so they do not overlap? Or did we divide the disorders in the wrong way to begin with, and need to rethink

▲ Gender bias may affect the diagnosis of clinicians who associate certain behavioural characteristics with one sex or the other.

Photos.com

TABLE 12.3 Diagnostic Overlap of Personality Disorders

	Percentage of People Qualifying for Other Personality Disorder Diagnoses									
Diagnosis	Paranoid	Schizoid	Schizotypal	Antisocial	Borderline	Histrionic	Narcissistic	Avoidant	Dependent	Obsessive-Compulsive
Paranoid		23.4	25.0	7.8	48.4	28.1	35.9	48.4	29.7	7.8
Schizoid	46.9		37.5	3.1	18.8	9.4	28.1	53.1	18.8	15.6
Schizotypal	59.3	44.4		3.7	33.3	18.5	33.3	59.3	29.6	11.1
Antisocial	27.8	5.6	5.6		44.4	33.3	55.6	16.7	11.1	0.0
Borderline	32.0	6.2	9.3	8.2		36.1	30.9	36.1	34.0	2.1
Histrionic	28.6	4.8	7.9	9.5	55.6		54.0	31.7	30.2	4.8
Narcissistic	35.9	14.1	14.1	15.6	46.9	53.1		35.9	26.6	10.9
Avoidant	39.2	21.5	20.3	3.8	44.3	25.3	29.1		40.5	16.5
Dependent	29.2	9.2	12.3	3.1	50.8	29.2	26.2	49.2		9.2
Obsessive-compulsive	21.7	21.7	13.0	0.0	8.7	13.0	30.4	56.5	26.1	

Source: *The American Journal of Psychiatry* by American Psychiatric Association. Copyright 1988. Reproduced with permission of AMERICAN PSYCHIATRIC ASSOCIATION (JOURNALS) in the format Textbook via Copyright Clearance Center.

the categories? Such questions about comorbidity are just a few of the important issues faced by researchers who study personality disorders.

Cluster A Disorders

Paranoid Personality Disorder

Although it is probably very adaptive to be a little wary of other people and their motives, being too distrustful can interfere with making friends, working with others, and getting through daily interactions in a functional way. People with **paranoid personality disorder** are excessively mistrustful and suspicious of others, without any justification. They assume other people are out to harm or trick them, and therefore they tend not to confide in others. Consider the case of Jake.

JAKE | *Victim of Conspiracy?*

Jake grew up in a middle-class neighbourhood, and although he never got in serious trouble, he had a reputation in high school for arguing with teachers and classmates. After high school he enrolled in the local community college but flunked out after the first year. Jake's lack of success in school was in part attributable to his failure to take responsibility for his poor grades. He began to develop conspiracy theories about fellow students and professors, believing they worked together to see him fail. Jake bounced from job to job, each time complaining that his employer was spying on him. His parents brought him to a psychologist, and he was diagnosed with paranoid personality disorder.

Clinical Description

The defining characteristic of people with paranoid personality disorder is a pervasive unjustified distrust (Edens, Marcus, & Morey, 2009). Certainly, there may be times when someone is deceitful and "out to get you"; however, people with paranoid personality disorder are suspicious in situations in which most other people would agree that their suspicions are unfounded. Even events that have nothing to do with them are interpreted as personal attacks (Bernstein & Useda, 2007). These people would view a neighbour's barking dog or a delayed airline flight as a deliberate attempt to annoy them. Unfortunately, such mistrust often extends to people close to them and makes meaningful relationships very difficult. Imagine what a lonely existence this must be! Suspiciousness and mistrust can show themselves in many ways. People with paranoid personality disorder may be argumentative, may complain, or may be quiet, but they are obviously hostile toward others. They often appear tense and are "ready to pounce" when they think they've been slighted by someone. These individuals are very sensitive to criticism and have an excessive need for autonomy (Bernstein & Useda, 2007). The *DSM-IV-TR* criteria are outlined in DSM Table 12.2.

Paranoid personality disorder bears relationship to two disorders we will discuss in more detail in Chapter 13: (1) the paranoid type of schizophrenia and (2) delusional disorder. Both of the latter disorders involve delusions—persistent beliefs that are out of touch with reality. Although individuals with paranoid personality disorder are very suspicious of others, their suspiciousness does not reach delusional proportions. Another difference between the paranoid type of schizophrenia and paranoid personality disorder is that the former also involves other psychotic symptoms like hallucinations (e.g., hearing voices), whereas paranoid personality disorder does not (see Chapter 13).

Table 12.2 Diagnostic Criteria for Paranoid Personality Disorder

A. A pervasive distrust and suspiciousness of others such that their motives are interpreted as malevolent, beginning by early adulthood and present in a variety of contexts, as indicated by four (or more) of the following:

1. Suspects, without sufficient basis, that others are exploiting, harming, or deceiving him or her

2. Is preoccupied with unjustified doubts about the loyalty or trustworthiness of friends or associates

3. Is reluctant to confide in others because of unwarranted fear that the information will be used maliciously against him or her

4. Reads hidden demeaning or threatening meanings into benign remarks or events

5. Persistently bears grudges (i.e., is unforgiving of insults, injuries, or slights)

6. Perceives attacks on his or her character or reputation that are not apparent to others and is quick to react angrily or to counterattack

7. Has recurrent suspicions, without justification, regarding fidelity of spouse or sexual partner

B. Does not occur exclusively during the course of schizophrenia, a mood disorder with psychotic features, or another psychotic disorder and is not due to the direct physiological effects of a general medical condition

Note: If criteria are met before the onset of schizophrenia, add "premorbid" (e.g., "paranoid personality disorder [premorbid])."

Source: Reprinted with permission from the *Diagnostic and Statistical Manual of Mental Disorders,* Fourth Edition, Text Revision, (Copyright © 2000). American Psychiatric Association.

Causes

Evidence for biological contributions to paranoid personality disorder is limited. Some research suggests the disorder may be slightly more common among the relatives of people who have schizophrenia, although the association does not seem to be strong (Tienari et al., 2003). In other words, relatives of individuals with schizophrenia may be more likely to have paranoid personality disorder than people who do not have a relative with schizophrenia. As you will see later with the other odd or eccentric personality disorders in Cluster A, there seems to be some relationship with schizophrenia, although its exact nature is not yet clear. In general, however, there appears to be a strong role for genetics in paranoid personality disorder (Kendler et al., 2006).

Psychological contributions to this disorder are even less certain, although some interesting speculations have been made. Retrospective research—asking people with this disorder to recall events from their childhood—suggests that early mistreatment or traumatic childhood experiences may play a role in the development of paranoid personality disorder (Natsuaki, Cicchetti, & Rogosch, 2009). Caution is warranted when interpreting these results because, clearly, there may be strong bias in the recall of these individuals, who are already prone to viewing the world as a threat.

Some psychologists point directly to the thoughts of people with paranoid personality disorder as a way of explaining their behaviour. One view is that people with this disorder have the following basic mistaken assumptions about others: "People are

malevolent and deceptive," "They'll attack you if they get the chance," and "You can be OK only if you stay on your toes" (Freeman, Pretzer, Fleming, & Simon, 1990). This is a maladaptive way to view the world, yet it seems to pervade every aspect of the lives of these individuals. Although we don't know why they develop these perceptions, some speculation is that the roots are in their early upbringing. Their parents may teach them to be careful about making mistakes and to impress on them that they are different from other people (Turkat & Maisto, 1985). This vigilance causes them to see signs that other people are deceptive and malicious (Carroll, 2009). It is certainly true that people are not always benevolent and sincere, and our interactions are sometimes ambiguous enough to make other people's intentions unclear. Looking too closely at what other people say and do can sometimes lead to misinterpretation.

Cultural factors have also been implicated in paranoid personality disorder. Certain groups of people such as prisoners, refugees, people with hearing impairments, and the elderly are thought to be particularly susceptible because of their unique experiences (Rogler, 2007). Imagine how you might view other people if you were an immigrant who had difficulty with the language and the customs of your new culture. Such innocuous things as other people laughing or talking quietly might be interpreted as somehow directed at you. We have seen how someone could misinterpret ambiguous situations as malevolent. Therefore, cognitive and cultural factors may interact to produce the suspiciousness observed in some people with paranoid personality disorder.

Treatment

Because people with paranoid personality disorder are mistrustful of everyone, they are unlikely to seek professional help when they need it and they have difficulty developing the trusting relationships necessary for successful therapy (Skodol & Gunderson, 2008). Establishing a meaningful therapeutic alliance between the client and the therapist therefore becomes an important first step (Bender, 2005). When they do seek therapy, the trigger is usually a crisis in their lives or other problems such as anxiety or depression, and not necessarily their personality disorder (Kelly, Casey, Dunn, Ayuso-Mateos, & Dowrick, 2007).

Therapists try to provide an atmosphere conducive to developing a sense of trust (Bender, 2005). They often use cognitive therapy to counter the person's mistaken assumptions about others, focusing on changing the person's beliefs that all people are malevolent and most people cannot be trusted (Skodol & Gunderson, 2008). Be forewarned, however, that to date there are no confirmed demonstrations that any form of treatment can significantly improve the lives of people with paranoid personality disorder. Nonetheless, a review of the literature by Québec researcher Stéphane Bouchard and his colleagues concluded that cognitive restructuring could be helpful in reducing paranoid beliefs (Bouchard, Vallieres, Roy, & Maziade, 1996). Unfortunately, an Australian survey of mental health professionals indicated that only 11 percent of therapists who treat paranoid personality disorder thought these individuals would continue in therapy long enough to be helped (Quality Assurance Project, 1990).

Schizoid Personality Disorder

Do you know someone who is a "loner"? Someone who would choose a solitary walk over an invitation to a party? A person who comes to class alone, sits alone, and leaves alone? Now, magnify this preference for isolation many times over and you can begin to grasp the impact of **schizoid personality disorder** (Cloninger & Svakic, 2009). People with this personality disorder show a pattern of detachment from social relationships and a very limited range of emotions in interpersonal situations (Phillips & Gunderson, 2000). They seem "aloof," "cold," and "indifferent" to other people (see DSM Table 12.3). The term *schizoid* is relatively old, having been used by Bleuler (1924) to describe people who have a tendency to turn inward and away from the outside world. These people were said to lack emotional expressiveness and pursued vague interests. Consider the case of Mr. Z.

MR. Z. | *All on His Own*

A 39-year-old scientist was referred after he returned from being stationed in Baffin Island where he had stopped cooperating with others, had withdrawn to his room, and begun drinking on his own. Mr. Z. was orphaned at age four, raised by an aunt until nine, and subsequently looked after by an aloof housekeeper. At university he excelled at physics, but chess was his only contact with others. Throughout his subsequent life he made no close friends and engaged primarily in solitary activities. Until his move to Baffin Island, he had been quite successful in his research work in physics. He was now, some months after his return, drinking at least a bottle of Schnapps each day and his work had continued to deteriorate. He presented as self-contained and unobtrusive, and he was difficult to engage effectively. He was at a loss to explain his colleagues' anger at his aloofness in Baffin Island and appeared indifferent to their opinion of him. He did not appear to require any interpersonal relations.

Source: Quality Assurance Project, 1990, p. 346.

Clinical Description

Individuals with schizoid personality disorder seem neither to desire nor enjoy closeness with others, including romantic or sexual relationships. As a result they appear cold, aloof, and detached (Loza & Hanna, 2006) and do not seem affected by praise or criticism. Unfortunately, homelessness appears to be prevalent among people with this personality disorder, perhaps because of their lack of close friendships and lack of dissatisfaction about not having a sexual relationship with another person (Rouff, 2000).

The social deficiencies of people with schizoid personality disorder are similar to those of people with paranoid personality disorder, although the deficiencies are more extreme. As Beck and Freeman (1990) put it, they "consider themselves to be observers rather than participants in the world around them" (p. 125). They do not seem to have the very unusual

---

DSM-IV-TR	**Table 12.3** Diagnostic Criteria for Schizoid Personality Disorder

A. A pervasive pattern of detachment from social relationships and a restricted range of expression of emotions in interpersonal settings, beginning by early adulthood and present in a variety of contexts, as indicated by four (or more) of the following:

1. Neither desires nor enjoys close relationships, including being part of a family
2. Almost always chooses solitary activities
3. Has little, if any, interest in having sexual experiences with another person
4. Takes pleasure in few, if any, activities
5. Lacks close friends or confidants other than first-degree relatives
6. Appears indifferent to the praise or criticism of others
7. Shows emotional coldness, detachment, or flattened affectivity

B. Does not occur exclusively during the course of schizophrenia, a mood disorder with psychotic features, another psychotic disorder, or a pervasive developmental disorder and is not due to the direct physiological effects of a general medical condition

Note: If criteria are met before the onset of schizophrenia, add "premorbid" (e.g., "schizoid personality disorder [premorbid]").

Source: Reprinted with permission from the *Diagnostic and Statistical Manual of Mental Disorders,* Fourth Edition, Text Revision, (Copyright © 2000). American Psychiatric Association.

---

thought processes that characterize the other disorders in Cluster A (Kalus, Bernstein, & Siever, 1993; see Table 12.3). For example, people with paranoid and schizotypal personality disorders often have *ideas of reference*, mistaken beliefs that meaningless events relate just to them. In contrast, those with schizoid personality disorder share the social isolation, poor rapport, and constricted affect (showing neither positive nor negative emotion) seen in people with paranoid personality disorder. We see in Chapter 13 that this distinction among psychotic-like symptoms is important to understanding people with schizophrenia, some of whom show the "positive" symptoms (actively unusual behaviours such as ideas of reference) and others only the "negative" symptoms (the more passive manifestations of social isolation or poor rapport with others).

TABLE 12.4 Grouping Schema for Cluster A Disorders

Cluster A Personality Disorder	Psychotic-Like Symptoms	
	"Positive" (e.g., ideas of reference, magical thinking, and perceptual distortions)	"Negative" (e.g., social isolation, poor rapport, and constricted affect)
Paranoid	Yes	Yes
Schizoid	No	Yes
Schizotypal	Yes	No

Source: Review of psychiatry by AMERICAN PSYCHIATRIC PRESS. Copyright 1992. Reproduced with permission of AMERICAN PSYCHIATRIC PRESS INC. in the format Textbook via Copyright Clearance Center.

Causes and Treatment

Extensive research on the genetic, neurobiological, and psychosocial contributions to schizoid personality disorder remains to be conducted (Phillips, Yen, & Gunderson, 2003). Childhood shyness is reported as a precursor to later adult schizoid personality disorder. It may be that this personality trait is inherited and serves as an important determinant in the development of this disorder. Abuse and neglect in childhood are also reported among individuals with this disorder (Johnson, Bromley, & McGeoch, 2005). Research over the past several decades point to biological causes of autism (a disorder we discuss in more detail in Chapter 14), and parents of children with autism are more likely to have schizoid personality disorder (Constantino et al., 2009). It is possible that a biological dysfunction found in both autism and schizoid personality disorder combines with early learning or early problems with interpersonal relationships to produce the social deficits that define schizoid personality disorder. For example, research on the neurochemical dopamine suggests that people with a lower density of dopamine receptors scored higher on a measure of "detachment" (Farde, Gustavsson, & Jonsson, 1997). It may be that dopamine (which seems to be involved with schizophrenia as well) may contribute to the social aloofness of people with schizoid personality disorder.

It is rare for a person with this disorder to request treatment except in response to a crisis such as extreme depression or losing a job (Kelly et al., 2007). Therapists often begin treatment by pointing out the value in social relationships. The person with the disorder may even need to be taught the emotions felt by others to learn empathy (Skodol & Gunderson, 2008). Because their social skills were never established or have atrophied through lack of use, people with schizoid personality disorder often receive social skills training. The therapist takes the part of a friend or significant other in a technique known as *role-playing* and helps the patient practise establishing and maintaining social relationships (Skodol & Gunderson, 2008). This type of social skills training is helped by identifying a social network—a person or people who will be supportive (Bender, 2005). Outcome research on this type of approach is unfortunately quite limited, so we must be cautious in evaluating the effectiveness of treatment for people with schizoid personality disorder.

Schizotypal Personality Disorder

People with **schizotypal personality disorder** are typically socially isolated, like those with schizoid personality disorder. In addition, they also behave in ways that would seem unusual to many of us, and they tend to be suspicious and to have odd beliefs (Cloninger & Svakic, 2009). Schizotypal personality disorder is considered by some to be on a continuum (i.e., on the same spectrum) with schizophrenia—the severe disorder we discuss in the Chapter 13—but without some of the more debilitating symptoms, such as hallucinations and delusions. Consider the case of Mr. S.

MR. S. | *Man with a Mission*

Mr. S. was a 35-year-old chronically unemployed man who had been referred by a physician because of a vitamin deficiency. This problem was thought to have eventuated because Mr. S. avoided any foods that "could have been contaminated by a machine." He had begun to develop alternative ideas about diet in his 20s and soon left his family and began to study an Eastern religion. "It opened my third eye; corruption is all about," he said.

He now lived by himself on a small farm in British Columbia, attempting to grow his own food, bartering for items he could not grow himself. He spent his days and evenings researching the origins and mechanisms of food contamination and, because of this knowledge, had developed a small band that followed his ideas. He had never married and maintained little contact with his family: "I've never been close to my father. I'm a vegetarian."

He said he intended to take an herbalism course to improve his diet before returning to his life on the farm. He had refused medication from the physician and became uneasy when the facts of his deficiency were discussed with him.

Source: Adapted from Quality Assurance Project, 1990, p. 344.

Clinical Description

People given a diagnosis of schizotypal personality disorder have psychotic-like (but not psychotic) symptoms (such as believing everything relates to them personally), social deficits, and sometimes cognitive impairments or paranoia (Cloninger & Svakic, 2009). These individuals are often considered "odd" or "bizarre" because of how they relate to other people, how they think and behave, and even how they dress. They have *ideas of reference*, which means they think insignificant events relate directly to them. For example, they may believe that somehow everyone on a passing city bus is talking about them, yet they may be able to acknowledge this is unlikely. Again, as we see in Chapter 13, some people with schizophrenia also have ideas of reference, but they are usually not able to "test reality" or see the illogic of their ideas.

Individuals with schizotypal personality disorder also have odd beliefs or engage in "magical thinking," believing, for example, that they are clairvoyant or telepathic. In addition, they report unusual perceptual experiences, including such *illusions* as feeling the presence of another person when they are alone. Notice the subtle but important difference between *feeling* as if someone else is in the room, and the more extreme perceptual distortion in people with schizophrenia who might report there is someone else in the room when there isn't. Only a small proportion of individuals with schizotypal personality disorder go on to develop schizophrenia (Wolff, Townshed, McGuire, & Weeks, 1991). Unlike people who simply have unusual interests or beliefs, those with schizotypal personality disorder tend to be suspicious and have paranoid thoughts, express little emotion, and may dress or behave in unusual ways (e.g., wear many layers of clothing in the summertime or mumble to themselves; Siever, Bernstein, & Silverman, 1991). Prospective research on children who later develop schizotypal personality disorder found that they tend to be passive and unengaged and are hypersensitive to criticism (Olin et al., 1997; see DSM Table 12.4).

Clinicians have to be warned that different cultural beliefs or practices may lead to a mistaken diagnosis of schizotypal personality disorder. For example, some people who practise certain religious rituals—such as speaking in tongues, practising voodoo, or mind reading—may do so with such obsessiveness as to make them seem extremely unusual, thus leading to a misdiagnosis (American Psychiatric Association, 2000a). Mental health workers have to be particularly sensitive to cultural practices that may differ from their own and can distort their view of certain seemingly unusual behaviours.

Causes

Historically, the word *schizotype* was used to describe people who were predisposed to develop schizophrenia (Meehl, 1962; Rado, 1962). Schizotypal personality disorder is viewed by some to be one phenotype of a schizophrenia genotype. Recall that a *phenotype* is one way a person's genetics is expressed. Your *genotype* is the gene or genes that make up a particular disorder. However, depending on a variety of other influences, the way you turn out—your phenotype—may vary from other people's phenotype, even if they have a similar genetic makeup to yours. Some people are thought to have "schizophrenia genes" (the genotype) and yet, because of the relative lack of biological influences (e.g., prenatal illnesses) or environmental stresses (e.g., poverty), some will have the less severe schizotypal personality disorder (the phenotype).

The idea of a relationship between schizotypal personality disorder and schizophrenia arises in part from the way people with the disorders behave. Many characteristics of schizotypal personality disorder, including ideas of reference, illusions, and paranoid thinking, are similar but milder forms of behaviours observed among people with schizophrenia. Genetic research also seems to support a relationship. Family, twin, and adoption studies, largely conducted in Norway, have shown an increased prevalence of schizotypal personality disorder among relatives of people with schizophrenia who do not also have schizophrenia themselves (Dahl, 1993; Torgersen, Onstad, Skre, Edvardsen, & Kringlen, 1993). However, these studies also tell us that the environment can strongly influence schizotypal personality disorder. For example, research from Britain suggests that a woman's exposure to influenza in pregnancy may increase the chance of schizotypal personality disorder in her children (Venables, 1996). It may be that a subgroup of people with schizotypal personality disorder has a similar genetic makeup when compared to people with schizophrenia.

Biological theories of schizotypal personality disorder are receiving empirical support. For example, cognitive assessment of persons with this disorder point to mild to moderate decrements in their ability to perform on tests involving memory and learning, suggesting some damage in the left hemisphere (Voglmaier et al., 2000). Research by Roger Graves, professor emeritus at the University of Victoria, suggests that abnormalities in semantic association abilities may contribute to the thinking oddities displayed by schizotypal individuals. Graves and his colleagues examined people with high levels of *magical ideation* (MI)—a thinking style similar to that of schizotypal patients. High-MI participants were found to consider unrelated words as more closely associated than low-MI participants. Thus, for schizotypal people, "loose associations" may not be loose after all (Mohr, Graves, Gianotti, Pizzagalli, & Brugger, 2001). Other research using magnetic resonance imaging (MRI) points to generalized brain abnormalities in patients with schizotypal personality disorder (Modinos et al., 2009).

DSM-IV-TR | **Table 12.4** Diagnostic Criteria for Schizotypal Personality Disorder

A. A pervasive pattern of social and interpersonal deficits marked by acute discomfort with, and reduced capacity for, close relationships as well as by cognitive or perceptual distortions and eccentricities of behaviour, beginning by early adulthood and present in a variety of contexts, as indicated by five (or more) of the following:

1. Ideas of reference (excluding delusions of reference)
2. Odd beliefs or magical thinking that influences behaviour and is inconsistent with subcultural norms (e.g., superstitiousness, belief in clairvoyance, telepathy, or "sixth sense"; in children and adolescents, bizarre fantasies or preoccupations)
3. Unusual perceptual experiences, including bodily illusions
4. Odd thinking and speech (e.g., vague, circumstantial, metaphorical, overelaborate, or stereotyped)
5. Suspiciousness or paranoid ideation
6. Inappropriate or constricted affect
7. Behaviour or appearance that is odd, eccentric, or peculiar
8. Lack of close friends or confidants other than first-degree relatives
9. Excessive social anxiety that does not diminish with familiarity and tends to be associated with paranoid fears rather than negative judgments about self

B. Does not occur exclusively during the course of schizophrenia, a mood disorder with psychotic features, another psychotic disorder, or a pervasive developmental disorder.

Note: If criteria are met prior to the onset of schizophrenia, add "premorbid" (e.g., "schizotypal personality disorder [premorbid]").

Source. Reprinted with permission from the *Diagnostic and Statistical Manual of Mental Disorders,* Fourth Edition, Text Revision, (Copyright © 2000). American Psychiatric Association.

Treatment

Some estimate that between 30 percent and 50 percent of the people with this disorder who request clinical help also meet the criteria for major depressive disorder. Treatment will obviously include some of the medical and psychological treatments for depression (Cloninger & Svakic, 2009; Mulder, Frampton, Luty, & Joyce, 2009).

Controlled studies of attempts to treat groups of people with schizotypal personality disorder are few, and, unfortunately, the results are modest at best. One general approach has been to teach social skills to help them reduce their isolation from and suspicion of others (O'Brien et al., 1993; Stone, 2001). A rather unusual tactic used by some therapists is not to encourage major changes at all; instead, the goal is to help the person accept and adjust to a solitary lifestyle (Stone, 1983).

Not surprisingly, medical treatment has been similar to that for people who have schizophrenia. In one study, haloperidol, often used with schizophrenia, was given to 17 people with schizotypal personality disorder (Hymowitz, Frances, Jacobsberg, Sickles, & Hoyt, 1986). There were some improvements in the group, especially with ideas of reference, odd communication, and social isolation. Unfortunately, because of the negative side effects of the medication, including drowsiness, many stopped taking their medication and dropped out of the study. About half the participants persevered through treatment but showed only mild improvement.

Further research on the treatment of people with this disorder is important for a variety of reasons. They tend not to improve over time and some evidence indicates that some will go on to develop the more severe characteristics of schizophrenia.

Cluster B Disorders

Antisocial Personality Disorder

People with **antisocial personality disorder** are among the most dramatic of the individuals a clinician will see in a practice and are characterized as having a history of failing to comply with social norms. They perform actions most of us would find unacceptable, such as stealing from friends and family. They also tend to be irresponsible, impulsive, and deceitful (Widiger & Corbitt, 1995). Robert Hare describes them as

> social predators who charm, manipulate, and ruthlessly plow their way through life, leaving a broad trail of broken hearts, shattered expectations, and empty wallets. Completely lacking in conscience and empathy, they selfishly take what they want and do as they please, violating social norms and expectations without the slightest sense of guilt or regret. (Hare, 1993, p. xi)

Of his work with psychopaths as a forensic psychologist in Vancouver, Hugues Hervé similarly notes that

> the psychopath's portrait consistently emerged as depicting a manipulative, grandiose, and superficial parasite who, devoid of emotional connections to the world, irresponsibly and selfishly drifts through life, only stopping long enough to callously, impulsively, and aggressively satisfy the urge of the moment. (Hervé, 2007, p. 45)

An epidemiological study conducted with individuals in Edmonton shows that about 3 percent of adults meet criteria for antisocial personality disorder (Swanson, Bland, & Newman, 1994). Just who are these people with antisocial personality disorder? Consider the case of Ryan.

RYAN | *The Thrill Seeker*

I first met Ryan on his 17th birthday. Unfortunately, he was celebrating the event in a psychiatric hospital. He had been truant from school for several months and had gotten into some trouble; the local judge who heard his case had recommended psychiatric evaluation one more time, though Ryan had been hospitalized six previous times, all for problems related to drug use and truancy. He was a veteran of the system and already knew most of the staff. I interviewed him to assess why he was admitted this time and to recommend treatment.

My first impression was that Ryan was cooperative and pleasant. He pointed out a tattoo on his arm that he had made himself, saying that it was a "stupid" thing to have done and that he now regretted it. In fact, he regretted many things and was looking forward to moving on with his life. I later found out that he was never truly remorseful for anything.

Our second interview was quite different. During those 48 hours, Ryan had done several things that showed why he needed a great deal of help. The most serious incident involved a 15-year-old girl named Ann who attended class with Ryan in the hospital school. Ryan had told her that he was going to get himself discharged, get in trouble, and be sent to the same correctional facility Ann's father was in, where he would rape her father. Ryan's threat so upset Ann that she hit her teacher and several of the staff. When I spoke to Ryan about this, he smiled slightly and said he was bored and that it was fun to upset Ann. When I asked whether it bothered him that his behaviour might extend her stay in the hospital, he looked puzzled and said, "Why should it bother me? She's the one who'll have to stay in this hellhole!"

Just before Ryan's admittance, a teenager in his town was murdered. A group of teens went to the local graveyard at night to perform satanic rituals, and a young man was stabbed to death, apparently over a drug purchase. Ryan was in the group, although he did not stab the boy. He told me that they occasionally dug up graves to get skulls for their parties; not because they really believed in the devil, but because it was fun and it scared the younger kids. I asked, "What if this was the grave of someone you knew, a relative or a friend? Would it bother you that strangers were digging up the remains?" He shook his head. "They're dead, man; they don't care. Why should I?"

Ryan told me he loved PCP, or "angel dust," and that he would rather be "dusted" than anything else. He routinely made the two-hour trip to Toronto to buy drugs in a particularly dangerous neighbourhood. He denied that he was ever nervous. This wasn't machismo; he really seemed unconcerned.

Ryan made little progress. I discussed his future in family therapy sessions and we talked about his pattern of showing supposed regret and remorse, and then stealing money from his parents and going back onto the street. In fact, most of our discussions centred on trying to give his parents the courage to say no to him and not to believe his lies.

One evening, after many sessions, Ryan said he had seen the "error of his ways" and that he felt bad that he had hurt his parents. If they would only take him home this one last time, he would be the son he should have been all these years. His speech moved his parents to tears, and they looked at me gratefully as if to thank me for curing their son. When Ryan finished talking, I smiled, applauded, told him it was the best performance I had ever seen. His parents turned on me in anger. Ryan paused for a second, then he too smiled and said, "It was worth a shot!" Ryan's parents were astounded that he had once again tricked them into believing him; he hadn't meant a word of what he had just said. Ryan was eventually discharged to a drug rehabilitation program. Within four weeks, he had convinced his parents to take him home, and within two days he had stolen all their cash and disappeared; he apparently went back to his friends and to drugs.

When he was in his 20s, after one of his many arrests for theft, Ryan was diagnosed as having antisocial personality disorder. His parents never summoned the courage to turn him out or refuse him money, and he continues to con them into providing him with a means of buying more drugs.

DSM-IV-TR	**Table 12.5** Diagnostic Criteria for Antisocial Personality Disorder

A. There is a pervasive pattern of disregard for and violation of the rights of others occurring since age 15, as indicated by three (or more) of the following:
  1. Failure to conform to social norms with respect to lawful behaviours as indicated by repeatedly performing acts that are grounds for arrest
  2. Deceitfulness, as indicated by repeated lying, use of aliases, or conning others for personal profit or pleasure
  3. Impulsivity or failure to plan ahead
  4. Irritability and aggressiveness, as indicated by repeated physical fights or assaults
  5. Reckless disregard for safety of self or others
  6. Consistent irresponsibility, as indicated by repeated failure to sustain consistent work behaviour or honour financial obligations
  7. Lack of remorse, as indicated by being indifferent to or rationalizing having hurt, mistreated, or stolen from another

B. The individual is at least age 18.

C. There is evidence of conduct disorder with onset before age 15.

D. The occurrence of antisocial behaviour is not exclusively during the course of schizophrenia or a manic episode.

Source: Reprinted with permission from the *Diagnostic and Statistical Manual of Mental Disorders,* Fourth Edition, Text Revision, (Copyright © 2000). American Psychiatric Association.

Clinical Description

Individuals with antisocial personality disorder tend to have long histories of violating the rights of others (De Brito & Hodgins, 2009). They are often described as being aggressive because they take what they want, indifferent to the concerns of other people. Lying and cheating seem to be second nature to them, and often they appear unable to tell the difference between the truth and the lies they make up to further their own goals (Hare, Forth, & Hart, 1989). They show no remorse or concern over the sometimes devastating effects of their actions. Substance abuse is common, occurring in 60 percent of people with antisocial personality disorder, and appears to be a lifelong pattern among these individuals (Taylor & Lang, 2006). The long-term outcome for people with antisocial personality disorder is usually poor, regardless of gender (Colman et al., 2009). One longitudinal study, for example, found that antisocial boys were more than twice as likely to die an unnatural death (e.g., accident, suicide, homicide) as their non-antisocial peers, which may be attributed to factors such as alcohol abuse and poor self-care (e.g., reckless behaviour; Laub & Vaillant, 2000).

Antisocial personality disorder has had a number of names over the years. Philippe Pinel (1801/1962) identified what he called *manie sans délire* (mania without delirium) to describe people with unusual emotional responses and impulsive rages but no deficits in reasoning ability (Charland, 2010). Other labels have included "moral insanity," "egopathy," "sociopathy," and "psychopathy." A great deal has been written about these labels; we focus on the two that have figured most prominently in psychological research: **psychopathy** and *DSM-IV-TR*'s antisocial personality disorder (see DSM Table 12.5). As you will see, there are important differences between the two.

Hervey Cleckley (1941/1982), a psychiatrist who spent much of his career working with the "psychopathic personality," identified a constellation of 16 major characteristics, most of which are personality traits and are sometimes referred to as the "Cleckley criteria" (Cleckley, 1982, p. 204):

1. Superficial charm and good intelligence
2. Absence of delusions and other signs of irrational thinking
3. Absence of "nervousness" and other psychoneurotic manifestations
4. Unreliability
5. Untruthfulness and insincerity
6. Lack of remorse or shame
7. Inadequately motivated antisocial behaviour
8. Poor judgment and failure to learn by experience
9. Pathologic egocentricity and incapacity for love
10. General poverty in major affective reactions
11. Specific loss of insight
12. Unresponsiveness in general interpersonal relations
13. Fantastic and uninviting behaviour
14. Suicide rarely carried out
15. Sex life impersonal, trivial, and poorly integrated
16. Failure to follow any life plan

Robert Hare and his colleagues, building on the descriptive work of Cleckley, researched the nature of psychopathy (e.g., Hare, 1970; Harpur, Hare, & Hakstian, 1989) and developed a 20-item checklist that serves as an assessment tool. Six of the criteria that Hare (1991) includes in his Revised Psychopathy Checklist (PCL-R) are as follows:

1. Glibness/superficial charm
2. Grandiose sense of self-worth
3. Proneness to boredom/need for stimulation
4. Pathological lying
5. Conning/manipulative
6. Lack of remorse

With some training, clinicians are able to gather information from interviews with a person, along with material from significant others or institutional files (e.g., prison records), and assign the person scores on the checklist. High scores indicate psychopathy (Hare & Neumann, 2006).

The *DSM-IV-TR* criteria for antisocial personality focus almost entirely on observable behaviours (e.g., "impulsively and repeatedly changes employment, residence, or sexual partners"). In contrast, the Cleckley/Hare criteria focus primarily on underlying personality traits (e.g., being self-centred or manipulative). The *DSM-IV-TR* and previous versions chose to use only observable behaviours so clinicians could reliably agree on a diagnosis. The framers of the criteria felt that trying to assess a personality trait—for example, whether someone was manipulative—would be more difficult than determining whether the person engaged in certain behaviours, such as repeated fighting.

Although Cleckley did not deny that many psychopaths are at greatly elevated risk for criminal and antisocial behaviours, he did emphasize that some have few or no legal or interpersonal difficulties. In other words, some psychopaths are not criminals and some do not display the aggressiveness that is a *DSM-IV-TR* criterion for antisocial personality disorder. Although the relationship between psychopathic personality and antisocial personality disorder is uncertain, the two syndromes clearly do not overlap perfectly (Hare, 1983). ■ Figure 12.2 illustrates the relative overlap among the characteristics of *psychopathy* as described by Cleckley and Hare, *antisocial personality disorder* as outlined in *DSM-IV-TR*, and *criminality*, which includes all people who get into trouble with the law. Despite much debate as to whether psychopathy or antisocial personality disorder is a more useful construct, a study with incarcerated Canadian offenders showed that measures of psychopathy and of antisocial personality disorder were similarly useful in identifying persistently antisocial offenders: violent reoffending was significantly predicted (and to the same degree) by the two measures (Skilling, Harris, Rice, & Quinsey, 2002).

Although psychopathy and antisocial personality disorder are both related to criminality, as you can see in Figure 12.2,

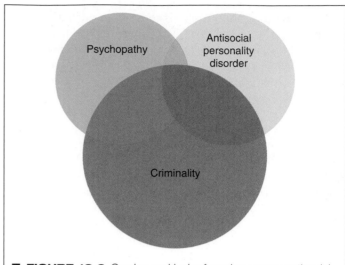

■ **FIGURE 12.2** Overlap and lack of overlap among antisocial personality disorder, psychopathy, and criminality

▲ University of British Columbia forensic psychologist Robert Hare has made extensive studies of people with psychopathic personalities.

not everyone who has psychopathy or antisocial personality disorder becomes involved with the legal system. What separates many in this group from those who get into trouble with the law may be IQ. In a prospective, longitudinal study, White, Moffit, and Silva (1989) followed almost 1000 children, beginning at age five, to see what predicted antisocial behaviour at age 15. They found that of the five-year-olds determined to be at high risk for later delinquent behaviour, 16 percent did indeed have run-ins with the law by the age of 15 and 84 percent did not. What distinguished these two groups? In general, the at-risk children with lower IQs were the ones who got in trouble. This finding suggests that having a higher IQ may help protect some people from developing more serious problems, or may at least prevent them from getting caught.

Some psychopaths function quite successfully in certain segments of society (e.g., politics, business, entertainment). Because of the difficulty in identifying these people, such "successful" or "subclinical" psychopaths (who meet some but not all the criteria for psychopathy) have not been the focus of much research. In a clever exception, Widom (1977) recruited a sample of subclinical psychopaths through advertisements in underground newspapers that invited many of the major personality characteristics of psychopathy. For example, one of the advertisements read as follows:

> Wanted: charming, aggressive, carefree people who are impulsively irresponsible but are good at handling people and at looking after number one.

Widom found that her sample appeared to possess many of the same characteristics as imprisoned psychopaths; for example, a large percentage of them received low scores on questionnaire measures of empathy and socialization and had high rates of parental psychopathology, including alcoholism. Moreover, many of these individuals had stable occupations and had managed to stay out of prison. Widom's study, although lacking a comparison group, shows that at least some individuals with psychopathic personality traits avoid repeated contact with the legal system and may even function successfully in society.

Identifying psychopaths among the criminal population seems to have important implications for predicting their future criminal behaviour (Hare, 1999). One study conducted in British Columbia by psychologist James Ogloff and his colleagues found that criminals who scored high on Hare's PCL-R put in less effort and showed fewer improvements in a therapy program than did criminals who were not psychopaths (Ogloff, Wong, & Greenwood, 1990). Other studies have shown that psychopathic criminals are more likely than nonpsychopathic criminals to repeat their criminal offences, especially those that are violent or sexual in nature (Langton, Barbaree, Harkins, & Peacock, 2006; Nicholls, Ogloff, & Douglas, 2004; Ogloff, 2006; Olver & Wong, 2006; Valliant, Gristey, Pottier, & Kosmyna, 1999).

Michael Woodworth and Stephen Porter (2002) examined characteristics of criminal homicides as a function of the offender's level of psychopathy. They ranked the characteristics of each offender's homicide on a scale ranging from purely instrumental (planned out) to purely reactive (spontaneous), which is one of the most relevant criteria in assessing risk for future violence and for predicting the outcome of treatment for criminal offenders (Eaves, Douglas, Webster, Ogloff, & Hart, 2000). The study showed that psychopaths rarely committed spontaneous "hot-blooded" murders. Rather, their murders were usually planned with a selfish goal in mind. This finding was intriguing because it contrasts with views of psychopaths as highly impulsive (Woodworth & Porter, 2002). Similarly, Flight and Forth (2007) found that incarcerated youth offenders who were classified as instrumentally violent scored higher in psychopathy than those who were not. This finding is further corroborated by the results of a study by Brown and Forth (1997): Psychopathy was associated with less (rather than more) intense negative emotions experienced before sexual offending among 60 incarcerated rapists. The rapes and homicides of children and young women by infamous criminals Paul Bernardo, Karla Homolka, and Clifford Olson exemplify the planning involved in the cold-blooded types of murders committed by psychopathic offenders. A more recent study by Porter, Woodworth, and Earle (2003) examined a group of individuals who were incarcerated for committing a sexual homicide. They found that about 85 percent of the sample scored in the moderate to high range on Hare's PCL-R. In addition, the homicides committed by psychopaths contained significantly higher levels of both gratuitous and sadistic violence (Porter et al., 2003).

The research of Stephen Porter and his colleagues is supportive of a subtype of psychopathic individual they refer to as a "sexual psychopath." Take, for example, the case of Mr. C.

MR. C. | *Sexual Predator*

Mr. C. is a middle-aged male currently incarcerated as a dangerous offender in a federal prison in British Columbia. In Canada, following a conviction for a "serious personal injury offence," whether it be either a sexual assault, or a violent or otherwise psychologically damaging offence, a Crown attorney can apply for a hearing to determine whether the offender's level of dangerousness warrants an indefinite period of incarceration (see Chapter 16). Mr. C's offences included repeatedly sexually assaulting three teen-aged girls over a one-year period in the context of a "master/slave" relationship. His previous sexual offences included the serial rapes of adult females, sexual assaults on children, and even bestiality. Mr. C.'s sexual crime pattern was to focus on one victim type for a long time and then to move on to another, admittedly "when [he] got bored."

Mr. C. had also been convicted of numerous other serious and sometimes violent nonsexual offences. In prison, he was suspected of sexually assaulting inmates and was often inappropriate with female staff. For example, he forwarded an envelope containing obscene material to a female parole officer before a parole hearing. It was reported in multiple psychological assessments that he was a "textbook psychopath." Recently, he was rated very high on the Revised Psychopathy Checklist (PCL-R; Hare, 1991) and was viewed as very high risk to reoffend. There was no evidence for paraphilia or an anger problem, two of the more common explanations for sexually deviant behaviour.

Source: Adapted from Porter, Hervé, Fairweather, & Birt, 1999.

Porter and his colleagues argue that individuals like Mr. C. represent a subtype of psychopath (i.e., sexual psychopath) who is devoid of conscience and empathy and whose thrill seeking is focused on victimizing multiple victim types in a sexual manner (Porter et al., 1999). In a scientific study, Porter and his colleagues (2000) investigated whether psychopathy would contribute to the understanding of sexual violence. A large sample of more than 300 Canadian federal sex offenders and non-sex offenders participated in the study. All sex offenders scored higher in the callous personality aspect of psychopathy relative to the non-sex offenders. However, the sex offenders varied in levels of psychopathy depending on the nature of their sexual offence backgrounds. Mixed rapist/molesters and rapists scored higher in psychopathy than did child molesters. In fact, a full 64 percent of sex offenders who had offended against both adults and children were psychopathic (Porter et al., 2000). This study illustrates the importance of assessing an inmate's levels of psychopathy when predicting the types of crimes he is likely to commit in the future.

As we review the literature on antisocial personality disorder, note that the people included in the research may be members of only one of the three groups we have described. For example, genetic research is usually conducted with criminals because they and their families are easier to identify than members of the other groups. As you now know, the criminal group may include people other than those with antisocial personality disorder or psychopathy. Keep this in mind as you read on.

Before we discuss causal factors, it is important to note the developmental nature of antisocial behaviour. The *DSM-IV-TR* provides a separate diagnosis for children who engage in behaviours that violate society's norms: *conduct disorder*. Many children with conduct disorder—most often diagnosed in boys—become juvenile offenders and tend to become involved with drugs (Durand, in press). Ryan fit into this category. More important, the research of Richard Tremblay and his colleagues supports a stable, lifelong pattern of antisocial behaviour in a subgroup of antisocial children. Specifically, a group of young children who display antisocial behaviour has been shown to likely continue these behaviours as the members grow older, while many others desist (Charlebois, LeBlanc, Gagnon, Larivée, & Tremblay, 1993). Some more recent longitudinal research from Tremblay and his colleagues shows that personality traits distinguish boys who show this stable pattern of antisocial behaviour over time. The most important personality characteristic that distinguished the boys who showed a stable and persistent pattern of physical aggression, theft, and vandalism, was "psychoticism" (Carrasco, Barker, Tremblay, & Vitaro, 2006). Not to be confused with the psychotic disorders like schizophrenia discussed in Chapter 13, psychoticism is an older label for a personality characterized by high impulsivity and low empathy (Carrasco et al., 2006).

Data from long-term follow-up research indicate that many adults with antisocial personality disorder or psychopathy had conduct disorder as children (Robins, 1978); the likelihood increases if the child has both conduct disorder and attention deficit/hyperactivity disorder (Lynam, 1996).

There is a tremendous amount of interest in studying a group that causes a great deal of harm to society. Research has been conducted for many years, and so we know a great deal more about antisocial personality disorder than about the other personality disorders.

Genetic Influences

Family, twin, and adoption studies all suggest a genetic influence on both antisocial personality disorder and criminality (Ferguson, 2010a). For example, Crowe (1974) examined adopted-away children of mothers who were felons and compared them with adopted-away children of normal mothers. All were separated from their mothers as newborns, minimizing the possibility that environmental factors from their biological families were responsible for the results. Crowe found that the adopted-away offspring of felons had significantly higher rates of arrests, conviction, and antisocial personality than did the adopted-away offspring of normal mothers, which suggests at least some genetic influence on criminality and antisocial behaviour.

However, Crowe (1974) also found something else quite interesting: The adopted children of felons who themselves later became criminals had spent more time in interim orphanages than either the adopted children of felons who did not become criminals or the adopted children of non criminal mothers. As Crowe points out, this suggests a gene–environment interaction; in other words, genetic factors may be important only in the presence of certain environmental influences (alternatively, certain environmental influences are important only in the presence of certain genetic predispositions). Genetic factors may present a vulnerability, but actual development of criminality may require environmental factors, such as a deficit in early, high-quality contact with parents or parent-surrogates.

This gene–environment interaction was demonstrated most clearly by Cadoret, Yates, Troughton, Woodworth, and Stewart (1995), who studied adopted children and their likelihood of developing conduct problems. If the children's biological parents had a history of antisocial personality disorder and their adoptive families exposed them to chronic stress through marital, legal, or psychiatric problems, the children were at greater risk for conduct problems. Again, research shows that genetic influence does not necessarily mean certain disorders are inevitable. Large-scale research on twins with conduct disorder supports the role of genetic and environmental influences on this disorder as well (Thomas, 2009).

Data from twin studies generally support those of adoption studies. Twin study researchers Kerry Jang, John Livesley, and Philip Vernon have shown that a personality characteristic called *dyssocial behaviour* (similar to the traits displayed by those with antisocial personality disorder) has a large genetic component (Jang, Vernon, & Livesley, 2001; Livesley, Jang, & Vernon, 1998). In a review of the major twin studies of criminality, Eysenck and Eysenck (1978) found that the average concordance rate for criminality among monozygotic twins was 55 percent, whereas among dizygotic twins it was only 13 percent, again suggesting a large genetic component. We must remember several limitations when we interpret findings on the genetics of criminality. First, "criminality" is an extremely heterogeneous category that includes people with and without antisocial personality disorder and psychopathy.

Genetics may influence one or more subtypes of criminality. Second, it is clear that environmental factors play a substantial role in many, if not all, cases of criminality. In the studies reviewed by Eysenck and Eysenck (1978), for example, the concordance rate of criminality among identical twins would be 100 percent if criminality were

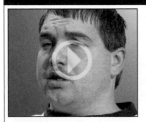

ABNORMAL PSYCHOLOGY Video

Antisocial Personality Disorder: George

"I have hatred inside me. I don't care how much I beat somebody.... The more I hear somebody, the more anger I get inside me.... I used drugs when I was... probably nine or ten years old... smoked marijuana.... First time I drank some alcohol I think I was probably about three years old.... I assaulted a woman.... I had so much anger.... I was just like a bomb.... It's just ticking... and the way I'm going, that bomb was going to blow up in me. I wouldn't be able to get away from it... going to be a lot of people hurt.... I'm not going out without taking somebody with me."

Go to Psychology CourseMate at www.abnormalpsych3ce.nelson.com to watch this video.

▲ Many prisons allow visits between inmates and their children, partly to help reduce later problems in those children.

caused entirely by genetic factors. Finally, the interaction between genes and environment may be important in the genesis of criminality (see Crowe, 1974, for example). Genetic factors may substantially contribute to criminal behaviour only in the presence of certain environmental factors (Rutter, 1997). Large-scale research on twins with conduct disorder supports the role of genetic and environmental influences on this disorder as well (Slutske et al., 1997, 1998).

Neurobiological Influences

A great deal of research has focused on neurobiological influences that may be specific to antisocial personality disorder. Some researchers have used neuropsychological tests to determine if there are to be specific cognitive deficits that might contribute to antisocial personality disorder or psychopathy. For example, a study by Thierry Pham at the Pinel Institute in Montréal looked at the neuropsychological function of psychopaths and did find evidence of differences between the executive functions and attention-related abilities of incarcerated psychopaths and incarcerated non-psychopathic controls. Specifically, Pham, Vanderstukken, Philippot, and Vanderlinden (2003) found that, relative to controls, psychopaths evidenced deficits in their abilities to maintain a plan and to inhibit irrelevant information. Similar results have been recently obtained by Blair et al. (2006), suggesting executive cognitive function deficits in psychopaths.

Two major neurobiological theories have attracted a great deal of attention in the area of psychopathy: (1) the *underarousal hypothesis* and (2) the *fearlessness hypothesis*. According to the underarousal hypothesis, psychopaths have abnormally low levels of *cortical arousal* (Sylvers, Ryan, Alden, & Brennan, 2009). There appears to be an inverted U-shaped relation between arousal and performance. The *Yerkes-Dodson* curve suggests that people with either very high or very low levels of arousal tend to experience negative affect and perform poorly in many situations, whereas individuals with intermediate levels of arousal tend to be relatively content and perform satisfactorily in most situations.

According to the underarousal hypothesis, the abnormally low levels of cortical arousal characteristic of psychopaths are the primary cause of their antisocial and risk-taking behaviours; they seek stimulation to boost their chronically low levels of arousal. This means that Ryan lied, took drugs, and dug up graves to achieve the same level of arousal we might get from talking on the phone with a good friend or watching television.

Low-frequency *theta waves* are found in brain wave measures of children and largely disappear in adulthood; their specific purpose is unknown. Evidence suggests that many psychopaths have excessive theta waves when they are awake. This finding led Robert Hare to generate another theory related to arousal levels, sometimes referred to as the *cortical immaturity hypothesis* of psychopathy (Hare, 1970). Hare's theory holds that the cerebral cortex of psychopaths is at a relatively primitive stage of development. This hypothesis may help explain why the behaviour of psychopaths is often childlike and impulsive: Their cerebral cortices, which play such a key role in the inhibition and control of impulses, may be insufficiently developed. But remember that many psychopaths are not impulsive, as indicated by the recent research of investigators like Adelle Forth and Stephen Porter discussed earlier (e.g., Brown & Forth, 1997; Woodworth & Porter, 2002).

The data on theta waves are open to an alternative and perhaps simpler explanation. Because theta waves also indicate states such as drowsiness or boredom, psychopaths' higher levels of theta waves may simply reflect their relative lack of concern regarding being hooked up to psychophysiological equipment! Picture yourself having your brain waves measured. You sit next to the intimidating polygraph machine, attached to a number of electrodes and wires. How will you react? As a nonpsychopath, you will probably feel anxiety and apprehension. In contrast, a psychopath, who is low in anxiety, will probably be bored, apathetic, and unresponsive. The excessive theta waves of psychopaths may simply reflect their relative absence of anxiety.

According to the *fearlessness hypothesis*, psychopaths possess a higher threshold for experiencing fear than most other individuals (Lykken, 1957, 1982). In other words, things that greatly frighten the rest of us have little or no effect on the psychopath. Remember that Ryan was unafraid of going alone to dangerous neighbourhoods to buy drugs. According to proponents of this hypothesis, the fearlessness of the psychopath gives rise to all the other major features of the syndrome.

Early evidence for the fearlessness hypothesis came from a series of studies by Lykken (1957) using prison inmates. In one such study, Lykken constructed a classical conditioning task involving painful electric shock. His primary dependent measure was galvanic skin response (GSR), a reaction marked by an increase in palmar sweating and typically interpreted as a sign of autonomic arousal. Lykken repeatedly paired a tone (the conditioned stimulus) with electric shock to the participants' fingertips (the unconditioned stimulus). Then, he presented the tone (conditioned stimulus) alone on multiple occasions. Nonpsychopaths showed a predictable and understandable pattern: When they heard the tone, their palms began to sweat, signalling that they expected the shock to come next. Moreover, their GSRs were quite slow to extinguish. In contrast, psychopaths showed a striking pattern: In most cases, they exhibited very weak GSRs to the tones alone, and their GSRs tended to extinguish rapidly.

This study by Lykken has important implications, suggesting that psychopaths may have difficulty associating certain cues or signals with impending punishment or danger, much as children are socialized to inhibit their behaviour. Most parents do not punish their children directly on every occasion for harmful or inappropriate behaviour, but instead rely on cues such as "No" or even a threatening stare to inhibit inappropriate behaviour. Largely because of classical conditioning, such cues tend to be quite effective substitutes for direct punishment. But if they have little or no impact on the prepsychopathic child, he or she will probably not acquire a well-developed capacity for impulse control.

Scientific research suggests the possibility that there may be a genetic component to one important aspect of psychopathy—namely aggression. Researchers in the Netherlands are cautiously optimistic after discovering that a gene mutation found in a large Dutch family may cause aggression (Brunner et al., 1993). Their study is important because it may tell us more about how genes affect behaviour. Brunner and his colleagues at the university hospital in Nijmegen have tracked the males of one family since 1978. Some of the men are prone to particularly violent outbursts. One raped his sister, two others were arsonists, and still another tried to run over his boss after being told his work wasn't good enough. None of the women in the family are given to violent outbursts.

The evidence for a genetic explanation of these behaviours is impressive. The observation that the condition occurs only in the males indicates the gene is probably on the X chromosome. Because men have only one X chromosome, any "bad" or mutated gene will show up. Because women have two X chromosomes, they tend to have a "good" or normal gene to balance the bad one.

To further narrow the location of the mutated gene, Brunner and his colleagues conducted a linkage study. As you may remember from Chapter 4, such studies try to identify marker genes that are inherited along with the gene you are trying to locate. Because we already know where the marker genes are, we can get a good idea of the approximate location of the mutated gene.

On the basis of the linkage study and biochemical analyses, Brunner and his fellow researchers believe the defect involves the gene that produces monoamine oxidase A, or MAOA. MAOA is an enzyme that helps break down neurotransmitters, specifically those involved in our "fight or flight" responses to threats and other stresses; they include serotonin, dopamine, and noradrenaline. If the MAOA enzyme isn't working properly, these neurotransmitters may build up and the affected people will have trouble handling stressful situations. For example, after the deaths of close relatives, the two arsonists in the Dutch family set fires. A subsequent study confirmed that MAOA is deficient only in the affected males (Brunner, Nelen, Breakefield, Ropers, & van Oost, 1993). The possible genetic vulnerability to react violently, in combination with certain stressors, may result in aggression. But remember that this defect, to date, has been found only in one family. It is unlikely that all or even most aggressive behaviour will be traced to the same cause. Finally, social, economic, and cultural factors determine the type and severity of stresses. What this research suggests, however, is that just the right (or wrong!) combination of genetic, neurobiological, and psychosocial contributions came together to create devastating outcomes in one Dutch family.

A more recent study by Caspi and colleagues (2002) in the United Kingdom found evidence suggesting that genetics may play a role in explaining why some males who are maltreated as children grow up to display antisocial behaviour, whereas others do not. There, researchers studied a large sample of male children from birth to adulthood. Once again, the genetic defect studied in this group involves the gene that produces the enzyme MAOA. Children who were maltreated but had the gene conferring high levels of MAOA expression (meaning they were less likely to have buildup of certain neurotransmitters during stress, and thus better able to handle stress) were less likely to develop antisocial problems than maltreated children without this genotype. The authors claim that their findings may help explain why some but not all victims of abuse grow up to victimize others (Caspi et al., 2002). The findings also once again show how genetic and environmental factors can interact in the development of various forms of psychopathology—antisocial personality in this case (Caspi et al., 2002).

Theorists have tried to connect what we know about the workings of the brain with clinical observations of people with antisocial personality disorder, especially those with psychopathy. Several theorists have applied British researcher Jeffrey Gray's (1987) model of brain functioning to this population (Fowles, 1988; Quay, 1993). According to Gray, three major brain systems influence learning and emotional behaviour: the behavioural inhibition system (BIS), the reward system (REW), and the fight-flight system (F/F). The BIS and the REW systems and the balance between the two may be involved in psychopathic behaviour. The BIS is responsible for our ability to stop or slow down when we are faced with impending punishment, nonreward, or novel situations, which leads to anxiety and frustration. The BIS is thought to be located in the septal-hippocampal area of the brain and involves the noradrenergic and serotonergic neurotransmitter systems. The REW system is responsible for our approach behaviour—in particular, our approach to positive rewards—and is associated with hope and relief. This system probably involves the dopaminergic neurotransmitter system in the mesolimbic area of the brain, which we previously noted as the "pleasure pathway" for its role in substance use and abuse (Chapter 11).

If you think about the behaviour of psychopaths, the possible malfunctioning of these two systems is clear. An imbalance between the BIS and REW may make the fear and anxiety produced by the BIS less apparent and the positive feelings associated with the REW more prominent (Levenston, Patrick, Bradley, & Lang, 2000; Quay, 1993). Theorists have proposed that this type of neurobiological dysfunction may explain why psychopaths aren't anxious about committing the antisocial acts that characterize their disorder.

Psychological and Social Dimensions

What goes on in the mind of a psychopath? In one of several studies of how psychopaths process reward and punishment, Newman, Patterson, and Kosson (1987) set up a card-playing task on a computer; they provided five-cent rewards and fines for correct and incorrect answers to psychopathic and non-psychopathic criminal offenders. The game was constructed so at first they were rewarded about 90 percent of the time and fined only about 10 percent of the time. Gradually, the odds changed until the probability of getting a reward was 0 percent.

Despite feedback that reward was no longer forthcoming, the psychopaths continued to play and lose. As a result of this and other studies, the researchers hypothesized that once psychopaths set their sights on a reward goal, they are less likely than nonpsychopaths to be deterred despite signs that the goal is no longer achievable (Dvorak-Bertscha, Curtin, Rubinstein, & Newman, 2009). Again, considering the reckless and daring behaviour of some psychopaths (robbing banks without a mask and getting caught immediately), failure to abandon an unattainable goal fits the overall picture.

Gerald Patterson's influential work suggests that aggression in such children may escalate, in part because of their interactions with their parents (Granic & Patterson, 2006; Patterson, 1982). He found that the parents often give in to the problems displayed by their children. For example, parents ask their son to make his bed and he refuses. One parent yells at the boy. He yells back and becomes abusive. At some point his interchange becomes so aversive that the parent stops fighting and walks away, thereby ending the fight but also letting the son not make his bed. Giving in to these problems results in short-term gains for both the parent (calm is restored in the house) and the child (he gets what he wants), but it results in continuing problems. The child has learned to continue fighting and not give up, and the parent learns that the only way to "win" is to withdraw all demands. This "coercive family process" combines with other factors, such as parents' inept monitoring of their child's activities and less parental involvement, to help maintain the aggressive behaviours (Chronis et al., 2007; Patterson, DeBaryshe, & Ramsey, 1989; Sansbury & Wahler, 1992).

Although little is known about which environmental factors play a direct role in causing antisocial personality disorder and psychopathy (as opposed to childhood conduct disorders), evidence from adoption studies strongly suggests that shared environmental factors—that tend to make family members similar—are important to the etiology of criminality and perhaps antisocial personality disorder. For example, in the Swedish adoption study by Sigvardsson, Cloninger, Bohman, and von-Knorring (1982), low social status of the adoptive parents increased the risk of nonviolent criminality among females. Like children with conduct disorders, individuals with antisocial personality disorder come from homes with inconsistent parental discipline (e.g., Robins, 1966). It is not known for certain, however, whether inconsistent discipline directly causes antisocial personality disorder; it is conceivable, for example, that parents have a genetic vulnerability to antisocial personality disorder that they pass on to their children but that also causes them to be inadequate parents.

One interesting study looked at the social environment and attitudes of neighbourhoods and their effect on violent crime. Sampson, Raudenbush, and Earls (1997) asked members of city neighbourhoods questions about the willingness of local residents to intervene for the common good, for example, whether neighbours would intervene if children were skipping school and hanging out on the street. The researchers found that the degree of mutual trust and solidarity in a neighbourhood was inversely related to violent crime. This study points out that factors outside the family can influence behaviours associated with antisocial personality disorder.

A final factor that has been implicated in antisocial personality disorder is the role of stress. One study found that trauma associated with combat may increase the likelihood of antisocial behaviour. In this study, more than 2000 army veterans of the Vietnam War were studied (Barrett et al., 1996). Even after adjusting for histories of childhood problems, the researchers found that those who had been exposed to the most traumatic events were most likely to engage in violence, illegal activities, lying, and using aliases. Stephen Porter has hypothesized that childhood trauma may play a role in the development of psychopathy. Specifically, when certain individuals are severely traumatized by loved ones, over time they might learn to "turn off" their emotions as a way of coping. The use of this maladaptive coping skill could contribute to the emotional deficits observed in psychopaths and even result in a psychopathic personality disorder (Porter, 1996). Consistent with this possibility, Campbell, Porter, and Santor (2004) found that higher psychopathy scores were associated with the experience of physical abuse in a large sample of male and female incarcerated adolescent offenders. Porter's (1996) intriguing hypothesis is thus deserving of further study.

Developmental Influences

The forms that antisocial behaviours take change as children move into adulthood, from truancy and stealing from friends to extortion, assaults, armed robbery, or other crimes (Forth & Mailloux, 2000; Hare, Forth, & Strachan, 1992). Fortunately, clinical lore, as well as scattered empirical reports (Robins, 1966), suggests that rates of antisocial behaviour begin to decline rather markedly around the age of 40. Hare et al. (1988) provided empirical support for this phenomenon. They examined the conviction rates of male psychopaths and male nonpsychopaths who had been incarcerated for a variety of crimes. The researchers found that between the ages of 16 and 45, the conviction rates of nonpsychopaths remained relatively constant. In contrast, the conviction rates of psychopaths remained relatively constant up until about 40, at which time they decreased markedly (see ■ Figure 12.3). Why antisocial behaviour often declines around middle age remains unanswered.

An Integrative Model

How can we put all this information together to get a better understanding of people with antisocial personality disorder? Remember that research in each area may involve people labelled as having antisocial personality disorder, people labelled as psychopathic, or criminals. Whatever the label, it appears these people have a genetic vulnerability to antisocial behaviours and personality traits. Perhaps this vulnerability results in underarousal or fearlessness. The genetic inheritance might be the propensity for weak inhibition systems (BIS) and overactive reward systems (REW) that could partially account for the evidence of differences in cognitive set (Newman & Wallace, 1993).

In a family that may already be under stress because of divorce or substance abuse (Hetherington, Stanley-Hagan, & Anderson, 1989; Patterson et al., 1989), there may be an interaction style that actually encourages antisocial behaviour on the part of the child

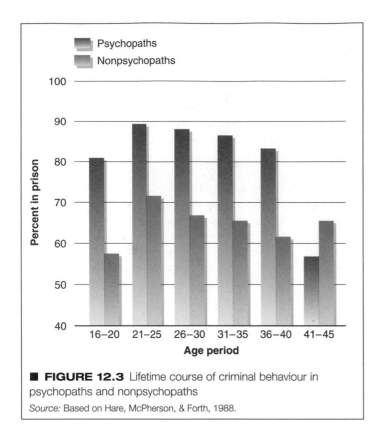

■ **FIGURE 12.3** Lifetime course of criminal behaviour in psychopaths and nonpsychopaths

Source: Based on Hare, McPherson, & Forth, 1988.

(Wootton, Frick, Shelton, & Silverthorn, 1997).The child's antisocial and impulsive behaviour alienates other children who might be good role models and attracts others who encourage antisocial behaviour (Vuchinich, Bank, & Patterson, 1992). These behaviours may also result in the child's dropping out of school and a poor occupational history in adulthood, which help create increasingly frustrating life circumstances that further incite acts against society (Caspi, Elder, & Bem, 1987).

This is, admittedly, an abbreviated version of a complex scenario. The important element is that in this integrative model of antisocial behaviour, biological, psychological, and cultural factors combine in intricate ways to create someone like Ryan or Mr. C.

Treatment

One of the major problems with treating people in this group is typical of numerous personality disorders: These people rarely identify themselves as needing treatment. Because of this, and because they can be very manipulative even with their therapists, most clinicians are pessimistic about the outcome of treatment for adults who have antisocial personality disorder, and there are few documented success stories (National Collaborating Centre for Mental Health, 2010). Antisocial behaviour is predictive of poor prognosis even in childhood (Kazdin & Mazurick, 1994). In general, therapists agree with incarcerating these people to deter future antisocial acts. Clinicians encourage identification of high-risk children so treatment can be attempted before they become adults (National Collaborating Centre for Mental Health, 2010; Patterson, 1982; Thomas, 2009).

The most common treatment strategy for children involves parent training (Patterson, 1986; Sanders, 1992). Parents are

taught how to recognize behaviour problems early and how to use praise and privileges to reduce problem behaviour and encourage prosocial behaviours. Treatment studies typically show that these types of programs can significantly improve the behaviours of many children who display antisocial behaviours (Conduct Problems Prevention Research Group, 2010; Fleischman, 1981; Patterson, Chamberlain, & Reid, 1982; Webster-Stratton & Hammond, 1997). A number of factors, however, put families at risk for either not succeeding in treatment or for dropping out early; these include cases with a high degree of family dysfunction, socioeconomic disadvantage, high family stress, parent's history of antisocial behaviour, and severe conduct disorder on the part of the child (Dumas & Wahler, 1983; Kaminski, Valle, Filene, & Boyle, 2008; Kazdin, Mazurick, & Bass, 1993).

Some researchers are now examining how a multifaceted approach to treatment can help reduce delinquent behaviour on the part of juvenile offenders. Programs that combine the behavioural approaches just described along with efforts to improve family relationships and providing services to the families in their communities are reporting some success. One study treating 155 violent and chronic juvenile offenders observed that by improving family relations and decreasing the child's

▲ Children with conduct disorder may become adults with antisocial personality disorder.

associations with delinquent peers, significant reductions in delinquent behaviour were obtained (Huey, Henggeler, Brondino, & Pickrel, 2000).

Prevention

Some programs address these problems even earlier, in an attempt to prevent problems from arising. Typically preschool programs, they combine teaching good parenting skills with a variety of supports for families with social and economic disadvantages (Zigler, Taussig, & Black, 1992). An obstacle to prevention efforts with this group is that we have relatively poor methods for identifying which children will grow up to have antisocial personality disorder (Bennett et al., 1999). It is too soon to assess the success of such programs in preventing the types of adult antisocial behaviours typically observed among people with this personality disorder. However, given the ineffectiveness of treatment for adults, prevention may be the best approach to this problem.

Borderline Personality Disorder

People with **borderline personality disorder** lead tumultuous lives. Their moods and relationships are unstable, and usually they have a very poor self-image. These people often feel empty and are at great risk of dying by their own hands. Consider the case of Claire.

CLAIRE | *A Stranger among Us*

I have known Claire for more than 40 years and have watched her through the good but mostly bad times of her often shaky and erratic life as a person with borderline personality disorder. Claire and I went to school together from Grade 8 through high school, and we've kept in touch periodically. My earliest memory of her is of her hair, which was cut short and rather unevenly. She told me that when things were not going well she cut her own hair severely, which helped to "fill the void." I later found out that the long sleeves she usually wore hid scars and cuts that she had made herself.

Claire was the first of our friends to smoke. What was unusual about this and her later drug use was not that they occurred (this was in the 1960s!) or that they began early; it was that she didn't seem to use them to get attention, like everyone else. Claire was also one of the first whose parents divorced, and both of them seemed to abandon her emotionally. She later told me that her father was an alcoholic who had regularly beaten her and her mother. She did poorly in school and had very low self-esteem. She frequently said she was stupid and ugly, yet she was obviously neither.

Throughout our school years, Claire left town periodically, without any explanation. I learned many years later that she was in psychiatric facilities to get help with her suicidal depression. She often threatened to kill herself, although we didn't guess that she was serious.

In our later teens we all drifted away from Claire. She had become increasingly unpredictable, sometimes berating us for a perceived slight ("You're walking too fast. You don't want to be seen with me!"), and at other times desperate to be around us. We were obviously confused by her behaviour. With some people, emotional outbursts can bring you closer together. Unfortunately for Claire, these incidents and her overall demeanour made us feel that we didn't know her at all. As we all grew older, the "void" she described in herself became overwhelming and eventually shut us all out.

Claire married twice, and both times had very passionate but stormy relationships interrupted by hospitalizations. She tried to stab her first husband during a particularly violent rage. She tried a number of drugs but mainly used alcohol to "deaden the pain."

Now, in her mid-50s, things have calmed down some, although she says she is rarely happy. Claire does feel a little better about herself and is doing well as a travel agent. Although she is seeing someone, she is reluctant to become very involved because of her personal history. Claire was ultimately diagnosed with depression and borderline personality disorder.

Clinical Description

Borderline personality disorder is one of the most common personality disorders observed in clinical settings; it is observed in every culture and is seen in about 1 percent to 2 percent of the general population. It is one of the most common personality disorders; in psychiatric settings, it accounts for about 15 percent of the population and about 50 percent of the patients with personality disorders (Widiger & Weissman, 1991). Claire's life illustrates the instability characteristic of people with borderline personality disorder (see DSM Table 12.6). They tend to have very turbulent relationships, fearing abandonment but lacking control over their emotions (Gunderson, Zanarini, & Kisiel, 1995). They frequently engage in suicidal or self-mutilative behaviours, cutting or burning or punching themselves. Claire sometimes used her cigarette to burn her palm or forearm, and she carved her initials in her arm. A significant proportion—about 6 percent—succeed at suicide (McGirr, Paris, Lesage, Renaud, & Turecki, 2009). On the positive side, the long-term outcome for people with borderline personality disorder is encouraging, with up to 88 percent achieving remission more than ten years after initial treatment (Zanarini et al., 2006).

People with this personality disorder are often very intense, going from anger to deep depression in a short time. They also are characterized by impulsivity; Paul Links and his colleagues at Saint Michael's Hospital in Toronto have argued that impulsivity is the core aspect of borderline personality disorder (Links, Heslegrave, & van Reekum, 1999). This impulsiveness can be seen in their drug abuse and self-mutilation. Although not so obvious as to why, the self-injurious behaviours such as cutting sometimes are described as tension reducing by people who engage in these behaviours (Bohus et al., 2000). Claire's empty feeling is also common; these people are sometimes described as chronically bored and have difficulties with their own identities (Wilkinson-Ryan & Westen, 2000). The mood disorders we discussed in Chapter 7 are common among people with borderline personality disorder, with 24 percent to 74 percent having major depression, and 4 percent to 20 percent having bipolar disorder (Widiger &

Rogers, 1989). Eating disorders are also common, particularly bulimia (see Chapter 8): Almost 25 percent of bulimics also have borderline personality disorder (Zanarini, Reichman, Frankenburg, Reich, & Fitzmaurice, 2010). Up to 67 percent of the people with this disorder are also diagnosed with at least one substance use disorder (Grant et al., 2008).

Research by University of British Columbia psychologist Don Dutton and his colleagues indicates a link between borderline personality disorder and spousal abuse; several studies by his team indicate that men who abuse their spouses are high in borderline characteristics (e.g., Dutton, 2007; Dutton & Starzomski, 1993; Tweed & Dutton, 1998). His more recent work suggests that about 40 percent of men who abuse their partners fit this borderline personality profile (Dutton, 2002). Dutton (1995) argues that men with borderline personality disorder are susceptible to abusing their partners because they set excessively high standards for others and blame their partners when things go wrong. Finally, there is evidence of changes in borderline features with aging. As with antisocial personality disorder, people with borderline personality disorder tend to improve during their 30s and 40s, although they may continue to have difficulties into old age (National Collaborating Centre for Mental Health, 2009; Rosowsky & Gurian, 1992).

▲ Toronto psychiatrist Paul Links and his colleagues have made many important contributions to understanding the nature, origins, and treatment of borderline personality disorder.

Causes

The results from almost 20 family studies suggest that borderline personality disorder is more prevalent in families with the disorder and is somehow linked with mood disorders (Baron, Gruen, Asnis, & Lord, 1985; Distel, Trull, & Boomsma, 2009; Zanarini, Gunderson, Marino, Schwartz, & Frankenburg, 1988). One such study was conducted by Paul Links and his colleagues (Links, Steiner, & Huxley, 1988). Just as schizotypal personality disorder seems to share a familial association with schizophrenia, borderline personality disorder may have a similar connection to mood disorders (Widiger & Trull, 1993). Although some traits may be inherited (e.g., impulsivity), there appears to be a great deal of room for environmental influences.

Cognitive factors in borderline personality disorder are just beginning to be explored. Here the question is, just how do people with this disorder process information, and does this contribute to their difficulties? One study that takes a look at the thought processes of these individuals asked people with and without borderline

▲ Borderline personality disorder is often accompanied by self-mutilation.

personality disorder to look at words projected on a computer screen and try to remember some of the words and try to forget others (Korfine & Hooley, 2000). When the words were not related to the symptoms of borderline personality disorder—for example, "celebrate," "charming," "collect"—both groups performed equally as well. However, when they were presented with words that might be relevant to the disorder—for example, "abandon," "suicidal," "emptiness"—individuals with borderline personality disorder remembered more of these words despite being instructed to forget them. This preliminary evidence for a memory bias may hold clues to the nature of this disorder and may someday be helpful in designing more effective treatment (Geraerts & McNally, 2008).

One psychosocial influence that has received a great deal of attention is the possible contribution of early trauma, especially sexual and physical abuse (Laporte & Guttman, 2001; Links & van Reekum, 1993; McLean & Gallop, 2003; Mitton, Links, & Durocher, 1997). Several studies have shown that people with this disorder are more likely to report abuse than are individuals with other psychiatric conditions (e.g., Goldman, D'Angelo, DeMaso, & Mezzacappa, 1992; Ogata et al., 1990). Wagner and Linehan (1994) found that among women with both borderline personality disorder and parasuicidal behaviour (which includes both serious and minor suicide attempts), 76 percent reported some type of childhood sexual abuse and had made the most serious attempts to commit suicide. In a large study, researchers found an even higher rate of abuse histories in individuals with borderline personality disorder, with 91 percent reporting abuse and 92 percent reporting being neglected before the age of 18 (Zanarini et al., 1997). Although we obviously do not know whether abuse and neglect cause later borderline personality disorder (data are based on recollection and a correlation between the two phenomena), they may be predisposing factors in at least some cases. If childhood abuse or neglect does lead to most cases of borderline personality disorder, the connection may well explain why women are affected more often than men. Girls are two or three times more likely to be sexually abused than are boys (Herman, Perry, & van der Kolk, 1989). Moreover, the work of Harriet MacMillan at McMaster University and the Canadian Centre for Studies of Children at Risk has shown that the association between a history of abuse in childhood and psychopathology in adulthood (including personality disorders) is stronger for women than for men (MacMillan et al., 2001).

Building on the possible link to abuse, Gunderson and Sabo (1993) argued that borderline personality disorder is similar to post-traumatic stress disorder (PTSD); they see many resemblances in the two behaviour patterns. Herman et al. (1989) have drawn similar parallels—for example, difficulties in the regulation of mood, impulse control, and interpersonal relationships. This discussion about borderline personality disorder and PTSD can be viewed from a political perspective. Some writers argue that what the mental health profession calls borderline personality disorder is simply a case of PTSD among women, and a diagnosis of PTSD puts the emphasis on the victimization of women rather than on their mental illness. This distinction in assigning a diagnosis is an important one and represents a debate that will continue for some time (Becker, 2000). These observations all seem to support the hypothesis that borderline personality disorder may be caused by early trauma. It is important to remember, however,

that not all cases of borderline personality disorder resemble PTSD (Zanarini et al., 1998).

Borderline personality disorder has been observed among people who have gone through rapid cultural changes. The problems of identity, emptiness, fears of abandonment, and low anxiety threshold have been found in child and adult immigrants (Laxenaire, Ganne-Vevonec, & Streiff, 1982; Skhiri, Annabi, Bi, & Allani, 1982). These observations further support the possibility that early trauma may, in some individuals, lead to borderline personality disorder.

Remember, however, that a history of childhood trauma, including sexual and physical abuse, occurs in a number of other disorders such as somatoform disorder (Chapter 6), panic disorder (Chapter 5), dissociative identity disorder (Chapter 6), and substance use disorders (Chapter 11). In addition, 20 percent to 40 percent of individuals with borderline personality disorder have no apparent history of such abuse (Gunderson & Sabo, 1993). Although childhood sexual and physical abuse seems to play some role in the etiology of borderline personality disorder, neither appears to be necessary or sufficient to produce the syndrome. Zanarini and Frankenberg (1997) attempt to integrate the different aspects of etiology in borderline personality disorder. They suggest that childhood trauma combines with a predisposing temperament or personality and a stressful triggering event causes the unstable behaviours. The individuals abused as children who do not develop the disorder may lack the biological predisposition that, in this case, may be a volatile or impulsive personality style (Figueroa & Silk, 1997).

Concept Check | 12.1

Which personality disorders are the following people displaying?

1. Homer, who seems eccentric, never shows much emotion. He does not have any close personal relationships and does not seek interactions with people.

   _____

2. Mohammed is 19 and has been in trouble with the law since he was 14. He lies to his parents, vandalizes buildings in his community, and, when caught, shows no remorse. He frequently fights with others and doesn't care whom he injures. _____

3. Russell trusts no one and incorrectly believes other people want to harm him or spoil his plans. He is sure his wife is having an affair. He no longer confides in friends for fear that the information will be used against him. He dwells for hours on harmless comments by co-workers. _____

4. Nick is involved in drugs and has casual sexual encounters. He feels empty unless he does dangerous and exciting things. He threatens to commit suicide if his girlfriend suggests getting help or if she talks about leaving him. He alternates between loving her and hating her. He has low self-esteem and has recently experienced high levels of stress. _____

Treatment

In contrast to the extensive research on the nature of borderline personality disorder, relatively few studies have examined the effects of treatment. Efforts to provide successful treatment for people with borderline personality disorder are complicated by problems with drug abuse, compliance with treatment, and suicide attempts. As a result, many clinicians are reluctant to work with borderline personality disorder clients.

In terms of pharmacotherapy, many people with borderline personality disorder appear to respond positively to a variety of medications, including tricyclic antidepressants, lithium, and even atypical antipsychotics (e.g., Soloff et al., 1989; Stone, 1986). For example, Paul Links and his colleagues have provided preliminary evidence on the efficacy of lithium therapy in the treatment of borderline personality disorder (Links, Steiner, Boiago, & Irwin, 1990). As another example, Québec researchers Evens Villeneuve and Sophie Lemelin (2005) have recently provided preliminary evidence that many symptoms of borderline personality disorder, including impulsivity, appear to respond favourably to treatment with the atypical antipsychotic quetiapine (see Chapter 13 for more information on the atypical antipsychotics).

Research on psychological treatment is also limited. In one exception, Linehan (1987, 1993) used an approach she called *dialectical behaviour therapy* (DBT), which involves helping people cope with the stressors that seem to trigger suicidal behaviours. Weekly individual sessions provide support, and patients are taught how to identify and regulate their emotions (Lau & McMain, 2005; McMain, Korman, & Dimeff, 2001). Problem solving is emphasized so that they can handle difficulties more effectively. In addition, they receive treatment similar to that used for people with post-traumatic stress disorder, in which prior traumatic events are re-experienced to help extinguish the fear associated with them (see Chapter 5). In the final stage of therapy, clients learn to trust their own responses rather than to depend on the validation of others, sometimes by visualizing themselves not reacting to criticism.

Preliminary results suggest that DBT may help reduce suicide attempts, dropouts from treatment, and hospitalizations (Linehan, Armstrong, Suarez, Allmon, & Heard, 1991; Linehan, Heard, & Armstrong, 1992). A follow-up of 39 women who received either dialectic behaviour therapy or general therapeutic support (called "treatment as usual") for one year showed that, during the first six months of follow-up, the women in the DBT group were less suicidal, less angry, and better adjusted socially (Linehan & Kehrer, 1993). Another study examined how treating these individuals with DBT in an inpatient setting—psychiatric hospital—for approximately three months before discharge to home would improve their outcomes (Bohus et al., 2000). The participants improved in several areas, such as with a reduction in self-injury (e.g., cutting themselves), depression, and anxiety. Additional work remains to be done on validating this approach to treatment including more follow-up data on long-term outcomes (Westen, 2000) and improving the feelings of hopelessness experienced by people with this disorder (Scheel, 2000), although the results so far make this type of treatment promising.

Innovative Approaches

When East Meets West

Dialectical behaviour therapy (DBT) as a treatment for borderline personality disorder combines traditional cognitive behavioural therapy techniques with concepts from Eastern spiritual traditions, including Buddhism (Linehan & Dexter-Mazza, 2008). In addition to incorporating treatment techniques we have described for other disorders—including teaching problem-solving skills and cognitive-behavioural therapy—DBT uses aspects of "mindfulness" (the act of directing attention to the experiences occurring in the present moment in a nonjudgmental accepting manner) (Baer & Krietemeyer, 2008). The idea of being mindful has a long tradition in Eastern spiritual practices, and is increasingly being incorporated into a variety of interventions currently being used to address other psychological problems. These problems include stress in survivors of breast cancer (mindfulness-based stress reduction; Lengacher et al., 2009), preventing relapse among people treated for major depression (mindfulness-based cogntive therapy; Mathew, Whitford, Kenny, & Denson, 2010), and reducing an individual's smoking (acceptance and commitment therapy; Bricker, Mann, Marek, Liu, & Peterson, 2010).

One of the advantages in practising mindfulness is that it encourages embracing your feelings and accepting them in a neutral way. If you recall back to Chapter 5 where we discussed treatments for anxiety-related disorders, you will remember that one of the most important aspects of treating anxiety is exposure to the anxiety-provoking stimuli. So, for example, if thoughts about being abandoned by a loved one (which are common in people with borderline personality disorder) make you upset, your natural tendency will be to avoid these thoughts and settings that might trigger them. However, by teaching someone to experience these thoughts in a relaxed manner, and accept them as natural but not dangerous, you increase the chance that the person will be exposed to these stimuli and therefore will have the opportunity to work toward reducing the anxiety surrounding them. We anticipate that many more approaches to helping people with complex problems will begin to incorporate Eastern concepts such as mindfulness as important therapeutic techniques.

Paul Links and Michelle Stockwell (2001) have recently suggested that, particularly given the pattern of unstable and intense interpersonal relationships characteristic of people with borderline personality disorder, couples therapy can be very beneficial for those borderline patients in a relationship. These authors identify three subtypes of borderline patients: (1) impulsive subtype (those with a history of impulsive, self-destructive, and treatment-threatening behaviours); (2) identity disturbance subtype (those with a markedly and persistently unstable self-image or sense of self); and (3) affective cluster (those with marked mood swings and difficulty controlling anger). They only recommend couples therapy for the latter two subtypes, and do not recommend that couples therapy be attempted for those in the impulsive subtype. Future research should evaluate the utility of this suggested subtyping scheme for borderline patients and evaluate the efficacy of couples treatment for the various subtypes (Links & Stockwell, 2001).

Histrionic Personality Disorder

Individuals with **histrionic personality disorder** tend to be overly dramatic and often seem almost to be acting, which is why the term *histrionic*, which means theatrical in manner, is used. Consider the case of Pat.

PAT | *Always Onstage*

When we first met, Pat seemed to radiate enjoyment of life. She was single, in her mid-30s, and was going to university part-time for her master's degree. She often dressed very flamboyantly. During the day she taught children with disabilities, and when she didn't have class in the evening she was often out late on a date. When I first spoke with her, she enthusiastically told me how impressed she was with my work in the field of developmental disabilities and that she had been extremely successful in using some of my techniques with her students. She was clearly overdoing the praise, but who wouldn't appreciate such flattering comments?

Because some of our research included children in her classroom, I saw Pat frequently. Over a period of weeks, however, our interactions grew strained. She frequently complained of various illnesses and injuries (falling in the parking lot, twisting her neck looking out a window) that interfered with her work. She was very disorganized, often leaving to the very last minute tasks that required considerable planning. Pat made promises to other people that were impossible to keep but seemed to be aimed at winning their approval; when she broke the promise, she usually made up a story designed to elicit sympathy and compassion. For example, she promised the mother of one of her students that she would put on a "massive and unique" birthday party for her daughter, but completely forgot about it until the mother showed up with cake and juice. On seeing her, Pat flew into a rage and blamed the school principal for keeping her late after school, although there was no truth to this accusation.

Pat often interrupted meetings about research to talk about her latest boyfriend. The boyfriends changed almost weekly, but her enthusiasm ("Like no other man I have ever met!") and optimism about the future ("He's the guy I want to spend the rest of my life with!") remained high for each of them. Wedding plans were seriously discussed with almost every one, despite their brief acquaintance. Pat was very ingratiating, especially to the male teachers, who often helped her out of trouble she got into because of her disorganization.

When it became clear that she would probably lose her teaching job because of her poor performance, Pat managed to manipulate several of the male teachers and the principal into recommending her for a new job in a nearby school district. A year later she was still at the new school but had been moved twice to different classrooms. According to teachers she worked with, Pat still lacked close interpersonal relationships, although she described her current relationship as "deeply involved." After a rather long period of depression, Pat sought help from a psychologist, who diagnosed her as also having histrionic personality disorder.

Clinical Description

People with histrionic personality disorder are inclined to express their emotions in an exaggerated fashion, for example, hugging someone they have just met or crying uncontrollably during a sad movie (Skodol & Gunderson, 2008). They also tend to be vain and self-centred, and uncomfortable when they are not in the limelight. They are often seductive in appearance and behaviour, and they are typically very concerned about their looks. (Pat, for example, spent a great deal of money on unusual jewellery and was sure to point it out to anyone who would listen.) In addition, people with histrionic personality disorder seek reassurance and approval constantly and may become upset or angry when others do not attend to them or praise them. People with histrionic personality disorder also tend to be impulsive and have great difficulty delaying gratification (see DSM Table 12.7).

DSM-IV-TR	**Table 12.7** Diagnostic Criteria for Histrionic Personality Disorder

A pervasive pattern of excessive emotionality and attention seeking, beginning by early adulthood and present in a variety of contexts, as indicated by five (or more) of the following:

1. Is uncomfortable in situations in which he or she is not the centre of attention
2. Interaction with others is often characterized by inappropriate sexually seductive or provocative behaviour
3. Displays rapidly shifting and shallow expression of emotions
4. Consistently uses physical appearance to draw attention to self
5. Has a style of speech that is excessively impressionistic and lacking in detail
6. Shows self-dramatization, theatricality, and exaggerated expression of emotion
7. Is suggestible (i.e., easily influenced by others or circumstances)
8. Considers relationships to be more intimate than they actually are

Source: Reprinted with permission from the *Diagnostic and Statistical Manual of Mental Disorders,* Fourth Edition, Text Revision, (Copyright © 2000). American Psychiatric Association.

▲ People with histrionic personality disorder tend to be vain, extravagant, and seductive.

onic personality and antisocial personality may be sex-typed alternative expressions of the same unidentified underlying condition. Females with the underlying condition may be predisposed to exhibit a predominantly histrionic pattern, whereas males with the underlying condition may be predisposed to exhibit a predominantly antisocial pattern. Whether this association exists remains a controversial issue, however, and further research on this potential relationship is needed (Dolan & Völlm, 2009; Salekin, Rogers, & Sewell, 1997). The overlap of histrionic personality disorder with other personality disorders (e.g., borderline, narcissistic, and dependent personality disorders) has caused some to question whether histrionic personality disorder should be reclassified in the *DSM-5* to be included under another personality disorder (such as narcissistic personality disorder) (Bakkevig & Karterud, 2010).

The cognitive style associated with histrionic personality disorder is impressionistic (Beck, Freeman, & Davis, 2007), characterized by a tendency to view situations in global, black-and-white terms. Speech is often vague, lacking in detail, and characterized by exaggeration (Nestadt et al., 2009). For example, when Pat was asked about a date she had had the night before, she might say it was "way cool" but fail to provide more detailed information.

The high rate of this diagnosis among women versus men raises questions about the nature of the disorder and its diagnostic criteria. As we first discussed in the beginning of this chapter, there is some thought that the features of histrionic personality disorder, such as overdramatization, vanity, seductiveness, and overconcern with physical appearance, are characteristic of the Western "stereotypical female" and may lead to an overdiagnosis among women. Sprock (2000) examined this important question and found some evidence for a bias among psychologists and psychiatrists to associate the diagnosis with women rather than men.

Causes

Despite its long history, very little research has been done on the causes or treatment of histrionic personality disorder. The ancient Greek philosophers believed that many unexplainable problems of women were caused by the uterus (*hysteria*) migrating within the body (Abse, 1987). As we have seen, however, histrionic personality disorder also occurs among men.

One hypothesis involves a possible relationship with antisocial personality disorder. Evidence suggests that histrionic personality and antisocial personality co-occur more often than chance would account for. Lilienfeld and colleagues (1986), for example, found that roughly two-thirds of people with a histrionic personality also met criteria for antisocial personality disorder. The evidence for this association has led to the suggestion (e.g., Cloninger, 1978; Lilienfeld, 1992) that histri-

Treatment

Although a great deal has been written about ways of helping people with this disorder, very little research demonstrates success (Cloninger & Svakic, 2009). Some therapists have tried to modify the attention-getting behaviour. Kass, Silvers, and Abrams (1972) worked with five women, four of whom had been hospitalized for suicide attempts and all of whom were later diagnosed with histrionic personality disorder. The women were rewarded for appropriate interactions and fined for attention-getting behaviour. The therapists noted improvement after an 18-month follow-up, but they did not collect scientific data to confirm their observation.

A large part of therapy for these individuals usually focuses on the problematic interpersonal relationships. They often manipulate others through emotional crises, using charm, sex, seductiveness, or complaining (Beck et al., 2007). People with histrionic personality disorder often need to be shown how the short-term gains derived from this interactional style result in long-term costs, and they need to be taught more appropriate ways of negotiating their wants and needs.

Narcissistic Personality Disorder

We all know people who think highly of themselves—perhaps exaggerating their real abilities. They consider themselves somehow different from others and deserving of special treatment. In **narcissistic personality disorder**, this tendency is taken to its extreme. In Greek mythology, Narcissus was a youth who spurned the love of Echo. So enamoured was he of his own beauty that he spent his days admiring his own image reflected in a pool of water. Psychoanalysts, including Sigmund Freud, used the term *narcissistic* to describe people who show an exaggerated sense of self-importance and are preoccupied with receiving attention (Cloninger & Svakic, 2009). Consider the case of David.

▲ In Greek mythology, Narcissus was so in love with his own image that he pined away and died of longing.

Clinical Description

People with narcissistic personality disorder have an unreasonable sense of self-importance and are so preoccupied with themselves that they lack sensitivity and compassion for other people (Miller, Campbell, & Pilkonis, 2007). They aren't comfortable unless someone is admiring them. Their exaggerated feelings and their fantasies of greatness, called grandiosity, create negative attributes. They require and expect a great deal of special attention—the best table in the restaurant, the illegal parking space in front of the movie theatre. They also tend to use or exploit others for their own interests and show little empathy. When confronted with other successful people, they can be extremely envious and arrogant. And because they often fail to live up to their own expectations, they are frequently depressed (see DSM Table 12.8).

Causes and Treatment

We start out as infants being self-centred and demanding, which is part of our struggle for survival. However, part of the socialization process involves teaching children empathy and altruism. Some writers, including Austrian native Heinz Kohut (1971, 1977), believe that narcissistic personality disorder arises largely from a profound failure of empathic "mirroring" by the parents very early in a child's development. Consequently, the child remains fixated at a self-centred, grandiose

---

DAVID | Taking Care of Number One

David was a lawyer in his early 40s when he sought treatment for depressed mood. He appeared to be an outgoing man who paid meticulous attention to his appearance. He made a point of asking for the therapist's admiration of his new designer suit, his winter tan, and his new foreign convertible. He also asked the therapist what kind of car he drove and how many VIP clients he dealt with. David wanted to make sure that he was dealing with someone who was the best in the business. David spoke of being an "ace" student and a "super" athlete, but could not provide any details that would validate a superior performance in these areas.

During law school, David became a workaholic, fuelled by fantasies of brilliant work and international recognition. He spent minimal time with his wife, and after their son was born, even less time with either of them. He waited until he felt reasonably secure in his first job so that he could let go of her financial support, and then he sought a divorce.

After his divorce, David decided he was totally free to just please himself. He loved spending all his money on himself, and he lavishly decorated his condominium and bought an attention-getting wardrobe. He constantly sought the companionship of different, attractive women.

David felt better when someone flattered him; when he was in a group social situation where he could easily grab the centre of attention; and when he could fantasize about obtaining a high-level position, being honoured for his great talent, or just being fabulously wealthy.

Source: Cases and excerpts from *Cognitive Therapy of Personality Disorders* by A. T. Beck and A. Freeman, 1990. Copyright © 1990 by Guilford Press. Reprinted by permission.

DSM-IV-TR	**Table 12.8** Diagnostic Criteria for Narcissistic Personality Disorder

A pervasive pattern of grandiosity (in fantasy or behaviour), need for admiration and lack of empathy, beginning by early adulthood and present in a variety of contexts, as indicated by five (or more) of the following:

1. Has a grandiose sense of self-importance (e.g., exaggerates achievements and talents, expects to be recognized as superior without commensurate achievements)
2. Is preoccupied with fantasies of unlimited success, power, brilliance, beauty, or ideal love
3. Believes that he or she is "special" and unique and can only be understood by, or should associate with, other special or high-status people (or institutions)
4. Requests excessive admiration
5. Has a sense of entitlement (i.e., unreasonable expectations of especially favourable treatment or automatic compliance with his or her expectations)
6. Is interpersonally exploitative (i.e., takes advantage of others to achieve his or her own ends)
7. Lacks empathy: is unwilling to recognize or identify with the feelings and needs of others
8. Is often envious of others or believes that others are envious of him or her
9. Shows arrogant, haughty behaviours or attitudes

Source: Reprinted with permission from the *Diagnostic and Statistical Manual of Mental Disorders,* Fourth Edition, Text Revision, (Copyright © 2000). American Psychiatric Association.

stage of development. In addition, the child (and later the adult) becomes involved in an essentially endless and fruitless search for the ideal person who will meet his or her unfulfilled empathic needs.

In a sociological view, Christopher Lasch (1978) wrote in his popular book *The Culture of Narcissism* that this personality disorder is increasing in prevalence in most Western societies, primarily as a consequence of large-scale social changes, including greater emphasis on short-term hedonism, individualism, competitiveness, and success. According to Lasch, the "me generation" has produced more than its share of individuals with narcissistic personality disorder. Indeed, reports confirm that narcissistic personality disorder is increasing in prevalence (Huang et al., 2009). However, this apparent rise may be a consequence of increased interest in and research on the disorder.

Some have questioned whether narcissism and psychopathy are redundant concepts. Researcher Delroy Paulhus and his colleagues at the University of British Columbia have conducted investigations of this issue. For example, a study by Paulhus and Williams (2002) administered measures of psychopathy and narcissism to 245 students along with other measures including a questionnaire measuring the features of the five-factor model of personality. It was found that although psychopaths and narcissists shared elevated disagreeableness on the five-factor measure and a tendency to be self-enhancers, they did not share any other features. The authors thus concluded that narcissism and psychopathy are overlapping but distinct constructs.

Treatment research is extremely limited in both the number of studies and the reports of success (Cloninger & Svakic, 2009; Dhawan, Kunik, Oldham, & Coverdale, 2010; Turkat & Maisto, 1985). When therapy is attempted with these individuals, it often focuses on their grandiosity, their hypersensitivity to evaluation, and their lack of empathy toward others (Beck et al., 2007). Cognitive therapy aims at replacing their fantasies with a focus on the day-to-day pleasurable experiences that are truly attainable. Coping strategies such as relaxation training are used to help them face and accept criticism. Helping them focus on the feelings of others is also a goal. Because individuals with this disorder are vulnerable to severe depressive episodes, particularly in middle age, treatment is often initiated for the depression. However, it is impossible to draw any conclusions about the impact of such treatment on the actual narcissistic personality disorder.

Cluster C Disorders

Avoidant Personality Disorder

As the name suggests, people with **avoidant personality disorder** are extremely sensitive to the opinions of others and therefore avoid most relationships. Their extremely low self-esteem, coupled with a fear of rejection, causes them to be limited in their friendships and very dependent on those they feel comfortable with. Consider the case of Jane.

JANE | *Not Worth Noticing*

Jane was raised by an alcoholic mother who had borderline personality disorder and who abused her verbally and physically. As a child she made sense of her mother's abusive treatment by believing that she (Jane) must be an intrinsically unworthy person to be treated so badly. As an adult in her late 20s, Jane still expected to be rejected when others found out that she was inherently unworthy and bad.

Jane was highly self-critical and predicted that she would not be accepted. She thought that people would not like her, that they would see she was a loser, and that she would not have anything to say. She became upset if she perceived that someone in even the most fleeting encounter was reacting negatively or neutrally. If a newspaper vendor failed to smile at her, or a sales clerk was slightly curt, Jane automatically thought it must be because she (Jane) was somehow unworthy or unlikable. She then felt quite sad. Even when she was receiving positive feedback from a friend, she discounted it. As a result, Jane had few friends and certainly no close ones.

Source: Cases and excerpts from *Cognitive Therapy of Personality Disorders* by A. T. Beck and A. Freeman, 1990. Copyright © 1990 by Guilford Press. Reprinted by permission.

Clinical Description

Millon (1981), who initially proposed this diagnosis, notes that it is important to distinguish between individuals who are asocial because they are apathetic, affectively flat, and relatively uninterested in interpersonal relationships (comparable to what the *DSM-IV-TR* terms *schizoid personality disorder*) and individuals who are asocial because they are interpersonally anxious and fearful of rejection. It is the latter who fit the criteria of avoidant personality disorder (Millon & Martinez, 1995). These individuals feel chronically rejected by others and are pessimistic about their future (see DSM Table 12.9).

Causes

Several theories have been proposed that integrate biological and psychosocial influences as the cause of avoidant personality disorder. Millon (1981), for example, suggests that these individuals may be born with a difficult temperament or personality characteristics. As a result, their parents may reject them, or at least not provide them with enough early, uncritical love. This rejection, in turn, may result in low self-esteem and social alienation, conditions that persist into adulthood. Limited support does exist for psychosocial influences. Stravynski, Elie, and Franche (1989) questioned a group of people with avoidant personality disorder and a group of control subjects about their early treatment by their parents. Those with the disorder remembered their parents as more rejecting, more guilt engendering, and less affectionate than the control group. Meyer and Carver (2000) found that these individuals were

Table 12.9 Diagnostic Criteria for Avoidant Personality Disorder

A pervasive pattern of social inhibition, feelings of inadequacy, and hypersensitivity to negative evaluation, beginning by early adulthood and present in a variety of contexts, as indicated by four (or more) of the following:

1. Avoids occupational activities that involve significant interpersonal contact, because of fears of criticism, disapproval, or rejection
2. Is unwilling to get involved with people unless certain of being liked
3. Shows restraint within intimate relationships because of the fear of being shamed or ridiculed
4. Is preoccupied with being criticized or rejected in social situations
5. Is inhibited in new interpersonal situations because of feelings of inadequacy
6. Views self as socially inept, personally unappealing, or inferior to others
7. Is unusually reluctant to take personal risks or to engage in any new activities because they may prove embarrassing

Source: Reprinted with permission from the *Diagnostic and Statistical Manual of Mental Disorders,* Fourth Edition, Text Revision, (Copyright © 2000). American Psychiatric Association.

more likely to report childhood experiences of isolation, rejection, and conflict with others.

In interpreting the results of these studies, some caution is in order. You probably noticed that these are retrospective studies, relying on the participants' memories for a report of what happened. The differences in the reports could be a consequence of differences in their ability to remember their childhoods rather than of actual differences in the ways the participants were treated. Also, it could be that people with avoidant personality disorder are more sensitive to the way they are treated, and therefore their memories are different from what actually happened. The findings are intriguing nonetheless and should be followed up as a possible contributor to our understanding of this disorder.

Some have suggested that, given its similarity to social phobia (see Chapter 5), avoidant personality disorder is part of a social anxiety spectrum (e.g., Schneider, Blanco, Antia, & Liebowitz, 2002). A growing body of research links *behavioural inhibition* (i.e., a heritable temperamental factor involving an avoidant response to unfamiliar situations; Brandon, 1995; Smoller et al., 2003) quite specifically to this social anxiety disorder spectrum, including avoidant personality disorder (see Schneider et al., 2002). For example, research by Kenneth Bruce and his colleagues at the Douglas Hospital in Montréal shows that women with comorbid avoidant personality disorder displayed more behavioural inhibition in response to threat, on a lab-based computer task (Bruce, Steiger, Koerner, Israel, & Young, 2004). We discussed the underlying biological basis of the behavioural inhibition system in detail in Chapter 5. Findings from a research group in Spain suggest that the behavioural inhibition system may be the core underlying vulnerability for Cluster C personality disorders more generally. More specifically, these researchers compared patients diagnosed with Cluster

C personality disorders (including avoidant personality disorder) with two comparison groups (patients diagnosed with other personality disorders and normal controls) on measures of behavioural inhibition. Overall, the results suggested that patients in the Cluster C personality disorders group showed scores on these measures suggesting an overactive behavioural inhibition system (Caseras, Torrubia, & Farre, 2001). Additional research is needed to determine the degree to which elevated behavioural inhibition is characteristic of avoidant personality disorder, specifically, or Cluster C personality disorders more generally.

Treatment

In contrast to the scarcity of research into most of the other personality disorders, several well-controlled studies exist on approaches to therapy for people with avoidant personality disorder. Lynn Alden and her colleagues have been at the forefront of the field, in developing effective approaches for treating individuals with avoidant personality disorder. Behavioural intervention techniques for anxiety and social skills problems have had some success (Alden, 1989; Alden & Capreol, 1993; Renneberg, Goldstein, Phillips, & Chambless, 1990; Stravynski, Lesage, Marcouiller, & Elie, 1989). In particular, Alden's work shows that social skills training within a support group is useful to help people with avoidant personality disorder become more assertive with others (e.g., Alden, 1989). Because the problems experienced by people with avoidant personality disorder resemble those of people with social phobia, many of the same treatments are used for both groups (see Chapter 5). For example, according to a recent review by Alden and her colleagues, the central element of cognitive behavioural treatment for avoidant personality disorder is graduated exposure to feared situations (Alden, Laposa, & Taylor, 2006).

Renneberg et al. (1990) identified areas that caused anxiety in a group of 17 people with avoidant personality disorder, including a fear of rejection, a fear of criticism, and anxiety about their appearance. In groups of five or six patients, they used *systematic desensitization*, which involves relaxing in the presence of feared situations (e.g., "You speak to a group of people at work, and you realize that your voice is not powerful enough; your voice is childish") and *behavioural rehearsal*, in which patients act out situations that cause anxiety. As a group, these people improved in such areas as fear of negative evaluation and social avoidance and distress. The improvements tended to be modest, although, given the usually poor outcomes found among people with personality disorders, even moderate improvement is encouraging.

Dependent Personality Disorder

We all know what it means to be dependent on another person. People with **dependent personality disorder**, however, rely on others to make ordinary decisions as well as important ones, which results in an unreasonable fear of abandonment. Consider the case of Karen.

KAREN | *Whatever You Say*

Karen was a 45-year-old married woman who was referred for treatment by her physician for problems with panic attacks. During the evaluation, she appeared to be very worried, sensitive, and naïve. She was easily overcome with emotion and cried on and off throughout the session. She was self-critical at every opportunity throughout the evaluation. For example, when asked how she got along with other people, she reported that "others think I'm dumb and inadequate," although she could give no evidence as to what made her think that. She reported that she didn't like school because "I was dumb," and that she always felt that she was not good enough.

Karen described staying in her first marriage for ten years, even though "it was hell." Her husband had affairs with many other women and was verbally abusive. She tried to leave him many times, but gave in to his repeated requests to return. She was finally able to divorce him, and shortly afterward she met and married her current husband, whom she described as kind, sensitive, and supportive. Karen stated that she preferred to have others make important decisions and agreed with other people in order to avoid conflict. She worried about being left alone without anyone to take care of her and reported feeling lost without other people's reassurance. She also reported that her feelings were easily hurt, so she worked hard not to do anything that might lead to criticism.

Source: Cases and excerpts from *Cognitive Therapy of Personality Disorders* by A. T. Beck and A. Freeman, 1990. Copyright © 1990 by Guilford Press. Reprinted by permission.

Clinical Description

Dependent personality disorder belongs in the anxious/fearful cluster of *DSM-IV-TR* personality disorders because their interpersonally dependent behaviour is motivated by anxiety (e.g., fear of abandonment; see, for example, Stewart, Knize, & Pihl, 1992). Individuals with dependent personality disorder sometimes agree with other people when their own opinion differs, so as not to be rejected (Cloninger & Svakic, 2009). Their desire to obtain and maintain supportive and nurturing relationships may lead to their other behavioural characteristics (Bornstein, 1997), including submissiveness, timidity, and passivity. People with this disorder are similar to those with *avoidant personality disorder* in their feelings of inadequacy, sensitivity to criticism, and need for reassurance. However, people with avoidant personality disorder respond to these feelings by avoiding relationships, whereas those with dependent personality disorder respond by clinging to relationships (Cloninger & Svakic, 2009; see DSM Table 12.10).

Causes and Treatment

We are all born dependent on other people for food, physical protection, and nurturance. Part of the socialization process involves helping us live independently (Bornstein, 1992). It is thought such disruptions as the early death of a parent or neglect or rejection by caregivers may cause people to grow up fearing

DSM-IV-TR | **Table 12.10** Diagnostic Criteria for Dependent Personality Disorder

A pervasive and excessive need to be taken care of that leads to submissive and clinging behaviour and fears of separation, beginning by early adulthood and present in a variety of contexts, as indicated by five (or more) of the following:

1. Has difficulty making everyday decisions without an excessive amount of advice and reassurance from others
2. Needs others to assume responsibility for most major areas of his or her life
3. Has difficulty expressing disagreement with others because of fear of loss of support or approval. *Note:* Do not include realistic fears of retribution.
4. Has difficulty initiating projects or doing things on his or her own (because of a lack of self-confidence in judgment or abilities rather than a lack of motivation or energy)
5. Goes to excessive lengths to obtain nurturance and support from others, to the point of volunteering to do things that are unpleasant
6. Feels uncomfortable or helpless when alone because of exaggerated fears of being unable to care for himself or herself
7. Urgently seeks another relationship as a source of care and support when a close relationship ends
8. Is unrealistically preoccupied with fears of being left to take care of himself or herself

Source: Reprinted with permission from the *Diagnostic and Statistical Manual of Mental Disorders,* Fourth Edition, Text Revision, (Copyright © 2000). American Psychiatric Association.

abandonment (Stone, 1993). This view comes from work in child development on "attachment," or how children learn to bond with their parents and other people who are important in their lives (Bowlby, 1977). If early bonding is interrupted, individuals may be constantly anxious that they will lose people close to them.

Research by David A. Clark and his colleagues suggests that certain personality traits may be quite relevant to the etiology of dependent personality disorder as well. In particular, these researchers have been investigating the role of the personality constructs of sociotropy and autonomy in the Cluster C personality disorders. *Sociotropy* refers to a personality orientation involving a strong investment in positive social interactions, whereas autonomy refers to a personality style involving a strong investment in independence from others, mobility, and freedom of choice (Beck, 1983, 1987). Clark and colleagues tested more than 2000 psychiatric outpatients on a self-report measure of sociotropy and autonomy and with a structured interview for establishing *DSM* diagnoses (Clark, Steer, Haslam, Beck, & Brown, 1997). They found the sample was characterized by four clusters of patients in terms of their responses to the sociotropy–autonomy measure: an autonomous group, a sociotropic group, an individualistic achievement group, and a group of low-scoring controls. They found that diagnoses of dependent personality disorder were significantly more common in the sociotropic group compared with the other three groups. Diagnoses of avoidant personality disorder were also significantly more common in the sociotropic group. Diagnoses of dependent personality disorder were significantly less common in the individualistic achievement group than in the other three groups.

No other differences in personality disorders were found across the four groups (Clark et al., 1997).

The treatment literature for this disorder is mostly descriptive; very little research exists to show whether a particular treatment is effective. On the surface, because of their attentiveness and eagerness to give responsibility for their problems to the therapist, people with dependent personality disorder can appear to be ideal patients. However, their submissiveness negates one of the major goals of therapy, which is to make the person more independent and personally responsible. Therapy therefore progresses gradually, as the patient develops confidence in his or her ability to make decisions independently (Beck & Freeman, 1990). There is a particular need for care that the patient does not become overly dependent on the therapist.

Concept Check | 12.2

Review your ability to differentiate among the personality disorders.

1. John is very reluctant to talk to anyone, not to mention a therapist. His reluctance and mistrust of others seem to be unlimited. John gives the impression that everyone is out to get him. _____

2. The therapist immediately notices that Milagros displays extreme emotional behaviour a great deal when she speaks, so much so that she seems to be acting. _____

3. Susan was brought in by her parents because they found her uncontrollable. She had been stealing from her parents and friends, and she's so impulsive her parents don't know what she might try next. Some people call her a "psychopath." _____

4. Jaikumar is especially anxious at even the thought of social interactions. He reacts excessively to criticism, which only feeds his pervasive feelings of inadequacy. _____

Obsessive-Compulsive Personality Disorder

People who have **obsessive-compulsive personality disorder** are characterized by a fixation on things being done "the right way." Although many might envy their persistence and dedication, this preoccupation with details prevents them from actually completing much of anything. Consider the case of Daniel.

DANIEL | Getting It Exactly Right

Each day at exactly 8 A.M., Daniel arrived at his office at the university where he was a graduate student in psychology. On his way, he always stopped at Tim Hortons to buy coffee. After arriving at his office, he drank his coffee and read *The Globe and Mail* from 8 to 9:15 A.M. At 9:15 he reorganized the files that held the hundreds of papers related to his doctoral dissertation, now several years overdue. From 10 A.M. until noon he read one of these papers, highlighting relevant passages. Then he took the paper bag that held his lunch (always a peanut butter and jelly sandwich and an apple) and went to the cafeteria to purchase a soft drink and eat by himself. From 1 P.M. until 5 P.M. he held meetings, organized his desk, made lists of things to do, and entered his references into a new database program on his computer. At home, Daniel had dinner with his wife, then worked on his dissertation until after 11 P.M., although much of the time was spent trying out new features of his home computer.

Daniel was no closer to completing his dissertation than he had been four-and-a-half years ago. His wife was threatening to leave him because he was equally rigid about everything at home and she didn't want to remain in this limbo of graduate school forever. When Daniel eventually sought help from a therapist for his anxiety over his deteriorating marriage, he was diagnosed as having obsessive-compulsive personality disorder.

Clinical Description

Like many with this personality disorder, Daniel is very work oriented, spending little time going to movies or parties or doing anything that isn't related to psychology. Because of their general rigidity, these people tend to have poor interpersonal relationships (Cloninger & Svakic, 2009; see DSM Table 12.11).

This personality disorder seems to be only distantly related to obsessive-compulsive disorder, one of the anxiety disorders we described in Chapter 5. People like Daniel tend not to have the obsessive thoughts and the compulsive behaviours seen in the like-named obsessive-compulsive disorder (OCD). Although people with the anxiety disorder sometimes show characteristics of the personality disorder, they also show the characteristics of other personality disorders as well (e.g., avoidant, histrionic, dependent; Eisen, Mancebo, Chiappone, Pinto, & Rasmussen, 2008).

An intriguing theory suggests that the psychological profiles of many serial killers point to the role of obsessive-compulsive personality disorder. Ferreira (2000) notes that these individuals do not often fit the definition of someone with a severe mental illness—such as schizophrenia—but are "masters of control" in manipulating their victims. Their need to control all aspects of the crime fits the pattern of people with obsessive-compulsive personality disorder, and some combination of this disorder and unfortunate childhood experiences may lead to this disturbing behaviour pattern. Obsessive-compulsive personality disorder may also play a role among some sex offenders—in particular, pedophiles. Brain-imaging research on pedophiles suggests that brain functioning in these individuals is similar to those with obsessive-compulsive personality disorder (Schiffer et al., 2007). At the other end of the behavioural spectrum, it is also common to find obsessive-compulsive personality disorder

DSM-IV-TR	**Table 12.11** Diagnostic Criteria for Obsessive-Compulsive Personality Disorder

A pervasive pattern of preoccupation with orderliness, perfectionism, and mental and interpersonal control, at the expense of flexibility, openness, and efficiency, beginning by early adulthood and present in a variety of contexts, as indicated by four (or more) of the following:

1. Is preoccupied with details, rules, lists, order, organization, or schedules to the extent that the major point of the activity is lost

2. Shows perfectionism that interferes with task completion (e.g., is unable to complete a project because his or her own overly strict standards are not met)

3. Is excessively devoted to work and productivity to the exclusion of leisure activities and friendships (not accounted for by obvious economic necessity)

4. Is overly conscientious, scrupulous, and inflexible about matters of morality, ethics, or values (not accounted for by cultural or religious identification)

5. Is unable to discard worn-out or worthless objects even when they have no sentimental value

6. Is reluctant to delegate tasks or to work with others unless they submit to exactly his or her way of doing things

7. Adopts a miserly spending style toward both self and others; money is viewed as something to be hoarded for future catastrophes

8. Shows rigidity and stubbornness

Source: Reprinted with permission from the *Diagnostic and Statistical Manual of Mental Disorders,* Fourth Edition, Text Revision, (Copyright © 2000). American Psychiatric Association.

among gifted children, whose quest for perfectionism can be quite debilitating (Nugent, 2000).

Causes and Treatment

There seems to be a weak genetic contribution to obsessive-compulsive personality disorder (Cloninger & Svakic, 2009). Some people may be predisposed to favouring structure in their lives, but to reach the level it did in Daniel may require parental reinforcement of conformity and neatness.

▲ People with obsessive-compulsive personality disorder are preoccupied with doing things "the right way."

We do not have much information on the successful treatment of individuals with this disorder. Therapy often attacks the fears that seem to underlie the need for orderliness. These individuals are often afraid that what they do will be inadequate, so they procrastinate and excessively ruminate about both important issues and minor details. Therapists help the individual relax or use distraction techniques to redirect the compulsive thoughts. Perfectionism (i.e., self-criticism, difficulty dealing with feedback, procrastination, and unrealistic goal setting) is an important aspect of obsessive-compulsive personality disorder, as indicated by the work of Toronto psychiatrists Allan Kaplan, Blake Woodside, and their colleagues (Halmi et al., 2005). A study by Alberta researchers Kirsten Ferguson and Margaret Rodway (1994) indicates that cognitive-behavioural therapy can be effective in treating this important feature of obsessive-compulsive personality disorder.

Concept Check | 12.3

Check your understanding of these additional personality disorders by identifying the patterns described here as (a) dependent, (b) narcissistic, (c) obsessive-compulsive, (d) schizoid, or (e) histrionic.

1. Katherine thinks she is the best candidate for any job, thinks her performance is always excellent, and looks for admiration from others. _____

2. Manon is afraid to be alone and seeks constant reassurance from her family. She won't make any decisions or do things on her own. She thinks that if she shows any resolve or initiative she will be abandoned and have to take care of herself. _____

3. The therapist discovers that Filipe has yet to fill out the information form, although he was given at least 15 minutes. Filipe says he first had to resharpen the pencil, then clean it of debris, then he noticed that the pencil sharpener wasn't very clean. The paper also wasn't properly placed on the clipboard. _____

4. George is overly dramatic about everyday occurrences and thinks the world revolves around him.

_____

Personality Disorders under Study

We started this chapter by noting difficulties in categorizing personality disorders; for example, there is much overlap of the categories, which suggests there may be other ways to arrange these pervasive difficulties of character. It shouldn't surprise you to learn that other personality disorders have been studied for inclusion in the *DSM*—for example, sadistic personality disorder, which includes people who receive pleasure by inflicting pain on others (Morey, Hopwood, & Klein, 2007), and self-defeating personality disorder, which includes people who are overly passive and accept the pain and suffering imposed by others (Skodol, 2005). However, few studies support the existence of these disorders, so they were not included in the *DSM-IV-TR* (Cloninger & Svakic, 2009).

Two new personality disorders are under study for inclusion in the *DSM-5*. *Depressive personality disorder* includes self-criticism, dejection, a judgmental stance toward others, and a tendency to feel guilt. Some evidence indicates this may indeed be a personality disorder distinct from dysthymic disorder (the mood disorder described in Chapter 7 that involves a persistently depressed mood lasting at least two years); research is continuing in this area (Orstavik, Kendler, Czajkowski, Tambs, & Reichborn-Kjennerud, 2007; Vachon, Sellbom, Ryder, Miller, & Bagby, 2009). *Passive-aggressive (negativistic) personality disorder* is characterized by passive aggression in which people adopt a negativistic attitude to resist routine demands and expectations. This category is an expansion of a previous *DSM-III-R* category, *passive-aggressive personality disorder*, and may be a subtype of a narcissistic personality disorder (Hopwood et al., 2009).

From the Inside

Let Me Make It Good: A Chronicle of My Life with Borderline Personality Disorder
by Jane Wanklin

Jane Wanklin grew up in Halifax, Nova Scotia, and London, Ontario. She lives with borderline personality disorder, making it extremely difficult to maintain stable relationships with family and friends. In her memoir, *Let Me Make It Good: A Chronicle of My Life with Borderline Personality Disorder*, Wanklin examines her life experiences, attempting to put her mental illness into perspective.

She describes her frequent psychiatric hospitalizations starting at age 16. Passages of her autobiography clearly illustrate classic symptoms of borderline personality disorder, such as her unstable self-image and impulsive behaviour (e.g., binge eating). Like many borderline patients, Wanklin reports that she experienced childhood trauma, which she believes contributed to her mental illness. In addition to her personality pathology, Wanklin also suffered with an eating disorder, which research shows is commonly comorbid with borderline personality disorder (see Chapter 8).

In many parts of the book, Wanklin describes her frequent angry outbursts and difficulties controlling her rage. She came up with a name to describe her anger, as she explains in the following excerpt:

That's what I termed my extreme anger: The Beast. It became my constant companion and would spring from me, seemingly out of nowhere, disrupting the entire ward and causing fear and apprehension in the hearts of the other patients. (Wanklin, 1998, p. 152)

In the opening passage of this textbook chapter, we chose a quote from Wanklin's book that captures the borderline patient's experience of, and motivations for, self-harm (see p. 438). Wanklin's elaborate self-harm rituals (which involved cutting) were limited by staff during stays in the psychiatric hospital:

My cutting rituals [caused] the staff [to] forbid me to sit alone with a can of pop and [I] had to throw it away in front of them. This didn't stop me, for I only became more sneaky. I would get [pop cans] from the canteen and then hide in the sub-basement and cut myself to pieces in private. (Wanklin, 1998, p. 180)

She also provides some excellent examples of the borderline tendency to alternate between extremes of idealization and devaluation within her interpersonal relationships. For instance, Wanklin details how this pattern of alternating between these two extremes applied in her relationship with her psychiatrist:

I grew hostile toward Dr. Milo, who I saw as my captor. I would spit and fume at him when he came into my room. "I hate you," I sputtered, hollering at him to "Get the f___ away from me!" ... [But]... by December, Dr. Milo was once again in my good books and we talked a lot out in the dayroom. Some of his other patients resented all the time he was devoting to me and it made me feel special. I basked in the glow of his attention and chatted to him about matters such as running, music, and... philosophy.... He had a wonderful sense of humour and I soon discovered that I was falling in love with him. (Wanklin, 1998, p. 180)

Let Me Make It Good is a moving and enlightening memoir that takes a stark, unflinching, and sometimes cynical look at what it's like to live with borderline personality disorder. The book helps in showing people with the disorder that they are not alone. Reading Wanklin's vivid description of the symptoms she suffered will help readers recognize and understand borderline personality disorder in themselves, family members, friends, or co-workers.

Source: From *Let Me Make It Good: A Chronicle of My Life with Borderline Personality Disorder* by Jane Wanklin (Mosaic Press, 1998).

We opened the chapter discussing the controversies surrounding the classification of the personality disorders. The great degree of overlap (comorbidity) of the disorders—for example, some people are diagnosed with three or more personality disorders—and the use of categories as opposed to dimensions continue to concern the researchers who study these disorders and the clinicians who care for these individuals (South et al., in press). For example, the organization that we use in the chapter (the three clusters of A, B, and C) is also used by the *DSM-IV* but is nothing more than a convenient way for clinicians to remember the disorders and is not based on any scientific evidence (Widiger, 2007). Perhaps the most anticipated change in this field is a radical redefinition of the disorders using dimensions, and we expect that the next version of the *DSM*— the *DSM-5*—will introduce this new approach and perhaps make us rethink how we view many of the other disorders we cover in this book (Krueger, Skodol, Livesley, Shrout, & Huang, 2008; Lopez, Compton, Grant, & Breiling, 2008; Widiger & Trull, 2007).

One way to introduce dimensions that is currently being discussed is to rate clients on six broad personality trait domains (negative emotionality, introversion, antagonism, disinhibition, compul-sivity, and schizotypy) (American Psychiatric Association, 2010). Each of these domains would include more specific "trait facets." For example, under the domain of "compulsivity" would be the facets of perfectionism, perseveration, rigidity, orderliness, and risk aversion. Clinicians would rate clients on a four-point scale as to the extent that these traits are present (from "very little or not at all" to "extremely descriptive"), therefore providing some indication of the dimensional quality of their difficulties. If and how this classification scheme will ultimately be incorporated into mainstream clinical work remains to be resolved.

Summary

An Overview

- The personality disorders represent long-standing and ingrained ways of thinking, feeling, and behaving that can cause significant distress. Because people may display two or more of these maladaptive ways of interacting with the world, considerable disagreement remains over how to categorize the personality disorders.

- The *DSM-IV-TR* includes ten personality disorders that are divided into three "clusters": Cluster A ("odd or eccentric") includes paranoid, schizoid, and schizotypal personality disorders; Cluster B ("dramatic, emotional, or erratic") includes antisocial, borderline, histrionic, and narcissistic personality disorders; Cluster C ("anxious or fearful") includes avoidant, dependent, and obsessive-compulsive personality disorder.

Specific Personality Disorders

- People with paranoid personality disorder are excessively mistrustful and suspicious of other people, without any justification. They tend not to confide in others and expect other people to do them harm.

- People with schizoid personality disorder show a pattern of detachment from social relationships and a very limited range of emotions in interpersonal situations. They seem aloof, cold, and indifferent to other people.

- People with schizotypal personality disorder are typically socially isolated and behave in ways that would seem unusual to most of us. Additionally, they tend to be suspicious and have odd beliefs about the world.

- People with antisocial personality disorder have a history of failing to comply with social norms. They perform actions most of us would find unacceptable, such as stealing from friends and family. They also tend to be irresponsible, impulsive, and deceitful.

- In contrast to the *DSM-IV-TR* criteria for antisocial personality, which focuses almost entirely on observable behaviours (e.g., impulsively and repeatedly changing employment, residence, or sexual partners), the related concept of psychopathy primarily reflects underlying personality traits (e.g., self-centredness, manipulativeness).

- People with borderline personality disorder lack stability in their moods and in their relationships with other people, and they usually have very poor self-esteem. These individuals often feel empty and are at great risk of suicide.

- Individuals with histrionic personality disorder tend to be overly dramatic and often appear almost to be acting.

- People with narcissistic personality disorder think highly of themselves—beyond their real abilities. They consider themselves somehow different from others and deserving of special treatment.

- People with avoidant personality disorder are extremely sensitive to the opinions of others and therefore avoid social relationships. Their extremely low self-esteem, coupled with a fear of rejection, causes them to reject the attention others crave.

- Individuals with dependent personality disorder rely on others to the extent of letting them make everyday decisions as well as major ones; this results in an unreasonable fear of being abandoned.

- People who have obsessive-compulsive personality disorder are characterized by a fixation on things being done "the right way." This preoccupation with details prevents them from actually completing much of anything.
- Treating people with personality disorders is often difficult because they usually do not see that their difficulties are a result of the way they relate to others.
- Personality disorders are important for the clinician to consider because they may interfere with efforts to treat more specific problems such as anxiety, depression, or substance abuse. Unfortunately, the presence of one or more personality disorders is associated with a poor treatment outcome and a generally negative prognosis.

Key Terms

antisocial personality disorder, 450

avoidant personality disorder, 466

borderline personality disorder, 459

dependent personality disorder, 468

histrionic personality disorder, 463

narcissistic personality disorder, 465

obsessive-compulsive personality disorder, 469

paranoid personality disorder, 446

personality disorders, 439

psychopathy, 451

schizoid personality disorder, 447

schizotypal personality disorder, 448

Answers to Concept Checks

12.1

1. schizoid personality disorder
2. antisocial personality disorder
3. paranoid personality disorder
4. borderline personality disorder

12.2

1. paranoid personality disorder
2. histrionic personality disorder
3. antisocial personality disorder
4. avoidant personality disorder

12.3

1. b 2. a 3. c 4. e

Media Resources

Access an integrated eBook, Abnormal Psychology Videos (formerly Abnormal Psych Live CD-ROM), chapter-specific interactive learning tools (flashcards, quizzes, learning modules), and more in your Psychology CourseMate, available at **www.abnormalpsych3ce.nelson.com**.

Abnormal Psychology Videos

Free Abnormal Psychology videos can be viewed on the website **www.abnormalpsych3ce.nelson.com**.

- *Antisocial Personality Disorder: George:* George describes his long history of violating people's rights.
- *Borderline Personality Disorders:* These women discuss the most troubling symptoms of their disorder.
- *Dialectical Behaviour Therapy:* Marsha Linehan discusses the effects of borderline personality disorders with a few clients.

Video Concept Reviews

CourseMate also contains Mark Durand's *Video Concept Reviews* on these challenging topics.

- Personality Disorders
- Paranoid Personality Disorder
- Schizoid Personality Disorder
- Schizotypal Personality Disorder
- Antisocial Personality Disorder
- Borderline Personality Disorder
- Histrionic Personality Disorder
- Narcissistic Personality Disorder
- Concept Check: Histrionic versus Narcissistic Personality Disorder
- Avoidant Personality Disorder
- Dependent Personality Disorder
- Obsessive-Compulsive Personality Disorder

Exploring Personality Disorders

> People with personality disorders think and behave in ways that cause distress to themselves and/or the people who care about them.

> There are three main groups, or clusters, of personality disorders, which usually begin in childhood.

CLUSTER A

Odd or Eccentric

Gazelle Technologies

Schizoid
social isolation

Psychological Influences

- Very limited range of emotions
- Apparently cold and unconnected
- Unaffected by praise or criticism

Causes

Biological Influences

- May be associated with lower density of dopamine receptors

Social/Cultural Influences

- Preference for social isolation
- Lack of social skills
- Lack of interest in close relationships, including romantic or sexual

Treatment

- Learning value of social relationships
- Social skills training with role playing

Paranoid
extreme suspicion

Psychological Influences

- Thoughts that people are malicious, deceptive, and threatening
- Behaviour based on mistaken assumptions about others

Causes

Biological Influences

- Possible but unclear link with schizophrenia

Social/Cultural Influences

- "Outsiders" may be susceptible because of unique experiences (e.g., prisoners, refugees, people with hearing impairments, and the elderly)
- Parents' early teaching may influence

Treatment

- Difficult because of client's mistrust and suspicion
- Cognitive work to change thoughts
- Low success rate

Schizotypal
suspicion and odd behaviour

Psychological Influences

- Unusual beliefs, behaviour, or dress
- Suspiciousness
- Believing insignificant events are personally relevant ("ideas of reference")
- Expressing little emotion
- Symptoms of major depressive disorder

Causes

Biological Influences

- Genetic vulnerability for schizophrenia but without the biological or environmental stresses present in that disorder

Social/Cultural Influences

- Preference for social isolation
- Excessive social anxiety
- Lack of social skills

Treatment

- Teaching social skills to reduce isolation and suspicion
- Medication (haloperidol) to reduce ideas of reference, odd communication, and isolation
- Low success rate

CLUSTER C

PhotoDisc/Getty Images

Anxious or Fearful

Dependent
pervasive need to be taken care of

Psychological Influences

- Early "loss" of caretaker (death, rejection, or neglect) leads to fear of abandonment
- Timidity and passivity

Causes

Biological Influences

- Each of us born dependent for protection, food, and nurturance

Social/Cultural Influences

- Agreement for the sake of avoiding conflict
- Similar to Avoidant in
  – inadequacy
  – sensitivity to criticism
  – need for reassurance
  BUT
for those same shared reasons
- Avoidants withdraw
- Dependents cling

Treatment

- Very little research
- Appear as ideal clients
- Submissiveness negates independence

CLUSTER B

Dramatic, Emotional, or Erratic

Note: Cluster B also includes Narcissistic Personality Disorder.

ThinkStock/Getty Images

Antisocial
violation of others' rights

Psychological Influences
- Difficulty learning to avoid punishment
- Indifferent to concerns of others

Causes

Biological Influences
- Genetic vulnerability combined with environmental influences
- Abnormally low cortical arousal
- High fear threshold

Social/Cultural Influences
- Criminality
- Stress/exposure to trauma
- Inconsistent parental discipline
- Socioeconomic disadvantage

Treatment
- Seldom successful (incarceration instead)
- Parent training if problems are caught early
- Prevention through preschool programs

Histrionic
excessively emotional

Psychological Influences
- Vain and self-centred
- Easily upset if ignored
- Vague and hyperbolic
- Impulsive; difficulty delaying gratification

Causes

Biological Influences
- Possible link to antisocial disorder
  – women histrionic/men antisocial

Social/Cultural Influences
- Overly dramatic behaviour attracts attention
- Seductive
- Approval-seeking

Treatment
- Little evidence of success
- Rewards and fines
- Focus on interpersonal relations

Borderline
tumultuous instability

Psychological Influences
- Suicidal
- Erratic moods
- Impulsivity

Causes

Biological Influences
- Familial link to mood disorders
- Possibly inherited tendencies (impulsivity or volatility)

Social/Cultural Influences
- Early trauma, especially sexual/physical abuse
- Rapid cultural changes (immigration) may trigger symptoms

Treatment
- Dialectical behaviour therapy (DBT)
- Medication:
  – tricyclic antidepressants
  – minor tranquilizers
  – lithium

Avoidant
inhibition

Psychological Influences
- Low self-esteem
- Fear of rejection, criticism leads to fear of attention
- Extreme sensitivity
- Resembles social phobia

Causes

Biological Influences
- Innate characteristics may cause rejection

Social/Cultural Influences
- Insufficient parental affection

Treatment
- Behavioural intervention techniques sometimes successful
  – systematic desensitization
  – behavioural rehearsal
- Improvements usually modest

Obsessive-compulsive
fixation on details

Psychological Influences
- Generally rigid
- Dependent on routines
- Procrastinating

Causes

Biological Influences
- Distant relation to OCD
- Probable weak genetic role
  – predisposition to structure combined with parental reinforcement

Social/Cultural Influences
- Very work-oriented
- Poor interpersonal relationships

Treatment
- Little information
- Therapy
  – attack fears behind need
  – relaxation or distraction techniques redirect compulsion to order

13 | Schizophrenia and Other Psychotic Disorders

Robert Daly/Stone/Getty Images

The next day I awake and go to the Laundromat. But why are these cars making gestures as though guns are at their heads. They must all hate me. Someone is going to kill me. Maybe it is a warning. Maybe it is Emillio's plan. I run to my apartment. My God, what am I going to do? These people want me dead for some reason. [...] I run from the Laundromat to my apartment. [...] I hide under my Parson's table. But what's this? Everyone is honking? Are they angry?
—Christina Alexandra, *Five Lost Years: A Personal Exploration of Schizophrenia*

Demonstrate knowledge and understanding representing appropriate breadth and depth in selected content areas of psychology:	> Biological bases of behaviour and mental processes, including physiology, sensation, perception, comparative, motivation, and emotion (APA SLO 1.2.a (3)) *(see textbook pages 479–485, 490–498)*
	> The history of psychology, including the evolution of methods of psychology, its theoretical conflicts, and its sociocultural contexts (APA SLO 1.2.b) *(see textbook pages 477–478)*
Use the concepts, language, and major theories of the discipline to account for psychological phenomena.	> Describe behaviour and mental processes empirically, including operational definitions (APA SLO 1.3.a) *(see textbook pages 477–488)*
Identify appropriate applications of psychology in solving problems, such as:	> Origin and treatment of abnormal behaviour (APA SLO 4.2.b) *(see textbook pages 489–506)*

* Portions of this chapter cover learning outcomes suggested by the American Psychological Association (2007) in their guidelines for the undergraduate psychology major. Chapter coverage of these outcomes is identified above by APA Goal and APA Suggested Learning Outcome (SLO).

A middle-aged man walks the streets of Toronto with aluminum foil on the inside of his hat so Martians can't read his mind. A young woman sits in her college classroom and hears the voice of God telling her she is a vile and disgusting person. You try to strike up a conversation with the supermarket bagger, but he stares at you vacantly and will say only one or two words in a flat, toneless voice. Each of these people may have **schizophrenia**, the startling disorder characterized by a broad spectrum of cognitive and emotional dysfunctions including delusions and hallucinations, disorganized speech and behaviour, and inappropriate emotions.

Schizophrenia is a complex syndrome that inevitably has a devastating effect on the lives of the person affected and on family members. This disorder can disrupt a person's perception, thought, speech, and movement—almost every aspect of daily functioning. And despite important advances in treatment, complete recovery from schizophrenia is rare. Obviously, this catastrophic disorder takes a tremendous emotional toll on everyone involved. In addition to the emotional costs, the financial drain is considerable. According to the Canadian National Outcomes Measurement Study in Schizophrenia, the majority of people with schizophrenia in our country are unemployed and living in poverty (Smith et al., 2006). The annual cost to Canadian society is in the billions of dollars when factors such as hospitalization, disability payments, welfare payments, and lost wages are considered (British Columbia Schizophrenia Society, 2001). Because schizophrenia is so widespread, affecting approximately 1 out of every 100 people at some point in their lives, and because its consequences are so severe, research on its causes and treatment has proliferated. Given the attention it has received, you would think that the question "What is schizophrenia?" would by now be answered easily. It is not.

In this chapter, we explore this intriguing disorder and review efforts to determine whether schizophrenia is distinct in itself or a combination of disorders. As noted by Walter Heinrichs and his colleagues at York University, the search is complicated by the presence of subtypes: different presentations and combinations of symptoms such as hallucinations, delusions, and disorders of speech, cognition, emotion, and socialization (Heinrichs, 1993; Heinrichs & Awad, 1993; Heinrichs, Ruttan, Zakzanis, & Case, 1997). After discussing the characteristics of people with schizophrenia, we describe research into its causes and treatment.

Perspectives on the Concept of Schizophrenia

Early Figures in Diagnosing Schizophrenia

Toward the end of the 19th century, the German psychiatrist Emil Kraepelin (1899) provided what stands today as the most enduring description and categorization of schizophrenia. Two of Kraepelin's accomplishments are especially important. First, he combined several symptoms of insanity that had usually been viewed as reflecting separate and distinct disorders: **catatonia** (alternating immobility and excited agitation), **hebephrenia** (silly and immature emotionality), and **paranoia** (delusions of grandeur or persecution). Kraepelin thought these symptoms shared similar underlying features and included them under the Latin term **dementia praecox**. Although the clinical manifestation might differ from person to person, Kraepelin believed an early onset at the heart of each disorder ultimately develops into "mental weakness."

In a second important contribution, Kraepelin (1898) distinguished dementia praecox from manic-depressive illness (bipolar disorder). For people with dementia praecox, an early age of onset and a poor outcome were characteristic; in contrast, these patterns were not essential to manic depression (Peters, 1991). Kraepelin also noted the numerous symptoms in people with dementia praecox, including hallucinations, delusions, negativism, and stereotyped behaviour.

A second major figure in the history of schizophrenia was Kraeplin's contemporary, Eugen Bleuler (1908), a Swiss psychiatrist who introduced the term *schizophrenia*. The label was significant because it signalled Bleuler's departure from Kraepelin on what he thought was the core problem. "Schizophrenia," which comes from the combination of the Greek words for "split" (*skhizein*) and "mind" (*phren*), reflected Bleuler's belief that underlying all the unusual behaviours shown by people with this disorder was an **associative splitting** of the basic functions of personality. This concept emphasized the "breaking of associative threads," or the destruction of the forces that connect one function to the next. Furthermore, Bleuler believed that difficulty keeping a consistent train of thought, characteristic of all persons with this

▲ Eugen Bleuler (1857–1939), a Swiss psychiatrist, introduced the term schizophrenia and was a pioneer in the field.

disorder, led to the many and diverse symptoms they displayed. Whereas Kraepelin focused on early onset and poor outcomes, Bleuler highlighted what he believed to be the universal underlying problem. Unfortunately, the concept of "split mind" inspired the common but incorrect use of the term *schizophrenia* to mean split or multiple personality.

Identifying Symptoms

It is not easy to point to one thing that makes a person "schizophrenic." As you read about different disorders in this book, you have learned that a particular behaviour, way of thinking, or emotion usually defines or is characteristic of each disorder. For example, depression always includes feelings of sadness, and panic disorder is always accompanied by intense feelings of anxiety. Surprisingly, this isn't the case for schizophrenia. Schizophrenia is actually a number of behaviours or symptoms that aren't necessarily shared by all the people who are given this diagnosis.

Despite significant variations, researchers have identified clusters of symptoms that make up the disorder of schizophrenia. Later, we describe these very dramatic symptoms, such as seeing or hearing things that others do not (hallucinations) or having beliefs that are unrealistic, bizarre, and not shared by others in the same culture (delusions). But first, consider the following case of an individual who had an intense but relatively rare short-term episode of psychotic behaviour.

ARTHUR | *Saving the Children*

We first met 22-year-old Arthur at an outpatient clinic in a psychiatric hospital. Arthur's family was extremely concerned and upset by his unusual behaviour and was desperately seeking help for him. They said that he was "sick" and "talking like a crazy man," and they were afraid he might harm himself.

Arthur had a normal childhood in a middle-class suburban neighbourhood. His parents had been happily married until his father's death several years earlier. Arthur was an average student throughout school and had completed an associate's degree in junior college. His family seemed to think he regretted not continuing on to receive a bachelor's degree. Arthur had worked in a series of temporary jobs, and his mother reported that he seemed satisfied with what he was doing. He lived and worked in a major city, some 15 minutes away from his mother and his married brother and sister.

Arthur's family said that about three weeks before he came to the clinic he had started speaking strangely. He had been laid off from his job a few days before because of cutbacks and hadn't communicated with any of his family members for several days. When they next spoke with him, his behaviour startled them. Although he had always been idealistic and anxious to help other people, he now talked about saving all the starving children in the world with his "secret plan." At first his family assumed this was just an example of Arthur's sarcastic wit, but his demeanour changed to one of extreme concern, and he spoke nonstop about his plans. He began carrying several spiral notebooks that he claimed contained his scheme for helping starving children; he said he would reveal it only at the right time to the right person. Suspecting that Arthur might be taking drugs, which could explain the sudden and dramatic change in his behaviour, his family searched his apartment. Although they didn't find any evidence of drug use, they did find his chequebook and noticed a number of strange entries. Over the past several weeks, Arthur's handwriting had deteriorated, and he had written notes instead of the usual cheque information ("Start to begin now"; "This is important!" "They must be saved"). He had also made unusual notes in several of his most prized books, a particularly alarming development given his reverence for these books.

As the days went on, Arthur showed dramatic changes in emotion, often crying and acting very apprehensive. He stopped wearing socks and underwear and, despite the extremely cold weather, wouldn't wear a jacket when he went outdoors. At the family's insistence, he moved into his mother's apartment. He slept little and kept the family up until the early morning. His mother said it was like being in a living nightmare. Each morning she would wake up with a knot in her stomach, not wanting to get out of bed because she felt so helpless to do anything to rescue Arthur from his obvious distress.

The family's sense of alarm grew as Arthur revealed more details of his plan. He said that he was going to the German embassy because that was the only place people would listen to him. He would climb the fence at night when everyone was asleep and present his plan to the German ambassador. Fearing that Arthur would be hurt trying to enter the embassy grounds, his family contacted a local psychiatric hospital, described Arthur's condition, and asked that he be admitted. Much to their surprise and disappointment, they were told that Arthur could commit himself, but they couldn't bring him in involuntarily unless he was in danger of doing harm to himself or others. The fear that Arthur might be harmed wasn't sufficient reason to admit him involuntarily.

His family finally talked Arthur into meeting the staff at the outpatient clinic. In our interview, it was clear he was delusional, firmly believing in his ability to help all starving children. After some cajoling, I finally convinced him to let me see his books. He had written random thoughts (e.g.,

"The poor, starving souls"; "The moon is the only place") and made drawings of rocket ships. Parts of his plan involved building a rocket ship that would go to the moon, where he would create a community for all malnourished children, a place where they could live and be helped. After a few brief comments on his plan, I began to ask him about his health.

"You look tired. Are you getting enough sleep?"

"Sleep isn't really needed," he noted. "My plans will take me through, and then they can all rest."

"Your family is worried about you," I said. "Do you understand their concern?"

"It's important for all concerned to get together, to join together," he replied.

With that, he got up and walked out of the room and out of the building, after telling his family that he would be right back. After five minutes they went to look for him, but he had disappeared. He was missing for two days, which caused his family a great deal of concern about his health and safety. In an almost miraculous sequence of events, they found him walking the streets of the city. He acted as if nothing had happened. Gone were his notebooks and the talk of his secret plan.

What caused Arthur to act so strangely? Was it being fired from his job? Was it the death of his father? Was it a genetic predisposition to have schizophrenia or another disorder that kicked in during a period of stress? Unfortunately, we will never know exactly what happened to Arthur to make him behave so bizarrely and then recover so quickly and completely. However, research that we discuss next may shed some light on schizophrenia and related disorders and potentially help other Arthurs and their families.

Clinical Description

The case of Arthur shows the range of problems experienced by people with schizophrenia or other psychotic disorders. The term **psychotic** has been used to characterize many unusual behaviours, although in its strictest sense it usually involves delusions (irrational beliefs) and hallucinations (sensory experiences in the absence of external events). Schizophrenia is one of the disorders that involve psychotic behaviour; we describe others in more detail later.

Schizophrenia can affect all the functions we rely on each day. Before we describe the symptoms, it is important to look carefully at the specific characteristics of people who exhibit these behaviours, partly because we constantly see distorted images of people with schizophrenia. Headlines such as "Ex-Mental Patient Kills Family" falsely imply that everyone with schizophrenia is dangerous and violent. A Québec survey found that the majority of respondents thought that people with schizophrenia were dangerous or violent (Stip, Caron, & Lane, 2001). But statistics show otherwise. A Canadian study examined nearly 700 cases from a forensic hospital and found that people with a schizophrenia diagnosis were far less likely to commit future violent crimes than those with a history of violent crime but no schizophrenia diag-

nosis (Noonan, 2003). Nonetheless, media portrayals continue to frequently depict people with schizophrenia as violent (Noonan, 2003). Like mistakenly assuming that "schizophrenia" means "split personality," the popular press also misrepresents abnormal psychology to the detriment of people who experience these debilitating disorders.

The *DSM-IV-TR* has a multiple-part process for determining whether someone has schizophrenia (see DSM Table 13.1). Later we discuss the symptoms the person experiences during the disorder (active phase symptoms), the course of the disorder, and the subtypes of schizophrenia currently in use.

Mental health workers typically distinguish between *positive* and *negative* symptoms of schizophrenia. A third dimension, *disorganized* symptoms, also appears to be an important aspect of the disorder (Lewis, Escalona, & Keith, 2009). There is not yet universal agreement about which symptoms should be included in these categories. Positive symptoms generally include the more active manifestations of abnormal behaviour, or an excess or distortion of normal behaviour, such as delusions and hallucinations (American Psychiatric Association, 2000a). Negative symptoms involve deficits in normal behaviour in such areas as speech and motivation (Carpenter, 1994; Earnst & Kring, 1997). Disorganized symptoms include rambling speech, erratic behaviour, and inappropriate affect (Ho, Black, & Andreasen, 2003). A diagnosis of schizophrenia requires that two or more positive, negative, or disorganized symptoms be present for at least one month. A great deal of research has focused on the different symptoms of schizophrenia, each of which is described here in some detail.

Positive Symptoms

We next describe the **positive symptoms** of schizophrenia, which are the more obvious signs of psychosis. These include the disturbing experiences of delusions and hallucinations. Between 50 percent and 70 percent of people with schizophrenia experience hallucinations, delusions, or both (Lindenmayer & Khan, 2006).

Delusions

A belief that would be seen by most members of a society as a misrepresentation of reality is called a *disorder of thought content* or a **delusion**. Because of its importance in schizophrenia, delusion has been called "the basic characteristic of madness" (Jaspers, 1963). If, for example, you believe that squirrels really are aliens sent to earth on a reconnaissance mission, you would be considered delusional. The media often portray people with schizophrenia as believing they are famous or important people (such as Napoleon or Jesus Christ). Arthur's belief that he could end starvation for all the world's children is also a *delusion of grandeur*.

A common delusion in people with schizophrenia is that others are "out to get them." Called *delusions of persecution*, these beliefs can be most disturbing. One of us worked with a world-class cyclist who was on her way to making the Olympic team. Tragically, however, she believed other competitors were determined to sabotage her efforts, which forced her to stop riding for years. She believed that opponents would spray her bicycle with chemicals that would take her strength away and that they would slow her down by putting small pebbles in the road that only she

A. Characteristic symptoms: Two (or more) of the following, each present for a significant portion of time during a one-month period (or less if successfully treated):

1. Delusions
2. Hallucinations
3. Disorganized speech (e.g., frequent derailment or incoherence)
4. Grossly disorganized or catatonic behaviour
5. Negative symptoms (i.e., affective flattening, alogia (the relative absence of speech), or avolition (inability to initiate and persist in activities)

Note: Only one Criterion A symptom is required if the delusions are bizarre, or the hallucinations consist of a voice keeping up a running commentary on the person's behaviour or thoughts or two or more voices conversing with each other.

B. Social/occupational dysfunction: For a significant portion of the time since the onset of the disturbance, one or more major areas of functioning such as work, interpersonal relations, or self-care are markedly below the level achieved before the onset (or when the onset is in childhood or adolescence, failure to achieve expected level of interpersonal, academic, or occupational achievement).

C. Duration: Continuous signs of the disturbance persist for at least six months. This six-month period must include at least one month of symptoms (or less if successfully treated) that meet Criterion A (i.e., active phase symptoms) and may include periods of prodromal symptoms (symptoms signalling the onset of the disease) or residual symptoms (symptoms remaining after the active phase of the illness). During these prodromal or residual periods, the signs of the disturbance may be manifested by only negative symptoms or two or more symptoms listed in Criterion A present in an attenuated form (e.g., odd beliefs, unusual perceptual experiences).

D. Schizoaffective and mood disorder exclusion: Schizoaffective disorder and mood disorder with psychotic features have been ruled out because either (1) no major depressive, manic, or mixed episodes have occurred concurrently with the active phase symptoms; or (2) if mood episodes have occurred during active phase symptoms, their total duration has been brief relative to the duration of the active and residual periods.

E. Substance/general medical condition exclusion: The disturbance is not due to the direct physiological effects of a substance (e.g., a drug of abuse, a medication) or a general medical condition.

F. Relationship to a pervasive developmental disorder: If there is a history of autistic disorder or another pervasive developmental disorder, the additional diagnosis of schizophrenia is made only if prominent delusions or hallucinations are also present for at least a month (or less if successfully treated).

Classification of longitudinal course (can be applied only after at least one year has elapsed since the initial onset of active phase symptoms):

Episodic with interepisode residual symptoms (episodes are defined by the re-emergence of prominent psychotic symptoms); also specify if with prominent negative symptoms

Episodic with no interepisode residual symptoms

Continuous (prominent psychotic symptoms are present throughout the period of observation); also specify if with prominent negative symptoms

Single episode in partial remission; also specify if with prominent negative symptoms

Single episode in full remission

Other or unspecified pattern

Source: Reprinted with permission from the *Diagnostic and Statistical Manual of Mental Disorders*, Fourth Edition, Text Revision, (Copyright © 2000). American Psychiatric Association.

would ride over. These thoughts created a great deal of anxiety, and she refused even to go near her bicycle for some time.

Other more unusual delusions include *Cotard's syndrome*, in which the person believes a part of his or her body (e.g., the brain) has changed in some impossible way, and *Capgras syndrome*, in which the person believes someone he or she knows has been replaced by a double (Black & Andreasen, 1999). A recent example of a celebrity who suffers from Capgras syndrome is the tragic case of comedian Tony Rosato, former star of *SCTV* and *Saturday Night Live* (Brean, 2007; Freed, 2007). Rosato was arrested in 2005 on charges of criminal harassment of his wife after repeatedly complaining to police that his wife Leah and their infant daughter had gone missing and had been replaced by imposters (Brean, 2007; Freed, 2007).

Why do delusions persist in the face of contradictory information? One possible explanation is that the new information is not properly integrated. J. Bruno Debruille and his colleagues at McGill University recently investigated this

The Maze by William Kurelek (1927–1977), photograph reproduced by kind permission of the Bethlem Art and History Collections Trust.

▲ Artist William Karelek was born in 1927 near Whitford, Alberta. He painted this piece during a psychiatric hospitalization in 1953 where he was treated for schizophrenia. "The Maze" is an introspective work in which Karelek portrays his persecutory and somatic delusions as scenes encapsulated within compartments in a human skull.

▲ Toronto comedian Tony Rosato, of *SCTV* and *Saturday Night Live* fame, suffers from the unusual delusions characteristic of Capgras syndrome.

Kingston Whig-Standard/Ian MacAlpine/Sun Media Corporation

and less depression, all of which seemed related to their delusional belief systems. Compare this with the opposite situation we discussed in Chapter 7, in which we found that people who were depressed seemed sadder but wiser. That delusions may serve an adaptive function is at present just a theory with little support, but it may help us understand the phenomenon and its effect on those who experience it.

Hallucinations

Did you ever think someone called your name, only to discover that no one was there? Did you ever think you saw something move by you, yet nothing did? We all have fleeting moments when we think we see or hear something that isn't there. However, for many people with schizophrenia, these perceptions are very real and occur on a regular basis. The experience of sensory events without any input from the surrounding environment is called a **hallucination** (Fischer et al., 2004). The case of David illustrates the phenomena of hallucinations and other disorders of thought that are common among people with schizophrenia.

possibility in a sample of patients with schizophrenia using event-related brain potential (ERP) recordings (see Chapter 3). The magnitude of a particular brain wave, called the N400, has been proposed as an index of integration of new information that is inconsistent with expectation. Imagine that your task is to decide if a series of words belong to the category "animal." You will produce a much larger N400 brain wave when you are presented with the word "broom" relative to when you are presented with the word "cat." Debruille et al. (2007) found that schizophrenic patients with more severe delusions produced smaller N400 brain waves to target words that were inconsistent with the expected category than did patients with less severe delusions. Future studies should test whether a deficit in the integration of new material could have a causal role in the persistence of delusions in people with schizophrenia (Debruille et al., 2007).

Another intriguing possibility is that delusions may serve a purpose for people with schizophrenia who are otherwise quite upset by the changes taking place within themselves. For example, Roberts (1991) studied 17 people who had elaborate delusions about themselves and the world, and compared them with a matched group of people who had previously had delusions but were now improving. The individuals with current delusions expressed a much stronger sense of purpose and meaning in life

DAVID | *Missing Uncle Bill*

David was 25 years old when I met him; he had been living in a psychiatric hospital for about three years. He was a little overweight and of average height; he typically dressed in a T-shirt and jeans and tended to be active. I first encountered him while I was talking to another man who lived on the same floor. David interrupted us by pulling on my shoulder. "My Uncle Bill is a good man. He treats me well." Not wanting to be impolite, I said, "I'm sure he is. Maybe after I've finished talking to Michael here, we can talk about your uncle." David persisted, "He can kill fish with a knife. Things can get awfully sharp in your mind, when you go down the river. I could kill you with my bare hands—taking things into my own hands.... I know you know!" He was now speaking very quickly and had gained emotionality along with speed as he spoke. I talked to him quietly until he calmed down for the moment. Later, I looked into David's file for some information about his background.

David was brought up on a farm by his Aunt Katie and Uncle Bill. His father's identity is unknown and his mother, who had mental retardation, couldn't care for him. David too was diagnosed as having mental retardation, although his functioning was only mildly impaired, and he attended school. The year David's Uncle Bill died, his high school teachers first reported unusual behaviour. David occasionally talked to his deceased Uncle Bill in class. Later, he became increasingly agitated and verbally aggressive toward others and was diagnosed as having schizophrenia. He managed to graduate from high school but never obtained a job after that; he lived at home with his aunt for several years. Although his aunt really wanted him to stay with her, his threatening behaviour escalated to the point that she requested he be seen at the local psychiatric hospital.

I spoke with David again and had a chance to ask him a few questions. "Why are you here in the hospital, David?"

"I really don't want to be here," he told me "I've got other things to do. The time is right, and you know, when opportunity knocks...."

He continued for a few minutes until I interrupted him. "I was sorry to hear that your Uncle Bill died a few years ago. How are you feeling about him these days?"

"Yes, he died. He was sick and now he's gone. He likes to fish with me, down at the river. He's going to take me hunting. I have guns. I can shoot you and you'd be dead in a minute."

David's conversational speech resembled a ball rolling down a rocky hill. Like an accelerating object, his speech gained momentum the longer he went on and, as if bouncing off obstacles, the topics almost always went in unpredictable directions. If he continued for too long, he often became agitated and spoke of harming others. David also told me that his uncle's voice spoke to him repeatedly. He heard other voices also, but he couldn't identify them or tell me what they said. We return to David's case later in this chapter when we discuss causes and treatments.

Hallucinations can involve any of the senses, although hearing things that aren't there, or *auditory hallucination*, is the most common form experienced by people with schizophrenia. David had frequent auditory hallucinations, usually of his uncle's voice. When David heard a voice that belonged to his Uncle Bill, he often couldn't understand what his uncle was saying; on other occasions the voice was clearer. "He told me to turn off the TV. He said, 'It's too damn loud, turn it down, turn it down.' Other times he talks about fishing. 'Good day for fishing. Got to go fishing.'" You could tell when David was hearing voices. He was usually unoccupied, and he sat and smiled as if listening to someone next to him, but no one was there. This behaviour is consistent with research, which suggests that people tend to experience hallucinations more frequently when they are unoccupied or restricted from sensory input (e.g., Margo, Hemsley, & Slade, 1981).

Exciting research on hallucinations uses sophisticated brain-imaging techniques to try to localize these phenomena in the brain. One theory of auditory verbal hallucinations states that people who are hallucinating are in fact not hearing the voices of others, but are listening to their own thoughts or their own voices and cannot recognize the difference. An alternative theory is that auditory verbal hallucinations arise from abnormal activation of the primary auditory cortex. A group of Montréal researchers (Ait Bentaleb, Beauregard, Liddle, & Stip, 2002)

tested a woman with schizophrenia using functional magnetic resonance imaging (fMRI) while she was experiencing her auditory verbal hallucinations and when she was listening to external speech; they compared her results to those of a matched control participant tested under the same conditions. They found that auditory verbal hallucinations were associated with increased metabolic activity in the left primary auditory cortex and in the right middle temporal gyrus. These results are consistent with both views regarding the origins of hallucinations (i.e., misinterpretation of inner speech and abnormal activation of the primary auditory cortex) and suggest that the two mechanisms are not necessarily mutually exclusive. More advanced imaging technology is allowing researchers to get a better view of just what is going on inside the brain during hallucinations and should help identify the role of the brain in the symptoms observed among people with schizophrenia (e.g., Silbersweig et al., 1995).

Regarding positive symptoms of schizophrenia more generally, a recent study by researchers in Toronto (Mizrahi et al., 2006) challenges the common assumption that positive symptoms represent a single dimension. Instead, their work shows that positive symptoms are multidimensional with some dimensions responding more readily than others to antipsychotic medications (Mizrahi et al., 2006).

Negative Symptoms

In contrast to the active presentations that characterize the positive symptoms of schizophrenia, the **negative symptoms** usually indicate the absence or insufficiency of normal behaviour. They include emotional and social withdrawal, apathy, and poverty of thought or speech (Carpenter, 1992). Approximately 25 percent of people with schizophrenia display these symptoms (Lewis et al., 2009).

Avolition

Combining the prefix *a*, meaning "without," and *volition*, which means "an act of willing, choosing, or deciding," **avolition** is the inability to initiate and persist in activities. People with this symptom (also referred to as *apathy*) show little interest in performing even the most basic daily functions, including those associated with personal hygiene.

ABNORMAL PSYCHOLOGY Video

Schizophrenia: Etta

"If anyone gets into the house, they say I'd get shot.... [Who said?] That's the eagle.... The eagle works through General Motors. They have something to do with my General Motors cheque I get every month.... When you do the 25 of the clock, it means that you leave the house 25 after one to mail letters so that they can check on you ... and they know where you're at. That's the eagle.... If you don't do something they tell you to do, Jesus makes the shotgun sound, and then ... not to answer the phone or the doorbell ... because you'd get shot [by the] eagle."

Go to Psychology CourseMate at www.abnormalpsych3ce.nelson.com to watch this video.

A recent study by researchers at the Centre for Addiction and Mental Health in Toronto examined the level of avolition in 28 patients with schizophrenia and its relationship to other symptoms of schizophrenia and to treatment outcome. These researchers found that levels of avolition were significantly higher in the patients with schizophrenia than in a matched group of control participants without schizophrenia. As expected, avolition was not related to positive symptoms of schizophrenia. Unexpectedly, avolition was not related to negative symptoms of schizophrenia other than emotional withdrawal. Finally, avolition was more highly associated with poor outcome than were other schizophrenia symptoms—positive or negative (Kiang, Christensen, Remington, & Kapur, 2003).

Alogia

Derived from the combination of *a* ("without") and *logos* ("words"), **alogia** refers to the relative absence of speech. A person with alogia may respond to questions with very brief replies that have little content and may appear uninterested in the conversation. For example, to the question, "Do you have any children?" most parents might reply, "Oh, yes, I have two beautiful children: a boy and a girl. My son is six and my daughter is twelve." In the following exchange, someone with alogia responds to the same question:

INTERVIEWER: Do you have any children?
CLIENT: Yes.
INTERVIEWER: How many children do you have?
CLIENT: Two.
INTERVIEWER: How old are they?
CLIENT: Six and twelve.

Such deficiency in communication is believed to reflect a negative thought disorder rather than inadequate communication skills. Some researchers, for example, suggest that people with alogia may have trouble finding the right words to formulate their thoughts (Alpert, Clark, & Pouget, 1994). Sometimes alogia takes the form of delayed comments or slow responses to questions. Talking with individuals who manifest this symptom can be extremely frustrating, making you feel as if you are "pulling teeth" to get them to respond.

Anhedonia

A related symptom is called **anhedonia,** which derives from the word *hedonic*, pertaining to pleasure. Anhedonia is the presumed lack of pleasure experienced by some people with schizophrenia. Like some mood disorders, anhedonia signals an indifference to activities that would typically be considered pleasurable, including eating, social interactions, and sexual relations. Given the similarities of the negative schizophrenia symptom of anhedonia to symptoms of depression, some researchers such as David Romney and Carmie Candido at the University of Calgary have questioned the distinctiveness of anhedonia and the mood disorders (e.g., Candido & Romney, 2002; Romney & Candido, 2001). A study by Ashok Malla at the University of Western Ontario and his colleagues provides mixed evidence on this issue. On the one hand, Malla et al. (2002) found a strong correlation between depression and a negative symptoms factor involving both anhedonia and avolition in a large sample of patients with schizophrenia. On the

other hand, they also found that negative symptoms were present at a relatively high rate even after excluding the influence of depression. Regardless of the dependence or independence from depression, anhedonia is clinically meaningful in that it relates to a delay in seeking treatment for schizophrenia (Malla et al., 2002).

Affective Flattening

Imagine that people wore masks at all times: You could communicate with them but you wouldn't be able to see their emotional reactions. Approximately two-thirds of the people with schizophrenia exhibit what is called **flat affect** (Malla et al., 2002). They are similar to people wearing masks because they do not show emotions when you would normally expect them to. They may stare at you vacantly, speak in a flat and toneless manner, and seem unaffected by things going on around them. However, although they do not react openly to emotional situations, they may indeed be responding inside.

Berenbaum and Oltmanns (1992) compared people with schizophrenia who had flat (or "blunted") affect with those who did not. The two groups were shown clips from films selected to create emotional reactions in the viewer. Berenbaum and Oltmanns found that the people with flat affect showed little change in facial expression, although they reported experiencing the appropriate emotions. The authors concluded that the flat affect in schizophrenia may represent difficulty expressing emotion, not a lack of feeling. In a more recent study, Montréal researchers Fahim et al. (2005) exposed schizophrenia patients with and without flat affect

▲ Negative symptoms of schizophrenia include social withdrawal and apathy.

to negative and neutral images. Like the Berenbaum and Oltmanns findings, both groups experienced unpleasant emotions in response to the negative pictures; however, the negative emotions experienced were less intense in the patients with flat affect (Fahim et al., 2005). More research is thus needed to determine if it is the expression of emotion, the experience of emotion, or both, that is aberrant in schizophrenia patients suffering flat affect.

Asociality

The severe deficits in social relationships, such as having few friendships, little interest in socializing, and poor social skills, shown by some people with schizophrenia are referred to collectively as *asociality*. A study by researchers Joel Goldberg and Louis Schmidt at McMaster University compared 23 patients with schizophrenia to 23 controls without schizophrenia on measures of current sociability and shyness as well as retrospectively reported inhibition in childhood (Goldberg & Schmidt, 2001). Patients were higher on all these characteristics than were the controls. Moreover, levels of asociality were associated with greater levels of other types of negative symptoms, supporting the grouping of asociality in this dimension of schizophrenia symptoms.

Research by University of Toronto researcher Jean Addington and her colleagues suggests that patients who have poor social or interpersonal functioning before the development of their psychosis also have greater levels of negative symptoms and greater social impairment at the time of their admission to a schizophrenia treatment program (Addington, van Mastrigt, & Addington, 2003). In a review of the literature, Peter Liddle at the University of British Columbia found that the best predictor of asociality in people with schizophrenia is chronic cognitive impairment, suggesting that difficulties in processing information may contribute significantly to the social skills deficits and other social difficulties displayed by many patients (Liddle, 2000).

Disorganized Symptoms

Perhaps the least studied and therefore the least understood symptoms of schizophrenia are referred to as the **disorganized symptoms**. These include a variety of erratic behaviours that affect speech, motor behaviour, and emotional reactions. The prevalence of these behaviours among those with schizophrenia is unclear.

Disorganized Speech

A conversation with someone who has schizophrenia can be particularly frustrating. If you want to understand what is bothering or upsetting this person, eliciting relevant information is especially difficult. For one thing, people with schizophrenia often lack insight, an awareness that they have a problem. In addition, they experience "associative splitting" (Bleuler, 1908) and "cognitive slippage" (Meehl, 1962). These phrases help describe the speech problems of people with schizophrenia: Sometimes they jump from topic to topic and at other times they talk illogically. The *DSM-IV-TR* uses the term **disorganized speech** to describe such communication problems (Kerns & Berenbaum, 2002). Let's go back to our conversation with David to demonstrate the symptom.

> THERAPIST: Why are you here in the hospital, David?
> DAVID: I really don't want to be here. I've got other things to do. The time is right, and you know, when opportunity knocks....

David didn't really answer the question he was asked. This type of response is called *tangentiality*—that is, going off on a tangent instead of answering a specific question (Andreasen, 1979). David also abruptly changed the topic of conversation to unrelated areas, a behaviour that has been called loose association or derailment (Cutting, 1985).

> THERAPIST: I was sorry to hear that your Uncle Bill died a few years ago. How are you feeling about him these days?
> DAVID: Yes, he died. He was sick, and now he's gone. He likes to fish with me, down at the river. He's going to take me hunting. I have guns. I can shoot you and you'd be dead in a minute.

Again, David didn't answer the question. The therapist could not tell whether he didn't understand the question, couldn't focus his attention, or found it too difficult to talk about his uncle. You can see why people spend a great deal of time trying to interpret all the hidden meanings behind this type of conversation. Unfortunately, however, such analyses have yet to provide us with useful information about the nature of schizophrenia or its treatment.

Concept Check | 13.1

Identify the following terms associated with schizophrenia: affective flattening, avolition, delusions, hallucinations.

1. Beliefs that most people would describe as a misrepresentation of reality, called a disorder of thought content: _____

2. Apathy, or an inability to initiate or persist in important activities: _____

3. Lack of visible emotional response or reactivity: _____

4. Perceptions of sensory events that do not originate in the surrounding environment: _____

Inappropriate Affect and Disorganized Behaviour

Occasionally, people with schizophrenia display **inappropriate affect**, laughing or crying at improper times. Sometimes they exhibit bizarre behaviours such as hoarding objects or acting in unusual ways in public. People with schizophrenia engage in several other "active" behaviours that are usually viewed as unusual. For example, catatonia is one of the most curious symptoms in some individuals with schizophrenia; it involves motor dysfunctions that range from wild agitation to immobility. On the active side of the continuum, some people pace excitedly or move their fingers or arms in stereotyped ways. At the other end of the extreme, people hold unusual postures, as if they are fearful of something terrible happening if they move (**catatonic immobility**). This manifestation can also involve *waxy flexibility*, or the tendency to keep their bodies and limbs in the position they are put in by someone else.

Again, to receive a diagnosis of schizophrenia, a person must display two or more positive, negative, or disorganized symptoms for a major portion of at least one month. Depending on the combination of symptoms displayed, two people could receive the same diagnosis but behave very differently, one having marked hallucinations and delusions and the other displaying disorganized speech and some of the negative symptoms. Proper treatment depends on differentiating individuals in terms of their varying symptoms.

Schizophrenia Subtypes

As we noted earlier, the search for subtypes of schizophrenia began before Kraepelin described his concept of schizophrenia. Three divisions have persisted: *paranoid* (delusions of grandeur or persecution), *disorganized* (or *hebephrenic*; silly and immature emotionality), and *catatonic* (alternate immobility and excited agitation). Although these categories continue to be used in the *DSM-IV-TR*, their usefulness is in question. We will discuss in the "On the Spectrum" feature at the end of the chapter that they may not be included in the *DSM-5* (American Psychiatric Association, 2010). And, as research advances on the underlying biological influences (endophenotypes) of this disorder, it is not clear that they will match these subtypes. In addition, a person's diagnosis can sometimes change over the course of his or her illness; so people can move from one category to another (Lewis et al., 2009). However, we describe the schizophrenia subtypes next for their historic value and because the current diagnostic system relies on these distinctions.

Paranoid Type

People with the **paranoid type of schizophrenia** stand out because of their delusions or hallucinations; at the same time, their cognitive skills and affect are relatively intact. They generally do not have disorganized speech or flat affect, and they typically have a better prognosis than people with other forms of schizophrenia. The delusions and hallucinations usually have a theme, such as grandeur or persecution. The *DSM-IV-TR* criteria for inclusion in this subtype specify preoccupation with one or more delusions or frequent auditory hallucinations but without a marked display of disorganized speech, disorganized or catatonic behaviour, or flat or inappropriate affect (American Psychiatric Association, 2000a; see DSM Table 13.2).

In a recent study by Jeffrey Carter and Richard Neufeld (2007) at the University of Western Ontario, patients with schizophrenia were less accurate at a facial emotion judgement task than controls. Those with the paranoid type of schizophrenia showed the longest latencies, suggesting particular deficits in social information processing among those with paranoid schizophrenia.

Disorganized Type

In contrast to the paranoid type of schizophrenia, people with the **disorganized type of schizophrenia** show marked disruption in their speech and behaviour; they also show flat or inappropriate

DSM-IV-TR	**Table 13.2** Diagnostic Criteria for Paranoid Type

A type of schizophrenia in which the following criteria are met:

A. Preoccupation with one or more delusions or frequent auditory hallucinations

B. None of the following is prominent: disorganized speech, disorganized or catatonic behaviour, or flat or inappropriate affect

Source: Reprinted with permission from the *Diagnostic and Statistical Manual of Mental Disorders*, Fourth Edition, Text Revision, (Copyright © 2000). American Psychiatric Association.

DSM-IV-TR	**Table 13.3** Diagnostic Criteria for Disorganized Type

A type of schizophrenia in which the following criteria are met:

A. All the following are prominent:
   1. Disorganized speech
   2. Disorganized behaviour
   3. Flat or inappropriate affect

B. The criteria are not met for catatonic type.

Source: Reprinted with permission from the *Diagnostic and Statistical Manual of Mental Disorders*, Fourth Edition, Text Revision, (Copyright © 2000). American Psychiatric Association.

affect, such as laughing in a silly way at the wrong times (American Psychiatric Association, 2000a; see DSM Table 13.3). They also seem unusually self-absorbed and may spend considerable amounts of time looking at themselves in the mirror (Ho et al., 2003). If delusions or hallucinations are present, they tend not to be organized around a central theme, as in the paranoid type, but are more fragmented. This subtype was previously called *hebephrenic*. Individuals with this diagnosis tend to show signs of

▲ Homeless people who suffer from paranoid schizophrenia often bear the additional burden of persecutory delusions, which interfere with outside efforts to help.

Clinical Description   **485**

difficulty early, and their problems are often chronic, lacking the remissions (improvement of symptoms) that characterize other forms of the disorder (Hardy-Bale, Sarfati, & Passerieux, 2003).

Catatonic Type

In addition to the unusual motor responses of remaining in fixed positions (waxy flexibility), engaging in excessive activity, and being oppositional by remaining rigid, individuals with the **catatonic type of schizophrenia** sometimes display odd mannerisms with their bodies and faces, including grimacing (American Psychiatric Association, 2000a; see DSM Table 13.4). They often repeat or mimic the words of others (*echolalia*) or the movements of others (*echopraxia*) (Cohen et al., 2005). There may be subtypes of catatonic schizophrenia, with some individuals showing primarily symptoms of labelled "negative withdrawal" (immobility, posturing, mutism), "automatic" (routine obedience, waxy flexibility), "repetitive/echo" (grimacing, perseveration, echolalia), and "agitated/resistive" (excitement, impulsivity, combativeness) (Ungvari, Goggins, Leung, & Gerevich, 2007).

Undifferentiated Type

People who do not fit neatly into these subtypes are classified as having an **undifferentiated type of schizophrenia**; they include people who have the major symptoms of schizophrenia but who do not meet the criteria for paranoid, disorganized, or catatonic types.

Residual Type

People who have had at least one episode of schizophrenia but who no longer manifest major symptoms are diagnosed as having the **residual type of schizophrenia**. Although they may not experience bizarre delusions or hallucinations, they may display residual or "leftover" symptoms, such as negative beliefs, or they may still have unusual ideas that are not fully delusional. Residual symptoms can include social withdrawal, bizarre thoughts, inactivity, and flat affect (see DSM Table 13.5). All versions of the *DSM* (from *DSM-I* through *DSM-IV-TR*) have included a residual type to describe the condition of individuals who have less severe problems associated with an episode of schizophrenia.

DSM-IV-TR	**Table 13.4** Diagnostic Criteria for Catatonic Type

A type of schizophrenia in which the clinical picture is dominated by at least two of the following:

1. Motoric immobility as evidenced by catalepsy (including waxy flexibility) or stupor
2. Excessive motor activity (that is apparently purposeless and not influenced by external stimuli)
3. Extreme negativism (an apparently motiveless resistance to all instructions or maintenance of a rigid posture against attempts to be moved) or mutism
4. Peculiarities of voluntary movement as evidenced by posturing (voluntary assumption of inappropriate or bizarre postures), stereotyped movements, prominent mannerisms, or prominent grimacing
5. Echolalia or echopraxia

Source: Reprinted with permission from the *Diagnostic and Statistical Manual of Mental Disorders*, Fourth Edition, Text Revision, (Copyright © 2000). American Psychiatric Association.

DSM-IV-TR	**Table 13.5** Diagnostic Criteria for Residual Type

A type of schizophrenia in which the following criteria are met:

A. There is an absence of prominent delusions, hallucinations, disorganized speech, and grossly disorganized or catatonic behaviour.
B. There is continuing evidence of the disturbance, as indicated by the presence of negative symptoms or two or more symptoms listed in Criterion A for schizophrenia, present in an attenuated form (e.g., odd beliefs, unusual perceptual experiences).

Source: Reprinted with permission from the *Diagnostic and Statistical Manual of Mental Disorders*, Fourth Edition, Text Revision, (Copyright © 2000). American Psychiatric Association.

Research suggests that the paranoid subtype may have a stronger familial link than the others and that these people may function better before and after episodes of schizophrenia than people diagnosed with other subtypes (Lewis et al., 2009). More work will determine whether dividing schizophrenia into five subtypes helps us understand and treat people.

An alternative system for subtyping schizophrenia, introduced in the mid-1970s by Strauss, Carpenter, and Bartko (1974), emphasizes the positive, negative, and, more recently, disorganized symptoms. Crow (1980, 1985) elaborated on this approach, suggesting that schizophrenia can be dichotomized into two types, based on a variety of characteristics, including symptoms, response to medication, outcome, and the presence or absence of intellectual impairment. Type I is associated with the positive symptoms of hallucinations and delusions, a good response to medication, an optimistic prognosis, and the absence of intellectual impairment. In contrast, Type II includes people with the negative symptoms of flat affect and poverty of speech (alogia), who show a poor response to medication, a pessimistic prognosis, and intellectual impairments. Although not without its critics (Andreasen & Carpenter, 1993), Crow's model has influenced current thinking regarding the nature of schizophrenia.

Other Psychotic Disorders

The psychotic behaviours of some individuals do not fit neatly under the heading of schizophrenia as we have just described. Several other categories of disorders depict these significant variations.

Schizophreniform Disorder

Some people experience the symptoms of schizophrenia for a few months only; they can usually resume normal lives. The symptoms sometimes disappear as the result of successful treatment, but often for unknown reasons. The label **schizophreniform disorder** classifies these symptoms, but because relatively few studies are available on this disorder, data on important aspects of it are sparse. It appears, however, that the lifetime prevalence is approximately 0.2 percent (American Psychiatric Association, 2000a). The *DSM-IV-TR* diagnostic criteria for schizophreniform disorder include onset of psychotic symptoms within four weeks of the first noticeable change in usual behaviour, confusion at the height of the psychotic episode, good premorbid social and occupational functioning, and the absence of blunted or flat affect (American Psychiatric Association, 2000a).

Schizoaffective Disorder

Historically, people who had symptoms of schizophrenia and who also exhibited the characteristics of mood disorders (e.g., depression or bipolar affective disorder) were lumped together in the category of schizophrenia. Now, however, this mixed bag of problems is diagnosed as **schizoaffective disorder** (Sikich, 2009). The prognosis is similar to the prognosis for people with schizophrenia—that is, individuals tend not to get better on their own and are likely to continue experiencing major life difficulties for many years. *DSM-IV-TR* criteria for schizoaffective disorder require that, in addition to the presence of a mood disorder, there have been delusions or hallucinations for at least two weeks in the absence of prominent mood symptoms (American Psychiatric Association, 2000a).

Delusional Disorder

Delusions are beliefs that are not generally held by other members of a society. The major feature of **delusional disorder** is a persistent belief that is contrary to reality, in the absence of other characteristics of schizophrenia. For example, a woman who believes without any evidence that co-workers are tormenting her by putting poison in her food and spraying her apartment with harmful gases has a delusional disorder. This disorder is characterized by a persistent delusion that is not the result of an organic factor such as brain seizures or of any severe psychosis. Individuals tend not to have flat affect, anhedonia, or other negative symptoms of schizophrenia; importantly, however, they may become socially isolated because they are suspicious of others. The delusions are often long-standing, sometimes persisting several years (Suvisaari et al., 2009).

The *DSM-IV-TR* recognizes the following delusional subtypes: erotomanic, grandiose, jealous, persecutory, and somatic. An *erotomanic* delusion is someone's mistaken belief that a higher-status and unsuspecting person is in love with him or her. This delusional belief often motivates the patient to engage in an unrelenting pursuit of the victim in attempts to communicate with him or her. There are several examples of celebrities who have been pursued by "stalkers" who likely have this form of delusional disorder. For example, in the 1980s, Canadian singer Anne Murray was relentlessly pursued by a Saskatchewan farmer named Charles Robert Kieling, despite several court orders that he stop attempting to contact her (MacFarlane, 1997). In another example, singer/songwriter Sarah McLachlan was pursued in the early 1990s by a computer programmer from Ottawa named Uwe Vandrei. He sent her flowers and hundreds of disturbing letters, and even made some comments to her in person. Vandrei took his own life in 1994, after he was unsuccessful in suing McLachlan for allegedly using his letters as the basis for her song "Possession" on her 1993 CD *Fumbling Toward Ecstasy* (Fitzgerald, 2000).

The *grandiose* type of delusion involves believing in one's inflated worth, power, knowledge, identity, or special relationship to a deity or famous person. A person with the *jealous* type of delusion believes a sexual partner is unfaithful. The persecutory type of delusion involves the person believing that he or she (or someone close) is being malevolently treated in some way. Finally, with the *somatic* type of delusion, the person feels afflicted by a physical defect or general medical condition. These delusions differ from the more bizarre types often found in people with schizophrenia because in delusional disorder the imagined events could be happening but aren't (e.g., mistakenly believing you are being followed); in schizophrenia, however, the imagined events aren't possible (e.g., believing your brain waves broadcast your thoughts to other people around the world).

Delusional disorder seems to be relatively rare, affecting 24 to 30 people out of every 100 000 in the general population (Suvisaari et al., 2009). Among those people with psychotic disorders in general, between 2 percent and 8 percent are thought to have delusional disorder (Vahia & Cohen, 2009). Researchers can't be confident about the percentages because they know that many of these individuals have no contact with the mental health system.

The onset of delusional disorder is relatively late: The average age of first admission to a psychiatric facility is between 40 and 49 (Vahia & Cohen, 2009). However, because many people with this disorder can lead relatively normal lives, they may not seek treatment until their symptoms become most disruptive. Delusional disorder seems to afflict more females than males (55 percent and 45 percent, respectively, of the affected population).

In a longitudinal study, Opjordsmoen (1989) followed 53 people with delusional disorder for an average of 30 years and found they tended to fare better in life than people with schizophrenia but not as well as those with some other psychotic disorders, such as schizoaffective disorder. About 80 percent of the 53 individuals had been married at some time, and half were employed, which demonstrates an ability to function relatively well despite delusions.

We know relatively little about either the biological or the psychosocial influences on delusional disorder (Vahia & Cohen, 2009). Research on families suggests that the characteristics of suspiciousness, jealousy, and secretiveness may occur more often among the relatives of people with delusional disorder than among the population at large, suggesting some aspect of this disorder may be inherited (Kendler & Walsh, 2007).

A number of other disorders can cause delusions, and their presence should be ruled out before diagnosing delusional disorder. For example, abuse of amphetamines, alcohol, and cocaine can cause delusions, as can brain tumours, Huntington's disease, and Alzheimer's disease (Vahia & Cohen, 2009).

Brief Psychotic Disorder

Recall the puzzling case of Arthur, who suddenly experienced the delusion that he could save the world and whose intense emotional swings lasted for only a few days. He would receive the *DSM-IV-TR* diagnosis of **brief psychotic disorder**, which is characterized by the presence of one or more positive symptoms such as delusions, hallucinations, or disorganized speech or behaviour lasting one month or less. Individuals like Arthur regain their previous ability to function well in day-to-day activities. Brief psychotic disorder is often precipitated by extremely stressful situations.

Shared Psychotic Disorder (Folie à Deux)

Relatively little is known about **shared psychotic disorder (folie à deux)**, the condition in which an individual develops delusions simply as a result of a close relationship with a delusional individual. The content and nature of the delusion originate with the partner and can range from the relatively bizarre, such as believing enemies are sending harmful gamma rays through your house, to the fairly ordinary, such as believing you are about to receive a major promotion despite evidence to the contrary. Although it was once thought that this disorder was more common among mother–daughter or sister–sister pairs, this does not appear to be the case (Shimizu, Kubota, Toichi, & Baba, 2007). Jose Silveira and Mary Seeman (1995) of the Hospital for Sick Children in Toronto reviewed 61 published case studies of individuals with shared psychotic disorder. On the basis of their review, they suggested that shared psychotic disorder occurs in predisposed individuals who become socially isolated with a psychotic person (Silveira & Seeman, 1995).

It is interesting to speculate whether the legal case of the couple Carline VandenElsen and Larry Finck might represent an example of this intriguing disorder. VandenElsen and Finck were arrested following an armed standoff with police in Halifax in May 2004 when the couple refused to give over their infant daughter to child protective services. Both had a history of losing access to their children following their involvement in separate abductions of their children from previous marriages. Following the armed standoff, Mr. Finck was diagnosed by a psychiatrist as suffering from chronic persecutory delusions (Hoare, 2005). But could their relationship together, and relative social isolation, have fuelled their shared persecutory ideas? According to media reports, the couple used the armed standoff to gain attention for their "theory" that various government agencies including the courts, police, and child protective services were plotting to sell children to childless parents (Brooks Arenburg, 2005; Hoare, 2005). More research is definitely warranted about the origins and treatment of this fascinating condition.

Republished with permission from The Halifax Herald Ltd.

▲ Larry Finck nails a sign to the front of his house during an armed standoff with the police in Halifax in 2004. Finck and his partner, Carline VandenElsen, appear to have held shared persecutory delusions.

Schizotypal Personality Disorder

This personality disorder, discussed in Chapter 12, is a related psychotic disorder. As you may recall, the characteristics are similar to those experienced by people with schizophrenia, but less severe. Some evidence also suggests that schizophrenia and schizotypal personality disorder may be genetically related as part of a "schizophrenia spectrum."

Remember that although people with related psychotic disorders display many of the characteristics of schizophrenia, these disorders differ significantly. We now examine the nature of schizophrenia and learn how researchers have attempted to understand and treat people who have it.

Statistics

Schizophrenia sometimes defies our desire for simplicity. We have seen how very different symptoms can be displayed by individuals who would all be considered to have the disorder; in some people the symptoms develop slowly, and in others they occur suddenly. Schizophrenia is generally chronic, and most people with the disorder have a very difficult time functioning in society. This is especially true of their ability to relate to others; they tend not to establish or maintain significant relationships, and therefore many people with schizophrenia never marry or have children. Unlike the delusions of people with other psychotic disorders, the delusions of people with schizophrenia are likely to be outside the realm of possibility. Finally, even when individuals with schizophrenia improve with treatment, they are likely to experience difficulties throughout their lives.

Worldwide, the lifetime prevalence rate of schizophrenia is roughly equivalent for men and women, and it is estimated from 0.2 percent to 1.5 percent in the general population (Ho et al., 2003), which means the disorder will affect around 1 percent of the population at some point. A recent study by Simon Fraser University researcher Elliot Goldner and his colleagues suggests that the one-year prevalence of schizophrenic disorders in the British Columbia population was 0.4 percent (Goldner, Jones, & Waraich, 2003). Life expectancy is slightly less than average, partly because of the higher rate of suicide and accidents among people with schizophrenia (Ho et al., 2003) but also because of higher rates of obesity, smoking, angina, and respiratory problems among those with schizophrenia (Seeman, 2007).

Concept Check | 13.2

Subtypes have been used for years to diagnose schizophrenia according to varying symptoms. Check your understanding by labelling each situation according to subtype.

1. Gary often has delusions and hallucinations that convince him enemies are out to persecute him.

   _____

2. Sabine displays motor immobility, and she often repeats words said by others around her. _____

3. Carrie had an episode of schizophrenia in the past, but she no longer displays the major symptoms of the disorder. She does, however, still have some negative, unusual ideas and displays flat affect on occasion.

_____

4. Tram has a type of schizophrenia that is identified by disruption and incoherence in his speech and behaviour. He also shows inappropriate affect, often laughing in sad or upsetting situations. _____

5. As a psych intern, you are assigned to interview a rather unremarkable-looking gentleman. He is quite pleasant and talkative. After exchanging a few pleasantries, he mentions something about someone listening in on the conversation. You see no one nearby. When you ask the man what he means, he reluctantly explains that spies with hidden cameras follow him constantly. He attributes this to the fact that he has developed a plan to move the earth's population to the planet Pluto. _____

6. You sit down next to a gentleman who suddenly giggles. When you ask what he's laughing at, he answers, but you can't make sense of what he says.

_____

7. Your next client is a woman who has been diagnosed as schizophrenic, but her behaviour patterns do not fit any of the identified subtypes. _____

8. As you enter the room of the institution, you see your patient in the opposite corner, standing in a fixed karate-like pose with a grimace on his face. _____

Although some disagreement exists about the distribution of schizophrenia between men and women, the difference between the sexes in age of onset is clear. For men, the likelihood of onset diminishes with age, but it can still first occur after the age of 75. The onset for women is lower than for men until age 36, when the relative risk for onset switches, with more women than men being affected later in life (Howard, Castle, Wessely, & Murray, 1993). Women appear to have more favourable outcomes than men (Ho et al., 2003).

Development

Increasing attention has been paid to the developmental course of schizophrenia (Asarnow, 1994; Walker, 1991), which may shed some light on its causes. Research suggests that children who later develop schizophrenia show some abnormal signs before they display the characteristic symptoms (Fish, 1987). Their emotional reactions may be abnormal, with less positive and more negative affect than their unaffected siblings (Walker, Grimes, Davis, & Smith, 1993). Remember that although the age of onset varies, schizophrenia is generally seen by early childhood. If the causative factors are present very early on, why does the disorder show itself only later in life?

It may be that brain damage very early in the developmental period causes later schizophrenia (McNeil, Cantor-Graae, & Weinberger, 2001). However, instead of resulting in an immediate progressive deterioration, the damage may lie dormant until later

in development when the signs of schizophrenia first appear. Some research finds that people with schizophrenia who demonstrate early signs of abnormality at birth and during early childhood tend to fare better than people who do not (Torrey, Bowler, Taylor, & Gottesman, 1994). One interpretation of these results is that the earlier the damage occurs, the more time the brain has to compensate for it, which results in milder symptoms.

A life-span perspective may at least partly reveal the development of schizophrenia (Belitsky & McGlashan, 1993). In one of the few studies that have followed people with schizophrenia into late life, Winokur, Pfohl, and Tsuang (1987) tracked 52 people over 40 years. Their general finding was that older adults tended to display fewer of the positive symptoms, such as delusions and hallucinations, and more of the negative symptoms, such as speech and cognitive difficulties.

The relapse rate must also be considered in discussing the course of schizophrenia. Unfortunately, a great many people who improve after an episode of schizophrenia later experience the symptoms again. In fact, most people with schizophrenia fluctuate between severe and moderate levels of impairment throughout their lives (Harrow, Sands, Silverstein, & Goldberg, 1997). ■ Figure 13.1 illustrates the data from one study that show the course of schizophrenia among four prototypical groups (Shepherd, Watt, Falloon, & Smeeton, 1989). As you can see, about 22 percent of the group had one episode of schizophrenia and improved without lasting impairment. However, the remaining 78 percent experienced several episodes, with differing degrees of impairment between them. Relapses are an important subject in the field of schizophrenia; we return to this phenomenon when we discuss causes and treatment.

Cultural Factors

Because schizophrenia is so complex, the diagnosis itself can be controversial. Some have argued that "schizophrenia" does not

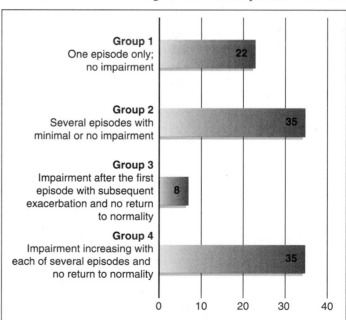

■ **FIGURE 13.1** The natural history of schizophrenia: A five-year follow-up

Source: Michael Shepherd, David Watt, Ian Falloon, and Nigel Smeeton, "The Natural History of Schizophrenia: A Five Year Follow-Up Study of Outcome and Prediction in a Representative Sample of Schizophrenia," *Psychological Medicine, 46 (Suppl. 15),* © 1989 by Cambridge University Press, reproduced with permission.

really exist but is a pejorative label for people who behave in ways outside the cultural norm (e.g., Laing, 1967; Szasz, 1961). Although the idea that schizophrenia exists only in the minds of mental health professionals is certainly provocative, this extreme view is contradicted by experience. As clinicians, we have had a great deal of contact with people who have this disorder and with their families and friends, and the tremendous amount of emotional pain resulting from schizophrenia gives definite credence to its existence. In addition, many people in extremely diverse cultures have the symptoms of schizophrenia, which supports the notion that it is a reality for many people worldwide (Ihara, Berrios, & McKenna, 2003; Patel & Andrade, 2003). Schizophrenia is thus universal, affecting all racial and cultural groups studied so far.

However, the course and outcome of schizophrenia vary from culture to culture. For example, in Colombia, India, and Nigeria, more people improve significantly or recover than in other countries (Leff, Sartorius, Jablensky, Korten, & Ernberg, 1992). These differences may be due to cultural variations or prevalent biological influences such as immunization, but we cannot yet explain these differences in outcomes.

Research from England suggests that proportionately more Blacks receive the diagnosis of schizophrenia than do whites. One possibility is that people from devalued ethnic minority groups (e.g., Afro-Caribbeans) may be victims of bias and stereotyping (Lewis, Croft-Jeffreys, & Anthony, 1990); in other words, they may be more likely to receive a diagnosis of schizophrenia than members of a dominant group. One prospective study of schizophrenia among different ethnic groups in London found that, although the outcomes of schizophrenia appear similar across various ethnic groups, Blacks were more likely to be detained against their will, brought to the hospital by police, and given emergency injections (Goater et al., 1999). A study by Eric Jarvis at McGill University similarly found that Black immigrants with schizophrenia were more likely to have police contact and be subject to compulsory hospital admissions, and that Afro-Caribbean immigrants had the highest rates of schizophrenia of all immigrant groups (Jarvis, 1998). The differing rates of schizophrenia, therefore, may to be due to *misdiagnosis* rather than due to any real cultural distinctions. Anthony Feinstein of the University of Toronto disagrees with this conclusion. He and his colleague conducted another study in England and again found minority ethnicity to be associated with an increased risk for psychiatric hospitalization (Feinstein & Holloway, 2002). However, they found no evidence that ethnic minority patients were being inappropriately admitted. They suggest instead that other factors (e.g., more frequent cannabis abuse) may contribute to the higher rates of psychiatric admissions among ethnic minorities. Later in this chapter, we discuss the possible role of cannabis use in the onset of schizophrenia.

Causes

Genetic Influences

We could argue that no other area of abnormal psychology so clearly illustrates the enormous complexity and intriguing mystery of genetic influences on behaviour than does the phenomenon of schizophrenia (Braff, Schork, & Gottesman, 2007).

Despite the possibility that schizophrenia may be several different disorders, we can safely make one generalization: *Genes are responsible for making some individuals vulnerable to schizophrenia.* We will look at a range of research findings from family, twin, adoption, offspring of twins, and linkage and association studies (Faraone, Tsuang, & Tsuang, 1999). We conclude by discussing the compelling reasons that no single gene is responsible for schizophrenia; rather, multiple genes combine to produce vulnerability. Gottesman (1991) has produced a detailed but highly readable discussion of this research in his book *Schizophrenia Genesis: The Origins of Madness.*

Family Studies

In 1938, German researcher Franz Kallmann published a major study on the families of people with schizophrenia (Kallmann, 1938). Kallmann examined family members of more than 1000 persons diagnosed with schizophrenia in a Berlin psychiatric hospital. Several of his observations continue to guide research on schizophrenia. Kallmann showed that the severity of the parent's disorder influenced the likelihood of the children having schizophrenia: The more severe the parent's schizophrenia, the more likely the children were to develop it also. Another observation was important: All forms of schizophrenia (e.g., catatonic, paranoid) were seen within the families. In other words, it does not appear that you inherit a predisposition for, say, paranoid schizophrenia. Instead, you may inherit a general predisposition for schizophrenia that manifests in the same form or a different one from that of your parent. More recent research from Ireland confirms this observation and suggests that families that have a member with schizophrenia are at risk not just for schizophrenia alone or for all psychological disorders; instead, there appears to be some familial risk for a spectrum of psychotic disorders related to schizophrenia (Kendler et al., 1993).

Gottesman (1991) summarized the data from about 40 studies of schizophrenia, as shown in ■ Figure 13.2. The most striking feature of this graph is its orderly demonstration that the risk of having schizophrenia varies according to how many genes an individual shares with someone who has the disorder. For example, you have the greatest chance (approximately 48 percent) of having schizophrenia if it has affected your identical (monozygotic) twin, a person who shares 100 percent of your genetic information. Your risk drops to about 17 percent with a fraternal (dizygotic) twin, who shares about 50 percent of your genetic information. And having any relative with schizophrenia makes you more likely to have the disorder than someone in the general population without such a relative (about 1 percent). Because family studies can't separate genetic influence from the impact of the environment, we use twin and adoption studies to help us evaluate the role of shared experiences in the cause of schizophrenia.

Twin Studies

If they are raised together, identical twins share 100 percent of their genes and 100 percent of their environment, whereas fraternal twins share only about 50 percent of their genes and 100 percent of their environment. If the environment is solely responsible for schizophrenia, we would expect little difference between identical and fraternal twins with regard to this disorder. If only genetic factors are relevant, both identical twins would always have

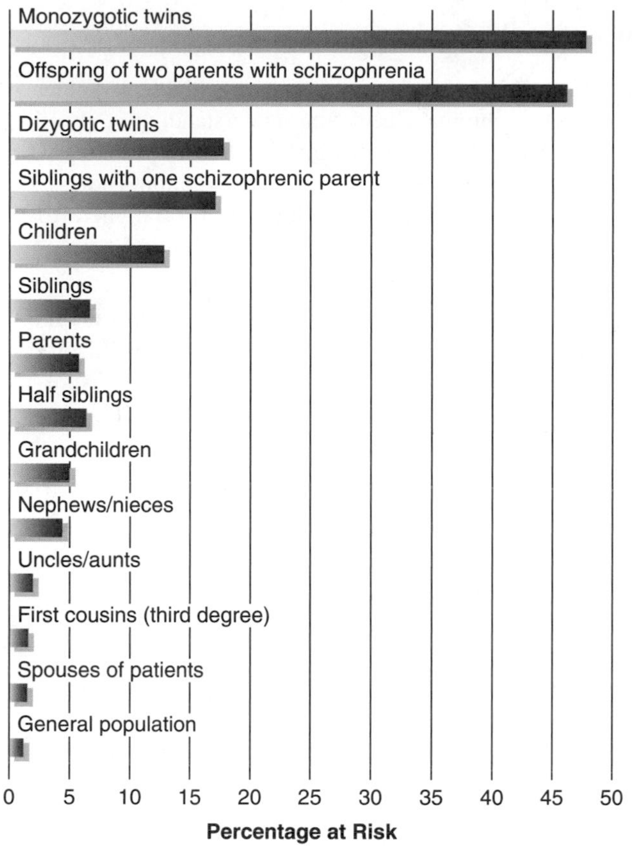
Monozygotic twins
Offspring of two parents with schizophrenia
Dizygotic twins
Siblings with one schizophrenic parent
Children
Siblings
Parents
Half siblings
Grandchildren
Nephews/nieces
Uncles/aunts
First cousins (third degree)
Spouses of patients
General population
0 5 10 15 20 25 30 35 40 45 50
Percentage at Risk

■ **FIGURE 13.2** Risk of developing schizophrenia

Source: Based on Gottesman, 1991.

schizophrenia (be concordant) and the fraternal twins would both have it about 50 percent of the time. Research from twin studies indicates that the truth is somewhere in the middle (Braff et al., 2007; Kendler & Diehl, 1993; Sherman et al., 1997).

In one of the most fascinating of "nature's experiments," identical quadruplets, all of whom have schizophrenia, have been studied extensively. Nicknamed the "Genain" quadruplets (from the Greek, meaning "dreadful gene"), these women have been followed by researchers for years (e.g., Mirsky et al., 2000; Rosenthal, 1963). In a sense, the women represent the complex interaction between genetics and the environment. All four shared the same genetic predisposition, and all were brought up in the same particularly dysfunctional household; yet the time of onset for schizophrenia, the symptoms and diagnoses, the course of the disorder, and, ultimately, their outcomes, differed significantly from sister to sister.

The case of the Genain quadruplets reveals an important consideration in studying genetic influences on behaviour—*unshared environments* (Plomin, 1990). We tend to think that siblings, and especially identical multiples, are brought up the same way. The impression is that "good" parents expose their children to favourable environments, and "bad" parents give them unstable experiences. However, even identical siblings can have very different prenatal and family experiences and therefore be exposed to varying degrees of biological and environmental stress. For example, Hester, one of the Genain sisters, was described by her disturbed parents as a habitual masturbator, and she had more social problems than her sisters as she grew up. Hester was the first to experience severe symptoms of schizophrenia, at age 18; her sister Myra was not hospitalized until six years later. This unusual case demonstrates that even siblings who are very close in every aspect of their lives can still have considerably different experiences physically and socially as they grow up, which may result in vastly different outcomes. A follow-up on the lives of these women showed the progression of their disorder stabilized and in some cases improved when they were assessed at age 66 (Mirsky et al., 2000).

Adoption Studies

Several adoption studies have distinguished the roles of the environment and genetics as they affect schizophrenia. These studies often span many years; because people often do not show the first signs of schizophrenia until middle age, researchers need to be sure all the offspring reach that point before drawing conclusions. Many schizophrenia studies are conducted in Europe, primarily because of the extensive and comprehensive records kept in many of these countries.

The largest adoption study is being conducted in Finland (Tienari, 1991). From a sample of almost 20 000 women with schizophrenia, the researchers found 190 children who had been given up for adoption. The data from this study support the idea that schizophrenia represents a spectrum of related disorders, all of which overlap genetically. If an adopted child had a biological mother with schizophrenia, he or she had about a 5 percent chance of having the disorder (compared with about only 1 percent in the general population). However, if the biological mother had schizophrenia or one of the related psychotic disorders (e.g., delusional disorder, schizophreniform disorder), the risk that the adopted child would have one of these disorders rose to about 22 percent (Tienari et al., 2003; Tienari, Wahlberg, & Wynne, 2006). Even when raised away from their biological parents, children of parents with schizophrenia have a much higher chance of having the disorder themselves. At the same time, there appears to be a protective factor if these children are brought up in healthy, supportive homes. In other words, a gene–environment interaction was observed in this study, with a good home environment reducing the risk of schizophrenia (Gilmore, 2010; Wynne et al., 2006).

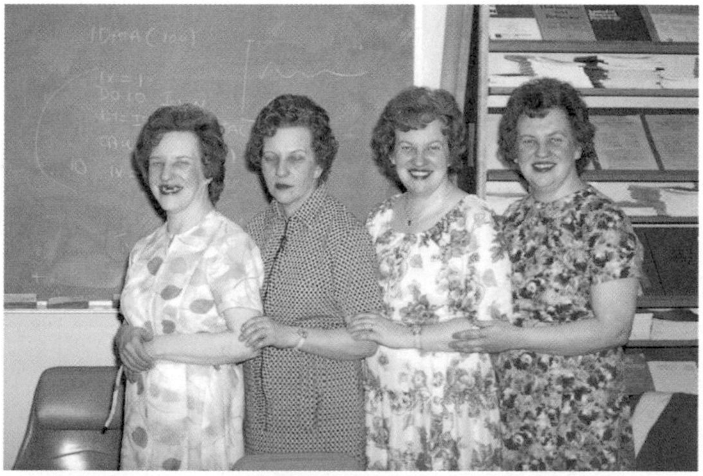

Dr. Allan F. Mirsky/National Institute of Mental Health

▲ The Genain quadruplets all had schizophrenia but exhibited different symptoms over the years.

The Offspring of Twins

Twin and adoption studies strongly suggest a genetic component for schizophrenia, but what about children who develop schizophrenia even though their parents do not? For example, the study by Tienari and colleagues (2003, 2006) we just discussed found that 1.7 percent of the children with nonschizophrenic parents developed schizophrenia. Does this mean you can develop schizophrenia without "schizophrenic genes"? Or are some people carriers, having the genes for schizophrenia but for some reason not showing the disorder themselves? An important clue to this question comes from research on the children of twins with schizophrenia.

In a study begun in 1971, 21 identical twin pairs and 41 fraternal twin pairs with a history of schizophrenia were identified along with their children (Fischer, 1971; Gottesman & Bertelsen, 1989). The researchers wanted to determine the relative likelihood that a child would have schizophrenia if his or her parent did, and if the parent's twin had schizophrenia but the parent did not. ■ Figure 13.3 illustrates the findings from this study. For example, if your parent is an identical (monozygotic) twin with schizophrenia, you have about a 17 percent chance of having the disorder yourself, a figure that holds if you are the child of an unaffected identical twin whose co-twin has the disorder.

Conversely, look at the risks for the child of a fraternal (dizygotic) twin. If your parent is the twin with schizophrenia, you have about a 17 percent chance of having schizophrenia yourself. However, if your parent does not have schizophrenia but your parent's fraternal twin does, your risk is only about 2 percent. The only way to explain this finding is through genetics. The data clearly indicate that you can have genes that predispose you to schizophrenia, not show the disorder yourself, but still pass on the genes to your children. In other words, you can be a "carrier" for schizophrenia. This is some of the strongest evidence yet that people are genetically vulnerable to schizophrenia. Remember, however, there is only a 17 percent chance of inheritance, meaning that other factors help determine who will have this disorder.

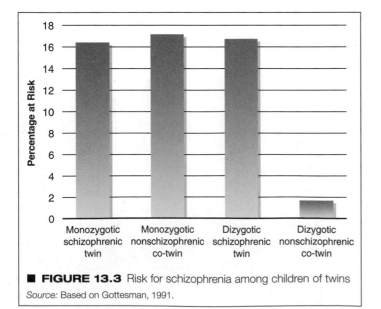

■ **FIGURE 13.3** Risk for schizophrenia among children of twins
Source: Based on Gottesman, 1991.

Gene–Environment Interactions

An interesting study by Caspi and colleagues (2005), conducted with the large New Zealand sample described in Chapter 2 (see page 38), extended the study of genetic factors to examine the possibility of a gene by environment interaction in the development of schizophrenia. Cannabis use in youth is an established but modest risk factor for psychosis in adulthood. Yet, clearly, most people who use marijuana do not develop psychosis! Caspi and colleagues tested whether there might be certain genetically vulnerable individuals who are particularly susceptible to the effects of cannabis initiating psychosis. Indeed, they found that the combination of a particular genetic profile (i.e., carriers of the catechol-*O*-methyltransferase [COMT] valine [VAL] 158 allele as compared to those with two copies of the methionine [MET] allele) were particularly likely to develop schizophrenia in adulthood. But this was only true if these individuals had used cannabis as teenagers. This study suggests the interesting possibility that certain genes may act as vulnerability factors that interact with specific environmental pathogens at crucial developmental stages, leading to the development of schizophrenia (Caspi et al., 2005).

Linkage and Association Studies

Genetic linkage and association studies rely on traits such as blood types (whose exact location on the chromosome is already known) that are inherited in families along with the disorder we are looking for—in this case, schizophrenia. Because we know the location of the genes for these traits (called *marker genes*), we can make a rough guess about the location of the disorder genes that are inherited along with them. To date, researchers have looked at several sites for genes that may be responsible for schizophrenia. For example, regions of chromosomes 1, 2, 3, 5, 6, 8, 10, 11, 13, 20, and 22 are implicated in this disorder (Kirov & Owen, 2009), and a particular genetic deficit (22q11 deletion syndrome) is being explored as the cause of a subtype of schizophrenia (Bassett et al., 2001; Hodgkinson, Murphy, O'Neill, Brzustowicz, & Bassett, 2001).

The Search for Markers

In the search for markers, researchers look for common traits other than the symptoms of the disorder itself. If some people have the positive symptoms of schizophrenia, others have the negative symptoms, and still others have a mixture of these symptoms, yet they all have a particular problem completing a certain task, the skill deficit would be very useful for identifying what else these people may have in common.

Several potential markers for schizophrenia have been studied over the years. As noted by McGill University psychologist Gillian O'Driscoll and her colleagues, one of the more highly researched markers is called *smooth-pursuit eye movement* or eye-tracking (O'Driscoll, Lenzenweger, & Holzman, 1998). While keeping your head still, you must be able to track a moving pendulum, back and forth, with your eyes. The ability to track objects smoothly across the visual field is deficient in many people who also have schizophrenia (e.g., Clementz & Sweeney, 1990); it does not appear to be the result of drug treatment or institutionalization (Lieberman et al., 1993). It also seems to be a problem for relatives of these people and is observed more frequently among people with schizophrenia than in others who do not have the disorder (Thaker & Avila, 2003). Although these eye-tracking deficits appear associated with both negative and positive symptoms, they are most strongly associated with positive symptoms (Holahan & O'Driscoll, 2005). When all these observations are combined, they suggest an eye-tracking deficit may be a marker for schizophrenia that could be used in further study (O'Driscoll et al., 1998).

Evidence for Multiple Genes

As we have seen, schizophrenia involves more than one gene, a phenomenon referred to as *quantitative trait loci* (Levinson et al., 1998; Plomin, Owen, & McGuffin, 1994). The schizophrenia we see most often is probably caused by several genes located at different sites throughout the chromosomes. This model would also clarify why there can be gradations of severity in people with the disorder (from mild to severe), and why the risk of having schizophrenia increases with the number of affected relatives in the family.

Neurobiological Influences

The belief that schizophrenia involves a malfunctioning brain goes back as far as the writings of Emil Kraepelin (1856–1926). It is therefore not surprising that a great deal of research has focused on the brain. Before we discuss some of this work, however, be forewarned: To study abnormalities in the brain for clues to the cause of schizophrenia is to face all the classic problems of doing correlational research which we discussed in Chapter 4. For example, if a person has schizophrenia and too much of a neurotransmitter, (1) does too much neurotransmitter cause schizophrenia, (2) does schizophrenia create too much of the neurotransmitter, or (3) does something else cause both the schizophrenia and the chemical imbalance? Keep this caveat in mind as you review the following research.

Dopamine

One of the most enduring yet still controversial theories of the cause of schizophrenia involves the neurotransmitter *dopamine* (Howes & Kapur, 2009). Before we consider the research, however, let's review briefly how neurotransmitters operate in the brain and how they are affected by neuroleptic medications, which reduce hallucinations and delusions. In Chapter 2 we discussed the sensitivity of specific neurons to specific neurotransmitters and described how they cluster throughout the brain. The top of ■ Figure 13.4 shows two neurons and the important synaptic gap that separates them. Neurotransmitters are released from the storage vessels (synaptic vesicles) at the end of the axon, cross the gap, and are taken up by receptors in the dendrite of the next axon. Chemical "messages" are transported in this way from neuron to neuron throughout the brain.

This process can be influenced in a number of ways, and the rest of Figure 13.4 illustrates some of them. The chemical messages can be increased by agonistic agents or decreased by antagonistic agents. (Remember the word *antagonistic* means hostile or unfriendly; in some way this is the effect of antagonistic agents on the chemical messenger service.) Antagonistic effects slow down or stop messages from being transmitted by preventing the release of the neurotransmitter, blocking uptake at the level of the dendrite, or causing leaks that reduce the amount of neurotransmitter ultimately released. Conversely, agonistic effects assist with the transference of chemical messages and, if extreme, can produce too much neurotransmitter activity by increasing production or release of the neurotransmitter, and by affecting more receptors at the dendrites.

What we've learned about antipsychotic medications points to the possibility that the dopamine system is too active in persons with schizophrenia. The simplified picture in Figure 13.4 does not show that there are actually different receptor sites and that a chemical such as dopamine produces different results depending on which of those sites it affects. In schizophrenia, attention has focused on two dopamine sites, referred to simply as D_1 and D_2. As we will see, D_2 is of particular interest to researchers in this field.

In a story that resembles a mystery plot, several pieces of "circumstantial evidence" are clues to the role of dopamine in schizophrenia:

1. Antipsychotic drugs (neuroleptics) that are often effective in treating people with schizophrenia are dopamine antagonists, partially blocking the brain's use of dopamine (Creese, Burt, & Snyder, 1976; Seeman, Lee, Chau-Wong, & Wong, 1976).
2. These drugs can produce negative side effects similar to those in Parkinson's disease, a disorder known to be due to insufficient dopamine.
3. The drug L-dopa, a dopamine agonist used to treat people with Parkinson's disease, produces schizophrenia-like symptoms in some people (Davidson et al., 1987).

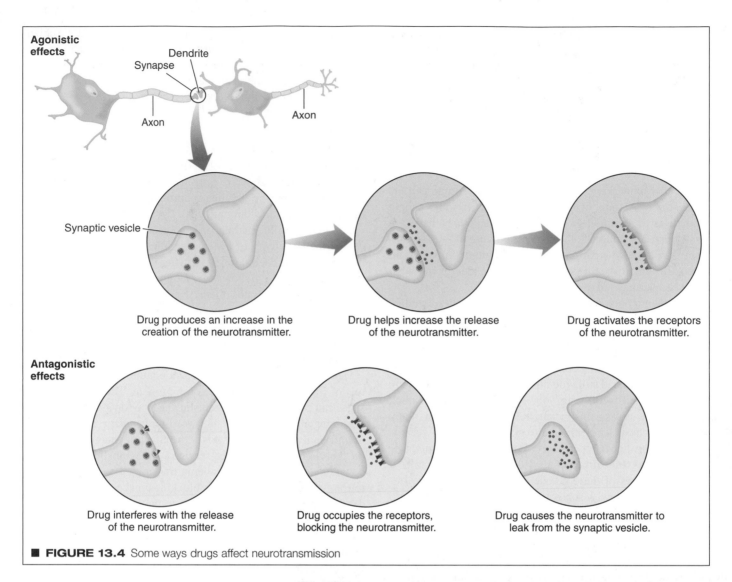

Agonistic effects

Dendrite
Synapse
Axon
Axon

Synaptic vesicle

Drug produces an increase in the creation of the neurotransmitter.

Drug helps increase the release of the neurotransmitter.

Drug activates the receptors of the neurotransmitter.

Antagonistic effects

Drug interferes with the release of the neurotransmitter.

Drug occupies the receptors, blocking the neurotransmitter.

Drug causes the neurotransmitter to leak from the synaptic vesicle.

■ **FIGURE 13.4** Some ways drugs affect neurotransmission

4. Amphetamines, which also activate dopamine, can make psychotic symptoms worse in some people with schizophrenia (van Kammen, Docherty, & Bunney, 1982).

In other words, when drugs are administered that are known to increase dopamine (agonists), there is an increase in schizophrenic behaviour; when drugs that are known to decrease dopamine activity (antagonists) are used, schizophrenic symptoms tend to diminish. Taking these observations together, researchers theorized that schizophrenia in some people was attributable to excessive dopamine activity.

Despite these observations, some evidence contradicts the dopamine theory (Javitt & Laruelle, 2006):

1. A significant number of people with schizophrenia are not helped by the use of dopamine antagonists.

2. Although the neuroleptics block the reception of dopamine quite quickly, the relevant

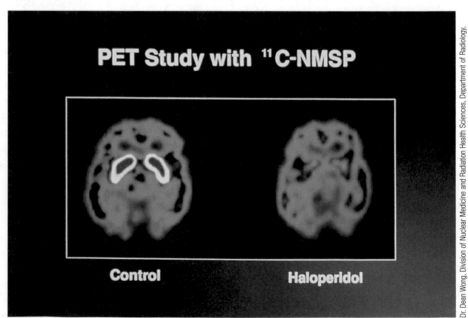

PET Study with ¹¹C-NMSP

Control

Haloperidol

▲ These PET images show the brain of a man with schizophrenia who had never been medicated (left) and after he received haloperidol (right). The red and yellow areas indicate activity in the D_2 receptors; haloperidol evidently reduced dopamine activity.

symptoms subside only after several days or weeks, much more slowly than researchers would expect.

3. These drugs are only partly helpful in reducing the negative symptoms (e.g., flat affect, anhedonia) of schizophrenia.

In addition to these concerns, there is evidence of a "double-edged sword" with respect to schizophrenia. A medication called clozapine is effective with many people who were not helped with traditional neuroleptic medications (Agid, Remington, Kapur, Arenovich, & Zipursky, 2007; Tauscher et al., 2004; Wahlbeck, Cheine, Essali, & Adams, 1999). That's the good news. But as pointed out by Shitij Kapur and his colleagues in Toronto, the bad news for the dopamine theory is that clozapine is one of the weakest dopamine antagonists by far, much less able to block the dopamine sites than other drugs (Kapur, Zipursky, & Remington, 1999). Why would a medication inefficient at blocking dopamine be effective as a treatment for schizophrenia if schizophrenia is caused by excessive dopamine activity?

The answer may be that, although dopamine is involved in the symptoms of schizophrenia, the relationship is more complicated than we once thought (Potter & Manji, 1993). Current thinking points to at least three specific neurochemical abnormalities simultaneously at play in the brains of people with schizophrenia.

Strong evidence now leads us to believe that schizophrenia is partially the result of excessive stimulation of striatal dopamine D_2 receptors (Laruelle, Kegeles, & Abi-Darham, 2003). Recall that the striatum is part of the basal ganglia found deep within the brain. These cells control movement, balance, and walking, and they rely on dopamine to function. Huntington's disease (which involves problems in motor function) involves deterioration in this brain area. How do we know that excessive stimulation of D_2 receptors is involved in schizophrenia? One clue is that most effective antipsychotic drugs all share dopamine D_2 receptor antagonism (Ho et al., 2003), meaning they help block the simulation of the D_2 receptors.

A second area of interest to scientists investigating the cause of schizophrenia is the observation of a deficiency in the stimulation of prefrontal D_1 receptors (Koh, Bergson, Undie, Goldman-Rakic, & Lidow, 2003). Therefore, although some dopamine sites may be overactive (e.g., striatal D_2), a second type of dopamine site in the part of the brain that we use for planning and organizing (prefrontal D_1 receptors) appears to be less active and may account for negative symptoms of schizophrenia such as avolition. As we discuss later in this chapter, lower prefrontal activity in people with schizophrenia is referred to as *hypofrontality*.

Finally, a third and more recent area of neurochemical interest involves research on alterations in prefrontal activity involving glutamate transmission (Goff & Coyle, 2001). Glutamate is an excitatory neurotransmitter that is found in all areas of the brain and is only now being studied in earnest. Like dopamine, glutamate has different types of receptors. The ones being studied for their role in schizophrenia are the *N*-methyl–D-aspartate (NMDA) receptors. The effects of certain drugs that affect NMDA receptors point to clues to schizophrenia. Two recreational drugs described in Chapter 11—phencyclidine (PCP) and ketamine—can result in psychotic-like behaviour in people without schizophrenia and can exacerbate psychotic symptoms in those with schizophrenia. Both PCP and ketamine are NMDA antagonists,

suggesting that a deficit in glutamate or blocking of NMDA sites may be involved in some of the symptoms of schizophrenia (Goff & Coyle, 2001).

You can see that research on these two neurotransmitters is complex and awaits further clarification. However, advances in technology are leading us closer to the clues behind this enigmatic disorder and closer still to better treatments.

Brain Structure

Evidence for neurological damage in people with schizophrenia comes from a number of observations. Many children with a parent who has the disorder, and who are therefore at risk, tend to show subtle but observable neurological problems, such as abnormal reflexes and inattentiveness (Wan, Abel, & Green, 2008). These difficulties are persistent: Adults who have schizophrenia show deficits in their ability to perform certain tasks and to attend during reaction time exercises (Cleghorn & Albert, 1990). Such findings suggest that brain damage or dysfunction may cause or accompany schizophrenia, although no single site is probably responsible for the whole range of symptoms (Belger & Dichter, 2006).

One of the most reliable observations about the brain in people with schizophrenia involves the size of the ventricles (see ■ Figure 13.5). As early as 1927, researchers noted that these liquid-filled cavities showed enlargement in some but not all of the brains examined in people with schizophrenia (Jacobi & Winkler, 1927). Since then, more sophisticated techniques have been developed for observing the brain, and in the dozens of studies conducted on ventricle size, the great majority show abnormally large lateral ventricles in people with schizophrenia (Shenton & Kubicki, 2009). Ventricle size in itself may not be a problem, but the dilation (enlargement) of the ventricles indicates that either adjacent parts of the brain have not developed fully or have atrophied, thus allowing the ventricles to become larger.

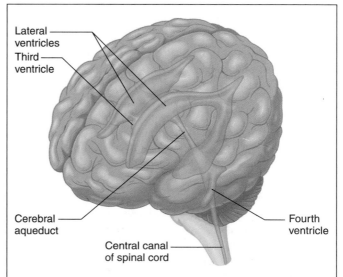

■ **FIGURE 13.5** Location of the cerebrospinal fluid in the human brain. This extracellular fluid surrounds and cushions the brain and spinal cord. It also fills the four interconnected cavities (cerebral ventricles) within the brain and the central canal of the spinal cord

Ventricle enlargement is not seen in everyone who has schizophrenia. Several factors seem to be associated with this finding. For example, enlarged ventricles are observed more often in men than in women (Goldstein & Lewine, 2000). Also, ventricles seem to enlarge in proportion to age and to the duration of the schizophrenia. One study found that individuals with schizophrenia who were exposed to influenza prenatally may be more likely to have enlarged ventricles (Takei, Lewis, Jones, Harvey, & Murray, 1996). (We describe the possible role of prenatal exposure to influenza and schizophrenia in the next section.)

In a study of ventricle size, researchers investigated the possible role of genetics (Staal et al., 2000). Using a brain-imaging technique called magnetic resonance imaging (MRI), investigators compared brain structure among people with schizophrenia, their same-sex siblings who did not have schizophrenia, and healthy volunteers. Both the people with schizophrenia and their otherwise unaffected siblings had enlargement of the third ventricle compared with the volunteers. This suggests that the enlargement of ventricles may be related to susceptibility to schizophrenia.

We touched on the concept of unshared environments in the section on genetics (Jang, 2005; Plomin, 1990). Although monozygotic twins are identical genetically, they can experience a number of environmental differences, even before they are born. For instance, in the intrauterine environment twins must compete for nutrients, and they may not be equally successful. In addition, birth complications, such as the loss of oxygen (anoxia), could affect only one of the twins (Jang, 2005). Obstetrical complications appear often among twins with schizophrenia in discordant identical pairs, and among the more severely affected if both twins have schizophrenia (McNeil, 1987). Different experiences among twins who are already predisposed to the disorder could damage the brain and cause the types of symptoms we associate with schizophrenia.

The frontal lobes of the brain have also interested people looking for structural problems associated with schizophrenia (Gur & Pearlson, 1993). This area may be less active in people with schizophrenia than in people without the disorder, a phenomenon known as *hypofrontality* (*hypo* means "less active" or "deficient"). Neuropsychological research by several Canadian teams has shown that patients with schizophrenia perform poorly relative to comparison groups on cognitive tasks known to be related to functioning of the frontal lobes (e.g., Zakzanis, Troyer, Rich, & Heinrichs, 2000). For example, James Everett and his colleagues at Laval University showed that patients with schizophrenia performed more poorly than healthy controls on a task called the Wisconsin Card Sorting Task—a test requiring planning and organization abilities subserved by the frontal lobes (Everett, Lavoie, Gagnon, & Gosselin, 2001). Further research suggests that deficient activity in a particular area of the frontal lobes, the dorsolateral prefrontal cortex (DLPFC), may be implicated in schizophrenia (e.g., Berman & Weinberger, 1990). When people with and without schizophrenia are given tasks that involve the DLPFC, less activity (measured by cerebral blood flow) is recorded in the brains of those with schizophrenia. A meta-analytic study showed that hypofrontality distinguishes about half of schizophrenia patients from nonschizophrenic people (Davidson & Heinrichs, 2003). Hypofrontality also seems to be associated with the negative symptoms of schizophrenia

(Andreasen et al., 1992) and with the eye-tracking deficits mentioned earlier (O'Driscoll et al., 1999).

It appears that several brain sites are implicated in the cognitive dysfunction observed among people with schizophrenia, especially the prefrontal cortex, various other related cortical regions, and subcortical circuits including the thalamus and the stratum (Shenton & Kubicki, 2009). Remember that this dysfunction seems to occur before the onset of schizophrenia. In other words, brain damage may develop progressively, beginning before the symptoms of the disorder are apparent, perhaps prenatally (Weinberger, 1995).

Viral Infection

A curious fact about schizophrenia is that, according to some authors, no adequate descriptions of people having this disorder appear earlier than about 1800 (e.g., Gottesman, 1991). If you look at historic records or read ancient literature, you can find people with such disorders as mental retardation, mania, depression, and senile dementia. Even William Shakespeare, who describes most human conditions, mentions nothing that resembles our current image of schizophrenia. Historically, such an obvious aberration of behaviour is puzzlingly absent. (However, there is now some evidence that at least a few cases of schizophrenia-like disorder may have existed as early as the 14th century; Heinrichs, 2003.)

One intriguing hypothesis is that schizophrenia is a recent phenomenon, appearing only during the past 200 years and that, like AIDS, it may involve some newly introduced virus (Gottesman, 1991). In other words, a "schizo-virus" could have caused some cases of this debilitating disorder (Torrey, 1988b). In fact, evidence suggests that a virus-like disease may account for some cases (Kirch, 1993). The higher prevalence of schizophrenia among men living in urban areas (Lewis et al., 1992) implies that they are more likely to have been exposed to infectious agents than are their peers in less populated areas.

Several studies have shown that schizophrenia may be associated with prenatal exposure to influenza. For example, Mednick and colleagues followed a large number of people after a severe Type A2 influenza epidemic in Helsinki, Finland, and found that those whose mothers were exposed to influenza during the second trimester of pregnancy were much more likely to have schizophrenia than others (Cannon, Barr, & Mednick, 1991). This observation has been confirmed by some researchers (e.g., O'Callaghan, Sham, Takei, Glover, & Murray, 1991; Venables, 1996) but not by others (e.g., Torrey, Rawlings, & Waldman, 1988).

Evidence that second-trimester developmental problems may be associated with schizophrenia has led researchers to look further into this area. Among the types of cells that normally migrate to the cortex during this period are the fingertip dermal cells, which are responsible for the number of fingerprint ridges. Although there is no such thing as an abnormal number of ridges, identical twins generally have the same number. However, if some interruption in second-trimester fetal development resulted in schizophrenia (when, according to the viral theory, a virus may have its effect), it would also affect the fingertip dermal cells. Researchers compared the fingerprint ridges of identical twins who were discordant for schizophrenia with those of identical twins without schizophrenia (Bracha, Torrey, Gottesman, Bigelow, & Cunniff, 1992). They found that the number of ridges on the fingertips of the twins without schizophrenia differed very little from each other; however, they differed a great deal among about one-third of the twin pairs who were discordant for schizophrenia. This study suggests that ridge count may be a marker of prenatal brain damage. Although there is no characteristic fingerprint for schizophrenia, this physical sign may add to our understanding of the second-trimester conditions that can trigger the genetic predisposition for schizophrenia (Weinberger, 1995).

Like the indications that virus-like diseases may cause damage to the fetal brain, which later may cause the symptoms of schizophrenia, the circumstantial evidence for the excessive dopamine hypothesis are interesting and may help explain why some people with schizophrenia behave the way they do (Mednick et al., 1998). However, there is not yet enough evidence to prove the existence of a "schizo-virus."

Psychological and Social Influences

That one identical twin may develop schizophrenia and the other may not suggests that schizophrenia involves something in addition to genes. We know that early brain trauma, perhaps resulting from a second-trimester virus-like attack or obstetrical complications, may generate physical stress that contributes to schizophrenia. All these observations show clearly that schizophrenia does not fall neatly into a few simple causal packages. For instance, not all people with schizophrenia have enlarged ventricles, nor do they all have hypofrontality or excessive activity in their dopamine systems. The causal picture may be further complicated by psychological and social factors. We next look at research into psychosocial factors. Do emotional stressors or family interaction patterns initiate the symptoms of schizophrenia? If so, how might those factors cause people to relapse after a period of improvement?

Stress

It is important to learn how much and what kind of stress makes a person with a predisposition for schizophrenia develop the disorder itself. Think back to the two cases we presented near the beginning of this chapter. Did you notice any precipitating events? Arthur's father had died several years earlier, and Arthur was laid off from his job right around the time his symptoms first appeared. David's uncle had died the same year David began acting strangely. Were these stressful events just coincidences, or did they contribute to the men's later problems?

Researchers have studied the effects of a variety of stressors on schizophrenia. Dohrenwend and Egri (1981), for instance, observed that otherwise healthy people who engage in combat during a war often display temporary symptoms that resemble those of schizophrenia. In an early study, Brown and Birley (1968; Birley & Brown, 1970) examined people whose onset of schizophrenia could be dated within a week. These individuals had experienced a high number of stressful life events in the three weeks just before they started showing signs of the disorder. In a large-scale study sponsored by the World Health Organization, researchers also looked at the role of life events in the onset of schizophrenia (Day et al., 1987). This cross-national study confirmed the findings of Brown and Birley across eight different research centres.

The *retrospective* nature of such research creates problems. Each study relies on after-the-fact reports, collected after the

person showed signs of schizophrenia. We always wonder whether such reports are biased in some way and therefore misleading (Hirsch, Cramer, & Bowen, 1992). One study used a *prospective* approach to examine the impact of stress on relapse. Ventura, Nuechterlein, Lukoff, and Hardesty (1989) identified 30 people with recent-onset schizophrenia and followed them for a year. The researchers interviewed the subjects every two weeks to learn whether they had experienced any stressful life events and whether their symptoms had changed. Notice that, unlike the previous studies, this research examines the factors that predict the recurrence of schizophrenic symptoms after a period of improvement. During the one-year assessment period, 11 of the 30 people had a significant relapse—that is, their symptoms returned or worsened. Like Brown and Birley, Ventura et al. (1989) found that relapses occurred when stressful life events increased during the previous month. Other research demonstrates that stressful life events can increase depression among people with schizophrenia, which in turn may contribute to relapse (Ventura, Nuechterlein, Subotnik, Hardesty, & Mintz, 2000). An important finding from the first study is that, although the people experienced more stressful events as a group just before their relapse, 55 percent did not have a major life event during the previous month. Other factors must account for the return of symptoms among these people (Bebbington et al., 1993; Ventura, Nuechterlein, Hardesty, & Gitlin, 1992).

Another important area in the study of the impact of stress on schizophrenia is research showing a significant negative correlation between social class and schizophrenia. In other words, there is a significant tendency for individuals with schizophrenia to be found in the lowest social classes. This finding has been replicated in a variety of cultures (e.g., Hollingshead & Redlich, 1958; Kohn, 1968). There are at least two possible explanations for this finding. The first explanation pertains to stress affecting schizophrenia rates: It could be that life in the lower social classes is stressful, predisposing those from the lower social classes to an increased likelihood of schizophrenia. This explanation is known as the *sociogenic hypothesis*. The second explanation pertains to the adverse effects of schizophrenia on a person's ability to hold a job. If the illness makes them less able to hold a job, individuals with schizophrenia may experience a downward social drift into the lower social classes. This second explanation is known as the *social selection hypothesis*. Although results have certainly been mixed, findings generally favour the social selection over the sociogenic hypothesis in terms of explaining the relation of social class and schizophrenia (see Dohrenwend et al., 1992). This should not be taken to mean that social environment does not play a role in schizophrenia, however. Take for example, the research on the role of social support, which we will examine next.

In Chapters 7 and 9, we examined how social support can exert a moderating influence in reducing the negative impact of stress in both physical and mental health disorders (i.e., mood disorders and chronic pain, respectively). Although investigations of social support in schizophrenia have been relatively sparse, some Canadian research supports its importance in this disorder as well. A longitudinal study by David Erickson and Morton Beiser at the University of Ottawa and the Centre for Addiction and Mental Health showed that higher levels of social support from non–family members in the social network predicted better outcomes five years later among patients experiencing their first episode of schizophrenia (Erickson, Beiser, & Iacono, 1998). But what of the role of family members? We look at this important influence next.

Families and Relapse

A great deal of research has studied how interactions within the family affect people who have schizophrenia. For example, the term **schizophrenogenic** was used for a time to describe a mother whose cold, dominant, and rejecting nature was thought to cause schizophrenia in her children (Fromm-Reichmann, 1948). In addition, the term **double bind** was used to portray a type of communication style that produced conflicting messages, which, in turn, caused schizophrenia to develop (Bateson, 1959). Here, the parent presumably communicates messages that have two conflicting meanings; for example, a mother responds coolly to her child's embrace, but says, "Don't you love me anymore?" when the child withdraws. Although these theories are no longer supported, they have been—and in some cases continue to be—destructive, producing guilt in parents who are persuaded that their early mistakes caused devastating consequences.

Recent work has focused more on how family interactions contribute, not to the onset of schizophrenia itself, but to relapse after initial symptoms are observed. Research has focused on a particular emotional communication style known as **expressed emotion (EE)**. This concept was formulated by Brown and colleagues in London, England. Following a sample of people who had been discharged from the hospital after an episode of schizophrenic symptoms, the researchers found that former patients who had limited contact with their relatives did better than patients who spent longer periods with their families (Brown, 1959). Additional research results indicated that if the level of criticism (disapproval), hostility (animosity), and emotional overinvolvement (intrusiveness) expressed by the families was high, patients tended to relapse (Brown, Monck, Carstairs, & Wing, 1962).

Other researchers, including John Cole of the London Psychiatric Hospital and Shahe Kazarian of the University of Western Ontario, have since found that ratings of high expressed emotion in a family are a good predictor of relapse among people with chronic schizophrenia (Bebbington, Bowen, Hirsch, & Kuipers, 1995; Kazarian, Malla, Cole, & Baker, 1990). In fact, if you have schizophrenia and live in a family with high expressed emotion, you are 3.7 times more likely to relapse than if you lived in a family with low expressed emotion (Kavanagh, 1992; Parker & Hadzi-Pavlovic, 1990). Here are examples of interviews that show how families of people with schizophrenia might communicate expressed emotion (Hooley, 1985).

High Expressed Emotion
- I always say, "Why don't you pick up a book, do a crossword or something like that to keep your mind off it." That's even too much trouble.
- I've tried to jolly him out of it and pestered him into doing things. Maybe I've overdone it, I don't know.

Low Expressed Emotion
- I know it's better for her to be on her own, to get away from me and try to do things on her own.
- Whatever she does suits me.
- I just tend to let it go because I know that when she wants to speak she will speak. (Hooley, 1985, pp. 148–149)

As is illustrated in the example, family communications involving high levels of expressed emotion are characterized by intrusiveness, high levels of emotional response, a negative attitude toward the illness on the part of family members, and low tolerance and unrealistic expectations of the patient (Cole & Kazarian, 1988). With respect to family members' low tolerance of and negative attitudes toward the patient's illness, research from Laval University researchers Helene Provencher and Frank Fincham demonstrates that, unfortunately, it is common for family members to see a schizophrenic patient's symptoms as being intentional (Provencher & Fincham, 2000). The literature on expressed emotion is valuable to our understanding of why symptoms of schizophrenia recur. It may also show us how to treat people with this disorder so they do not experience further psychotic episodes (Mueser et al., 1993).

An interesting issue that arises when studying family influences is whether what we see is unique to our culture or is universal. Looking at expressed emotion across different cultures may help us learn whether it is a cause of schizophrenia. Remember that schizophrenia is observed at about the same rate worldwide, with a prevalence of about 1 percent in the global population. If a factor like high expressed emotion in families is a causal agent, we should see the same rates in families across cultures; in fact, however, they differ, as you can see in ■ Figure 13.6. These data come from an analysis of the concept of expressed emotion in several studies, from India, Mexico, Great Britain, and North America (Jenkins & Karno, 1992). The differences suggest there are cultural variations in how families react to someone with schizophrenia, and their reactions do not cause the disorder (Weisman, 1997; Weisman & Lopez, 1997). However, critical and hostile environments clearly provide additional stressors that can in turn lead to more relapses. However, as pointed out by the research of Suzanne King at the Douglas Hospital in Montréal, it is also very important to consider the possibility that critical comments and emotional overinvolvement may be family responses to a schizophrenic patient's unusual and disturbing behaviour rather than a cause (King, 2000). In fact, research does show that certain kinds of patient behaviours do evoke hostility in family members, supporting the position that the relation between the behaviour of

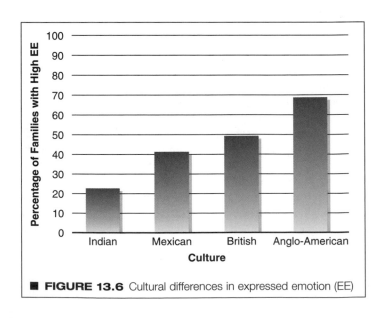

■ **FIGURE 13.6** Cultural differences in expressed emotion (EE)

patients with schizophrenia and expressed emotion in family members is indeed a reciprocal process (e.g., Cook, Strachan, Goldstein, & Miklowitz, 1989; Miklowitz et al., 1989).

Treatment

If you remember our descriptions of Arthur and David, you will recall their families' concern for them. Arthur's mother spoke of the "living nightmare" and David's aunt expressed concern for both her safety and David's. In each case the family was desperate to help, but what do you do for someone who has delusions, hears his dead uncle's voice, or can't communicate complete thoughts? The search for help has taken many paths, sometimes down some very disturbing roads; for example, in the 16th century, primitive surgery was conducted to remove the "stone of madness," which was thought to cause disturbed behaviour. As barbaric as this practice may seem today, it is not very different from the prefrontal lobotomies performed on people with schizophrenia as late as the 1950s. This procedure severed the frontal lobes from the lower portion of the brain, which sometimes calmed the patient but also caused cognitive and emotional deficits. Even today, some societies use crude surgical procedures to eliminate the symptoms of schizophrenia. In Kenya, for instance, Kisii tribal doctors listen to their patients to find the location of the noises in the patients' heads (hallucinations), then get them drunk, cut out a piece of scalp, and scrape the skull in the area of the voices (Mustafa, 1990).

In the Western world today, treatment usually begins with one of the neuroleptic drugs that are invaluable in reducing the symptoms of schizophrenia for many people. They are typically used in combination with a variety of psychosocial treatments to reduce relapse, compensate for skills deficits, and improve cooperation for taking the medications (American Psychiatric Association, 2000b).

Biological Interventions

Researchers have assumed for more than a century that schizophrenia requires some form of biological intervention. Emil Kraepelin, who so eloquently described dementia praecox in the late 19th century, saw the disorder as a brain disease. Lacking a biological treatment, he routinely recommended that the physician use "good patience, kindly disposition, and self-control" to calm excited patients (Nagel, 1991). This approach was seen as only a temporary way of helping the person through disturbing times and was not thought to be an actual treatment.

During the 1930s, several novel biological treatments were tried. One approach was to inject massive doses of insulin—the drug that given in smaller doses is used to treat diabetes—to induce comas in people who have schizophrenia. Insulin coma therapy was thought for a time to be helpful, but closer examination showed it carried great risk of serious illness and death. During this time psychosurgery, including prefrontal lobotomies, was introduced; and in the late 1930s, electroconvulsive therapy (ECT) was advanced as a treatment for schizophrenia. As with earlier drastic treatments, initial enthusiasm for ECT faded because it was found not to be beneficial for most people with schizophrenia—although it is still used with a limited number of

The Surgeon by Jan Sanders van Hemessen/Museo del Prado, Madrid, Spain/Bridgeman Art Library

▲ An early 16th-century painting of psychosurgery, in which part of the brain is removed to treat mental illness

people today (Fink & Sackeim, 1996). As we explained in Chapter 7, ECT is sometimes recommended for people who experience very severe episodes of depression.

A breakthrough in the treatment of schizophrenia came during the 1950s with the introduction of several drugs that relieved symptoms in many people (Lehmann & Ban, 1997; Potkin et al., 1993). Called neuroleptics (meaning "taking hold of the nerves"), these medications provided the first real hope that help was available for people with schizophrenia. The late psychiatrist Heinz Lehmann of McGill University is credited by many (e.g., Dongier, 1999) with introducing neuroleptic medications for the treatment of schizophrenia to North America. Lehmann conducted a study demonstrating the effectiveness of chlorpromazine with about 200 patients who had schizophrenia at the Douglas Hospital in Montréal (Lehmann & Hanrahan, 1954). When they are effective, neuroleptics help people think more clearly and reduce or eliminate hallucinations and delusions. They work by affecting the positive symptoms (delusions, hallucinations, agitation) and to a lesser extent the negative and disorganized ones, such as social deficits. Table 13.1 shows the classes of these drugs (based on their chemical structure) and their trade names (Potkin et al., 1993).

Recall from our discussion of the dopamine theory of

Courtesy of Douglas Hospital, Montreal

▲ The late psychiatrist Heinz Lehmann is credited with introducing neuroleptic medications in the treatment of schizophrenia to North America in the 1950s. During his influential career, Lehmann was employed at the Douglas Hospital and McGill University in Montréal.

TABLE 13.1 Antipsychotic Medications

Class	Example*	Degree of Extrapyramidal Side Effects
Conventional Antipsychotics		
Phenothiazines		
	Fluphenazine/*Prolixin*	High
	Trifluoperazine/*Stelazine*	High
	Perphenazine/*Trilafon*	High
	Mesoridazine/*Serentil*	Low
	Chlorpromazine/*Thorazine*	Moderate
	Thioridazine/*Mellaril*	Low
Butyrophenone	Haloperidol/*Haldol*	High
Others		
	Thiothixene/*Navane*	High
	Molindone/*Moban*	Low
	Loxapine/*Loxitane*	High
New Antipsychotics		
	Clozapine/*Clozaril*	Low
	Risperidone/*Risperdal*	Low
	Olanzapine/*Zyprexa*	Low
	Sertindole/*Serlect*	Low
	Quetiapine/*Seroquel*	Low

Note: * The trade names are in italics.

Source: The American Journal of Psychiatry by American Psychiatric Association. Copyright 1997. Reproduced with permission of AMERICAN PSYCHIATRIC ASSOCIATION (JOURNALS) in the format Textbook via Copyright Clearance Center.

schizophrenia that the neuroleptics are dopamine antagonists. One of their major actions in the brain is to interfere with the dopamine neurotransmitter system. However, they can also affect other systems, such as the serotonergic system. We are just beginning to understand the mechanisms by which these drugs work.

In general, each drug is effective with some people and not with others. Clinicians and patients often must go through a trial-and-error process to find the medication that works best, and some individuals do not benefit significantly from any of them. The earliest neuroleptic drugs, called conventional antipsychotics, are effective for approximately 60 percent of persons who try them (American Psychiatric Association, 2000b). However, many people are not helped by antipsychotics or experience unpleasant side effects. Fortunately, some people respond well to newer medications; the most common are clozapine, risperidone, and olanzapine. First marketed in 1990, clozapine is now used widely, and risperidone and other newer drugs hold promise for helping patients who were previously unresponsive to medications (American Psychiatric Association, 2000b; Iskedjian, Hux, & Remington, 1998;

Malla, Norman, Scholten, Zirul, & Kotteda, 2001; Wahlbeck et al., 1999). These newer antipsychotics are now prescribed to more than three-quarters of patients with schizophrenia in Canada (Smith et al., 2006). They tend to have fewer serious side effects than the conventional antipsychotics (Black & Andreasen, 1999; Levy, Margolese, Annable, & Chouinard, 2004). In fact, evidence from Howard Margolese and colleagues at McGill University shows that treatment with these newer antipsychotics can reduce the severity of long-standing *tardive dyskinesia* (Margolese et al., 2005).

There is also some limited evidence that these newer antipsychotics may also be more effective than conventional antipsychotics in reducing both negative and positive symptoms (e.g., Chouinard et al., 1993). For example, University of Montréal researcher Emmanuel Stip and his colleagues have recently shown that the newer antipsychotic, quetiapine, may be effective in treating the negative symptom of flat affect (Stip et al., 2005). Moreover, research by Kimberly Good and colleagues at Dalhousie University provides preliminary evidence that these newer medications may be helpful in improving cognitive functioning, at least among patients experiencing their first episode of psychosis (Good et al., 2002; Kopala et al., 2006).

Despite the optimism generated by the effectiveness of antipsychotics, they work only when they are taken properly, and many people with schizophrenia do not routinely take their medication. David frequently "cheeked" the Haldol pills that were helpful in reducing his hallucinations, holding them in his mouth until he was alone, then spitting them out. Approximately 7 percent of the people prescribed antipsychotic medication refuse to take it at all (Hoge et al., 1990). Research on the prevalence of occasional noncompliance suggests that a majority of people with schizophrenia stop taking their medication periodically. A follow-up study, for example, found that over a two-year period, three out of four patients studied refused to take their antipsychotic medication for at least one week (Weiden et al., 1991).

Several factors seem to be related to patients' noncompliance with a medication regimen, including negative doctor–patient relationships, cost of the medication, and poor social support (Weiden et al., 1991). Not surprisingly, negative side effects are a major factor in patient refusal. Antipsychotics can produce a number of unwanted physical symptoms, such as grogginess, blurred vision, and dryness of the mouth. Because the drugs affect neurotransmitter systems, more serious side effects, called *extrapyramidal symptoms*, can also result (Umbricht & Kane, 1996). These symptoms include the motor difficulties similar to those experienced by people with Parkinson's disease, sometimes called *parkinsonian symptoms* (Lévy et al., 2004). *Akinesia* is one of the most common; it includes an expressionless face, slow motor activity, and monotonous speech (Blanchard & Neale, 1992). Another extrapyramidal symptom is *tardive dyskinesia*, which involves involuntary movements of the tongue, face, mouth, or jaw, and can include protrusions of the tongue, puffing of the cheeks, puckering of the mouth, and chewing movements. Tardive dyskinesia seems to result from long-term use of high doses of antipsychotic medication and is often irreversible. During the first five years of use, 3 percent to 5 percent of people taking this medication display tardive dyskinesia, with the risk increasing over time (Kane, 2006). These serious negative side effects have justifiably concerned people who otherwise benefit from the drugs.

To learn what patients themselves say, Windgassen (1992) questioned 61 people who had had recent onsets of schizophrenia. About half reported the feeling of sedation or grogginess as an unpleasant side effect: "I always have to fight to keep my eyes open," "I felt as though I was on drugs ... drowsy, and yet really wound up" (p. 407). Other complaints included deterioration in the ability to think or concentrate (18 percent), problems with salivation (16 percent), and blurred vision (16 percent). Although a third of the patients felt the medications were beneficial, about 25 percent had a negative attitude toward them. A significant number of people who could benefit from antipsychotic medications find them unacceptable as a treatment, which may explain the relatively high rates of refusal and noncompliance (Pratt, Mueser, Driscoll, Wolfe, & Bartels, 2006; Yamada et al., 2006).

Concept Check | 13.4

Read the descriptions and then match them to the following words: (a) clozapine, (b) extrapyramidal symptoms, (c) serotonin, and (d) dopamine.

1. Recent studies sometimes indicate that the relationship of the neurotransmitters _____ and _____ may explain some of the positive symptoms of schizophrenia.

2. Difficult cases of schizophrenia seem to improve with a serotonin and dopamine antagonist called

   _____.

3. Because antipsychotic medication may cause serious side effects, some patients stop taking them. One serious side effect is called _____, which may have parkinsonian symptoms.

▲ One of the major obstacles to drug treatment for schizophrenia is compliance. Patients discontinue their medication for a variety of reasons, including the negative side effects.

Researchers have made this a major treatment issue in schizophrenia, realizing that medications can't be successful if they aren't taken regularly. Clinicians hoped that the new antipsychotics such as clozapine, which produce fewer negative side effects, would allay some legitimate concerns. However, even clozapine produces undesirable effects, and its use must be monitored closely to avoid rare effects that are potentially life threatening (Umbricht & Kane, 1996). Researchers hoped that compliance rates would improve with the introduction of injectable medications. Instead of taking an oral antipsychotic every day, patients can have their medications injected every few weeks. Unfortunately, noncompliance remains an issue, primarily because patients do not return to the hospital or clinic for repeated doses (Kane, Stroup, & Marder, 2009). Psychosocial interventions are now used not only to treat schizophrenia but also to increase medication-taking compliance by helping patients communicate better with professionals about their concerns.

An interesting, but as yet not well-validated, treatment for the hallucinations experienced by many persons with schizophrenia involves exposing the individual to magnetic fields. Called *transcranial magnetic stimulation* (TMS), this technique uses wire coils to repeatedly generate magnetic fields—up to 50 times per second—that pass through the skull to the brain (see review by Daskalakis, Christensen, Fitzgerald, & Chen, 2002). This input seems to interrupt the normal communication temporarily to that part of the brain. Hoffman and colleagues (2000) used this technique to stimulate the area of the brain involved in hallucinations for 12 individuals with schizophrenia who experienced auditory hallucinations. They found that many of the individuals experienced improvement following transcranial magnetic stimulation. Again, more research is required to assess the true value of this technique for people with hallucinations. A more recent study by Jeff Daskalakis at the Centre for Addiction and Mental Health in Toronto and his colleagues produced less promising results. They investigated whether TMS could help individuals with treatment-resistant auditory hallucinations. Unfortunately, TMS was generally ineffective in treating the auditory hallucinations except in decreasing their loudness (Fitzgerald et al., 2005).

Psychosocial Interventions

Historically, a number of psychosocial treatments have been tried for schizophrenia, reflecting the belief that the disorder results from problems in adapting to the world because of early experiences (Tenhula, Bellack, & Drake, 2009). Many therapists have thought that individuals who could achieve insight into the presumed role of their personal histories could be safely led to deal with their existing situations. Although clinicians who take a psychodynamic or psychoanalytic approach to therapy continue to use this type of treatment, research suggests that their efforts at best may not be beneficial and at worst may be harmful (Mueser & Berenbaum, 1990; Scott & Dixon, 1995b).

Using Virtual Reality in Assessment and Treatment

Is there a role for new technologies in the diagnosis and treatment of schizophrenia? Creative researchers are answering this question in a number of exciting developments for the field. One study looked to improve the understanding of schizophrenia by using virtual reality technology to simulate multiple cognitive tasks (Sorkin, Weinshall, Modai, & Peled, 2006). Researchers created a gamelike task to test aspects of working memory and perseveration (focusing on the same things repeatedly) and found not only that this approach could create real-life simulations that revealed deficits but also that the tasks could be fun. A study carried out at King's College in London, England, tested the nature of paranoia in a virtual reality environment among groups with low paranoia, nonclinical paranoia, and those with persecutory delusions (Freeman, Pugh, Vorontsova, Antley, & Slater, 2010). Researchers constructed a virtual scene that depicts a London subway and created avatars as passengers that at times would look at the study participant (see accompanying photos).

Across the groups there were meaningful differences in levels of anxiety, worry, interpersonal sensitivity, and depression according to their previous levels of paranoia. This type of assessment provided a safe environment in which to assess and study persecutory paranoia in the groups. Other research is using this technology to assist older persons with schizophrenia improve their cognitive and general motor skills (e.g., by having them push away colourful balls that are floating toward them in a virtual world) (Chan, Ngai, Leung, & Wong, 2010). Again, these virtual assessments and treatments provide clinicians with controllable and safer environments in which to study and treat persons with schizophrenia.

▲ Researchers are using virtual reality technology to better understand the complexity of schizophrenia. The photo at the top illustrates a participant in a study of paranoia. The bottom photo shows what the participants see. This technology allows researchers to closely control positions and facial expressions of the virtual people on the train.

Today, few believe that psychological factors cause people to have schizophrenia or that traditional psychotherapeutic approaches will cure them. We will see, however, that psychological methods do have an important role (American Psychiatric Association, 2000b). Despite the great promise of drug treatment, the problems with ineffectiveness, inconsistent use, and relapse suggest that, by themselves, drugs may not be effective with many people. As with several other disorders discussed in this text, recent work in the area of psychosocial intervention has suggested the value of an approach that uses both kinds of treatment (Mueser & Marcello, 2010; Tarrier et al., 1999, 2000).

Until relatively recently, most people with severe and chronic cases of schizophrenia were treated in hospital settings. During the 19th century, inpatient care involved "moral treatment," which emphasized improving patients' socialization, helping them establish routines for self-control, and showing them the value of work and religion (Tenhula et al., 2009). Various types of such "milieu" treatment have been popular but, with one important exception, none seems to have helped people with schizophrenia (Tucker, Ferrell, & Price, 1984).

In the 1970s, Gordon Paul and Robert Lentz (1977) conducted pioneering work that borrowed from the behavioural approaches used by Ted Ayllon and Nate Azrin (1968). Paul and Lentz designed an environment for inpatients that encouraged appropriate socialization, participation in group sessions, and self-care such as bed-making, while discouraging violent outbursts. They set up an elaborate **token economy**, in which residents could earn access to meals and small luxuries by behaving appropriately. A patient could, for example, buy cigarettes with the tokens earned for keeping his or her room neat. Conversely, a patient would be fined (lose tokens) for being disruptive or otherwise acting inappropriately. This incentive system was combined with a full schedule of daily activities. Paul and Lentz compared the effectiveness of applied behavioural (or social learning) principles with traditional inpatient environments. In general, they found that patients who went through their program did better than others on social, self-care, and vocational skills, and more of them could be discharged from the hospital. This study was one of the first to show that people experiencing the debilitating effects of schizophrenia can learn to perform some of the skills they need to live more independently.

Since 1955, many efforts have combined to halt the routine institutionalization of people with schizophrenia in both Canada and the United States (Bachrach, 1994; Barnes & Toews, 1983; Talbott, 1990). This trend has occurred in part because of court rulings that limit involuntary hospitalization (as we saw in Arthur's case), in part because of the relative success of antipsychotic medication and in part because of fiscal crisis and ensuing cutbacks in health care (Hanna, 2001). In Canada, provincial mental hospitals released thousands of patients and closed down more than 32 500 beds between 1960 and 1976, and this trend continues to the present day (Nichols, 1995). The bad news is that policies of deinstitutionalization have often been ill conceived, so that the process has sometimes resulted in problems (Barnes & Toews, 1983). For example, as a consequence of deinstitutionalization, many people who have schizophrenia or other serious psychological disorders are homeless (e.g., Stuart & Arboleda-Florez, 2000). See Chapter 16 for an in-depth discussion of the problem of homelessness in Canada and of the relation of deinstitutionalization to homelessness. As another example, women (and other family members) are increasingly expected to bear the burden of caring for a family member who has a mental illness (Hanna, 2001). The good news is that more attention is being focused on supporting these people in their communities, among their friends and families (Richman & Harris, 1982–1983; Uditsky, 1994). In fact, when adequate community support is provided, these people fare no worse and sometimes fare better in the community than in institutions (Barnes & Toews, 1983). Thus, the trend is away from creating better hospital environments and toward the perhaps more difficult task of addressing complex problems in the less predictable and insecure world outside. So far, only a small fraction of the growing number of homeless individuals with mental disorders are being helped.

One of the more insidious effects of schizophrenia is its negative impact on a person's ability to relate to other people. Although not as dramatic as hallucinations and delusions, this problem can be the most visible impairment displayed by people with schizophrenia and can prevent them from getting and keeping jobs and making friends. Clinicians attempt to reteach social skills such as basic conversation, assertiveness, and relationship building to people with schizophrenia (Dobson,

▲ A mother is glad to have her daughter home from a psychiatric hospital, but she acknowledges that "now the real struggle begins."

McDougall, Busheikin, & Aldous, 1995; Mueser & Marcello, 2010; Smith, Bellack, & Liberman, 1996).

Therapists divide complex social skills into their component parts, which they model. Then the clients role-play and ultimately practise their new skills in the "real world," all the while receiving feedback and encouragement at signs of progress. This isn't as easy as it may sound. For example, how would you teach someone to make a friend? Many skills are involved, such as maintaining eye contact when you talk to someone and providing the prospective friend with some (but not too much!) positive feedback on his or her own behaviour ("I really enjoy talking to you"). Such individual skills are practised and then combined until they can be used naturally (Swartz, Lauriello, & Drake, 2006). Basic skills can be taught to people with schizophrenia, but there is some disagreement about how ultimately successful the treatment is (Bellack & Mueser, 1992; Hogarty et al., 1992). The problem is that the positive results of social skills training may fade after the training is over (Scott & Dixon, 1995b). The challenge of teaching social skills, as with all therapies, is to maintain the effects over a long time.

In addition to social skills, programs often teach a range of ways that people can adapt to their disorder yet still live in the community. In the Independent Living Skills Program developed by Eckman and colleagues (1992), the focus is on helping people take charge of their own care by such methods as identifying signs that warn of a relapse and learning how to manage their medication (Corrigan, Wallace, Schade, & Green, 1994; Eckman et al., 1992). Preliminary evidence indicates that this type of training may help prevent the relapses of people with schizophrenia. For example, Ross Norman and his colleagues at the University of Western Ontario added a stress-management intervention to an existing medical and psychosocial treatment program for individuals with schizophrenia. Patients who participated in the stress management program had fewer hospitalizations in the following year, particularly those who showed a high level of attendance at treatment sessions (Norman et al., 2002). Longer-term outcome research is needed to see how long these effects last. To address some of the obstacles to this much-desired maintenance, such programs combine skills training with the support of a multidisciplinary team that provides services directly in the community, which seems to reduce hospitalization (Scott & Dixon, 1995a). The more time and effort given to these services, the more likely the improvement (Brekke, Long, Nesbitt, & Sobell, 1997).

In our discussion of the psychosocial influences on schizophrenia, we reviewed some of the work linking the person's social and emotional environments to the recurrence of schizophrenic episodes (McNab, Haslam, & Burnett 2007). It is logical to ask whether families could be helped by learning to reduce their level of expressed emotion, and whether this would result in fewer relapses and better overall functioning for people with schizophrenia. Several studies have addressed these issues in a variety of ways (Falloon et al., 1985; Hogarty et al., 1986; Hogarty et al., 1991), and behavioural family therapy has been used to teach the families of persons with schizophrenia to be more supportive (Dixon & Lehman, 1995; Mueser, Liberman, & Glynn, 1990). Research on professionals who provide care for people who have schizophrenia, and who may also display high levels of expressed emotion, is also an active area of study (Barrowclough & Tarrier, 1998; Tattan & Tarrier, 2000).

In contrast to traditional therapy, behavioural family therapy resembles classroom education (Lefley, 2009). Family members are informed about schizophrenia and its treatment, relieved of the myth that they caused the disorder, and taught practical facts about antipsychotic medications and their side effects. They are also helped with communication skills so they can become more empathic listeners, and they learn constructive ways of expressing negative feelings to replace the harsh criticism that characterizes some family interactions. In addition, they learn problem-solving skills to help them resolve conflicts that arise. Like the research on social skills training, outcome research suggests that the effects of behavioural family therapy are significant during the first year, but less robust two years after intervention (Montero, Masanet, Bellver, & Lacruz, 2006; Montero et al., 2005). This type of therapy, therefore, must be ongoing if patients and their families are to benefit from it.

Adults with schizophrenia face great obstacles to maintaining gainful employment. Their social skills deficits make reliable job performance and adequate employee relationships a struggle. To address these difficulties, some programs focus on vocational rehabilitation, such as supportive employment (Bustillo, Lauriello, Horan, & Keith, 2001). Providing coaches who give on-the-job training may help some people with schizophrenia maintain meaningful jobs (Bond, Drake, Mueser, & Becker, 1997; Drake, McHugo, Becker, Anthony, & Clark, 1996; Lehman, 1995). Social skills training, family intervention, and vocational rehabilitation may be helpful additions to biological treatments for schizophrenia, in terms of avoiding or delaying relapse. A review by Falloon, Brooker, and Graham-Hole (1992) showed that multi-level treatments reduce the number of relapses among persons receiving drug therapy in comparison with simple social support or educational efforts (see ■ Figure 13.7).

A general trend in the treatment of schizophrenia today is toward early intervention. It is increasingly becoming recognized that intervening early can be important in affecting the course of the disorder over time. Getting help in the early stages of the illness is critical. In fact, research has shown that getting patients onto the right medications and into effective psychotherapy as

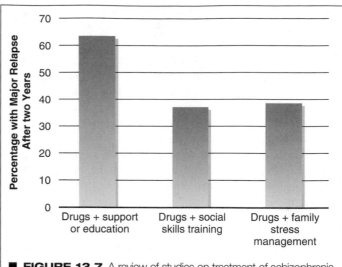

■ **FIGURE 13.7** A review of studies on treatment of schizophrenia

Source: Adapted from "Psychosocial interventions for schizophrenia" by I. R. H. Falloon, C. Brooker, & V. Graham-Hole, 1992, *Behavior Change, 9,* 238–245.

soon as possible, and providing information and support to affected families right away, can actually reduce the severity of future relapses (e.g., Drury, Birchwood, Cochrane, & MacMillan, 1996). The key elements of early intervention are outlined in Table 13.2. Early psychosis clinical programs have now been developed at 11 sites across Canada (e.g., Halifax, Toronto, London, Hamilton, and Calgary; Lines, 2001). The first such centre, the First Episode Psychosis Clinic/Early Psychosis Unit, was developed at the Centre for Addiction and Mental Health in Toronto (Nichols, 1995). It is designed to meet the needs of individuals experiencing a first episode of psychosis and assists such individuals and their families with the initial period of adjustment and recovery. The clinic provides a full assessment and psychosocial intervention to help such patients on an outpatient basis; inpatient services are also available. Priority is given to adults (aged 18 to 45) who have not yet received any antipsychotic treatment. (More information can be found at http://www.camh.net/About_CAMH/Guide_to_CAMH/Mental_Health_Programs/Schizophrenia_Program/guide_first_episode_program.html.)

A relatively newer approach to the treatment of schizophrenia that has been applied over the past 15 years is cognitive-behavioural therapy (CBT; see reviews by Bouchard et al., 1996; Norman & Townsend, 1999; Rector & Beck, 2001). For example, British researchers David Kingdon and Douglas Turkington (1994) argue that people with schizophrenia are not inherently irrational, but instead have a particular set of irrational beliefs that are amenable to intervention with cognitive and behavioural techniques. CBT has usually been applied to auditory hallucinations and delusions (i.e., positive symptoms; Birchwood et al., 1994; Norman & Townsend, 1999), although CBT strategies have been developed to treat both positive and negative symptoms (Beck & Rector, 2000). CBT strategies developed to treat symptoms of schizophrenia are essentially adaptations of CBT strategies successfully used in the treatment of depression and anxiety (Rector & Beck, 2002). Take the following case example described by clinical psychologist Neil Rector—a case that was treated by Aaron Beck over 50 years ago, in the first application of CBT to the treatment of delusions (Rector & Beck, 2002).

TABLE 13.2 Key Elements of Early Intervention

- Reduction of duration of untreated psychosis (DUP) through education. Raising psychosis awareness through educational initiatives with health professionals, teachers, families, and community members is a necessary step towards the reduction of DUP.

- Assessment and the context of care: building a therapeutic alliance. Once a psychosis is suspected, careful and comprehensive assessment of the individual by skilled professionals is the next step. For many, this will be the individual's first contact with the mental health system. This situation provides a significant opportunity for practitioners to begin to develop a positive, honest, mutually respectful relationship—a "therapeutic alliance"—with the young client and his or her family.

- Family engagement and support. Most young people experiencing psychosis for the first time are living in the family home. The family can play a significant role in promoting the recovery of their family member. But, in order to do so, the family also requires education, support, and inclusion in the therapeutic process.

- Comprehensive, phase-specific, individualized treatment including low-dose antipsychotic medications, psychoeducation, and psychosocial support. These three main components, when offered in the context of a therapeutic alliance with an attitude of "realistic optimism" are demonstrating positive outcomes in the lives of young people who experience psychosis.

- Prolonged engagement to sustain gains. Psychosis is a serious physiological event. Recovery takes time. Early psychosis intervention, even at its best, is not a magic bullet. Clients may need to receive services on an outpatient basis from an early psychosis clinical program for two years or more.

Source: Adapted from "Youth and Mental Illness: Early Intervention Project," an initiative of the CMHA National Office.

THOMAS | *Examining the Evidence for a Conspiracy*

At the time he was seen by Beck, Thomas was a 28-year-old veteran of World War II who presented with a paranoid delusion that he had held for the last seven years. When he returned home from the war, he came to believe that members of his unit in the armed forces were working secretly with the government to monitor his activities. In treatment, Beck worked with Thomas to help him identify the antecedents or triggers of his delusional beliefs and to apply this knowledge to his current delusional system. Thomas's misperceptions of everyday events that were taken as evidence of this conspiracy (e.g., a stranger looking at him while he was on the bus) were identified by the therapist and gently questioned. The repeated questioning and testing of alternative explanations for such everyday events eventually led to changes in Thomas's beliefs. By the end of therapy, every time Thomas began to become suspicious that he was being watched, he was able to stand back and reason himself out of his erroneous thinking patterns. Thomas was taught to carefully question the evidence that supported his delusion both in the therapy session and between sessions. Through this careful examination of the evidence, he was eventually able to see his delusions as "hypotheses" about the meaning of things that happened in his life rather than as absolute, rigid "truths."

Source: Adapted from Rector, N. A., & Beck, A. T. (2002). "Cognitive Therapy for Schizophrenia: From Conceptualization to Intervention." *Canadian Journal of Psychiatry, 47:*39–48.

In the following excerpt, a patient from the Royal Ottawa Hospital, J. P. Lee, who has been living with schizophrenia for 20 years, describes how he learned to use CBT to effectively challenge his delusional paranoid thoughts:

> I will attempt to describe [a] scenario where I used CBT to modify the sequence of [my] reactions.... My stimulating problematic thought may be that I am suspicious that my friends may be secretly criticizing and ridiculing me and doing that in my presence using cryptic language with each other. My interpretation is that my friends don't really like me and my reaction is one of resentment of this behavior. The consequence is that I am angry at my friends and choose not to socialize so much with them. Having recognized this pattern, I now attempt CBT. I will respond ... with a different interpretation and reaction.... I will consider as a real possibility that my friends have not been ridiculing me using cryptic language. I will try harder not to sink into my paranoia but instead talk and interact with them and engage more enthusiastically with the activities at hand.... The consequence is that I am no longer angry but more in synchrony with my friends. Having done one CBT exercise, I can mentally rehearse my way through future potential problematic/delusional thoughts in order to bypass the ravages of paranoid thinking. The next time when such stimuli trigger my mind I can quickly recognize the pattern and ... relieve myself of confusion and harmful emotions. Hence, I am in charge of my symptoms, I am free from the strangulation of mental processes by excessive medication, and I am also free from the control of delusional thoughts. (Lee, 2005, p. 74)

Despite a good deal of initial skepticism as to whether symptoms of a disorder with such a strong physiological basis could be amenable to "talk therapy" (e.g., Patience, 1994, versus John, Turkington, & Kingdon, 1994), more recent reviews of the literature are unanimous in supporting the potential of this approach in the treatment of patients with schizophrenia. For example, in a review of the literature conducted with CBT developer Aaron Beck, University of Toronto psychologist Neil Rector found that CBT produces large clinical effects on both positive and negative symptoms of schizophrenia (Rector & Beck, 2001). In one such study by Rector and his colleagues, 42 patients with schizophrenia were randomly assigned to either a treatment-as-usual control condition (i.e., specialized schizophrenia treatment services) or to treatment as usual with an additional 20 sessions of CBT. For patients in the experimental group receiving adjunctive CBT, significant benefits of treatment were observed at a six-month follow-up for positive symptoms, negative symptoms, and overall severity of the disorder. The most pronounced effect of the addition of CBT relative to the treatment-as-usual control group was in the reduction of negative symptoms at follow-up (Rector, Seeman, & Segal, 2003). In another example, Garety and colleagues at the Institute of Psychiatry in London, England, reported excellent outcome of a controlled trial of CBT for patients with schizophrenia who had not responded well to drug treatment in the past. They found that the treatment group improved more than the controls on the degree of conviction in their delusional beliefs, the severity of their overall symptoms, and their depression levels (Garety Kuipers, Fowler, Chamberlain, & Dunn, 1994). Results such as these suggest promise for the impact of CBT in the treatment of schizophrenia.

Courtesy of Neil A. Rector

▲ Neil Rector of the Centre for Addiction and Mental Health and the University of Toronto has worked closely with cognitive-behavioural therapy (CBT) originator Aaron Beck to develop and test the efficacy of CBT in the treatment of schizophrenia.

The locus of treatment has expanded over the years from locked wards in large mental hospitals to family homes to local communities. In addition, the services have expanded to include self-advocacy and self-help groups. Former patients have organized programs to provide mutual support (Beard, Propst, & Malamud, 1982). Psychosocial clubs have differing models, but all are "person centred" and focus on obtaining positive experiences through employment opportunities, friendship, and empowerment. Some research indicates that participation in such programs may help reduce relapses (Beard, Malamud, & Rossman, 1978), but as it is also possible that those who participate may be a special group of individuals, it is difficult to interpret improvements (Mueser et al., 1990).

Treatment across Cultures

Treatment of schizophrenia and its delivery differ from one country to another and across cultures within countries. In China, for example, the most frequently used treatment is antipsychotic medication, although 7 percent to 9 percent of patients also receive traditional herbal medicine and acupuncture (Mingdao & Zhenyi, 1990). For financial and cultural reasons, more people in China are treated outside the hospital than are in Western societies. The vast majority of the Xhosa people of South Africa who have schizophrenia report using traditional healers who sometimes recommend the use of oral treatments to induce vomiting, enemas, and the slaughter of cattle to appease the spirits (Koen, Niehaus, Muller, & Laurent, 2008). In one interesting study, beliefs about symptoms and treatments were compared between British and Chinese populations (Furnham & Wong, 2007). Native Chinese hold more religious beliefs about both the causes and the treatments of schizophrenia than those living in England—for example, endorsing statements such as, "Schizophrenia is due to evil done in a previous life" and "Ancestor worship (burning candles and joss sticks) will help treat schizophrenia." These different beliefs translate into practice—with the British using more biological, psychological, and community treatments and the Chinese relying more on alternative medicine (Furnham & Wong, 2007). Supernatural beliefs about the cause of schizophrenia among family members in Bali lead to limited use of antipsychotic medication in treatment (Kurihara, Kato, Reverger, & Gusti Rai Tirta, 2006). In many countries in Africa, people with schizophrenia are kept in prisons, primarily because of the lack of adequate alternatives (Mustafa, 1990). In general, the movement from housing people in large institutional settings to community care is ongoing in most Western countries.

Prevention

One strategy for preventing a disorder such as schizophrenia—which typically first shows itself in early adulthood—is to identify and treat children who may be at risk for getting the disorder later in life. In our discussion of genetics, we noted that approximately 13 percent of the children born to parents who have schizophrenia are likely themselves to develop the disorder. These high-risk children have been the focus of several studies, both *prospective* (before and during an expected situation) and longitudinal (over long periods).

A classic at-risk study was initiated in the 1960s by Mednick and Schulsinger (1965, 1968) in Denmark. They identified 207 Danish children of mothers who had severe cases of schizophrenia and 104 control children born to mothers who had no history of the disorder. The average age of these children was about 15 when they were first identified, and the researchers followed them for ten more years to determine whether any factors had predicted who would and would not develop schizophrenia. We have already discussed pregnancy and delivery-related complications. Mednick and Schulsinger also identified *instability of the early family-rearing environment,* which suggests that environmental influences may trigger the onset of schizophrenia (Cannon et al., 1991). Poor parenting may place additional strain on a vulnerable person who is already at risk. When the at-risk children in the Danish study enter middle age, we will know the eventual outcomes for all of them; until then we cannot draw strong conclusions from the study (Mirsky, 1995).

As we await the outcomes of long-term studies, other approaches may prove valuable for reducing the rates of this disorder. For example, we have seen that factors such as birth complications and certain early illnesses (e.g., viruses) may trigger the onset of schizophrenia, especially among those individuals who are genetically predisposed. Therefore, interventions such as vaccinations against viruses for women of childbearing age and interventions related to improving prenatal nutrition and care may be effective preventive measures (McGrath, 2010).

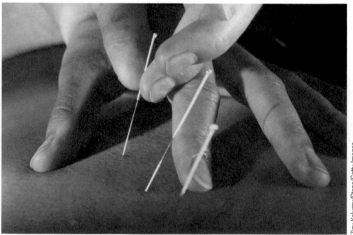

Zigy Kaluzny/Stone/Getty Images

▲ In China, acupuncture and herbal medicine are often used with antipsychotic medications for schizophrenia.

On Second Thought: Eliminating Paranoid Delusions in Schizophrenia
by Robert K. Chapman

For Robert K. Chapman, entering his 20s did not herald the beginning of exciting new adult pursuits, but rather the onset of symptoms of a major mental illness. Specifically, he was diagnosed with the paranoid type of schizophrenia. He struggled with this illness for more than a decade.

On Second Thought is a personal account of Chapman's struggles with many of the classic symptoms of paranoid schizophrenia. For example, he experienced delusions of influence, telepathy-like delusions of persecution, and problems with reality monitoring. Chapman also believed that his thoughts were being transmitted and that others could read his mind.

Not only does Chapman provide a lucid (and often humorous) account of his illness, but he also provides the reader with insights into the continuing social stigma associated with schizophrenia. He illustrates with examples from his own experience how people who have been diagnosed with this illness can be subject to such stigma, even after they have recovered. For Chapman, after he had recovered from schizophrenia, it took another two years to recuperate from the negative effects of the social stigma attached to mental illness.

Robert Chapman is now fully recovered from schizophrenia and resides in Ontario. He has been off antipsychotic medications for more than 15 years. His book contains a strong message of hope for those who have this disorder, their family members, and even for mental health professionals who work with clients who have schizophrenia. *On Second Thought* is largely a personal account of his courageous journey to full recovery. Chapman clearly describes how he made use of cognitive-behavioural therapy techniques to eliminate his paranoid delusions.

Having successfully employed cognitive-behavioural techniques to combat his illness, Chapman is dedicated to bringing a message of hope to others who are enduring this devastating disorder. In addition to *On Second Thought*, he has written, researched, and illustrated several books on this subject. He also provides workshops and lectures at which he speaks about how he eliminated his paranoid delusions using cognitive-behavioural coping strategies such as counterarguing against mind-reading ideas. He has given presentations from Ottawa, Ontario, to Oakland, California. A study conducted by researchers at McMaster University provides objective evidence that Chapman's message inspires hope for recovery among those who have schizophrenia. Specifically, the study showed that having a consumer like Chapman speak about cognitive-behavioural therapy is more effective in instilling hope for recovery than is having a mental health professional provide the same type of lecture (Zacharias, Goldberg, & Chapman, 1997).

Source and photo: From On Second Though: Eliminating Paranoid Delusions in Schizophrenia *by Robert K. Chapman, 1999. Reprinted with permission of Chapman Graphics.*

On the Spectrum

Emerging Views of Schizophrenia

Although the *DSM-IV-TR* does not use this language, there is a recognition in the field of schizophrenia that the group of diagnoses that we cover in this chapter (and in others) constitute *schizophrenia spectrum disorders*. In fact, Eugen Bleuler, who coined the term *schizophrenia* in his book *Dementia Praecox or the Group of Schizophrenias* (1911), identified the different variants that were all included within this spectrum (Heckers, 2009). The *DSM* has struggled with this concept in its varied presentations over the years, and, as we describe in this chapter, the *DSM-IV-TR* currently lists five subtypes of schizophrenia (paranoid, disorganized, catatonic, undifferentiated, and residual) as well as other related psychotic disorders that fall under this heading (schizophreniform, schizoaffective, delusional, brief psychotic, and shared psychotic disorders). In addition, a personality disorder (schizotypal personality disorder, discussed in Chapter 12) and possibly two mood disorders (psychotic bipolar disorder and psychotic depression) are also considered by some to be included under this umbrella category of schizophrenia spectrum disorders. All of these difficulties seem to share features of extreme reality distortion (e.g., hallucinations and delusions).

Discussions for the *DSM-5* include the possible removal of the subtypes of schizophrenia and instead adding a dimensional rating for some of the core symptoms of schizophrenia (American Psychiatric Association, 2010). For example, one possibility being discussed is to rate the extent to which an individual has and is distressed by the following dimensions: hallucinations, delusions, disorganization, abnormal psychomotor behaviour, restricted emotional expression, avolition, impaired cognition, depression, and mania. This would allow clinicians the ability to provide a richer description of the complex problems faced by an individual that often go unspecified within single labels (e.g., paranoid schizophrenia) that people are assigned. What is required is a thorough study of the soundness of these types of dimensional structures and a determination of whether or not they represent valid diagnoses.

Summary

Clinical Description, Symptoms, and Subtypes

- Schizophrenia is characterized by a broad spectrum of cognitive and emotional dysfunctions that include delusions and hallucinations, disorganized speech and behaviour, and inappropriate emotions.

- The symptoms of schizophrenia can be divided into "positive," "negative," and "disorganized." Positive symptoms are active manifestations of abnormal behaviour, or an excess or distortion of normal behaviour, and include delusions and hallucinations. Negative symptoms involve deficits in normal behaviour on such dimensions as affect, speech, and motivation. Disorganized symptoms include rambling speech, erratic behaviour, and inappropriate affect.

- The *DSM-IV-TR* divides schizophrenia into five subtypes. People with the *paranoid type* of schizophrenia have prominent delusions or hallucinations while their cognitive skills and affect remain relatively intact. People with the *disorganized type* of schizophrenia tend to show marked disruption in their speech and behaviour; they also show flat or inappropriate affect. People with the *catatonic type* of schizophrenia have unusual motor responses, such as remaining in fixed positions (waxy flexibility), excessive activity, and being oppositional by remaining rigid. In addition, they display odd mannerisms with their bodies and faces, including grimacing. People who do not fit neatly into these subtypes are classified as having an *undifferentiated type* of schizophrenia. Some people who have had at least one episode of schizophrenia, but who no longer have major symptoms, are diagnosed as having the *residual type of schizophrenia.*

- Several other disorders are characterized by psychotic behaviours such as hallucinations and delusions; these include *schizophreniform disorder* (which includes people who experience the symptoms of schizophrenia for less than six months); *schizoaffective disorder* (which includes people who have symptoms of schizophrenia and who also exhibit the characteristics of mood disorders such as depression and bipolar affective disorder); *delusional disorder* (which includes people with a persistent belief that is contrary to reality, in the absence of the other characteristics of schizophrenia); *brief psychotic disorder* (which includes people with one or more positive symptoms such as delusions, hallucinations, or disorganized speech or behaviour over the course of less than a month); and *shared psychotic disorder* (which includes individuals who develop delusions simply as a result of a close relationship with a delusional individual).

Prevalence and Causes of Schizophrenia

- A number of causative factors have been implicated for schizophrenia, including genetic influences, neurotransmitter imbalances, structural damage to the brain caused by a prenatal viral infection or birth injury, and psychological stressors.

- Relapse appears to be triggered by hostile and critical family environments characterized by high expressed emotion.

Treatment of Schizophrenia

- Successful treatment for people with schizophrenia rarely includes complete recovery. However, the quality of life for these individuals can be meaningfully affected by combining antipsychotic medications with psychosocial approaches, employment support, and community-based and family interventions.

- Treatment typically involves antipsychotic drugs that are usually administered in combination with a variety of psychosocial treatments, with the goal of reducing relapse and improving skills in deficits and compliance in taking the medications. The effectiveness of treatment is limited, as schizophrenia is typically a chronic disorder.

Key Terms

alogia, 483

anhedonia, 483

associative splitting, 477

avolition, 482

brief psychotic disorder, 487

catatonia, 477

catatonic immobility, 484

catatonic type of
   schizophrenia, 486

delusion, 479

delusional disorder, 487

dementia praecox, 477

disorganized speech, 484

disorganized symptoms, 484

disorganized type of
   schizophrenia, 485

double bind, 498

expressed emotion (EE), 498

flat affect, 483

folie à deux, 487

hallucination, 481

hebephrenia, 477

inappropriate affect, 484

negative symptoms, 482

paranoia, 477

paranoid type of
   schizophrenia, 485

positive symptoms, 479

psychotic, 479

residual type of
   schizophrenia, 486

schizoaffective disorder, 487

schizophrenia, 477

schizophreniform disorder, 486

schizophrenogenic, 498

shared psychotic disorder, 487

token economy, 503

undifferentiated type of
   schizophrenia, 486

Answers to Concept Checks

13.1

1. delusions 2. avolition
3. affective flattening
4. hallucinations

13.2

1. paranoid 2. catatonic
3. residual 4. disorganized
5. paranoid 6. disorganized
7. undifferentiated 8. catatonic

13.3

1. d, i 2. f, a 3. a, a

13.4

1. c, d 2. a 3. b

Media Resources

CourseMate

Access an integrated eBook, Abnormal Psychology Videos (formerly Abnormal Psych Live CD-ROM), chapter-specific interactive learning tools (flashcards, quizzes, learning modules), and more in your Psychology CourseMate, available at **www.abnormalpsych3ce.nelson.com**.

Abnormal Psychology Videos

Free Abnormal Psychology videos can be viewed on the website **www.abnormalpsych3ce .nelson.com**.

- *Schizophrenia: Etta:* An example of a lower-functioning patient with schizophrenia.
- *Positive versus Negative Symptoms:* A team of clinicians describe the differences between positive and negative symptoms.
- *Common Symptoms of Schizophrenia:* A clinician reviews the most common psychotic symptoms in schizophrenia, and his discussion is interspersed with patients who exemplify these symptoms.

Video Concept Reviews

CourseMate also contains Mark Durand's *Video Concept Reviews* on these challenging topics.

- Schizophrenia
- Positive Symptoms
- Delusions
- Hallucinations
- Negative Symptoms
- Avolition, Alogia, Anhedonia and Flat Affect
- Disorganized Symptoms

- Paranoid Type of Schizophrenia
- Catatonic Type of Schizophrenia
- Delusional Disorder
- Brief Psychotic Disorder and Shared Psychotic Disorder
- Expressed Emotion and Stress
- Schizophrenia Treatment

Exploring Schizophrenia

> Schizophrenia disrupts perception of the world, thought, speech, movement, and almost every other aspect of daily functioning.

> Usually chronic with a high relapse rate; complete recovery from schizophrenia is rare.

- Stressful, traumatic life event
- High expressed emotion (family criticism, hostility, and/or intrusion)
- Sometimes no obvious trigger

Trigger

Biological Influences

- Inherited tendency (multiple genes) to develop disease
- Prenatal/birth complications—viral infection during pregnancy/birth injury affects child's brain cells
- Brain chemistry (abnormalities in the dopamine and glutamate systems)
- Brain structure (enlarged ventricles)

Social Influences

- Environment (early family experiences) can trigger onset
- Culture influences interpretation of disease/symptoms (hallucinations, delusions)

PhotoDisc/Getty Images

Causes

Dynamic Graphics

Behavioural Influences

- **Positive symptoms:**
  —Active manifestations of abnormal behaviour (delusions, hallucinations, disorganized speech, odd body movements, or catatonia)
- **Negative symptoms:**
  —Flat affect (lack of emotional expression)
  —Avolition (lack of initiative, apathy)
  —Alogia (relative absence in amount or content of speech)

Emotional and Cognitive Influences

- Interaction styles that are high in criticism, hostility, and emotional overinvolvement can trigger a relapse

TREATMENT OF SCHIZOPHRENIA

Treatment		
Individual, Group, and Family Therapy		• Can help patient and family understand the disease and symptom triggers • Teaches families communication skills • Provides resources for dealing with emotional and practical challenges
Social Skills Training		• Can occur in hospital or community settings • Teaches the person with schizophrenia social, self-care, and vocational skills

Medications		• Taking neuroleptic medications may help people with schizophrenia to:
		  —Clarify thinking and perceptions of reality
		  —Reduce hallucinations and delusions
		• Drug treatment must be consistent to be effective. Inconsistent dosage may aggravate existing symptoms or create new ones

PhotoDisc/Getty Images

SYMPTOMS OF SCHIZOPHRENIA

People with schizophrenia do not all show the same kinds of symptoms. Symptoms vary from person to person and may be cyclical. Common symptoms include:

Symptoms		
Delusions		• Unrealistic and bizarre beliefs not shared by others in the culture • May be delusions of grandeur (that you are really Mother Teresa or Napoleon) or delusions of persecution (the cyclist who believed her competitors were sabotaging her by putting pebbles in the road)
Hallucinations		• Sensory events that aren't based on any external event (hearing voices, seeing people who have died) • Many have auditory hallucinations (David hears his dead uncle talking to him)
Disorganized Speech		• Jumping from topic to topic • Talking illogically (not answering direct questions, going off on tangents) • Speaking in unintelligible words and sentences
Behavioural Problems		• Pacing excitably, wild agitation • Catatonic immobility • Waxy flexibility (keeping body parts in the same position when they are moved by someone else) • Inappropriate dress (coats in the summer, shorts in the winter) • Inappropriate affect • Ignoring personal hygiene
Withdrawal		• Lack of emotional response (flat speech, little change in facial expressions) • Apathy (little interest in day-to-day activities) • Delayed and brief responses in conversation • Loss of enjoyment in pleasurable activities (eating, socializing, sex)

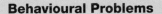

PhotoDisc/Getty Images — Corbis Canada — © Dynamic Graphics — PhotoDisc/Getty Images

TYPES OF SCHIZOPHRENIA

Paranoid	Disorganized	Catatonic	Residual	Undifferentiated
• Delusions of grandeur or persecution • Hallucinations (especially auditory) • Higher level of functioning between episodes • May have stronger familial link than other types	• Disorganized speech and/or behaviour • Immature emotionality (inappropriate affect) • Chronic and lacking in remissions	• Alternating immobility and excited agitation • Unusual motor responses (waxy flexibility, rigidity) • Odd facial or body mannerisms (often mimicking others) • Rare	• Has had at least one schizophrenic episode but no longer shows major symptoms • Still shows "leftover" symptoms (social withdrawal, bizarre thoughts, inactivity, flat affect)	• Symptoms of several types that taken together do not neatly fall into one specific category

14 | Developmental Disorders

© moodboard/Corbis

*Staring into nothingness since time began,
There and yet not there she stood.
In a world of dreams, shadows, and fantasy,
Nothing more complex than colour and indiscernible sound.
With the look of an angel no doubt,
But also without the ability to love or
Feel anything more complex than the sensation of cat's fur
Against her face.*

—Australian author Donna Williams, *Nobody Nowhere: The Extraordinary
Autobiography of an Autistic*

Demonstrate knowledge and understanding representing appropriate breadth and depth in selected content areas of psychology:	› Biological bases of behaviour and mental processes, including physiology, sensation, perception, comparative, motivation, and emotion (APA SLO 1.2.a (3)) *(see textbook pages 536–539)*
Use the concepts, language, and major theories of the discipline to account for psychological phenomena.	› Describe behaviour and mental processes empirically, including operational definitions (APA SLO 1.3.a) *(see textbook pages 514–517, 520, 524–528, 533–536)*
Identify appropriate applications of psychology in solving problems, such as:	› Origin and treatment of abnormal behaviour (APA SLO 4.2.b) *(see textbook pages 517–520, 522–524, 529–533, 536–540)*

* Portions of this chapter cover learning outcomes suggested by the American Psychological Association (2007) in their guidelines for the undergraduate psychology major. Chapter coverage of these outcomes is identified above by APA Goal and APA Suggested Learning Outcome (SLO).

Almost all the disorders described in this book are developmental disorders in the sense that they change over time. Most disorders originate in childhood, although the full presentation of the problem may not manifest until much later. Disorders that show themselves early in life often persist as the person grows older, so the term *childhood disorder* may be misleading. In this chapter, we cover those disorders that are revealed in a clinically significant way during a child's developing years and that are of concern to families and the educational system (Mash & Wolfe, 2003). Remember, however, that these difficulties often persist through adulthood and are typically lifelong problems, not ones unique to children.

Again, several difficulties and, indeed, distinct disorders begin in childhood. In certain disorders, some children are fine except for difficulties with talking. Others have problems relating to their peers. Still other children have a combination of conditions that significantly hinder their development.

Before we discuss specific disorders, we need to address the broad topic of development in relation to disorders usually first diagnosed in infancy, childhood, or adolescence. Does it matter when in the developmental period certain problems arise? Are disruptions in development permanent, thus making any hope for treatment doubtful?

Perspectives

Recall that in Chapter 2 we described developmental psychopathology as the study of how disorders arise and how they change with time. Childhood is considered particularly important because the brain changes significantly for several years after birth; this is also the time when critical developments occur in social, emotional, cognitive, and other important competency areas. For the most part, these changes follow a pattern: The child develops one skill before acquiring the next. Although this pattern of change is only one aspect of development, it is an important concept for us at this point because it implies that any disruption in the development of early skills will, by the very nature of this sequential process, disrupt the development of later skills. For example, some researchers believe that people with autism suffer from a disruption in early social development, which prevents them from developing important social relationships, even with their parents. From a developmental perspective, the absence of early and meaningful social relationships has serious consequences. Children whose motivation to interact with others is disrupted may have a more difficult time learning to communicate; that is, they may not want to learn to speak if other people are not important to them. We don't know whether a disruption in communication skills is a direct outcome of the disorder or a byproduct of disrupted early social development.

Understanding this type of developmental relationship is important for several reasons. Knowing what processes are disrupted will help us understand the disorder better and may lead to more appropriate intervention strategies. It may be important to identify children with attention deficit/hyperactivity disorder, for example, because their problems with impulsivity may interfere with their ability to create and maintain friendships, an important developmental consideration. Similarly, identifying a disorder such as autism at an early age is important for these children so their social deficits can be addressed before they affect other skill domains, such as language and communication. Too often, people see early and pervasive disruptions in developmental skills and expect a negative prognosis, with the problems predetermined and permanent. Remember that biological and psychosocial influences continuously interact with each other. Therefore, even for disorders such as attention deficit/hyperactivity disorder and autism that have clear biological bases, the presentation of the disorder is different for each individual. Changes at the biological or the psychosocial level may reduce the impact of the disorder.

One note of caution is appropriate here. There is real concern in the profession, especially among developmental psychologists, that some workers in the field may view aspects of normal development as symptoms of abnormality. For example, *echolalia*, which involves repeating the speech of others, was once thought to be a sign of autism. However, when we study the development of speech in children without disorders, we find that repeating what someone else says is an intermediate step in language development. In children with autism, therefore, echolalia is just a sign of relatively delayed language skills and not a symptom of their disorder (Tager-Flusberg et al., 2009). Thus, as noted by developmental psychologist and autism expert Jacob Burack from McGill University, knowledge of normal development is important for understanding the nature of childhood psychological disorders such as autism (Burack, Iarocci, Bowler, & Mottron, 2002).

With that caveat in mind, we now examine several of the disorders usually diagnosed first in infancy, childhood, or adolescence, including *attention deficit/hyperactivity disorder* (ADHD), which involves characteristics of inattention or hyperactivity and impulsivity, and learning disorders, which are characterized by one or more difficulties in areas such as reading and writing. We then focus on *autism*, a more severe disability, in which a child shows significant impairment in social interactions and communication and restricted patterns of behaviour, interest, and activities. Finally, we examine *intellectual disability*, which involves significant deficits in cognitive abilities.

Attention Deficit/Hyperactivity Disorder

Do you know people who flit from activity to activity, who start many tasks but seldom finish one, who have trouble concentrating, and who don't seem to pay attention when others speak? These people may have **attention deficit/hyperactivity disorder (ADHD)**, one of the most common reasons children are referred for mental health services (Popper, Gammon, West, & Bailey, 2003). The primary characteristics of such people include a pattern of inattention, such as not paying attention to school- or work-related tasks, or of hyperactivity and impulsivity. These deficits can significantly disrupt academic efforts as well as social relationships. Consider the case of Danny.

DANNY | *The Boy Who Couldn't Sit Still*

Danny, a handsome nine-year-old boy, was referred to us because of the significant difficulties he was experiencing at school and at home. Danny had a great deal of energy and loved playing most sports, especially baseball. Academically, he was experiencing substantial difficulties with his grades. His teacher reported that Danny's performance was diminishing and she believed he would do better if he paid more attention in class. Danny rarely spent more than a few minutes on a task without some interruption: He would get up out of his seat, rifle through his desk, or constantly ask questions. His peers were frustrated with him because he was equally impulsive during their interactions: He never finished a game, and in sports he tried to play all the positions simultaneously.

At home, Danny was considered quite a handful. His room was in a constant mess because he became engaged in a game or activity only to drop it and initiate something else. Danny's parents reported that they often scolded him for not carrying out some task, although the reason seemed to be that he forgot what he was doing rather than that he deliberately tried to defy them. They also said that, out of their own frustration, they sometimes grabbed him by the shoulders and yelled "Slow down!" because his hyperactivity drove them crazy.

Clinical Description

Danny has many of the characteristics of ADHD. Like Danny, people with this disorder have a great deal of difficulty sustaining their attention on a task or activity (Popper et al., 2003). As a result, their tasks are frequently unfinished and they often seem not to be listening when someone else is speaking. In addition to this serious disruption in attention, some people with ADHD also display motor hyperactivity (Mariani & Barkley, 1997). Children with this disorder are often described as fidgety in school, unable to sit still for more than a few minutes. Danny's restlessness in his classroom was a considerable source of concern for his teacher and peers, who were frustrated by his impatience. In addition to hyperactivity and problems sustaining attention, impulsivity— acting apparently without thinking—is a common complaint made about people with ADHD. For instance, during meetings of his baseball team, Danny often shouted out responses to the coach's questions even before the coach had finished his sentence.

For ADHD, the *DSM-IV-TR* differentiates two types of symptoms (see DSM Table 14.1). The first includes problems of *inattention*. People may appear not to listen to others; they may lose necessary school assignments, books, or tools; and they may not pay enough attention to details, making careless mistakes. The second type of symptom includes *hyperactivity*, which includes fidgeting, having trouble sitting for any length of time, always being on the go, and *impulsivity*, which includes blurting out answers before questions have been completed and having trouble waiting turns. Either the first (inattention) or the second (hyperactivity and impulsivity) type of symptom must be present for someone to be diagnosed with ADHD. The work of clinical psychologist Virginia Douglas at McGill University was largely responsible for recognition that problems of inattention often accompany symptoms of hyperactivity (Douglas, 1972). Her work led to changes in the conceptualization of and diagnostic criteria for this disorder, which used to be called "hyperactive child syndrome." These two clusters of ADHD symptoms appear to be consistent across different cultural groups (Beiser, Dion, & Gotowiec, 2000).

Inattention, hyperactivity, and impulsivity often cause other problems that appear secondary to ADHD. Academic performance tends to suffer, especially as the child progresses in school. The cause of this poor performance is not known. It could be a result of the problems with attention and impulsivity characteristic of ADHD, or it could be caused by factors such as brain impairment that may be responsible for the disorder itself (Frick, Strauss, Lahey, & Christ, 1993). And because they engage in more frequent dangerous and risky behaviours, children with ADHD are at an increased risk for minor injuries, thus causing their parents more worry (Byrne, Bawden, Beattie, & DeWolfe, 2003). Children with ADHD are also likely to be unpopular and rejected by their peers (Erhardt & Hinshaw, 1994; Ohan & Johnston, 2007). Here, however, the difficulty appears to be directly related to the behaviours symptomatic of ADHD, because inattention, impulsivity, and hyperactivity get in the way of establishing and maintaining friendships. Research by University of British Columbia clinical psychologist Charlotte Johnston and her colleagues indicates that problems with peers combined with frequent negative feedback from parents and teachers often result in low self-esteem among these children (Johnston, Pelham, & Murphy, 1985).

A. Either (1) or (2):

   1. Six (or more) of the following symptoms of inattention have persisted for at least six months to a degree that is maladaptive and inconsistent with developmental level:

   Inattention

   a. often fails to give close attention to details or makes careless mistakes in schoolwork, work, or other activities

   b. often has difficulty sustaining attention in tasks or play activities

   c. often does not seem to listen when spoken to directly

   d. often does not follow through on instructions and fails to finish schoolwork, chores, or duties in the workplace (not because of oppositional behaviour or failure to understand instructions)

   e. often has difficulty organizing tasks and activities

   f. often avoids, dislikes, or is reluctant to engage in tasks that require sustained mental effort (such as schoolwork or homework)

   g. often loses things necessary for tasks or activities (e.g., toys, school assignments, pencils, books, or tools)

   h. is often easily distracted by extraneous stimuli

   i. is often forgetful in daily activities

   2. Six (or more) of the following symptoms of hyperactivity/impulsivity have persisted for at least six months to a degree that is maladaptive and inconsistent with developmental level:

   Hyperactivity

   a. often fidgets with hands or feet or squirms in seat

   b. often leaves seat in classroom or in other situations in which remaining seated is expected

   c. often runs about or climbs excessively in situations in which it is inappropriate (in adolescents or adults, may be limited to subjective feelings of restlessness)

   d. often has difficulty playing or engaging in leisure activities quietly

   e. is often "on the go" or often acts as if "driven by a motor"

   f. often talks excessively

   Impulsivity

   g. often blurts out answers before questions have been completed

   h. often has difficulty awaiting turn

   i. often interrupts or intrudes on others (e.g., butts into conversations or games)

B. Some hyperactive-impulsive or inattentive symptoms that caused impairment were present before age seven.

C. Some impairment from the symptoms is present in two or more settings (e.g., at school [or work] and at home).

D. There must be clear evidence of clinically significant impairment in social, academic, or occupational functioning.

E. The symptoms do not occur exclusively during the course of a pervasive developmental disorder, schizophrenia, or other psychotic disorder and are not better accounted for by another mental disorder (e.g., mood disorder, anxiety disorder, dissociative disorder, or a personality disorder).

Source: Reprinted with permission from the *Diagnostic and Statistical Manual of Mental Disorders,* Fourth Edition, Text Revision, (Copyright © 2000). American Psychiatric Association.

ABNORMAL PSYCHOLOGY Video

Edward: ADHD in a Gifted Student

"He's very, very intelligent; his grades don't reflect that because he will just neglect to do a 240-point assignment if somebody doesn't stay behind it....What I try to do with him is come in and cut it down to 'this is what I want by tomorrow, this is what I want day after tomorrow.'"

Go to Psychology CourseMate at www.abnormalpsych3ce.nelson.com to watch this video.

Statistics

ADHD is estimated to occur in about 6 percent of school-aged children (Popper et al., 2003). Research by Rosemary Tannock of Toronto's Hospital for Sick Children has demonstrated the importance of the *DSM-IV-TR* requirement that at least some ADHD symptoms be present in childhood, before the age of seven (Rucklidge & Tannock, 2002). With respect to gender distribution, boys outnumber girls roughly four to one (Popper et al., 2003). The reason for this large gender difference is unknown. It may be that adults are more tolerant of hyperactivity among girls with ADHD, who tend to be less active than boys with ADHD. Whether ADHD has a different presentation in girls is as yet unknown, but this may account for the different prevalence rates for girls and boys. Children with ADHD are first identified as different from their peers around age three or four; their parents describe them as very active, mischievous, slow to toilet train, and oppositional (Conners, March, Frances, Wells, & Ross, 2001). The symptoms of inattention, impulsivity, and hyperactivity become increasingly obvious during the school years. Despite the perception that children grow out of ADHD, their problems usually continue: 68 percent of children with ADHD have ongoing difficulties through adulthood (Faraone, 2000). Over time, children with ADHD seem to be less impulsive, although inattention persists (Hart, Lahey, Loeber, Applegate, & Frick, 1995). Research shows that adults with ADHD are more likely than individuals without ADHD to have driving difficulties such as crashes, and they are more likely to be cited for speeding and to have their licences suspended (Barkley, Murphy, & Kwasnik, 1996; Faraone et al., 2000). In short, although the manifestations of ADHD change as people grow older, many of the problems persist.

In addition to the gender differences among children with ADHD, children are more likely to receive the label of ADHD in North America than anywhere else (Popper et al., 2003). This had led to concerns about overdiagnosis of ADHD in North America along with efforts to develop more objective measures (such as reaction time tasks) that might assist in the diagnostic process (e.g., Leth-Steensen,

ABNORMAL PSYCHOLOGY Video

ADHD: Sean

He would never think before he did stuff. And actually, the thing that really made me go, 'Something is desperately wrong here'—we had a little puppy. Real tiny little dog. And Sean was upstairs playing with it. And my daughter had gone upstairs, and went, 'Mom, something's wrong with the dog's paw.' And I looked and this poor little dog had a broken paw. Sean had dropped her. But didn't say anything to anyone. Just left the poor little dog sitting there. And I thought, 'Wow. This is just not normal.'"

Go to Psychology CourseMate at www.abnormalpsych3ce.nelson.com to watch this video.

Elbaz, & Douglas, 2000). However, with improvements in diagnosis worldwide, countries that previously reported lower rates of ADHD are finding similar numbers of these children being brought to the attention of helping professionals (Montiel-Nava, Pena, & Montiel-Barbero, 2003). This change suggests that the disorder may not simply be a reflection of a "lack of tolerance" on

Catherine Ledner/Taxi/Getty Images

▲ A child with ADHD is likely to behave inappropriately regardless of the setting.

Toby Maudsley/The Image Bank/Getty Images

▲ ADHD is often comorbid with other disruptive behaviour disorders such as conduct disorder, the childhood precursor to antisocial personality disorder.

the part of North American teachers or parents for active or impulsive children, but rather an indication that ADHD is a disorder that affects a significant number of children all over the world.

ADHD is frequently comorbid with other disruptive behaviour disorders, including *oppositional defiant disorder* (a pattern of negative, defiant, and hostile behaviour; e.g., refusing to obey adult, angry, argumentative) and conduct disorder (Waschbusch, 2002)—the childhood precursor to antisocial personality disorder that we discussed in Chapter 12. Additionally, research by Lily Hechtman and Gabrielle Weiss at the Montréal Children's Hospital and McGill University suggests that ADHD is a risk factor for antisocial outcomes in boys but not in girls (Herrero, Hechtman, & Weiss, 1994). ADHD is also frequently comorbid with learning disorders (Offord, 1989)—a category of childhood disorder we discuss shortly.

Causes

As with many other disorders, we are at a period when important information about the genetics of ADHD is beginning to be uncovered (Kebir, Tabbane, Sengupta, & Joober, 2009; Waldman & Gizer, 2006). Researchers have known for some time that ADHD is more common in families in which one person has the disorder. For example, the relatives of children with ADHD have been found to be more likely to have ADHD themselves than would be expected in the general population (Fliers et al., 2009). It is important to note that these families display an increase in psychopathology in general, including conduct disorder, mood disorders, anxiety disorders, and substance abuse (Faraone et al., 2000). This research and the comorbidity in the children themselves suggest that some shared genetic deficits may contribute to the problems experienced by individuals with these disorders (Brown, 2009).

ADHD is considered to be highly influenced by genetics, with a relatively small role played by environmental influences in the cause of the disorder when compared to many other disorders we discuss in this book. As with other disorders, researchers are finding that multiple genes are responsible for ADHD (Nikolas & Burt, 2010). Research in this area is following the same progression as for other disorders and involves large collaborative studies across many laboratories worldwide. Most attention to date focuses on genes associated with the neurochemical dopamine, although norepinephrine, serotonin, and gamma aminobutyric acid (GABA) are also implicated in the cause of ADHD. More specifically, there is strong evidence that ADHD is associated with the dopamine D4 receptor gene, the dopamine transporter gene (DAT1), and the dopamine D5 receptor gene. DAT1 is of particular interest because methylphenidate (Ritalin)—one of the most common medical treatments for ADHD—inhibits this gene and increases the amount of dopamine available. Such research helps us understand at a microlevel what might be going wrong and how to design new interventions.

As with several other disorders we've discussed, researchers are looking for endophenotypes, those basic deficits—such as specific attentional problems—characteristic of ADHD. The goal is to link these deficits to specific brain dysfunctions. Not surprisingly, specific areas of current interest for ADHD are the brain's attention system, working memory functions, inattentiveness, and impulsivity. Researchers are now trying to tie specific genetic

defects to these cognitive processes to make the link between genes and behaviour. Some research indicates that poor "inhibitory control" (the ability to stop responding to a task when signalled) may be common among both children with ADHD and their unaffected family members (siblings and parents) and may be one genetic marker (an endophenotype) for this disorder (Goos, Crosbie, Payne, & Schachar, 2009).

The strong genetic influence in ADHD does not rule out any role for the environment (Ficks & Waldman, 2009). In one of a growing number of gene–environment interaction studies of ADHD, for example, researchers found that children with a specific mutation involving the dopamine system (called the DAT1 genotype) were more likely to exhibit the symptoms of ADHD if their mothers smoked during pregnancy (Kahn, Khoury, Nichols, & Lanphear, 2003). Prenatal smoking seemed to interact with this genetic predisposition to increase the risk for hyperactive and impulsive behaviour. Other research is now pointing to additional environmental factors, such as low socio-economic status and parental marital instability and discord, as involved in these gene–environment interactions (Ficks & Waldman, 2009).

For several decades, ADHD has been thought to involve brain damage, and this notion is reflected in the previous use of labels such as "minimal brain damage" or "minimal brain dysfunction" (Ross & Pelham, 1981). In recent years, scanning technology has permitted a sophisticated assessment of the validity of this assumption. One thing is clear—there are likely several different brain mechanisms that can lead to the attention deficits, along with the impulsivity and hyperactivity seen in individuals with ADHD. A general finding from brain-imaging studies of those with and without ADHD is that although no major damage is found in the brains of those with ADHD, there are subtle differences. One of the more reliable findings is that the volume (or overall size) of the brain is smaller in children with ADHD (Castellanos et al., 2003; Hill et al., 2003). Three areas of the brain appear smaller than is typical—the frontal cortex (in the outer portion of the brain), the basal ganglia (deep within the brain), and the cerebellar vermis (part of the cerebellum in the back of the brain; Popper et al., 2003). This smaller volume seems to occur early in the development of the brain, meaning that general progressive damage is not occurring in these individuals. Researchers are actively engaged in narrowing down just what parts of the brain are involved and how they may contribute to the symptoms we see in ADHD.

A variety of such toxins as allergens and food additives have been considered as possible causes of ADHD over the years, although very little evidence supports the association. The theory that food additives such as artificial colours, flavourings, and preservatives are responsible for the symptoms of ADHD has had a substantial impact. Feingold (1975) presented this view along with recommendations for eliminating these substances as a treatment for ADHD. Hundreds of thousands of families have put their children on the Feingold diet, despite evidence that it has little or no effect on the symptoms of ADHD (Barkley, 1990). However, some large-scale research now suggests that there may be a small but measurable impact of artificial food colours and additives on the behaviour of young children. One study found that three-year-old and eight- to nine-year-old children who consumed typical amounts of preservatives (sodium benzoate) and food colourings had increased levels of hyperactive behaviours (inattention,

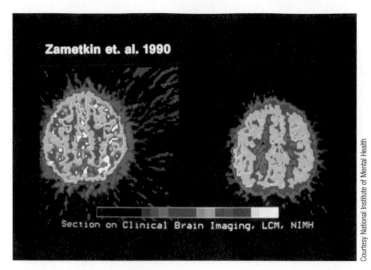

Courtesy National Institute of Mental Health

▲ Thanks to brain scan technology, we are beginning to understand the neurological aspects of ADHD.

impulsivity, and overactivity) (McCann et al., 2007). Other research now points to the possible role of the pesticides found in foods as contributing to an increased risk of ADHD (Bouchard, Bellinger, Wright, & Weisskopf, 2010).

As you saw in the discussion of genetics, one of the more consistent findings among children with ADHD involves its association with maternal smoking. In addition, a variety of other pregnancy complications (e.g., maternal alcohol consumption and low birth weight) may play a role in increasing the chance that a child with a genetic predisposition for ADHD will display the symptoms characteristic of this disorder (Barkley, 2006). Unfortunately, many of the studies in this area confound socio-economic and genetic factors (e.g., there is an increased likelihood of smoking among women who also have low socio-economic status), and there may not be a direct link between maternal smoking and ADHD (Lindblad & Hjern, 2010).

Psychological and social dimensions of ADHD further influence the disorder. Negative responses by parents, teachers, and peers to the affected child's impulsivity and hyperactivity may contribute to his or her feelings of low self-esteem, especially in children who are also depressed (Anastopoulos, Sommer, & Schatz, 2009). Years of constant reminders by teachers and parents to behave, sit quietly, and pay attention may create a negative self-image in these children, which, in turn, can have a negative impact on their ability to make friends. Thus, the possible biological influences on impulsivity, hyperactivity, and attention, combined with attempts to control these children, may lead to their being rejected and to their consequent poor self-image. An integration of the biological and psychological influences on ADHD suggests that both need to be addressed when designing effective treatments (Rapport, 2001).

Treatment

Treatment for ADHD has proceeded on two fronts: biological and psychosocial interventions (Biederman, Spencer, Wilens, & Greene, 2001). Typically, the goal of biological treatments is to reduce the children's impulsivity and hyperactivity and to improve their attentional skills. Psychosocial treatments generally focus on broader issues such as improving academic performance, decreasing disruptive behaviour, and improving social skills. Although these two kinds of approaches have typically developed independently, recent efforts combine them in order to have a broader impact on people with ADHD.

Since the use of stimulant medication with children with ADHD was first described (Bradley, 1937), hundreds of studies have documented the effectiveness of this kind of medication in reducing the core symptoms of the disorder. Drugs such as methylphenidate (Ritalin, Metadate, Concerta), D-amphetamine (Dexedrine, Dextrostat), and pemoline (Cylert) have proven helpful for approximately 70 percent of cases in at least temporarily reducing hyperactivity and impulsivity and improving concentration on tasks (e.g., Berman, Douglas, & Barr, 1999; Brodeur & Pond, 2001). A recent study by Gillian O'Driscoll and her colleagues (2005) showed that Ritalin improved both motor planning and response inhibition performance in children with ADHD. Cylert has a greater likelihood of negative side effects, so it is currently discouraged from routine use. Adderall, which is a longer-acting version of these psychostimulants, reduces the need for children to take multiple doses during the day but has similar positive effects (Grcevich, Rowane, Marcellino, & Sullivan-Hurst, 2001).

Research suggests that other drugs, such as certain antidepressants (bupropion, imipramine) and a drug used for treating high blood pressure (clonidine), may have similar effects on people with ADHD (Popper et al., 2003). All these drugs seem to improve compliance and decrease negative behaviours in many children, but they do not appear to produce substantial improvement in learning and academic performance, and their effects do not usually last over the long term when the drugs are discontinued.

Originally, it seemed paradoxical or contrary to expectation that children would calm down after taking a stimulant. However, on the same low doses, children and adults with and without ADHD react in the same way. It appears that stimulant medications reinforce the brain's ability to focus attention during problem-solving tasks (Volkow & Swanson, 2003). Without stimulant medications, children with ADHD perform more poorly on a variety of cognitive tasks than do children with other disorders, including anxiety or mood disorders (Szatmari, Offord, Siegel, Finlayson, & Tuff, 1990). Although the use of stimulant medications remains controversial, especially for children, most clinicians rec-

Photo by Ed Shapiro, Westmount Studio of Photography/Courtesy of Virginia Douglas

▲ Virginia Douglas is a clinical psychologist at McGill University. Her research has contributed substantially to our understanding of the nature of ADHD and the best ways to treat this childhood disorder.

ommend them temporarily, in combination with psychosocial interventions, to help improve children's social and academic skills (e.g., Douglas, Barr, Desilets, & Sherman, 1995).

There are two main concerns about the use of stimulant medications in the treatment of children with ADHD. The first concern pertains to stimulant drugs' potential for abuse. We saw in Chapter 11 that drugs such as methylphenidate are sometimes abused for their ability to create elation and reduce fatigue (Volkow & Swanson, 2003). This is of particular concern for children with ADHD because they are at increased risk for later substance abuse (Molina & Pelham, 2003). A second concern is that these medications may be overprescribed and their long-term effects are not well understood (Evenson, 2001). A study by Elisa Romano and her colleagues at the University of Montréal found that methylphenidate (Ritalin) use increased 36 percent among Canadian children over a two-year period (Romano, Baillargeon, Wu, Robaey, & Tremblay, 2002). Their more recent research suggests that methylphenidate use is highest in school-aged boys compared with younger children and girls (Romano et al., 2005; see ■ Figure 14.1). Another survey showed that 80 percent of Canadian physicians had seen a patient with ADHD, 84 percent had prescribed methylphenidate, and 39 percent felt pressured to prescribe methylphenidate (Health Canada, 1999). A concern related to methylphenidate overprescription pertains to the medication's side effects, such as insomnia, irritability, and appetite suppression (Schachter, Pham, King, Langford, & Moher, 2001). A recent longitudinal study by Alice Charach and her colleagues at the Hospital for Sick Children in Toronto further suggests that long-term use of high doses of stimulants is likely to have measurable adverse effects on the growth of

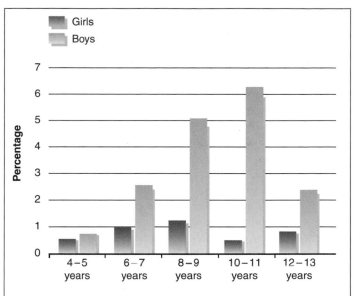

■ **FIGURE 14.1** Methylphenidate use among girls and boys in different age groups from data collected in the 1996–97 National Longitudinal Survey of Children and Youth. Bars represent prevalence rates (%).

Source: Adapted and redrawn from Elisa Romano et al. (2005). "Individual change in methylphenidate use in a national sample of children aged 2 to 11 years." *Canadian Journal of Psychiatry, 50 (3),* 144–152. The figure is drawn from material in Table 2, p.149.

school-aged children with ADHD (Charach, Figueroa, Chen, Ickowica, & Schachar, 2006).

In addition to these concerns, some portion of children with ADHD do not respond to medications, and most children who do

Innovative Approaches

Helpful "Designer Drugs"

Get ready to learn a new word—psychopharmacogenetics

Psychopharmacogenetics is the study of how your genetic makeup influences your response to certain drugs. The hope for this field is that medications can be matched or even "designed" for individuals to better complement their specific needs (Weinshilboum, 2003). For example, one study looked at the use of methylphenidate (Ritalin) for children and adolescents with ADHD (Polanczyk et al., 2007). For those who had a specific gene defect—the adrenergic alpha-2A receptor gene (ADRA2A)—methylphenidate had a strong positive effect, especially on their problems with inattention. This was not the case for those with ADHD who did not have the ADRA2A gene defect. Currently, the use of drug treatments tends to be by trial and error: A medication is attempted at a particular dose; if it is not effective, the dose is changed. If that does not work, a different medication is tried. This new study holds the promise of potentially eliminating this guesswork and tailoring the treatment to the individual.

This exciting new approach to medical treatment for mental illness brings with it some weighty concerns. Central to these concerns are issues of privacy and confidentiality. Genetic screening to identify defects is likely to identify any number of potential genetic problems in each of us. How will schools, employment sites, and insurance companies view this information if they have access? The concern is that people will be discriminated against based on this information (e.g., having the genes that may or may not lead to having ADHD or another disorder). Will the desire to better target drug treatments outweigh these types of ethical concerns? Most new technical advances, like those promised with psychopharmacogenetics, also uncover new problems, and it is essential that ethical issues be part of the discussion as researchers move forward in this area.

Attention Deficit/Hyperactivity Disorder

respond do not show gains in the important areas of academics and social skills (Biederman et al., 2001; Pelham, Waschbusch, Hoza, Pillow, & Gnagy, 2001). Because of these findings, researchers have applied various behavioural interventions to help these children at home and in school (Fiore, Becker, & Nero, 1993; Garber, Garber, & Spizman, 1996; Waschbusch, Pelham, & Massetti, 2005). In general, the programs set such goals as increasing the amount of time the child remains seated, increasing the number of math papers completed, or engaging in appropriate play with peers. Reinforcement programs reward the child for improvements and, at times, punish misbehaviour with loss of rewards (Braswell & Bloomquist, 1994). Other programs incorporate parent training to teach families how to respond constructively to their child's behaviours and how to structure the child's day to help prevent difficulties (Sonuga-Barke, Daley, Thompson, Laver-Bradbury, & Weeks, 2001). Although many children have benefited from these types of programs, others have not, and we have no way to predict which children will respond positively (Fiore et al., 1993). In sum, both medication and behavioural interventions have shortcomings. Most clinicians typically recommend a combination of approaches designed to individualize treatments for children with ADHD (e.g., Waschbusch, Kipp, & Pelham, 1998), targeting both short-term management issues (decreasing hyperactivity and impulsivity) and long-term concerns (preventing and reversing academic decline and improving social skills).

To determine whether a combined approach to treatment is the most effective, a large-scale study was conducted by six teams of researchers (Jensen et al., 2001). Labelled the Multimodal Treatment of Attention-Deficit Hyperactivity Disorder Study, this project included 579 children who were randomly assigned to one of four groups. One group of the children received routine care without medication or specific behavioural interventions (community care, CC). The three treatment groups consisted of medication management (MedMgt; usually methylphenidate), intensive behavioural treatment (Beh), and a combination (Comb), and the study lasted 14 months. Initial reports from the study suggested that Comb and MedMgt alone were superior to Beh alone and CC interventions for ADHD symptoms. For problems that went beyond the specific symptoms of ADHD, such as social skills, academics, parent–child relations, oppositional behaviour, and anxiety or depression (see Schachar et al., 2002), results suggested advantages of Comb over single treatments (MedMgt, Beh) and CC.

Some controversy surrounds the interpretation of these findings; specifically, whether Comb is superior to MedMgt alone (Pelham, 1999; Schachar et al., 2002). Practically speaking, if there is no difference between these treatments, most parents and therapists would opt for simply providing medication for these children. As we mentioned previously, behavioural interventions have the added benefit of improving aspects of the child and family that are not directly affected by medication. Reinterpretations of the data from this large-scale study continue, and more research is likely needed to clarify the combined and separate effects of these two approaches to treatment (Conners et al., 2001). Despite these advances, however, children with ADHD continue to pose a considerable challenge to their families and to the educational system.

Concept Check | 14.1

Check your understanding of the different clusters of symptoms that can accompany a diagnosis of attention deficit/hyperactivity disorder. Assign a label of (a) ADHD or (b) ADHD without hyperactivity to each of the following cases.

1. Ten-year-old Michael is frequently off-task in school. He often forgets to bring his homework to school and typically comes home without an important book. He works quickly and makes careless mistakes. _____

2. Nine-year-old Evan can be very frustrating to his parents, teachers, and friends. He often calls out answers in school, sometimes before the complete question is asked. He has trouble waiting his turn during games and does things seemingly without thinking. _____

3. Nine-year-old Cathy is described by everyone as a "handful." She fidgets constantly in class, drumming her fingers on the desk, squirming around in her chair, and getting up and down. She has trouble waiting her turn at work or at play, and she sometimes has violent outbursts. _____

Learning Disorders

Academic achievement is highly valued in our society. Because parents often invest a great deal of time and emotional energy in ensuring their children's academic success, it can be extremely upsetting when a child with no obvious intellectual deficits does not achieve as expected. In this section we describe **learning disorders** in reading, mathematics, and written expression—all characterized by performance that is substantially below what would be expected given the person's age, IQ, and education. We also look briefly at disorders that involve how we communicate. Consider the case of Alice.

ALICE | *Taking a Reading Disorder to College*

Alice, a 20-year-old college student, sought help because of her difficulty in several of her classes. She reported that she had enjoyed school and had been a good student up until about the sixth grade, when her grades suffered significantly. Her teacher informed her parents that Alice wasn't working up to her potential and that she needed to be better motivated. Alice had always worked hard in school but promised to try harder. However, with each report card her mediocre grades made her feel worse about herself. She managed to graduate from high school, but by that time she felt she was not as bright as her friends.

Alice enrolled in the local community college and again found herself struggling with the work. Over the years, she had learned several tricks that seemed to help her study and at least get passing grades. She read the material in her textbooks aloud to herself; she had earlier discovered that she could recall the material much better this way than if she just read silently to herself. In fact, reading silently, she could barely remember any of the details just minutes later.

After her second year in community college, Alice transferred to university, which she found even more demanding and where she failed most of her classes. After our first meeting, I suggested that she be formally assessed to identify the source of her difficulty. As suspected, Alice had a learning disability. Scores from an IQ test placed her above average, but she was also found to have significant difficulties with reading. Her comprehension was poor, and she could not remember most of the content of what she read. We recommended that she continue with her trick of reading aloud (Hinchley & Levy, 1988), because her comprehension for what she heard was adequate. In addition, Alice was taught how to analyze her reading—that is, how to outline and take notes. She was even encouraged to audiotape her lectures and play them back to herself as she drove around in her car. Although Alice did not become an A student, she was able to graduate from university, and she now works with young children who have learning disabilities.

Clinical Description

According to *DSM-IV-TR* criteria (see DSM Table 14.2), Alice would be diagnosed as having a **reading disorder**, which is defined as a significant discrepancy between a person's reading achievement and what would be expected for someone of the same age (American Psychiatric Association, 2000a). This particular learning disorder is also known as *dyslexia*. More specifically, the criteria require that the person read at a level significantly below that of a typical person of the same age, cognitive ability (as measured on an IQ test), and educational background. In addition, this disability cannot be caused by a sensory difficulty such as trouble with sight or hearing. Similarly, the *DSM-IV-TR* (DSM Table 14.2) defines a **mathematics disorder** as achievement below expected performance in mathematics and a **disorder of**

Table 14.2 Diagnostic Criteria for Learning Disorders*

DSM-IV-TR

for Reading Disorder (Developmental Reading Disorder), Mathematics Disorder (Developmental Arithmetic Disorder), and Disorder of Written Expression (Developmental Expressive Writing Disorder)

A. Reading achievement or mathematical ability or writing skill, as measured by individually administered standardized tests, is substantially below that expected given the person's chronological age, measured intelligence, and age-appropriate education.

B. The disturbance in Criterion A significantly interferes with academic achievement or activities of daily living that require reading skills or mathematical ability or composition of written texts.

C. If a sensory deficit is present, the learning difficulties are in excess of those usually associated with it.

Source: Reprinted with permission from the *Diagnostic and Statistical Manual of Mental Disorders,* Fourth Edition, Text Revision, (Copyright © 2000). American Psychiatric Association.

written expression as achievement below expected performance in writing. In each of these disorders, the difficulties are sufficient to interfere with the students' academic achievement and to disrupt their daily activities.

Statistics

Estimates of how prevalent learning disorders are range from 5 percent to 10 percent (Young & Beitchman, 2001), although the frequency of this diagnosis appears to increase in wealthier regions. According to school principals who participated in the National Longitudinal Survey of Children and Youth, an average of 12 percent of children in their schools had a learning disorder (Statistics Canada, 1996). According to Statistics Canada's *A Profile of Disability in Canada*, learning disability is one of the two most common disabilities suffered by children up to 14 years of age (Statistics Canada, 2001). In fact, more than half of all Canadian school children classified as having a disability have a learning disability (Statistics Canada, 1996; see ■ Figure 14.2).

Difficulties with reading are the most common of the learning disorders and occur in approximately 5 percent to 15 percent of the general population (Beitchman & Young, 1997; Popper et al., 2003). Mathematics disorder appears in approximately 6 percent of the population (Gross-Tsur, Manor, & Shalev, 1996), but we have very limited information about the prevalence of disorder of written expression among children and adults. Early studies suggested that boys were more likely to have a reading disorder than were girls, although more contemporary research indicates that boys and girls may be equally affected by this disorder (Wadsworth, DeFries, Stevenson, Gilger, & Pennington, 1992).

A learning disorder can lead to several different outcomes, depending on the extent of the disability and the extent of available support. One study found that about 32 percent of students with learning disabilities dropped out of school (Wagner, 1990). In addition, employment rates for students with learning disorders tend to be discouragingly low, ranging from 60 percent to 70 percent (Shapiro & Lentz, 1991). The low figure may be due in part to the students' low expectations; one study reported that only 50 percent of high school students with learning disabilities had post-graduation plans (Shapiro & Lentz, 1991). The low figure may also be due in part to difficulties these individuals have in holding a job. According to the Handicapped Employment Program of the Ontario Ministry of Labour, adults with learning disabilities who have not received appropriate education or training typically hold a job for only three months. Additionally, learning disorders may be related to the later development of other mental health problems. For example, a study by Toronto-based researcher Joseph Beitchman and his colleagues suggests that adolescents with learning disorders are at increased risk for substance use disorders (Beitchman, Wilson, Douglas, Young, & Adlaf, 2001a). Another longitudinal study by this team showed that children with language disorders were at increased risk for the later development of psychiatric disorders (Beitchman et al., 2001b).

Some individuals with learning disorders do attain their education or career goals (Spreen, 1988). Psychologist Maggie Bruck notes that individuals with reading disorders can succeed in college or university if they are provided with instructional supports such as tutors, tape-recorded lectures, and tests without time limits (Bruck, 1987). However, completing college or university

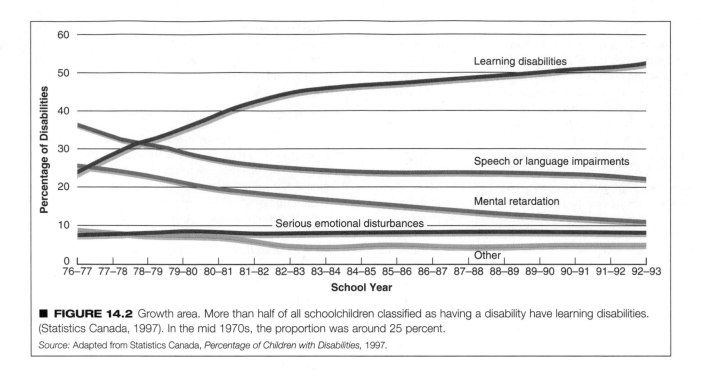

■ **FIGURE 14.2** Growth area. More than half of all schoolchildren classified as having a disability have learning disabilities. (Statistics Canada, 1997). In the mid 1970s, the proportion was around 25 percent.

Source: Adapted from Statistics Canada, *Percentage of Children with Disabilities,* 1997.

appears to be more difficult for people with severe learning disorders (Spreen, 1988). Interviews with adults who have learning disabilities reveal that their school experiences were generally negative, and the effects often lasted beyond graduation. One man who did not have special assistance during school reports the following:

> I faked my way through school because I was very bright. I resent most that no one picked up my weaknesses. Essentially I judge myself on my failures.... [I] have always had low self-esteem. In hindsight I feel that I had low self-esteem in college.... I was afraid to know myself. A blow to my self-esteem when I was in school was that I could not write a poem or a story.... I could not write with a pen or pencil. The computer has changed my life. I do everything on my computer. It acts as my memory. I use it to structure my life and for all of my writing since my handwriting and written expression has always been so poor. (Polloway, Schewel, & Patton, 1992, p. 521)

A group of disorders loosely identified as verbal or communication disorders seem closely related to learning disorders. These disorders can appear deceptively benign, yet their presence early in life can cause wide-ranging problems later on. For a brief overview of these disorders, which include **stuttering**, **expressive language disorder**, **selective mutism**, and **tic disorders**, see Box 14.1.

Causes

Theories about the etiology of learning disorders assume a diverse and complex origin, and include genetic, neurobiological, and environmental factors. For example, some disorders of reading may have a genetic basis; the parents and siblings of people with reading disorders are more likely to display these disorders than are relatives of people without reading problems (Popper et al., 2003). When identical twins are studied, if one twin receives a diagnosis of reading disorder, there appears to be an almost 100 percent chance that the second twin will receive the same diagnosis (100 percent concordance), further supporting a genetic influence (Vandenberg, Singer, & Pauls, 1986). As we saw with ADHD, the genetics of disorders of reading are complex, and genes on chromosomes 2, 3, 6, 15, and 18 have all been repeatedly linked to these difficulties (Kaminen et al., 2003). Remember, however, that problems in learning are extremely diverse, and undoubtedly are influenced by multiple biological and psychosocial influences.

Various forms of subtle brain damage have also been thought responsible for learning disabilities; some of the earliest theories involve a neurological explanation (Hinshelwood, 1896). Studies show a link between phonologial processing problems and reading disabilities in both children and adults (e.g., Bruck, 1992; Chiappe, Stringer, Siegel, & Stanovich, 2002; Helenius et al., 2002; Stringer & Stanovich, 2000). For example, research by Ron Stringer at McGill University indicates that participants with dyslexia have difficulties performing a task in which they are asked to delete syllables from words spoken by the experimenter. For instance, they might be asked to delete a single phoneme from the initial or final position in a word (e.g., delete "bi" from "bicycle"; Stringer & Stanovich, 2000). Research suggests structural as well as functional differences in the brains of people with learning disabilities. For example, the research of John Connolly and his colleagues at Dalhousie University shows weaker and delayed neural responses during reading of sentences among dyslexic readers compared with controls (Helenius, Salmelin, Service, & Connolly, 1999). Such findings imply a neuropsychological deficit that interferes with the processing of certain essential language information. However, such physiological deficits are not consistent across individuals (Hynd & Semrud-Clikeman, 1989), which is not surprising, given that people with learning disorders display very different types of cognitive problems and therefore probably

BOX 14.1

Communications and Related Disorders

STUTTERING

Clinical Description

A disturbance in speech fluency that includes a number of problems with speech, such as repeating syllables or words, prolonging certain sounds, making obvious pauses, or substituting words to replace ones that are difficult to articulate.

Statistics

Occurs twice as frequently among boys as among girls; begins most often in children under the age of three (Yairi & Ambrose, 1992); 98 percent of cases occur before the age of ten (Mahr & Leith, 1992); approximately 80 percent of children who stutter before they enter school will no longer stutter after they have been in school a year or so (Yairi & Ambrose, 1992).

Causes

Rather than anxiety causing stuttering, stuttering makes people anxious (Miller & Watson, 1992); multiple brain pathways appear to be involved (Fox et al., 1996); genetic influences also may be a factor (Andrews, Morris-Yates, Howie, & Martin, 1991).

Treatment

Psychological: Parents are counselled about how to talk to their children; as noted by Mireille Gagnon and Robert Ladouceur, the *regulated-breathing method* is a promising behavioural treatment in which the person is instructed to stop speaking when a stuttering episode occurs and then to take a deep breath (exhale, then inhale) before proceeding (Gagnon & Ladouceur, 1992); work by Marilyn Langevin of the University of Alberta and her colleagues suggests promise for an approach combining speech therapy with cognitive-behavioural therapy aimed at improving negative emotions surrounding the speech impediment (Huinck et al., 2006).

Pharmacological: The serious side effects of haloperidol outweigh any benefit it may offer; verapamil may decrease the severity of stuttering in some individuals (Brady, 1991).

EXPRESSIVE LANGUAGE DISORDER

Clinical Description

Limited speech in all situations; expressive language (what is said) is significantly below their usually average receptive language (what is understood).

Statistics

Approximately 2.2 percent of three-year-olds experience this disorder (Silva, 1980); boys are almost five times as likely as girls to be affected (Whitehurst et al., 1988).

Causes

An unfounded psychological explanation is that the children's parents may not speak to them enough; a biological theory is that middle ear infection is a contributory cause.

Treatment

May be self-correcting and may not require special intervention.

SELECTIVE MUTISM

Clinical Description

Persistent failure to speak in very specific situations—such as school—despite the ability to do so.

Statistics

Less than 1 percent of children; more prevalent among girls than boys; most common between the ages of five and seven.

Causes

Not much is known; anxiety is one possible cause (Wilkins, 1985), particularly social anxiety (Cunningham, McHolm, & Boyle, 2006).

Treatment

Contingency management: Giving children praise and reinforcers for speaking while ignoring their attempts to communicate in other ways.

TIC DISORDERS

Clinical Description

Involuntary motor movements (tics), such as head twitching, or vocalizations, such as grunts, that often occur in rapid succession, come on suddenly, and happen in idiosyncratic or stereotyped ways. In one type, Tourette's disorder, vocal tics often include the involuntary repetition of obscenities.

Statistics

Of all children, 12 percent to 24 percent show some tics during their growing years (Ollendick & Ollendick, 1990); 2 to 8 children out of every 10 000 have Tourette's disorder (Leckman et al., 1997b); usually develops before the age of 14; high comorbidity with obsessive-compulsive behaviour.

Causes

Inheritance may be through a dominant gene or genes (Bowman & Nurnberger, 1993; Wolf et al., 1996); a study of a large family in eastern Québec with a high incidence of tic disorders found significant evidence for genetic linkage (Mérette et al., 2000).

Treatment

Psychological: Self-monitoring, relaxation training, and habit reversal.
Pharmacological: Haloperidol and more recently pimozide and clonidine.

represent a number of etiological subgroups (Beitchman & Young, 1997; Popper et al., 2003; Young et al., 2002).

We saw that Alice persisted despite the obstacles caused by her learning disorder, as well as by the reactions of teachers and others. What helped her continue toward her goal when others choose, instead, to drop out of school? Psychological and motivational factors that have been reinforced by others seem to play an important role in the eventual outcome for people with learning disorders. Factors such as socio-economic status, cultural expectations, parental interactions and expectations, and child management practices, together with existing neurological deficits and the types of support provided in the school, seem to determine outcome (Tannock, 2009b).

Treatment

Before beginning treatment, an assessment must be conducted, typically by a school psychologist. The most common method of assessing learning disorders is to administer two types of tests (i.e., intelligence tests and achievement tests) and compare the scores on each. Intelligence tests such as the Wechsler Intelligence Scales (see Chapter 3) are thought to tap academic aptitude or potential, whereas achievement tests tap performance in particular areas (reading, writing, math). If a significant discrepancy exists between aptitude and actual achievement in a particular subject, then a specific learning disorder is diagnosed (Kaufman & Kaufman, 2001). For example, when Alice was assessed, she scored one standard deviation above average on an intelligence test (IQ = 115) but one standard deviation below average on an achievement test tapping her reading performance. Thus, Alice

was diagnosed with a reading disorder (dyslexia) and a treatment was planned with this diagnosis in mind.

As we will see in the case of intellectual disability, learning disorders primarily require educational intervention. Biological treatment is typically restricted to those individuals who may also have ADHD, which we have seen involves impulsivity and an inability to sustain attention, and which can be helped with certain stimulant medications such as methylphenidate (Ritalin). Educational efforts can be broadly categorized into (1) efforts to remediate directly the underlying basic processing of problems (e.g., by teaching students visual and auditory perception skills); (2) efforts to improve *cognitive* skills through general instruction in listening, comprehension, and memory; and (3) targeting the *behavioural* skills needed to compensate for specific problems the student may have with reading, mathematics, or written expression—such as those we discussed in the case of Alice (Reeve & Kauffman, 1988). For example, Alice's reading disorder was helped by the behavioural skill of reading aloud (Hinchley & Levy, 1988).

For children with learning disorders who have difficulties processing language, treatment using exercises such as specially designed computer games that help children distinguish among sounds appears to be helpful (Merzenich et al., 1996). Considerable research also supports the usefulness of teaching the behavioural skills necessary to improve academic skills (Hammill, 1993). Maureen Lovett and her colleagues at the Hospital for Sick Children in Toronto have developed a new integrated program called the Phonology and Strategy Training Program (Lovett et al., 2000). They showed this combined program to be more effective than either phonological skills training or strategies training alone, in treating children with reading disorder (Lovett et al., 2000).

PATTERN   MOTION
CONTROLS
V1/V2   V5/MT
DYSLEXICS
V1/V2

Courtesy National Institute of Mental Health

▲ These functional MRI scans of composite data from six dyslexic adults and eight controls show a horizontal slice through the brain, with the face at the top. Imaging shows atypical brain activity associated with dyslexia. The scans were performed while subjects tracked a pattern of moving dots on a computer screen. A brain area (V5/MT) normally active during such motion tasks did not switch on in dyslexic subjects (right). Their brain activity was more similar to that of controls during a pattern recognition task (left).

Pervasive Developmental Disorders

People with **pervasive developmental disorders** all experience problems with language, socialization, and cognition (Durand & Mapstone, 1999). The word pervasive means that these problems are not relatively minor and significantly affect individuals throughout their lives. Included under the heading of pervasive developmental disorders are **autistic disorder** (or autism), **Asperger's disorder**, **Rett's disorder**, **childhood disintegrative disorder**, and **pervasive developmental disorder—not otherwise specified**. We focus on one of the more prevalent pervasive developmental disorders—autistic disorder—with the other disorders highlighted in Box 14.2. Note that discussions are under way to possibly reorganize these disorders under the title "autism spectrum disorders" in the *DSM-5*, this spectrum of disorders would include autistic disorder (autism), Asperger's disorder, childhood disintegrative disorder, and pervasive developmental disorder not otherwise specified (American Psychiatric Association, 2010a).

Autistic Disorder

Autistic disorder, or *autism*, is a childhood disorder characterized by significant impairment in social interactions and communication and by restricted patterns of behaviour, interest, and activities (Durand, 2004). Individuals have a puzzling array of symptoms. Consider the case of Amy.

BOX 14.2 Additional Pervasive Developmental Disorders

ASPERGER'S DISORDER

Clinical Description

Impaired social relationships and restricted or unusual behaviours or activities, but without the language delays associated with autism; few severe cognitive impairments; IQ usually in the average range; often exhibit clumsiness and poor coordination; some researchers think it may be a mild form of autism (see review in Szatmari et al., 2000).

Statistics

Prevalence uncertain; estimated at between 1 and 36 per 10 000 (Volkmar & Klin, 2000); believed to occur more often in boys than girls (Volkmar & Cohen, 1991).

Causes

Limited causal research conducted to date; some evidence suggests that it runs in families, so a genetic contribution is suspected (Folstein & Santangelo, 2000).

Treatment

Similar to that for autism; less need to work on communication and academic skills; should focus on helping improve social skills (Koning & Magill-Evans, 2001; Starr, Szatmari, Bryson, & Zwaigenbaum, 2003).

RETT'S DISORDER

Clinical Description

A progressive neurological disorder that primarily affects girls; characterized by constant hand wringing, increasingly severe intellectual disability, and impaired motor skills, all of which appear after an apparently normal start in development (Van Acker, 1991); motor skills deteriorate progressively over time; social skills, however, develop normally at first, decline between the ages of one and three, and then partially improve. May be removed from the *DSM-5* because it is minimally related to autism.

Statistics

Relatively rare; occurs in approximately 1 per 12 000 to 15 000 live female births.

Causes

Unlikely that psychological factors play a role in causation; more likely, a genetic disorder involving the X chromosome.

Treatment

Focuses on teaching self-help and communication skills and on efforts to reduce problem behaviours.

CHILDHOOD DISINTEGRATIVE DISORDER

Clinical Description

Involves severe regression in language, adaptive behaviour, and motor skills after a two- to four-year period of normal development (Malhotra & Gupta, 1999; Zwaigenbaumet et al., 2000).

Statistics

Rare, occurring once in approximately every 100 000 births (Kurita, Kita, & Miyake, 1992); 60 times less common than autism; occurs more frequently in males (Fombonne, 2002).

Causes

Although no specific cause has been identified, several factors suggest a neurological origin, with abnormal brain activity in almost half the cases; incidence of seizures is about 10 percent and may rise to nearly 25 percent in teenagers (Hill & Rosenbloom, 1986).

Treatment

Typically involves behavioural interventions to regain lost skills and behavioural and pharmacological treatments to help reduce behavioural problems.

PERVASIVE DEVELOPMENTAL DISORDER NOT OTHERWISE SPECIFIED)

Clinical Description

Severe and pervasive impairments in social interactions that do not meet all the criteria for autistic disorder; may not display the early avoidance of social interaction, but still may exhibit significant social problems; exhibit fewer repetitive stereotyped behaviours than autistic children (Walker et al., 2004); problems may become more obvious later than three years of age.

Statistics

A relatively large category within the pervasive developmental disorders, with a prevalence of 21 per 10 000 (Fombonne, 2005).

Causes

Likely that some of the same genetic influences (Chudley, Gutierrez, Jocelyn, & Chodirker, 1998) and neurobiological impairments common in autism are involved in these individuals as well (Juul-Dam, Townsend, & Courchesne, 2001).

Treatment

Focuses on teaching socialization and communication skills and on efforts to reduce problem behaviours.

Amy | *In Her Own World*

Amy, three years old, spends much of her day picking up pieces of lint. She drops the lint in the air and then watches intently as it falls to the floor. She also licks the back of her hands and stares at the saliva. She hasn't spoken yet and can't feed or dress herself. Several times a day she screams so loudly that the neighbours at first thought she was being abused. She doesn't seem to be interested in her mother's love and affection but will take her mother's hand to lead her to the refrigerator. Amy likes to eat butter—whole pats of it, several at a time. Her mother uses the pats of butter that you get at some restaurants to help Amy learn and to keep her well behaved. If Amy helps with dressing herself, or if she sits quietly for several minutes, her mother gives her some butter. Amy's mother knows that the butter isn't good for her, but it is the only thing that seems to get through to the child. The family's pediatrician has been concerned about Amy's developmental delays for some time and has recently suggested that she be evaluated by specialists. The pediatrician thinks Amy may have autism and the child and her family will probably need extensive support.

Courtesy of Dalhousie University

▲ Susan Bryson holds an endowed chair in autism research at Dalhousie University. Her research efforts have contributed substantially to the understanding and treatment of autism and other pervasive developmental disorders.

Clinical Description

Three major characteristics of autism are expressed in the *DSM-IV-TR*: impairment in social interactions, impairment in communication, and restricted behaviour, interests, and activities (American Psychiatric Association, 2000a; see DSM Table 14.3). Recent research by Peter Szatmari, Susan Bryson, and their colleagues examined the components of autism scientifically and found evidence for three major sets of symptoms, although these are slightly different from the three outlined in the *DSM-IV-TR*: social-communication deficits, inflexible language and behaviour, and repetitive sensory and motor behaviour (Georgiades

et al., 2007). We nonetheless organize our discussion of autism symptoms around the three categories outlined in the *DSM-IV-TR* since most previous research has used this organizational structure.

Impairment in Social Interactions One of the defining characteristics of people with autistic disorder is that they do not develop the types of social relationships expected for their age (Durand, 2004). Amy never made any friends among her peers and often limited her contact with adults to using them as tools—for example, taking the adult's hand to reach for something she wanted. For young children, the signs of social problems usually include a failure to engage in skills such as joint attention (Dawson et al., 2004;

DSM-IV-TR	**Table 14.3** Diagnostic Criteria for Autistic Disorder

A. At least six items from (1), (2), and (3), with at least two from (1), and one each from (2) and (3):

1. Qualitative impairment in social interaction, as manifested by at least two of the following:
   a. marked impairment in the use of multiple nonverbal behaviours such as eye-to-eye gaze, facial expression, body postures, and gestures to regulate social interaction
   b. failure to develop peer relationships appropriate to developmental level
   c. a lack of spontaneous seeking to share enjoyment, interests, or achievements with other people (e.g., by a lack of showing, bringing, or pointing out objects of interest)
   d. lack of social or emotional reciprocity

2. Qualitative impairments in communication as manifested by at least one of the following:
   a. delay in, or total lack of, the development of spoken language (not accompanied by an attempt to compensate through alternative modes of communication such as gesture or mime)
   b. in individuals with adequate speech, marked impairment in the ability to initiate or sustain a conversation with others
   c. stereotyped and repetitive use of language or idiosyncratic language
   d. lack of varied, spontaneous make-believe play or social imitative play appropriate to developmental level

3. Restricted, repetitive, and stereotyped patterns of behaviour, interests, and activities, as manifested by at least one of the following:
   a. encompassing preoccupation with one or more stereotyped and restricted patterns of interest that is abnormal either in intensity or focus
   b. apparently inflexible adherence to specific, nonfunctional routines or rituals
   c. stereotyped and repetitive motor mannerisms (e.g., hand or finger flapping or twisting, or complex whole-body movements)
   d. persistent preoccupation with parts of objects

B. The person experiences delays or abnormal functioning in at least one of the following areas, with onset before age three: (1) social interaction, (2) language as used in social communication, or (3) symbolic or imaginative play.

C. The disturbance is not better accounted for by Rett's disorder or childhood disintegrative disorder

Source: Reprinted with permission from the *Diagnostic and Statistical Manual of Mental Disorders,* Fourth Edition, Text Revision, (Copyright © 2000). American Psychiatric Association.

Leekam, Lopez, & Moore, 2000). As Dalhousie University developmental psychologist Chris Moore and his colleagues explain, when sitting with a parent in front of a favourite toy, young children will typically look back and forth between the parent and the toy, smiling, in an attempt to engage the parent with the toy. However, this skill in joint attention is noticeably absent in children with autism (Leekam & Moore, 2001; Leekam et al., 2000).

Research using sophisticated eye-tracking technology shows how this social awareness problem evolves as the children grow older. In one study, scientists showed an adult man with autism scenes from some movies and compared how he looked at social scenes with how a man without autism did so (Klin, Jones, Schultz,

▲ Researchers are exploring how people with autism view social interactions among other people.

▲ Specially designed computer games may help children with learning disorders improve their language skills.

Volkmar, & Cohen, 2002). You can see from the photo that the man with autism (indicated by the red lines) scanned nonsocial aspects of the scene (the actor's mouth and jacket), while the man without autism looked at the socially meaningful sections (looking from eye to eye of the people conversing). This research suggests that people with autism—for reasons not yet fully understood—may not be interested in social situations and therefore may not enjoy meaningful relationships with others or have the ability to develop them.

One current view on the social deficits of people with autism is that they lack a theory of mind (i.e., the ability to appreciate that others have a point of reference that differs from their own; Baron-Cohen, Tager-Flusberg, & Cohen, 1994). However, some have been critical of the theory of mind perspective on autism. For example, Philip Zelazo Jr. of the University of Toronto and Sophie Jacques of Dalhousie University have argued that autistic individuals' poor performance on theory of mind tasks may instead be attributed to more general difficulties with executive functioning (i.e., planning, organizing, sequencing, abstracting; e.g., Zelazo, Burack, Boseovski, Jacques, & Frye, 2001; Zelazo, Jacques, Burack, & Frye, 2002).

Impairment in Communication People with autism nearly always have severe problems with communicating (Mundy, Sigman, & Kasari, 1990). These language and communication impairments are visible very early in life, even before diagnosis (Mitchell, Walters, & Stewart, 2006; Zwaigenbaum et al., 2005). About 50 percent of those with autism never acquire useful speech (Rutter, 1978; Volkmar et al., 1994). In those with some speech, much of their communication is unusual. Some repeat the speech of others, a pattern called echolalia we referred to earlier as a sign of

delayed speech development. If you say, "My name is Eileen. What's yours?" they will repeat all or part of what you said: "Eileen, what's yours?" Often, not only are your words repeated, but so is your intonation. Some who can speak are unable or unwilling to carry on conversations with others. Another aspect of the communication deficits of autistic children is a lack of spontaneous pretend play or social imitative play appropriate to the child's development level, as shown in the work of Mel Rutherford and his colleagues at McMaster University (Rutherford & Rogers, 2003).

Restricted Behaviour, Interests, and Activities The more striking characteristics of autism include restricted patterns of behaviour, interests, and activities. The work of McMaster University's Peter Szatmari and his colleagues has shown that this broader category consists of two distinct dimensions: maintenance of sameness, and stereotyped and ritualistic behaviours (Szatmari et al., 2006). Exemplifying the first of these two dimensions, Amy appeared to like things to stay the same: She became extremely upset if even a small change was introduced (such as moving her toys in her room). This intense preference for the status quo has been called maintenance of sameness. One parent related that her son with autism liked one particular helicopter from a toy set. She contacted the manufacturer and obtained more than 50 identical helicopters for her son. He would spend hours lining them up, and his mother reported that he could immediately tell if even one of the 50 was removed.

ABNORMAL PSYCHOLOGY Video

Autism: Christina

"Last year she used [the communication book] a lot more in communicating with us. We have different pictures in the book. They're called picture symbols to represent what she might want, what she might need, what she's asking of us."

Go to Psychology CourseMate at www.abnormalpsych3ce.nelson.com to watch this video.

▲ In a pose typical of autism, a boy's gaze is fixed on an overhead light.

Often, people with autism spend countless hours in stereotyped and ritualistic behaviours, making such stereotyped movements as spinning around in circles, waving their hands in front of their eyes with their heads cocked to one side, or biting their hands. The rituals are often complex: Some people must touch each door as they walk down a hall; others touch each desk in a classroom. If they are interrupted or prevented from completing the ritual, they may have a severe tantrum.

Statistics

Autism was once thought to be a rare disorder, although more recent estimates of its occurrence seem to show an increase in its prevalence. Previous estimates found a rate of 2 to 20 per 10 000 people, although it is now believed to be as high as one in every 500 births (Shattuck, 2006). The prevalence of autism spectrum disorders (which include autistic disorder, pervasive developmental disorder not otherwise specified, and Asperger's disorder) is estimated as high as one in every 110 births (Centers for Disease Control and Prevention, 2009). This rise in the rates may be the result of increased awareness on the part of professionals who now distinguish the pervasive developmental disorders from intellectual disability. However, other environmental factors (such as exposure to toxic chemicals) cannot as yet be ruled out as contributing to this rise.

Gender differences for autism vary depending on the IQ level of the person affected. For people with IQs under 35, autism is more prevalent among females; in the higher IQ range, it is more prevalent among males. The reason for these differences is not known (Centers for Disease Control and Prevention, 2009). Autistic disorder appears to be a universal phenomenon, identified in every part of the world, including Sweden (Gillberg, 1984), Japan (Sugiyama & Abe, 1989), Russia (Lebedinskaya & Nikolskaya, 1993), and China (Chung, Luk, & Lee, 1990). Most people with autism develop the associated symptoms before the age of 36 months (American Psychiatric Association, 2000a).

People with autism have a range of IQ scores. Earlier estimates placed the rate of intellectual disability among children with autism as high as 75 percent, although more recent work—using more appropriate tests for these children—indicates the range between 40 percent and 55 percent (Chakrabarti & Fombonne, 2001; Edelson, 2006). This means that 45 percent to 60 percent of people with autism have average or above average IQs.

▲ Football quarterback Doug Flutie was voted most valuable player in the Canadian Football League six times and led Calgary and Toronto to three Grey Cup titles in the 1990s. His son has autistic disorder. In 2001, he and his wife started the Doug Flutie, Jr., Foundation for Autism to honour their son and to help other families facing childhood autism through support and education.

▲ Timothy plays violin and piano as well as baseball. Autistic disorder occurs in all cultures and races.

IQ measures are used to determine prognosis: The higher children score on IQ tests, the less likely they are to need extensive support by family members or people in the helping professions. Conversely, young children with autistic disorder who score poorly on IQ tests are more likely to be severely delayed in acquiring communication skills and to need a great deal of educational and social support as they grow older. Usually, language abilities and IQ scores are reliable predictors of how children with autistic disorder will fare later in life: the better the language skills and IQ test performance, the better the prognosis (Ben Itzchak, Lahat, Burgin, & Zachor, 2008).

Causes

Autism is a puzzling condition, so we should not be surprised to find numerous theories of why it develops. One generalization is that autistic disorder probably does not have a single cause (Rutter, 1978; Szatmari, 2003). Instead, a number of biological contributions may combine with psychosocial influences to result in the unusual behaviours of people with autism.

Biological Dimensions

Biological theories about the origins of autism have received much empirical support. Several different medical conditions have been associated with autism, including congenital rubella (German measles), hypsarrhythmia (a type of brain wave abnormality sometimes observed in infants), tuberous sclerosis (a genetic disease characterized by benign tumour-like nodules in the brain, intellectual disability, and seizures), cytomegalovirus (an infection caused by a specific type of herpes virus), and difficulties during pregnancy and labour. However, although a small percentage of mothers exposed to the rubella virus have children with autism, most often no autism is present. Research by Lonnie Zwaigenbaum at McMaster University and his colleagues has similarly raised questions about the association of pregnancy and birth complications in autism, suggesting that the association is not likely causal (Zwaigenbaum et al., 2002). Thus, more research is required about the role of various medical conditions in causing autism.

Genetic Influences It is now clear that autism has a genetic component (Volkmar, Klin, & Schultz, 2005). Families that have one child with autism have a 5 percent to 10 percent risk of having another child with the disorder. This rate is 50 to 200 times the risk in the general population, providing strong evidence of a genetic component in the disorder. The exact genes involved in the development of autism remain elusive. There is evidence for some involvement with numerous chromosomes, and work is ongoing in this complex field (Autism Genome Project Consortium, 2007). One area that is receiving attention involves the genes responsible for the brain chemical oxytocin. Because oxytocin is shown to have a role in how we bond with others and in our social memory, researchers are looking for whether genes responsible for this neurochemical are involved with the disorder. Preliminary work identifies an association between autism and an oxytocin receptor gene (Wermter et al., 2010), and researchers expect more connections will be identified in the coming years.

ABNORMAL PSYCHOLOGY Video

Rebecca: A First-Grader with Autistic Disorder

"Getting her out of her routine is something that sets her off.... Routine is extremely, extremely important with her."

Go to Psychology CourseMate at www.abnormalpsych3ce.nelson.com to watch this video.

Concept Check | 14.2

Determine how well you are able to diagnose the disorder in each of the following situations by labelling them autistic disorder, Asperger's disorder, Rett's disorder, Tourette's disorder, selective mutism, or attention deficit/hyperactivity disorder.

1. Five-year-old Sharmila has a low IQ and enjoys sitting in a corner by herself, where she arranges her blocks in little lines or watches the pump bubble in the fish tank. She cannot communicate verbally, but she throws temper tantrums when her parents try to get her to do something she doesn't want to do. _____

2. Mike's developmental disorder is characterized by uncontrollable yelps, sniffs, and grunting noises. _____

3. Three-year-old Abby has severe intellectual disability and trouble walking on her own. One of the characteristics of her disorder is constant hand wringing. _____

4. Aaron started the crossword puzzle. Before getting very far, he turned on the TV and flipped through all the channels a few times. Then he pulled out the model he had started a few weeks ago. After a few minutes, he decided to go for a walk. _____

5. Brad's parents first noticed when he was an infant that he did not like to play with the other children or to be touched or held. He spent most of his time in his playpen by himself. His speech development, however, was not delayed. _____

6. At home, eight-year-old Hanna has been excitedly telling her cousins about a recent trip to a theme park. This would surprise her teachers, who have never heard her speak. _____

Neurobiological Influences As in the area of genetics, many neurobiological influences are being studied to help explain the social and communication problems observed in autism (Volkmar, Klin, Schultz, & State, 2009). One intriguing theory involves research on the amygdala—the area of the brain that, as you saw in Chapter 5, is involved in emotions such as anxiety and fear. Researchers studying the brains of people with autism after they died note that adults with and without the disorder have amygdalae of about the same size but that those with autism have fewer neurons in this structure (Schumann & Amaral, 2006). Earlier research showed that young children with autism actually have a larger amygdala. The theory being proposed is that the amygdala in children with autism is enlarged early in life—causing excessive anxiety and fear (perhaps contributing to their social withdrawal). With continued stress, the release of the stress hormone cortisol damages the amygdala, causing the relative absence of these neurons in adulthood. The damaged amygdala may account for the different way people with autism respond to social situations (Lombardo, Chakrabarti, & Baron-Cohen, 2009).

Other evidence that autism is associated with some form of organic (brain) damage comes most obviously from the prevalence of data showing that a large percentage of people with autism also have some level of intellectual disability. In addition, it has been estimated that between 30 percent and 75 percent of these people display some neurological abnormality such as clumsiness and abnormal posture or gait (Tsai & Ghaziuddin, 1992). These observations provide suggestive but only correlational evidence that autism is physical in origin. With modern brain imaging and scanning technologies, a clearer picture is evolving of the possible neurological dysfunctions in people with autism (Peterson, 1995). Researchers using CT and MRI technologies have found abnormalities of the cerebellum, including reduced size, among people with autism. Courchesne and colleagues examined the brain of a 21-year-old man who had a diagnosis of autism but no other neurological disorders and a tested IQ score in the average range (Courchesne, Hesselink, Jernigan, & Yeung-Courchesne, 1987). He was selected as a subject because he did not have the severe cognitive deficits seen in three-quarters of people with autism. Hence, the researchers could presume that he was free of any brain damage associated with intellectual disability but not necessarily with autism. After obtaining the informed consent of this man and his parents, they conducted an MRI scan of his brain.

As seen in the photo below, the most striking finding was that the cerebellum of the subject was abnormally small compared with that of a person without autism. Although this kind of abnormality has not been found in every study using brain imaging, it appears to be one of the more reliable findings of brain involvement in autism to date (Courchesne, 1991), and it may point to an important subtype of people with autism.

An additional neurobiological influence we mentioned in the section on genetics involves the neuropeptide oxytocin. Remember that this is an important social neurochemical that influences bonding and is found to increase trust and reduce fear. Some research on children with autism found lower levels of oxytocin in their blood (Modahl et al., 1998), and giving people with autism oxytocin improved their ability to remember and process information with emotion content (such as remembering happy faces), a problem that is symptomatic of autism (Guastella et al., 2010). This is one of a number of theories being explored as possible contributors to this puzzling disorder.

One highly controversial theory is that mercury—specifically, the mercury previously used as a preservative in childhood vaccines (thimerosal)—is responsible for the increases seen in autism over the last decade. Large epidemiological studies conducted in Denmark show that there is no increased risk of autism in children who are vaccinated (Madsen et al., 2002; Parker, Schwartz, Todd, & Pickering, 2004). Despite this and other convincing evidence, the correlation between when a child is vaccinated for measles, mumps, and rubella (12–15 months) and when the symptoms of autism first become evident (before three years), continues to fuel the belief by many families that there must be some connection.

Psychological and Social Dimensions

Because historical context is important to research, it is helpful to examine past as well as more recent theories of autism. Historically, autistic disorder was seen as the result of failed parenting (Bettelheim, 1967; Ferster, 1961; Tinbergen & Tinbergen, 1972). Mothers and fathers of children with autism were characterized as perfectionistic, cold, and aloof (Kanner, 1949), with relatively high socioeconomic status (Allen, DeMyer, Norton, Pontius, & Yang, 1971; Cox, Rutter, Newman, & Bartak, 1975) and higher IQs than the general population (Kanner, 1943). Descriptions such as these have inspired theories that hold parents responsible for their children's unusual behaviours. These views were devastating to a generation of parents, who felt guilty and responsible for their children's problems. Imagine being accused of such coldness toward your own child as to cause serious and permanent disabilities! Later research contradicts these studies, suggesting that on a variety of personality measures, the parents of individuals with autism may not differ substantially from parents of children without disabilities (Koegel, Schreibman, O'Neill, & Burke, 1983; McAdoo & DeMyer, 1978).

Other theories about the origins of autism were based on the unusual speech patterns of some individuals—namely, their tendency to avoid first-person pronouns such as *I* and *me* and to use *he* and *she* instead. For example, if

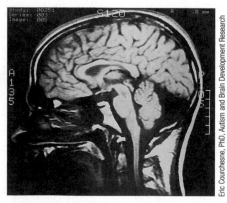

▲ MRIs of two different brains: The person on the left has no neurological disorders, and the person on the right has autism. Note (lower right) that the cerebellum is smaller in the person with autism.

Eric Courchesne, PhD, Autism and Brain Development Research Laboratory, LaJolla, CA you ask a child with autism, "Do you want something to drink?" he might say, "He wants something to drink" (meaning "I want something to drink"). This observation led some theorists to wonder whether autism involves a lack of self-awareness (Goldfarb, 1963; Mahler, 1952). Imagine, if you can, not understanding that your existence is distinct. There is no "you," only "them"! Such a debilitating view of the world was used to explain the unusual ways people with autism behaved. Theorists suggested that the withdrawal seen among people with autistic disorder reflected a lack of awareness of their own existence.

However, later research has shown that some people with autistic disorder do seem to have self-awareness (Dawson & McKissick, 1984; Spiker & Ricks, 1984), and it follows a developmental progression. Just like children without a disability, those with cognitive abilities below the level expected for a child of 18 to 24 months show little or no self-recognition, but people with more advanced abilities do demonstrate self-awareness. Self-concept may be lacking when people with autism also have cognitive disabilities or delays and not because of autism itself.

Myths about people with autism are perpetuated when the idiosyncrasies of the disorder are highlighted. These perceptions are furthered by portrayals such as Dustin Hoffman's in *Rain Man*—his character could, for instance, instantaneously and accurately count hundreds of toothpicks falling to the floor. This type of ability—referred to as *savant skills*—is just not typical with autism. It is important always to separate myth from reality and to be aware that such portrayals do not accurately represent the full range of manifestations of this complex disorder.

The phenomenon of *echolalia*, repeating a word or phrase spoken by another person, was once believed to be an unusual characteristic of this disorder. Subsequent work in developmental psychopathology, however, has demonstrated that repeating the speech of others is part of the normally developing language skills observed in most young children (Koegel, 1995; Prizant & Wetherby, 1989). Even a behaviour as disturbing as the self-injurious behaviour sometimes seen in people with autism is observed in milder forms, such as head banging, among typically developing infants (de Lissovoy, 1961). This type of research has helped workers isolate the facts from the myths about autism and clarify the role of development in the disorder. Primarily, it appears that what clearly distinguishes people with autism from others are social deficiencies.

At present, few workers in the field of autism believe that psychological or social influences play a major role in the development of this disorder. To the relief of many families, it is now clear that poor parenting is not responsible for autism. Deficits in such skills as socialization and communication appear to be more biological in origin. However, the study of autism is a relatively young field and still awaits an integrative theory. It is likely that further research will identify psychological and social factors that interact very early with the biological influences, producing the deficits in socialization and communication as well as the characteristic unusual behaviours of individuals with autism.

Treatment

Most of the treatment research has focused on children with autism, so we primarily discuss treatment research for these individuals. However, because treatment for all the pervasive developmental disorders relies on a similar approach, this research should be relevant across disorders. One generalization that can be made about autism as well as the other pervasive developmental disorders is that no completely effective treatment exists. We have not been successful in eliminating the social problems experienced by these individuals. Rather, like the approach to individuals with intellectual disability, most efforts at treating people with pervasive developmental disorders focus on enhancing their communication and daily living skills and on reducing problem behaviours such as tantrums and self-injury (Durand, 1999b). We describe some of these approaches next, including work on early intervention for young children with autism.

Psychosocial Treatments

Early psychodynamic treatments were based on the belief that autism is the result of improper parenting, and these treatments encouraged ego development (Bettelheim, 1967). Given our current understanding about the nature of the disorder, we should not be surprised to learn that treatments based solely on ego development have not had a positive impact on the lives of people with autism (Kanner & Eisenberg, 1955). Greater success has been achieved with behavioural approaches that focus on skill building and behavioural treatment of problem behaviours. A review by Susan Bryson and her colleagues concludes that the types of psychosocial interventions that are most successful are those that are very systematic and dedicated to teaching a specific skill (Bryson, Rogers, & Fombonne, 2003). Behavioural approaches are based on the early work of Ferster and Lovaas (e.g., Ferster, 1961; Lovaas, 1977). Although the work of these researchers has been greatly refined over the past 40 years, the basic premise— that people with autism can learn and that they can be taught some of the skills they lack—remains central. There is a great deal of overlap between the treatment of autism and the treatment of intellectual disability. With that in mind, we highlight several treatment areas that are particularly important for people with autism, including communication and socialization.

Communication Problems with communication and language are among the defining characteristics of this disorder. People with autism often do not acquire meaningful speech; they tend to have either very limited speech or use unusual speech such as echolalia. Teaching people to speak in a useful way is difficult. Think about how we teach languages: It mostly involves imitation. Imagine how you would teach a young girl to say the word *spaghetti*. You could wait for several days until she said a word that sounded something like "spaghetti" (maybe "confetti"), and then reinforce her. You could then spend several weeks trying to shape "confetti" into something closer to "spaghetti." Or you could just prompt, "Say 'spaghetti.'" Fortunately, most children can imitate and learn to communicate very efficiently. But a child who has autism can't or won't imitate.

In the mid-1960s, Lovaas and colleagues took a monumental first step toward addressing the difficulty of getting children with autism to respond. They used the basic behavioural procedures of *shaping* and *discrimination training* to teach these nonspeaking children to imitate others verbally (Lovaas, Berberich, Perloff, & Schaeffer, 1966). The first skill the researchers taught them was to imitate other people's speech. They began by reinforcing a child with food and praise for making any sound while watching the teacher. After the child had mastered that step, they reinforced the child only if she or he made a sound after the teacher made a request—such as the phrase "Say 'ball'" (a procedure known as discrimination training). Once the child reliably made some sound after the teacher's request, the teacher used shaping to reinforce only approximations of the requested sound, such as the sound of the letter "b." Sometimes the teacher helped the child with physical prompting—in this case, by gently holding the lips together to help the child make the sound of "b." Once the child had responded successfully, a second word was introduced—such as "mama"—and the procedure was repeated. This continued until the child could correctly respond to multiple requests, demonstrating imitation by copying the words or phrases made by the teacher.

Once a child could imitate, speech was easier, and progress was made in teaching some children to use labels, plurals, sentences, and other more complex forms of language (Lovaas, 1977). Despite the success of some children in learning speech, other children do not respond to this training, and workers sometimes use alternatives to vocal speech such as sign language and devices that have vocal output and can literally "speak" for the child (Johnson, Baumgart, Helmstetter, & Curry, 1996). One such alternative is the Picture Exchange Communication System (PECS) recently developed by Bondy and Frost (2001, 2002) to teach functional communication to individuals with limited speech, such as children with autism spectrum disorders. This interesting new approach teaches children to initiate communicative interactions within a social framework. Children are taught to exchange a single picture for a desired item. Eventually, they learn to construct picture-based sentences and to use a variety of attributes in their requests (Bondy & Frost, 2001, 2002).

Socialization One of the most striking features of people with autism is their unusual reaction to other people. One study compared rates of adolescent interaction among children with autism, those with Down syndrome, and those developing normally; the

▲ The communication deficits typical of autism often lead to social isolation.

adolescents with autism showed significantly fewer interactions with their peers (Attwood, Frith, & Hermelin, 1988). Although social deficits are among the more obvious problems experienced by people with autism, limited progress has been achieved in developing social skills. Behavioural procedures have increased behaviours such as playing with toys or with peers, although the quality of these interactions appears to remain limited (Durand & Carr, 1988). In other words, behavioural clinicians have not found a way of teaching people with autism the subtle social skills that are important for interactions with peers—including how to initiate and maintain social interactions that lead to meaningful friendships.

Timing and Settings for Treatment Lovaas and colleagues reported on their early intervention efforts with very young children (Lovaas, 1987). They used intensive behavioural treatment for communication and social skills problems for 40 hours or more per week, which seemed to improve intellectual and educational functioning. Follow-up suggests that these improvements are long lasting (McEachin, Smith, & Lovaas, 1993).

Lovaas found that the children who improved most had been placed in regular classrooms, and children who did not do well had been placed in separate special education classes. As we will see in our discussion of intellectual disability, children with even the most severe disabilities are now being taught in regular classrooms. In addition, *inclusion*—helping children fully participate in the social and academic life of their peers—applies not only to school but also to all aspects of life. Many different models are being used to integrate people with autism in order to normalize their experiences (Durand, 1999b). For instance, community homes are being recommended over separate residential settings, including special foster care programs (Smith, 1992), and supported employment options are being tested that would let individuals with autism have regular jobs. The behavioural interventions discussed are essential to easing this transition to fully integrated settings.

Biological Treatments

No one medical treatment has been found to cure autism. In fact, medical intervention has had little success. A variety of pharmacological treatments are used to decrease agitation, and the major tranquilizers and serotonin-specific reuptake inhibitors seem helpful here (Volkmar et al., 2009). While psychotropic drugs may help to reduce some symptoms of autism, Susan Bryson and her colleagues (2003) warn that they are neither curative nor a substitute for other forms of support and intervention. Although vitamins and dietary changes have been promoted as one approach to treating autism and initial reports were very optimistic, research to date has found little support that they significantly help children with autism (Holm & Varley, 1989).

Because autism may result from a variety of different deficits, it is unlikely that one drug will work for everyone with this disorder. Much current work is focused on finding pharmacological treatments for specific behaviours or symptoms.

Integrating Treatments

The treatment of choice for people with pervasive developmental disorder combines various approaches to the many facets of this disorder. For children, most therapy consists of school education combined with special psychological supports for problems with communication and socialization. Behavioural approaches have been most clearly documented as benefiting children in this area. Pharmacological treatments can help some of them temporarily. Parents also need support because of the great demands and stressors involved in living with and caring for such children. As children with autism grow older, intervention focuses on efforts to integrate them into the community, often with supported living arrangements and work settings. Because the range of abilities of people with autism is so great, however, these efforts differ dramatically. Some people are able to live in their own apartments with only minimal support from family members. Others, with more severe forms of intellectual disability, require more extensive efforts to support them in their communities.

Intellectual Disability

Intellectual disability (previously referred to as *mental retardation*) is a disorder evidenced in childhood as significantly below-average intellectual and adaptive functioning (Toth & King, 2010). People with intellectual disability experience difficulties with day-to-day activities, to an extent that reflects both the severity of their cognitive deficits and the type and amount of assistance they receive. Perhaps more than any other group we have studied, people with intellectual disability have throughout history received treatment that can best be described as shameful (Scheerenberger, 1983). With notable exceptions, societies throughout the ages have devalued individuals whose intellectual abilities are deemed less than adequate. Although the *DSM-IV-TR* uses the term "mental retardation," we use "intellectual disability" throughout this chapter to be consistent with changes in terminology in this field and possible changes in the *DSM-5* (American Psychiatric Association, 2010b).

The field of intellectual disability has undergone dramatic and fundamental changes during the past two decades. What it means to have an intellectual disability, how to define it, how to label it, and how people with this disorder are treated have been scrutinized, debated, and fought over by a variety of concerned groups. We describe the disorder in the context of these important changes, explaining both the status of people who have intellectual disabilities and our current understanding of its causes and treatment.

The manifestations of intellectual disability are varied. Some individuals function quite well, even independently, in our complex society, such as Canadian artist Jane Cameron, whose tapestries are found in galleries around the world. Also, American actor Lauren Potter (who has Down syndrome) plays a cheerleader in the television show *Glee*. Others with intellectual disability have significant cognitive and physical impairments and require considerable assistance to carry on daily activities. Consider the case of James.

JAMES | *Up to the Challenge*

James's mother contacted us because he was disruptive at school and at work. James was 17 and attended the local high school. He had Down syndrome and was described as very likable and, at times, mischievous. He enjoyed skiing, bike riding, and many other activities common among teenage boys. In fact, his desire to participate was a source of some conflict between him and his mother: He wanted to take the driver's education course at school, which his mother felt would set him up for failure; and he had a girlfriend he wanted to date, a prospect that also caused his mother concern.

School administrators complained because James didn't participate in activities such as physical education, and at the work site that was part of his school program, he was often sullen, sometimes lashing out at the supervisors. They were considering moving him to a program with more supervision and less independence.

James's family had moved frequently during his youth, and they had experienced striking differences in the way each community responded to James and his intellectual disability. In some school districts, he was immediately placed in classes with other children of his age and his teachers were provided with additional assistance and consultation. In others, it was just as quickly recommended that he be taught separately. Sometimes the school district had a special classroom in the local school for children with intellectual disabilities. Other districts had programs in other towns, and James would have to travel an hour to and from school each day. Every time he was assessed in a new school, the evaluation was similar to earlier ones. He received scores on his IQ tests in the range of 40 to 50, which placed him in the moderate range of intellectual disability. Each school gave him the same diagnosis: Down syndrome with moderate intellectual disability. At each school, the teachers and other professionals were competent and caring individuals who wanted the best for James and his mother. Yet some believed that in order to learn skills, James needed a separate program with specialized staff. Others felt they could provide a comparable education in a regular classroom and that to have peers without disabilities would be an added benefit.

In high school, James had several academic classes in a separate classroom for adolescents with learning problems, but he participated in some classes, such as gym, with students who did not have intellectual disabilities. His current difficulties in gym (not participating) and at work (being oppositional) were jeopardizing his placement in both programs. When I spoke with James's mother, she expressed frustration that the work program was beneath him because he was asked to do boring, repetitive work such as folding paper. James expressed a similar frustration, saying that he was treated like a baby. He could communicate fairly well when he wanted to, although he sometimes would get confused about what he wanted to say, and it was difficult to understand everything he tried to articulate. On observing him at school and at work, and after speaking with his teachers, we realized that a common paradox had developed. James resisted work he thought was too easy. His teachers interpreted his resistance to mean that the work was too hard for him, and they gave him even simpler tasks. He resisted or protested more vigorously, and they responded with even more supervision and structure.

▲ The colourful tapestries of Canadian artist Jane Cameron, who has Down syndrome, hang in galleries all over the world. She has flourished both as an artist and as a swimmer in the Special Olympics.

Later, when we discuss treatment, we return to James, showing how we intervened at school and work to help him progress and become more independent.

Clinical Description

People with intellectual disability display a broad range of abilities and personalities. Individuals like James, who have mild or moderate impairments, can, with proper preparation, carry out most of the day-to-day activities expected of any of us. Many can learn to use mass transportation, purchase groceries, and hold a variety of jobs. Those with more severe impairments may need help to eat, bathe, and dress themselves, although with proper training and support they can achieve a degree of independence. These individuals experience impairments that affect most areas of functioning. Language and communication skills are often the most obvious. James was only mildly impaired in this area, needing help with articulation. In contrast, people with more severe forms of intellectual disability may never learn to use speech as a form of communication, requiring alternatives such as sign language or special communication devices to express even their most basic needs. Because many cognitive processes are adversely affected, individuals with intellectual disability have difficulty learning. The level of challenge depends on how extensive the cognitive disability is.

Before examining the specific criteria for intellectual disability, note that, like the personality disorders we described in Chapter 12, intellectual disability is included on Axis II of the *DSM-IV-TR*. Remember that separating disorders by axes serves two purposes: first, indicating that disorders on Axis II tend to be more chronic and less amenable to treatment, and second, reminding clinicians to consider whether these disorders, if present, are affecting an Axis I disorder. People can be diagnosed on both Axis I (e.g., generalized anxiety disorder) and Axis II (e.g., mild intellectual disability).

The *DSM-IV-TR* criteria for intellectual disability are in three groups (see DSM Table 14.4). First, a person must have *significantly subaverage intellectual functioning*, a determination made with one of several IQ tests with the cutoff score set by *DSM-IV-TR* at approximately 70 or below. Roughly 2 percent to 3 percent of the population score at 70 or below on these tests. The American Association on Intellectual and Developmental Disabilities (AAIDD), which has its own, similar definition of intellectual disability, has a cutoff score of approximately 70 to 75 (Thompson et al., 2009; Toth & King, 2010).

The second criterion of both the *DSM-IV-TR* and AAIDD definitions for intellectual disability calls for *concurrent deficits or impairments in adaptive functioning*. In other words, scoring "approximately 70 or below" on an IQ test is not sufficient for a diagnosis of intellectual disability; a person must also have significant difficulty in at least two of the following areas: communication, self-care, home living, social and interpersonal skills, use of community resources, self-direction, functional academic skills, work, leisure, health, and safety. To illustrate, although James had many strengths, such as his ability to communicate and his social and interpersonal skills (he had several good friends), he was not as proficient as other teenagers at caring for himself in areas such as home living, health, and safety, or in academic areas. This aspect of the definition is important because it excludes people who can function quite well in society but for various reasons do poorly on IQ tests. For instance, someone whose primary language is not English may do poorly on an IQ test but may still function at a level comparable to his or her peers. This person would not be considered to have intellectual disability even if he or she scored below 70 on the IQ test.

The final criterion for intellectual disability is the *age of onset*. The characteristic below-average intellectual and adaptive abilities must be evident before the person is 18. This cutoff is designed to identify affected individuals during the developmental period,

DSM-IV-TR	**Table 14.4** Diagnostic Criteria for Intellectual Disability (Mental Retardation)

A. Significantly subaverage intellectual functioning, an IQ of approximately 70 or below on an individually administered IQ test (for infants, a clinical judgment of significantly subaverage intellectual functioning)

B. Concurrent deficits or impairments in present adaptive functioning (i.e., the person's effectiveness in meeting the standards expected for his or her age by his or her cultural group) in at least two of the following areas: communication, self-care, home living, social/interpersonal skills, use of community resources, self-direction, functional-academic skills, work, leisure, health, and safety

C. The onset is before age 18

Code based on degree of severity reflecting level of intellectual impairment:

Mild intellectual disability: IQ level 50–55 to approximately 70

Moderate intellectual disability: IQ level 35–40 to 50–55

Severe intellectual disability: IQ level 20–25 to 35–40

Profound intellectual disability: IQ level below 20 or 25

Intellectual disability, severity unspecified: When there is strong presumption of intellectual disability but the person's intelligence is untestable by standard tests

Source: Reprinted with permission from the *Diagnostic and Statistical Manual of Mental Disorders*, Fourth Edition, Text Revision, (Copyright © 2000). American Psychiatric Association.

when the brain is developing and therefore when any problems should become evident. The age criterion rules out the diagnosis of intellectual disability for adults who suffer from brain trauma or forms of dementia that impair their abilities. The age of 18 is somewhat arbitrary, but it is the age at which most children leave school and when our society considers a person an adult.

The imprecise definition of intellectual disability points to an important issue: Intellectual disability, perhaps more than any of the other disorders, is defined by society. The cutoff score of 70 or 75 is based on a statistical concept (two or more standard deviations from the mean) and not on qualities inherent in people who supposedly have intellectual disability. There is little disagreement about the diagnosis for people with the most severe disabilities; however, the majority of people diagnosed with intellectual disability are in the mild range of cognitive impairment. They need some support and assistance, but remember that the criteria for using the label of "intellectual disability" are based partly on a somewhat arbitrary cutoff score for IQ that can (and does) change with changing social expectations.

People with intellectual disability differ significantly in their degree of disability. Almost all classification systems have differentiated these individuals in terms of their ability or on the cause of the intellectual disability (Toth & King, 2010). Traditionally (and still evident in the *DSM-IV-TR*), classification systems have identified four levels of intellectual disability: *mild*, which is identified by an IQ score between 50 or 55 and 70; *moderate*, with a range of 35–40 to 50–55; *severe*, ranging from 20–25 up to 35–40; and *profound*, which includes people with IQ scores below 20–25. It is difficult to categorize each level of intellectual disability according to "average" individual achievements by people at each level. A person with severe or profound intellectual disability tends to have extremely limited formal communication skills (no spoken speech or only one or two words) and may require great or even total assistance in dressing, bathing, and eating. Yet people with these diagnoses have a wide range of skills that depend on training and the availability of other supports. Similarly, people like James, who have mild or moderate intellectual disability, should be able to live independ-

ently or with minimal supervision; again, however, their achievement depends in part on their education and the community support available to them.

Perhaps the most controversial change being suggested in the new AAIDD definition of intellectual disability is its description of different levels of this disorder, which are based on the level of support or assistance people need: *intermittent, limited, extensive,* or *pervasive* (Thompson et al., 2009). The important difference is that the AAIDD system identifies the role of "needed supports" in determining level of functioning, whereas the *DSM-IV-TR* implies that the ability of the person is the sole determining factor. The AAIDD system focuses on specific areas of assistance a person needs that can then be translated into training goals. Whereas his *DSM-IV-TR* diagnosis might be "moderate intellectual disability," James might receive the following AAIDD diagnosis: "a person with intellectual disability who needs limited supports in home living, health and safety, and in academic skills." The AAIDD definition emphasizes the types of support James and others require, and it highlights the need to identify what assistance is available when considering a person's abilities and potential. However, at this writing, the AAIDD system has not been assessed empirically to determine whether it has greater value than traditional (*DSM*) systems.

An additional method of classification has been used in the educational system to identify the abilities of students with intellectual disability. It relies on three categories: *educable intellectual disability* (based on an IQ of 50 to approximately 70–75), *trainable intellectual disability* (IQ of 30 to 50), and *severe intellectual disability* (IQ below 30) (Cipani, 1991). The assumption is that students with educable intellectual disability (comparable to mild intellectual disability) could learn basic academic skills; students with trainable intellectual disability (comparable to moderate intellectual disability) could not master academic skills but could learn rudimentary vocational skills; and students with severe intellectual disability (comparable to severe and profound intellectual disability) would not benefit from academic or vocational instruction. Built into this categorization system is the automatic negative assumption that certain individuals cannot

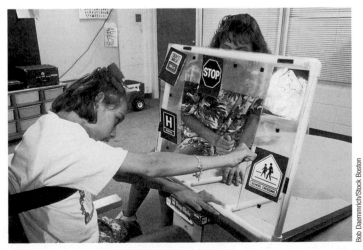
▲ Although she cannot speak, this girl is learning to communicate with an eye-gaze board, pointing to or simply looking at the image that conveys her message.

▲ Intellectual disability can be defined in terms of the level of support people need.

benefit from certain types of training. This system and the potentially stigmatizing and limiting *DSM-IV-TR* categories (mild, moderate, severe, and profound intellectual disability) inspired the AAIDD categorization of needed supports. Current trends are away from the educational system of classification, because it inappropriately creates negative expectations in teachers. Clinicians continue to use the *DSM-IV-TR* system; time will tell whether the AAIDD categories will be widely adopted.

Statistics

Approximately 90 percent of people with intellectual disability fall under the label of mild intellectual disability (IQ of 50 to 70). When you add individuals with moderate, severe, and profound intellectual disability (IQ below 50), the total population of people with this disorder represents 1 percent to 3 percent of the general population (Toth & King, 2010). In Canada, current statistics suggest that 70 babies a week are born with intellectual disability (Goldner, 2003). A study conducted with Ontario adolescents suggests that while the prevalence of severe intellectual disability is similar in Canada to rates obtained in studies conducted around the world, the rates of mild intellectual disability appear lower in Canada than in the United States, and more similar to rates found in the Scandinavian countries (Bradley, Thompson, & Bryson, 2002).

The course of intellectual disability is chronic, meaning that people do not recover. However, the prognosis for people with this disorder varies considerably. Given appropriate training and support, individuals with less severe forms can live relatively independent and productive lives. People with more severe impairments require more assistance in order to participate in work and community life. Intellectual disability is observed more often among males, with a male-to-female ratio of about 1.6 to 1 (Laxova, Ridler, & Bowen-Bravery, 1977). This difference may be present mainly among people with mild intellectual disability; no gender differences are found among people with severe forms (Richardson, Katz, & Koller, 1986).

Causes

There are literally hundreds of known causes of intellectual disability, including the following:

- *Environmental*: for example, deprivation, abuse, and neglect
- *Prenatal*: for instance, exposure to disease or drugs while still in the womb
- *Perinatal*: such as difficulties during labour and delivery
- *Postnatal*: for example, infections, head injury

As we mentioned in Chapter 11, heavy use of alcohol among pregnant women can produce a disorder in their children called *fetal alcohol syndrome*, a condition that can lead to severe learning disabilities. Other prenatal factors that can produce intellectual disability include a pregnant woman's exposure to disease and chemicals, and poor nutrition. In addition, lack of oxygen (anoxia) during birth, and insults such as malnutrition and head injuries during the developmental period, can lead to severe cognitive impairments. Despite the rather large number of known causes of intellectual disability, keep one fact in mind: Nearly 25 percent of cases either cannot be attributed to any known cause or are thought to be the result of social and environmental influences (Toth & King, 2010).

Biological Dimensions

Genetic Influences Almost 300 genes have been identified as having the potential to contribute to intellectual disability, and it is expected that there are many more (Inlow & Restifo, 2004). A portion of the people with more severe intellectual disability have identifiable single-gene disorders, involving a *dominant gene* (expresses itself when paired with a normal gene), a *recessive gene* (expresses itself only when paired with another copy of itself), or an *X-linked gene* (present on the X or sex chromosome).

Only a few dominant genes result in intellectual disability, probably as a result of natural selection: Someone who carries a dominant gene that results in intellectual disability is less likely to have children and thus less likely to pass the gene to offspring. Therefore, this gene becomes less likely to continue in the population. However, some people, especially those with mild intellectual disability, do marry and have children, thus passing on their genes. One example of a dominant gene disorder, *tuberous sclerosis*, is relatively rare, occurring in one of approximately every 30 000 births. About 60 percent of the people with this disorder have intellectual disability, and most have seizures (uncontrolled electrical discharges in the brain) and characteristic bumps on the skin that during their adolescence resemble acne (Curatolo, Bombardieri, & Jozwiak, 2008).

A recessive disorder called *phenylketonuria*, or PKU, affects one of every 14 000 newborns and is characterized by an inability to break down a chemical in our diets called phenylalanine (Smith, Klim, & Hanley, 2000). For example, diet soft drinks contain phenylalanine. Until the mid-1960s, the majority of people with PKU had intellectual disability, seizures, and behaviour problems, resulting from high levels of this chemical. However, researchers developed a screening technique that identifies the existence of PKU; infants are now routinely tested at birth, and any individuals identified with PKU can be successfully treated with a special diet that avoids the chemical phenylalanine. This is a rare example of the successful prevention of one form of intellectual disability.

Ironically, successful early identification and treatment of people with PKU during the past three decades has some worried that an outbreak of PKU-related intellectual disability will recur. The special diet to prevent symptoms is necessary only until the person reaches age six or seven. At this point, people tend to become lax and eat a regular diet—fortunately, with no harmful consequences for themselves. Because untreated maternal PKU can harm the developing fetus (Lenke & Levy, 1980), there is concern now that women with PKU who are of childbearing age may not stick to their diets and inadvertently cause PKU-related intellectual disability in their children before birth. Many physicians recommend dietary restriction through the person's lifetime, and especially during the childbearing period—thus the warnings on products with phenylalanine (Widaman, 2009).

Lesch-Nyhan syndrome, an X-linked disorder, is characterized by intellectual disability, signs of cerebral palsy (spasticity or tightening of the muscles), and self-injurious behaviour, including finger and lip biting (Nyhan, 1978). Only males are affected, because a recessive gene is responsible; when it is on the X chromosome in males it does not have a normal gene to balance it, because males do not have a second X chromosome. Women with this gene are carriers and do not show any of the symptoms.

As our ability to detect genetic defects improves, more disorders will be identified genetically. The hope is that our increased knowledge will be accompanied by improvements in our ability to treat or, as in the case of PKU, prevent intellectual disability and other negative outcomes.

Chromosomal Influences It was only about 50 years ago that the number of chromosomes—46—was correctly identified in human cells (Tjio & Levan, 1956). Three years later, researchers found that people with Down syndrome (the disorder James displayed) had an additional small chromosome (Lejeune, Gauthier, & Turpin, 1959). Since that time, a number of other chromosomal aberrations that result in intellectual disability have been identified. We describe Down syndrome and fragile X syndrome in some detail, but there are hundreds of other ways in which abnormalities among the chromosomes can lead to intellectual disability.

Down syndrome, the most common chromosomal form of intellectual disability, was first identified by the British physician Langdon Down in 1866. Down had tried to develop a classification system for people with intellectual disability based on their resemblance to people of other races; he described individuals with this particular disorder as "mongoloid" because they resembled people from Mongolia (Scheerenberger, 1983). The term *mongoloidism* was used for some time but has been replaced with the term *Down syndrome*. The disorder is caused by the presence of an extra 21st chromosome and is therefore sometimes referred to as trisomy 21. For reasons we don't completely understand, during cell division two of the 21st chromosomes stick together (a condition called *nondisjunction*), creating one cell with one copy that dies, and one cell with three copies that divide to create a person with *Down syndrome*.

People with Down syndrome have characteristic facial features, including folds in the corners of their upwardly slanting eyes, a flat nose, and a small mouth with a flat roof that makes the tongue protrude somewhat. Like James, they tend to have congenital heart malformations. Tragically, nearly all adults with Down syndrome past the age of 40 show signs of dementia of the Alzheimer's type, a degenerative brain disorder that causes impairments in memory and other cognitive disorders (Wiseman, Alford, Tybulewicz, & Fisher, 2009). This disorder among people with Down syndrome occurs earlier than usual (sometimes in their early 20s) and has led to the finding that at least one form of Alzheimer's disease is attributable to a gene on the 21st chromosome.

According to the Canadian Down Syndrome Society, 35 000 Canadians have Down syndrome (Canadian Down Syndrome Society, 2007). The incidence of this syndrome is about one in 800 births (Canadian Down Syndrome Society, 2007). The incidence of children born with Down syndrome has been tied to maternal age. As shown in ■ Figure 14.3, as the age of the mother increases, so does her chance of having a child with this disorder (Evans & Hammerton, 1985; Hook, 1982). A woman at age 20 has a one in 2000 chance of having a child with Down syndrome; at the age of 35 this risk increases to one in 500, and at the age of 45 it increases again to one in every 30 births (Hook, 1982). Despite these numbers, many more children with Down syndrome are born to younger mothers because, as women get older, they tend to have fewer children. The reason for the rise in incidence with maternal age is not clear. Some suggest that because a woman's ova (eggs) are all produced in youth, the older ones have been exposed to toxins, radiation, and other harmful substances over longer periods of time. This exposure may interfere with the normal meiosis (division) of the chromosomes, creating an extra 21st chromosome (Pueschel & Goldstein, 1991). Others believe the hormonal changes that occur as women age are responsible for this error in cell division (Crowley, Hayden, & Gulati, 1982).

For some time it has been possible to detect the presence of Down syndrome—but not the degree of intellectual disability—through **amniocentesis**, a procedure that involves removing and testing a sample of the fluid that surrounds the fetus in the amniotic sac. Down syndrome and a number of other disorders can be detected through amniocentesis.

Fragile X syndrome is a second common chromosomally related cause of intellectual disability (Toth & King, 2010). As its name suggests, this disorder is caused by an abnormality on the X chromosome, a mutation that makes the tip of the chromosome look as though it were hanging from a thread, giving it the appearance of fragility. As with Lesch-Nyhan syndrome, which also involves the X chromosome, fragile X primarily affects males because they do not have a second X chromosome with a normal gene to balance out the mutation. Unlike Lesch-Nyhan carriers, however, women who carry fragile X syndrome commonly display mild to severe learning disabilities (Koukoui & Chaudhuri, 2007). Men with the disorder display moderate to severe levels of intellectual disability and have higher rates of hyperactivity, short attention spans, gaze avoidance, and perseverative speech (repeating the same words again and again). In addition, such physical characteristics as large ears, testicles, and head circumference are common. Estimates are that 1 of every 4000 males and 1 of every 8000 females are born with fragile X syndrome (Toth & King, 2010).

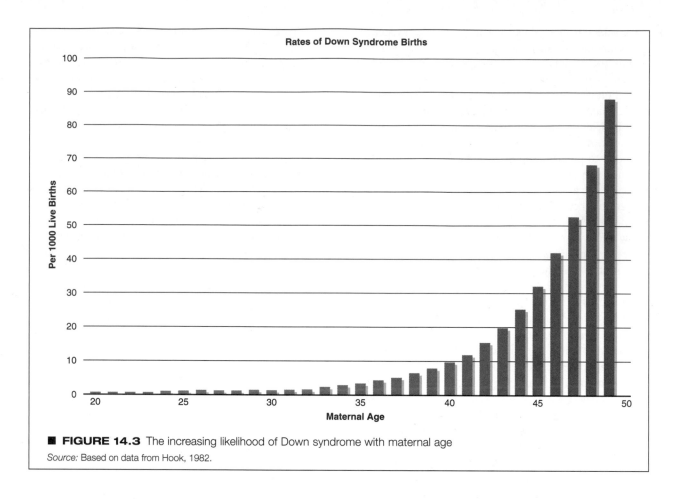

Rates of Down Syndrome Births

Per 1000 Live Births (y-axis) vs *Maternal Age* (x-axis)

■ **FIGURE 14.3** The increasing likelihood of Down syndrome with maternal age

Source: Based on data from Hook, 1982.

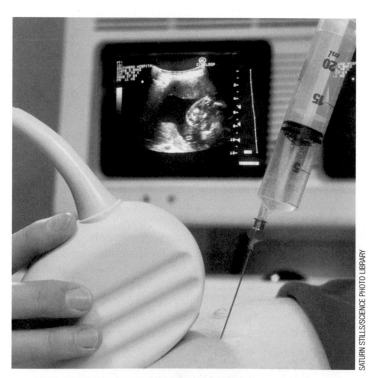

▲ Amniocentesis can detect the presence of Down syndrome in a fetus. Guided by an ultrasound image, the doctor withdraws amniotic fluid for analysis.

Psychological and Social Dimensions

Up to 25 percent of the cases of intellectual disability fall in the mild range and are not associated with any obvious genetic or physical disorders. Sometimes referred to as **cultural-familial intellectual disability**, people with these characteristics are thought to have cognitive impairments that result from a combination of psychosocial and biological influences, although the specific mechanisms that lead to this type of intellectual disability are not yet understood. The cultural influences that may contribute to this condition include abuse, neglect, and social deprivation.

It is sometimes useful to consider people with intellectual disability in two distinct groups: those with cultural-familial and those with biological (or "organic") forms of intellectual disability. People in the latter group have more severe forms of intellectual disability that are usually traceable to known causes such as fragile X syndrome. ■ Figure 14.4 shows that the cultural-familial group is composed primarily of individuals at the lower end of the IQ continuum (in other words, just part of the normal distribution), whereas in the organic group, genetic, chromosomal, and other factors affect intellectual performance which explains the "bump" in their numbers at that end of the distribution. The organic group increases the number of people at the lower end of the IQ continuum so that it exceeds the expected rate for a normal distribution (Toth & King, 2010).

Two views of cultural-familial intellectual disability further our understanding of this phenomenon. The difference view holds that those with cultural-familial intellectual disability have a subset of deficits, such as attentional (Fisher & Zeaman, 1973) or memory

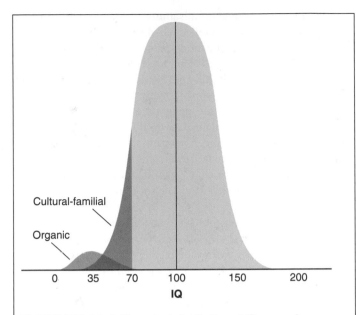

■ FIGURE 14.4 The actual distribution of IQ scores for individuals with cultural-familial intellectual disability and organic intellectual disability. Note that the cultural-familial group represents the normal expected lower end of the continuum, but the organic group is a separate and overlapping group.

Source: Adapted from *Understanding Mental Retardation* by E. Zigler and R. M. Hodapp. © 1986 by Cambridge University Press. Reprinted by permission.

problems (Ellis, 1970), that represent a limited portion of the larger set of deficiencies experienced by people with more severe forms of intellectual disability. In other words, these individuals *differ* from people without intellectual disability in terms of specific damage, and they are similar to people with more severe intellectual disability. In contrast, the developmental view sees the mild intellectual disability of people with cultural-familial intellectual disability as simply a difference in the rate and ultimate ceiling of an otherwise normal developmental sequence (Zigler & Balla, 1982). Put another way, as children these individuals go through the same developmental stages as people without intellectual disability, but they do so at a slower pace and do not attain all the skills they probably would have developed in a more supportive environment (Zigler & Stevenson, 1993). Support is mixed for both these views of the nature of cultural-familial intellectual disability. Much is still not understood about people with cultural-familial intellectual disability; future work may reveal important subgroups among them.

Treatment

Direct biological treatment of intellectual disability is currently not a viable option. Generally, the treatment of individuals with intellectual disability parallels that of people with pervasive developmental disorders, attempting to teach them the skills they need to become more productive and independent. For individuals with mild intellectual disability, intervention is similar to that for people with learning disorders. Specific learning deficits are identified and addressed to help the person improve such skills as reading and writing. At the same time, these individuals often need additional support to live in the community. For people with more severe disabilities, the general goals are the same; however, the level of assistance they need is frequently more extensive. Remember that the expectation for all people with intellectual disability is that they will in some way participate in community life, attend school, and later hold a job, and have the opportunity for meaningful social relationships. Advances in electronic and educational technologies have made this goal realistic even for people with profound intellectual disability.

People with intellectual disability can acquire skills through the many behavioural innovations first introduced in the early 1960s to teach such basic self-care as dressing, bathing, feeding, and toileting to persons with even the most severe disabilities (Reid, Wilson, & Faw, 1991). The skill is broken into its component parts (a procedure called a *task analysis*) and the person is taught each part in succession until he or she can perform the whole skill. Performance on each step is encouraged by praise and by access to objects or activities the person desires (reinforcers). Success in teaching these skills is usually measured by the level of independence the person can attain by using them. Typically, most individuals, regardless of their disability, can be taught to perform some skills.

Communication training is very important for people with intellectual disability. Making their needs and wants known is essential for personal satisfaction and for participation in most social activities. The goals of communication training differ, depending on the existing skills. For people with mild levels of intellectual disability, the goals may be relatively minor (e.g., improving articulation) or more extensive (e.g., organizing a conversation; Sigafoos, Arthur-Kelly, & Butterfield, 2006). Some, like James, have communication skills that are already adequate for day-to-day needs.

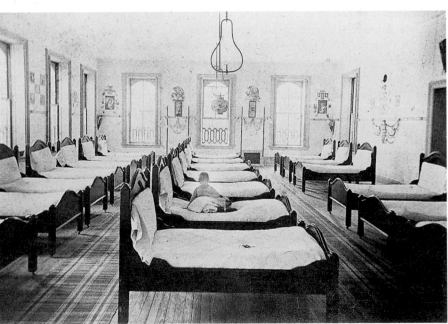

▲ In the 19th century, children with intellectual disability were housed in asylums for the "feeble-minded" like the one illustrated here. Today, great efforts are made to keep children with intellectual disability in their homes and communities.

Intellectual Disability **539**

For individuals with the most severe disabilities, this type of training can be particularly challenging, because they may have multiple physical or cognitive deficits that make spoken communication difficult or impossible (Warren & Reichle, 1992). Creative researchers, however, use alternative systems that may be easier for these individuals, including the sign language used primarily by people with hearing disabilities and *augmentative communication strategies*. Augmentative strategies may use picture books, teaching the person to make a request by pointing to a picture—for instance, pointing to a picture of a cup to request a drink (Sigafoos et al., 2009). A variety of computer-assisted devices can be programmed so that the individual presses a button to produce complete spoken sentences (e.g., "Would you come here? I need your help"). People with very limited communication skills can be taught to use these devices, which helps them reduce the frustration of not being able to relate their feelings and experiences to other people (Durand, 1993).

Concern is often expressed by parents, teachers, and employers that some people with intellectual disability can be physically or verbally aggressive or may hurt themselves. Considerable debate has ensued over the proper way to reduce these behaviour problems; the most heated discussions involve whether to use painful punishers (Repp & Singh, 1990). Alternatives to punishment that may be equally effective in reducing behaviour problems such as aggression and self-injury (Durand, 1999a) include teaching people how to communicate their need or desire for such things as attention that they seem to be getting with their problem behaviours. To date, however, no treatment or treatment package has proven successful in all cases, although important advances are being made in significantly reducing even severe behaviour problems for some people.

In addition to ensuring that people with intellectual disability are taught specific skills, caretakers focus on the important task of supporting them in their communities. "Supported employment" involves helping an individual find and participate satisfactorily in a competitive job (Hall, Butterworth, Winsor, Gilmore, & Metzel, 2007). Research has shown not only that people with intellectual disability can be placed in meaningful jobs but also that, despite the costs associated with supported employment, it can be cost-effective (Sandys, 2007). The benefits to people who achieve the satisfaction of being a productive part of society are incalculable.

There is general agreement about *what* should be taught to people with intellectual disability. The controversy in recent years has been over *where* this teaching should take place. Should people with intellectual disability, especially the severe forms, be taught in specially designed separate classrooms or workshops, or should they attend their neighbourhood public schools and work at local businesses? Increasingly, teaching strategies to help these students learn are being used in regular classrooms and in preparing them to work at jobs in the community (Frankel & Gold, 2007). There is at present no cure for intellectual disability, but the current prevention and treatment efforts suggest that meaningful changes can be achieved in the lives of those with intellectual disability.

Prevention of Developmental Disorders

Unfortunately, Canada has a rather dark history in terms of the types of efforts that were undertaken to prevent certain developmental disorders. In particular, "eugenics" advocates argued for the prevention of intellectual disability through sexual sterilization of individuals with intellectual disability. Eugenics was a movement involving applications of genetics knowledge at the time, for which the goal was to improve the human race through better breeding. In the 1920s and 1930s, British Columbia and Alberta introduced legislation allowing for sterilization of the "feeble-minded," without the patient's consent, to improve the gene pool by preventing intellectual disability. Sterilizations were performed in other provinces as well, despite the absence of similar legislation. Provincial sterilization laws were repealed in the 1970s, and today, the rights of individuals with intellectual disability are protected under the Charter of Rights and Freedoms (McLaren, 1990).

Current efforts to prevent developmental disorders are in their early stages. One such effort—early intervention—has been described for the pervasive developmental disorders and appears to hold considerable promise for some children. Additionally, early interventions combining educational, medical, and social supports can target and assist children and their families where the child is at risk for developing cultural-familial intellectual disability because of an inadequate environment (Eldevik, Jahr, Eikeseth, Hastings, & Hughes, 2010). One such effort at early intervention identified a group of children shortly after birth and provided them with an intensive preschool program, along with medical and nutritional supports. This intervention continued until the children began formal education (Martin, Ramey, & Ramey, 1990). The authors of this study found that for all but one of the children in a control group who received medical and nutritional support but not the intensive educational experiences, each had an IQ score below 85 at age three. The children in the experimental group all tested above 85 at age three. Obviously, such findings are important because they show the potential for creating a lasting impact on the lives of these children and their families.

Although it appears that many children can make significant progress if interventions are initiated early in life (Eldevik et al., 2010), a number of important questions remain regarding early intervention efforts. Not all children, for example, benefit significantly from such efforts, and future research will need to resolve a number of lingering concerns. For example, researchers need to determine how best to identify children and families who will benefit from such programs, how early in the child's development programs should begin, and how long to continue these early intervention programs to produce desirable outcomes.

Given recent advances in genetic screening and technology, it may someday be possible to detect and correct genetic and chromosomal abnormalities; related ongoing research could fundamentally change our approach to children with developmental disorders. For example, one study used mice that were genetically engineered to model fragile X syndrome found in many individuals with intellectual disability (Suvrathan, Hoeffer, Wong, Klann, & Chattarji, 2010). Researchers found that they could improve the functioning of certain glutamate receptors in the amygdala of the mice with a drug that blocks these receptors. This resulted in more normalized functioning between these neurons, a potential early medical intervention for children with fragile X disorder (Suvrathan et al., 2010). Someday, it may be possible for similar research to be performed prenatally on children identified as having syndromes associated with intellectual disability.

For example, it may soon be possible to conduct prenatal gene therapy, where a developing fetus that has been screened for a genetic disorder may be the target of intervention before birth (Ye, Mitchell, Newman, & Batshaw, 2001). This prospect is not without its difficulties, however (Durand, 2001).

One cause of concern is the reliability of gene therapy. This technology is not sufficiently advanced to produce the intended results consistently. Currently, any such intervention may cause unwanted mutations or other complications, which in turn could be fatal to the fetus. Gene therapy will probably not be practical for those disorders that involve numerous genes, but rather may be limited to single-gene disorders such as phenylketonuria.

Advances in biomedical technology will need support from psychological researchers to make sure that any needed treatments are carried out properly. For example, biological risk factors for several developmental disorders include malnutrition and exposure to toxins such as lead and alcohol. Although medical researchers can identify the role of these biological events in cognitive development, psychologists will need to support these efforts. Behavioural intervention for safety training (e.g., involving lead-based paints in older homes), substance-use treatment and prevention, and behavioural medicine (e.g., "wellness" efforts) are examples of crucial roles played by psychologists in helping to prevent certain forms of developmental disorders.

From the Inside

Nobody Nowhere: The Extraordinary Autobiography of an Autistic
by Donna Williams

This is a rare firsthand account by one of the fortunate few who can express what it is like to grow up with autism. Australian author Donna Williams courageously reveals the unique perspectives associated with her condition. As a child, she spent her time "making miniature worlds, full of bits of coloured things and fluff and things that I might get under or climb over if I could somehow get myself into that tiny place" (p. 21). Her childhood was filled with despair: "Anything I tried to learn, unless it was something I sought and taught myself, closed me out and became hard to comprehend, just like any other intrusion from 'the world'" (p. 43).

Although autism is no longer associated with poor parenting, Donna's mother was almost unbelievably hostile and made no effort to understand her daughter's disorder: "I would walk up to the faces of family members, lunge forward and weave my hands back and forth in repetitive figure eights. Slap! came the response again and again, and I smiled with

every hit" (p. 67). Williams retreated into separate personalities in order to deal with the harsh realities of her life. She believes that her dissociation was in large part an effort to protect herself from the intense pain most emotions brought her; at the same time, she instinctively knew that she needed to feel: "I, like so many 'disturbed' people, began to hurt myself in order to feel something" (p. 56). (She later wanted to cut a doll open to see whether it had feelings inside.)

Williams reveals a strong need to control her life in a world fighting to control her, and she manages to leave home, survive on her own, and graduate from college. Not "cured," Donna Williams learned through sheer force of will and intelligence to live in the world she had feared. Although her experience may not be typical of autism, her account is fascinating, impressive, and very moving.

Source: From *Nobody Nowhere* by Donna Williams, © 1992 by Donna Williams. Used by permission of the author. www.donnawilliams.ne

On the Spectrum

Emerging Views of Developmental Disorders

The disorders described in this chapter represent a broad range of problems first evident in childhood (Durand, 2010). Some of the disorders discussed may be considered part of a spectrum of disorders. For instance, some of the pervasive developmental disorders are being studied under the category of "autism spectrum disorders" and this change is being discussed for possible inclusion in the *DSM-5*. Autistic disorder and Asperger's disorder are thought to be related in

the spectrum, although research continues on the co-occurrence of childhood disintegrative disorder and pervasive developmental disorder—not otherwise specified (PDD-NOS) (Swedo, Thorsen, & Pine, 2008).

Two other major disorders—conduct disorder (CD) and oppositional defiant disorder (ODD)—may be part of a spectrum of "disruptive behaviour disorders," although this research is in a beginning stage (Shaffer, Leibenluft, Rohde,

Sirovatka, & Regier, 2009). There is also considerable comorbidity among attention deficit disorder, CD, and ODD, although any conclusion about their being part of a spectrum of disorders is premature. To move this research ahead in the coming years, researchers are examining the complex genetics of CD and ODD to see if there are meaningful ways to view these childhood problems and their apparent overlap (some children have some symptoms of both disorders).

SUMMARY

Normal and Abnormal Development

- Developmental psychopathology is the study of how disorders arise and change with time. These changes usually follow a pattern, with the child mastering one skill before acquiring the next. This aspect of development is important, because it implies that any disruption in the acquisition of early skills will, by the very nature of the developmental process, also disrupt the development of later skills.

Attention Deficit/Hyperactivity Disorder

- The primary characteristics of people with attention deficit/hyperactivity disorder are a pattern of inattention (such as not paying attention to school- or work-related tasks) or hyperactivity-impulsivity, or both. These deficits can significantly disrupt academic efforts and social relationships.

Learning Disorders

- The *DSM-IV-TR* groups the learning disorders as reading disorder, mathematics disorder, and disorder of written expression. All are defined by performance that falls far short of expectations based on intelligence and school preparation.
- Verbal or communication disorders seem closely related to learning disorders. They include stuttering, a disturbance in speech fluency; expressive language disorder, very limited speech in all situations but without the types of cognitive deficits that lead to language problems in people with intellectual disability or one of the pervasive developmental disorders; selective mutism, refusal to speak despite having the ability to do so; and tic disorders, which include involuntary motor movements such as head twitching and vocalizations such as grunts that occur suddenly, in rapid succession, and in very idiosyncratic or stereotyped ways.

Pervasive Developmental Disorders

- People with pervasive developmental disorder all experience trouble progressing in language, socialization, and cognition. The use of the word pervasive means these are not relatively minor problems (like learning disabilities) and are conditions that significantly affect how individuals live. Included in this group are autistic disorder, Rett's disorder, Asperger's disorder, and childhood disintegrative disorder.

- Autistic disorder, or autism, is a childhood disorder characterized by significant impairment in social interactions, gross and significant impairment in communication, and restricted patterns of behaviour, interest, and activities. It probably does not have a single cause; instead, a number of biological conditions may contribute, and these, in combination with psychosocial influences, result in the unusual behaviours displayed by people with autism.
- Asperger's disorder is characterized by impairments in social relationships and restricted or unusual behaviours or activities, but it does not present the language delays observed in people with autism.
- Rett's disorder, almost exclusively observed in females, is a progressive neurological disorder characterized by constant hand-wringing, intellectual disability, and impaired motor skills.
- Childhood disintegrative disorder involves severe regression in language, adaptive behaviour, and motor skills after two to four years of normal development.
- Pervasive developmental disorder—not otherwise specified is a childhood disorder characterized by significant impairment in social interactions, gross and significant impairment in communication, and restricted patterns of behaviour, interest, and activities. These children are similar to those with autism but may not meet the age criterion or may not meet the criteria for the other symptoms.

Intellectual Disability

- The definition of intellectual disability has three parts: significantly subaverage intellectual functioning, concurrent deficits or impairments in present adaptive functioning, and an onset before the age of 18.
- Down syndrome is a type of intellectual disability caused by the presence of an extra 21st chromosome. It is possible to detect the presence of Down syndrome in utero through a process known as amniocentesis.
- Two other types of intellectual disability are common: fragile X syndrome, which is caused by a chromosomal abnormality of the tip of the X chromosome, and cultural-familial intellectual disability, the presumed cause, possibly by a combination of psychosocial and biological factors, of up to 75 percent of intellectual disability.

Key Terms

Answers to Concept Checks

14.1

1. ADHD without hyper-activity
2. ADHD 3. ADHD

14.2

1. autistic disorder
2. Tourette's disorder
3. Rett's disorder
4. attention deficit/hyper-activity disorder
5. Asperger's disorder
6. selective mutism

14.3

1. Moderate/limited support
2. Profound/pervasive support
3. Mild/intermittent support
4. Severe/extensive support

Media Resources

 CourseMate

Access an integrated eBook, Abnormal Psychology Videos (formerly Abnormal Psych Live CD-ROM), chapter-specific interactive learning tools (flashcards, quizzes, learning modules), and more in your Psychology CourseMate, available at **www.abnormalpsych3ce.nelson.com**.

Abnormal Psychology Videos

Free Abnormal Psychology videos can be viewed on the website **www.abnormalpsych3ce .nelson.com**.

- *ADHD: Sean:* This child's mother and psychologists describe and discuss Sean's behaviour before his treatment with a behaviour modification program at school and at home. The eminent clinician Jim Swanson also discusses what we believe is involved in ADHD.

- *Edward: ADHD in a Gifted Student:* This segment shows interviews with Edward, who suffers from ADHD, and his teacher, who describes Edward's struggles in school and the various strategies to help his grades reflect his high level of intelligence.

- *Life Skills Training:* This segment shows an empirically validated program that teaches anger management to reduce violence in school-age and adolescent students.

- *Bullying Prevention:* This segment features an empirically validated program that shows how to teach students specific strategies for dealing with bullying behaviours in school.

- *Autism: The Nature of the Disorder:* Mark Durand's research program deals with the motivation behind problem behaviours and how communication training can be used to lessen such behaviours.

- *Autism: Christina:* This clip shows Christina's school, where you see how she spends a typical day in a mainstreamed classroom. There are interviews with her teacher's aide and a background interview with Mark Durand to describe functional communication issues and other cutting-edge research trends in autism.

- *Rebecca: A First-Grader with Autistic Disorder:* This segment shows an autistic child in a mainstreamed first-grade classroom and interviews her teachers about what strategies work best in helping Rebecca learn and control her behaviour.

- *Lauren: A Kindergartner with Down Syndrome:* The teacher and mother of a kinder-gartner with Down syndrome are interviewed to discuss strategies for teaching her new skills and managing her behaviour difficulties.

Video Concept Reviews

CourseMate also contains Mark Durand's *Video Concept Reviews* on these challenging topics.

- Attention-Deficit/Hyperactivity Disorder (ADHD)
- Reading Disorder
- Mathematics Disorder
- Pervasive Developmental Disorders
- Autistic Disorder (Autism)
- Asperger's Disorder
- Intellectual Disability

Exploring Developmental Disorders

Disorders that appear early in life disrupt the normal course of development.

> Interrupting or preventing the development of one skill impedes mastery of the skill that is normally acquired next.

> Knowing what skills are disrupted by a particular disorder is essential to developing appropriate intervention strategies.

COGNITION

LANGUAGE

SOCIALIZATION

Infancy **Childhood** **Adolescence**

TYPES OF DEVELOPMENTAL DISORDERS

		Description	Causes	Treatment
Attention Deficit/ Hyperactivity Disorder (ADHD)		• Inattentive, overactive, and impulsive behaviour • Disrupted schooling and relationships • Symptoms may change with maturity, but problems persist • More prevalent in boys than girls	• Research suggests hereditary factor • Abnormal neurology • Possible link with maternal smoking • Negative responses by others create low self-esteem	• Biological (medication) – improves compliance – decreases negative behaviours – effects not long term • Psychological (behavioural) – goal setting and reinforcement
Learning Disorders		• Reading, math, and written expression fall behind IQ, age, and education • May also be accompanied by ADHD	• Theories assume genetic, neurobiological, and environmental factors	• Education intervention – basic processing – cognitive and behavioural skills

Catherine Ledner/Taxi/Getty Images

Used with permission of Laureate Learning Systems, Inc.

		Types	Description	Treatment
Communication Disorders Closely related to learning disorders, but comparatively benign. Early appearance, wide range of problems later in life.		Stuttering	Disturbance in speech fluency (repeating words, prolonging sounds, extended pauses)	• Psychological • Pharmacological
		Expressive Language Disorders	Limited speech in all situations	• May be self-correcting
		Selective Mutism	Failure to speak in specific situations (e.g., school)	• Contingency management
		Tic Disorders	Involuntary motor movements (tics), such as physical twitches or vocalizations	• Psychological • Pharmacological

PhotoDisc/Getty Images

PERVASIVE DEVELOPMENTAL DISORDERS

	Description	Causes	Treatment

Autistic Disorder	• Severely impaired socialization and communication
	• Restricted behaviour, interests, and activities
	  – echolalia
	  – maintenance of sameness
	  – stereotyped, ritualistic behaviours
	• Symptoms almost always develop before 36 months of age.
		• Little conclusive data
		• Numerous biological factors
		  – clear genetic component
		  – evidence of brain damage (cognitive deficits)
		combined with psychosocial influences
			• Behavioural focus
			  – communication
			  – socialization
			  – living skills
			• Inclusive schooling
			• Temporary benefits from medication

Asperger's Disorder	Impaired socialization and restricted/unusual behaviours, but without language delays • Few cognitive impairments (average IQ) • May be mild autism, not separate disorder		
Rett's Disorder	Progressive neurological disorder after apparently normal early development • Primarily affects girls • Intellectual disability • Deteriorating motor skills • Constant hand-wringing		
Childhood Disintegrative Disorder	Severe regression after 2–4 years normal development • Affects language, adaptive behaviour, and motor skills • Evidence of neurological origin		

PhotoDisc/Getty Images

© moodboard/Corbis

Paul Conklin/PhotoEdit

INTELLECTUAL DISABILITY

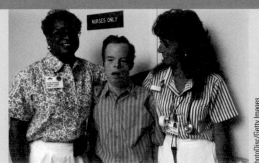

PhotoDisc/Getty Images

Description	Causes	Treatment

• Adaptive and intellectual functioning significantly below average
  – language and communication impairments
• Wide range of impairment—from mild to profound—in daily activities (90 percent of affected individuals have mild impairments.)
	• Hundreds of identified factors
	  – genetic
	  – prenatal
	  – perinatal
	  – postnatal
	  – environmental
	• Nearly 75 percent of cases cannot be attributed to any known cause
		• No biological intervention
		• Behavioural focus similar to that for autism
		• Prevention
		  – genetic counselling
		  – biological screening
		  – maternal care

15 | Cognitive Disorders

© Gabriela Medina/Blend Images/Getty Images

> *As my grip upon the present slips, more and more comfort is found within my memories of the past. Childhood nostalgia is so keen I can actually smell the aroma of the small town library where I spent so many childhood hours.*
>
> —Diana Friel McGowin, *Living in the Labyrinth: A Personal Journey, Through the Maze of Alzheimer's*

Demonstrate knowledge and understanding representing appropriate breadth and depth in selected content areas of psychology:	› Biological bases of behaviour and mental processes, including physiology, sensation, perception, comparative, motivation, and emotion (APA SLO 1.2.a (3)) *(see textbook pages 558–561)*
Use the concepts, language, and major theories of the discipline to account for psychological phenomena.	› Describe behaviour and mental processes empirically, including operational definitions (APA SLO 1.3.a) *(see textbook pages 548–552)* › Identify antecedents and consequences of behaviour and mental processes (APA SLO 1.3.b) *(see textbook pages 558–561)*
Identify appropriate applications of psychology in solving problems, such as:	› Origin and treatment of abnormal behaviour (APA SLO 4.2.b) *(see textbook pages 558–565)*

* Portions of this chapter cover learning outcomes suggested by the American Psychological Association (2007) in their guidelines for the undergraduate psychology major. Chapter coverage of these outcomes is identified above by APA Goal and APA Suggested Learning Outcome (SLO).

Research on the brain and its role in psychopathology has increased at a rapid pace, and we have described many of the latest advances throughout this book. All the disorders we have reviewed are in some way influenced by the brain. You have seen, for example, that relatively subtle changes in neurotransmitter systems can significantly affect mood, cognition, and behaviour. Unfortunately, the brain is sometimes affected profoundly, and when this happens, drastic changes occur. In earlier editions of this book, the tone of this chapter was quite dark given the lack of information on these cognitive disorders that impair all aspects of mental functioning. The typically poor prognosis of the people afflicted led to pessimistic conclusions. However, a great deal of new research is leading us to be more optimistic about the future. For example, we used to think that once neurons died there was no hope of any replacement, yet we now know brain cells can regenerate even in the aging brain (Stellos et al., 2010). In this chapter, we examine this exciting new work related to the brain disorders that affect cognitive processes such as learning, memory, and consciousness.

Perspectives

Whereas intellectual disability and other learning disorders are believed to be present from birth (see Chapter 14), most cognitive disorders develop much later in life. In this section we review three classes of cognitive disorders: *delirium*, an often temporary condition displayed as confusion and disorientation; *dementia*, a progressive condition marked by gradual deterioration of a broad range of cognitive abilities; and *amnestic disorders*, dysfunctions of memory due to a medical condition or a drug or toxin.

The *DSM-IV-TR* label of "cognitive disorders" reflects a shift in the way these disorders are viewed (Weiner, 2003). In previous editions of the *DSM* they were defined as "organic mental disorders," along with mood, anxiety, personality, hallucinosis, and delusional disorders. The word "organic" indicated that brain damage or dysfunction was believed to be involved. Although brain dysfunction is still thought to be the primary cause, we now know that some dysfunction in the brain is involved in most disorders described in the *DSM-IV-TR* (American Psychiatric Association, 2000a).

We have repeatedly emphasized the complex relationship between neurological and psychosocial influences in many, if not all, psychological disorders. Few people would disagree, for example, that schizophrenia involves some damage to the brain. In one sense, then, most disorders are "organic." This fundamental shift in perspective immediately affected the categorizing of disorders. Obviously, the term *organic mental disorders* now covered so many as to make any distinction meaningful. Consequently, the traditional organic disorders— delirium, dementia, and amnestic disorders—were kept together, and the others—organic mood, anxiety, personality, hallucinosis, and delusional disorders—were categorized with disorders that shared their symptoms (such as anxiety and mood disorders).

Once the term *organic* was dropped, attention moved to developing a better label for delirium, dementia, and the amnestic disorders. The label "cognitive disorders" signifies that their predominant feature is the impairment of such cognitive abilities as memory, attention, perception, and thinking. Although disorders such as schizophrenia and depression also involve cognitive problems, cognitive issues are not believed to be primary characteristics. Problems still exist with this term, however, because although the cognitive disorders usually first appear in older adults, intellectual disability and learning disorders (which are apparent early) also have cognitive impairment as a predominant characteristic. Currently, discussions are under way for the *DSM-5* to keep the label "delirium" but to combine the other cognitive disorders (such as dementia and amnestic disorders) and call them "neurocognitive disorders"; their dimensional quality would be specified as either the "major" or "minor" subtype (American Psychiatric Association, 2010). In part, this may be the result of the overlap of the different types of dementia (e.g., Alzheimer's disorder) and amnestic disorder found in people such that one person may actually suffer from multiple types of neurocognitive problems (Sweet, 2009).

■ Figure 15.1 illustrates how the incidence of disability due to cognitive functions (memory and speech) rises with increasing age, with rates being highest for these types of disability in those aged 65 years and older. In contrast, the prevalence of disability due to psychological problems does not follow this age pattern

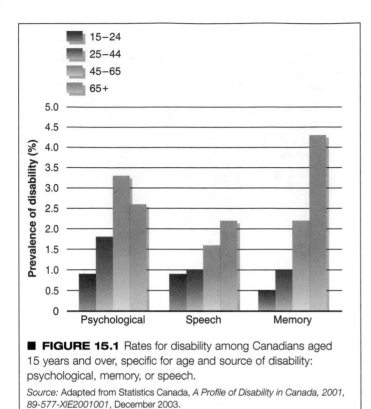

FIGURE 15.1 Rates for disability among Canadians aged 15 years and over, specific for age and source of disability: psychological, memory, or speech.

Source: Adapted from Statistics Canada, *A Profile of Disability in Canada, 2001*, 89-577-XIE2001001, December 2003.

Mr. J. | *Sudden Distress*

Mr. J., an older gentleman, was brought to the hospital emergency room. He didn't know his own name and at times he didn't seem to recognize his daughter, who was with him. Mr. J. appeared confused, disoriented, and a little agitated. He had difficulty speaking clearly and could not focus his attention to answer even the most basic questions. Mr. J.'s daughter reported that he had begun acting this way the night before, had been awake most of the time since then, was frightened, and seemed even more confused today. She told the nurse that this behaviour was not normal for him and she was worried that he was becoming senile. She mentioned that his doctor had just changed his hypertension medication and wondered whether the new medication could be causing her father's distress. Mr. J. was ultimately diagnosed as having substance-induced delirium (a reaction to his new medication); once the medication was stopped, he improved significantly over the next two days. This scenario is played out daily in most major metropolitan hospital emergency rooms.

Clinical Description and Statistics

People with delirium appear confused, disoriented, and out of touch with their surroundings. They cannot focus and sustain their attention on even the simplest tasks. They have marked impairments in memory and language. Mr. J. had trouble speaking; he was not only confused but also couldn't remember basic facts such as his own name. As we saw, the symptoms of delirium do not come on gradually; they develop over hours or a few days, and they can vary over the course of a day.

Delirium is estimated to be present in as many as 10 percent to 30 percent of the people who come into acute care facilities such as emergency rooms (American Psychiatric Association, 2000e). A study by Michel Elie and his colleagues at McGill University determined the prevalence of delirium in emergency department patients aged 65 years and above to be about 10 percent (Elie, Rousseau, Cole, Primeau, McCusker, & Bellavance, 2000). It is most prevalent among older adults, people undergoing medical procedures, cancer patients, and people with acquired immune deficiency syndrome (AIDS; Bourgeois, Seaman, & Servis, 2003). According to a study by a group of researchers in Québec, common risk factors for delirium in older patients include dementia (a cognitive disorder to be discussed in the next section of this chapter), medication, and medical illness (Voyer, McCusker, Cole, St-Jacques, & Khomenko, 2007). Delirium subsides relatively quickly, with full recovery expected in most cases within several weeks. A minority of individuals continue to have problems on and off; some even lapse into a coma and may die. In fact, the symptoms of delirium are often present during the last several hours of life among terminally ill patients (Rockwood & Lindesay, 2002).

Many medical conditions that impair brain function have been linked to delirium, including intoxication by drugs and poisons; withdrawal from drugs such as alcohol and sedative, hypnotic, and anxiolytic drugs; infections; head injury; and various other

and rates decline after age 65 (Statistics Canada, 2001b). As our life expectancy increases, cognitive disorders become more prevalent and have emerged as a major concern for mental health professionals.

As with certain other disorders, it may be useful to clarify why cognitive disorders are discussed in a textbook on abnormal psychology. Because they so clearly have organic causes, you could argue that they are purely medical concerns. We will see, however, that the consequences of a cognitive disorder often include profound changes in a person's behaviour and personality. Intense anxiety or depression is common, especially among people with dementia. In addition, paranoia is frequently reported, as are extreme agitation and aggression. Families and friends are also profoundly affected by such changes. Imagine your emotional distress as a loved one is transformed into a different person, often one who no longer remembers who you are or your history together. The deterioration of cognitive ability, behaviour, and personality and the effects on others are a major concern for mental health professionals.

Delirium

The disorder known as **delirium** is characterized by impaired consciousness and cognition during the course of several hours or days (Cole, 2004; Conn & Lieff, 2001; Rahkonen et al., 2000). Delirium is one of the earliest recognized mental disorders: Descriptions of people with these symptoms were written more than 2500 years ago (Lipowski, 1990). Consider the case of Mr. J.

types of brain trauma (Fearing & Inouye, 2009). The *DSM-IV-TR* (see DSM Table 15.1) recognizes several causes of delirium among its subtypes. The criteria for delirium due to a general medical condition include a disturbance of consciousness (reduced awareness of the environment) and a change in cognitive abilities such as memory and language skills, occurring over a short period and brought about by a general medical condition. Other subtypes include the diagnosis received by Mr. J.—substance-induced delirium—as well as delirium due to multiple etiologies and delirium not otherwise specified. The last two categories indicate the often complex nature of delirium.

DSM-IV-TR	**Table 15.1** Diagnostic Criteria for Delirium Due to… [Indicate the General Medical Condition]

A. Disturbance of consciousness (i.e., reduced clarity of awareness of the environment) with reduced ability to focus, sustain, or shift attention.

B. A change in cognition (such as memory deficit, disorientation, language disturbance) or the development of a perceptual disturbance that is not better accounted for by a pre-existing, established, or evolving dementia.

C. The disturbance develops over a short period (usually hours to days) and tends to fluctuate during the course of the day.

D. There is evidence from the history, physical examination, or laboratory findings that the disturbance is caused by the direct physiological consequences of a general medical condition.

Source: Reprinted with permission from the *Diagnostic and Statistical Manual of Mental Disorders*, Fourth Edition, Text Revision, (Copyright © 2000). American Psychiatric Association.

That delirium can be brought on by the improper use of medication can be a particular problem for older adults, because they tend to use prescription medications more than any other age group (Cole, 2004). Medications with anticholinergic effects (e.g., those used to counteract extrapyramidal side effects of neuroleptic medications; see Chapter 13) appear particularly associated with severe delirium in the elderly (Han et al., 2001). This suggests the possibility that a cholinergic deficit may contribute to delirium. Moreover, the elderly also tend to be multiple medication users (Millar, 1998), putting them at risk for adverse drug interactions. The risk of problems among the elderly is increased further because they tend to eliminate drugs from their systems less efficiently than younger individuals. It is not surprising, then, that adverse drug reactions resulting in hospitalization are almost six times higher among elderly people than in other age groups (Olivier et al., 2009). And it is believed that delirium is responsible for many of the falls that cause debilitating hip fractures in the elderly (Stenvall et al., 2006). Although there has been some improvement in the use of medication among older adults, with physicians using more care with drug dosages and the use of multiple drugs, improper use continues to produce serious side effects, including symptoms of delirium (Olivier et al., 2009). Because possible combinations of illnesses and medications are so numerous, determining the cause of delirium is extremely difficult (Solai, 2009).

Delirium may be experienced by children who have high fevers or who are taking certain medications and is often mistaken for noncompliance (Smeets et al., 2010). It often occurs during the course of dementia; as many as 50 percent of people with dementia suffer at least one episode of delirium (Kwok, Lee, Lam, & Woo, 2008). Because many of the primary medical conditions can be treated, delirium is often reversed within a relatively short time. Yet, in about a quarter of cases, delirium can be a sign of the end of life (Wise, Hilty, & Cerda, 2001).

Factors other than medical conditions can trigger delirium. Age itself is an important factor; older adults are more susceptible to developing delirium as a result of mild infections or medication changes (Fearing & Inouye, 2009). Sleep deprivation, immobility, and excessive stress can also cause delirium (Solai, 2009).

Environmental factors can also play a role in the risk for severe delirium in hospitalized elderly people. In a prospective study of hospitalized elderly individuals, Jane McCusker of McGill University and her colleagues found environmental variables such as the number of room changes, and absence of a clock, watch, or reading glasses, were related to an increase in delirium severity over time. Hospital room changes, for example, can disrupt older patients' ability to correctly perceive environmental cues, resulting in their misinterpretation of stimuli around them (McCusker et al., 2001). Since these environmental factors are modifiable, they can be targeted in treatment or prevention.

Treatment

Rapid treatment of delirium is important, as quicker in-hospital recovery is associated with better long-term outcomes (Cole & McCusker, 2002). Acute delirium and delirium brought on by withdrawal from alcohol or other drugs is usually treated with haloperidol or other antipsychotic medications, which help calm the individual. Infections, brain injury, and tumours are given the necessary and appropriate medical intervention, which often then resolves the accompanying delirium. The antipsychotic drug haloperidol is also prescribed for individuals in acute delirium when the cause is unknown (Fearing & Inouye, 2009).

The recommended first line of treatment for a person experiencing delirium is psychosocial intervention. The goal of nonmedical treatment is to reassure the individual to help him or her deal with the agitation, anxiety, and hallucinations of delirium. A person in the hospital may be comforted by familiar personal belongings such as family photographs (Fearing & Inouye, 2009). Also, a patient who is included in all treatment decisions retains a sense of control (Katz, 1993). This type of psychosocial treatment can help the person manage during this disruptive period until the medical causes are identified and addressed. Some evidence suggests that this type of support can also delay institutionalization for elderly patients (Rahkonen et al., 2001).

Prevention

Preventive efforts may be most successful in assisting people who are susceptible to delirium. Proper medical care for illnesses and therapeutic drug monitoring can play a significant role in preventing delirium. According to Montréal psychiatrist Martin Cole

(2004), the evidence suggests that a broad spectrum of interventions (education, support, reorientation, anxiety-reduction, preoperative medical assessment) may be moderately effective in preventing delirium in surgical patients.

Dementia

Few things are more frightening than the possibility that you will one day not recognize those you love, that you will not be able to perform the most basic of tasks, and, worse yet, that you will be acutely aware of this failure of your mind. And when family members show these signs, adult children often deny any difficulty, coming up with excuses ("I forget things too") for their parents' failing abilities. Dementia is the cognitive disorder that makes these fears real: a gradual deterioration of brain functioning that affects judgment, memory, language, and other advanced cognitive processes. **Dementia** is caused by several medical conditions and by the abuse of drugs or alcohol that cause negative changes in cognitive functioning. Some of these conditions—for instance, infection or depression—can cause dementia, although it is often reversible through treatment of the primary condition. Some forms of the disorder, such as Alzheimer's disease, are at present irreversible. Although delirium and dementia can occur together, dementia has a gradual progression as opposed to delirium's acute onset; people with dementia are not disoriented or confused in the early stages, unlike people with delirium. Like delirium, however, dementia has many causes, including a variety of insults to the brain such as stroke (which destroys blood vessels), the infectious diseases of syphilis and HIV, severe head injury, the introduction of certain toxic or poisonous substances, and diseases such as Parkinson's, Huntington's, and the most common cause of dementia, Alzheimer's disease. Consider the rare personal account by Diana, a woman who poignantly writes of her experiences with this disorder (McGowin, 1993).

DIANA | *Humiliation and Fear*

At the age of 45, Diana Friel McGowin was a successful legal assistant, wife, and mother, but she was beginning to experience "lapses." She writes about developing these problems just before the party she was planning for her family.

> Nervously, I checked off the table appointments on a list retrieved from my jumpsuit pocket. Such a list had never been necessary before, but lately I noticed frequent little episodes of confusion and memory lapses.
>
> I had decided to "cheat" on this family buffet and have the meal prepared on a carry-out basis. Cooking was also becoming increasingly difficult, due to what my children and my husband Jack teasingly referred to as my "absentmindedness." (pp. 1–2)

In addition to memory difficulties, other problems began at this time, including brief dizzy spells. Diana wrote of her family's growing awareness of the additional symptoms.

> Shaun walked past me on his way to the kitchen, and paused. "Mom, what's up? You look ragged," he commented sleepily. "Late night last night, plenty of excitement, and then up early to get your father off to work," I answered. Shaun laughed disconcertingly. I glanced up at him ruefully. "What is so funny?" I demanded. "You, Mom! You are talking as though you are drunk or something! You must really be tired!" (pp. 4–5)

In the early stages of her dementia, Diana tended to explain these changes in herself as temporary, with such causes as tension at work. However, the extent of her dysfunction continued to increase, and she had more frightening experiences. In one episode, she describes an attempt to drive home from a brief errand.

> Suddenly, I was aware of car horns blowing. Glancing around, nothing was familiar. I was stopped at an intersection and the traffic light was green. Cars honked impatiently, so I pulled straight ahead, trying to get my bearings. I could not read the street sign, but there was another sign ahead; perhaps it would shed some light on my location. A few yards ahead, there was a park ranger building. Trembling, I wiped my eyes, and breathing deeply, tried to calm myself. Finally, feeling ready to speak, I started the car again and approached the ranger station. The guard smiled and inquired how he could assist me. "I appear to be lost," I began, making a great effort to keep my voice level, despite my emotional state. "Where do you need to go?" the guard asked politely. A cold chill enveloped me as I realized I could not remember the name of my street. Tears began to flow down my cheeks. I did not know where I wanted to go. (pp. 7–8)

Diana's difficulties continued. She sometimes forgot the names of her children, and once astounded her nephew when she didn't recognize him. If she left home, she almost invariably got lost. She learned to introduce herself as a tourist from out of town, because people would give her better directions. She felt as if there "was less of me every day than there was the day before."

During initial medical examinations, Diana didn't recall this type of problem in her family history. However, a look through some of her late mother's belongings revealed that Diana was not the first to experience symptoms of dementia.

> Then I noticed the maps. After mother's death I had found mysterious hand drawn maps and bits of directions scribbled on note papers all over her home. They were in her purses, in bureau drawers, in the desks, seemingly everywhere. Too distraught at the time to figure out their purpose, I simply packed them all away with other articles in the box. Now I smoothed out each map and scrawled note, and placed them side by side. They covered the bedroom floor. There were maps to every place my mother went about town, even to my home and my

brother's home. As I deciphered each note and map, I began recollecting my mother's other eccentric habits. She would not drive out of her neighborhood. She would not drive at night. She was teased by both myself and my brother about "memory goofs" and would become irate with both of her children over their loving teasing.

Then with a chill, I recalled one day when I approached my mother to tell her something, and she did not recognize me. (p. 52)

After several evaluations, which included an MRI showing some damage in several parts of her brain, Diana's neurologist concluded that she had dementia. The cause could be a stroke she had had several years before that had damaged several small areas of her brain by breaking or blocking several blood vessels. The dementia could also indicate Alzheimer's disease. People at the same stage of decline as Diana Friel McGowin will continue to deteriorate and eventually may die from complications of their disorder.

Clinical Description and Statistics

Depending on the individual and the cause of the disorder, the gradual progression of dementia may have somewhat different symptoms, although all aspects of cognitive functioning are eventually affected. In the initial stages, memory impairment is typically seen as an inability to register ongoing events. In other words, a person can remember how to talk and may remember events from many years ago, but have trouble remembering what happened in the past hour. For example, Diana still knew how to use the stove, but couldn't remember whether she had turned it on or off.

Diana couldn't find her way home because *visuospatial* skills are impaired among people with dementia. **Agnosia**, the inability to recognize and name objects, is one of the most familiar symptoms. **Facial agnosia**, the inability to recognize even familiar faces, can be extremely distressing to family members. Diana

▲ People with facial agnosia, a common symptom of dementia, are unable to recognize faces, even of their closest friends and relatives.

failed to recognize not only her nephew but also co-workers whom she had seen every day for years. A general deterioration of intellectual function results from impairment in memory, planning, and abstract reasoning.

Perhaps because victims of dementia are aware that they are deteriorating mentally, emotional changes often occur as well. Common side effects are delusions (irrational beliefs), depression, agitation, aggression, and apathy (Richards & Sweet, 2009). Again, it is difficult to establish the cause-and-effect relationship. We don't know how much behavioural change is due to progressive brain deterioration directly and how much is a result of the frustration and discouragement that inevitably accompany the loss of function and the isolation of "losing" loved ones. Cognitive functioning continues to deteriorate until the person requires almost total support to carry out day-to-day activities. Ultimately, death occurs as the result of inactivity combined with the onset of other illnesses such as pneumonia.

Dementia can occur at almost any age, although dementia of the Alzheimer's type rarely occurs in people under 45 years of age (American Psychiatric Association, 2000f). The incidence of dementia is highest in older adults. According to the Canadian Study of Health and Aging (Rockwood, Wolfson, & McDowell, 2001), about 8 percent of Canadians over the age of 65 are affected by Alzheimer's disease and related dementias (Lindsay, Sykes, McDowell, Verreault, & Laurin, 2004). This study found a prevalence of 2 percent in people between the ages of 65 and 74; this rate increased to a little over 10 percent in those aged 75 to 84 and to more than 30 percent in people 85 and older (see ■ Figure 15.2; Lindsay et al., 2004).

The actual rate may be considerably higher, however, especially among older adults. Evans and colleagues (1989) found that as many as 47 percent of adults over the age of 85 may have dementia of the Alzheimer's type, and a study of centenarians (people 100 years and older) found that almost 90 percent showed signs of dementia (Blansjaar, Thomassen, & Van Schaick, 2000). Thus,

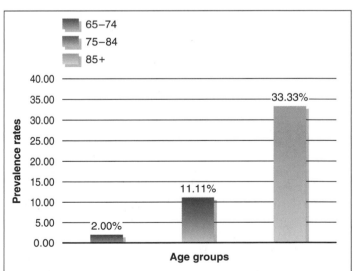

■ **FIGURE 15.2** Prevalence of dementia in three age groups of elderly Canadians

Source: Adapted from Freedman, M., Leach, L., Kaplan, E., Winocur, G., Shulman, K. I., & Delis, D. C. (1994). *Clock drawing: A neuropsychological analysis.* New York: Oxford University Press.

▲ Kenneth Rockwood is a professor of geriatric medicine and neurology and the Kathryn Allen Weldon Professor of Alzheimer Research at Dalhousie University. He is also a staff internist and geriatrician at the Capital District Health Authority in Halifax. He has published seven books and more than 300 articles on various aspects of geriatric medicine, dementia, and delirium.

prevalence rates have varied considerably across studies. This discrepancy in estimates may result from several factors. Using data from the Canadian Study of Health and Aging, researchers at the University of Western Ontario and the London Health Sciences Centre have demonstrated how the use of different diagnostic criteria can dramatically affect prevalence estimates for dementia (Erkinjuntti, Ostbye, Steenhuis, & Hachinski, 1997).

An additional problem with confirming prevalence figures for dementia is that survival rates alter the outcomes. Incidence studies, which count the number of new cases in a year, may thus be the most reliable method for assessing the frequency of dementia, especially among the elderly. In one study, the annual incidence rates for dementia were 2.3 percent for people 75 to 79 years of age, 4.6 percent for people 80 to 84 years of age, and 8.5 percent for those 85 and older (Paykel et al., 1994). The research showed that the rate for new cases doubled with every five years of age. In addition, the rate for dementia was comparable for men and women and was equivalent across educational level and social class. Many other studies, however, find greater increases of dementia among women (e.g., Canadian Study of Health and Aging Working Group, 2000), although this difference may be due to the tendency of women to live longer. Dementia of the Alzheimer's type may, as we discuss later, be more prevalent among women. Together, results suggest that dementia is a relatively common disorder among older adults, and the chances of developing it increase rapidly after the age of 75.

In addition to the human costs of dementia, the medical costs are staggering (Getsios, Caro, Caro, & Ishak, 2001). For example, the Canadian Study of Health and Aging conservatively estimated that $3.9 billion was spent on caring for people with dementia in 1991 (Lindsay et al., 2004). But direct medical costs (e.g., hospital and doctor's visits, medication) are only a fraction of the total financial burden of caring for a person with dementia. Yearly nursing home costs are astounding. Often family members care for an afflicted person around the clock, which is an inestimable personal and financial commitment (Hermann et al., 2006). In a review of the literature, a team of researchers in Hong Kong found that the economic costs associated with the care of individuals with dementia of the Alzheimer's type were highly variable across studies. This variation was mostly due to differences in the methods that researchers used to calculate economic costs and to variations in care patterns in different areas of the world. The researchers concluded, however, that there is little doubt that the economic impact of dementia is substantial (Leung, Yeung, Chi, & Chu, 2003). The economic impact is likely to worsen worldwide as a greater proportion of the world's population becomes elderly.

The statistics on prevalence and incidence cover dementias that arise from a variety of etiologies. The *DSM-IV-TR* groups are based on presumed cause, but determining the cause of dementia is an inexact process. Sometimes, as with dementia of the Alzheimer's type, clinicians rely on ruling out alternative explanations—identifying all the things that are not the cause—instead of determining the precise origin.

Five classes of dementia based on etiology have been identified: (1) dementia of the Alzheimer's type, (2) vascular dementia, (3) dementia due to other general medical conditions, (4) substance-induced persisting dementia, and (5) dementia due to multiple etiologies. A sixth, called dementia not otherwise specified, is included when etiology cannot be determined. We emphasize dementia of the Alzheimer's type because of its prevalence (almost half of those with dementia exhibit this type) and the relatively large amount of research conducted on its etiology and treatment.

Dementia of the Alzheimer's Type

Description and Statistics

In 1906 the German psychiatrist Alois Alzheimer first described the disorder that bears his name. He wrote of a 51-year-old woman who had a "strange disease of the cerebral cortex" that manifested as a progressive memory impairment and other behavioural and cognitive problems including suspiciousness (Richards & Sweet, 2009). He called the disorder an "atypical form of senile dementia," and thereafter it was referred to as **Alzheimer's disease**.

The *DSM-IV-TR* diagnostic criteria for **dementia of the Alzheimer's type** include multiple cognitive deficits that develop gradually and steadily. Predominant is the impairment of *memory, orientation, judgment,* and *reasoning.* The inability to integrate new information results in failure to learn new associations. Individuals with Alzheimer's disease forget important events and lose objects. Their interest in nonroutine activities narrows. They tend to lose interest in others and, as a result, become more socially isolated. As the disorder progresses, they can become agitated, confused, depressed, anxious, or even combative (see DSM Table 15.2). Many of these difficulties become more pronounced late in the day—in a phenomenon referred to as "sundowner syndrome"—perhaps as a result of fatigue or a disturbance in the brain's biological clock (Lemay & Landreville, 2010).

As noted in a review by University of Western Ontario researchers Edward Helmes and Truls Ostbye (2002), people with dementia of the Alzheimer's type also display one or more other cognitive disturbances, including **aphasia** (difficulty with language), *apraxia* (impaired motor functioning), *agnosia* (failure to recognize objects), or difficulty with activities such as planning, organizing, sequencing, or abstracting information. One example of the language difficulties experienced by people with Alzheimer's disease is *anomia* (problems with naming objects; Auchterlonie, Phillips, & Chertkow, 2002). These cognitive impairments also have a serious negative impact on social and occupational functioning, and they represent a significant decline from previous abilities.

A definitive diagnosis of Alzheimer's disease can be made only after an autopsy determines that certain characteristic

DSM-IV-TR

Table 15.2 Diagnostic Criteria for Dementia of the Alzheimer's Type

A. The development of multiple cognitive deficits manifested by both

  1. memory impairment (impaired ability to learn new information or to recall previously learned information)

  2. one (or more) of the following cognitive disturbances:

    a. aphasia (language disturbance)

    b. apraxia (impaired ability to carry out motor activities despite intact motor function)

    c. agnosia (failure to recognize or identify objects despite intact sensory function)

    d. disturbance in executive functioning (i.e., planning, organizing, sequencing, abstracting)

B. The cognitive deficits in Criteria A1 and A2 each cause significant impairment in social or occupational functioning and represent a significant decline from a previous level of functioning.

C. The course is characterized by gradual onset and continuing cognitive decline.

D. The cognitive deficits in Criteria A1 and A2 are not due to any of the following:

  1. other central nervous system conditions that cause progressive deficits in memory and cognition (e.g., cerebrovascular disease, Parkinson's disease, Huntington's disease, subdural hematoma, normal-pressure hydrocephalus, brain tumour)

  2. systemic conditions that are known to cause dementia (e.g., hypothyroidism, vitamin B_{12} or folic acid deficiency, niacin deficiency, hypercalcemia, neurosyphillis, HIV infection)

  3. substance-induced conditions

E. The deficits do not occur exclusively during the course of a delirium.

F. The disturbance is not better accounted for by another Axis I disorder (e.g., major depressive disorder, schizophrenia).

Without Behavioural Disturbance: in the cognitive disturbance is not accompanied by any clinically significant behavioural disturbance.

With Behavioural Disturbance: if the cognitive disturbance is accompanied by a clinically significant behavioural disturbance (e.g., wandering, agitation).

Specify subtype:

With Early Onset: if onset is at age 65 years or below.

With Late Onset: if onset is after age 65 years.

Source: Reprinted with permission from the *Diagnostic and Statistical Manual of Mental Disorders,* Fourth Edition, Text Revision, (Copyright © 2000). American Psychiatric Association.

types of damage are present in the brain, although clinicians are accurate in identifying this condition in living patients 70 percent to 90 percent of the time (Bourgeois et al., 2003). To make a diagnosis without direct examination of the brain, a simplified version of a mental status exam, called the Mini Mental State Examination (Folstein, Folstein, & McHugh, 1975), is used to assess language and memory problems. This simple exam has been shown to be quite accurate in identifying people with dementia (Mcdowell, Kristjanson, Hill, & Hebert, 1997).

A test that is often used to supplement the mental status exam for detecting dementia and Alzheimer's disease (Shulman, 2000) is the clock-drawing subtest of the Clock Test (Tuokko,

Hadjistavropoulos, Rae, & O'Rourke, 2000; Tuokko, Kristjansson, & Miller, 1995). In this test, the patient is presented with a drawing of a circle and is instructed to imagine that the circle is a clock. The patient is then asked to put the numbers on the clock and to place the clock's hands in the position to show the time as 11:10. The test is scored according to the number and types of errors that the patient makes to assist in identifying patients with Alzheimer's disease (Shulman, Shedletsky, & Silver, 1986). Patients with Alzheimer's disease make more errors of omission and misplacements of numbers, as compared to controls (Tuokko, Hadjistavropoulos, Miller, & Beattie, 1992). Samples of clocks drawn by three Alzheimer's disease patients are displayed in ■ Figure 15.3. These examples come from a book entitled *Clock Drawing: A Neuropsychological Analysis* by Toronto neurologist Morris Freedman and his colleagues (1994). Additionally, longitudinal research suggests that scores on the Clock Test may also be useful in identifying which elderly individuals will develop dementia in the future (O'Rourke, Tuokko, Hayden, & Beattie, 1997).

In an interesting, somewhat controversial study, the writings of a group of Catholic nuns collected over several decades appeared to indicate early in life which women were most likely to develop Alzheimer's disease later (Massie et al., 1996). Researchers observed that samples from the nuns' journals over the years

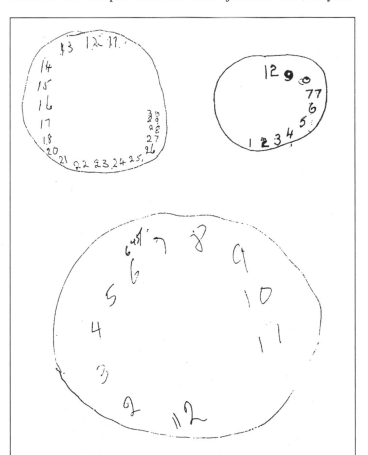

■ **FIGURE 15.3** Samples of the clock drawing subtest of the Clock Test developed by Holly Tuokko, as drawn by three patients with Alzheimer's disease.

Source: Adapted from Freedman, M., Leach, L., Kaplan, E., Winocur, G., Shulman, K. I., & Delis, D. C. (1994). Clock drawing: *A neuropsychological analysis.* New York: Oxford University Press.

Courtesy of Holly Tuokko

▲ Holly Tuokko at the University of Victoria has conducted considerable research on various aspects of dementia and Alzheimer's disease. She is probably best known for her work in developing and evaluating the Clock Test (Tuokko et al., 1992, 1995, 2000) as a measure for detecting dementia and Alzheimer's disease.

differed in the number of ideas each contained, which the scientists called "idea density." Some of the sisters described events in their lives very simply: "I was born in Eau Claire on May 24, 1913, and was baptized in St. James Church." Others were more elaborate in their prose: "The happiest day of my life so far was my First Communion Day, which was in June nineteen hundred and twenty when I was but eight years of age, and four years later in the same month I was confirmed by Bishop D. D. McGavich." When autopsy findings on 14 of the nuns were correlated with idea density, the very simple writing (low idea density) occurred among all five of the nuns with Alzheimer's disease (Massie et al., 1996). This is an elegant research study because the daily lives of the nuns were similar on a day-to-day basis, which ruled out many other possible causes. However, we must be cautious in depending on this study, because only a small number of people were examined. It is not yet clear that dementia of the Alzheimer's type has such early signs, but research continues in the hope of early detection so that early intervention can be developed (Tyas et al., 2007).

Cognitive deterioration of the Alzheimer's type is slow during the early and later stages but more rapid during the middle stages (Richards & Sweet, 2009). Although it was once thought that the average survival time was about eight years (Report of the Advisory Panel on Alzheimer's Disease, 1995), more recent Canadian data suggest that the survival time may be much shorter. Christina Wolfson of McGill University and her colleagues made use of data from the Canadian Study of Health and Aging and found that the median survival after the onset of Alzheimer's disease was only three years (Wolfson et al., 2001). In some forms, the disease can occur relatively early, during the 40s or 50s (sometimes referred to as *presenile dementia*), but it usually appears during the 60s or 70s (Wise, Gray, & Seltzer, 1999). Approximately 50 percent of the cases of dementia are ultimately found to be the result of Alzheimer's disease, which is believed to afflict 238 000 Canadians over age 65 and many millions more worldwide (Canadian Study of Health and Aging Working Group, 2001).

Some research on prevalence suggests that Alzheimer's disease may occur most often in people who are poorly educated (Fratiglioni et al., 1991; Korczyn, Kahana,

& Galper, 1991). Greater impairment among uneducated people might indicate a much earlier onset, suggesting that Alzheimer's disease causes intellectual dysfunction that in turn hampers educational efforts. Or there could be something about intellectual achievement that prevents or delays the onset or symptoms of the disorder. To address these issues, Stern et al. (1994) examined the incidence of Alzheimer's-type dementia to learn whether educational levels affected who would and who would not later be diagnosed with the disorder. They found that those with the least amount of formal education were more likely to develop dementia than those with more education. It is important that the researchers were able to study living subjects before they could be identified as having dementia; such a prospective study rules out many alternative explanations for the results. Stern and colleagues concluded that educational attainment may somehow create a mental "reserve," a learned set of skills that helps someone cope for longer with the cognitive deterioration that marks the beginning of dementia. Like Diana's mother, who made copious notes and maps to help her function despite her cognitive deterioration, some people may adapt more successfully than others and thus escape detection longer. Brain deterioration may thus be comparable for both groups, but better educated individuals may be able to function successfully on a day-to-day basis for a longer period. This tentative hypothesis may prove useful in designing treatment strategies, especially during the early stages of the disorder.

A biological version of this theory—called the *cerebral reserve hypothesis*—suggests that the more synapses a person develops throughout life, the more neuronal death must take place before the signs of dementia are obvious (Stern, 2009). Mental activity that occurs with education presumably builds up this reserve of synapses and serves as a protective factor in the development of the disorder. It is likely that both skill development and the changes in the brain with education may contribute to how quickly the disorder progresses.

Research suggests that Alzheimer's disease may be more prevalent among women (Craig & Murphy, 2009), even when women's higher survival rate is factored into the statistics. In other words, because women live longer than men on average, they are more likely to experience Alzheimer's and other diseases, but longevity alone does not account for the higher prevalence of the disorder among women. A tentative explanation involves the hormone estrogen. Women lose estrogen as they grow older, so perhaps estrogen is protective against the

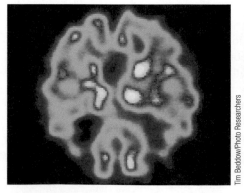
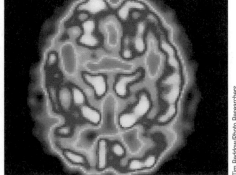

▲ The PET scan of a brain afflicted with Alzheimer's disease (left) shows significant tissue deterioration in comparison with a normal brain (right).

disease. A large and important study—the Women's Health Initiative Memory Study—looked at hormone use among women and its effect on Alzheimer's disease (Shumaker et al., 2004). In its initial findings, the study followed women over age 65 using a type of combined estrogen plus progestin known as Prempro and, contrary to the belief that giving women estrogen would decrease their chance of developing dementia, they observed an *increased* risk for Alzheimer's disease (Coker et al., 2010). More research is ongoing into the individual effects of these two types of hormones on dementia.

Finally, there appear to be questions about the prevalence of Alzheimer's disease according to racial identity. Early research seemed to suggest that certain populations (such as those with Japanese, Nigerian, certain First Nation, and Amish backgrounds) were less likely to be affected (e.g., see Pericak-Vance et al., 1996; Rosenberg et al., 1996). However, more recent work indicates that some of these differences may have been the result of differences in who seeks assistance (which is seen as unacceptable in some cultural groups), as well as differences in education (which we saw may delay the onset of obvious symptoms) (Wilson et al., 2010). Alzheimer's disease is found in roughly the same numbers across all ethnic groups, with one study finding a slightly lower rate among First Nations groups (Weiner, Hynan, Beekly, Koepsell, & Kukull, 2007). As you will see, findings like these help bring us closer to understanding the causes of this devastating disease.

Concept Check | 15.1

Dementia (a) and delirium (b) are two of the cognitive disorders identified in the *DSM-IV-TR*. Review what you have just learned by providing a tentative diagnosis for the individuals described.

1. Your grandfather's occasional memory slips seem to be getting worse. _____

2. A neighbour was found incoherent, confused, and disoriented after taking a new hypertension medication. _____

3. An older uncle no longer recognizes you or any other family members, and he forgets things he heard just minutes ago. _____

Check your understanding of some of the symptoms of dementia by identifying them from the following list:
(a) facial agnosia, (b) agnosia, and (c) aphasia.

4. Your elderly Aunt Bessie can no longer form complete, coherent sentences. _____

5. She does not recognize her own home any longer. _____

6. Aunt Bessie no longer recognizes you when you visit, even though you are her favourite niece. _____

Vascular Dementia

Description and Statistics

Each year, thousands of people die from strokes (any diseases or insults to the brain that result in restriction or cessation of blood flow). Although stroke is one of the top causes of death in Canadian seniors (Statistics Canada, 2000), many people survive, but one potential long-term consequence can be severely debilitating. According to University of Toronto neuropsychologist Donald Stuss, **vascular dementia** is a progressive brain disorder that is second only to Alzheimer's disease as a cause of dementia (Stuss & Cummings, 1990). The word *vascular* refers to blood vessels. When the blood vessels in the brain are blocked or damaged and no longer carry oxygen and other nutrients to certain areas of brain tissue, damage results. MRI scans of Diana Friel McGowin's brain showed a number of damaged areas, or multiple infarctions, left by a stroke several years earlier; this was one probable cause of her dementia. Because multiple sites in the brain can be damaged, the profile of degeneration—the particular pattern of skills that are impaired—differs from person to person. The *DSM-IV-TR* lists as criteria for vascular dementia the memory and other cognitive disturbances that are identical to those for dementia of the Alzheimer's type. However, certain neurological signs of brain tissue damage, such as abnormalities in walking and weakness in the limbs, are observed in many people with vascular dementia but not in people in the early stages of dementia of the Alzheimer's type (see DSM Table 15.3 on page 556).

In comparison with research on dementia of the Alzheimer's type, there are fewer studies on vascular dementia, perhaps because of its lower incidence rates. One study of people living in a Swedish city suggests that the lifetime risk of having vascular dementia is 4.7 percent among men and 3.8 percent among women (Hagnell et al., 1992). The higher risk for men is typical for this disorder, in contrast with the higher risk among women for Alzheimer's-type dementia (Alzheimer's Society of Canada, 2004). The relatively high rate of cardiovascular disease among men in general may account for their increased risk of vascular dementia. The onset of vascular dementia is typically more sudden than for the Alzheimer's type (King, Devichand, & Rockwood, 2005; King, Song, & Rockwood, 2006), probably because the disorder is the result of stroke, which inflicts brain damage immediately. The outcome, however, is similar for people with both types: Ultimately, they will require formal nursing care until they succumb to an infectious disease such as pneumonia.

Dementia Due to Other General Medical Conditions

Descriptions and Statistics

In addition to Alzheimer's disease and vascular damage, several other neurological and biochemical processes can lead to dementia. The *DSM-IV-TR* lists several other types with specific causes, including dementia due to HIV disease, dementia due to head trauma, dementia due to Parkinson's disease, dementia due to Huntington's disease, dementia due to Pick's disease, and dementia due to Creutzfeldt-Jakob disease (see DSM Table 15.4 on page 556). Each of these types is discussed here. Other

DSM-IV-TR **Table 15.3** Diagnostic Criteria for Vascular Dementia

A. The development of multiple cognitive deficits manifested by both

1. memory impairment (impaired ability to learn new information or to recall previously learned information)

2. one (or more) of the following cognitive disturbances:

 a. aphasia (language disturbance)

 b. apraxia (impaired ability to carry out motor activities despite intact motor function)

 c. agnosia (failure to recognize or identify objects despite intact sensory function)

 d. disturbance in executive functioning (i.e., planning, organizing, sequencing, abstracting)

B. The cognitive deficits in Criteria A1 and A2 each cause significant impairment in social or occupational functioning and represent a significant decline from a previous level of functioning.

C. Focal neurological signs and symptoms (e.g., exaggeration of deep tendon reflexes, extensor plantar response, pseudobulbar palsy, gait abnormalities, weakness of an extremity) or laboratory evidence indicative of cerebrovascular disease (e.g., multiple infarctions involving cortex and underlying white matter) that are judged to be etiologically related to the disturbance.

D. The deficits do not occur exclusively during the course of a delirium.

With Delirium: if delirium is superimposed on the dementia.

With Delusions: if delusions are the predominant feature.

With Depressed Mood: if depressed mood (including presentations that meet full symptom criteria for a major depressive episode) is the predominant feature. A separate diagnosis of mood disorder Due to a General Medical Condition is not given.

Uncomplicated: if none of the above predominates in the current clinical presentation.

Specify if:

With Behavioural Disturbance

Source: Reprinted with permission from the *Diagnostic and Statistical Manual of Mental Disorders,* Fourth Edition, Text Revision, (Copyright © 2000). American Psychiatric Association.

DSM-IV-TR **Table 15.4** Diagnostic Criteria for Dementia Due to Other General Medical Conditions

A. The development of multiple cognitive deficits manifested by both

1. memory impairment (impaired ability to learn new information or to recall previously learned information)

2. one (or more) of the following cognitive disturbances:

 a. aphasia (language disturbance)

 b. apraxia (impaired ability to carry out motor activities despite intact motor function)

 c. agnosia (failure to recognize or identify objects despite intact sensory function)

 d. disturbance in executive functioning (i.e., planning, organizing, sequencing, abstracting)

B. The cognitive deficits in Criteria A1 and A2 each cause significant impairment in social or occupational functioning and represent a significant decline from a previous level of functioning.

C. There is evidence from the history, physical examination, or laboratory findings that the disturbance is the direct physiological consequence of a general medical condition other than Alzheimer's disease or cerebrovascular disease (e.g., HIV infection, traumatic brain injury, Parkinson's disease, Huntington's disease, Pick's disease, Creutzfeldt-Jakob disease, normal-pressure hydrocephalus, hypothyroidism, brain tumor, or vitamin B_{12} deficiency).

D. The deficits do not occur exclusively during the course of a delirium.

Without Behavioural Disturbance: if the cognitive disturbance is not accompanied by any clinically significant behavioural disturbance.

With Behavioural Disturbance: if the cognitive disturbance is accompanied by a clinically significant behavioural disturbance (e.g., wandering, agitation).

Source: Reprinted with permission from the *Diagnostic and Statistical Manual of Mental Disorders,* Fourth Edition, Text Revision, (Copyright © 2000). American Psychiatric Association.

---

medical conditions that can lead to dementia include normal-pressure hydrocephalus (excessive water in the cranium, due to brain shrinkage), hypothyroidism (an underactive thyroid gland), brain tumour, and vitamin B12 deficiency. In their effect on cognitive ability, these disorders are comparable to the other forms of dementia we have discussed so far.

The human immunodeficiency virus-type-1, which causes acquired immune deficiency syndrome (AIDS), can also cause dementia (i.e., **HIV-1 disease**; Perry, 1993; Robinson & Qaqish, 2002). This impairment seems to be independent of the other infections that accompany HIV; in other words, the HIV infection itself seems to be responsible for the neurological impairment (Bourgeois et al., 2003). The early symptoms of dementia due to HIV are cognitive slowness, impaired attention, and

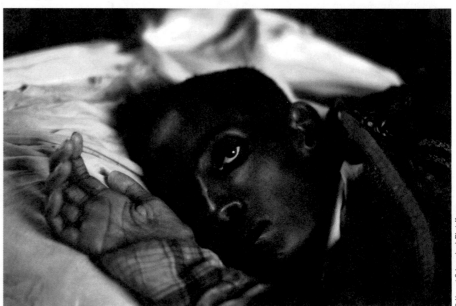

▲ The AIDS virus may cause dementia in the later stages.

© Harmut Schwarzbach/Photolibrary

forgetfulness. Affected individuals also tend to be clumsy, to show repetitive movements such as tremors and leg weakness, and to become apathetic and socially withdrawn (Navia, 1990).

People with HIV seem particularly susceptible to cognitive impairments in the later stages of HIV infection, although significant impairment of cognitive abilities may occur earlier (Heaton et al., 1994). Cognitive impairments are observed in 29 percent to 87 percent of people with AIDS (Lipton & Weiner, 2003), and approximately one-third of the infected people ultimately meet the criteria for dementia due to HIV disease (Day et al., 1992; Price & Brew, 1988). HIV disease accounts for a relatively small percentage of people with dementia compared with Alzheimer's disease and vascular causes, but its presence complicates an already devastating and ultimately fatal set of conditions.

Like dementia from Parkinson's disease, Huntington's disease, and several other causes, dementia resulting from HIV is sometimes referred to as subcortical dementia, because it affects primarily the inner areas of the brain, below the outer layer called the *cortex* (Bourgeois et al., 2003). The distinction between "cortical" (including dementia of the Alzheimer's type) and "subcortical" is important because of the different expressions of dementia in these two categories. Aphasia, which involves impaired language skills, occurs among people with dementia of the Alzheimer's type, but not among people with subcortical dementia. In contrast, people with subcortical dementia are more likely to experience severe depression and anxiety than those with dementia of the Alzheimer's type. In general, motor skills including speed and coordination are impaired early on among those with subcortical dementia. The differing patterns of impairment can be attributed to the different areas of the brain affected by the disorders.

Head trauma, injury to the head and therefore to the brain, is typically caused by accidents and can lead to cognitive impairments in both children and adults. Memory loss is the most common symptom (Lipton & Weiner, 2003).

Parkinson's disease is a degenerative brain disorder that affects about one out of every 1000 people worldwide (Marsh & Margolis, 2009). Nearly 100 000 people in Canada have Parkinson's (Parkinson Society of Canada, 2002). Motor problems are characteristic among people with Parkinson's disease, who tend to have stooped posture, slow body movements (called *bradykinesia*), tremors, and jerkiness in walking. The voice is also affected; afflicted individuals speak in a very soft monotone. The changes in motor movements are the result of damage to dopamine pathways. Because dopamine is involved in complex movement, a reduction in this neurotransmitter makes affected individuals increasingly unable to control their muscle movements, which leads to tremors

and muscle weakness. Some people with Parkinson's develop dementia (La Rue, 1992); conservative estimates place the rate at twice that found in the general population (Gibb, 1989). The pattern of impairments for these individuals fits the general pattern of subcortical dementia.

Huntington's disease is a genetic disorder that initially affects motor movements, typically in the form of *chorea*, involuntary limb movements (Marsh & Margolis, 2009). People with Huntington's can live for 20 years after the first signs of the disease appear, although skilled nursing care is often required during the last stages. Just as with Parkinson's disease, only a portion of persons with Huntington's disease go on to display dementia— somewhere between 20 percent and 80 percent—although some researchers believe that all Huntington's patients would eventually display dementia if they lived long enough (Marsh & Margolis, 2009). Dementia due to Huntington's disease also follows the subcortical pattern.

The search for the gene responsible for Huntington's disease is like a detective story. For some time, researchers have known that the disease is inherited as an autosomal dominant disorder, meaning that approximately 50 percent of the offspring of an adult with Huntington's will develop the disease. Since 1979, behavioural scientist Nancy Wexler and a team of researchers have been studying the largest known extended family in the world afflicted by Huntington's disease, in small villages in Venezuela. The villagers have cooperated with the research, partly because Wexler herself lost her mother, three uncles, and her maternal grandfather to Huntington's disease, and she,

▲ Actor Michael J. Fox provides his time and celebrity status to efforts to cure Parkinson's disease, a degenerative disease that is severely affecting his life. Despite his worsening symptoms, Fox continues his advocacy efforts to this day. More detail on his struggles with Parkinson's disease can be found in his autobiography, described in this chapter's From the Inside box on page 567.

too, may develop the disorder (Wexler & Rawlins, 2005). Using genetic linkage analysis techniques (see Chapter 4), these researchers first mapped the deficit to an area on chromosome 4 (Gusella et al., 1983), and then identified the elusive gene (Huntington's Disease Collaborative Research Group, 1993). Finding that one gene causes a disease is exceptional; research on other inherited mental disorders typically points to multiple gene (polygenic) influences.

Pick's disease is a rare neurological condition that produces a cortical dementia similar to that of Alzheimer's disease. The course of this disease is believed to last from five to ten years, although its cause is as yet unknown (Richards & Sweet, 2009). Like Huntington's disease, Pick's disease usually occurs relatively early in life—during a person's 40s or 50s—and is therefore considered an example of presenile dementia. An even rarer condition, **Creutzfeldt-Jakob disease**, is believed to affect only one in every million individuals (Edwards, 1994). An alarming development in the study of Creutzfeldt-Jacob disease is the finding of ten cases of a new variant that may be linked to bovine spongiform encephalopathy (BSE), more commonly referred to as "mad cow disease" (Smith & Cousens, 1996). This discovery led to a ban on exporting beef from the United Kingdom, because the disease might be transmitted from infected cattle to humans. More recently, we have experienced similar problems in our country. In May 2003, veterinary officials in Alberta identified a single sick cow. This announcement led the United States and Mexico to institute a ban on Canadian beef, which resulted in a severe slump in the Canadian beef industry (CBC News Online, 2004b); the U.S. ban continued for more than two years (CBC News Online, 2007). We do not yet have definitive information about the link between mad cow disease and the new form of Creutzfeldt-Jacob disease.

Substance-Induced Persisting Dementia

Description and Statistics

Prolonged drug use, especially in combination with poor diet, can damage the brain and, in some circumstances, can also lead to dementia. As many as 7 percent of individuals who are dependent on alcohol meet the criteria for dementia (Oslin & Cary, 2003). The *DSM-IV-TR* identifies several drugs that can lead to symptoms of dementia, including alcohol, inhalants such as glue or gasoline (which some people inhale for the euphoric feeling they produce), and the sedative, hypnotic, and anxiolytic drugs (see Chapter 11). These drugs pose a threat because they create dependence, making it difficult for a user to stop ingesting them. The resulting brain damage can be permanent and can cause the same symptoms seen in dementia of the Alzheimer's type (Parsons & Nixon, 1993). The *DSM-IV-TR* criteria for substance-induced persisting dementia are essentially the same as for the other forms of dementia; they include memory impairment and at least one of the following cognitive disturbances: aphasia (language disturbance), apraxia (inability to carry out motor activities despite intact motor function), agnosia (failure to recognize or identify objects despite intact sensory function), or a disturbance in executive functioning (such as planning, organizing, sequencing, and abstracting; see DSM Table 15.5).

Table 15.5 Diagnostic Criteria for Substance-Induced Persisting Dementia — **DSM-IV-TR**

A. The development of multiple cognitive deficits manifested by both
  1. memory impairment (impaired ability to learn new information or to recall previously learned information)
  2. one (or more) of the following cognitive disturbances:
     a. aphasia (language disturbance)
     b. apraxia (impaired ability to carry out motor activities despite intact motor function)
     c. agnosia (failure to recognize or identify objects despite intact sensory function)
     d. disturbance in executive functioning (i.e., planning, organizing, sequencing, abstracting)
B. The cognitive deficits in Criteria A1 and A2 each cause significant impairment in social or occupational functioning and represent a significant decline from a previous level of functioning.
C. The deficits do not occur exclusively during the course of a delirium and persist beyond the usual duration of Substance Intoxication or Withdrawal.
D. There is evidence from the history, physical examination, or laboratory findings that the deficits are etiologically related to the persisting effects of substance use (e.g., a drug of abuse, a medication).

Source: Reprinted with permission from the *Diagnostic and Statistical Manual of Mental Disorders,* Fourth Edition, Text Revision, (Copyright © 2000). American Psychiatric Association.

Causes

As our technology for studying the brain advances, so does our understanding of the many and varied causes of dementia. A complete description of what is known about the origins of this type of brain impairment is beyond the scope of this book, but we highlight some insights available for more common forms of dementia.

Biological Influences

Cognitive abilities can be adversely compromised in many ways. As we have seen, dementia can be caused by a number of processes: Alzheimer's disease, Huntington's disease, Parkinson's disease, head trauma, substance abuse, and others. The most common cause of dementia, Alzheimer's disease, is also the most mysterious. Because of its prevalence and our relative ignorance about the factors responsible for it, Alzheimer's disease has held the attention of a great many researchers who are trying to find the cause and ultimately a treatment or cure for this devastating condition.

Findings from Alzheimer's research seem to appear almost daily. We should be cautious when interpreting the output of this fast-paced and competitive field; too often, as we have seen in other areas, findings are heralded prematurely as conclusive and important. Remember that "discoveries" of a single gene for bipolar disorder, schizophrenia, and alcoholism were later shown to be based on overly simplistic accounts. Similarly, findings from Alzheimer's research are sometimes too quickly sanctioned as accepted truths before they have been replicated, an essential validation process.

▲ Maureen Forrester, a famous Canadian opera singer who died in 2010, suffered from a form of dementia brought on by prolonged alcohol abuse.

One lesson in scientific caution comes from research that demonstrates a negative correlation between cigarette smoking and Alzheimer's disease (Brenner et al., 1993). In other words, the study found that smokers are less likely than nonsmokers to develop Alzheimer's disease. Does this mean smoking has a protective effect, shielding a person against the development of this disease? On close examination, the finding may instead be the result of the differential survival rates of those who smoke and those who do not. In general, nonsmokers tend to live longer and are thereby more likely to develop Alzheimer's disease, which appears later in life. Some believe the relative inability of cells to repair themselves, a factor that may be more pronounced among people with Alzheimer's disease, may interact with cigarette smoking to shorten the lives of smokers who are at risk for Alzheimer's (Riggs, 1993). Put another way, smoking may exacerbate the degenerative process of Alzheimer's disease, causing people with the disease who also smoke to die much earlier than nonsmokers who have Alzheimer's. These types of studies and the conclusions drawn from them should make us sensitive to the complicated nature of the disorders we study.

Another theory about Alzheimer's disease that remains largely unsubstantiated is the aluminum hypothesis, which asserts that exposure to aluminum (e.g., through occupational exposure) is involved in causing Alzheimer's disease. However, many studies, such as the large-scale Canadian Study of Health and Aging, have failed to support a strong role of aluminum exposure as a risk factor (Canadian Study of Health and Aging Working Group, 1994). Most scientists now conclude that if aluminum exposure plays any role in Alzheimer's disease, the role is small (Alzheimer's Association, 2004).

What do we know about Alzheimer's disease, the most common cause of dementia? After the death of the patient he described as having a "strange disease of the cerebral cortex," Alois Alzheimer performed an autopsy. He found that the brain contained large numbers of tangled, strand-like filaments (referred to as *neurofibrillary tangles*). This type of damage occurs in everyone with Alzheimer's disease, although we do not know what causes it. A second type of degeneration results from gummy protein deposits—called *amyloid plaque*s (also called *senile* or *neuritic plaques*)—that accumulate in the brains of people with this disorder. Amyloid plaques are also found in older adults who do not have symptoms of dementia, but they have far fewer of them than individuals with Alzheimer's disease (Richards & Sweet, 2009). Both forms of damage—neurofibrillary tangles and amyloid plaques—accumulate over the years and are believed to produce the characteristic cognitive disorders we have been describing.

These two types of degeneration affect extremely small areas and can be detected only by a microscopic examination of the brain. Even sophisticated brain-scan techniques are not yet powerful enough to observe these changes in the living brain, which is why a definitive diagnosis of Alzheimer's disease requires an autopsy (Weiner et al., 2010). In addition to having neurofibrillary tangles and amyloid plaques, over time the brains of many people with Alzheimer's disease atrophy (shrink) to a greater extent than would be expected through normal aging (Richards & Sweet, 2009). Because brain shrinkage has many causes, however, only by observing the tangles and plaques can a diagnosis of Alzheimer's disease be properly made.

Rapid advances are being made toward uncovering the genetic bases of Alzheimer's disease (e.g., Seshadri et al., 2010). Because important discoveries happen almost daily, we cannot speak conclusively; however, certain overall themes have arisen from genetic research. As with most of the other behavioural disorders we have examined, multiple genes seem to be involved in the development of Alzheimer's disease. Table 15.1 on page 560 illustrates what we know so far. Genes on chromosomes 21, 19, 14, 12, and 1 have all been linked to certain forms of Alzheimer's disease (Devi et al., 2000; Marx, 1998; Rogaeva, Tandon, & St. George-Hyslop, 2001). The link to chromosome 21 was discovered first and resulted from the unfortunate observation that individuals with Down syndrome, who have three copies of chromosome 21 instead of the usual two, developed the disease at an unusually high rate (Report of the Advisory Panel on Alzheimer's Disease, 1995). More recent work has located relevant genes on other chromosomes. These discoveries indicate that there is more than one genetic cause of Alzheimer's disease. Some forms, including the one associated with chromosome 14, have an early onset. A team of researchers at the University of Toronto headed by geneticist and neurologist Peter St. George-Hyslop were the first to uncover gene mutations on chromosome 14 in the early-onset familial form of Alzheimer's disease (Jeffrey, 1995; Sherrington et al., 1995). Diana Friel McGowin may have an early-onset form, because she started noting symptoms at

TABLE 15.1 Genetic Factors in Alzheimer's Disease

Gene	Chromosome	Age of Onset
APP	21	45 to 66
Presenilin 1	14	28 to 62
Presenilin 2	1	40 to 85
apoE-4	19	19
A2M	12	12

Source: Adapted from Marx, 1998, and Rogaeva et al., 2001.

the age of 45. In contrast, Alzheimer's disease associated with chromosome 19 seems to be a late-onset form of the disease that has an effect only after about age 60.

Some genes that are now identified are **deterministic**, meaning that if you have one of these genes you have a nearly 100 percent chance of developing Alzheimer's disease (Bettens, Sleegers, & Van Broeckhoven, 2010). Deterministic genes such as the precursor gene for small proteins called *amyloid beta peptides* (also referred to as beta-amyloid or Aβ) and the *Presenilin 1* and *Presenilin 2* genes will inevitably lead to Alzheimer's disease, but, fortunately, these genes are also rare in the general population. For treatment purposes, this means that even if researchers can find a way to prevent these genes from leading to Alzheimer's disease, it will only help a relatively small number of people. On the other hand, some genes—including the *apolipoprotein E4 (apo E4)* gene—are known as **susceptibility** genes. These genes only slightly increase the risk of developing Alzheimer's disease, but in contrast to the deterministic genes, these are more common in the general population (Bettens et al., 2010). If future research can find ways to interfere with the apo E4 gene, many people will be helped.

Although closing in on the genetic origins of Alzheimer's disease has not brought immediate treatment implications, researchers are nearer to understanding how the disease develops, which may result in medical interventions. Genetic research has advanced our knowledge of how the amyloid plaques develop in the brains of people with Alzheimer's disease and may hold a clue to its origins. In the core of the plaques is a solid waxy substance made up of Aβ. Just as cholesterol buildup on the walls of blood vessels chokes the blood supply, deposits of Aβ are believed by some researchers to cause the cell death associated with Alzheimer's disease (Gatz, 2007). An important question, then, is: Why does this protein accumulate in the brain cells of some people but not of others?

Two mechanisms that may account for amyloid protein buildup are being studied. The first involves *amyloid precursor protein* (APP), a large protein that is eventually broken down into the *amyloid protein* found in the amyloid plaques. Important work resulted in identifying the gene responsible for producing APP, on chromosome 21 (Richards & Sweet, 2009). This finding may help integrate two observations about Alzheimer's disease: (1) APP produces the amyloid protein found in the amyloid plaques, and (2) Down syndrome, associated with an extra 21st chromosome, results in a higher incidence of the disease (see Chapter 14). The

gene responsible for producing APP and, ultimately, amyloid protein, may be responsible for the relatively infrequent early-onset form of the disease, and its location could explain why people with Down syndrome—who have an extra 21st chromosome and therefore an extra APP gene—are more likely than the general population to develop Alzheimer's disease.

A second, more indirect way that amyloid protein may build up in brain cells is through apolipoprotein E (apo E), which normally helps transport cholesterols, including amyloid protein, through the bloodstream. There are at least three forms of this transporter protein: apo E2, apo E3, and apo E4. Individuals who have late-onset Alzheimer's disease, the most common form, are likely to carry the gene associated with apo E4, located on chromosome 19. Researchers have found that the majority of people with Alzheimer's disease who also have a family history of the disease will have at least one gene for apo E4 (Richards & Sweet, 2009). In contrast, approximately 64 percent of individuals with Alzheimer's disease who have no family history of the disease have at least one gene for apo E4, and only 31 percent of nonaffected individuals have the gene. Having two genes for apo E4 (one on each member of the chromosome 19 pair) increases the risk for Alzheimer's disease: As many as 90 percent of people with two genes developed Alzheimer's disease (Reiman et al., 2007). In addition, having two apo E4 genes seemed to decrease the mean age of onset from 84 years to 68 years. These results suggest that apo E4 may be responsible for late-onset Alzheimer's disease and that a gene on chromosome 19 is responsible. What is still not completely understood is how apo E4 causes amyloid proteins to build up in the neurons of people who ultimately exhibit Alzheimer's disease and whether this process is responsible for the disease.

Researchers are just beginning to try to examine potential gene–environment interactions in Alzheimer's disease. Several isolated studies suggest a few areas of promise. For example, one study found that among those of African descent, having low levels of cholesterol seemed to reduce risk of Alzheimer's disease—but only among those who did not carry the apo E4 gene (Evans et al., 2000). In another study, physical exercise reduced the likelihood of developing the disease but, like the previous study, only among those without the apo E4 gene (Podewils et al., 2005). This type of research holds the potential for better understanding the complex nature of Alzheimer's disease and may lead to important prevention strategies (such as lowering cholesterol levels and exercising regularly) (Pedersen, 2010).

For all disorders described in this book, we have identified the role of biological, psychological, or both types of stressors as partially responsible for the onset of the disorder. Does dementia of the Alzheimer's type—which appears to be a strictly biological event—follow the same pattern? One of the leading candidates for an external contributor to this disorder is head trauma. As we have seen, it appears that repeated blows to the head can bring on *dementia pugilistica,* named after the boxers who suffer from this type of dementia. Fighters who carry the apo E4 gene may be at greater risk for developing dementia attributed to head trauma (Jordan et al., 1997). In addition to boxers, news accounts suggest links to the trauma experienced by football players and the development of dementia in these former athletes (Schwarz,

2007). Because it is now known that not only boxers are affected by this type of dementia, the disorder is now termed *chronic traumatic encephalopathy (CTE)*. Head trauma may be one of the stressors that initiates the onset of dementias of varying types. Other such stressors include having diabetes, high blood pressure, or herpes simplex virus-1 (Richards & Sweet, 2009). As with each of the disorders discussed, psychological and biological stressors may interact with physiological processes to produce Alzheimer's disease.

Psychological and Social Influences

For the most part, research has focused on the biological conditions that produce dementia. Although few would claim that psychosocial influences directly cause the type of brain deterioration seen in people with dementia, they may help determine onset and course. For example, a person's lifestyle may involve contact with factors that can cause dementia. We saw, for instance, that substance abuse can lead to dementia and, as we discussed previously (see Chapter 11), whether a person abuses drugs is determined by a combination of biological and psychosocial factors. In the case of vascular dementia, a person's biological vulnerability to vascular disease will influence the chances of strokes that can lead to this form of dementia. Lifestyle issues such as diet, exercise, and stress influence cardiovascular disease, and therefore help determine who ultimately experiences vascular dementia.

Cultural factors may also affect this process. For example, hypertension and strokes are prevalent among those of African and Asian heritage (Cruickshank & Beevers, 1989), which may explain why vascular dementia is most often observed in members of these groups (de la Monte, Hutchins, & Moore, 1989). In an extreme example, exposure to a viral infection can lead to dementia similar in form to Creutzfeldt-Jakob disease and to mad cow disease (both of which were discussed in more detail earlier in the chapter) through a condition known as *kuru*. Kuru is a fatal disease of the nervous system that is caused by a slow-acting virus. The virus causing kuru is passed on through a ritual form of cannibalism practised in Papua New Guinea as a part of mourning (Gajdusek, 1977). In yet another example of how cultural factors may play a role, dementia caused by head trauma and malnutrition are relatively prevalent in preindustrial rural societies (Lin, 1986; Westermeyer, 1989), which suggests that social engineering in the form of occupational safety and economic conditions influencing diet also affect the prevalence of certain forms of dementia. It is apparent that psychosocial factors help influence who does and who does not develop certain forms of dementia. Brain deterioration is a biological process but, as we have seen throughout this text, even biological processes are influenced by psychosocial factors.

Psychosocial factors also influence the course of dementia. Recall that educational attainment may affect the onset of dementia (Richards & Sweet, 2009). Having certain skills may help some people cope better than others with the early stages of dementia. As we saw earlier, Diana Friel McGowin's mother was able to carry on her daily activities by making maps and using other tricks to help compensate for her failing abilities. The early stages of confusion and memory loss may be better tolerated in cultures with lowered expectations of older adults. In certain cultures, including the Chinese, younger people are expected to take the demands of work and care from older adults after a certain age, and symptoms of dementia are viewed as a sign of normal aging (Gallagher-Thompson et al., 2006; Hinton, Guo, Hillygus, & Levkoff, 2000). Dementia may go undetected for years in these societies.

Much remains to be learned about the cause and course of most types of dementia. As we saw in Alzheimer's and Huntington's disease, certain genetic factors make some individuals vulnerable to progressive cognitive deterioration. In addition, brain trauma, some diseases, and exposure to certain drugs such as alcohol, inhalants, and sedative, hypnotic, and anxiolytic drugs can cause the characteristic decline in cognitive abilities. We also noticed that psychosocial factors can help determine who is subject to these causes and how they cope with the condition. Looking at dementia from this integrative perspective should help us view treatment approaches in a more optimistic light. It may be possible to protect people from conditions that lead to dementia and to support them in dealing with the devastating consequences of having it. We next review attempts to help from both biological and psychosocial perspectives.

Treatment: An Overview

For many of the disorders we have considered, treatment prospects are fairly good. Clinicians can combine various strategies to reduce suffering significantly. Even when treatment does not bring expected improvements, mental health professionals have usually been able to stop problems from progressing. This is not the case in the treatment of dementia.

One factor preventing major advances in the treatment of dementia is the nature of the damage caused by this disorder. The brain contains billions of neurons, many more than are used. Damage to some can be compensated for by others, due to plasticity. However, there is a limit to where and how many neurons can be destroyed before vital functioning is disrupted. Researchers are closing in on how to use the brain's natural process of regeneration to potentially reverse the damage caused in dementia (Khachaturian, 2007). Currently, however, with extensive brain damage, no known treatment can restore lost abilities. The goals of treatment therefore become (1) trying to prevent certain conditions, such as substance abuse, that may bring on dementia; (2) trying to delay the onset of symptoms to provide better quality of life; and (3) attempting to help these individuals and their caregivers cope with the advancing deterioration. Most efforts in treating dementia have focused on the second and third goals, with biological treatments aimed at stopping the cerebral deterioration and psychosocial treatments directed at helping patients and caregivers cope.

A troubling statistic further clouds the tragic circumstances of dementia: More than half the caregivers of people with dementia— usually relatives—eventually become clinically depressed (Burns, 2000; Clyburn, Stones, Hadjistavropoulos, & Tuokko, 2000).

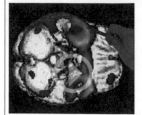
Compared with the general public, these caregivers are twice as likely to develop depression (Canadian Study of Health and Aging Working Group, 1994; O'Rourke, Cappeliez, & Guindon, 2003), and they use more psychotropic medications and report stress symptoms at three times the normal rate (George, 1984). Caring for people with dementia, especially in its later stages, is clearly an especially trying experience (O'Rourke & Cappeliez, 2002). The stress experienced by such caregivers is illustrated in the film *Away from Her* (Polley, 2006)—a film that depicts the decline of Fiona (played by Julie Christie) as her cognitive abilities become increasingly compromised by Alzheimer's disease. The film is particularly compelling in its depiction of the caregiver burden experienced by her loving husband Grant (played by Gordon Pinsent) and the couple's ultimate decision to place Fiona in a nursing home specializing in dementia, to relieve Grant of the burden of caring for her on his own. Clinicians are becoming increasingly sensitive to the needs of caregivers, and research is now exploring interventions to help them to care for people with dementia (Lee, Czaja, & Schulz, 2010).

Biological Treatments

Dementia due to known infectious diseases, nutritional deficiencies, and depression can be treated if it is caught early. Unfortunately, however, no known treatment exists for most of the different types of dementia that are responsible for the vast majority of cases. Dementia due to stroke, HIV, Parkinson's disease, and Huntington's disease is not currently treatable because we have no effective treatment for the primary disorder. However, new research in several related areas has brought us closer to helping individuals with these forms of dementia. Substances that may help preserve and perhaps restore neurons—called *glial cell-derived neurotrophic factor*, or *GDNF*—may someday be used to help reduce or reverse the progression of degenerative brain diseases (Zuccato & Cattaneo, 2009). Researchers are also looking into the possible benefits of transplanting stem cells (from fetal brain tissue) into the brains of people with such diseases. Initial results from these studies are still preliminary but appear promising (Arenas, 2010). Dementia brought on by strokes may now be more preventable by new drugs that help prevent much of the damage inflicted by the blood clots characteristic of stroke (Richards & Sweet, 2009). Most current attention is on a treatment for dementia of the Alzheimer's type, because it affects so many people. Here, too, however, success has been modest at best.

Much work has been directed at developing drugs that will enhance the cognitive abilities of people with dementia of the Alzheimer's type. Many seem to be effective initially, but long-term improvements have not been observed in placebo-controlled studies (Richards & Sweet, 2009). Several drugs (called *cholinesterase inhibitors*) have had a modest impact on cognitive abilities in some patients and include donepezil (Aricept), rivastigmine (Exelon), and galantamine (Reminyl). *Tacrine hydrochloride* (Cognex), another in this family of drugs, is rarely used today because of the potential for liver damage (Rabins, 2006). These drugs prevent the breakdown of the neurotransmitter acetylcholine (which is deficient in people with Alzheimer's disease), thus making more acetylcholine available to the brain. Research suggests that, when using these drugs, people's cognitive abilities improve to the point where they were six months earlier (Lyketos, 2009). But the gain is not permanent. Even people who respond positively do not stabilize but continue to experience the cognitive decline associated with Alzheimer's disease. In addition, if they stop taking the drug—as almost three-quarters of the patients do because of negative

▲ The film *Away from Her* (2006) is a beautiful and moving love story about a couple dealing with the wife's cognitive decline as she becomes increasingly debilitated by Alzheimer's disease. Directed by Sarah Polley, and starring Gordon Pinsent and Julie Christie, the film is a screenplay adaptation of celebrated author Alice Munro's 1999 short story "The Bear Came over the Mountain."

The Film Farm/Foundry Films Inc./The Kobal Collection/Art Resource side effects such as liver damage and nausea—they lose even that six-month gain (Lyketos, 2009). Newer drugs are now being investigated for the treatment of Alzheimer's disease. These include drugs that target the beta-amyloid (plaques) in the brain, and it is hoped that these advances will finally provide a positive prognosis for this devastating disease (Rafii & Aisen, 2009).

Several other medical approaches are being explored to slow the course of Alzheimer's disease, but initial excitement generated by these approaches has waned with the findings from researchers. For example, most of you have heard of using *Ginkgo biloba* (maidenhair) to improve memory. Initial research suggested that this herbal remedy may produce modest improvements in the memory of people with Alzheimer's disease, but other studies have not replicated this benefit (DeKosky et al., 2008). Similarly, the effects of vitamin E have been evaluated. One large study found that among individuals with moderately severe impairment, high doses of the vitamin (2000 international units per day) delayed progression compared to a placebo (Sano et al., 1997), but it did not prevent the development of the disease. Further research, in fact, indicates that taking high doses of vitamin E may actually increase mortality and therefore this intervention is no longer recommended (Richards & Sweet, 2009). Modest slowing of the progression of the disease also may be obtained by introducing exercise to patients (Rockwood & Middleton, 2007; Teri et al., 2003). To date, however, no medical interventions are available that directly treat and therefore stop the progression of the conditions that cause the cerebral damage in Alzheimer's disease.

Medical interventions for dementia also include the use of drugs to help with some associated symptoms. A variety of antidepressants—such as serotonin-specific reuptake inhibitors—are commonly recommended to alleviate the depression and anxiety that too often accompany the cognitive decline. Antipsychotic medication is sometimes used for those who become unusually agitated (Richards & Sweet, 2009).

Psychosocial Treatments

Psychosocial treatments are now receiving a great deal of attention for their ability to delay the onset of severe cognitive decline. These efforts focus on enhancing the lives of people with dementia, as well as those of their families. People with dementia can be taught skills to compensate for their lost abilities. Recall that Diana's mother learned on her own to make maps to help her get from place to place. Diana herself began making lists so she would not forget important things. Some researchers have evaluated more formal adaptations to help people in the early stages of dementia. Bourgeois (1992, 1993) created "memory wallets" to help people with dementia carry on conversations. On white index cards inserted into a plastic wallet are printed declarative statements such as "My husband John and I have three children," or "I was born on January 6, 1921, in Winnipeg." In one study, Bourgeois (1992) found that six adults with dementia could, with minimal training, use

this memory aid to improve their conversations with others. Three of the adults used their memory wallets with people who had initially not been involved in the training, such as children and grandchildren. (One participant withdrew from the training after several weeks, which seemed to coincide with a substantial decline in her cognitive abilities during that time.) Other researchers have used similar devices to help people orient themselves in time and place, another ability disrupted by dementia (Hanley, 1986; Hanley & Lusty, 1984). Adaptations such as these help people communicate with others and remain aware of their surroundings, and the aids can also reduce the frustration that people experience with the awareness of their own decline.

Cognitive stimulation—encouraging people with dementia to practise learning and memory skills—seems to be an effective method for delaying the onset of the more severe cognitive effects of this disorder (Knowles, 2010). These activities include word games, tests of memory of famous and familiar faces, and practice with numbers (e.g., how much change back you would receive from a purchase). These types of skill-building exercises can maintain cognitive activity and improve the quality of life in those patients when compared to controls.

What impact do the medical and nonmedical treatments have on those with Alzheimer's disease? ■ Figure 15.4 illustrates how these interventions may delay the worst of the symptoms—essentially compressing the time when the person is most impaired (Becker, Mestre, Ziolko, & Lopez, 2007). The red line illustrates the typical course of the disease, which results in three to five years of severe impairment before death. However, with the interventions we highlighted (illustrated by the purple line), people are able to live more fully for a longer period, despite the still-inevitable impairment and death. Families find this extra time with their loved ones to be invaluable, and hopefully with more advancements we will see progress on improving mortality rates of this progressive disease.

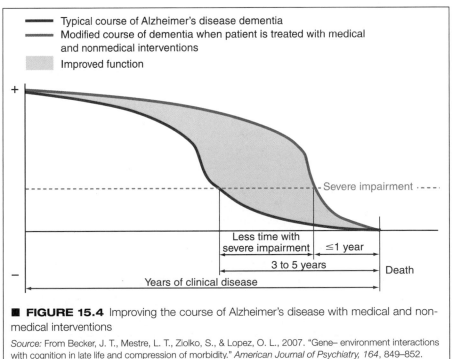

■ **FIGURE 15.4** Improving the course of Alzheimer's disease with medical and non-medical interventions

Source: From Becker, J. T., Mestre, L. T., Ziolko, S., & Lopez, O. L., 2007. "Gene– environment interactions with cognition in late life and compression of morbidity." *American Journal of Psychiatry, 164,* 849–852.

Individuals with advanced dementia are not able to feed, bathe, or dress themselves. They cannot communicate with or recognize even familiar family members. They may wander away from home and become lost. Because they are no longer aware of social stigma, they may engage in public displays of sexual behaviour such as masturbation. They may be frequently agitated or even physically violent. To help both the person with dementia and the caregiver, researchers have explored interventions for dealing with these consequences of the disorder (Richards & Sweet, 2009). For example, some research indicates that a combination of exercise for patients and instruction for caregivers on how to handle behaviour problems can improve the overall health and the depression in people with Alzheimer's disease (Logsdon, McCurry, Pike, & Teri, 2009; Teri et al., 2003).

Of great concern is the tendency of people with dementia to wander. Sometimes they wind up in places or situations that may be dangerous (e.g., stairwells, the street). This tendency to wander was depicted in a scene in the film *Away from Her*, where the central character, Fiona, wanders away from her home, sending her caregiver husband, Grant, on a frantic search to find her (Polley, 2006). Often, the person with dementia is tied to a chair or bed, or sedated, to prevent roaming. Unfortunately, physical and medical restraints have their own risks, including additional medical complications; they also add greatly to the loss of control and independence that already plague the person with dementia. Psychological treatment as an alternative to restraint sometimes involves providing cues for people to help them safely navigate around their home or other areas. New innovations in surveillance technology—creating a "smart home" that can monitor the location of the patient and warn caregivers—may provide more piece of mind for those who care for these patients. At the same time, ethical concerns are being raised about the use of this technology because of its ability to invade privacy (Bharucha et al., 2009; Mahoney et al., 2007).

Someone with dementia can become agitated and is sometimes verbally and physically aggressive. This behaviour is understandably very stressful for people trying to provide care. In these situations, medical intervention is often used, although frequently with only modest results (Testad, Ballard, Brønnick, & Aarsland, 2010). Caregivers are often given assertiveness training to help them deal with hostile behaviours (see Table 15.2). Otherwise, caregivers may either passively accept all the criticism inflicted by the person with dementia, which increases stress, or become

angry and aggressive in return. This last response is of particular concern because of the potential for *elder abuse*. Four percent or approximately 100 000 elderly persons living in private dwellings in Canada have suffered elder abuse (Alberta Family and Social Services, 1990). About half the time, the victimization of seniors is perpetrated by a family member (most often an adult child or spouse) (Statistics Canada, 2004, 2007). A group at particular risk for elder abuse is seniors with cognitive impairments (Vida, Monks, & des Rosiers, 2002). Withholding food or medication or inflicting physical abuse is most common among caregivers of elderly people who have cognitive deficits (Sachs & Cassel, 1989). Given the established role of caregiver stress in many such cases of elder abuse (Statistics Canada, 2004), it is important to teach caregivers how to handle stressful circumstances so they do not escalate into abusive situations. Little objective evidence supports the usefulness of assertiveness training for reducing caregiver stress, and we await research to guide future efforts.

In general, families of people with dementia can benefit from supportive counselling to help them cope with the frustration, depression, guilt, and loss that take a heavy emotional toll. One group, which conducted a large-scale study of 555 principal caregivers over three years, identified a number of steps that can be taken to support caregivers through this difficult time (Aneshensel, Pearlin, Mullan, Zarit, & Whitlatch, 1995). Early on, caregivers need basic information on the causes and treatment of dementia, as well as on financial and legal issues, and on locating help for the patient and the family. As the dementia progresses, and the affected person requires more and more assistance, caregivers will need help managing behavioural difficulties (wandering away, violent outbursts) and developing effective ways to communicate with the patient. Clinicians also assist the family with decisions about hospitalizations and, finally, help them adjust during bereavement (Peeters, Van Beek, Meerveld, Spreeuwenberg, & Francke, 2010).

Overall, the outlook for slowing (but not stopping) the cognitive decline characteristic of dementia is optimistic. The best available medications provide some recovery of function, but they do not stop the progressive deterioration. Psychological interventions may help people cope more effectively with the loss of cognitive abilities, especially in the earlier stages of this disorder. In addition, emphasis is placed on helping caregivers—the other victims of dementia—as the person they care for continues to decline.

TABLE 15.2 Sample Assertive Responses

Patient Behaviour	Assertive Response
	Calmly but firmly say the following:
1. The patient refuses to eat, bathe, or change clothes.	"We agreed to do this at this time so that we will be able to (give specific activity or reward)."
2. The patient says she or he wants to go home.	"I know you miss some of the places we used to be. This is our home now and together we are safe and happy here."
3. The patient demands immediate gratification.	"It's not possible to have everything we want. As soon as I've finished (describe your task or actions), we can discuss other things we want to do."
4. The patient accuses the caregiver of taking his or her possessions.	"We both enjoy our own things. I'll help you look for (specific item missing) so you can enjoy it, just as soon as I have finished (describe specific task or action)."
5. The patient is angry or rebellious.	"I like to be treated fairly just as you do. Let's discuss what's bothering you so we can go back to our usual good relationship."

Source: Adapted from *When Memory Fails: Helping the Alzheimer's and Dementia Patient* by Allen Jack Edwards, p. 174. Copyright © 1994 Allen Jack Edwards. Reprinted by permission of Da Capo Press, a member of the Perseus Books Group.

Are We Close to an Alzheimer's Vaccine?

We described in Chapter 11 how researchers are striving to create a vaccine that would use the immune system to fight drugs such as heroin, just as your body attacks infectious bacteria. Other researchers are targeting vaccines that would potentially treat and prevent—rather than just delay—the symptoms of Alzheimer's disease. Much of the research is attempting to get the immune system to attack the process that overproduces the small proteins (Aβ) that lead to cell death. Prior efforts had to be abandoned because of the severe negative side effects of the vaccine, which included serious brain inflammation. More recent research with humans and animals indicates that there may be several vaccines that could be effective in preventing the damage caused by Aβ formation and therefore represent the first glimmer of hope for patients and their families

(Subramanian, Bandopadhyay, Mishra, Mathew, & John, 2010).

This type of research currently begins with transgenic mice—mice in which the DNA has been altered. In the case of testing an Alzheimer's vaccine, the mice DNA is engineered to produce the same small proteins thought to be responsible for the dementia. Mice are good subjects because they age rapidly, with a 22-month-old mouse equivalent to a 65-year-old human (Morgan, 2007). This allows researchers to study how the brain reacts to the potential vaccine if it has already started the progression of Alzheimer's. If the results are promising in these transgenic mice, only then do researchers try small studies with humans. Researchers are optimistic that there may finally be intervention approaches that would reverse the current trend of increasing numbers of people with dementia.

Prevention

Without treatment, we need to rely even more heavily on prevention strategies for dementia. You can imagine that it is difficult to study prevention efforts for dementia because of the need to follow individuals for long periods to see whether the efforts are effective. One major study conducted in Sweden looked at many of the risk factors (those factors that increase the chance of having dementia) and protective factors (those that decrease the risk) under study today (Fratiglioni, Winblad, & von Strauss, 2007). They looked at the medical records of 1810 participants who were older than 75 at the time and followed them for about 13 years. Through interviews and medical histories, they came to two major conclusions: control your blood pressure, and lead an active physical and social life! These two recommendations came out as the major factors that individuals can change—because you cannot change your genetics, for example—that will decrease the chances of developing dementia. Additional prevention research is ongoing, and there may be other potentially fruitful research areas that can lead to the successful prevention of this devastating disorder.

Amnestic Disorder

Say these three words to yourself: *apple, bird, roof.* Try to remember them, and then count backward from 100 by threes. After about 15 seconds of counting, can you still recall the three words? Probably so. However, people with amnestic disorder will not remember them, even after such a short time (Bourgeois, Seaman, & Servis, 2008). The loss of this type of memory, which we described as a primary characteristic of dementia, can occur without the loss of other high-level cognitive functions. The main deficit of **amnestic disorder** appears to be the inability to transfer information like the list we just described into long-term memory, which can cover minutes, hours, or years. This disturbance in memory is due either to the physiological effects of a medical condition, such as head trauma,

or to the long-term effects of a drug. Consider the case of S. T. described by Martin Cole and his colleagues.

S. T. | *Remembering Fragments*

S. T., a 67-year-old white woman, suddenly fell, without loss of consciousness. She appeared bewildered and anxious but oriented to person and place yet not to time. Language functioning was normal. She was unable to recall her birthplace, the ages of her children, or any recent Canadian prime ministers. She could not remember three objects for one minute, nor recall what she had eaten for her last meal. She could not name the colour of any object shown to her but could correctly name the colour related to certain words—for example, "grass," "sky." Object naming was normal. Examined one year later, she could repeat five digits forward and backward but could not recall her wedding day, the cause of her husband's death, or her children's ages. She did not know her current address or phone number and remembered zero out of three objects after five minutes. Although she was described by her family as extremely hard-working before her illness, after hospitalization she spent most of her time sitting and watching television. She was fully oriented, displayed normal language function, and performed simple calculations without error.

Source: "Thalamic amnesia: Korsakoff syndrome due to left thalamic infarction," by M. Cole, M. D. Winkelman, J. C. Morris, J. E. Simon, T. A. Boyd, *Journal of the Neurological Sciences (1992),* Volume: 110, Issue: 1–2, Pages: 62–67 with permission from Elsevier.

The *DSM-IV-TR* criteria for amnestic disorder describe the inability to learn new information or to recall previously learned information (see DSM Table 15.6 on page 566). As with all cognitive disorders, memory disturbance causes significant impairment in social and occupational functioning. The woman we just described (S. T.) was diagnosed with a type of amnestic disorder called *Wernicke-Korsakoff* syndrome, which is caused by damage to the thalamus, a small region deep inside the brain that acts as a relay station for information from many other parts of the brain. In her case, the damage to the thalamus was believed to be due to a stroke that caused vascular damage. Another common cause of the Wernicke-Korsakoff syndrome is chronic heavy alcohol use. As you saw, S. T. had pronounced difficulty recalling information presented just minutes before. Although she could repeat a series of numbers, she couldn't remember three objects that had been presented to her moments earlier. As with other people with amnestic disorder, despite these obvious deficits with her memory, her language command was fine and she could perform simple chores. Yet these individuals are often significantly impaired in social or vocational functioning because of the importance of memory to such activities.

As we saw with the other cognitive impairments, a wide range of insults to the brain can cause permanent amnestic disorders. Recent research has focused on attempting to prevent the damage associated with Wernicke-Korsakoff syndrome. Specifically, a deficiency in thiamine (vitamin B1) due to alcohol abuse in persons developing Wernicke-Korsakoff syndrome is leading researchers to try supplementing this vitamin, especially for very heavy drinkers (Sechi & Serra, 2007).

One promising cognitive approach to treating people with amnestic disorders was recently reported by researchers at York University and the Baycrest Centre for Geriatric Care in Toronto. Specifically, Karantzoulis, Rich, and Mangels (2006) had patients with amnestic disorder and healthy controls complete an enactment task. In addition to saying the object-action association that needs to be remembered, participants were also asked to perform the action, thus providing another route (i.e., episodic as well as semantic) for memory retrieval. Some of the object-action pairs were familiar and semantically meaningful ("Pet the cat") and some were novel and semantically meaningless ("Pet the compass"). They found that the enactment task improved memory for both the amnestic patients and the controls, and that it even enhanced memory for the novel but semantically meaningless object-action pairs. The results showed that enactment facilitates memory even among those who have particular difficulties in forming new associations, suggesting its potential utility as part of treatment for those with amnestic disorders (Karantzoulis et al., 2006).

DSM-IV-TR	**Table 15.6** Diagnostic Criteria for Amnestic Disorder due to ... [Indicate the General Medical Condition]

A. The development of memory impairment as manifested by impairment in the ability to learn new information or the inability to recall previously learned information.

B. The memory disturbance causes significant impairment in social or occupational functioning and represents a significant decline from a previous level of functioning.

C. The memory disturbance does not occur exclusively during the course of a delirium or a dementia.

D. There is evidence from the history, physical examination, or laboratory findings that the disturbance is the direct physiological consequence of a general medical condition (including physical trauma).

Specify if:

Transient: if memory impairment lasts for one month or less

Chronic: if memory impairment lasts for more than one month

Source: Reprinted with permission from the *Diagnostic and Statistical Manual of Mental Disorders,* Fourth Edition, Text Revision, (Copyright © 2000). American Psychiatric Association.

Concept Check | 15.2

Identify the cognitive disorders described.

1. Decline in cognitive functioning that is gradual and continual and has been associated with neurofibrillary tangles and amyloid plaques. _____

2. The apparent loss of ability to transfer information to long-term memory without loss of other high-level cognitive functions. _____

3. José is a recovering alcoholic. Ask him about his wild partying days, and his stories usually end quickly because he can't remember the whole tale. He even has to write down things he has to do in a notebook; otherwise, he's likely to forget. _____

4. Grandpa has had several strokes but can still care for himself. However, his ability to remember important things has been declining steadily for the past few years. _____

Lucky Man: A Memoir
by Michael J. Fox

In 1998, during an interview with Barbara Walters, Canadian actor Michael J. Fox first revealed to the public that he had been diagnosed with Parkinson's disease (PD) seven years earlier. Although Fox initially attempted to hide the symptoms of his illness from his co-workers and fans, he is now using his celebrity status to give hope to those with the illness and to attempt to find a cure. *Lucky Man* is his autobiography in which he courageously shares with his readers many of the problems he has faced—problems that many PD patients face. He describes not only the debilitating physical effects of the disease, but also the sense of mourning he experienced on the discovery of his illness. The book is an engaging read as is illustrated by the following excerpts:

I need to explain the "on-off" phenomenon. This Jekyll-and-Hyde melodrama is a constant vexation for the PD patient, especially one as determined as I was to remain closeted. "On" refers to the time when the medication is telling my brain everything it wants to hear. I'm relatively loose and fluid, my mind clear and movements under control. Only a trained observer could detect my Parkinson's....

When I'm "off," the disease has complete authority over my physical being. I'm utterly in its possession. Sometimes there are flashes of function, and I can be effective at performing basic physical tasks, certainly feeding and dressing myself (though I'll lean toward loafers and pullover sweaters), as well as any chore calling for more brute force than manual dexterity. In my very worse "off" times I experience the full panoply of classic parkinsonian symptoms: rigidity, shuffling, tremors, lack of balance,

diminished small motor control, and the insidious cluster of symptoms that makes communication—written as well as spoken—difficult and sometimes impossible....

My ability to form thoughts and ideas into words and sentences is not impaired; the problem is translating those words and sentences into articulate speech. My lips, tongue, and jaw muscles simply won't cooperate. What words I do smuggle through the blockade can be heard, though not always comprehended. Try as I might, I can't inflect my speech to reflect my state of mind. And it's not like I can liven up my halting monotone with a raised eyebrow; my face, utterly expressionless, simply won't respond. (excerpts from Chapter 8: "Unwrapping the Gift")

Another aspect of his experience that Fox makes clear in his book is the impressive social support that members of the PD community provide to one another. He also describes the importance of family for people with this debilitating condition. His wife, Tracy Pollan, clearly has served as a monumental support to Fox throughout the stages of his illness and has assisted him in making the transition from initial mourning over his losses to his current sense of growth, empowerment, and acceptance.

Source: From *Lucky Man* by Michael Fox. Copyright © 2000 Michael Fox.

Toward a Dimensional Approach to Cognitive Disorders

Discussions about any changes in the category of cognitive disorders in the *DSM-5* are focused on ways to incorporate a dimensional approach. Although there are as yet no final changes, one of the proposals is to separate the disorders involving dementia and amnesia into Major and Minor Neurocognitive Disorders categories (American Psychiatric Association, 2010). The distinction between "major" and "minor" neurocognitive disorders is a difficult one to make, although it is assumed that minor cognitive deficits would include problems such as memory difficulties that are not sufficient to interfere with the person's ability to live independently. The neurocognitive disorders would be defined based on a decline from a previous level of cognitive functioning, which would include the loss of a person's ability to carry out important daily living activities independently (cooking, dressing, etc.).

This proposed distinction is consistent with some of the breakthroughs in diagnoses involving improved brain scanning that we covered earlier in this chapter (Weiner et al., 2010). Researchers are becoming more sophisticated in their ability to identify beginning signs of dementia, which not only allows for early diagnosis (e.g., minor neurocognitive disorder) but also can highlight for clinicians the need to track cognitive abilities over time. It is important to monitor cognitive abilities to see if the changes remain stable (as you would see in traumatic brain injury or stroke), if they improve (which can occur with dementia related to properly treated HIV or substance abuse), or if they continue to decline (such as with Alzheimer's disease). This is a beginning step designed to assist diagnostic efforts by including a dimensional approach to identifying the range of neurocognitive disorders (such as dementia and amnestic disorder). For example, being able to identify minor problems may someday lead to differential treatment, along the lines of the Alzheimer's vaccine discussed previously.

Summary

Delirium

- Delirium is a temporary state of confusion and disorientation that can be caused by brain trauma, intoxication by drugs or poisons, surgery, and a variety of other stressful conditions, especially among older adults.

Dementia

- Dementia is a progressive and degenerative condition marked by gradual deterioration of a broad range of cognitive abilities including memory; language; and planning, organizing, sequencing, and abstracting information.
- Alzheimer's disease is the leading cause of dementia; there is currently no known cause or cure.

- To date, there is no effective treatment for the irreversible dementias caused by Alzheimer's disease, Parkinson's disease, Huntington's disease, and the various other less common conditions that produce this progressive cognitive impairment. Treatment often focuses on helping the patient cope with the continuing loss of cognitive skills and helping caregivers deal with the stress of caring for the affected individuals.

Amnestic Disorder

- Amnestic disorders involve a dysfunction in the ability to recall recent and past events. The most common is Wernicke-Korsakoff syndrome, a memory disorder usually associated with chronic alcohol abuse.

Key Terms

agnosia, 551
Alzheimer's disease, 552
amnestic disorder, 565
aphasia, 552
Creutzfeldt-Jakob disease, 558

delirium, 548
dementia, 550
dementia of the Alzheimer's
 type, 552
deterministic, 560

facial agnosia, 551
head trauma, 557
HIV-1 disease, 556
Huntington's disease, 557
Parkinson's disease, 557

Pick's disease, 558
susceptibility, 560
vascular dementia, 555

Answers to Concept Checks

15.1

1. dementia (a)
2. delirium (b)
3. dementia (a)

4. aphasia (c)
5. agnosia (b)
6. facial agnosia (a)

15.2

1. dementia of the Alzheimer's type
2. amnestic disorder

3. Wernicke-Korsakoff syndrome
4. vascular dementia

Media Resources

CourseMate

Access an integrated eBook, Abnormal Psychology Videos (formerly Abnormal Psych Live CD-ROM), chapter-specific interactive learning tools (flashcards, quizzes, learning modules), and more in your Psychology CourseMate, available at **www.abnormalpsych3ce .nelson.com**.

Abnormal Psychology Videos

Free Abnormal Psychology videos can be viewed on the website **www.abnormalpsych3ce .nelson.com**.

- *Computer Simulations and Senile Dementia:* In this clip, James McClelland proposes that computer simulations of the brain's neural networks can reveal how human cognition works—and even how cognition fails in dementia.

- *Alzheimer's Disease: Tom:* This is a rather moving clip in which Tom's family talks about him and you see a surprising example of memory that still works.

- *Amnestic Disorder: Mike:* Following an accident, Mike struggles with memory problems that affect his employment, his relationship, and his sense of self. You'll notice how he expresses himself both in his language and in the flatness of his emotion.

Video Concept Reviews

CourseMate also contains Mark Durand's *Video Concept Reviews* on these challenging topics.

- Delirium
- Dementia
- Agnosia
- Dementia of the Alzheimer's Type
- Vascular Dementia
- Human Immunodeficiency Virus Type 1 (HIV-1)
- Head Trauma
- Amnestic Disorder

Exploring Cognitive Disorders

> When the brain is damaged, the effects are irreversible, accumulating until learning, memory, or consciousness are obviously impaired.

> Cognitive disorders develop much later than intellectual disability and other learning disorders, which are believed to be present at birth.

TYPES OF COGNITIVE DISORDERS

		Description	Causes (subtypes)	Treatment

Delirium	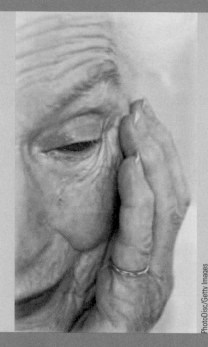	• Impaired consciousness and cognition for several hours or days
		  – confusion, disorientation, inability to focus
		• Most prevalent among older adults, people with AIDS, and patients on medication
			• Delirium due to a general medical condition
			• Substance-induced delirium
			• Delirium due to multiple etiologies
			• Delirium not otherwise specified
				• Pharmacological
				  – benzodiazepines
				  – antipsychotics
				• Psychosocial
				  – reassurance
				  – presence of personal objects
				  – inclusion in treatment decisions

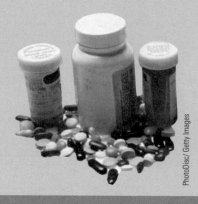

PhotoDisc/Getty Images

PhotoDisc/ Getty Images

		Description	Causes	Treatment

Amnestic Disorder		• Permanent short-term memory loss without impairment of other cognitive functions
		  – inability to learn new information or recall previously learned information
		  – significant impairment in social and occupational functioning
			• Medical condition such as head trauma
			• Lasting effects of a drug, even after the substance is no longer ingested
				• Prevention: proper medical care and drug monitoring
				• No long-term success at combating damage

Subtype

Wernicke/Korsakoff Syndrome

Caused by damage to the thalamus from injury (stroke) or chronic heavy alcohol use (thiamine depletion)

PhotoDisc/Getty Images

Dementia

> Gradual deterioration of brain functioning that affects judgment, memory, language, and other advanced cognitive processes
> Caused by medical condition or drug abuse
> Some forms are irreversible, some are resolved by treatment of primary condition.

TYPES OF DEMENTIA

		Description	Causes	Treatment
Dementia of the Alzheimer's Type	 Gabrie a Medina/Blend Images/Getty Images	• Increasing memory impairment and other multiple behavioural and cognitive deficits, affecting language, motor functioning, ability to recognize people or things, and/or planning • Most prevalent dementia • Subject of most research	• Progressive brain damage, evident in neurofibrillary tangles and neuritic plaque, confirmed by autopsy but assessed by simplified mental status exam • Involves multiple genes	• No cure so far, but hope lies in genetic research and amyloid protein in neurine plaques. • Management may include lists, maps, and notes to help maintain orientation. • New medications that prevent acetylcholine breakdown and vitamin therapy show promise.
Substance-Induced Persisting Dementia	 PhotoDisc/Getty Images	• Caused by brain damage due to prolonged drug use, especially in combination with poor diet, as in alcohol dependency; other substances may include inhalants, and the sedative, hypnotic, and anxiolytic drugs • Treatment focuses on prevention.		
Vascular Dementia	PhotoDisc/Getty Images	• Permanent deterioration due to blocked or damaged blood vessels in the brain (stroke) • Symptoms identical to Alzheimer's and may also include problems with walking and weakness of limbs • Treatment focuses on coping.		
Dementia Due to Other General Medical Conditions	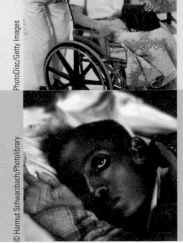 © Harmut Schwarzbach/Photolibrary	• Similar in effect to other cognitive disorders, but caused by: – head trauma – HIV, Parkinson's, Huntington's, Pick's, or Creutzfeldt-Jakob disease – hydrocephalus, hypothyroidism, brain tumour, and vitamin B_{12} deficiency • Treatment of primary condition is sometimes possible.		

16 | Mental Health Services: Legal and Ethical Issues

Government Gouvernement
of Canada du Canada

The Human Face of Mental Health and Mental Illness in Canada 2006

Canadä

The Human Face of Mental Health and Mental Illness in Canada. Public Health Agency of Canada, 2006. Reproduced with the permission of the Minister of Health, 2011.

Mind is the great lever of all things: human thought is the process by which human ends are ultimately answered.
—Daniel Webster

Identify appropriate applications of psychology in solving problems, such as:	› Psychology-based interventions in clinical, counselling, educational, industrial/organizational, community, and other settings and their empirical evaluation (APA SLO 4.2.d) *(see textbook pages 559–562, 569–574)*
Articulate how psychological principles can be used to explain social issues and inform public policy.	› Use psychological principles to explain social issues and inform public policy (APA SLO 4.3) *(see textbook pages 562–569)*

* Portions of this chapter cover learning outcomes suggested by the American Psychological Association (2007) in their guidelines for the undergraduate psychology major. Chapter coverage of these outcomes is identified above by APA Goal and APA Suggested Learning Outcome (SLO).

We begin this chapter with a return to Arthur, who we described in Chapter 13 as having psychotic symptoms. Revisiting the case from his family's perspective reveals the complexities of mental health law and the ethical aspects of working with people who have psychological disorders.

ARTHUR | *A Family's Dilemma*

As you remember, Arthur's family members brought him to one of our clinics because he was speaking and acting strangely. He talked incessantly about his "secret plan" to save all the starving children in the world. His family's concern intensified when Arthur said he was planning to break into the German embassy and present his plan to the German ambassador. Alarmed by his increasingly inappropriate behaviour and fearing he would be hurt, the family was astounded to learn they could not force him into a psychiatric hospital. Arthur could admit himself—which was not likely, given his belief that nothing was wrong with him—but they had no power to admit him involuntarily unless he was in danger of doing harm to himself or others. The family coped with this emergency as best they could for several weeks until the worst of Arthur's behaviours began to diminish.

Arthur experienced what is known as brief psychotic disorder (see Chapter 13). Fortunately for him, this is one of the few psychotic disorders that are not chronic. What is important here is to see how the mental health system responded. Because Arthur had not hurt himself or someone else, he had to seek help on his own before the hospital would assist him, even though everyone involved realized that such action on his part was very unlikely. This response by the mental health system added one more layer of helplessness to the family's already desperate emotional state.

Why wouldn't the mental health facility admit Arthur, who was clearly out of touch with reality and in need of help? Why couldn't his family authorize the mental health facility to act? What would have happened if Arthur had entered the German embassy and hurt or, worse, killed someone? Would he have gone to jail, or would he have finally received help from the mental health community? Would Arthur have been held responsible if he hurt other people while he was delusional? These are just a few of the many issues that surface when we try to balance the rights of people who have psychological disorders with the responsibilities of society to provide care.

Mental health professionals face such questions daily. They must both diagnose and treat people and consider individual and societal rights and responsibilities. As we describe how systems of ethics and legal concepts have developed, remember that they change with time and with shifting societal and political perspectives on mental illness. How we treat people with psychological disorders is in part a function of how society views them. For example, do people with mental illness need help and protection, or does society need protection from them? As public opinion of people with mental illness changes, so do the laws affecting them, and legal and ethical issues have an effect on both research and practice. As you will see, the issues affecting research and practice are often complementary. For example, confidentiality (i.e., that no information will be released to a third party) is required to protect the identity of a participant in a research study and of a patient seeking help for a psychological disorder. Because people who receive mental health services often simultaneously participate in research studies, we must consider the concerns of both constituencies.

Civil Commitment

The legal system exercises significant influence over the mental health system, for better or for worse. Laws have been designed to protect people who display abnormal behaviour and to protect society. Often, achieving this protection is a delicate balancing act, with the scales sometimes thought to be tipped in favour of the rights of individuals and at other times in favour of society as a whole. For example, each province and territory has **civil commitment laws** under the provincial or territorial Mental Health Acts that detail when a person can be legally detained in a psychiatric institution—even against his or her will (Douglas & Koch, 2001). When Arthur's family tried to have him involuntarily committed to a mental health facility, hospital officials decided that because he was not in imminent danger of hurting himself or others, he could not be committed against his will. In this case, the laws of his provincial Mental Health Act protected Arthur from involuntary commitment, but they also put him and others at potential risk by not compelling him to get help. In civil commitment law, the rights of people are pitted against the responsibility of the government (in this case the provinces and territories) to care for its citizens (Douglas & Koch, 2001).

Criteria for Civil Commitment

Although there is variability across provinces and territories, as outlined in Table 16.1 on page 574, most provincial legislation permits commitment when the following three conditions have been met: (1) The person has a "mental disorder," (2) the person

TABLE 16.1 A Comparison of Civil Commitment Legislation across Canadian Jurisdictions

Specified Statutory Factors												
BC	YT	AB	NT	NU	SK	MB	ON	QC	NB	NS	PE	NL
Requirement of mental disorder												
yes	yes	yes	yes	yes	yes	yes	yes	no	yes	yes	yes	yes
Functional definition of mental illness												
yes	yes	yes	yes	yes	yes	yes	no	no	yes	yes	yes	yes
Requirement of danger to self or others												
yes	yes	yes	yes	yes	yes	yes	yes	yes	yes	yes	yes	yes
Strict definition of danger												
no	yes	no	yes	yes	no	yes	yes	no	no	yes	no	yes
Requirement of need for treatment												
yes	no	no	no	yes	yes	yes	yes	no	yes	yes	yes	yes
Right to refuse or consent to treatment												
no	no	yes	no	no	yes	yes	yes	yes	yes	yes	yes	no
Right to be informed of reasons for detention												
yes	yes	yes	yes	yes	yes	yes	yes	no	yes	yes	yes	yes
Specified right to legal counsel												
yes	yes	no	yes	yes	no	yes	yes	yes	yes	yes	yes	yes
Provision for apprehension by peace officer												
yes	yes	yes	yes	yes	yes	yes	yes	yes	yes	yes	yes	yes
Length of short-term commitment order												
48 h	24 h	24 h	48 h	48 h	24 h	72 h	72 h	72 h	72 h	72 h	72 h	72 h
Length of initial commitment certificate												
1 mo	21 d	1 mo	14 d	14 d	21 d	3 wk	2 wk	21 d	1 mo	1 mo	28 d	1 mo
Length of second commitment certificate												
1 mo	21 d	1 mo	1 mo	1 mo	21 d	3 mo	1 mo	21 d	2 mo	1 mo	30 d	30 d
Length of further commitment certificate												
3, 6 mo	21 d	1 6 mo	1, 3, 6 mo	1, 3, 6 mo	21 d, 1 y	3 mo	2, 3 mo	3 mo	3 mo	2, 3 mo	90 d, 12 mo	60, 90 d
Discharge criteria specified												
yes	yes	yes	yes	yes	yes	yes	yes	yes	yes	no	yes	yes
Statutory presence of review panel												
yes	yes	yes	no	no	yes	yes	yes	yes*	yes	yes	yes	yes
Director may give treatment consent												
yes	yes	yes	no	no	yes	yes	yes	no	yes	no	yes	yes
Specified right to appeal court												
yes	yes	yes	yes	yes	yes	yes	yes	no	no	yes	no	yes
Any person may bring issue before court												
yes	yes	yes	yes	yes	yes	yes	yes	no	no	yes	yes	yes

Notes: The table from Douglas and Koch (2001) was updated to include information from the new provincial and territorial Mental Health Acts, as amended by annual provincial or territorial legislation since the time the original table was constructed.

* In the Québec legislation, the Administrative Tribunal of Québec seems to be the functional equivalent of statutorily created review panels in other provinces' schemes. As such, although Québec does not have a statutory review panel per se, it has a body that serves some of the same purposes (e.g., to review the legitimacy of detention). Statutes:

BC: Mental Health Act, R.S.B.C. 1996, C. 288

YT: Mental Health Act, R.S.Y. 2002, C. 150

AB: Mental Health Act, R.S.A. 2000, c. M-13

NT: Mental Health Act, R.S.N.W.T. 1988, c. M-10

NU: Mental Health Act, R.S.N.W.T. 1988, c. M-10 (as amended since by NU); SK: Mental Health Services Act, S.S. 1984–85–86, c. M-13.1

MB: Mental Health Act, C.C.S.M. 1998, c M110

ON: Mental Health Act, R.S.O. 1990, c. M.7

QC: Act Respecting the Protection of Persons Whose Mental State Presents a Danger to Themselves or to Others, R.S.Q. 1997, c. P-38.001

NB: An Act to Amend the Mental Health Act, S.N.B. 2006, c. M-10

NS: Mental Health Act (Bill 109—not yet a statute, 2004); PE: Mental Health Act, S.P.E.I. 2005, c. M-6.1

NL: Mental Health Care and Treatment Act, S.N.L. 2006, c. M-9.1.

Source: From "Civil Commitment and Civil Competence: Psychological Issues" by Kevin S. Douglas and William J. Koch. In Schuller, R. A. (Ed.); Ogloff, J. R. P. (Ed.); 2001. *Introduction to Psychology and Law: Canadian Perspectives.* Toronto, ON: University of Toronto Press. pp. 353–374. Adapted with permission from University of Toronto Press.

is dangerous to himself or herself or others, and (3) the person is in need of treatment (Douglas & Koch, 2001). All Canadian jurisdictions require the second of these three criteria and some, but not all, also require the first and third (see Table 16.1). Although every Canadian jurisdiction but one (i.e., Québec) requires that a person have a mental illness before he or she can be detained under civil commitment legislation, the definition of "mental illness" differs across jurisdictions, as we will see in the next section of this chapter. Similarly, although every Canadian jurisdiction also requires that a person be a danger to himself or herself or others, or that the person needs to be hospitalized for his or her safety or protection or for the safety or protection of others, the provinces and territories vary considerably in how they define "safety" and "protection" (Douglas & Koch, 2001).

For example, British Columbia defines these terms very broadly (i.e., the person requiring hospitalization to prevent his or her substantial mental or physical deterioration). Broad definitions such as this one can require a great deal of subjective judgment from the court and from mental health professionals. In contrast, Ontario defines these terms much more strictly (i.e., requiring that the person's mental disorder will likely result in serious bodily harm or imminent and serious physical impairment to himself or herself or to another person; see Douglas & Koch, 2001). With these differences across jurisdictions in how strictly dangerousness is defined, you can see how it would have been easier for Arthur to have been committed under the legislation in British Columbia than under the legislation in Ontario. Some have argued that more liberal definitions of dangerousness are actually in the patient's best interest. For example, John Gray and Richard O'Reilly of the British Columbia Ministry of Health and the University of Western Ontario, respectively, argue that if a patient cannot be legally admitted until he or she has demonstrated dangerousness, not only will the patient's prognosis be worse for the lost treatment time, but the patient will also likely have legal issues to deal with because he or she has broken the law (Gray & O'Reilly, 2001). But others, such as the Québec patient advocacy group Action Autonomie, have argued that more liberal definitions of dangerousness can result in decisions that compromise a patient's autonomy. For example, a liberal definition of dangerousness could result in a psychiatrist deciding to detain a schizophrenic patient because he refuses to take his medications. This could happen if the psychiatrist feels the medication noncompliance could result in the patient directing traffic, for example, thus putting the patient and others in danger—even when the patient is not actually actively dangerous to others in the sense of wanting to kill someone (Bratulic, 2007).

The Canadian jurisdictions also differ on several other issues pertaining to civil commitment, such as whether the patient has the right to refuse treatment, the right to be informed of the reasons for the hospital detention, the right to apply to a review panel that can grant a discharge from the hospital, and the specified right to legal counsel. These safeguards are built into the civil commitment process to guarantee the rights of the person being examined and to ensure that no one is involuntarily committed to a psychiatric facility for other than legitimate reasons. The legislations relevant to civil commitment across Canada also vary in terms of how long a person can be detained (see Table 16.1).

How the conditions for civil commitment are interpreted has varied over the years and has always been controversial. It is important to see that the government justifies its right to act against the wishes of an individual—in this case, to commit someone to a mental health facility—under two types of authority: police power and *parens patriae* ("state as the parent") power. Under police power, the government takes responsibility for protecting the public health, safety, and welfare and can create laws and regulations to ensure this protection. Criminal offenders are held in custody if they are a threat to society. This first rationale for civil commitment has a long history under Canadian law. Even as Europeans were settling Canada, people with mental illnesses could be detained in order to prevent them from harming others. The provinces and territories apply the second rationale for civil commitment—*parens patriae* power—in circumstances in which citizens are not likely to act in their own best interest. For example, it is used to commit individuals with severe mental illness to mental health facilities when it is believed that they might be harmed because they are unable to secure the basic necessities of life, such as food and shelter, or because they do not recognize their need for treatment (Perlin, 2000). Under *parens*

▲ The government can exert *parens patriae* to protect people from hurting themselves.

Civil Commitment

▲ People with mental illness are treated differently in different cultures.

patriae power, the government acts as a surrogate parent, presumably in the best interests of a person who needs help.

A person in need of help can always voluntarily request admission to a mental health facility; after an evaluation by a mental health professional, he or she may be accepted for treatment. However, when an individual does not voluntarily seek help, but others feel that treatment or protection is necessary, the process of civil commitment may be initiated. The specifics of this process differ from province to province, but typically one or two physicians or psychiatrists must conduct an assessment and agree that the person meets the criteria for commitment outlined in the relevant jurisdiction's legislation (Douglas & Koch, 2001).

In Canada, people deemed suitable for commitment are not necessarily committed to a hospital. Instead, there are also options for compulsory community treatments (CCT) for the mentally ill (Gray & O'Reilly, 2005). CCT's main goals are to prevent relapse, and to provide care in a less restrictive environment (Gray & O'Reilly, 2005). Unlike Australia where CCT is allowed as a first form of treatment, CCT is not permitted in Canada until there has already been previous inpatient treatment. The necessary criteria for CCT in Canadian jurisdictions are that the patient must have some risk of increased mental deterioration, or possibly pose harm to himself or herself or others (Gray & O'Reilly, 2005).

Defining Mental Illness

The concept of mental illness figures prominently in civil commitment, and it is important to understand how it is defined. **Mental illness** is a legal concept, typically meaning severe emotional or thought disturbances that negatively affect an individual's health and safety. As we mentioned earlier, each Canadian jurisdiction has its own definition. For example, in Saskatchewan, mental illness means "a disorder of thought, perceptions, feelings or behaviour that seriously impairs a person's judgement, capacity to recognize reality, ability to associate with others, or ability to meet the ordinary demands of life, in respect of which treatment is advisable" (Douglas & Koch, 2001, p. 355). Robertson (1994) refers to this type of definition of mental illness as a functional definition, because it specifies the effect of the illness on the patient's thoughts and behaviour. In contrast, some other provinces like Ontario (see Table 16.1 on page 574) do not use a functional definition of mental illness; they instead define mental disorder more traditionally as a "disease or disability of the mind" (Douglas & Koch, 2001, p. 355).

Mental illness is *not* synonymous with psychological disorder; in other words, receiving a *DSM-IV-TR* diagnosis does not necessarily mean that a person fits the legal definition of someone having a mental illness. Although the *DSM* is quite specific about criteria that must be met for diagnosis, considerable ambiguity exists about what constitutes a "disease or disability of the mind" or what are "adverse effects on a person's ability to function" as required in a functional definition of mental illness. This ambiguity allows for flexibility in making decisions about individual cases, but it also creates the possibility of subjective impression and bias influencing these decisions.

Dangerousness

Assessing whether someone is a danger to himself, herself, or others is a critical determinant of the civil commitment process. **Dangerousness** is a particularly controversial concept for people with mental illnesses: Popular opinion tends to be that people who have a mental illness are more dangerous than those who do not. Though this conclusion is questionable, the belief is still widespread, in part because of sensational media reports. Such views are important to the process of civil commitment if they bias a determination of dangerousness and unfairly link it with severe mental illness.

There is a widespread popular belief that mental illness causes a person to be violent (Kobau, DiIorio, Chapman, & Delvecchio, 2010). The results of research on dangerousness and mental illness are often mixed, but evidence points to a moderately increased rate of violence among people with mental illness (Elbogen & Johnson, 2009). Closer examination of this kind of research reveals that although having a mental illness generally does increase the likelihood of future violence, specific symptoms (such as hallucinations, delusions, or having a comorbid personality disorder) appear to be associated with people at increased risk of violence (Lurigio & Harris, 2009). Even previously violent individuals with mental illness are not necessarily going to commit violent crimes after they are released, although the presence of certain symptoms may increase the risk.

Unfortunately, the widely held misperception that people with mental illness in general are more dangerous may differentially affect ethnic minorities and women. Women, for example, are likely to be viewed as more dangerous than are men when they engage in similar aggressive behaviours (Coughlin, 1994). Black males are often perceived as dangerous, even when they don't exhibit any violent behaviour (Bond, DeCandia, & MacKinnon, 1988).

Photo by Christopher J. Koegl/Courtesy of Dr. Christopher D. Webster

▲ Forensic psychologist Christopher Webster, professor emeritus at both the University of Toronto and Simon Fraser University, is an internationally acclaimed expert in the assessment of risk for violence.

To return to the general issue, how do you determine whether a person is dangerous to others? How accurate are mental health professionals at predicting who will and who will not later be violent? The answers directly affect the process of civil commitment as well as the protection of society. If we can't accurately predict dangerousness, how can we justify involuntary commitment?

Early research on this issue suggested that psychologists were actually rather poor at predicting dangerousness (see reviews by Douglas & Webster, 1999; Webster, Douglas, Eaves, & Hart, 1997a, 1997b). However, more recent research has shown that accurate predictions of the risk for violence are indeed possible (Douglas & Webster, 1999; Ogloff & Daffern, 2006; Rice, 1997). Many advances in predicting dangerousness have been made by Canadian research teams. One example is a study conducted at Simon Fraser University by Douglas, Ogloff, and Hart (2003) in which a model of violence risk assessment, called the HCR-20, was evaluated among forensic psychiatric patients. The HCR-20 has professional clinicians assess 20 established risk factors in a structured fashion. The researchers applied the HCR-20 to 100 forensic psychiatric patients who had been found "not guilty by reason of a mental disorder" (a concept described later in this chapter) and who were subsequently released into the community. Risk judgments made on the basis of the HCR-20 were significantly predictive of post-release community violence, supporting the validity of the authors' structured professional judgment model of risk assessment (Douglas et al., 2003). Canadian teams have also recently made important advances in the prediction of violence in women (e.g., Nicholls, Ogloff, Brink, & Spidel, 2005).

Similarly, since risk for self-harm is one of the common criteria used for decisions about civil commitment, one might ask whether psychologists can accurately predict risk for suicidal behaviour. The job of assessing patients' risk for suicide and other self-harm is an important and common activity for many mental health professionals. A good deal of research, again much of which has been done by Canadian teams (e.g., Cochrane-Brink, Lofchy, & Sakinofsky, 2000), shows that several important variables should be assessed in evaluating a patient's risk for self-injury. For example, a study done by forensic psychologist James Ogloff and his colleagues investigated nearly 300 psychiatric patients who had been involuntarily committed to the Riverview Psychiatric Hospital in British Columbia. These researchers investigated what variables predicted which patients would display self-injurious behaviour while in hospital. They found that those patients who reported suicidal thoughts while in the hospital, those who showed verbal and physical aggression toward others in the hospital, those with a history of self-harm, and those who had engaged in a suicide attempt or other form of self-injurious behaviour within the two weeks before being committed to hospital were most likely to harm themselves while in hospital (Jack, Nicholls, & Ogloff, 1998; Nicholls, Jack, & Ogloff, 1998). More recently, a scale called the Suicide Risk Assessment Scale (SRAS) for prisoners was developed by a group of researchers at the Correctional Service of Canada (Wichmann, Serin, & Motiuk, 2000). The SRAS was subsequently validated by a research group in Trois-Rivières, Québec. Specifically, the SRAS performed better than a more elaborate test in predicting suicide risk in two samples of inmates (Daigle, Labelle, & Côté, 2006). Research like this has led to guidelines to help clinicians make decisions about predicting self-harm that are more accurate than clinicians' global judgments and far better than chance (Douglas & Koch, 2001; Murray & Wright, 2006).

Deinstitutionalization and Homelessness

Two trends have influenced the number of people in Canada who are involuntarily committed each year: (1) the increase in the number of people who were homeless and (2) **deinstitutionalization**, the movement of people with severe mental illness out of institutions. Homelessness, although not exclusively a problem of the mentally ill, is largely determined by social views of people with mental illness. Estimates from social action agencies in the late 1980s placed the number of homeless people at between 100 000 and 250 000 in Canada alone (Hargrave, 1999). According to the 2001 census, more than 14 000 Canadians live in homeless shelters (Statistics Canada, 2002). The vast majority of these people are aged 35 to 64 (47 percent) or aged 15 to 34 (33 percent); almost 11 percent are minors. Stuart and Arboldea-Florez (2000) from Queen's University interviewed homeless people using inner-city shelters in Calgary in the late summer of 1997. Three-quarters of them had some kind of mental health issue, with 33 percent displaying significant mental health problems. Lifetime alcohol abuse was evident for one-third. Those with mental health problems were having a harder time living on the streets (e.g., being victimized, stressed, having a harder time finding food and work) than those without mental health problems. Theses researchers also reported that the face of the homeless person in Canada has changed from the image of an older male with an alcohol use disorder; today, there are also many younger people, women, and families living on the streets (Stuart & Arboldea-Florez, 2000). First Nations people, refugees, and ethnic minorities are overrepresented among the Canadian homeless (Hargrave, 1999).

Information on the characteristics of people who are homeless is important because it provides us with clues about the reasons that people become homeless, and it dispels the notion that all homeless people have mental health problems. For a time, homelessness was blamed on strict civil commitment criteria and deinstitutionalization (Perlin, 1996; Torrey, 1988a); that is, policies to limit severely who can be involuntarily committed, the limits placed on the stays of people with severe mental illness, and the concurrent closing of large psychiatric hospitals were held responsible for the substantial increase in homelessness during the 1980s. Although a sizable percentage of homeless people do have mental illness, the rise in homelessness is also due to such economic factors as increased unemployment and a shortage of low-income housing (Hargrave, 1999).

Deinstitutionalization—the closing of many large psychiatric hospitals—is one factor that many believe has contributed to increasing rates of homelessness in Canada (Turkheimer & Parry, 1992). Deinstitutionalization had two goals: (1) to downsize or even close the large provincial and territorial mental hospitals and (2) to create a network of community mental health services in which the released individuals could be treated. As noted by Douglas and Koch (2001), the deinstitutionalization movement led to the rapid downsizing of psychiatric facilities across Canada. In 1957, some 70 300 persons were detained in psychiatric institutions in Canada (Dominion Bureau of Statistics, 1955–1957). In 1975, this figure was down to 44 847 inpatients (Statistics Canada, 1975). Further decreases ensued. For example, in 1992–1993 alone, 29 991 patients were discharged from psychiatric hospitals, and the number detained was even lower (Douglas & Koch, 2001; Statistics Canada, 1995). Some argue that the deinstitutionalization movement continues into the present-day era of "community integration" (Jones, 2007).

▲ People become homeless because of many factors, including economic conditions, mental health status, and alcohol or other drug abuse.

As we can see, the first goal of the deinstitutionalization movement (i.e., downsizing or closing the large provincial/territorial mental hospitals) appears to have been substantially accomplished. However, the second goal of providing alternative community care has not. Instead, there was **transinstitutionalization**, or the movement of people with severe mental illness from large psychiatric hospitals to nursing homes or other group residences, including jails and prisons, many of which provide only marginal services (Sealy & Whitehead, 2004). Because of the deterioration in care for many people who had previously been served by the provincial or territorial mental hospital system, deinstitutionalization is largely considered a failure. Although many praise the ideal of providing community care for people with severe mental illness, the support needed to provide this type of care has been severely deficient. And many remain concerned about continuity of care (i.e., how the many different agencies and services should best work together) in this new era of community integration (e.g., Durbin, Goering, Streiner, & Pink, 2006).

As noted by Patricia Sealy and Paul Whitehead (2004) of the University of Western Ontario, since the deinstitutionalization movement began over 40 years ago to the present day, community care continues to grow and the number of hospital beds continues to decrease. They fear this trend will continue until the appropriate balance of community care and inpatient psychiatric services is definitively determined (Sealy & Whitehead, 2004). However, others argue that deinstitutionalization does not lead to homelessness or patient abandonment in the community. For example, a study by researchers at the University of Montréal examined the effects of deinstitutionalization in a sample of 96 patients discharged from Louis H. Lafontaine Hospital between 1989 and 1998, as compared to a control sample of 96 patients who were hospitalized during the same interval. They did not find higher rates of homelessness in the deinstitutionalized sample (only two ended up on the streets). Most discharged patients moved to some form of group residential supervised care in the community (Lesage, Morisette, Fortier, Reinharz, & Contandriopoulos, 2000).

An Overview of Civil Commitment

What should the criteria be for involuntarily committing someone with severe mental illness to a mental health facility? Should imminent danger to self or others be the only justification, or should society paternalistically coerce people who appear to be in distress and in need of asylum or safety? How do we address the concerns of families like Arthur's, who see their loved ones overcome by psychological problems? And what of our need not to be harassed by homeless people with mental illness? When do these rights take precedence over the rights of an individual to be free from unwanted incarceration? It is clearly difficult to strike the appropriate balance between individual rights and the government's responsibility to care for its citizens. The mental health laws pertaining to civil commitment across Canadian jurisdictions have attempted to do just that. With high rates of Canadian people homeless due to factors such as strict civil commitment laws and the deinstitutionalization movement, it is tempting to conclude that the Canadian legal system has failed to strike this balance. However, the fact that laws can be changed should make us optimistic that the needs of individuals and of society can ultimately be addressed through the courts.

Criminal Commitment

What would have happened if Arthur had been arrested for trespassing on embassy grounds or, worse yet, if he had hurt or killed someone in his effort to present his plan for saving the world? Would he have been held responsible for his actions, given his obviously disturbed mental state? How would a jury have responded to him when he seemed fine just several days later? If he was not responsible for his behaviour then, why does he seem so normal now?

These questions are of enormous importance as we debate whether people should be held responsible for their criminal behaviour despite the possible presence of mental illness. For example, Nova Scotian Jane Hurshman admitted to shooting her common-law husband, Billy Stafford, to death but claimed

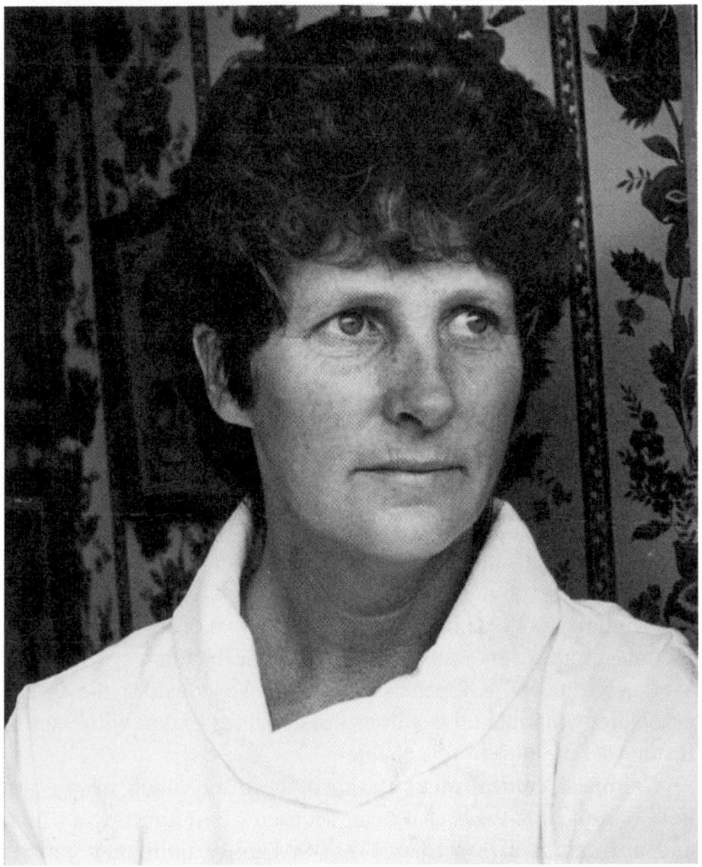

Republished with permission from The Halifax Herald Ltd.

▲ Nova Scotian Jane Hurshman was severely abused over a number of years by her common-law husband, Billy Stafford, whom she eventually killed. Cases like Hurshman's led to the acceptance of the battered woman syndrome as a murder defence in Canadian courts in 1990.

she was driven to it by years of severe abuse perpetrated by Stafford (Vallee, 1986). She was acquitted by a jury, but on appeal, a new trial was ordered. Rather than go though another trial, Hurshman pleaded guilty to manslaughter and served a short jail term. Cases such as this have ignited considerable controversy about the conditions under which people should be responsible for criminal behaviour. Jane Hurshman's experience and other similar cases (e.g., *Regina v. Lavallee*; see Regehr & Glancy, 1995) led to the recognition of *battered woman syndrome* in Canadian law (Schuller & Yarmey, 2001).

Battered woman syndrome is not recognized in the *DSM-IV-TR*. The term refers to a state of learned helplessness (see Chapter 7) or post-traumatic stress (see Chapter 5) that results from chronic abuse within a relationship such that a woman feels unable to leave (Walker, 1979). The Supreme Court of Canada has acknowledged that in certain extreme cases involving battered woman syndrome, an accused may well be under a reasonable apprehension of death even though she is not in danger of "imminent or immediate harm" at the moment that force is used to protect herself. This is an expansion of the self-defence legal defence that is always available to any person accused of murder who reasonably believes that his or her life was in danger from an assault. A battered woman's apprehension about dying may be quite realistic; one study conducted in Ontario found that nearly 80 percent of female murder victims are killed by their spouses or intimate partners (Crawford & Gartner, 1992). Nonetheless, the battered woman syndrome defence has its critics, with some calling it the "abuse excuse" (e.g., Dershowitz, 1994).

An interesting recent experiment by Regina Schuller and her colleagues (2004) examined what were the different verdicts reached by mock jurors in a murder case involving a battered woman as the defendant. The researchers found that the verdicts varied on the basis of (1) whether the defendant had killed her spouse during a fight (imminent threat) or while he was sleeping (no - nimminent threat), and (2) whether expert witness testimony on battered woman syndrome or the social context of battered women was provided. Results showed that mock jurors were more likely to find the defendant guilty of murder if the spouse was asleep than if the death occurred during a fight (see ■ Figure 16.1). However, the harsher verdicts evidenced in the non-imminent threat condition were more pronounced when no expert testimony was provided than when expert testimony was provided (see Figure 16.1). Thus, expert testimony appears beneficial to victims of abuse in cases like that of Jane Hurshman (Schuller, Wells, Rzepa, & Klippenstine, 2004). We consider the issues associated with mental health professionals as expert witnesses in further detail, later in this chapter.

Criminal commitment is the process by which people are held because (1) they have been accused of committing a crime and are detained in a mental health facility until they can be assessed as fit or unfit to participate in legal proceedings against them, or (2) they have been found not criminally responsible on account of a mental disorder (NCRMD).

The Insanity Defence

Not all people are punished for criminal behaviour. Why not? Because the law recognizes that, under certain circumstances, people are not responsible for their behaviour and it would be unfair and perhaps ineffective to punish them. Current views originate from a case recorded more than 150 years ago in England. Daniel M'Naghten today might receive the diagnosis of paranoid schizophrenia (see Chapter 13). He held the delusion that the English Tory party was persecuting him, and he set out to kill the British prime minister. He mistook the man's secretary for the prime minister himself and killed the secretary instead. In what has become known as the M'Naghten rule, the English court decreed that people are not responsible for their criminal behaviour if they do not know what they are doing or if they don't know that what they are doing is wrong. An adaptation of this standard became part of Canadian law in 1894.

The M'Naghten rule was the most common insanity defence standard used in the last half of the 19th century and well into the 20th century. The requirements of the M'Naghten rule are still being used by numerous jurisdictions worldwide, including in Canada and in many states in the United States (Ogloff & Whittemore, 2001). Other standards have been proposed in the United States to modify the M'Naghten rule, because many critics feel that simply relying on an accused person's knowledge of right or wrong is too limiting and a broader definition is needed (Guttmacher & Weihofen, 1952). For example, a person with a compulsion may know what he or she is doing is considered wrong by society and yet not be able to resist the compulsion. These proposed American alternatives to the M'Naghten rule are summarized in Table 16.2.

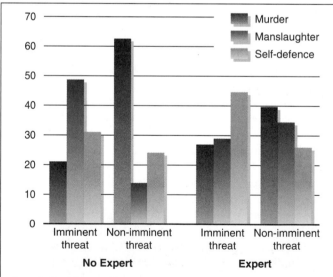

■ FIGURE 16.1 Verdicts rendered in mock juror study of a hypothetical murder trial involving a battered woman as defendant, as function of imminence of threat (imminent vs. non-imminent) and expert witness testimony (expert vs. no expert)

Source: Adapted from "Rethinking Battered Woman Syndrome Evidence: The Impact of Alternative Forms of Expert Testimony on Mock Jurors' Decisions" Regina Schuller et al, *Canadian Journal of Behavioural Science, 2004, 36 (2)* 127–136.

TABLE 16.2 The M'Naghten Rule and Proposed Alternative Standards for the Insanity Defence

The M'Naghten Rule 1843

It must be clearly proved that at the time of committing the act, the party accused was labouring under such a defect of reason, from disease of the mind, as not to know the nature and quality of the act he was doing; or if he did know it, that he did not know he was doing what was wrong. [101 Cl. & F. 200, 8 Eng. Rep. 718 (H.L. 1843)]

The Durham Rule 1954

An accused is not criminally responsible if his unlawful act was the product of mental disease or mental defect. [*Durham v. United States*, 214 F.2d 862, 876 (D.C. Cir. 1954)]

American Law Institute (ALI) Rule 1962

1. A person is not responsible for criminal conduct if at the time of such conduct as a result of mental disease or defect he lacks substantial capacity either to appreciate the criminality (wrongfulness) of his conduct or to conform his conduct to the requirements of law.

2. As used in the Article, the terms "mental disease or defect" do not include an abnormality manifested only by repeated criminal or otherwise antisocial conduct. [American Law Institute (1962). *Model penal code: Proposed official draft.* Philadelphia: Author.]

Source: From "Fitness to Stand Trial and Criminal Responsibility" by James R. P. Ogloff and Karen E. Whittemore. In Schuller, R. A. (Ed.); Ogloff, J. R. P. (Ed.); 2001. *Introduction to Psychology and Law: Canadian Perspectives.* Toronto, ON: University of Toronto Press. pp. 283–313. Adapted with permission.

Concept Check | 16.1

Commitment laws determine the conditions under which a person is certified to have a mental disorder and therefore placed in a hospital, sometimes in conflict with the person's own wishes. The following paragraph is about civil commitment, criminal commitment, and the two types of authority by which the state takes control of its citizens. Check your understanding by filling in the blanks.

Several conditions must be met before the government is permitted to commit a person involuntarily: The person has a(n) (1) _____; the person is considered (2) _____ to herself or himself or others, and the person is in need of (3) _____. In the case of criminal commitment, people are held for two reasons: (4) _____ or (5) _____.

There have been changes to the insanity defence in Canada as well. Originally, under the 1985 Canadian Criminal Code, a person found not guilty by reason of insanity (NGRI) would be automatically detained in a psychiatric hospital until the mental disorder improved sufficiently to justify the patient's release. The purpose of this criminal commitment was to protect the public and to allow the patient to recover from his or her mental disorder. However, concerns were raised about whether patients detained under criminal commitment were actually receiving sufficient treatment. Concerns were also expressed that the detention periods in psychiatric facilities were often much longer than the prison sentence the person would have served if he or she had been convicted of the offence (Gelinas, 1994). Thus, in 1991, in the case of *Regina v. Swain* (1991), the Supreme Court ruled that this indeterminate detention infringed on the rights of the accused. There were also changes in the insanity defence. Specifically, the name of the defence was changed from not guilty by reason of insanity (NGRI) to not criminally responsible on account of mental disorder (NCRMD). The wording of the standard was also revised, as follows:

> No person is criminally responsible for an act committed or an omission made while suffering from a mental disorder that rendered the person incapable of appreciating the nature and quality of the act or omission or of knowing that it was wrong. (Criminal Code of Canada, Section 16, 1992)

There are three main differences between the NGRI and the NCRMD defences. First, the term "insanity" has been replaced by "mental disorder." Second, the defendant is now considered "not criminally responsible" as opposed to "not guilty." This difference may appear subtle, but the change recognizes explicitly that the defendant did commit the crime as opposed to being "not guilty" of the crime. Finally, the meaning of "wrong" has changed from NGRI to NCRMD. Unlike NGRI, which was concerned only with legal wrongs, NCRMD judgments can be made if the person is incapable of knowing that his or her actions were either legally or morally wrong (Davis, 1993).

A well-known example of the successful use of the NCRMD defence in Canada is the case of André Dallaire in 1995. In November of that year, Dallaire attempted to assassinate the Canadian prime minister at the time, Jean Chrétien. Dallaire broke into the prime minister's home armed with a knife, intending to slit Chrétien's throat. Chrétien and his wife were able to hide safely in a locked bedroom until the police came to arrest Dallaire. A psychiatric assessment revealed that Dallaire was suffering from a psychotic disorder, specifically paranoid schizophrenia (see Chapter 13). His hallucinations consisted of hearing voices that commanded him to kill the prime minister. He also displayed delusions of grandeur that he was a secret agent with a mission to avenge the outcome of the Québec independence referendum (Fisher, 1996). Although Dallaire was found guilty of the crime of attempted murder of the prime minister, he was also found not to be criminally responsible for his actions because his intention to kill the prime minister was ruled to be the product of a mental disorder and because his mental disorder prevented him from comprehending the nature of his actions or the fact that his actions were wrong (Fisher, 1996). He was committed to the Royal Ottawa

▲ In his 1995 trial for the attempted assassination of Prime Minister Jean Chrétien, André Dallaire successfully used the NCRMD defence, as he was suffering from paranoid schizophrenia at the time.

Hospital, where he received treatment including antipsychotic medication. Once Dallaire was no longer delusional or hallucinating, he was conditionally released to a group home and finally into the community with continued psychiatric care (Fisher, 1996).

Another more recent example is that of David Carmichael, a well-known fitness expert who strangled his 11-year-old son Ian in a London, Ontario, hotel room in July 2004. He was charged with first-degree murder. Two leading forensic psychiatrists assessed Carmichael as having been in a major depression with psychotic features, including delusions, at the time when he killed his son. Carmichael was judged to be NCRMD and was sentenced to the Brockville Psychiatric Hospital where he received the treatment he needed. One year later, he was released into the community where he continues as an outpatient and where he is working with his wife and daughter to rebuild their family (Mandel, 2007).

A third example of the successful use of the NCRMD defence is described by James Ogloff and Karen Whittemore.

WAYNE SULLIVAN | *Not Criminally Responsible or Getting Off Easy?*

On January 18, 1992, Wayne Sullivan, his wife, Maureen Sullivan, and a friend of Maureen's (Mrs. W.) were drinking at a pub in Prince George, British Columbia. Sometime after midnight, Mrs. W. drove the Sullivans home because the Sullivans were too drunk to drive. When they reached the Sullivans' home, Mrs. W. joined the Sullivans for a drink. Once they were all inside, Mr. Sullivan made several advances toward Mrs. W. when his wife was not there. Mr. Sullivan suggested that they have a "threesome." Mrs. W. declined. When Mrs. Sullivan rejoined them, she helped her husband to his room. The accused claims that while in the bedroom his wife said that she no longer loved him and that she was in love with Mrs. W.

After Mr. Sullivan had been taken to his bedroom, the women had talked for a few minutes and then Mrs. W. decided to leave. As she gathered her belongings, she saw both of the Sullivans at the front door. Mrs. W. said that she saw a bright flash, heard a loud noise, and saw Mrs. Sullivan fall. Mr. Sullivan was standing over his wife and he had a gun in his hand. When Mrs. W asked Mr. Sullivan if he had shot Maureen, he replied that he had. Mr. Sullivan then pointed the gun at Mrs. W. and ordered her to go to the bedroom and disrobe. An argument ensued. Finally, Mr. Sullivan called 911.

At trial, Mr. Sullivan raised the defence of legal insanity—specifically, that he was not criminally responsible on account of a mental disorder. A psychologist and a psychiatrist provided expert testimony for the defence that Mr. Sullivan was in a dissociative state (see Chapter 6) at the time of the shooting. The experts noted that while in this dissociative state, Mr. Sullivan would not have had the ability to appreciate the nature and consequences of his behaviour. In marked contrast, the psychiatrist called by the Crown stated that he doubted Mr. Sullivan had experienced dissociation. Instead, he testified that Mr. Sullivan's heavy drinking just before and at the time of the crime likely contributed to his behaviour.

At the completion of the trial, the jury found Mr. Sullivan not criminally responsible on account of a mental disorder. Mr. Sullivan spent a short time in hospital and is now living in the community.

Source: Adapted from Ogloff & Whittemore, 2001.

Reactions to the Insanity Defence

The NCRMD and the earlier NGRI legal defences represent an effort by the legal system to focus on the needs of people with mental illness who also break the law by providing mental health treatment instead of punishment. However, the successful use of concepts such as insanity or mental disorder in criminal cases alarmed large segments of the population, just as have defences involving battered woman syndrome discussed earlier in this chapter. As noted by Ogloff and Whittemore (2001), when someone is found NCRMD, there is often a public outcry that the person has "got off" too easily. Research supports that the public often holds negative perceptions about the NCRMD defence. One telephone survey study found that 91 percent of people who responded agreed with the statement that "judges and juries have a hard time telling whether the defendants are really sane or insane" (Hans, 1986). Almost 90 percent agreed the "insanity plea is a loophole that allows too many guilty people to go free." In a similar study, 90 percent of people agreed that "the insanity plea is used too much. Too many people escape responsibilities for crimes by pleading insanity" (Pasewark & Seidenzahl, 1979). Do you think that Dallaire, Carmichael, or Sullivan "got off too easily"? Is there hard evidence that the insanity defence is used too often?

You will probably be surprised to learn that the old NGRI defence was used relatively infrequently in Canadian courts. For example, in 1991, only about 1000 individuals who had been found NGRI were being held in institutions across Canada (Roesch et al., 1997). Although the NCRMD defence is used more often than the old NGRI defence (Livingston, Wilson, Tien, & Bond, 2003), its use is still relatively uncommon (Roesch et al., 1997). For example, in British Columbia, in the two years following the legal change to the NCRMD defence, among those cases remanded for assessment of criminal responsibility, psychiatrists' recommendations favoured NCRMD only 28.6 percent of the time—a total of only 53 cases over two years. Moreover, individuals remanded for assessment of criminal responsibility in 1993–1994 were more likely to be recommended NCRMD by the assessing psychiatrists than those remanded for assessment in 1992–1993 (the year immediately after the change to the NCRMD defence). Together these findings show that although the use of this newer defence is increasing, it is still fairly uncommon (Roesch et al., 1997). In a study conducted in British Columbia, Livingston et al. (2003) found that after the change from the

NGRI to the NCRMD defence, the NCRMD population contained many fewer serious charges (e.g., murder) and many more minor offence charges.

Negative public perceptions of the NCRMD defence reflect a lack of appreciation by the public about just how serious the consequences are of using this defence (Ogloff & Whittemore, 2001). Although the NCRMD defence does not entail automatic detention in a psychiatric hospital, some defendants end up being incarcerated in psychiatric institutions for much longer periods than they would have been sentenced to prison if they had not employed this defence (Davis, 1994; Holley, Arboleda-Florez, & Crisanti, 1998). People with mental illness apparently do not often "beat the rap" as a result of being judged NCRMD.

An important issue around the NCRMD defence concerns where such people should be cared for once they have been judged NCRMD. A recent Canadian review suggests that forensic community programs are generally one of the best tools for helping people deemed NCRMD (Woodworth, Peace, O'Donnell, & Porter, 2003). These authors recommend that, in order to best implement such community-based programs for NCRMD individuals, people in the community must be aware of the program and be appropriately educated about the risk that these individuals pose, and that there be high levels of monitoring of these individuals, assessment of psychopathic traits (see Chapter 12), and routine use made of validated risk assessment tools such as those discussed earlier in this chapter (Woodworth et al., 2003).

A final issue relates to the legal concept of burden of proof, the weight of evidence needed to win a case. With respect to the defence of NCRMD, according to Canadian law, the defendant can raise the issue of NCRMD at any time. In contrast, the prosecution can only raise the possibility of NCRMD after the defendant has been found guilty or after the defence, for any reason, raises the issue of the defendant's mental state (Ogloff & Whittemore, 2001).

Society has long recognized the need to identify criminals who may not be in control of their behaviour and who may not benefit from simple incarceration. The challenge is in trying to do what may be impossible: determining whether the person knew what he or she was doing, knew right from wrong, and could control his or her behaviour. Mental health professionals cannot assess mental health retrospectively. An additional dilemma is the desire, on the one hand, to provide care to people with mental illness and, on the other, to treat them as responsible individuals. Finally, we must resolve the simultaneous and conflicting interests of wanting to assist people with mental illness and wanting to be protected from them. By evaluating the effects of various consequences, science may be able to help resolve some of these issues. We must reach a national consensus about the basic value of people with mental illness in order to decide how they should be dealt with legally. Concerns about law and order must be balanced with the rights of people with mental illness, providing adequate attention to both concerns.

Fitness to Stand Trial

Before people can be tried for a criminal offence, they must be able to understand the charges against them and to assist with their own defence, criteria outlined by the Canadian Criminal

Code in 1992. Thus, in addition to interpreting a person's state of mind during the criminal act, experts must also anticipate his or her state of mind during the subsequent legal proceedings. A person could be ruled NCRMD because of his or her mental illness at the time of the criminal act yet still be fit to stand trial.

The classic case for the determination of fitness in Canada is *Regina v. Pritchard* (1836). Lindsay (1977) describes three issues emerging from the criteria defined in the *Pritchard* ruling that need to be tapped in a fitness assessment: (1) Is the accused able to assist in his or her defence? (2) Does the accused understand his or her role in the proceedings? (3) Does the accused understand the nature or object of the proceedings? According to the Canadian Criminal Code: "Unfit to stand trial means ... in particular, unable on account of mental disorder to: (a) understand the nature or object of the proceedings, (b) understand the possible consequences of the proceedings, or (c) communicate with counsel" (Ogloff & Whittemore, 2001, p. 294).

A person determined not fit to stand trial typically loses the authority to make decisions and faces commitment. If the defendant is found to be unfit to stand trial, the court may decide the next step (e.g., detention in hospital) if it can do so readily, and if not, a review board must reach a decision in 45 days. The review board's three options are (1) conditionally discharge the accused, (2) detain the accused in hospital, or (c) order that the accused receive treatment (Ogloff & Whittemore, 2001).

Canadian researchers have contributed substantially to developing sound instruments and methods for assessing a defendant's **fitness to stand trial** (Ogloff & Whittemore, 2001). For example, the Fitness Interview Test–Revised is a three-part instrument developed by Christopher Webster and his colleagues (Roesch, Zapf, Webster, & Eaves, 1999) that specifies the particular abilities required by an individual to demonstrate that he or she is fit to stand trial. In the first section, the individual's understanding of the nature and object of the proceedings is assessed (e.g., does the individual understand key components such as the arrest process, pleas available, court procedures?).

Concept Check | 16.2

The legal system has evolved to incorporate the idea that some people cannot be held responsible for their criminal actions due to mental disorder. Check your understanding of this idea by identifying the following concepts. Pick your answers from (a) fitness to stand trial, (b) American Law Institute rule, (c) the Durham rule, and (d) the M'Naghten rule.

1. The person could not distinguish between right and wrong at the time of the crime. _____

2. The person is not criminally responsible if the crime was due to "mental disease or mental defect.". _____

3. The person is not responsible for the crime if he or she is not able to appreciate wrongfulness of behaviour due to mental disease or defect. _____

4. The defendant does not go to trial because he or she is unable to understand the proceedings and assist in the defence. _____

In the second section, the individual's understanding of the possible consequences of the proceedings is measured (e.g., the range of possible penalties, legal defences available). In the final section, the individual's capacity to contribute to his or her own defence is tapped (e.g., can he or she communicate with a lawyer, plan a legal strategy?). Research has shown that this test reliably screens out those individuals who are clearly fit to stand trial (Viljoen, Roesch, & Zapf, 2002; Zapf, 2001; Zapf & Roesch, 1997).

Duty to Warn

Do mental health professionals have any responsibility for the actions of the people they serve? This question is especially important when we consider the dangerous behaviour exhibited by a minority of people with severe mental illness. What are the responsibilities of professionals who suspect that someone with whom they are working may hurt or even kill another person? Must they contact the appropriate authority or the person who may be harmed, or are they forbidden to discuss information disclosed during therapy sessions?

These issues are the subject of a tragic case in the United States known as *Tarasoff v. Regents of the University of California* (1974, 1976). In 1969, Prosenjit Poddar, a graduate student at the University of California, killed a fellow student, Tatiana Tarasoff, who had previously rejected his romantic advances. At the time of the murder, he was being seen by two therapists at the University Health Center and had received a diagnosis of paranoid schizophrenia. At his last session, Poddar hinted that he was going to kill Tarasoff. His therapist believed this threat was serious and contacted the campus police, who investigated the allegation and received assurances from Poddar that he would leave Tarasoff alone. Weeks later, after repeated attempts to contact her, Poddar shot and stabbed Tarasoff until she died.

After learning of the therapists' role in the case, Tatiana Tarasoff's family sued the university, the therapists, and the university police, saying they should have warned Tatiana that she was in danger. The court agreed, and the *Tarasoff* case has been used ever since as a standard in the United States for therapists concerning their **duty to warn** a client's potential victims. Nonetheless, it is still difficult for therapists to know their exact responsibilities for protecting third parties from their clients. Good clinical practice dictates that any time they are in doubt, they should consult with colleagues. A second opinion can be just as helpful to a therapist as to a client. We have not had a legal precedent in Canada like the ruling in the *Tarasoff* case in the United States (Birch, 1992). Nonetheless, the Alberta Court of Queen's Bench stated in *Wenden v. Trikha* (1991) that a duty to warn might be imposed for psychologists under some circumstances (Lyon, Hart, & Webster, 2001; Schuller & Ogloff, 2001).

In addition to this legal warning, the code of ethics of the Canadian Psychological Association (see Chapter 4) dictates how mental health practitioners should behave in such cases. The code is quite clear that psychologists have an ethical duty to warn a third party of impending danger from a client, very similar to the legal requirements imposed by the ruling in the *Tarasoff* case in the United States (Ogloff & Olley, 1998). Specifically, the Canadian Psychological Association Code requires that psychologists should do everything within reason to stop or offset the harmful

or lethal consequences of a client's actions. According to the Code, the ethical response can include making a report to appropriate authorities (e.g., the police) or warning an intended victim. Moreover, the psychologist should take such actions even when a confidential relationship, like a patient–therapist relationship, is involved (Canadian Psychological Association [CPA], 2000).

Communications between a therapist and client are required to be held completely confidential, except in a very few exceptional situations (CPA, 2000). These exceptions are called "limits to confidentiality." One such limit to confidentiality occurs when the psychologist must break confidentiality to allow for the protection of identifiable third parties at risk for harm (Schuller & Ogloff, 2001). Another such limit to confidentiality involves suspected cases of child abuse. In virtually every Canadian jurisdiction, psychologists have an affirmative duty to report suspected cases of child abuse, even when information pertaining to this suspicion was obtained within the otherwise confidential patient–therapist relationship (Schuller & Ogloff, 2001). A further situation in which limits to confidentiality apply occurs when the psychologist judges the patient to be a risk to himself or herself (Schuller & Ogloff, 2001). The therapist may need to break confidentiality in order to arrange for proper care for a highly suicidal patient who does not want to enter hospital, for example.

Mental Health Professionals as Expert Witnesses

As we discussed earlier in the context of the mock juror experiment in the hypothetical murder case involving an abused woman as defendant (Schuller et al., 2004), judges and juries often have to rely on **expert witnesses**, individuals who have specialized knowledge, to assist them in making decisions (O'Connor, Sales, & Shuman, 1996). The Canadian legal system has been relying increasingly often on expert witness testimony in such areas as child custody disputes (Austin, Jaffe, & Friedman, 1994). We have alluded to several instances in which mental health professionals serve as experts, providing information about a person's dangerousness or ability to understand and participate in the defence. The public's perception of expert witnesses is characterized by ambivalence. On one hand, they see the value of persuasive expert testimony in educating a jury; on the other, they see expert witnesses as "hired guns" whose opinions suit the side that pays their bills (Hollien, 1990). How reliable are the judgments of mental health professionals who act as expert witnesses?

Courtesy of Dr. John C. Yuille

▲ Dr. John Yuille, a forensic psychologist at the University of British Columbia and an expert in human memory, has provided a good deal of expert witness testimony in his areas of expertise. For example, he testified for the defence during the trial of a group of childcare workers in Martensville, Saskatchewan, in the early 1990s, who were alleged to have perpetrated multiple counts of child abuse.

To take one example, in deciding whether someone should be civilly committed, the assessor must determine the person's potential for future violence. As we discussed earlier in this chapter, research suggests that mental health professionals can now make reliable predictions of dangerousness using appropriate tools (Douglas & Webster, 1999; Ogloff & Daffern, 2006; Rice, 1997). A second area in which mental health professionals are frequently asked to provide consultation is in assigning a diagnosis. In Chapter 3, we discussed the development of systems to ensure the reliability of diagnoses. Recent revisions of diagnostic criteria, including the *DSM-IV-TR*, have addressed this issue directly, thus helping clinicians make diagnoses that are generally reliable. Remember, however, that the legal definition of mental illness is not matched by a comparable disorder in the *DSM-IV-TR*. Therefore, statements about whether someone has a "mental illness" reflect determinations made by the court and not by mental health professionals.

Mental health professionals appear to have expertise in identifying **malingering** and in assessing competence. Remember, as we discussed in Chapter 6, that to malinger is to fake or grossly exaggerate symptoms, usually to be absolved from blame. For example, a person might claim to have been actively hallucinating at the time of the crime and therefore not be responsible. A good deal of research suggests that malingering is readily detected using validated instruments like the Minnesota Multiphasic Personality Inventory (MMPI; e.g., Bacchiochi & Bagby, 2006; Bagby, Marshall, & Bacchiochi, 2005; Bagby, Nicholson, Bacchiochi, Ryder, & Bury, 2002). For example, research indicates that the MMPI test is almost 90 percent accurate in revealing malingering in people claiming to have post-traumatic stress disorder (PTSD; McCaffrey & Bellamy-Campbell, 1989). However, recent work cautions that people who have knowledge about the MMPI validity scales (see Chapter 3) can be quite successful in avoiding detection that they are faking PTSD (Bury & Bagby, 2002). Mental health professionals also appear capable of providing reliable information about a person's competence or ability to understand and assist with a defence (Melton, Petrila, Poythress, & Slobogin, 1987). Overall, mental health professionals can provide judges and juries with reliable and useful information in certain specific areas (Gacono, 2000).

The research described here does not indicate how accurate expert testimony actually is under everyday conditions. In other words, under the right circumstances, experts can make accurate determinations of the short-term risks that a person will commit an act of violence, is faking certain symptoms, or is fit to stand trial, and of what diagnosis should be made. Yet other factors conspire to influence expert testimony. Personal and professional opinions that exceed the competence of the expert witness can influence what information is or is not presented, as well as how it is relayed to the court (Simon, 2003). For instance, if the expert witness believes in general that people should not be involuntarily committed to mental health facilities, this opinion will likely influence how the witness presents clinical information in civil commitment court proceedings.

Ethics and Treatment of Mental Illness

Psychologists who are providing treatment to individuals with mental disorders are bound by the ethical principles set out by their professional organization to protect the dignity of the individuals they are treating and to ensure that caring for them occurs in a responsible fashion. As we mentioned in Chapter 4, Canadian psychologists follow the ethical principles laid out in the Canadian Code of Ethics for Psychologists, published by the CPA (2000). These ethical principles cover a variety of issues including boundary issues, the requirement that the psychologist do no harm, and the need for psychologists to practise within their areas of competence. Let us first turn our attention to a case in which two of these principles were broken.

The ethical principles of maintaining clear boundaries with patients and doing no harm were breached in a case that occurred in Toronto in the 1980s. Psychologist David Garner lost his licence to practise in Ontario after engaging in sexual relations with two clients he was treating for eating disorders. You may remember Garner's name from Chapter 8, as he was, and continues to be, a very productive researcher in the area of eating disorders. The College of Psychologists of Ontario removed Garner's licence to practise in 1989 because it was learned that he had been having sexual relations with a client while he was operating the eating disorders clinic at the Toronto General Hospital.

At the time his licence to practise was revoked, Garner was already serving a two-year suspension of his registration after it was learned that he had been engaging in sexual relations with another 18-year-old client with anorexia nervosa in 1985. The original two-year suspension of Garner's licence forced him to resign from his position as a clinical psychologist at the Toronto General Hospital and from his academic appointment at the University of Toronto. He moved to the United States, where he engaged in research until he was once again given a licence to practise psychology by the Ohio psychology board in 1994 (Goodman, 2003; Mahr, 2003).

Boundary Issues

The Canadian Code of Ethics for Psychologists clarifies that psychologists must be clear about professional boundaries with their clients to avoid situations involving conflict of interest. This means that psychologists should avoid dual relationships (e.g., acting as therapist to someone they have interactions with in another context) whenever possible. It also means that psychologists must not exploit any relationship established with them as psychologists to further their own personal, business, or political interests at the expense of the best interests of their client. This means a psychologist cannot take advantage of a client's trust or dependency to encourage or engage in sexual relations with clients or with a client's partner or relatives. The lack of attention to boundary issues with his two clients was one reason that Garner lost his licence to practise in Ontario.

Do No Harm

Psychologists are also bound by the ethical principle of minimizing harm to their clients. This is quite a broad ethical principle that applies to such activities as record keeping (not recording information that could be misinterpreted and misused), psychological report writing (using clear language in reports that can be understood by the person who receives the report), and making referrals to other mental health professionals (giving reasonable assistance to help a person secure needed services if a therapist is unable to treat the person himself or herself). The do-no-harm imperative also prohibits sexual intimacy between a therapist and a client. The Canadian Code of Ethics for Psychologists stipulates that the psychologist must be "acutely aware of the power relationship in therapy and therefore not encourage or engage in sexual intimacy with therapy clients" (CPA, 2000, principle II.27, p. 65). This prohibition against sexual relations with therapy clients applies not only to the period while therapy is taking place, but also to any period after therapy has ended when the power relationship could reasonably be expected to still be influencing the client's decision making. It was also his failure to attend to the power relationship that was present with his two female clients, and his consequent failure to minimize harm to them by engaging in sexual relations with them despite the power relationship, that resulted in the revoking of Garner's psychologist's licence in Ontario.

Recognizing Limits of Competence

According to the Canadian Code of Ethics for Psychologists (CPA, 2000), psychologists must practise within the limits of their competence. A neuropsychologist would not treat an individual with a substance use disorder, unless he or she had the proper training to work with a client with addictions, for example. Psychologists must obtain specific training (coursework, research, individual study, applied training, or supervision) in the particular areas of expertise in which they provide clinical services. If a neuropsychologist wanted to begin working with clients with substance use disorders, he or she would need to obtain specialized training in this new area to establish competence before he or she could begin providing clinical services in this new area. Clients have the right to receive treatment from competent and well-trained professionals. This brings us to a discussion of specific examples of patients' rights and how they are, and have come to be, protected by law in Canada today.

Patients' Rights

Until about 30 years ago, people in mental health facilities were accorded few rights. What treatment they received, and whether they could make phone calls, send and receive mail, or have visitors was typically decided by hospital personnel who rarely consulted with the patient. However, abuses of this authority led to legal action and subsequent rulings by the courts concerning the rights of people in these facilities. Over the past three decades, constitutional protection of the rights of Canadian citizens has been explicitly extended to patients in psychiatric institutions (Olley & Ogloff, 1995).

The Right to Treatment

One of the most fundamental rights of people in mental health facilities is, obviously, the right to treatment. For too many and for too long, conditions were poor and treatment was lacking in numerous large mental health facilities. In Canada, the right to treatment of people with mental illness and intellectual disability

has been more explicitly recognized in Canadian law over the last three decades (Olley & Ogloff, 1995).

A related but separate right is the right to treatment in the least restrictive setting possible (Olley & Ogloff, 1995). For example, those with intellectual disability should have a right to the least restrictive conditions necessary to achieve the purpose of habilitation (i.e., maximizing their independence). This right was established by a landmark case in the United States, *Wyatt v. Stickney* (1972). This case grew out of a lawsuit filed by the employees of large institutions in Alabama who were fired because of funding difficulties. The case mandated that facilities make positive efforts to attain treatment goals for their patients. To this end, it was ruled that institutions should make every attempt to move residents with mental retardation from (1) more to less structured living, (2) large to smaller facilities, (3) large to smaller living units, (4) group to individual residences, (5) segregated from the community to integrated into the community, and (6) dependent living to independent living. In Canada, advocacy efforts and constitutional provisions (e.g., the Canadian Charter of Rights and Freedoms, 1982) protect the rights of people with mental illness, such as the right to treatment in the least restrictive environment and the right to refuse treatment, which we discuss next (Olley & Ogloff, 1995).

The Right to Refuse Treatment

One of the most controversial issues in mental health today is the right of people, especially those with severe mental illness, to refuse treatment (Simon, 1999; Winick, 1997). Along with the development of the Canadian Charter of Rights and Freedoms in 1982, provinces like Manitoba and Ontario now explicitly recognize the right of involuntary but competent patients (e.g., someone who is involuntarily committed because of suicidality who nonetheless understands the risks and benefits of a proposed treatment) to refuse treatment (Gratzer & Matas, 1994). Some provinces such as British Columbia continue to fail to recognize this right and leave the decision in the hands of individual physicians treating a given patient. It should be noted that this condition arises rarely: fewer than 10 percent of involuntary patients persist in refusing treatment (Gratzer & Matas, 1994). Nonetheless, the issues involved can be quite complex when an involuntary patient does persist in refusing treatment, as is illustrated in the following case described by Douglas and Koch (2001).

GEORGE REID | *Asserting the Right to Refuse Treatment*

In the early 1980s, George Reid committed a violent robbery, was arrested, and later found not guilty by reason of insanity. He was held in a maximum-security psychiatric facility, having been declared under the Ontario Mental Health Act to be an involuntary patient who was incompetent to make treatment decisions for himself. He was diagnosed with schizophreniform psychosis. His psychiatrist, Dr. Russell Fleming, proposed to treat him with antipsychotic medication. Such medication usually has a beneficial effect on symptoms of psychosis, as well on restoring cognitive capacity to some extent. However, it also has side effects that many people find highly undesirable.

Under the legislation at the time, a "substitute decision maker," in this case a designate of the province, could provide consent to treatment on the behalf of an incompetent person. The psychiatrist applied to this person for consent to treat Mr. Reid. The substitute decision maker refused, as Mr. Reid had earlier expressed (when he was competent) that he did not want to take psychotropic medication. The psychiatrist appealed this decision to the psychiatric review board in Ontario, which granted consent to treatment. This decision was upheld by the Ontario District Court but later overturned by the Ontario Court of Appeal. The Court of Appeal held that treatment provided against the consent (even if given earlier) of a person is unconstitutional, violating the right to security of the person under section 7 of the Canadian Charter of Rights and Freedoms.

This decision introduced a conundrum into the law: Although people could be admitted to hospital involuntarily, the mental illness that gave rise to their involuntary hospitalization could not be treated. Without treatment, patients' illnesses may never remit, and patients could then be hospitalized indefinitely. Although Ontario has dealt with this problem by revising its legislation, the Fleming case has dramatic implications for other provinces that may treat patients without their consent, or even against their express wishes. The inherent dilemma is that to provide treatment may be unconstitutional, but to withhold it may give rise to indefinite hospitalization, because the very basis for hospitalization—mental illness—may not remit without treatment.

Source: Adapted from Douglas & Koch, 2001, pp. 353–354.

As illustrated in the case above, today, the argument about patients' rights to refuse treatment has often centred on the use of antipsychotic medications. On one side of the issue is the mental health professional who believes that, under certain circumstances, people with severe mental illness are not capable of making a decision in their own best interest and that the clinician is therefore responsible for providing treatment despite the protestations of the affected person. On the other side, patients and their advocates argue that all people have a fundamental right to make decisions about their own treatment, even if doing so is not in their own best medical interests. This controversy is not yet completely resolved.

Ethics of Research Involving Human Participants

Throughout this text we have described research conducted worldwide with people who have psychological disorders; and we touched briefly in Chapter 4 on the issue of

the ethical issues involved in conducting research with these individuals. In general, research involving human participants should be guided by the following ethical principles (Public Works and Government Services Canada, 2003):

1. Respect for human dignity
2. Respect for free and informed consent
3. Respect for vulnerable persons
4. Respect for privacy and confidentiality
5. Respect for justice and inclusiveness
6. Balance of harm and benefits
7. Minimization of harm
8. Maximization of benefit

According to the principles outlined in the Tri-Council policy statement (Public Works and Government Services Canada, 2003), the researcher must be respectful of the dignity of his or her research participants, as noted in principle 1. Protecting participants' dignity is particularly important for people with psychological disorders who may not be able to understand the research fully, as noted in principle 3. One of the most important concepts in research is that those who participate must be fully informed about the risks and benefits of the study, as noted in principle 2. Simple consent is not sufficient; it must be **informed consent**, or formal agreement by the subject to participate after being fully apprised of all important aspects of the study, including any possibility of harm.

Unfortunately, there are many examples in history where researchers have not followed ethical principles in the conduct of their research on various forms of abnormal behaviour. Take, for example, the brainwashing research of Dr. Ewan Cameron, which was conducted on psychiatric patients at the Allan Memorial Institute in Montréal in the 1950s and 1960s. As mentioned in Chapter 4, patients and their families were not asked for their consent to participate in Cameron's studies on experimental

▲ The Allan Memorial Institute in Montréal was the site of the notorious brainwashing research of Dr. Ewan Cameron in the 1950s and 1960s. His "psychic driving" experiments resulted in horrific consequences for many of his psychiatric patient participants who did not provide informed consent for their participation in Cameron's research.

treatments for mental illness, nor were they adequately informed that his treatments were experimental and not standard practice. His treatments included multiple courses of shock treatment daily and a technique called "psychic driving," where patients listened to subliminal messages repeatedly while in a drug-induced coma. Although well intentioned, these experimental procedures unfortunately resulted in horrific consequences for many, including patients becoming confused, unable to feed themselves, and unable to control their bladders (Collins, 1988). The ethical principles outlined in the Tri-Council policy statement (Public Works and Government Services Canada, 2003), such as the respect for free and informed consent, help to ensure that this extreme type of tragic case does not happen in Canada again.

Concept Check | 16.3

Psychological professionals assume many roles and responsibilities. Identify the following situations using one of these terms: (a) informed consent, (b) duty to warn, (c) expert witness, (d) deinstitutionalization, (e) malingering.

1. Dr. X testified in court that the defendant was faking and exaggerating symptoms to evade responsibility. Dr. X is acting as a(n) _____ and the defendant is _____.

2. The therapist has learned he is required to release more mentally ill patients from the hospital. He is worried that many of them will end up homeless and without continuing treatment as a result of _____ .

3. One of my clients threatened his mother's life during his session today. Now I must decide whether I have a(n) _____ .

4. The clinical researcher knows the potential for harm of the participants is very slight, but is nevertheless careful to tell them about it and asks them whether they agree to give their _____ .

Clinical Practice Guidelines

Over the past two decades, there have been attempts made to establish greater uniformity in the delivery of effective mental health care and to better communicate the latest developments in treating certain disorders effectively to practitioners. A greater emphasis has also been placed on research focused on improving systems for the delivery of mental health services.

To accomplish these goals, some clinical practice guidelines have been published for specific health problems, including sickle cell disease, management of cancer pain, unstable angina, and depression in primary care settings. The hope is not only to reduce costs by eliminating unnecessary or ineffective treatments but also to facilitate the dissemination of effective interventions based on the latest research evidence. Treating people effectively—alleviating their pain and distress—is ultimately the most important way to reduce health care costs, because these individuals will no longer request one treatment after another in an unending search for relief.

A task force of the American Psychological Association (APA) composed a template, or set, of principles for constructing and evaluating guidelines for clinical interventions for both psychological disorders and psychosocial aspects of physical disorders, which were published in 1995. These principles help ensure that future clinical practice guidelines will be comprehensive and consistent. As envisioned by the APA task force, the guidelines developed from this template should help both the practitioner and the patient make decisions about appropriate treatment interventions for psychological disorders, as well as psychosocial aspects of physical disorders.

The CPA has been engaging in a similar exercise. Specifically, the clinical psychology section of the CPA has developed a task force on empirically supported treatments. It has developed recommendations for Canadian professional psychologists regarding the use of empirically supported treatments in psychology (see http://www.cpa.ca/documents /empiric_toc.html).

The APA task force decided that clinical practice guidelines for specific disorders should be constructed on the basis of two simultaneous considerations, or axes. The **clinical efficacy** axis is a thorough consideration of the scientific evidence to determine whether the intervention in question is effective. This evidence would answer the question: "Is the treatment effective when compared with an alternative treatment or to no treatment in a controlled clinical research context?" In Chapter 4, we reviewed the various research strategies used to determine whether an intervention is effective. For many reasons a treatment might seem effective when it is not effective at all. For instance, if patients improve on their own while being treated simply because of the passage of time or the natural healing process, the treatment had little to do with the improvement. It is possible that nonspecific effects of the treatment—perhaps just meeting with a caring health professional—are enough to make someone feel better without any contribution from the particular treatment technique.

To determine clinical efficacy, experiments must establish whether the intervention in question is better than no therapy, better than a nonspecific therapy, or better than an alternative therapy. (The latter finding provides the highest level of evidence for a treatment's effectiveness.) We might also rely on information collected from various clinics in which a large number of practitioners are treating the disorder in question. If these clinicians collect systematic data on the outcomes of their patients, they can ascertain how many are "cured," how many improve somewhat without recovering totally, and how many fail to respond to the intervention. Such data are referred to as quantified clinical observations or clinical replication series. Finally, a clinical consensus of leading experts is also a valuable additional source of information.

The **clinical utility** axis is concerned with the effectiveness of the intervention in the practice setting in which it is to be applied; in other words, will an intervention with proven efficacy in a research setting also be effective in the various frontline clinical settings in which it will be most frequently applied? For example, randomized controlled trials of therapy efficacy are often conducted with a very homogeneous group of patients who only have the disorder in question; those patients with comorbid disorders are typically excluded. But as we have discussed throughout this textbook, co-occurrence of more than one disorder (i.e., comorbidity) is a common phenomenon, making it difficult to know whether the results of the randomized controlled trial generalize to more complicated types of patients seen in frontline clinical settings. Also, is application of the intervention in the settings where it is needed feasible and cost effective? This axis is concerned with external validity, the extent to which an internally valid intervention is effective in different settings or under different circumstances from those under which it was tested.

The first major issue to consider on the clinical utility axis is feasibility. Will patients accept the intervention and comply with its requirements, and is it relatively easy to administer? As noted in Chapter 7, electroconvulsive therapy (ECT) is an effective treatment for very severe depression in many cases, but it is extremely frightening to patients, many of whom refuse it. The treatment also requires sophisticated procedures and close supervision by medical personnel, usually in a hospital setting. Therefore, it is not particularly feasible.

A second issue on the clinical utility axis is generalizability—the extent to which an intervention is effective with patients of differing backgrounds (ethnicity, age, sex) as well as in different settings (inpatient, outpatient, community) or with different therapists. Once again, an intervention could be very effective in a research setting with one group of patients but generalize very poorly across different ethnic groups.

In reading the chapters on various disorders, you will have noted a number of effective treatments, both psychosocial and medical. In the future, we will see a great deal of additional research to establish both the clinical efficacy and the clinical utility of various interventions for psychological disorders, and the development of ever more sophisticated clinical practice guidelines. In 2010, the American Psychological Association decided to develop its own set of clinical practice guidelines on providing the best evidence-based psychological care for people with psychological disorders.

In Chapter 1, we reviewed various activities that make up the role of scientist-practitioners in the mental health professions, who take a scientific approach to their clinical work to provide the most effective assessment procedures and interventions. Changes in the delivery of mental health services are likely to be accompanied by considerable disruption, because this is a major system that affects millions of people. But the change will also bring opportunities. Scientist-practitioners will contribute to the process of guidelines development in several ways. For example, most of the information relevant to clinical utility or external validity of interventions will be collected by mental health professionals in the course of their practice. Thus, they will truly fulfill the scientist-practitioner role to the benefit of patients in our field.

Conclusions

Therapy and scientific progress do not occur in a vacuum. People who study and treat abnormal behaviour are responsible not only for mastering the wealth of information we have only touched on in this book but also for understanding and appreciating their role in Canadian society and in the world at large. Every facet of life—from the biological to the social, political, and legal—interacts with every other; if we are to help people, we must appreciate this complexity.

We hope we have given you a good sense of the challenges faced by workers in the field of mental health and have spurred some of you to join us in this rewarding work.

Summary

- Mental health law must balance a commitment to individual rights and fairness against majority concerns and a commitment to law and order.

Civil Commitment

- Civil commitment laws determine the conditions under which a person may be certified legally to have a mental illness and therefore to be placed in a hospital, sometimes in conflict with the person's own wishes.
- Most Canadian jurisdictions permit commitment when several conditions have been met: (1) the person has a mental illness, (2) the person is dangerous to himself or herself or to others, and (3) the person is in need of treatment.
- "Mental illness" as used in legal system language is not synonymous with "psychological disorder"; each Canadian jurisdiction has its own definition of mental illness. Those provinces using functional definitions of mental illness include people with very severe disturbances that negatively affect their health and safety.
- Having a severe mental illness seems to increase the likelihood of dangerousness, that is, that a person will commit violent acts in the future. In particular, having symptoms of hallucinations and delusions seems to indicate more risk for behaving violently.
- Strict civil commitment laws were designed to protect individual rights and freedoms. However, the combination of strict civil commitment laws and the lack of success with deinstitutionalization has resulted instead in transinstitutionalization and a rise in homelessness.

Criminal Commitment

- Criminal commitment is the process by which people are held for one of two reasons: (1) they have been accused of committing a crime and are detained in a mental health facility until they can be determined as fit or unfit to participate in legal proceedings against them, or (2) they have been found not criminally responsible on account of a mental disorder (NCRMD).
- The insanity defence in Canada is currently the not criminally responsible on account of a mental disorder (NCRMD) defence. It is primarily determined by the following legal ruling from a historical case in England: The M'Naghten rule states that people are not responsible for criminal behaviour if they do not know what they are doing, or if they do know what they are doing but don't know it is wrong. Other rulings have influenced the insanity defence in the United States.

- A determination of fitness must be made before an individual can be tried for a criminal offence: To stand trial, people must be fit to do so—able to understand the charges against them and to assist with their own defence.

Duty to Warn

- Duty to warn is an American legal standard and Canadian professional ethical standard that sets forth the responsibility of the therapist to warn potential victims that a client may attempt to hurt or kill them.

Mental Health Professionals as Expert Witnesses

- Individuals who have specialized knowledge and who assist judges and juries in making decisions, especially about such issues as competence and malingering, are called expert witnesses.

Patients' Rights

- One of the more fundamental rights of patients in mental facilities is their right to treatment; that is, they have a legal right to some sort of ongoing effort to both define and strive toward treatment goals. By contrast, a great deal of controversy exists over whether all patients are capable of making a decision to refuse treatment. This is an especially difficult dilemma in the case of antipsychotic medications that may improve patients' symptoms but also bring with them severe negative side effects.

Ethics of Research Involving Human Participants

- Those who participate in any research study must be fully informed of the risks and benefits and formally give their informed consent to indicate so.

Clinical Practice Guidelines

- Clinical practice guidelines can play a major role in providing information about types of interventions that are likely to be effective for a specific disorder. Critical to such a determination are measures of clinical efficacy (internal validity) and clinical utility (external validity); in other words, the former is a measure of whether a treatment works, and the latter is a measure of whether the treatment is effective in a variety of settings.

Key Terms

Answers to Concept Checks

16.1

1. mental disorder
2. dangerous
3. treatment

4. They have been accused of committing crimes and they are waiting for their mental fitness to stand trial to be assessed.

5. They have been found not criminally responsible on account of a mental disorder (NCRMD).

16.2

1. e 2. d 3. c 4. b 5. a

16.3

1. c, e 2. d 3. b 4. a

Media Resources

CourseMate

Access an integrated eBook, Abnormal Psychology Videos (formerly Abnormal Psych Live CD-ROM), chapter-specific interactive learning tools (flashcards, quizzes, learning modules), and more in your Psychology CourseMate, available at **www.abnormalpsych3ce.nelson.com**

Abnormal Psychology Videos

Free Abnormal Psychology videos can be viewed on the website **www.abnormalpsych3ce.nelson.com**.

- *False Memory Research:* This clip of Elizabeth Loftus raises a host of questions about the use of therapy-related testimony in trials related to child abuse.

Video Concept Reviews

CourseMate also contains Mark Durand's *Video Concept Reviews* on these challenging topics.

- Civil Commitment Laws
- *Parens Patriae* and Police Power
- Mental Illness
- Dangerousness
- Criminal Commitment
- Concept Check: How Can Juries Decide Insanity?
- The Insanity Defence
- Competence

Glossary

acute pain Pain that typically follows an injury and disappears once the injury heals or is effectively treated. (328)

acute stress disorder Severe reaction immediately following a terrifying event, often including amnesia about the event, emotional numbing, and **derealization**. Many victims later develop **post-traumatic stress disorder**. (163)

adoption studies In genetics research, the study of first-degree relatives reared in different families and environments. If they share common characteristics, such as a disorder, this finding suggests that those characteristics have a genetic component. (117)

affect Conscious, subjective aspect of an **emotion** that accompanies an action at a given time. (61)

agnosia Inability to recognize and name objects; may be a symptom of **dementia** or other brain disorders. (551)

agonist Chemical substance that effectively increases the activity of a **neurotransmitter** by imitating its effects. (48)

agonist substitution Replacement of a drug on which a person is dependent with one having a similar chemical makeup, an **agonist**. Used as a treatment for **substance dependence**. (423)

agoraphobia Anxiety about being in places or situations from which escape might be difficult. (140)

AIDS-related complex (ARC) Group of minor health problems such as weight loss, fever, and night sweats that appears after HIV infection but before development of full-blown AIDS. (320)

alcohol dehydrogenase (ADH) Enzyme that helps humans metabolize alcohol. Different levels of its subtypes may account for different susceptibilities to disorders such as **fetal alcohol syndrome (FAS)**. (417)

alcohol use disorders Cognitive, biological, behavioural, and social problems associated with alcohol use and abuse. (400)

alogia Deficiency in the amount or content of speech; a disturbance often seen in people with **schizophrenia**. (483)

alters Shorthand term for alter **egos**, the different personalities or identities in **dissociative identity disorder**. (205)

Alzheimer's disease The "strange disease of the cerebral cortex" that causes an "atypical form of senile **dementia**," discovered in 1906 by the German psychiatrist Alois Alzheimer. (552)

amnestic disorder Deterioration in the ability to transfer information from short-term to long-term memory, in the absence of other **dementia** symptoms, as a result of **head trauma** or drug abuse. (565)

amniocentesis Prenatal medical procedure that allows the detection of abnormalities (e.g., **Down syndrome**) in the developing fetus. It involves removal and analysis of amniotic fluid from the mother. (537)

amphetamine use disorders Psychological, biological, behavioural, and social problems associated with amphetamine use and abuse. (407)

analogue model Approach to research employing subjects who are similar to clinical clients, allowing replication of a clinical problem under controlled conditions. (107)

anhedonia Inability to experience pleasure, associated with some schizophrenic and **mood disorders**. (483)

animal phobia Unreasonable, enduring **fear** of animals or insects that usually develops early in life. (152)

anorexia nervosa Eating disorder characterized by recurrent food refusal leading to dangerously low body weight. (269)

antagonist In neuroscience, a chemical substance that decreases or blocks the effects of a **neurotransmitter**. (48)

antagonist drugs Medications that block or counteract the effects of psychoactive drugs. (424)

antidepressants Medications used to treat depressive disorders such as tricyclic antidepressants, monoamine oxidase (MAO) inhibitors, and selective serotonin reuptake inhibitors. (247)

antigens Foreign materials that enter the body, including bacteria and parasites. (318)

antisocial personality disorder Cluster B (dramatic, emotional, or erratic) **personality disorder** involving a pervasive pattern of disregard for and violation of the rights of others. Similar to the non-*DSM*-label **psychopathy**, but with greater emphasis on overt behaviour rather than on personality traits. (450)

anxiety Mood state characterized by marked negative **affect** and bodily symptoms of tension in which a person apprehensively anticipates future danger or misfortune. Anxiety may involve feelings, behaviours, and physiological responses. (129)

aphasia Impairment or loss of language skills resulting from brain damage caused by **stroke, Alzheimer's disease**, or other illness or trauma. (552)

Asperger's disorder Pervasive developmental disorder characterized by impairments in social relationships and restricted or unusual behaviours, but without language delays seen in autism. (524)

association studies Research strategies for comparing **genetic markers** in groups of people with and without a particular disorder. (118)

associative splitting Separation among basic functions of human personality (e.g., cognition, **emotion**, perception) that is seen by some as the defining characteristic of **schizophrenia**. (477)

attention deficit/hyperactivity disorder (ADHD) Developmental disorder featuring maladaptive levels of inattention, excessive activity, and impulsiveness. (514)

autistic disorder (autism) Pervasive developmental disorder characterized by significant impairment in social interactions and communication, and restricted patterns of behaviour, interest, and activity. (524)

autoimmune disease Condition in which the body's **immune system** attacks healthy tissue rather than **antigens**. (319)

avoidant personality disorder Cluster C (anxious or fearful) **personality disorder** featuring a pervasive pattern of social inhibition, feelings of inadequacy, and hypersensitivity to criticism. (466)

avolition Apathy, or the inability to initiate or persist in important activities. (482)

barbiturates Sedative (and addictive) drugs including Amytal, Seconal, and Nembutal that are used as sleep aids. (405)

baseline Measured rate of a behaviour before introduction of an intervention that allows comparison and assessment of the effects of the intervention. (114)

behaviour therapy Array of therapy methods based on the principles of behavioural and **cognitive science** as well as principles of learning as applied to clinical problems. It considers specific behaviours rather than inferred conflict as legitimate targets for change. (25)

behavioural assessment Measuring, observing, and systematically evaluating (rather than inferring) the client's thoughts, feelings, and behaviour in the actual problem situation or context. (79)

behavioural inhibition system (BIS) Brain circuit in the limbic system that responds to threat signals by inhibiting activity and causing **anxiety**. (132)

behavioural medicine Interdisciplinary approach applying behavioural science to the prevention, **diagnosis**, and treatment of medical problems. (314)

behavioural model Explanation of human behaviour, including dysfunction, based on principles of learning and adaptation derived from experimental psychology. (23)

behaviourism Explanation of human behaviour, including dysfunction, based on principles of learning and adaptation derived from experimental psychology. (17)

benzodiazepines Anti-anxiety drugs, including Valium, Xanax, Dalmane, and Halcion, also used to treat insomnia. Effective against **anxiety** (and, at high potency, panic disorder), they show some side effects, such as some cognitive and motor impairment, and may result in dependence and addiction. Relapse rates are extremely high when the drug is discontinued. (405)

binge Relatively brief episode of uncontrolled, excessive consumption, usually of food or alcohol. (269)

binge-eating disorder (BED) Pattern of eating involving distress-inducing **binges** not followed by purging behaviours; being considered as a new *DSM* diagnostic category. (270)

biofeedback Use of physiological monitoring equipment to make individuals aware of their own bodily functions, such as blood pressure or brain waves, that they cannot normally access, with the purpose of controlling these functions. (333)

bipolar I disorder Alternation of **major depressive** episodes with full manic episodes. (226)

bipolar II disorder Alternation of **major depressive** episodes with **hypomanic episodes** (not full manic episodes). (226)

blood-injury-injection phobia Unreasonable **fear** and avoidance of exposure to blood, injury, or the possibility of an injection. Victims experience fainting and a drop in blood pressure. (151)

body dysmorphic disorder (BDD) Somatoform disorder featuring a disruptive preoccupation with some imagined defect in appearance ("imagined ugliness"). (196)

borderline personality disorder Cluster B (dramatic, emotional, or erratic) **personality disorder** involving a pervasive pattern of instability of interpersonal relationships, self-image, **affects**, and control over impulses. (459)

brain circuits **Neurotransmitter** currents or neural pathways in the brain. (48)

breathing-related sleep disorders Sleep disruption leading to excessive sleepiness or insomnia, caused by a breathing problem such as interrupted (apnea) or laboured (hypoventilation) breathing. (297)

brief psychotic disorder Psychotic disturbance involving **delusions**, **hallucinations**, or **disorganized speech** or behaviour, but lasting less than one month; often occurs in reaction to a stressor. (487)

bulimia nervosa Eating disorder involving recurrent episodes of uncontrolled excessive (**binge**) eating followed by compensatory actions to remove the food (e.g., deliberate vomiting, laxative abuse, excessive exercise). (269)

caffeine use disorders Cognitive, biological, behavioural, and social problems associated with the use and abuse of caffeine. (410)

cancer Category of often-fatal medical conditions involving abnormal cell growth and malignancy. (322)

cardiovascular disease Afflictions in the mechanisms, including the heart, blood vessels, and their controllers, that are responsible for transporting blood to the body's tissues and organs. Psychological factors may play important roles in such diseases and their treatments. (324)

case study method Research procedure in which a single person or small group is studied in detail. The method does not allow conclusions about cause-and-effect relationships, and findings can be generalized only with great caution. (108)

catatonia Disorder of movement involving immobility or excited agitation. (477)

catatonic immobility Disturbance of motor behaviour in which the person remains motionless, sometimes in an awkward posture, for extended periods of time. (484)

catatonic type of schizophrenia Type of **schizophrenia** in which motor disturbances (rigidity, agitation, odd mannerisms) predominate. (486)

catharsis Rapid or sudden release of emotional tension thought to be an important factor in psychoanalytic therapy. (18)

cerebral vascular accident (CVA) Temporary blockage of blood vessels supplying the brain, or a rupture of vessels in the brain, resulting in temporary or permanent loss of brain functioning. Also called a **stroke**. (324)

childhood disintegrative disorder Pervasive developmental disorder involving severe regression in language, adaptive behaviour, and motor skills after a two-year to four-year period of normal development. (524)

chronic fatigue syndrome (CFS) Incapacitating exhaustion following only minimal exertion, accompanied by fever, headaches, muscle and joint pain, depression, and **anxiety**. (331)

chronic pain Enduring pain that does not decrease over time; may occur in muscles, joints, and the lower back, and may be due to enlarged blood vessels, or degenerating or cancerous tissue. Other significant factors are social and psychological. (328)

circadian rhythm sleep disorder Sleep disturbance resulting in sleepiness or insomnia caused by the body's inability to synchronize its sleep patterns with the current pattern of day and night. (298)

civil commitment laws Legal proceedings that determine a person has a mental disorder and may be hospitalized, even involuntarily. (573)

classical categorical approach Classification method founded on the assumption of clear-cut differences among disorders, each with a different known cause. (90)

classical conditioning Fundamental learning process first described by Ivan Pavlov. An event that automatically elicits a response is paired with another stimulus event that does not (a neutral stimulus). After repeated pairings, the neutral stimulus becomes a conditioned stimulus that by itself can elicit the desired response. (24)

classification Assignment of objects or people to categories on the basis of shared characteristics. (89)

clinical assessment Systematic evaluation and measurement of psychological, biological, and social factors in a person presenting with a possible **psychological disorder**. (73)

clinical description Details of the combination of behaviours, thoughts, and feelings of an individual that make up a particular disorder. (8)

clinical efficacy (axis) One of a proposed set of guidelines for evaluating clinical interventions on the evidence of their effectiveness. (588)

clinical significance Degree to which research findings have useful and meaningful applications to real problems. (107)

clinical utility (axis) One of a proposed set of guidelines for evaluating clinical interventions by whether they can be applied effectively and cost effectively in real clinical settings. (588)

cocaine use disorders Cognitive, biological, behavioural, and social problems associated with the use and abuse of cocaine. (407)

cognitive science Field of study that examines how humans and other animals acquire, process, store, and retrieve information. (55)

cognitive therapy Treatment approach that involves identifying and altering negative thinking styles related to **psychological disorders**, such as depression and **anxiety**, and replacing them with more positive beliefs and attitudes and, ultimately, more adaptive behaviour and coping styles. (252)

cognitive-behavioural therapy (CBT) Group of treatment procedures aimed at identifying and modifying faulty thought processes, attitudes and attributions, and problem behaviours; often used synonymously with **cognitive therapy**. (59)

cohort Participants in each age group of a cross-sectional research study. (119)

cohort effect Observation that people of different age groups also differ in their values and experiences. (120)

comorbidity The presence of two or more disorders in an individual at the same time. (96)

comparative treatment research Outcome research that contrasts two or more treatment methods to determine which is most effective. (112)

compulsions Repetitive, ritualistic, time-consuming behaviours or mental acts a person feels driven to perform. (169)

confound Any factor occurring in a research study that makes the results uninterpretable because its effects cannot be separated from those of the variables being studied. (106)

control group Group of individuals in a research study who are similar to the experimental subjects in every way but are not exposed to the treatment received by the experimental group; their presence allows for a comparison of the differential effects of the treatment. (107)

controlled drinking An extremely controversial treatment approach to alcohol dependence in which severe abusers are taught to drink in moderation. (426)

conversion disorder Physical malfunctioning, such as blindness or paralysis, suggesting neurological impairment, with no organic pathology to account for it. (189)

coronary heart disease (CHD) Blockage of the arteries supplying blood to the heart muscle, a major cause of death in Western culture, with social and psychological factors involved. (326)

correlation Degree to which two variables are associated. In a **positive correlation**, the two variables increase or decrease together; in a **negative correlation**, one variable decreases as the other increases. (109)

correlation coefficient Computed statistic reflecting the strength and direction of any association between two variables. It can range from +1.00 through zero (indicating no association) to –1.00, with the absolute value indicating the strength, and the sign reflecting the direction. (109)

course Pattern of development and change of a disorder over time. (8)

covert desensitization Cognitive-behavioural intervention to reduce unwanted behaviours by having clients imagine the extremely aversive consequences of the behaviours and establish negative rather than positive associations with them. (384)

Creutzfeldt-Jakob disease Extremely rare condition that causes **dementia**. (558)

criminal commitment Legal procedure by which a person who is found not criminally responsible on account of a mental disorder must be confined in a psychiatric hospital. (580)

cross-generational effect Limit to the **generalizability** of longitudinal research because the group under study may differ from others in culture and experience. (121)

cross-sectional design Methodology to examine a characteristic by comparing different individuals of different ages. Contrast with **longitudinal design**. (119)

cultural-familial intellectual disability Mild intellectual disability that may be caused largely by environmental influences. (538)

cyclothymic disorder Chronic (at least two years) **mood disorder** characterized by alternating **mood** elevation and depression levels that are not as severe as manic or **major depressive episodes**. (227)

dangerousness Tendency to violence that, contrary to popular opinion, is not more likely among mental patients. (577)

defence mechanisms Common patterns of behaviour, often adaptive coping styles when they occur in moderation, observed in response to particular situations. In **psychoanalysis**, these are thought to be **unconscious** processes originating in the **ego**. (20)

deinstitutionalization Systematic removal of people with severe **mental illness** or intellectual disability from institutions like psychiatric hospitals. (577)

delirium Rapid-onset reduced clarity of consciousness and cognition, with confusion, disorientation, and deficits in memory and language. (548)

delirium tremens (DTs) Frightening **hallucinations** and body tremors that result when a heavy drinker withdraws from alcohol. Also called **withdrawal delirium**. (401)

delusion Psychotic symptom involving disorder of thought content and presence of strong beliefs that are misrepresentations of reality. (479)

delusional disorder Psychotic disorder featuring a persistent belief contrary to reality (**delusion**) but no other symptoms of **schizophrenia** (487).

dementia Gradual-onset deterioration of brain functioning, involving memory loss,

inability to recognize objects or faces, and problems in planning and abstract reasoning. These are associated with frustration and discouragement. (550)

dementia of the Alzheimer's type Gradual onset of cognitive deficits caused by **Alzheimer's disease**, principally identified by a person's inability to recall newly or previously learned material. The most common form of **dementia**. (552)

dementia praecox Latin term meaning "premature loss of mind," an early label for what is now called **schizophrenia**, emphasizing the disorder's frequent appearance during adolescence. (477)

dependent personality disorder Cluster C (anxious or fearful) **personality disorder** characterized by a person's pervasive and excessive need to be taken care of, a condition that leads to submissive and clinging behaviour and **fears** of separation. (468)

dependent variable In an experimental research study, the phenomenon that is measured and expected to be influenced. (105)

depersonalization disorder Dissociative disorder in which feelings of depersonalization are so severe that they dominate the client's life and prevent normal functioning. (201)

depressants Psychoactive substances that result in behavioural sedation, including alcohol and the sedative, hypnotic, and anxiolytic drugs. (399)

depressive cognitive triad Aaron T. Beck's theory that depression may result from a tendency to think negatively about three areas: oneself, one's immediate world, and one's future. (242)

derealization Situation in which the individual loses his or her sense of the reality of the external world. (200)

diagnosis Process of determining whether a **presenting problem** meets the established criteria for a specific **psychological disorder**. (73)

diathesis–stress model Hypothesis that both an inherited tendency (a vulnerability) and specific stressful conditions are required to produce a disorder. (38)

dimensional approach Method of categorizing characteristics on a continuum rather than on a binary, either-or, or all-or-none basis. (90)

directionality The possibility that, when two variables, A and B, are correlated, variable A causes variable B, or that B causes A. (110)

disorder of written expression Condition in which a person's writing performance is significantly below age norms. (520)

disorganized speech Style of talking often seen in people with **schizophrenia** that involves incoherence and a lack of typical logic patterns. (484)

disorganized type of schizophrenia Type of **schizophrenia** featuring disrupted speech and behaviour, disjointed **delusions**, and **hallucinations**, and silly or **flat affect**. (485)

dissociative amnesia Dissociative disorder featuring the inability to recall personal information, usually of a stressful or traumatic nature. (202)

dissociative disorders Disorder in which individuals feel detached from themselves or their surroundings, and reality, experience, and identity may disintegrate. (181)

dissociative fugue Dissociative disorder featuring sudden, unexpected travel away from home, along with an inability to recall the past, sometimes with assumption of a new identity. (203)

dissociative identity disorder (DID) Formerly known as multiple **personality disorder**, a disorder in which as many as one hundred personalities or fragments of personalities coexist within one body and mind. (204)

dissociative trance disorder (DTD) Altered state of consciousness in which the person believes firmly that he or she is possessed by spirits; considered a disorder only where there is distress and dysfunction. (204)

dopamine Neurotransmitter whose generalized function is to activate other neurotransmitters and to aid in exploratory and pleasure-seeking behaviours (thus balancing **serotonin**). A relative excess of dopamine is implicated in **schizophrenia** (though contradictory evidence suggests the connection is not simple) and its deficit is involved in **Parkinson's disease.** (51)

double-bind communication According to an obsolete, unsupported theory, the practice of transmitting conflicting messages that was thought to cause **schizophrenia.** (498)

double-blind control Procedure in outcome studies that prevents bias by ensuring that neither the subjects nor the providers of the experimental treatment know who is receiving treatment and who is receiving placebo. (112)

double depression Severe **mood disorder** typified by **major depressive episodes** superimposed over a background of dysthymic disorder. (223)

Down syndrome Type of intellectual disability caused by a chromosomal aberration (on chromosome 21) and involving characteristic physical appearance. (537)

dream analysis Psychoanalytic therapy method in which dream contents are examined as symbolic of **id** impulses and **intrapsychic conflicts.** (22)

duty to warn Mental health professionals' responsibility to break confidentiality and notify the potential victim whom a client has specifically threatened. (584)

dyspareunia Recurring genital pain in either males or females before, during, or after sexual intercourse. Also called **sexual pain disorder.** (365)

dysphoric manic or mixed episode See **mixed manic episode.** (221)

dyssomnias Problems in getting to sleep or in obtaining sufficient quality sleep. (292)

dysthymic disorder Mood disorder involving persistently depressed **mood,** with low self-esteem, withdrawal, pessimism or despair, present for at least two years, with no absence of symptoms for more than two months. (222)

ego In **psychoanalysis**, the psychical entity responsible for finding realistic and practical ways to satisfy **id** drives. (19)

ego psychology Derived from **psychoanalysis,** this theory emphasizes the role of the **ego** in development and attributes **psychological disorders** to failure of the ego to manage impulses and internal conflicts. (21)

electroconvulsive therapy (ECT) Biological treatment for severe, chronic depression involving the application of electrical impulses through the brain to produce seizures. The reasons for its effectiveness are unknown. (250)

electroencephalogram (EEG) Measure of electrical activity patterns in the brain taken through electrodes placed on the scalp. (88)

emotion Pattern of action elicited by an external event and a feeling state, accompanied by a characteristic physiological response. (61)

endogenous opioids Substances occurring naturally throughout the body that function like **neurotransmitters** to shut down pain sensation even in the presence of marked tissue damage. These may contribute to psychological problems such as eating disorders. Also known as endorphins or enkephalins. (331)

epidemiology Psychopathology research method examining the **prevalence**, distribution, and consequences of disorders in populations. (110)

epigenetics The study of factors other than inherited DNA sequence, such as new learning or **stress,** that alter the phenotypic expression of **genes.** (41)

equifinality Developmental **psychopathology** principle that a behaviour or disorder may have several different causes. (67)

essential hypertension High blood pressure with no verifiable physical cause, which makes up the overwhelming majority of high blood pressure cases. (324)

etiology Cause or source of a disorder. (8)

exhibitionism Sexual gratification attained by exposing the genitals to unsuspecting strangers. (377)

experiment Research method that can establish causation by manipulating the variables in question and controlling for other alternative explanations of any observed effects. (111)

expert witness Person who because of special training and experience is allowed to offer opinion testimony in legal trials. (584)

expressed emotion (EE) The hostility, criticism, and overinvolvement demonstrated by some families toward a family member with a **psychological disorder;** this can often contribute to the person's relapse. (498)

expressive language disorder Person's problems in spoken communication, as measured by significantly low scores on standardized tests of expressive language relative to nonverbal intelligence test scores. Symptoms may include a markedly limited vocabulary or errors in verb tense. (522)

external validity Extent to which research study findings generalize, or apply, to people and settings not involved in the study. (106)

extinction Learning process in which a response maintained by **reinforcement** in operant conditioning or pairing in **classical conditioning** decreases when that reinforcement or pairing is removed; also the procedure of removing that reinforcement or pairing. (24)

facial agnosia Type of **agnosia** characterized by a person's inability to recognize even familiar faces. (551)

factitious disorders Nonexistent physical or **psychological disorders** deliberately faked for no apparent gain except possibly sympathy and attention. (190)

false negative Assessment error in which no pathology is noted (i.e., test results are negative) when it is actually present. (86)

false positive Assessment error in which pathology is reported (i.e., test results are positive) when none is actually present. (86)

family studies Genetic studies that examine patterns of traits and behaviours among relatives. (117)

fear Emotion of an immediate alarm reaction to present danger or life-threatening emergencies. (130)

female orgasmic disorder Recurring delay or absence of orgasm in some women following a normal sexual excitement phase, relative to their prior experience and current stimulation. Also known as inhibited female orgasm. (363)

female sexual arousal disorder Recurrent inability in some women to attain or maintain adequate lubrication and swelling sexual excitement responses until completion of sexual activity. (362)

fetal alcohol syndrome (FAS) Pattern of problems including learning difficulties, behaviour deficits, and characteristic physical flaws, resulting from heavy drinking by the victim's mother when she was pregnant with the victim. (402)

fetishism Long-term, recurring, intense, sexually arousing urges, fantasies, or behaviour involving the use of nonliving, unusual objects, which cause distress or impairment in life functioning. (377)

fight-flight system (FFS) Brain circuit in animals that, when stimulated, causes an immediate alarm and escape response resembling human **panic**. (132)

fight-or-flight response See **flight-or-fight response**.

fitness to stand trial To stand trial, people must be able to understand the charges against them and to assist with their own defence. (583)

flat affect Apparently emotionless demeanour (including toneless speech and vacant gaze) when a reaction would be expected. (483)

flight-or-fight response Biological reaction to alarming stressors that musters the body's resources (e.g., blood flow, respiration) to resist or flee the threat. (60)

folie à deux Psychotic disturbance in which an individual develops a **delusion** similar to that of a person with whom he or she shares a close relationship. Also called **shared psychotic** disorder. (487)

fragile X syndrome Pattern of abnormality caused by a defect in the X chromosome that results in intellectual disability, learning problems, and unusual physical characteristics. (537)

free association Psychoanalytic therapy technique intended to explore threatening material repressed into the **unconscious**. The patient is instructed to say whatever comes to mind without censoring. (22)

gamma aminobutyric acid (GABA) Neurotransmitter that reduces activity across the synapse and thus inhibits a range of behaviours and **emotions**, especially generalized **anxiety**. (49)

gamma aminobutyric acid (GABA) system Inhibitory **neurotransmitter** system that is thought to be associated with excessive **anxiety**. (401)

gender identity disorder Psychological dissatisfaction with own biological gender, a disturbance in the sense of identity as a male or female. The primary goal is not sexual arousal but rather to live the life of the opposite gender. (354)

general adaptation syndrome (GAS) Sequence of reactions to sustained **stress** described by Hans Selye. These stages are alarm, resistance, and exhaustion, which may lead to death. (315)

generalizability Extent to which research results apply to a range of individuals not included in the study. (107)

generalized amnesia Condition in which a person loses memory of all personal information, including his or her own identity. (202)

generalized anxiety disorder (GAD) Anxiety disorder characterized by intense,

uncontrollable, unfocused, chronic, and continuous worry that is distressing and unproductive accompanied by physical symptoms of tenseness, irritability, and restlessness. (135)

genes Long deoxyribonucleic acid (DNA) molecules, the basic physical units of heredity, that appear as locations on chromosomes. (35)

genetic linkage analysis Studies that seek to match the inheritance pattern of a disorder to that of a **genetic marker**; this helps researchers establish the location of the **gene** responsible for the disorder. (118)

genetic marker Inherited characteristic for which the chromosomal location of the responsible **gene** is known. (118)

genotype Specific genetic makeup of an individual. (116)

glutamate Amino acid neurotransmitter that excites many different neurons, leading to action. (49)

hallucination Psychotic symptom of a perceptual disturbance in which things are seen or heard or otherwise sensed although they are not real or actually present. (481)

hallucinogen use disorders Cognitive, biological, behavioural, and social problems associated with the use and abuse of hallucinogenic substances. (412)

hallucinogens Any **psychoactive substances** such as **LSD** or **marijuana** that can produce **delusions**, **hallucinations**, **paranoia**, and altered sensory perception. (399)

harm reduction Approach to **substance abuse** prevention and treatment that seeks to minimize the harm associated with substance use as its primary goal (e.g., **controlled drinking** interventions, safe injection sites for injection drug users). (423)

head trauma Injury to the head and therefore to the brain, typically caused by accidents; can lead to cognitive impairments, including memory loss. (557)

health psychology Subfield of **behavioural medicine** that studies psychological factors important in health promotion and maintenance. (314)

hebephrenia Silly and immature emotionality, a characteristic of some types of **schizophrenia**. (477)

histrionic personality disorder Cluster B (dramatic, emotional, or erratic) **personality disorder** involving a pervasive pattern of excessive emotionality and attention seeking. (463)

HIV-l disease Human immunodeficiency virus-type-1 that causes AIDS. (556)

hormone Chemical messenger produced by the endocrine glands. (46)

human genome project Ongoing scientific attempt to develop a comprehensive map of all human **genes**. (116)

Huntington's disease Genetic disorder marked by involuntary limb movements and progressing to **dementia**. (557)

hypersomnia Abnormally excessive sleep; a person with this condition will fall asleep several times a day. (296)

hypertension Also known as high blood pressure; a major risk factor for **stroke** and heart and kidney disease that is intimately related to psychological factors. (324)

hypoactive sexual desire disorder Apparent lack of interest in sexual activity or fantasy that would be expected considering the person's age and life situation. (360)

hypochondriasis Somatoform disorder involving severe **anxiety** over the belief that the person has a disease process without any evident physical cause. (181)

hypomanic episode Less severe and less disruptive version of a manic episode that is one of the criteria for several **mood disorders**. (221)

hypothesis Educated guess or statement to be tested by research. (105)

id In **psychoanalysis**, the **unconscious** psychical entity present at birth representing basic drives. (19)

immune system Body's means of identifying and eliminating any foreign materials (e.g., bacteria, parasites, even transplanted organs) that enter. (318)

impacted grief reaction Extreme reaction to the death of a loved one that involves psychotic features, **suicidal ideation**, or severe loss of weight or energy, or that persists more than two months. Also called **pathological grief reaction**. (225)

implicit cognition Unconscious cognitive processes that are difficult to measure because people cannot verbalize them, as they are not even aware of them. (58)

implicit memory Condition of memory in which a person cannot recall past events even though he or she acts in response to them. (58)

inappropriate affect Emotional displays that are improper for the situation. (484)

incest Deviant sexual attraction (**pedophilia**) directed toward a family member; often the attraction of a father toward a daughter who is maturing physically. (380)

incidence Number of new cases of a disorder appearing during a specific time period (compare with **prevalence**). (8, 110)

independent variable Phenomenon that is manipulated by the experimenter in a research study and expected to influence the **dependent variable**. (105)

informed consent Ethical requirement whereby research subjects agree to participate in a research study only after they receive full disclosure about the nature of the study and their own role in it. (124, 587)

inhibited orgasm Inability to achieve orgasm despite adequate sexual desire and arousal; commonly seen in women but relatively rare in men. (363)

intellectual disability (intellectual disability) Significantly subaverage intellectual functioning paired with deficits in adaptive functioning such as self-care or occupational activities, appearing before age 18. (533)

intelligence quotient (IQ) Score on an intelligence test, abbreviated IQ, estimating a person's deviation from average test performance. (85)

internal validity Extent to which the results of a research study can be attributed to the **independent variable** after confounding alternative explanations have been ruled out. (106)

interpersonal psychotherapy (IPT) Newer brief treatment approach that emphasizes resolution of interpersonal problems and stressors such as role disputes in marital conflict, or forming relationships in marriage or a new job. It has demonstrated effectiveness for such problems as depression. (66, 253)

intrapsychic conflict In **psychoanalysis**, the struggles among the **id**, **ego**, and **superego**. (19)

introspection Early, nonscientific approach to the study of psychology involving systematic attempts to report thoughts and feelings that specific stimuli evoked. (24)

inverse agonist Chemical substance that produces effects opposite those of a particular **neurotransmitter**. (48)

labelling Applying a name to a phenomenon or a pattern of behaviour. The label may acquire negative connotations or be applied erroneously to the person rather than his or her behaviours. (96)

learned helplessness A condition in which a person begins to believe that he or she has no control over his or her life. (56)

learned helplessness theory of depression Seligman's theory that people become anxious and depressed when they make an attribution that they have no control over the **stress** in their lives (whether in reality they do or not). (241)

learning disorders Reading, mathematics, or written expression performance substantially below levels expected relative to the person's age, IQ, and education. (520)

level Degree of behaviour change with different interventions (e.g., high, low). (114)

localized amnesia Memory loss limited to specific times and events, particularly traumatic events. Also known as **selective amnesia**. (202)

longitudinal design Systematic study of changes in the same individual or group examined over time. (120)

LSD (d-lysergic acid diethylamide) Most common hallucinogenic drug; a synthetic version of the grain fungus ergot. (414)

maintenance treatment Combination of continued **psychosocial** treatment or medication designed to prevent relapse following therapy. (254)

major depressive disorder, single or recurrent episode Mood disorder involving one (single episode) or more (separated by at least two months without depression—recurrent) **major depressive episodes**. (222)

major depressive episode Most common and severe experience of depression, including feelings of worthlessness, disturbances in bodily activities such as sleep, loss of interest, and the inability to experience pleasure, persisting at least two weeks. (220)

male erectile disorder Recurring inability in some men to attain or maintain adequate penile erection until completion of sexual activity. (362)

male orgasmic disorder Recurring delay in or absence of orgasm in some men following a normal sexual excitement phase, relative to age and current stimulation. Also known as inhibited male orgasm. (364)

malingering Deliberate faking of a physical or **psychological disorder** motivated by gain. (190, 588)

mania Period of abnormally excessive elation or euphoria, associated with some **mood disorders**. (221)

marijuana (*Cannabis sativa*) Dried part of the hemp plant, a **hallucinogen** that is the most widely used illegal substance. (412)

mathematics disorder Mathematics performance significantly below age norms. (520)

mental hygiene movement Mid-19th-century effort to improve care of the mentally disordered by informing the public of their mistreatment. (16)

mental illness Term formerly used to mean **psychological disorder** but less preferred because it implies that the causes of the disorder can be found in a medical disease process. (576)

mental status exam Relatively coarse preliminary test of a client's judgment, orientation to time and place, and emotional and mental state; typically conducted during an initial interview. (75)

microsleeps Short, seconds-long periods of sleep that occur in people who have been deprived of sleep. (293)

mixed episode Condition in which the individual experiences both elation and depression or **anxiety** at the same time. Also known as **dysphoric manic episode**. (221)

modelling (also known as **observational learning**) Learning through observation and imitation of the behaviour of other individuals and the consequences of that behaviour. (57)

mood Enduring period of emotionality. (61)

mood disorders Group of disorders involving severe and enduring disturbances in emotionality ranging from elation to severe depression. (220)

moral therapy Nineteenth-century **psychosocial** approach to treatment that involved treating patients as normally as possible in normal environments. (15)

multidimensional integrative approach Approach to the study of **psychopathology** that holds that **psychological disorders** are always the products of multiple interacting causal factors. (33)

multiple baseline Single-case experimental design in which measures are taken on two or more behaviours, or on a single behaviour in two or more situations. A particular intervention is introduced for each at different times. If behaviour change is coincident with each introduction, this is strong evidence the intervention caused the change. (115)

narcissistic personality disorder Cluster B (dramatic, emotional, or erratic) **personality disorder** involving a pervasive pattern of grandiosity in fantasy or behaviour, need for admiration, and lack of empathy. (465)

narcolepsy Sleep disorder involving sudden and irresistible sleep attacks. (296)

natural environment phobia Fear of situations or events in nature, especially heights, storms, and water. (152)

negative correlation Association between two variables in which one increases as the other decreases. (110)

negative symptoms Less outgoing symptoms, such as **flat affect** and poverty of speech, displayed by some people with **schizophrenia**. (482)

neurohormones Hormones that affect the brain and are increasingly the focus of study in **psychopathology**. (239)

neuroimaging Sophisticated computer-aided procedures that allow nonintrusive examination of nervous system structure and function. (86)

neurons Individual nerve cells that are responsible for transmitting information. (43)

neuropsychological testing Assessment of brain and nervous system functioning by testing an individual's performance on behavioural tasks. (86)

neuroscience Study of the nervous system and its role in behaviour, thoughts, and **emotions**. (42)

neuroses Obsolete psychodynamic term for **psychological disorders** thought to result from **unconscious** conflicts and the **anxiety** they cause. Singular is neurosis. (21)

neurotransmitters Chemicals that cross the **synaptic cleft** between nerve cells to transmit impulses from one **neuron** to the next. Their relative excess or deficiency is involved in several **psychological disorders**. (44)

nicotine use disorders Cognitive, biological, behavioural, and social problems associated with the use and abuse of nicotine. (409)

nightmares Frightening and **anxiety**-provoking dreams occurring during **rapid eye** movement (REM) sleep. The individual recalls the bad dreams and recovers alertness and orientation quickly. (303)

nomenclature In a naming system or **nosology**, the actual labels or names that are applied. In **psychopathology** these include, for example, **mood disorders** or eating disorders. (89)

noradrenaline See **norepinephrine**.

norepinephrine (also **noradrenaline**) Neurotransmitter that is active in the central and peripheral nervous systems controlling heart rate, blood pressure, and respiration, among other functions. Because of its role in the body's alarm reaction, it may also contribute in general and indirectly to **panic attacks** and other disorders. (50)

nosology Classification and naming system for medical and psychological phenomena. (89)

object relations Modern development in psychodynamic theory involving the study of how children incorporate the memories and values of people who are close and important to them. (21)

observational learning Type of learning that does not require direct experience; rather, an organism can learn by observing what happens to another organism and later imitating the other organism's behaviour (also known as **modelling**). (57)

obsessions Recurrent intrusive thoughts or impulses the client seeks to suppress or neutralize while recognizing they are not imposed by outside forces. (169)

obsessive-compulsive disorder (OCD) **Anxiety** disorder involving unwanted, persistent, intrusive thoughts and impulses as well as repetitive actions intended to suppress them. (168)

obsessive-compulsive personality disorder Cluster C (anxious or fearful) **personality disorder** featuring a pervasive pattern of preoccupation with orderliness, perfectionism, and mental and interpersonal control at the expense of flexibility, openness, and efficiency. (469)

opiates Addictive **psychoactive substances** such as heroin, opium, and morphine that cause temporary euphoria and analgesia (pain reduction). (399)

opioid use disorders Cognitive, biological, behavioural, and social problems associated with the use and abuse of **opiates** and their synthetic variants. (411)

orgasmic reconditioning Learning procedure to help clients strengthen appropriate patterns of sexual arousal by pairing appropriate stimuli with the pleasurable sensations of masturbation. (385)

pain catastrophizing An exaggerated negative response during an actual or anticipated painful experience. Catastrophizers ruminate on and magnify the pain, and they often feel helpless in the face of the pain. (329)

pain disorder A **somatoform disorder** featuring true pain, but for which psychological factors play an important role in onset, severity, or maintenance. (195)

panic Sudden overwhelming fright or terror. (130)

panic attack Abrupt experience of intense **fear** or discomfort accompanied by physical symptoms such as dizziness or heart palpitations. (130)

panic control treatment (PCT) Cognitive-behavioural treatment for **panic attacks**, involving gradual exposure to feared somatic sensations and modification of perceptions and attitudes about them. (147)

panic disorder with agoraphobia (PDA) Fear and avoidance of situations the person believes might induce a dreaded **panic attack**. (140)

panic disorder without agoraphobia (PD) **Panic attacks** experienced without development of **agoraphobia**. (141)

paranoia Person's irrational beliefs that he or she is especially important (**delusions** of grandeur) or that other people are seeking to do him or her harm. (477)

paranoid personality disorder Cluster A (odd or eccentric) **personality disorder** involving pervasive distrust and suspiciousness of others such that their motives are interpreted as malevolent. (446)

paranoid type of schizophrenia Type of **schizophrenia** in which symptoms primarily involve **delusions** and **hallucinations**; speech and motor and emotional behaviour are relatively intact. (485)

paraphilias Sexual disorders and deviations in which sexual arousal occurs almost exclusively in the context of inappropriate objects or individuals. (376)

parasomnias Abnormal behaviours such as **nightmares** or **sleepwalking** that occur during sleep. (292)

Parkinson's disease Degenerative brain disorder principally affecting motor performance (e.g., tremors, stooped posture) associated with reduction in **dopamine**. **Dementia** may be a result as well. (557)

pathological grief reaction Extreme reaction to the death of a loved one that involves psychotic features, **suicidal ideation**, or severe loss of weight or energy, or that persists more than two months. Also called **impacted grief reaction**. (225)

pedophilia **Paraphilia** (sexual deviation) involving strong sexual attraction toward children. (380)

personality disorders Enduring maladaptive patterns for relating to the environment and oneself, exhibited in a wide range of

contexts that cause significant functional impairment or subjective distress. (439)

personality inventories Self-report questionnaires that assess personal traits by asking respondents to identify descriptions that apply to them. (83)

person-centred therapy Therapy method in which the client, rather than the counsellor, primarily directs the course of discussion, seeking self-discovery and self-responsibility. (23)

pervasive developmental disorder—not otherwise specified (PDD-NOS) Severe and pervasive impairments in social interactions that do not meet all the diagnostic criteria for **autistic disorder**. (524)

pervasive developmental disorders Wide-ranging, significant, and long-lasting dysfunctions that appear before the age of 18. (524)

phenotype Observable characteristics or behaviours of an individual. (116)

phobia **Psychological disorder** characterized by marked and persistent **fear** of an object or situation. (3)

phototherapy Treatment of **seasonal affective disorder** with large doses of exposure to bright light. (251)

Pick's disease Very rare neurological disorder that results in presenile (early onset) **dementia**. (558)

placebo control group In an outcome **experiment**, a **control group** that does not receive the experimental manipulation but is given a similar procedure with an identical expectation of change, allowing the researcher to assess any **placebo effect**. (112)

placebo effect Behaviour change resulting from the person's expectation of change rather than from the experimental manipulation itself. (112)

polysomnographic (PSG) evaluation Assessment of sleep disorders in which a client sleeping in the lab is monitored for heart, muscle, respiration, brain wave, and other functions. (292)

polysubstance use Use of multiple mind-altering and behaviour-altering substances, such as drugs. (393)

positive correlation Association between two variables in which one increases as the other increases. (109)

positive symptoms More overt symptoms, such as **delusions** and **hallucinations**, displayed by some people with **schizophrenia**. (479)

post-traumatic stress disorder (PTSD) Enduring, distressing emotional disorder that follows exposure to a severe helplessness- or **fear**-inducing threat. The victim re-experiences the trauma, avoids stimuli associated with it, and develops a numbing of responsiveness and an increased vigilance and arousal. (161)

premature ejaculation Recurring ejaculation before the person wants it, with minimal sexual stimulation. (364)

prepared learning Certain associations can be learned more readily than others because this ability has been adaptive for evolution. (57)

presenting problem Original complaint reported by the client to the therapist. The actual treated problem may sometimes be a modification derived from the presenting problem. (8)

prevalence Number of people displaying a disorder in the total population at any given time (compare with **incidence**). (8, 110)

primary insomnia Difficulty in initiating, maintaining, or gaining from sleep; not related to other medical or psychological problems. (293)

proband In genetics research, the individual displaying the trait or characteristic being studied. Also known as index case. (117)

prognosis Predicted future development of a disorder over time. (8)

projective tests Psychoanalytically based measures that present ambiguous stimuli to clients on the assumption that their responses will reveal their **unconscious** conflicts. Such tests are very inferential and lack high **reliability** and **validity**. (81)

prototypical approach System for categorizing disorders using both essential, defining characteristics and a range of variation on other characteristics. (90)

psychoactive substances Substances, such as drugs, that alter **mood** or behaviour. (394)

psychoanalysis Psychoanalytic assessment and therapy, which emphasizes exploration of, and insight into, **unconscious** processes and conflicts, pioneered by Sigmund Freud. (17)

psychoanalyst Therapist who practises **psychoanalysis** after earning either an M.D. or Ph.D. degree and then receiving additional specialized postdoctoral training. (22)

psychoanalytic model Complex and comprehensive theory originally advanced by Sigmund Freud that seeks to account for the development and structure of personality, as well as the origin of abnormal behaviour, based primarily on inferred inner entities and forces. (19)

psychodynamic psychotherapy Contemporary version of **psychoanalysis** that still emphasizes **unconscious** processes and conflicts but is briefer and more focused on specific problems. (22)

psychological autopsy Post-mortem psychological profile of a suicide victim constructed from interviews with people who knew the person before death. (259)

psychological disorder Psychological dysfunction associated with distress or impairment in functioning that is not a typical or culturally expected response. (3)

psychoneuroimmunology (PNI) Study of psychological influences on the neurological responding involved in the body's immune response. (319)

psycho-oncology Study of psychological factors involved in the **course** and treatment of **cancer**. (322)

psychopathology Scientific study of **psychological disorders**. (6)

psychopathy Non-*DSM* category similar to **antisocial personality disorder** but with less emphasis on overt behaviour; indicators include superficial charm, lack of remorse, and other personality characteristics. (451)

psychophysiological assessment Measurement of changes in the nervous system reflecting psychological or emotional events such as **anxiety**, **stress**, and sexual arousal. (88)

psychosexual stages of development In **psychoanalysis**, the sequence of phases a person passes through during development. Each stage is named for the location on the body where **id** gratification is maximal at that time. (20)

psychosocial Social and cultural factors (such as family experience) and psychological influences. (15)

psychotic disorder Disorder involving **delusions**, **hallucinations**, loss of contact with reality, or **disorganized speech** or behaviour. (479)

purging techniques In the eating disorder **bulimia nervosa**, the self-induced vomiting or laxative abuse used to compensate for excessive food ingestion. (272)

randomization Method for placing individuals into research groups that assures each one of an equal chance of being assigned to any group, to eliminate any systematic differences across groups. (107)

rapid eye movement (REM) sleep Periodic intervals of sleep during which the eyes move rapidly from side to side, and dreams occur, but the body is inactive. (291)

reading disorder Reading performance significantly below age norms. (520)

rebound insomnia In a person with insomnia, the worsened sleep problems that can occur when medications are used to treat insomnia and then withdrawn. (295)

reciprocal gene–environment model Hypothesis that people with a genetic predisposition for a disorder may also have a genetic tendency to create environmental risk factors that promote the disorder. (39)

reinforcement In operant conditioning, consequences for behaviour that strengthen it or increase its frequency. Positive reinforcement involves the contingent delivery of a desired consequence; negative reinforcement is the contingent escape from an aversive consequence. Unwanted behaviours may result from their **reinforcement**, or the failure to reinforce desired behaviours. (26)

relapse prevention Extending therapeutic progress by teaching the client how to cope with future troubling situations. (385, 427)

relaxation response Active components of meditation methods, including repetitive thoughts of a sound to reduce distracting thoughts, and closing the mind to other intruding thoughts, that decrease the flow of stress **hormones** and **neurotransmitters** and cause a feeling of calm. (334)

reliability Degree to which a measurement is consistent—for example, over time or among different raters. (74)

research design Plan of experimentation used to test a **hypothesis**. (105)

residual type of schizophrenia Diagnostic category for people who have experienced at least one episode of **schizophrenia**, and who no longer display its major symptoms but still show some bizarre thoughts or social withdrawal. (486)

retrospective information Literally "the view back," data collected by examining records or recollections of the past. It is limited by the accuracy, **validity**, and thoroughness of the sources. (120)

Rett's disorder Progressive neurological developmental disorder featuring constant hand-wringing, intellectual disability, and impaired motor skills. (524)

reuptake Action by which a **neurotransmitter** is quickly drawn back into the discharging **neuron** after being released into a **synaptic cleft**. (48)

rheumatoid arthritis Painful, degenerative disease in which the **immune system** essentially attacks itself, resulting in stiffness, swelling, and even destruction of the joints. Cognitive-behavioural treatments can help relieve pain and stiffness. (319)

schizoaffective disorder Psychotic disorder featuring symptoms of both **schizophrenia** and major **mood disorder**. (487)

schizoid personality disorder Cluster A (odd or eccentric) **personality disorder** featuring a pervasive pattern of detachment from social relationships and a restricted range of expression of **emotions**. (447)

schizophrenia Devastating **psychotic disorder** that may involve characteristic disturbances in thinking (**delusions**), perception (**hallucinations**), speech, **emotions**, and behaviour. (477)

schizophreniform disorder Psychotic disorder involving the symptoms of **schizophrenia** but lasting less than six months. (486)

schizophrenogenic According to an obsolete, unsupported theory, a cold, dominating, an rejecting parent who was thought to cause **schizophrenia** in his or her offspring. (498)

schizotypal personality disorder Cluster A (odd or eccentric) **personality disorder** involving a pervasive pattern of interpersonal deficits featuring acute discomfort with, and reduced capacity for, close relationships, as well as by cognitive or perceptual distortions and eccentricities of behaviour. (448)

scientist-practitioner model Expectation that mental health professionals will apply scientific methods to their work. They must keep current in the latest research on **diagnosis** and treatment, they must evaluate their own methods for effectiveness, and they may generate their own research to discover new knowledge of disorders and their treatment. (7)

seasonal affective disorder (SAD) Mood disorder involving a cycling of episodes corresponding to the seasons of the year, typically with depression occurring during the winter. (230)

selective mutism Developmental disorder characterized by the individual's consistent failure to speak in specific social situations despite speaking in other situations. (522)

selective amnesia Memory loss limited to specific times and events, particularly traumatic events. Also known as **localized amnesia**. (202)

self-actualizing Process emphasized in humanistic psychology in which people strive to achieve their highest potential against difficult life experiences. (23)

self-efficacy Person's perception that he or she has the ability to cope with **stress** or challenges. (317)

separation anxiety disorder Excessive enduring **fear** in some children that harm will come to them or their parents while they are apart. (152)

sequential design Combination of the cross-sectional and longitudinal research methods involving repeated study of different **cohorts** over time. (121)

serotonin A **neurotransmitter** involved in processing information and coordination of movement as well as inhibition and restraint; it also assists in the regulation of eating, sexual, and aggressive behaviours, all of which may be involved in different **psychological disorders**. Its interaction with **dopamine** is implicated in **schizophrenia**. (49)

sex reassignment surgery Surgical procedures to alter a person's physical anatomy to conform to that person's psychological gender identity. (357)

sexual aversion disorder Extreme and persistent dislike of sexual contact or similar activities. (361)

sexual dysfunction Sexual disorder in which the client finds it difficult to function adequately while having sex. (359)

sexual masochism A **paraphilia** in which sexual arousal is associated with experiencing pain or humiliation. (379)

sexual pain disorder Recurring genital pain in either males or females before, during, or after sexual intercourse. Also called **dyspareunia**. (365)

sexual sadism A **paraphilia** in which sexual arousal is associated with inflicting pain or humiliation. (379)

shaping In operant conditioning, the development of a new response by reinforcing successively more similar versions of that response. Both desirable and undesirable behaviours may be learned in this manner. (26)

shared psychotic disorder Psychotic disturbance in which an individual develops a **delusion** similar to that of a person with whom he or she shares a close relationship. Also called **folie à deux**. (487)

single-case experimental design Research tactic in which an **independent variable** is manipulated for a single individual, allowing cause-and-effect conclusions, but with limited **generalizability** (contrast with **case study method**). (113)

situational phobia **Anxiety** involving enclosed places (e.g., claustrophobia) or public transportation (e.g., **fear** of flying). (152)

sleep apnea Disorder involving brief periods when breathing ceases during sleep. (296)

sleep efficiency (SE) Percentage of time actually spent sleeping of the total time spent in bed. (293)

sleep terrors Episodes of apparent awakening from sleep, accompanied by signs of **panic**, followed by disorientation and amnesia for the incident. These occur during NREM sleep and so do not involve frightening dreams. (303)

sleepwalking (or **somnambulism**) A **parasomnia** that involves leaving the bed during NREM—deep, nondreaming—sleep. (304)

social phobia Extreme, enduring, irrational **fear** and avoidance of social or performance situations. (156)

somatization disorder Somatoform disorder involving extreme and long-lasting focus on multiple physical symptoms for which no medical cause is evident. (185)

somatoform disorders Pathological concern of individuals with the appearance or functioning of their bodies, usually in the absence of any identifiable medical condition. (181)

specific phobia Unreasonable **fear** of a specific object or situation that markedly interferes with daily life functioning. (150)

standardization Process of establishing specific norms and requirements for a measurement technique to ensure it is used consistently across measurement occasions. This includes

instructions for administering the measure, evaluating its findings, and comparing these to data for large numbers of people. (75)

statistical significance Probability that obtaining the observed research findings merely by chance is small. (107)

stimulants Psychoactive substances that elevate **mood**, activity, and alertness, including amphetamines, caffeine, cocaine, and nicotine. (399)

stress Body's physiological response to a stressor, which is any event or change that requires adaptation. (315)

stroke Temporary blockage of blood vessels supplying the brain, or a rupture of vessels in the brain, resulting in temporary or permanent loss of brain functioning. Also called a **cerebral vascular accident (CVA)**. (324)

stuttering Disturbance in the fluency and time patterning of speech (e.g., sound and syllable repetitions or prolongations). (522)

substance abuse Pattern of **psychoactive substance** use leading to significant distress or impairment in social and occupational roles, and in hazardous situations. (394)

substance dependence Maladaptive pattern of substance use characterized by the need for increased amounts to achieve the desired effect, negative physical effects when the substance is withdrawn, unsuccessful efforts to control its use, and substantial effort expended to seek it or recover from its effects. (395)

substance intoxication Physiological reactions, such as impaired judgment and motor ability as well as **mood** changes, resulting from the ingestion of **psychoactive substances**. (394)

substance-related disorders Range of problems associated with the use and abuse of drugs such as alcohol, cocaine, heroin, and other substances people use to alter the way they think, feel, and behave. These are extremely costly in human and financial terms. (393)

suicidal attempts Efforts made to kill oneself. (258)

suicidal ideation Serious thoughts about committing suicide. (258)

superego In **psychoanalysis**, the psychical entity representing the internalized moral standards of parents and society. (19)

synaptic cleft Space between nerve cells where chemical transmitters act to move impulses from one **neuron** to the next. (43)

systematic desensitization Behavioural therapy technique to diminish excessive **fears**, involving gradual exposure to the feared stimulus paired with a positive coping experience, usually relaxation. (25)

taxonomy System of naming and classification (e.g., of specimens) in science. (89)

testability Ability of a **hypothesis**, for example, to be subjected to scientific scrutiny and to be accepted or rejected, a necessary condition for the hypothesis to be useful. (106)

tic disorder Disruption in early development involving involuntary motor movements or vocalizations. (522)

token economy Social learning behaviour modification system in which individuals earn items they can exchange for desired rewards by displaying appropriate behaviours. (503)

tolerance Need for increased amounts of a substance to achieve the desired effect, and a diminished effect with continued use of the same amount. (395)

transference Psychoanalytic concept suggesting that clients may seek to relate to the therapist as they do to important authority figures, particularly their parents. (22)

transinstitutionalization Movement of people with severe **mental illness** from large psychiatric hospitals to smaller group residences. (578)

transvestic fetishism Paraphilia in which individuals, usually males, are sexually aroused or receive gratification by wearing clothing of the opposite sex. (378)

treatment outcome research Studies of the effectiveness of clinical interventions, including the comparison of competing treatments.

trend The direction of change of a behaviour or behaviours (e.g., increasing, decreasing). (114)

twin studies In genetics research, the comparison of twins with unrelated or less closely related individuals. If twins, particularly monozygotic twins who share identical **genotypes**, share common characteristics such as a disorder, even if they were reared in different environments, this is strong evidence of genetic involvement in those characteristics. (118)

type A behaviour pattern Cluster of behaviours including excessive competitiveness, time-pressured impatience, accelerated speech, and anger, originally thought to promote high risk for heart disease. (326)

type B behaviour pattern Cluster of behaviours including a relaxed attitude, indifference to time pressure, and less forceful ambition; originally thought to cause low risk for heart disease. (326)

unconditional positive regard Acceptance by the counsellor of the client's feelings and actions without judgment or condemnation. (23)

unconscious Part of the psychic makeup that is outside the person's awareness. (18)

undifferentiated type of schizophrenia Category for individuals who meet the criteria for **schizophrenia** but not for any one of the defined subtypes. (486)

vaginismus Recurring involuntary muscle spasms in the outer third of the vagina that interfere with sexual intercourse. (366)

validity Degree to which a technique actually measures what it purports to measure. (75)

variability Degree of change in a phenomenon over time. (114)

vascular dementia Progressive brain disorder involving loss of cognitive functioning, caused by blockage of blood flow to the brain, that appears concurrently with other neurological signs and symptoms. (555)

voyeurism Paraphilia in which sexual arousal is derived from observing unsuspecting individuals undressing or naked. (377)

vulnerability Susceptibility or tendency to develop a disorder. (38)

withdrawal Severely negative physiological reaction to removal of a **psychoactive substance**, which can be alleviated by the same or a similar substance. (395)

withdrawal delirium Frightening **hallucinations** and body tremors that result when a heavy drinker withdraws from alcohol. Also called **delirium tremens (DTs)**. (401)

withdrawal design Removing a treatment to note whether it has been effective. In single-case experimental designs, a behaviour is measured (**baseline**), an **independent variable** is introduced (intervention), and then the intervention is withdrawn. Because the behaviour continues to be measured throughout (repeated measurement), any effects of the intervention can be noted. Also called reversal design. (114)

References

Abad, V., & Guilleminault, C. (2009). Treatment options for obstructive sleep apnea. *Current Treatment Options in Neurology, 11*(5), 358–367.

Abbeduto, L., & Rosenberg, S. (1992). Linguistic communication in persons with mental retardation. In S. F. Warren & J. Reichle (Eds.), *Causes and effects in communication and language intervention* (pp. 331–359). Baltimore: Paul H. Brookes.

Abbey, S. E. (2005). Somatization and somatoform disorders. In J. L. Levenson (Ed.), *The American psychiatric publishing textbook of psychosomatic medicine* (pp. 271–296). Washington, DC: American Psychiatric Publishing, Inc.

Abbey, S. E., & Garfinkel, P. E. (1991a). Neurasthenia and chronic fatigue syndrome: The role of culture in the making of a diagnosis. *American Journal of Psychiatry, 148,* 1638–1646.

Abbey, S. E., & Garfinkel, P. E. (1991b). Chronic fatigue syndrome and depression: Cause, effect, or covariate? *Reviews of Infectious Diseases, 13*(1), 73–83.

Abbott, D. W., de Zwaan, M., Mussell, M. P., Raymond, N. C., Seim, H. C., Crow, S. J., ... Mitchell, J. E. (1998). Onset of binge eating and dieting in overweight women: Implications for etiology, associated features and treatment. *Journal of Psychosomatic Research, 44,* 367–374.

Abel, G. G. (1989). Behavioral treatment of child molesters. In A. J. Stunkard & A. Baum (Eds.), *Perspectives in behavioral medicine: Eating, sleeping and sex* (pp. 223–242). Hillsdale, NJ: Erlbaum.

Abel, G. G., Becker, J. V., Cunningham-Rathner, J., Mittelman, M., & Rouleau, J. L. (1988). Multiple paraphilic diagnoses among sex offenders. *Bulletin of the American Academy of Psychiatry and Law, 16,* 153–168.

Abel, G. G., Becker, J. V., Mittelman, M., Cunningham-Rathner, J., Rouleau, J. L., & Murphy, W. E. (1987). Self-reported sex crimes of nonincarcerated paraphiliacs. *Journal of Interpersonal Violence, 2,* 3–25.

Abela, J. R. Z., Aydin, C., & Auerbach, R. P. (2006). Operationalizing the "vulnerability" and "stress" components of the hopelessness theory of depression: A multi-wave longitudinal study. *Behaviour Research and Therapy, 44,* 1565–1583.

Abela, J. R. Z., Payne, A. V. L., & Moussaly, N. (2003). Cognitive vulnerability to depression in individuals with borderline personality disorder. *Journal of Personality Disorders, 17,* 319–329.

Abela, J. R. Z., & Sarin, S. (2002). Cognitive vulnerability to hopelessness depression: A chain is only as strong as its weakest link. *Cognitive Therapy & Research, 26,* 811–829.

Abramson, L. Y., Bardone-Cone, A. M., Vohs, K. D., Joiner, T. E., Jr., & Heatherton, T. F. (2006). Cognitive vulnerability to bulimia. In L. B. Alloy & J. H. Riskind (Eds.), *Cognitive vulnerability to emotional disorders* (pp. 329–364).

Mahwah, NJ: Lawrence Erlbaum Associates Publishers.

Abramson, L. Y., Metalsky, G. I., & Alloy, L. B. (1989). Hopelessness depression: A theory-based subtype of depression. *Psychological Review, 96*(2), 358–372.

Abramson, L. Y., Seligman, M. E. P., & Teasdale, J. D. (1978). Learned helplessness in humans: Critique and reformulation. *Journal of Abnormal Psychology, 87,* 49–74.

Abse, D. W. (1987). *Hysteria and related mental disorders: An approach to psychological medicine.* Bristol: Wright.

Abuelo, D. N. (1991). Genetic disorders. In J. L. Matson & J. A. Mulick (Eds.), *Handbook of mental retardation* (2nd ed., pp. 97–114). Elmsford, NY: Pergamon Press.

Adachi, Y., Sato, C., Nishino, N., Ohryoji, F., Hayama, J., & Yamagami, T. (2009). A brief parental education for shaping sleep habits in 4-month-old infants. *Clinical Medicine & Research, 7*(3), 85–92.

Adair, R., Bauchner, H., Philipp, B., Levenson, S., & Zuckerman, B. (1991). Night waking during infancy: Role of parent presence at bedtime. *Pediatrics, 87,* 500–504.

Adams, M., Kutcher, S., Antoniw, E., & Bird, D. (1996). Diagnostic utility of endocrine and nero imaging screening tests in first-onset adolescent psychosis. *Journal of the American Academy of Child & Adolescent Psychiatry, 35,* 67–73.

Addington, J., van Mastrigt, S., & Addington, D. (2003). Patterns of premorbid functioning in first-episode psychosis: Initial presentation. *Schizophrenia Research, 62,* 23–30.

Addis, M. E. (2008). Gender and depression in men. *Clinical Psychology: Science and Practice, 15*(3), 153–168.

Ader, R., & Cohen, N. (1975). Behaviorally conditioned immunosuppression. *Psychosomatic Medicine, 37,* 333–340.

Ader, R., & Cohen, N. (1993). Psychoneuroimmunology: Conditioning and stress. *Annual Review of Psychology, 44,* 53–85.

Adler, C. M., Côte, G., Barlow, D. H., & Hillhouse, J. J. (1994). *Phenomenological relationships between somatoform, anxiety, and psychophysiological disorders.* Unpublished manuscript.

Adler, P. S. J., Ditto, B., France, C., & France, J. (1994). Cardiovascular reactions to blood donation in offspring of hypertensives and normotensives. *Journal of Psychosomatic Research, 38,* 429–439.

Adler, R. H., Zamboni, P., Hofer, T., & Hemmeler, W. (1997). How not to miss a somatic needle in the haystack of chronic pain. *Journal of Psychosomatic Research, 42,* 499–505.

Agid, O., Remington, G. Kapur, S., Arenovich, T., & Zipursky, R. B. (2007). Early use of clozapine for poorly responding first-episode psychosis. *Journal of Clinical Psychopharmacology, 27*(4), 369–373.

Agras, W. S. (1987). *Eating disorders: Management of obesity, bulimia, and anorexia nervosa.* Elmsford, NY: Pergamon Press.

Agras, W. S. (2001). The consequences and costs of eating disorders. *Psychiatric Clinics of North America, 24,* 371–379.

Agras, W. S., Barlow, D. H., Chapin, H. N., Abel, G. G., & Leitenberg, H. (1974). Behavior modification of anorexia nervosa. *Archives of General Psychiatry, 30,* 279–286.

Agras, W. S., & Kirkley, B. G. (1986). Bulimia: Theories of etiology. In K. D. Brownell & J. P. Foreyt (Eds.), *Handbook of eating disorders: Physiology, psychology, and treatment of obesity, anorexia, and bulimia* (pp. 367–378). New York: Basic Books.

Agras, W. S., Schneider, J. A., Arnow, B., Raeburn, S. D., & Telch, C. F. (1989). Cognitive-behavioral and response-prevention treatments for bulimia nervosa. *Journal of Consulting and Clinical Psychology, 57,* 215–221.

Agras, W. S., Sylvester, D., & Oliveau, D. (1969). The epidemiology of common fears and phobia. *Comprehensive Psychiatry, 10,* 151–156.

Agras, W. S., Telch, C. F., Arnow, B., Eldredge, K., & Marnell, M. (1997). One year follow-up of cognitive-behavioral therapy of obese individuals with binge eating disorder. *Journal of Consulting and Clinical Psychology, 65,* 343–347.

Agras, W. S., Walsh, B. T., Fairburn, C. G., Wilson, G. T., & Kraemer, H. C. (2000). A multicenter comparison of cognitive-behavioral therapy and interpersonal psychotherapy for bulimia nervosa. *Archives of General Psychiatry, 57,* 459–466.

Agrawal, P. (1978). Diazepam addiction: A case report. *Canadian Psychiatric Association Journal, 23,* 35–37.

Ahmed, M., Westra, H. A., & Stewart, S. H. (2008). A self-help handout for benzodiazepine discontinuation using cognitive behavioural therapy. *Cognitive and Behavioral Practice, 15*(3), 317–324.

Aigner, M., & Bach, M. (1999). Clinical utility of DSM-IV pain disorder. *Comprehensive Psychiatry, 40*(5), 353–357.

Ait Bentaleb, L., Beauregard, M., Liddle, P., & Stip, E. (2002). Cerebral activity associated with auditory verbal hallucinations: A functional magnetic resonance imaging case study. *Journal of Psychiatry & Neuroscience, 27,* 110–115.

Akiskal, H. S. (1997). Overview of chronic depressions and their clinical management. In H. S. Akiskal & G. B. Cassano (Eds.), *Dysthymia and the spectrum of chronic depressions* (pp. 1–34). New York: Guilford Press.

Akiskal, H. S. (2009). Dysthymia, cyclothymia, and hyperthymia. In M. G. Gelder, N. C. Andreasen, J. J. López-Ibor, Jr., & J. R. Geddes (Eds.), *New Oxford textbook of psychiatry* (Vol. 1, 2nd ed., pp. 680–692). Oxford: Oxford University Press.

Akiskal, H. S., & Cassano, G. B. (Eds.). (1997). *Dysthymia and the spectrum of chronic depressions.* New York: Guilford Press.

Akiskal, H. S., Khani, M. K., & Scott-Strauss, A. (1979). Cyclothymic temperamental disorders. *Psychiatric Clinics of North America, 2,* 527–554.

Akiskal, H. S., & Pinto, O. (1999). The evolving spectrum: Prototypes I, II, III, and IV. *The Psychiatric Clinics of North America, 22*(3), 517–534.

Aktar, S., & Brenner, I. (1979). Differential diagnosis of fugue-like states. *Journal of Clinical Psychiatry, 40,* 381–385.

Alarcon, R. D., Bell, C. C., Kirmayer, L. J., Ling, K., Bedirhan, U., & Wisner, K. L. (2002). Beyond the funhouse mirrors: Research agenda on culture and psychiatric diagnosis. In D. Kupfer, M. First, & D. Regier (Eds.), *A research agenda for DSM-V* (pp. 219–281). Washington, DC: American Psychiatric Association.

Albano, A., Pincus, D. B., Tracey, S., & Barlow, D. H. (in preparation). Cognitive behavioral group treatment of social phobia in adolescents: Importance of parent inclusion in treatment. Manuscript in preparation.

Albano, A. M., & Barlow, D. H. (1996). Breaking the vicious cycle: Cognitive-behavioral group treatment for socially anxious youth. In E. D. Hibbs & P. S. Jensen (Eds.), *Psychosocial treatment research and adolescent disorders* (pp. 43–62). Washington, DC: APA Press.

Albano, A. M., Chorpita, B. F., & Barlow, D. H. (1996). Childhood anxiety disorders. In E. J. Mash & R. A. Barkley (Eds.), *Child psychopathology* (pp. 196–241). New York: Guilford Press.

Albano, A. M., DiBartolo, P. M., Heimberg, R. G., & Barlow, D. H. (1995). Children and adolescents: Assessment and treatment. In R. G. Heimberg, M. R. Liebowitz, D. A. Hope, & F. R. Schneier (Eds.), *Social phobia: Diagnosis, assessment and treatment* (pp. 387–426). New York: Guilford Press.

Albano, A. M., & Hack, S. (2004). Children and adolescents. In R. G. Heimberg, C. L. Turk, & D. S. Mennin (Eds.), *Generalized anxiety disorder: Advances in research and practice* (pp. 383–408). New York: Guilford Press.

Albano, A. M., Miller, P. P., Zarate, R., Côté, G., & Barlow, D. H. (1997). Behavioral assessment and treatment of PTSD in prepubertal children: Attention to developmental factors and innovative strategies in the case study of a family. *Cognitive & Behavioral Practice, 4,* 245–262.

Albee, G. W. (1998). Fifty years of clinical psychology: Selling our soul to the devil. *Applied & Preventive Psychology, 7,* 189–194.

Albee, G. W. (2000). The Boulder model's fatal flaw. *American Psychologist, 55,* 247–248.

Albert, C., Chae, C., Rexrode, K., Manson, J., & Kawachi, I. (2005). Phobic anxiety and risk of coronary heart disease and sudden cardiac among women. *Circulation, 111,* 480–487.

Alberta Family and Social Services. (1990). *Elder abuse: What is it? What to do about it?* Retrieved November 24, 2003, from http://www.acjnet.org/docs/eldabpfv.html

Albertini, R. S., & Phillips, K. A. (1999). Thirty-three cases of body dysmorphic disorder in children and adolescents. *Journal of the American Academy of Child and Adolescent Psychiatry, 38*(4), 453–459.

Alcoholics Anonymous. (1990). Comments on A. A.'s triennial surveys. New York: Alcoholics Anonymous World Services.

Alden, L. (1989). Short-term structured treatment for avoidant personality disorder. *Journal of Consulting and Clinical Psychology, 57,* 756–764.

Alden, L. E. (2001). Interpersonal perspectives on social phobia. In W. R. Crozier & L. E. Alden (Eds.), *International handbook of social anxiety: Research and interventions* (pp. 381–404). New York: Wiley.

Alden, L. E., Bieling, P. J., & Meleshko, K. G. (1995). An interpersonal comparison of depression and social anxiety. In K. Craig & K. S. Dobson (Eds.), *Anxiety and depression in adults and children* (pp. 57–81). Thousand Oaks, CA: Sage.

Alden, L. E., & Capreol, M. J. (1993). Avoidant personality disorder: Interpersonal problems as predictors of treatment response. *Behavior Therapy, 24,* 357–376.

Alden, L. E., Laposa, J. M., & Taylor, C. T. (2006). Avoidant personality disorder. In J. E. Fisher & W. T. O'Donohue (Eds.), *Practitioner's guide to evidence-based psychotherapy* (pp. 115–121). New York Springer Science + Business Media.

Alden, L. E., & Taylor, C. T. (2004). Interpersonal processes in social phobia [Special issue: Social phobia and social anxiety]. *Clinical Psychology Review, 24,* 857–882.

Alden, L. E., & Wallace, S. T. (1995). Social phobia and social appraisal in successful and unsuccessful interactions. *Behaviour Research and Therapy, 33,* 497–506.

Alexander, F. (1950). *Psychosomatic medicine.* New York: Norton.

Alexander, F. G. (1939). Emotional factors in essential hypertension: Presentation of a tentative hypothesis. *Psychosomatic Medicine, 1,* 175–179.

Alexander, F. G., & Selesnick, S. T. (1966). *The history of psychiatry: An evaluation of psychiatric thought and practice from prehistoric times to the present.* New York: Harper & Row.

Alexandra, C. (2000). *Five lost years: A personal exploration of schizophrenia.* Roseville, CA: Dry Bones Press.

Allen, D., & Midwinter, J. (1990, September 30). The debunking of a myth. *Satanic MediaWatch and News Exchange.* Retrieved November 1, 2007, from http://www.smwane.dk/content/view/173/34/

Allen, J., DeMyer, M., Norton, J., Pontius, W., & Yang, G. (1971). Intellectuality in parents of psychotic, subnormal, and normal children. *Journal of Autism and Childhood Schizophrenia, 1,* 311–326.

Allen, J. M., Lam, R. W., Remick, R. A., & Sadovnick, A. D. (1993). Depressive symptoms and family history in seasonal and nonseasonal mood disorders. *American Journal of Psychiatry, 150*(3), 443–448.

Allen, K., Blascovich, J., & Mendes, W. B. (2002). Cardiovascular reactivity in the presence of pets, friends, and spouses: The truth about cats and dogs. *Psychosomatic Medicine, 64,* 727–739.

Allen, L. B., White, K. S., Barlow, D. H., Shear, M. K., Gorman, J. M., & Woods, S. W. (2010). Cognitive-behavior therapy (CBT) for panic disorder: Relationship of anxiety and depression comorbidity with treatment outcome. *Journal of Psychopathology & Behavioral Assessment, 32*(2), 185–192.

Allen, L. S., & Gorski, R. A. (1992). Sexual orientation and the size of the anterior commissure in the human brain. *Proceedings of the National Academy of Science, 89,* 7199–7202.

Allin, M., Streeruwitz, A., & Curtis, V. (2005). Progress in understanding conversation disorder. *Neuropsychiatric Disease and Treatment, 3,* 1–5.

Alloy, L., & Abramson, L. (2001). Cyclothymic personality. In W. E. Craighead & C. B. Nemeroff (Eds.), *The Corsini encyclopedia of psychology and behavioral science* (3rd ed., pp. 417–418). New York: John Wiley & Sons.

Alloy, L., & Abramson, L. (2006). Prospective incidence of first onsets and recurrences of depression individuals at high and low cognitive risk for depression. *Journal of Abnormal Psychology, 115,* 145–156.

Alloy, L. B., Kelly, K. A., Mineka, S., & Clements, C. M. (1990). Comorbidity of anxiety and depressive disorders: A helplessness-hopelessness perspective. In J. D. Maser & C. R. Cloninger (Eds.), *Comorbidity of mood and anxiety disorders* (pp. 499–543). Washington, DC: American Psychiatric Press.

Alpert, M., Clark, A., & Pouget, E. R. (1994). The syntactic role of pauses in the speech of schizophrenic patients with alogia. *Journal of Abnormal Psychology, 103,* 750–757.

Althof, S. (2006). The psychology of premature ejaculation: Therapies and consequences. *Journal of Sexual Medicine, 3,* 324–331.

Alzheimer's Association. (2004). *Aluminum and Alzheimer: Does aluminum play a role in causing Alzheimer's disease?* Retrieved May 21, 2004, from http://www.corrosion-doctors.org/Pollution/Alumin-Alzheimer.htm

Alzheimer's Society of Canada. (2004). *People with Alzheimer disease and related dementias.* Retrieved August 17, 2004, from http://www.alzheimers.ca/english/disease/stats-people.htm

Amat, J., Baratta, B. V., Paul, E., Bland, S. T., Watkins, L. R., & Maier, S. F. (2005). Medial prefrontal cortex determines how stressor controllability affects behavior and dorsal raphe nucleus. *Nature Neuroscience, 8,* 365–371.

American College of Obstetricians and Gynecologists. (2002). Clinical management guidelines for obstetricians-gynecologists: Premenstrual syndrome. *ACOG Practice Bulletin.* No. 15. Washington, DC: American College of Obstetricians and Gynecologists.

American Psychiatric Association. (1980). *Diagnostic and statistical manual of mental disorders* (3rd ed.). Washington, DC: Author.

American Psychiatric Association. (1987). *Diagnostic and statistical manual of mental disorders* (3rd ed. rev.). Washington, DC: Author.

American Psychiatric Association. (1990). *Benzodiazepine dependence, toxicity, and abuse: A task force report of the American Psychiatric Association.* Washington, DC: Author.

American Psychiatric Association. (1993). Practice guidelines for eating disorders. *American Journal of Psychiatry, 150*(2), 212–228.

American Psychiatric Association. (1994). *Diagnostic and statistical manual of mental disorders* (4th ed.). Washington, DC: Author.

American Psychiatric Association. (2000a). *Diagnostic and statistical manual of mental disorders* (4th ed., Text Revision). Washington, DC: Author.

American Psychiatric Association. (2000b). Practice guidelines for the treatment of patients with major depressive disorder (revision). Supplement to *The American Journal of Psychiatry, 157*(4).

American Psychiatric Association. (2000c). Substance use disorders: Alcohol, cocaine, opioids. In *Practice guidelines for the treatment of psychiatric disorders: Compendium 2000* (pp. 139–238). Washington, DC: Author.

American Psychiatric Association. (2000d). Schizophrenia. In *Practice guidelines for the treatment of psychiatric disorders: Compendium 2000* (pp. 200–412). Washington, DC: Author.

American Psychiatric Association. (2000e). *Practice guidelines for the treatment of patients with delirium: Compendium 2000* (pp. 31–68). Washington, DC: Author.

American Psychiatric Association. (2000f). *Practice guidelines for the treatment of patients with Alzheimer's disease and other dementias of late life: Compendium 2000* (pp. 69–137). Washington, DC: Author.

American Psychiatric Association. (2003). Practice guideline for the assessment and treatment of patients with suicidal behaviors. *American Journal of Psychiatry, 160*(Suppl.), 1–44.

American Psychiatric Association. (2006). Practice guideline for the psychiatric evaluation of adults (2nd ed.). *American Journal of Psychiatry, 163*(Suppl.), 1–36.

American Psychiatric Association. (2010a). *APA practice guidelines for treatment of patients with eating disorders* (3rd ed.). Retrieved from http://www.psychiatryonline.com/content.aspx?aID5138866

American Psychiatric Association. (2010b). *DSM-5 development: Personality and personality disorders.* Retrieved from http://www.dsm5.org/ProposedRevisions/Pages/PersonalityandPersonalityDisorders.aspx

American Sleep Disorders Association. (1990). *The international classification of sleep disorders: Diagnostic and coding manual.* Rochester, MN: Author.

Amering, M., & Katschnig, H. (1990). Panic attacks and panic disorder in cross-cultural perspective. *Psychiatric Annals, 20,* 511–516.

Amir, N., Cashman, L., & Foa, E. B. (1997). Strategies of thought control and obsessive-compulsive disorder. *Behaviour Research and Therapy, 35,* 775–777.

Anastasi, A. (1988). *Psychological testing* (6th ed.). New York: Oxford University Press.

Anastopoulos, A., Sommer, J., & Schatz, N. (2009). ADHD and family functioning. *Current Attention Disorders Reports, 1*(4), 167–170.

Anch, A. M., Browman, C. P., Mitler, M. M., & Walsh, J. K. (1988). *Sleep: A scientific perspective.* Englewood Cliffs, NJ: Prentice-Hall.

Ancoli-Israel, S. (2000). Insomnia in the elderly: A review for the primary care practitioner. *Sleep 23*(Suppl. 1), S23–S30.

Ancoli-Israel, S., & Ayalon, L. (2009). Diagnosis and treatment of sleep disorders in older adults. *Focus: The Journal of Lifelong Learning in Psychiatry, 7*(1), 98–105.

Andersen, B. L., & Cyranowski, J. M. (1994). Women's sexual self-schema. *Journal of Personality and Social Psychology, 67*(6), 1079–1100.

Andersen, B. L., Cyranowski, J. M., & Espindle, D. (1999). Men's sexual self-schema. *Journal of Personality and Social Psychology, 76*(4), 645–661.

Andersen, B. L., Kiecolt-Glaser, J. K., & Glaser, R. (1994). A biobehavioral model of cancer stress and disease course. *American Psychologist, 49,* 389–404.

Anderson, B., & Baum, A. (2001). *Psychosocial intervention for cancer.* Washington, DC: American Psychological Association.

Anderson-Fye, E. (2009). Cross-cultural issues in body image among children and adolescents. In L. Smolak & J. K. Thompson (Eds.), *Body image, eating disorders, and obesity in youth: Assessment, prevention, and treatment* (2nd ed., pp. 113–133). Washington, DC: American Psychological Association.

Andrade, L., Caraveo-Anduaga, J. J., Berglund, P., Bijl, R. V., de Graaf, R., Vollegergh, W., … Wittchen, H. U. (2003). The epidemiology of major depressive episodes: results from the International Consortium of Psychiatric Epidemiology (ICPE) Surveys. *International Journal of Methods in Psychiatric Research, 12*(1), 3–21.

Andrasik, F. (2000). Biofeedback. In D. I. Mostofsky & D. H. Barlow (Eds.), *The management of stress and anxiety in medical disorders* (pp. 66–83). Needham Heights, MA: Allyn & Bacon.

Andreasen, N. C. (1979). Thought, language, and communication disorders: I. Clinical assessment, definition of terms, and evaluation of their reliability. *Archives of General Psychiatry, 36,* 1315–1321.

Andreasen, N. C., & Bardach, J. (1977). Dysmorphophobia: Symptom or disease? *American Journal of Psychiatry, 134,* 673–676.

Andreasen, N. C., & Carpenter, W. T., Jr. (1993). Diagnosis and classification of schizophrenia. *Schizophrenia Bulletin, 19*(2), 199–214.

Andreasen, N. C., & Swayze, V. W. (1993). Neuroimaging. In J. A. Costae Silva & C. C. Nadelson (Eds.), *International review of psychiatry* (Vol. 1). Washington, DC: American Psychiatric Press.

Andreasen, N. C., Rezai, K., Alliger, R., Swayze, V. W., Flaum, M., Kirchner, P., … O'Leary, D. S. (1992). Hypofrontality in neuroleptic-naive patients and in-patients with chronic schizophrenia: Assessment with xenon 133 single-photon emission computed tomography with the Tower of London. *Archives of General Psychiatry, 49,* 943–958.

Andrews, G., Hobbs, M. J., Borkovec, T. D., Beesdo, K., Craske, M. G., Heimberg, R. G., … Stanley, M. A. (2010). Generalized worry disorder: A review of DSM-IV generalized anxiety disorder and options for DSM-V. *Depression and Anxiety, 27*(2), 134–147.

Andrews, G., Morris-Yates, A., Howie, P., & Martin, N. G. (1991). Genetic factors in stuttering confirmed. *Archives of General Psychiatry, 48,* 1034–1035.

Aneshensel, C. S., Pearlin, L. I., Mullan, J. T., Zarit, S. H., & Whitlatch, C. J. (1995). *Profiles in caregiving: The unexpected career.* San Diego, CA: Academic Press.

Angst, A., Angst, F., Gerber-Werder, R., & Gamma, A. (2005). Suicide in 406 mood disordered patients with and without long-term medication: A 40 to 44 years' follow-up. *Archives Suicide Research, 9,* 279–300.

Angst, J. (1988). Clinical course of affective disorders. In T. Helgason & R. J. Daly (Eds.), *Depressive illness: Prediction of course and outcome* (pp. 1–44). Berlin: Springer-Verlag.

Angst, J. (2009). Course and prognosis of mood disorders. In M. G. Gelder, N. C. Andreasen, J. J. López-Ibor, Jr., & J. R. Geddes (Eds.), *New Oxford textbook of psychiatry* (Vol. 1, 2nd ed., pp. 665–669). Oxford: Oxford University Press.

Angst, J., & Preizig, M. (1996). Course of a clinical cohort of unipolar, bipolar and schizoaffective patients: Results of a prospective study from 1959 to 1985. *Schweizer Archiv fur Neurologie und Psychiatrie, 146,* 1–16.

Angst, J., & Sellaro, R. (2000). Historical perspectives and natural history of bipolar disorder. *Biological Psychiatry, 48*(6), 445–457.

Angst, J., Sellaro, R., Stolar, M., Merikangas, K. R., & Endicott, J. (2001). The epidemiology of premenstrual psychological symptoms. *Acta Psychiatrica Scandinavica, 104,* 110–116.

Anisman, H., Zaharia, M. D., Meaney, M. J., & Merali, Z. (1998). Do early life events permanently alter behavioral and hormonal responses to stressors? *International Journal of Developmental Neuroscience, 16,* 149–164.

Anthenelli, R. M., & Schuckit, M. A. (1997). Genetics. In J. H. Lowinson, P. Ruiz, R. B. Millman, & J. G. Langrod (Eds.), *Substance abuse: A comprehensive textbook* (pp. 41–51). Baltimore: Williams & Wilkins.

Antle, M. C., & Silver, R. (2005). Orchestrating time: Arrangements of the brain circadian clock. *Trends in Neurosciences, 28,* 145–151.

Anton, B., & Leff, L. P. (2006). A novel bivalent morphine/heroin vaccine that prevents relapse to heroin addiction in rodents. *Vaccine, 24*(16), 3232–3240.

Anton, R. F. (1999). What is craving? Models and implications for treatment. *Alcohol Research & Health, 23*(3), 165–173.

Anton, R. F., O'Malley, S. S., Ciraulo, D. A., Cisler, R. A., Couper, D., Donovan, D. M., … Zweben, A. for the COMBINE Study Research Group. (2006). Combined pharmacotherapies and behavioral interventions for alcohol dependence: The COMBINE Study: A randomized controlled trial. *JAMA, 295,* 2003–2017.

Antoni, M. H., Baggett, L., Ironson, G., LaPerriere, A., August, S., Klimas, N., … Fletcher, M. A. (1991). Cognitive-behavioral stress management intervention buffers distress responses and immunologic changes following notification of HIV-1 seropositivity. *Journal of Consulting and Clinical Psychology, 59*(6), 906–915.

Antoni, M. H., Cruess, D. G., Cruess, S., Lutgendorf, S., Kumar, M., Ironson, G., … Schneiderman, N. (2000). Cognitive-behavioral stress management intervention effects on anxiety, 24-hr urinary norepinephrine output, and T-cytotoxic/suppressor cells over time among symptomatic HIV-infected gay men. *Journal of Consulting and Clinical Psychology, 68,* 31–45.

Antony, M. M., & Barlow, D. H. (2002). Specific phobias. In D. H. Barlow (Ed.), *Anxiety and its disorders: The nature and treatment of anxiety and panic* (2nd ed., pp. 380–417). New York, NY: Guilford Press.

Antony, M. M., Brown, T. A., & Barlow, D. H. (1997a). Heterogeneity among specific phobia types in DSM-IV. *Behavior Research and Therapy, 35,* 1089–1100.

Antony, M. M., Brown, T. A., & Barlow, D. H. (1997b). Response to hyperventilation and 5.5% CO$_2$ inhalation of subjects with types of specific phobia, panic disorder, or no mental disorder. *The American Journal of Psychiatry, 154,* 1089–1095.

Antony, M. M., Craske, M. G., & Barlow, D. H. (1995). *Mastery of your specific phobia, client workbook.* San Antonio, TX: Graywind Publications Incorporated/The Psychological Corporation.

Antony, M. M., & McCabe, R. E. (2002). Empirical basis of panic control treatment. *Scientific Review of Mental Health Practice, 1,* 189–194.

Antony, M. M., McCabe, R. E., Leeuw, I., Sano, N., & Swinson, R. P. (2001). Effect of distraction and coping style on in vivo exposure for specific phobia of spiders. *Behaviour Research and Therapy, 39,* 1137–1150.

Antony, M. M., Rowa, K., Liss, A., Swallow, S. R., & Swinson, R. P. (2005). Social comparison processes in social phobia. *Behavior Therapy, 36,* 65–75.

Anzengruber, D., Klump, K. L., Thornton, L., Brandt, H., Crawford, S., Fichter, M. M., ... Bulik, C. M. (2006). Smoking in eating disorders. *Eating Behaviors, 7,* 291–299.

Aouizerate, B., Rotge, J., Martin-Guehl, C., Cuny, E., Rougier, A., Guehl, D., ... Tignol, J. (2006). A systematic review of psychsurgical treatments for obsessive-compulsive disorder: Does deep brain stimulation represent the future trend in psychosurgery? *Clinical Neuropsychiatry, 3*(6), 391–403.

Apfelbaum, B. (2000). Retarded ejaculation: A much misunderstood syndrome. In S. R. Leiblum & R. C. Rosen (Eds.), *Principles and practice of sex therapy* (3rd ed., pp. 205–241). New York: Guilford Press.

Archer, R. P., & Krishnamurthy, R. (1996). The Minnesota Multiphasic Personality Inventory-Adolescent (MMPI-A). In C. S. Newmark (Ed.), *Major psychological assessment instruments* (pp. 59–107). Boston: Allyn & Bacon.

Arai, J. A., Li, S., Hartley, D. M., & Feig, L. A. (2009). Transgenerational rescue of a genetic defect in long-term potentiation and memory formation by juvenile enrichment. *The Journal of Neuroscience, 29*(5), 1496–1502.

Arenas, E. (2010). Towards stem cell replacement therapies for Parkinson's disease. *Biochemical and Biophysical Research Communications, 396*(1), 152–156.

Arendt, J., Stone, B., & Skene, D. (2000). Jet lag and sleep disruption. In M. H. Kryger, T. Roth, & W. C. Dement (Eds.), *Principles and practice of sleep medicine* (3rd ed., pp. 591–599). Philadelphia: W. B. Saunders.

Arenkiel, B. R., & Ehlers, M. D. (2009). Molecular genetics and imaging technologies for circuit-based neuroanatomy. *Nature, 461*(7266), 900–907.

Armbruster, D., Mueller, A., Moser, D. A., Lesch, K. P., Brocke, B., & Kirschbaum, C. (2009). Interaction effect of D4 dopamine receptor gene and serotonin transporter promoter polymorphism on the cortisol stress response. *Behavioral Neuroscience, 123*(6), 1288–1295.

Armstrong, H. E. (1993). Review of psychosocial treatments for schizophrenia. In D. L. Dunner (Ed.), *Current psychiatric therapy* (pp. 183–188). Philadelphia: W. B. Saunders.

Arrindell, W. A., Eisemann, M., Richter, J., Oei, T. P. S., Caballo, V. E., van der Ende, J., ... Hudson, B. L. (2003). Phobic anxiety in 11 nations Part I: Dimensional constancy of the five-factor model. *Behaviour Research and Therapy, 41,* 461–479.

Asarnow, J. R. (1994). Annotation: Childhood-onset schizophrenia. *Journal of Child Psychology and Psychiatry, 35,* 1345–1371.

Asberg, M., Nordstrom, P., & Traskman-Bendz, L. (1986). Cerebrospinal fluid studies in suicide: An overview. *Annals of the American Academy of Science, 487,* 243–255.

Aschoff, J., & Wever, R. (1962). Spontanperiodik des Menschen die Ausschulus aller Zeitgeber. *Die Naturwissenschaften, 49,* 337–342.

Ashbaugh, A. R., Antony, M. M., & McCabe, R. E. (2005). Self-evaluative biases in social anxiety. *Cognitive Therapy and Research, 29,* 387–398.

Asmundson, G. J., & Carleton, R. N. (2009). Fear of pain. In M. M. Antony & M. B. Stein (Eds.), *Oxford handbook of anxiety and related disorders* (pp. 551–561). Oxford, UK: Oxford University Press.

Asmundson, G. J. G., Carleton, R. N., Wright, K. D., & Taylor, S. (2004). Psychological sequelae of remote exposure to the September 11th terrorist attacks in Canadians with and without panic. *Cognitive Behaviour Therapy, 33*(2), 49–50.

Asmundson, G. J. G., Jacobson, S. J., Allerdings, M. D., & Norton, G. R. (1996). Social phobia in disabled workers with chronic musculoskeletal pain. *Behaviour Research & Therapy, 34,* 939–943.

Asmundson, G. J. G., Norton, G. R., & Stein, M. B. (2002). *Clinical research in mental health: A practical guide.* Thousand Oaks, CA: Sage.

Asmundson, G. J. G., & Stein, M. B. (1994). Selective processing of social threat in patients with generalized social phobia: Evaluation using a dot-probe paradigm. *Journal of Anxiety Disorders, 8,* 107–117.

Asmundson, G. J. G., & Taylor, S. (2005). *It's not all in your head: How worrying about your health could be making you sick—and what you can do about it.* New York: Guilford.

Asmundson, G. J. G., Taylor, S., & Cox, B. J. (Eds.). (2001). *Health anxiety: Clinical and research perspectives on hypochondriasis and related disorders.* New York: John Wiley & Sons.

Asmundson, G. J. G., Taylor, S., Sevgur, S., & Cox, B. J. (2001). Health anxiety: Conceptual, diagnostic, and epidemiological issues. In G. J. G. Asmundson, S. Taylor, & B. J. Cox (Eds.), *Health anxiety: Clinical and research perspectives on hypochondriasis and related disorders* (pp. 3–21). London: Wiley.

Attia, E., Haiman, C., Walsh, B. T., & Flater, S. R. (1998). Does fluoxetine augment the inpatient treatment of anorexia nervosa? *American Journal of Psychiatry, 155*(4), 548–551.

Attia, E., & Roberto, C. A. (2009). Should amenorrhea be a diagnostic criterion for anorexia nervosa? *International Journal of Eating Disorders, 42*(7), 581–589.

Attie, I., & Brooks-Gunn, J. (1995). The development of eating regulation across the life span. In D. Cicchetti & D. J. Cohen (Eds.), *Developmental psychopathology* (Vol. 2). New York: Wiley.

Attwood, A., Frith, U., & Hermelin, B. (1988). The understanding and use of interpersonal gesture by autistic and Down syndrome children. *Journal of Autism and Developmental Disorders, 18,* 241–258.

Auchterlonie, S., Phillips, N. A., & Chertkow, H. (2002). Behavioral and electrical brain measures of semantic priming in patients with Alzheimer's disease: Implications for access failure versus deterioration hypotheses. *Brain & Cognition, 48,* 264–267.

Austin, G. W., Jaffe, P., & Friedman, B. (1994). Custody and access assessors: Effects of background and experience on analogue case judgement. *Canadian Journal of Behavioural Science, 26,* 463–475.

Ausubel, D. (1971). The peer group and adolescent conformity. *Delta* (Nov), 50–64.

Autism Genome Project Consortium. (2007). Mapping autism risk loci using genetic linkage and chromosomal rearrangements. *Nature Genetics, 39,* 319–328.

Ayala, E. S., Meuret, A. E., & Ritz, T. (2009). Treatments for blood-injury-injection phobia: A critical review of current evidence. *Journal of Psychiatric Research, 43*(15), 1235–1242.

Ayers, C. R., Thorp, S. R., & Wetherell, J. L. (2009). Anxiety disorders and hoarding in older adults. In M. M. Antony & M. B. Stein (Eds.), *Oxford handbook of anxiety and related disorders* (pp. 625–635). New York: Oxford University Press.

Ayllon, T., & Azrin, N. H. (1968). *The token economy: A motivational system for therapy and rehabilitation.* New York: Appleton-Century-Crofts.

Ayllon, T., & Michael, J. (1959). The psychiatric nurse as a behavioral engineer. *Journal of the Experimental Analysis of Behavior, 2,* 323–334.

Azmitia, E. C. (1978). The serotonin-producing neurons of the midbrain median and dorsal raphe nuclei. In L. Iverson, S. Iverson, & S. Snyder (Eds.), *Handbook of psychopharmacology: Vol. 9. Chemical pathways in the brain* (pp. 233–314). New York: Plenum Press.

Bacchiochi, J. R., & Bagby, R. M. (2006). Development and validation of the malingering discriminant function index for the MMPI-2. *Journal of Personality Assessment, 87,* 51–61.

Bach, A. K., Brown, T. A., & Barlow, D. H. (1999). The effects of false negative feedback on efficacy expectancies and sexual arousal in sexually functional males. *Behavior Therapy, 30,* 79–95.

Bach, A. K., Wincze, J. P., & Barlow, D. H. (2001). Sexual dysfunction. In D. H. Barlow (Ed.), *Clinical handbook of psychological disorders: A step-by-step treatment manual* (3rd ed.). New York: Guilford Press.

Bachrach, L. L. (1994). Deinstitutionalization and service priorities in Canada and the United States. In L. L. Bachrach & P. Goering (Eds.), *Mental health care in Canada* (pp. 3–9). San Francisco: Jossey-Bass.

Baer, D. M., Wolf, M. M., & Risley, T. R. (1968). Some current dimensions of applied behavior analysis. *Journal of Applied Behavior Analysis, 1,* 91–97.

Baer, R. A., & Krietemeyer, J. (2008). Overview of mindfulness- and acceptance-based treatment approaches. In R. A. Baer (Ed.), *Mindfulness-based treatment approaches: Clinician's guide to evidence base and applications* (pp. 3–27). Burlington, MA: Academic Press.

Bagby, R. M., Joffe, R. T., Parker, J. D. A., & Schuller, D. R. (1993). Re-examination of the evidence for the DSM-III personality disorder clusters. *Journal of Personality Disorders, 7,* 320–328.

Bagby, R. M., Marshall, M. B., & Bacchiochi, J. R. (2005). The validity and clinical utility of the MMPI-2 malingering depression scale. *Journal of Personality Assessment, 85,* 304–311.

Bagby, R. M., Marshall, M. B., & Georgiades, S. (2005). Dimensional personality traits and the prediction of DSM-IV personality disorder symptom counts in a nonclinical sample. *Journal of Personality Disorders, 19,* 53–67.

Bagby, R. M., Nicholson, R. A., Bacchiochi, J. R., Ryder, A. G., & Bury, A. S. (2002). The predictive capacity of the MMPI-2 and PAI validity scales and indexes to detect coached and uncoached feigning. *Journal of Personality Assessment, 78,* 69–86.

Bagby, R. M., Ryder, A. G., & Cristi, C. (2002). Psychosocial and clinical predictors of response to pharmacotherapy for depression. *Journal of Psychiatry & Neuroscience, 27,* 250–257.

Bailey, J. A. (2009). Addressing common risk and protective factors can prevent a wide range of adolescent risk behaviors. *Journal of Adolescent Health, 45*(2), 107–108.

Bailey, J. M. (2003). *The man who would be queen: The science of gender-bending and transsexualism.* Washington, DC: National Academy Press.

Bailey, J. M., & Benishay, D. S. (1993). Familial aggregation of female sexual orientation. *American Journal of Psychiatry, 150*(2), 272–277.

Bailey, J. M., & Pillard, R. C. (1991). A genetic study of male sexual orientation. *Archives of General Psychiatry, 48,* 1089–1096.

Bailey, J. M., Pillard, R. C., Dawood, K., Miller, M. B., Farrer, L. A., Trivedi, S., & Murphy, R. L. (1999). A family history study of male sexual orientation using three independent samples. *Behavior Genetics, 29,* 79–86.

Bailey, J. M., Pillard, R. C., Neale, M. C., & Agyei, Y. (1993). Heritable factors influence sexual orientation in women. *Archives of General Psychiatry, 50,* 217–223.

Baker, A., van Kesteren, P. J., Gooren, L. J. G., & Bezemer, P. D. (1993). The prevalence of trans-sexualism in The Netherlands. *Acta Psychiatrica Scandinavica, 87,* 237–238.

Baker, B., Richter, A., & Anand, S. S. (2001). From the heartland: Culture, psychological factors, and coronary heart disease. In S. S. Kazarian & D. R. Evans (Eds.), *Handbook of cultural health psychology* (pp. 141–162), San Diego, CA: Academic Press.

Baker, C. D., & DeSilva, P. (1988). The relationship between male sexual dysfunction and belief in Zilbergeld's myths: An empirical investigation. *Sexual and Marital Therapy, 3*(2), 229–238.

Bakkevig, J. F., & Karterud, S. (2010). Is the Diagnostic and Statistical Manual of Mental Disorders, Fourth Edition, histrionic personality disorder category a valid construct? *Comprehensive Psychiatry, 51*(5), 462–470.

Baldessarini, R. J. (1989). Current status of anti-depressants: Clinical pharmacology and therapy. *Journal of Clinical Psychiatry, 50*(4), 117–126.

Baldwin, J. D., & Baldwin, J. I. (1989). The socialization of homosexuality and heterosexuality in a non-Western society. *Archives of Sexual Behavior, 18,* 13–29.

Balfour, L., Kowal, J., Silverman, A., Tasca, G. A., Angel, J. B., Macpherson, P. A., ... Cameron, D. W. (2006). A randomized controlled psycho-education intervention trial: Improving psychological readiness for successful HIV medication adherence and reducing depression before initiating HAART. *AIDS Care, 18*(7), 830–838.

Ball, J. C., & Ross, A. (1991). *The effectiveness of methadone maintenance treatment.* New York: Springer-Verlag.

Ballenger, J. C., Burrows, G. D., DuPont, R. L., Lesser, I. M., Noyes, R., Pecknold, J. C., ... Swinson, R. P. (1988). Alprazolam in panic disorder and agoraphobia: Results from a multi-center trial: I. Efficacy in short-term treatment. *Archives of General Psychiatry, 45,* 413–422.

Balon, R. (2006). SSRI-associated sexual dysfunction. *American Journal of Psychiatry, 163,* 1504–1512.

Balon, R., Segraves, R., & Clayton, A. (2007). Issues for DSM-V: Sexual dysfunction, disorder, or variation along normal distribution—Toward rethinking DSM criteria of sexual dysfunctions. *American Journal of Psychiatry, 164,* 198–200.

Bancroft, J. (1989). *Human sexuality and its problems* (2nd ed.). Edinburgh: Churchill Livingstone.

Bancroft, J. (1994). Homosexual orientation: The search for a biological basis. *British Journal of Psychiatry, 164,* 437–440.

Bancroft, J. (1997). Sexual problems. In D. M. Clark & C. G. Fairburn (Eds.), *Science and practice of cognitive behavior therapy* (pp. 243–257). New York: Oxford University Press.

Bandura, A. (1973). *Aggression: A social learning analysis.* Englewood Cliffs, NJ: Prentice-Hall.

Bandura, A. (1986). *Social foundations of thought and action: A social cognitive theory.* Englewood Cliffs, NJ: Prentice-Hall.

Bandura, A., & McDonald, F. J. (1963). Influence of social reinforcement and the behavior of models in shaping children's moral judgment. *Journal of Abnormal & Social Psychology, 67,* 274–281.

Bandura, A., Jeffery, R., & Bachicha, D. L. (1974). Analysis of memory codes and cumulative rehearsal in observational learning. *Journal of Research in Personality, 7,* 295–305.

Bandura, A., O'Leary, A., Taylor, C. B., Gauthier, J., & Gossard, D. (1987). Perceived self-efficacy and pain control: Opioid and nonopioid mechanisms. *Journal of Personality and Social Psychology, 53,* 563–571.

Bandura, A., Ross, D., & Ross, S. A. (1961). Transmission of aggression through imitation of aggressive models. *Journal of Abnormal & Social Psychology, 63,* 575–582.

Bandura, A., Ross, D., & Ross, S. A. (1963). Imitation of film-mediated aggressive models. *Journal of Abnormal & Social Psychology, 66,* 3–11.

Bankert, E. A., & Amdur, R. J. (2006). *Institutional Review Board: Management and function.* Boston: Jones and Bartlett Publishers.

Barbaree, H. E., & Seto, M. C. (1997). Pedophilia: Assessment and treatment. In D. R. Laws & W. O. O'Donohue (Eds.), *Sexual deviance: Theory, assessment, and treatment* (pp. 175–193). New York: Guilford Press.

Bargh, J. A., & Chartrand, T. L. (1999). The unbearable automaticity of being. *American Psychologist, 54,* 462–479.

Barinaga, M. (1997, June 27). New imaging methods provide a better view into the brain. *Science, 276,* 1974–1976.

Barker, E. T., Williams, R. L., & Galambos, N. L. (2006). Daily spillover to and from Binge Eating in First-Year University Females. *Eating Disorders, 14,* 229–242.

Barkley, R. A. (1989). Attention deficit-hyperactivity disorder. In E. J. Mash & R. A. Barkley (Eds.), *Treatment of childhood disorders* (pp. 39–72). New York: Guilford Press.

Barkley, R. A. (1990). *Attention deficit hyperactivity disorder: A handbook for diagnosis and treatment.* New York: Guilford Press.

Barkley, R. A. (2006). Etiologies. In R. A. Barkley (Ed.), *Attention-deficit hyperactivity disorder: A handbook for diagnosis and treatment* (3rd ed., pp. 219–247). New York: Guilford Press.

Barkley, R. A., Murphy, K. R., & Kwasnik, D. (1996). Motor vehicle driving competencies and risks in teens and young adults with attention deficit hyperactivity disorder. *Pediatrics, 98,* 1089–1095.

Barlow, D. H. (1986). Causes of sexual dysfunction: The role of anxiety and cognitive interference. *Journal of Consulting and Clinical Psychology, 54,* 140–148.

Barlow, D. H. (1988). *Anxiety and its disorders: The nature and treatment of anxiety and panic.* New York: Guilford Press.

Barlow, D. H. (1991). Disorders of emotion. *Psychological Inquiry, 2*(1), 58–71.

Barlow, D. H. (1993). Covert sensitization for paraphilia. In J. R. Cautela & A. J. Kearney (Eds.), *Covert conditioning casebook* (pp. 187–198). Pacific Grove, CA: Brooks/Cole.

Barlow, D. H. (2000). Unraveling the mysteries of anxiety and its disorders from the perspective of emotion theory. *American Psychologist, 55,* 1245–1263.

Barlow, D. H. (2002). *Anxiety and its disorders: The nature and treatment of anxiety and panic* (2nd ed.). New York: Guilford Press.

Barlow, D. H., Abel, G. G., & Blanchard, E. B. (1979). Gender identity change in transsexuals: Follow-up and replications. *Archives of General Psychiatry, 36,* 1001–1007.

Barlow, D. H., Allen, L. B., & Choate, M. L. (2004). Toward a unified treatment for emotional disorders. *Behavior Therapy, 35,* 205–230.

Barlow, D. H., Becker, R., Leitenberg, H., & Agras, W. S. (1970). A mechanical strain gauge for recording penile circumference change. *Journal of Applied Behavior Analysis, 3,* 73–76.

Barlow, D. H., Brown, T. A., & Craske, M. G. (1994). Definitions of panic attacks and panic disorder in DSM-IV: Implications for research. *Journal of Abnormal Psychology, 103,* 553–554.

Barlow, D. H., Chorpita, B. F., & Turovsky, J. (1996). Fear, panic, anxiety, and disorders of emotion. In D. A. Hope (Ed.), The 43rd Annual Nebraska Symposium on Motivation. *Perspectives on anxiety, panic and fear* (pp. 251–328). Lincoln: Nebraska University Press.

Barlow, D. H., & Craske, M. G. (1989). *Mastery of your anxiety and panic.* Albany, NY: Graywind.

Barlow, D. H., & Craske, M. G. (2000). *Mastery of your anxiety and panic: Client workbook for anxiety and panic* (3rd ed.). San Antonio, TX: Graywind Publications/ Psychological Corporation.

Barlow, D. H., Gorman, J. M., Shear, K. M., & Woods, S. W. (2000). Cognitive-behavioral therapy, imipramine, or their combination for panic disorder: A randomized controlled trial. *JAMA, 283*(19), 2529–2536.

Barlow, D. H., Hayes, S. C., & Nelson, R. O. (1984). *The scientist practitioner: Research and accountability in clinical and educational settings.* Boston: Allyn & Bacon.

Barlow, D. H., Hayes, S. C., Nelson, R. O., Steele, D. L., Meeler, M. E., & Mills, J. R. (1979). Sex role motor behavior: A behavioral checklist. *Behavioral Assessment, 1,* 119–138.

Barlow, D. H., & Hersen, M. (1984). *Single case experimental design: Strategies for studying behavior change.* Elmsford, NY: Pergamon Press.

Barlow, D. H., & Lehman, C. L. (1996). Advances in the psychosocial treatment of anxiety disorders: Implications for national health care. *Archives of General Psychiatry, 53,* 727–735.

Barlow, D. H., & Liebowitz, M. R. (1995). Specific and social phobias. In H. I. Kaplan & B. J. Sadock (Eds.), *Comprehensive textbook of psychiatry: VI* (pp. 1204–1217). Baltimore: Williams & Wilkins.

Barlow, D. H., Nock, M. K., & Hersen, M. (2009). *Single case experimental designs: Strategies for studying behavior change* (3rd ed.). New York: Allyn & Bacon.

Barlow, D. H., Pincus, D. B., Heinrichs, N., & Choate, M. (2003). Anxiety disorders: A Lifespan developmental perspective. In I. Weiner (Ed.), *Comprehensive Handbook of Psychology* (Vol. 8, pp.119–147). New York: John Wiley & Sons.

Barlow, D. H., Rapee, R. M., & Reisner, L. C. (2001). *Mastering stress 2001: A lifestyle approach.* Dallas, TX: American Health.

Barlow, D. H., Reynolds, E. J., & Agras, W. S. (1973). Gender identity change in a transsexual. *Archives of General Psychiatry, 28,* 569–576.

Barlow, D. H., & Wincze, J. P. (1980). Treatment of sexual deviations. In S. R. Leiblum & L. A. Pervin (Eds.), *Principles and practice of sex therapy* (pp. 347–375). New York: Guilford Press.

Barnard, A. (2000, September 12). When plastic surgeons should just say "no." *Boston Globe*, pp. E1, E3.

Barnes, G. E., & Toews, J. (1983). Deinstitutionalization of chronic mental patients in the Canadian context. *Canadian Psychology, 24,* 22–36.

Barnes, J. (1981). Non-consummation of marriage. *Irish Medical Journal, 74,* 19–21.

Barnes, J., Bowman, E. P., & Cullen, J. (1984). Biofeedback as an adjunct to psychotherapy in the treatment of vaginismus. *Biofeedback and Self-Regulation, 9,* 281–289.

Barnett, P. A., & Gotlib, I. H. (1988). Psychosocial functioning and depression: Distinguishing among antecedents, concomitants and consequences. *Psychological Bulletin, 104*(1), 97–126.

Baron, M., Gruen, R., Asnis, L., & Lord, S. (1985). Familial transmission of schizotypal and borderline personality disorders. *American Journal of Psychiatry, 142,* 927–934.

Baron, M., Risch, N., Hamburger, R., Mandel, B., Kushner, S., Newman, M., ... Belmaker, R. H. (1987). Genetic linkage between X-chromosome markers and bipolar affective illness. *Nature, 326,* 289–292.

Baron-Cohen, S., Tager-Flusberg, H., & Cohen, D. J. (Eds.). (1994). *Understanding other minds: Perspectives from autism.* London: Oxford University Press.

Barr, H. M., & Streissguth, A. P. (2001). Identifying maternal self-reported alcohol use associated with fetal alcohol spectrum disorders. *Alcoholism, Clinical and Experimental Research, 25,* 283–287.

Barrett, D. H., Resnick, H. S., Foy, D. W., Dansky, B. S., Flanders, W. D., & Stroup, N. E. (1996). Combat exposure and adult psychosocial adjustment among U.S. army veterans serving in Vietnam, 1965–1971. *Journal of Abnormal Psychology, 105,* 575–581.

Barrett, J. E., Barrett, J. A., Oxman, T. E., & Gerber, P. D. (1988). The prevalence of psychiatric disorders in a primary care practice. *Archives of General Psychiatry, 45,* 1100–1106.

Barrett, P. M., Dadds, M. R., & Rapee, R. M. (1996). Family treatment of childhood anxiety: A controlled trial. *Journal of Consulting and Clinical Psychology, 64,* 333–342.

Barrett, R., Loa, P., Jerah, E., Nancarrow, D., Chant, D., & Mowry, B. (2005). Rates of treated schizophrenia and its clinical and cultural features in the population isolate of the Iban of Sarawak: A tri-diagnostic approach. *Psychological Medicine, 35,* 281–293.

Barrett, S. P., Darredeau, C., & Pihl, R. O. (2006a). Patterns of simultaneous polysubstance use in drug using university students. *Human Psychopharmacology: Clinical and Experimental, 21*(4), 255–263.

Barrett, S. P., Tichauer, M., Leyton, M., & Pihl, R. O. (2006b). Nicotine increases alcohol self-administration in non-dependent male smokers. *Drug and Alcohol Dependence, 81*(2), 197–204.

Barrowclough, C., & Tarrier, N. (1998). The application of expressed emotion to clinical work in schizophrenia. *In Session: Psychotherapy in Practice, 4*(3), 7–23.

Barsky, A. J., Fama, J. M., Bailey, E. D., & Ahern, D. K. (1998). A prospective 4 to 5 year study

of DSM-III-R hypochondriasis. *Archives of General Psychiatry, 55*(8), 737–744.

Barsky, A. J., Frank, C. B., Cleary, P. D., Wyshak, G., & Klerman, G. L. (1991). The relation between hypochondriasis and age. *American Journal of Psychiatry, 148,* 923–928.

Barsky, A. J., & Wyshak, G. (1990). Hypochondriasis and somatosensory amplification. *British Journal of Psychiatry, 157,* 404–409.

Barsky, A. J., Wyshak, G., & Klerman, G. L. (1986). Hypochondriasis: An evaluation of the DSM-III criteria in medical outpatients. *Archives of General Psychiatry, 43,* 493–500.

Barsky, A. J., Wyshak, G., Klerman, G. L., & Latham, K. S. (1990). The prevalence of hypochondriasis in medical outpatients. *Social Psychiatry and Psychiatric Epidemiology, 25*(2), 89–94.

Bartlett, N. H., Vasey, P. L., & Bukowski, W. M. (2000). Is gender identity disorder in children a mental disorder? *Sex Roles, 43,* 753–785.

Bartlik, B., & Goldberg, J. (2000). Female sexual arousal disorder. In S. R. Leiblum & R. C. Rosen (Eds.), *Principles and practice of sex therapy* (3rd ed., pp. 85–117). New York: Guilford Press.

Basoglu, M., Marks, I., Livanou, M., & Swinson, R. (1997). Double-blindness procedures, rater blindness, and ratings of outcome: Observations from a controlled trial. *Archives of General Psychiatry, 54,* 744–748.

Bassett, A. S., Chow, E. W., Waterworth, D. M., & Brzustowicz, L. (2001). Genetic insights into schizophrenia. *Canadian Journal of Psychiatry, 46*(2), 131–137.

Bassetti, C., & Aldrich, M. (1996). Narcolepsy. *Neurology Clinics, 14,* 545–571.

Bassiri, A. G., & Guilleminault, C. (2000). Clinical features and evaluation of obstructive sleep apnea-hypopnea syndrome. In M. H. Kryger, T. Roth, & W. C. Dement (Eds.), *Principles and practice of sleep medicine* (3rd ed., pp. 869–878). Philadelphia: W. B. Saunders.

Basson, R. (2001). Using a different model for female sexual response to address women's problematic low sexual desire. *Journal of Sex & Marital Therapy, 27,* 395–403.

Basson, R. (2006). Sexual desire and arousal disorders in women. *New England Journal of Medicine, 354,* 1497–1506.

Basson, R. (2007). Sexual desire/arousal disorders in women. In S. R. Leiblum (Ed.), *Principles and practice of sex therapy* (4th ed., pp. 25–53). New York: Guilford Press.

Basson, R., Althof, S., Davis, S., Fugl-Meyer, K., Goldstein, I., Leiblum, S., ... Wagner, G. (2004a). Summary of the recommendations on sexual dysfunctions in women. *Journal of Sexual Medicine, 1,* 24–34.

Basson, R., Brotto, L. A., Laan, E., Redmond, G., & Utian, W. H. (2005). Assessment and management of women's sexual dysfunctions: Problematic desire and arousal. *Journal of Sexual Medicine, 2,* 291–300.

Basson, R., Leiblum, S., Brotto, L., Derogatis, L., Fourcroy, J., Fugl-Meyer, K., ... Weijmar Schultz, W. (2004b). Definitions of women's sexual dysfunction reconsidered: Advocating expansion and revision. *Journal of Psychosomatic Obstetrics & Gynecology, 24,* 221–229.

Bastien, C. H., Vallières, A., & Morin, C. M. (2004). Precipitating factors of insomnia. *Behavioral Sleep Medicine, 2,* 50–62.

Bateson, G. (1959). Cultural problems posed by a study of schizophrenic process. In A. Auerback (Ed.), *Schizophrenia: An integrated approach.* New York: Ronald Press.

Bauer, M. S., Calabrese, J., Dunner, D. L., Post, R., Whybrow, P. C., Gyulai, L., ... Price, R. A. (1994). Multisite data reanalysis of the validity of rapid cycling as a course modifier for bipolar disorder in DSM-IV. *American Journal of Psychiatry, 151,* 506–515.

Baxter, L. R., Guze, B. H., & Reynolds, C. A. (1993). Neuroimaging: Uses in psychiatry. In D. L. Dunner (Ed.), *Current psychiatric therapy.* Philadelphia: W. B. Saunders.

Baxter, L. R., Jr., Schwartz, J. M., Bergman, K. S., Szuba, M. P., Guze, B. H., Mazziotta, J. C., ... Phelps, M. E. (1992). Caudate glucose metabolic rate changes with both drug and behavior therapy for obsessive-compulsive disorder. *Archives of General Psychiatry, 49,* 681–689.

Bayer, R. (1987). *Homosexuality and American psychiatry: The politics of diagnosis.* Princeton, NJ: University Press.

Baylé, F. J., Caci, H., Millet, B., Richa, S., & Olié, J. P. (2003). Psychopathology and comorbidity of psychiatric disorders in patients with kleptomania. *American Journal of Psychiatry, 160,* 1509–1513.

Bazana, G. (1999). *Geographic locations survey of clinical psychologists in Canada.* Canadian Psychological Association. Retrieved August 13, 2007, from http://www.cpa.ca/documents/geo-graphic_survey.html

BBC. (2004). *1988: Johnson stripped of Olympic gold.* Retrieved August 17, 2004, from http://news.bbc.co.uk/onthisday/hi/dates/stories/september/27/newsid_2539000/2539525.stm

Beach, S. R. H., Jones, D. J., & Franklin, K. J. (2009). Marital, family, and interpersonal therapies for depression in adults. In I. H. Gotlib & C. L. Hammen (Eds.), *Handbook of depression* (2nd ed., pp. 624–641). New York: Guilford Press.

Beach, S. R. H., Sandeen, E. E., & O'Leary, K. D. (1990). Depression in marriage: A model for etiology and treatment. In D. H. Barlow (Ed.), *Treatment manuals for practitioners.* New York: Guilford Press.

Beard, G. M. (1869). Neurasthenia or nervous exhaustion. *Boston Medical Surgical Journal, 3,* 217–221.

Beard, J. H., Malamud, T. J., & Rossman, E. (1978). Psychiatric rehabilitation and long-term rehospitalization rates: The findings of two research studies. *Schizophrenia Bulletin, 4,* 622–635.

Beard, J. H., Propst, R. N., & Malamud, T. J. (1982). The Fountain House model of psychiatric rehabilitation. *Psychosocial Rehabilitation Journal, 5,* 47–53.

Beardslee, W. R., Salt, P., Versage, E. M., Gladstone, T. R. G., Wright, E. J., & Rothberg, P. C. (1997). Sustained change in parents receiving preventive interventions for families with depression. *American Journal of Psychiatry, 154*(4), 510–515.

Bebbington, P. E., Bowen, J., Hirsch, S. R., & Kuipers, E. A. (1995). Schizophrenia and psychosocial stresses. In S. R. Hirsch and D. R. Weinberger (Eds.), *Schizophrenia* (pp. 587–604). Oxford: Blackwell Science.

Bebbington, P. E., Brugha, T., MacCarthy, B., Potter, J., Sturt, E., Wykes, T., ... McGuffin, P. (1988). The Camberwell Collaborative Depression Study: I. Depressed probands: Adversity and the form of depression. *British Journal of Psychiatry, 152,* 754–765.

Bebbington, P., Wilkins, S., Jones, P., Foerster, A., Murray, R., Toone, B., & Lewis, S. (1993). Life events and psychosis: Initial results from the

Camberwell Collaborative Psychosis Study. *British Journal of Psychiatry, 162,* 72–79.

Bech, P. (2009). Clinical features of mood disorders and mania. In M. G. Gelder, N. C. Andreasen, J. J. López-Ibor, Jr., & J. R. Geddes (Eds.), *New Oxford textbook of psychiatry* (Vol. 1, 2nd ed., pp. 632–637). Oxford: Oxford University Press.

Beck, A. T. (1967). *Depression: Clinical, experimental and theoretical aspects.* New York: Harper & Row.

Beck, A. T. (1976). *Cognitive therapy and the emotional disorders.* New York: International Universities Press.

Beck, A. T. (1983). Cognitive therapy of depression: New perspectives. In P. Clayton & J. E. Barrett (Eds.), *Treatment of depression: Old controversies and new approaches* (pp. 265–290). New York: Raven Press.

Beck, A. T. (1986). Hopelessness as a predictor of eventual suicide. *Annals of the New York Academy of Science, 487,* 90–96.

Beck, A. T. (1987). Cognitive models of depression. *Journal of Cognitive Psychotherapy, 1,* 5–37.

Beck, A. T., Epstein, N., & Harrison, R. (1983). Cognitions, attitudes and personality dimensions in depression. *British Journal of Cognitive Psychotherapy,* 1(1), 1–16.

Beck, A. T., & Freeman, A. (1990). *Cognitive therapy of personality disorders.* New York: Guilford Press.

Beck, A. T., Freeman, A., & Davis, D. D. (2007). *Cognitive therapy of personality disorders* (2nd ed.). New York: Guilford Press.

Beck, A. T., Hollon, S. D., Young, J. E., Bedrosian, R. C., & Budenz, D. (1985). Treatment of depression with cognitive therapy and amitriptyline. *Archives of General Psychiatry, 42,* 142–148.

Beck, A. T., & Rector, N. A. (2000). Cognitive therapy of schizophrenia: A new therapy for the new millennium. *American Journal of Psychotherapy, 54,* 291–300.

Beck, A. T., Steer, R., Kovacs, M., & Garrison, B. (1985). Hopelessness and eventual suicide: A 10-year prospective study of patients hospitalized with suicidal ideation. *American Journal of Psychiatry, 142,* 559–563.

Beck, A. T., & Young, J. E. (1985). Depression. In D. H. Barlow (Ed.), *Clinical handbook of psychological disorders.* New York: Guilford Press.

Beck, C. A., Patten, S. B., Williams, J. V. A., Wang, J. L., Currie, S. R., Maxwell, C. J., & El-Guebaly, N. (2005). Anti-depressant utilization in Canada. *Social Psychiatry and Psychiatric Epidemiology, 40,* 799–807.

Beck, C. A., Williams, J. V. A., Wang, J. L., Kassam, A., El-Guebaly, N., Currie, S. R., … Patten, S. B. (2005). Psychotropic medication use in Canada [Special issue: The Canadian Academy of Psychiatric Epidemiology (CAPE) look at the Canadian Community Health Survey, Cycle 1. 2]. *Canadian Journal of Psychiatry, 50,* 605–613.

Beck, J. G. (1993). Vaginismus. In W. O'Donohue & J. H. Geer (Eds.), *Handbook of sexual dysfunctions: Assessment and treatment* (pp. 381–397). Boston: Allyn & Bacon.

Beck, J. G., & Averill, P. M. (2004). Older adults. In R. G. Heimberg, C. L. Turk, & D. S. Mennin (Eds.), *Generalized anxiety disorder: Advances in research and practice* (pp. 409–433). New York: Guilford Press.

Beck, J. G., & Barlow, D. H. (1984). Unraveling the nature of sex roles. In E. A. Blechman (Ed.), *Behavior modification with women* (pp. 34–59). New York: Guilford Press.

Beck, J. G., & Stanley, M. A. (1997). Anxiety disorders in the elderly: The emerging role of behavior therapy. *Behavior Therapy, 28,* 83–100.

Becker, D. (2000). When she was bad: Borderline personality disorder in a posttraumatic age. *American Journal of Orthopsychiatry, 70,* 422–432.

Becker, J. T., Mestre, L. T., Ziolko, S., & Lopez, O. L. (2007). Gene-environment interactions with cognition in late life and compression of morbidity. *American Journal of Psychiatry, 164*(6), 849–852.

Behl, P., Lanctôt, K. L., Streiner, D. L., Guimont, I., & Black, S. E. (2006). Cholinesterase inhibitors slow decline in executive functions, rather than memory, in Alzheimer's disease: A 1-year observational study in the Sunnybrook dementia cohort. *Current Alzheimer Research, 3,* 147–156.

Beiser, M., Dion, R., & Gotowiec, A. (2000). The structure of attention-deficit and hyperactivity symptoms among Native and non-Native elementary school children. *Journal of Abnormal Child Psychology, 28,* 425–437.

Beiser, M., & Gotowiec, A. (2000). Accounting for Native/non-Native differences in IQ scores. *Psychology in the Schools, 3*(3), 237–252.

Beitchman, J. H., Wilson, B., Douglas, L., Young, A., & Adlaf, E. (2001a). Substance use disorders in young adults with and without LD: Predictive and concurrent relationships. *Journal of Learning Disabilities, 34,* 317–332.

Beitchman, J. H., Wilson, B., Johnson, C. J., Atkinson, L., Young, A., Adlaf, E., … Douglas, L. (2001b). Fourteen-year follow-up of speech/language-impaired and control children: Psychiatric outcome. *Journal of the American Academy of Child & Adolescent Psychiatry, 40,* 75–82.

Beitchman, J. H., & Young, A. R. (1997). Learning disorders with a special emphasis on reading disorders: A review of the past 10 years. *Journal of the American Academy of Child & Adolescent Psychiatry, 36,* 1020–1032.

Bélanger, L., Savard, J., & Morin, C. M. (2006). Clinical management of insomnia using cognitive therapy. *Behavioral Sleep Medicine, 4,* 179–202.

Belger, A., & Dichter, G. (2006). Structural and functional neuroanatomy. In J. A. Lieberman, T. S. Stroup, & D. O. Perkins (Eds.), *The American Psychiatric Publishing textbook of schizophrenia* (pp. 167–185). Washington, DC: American Psychiatric Publishing.

Belik, S. L., Sareen, J., & Stein, M. B. (2009). Anxiety disorders and physical comorbidity. In M. M. Antony & M. B. Stein (Eds.), *Oxford handbook of anxiety and related disorders* (pp. 596–610). New York: Oxford University Press.

Belitsky, C. A., Toner, B. B., Ali, A., Yu, B., Osborne, S. L., & deRooy, E. (1996). Sex-role attitudes and clinical appraisal in psychiatry residents. *Canadian Journal of Psychiatry, 41,* 503–508.

Belitsky, R., & McGlashan, T. H. (1993). The manifestations of schizophrenia in late life: A dearth of data. *Schizophrenia Bulletin, 19,* 683–685.

Belke, T. W., Pierce, W. D., & Duncan, I. D. (2006). Reinforcement value and substitutability of sucrose and wheel running: Implications for a activity anorexia. *Journal of the Experimental Analysis of Behavior, 86*(2), 131–158.

Bell, C. C., Dixie-Bell, D. D., & Thompson, B. (1986). Further studies on the prevalence of isolated sleep paralysis in black subjects. *Journal of the National Medical Association, 75,* 649–659.

Bell, I. R. (1994). Somatization disorder: Health care costs in the decade of the brain. *Biological Psychiatry, 35,* 81–83.

Bellack, A. S., & Mueser, K. T. (1992). Social skills training for schizophrenia? *Archives of General Psychiatry, 49,* 76.

Bellak, L. (1975). *The thematic apperception test, the children's apperception test, and the senior apperception technique in clinical use* (3rd ed.). New York: Grune & Stratton.

Bellamy, G. T., Rhodes, L. E., Mank, D. M., & Albin, J. M. (1988). *Supported employment: A community implementation guide.* Baltimore: Paul H. Brookes.

Bellis, D. J. (1981). *Heroin and politicians: The failure of public policy to control addiction in America.* Westport, CT: Greenwood Press.

Bem, D. J. (1996). Exotic becomes erotic: A developmental theory of sexual orientation. *Psychological Review, 103,* 320–335.

Ben Itzchak, E., Lahat, E., Burgin, R., & Zachor, A. D. (2008). Cognitive, behavior and intervention outcome in young children with autism. *Research in Developmental Disabilities, 29*(5), 447–458.

Benbadis, R. R., & Allen-Hauser, W. (2000). An estimate of the prevalence of psychogenic non-epileptic seizures. *Seizure, 9*(4), 280–281.

Benca, R. M., Obermeyer, W. H., Thisted, R. A., & Gillin, J. C. (1992). Sleep and psychiatric disorders: A meta-analysis. *Archives of General Psychiatry, 49,* 651–668.

Bender, D. S. (2005). Therapeutic alliance. In J. M. Oldham, A. E. Skodol, & D. S. Bender (Eds.), *Textbook of personality disorders* (pp. 405–420). Washington, DC: American Psychiatric Publishing.

Benedetti, A., Perugi, G., Toni, C., Simonetti, B., Mata, B., & Cassano, G. B. (1997). Hypochondriasis and illness phobia in panic-agoraphobic patients. *Comprehensive Psychiatry, 38*(2), 124–131.

Benight, C. C., & Bandura, A. (2004). Social cognitive theory of posttraumatic recovery: The role of perceived self-efficacy. *Behaviour Research and Therapy, 42*(10), 1129–1148.

Bennett, A. H. (1988). Venous arterialization for erectile impotence. *Urologic Clinics of North America, 15,* 111–113.

Bennett, K. J., Lipman, E. L., Brown, S., Racine, Y., Boyle, M. H., & Offord, D. R. (1999). Predicting conduct problems: Can high-risk children be identified in kindergarten and grade 1? *Journal of Consulting and Clinical Psychology, 67,* 470–480.

Bennett-Branson, S. M., & Craig, K. D. (1993). Postoperative pain in children: Developmental and family influences on spontaneous coping strategies. *Canadian Journal of Behavioural Science, 25,* 355–383.

Benowitz, N. L. (1996). Pharmacology of nicotine: Addiction and therapeutics. *Annual Review of Pharmacology and Toxicology, 36,* 597–613.

Benson, H. (1975). *The relaxation response.* New York: William Morrow.

Benson, H. (1984). *Beyond the relaxation response.* New York: Times Books.

Berenbaum, H., & Oltmanns, T. F. (1992). Emotional experience and expression in schizophrenia and depression. *Journal of Abnormal Psychology, 101,* 37–44.

Berkman, L. F., & Syme, S. L. (1979). Social networks, host resistance, and mortality: A nine-year follow-up study of Alameda county residents. *American Journal of Epidemiology, 109,* 186.

Berman, A. L. (2009). Depression and suicide. In I. H. Gotlib & C. L. Hammen (Eds.), *Handbook of depression* (2nd ed., pp. 510 -530). New York: Guilford Press.

Berman, A. L., & Jobes, D. A. (1991). *Adolescent suicide: Assessment and intervention*. Washington, DC: American Psychological Association.

Berman, K. F., & Weinberger, D. R. (1990). Lateralization of cortical function during cognitive tasks: Regional cerebral blood flow studies of normal individuals and patients with schizophrenia. *Journal of Neurology, Neurosurgery and Psychiatry, Neurology, 53,* 150–160.

Berman, T., Douglas, V. I., & Barr, R. G. (1999). Effects of methylphenidate on complex cognitive processing in attention-deficit hyperactivity disorder. *Journal of Abnormal Psychology, 108,* 90–105.

Bernat, J. A., Calhoun, K. S., & Adams, H. E. (1999). Sexually aggressive and nonaggressive men: Sexual arousal and judgments in response to acquaintance rape and consensual analogues. *Journal of Abnormal Psychology, 108,* 662–673.

Berney, A., Sookman, D., Leyton, M., Young, S. N., & Benkelfat, C. (2006). Lack of effects on core obsessive-compulsive symptoms of tryptophan depletion during symptom provocation in remitted obsessive-compulsive disorder patients. *Biological Psychiatry, 59,* 853–857.

Bernstein, D. A., & Borkovec, T. D. (1973). *Progressive relaxation training: A manual for the helping professions.* Champaign, IL: Research Press.

Bernstein, D. A., Borkovec, T. D., & Hazlett-Stevens, H. (2000). *New directions in progressive relaxation training: A guidebook for helping professionals.* Westport, CT: Praeger.

Bernstein, D. M., & Loftus, E. F. (2009). How to tell if a particular memory is true or false. *Perspectives on Psychological Science, 4*(4), 370–374.

Bernstein, D. P., & Useda, J. (2007). Paranoid personality disorder. In W. O'Donohue, K. Fowler, & S. Lilienfeld (Eds.), *Personality disorders: Toward the DSM-V* (pp. 41–62). Thousand Oaks, CA: Sage.

Bernstein, D. P., Useda, D., & Siever, L. J. (1993). Paranoid personality disorder: Review of the literature and recommendations for DSM-IV. *Journal of Personality Disorders, 7,* 53–62.

Bernstein, J., Adlaf, E., & Paglia, A. (2002). *Drug use in Toronto—2000.* Retrieved October 25, 2003, from http://www.city.toronto.on.ca/drugcentre/rgdu00/rgdu1.htm

Berry, J. W. (2003). Origins of cross-cultural similarities and differences in human behavior: An ecocultural perspective. In A. Toomela (Ed.), *Cultural guidance in the development of the human mind* (pp. 97–109). Westport, CT: Ablex.

Berthiaume, L. (2006, May 6). Margaret Trudeau's secret war. *Canada.com.* Retrieved September 22, 2007, from http://www.canada.com/topics/bodyandhealth/story.html?id8cf493ee-f0d4-421c-bfce-92adb8b2ea0b&k22306

Bettelheim, B. (1967). *The empty fortress.* New York: Free Press.

Bettens, K., Sleegers, K., & Van Broeckhoven, C. (2010). Current status on Alzheimer disease molecular genetics: From past, to present, to future. *Human Molecular Genetics, 19*(R1), R4–R11.

Bhagwanjee, A., Parekh, A., Parvk, Z., Petersen, I., & Subedar, H. (1998). Prevalence of minor psychiatric disorders in an adult African rural community in South Africa. *Psychological Medicine, 28,* 1137–1147.

Bharucha, A., Anand, V., Forlizzi, J., Dew, M., Reynolds, C., III, Stevens, S., & Wactlar, M. S. (2009). Intelligent assistive technology applications to dementia care: Current capabilities, limitations, and future challenges. *The American Journal of Geriatric Psychiatry: Official Journal of the American Association for Geriatric Psychiatry, 17*(2), 88.

Biederman, J., Faraone, S. V., Keenan, K., Benjamin, J., Krifcher, B., Moore, C., ... Tsuang, M. T. (1992). Further evidence for family-genetic risk factors in attention deficit hyperactivity disorder: Patterns of comorbidity in probands and relatives in psychiatrically and pediatrically referred samples. *Archives of General Psychiatry, 49,* 728–738.

Biederman, J., Mick, E., Faraone, S. V., Spencer, T., Wilens, T. E., & Wozniak, J. (2000). Pediatric mania: A developmental subtype of bipolar disorder? *Biological Psychiatry, 48*(6), 458–466.

Biederman, J., Munir, K., Knee, D., Armentano, M., Autor, S., Waternaux, C., & Tsuang, M. (1987). High rate of affective disorders in probands with attention deficit disorder and in their relatives: A controlled family study. *American Journal of Psychiatry, 144*(3), 330–333.

Biederman, J., Rosenbaum, J. F., Hirshfeld, D. R., Farone, S. V., Bolduc, E. A., Gersten, M., ... Reznick, J. S. (1990). Psychiatric correlates of behavioral inhibition in young children of parents with and without psychiatric disorders. *Archives of General Psychiatry, 47,* 21–26.

Biederman, J., Spencer, T., Wilens, T., & Greene, R. (2001). Attention-deficit/hyperactivity disorder. In G. O. Gabbard (Ed.), *Treatment of psychiatric disorders* (Vol. 1, 3rd ed., pp. 145–176). Washington, DC: American Psychiatric Press.

Bierut, L. J., Heath, A. C., Bucholz, K. K., Dinwiddie, S. H., Madden, P. A., Statham, D. J., ... Martin, N. G. (1999). Major depressive disorder in a community-based twin sample: Are there different genetic and environmental contributions for men and women? *Archives of General Psychiatry, 56*(6), 557–563.

Biglan, A., Hops, H., Sherman, L., Friedman, L. S., Arthur, J., & Osteen, V. (1985). Problem solving interactions of depressed women and their husbands. *Behavior Therapy, 16,* 431–451.

Billingsley, R. L., McAndrews, M. P., & Smith, M. L. (2002). Intact perceptual and conceptual priming in temporal lobe epilepsy: Neuroanatomical and methodological implications. *Neuropsychology, 16*(1), 92–101.

Billingsley, R. L., Smith, M. L., & McAndrews, M. P. (2002). Developmental patterns in priming and familiarity in explicit recollection. *Journal of Experimental Child Psychology, 82,* 251–277.

Binder, E. B., Bradley, R. G., Liu, W., Epstein, M. P., Deveau, T. C., Mercer, K. B., ... Ressler, K. J. (2008). Association of FKBP5 polymorphisms and childhood abuse with risk of posttraumatic stress disorder symptoms in adults. *JAMA, 299*(11), 1291–1305.

Binik, Y. M. (2005). Should dyspareunia be retained as a sexual dysfunction in DSM-V? A painful classification decision. *Archives of Sexual Behavior, 34,* 11–21.

Binik, Y. M. (2010). The DSM diagnostic criteria for dyspareunia. *Archives of Sexual Behavior, 39,* 292–303.

Binik, Y. M., Bergeron, S., & Khalife, S. (2000). Dyspareunia. In S. R. Leiblum & R. C. Rosen (Eds.), *Principles and practice of sex therapy* (3rd ed., pp. 154–180). New York: Guilford Press.

Binzer, M., Andersen, P. M., & Kullgren, G. (1997). Clinical characteristics of patients with motor disability due to conversion disorder: A prospective control group study. *Journal of Neurology, Neurosurgery, and Psychiatry, 63*(1), 83–88.

Birch, D. E. (1992). Duty to protect: Update and Canadian perspective. *Canadian Psychology, 33,* 94–104.

Birchwood, M., Smith, J., Drury, V., Healy, J., MacMillan, F., & Slade, M. A. (1994). A self-report insight scale for psychosis: Reliability, validity and sensitivity to change. *Acta Psychiatrica Scandinavica, 89,* 62–67.

Bird, J. M. (1985). Computed tomographic brain studies and treatment response in schizophrenia. *Canadian Journal of Psychiatry, 30,* 251–254.

Birley, J., & Brown, G. W. (1970). Crisis and life changes preceding the onset or relapse of acute schizophrenia: *Clinical aspects. British Journal of Psychiatry, 16,* 327–333.

Bjorklund, D. F. (1989). *Children's thinking: Developmental function and individual differences.* Pacific Grove, CA: Brooks/Cole.

Bjorvatn, B., & Pallesen, S. (2009). A practical approach to circadian rhythm sleep disorders. *Sleep Medicine Reviews, 13*(1), 47–60.

Black, D. W., & Andreasen, N. C. (1999). Schizophrenia, schizophreniform disorder, and delusional (paranoid) disorders. In R. E. Hales, S. C. Yudofsky, & J. A. Talbott (Eds.), *Textbook of psychiatry* (3rd ed., pp. 425–477). Washington, DC: American Psychiatric Press.

Black, D. W., Monahan, P., Gable, J., Blum, N., Clancy, G., & Baker, P. (1998). Hoarding and treatment response in 38 nondepressed subjects with obsessive compulsive disorder. *Journal of Clinical Psychiatry, 5,* 420–425.

Black, D. W., Winokur, G., & Nasrallah, A. (1987). The treatment of depression: Electroconvulsive therapy vs. antidepressants: A naturalistic evaluation of 1,495 patients. *Comprehensive Psychiatry, 28*(2), 169–182.

Black, S. E., Patterson, C., & Feightner, J. (2001). Preventing dementia. *Canadian Journal of Neurological Science, 28*(Suppl. 1), S56.

Blackburn, I. M., & Moore, R. G. (1997). Controlled acute and follow-up trial of cognitive therapy and pharmacotherapy in outpatients with recurrent depression. *British Journal of Psychiatry, 171,* 328–334.

Blacker, D. (2005). Psychiatric rating scales. In B. J. Sadock & V. A. Sadock (Eds.), *Kaplan & Sadock's comprehensive textbook of psychiatry* (pp. 929–955). Philadelphia: Lippincott Williams & Wilkins.

Blackshaw, S., Chadarana, P., Garneau, Y., Merskey, H., & Mescarello, R. (1996). Adult recovered memories of childhood sexual abuse. *The Canadian Journal of Psychiatry, 41,* 305–306.

Blagys, M. D., & Hilsenroth, M. J. (2000). Distinctive features of short-term psychodynamic-interpersonal psychotherapy: A review of the comparative psychotherapy process literature. *Clinical Psychology: Science and Practice, 7,* 167–188.

Blair, K., Shaywitz, J., Smith, B. W., Rhodes, R., Geraci, M., Jones, M., ... Pine, D. S. (2008). Response to emotional expressions in generalized social phobia and generalized anxiety disorder: Evidence for separate disorders. *American Journal of Psychiatry, 165*(9), 1193–1202.

Blair, K. S., Newman, C., Mitchell, D. G. V., Richell, R. A., Leonard, A., Morton, J., & Blair, R. J. R. (2006). Differentiating among prefrontal substrates in psychopathy: neuropsychological test findings. *Neuropsychology, 20,* 153–165.

Blais, S. (2007, March 14). Pharmacist praises changes in how tobacco can be displayed. *Coquitlam Now,* p. 20.

Blanchard, C. G., Blanchard, E. B., & Becker, J. V. (1976). The young widow: Depressive symptomatology throughout the grief process. *Psychiatry, 39,* 394–399.

Blanchard, E. B. (1987). Long-term effects of behavioral treatment of chronic headache. *Behavior Therapy, 18,* 375–385.

Blanchard, E. B. (1992). Psychological treatment of benign headache disorders. [Special issue: Behavioral medicine: An update for the 1990s]. *Journal of Consulting and Clinical Psychology, 60*(4), 537–551.

Blanchard, E. B., & Andrasik, F. (1982). Psychological assessment and treatment of headache: Recent developments and emerging issues. *Journal of Consulting and Clinical Psychology, 50*(6), 859–879.

Blanchard, E. B., Andrasik, F., Ahles, T. A., Teders, S. J., & O'Keefe, D. (1980). Migraine and tension headache: A meta-analytic review. *Behavior Therapy, 11,* 613–631.

Blanchard, E. B., Appelbaum, K. A., Radnitz, C. L., Michultka, D., Morrill, B., Kirsh, C., ... Dentinger, M. P. (1990). Placebo-controlled evaluation of abbreviated progressive muscle relaxation combined with cognitive therapy in the treatment of tension headache. *Journal of Consulting and Clinical Psychology, 58*(2), 210–215.

Blanchard, E. B., & Epstein, L. H. (1977). *A biofeedback primer.* Reading, MA: Addison-Wesley.

Blanchard, E. B., Kuhn, E., Rowell, D. L., Hickling, E. J., Wittrock, D., Rogers, R. L., ... Steckler, D. C. (2004). Studies of the vicarious traumatization of college students by the September 11th attacks: Effects of proximity, exposure and connectedness. *Behaviour Research & Therapy, 42,* 191–205.

Blanchard, E. B., Martin, J. E., & Dubbert, P. M. (1988). *Non-drug treatments for essential hypertension.* Elmsford, NY: Pergamon Press.

Blanchard, J. J., & Neale, J. M. (1992). Medication effects: Conceptual and methodological issues in schizophrenia research. *Clinical Psychology Review, 12,* 345–361.

Blanchard, R. (2008). Sex ration of older siblings in heterosexual and homosexual, right-handed and non-right-handed men. *Archives of Sexual Behavior, 37,* 977–981.

Blanchard, R., & Bogaert, A. (1998). Birth order in homosexual versus heterosexual sex offenders against children, pubescents, and adults. *Archives of Sexual Behavior, 27*(6), 595–603.

Blanchard, R., & Bogaert, A. F. (1996). Homosexuality in men and number of older brothers. *American Journal of Psychiatry, 153,* 27–31.

Blanchard, R., Cantor, J. M., Bogaert, A. F., Breedlove, M., & Ellis, L. (2006). Interaction of fraternal birth order and handedness in the development of male homosexuality. *Hormones and Behavior, 49,* 405–414.

Blanchard, R., & Steiner, B. W. (Eds.). (1990). *Clinical management of gender identity disorders in children and adults.* Washington, DC: American Psychiatric Association.

Blanchard, R., Zucker, K. J., Cohen-Kettenis, P. T., Gooren, L. J. G., & Bailey, M. J. (1996). Birth order and sibling sex ratio in two samples of Dutch genderdysphoric homosexual males. *Archives of Sexual Behavior, 25,* 495–514.

Blanco, C., Heimberg, R. G., Schneier, F. R., Fresco, D. M., Chen, H., Turk, C. L., ... Liebowitz, M. R. (2010). A placebo-controlled trial of phenelzine, cognitive behavioral group therapy, and their combination for social anxiety disorder. *Archives of General Psychiatry, 67*(3), 286–295.

Bland, R. C. (1997). Epidemiology of affective disorders: A review. *Canadian Journal of Psychiatry, 42,* 367–377.

Bland, R. C., Newman, S. C., & Orn, H. (1988). Period prevalence of psychiatric disorders in Edmonton. *Acta Psychiatrica Scandanavica, 77*(Suppl. 338), 33–42.

Blansjaar, B. A., Thomassen, R., & Van Schaick, H. W. (2000). Prevalence of dementia in centenarians. *International Journal of Geriatric Psychiatry, 15*(3), 219–225.

Blashfield, R. K., & Livesley, W. J. (1991). Metaphorical analysis of psychiatric classification as a psychological test. *Journal of Abnormal Psychology, 100*(3), 262–270.

Blatchford, C., Lowson, G., & Hershorn, G. (2001, September 1). Maureen Forrester's life out of the spotlight. *The National Post.* Article posted to UC Davis electronic mailing list by Moore, P. (2001, September 2). Canada's Maureen Forrester—Read it and weep. Retrieved from http://listproc.ucdavis.edu/archives/mlist/log0109/0001.html

Blazer, D. (1999). Geriatric psychiatry. In R. E. Hales, S. C. Yudofsky, & J. A. Talbot (Eds.), *Textbook of psychiatry* (3rd ed., pp. 1447–1462). Washington, DC: American Psychiatric Press.

Blazer, D. G. (1989). Current concepts: Depression in the elderly. *New England Journal of Medicine, 320,* 164–166.

Blazer, D. G., George, L., & Hughes, D. (1991). The epidemiology of anxiety disorders: An age comparison. In C. Salzman & B. Liebowitz (Eds.), *Anxiety disorders in the elderly* (pp. 17–30). New York: Springer.

Blazer, D. G., Hughes, D., George, L. K., Swartz, M., & Boyer, R. (1991). Generalized anxiety disorder. In L. N. Robins & D. A. Regier (Eds.), *Psychiatric disorders in America* (pp. 180–203). New York: Free Press.

Bleackley, C., Green, D., Lockshin, R. A., Melino, G., & Zakeri, Z. (2001). *Arnold H. Greenberg, 1941–2001.* Retrieved June 25, 2004, from http:// www.celldeath-apoptosis.org/arnold_h.htm

Blehar, M. C., & Rosenthal, N. E. (1989). Seasonal affective disorders and phototherapy. *Archives of General Psychiatry, 46,* 469–474.

Bleiberg, K. L., & Markowitz, J. C. (2008). Interpersonal psychotherapy for major depressive disorder. In D. H. Barlow (Ed.), *Clinical handbook of psychological disorders* (4th ed.). New York: Guilford Press.

Bleuler, E. (1908). Die Prognoser Dementia praecox (Schizophreniegruppe). *Allgemeine Zeitschrift für Psychiatrie, 65,* 436–464.

Bleuler, E. (1924). *Textbook of psychiatry* (A. A. Brill, Trans.). New York: Macmillan.

Bliss, E. L. (1984). A symptom profile of patients with multiple personalities including MMPI results. *Journal of Nervous and Mental Diseases, 172,* 197–211.

Bliss, E. L. (1986). *Multiple personality allied disorders and hypnosis.* New York: Oxford University Press.

Bloch, M. H., Landeros-Weisenberger, A., Rosario, M. C., Pittenger, C., & Leckman, J. F. (2008). Meta-analysis of the symptom structure of obsessive-compulsive disorder. *American Journal of Psychiatry, 165*(12), 1532–1542.

Block, J. J. (2008). Issues for DSM-V: Internet addiction. *American Journal of Psychiatry, 165*(3), 306–307.

Bloom, F. E., & Kupfer, D. J. (1995). *Psychopharmacology: The fourth generation of progress.* New York: Raven Press.

Bloom, F. E., Nelson, C. A., & Lazerson, A. (2001). *Brain, mind, and behavior* (3rd ed.). New York: Worth.

Blue, A. V., & Gaines, A. D. (1992). The ethnopsychiatric répertoire: A review and overview of ethnopsychiatric studies. In A. D. Gaines (Ed.), *Ethnopsychiatry: The cultural construction of professional and folk psychiatries* (pp. 397–484). Albany: State University of New York Press.

Blum, K., Noble, E. P., Sheridan, P. J., Montgomery, A., Ritchie, T., Jagadeeswaran, P., ... Cohn, J. B. (1990). Allelic association of human dopamine D2 receptor gene in alcoholism. *JAMA, 263,* 2055–2060.

Blumenthal, J. A., Sherwood, A., Babyak, M. A., Watkins, L. L., Waugh, R., Georgiades, A., ... Hinderliter, A. (2005). Effects of exercise and stress management training on markers of cardiovascular risk in patients with ischemic heart disease: A randomized controlled trial. *JAMA, 293*(13), 1626–1634.

Blumenthal, S. J. (1990). An overview and synopsis of risk factors, assessment, and treatment of suicidal patients over the life cycle. In S. J. Blumenthal & D. J. Kupfer (Eds.), *Suicide over the life cycle: Risk factors, assessment and treatment of suicidal patients.* Washington, DC: American Psychiatric Press.

Blumenthal, S. J., & Kupfer, D. J. (1988). Overview of early detection and treatment strategies for suicidal behavior in young people. *Journal of Youth & Adolescence, 17,* 1–23.

Boachie, A., Goldfield, G. S., & Spettigue, W. (2003). Olanzapine use as an adjunctive treatment for hospitalized children with anorexia nervosa: Case reports. *International Journal of Eating Disorders, 33,* 98–103.

Bock, G. R., & Goode, J. A. (Eds.). (1996). *Genetics of criminal and antisocial behaviour* (Ciba Foundation, Vol. 194). Chichester: Wiley.

Bockoven, J. S. (1963). *Moral treatment in American psychiatry.* New York: Springer.

Bodlund, O., & Kullgren, G. (1996). Transsexualism—general outcome and prognostic factors: A five-year follow-up study of nineteen transsexuals in the process of changing sex. *Archives of Sexual Behavior, 25,* 303–316.

Bögels, S. M., Alden, L., Beidel, D. C., Clark, L. A., Pine, D. S., Stein, M. B., & Voncken, M. (2010). Social anxiety disorder: Questions and answers for the DSM-V. *Depression and Anxiety, 27*(2), 168–189.

Bohman, M., Cloninger, C. R., von Knorring, A. L., & Sigvardsson, S. (1984). An adoption study of somatoform disorders: III. Cross-fostering analysis and genetic relationship to alcoholism and criminality. *Archives of General Psychiatry, 41,* 872–878.

Bohus, M., Haaf, B., Stiglmayr, C., Pohl, U., Bohme, R., & Linehan, M. (2000). Evaluation of inpatient dialectical-behavioral therapy for borderline personality disorder—a prospective study. *Behavior Research and Therapy, 38*(9), 875–887.

Boileau, I., Dagher, A., Leyton, M., Gunn, R. N., Baker, G. B., Diksic, M., & Benkelfat, C. (2006). Modelings sensitization to stimulants in humans: An [^{11}C]raclopride/positron emission tomography study in healthy men. *Archives of General Psychiatry, 63*(12), 1386–1395.

Boivin, D. B. (2000). Influence of sleep-wake and circadian rhythm disturbances in psychiatric disorders. *Journal of Psychiatry & Neuroscience, 25,* 446–458.

Boivin, D. B., Czeisler, D. A., Dijk, D. J., Duffy, J. E., Folkard, S., Minors, D. S., ... Waterhouse, J. M.

(1997). Complex interaction of the sleep-wake cycle and circadian phase modulates mood in healthy subjects. *Archives of General Psychiatry, 54,* 145–152.

Boivin, D. B., & James, F. O. (2003). Insomnia due to circadian rhythm disturbances. In M. P. Szuba, J. D. Kloss, & D. F. Dinges (Eds.), *Insomnia: Principles and management* (pp. 155–191). New York: Cambridge University Press.

Boland, R. J., & Keller, M. B. (2009). Course and outcome of depression. In I. H. Gotlib & C. L. Hammen (Eds.), *Handbook of depression* (2nd ed., pp. 23–43). New York: Guilford Press.

Boll, T. J. (1985). Developing issues in clinical neuropsychology. *Journal of Clinical and Experimental Neuropsychology, 7*(5), 473–485.

Bonanno, G. A., & Kaltman, S. (1999). Toward an integrative perspective on bereavement. *Psychological Bulletin, 125*(6), 1004–1008.

Bonanno, G. A., Wortman, C. B., Lehman, D. R., Tweed, R. G., Haring, M., Sonnega, J., … Nesse, R. M. (2002). Resilience to loss and chronic grief: A prospective study from preloss to 18-months postloss. *Journal of Personality and Social Psychology, 83,* 1150–1164.

Bond, A., & Lader, M. L. (1979). Benzodiazepines and aggression. In M. Sandler (Ed.), *Psychopharmcology of aggression.* New York: Raven Press.

Bond, C. F., DeCandia, C. G., & MacKinnon, J. (1988). Responses to race in a psychiatric setting: The role of patient's race. *Personality and Social Psychology Bulletin, 14,* 448–458.

Bond, G. R., Drake, R. E., Mueser, K. T., & Becker, D. R. (1997). An update on supported employment for people with severe mental illness. *Psychiatric Services, 48,* 335–346.

Bondy, A., & Frost, L. (2001). The picture exchange communication system. *Behavior Modification, 25,* 725–744.

Bondy, A., & Frost, L. (2002). *A picture's worth: PECS and other visual communication strategies in autism.* Bethesda, MD: Woodbine House.

Bongaarts, J., & Over, M. (2010). Global HIV/AIDS policy in transition. *Science, 328,* 1359–1360.

Bonnet, M. H. (2000). Sleep deprivation. In M. H. Kryger, T. Roth, & W. C. Dement (Eds.), *Principles and practice of sleep medicine* (3rd ed., pp. 53–71). Philadelphia: W. B. Saunders.

Book, A. S., Clark, H. J., & Forth, A. E. (2006). The psychopathy checklist-revised and the psychopathy checklist: Youth version. In R. P. Archer (Ed.), *Forensic uses of clinical assessment instruments* (pp. 147–179). Mahwah, NJ: Lawrence Erlbaum Associates Publishers.

Boon, S., & Draijer, N. (1991). Diagnosing dissociative disorders in the Netherlands: A pilot study with the Structured Clinical Interview for DSM-III-R dissociative disorders. *American Journal of Psychiatry, 148,* 458–462.

Boon, S., & Draijer, N. (1993). Multiple personality disorder in the Netherlands: A clinical investigation of 71 cases. *American Journal of Psychiatry, 150,* 489–494.

Boothroyd, L. J., Kirmayer, L. J., Spreng, S., Malus, M., & Hodgins, S. (2001). Completed suicides among the Inuit of northern Québec, 1982–1996: A case-control study. *Canadian Medical Association Journal, 165,* 749–755.

Bootzin, R. R., Manber, R., Perlis, M. L., Salvio, M., & Wyatt, J. K. (1993). Sleep disorders. In P. B. Sutker & H. E. Adams (Eds.), *Comprehensive handbook of psychopathology* (2nd ed., pp. 531–561). New York: Plenum Press.

Bootzin, R. R., & Nicassio, P. M. (1978). Behavioral treatments of insomnia. In M. Hersen, R. Eisler, & P. M. Miller (Eds.), *Progress in behavior modification* (Vol. 6, pp. 1–45). New York: Academic Press.

Borckardt, J. J., Nash, M. R., Murphy, M. D., Shaw, D., O'Neil, P., & Moore, M. (2008). Clinical practice as natural laboratory for psychotherapy research: A guide to case-based time-series analysis. *American Psychologist, 63*(2), 77–95.

Borkovec, T. D., Alcaine, O. M., & Behar, E. (2004). Avoidance theory of worry and generalized anxiety disorder. In R. G. Heimberg, C. L. Turk, & D. S. Mennin (Eds.), *Generalized anxiety disorder: Advances in research and practice* (pp. 77–108). New York: Guilford Press.

Borkovec, T. D., & Costello, E. (1993). Efficacy of applied relaxation and cognitive-behavioral therapy in the treatment of generalized anxiety disorder. *Journal of Consulting and Clinical Psychology, 61*(4), 611–619.

Borkovec, T. D., & Hu, S. (1990). The effect of worry on cardiovascular response to phobic imagery. *Behaviour Research and Therapy, 28,* 69–73.

Borkovec, T. D., & Inz, J. (1990). The nature of worry in generalized anxiety disorder: A predominance of thought activity. *Behaviour Research and Therapy, 28,* 153–158.

Borkovec, T. D., Newman, M. G., Pincus, A. L., & Lytle, R. (2002). A component analysis of cognitive-behavioral therapy for generalized anxiety disorder and the role of interpersonal problems. *Journal of Consulting and Clinical Psychology, 70,* 288–298.

Borkovec, T. D., & Ruscio, A. (2001). Psychotherapy for generalized anxiety disorder. *Journal of Clinical Psychiatry, 62,* 37–45.

Borkovec, T. D., Shadick, R., & Hopkins, M. (1991). The nature of normal and pathological worry. In R. M. Rapee & D. H. Barlow (Eds.), *Chronic anxiety, generalized anxiety disorder, and mixed anxiety depression.* New York: Guilford Press.

Borkovec, T. D., & Whisman, M. A. (1996). Psychosocial treatment for generalized anxiety disorder. In M. R. Mavissakalian & R. F. Prien (Eds.), *Long-term treatments of anxiety disorders.* Washington, DC: American Psychiatric Press.

Bornath, L. M. (2002). *Elaine Tanner: Best female Canadian swimmer in the late 1960s.* Retrieved June 25, 2004, from http://www.almostfabulous.com/canadians/name/t/tannerelaine.php

Bornstein, R. F. (1992). The dependent personality: Developmental, social, and clinical perspectives. *Psychological Bulletin, 112,* 3–23.

Bornstein, R. F. (1997). Dependent personality disorder in the DSM-IV and beyond. *Clinical Psychology: Science and Practice, 4,* 175–187.

Borodinsky, L. N., Root, C. M., Cronin, J. A., Sann, S. B., Gu, X., & Spitzer, N. C. (2004). Activity-dependent homeostatic specification of transmitter expression in embryonic neurons. *Nature, 429,* 523–530.

Boskind-Lodahl, M. (1976). Cinderella's stepsisters: A feminist perspective on anorexia nervosa and bulimia. *Signs, 2,* 342–356.

Bouchard, M. F., Bellinger, D. C., Wright, R. O., & Weisskopf, M. G. (2010). Attention-deficit/hyperactivity disorder and urinary metabolites of organophosphate pesticides. *Pediatrics, 125*(6), e1270–e1277.

Bouchard, S., Gauthier, J., Nouwen, A., Ivers, H., Vallieres, A., Simard, S., & Fournier, T. (2007).

Temporal relationship between dysfunctional beliefs, self-efficacy, and panic apprehension in the treatment of panic disorders with agoraphobia. *Journal of Behavior Therapy and Experimental Psychiatry, 38,* 275–292.

Bouchard, S., Vallieres, A., Roy, M. A., & Maziade, M. (1996). Cognitive restructuring in the treatment of psychotic symptoms in schizophrenia: A critical analysis. *Behavior Therapy, 27,* 257–277.

Bouchard, T. J., Jr., Lykken, D. T., McGue, M., Segal, N. L., & Tellegen, A. (1990). Sources of human psychological differences: The Minnesota study of twins reared apart. *Science, 250,* 223–228.

Boulos, C., Kutcher, S., Marton, P., Simeon, J., Ferguson, B., & Roberts, N. (1991). Response to desipramine treatment in adolescent major depression. *Pscyhopharmacology Bulletin, 27,* 59–65.

Bourgeois, J. A., Seaman, J. S., & Servis, M. E. (2003). Delirium, dementia, and amnestic disorders. In R. E. Hales & S. C. Yudofsky (Eds.), *Textbook of clinical psychiatry* (4th ed., pp. 259–308). Washington, DC: American Psychiatric Press.

Bourgeois, J. A., Seaman, J. S., & Servis, M. E. (2008). Delirium, dementia, and amnestic and other cognitive disorders. In R. E. Hales, S. C. Yudofsky, & G. O. Gabbard (Eds.), *The American Psychiatric Publishing textbook of psychiatry* (5th ed., pp. 303–364). Arlington, VA: American Psychiatric Publishing, Inc.

Bourgeois, M. S. (1992). Evaluating memory wallets in conversations with persons with dementia. *Journal of Speech and Hearing Research, 35,* 1344–1357.

Bourgeois, M. S. (1993). Effects of memory aids on the dyadic conversations of individuals with dementia. *Journal of Applied Behavior Analysis, 26,* 77–87.

Bouton, M. E. (2005). Behavior systems and the contextual control of anxiety, fear, and panic. In L. Feldman-Barrett, P. Niedenthal, & P. Winkielman (Eds.), *Emotion: Conscious and unconscious* (pp. 205–227). New York: Guilford Press.

Bouton, M. E., Mineka, S., & Barlow, D. H. (2001). A modern learning-theory perspective on the etiology of panic disorder. *Psychological Review, 108,* 4–32.

Bowden, S., Bardenhagen, F., Ambrose, M., & Whelan, G. (1994). Alcohol, thiamin deficiency, and neuropsychological disorders. *Alcohol and Alcoholism Supplement, 2,* 267–272.

Bower, G. H. (1981). Mood and memory. *American Psychologist, 36,* 129–148.

Bowlby, J. (1977). The making and breaking of affectionate bonds. *British Journal of Psychiatry, 130,* 201–210.

Bowman, E. S., & Nurnberger, J. I. (1993). Genetics of psychiatric diagnosis and treatment. In D. L. Dunner (Ed.), *Current psychiatric therapy* (pp. 46–53). Philadelphia: W. B. Saunders.

Boyce, W., Doherty-Poirier, M., MacKinnon, D., Fortin, C., Saab, H., King, M., & Gallupe, O. (2006). Sexual health of Canadian youth: Findings from the Canadian youth, sexual health and HIV/AIDS study. *Canadian Journal of Human Sexuality, 15,* 59–68.

Boyer, P. S., & Nissenbaum, S. (1974). *Salem possessed: The social origins of witchcraft.* Cambridge, MA: Harvard University Press.

Boyle, W., Doherty, M., Fortin, C., & MacKinnon, D. (2002). *Canadian youth, sexual health and*

AIDS study. Toronto, ON: Council Ministers of Education Canada.

Bracha, H. S., Torrey, E. F., Gottesman, I. I., Bigelow, L. B., & Cunniff, C. (1992). Second-trimester markers of fetal size in schizophrenia: A study of monozygotic twins. *American Journal of Psychiatry, 149,* 1355–1361.

Bradford, A., & Meston, C. M. (2006). The impact of anxiety on sexual arousal in women. *Behaviour Research and Therapy, 44,* 1067–1077.

Bradford, J. (1997). Medical interventions in sexual deviance. In D. R. Laws & W. O'Donohue (Eds.), *Sexual deviance: Theory, assessment and treatment* (pp. 449–464). New York: Guilford Press.

Bradley, B. P., & Mathews, A. (1988). Memory bias in recovered clinical depressives. [Special issue: Information processing and the emotional disorders]. *Cognition and Emotion, 2*(3), 235–245.

Bradley, B. P., Mogg, K., White, J., Groom, C., & de Bono, J. (1999). Attentional bias for emotional faces in generalized anxiety disorder. *British Journal of Clinical Psychology, 38,* 267–278.

Bradley, E. A., Thompson, A., & Bryson, S. E. (2002). Mental retardation in teenagers: Prevalence data from the Niagara region, Ontario. *Canadian Journal of Psychiatry, 47,* 652–659.

Bradley, R. G., Binder, E. B., Epstein, M. P., Tang, Y., Nair, H. P., Liu, W., ... Ressler, K. J. (2008). Influence of child abuse on adult depression: Moderation by the corticotropin-releasing hormone receptor gene. *Archives of General Psychiatry, 65*(2), 190–200.

Bradley, S. J., Oliver, G. D., Chernick, A. B., & Zucker, K. J. (1998). Experiment of nurture: ablatio penis at 2 months, sex reassignment at 7 months, and a psychosexual follow-up in young adulthood. *Pediatrics, 102*(1), E9.

Bradley, S. J., & Zucker, K. J. (1997). Gender identity disorder: A review of the past 10 years. *Journal of the American Academy of Child & Adolescent Psychiatry, 36,* 872–880.

Bradley, W. (1937). The behavior of children receiving benzedrine. *American Journal of Psychiatry, 94,* 577–585.

Brady, J. P. (1991). The pharmacology of stuttering: A critical review. *American Journal of Psychiatry, 148,* 1309–1316.

Brady, J. P., & Lind, D. L. (1961). Experimental analysis of hysterical blindness. *Archives of General Psychiatry, 4,* 331–339.

Braff, D., Schork, N. J., & Gottesman, I. I. (2007). Endophenotyping schizophrenia. *American Journal of Psychiatry, 164,* 705–707.

Brand, B., Classen, C., Lanins, R., Loewenstein, R., McNary, S., Pain, C., & Putnam, F. (2009). A naturalistic study of dissociative identity disorder and dissociative disorder not otherwise specified patients treated by community clinicians. *Psychological Trauma: Theory, Research, Practice, and Policy, 1*(2), 153–171.

Brandon, K. O. (1995). A multivariate twin family study of the genetic and environmental structure of personality, beliefs, and alcohol use. *Dissertation Abstracts International: Section B: The Sciences & Engineering, 55*(10-B), 4599.

Brandon, S., Cowley, P., McDonald, C., Neville, P., Palmer, R., & Wellstood-Eason, S. (1984). Electroconvulsive therapy: Results in depressive illness from the Leicestershire trial. *British Medical Journal, 288*(6410), 22–25.

Brandon, T. H., & Baker, T. B. (1992). The smoking consequences questionnaire: The subjective utility of smoking in college students. *Psychological Assessment: A Journal of Consulting and Clinical Psychology, 3,* 484–491.

Brannon, L., & Feist, J. (1997). *Health psychology: An introduction to behavior and health.* Pacific Grove, CA: Brooks/Cole.

Braswell, L., & Bloomquist, M. (1994). *Cognitive behavior therapy of ADHD.* New York: Guilford Press.

Bratulic, A. (2007, October 3). Law used for medical blackmail: Rights group. *The Suburban.* Retrieved October 12, 2007, from http://thesuburban.com/content.jsp?sid 1630869967586300301913424001 2&ctid10000 00&cnid1013020

Brazeau, R., & Burr, N. (1992). *International survey: Alcoholic beverage taxation and control policies.* Ottawa, Canada ON: Brewers Association of Canada.

Brean, J. (2007, September 6). Judge's verdict reveals comic's sad descent. *National Post.* Retrieved October 1, 2007, from http://www.nationalpost. com/news/story.html?id2fc21502-f905-4409-8a86-603c4632f2e9&k48220

Brechtl, J. R., Breitbart, W., Galietta, M., Krivo, S., & Rosenfeld, B. (2001). The use of highly active antiretroviral therapy (HAART) in patients with advanced HIV infection: Impact on medical, palliative care, and quality of life outcomes. *Journal of Pain Symptom Management, 21,* 41–51.

Breier, A., Buchanan, R. W., Kirkpatrick, B., Davis, O. R., Irish, D., Summerfelt, A., & Carpenter, W. T. (1994). Effects of clozapine on positive and negative symptoms in outpatients with schizophrenia. *American Journal of Psychiatry, 151,* 20–26.

Breiner, M. J., Stritzke, W. G. K., & Lang, A. R. (1999). Approaching avoidance: A step essential to the understanding of craving. *Alcohol Research & Health, 23*(3), 197–206.

Brekke, J. S., Long, J. D., Nesbitt, N., & Sobell, E. (1997). The impact of service characteristics on functional outcomes from community support programs for persons with schizophrenia: A growth curve analysis. *Journal of Consulting and Clinical Psychology, 65,* 464–475.

Bremner, J. D. (1999). Does stress damage the brain? *Biological Psychiatry, 45,* 797–805.

Bremner, J. D., Licinio, J., Darnell, A., Krystal, A. H., Owens, M. J., Southwick, S. M., ... Charney, D. S. (1997). Elevated CSF corticotropin-releasing factor concentrations in posttraumatic stress disorder. *American Journal of Psychiatry, 154,* 624–629.

Bremner, J. D., Randall, P. R., Scott, T. M., Bronen, R. A., Seibyl, J. P., Southwick, S. M., ... Innis, R. B. (1995). MRI-based measurement of hippocampal volume in patients with combat-related posttraumatic stress disorder. *American Journal of Psychiatry, 152,* 973–981.

Bremner, J. D., Vermetten, E., Southwick, S. M., Krystal, J. H., & Charney, D. S. (1998). Trauma, memory, and dissociation: An integrative formulation. In J. D. Bremner & C. Marmar (Eds.), *Trauma, memory, and dissociation.* Washington, DC: American Psychiatric Press.

Brener, N. D., Hassan, S. S., & Barrios, L. C. (1999). Suicidal ideation among college students in the United States. *Journal of Consulting & Clinical Psychology, 67,* 1004–1008.

Brenner, D. E., Kukull, W. A., van Belle, G., Bowen, J. D., McCormick, W. C., Teri, L., & Larson, E. B. (1993). Relationship between cigarette smoking and Alzheimer's disease in a population-based case-control study. *Neurology, 43,* 293–300.

Brent, D. A., Kerr, M. M., Goldstein, C., Bozigar, J., Wartella, M., & Allan, M. J. (1989). An outbreak of suicide and suicidal behavior in a high school. *Journal of the American Academy of Child and Adolescent Psychiatry, 28*(6), 918–924.

Brent, D. A., & Kolko, D. J. (1990). The assessment and treatment of children and adolescents at risk for suicide. In S. J. Blumenthal & D. J. Kupfer (Eds.), *Suicide over the life cycle: Risk factors, assessment and treatment of suicidal patients.* Washington, DC: American Psychiatric Press.

Brent, D. A., Perper, J. A., Goldstein, C. E., Kolko, D. J., Allan, M. J., Allman, C. J., & Zelenak, J. P. (1988). Risk factors for adolescent suicide: A comparison of adolescent suicide victims with suicidal inpatients. *Archives of General Psychiatry, 45,* 581–588.

Breslau, N., Davis, G. C., & Andreski, M. A. (1995). Risk factors for PTSD-related traumatic events: A prospective analysis. *American Journal of Psychiatry, 152,* 529–535.

Breslau, N., Kilbey, M. M., & Andreski, P. (1993). Nicotine dependence and major depression: New evidence from a prospective investigation. *Archives of General Psychiatry, 50,* 31–35.

Breslau, N., Lucia, V. C., & Alvarado, G. F. (2006). Intelligence and other predisposing factors in exposure to trauma and posttraumatic stress disorder. *Archives of General Psychiatry, 63,* 1238–1245.

Breuer, J., & Freud, S. (1957). *Studies on hysteria.* New York: Basic Books. (Original work published 1895).

Brewin, C. R., Andrews, B., & Gotlib, I. H. (1993). Psychopathology in early experience: A reappraisal of retrospective reports. *Psychological Bulletin, 113,* 82–98.

Bricker, J., Mann, S., Marek, P., Liu, J., & Peterson, A. (2010). Telephone-delivered Acceptance and Commitment Therapy for adult smoking cessation: A feasibility study. *Nicotine & Tobacco Research: Official Journal of the Society for Research on Nicotine and Tobacco, 12*(4), 454–458.

Bridges, F. S., & Kunselman, J. C. (2005). Premature mortality due to suicide, homicide, and motor vehicle accidents in health service delivery areas: Comparison of status Indians in British Columbia, Canada, with all other residents. *Psychological Reports, 97*(3), 739–749.

Briere pleads guilty to Holly Jones's murder. (2004). *The Globe and Mail.* Retrieved August 5, 2004, from http://www.theglobeandmail.com/servlet/story/RTGAM.20040617.wbrier0617B/BNStory/Nationl

Brinker, J. K., Harris, J. A., Guyitt, B., & Dozois, D. J. A. (2006). The importance of importance: Self-descriptors in dysphoria. *Journal of Individual Differences, 27,* 193–198.

British Columbia Schizophrenia Society. (2001). *Basic facts about schizophrenia.* Retrieved November 3, 2004, from http://www.mentalhealth.com/book/p40-sc02.html

Britton, J. C. & Rauch, S. L. (2009). Neuroanatomy and neuroimaging of anxiety disorders. In M. M. Antony & M. B. Stein (Eds.), *Oxford handbook of anxiety and related disorders* (pp. 97–110). Oxford: Oxford University Press.

Broadhead, W. E., Kaplan, B. H., & James, S. A. (1983). The epidemiologic evidence for a relationship between social support and health. *American Journal of Epidemiology, 117,* 521–537.

Brodeur, D. A., & Pond, M. (2001). The development of selective attention in children with attention deficit hyperactivity disorder. *Journal of Abnormal Child Psychology, 29,* 229–239.

Brody, A. L., Saxena, S., Stoessel, P., Gillies, L. A., Fairbanks, L. A., Alborzian, S., … Baxter, L. R., Jr. (2001). Regional brain metabolic changes in patients with major depression treated with either paroxetine or interpersonal therapy. *Archives of General Psychiatry, 48,* 631–640.

Brondolo, E., Rieppi, R., Erckson, Erickson, S. A., Bagiella, E., Shapiro, P. A., McKinley, P., & Sloan, R. P. (2003). Hostility, interpersonal interactions, and ambulatory blood pressure. *Psychosomatic Medicine, 65,* 1003–1011.

Brooks, P. (2005, June 25). *Long road to lost children.* Retrieved September 1, 2007, from The Dufferin Voices of Children Alliance; http://www.fixcas.com/news/halif ax/recap.htm

Brotto, L. A. (2010a). The DSM diagnostic criteria for hypoactive sexual desire disorder in women. *Archives of Sexual Behavior, 39,* 222–239.

Brotto, L. A. (2010b). The DSM diagnostic criteria for sexual aversion disorder. *Archives of Sexual Behavior, 39,* 271–277.

Brotto, L. A., Chik, H. M., Ryder, A. G., Gorzalka, B. B., & Seal, B. N. (2005). Acculturation and sexual function in Asian women. *Archives of Sexual Behavior, 34,* 613–626.

Broude, G. J., & Greene, S. J. (1980). Cross-cultural codes on 20 sexual attitudes and practices. In H. Barry, III & A. Schlegel (Eds.), *Cross-cultural samples and codes* (pp. 313–333). Pittsburgh: University of Pittsburgh Press.

Broughton, R. J. (2000). NREM arousal parasomnias. In M. H. Kryger, T. Roth, & W. C. Dement (Eds.), *Principles and practice of sleep medicine* (3rd ed., pp. 693–706). Philadelphia: W. B. Saunders.

Broughton, R., Billings, R., & Cartwright, R. (1994). Homicidal somnabulism: A case report. *Sleep, 17,* 253–264.

Brown, G. K., Beck, A. T., Steer, R. A., & Grisham, J. R. (2000). Risk factor for psychiatric outpatients: A 20-year perspective study. *Journal of Consulting and Clinical Psychology, 63*(3), 371–377.

Brown, G. W. (1959). Experiences of discharged chronic schizophrenic mental hospital patients in various types of living group. *Millbank Memorial Fund Quarterly, 37,* 105–131.

Brown, G. W. (1989). Depression. In G. W. Brown & T. O. Harris (Eds.), *Life events and illness* (pp. 49–93). New York: Guilford Press.

Brown, G. W., & Birley, J. L. T. (1968). Crisis and life change and the onset of schizophrenia. *Journal of Health and Social Behavior, 9,* 203–214.

Brown, G. W., & Harris, T. O. (1978). Social origins of depression: A study of psychiatric disorder in women. London: Tavistock.

Brown, G. W., Harris, T. O., & Hepworth, C. (1994). Life events and endogenous depression. *Archives of General Psychiatry, 51,* 525–534.

Brown, G. W., Monck, E. M., Carstairs, G. M., & Wing, J. K. (1962). Influence of family life on the course of schizophrenic illness. *British Journal of Preventive and Social Medicine, 16,* 55–68.

Brown, J., & Finn, P. (1982). Drinking to get drunk: Findings of a survey of junior and senior high school students. *Journal of Alcohol and Drug Education, 27,* 13–25.

Brown, R. E. (1994). *An introduction to neuroendocrinology.* Cambridge, NY: Cambridge University Press.

Brown, S. L., & Forth, A. E. (1997). Psychopathy and sexual assault: Static risk factors, emotional precursors, and rapist subtypes. *Journal of Consulting & Clinical Psychology, 65,* 848–857.

Brown, T. A., & Barlow, D. H. (2002). Classification of anxiety and mood disorders. In D. H. Barlow (Ed.), *Anxiety and its disorders: The nature and treatment of anxiety and panic* (2nd ed.). New York: Guilford Press.

Brown, T. A., & Barlow, D. H. (2005). Dimensional versus categorical classification of mental disorders in the fifth edition of the diagnostic and statistical manual of mental disorders and beyond: Comment on the special section. [Special issue: Toward a dimensionally based taxonomy of psychopathology]. *Journal of Abnormal Psychology, 114*(4), 551–556.

Brown, T. A., & Barlow, D. H. (2009). A proposal for a dimensional classification system based on the shared features of the DSM-IV anxiety and mood disorders: Implications for assessment and treatment. *Psychological Assessment, 21*(3), 256–271.

Brown, T. A., Barlow, D. H., & Liebowitz, M. R. (1994). The empirical basis of generalized anxiety disorder. *American Journal of Psychiatry, 15*(9), 1272–1280.

Brown, T. A., Campbell, L. A., Lehman, C. L., Grisham, J. R., & Mancill, R. B. (2001). Current and lifetime comorbidity of the DSM-IV anxiety and mood disorders in a large clinical sample. *Journal of Abnormal Psychology.*

Brown, T. A., Chorpita, B. F., & Barlow, D. H. (1998). Structural relationships among dimensions of the DSM-IV anxiety and mood disorders and dimensions of negative affect, positive affect, and autonomic arousal. *Journal of Abnormal Psychology, 107*(2), 179–192.

Brown, T. A., Marten, P. A., & Barlow, D. H. (1995). Discriminant validity of the symptoms comprising the DSM-III-R and DSM-IV associated symptom criterion of generalized anxiety disorder. *Journal of Anxiety Disorders, 9,* 317–328.

Brown, T. E. (Ed.). (2009). *ADHD comorbidities: Handbook for ADHD complications in children and adults.* Arlington, VA: American Psychiatric Publishing.

Brown, T. G., Dongier, M., Latimer, E., Legault, L., Seraganian, P., Kokin, M., & Ross, D. (2007). Group-delivered brief intervention versus standard care for mixed alcohol/other drug problems: A preliminary study. *Alcoholism Treatment Quarterly, 24*(4), 23–40.

Brown, T. M. (2001). Substance-induced delirium and related encephalopathies. In G. O. Gabbard (Ed.), *Treatment of psychiatric disorders* (Vol. 1, 3rd ed., pp. 423–479). Washington, DC: American Psychiatric Press.

Brownell, K. D. (1991). Dieting and the search for the perfect body: Where physiology and culture collide. *Behavior Therapy, 22,* 1–12.

Brownell, K. D., & Fairburn, C. G. (Eds.). (1995). *Eating disorders and obesity: A comprehensive handbook.* New York: Guilford Press.

Brownell, K. D., & Fairburn, C. G. (2002). *Eating disorders and obesity: A comprehensive handbook* (2nd ed.). New York: Guildford Press.

Brownell, K. D., Hayes, S. C., & Barlow, D. H. (1977). Patterns of appropriate and deviant sexual arousal: The behavioral treatment of multiple sexual deviations. *Journal of Consulting and Clinical Psychology, 45*(6), 1144–1155.

Brownell, K. D., & Rodin, J. (1994). The dieting maelstrom: Is it possible and advisable to lose weight? *American Psychologist, 49*(9), 781–791.

Brownlee, K., Devins, G. M., Flanigan, M., Fleming, J. A. E., Morehouse, R., Moscovitch, A., … Shapiro, C. M. (2003). Are there gender differences in the prescribing of hypnotic medications for insomnia? *Human Psychopharmacology Clinical and Experimental, 18,* 69–73.

Brownmiller, S. (1984). *Femininity.* New York: Ballantine Books.

Brownridge, D. A. (2003). Male partner violence against Aboriginal women in Canada: An empirical analysis. *Journal of Interpersonal Violence, 18*(1), 65–83.

Bruce, K. R., Koerner, N. M. Steiger, H., & Young, S. N. (2003). Laxative misuse and behavioral disinhibition in bulimia nervosa. *International Journal of Eating Disorders, 33,* 92–97.

Bruce, K. R., Steiger, H., Koerner, N. M., Israel, M., & Young, N. (2004). Bulimia nervosa with co-morbid avoidant personality disorder: Behavioural characteristics and serotonergic function. *Psychological Medicine, 34,* 113–124.

Bruce, M. L., & Kim, K. M. (1992). Differences in the effects of divorce on major depression in men and women. *American Journal of Psychiatry, 149*(7), 914–917.

Bruce, S. E., Yonkers, K. A., Otto, M. W., Eisen, J. L., Weisberg, R. B., Pagano, M., … Keller, M. B. (2005). Influence of psychiatric comorbidity on recovery and recurrence in generalized anxiety disorder, social phobia, and panic disorder: A 12-year prospective study. *American Journal of Psychiatry, 162,* 1179–1187.

Bruch, H. (1973). *Eating disorders: Obesity, anorexia nervosa, and the person within.* New York: Basic Books.

Bruch, H. (1985). Four decades of eating disorders. In D. M. Garner & P. E. Garfinkel (Eds.), *Handbook of psychotherapy for anorexia nervosa and bulimia* (pp. 7–18). New York: Guilford Press.

Bruch, H. (1986). Anorexia nervosa: The therapeutic task. In K. D. Brownell & J. P. Foreyt (Eds.), *Handbook of eating disorders: Physiology, psychology, and treatment of obesity, anorexia, and bulimia* (pp. 328–332). New York: Basic Books.

Bruch, M. A., & Heimberg, R. G. (1994). Differences in perceptions of parental and personal characteristics between generalized and non-generalized social phobics. *Journal of Anxiety Disorders, 8,* 155–168.

Bruck, M. (1987). The adult outcomes of children with learning disabilities. *Annals of Dyslexia, 37,* 252–263.

Bruck, M. (1992). Persistence of dyslexics' phonological deficits. *Developmental Psychology, 28,* 874–886.

Brunner, H. G., Nelen, M., Breakefield, X. O., Ropers, H. H., & van Oost, B. A. (1993). Abnormal behavior associated with a point mutation in the structural gene for monoamine oxidase A. *Science, 262,* 578–580.

Brunner, H. G., Nelen, M. R., Van Zandvoort, P., Abeling, N. G. G. M., van Gennip, A. H., Wolters, E. C., … van Oost, B. A. (1993). X-linked borderline mental retardation with prominent behavioral disturbance: Phenotype, genetic localization, and evidence for disturbed monoamine metabolism. *American Journal of Human Genetics, 52,* 1032–1039.

Bryant, D. M., & Maxwell, K. L. (1999). The environment and mental retardation. *International Review of Psychiatry, 11,* 56–67.

Bryant, R. A., Moulds, M. L., & Nixon, R. V. D. (2003). Cognitive behavior therapy of acute stress disorder: A four-year follow-up. *Behaviour Research and Therapy, 41,* 489–494.

Bryson, S., Rogers, S. J., & Fombonne, E. (2003). Autism spectrum disorders: Early detection, intervention, education, and psychopharmacological management. *Canadian Journal of Psychiatry, 48,* 506–516.

Bryson, S. E., & Smith, I. M. (1998). Epidemiology of autism: Prevalence, associated characteristics, and implications for research and service delivery. *Mental Retardation & Developmental Disabilities Research Reviews, 4,* 97–103.

Buchwald, A. M., & Rudick-Davis, D. (1993). The symptoms of major depression. *Journal of Abnormal Psychology, 102*(2), 197–205.

Buda, M., & Tsuang, M. T. (1990). The epidemiology of suicide: Implications for clinical practice. In S. J. Blumenthal & D. J. Kupfer (Eds.), *Suicide over the life cycle: Risk factors, assessment and treatment of suicidal patients.* Washington, DC: American Psychiatric Press.

Buehler, R. E., Patterson, G. R., & Furniss, J. M. (1966). The reinforcement of behavior in institutional settings. *Behavior, Research, and Therapy, 4,* 157–167.

Buffett-Jerrott, S., & Stewart, S. H. (2002). Cognitive and sedative effects of benzodiazepine use. *Current Pharmaceutical Design, 8,* 45–58.

Buffett-Jerrott, S. E., Stewart, S. H., Finley, G. A., & Loughlan, H. L. (2003). Effects of benzodiazepines on explicit memory in a paediatric surgery setting. *Psychopharmacology, 168,* 377–386.

Buffett-Jerrott, S. E., Stewart, S. H., & Teehan, M. D. (1998). A further examination of the time-dependent effects of oxazepam and lorazepam on implicit and explicit memory. *Psychopharmacology, 138,* 344–353.

Buffum, J. (1982). Pharmacosexology: The effects of drugs on sexual function—a review. *Journal of Psychoactive Drugs, 14,* 5–44.

Bulik, C. M., Sullivan, P. F., & Kendler, K. S. (2000). An empirical study of the classification of eating disorders. *American Journal of Psychiatry, 157*(6), 886–895.

Bumpass, E. R., Fagelman, F. D., & Brix, R. J. (1983). Intervention with children who set fires. *American Journal of Psychotherapy, 37*(3), 328–345.

Burack, J. A., Iarocci, G., Bowler, D., & Mottron, L. (2002). Benefits and pitfalls in the merging of disciplines: The example of developmental psychopathology and the study of persons with autism. *Development & Psychopathology, 14,* 225–237.

Burke, K. C., Burke, J. D., Jr., Regier, D. A., & Rae, D. S. (1990). Age at onset of selected mental disorders in five community populations. *Archives of General Psychiatry, 47,* 511–518.

Burns, A. (2000). The burden of Alzheimer's disease. *International Journal of Neuropsychopharmacology, 3*(7), 31–38.

Burton, R. (1977). *Anatomy of melancholy* (reprinted.). New York: Random House. (Original work published 1621).

Bury, A. S., & Bagby, R. M. (2002). The detection of feigned uncoached and coached posttraumatic stress disorder with the MMPI-2 in a sample of workplace accident victims. *Psychological Assessment, 14,* 472–484.

Buscher, A. L., & Giordano, T. P. (2010). Gaps in knowledge in caring for HIV survivors long-term. *JAMA, 304,* 340–341.

Bushman, B. J. (1993). Human aggression while under the influence of alcohol and other drugs: An integrative research review. *Psychological Science, 2,* 148–152.

Bushnell, J. A., Wells, J. E., Hornblow, A. R., Oakley-Browne, M. A., & Joyce, P. (1990). Prevalence of three bulimia syndromes in the general population. *Psychological Medicine, 20,* 671–680.

Bustillo, J., Lauriello, J., Horan, W., & Keith, S. (2001). The psychosocial treatment of schizophrenia: An update. *American Journal of Psychiatry, 158*(2), 163–175.

Butcher, J. N. (2009). Clinical personality assessment: History, evolution, contemporary models, and practical applications. In J. N. Butcher (Ed.), *Oxford handbook of personality assessment* (pp. 5–21). New York: Oxford University Press.

Butcher, J. N., Graham, J. R., Williams, C. L., & Ben-Porath, Y. S. (1990). *Development and use of the MMPI-2 content scales.* Minneapolis: University of Minnesota Press.

Butler, G., & Mathews, A. (1983). *Cognitive processes in anxiety. Advances in Behaviour Research and Therapy, 5,* 51–62.

Butler, L. D., Duran, R. E. F., Jasiukaitis, P., Koopman, C., & Spiegel, D. (1996). Hypnotizability and traumatic experience: A diathesis stress model of dissociative symptomatology. *American Journal of Psychiatry, 153,* 42–63.

Buxton, J. (2005). *Vancouver Drug Use Epidemiology: Vancouver site report for the Canadian Community Epidemiology Network on Drug Use (CCENDU).* Ottawa, ON: Canadian Community Epidemiology Network on Drug Use. Retrieved December 1, 2007, from http://www.ccsa.ca/NR/rdonlyres/E8864A4A-6225-4EF9-B4A9-9C391AC60B91/0/CCENDUVancouverhighlights2005e.pdf

Buysse, D. J., Reynolds, C. F., & Kupfer, D. J. (1993). Classification of sleep disorders: A preview of the DSM-IV. In D. L. Dunner (Ed.), *Current psychiatric therapy* (pp. 360–361). Philadelphia: W. B. Saunders.

Buysse, D. J., Strollo, P. J., Black, J. E., Zee, P. G., & Winkelman, J. W. (2008). Sleep disorders. In R. E. Hales, S. C. Yudofsky, & G. O. Gabbard (Eds.), *The American Psychiatric Publishing Textbook of Psychiatry* (5th ed., pp. 921–969). Arlington, VA: American Psychiatric Publishing.

Bye, E. K. (2007). Alcohol and violence: Use of possible confounders in a time-series analysis. *Addiction, 102,* 369–376.

Byne, W., Lasco, M. S., Kemether, E., Edgar, M. A., Morgello, S., Jones, L. B., & Tobet, S. (2000). The interstitial nuclei of the human anterior hypothalamus: An investigation of sexual variation in volume and cell size, number and density. *Brain Research, 856,* 254–258.

Byne, W., & Parsons, B. (1993). Human sexual orientation: The biologic theories reappraised. *Archives of General Psychiatry, 50,* 228–239.

Byrne, D., & Schulte, L. (1990). Personality dispositions as mediators of sexual responses. *Annual Review of Sex Research, 1,* 93–117.

Byrne, J. M., Bawden, H. N., Beattie, T., DeWolfe, N. A. (2003). Risk for injury in preschoolers: Relationship to attention deficit hyperactivity disorder. *Child Neuropsychology, 9,* 142–151.

Cabeza, R., & Nyberg, L. (2000). Imaging cognition II: An empirical review of 275 PET and fMRI studies. *Journal of Cognitive Neuroscience, 12*(1), 1–47.

Cacioppo, J. T., Amaral, D. G., Blanchard, J. J., Cameron, J. L., Carter, C. S., Crews, D., ... Quinn, K. J. (2007). Social neuroscience: Progress and implications for mental health. *Perspectives on Psychological Science, 2*(2), 99–123.

Cadoret, R. J. (1978). Psychopathology in the adopted-away offspring of biologic parents with antisocial behavior. *Archives of General Psychiatry, 35,* 176–184.

Cadoret, R. J., Yates, W. R., Troughton, E., Woodworth, G., & Stewart, M. A. (1995). Genetic-environment interaction in the genesis of aggressivity and conduct disorders. *Archives of General Psychiatry, 52,* 916–924.

Cafri, G., Yamamiya, Y., Brannick, M., & Thompson, J. K. (2005). The influence of sociocultural factors on body image: A meta-analysis. *Clinical Psychology: Science and Practice, 12,* 421–433.

Cairney, J., Thorpe, C., Rietschlin, J., & Avison, W. R. (1999). 12-month prevalence of depression among single and married mothers in the 1994 National Population Health Survey. *Canadian Journal of Public Health, 90,* 320–324.

Calabrese, J., Shelton, M, Rapport, D., Youngstrom, E., Jackson, K., Bilali, S., ... Findling, R. L. (2005). A 20-month, double-blind, maintenance trial of lithium versus divalproex, in rapid-cycling bipolar disorder. *American Journal of Psychiatry, 162,* 2152–2161.

Calamari, J. E., Wiegartz, P. S., Riemann, B. C., Cohen, R. J., Greer, A., Jacobi, D. M., ... Carmin, C. (2004). Obsessive-compulsive disorder subtypes: An attempted replication and extension of symptom-based taxonomy. *Behavior Research and Therapy, 42,* 647–670.

Cameron, N. M., Champagne, F. A., Parent, C., Fish, E. W., Ozaki-Kuroda, K., & Meaney, M. J. (2005). The programming of individual differences in defensive responses and reproductive strategies in the rat through variations in maternal care. *Neuroscience and Biobehavioral Reviews, 29,* 843–865.

Campbell, D. (2003, January 15). Pcp pills blamed in friendly fire case. *The Guardian.* Retrieved October 25, 2003, from http://www.guardian.co.uk/afghanistan/story/0,1284,874923,00.html

Campbell, M. A., Porter, S., & Santor, D. (2004). Psychopathic traits in adolescent offenders: An evaluation of criminal history, clinical, and psychosocial correlates. *Behavioral Sciences & the Law, 22,* 23–47.

Campbell-Sills, L., & Barlow, D. H. (2007). Incorporating emotion regulation into conceptualization and treatment of anxiety and mood disorders. In J. J. Gross (Ed.), *Handbook of emotion regulation* (pp. 542–560). New York: Guilford Press.

Campisi, T. A. (1995). Exposure and response prevention in the treatment of body dysmorphic disorder. *Dissertation Abstracts International: Section B: The Sciences and Engineering, 56,* 7036.

Campo, J. V., & Negrini, B. J. (2000). Case study: Negative reinforcement and behavioral management of conversion disorder. *Journal of the American Academy of Child and Adolescent Psychiatry, 39*(6), 787–790.

Canada Online. (2003, May 26). *The issue—Decriminalization of marijuana in Canada: Canadian government plans to ease marijuana laws.* Retrieved October 26, 2003, from http://canadaonline.about.com/library/issues/blimj.htm

Canadian Centre for Substance Abuse. (1999). *Canadian Profile 1999. Alcohol: Highlights.* Retrieved November 15, 2002, from http://www.ccsa.ca/profile/cp99alc.htm

Canadian Centre for Substance Abuse. (2004, November). *A national survey of Canadians' use of alcohol and other drugs: Prevalence of use and related harms.* Retrieved March 3, 2008, from http://www.ccsa.ca/NR/rdonlyres/B2C820A2-C987-4F08-8605 2BE999FE4DFC/0/ccsa0048042004.pdf

Canadian Charter of Rights and Freedoms, being Part I of the Constitution Act, 1982, enacted by the Canada Act 1982 (U.K.), c. 11, Sched. B. (R. S. C. (1985), Appendix II, No. 44).

Canadian Council on Smoking & Health and Physicians for a Smoke-Free Canada. (2003). *Number of deaths in Canada caused by smoking.* Retrieved August 16, 2003, from http://www.mediaawareness.ca/english/resources/educational/handouts/tobacco_advertising/number_of_deaths.cfm

Canadian Down Syndrome Society. (2000). New Down syndrome statistics. *CDSS Quarterly, 13.* Retrieved May 20, 2004, from http://www.cdss.ca/Newsletter%20Articles/medical%20and%20health/2000vol13–1,8.html

Canadian Press. (2003, December 30). *Questions about the herb ephedra and its ban by the FDA.* Retrieved August 6, 2004, from http://www.medbroadcast.com/channel_health_news_details.asp?news_channel_id1000&news_id2957&channel_id1012&relation_id0

Canadian Press. (2004, May 11). Boy raised as girl has tragic demise: Doctor advised gender switch. *The Chronicle Herald, 56,* A1–A2.

Canadian Psychological Association. (1999). *Geographic locations survey of clinical psychologists in Canada.* Ottawa, ON: Canadian Psychological Association.

Canadian Psychological Association. (2000). *Canadian code of ethics for psychologists* (3rd ed.). Ottawa, ON: Canadian Psychological Association.

Canadian Psychological Association. (2004). *Deciding to see a psychologist: How to choose one and what to expect.* Retrieved July 5, 2004, from http://www.cpa.ca/Psychologist/psychologist.htm

Canadian Study of Health and Aging Working Group. (1994). Canadian Study of Health and Aging: Study methods and prevalence of dementia. *Canadian Medical Association Journal, 150,* 899–913.

Canadian Study of Health and Aging Working Group. (2000). The incidence of dementia in Canada. *Neurology, 55,* 66–73.

Canadian Study of Health and Aging Working Group. (2001). Disability and frailty among elderly Canadians: A comparison of six surveys. *International Journal of Psychogeriatrics, 13*(Suppl. 1), 159–167.

Candido, C. L., & Romney, D. M. (2002). Depression in paranoid and nonparanoid schizophrenic patients compared with major depressive disorder. *Journal of Affective Disorders, 70,* 261–271.

Cannon, T. D., Barr, C. E., & Mednick, S. A. (1991). Genetic and perinatal factors in the etiology of schizophrenia. In E. F. Walker (Ed.), *Schizophrenia: A life-course developmental perspective* (pp. 9–31). New York: Academic Press.

Cannon, W. B. (1929). *Bodily changes in pain, hunger, fear and rage* (2nd ed.). New York: Appleton-Century-Crofts.

Cannon, W. B. (1942). Voodoo death. *American Anthropologist, 44,* 169–181.

Canter, A. (1996). The Bender-Gesalt Test (BGT). In C. S. Newmark (Ed.), *Major psychological assessment instruments* (pp. 400–430). Boston: Allyn & Bacon.

Canterbury Farms. (1997). *The new wonder herb that has been around for 2500 years!* Retrieved July 7, 2004, from http://www.nwgardening.com/stjohnswort.html

CanWest News Service. (2006, October 26). First look at conjoined twins. *Canada.com.* Retrieved

November 1, 2006, from http://www.canada.com/cityguides/toronto/story.html?id0e49832c-7a4f-4ab7-a804-e7cc03c9978f&k13358

Cappell, H., & Greeley, J. (1987). Alcohol and tension reduction: An update on research and theory. In H. T. Blane & K. E. Leonard (Eds.), *Psychological theories of drinking and alcoholism* (pp. 15–54). New York: Guilford Press.

Caprara, D. L., Nash, K., Greenbaum, R., Rovet, J., & Koren, G. (2007). Novel approaches to the diagnosis of fetal alcohol spectrum disorder. *Neuroscience & Biobehavioral Reviews, 31*(2), 254–260.

CARE Study Group. (2008). Maternal caffeine intake during pregnancy and risk of fetal growth restriction: A large prospective observational study. *BMJ, 337,* 1334–1338.

Cardeña, E., Lewis-Fernandez, R., Bear, D., Pakianathan, I., & Spiegel, D. (1996). Dissociative disorders. In T. A. Widiger, A. J. Frances, H. A. Pincus, R. Ross, et al. (Eds.), *DSM-IV sourcebook* (Vol. 2, pp. 973–1005). Washington, DC: American Psychiatric Press.

Cardeña, E. A., & Gleaves, D. H. (2003). Dissociative disorders: Phantoms of the self. In M. Hersen & S. M. Turner (Eds.), *Adult psychopathology and diagnosis* (4th ed., pp. 476–505). New York: John Wiley & Sons.

Carey, G. (1992). Twin imitation for antisocial behavior: Implications for genetic and family environment research. *Journal of Abnormal Psychology, 101,* 18–25.

Carey, M. P., & Johnson, B. T. (1996). Effectiveness of yohimbine in the treatment of erectile disorder: Four meta-analytic integrations. *Archives of Sexual Behavior, 25,* 341–360.

Carey, M. P., Wincze, J. P., & Meisler, A. W. (1993). Sexual dysfunction: Male erectile disorder. In D. H. Barlow (Ed.), *Clinical handbook of psychological disorders* (2nd ed., pp. 442–480). New York: Guilford Press.

Carlat, D. J., & Camargo, C. A. (1991). Review of bulimia nervosa in males. *American Journal of Psychiatry, 148,* 831–843.

Carlat, D. J., Camargo, C. A., Jr., & Herzog, D. B. (1997). Eating disorders in males: A report on 135 patients. *American Journal of Psychiatry, 154,* 1127–1132.

Carlbring, P., Westling, B. E., Ljungstrand, P., Ekselius, L., & Andersson, G. (2001). Treatment of panic disorder via the Internet: A randomized trial of a self-help program. *Behavior Therapy, 32,* 751–764.

Carlson, E. B., & Putnam, F. W. (1989). Integrating research on dissociation and hypnotizability: Are there two pathways to hypnotizability? *Dissociation, 2,* 32–38.

Carlson, G. A. (1990). Annotation: Child and adolescent mania—diagnostic considerations. *Journal of Child Psychology and Psychiatry, 31*(3), 331–341.

Carlson, L. E., & Garland, S. N. (2005). Impact of mindfulness-based stress reduction (MBSR) on sleep, mood, stress and fatigue symptoms in cancer outpatients. *International Journal of Behavioral Medicine, 12*(4), 278–285.

Carlson, L. E., Speca, M., Patel, K. D., & Goodey, E. (2004). Mindfulness-based stress reduction in relation to quality of life, mood, symptoms of stress and levels of cortisol, dehydroepiandrosterone sulfate (DHEAS) and melatonin in breast and prostate cancer outpatients. *Psychoneuroendocrinology, 9*(4), 448–474.

Carlsson, A. (1995). The dopamine theory revisited. In S. R. Hirsch and D. R. Weinberger (Eds.),

Schizophrenia (pp. 379–400). Oxford: Blackwell Science.

Carmody, D. L., & Carmody, J. T. (1993). *Native American Religions.* Mahwah, NJ: Paulist Press.

Caron, C., & Rutter, M. (1991). Comorbidity in childhood psychopathology: Concepts, issues, and research strategies. *Journal of Child Psychology and Psychiatry, 32,* 1063–1080.

Carpenter, W. T. (1992). The negative symptom challenge. *Archives of General Psychiatry, 49,* 236–237.

Carpenter, W. T. (1994). The deficit syndrome. *American Journal of Psychiatry, 151,* 327–329.

Carr, E. G., & Durand, V. M. (1985). Reducing behavior problems through functional communication training. *Journal of Applied Behavior Analysis, 18,* 111–126.

Carrasco, M., Barker, E. D., Tremblay, R. E., & Vitaro, F. (2006). Eysenck's personality dimensions as predictors of male adolescent trajectories of physical aggression, theft and vandalism. *Personality and Individual Differences, 41,* 1309–1320.

Carrico, A. W., & Antoni, M. H. (2008). Effects of psychological interventions on neuroendocrine hormone regulation and immune states in HIV-positive persons: A review of randomized controlled trials. *Psychosomatic Medicine, 70,* 575–584.

Carrier, S., Brock, G. B., Pommerville, P. J., Shin, J., Anglin, G., Whittaker, S., & Beasley, C. M., Jr. (2005). Efficacy and safety of oral tadalafil in the treatment of men in Canada with erectile dysfunction: A randomized, double-blind, parallel, placebo-controlled clinical trial. *Journal of Sexual Medicine, 2,* 685–698.

Carrigg, D., & Luymes, G. (2007, July 11). Decriminalize pot: Campbell, B. C. senator and ex-mayor says possession should result in fine. *The Province,* p. A.3.

Carrington, P. J. (1999). Gender, gun control, suicide and homicide in Canada. *Archives of Suicide Research, 5,* 71–75.

Carroll, A. (2009). Are you looking at me? Understanding and managing paranoid personality disorder. *Advances in Psychiatric Treatment, 15*(1), 40.

Carroll, B. J., Feinberg, M., Greden, J. F., Haskett, R. F., James, N. M., Steiner, M., & Tarika, J. (1980). Diagnosis of endogenous depression: Comparison of clinical, research, and neuroendocrine criteria. *Journal of Affective Disorders, 2,* 177–194.

Carroll, B. J., Martin, F. I., & Davies, B. (1968). Resistance to suppression by dexamethasome of plasma 11-O.H.C.S. levels in severe depressive illness. *British Medical Journal, 3,* 285–287.

Carroll, E. M., Rueger, D. B., Foy, D. W., & Donahoe, C. P. (1985). Vietnam combat veterans with post-traumatic stress disorder: Analysis of marital and cohabitating adjustment. *Journal of Abnormal Psychology, 94,* 329–337.

Carroll, K. M. (1992). Psychotherapy for cocaine abuse: Approaches, evidence, and conceptual models. In T. R. Kosten & H. D. Kleber (Eds.), *Clinician's guide to cocaine addiction: Theory, research, and treatment* (pp. 290–313). New York: Guilford Press.

Carroll, R. A. (2000). Assessment and treatment of gender dysphoria. In S. R. Leiblum & R. C. Rosen (Eds.), *Principles and practice of sex therapy* (3rd ed., pp. 368–397). New York: Guilford Press.

Carroll, R. A. (2007). Gender dysphoria and transgender experiences. In S. R. Leiblum (Ed.), *Principles and practice of sex therapy* (4th ed., pp. 477–508). New York: Guilford Press.

Carson, R. C. (1991). Discussion: Dilemmas in the pathway of DSM-IV. *Journal of Abnormal Psychology, 100,* 302–307.

Carson, R. C. (1996). Aristotle, Galileo, and the DSM taxonomy: The case of schizophrenia. *Journal of Consulting and Clinical Psychology, 64*(6), 1133–1139.

Carson, R. C., & Sanislow, C. A. (1993). The schizophrenias. In P. B. Sutker & H. E. Adams (Eds.), *Comprehensive handbook of psychopathology* (pp. 295–333). New York: Plenum Press.

Carstensen, L. L., Charles, S. T., Isaacowitz, D., & Kennedy, Q. (2003). Life-span personality development and emotion. In R. J. Davidson, K. Scherer, & H. H. Goldsmith (Eds.), *Handbook of affective sciences* (pp. 726–746). Oxford: Oxford University Press.

Carter, J. C., & Fairburn, C. G. (1998). Cognitive-behavioral self-help for binge eating disorder: A controlled effectiveness study. *Journal of Consulting and Clinical Psychology, 66,* 616–623.

Carter, J. R., & Neufeld, R. W. J. (1998). Cultural aspects of understanding people with schizophrenic disorders. In S. S. Kazarian & D. R. Evans (Eds.), *Cultural clinical psychology: Theory, research, and practice* (pp. 246–266). London: Oxford University Press.

Carter, J. R., & Neufeld, R. W. J. (2007). Cognitive processing of facial affect: Connectionist model of deviations in schizophrenia. *Journal of Abnormal Psychology, 116*(2), 290–305.

Cartwright, R. D. (2006). Sleepwalking. In T. Lee Chiong (Ed.), *Sleep: A comprehensive handbook* (pp. 429–433). Hoboken, NJ: John Wiley & Sons.

Carver, C. S., Johnson, S. L., & Joormann, J. (2009). Two-mode models of self-regulation as a tool for conceptualizing effects of the serotonin system in normal behavior and diverse disorders. *Current Directions in Psychological Science, 18*(4), 195–199.

Caseras, X., Torrubia, R., & Farre, J. M. (2001). Is the behavioral inhibition system the core vulnerability for cluster C personality disorders? *Personality and Individual Differences, 31,* 349–359.

Cash, T. F., & Pruzinsky, T. (2002). Understanding body images. In T. F. Cash & T. Pruzinsky (Eds.), *Body image: A handbook of theory, research and clinical practice* (pp. 3–12). New York: Guildford Press.

Casper, R. C. (1982). Treatment principles in anorexia nervosa. *Adolescent Psychiatry, 10,* 431–454.

Caspi, A., Elder, G. H., Jr., & Bem, D. L. (1987). Moving against the world: Life-course patterns of explosive children. *Developmental Psychology, 23,* 308–313.

Caspi, A., McClay, J., Moffitt, T., Mill, J., Martin, J., Craig, I. W., . . . Poulton, R. (2002). Role of genotype in the cycle of violence in maltreated children. *Science, 297,* 851–854.

Caspi, A., Moffitt, T. E., Cannon, M., McClay, J., Murray, R., Harrington, H. L., . . . Craig, I. W. (2005). Moderation of the effect of adolescent-onset cannabis use on adult psychosis by a functional polymorphism in the catechol-*o*-methyltransferase gene: Longitudinal evidence of a gene X environment interaction. *Biological Psychiatry, 57,* 1117–1127.

Caspi, A., Sugden, K., Moffitt, T. E., Taylor, A., Craig, I. W., Harrington, H., . . . Poulton, R. (2003). Influence of life stress on depression: Moderation by a polymorphism in the 5-HTT gene. *Science, 301,* 386–389.

Cassidy, F., Forest, K., Murry, E., & Carroll, B. J. (1998). A factor analysis of the signs and symptoms of mania. *Archives of General Psychiatry, 55,* 27–32.

Cassin, S. E., & von Ranson, K. M. (2005). Personality and eating disorders: A decade in review. *Clinical Psychology Review, 25,* 895–916.

Castellanos, F. X., Sharp, W. S., Gottesman, R. F, Greenstein, D. K., Giedd, J. N., & Rapoport, J. L. (2003). Anatomic brain abnormalities in monozygotic twins discordant for attention deficit hyperactivity disorder. *American Journal of Psychiatry, 160,* 1693–1696.

Castonguay, L. G., Eldredge, K. L., & Agras, W. S. (1995). Binge eating disorder: Current state and directions. *Clinical Psychology Review, 15,* 815–890.

Catania, J. A., Morin, S. F., Canchola, J., Pollack, L., Chang, J., & Coates, T. J. (2000). U.S. priorities—HIV prevention. *Science, 290,* 717.

Cautela, J. R. (1966). Treatment of compulsive behavior by covert sensitization. *Psychological Record, 16,* 33–41.

Cautela, J. R. (1967). Covert sensitization. *Psychological Reports, 20,* 459–468.

Cavior, N., & Marabotto, C. M. (1976). Monitoring verbal behaviors in a dyadic interaction: Valence of target behaviors, type, timing, and reactivity of monitoring. *Journal of Consulting and Clinical Psychology, 44,* 68–76.

CBC News Online. (2003a, June 21). *Police lay murder charge in Holly Jones case.* Retrieved August 5, 2004, from http://www.cbc.ca/stories/2003/06/20/holly030620

CBC News Online. (2003b, June 20). *Holly Jones timeline.* Retrieved August 5, 2004, from http://www.cbc.ca/news/indepth/background/jones_holly_timeline.html

CBC News Online. (2004a, June 17). *Killer of Holly Jones pleads guilty.* Retrieved August 5, 2004, from http://www.cbc.ca/stories/2004/06/17/canada/holly040617

CBC News Online. (2004b, August 5). *Timeline of BSE in Canada and the U.S.* Retrieved August 11, 2004, from http://www.cbc.ca/news/background/madcow/timeline.html

CBC News Online. (2007, September 14). *U.S. to allow import of older Canadian cows as of November.* Retrieved September 28, 2007, from http://www.cbc.ca/canada/story/2007/09/14/usda-ruling.html

CBC Saskatchewan News Staff. (2003). *Possible Mackay forgets burning body: Expert.* CBC Saskatchewan. Retrieved June 8, 2003, from http://sask.cbc.ca/regional/servlet/View?filenamemackay020608

CBCnews.ca. (2008, January 24). *Crown, defence disagree on date for Pickton's 2nd trial.* Retrieved January 31, 2008, from http://www.cbc.ca/canada/british-columbia/story/2008/01/24/bc-pickton.html

CBS News. (1999, February 25). *Obsessions* [Television series episode]. Retrieved from http://www.ocfoundation.org/ocf1420q.htm

Celio, A. A., Zabinski, M. F., & Wilfley, D. E. (2002). African-American body images. In T. F. Cash & T. Pruzinsky (Eds.), *Body image: A handbook of theory, research and clinical practice* (pp. 234–242). New York: Guildford Press.

Centers for Disease Control. (1994, September). *HIV/AIDS surveillance.* Atlanta, GA: U.S. Department of Health and Human Services, Public Health Services.

Centers for Disease Control. (2003). *Deaths, percent of total deaths, and death rates for the 15 leading causes of death in 5-year age groups, by race and sex: United States, 2000.* Centers for Disease Control and National Center for Health Statistics, National Vital Statistics System.

Centers for Disease Control and Prevention. (2009). Prevalence of autism spectrum disorders—Autism and developmental disabilities monitoring network: United States, 2006. *Morbidity and Mortality Weekly Report, 58*(SS10), 1–20.

Centre for Addiction and Mental Health. (2007). *First Episode Psychosis Clinic.* Retrieved January 7, 2008, from http://www.camh.net/About_CAMH/Guide_to_CAMH/MentalHealth_Programs/Schizophrenia_Program/guide_first_episode_program.html

Cepeda-Benito, A. (1993). Meta-analytical review of the efficacy of nicotine chewing gum in smoking treatment programs. *Journal of Consulting and Clinical Psychology, 61,* 822–830.

Chakrabarti, S., & Fombonne, E. (2001). Pervasive developmental disorders in preschool children. *JAMA, 285,* 3093–3099.

Chalder, T., Cleare, A., & Wessely, S. (2000). The management of stress and anxiety in chronic fatigue syndrome. In D. I. Mostofsky & D. H. Barlow (Eds.), *The management of stress and anxiety in medical disorders* (pp. 160–179). Needham Heights, MA: Allyn & Bacon.

Chamberlain, S. R., Menzies, L., Hampshire, A., Suckling, J., Fineberg, N. A., del Campo N., . . . Sahakian, B. J. (2008). Orbitofrontal dysfunction in patients with obsessive-compulsive disorder and their unaffected relatives. *Science, 321,* 421–422.

Chamberlain, S. R., Menzies, L., Sahakian, B. J., & Fineberg, N. A. (2007). Lifting the veil on trichotillomania. *American Journal of Psychiatry, 164,* 568–574.

Chan, C., Ngai, E., Leung, P., & Wong, S. (2010). Effect of the adapted virtual reality cognitive training program among Chinese older adults with chronic schizophrenia: A pilot study. *International Journal of Geriatric Psychiatry, 25*(6), 643–649.

Chandler, M. J., & Lalonde, C. (1998). Cultural continuity as a hedge against suicide in Canada's First Nations. *Transcultural Psychiatry, 35,* 191–219.

Charach, A., Figueroa, M., Chen, S., Ickowicz, A., & Schachar, R. (2006). Stimulant treatment over 5 years: Effects on growth. *Journal of the American Academy of Child and Adolescent Psychiatry, 45,* 415–421.

Charbonneau, J., & O'Connor, K. (1999). Depersonalization in a non-clinical sample. *Behavioural and Cognitive Psychotherapy, 27,* 377–381.

Charland, L. C. (2010). Science and morals in the affective psychopathology of Philippe Pinel. *History of Psychiatry, 21*(1), 38–53.

Charlebois, P., LeBlanc, M., Gagnon, C., Larivée, S., & Tremblay, R. (1993). Age trends in early behavioral predictors of serious antisocial behaviors. *Journal of Psychopathology and Behavioral Assessment, 15,* 23–41.

Charney, D. S., Barlow, D. H., Botteron, K., Cohen, J. D., Goldman, D., Gur, R. E., . . . Zalcman, S. J. (2002). Neuroscience research agenda to guide development of a pathophysiologically based classification system. In D. J. Kupfer, M. B. First, & D. A. Regier (Eds.), *A research agenda for DSM-V* (pp. 31–83). Washington, DC: American Psychiatric Association.

Charney, D. S., Deutch, A. Y., Krystal, J. H., Southwick, S. M., & Davis, M. (1993). Psychobiological mechanisms of posttraumatic stress disorder. *Archives of General Psychiatry, 50,* 294–305.

Charney, D. S., & Drevets, W. C. (2002). Neurobiological basis of anxiety disorders.

In K. L. Davis, D. Charney, J. T. Coyle, & C. Nemeroff (Eds.), *Neuropsychopharmacology: The fifth generation of progress* (pp. 901–951). Philadelphia: Lippincott Williams & Wilkins.

Charney, D. S., Woods, S. W., Price, L. H., Goodman, W. K., Glazer, W. M., & Heninger, G. R. (1990). Noradrenergic dysregulation in panic disorder. In J. C. Ballenger (Ed.), *Neurobiology of panic disorder* (pp. 91–105). New York: Wiley-Liss.

Chassin, L., Pillow, D. R., Curran, P. J., Molina, B. S. G., & Barrera, M. (1993). Relation of parental alcoholism to early adolescent substance use: A test of three mediating mechanisms. *Journal of Abnormal Psychology, 102,* 3–19.

Chavez, M., & Insel, T. R. (2007). Eating disorders: National Institute of Mental Health perspective. *American Psychologist, 62,* 159–166.

Check, J. R. (1998). Munchausen syndrome by proxy: An atypical form of child abuse. *Journal of Practical Psychology and Behavioral Health, 4,* 340–345.

Cheng, C., & Tang, C. S.-K. (2004). The psychology behind the masks: Psychological responses to the severe acute respiratory syndrome outbreak in different regions [Special issue: Special issue on psychology of severe acute respiratory syndrome (SARS)]. *Asian Journal of Social Psychology, 7,* 3–7.

Chesney, M. A. (1986, November). Type A behavior: The biobehavioral interface. Keynote address presented at the annual meeting of the Association for Advancement of Behavior Therapy, Chicago.

Chiappe, P., Stringer, R., Siegel, L. S., & Stanovich, K. E. (2002). Why the timing deficit hypothesis does not explain reading disability in adults. *Reading and Writing, 15,* 73–107.

Chilcott, L. A., & Shapiro, C. M. (1996). The socio-economic impact of insomnia: An overview. *Pharmacoeconomics, 10,* 1–14.

China U.N. Theme Group on HIV/AIDS for the U.N. Country team in China. (2001). *HIV/AIDS: China's titanic peril. In 2001 update of the AIDS situation and needs assessment report.* Beijing: UNAIDS.

Ching, S., Thoma, A., McCabe, R., & Antony, M. (2003). Measuring outcomes in aesthetic surgery: A comprehensive review of the literature. *Canadian Journal of Plastic Surgery, 111*(1), 469–480.

Chivers, M. L., & Bailey, J. M. (2000). Sexual orientation of female-to-male transsexuals: A comparison of homosexual and nonhomosexual types. *Archives of Sexual Behavior, 29*(3), 259–279.

Cho, H. J., Lavretsky, H., Olmstead, R., Levin, M. J., Oxman, M. N., & Irwin, M. R. (2008). Sleep disturbance and depression recurrence in community-dwelling older adults: A prospective study. *American Journal of Psychiatry, 165*(12), 1543–1550.

Choate, M. L., Pincus, D. B., Eyberg, S. M., & Barlow, D. B. (2005). Parent–child interaction therapy for treatment of separation anxiety disorder: A pilot study. *Cognitive and Behavioral Practice, 12*(1), 126–135.

Chodoff, P. (1974). The diagnosis of hysteria: An overview. *American Journal of Psychiatry, 131,* 1073–1078.

Chodoff, P. (1982). Hysteria in women. *American Journal of Psychiatry, 139,* 545–551.

Chorpita, B. F., & Barlow, D. H. (1998). The development of anxiety: The role of control in the early environment. *Psychological Bulletin, 124*(1), 3–21.

Chorpita, B. F., Brown, T. A., & Barlow, D. H. (1998). Perceived control as a mediator of family environment in etiological models of childhood anxiety. *Behavior Therapy, 29,* 457–476.

Chosak, A., Marques, L., Greenberg, J. L., Jenike, E., Dougherty, D. D., & Wilhelm, S. (2008). Body dysmorphic disorder and obsessive-compulsive disorder: Similarities, differences and the classification debate. Expert Review of *Neurotherapeutics, 8*(8), 1209–1218.

Chouinard, G., Jones, B., Remington, G., Bloom, D., Addington, D., MacEwan, G. W., … Arnott, W. (1993). A Canadian multicenter placebo-controlled study of fixed doses of risperidone and haloperidol in the treatment of chronic schizophrenic patients. *Journal of Clinical Psychopharmacology, 13,* 25–40.

Christenson, R., & Blazer, D. (1984). Epidemiology of persecutory ideation in an elderly population in the community. *American Journal of Psychiatry, 141,* 1088–1091.

Christiansen, B. A., Smith, G. T., Roehling, P. V., & Goldman, M. S. (1989). Using alcohol expectancies to predict adolescent drinking behavior after one year. *Journal of Consulting and Clinical, 57,* 93–99.

Chronic Pain Association of Canada. (2003). *Painful facts.* Retrieved July 15, 2004, from http://ecn.ab.ca/cpac/page5.html

Chronis, A. M., Lahey, B. B., Pelham, W. E., Jr., Williams, S. H., Baumann, B. L., Kipp, H., … Rathouz, P. J. (2007). Maternal depression and early positive parenting predict future conduct problems in young children with attention-deficit/hyperactivity disorder. *Developmental Psychology, 43,* 70–82.

Chudley, A. E., Gutierrez, E., Jocelyn, L. J., & Chodirker, B. N. (1998). Outcomes of genetic evaluation in children with pervasive developmental disorder. *Journal of Developmental and Behavioral Pediatrics, 19*(5), 321–325.

Chung, S. Y., Luk, S. L., & Lee, P. W. H. (1990). A follow-up study of infantile autism in Hong Kong. *Journal of Autism and Developmental Disorders, 20,* 221–232.

Cicchetti, D. (1991). A historical perspective on the discipline of developmental psychopathology. In J. Rolf, A. S. Masten, D. Cicchetti, K. H. Nuechterlein, et al. (Eds.), *Risk and protective factors in the development of psychopathology* (pp. 2–28). New York: Cambridge University Press.

Cipani, E. (1991). Educational classification and placement. In J. L. Matson & J. A. Mulick (Eds.), *Handbook of mental retardation* (2nd ed., pp. 181–191). Elmsford, NY: Pergamon Press.

Ciraulo, D. A., & Sarid-Segal, O. (2009). Sedative-, hypnotic-, or anxiolytic-related disorders. In B. J. Sadock, V. A. Sadock, & P. Ruiz (Eds.), *Kaplan & Sadock's comprehensive textbook of psychiatry* (Vol. I, 9th ed., pp. 1397–1418). Philadelphia: Lippincott Williams & Wilkins.

Clark, D. A. (2001). The persistent problem of negative cognition in anxiety and depression: New perspectives and old controversies. *Behavior Therapy, 32,* 3–12.

Clark, D. A., Beck, A. T., & Alford, B. A. (1999). *Scientific foundations of cognitive theory and therapy of depression.* New York: John Wiley & Sons.

Clark, D. A., & O'Connor, K. (2005). Thinking is believing: Ego-dystonic intrusive thoughts in obsessive-compulsive disorder. In D. A. Clark (Ed.), *Intrusive thoughts in clinical disorders* (pp. 145–174). New York: Guilford Press.

Clark, D. A., & Purdon, C. L. (1995). The assessment of unwanted intrusive thoughts: A review and critique of the literature. *Behaviour Research and Therapy, 33,* 967–976.

Clark, D. A., Steer, R. A., Haslam, N., Beck, A. T., & Brown, G. K. (1997). Personality vulnerability, psychiatric diagnoses, and symptoms: Cluster analyses of the sociotropy-autonomy subscales. *Cognitive Therapy & Research, 21,* 267–283.

Clark, D. M. (1986). A cognitive approach to panic. *Behaviour Research and Therapy, 24,* 461–470.

Clark, D. M. (1996). Panic disorder: From theory to therapy. In P. Salkovskis (Ed.), *Frontiers of cognitive therapy* (pp. 318–344). New York: Guilford Press.

Clark, D. M., Ehlers, A., McManus, F., Hackman, A., Fennell, M. J. V., Campbell, H., … Louis, B. (2003). Cognitive therapy versus fluoxetine in generalized social phobia: A randomized placebo-controlled trial. *Journal of Consulting and Clinical Psychology, 71,* 1058–1067.

Clark, D. M., Salkovskis, P. M., Hackmann, A., Middleton, H., Anastasiades, P., & Gelder, M. (1994). A comparison of cognitive therapy, applied relaxation and imipramine in the treatment of panic disorder. *British Journal of Psychiatry, 164*(6), 759–769.

Clark, D. M., Salkovski, P. M. N., Hackmann, A., Wells, A., Fennell, M., Ludgate, S., … Gelder, M. (1998). Two psychological treatments for hypochondriasis: A randomised controlled trial. *British Journal of Psychiatry, 173,* 218–225.

Clark, L. A. (1993). *Manual for the Schedule of Non-adaptive and Adaptive Personality.* Minneapolis: University of Minnesota Press.

Clark, L. A. (1999). Introduction to the special section on the concept of disorder. *Journal of Abnormal Psychology, 108,* 371–373.

Clark, L. A. (2005). Temperament as a unifying basis for personality and psychopathology [Special issue]. *Journal of Abnormal Psychology, 114,* 505–521.

Clark, R. (2003). Parental history of hypertension and coping responses predict blood pressure changes in black college volunteers undergoing a speaking task about perceptions of racism. *Psychosomatic Medicine, 65,* 1012–1019.

Clarke, C. E. (1999). Does the treatment of isolated systolic hypertension prevent dementia? *Journal of Human Hypertension, 13*(6), 357–358.

Clarkin, J. F., Haas, G. L., & Glick, I. D. (1988). *Affective disorders in the family.* New York: Guilford Press.

Clarkin, J. F., Howieson, D. B., & McClough, J. (2008). The role of psychiatric measures in assessment and treatment. In R. E. Hales, S. C. Yudofsky, & G. O. Gabbard (Eds.), *The American Psychiatric Publishing textbook of psychiatry* (5th ed., pp. 73–110). Arlington, VA: American Psychiatric Publishing, Inc.

Classen, C., Sephton, S. E., Diamond, S., & Spiegel, D. (1998). Studies of life-extending psychosocial interventions. In J. Holland (Ed.), *Psychooncology* (pp. 730–742). Oxford: Oxford University Press.

Clayton, P. J., & Darvish, H. S. (1979). Course of depressive symptoms following the stress of bereavement. In J. E. Barrett (Ed.), *Stress and mental disorder.* New York: Raven Press.

Cleckley, H. M. (1982). *The mask of sanity* (6th ed.). St. Louis, MO: Mosby. (Original work published 1941).

Cleghorn, J. M., & Albert, M. L. (1990). Modular disjunction in schizophrenia: A framework for a pathological psychophysiology. In A. Kales, C. N. Stefanis, & J. A. Talbot (Eds.), *Recent advances in schizophrenia* (pp. 59–80). New York: Springer-Verlag.

Clement, U. (1990). Surveys of heterosexual behavior. *Annual Review of Sex Research, 1,* 45–74.

Clementz, B. A., & Sweeney, J. A. (1990). Is eye movement dysfunction a biological marker for schizophrenia? A methodological review. *Psychoogical Bulletin, 108,* 77–92.

Cloninger, C. R. (1978). The link between hysteria and sociopathy: An integrative model of pathogenesis based on clinical, genetic, and neurophysiological observations. In H. S. Akiskal & W. L. Webb (Eds.), *Psychiatric diagnosis: Exploration of biological predictors* (pp. 189–218). New York: Spectrum.

Cloninger, C. R. (1987). A systematic method for clinical description and classification of personality variants: A proposal. *Archives of General Psychiatry, 44,* 573–588.

Cloninger, C. R. (1989). Establishment of diagnostic validity in psychiatric illness: Robins and Guze's method revisited. In L. N. Robins & J. E. Barrett (Eds.), *The validity of psychiatric diagnosis* (pp. 9–16). New York: Raven Press.

Cloninger, C. R. (1996). *Somatization disorder. Literature review for DSM-IV sourcebook.* Washington, DC: American Psychiatric Press.

Cloninger, C. R., & Svakic, D. M. (2009). Personality disorders. In B. J. Sadock, V. A. Sadock, & P. Ruiz (Eds.), *Kaplan & Sadock's comprehensive textbook of psychiatry* (Vol. II, 9th cd., pp. 2197–2240). Philadelphia: Lippincott Williams & Wilkins.

Closser, M. H. (1992). Cocaine epidemiology. In T. R. Kosten & H. D. Kleber (Eds.), *Clinician's guide to cocaine addiction: Theory, research, and treatment* (pp. 225–240). New York: Guilford Press.

Clyburn, L. D., Stones, M. J., Hadjistavropoulos, T., & Tuokko, H. (2000). Predicting caregiver burden and depression in Alzheimer's disease. *Journals of Gerontology Series B: Psychological Sciences and Social Sciences, 55,* 2–13.

c-News News Staff. (2003). Husband of "missing" alderwoman disputes media claims. *CNEWS Canada.* Retrieved May 12, 2003, from http://cnews.canoe.ca/CNEWS/Canada/2003/05/09/83590–cp.html.

Cobb, S. (1976). Social support as a moderator of life stress. *Psychosomatic Medicine, 38,* 300.

Coccaro, E., & McCloskey, M. (2010). Intermittent explosive disorder: Clinical aspects. In E. Aboujaoude & L. M. Koran (Eds.), *Impulse control disorders* (pp. 221–232). New York: Cambridge University Press.

Cochran, S. D. (1984). Preventing medical noncompliance in the outpatient treatment of bipolar affective disorders. *Journal of Consulting and Clinical Psychology, 52*(5), 873–878.

Cochrane-Brink, K. A., Lofchy, J. S., & Sakinofsky, I., (2000). Clinical rating scales in suicide risk assessment. *General Hospital Psychiatry, 22,* 445–451.

Cocores, J. A., Miller, N. S., Pottash, A. C., & Gold, M. S. (1988). Sexual dysfunction in abusers of cocaine and alcohol. *American Journal of Drug and Alcohol Abuse, 14,* 169–173.

Coderre, T. J., Katz, J., Vaccarino, A. L., & Melzack, R. (1993). Contribution of central neuroplasticity to pathological pain: Review of clinical and experimental evidence. *Pain, 52,* 259–285.

Cohen, D., Nicolas, J-D., Flament, M. F., Périsse, D., Dubos, P-F., Bonnot, O., ... Mazet, P. (2005). Clinical relevance of chronic catatonic schizophrenia in children and adolescents: Evidence from a prospective naturalistic study. *Schizophrenia Research, 76*(2–3), 301–308.

Cohen, D., & Pressman, S. D. (2006). Positive affect and health. *Current Directions in Psychological Science, 15,* 122–125.

Cohen, J. (1992). A power primer. *Psychological Bulletin, 112,* 155–159.

Cohen, J. (1997, July 4). The daunting challenge of keeping HIV suppressed. *Science, 277,* 32–33.

Cohen, J. (2002). Confronting the limits of success. *Science, 296,* 2320–2324.

Cohen, J. (2006). The overlooked epidemic. *Science Magazine, 313,* 468–469.

Cohen, J. B., & Reed, D. (1985). Type A behavior and coronary heart disease among Japanese men in Hawaii. *Journal of Behavioral Medicine, 8,* 343–352.

Cohen, M. S., Rosen, B. R., & Brady, T. J. (1992). Ultrafast MRI permits expanded clinical role. *Magnetic Resonance, 2,* 26–37.

Cohen, S. (1996). Psychological stress, immunity, and upper respiratory infections. *Current Directions in Psychological Science, 5,* 86–90.

Cohen, S., Doyle, W. J., & Skoner, D. P. (1999). Psychological stress, cytokine production, and severity of upper respiratory illness. *Psychosomatic Medicine, 61,* 175–180.

Cohen, S., Doyle, W. J., Skoner, D. P., Fireman, P., Gwaltney, J. M., Jr., & Newsome, J. T. (1995). State and trait negative affect as predictors of objective and subjective symptoms of respiratory viral infections. *Journal of Personality and Social Psychology, 68,* 159–169.

Cohen, S., Doyle, W.J., Skoner, D. P., Rabin, B. S., & Gwaltney, J. M. (1997). Social ties and susceptibility to the common cold. *JAMA, 277,* 1940–1944.

Cohen, S., Doyle, W. J., Turner, R., Alper, C. M., & Skoner, D. P. (2003). Sociability and susceptibility to the common cold. *Psychological Science, 14*(5), 389–395.

Cohen, S., & Herbert, T. B. (1996). Health psychology: Psychological factors and physical disease from the perspective of human psychoneuroimmunology. *Annual Review of Psychology, 47,* 113–142.

Cohen, S., & Janicki-Deverts, D. (2009). Can we improve our physical health by altering our social networks? *Perspectives on Psychological Science, 4,* 375–378.

Cohen, S., Tyrrell, D. A., & Smith, A. P. (1991). Psychological stress and susceptibility to the common cold. *New England Journal of Medicine, 325,* 606–612.

Cohen, S., Tyrrell, D. A., & Smith, A. P. (1993). Negative life events, perceived stress, negative affect, and susceptibility to the common cold. *Journal of Personality and Social Psychology, 64*(1), 131–140.

Cohen-Kettenis, P. T., & Pfäfflin, F. (2010). The DSM diagnostic criteria for gender identity disorder in adolescents and adults. *Archives of Sexual Behavior, 39,* 499–513.

Coker, L. H., Espeland, M. A., Rapp, S. R., Legault, C., Resnick, S. M., Hogan, P., ... Shumaker, S. A. (2010). Postmenopausal hormone therapy and cognitive outcomes: The Women's Health Initiative Memory Study (WHIMS). *The Journal of Steroid Biochemistry and Molecular Biology, 118*(4–5), 304–310.

Col, N., Fanale, J. E., & Kronholm, P. (1990). The role of medical noncompliance and adverse drug reactions in hospitalizations of the elderly. *Archives of Internal Medicine, 150,* 841–845.

Colapinto, J. (2001). *As nature made him: The boy who was raised as girl.* New York: HarperCollins.

Cole, J. D., & Kazarian, S. S. (1988). The Level of expressed emotion scale: A new measure of expressed emotion. *Journal of Clinical Psychology, 44,* 392–397.

Cole, J. T., Mitala, C. M., Kundu, S., Verma, A., Elkind, J. A., Nissim, I., & Cohen, A. S. (2010). Dietary branched chain amino acids ameliorate injury-induced cognitive impairment. *Proceedings of the National Academy of Sciences, 107,* 366–371.

Cole, M., Winkelman, M. D., Morris, J. C., Simon, J. E., & Boyd, T. A. (1992). Thalamic amnesia: Korsakoff syndrome due to left thalamic infarction. *Journal of the Neurological Sciences, 110,* 62–67.

Cole, M. G. (2004). Delirium in elderly patients. *American Journal of Geriatric Psychiatry, 12,* 7–21.

Cole, M. G., & McCusker, J. (2002). Treatment of delirium in older medical inpatients: A challenge for geriatric specialists [Letter to the Editor]. *Journal of the American Geriatrics Society, 50,* 2101–2103.

Cole, S. W. (2008). Psychosocial influences on HIV-1 disease progression: Neural, endocrine, and virologic mechanisms. *Psychosomatic Medicine, 70,* 562–568.

Coleman, E., Bockting, W. O., & Gooren, L. (1993). Homosexual and bisexual identity in sex-reassigned female-to-male transsexuals. *Archives of Sexual Behavior, 22,* 37–50.

Coleman, H., Charles, G., & Collins, J. (2001). Inhalant use by Canadian aboriginal youth. *Journal of Child & Adolescent Substance Abuse, 10*(3), 1–20.

Collins, A. (1988). *In the sleeproom: The story of the CIA brainwashing experiments in Canada.* Toronto, ON: Lester and Orpen Dennys Limited.

Collins, W. A., Maccoby, E. E., Steinberg, L., Hetherington, E. M., & Bornstein, M. H. (2000). Contemporary research on parenting: The case for nature and nurture. *American Psychologist, 55,* 218–232.

Colman, I., Murray, J., Abbott, R., Maughan, B., Kuh, D., Croudace, T., & Jones, P. B. (2009). Outcomes of conduct problems in adolescence: 40 year follow-up of national cohort. *BMJ, 338,* a2981.

Colp, R. (2009). History of psychiatry. In B. J. Sadock, V. A. Sadock, & P. Ruiz (Eds.), *Kaplan & Sadock's comprehensive textbook of psychiatry* (Vol. II, 9th ed., pp. 4474–4509). Philadelphia: Lippincott Williams & Wilkins.

Comas-Diaz, L. (1981). Puerto Rican espiritismo and psychotherapy. *American Journal of Orthopsychiatry, 51*(4), 636–645.

Compas, B. E., Boyer, M., Stanger, C., Colletti, R., & Thomsen, A. (2006). Latent variable analysis of coping, anxiety/depression, and somatic symptoms in adolescents with chronic pain. *Journal of Consulting and Clinical Psychology, 74,* 1132–1142.

Compas, B. E., Oppedisano, G., Connor, J. K., Gerhardt, C. A., Hinden, B. R., Achenbach, T. M., & Hammen, C. (1997). Gender differences in depressive symptoms in adolescence: Comparison of national samples of clinically referred and nonreferred youths. *Journal of Consulting and Clinical Psychology, 65,* 617–626.

Compton, W. M., Cottler, L. B., Jacobs, J. L., Ben-Abdallah, A., & Spitznagel, E. L. (2003). The role of psychiatric disorders in predicting drug dependence treatment outcomes. *American Journal of Psychiatry, 160,* 890–895.

Condelli, W. S., Fairbank, J. A., Dennis, M. L., & Rachal, J. V. (1991). Cocaine use by clients in methadone programs: Significance, scope, and behavioral interventions. *Journal of Substance Abuse Treatment, 8,* 203–212.

Condon, W., Ogston, W., & Pacoe, L. (1969). Three faces of Eve revisited: A study of transient microstrabismus. *Journal of Abnormal Psychology, 74,* 618–620.

Conduct Problems Prevention Research Group. (2010). The effects of a multiyear universal social-emotional learning program: The role of student and school characteristics. *Journal of Consulting and Clinical Psychology, 78*(2), 156–168.

Conjoined B.C. twins in stable condition. (2006, October, 26). *CanWest News Service.* Retrieved January 4, 2008, from http://www.canada.com/nationalpost/news/story.html?id0e49832c-7a4f-4ab7-a804-e7cc03c9978f&k13358

Conn, D. K., & Lieff, S. (2001). Diagnosing and managing delirium in the elderly. *Canadian Family Physician, 47,* 101–108.

Conners, C. K., March, J. S., Frances, A., Wells, K. C., & Ross, R. (Eds.). (2001). Treatment of attention-deficit/hyperactivity disorder: Expert consensus guidelines [Special issue]. *Journal of Attention Disorders, 4*(Suppl. 1).

Conrod, P. J., Peterson, J. B., Pihl, R. O., & Mankowski, S. (1997). Biphasic effects of alcohol on heart rate are influenced by alcoholic family history and rate of alcohol ingestion. *Alcoholism: Clinical & Experimental Research, 21,* 140–149.

Conrod, P. J., Pihl, R. O., Stewart, S. H., & Dongier, M. (2000a). Validation of a system of classifying female substance abusers on the basis of personality and motivational risk factors for substance abuse. *Psychology of Addictive Behaviors, 14,* 243–256.

Conrod, P. J., & Stewart, S. H. (2005). A critical look at dual-focused cognitive-behavioural treatment for comorbid substance abuse and psychiatric disorders: Strengths, limitations and future directions. *Journal of Cognitive Psychotherapy, 19,* 265–289.

Conrod, P. J., Stewart, S. H., Pihl, R. O., Côté, S., Fontaine, V., & Dongier, M. (2000b). Efficacy of brief coping skills interventions that match different personality profiles of female substance abusers. *Psychology of Addictive Behaviors, 14,* 231–242.

Constantino, J., Abbacchi, A., Lavesser, P., Reed, H., Givens, L., Chiang, L., ... Todd, R. D. (2009). Developmental course of autistic social impairment in males. *Development and psychopathology, 21*(1), 127–138.

Conti, C. R., Pepine, C. J., & Sweeney, M. (1999). Efficacy and safety of sildenafil citrate in the treatment of erectile dysfunction in patients with ischemic heart disease. *American Journal of Cardiology, 83,* 29C–34C.

Conwell, Y., Duberstein, P. R., & Caine, E. D. (2002). Risk factors for suicide in later life. *Biological Psychiatry, 52,* 193–204.

Conwell, Y., Duberstein, P. R., Cox, C., Herrmann, J. H., Forbes, N. T., & Caine, E. D. (1996). Relationships of age and axis I diagnoses in victims of completed suicide: A psychological autopsy study. *American Journal of Psychiatry, 153,* 1001–1008.

Cook, E. H., Jr. (2001). Genetics of autism. *Child and Adolescent Psychiatric Clinics of North America, 10*(2), 333–350.

Cook, E. H., Jr., Courchesne, R. Y., Cox, N. J., Lord, C., Gonen, D., Guter, S. J., ... Courchesne, E. (1998). Linkage-disequilibrium mapping of autistic disorder, with 15q11-13 markers. *American Journal of Human Genetics, 62*(5), 1077–1083.

Cook, E. W., III, Hodes, R. L., & Lang, P. J. (1986). Preparedness and phobia: Effects of stimulus content on human visceral conditioning. *Journal of Abnormal Psychology, 95,* 195–207.

Cook, W. L., Strachan, A. M., Goldstein, M. J., & Miklowitz, D. J. (1989). Expressed emotion and reciprocal affective relationships in families of disturbed adolescents. *Family Process, 28,* 337–348.

Coolidge, F., Thede, L., & Young, S. (2002). The heritability of gender identity disorder in a child and adolescent twin sample. *Behavior Genetics, 32,* 251–257.

Coon, P. M. (1986). Treatment progress in 20 patients with multiple personality disorder. *Journal of Nervous and Mental Disease, 174,* 715–721.

Cooney, N. L., Litt, M. D., Morse, P. A., Bauer, L. O., & Gaupp, L. (1997). Alcohol cue reactivity, negative-mood reactivity, and relapse in treated alcoholic men. *Journal of Abnormal Psychology, 106,* 243–250.

Coons, P. M. (1994). Confirmation of childhood abuse in child and adolescent cases of multiple personality disorder not otherwise specified. *Journal of Nervous & Mental Disease, 182,* 461–464.

Coons, P. M., Bowman, E. S., Kluft, R. P., & Milstein, V. (1991). The cross cultural occurrence of NPD: Additional cases from a recent survey. *Dissociation, 4,* 124–128.

Coons, W. H. (1957). Interaction and insight in group psychotherapy. *Canadian Journal of Psychology, 11,* 1–8.

Coons, W. H. (1967). The dynamics of change in psychotherapy. *Canadian Psychiatric Association Journal, 12,* 239–245.

Coons, W. H., & Peacock, E. P. (1970). Interpersonal interaction and personality change in group psychotherapy. *Canadian Psychiatric Association Journal, 15,* 347–355.

Cooper, A. J. (1988). Sexual dysfunction and cardiovascular disease. *Stress Medicine, 4,* 273–281.

Cooper, A. M., & Ronningstam, E. (1992). Narcissistic personality disorder. In A. Tasman & M. B. Riba (Eds.), *Review of psychiatry* (Vol. 11, pp. 80–97). Washington, DC: Psychiatric Press.

Cooper, J., Kapur, N., Webb, R., Lawlor, M., Guthrie, E., Mackway-Jones, K., & Appleby, L. (2005). Suicide after deliberate self-harm: A 4-year cohort study. *American Journal of Psychiatry, 162,* 297–303.

Cooper, M., Corrado, R., Karlberg, A. M., & Adams, L. P. (1992). Aboriginal suicide in British Columbia: An overview. *Canada's Mental Health, 40*(3), 19–23.

Cooper, M. L., Russell, M., & George, W. H. (1988). Coping, expectancies, and alcohol abuse: A test of social learning formulations. *Journal of Abnormal Psychology, 97,* 218–230.

Cooper, M. L., Russell, M., Skinner, J. B., Frone, M. R., & Mudar, P. (1992). Stress and alcohol use: Moderating effects of gender, coping, and alcohol expectancies. *Journal of Abnormal Psychology, 101,* 139–152.

Cooperstock, R., & Hill, J. (1982). *The effects of tranquillization: Benzodiazepine use in Canada.* Ottawa, ON: Health Canada.

Copeland, W., Shanahan, L., Costello, E., & Angold, A. (2009). Childhood and adolescent psychiatric disorders as predictors of young adult disorders. *Archives of General Psychiatry, 66*(7), 764.

Coplan, J. D., Andrews, M. W., Rosenblum, L. A., Owens, M. J., Friedman, S., Gorman, J. M., & Nemeroff, C. B. (1996). Persistent elevations of cerebrospinal fluid concentrations of corticotropin releasing factor in adult non-human primates exposed to early life stressors: Implications for the pathophysiology of mood and anxiety disorders. *Proceedings of the National Academy of Sciences, 93,* 1619–1623.

Coplan, J. D., Trost, R. C., Owens, M. J., Cooper, T. B., Gorman, J. M., Nemeroff, C. B., & Rosenblum, L. A. (1998). Cerebrospinal fluid concentrations of somatostatin and biogenic amines in grown primates reared by mothers exposed to manipulated foraging conditions. *Archives of General Psychiatry, 55,* 473–477.

Coren, S. (1996). *Sleep thieves :An eye-opening exploration into the science and mysteries of sleep.* New York: Free Press.

Corkum, P., Tannock, R., & Moldofsky, H. (1998). Sleep disturbances in children with attention-deficit/hyperactivity disorder. *Journal of the American Academy of Child & Adolescent Psychiatry, 37,* 637–646.

Corneil, T. A., Kuyper, L. M., Shoveller, J., Hogg, R. S., Li, K., Spittal, M. M., ... Wood, E. (2006). Unstable housing, associated risk behaviour, and increased risk for HIV infection among injection drug users. *Health & Place, 12,* 79–85.

Corrigan, P. W., Wallace, C. J., Schade, M. L., & Green, M. F. (1994). Learning medication self-management skills in schizophrenia: Relationships with cognitive deficits and psychiatric symptoms. *Behavior Therapy, 25,* 5–15.

Coryell, W. H., & Zimmerman, M. (1989). Personality disorder in the families of depressed, schizophrenic, and never-ill probands. *American Journal of Psychiatry, 146,* 496–502.

Coryell, W., Endicott, J., & Keller, M. (1992). Rapid cycling affective disorder: Demographics, diagnosis, family history, and course. *Archives of General Psychiatry, 49,* 126–131.

Coryell, W., Endicott, J., Maser, J. D., Keller, M. B., Leon, A. C., & Akiskal, H. S. (1995). Long-term stability of polarity distinctions in the affective disorders. *American Journal of Psychiatry, 152,* 385–390.

Coryell, W., Solomon, D., Turvey, C., Keller, M., Leon, A. C., Endicott, J., ... Mueller, T. (2003). The long-term course of rapid-cycling bipolar disorder. *Archives of General Psychiatry, 60,* 914–920.

Costa, E. (1985). Benzodiazepine-GABA interactions: A model to investigate the neurobiology of anxiety. In A. H. Tuma & J. D. Maser (Eds.), *Anxiety and the anxiety disorders.* Hillsdale, NJ: Erlbaum.

Costa, P. T., & Widiger, T. A. (2002). Introduction: Personality disorders and the five-factor model of personality. In P. T. Costa & T. A. Widiger (Eds.), *Personality disorders and the five-factor model of personality* (2nd ed.). Washington, DC: American Psychological Association.

Costa, P. T., Jr., & McCrae, R. R. (1990). Personality disorders and the five-factor model of personality. *Journal of Personality Disorders, 4,* 362–371.

Costa, P. T., Jr., & Widiger, T. A. (Eds.). (1994). *Personality disorders and the five-factor model of personality.* Washington, DC: American Psychological Association.

Costa e Silva, J. A., & DeGirolamo, G. (1990). Neurasthenia: History of a concept. In N. Sartorious, D. Goldberg, G. DeGirolamo, J. A. Costa e Silva, et al. (Eds.), *Psychological disorders in general medical settings* (pp. 699–781). Toronto, ON: Hogrefe and Huber.

Côté, G., O'Leary, T., Barlow, D. H., Strain, J. J., Salkovskis, P. M., Warwick, H. M. C., ... Rasmussen, S. A. (1996). Hypochondriasis. In T. A. Widiger,

A. J. Frances, H. A. Pincus, R. Ross, et al. (Eds.), *DSM-IV sourcebook* (Vol. 2, pp. 933–947). Washington, DC: American Psychiatric Association.

Côté, J. K., & Pepler, C. (2002). A randomized trial of a cognitive coping intervention for acutely ill HIV-positive men. *Nursing Research, 51,* 237–244.

Coughlin, A. M. (1994). Excusing women. *California Law Review, 82,* 1–93.

Courchesne, E. (1991). Neuroanatomic imaging in autism. *Pediatrics, 87,* 781–790.

Courchesne, E., Hesselink, J. R., Jernigan, T. L., & Yeung-Courchesne, R. (1987). Abnormal neuroanatomy in a nonretarded person with autism: Unusual findings with magnetic resonance imaging. *Archives of Neurology, 44,* 335–341.

Courneya, K. S., Friedenreich, C. M., Sela, R. A., Quinney, H. A., Rhodes, R. E., & Handman, M. (2003). The group psychotherapy and home-based physical exercise (group-hope) trial in cancer survivors: Physical fitness and quality of life outcomes. *Psycho-oncology, 12,* 357–374.

Couturier, J. L., & Lock, J. (2006). Denial and minimization in adolescents with anorexia nervosa. *International Journal of Eating Disorders, 39,* 212–216.

Cox, A., Rutter, M., Newman, S., & Bartak, L. (1975). A comparative study of infantile autism and specific developmental receptive language disorder: II. Parental characteristics. *British Journal of Psychiatry, 126,* 146–159.

Cox, A. C., Weed, N. C., & Butcher, J. N. (2009). The MMPI-2: History, interpretation, and clinical issues. In J. N. Butcher (Ed.), *Oxford handbook of personality assessment* (pp. 250–276). New York: Oxford University Press.

Cox, B. J., Borger, S. C., & Enns, M. W. (1999). Anxiety sensitivity and emotional disorders: Psychometric studies and their theoretical implications. In S. Taylor (Ed.), *Anxiety sensitivity: Theory, research, and treatment of the fear of anxiety* (pp. 115–148). Mahwah, NJ: Lawrence Erlbaum.

Cox, B. J., Endler, N. S., & Norton, G. R. (1994). Levels of "nonclinical panic." *Journal of Behavior Therapy & Experimental Psychiatry, 25,* 35–40.

Cox, B. J., Endler, N. S., & Swinson, R. P. (1991). Clinical and nonclinical panic attacks: An empirical test of a panic-anxiety continuum. *Journal of Anxiety Disorders, 5,* 21–34.

Cox, B. J., Enns, M. W., Walker, J. R., Kjernisted, K., & Pidlubny, S. R. (2001). Psychological vulnerabilities in patients with major depression vs panic disorder. *Behaviour Research & Therapy, 39,* 567–573.

Cox, B. J., Norton, G. R., Swinson, R. P., & Endler, N. S. (1990). Substance abuse and panic related anxiety: A critical review. *Behaviour Research and Therapy, 28,* 385–393.

Cox, B. J., Swinson, R. P., Schulman, I. D., Kuch, K., & Reichman, J. T. (1993). Gender effects in alcohol use in panic disorder with agoraphobia. *Behaviour Research & Therapy, 31,* 413–416.

Cox, B. J., Walker, J. R., Enns, M. W., & Karpinski, D. C. (2002). Self-criticism in generalized social phobia and response to cognitive-behavioral treatment. *Behavior Therapy, 33,* 479–491.

Cox, B. J., Yu, N., Afifi, T. O., & Ladouceur, R. (2005). A national survey of gambling problems in Canada. *Canadian Journal of Psychiatry, 50*(4), 213–217.

Coyne, J. C. (1976). Toward an interactional description of depression. *Psychiatry, 39*(1), 28–40.

Crabbe, J. C., Belknap, J. K., & Buck, K. J. (1994). Genetic animal models of alcohol and drug abuse. *Science, 264,* 1715–1723.

Crabbe, J. C., Wahlsten, D., & Dudek, B. C. (1999). Genetics of mouse behavior: Interactions with laboratory environment. *Science, 284,* 1670–1672.

Craddock, N., & Jones, I. (2001). Molecular genetics of bipolar disorder. *British Journal of Psychiatry, 41,* 128–133.

Crafti, N. A. (2002). Integrating cognitive-behavioural and interpersonal approaches in a group program for the eating disorders: Measuring effectiveness in a naturalistic setting. *Behaviour Change, 19,* 22–38.

Crago, M., Shisslak, C. M., & Estes, L. S. (1997). Eating disturbances among American minority groups: A review. *The International Journal of Eating Disorders, 19,* 239–248.

Craig, M. C., & Murphy, D. G. M. (2009). Alzheimer's disease in women. *Best Practice & Research Clinical Obstetrics & Gynaecology, 23*(1), 53–61.

Craighead, L. W., & Agras, W. S. (1991). Mechanisms of action in cognitive-behavioral and pharmacological interventions for obesity and bulimia nervosa. *Journal of Consulting and Clinical Psychology, 59,* 115–125.

Craighead, W. E., Ilardi, S. S., Greenberg, M. P., & Craighead, L. W. (1997). Cognitive psychology: Basic theory and clinical implications. In A. Tasman, J. Key, & J. A. Lieberman (Eds.), *Psychiatry* (Vol. 1, pp. 350–368). Philadelphia: W. B. Saunders.

Craske, M. G. (1999). *Anxiety disorders: Psychological approaches to theory and treatment.* Boulder, CO: Westview Press.

Craske, M. G., Antony, M. M., & Barlow, D. H. (1997). *Mastery of your specific phobia, therapist guide.* San Antonio, TX: Graywind Publications/The Psychological Corporation.

Craske, M. G., Antony, M. M., & Barlow, D. H. (2006). *Mastering your fears and phobias: Therapist guide.* New York: Oxford University Press.

Craske, M. G., & Barlow, D. H. (1988). A review of the relationship between panic and avoidance. *Clinical Psychology Review, 8,* 667–685.

Craske, M. G., & Barlow, D. H. (2001). Panic disorder and agoraphobia. In D. H. Barlow (Ed.), *Clinical Handbook of Psychological Disorders* (3rd ed.). New York: Guilford Press.

Craske, M.G., & Barlow, D.H. (2006). *Mastery of your anxiety and worry.* New York: Oxford University Press.

Craske, M. G., & Barlow, D. H. (2008). Panic disorder and agoraphobia. In D. H. Barlow (Ed.), *Clinical handbook of psychological disorders: A step-by-step treatment manual* (4th ed.). New York: Guilford Press.

Craske, M. G., Barlow, D. H., Clark, D. M., Curtis, G. C., Hill, E. M., Himle, J. A., … Warwick, H. M. C. (1996). Specific (simple) phobia. In T. A. Widiger, A. J. Frances, H. A. Pincus, R. Ross, et al. (Eds.), *DSM-IV sourcebook* (Vol. 2, pp. 473–506). Washington, DC: American Psychiatric Association.

Craske, M. G., Barlow, D. H., & O'Leary, T. A. (1992). *Mastery of your anxiety and worry.* Albany, NY: Graywind Publications.

Craske, M. G., Brown, T. A., & Barlow, D. H. (1991). Behavioral treatment of panic disorder: A two-year follow-up. *Behavior Therapy, 22,* 289–304.

Craske, M. G., Golinelli, D., Stein, M. B., Roy-Byrne, P., Bystritsky, A., Sherbourne, C. (2005). Does the addition of cognitive behavioral therapy improve panic disorder treatment outcome relative to medication alone in the primary-care setting? *Psychological Medicine, 35*(11), 1645–1654.

Craske, M. G., Kircanski, K., Epstein, A., Wittchen, H.-U., Pine, D. S., Lewis-Fernández, R., & Hinton, D. (2010). Panic disorder: A review of DSM-IV panic disorder and proposals for DSM-V. *Depression and Anxiety, 27*(2), 93–112.

Craske, M. G., Lang, A. J., Mystkowski, J. L., Zucker, B. G., & Bystritsky, A. (2002). Does nocturnal panic represent a more severe form of panic disorder? *Journal of Nervous and Mental Disease, 190,* 611–618.

Craske, M. G., Rapee, R. M., & Barlow, D. H. (1988). The significance of panic expectancy for individual patterns of avoidance. *Behavior Therapy, 19,* 577–592.

Craske, M. G., & Rowe, M. K. (1997). Nocturnal panic. *Clinical Psychology: Science & Practice, 4,* 153–174.

Crawford, M., & Garnter, R. (1992). *Woman killing: Intimate femicide in Ontario, 1974–1990.* Toronto, ON: Women We Honour Action Committee.

Creed, F., & Barsky, A. (2004). A systematic review of the epidemiology of somatisation disorder and hypochondriasis. *Journal of Psychosomatic Research, 56,* 391–408.

Creese, I., Burt, D. R., & Snyder, S. H. (1976). Dopamine receptor binding predicts clinical and pharmacological potencies of antischizophrenic drugs. *Science, 192,* 481–483.

Cremniter, D., Jamin, S., Kollenbach, K., Alvarez, J. C., Lecruibier, Y., Gilton, A., … Spreux-Varoquaux, O. (1999). CSF 5–HIAA levels are lower in impulsive as compared to nonimpulsive violent suicide attempts and control subjects. *Biological Psychiatry, 45*(12), 1572–1579.

Crerand, C., Sarwer, D., Magee, L., Gibbons, L., Lowe, M., Bartlett, S., … Whitaker, L. A. (2004). Rate of body dysmorphic disorder among patients seeking facial plastic surgery. *Psychiatric Annals, 34,* 958–965.

Crichton, P., & Morey, S. (2003). Treating pain in cancer patients. In D. C. Turk & R. J. Gatchel (Eds.), *Psychological approaches to pain management: A practitioner's handbook* (2nd ed., pp. 501–514). New York: Guilford Press.

Crisp, A. H., Callender, J. S., Halek, C., & Hsu, L. K. G. (1992). Long-term mortality in anorexia nervosa: A 20-year follow-up of the St. George's and Aberdeen cohorts. *British Journal of Psychiatry, 161,* 104–107.

Crockford, D. N., & el-Guebaly, N. (1998). Psychiatric comorbidity in pathological gambling: A critical review. *Canadian Journal of Psychiatry, 43,* 43–50.

Cross-National Collaborative Panic Study, Second Phase Investigators. (1992). Drug treatment of panic disorder. Comparative efficacy of alprazolam, imipramine, and placebo. *British Journal of Psychiatry, 160,* 191–202.

Crow, S. J., Mitchell, J. E., Roerig, J. D., & Steffen, K. (2009). What potential role is there for medication treatment in anorexia nervosa? *International Journal of Eating Disorders, 42*(1), 1–8.

Crow, S. J., Thuras, P., Keel, P. K., & Mitchell., J. E. (2002). Long-term menstrual and reproductive function in patients with bulimia nervosa. *American Journal of Psychiatry, 159,* 1048–1050.

Crow, T. J. (1980). Molecular pathology of schizophrenia: More than one dimension of pathology? *British Medical Journal, 280,* 66–68.

Crow, T. J. (1985). The two-syndrome concept: Origins and current status. *Schizophrenia Bulletin, 11,* 471–486.

Crowe, L. C., & George, W. H. (1989). Alcohol and human sexuality: Review and integration. *Psychological Bulletin, 105*(3), 374–386.

Crowe, R. R. (1974). An adoption study of antisocial personality. *Archives of General Psychiatry, 31,* 785–791.

Crowe, R. R. (1984). Electroconvulsive therapy: A current perspective. *New England Journal of Medicine, 311,* 163–167.

Crowley, P. H., Hayden, T. L., & Gulati, D. K. (1982). Etiology of Down syndrome. In S. M. Pueschel & J. E. Rynders (Eds.), *Down syndrome: Advances in biomedicine and behavioral sciences* (pp. 89–131). Cambridge, MA: Ware Press.

Cruickshank, J. K., & Beevers, D. G. (1989). *Ethnic factors in health and disease.* London: Wright.

CTV. ca News Staff. (2003). Alderwoman to seek therapy to avoid charges. *CTV News, Shows and Sports,* May 21, 2003. Retrieved June 10, 2004, from http://www.ctv.ca/servlet/ArticleNews/story/CTVNews/1053451733897_24//

Culos-Reed, S. N., Carlson, L. E., Daroux, L. M., & Hately-Aldous, S. (2006). A pilot study of yoga for breast cancer survivors: Physical and psychological benefits. *Psycho-oncology, 15*(10), 891–897.

Cummings, J. L. (1990). *Subcortical dementia.* New York: Oxford University Press.

Cunningham, C., McHolm, A., & Boyle, M. (2006). Social phobia, anxiety, oppositional behavior, social skills, and self-concept in children with specific selective mutism, generalized selective mutism, and community controls. *European Child and Adolescent Psychiatry, 15,* 245–255.

Cunningham, J., Yonkers, K. A., O'Brien, S., & Eriksson, E. (2009). Update on research and treatment of premenstrual dysphoric disorder. *Harvard Review of Psychiatry, 17*(2), 120–137.

CUPE. (2005, November 17). Ontario tribunal rules on sex reassignment surgery. *CUPE News.* Retrieved July 1, 2007, from http://www.cupe.ca/www/news/stonehouse_tribunal

Curatolo, P., Bombardieri, R., & Jozwiak, S. (2008). Tuberous sclerosis. *The Lancet, 372*(9639), 657–668.

Curtis, G. C., Hill, E. M., & Lewis, J. A. (1990). *Heterogeneity of DSM-III-R simple phobia and the simple phobia/agoraphobia boundary: Evidence from the ECA study.* Preliminary report to the Simple Phobia subcommittee of the DSM-IV Anxiety Disorders Work Group.

Cutler, S. J., & Hodgson, L. G. (2003). To test or not to test: Interest in genetic testing for Alzheimer's disease among middle-aged adults. *American Journal of Alzheimer's Disease & Other Dementias, 18,* 9–20.

Cutrona, C. E. (1984). Social support and stress in the transition to parenthood. *Journal of Abnormal Psychology, 93*(4), 378–390.

Cutting, J. (1985). *The psychology of schizophrenia.* New York: Churchill Livingstone.

Cyranowski, J. M., Aarestad, S. L., & Andersen, B. L. (1999). The role of sexual self-schema in a diathesis-stress model of sexual dysfunction. *Applied & Preventative Psychology, 8,* 217–228.

Czeisler, C. A., & Allan, J. S. (1989). Pathologies of the sleep-wake schedule. In R. L. Williams, I. Karacan, & C. A. Morre (Eds.), *Sleep disorders: Diagnosis and treatment* (pp. 109–129). New York: John Wiley & Sons.

Czeisler, C. A., Richardson, G. S., Coleman, R. M., Zimmerman, J. C., Moore-Ede, M. C., Dement, W. C., & Weitzman, E. D. (1981). Chronotherapy: Resetting the circadian clocks of patients with delayed sleep phase insomnia. *Sleep, 4,* 1–21.

D'Hulst, C., Atack, J. R., & Kooy, R. F. (2009). The complexity of the GABAA receptor shapes unique pharmacological profiles. *Drug Discovery Today, 14*(17–18), 866–875.

D'Onofrio, B. M., Turkheimer, E., Emery, R. E., Slutske, W. S., Heath, A. C., Madden, P. A., & Martin, N. G. (2006). A genetically informed study of the processes underlying the association between parental marital instability and offspring adjustment. *Developmental Psychology, 42,* 486–499.

Dadds, M. R., Sanders, M. R., Morrison, M., & Rebgetz, M. (1992). Childhood depression and conduct disorder: II. An analysis of family interaction patterns in the home. *Journal of Abnormal Psychology, 101*(3), 505–513.

Dagan, Y., Dela, H., Omer, H., Hallis, D., & Dar, R. (1996). High prevalence of personality disorders among circadian rhythm sleep disorders (CRSD) patients. *Journal of Psychosomatic Research, 41,* 357–363.

Dahl, A. A. (1993, Spring). The personality disorders: A critical review of family, twin, and adoption studies. *Journal of Personality Disorders,* Supplement, 86–99.

Daigle, M. S., Labelle, R., & Coté, G., (2006). Further evidence of the validity of the suicide risk assessment scale for prisoners. *International Journal of Law and Psychiatry, 29,* 343–354.

Dailey, R. C. (1968). The role of alcohol among North American Indian Tribes as reported in the Jesuit Relations. *Anthropologia, 10,* 45–49.

Dalack, G. W., Glassman, A. H., & Covey, L. S. (1993). Nicotine use. In D. L. Dunner (Ed.), *Current psychiatric therapy* (pp. 114–118). Philadelphia: W. B. Saunders.

Dallaire, R. (2003a). PTSD and military peacekeeping. Invited address at the Annual Meeting of the Anxiety Disorders Association of America, Toronto, March.

Dallaire, R. (2003b). *Shake hands with the Devil: The failure of humanity in Rwanda.* Toronto, ON: Random House Canada.

Dana, R. H. (1996). The thematic apperception test (TAT). In C. S. Newmark (Ed.), *Major psychological assessment instruments* (pp. 166–205). Boston: Allyn & Bacon.

Daniels, A., Adams, N., Carroll, C., & Beinecke, R. (2009). A conceptual model for behavioral health and primary care integration: Emerging challenges and strategies for improving international mental health services. *International Journal of Mental Health, 38*(1), 100–112.

Darwin, C. R. (1872). *The expression of emotions in man and animals.* London: John Murray.

Daskalakis, Z. J., Christensen, B. K., Fitzgerald, P. B., Chen, R. (2002). Transcranial magnetic stimulation: A new investigational and treatment tool in psychiatry. *Journal of Neuropsychiatry & Clinical Neurosciences, 14*(4), 406–415.

Davidson, A. J., Sellix, M. T., Daniel, J., Yamazaki, S., Menaker, M., & Block, G. D. (2006). Chronic jet-lag increases mortality in aged mice. *Current Biology, 16,* R914–R916.

Davidson, J., & Robertson, E. (1985). A follow-up study of postpartum illness, 1946–1978. *Acta Psychiatrica Scandinavica, 71*(15), 451–457.

Davidson, J. R. T., Hughes, D. L., Blazer, D. G., & George, L. K. (1991). Posttraumatic stress in the community: An epidemiological study. *Journal of Psychological Medicine, 21,* 713–721.

Davidson, K., MacGregor, M. W., Stuhr, J., Dixon, K., & MacLean, D. (2000). Constructive anger verbal behavior predicts blood pressure in a population-based sample. *Health Psychology, 19,* 55–64.

Davidson, L. L., & Heinrichs, R. W. (2003). Quantification of frontal and temporal lobe brain-imaging findings in schizophrenia: a meta-analysis. *Psychiatry Research: Neuroimaging, 122,* 69–87.

Davidson, M., Keefe, R. S. E., Mohs, R. C., Siever, L. J., Losonczy, M. F., Horvath, T. B., & Davis, K. L. (1987). L-Dopa challenge and relapse in schizophrenia. *American Journal of Psychiatry, 144,* 934–938.

Davidson, R. D. (1993). The neuropsychology of emotion and affective style. In M. Lewis & J. Haviland (Eds.), *Handbook of emotions* (pp. 143–154). New York: Guilford Press.

Davidson, R. J. (1993). Cerebral asymmetry and emotion: Methodological conundrums. *Cognition and Emotion, 7,* 115–138.

Davies, L. (2007, November 28). Politics of fear: Harper's "war on drugs." *Rabble News.* Retrieved December 1, 2007, from http://www.rabble.ca/news_full_story.shtml?x64925

Davila, J., Stroud, C. B., & Starr, L. R. (2009). Depression in couples and families. In I. H. Gotlib & C. L. Hammen (Eds.), *Handbook of depression* (2nd ed., pp. 467–491). New York: Guilford Press.

Davis, C. (1997). Normal and neurotic perfectionism in eating disorders: An interactive model. *International Journal of Eating Disorders, 22,* 421–426.

Davis, C., Blackmore, E., Katzman, D. K., & Fox, J. (2005). Female adolescents with anorexia nervosa and their parents: A case-control study of exercise attitudes and behaviours. *Psychological Medicine, 35,* 377–386.

Davis, C., Katzman, D. K., Kaptein, S., Kirsh, C., Brewer, H., Kalmbach, K., … Kaplan, A. S. (1997). The prevalence of high-level exercise in the eating disorders: Etiological implications. *Comprehensive Psychiatry, 38,* 321–326.

Davis, C., Shuster, B., Blackmore, E., & Fox, J. (2004). Looking good: Family focus on appearance and the risk for eating disorders. *International Journal of Eating Disorders, 35,* 136–144.

Davis, C., & Strachan, S. (2001). Elite female athletes with eating disorders: A study of psychopathological characteristics. *Journal of Sport & Exercise Psychology, 23,* 245–253.

Davis, K. L., Kahn, R. S., Ko, G., & Davidson, M. (1991). Dopamine in schizophrenia: A review and reconceptualization. *American Journal of Psychiatry, 148,* 1474–1486.

Davis, M. (1992). The role of the amygdala in fear and anxiety. *Annual Review of Neuroscience, 15,* 353–375.

Davis, M. (2002). Neural circuitry of anxiety and stress disorders. In K. L. Davis, D. harney, J. T. Coyle, & C. Nemeroff (Eds.), *Neuropsychopharmacology: The fifth generation of progress* (pp. 901–930). Philadelphia: Lippincott Williams & Wilkins.

Davis, R., Freeman, R. J., & Garner, D. M. (1988). A naturalistic investigation of eating behavior in bulimia nervosa. *Journal of Consulting & Clinical Psychology, 56,* 273–279.

Davis, R., McVey, G., Heinmaa, M., Rockert, W., & Kennedy, S. (1999). Sequencing of cognitive-behavioral treatments for bulimia nervosa. *International Journal of Eating Disorders, 25,* 361–374.

Davis, R., & Olmsted, M. P. (1992). Cognitive-behavioral group treatment for bulimia nervosa: Integrating psychoeducation and psychotherapy. In H. Harper-Giuffre & K. R. MacKenzie (Eds.), *Group psychotherapy for eating disorders* (pp. 71–103). Washington, DC: American Psychiatric Association.

Davis, R., Olmsted, M. P., & Rockert, W. (1990). Brief group psychoeducation for bulimia nervosa: Assessing the clinical significance of change. *Journal of Consulting & Clinical Psychology, 58,* 882–885.

Davis, R., Olmsted, M. P., & Rockert, W. (1992). Brief group psychoeducation for bulimia nervosa: II. Prediction of clinical outcome. *International Journal of Eating Disorders, 11,* 205–211.

Davis, S. (1993). Changes to the Criminal Code provisions for mentally disordered offenders and their implications for Canadian psychiatry. *Canadian Journal of Psychiatry, 38,* 122–126.

Davis, S. (1994). Fitness to stand trial in Canada in light of the recent Criminal Code amendments. *International Journal of Law and Psychiatry, 17,* 319–329.

Davison, G. C. (1968). Elimination of a sadistic fantasy by a client-controlled counter-conditioning technique: A case study. *Journal of Abnormal Psychology, 73,* 91–99.

Dawson, G., & McKissick, F. C. (1984). Self-recognition in autistic children. *Journal of Autism and Developmental Disorders, 14,* 383–394.

Dawson, G., Toth, K., Abbott, R., Osterling, J., Munson, J., Estes, A., & Liaw, J. (2004). Early social attention impairments in autism: Social orienting, joint attention, and attention to distress. *Developmental Psychology, 40,* 271–283.

Day, J. J., Grant, I., Atkinson, J. H., Brysk, L. T., McCutchan, J. A., Hesselink, J. R., … Richman, D. D. (1992). Incidence of AIDS dementia in a two-year follow-up of AIDS and ARC patients on an initial phase II AZT placebo-controlled study: San Diego cohort. *Journal of Neuropsychiatry and Clinical Neuroscience, 4,* 15–20.

Day, R., Nielsen, J. A., Korten, A., Ernberg, G., Dube, K. C., Gebhart, J., … Olatawura, M. (1987). Stressful life events preceding the acute onset of schizophrenia: A cross-national study from the World Health Organization. *Cultural Medicine and Psychiatry, 11,* 123–205.

de Almeidia-Filho, N., Santana, V. S., Pinto, I. M., & de Carvalho-Neto, J. A. (1991). Is there an epidemic of drug misuse in Brazil? A review of the epidemiological evidence (1977–1988). *International Journal of the Addictions, 26,* 355–369.

De Brito, S. A., & Hodgins, S. (2009). Antisocial personality disorder. In M. McMurran & R. C. Howard (Eds.), *Personality, personality disorder and violence: An evidence based approach* (pp. 133–154). New York: Wiley.

de la Fuente-Fernández, R., & Stoessl, A. J. (2004). The biochemical bases of the placebo effect. *Science & Engineering Ethics, 10*(1), 143–150.

de la Monte, S. M., Hutchins, G. M., & Moore, G. W. (1989). Racial differences in the etiology of dementia and frequency of Alzheimer lesions in the brain. *Journal of the National Medical Association, 81,* 644–652.

de Lissovoy, V. (1961). Head banging in early childhood. *Child Development, 33,* 43–56.

De Marco, R. R. (2000). The epidemiology of major depression: implications of occurrence, recurrence, and stress in a Canadian community sample. *Canadian Journal of Psychiatry, 45,* 67–74.

de Silva, P., Rachman, S., & Seligman, M. E. (1977). Prepared phobias and obsessions: Therapeutic outcome. *Behaviour Research and Therapy, 15*(1), 65–77.

de Zwann, M., Roerig, J. L., & Mitchell, J. E. (2004). Pharmacological treatment of anorexia nervosa, bulimia nervosa and binge eating disorder. In J.. K. Thompson (Ed.), *Handbook of eating disorders and obesity* (pp. 186–217). New York: John Wiley & Sons.

Deakin, J. F. W., & Graeff, F. G. (1991). Critique: 5-HT and mechanisms of defence. *Journal of Psychopharmacology, 5*(4), 305–315.

Deale, A., Chalder, T., Marks, I., & Wessely, S. (1997). Cognitive behavior therapy for chronic fatigue syndrome: A randomized controlled trial. *American Journal of Psychiatry, 154,* 408–414.

Dean, R. R., Kelsey, J. E., Heller, M. R., & Ciaranello, R. D. (1993). Structural foundations of illness and treatment: Receptors. In D. L. Dunner (Ed.), *Current psychiatric therapy.* Philadelphia: W. B. Saunders.

DeBacker, G., Kittel, F., Kornitzer, M., & Dramaix, M. (1983). Behavior, stress, and psychosocial traits as risk factors. *Preventative Medicine, 12,* 32–36.

Debruille, J. B., Kumar, N., Saheb, D., Chintoh, A., Gharghi, D., Lionnet, C., & King, S. (2007). Delusions and processing of discrepant information: An event-related brain potential study. *Schizophrenia Research, 89*(1–3), 261–277.

DeBuono, B. A., Zinner, S. H., Daamen, M., & McCormack, W. M. (1990). Sexual behavior of college women in 1975, 1986 and 1989. *New England Journal of Medicine, 322*(12), 821–825.

DeKosky, S. T., Williamson, J. D., Fitzpatrick, A. L., Kronmal, R. A., Ives, D. G., Saxton, J. A., … Furberg, C. D. (2008). Ginkgo biloba for prevention of dementia: A randomized controlled trial. *JAMA, 300*(19), 2253–2262.

DeLamater, J., & Sill, M. (2005). Sexual desire in latter life. *Journal of Sex Research, 42,* 138–149.

Delano-Wood, L., & Abeles, N. (2005). Late-life depression: Detection, risk, reduction, and somatic intervention. *Clinical Psychology Science Practice, 12,* 207–217.

Delizonna, L. L., Wincze, J. P., Litz, B. T., Brown, T. A., & Barlow, D. H. (2001). A comparison of subjective and physiological measures of mechanically produced and erotically produced erections. (Or, is an erection an erection?). *Journal of Sex and Marital Therapy, 27,* 21–31.

Dell, P. F. (1998). Axis II pathology in outpatients with dissociative identity disorder. *Journal of Nervous and Mental Disease, 186*(6), 352–356.

Dembroski, T. M., & Costa, P. T., Jr. (1987). Coronary prone behavior: Components of the type A pattern and hostility. *Journal of Personality, 55*(2), 211–235.

Denton, F. T., Feaver, C. H., & Spencer, B. G. (1998). The future population of Canada, its age distribution and dependency relations. *Canadian Journal on Aging, 17,* 83–109.

Denzin, N. K. (1987). *The recovering alcoholic.* Newbury Park, CA: Sage.

Department of Justice, Canada. (2007, November). *National Anti-Drug Strategy.* Retrieved March 3, 2008, from http://www.justice.gc.ca/en/news/nr/2007/doc_32176.html

Depression Guideline Panel. (1993, April). Depression in primary care: Vol. 1. Detection and diagnosis (AHCPR Publication No. 93–0550). *Clinical practice guideline, No. 5.* Rockville, MD: U.S. Department of Health and Human Services, Public Health Service, Agency for Health Care Policy and Research.

Deptula, D., & Pomara, N. (1990). Effects of antidepressants on human performance: A review. *Journal of Clinical Psychopharmacology, 10,* 105–111.

Depue, R. A., & Iacono, W. G. (1989). Neurobehavioral aspects of affective disorders. *Annual Review of Psychology, 40,* 457–492.

Depue, R. A., Luciana, M., Arbisi, P., Collins, P., & Leon, A. (1994). Dopamine and the structure of personality: Relation of agonist-induced dopamine activity to positive emotionality. *Journal of Personality and Social Psychology, 67,* 485–498.

Depue, R. A., Slater, J. F., Wolfstetter-Kausch, H., Klein, D., Goplerud, E., & Farr, D. (1981). A behavioral paradigm for identifying persons at risk for bipolar depressive disorder: A conceptual framework and five validation studies. *Journal of Abnormal Psychological Monographs, 90,* 381–437.

Depue, R. A., & Spoont, M. R. (1986). Conceptualizing a serotonin trait: A behavioral dimension of constraint. *Annals of the New York Academy of Sciences, 487,* 47–62.

Depue, R. A., & Zald, D. (1993). Biological and environmental processes in nonpsychotic psychopathology: A neurobehavioral system perspective. In C. Costello (Ed.), *Basic issues in psychopathology.* New York: Guilford Press.

Derry, P. A., & Kuiper, N. A. (1981). Schematic processing and self-reference in clinical depression. *Journal of Abnormal Psychology, 90,* 286–297.

Dersh, J., Polatin, P. B., & Gatchel, R. J. (2002). Chronic pain and psychopathology: Research findings and theoretical considerations. *Psychosomatic Medicine, 64,* 773–786.

Dershewitz, R. A., & Williamson, J. W. (1977). Prevention of childhood household injuries: A controlled clinical trial. *American Journal of Public Health, 67,* 1148–1153.

Dershowitz, A. (1994). *The abuse excuse and other cop-outs, sob stories, and evasions of responsibility.* Boston: Little Brown.

DeRubeis, R. J., Gelfand, L. A., Tang, T. Z., & Simons, A. D. (1999). Medications versus cognitive behavior therapy for severely depressed outpatients: Mega-analysis of four randomized comparisons. *American Journal of Psychiatry, 156,* 1007–1013.

Deveci, A., Taskin, O., Dinc, G., Yilmaz, H., Demet, M. M., Erbay-Dundar, P., … Ozmen, E. (2007). Prevalence of pseudoneurologic conversion disorder in an urban community in Manisa, Turkey. *Social Psychiatry and Psychiatric Epidemiology, 42*(11), 857–864.

Devi, G., Fotiou, A., Jyrinji, D., Tycko, B., DeArmand, S., Rogaeva, E., … Mayeux, R. (2000). Novel presenilin 1 mutations associated with early onset of dementia in a family with both early-onset and late-onset Alzheimer disease. *Archives of Neurology, 57,* 1454–1457.

Devins, G. M., Flanigan, M., Fleming, J. A. E., Morehouse, R., Moscovitch, A., Plamondon, J., … Shapiro, C. (1995). Differential illness intrusiveness associated with sleep-promoting medications. *European Psychiatry, 10*(Suppl. 3), 153–159.

Devinsky, O., Feldman, E., Burrowes, K., & Bromfield, E. (1989). Autoscopic phenomena with seizures. *Archives of Neurology, 46*(10), 1080–1088.

DeWit, D. J., Adlaf, E. M., Offord, D. R., & Ogborne, A. C. (2000). Age at first alcohol use: A risk factor for the development of alcohol disorders. *American Journal of Psychiatry, 157,* 745–750.

Dhawan, N., Kunik, M. E., Oldham, J., & Coverdale, J. (2010). Prevalence and treatment of narcissistic personality disorder in the community:

A systematic review. *Comprehensive Psychiatry, 51*(4), 333–339.

Di Giulio, G., & Reissing, E. D. (2006). Premenstrual dysphoric disorder: Prevalence, diagnostic considerations, and controversies. *Journal of Psychosomatic Obstetrics & Gynecology, 27*(4), 201–210.

Diamond, L. M. (2007). A dynamical systems approach to the development and expression of female same-sex sexuality. *Perspectives on Psychological Science, 2*, 142–161.

Diamond, L. M., Butterworth, M. R., & Savin-Williams, R. C. (in press). Working with sexual-minority individuals. In D. H. Barlow (Ed.), *Oxford handbook of clinical psychology*. New York: Oxford University Press.

Diamond, M. (1995). Biological aspects of sexual orientation and identity. In L. Diamant & R. D. McAnulty (Eds.), *The psychology of sexual orientation, behavior, and identity*. Westport, CT: Greenwood Press.

Diamond, M., & Sigmundson, K. (1997). Sex reassignment at birth: Long-term review and clinical implications. *Archives of Pediatric and Adolescent Medicine, 151*, 298–304.

DiBartolo, P. M., Brown, T. A., & Barlow, D. H. (1997). Effects of anxiety on attentional allocation and task performance: An information processing analysis. *Behaviour Research and Therapy, 35*, 1101–1111.

Dick, D. M., Aliev, F., Wang, J. C., Grucza, R. A., Schuckit, M., Kuperman, S., … Goate, A. (2008). Using dimensional models of externalizing psychopathology to aid in gene identification. *Archives of General Psychiatry, 65*(3), 310–318.

Dickey, C. C., Shenton, M. E., Hirayasu, Y., Fischer, I., Voglmaier, M. M., Niznikiewicz, M. A., … McCarley, R. W. (2000). Large CSF volume is not attributable to ventricular volume in schizotypal personality disorder. *American Journal of Psychiatry, 157*, 48–54.

DiClemente, R. J., Crittenden, C. P., Rose, E., Sales, J. M., Wingood, G. M., Crosby, R. A., & Salazar, L. F. (2008). Psychosocial predictors of HIV-associated sexual behaviors and the efficacy of prevention interventions in adolescents at-risk for HIV infection: What works and what doesn't work? *Psychosomatic Medicine, 70*, 598–605.

DiClemente, R. J., Wingood, G. M., Harrington, K. F., Lang, D. L., Davies, S. L., Hook, E. W., … Robillard, A. (2004). Efficacy of an HIV prevention intervention for African American adolescent girls: A randomized controlled trial. *JAMA, 292*, 171–179.

Diener, E. (2000). Subjective well-being: The science of happiness and a proposal for a national index. *American Psychologist, 55*, 34–43.

Diener, E., Oishi, S., & Lucas, R. E. (2003). Personality, culture, and subjective well-being: Emotional and cognitive evaluations of life. *Annual Review of Psychology, 54*, 403–425.

DiLalla, L. F., & Gottesman, I. I. (1991). Biological and genetic contributors to violence—Widom's untold tale. *Psychological Bulletin, 109*, 125–129.

Dimberg, U., & Öhman, A. (1983). The effects of directional facial cues on electrodermal conditioning to facial stimuli. *Psychophysiology, 20*, 160–167.

Dimeff, L. A., Baer, J. S., Kivlahan, D. R., & Marlatt, G. A. (2002). Brief alcohol screening and intervention for college students (BASICS): A harm reduction approach. *Journal of Psychiatry & Law, 30*, 275–278.

Dimidjian, S., Martell, C. R., Addis, M. E., & Herman-Dunn, R. (2008). Behavioral activation for depression. In D. H. Barlow (Ed.), *Clinical handbook of psychological disorders: A step-by-step treatment manual* (4th ed., pp. 328–364). New York: Guilford Press.

DiNardo, P. A., & Barlow, D. H. (1990). Syndrome and symptom comorbidity in the anxiety disorders. In J. D. Maser & C. R. Cloninger (Eds.), *Comorbidity of mood and anxiety disorders* (pp. 205–230). Washington, DC: American Psychiatric Press.

DiNardo, P. A., Brown, T. A., & Barlow, D. H. (1994). *Anxiety disorders interview schedule for DSM-IV (ADIS-IV)*. Albany, NY: Graywind Publications.

DiNardo, P. A., Moras, K., Barlow, D. H., Rapee, R. M., & Brown, T. A. (1993). Reliability of DSM-III-R anxiety disorder categories: Using the anxiety disorders interview schedule-revised (ADIS-R). *Archives of General Psychiatry, 50*, 251–256.

DiNardo, P. A., O'Brien, G. T., Barlow, D. H., Waddell, M. T., & Blanchard, E. B. (1983). Reliability of DSM-III anxiety disorder categories using a new structured interview. *Archives of General Psychiatry, 40*, 1070–1074.

Dineen, T. (2002, August 15). Peggy Claude-Pierre: Angel for anorexics or misguided amateur? *The Vancouver Sun*. Retrieved June 24, 2004, from http://tanadineen.com/COLUMNIST/Columns/MontreuxClinic.htm

Dinnel, D. L., Kleinknecht, R. A., & Tanaka-Matsumi, J. (2002). A cross-cultural comparison of social phobia symptoms. *Journal of Psychopathology and Behavioral Assessment, 24*, 75–84.

Dishion, T. J., Patterson, G. R., & Reid, J. R. (1988). Parent and peer factors associated with drug sampling in early adolescence: Implications for treatment. In E. R. Rahdert & J. Gabowski (Eds.), *Adolescent drug abuse: Analyses of treatment research* (NIDA Research Monograph No. 77, DHHS Publication No. ADM88–1523, pp. 69–93). Rockville, MD: National Institute on Drug Abuse.

Distel, M. A., Trull, T. J., & Boomsma, D. I. (2009). Genetic epidemiology of borderline personality disorder. In M. H. Jackson & L. F. Westbrook (Eds.), *Borderline personality disorder: New research* (pp. 1–31). Hauppage, NY: Nova Science Publishers.

Ditto, B., Wilkins, J.-A., France, C. R., Lavoie, P., & Adler, P. S. (2003). On-site training in applied muscle tension to reduce vasovagal reactions to blood donation. *Journal of Behavioral Medicine, 26*, 53–65.

Dixon, J. C. (1963). Depersonalization phenomena in a sample population of college students. *British Journal of Psychiatry, 109*, 371–375.

Dixon, L. B., & Lehman, A. F. (1995). Family interventions for schizophrenia. *Schizophrenia Bulletin, 21*, 631–643.

Dobson, D. J. G., McDougall, G., Busheikin, J., & Aldous, J. (1995). Effects of social skills training and social milieu treatment on symptoms of schizophrenia. *Psychiatric Services, 46*, 376–380.

Dobson, K. (2003). *Frequently asked questions about clinical psychology*. Retrieved June 24, 2004, from University of Calgary website: http://www.psych.ucalgary.ca/students/careers/clin-ical_faq.html

Dobson, K. S., & Dozois, D. J. A. (2004). Attentional biases in eating disorders: A meta-analytic review of Stroop performance. *Clinical Psychology Review, 23*, 1001–1022.

Dobson, K. S., & Shaw, B. F. (1987). Specificity and stability of self-referent encoding in clinical depression. *Journal of Abnormal Psychology, 96*, 34–40.

Docter, R. F., & Prince, V. (1997). Transvestism: A survey of 1032 cross-dressers. *Archives of Sexual Behavior, 26*, 589–605.

Doghramji, K. (2000). The need for flexibility in dosing of hypnotic agents. *Sleep, 23*(Suppl. 1), S16–S20.

Dohrenwend, B. P., & Dohrenwend, B. S. (1981). Socioenvironmental factors, stress and psychopathology. *American Journal of Community Psychology, Journal of Community Psychology, 9*(2), 128–164.

Dohrenwend, B. P., & Egri, G. (1981). Recent stressful life events and episodes of schizophrenia. *Schizophrenia Bulletin, 7*, 12–23.

Dohrenwend, B. P., Levav, I., Shrout, P. E., Schwartz, S., Naveh, G., Link, B. G., … Stueve, A. (1992). Socioeconomic status and psychiatric disorders: The causation-selection issue. *Science, 255*, 946–952.

Dohrenwend, B. P., Turner, J. B., & Turse, N. A. (2006). The psychological risks of Vietnam for U.S. veterans: A revisit with new data and methods. *Science, 313*, 979–982.

Doidge, N., Simon, B., Brauer, L., Grant, D. C., First, M., Brunshaw, J., … Mosher, P. (2002). Psychoanalytic patients in the U.S., Canada, and Australia: I. DSM-III-R disorders, indications, previous treatment, medications, and length of treatment. *Journal of the American Psychoanalytic Association, 50*, 575–614.

Dolan, M., & Völlm, B. (2009). Antisocial personality disorder and psychopathy in women: A literature review on the reliability and validity of assessment instruments. *International Journal of Law and Psychiatry, 32*(1), 2–9.

Dominion Bureau of Statistics. (1955–1957). *Mental health statistics: Patients in institutions*. Ottawa, ON: Minister of Trade and Commerce.

Dongier, M. (1999). In memoriam—Heinz E. Lehmann, 1911–1999. *Journal of Psychiatry and Neuroscience, 24*, 362.

Douglas, K. S., & Hart, S. D. (1996, March). *Major mental disorder and violent behaviour: A meta-analysis of study characteristics and substantive factors influencing effect size*. Poster presented at the biennial conference of the American Psychology-Law Society's, Hilton Head, South Carolina.

Douglas, K. S., & Koch, W. J. (2001). Civil commitment and civil competence: Psychological issues. In R. A. Schuller & J. R. P. Ogloff (Eds.), *Introduction to psychology and law: Canadian perspectives* (pp. 353–374). Toronto, ON: University of Toronto Press.

Douglas, K. S., & Webster, C. D. (1999). Predicting violence in mentally and personality disordered individuals. In R. Roesch & S. D. Hart (Eds.), *Psychology and law: The state of the discipline* (pp. 175–239). Dordrecht, The Netherlands: Kluwer.

Douglas, K. S., Ogloff, J. R. P., & Hart, S. D. (2003). Evaluation of a model of violence risk assessment among forensic psychiatric patients. *Psychiatric Services, 54*, 1372–1379.

Douglas, V. I. (1972). Stop, look and listen: The problem of sustained attention and impulse control in hyperactive and normal children. *Canadian Journal of Behavioural Science, 4*, 259–282.

Douglas, V. L., Barr, R. G., Desilets, J., & Sherman, E. (1995). Do high doses of stimulants impair flexible thinking in attention-deficit hyperactivity disorder? *Journal of the American Academy of Child & Adolescent Psychiatry, 34,* 877–885.

Dougherty, D. D., Baer, L., Cosgrove, G. R., Cassem, E. H., Price, B. H., Nierenberg, A. A., ... Rauch, S. L. (2002). Prospective long-term follow-up of 44 patients who received cingulotomy for treatment-refractory obsessive-compulsive disorder. *The American Journal of Psychiatry, 159*(2), 269–275.

Dowling, N., Smith, D., & Thomas, T. (in press). A comparison of individual and group cognitive-behavioural treatment for female pathological gambling. *Behaviour Research and Therapy.*

Dozois, D. J. A., & Dobson, K. S. (2001). Information processing and cognitive organization in unipolar depression: Specificity and comorbidity issues. *Journal of Abnormal Psychology, 110,* 236–246.

Dozois, D. J. A., & Dobson, K. S. (2003). The structure of the self-schema in clinical depression: Differences related to episode recurrence. *Cognition & Emotion, 17,* 933–941.

Dozois, D. J. A., Frewen, P. A., & Covin, R. (2006). Cognitive theories. In J. C. Thomas, D. L. Segal, & M. Hersen (Eds.), *Comprehensive handbook of personality and psychopathology: Personality and everyday functioning* (Vol. 1, pp. 173–191). Hoboken, NJ: John Wiley & Sons.

Drake, R. E., McHugo, G. J., Becker, D. R., Anthony, W. A., & Clark, R. E. (1996). The New Hampshire study of supported employment for people with severe mental illness. *Journal of Consulting and Clinical Psychology, 64,* 391–399.

Drury, V., Birchwood, M., Cochrane, R., & MacMillan, F. (1996). Cognitive therapy and recovery from acute psychosis: A controlled trial: II. Impact on recovery time. *British Journal of Psychiatry, 169,* 602–607.

Dubovsky, S. L. (1983). Psychiatry in Saudi Arabia. *American Journal of Psychiatry, 140,* 1455–1459.

Duddu, V., Isaac, M. K., & Chaturvedi, S. K. (2006). Somatization, somatosensory amplification, attribution styles and illness behaviour: A review [Special issue]. *International Review of Psychiatry, 18,* 25–33.

Dugas, M. J., Freeston, M. H., & Ladouceur, R. (1997). Intolerance of uncertainty and problem orientation in worry. *Cognitive Therapy & Research, 21,* 593–606.

Dugas, M. J., Gagnon, F., Ladouceur, R., & Freeston, M. H. (1998). Generalized anxiety disorder: A preliminary test of a conceptual model. *Behaviour Research and Therapy, 36,* 215–226.

Dugas, M. J., & Koerner, N. (2005). Cognitive-behavioral treatment for generalized anxiety disorder: Current status and future directions. *Journal of Cognitive Psychotherapy, 19,* 61–81.

Dugas, M. J., Ladouceur, R., Leger, E., Freeston, M. H., Langlois, F., Provencher, M., & Boisvert, J. M. (2003). Group cognitive-behavioral therapy for generalized anxiety disorder: Treatment outcome and long-term follow-up. *Journal of Consulting and Clinical Psychology, 71,* 821–825.

Dugas, M. J., Marchand, A., & Ladouceur, R. (2005). Further validation of a cognitive-behavioral model of generalized anxiety disorder: Diagnostic and symptom specificity. *Journal of Anxiety Disorders, 19,* 329–343.

Dulit, R. A., Marin, D. B., & Frances, A. J. (1993). Cluster B personality disorders. In D. L. Dunner (Ed.), *Current psychiatric therapy* (pp. 405–411). Philadelphia: W. B. Saunders.

Dumas, J., & Wahler, R. G. (1983). Predictors of treatment outcome in parent training: Mother insularity and socioeconomic disadvantage. *Behavioral Assessment, 5,* 301–313.

Dunkley, D. M., & Grilo, C. M. (2007). Self-criticism, low self-esteem, depressive symptoms, and over-evaluation of shape and weight in binge eating disorder patients. *Behaviour Research and Therapy, 45,* 139–149.

Dunlop, B. W., & Nemeroff, C. B. (2007). The role of dopamine in the pathophysiology of depression. *Archives of General Psychiatry, 64*(3), 327–337.

Dunn, E. C., Neighbors, C., & Larimer, M. E. (2006). Motivational enhancement therapy and self-help treatment for binge eaters. *Psychology of Addictive Behaviors, 20,* 44–52.

Dunner, D. D., & Fieve, R. (1974). Clinical factors in lithium carbonate prophylaxis failure. *Archives of General Psychiatry, 30,* 229–233.

Durand, V. M. (1990). *Severe behavior problems: A functional communication training approach.* New York: Guilford Press.

Durand, V. M. (1993). Functional communication training using assistive devices: Effects on challenging behavior and affect. *Augmentative and Alternative Communication, 9,* 168–176.

Durand, V. M. (1998). *Sleep better: A guide to improving the sleep of children with special needs.* Baltimore: Paul H. Brookes.

Durand, V. M. (1999a). Functional communication training using assistive devices: Recruiting natural communities of reinforcement. *Journal of Applied Behavior Analysis, 32,* 247–267.

Durand, V. M. (1999b). New directions in educational programming for students with autism. In D. Zager (Ed.), *Autism: Identification, education, and treatment* (2nd ed., pp. 323–343). Hillsdale, NJ: Erlbaum.

Durand, V. M. (2001). Future directions for children and adolescents with mental retardation. *Behavior Therapy, 32*(4), 633–650.

Durand, V. M., (2004). Past, present and emerging directions in education. In D. Zager (Ed.), *Autism: Identification, education, and treatment* (3rd ed.). Hillsdale, NJ: Erlbaum.

Durand, V. M. (2008). *When children don't sleep well: Interventions for pediatric sleep disorders, therapist guide.* New York: Oxford University Press.

Durand, V. M., Blanchard, E. B., & Mindell, J. A. (1988). Training in projective testing: A survey of clinical training directors and internship directors. *Professional psychology: Research and Practice, 19,* 236–238.

Durand, V. M., & Carr, E. G. (1988). Autism. In V. B. Van Hasselt, P. S. Strain, & M. Hersen (Eds.), *Handbook of developmental and physical disabilities* (pp. 195–214). New York: Pergamon Press.

Durand, V. M., & Carr, E. G. (1992). An analysis of maintenance following functional communication training. *Journal of Applied Behavior Analysis, 25,* 777–794.

Durand, V. M., & Crimmins, D. B. (1988). Identifying the variables maintaining self-injurious behavior. *Journal of Autism and Developmental Disorders, 18,* 99–117.

Durand, V. M., Hieneman, M., Clarke, S., & Zona, M. (2009). Optimistic parenting: Hope and help for parents with challenging children. In W. Sailor, G. Dunlap, G. Sugai, & R. H. Horner (Eds.), *Handbook of positive behavior support* (pp. 233–256). New York: Springer.

Durand, V. M., & Mapstone, E. (1999). Pervasive developmental disorders. In W. K. Silverman & T. H. Ollendick (Eds.), *Developmental issues in the clinical treatment of children* (pp. 307–317). Needham Heights, MA: Allyn & Bacon.

Durand, V. M., & Mindell, J. A. (1990). Behavioral treatment of multiple childhood sleep disorders. *Behavior Modification, 14,* 37–49.

Durand, V. M., & Mindell, J. A. (1999). Behavioral intervention for childhood sleep terrors. *Behavior Therapy, 30,* 705–715.

Durand, V. M., Mindell, J., Mapstone, E., & Gernert-Dott, P. (1995). Treatment of multiple sleep disorders in children. In C. E. Schaefer (Ed.), *Clinical handbook of sleep disorders in children* (pp. 311–333). Northvale, NJ: Jason Aronson.

Durand, V. M., Mindell, J., Mapstone, E., & Gernert-Dott, P. (1998). Sleep problems. In T. S. Watson & F. M. Gresham (Eds.), *Handbook of child behavior therapy* (pp. 203–219). New York: Plenum Press.

Durand, V. M., & Wang, M. (in press). Clinical trials. In J. C. Thomas & M. Hersen (Eds.), *Understanding research in clinical and counseling psychology.* New York: Routledge.

Durbin, J., Goering, P., Streiner, D. L., & Pink, G. (2006). Does systems integration affect continuity of mental health care? *Administration and Policy in Mental Health and Mental Health Services Research, 33,* 705–717.

Durham v. United States. (1954). 214 F. 2d, 862, 874–875 (D. C. Cir.).

Durkheim, E. (1951). *Suicide: A study in sociology* (J. A. Spaulding & G. Simpson, Trans.). New York: Free Press.

Dusseldorp, E., van Elderen, T., Maes, S., Meulman, J., & Kraaij, V. (1999) A meta-analysis of psychoeducational programs for coronary heart disease patients. *Health Psychology, 18,* 506–519.

Dutton, D. G. (1995). Male abusiveness in intimate relationships. *Clinical Psychology Review, 15,* 567–581.

Dutton, D. G. (2002). Personality dynamics of intimate abusiveness. *Journal of Psychiatric Practice, 8,* 216–228.

Dutton, D. G. (2007). *The abusive personality: Violence and control in intimate relationships* (2nd ed.). New York: Guilford Press.

Dutton, D. G., & Starzomski, A. J. (1993). Borderline personality in perpetrators of psychological and physical abuse. *Violence & Victims, 8,* 327–337.

Dvorak-Bertscha, J., Curtin, J., Rubinstein, T., & Newman, J. (2009). Psychopathic traits moderate the interaction between cognitive and affective processing. *Psychophysiology, 46*(5), 913.

Dwyer, E. (1992). Attendants and their world of work. In A. D. Gaines (Ed.), *Ethnopsychiatry: The cultural construction of professional and folk psychiatries* (pp. 291–305). Albany: State University of New York Press.

Dwyer, J. T., Feldman, J. J., Seltzer, C. C., & Mayer, J. (1969). Body image in adolescents: Attitudes toward weight and perception of appearance. *American Journal of Clinical Nutrition, 20,* 1045–1056.

Dyck, R. J., & White, J. (1998). Suicide prevention in Canada: Work in progress. In A. A. Leenars, S. Wenckstern, I. Sakinofsky, R. J. Dyck, et al. (Eds.), *Suicide in Canada* (pp. 256–274). Toronto, ON: University of Toronto Press.

Dykens, E., Leckman, J., Paul, R., & Watson, M. (1988). Cognitive, behavioral, and adaptive functioning in fragile X and non-fragile X retarded men. *Journal of Autism and Developmental Disorders, 18,* 41–52.

Eagles, J. M., Johnston, M. I., Hunter, D., Lobban, M., & Millar, H. R. (1995). Increasing incidence of anorexia nervosa in the female population of northeast Scotland. *American Journal of Psychiatry, 152,* 1266–1271.

Eaker, E. D., Pinsky, J., & Castelli, W. P. (1992). Myocardial infarction and coronary death among women: Psychosocial predictors from a 20-year follow-up of women in the Framingham study. *American Journal of Epidemiology, 135,* 854–864.

Earnst, K. S., & Kring, A. M. (1997). Construct validity of negative symptoms. *Clinical Psychology Review, 17,* 167–189.

Eastman, C. I., Young, M. A., Fogg, L. F., Liu, L., & Meaden, P. M. (1998). Bright light treatment of winter depression: A placebo-controlled trial. *Archives of General Psychiatry, 55*(10), 883–889.

Eaton, W. W., Anthony, J. C., Gallo, J., Cai, G., Tien, A., Romanoski, A., ... Chen, L. S. (1997). Natural history of diagnostic interview schedule/DSM-IV major depression: The Baltimore Epidemiologic Catchment Area follow-up. *Archives of General Psychiatry, 54,* 993–999.

Eaton, W. W., Kessler, R. C., Wittchen, H. U., & Mcgee, W. J. (1994). Panic and panic disorder in the United States. *American Journal of Psychiatry, 151,* 413–420.

Eaton, W. W., Shao, H., Nestadt, G., Lee, H. B., Bienvenu, O. J., & Zandi, P. (2008). Population-based study of first onset and chronicity in major depressive disorder. *Archives of General Psychiatry, 65*(5), 513–520.

Eaves, D., Douglas, K. S., Webster, C. D., Ogloff, J. R. P., & Hart, S. D. (2000). *Dangerous and long-term offenders: An assessment guide.* Burnaby, BC: Simon Fraser University, Mental Health, Law, and Policy Institute.

Ebben, M., & Spielman, A. (2009). Non-pharmacological treatments for insomnia. *Journal of Behavioral Medicine, 32*(3), 244–254.

Ebigno, P. (1982). Development of a culture-specific screening scale of somatic complaints indicating psychiatric disturbance. *Culture, Medicine, and Psychiatry, 6,* 29–43.

Ebigno, P. O. (1986). A cross sectional study of somatic complaints of Nigerian females using the Enugu Somatization Scale. *Culture, Medicine, and Psychiatry, 10,* 167–186.

Eckman, T. A., Wirshing, W. C., Marder, S. R., Liberman, R. P., Johnston-Cronk, K., Zimmermann, K., & Mintz, J. (1992). Techniques for training schizophrenic patients in illness self-management: A controlled trial. *American Journal of Psychiatry, 149,* 1549–1555.

Eddy, K. T., Dorer, D. J., Franko, D. L., Tahilani, K., Thompson-Brenner, H., & Herzog, D. B. (2008). Diagnostic crossover in anorexia nervosa and bulimia nervosa: Implications for DSM-V. *American Journal of Psychiatry, 165*(2), 245–250.

Eddy, K. T., Keel, P. K., Dorer, D. J., Delinsky, S. S., Franko, D. L., & Herzog, D. B. (2002). Longitudinal comparison of anorexia nervosa subtypes. *International Journal of Eating Disorders, 31,* 191–201.

Edelson, M. G. (2006). Are the majority of children with autism mentally retarded? *Focus on Autism and other Developmental Disabilities, 21,* 66–83.

Edens, J. F., Marcus, D. K., & Morey, L. C. (2009). Paranoid personality has a dimensional latent structure: Taxometric analyses of community and clinical samples. *Journal of Abnormal Psychology, 118*(3), 545–553.

Eder, H., Fischer, G., Gombas, W., Jagsch, R., Stuhlinger, G., & Kasper, S. (1998). Comparison of buprenorphine and methadone maintenance in opiate addicts. *European Addiction Research, 4*(Suppl. 1), 3–7.

Edwards, A. J. (1994). *When memory fails: Helping the Alzheimer's and dementia patient.* New York: Plenum Press.

Edwards, R. R., Campbell, C., Jamison, R. N., & Wiech, K. (2009). The neurobiological underpinnings of coping with pain. *Current Directions in Psychological Science, 18,* 237–241.

Efon, S. (1997, October 19). Tsunami of eating disorders sweeps across Asia. *San Francisco Examiner,* p. A27.

Egale Canada. (2003, September 26). *De-listing of sex reassignment surgery (SRS) an injury to public health: Access to SRS by transsexuals is crucial to ensuring full dignity and participation.* Retrieved May 16, 2004, from http://egale.ca/index.asp?langE&menu39&item427

Egale Canada. (2004, October 1). *Sex reassignment surgery (SRS) backgrounder.* Retrieved June 30, 2007. from http://www.egale.ca/index.asp?langE&item1086

Egeland, J. A., Gerhard, D. S., Pauls, D. L., Sussex, J. N., Kidd, K. K., Allen, C. R., ... Housman, D. E. (1987). Bipolar affective disorders linked to DNA markers on chromosome 11. *Nature, 325*(6107), 783–787.

Ehlers, A., & Breuer, P. (1992). Increased cardiac awareness in panic disorder. *Journal of Abnormal Psychology, 101*(3), 371–382.

Ehlers, A., Clark, D. M., Hackmann, A., McManus, F., Fennell, M., Herbert, C., & Mayou, R. (2003). A randomized controlled trial of cognitive therapy, a self-help booklet, and repeated assessments as early interventions for posttraumatic stress disorder. *Archives of General Psychiatry, 60,* 1024–1032.

Ehlers, C., Gizer, I., Vieten, C., Gilder, D., Stouffer, G., Lau, P., & Wilhelmsen, K. C. (2010). Cannabis dependence in the San Francisco Family Study: Age of onset of use, DSM-IV symptoms, withdrawal, and heritability. *Addictive Behaviors, 35*(2), 102–110.

Ehrhardt, A. A., & Meyer-Bahlburg, H. F. L. (1981). Effects of prenatal sex hormones on gender-related behavior. *Science, 211,* 1312–1318.

Ehrhardt, A. A., Meyer-Bahlburg, H. F. L., Rosen, L. R., Feldman, J. F., Veridiano, N. P., Zimmerman, I., & McEwen, B. S. (1985). Sexual orientation after prenatal exposure to exogenous estrogen. *Archives of Sexual Behavior, 14*(1), 57–77.

Eich, E., Macaulay, D., Loewenstein, R. J., & Dihle, P. H. (1997a). Implicit memory, interpersonality amnesia, and dissociative identity disorder: Comparing patients with simulators. In D. Read & S. Lindsay (Eds.), *Recollections of trauma* (pp. 469–474). New York: Plenum.

Eich, E., Macaulay, D., Loewenstein, R. J., & Dihle, P. H. (1997b). Memory, amnesia, and dissociative identity disorder. *Psychological Science, 8,* 417–422.

Eisen, J., & Steketee, G. (1998). Course of illness in obsessive-compulsive disorder. In L. J. Dickstein, M. B. Riba, & J. M. Oldham (Eds.), *Review of psychiatry* (Vol. 16). Washington, DC: American Psychiatric Press.

Eisler, I., Dare, C., Russell, G. F. M., Szmukler, G., le Grange, D., & Dodge, E. (1997). Family and individual therapy in anorexia nervosa: A five-year follow-up. *Archives of General Psychiatry, 54,* 1025–1030.

Elbogen, E., & Johnson, S. (2009). The intricate link between violence and mental disorder: Results from the National Epidemiologic Survey on Alcohol and Related Conditions. *Archives of General Psychiatry, 66*(2), 152.

Eldevik, S., Hastings, R., Hughes, J., Jahr, E., Eikeseth, S., & Cross, S. (2009). Meta-analysis of early intensive behavioral intervention for children with autism. *Journal of Clinical Child & Adolescent Psychology, 38*(3), 439–450.

Eldredge, K. L., & Agras, W. S. (1996). Weight and shape overconcern and emotional eating in binge eating disorder. *International Journal of Eating Disorders, 19,* 73–82.

Elie, M., Rousseau, F., Cole, M., Primeau, F., McCusker, J., & Bellavance, F. (2000). Prevalence and detection of delirium in elderly emergency department patients. *Canadian Medical Association Journal, 163,* 977–81.

Elkin, I., Gibbons, R. D., Shea, M. T., Sotsky, S. M., Watkins, J. T., Pilkonis, P. A., & Hedeker, D. (1995). Initial severity and differential treatment outcome in the National Institute of Mental Health Treatment of Depression Collaborative Research Program. *Journal of Consulting and Clinical Psychology, 63,* 841–847.

Elkin, I., Shea, M. T., Watkins, J. T., Imber, S. D., Sotsky, S. M., Collins, J. F., ... Parloff, M. B. (1989). National Institute of Mental Health Treatment of Depression Collaborative Research Program: General effectiveness of treatments. *Archives of General Psychiatry, 46*(11), 971–982.

Ellason, J. W., & Ross, C. A. (1997). Two-year follow up of inpatients with dissociative identity disorder. *American Journal of Psychiatry, 154,* 832–839.

Ellery, M., Stewart, S. H., & Loba, P. (2005). Alcohol's effects on risk-taking during video lottery terminal (VLT) play among probable pathological and non-pathological gamblers. *Journal of Gambling Studies, 21*(3), 299–324.

Ellicott, A. G. (1988). *A prospective study of stressful life events and bipolar illness.* Unpublished doctoral dissertation, University of California, LA.

Elliot, D. M. (1997). Traumatic events: Prevalence and delayed recall in the general population. *Journal of Consulting and Clinical Psychology, 65,* 811–820.

Elliott, R., Malkin, I., & Gold, J. (2002). *Establishing safe injection sites in Canada: Legal and ethical issues.* Montreal, QC: Canadian HIV/AIDS Legal Network.

Ellis, A. (1962). *Reason and emotion in psychotherapy.* Secaucus, NJ: Prentice-Hall.

Ellis, N. R. (Ed.) (1970). Memory processes in retardates and normals. In *International review of research in mental retardation* (Vol. 4, pp. 1–32). New York: Academic Press.

Elovainio, M., Kivimaki, M., Viikari, J., Ekelund, J., & Keltikangas-Jarvinen, L. (2005). The mediating role of novelty seeking in the association between the type 4 dopamine receptor gene polymorphism and cigarette-smoking behavior. *Personality and Individual Differences, 38,* 639–645.

Emrick, C. D. (1999). Alcoholics Anonymous and other 12-step groups. In M. Galanter & H. D. Kleber (Eds.), *Textbook of substance abuse treatment* (2nd ed., pp. 403–411). Washington, DC: American Psychiatric Press.

Emrick, C. D., Tonigan, J. S., Montgomery, H., & Little, L. (1993). Alcoholics Anonymous: What is currently known? In B. S. McCrady & W. R. Miler (Eds.), *Research on Alcoholics Anonymous: Opportunities and alternatives* (pp. 41–76). New Brunswick, NJ: Rutgers Center of Alcohol Studies.

Emslie, G. J., Rush, A. J., Weinberg, W. A., Rintelmann, J. W., & Roffwarg, H. P. (1994). Sleep EEG features of adolescents with major depression. *Biological Psychiatry, 36,* 573–581.

Endler, N. S. (1990). *Holiday of darkness.* Toronto, ON: Wall & Emerson.

Endler, N. S., & Flett, G. L. (2002). *Endler Multidimensional Anxiety Scales (EMAS)— Social Anxiety Scales (SAS): Manual.* Los Angeles: Western Psychological Services.

Endler, N. S., Macrodimitris, S. D., & Kocovski, N. L. (2003). Anxiety and depression: Congruent, separate or both? *Journal of Applied Biobehavioral Research, 8,* 42–60.

Endler, N. S., Parker, J. D. A., & Summerfeldt, L. J. (1998). Coping with health problems: Developing a reliable and valid multidimensional measure. *Psychological Assessment, 10,* 195–205.

Engelberg, M. J., Gauvin, L., & Steiger, H. (2005). A naturalistic evaluation of the relation between dietary restraint, the urge to binge, and actual binge eating: A clarification. *International Journal of Eating Disorders, 38,* 355–360.

Enns, M. W., Cox, B. J., Levitt, A. J., Levitan, R. D., Morehouse, R., Michalak, E. E., & Lam, R. W. (2006). Personality and seasonal affective disorder: Results from the CAN-SAD study. *Journal of Affective Disorders, 93,* 35–42.

Enns, M. W., Inayatulla, M., Cox, B., & Cheyne, L. (1997). Prediction of suicide intent in Aboriginal and non-Aboriginal adolescent inpatients: A research note. *Suicide & Life-Threatening Behavior, 27,* 218–224.

Enns, M. W., Kjernisted, K., & Lander, M. (2001). Pharmacological management of hypochondriasis and related disorders. In G. J. G. Asmundson, S. Taylor, & B. J. Cox (Eds.), *Health anxiety: Clinical and research perspectives on hypochondriasis and related conditions* (pp. 193–219). New York: Wiley.

Epling, W. F., & Pierce, W. D. (1992). *Solving the anorexia puzzle.* Toronto, ON: Hogrefe & Huber.

Eppright, T. D., Kashani, J. H., Robison, B. D., & Reid, J. C. (1993). Comorbidity of conduct disorder and personality disorders in an incarcerated juvenile population. *American Journal of Psychiatry, 150,* 1233–1236.

Eranti, S., Mogg, A., Pluck, G., Landau, S., Purvis, R., Brown, R. G., ... McLoughlin, D. M. (2007). A randomized, controlled trial with 6-month follow-up of repetitive transcranial magnetic stimulation and electroconvulsive therapy for severe depression. *American Journal of Psychiatry, 164*(1), 73–81.

Erath, S. A., Bierman, K. L., & Conduct Problems Prevention Research Group. (2006). Aggressive marital conflict, maternal harsh punishment, and child aggressive-disruptive behavior: Evidence for direct and mediated relations. *Journal of Family Psychology, 20,* 217–226.

Erdberg, P. (2000). Rorschach assessment. In G. Goldstein & M. Hersen (Eds.), *Handbook of psychological assessment* (pp. 437–449). New York: Pergamon Press.

Erhardt, D., & Hinshaw, S. P. (1994). Initial sociometric impressions of attention-deficit hyperactivity disorder and comparison boys: Predictions from social behaviors and from non-behavioral variables. *Journal of Consulting and Clinical Psychology, 62,* 833–842.

Erickson, D. H., Beiser, M., & Iacono, W. G. (1998). Social support predict 5-year outcome in 1st episode schizophrenia. *Journal of Abnormal Psychology, 107,* 681–685.

Erikson, E. (1982). *The life cycle completed.* New York: Norton.

Erkinjuntti, T., Ostbye, T., Steenhuis, R., & Hachinski, V. (1997). The effect of different diagnostic criteria on the prevalence of dementia. *New England Journal of Medicine, 337,* 1667–1674.

Ertekin, C., Colakoglu, Z., & Altay, B. (1995). Hand and genital sympathetic skin potentials in flaccid and erectile penile states in normal potent men and patients with premature ejaculation. *The Journal of Urology, 153,* 76–79.

Escobar, J. I., & Canino, G. (1989). Unexplained physical complaints: Psychopathology and epidemiological correlates. *British Journal of Psychiatry, 154,* 24–27.

Escobar, J. I., Waitzkin, H., Silver, R., Gara, M., & Holman, A. (1998). Abridged somatization: A study in primary care. *Psychosomatic Medicine, 60,* 466–472.

Eser, D., Schule, C., Baghai, T. C., Romeo, E., & Rupprecht, R. (2006). Neuroactive steroids in depression and anxiety disorders: Clinical studies. *Neuroendocrinology, 84*(4), 244–254.

Eslinger, P. J., & Damasio, A. R. (1985). Severe disturbance of higher cognition after bilateral frontal lobe ablation: Patient EVR. *Neurology, 35,* 1731–1741.

Esposito, C. L., & Clum, G. A. (2003). The relative contribution of diagnostic and psychosocial factors in the prediction of adolescent suicidal ideation. *Journal of Clinical Child and Adolescent Psychology, 32,* 386–395.

Essex, M. J., Klein, M. H., Slattery, M. J., Goldsmith, H. H., & Kalin, N. H. (2010). Early risk factors and developmental pathways to chronic high inhibition and social anxiety disorder in adolescence. *American Journal of Psychiatry, 167*(1), 40–46.

Eth, S. (1990). Posttraumatic stress disorder in childhood. In M. Hersen & C. G. Last (Ed.), *Handbook of child and adult psychopathology : A longitudinal perspective.* Elmsford, NY: Pergamon Press.

Etter, J. (2009). Dependence on the nicotine gum in former smokers. *Addictive Behaviors, 34*(3), 246–251.

Evans, D. A., Funkenstein, H. H., Albert, M. S., Scherr, P. A., Cook, N. R., Chown, M. J., ... Taylor, J. O. (1989). Prevalence of Alzheimer's disease in a community population of older persons. *JAMA, 262,* 2551–2556.

Evans, J. A., & Hammerton, J. L. (1985). Chromosomal anomalies. In A. M. Clarke, A. D. B. Clarke, & J. M. Berg (Eds.), *Mental deficiency: The changing outlook* (4th ed., pp. 213–266). New York: Free Press.

Evans, M. D., Hollon, S. D., DeRubeis, R. J., Pinsecki, J. M., Grove, W. M., Garvey, M. J., & Tuason, V. B. (1992). Differential relapse following cognitive therapy and pharmacotherapy for depression. *Archives of General Psychiatry, 49*(10), 802–808.

Evenson, B. (2001, April 3). Scientology leads backlash. *National Post.* Retrieved May 20, 2004, from http://www.rickross.com/reference/scientology/scien300.html.

Everaerd, W., Laan, E. T. M., Roth, S., & van der Velde, J. (2000). Female sexuality. In L. T. Szuchman & F. Muscarella (Eds.), *Psychological perspectives on human sexuality* (pp. 101–146). New York: Wiley.

Everett, J., Lavoie, K., Gagnon, J.-F., & Gosselin, N. (2001). Performance of patients with schizophrenia on the Wisconsin Card Sorting Test (WCST). *Journal of Psychiatry & Neuroscience, 26,* 123–130.

Exner, J. E. (1974). *The Rorschach: A comprehensive system* (Vol. 1). New York: John Wiley & Sons.

Exner, J. E. (1978). *The Rorschach: A comprehensive system: Current research and advanced interpretation* (Vol. 2). New York: John Wiley & Sons.

Exner, J. E. (1986). *The Rorschach: A comprehensive system* (Vol. 1, 2nd ed.). New York: John Wiley & Sons.

Exner, J. E. (2003). The Rorschach: A comprehensive system. *Basic foundations and principles of interpretation* (4th ed.). New York: Wiley.

Exner, J. E., & Weiner, I. B. (1982). *The Rorschach: A comprehensive system: Assessment of children and adolescents* (Vol. 3). New York: John Wiley & Sons.

Eysenck, H. J. (Ed.). (1967). *The biological basis of personality.* Springfield, IL: Charles C Thomas.

Eysenck, H. J., & Eysenck, S. B. G. (1975). *Manual for the Eysenck Personality Questionnaire.* London: Hodder & Stoughton.

Eysenck, H. J., & Eysenck, S. B. G. (1978). Psychopathy, personality, and genetics. In R. D. Hare & D. Schalling (Eds.), *Psychopathic behaviour: Approaches to research* (pp. 197–223). Chicheste: John Wiley & Sons.

Eysenck, M. W. (1992). *Anxiety: The cognitive perspective.* Hove, UK: Erlbaum.

Ezzel, C. (1993). On borrowed time: Long-term survivors of HIV-1 infection. *Journal of NIH Research, 5,* 77–82.

Faden, R. R. (1987). Health psychology and public health. In G. L. Stone, S. M. Weiss, J. D. Matarazzo, N. E. Miller, J. Rodin, C. D. Belar, et al. (Eds.), *Health psychology: A discipline and a profession.* Chicago: University of Chicago Press.

Fahim, C., Stip, E., Mancini-Marïe, A., Mensour, B., Boulay, L. J., Leroux, J.-M., ... Beauregard, M. (2005). Brain activity during emotionally negative pictures in schizophrenia with and without flat affect: An fMRI study. *Psychiatry Research: Neuroimaging, 140*(1), 1–15.

Fahrner, E. M. (1987). Sexual dysfunction in male alcohol addicts: Prevalence and treatment. *Archives of Sexual Behavior, 16*(3), 247–257.

Fairburn, C. G. (1985). Cognitive-behavioral treatment for bulimia. In D. M. Garner & P. E. Garfinkel (Eds.), *Handbook of psychotherapy for anorexia nervosa and bulimia* (pp. 160–192). New York: Guilford Press.

Fairburn, C. G., Agras, W. S., & Wilson, G. T. (1992). The research on the treatment of bulimia nervosa: Practical and theoretical implications. In G. H. Anderson & S. H. Kennedy (Eds.), *The biology of feast and famine: Relevance to eating disorders* (pp. 317–340). New York: Academic Press.

Fairburn, C. G., & Beglin, S. J. (1990). Studies of the epidemiology of bulimia nervosa. *American Journal of Psychiatry, 147*(4), 401–409.

Fairburn, C. G., & Cooper, Z. (1993). The eating disorder examination. In C. G. Fairburn & G. T. Wilson (Eds.), *Binge eating: Nature, assessment, and treatment* (pp. 317–360). New York: Guilford Press.

Fairburn, C. G., Cooper, Z., & Cooper, P. J. (1986). The clinical features and maintenance of bulimia nervosa. In K. D. Brownell & J. P. Foreyt (Eds.), *Handbook of eating disorders: Physiology, psychology, and treatment of obesity, anorexia, and bulimia* (pp. 389–404). New York: Basic Books.

Fairburn, C. G., Cooper, Z., Doll, H. A., Norman, P., & O'Connor, M. (2000). The natural course of bulimia nervosa and binge eating disorder in young women. *Archives of General Psychiatry, 57,* 659–665.

Fairburn, C. G., Cooper, Z., Doll, H. A., & Welch, S. L. (1999). Risk factors for anorexia nervosa. Three integrated case-control comparisons. *Archives of General Psychiatry, 56,* 468–476.

Fairburn, C. G., Cooper, Z., Shafran, R., & Wilson, G. T. (2008). Eating disorders: A transdiagnostic protocol. In D. H. Barlow (Ed.), *Clinical handbook of psychological disorders: A step-by-step treatment manual* (4th ed., pp. 578–614). New York: Guilford Press.

Fairburn, C. G., Cowen, P. J., & Harrison, P. J. (1999). Twin studies and the etiology of eating disorders. *International Journal of Eating Disorders, 26*(4), 349–358.

Fairburn, C. G., Doll, H. A., Welch, S. L., Hay, P. J., Davies, B. A., & O'Connor, M. E. (1998). Risk factors for binge eating disorder. *Archives of General Psychiatry, 55*, 425–432.

Fairburn, C. G., Hay, P. J., & Welch, S. L. (1993). Binge eating and bulimia nervosa: Distribution and determinants. In C. G. Fairburn & G. T. Wilson (Eds.), *Binge eating: Nature, assessment, and treatment*. New York: Guilford Press.

Fairburn, C. G., Jones, R., Peveler, R. C., Hope, R. A., & O'Connor, M. (1993). Psychotherapy and bulimia nervosa: The longer-term effects of interpersonal psychotherapy, behaviour therapy and cognitive behaviour therapy. *Archives of General Psychiatry, 50*, 419–428.

Fairburn, C. G., Marcus, M. D., & Wilson, G. T. (1993). Cognitive behaviour therapy for binge eating and bulimia nervosa: A comprehensive treatment manual. In C. G. Fairburn & G. T. Wilson (Eds.), *Binge eating: Nature, assessment, and treatment*. New York: Guilford Press.

Fairburn, C. G., Norman, P. A., Welch, S. L., O'Connor, M. E., Doll, H., & Peveler, R. C. (1995). A prospective study of outcome in bulimia nervosa and the long-term effects of three psychological treatments. *Archives of General Psychiatry, 52*, 304–312.

Fairburn, C. G., Shafran, R., & Cooper, Z. (1999). A cognitive behavioural theory of anorexia nervosa. *Behaviour Research and Therapy, 37*, 1–13.

Fairburn, C. G., Stice, E., Cooper, Z., Doll, H. A., Norman, P. A., & O'Connor, M. E. (2003). Understanding persistence in bulimia nervosa: A 5-year naturalistic study. *Journal of Consulting and Clinical Psychology, 71*, 103–109.

Fairburn, C. G., Welch, S. L., Doll, S. A., Davies, B. A., & O'Connor, M. E. (1997). Risk factors for bulimia nervosa: A community-based case-control study. *Archives of General Psychiatry, 54*, 509–517.

Fairholme, C. P., Boisseau, C. L., Ellard, K. K., Ehrenreich, J. T., & Barlow, D. H. (2010). Emotions, emotion regulation, and psychological treatment: A unified perspective. In A. M. Kring & D. M. Sloan (Eds.), *Emotion regulation and psychopathology: A transdiagnostic approach to etiology and treatment* (pp. 283–309). New York: Guilford Press.

Fallon, A. (1990). Culture in the mirror: Sociocultural determinants of body image. In T. F. Cash & T. Pruzinsky (Eds.), *Body images: Development, deviance, and change* (pp. 80–109). New York: Guilford Press.

Fallon, A. E., & Rozin, P. (1985). Sex differences in perceptions of desirable body shape. *Journal of Abnormal Psychology, 94*, 102–105.

Falloon, I. R. H., Boyd, J. L., McGill, C. W., Williamson, M., Razani, J., Moss, H. B., ... Simpson, G. M. (1985). Family management in the prevention of morbidity of schizophrenia. *Archives of General Psychiatry, 42*, 887–896.

Falloon, I. R. H., Brooker, C., & Graham-Hole, V. (1992). Psychosocial interventions for schizophrenia. *Behaviour Change, 9*, 238–245.

Faraone, S. V. (2000). Attention deficit hyperactivity disorder in adults: Implications for theories of diagnosis. *Current Directions in Psychological Science, 9*, 33–36.

Faraone, S. V. (2003). Report from the 4th international meeting of the attention deficit hyperactivity disorder molecular genetics network. *American Journal of Medical Genetics, 121*, 55–59.

Faraone, S. V., Biederman, J., Mick, E., Williamson, S., Wilens, T., Spencer, T., ... Zallen, B. (2000). Family study of girls with attention deficit hyperactivity disorder. *American Journal of Psychiatry, 157*(7), 1077–1083.

Faraone, S. V., Biederman, J., Woznaik, J., Mundy, E., Mennin, D., & O'Donnell, D. (1997). Comorbidity w/ADHD a marker for juvenile onset mania? *Journal of the American Academy of Child and Adolescent Psychiatry, 36*(8), 1046–1055.

Faraone, S. V., Tsuang, M. T., & Tsuang, D. W. (1999). *Genetics of mental disorders: A guide for students, clinicians, and researchers*. Baltimore: Guilford Press.

Farde, L., Gustavsson, J. P., & Jonsson, E. (1997). D2 dopamine receptors and personality traits. *Nature, 385*, 590.

Fausto-Sterling, A. (2000a). The five sexes, revisited. *The Sciences, 40*(4), 19–23.

Fausto-Sterling, A. (2000b). *Sexing the body*. New York: Basic.

Fava, G. A., Grandi, S., Zielezny, M., Rafanelli, C., & Canestrari, R. (1996). Four-year outcome for cognitive behavioral treatment of residual symptoms in major depression. *American Journal of Psychiatry, 153*, 945–947.

Fava, G. A., Rafanelli, C., Grandi, S., Conti, S., & Belluardo, P. (1998). Prevention of recurrent depression with cognitive behavioral therapy: Preliminary finding. *Archives of General Psychiatry, 55*(9), 816–820.

Fava, M., & Rosenbaum, J. F. (1991). Suicidality and fluoxetine: Is there a relationship? *Journal of Clinical Psychiatry, 52*(3), 108–111.

Fawzy, F. I., Cousins, N., Fawzy, N. W., Kemeny, M. E., Elashoff, R., & Morton, D. (1990). A structured psychiatric intervention for cancer patients: I. Changes over time in methods of coping and affective disturbance. *Archives of General Psychiatry, 47*, 720–728.

Fearing, M. A., & Inouye, S. K. (2009). Delirium. In D. G. Blazer & D. C. Steffens (Eds.), *The American Psychiatric Publishing textbook of geriatric psychiatry* (4th ed., pp. 229–242). Arlington, VA: American Psychiatric Publishing.

Fears, S. C., Mathews, C. A., & Freimer, N. B. (2009). Genetic linkage analysis of psychiatric disorders. In B. J. Sadock, V. A. Sadock, & P. Ruiz (Eds.), *Kaplan & Sadock's comprehensive textbook of psychiatry* (Vol. I, 9th ed., pp. 320–333). Philadelphia: Lippincott Williams & Wilkins.

Fedoroff, I. C., & Taylor, S. (2001). Psychological and pharmacological treatments of social phobia: A meta-analysis. *Journal of Clinical Psychopharmacology, 21*, 311–324.

Fedoroff, I. C., Taylor, S., Asmundson, G. J. G., & Koch, W. J. (2000). Cognitive factors in traumatic stress reactions: Predicting PTSD symptoms from anxiety sensitivity and beliefs about harmful events. *Behavioural and Cognitive Psychotherapy, 28*, 5–15.

Fedoroff, J. P. (2003). The paraphilic world. In S. B. Levine, C. B. Risen, & S. E. Althof (Eds.), *Handbook of clinical sexuality for mental health professionals* (pp. 333–356). New York: Brunner-Routledge.

Fedoroff, J. P., Fishell, A., & Fedoroff, B. (1999). A case series of women evaluated for paraphilic sexual disorders. *Canadian Journal of Human Sexuality, 8*(2), 127–140.

Fein, G., & Callaway, E. (1993). Electroencephalograms and event-related potentials in clinical psychiatry. In D. L. Dunner (Ed.), *Current psychiatric therapy* (pp. 18–26). Philadelphia: W. B. Saunders.

Feinberg, M., & Carroll, B. J. (1984). Biological "markers" for endogenous depression: Effect of age, severity of illness, weight loss and polarity. *Archives of General Psychiatry, 41*, 1080–1085.

Feingold, B. F. (1975). *Why your child is hyperactive*. New York: Random House.

Feinstein, A., & Holloway, F. (2002). Evaluating the use of a psychiatric intensive care unit: Is ethnicity a risk factor for admission? *International Journal of Social Psychiatry, 48*(1), 38–46.

Feinstein, A., Stergiopoulos, V., Fine, J., & Lang, A. E. (2001). Psychiatric outcome in patients with a psychogenic movement disorder. *Neuropsychiatry, Neuropsychology, and Behavioral Neurology, 14*, 169–176.

Feldman, H. A., Goldstein, I., Hatzichristou, D. G., Krane, R. J., & McKunlay, J. B. (1994). Impotence and its medical and psychosocial correlates: Results of the Massachusetts male aging study. *Journal of Urology, 151*, 54–61.

Feldman, M. B., & Meyer, I. H. (2007). Childhood abuse and eating disorders in gay and bisexual men. *International Journal of Eating Disorders, 40*(5), 418–423.

Feldner, M. T., Smith, R. C., Babson, K. A., Sachs-Ericsson, N., Schmidt, N. B., & Zvolensky, M. J. (2009). Test of the role of nicotine dependence in the relation between posttraumatic stress disorder and panic spectrum problems. *Journal of Traumatic Stress, 22*, 36–44.

Ferber, R. (1985). *Solve your child's sleep problems*. New York: Simon & Schuster.

Ferguson, C. (2010a). A meta-analysis of normal and disordered personality across the life span. *Journal of Personality and Social Psychology, 98*(4), 659–667.

Ferguson, C. (2010b). Genetic contributions to antisocial personality and behavior: A meta-analytic review from an evolutionary perspective. *The Journal of Social Psychology, 150*(2), 160–180.

Ferguson, K. L., & Rodway, M. R. (1994). Cognitive behavioral treatment of perfectionism: Initial evaluation studies. *Research on Social Work Practice, 4*, 283–308.

Fernandez, F., Levy J. K., Lachar, B. L., & Small, G. W. (1995). The management of depression and anxiety in the elderly. *Journal of Clinical Psychiatry, 56*(Suppl. 2), 20–29.

Fernandez, Y. M., & Marshall, W. L. (2003). Victim empathy, social self-esteem, and psychopathy in rapists. *Sexual Abuse: Journal of Research & Treatment, 15*, 11–26.

Fernandez, Y. M., Marshall, W. L., Lightbody, S., & O'Sullivan, C. (1999). The child molester empathy measure: Description and examination of its reliability and validity. *Sexual Abuse: Journal of Research & Treatment, 11*, 17–32.

Ferreira, C. (2000). Serial killers: Victims of compulsion or masters of control? In D. H. Fishbein (Ed.), *The science, treatment, and prevention of antisocial behaviors: Application to the criminal justice system* (pp. 15-1–15-18). Kingston, NJ: Civic Research Institute.

Ferster, C. B. (1961). Positive reinforcement and behavioral deficits of autistic children. *Child Development, 32*, 437–456.

Ferster, C. B., & Skinner, B. F. (1957). *Schedules of reinforcement.* New York: Appleton-Century-Crofts.

Feske, U., & Chambless, D. L. (1995). Cognitive behavioral versus exposure only treatment for social phobia: A meta-analysis. *Behavior Therapy, 26,* 695–720.

Feusner, J., Phillips, K, & Stein, D. (2010). Olfactory reference syndrome: Issues for DSM-V. *Depression and Anxiety, 27*(6), 592–599.

Fewell, R. R., & Glick, M. P. (1996). Program evaluation findings of an intensive early intervention program. *American Journal on Mental Retardation, 101,* 233–243.

Ficks, C., & Waldman, I. (2009). Gene-environment interactions in attention-deficit/hyperactivity disorder. *Current Psychiatry Reports, 11*(5), 387–392.

Field, A. E., Camargo, C. A., Taylor, C. B., Bekey, C. S., Roberts, S. B., & Colditz, G. A. (2001). Peer, parent and media influences on the development of weight concerns and frequent dieting among preadolescent and adolescent girls and boys. *Pediatrics, 107,* 54–60.

Field, T., Healy, B., Goldstein, S., Perry, S., Bendell, D., Schanberg, S., ... Kuhn, C. (1988). Infants of depressed mothers show "depressed" behavior even with nondepressed adults. *Child Development, 59*(6), 1569–1579.

Fiester, S. J. (1995). Self-defeating personality disorder. In W. J. Livesley (Ed.), *The DSM-IV personality disorders* (pp. 341–358). New York: Guilford Press.

Fiester, S. J., & Gay, M. (1995). Sadistic personality disorder. In W. J. Livesley (Ed.), *The DSM-IV personality disorders* (pp. 329–340). New York: Guilford Press.

Figueroa, E., & Silk, K. R. (1997). Biological implications of childhood sexual abuse in borderline personality disorder. *Journal of Personality Disorders, 11,* 71–92.

Fils-Aime, M. L. (1993). Sedative-hypnotic abuse. In D. L. Dunner (Ed.), *Current psychiatric therapy* (pp. 124–131). Philadelphia: W. B. Saunders.

Fincham, F. D., Beach, S. R. H., Harold, G. T., & Osborne, L. N. (1997). Marital satisfaction and depression: Different causal relationships for men and women? *Psychological Science, 8*(5), 351–357.

Fineberg, N. A., Potenza, M. N., Chamberlain, S. R., Berlin, H. A., Menzies, L., Bechara, A., ... Hollander, E. (2010). Probing compulsive and impulsive behaviors, from animal models to endophenotypes: A narrative review. *Neuropsychopharmacology, 35*(3), 591–604.

Fink, M., & Sackeim, H. A. (1996). Convulsive therapy in schizophrenia? *Schizophrenia Bulletin, 22,* 27–39.

Finn, P. R., Sharkansky, E. J., Brandt, K. M., & Turcotte, N. (2000). The effects of family risk, personality, and expectancies on alcohol use and abuse. *Journal of Abnormal Psychology, 109,* 122–133.

Finney, M. L., Stoney, C. M., & Engebretson, T. O. (2002). Hostility and anger expression in African American and European American men is associated with cardiovascular and lipid reactivity. *Psychophysiology, 39,* 340–349.

Fiore, T. A., Becker, E. A., & Nero, R. C. (1993). Educational interventions for students with attention deficit disorder. *Exceptional Children, 60,* 163–173.

Fiorino, A. S. (1996). *Sleep,* genes and death: Fatal familial insomnia. *Brain Research Reviews, 22,* 258–264.

Firestone, P., Bradford, J. M., Greenberg, D. M., & Nunes, K. L. (2000). Differentiation of homicidal child molesters, nonhomicidal child molesters, and nonoffenders by phallometry. *American Journal of Psychiatry, 157,* 1847–1850.

First, M. B., Bell, C. C., Cuthbert, B., Krystal, J. H., Malison, R., Offord, D. R., ... Wisner, K. L. (2002). Personality disorders and relational disorders: A research agenda for addressing crucial gaps in DSM. In D. J. Kupfer, M. B. First, & D. A. Regier (Eds.), *A research agenda for DSM-V* (pp. 123–199). Washington, DC: American Psychiatric Association.

First, M. B., & Pincus, H. A. (2002). The DSM-IV text revision: Rationale and potential impact on clinical practice. *Psychiatric Services, 53,* 288–292.

Fischer, C. E., Marchie, A., & Norris, M. (2004). Musical and auditory hallucinations: A spectrum. *Psychiatry and Clinical Neurosciences, 58*(1), 96–98.

Fischer, M. (1971). Psychoses in the offspring of schizophrenic monozygotic twins and their normal co-twins. *British Journal of Psychiatry, 118,* 43–52.

Fish, B. (1977). Neurobiological antecedents of schizophrenia in children: Evidence for an inherited, congenital, neurointegrative defect. *Archives of General Psychiatry, 34,* 1297–1313.

Fish, B. (1987). Infant predictors of the longitudinal course of schizophrenic development. *Schizophrenia Bulletin, 13,* 395–410.

Fishbain, D. A. (1987). Kleptomania as risk-taking behavior in response to depression. *American Journal of Psychotherapy, 41,* 598–603.

Fisher, J. D., Fisher, W. A., Bryan, A. D., & Misovich, S. J. (2002). Information-motivation-behavioral skills model-based HIV risk behavior change intervention for inner-city high school youth. *Health Psychology, 21,* 177–186.

Fisher, J. E., & Carstensen, L. L. (1990). Behavior management of the dementias. *Clinical Psychology Review, 10,* 611–629.

Fisher, L. (1996). Bizarre right from Day 1. *Maclean's, 109*(28), 14.

Fisher, M., & Zeaman, D. (1973). An attention-retention theory of retardate discrimination learning. In N. R. Ellis (Ed.), *International review of research in mental retardation* (Vol. 6, pp. 169–256). New York: Academic Press.

Fitts, S. N., Gibson, P., Redding, C. A., & Deiter, P. J. (1989). Body dysmorphic disorder: Implications for its validity as a DSM-III-R clinical syndrome. *Psychological Reports, 64,* 655–658.

Fitzgerald, J. (2000). *Sarah McLachlan: Building a mystery.* Kingston, ON: Quarry Press.

Fitzgerald, P. B., Benitez, J., Daskalakis, J. Z., Brown, T. L., Marston, N. A. U., de Castella, A., & Kulkarni, J. (2005). A double-blind sham-controlled trial of repetitive transcranial magnetic stimulation in the treatment of refractory auditory hallucinations. *Journal of Clinical Psychopharmacology, 25*(4), 358–362.

Fitzpatrick, A. L., Kuller, L. H., Ives, D. G., Lopez, L., Jagust, W., Breitner, J. C., ... Dulberg, C. (2004). Incidence and prevalence of dementia in the cardiovascular health study. *Journal of the American Geriatric Society, 52,* 195–204.

Flament, M. F., Furino, C., & Godart, N. (2005). Evidence-based pharmacotherapy of eating disorders. In D. J. Stein, B. Lerer, & S. Stahl (Eds.), *Evidence-based psychopharmacology* (pp. 204–254). New York: Cambridge University Press.

Fleischman, M. J. (1981). A replication of Patterson's "Intervention for boys with conduct problems." *Journal of Consulting and Clinical Psychology, 49,* 342–351.

Fleming, J. E., Boyle, M. H., & Offord, D. R. (1993). The outcome of adolescent depression in the Ontario child health study follow-up. *Journal of the American Academy of Child and Adolescent Psychiatry, 32*(1), 28–33.

Fliers, E., Vermeulen, S., Rijsdijk, F., Altink, M., Buschgens, C., Rommelse, N., ... Franke, B. (2009). ADHD and poor motor performance from a family genetic perspective. *Journal of the American Academy of Child & Adolescent Psychiatry, 48*(1), 25–34.

Flight, J. I., & Forth, A. E. (2007). Instrumentally violent youths: The roles of psychopathic traits, empathy, and attachment. *Criminal Justice and Behavior, 34,* 739–751.

Flint, A. J. (1994). Epidemiology and co-morbidity of anxiety disorders in the elderly. *American Journal of Psychiatry, 151,* 640–649.

Flint, J. (2009). Molecular genetics. In M. G. Gelder, N. C. Andreasen, J. J. Lopez-Ibor, Jr., & J. R. Geddes (Eds.), *New Oxford textbook of psychiatry* (Vol. 1, 2nd ed., pp. 222–233). Oxford: Oxford University Press.

Flor, H., Elbert, T., Knecht, S., Weinbruch, C., Pantev, C., Birbaumer, N., ... Taub, E. (1995). Phantom limb pain as a perceptual correlate of corticol reorganization following arm amputation. *Nature, 375,* 482–484.

Foa, E. B., & Franklin, M. E. (2001). Obsessive compulsive disorder. In D. H. Barlow (Ed.), *Clinical handbook of psychological disorders* (3rd ed., pp. 209–263). New York: Guilford Press.

Foa, E. B., Jenike, M., Kozak, M. J., Joffe, R., Baer, L., Pauls, D., ... Turner, S. M. (1996). Obsessive-compulsive disorder. In T. A. Widiger, A. J. Frances, H. A. Pincus, M. R. Ross, M. B. First, & W. W. Davis (Eds.), *DSM-IV source-book* (Vol. 2, pp. 549–576). Washington, DC: American Psychiatric Association.

Foa, E. B., Liebowitz, M. R., Kozak, M. J., Davies, S., Campeas, R., Franklin, M. E., ... Tu, X. (2005). Randomized, placebo-controlled trial of exposure and ritual prevention, clomipramine, and their combination in the treatment of obsessive-compulsive disorder. *American Journal of Psychiatry, 162,* 151–161.

Foa, E. B., & Meadows, E. A. (1997). Psychosocial treatments for posttraumatic stress disorder: A critical review. *Annual Review of Psychology, 48,* 449–480.

Foley, D. J., Monjan, A. A., Simonsick, E. M., Wallace, R. B., & Blazer, D. G. (1999). Incidence and remission of insomnia among elderly adults: An epidemiologic study of 6800 persons over three years. *Sleep, 22* (Suppl. 2), S366–S372.

Folks, D. G., Ford, C. U., & Regan, W. M. (1984). Conversion symptoms in a general hospital. *Psychosomatics, 25*(4), 285–295.

Follette, W. C., & Houts, A. C. (1996). Models of scientific progress and the role of theory in taxonomy development: A case study of the DSM. *Journal of Consulting and Clinical Psychology, 64*(6), 1120–1132.

Follman, M. (2003, September 8). Canada's safe haven for junkies. *Salon.com.* Retrieved October 27, 2003, from http://www.salon.com/news/feature/2003/09/08/vancouver/index_np.html

Folstein, M. F., Folstein, S. E., & McHugh, P. R. (1975). Mini-mental state: A practical method for grading the cognitive state of patients for the clinician. *Journal of Psychiatric Research, 12,* 189–198.

Folstein, S. E., Brandt, J., & Folstein, M. F. (1990). Huntington's disease. In J. L. Cummings (Ed.), *Subcortical dementia* (pp. 87–107). New York: Oxford University Press.

Folstein, S. E., & Folstein, M. F. (1998). Genetic counseling in Alzheimer's disease and Huntington's disease: Principles and practice. In M. F. Folstein (Ed.), *Neurobiology of primary dementia* (pp. 329–364). New York: Association for Research in Nervous and Mental Disease.

Folstein, S. E., & Santangelo, S. L. (2000). Does Asperger syndrome aggregate in families? In A. Klin, F. R. Volkmar, & S. S. Sparrow (Eds.), *Asperger syndrome* (pp. 159–171). New York: Guilford Press.

Fombonne, E. (1999). The epidemiology of autism: A review. *Psychological Medicine, 29,* 769–786.

Fombonne, E. (2002). Prevalence of childhood disintegrative disorder. *Autism, 6,* 149–157.

Fombonne, E. (2003a). Epidemiological surveys of autism and other pervasive developmental disorders: An update. *Journal of Autism & Developmental Disorders, 33,* 365–382.

Fombonne, E. (2003b). The prevalence of autism. *JAMA, 289,* 87–89.

Fombonne, E. (2005). The changing epidemiology of autism. *Journal of Applied Research in Intellectual Disabilities, 18,* 281–294.

Foot, M., & Koszycki, D. (2004). Gender differences in anxiety-related traits in patients with panic disorder. *Depression and Anxiety, 20,* 123–130.

Ford, C. V. (1985). Conversion disorders: An overview. *Psychosomatics, 26,* 371–383.

Ford, D. E., & Kamerow, D. B. (1989). Epidemiologic study of sleep disturbances and psychiatric disorder: An opportunity for prevention? *JAMA, 262,* 1479–1484.

Ford, M. R., & Widiger, T. A. (1989). Sex bias in the diagnosis of histrionic and antisocial personality disorders. *Journal of Consulting and Clinical Psychology, 57,* 301–305.

Fordyce, W. E. (1976). *Behavioral methods in chronic pain and illness.* St. Louis, MO: Mosby.

Fordyce, W. E. (1988). Pain and suffering: A reappraisal. *American Psychologist, 43*(4), 276–283.

Forestell, C. A., Humphrey, T. M., & Stewart, S. H. (2004). Involvement of body weight and shape factors in ratings of attractiveness by women: A replication and extension of Tassinary and Hansen (1998). *Personality & Individual Differences, 36,* 295–305.

Forth, A. E., & Mailloux, D. L. (2000). Psychopathy in youth: What do we know? In C. B. Gacono (Ed.), *Clinical and forensic assessment of psychopathy: A practitioner's guide* (pp. 25–54). Mahwah, NJ: Lawrence Erlbaum.

Fortier, P., Mottard, J.-P., & Trudel, G. (2003). Study of sexuality-related characteristics in young adults with schizophrenia treated with novel neuroleptics and in a comparison group of young adults. *Schizophrenia Bulletin, 29,* 559–572.

Fossati, A., Maffei, C., Bagnato, M., Donati, D., Donini, M., Fiorilli, M., & Novella, L. (2000). A psychometric study of DSM-IV passive aggressive (negativistic) personality disorder criteria. *Journal of Personality Disorders, 14,* 72–83.

Fossey, M., Libman, E., Bailes, S., Baltzan, M., Schondorf, R., Amsel, R., & Fichten, C. S. (2004). Sleep quality and psychological adjustment in chronic fatigue syndrome. *Journal of Behavioral Medicine, 27*(6), 581–605).

Foster, J. D. (2004, April 6). *Corson getting one more shot at the title.* Retrieved July 15, 2004, from http://www.dallasstars.com/news/news-Detail.jsp?id2121

Fouts, G., & Burggraf, K. (2000). Television situation comedies: Female weight, male negative comments, and audience reactions. *Sex Roles, 42,* 925–932.

Fowles, D. C. (1988). Psychophysiology and psychopathy: A motivational approach. *Psychophysiology, 25,* 373–391.

Fowles, D. C. (1993). A motivational theory of psychopathology. In W. Spaulding (Ed.), *Nebraska symposium on motivation: Integrated views of motivation, cognition, and emotion* (Vol. 41, pp. 181–238). Lincoln: University of Nebraska Press.

Fox, M. J. (2002). *Lucky man: A memoir.* New York: Hyperion Books.

Fox, P. T., Ingham, R. J., Ingham, J. C., Hirsch, T. B., Downs, J. H., Martin, C., … Lancaster, J. L. (1996). A PET study of the neural systems of stuttering. *Nature, 382,* 158–161.

Foy, D. W., Resnick, H. S., Sipprelle, R. C., & Carroll, E. M. (1987). Premilitary, military and postmilitary factors in the development of combat related posttraumatic stress disorder. *The Behavior Therapist, 10,* 3–9.

Foy, D. W., Sipprelle, R. C., Rueger, D. B., & Carroll, E. M. (1984). Etiology of posttraumatic stress disorder in Vietnam veterans: Analysis of premilitary, military, and combat exposure influences. *Journal of Consulting and Clinical Psychology, 52,* 79–87.

Frances, A. (2009). Whither DSM-V? *British Journal of Psychiatry, 195,* 391–392.

Frances, A., & Blumenthal, S. J. (1989). Personality disorders and characteristics in youth suicide. In *Alcohol, drug abuse and mental health administration. Report of the secretary's task force on youth suicide: Vol. 12, risk factors for youth suicide* (DHHS Publication No. ADM89–1622, pp. 172–185). Washington, DC: U.S. Government Printing Office.

Frances, R., Franklin, J., & Flavin, D. (1986). Suicide and alcoholism. *Annals of the New York Academy of Science, 287,* 316–326.

Francis, D., Diorio, J., Liu, D., & Meaney, M. J. (1999). Nongenomic transmission across generations of maternal behavior and stress responses in the rat. *Science, 286,* 1155–1158.

Francis, G., & Hart, K. J. (1992). Depression and suicide. In V. B. Van Hasselt & D. J. Kolko (Eds.), *Inpatient behavior therapy for children and adolescents* (pp. 93–111). New York: Plenum Press.

Francis, J. A., Stewart, S. H., & Hounsell, S. (1997). Dietary restraint and the selective processing of forbidden and nonforbidden food words. *Cognitive Therapy & Research, 21,* 633–646.

Frank, E., Anderson, C., & Rubinstein, D. (1978). Frequency of sexual dysfunction in "normal" couples. *New England Journal of Medicine, 299,* 111–115.

Frank, E., Kupfer, D. J., Perel, J. M., Cornes, C., Jarrett, D. B., Mallinger, A. G., … Grochocinski, V. J. (1990). Three-year outcomes for maintenance therapies in recurrent depression. *Archives of General Psychiatry, 47*(12), 1093–1099.

Frank, E., Swartz, H. A., Mallinger, A. G., Thase, M. E., Weaver, E. V., & Kupfer, D. J. (1999). Adjunctive psychotherapy for bipolar disorder: Effects of changing treatment modality. *Journal of Abnormal Psychology, 108*(4), 579–587.

Frankel, E. B., & Gold, S. (2007). Principles and practices of early intervention. In I. Brown & M. Percy (Eds.), *A comprehensive guide to intellectual & developmental disabilities* (pp. 451–466). Baltimore: Paul H. Brookes.

Franklin, D. (1990, November/December). Hooked-not hooked: Why isn't everyone an addict? *Health,* 39–52.

Franklin, J. E., & Frances, R. J. (1999). Alcohol and other psychoactive substance use disorders. In R. E. Hales, S. C. Yudofsky, & J. A. Talbott (Eds.), *Textbook of psychiatry* (3rd ed., pp. 363–423). Washington, DC: American Psychiatric Press.

Franko, D. L., Wonderlich, S. A., Little, D., & Herzog, D. B. (2004). Diagnosis and classification of eating disorders. In J. K. Thompson (Ed.), *Handbook of eating disorders and obesity* (pp. 58–80). New York: John Wiley & Sons.

Fraser, G. A. (1994). Dissociative phenomena and disorders: Clinical presentations. In R. M. Klei & B. K. Doane (Eds.), *Psychological concepts and dissociative disorders* (pp. 131–151). Hillside, NJ: Erlbaum.

Frasure-Smith, N., & Lesperance, F. (2005). Depression and coronary heart disease: Complex synergism of mind, body, and environment. *Current Directions in Psychological Science, 14,* 39–43.

Frasure-Smith, N., Lesperance, F., Juneau, M., Talajic, M., & Bourassa, M. G. (1999). Gender, depression, and one-year prognosis after myocardial infarction. *Psychosomatic Medicine, 61,* 26–37.

Fratiglioni, L., Grut, M., Forsell, Y., Viitanen, M., Grafstrom, M., & Holmen, K., … Winblad, B. (1991). Prevalence of Alzheimer's disease and other dementias in an elderly urban population: Relationship with age, sex and education. *Neurology, 41,* 1886–1892.

Fratiglioni, L., Winblad, B., & von Strauss, E. (2007). Prevention of Alzheimer's disease and dementia: Major findings from the Kungsholmen Project. *Physiology & Behavior, 92*(1–2), 98–104.

Frecska, E., Perenyi, A., & Arato, M. (2003). Blunted prolactin response to fentanyl in depression. Normalizing effect of partial sleep deprivation. *Psychiatry Research, 118,* 155–164.

Fredrikson, M., Annas, P., & Wik, G. (1997). Parental history, aversive exposure and the development of snake and spider phobia in women. *Behavior Research and Therapy, 35,* 23–28.

Fredrikson, M., & Matthews, K. A. (1990). Cardiovascular responses to behavioral stress and hypertension: A meta-analytic review. *Annals of Behavioral Medicine, 12*(1), 30–39.

Freed, D. A. (2007, May 13). From jokester to jailbird. *The Toronto Star.* Retrieved June 9, 2007, from http://www.thestar.com/article/213298

Freedman, M. (1990). Parkinson's disease. In J. L. Cummings (Ed.), *Subcortical dementia* (pp. 108–122). New York: Oxford University Press.

Freedman, M., Leach, L., Kaplan, E., Winocur, G., Shulman, K. I., & Delis, D. C. (1994). *Clock drawing: A neuropsychological analysis.* New York: Oxford University Press.

Freeman, A., Pretzer, J., Fleming, B., & Simon, K. M. (1990). *Clinical applications of cognitive therapy.* New York: Plenum Press.

Freeman, D., Pugh, K., Vorontsova, N., Antley, A., & Slater, M. (2010). Testing the continuum of delusional beliefs: An experimental study using virtual reality. *Journal of Abnormal Psychology, 119*(1), 83–92.

Freeman, E. W., Rickels, K., Sammel, M. D., Lin, H., & Sondheimer, S. J. (2009). Time to relapse after short- or long-term treatment of severe premenstrual syndrome with sertraline. *Archives of General Psychiatry, 66*(5), 537–544.

Freeman, M. P., & McElroy, S. L. (1999). Clinical picture and etiological models of mixed states. *Psychiatric Clinics of North America, 22*(3), 535–546.

French-Belgian Collaborative Group. (1982). Ischemic heart disease and psychological patterns: Prevalence and incidence studies in Belgium and France. *Advances in Cardiology, 29,* 25–31.

Freud, A. (1946). *Ego and the mechanisms of defense.* New York: International Universities Press.

Freud, S. (1957). Mourning and melancholia. In J. Strachey (Ed. and Trans.), *The standard edition of the complete psychological works of Sigmund Freud* (Vol. 14). London: Hogarth Press. (Original work published 1917).

Freud, S. (1962). The neuropsychoses of defence. In J. Strachey (Ed.), *The complete psychological works* (Vol. 3, pp. 45–62). London: Hogarth Press. (Original work published 1894).

Freund, K., Seto, M. C., & Kuban, M. (1996). Two types of fetishism. *Behaviour Research and Therapy, 34,* 687–694.

Frick, P. J., Strauss, C. C., Lahey, B. B., & Christ, M. A. G. (1993). Behavior disorders of children. In P. B. Sutker & H. E. Adams (Eds.), *Comprehensive handbook of psychopathology* (pp. 765–789). New York: Plenum.

Friedl, M. C., & Draijer, N. (2000). Dissociative disorders in Dutch psychiatric inpatients. *American Journal of Psychiatry, 157*(6), 1012–1013.

Friedman, J. M. (2009). Obesity: Causes and control of excess body fat. *Nature, 459*(7245), 340–342.

Friedman, M., & Rosenman, R. H. (1959). Association of specific overt behavior pattern with blood and cardiovascular findings. *JAMA, 169,* 1286.

Friedman, M., & Rosenman, R. H. (1974). *Type A behavior and your heart.* New York: Knopf.

Friedman, S., Jones, J. C., Chernen, L., & Barlow, D. H. (1992). Suicidal ideation and suicide attempts among patients with panic disorder: A survey of two outpatient clinics. *American Journal of Psychiatry, 149*(5), 680–685.

Fromm-Reichmann, F. (1948). Notes on the development of treatment of schizophrenics by psychoanalytic psychotherapy. *Psychiatry, 11,* 263–273.

Frost, R. O., Sher, K. J., & Geen, T. (1986). Psychotherapy and personality characteristics of non-clinical compulsive checkers. *Behaviour Research and Therapy, 24,* 133–143.

Frost, R. O., Steketee, G., & Williams, L. (2002). Compulsive buying, compulsive hoarding, and obsessive-compulsive disorder. *Behavior Therapy, 33,* 201–214.

Frost, S., Myers, L. B., & Newman, S. P. (2001). Genetic screening for Alzheimer's disease: What factors predict intentions to take a test? *Behavioral Medicine, 27,* 101–109.

Fugl-Meyer, A. R., & Sjogren Fugl-Meyer, K. (1999). Sexual disabilities, problems, and satisfaction in 18–74 year old Swedes. *Scandinavian Journal of Sexology, 3,* 79–105.

Fukuda, K., Straus, S. E., Hickie, I., Sharpe, M. B., Dobbins, J. G., & Komaroff, A. L. (1994). Chronic fatigue syndrome: A comprehensive approach to its diagnosis and management. *Annals of Internal Medicine, 121,* 953–959.

Furer, P., & Walker, J. R. (2005). Treatment of hypochondriasis with exposure. *Journal of Contemporary Psychotherapy, 35,* 251–267.

Furer, P., Walker, J. R., Chartier, M., & Stein, M. B. (1997). Hypochondriacal concerns and somatization in panic disorder. *Depression and Anxiety, 6,* 78–85.

Furer, P., Walker, J. R., & Freeston, M. H. (2001). Approach to integrated cognitive-behavior therapy for intense illness worries. In G. J. G. Asmundson, S. Taylor, & B. J. Cox (Eds.), *Health anxiety: Clinical and research perspectives on hypochondriasis and related conditions* (pp. 161–192). New York: Wiley.

Furer, P., Walker, J. R., & Stein, M. B. (2007). *Treating health anxiety and fear of death: A practitioner's guide.* New York: Springer Publishing.

Furnham, A., & Wong, L. (2007). A cross-cultural comparison of British and Chinese beliefs about the causes, behaviour manifestations and treatment of schizophrenia. *Psychiatry Research, 151,* 123–138.

Furr, J. M., Tiwari, S., Suveg, C., & Kendall, P. C. (2009). Anxiety disorders in children and adolescents. In M. M. Antony & M. B. Stein (Eds.), Oxford handbook of anxiety and related disorders (pp. 636–656). New York: Oxford University Press.

Fyer, A., Liebowitz, M., Gorman, J., Compeas, R., Levin, A., Davies, S., ... Klein, D. F. (1987). Discontinuation of alprazolam treatment in panic patients. *American Journal of Psychiatry, 144,* 303–308.

Fyer, A. J., Mannuzza, S., Chapman, T. F., Liebowitz, M. R., & Klein, D. F. (1993). A direct interview family study of social phobia. *Archives of General Psychiatry, 50,* 286–293.

Fyer, A. J., Mannuzza, S., Gallops, M. S., Martin, L. Y., Aaronson, C., Gorman, J. M., ... Klein, D. F. (1990). Familial transmission of simple phobias and fears: A preliminary report. *Archives of General Psychiatry, 47,* 252–256.

Gacono, C. B. (Ed.). (2000). The *clinical and forensic assessment of psychopathy: A practitioner's guide.* Mahwah, NJ: Earlbaum.

Gadsby, J. (2001, October 9). *Benzodiazepines: Responsible prescribing & informed use.* Retrieved August 17, 2004, from http://www.benzo.org.uk/jegres.htm.

Gadsby, J. E. (2000). *Addiction by prescription. One woman's triumph and fight for change.* Toronto, ON: Key Porter Books.

Gagliese, L., & Katz, J. (2000). Medically unexplained pain is not caused by psychopathology. *Pain Research and Management, 5,* 251–257.

Gagnon, J. H. (1990). The explicit and implicit use of the scripting perspective in sex research. *Annual Review of Sex Research, 1,* 1–43.

Gagnon, M., & Ladouceur, R. (1992). Behavioral treatment of child stutterers: Replication and extension. *Behavior Therapy, 23,* 113–129.

Gajdusek, D. C. (1977). Unconventional viruses and the origin and disappearance of Kuru. *Science, 197,* 943.

Galambos, N. L., Barker, E. T., & Almeida, D. M. (2003). Parents do matter: Trajectories of change in externalizing and internalizing problems in early adolescence. *Child Development, 74,* 578–594.

Galambos, N. L., & Leadbeater, B. J. (2002). Transitions in adolescent research. In W. W. Hartup & R. K. Silbereisen (Eds.), *Growing points in developmental science: An introduction* (pp. 287–306). Philadelphia: Psychology Press.

Gallagher-Thompson, D., & Osgood, N. J. (1997). Suicide later in life. *Behavior Therapy, 28,* 23–41.

Gallagher-Thompson, D., Rabinowitz, Y., Tang, P., Tse, C., Kwo, E., Hsu, S., ... Thompson, L. W. (2006). Recruiting Chinese Americans for dementia caregiver intervention research: Suggestions for success. *American Journal of Geriatric Psychiatry, 14*(8), 676.

Gallant, D. (1999). Alcohol. In M. Galanter & H. D. Kleber (Eds.), *Textbook of substance abuse treatment* (2nd ed., pp. 151–164). Washington, DC: American Psychiatric Press.

Gallup, G. G., & Frederick, D. A. (2010). The science of sex appeal: An evolutionary perspective. *Review of General Psychology, 14,* 240–250.

Gansler, D. A., McLaughlin, N. C., Iguchi, L., Jerram, M., Moore, D. W., Bhadelia, R., & Fulwiler, C. (2009). A multivariate approach to aggression and the orbital frontal cortex in psychiatric patients. *Psychiatry Research: Neuroimaging, 171*(3), 145–154.

Gao, Y., Raine, A., Venables, P. H., Dawson, M. E., & Mednick, S. A. (2010). Association of poor childhood fear conditioning and adult crime. *American Journal of Psychiatry, 167*(1), 56–60.

Garber, S. W., Garber, M. D., & Spizman, R. F. (1996). *Beyond Ritalin: Facts about medication and other strategies for helping children, adolescents, and adults with attention deficit disorders.* New York: Villard.

Garcia, J., McGowan, B. K., & Green, K. F. (1972). Biological constraints on conditioning. In A. H. Black & W. F. Prokasy (Eds.), *Classical conditioning II: Current research and theory.* New York: Appleton-Century-Crofts.

Gardner, E. L. (1997). Brain reward mechanisms., In J. H. Lowinson, P. Ruiz, R. B. Millman, & J. G. Langrod (Eds.), *Substance abuse: A comprehensive textbook* (pp. 51–85). Baltimore: Williams & Wilkins.

Garety, P. A., Kuipers, L., Fowler, D., Chamberlain, F., & Dunn, G. (1994). Cognitive behavioural therapy for drug-resistant psychosis. *British Journal of Medical Psychology, 67,* 259–271.

Garfield, A. F., & Zigler, E. (1993). Adolescent suicide prevention: Current research and social policy implications. *American Psychologist, 48*(2), 169–182.

Garfinkel, P. E. (1992). Evidence in support of attitudes to shape and weight as a diagnostic criterion of bulimia nervosa. *International Journal of Eating Disorders, 11*(4), 321–325.

Garfinkel, P. E. (2002). Guest editorial: Eating disorders. *Canadian Journal of Psychiatry, 47,* 225–226.

Garfinkel, P. E., & Dorian, B. J. (2001). Improving understanding and care for the eating disorders. In R. H. Striegel-Moore & L. Smolak (Eds.), *Eating disorders: Innovative directions in research and practice* (pp. 9–26). Washington, DC: American Psychological Association.

Garfinkel, P. E., & Garner, D. M. (1982). *Anorexia nervosa: A multidimensional perspective.* New York: Brunner/Mazel.

Garfinkel, P. E., Kennedy, S. H., & Kaplan, A. S. (1995). Views on classification and diagnosis of eating disorders. *Canadian Journal of Psychiatry, 40,* 445–456.

Garfinkel, P. E., Lin, E., Goering P., Spegg, C., Goldbloom, D. S., Kennedy, S., ... Woodside, D. B. (1995). Bulimia nervosa in a Canadian community sample: Prevalence in comparison of subgroups. *American Journal of Psychiatry, 152,* 1052–1058.

Garfinkel, P. E., Lin, E., Goering, P., Spegg, C., Goldbloom, D. S., Kennedy, S., ... Woodside, D. B. (1996). Purging and nonpurging forms of bulimia nervosa in a community sample. *International Journal of Eating Disorders, 20,* 231–238.

Garfinkel, P. E., Moldofsky, H., & Garner, D. M. (1979). The heterogeneity of anorexia nervosa: Bulimia as a distinct subgroup. *Archives of General Psychiatry, 37,* 1036–1040.

Garlow, S., & Nemeroff, C. B. (2003). Neurobiology of depressive disorders. In R. J. Davidson, K. R. Scherer, & H. H. Goldsmith (Eds.), *Handbook of affective sciences* (pp. 1021–1043). New York: Oxford University Press.

Garmezy, N., & Rutter, M. (Eds.). (1983). *Stress, coping and development in children.* New York: McGraw-Hill.

Garner, D. M., & Fairburn, C. G. (1988). Relationship between anorexia nervosa and bulimia nervosa: Diagnostic implications. In D. M. Garner & P. E. Garfinkel (Eds.), *Diagnostic issues in anorexia nervosa and bulimia nervosa.* New York: Brunner/ Mazel.

Garner, D. M., Fairburn, C. G., & Davis, R. (1987). Cognitive-behavioral treatment of bulimia nervosa: A critical appraisal. *Behavior Modification, 11,* 398–431.

Garner, D. M., & Garfinkel, P. E. (Eds.). (1985). *Handbook of psychotherapy for anorexia nervosa and bulimia.* New York: Guilford Press.

Garner, D. M., Garfinkel, P. E., & O'Shaughnessy, M. (1985). The validity of the distinction between bulimics with and without anorexia nervosa. *American Journal of Psychiatry, 142,* 581–587.

Garner, D. M., Garfinkel, P. E., Rockert, W., & Olmsted, M. P. (1987). A prospective study of eating disturbances in the ballet. Ninth World Congress of the International College of Psychosomatic Medicine, Sydney, Australia. *Psychotherapy and Psychosomatics, 48,* 170–175.

Garner, D. M., Garfinkel, P. E., Schwartz, D., & Thompson, M. (1980). Cultural expectation of thinness in women. *Psychological Reports, 47,* 483–491.

Garner, D. M., & Needleman, L. D. (1996). Step care and the decision-tree models for treating eating disorders. In J. K. Thompson (Ed.), *Body image, eating disorders and obesity* (pp. 225–252). Washington, DC: American Psychological Association.

Garner, D. M., Olmstead, M. P., & Polivy, J. (1983). Development and validation of a multidimensional eating disorder inventory for anorexia nervosa and bulimia. *International Journal of Eating Disorders, 2*(2), 15–34.

Garre-Olmo, J., López-Pousa, S., Vilata-Franch, J., Turon-Estrada, A., Lozano-Gallego, M., Hernández-Ferrándiz, M., ... Peralta-Rodríguez, J. (2004). Neuropsychological profile of Alzheimer's disease in women: Moderate and moderately severe cognitive decline. *Archives of Women's Mental Health, 7,* 27–36.

Garry, M., & Wade, K. A. (2005). Actually, a picture is worth less than 45 words: Narratives produce more false memories than photographs do. *Psychonomic Bulletin and Review, 12,* 359–366.

Gatchel, R. (2005). *Clinical essentials of pain management.* Washington, DC: American Psychological Association.

Gatchel, R. J., Peng, Y. B., Peters, M. L., Fuchs, P. N., & Turk, D. C. (2007). The biopsychosocial approach to chronic pain: Scientific advances and future directions. *Psychological Bulletin, 133,* 581–624.

Gatchel, R. J., & Turk, D. C. (Eds.). (1996). *Psychological approaches to pain management: A practitioner's handbook.* New York: Guilford Press.

Gatchel, R. J., & Turk, D. C. (Eds.). (1999). *Psychosocial factors in pain: Critical perspectives.* New York: Guilford Press.

Gatz, M. (2007). Genetics, dementia, and the elderly. *Current Directions in Psychological Science, 16,* 123–127.

Gatz, M., & Smyer, M. A. (1992). The mental health system and older adults in the 1990s. *American Psychologist, 47*(6), 741–751.

Gaw, A. C. (2008). Cultural issues. In R. E. Hales, S. C. Yudofsky, & G. O. Gabbard (Eds.), *The American Psychiatric Publishing textbook of psychiatry* (5th ed., pp. 1529–1547). Arlington, VA: American Psychiatric Publishing, Inc.

Gawin, F. H., Kleber, H. D., Byck, R., Rounsaville, B. J., Kosten, T. R., Jatlow, P. I., & Morgan, C. (1989). Desipramine facilitation of initial cocaine abstinence. *Archives of General Psychiatry, 46,* 117–121.

Gearhart, J. P. (1989). Total ablation of the penis after circumcision electrocautery: A method of management and long term follow-up. *Journal of Urology, 42,* 789–801.

Geer, J. H., Morokoff, P., & Greenwood, P. (1974). Sexual arousal in women: The development of a measurement device for vaginal blood volume. *Archives of Sexual Behavior, 3,* 559–564.

Geist, R., Heinmaa, M., Stephens, D., Davis, R., & Katzman, D. K. (2000). Comparison of family therapy and family group psycho-education in adolescents with anorexia nervosa. *Canadian Journal of Psychiatry, 45,* 173–178.

Gelernter, J., & Stein, M. B. (2009). Heritability and genetics of anxiety disorders. In M. M. Antony & M. B. Stein (Eds.), *Oxford handbook of anxiety and related disorders.* Oxford: Oxford University Press.

Gelinas, L. (1994). The new rights of persons held in psychiatric institutions following the commission of a criminal offence: The Criminal Code revised and corrected. *Canada's Mental Health, 42*(1), 10–16.

Geller, B., Cooper, T. B., Graham, D. L., Fetaer, H. M., Marsteller, F. A., & Wells, J. M. (1992). Pharmacokinetically designed double blind placebo controlled study of nortriptyline in 6–12 year olds with major depressive disorder: Outcome: Nortriptyline and hydroxy-nortriptyline plasma levels; EKG, BP and side effect measurements. *Journal of the American Academy of Child and Adolescent Psychiatry, 31,* 33–44.

Geller, J. (2002). Estimating readiness for change in anorexia nervosa: Comparing clients, clinicians and research assessors. *International Journal of Eating Disorders, 31,* 251–260.

Gellis, L. A., & Lichstein, K. L. (2009). Sleep hygiene practices of good and poor sleepers in the united states: An Internet-based study. *Behavior Therapy, 40*(1), 1–9.

Generations United. (2006). Meth and child welfare: Promising solutions for children, their parents and grandparents. Washington, DC: Author.

George, C., Alary, M., Hogg, R. S., Otis, J., Remis, R. S., Mâsse, B., ... Schechter, M. T. (2007). HIV and ethnicity in Canada: Is the HIV risk-taking behaviour of young foreign-born MSM similar to Canadian born MSM? *AIDS Care, 19*(1), 9–16

George, L. K. (1984). *The burden of caregiving: Center reports of advances in research* (Vol. 8). Durham, NC: Duke University Center for the Study of Aging and Human Development.

George, M. S., Lisanby, S. H., & Sackheim, H. A. (1999). Transcranial magnetic stimulation. *Archives of General Psychiatry, 56,* 300–311.

Georgiades, K., Lewinsohn, P. M., Monroe, S. M., & Seeley, J. R. (2006). Major depressive disorder in adolescence: The role of subthreshold symptoms. *Journal of the American Academy of Child & Adolescent Psychiatry, 45,* 936–944.

Georgiades, S., Szatmari, P., Zwaigenbaum, L., Duku, E., Bryson, S., Roberts, W., ... Mahoney, W. (2007). Structure of the autism symptom phenotype: A proposed multidimensional model. *Journal of the American Academy of Child and Adolescent Psychiatry, 46,* 188–196.

Geraerts, E., Lindsay, D. S., Merckelbach, H., Jelicic, M., Raymaekers, L., Arnold, M. M., & Schooler, J. W. (2009). Cognitive mechanisms underlying recovered memory experiences of childhood sexual abuse. *Psychological Science, 20,* 92–98.

Geraerts, E., & McNally, R. (2008). Forgetting unwanted memories: Directed forgetting and thought suppression methods. *Acta psychologica, 127*(3), 614–622.

Geremia, G., & Neziroglu, F. (2001). Cognitive therapy in the treatment of body dysmorphic disorder. *Clinical Psychology and Psychotherapy, Clinical Psychology and Psychotherapy, 8,* 243–251.

Gerin, W., Pickering, T. G., Glynn, L., Christenfeld, N., Schwartz, A., Carroll, D., & Davidson, K. (2000). An historical context for behavioral models of hypertension. *Journal of Psychosomatic Research, 48,* 369–377.

Gershon, E. S. (1990). Genetics. In F. K. Goodwin & K. R. Jamison (Eds.), *Manic-depressive illness* (pp. 373–401). New York: Oxford University Press.

Gershon, E. S., Kelsoe, J. R., Kendler, K. S., & Watson, J. D. (2001). It's time to search for susceptibility genes for major mental illnesses. *Science, 294,* 5.

Gervais, S., Dupuis, G., Véronneau, F., Bergeron, Y., Millette, D., & Avard, J. (1991). Predictive model to determine cost/benefit of early detection and intervention in occupational low back pain. *Journal of Occupational Rehabilitation, 1,* 113–131.

Getsios, D., Caro, J. J., Caro, G., & Ishak, K. (2001). Assessment of health economics in Alzheimer's disease (AHEAD). Galantamine treatment in Canada. *Neurology, 57,* 972–978.

Ghadirian, A.-M., Gregoire, P., & Kosmidis, H. (2001). Creativity and the evolution of psychopathologies. *Creativity Research Journal, 13,* 145–148.

Giacomuzzi, S. M., Riemer, Y., Ertl, M., Kemmler, G., Rossler, H., Hinterhuber, H., & Kurz, M. (2003). Buprenorphine versus methadone maintenance treatment in an ambulant setting: a health-related quality of life assessment. *Addiction, 98,* 693–702.

Gianoulakis, C. (2001). Influence of the endogenous opioid system on high alcohol consumption and genetic predisposition to alcoholism. *Journal of Psychiatry & Neuroscience, 26* 304–318.

Gibb, W. R. G. (1989). Dementia and Parkinson's disease. *British Journal of Psychiatry, 154,* 596–614.

Gibbons, J. L. (1964). Cortisol secretion rates in depressive illness. *Archives of General Psychiatry, 10,* 572–575.

Gidron, Y., Davidson, K., & Bata, I. (1999). The short-term effects of a hostility-reduction intervention on male coronary heart disease patients. *Health Psychology, 18,* 416–420.

Giesbrecht, T., Lynn, S. J., Lilienfeld, S. O., & Merckelbach, H. (2008). Cognitive processes in dissociation: An analysis of core theoretical assumptions. *Psychological Bulletin, 134*(5), 617–647.

Giesbrecht, T., Smeets, T., Leppink, J., Jelicic, M., & Merckelbach, H. (2007). Acute dissociation after 1 night of sleep loss. *Journal of Abnormal Psychology, 116*(3), 599–606.

Gieser, L., & Stein, M. I. (Eds.). (1999). *Evocative images: The Thematic Apperception Test and the art of projection.* Washington, DC: American Psychological Association.

Gil, K., Williams, D., Keefe, F., & Beckham, J. (1990). The relationship of negative thoughts to pain and psychological distress. *Behavior Therapy, 21,* 349–362.

Gilham, J. E., Reivich, K. J., Jaycox, L. H., & Seligman, M. E. P. (1995). Prevention of depressive symptoms in schoolchildren: Two-year follow-up. *Psychological Science, 6*(6), 343–351.

Gillberg, C. (1984). Infantile autism and other childhood psychoses in a Swedish urban region: Epidemiological aspects. *Journal of Child Psychology and Psychiatry, 25,* 35–43.

Gillies, L. A. (2001). Interpersonal psychotherapy for depression and other disorders. In D. H. Barlow (Ed.), *Clinical handbook of psychological disorders* (3rd ed., pp. 309–331). New York: Guilford Press.

Gillin, J. C. (1993). Clinical sleep-wake disorders in psychiatric practice: Dyssomnias. In D. L. Dunner (Ed.), *Current psychiatric therapy* (pp. 373–380). Philadelphia: W. B. Saunders.

Gilmore, J. H. (2010). Understanding what causes schizophrenia: A developmental perspective. *American Journal of Psychiatry, 167*(1), 8–10.

Ginsburg, G. S., & Silverman, W. K. (2000). Gender role orientation and fearfulness in children with anxiety disorders. *Journal of Anxiety Disorders, 14*(1), 57–67.

Girault, J. A., & Greengard, P. (2004). The neurobiology of dopamine signaling. *Archives of Neurology, 61*(5), 641–644.

Gitlin, M. J. (2009). Pharmacotherapy and other somatic treatments for depression. In I. H. Gotlib & C. L. Hammen (Eds.), *Handbook of depression* (2nd ed., pp. 554–585). New York: Guilford Press.

Gitlin, M. J., Swendsen, J., Heller, T. L., & Hammen, C. (1995). Relapse and impairment in bipolar disorder. *American Journal of Psychiatry, 152,* 1635–1640.

Gladue, B. A., Green, R., & Hellman, R. E. (1984). Neuroendocrine response to estrogen and sexual orientation. *Science, 225,* 1496–1499.

Glaser, R., Kennedy, S., Lafuse, W. P., Bonneau, R. H., Speicher, C. E., Hillhouse, J., & Kiecolt-Glaser, J. K. (1990). Psychological stress-induced modulation of IL-2 receptor gene expression and IL-2 production in peripheral blood leukocytes. *Archives of General Psychiatry, 47,* 707–712.

Glaser, R., Rice, J., Sheridan, J., Fertel, R., Stout, J., Speicher, C., … Beck, M. (1987). Stress-related immune suppression: Health implications. *Brain, Behavior, and Immunity, 1,* 7–20.

Glass, J., Lanctôt, K., Herrmann, N., Sproule, B. A., & Busto, U. E. (2005). Sedative-hypnotics in older people with insomnia: Meta-analysis of risks and benefits. *BMJ, 331,* 1169–1175.

Glatt, A. E., Zinner, S. H., & McCormack, W. M. (1990). The prevalence of dyspareunia. *Obstetrics and Gynecology, 75,* 433–436.

Gleason, O. C. (2003). Delirium. *American Family Physicians, 67,* 1027–1034.

Gleaves, D. H. (1996). The sociocognitive model of dissociative identity disorder: A re-examination of the evidence. *Psychological Bulletin, 120,* 42–59.

Gleaves, D. H., Lowe, M. R., Snow, A. C., Green, B. A., & Murphy-Eberenz, K. P. (2000). Continuity and discontinuity models of bulimia nervosa: A taxometric investigation. *Journal of Abnormal Psychology, 109*(1), 56–68.

Gleaves, D. H., Smith, S. M., Butler, L. D., & Spiegel, D. (2004). False and recovered memories in the laboratory and clinic: A review of experimental and clinical evidence. *Clinical Psychology: Science and Practice, 11*(1), 3–28.

Goater, N., King, M., Cole, E. Leavey, G., Johnson-Sabine, E., Blizard, R., & Hoar, A. (1999). Ethnicity and outcomes of psychosis. *British Journal of Psychiatry, 175,* 34–42.

Goering, P., Wasylenki, D., & Durbin, J. (2000). Canada's mental health system. *International Journal of Law & Psychiatry, 23,* 345–359.

Goff, D. C., & Coyle, J. T. (2001). The emerging role of glutamate in the pathophysiology and treatment of schizophrenia. *American Journal of Psychiatry, 158,* 1367–1377.

Gold, J. H. (1997a). Premenstrual dysphoric disorder: What's that? *JAMA, 278,* 1024–1025.

Gold, J. H. (1999). Premenstrual dysphoric disorder: An update. *Journal of Practical Psychiatry and Behavioral Health, 5,* 209–215.

Gold, J. H., Endicott, J., Parry, B. L., Severino, S. K., Stotland, N., & Frank, E. (1996). Late luteal phase dysphoric disorder. In T. A. Widiger, A. J. Frances, H. A. Pincus, R. Ross, et al. (Eds.), *DSM-IV sourcebook* (Vol. 2, pp. 317–394). Washington, DC: American Psychiatric Association.

Gold, M. S. (1997b). Cocaine (and crack): Clinical aspects. In J. H. Lowinson, P. Ruiz, R. B. Millman, & J. G. Langrod (Eds.), *Substance abuse: A comprehensive textbook* (pp. 181–199). Baltimore: Williams & Wilkins.

Gold, P. W., Goodwin, F. K., & Chrousos, G. P. (1988). Clinical and biochemical manifestations of depression: Relation to the neurobiology of stress. *New England Journal of Medicine, 319,* 348–353.

Gold, S. N., & Seibel, S. L. (2009). Treating dissociation: A contextual approach. In P. F. Dell & J. A. O'Neil (Eds.), *Dissociation and the dissociative disorders: DSM-V and beyond* (pp. 625–636). New York: Routledge/Taylor & Francis Group.

Goldapple, K., Segal, Z., Garson, C., Lau, M., Bieling, P., Kennedy, S., & Mayberg, H. (2004). Modulation of cortical-limbic pathways in major depression. *Archives of General Psychiatry, 61,* 34–41.

Goldberg, J. F., Harrow, M., & Grossman, L. S. (1995). Course and outcome in bipolar affective disorder: A longitudinal follow-up study. *American Journal of Psychiatry, 152,* 379–384.

Goldberg, J. F., Perlis, R. H., Bowden, C. L., Thase, M. E., Miklowitz, D. J., Marangell, L. B., … Sachs, G. S. (2009). Manic symptoms during depressive episodes in 1,380 patients with bipolar disorder: Findings from the STEP-BD. *American Journal of Psychiatry, 166*(2), 173–181.

Goldberg, J. O., & Schmidt, L. A. (2001). Shyness, sociability, and social dysfunction in schizophrenia. *Schizophrenia Research, 48,* 343–349.

Goldberg, L. (1993). The structure of phenotypic personality traits. *American Psychologist, 48,* 26–34.

Goldberg, S. C., Schultz, C., Resnick, R. J., Hamer, R. M., & Schultz, P. M. (1987). Differential prediction of response to thiothixene and placebo in borderline and schizotypal personality disorders. *Psychopharmacology Bulletin, 23,* 342–346.

Golden, C. J., Hammeke, T. A., & Purisch, A. D. (1980). *The Luria-Nebraska battery manual.* Palo Alto, CA: Western Psychological Services.

Goldfarb, W. (1963). Self-awareness in schizophrenic children. *Archives of General Psychiatry, 8,* 63–76.

Goldin, P. R., Manber, T., Hakimi, S., Canli, T., & Gross, J. J. (2009). Neural bases of social anxiety disorder: Emotional reactivity and cognitive regulation during social and physical threat. *Archives of General Psychiatry, 66*(2), 170–180.

Goldman, M. S., Del Boca, F. K., & Darkes, J. (1999). Alcohol expectancy theory: The application of cognitive neuroscience. In H. Blane & K. Leonard (Eds.), *Psychological theories of drinking and alcoholism* (pp. 203–246). New York: Guilford Press.

Goldman, M. S., & Rather, B. C. (1993). Substance use disorders: Cognitive models and architecture. In K. S. Dobson & P. C. Kendall (Eds.), *Psychopathology and cognition* (pp. 245–292). New York: Academic Press.

Goldman, N., Glei, D. A., Lin, Y., & Weinstein, M. (2010). The serotonin transporter polymorphism (5-HTTLPR): Allelic variation and links with depressive symptoms. *Depression and Anxiety, 27*(3), 260–269.

Goldman, R., Greenberg, L., & Angus, L. (2006) The effects of adding emotion-focused interventions to the therapeutic relationship in the treatment of depression. *Psychotherapy Research, 16,* 537–549.

Goldman, S. J., D'Angelo, E. J., DeMaso, D. R., & Mezzacappa, E. (1992). Physical and sexual abuse histories among children with borderline personality disorder. *American Journal of Psychiatry, 149,* 1723–1726.

Goldner, E. (1989). Treatment refusal in anorexia nervosa. *International Journal of Eating Disorders, 8,* 297–306.

Goldner, E. M., Cockell, S. J., & Srikameswaran, S. (2002). Perfectionism and eating disorders. In G. L. Flett & P. L. Hewitt (Eds.), *Perfectionism: Theory, research, and treatment* (pp. 319–340). Washington, DC: American Psychological Association.

Goldner, E. M., Geller, J., Birmingham, C. L., & Remick, R. A. (2000). Comparison of shoplifting behaviours in patients with eating disorders, psychiatric control subjects, and undergraduate control subjects. *Canadian Journal of Psychiatry, 45,* 471–475.

Goldner, E. M., Jones, W., & Waraich, P. (2003). Using administrative data to analyze the prevalence and distribution of schizophrenic disorders. *Psychiatric Services, 54,* 1017–1021.

Goldner, E. M., Srikameswaran, S., Schroeder, M. L., Livesley, W. J., & Birmingham, C. L. (1999). Dimensional assessment of personality pathology in patients with eating disorders. *Psychiatry Research, 85,* 151–159.

Goldner, V. (2003). Ironic gender/authentic sex. *Studies in Gender & Sexuality, 4,* 113–139.

Goldstein, A. (1994). *Addiction: From biology to drug policy.* New York: W. H. Freeman.

Goldschmidt, A. B., Hilbert, A., Manwaring, J. L., Wilfley, D. E., Pike, K. M., Fairburn, C. G., ... Striegel-Moore, R. H. (2010). The significance of overvaluation of shape and weight in binge eating disorder. *Behaviour Research and Therapy, 48*(3), 187–193.

Goldstein, B. I. (2006). Why do women get depressed and men get drunk? An examination of attributional style and coping style in response to negative life events among Canadian young adults. *Sex Roles, 54*(1/2), 27–37.

Goldstein, G. (2000). Comprehensive neuropsychological assessment batteries. In G. Goldstein & M. Hersen (Eds.), *Handbook of psychological assessment* (pp. 231–261). New York: Pergamon Press.

Goldstein, I., Lue, T. F., Padma-Nathan, H., Rosen, R. C., Steers, W. D., & Wicker, P. A., for the Sildenafil Study Group. (1998). Oral sildenafil in the treatment of erectile dysfunction. *New England Journal of Medicine, 338,* 1397–1404.

Goldstein, J. M., & Lewine, R. R. J. (2000). Overview of sex differences in schizophrenia: Where have we been and where do we go from here? In D. J. Castle, J. McGrath, & J. Kulkarni (Eds.), *Women and schizophrenia* (pp. 111–143). Cambridge: Cambridge University Press.

Golier, J., Yehuda, R., Lupien, S., Harvey, P., Grossman, R., & Elkin, A. (2002). Memory performance in Holocaust survivors with posttraumatic stress disorder. *American Journal of Psychiatry, 159,* 1682–1688.

Gomez-Caminero, A., Blumentals, W. A., Russo, L., Brown, R. R., & Castilla-Puentes, R. (2005). Does panic disorder increase the risk of coronary heart disease? A cohort study of a national managed care database. *Psychosomatic Medicine, 67,* 688–691.

Gomez-Gil, E., Steva, I., Almaraz, M. C., Pasara, E., Segovia, S., & Guillamon, A. (2010). Familiality of gender identity disorder in non-twin siblings. *Archives of Sexual Behavior, 39,* 546–552.

Gomez-Perez, J. C., Marks, I. M., & Gutierrez-Fisac, J. L. (1994). Dysmorphophobia: Clinical features and outcome with behaviour therapy. *European Psychiatry, 9,* 229–235.

Gonzalez-Lavin, A., & Smolak, L. (1995, March). *Relationships between television and eating problems in middle school girls.* Paper presented at the meeting of the Society for Research in Child Development, Indianapolis, IN.

Good, B. J., & Kleinman, A. M. (1985). Culture and anxiety: Cross-cultural evidence for the patterning of anxiety disorders. In A. H. Tuma & J. D. Maser (Eds.), *Anxiety and the anxiety disorders.* Hillsdale, NJ: Erlbaum.

Good, K. P., Kiss, I., Buiteman, C., Woodley, H., Rui, Q., Whitehorn, D., & Kopala, L. (2002). Improvement in cognitive functioning in patients with first-episode psychosis during treatment with quetiapine: An interim analysis. *British Journal of Psychiatry, 181*(Suppl. 43), 45–49.

Goodman, J. T. (2000). Three decades of professional psychology: Reflections and future challenges. *Canadian Psychology, 41,* 25–33.

Goodman, L. A. (2003, December 11). Canadian psychologist stripped of licence faces misconduct charges in Ohio. *CNEWS Canada.* Retrieved May 21, 2004, from http://cnews. canoe. ca/CNEWS/Canada/2003/12/11/284357-cp.html

Goodman, S. H., & Gotlib, I. H. (1999). Risk for psychopathology in the children of depressed mothers: A developmental model for understanding mechanisms of transmission. *Psychological Review, 106*(3), 458–490.

Goodwin, D. W., & Gabrielli, W. F. (1997). Alcohol: Clinical aspects. In J. H. Lowinson, P. Ruiz, R. B. Millman, & J. G. Langrod (Eds.), *Substance abuse: A comprehensive textbook* (pp. 142–148). Baltimore: Williams & Wilkins.

Goodwin, D. W., & Guze, S. B. (1984). *Psychiatric diagnosis* (3rd ed.). New York: Oxford University Press.

Goodwin, F. K., Fireman, B., Simon, G. E., Hunkeler, E. M., Lee, J., & Revicki, D. (2003). Suicide risk in bipolar disorder during treatment with lithium and divalproex. *JAMA, 290,* 1467–1473.

Goodwin, F. K., & Ghaemi, S. N. (1998). Understanding manic-depressive illness. *Archives of General Psychiatry, 55*(1), 23–25.

Goodwin, F. K., & Jamison, K. R. (1990). *Manic depressive illness.* New York: Oxford University Press.

Goodwin, F. K., & Jamison, K. R. (Eds.) (2007). *Manic depressive illness: Bipolar disorders and recurrent depression* (2nd ed.). New York: Oxford University Press.

Goodwin, G. M. (2009). Neurobiological aetiology of mood disorders. In M. G. Gelder, N. C. Andreasen, J. J. Lopez-Ibor, Jr., & J. R. Geddes (Eds.), *New Oxford textbook of psychiatry* (Vol. 1, 2nd ed., pp. 658–664). Oxford, UK: Oxford University Press.

Goos, L. M., Crosbie, J., Payne, S., & Schachar, R. (2009). Validation and extension of the endophenotype model in ADHD patterns of inheritance in a family study of inhibitory control. *American Journal of Psychiatry, 166*(6), 711–717.

Gootenberg, P. (2009). *Andean cocaine: The making of a global drug.* Chapel Hill, NC: The University of North Carolina Press.

Gordis, E. (2000a). Alcohol, the brain, and behavior: Mechanisms of addiction. *Alcohol Research & Health, 24*(1), 12–15.

Gordis, E. (2000b). Why do some people drink too much? The role of genetic and psychosocial influences. *Alcohol Research & Health, 24*(1), 17–26.

Gordis, E. (2000c). Latest approaches to preventing alcohol abuse and alcoholism. *Alcohol Research & Health, 24*(1), 42–51.

Gordis, E. (2000d). Research refines alcohol treatment options. *Alcohol Research & Health, 24*(1), 53–61.

Gordon, J. A. (2002). Anxiolytic drug targets: Beyond the usual suspects. *Journal of Clinical Investigation, 110*(7), 915–917.

Gore-Felton, C., & Koopman, C. (2008). Behavioral mediation of the relationship between psychosocial factors and HIV disease progression. *Psychosomatic Medicine, 70,* 569–574.

Gorenstein, E. E. (1984). Debating mental illness: Implications for science, medicine, and social policy. *American Psychologist, 39,* 50–56.

Gorenstein, E. E., & Newman, J. P. (1980). Disinhibitory psychopathology: A new perspective and a model for research. *Psychological Review, 87,* 301–315.

Gosselin, P., Ladouceur, R., Morin, C. M., Dugas, M. J., & Baillargeon, L. (2006). Benzodiazepine discontinuation among adults with GAD: A randomized trial of cognitive-behavioral therapy. *Journal of Consulting and Clinical Psychology, 74,* 908–919.

Gosselin, P., Langlois, F., Freeston, M. H., Laberge, M., & Lemay, D. (2007). Cognitive variables related to worry among adolescents: Avoidance strategies and faulty beliefs about worry. *Behaviour Research and Therapy, 45,* 225–233.

Gotlib, I. H., & Abramson, L. Y. (1999). Attributional theories of emotion. In T. Dagleish & M. J. Power (Eds.), *Handbook of cognition and emotion.* Chichester: John Wiley.

Gotlib, I. H., & Beach, S. R. H. (1995). A marital/family discord model of depression: Implications for therapeutic intervention. In N. S. Jacobson & A. S. Gurman (Eds.), *Clinical handbook of couple therapy* (pp. 411–436). New York: Guilford Press.

Gotlib, I. H., Lewinsohn, P. M., Seeley, J. R., Rohde, P., & Redner, J. E. (1993). Negative cognitions and attributional style in depressed adolescents: An examination of stability and specificity. *Journal of Abnormal Psychology, 102,* 607–615.

Gotlib, I. H., & Nolan, S. A. (2000). Depression. In A. S. Bellack & M. Hersen (Eds.), *Psychopathology in adulthood* (2nd ed., pp. 252–277). Boston: Allyn & Bacon.

Gotlib, I. H., Ranganath, C., & Rosenfeld, J. P. (1998). Frontal EEG alpha asymmetry, depression, and cognitive functioning. *Cognition and Emotion, 12,* 449–478.

Gotlib, I. H., Roberts, J. E., & Gilboa, E. (1996). Cognitive interference in depression. In I. G. Sarason, G. R. Pierce, & B. R. Sarason (Eds.), *Cognitive interference: Theories, methods, and findings* (pp. 347–377). Mahwah, NJ: Erlbaum.

Gotowiec, A., & Beiser, M. (1993–1994). Aboriginal children's mental health: Unique challenges. *Canada's Mental Health, 41*(4), 7–11.

Gottesman, I. I. (1991). *Schizophrenia genesis: The origins of madness.* New York: W. H. Freeman.

Gottesman, I. I. (1997, June 6). Twins: En route to QTLs for cognition. *Science, 276,* 1522–1523.

Gottesman, I. I., & Bertelsen, A. (1989). Dual mating studies in psychiatry—offspring of inpatients with examples from reactive (psychogenic) psychoses. *International Review of Psychiatry, 1,* 287–296.

Gottlieb, B. H., & Johnson, J. (2000). Respite programs for caregivers of persons with dementia: A review with practice implications. *Aging & Mental Health, 4,* 119–129.

Gottlieb, G. (1998). Normally occurring environmental and behavioral influences on gene activity: From central dogma to probabilistic epigenesis. *Psychological Review, 105,* 492–802.

Gould, M. S. (1990). Suicide clusters and media exposure. In S. J. Blumenthal & D. J. Kupfer (Eds.), *Suicide over the life cycle: Risk factors, assessment and treatment of suicidal patients.* Washington, DC: American Psychiatric Press.

Gould, M. S., Greenberg, T., Velting, D. M., & Shaffer, D. (2003). Youth suicide risk and preventive interventions: A review of the past 10 years. *Journal of the American Academy of Child and Adolescent Psychiatry, 42*(4), 386–405.

Gould, R. A., Buckminster, S., Pollack, M. H., Otto, M. W., & Yap, L. (1997a). Cognitive-behavioral and pharmacological treatment for social phobia: A meta-analysis. *Clinical Psychology: Science and Practice, 4,* 291–306.

Gould, R. A., Otto, M. W., Pollack, M. H., & Yap, L. (1997b). Cognitive behavioral and pharmacological treatment of generalized anxiety disorder: A preliminary meta-analysis. *Behavior Therapy, 28,* 285–305.

Grabbe, K. L., & Bunnell, R. (2010). Reframing HIV prevention in sub-saharan Africa using couple-centered approaches. *JAMA, 304,* 346–347.

Grabe, H. J., Meyer, C., Hapke, U., Rumpf, H. J., Freyberger, H. J., Dilling, H., & John, U. (2003). Somatoform pain disorder in the general population. *Psychotherapy and Psychosomatics, 72,* 88–94.

Grabe, S., Ward, L. M., & Hyde, J. S. (2008). The role of the media in body image concerns among women: A meta-analysis of experimental and correlational studies. *Psychological Bulletin, 134*(3), 460–476.

Grados, M. A., Riddle, M. A., Samuels, J. F., Liang, K.-Y., Hoehn-Saric, R., Bienvenu, O. J., ... Nestadt, G. (2001). The familial phenotype of obsessive-compulsive disorder in relation to tic disorders: The Hopkins OCD family study. *Biological Psychiatry, 50,* 559–565.

Grady-Weliky, T. (2003). Premenstrual dysphoric disorder. *New England Journal of Medicine, 345,* 433–438.

Graeff, F. G. (1987). The anti-aversive action of drugs. In T. Thompson, P. B. Dews, & J. Barrett (Eds.), *Advances in behavioral pharmacology* (Vol. 6). Hillside, NJ: Erlbaum.

Graeff, F. G. (1993). Role of 5-ht in defensive behavior and anxiety. *Review in the Neurosciences, 4,* 181–211.

Graf, P., Squire, L. R., & Mandler, G. (1984). The information that amnesic patients do not forget. *Journal of Experimental Psychology: Learning, Memory, and Cognition, 10,* 164–178.

Graham, C. A. (2010). The DSM criteria for female orgasmic disorder. *Archives of Sexual Behavior, 39,* 256–270.

Grandy, T. (1995). *New occupational hazards of career addicts: Main line intravenous needs assessment (MINA).* Document prepared by Main Line Needle Exchange with funding from Health Canada.

Granic, I., & Patterson, G. R. (2006). Toward a comprehensive model of antisocial development: A dynamic systems approach. *Psychological Review, 113,* 101–131.

Grant, A. (1996). *No end of grief: Indian residential schools in Canada.* Winnipeg, MB: Pemmican.

Grant, B., Chou, S., Goldstein, R., Huang, B., Stinson, F., Saha, T., ... Ruan, W. J. (2008). Prevalence, correlates, disability, and comorbidity of DSM-IV borderline personality disorder: Results from the Wave 2 National Epidemiologic Survey on Alcohol and Related Conditions. *The Journal of Clinical Psychiatry, 69*(4), 533.

Grant, B. F., & Dawson, D. A. (1999). Alcohol and drug use, abuse, and dependence: Classification, prevalence, and comorbidity. In B. S. McCrady & E. E. Epstein (Eds.), *Addictions: A comprehensive guidebook* (pp. 9–29). New York: Oxford University Press.

Grant, I., Patterson, T. L., & Yager, J. (1988). Social supports in relation to physical health and symptoms of depression in the elderly. *American Journal of Psychiatry, 145,* 1254–1258.

Grant, J. E., Correia, S., & Brennan-Krohn, T. (2006). White matter integrity in kleptomania: A pilot study. *Psychiatry Research: Neuroimaging, 147,* 233–237.

Grant, J. E., & Kim, S. W. (2002). Temperament and early environmental influences in kleptomania. *Comprehensive Psychiatry, 43,* 223–229.

Grant, K. E., Compas, B. E., Thurm, A. E., McMahon, S. D., & Gipson, P. Y. (2004). Stressors and child and adolescent psychopathology: Measurement issues and prospective effects. *Journal of Clinical Child and Adolescent Psychology, 33*(2), 412–425.

Grassick, P. (1990). The fear behind the fear: A case study of apparent simple injection phobia.

Journal of Behavior Therapy and Experimental Psychiatry, 21, 281–287.

Gratzer, T. G., & Matas, M. (1994). The right to refuse treatment: Recent Canadian developments. *Bulletin of the American Academy of Psychiatry & the Law, 22,* 249–256.

Gray, J. A. (1982). *The neuropsychology of anxiety.* New York: Oxford University Press.

Gray, J. A. (1985). Issues in the neuropsychology of anxiety. In A. H. Tuma & J. D. Maser (Eds.), *Anxiety and the anxiety disorders* (pp. 5–25). Hillside, NJ: Erlbaum.

Gray, J. A. (1987). *The psychology of fear and stress* (2nd ed.). New York: Cambridge University Press.

Gray, J. A., & Buffery, A. W. H. (1971). Sex differences in emotional and cognitive behavior in mammals including man: Adaptive and neural bases. *Acta Psychologica, 35,* 89–111.

Gray, J. A., & McNaughton, N. (1996). The neuropsychology of anxiety: Reprise. In D. A. Hope (Ed.), *Perspectives on anxiety, panic and fear* (the 43rd Annual Nebraska Symposium on Motivation, pp. 61–134). Lincoln: Nebraska University Press.

Gray, J. E., & O'Reilly, R. L. (2001). Clinically significant differences among Canadian mental health acts. *Canadian Journal of Psychiatry, 46,* 315–321.

Gray, J. E., & O'Reilly, R. L. (2005). Canadian compulsory community treatment laws: Recent reforms. *International Journal of Law and Psychiatry, 28,* 13–22.

Graziottin, A., & Brotto, L. A. (2004). Vulvar vestibulitis syndrome: A clinical approach. *Journal of Sex & Marital Therapy, 30,* 125–139.

Grcevich, S., Rowane, W. A., Marcellino, B., & Sullivan-Hurst, S. (2001). Retrospective comparison of Adderall and methylphenidate in the treatment of attention deficit hyperactivity disorder. *Journal of Child and Adolescent Pscyhopharmacology, 11,* 35–41.

Grebb, J. A., & Carlsson, A. (2009). Introduction and considerations for a brain-Based diagnostic system in psychiatry. In B. J. Sadock, V. A. Sadock, & P. Ruiz (Eds.), *Kaplan & Sadock's comprehensive textbook of psychiatry* (Vol. I, 9th ed., pp. 1–5). Philadelphia: Lippincott Williams & Wilkins.

Greden, J. F., & Walters, A. (1997). Caffeine. In J. H. Lowinson, P. Ruiz, R. B. Millman, & J. G. Langrod (Eds.), *Substance abuse: A comprehensive textbook* (pp. 294–307). Baltimore: Williams & Wilkins.

Green, A. I., Mooney, J. J., Posener, J. A., & Schildkraut, J. J. (1995). Mood disorders: Biochemical aspects. In H. I. Kaplan & B. J. Sadock (Eds.), *Comprehensive textbook of psychiatry* (6th ed., pp. 1089–1101). Baltimore: Williams & Wilkins.

Green, B. L., Grace, M. C., Lindy, J. D., Titchener, J. L., & Lindy, J. G. (1983). Levels of functional impairment following a civilian disaster: The Beverly Hills Supper Club fire. *Journal of Consulting and Clinical Psychology, 51,* 573–580.

Green, R. (1987). *The "sissy boy syndrome" and the development of homosexuality.* New Haven, CT: Yale University Press.

Green, R., & Fleming, D. T. (1990). Transsexual surgery follow-up: Status in the 1990s. *Annual Review of Sex Research, 1,* 163–174.

Green, R., & Money, J. (1969). *Transsexualism and sex reassignment.* Baltimore: Johns Hopkins Press.

Greenberg, A. H. (1994). The origins of the NK cell, or a Canadian in King Ivan's court. *Clinical and Investigative Medicine, 17,* 626–631.

Greenberg, H. R. (2005). Impulse-control disorders not elsewhere classified. In B. J. Sadock & V. A. Sadock (Eds.), *Kaplan & Sadock's comprehensive textbook of psychiatry* (8th ed., pp. 2035–2054). Philadelphia: Lippincott Williams & Wilkins.

Greenberg, L. (2004). Introduction to emotion-focused therapy [Special issue]. *Clinical Psychology and Psychotherapy, 11,* 1–2.

Greenberg, L., Elliott, R., & Lietaer, G. (2003). Humanistic-Experiential Psychotherapy. In G. Stricker & T. Widiger (Eds.) *Handbook of psychology: Clinical psychology* (Vol. 8, pp. 301–326) Hoboken, NJ: John Wiley & Sons.

Greenberg, L., & Watson, J. (2005). *Emotion-focused therapy of Depression.* Washington, DC: APA Press.

Greenberg, M. S., & Beck, A. T. (1989). Depression versus anxiety: A test of the content specificity. *Journal of Abnormal Psychology, 98*(1), 9–13.

Greene, R. W., & Ollendick, T. H. (2000). Behavioral assessment of children. In G. Goldstein & M. Hersen (Eds.), *Handbook of psychological assessment* (pp. 453–470). New York: Pergamon Press.

Greenough, W. T., Withers, G. S., & Wallace, C. S. (1990). Morphological changes in the nervous system arising from behavioral experience: What is the evidence that they are involved in learning and memory? In L. R. Squire & E. Lindenlaub (Eds.), *The biology of memory, Symposia Medica Hoescht 23* (pp. 159–183). Stuttgart/New York: Schattauer Verlag.

Greer, S. (1999). Mind-body research in psychoncology. *Advances in Mind-Body-Medicine, 15,* 236–244.

Gregoire, A. (1992). New treatments for erectile impotence. *British Journal of Psychiatry, 160,* 315–326.

Greist, J. H. (1990). Treatment of obsessive compulsive disorder: Psychotherapies, drugs, and other somatic treatments. *Journal of Clinical Psychiatry, 51,* 44–50.

Grenier, G., & Byers, E. S. (2001). Operationalizing premature or rapid ejaculation. *Journal of Sex Research, 38,* 369–378.

Griffin, J. (1989). *In search of sanity: a chronicle of the Canadian Mental Health Association, 1918–1988.* London, ON: Third Eye Publications.

Griffith, E. E. H., English, T., & Mayfield, U. (1980). Possession, prayer and testimony: Therapeutic aspects of the Wednesday night meeting in a black church. *Psychiatry, 43*(5), 120–128.

Griffith, E. E. H., González, C. A., & Blue, H. C. (1999). The basics of cultural psychiatry. In R. E. Hales, S. C. Yudofsky, & J. A. Talbott (Eds.), *The American Psychiatric Press textbook of psychiatry* (3rd ed., pp. 1463–1492). Washington, DC: American Psychiatric Press.

Grilo, C. M., Masheb, R. M., & White, M. A. (2010). Significance of overvaluation of shape/weight in binge-eating disorder: Comparative study with overweight and bulimia nervosa. *Obesity, 18,* 499–504.

Grinspoon, L., & Bakalar, J. B. (1980). Drug dependence: Non-narcotic agents. In H. I. Kaplan, A. M. Freedman, & B. J. Sadock (Eds.), *Comprehensive textbook of psychiatry* (3rd ed., pp. 1614–1629). Baltimore: Williams & Wilkins.

Grinspoon, L., & Bakalar, J. B. (1997). Marihuana. In J. H. Lowinson, P. Ruiz, R. B. Millman, &

J. G. Langrod (Eds.), *Substance abuse: A comprehensive textbook* (pp. 199–206). Baltimore: Williams & Wilkins.

Grisham, J., Frost, R. O., Steketee, G., Kim, H. J., & Hood, S. (2006). Age of onset of compulsive hoarding. *Journal of Anxiety Disorders, 20,* 675–686.

Grisham, J. R., & Barlow, D. H. (2005). Compulsive hoarding: Current research and theory. *Journal of Psychopathology and Behavioral Assessment, 27,* 45–52.

Grub, C. S., & Poland, R. E. (1997). In J. H. Lowinson, P. Ruiz, R. B. Millman, & J. G. Langrod (Eds.), *Substance abuse: A comprehensive textbook* (pp. 269–275). Baltimore: Williams & Wilkins.

Gross, J., & Rosen, J. C. (1988). Bulimia in adolescents: Prevalence and psychosocial correlates. *International Journal of Eating Disorders, 7,* 51–61.

Gross, J. J. (1999). Emotion and emotion regulation. In L. A. Pervin & O. P. John (Eds.), *Handbook of personality: Theory and research* (2nd ed., pp. 525–552). New York: Guilford Press.

Gross, J. J. (Ed.). (2007). *Handbook of emotion regulation.* New York: Guilford Press.

Gross, J. J., & John, O. P. (2003). Individual differences in two emotion regulation processes: Implications for affect, relationships, and well-being. *Journal of Personality & Social Psychology, 85,* 348–362.

Gross, J. J., & Muñoz, R. F. (1995). Emotion regulation and mental health. *Clinical Psychology: Science and Practice, 2,* 151–164.

Gross, S. R., Barrett, S. P., Shestowsky, J. S., & Pihl, R. O. (2002). Ecstasy and drug consumption patterns: A Canadian rave population study. *The Canadian Journal of Psychiatry/La Revue canadienne de psychiatrie, 47*(6), 546–551.

Gross-Tsur, V., Manor, O., & Shalev, R. S. (1996). Developmental dyscalcula: Prevalence and demographic features. *Developmental Medicine and Child Neurology, 38,* 25–33.

Grosz, H. J., & Zimmerman, J. (1965). Experimental analysis of hysterical blindness: A follow-up report and new experimental data. *Archives of General Psychiatry, 13,* 255–260.

Grosz, H. J., & Zimmerman, J. (1970). A second detailed case study of functional blindness: Further demonstration of the contribution of objective psychological laboratory data. *Behavior Therapy, 1,* 115–123.

Grove, W. M., & Tellegen, A. (1991). Problems in the classification of personality disorders. *Journal of Personality Disorders, 5,* 31–42.

Gruder, C. L., Mermelstein, R. J., Kirkendol, S., Hedeker, D., Wong, S. C., Schreckengost, J., … Miller, T. Q. (1993). Effects of social support and relapse prevention training as adjuncts to a televised smoking-cessation intervention. *Journal of Consulting and Clinical Psychology, 61,* 113–120.

Guastella, A. J., Einfeld, S. L., Gray, K. M., Rinehart, N. J., Tonge, B. J., Lambert, T. J., & Hickie, I. B. (2010). Intranasal oxytocin improves emotion recognition for youth with autism spectrum disorders. *Biological Psychiatry, 67*(7), 692–694.

Guillem, F., Bicu, M., Semkovska, M., & Bebruille, J. B. (2002). The dimensional symptom structure of schizophrenia and its association with temperament and character. *Schizophrenia Research, 56*(1–2), 137–147.

Guilleminault, C. (1989). Clinical features and evaluation of obstructive sleep apnea. In M. H. Kryger, T. Roth, & W. C. Dement (Eds.),

Principles and practice of sleep medicine (pp. 552–558). Philadelphia: W. B. Saunders.

Guilleminault, C., & Anagnos, A. (2000). Narcolepsy. In M. H. Kryger, T. Roth, & W. C. Dement (Eds.), *Principles and practice of sleep medicine* (3rd ed., pp. 676–686). Philadelphia: W. B. Saunders.

Guilleminault, C., & Dement, W. C. (1988). Sleep apnea syndromes and related sleep disorders. In R. L. Williams, I. Karacan, & C. A. Moore (Eds.), *Sleep disorders: Diagnosis and treatment* (pp. 47–71). New York: John Wiley & Sons.

Guilleminault, C., & Pelayo, R. (2000). Idiopathic central nervous system hypersomnia. In M. H. Kryger, T. Roth, & W. C. Dement (Eds.), *Principles and practice of sleep medicine* (3rd ed., pp. 687– 692). Philadelphia: W. B. Saunders.

Gunderson, J. G. (1992). Diagnostic controversies. In A. Tasman & M. B. Riba (Eds.), *Review of psychiatry* (Vol. 11, pp. 9–24). Washington, DC: American Psychiatric Press.

Gunderson, J. G., Ronningstam, E., & Smith, L. E. (1991). Narcissistic personality disorder: A review of data on DSM-III-R descriptions. *Journal of Personality Disorders, 5,* 167–177.

Gunderson, J. G., Ronningstam, E., & Smith, L. E. (1995). Narcissistic personality disorder. In W. J. Livesley (Ed.), *The DSM-IV personality disorders* (pp. 201–212). New York: Guilford Press.

Gunderson, J. G., & Sabo, A. N. (1993). The phenomenological and conceptual interface between borderline personality disorder and PTSD. *American Journal of Psychiatry, 150,* 19–27.

Gunderson, J. G., Zanarini, M. C., & Kisiel, C. L. (1995). Borderline personality disorder. In W. J. Livesley (Ed.), *The DSM-IV personality disorders* (pp. 141–157). New York: Guilford Press.

Gunnar, M. R., & Fisher, P. A. (2006). Bringing basic research on early experience and stress neurobiology to bear on preventive interventions for neglected and maltreated children. *Development and Psychopathology, 18*(3), 651–677.

Gupta, M. A., Chaturvedi, S. K., Chandarana, P. C., & Johnson, A. M. (2001). Weight-related body image concerns among 18–24-year-old women in Canada and India: An empirical comparative study. *Journal of Psychosomatic Research, 50,* 193–198.

Gur, R. E., & Pearlson, G. D. (1993). Neuroimaging in schizophrenia research. *Schizophrenia Bulletin, 19,* 337–353.

Guralnik, O., Schmeidler, J., & Simeon, D. (2000). Feeling unreal: Cognitive processes in depersonalization. *American Journal of Psychiatry, 157*(1), 103–109.

Gureje, O., Simon, G. E., Ustun, T. B., & Goldberg, D. P. (1997). Somatization in cross-cultural perspective: A World Health Organization study in primary care. *American Journal of Psychiatry, 154,* 989–995.

Gurvits, T. V., Shenton, M. E., Hokama, H., Ohta, H., Lasko, N. B., Gilbertson, M. W., … Pitman, R. K. (1996). Magnetic resonance imaging study of hippocampal volume in chronic, combat related posttraumatic stress disorder. *Biological Psychiatry, 40,* 1091–1099.

Gusella, J., Butler, G., Nichols, L., & Bird, D. (2003). A brief questionnaire to assess readiness to change in adolescents with eating disorders: Its application to group therapy. *European Eating Disorders Review, 11,* 58–71.

Gusella, J. F., Wexler, N. S., Conneally, P. M., Naylor, S. L., Anderson, M. A., Tanzi, R. E., …

Martin, J. B. (1983). A polymorphic DNA marker genetically linked to Huntington's disease. *Nature, 306,* 234–239.

Gustad, J., & Phillips, K. A. (2003). Axis I comorbidity in body dysmorphic disorder. *Comprehensive Psychiatry, 44,* 270–276.

Guttmacher, M. S., & Weihofen, H. (1952). *Psychiatry and the law.* New York: Norton.

Guydish, J., Sorensen, J. L., Chan, M., Werdegar, D., & Acampora, A. (1999). A randomized trial comparing day and residential drug abuse treatment: 18-month outcomes. *Journal of Consulting and Clinical Psychology, 67*(3), 428–434.

Guyton, A. (1981). *Textbook of medical physiology.* Philadelphia: W. B. Saunders.

Guze, S. B., Cloninger, C. R., Martin, R. L., & Clayton, P. J. (1986). A follow-up and family study of Briquet's syndrome. *British Journal of Psychiatry, 149,* 17–23.

Haas, A. P., & Hendin, H. (1987). The meaning of chronic marijuana use among adults: A psychosocial perspective. *Journal of Drug Issues, 17,* 333–348.

Hackett, T. P., & Cassem, N. H. (1973). Psychological adaptation to convalescence in myocardial infarction patients. In J. P. Naughton, H. K. Hellerstein, & I. C. Mohler (Eds.), *Exercise testing and exercise training in coronary heart disease.* New York: Academic Press.

Haenen, M. A., de Jong, P. J., Schmidt, A. J. M., Stevens, S., & Visser, L. (2000). Hypochondriacs' estimation of negative outcomes: Domain-specificity and responsiveness to reassuring and alarming information. *Behaviour Research and Therapy, 38,* 819–833.

Haggarty, J. M., Cernovsky, Z., Husni, M., Minor, K., Kermeen, P., & Merskey, H. (2002). Seasonal affective disorder in an Arctic community. *Acta Psychiatrica Scandinavica, 105,* 378–384.

Haggarty, J. M., Cernovsky, Z., Kermeen, P., & Merskey, H. (2000). Psychiatric disorders in an Arctic community. *Canadian Journal of Psychiatry, 45,* 357–362.

Hagnell, O., Franck, A., Grasbeck, A., Ohman, R., Ojesjo, L., Otterbeck, L., & Rorsman, B. (1992). Vascular dementia in the Lundby study: I. A prospective, epidemiological study of incidence and risk from 1957 to 1972. *Neuropsychobiology, 26,* 43–49.

Haig-Brown, C. (1988). *Resistance and renewal: Surviving the Indian residential school.* Vancouver, BC: Tillacum Library.

Hall, A. C., Butterworth, J., Winsor, J., Gilmore, D., & Metzel, D. (2007). Pushing the employment agenda: Case study research of high performing states in integrated employment. *Intellectual and Developmental Disabilities, 45,* 182–198.

Hall, D. E., Eubanks, L., Meyyazhagan, S., Kenney, R. D., & Johnson, S. (2000). Evaluation of covert video surveillance in the diagnosis of Munchausen syndrome by proxy: Lessons from 41 cases. *Pediatrics, 6,* 1305–1312.

Hall, G. C. N. (1995). The preliminary development of theory-based community treatment for sexual offenders. *Professional Psychology: Research and Practice, 26*(5), 478–483.

Hall, J. (2007, June 1). Retailers juggle restrictions with curtains, separate entrances. *Edmonton Journal,* p. A.2.

Hall, S. M., Muñoz, R. F., Reus, V. I., & Sees, K. L. (1993). Nicotine, negative affect, and depression. *Journal of Consulting and Clinical Psychology, 61,* 761–767.

Hall, S. M., Muñoz, R. F., Reus, V. I., Sees, K. L., Duncan, C., Humfleet, G. L., & Hartz, D. T.

(1996). Mood management and nicotine gum in smoking treatment: A therapeutic contact and placebo-controlled study. *Journal of Consulting and Clinical Psychology, 64,* 1003–1009.

Halmi, K. A., Tozzi, F., Thornton, L. M., Crow, S., Fichter, M. M., Kaplan, A. S., ... Bulik, C. M. (2005). The relation among perfectionism, obsessive-compulsive personality disorder and obsessive-compulsive disorder in individuals with eating disorders. *International Journal of Eating Disorders, 38,* 371–374.

Halsey, N. A., & Hyman, S. L. (2001). Measles-mumps-rubella vaccine and autistic spectrum disorder: Report from the new challenges in childhood immunizations conference convened in Oak Brook, Illinois, June 12–13, 2000. *Pediatrics, 107*(5), E84.

Hamer, D. H., Hu, S., Magnuson, V. L., Hu, N., & Pattatucci, A. M. (1993). A linkage between DNA markers on the X chromosome and male sexual orientation. *Science, 261,* 321–327.

Hamilton, D. A., Kodituwakku, P., Sutherland, R. J., & Savage, D. D. (2003). Children with fetal alcohol syndrome are impaired at place learning but not cued-navigation in a virtual Morris water task. *Behavioural Brain Research, 143*(1), 85–94.

Hammen, C. (2005). Stress and depression. *Annual Review of Clinical Psychology, 1,* 293–319.

Hammen, C., Burge, D., Burney, E., & Adrian, C. (1990). Longitudinal study of diagnoses in children of women with unipolar and bipolar affective disorder. *Archives of General Psychiatry, 47*(12), 1112–1117.

Hammen, C., Marks, T., Mayol, A., & DeMayo, R. (1985). Depressive self-schemas, life stress, and vulnerability to depression. *Journal of Abnormal Psychology, 94,* 308–319.

Hammer, S., Saag, M., Scheechter, M., Montaner, J., Schooley, R., Jacobsen, D., ... Volberding, P. A. (2006). Treatment for adult HIV infection: 2006 recommendations of the International AIDS Society-USA Panel. *JAMA, 296,* 827–843.

Hammill, D. D. (1993). A brief look at the learning disability movement in the United States. *Journal of Learning Disabilities, 26,* 295–310.

Han, L., McCusker, J., Cole, M., Abrahamowicz, M., Primeau, F., & Élie, M. (2001). Use of medications with anticholinergic effect predicts clinical severity of delirium symptoms in older medical inpatients. *Archives of Internal Medicine, 161,* 1099–1105.

Hankin, B. L., Abramson, L. Y., Moffitt, T. E., Silva, P. A., McGee, R., & Angell, K. E. (1998). Development of depression from preadolescence to young adulthood: Emerging gender differences in a 10-year longitudinal study. *Journal of Abnormal Psychology, 107,* 128–140.

Hankins, C. (1997). Recognizing and countering the psychological and economic impact of HIV on women in developing countries. In J. Catalan & L. Sherr (Eds.), *Impact of AIDS: Psychological and social aspects of HIV infection* (pp. 127–135). Amsterdam: Harwood Academic Publishers.

Hanley, I. (1986). Reality orientation in the care of the elderly patient with dementia—Three case studies. In I. Hanley & M. Gilhooly (Eds.), *Psychological therapies for the elderly* (pp. 65–79). New York: New York University Press.

Hanley, I. G., & Lusty, K. (1984). Memory aids in reality orientation: A single-case study. *Behavior Research and Therapy, 22,* 709–712.

Hanna, G. L. (1995). Demographic and clinical features of obsessive-compulsive disorder in children and adolescents. *Journal of the American Academy of Child and Adolescent Psychiatry, 34,* 19–27.

Hanna, L. (2001). *Deinstitutionalization in Canada of the chronically mentally ill: Women as primary family caregivers and the governance of madness.* Retrieved November 6, 2003, from International Academy of Law and Mental Health Website: http://www.ialmh.org/Montreal2001/sessions/ governance_of_madness.htm

Hans, S. L., & Marcus, J. (1991). Neurobehavioral development of infants at risk for schizophrenia: A review. In E. F. Walker (Ed.), *Schizophrenia: A life-course developmental perspective* (pp. 33–57). New York: Academic Press.

Hans, V. P. (1986). An analysis of public attitudes toward the insanity defense. *Criminology, 4,* 393–415.

Hantouche, E., Akiskal, H., Azorin, J., Chatenet-Duchene, L., & Lancrenon, S. (2006). Clinical and psychometric characterization of depression in mixed mania: A report from the French National Cohort of 1090 manic patients. *Journal of Affective Disorders, 96,* 225–232.

Harbert, T. L., Barlow, D. H., Hersen, M., & Austin, J. B. (1974). Measurement and modification of incestuous behavior: A case study. *Psychological Reports, 34,* 79–86.

Harburg, E., Kaciroti, N., Gleiberman, L., Julius, M., & Schork, M. A. (2008). Marital pair anger-coping types may act as an entity to affect mortality: Preliminary findings from a prospective study (Tecumseh, Michigan, 1971–1988). *Journal of Family Communication, 8*(1), 44–61.

Hardy-Bale, M. C., Sarfati, Y., & Passerieux, C. (2003). The cognitive basis of disorganization symptomatology in schizophrenia and its clinical correlates: Toward a pathogenetic approach to disorganization. *Schizophrenia Bulletin, 20,* 459–471.

Hare, R. D. (1970). *Psychopathy: Theory and research.* New York: John Wiley & Sons.

Hare, R. D. (1983). Diagnosis of antisocial personality disorder in two prison populations. *American Journal of Psychiatry, 140,* 887–890.

Hare, R. D. (1991). *Manual for the Revised Psychopathy Checklist.* Toronto, ON: Multi-Health Systems.

Hare, R. D. (1993). *Without conscience: The disturbing world of the psychopaths among us.* New York: Pocket Books.

Hare, R. D. (1999). Psychopathy as a risk factor for violence. *Psychiatric Quarterly, 70,* 181–197.

Hare, R. D., Forth, A. E., & Hart, S. D. (1989). The psychopath as prototype for pathological lying and deception. In J. C. Yule (Ed.), *Credibility assessment* (pp. 25–49). New York: Kluwer Academic/Plenum.

Hare, R. D., Forth, A. E., & Strachan, K. E. (1992). Psychopathy and crime across the life span. In R. D. Peters & R. J. McMahon (Eds.), *Aggression and violence throughout the life span* (pp. 285–300). Thousand Oaks, CA: Sage.

Hare, R. D., McPherson, L. M., & Forth, A. E. (1988). Male psychopaths and their criminal careers. *Journal of Consulting and Clinical Psychology, 56,* 710–714.

Hare, R. D., & Neumann, C. S. (2006). The PCL-R Assessment of psychopathy: Development, structural properties, and new directions. In C. J. Patrick (Ed.), *Handbook of the psychopathy* (pp. 58–88). New York: Guilford Press.

Hargrave, C. (1999). Homelessness in Canada: From housing to shelters to blankets. *Share International.* Retrieved February 14, 2004, from http://www.shareintl.org/archives/homelessness/hl-ch_Canada.htm

Hariri, A. R., Mattay, V. S., Tessitore, A., Kolachana, B., Fera, F., Goldman, D., ... Weinberger, D. R. (2002). Serotonin transporter genetic variation and the response of the human amygdala. *Science, 297,* 400–402.

Harmer, C. J. (2008). Serotonin and emotional processing: Does it help explain antidepressant drug action? *Neuropharmacology, 55*(6), 1023–1028.

Harmer, C. J., O'Sullivan, U., Favaron, E., Massey-Chase, R., Ayres, R., Reinecke, A., ... Cowen, P. J. (2009). Effect of acute antidepressant administration on negative affective bias in depressed patients. *The American Journal of Psychiatry, 166*(10), 1178–1184.

Harper, L. V. (2005). Epigenetic inheritance and the intergenerational transfer of experience. *Psychological Bulletin, 131,* 340–360.

Harpur, T. J., Hare, R. D., & Hakstian, A. R. (1989). Two-factor conceptualization of psychopathy: Construct validity and assessment implications. *Psychological Assessment: A Journal of Consulting and Clinical Psychology, 1,* 6–17.

Harpur, T. J., Hart, S. D., & Hare, R. D. (2002). Personality of the psychopath. In P. T. Costa & T. A. Widiger, (Eds.), *Personality disorders and the five-factor model of personality* (2nd ed., pp. 299–324). Washington, DC: American Psychological Association.

Harrington, C. (2003). Great Falls residents caught up in Heatherington story. C News., Retrieved May 8, 2003, from at http://cnews.canoe.ca/CNEWS/ Canada/2003/05/08/82654–cp.html

Harris, B. (1979). Whatever happened to little Albert? *American Psychologist, 34,* 151–160.

Harris, E. C., & Barraclough, B. (1998). Excess mortality of mental disorder. *British Journal of Psychiatry, 173,* 11–53.

Harrist, A. W., & Ainslie, R. C. (1998). Marital discord and child behavior problems: Parent-child relationship quality and child interpersonal awareness as mediators. *Journal of Family Issues, 19,* 140–163.

Harrow, M., Sands, J. R., Silverstein, M. L., & Goldberg, J. F. (1997). Course and outcome for schizophrenia versus other psychotic patients: A longitudinal study. *Schizophrenia Bulletin, 23,* 287–303.

Hart, E. L., Lahey, B. B., Loeber, R., Applegate, B., & Frick, P. J. (1995). Developmental change in attention-deficit hyperactivity disorder in boys: A four-year longitudinal study. *Journal of Abnormal Child Psychology, 23,* 729–749.

Hartenbaum, N., Collop, N., Rosen, I. M., Phillips, B., George, C. F. P., Rowley, J. A., ... Moffitt, G. L. (2006). Sleep apnea and commercial motor vehicle operators: Statement from the Joint Task Force of the American College of Occupational and Environmental Medicine and the National Sleep Foundation. *Chest, 130,* 902–905.

Hartlage, S., & Gehlert, S. (2001). Differentiating premenstrual dysphoric disorder from premenstrual exacerbations of other disorders: A methods dilemma. *Clinical Psychology: Science and Practice, 8*(2), 242–253.

Harvey, A. G., & Bryant, R. A. (1998). The relationship between acute stress disorder and posttraumatic stress disorder: A prospective evaluation of motor vehicle accident survivors. *Journal of Consulting and Clinical Psychology, 66,* 507–512.

Harvey, L., Inglis, S. J., & Espie, C. (2002). Insomniacs' reported use of CBT components and relationship to long-term clinical outcome. *Behaviour Research and Therapy, 40,* 75–83.

Hasin, D. S., Goodwin, R. D., Stinson, F. S., & Grant, B. F. (2005). Epidemiology of major depressive disorder: Results from the National

Epidemiologic Survey on alcoholism and related conditions. *Archives of General Psychiatry, 62* (10), 1097–1106.

Hatfield, E., Sprecher, S., Pillemer, J. T., Greenberger, D., & Wexler, P. (1988). Gender differences in what is desired in the sexual relationship. *Journal of Psychology and Human Sexuality, 1*(2), 39–52.

Hathaway, S. R., & McKinley, J. C. (1943). *Manual for the Minnesota Multiphasic Personality Inventory.* New York: Psychological Corporation.

Hathaway, S. R., & McKinley, J. C. (1983). *Manual for the Minnesota Multiphasic Personality Inventory* (3rd ed.). New York: Psychological Corporation.

Hatsukami, D. K., Grillo, M., Boyle, R., Allen, S., Jensen, J., Bliss, R., & Brown, S. (2000). Treatment of spit tobacco users with transdermal nicotine system and mint snuff. *Journal of Consulting and Clinical Psychology, 68*(2), 241–249.

Hauri, P. (1982). *The sleep disorders* (2nd ed.). Kalamazoo, MI: Upjohn Company.

Hauri, P. J. (1991). Sleep hygiene, relaxation therapy, and cognitive interventions. In P. J. Hauri (Ed.), *Case studies in insomnia* (pp. 65–84). New York: Plenum Medical Books Company.

Hawkins, R. P. (1979). The functions of assessment: Implications for selection and development of devices for assessing repertoires in clinical, educational, and other settings. *Journal of Applied Behavior Analysis, 12,* 501–516.

Hawkley, L. C., & Cacioppo, J. T. (2007). Aging and loneliness: Downhill quickly? *Current Directions in Psychological Science, 16,* 187–191.

Hawton, K. (1995). Treatment of sexual dysfunctions of sex therapy and other approaches. *British Journal of Psychiatry, 167,* 307–314.

Hawton, K., Houston, K., Haw, C., Townsend, E., & Harriss, L. (2003). Comorbidity of axis I and axis II disorders in patients who attempted suicide. *American Journal of Psychiatry, 160,* 1494–1500.

Hay, P., & Fairburn, C. (1998). The validity of the DSM-IV scheme for classifying bulimic eating disorders. *International Journal of Eating Disorders, 23,* 7–15.

Hay, P. J., & Hall, A. (1991). The prevalence of eating disorders in recently admitted psychiatric in-patients. *British Journal of Psychiatry, 159,* 562–565.

Hayes, S. C., Barlow, D. H., & Nelson-Gray, R. O. (1999). *The scientist practitioner: Research and accountability in the age of managed care* (2nd ed.). Needham Heights, MA: Allyn & Bacon.

Hayes, S. C., Wilson, K. G., Gifford, E. V., Follette, V. M., & Strosahl, K. (1996). Experiential avoidance and behavior disorders: A functional dimensional approach. *Journal of Consulting and Clinical Psychology, 64*(6), 1152–1168.

Hayman-Abello, B. A., Hayman-Abello, S. E., & Rourke, B. P. (2003). Human neuropsychology in Canada: The 1990s (a review of research by Canadian neuropsychologists conducted over the past decade). *Canadian Psychology, 44,* 100–138.

Haynes, S. G., Feinleib, M., & Kannel, W. B. (1980). The relationship of psychosocial factors to coronary heart disease in the Framingham study: III. Eight-year incidence of coronary heart disease. *American Journal of Epidemiology, 111,* 37–58.

Haynes, S. G., & Matthews, K. A. (1988). Area review: Coronary-prone behavior: Continuing evolution of the concept: Review and methodologic critique of recent studies on type A behavior and cardiovascular disease. *Annals of Behavioral Medicine, 10*(2), 47–59.

Haynes, S. N. (2000). Behavioral assessment of adults. In G. Goldstein & M. Hersen (Eds.),

Handbook of psychological assessment (pp. 471–502). New York: Pergamon Press.

Haynes, S. N., Yoshioka, D. T., Kloezeman, K., & Bello, I. (2009). Clinical applications of behavioral assessment. In J. N. Butcher (Ed.), *Oxford Handbook of Personality Assessment* (pp. 226–249). New York: Oxford University Press.

Hayward, C., Killen, J. D., Kraemer, H. C., & Taylor, C. B. (2000). Predictors of panic attacks in adolescents. *Journal of the American Academy of Child and Adolescent Psychiatry, 39*(2), 1–8.

Hayward, G., Killen, J. D., Hammer, L. D., Litt, I. F., Wilson, D. M., Simmonds, B., & Taylor, C. B. (1992). Pubertal stage and panic attack history in sixth- and seventh-grade girls. *American Journal of Psychiatry, 149,* 1239–1243.

Hazell, P., O'Connell, D., Heathcote, D., Robertson, J., & Henry, D. (1995). Efficacy of tricyclic drugs in treating child and adolescent depression: a meta-analysis. *BMJ, 310,* 897–901.

Health Canada. (1999). *New report highlights HIV prevention for youth.* News release #1999–94. Retrieved May 14, 2004, from http://.hc-sc.gc.ca/english/media/releases/1999/99_94e.htm

Health Canada. (2000a). *Risk of important drug interactions between St. John's Wort and other prescription drugs.* Retrieved July 13, 2003, from http://.hc-sc.gc.ca/hpfb-dgpsa/tpd-dpt/st_johns_wort_e.html

Health Canada. (2000b). *Leading causes of death and hospitalization in Canada.* Ottawa, ON: Population and Public Health Branch.

Health Canada. (2002a). *A report on mental illnesses in Canada.* Ottawa, ON: Author.

Health Canada. (2002b). *HIV and AIDS in Canada: Surveillance report to June 30, 2002.* Ottawa, ON: Population and Public Health Branch: Division of HIV/ AIDS Epidemiology and Surveillance, Centre for Infectious Disease Prevention and Control.

Heatherton, T. F., & Baumeister, R. F. (1991). Binge eating as escape from self-awareness. *Psychological Bulletin, 110,* 86–108.

Heaton, R. K., Velin, R. A., McCutchan, A., Gulevich, S. J., Atkinson, J. H., Wallace, M. R. ... Grant, I. (1994). Neuropsychological impairment in human immunodeficiency virus-infection: Implications for employment. *Psychosomatic Medicine, 56,* 8–17.

Heim, C., & Nemeroff, C. B. (1999). The impact on early adverse experiences on brain systems involved in the pathophysiology of anxiety and affective disorders. *Biological Psychiatry, 46*(11), 1509–1522.

Heiman, J. R., (2000). Orgasmic disorders in women. In S. R. Leiblum & R. C. Rosen (Eds.), *Principles and practice of sex therapy* (3rd ed., pp. 118–153). New York: Guilford Press.

Heiman, J. R., & LoPiccolo, J. (1983a). Clinical outcome of sex therapy: Effects of daily versus weekly treatment. *Archives of General Psychiatry, 40,* 443–449.

Heiman, J. R., & LoPiccolo, J. (1983b). Effectiveness of daily versus weekly therapy in the treatment of sexual dysfunction. Unpublished manuscript, State University of New York at Stony Brook.

Heiman, J. R., & LoPiccolo, J. (1988). *Becoming orgasmic: A sexual and personal growth program for women* (rev. ed.). New York: Prentice Hall.

Heiman, J. R., & Meston, C. M. (1997). Empirically validated treatment for sexual dysfunction. *Annual Review of Sex Research, 8,* 148–195.

Heimberg, R. G., Dodge, C. S., Hope, D. A., Kennedy, C. R., Zollo, L., & Becker, R. E. (1990). Cognitive behavioral group treatment for social

phobia: Comparison to a credible placebo control. *Cognitive Therapy and Research, 14,* 1–23.

Heimberg, R. G., Klosko, J. S., Dodge, C. S., & Shadick, R. (1989). Anxiety disorders, depression and attributional style: A further test of the specificity of depressive attributions. *Cognitive Therapy and Research, 13*(1), 21–36.

Heimberg, R. G., Liebowitz, M. R., Hope, D. A., Schneier, F. R., Holt, C. S., Welkowitz, L. A., ... Klein, D. F. (1998). Cognitive behavioral group therapy vs. phenelzine therapy for social phobia. *Archives of General Psychiatry, 55,* 1133–1141.

Heimberg, R. G., Salzman, D. G., Holt, C. S., & Blendell, K. A. (1993). Cognitive-behavioral group treatment for social phobia: Effectiveness at five-year follow-up. *Cognitive Therapy and Research, 17,* 325–339.

Heinrichs, N., Rapee, R. M., & Alden, L. A. (2006). Cultural differences in perceived social norms and social anxiety. *Behaviour Research and Therapy, 44,* 1187–1197.

Heinrichs, N., Rapee, R. M., Alden, L. A., Bogels, S., Hofmann, S. G., Oh, K. J., & Sakano, Y. (2006). Cultural differences in perceived social norms and social anxiety. *Behaviour Research and Therapy, 44*(8), 1187–1197.

Heinrichs, R. W. (1993). Schizophrenia and the brain: Conditions for a neuropsychology of madness. *American Psychologist, 48,* 221–233.

Heinrichs, R. W. (2003). Historical origins of schizophrenia: Two early madmen and their illness. *Journal of the History of the Behavioral Sciences, 39,* 349–363.

Heinrichs, R. W., & Awad, A. G. (1993). Neurocognitive subtypes of chronic schizophrenia. *Schizophrenia Research, 9,* 49–58.

Heinrichs, R. W., Ruttan, L., Zakzanis, K. K., & Case, D. (1997). Parsing schizophrenia in neurocognitive tests: Evidence of stability and validity. *Brain & Cognition, 35,* 207–224.

Helenius, P., Salmelin, R., Service, E., & Connolly, J. F. (1999). Semantic cortical activation in dyslexic readers. *Journal of Cognitive Neuroscience, 11,* 535–550.

Helenius, P., Salmelin, R., Service, E., Connolly, J., Leinonen, S., & Lyytinen, H. (2002). Cortical activation during spoken-words segmentation in non-reading-impaired and dyslexic adults. *The Journal of Neuroscience, 22,* 2936–2944.

Hellekson, K. L. (2001). NIH consensus statement on phenylketonuria. *American Family Physician, 63*(7), 1430–1432.

Heller, W., & Nitschke, J. B. (1997). Regional brain activity in emotion: A framework for understanding cognition in depression. *Cognition and Emotion, 11*(5–6), 737–661.

Heller, W., Nitschke, J. B., & Miller, G. A. (1998). Lateralization in emotion and emotional disorders. *Current Directions in Psychological Science, 7,* 26–27.

Hellstrom, K., Fellenius, J., & Osst, L. G. (1996). One versus five sessions of applied tension in the treatment of blood phobia. *Behaviour Research and Therapy, 34,* 101–112.

Helmes, E., & Ostbye, T. (2002). Beyond memory impairment: Cognitive changes in Alzheimer's disease. *Archives of Clinical Neuropsychology, 17,* 179–193.

Helmes, E., & Reddon, J. R. (1993). A perspective on developments in assessing psychopathology: A critical review of the MMPI and MMPI-2. *Psychological Bulletin, 113,* 453–471.

Helweg-Larsen, M., & Collins, B. E. (1997). A social psychological perspective on the role of knowledge about AIDS in AIDS prevention.

Current Directions in Psychological Science, 6, 23–26.

Helzer, J. E., Kraemer, H. C., Krueger, R. F., Wittchen, H.-U., Sirovatka, P. J., & Regier, D. A. (2008). *Dimensional approaches in diagnostic classification: Refining the research agenda for DSM-V.* Washington, DC: American Psychiatric Association.

Henderson, K. E. (2004). Functional analysis of binge eating in the obese. (Doctoral Dissertation, Queen's University, 2004). *Dissertation Abstracts International: Section B: The Sciences and Engineering, 64,* 3525.

Hepburn, K. W., Tornatore, J., Center, B., & Ostwald, S. W. (2001). Dementia family caregiver training: Affecting beliefs about caregiving and caregiver outcomes. *Journal of the American Geriatric Society, 49*(4), 450–457.

Herbert, T. B., & Cohen, S. (1993). Depression and immunity: A meta-analytic review. *Psychological Bulletin, 113*(3), 472–486.

Herdt, G. H. (1987). *The Sambia: Ritual and gender in New Guinea.* New York: Holt, Rinehart and Winston.

Herdt, G. H., & Stoller, R. J. (1989). Commentary to "The socialization of homosexuality and heterosexuality in a non-Western society." *Archives of Sexual Behavior, 18,* 31–34.

Herlitz, C. A., & Forsberg, M. (2010). Sexual behavior and risk assessment in different age cohorts in the general population of Sweden (1989-2007). *Scandinavian Journal of Public Health, 38,* 32–39.

Herman, J. L., Perry, C., & van der Kolk, B. A. (1989). Childhood trauma in borderline personality disorder. *American Journal of Psychiatry, 146,* 490–495.

Hermann, N., Lanctôt, K. L., Sambrook, R., Lesnikova, N., Hébert, R., McCracken, P., … Nguyen, E. (2006). The contribution of neuropsychiatric symptoms to the cost of dementia care. *International Journal of Geriatric Psychiatry, 21,* 972–976.

Herrero, M. E., Hechtman, L., & Weiss, G. (1994). Antisocial disorders in hyperactive subjects from childhood to adulthood: Predictive factors and characterization of subgroups. *American Journal of Orthopsychiatry, 64,* 510–521.

Hervé, H. (2007). Psychopathy across the ages: A history of the Hare psychopath. In H. Hervé & J. C. Yuille (Eds.), *The psychopath: Theory, research, and practice* (pp. 31–55). Mahwah, NJ: Lawrence Erlbaum Associates Publishers.

Herz, M. I. (1985). Prodromal symptoms and prevention of relapse in schizophrenia. *Journal of Clinical Psychiatry, 46*(11), 22–25.

Herzog, D. B. (1988). Eating disorders. In A. M. Nicoli, Jr. (Ed.), *The new Harvard guide to psychiatry* (pp. 434–445). Boston: Harvard University Press.

Herzog, D. B., Dorer, D. J., Keel, P. K., Selwyn, S. E., Ekeblad, E. R., Flores, A. T., … Keller, M. B. (1999). Recovery and relapse in anorexia and bulimia nervosa: A 7. 5-year follow-up study. *Journal of the American Academy of Child and Adolescent Psychiatry, 38*(7), 829–837.

Hetherington, E. M., & Blechman, E. A. (Eds.). (1996). *Stress, coping and resiliency in children and families.* Mahwah, NJ: Erlbaum.

Hetherington, E. M., Stanley-Hagan, M., & Anderson, E. R. (1989). Marital transitions: A child's perspective. *American Psychologist, 44,* 303–312.

Hettema, J. M., Prescott, C. A., Myers, J. M., Neale, M. C., & Kendler, K. S. (2005). The structure of genetic and environmental risk factors for anxiety disorders in men and women. *Archives of General Psychiatry, 62,* 182–189.

Hewitt, P. L., Flett, G. L., & Ediger, E. (1995). Perfectionism traits and perfectionistic self-presentation in eating disorder attitudes, characteristics, and symptoms. *International Journal of Eating Disorders, 18,* 317–326.

Higgins, S. T., Budney, A. J., Bickel, W. K., Hughes, J. R., Foerg, F., & Badger, G. (1993). Achieving cocaine abstinence with a behavioral approach. *American Journal of Psychiatry, 150,* 763–769.

Higgins, S. T., Heil, S. H., Dantona, R., Donham, R., Matthews, M., & Badger, G. J. (2006). Effects of varying the monetary value of voucher-based incentives on abstinence achieved during and following treatment among cocaine-dependent outpatients. *Addiction, 102,* 271–281.

Higgins, S. T., & Petry, N. M. (1999). Contingency management: Incentives for sobriety. *Alcohol Research & Health, 23*(2), 122–127.

Higgins, S. T., Sigmon, S. C., & Heil, S. H. (2008). Drug abuse and dependence. In D. H. Barlow (Ed.), *Clinical handbook of psychological disorders* (4th ed., pp. 547–577). New York: Guilford Press.

Hilgard, E. R. (1992). Divided consciousness and dissociation. *Consciousness & Cognition, 1,* 16–31. A. E. Hill & L. Rosenbloom (1986). Disintegrative psychosis of childhood: Teenage follow-up. *Developmental Medicine and Child Neurology, 28,* 34–40.

Hill, D. E., Yeo, R. A., Campbell, R. A., Hart, B., Vigil, J., & Brooks, W. (2003). Magnetic resonance imaging correlates of attention-deficit/hyperactivity disorder in children. *Neuropsychology, 17,* 496–506.

Hillman, E., Kripke, D. F., & Gillin, J. C. (1990). Sleep restriction, exercise, and bright lights: Alternate therapies for depression. In A. Tasman, C. Kaufman, & S. Goldfinger (Eds.), *American Psychiatric Press review of psychiatry: Section I: Treatment of refractory affective disorder* (R. Post, section ed., Vol. 9, pp. 132–144). Washington, DC: American Psychiatric Press.

Hinchley, J., & Levy, B. A. (1988). Developmental and individual differences in reading comprehension. *Cognition & Instruction, 5,* 3–47.

Hindmarch, I. (1990). Cognitive impairment with anti-anxiety agents: A solvable problem? In D. Wheatley (Ed.), *The anxiolytic jungle: Where, next?* (pp. 49–61). Chichester, UK: John Wiley & Sons.

Hinshelwood, J. A. (1896). A case of dyslexia: A peculiar form of word-blindness. *Lancet, 2,* 1451–1454.

Hinton, L., Guo, Z., Hillygus, J., & Levkoff, S. (2000). Working with culture: A qualitative analysis of barriers to the recruitment of Chinese-American family caregivers for dementia research. *Journal of Cross-Cultural Gerontology, 15*(2), 119–137.

Hirsch, S., Cramer, P., & Bowen, J. (1992). The triggering hypothesis of the role of life events in schizophrenia. *British Journal of Psychiatry, 161,* 84–87.

Hirschfeld, D. R., Rosenbaum, J. F., Biederman, J., Bolduc, E. A., Farone, S. V., Snidman, N., … Kagan, J. (1992). Stable behavioral inhibition and its association with anxiety disorder. *Journal of the American Academy of Child and Adolescent Psychiatry, 31,* 103–111.

Hirschfeld, R. M., Keller, M., Panico, S., Arons, B. S., Barlow, D., Davidoff, F., … Wyatt, R. J. (1997). The national depressive and manic-depressive association consensus statement on the undertreatment of depression. *JAMA, 277,* 333–340.

Hirschfeld, R. M., Shea, M. T., & Weise, R. E. (1991). Dependent personality disorder:

Perspectives for DSM-IV. *Journal of Personality Disorders, 5,* 135–149.

Hirschfeld, R. M. A., Shea, M. T., & Weise, R. (1995). Dependent personality disorder. In W. J. Livesley (Ed.), *The DSM-IV personality disorders* (pp. 239–256). New York: Guilford Press.

Hirshkowitz, M., Seplowitz, R. G., & Sharafkhaneh, A. (2009). Sleep disorders. In B. J. Sadock, V. A. Sadock, & P. Ruiz (Eds.), *Kaplan & Sadock's Comprehensive Textbook of Psychiatry* (Vol. I, 9th ed., pp. 2150–2177). Philadelphia: Lippincott Williams & Wilkins.

Hitchcock, P. B., & Mathews, A. (1992). Interpretation of bodily symptoms in hypochondriasis. *Behaviour Research and Therapy, 30*(3), 223–234.

Ho, B. C., Black, D. W., & Andreasen, N. C. (2003). Schizophrenia and other psychotic disorders. In R. E. Hales & S. C. Yudofsky (Eds.), *Textbook of clinical psychiatry* (4th ed., pp. 379–438). Washington, DC: American Psychiatric Press.

Hoaken, P. N. S., Shaughnessy, V. K., & Pihl, R. O. (2003). Executive cognitive functioning and aggression: Is it an issue of impulsivity? *Aggressive Behavior, 29*(1), 15–30.

Hoaken, P. N. S., & Stewart, S. H. (2003). Drugs of abuse and the elicitation of human aggressive behavior. *Addictive Behaviors, 28,* 1533–1554.

Hoare, E. (2005, June 27). Fighting the system. *TheHalifax Herald.* Retrieved June 27, 2006, from http://www.fi xcas.com/news/halifax/recap.htm

Hockey Hall of Fame and Museum. (2001). *Shayne Corson.* Retrieved July 15, 2004, from http://www.legendsofhockey.net:8080/LegendsOfHockey/jsp/SearchPlayer.jsp?player10297

Hoehn-Saric, R., McLeod, D. R., & Zimmerli, W. D. (1989). Somatic manifestations in women with generalized anxiety disorder: Psychophysiological responses to psychological stress. *Archives of General Psychiatry, 46,* 1113–1119.

Hodapp, R. M., & Dykens, E. M. (1994). Mental retardation's two cultures of behavioral research. *American Journal of Mental Retardation, 98,* 675–687.

Hodgins, D. C., Currie, S., & el-Guebaly, N. (2001). Motivational enhancement and self-help treatments for problem gambling. *Journal of Consulting and Clinical Psychology, 69*(1), 50–57.

Hodgins, D. C., Currie, S., el-Guebaly, N., & Peden, N. (2004). Brief motivational treatment for problem gambling: A 24-month follow-up. *Psychology of Addictive Behaviors, 18*(3), 293–296.

Hodgkinson, K. A., Murphy, J. O'Neill, S, Brzustowicz, L., & Bassett, A. S. (2001). Genetic counselling for schizophrenia in the era of molecular genetics. *Canadian Journal of Psychiatry, 46* (2), 123–130.

Hoehn-Saric, R., McLeod, D. R., & Zimmerli, W. D. (1989). Somatic manifestations in women with generalized anxiety disorder: Psychophysiological responses to psychological stress. *Archives of General Psychiatry, 46,* 1113–1119.

Hoek, H. W. (2002). The distribution of eating disorders. In K. D. Brownell & C. G. Fairburn (Eds.), *Eating disorders and obesity: A comprehensive handbook* (2nd ed., pp. 207–211).

Hoek, H. W., Bartelds, A. I. M., Bosveld, J. J. F., van der Graaf, Y., Limpens, V. E. L., Maiwald, M., & Spaaij, C. J. (1995). Impact of urbanization on detection rates of eating disorders. *American Journal of Psychiatry, 152,* 1272–1278.

Hoffman, B., Papas, R., Chatkoff, D., & Kerns, R. (2007). Meta-analysis of psychological interventions for chronic low back pain. *Health Psychology, 26,* 1–9.

Hoffman, R. E., Boutros, N. N., Hu, S., Berman, R. M., Krystal, J. H., & Charney, D. S. (2000). Transcranial magnetic stimulation and auditory hallucinations in schizophrenia. *Lancet, 355,* 1073–1075.

Hofmann, S., & Barlow, D. H. (2002). Social phobia (social anxiety disorder). In D. H. Barlow (Ed.), *Anxiety and its disorders: The nature and treatment of anxiety and panic* (2nd ed.). New York: Guilford Press.

Hofmann, S., Richey, J., Kashdan, T., & McKnight, P. (2009). Anxiety disorders moderate the association between externalizing problems and substance use disorders: Data from the National Comorbidity Survey-Revised. *Journal of Anxiety Disorders, 23*(4), 529–534.

Hofmann, S. G., Lehman, C. L., & Barlow, D. H. (1997). How specific are specific phobias? *Journal of Behavior Therapy and Experimental Psychiatry, 28,* 233–240.

Hogarty, G. E., Anderson, C. M., Reiss, D. J., Kornblith, S. J., Greenwald, D. P., Javna, C. D., & Madonia, M. J. (1986). Family psychoeducation, social skills training, and maintenance chemotherapy in the aftercare treatment of schizophrenia: I. One year effects of a controlled study on relapse and expressed emotion. *Archives of General Psychiatry, 43,* 633–642.

Hogarty, G. E., Anderson, C. M., Reiss, D. J., Kornblith, S. J., Greenwald, D. P., Ulrich, R. F., Carter, M., & The Environmental-Personal Indicators in the Course of Schizophrenia (EPICS) Research Group. (1991). Family psychoeducation, social skills training, and maintenance chemotherapy in the aftercare treatment of schizophrenia. *Archives of General Psychiatry, 48,* 340–347.

Hogarty, G. E., Reis, D., Kornblith, S. J., Greenwald, D., Ulrich, R., & Carter, M. (1992). In reply. *Archives of General Psychiatry, 49,* 76–77.

Hoge, S. K., Appelbaum, P. S., Lawler, T., Beck, J. C., Litman, R., Greer, A., … Kaplan, E. (1990). A prospective, multicenter study of patients' refusal of antipsychotic medication. *Archives of General Psychiatry, 47,* 949–956.

Hokanson, J. E., Rubert, M. P., Welker, R. A., Hollander, G. R., & Hedeen, C. (1989). Interpersonal concomitants and antecedents of depression among college students. *Journal of Abnormal Psychology, 98*(3), 209–217.

Holahan, A.-L. V., & O'Driscoll, G. A. (2005). Anti-saccade and smooth pursuit performance in positive- and negative-symptom schizotype. *Schizophrenia Research, 76*(1), 43–54.

Holder, H. D., Gruenewald, P. J., Ponicki, W. R., Treno, A. J., Grube, J. W., Saltz, R. F., … Roeper, P. (2000). Effect of community-based interventions on high-risk drinking and alcohol-related injuries. *JAMA, 284,* 2341–2347.

Hollander, E., Allen, A., Kwon, J., Aronwoitz, B., Schmeidler, J., Wong, C., & Simeon, D. (1999). Clomipramine vs desipramine crossover trial in body dysmorphic disorder: Selective efficacy of a serotonin reuptake inhibitor in imagined ugliness. *Archives of General Psychiatry, 56*(11), 1033–1039.

Hollander, E., Berlin, H. A., & Stein, D. J. (2009). Impulse-control disorders not elsewhere classified. In J. A. Bourgeois, R. E. Hales, J. S. Young, & S. C. Yudofsky (Eds.), *The American psychiatric publishing board review guide for psychiatry* (pp. 469–482). Arlington, VA: American Psychiatric Publishing.

Hollander, E., Cohen, L. J., Simeon, D., & Rosen, J. (1994). Fluvoxamine treatment of body dysmorphic disorder. *Journal of Clinical Psychopharmacology, 14,* 75–77.

Hollander, E., Liebowitz, M. R., Winchel, R., Klumker, A., & Klein, D. F. (1989). Treatment of body-dysmorphic disorder with serotonin reuptake blockers. *American Journal of Psychiatry, 146,* 768–770.

Holley, H., Arboleda-Florez, J., & Crisanti, A. (1998). Do forensic offenders receive harsher sentences? An examination of legal outcomes. *International Journal of Law & Psychiatry, 21,* 43–57.

Hollien, H. (1990). The expert witness: Ethics and responsibilities. *Journal of Forensic Sciences, 35,* 1414–1423.

Hollifield, M., Katon, W., Spain, D., & Pule, L. (1990). Anxiety and depression in a village in Lesotho, Africa: A comparison with the United States. *British Journal of Psychiatry, 156,* 343–350.

Hollingshead, A. B., & Redlich, F. C. (1958). *Social class and mental illness.* Oxford, UK: Wiley.

Hollis, J. F., Connett, J. E., Stevens, V. J., & Greenlick, M. R. (1990). Stressful life events, type A behavior, and the prediction of cardiovascular and total mortality over six years. *Journal of Behavioral Medicine, 13*(3), 263–280.

Hollon, S. D. (1993). Review of psychosocial treatments for mood disorders. In D. L. Dunner (Ed.), *Current psychiatric therapy.* Philadelphia: W. B. Saunders.

Hollon, S. D., DeRubeis, R. J., Evans, M. D., Wiener, M. J., Garvey, M. J., Grove, W. M., & Tuason, V. B. (1992). Cognitive therapy and pharmacotherapy for depression: Singly and in combination. *Archives of General Psychiatry, 49*(10), 772–781.

Hollon, S. D., Kendall, P. C., & Lumry, A. (1986). Specificity of depressotypic cognitions in clinical depression. *Journal of Abnormal Psychology, 95,* 52–59.

Hollon, S. D., Shelton, R. C., & Loosen, P. T. (1991). Cognitive therapy and pharmacotherapy for depression. *Journal of Consulting and Clinical Psychology, 59*(1), 88–99.

Holm, V. A., & Varley, C. K. (1989). Pharmacological treatment of autistic children. In G. Dawson (Ed.), *Autism: Nature, diagnosis, and treatment* (pp. 386–404). New York: Guilford Press.

Holroyd, K. A., & Penzien, D. B. (1986). Client variables in the behavioral treatment of current tension headache: A meta-analytic review. *Journal of Behavioral Medicine, 9,* 515–536.

Holroyd, K. A., Andrasik, F., & Noble, J. (1980). A comparison of EMG biofeedback and a credible pseudotherapy in treating tension headache. *Journal of Behavioral Medicine, 3,* 29–39.

Holroyd, K. A., Nash, J. M., Pingel, J. D., Cordingley, G. E., & Jerome, A. (1991). A comparison of pharmacological (amitriptyline HCL) and non-pharmacological (cognitive-behavioral) therapies for chronic tension headaches. *Journal of Consulting and Clinical Psychology, 59*(3), 387–393.

Holroyd, K. A., Penzien, D. B., Hursey, K. G., Tobin, D. L., Rogers, L., Holm, J. E., … Chila, A. G. (1984). Change mechanisms in EMG biofeedback training. Cognitive changes underlying improvements in tension headache. *Journal of Consulting and Clinical Psychology, 52,* 1039–1053.

Hommer, D. W. (1999). Functional imaging of craving. *Alcohol Research & Health,* 23(3), 187–196.

Hong, R. Y. (2007). Worry and rumination: Differential associations with anxious and depressive symptoms and coping behavior. *Behaviour Research and Therapy, 45,* 277–290.

Hook, E. B. (1982). Epidemiology of Down syndrome. In S. M. Pueschel & J. E. Rynders (Eds.), *Down syndrome: Advances in biomedicine and the behavioral sciences* (pp. 11–88). Cambridge, MA: Ware Press.

Hooley, J. M. (1985). Expressed emotion: A review of the critical literature. *Clinical Psychology Review, 5,* 119–139.

Horen, S. A., Leichner, P. P., & Lawson, J. S. (1995). Prevalence of dissociative symptoms and disorders in an adult psychiatric inpatient population in Canada. *Canadian Journal of Psychiatry, 40,* 185–191.

Horgan, M. M., Sparrow, M. D., & Brazeau, R. (1986). *Alcoholic beverage taxation and control policies* (6th ed.). Ottawa, ON: Brewers Association of Canada.

Horikoshi, H. (1980). Asrama: An Islamic psychiatric institution in West Java. *Social Science and Medicine, 14,* 157–165.

Hornby, L. (2001, October 21). Panic hit Corson on leaf's bench. *Toronto Sun.* Retrieved June 21, 2004, from http://www.canoe.ca/Health0110/18_corson-sun.html

Horney, K. (1967). *Feminine psychology.* New York: W. W. Norton.

Hornig, C. D., & McNally, R. J. (1995). Panic disorder and suicide attempt: A reanalysis of data from the Epidemiologic Catchment Area Study. *British Journal of Psychiatry, 167,* 76–79.

Horowitz, M. J., Siegel, B., Holen, A., Bonanno, G. A., Milbrath, C., & Stinson, C. H. (1997). Diagnostic criteria for complicated grief disorder. *American Journal of Psychiatry, 154,* 904–910.

Horsfall, J., Cleary, M., Hunt, G., & Walter, G. (2009). Psychosocial treatments for people with co-occurring severe mental illnesses and substance use disorders (dual diagnosis): A review of empirical evidence. *Harvard Review of Psychiatry, 17*(1), 24–34.

Horwath, E., & Weissman, M. (1997). Epidemiology of anxiety disorders across cultural groups. In S. Friedman (Ed.), *Cultural issues in the treatment of anxiety* (pp. 21–39). New York: Guilford Press.

Horwitz, A. V. (2002). *Creating mental illness.* Chicago: University Press.

House, J. S., Landis, K. R., & Umberson, D. (1988). Social relationships and health. *Science, 241,* 540–545.

House, J. S., Robbins, C., & Metzner, H. M. (1982). The association of social relationships and activities with mortality: Prospective evidence from the Tecumseh community health study. *American Journal of Epidemiology, 116,* 123.

Houston, B. K., Chesney, M. A., Black, G. W., Cates, D. S., & Hecker, M. H. L. (1992). Behavioral clusters and coronary heart disease risk. *Psychosomatic Medicine, 54*(4), 447–461.

Howard, R., Castle, D., Wessely, S., & Murray, R. (1993). A comparative study of 470 cases of early-onset and late-onset schizophrenia. *British Journal of Psychiatry, 163,* 352–357.

Howes, J. L., & Vallis, T. M. (1996). Cognitive therapy with nontraditional populations: Application to post-traumatic stress disorder and personality disorders. In K. S. Dobson & K. D. Craig (Eds.), *Advances in cognitive-behavioral therapy* (Vol. 2, pp. 237–271). Thousand Oaks, CA: Sage.

Howes, O. D., & Kapur, S. (2009). The dopamine hypothesis of schizophrenia: Version III—The final common pathway. *Schizophrenia Bulletin, 35*(3), 549–562.

Hrabosky, J. I., Masheb, R. M., White, M. A., & Grilo, C. M. (2007). Overvaluation of shape and weight in binge eating disorder. *Journal of Consulting and Clinical Psychology, 75,* 175–180.

Hser, Y., Anglin, M. D., & Powers, K. (1993). A 24-year follow-up of California narcotics addicts. *Archives of General Psychiatry, 50,* 577–584.

Hsu, L. K. G. (1988). The outcome of anorexia nervosa: A reappraisal. *Psychological Medicine, 18,* 807–812.

Hsu, L. K. G. (1990). *Eating disorders.* New York: Guilford Press.

Hsu, L. M. (1989). Random sampling, randomization, and equivalence of contrasted groups in psychotherapy outcome research. *Journal of Consulting and Clinical Psychology, 57,* 131–137.

Hubert, N. C., Jay, S. M., Saltoun, M., & Hayes, M. (1988). Approach-avoidance and distress in children undergoing preparation for painful medical procedures. *Journal of Clinical Child Psychology, 17,* 194–202.

Hucker, S. J. (1997). Sexual sadism: Psychopathology and theory. In D. R. Laws & W. T. O'Donohue (Eds.), *Sexual deviance: Theory, assessment, and treatment* (pp. 194–209). New York: Guilford Press.

Hudson, J., Pope, H., Jonas, J. M., & Yurgelun-Todd, D. (1983). Family history study of anorexia nervosa and bulimia. *British Journal of Psychiatry, 142,* 133–138.

Huey, S. J., Henggeler, S. W., Brondino, M. J., & Pickrel, S. G. (2000). Mechanisms of change in multisystem therapy: Reducing delinquent behavior through therapist adherence and improved family and peer functioning. *Journal of Consulting and Clinical Psychology, 68,* 451–467.

Hufford, D. J. (1982). *The terror that comes in the night: An experience centered study of supernatural assault traditions.* Philadelphia: University of Pennsylvania Press.

Hughes, J. R. (1993). Pharmacotherapy for smoking cessation: Unvalidated assumptions, anomalies, and suggestions for future research. *Journal of Consulting and Clinical Psychology, 61,* 751–760.

Hughes, J. R. (2009). Nicotine-related disorders. In B. J. Sadock, V. A. Sadock, & P. Ruiz (Eds.), *Kaplan & Sadock's comprehensive textbook of psychiatry* (Vol. I, 9th ed., pp. 1353–1360). Philadelphia: Lippincott Williams & Wilkins.

Hughes, J. R., Gust, S. W., Skoog, K., Keenan, R. M., & Fenwick, J. W. (1991). Symptoms of tobacco withdrawal: A replication and extension. *Archives of General Psychiatry, 48,* 52–61.

Huinck, W. J., Langevin, M., Kully, D., Graamans, K., Peters, H. F. M., & Hulstijn, W. (2006). The relationship between pre-treatment clinical profile and treatment outcome in an integrated stuttering program. *Journal of Fluency Disorders, 31,* 43–63.

Humphrey, L. L. (1986). Structural analysis of parent-child relationships in eating disorders. *Journal of Abnormal Psychology, 95,* 395–402.

Humphrey, L. L. (1988). Relationships within subtypes of anorexic, bulimic, and normal families. *Journal of the American Academy of Child and Adolescent Psychiatry, 27,* 544–551.

Humphrey, L. L. (1989). Observed family interactions among subtypes of eating disorders using structural analysis of social behavior. *Journal of Consulting and Clinical Psychology, 57,* 206–214.

Hunicutt, C. P., & Newman, I. A. (1993). Adolescent dieting practices and nutrition knowledge. *Health Values: The Journal of Health Behavior, Education and Promotion, 17*(4), 35–40.

Hunsley, J., & Bailey, J. M. (1999). The clinical utility of the Rorschach: Unfulfilled promises and an uncertain future. *Psychological Assessment, 11,* 266–277.

Hunsley, J., & Johnston, C. (2000). The role of empirically supported treatments in evidence-based psychological practice: A Canadian perspective. *Clinical Psychology: Science & Practice, 7,* 269–272.

Hunsley, J., Lee, C. M., & Aubry, T. (1999). Who uses psychological services in Canada? *Canadian Psychology, 40,* 232–240.

Hunt, M. (2007). Borderline personality disorder across the life span. *Journal of Women & Aging, 19*(1), 173–191.

Hunt, W. A. (1980). History and classification. In A. E. Kazdin, A. S. Bellack, & M. Hersen (Eds.), *New perspectives in abnormal psychology.* New York: Oxford University Press.

Hunter, J. A., Jr., & Mathews, R. (1997). Sexual deviance in females. In D. R. Laws & W. T. O'Donohue (Eds.), *Sexual deviance: Theory, assessment, and treatment* (pp. 465–490). New York: Guilford Press.

Huntington's Disease Collaborative Research Group. (1993). A novel gene containing a trinucleotide repeat that is expanded and unstable on Huntington's disease chromosomes. *Cell, 72,* 971–983.

Huot, I., Paradis, G., & Ledoux, M. (2004). Effects of the Quebec Heart Health Demonstration Project on adult dietary behaviours. Quebec Heart Health Demonstration Project Research Group. *Preventive Medicine: An International Journal Devoted to Practice and Theory, 38*(2), 137–148.

Hurd, H. M., Drewry, W. F., Dewey, R., Pilgrim, C. W., Blumer, G. A., & Burgess, T. J. W. (1916). *The institutional care of the insane in the United States and Canada.* Oxford, UK: Johns Hopkins Press.

Hurt, S. W., Schnurr, P. P., Severino, S. K., Freeman, E. W., Gise, L. H., Rivera-Tovar, A., & Steege, J. F. (1992). Late luteal phase dysphoric disorder in 670 women evaluated for premenstrual complaints. *American Journal of Psychiatry, 149,* 525–530.

Hussian, R. A., & Brown, D. C. (1987). Use of two dimensional grid patterns to limit hazardous ambulation in demented patients. *Journal of Gerontology, 42,* 558–560.

Hutchinson, B. (2007, February 6). I was kept in a chicken coop: Pickton Jurors hear tape from undercover RCMP officer. *National Post.* Retrieved August 14, 2007, from http://www.canada.com/nationalpost/pickton/story.html?id 59e39423-9262-416e-be4e20430931d80f

Hyler, S. E., Williams, J. B. W., & Spitzer, R. L. (1982). Reliability in the DSM-III field trials: Interview v. case summary. *Archives of General Psychiatry, 39,* 1275–1278.

Hyman, S. E. (2009). How adversity gets under the skin. *Nature Neuroscience, 12*(3), 241–243

Hyman, S. E., & Shore, D. (2000). An NIMH perspective on the use of placebos. *Biological Psychiatry, 47*(8), 689–691.

Hymowitz, P., Frances, A., Jacobsberg, L., Sickles, M., & Hoyt, R. (1986). Neuroleptic treatment of schizotypal personality disorder. *Comprehensive Psychiatry, 27,* 267–271.

Hynd, G. W., & Semrud-Clikeman, M. (1989). Dyslexia and brain morphology. *Psychological Bulletin, 106,* 447–482.

Hypericum Depression Trial Study Group. (2002). Effect of *Hypericum performatum* (St. John's Wort) in major depressive disorder: A randomized controlled trial. *JAMA, 287,* 1807–1814.

Iguchi, M. Y., Griffiths, R. R., Bickel, W. K., Handelsman, L., Childress, A. R., & McLellan, A. T. (1990). *Relative abuse liability of benzodiazepines in methadone maintenance populations in three cities. Problems of drug dependence* (pp. 364–365, NIDA Publication No. ADM 90–1663). Washington, DC: U.S. Government Printing Office.

Ihara, H., Berrios, G. E., & McKenna, P. J. (2003). The association between negative and dysexecutive syndromes in schizophrenia: A cross-cultural study. *Behavioral Neurology, 14,* 63–74.

Ikels, C. (1991). Aging and disability in China: Cultural issues in measurement and interpretation. *Social Science Medicine, 32,* 649–665.

Imber, S. D., Glanz, L. M., Elkin, I., Sotsky, S. M., Boyer, J. L., & Leber, W. R. (1986). Ethical issues in psychotherapy research: Problems in a collaborative clinical trials study. *American Psychologist, 41,* 137–146.

Imperato-McGinley, J., Peterson, R. E., Gautier, T., & Sturla, E. (1979). Androgens and the evolution of male-gender identity among male pseudohermaphrodites with 5-alphareductase deficiency. *New England Journal of Medicine, 300,* 1233–1237.

IMS Health Canada. (2004a). *A health information update from IMS health.* Retrieved August 5, 2004, from http://www.imshealthcanada.com/htmen/3_1_39.htm

IMS Health Canada. (2004b). *Early figures show Viagra expanding erectile dysfunction market.* Retrieved August 5, 2004, from http://www.imshealthcanada.com/htmen/4_2_1_13.htm

Inlow, J. K., & Restifo, L. L. (2004). Molecular and comparative genetics of mental retardation. *Genetics, 166,* 835–881.

Insel, T. R. (Ed.). (1984). *New findings in obsessive-compulsive disorder.* Washington, DC: American Psychiatric Press.

Insel, T. R. (1992). Toward a neuroanatomy of obsessive-compulsive disorder. *Archives of General Psychiatry, 49,* 739–744.

Insel, T. R., Scanlan, J., Champoux, M., & Suomi, S. J. (1988). Rearing paradigm in a nonhuman primate affects response to B-CCE challenge. *Psychopharmacology, 96,* 81–86.

Institut de la statistique du Québec. (2001). *Enquête sociale et de santé 1998.* Québec, QC: Institut de la statistique du Québec.

Institute of Medicine. (2002). *Reducing suicide: A national imperative.* Washington, DC: National Academic Press.

International Interdisciplinary Conference on Hypertension in Blacks. (1999, July 9). *Linking race and genetics to cardiovascular disease for improved health among ethnic populations.* Retrieved July 15, 2004, from http://www.ishib.org/main/newsrel_lead_i99.htm

Iribarren, C., Sidney, S., Bild, D. E., Liu, K., Markovitz, J. H., Roseman, J. M., & Matthews, K. (2000). Association of hostility with coronary artery calcification in young adults. *JAMA, 283*(19), 2546–2551.

Ironson, G., Friedman, A., Klimas, N., Antoni, M., Fletcher, M. A., Laperriere, A., ... Schneiderman, N. (1994). Distress, denial, and low adherence to behavioral interventions predict faster disease progression in gay men infected with human immunodeficiency virus. *International Journal of Behavioral Medicine, 1,* 90–105.

Ironson, G., Taylor, C. B., Boltwood, M., Bartzokis, T., Dennis, C., Chesney, M., ... Segall, G. M. (1992). Effects of anger on left ventricular ejection fraction in coronary artery disease. *American Journal of Cardiology, 70,* 281–285.

Irvin, J. E., Bowers, C. A., Dunn, M. E., & Wang, M. C. (1999). Efficacy of relapse prevention: A meta-analytic review. *Journal of Consulting and Clinical Psychology, 67*(4), 563–570.

Irwin, M., Mascovich, A., Gillin, J. C., Willoughby, R., Pike, J., & Smith, T. L. (1994). Partial sleep deprivation reduces natural killer cell activity in humans. *Psychosomatic Medicine, 56,* 493–498.

Isaacowitz, D. M., Smith, T. B., & Carstensen, L. L. (2003). Socioemotional selectivity and mental health among trauma survivors in old age. *Ageing International, 28,* 181–199.

Iskedjian, M., Hux, M., & Remington, G. J. (1998). The Canadian experience with risperidone for the treatment of schizophrenia: An overview. *Journal of Psychiatry & Neuroscience, 23,* 229–239.

Israeli, A. L., & Stewart, S. H. (2001). Memory bias for forbidden food cues in restrained eaters. *Cognitive Therapy & Research, 25,* 37–47.

Ivanov, I. (2009). Disulfiram and acamprosate. In B. J. Sadock, V. A. Sadock, & P. Ruiz (Eds.), *Kaplan & Sadock's comprehensive textbook of psychiatry* (Vol. II, 9th ed., pp. 3099–3105). Philadelphia: Lippincott Williams & Wilkins.

Iversen, L. L. (2000). *The science of marijuana.* New York: Oxford University Press.

Izard, C. E. (1992). Basic emotions, relations among emotions, and emotion-cognition relations. *Psychological Review, 99*(3), 561–565.

Jack, L., Nicholls, T., & Ogloff, J. R. P. (1998, March). *An investigation of inpatient self-injurious behavior among involuntarily hospitalized patients.* Poster presented at the Biennial Meeting of the American Psychology Law Society, Redondo Beach, CA.

Jackson, G., Rosen, R., Kloner, R., & Kostis, J. (2006). The second Princeton consensus on sexual dysfunction and cardiac risk: New guidelines for sexual medicine. *Journal of Sexual Medicine, 3,* 28–36.

Jacobi, W., & Winkler, H. (1927). Encephalographsche Studien an chronischen Schizophrenen. *Archiv für Psychiatrie und Nervenkrankheiten, 81,* 299–332.

Jacobs, S. (1993). *Pathologic grief: Maladaptation to loss.* Washington, DC: American Psychiatric Press.

Jacobs, S., Hansen, F., Berkman, L., Kasl, S., & Ostfeld, A. (1989). Depressions of bereavement. *Comprehensive Psychiatry, 30*(3), 218–224.

Jacobs, S.-E., Thomas, W., & Lang, S. (Eds.). (1997). *Two-spirit people: Native American gender identity, sexuality, and spirituality.* Chicago: University of Illinois Press.

Jacobson, E. (1938). *Progressive relaxation.* Chicago: University of Chicago Press.

Jacobson, N. S., & Hollon, S. D. (1996a). Cognitive behavior therapy vs. pharmacotherapy: Now that the jury's returned its verdict, it's time to present the rest of the evidence. *Journal of Consulting and Clinical Psychology, 64,* 74–80.

Jacobson, N. S., & Hollon, S. D. (1996b). Prospects for future comparisons between drugs and psychotherapy: Lessons from the CBT vs. pharmacotherapy exchange. *Journal of Consulting and Clinical Psychology, 64,* 104–108.

Jacobson, N. S., Martell, C. R., & Dimidjian, S. (2001). Behavioral activation treatment for depression: Returning to contextual roots. *Clinical Psychology: Science and Practice, 8*(3), 255–270.

Jacobson, N. S., & Truax, P. (1991). Clinical significance: A statistical approach to defining meaningful change in psychotherapy research. *Journal of Consulting and Clinical Psychology, 59,* 12–19.

Jaffe, A. J., Rounsaville, B., Chang, G., Schottenfeld, R. S., Meyer, R. E., & O'Malley, S. O. (1996). Naltrexone, relapse prevention, and supportive therapy with alcoholics: An analysis of patient treatment matching. *Journal of Consulting and Clinical Psychology, 64,* 1044–1053.

Jaffe, J. H., Knapp, C. M., & Ciraulo, D. A. (1997). Opiates: Clinical aspects. In J. H. Lowinson, P. Ruiz, R. B. Millman, & J. G. Langrod (Eds.), *Substance abuse: A comprehensive textbook* (pp. 158–166). Baltimore: Williams & Wilkins.

Jaffe, J. H., & O'Keeffe, C. (2003). From morphine clinics to buprenorphine: Regulating opioid agonist treatment of addiction in the United States. *Drug & Alcohol Dependence, 70* (Suppl. 2), 3–11.

Jaffe, J. H., Rawson, R. A., & Ling, W. (2005). Cocaine-related disorders. In B. J. Sadock & V. A. Sadock (Eds.), *Kaplan & Sadock's comprehensive textbook of psychiatry* (8th ed., pp. 1220–1238). Philadelphia: Lippincott Williams & Wilkins.

Jaffe, S. E. (2000). Sleep and infectious disease. In M. H. Kryger, T. Roth, & W. C. Dement (Eds.), *Principles and practice of sleep medicine* (3rd ed., pp. 1093–1102). Philadelphia: W. B. Saunders.

Jamison, K. R. (1989). Mood disorders and patterns of creativity in British writers and artists. *Psychiatry, 52,* 125–134.

Jamison, R. N., & Virts, K. L. (1990). The influence of family support on chronic pain. *Behaviour Research and Therapy, 28*(4), 283–287.

Jamner, L. D., Shapiro, D., Goldstein, I. B., & Hug, R. (1991). Ambulatory blood pressure and heart rate in paramedics: Effects of cynical hostility and defensiveness. *Psychosomatic Medicine, 53,* 393–406.

Jane, J. S., Oltmanns, T. F., South, S. C., & Turkheimer, E. (2007). Gender bias in diagnostic criteria for personality disorders: An item response theory analysis. *Journal of Abnormal Psychology, 116,* 166–175.

Jang, K. L. (2005). *The behavioral genetics of psychopathology: A clinical guide.* Mahwah, NJ: Lawrence Erlbaum Associates.

Jang, K. L., Livesley, W. J., Angleitner, A., Riemann, R., & Vernon, P. A. (2002). Genetic and environmental influences on the covariance of facets defining the domains of the five-factor model of personality. *Personality & Individual Differences, 33,* 83–101.

Jang, K. L., Paris, J., Zweig-Frank, H., & Livesley, W. J. (1998). Twin study of dissociative experience. *Journal of Nervous and Mental Disease, 186,* 345–351.

Jang, K. L., Vernon, P. A., & Livesley, W. J. (2001). Behaviouralgenetic perspectives on personality function. *Canadian Journal of Psychiatry, 46,* 234–244.

Jarrett, R. B., Kraft, D., Doyle, J., Foster, B. M., Eaves, G. G., & Silver, P. C. (2001). Preventing recurrent depression using cognitive therapy with and without a continuation phase. *Archives of General Psychiatry, 58,* 381–388.

Jarvis, E. (1998). Schizophrenia in British immigrants: Recent findings, issues and implications. *Transcultural Psychiatry, 35*(1), 39–74.

Jason, L. A., Fennell, P. A., & Taylor, R. R. (2003). *Handbook of chronic fatigue syndrome.* Hoboken, NJ: John Wiley & Sons.

Jaspers, K. (1963). *General psychopathology* (J. Hoenig & M. W. Hamilton, Trans.). Manchester, UK: Manchester University Press.

Javitt, D. C., & Laruelle, M. (2006). Neurochemical theories. In J. A. Lieberman, T. S. Stroup, & D. O. Perkins (Eds.), *The American Psychiatric Publishing textbook of schizophrenia* (pp. 85–116). Washington, DC: American Psychiatric Publishing.

Jeffrey, S. (1995, July 4). Toronto team uncovers Alzheimer's gene. *The Medical Post.* Retrieved May 21, 2004, from http://www.mentalhealth.com/mag1/p5m-alz1.html

Jellinek, E. M. (1946). Phases in the drinking histories of alcoholics. *Quarterly Journal of Studies on Alcohol, 7,* 1–88.

Jellinek, E. M. (1952). Phases of alcohol addiction. *Quarterly Journal of Studies on Alcohol, 13,* 673–684.

Jellinek, E. M. (1960). *The disease concept of alcohol.* New Brunswick, NJ: Hillhouse Press.

Jenike, M. A., Baer, L., Ballantine, H. T., Martuza, R. L., Tynes, S., Giriunas, I., ... Cassem, N. H. (1991). Cingulotomy for refractory obsessive-compulsive disorder: A long-term follow-up of 33 patients. *Archives of General Psychiatry, 48,* 548–555.

Jenike, M. A., Baer, L., & Minichiello, W. E. (Eds.). (1986). *Obsessive-compulsive disorders: Theory and management.* Littleton, MA: PSG Publishing.

Jenkins, J. H., & Karno, M. (1992). The meaning of expressed emotion: Theoretical issues raised by cross-cultural research. *American Journal of Psychiatry, 149,* 9–21.

Jenkins, J. H., Kleinman, A., & Good, B. J. (1990). Cross-cultural studies of depression. In J. Becker & A. Kleinman (Eds.), *Psychosocial aspects of depression.* Hillsdale, NJ: Erlbaum.

Jennum, P., & Riha, R. L. (2009). Epidemiology of sleep apnoea/hypopnoea syndrome and sleep-disordered breathing. *The European Respiratory Journal - The Official Journal of the European Respiratory Society, 33*(4), 907–914.

Jensen, E. J., Schmidt, E., Pedersen, B., & Dahl, R. (1991). Effect on smoking cessation of silver acetate, nicotine and ordinary chewing gum. *Psychopharmacology, 104,* 470–474.

Jensen, P. S., Hinshaw, S. P., Swanson, J. M., Greenhill, L. L., Conners, C. K., Arnold, L. E., ... Wigal, T. (2001). Findings from the NIMH Multimodal Treatment Study of ADHD (MTA): Implications and applications for primary care providers. *Journal of Developmental & Behavioral Pediatrics, 22,* 60–73.

Jilek, W. G. (1982). Altered states of consciousness in North American Indian ceremonials. *Ethos, 10*(4), 326–343.

Joe, S., Baser, R., Breeden, G., Neighbors, H., & Jackson, J. (2006). Prevalence of and risk factors for lifetime suicide attempts among blacks in the United States. *JAMA, 296,* 2112–2123.

Joffe, R., Segal, Z., & Singer, W. (1996). Change in thyroid hormone levels following response to cognitive therapy for major depression. *American Journal of Psychiatry, 153,* 411–413.

John, C., Turkington, D., & Kingdon, D. (1994). Cognitive-behavioural therapy for schizophrenia: Reply. *British Journal of Psychiatry, 165,* 695.

Johns, M. B., Hovell, M, F., Ganiatis, T., Peddecord, K. M., & Agras, W. S. (1987). Primary care and health promotion: A model for preventive medicine. *American Journal of Preventive Medicine, 3*(6), 351.

Johnson, B. A. (1991). Cannabis. In I. B. Glass (Ed.), *International handbook of addiction behaviour* (pp. 69–76). London: Tavistock/Routledge.

Johnson, B. A., Roache, J. D., Javors, M. A., DiClemente, C. C., Cloninger, C. R., Prihoda, T. J., … Hensler, J. (2000a). Ondansetron for reduction of drinking among biologically predisposed alcoholic patients. *JAMA, 284*(8), 963–971.

Johnson, J., Weissman, M. M., & Klerman, G. L. (1990). Panic disorder, comorbidity and suicide attempts. *Archives of General Psychiatry, 47,* 805–808.

Johnson, J. G., Bromley, E., & McGeoch, P. G. (2005). Role of childhood experiences in the development of maladaptive and adaptive traits. In J. M. Oldham, A. E. Skodol, & D. S. Bender (Eds.), *Textbook of personality disorders* (pp. 209–221). Washington, DC: American Psychiatric Publishing.

Johnson, J. G., Cohen, P., Pine, D. S., Klein, D. F., Kasen, S., & Brook, J. S. (2000b). Association between cigarette smoking and anxiety disorders during adolescence and early adulthood. *JAMA, 284,* 2348–2351.

Johnson, J. M., Baumgart, D., Helmstetter, E., & Curry, C. (1996). *Augmenting basic communication in natural contexts.* Baltimore: Paul H. Brookes.

Johnson, S. L., Gruber, J. L., & Eisner, L. R. (2007). Emotion and bipolar disorder. In J. Rottenberg & S. L. Johnson (Eds.), *Emotion and psychopathology* (pp. 123–150). Washington, DC: American Psychological Association.

Johnson, S. L., & Miller, I. (1997). Negative life events and time to recovery from episodes of bipolar disorder. *Journal of Abnormal Psychology, 106*(3), 449–457.

Johnson, S. L., & Roberts, J. E. (1995). Life events and bipolar disorder: Implications from biological theories. *Psychological Bulletin, 117*(3), 434–449.

Johnson, S. L., Winett, C. A., Meyer, B., Greenhouse, W. J., & Miller, I. (1999). Social support and the course of bipolar disorder. *American Psychological Association, 180*(4), 558–566.

Johnston, C., Pelham, W. E., & Murphy, H. A. (1985). Peer relationships in ADHD and normal children: A developmental analysis of peer and teacher ratings. *Journal of Abnormal Child Psychology, 13,* 89–100.

Johnston, L., Bachman, J., & Schulenberg, J. (2005). *Monitoring the Future National Results on Adolescent Drug Use: Overview of Key Findings, 2004.* Substance Abuse and Mental Health Services Administration.

Joiner, T. E., & Rudd, D. M. (1996). Toward a categorization of depression-related psychological constructs. *Cognitive Therapy and Research, 20,* 51–68.

Joiner, T. E., Jr. (1997). Shyness and low social support as interactive diatheses, with loneliness as mediator: Testing an interpersonal–personality view of vulnerability to depressive symptoms. *Journal of Abnormal Psychology, 106*(3), 386–394.

Joiner, T. E., Jr. (1999). A test of interpersonal theory of depression in youth psychiatric inpatients. *Journal of Abnormal Child Psychology, 27*(1), 77–85.

Joiner, T. E., Jr., Heatherton, T. F., & Keel, P. K. (1997). Ten year stability and predictive validity of five bulimia-related indicators. *American Journal of Psychiatry, 154,* 1133–1138.

Joiner, T. E., Jr., & Rudd, M. D. (2000). Intensity and duration of suicidal crises vary as a function of previous suicide attempts and negative life events. *Journal of Consulting and Clinical Psychology, 68*(5), 909–916.

Jones, A. (2007, October 3). Ont. Closing facilities for intellectually disabled in wrong way: opposition. *The Daily News.* Retrieved January 3, 2008, from http://www.hfxnews.ca/index .cfm?pid 1305&cpcatelection&stry62017026

Jones, H. (2004, October 22). *Lazing in the afterglow. icWales.co.uk.* Retrieved July 10, 2007, from http://icwales.icnetwork.co.uk/0 900entertainment/0050artsnews/tm_objectid 14786275&methodfull&siteid50082&hea dlinelazing-in-the-afterglow-name_page. html#story_continue

Jones, J. C., & Barlow, D. H. (1990). The etiology of posttraumatic stress disorder. *Clinical Psychology Review, 10,* 299–328.

Jones, K. L., & Smith, D. W. (1973). Recognition of the fetal alcohol syndrome in early infancy. *Lancet, 2,* 999–1001.

Jones, M. B., & Blanchard, R. (1998). Birth order and male homosexuality: An extension of Slater's index. *Human Biology, 70,* 775–787.

Jones, M. C. (1924a). The elimination of children's fears. *Journal of Experimental Psychology, 7,* 383–390.

Jones, M. C. (1924b). A laboratory study of fear. The case of Peter. *Pedagogical Seminary, 31,* 308–315.

Jones, R. T., & Haney, J. I. (1984). A primary preventive approach to the acquisition and maintenance of fire emergency responding: Comparison of external and self-instruction strategies. *Journal of Community Psychology, 12*(2), 180–191.

Jones, R. T., & Kazdin, A. E. (1980). Teaching children how and when to make emergency telephone calls. *Behavior Therapy, 11*(4), 509–521.

Jordan, B. D., Relkin, N. R., Ravdin, L. D., Jacobs, A. R., Bennett, A., & Gandy, S. (1997). Apolipoprotein E Epsilon 4 associated with chronic traumatic brain injury in boxing. *JAMA, 278,* 136–140.

Joshi, G., & Wilens, T. (2009). Comorbidity in pediatric bipolar disorder. *Child and Adolescent Psychiatric Clinics of North America, 18*(2), 291–319.

Juby, H., & Farrington, D. P. (2001). Disentangling the link between disrupted families and delinquency. *British Journal of Criminology, 41*(1), 22–40.

Judd, L. (2000). Course and chronicity of unipolar major depressive disorder: Commentary on Joiner. *Child Psychology Science and Practice, 7*(2), 219–223.

Judd, L. L. (1997). The clinical course of unipolar major depressive disorders. *Archives of General Psychiatry, 54,* 989–991.

Judd, L. L., Akiskal, H. S., Maser, J. D., Zeller, P. J., Endicott, J., Coryell, W., … Keller, M. B. (1998a). A prospective 12-year study of subsyndromal and syndromal depressive symptomatology in 431 patients with unipolar major depressive disorder. *Archives of General Psychiatry, 55,* 694–700.

Judd, L. L., Akiskal, H. S., Maser, J. D., Zeller, P. J., Endicott, J., Coryell, W., … Keller, M. B. (1998b). Major depressive disorder: A prospective study of residual subthreshold depressive symptoms as predictor of rapid release. *Journal of Affective Disorders, 50,* 97–108.

Juliano, L. M., & Griffiths, R. R. (2009). Caffeine-related disorders. In B. J. Sadock, V. A. Sadock, & P. Ruiz (Eds.), *Kaplan & Sadock's comprehensive textbook of psychiatry* (Vol. I, 9th ed., pp. 1296–1309). Philadelphia: Lippincott Williams & Wilkins.

Junginger, J. (1997). Fetishism: Assessment and treatment. In D. R. Laws & W. O'Donohue (Eds.), *Sexual deviance: Theory, assessment and treatment* (pp. 92–110). New York: Guilford Press.

Juul-Dam, N., Townsend, J., & Courchesne, E. (2001). Prenatal, perinatal, and neonatal factors in autism, pervasive developmental disorder—not otherwise specified, and the general population. *Pediatrics, 107*(4), E63.

Kafka, M. P. (1997). A monoamine hypothesis for the pathophysiology of paraphilic disorders. *Archives of Sexual Behavior, 26,* 343–358.

Kagan, J. (1994). *Galen's prophesy.* New York: Basic Books.

Kagan, J. (1997). Temperament and the reactions to unfamiliarity. *Child Development, 68,* 139–143.

Kagan, J., Reznick, J. S., & Snidman, N. (1988). The physiology and psychology of behavioral inhibition in children. *Annual Progress in Child Psychiatry & Child Development,* 102–127.

Kagan, J., & Snidman, N. (1991). Infant predictors of inhibited and uninhibited profiles. *Psychological Science, 2,* 40–44.

Kagan, J., & Snidman, N. (1999). Early childhood predictors of adult anxiety disorders. *Biological Psychiatry, 46,* 1536–1541.

Kahn, R. S., Khoury, J., Nichols, W. C., & Lanphear, B. P. (2003). Role of dopamine transporter genotype and maternal prenatal smoking in childhood hyperactive-impulsive, inattentive, and oppositional behaviors. *The Journal of Pediatrics, 143*(1), 104–110.

Kahn, S. (2001). Golden girl Uma admits to having body dysmorphic disorder (BDD). *Talk Surgery, Inc.* Retrieved May 15, 2001, from http://canoe. talksurgery. com/consumer/new/ new00000056_1.html

Kaiser, J. (2006). Differences in immune cell "brakes" may explain chimp–human split on AIDS. *Science Magazine, 312,* 672–673.

Kalat, J. W. (Ed.). (2001). *Biological psychology* (7th ed.). Belmont, CA: Wadsworth/Thomson Learning.

Kales, A., Soldatos, C. R., Caldwell, A., Kales, J., Humphrey, F., Charney, D., & Schweitzer, P. K. (1980). Somnabulism: Clinical characteristics and personality patterns. *Archives of General Psychiatry, 37,* 1406–1410.

Kalivas, P. W. (2005). New directions pharmacotherapy for addiction or can we forget to be addicted? *Clinical Neuroscience Research, 5,* 147–150.

Kallmann, F. J. (1938). *The genetics of schizophrenia.* New York: Augustin.

Kalus, O., Bernstein, D. P., & Siever, L. J. (1993). Schizoid personality disorder: A review of current status and implications for DSM-IV. *Journal of Personality Disorders, 7,* 43–52.

Kalus, O., Bernstein, D. P., & Siever, L. J. (1995). Paranoid personality disorder. In W. J. Livesley (Ed.), *The DSM-IV personality disorders* (pp. 58–70). New York: Guilford Press.

Kamb, L., & Barber, M. (2002, February 9). B. C. police were told years ago of pig farm: Mother says she hopes they find bodies there. *Seattle Post-Intelligencer.* Retrieved August 14, 2007, from http://seattlepi.nwsource.com/local/57736_vancouver09.shtml

Kaminen, N., Hannula-Jouppi, K., Kestila, M., Lahermo, P., Muller, K., Kaaranen, M., ... Kere, J. (2003). A genome scan for developmental dyslexia confirms linkage to chromosome 2p11 and suggests a new locus on 7q32. *Journal of Medical Genetics, 40,* 340–345.

Kandel, D. B., Wu, P., & Davies, M. (1994). Maternal smoking during pregnancy and smoking by adolescent daughters. *American Journal of Public Health, 84,* 1407–1413.

Kandel, E. R. (1983). From metapsychology to molecular biology: Explorations into the nature of anxiety. *American Journal of Psychiatry, 140,* 1277–1293.

Kandel, E. R., Jessell, T. M., & Schacter, S. (1991). Early experience and the fine tuning of synaptic connections. In E. R. Kandel, J. H. Schwartz, & T. M. Jessell (Eds.), *Principles of neural science* (3rd ed., pp. 945–958). New York: Elsevier.

Kandel, E. R., Schwartz, J. H., & Jessell, T. M. (Eds.). (2000). *Principles of neural science* (4th ed.). New York: McGraw-Hill.

Kane, J. M. (2006). Tardive dyskinesia circa 2006. *American Journal of Psychiatry, 163,* 1316–1318.

Kanigel, R. (1988, October/November). Nicotine becomes addictive. *Science Illustrated,* pp. 12–14, 19–21.

Kanner, L. (1943). Autistic disturbances of affective contact. *Nervous Child, 2,* 217–250.

Kanner, L. (1949). Problems of nosology and psychodynamics of early infantile autism. *American Journal of Orthopsychiatry, 19,* 416–426.

Kanner, L., & Eisenberg, L. (1955). Notes on the follow-up studies of autistic children. In P. Hoch & J. Zubin (Eds.), *Psychopathology of childhood* (pp. 227–239). New York: Grune & Stratton.

Kaplan, A. S., & Garfinkel, P. E. (1999). Difficulties in treating patients with eating disorders: A review of patient and clinician variables. *Canadian Journal of Psychiatry, 44,* 665–670.

Kaplan, H. S. (1979). *Disorders of sexual desire.* New York: Brunner/Mazel.

Kaplan, H. S. (1987). *Sexual aversion, sexual phobias, and panic disorder.* New York: Brunner/Mazel.

Kaplan, M. (1983). A woman's view of DSM-III. *American Psychologist, 38,* 786–792.

Kaplan, N. M. (1980). The control of hypertension: A therapeutic breakthrough. *American Scientist, 68,* 537–545.

Kaplan, S. A., Reis, R. B., Kohn, I. J. Ikeguchi, E. F., Laor, E., Te, A. E., & Martins, A. C. (1999). Safety and efficacy of sildenafil in postmenopausal women with sexual dysfunction. *Urology, 53,* 481–486.

Kapur, S., Zipursky, R. B., & Remington, G. (1999). Clinical and theoretical implications of 5-HT2 and D2 receptor occupancy of clozapine, risperidone, and olanzapine in schizophrenia. *American Journal of Psychiatry, 156,* 286–293.

Karantzoulis, S., Rich, J. B., & Magels, J. A. (2006). Subject-performed tasks improve associative learning in amnestic mild cognitive impairment. *Journal of the International Neuropsychological Society, 12,* 493–501.

Karno, M., & Golding, J. M. (1991). Obsessive-compulsive disorder. In L. N. Robins & D. A. Regier (Eds.), *Psychiatric disorders in America: The epidemiologic catchment area study* (pp. 204–219). New York: Free Press.

Kashani, J. H., Hoeper, E. W., Beck, N. C., & Corcoran, C. M. (1987). Personality, psychiatric disorders, and parental attitude among a community sample of adolescents. *Journal of the American Academy of Child and Adolescent Psychiatry, 26*(6), 879–885.

Kashani, J. H., McGee, R. O., Clarkson, S. E. A., Walton, L. A., Williams, S., Silva, P. A., ... McKnew, D. H. (1983). Depression in a sample of 9-year-old children: Prevalence and associated characteristics. *Archives of General Psychiatry, 40,* 1217–1223.

Kashner, T. M., Rost, K., Cohen, B., Anderson, M., & Smith, G. R. (1995). Enhancing the health of somatization disorder patients: Effectiveness of short-term group therapy. *Psychosomatics, 36,* 462–470.

Kass, D. J., Silvers, F. M., & Abrams, G. M. (1972). Behavioral group treatment of hysteria. *Archives of General Psychiatry, 26,* 42–50.

Katon, W., Lin, E., Von Korff, M., Russo, J., Lipscomb, P., & Bush, T. (1991). Somatization: A spectrum of severity. *American Journal of Psychiatry, 148,* 34–40.

Katon, W., & Roy-Byrne, P. P. (1991). Mixed anxiety and depression. *Journal of Abnormal Psychology, 100,* 337–345.

Katon, W. J. (2003). Clinical and health services relationships between major depression, depressive symptoms, and general medical illness. *Biological Psychiatry, 54,* 216–226.

Katschnig, H. (1999). Anxiety neurosis, panic disorder or what? In D. J. Nutt, C. Ballenger, & J. P., Lépine (Eds.), *Panic disorder: Clinical diagnosis, management and mechanisms* (pp. 1–8). London: Dunitz.

Katschnig, H., & Amering, M. (1990). Panic attacks and panic disorder in cross-cultural perspective. In J. C. Ballenger (Ed.), *Clinical aspects of panic disorder* (pp. 67–80). New York: Wiley.

Katz, I. R. (1993). Delirium. In D. L. Dunner (Ed.), *Current psychiatric therapy* (pp. 65–73). Philadelphia: W. B. Saunders.

Katz, I. R., Leshen, E., Kleban, M., & Jethanandani, V. (1989). Clinical features of depression in the nursing home. *International Psychogeriatrics, 1,* 5–15.

Katz, J., & Gagliese, L. (1999). Phantom limb pain: A continuing puzzle. In R. J. Gatchel & D. C. Turk (Eds.), *Psychosocial factors in pain: Critical perspectives* (pp. 284–300). New York: Guilford Press.

Katz, J. L., Weiner, H., Gallagher, T. F., & Hellman, I. (1970). Stress, distress, and ego defenses: Psychoendocrine response to impending breast tumor biopsy. *Archives of General Psychiatry, 23,* 131–142.

Katz, R., & McGuffin P. (1993). The genetics of affective disorders. *Progress in Experimental Personality and Psychopathology Research, 16,* 200–221.

Kaufman, A. S., & Kaufman, N. L. (Eds.). (2001). *Specific learning disabilities and difficulties in children and adolescents: Psychological assessment and evaluation.* New York: Cambridge University Press.

Kavanagh, D. J. (1992). Recent developments in expressed emotion and schizophrenia. *British Journal of Psychiatry, 160,* 601–620.

Kawamura, K. Y. (2002). Asian American body images. In T. F. Cash & T. Pruzinsky (Eds.), *Body image: A handbook of theory, research and clinical practice* (pp. 243–249). New York: Guilford Press.

Kaye, W., Strober, M., Stein, D., & Gendall, K. (1999). New directions in treatment research of anorexia and bulimia nervosa. *Biological Psychiatry, 45,* 1285–1292.

Kaye, W. H., Greeno, C. G., Moss, H., Fernstrom, J., Fernstrom, M., Lilenfeld, L. R., ... Mann, J. J. (1998). Alterations in serotonin activity and psychiatric symptoms after recovery from bulimia nervosa. *Archives of General Psychiatry, 55,* 927–935.

Kaye, W. H., Weltzin, T. E., Hsu, L. K. G., McConaha, C. W., & Bolton, B. (1993). Amount of calories retained after binge eating and vomiting. *American Journal of Psychiatry, 150*(6), 969–971.

Kazarian, S. S., & Evans, D. R. (Eds.) (2001). Health psychology and culture: Embracing the 21st century. In *Handbook of cultural health psychology* (pp. 3–43). San Diego, CA: Academic Press.

Kazarian, S. S., Malla, A. K., Cole, J. D., & Baker, B. (1990). Comparisons of two expressed emotion scales with the Camberwell Family Interview. *Journal of Clinical Psychology, 46,* 306–309.

Kazdin, A. E. (1979). Unobtrusive measures in behavioral assessment. *Journal of Applied Behavior Analysis, 12,* 713–724.

Kazdin, A. E. (1981). Drawing valid inferences from case studies. *Journal of Consulting and Clinical Psychology, 49,* 183–192.

Kazdin, A. E. (1983). Hopelessness, depression, and suicidal intent among psychiatrically disturbed inpatient children. *Journal of Consulting and Clinical Psychology, 51*(4), 504–510.

Kazdin, A. E., & Mazurick, J. L. (1994). Dropping out of child psychotherapy: Distinguishing early and late dropouts over the course of treatment. *Journal of Consulting and Clinical Psychology, 62,* 1069–1074.

Kazdin, A. E., Mazurick, J. L., & Bass, D. (1993). Risk for attrition in treatment of antisocial children and families. *Journal of Child Clinical Psychology, 22,* 2–16.

Keane, T. M., & Barlow, D. H. (2002). Post traumatic stress disorder. In D. H. Barlow (Ed.), *Anxiety and its disorders: The nature and treatment of anxiety and panic* (2nd ed.). New York: Guilford Press.

Kearney, A. J. (2006). A primer of covert sensitization. *Cognitive and Behavioral Practice, 13*(2), 167–175.

Kebir, O., Tabbane, K., Sengupta, S., & Joober, R. (2009). Candidate genes and neuropsychological phenotypes in children with ADHD: Review of association studies. *Journal of Psychiatry & Neuroscience, 34*(2), 88.

Keefe, F. J., Crisson, J., Urban, B. J., & Williams, D. A. (1990). Analyzing chronic low back pain: The relative contribution of pain coping strategies. *Pain, 40,* 293–301.

Keefe, F. J., & France, C. R. (1999). Pain: Biopsychosocial mechanisms and management. *Current Directions in Psychological Science, 8,* 137–141.

Keel, P. K., Dorer, D. J., Eddy, K. T., Franko, D., Charatan, D. L., & Herzog, D. B. (2003).

Predictors of mortality in eating disorders. *Archives of General Psychiatry, 60,* 179–183.

Keel, P. K., & Mitchell, J. E. (1997). Outcome in bulimia nervosa. *American Journal of Psychiatry, 154,* 313–321.

Keel, P. K., Mitchell, J. E., Miller, K. B., Davis, T. L., & Crow, S. J. (1999). Long-term outcome of bulimia nervosa. *Archives of General Psychiatry, 56,* 63–69.

Keel, P. K., Mitchell, J. E., Miller, K. B., Davis, T. L., & Crow, S. J. (2000). Predictive validity of bulimia nervosa as a diagnostic strategy. *American Journal of Psychiatry, 157*(1), 136–138.

Keitner, G. I., Ryan, C. E., Miller, I. W., Kohn, R., Bishop, D. S., & Epstein, N. B. (1995). Role of the family in recovery and major depression. *American Journal of Psychiatry, 152,* 1002–1008.

Keller, M. B., Baker, L. A., & Russell, C. W. (1993). Classification and treatment of dysthymia. In D. L. Dunner (Ed.), *Current psychiatric therapy.* Philadelphia: W. B. Saunders.

Keller, M. B., Hirschfeld, R. M. A., & Hanks, D. L. (1997). Double depression: A distinctive subtype of unipolar depression. *Journal of Affective Disorders, 45,* 65–73.

Keller, M. B., Klein, D. N., Hirschfeld, R. M. A., Kocsis, J. H., McCullough, J. P., ... Miller, I., Marin, D. B. (1995). Results of the DSM-IV mood disorders field trial. *American Journal of Psychiatry, 152,* 843–849.

Keller, M. B., Lavori, P. W., Endicott, J., Coryell, W., & Klerman, G. L. (1983). Double depression: Two year follow-up. *American Journal of Psychiatry, 140*(6), 689–694.

Keller, M. B., Lavori, P. W., Mueller, T. I., Endicott, J., Coryell, W., Hirschfeld, R. M. A., & Shea, T. (1992). Time to recovery, chronicity, and levels of psychopathology in major depression. *Archives of General Psychiatry, 49,* 809–816.

Keller, M. B., McCollough, J. P., Klein, D. N., Arnow, B., Dunner, D. L., Gelenberg, A. J., ... Zajecka, J. (2000). A comparison of nefazodone, the cognitive behavioral-analysis system of psychotherapy, and their combination for the treatment of chronic depression. *New England Journal of Medicine, 342*(20), 1462–1470.

Keller, M. B., & Wunder, J. (1990). Bipolar disorder in childhood. In M. Hersen & C. G. Last (Eds.), *Handbook of child and adult psychopathology: A longitudinal perspective.* Elmsford, NY: Pergamon Press.

Kellner, R. (1985). Functional somatic symptoms and hypochondriasis: A survey of empirical studies. *Archives of General Psychiatry, 42,* 821–833.

Kellner, R. (1986). *Somatization and hypochondriasis.* New York: Praeger-Greenwood.

Kellner, R., Hernandez, J., & Pathak, D. (1992). Hypochondriacal fears and beliefs, anxiety, and somatization. *British Journal of Psychiatry, 160,* 525–532.

Kelly, B. D., Casey, P., Dunn, G., Ayuso-Mateos, J. L., & Dowrick, C. (2007). The role of personality disorder in "difficult to reach" patients with depression: Findings from the ODIN study. *European Psychiatry, 22,* 153–159.

Kelly, M. P., Strassberg, D. S., & Kircher, J. R. (1990). Attitudinal and experiential correlates of anorgasmia. *Archives of Sexual Behavior, 19*(2), 165–177.

Kemeny, M. E. (2003). The psychobiology of stress. *Current Directions in Psychological Science, 12*(4), 124–129.

Kemp, S. (1990). *Medieval psychology.* New York: Greenwood Press.

Kendall, P. C., Flannery-Schroeder, E., Panichelli-Mindell, M., Southam-Gerow, M., Henin, A., & Warman, M. (1997). Therapy for youths with anxiety disorder: A second randomized clinical trial. *Journal of Consulting and Clinical Psychology, 65,* 366–380.

Kendall, P. C., Flannery-Schroeder, E., Panichelli-Mindell, M., Southam-Gerow, M., Henin, A., & Warman, M. (1997). Therapy for youths with anxiety disorder: A second randomized clinical trial. *Journal of Consulting and Clinical Psychology, 65,* 366–380.

Kendler, K. S. (2001). Twin studies of psychiatric illness. *Achieves of General Psychiatry, 58,* 1005–1013.

Kendler, K. S. (2006). Reflections on the relationship between psychiatric genetics and psychiatric nosology. *American Journal of Psychiatry, 163,* 1138–1146.

Kendler, K. S., Czajkowski, N., Tambs, K., Torgersen, S., Aggen, S. H., Neale, M. C., & Reichborn-Kjennerud, T. (2006). Dimensional representations of DSM-IV cluster A personality disorders in a population-based sample of Norwegian twins: A multivariate study. *Psychological Medicine, 36,* 1583–1591.

Kendler, K. S., & Diehl, S. R. (1993). The genetics of schizophrenia: A current, genetic-epidemiologic perspective. *Schizophrenia Bulletin, 19,* 261–285.

Kendler, K. S., & Gruenberg, A. M. (1982). Genetic relationship between paranoid personality disorder and the "schizophrenic spectrum" disorders. *American Journal of Psychiatry, 139,* 1185–1186.

Kendler, K. S., Heath, A. C., Martin, N. G., & Eaves, L. J. (1987). Symptoms of anxiety and symptoms of depression: Same genes, different environments? *Archives of General Psychiatry, 44*(5), 451–457.

Kendler, K. S., Jacobson, K. C., Prescott, C. A., & Neale, M. C. (2003). Specificity of genetic and environmental risk factors for use and abuse/dependence of cannabis, cocaine, hallucinogens, sedatives, stimulants, and opiates in male twins. *American Journal of Psychiatry, 160,* 687–695.

Kendler, K. S., Karkowski, L. M., & Prescott, C. A. (1999a). The assessment of dependence in the study of stressful life events: Validation using a twin design. *Psychological Medicine, 29*(6), 1455–1460.

Kendler, K. S., Karkowski, L. M., & Prescott, C. A. (1999b). Causal relationship between stressful life events and the onset of major depression. *American Journal of Psychiatry, 156*(6), 837–841.

Kendler, K. S., Kessler, R. C., Neale, M. C., Heath, A. C., & Eaves, L. J. (1993). The prediction of major depression in women: Toward an integrated etiologic model. *American Journal of Psychiatry, 150,* 1139–1148.

Kendler, K. S., Kessler, R. C., Walters, E. E., MacLean, C., Neale, M. C., Heath, A. C., & Eaves, L. J. (1995). Stressful life events, genetic liability, and onset of an episode of major depression in women. *American Journal of Psychiatry, 152,* 833–842.

Kendler, K. S., MacLean, C., Neale, M., Kessler, R., Heath, A., & Eaves, L. (1991). The genetic epidemiology of bulimia nervosa. *American Journal of Psychiatry, 148*(12), 1627–1637.

Kendler, K. S., McGuire, M., Gruenberg, A. M., O'Hare, A., Spellman, M., & Walsh, D. (1993). The Roscommon Family Study: I. Methods, diagnosis of probands, and risk of schizophrenia in relatives. *Archives of General Psychiatry, 50,* 527–540.

Kendler, K. S., Myers, J., & Zisook, S. (2008). Does bereavement-related major depression differ from major depression associated with other stressful life events? *American Journal of Psychiatry, 165*(11), 1449–1455.

Kendler, K. S., Neale, M. C., Kessler, R. C., Heath, A. C., & Eaves, L. J. (1992a). Generalized anxiety disorder in women: A population-based twin study. *Archives of General Psychiatry, 49,* 267–272.

Kendler, K. S., Neale, M. C., Kessler, R. C., Heath, A. C., & Eaves, L. J. (1992b). Major depression and generalized anxiety disorder: Same genes, (partly) different environments? *Archives of General Psychiatry, 49,* 716–722.

Kendler, K. S., Neale, M. C., Kessler, R. C., Heath, A. C., & Eaves, L. J. (1993). A longitudinal twin study of 1-year prevalence of major depression in women. *Archives of General Psychiatry, 50,* 843–852.

Kendler, K., & Walsh, D. (2007). Schizophreniform disorder, delusional disorder and psychotic disorder not otherwise specified: Clinical features, outcome and familial psychopathology. *Acta Psychiatrica Scandinavica, 91*(6), 370–378.

Kennard, B. D., Clarke, G. N., Weersing, V. R., Asarnow, J. R., Shamseddeen, W., Porta, G., ... Brent, D. A. (2009). Effective components of TORDIA cognitive–behavioral therapy for adolescent depression: Preliminary findings. *Journal of Consulting and Clinical Psychology, 77*(6), 1033–1041.

Kennedy, K. (2001, October 22). Brotherly love. *Sports Illustrated.* Retrieved June 21, 2004, from http://www.macanxiety.com/corson.htm

Kennedy, S. (2000). Psychological factors and immunity in HIV infection: Stress, coping, social support, and intervention outcomes. In D. I. Mostofsky & D. H. Barlow (Eds.), *The management of stress and anxiety in medical disorders* (pp. 194–205). Needham Heights, MA: Allyn & Bacon.

Kennedy, S. H., & Goldbloom, D. S. (1996). Eating disorders. In Q. Rae-Grant (Ed.), *Images in psychiatry: Canada* (pp. 229–234). Washington, DC: American Psychiatric Press.

Kennedy, S. H., Katz, R., Neitzert, C. S., Ralevski, E., & Mendlowitz, S. (1995). Exposure with response prevention treatment of anorexia nervosa-bulimic subtype and bulimia nervosa. *Behaviour Research & Therapy, 33,* 685–689.

Kennedy, S. H., McVey, G., & Katz, R. (1990). Personality disorders in anorexia nervosa and bulimia nervosa. *Journal of Psychiatric Research, 24,* 259–269.

Kerns, J. (2009). Distinct conflict resolution deficits related to different facets of schizophrenia. *Psychological Research, 73*(6), 786–793.

Kerns, J. G., & Berenbaum, H. (2002). Cognitive impairments associated with formal thought disorder in people with schizophrenia. *Journal of Abnormal Psychology, 111*(2), 211–224.

Kerns, K., Don, A., Mateer, C. A., & Streissguth, A. P. (1997). Cognitive deficits in nonretarded adults with fetal alcohol syndrome. *Journal of Learning Disabilities, 30*(6), 685–693.

Kerns, R., Southwick, S., Giller, E., Haythornwaite, J., Jacob, M., & Rosenberg, R. (1991). The relationship between reports of pain-related social interactions and expressions of pain and affective distress. *Behavior Therapy, 22,* 101–111.

Kerr, G., Berman, E., & de Souza, M. J., (2006). Disordered eating in women's gymnastics:

Perspectives of athletes, coaches, parents, and judges. *Journal of Applied Sport Psychology, 18,* 28–43.

Kertzner, R. M., & Gorman, J. M. (1992). Psychoneuroimmunology and HIV infection. In A. Tashan & M. B. Riba (Eds.), *Review of psychiatry* (Vol. 11). Washington, DC: American Psychiatric Press.

Kessler, R. C. (1997). The effects of stressful life events on depression. *Annual Review of Psychology, 48,* 191–214.

Kessler, R. C., Avenevoli, S., & Ries Merikangas, K. (2001). Mood disorders in children and adolescents: An epidemiologic perspective. *Biological Psychiatry, 49*(12), 1002–1014.

Kessler, R. C., Berglund, P., Demler, O., Jin, R., Koretz, D., Merikangas, K. R., … Wang, P. S. (2003). The epidemiology of major depressive disorder: Results from the National Comorbidity Survey Replication (NCS-R). *JAMA, 289,* 3095–3105.

Kessler, R. C., McGonagle, K. A., Zhao, S., Nelson, C. B., Hughes, M., Eshleman, S., … Kendler, K. S. (1994). Lifetime and 12-month prevalence of DSM-III-R psychiatric disorders among persons aged 15–54 in the United States: Results from the national comorbidity survey. *Archives of General Psychiatry, 51*(1), 8–19.

Kessler, R. C., Nelson, C. B., McGonagle, K. A., Liu, J., Swartz, M., & Blazer, D. G. (1996). Comorbidity of DSM-III-R major depressive disorder in the general population: Results from the US national comorbidity survey. *British Journal of Psychiatry, 168*(Suppl. 30), 17–30.

Kessler, R. C., Sonnega, A., Bromet, E., Hughes, M., & Nelson, C. B. (1995). Posttraumatic stress disorder in the national comorbidity survey. *Archives of General Psychiatry, 52,* 1048–1060.

Kessler, R. C., & Wang, P. S. (2009). Epidemiology of depression. In I. H. Gotlib & C. L. Hammen (Eds.), *Handbook of depression* (2nd ed., pp. 5–22). New York: Guilford Press.

Kety, S. S. (1990). Genetic factors in suicide: Family, twin, and adoption studies. In S. J. Blumenthal & D. J. Kupfer (Eds.), *Suicide over the life cycle: Risk factors, assessment and treatment of suicidal patients* (pp. 127–133). Washington, DC: American Psychiatric Press.

Keys, A., Brozek, J., Henschel, A., Michelson, O., & Taylor, H. L. (1950). *The biology of human starvation* (Vol. 1). Minneapolis: University of Minnesota Press.

Khachaturian, Z. S. (2007). Alzheimer's 101. *Alzheimer's and Dementia, 3,* 1–2.

Khantzian, E. J., Gawin, F., Kleber, H. D., & Riordan, C. E. (1984). Methyl-phenidate (Ritalin) treatment of cocaine dependence: A preliminary report. *Journal of Substance Abuse Treatment, 1,* 107–112.

Khemlani-Patel, S. (2001). Cognitive and behaviour therapy for body dysmorphic disorder: A comparative investigation. *Dissertation Abstracts International: Section B: The Sciences and Engineering, 62,* 1087.

Khokhar, J., Ferguson, C., Zhu, A., & Tyndale, R. (2010). Pharmacogenetics of drug dependence: Role of gene variations in susceptibility and treatment. *Annual Review of Pharmacology and Toxicology, 50*(1), 39–61.

Kiang, M., Christensen, B. K., Remington, G., & Kapur, S. (2003). Apathy in schizophrenia: Clinical correlates and association with functional outcome. *Schizophrenia Research, 63,* 79–88.

Kiecolt-Glaser, J. K., & Glaser, R. (1987). Chronic stress and immunity in family caregivers of Alzheimer's disease victims. *Psychosomatic Medicine, 49*(5), 523–535.

Kiecolt-Glaser, J. K., & Glaser, R. (1992). Psychoneuroimmunology: Can psychological interventions modulate immunity? [Special issue: Behavioral medicine: An update for the 1990s]. *Journal of Consulting and Clinical Psychology, 60*(4), 569–575.

Kiecolt-Glaser, J. K., Loving, T., Stowell, J., Malarkey, W., Lemeshow, S., & Dickinson, S., & Glaser, R. (2005). Hostile marital interactions, proinflammatory cytokine production, and wound healing. *Archives of General Psychiatry, 62,* 1377–1384.

Kiecolt-Glaser, J. K., & Newton, T. L. (2001). Marriage and health: His and hers. *Psychological Bulletin, 127,* 475–503.

Kiehl, K. A., Smith, A. M., Hare, R. D., Mendrek, A., Forster, B. B., Brink, J., & Liddle, P. F. (2001). Limbic abnormalities in affective processing by criminal psychopaths as revealed by functional magnetic resonance imaging. *Biological Psychiatry, 50,* 677–684.

Kiesler, D. J. (1966). Some myths of psychotherapy research and the search for a paradigm. *Psychological Bulletin, 65,* 110–136.

Kihlstrom, J. F. (1992). Dissociation and dissociations: A commentary on consciousness and cognition. *Consciousness & Cognition, 1,* 47–53.

Kihlstrom, J. F. (1994). One hundred years of hysteria. In S. J. Lynn & J. W. Rhue (Eds.), *Dissociation: Clinical and theoretical perspectives.* New York: Guilford Press.

Kihlstrom, J. F. (1997). Memory, abuse, and science. *American Psychologist, 52,* 994–995.

Kihlstrom, J. F., Barnhardt, T. M., & Tataryn, D. J. (1992). The Psychological unconscious: Found, lost, and regained. *American Psychologist, 47*(6), 788–791.

Kihlstrom, J. F., Glisky, M. L., & Anguilo, M. J. (1994). Dissociative tendencies and dissociative disorders. *Journal of Abnormal Psychology, 103,* 117–124.

Killen, J. D. (1996). Development and evaluation of a school-based eating disorder symptoms prevention program. In L. Smolak, M. P. Levine, & R. Striegel-Moore (Eds.), *The developmental psychopathology of eating disorders: Implications for research, prevention, and treatment* (pp. 313–339). Mahwah, NJ: Erlbaum.

Killen, J. D., Taylor, C. B., Hayward, C., Haydel, F., Wilson, D. M., Hammer, L. D., … Strachowski, D. (1996). Weight concerns influence the development of eating disorders: A four-year prospective study. *Journal of Consulting and Clinical Psychology, 64,* 936–940.

Killen, J. D., Taylor, C. B., Hayward, C., Wilson, D. M., Hammer, L. D., Robinson, T. N., … Varady, A. (1994). Pursuit of thinness and onset of eating disorder symptoms in a community sample of adolescent girls: A three-year prospective analysis. *International Journal of Eating Disorders, 16,* 227–238.

KilPatrick, D. G., Best, C. L., Veronen, L. J., Amick, A. E., VillePonteaux, L. A., & Ruff, G. A. (1985). Mental health correlates of criminal victimization: A random community survey. *Journal of Consulting and Clinical Psychology, 53,* 866–873.

KilPatrick, K., & Lavoie-Tremblay, M. (2006). Shift-work: what health care managers need to know. *Health Care Manager, 25,* 160–166.

Kilzieh, N., & Akiskal, H. S. (1999). Rapid-cycling bipolar disorder: An overview of research and clinical experience. *Psychiatric Clinics of North America, 22*(3), 585–607.

Kim, E. D., & Lip Shultz, L. I. (1997, April 15). Advances in the treatment of organic erectile dysfunction. *Hospital Practice,* 101–120.

Kindon, S. L., Pain, R., & Kesby, M. (Eds.). (2007). *Participatory action research approaches and methods: Connecting people, participation and place.* New York: Routledge.

King, A. C. Taylor, C. B., Albright, C. A., & Haskell, W. L. (1990). The relationship between repressive and defensive coping styles and blood pressure responses in healthy, middle-aged men and women. *Journal of Psychosomatic Research, 34,* 461–471.

King, D. W., King, L. A., Foy, D. W., & Gudanowski, D. M. (1996). Prewar factors in combat related posttraumatic stress disorder: Structural equation modeling with a national sample of female and male Vietnam veterans. *Journal of Consulting and Clinical Psychology, 64,* 520–531.

King, G. R., & Ellinwood, E. H. (1997). Amphetamines and other stimulants. In J. H. Lowinson, P. Ruiz, R. B. Millman, & J. G. Langrod (Eds.), *Substance abuse: A comprehensive textbook* (pp. 207– 223). Baltimore: Williams & Wilkins.

King, N. J. (1993). Simple and social phobias. In T. H. Ollendick & R. J. Prinz (Eds.), *Advances in clinical child psychology* (Vol. 15, pp. 305–341). New York: Plenum Press.

King, P., Devichand, P., & Rockwood, K. (2005). Dementia of acute onset in the Canadian study of health and aging. *International Psychogeriatrics, 17,* 451–459.

King, P., Song, X., Rockwood, K. (2006). Cognitive impairment of acute onset in the consortium to investigate vascular impairment of cognition (CIVIC) study: Occurrences, correlates, and outcomes. *American Journal of Geriatric Psychiatry, 14,* 893–896.

King, S. (2000). Is expressed emotion cause or effect in the mothers of schizophrenic young adults? *Schizophrenia Research, 45,* 65–78.

King, S. A., & Strain, J. J. (1991). *Pain disorders: A proposed classification for DSM-IV.* Paper presented at the 144th annual meeting of the American Psychiatric Association, New Orleans.

Kingdon, D. G., & Turkington, D. (1994). *Cognitive-behavioral therapy of schizophrenia.* New York: Guilford Press.

Kingsley, J. (1998, February 12). Snowboarder Rebagliati wins appeal. *Canadian Press NewsWire.* Retrieved December 1, 2007, from http://Proquest.umi.com/pqdweb?did 391930131&sid11&Fmt3&clientId15814&RQT 309&VNamePQD

Kinsey, A. C., Pomeroy, W. B., & Martin, C. E. (1948). *Sexual behavior in the human male.* Philadelphia: W. B. Saunders.

Kinsey, A. C., Pomeroy, W. B., Martin, C. E., & Gebhard, P. H. (1953). *Sexual behavior in the human female.* Philadelphia: W. B. Saunders.

Kinzie, J. D., Leung, P. K., Boehnlein, J., & Matsunaga, D. (1992). Psychiatric epidemiology of an Indian village: A 19-year replication study. *Journal of Nervous and Mental Disease, 180*(1), 33–39.

Kirch, D. G. (1993). Infection and autoimmunity as etiologic factors in schizophrenia: A review and reappraisal. *Schizophrenia Bulletin, 19,* 355–370.

Kirmayer, L. J. (1991). The place of culture in psychiatric nosology: Taijin kyofusho and DSM-III-R. *Journal of Nervous and Mental Disease, 179,* 19–28.

Kirmayer, L. J. (2001). Cultural variations in the clinical presentation of depression and anxiety: Implications for diagnosis and treatment. *Journal of Clinical Psychiatry, 62*(Suppl. 13), 22–28.

Kirmayer, L. J. (2002). Psychopharmacology in a globalizing world: The use of antidepressants in Japan. *Transcultural Psychiatry, 39*(3), 295–322.

Kirmayer, L. J., Boothroyd, L. J., Tanner, A., Adelson, N., & Robinson, E. (2000). Psychological distress among the Cree of James Bay. *Transcultural Psychiatry, 37,* 35–56.

Kirmayer, L. J., & Groleau, D. (2001). Affective disorders in cultural context. *Psychiatric Clinics of North America, 24,* 465–478.

Kirmayer, L. J., Groleau, D., LooPer, K. J., & Dao, M. D. (2004). Explaining medically unexplained symptoms. *Canadian Journal of Psychiatry, 49,* 663–672.

Kirmayer, L. J., & Jarvis, G. E. (2006). Depression across cultures. In D. J. Stein, D. J. Kupfer, & A. F. Schatzberg (Eds.), *The American Psychiatric Publishing textbook of mood disorders* (pp. 699–715). Washington, DC: American Psychiatric Publishing, Inc.

Kirmayer, L. J., LooPer, K. J., & Taillefer, S. (2003). Somatoform disorders. In M. Hersen & S. M. Turner (Eds.), *Adult psychopathology and diagnosis* (4th ed. pp. 420–475). New York: John Wiley & Sons.

Kirmayer, L. J., Malus, M., & Boothroyd, L. J. (1996). Suicide attempts among Inuit youth: A community survey of prevalence and risk factors. *Acta Psychiatrica Scandinavia, 94,* 8–17.

Kirmayer, L. J., & Robbins, J. M. (1991). Three forms of somatization in primary care: Prevalence, co-occurrence, and sociodemographic characteristics. *Journal of Nervous and Mental Disease, 179,* 647–655.

Kirmayer, L. J., Robbins, J. M., & Paris, J. (1994). Somatoform disorders: personality and the social matrix of somatic distress. *Journal of Abnormal Psychology, 103,* 125–136.

Kirmayer, L. J., Simpson, C., & Cargo, M (2003). Healing traditions: Culture, community and mental health promotion with Canadian Aboriginal peoples. *Australasian Psychiatry, 11*(Suppl. 1), S15–S23.

Kirmayer, L. J., & Weiss, M. (1993). On cultural considerations for somatoform disorders in the DSM-IV. *In cultural proposals and supporting papers for DSM-IV.* Submitted to the DSM-IV Task Force by the Steering Committee, NIMH—Sponsored Group on Culture and Diagnosis.

Kirov, G., & Owen, M. J. (2009). Genetics of schizophrenia. In B. J. Sadock, V. A. Sadock, & P. Ruiz (Eds.), *Kaplan & Sadock's comprehensive textbook of psychiatry* (Vol. I, 9th ed., pp. 1462–1475). Philadelphia: Lippincott Williams & Wilkins.

Kirschenbaum, B., Nedergaard, M., Preuss, A., Barami, K., Fraser, R. A., & Goldman, S. A. (1994). In vitro neuronal production and differentiation by precursor cells derived from the adult human forebrain. *Cerebral Cortex, 4,* 576–589.

Kjernisted, K. D., Enns, M. W., & Lander, M. (2002). An open-label clinical trial of nefazodone in hypochondriasis. *Psychosomatics: Journal of Consultation Liaison Psychiatry, 43,* 290–294.

Kleber, H. D. (1999). Opioid: Detoxification. In M. Galanter & H. D. Kleber (Eds.), *Textbook of substance abuse treatment* (2nd ed., pp. 251–279). Washington, DC: American Psychiatric Press.

Klein, D. F. (1999). Harmful dysfunction, disorder, disease, illness, and evolution. *Journal of Abnormal Psychology, 108,* 421–429.

Klein, D. N. (2010). Chronic depression: Diagnosis and classification. *Current Directions in Psychological Science, 19*(2), 96–100.

Klein, D. N., Lewinsohn, P., Rohde, P., Seeley, J., & Durbin, C. E. (2002). Clinical features of major depressive disorder in adolescents and their relatives: Impact on familial aggregation, implications for phenotype definition, and specificity of transmission. *Journal of Abnormal Psychology, 111,* 98–106.

Klein, D. N., Lewinsohn, P. M., & Seeley, J. R. (1997). Psychosocial characteristics of adolescents with a past history of dysthymic disorder: Comparison with adolescents with past histories of major depressive and non-affective disorders, and never mentally ill controls. *Journal of Affective Disorders, 42,* 127–135.

Klein, D. N., Schwartz, J. E., Rose, S., & Leader, J. B. (2000). Five-year course and outcome of dysthymic disorder: A prospective, naturalistic follow-up study. *American Journal of Psychiatry, 157*(6), 931–939.

Klein, D. N., Shankman, S., & Rose, S. (2006). Ten-year prospective follow-up study of the naturalistic course of dysthymic disorder and double depression. *American Journal of Psychiatry, 163,* 872–880.

Klein, D. N., Taylor, E. B., Dickstein, S., & Harding, K. (1988). The early-late onset distinction in DSM-III-R dysthymia. *Journal of Affective Disorders, 14*(1), 25–33.

Kleinknecht, R. A., Dinnel, D. L., Kleinknecht, E. E., Hiruma, N., & Harada, N. (1997). Cultural factors in social anxiety: A comparison of social phobia symptoms and taijin kyofusho. *Journal of Anxiety Disorders, 11,* 157–177.

Kleinman, A. (1986). *Social origins of distress and disease: Depression neurasthenia, and pain in modern China.* New Haven, CT: Yale University Press.

Klerman, G. L. (1988). Depression and related disorders of mood (affective disorders). In A. M. Nicholi, Jr. (Ed.), *The new Harvard guide to psychiatry.* Cambridge, MA: Harvard University Press.

Klerman, G. L., & Weissman, M. M. (1989). Increasing rates of depression. *JAMA, 261,* 2229–2235

Klerman, G. L., Weissman, M. M., Rounsaville, B. J., & Chevron, E. S. (1984). *Interpersonal psychotherapy of depression.* New York: Basic Books.

Klimas, N., Koneru, A. O., & Fletcher, M. A. (2008). Overview of HIV. *Psychosomatic Medicine, 70,* 523–530.

Klosko, J. S., Barlow, D. H., Tassinari, R., & Cerny, J. A. (1990). A comparison of alprazolam and behavior therapy in treatment of panic disorder. *Journal of Consulting and Clinical Psychology, 58,* 77–84.

Kluft, R. (1995). Current controversies surrounding dissociative identity disorder. In L. Cohen, J. Berzoff, & M. Elin (Eds.), *Dissociative identity disorder* (p. 351). Northvale, NJ: Jason Aronson, Inc.

Kluft, R. P. (1984). Treatment of multiple personality disorder. *Psychiatric Clinics of North America, 7,* 9–29.

Kluft, R. P. (1991). Multiple Personality disorder. In A. Tasman & S. W. Goldinger (Eds.), *Review of psychiatry* (Vol. 10). Washington, DC: American Psychiatric Press.

Kluft, R. P. (1996). Treating the traumatic memories of patients with dissociative identity disorder. *American Journal of Psychiatry, 153,* 103–110.

Kluft, R. P. (1999). Current issues in dissociative identity disorder. *Journal of Practical Psychology and Behavioral Health, 5,* 3–19.

Klump, K. L., Kaye, W. H., & Strober, M. (2001). The evolving genetic foundations of eating disorders. *The Psychiatric Clinics of North America, 24,* 215–225.

Knight, L. J., & Boland, F. J. (1989). Restrained eating: An experimental disentanglement of the disturbing variables of perceived calories and food type. *Journal of Abnormal Psychology, 98,* 412–420.

Knight, R. A., & Prentky, R. A. (1990). Classifying sexual offenders: The development and corroboration of taxonomic models. In W. L. Marshall, D. R. Laws, & H. E. Barbaree (Eds.), *Handbook of sexual assault: Issues, theories and treatment of the offender* (pp. 23–52). New York: Plenum Press.

Knoll, B., Lassman, B., & Temesgen, Z. (2007). Current status of HIV infection: A review for non-HIV-treating physicians. *International Journal of Dermatology, 46,* 1219–1228.

Knowles, J. (2010). Cognitive stimulation therapy: Why it deserves better awareness and availability. *Journal of Care Services Management, 4*(2), 188–194.

Ko, H.-C., Lee, L.-R., Chang, F.-M., Lu, R. B., & Huang, K.-E. (1996). Comorbidity of premenstrual depression and postpartum blues among Chinese women. *Biological Psychiatry, 39,* 648.

Kobau, R., DiIorio, C., Chapman, D., & Delvecchio, P. (2010). Attitudes about mental illness and its treatment: Validation of a generic scale for public health surveillance of mental illness associated stigma. *Community Mental Health Journal, 46*(2), 164–176.

Koegel, L. K. (1995). Communication and language intervention. In R. L. Koegel and L. K. Koegel (Eds.), *Teaching children with autism: Strategies for initiating positive interactions and improving learning opportunities* (pp. 17–32). Baltimore: Paul H. Brookes.

Koegel, R. L., Schreibman, L., O'Neill, R. E., & Burke, J. C. (1983). The personality and family interaction characteristics of parents of autistic children. *Journal of Consulting and Clinical Psychology, 51,* 683–692.

Koen, L., Niehaus, D., Muller, J., & Laurent, C. (2008). Use of traditional treatment methods in a Xhosa schizophrenia population. *South African Medical Journal, 93*(6), 443.

Koh, P. O., Bergson, C., Undie, A. S., Godlman-Rakic, P. S., & Lidow, M. S. (2003). UP-regulation of the D1 dopamine receptor-interacting protein, calcyon, in patients with schizophrenia. *Archives of General Psychiatry, 60,* 311–319.

Kohn, M. L. (1968). Social class and schizophrenia: A critical review. In D. Rosenthal & S. S. Kety (Eds.), *The transmission of schizophrenia.* Elmsford, NY: Pergamon.

Kohut, H. (1971). *The analysis of self.* New York: International Universities Press.

Kohut, H. (1977). *The restoration of the self.* New York: International Universities Press.

Kokko, K., Tremblay, R. E., Lacourse, E., Nagin, D. S., & Vitaro, F. (2006). Trajectories of prosocial behavior and physical aggression in middle childhood: Links to adolescent school dropout and physical violence. *Journal of Research on Adolescence, 16*(3), 403–428.

Kolb, B., Gibb, R., & Gorny, G. (2003). Experience-dependent changes in dendritic arbor and spine density in neocortex vary qualitatively with age and sex. *Neurobiology of Learning & Memory, 79,* 1–10.

Kolb, B., Gibb, R., & Robinson, T. E. (2003). Brain plasticity and behavior. *Current Directions in Psychological Science, 12,* 1–5.

Kolb, B., & Whishaw, I. Q. (1998). Brain plasticity and behavior. *Annual Review of Psychology, 49,* 43–64.

Kolb, B., & Whishaw, I. Q. (2003). *Fundamentals of human neuropsychology* (5th ed.). New York: Worth/Freeman.

Koning, C., & Magill-Evans, J. (2001). Social and language skills in adolescent boys with Asperger syndrome. *Autism, 5,* 23–36.

Koocher, G. P. (1996). Pediatric oncology: Medical crisis intervention. In R. J. Resnick & R. H. Rozensky (Eds.), *Health psychology through the lifespan: Practice and research opportunities* (pp. 213–225). Washington, DC: American Psychological Association.

Kopala, L., Smith, G., Malla, A., Williams, R., Love, L., Talling, D., & Balshaw, R. (2006). Resource utilization in a Canadian national study of people with schizophrenia and related psychotic disorders. *Acta Psychiatrica Scandinavica, 113*(430), 29–39.

Kopala, L. C., Good, K. P., Milliken, H., Buiteman, C., Woodley, H., Rui, Q., … Honer, W. G. (2006). Treatment of a first episode of psychotic illness with quetiapine: An analysis of 2 year outcomes. *Schizophrenia Research, 81*(1), 29–39.

Kopyov, O. V., Jacques, D., Lieberman, A., Duma, C. M., & Rogers, R. L. (1996). Clinical study of fetal mesencephalic intracerebral transplants for the treatment of Parkinson's disease. *Cell Transplantation, 5,* 327–337.

Korczyn, A. D., Kahana, E., & Galper, Y. (1991). Epidemiology of dementia in Ashkelon, Israel. *Neuroepidemiology, 10,* 100.

Korenman, S. G., & Barchas, J. D. (1993). *Biological basis of substance abuse.* New York: Oxford University Press.

Korfine, L., & Hooley, J. M. (2000). Directed forgetting of emotional stimuli in borderline personality disorder. *Journal of Abnormal Psychology, 109,* 214–221.

Korol, C. T., & Craig, K. D. (2001). Pain from the perspectives of health psychology and culture. In S. S. Kazarian & D. R. Evans (Eds.), *Handbook of cultural health psychology* (pp. 241–265). San Diego, CA: Academic Press.

Kotsaftis, A., & Neale, J. M. (1993). Schizotypal personality disorder I: The clinical syndrome. *Clinical Psychology Review, 13,* 451–472.

Koukoui, S. D., & Chaudhuri, A. (2007). Neuroanatomical, molecular genetic, and behavioral correlates of fragile X syndrome. *Brain Research Reviews, 53,* 27–38.

Kovacs, M., Akiskal, H. S., Gatsonis, C., & Parrone, P. L. (1994). Childhood-onset dysthymic disorder. *Archives of General Psychiatry, 51,* 365–374.

Kovacs, M., Gatsonis, C., Paulauskas, S. L., & Richards, C. (1989). Depressive disorders in childhood: IV. A longitudinal study of comorbidity with and risk for anxiety disorders. *Archives of General Psychiatry, 46*(9), 776–782.

Kovacs, M., Goldston, D., & Gatsonis, C. (1993). Suicidal behaviors and childhood-onset depressive disorders: A longitudinal investigation. *Journal of the American Academy of Child and Adolescent Psychiatry, 32,* 8–20.

Kovacs, M., Rush, A. J., Beck, A. T., & Hollon, S. D. (1981). Depressed outpatients treated with cognitive therapy or Pharmacotherapy: A one-year follow-up. *Archives of General Psychiatry, 38*(1), 33–39.

Kozak, J. M., Leibowitz, M. R., & Foa, E. B. (2000). Cognitive behavior therapy for obsessive-compulsive disorder: The NIMH sponsored collaborative study. In W. K. Goodman & M. V. Rudorfer (Eds.), *Obsessive-compulsive disorder: Contemporary issues in treatment. Personality and clinical psychology series* (pp. 501–530). Mahwah, NJ: Erlbaum.

Kraepelin, E. (1898). *The diagnosis and prognosis of dementia praecox.* Paper presented at the 29th Congress of Southwestern German Psychiatry, Heidelberg.

Kraepelin, E. (1899). *Kompendium der Psychiatrie* (6th ed.). Leipzig: Abel.

Kraepelin, E. (1913). *Psychiatry: A textbook.* Leipzig: Barth.

Krambeer, L. L., von McKnelly, W., Jr., Gabrielli, W. F., Jr., & Penick, E. C. (2001). Methadone therapy for opioid dependence. *American Family Physician, 15,* 2404–2410.

Krank, M., & Wall, A.-M. (2006). Context and retrieval effects on implicit cognition for substance use. In R. W. Wiers & A. W. Stacy (Eds.), *Handbook on implicit cognition and addiction* (pp. 281–292). Thousand Oaks, CA: Sage.

Krank, M., Wall, A. M., Stewart, S. H., Wiers, R., & Goldman, M. S. (2005). Context effects on alcohol cognitions . *Alcoholism: Clinical and Experimental Research, 29,* 196–206.

Krantz, D. S., & Deckel, A. W. (1983). Coping with coronary heart disease and stroke. In T. G. Burish & L. A. Bradley (Eds.), *Coping with chronic disease: Research and applications.* New York: Academic Press.

Kranzler, H. R. (2000). Medications for alcohol dependence: New vistas. *JAMA, 284*(8), 1016–1017.

Kripke, D. F. (1998). Light treatment for nonseasonal depression: Speed, efficiency, and combined treatment. *Journal of Affective Disorder, 49,* 109–117.

Krishnan, K. R., Doraiswamy, P. M., Venkataraman, S., Reed, D., & Richie, J. C. (1991). Current concepts in hypothalamo-pituitary-adrenal axis regulation. In J. A. McCubbin, P. G. Kaufmann, & C. B. Nemeroff (Eds.), *Stress, neuropeptides, and systemic disease* (pp. 19–35). San Diego, CA: Academic Press.

Kristiansen, C. M., Gareau, C., Mittlehold, J., DeCourville, N. H., & Hovdestad, W. E. (1999). The sociopolitical context of the delayed memory debate. In L. M. Williams & V. L. Banyard (Eds.), *Trauma and recovery* (pp. 331–347). Thousand Oaks, CA: Sage.

Kroenke, K. (2007). Efficacy of treatment for somatoform disorders: A review of randomized controlled trials. *Psychosomatic Medicine, 69*(9), 881–888.

Krueger, R. B. (2010). The DSM diagnostic criteria for sexual sadism. *Archives of Sexual Behavior, 39,* 325–345.

Krueger, R. F., Caspi, A., Moffitt, T. E., Silva, P. A., & McGee, R. (1996). Personality traits are differentially linked to mental disorders: A multitrait-multidiagnosis study of an adolescent birth cohort. *Journal of Abnormal Psychology, 105,* 299–312.

Krueger, R. F., Markon, K. E., Patrick, C. J., & Iacono, W. G. (2005). Externalizing psychopathology in adulthood: A dimensional-spectrum conceptualization and its implications for DSM-V. *Journal of Abnormal Psychology, 114*(4), 537–550.

Krueger, R. F., Watson, D., & Barlow, D. H. (2005). Introduction to the special section: Toward a dimensionally based taxonomy of psychopathology [Special issue]. *Journal of Abnormal Psychology, 114,* 491–493.

Krug, E. G., Kresnow, M. J., Peddicord, J. P., Dahlberg, L. L., Powell, K. E., Crosby, A. E., & Annest, J. L. (1998). Suicide after natural disasters. *New England Journal of Medicine, 338*(6), 373–378.

Kruger, S., & Kennedy, S. H. (2000). Psychopharmacotherapy of anorexia nervosa, bulimia nervosa and binge-eating disorder. *Journal of Psychiatry and Neuroscience, 25,* 497–508.

Kryger, M. H. (2000). Management of obstructive sleep apnea-hypoapnea syndrome: Overview. In M. H. Kryger, T. Roth, & W. C. Dement (Eds.), *Principles and practice of sleep medicine* (3rd ed., pp. 940–954). Philadelphia: W. B. Saunders.

Kuban, M., Barbaree, H. E., & Blanchard, R. (1999). A comparison of volume and circumference phallometry: Response magnitude and method agreement. *Archives of Sexual Behavior, 28,* 345–359.

Kuiper, B., & Cohen-Kettenis, P. (1988). Sex reassignment surgery: A study of 141 Dutch transsexuals. *Archives of Sexual Behaviour, 17,* 439–457.

Kuo, M., Adlaf, E. M., Lee, H., Gliksman, L., Demers, A., & Wechsler, H. (2002). More Canadian students drink but American students drink more: Comparing college alcohol use in two countries. *Addiction, 97,* 1583–1592.

Kuo, M. Adlaf, E. M., Lee, H., Gliksman, L., Demers, A., & Wechsler, H. (2003). More Canadian students drink but American students drink more: comparing college alcohol use in two countries: Corrigendum. *Addiction, 98,* 373.

Kupfer, D. J. (1995). Sleep research in depressive illness: Clinical implications—A tasting menu. *Biological Psychiatry, 38,* 391–403.

Kupfer, D. J., First, M. B., & Regier, D. A. (Eds.). (2002). *A research agenda for DSM-V.* Washington, DC: American Psychiatric Association.

Kurihara, T., Kato, M., Reverger, R., & Gusti Rai Tirta, I. (2006). Beliefs about causes of schizophrenia among family members: A community-based survey in Bali. *Psychiatric Services, 57,* 1795–1799.

Kurita, H., Kita, M., & Miyake, Y. (1992). A comparative study of development and symptoms among disintegrative psychosis and infantile autism with and without speech loss. *Journal of Autism and Developmental Disorders, 22,* 175–188.

Kushner, M. G., Abrams, K., & Borchardt, C. (2000). The relationship between anxiety disorders and alcohol use disorders: A review of major perspectives and findings. *Clinical Psychology Review, 20,* 149–171.

Kushner, M. G., Sher, K. J., & Beitman, B. D. (1990). The relation between alcohol problems and the anxiety disorders. *American Journal of Psychiatry, 147,* 685–695.

Kwok, T., Lee, J., Lam, L., & Woo, J. (2008). Vitamin B12 supplementation did not improve cognition but reduced delirium in demented patients with vitamin B12 deficiency. *Archives of Gerontology and Geriatrics, 46*(3), 273–282.

La Rue, A. (1992). *Aging and neuropsychological assessment.* New York: Plenum Press.

Lacey, J. H. (1992). The treatment demand for bulimia: A catchment area report of referral rates and demography. *Psychiatric Bulletin, 16,* 203–205.

Lack, L. C., Gradisar, M., Van Someren, E. J. W., Wright, H. R., & Lushington, K. (2008). The relationship between insomnia and body temperatures. *Sleep Medicine Reviews, 12*(4), 307–317.

Lacks, P., & Morin, C. M. (1992). Recent advances in the assessment and treatment of insomnia. *Journal of Consulting and Clinical Psychology, 60,* 586–594.

Ladd, C. O., Huot, R. L., Thrivikraman, K. V., Nemeroff, C. B., Meaney, M. J., & Plotsky, P. M. (2000). Long-term behavioral and neuroendocrine adaptations to adverse early experience. In E. A. Mayer & C. B. Saper (Eds.), *Progress in brain research: The biological basis for mind body interactions* (Vol. 122, pp. 81–103). Amsterdam: Elsevier.

Ladd, C. O., Owens, M. J., & Nemeroff, C. B. (1996). Persistent changes in corticotropin-releasing factor neuronal systems induced by maternal deprivation. *Endocrinology, 137*(4), 1212–1218.

Ladee, G. A. (1966). *Hypochondriacal syndromes.* New York: Elsevier.

Lader, M., & Sartorius, N. (1968). Anxiety in Patients with hysterical conversion symptoms. *Journal of Neurology, Neurosurgery, and Psychiatry, 31,* 490–495.

Lader, M. H. (1975). *The psychophysiology of mental illness.* London: Routledge & Kegan Paul.

Lader, M. H., & Wing, L. (1964). Habituation of the psycho-galvanic reflex in patients with anxiety states and in normal subjects. *Journal of Neurology, Neurosurgery, and Psychiatry, 27,* 210–218.

Ladouceur, R. (1982). In vivo cognitive desensitization of flight phobia: A case study. *Psychological Reports, 50,* 459–462.

Ladouceur, R. (1996). The prevalence of pathological gambling in Canada. *Journal of Gambling Studies, 12,* 129–142.

Ladouceur, R., Dugas, M. J., Freeston, M. H., Rheaume, J., Blais, F., Gagnon, F., & Thibodeau, N. (1999). Specificity of generalized anxiety disorder symptoms and processes. *Behavior Therapy, 30,* 191–207.

Ladouceur, R., Gosselin, P., & Dugas, M. J. (2000). Experimental manipulation of intolerance of uncertainty: A study of a theoretical model of worry. *Behaviour Research and Therapy, 38,* 933–941.

Ladouceur, R., & Lachance, S. (2007). *Overcoming pathological gambling: Therapist guide.* New York: Oxford University Press.

Laing, R. D. (1967). *The politics of experience.* New York: Pantheon.

Lakin, M. M., Montague, D. K., Vanderbrug Medendorp, S., Tesar, L., & Schover, L. R. (1990). Intracavernous injection therapy: Analysis of results and complications. *Journal of Urology, 143,* 1138–1141.

Lalonde, J. K., Hudson, J. I., Gigante, R. A., & Pope, H. G. (2001). Canadian and American psychiatrists' attitudes toward dissociative disorders diagnoses. *Canadian Journal of Psychiatry, 46,* 407–412.

Lalumière, M. L. Blanchard, R., & Zucker, K. J. (2000). Sexual orientation and handedness in men and women: A meta-analysis. *Psychological Bulletin, 126,* 575–592.

Lam, D. H., Watkins, E. R., Hayward, P., Bright, J., Wright, K., Kerr, N., ... Sham, P. (2003). A randomized controlled study of cognitive therapy for relapse prevention for bipolar affective disorder: Outcome of the first year. *Archives of General Psychiatry, 60,* 145–152.

Lam, R. W. (1994). Morning light therapy for winter depression: Predictors of response. *Acta Psychiatrica Scandinavica, 89,* 97–101.

Lam, R. W., & Levitt, A. J. (1999). *Clinical guidelines for the treatment of seasonal affective disorder.* Vancouver, BC: Clinical & Academic Publishing.

Lam, R. W., Tam, E. M., Shiah, I.-S., Yatham, L. N., & Zis, A. P. (2000). Effects of light therapy on suicidal ideation in patients with winter depression. *Journal of Clinical Psychiatry, 61,* 30–32.

Lambert, M. C., Coyle, N., & Lendon, C. (2004). The allelic modulation of apolipoprotein E expression by oestrogen: Potential relevance for Alzheimer's disease. *Journal of Medical Genetics, 41,* 104–112.

Lambert, M. C., Weisz, J. R., Knight, F., Desrosiers, M., Overly, K., & Thesiger, C. (1992). Jamaican and American adult perspectives on child psychopathology: Further explorations of the threshold model. *Journal of Consulting and Clinical Psychology, 60,* 146–149.

Lambert, M. J., Shapiro, D. A., & Bergin, A. E. (1986). The effectiveness of psychotherapy. In S. L. Garfield & A. E. Bergin (Eds.), *Handbook of psychotherapy and behavior change* (3rd ed.). New York: John Wiley & Sons.

Landis, S., & Insel, T. R. (2008, November 7). The "neuro" in neurogenetics. *Science, 322,* 821.

Landis, S. E., Earp, J. L., & Koch, G. G. (1992). Impact of HIV testing and counseling on subsequent sexual behavior. *AIDS Education and Prevention, 4*(1), 61–70.

Lang, P. J. (1985). The cognitive psychophysiology of emotion: Fear and anxiety. In A. H. Tuma & J. D. Maser (Eds.), *Anxiety and the anxiety disorders.* Hillsdale, NJ: Erlbaum.

Lang, P. J. (1995). The emotion probe: Studies of motivation and attention. *American Psychologist, 50,* 372–385.

Lang, P. J., Bradley, M. M., & Cuthbert, B. N. (1998). Emotion, motivation, and anxiety: Brain mechanisms and psychophysiology. *Biological Psychiatry, 44,* 1248–1263.

Langewisch, M. W. J., & Frisch, G. R. (1998). Gambling behavior and pathology in relation to impulsivity, sensation seeking, and risk behavior in male college students. *Journal of Gambling Studies, 14,* 245–262.

Langille, D. (2000). *Adolescent sexual health services and education: Options for Nova Scotia.* [Policy discussion series paper #8]. Halifax, NS: Maritime Centre of Excellence for Women's Health.

Langlois, F., & Ladouceur, R. (2004). Adaptation of a GAD treatment for hypochondriasis. *Cognitive and Behavioral Practice, 11,* 393–404.

Langlois, F., Pelletier, O., Ladouceur, R., & Boucher, O. (2005). Hypocondrie et Anxiété à l'égard de la santé. [Hypochondriasis and health anxiety.] *Revue Francophone de Clinique Comportementale et Cognitive, 10,* 1–10.

Langosch, W., Budde, H.-G, & Linden, W. (2007). Psychological interventions for coronary heart disease: Stress management, relaxation, and Ornish groups. In J. Jordan, B. Bardé, & A. M. Andreas (Eds.), *Contributions toward evidence-based psychocardiology: A systematic review of the literature* (pp. 231–254). Washington, DC: American Psychological Association.

Långström, N., Rahman, Q., Carlström, E., & Lichtenstein, P. (2010). Genetic and environmental effects on same-sex sexual behavior: A population study of twins in Sweden. *Archives of Sexual Behavior, 39,* 75–80.

Långström, N., & Seto, M. C. (2006). Exhibitionistic and voyeuristic behavior in a Swedish national population survey. *Archives of Sexual Behavior, 35,* 427–435.

Langton, C. M., Barbaree, H. E., Harkins, L., & Peacock, E. J. (2006). Sex offenders' response to treatment and its association with recidivism as a function of psychopathy. *Sexual Abuse: Journal of Research and Treatment, 18,* 99–120.

Lanius, R. A., Bluhm, R., Lanius, U., & Pain, C. (2006). A review of neuroimaging studies in PTSD: Heterogeneity of response to symptom provocation. *Journal of Psychiatric Research, 40*(8), 709–729.

LaPierre, Y. D. (1994). Pharmacological therapy of dysthymia. *Acta Psychiatrica Scandinavica Supplemental, 89*(383), 42–48.

LaPorte, L., & Guttman, H. (2001). Abusive relationships in families of women with borderline personality disorder, anorexia nervosa and a control group. *Journal of Nervous and Mental Disease, 189,* 522–531.

Larson, S. A., Lakin, K. C., Anderson, L., Kwak, N., Lee, J. H., & Anderson, D. (2001). Prevalence of mental retardation and developmental disabilities: Estimates from the 1994/1995 National Health Interview Survey Disability Supplements. *American Journal on Mental Retardation, 106,* 231–252.

Laruelle, M., Kegeles, L. S., & Abi-Darham, A. (2003). Glutamate, dopamine, and schizophrenia: From pathophysiology to treatment. *Annals of the New York Academy of Sciences, 1003,* 138–158.

Lasch, C. (1978). *The culture of narcissism: American life in an age of diminishing expectations.* New York: W. W. Norton.

Lau, M. A., & McMain, S. F. (2005). Integrating mindfulness meditation with cognitive and behavioural therapies: The challenge of combining acceptance- and change-based strategies. *The Canadian Journal of Psychiatry, 50,* 863–869.

Lau, M. A., & Segal, Z. V. (2003). Depression in context: Strategies for guided action. *Journal of Cognitive Psychotherapy, 17,* 94–97.

Laub, J. H., &Vaillant, G. E. (2000). Delinquency and mortality: A 50-year follow-up study of 1,000 delinquent and nondelinquent boys. *American Journal of Psychiatry, 157,* 96–102.

Laumann, E., Gagnon, J., Michael, R., & Michaels, S. (1994). *The social organization of sexuality: Sexual practices in the United States.* Chicago: University of Chicago Press.

Laumann, E. O., Paik, A., & Rosen, R. C. (1999). Sexual dysfunction in the United States. Prevalence and predictors. *JAMA, 281,* 537–544.

Lavallee, C., Robinson, E., & Laverdure, J. (1991). Description de la clientèle et des services de santé mentale au sein de la Población crie du nord québécois. *Santé Culture Health, 8*(3), 265–284.

Lavoie, K. L., Fleet, R. P., Laurin, C., Arsenault, A., Miller, S. R., & Bacon, S. L. (2004). Heart rate variability in coronary artery disease patients with and without panic disorder. *Psychiatry Research, 128*(3), 289–299.

Lawrence, A. (2005). Sexuality before and after male-to-female sex reassignment surgery. *Archives of Sexual Behavior, 34,* 147–166.

Laws, D. R. (Ed.). (1989). *Relapse prevention with sex offenders.* New York: Guilford Press.

Laws, D. R., & O'Donohue, W. (Eds.). (1997). *Sexual deviance: Theory, assessment and treatment.* NewYork: Guilford Press.

Laxenaire, M., Ganne-Vevonec, M. O., & Streiff, O. (1982). Les Problèmes d'identité chez les enfants des migrants. *Annales Medico-Psychologiques, 140,* 602–605.

Laxova, R., Ridler, M. A. C., & Bowen-Bravery, M. (1977). An etiological survey of the severely retarded Hertfordshire children who were born between January 1, 1965, and December 31, 1967. *American Journal of Medical Genetics, 1,* 75–86.

Lazarus, R. S. (1968). Emotions and adaptation: Conceptual and empirical relations. In W. J. Arnold (Ed.), *Nebraska Symposium on Motivation* (Vol. 16). Lincoln: University of Nebraska Press.

Lazarus, R. S. (1991). Progress on a cognitive-motivational relational theory of emotion. *American Psychologist, 46*(8), 819–834.

Lazarus, R. S. (1995). Psychological stress in the workplace. In R. Crandall & P. L. Perrewe (Eds.), *Occupational stress: A handbook* (pp. 3–14). Philadelphia: Taylor & Francis.

Leach, L. S., & Christensen, H. (2006). A systematic review of telephone-based interventions for mental disorders. *Journal of Telemedicine and Telecare, 12,* 122–129.

Leamon, M. H., Wright, T. M., & Myrick, H. (2008). Substance-related disorders. In R. E. Hales, S. C. Yudofsky, & G. O. Gabbard (Eds.), *The American Psychiatric Publishing textbook of psychiatry* (5th ed., pp. 365–406). Arlington, VA: American Psychiatric Publishing.

LeBeau, R. T., Glenn, D., Liao, B., Wittchen, H.-U., Beesdo-Baum, K., Ollendick, T., & Craske, M. G. (2010). Specific phobia: A review of DSM-IV specific phobia and preliminary recommendations for DSM-V. *Depression and Anxiety, 27*(2), 148–167.

Lebedinskaya, K. S., & Nikolskaya, O. S. (1993). Brief report: Analysis of autism and its treatment in modern Russian defectology. *Journal of Autism and Developmental Disorders, 23,* 675–697.

Leccese, A. P. (1991). *Drugs and society: Behavioral medicines and abusable drugs.* Englewood Cliffs, NJ: Prentice Hall.

Leckman, J. F., Denys, D., Simpson, H. B., Mataix-Cols, D., Hollander, E., Saxena, S., ... Stein, D. J. (2010). Obsessive-compulsive disorder: A review of the diagnostic criteria and possible subtypes and dimensional specifiers for DSM-V. *Depression and Anxiety, 27*(6), 507–527.

Leckman, J. F., Grice, D. E., Boardman, J., Zhang, H., Vitali, A., Bondi, C., ... Pauls, D. L. (1997a). Symptoms of obsessive-compulsive disorder. *American Journal of Psychiatry, 154,* 911–917.

Leckman, J. F., Peterson, B. S., Anderson, G. M., Arnstein, A. F. T., Pauls, D. L., & Cohen, D. J. (1997b). Pathogenesis of Tourette's syndrome. *Journal of Child Psychology and Psychiatry, 38,* 119–142.

Leckman, J. F., Weissman, M. M., Merikangas, K. R., Pauls, D. L., & Prusoff, B. A. (1983). Panic disorder and major depression. *Archives of General Psychiatry, 40,* 1055–1060.

Leclerc, J., Rahn, M., & Linden, W. (2006). Does personality predict blood pressure over a 10-year period? *Personality and Individual Differences, 40*(6), 1313–1321.

Lecrubier, Y., Bakker, A., Dunbar, G., & Judge, R. (1997). A comparison of paroxetine, clomipramine and placebo in the treatment of panic disorder. *Acta psychiatrica Scandinavica, 95,* 145–152.

Lecrubier, Y., & Judge, R. (1997). Long term evaluation of paroxetine, clomipramine and placebo in panic disorder. *Acta Psychiatrica Scandinavica, 95,* 153–160.

Lederman, J., Petitto, J. M., Golden, R. N., Gaynes, B. N., Gu, H., Perkins, D. O., ... Evans, D. L. (2000). Impact of stressful life events, depression, social support, coping, and cortisol on progression to AIDS. *American Journal of Psychiatry, 157,* 1221–1228.

LeDoux, J. E. (1996). *The emotional brain: The mysterious underpinnings of emotional life.* New York: Simon & Schuster.

LeDoux, J. E. (2002). Synaptic self: *How our brains become who we are.* New York: Penguin Books.

LeDoux, J. E. (2003). The self: Clues from the brain. In J. E. LeDoux, J. Debiec, & H. Moss (Eds.), The self: From soul to brain. *Annals of the New York Academy of Sciences, 1001,* 295–304.

Lee, C. C., Czaja, S. J., & Schulz, R. (2010). The moderating influence of demographic characteristics, social support, and religious coping on the effectiveness of a multicomponent psychosocial caregiver intervention in three racial ethnic groups. *The Journals of Gerontology Series B: Psychological Sciences and Social Sciences, 65B*(2), 185–194.

Lee, C. K. (1992). Alcoholism in Korea. In J. Helzer & G. Canino (Eds.), *Alcoholism—North America, Europe and Asia: A coordinated analysis of population data from ten regions* (pp. 247–262). London: Oxford University Press.

Lee, J. P. (2005). Hearing voices and seeing pictures. *Psychiatric Rehabilitation Journal, 29*(1), 73–76.

Lee, K. (1992). Pattern of night waking and crying of Korean infants from 3 months to 2 years old and its relation with various factors. *Journal of Developmental & Behavioral Pediatrics, 13,* 326–330.

Lee, K. K. (2000). *Urban poverty in Canada: A statistical profile.* Ottawa, ON: Canadian Council on Social Development.

Lee, M. A., & Shlain, B. (1985). *Acid dreams.* New York: Grove Weidenfeld.

Lee, S. (1993). How abnormal is the desire for slimness? A survey of eating attitudes and behavior among Chinese undergraduates in Hong Kong. *Psychological Medicines, 23,* 437–451.

Lee, S., Hsu, L. K. G., & Wing, Y. K. (1992). Bulimia nervosa in Hong Kong Chinese patients. *British Journal of Psychiatry, 161,* 545–551.

Lee, S., Leung, C. M., Wing, Y. K., Chiu, H. F., & Chen, C. N. (1991). Acne as a risk factor for anorexia nervosa in Chinese. *Australian and New Zealand Journal of Psychiatry, 25*(1), 134–137.

Lee, T. M., Chen, E. Y., Chan, C. C., Paterson, J. G., Janzen, H. L., & Blashko, C. A. (1998). Seasonal affective disorder. *Clinical Psychology: Science and Practice, 5,* 275–290.

Lee-Baggley, D., DeLongis, A., Voorhoeave, P., & Greenglass, E. (2004). Coping with the threat of severe acute respiratory syndrome: Role of threat appraisals and coping responses in health behaviors. *Asian Journal of Social Psychology, 7,* 9–23.

Leekam, S. R., Lopez, B., & Moore, C. (2000). Attention and joint attention in preschool children with autism. *Developmental Psychology, 36,* 261–273.

Leekam, S. R., & Moore, C. R. (2001). The development of attention and joint attention in children with autism. In J. A. Burack, T. Charman, N. Yirmiya, & P. R. Zelazo (Eds.), *The development of autism: Perspectives from theory and research.* Mahwah, NJ: Lawrence Erlbaum Associates Publishers.

Leenaars, A. A., & Lester, D. (1996). Gender and the impact of gun control on suicide and homicide. *Archives of Suicide Research, 2,* 223–234.

Leff, J., Sartorius, N., Jablensky, A., Korten, A., & Ernberg, G. (1992). The International Pilot Study of Schizophrenia: Five-year follow-up findings. *Psychological Medicine, 22,* 131–145.

Lefley, H. (2009). *Family psychoeducation in serious mental illness: Models, outcomes, applications.* New York: Oxford University Press.

Lehman, A. F. (1995). Vocational rehabilitation in schizophrenia. *Schizophrenia Bulletin, 21,* 645–656.

Lehmann, H. E., & Ban, T. A. (1997). The history of the psychopharmacology of schizophrenia. *Canadian Journal of Psychiatry, 42,* 152–162.

Lehmann, H. E., & Hanrahan, G. E. (1954). Chlorpromazine: New inhibiting agent for psychomotor excitement and manic states. *AMA Archives of Neurology and Psychiatry, 71,* 227–237.

Leiblum, S. R. (2000). Vaginismus: A most perplexing problem. In S. R. Leiblum & R. C. Rosen (Eds.), *Principles and practice of sex therapy* (3rd ed., pp. 181–202). New York: Guilford Press.

Leiblum, S. R., & Rosen, R. C. (Eds.). (2000). *Principles and practice of sex therapy* (3rd ed.). New York: Guilford Press.

Lejeune, J., Gauthier, M., & Turpin, R. (1959). Étude des chromosomes somatiques de neuf enfants mongoliens. *Comptes Rendus Hebdomadaires des Séances de l'Académie des Sciences. D: Sciences Naturelles* (Paris), *248,* 1721–1722.

Lejoyeux, M., McLoughlin, M., & Ades, J. (2006). Pyromania. In E. Hollander & C. Stein (Eds.), *Clinical manual of impulse-control disorders* (pp. 229–250). Arlington, VA: American Psychiatric Publishing.

Lemay, M., & Landreville, P. (2010). Verbal agitation in dementia: The role of discomfort. *American Journal of Alzheimer's Disease and Other Dementias, 25*(3), 193-201.

Lemoine, P., Harousseau, H., Borteyru, J. P., & Menuet, J. C. (1968). Les enfants de Parents alcooliques: Anomalies observées. À Propos de 127 cas [Children of alcoholic Parents: Anomalies observed in 127 cases]. *Quest Medicine, 21,* 476–482.

Lengacher, C., Johnson-Mallard, V., Post-White, J., Moscoso, M., Jacobsen, P., Klein, T., ... Kip, K. E. (2009). Randomized controlled trial of mindfulness-based stress reduction (MBSR) for survivors of breast cancer. *Psycho-Oncology, 18*(12), 1261–1272.

Lenke, R. R., & Levy, H. (1980). Maternal phenyl-ketonuria and hyperphenylalanemia: An international survey of the outcome of untreated and treated pregnancies. *New England Journal of Med cine, 303,* 1202–1208.

Lenze, E. J., Mulsant, B. H., Shear, K. M., Schulberg, H. C., Dew, M. A., Begley, A. E., ... Reynolds, C. F. (2000). Comorbid anxiety disorders in depressed elderly patients. *American Journal of Psychiatry, 157*(5), 722–728.

Lenzenweger, M. F. A., & Dworkin, R. H. (1996). The dimensions of schizophrenia phenomenology. Note one or two, at least three, perhaps four. *British Journal of Psychiatry, 168,* 432–440.

Lerman, C., Caporaso, N. E., Audrain, J., Main, D., Bowman, E. D., Lockshin, B., ... Shields, P. G. (1999). Evidence suggesting the role of specific genetic factors in cigarette smoking. *Health Psychology, 18*(1), 14–20.

Lesage, A. D., Morissette, R., Fortier, L., Rienharz, D., & Contandriopoulos, A. P. (2000). Downsizing psychiatric hospitals: Needs for care and services of current and discharged long-stay inpatients. *Canadian Journal of Psychiatry, 45,* 526–531.

Lesch, K.-P., Bengel, D., Heils, A., Sabol, S. Z., Greenberg, B. D., Petri, S., ... Murphy, D. L. (1996, November 29). Association of anxiety-related traits with a polymorphism in the serotonin transporter gene regulatory region. *Science, 274,* 1527–1531.

Leserman, J., Petitto, J. M., Golden, R. N., Gaynes, B. N., Gu, H., Perkins, D. O., ... Evans, D. L. (2000). Impact of stressful life events, depression, social support, coping, and cortisol on progression to AIDS. *American Journal of Psychiatry, 157,* 1221–1228.

Lester, D. (1991). Do suicide prevention centres prevent suicide? *Homeostasis in Health and Disease, 33,* 190–194.

Leth-Steensen, C., Elbaz, Z. K., & Douglas, V. I. (2000). Mena response times, variability, and skew in the responding of ADHD children: A response time distributional approach. *Acta Psychologica, 104,* 167–190.

Lett, H., Blumenthal, J., Babyak, M., Strauman, T., Robins, C., & Sherwood, A. (2005). Social support and coronary heart disease: Epidemiologic evidence and implications for treatment. *Psychosomatic Medicine, 67,* 869–878.

Leuchter, A. F., Cook, I. A., Witte, E. A., Morgan, M., & Abrams, M. (2002). Changes in brain function of depressed subjects during treatment with placebo. *American Journal of Psychiatry, 159,* 122–129.

Leung, F., Lam, S., & Sze, S. (2001). Cultural expectations of thinness in Chinese women. *Journal of Treatment and Prevention, 9,* 339–350.

Leung, F., Schwartzman, A., & Steiger, H. (1996). Testing a dual-process family model in understanding the development of eating pathology: A structural equation modeling analysis. *International Journal of Eating Disorders, 20,* 367–375.

Leung, G. M., Yeung, R. Y., Chi, I., & Chu L. W. (2003). The economics of Alzheimer disease. *Dementia & Geriatric Cognitive Disorders, 15,* 34–43.

LeVay, S. (1991). A difference in hypothalamic structure between heterosexual and homosexual men. *Science, 253,* 1034 1037.

Levenston, G. K., Patrick, C. J., Bradley, M. M., & Lang, P. J. (2000). The psychopath as observer: Emotion and attention in picture processing. *Journal of Abnormal Psychology, 109,* 373–385.

Leventhal, A. M., Kahler, C. W., Ray, L. A., & Zimmerman, M. (2009). Refining the depression-nicotine dependence link: Patterns of depressive symptoms in psychiatric outpatients with current, past, and no history of nicotine dependence. *Addictive Behaviors, 34*(3), 297–303.

Levin, A., & Hyler, S. (1986). DSM-III personality diagnosis in bulimia. *Comprehensive Psychiatry, 27,* 47.

Levine, M. N., Guyatt, G. H., Gent, M., DePauw, S., Goodyear, M. D., Hryniuk, W. M., ... Bramwell, V. H. (1988). Quality of life in stage II breast cancer: An instrument for clinical trials. *Journal of Clinical Oncology, 6,* 1798–1810.

Levine, M. P., & Smolak, L. (1996). Media as a context for the development of disordered eating. In L. Smolak, M. P. Levine, & R. Striegel-Moore (Eds.), *The developmental psychopathology of eating disorders: Implications for research, prevention, and treatment* (pp. 235–257). Mahwah, NJ: Erlbaum.

Levinson, D. F. (2009). Genetics of major depression. In I. H. Gotlib & C. L. Hammen (Eds.), *Handbook of depression* (2nd ed., pp. 165–186). New York: Guilford Press.

Levinson, D. F., Mahtami, M. M., Nancarrow, D. J., Brown, D., Kruglyak, L., Kirby, A., ... Mowry, B. J. (1998). Genome scan of schizophrenia. *American Journal of Psychiatry, 155*(6), 741–750.

Levitan, R. D., Parikh, S. V., Lesage, A. D., Hegadoren, K. M., Adams, M., Kennedy, S. H., & Goering, P. N. (1998). Major depression in individuals with a history of childhood physical or sexual abuse: Relationship to neurovegetative features, mania, and gender. *American Journal of Psychiatry, 155,* 1746–1752.

Levitan, R. D., Rector, N. A., Sheldon, T., & Goering, P. (2003). Childhood adversities associated with major depression and/or anxiety disorders in a community sample of Ontario: Issues of comorbidity and specificity. *Depression and Anxiety, 17,* 34–42.

Levitsky, A., & Perls, F. S. (1970). The rules and games of Gestalt therapy. In J. Fagan & I. L. Shepherd (Eds.), *Gestalt therapy now: Theory, techniques, applications.* Palo Alto, CA: Science & Behavior Books.

Levitt, A. J., Boyle, M. H., Joffe, R. T., & Baumal, Z. (2000). Estimated prevalence of the seasonal subtype of major depression in a Canadian community sample. *Canadian Journal of Psychiatry, 45,* 650–654.

Levitt, A. J., Joffe, R. T., Moul, D. F., Lam, R. W., Teicher, M. H., Lebegue, B., ... Buchanan, A. (1993). Side effects of light therapy in seasonal affective disorder. *American Journal of Psychiatry, 150,* 650–652.

Levitt, A. J., Lam, R. W., & Levitan, R. (2002). A comparison of open treatment of seasonal major and minor depression with light therapy. *Journal of Affective Disorders, 71,* 243–248.

Levy, B. R., Slade, M. D., Kunkel, S. R., & Kasl, S. V. (2002). Longevity increased by positive self-perceptions of aging. *Journal of Personality & Social Psychology, 83,* 261–270.

Lévy, E., Margolese, H. C., Annable, L., Chouinard, G. (2004). Diabetes, tardive dyskinesia, Parkinsonism, and akathisia in schizophrenia: A retrospective study applying 1998 diabetes health care guidelines to antipsychotic use. *The Canadian Journal of Psychiatry, 49*(6), 398–402.

Lewinsohn, P. M., Allen, N. B., Seeley, J. R., Gotlib, I. H. (1999). First onset versus recurrence of depression: Differential processes of psychosocial risk. *Journal of Abnormal Psychology, 108*(3), 483–489.

Lewinsohn, P. M., & Gotlib, I. H. (1995). Behavioral therapy and treatment of depression. In E. E. Beckham & W. R. Leber (Eds.), *Handbook of depression* (pp. 352–375). New York: Guilford Press.

Lewinsohn, P. M., Gotlib, I. H., & Seeley, J. R. (1997). Depression-related psychosocial variables: Are they specific to depression in adolescents? *Journal of Abnormal Psychology, 106*(3), 365–375.

Lewinsohn, P. M., Hops, H., Roberts, R. E., Seeley, J. R., & Andrews, J. A. (1993). Adolescent Psychopathology: I. Prevalence and incidence of depression and other DSM-III-R disorders in high school students. *Journal of Abnormal Psychology, 102*(1), 133–144.

Lewinsohn, P. M., Rohde, P., & Seeley, J. R. (1993). Psychosocial characteristics of adolescents with a history of suicide attempt. *Journal of the American Academy of Child and Adolescent Psychiatry, 32*(1), 60–68.

Lewinsohn, P. M., Rohde, P., Seeley, J. R., & Fischer, S. A. (1993). Age-cohort changes in the lifetime occurrence of depression and other mental disorders. *Journal of Abnormal Psychology, 102*(1), 110–120.

Lewinsohn, P. M., Rohde, P., Seeley, J. R., Klein, D. N., & Gotlib, I. H. (2000). Natural course of adolescent major depressive disorder on community sample: Predictors of recurrence in young adults. *American Journal of Psychiatry, 157*(10), 1584–1591.

Lewinsohn, P. M., Rohde, P., Seeley, J. R., Klein, D. N., & Gotlib, I. H. (2003). Psychosocial functioning of young adults who have experienced and recovered from major depressive disorder during adolescence. *Journal of Abnormal Psychology, 112,* 353–363.

Lewinsohn, P. M., Rohde, P., Seeley, J. R., Klein, D. N., & Gotlib, I. H. (2006). The consequences of adolescent major depressive disorder on young adults. In T. E. Joiner, J. S. Brown, & J. Kistner (Eds.), *The interpersonal, cognitive, and social nature of depression* (pp. 43–68). Mahwah, NJ: Lawrence Erlbaum Associates Publishers.

Lewis, D. O., Yeager, C. A., Swica, Y., Pincus, J. H., & Lewis, M. (1997). Objective documentation of child abuse and dissociation in 12 murderers with dissociative identity disorder. *American Journal of Psychiatry, 154,* 1703–1710.

Lewis, G., Croft-Jeffreys, C., & Anthony, D. (1990). Are British psychiatrists racist? *British Journal of Psychiatry, 157,* 410–415.

Lewis, G., David, A., Andreasson, S., & Allsbeck, P. (1992). Schizophrenia and city life. *Lancet, 340,* 137–140.

Lewis, G., Hawton, K., & Jones, P. (1997). Strategies for preventing suicide. *British Journal of Psychiatry, 171,* 351–354.

Lewy, A. J. (1993). Seasonal mood disorders. In D. L. Dunner (Ed.), *Current psychiatric therapy* (pp. 220–225). Philadelphia: W. B. Saunders.

Lewy, A. J., Bauer, V. K., Cutler, N. L., Ahmed, S., Thomas, K. H., Blood, M. L., & Jackson, J. M. (1998). Morning vs evening light treatment of patients with winter depression. *Archives of General Psychiatry, 55,* 890–896.

Lewy, A. J., Kern, H. E., Rosenthal, N. E., & Wehr, T. A. (1982). Bright artificial light treatment of a manic-depressive patient with a seasonal mood cycle. *American Journal of Psychiatry, 139,* 1496–1498.

Lewy, A. J., & Sack, R. L. (1987). Light therapy of chronobiological disorders. In A. Halaris (Ed.), *Chronobiology an psychiatric disorders* (pp. 181– 206). New York: Elsevier.

Leykin, Y., & DeRubeis, R. J. (2009). Allegiance in psychotherapy outcome research: Separating association from bias. *Clinical Psychology: Science and Practice, 16*(1), 54–65.

Li, H. Z., & Browne, A. J. (2000). Defining mental illness and accessing mental health services: Perspectives of Asian Canadians. *Canadian Journal of Community Mental Health, 19,* 143–159.

Liberman, R. P., DeRisi, W. D., & Mueser, K. T. (1989). *Social skills training for psychiatric patients.* Boston: Allyn & Bacon.

Lidbeck, J. (1997). Group therapy for somatization disorders in general practice: Effectiveness of a short cognitive-behavioral treatment model. *Acta Psychiatrica Scandinavica, 96,* 14–24.

Liddle, P. F. (2000). Schizophrenic syndromes. In M. S. Lidow (Ed.), *Neurotransmitter receptors in actions of antipsychotic medications* (pp. 1–15). Boca Raton, FL: CRC Press.

Lieb, R., Wittchen, H.-U., Hofler, M., Fuetsch, M., Stein, M. B., & Merikangas, K. R. (2000). Parental psychopathology, parenting styles, and the risk of social phobia in offspring. *Archives of General Psychiatry, 57,* 859–866.

Lieb, R., Zimmermann, P., Friis, R. H., Hofler, M., Tholen, S., & Wittchen, H. U. (2002). The natural course of DSM-IV somatoform disorders and syndromes among adolescents and young adults: A prospective-longitudinal community study. *European Psychiatry, 17,* 321–331.

Lieberman, J. A., Jody, D., Alvir, J. M. J., Ashtari, M., Levy, D. L., Bogerts, B., ... Cooper, T. (1993). Brain morphology, dopamine, and eye-tracking abnormalities in first-episode schizophrenia. *Archives of General Psychiatry, 50,* 357–368.

Liebeskind, J. (1991). Pain can kill. *Pain, 44,* 3–4.

Liebowitz, M. R., Heimberg, R. G., Schneier, F. R., Hope, D. A., Davies, S., Holt, C. S., ... Klein, D. F. (1999). Cognitive-behavioral group therapy versus phenelzine in social phobia: Long-term outcome. *Depression and Anxiety, 10,* 89–98.

Liebowitz, M. R., Salman, E., Jusino, C. M., Garfinkel, R., Street, L., Cardenas, D. L., ... Davies, S. (1994). Ataque de nervios and panic disorder. *American Journal of Psychiatry, 151,* 871–875.

Liebowitz, M. R., Schneier, F., Campeas, R., Hollander, E., Hatterer, J., Fyer, A., ... Gully, R. (1992). Phenelzine vs. atenolol in social phobia: A placebo controlled comparison. *Archives of General Psychiatry, 49,* 290–300.

Liggett, J. (1974). *The human face.* New York: Stein and Day.

Lilienfeld, S. O. (1992). The association between antisocial personality and somatization disorders: A review and integration of theoretical models. *Clinical Psychology Review, 12,* 641–662.

Lilienfeld, S. O., & Hess, T. H. (2001). Psychopathic personality traits and somatization: Sex differences and the mediating role of negative emotionality. *Journal of Psychopathology and Behavioral Assessment, 23,* 11–24.

Lilienfeld, S. O., Kirsch, I., Sarbin, T. R., Lynn, S. J., Chaves, J. F., & Ganaway, G. K. (1999). Dissociative identity disorder and the sociocognitive model: Recalling the lessons of the past. *Psychological Bulletin, 125*(5), 507–523.

Lilienfeld, S. O., & Marino, L. (1995). Mental disorder as a Roschian concept: A critique of Wakefield's "harmful dysfunction" analysis. *Journal of Abnormal Psychology, 104,* 411–420.

Lilienfeld, S. O., & Marino, L. (1999). Essentialism revisited: Evolutionary theory and the concept of mental disorder. *Journal of Abnormal Psychology, 108,* 400–411.

Lilienfeld, S. O., VanValkenburg, C., Larntz, K., & Akiskal, H. S. (1986). The relationship of histrionic personality to antisocial personality and somatization disorders. *American Journal of Psychiatry, 143,* 718–722.

Lin, K. M. (1986). Psychopathology and social disruption in refugees. In C. L. Williams & J. Westermeyer (Eds.), *Refugee mental health in resettlement countries* (pp. 61–73). Washington, DC: Hemisphere.

Lin, N., & Ensel, W. M. (1984). Depression-mobility and its social etiology: The role of life events and social support. *Journal of Health and Social Behavior, 25*(2), 176–188.

Lindblad, F., & Hjern, A. (2010). ADHD after fetal exposure to maternal smoking. *Nicotine & Tobacco Research, 12*(4), 408–415.

Linden, W., Gerin, W., & Davidson, K. (2003). Cardiovascular reactivity: Status quo and a research agenda for the new millennium. *Psychosomatic Medicine, 65,* 5–8.

Linden, W., & Moseley, J. V. (2006). The efficacy of behavioral treatments for hypertension. *Applied Psychophysiology and Biofeedback, 31*(1), 51–63.

Lindenmayer, J. P., & Khan, A. (2006). Psychopathology. In J. A. Lieberman, T. S. Stroup, & D. O. Perkins (Eds.), *The American Psychiatric Publishing textbook of schizophrenia* (pp. 187–221). Washington, DC: American Psychiatric Publishing.

Lindquist, P., & Allebeck, P. (1990). Schizophrenia and crime: A longitudinal followup of 644 schizophrenics in Stockholm. *British Journal of Psychiatry, 157,* 345–350.

Lindsay, J., Sykes, E., McDowell, I., Verreault, R., & Laurin, D. (2004). More than the epidemiology of Alzheimer's disease: Contributions of the Canadian study of health and aging. *Canadian Journal of Psychiatry, 49,* 83–91.

Lindsay, P. S. (1977). Fitness to stand trial in Canada: An overview in light of the recommendations of the law reform commission of Canada. *Criminal Law Quarterly, 19,* 303–348.

Lindsey, S. (2007, July 20). Oxycontin maker and executives fined $634. 5M for misleading public. *The Cape Breton Post.* Retrieved December 1, 2007, from http://www.capebretonpost.com/index .cfm?pid1875&cpcatbusiness&stry31849023

Linehan, M. M. (1987). Dialectical behavior therapy for borderline personality disorder: Theory and method. *Bulletin of the Menninger Clinic, 51,* 261–276.

Linehan, M. M. (1993). *Cognitive behavioral treatment of borderline personality disorder.* NewYork: Guilford Press.

Linehan, M. M., Armstrong, , H. E., Suarez, A., Allmon, D., & Heard, H. L. (1991). Cognitive-behavioral treatment of chronically parasuicidal borderline patients. *Archives of General Psychiatry, 48,* 1060–1064.

Linehan, M. M., & Dexter-Mazza, E. T. (2008). Dialectical behavior therapy for borderline personality disorder. In D. H. Barlow (Ed.), *Clinical handbook of psychological disorders* (4th ed., pp. 365–420). New York: Guilford Press.

Linehan, M. M., Heard, H. L., & Armstrong, H. E. (1992). *Naturalistic follow-up of a behavioral treatment for chronically parasuicidal borderline patients.* Unpublished manuscript, University of Washington, Seattle.

Linehan, M. M., & Kehrer, C. A. (1993). Borderline personality disorder. In D. H. Barlow (Ed.), *Clinical handbook of psychological disorders: A step by step treatment manual.* New York: Guilford Press.

Lines, E. (2001). *Early Psychosis Intervention.* Retrieved January 7, 2008, from http://www. cmha.ca/english/intrvenLinks

Links, P., Steiner, M., & Huxley, G. (1988). The occurrence of borderline personality disorder in families of borderline patients. *Journal of Personality Disorders, 2,* 14–20.

Links, P. S., Heslegrave, R, & van Reekum, R. (1998). Prospective follow-up study of borderline personality disorder: Prognosis, prediction outcome, and axis II comorbidity. *Canadian Journal of Psychiatry, 43,* 265–270.

Links, P. S., Heslegrave, R., & van Reekum, R. (1999). Impulsivity: Core aspect of borderline personality disorder. *Journal of Personality Disorders, 13,* 1–9.

Links, P. S., Steiner, M., Boiago, I., & Irwin, D. (1990). Lithium therapy for borderline patients: Preliminary findings. *Journal of Personality Disorders, 4,* 173–181.

Links, P. S., & Stockwell, M. (2001). Is couple therapy indicated for borderline personality disorder? *American Journal of Psychotherapy, 55,* 491–506.

Links, P. S., & van Reekum, R. (1993). Childhood sexual abuse, parental impairment and the development of borderline personality disorder. *Canadian Journal of Psychiatry, 38,* 472–474.

Linnet, K. M., Dalsgaard, S., Obel, C., Wisborg, K., Henriksen, T. B., Rodriguez, A., ... Jarvelin, M. R. (2003). Maternal lifestyle factors in pregnancy risk of attention deficit hyperactivity disorder and associated behaviors: Review of the current evidence. *American Journal of Psychiatry, 160,* 1028–1040.

Litz, B. T., Gray, M. J., Bryant, R. A., & Adler, A. B. (2002). Early intervention for trauma: Current status and future directions. *Clinical Psychology: Science & Practice, 9,* 112–134.

Lipowski, Z. J. (1990). *Delirium: Acute confusional states.* New York: Oxford University Press.

Lipton, A. M., & Weiner, M. F. (2003). Differential diagnosis. In M. F. Weiner & A. M. Lipton (Eds.), *The dementias: Diagnosis, treatment and research* (3rd ed., pp. 137–180). Washington, DC: American Psychiatric Press.

Lisspers, J., & Öst, L. (1990). Long-term followup of migraine treatment: Do the effects remain up to six years? *Behaviour Research and Therapy, 28,* 313–322.

Liu, D., Diorio, J., Day, J. C., Francis, D. D., & Meaney, M. J. (2000). Maternal care, hippocampal synaptogenesis and cognitive development in rats. *Nature Neuroscience, 3*(8), 799–806.

Livesley, W. J. (2006). The dimensional assessment of personality pathology (DAPP) approach to personality disorder. In Strack, S. (Ed.), *Differentiating normal and abnormal personality* (2nd ed., pp. 401–429). New York: Springer Publishing Co.

Livesley, W. J. (2007). A framework for integrating dimensional and categorical classifications of personality disorder. *Journal of Personality Disorders, 21,* 199–224.

Livesley, W. J., & Jang, K. L. (2000). Toward an empirically based classification of personality disorder. *Journal of Personality Disorders, 14,* 137–151.

Livesley, W. J., & Jang, K. L. (2008). The behavioral genetics of personality disorder. *Annual Review of Clinical Psychology, 4,* 247–274.

Livesley, W. J., Jang, K. L., & Thordarson, D. S. (2005). Etiological relationships between eating disorder symptoms and dimensions of personality disorder [Special issue: Personality Disorders & Eating Disorders]. *Eating Disorders: The Journal of Treatment & Prevention, 13*(1), 23–35.

Livesley, W. J., Jang, K. L., & Vernon, P. A. (1998). Phenotypic and genotypic structure of traits delineating personality disorder. *Archives of General Psychiatry, 55,* 941–948.

Livesley, W. J., Schroeder, M. L., Jackson, D. N., & Jang, K. L. (1994). Categorical distinctions in the study of personality disorder: Implications for classification. *Journal of Abnormal Psychology, 103,* 6–17.

Livingston, J. D., Wilson, D., Tien, G., & Bond, L. (2003). A follow-up study of persons found not criminally responsible on account of mental disorder in British Columbia. *Canadian Journal of Psychiatry, 48,* 408–415.

Loeb, K. L., Wilson, G. T., Gilbert, J. S., & Labouvie, E. (2000). Guided and unguided self-help for binge eating. *Behaviour Research and Therapy, 38*(3), 259–272.

Loebel, J. P., Dager, S. R., & Kitchell, M. A. (1993). Alzheimer's disease. In D. L. Dunner (Ed.), *Current psychiatric therapy* (pp. 59–65). Philadelphia: W. B. Saunders.

Loehlin, J. C. (1992). *Genes and environment in personality development*. Newbury Park, CA: Sage.

Loewenstein, R. J. (1991). Psychogenic amnesia and psychogenic fugue: A comprehensive review. In A. Tasman & S. M. Goldfinger (Eds.), *American Psychiatric Press review of psychiatry* (Vol. 10, pp. 189–222). Washington, DC: American Psychiatric Association.

Loftus, E. F., Coan, J. A., & Pickrell, J. E. (1996). Manufacturing false memories using bits of reality. In L. Reder (Ed.), *Implicit memory and metacognition* (pp. 195–220). Mahwah, NJ: Erlbaum.

Logan, C. (2009). Sexual deviance in females: Psychopathology and theory. In D. R. Laws & W. T. O'Donohue (Eds.), *Sexual deviance: Theory, assessment, and treatment* (2nd ed., pp. 486–507). New York: Guilford Press.

Logsdon, R., McCurry, S., Pike, K., & Teri, L. (2009). Making physical activity accessible to older adults with memory loss: A feasibility study. *The Gerontologist, 49*(S1), S94.

Lombardo, M. V., Chakrabarti, B., & Baron-Cohen, S. (2009). The amygdala in autism: not adapting to faces? *American Journal of Psychiatry, 166*(4), 395–397.

Lonczak, H. S. P., Abbott, R. D. P., Hawkins, J. D. P., Kosterman, R. P., & Catalano, R. F. P. (2002). Effects of the Seattle Social Development Project on sexual behavior, pregnancy, birth, and sexually transmitted disease outcomes by age 21 years. *Archives of Pediatrics & Adolescent Medicine, 156*(5), 438–447.

Long, J. C., Knowler, W. C., Hanson, R. L., Robin, R. W., Urbanek, M., Moore, E., ... Goldman, D. (1998). Evidence for genetic linkage to alcohol dependence on chromosomes 4 and 11 from an autosome-wide scan in an American Indian population. *American Journal of Medicine and Genetics, 81,* 216–221.

Loo, C., Mitchell, P., Sachdev, P., McDarmont, B., Parker, G., & Gandevia, S. (1999). Double-blind controlled investigation of transcranial magnetic stimulation for the treatment of resistant major depression. *American Journal of Psychiatry, 156*(6), 946–948.

Looman, J., & Marshall, W. L. (2001). Phallometric assessments designed to detect arousal to children: The responses of rapists and child molesters. *Sexual Abuse: Journal of Research & Treatment, 13,* 3–13.

Looper, K. J., & Kirmayer, L. J. (2002). Behavioral medicine approaches to somatoform disorders. *Journal of Consulting and Clinical Psychology, 70,* 810–827.

Looper, K. J., & Paris, J. (2000). What dimensions underlie Cluster B personality disorders? *Comprehensive Psychiatry, 41,* 432–437.

LoPiccolo, J., Heiman, J. R., Hogan, D. R., & Roberts, C. W. (1985). Effectiveness of single therapists versus cotherapy teams in sex therapy. *Journal of Consulting and Clinical Psychology, 53*(3), 287–294.

LoPiccolo, J., & Stock, W. E. (1987). Sexual function, dysfunction and counseling in gynecological practice. In Z. Rosenwaks, F. Benjamin, & M. L. Stone (Eds.), *Gynecology*. New York: Macmillan.

Lovaas, O. I. (1977). *The autistic child: Language development through behavior modification.* New York: Irvington.

Lovaas, O. I. (1987). Behavioral treatment and normal educational and intellectual functioning in young autistic children. *Journal of Consulting and Clinical Psychology, 55,* 3–9.

Lovaas, O. I., Berberich, J. P., Perloff, B. F., & Schaeffer, B. (1966). Acquisition of imitative speech by schizophrenic children. *Science, 151,* 705–707.

Lovett, M. W., Lacerenza, L., Borden, S. L., Frijters, J. C., Steinbach, K. A., & De Palma, M. (2000). Components of effective remediation for developmental reading disabilities: Combining phonological and strategy-based instruction to improve outcomes. *Journal of Educational Psychology, 92,* 263–283.

Loza, W., & Hanna, S. (2006). Is schizoid personality a forerunner of homicidal or suicidal behavior? A case study. *International Journal of Offender Therapy and Comparative Criminology, 50,* 338–343.

Lubit, R. H. (2009). Ethics in psychiatry. In B. J. Sadock, V. A. Sadock, & P. Ruiz (Eds.), *Kaplan & Sadock's comprehensive textbook of psychiatry* (Vol. II, 9th ed., pp. 4439–4448). Philadelphia: Lippincott Williams & Wilkins.

Lucas, A. R., Beard, C. M., O'Fallon, W. M., & Kurlan, L. T. (1991). 50-year trends in the incidence of anorexia nervosa in Rochester, Minn. : A population-based study. *American Journal of Psychiatry, 148,* 917–922.

Luckasson, R., Coulter, D. L., Polloway, E. A., Reiss, S., Schalock, R. L., Snell, M. E., ... Stark, J. (1992). *Mental retardation: Definition, classification, and systems of supports* (9th ed.). Washington, DC: American Association on Mental Retardation.

Ludescher, B., Leitlein, G., Schaefer, J. E., Vanhoeffen, S., Baar, S., Machann, J., ... Eschweiler, G. W. (2009). Changes of body composition in bulimia nervosa: Increased visceral fat and adrenal gland size. *Psychosomatic Medicine, 71*(1), 93–97.

Ludwig, A., Brandsma, J., Wilbur, C., Bendfeldt, F., & Jameson, D. (1972). The objective study of a multiple personality. *Archives of General Psychiatry, 26,* 298–310.

Ludwig, A. M. (1985). Cognitive processes associated with "spontaneous" recovery from alcoholism. *Journal of Studies on Alcohol, 46,* 53–58.

Lundh, L.-G., & Öst, L.-G. (1996). Recognition bias for critical faces in social phobics. *Behaviour Research and Therapy, 34,* 787–794.

Lundstrom, B., Pauly, I., & Walinder, J. (1984). Outcome of sex reassignment surgery. *Acta Psychiatrica Scandinavica, 70,* 289–294.

Lurigio, A., & Harris, A. (2009). Mental illness, violence, and risk assessment: An evidence-based review. *Victims & Offenders, 4*(4), 341–347

Lussier, P., & Piché, L. (2008). Frotteurism: Psychopathology and theory. In D. R. Laws & W. T. O'Donohue (Eds.), *Sexual deviance: Theory, assessment, and treatment* (2nd ed., pp. 131–149). New York: Guilford Press.

Lutgendorf, S. K., Antoni, M. H., Ironson, G., Klimas, N., Kumar, M., Starr, K., ... Schneiderman, N. (1997). Cognitive-behavioral stress management decreases dysphoric mood and herpes simplex virus-type 2 antibody titers in symptomatic HIV-seropositive gay men. *Journal of Consulting and Clinical Psychology, 65,* 31–43.

Lyden, J. (2002, February 27). *Genetic screening and Alzheimer's*. Retrieved May 21, 2004, from http:// www.npr.org/features/feature.php?wfId 1138834

Lydiard, R. B., Brawman-Mintzer, O., & Ballenger, J. C. (1996). Recent developments in the psychopharmacology of anxiety disorders. *Journal of Consulting & Clinical Psychology, 64,* 660–668.

Lyketos, C. G. (2009). Dementia and milder cognitive syndromes. In D. G. Blazer & D. C. Steffens (Eds.), *The American Psychiatric Publishing textbook of geriatric psychiatry* (4th ed., pp. 243–260). Arlington, VA: American Psychiatric Publishing.

Lyketsos, C. G., Steinberg, M., Tschanz, J. T., Norton, M. C., Steffens, D. C., & Breitner, J. C. S. (2000). Mental and behavioral disturbances in dementia: Findings from the Cache County study on memory and aging. *American Journal of Psychiatry, 157,* 708–714.

Lykken, D. T. (1957). A study of anxiety in the sociopathic personality. *Journal of Abnormal and Social Psychology, 55,* 6–10.

Lykken, D. T. (1982). Fearlessness: Its carefree charms and deadly risks. *Psychology Today, 16,* 20–28.

Lynch, S. K., Turkheimer, E., D'Onofrio, B. M., Mendle, J., Emery, R. E., Slutske, W. S., & Martin, N. G. (2006). A genetically informed study of the association between harsh punishment and offspring behavioral problems. *Journal of Family Psychology, 20,* 190–198.

Lynam, D. R. (1996). Early identification of chronic offenders: Who is a fledgling psychopath? *Psychological Bulletin, 120,* 209–234.

Lyon, D. R., Hart, S. D., & Webster, C. D. (2001). Violence and risk assessment. In R. A. Schuller & J. R. P. Ogloff (Eds.), *Introduction to psychology and law: Canadian perspectives* (pp. 314–350). Toronto, ON: University of Toronto Press.

Lyons, M. J., Eisen, S. A., Goldberg, J., True, W., Lin, N., Meyer, J. M., ... Tsuang, M. T. (1998). A registry-based twin study of depression in men. *Archives of General Psychiatry, 55,* 468–472.

Lyons, M. J., York, T. P., Franz, C. E., Grant, M. D., Eaves, L. J., Jacobson, K. C., ... Kremen, W. S. (2009). Genes determine stability and the environment determines change in cognitive ability during 35 years of adulthood. *Psychological Science, 20*(9), 1146–1152.

Lyubomirsky, S. (2001). Why are some people happier than others? The role of cognitive and motivational processes in well-being. *American Psychologist, 56,* 239–249.

Maas, J. W., Bowden, C. L., Miller, A. L., Javors, M. A., Funderburg, L. G., Berman, N., & Weintraub, S. T. (1997). Schizophrenia, psychosis, and cerebral spinal fluid homovanillic acid concentrations. *Schizophrenia Bulletin, 23,* 147–154.

Macciocchi, S. N., & Barth, J. T. (1996). The Halstead-Reitan Neuropsychological Test Battery (HRNTB). In C. S. Newmark (Ed.), *Major psychological assessment instruments* (pp. 431–459). Boston: Allyn & Bacon.

MacDonald, A. B., Baker, J. M., Stewart, S. H., & Skinner, M. (2000). Effects of alcohol on the response to hyperventilation of participants high and low in anxiety sensitivity. *Alcoholism: Clinical and Experimental research, 24,* 1656–1665.

MacDonald, A. B., Stewart, S. H., Hutson, R., Rhyno, E., & Loughlin, H. L. (2001). The roles of alcohol and alcohol expectancy in the dampening of responses to hyperventilation among high anxiety sensitive young adults. *Addictive Behaviors, 26,* 841–867.

Macdonald, P. T., Waldorf, D., Reinarman, C., & Murphy, S. (1988). Heavy cocaine use and sexual behavior. *Journal of Drug Issues, 18,* 437–455.

MacDonald, T. K., Fong, G. T., Zanna, M. P., & Martineau, A. M. (2000). Alcohol myopia and condom use: Can alcohol intoxication be associated with more prudent behavior? *Journal of Personality & Social Psychology, 78,* 605–619.

MacDonald, T. K., MacDonald, G., Zanna, M. P., & Fong, G. (2000). Alcohol, sexual arousal, and intentions to use condoms in young men: Applying alcohol myopia theory to risky sexual behavior. *Health Psychology, 19,* 290–298.

MacDonald, T. K., Zanna, M. P., & Fong, G. T. (1996). Why common sense goes out the window: Effects of alcohol on intentions to use condoms. *Personality & Social Psychology Bulletin, 22,* 763–775.

MacDonald, T. K., Zanna, M. P., & Fong, G. T. (1998). Alcohol and intentions to engage in risky health-related behaviors: Experimental evidence for a causal relationship. In J. G. Adair & D. Belanger (Eds.), *Advances in psychological science* (Vol. 1, pp. 407–428). Hove, UK: Psychology Press/Erlbaum.

MacDougall, J. M., Dembroski, T. M., Dimsdale, J. E., & Hackett, T. P. (1985). Components of Type A, hostility, and anger-in: Further relationships to angiographic findings. *Health Psychology, 4*(2), 137–152.

Mace, C. J. (1992). Hysterical conversion II: A critique. *British Journal of Psychiatry, 161,* 378–389.

MacFarlane, B. A. (1997). *People who stalk people.* Retrieved November 5, 2003, from http://canadiancriminallaw.com/PDF/PEOPLE%20WHO%20STALK%20PEOPLE.pdf.

MacGregor, M. W., Davidson, K. W., Rowan, P., Barksdale, C., & MacLean, D. (2003). The use of defenses and physician health care costs: Are physician health care costs lower in persons with more adaptive defense profiles? *Psychotherapy & Psychosomatics, 72,* 315–323.

Mack, A. H., Franklin, J. E., & Frances, R. J. (2003). Substance use disorders. In R. E. Hales & S. C. Yudofsky (Eds.), *Textbook of clinical psychiatry* (4th ed., pp. 309–377). Washington, DC: American Psychiatric Publishing.

MacLeod, C., Mathews, A., & Tata, P. (1986). Attentional bias in emotional disorders. *Journal of Abnormal Psychology, 95,* 15–20.

MacLeod, C., & Mathews, A. M. (1991). Cognitive-experimental approaches to the emotional disorders. In P. R. Martin (Ed.), *Handbook of behavior therapy and psychological science: An integrative approach* (pp. 116–150). Elmsford, NY: Pergamon Press.

MacMartin, C., & Yarmey, A. D. (1999). Rhetoric and the recovered memory debate. *Canadian Psychology, 40,* 343–358.

MacMillan, H. L., Fleming, J. E., Streiner, D. L., Lin, E., Boyle, M. H., Jamieson, E., ... Beardslee, W. R. (2001). Childhood abuse and lifetime psychopathology in a community sample. *American Journal of Psychiatry, 158,* 1878–1883.

MacPherson, P. S. R., Stewart, S. H., & McWilliams, L. A. (2001). Parental problem drinking and anxiety disorder symptoms in adult offspring: Examining the mediating role of anxiety sensitivity. *Addictive Behaviors, 26,* 917–934.

Madsen, K. M., Hviid, A., Vestergaard, M., Schendel, D., Wohlfahrt, J., Thorsen, P., ... Melbye, M. (2002). A population-based study of measles, mumps, and rubella vaccination and autism. *New England Journal of Medicine, 347,* 1477–1482.

Magee, W. J., Eaton, W. W., Wittchen, H. U., McGonagle, K. A., & Kessler, R. C. (1996). Agoraphobia, simple phobia, and social phobia in the National Comorbidity Survey. *Archives of General Psychiatry, 53,* 159–168.

Magne-Ingvar, U., Ojehagen, A., & Traskman-Bendz, L. (1992). The social network of people who attempt suicide. *Acta Psychiatrica Scandinavica, 86,* 153–158.

Magnusson, A., & Axelsson, J. (1993). The prevalence of seasonal affective disorder is low among descendants of Icelandic emigrants in Canada. *Archives of General Psychiatry, 50,* 947–951.

Maher, B. A., & Maher, W. B. (1985a). Psychopathology: I. From ancient times to the eighteenth century. In G. A. Kimble & K. Schlesinger (Eds.), *Topics in the history of psychology* (pp. 251–294). Hillsdale, NJ: Erlbaum.

Maher, B. A., & Maher, W. B. (1985b). Psychopathology: II. From the eighteenth century to modern times. In G. A. Kimble & K. Schlesinger (Eds.), *Topics in the history of psychology* (pp. 295–329). Hillsdale, NJ: Erlbaum.

Maher, J. J. (1997). Exploring alcohol's effects on liver function. *Alcohol Health & Research World, 21,* 5–12.

Mahler, M. S. (1952). On childhood psychosis and schizophrenia: Autistic and symbiotic infantile psychosis. *Psychoanalytic Study of the Child, 7,* 286–305.

Mahoney, D. F., Purtilo, R. B., Webbe, F. M., Alwan, M., Bharucha, A. J., Adlam, T. D., ... Becker, S. A. (2007). In-home monitoring of persons with dementia: Ethical guidelines for technology research and development. *Alzheimer's & Dementia, 3*(3), 217–226.

Mahowald, M. W., & Schenck, C. H. (2000). Violent parasomnias: Forensic medical issues. In M. H. Kryger, T. Roth, & W. C. Dement (Eds.), *Principles and practice of sleep medicine* (3rd ed., pp. 786–795). Philadelphia: W. B. Saunders.

Mahr, G., & Leith, W. (1992). Psychogenic stuttering of adult onset. *Journal of Speech and Hearing Research, 35,* 283–286.

Mahr, J. (2003, December 13). *Trouble revisits local psychologist as counselor admits affair; state cities ethics breaches.* Retrieved May 21, 2004, from http://www.talkaboutsupport.com/group/alt.support.eatingdisord/messages/237228.html

Maier, S. F. (1997, September). *Stressor controllability, anxiety, and serotonin.* Paper presented at the National Institute of Mental Health Workshop on Cognition and Anxiety, Rockville, MD.

Mailloux, D. L., Forth, A. E., & Kroner, D. G. (1997). Psychopathy and substance use in adolescent male offenders. *Psychological Reports, 81,* 529–530.

Makarchuk, K., Hodgins, D. C., & Peden, N. (2002). Development of a brief intervention for concerned significant others of problem gamblers. *Addictive Disorders & Their Treatment, 1*(4), 126–134.

Malatesta, V. J., & Adams, H. E. (1984). The sexual dysfunctions. In H. E. Adams & P. B. Sutker (Eds.), *Comprehensive handbook of psychopathology* (pp. 725–775). New York: Plenum Press.

Malchy, B., Enns, M. W., Young, T. K., & Cox, B. J. (1997). Suicide among Manitoba's aboriginal people, 1988 to 1994. *Canadian Medical Association Journal, 156,* 1133–1138.

Maldonado, J. R., Butler, L. D., & Spiegel, D. (1998). Treatments for dissociative disorders. In P. E. Nathan & J. M. Gorman (Eds.), *A guide to treatments that work.* New York: Oxford University Press.

Maletzky, B. M. (1991). *Treating the sexual offender.* Newbury Park, CA: Sage.

Maletzky, B. M. (1998). The paraphilias: Research and treatment. In P. E. Nathan & J. M. Gorman (Eds.), *A guide to treatments that work* (pp. 472–500). New York: Oxford University Press.

Malhotra, S., & Gupta, N. (1999). Childhood disintegrative disorder. *Journal of Autism and Developmental Disorders, 29,* 491–498.

Malla, A. K., Norman, R. M. G., Scholten, D. J., Zirul, S., & Kotteda, V. (2001). A comparison of long-term outcome in first-episode schizophrenia following treatment with risperidone or a typical antipsychotic. *Journal of Clinical Psychiatry, 62,* 179–184.

Malla, A. K., Takhar, J. J., Norman, R. M. G., Manchanda, R., Cortese, L., Haricharan, R., ... Ahmed, R. (2002). Negative symptoms in first episode non-affective psychosis. *Acta Psychiatrica Scandinavica, 105*(6), 431–439.

Malpass, R. S., & Poortinga, Y. H. (1986). Strategies for design and analysis. In W. J. Lonner & J. W. Berry (Eds.), *Field methods in cross-cultural research* (pp. 47–83). Beverly Hills, CA: Sage.

Mancuso, S., Knoesen, N., & Castle, D.J. (in press). Delusional vs. nondelusional body dysmorphic disorder. *Comprehensive Psychiatry.*

Mandalos, G. E., & Szarek, B. L. (1990). Dose-related paranoid reaction associated with fluoxetine. *Journal of Nervous and Mental Disease, 178*(1), 57–58.

Mandel, M. (2007, October 21). A man who killed his 11-year-old son because of a mental disorder shares his pain—and his insight. *The Toronto Sun.* Retrieved October 22, 2007, from http://www.torontosun.com/News/Columnists/Mandel_Michele/2007/10/21/4593856-sun.php

Mandell, A. J., & Knapp, S. (1979). Asymmetry and mood, emergent properties of seratonin regulation: A proposed mechanism of action of lithium. *Archives of General Psychiatry, 36*(8), 909–916.

Mann, J., Apter, A., Bertolote, J., Beautrais, A., Currier, D., Haas, A., ... Hendin, H. (2005). Suicide prevention strategies: A systematic review. *JAMA, 294,* 2064–2074.

Mann, J. J., Brent, D. A., & Arango, V. (2001). The neurobiology and genetics of suicide and attempted suicide: a focus on the serotonergic system. *Neuropsychopharmacology, 24*(5), 467–477.

Mann, J. J., Malone, K. M., Diehl, D. J., Perel, J., Cooper, T. B., & Mintun, M. A. (1996). Demonstration in vivo of reduced serotonin responsivity in the brain of untreated depressed patients. *American Journal of Psychiatry, 153,* 174–182.

Mann, J. J., Waternaux, C., Haas, G. L., & Malone, K. M. (1999). Toward a clinical model of suicidal behavior in psychiatric patients. *American Journal of Psychiatry, 156*(2), 181–189.

Mann, K., Klingler, T., Noe, S., Röschke, J., Müller, S., & Benkert, O. (1996). Effects of yohimbine on sexual experiences and nocturnal penile tumescence and rigidity in erectile dysfunction. *Archives of Sexual Behavior, 25,* 1–16.

Manni, R., Ratti, M. T., & Tartara, A. (1997). Nocturnal eating: Prevalence and features in 120 insomniac referrals. *Sleep, 20,* 734–738.

Mannino, D. M., Klevens, R. M., & Flanders, W. D. (1994). Cigarette smoking: An independent risk factor for impotence? *American Journal of Epidemiology, 140,* 1003–1008.

Manson, S. M., & Good, B. J. (1993, January). Cultural considerations in the diagnosis of DSM-IV mood disorders. *Cultural proposals and supporting papers for DSM-IV.* Submitted to the DSM-IV Task Force by the Steering Committee, NIMH-Sponsored Group on Culture and Diagnosis.

Marangell, L., Rush, A., George, M., Sackheim, H., Johnson, C, Husain, M., … Lisanby, S. H. (2002). Vagus nerve stimulation (VNS) for major depressive episodes: One year outcomes. *Biological Psychiatry, 51,* 280–287.

Marcopulos, B. A., & Graves, R. E. (1990). Antidepressant effect on memory in depressed older persons. *Journal of Clinical and Experimental Neuropsychology, 12*(5), 655–663.

Marcus, M. D., Wing, R. R., Ewing, L., Keern, E., Gooding, W., & McDermott, M. (1990). Psychiatric disorders among obese binge eaters. *International Journal of Eating Disorders, 9,* 69–77.

Marcus, M. D., Wing, R. R., & Hopkins, J. (1988). Obese binge eaters: Affect, cognitions, and response to behavioral weight control. *Journal of Consulting and Clinical Psychology, 3,* 433–439.

Margo, A., Hemsley, D. R., & Slade, P. D. (1981). The effects of varying auditory input on schizophrenic hallucinations. *British Journal of Psychiatry, 139,* 122–127.

Margolese, H. C., Chouinard, G., Kolivakis, T. T., Beauclair, L., Miller, R., & Annable, L. (2005). Tardive dyskinesia in the era of typical and atypical antipsychotics. Part 2: Incidence and management strategies in patients with schizophrenia. *The Canadian Journal of Psychiatry/La Revue canadienne de psychiatrie, 50*(11), 703–713.

Mariani, M. A., & Barkley, R. A. (1997). Neuropsychological and academic functioning in preschool boys with attention deficit hyperactivity disorder. *Developmental Neuropsychology, 13,* 111–129.

Marks, I. M. (1969). *Fears and phobias.* New York: Academic.

Marks, I. M. (1985). Behavioural treatment of social phobia. *Psychopharmacology Bulletin, 21,* 615–618.

Marks, I. M. (1988). Blood-injury phobia: A review. *American Journal of Psychiatry, 145,* 1207–1213.

Marlatt, G. A. (1985). Relapse prevention: Theoretical rationale and overview of the model. In G. A. Marlatt & J. R. Gordon (Eds.), *Relapse prevention: Maintenance strategies in the treatment of addictive behaviors* (pp. 3–70). New York: Guilford Press.

Marlatt, G. A. (Ed.). (1998). *Harm reduction: Pragmatic strategies for managing high-risk behaviors.* New York: Guilford Press.

Marlatt, G. A., & Gordon, J. R. (1985). *Relapse prevention: Maintenance strategies in the treatment of addictive behaviors.* New York: Guilford Press.

Marlatt, G. A., Larimer, M. E., Baer, J. S., & Quigley, L. A. (1993). Harm reduction for alcohol problems: Moving beyond the controlled drinking controversy. *Behavior Therapy, 24,* 461–504.

Marmot, M. G., & Syme, S. L. (1976). Acculturation and coronary heart disease in Japanese Americans. *American Journal of Epidemiology, 104,* 225–247.

Marsden, C. D. (1986). Hysteria—A neurologist's view. *Psychological Medicine, 16,* 277–288.

Marsh, L., & Margolis, R. L. (2009). Neuropsychiatric aspects of movement disorders. In B. J. Sadock, V. A. Sadock, & P. Ruiz (Eds.), *Kaplan & Sadock's comprehensive textbook of psychiatry* (Vol. I, 9th ed., pp. 481–503). Philadelphia: Lippincott Williams & Wilkins.

Marshall, W. L. (1997). Pedophilia: Psychopathology and theory. In D. R. Laws & W. O'Donohue (Eds.), *Sexual deviance: Theory, assessment and treatment* (pp. 152–174). New York: Guilford Press.

Marshall, W. L. (1999). Current status of North American assessment and treatment programs for sexual offenders. *Journal of Interpersonal Violence, 14,* 221–239.

Marshall, W. L., Barbaree, H. E., & Christophe, D. (1986). Sexual offenders against female children: Sexual preferences for age of victims and type of behavior. *Canadian Journal of Behavioral Science, 18,* 424–439.

Marshall, W. L., Hamilton, K., & Fernandez, Y. (2001). Empathy deficits and cognitive distortions in child molesters. *Sexual Abuse: Journal of Research & Treatment, 13,* 123–130.

Marshall, W. L., & Hucker, S. J. (2006). Severe sexual sadism: Its features and treatment. In R. D. McAnulty & M. M. Burnette (Eds.), *Sex and sexuality, Vol 3: Sexual deviation and sexual offenses* (pp. 227–250). Westport, CT: Praeger Publishers/Greenwood Publishing Group.

Marshall, W. L., & Moulden, H. (2001). Hostility toward women and victim empathy in rapists. *Sexual Abuse: Journal of Research & Treatment, 13,* 249–255.

Marten, P. A., Brown, T. A., Barlow, D. H., Borkovec, T. D., Shear, M. K., & Lydiard, M. B. (1993). Evaluation of the ratings comprising the associated symptom criterion of DSM-III-R generalized anxiety disorder. *Journal of Nervous and Mental Disease, 181,* 676–682.

Martin, C. S., Chung, T., & Langenbucher, J. W. (2008). How should we revise diagnostic criteria for substance use disorders in the DSM-V? *Journal of Abnormal Psychology, 117*(3), 561–575.

Martin, I. (1983). Human classical conditioning. In A. Gale & J. A. Edward (Eds.), *Physiological correlates of human behavior: Vol. 2. Attention and performance.* London: Academic Press.

Martin, P. R., Pekovich, S. R., McCool, B. A., Whetsell, W. O., & Singleton, C. K. (1994). Thiamine utilization in the pathogenesis of alcohol-induced brain damage. *Alcohol and Alcoholism Supplement, 2,* 273–279.

Martin, S. D., Martin, E., Rai, S. S., Richardson, M. A., & Royall, R. (2001). Brain blood flow changes in depressed patients treated with interpersonal psychotherapy or venlafaxine hydrochloride. *Archives of General Psychiatry, 58,* 641–648.

Martin, S. L., Ramey, C. T., & Ramey, S. L. (1990). The prevention of intellectual impairment in children of impoverished families: Findings of a randomized trial of educational daycare. *American Journal of Public Health, 80,* 844–847.

Martin-Cook, K., Svetlik, D., & Weiner, M. F. (2003). Supporting family caregivers. In M. F. Weiner & A. M. Lipton (Eds.), *The dementias: Diagnosis, treatment and research* (3rd ed., pp. 321–340). Washington, DC: American Psychiatric Press.

Marx, J. (1998). New gene tied to common form of Alzheimer's. *Science, 281,* 507–509.

Maser, J. D. (1985). List of phobias. In A. H. Tuma & J. D. Maser (Eds.), *Anxiety and the anxiety disorders.* Hillsdale, NJ: Erlbaum.

Maser, J. D., Kaelber, C., & Weise, R. E. (1991). International use and attitudes toward DSM-III and DSM-III-R: Growing consensus in psychiatric classification. *Journal of Abnormal Psychology, 100*(3), 271–279.

Mash, E. J., & Wolfe, D. A. (2003). Disorders of childhood and adolescence. In G. Stricker & T. A. Widiger (Eds.), *Handbook of psychology: Clinical psychology* (Vol. 8, pp. 27–63). New York: John Wiley & Sons.

Mason, F. L. (1997). Fetishism: Psychopathology and theory. In D. R. Laws & W. O'Donohue (Eds.), *Sexual deviance: Theory, assessment and treatment* (pp. 75–91). New York: Guilford Press.

Massie, H. N., Miranda, G., Snowdon, D. A., Greiner, L. H., Wekstein, D. R., Danner, D., … Mortimer, J. A. (1996). Linguistic ability in early life and Alzheimer disease in late life. *JAMA, 275,* 1879.

Master, S. L., Eisenberger, N. I., Taylor, S. E., Naliboff, B. D., Shirinyan, D., & Lieberman, M. D. (2009). A picture's worth: Partner photographs reduce experimentally induced pain. *Psychological Science, 20,* 1316–1318.

Masters, W. H., & Johnson, V. E. (1966). *Human sexual response.* Boston: Little, Brown.

Mathew, K., Whitford, H., Kenny, M., & Denson, L. (2010). The long-term effects of mindfulness-based cognitive therapy as a relapse prevention treatment for major depressive disorder. *Behavioural and Cognitive Psychotherapy, 7,* 1–16.

Mathew, S. J., & Hoffman, E. J. (2009). Pharmacotherapy for generalized anxiety disorder. In M. M. Antony & M. B. Stein (Eds.), *Oxford handbook of anxiety and related disorders* (pp. 350–363). New York: Oxford University Press.

Mathews, A. (1997). Information processing biases in emotional disorders. In D. M. Clark & C. G. Fairburn (Eds.), *Science and practice of cognitive-behavior therapy* (pp. 47–66). Oxford: Oxford University Press.

Mathews, A., & MacLeod, C. (1994). Cognitive approaches to emotion and emotional disorders. *Annual Review of Psychology, 45,* 25–50.

Mathews, A., Mogg, K., Kentish, J., & Eysenck, M. (1995). Effective psychological treatment on cognitive bias and generalized anxiety disorder. *Behavior Research and Therapy, 33,* 293–303.

Mathews, C.A. (2009). Phenomenology of obsessive-compulsive disorder. In M. M. Antony & M. B. Stein (Eds.), *Oxford handbook of anxiety and related disorders.* Oxford, UK: Oxford University Press.

Mathews, K. A. (1988). Coronary heart disease and Type A behaviors: Update on and alternative to the Booth-Kewley and Friedman (1987) quantitative review. *Psychological Bulletin, 104*(3), 373–380.

Maticka-Tyndale, E. (2001). Sexual Health and Canadian youth: How do we measure up? *Canadian Journal of Human Sexuality, 10,* 1–17.

Maticka-Tyndale, E., McKay, A., & Barrett, F. M. (2001). *Teenage sexual and reproductive behavior in developed countries: Country report for Canada.* Occasional Report No. 4, November, 2001, Alan Guttmacher Institute, New York, p. 52.

Matsumoto, D. (1994). *People: Psychology from a cultural perspective.* Pacific Grove, CA: Brooks/Cole.

Matsumoto, D. (1996). *Culture and psychology.* Pacific Grove, CA: Brooks/Cole.

Matthews, K. (2005). Psychological perspectives on the development of coronary heart disease. *American Psychologist, 60,* 780–796.

Mattis, S. G., & Ollendick, T. H. (2002). Nonclinical panic attacks in late adolescence prevalence and associated psychopathology. *Journal of Anxiety Disorders, 16,* 351–367.

Mayberg, H., Lozano, A., Voon, V., McNeely, H., Seminowicz, D., Hanani, C., ... Kennedy, S. H. (2005). Deep brain stimulation for treatment resistant depression. *Neuron, 45,* 651–660.

Mayou, R., Phil, M., Kirmayer, L., Simon, G., Kroenke, G., & Sharpe, M. (2005). Somato-form disorders: Time for a new approach in DSM-V. *American Journal of Psychiatry, 162,* 847–855.

Mayville, S., Katz, R. C., Gipson, M. T., & Cabral, K. (1999). Assessing the prevalence of body dysmorphic disorder in an ethically diverse group of adolescents. *Journal of Child and Family Studies, 8*(3), 357–362.

Mazure, C. M. (1998). Life stressors as risk factors in depression. *Clinical Psychology: Science and Practice, 5*(3), 291–313.

Mazure, C. M., Bruce, M. L., Maciejewski, P. K., & Jacobs, S. C. (2000). Adverse life events and cognitive-personality characteristics in the prediction of major depression and antidepressant response. *American Journal of Psychiatry, 157*(6), 896–903.

McAdoo, W. G., & DeMyer, M. K. (1978). Research related to family factors in autism. *Journal of Pediatric Psychology, 2,* 162–166.

McCabe, M., & Wauchope, M. (2005). Behavioral characteristics of men accused of rape: Evidence for different types of rapists. *Archives of Sexual Behavior, 34,* 241–253.

McCabe, R. E. (2003). *SARS and illness phobia.* Presented at a symposium on "Clinical issues in the assessment and treatment of health anxiety: A case-based panel discussion (Chair: R. E. McCabe) at the Annual Meeting of the Anxiety Disorders Association of America, Toronto, March.

McCabe, R. E., & Antony, M. M. (2002). Specific and social phobia. In M. M. Antony & D. H. Barlow (Eds.), *Handbook of assessment and treatment planning for psychological disorders* (pp. 113–146). New York: Guilford Press.

McCabe, R. E., Antony, M. M., Summerfeldt, L. J., Liss, A., & Swinson, R. P. (2003). A preliminary examination of the relationship between anxiety disorders in adults and self-reported history of teasing or bullying experiences. *Cognitive Behaviour Therapy, 32*(4), 187–193.

McCabe, R. E., McFarlane, T., Polivy, J., & Olmsted, M. P. (2001). Eating disorders, dieting, and the accuracy of self-reported weight. *International Journal of Eating Disorders, 29,* 59–64.

McCaffrey, R. J., & Bellamy-Campbell, R. (1989). Psychometric detection of fabricated symptoms of combat-related posttraumatic stress disorder: A systematic replication. *Journal of Clinical Psychology, 45,* 76–79.

McCann, D., Barrett, A., Cooper, A., Crumpler, D., Dalen, L., Grimshaw, K., ... Stevenson, J. (2007). Food additives and hyperactive behaviour in 3-year-old and 8/9-year-old children in the community: A randomised, double-blinded, placebo-controlled trial. *The Lancet, 370*(9598), 1560–1567.

McCann, U. D., & Ricaurte, G. A. (2009). Amphetamine (or amphetamine-like)-related disorders. In B. J. Sadock, V. A. Sadock, & P. Ruiz (Eds.), *Kaplan & Sadock's comprehensive textbook of psychiatry* (Vol. I, 9th ed., pp. 1288–1296). Philadelphia: Lippincott Williams & Wilkins.

McCaughrin, W. B. (1988). *Longitudinal trends of competitive employment for developmentally disabled adults: A benefit-cost analysis.* Unpublished doctoral dissertation, University of Illinois at Urbana-Champaign.

McClearn, G. E., Johansson, B., Berg, S., Pedersen, N. L., Ahern, F., Petrill, S. A., & Plomin, R. (1997). Substantial genetic influence on cognitive abilities in twins 80 or more years old. *Science, 276,* 1560–1563.

McCloskey, M. S., Noblett, K. L., Deffenbacher, J. L., Gollan, J. K., & Coccaro, E. F. (2008). Cognitive-behavioral therapy for intermittent explosive disorder: A pilot randomized clinical trial. *Journal of Consulting and Clinical Psychology, 76*(5), 876–886.

McCrae, R., & Costa, P., Jr. (2008). The five-factor theory of personality. In O. P. John, R. W. Robins, & L. A. Pervin (Eds.), *Handbook of personality: Theory and research* (3rd ed., pp. 159–181). New York: Guilford Press.

McCrae, R. R., & Costa, P. T. (1997). Personality trait structure as a human universal. *American Psychologist, 52,* 509–516.

McCreery, J. M., & Walker, R. D. (1993). Alcohol problems. In D. L. Dunner (Ed.), *Current psychiatric therapy* (pp. 92–98). Philadelphia: W. B. Saunders.

McCullough, J. P., Jr., Klein, D. N., Keller, M. B., Holzer, C. E., III, Davis, S. M., Kornstein, S. G., ... Harrison, W. M. (2000). Comparison of DSM-II-R chronic major depression and major depression superimposed on dysthymia (double depression): Validity of the distinction. *Journal of Abnormal Psychology, 109,* 419–427.

McCusker, J., Cole, M., Abrahamowicz, M., Han, L., Podoba, J. E., & Ramman-Haddad, L. (2001). Environmental risk factors for delirium in hospitalized older people. *Journal of the American Geriatrics Society, 49,* 1327–1334.

McDaniel, K. (1990). Thalmic degeneration. In J. L. Cummings (Ed.), *Subcortical dementia* (pp. 132–144). New York: Oxford University Press.

McDonough, J. (2002). *Shakey: Neil Young's biography.* Toronto, ON: Random House.

McDowell, D. M. (1999). MDMA, ketamine, GHB, and the "club drug" scene. In M. Galanter & H. D. Kleber (Eds.), *Textbook of substance abuse treatment* (2nd ed., pp. 295–305). Washington, DC: American Psychiatric Press.

Mcdowell, I., Kristjanson, B., Hill, G. B., & Hébert, R. (1997). Community screening for dementia: the Mini Mental State Exam (MMSE) and Modified Mini Mental State Exam (3MS) compared. *Journal of Clinical Epidemiology, 50,* 377–383

McEachin, J. J., Smith, T., & Lovaas, O. I. (1993). Long-term outcome for children with autism who received early intensive behavioral treatment. *American Journal on Mental Retardation, 97,* 359–372.

McElroy, S. L., & Arnold, L. M. (2001). Impulse-control disorders. In G. O. Gabbard (Ed.), *Treatment of psychiatric disorders* (Vol. 1, 3rd ed., pp. 2435–2471). Washington, DC: American Psychiatric Publishing.

McElroy, S. L., & Keck, P. E. (1993). Rapid cycling. In D. L. Dunner (Ed.), *Current psychiatric therapy* (pp. 226–231). Philadelphia: W. B. Saunders.

McEwen, B. S., & Magarinos, A. M. (2004). Does Stress Damage the Brain? In J. M. Gorman, *Fear and anxiety: The benefits of translational research* (pp. 23–45). Washington, DC: American Psychiatric Publishing.

McEwen, B. S., & Stellar, E. (1993). Stress and the individual: Mechanisms leading to disease. *Archives of Internal Medicine, 153,* 2093–2101.

McGee, B. J., Hewitt, P. L., Sherry, S. B., Parkin, M., & Flett, G. L. (2005). Perfectionistic self-presentation, body image, and eating disorder symptoms. *Body Image, 2,* 29–40.

McGehee, D. S., Heath, M. J. S., Gelber, S., Devay, P., & Role, L. W. (1995). Nicotine enhancement of fast excitatory synaptic transmission in CNS by presynaptic receptors. *Science, 269,* 1692–1696.

McGinnis, J. M., & Foege, W. H. (1993). Actual causes of death in the United States. *JAMA, 270*(18), 2207–2212.

McGirr, A., Paris, J., Lesage, A., Renaud, J., & Turecki, G. (2009). An examination of DSM-IV borderline personality disorder symptoms and risk for death by suicide: A psychological autopsy study. *Canadian Journal of Psychiatry, 54*(2), 87.

McGlashan, T. H., & Fenton, W. S. (1991). Classical subtypes for schizophrenia: Literature review for DSM-IV. Schizophrenia Bulletin, 17, 609–623.

McGoldrick, M., Loonan, R., & Wohlsifer, D. (2007). Sexuality and culture. In S. R. Leiblum (Ed.), *Principles and practice of sex therapy* (4th ed., pp. 416–441). New York: Guilford Press.

McGovern, M. P., Xie, H., Segal, S. R., Siembab, L., & Drake, R. E. (2006). Addiction treatment services and co-occurring disorders: Prevalence estimates, treatment practices, and barriers. *Journal of Substance Abuse Treatment, 31,* 267–275.

McGowin, D. F. (1993). *Living in the labyrinth: A personal journey through the maze of Alzheimer's.* New York: Delacorte Press.

McGrath, J. (2000). Universal interventions for the primary prevention of schizophrenia. *Australian and New Zealand Journal of Psychiatry, 34*(Suppl.), S58.

McGrath, J. (2010). Is it time to trial vitamin D supplements for the prevention of schizophrenia? *Acta Psychiatrica Scandinavica, 121*(5), 321–324.

McGrath, P., Marshall, P. G., & Prior, K. (1979). A comprehensive treatment program for a fire setting child. *Journal of Behavior Therapy and Experimental Psychiatry, 10*(1), 69–72.

McGrath, P. A., & DeVeber, L. L. (1986). The management of acute pain evoked by medical procedures in children with cancer. *Journal of Pain and Symptom Management, 1,* 145–150.

McGrath P. J., Finley G. A., & Turner C. J. (1992). *Making cancer less painful: A handbook for parents.* Halifax, NS: IWK Children's Hospital.

McGregor, I., Zanna, M. P., Holmes, J. G., & Spencer, S. J. (2001). Compensatory conviction in the face of personal uncertainty: Going to extremes and being oneself. *Journal of Personality & Social Psychology, 80,* 472–488.

McGue, M. (1999). The behavioral genetics of alcoholism. *Current Directions in Psychological Science, 8*(4), 109–115.

McGue, M., & Christensen, K. (1997). Genetic and environmental contributions to depression symptomatology: Evidence from Danish twins 75 years of age and older. *Journal of Abnormal Psychology, 106*(3), 439–448.

McGue, M., & Lykken, D. T. (1992). Genetic influence on risk of divorce. *Psychological Science, 3*(6), 368–373.

McGue, M., Pickens, R. W., & Svikis, D. S. (1992). Sex and age effects on the inheritance of alcohol problems: A twin study. *Journal of Abnormal Psychology, 101,* 3–17.

McGuffin, P., & Katz, R. (1989). The genetics of depression and manic-depressive disorder. *British Journal of Psychiatry, 155,* 294–304.

McGuffin, P., & Katz, R. (1993). Genes, adversity and depression. In R. Plomin & G. E. McClearn

(Eds.), *Nature, nurture & psychology* (pp. 217–230). Washington, DC: American Psychological Association.

McGuffin, P., Katz, R., & Bebbington, P. (1988). The Camberwell Collaborative Depression Study: III. Depression and adversity in the relatives of depressed probands. *British Journal of Psychiatry, 152,* 775–782.

McGuffin, P., Rijsdijk, F., Andrew, M., Sham, P., Katz, R., & Cardno, A. (2003). The heritability of bipolar affective disorder and the genetic relationship to unipolar depression. *Archives of General Psychiatry, 60,* 497–502.

McHugh, R. K., & Barlow, D. H. (2010). The dissemination and implementation of evidence-based psychological treatments: A review of current efforts. *American Psychologist, 65,* 73–84.

McIntosh, J. L., Santos, J. F., Hubbard, R. W., & Overholser, J. C. (1994). *Elder suicide: Research, theory and treatment.* Washington, DC: American Psychological Association.

McIsaac, H. K., Thordarson, D. S., Shafran, R., Rachman, S., & Poole, G. (1998). Claustrophobia and the magnetic resonance imaging procedure. *Journal of Behavioral Medicine, 21,* 255–268.

McKay, A. (2005). Sexuality and substance use: The impact of tobacco, alcohol, and selected recreational drugs on sexual function. *Canadian Journal of Human Sexuality, 14,* 47–56.

McKay, D., Todaro, J., Neziroglu, F., Campisi, T., Moritz, E. K., & Yaryura-Tobias, J. A. (1997). Body dysmorphic disorder: A preliminary evaluation of treatment and maintenance using exposure with response prevention. *Behaviour Research and Therapy, 35,* 67–70.

McKenzie, S. J., Williamson, D. A., & Cubic, B. A. (1993). Stable and reactive body image disturbances in bulimia nervosa. *Behavior Therapy, 24,* 195–207.

McKeon, P., & Murray, R. (1987). Familial aspects of obsessive-compulsive neuroses. *British Journal of Psychiatry, 151,* 528–534.

McKim, W. A. (1991). *Drugs and behavior: An introduction to behavioral pharmacology* (2nd ed.). Englewood Cliffs, NJ: Prentice Hall.

McKinnon, W., Weisse, C. S., Reynolds, C. P., Bowles, C. A., & Baum, A. (1989). Chronic stress, leukocyte subpopulations, and hormonal response to latent viruses. *Health Psychology, 8,* 399–402.

McKnight, D. L., Nelson-Gray, R. O., & Barnhill, J. (1992). Dexamethasone suppression test and response to cognitive therapy and antidepressant medication. *Behavior Therapy, 23,* 99–111.

McLaren, A. (1990). *Our own master race: Eugenics in Canada 1885–1945.* Toronto, ON: McClelland & Stewart.

McLean, L. M., & Gallop, R. (2003). Implications of childhood sexual abuse for adult borderline personality disorder and complex posttraumatic stress disorder. *American Journal of Psychiatry, 160,* 369–371.

McLean, P., & Taylor, S. (1992). Severity of unipolar depression and choice of treatment. *Behaviour Research and Therapy, 30,* 443–451.

McLean, P. D., Whittal, M. L., Thordarson, D. S., Taylor, S., Socting, I., Koch, W. J., ... Anderson, K. W. (2001). Cognitive versus behavior therapy in the group treatment of obsessive-compulsive disorder. *Journal of Consulting and Clinical Psychology, 69,* 205–214.

McLeod, J. D., Kessler, R. C., & Landis, K. R. (1992). Speed of recovery from major depressive episodes in a community sample of married men and women. *Journal of Abnormal Psychology, 101*(2), 277–286.

McLewin, L. A., & Muller, R. T. (2006). Childhood trauma, imaginary companions, and the development of pathological dissociation. *Aggression and Violent Behavior, 11,* 531–545.

McLintock, B. (2002, July 22). Montreux clinic under fire. *The Province,* A14. Retrieved June 24, 2004, from http://www.anorexiasfallenangel.com/news/22072002.htm

McMain, S., Korman, L. M., & Dimeff, L. (2001). Dialectical behavior therapy and the treatment of emotion dysregulation. *Journal of Clinical Psychology, 57,* 183–196.

McNally, R. J. (1996). Cognitive bias in the anxiety disorders. In D. A. Hope (Ed.), *Perspectives on anxiety, panic and fear* (the 43rd Annual Nebraska Symposium on Motivation, pp. 211–250). Lincoln: Nebraska University Press.

McNally, R. J. (1999a). EMDR and mesmerism: A comparative historical analysis. *Journal of Anxiety Disorders, 13,* 225–236.

McNally, R. J. (1999b). Panic and phobias. In T. Dalgleish & M. J. Power (Eds.), *Handbook of cognition and emotion* (pp. 479–496). Chichester, UK: John Wiley & Sons.

McNaughton, N., & Gray, J. H. (2000). Anxiolytic action on the behavioral inhibition system implies multiple types of arousal contribute to anxiety. *Journal of Affective Disorders, 61*(3), 161–176.

McNeil, T. F. (1987). Perinatal influences in the development of schizophrenia. In H. Helmchen & F. A. Henn (Eds.), *Biological perspectives of schizophrenia* (pp. 125–138). New York: John Wiley & Sons.

McNeil, T. F., Cantor-Graae, E., & Weinberger, D. R. (2001). Relationship of obstetric complications and differences in brain structures in monozygotic twin pairs discordant for schizophrenia. *American Journal of Psychiatry, 157*(2), 203–212.

McQueen, A. M. (2005, June 29). Alanis battled anorexia, bulimia. *Ottawa Sun.* Retrieved June 30, 2007, from http://jam.canoe.ca/Music/2005/06/ 29/1109259.html

McTeer, M. (2003). *In my own name.* Toronto, ON: Random House of Canada.

McVey, G. L., Davis, R., Tweed, S., & Shaw, B. (2004). An evaluation of a school-based program designed to improve body image satisfaction, global self-esteem, and eating attitudes and behaviours: A replication study. *International Journal of Eating Disorders, 36,* 1–11.

McVey, G. L., Pepler, D., Davis, R., Flett, G. L., & Abdolell, M. (2002). Risk and protective factors associated with disordered eating during early adolescence. *Journal of Early Adolescence, 22,* 75–95.

McWilliams, L. A., & Asmundson, G. J. G. (2001). Is there a negative association between anxiety sensitivity and arousal-increasing substances and activities? *Journal of Anxiety Disorders, 15,* 161–170.

Meana, M., Binik, I., Khalife, S., & Cohen, D. (1998). Affect and marital adjustment in women's rating of dyspareunic pain. *Canadian Journal of Psychiatry, 43,* 381–385.

Meana, M., & Nunnink, S. E. (2005). Gender differences in the content of cognitive distraction during sex [Special issue: Scientific Abstracts, World Congress of Sexology]. *Journal of Sex Research, 43,* 59–67.

Meaney, M. J. (2001). Maternal care, gene expression, and the transmission of individual differences in stress reactivity across generations. *Annual Review of Neuroscience, 24,* 1161–1192.

Meaney, M. J., & Szyf, M. (2005). Maternal care as a model for experience-dependent chromatin plasticity? *Trends in Neurosciences, 28*(9), 456–463.

Mednick, S. A., & Schulsinger, F. (1965). A longitudinal study of children with a high risk for schizophrenia: A preliminary report. In S. Vandenberg (Ed.), *Methods and goals in human behavior genetics* (pp. 255–296). New York: Academic Press.

Mednick, S. A., & Schulsinger, F. (1968). Some premorbid characteristics related to breakdown in children with schizophrenic mothers. *Journal of Psychiatric Research, 6,* 267–291.

Mednick, S. A., Watson, J. B., Huttunen, M., Cannon, T. D., Katila, H., Machon, R., ... Wang, X. (1998). A two-hit working model of the etiology of schizophrenia. In M. F. Lenzenweger & R. H. Dworkin (Eds.), *Origins and development of schizophrenia: Advances in experimental psychopathology* (pp. 27–66). Washington, DC: American Psychological Association.

Meehan, P. J., Lamb, J. A., Saltzman, L. E., & O'Carroll, P. W. (1992). Attempted suicide among young adults: Progress toward a meaningful estimate of prevalence. *American Journal of Psychiatry, 149*(1), 41–44.

Meehl, P. E. (1962). Schizotaxia, schizotypy, schizophrenia. *American Psychologist, 17,* 827–838.

Meehl, P. E. (1989). Schizotaxia revisited. *Archives of General Psychiatry, 46,* 935–944.

Meichenbaum, D. (1977). Dr. Ellis, please stand up. *Counseling Psychologist, 7,* 43–44.

Meichenbaum, D. (2006). Resilience and posttraumatic growth: A constructive narrative perspective. In L. G. Calhoun & R. G. Tedeschi (Eds.), *Handbook of posttraumatic growth: Research & practice* (pp. 355–367). Mahwah, NJ: Erlbaum.

Meichenbaum, D., & Cameron, R. (1973). Training schizophrenics to talk to themselves: A means of developing attentional controls. *Behavior Therapy, 4,* 515–534.

Meichenbaum, D., & Cameron, R. (1974). The clinical potential of modifying what clients say to themselves. *Psychotherapy: Theory, Research & Practice, 11,* 103–117.

Meichenbaum, D. H. (1971). Nature and modification of impulsive children: Training impulsive children to talk to themselves. *Catalog of Selected Documents in Psychology, 1,* 15–16.

Meichenbaum, D. H. (1994). *A clinical handbook/practical therapist manual for assessing and treating adults with posttraumatic stress disorder.* Waterloo, ON: Institute Press.

Meichenbaum, D. H. (1995). Cognitive-behavioral therapy in historical perspective. In B. M. Bongar & L. E. Beutler (Eds.), *Comprehensive textbook of psychotherapy: Theory and practice* (pp. 140–158). London: Oxford University Press.

Meichenbaum, D. H., & Goodman, J. (1971). Training impulsive children to talk to themselves: A means of developing self-control. *Journal of Abnormal Psychology, 77,* 115–126.

Meleshko, K. A., & Alden, L. E. (1993). Anxiety and self-disclosure: Toward a motivational model. *Journal of Personality and Social Psychology, 64,* 1000–1009.

Mellinger, G. D., Balter, M. B., & Uhlenhuth, E. H. (1985). Insomnia and its treatment: Prevalence and correlates. *Archives of General Psychiatry, 42,* 225–232.

Melton, G. B., Petrila, J., Poythress, N. G., & Slobogin, C. (1987). *Psychological evaluations for the courts.* New York: Guilford Press.

Meltzer, E. S., & Kumar, R. (1985). Puerperal mental illness, clinical features and classification: A study of 142 mother-and-baby admissions. *British Journal of Psychiatry, 147,* 647–654.

Melzack, R. (1999). From the gate to the neuromatrix. *Pain* (Suppl. 6), S121–S126.

Melzack, R. (2005). Evolution of the neuromatrix theory of pain. *Pain Practice, 5,* 85–94.

Melzack, R., & Katz, J. (2004). The gate control theory: Reaching for the brain. In T. Hadjistavropoulos & K. D. Craig (Eds.), *Pain: Psychological perspectives* (pp. 13–34). Mahwah, NJ: Lawrence Erlbaum Associates Publishers.

Melzack, R., & Katz, J. (2007). The gate control theory: Reaching for the brain. In T. Hadjistavropoulos & K. D. Craig (Eds.), *Pain: Psychological perspectives* (pp. 13–34). Mahwah, NJ: Lawrence Erlbaum Associates Publishers.

Melzack, R., & Wall, P. D. (1965). Pain mechanisms: A new theory. *Science, 150,* 971–979.

Melzack, R., & Wall, P. D. (1982). *The challenge of pain.* New York: Basic Books.

Mendelson, W. (2005). Sleep disorders. In B. J. Sadock & V. A. Sadock (Eds.), *Kaplan & Sadock's comprehensive textbook of psychiatry* (pp. 2022–2034). Philadelphia: Lippincott Williams & Wilkins.

Mendlewicz, J., & Rainer, J. D. (1977). Adoption study supporting genetic transmission in manic depressive illness. *Nature, 268*(5618), 327–329.

Merens, W., Willem Van der Does, A. J., & Spinhoven, P. (2007). The effects of serotonin manipulations on emotional information processing and mood. *Journal of Affective Disorders, 103*(1–3), 43–62.

Mérette, C., Brassard, A., Potvin, A., Bouvier, H., Rousseau, F., Émond, C., ... Caron, C. (2000). Significant linkage for Tourette syndrome in a large French Canadian family. *American Journal of Human Genetics, 67,* 1008–1013.

Merikangas, K. R., Mehta, R. L., Molnar, B. E., Walters, E. E., Swendsen, J. D., Auilar-Gaziola, S., ... Kessler, R. C. (1998). Comorbidity of substance use disorders with mood and anxiety disorders: Results of the international consortium in psychiatric epidemiology. *Addictive Behaviors, 23,* 893–908.

Merikangas, K. R., & Pato, M. (2009). Recent developments in the epidemiology of bipolar disorder in adults and children: Magnitude, correlates, and future directions. *Clinical Psychology: Science and Practice, 16*(2), 121–133.

Merikangas, K. R., & Risch, N. (2003). Will the genomics revolution revolutionize psychiatry? *American Journal of Psychiatry, 160,* 625–635.

Merzenich, M. M., Jenkins, W. M., Johnston, P., Schreiner, C., Miller, S. L., & Tallal, P. (1996). Temporal processing deficits of language-learning impaired children ameliorated by training. *Science, 271,* 77–81.

Messenger, O. J., & Messenger, D. R. (1995). *Borrowed time: A surgeon's struggle with transfusion-induced AIDS.* New York: Mosaic Press.

Meston, C. M. (2000). The psycho physiological assessment of female sexual function. *Journal of Sex Education & Therapy, 25,* 6–16.

Meston, C. M., & Gorzalka, B. B. (1996). The effects of immediate, delayed, and residual sympathetic activation on sexual arousal in women. *Behaviour Research & Therapy, 34,* 143–148.

Meston, C. M., & Heiman, J. R. (2000). Sexual abuse and sexual function: An examination of sexually relevant cognitive processes. *Journal of Consulting & Clinical Psychology, 68,* 399–406.

Meston, C. M., Trapnell, P. D., & Gorzalka, B. B. (1996). Ethnic and gender differences in sexuality: Variations in sexual behavior between Asian and non-Asian university students. *Archives of Sexual Behavior, 25,* 33–72.

Meston, C. M., Trapnell, P. D., & Gorzalka, B. B. (1998). Ethnic, gender, and length-of-residency influences on sexual knowledge and attitudes. *Journal of Sex Research, 35,* 176–188.

Meston, C. M., & Worcel, M. (2002). The effects of yohimbine plus L-arginine glutamate on sexual arousal in postmenopausal women with sexual arousal disorder. *Archives of Sexual Behavior, 31,* 323–332.

Meyer, A. J., Nash, J. D., McAlister, A. L., Maccoby, M., & Farquhar, J. W. (1980). Skills training in a cardiovascular health education campaign. *Journal of Consulting and Clinical Psychology, 2,* 129–142.

Meyer, B., & Carver, C. S. (2000). Negative childhood accounts, sensitivity and pessimism: A study of avoidant personality disorder features in college students. *Journal of Personality Disorders, 14,* 233–248.

Meyer, L. H., Peck, C. A., & Brown, L. (1991). *Critical issues in the lives of people with severe disabilities.* Baltimore: Paul H. Brookes.

Meyerowitz, B. E. (1983). Postmastectomy coping strategies and quality of life. *Health Psychology, 2,* 117–132.

Meyers, A. (1991). Biobehavioral interactions in behavioral medicine. *Behavior Therapy, 22,* 129–131.

Meyers, R. J., Villanueva, M., & Smith, J. E. (2005). The community reinforcement approach: History and new directions. *Journal of Cognitive Psychotherapy, 19,* 251–264.

Mezzich, J. E., Good, B. J., Lewis-Fernandez, R., Guarnaccia, P., Lin, K. M., Parron, D., ... Hughes, C. (1993, September). *Cultural formulation guidelines.* Revised cultural proposals for DSM-IV. Submitted to the DSM-IV Task Force by the Steering Committee, NIMH-Sponsored Group on Culture and Diagnosis.

Mezzich, J. E., Kirmayer, L. J., Kleinman, A., Fabrega, H., Jr., Parron, D. L., Good, B. J., ... Manson, S. M. (1999). The place of culture in DSM-IV. *Journal of Nervous and Mental Disease, 187,* 457–464.

Mezzich, J. E., Kleinman, A., Fabrega, H., Jr., Good, B., Johnson-Powell, G., Lin, K. M., ... Parron, D. (1992). *Cultural proposals for DSM-IV.* Submitted to the DSM-IV Task Force by the Steering Committee, NIMH-Sponsored Group on Culture and Diagnosis.

Miaskowski, C. (1999). The role of sex and gender in pain perception and responses to treatment. In R. J. Gatchel & D. C. Turk (Eds.), *Psychosocial factors in pain: Critical perspectives* (pp. 401–411). New York: Guilford Press.

Michultka, D. M., Blanchard, E. B., Appelbaum, K. A., Jaccard, J., & Dentinger, M. P. (1989). The refractory headache patient: II. High medication consumption (analgesic rebound) headache. *Behaviour Research and Therapy, 27,* 411–420.

Middleton, W., Burnett, P., Raphael, B., & Martinek, N. (1996). The bereavement response: A cluster analysis. *British Journal of Psychiatry, 169,* 167–171.

Mignot, E. (2000). Pathophysiology of narcolepsy. In M. H. Kryger, T. Roth, & W. C. Dement (Eds.), *Principles and practice of sleep medicine* (3rd ed., pp. 663–675). Philadelphia: W. B. Saunders.

Miklowitz, D. J. (2001). Bipolar disorder. In D. H. Barlow (Ed.), *Clinical handbook of psychological disorders* (3rd ed., pp. 523–561). New York: Guilford Press.

Miklowitz, D. J., & Goldstein, M. J. (1997). *Bipolar disorder: A family focused treatment approach.* New York: Guilford Press.

Miklowitz, D. J., Goldstein, M. J., Doane, J. A., Nuechterlein, K. H., Strachan, A. M., Snyder, K. S., & Magaña-Amato, A. (1989). Is expressed emotion an index of a transactional process? I. Parents' affective style. *Family Process, 28,* 153–167.

Miklowitz, D. J., & Johnson, S. (2006). The psychopathology and treatment of bipolar disorder. In S. Nolen-Hoeksema, T. D. Cannon, & T. Widiger (Eds.), *Annual Review of Clinical Psychology* (pp. 199–235). Palo Alto, CA: Annual Reviews.

Miklowitz, D. J., Simoneau, T. L., George, E. L., Richards, J. A., Kalbag, A., Sachs-Ericsson, N., & Suddath, R. (2000). Family-focused treatment of bipolar disorder: 1-year effects of a psychoeducational program in conjunction with pharmacotherapy. *Biological Psychiatry, 48,* 582–592.

Miklowitz, D. J., Simoneau, T. L., Sachs-Ericsson, N., Warner, R., & Suddath, R. (1996). Family risk indicators in the course of bipolar affective disorder. In C. Mundt, M J. Goldstein, K. Hahlweg, P. Fiedler, et al. (Eds.), *Interpersonal factors in the origin and course of affective disorders* (pp. 204–217). London: Gaskell Press.

Milby, J. B., Williams, V., Hall, J. N., Khuder, S., McGill, T., & Wooten, V. (1993). Effectiveness of combined triazolam-behavior therapy for primary insomnia. *American Journal of Psychiatry, 150,* 1259–1260.

Millar, W. J. (1998). Multiple medication use among seniors. *Health Reports, 9*(4), 11–17.

Miller, G., & Blackwell, E. (2006). Turning up the heat: Inflammation as a mechanism linking chronic stress, depression, and heart disease. *Current Directions in Psychological Science, 15,* 269–277.

Miller, I. W., Keitner, G. I., Epstein, N. B., Bishop, D. S., & Ryan, C. E. (1991). *Families of bipolar patients: Dysfunction, course of illness, and pilot treatment study.* Paper presented at the annual meeting of the Association for the Advancement of Behavior Therapy, New York.

Miller, I. W., & Norman, W. H. (1979). Learned helplessness in humans: A review and attribution-theory model. *Psychological Bulletin, 86*(1), 93–118.

Miller, I. W., Norman, W. H., & Keitner, G. I. (1989). Cognitive-behavioral treatment of depressed inpatients: Six- and twelve-month follow-up. *American Journal of Psychiatry, 146,* 1274–1279.

Miller, I. W., Norman, W. H., Keitner, G. I., Bishop, S. B., & Down, M. G. (1989). Cognitive-behavioral treatment of depressed inpatients. *Behavior Therapy, 20*(1), 25–47.

Miller, J. D., Campbell, W. K., & Pilkonis, P. A. (2007). Narcissistic personality disorder: Relations with distress and functional impairment. *Comprehensive Psychiatry, 48,* 170–177.

Miller, N. E. (1969). Learning of visceral and glandular responses. *Science, 163,* 434–445.

Miller, N. S., Gold, M. S., & Pottash, A. C. (1989). A 12-step treatment approach for marijuana (*Cannabis*) dependence. *Journal of Substance Abuse Treatment, 6,* 241–250.

Miller, P. M., Smith, G. T., & Goldman, M. S. (1990). Emergence of alcohol expectancies in childhood: A possible critical period. *Journal of Studies on Alcohol, 51,* 343–349.

Miller, S., & Watson, B. C. (1992). The relationship between communication attitude, anxiety, and depression in stutterers and nonstutterers. *Journal of Speech and Hearing Research, 35,* 789–798.

Miller, S. D. (1989). Optical differences in cases of multiple personality disorder. *Journal of Nervous and Mental Disease, 177*(8), 480–486.

Miller, T. J., McGlashan, T. H., Rosen, J. L., Somjee, L., Markovich, P. J., Stein, K., & Woods, S. W. (2002). Prospective diagnosis of the initial prodrome for schizophrenia based on the Structured Interview for Prodromal Syndromes: Preliminary evidence of interrater reliability and predictive validity. *American Journal of Psychiatry, 159,* 863–865.

Miller, T. Q., Smith, T. W., Turner, C. W., Guijarro, M. L., & Hallet, A. J. (1996). A meta-analytic review of research on hostility and physical health. *Psychological Bulletin, 119*(2), 322–348.

Miller, W. R. (1985). Motivation for treatment: A review with special emphasis on alcoholism. *Psychological Bulletin, 98,* 84–107.

Miller, W. R., & Hester, R. K. (1986). Inpatient alcoholism treatment: Who benefits? *American Psychologist, 41,* 794–805.

Miller, W. R., & McCrady, B. S. (1993). The importance of research on Alcoholics Anonymous. In B. S. McCrady & W. R. Miller (Eds.), *Research on Alcoholics Anonymous: Opportunities and alternatives* (pp. 3–11). New Brunswick, NJ: Rutgers Center of Alcohol Studies.

Miller, W. R., Meyers, R. J., & Hiller-Sturmhöfel, S. (1999). The community-reinforcement approach. *Alcohol Research & Health, 23*(2), 116–121.

Miller, W. R., & Rollnick, S. (2002). *Motivational interviewing: Preparing people for change* (2nd ed.). New York: Guilford Press.

Millon, T. (1981). *Disorders of personality: DSM-III, Axis II.* New York: John Wiley & Sons.

Millon, T. (1986). Schizoid and avoidant personality disorders in DSM-III. *American Journal of Psychiatry, 143,* 1321–1322.

Millon, T. (1991). Classification in psychopathology: Rationale, alternatives, and standards. *Journal of Abnormal Psychology, 100*(3), 245–261.

Millon, T. (2004). *Masters of the mind.* Hoboken, NJ: John Wiley & Sons.

Millon, T., & Martinez, A. (1995). Avoidant personality disorder. In W. J. Livesley (Ed.), *The DSM-IV personality disorders* (pp. 218–233). New York: Guilford Press.

Mills, J. L., Holmes, L. B., Aarons, J. H., Simpson, J. L., Brown, Z. A., Jovanovic-Peterson, L. G., … Metzger, B. E. (1993). Moderate caffeine use and the risk of spontaneous abortion and intrauterine growth retardation. *JAMA, 269,* 593–597.

Mills, P. J., Adler, K. A., Dimsdale, J. E., Perez, C. J., Ziegler, M. G., Ancoli-Israel, S., … Grant, I. (2004). Vulnerable caregivers of Alzheimer disease patients have a deficit in beta 2-adrenergic receptor sensitivity and density. *American Journal of Geriatric Psychiatry, 12,* 281–286.

Millson, P., Challacombe, L., Villeneuve, P. J., Strike, C. J., Fischer, B., Myers, T., … Hopkins, S. (2007). Reduction in the injection-related HIV risk after 6 months in a low-threshold methadone treatment program. *AIDS Education and Prevention, 19*(2), 124–136.

Milner, C., Fogel, S., & Cote, K. (2006). Experience with napping moderates motor performance improvements following a short daytime nap. *Biological Psychology, 73,* 141–156.

Mindell, J. A. (1993). Sleep disorders in children. *Health Psychology, 12,* 152–163.

Mindell, J. A., & Owens, J. A. (2009). *A clinical guide to pediatric sleep: Diagnosis and management of sleep problems* (2nd ed.). Philadelphia: Lippincott Williams & Wilkins.

Mineka, S. (1985). The frightful complexity of the origins of fears. In F. R. Bruch & J. B. Overmier (Eds.), *Affect, conditioning, and cognition: Essays on the determinants of behavior.* Hillsdale, NJ: Erlbaum.

Mineka, S., & Kelly, K. A. (1989). The relationship between anxiety, lack of control and loss of control. In A. Steptoe & A. Appels (Eds.), *Stress, personal control and worker health.* New York: John Wiley & Sons.

Mineka, S., Watson, D., & Clark, L. A. (1998). Comorbidity of anxiety and unipolar mood disorders. *Annual Review of Psychology, 49,* 377–412.

Mineka, S., & Zinbarg, R. (1998). Experimental approaches to understanding the mood and anxiety disorders. In J. Adair (Ed.), *Advances in psychological research: Social, personal, and cultural aspects* (Vol. 2, pp. 429–454). Hove, UK: Psychology Press/Erlbaum.

Mineka, S., & Zinbarg, R. (2006). A contemporary learning theory perspective on the etiology of anxiety disorders. *American Psychologist, 61,* 10–26.

Mineka, S., & Zinbarg, R. E. (1995). Animal-ethological models of social phobia. In R. Heimberg, M. Leibowitz, D. Hope, & F. Schneier (Eds.), *Social phobia: Diagnosis, assessment and treatment* (pp. 134–162). New York: Guilford Press.

Mineka, S., & Zinbarg, R. E. (1996). Conditioning and ethological models of anxiety disorders: Stress-in-dynamic-context anxiety models. In D. A. Hope (Ed.), *Perspectives on anxiety, panic and fear* (the 43rd Annual Nebraska Symposium on Motivation, pp. 135–210). Lincoln: Nebraska University Press.

Mingdao, Z., & Zhenyi, X. (1990). Delivery systems and research for schizophrenia in China. In A. Kales, C. N. Stefanis, & J. A. Talbott (Eds.), *Recent advances in schizophrenia* (pp. 373–395). New York: Springer-Verlag.

Minuchin, S., Rosman, B. L., & Baker, L. (1978). *Psychosomatic families.* Cambridge, MA: Harvard University Press.

Mirsky, A. F. (1995). Israeli High-Risk Study: Editor's introduction. *Schizophrenia Bulletin, 21,* 179–182.

Mirsky, A. F., Bieliauskas, L. A., French, L. M., Van Kammen, D. P., Joensson, E., & Sedvall, G. (2000). A 39-year followup on the Genain quadruplets. *Schizophrenia Bulletin, 26,* 699–708.

Mishara, B. L. (1999). Suicide in the Montreal subway system. Characteristics of the victims, antecedents, and implications for prevention. *Canadian Journal of Psychiatry, 44,* 690–696.

Misri, S., Kostaras, X., Fox, D., & Kostaras, D. (2000). The impact of partner support in the treatment of postpartum depression. *Canadian Journal of Psychiatry, 45,* 554–558.

Mistlberger, R. E., & Rusak, B. (2005). Circadian rhythms in mammals: Formal properties and environmental influences. In M. H. Kryger, T. Roth, & W. C. Dement (Eds.), *Principles and practice of sleep medicine* (4th ed.). Philadelphia: W. B. Saunders.

Mitchell, J. E., & Pyle, R. L. (1988). The diagnosis and clinical characteristics of bulimia. In B. J. Blinder, B. F. Chaitin, & R. S. Goldstein (Eds.), *The eating disorders: Medical and psychological bases of diagnosis and treatment* (pp. 267–273). New York: PMA.

Mitchell, T., Stewart, S. H., Griffin, K., & Loba, P. (2004). "We Will Never Ever Forget…": The Swissair Flight 111 disaster and its impact on volunteers and communities. *Journal of Health Psychology, 9,* 245–262.

Mitchell, T. L., Walters, W., & Stewart, S. H. (2006). Swissair Flight 111 disaster response impacts: Lessons learned from the voices of disaster volunteers. *Brief Treatment and Crisis Intervention, 6,* 154–170.

Mitton, M. J. E., Links, P. S., & Durocher, G. (1997). A history of childhood sexual abuse and the course of borderline personality disorder. In M. C. Zanarini (Ed.), *Role of sexual abuse in the etiology of borderline personality disorder* (pp. 181–202). Washington, DC: American Psychiatric Association.

Mizrahi, R., Kiang, M., Mamo, D. C., Arenovich, T., Bagby, R. M., Zipursky, R. B., & Kapur, S. (2006). The selective effect of antipsychotics on the different dimensions of the experience of psychosis in schizophrenia spectrum disorders. *Schizophrenia Research, 88*(1–3), 111–118.

Moak, D. H., & Anton, R. F. (1999). Alcohol. In B. S. McCrady & E. E. Epstein (Eds.), *Addictions: A comprehensive guidebook* (pp. 75–94). New York: Oxford University Press.

Modahl, C., Green, L., Fein, D., Morris, M., Waterhouse, L., Feinstein, C., & Levin, H. (1998). Plasma oxytocin levels in autistic children. *Biological Psychiatry, 43,* 270–277.

Modinos, G., Mechelli, A., Ormel, J., Groenewold, N., Aleman, A., & McGuire, P. (2009). Schizotypy and brain structure: A voxel-based morphometry study. *Psychological Medicine, 40,* 1423–1431.

Moeller, F. G. (2009). Impulse-control disorders not elsewhere classified. In B. J. Sadock, V. A. Sadock, & P. Ruiz (Eds.), *Kaplan & Sadock's comprehensive textbook of psychiatry* (Vol. I, 9th ed., pp. 2178–2186). Philadelphia: Lippincott Williams & Wilkins.

Moene, F. C., Spinhoven, P., Hoogduin, K. A., & van Dyck, R. (2002). A randomised controlled clinical trial on the additional effect of hypnosis in a comprehensive treatment programme for in-patients with conversion disorder of the motor type. *Psychotherapy and Psychosomatics, 71,* 66–76.

Mogg, K., Bradley, B. P., Millar, N., & White, J. (1995). A follow-up study of cognitive bias in generalized anxiety disorder. *Behaviour Research & Therapy, 33,* 927–935.

Mogg, K., Mathews, A., & Weinman, J. (1989). Selective processing of threat cues in anxiety states: A replication. *Behaviour Research and Therapy, 27,* 317–323.

Mogg, K., Philippot, P., & Bradley, B. P. (2004). Selective attention to angry faces in clinical social phobia. *Journal of Abnormal Psychology, 113,* 160–165.

Mogil, J. S., Sternberg, W. F., Kest, B., Marek, P., & Liebeskind, J. C. (1993). Sex differences in the antagonism of non-opioid swim stress-induced analgesia: Effects of gonadectomy and estrogen replacement. *Pain, 53,* 17–25.

Mohr, C., Graves, R. E., Gianotti, L. R. R., Pizzagalli, D., & Brugger, P. (2001). Loose but normal: A semantic association study. *Journal of Psycholinguistic Research, 30,* 475–483.

Mohr, D. C., & Beutler, L. E. (1990). Erectile dysfunction: A review of diagnostic and treatment procedures. *Clinical Psychology Review, 10*(1), 123–150.

Molina, B. S., & Pelham, W. E. (2003). Childhood predictors of adolescent substance use in a longitudinal study of children with ADHD. *Journal of Abnormal Psychology, 112,* 497–507.

Moller-Madsen, S., & Nystrup, J. (1992). Incidence of anorexia nervosa in Denmark. *Acta Psychiatrica Scandinavica, 86,* 197–200.

Monahan, J. (1992). "A terror to their neighbors": Beliefs about mental disorder and violence in historical and cultural perspective. *Bulletin of the American Academy of Psychiatry & the Law, 20,* 191–195.

Money, J., & Ehrhardt, A. (1972). *Man and woman, boy and girl.* Baltimore: Johns Hopkins University Press.

Monk, T. H. (2000). Shift work. In M. H. Kryger, T. Roth, & W. C. Dement (Eds.), *Principles and practice of sleep medicine* (3rd ed., pp. 600–605). Philadelphia: W. B. Saunders.

Monk, T. H., Buysse, D. J., & Rose, L. R. (1999). Wrist actigraphic measures of sleep in space. *Sleep, 22,* 948–954.

Monk, T. H., & Moline, M. L. (1989). The timing of bedtime and waketime decisions in free-running subjects. *Psychophysiology, 26,* 304–310.

Monroe, S. M., Bromet, E. J., Connell, M. M., & Steiner, S. C. (1986). Social support, life events, and depressive symptoms: A 1-year prospective study. *Journal of Consulting and Clinical Psychology, 54*(4), 424–431.

Monroe, S. M., Imhoff, D. F., Wise, B. D., & Harris, J. E. (1983). Prediction of psychological symptoms under high-risk psychosocial circumstances: Life events, social support, and symptom specificity. *Journal of Abnormal Psychology, 92*(2), 338–350.

Monroe, S. M., Kupfer, D. J., & Frank, E. (1992). Life stress and treatment course of recurrent depression: I. Response during index episode. *Journal of Consulting and Clinical Psychology, 60*(5), 718–724.

Monroe, S. M., & Reid, M. W. (2009). Life stress and major depression. *Current Directions in Psychological Science, 18*(2), 68–72.

Monroe, S. M., & Roberts, J. E. (1990). Conceptualizing and measuring life stress: Problems, principles, procedures, progress. [Special issue: II–IV. Advances in measuring life stress]. *Stress Medicine, 6*(3), 209–216.

Monroe, S. M., Roberts, J. E., Kupfer, D. J., & Frank, E. (1996). Life stress and treatment course of recurrent depression: II. Postrecovery associations with attrition, symptom course, and recurrence over 3 years. *Journal of Abnormal Psychology, 105*(3), 313–328.

Monroe, S. M., Rohde, P., Seeley, J. R., & Lewinsohn, P. M. (1999). Life events and depression in adolescence: For first onset of major depressive disorder. *Journal of Abnormal Psychology, 108*(4), 606–614.

Monroe, S. M., Slavich, G. M., & Georgiades, K. (2009). The social environment and life stress in depression. In I. H. Gotlib & C. L. Hammen (Eds.), Handbook of depression (2nd ed., pp. 340–360). New York: Guilford Press.

Montejo-Gonzalez, A. L., Liorca, G., Izquierdo, J. A., Ledesma, A., Bousono, M., Calcedo, A., ... Vicens, E. (1997). SSRI-Induced sexual dysfunction: Fluoxetine, paroxetine, sertraline, and fluvoxamine in a prospective, multi-center, and descriptive clinical study of 344 patients.

Journal of Sex and Marital Therapy, 23, 176–194.

Montero, I., Hernandez, I., Asencio, A., Bellver, F., LaCruz, M., & Masanet, M. J. (2005). Do all people with schizophrenia receive the same benefit from different family intervention programs? *Psychiatry Research, 133*(2–3), 187–195.

Montero, I., Masanet, M. J., Bellver, F., & Lacruz, M. (2006). The long-term outcome of two family intervention strategies in schizophrenia. *Comprehensive Psychiatry, 47*(5), 362–367.

Montiel-Nava, C., Pena, J. A., & Montiel-Barbero, I. (2003). Epidemiological data about attention deficit hyperactivity disorder in a sample of Marabino children. *Revista de Neurologia, 37,* 815–819.

Moore, D. S. (2001). *The dependent gene: The fallacy of "nature vs. nurture."* New York: Henry Holt & Company, LLC.

Moore, R. Y. (1999). Circadian rhythms: A clock for the ages. *Science, 284,* 2102–2103.

Moras, K., Clark, L. A., Katon, W., Roy-Byrne, P., Watson, D., & Barlow, D. H. (1996). Mixed anxiety-depression. In T. A. Widiger, A. J. Frances, H. A. Pincus, R. Ross, et al. (Eds.), *DSM-IV sourcebook* (Vol. 2, pp. 623–643). Washington, DC: American Psychiatric Association.

Morelli, G. A., Rogoff, B., Oppenheim, D., & Goldsmith, D. (1992). Cultural variation in infants' sleeping arrangements: Questions of independence. *Developmental Psychology, 28,* 604–613.

Moreno, A., Azar, M., Warren, N., Dickerson, T., Koob, G., & Janda, K. (2010). A critical evaluation of a nicotine vaccine within a self-administration behavioral model. *Molecular pharmaceutics, 7*(2), 431–441.

Moretti, M. M., Segal, Z. V., McCann, C. D., Shaw, B. F., Miller, D. T., & Vella, D. (1996). Self-referent versus other-referent information processing in dysphoric, clinically depressed, and remitted depressed subjects. *Personality & Social Psychology Bulletin, 22,* 68–80.

Morey, L. C. (1988). Personality disorders in DSM-III and DSM-III-R: Convergence, coverage, and internal consistency. *American Journal of Psychiatry, 145,* 573–577.

Morey, L. C., Alexander, G. M., & Boggs, C. (2005). Gender. In J. M. Oldham, A. E. Skodol, & D. S. Bender (Eds.), *Textbook of personality disorders* (pp. 541–559). Washington, DC: American Psychiatric Publishing.

Morey, L. C., Hopwood, C. J., & Klein, D. (2007). Depressive, passive-aggressive, and sadistic personality disorders. In W. O'Donohue, K. A. Fowler, & S. O. Lilienfeld (Eds.), *Personality disorders: Toward the DSM-V* (pp. 353–374). Thousand Oaks, CA: Sage Publications.

Morey, L. C., & Kurtz, J. E. (1989). *The place of neurasthenia in the DSM-IV.* Unpublished report to the DSM-IV subgroup on generalized anxiety disorder and mixed anxiety depression.

Morey, L. C., & Ochoa, E. S. (1989). An investigation of adherence to diagnostic criteria: Clinical diagnosis of the DSM-III personality disorders. *Journal of Personality Disorders, 3*(3), 180–192.

Morgan, D. (2007). The rationale for an immunological approach to Alzheimer's therapeutics. In A. C. Cuello (Ed.), *Pharmacological mechanisms in Alzheimer's therapeutics* (pp. 141–148). New York: Springer.

Morgan, D. L., & Morgan, R. K. (2001). Single-participant research design: Bringing science

to managed care. *American Psychologist, 56,* 119–127.

Morgan, H. W. (1981). *Drugs in America: A social history, 1800–1980.* Syracuse, NY: Syracuse University Press.

Morgan, J. P. (1997). Designer drugs. In J. H. Lowinson, P. Ruiz, R. B. Millman, & J. G. Langrod (Eds.), *Substance abuse: A comprehensive textbook* (pp. 264–269). Baltimore: Williams & Wilkins.

Morgenstern, H., & Glazer, W. M. (1993). Identifying risk factors for tardive dyskinesia among long-term outpatients maintained with neuroleptic medications: Results of the Yale tardive dyskinesia study. *Archives of General Psychiatry, 50,* 723–733.

Morgenthaler, T. I., & Silber, M. H. (2002). Amnestic sleep-related eating disorder associated with zolpidem. *Sleep Medicine, 3,* 323–327.

Morin, C. M. (1993). *Insomnia: Psychological assessment and management.* New York: Guilford Press.

Morin, C. M., & Azrin, N. H. (1988). Behavioral and cognitive treatments of geriatric insomnia. *Journal of Consulting and Clinical Psychology, 56,* 748–753.

Morin, C. M., Colecchi, C., Stone, J., Sood, R., & Brink, D. (1999). Behavioral and pharmacological therapies for late-life insomnia: A randomized controlled trial. *JAMA, 281,* 991–999.

Morin, C. M., & Edinger, J. D. (2003). Sleep disorders: Evaluation and diagnosis. In M. Hersen & S. M. Turner (Eds.), *Adult psychopathology and diagnosis* (4th ed., pp. 583–612). New York: John Wiley & Sons.

Morin, C. M., Kowatch, R. A., Barry, T., & Walton, E. (1993). Cognitive-behavior therapy for late-life insomnia. *Journal of Consulting and Clinical Psychology, 61,* 137–146.

Morin, C. M., Rodrigue, S., & Ivers, H. (2003). Role of stress, arousal, and coping skills in primary insomnia. *Psychosomatic Medicine, 65,* 259–267.

Morin, C. M., Savard, J., Ouellet, M. C., & Daley, M. (2003). Insomnia: *Nature, epidemiology and* treatment. In A. M. Nezu, C. M. Nezu, & P. A. Geller (Eds.), *Handbook of psychology: Health psychology* (Vol. 9, pp. 317–337). New York: John Wiley & Sons.

Morin, C. M., Stone, J., Trinkle, D., Mercer, J., & Remsberg, S. (1993). Dysfunctional beliefs and attitudes about sleep among older adults with and without insomnia complaints. *Psychology and Aging, 8,* 463–467.

Morin, C. M., & Wooten, V. (1996). Psychological and pharmacological approaches to treating insomnia: Critical issues in assessing their separate and combined effects. *Clinical Psychology Review, 16,* 521–542.

Morokoff, P. J. (1993). Female sexual arousal disorder. In W. O'Donohue & J. H. Geer (Eds.), *Handbook of sexual dysfunctions: Assessment and treatment* (pp. 157–199). Boston: Allyn & Bacon.

Morris, D. (1985). *Body watching: A field guide to the human species.* New York: Crown.

Morris, J. K., Cook, D. G., & Shaper, A. G. (1994). Loss of employment and mortality. *BMJ, 308,* 1135–1139.

Morris, J. S., Öhman, A., & Dolan, R. J. (1998). Conscious and unconscious emotion learning in the human amygdala. *Nature, 393,* 467–470.

Morris, M., Lack, L., & Dawson, D. (1990). Sleep-onset insomniacs have delayed temperature rhythms. *Sleep, 13,* 1–14.

Morrow, G. R., & Dobkin, P. L. (1988). Anticipatory nausea and vomiting in cancer patients undergoing chemotherapy treatment: Prevalence, etiology, and behavioral interventions. *Clinical Psychology Review, 8,* 517–556.

Morton, A. (1992). *Diana: Her true story.* New York: Pocket Books.

Mosher, D. L., & Sirkin, M. (1984). Measuring a macho personality constellation. *Journal of Research in Personality, 18,* 150–163.

Mosko, S., Richard, C., & McKenna, J. C. (1997). Maternal sleep and arousals during bedsharing with infants. *Sleep, 20,* 142–150.

Moss, A. R., & Bacchetti, P. (1989). Natural history of HIV infection. *AIDS, 3,* 55–61.

Mostofsky, D. I., & Barlow, D. H. (Eds.). (2000). *The management of stress and anxiety in medical disorders.* Needham Heights, MA: Allyn & Bacon.

Moulton, D. (2004, April 27). N.S.'s concern over oxycontin use rises: Government and college step in to stem narcotic abuse. *Medical Post, 40*(17). Retrieved May 17, 2004, from http://www.medicalpost.com/mpcontent/article .jsp?content 20040425_093635_5176

Mucha, T. F., & Reinhardt, R. F. (1970). Conversion reactions in student aviators. *American Journal of Psychiatry, 127,* 493–497.

Mueller, T., Keller, M. B., Leon, A. C., Solomon, D. A., Shea, M. T., Coryell, W., & Endicott, J. (1996). Recovery after 5 years of unremitting major depressive disorder. *Archives of General Psychiatry, 53,* 794–799.

Mueller, T. I., Leon, A. C., Keller, M. B., Solomon, D. A., Endicott, J., Coryell, W., ... Maser, J. D. (1999). Recurrence after recovery from major depressive disorder during 15 years of observational follow-up. *American Journal of Psychiatry, 156*(7), 1000–1006.

Mueser, K. T., Bellack, A. S., Wade, J. H., Sayers, S. L., Tierney, A., & Haas, G. (1993). Expressed emotion, social skill, and response to negative affect in schizophrenia. *Journal of Abnormal Psychology, 102,* 339–351.

Mueser, K. T., & Berenbaum, H. (1990). Psycho-dynamic treatment of schizophrenia: Is there a future? *Psychological Medicine, 20,* 253–262.

Mueser, K. T., Liberman, R. P., & Glynn, S. M. (1990). Psychosocial interventions in schizo-phrenia. In A. Kales, C. N. Stefanis, & J. A. Talbott (Eds.), *Recent advances in schizophrenia* (pp. 213–235). New York: Springer-Verlag.

Mueser, K. T., & Marcello, S. (2010). Schizophrenia. In D. H. Barlow (Ed.), *Oxford handbook of clinical psychology.* New York: Oxford University Press.

Mueser, K. T., Sengupta, A., Schooler, N. R., Bellack, A. S., Xie, H., Glick, I. D., & Keith, S. J. (2001). Family treatment and medication dosage reduction in schizophrenia: Effects on patient social func-tioning, family attitudes, and burden. *Journal of Consulting and Clinical Psychology, 69*(1), 3–12.

Mulder, R., Frampton, C., Luty, S., & Joyce, P. (2009). Eighteen months of drug treatment for depres-sion: *Predicting relapse and recovery. Journal of Affective Disorders, 114*(1–3), 263–270.

Mullane, J., & Corkum, P. (2006). Case series: Evaluation of a behavioral sleep intervention for three children with attention-deficit/hyperactivity disorder and dyssomnia. *Journal of Attention Disorders, 10,* 217–227.

Mullane, J. C., Stewart, S. H., Rhyno, E., Steeves, D., Watt, M., & Eisner, A. (2008). *Anxiety sensi-tivity and difficulties with smoking cessation.* In F. Columbus (Ed.), *Advances in Psychology Research.* Hauppauge, NY: Nova Science Publishers.

Mumford, D. B., Whitehouse, A. M., & Platts, M. (1991). Sociocultural correlates of eating disorders among Asian schoolgirls in Bradford. *British Journal of Psychiatry, 158,* 222–228.

Mundy, P., Sigman, M., & Kasari, C. (1990). A longitudinal study of joint attention and language development in autistic children. *Journal of Autism and Developmental Disorders, 20,* 115–128.

Munjack, D. J. (1984). The onset of driving phobias. *Journal of Behavior Therapy and Experimental Psychiatry, 15,* 305–308.

Muñoz, R. F. (1993). The prevention of depres-sion: Current research and practice. *Applied and Preventative Psychology, 2,* 21–33.

Munro, A. (1999). *Delusional disorder: Paranoia and related illnesses.* New York: Cambridge University Press.

Murdoch, D., Pihl, R. O., & Ross, D. (1990). Alcohol and crimes of violence: Present issues. *International Journal of the Addictions, 25,* 1065–1081.

Murphy, A., Lehrer, P., & Jurish, S. (1990). Cognitive coping skills training and relaxation training as treatments for tension headaches. *Behavior Therapy, 21,* 89–98.

Murphy, W. D., & Page, I. J. (2008). Exhibitionism: Psychopathology and theory. In D. R. Laws & W. T. O'Donohue (Eds.), *Sexual deviance: Theory, assessment, and treatment* (2nd ed., pp. 61–75). New York: Guilford Press.

Murray, B. L., & Wright, K. (2006). Integration of a suicide risk assessment and intervention approach: The perspective of youth. *Journal of Psychiatric and Mental Health Nursing, 13,* 157–164.

Murray, C. J. L. (1996). *Global health statistics.* Cambridge, MA: Harvard University Press.

Murray, C. J. L., & Lopez, A. (Eds.). (1996). *The global burden of disease.* Cambridge, MA: Harvard University Press.

Murray, J. B. (1998). Effectiveness of methadone maintenance for heroin addiction. *Psychological Reports, 83,* 295–302.

Mushquash, C., & Bova, D. (2007). Cross-cultural measurement and assessment issues. *Journal on Developmental Disabilities, 12,* 53–66.

Mustafa, G. (1990). Delivery systems for the care of schizophrenic patients in Africa—Sub-Sahara. In A. Kales, C. N. Stefanis, & J. A. Talbot (Eds.), *Recent advances in schizophrenia* (pp. 353–371). New York: Springer-Verlag.

Mustanski, B. S., Chivers, M. L., & Bailey, J. M. (2002). A critical review of recent biological research on human sexual orientation. *Annual Review of Sex Research, 13,* 89–140.

Musto, D. F. (1992). America's first cocaine epi-demic: What did we learn? In T. R. Kosten & H. D. Kleber (Eds.), *Clinician's guide to cocaine addiction: Theory, research, and treatment* (pp. 3–15). New York: Guilford Press.

Myers, J. K., Weissman, M. M., Tischler, C. E., Holzer, C. E., III, Orvaschel, H., Anthony, J. C., ... Stoltzman, R. (1984). Six-month prevalence of psychiatric disorders in three com-munities: 1980 to 1982. *Archives of General Psychiatry, 41,* 959–967.

Myers, K., & Collett, B. (2006). Rating scales. In M. K. Dulcan & J. M. Wiener (Eds.), *Essentials of child and adolescent psychiatry* (pp. 81–97). Washington, DC: American Psychiatric Publishing.

Nachmias, M., Gunnar, M., Mangelsdorf, S., Parritz, R. H., & Buss, K. (1996). Behavioral inhibition and stress reactivity: The moderating role of attachment security. *Child Development, 67*(2), 508–522.

Nagasaki, Y., Matsubara, Y., Takano, H., Fujii, K., Senoo, M., Akanuma, J., ... Narisawa, K. (1999). Reversal of hypopigmentation in phenylketon-uria mice by adenovirus-mediated gene transfer. *Pediatric Research, 45,* 465–473.

Nagel, D. B. (1991). Psychotherapy of schizophrenia: 1900–1920. In J. G. Howells (Ed.), *The concept of schizophrenia: Historical perspectives* (pp. 191–201). Washington, DC: American Psychiatric Press.

Nagin, D., & Tremblay, R. E. (1999). Trajectories of boys' physical aggression, opposition, and hyperactivity on the path to physically violent and nonviolent juvenile delinquency. *Child Development, 70,* 1181–1196.

Nagin, D. S., & Tremblay, R. E. (2001). Parental and early childhood predictors of persistent physical aggression in boys from kindergarten to high school. *Archives of General Psychiatry, 58,* 389–394.

Najavits, L. M. (2007). Psychosocial treatments for posttraumatic stress disorder. In P. E. Nathan & J. M. Gorman (Eds.), *A guide to treatments that work* (3rd ed.). New York: Oxford University Press.

NAMHC Workgroup on Mental Disorders Prevention Research. (1998). *Priorities for Prevention Research at NIMH* (NIH Publication No. 98–4321). Bethesda, MD: National Institutes of Health.

Nasser, M. (1986). Comparative study of the preva-lence of abnormal eating attitudes among Arab female students of both London and Cairo uni-versities. *Psychological Medicine, 16,* 621–625.

Nasser, M. (1988). Eating disorders: The cultural dimension. *Social Psychiatry and Psychiatric Epidemiology, 23,* 184–187.

Nathan, P. E. (1993). Alcoholism: Psychopathology, eti-ology, and treatment. In P. B. Sutker & H. E. Adams (Eds.), *Comprehensive handbook of psycho-pathology* (pp. 451–476). New York: Plenum Press.

National Center for Health Statistics. (1993). *Advance report of final mortality statistics, 1990* (Monthly Vital Statistics Report, Vol. 41, No. 7, Suppl.). Hyattsville, MD: Public Health Service.

National Sleep Foundation. (2005). *2005 Sleep in America Poll.* Washington, DC: Author.

Natsuaki, M., Cicchetti, D., & Rogosch, F. (2009). Examining the developmental history of child maltreatment, peer relations, and externalizing problems among adolescents with symptoms of paranoid personality disorder. *Development and Psychopathology, 21*(4), 1181–1193.

Navarrete, C. D., Olsson, A., Ho, A. K., Mendes, W. B., Thomsen, L., & Sidanius, J. (2009). Fear extinction to an out-group face: The role of target gender. *Psychological Science, 20*(2), 155–158.

Navia, B. A. (1990). The AIDS dementia complex. In J. L. Cummings (Ed.), *Subcortical dementia* (pp. 181–198). New York: Oxford University Press.

Neighbors, H. W., Jackson, J. S., Campbell, L., & Williams, D. (1989). The influence of racial factors on psychiatric diagnosis: A review and suggestions for research. *Community Mental Health Journal, 25*(4), 301–311.

Neill, M., & Sider, D. (1992, April 27). On the rebound. *People, 97.* Retrieved June 24, 2004, from http://www.eatingdisorderresources.com/peoplemag/042792carlingbassett.htm

Nelles, W. B. N., & Barlow, D. H. (1988). Do children panic? *Clinical Psychology Review, 8*(4), 359–372.

Nelson, R. O., & Barlow, D. H. (1981). Behavioral assessment: Basic strategies and initial procedures. In D. H. Barlow (Ed.), *Behavioral assessment of adult disorders.* New York: Guilford Press.

Nemeroff, C. (2006). The burden of severe depres-sion: A review of diagnostic challenges and treatment alternatives. *Journal of Psychiatric Research, 41*(3–4), 189–206.

Nestadt, G., Romanoski, A. J., Chahal, R., Merchant, A., Folstein, M. F., Gruenberg, E. M., & McHugh, P. R. (1990). An epidemiological study of histrionic personality disorder. *Psychological Medicine, 20,* 413–422.

Nestler, E. J., Hyman, S. E., & Malenka, R. C. (2008). *Molecular neuropharmacology* (2nd ed.). New York: McGraw-Hill.

Nestor, P. G. (2002). Mental disorder and violence: Personality dimensions and clinical features. *American Journal of Psychiatry, 159,* 1973–1978.

Neutel, C. I. (2005). The epidemiology of long-term benzodiazepine use. *International Review of Psychiatry, 17*(3), 189–197.

Newfoundland brother gets 4 years. (1992, February 8). *Spectator.* Retrieved August 23, 2003, from http://members.fortunecity.com/foul2/can.htm.

Newlin, D. B. (1989). The skin-flushing response: Autonomic, self-report, and conditioned responses to repeated administrations of alcohol in Asian men. *Journal of Abnormal Psychology, 98,* 421–425.

Newman, J. P., Patterson, C. M., & Kosson, D. S. (1987). Response perseveration in psychopaths. *Journal of Abnormal Psychology, 96,* 145–148.

Newman, J. P., & Wallace, J. F. (1993). Psychopathy and cognition. In K. S. Dobson & P. C. Kendall (Eds.), *Psychopathology and cognition* (pp. 293–349). New York: Academic Press.

Newman, J. P., Widom, C. S., & Nathan, S. (1985). Passive-avoidance in syndromes of disinhibition: Psychopathy and extraversion. *Journal of Personality and Social Psychology, 50,* 624–630.

Newman, S. C., & Bland, R. C. (1994). Life events and the 1-year prevalence of major depressive episode, generalized anxiety disorder, and panic disorder in a community sample. *Comprehensive Psychiatry, 35,* 76–82.

Newmark, C. S., & McCord, D. M. (1996). The Minnesota Multiphasic Personality Inventory-2 (MMPI-2). In C. S. Newmark (Ed.), *Major psychological assessment instruments* (pp. 1–58). Boston: Allyn & Bacon.

Neylan, T. C., Reynolds, C. F., III, & Kupfer, D. J. (2003). Sleep disorders. In R. E. Hales & S. C. Yudofsky (Eds.), *Textbook of clinical psychiatry* (4th ed., pp. 975–1000). Washington, DC: American Psychiatric Publishing.

Nezami, E., & Butcher, J. N. (2000). Objective personality assessment. In G. Goldstein & M. Hersen (Eds.), *Handbook of psychological assessment* (pp. 413–435). New York: Pergamon Press.

Neziroglu, F., McKay, D., Todaro, J., & Yaryura-Tobias, J. A. (1996). Effect of cognitive behaviour therapy on persons with body dysmorphic disorder and comorbid axis II diagnosis. *Behaviour Therapy, 27,* 67–77.

Nezu, C. M., Nezu, A. M., Friedman, S. H., Houts, P. S., DelliCarpini, L., Bildner, C., & Faddis, S. (1999). Cancer and psychological distress: Two investigations regarding the role of social problem-solving. *Journal of Psychosocial Oncology, 16*(3–4), 27–40.

Nicholls, T., Jack, L., & Ogloff, J. R. P. (1998, March). *Comorbidity of violence against self and violence against others in a civil psychiatric population.* Poster presented at the Biennial Meeting of the American Psychology Law Society, Redondo Beach, CA.

Nicholls, T. L., Ogloff, J. R. P., Brink, J., & Spidel, A. (2005). Psychopathology in women: A review of its clinical usefulness for assessing risk for aggression and criminality. *Behavioral Sciences and the Law, 23,* 779–802.

Nicholls, T. L., Ogloff, J. R. P., & Douglas, K. S. (2004). Assessing risk for violence among male and female civil psychiatric patients: The HCR-20, PCL:SV, and VSC. *Behavioral Sciences & the Law, 22,* 127–158.

Nichols, M. (with S. Dolye Driedger & D. Ballon). (1995, January 30). Schizophrenia: Hidden torment. *Maclean's.* Retrieved December 11, 2006, from http://www.mentalhealth.com/mag1/p51-sc01.html

Nicolosi, A., Laumann, E. O., Glasser, D. B., Brock, G., King, R., & Gingell, C. (2006). Sexual activity, sexual disorders and associated help-seeking behavior among mature adults in five anglophone countries from the global survey of sexual attitudes and behaviors (GSSAB). *Journal of Sex & Marital Therapy, 32,* 331–342.

Nicolson, R., & Szatmari, P. (2003). Genetic and neurodevelopmental influences in autistic disorder. *Canadian Journal of Psychiatry, 48,* 526–537.

Nielsen, T. A., Stenstrom, P., & Levin, R. (2006). Nightmare frequency as a function of age, gender, and September 11, 2001: Findings from an internet questionnaire. *Dreaming, 16,* 145–158.

Nikolas, M., & Burt, S. (2010). Genetic and environmental influences on ADHD symptom dimensions of inattention and hyperactivity: A meta-analysis. *Journal of Abnormal Psychology, 119*(1), 1.

Nisbett, R. E., & Ross, L. (1980). *Human inference: Strategies and shortcomings in social judgement.* New York: Century.

Nock, M. K., Borges, G., Bromet, E. J., Cha, C. B., Kessler, R. C., & Lee, S. (2008). Suicide and suicidal behavior. Epidemiologic Reviews, 30, 133–154.

Nock, M. K., Hwang, I., Sampson, N. A., & Kessler, R. C. (2009). Mental disorders, comorbidity and suicidal behavior: *Results from the National Comorbidity Survey Replication. Molecular Psychiatry, 15,* 868–876.

Nofzinger, E. A., Schwartz, C. F., Reynolds, C. F., Thase, M. E., Jennings, J. R., Frank, E., … Kupfer, D. J. (1994). Affect intensity and phasic REM sleep in depressed men before and after treatment with cognitive-behavior therapy. *Journal of Consulting and Clinical Psychology, 62,* 83–91.

Nolen-Hoeksema, S. (1987). Sex differences in unipolar depression: Evidence and theory. *Psychological Bulletin, 101*(2), 259–282.

Nolen-Hoeksema, S. (1990). *Sex differences in depression.* Stanford, CA: Stanford University Press.

Nolen-Hoeksema, S. (2000a). Further evidence for the role of psychosocial factors in depression chronicity. *Clinical Psychology: Science and Practice, 7*(2), 224–227.

Nolen-Hoeksema, S. (2000b). The role of rumination in depressive disorders and mixed anxiety/depressive symptoms. *Journal of Abnormal Psychology, 109,* 504–511.

Nolen-Hoeksema, S., Girgus, J. S., & Seligman, M. E. P. (1992). Predictors and consequences of childhood depressive symptoms: A 5-year longitudinal study. *Journal of Abnormal Psychology, 101*(3), 405–422.

Nolen-Hoeksema, S., Larson, J., & Grayson, C. (1999). Explaining the gender differences in depressive symptoms. *Journal of Personality and Social Psychology, 77*(5), 1061–1072.

Nolen-Hoeksema, S., Wisco, B. E., & Lyubomirsky, S. (2008). *Rethinking rumination.* Perspectives on Psychological Science, 3(5), 400–424.

Nolen-Hoeksema, S., Wolfson, A., Mumme, D., & Guskin, K. (1995). Helplessness in children of depressed and nondepressed mothers. *Developmental Psychology, 31,* 377–387.

Noonan, D. (2003). Exposing the myth of violence. *Schizophrenia Digest.* Retrieved November 10, 2003, from www.schizophreniadigest.com/images/archive/phpVQLG8H.pdf

Norman, R. M. G., Malla, A. K., McLean, T. S., McIntosh, E. M., Neufeld, R. W. J., Voruganti, L. P., & Cortese, L. (2002). An evaluation of a stress management program for individuals with schizophrenia. *Schizophrenia Research, 58*(2–3), 293–303.

Norman, R. M. G., & Townsend, L. A. (1999). Cognitive-behavioural therapy for psychosis: A status report. *Canadian Journal of Psychiatry, 44,* 245–252.

Normile, D. (2009). Asia grapples with unexpected wave of HIV infections. *Science, 27,* 1174.

Norrholm, S. D., & Ressler, K. J. (2009). Genetics of anxiety and trauma-related disorders. *Neuroscience, 164*(1), 272–287.

Norton, G. R., Cox, B. J., & Malan, J. (1992). Nonclinical panickers: A critical review. *Clinical Psychology Review, 12,* 121–139.

Norton, G. R., Dorward, J., & Cox, B. J. (1986). Factors associated with panic attacks in nonclinical subjects. *Behavior Therapy, 17,* 239–252.

Norton, G. R., Harrison, B., Hauch, J., & Rhodes, L. (1985). Characteristics of people with infrequent panic attacks. *Journal of Abnormal Psychology, 94,* 216–221.

Norton, G. R., Norton, P. J., Cox, B. J., & Belik, S. (2008). Panic spectrum disorders and substance use. In S. H. Stewart & P. J. Conrod (Eds.), *Anxiety and substance abuse disorders: The vicious cycle of comorbidity.* New York: Springer.

Noyes, R., Clarkson, C., Crowe, R. R., Yates, W. R., & McChesney, C. M. (1987). A family study of generalized anxiety disorder. *American Journal of Psychiatry, 144,* 1019–1024.

Noyes, R., Garvey, M. J., Cook, B., & Suelzer, M. (1991). Controlled discontinuation of benzodiazepine treatment for patients with panic disorder. *American Journal of Psychiatry, 148,* 517–523.

Noyes, R., Hoenk, P., Kuperman, S., & Slymen, D. (1977). Depersonalization in accident victims and psychiatric patients. *Journal of Nervous and Mental Disease, 164,* 401–407.

Noyes, R., & Kletti, R. (1977). Depersonalization in response to life-threatening danger. *Comprehensive Psychiatry, 18,* 375–384.

Noyes, R., Stuart, S. P., Langbehn, D. R., Happel, R. L., Longley, S. L., Muller, B. A., & Yagla, S. J. (2003). Test of an interpersonal model of hypochondriasis. *Psychosomatic Medicine, 65,* 292–300.

Noyes, R., Woodman, C., Garvey, M. J., Cook, B. L., Suelzer, M., Clancy, J., & Anderson, D. J. (1992). Generalized anxiety disorder vs. panic disorder: Distinguishing characteristics and patterns of comorbidity. *Journal of Nervous and Mental Disease, 180,* 369–379.

Noyes, R., Jr., Stuart, S. P., & Watson, D. B. (2008). A reconceptualization of the somatoform disorders. *Psychosomatics, 49*(1), 14–22.

Nugent, S. A. (2000). Perfectionism: Its manifestations and classroom-based interventions. *Journal of Secondary Gifted Education, 11,* 215–221.

Nurnberg, H. G., Raskin, M., Levine, P. E., Pollack, S., Siegel, O., & Prince, R. (1991). The comorbidity of borderline personality and other DSM-III-R Axis II personality disorders. *American Journal of Psychiatry, 148,* 1371–1377.

Nurnberger, J. I., & Gershon, E. S. (1992). Genetics. In E. S. Paykel (Ed.), *Handbook of affective disorders* (pp. 126–145). New York: Guilford Press.

Nurnberger, J. I., Jr., Berrettini, W., Tamarkin, L., Hamovit, J., Norton, J., & Gershon, E. S. (1988). Supersensitivity to melatonin suppression by light in young people at high risk for affective disorder: A preliminary report. *Neuropsychopharmacology, 1,* 217–223.

Nyhan, W. L. (1978). The Lesch-Nyhan syndrome. *Developmental Medicine and Child Neurology, 20,* 376–387.

Oades, R. D. (1985). The role of noradrenaline in tuning and dopamine in switching between signals in the CNS. *Neuroscience and Biobehavioral Reviews, 9,* 261–282.

O'Brien, C. P. (1996). Recent developments in the pharmacotherapy of substance abuse. *Journal of Consulting and Clinical Psychology, 64,* 677–686.

O'Brien, C. P., & Cornish, J. W. (1999). Opioids: Antagonists and partial agonists. In M. Galanter & H. D. Kleber (Eds.), *Textbook of substance abuse treatment* (2nd ed., pp. 281–294). Washington, DC: American Psychiatric Press.

O'Brien, K. M., & Vincent, N. K. (2003). Psychiatric comorbidity in anorexia and bulimia nervosa: Nature, prevalence and causal relationships. *Clinical Psychology Review, 23,* 57–74.

O'Brien, M. E., Clark, R. A., Besch, C. L., Myers, L., & Kissinger, P. (2003). Patterns and correlates of discontinuation of the initial HAART regimen in an urban outpatient cohort. *Journal of Acquired Immune Deficiency Syndrome, 34*(4), 407–414.

O'Brien, M. M., Trestman, R. L., & Siever, L. J. (1993). Cluster A personality disorders. In D. L. Dunner (Ed.), *Current psychiatric therapy* (pp. 399–404). Philadelphia: W. B. Saunders.

O'Callaghan, E., Sham, P., Takei, N., Glover, G., & Murray, R. M. (1991). Schizophrenia after prenatal exposure to 1957 A2 influenza epidemic. *Lancet, 337,* 1248–1250.

O'Carroll, P. W. (1990). Community strategies for suicide prevention and intervention. In S. J. Blumenthal & D. J. Kupfer (Eds.), *Suicide over the life cycle: Risk factors, assessment and treatment of suicidal patients.* Washington, DC: American Psychiatric Press.

O'Connor, B. P. (2005). A search for consensus on the dimensional structure of personality disorders. *Journal of Clinical Psychology, 61*(3), 323–345.

O'Connor, M., Sales, B. D., & Shuman, D. W. (1996). Mental health professional expertise in the courtroom. In B. D. Sales & D. W. Shuman (Eds.), *Law, mental health, and mental disorder* (pp. 40–59). Pacific Grove, CA: Brooks/Cole.

Ochsner, K. N., Ray, R. R., Hughes, B., McRae, K., Cooper, J. C., Weber, J., ... Gross, J. J. (2009). Bottom-up and top-down processes in emotion generation: Common and distinct neural mechanisms. *Psychological Science, 20*(11), 1322–1331.

O'Driscoll, G. A., Benkelfat, C., Florencio, P. S., Wolff, A. L. V. G., Joober, R., Lal, S., & Evans, A. C. (1999). Neural correlates of eye tracking deficits in first-degree relatives of schizophrenic patients: A positron emission tomography study. *Archives of General Psychiatry, 56,* 1127–1134.

O'Driscoll, G. A., Departié, L., Holahan, A. L. V., Savion-Lemieux, T., Barr, R. G., Jolicoeur, C., & Douglas, V. I. (2005). Executive functions and methylphenidate response in subtypes of attentiondeficit/hyperactivity disorder. *Biological Psychiatry, 57,* 1452–1460.

O'Driscoll, G. A., Lenzenweger, M. F., & Holzman, P. S. (1998). Antisaccades and smooth pursuit eye tracking and schizotypy. *Archives of General Psychiatry, 55,* 837–843.

Offman, A., & Kleinplatz, P. J. (2004). Does PMDD belong in the DSM? Challenging the medicalization of women's bodies. *Canadian Journal of Human Sexuality, 13*(1), 17–27.

Offord, D. R. (1989). *Ontario Child Health Study: Children at risk.* Toronto, ON: Ontario Ministry of Community and Social Services.

Offord, D. R., Boyle, M. H., Campbell, D., Goering, P., Lin, E., Wong, M., & Racine, Y. A. (1996). One-year prevalence of psychiatric disorder in Ontarians 15 to 64 years of age. *Canadian Journal of Psychiatry, 41,* 559–563.

Offord, D. R., Boyle, M. H., Szatmari, P., Rae-Grant, N. I., Links, P. S., Cadman, D. T., ... Woodward, C. A. (1987). Ontario Child Health Study: II. Six-month prevalence of disorder and rates of service utilization. *Archives of General Psychiatry, 44,* 832–836.

Ogata, S. N., Silk, K. R., Goodrich, S., Lohr, N. E., Westen, D., & Hill, E. M. (1990). Childhood sexual and physical abuse in adult patients with borderline personality disorder. *American Journal of Psychiatry, 147,* 1008–1013.

Ogloff, J. R. P. (2006). Psychopathy/antisocial personality disorder conundrum. *Australian and New Zealand Journal of Psychiatry, 40,* 519–528.

Ogloff, J. R. P., & Daffern, M. (2006). The dynamic appraisal of situational aggression: An instrument to assess risk for imminent aggression in psychiatric patients. *Behavioral Sciences and the Law, 4,* 799–813.

Ogloff, J. R. P., & Olley, M. C. (1998). The interaction between ethics and the law: The ongoing refinement of ethical standards for psychologists in Canada. *Canadian Psychology, 39,* 221–230.

Ogloff, J. R. P., & Whittemore, K. E. (2001). Fitness to stand trial and criminal responsibility in Canada. In R. A. Schuller & J. R. P. Ogloff (Eds.), *Introduction to psychology and law: Canadian perspectives* (pp. 283–313). Toronto, ON: University of Toronto Press.

Ogloff, J. R. P., Wong, S., & Greenwood, A. (1990). Treating criminal psychopaths in a therapeutic community program. *Sciences and the Law, 8,* 81–90.

Ogrodniczuk, J. S., & Piper, W. E. (2001). Day treatment for personality disorders: A review of research findings. *Harvard Review of Psychiatry, 9,* 105–117.

Ogrodniczuk, J. S., Piper, W. E., & Joyce, A. S. (2003). Differentiating symptoms of complicated grief and depression among psychiatric outpatients. *The Canadian Journal of Psychiatry, 48,* 87–93.

Ogrodniczuk, J. S., Piper, W. E., Joyce, A. S., Weideman, R., McCallum, M., Azim, H. F., & Rosie, J. S. (2003). Differentiating symptoms of complicated grief and depression among psychiatric outpatients. *Canadian Journal of Psychiatry, 48,* 87–93.

O'Hagan, S. (1992, February 22). Raving madness. *The Times Saturday Review,* pp. 10–12.

Ohan, J. L., & Johnston, C. (2007). What is the social impact of ADHD in girls? A multimethod assessment. *Journal of Abnormal Child Psychology, 35,* 239–250.

O'Hanlon, J. F., Haak, J. W., Blaauw, G. J., & Riemersma, J. B. J. (1982). Diazepam impairs lateral position control in highway driving. *Science, 27,* 79–81.

O'Hara, A. (2004). *Missing/murdered First Nations (Native) women.* Retrieved July 4, 2004, from http://www.missingnativewomen.ca/index.html

O'Hara, M. W. (1986). Social support, life events and depression during pregnancy and the puerperium. *Archives of General Psychiatry, 43*(6), 569–575.

O'Hara, M. W., Stuart, S., Gorman, L. L., & Wenzel, A. (2000). Efficacy of interpersonal psychotherapy for postpartum depression. *Archives of General Psychiatry, 57,* 1039–1045.

O'Hara, M. W., Zekoski, E. M., Philipps, L. H., & Wright, E. J. (1990). Controlled prospective study of postpartum mood disorders: Comparison of child bearing and nonbearing women. *Journal of Abnormal Psychology, 99*(1), 3–15.

Ohayon, M. M., & Schatzberg, A. F. (2003). Using chronic pain to predict depressive morbidity in the general population. *Archives of General Psychiatry, 60,* 39–47.

Öhman, A. (1986). Face the beast and fear the face: Animal and social fears as prototypes for evolutionary analyses of emotion. *Psychophysiology, 23,* 123–145.

Öhman, A. (1996). Preferential pre-attentive processing of threat in anxiety: Preparedness and attentional biases. In R. Rapee (Ed.), *Current controversies in the anxiety disorders* (pp. 253–290). New York: Guilford Press.

Öhman, A., & Dimberg, U. (1978). Facial expressions as conditioned stimuli for electrodermal responses: A case of preparedness? *Journal of Personality and Social Psychology, 36*(11), 1251–1258.

Öhman, A., Flykt, A., & Lundqvist, D. (2000). Unconscious emotion: Evolutionary perspective, psychophysiological data, and neuropsychological mechanisms. In R. Lane & L. Nadel (Eds.), *The cognitive neuroscience of emotion* (pp. 296–327). New York: Oxford University Press.

Öhman, A., & Mineka, S. (2001). Fears, phobias, and preparedness: Toward an evolved model of fear and fear learning. *Psychological Review, 108*(3), 483–522.

olde Hartman, T. C., Borghuis, M. S., Lucassen, P. L., van de Laar, F. A., Speckens, A. E., & van Weel, C. (2009). Medically unexplained symptoms, somatisation disorder and hypochondriasis: Course and prognosis. A systematic review. *Journal of Psychosomatic Research, 66*(5), 363–377.

Olds, J. (1956). Pleasure centers in the brain. *Scientific American, 195,* 105–116.

Olds, J., & Milner, P. M. (1954). Positive reinforcement produced by electrical stimulation of septal area and other regions of rat brain. *Journal of Comparative and Physiological Psychology, 47,* 419–427.

O'Leary, A. (1990). Stress, emotion, and human immune function. *Psychological Bulletin, 108*(3), 363–382.

Olin, S. S., Raine, A., Cannon, T. D., Parnas, J., Schulsinger, F., & Mednick, S. A. (1997). Childhood behavior precursors of schizotypal personality disorder. *Schizophrenia Bulletin, 23,* 93–103.

Oliver, M. B., & Hyde, J. S. (1993). Gender differences in sexuality: A meta-analysis. *Psychological Bulletin, 114*(1), 29–51.

Olivier, P., Bertrand, L., Tubery, M., Lauque, D., Montastruc, J.-L., & Lapeyre-Mestre, M. (2009). Hospitalizations because of adverse drug reactions in elderly patients admitted through the emergency department: A prospective survey. *Drugs & Aging, 26*(6), 475–482.

Ollendick, T. H., & Huntzinger, R. M. (1990). Separation anxiety disorder in childhood. In M. Hersen & C. G. Last (Eds.), *Handbook of child and adult psychopathology: A longitudinal perspective.* Elmsford, NY: Pergamon Press.

Ollendick, T. H., & Ollendick, D. G. (1990). Tics and Tourette syndrome. In A. M. Gross & R. S. Drabman (Eds.), *Handbook of clinical behavioral pediatrics* (pp. 243–252). New York: Plenum Press.

Olley, M. C., & Ogloff, J. R. P. (1995). Patients' rights advocacy: Implications for program design and implementation. *Journal of Mental Health Administration, 22,* 368–376.

Olver, M. E., & Wong, S. C. P. (2006). Psychopathy, sexual deviance, and recidivism among sex offenders. *Sexual Abuse: Journal of Research and Treatment, 18,* 65–82.

O'Malley, M., & Missio, E. (2003, January 13). Gordon Campbell's predicament. *CBC News Online.* Retrieved June 24, 2004, from http://www.cbc.ca/news/features/campbell_gordon.html

O'Malley, S. S. (1996). Opioid antagonists in the treatment of alcohol dependence. Clinical efficacy and prevention of relapse. *Alcohol and Alcoholism, 31*(Suppl. 1), 77–81.

O'Malley, S. S., Jaffe, A. J., Chang, G., Schottenfeld, R. S., Meyer, R. E., & Rounsaville, B. (1992). Naltrexone and coping skills therapy for alcohol dependence: A controlled study. *Archives of General Psychiatry, 49,* 881–887.

O'Neill, P. (1998a). Communities, collectivities, and the ethics of research. *Canadian Journal of Community Mental Health, 17,* 67–78.

O'Neill, P. (1998b). Teaching ethics: The utility of the CPA code. *Canadian Psychology, 39,* 194–201.

Opjordsmoen, S. (1989). Delusional disorders: I. Comparative long-term outcome. *Acta Psychiatrica Scandinavica, 80,* 603–612.

Orbach, I. (1997). A taxonomy of factors related to suicidal behavior. *Clinical Psychology: Science and Practice, 4,* 205–224.

Orne, M. T., Dinges, D. F., & Orne, E. C. (1984). On the differential diagnosis of multiple personality in the forensic context. *International Journal of Clinical and Experimental Hypnosis, 32,* 118–169.

O'Rourke, N., & Cappeliez, P. (2002). Perceived control, coping, and expressed burden among spouses of suspected dementia patients: Analysis of the goodness-of-fit hypothesis. *Canadian Journal on Aging, 21,* 385–392.

O'Rourke, N., Cappeliez, P., & Guindon, S. (2003). Depressive symptoms and physical health of caregivers of persons with cognitive impairment: Analysis of reciprocal effects over time. *Journal of Aging and Health, 15,* 688–712.

O'Rourke, N., Tuokko, H., Hayden, S., & Beattie, B. L. (1997). Early identification of dementia: predictive validity of the clock test. *Archives of Clinical Neuropsychology, 12,* 257–267.

Orth, U., Robins, R. W., Trzesniewski, K. H., Maes, J., & Schmitt, M. (2009). Low self-esteem is a risk factor for depressive symptoms from young adulthood to old age. *Journal of Abnormal Psychology, 118*(3), 472–478.

Ortiz, A., & Medicna-Mora, M. E. (1988). *Research on drugs in Mexico: Epidemiology of drug abuse and issues among Native American populations.* In Community Epidemiology Work Group Proceedings, December 1987. (Contract No. 271–87–8321). Washington, DC: U.S. Government Printing Office.

Oscar-Berman, M., Shagrin, B., Evert, D. L., & Epstein, C. (1997). Impairments of brain and behavior: The neurological effects of alcohol. *Alcohol Health & Research World, 21,* 65–75.

Oslin, D. W., & Cary, M. S. (2003). Alcohol-related dementia: Validation of diagnostic criteria. *American Journal of Geriatric Psychiatry, 11,* 441–447.

Öst, L. G. (1985). Mode of acquisition of phobias. *Acta Universitatis Uppsaliensis* (Abstracts of Uppsala Dissertations from the Faculty of Medicine) *529,* 1–45.

Öst, L. G. (1987). Age at onset in different phobias. *Journal of Abnormal Psychology, 96,* 223–229.

Öst, L. G. (1989). *Blood phobia: A specific phobia subtype in DSM-IV.* Paper requested by the Simple Phobia subcommittee of the DSM-IV Anxiety Disorders Work Group.

Öst, L. G. (1992). Blood and injection phobia: Background and cognitive, physiological, and behavioral variables. *Journal of Abnormal Psychology, 101*(1), 68–74.

Öst, L. G., Ferebee, I., & Furmark, T. (1997). One session group therapy of spiderphobia: Direct vs. indirect treatments. *Behaviour Research and Therapy, 35,* 721–732.

Öst, L. G., Svensson, L., Hellström, K., & Lindwall, R. (2001). One-session treatment of specific phobia in youths: A randomized clinical trial. *Journal of Consulting and Clinical Psychology, 69,* 814–824.

Öst, L. G., & Sterner, U. (1987). Applied tension: A specific behavioural method for treatment of blood phobia. *Behaviour Research and Therapy, 25,* 25–30.

O'Sullivan, K. (1979). Observations on vaginismus in Irish women. *Archives of General Psychiatry, 36,* 824–826.

Otis, J. D., & Pincus, D. B. (2008). Chronic pain. In B. A. Boyer & I. Paharia (Eds.), *Comprehensive handbook of clinical health psychology* (pp. 349–370). Hoboken, NJ: John Wiley & Sons.

Otto, M. W. & Applebaum, A. J. (in press). The nature and treatment of bipolar disorder and the bipolar spectrum. In D. H. Barlow (Ed.), *Handbook of clinical psychology.* New York: Oxford University Press.

Otto, M. W., Behar, E., Smits, J. A. J., & Hofmann, S. G. (2009). Combining pharmacological and cognitive behavioral therapy in the treatment of anxiety disorders. In M. M. Antony & M. B. Stein (Eds.), *Oxford handbook of anxiety and related disorders* (pp. 429–440). New York: Oxford University Press.

Ouellet-Morin, I., Boivin, M., Dionne, G., Lupien, S. J., Arsenault, L., Barr, R. G., … Tremblay, R. E. (2008). Variations in heritability of cortisol reactivity to stress as a function of early familial adversity among 19-month-old twins. *Archives of General Psychiatry, 65*(2), 211–218.

Ouimette, P. C., Finney, J. W., & Moos, R. H. (1997). Twelve-step and cognitive-behavioral treatment for substance abuse: A comparison of treatment effectiveness. *Journal of Consulting and Clinical Psychology, 65,* 230–240.

Overall, J. E., & Hollister, L. E. (1982). Decision rules for phenomenological classification of psychiatric patients. *Journal of Consulting and Clinical Psychology, 50,* 535–545.

Owens, K. M. B., Asmundson, G. J. G., Hadjistavro-poulos, T., & Owens, T. J. (2004). Attentional bias toward illness threat in individuals with elevated health anxiety. *Cognitive Therapy and Research, 28*(1), 57–66.

Owens, M. J., Mulchahey, J. J., Stout, S. C., & Plotsky, P. M. (1997). Molecular and neuro-biological mechanisms in the treatment of psychiatric disorders. In A. Tasman, J. Kay, & J. A. Lieberman (Eds.), *Psychiatry* (Vol. 1, pp. 210–257). Philadelphia: W. B. Saunders.

Oyama, O., & Andrasik, F. (1992). Behavioral strategies in the prevention of disease. In S. M.

Turner, K. S. Calhoun, & H. E. Adams (Eds.), *Handbook of clinical behavior therapy* (2nd ed., pp. 397–413). New York: John Wiley & Sons.

Pagani, L., Tremblay, R. E., Vitaro, F., Kerr, M., & McDuff, P. (1998). The impact of family transition on the development of delinquency in adolescent boys: A 9-year longitudinal study. *Journal of Child Psychology & Psychiatry & Allied Disciplines, 39,* 489–499.

Page, A. C. (1994). Blood-injury phobia. *Clinical Psychology Review, 14,* 443–461.

Page, A. C. (1996). Blood-injury-injection fears in medical practice. *Medical Journal of Australia, 164,* 189.

Page, A. C., & Martin, N. G. (1998). Testing a genetic structure of blood-injury-injection fears. *American Journal of Medical Genetics Part B: Neuropsychiatric Genetics, 81,* 377–384.

Page, G. G., Ben-Eliyahu, S., Yirmiya, R., & Liebeskind, J. C. (1993). Morphine attenuates surgery-induced enhancement of metastatic colonization in rats. *Pain, 54*(1), 21–28.

Pagel, J. F. (2006). Medications that induce sleepiness. In T. Lee-Chiong (Ed.), *Sleep: A comprehensive handbook* (pp. 175–182). Hoboken, NJ: John Wiley & Sons.

Pahl, J. J., Swayze, V. W., & Andreasen, N. C. (1990). Diagnostic advances in anatomical and functional brain imaging in schizophrenia. In A. Kales, C. N. Stefanis, & J. A. Talbott (Eds.), *Recent advances in schizophrenia* (pp. 163–189). New York: Springer-Verlag.

Pajer, K. A. (1998). What happens to "bad" girls? A review of the adult outcomes of antisocial adolescent girls. *American Journal of Psychiatry, 155,* 862–870.

Pandina, R., & Hendren, R. (1999). Other drugs of abuse: Inhalants, designer drugs, and steroids. In B. S. McCrady & E. E. Epstein (Eds.), *Addictions: A comprehensive guidebook* (pp. 171–184). New York: Oxford University Press.

Pantaleo, G., Graziosi, C., & Fauci, A. S. (1993). The immunopathogenesis of human immuno-deficiency virus infection. *New England Journal of Medicine, 328,* 327–335.

Pantony, K. L., & Caplan, P. J. (1991). Delusional dominating personality disorder: A modest proposal for identifying some consequences of rigid masculine socialization. *Canadian Psychology, 32,* 120–135.

Papadopoulos, F. C., Ekbom, A., Brandt, L., & Ekselius, L. (2009). Excess mortality, causes of death and prognostic factors in anorexia nervosa. *British Journal of Psychiatry, 194*(1), 10–17.

Papillo, J. F., & Shapiro, D. (1990). The cardio-vascular system. In J. T. Cacioppo & L. G. Tassinaryo (Eds.), *Principles of psychophysiology: Physical, social, and inferential elements.* New York: Cambridge University Press.

Papsdorf, M. P., & Alden, L. E. (1998). Mediators of social rejection in socially anxious individuals. *Journal of Research in Personality, 32,* 351–369.

Paquette, V., Lévesque, J., Mensour, B., Leroux, J.M., Beudoin, G., Bourgouin, P., & Beauregard, M. (2003). "Change the mind and you change the brain": Effects of cognitive-behavioral therapy on the neural correlates of spider phobia. *Neuroimage, 18,* 401–409.

Park, D. C. (2007). Eating disorders: A call to arms. *American Psychologist, 62,* 158.

Park, J. (2000). *Genetic screening in Alzheimer's disease.* Retrieved May 21, 2004, from http://www.fcs.okstate.edu/publications/resource-update/09–00/ger3–1.htm

Parker, G., & Hadzi-Pavlovic, D. (1990). Expressed emotion as a predictor of schizophrenic relapse: An analysis of aggregated data. *Psychological Medicine, 20,* 961–965.

Parker, S., Schwartz, B., Todd, J., & Pickering, L. (2004). Thimerosal-containing vaccines and autistic spectrum disorder: A critical review of published original data. *Pediatrics, 114*(3), 793.

Parkes, J. D., & Block, C. (1989). Genetic factors in sleep disorders. *Journal of Neurology, Neurosurgery, and Psychiatry, 52,* 101–108.

Parkinson, L., & Rachman, S. (1981a). Intrusive thoughts: The effects of an uncontrived stress. *Advances in Behaviour Research and Therapy, 3,* 111–118.

Parkinson, L., & Rachman, S. (1981b). Speed of recovery from an uncontrived stress. *Advances in Behaviour Research and Therapy, 3,* 119–123.

Parkinson Society of Canada. (2002). *Parkinson's disease: Frequently asked questions.* Retrieved November 24, 2003, from http://www.parkinson.ca/pd/faq.html

Parry-Jones, B., & Parry-Jones, W. L. (2002). History of bulimia and bulimia nervosa. In K. D. Brownell & C. G. Fairburn (Eds.), Eating disorders and obesity: *A comprehensive handbook* (2nd ed., pp. 145–150). New York: Guilford Press.

Parry-Jones, W. Li., & Parry-Jones, B. (1994). Implications of historical evidence for the classification of eating disorders. *British Journal of Psychiatry, 165,* 287–292.

Parsons, O. A., & Nixon, S. J. (1993). Behavioral disorders associated with central nervous system dysfunction. In P. B. Sutker & H. E. Adams (Eds.), *Comprehensive handbook of psychopathology* (pp. 689–733). New York: Plenum Press.

Pasewark, R. A., & Seidenzahl, D. (1979). Opinions concerning the insanity plea and criminality among mental patients. *Bulletin of the American Academy of Psychiatry and Law, 7,* 199–202.

Pataki, C. S., & Carlson, G. A. (1990). Major depression in childhood. In M. Hersen & C. Last (Eds.), *Handbook of child and adult psychopathology: A longitudinal perspective.* Elmsford, NY: Pergamon Press.

Patel, V., & Andrade, C. (2003). Pharmacological treatment of severe psychiatric disorders in the developing world: Lessons from India. *CNS Drugs, 17,* 1071–1080.

Patience, D. A. (1994). Cognitive-behavioural therapy for schizophrenia. *British Journal of Psychiatry, 165,* 266–267.

Patten, S. B. (2000). Major depression prevalence in Calgary. *Canadian Journal of Psychiatry, 45,* 923–926.

Patten, S. B. (2002). Progress against major depression in Canada. *Canadian Journal of Psychiatry, 47,* 775–780.

Patten, S. B., & Charney, D. A. (1998). Alcohol consumption and major depression in the Canadian population. *Canadian Journal of Psychiatry, 43,* 502–506.

Patten, S. B., Wang, J. L., Williams, J. V. A., Currie, S., Beck, C. A., Maxwell, C. J., & El-Guebaly, N. (2006). Descriptive epidemiology of major depression in Canada. *Canadian Journal of Psychiatry, 51,* 84–90.

Patterson, G. R. (1982). *Coercive family process.* Eugene, OR: Castalia.

Patterson, G. R. (1986). Performance models for antisocial boys. *American Psychologist, 41,* 432–444.

Patterson, G. R., Chamberlain, P., & Reid, J. B. (1982). A comparative evaluation of a parent training program. *Behavior Therapy, 13,* 638–650.

Patterson, G. R., Cobb, J. A., & Ray, R. S. (1972). Direct intervention in the classroom: A set of procedures for the aggressive child. In F. Clark, D. Evans, & L. Hamerlynck (Eds.), *Implementing behavioral programs for schools and clinics.* Champaign, IL: Research Press.

Patterson, G. R., DeBaryshe, B. D., & Ramsey, E. (1989). A developmental perspective on antisocial behavior. *American Psychologist, 44,* 329–335.

Patterson, G. R., & Fleischman, M. J. (1979). Maintenance of treatment effects: Some considerations concerning family systems and follow-up data. *Behavior Therapy, 10,* 168–185.

Patton, G. C. (1988). Mortality in eating disorders. *Psychological Medicine, 18*(4), 947–951.

Patton, G. C., Johnson-Sabine, E., Wood, K., Mann, A. H., & Wakeling, A. (1990). Abnormal eating attitudes in London school girls—A prospective epidemiological study: Outcome at twelve month follow up. *Psychological Medicine, 20,* 383–394.

Paul, G. L., & Lentz, R. J. (1977). *Psychosocial treatment of chronic mental patients: Milieu versus social learning programs.* Cambridge, MA: Harvard University Press.

Paulhus, D. L., & Morgan, K. L. (1997). Perceptions of intelligence in leaderless groups: The dynamic effects of shyness and acquaintance. *Journal of Personality and Social Psychology, 71,* 581–591.

Paulhus, D. L., & Williams, K. M. (2002). The Dark Triad of personality: Narcissism, Machiavellianism and psychopathy. *Journal of Research in Personality, 36,* 556–563.

Pauli, P., & Alpers, G. W. (2002). Memory bias in patients with hypochondriasis and somatoform pain disorder. *Journal of Psychosomatic Research, 52,* 45–53.

Pavalko, E. K., Elder, G. H., Jr., & Clipp, E. C. (1993). Work lives and longevity: Insights from a life course perspective. *Journal of Health and Social Behavior, 34,* 363–380.

Paxton, S. J., Schutz, H. K., Wertheim, E. H., & Muir, S. L. (1999). Friendship clique and peer influences on body image concerns, dietary restraint, extreme weight-loss behaviors, and binge eating in adolescent girls. *Journal of Abnormal Psychology, 108*(2), 255–266.

Paykel, E. S., Brayne, C., Huppert, F. A., Gill, C., Barkley, C., Gehlhaar, E., … O'Connor, D. (1994). Incidence of dementia in a population older than 75 years in the United Kingdom. *Archives of General Psychiatry, 51,* 325–332.

Paykel, E. S., & Weissman, M. M. (1973). Social adjustment and depression: A longitudinal study. *Archives of General Psychiatry, 28,* 659–663.

Payne, K. A., Reissing, E. D., Lahaie, M. A., Yitzchak M. B., Rhonda A., & Samir K. (2005). What is sexual pain? A critique of DSM's classification of dyspareunia and vaginismus. *Journal of Psychology & Human Sexuality, 17,* 141–154.

Pearlstein, T., & Steiner, M. (2008). Premenstrual dysphoric disorder: Burden of illness and treatment update. *Journal of Psychiatry & Neuroscience, 33*(4), 291–301.

Pearlstein, T., Yonkers, K. A., Fayyad, R., & Gillespie, J. A. (2005). Pretreatment pattern of symptom expression in premenstrual dysphoric disorder. *Journal of Affective Disorder, 85,* 275–282.

Pearson, C. (2002, October 31). MDs refuse to prescribe medicinal pot. *Windsor Star* [Online].

Retrieved October 26, 2003, from http://www.medicalmarihuana.ca/refusal.html

Peat, C., Mitchell, J. E., Hoek, H. W., & Wonderlich, S. A. (2009). Validity and utility of subtyping anorexia nervosa. International Journal of Eating Disorders, 42(7), 590–594.

Pechnick, R. N., & Ungerleider, J. T. (1997). Hallucinogens. In J. H. Lowinson, P. Ruiz, R. B. Millman, & J. G. Langrod (Eds.), *Substance abuse: A comprehensive textbook* (pp. 230–238). Baltimore: Williams & Wilkins.

Pedersen, N. L. (2010). Reaching the limits of genome-wide significance in Alzheimer disease: Back to the environment. *JAMA, 303*(18), 1864–1865.

Peeters, J., Van Beek, A., Meerveld, J., Spreeuwenberg, P., & Francke, A. (2010). Informal caregivers of persons with dementia, their use of and needs for specific professional support: A survey of the National Dementia Programme. *BMC Nursing, 9*(1), 9.

Pelham, W. E., Jr. (1999). The NIMH Multimodal Treatment Study for attention-deficit hyperactivity disorder: Just say yes to drugs alone? *Canadian Journal of Psychiatry, 44,* 981–990.

Pelham, W. E., Jr., Waschbusch, D. A., Hoza, B., Pillow, D. R., & Gnagy, E. M. (2001). Effects of methylphenidate and expectancy on performance, self-evaluations, persistence, and attributions on a social task in boys with ADHD. *Experimental & Clinical Psychopharmacology, 9,* 425–437.

Pelletier, J., Moisan, J., Roussel, R., & Gilbert, M. (1997). Heart health promotion: A community development experiment in a rural area of Quebec, Canada. *Health Promotion International, 12*(4), 291–298.

Pendery, M. L., Maltzman, I. M., & West, L. J. (1982). Controlled drinking by alcoholics? New findings and a reevaluation of a major affirmative study. *Science, 217,* 169–175.

Pentz, M. A. (1999). Prevention. In M. Galanter & H. D. Kleber (Eds.), *Textbook of substance abuse treatment* (2nd ed., pp. 535–544). Washington, DC: American Psychiatric Press.

"People's Courtney, The" (1995). Retrieved November 1, 2006, from http://www.geocities.com/ SunsetStrip/4925/Alanis/Articles/art9.html

Pepler, D. J., Craig, W. M., Connolly, J. A., Yuile, A., McMaster, L., & Jiang, D. (2006). A developmental perspective on bullying. *Aggressive Behavior, 32*(4), 376–384.

Pepper, C. M., Klein, D. N., Anderson, R. L., Riso, L. P., Ouimette, P. C., & Lizardi, H. (1995). DSM-III-R Axis II comorbidity in dysthymia and major depression. *American Journal of Psychiatry, 152,* 239–247.

Pericak-Vance, M. A., Johnson, C. C., Rimmler, J. B., Saunders, A. M., Robinson, L. C., D'Hondt, E. G., … Haines, J. L. (1996). Alzheimer's disease and apolipoprotein E-4 allele in an Amish population. *Annals of Neurology, 39,* 700–704.

Perlin, M. L. (1996). The voluntary delivery of mental health services in the community. In B. D. Sales and D. W. Shuman (Eds.), *Law, mental health, and mental disorder* (pp. 150–177). Pacific Grove, CA: Brooks/Cole.

Perlin, M. L. (2000). The hidden prejudice: Mental disability on trial. Washington, DC: *American Psychological Association.*

Perls, F. S. (1969). *Gestalt therapy verbatim.* Moab, UT: Real People Press.

Perry, A., Tarrier, N., Morriss, R., McCarthy, E., & Limb, K. (1999). Randomized controlled trial of efficacy of teaching patients with bipolar disorder to identify early symptoms of relapse and obtain treatment. *BMJ, 318,* 149–153.

Perry, J. C. (1993). Longitudinal studies of personality disorders. *Journal of Personality Disorders, 7,* 63–85.

Perry, J. C., Banon, E., & Ianni, F. (1999). Effectiveness of psychotherapy for personality disorders. *American Journal of Psychiatry, 156,* 1312–1321.

Perry, S. (1993). Psychiatric treatment of adults with human immunodeficiency virus infection. In D. L. Dunner (Ed.), *Current psychiatric therapy* (pp. 475– 482). Philadelphia: W. B. Saunders.

Person, D. C., & Borkevec, T. D. (1995, August). *Anxiety disorders among the elderly: Patterns and issues.* Paper presented at the 103rd annual meeting of the American Psychological Association. New York, NY.

Perugi, G., Giannotti, D., Di Vaio, S., Frare, F., Saettoni, M., & Cassano, G. B. (1996). Fluvoxamine in the treatment of body dysmorphic disorder (dysmorphophobia). *International Clinical Psychopharmacology, 11,* 247–254.

Peselow, E. D., Fieve, R. R., Difiglia, C., & Sanfilipo, M. P. (1994). Lithium prophylaxis of bipolar illness: The value of combination treatment. *British Journal of Psychiatry, 164,* 208–214.

Peters, C. P. (1991). Concepts of schizophrenia after Kraepelin and Bleuler. In J. G. Howells (Ed.), *The concept of schizophrenia: Historical perspectives* (pp. 93–107). Washington, DC: American Psychiatric Press.

Petersen, A. C., Compas, B. E., Brooks-Gunn, J., Stemmler, M., Ey, S., & Grant, K. E. (1993). Depression in adolescence. *American Psychologist, 48*(2), 155–168.

Peterson, B. S. (1995). Neuroimaging in child and adolescent neuropsychiatric disorders. *Journal of the American Academy of Child and Adolescent Psychiatry, 34,* 1560–1576.

Peterson, C. B., Mitchell, J. E., Engbloom, S., Nugent, S., Mussell, M. P., & Miller, J. P. (1998). Group cognitive-behavioral treatment of binge eating disorders: A comparison of therapist-led versus self-help formats. *International Journal of Eating Disorders, 24,* 125–136.

Peterson, D. R. (1968). *The clinical study of social behavior.* New York: Appleton-Century-Crofts.

Peterson, J. B., Conrod, P., Vassileva, J., Gianoulakis, C., & Pihl, R. O. (2006). Differential effects of naltrexone on cardiac, subjective and behavioural reactions to acute ethanol intoxication. *Journal of Psychiatry & Neuroscience, 31*(6), 386–393.

Peterson, J. B., Pihl, R. O., Gianoulakis, C., Conrod, P., Finn, P. R., Stewart, S. H., … Bruce, K. R. (1996). Ethanol-induced change in cardiac and endogenous opiate function and risk for alcoholism. *Alcoholism: Clinical & Experimental Research, 20,* 1542–1552.

Peterson, J. B., Pihl, R. O., Seguin, J. R., Finn, P. R., & Stewart, S. H. (1993). Heart rate re   activity and alcohol consumption among sons of male alcoholics and sons of non-alcoholics. *Journal of Psychiatry and Neuroscience, 18,* 190–198.

Peterson, L., Farmer, J., & Kashani, J. H. (1990). Parental injury prevention endeavors: A function of health beliefs? *Health Psychology, 9*(2), 177–191.

Peterson, L., & Roberts, M. C. (1992). Complacency, misdirection, and effective prevention of children's injuries. *American Psychologist, 47*(8), 1040–1044.

Peterson, L., & Thiele, C. (1988). Home safety at school. *Child and Family Behavior Therapy, 10*(1), 1–8.

Peto, R., Lopez, A. D., Boreham, J., & Thun, T. (2006). *Mortality from Smoking in Developed Countries 1950–2000.* Retrieved January 7, 2008, from http://www.deathsfromsmoking.net/countries.html

Petrovic, P., Kalso, E., Petersson, K. M., & Ingvar, M. (2002). Placebo and opioid analgesia: Imaging a shared neuronal network. *Science, 295,* 1737–1740.

Petry, N. M., Martin, B., Cooney, J. L., & Kranzler, H. R. (2000). Give them prizes, and they will come: Contingency management for treatment of alcohol dependence. *Journal of Consulting and Clinical Psychology, 68*(2), 250–257.

Pfohl, B. (1991). Histrionic personality disorder: A review of available data and recommendations for DSM-IV. *Journal of Personality Disorders, 5,* 150–166.

Pfohl, B. (1993). Proposed DSM-IV criteria for personality disorders. In D. L. Dunner (Ed.), *Current psychiatric therapy* (pp. 397–399). Philadelphia: W. B. Saunders.

Pfohl, B. (1995). Histrionic personality disorder. In W. J. Livesley (Ed.), *The DSM-IV personality disorders* (pp. 173–192). New York: Guilford Press.

Pfohl, B., & Blum, N. (1995). Obsessive-compulsive personality disorder. In W. J. Livesley (Ed.), *The DSM-IV personality disorders* (pp. 261–276). New York: Guilford Press.

Pham, T. H., Vanderstukken, O., Philippot, P., & Vanderlinden, M. (2003). Selective attention and executive functions deficits among criminal psychopaths. *Aggressive Behavior, 29,* 393–405.

Pharmacists. ca. (2003). *Products discontinued from the market.* Retrieved August 6, 2004, from http://www.pharmacists.ca/content/hcp/tools/drugnews/discontinued.htm

Phifer, J. F., & Murrell, S. A. (1986). Etiologic factors in the onset of depressive symptoms in older adults. *Journal of Abnormal Psychology, 95,* 282–291.

Philips, H. C., & Grant, L. (1991). Acute back pain: A psychological analysis. *Behaviour Research and Therapy, 29,* 429–434.

Phillip, M. (2003). When women run away from their lives. *The Globe and Mail,* May 9, 2003. Retrieved June 17, 2004, from http://www.globeandmail.com/servlet/ArticleNews/TPPrint/LAC/20030509/UAMNEN

Phillips, K. A. (1991). Body dysmorphic disorder: The distress of imagined ugliness. *American Journal of Psychiatry, 148,* 1138–1149.

Phillips, K. A. (2000). Quality of life for patients with body dysmorphic disorder. *Journal of Nervous and Mental Disease, 188*(3), 170–175.

Phillips, K. A., Albertini, R. S., & Rasmussen, S. A. (2002). A randomized placebo-controlled trial of fluoxetine in body dysmorphic disorder. *Archives of General Psychiatry, 59,* 381–388.

Phillips, K. A., Dwight, M. M., & McElroy, S. L. (1998). Efficacy and safety of fluvoxamine in body dysmorphic disorder. *Journal of Clinical Psychiatry, 59*(4), 165–171.

Phillips, K. A., & Gunderson, J. G. (2000). Personality disorders. In M. H. Kryger, T. Roth, & W. C. Dement (Eds.), *Principles and practice of sleep medicine* (3rd ed., pp. 795–823). Philadelphia: W. B. Saunders.

Phillips, K. A., Gunderson, J. G., Triebwasser, J., Kimble, C. R., Faedda, G., Lyoo, I. K., & Renn, J. (1998). Reliability and validity of depressive personality disorder. *American Journal of Psychiatry, 155,* 1044–1048.

Phillips, K. A., McElroy, S. L., Keck, P. E., Jr., Pope, H. G., Jr., & Hudson, J. I. (1993). Body dys-

morphic disorder: 30 cases of imagined ugliness. *American Journal of Psychiatry, 150,* 302–308.

Phillips, K. A., Menard, W., Pagano, M., Fay, C., & Stout, R. (2006). Delusional versus non-delusional body dysmorphic disorder: Clinical features and course of illness. *Journal of Psychiatric Research, 40,* 95–104.

Phillips, K. A., & Najjar, F. (2003). An open-label study of citalopram in body dysmorphic disorder. *Journal of Clinical Psychiatry, 64,* 715–720.

Phillips, K. A., Pagano, M., Menard, W., & Stout, R. (2006). A 12-month follow-up study of the course of body dysmorphic disorder. *American Journal of Psychiatry, 163,* 907–912.

Phillips, K. A., & Stout, R. (2006). Association in the longitudinal course of body dysmorphic disorder with major depression, obsessive compulsive disorder, and social phobia. Journal of *Psychiatric Research, 40,* 360–369.

Phillips, K. A., Wilhelm, S., Koran, L. M., Didie, E., Fallon, B., Feusner, J., & Stein, D. J. (2010). Body dysmorphic disorder: Some key issues for DSM-V. *Depression and Anxiety, 27,* 573–591.

Phillips, K. A., Yen, S., & Gunderson, J. G. (2003). Personality disorders. In R. E. Hales & S. C. Yudofsky (Eds.), *Textbook of clinical psychiatry* (4th ed., pp. 804–832). Washington, DC: American Psychiatric Press.

Phillips, L. J., Francey, S. M., Edwards, J., & McMurray, N. (2007). Stress and psychosis: Towards the development of new models of investigation. *Clinical Psychology Review, 27,* 307–317.

Physicians for a Smoke-Free Canada. (2002). *Percentage of Canadians who smoke (on either a daily or occasional basis), federal surveys, 1965–2003.* Retrieved October 26, 2003, from http://www.smoke-free.ca/factsheets/pdf/prevalence.pdf

Piasecki, T. M., Hufford, M. R., Solhan, M., & Trull, T. J. (2007). Assessing clients in their natural environments with electronic diaries: Rationale, benefits, limitations, and barriers. *Psychological Assessment, 19,* 25–43.

Pickens, R. W., Svikis, D. S., McGue, M., Lykken, D. T., Heston, L. L., & Clayton, P. J. (1991). Heterogeneity in the inheritence of alcoholism. *Archives of General Psychiatry, 48,* 19–28.

Pierce, J. P., & Gilpin, E. A. (1995). A historical analysis of tobacco marketing and the uptake of smoking by youth in the United States: 1890–1977. *Health Psychology, 14,* 500–508.

Pierce, K. A., & Kirkpatrick, D. R. (1992). Do men lie on fear surveys? *Behaviour Research and Therapy, 30,* 415–418.

Pierce, W. D., & Epling, W. F. (1994). Activity anorexia: An interplay between basic and applied behavior analysis. *Behavior Analyst, 17,* 7–23.

Pierce, W. D., & Epling, F. W. (1996). Theoretical developments in activity anorexia. In W. F. Epling & W. D. Pierce (Eds.), *Activity anorexia: Theory research, and treatment* (pp. 23–41). Mahwah, NJ: Erlbaum.

Pihl, R. O., Assaad, J. M., & Hoaken, P. N. S. (2003). The alcohol-aggression relationship and differential sensitivity to alcohol. *Aggressive Behavior, 29*(4), 302–315.

Pihl, R. O., Peterson, J. B., & Lau, M. A. (1993). A biosocial model of the alcohol-aggression relationship. *Journal of Studies on Alcohol,* (Suppl. 11) 128–139.

Piira, T., Hayes, B., Goodenough, B., & von Baeyer, C. L. (2006). Effects of attentional direction, age, and coping style on cold-pressor pain in children.

Behaviour Research and Therapy, 44(6), 835–848.

Pike, K. M., Devlin, M. J, & Loeb, C. (2004). Cognitive-behavioral therapy in the treatment of anorexia nervosa, and binge eating disorder. In J. K. Thompson (Ed.), *Handbook of eating disorders and obesity* (pp. 130–162). New York: John Wiley & Sons.

Pike, K. M., Loeb, K., & Vitousek, K. (1996). Cognitive-behavioral therapy for anorexia nervosa and bulimia nervosa. In J. K. Thompson (Ed.), *Body image, eating disorders and obesity* (pp. 253–302). Washington, DC: American Psychological Association.

Pike, K. M., & Rodin, J. (1991). Mothers, daughters, and disordered eating. *Journal of Abnormal Psychology, 100*(2), 198–204.

Pike, K. M., Walsh, B. T., Vitousek, K., Wilson, G. T., & Bauer, J. (2003). Cognitive behavior therapy in the post-hospitalization treatment of anorexia nervosa. *American Journal of Psychiatry, 160*, 2046–2048.

Pilowsky, I. (1970). Primary and secondary hypochondriasis. *Acta Psychiatrica Scandinavica, 46*, 273–285.

Pincus, D. B., Santucci, L. C., Ehrenreich, J. T., & Eyberg, S. M. (2008). The implementation of modified parent-child interaction therapy for youth with separation anxiety disorder. *Cognitive and Behavioral Practice, 15*(2), 118–125.

Pinel, J. P. J., Assanand, S., & Lehman, D. R. (2000). Hunger, eating, and ill health. *American Psychologist, 55*, 1105–1116.

Pinel, P. (1962). *A treatise on insanity*. New York: Hafner. (Original work published in 1801).

Piper, A., & Merskey, H. (2004). The persistence of folly: Critical examination of dissociative identity disorder. Part I. The excesses of an improbable concept. *Canadian Journal of Psychiatry, 49*, 678–683.

Piran, N. (1997). Prevention of eating disorders: Directions for future research. *Psychopharmacology Bulletin, 33*, 419–423.

Piran, N. (1998). A participatory approach to the prevention of eating disorders in a school. In W. Vandereycken & G. Noordenbos (Eds.), *Prevention of eating disorders* (pp. 173–186). New York: University Press.

Piran, N. (1999). Eating disorders: A trial of prevention in a high risk school setting. *Journal of Primary Prevention, 20*, 75–90.

Piran, N. (2004). Teachers: On "being" (rather than "doing") prevention. *Eating Disorders: The Journal of Treatment & Prevention, 12*, 1–9.

Piran, N. V. (2001). Reinhabiting the body. *Feminism & Psychology, 11*, 172–176

Pirke, K. M., Schweiger, U., & Fichter, M. M. (1987). Hypothalamic-pituitary-ovarian axis in bulimia. In J. I. Hudson & H. G. Pope (Eds.), *The psychobiology of bulimia* (pp. 15–28). Washington, DC: American Psychiatric Press.

Pithers, W. D., Martin, G. R., & Cumming, G. F. (1989). Vermont treatment program for sexual aggressors. In D. R. Laws (Ed.), *Relapse prevention with sex offenders* (pp. 292–310). New York: Guilford Press.

Pliner, P., & Haddock, G. (1996). Perfectionism in weight-concerned and unconcerned women: An experimental approach. *International Journal of Eating Disorders, 19*, 381–389.

Plomin, R. (1990). The role of inheritance in behavior. *Science, 248*, 183–188.

Plomin, R., & Davis, O. S. P. (2009). The future of genetics in psychology and psychiatry: Microarrays, genome-wide association, and

non-coding RNA. *Journal of Child Psychology and Psychiatry, 50*(1–2), 63–71.

Plomin, R., DeFries, J. C., McClearn, G. E., & Rutter, M. (1997). *Behavioral genetics: A primer* (3rd ed.). New York: Freeman.

Plomin, R., McClearn, G. E., Smith, D. L., Skuder, P., Vignetti, S., Chorney, M. J., ... McGuffin, P. (1995). Allelic association between 100 DNA markers and high versus low IQ. *Intelligence, 21*, 31–48.

Plomin, R., Owen, M. J., & McGuffin, P. (1994). The genetic basis of complex human behaviors. *Science, 264*, 1733–1739.

Podewils, L. J., Guallar, E., Kuller, L. H., Fried, L. P., Lopez, O. L., Carlson, M., & Lyketsos, C. G. (2005). Physical activity, APOE genotype, and dementia risk: Findings from the Cardiovascular Health Cognition Study. *American Journal of Epidemiology, 161*, 639–651.

Poirier, M.-F., Laqueille, X., Jalfre, V., Willard, D., Bourdel, M. C., Fermanian, J., & Olié, J. P. (2004). Clinical profile of responders to buprenorphine as a substitution treatment in heroin addicts: Results of a multicenter study of 73 patients. *Progress in Neuro-Psychopharmacology & Biological Psychiatry, 28*, 267–272.

Polanczyk, G., Zeni, C., Genro, J. P., Guimaraes, A. P., Roman, T., Hutz, M. H., & Rohde, L. A. (2007). Association of the adrenergic α-2A receptor gene with methylphenidate improvement of inattentive symptoms in children and adolescents with attention-deficit/hyperactivity disorder. *Archives of General Psychiatry, 64*, 218–224.

Polivy, J. (2001). The false hope syndrome: unrealistic expectations of self-change. *International Journal of Obesity and Related Metabolic Disorders, 25*(Suppl. 1), 80–84.

Polivy, J., & Herman, C. P. (2002). If at first you don't succeed. False hopes of self-change. *American Psychologist, 57*, 677–689.

Polivy, J., Herman, C. P., Mills, J., & Brock, H. (2003). Eating disorders in adolescence. In G. R. Adams & M. D. Berzonsky (Eds.), *Blackwell handbook of adolescence* (pp. 523–549). Malden, MA: Blackwell.

Polivy, J. M., & Herman, C. P. (1985). Dieting and binging: A causal analysis. *American Psychologist, 40*, 193–201.

Polivy, J. M., & Herman, C. P. (1993). Etiology of binge eating: Psychological mechanisms. In C. G. Fairburn & G. T. Wilson (Eds.), *Binge eating: Nature, assessment, and treatment*. New York: Guilford Press.

Pollack, C., & Andrews, G. (1989). Defense styles associated with specific anxiety disorders. *American Journal of Psychiatry, 146*, 1500–1502.

Pollack, M. H. (2005). The pharmacotherapy of panic disorder. *Journal of Clinical Psychiatry, 66*, 23–27.

Pollack, M. H., & Simon, N. M. (2009). Pharmacotherapy for panic disorder and agoraphobia. In M. M. Antony & M. B. Stein (Eds.), *Oxford handbook of anxiety and related disorders* (pp. 295–307). New York: Oxford University Press.

Polley, S. (Director/Writer). (2006). *Away from her* [Motion picture]. Canada: Capri Films.

Polloway, E. A., Schewel, R., & Patton, J. R. (1992). Learning disabilities in adulthood: Personal perspectives. *Journal of Learning Disabilities, 25*, 520–522.

Polonsky, D. C. (2000). Premature ejaculation. In S. R. Leiblum & R. C. Rosen (Eds.), *Principles and practice of sex therapy* (3rd ed., pp. 305–332). New York: Guilford Press.

Pomeroy, C. (2004). Assessment of medical status and physical factors. In Thompson, J. K. (Ed.), *Handbook of eating disorders and obesity* (pp. 81–111). New York: John Wiley & Sons.

Poorsattar, S., & Hornung, R. (2010). Tanning addiction: Current trends and future treatment. *Expert Review of Dermatology, 5*(2), 123–125.

Pope, H. D., Jr., Oliva, P. S., Hudson, J. I., Bodkin, J. A., & Gruber, A. J. (1999). Attitudes toward DSM-IV dissociative disorders diagnoses among board-certified American psychiatrists. *American Journal of Psychiatry, 156*(2), 321–323.

Pope, H. G., Jr., Gruber, A. J., Mangweth, B., Bureau, B., deCol, C., Jouvent, R., & Hudson, J. I. (2000). Body image perception among men in three countries. *American Journal of Psychiatry, 157*, 1297–1301.

Pope, K. S. (1996). Memory, abuse and science: Questioning claims about the false memory syndrome epidemic. *American Psychologist, 51*, 957–974.

Pope, K. S. (1997). Science as careful questioning: Are claims of a false memory syndrome epidemic based on empirical evidence? *American Psychologist, 52*, 997–1006.

Popper, C., & West, S. A. (1999). Disorders usually first diagnosed in infancy, childhood, or adolescence. In R. E. Hales, S. C. Yudofsky, & J. A. Talbott (Eds.), *Textbook of psychiatry* (3rd ed., pp. 825–954). Washington, DC: American Psychiatric Press.

Portenoy, R., & Mathur, G. (2009). Cancer pain. In S.-C. J. Yeung, C. P. Escalante, & R. F. Gagel (Eds.), *Medical care of the cancer patient* (pp. 60–71). Shelton, CT: PMPH USA Ltd.

Portenoy, R. K., & Payne, R. (1997). Acute and chronic pain. In J. H. Lowinson, P. Ruiz, R. B. Millman, & J. G. Langrod (Eds.), *Substance abuse: A comprehensive textbook* (pp. 563–589). Baltimore: Williams & Wilkins.

Porter, S. (1996). Without conscience or without active conscience? The etiology of psychopathy revisited. *Aggression and Violent Behavior, 1*, 179–189.

Porter, S., Campbell, M. A., Birt, A. R., & Woodworth, M. T. (2003). "He said, she said": A psychological perspective on historical memory evidence in the courtroom. *Canadian Psychology, 44*, 190–206.

Porter, S., Fairweather, D., Drugge, J., Hervé, H., Birt, A., & Boer, D. P. (2000). Profiles of psychopathy in incarcerated sexual offenders. *Criminal Justice & Behavior, 27*, 216–233.

Porter, S., Hervé, H., Fairweather, D., & Birt, A. R. (November, 1999). *Patterns of psychopathy in sexually violent offenders: Is the sexual psychopath a valid entity?* Paper presented at the Conference on Risk Assessment and Management, BC Institute of Family Violence, Vancouver, BC.

Porter, S., Spencer, L., & Birt, A. R. (2003). Blinded by emotion? Effect of the emotionality of a scene on susceptibility to false memories. *Canadian Journal of Behavioural Science, 35*, 165–175.

Porter, S., Woodworth, M., Earle, J., Drugge, J., & Boer, D. (2003). Characteristics of sexual homicides committed by psychopathic and nonpsychopathic offenders. *Law and Human Behavior, 27*, 459–470.

Porter, S., Yuille, J. C., & Lehman, D. R. (1999). The nature of real, implanted, and fabricated memories for emotional childhood events: Implications for the recovered memory debate. *Law and Human Behavior, 23*, 517–537.

Post, R. M. (1992). Transduction of psychosocial stress into the neurobiology of recurrent affective disorder. *American Journal of Psychiatry, 149*(8), 999–1010.

Post, R. M., Rubinow, D. R., Uhde, T. W., Roy-Byrne, P. P., Linnoila, M., Rosoff, A., & Cowdry, R. (1989). Dysphoric mania: Clinical and biological correlates. *Archives of General Psychiatry, 46,* 353–358.

Potenza, M. N. (2001). The neurobiology of pathological gambling. *Seminars in Clinical Neuropsychiatry, 6,* 217–226.

Potkin, S. G., Albers, L. J., & Richmond, G. (1993). Schizophrenia: An overview of pharmacological treatment. In D. L. Dunner (Ed.), *Current psychiatric therapy* (pp. 142–154). Philadelphia: W. B. Saunders.

Potter, S. M., Zelazo, P. R., Stack, D. M., & Papageorgiou, A. N. (2000). Adverse effects of fetal cocaine exposure on neonatal auditory information processing. *Pediatrics, 105*(3), E40.

Potter, W. Z., & Manji, H. K. (1993). Are mono-amine metabolites in cerebral spinal fluid worth measuring? *Archives of General Psychiatry, 50,* 653–656.

Powell, R. A., & Howell, A. J., (1998). Effectiveness of treatment for dissociative identity disorder. *Psychological Reports, 83,* 483–490.

Poznanski, E. O., Israel, M. C., & Grossman, J. A. (1984). Hypomania in a four year old. *Journal of the American Academy of Child Psychiatry, 23*(1), 105–110.

Prapavessis, H., Cameron, L., Baldi, J. C., Robinson, S., Borrie, K., Harper, T., & Grove, R. J. (2007). The effects of exercise and nicotine replacement therapy on smoking rates in women. *Addictive Behaviors, 32*(7), 1416–1432.

Prelior, E. F., Yutzy, S. H., Dean, J. T., & Wetzel, R. D. (1993). Briquet's syndrome, dissociation and abuse. *American Journal of Psychiatry, 150,* 1507–1511.

Prescott, C. A., & Kendler, K. S. (1999). Genetic and environmental contributions to alcohol abuse and dependence in a population-based sample of male twins. *American Journal of Psychiatry, 156,* 34–40.

Preskorn, S. H. (1995). Comparison of the toler-ability of bupropion, fluoxetine, imipramine, nefazodone, paroxetine, sertraline, and ven-lafaxine. *Journal of Clinical Psychiatry, 56*(Suppl. 6), 12–21.

Price, R., & Brew, B. (1988). The AIDS dementia complex. *Journal of Infectious Diseases, 158,* 1079–1083.

Pridal, C. G., & LoPiccolo, J. (2000). Multielement treatment of desire disorders: Integration of cognitive, behavioral and systemic therapy. In S. R. Leiblum & R. C. Rosen (Eds.), *Principles and practice of sex therapy* (3rd ed., pp. 57–81). New York: Guilford Press.

Prien, R. F., & Kupfer, D. J. (1986). Continuation drug therapy for major depressive episodes: How long should it be maintained? *American Journal of Psychiatry, 143*(1), 18–23.

Prien, R. F., Kupfer, D. J., Mansky, P. A., Small, J. G., Tuason, V. B., Voss, C. B., & Johnson, W. E. (1984). Drug therapy in the preven-tion of recurrences in unipolar and bipolar affective disorders: Report of the NIMH col-laborative study group comparing lithium carbonate, imipramine and a lithium carbonate-imipramine combination. *Archives of General Psychiatry, 41,* 1096–1104.

Prien, R. F., & Potter, W. Z. (1993). Maintenance treatment for mood disorders. In D. L. Dunner (Ed.), *Current psychiatric therapy* (pp. 255–260). Philadelphia: W. B. Saunders.

Priest, L. (2003). Children's Aid closes suspected case of Munchausen's syndrome. June 25, 2003, *The Globe*. Retrieved June 21, 2004, from http://www.msbp.com/DeSousa.htm

Prince, M. (1906–1907). Hysteria from the point of view of dissociated personality. *Journal of Abnormal Psychology, 1,* 170–187.

Prins, J., van der Meer, J., & Bleijenberg, G. (2006). Chronic fatigue syndrome. *Lancet, 367,* 346–355.

Pritchett, D. B., Lüddens, H., & Seeburg, P. H. (1989). Importance of a novel GABA receptor subunit for benzodiazepine pharmacology. *Nature, 338,* 582–585.

Privacy Commissioner of Canada (1995). *Genetic testing and privacy*. Ottawa, ON: Minister of Supply and Services Canada.

Prizant, B. M., & Wetherby, A. M. (1989). Enhancing language and communication in autism: From theory to practice. In G. Dawson (Ed.), *Autism: Nature, diagnosis, and treatment* (pp. 282–309). New York: Guilford Press.

Prochaska, J. O., DiClemente, C. C., & Norcross, J. C. (1997). In search of how people change: Applications to addictive behaviors. In G. A. Marlatt & G. R. VandenBos (Eds.), *Addictive behaviors: Readings on etiology, prevention, and treatment* (pp. 671–696). Washington, DC: American Psychological Association.

Project MATCH Research Group. (1993). Project MATCH: Rationale and methods for a mult-isite clinical trial matching patients to alco-holism treatment. *Alcoholism: Clinical and Experimental Research, 17,* 1130–1145.

Project MATCH Research Group. (1997). Matching alcoholism treatments to client heterogeneity: Project MATCH: Posttreatment drinking out-comes. *Journal of Studies on Alcohol, 58,* 7–29.

Project MATCH Research Group. (1998). Matching alcoholism treatments to client heterogeneity: Treatment main effects and matching effects on drinking during treatment. *Journal of Studies on Alcohol, 59,* 631–639.

Proulx, E. A. (2001). *The shipping news*. New York: Simon & Schuster.

Proulx, T., & Heine, S. J. (2009). Connections from Kafka: Exposure to meaning threats improves implicit learning of an artificial grammar. *Psychological Science, 20*(9), 1125–1131.

Prout, P. I., & Dobson, K. S. (1998). Recovered memories of childhood sexual abuse: Searching for the middle ground in clinical practice. *Canadian Psychology, 39,* 257–265.

Provencher, H. L., & Fincham, F. D. (2000). Attributions of causality, responsibility and blame for positive and negative symptom behaviours in caregivers of persons with schizo-phrenia. *Psychological Medicine, 30,* 899–910.

Province-wide smoking ban adopted. (2005, July/August). *Human Resources Advisor Newsletter*, p. 3. Retrieved September 15, 2007, from http://proquest.umi.com/pqdweb?index1&did8704995 91&SrchMode1&sid5&Fmt3&VInstPROD&VT ypePQD&RQT309&VNamePQD&TS11862539 21&clientId6993

Prudic, J., Sackeim, H. A., & Devanand, D. P. (1990). Medication resistance and clinical response to electroconvulsive therapy. *Psychiatry Research, 31,* 287–296.

Public Works and Government Services Canada. (2003). *Tri-council policy statement: Ethical conduct for research involving humans*. Ottawa, ON: Medical Research Council of Canada.

Pueschel, S. M., & Goldstein, A. (1991). Genetic counseling. In J. L. Matson & J. A. Mulick (Eds.), *Handbook of mental retardation* (2nd ed., pp. 279–291). Elmsford, NY: Pergamon Press.

Puhan, M. A., Suarez, A., Lo Cascio, C., Zahn, A., Heitz, M., & Braendli, O. (2006). Didgeridoo playing as alternative treatment for obstructive sleep apnoea syndrome: Randomised controlled trial. *British Medical Journal, 332,* 266–270.

Puig-Antich, J. (1982). Major depression and conduct disorder in prepuberty. *Journal of the American Academy of Child Psychiatry, 21,* 118–128.

Puig-Antich, J., & Rabinovich, H. (1986). Relationship between affective and anxiety disorders in childhood. In R. G. Helman (Ed.), *Anxiety disorders of childhood* (pp. 136–156). New York: John Wiley & Sons.

Purdon, C. (1999). Thought suppression and psycho-pathology. *Behaviour Research and Therapy, 37,* 1029–1054.

Purdon, C. (2004). Empirical investigations of thought suppression in OCD. *Journal of Behavior Therapy and Experimental Psychiatry, 35,* 121–136.

Purdon, C. (2009). Psychological approaches to understanding obsessive-compulsive disorder. In M. M. Antony & M. B. Stein (Eds.), *Oxford handbook of anxiety and related disorders* (pp. 238–249). New York: Oxford University Press.

Purdon, C., Antony, M., Monteiro, S., & Swinson, R. P. (2001). Social anxiety in college students. *Journal of Anxiety Disorders, 15,* 203–215.

Purdon, C., & Clark, D. A. (2000). White bears and other elusive intrusions: Assessing the relevance of thought suppression for obsessional phenomena. *Behavior Modification, 24,* 425–453.

Purdy, D., & Frank, E. (1993). Should postpartum mood disorders be given a more prominent or distinct place in DSM-IV? *Depression, 1,* 59–70.

Pury, C. L. S., & Mineka, S. (1997). Covariation bias for blood-injury stimuli and aversion outcomes. *Behavior Research and Therapy, 35,* 35–47.

Putnam, F. W. (1989). *Diagnosis and treatment of multiple personality disorder*. New York: Guilford Press.

Putnam, F. W. (1991). Dissociative phenomena. In A. Tasman & S. M. Goldinger (Eds.), *American Psychiatric Press review of psychiatry* (Vol. 10). Washington, DC: American Psychiatric Press.

Putnam, F. W. (1992). Altered states: Peeling away the layers of a multiple personality. *Sciences, 32*(6), 30–36.

Putnam, F. W. (1994). The switch process in mul-tiple personality disorder and other state-change disorders. In R. M. Klein & B. K. Doane (Eds.), *Psychological concepts and dissociative disorders* (pp. 283–304). Hillside, NJ: Erlbaum.

Putnam, F. W. (1997). *Dissociation in children and adolescents: A developmental perspective*. New York: Guilford Press.

Putnam, F. W., & Loewenstein, R. J. (1993). Treatment of multiple personality disorder: A survey of cur-rent practices. *American Journal of Psychiatry, 150,* 1048–1052.

Putnam, F. W., Guroff, J. J., Silberman, E. K., Barban, L., & Post, R. M. (1986). The clinical phenomenology of multiple personality disorder: Review of 100 recent cases. *Journal of Clinical Psychiatry, 47,* 285–293.

Quality Assurance Project. (1990). Treatment out-lines for paranoid, schizotypal and schizoid per-sonality disorders. *Australian and New Zealand Journal of Psychiatry, 24,* 339–350.

Quay, H. C. (1965). Psychopathic personality as pathological stimulation seeking. *American Journal of Psychiatry, 122,* 180–183.

Quay, H. C. (1993). The psychobiology of under-socialized aggressive conduct disorder: A theoretical perspective. *Development and Psychopathology, 5,* 165–180.

Quinsey, V. L. (2010). Coercive paraphilic disorder. *Archives of Sexual Behavior, 39,* 405–410.

Quinsey, V. L., Khanna, A., & Malcolm, P. B. (1998). A retrospective evaluation of the regional treatment centre sex offender treatment program. *Journal of Interpersonal Violence, 13,* 621–644.

Quist, J. F., Barr, C. L., Schachar, R., Roberts, W., Malone, M., Tannock, R., … Kennedy, J. L. (2003). The serotonin 5-HT1B receptor gene and attention deficit hyperactivity disorder. *Molecular Psychiatry, 8,* 98–102.

Quitkin, F. M., Rabkin, J. G., Gerald, J., Davis, J. M., & Klein, D. F. (2000). Validity of clinical trials of antidepressants. *American Journal of Psychiatry, 157,* 327–337.

Rabe, S., Zoellner, T., Beauducel, A., Maercker, A., & Karl, A. (2008). Changes in brain electrical activity after cognitive behavioral therapy for posttraumatic stress disorder in patients injured in motor vehicle accidents. *Psychosomatic Medicine, 70*(1), 13–19.

Rabins, P. V. (2006). Guideline watch: Practice guidelines for the treatment of patients with *Alzheimer's disease and other dementias of late life.* Washington, DC: American Psychiatric Association.

Rachman, S. (1978). *Fear and courage.* San Francisco: W. H. Freeman.

Rachman, S. (1991). Neo-conditioning and the classical theory of fear acquisition. *Clinical Psychology Review, 11,* 155–173.

Rachman, S. (1998). A cognitive theory of obsessions. In E. Sanavio (Ed.), *Behavior and cognitive therapy today: Essays in honor of Hans J. Eysenck* (pp. 209–222). Oxford, UK: Elsevier Science Ltd.

Rachman, S. (2003). *The treatment of obsessions.* New York: Oxford University Press.

Rachman, S. (2006). *Fear of contamination.* New York: Oxford University Press.

Rachman, S., & de Silva, P. (1978). Abnormal and normal obsessions. *Behaviour Research & Therapy, 16,* 233–248.

Rachman, S., & Hodgson, R. (1968). Experimentally induced "sexual fetishism": Replication and development. *Psychological Record, 18*(1), 25–27.

Rachman, S., & Philips, C. (1980). *Psychology and behavioral medicine.* Cambridge, NY: Cambridge University Press.

Rachman, S., & Shafran, R. (1998). Cognitive and behavioral features of obsessive-compulsive disorder. In R. P. Swinson & M. M. Antony (Eds.), *Obsessive-compulsive disorder: Theory, research, and treatment* (pp. 51–78). New York: Guilford Press.

Rachman, S. J. (1977). The conditioning theory of fear-acquisition: A critical examination. *Behaviour Research and Therapy, 15,* 375–387.

Rachman, S. J. (1984). Agoraphobia: A safety-signal perspective. *Behaviour Research and Therapy, 22,* 59–70.

Rachman, S. J. (1988). Panics and their consequences: A review and prospect. In S. J. Rachman & J. D. Maser (Eds.), *Panic: Psychological perspectives* (pp. 259–304). Hillsdale, NJ: Erlbaum.

Rachman, S. J., & de Silva, P. (2004). *Obsessive compulsive disorder: The facts* (3rd ed.). New York: Oxford University Press.

Radnitz, C. L., Appelbaum, K. A., Blanchard, E. B., Elliott, L., & Andrasik, F. (1988). The effect of self-regulatory treatment on pain behavior in chronic headache. *Behaviour Research and Therapy, 26,* 253–260.

Rado, S. (1962). Theory and therapy: The theory of schizotypal organization and its application to the treatment of decompensated schizotypal behavior. In S. Rado (Ed.), *Psychoanalysis of behavior* (Vol. 2, pp. 127–140). New York: Grune & Stratton.

Radomsky, A. S., & Otto, M. W. (2001). Cognitive behavioral therapy for social anxiety disorder. *Psychiatric Clinics of North America, 24,* 805–815.

Radomsky, A. S., Rachman, S. J., Thordarson, D. S., McIsaac, H. K., & Teachman, B. A. (2001). The Claustrophobia Questionnaire. *Journal of Anxiety Disorders, 15,* 287–297.

Radomsky, A. S., & Taylor, S. (2005). Subtyping OCD: *Prospects and problems. Behavior Therapy, 36,* 371–379.

Rafii, M., & Aisen, P. (2009). Recent developments in Alzheimer's disease therapeutics. *BMC Medicine, 7*(1), 7.

Rahkonen, T., Eloniemi-Sulkava, U., Paanila, S., Halonen, P., Sivenius, J., & Sulkava, R. (2001). Systematic intervention for supporting community care of elderly people after a delirium episode. *International Psychogeriatrics, 13,* 37–49.

Rahkonen, T., Makela, H., Paanila, S., Halonen, P., Sivenius, J., & Sulkava, R. (2000). Delirium in elderly people without severe predisposing disorders: Etiology and 1-year prognosis after discharge. *International Psychogeriatrics, 12,* 473–481.

Raich, R. M., Rosen, J. C., Deus, J., Perez, O., Requiena, A., & Gross, J. (1992). Eating disorder symptoms among adolescents in the United States and Spain: A comparative study. *International Journal of Eating Disorders, 11,* 63–72.

Rainville, P., & Duncan, G. H. (2006). Functional brain imaging of placebo analgesia: Methodological challenges and recommendations. *Pain, 121*(3), 177–180.

Raj, A., Amaro, H., & Reed, E. (2001). Culturally tailoring HIV/AIDS prevention programs: Why, when, and how. In S. S. Kazarian & D. R. Evans (Eds.), *Handbook of cultural health psychology* (pp. 195–239). San Diego, CA: Academic Press.

Ramacciotti, C. E., Dell'Osso, L., Paoli, R. A., Ciapparelli, A., Coli, E., Kaplan, A. S., & Garfinkel, P. E. (2002). Characteristics of eating disorder patients without a drive for thinness. *International Journal of Eating Disorders, 32,* 206–212.

Ramachandran, V. S. (1993). Filling in the gaps in perception II: Scotomas and phantom limbs. *Current Directions in Psychological Science, 2,* 56–65.

Ramey, C. T., & Ramey, S. L. (1992). Effective early intervention. *Mental Retardation, 30,* 337–345.

Ramey, C. T., & Ramey, S. L. (1994). Which children benefit the most from early intervention? *Pediatrics, 94,* 1064–1066.

Ramey, C. T., & Ramey, S. L. (1998). Prevention of intellectual disabilities: Early interventions to improve cognitive development. *Preventive Medicine, 27*(2), 224–232.

Ramsawh, H. J., Morgentaler, A., Covino, N., Barlow, D. H., & DeWolf, W. C. (2005). Quality of life following simultaneous placement of penile prosthesis with radical prostatectomy. *Journal of Urology, 174*(4, Part 1 of 2), 1395–1398.

Ramsey, M. (2003, July 28). Bar goers wary of rape drug. *The Vancouver Sun,* p. B.1.

Ranson, M. B., Nichols, D. S., Rouse, S. V., & Harrington, J. L. (2009). Changing or replacing an established psychological assessment standard: Issues, goals, and problems with special reference to recent developments in the MMPI-2. In J. N. Butcher (Ed.), *Oxford handbook of personality assessment* (pp. 112–139). New York: Oxford University Press.

Rao, U., Hammen, C., & Poland, R. (2009). Mechanisms underlying the comorbidity between depressive and addictive disorders in adolescents: Interactions between stress and HPA activity. *American Journal of Psychiatry, 166*(3), 361.

Rapee, R. M., & Melville, L. F. (1997). Recall of family factors in social phobia and panic disorder: Comparison of mother and offspring reports. *Depression and Anxiety, 5,* 7–11.

Rapkin, A. J., Chang, L. C., & Reading, A. E. (1989). Mood and cognitive style in premenstrual syndrome. *Obstetrics and Gynecology, 74,* 644–649.

Rapp, S. R., Parisi, S. A., & Wallace, C. E. (1991). Comorbid psychiatric disorders in elderly medical patients: A l-year prospective study. *Journal of the American Geriatrics Society, 39*(2), 124–131.

Rapport, M. D. (2001). Bridging theory and practice: Conceptual understanding of treatments for children with attention deficit hyperactivity disorder (ADHD), obsessive-compulsive disorder (OCD), autism, and depression. *Journal of Clinical Child Psychology, 30*(1), 3–7.

Rasmussen, S. A., & Eisen, J. L. (1990). Epidemiology of obsessive compulsive disorder. *Journal of Clinical Psychiatry, 51,* 10–14.

Rasmussen, S. A., & Tsuang, M. T. (1984). The epidemiology of obsessive-compulsive disorder. *Journal of Clinical Psychiatry, 45,* 450–457.

Rasmussen, S. A., & Tsuang, M. T. (1986). Clinical characteristics and family history in DSM-III obsessive-compulsive disorder. *American Journal of Psychiatry, 143,* 317–322.

Rasmusson, A. M., Anderson, G. M., Krishnan-Sarin, S., Wu, R., & Paliwal, P. (2006). A decrease in plasma DHEA to cortisol ratio during smoking abstinence may predict relapse: *A preliminary study. Psychopharmacology, 186,* 473–480.

Rauch, S. L., Phillips, K. A., Segal, E., Markis, N., Shin, L. M., Whalen, P. J., … Kennedy, D. N. (2003). A preliminary morphometric magnetic resonance imaging study of regional brain volumes in body dysmorphic disorder. *Psychiatry Research, 122,* 13–19.

Ray, W. A., Fought, R. L., & Decker, M. D. (1992). Psychoactive drugs and the risk of injurious motor vehicle crashes in elderly drivers. *American Journal of Epidemiology, 136,* 873–883.

Ray, W. A., Griffin, M. R., Schaffner, W., Baugh, D. K., & Melton, L. J. (1987). Psychotropic drug use and the risk of hip fracture. *New England Journal of Medicine, 316,* 363–369.

Ray, W. A., Gurwitz, J., Decker, M. D., & Kennedy, D. L. (1992). Medications and the safety of the older driver: Is there a basis for concern? [Special issue: Safety and mobility of elderly drivers: ll]. *Human Factors, 34*(1), 33–47.

Ray, W. A., Thapa, P. B., & Gideon, P. (2000). Benzodiazepines and the risk of falls in nursing home residents. *Journal of the American Geriatrics Society, 48,* 682–685.

Raymond, N. C., Coleman, E., Ohlerking, F., Christenson, G. A., & Miner, M. (1999).

Psychiatric comorbidity in pedophilic sex offenders. *American Journal of Psychiatry, 156,* 786–788.

Razran, G. (1961). The observable unconscious and the inferable conscious in current Soviet psychophysiology: Interoceptive conditioning, semantic conditioning, and the orienting reflex. *Psychological Review, 68,* 81–150.

Rector, N. A., & Beck, A. T. (2001). Cognitive behavioral therapy for schizophrenia: An empirical review. *Journal of Nervous & Mental Disease, 189,* 278–287.

Rector, N. A., & Beck, A. T. (2002). Cognitive therapy for schizophrenia: From conceptualization to intervention. *Canadian Journal of Psychiatry, 47,* 41–50.

Rector, N. A., Seeman, M. V., & Segal, Z. V. (2003). Cognitive therapy for schizophrenia: A preliminary randomized controlled trial. *Schizophrenia Research, 63,* 1–11.

Rector, N. A., Segal, Z. V., & Gemar, M. (1998). Schema research in depression: A Canadian perspective. *Canadian Journal of Behavioural Science, 30,* 213–224.

Redd, W. H., & Andrykowski, M. A. (1982). Behavioral intervention in cancer treatment: Controlling aversion reactions to chemotherapy. *Journal of Consulting and Clinical Psychology, 50,* 1018–1029.

Reeve, R. E., & Kauffman, J. M. (1988). Learning disabilities. In V. B. Van Hasselt, P. S. Strain, & M. Hersen (Eds.), *Handbook of developmental and physical disabilities* (pp. 316–335). Elmsford, NY: Pergamon Press.

Regehr, C., & Glancy, G. (1995). Battered woman syndrome defense in Canadian courts. *Canadian Journal of Psychiatry, 40,* 130–135.

Regier, D. A., Narrow, W. E., Kuhl, E. A., & Kupfer, D. J. (2009). The conceptual development of DSM-V. *American Journal of Psychiatry, 166*(6), 645–650

Regina v. Lavallee (1988), 65 C. R. 3d 387.

Regina v. Prichard (1836), 7 Car., and P. 304.

Regina v. Swain (1991), 63 C. C. C. (3d) 481 (S. C. C.).

Reich, J. (1987). Sex distribution of DSM-III personality disorders in psychiatric outpatients. *American Journal of Psychiatry, 144,* 485–488.

Reich, J., Yates, W., & Nduaguba, M. (1989). Prevalence of DSM-III personality disorders in the community. *Social Psychiatry and Psychiatric Epidemiology, 24,* 12–16.

Reich, T., Edenberg, H. J., Goate, A., Williams, J. T., Rice, J. P., Van Eerdewegh, P., … Begleiter, H. (1998). Genome-wide search for genes affecting the risk of alcohol dependence. *American Journal of Medicine and genetics, 81,* 207–215.

Reichardt, C. S. (2006). The principle of parallelism in the design of studies to estimate treatment effects. *Psychological Methods, 11,* 1–18.

Reichle, J., Mirenda, P., Locke, P., Piche, L., & Johnston, S. (1992). Beginning augmentative communication systems. In S. F. Warren & J. Reichle (Eds.), *Causes and effects in communication and language intervention* (pp. 131–156). Baltimore: Paul H. Brookes.

Reid, D. H., Wilson, P. G., & Faw, G. D. (1991). Teaching self-help skills. In J. L. Matson & J. A. Mulick (Eds.), *Handbook of mental retardation* (2nd ed., pp. 436–450). Elmsford, NY: Pergamon Press.

Reid, G. J., Chambers, C. T., McGrath, P. J., & Finley, G. A. (1997). Coping with pain and surgery: Children's and parents' perspectives. *International Journal of Behavioral Medicine, 4,* 339–363.

Reid, W. J., & Crisafulli, A. (1990). Marital discord and child behavior problems: A meta-analysis. *Journal of Abnormal Child Psychology, 18,* 105–117.

Reik, T. (1964). *Pagan rites in Judaism.* New York: Farrar, Strauss.

Reilly-Harrington, N. A., Alloy, L. B., Fresco, D. M., & Whitehouse, W. G. (1999). Cognitive styles and life events interact to predict bipolar and unipolar symptomatology. *Journal of Abnormal Psychology, 108*(4), 567–578.

Reiman, E. M., Webster, J. A., Myers, A. J., Hardy, J., Dunckley, T., Zismann, V. L., … Stephan, D. A. (2007). GAB2 alleles modify Alzheimer's risk in APOE ε4 Carriers. Neuron, 54(5), 713–720.

Reiss, S., Peterson, R. A., Gursky, D. M., & McNally, R. J. (1986). Anxiety sensitivity, anxiety frequency, and the prediction of fearfulness. *Behaviour Research and Therapy, 24,* 1–8.

Reissing, E. D., Binik, Y. M., & Khalife, S. (1999). Does vaginismus exist? A critical review of the literature. *Journal of Nervous & Mental Disease, 187,* 261–274.

Reissing, E. D., Binik, Y. M., Khalifé, S., Cohen, D., & Amsel, R. (2004). Vaginal spasm, pain, and behavior: An empirical investigation of the diagnosis of vaginismus. *Archives of Sexual Behavior, 33,* 5–17.

Reitan, R. M., & Davison, I. A. (1974). *Clinical neuropsychology: Current status and applications.* Washington, DC: V.H. Winston.

Rekers, G. A., Kilgus, M., & Rosen, A. C. (1990). Long-term effects of treatment for gender identity disorder of childhood. *Journal of Psychology & Human Sexuality, 3*(2), 121–153.

Renaud, C. A., & Byers, E. S. (2001). Positive and negative sexual cognitions: Subjective experience and relationships to sexual adjustment. *Journal of Sex Research, 38,* 252–262.

Rende, R., & Plomin, R. (1992). Diathesis-stress models of psychopathology: A quantitative genetic perspective. *Applied & Preventive Psychology, 1,* 177–182.

Renneberg, B., Goldstein, A. J., Phillips, D., & Chambless, D. L. (1990). Intensive behavioral group treatment of avoidant personality disorder. *Behavior Therapy, 21,* 363–377.

Report of the Advisory Panel on Alzheimer's Disease. (1995). *Alzheimer's disease and related dementias: Biomedical update.* Department of Health and Human Services.

Repp, A. C., & Singh, N. N. (1990). *Perspectives on the use of nonaversive and aversive interventions for persons with developmental disabilities.* Sycamore, IL: Sycamore Publishing.

Rescorla, R. A. (1988). Pavlovian conditioning: It's not what you think it is. *American Psychologist, 43*(3), 151–160.

Resick, P. A., Monson, C. M., & Rizvi, S. L. (2008). Posttraumatic stress disorder. In D. H. Barlow (Ed.), *Clinical handbook of psychological disorders* (4th ed.). New York: Guilford Press.

Resner, J., & Hartog, J. (1970). Concepts and terminology of mental disorders among Malays. *Journal of Cross-Cultural Psychology, 1,* 369–381.

Resnick, H. S., Kilpatrick, D. G., Dansky, B. S., Saunders, B. E., & Best, C. L. (1993). Prevalence of civilian trauma in posttraumatic stress disorder in a representative national sample of women. *Journal of Consulting and Clinical Psychology, 61,* 984–991.

Rice, D. P., & MacKenzie, E. J. (1989). *Cost of injury in the United States: A report to Congress.*

San Francisco: University of California and Injury Prevention Center, Institute for Health and Aging, and the Johns Hopkins University.

Rice, M. E. (1997). Violent offender research and implications for the criminal justice system. *American Psychologist, 52,* 414–423.

Richards, R., Kinney, D. K., Lunde, I., Benet, M., & Merzel, A. P. C. (1988). Creativity in manic depressives, cyclothymes, their normal relatives, and control subjects. *Journal of Abnormal Psychology, 97*(3), 281–288.

Richards, S. S., & Sweet, R. A. (2009). Dementia. In B. J. Sadock, V. A. Sadock, & P. Ruiz (Eds.), *Kaplan & Sadock's comprehensive textbook of psychiatry* (Vol. I, 9th ed., pp. 1167–1198). Philadelphia: Lippincott Williams & Wilkins.

Richardson, G. S. (2006). Shift work sleep disorder. In T. Lee-Chiong (Ed.), Sleep: *A comprehensive handbook* (pp. 395–399). Hoboken, NJ: John Wiley & Sons.

Richardson, S. A., Katz, M., & Koller, H. (1986). Sex differences in number of children administratively classified as mildly mentally retarded: An epidemiological review. *American Journal of Mental Deficiency, 91,* 250–256.

Richman, A., & Harris, P. (1982–1983). Mental hospital deinstitutionalization in Canada: A national perspective with some regional examples. *International Journal of Mental Health, 11*(4), 64–83.

Richters, J. E. (1993). Community violence and children's development: Toward a research agenda for the 1990's. *Psychiatry, 56,* 3–6.

Rickels, K., Downing, R., Schweizer, E., & Hassman, H. (1993). Antidepressants for the treatment of generalized anxiety disorder. *Archives of General Psychiatry, 50,* 884–895.

Rickels, K., Rynn, M., Ivengar, M., & Duff, D. (2006). Remission of generalized anxiety disorder: A review of the paroxetine clinical trials database. *Journal of Clinical Psychiatry, 67,* 41–47.

Rickels, K., Schweizer, E., Case, W. G., & Greenblatt, D. J. (1990). Long-term therapeutic use of benzodiazepines: I. Effects of abrupt discontinuation. *Archives of General Psychiatry, 47,* 899–907.

Riding, A. (1992, November 17). New catechism for Catholics defines sins of modern world. *New York Times,* p. A14.

Rief, W., Hiller, W., & Margraf, J. (1998). Cognitive aspects of hypochondriasis and the somatization syndrome. *Journal of Abnormal Psychology, 107,* 587–595.

Riggs, J. E. (1993). Smoking and Alzheimer's disease: Protective effect or differential survival bias? *Lancet, 342,* 793–794.

Rihmer, Z., & Pestality, P. (1999). Bipolar II disorder and suicidal behavior. *The Psychiatric Clinics of North America, 22*(3), 667–674.

Ritenbaugh, C., Shisstak, C., Teufel, N., Leonard-Green, T. K., & Prince, R. (1993). Eating disorders: A cross-cultural review in regard to DSM-IV. In J. E. Mezzich, A. Kleinman, H. Fabrega, B. Good, et al. (Eds.), Cultural proposals and supporting papers for DSM-IV.

Rivera-Tovar, A. D., & Frank, E. (1990). Late luteal phase dysphoric disorder in young women. *American Journal of Psychiatry, 147,* 1634–1636.

Rivera-Tovar, A. D., Pilkonis, P., & Frank, E. (1992). Symptom patterns in late luteal-phase dysphoric disorder. *Journal of Psychopathology and Behavioral Assessment, 14,* 189–199.

Ro, E., & Clark, L. A. (2009). Psychosocial functioning in the context of diagnosis: Assessment and theoretical issues. *Psychological Assessment, 21*(3), 313–324.

Roberts, G. A. (1991). Delusional belief and meaning in life: A preferred reality? *British Journal of Psychiatry, 159,* 20–29.

Roberts, L. J., & Marlatt, G. A. (1999). Harm reduction. In P. J. Ott & R. F. Tarter (Eds.), *Sourcebook on substance abuse: Etiology, epidemiology, assessment, and treatment* (pp. 389–398). Needham Heights, MA: Allyn & Bacon.

Roberts, L. W., Hoop, J. G., & Dunn, L. B. (2008). Ethical aspects of psychiatry. In R. E. Hales, S. C. Yudofsky, & G. O. Gabbard (Eds.), *The American Psychiatric Publishing textbook of psychiatry* (5th ed., pp. 1601–1636). Arlington, VA: American Psychiatric Publishing Inc.

Roberts, R. F., Kaplan, G. A., Shema, S. J., & Strawbridge, W. J. (1997). Does growing old increase the risk for depression? *American Journal of Psychiatry, 154,* 1384–1390.

Roberts, T. B., & Hruby, P. J. (1984). *Religion and psychoactive sacraments: An entheogen chrestomathy.* Retrieved October 26, 2003, from http://www.csp.org/chrestomathy/pass_it_on.html

Robertson, G. B. (1994). *Mental disability in the law in Canada* (2nd ed.). Scarborough, ON: Carswell.

Robertson, N. (1988). *Getting better: Inside Alcoholics Anonymous.* New York: William Morrow.

Robillard, G., Bouchard, S., Fournier, T., & Renaud, P. (2003). Anxiety and presence during VR immersion: A comparative study of the reactions of phobic and non-phobic participants in therapeutic virtual environments derived from computer games. *CyberPsychology and Behavior, 6,* 467–476.

Robins, L. N. (1966). *Deviant children grown up: A sociological and psychiatric study of sociopathic personality.* Baltimore: Williams & Wilkins.

Robins, L. N. (1978). Sturdy childhood predictors of adult antisocial behavior: Replications from longitudinal studies. *Psychological Medicine, 8,* 611–622.

Robins, L. N., Helzer, J. F., & Davis, D. H. (1975). Narcotic use in Southeast Asia and afterwards. *Archives of General Psychiatry, 32,* 955–961.

Robins, R. W., Gosling, S. D., & Craik, K. H. (1999). An empirical analysis of trends in psychology. *American Psychologist, 54,* 117–128.

Robins, S., & Novaco, R. W. (2000). Anger control as a health promotion mechanism. In D. I. Mostofsky & D. H. Barlow (Eds.), *The management of stress and anxiety in medical disorders* (pp. 361–377). Needham Heights, MA: Allyn & Bacon.

Robinson, G. E., Fernald, R. D., & Clayton, D. F. (2008, November 7). Genes and social behavior. *Science, 322,* 896–899.

Robinson, M. J., & Qaqish, R. B. (2002). Practical psychopharmacology in HIV-1 and acquired immunodeficiency syndrome. *Psychiatric Clinics of North America, 25,* 149–175.

Robles, T., Glaser, R., & Kiecolt-Glaser, J. (2005). Out of balance: A new look at chronic stress, depression, and immunity. *Current Directions in Psychological Science, 14,* 111–115.

Rockwood, K., & Joffres, C. (2002). Improving clinical descriptions to understand the effects of dementia treatment: Consensus recommendations. *International Journal of Geriatric Psychiatry, 17,* 1006–1011.

Rockwood, K., & Lindesay, J. (2002). Delirium and dying. *International Psychogeriatrics, 14,* 235–238.

Rockwood, K., & Middleton, L. (2007). Physical activity and the maintenance of cognitive function. Alzheimer's & Dementia: *The Journal of the Alzheimer's Association, 3(2),* S38–S44.

Rockwood, K., Stolee, P., & Brahim, A. (1991). Outcomes of admission to a psychogeriatric service. *Canadian Journal of Psychiatry, 36*(4), 275–279.

Rockwood, K., Wolfson, C., & McDowell, l. (2001). The Canadian Study of Health and Aging: Organizational lessons from a national, multicenter, epidemiologic study. *International Psychogeriatrics, 13*(Suppl. 1), 233–237.

Rodin, J., & Langer, E. J. (1977). Long-term effects of a controlled relevant intervention with the institutionalized aged. *Journal of Personality and Social Psychology, 35*(12), 897–902.

Rodin, J., & Salovey, P. (1989). Health psychology. *Annual Review of Psychology, 40,* 533–579.

Roehrich, L., & Kinder, B. N. (1991). Alcohol expectancies and male sexuality: Review and implications for sex therapy. *Journal of Sex and Marital Therapy, 17*(1), 45–54.

Roehrs, T., Carskadon, M. A., Dement, W. C., & Roth, T. (2000). Daytime sleepiness & alertness. In M. H. Kryger, T. Roth, & W. C. Dement (Eds.), *Principles and practice of sleep medicine* (3rd ed., pp. 43–52). Philadelphia: W. B. Saunders.

Roehrs, T., & Roth, T. (2000). Hypnotics: Efficacy & adverse effects. In M. H. Kryger, T. Roth, & W. C. Dement (Eds.), *Principles and practice of sleep medicine* (3rd ed., pp. 414–418). Philadelphia: W. B. Saunders.

Roelofs, K., Keijsers, G. P., Hoogduin, K. A., Naring, G. W., & Moene, F. C. (2002). Childhood abuse in patients with conversion disorder. *American Journal of Psychiatry, 159,* 1908–1913.

Roemer, L., & Borkovec, T. D. (1993). Worry: Unwanted cognitive activity that controls unwanted somatic experience. In D. M. Wegner & J. W. Pennebaker (Eds.), *Handbook of mental control.* Englewood Cliffs, NJ: Prentice Hall.

Roemer, L., & Orsillo, S. M. (2002). Expanding our conceptualization of and treatment for generalized anxiety disorder: Integrating mindfulness/acceptance-based approaches with existing cognitive-behavioral models. *Clinical Psychology: Science and Practice, 9,* 54–68.

Roemer, L., & Orsillo, S. M. (2007). An open trial of an acceptance-based behavior therapy for generalized anxiety disorder. *Behavior Therapy, 38*(1), 72–85.

Roemer, L., Orsillo, S. M., & Barlow, D. H. (2002). Generalized anxiety disorder. In D. H. Barlow (Ed.), *Anxiety and its disorders: The nature and treatment of anxiety and panic* (2nd ed.). New York: Guilford Press.

Roesch, R., Ogloff, J. R. P., Hart, S. D., Dempster, R. J., Zapf, P. A., & Whittemore, K. F. (1997). The impact of Canadian criminal code changes on remands and assessments of fitness to stand trial and criminal responsibility in British Columbia. *Canadian Journal of Psychiatry, 42,* 509–514.

Roesch, R., Zapf, P., Webster, C. D., & Eaves, D. (1999). *The Fitness Interview Test.* Burnaby, BC: Simon Fraser University, Mental Health Law & Policy Institute.

Roffman, R. A., & Barnhart, R. (1987). Assessing need for marijuana dependence treatment through an anonymous telephone interview. *International Journal of the Addictions, 22,* 639–651.

Rogaeva, F., Tadon, A., & St George-Hyslop, P. (2001). Genetic markers in the diagnosis of Alzheimer's disease. *Journal of Alzheimer's Disease, 3,* 293–304.

Rogers, C. R. (1961). *On becoming a person.* Boston: Houghton Mifflin.

Rogers, S. J. (2009). What are infant siblings teaching us about autism in infancy? *Autism Research, 2*(3), 125–137.

Rogers, S. L., & Friedhoff, L. T. (1996). The efficacy and safety of donepezil in patients with Alzheimer's disease: Results of a US multicentre, randomized, double-blind, placebo-controlled trial. *The Donepezil Study Group. Dementia, 7,* 293–303.

Rogler, L. (2007). Framing research on culture in psychiatric diagnosis. In J. E. Mezzich & G. Caracci (Eds.), Cultural formulation: *A reader for psychiatric diagnosis* (pp. 151–166). Lanham, MD: Jason Aronson Inc.

Roitt, I. (1988). *Essential immunology* (6th ed.). Oxford, UK: Blackwell.

Rojo, L., Conesa, L., Bermudez, O., & Livianos, L. (2006). Influence of stress in the onset of eating disorders: Data from a two stage epidemiologic controlled study. (2006). *Psychosomatic Medicine, 68,* 628–635.

Roland, C. G. (1990). *Clarence Hincks: mental health crusader.* Toronto, ON: Hannah Institute & Dundurn Press.

Roma, P. G., Champoux, M., & Suomi, S. J. (2006). Environmental control, social context, and individual differences in behavioral and cortisol responses to novelty in infant rhesus monkeys. *Child Development, 77,* 118–131.

Romano, F., Baillargeon, R. H., Fortier, I., Wu, H.-X, Robaey, P., Zoccolillo, M., & Tremblay, R. E. (2005). Individual change in methylphenidate use in a national sample of children aged 2 to 11 years. *Canadian Journal of Psychiatry, 50,* 144–152.

Romano, F., Baillargeon, R. H., Wu, H. X., Robaey, P., & Tremblay, R. F. (2002). Prevalence of methylphenidate use and change over a two-year period: A nationwide study of 2- to 11-year-old Canadian children. *Journal of Pediatrics, 141,* 71–75.

Romano, J. M., Jensen, M. P., Turner, J. A., Good, A. B., & Hops, H. (2000). Chronic pain patient-partner interactions: Further support for a behavioral model of chronic pain. *Behavior Therapy, 31,* 415–440.

Romney, D. M., & Candido, C. L. (2001). Anhedonia in depression and schizophrenia: a reexamination. *Journal of Nervous & Mental Disease, 189,* 735–740.

Room, R. (1993). Alcoholics Anonymous as a social movement. In B. S. McCrady & W. R. Miller (Eds.), *Research on Alcoholics Anonymous: Opportunities and alternatives* (pp. 167–187). New Brunswick, NJ: Rutgers Center of Alcohol Studies.

Root, T. L., Pinheiro, A. P., Thornton, L., Strober, M., Fernandez-Aranda, F., Brandt, H., . . . Bulik, C. M. (2010). Substance use disorders in women with anorexia nervosa. *International Journal of Eating Disorders, 43*(1), 14–21.

Rorschach, H. (1951). *Psychodiagnostics.* New York: Grune & Stratton. (Original work published 1921).

Rosa-Neto, P., Diksic, M., Okazawa, H., Leyton, M., Ghadirian, N., Mzengeza, S., . . . Benkelfat, C. (2004). Measurement of brain regional [^{11}C] Methyl-L-Tryptophan trapping as a measure of serotonin synthesis in medication-free patients with major depression. *Archives of General Psychiatry, 61,* 556–563.

Rosebush, P., & Mazurek, M. F. (2006). Treatment of conversion disorder. In M. Hallett, S. Fahn, J. Jankovic, A. F. Lang, et al. (Eds.), *Psychogenic movement disorders: Neurology* and neuropsychiatry (pp. 289–301). Philadelphia: Lippincott Williams & Wilkins Publishers.

Rosen, J. C., & Leitenberg, H. (1985). Exposure plus response prevention treatment of bulimia. In D. M. Garner & P. F. Garfinkel (Eds.), Handbook of psychotherapy for anorexia nervosa and bulimia (pp. 193–209). New York: Guilford Press.

Rosen, J. C., Reiter, J., Orosan, P. (1995). Cognitive-behavioral body image therapy for body dysmorphic disorder. Journal of Consulting Clinical Psychology, 63, 263–269.

Rosen, R. C. (2000). Medical and psychological interventions for erectile dysfunction: Toward a combined treatment approach. In S. R. Leiblum & R. C. Rosen (Eds.), Principles and practice of sex therapy (3rd ed., pp. 276–304). New York: Guilford Press.

Rosen, R. C. (2007). Erectile dysfunction: Integration of medical and psychological approaches. In S. R. Leiblum (Ed.), Principles and practice of sex therapy (4th ed., pp. 277–312). New York: Guilford Press.

Rosen, R. C., & Beck, J. G. (1988). Patterns of sexual arousal: Psychophysiological processes and clinical applications. New York: Guilford Press.

Rosen, R. C., & Leiblum, S. R. (1995). Treatment of sexual disorders in the 1990's: An integrated approach. Journal of Consulting and Clinical Psychology, 63, 877–890.

Rosenbaum, M. (2000). Psychogenic seizures—why women? Psychosomatics, 41(2), 147–149.

Rosenberg, H. (1993). Prediction of controlled drinking by alcoholics and problem drinkers. Psychological Bulletin, 113, 129–139.

Rosenberg, H., & Melville, J. (2005). Controlled drinking and controlled drug use as outcome goals in British treatment services. Addiction Research and Theory, 13(1), 85–92.

Rosenberg, R. N., Richter, R. W., Risser, R. C., Taubman, K., Prado-Farmer, I., Ebalo, F., . . . Schellenberg, G. D. (1996). Genetic factors for the development of Alzheimer's disease in the Cherokee Indian. Archives of Neurology, 53, 997–1000.

Rosengren, A., Tibblin, G., & Wilhelmsen, L. (1991). Self-perceived psychological stress and incidence of coronary artery disease in middle-aged men. American Journal of Cardiology, 68, 1171–1175.

Rosenman, R. H., Brand, R. J., Jenkins, C. D., Friedman, M., Straus, R., & Wurm, M. (1975). Coronary heart disease in the Western Collaborative Group Study: Final follow-up experience of 8 years. JAMA, 233, 872–877.

Rosenthal, D. (Ed.). (1963). The Genain quadruplets: A case study and theoretical analysis of heredity and environment in schizophrenia. New York: Basic Books.

Rosenthal, P. A., & Rosenthal, S. (1984). Suicidal behavior by preschool children. American Journal of Psychiatry, 141, 520–525.

Rösler, A., & Witztum, F. (1998). Treatment of men with paraphilia with a long-acting analogue of gonadotropin-releasing hormone. New England Journal of Medicine, 338, 416–422.

Rösler, A., & Witztum, F. (2000). Pharmacotherapy of paraphilias in the next millennium. Behavioral Sciences & the Law, 18, 43–56.

Rosowsky, F., & Gurian, B. (1992). Impact of borderline personality disorder in late life on systems of care. Hospital and Community Psychiatry, 43, 386–389.

Ross, A. O., & Pelham, W. F. (1981). Child psychopathology. Annual Review of Psychology, 32, 243–278.

Ross, C. A. (1991). Epidemiology of multiple personality disorder and dissociation. Psychiatric Clinics of North America, 14, 503–517.

Ross, C. A. (1997). Dissociative identity disorder. New York: John Wiley & Sons.

Ross, C. A. (2009). Dissociative amnesia and dissociative fugue. In P. F. Dell & J. A. O'Neil (Eds.), Dissociation and the dissociative disorders (pp. 429–434). New York: Routledge.

Ross, C. A., Anderson, G., Fleisher, W. P., & Norton, G. R. (1991). The frequency of multiple personality disorder among psychiatric inpatients. American Journal of Psychiatry, 148, 1717–1720.

Ross, C. A., Miller, S. D., Reagor, P., Bjornson, L., Fraser, G. A., & Anderson, G. (1990). Structured interview data on 102 cases of multiple personality disorder from four centers. American Journal of Psychiatry, 147, 596–601.

Ross, C. A., Norton, G. R., & Wozney, K. (1989). Multiple personality disorder: An analysis of 236 cases. Canadian Journal of Psychiatry, 34, 413–418.

Ross, M. W., Walinder, J., Lundstrom, B., & Thuwe, I. (1981). Cross-cultural approaches to trans-sexualism: A comparison between Sweden and Australia. Acta Psychiatrica Scandinavica, 63, 75–82.

Rost, K., Kashner, T. M., & Smith, G. R. Jr. (1994). Effectiveness of psychiatric intervention with somatization disorder patients: Improved outcomes at reduced costs. General Hospital Psychiatry, 16, 381–387.

Rothbaum, B. O., Hodges, L., & Kooper, R. (1997). Virtual reality exposure therapy. Journal of Psychotherapy Practice & Research, 6, 219–226.

Rothblum, F. D. (2002). Gay and lesbian body images. In T. F. Cash & T. Pruzinsky (Eds.), Body image: A handbook of theory, research and clinical practice (pp. 257–265). New York: Guilford Press.

Rottenberg, J., Gross, J. J., Wilhelm, F. H., Najmi, S., & Gotlib, I. H. (2002). Crying threshold and intensity in major depressive disorder. Journal of Abnormal Psychology, 111, 302–312.

Rottenberg, J., & Johnson, S. L. (2007). Emotion and psychopathology: Bridging affective and clinical science. Washington, DC: American Psychological Association.

Rouff, L. (2000). Schizoid personality traits among the homeless mentally ill: A quantitative and qualitative report. Journal of Social Distress and the Homeless, 9, 127–141.

Rounsaville, B. J., Alarcon, R. D., Andrews G., Jackson, J. S., Kendell, R. F., & Kendler, K. (2002). Basic nomenclature issues for DSM-V. In D. J. Kupfer, M. B. First, & D. A. Regier (Eds.), A research agenda for DSM-V (pp. 1–29). Washington, DC: American Psychiatric Association.

Rounsaville, B. J., Sholomskas, D., & Prusoff, B. A. (1988). Chronic mood disorders in depressed outpatients: Diagnosis and response to pharmacotherapy. Journal of Affective Disorders, 2, 72–88.

Roush, W. (1997). Herbert Benson: Mind-body maverick pushes the envelope. Science, 276, 357–359.

Rowa, K., McCabe, R. F., & Antony, M. M. (2006). Specific phobias. In F. Andrasik (Ed.), Comprehensive handbook of personality and psychopathology: Adult Psychopathology (Vol. 2, pp. 154–168). Hoboken, NJ: Wiley.

Rowe, J. B. (2010). Conversion disorder: Understanding the pathogenic links between emotion and motor systems in the brain. Brain, 133(Pt 5), 1295–1297.

Roy, A., Segal, N. L., & Sarchiapone, M. (1995). Attempted suicide among living co-twins of twin suicide victims. American Journal of Psychiatry, 152, 1075–1076.

Roy-Byrne, P. P., & Katon, W. (2000). Anxiety management in the medical setting: Rationale, barriers to diagnosis and treatment, and proposed solutions. In D. I. Mostofsky & D. H. Barlow (Eds.), The management of stress and anxiety in medical disorders (pp. 1–14). Needham Heights, MA: Allyn & Bacon.

Rubenstein, S., & Caballero, B. (2000). Is Miss America an undernourished role model? JAMA, 283, 1569.

Rubin, R. T. (1982). Koro (Shook Yang): A culture-bound psychogenic syndrome. In C. T. H. Friedmann & R. A. Fauger (Eds.), Extraordinary disorders of human behavior (pp. 155–172). New York: Plenum Press.

Rubonis, A. V., Colby, S. M., Monti, P. M., Rohsenow, D. J., Gulliver, S. B., & Sirota, A. D. (1994). Alcohol cue reactivity and mood induction in male and female alcoholics. Journal of Studies on Alcohol, 55, 487–494.

Rucklidge, J. J., & Tannock, R. (2002). Neuropsychological profiles of adolescents with ADHD: Effects of reading difficulties and gender. Journal of Child Psychology & Psychiatry & Allied Disciplines, 43, 988–1003.

Rudaz, M., Craske, M. G., Becker, E. S., Ledermann, T., & Margraf, J. (2010). Health anxiety and fear of fear in panic disorder and agoraphobia vs. social phobia: A prospective longitudinal study. Depression and Anxiety, 27, 404–411.

Rudd, M. D., Joiner, Y., & Rajab, M. H. (2001). Treating suicidal behavior. An effective, time-limited approach. New York: Guilford Press.

Rudd, M. D., Rajab, M. H., Orman, D. T., Stulman, D. A., Joiner, T., & Dixon, W. (1996). Effectiveness of an outpatient intervention targeting suicidal young adults: Preliminary results. Journal of Consulting and Clinical Psychology, 64, 179–190.

Ruiz, I., Offermanns, J., Lanctot, K. L., & Busto, U. (1993). Comparative study on benzodiazepine use in Canada and Chile. Journal of Clinical Pharmacology, 33, 124–129.

Rupprecht, R., Rammes, G., Eser, D., Baghai, T. C., Schule, C., Nothdurfter, C., . . . Kucher, K. (2009). Translocator protein (18 kD) as target for anxiolytics without benzodiazepine-like side effects. Science, 325(5939), 490–493.

Ruscio, J. (2004). Diagnoses and the behaviors they denote: A critical evaluation of the labeling theory of mental illness. Scientific Review of Mental Health Practice, 3, 5–22.

Rush, A. J., Giles, D. F., Schlesser, M. A., Orsulak, P. J., Weissenburger, J. F., Fulton, C. L., . . . Roffwarg, H. P. (1997). Dexamethasone response, thyrotropin-releasing hormone stimulation, rapid eye movement latency, and subtypes of Depression. Biological Psychiatry, 41, 915–928.

Rush, J. A. (1993). Mood disorders in DSM-IV. In D. L. Dunner (Ed.), Current psychiatric therapy (pp. 189–195). Philadelphia: W. B. Saunders.

Russell, G. F. M. (1979). Bulimia nervosa: An ominous variant of anorexia nervosa. Psychological Medicine, 9, 429–448.

Russell, G. F. M., Szmukler, G. I., Dare, C., & Fisler, I. (1987). An evaluation of family therapy in anorexia nervosa and bulimia nervosa. *Archives of General Psychiatry, 44,* 1047–1056.

Rutherford, J., McGuffin, P., Katz, R. J., & Murray, R. M. (1993). Genetic influences on eating attitudes in a normal female twin population. *Psychological Medicine, 23,* 425–436.

Rutherford, M. D., & Rogers, S. J. (2003). Cognitive underpinnings of pretend play in autism. *Journal of Autism & Developmental Disorders, 33,* 289–302.

Rutter, M. (1978). Diagnosis and definition of childhood autism. *Journal of Autism and Childhood Schizophrenia, 8,* 139–161.

Rutter, M. (2002). The interplay of nature, nurture, and developmental influences: The challenge ahead for mental health. *Archives of General Psychiatry, 59,* 996–1000.

Rutter, M. (2006). *Genes and behavior: Nature–nurture interplay.* Oxford, UK: Blackwell.

Rutter, M. (2010). Gene-environment interplay. *Depression and Anxiety, 27*(1), 1–4.

Rutter, M., & Giller, H. (1984). *Juvenile delinquency: Trends and perspectives.* New York: Guilford Press.

Rutter, M., Macdonald, H., Le Couteur, A., Harrington, R., Bolton, P., & Baily, A. (1990). Genetic factors in child psychiatric disorders: II. Empirical findings. *Journal of Child Psychology and Psychiatry, 31,* 39–83.

Rutter, M., Moffitt, T. E., & Caspi, A. (2006). Gene–environment interplay and psychopathology: Multiple varieties but real effects. *Journal of Child Psychology and Psychiatry, 47,* 226–261.

Rutter, M. L. (1997). Nature-nurture integration: The example of antisocial behavior. *American Psychologist, 52,* 390–398.

Ryan, J. D., & Cohen, N. J. (2003). Evaluating the neuropsychological dissociation evidence for multiple memory systems. *Cognitive, Affective & Behavioral Neuroscience, 3*(3), 168–185.

Ryan, W. D. (1992). The pharmacologic treatment of child and adolescent depression. *Psychiatric Clinics of North America, 15,* 29–40.

Ryder, A. G., Yang, J., Zhu, X., Yao, S., Yi, J., Heine, S. J., & Bagby, R. M. (2008). The cultural shaping of depression: Somatic symptoms in China, psychological symptoms in North America? *Journal of Abnormal Psychology, 117*(2), 300–313.

Saab, P. G., Llabre, M. M., Hurwitz, B. F., Frame, C. A., Reineke, I., Fins, A. I., ... Schneiderman, N. (1992). Myocardial and peripheral vascular responses to behavioral challenges and their stability in black and white Americans. *Psychophysiology, 29*(4), 384–397.

Sachs, G. A., & Cassel, C. K. (1989). Ethical aspects of dementia. *Neurologic Clinics, 7,* 845–858.

Sachs, G. S., & Rush, A. J. (2003). Response, remission, and recovery in bipolar disorders: What are the realistic treatment goals? *Journal of Clinical Psychiatry, 64,* 18–22.

Sack, R. L., & Lewy, A. J. (1993). Human circadian rhythms: Lessons from the blind. *Annals of Medicine, 25,* 303–305.

Sackeim, H. A., & Devanand, D. P. (1991). Dissociative disorders. In M. Hersen & S. M. Turner (Eds.), *Adult psychopathology & diagnosis* (2nd ed., pp. 279–322). New York: John Wiley & Sons.

Sackeim, H. A., Nordlie, J. W., & Gur, R. C. (1979). A model of hysterical and hypnotic blindness: Cognition, motivation and awareness. *Journal of Abnormal Psychology, 88,* 474–489.

Sadeh, A., Raviv, A., & Gruber, R. (2000). Sleep patterns and sleep disruptions in school-age children. *Developmental Psychology, 36,* 291–301.

Sadovnick, A. D. (2001). Genetic counselling and genetic screening for Alzheimer's disease and other dementias. *Canadian Journal of Neurological Science, 28*(Suppl. 1), 52–55.

Sahay, S., Piran, N., & Maddocks, S. (2000). Sexual victimization and clinical challenges in women receiving hospital treatment for depression. *Canadian Journal of Community Mental Health, 19,* 161–174.

Sakel, M. (1958). *Schizophrenia.* New York: Philosophical Library.

Sakheim, D. K., Barlow, D. H., Abrahamson, D. J., & Beck, J. G. (1987). Distinguishing between organogenic and psychogenic erectile dysfunction. *Behaviour Research and Therapy, 25,* 379–390.

Sakinofsky, I. (1998). The epidemiology of suicide in Canada. In A. A. Leenars, S. Wenckstern, I. Sakinofsky, R. J. Dyck, et al. (Eds.), *Suicide in Canada* (pp. 37–66). Toronto, ON: University of Toronto Press.

Saklofske, D. H., Hildebrand, D. K., & Gorsuch, R. L. (2000). Replication of the factor structure of the Wechsler Adult Intelligence Scale—Third edition with a Canadian sample. *Psychological Assessment, 12,* 436–439.

Salekin, R. T., Rogers, R., & Sewell, K. W. (1997). Construct validity of psychopathy in a female offender sample: A multitrait–multimethod evaluation. *Journal of Abnormal Psychology, 106*(4), 576–585.

Salkovskis, P., Shafran, R., Rachman, S., & Freeston, M. H. (1999). Multiple pathways to inflated responsibility beliefs in obsessional problems: Possible origins and implications for therapy and research. *Behaviour Therapy and Research, 37,* 1055–1072.

Salkovskis, P. M., Atha, C., & Storer, D. (1990). Cognitive-behavioural problem solving in the treatment of patients who repeatedly attempt suicide: A controlled trial. *British Journal of Psychiatry, 157,* 871–876.

Salkovskis, P. M., & Campbell, P. (1994). Thought suppression induces intrusion in naturally occurring negative intrusive thoughts. *Behaviour Research and Therapy, 32*(1), 1–8.

Salkovskis, P. M., & Clark, D. M. (1993). Panic disorder and hypochondriasis. *Advances in Behaviour Research & Therapy, 15,* 23–48.

Salkovskis, P. M., & Warwick, H. M. C. (2001). Making sense of hypochondriasis: A cognitive theory of health anxiety. In G. J. G. Asmundson, S. Taylor, & B. J. Cox (Eds.), *Health anxiety: Clinical and research perspectives on hypochondriasis and related conditions* (pp. 46–64). New York: Wiley.

Saln-Pascual, R. J., Castao, A., Shiromani, P. J., Valencia-Flores, M., & Campos, R. M. (2006). Caffeine challenge in insomniac patients after total sleep deprivation. *Sleep Medicine, 7,* 141–145.

Salzman, C. (1991). Pharmacologic treatment of the anxious elderly patient. In C. Salzman & B. D. Lebowitz (Eds.), *Anxiety in the elderly: Treatment and research* (pp. 149–173). New York: Springer.

Sameroff, A. J., & Seifer, R. (1990). Early contributors to developmental risk. In J. Rolf, A. S. Masten, D. Cicchetti, K. H. Nuechterlein, et al. (Eds.), *Risk and protective factors in the development of psychopathology* (pp. 52–66). Cambridge: Cambridge University Press.

Sampson, R. J., Raudenbush, S. W., & Earls, F. (1997). Neighborhoods and violent crime: A multilevel study of collective efficacy. *Science, 277,* 918–924.

Samson, J. A., Mirin, S. M., Hauser, S. T., Fenton, B. T., & Schildkraut, J. J. (1992). Learned helplessness and urinary MHPG levels in unipolar depression. *American Journal of Psychiatry, 149*(6), 806–809.

Samuels, J., Bienvenu, O. J., III, Riddle, M. A., Cullen, B. A. M., Grados, M. A., Liang, K.-Y., ... Nestadt, G. (2002). Hoarding in obsessive compulsive disorder: Results from a case-control study. *Behaviour Research Therapy, 40,* 517–528.

Samuels, S. C., & Davis, K. L. (1997). A risk-benefit assessment of tacrine in the treatment of Alzheimer's disease. *Drug Safety, 16,* 66–77.

Sandberg, O., Franklin, K. A., Bucht, G., & Gustafson, Y. (2001). Sleep apnea, delirium, depressed mood, cognition, and ADL ability after stroke. *Journal of the American Geriatric Society, 49*(4), 391–397.

Sanders, M. R. (1992). Enhancing the impact of behavioural family intervention with children: Emerging perspectives. *Behaviour Change, 9,* 115–119.

Sanders, M. R., Dadds, M. R., Johnston, B. M., & Cash, R. (1992). Childhood depression and conduct disorder: I. Behavioral, affective and cognitive aspects of family problem solving interactions. *Journal of Abnormal Psychology, 101*(3), 495–504.

Sanderson, C., & Clarkin, J. F. (1994). Use of the NFO-Pl personality dimensions in differential treatment planning. In P. T. Costa & T. A. Widiger (Eds.), *Personality disorders and the five-factor model of personality* (pp. 219–235). Washington, DC: American Psychological Association.

Sanderson, W. C., & Barlow, D. H. (1990). A description of patients diagnosed with DSM-III-R generalized anxiety disorder. *Journal of Nervous and Mental Disease, 178,* 588–591.

Sanderson, W. C., DiNardo, P. A., Rapee, R. M., & Barlow, D. H. (1990). Syndrome comorbidity in patients diagnosed with a DSM-III-R anxiety disorder. *Journal of Abnormal Psychology, 99,* 308–312.

Sandys, J. (2007). Work and employment for people with intellectual and developmental disabilities. In I. Brown & M. Percy (Eds.), *A comprehensive guide to intellectual & developmental disabilities* (pp. 527–543). Baltimore: Paul H. Brookes.

Sano, M., Ernesto, C., Thomas, R. G., Klauber, M. R., Schafer, K., Grundman, M., ... Thal, L. J. (1997). A controlled trial of selegiline, alphatocopherol, or both as treatment for Alzheimer's disease. *New England Journal of Medicine, 336,* 1216–1222.

Sansbury, L. L., & Wahler, R. G. (1992). Pathways to maladaptive parenting with mothers and their conduct disordered children. *Behavior Modification, 16,* 574–592.

Santor, D. A., & Kusumakar, V. (2001). Open trial of interpersonal therapy in adolescents with moderate to severe major depression: Effectiveness of novice IPT therapists. *Journal of the American Academy of Child & Adolescent Psychiatry, 40,* 236–240.

Santor, D. A., & Yazbek, A. A. (2006). Soliciting unfavourable social comparison: Effects of self-criticism. *Personality and Individual Differences, 40,* 545–556.

Santucci, L. C., Ehrenreich, J. T., Trosper, S. E., Bennett, S. M., & Pincus, D. B. (2009). Development and preliminary evaluation of a one-week summer treatment program for separation anxiety disorder. *Cognitive and Behavioral Practice, 16,* 317–331.

Sapolsky, R. M. (1990, January). Stress in the wild. *Scientific American*, pp. 116–123.

Sapolsky, R. M. (2000a). Genetic hyping. *The Sciences, 40*(2), 12–15.

Sapolsky, R. M. (2000b). Glucocorticoids and hippocampal atrophy in neuropsychiatric disorders. *Archives of General Psychiatry, 57*, 925–935.

Sapolsky, R. M. (2000c). *Why zebras don't get ulcers: An updated guide to stress, stress-related diseases, and coping*. New York: Barnes & Noble.

Sapolsky, R. M. (2002). *A primate's memoir*. New York: Simon & Schuster.

Sapolsky, R. M. (2007). Stress, stress-related disease, and emotional regulation. In J. J. Gross (Ed.), *Handbook of emotion regulation* (pp. 606–615). New York: Guilford Press.

Sapolsky, R. M., & Meaney, M. J. (1986). Maturation of the adrenal stress response: Neuroendocrine control mechanisms and the stress hyporesponsive period. *Brain Research Review, 11*, 65–76.

Sapolsky, R. M., & Ray, J. C. (1989). Styles of dominance and their endocrine correlates among wild, live baboons. *American Journal of Primatology, 18*(1), 1–13.

Sareen, J., Chartier, M., Paulus, M. P., & Stein, M. B. (2006). Illicit drug use and anxiety disorders: Findings from two community surveys. *Psychiatry Research, 142*, 11–17.

Sareen, J., Cox, B. J., Afifi, T. O., de Graaf, R., Asmundson, G. J. G., ten Have, M., & Stein, M. B. (2005). Anxiety disorders and risk for suicidal ideation and suicide attempts: A population-based longitudinal study of adults. *Archives of General Psychiatry, 62*, 1249–1257.

Sareen, J., Houlahan, T., Cox, B. J., & Asmundson, G. J. G. (2005). Anxiety disorders associated with suicidal ideation and suicide attempts in the National Comorbidity Survey. *Journal of Nervous and Mental Disease, 193*, 450–454.

Sarwer, D. B., & Durlak, J. A. (1997). A field trial of the effectiveness of behavioral treatment for sexual dysfunctions. *Journal of Sex and Marital Therapy, 23*, 87–97.

Sass, K. J., Sass, A., Westerveld, M., Lencz, T., Novelly, R. A., Kim, J. H., & Spencer, D. D. (1992). Specificity in the correlation of verbal memory and hippocampal neuron loss: Dissociation of memory, language, and verbal intellectual ability. *Journal of Clinical and Experimental Neuropsychology, 14*(5), 662–672.

Satel, S. (1992). Craving for and fear of cocaine: A phenomenologic update on cocaine craving and paranoia. In T. R. Kosten & H. D. Kleber (Eds.), *Clinician's guide to cocaine addiction: Theory, research, and treatment* (pp. 172–192). New York: Guilford Press.

Saudino, J. J., Pedersen, N. L., Lichenstein, P., McClearn, G. F., & Plomin, R. (1997). Can personality explain genetic influence on life events? *Journal of Personality & Social Psychology, 72*(1), 196–206.

Saudino, K. J., & Plomin, R. (1996). Personality and behavioral genetics: Where have we been and where are we going? *Journal of Research in Personality, 30*, 335–347.

Saudino, K. J., Plomin, R., & DeFries, J. C. (1996). Tester-rated temperament at 14, 20, and 24 months: Environmental change and genetic continuity. *British Journal of Developmental Psychology, 14*, 129–144.

Savard, J., Laroche, L., Simard, S., Ivers, H., & Morin, C. M. (2003). Chronic insomnia and immune functioning. *Psychosomatic Medicine, 65*, 211–221.

Savin-Williams, R. (2006). Who's gay? Does it matter? *Current Directions in Psychological Science, 15*, 40–44.

Sawa, A., & Snyder, S. H. (2002). Schizophrenia: Diverse approaches to a complex disease. *Science, 296*, 692–695.

Saxe, G. N., Stoddard, F., Hall, E., Chawla, N., Lopez, C., Sheridan, R., … Yehuda, R. (2005). Pathways to PTSD: Part I. Children with burns. *American Journal of Psychiatry, 162*, 1299–1304.

Saxe, G. N., van der Kolk, B. A., Berkowitz, R., Chinman, G., Hall, K., Leiberg, G., & Schwartz, J. (1993). Dissociative disorders in psychiatric inpatients. *American Journal of Psychiatry, 150*, 1037–1042.

Saxena, S., & Prasad, K. (1989). DSM-III subclassifications of dissociative disorders applied to psychiatric outpatients in India. *American Journal of Psychiatry, 146*, 261–262.

Sayar, K., Kirmayer, L. J., & Taillefer, S. S. (2003). Predictors of somatic symptoms in depressive disorder. *General Hospital Psychiatry, 25*, 108–114.

Sbrocco, T., & Barlow, D. H. (1996). Conceptualizing the cognitive component of sexual arousal: Implications for sexuality research and treatment. In P. M. Salkovskis (Ed.), *Frontiers of cognitive therapy* (pp. 419–449). New York: Guilford Press.

Schachar, R., Jadad, A. R., Gauld, M., Boyle, M., Booker, L., Snider, A., … Cunningham, C. (2002). Attention-deficit hyperactivity disorder: Critical appraisal of extended treatment studies. *Canadian Journal of Psychiatry, 47*, 337–348.

Schachter, H. M., Pham, B., King, J., Langford, S., & Moher, D. (2001). How efficacious and safe is short-acting methylphenidate for the treatment of attention-deficit disorder in children and adolescents? A metaanalysis. *Canadian Medical Association Journal, 165*, 1475–1488.

Schacter, D. L. (Ed.). (1995). *Memory distortion: How minds, brains, and societies reconstruct the past*. Cambridge, MA: Harvard University Press.

Schacter, D. L., Chiu, P., & Ochsner, K. N. (1993). Implicit memory: A selective review. *Annual Review of Neuroscience, 16*, 159–182.

Schafer, J., & Brown, S. A. (1991). Marijuana and cocaine effect expectancies and drug use patterns. *Journal of Consulting and Clinical Psychology, 59*, 558–565.

Schatzberg, A. F. (2000). New indications for antidepressants. *Journal of Clinical Psychiatry, 61* (Suppl. 11), 9–17.

Scheel, K. R. (2000). The empirical basis of dialectical behavior therapy: Summary, critique, and implications. *Clinical Psychology: Science and Practice, 7*, 68–86.

Scheerenberger, R. C. (1983). *A history of mental retardation*. Baltimore: Paul H. Brookes.

Scheier, M. F., Matthews, K. A., Owens, J. F., Magovern, G. J., Sr., Lefebvre, R. C., Abbott, R. A., & Carver, C. S. (1989). Dispositional optimism and recovery from coronary artery bypass surgery: The beneficial effects on physical and psychological well-being. *Journal of Personality and Social Psychology, 57*(6), 1024–1040.

Schenk, L., & Bear, D. (1981). Multiple personality and related dissociative phenomena in patients with temporal lobe epilepsy. *American Journal of Psychiatry, 138*, 1311–1316.

Scherer, S., Tsui, L. C., & Rommens, J. (2003). *The chromosome 7 annotation project*. Retrieved June 21, 2004, from http://www.chr7.org/

Schiavi, R. C. (1990). Chronic alcoholism and male sexual dysfunction. *Journal of Sex and Marital Therapy, 16*, 23–33.

Schiavi, R. C., White, D, Mandeli, J., & Levine, A. C. (1997). Effect of testosterone administration on sexual behavior and mood in men with erectile dysfunction. *Archives of Sexual Behavior, 26*, 231–241.

Schiffer, B., Peschel, T., Paul, T., Gizewski, E., Forsting, M., Leygraf, N., … Krueger, T. H. (2007). Structural brain abnormalities in the frontostriatal system and cerebellum in pedophilia. *Journal of Psychiatric Research, 41*, 753–762.

Schildkraut, J. J. (1965). The catecholamine hypothesis of affective disorders: A review of supporting evidence. *American Journal of Psychiatry, 122*, 509–522.

Schizophrenia Collaborative Linkage Group (Chromosome 22). (1996). A combined analysis of D22S278 marker alleles in affected sib-pairs: Support for a susceptibility locus at chromosome 22ql2. *American Journal of Medical Genetics, Neuro-psychiatric Genetics, 67*, 40–45.

Schleifer, S. J., Keller, S. F., Bond, R. N., Cohen, J., & Stein, M. (1989). Major depressive disorder and immunity: Role of age, sex, severity, and hospitalization. *Archives of General Psychiatry, 46*, 81–87.

Schlundt, O. G., & Johnson, W. G. (1990). *Eating disorders: Assessment and treatment*. Boston: Allyn & Bacon.

Schmidt, N. B., & Koselka, M. (2000). Gender differences in patients with panic disorder: Evaluating cognitive mediation of phobic avoidance. *Cognitive Therapy and Research, 24*, 533–550.

Schmidt, N. B., Lerew, D. R., & Jackson, R. J. (1997). The role of anxiety sensitivity in the pathogenesis of panic: Projective evaluation of spontaneous panic attacks during acute stress. *Journal of Abnormal Psychology, 106*, 355–364.

Schmidt, N. B., Lerew, D. R., & Jackson, R. J. (1999). Prospective evaluation of anxiety sensitivity in the pathogenesis of panic: Replication and extension. *Journal of Abnormal Psychology, 108*, 532–537.

Schmitz, J. M., Schneider, N. G., & Jarvik, M. F. (1997). Nicotine. In J. H. Lowinson, P. Ruiz, R. B. Millman, & J. G. Langrod (Eds.), *Substance abuse: A comprehensive textbook* (pp. 276–294). Baltimore: Williams & Wilkins.

Schneck, C., Miklowitz, D., Calabrese, J., Allen, M., Thomas, M., Wisniewski, S., … Sachs, G. S. (2004). Phenomenology of rapid-cycling bipolar disorder: Data from the first 500 participants in the systematic treatment enhancement program. *American Journal Psychiatry, 161*, 1902–1908.

Schneider, F. R., Blanco, C., Antia, S. X., & Liebowitz, M. R. (2002). The social anxiety spectrum. *Psychiatric Clinics of North America, 25*, 757–774.

Schneiderman, N., Antoni, M. H., Ironson, G., LaPerriere, A., & Fletcher, M. A. (1992). Applied psychological science and HIV-1 spectrum disease. *Applied and Preventive Psychology, 1*, 67–82.

Schneier, F. R., Garfinkel, R., Kennedy, B., Campeas, R., Fallon, B., Marshall, R., … Liebowitz, M. R. (1996). Ondansetron in the treatment of panic disorder. *Anxiety, 2*, 199–202.

Schneier, F. R., Liebowitz, M. R., Beidel, D. C., Fyer, A. J., George, M. S., Heimberg, R. G., … Versiani, M. (1996). Social phobia. In T. A. Widiger, A. J. Frances, H. A. Pincus, R. Ross, et al. (Eds.), *DSM-IV sourcebook* (Vol. 2, pp. 507–548). Washington, DC: American Psychiatric Association.

Schoenbach, V. J., Kaplan, B. H., Fredman, L., & Kleinbaum, D. G. (1986). Social ties and mortality in Evans County, Georgia. *American Journal of Epidemiology, 123,* 577.

Schoeneman, T. J. (1977). The role of mental illness in the European witchhunts of the sixteenth and seventeenth centuries: An assessment. *Journal of the History of the Behavioral Sciences, 13,* 337–351.

Schover, L. R., & Jensen, S. B. (1988). *Sexuality and chronic illness: A comprehensive approach.* New York: Guilford Press.

Schreiber, F. R. (1973). *Sybil.* Chicago: Regnery.

Schreiner-Engel, P., & Schiavi, R. C. (1986). Lifetime psychopathology in individuals with low sexual desire. *Journal of Nervous and Mental Disease, 174,* 646–651.

Schroeder, M. L., Wormworth, J. A., & Livesley, W. J. (1993). Dimensions of personality disorder and the five-factor model of personality. In P. T. Costa, Jr., & T. A. Widiger (Eds.), *Personality disorders and the five-factor model of personality* (pp. 117–127). Washington, DC: American Psychological Association.

Schuckit, M. A. (2009a). Alcohol-related disorders. In B. J. Sadock, V. A. Sadock, & P. Ruiz (Eds.), *Kaplan & Sadock's comprehensive textbook of psychiatry* (Vol. I, 9th ed., pp. 1268–1288). Philadelphia: Lippincott Williams & Wilkins.

Schuckit, M. A. (2009b). Alcohol-use disorders. *The Lancet, 373*(9662), 492–501.

Schuckit, M. A., Smith, T. L., Anthenelli, R., & Irwin, M. (1993). Clinical course of alcoholism in 636 male inpatients. *American Journal of Psychiatry, 150,* 786–792.

Schulberg, H. C., Block, M. R., Madonia, M. J., Scott, C. P., Rodriguez, F., Imber, S. D., ... Coulehan, J. L. (1996). Treating major depression in primary care practice: Eight-month clinical outcomes. *Archives of General Psychiatry, 53,* 913–919.

Schuller, R. A., & Ogloff, J. R. P. (2001). An introduction to psychology and law. In R. A. Schuller & J. R. P. Ogloff (Eds.), *Introduction to psychology and law: Canadian perspectives* (pp. 3–28). Toronto, ON: University of Toronto Press.

Schuller, R. A., Wells, F., Rzepa, S., & Klippenstine, M. A. (2004). Rethinking battered woman syndrome evidence: The impact of alternative forms of expert testimony on mock jurors' decisions. *Canadian Journal of Behavioural Science, 36,* 127–136.

Schuller, R. A., & Yarmey, M. (2001). The jury: Deciding guilt and innocence. In R. A. Schuller & J. R. P. Ogloff (Eds.), *Introduction to psychology and law: Canadian perspectives* (pp. 157–187). Toronto, ON: University of Toronto Press.

Schulsinger, F., Kety, S. S., & Rosenthal, D. (1979). A family study of suicide. In M. Schou & F. Stromgren (Eds.), *Origin, prevention, and treatment of affective disorders.* New York: Academic Press.

Schultz, W. W., Basson, R., Binik, Y., Eschenbach, D., Wesselmann, U., & Van Lankveld, J. (2005). Women's sexual pain and its management. *Journal of Sexual Medicine, 2,* 301–316.

Schulz, R., Drayer, R. A., & Rollman, B. L. (2002). Depression as a risk factor for non-suicide mortality in the elderly. *Biological Psychiatry, 52,* 204–225.

Schumann, C. M., & Amaral, D. G. (2006). Stereological analysis of amygdala neuron number in autism. *Journal of Neuroscience, 26,* 7674–7679.

Schutter, D. J. (2009). Antidepressant efficacy of high-frequency transcranial magnetic stimulation over the left dorsolateral prefrontal cortex in double-blind sham-controlled designs: A meta-analysis. *Psychological Medicine, 39*(1), 65–75.

Schwalberg, M. D., Barlow, D. H., Alger, S. A., & Howard, L. J. (1992). Comparison of bulimics, obese binge eaters, social phobics, and individuals with panic disorder or comorbidity across DSM-III-R anxiety. *Journal of Abnormal Psychology, 101,* 675–681.

Schwartlander, B., Garnett, G., Walker, N., & Anderson, R. (2000). AIDS in a new millennium. *Science, 289,* 64–67.

Schwartz, A. J., & Whitaker, L. C. (1990). Suicide among college students: Assessment, treatment, and intervention. In S. J. Blumenthal & D. J. Kupfer (Eds.), *Suicide over the life cycle: Risk factors, assessment and treatment of suicidal patients.* Washington, DC: American Psychiatric Press.

Schwartz, G. F., & Weiss, S. M. (1978). Behavioral medicine revisited: An amended definition. *Journal of Behavioral Medicine, 1,* 249–252.

Schwartz, I. M. (1993). Affective reactions of American and Swedish women to the first premarital coitus: A cross-cultural comparison. *Journal of Sex Research, 30*(1), 18–26.

Schwartz, P. J., Brown, C., Wehr, T. A., & Rosenthal, N. F. (1996). Winter seasonal affective disorder: A follow-up study of the first 59 patients of the National Institute of Mental Health seasonal studies program. *American Journal of Psychiatry, 153,* 1028–1036.

Schwarz, A. (2007, March 14). Wives united by husband's post-NFL trauma. *New York Times,* p. A1. Retrieved from http://www.nytimes.com

Schweizer, E., & Rickels, K. (1996). Pharmacological treatment for generalized anxiety disorder. In M. R. Mavissakalian & R. F. Prien (Eds.), *Long-term treatments of anxiety disorders.* Washington, DC: American Psychiatric Press.

Scott, C. L., Hilty, D. M., & Brook, M. (2003). Impulse-control disorders not elsewhere classified. In R. E. Hales & S. C. Yudofsky (Eds.), *Textbook of clinical psychiatry* (4th ed., pp. 781–802). Washington, DC: American Psychiatric Publishing.

Scott, J. (1995). Psychotherapy for bipolar disorder. *British Journal of Psychiatry, 167,* 581–588.

Scott, J. F., & Dixon, L. B. (1995a). Assertive community treatment and case management for schizophrenia. *Schizophrenia Bulletin, 21,* 657–668.

Scott, J. F., & Dixon, L. B. (1995b). Psychological interventions for schizophrenia. *Schizophrenia Bulletin, 21,* 621–630.

Sealy, P., & Whitehead, P. C. (2004). Forty years of deinstitutionalization of psychiatric services in Canada: An empirical assessment. *Canadian Journal of Psychiatry, 49,* 249–257.

Secko, D. (2005). Depression: More than just serotonin. *Canadian Medical Association Journal, 172,* 1551.

Seeman, M. V. (2007). An outcome measure in schizophrenia: Mortality. *The Canadian Journal of Psychiatry/La Revue canadienne de psychiatrie, 52*(1), 55–60.

Seeman, P., Lee, T., Chau Wong, M., & Wong, K. (1976). Antipsychotic drug doses and neuroleptic/dopamine receptors. *Nature, 261,* 717–719.

Segal, S. (1978). Attitudes toward the mentally ill: A review. *Social Work, 23,* 211–217.

Segal, Z., Vincent, P., & Levitt, A. (2002). Efficacy of combined, sequential and crossover psychotherapy and pharmacotherapy in improving outcomes in depression. *Journal of Psychiatry & Neuroscience, 27,* 281–290.

Segal, Z. V., Hood, J. F., Shaw, B. F., & Higgins, F. (1988). A structural analysis of the self-schema construct in major depression. *Cognitive Therapy and Research, 12*(5), 471–485.

Segal, Z. V., Williams, J. M. G., & Teasdale, J. D. (2002). *Mindfulness-based cognitive therapy for depression: A new approach to preventing relapse.* New York: Guilford Press.

Segerstrom, S. C., & Sephton, S. E. (2010). Optimistic expectancies and cell-mediated immunity: The role of positive affect. *Psychological Science, 21,* 448–455.

Segraves, R. T., & Althof, S. (1998). Psychotherapy and pharmacotherapy of sexual dysfunctions. In P. F. Nathan & J. M. Gorman (Eds.), *A guide to treatments that work* (pp. 447–471). New York: Oxford University Press.

Seligman, M. F. P. (1971). Phobias and preparedness. *Behavior Therapy, 2,* 307–320.

Seligman, M. F. P. (1975). *Helplessness: On depression, development and death.* San Francisco: W. H. Freeman.

Seligman, M. F. P. (1998). The prediction and prevention of depression. In D. K. Routh & R. J. DeRubeis (Eds.), *Science of clinical psychology: Accomplishments and future directions* (pp. 201–214). Washington, DC: American Psychological Association.

Seligman, M. F. P. (2002). Positive psychology, positive prevention, and positive therapy. In C. R. Snyder & S. J. Lopez (Eds.), *Handbook of positive psychology* (pp. 3–9). London: Oxford University Press.

Seligman, M. F. P., & Binik, Y. (1977). The safety signal hypothesis. In H. Davis & H. Horowitz (Eds.), *Operant-Pavlovian interaction.* Hillsdale, NJ: Erlbaum.

Seligman, M. F. P., Schulman, P., DeRubeis, R. J., & Hollon, S. D. (1999). The prevention of depression and anxiety. *Prevention and Treatment, 2,* 8.

Sellick, S. M., & Zaza, C. (1998). Critical review of 5 nonpharmacologic strategies for managing cancer pain. *Cancer Prevention and Control, 2,* 7–14.

Selye, H. (1936). A syndrome produced by diverse noxious agents. *Nature, 138,* 32.

Selye, H. (1950). *The physiology and pathology of exposure to stress.* Montreal: Acta.

Semans, J. H. (1956). Premature ejaculation: A new approach. *Southern Medical Journal, 49,* 353–358.

Seshadri, S., Fitzpatrick, A. L., Ikram, M. A., DeStefano, A. L., Gudnason, V., Boada, M., ... Breteler, M. M. B. (2010). Genome-wide analysis of genetic loci associated with Alzheimer disease. *JAMA, 303*(18), 1832–1840.

Seto, M. C. (2009). Pedophilia. In S. Nolen-Hoeksema, T. D. Cannon, & T. Widiger, T. (Eds.), *Annual review of clinical psychology* (Vol. 5, pp. 391–408). Palo Alto, CA: Annual Reviews.

Seto, M. C., Cantor, J. M., & Blanchard, R. (2006). Child pornography offenses are a valid diagnostic indicator of pedophilia. *Journal of Abnormal Psychology, 115,* 610–615.

Severino, S. K., & Moline, M. L. (1989). *Premenstrual syndrome: A clinician's guide.* New York: Guilford Press.

Sexton, M. M. (1979). Behavioral epidemiology. In O. F. Pomerleau & J. P. Brady (Eds.), *Behavioral medicine: Theory and practice* (pp. 3–21). Baltimore: Williams & Wilkins.

Seyfort, B., Spreen, O., & Lahmer, V. (1980). A critical look at the WISC-R with Native Indian children. *Alberta Journal of Educational Research, 26,* 14–24.

Shabecoff, P. (1987, October 14). Stress and the lure of harmless remedies. *New York Times*, p. 12.

Shaffer, D., Garland, A., Gould, M., Fisher, P., & Trautmen, P. (1988). Preventing teenage suicide: A critical review. *Journal of the American Academy of Child and Adolescent Psychiatry, 27*, 675–687.

Shaffer, D., Garland, A., Vieland, V., Underwood, M., & Busner, C. (1991). The impact of curriculum based suicide prevention programs for teenagers. *Journal of the American Academy of Child and Adolescent Psychiatry, 30*(4), 588–596.

Shaffer, D., Leibenluft, E., Rohde, L. A., Sirovatka, P., & Regier, D. A. (Eds.). (2009). *Externalizing disorders of childhood: Refining the research agenda for DSM-V*. Arlington, VA: American Psychiatric Association.

Shaffer, D. R. (1993). *Developmental psychology: Childhood and adolescence* (3rd ed.). Pacific Grove, CA: Brooks/Cole.

Shafran, R., Thordarson, D. S., & Rachman, S. (1996). Thought-action fusion in obsessive compulsive disorder. *Journal of Anxiety Disorders, 10*, 379–391.

Shakespeare, W. (2002). *Macbeth*. New York: Dover Publications.

Shapiro, D. (1965). *Neurotic styles*. New York: Basic Books.

Shapiro, D. A., Rees, A., Barkham, M., Hardy, G., Reynolds, S., & Startup, M. (1995). Effects of treatment duration and severity of depression on the maintenance of gains after cognitive-behavioral and psychodynamic-interpersonal psychotherapy. *Journal of Consulting and Clinical Psychology, 63*, 378–387.

Shapiro, F. (1995). *Eye movement desensitization and reprocessing: Basic principles, protocols, and procedures*. New York: Guilford Press.

Shapiro, F. (1999). Eye movement desensitization and reprocessing (FMDR) and the anxiety disorders: Clinical and research implications of an integrated psychotherapy treatment. *Journal of Anxiety Disorders, 13*, 35–67.

Shapiro, F. S., & Lentz, F. F. (1991). Vocational-technical programs: Follow-up of students with learning disabilities. *Exceptional Children, 58*, 47–59.

Sharp, T. (2009). Neurotransmitters and signalling. In M. G. Gelder, N. C. Andreasen, J. J. Lopez-Ibor, Jr., & J. R. Geddes (Eds.), *New Oxford textbook of psychiatry* (Vol. 1, 2nd ed., pp. 168–176). Oxford, UK: Oxford University Press.

Sharpe, M. (1992). Fatigue and chronic fatigue syndrome. *Current Opinion in Psychiatry, 5*, 207–212.

Sharpe, M. (1993). *Chronic fatigue syndrome* (pp. 298–317). Chichester, UK: John Wiley & Sons.

Sharpe, M. (1997). Chronic fatigue. In D. M. Clark & C. G. Fairburn (Eds.), *Science and practice of cognitive behavior therapy* (pp. 381–414). Oxford, U.K.: Oxford University Press.

Sharpe, M., Clements, A., Hawton, K., Young, A., Sargent, P., & Cowen, P. (1996). Increased prolactin response to buspirone in chronic fatigue syndrome. *Journal of Affective Disorders, 41*, 71–76.

Shatkin, J. P., & Ivanenko, A. (2009). Pediatric sleep disorders. In B. J. Sadock, V. A. Sadock & P. Ruiz (Eds.), *Kaplan & Sadock's comprehensive textbook of psychiatry* (Vol. I, 9th ed., pp. 3903–3908). Philadelphia: Lippincott Williams & Wilkins.

Shattuck, P. T. (2006). The contribution of diagnostic substitution to the growing administrative prevalence of autism in U.S. special education. *Pediatrics, 117*, 1028–1037.

Shaywitz, S. (2003). *Overcoming dyslexia: A new and complete science-based program for reading problems at any level*. New York: Alfred A. Knopf.

Shea, M. T., Elkin, I., Imber, S. D., Sotsky, S. M., Watkins, J. T., Collins, J. F., ... Dolan, R. T. (1992). Course of depressive symptoms over follow-up: Findings from the National Institute of Mental Health Treatment of Depression Collaborative Research Program. *Archives of General Psychiatry, 49*(10), 782–787.

Shea, M. T., Pilkonis, P. A., Beckham, F., Collins, J. F., Elkin, I., Sotsky, S. M., & Docherty, J. P. (1990). Personality disorders and treatment outcome in the NIMH treatment of depression collaborative research program. *American Journal of Psychiatry, 147*, 711–718.

Sheaffer, R. (1986). *The UFO verdict: Examining the evidence*. Buffalo, NY: Prometheus Books.

Shear, K. (2006). Adapting imaginal exposure to the treatment of complicated grief. In Rothbaum, B. (Ed.), Pathological anxiety: *Emotional processing in etiology and treatment* (pp. 215–226). New York: Guilford Press.

Shear, K., Jin, R., Ruscio, A. M., Walters, E. E., & Kessler, R. C. (2006). Prevalence and correlates of estimated DSM-IV child and adult separation anxiety disorder in the National Comorbidity Survey Replication. *American Journal of Psychiatry, 163*(6), 1074–1083.

Shear, M. K., Brown, T. A., Barlow, D. H., Money, R., Sholomskas, D. F., Woods, S. W., ... Papp, L. A. (1997). Multicenter collaborative panic disorder severity scale. *American Journal of Psychiatry, 154*, 1571–1575.

Sheikh, J. I. (1992). Anxiety and its disorders in old age. In J. F. Birren, K. Sloan, & G. D. Cohen (Eds.), *Handbook of mental health and aging* (pp. 410–432). New York: Academic Press.

Shen, F. K., Alden., L. F., Söchting, I., & Tsang, P. (2006). Clinical observations of a Cantonese Cognitive-Behavioral Treatment Program for Chinese immigrants [Special issue]. *Psychotherapy: Theory, Research, Practice, Training, 43*(4), 518–530.

Shenton, M. E., & Kubicki, M. (2009). Structural brain imaging in schizophrenia. In B. J. Sadock, V. A. Sadock, & P. Ruiz (Eds.), *Kaplan & Sadock's comprehensive textbook of psychiatry* (Vol. I, 9th ed., pp. 1494–1507). Philadelphia: Lippincott Williams & Wilkins.

Shepard, B., O'Neill, L., & Guenette, F. (2006). Counselling with First Nations women: Considerations of oppression and renewal. *International Journal for the Advancement of Counselling, 28*(3), 227–240.

Shepertycky, M. R., Banno, K., & Kryger, M. H. (2005). Differences between men and women in clinical presentation of patients diagnosed with obstructive sleep apnea syndrome. *Sleep, 28*, 309–314.

Shepherd, J. F. (2001). Effects of estrogen on cognition, mood, and degenerative brain diseases. *Journal of the American Pharmacological Association* (Wash.), *41*(2), 221–228.

Shepherd, M., Watt, D., Falloon, I., & Smeeton, N. (1989). The natural history of schizophrenia: a five-year follow-up study of outcome and prediction in a representative sample of schizophrenics. *Psychological Medicine Monograph, 15*(Suppl.), 1–46.

Sher, K. J., Martinez, J. A., & Littlefield, A. K. (in press). Alcohol use and alcohol use disorders. In D. H. Barlow (Ed.), *Oxford handbook of clinical psychology*. New York: Oxford University.

Sherbourne, C. D., Hays, R. D., & Wells, K. B. (1995). Personal and psychosocial risk factors for physical and mental health outcomes and course of depression among depressed patients. *Journal of Consulting and Clinical Psychology, 63*, 345–355.

Sherman, A. C., Leszcz, M., Mosier, J., Burlingame, G. M., Cleary, T., Ulman, K. H., ... Hazelton, L. (2004). Group interventions for patients with cancer and HIV disease: Part II. Effects on immune, endocrine, and disease outcomes at different phases of illness. *International Journal of Group Psychotherapy, 54*(2), 203–233.

Sherman, S. L., DeFries, J. C., Gottesman, I. I., Loehlin, J. C., Meyer, J. M., Pelias, M. Z., ... Waldman, I. (1997). Recent developments in human behavioral genetics: Past accomplishments and future directions. *American Journal of Human Genetics, 60*, 1265–1275.

Sherrington, R., Rogaev, F. I., Liang, Y., Rogaeva, F. A., Levesque, G., Ikeda, M., ... St. George-Hyslop, P. H. (1995). Cloning of a gene bearing missense mutations in early-onset familial Alzheimer's disease. *Nature, 375*, 754–60.

Shiah, I., & Yatham, L. N. (2000). Serotonin in mania and in the mechanism of action of mood stabilizers: A review of clinical studies. *Bipolar Disorders, 2*(2), 77–92.

Shiffman, S., Hickcox, M., Paty, J. A., Gnys, M., Kassel, J. D., & Richards, T. J. (1996). Progression from a smoking lapse to relapse: Prediction from abstinence violation effects, nicotine dependence, and lapse characteristics. *Journal of Consulting and Clinical Psychology, 64*, 993–1002.

Shimizu, M., Kubota, Y., Toichi, M., & Baba, H. (2007). Folie à deux and shared psychotic disorder. *Current Psychiatry Reports, 9*(3), 200–205.

Shin, L. M., Lasko, N. B., Macklin, M. L., Karpf, R. D., Milad, M. R., Orr, S. P., ... Pitman, R. K. (2009). Resting metabolic activity in the cingulate cortex and vulnerability to posttraumatic stress disorder. *Archives of General Psychiatry, 66*(10), 1099–1107.

Shin, L. M., Shin, P. S., Heckers, S., Krangel, T. S., Macklin, M. L., Orr, S. P., ... Rauch, S. L. (2004). Hippocampal function in posttraumatic stress disorder. *Hippocampus, 14*, 292–300.

Shneidman, F. S. (1989). Approaches and commonalities of suicide. In R. F. W. Diekstra, R. Mariss, S. Platt, A. Schmidtke, et al. (Eds.), *Suicide and its prevention: The role of attitude and imitation. Advances in Suicidology* (Vol. 1). Leiden, The Netherlands: F. J. Brill.

Shneidman, F. S., Farberow, N. L., & Litman, R. F. (Eds.). (1970). *The psychology of suicide*. New York: Science House.

Show, M. (1985). Practical problems of lithium maintenance treatment. *Advances in Biochemical Psychopharmacology, 40*, 131–138.

Shulman, K. I. (2000). Clock-drawing: Is it the ideal cognitive screening test? *International Journal of Geriatric Psychiatry, 15*, 548–561.

Shulman, K. I., Shedletsky, R., & Silver, I. (1986). The challenge of time: Clock drawing and cognitive function in the elderly. *International Journal of Geriatric Psychiatry, 1*, 135–140.

Shumaker, S. A., Legault, C., Kuller, L., Rapp, S. R., Thal, L., Lane, D. S., ... Coker, L. H., & Women's Health Initiative Memory Study. (2004). Conjugated equine estrogens and incidence of probable dementia and mild cognitive impairment in postmenopausal women: Women's Health Initiative Memory Study. *JAMA, 291*, 3005–3007.

Sibley, D. C., & Blinder, B. J. (1988). Anorexia nervosa. In B. J. Blinder, B. F. Chaitin, & R. S. Goldstein (Eds.), *The eating disorders: Medical and psychological bases of diagnosis and treatment* (pp. 247–258). New York: PMA.

Sieck, W. A., & McFall, R. M. (1976). Some determinants of self-monitoring effects. *Journal of Consulting and Clinical Psychology, 44*, 958–965.

Siegel, S. (1982). Opioid expectation modifies opioid effects. *Federation Proc, 41*, 2339–2343.

Siegel, S., Hinson, R. F., Krank, M. D., & McCully, J. (1982). Heroin "overdose" death: Contribution of drug-associated environmental cues. *Science, 216*, 436–437.

Sierra, M., & Berrios, G. F. (1998). Depersonalization: Neurobiological perspectives. *Society of Biological Psychiatry, 44*, 898–908.

Sierra, M., Senior, C., Dalton, J., McDonough, M., Bond, A., Phillips, M. L., … David, A. S. (2002). Autonomic response in depersonalization disorder. *Archives of General Psychiatry, 59*, 833–838.

Siever, L. J. (1992). Schizophrenia spectrum personality disorders. In A. Tasman & M. B. Riba (Eds.), *Review of psychiatry* (Vol. 11, pp. 25–42). Washington, DC: American Psychiatric Press.

Siever, L. J., Bernstein, D. P., & Silverman, J. M. (1991). Schizotypal personality disorder: A review of its current status. *Journal of Personality Disorders, 5*, 178–193.

Siever, L. J., Bernstein, D. P., & Silverman, J. M. (1995). Schizotypal personality disorder. In W. J. Livesley (Ed.), *The DSM-IV personality disorders* (pp. 71–90). New York: Guilford Press.

Siever, L. J., Davis, K. L., & Gorman, L. K. (1991). Pathogenesis of mood disorders. In K. Davis, H. Klar, & J. T. Coyle (Eds.), *Foundations of psychiatry*. Philadelphia: W. B. Saunders.

Siffre, M. (1964). *Beyond time* (H. Briffault, Ed. and Trans.). New York: McGraw-Hill.

Sigafoos, J., Arthur-Kelly, M., & Butterfield, N. (2006). *Enhancing everyday communication for children with disabilities*. Baltimore, MD: Paul H. Brookes.

Sigafoos, J., Green, V. A., Schlosser, R., O'Reilly, M. F., Lancioni, G. E., Rispoli, M., & Lang, R. (2009). Communication intervention in Rett syndrome: A systematic review. *Research in Autism Spectrum Disorders, 3*(2), 304–318.

Sigvardsson, S., Cloninger, C. R., Bohman, M., & von-Knorring, A. L. (1982). Predisposition to petty criminality in Swedish adoptees. *Archives of General Psychiatry, 39*, 1248–1253.

Sikich, L. (2009). Early onset psychotic disorders. In B. J. Sadock, V. A. Sadock, & P. Ruiz (Eds.), *Kaplan & Sadock's comprehensive textbook of psychiatry* (Vol. II, 9th ed., pp. 3699–3706). Philadelphia: Lippincott Williams & Wilkins.

Silbersweig, D. A., Stern, E., Frith, C., Cahill, C., Holmes, A., Grootoonk, S., … Frackowiak, R. S. J. (1995). A functional neuroanatomy of hallucinations in schizophrenia. *Nature, 378*, 176–179.

Silove, D. M., Marnane, C. L., Wagner, R., Manicavasagar, V. L., & Rees, S. (2010). The prevalence and correlates of adult separation anxiety disorder in an anxiety clinic. *BMC Psychiatry, 10*, 21.

Silva, P. A. (1980). The prevalence, stability and significance of developmental language delay in preschool children. *Developmental Medicine and Child Neurology, 22*, 768–777.

Silveira, J. M., & Seeman, M. V. (1995). Shared psychotic disorder: A critical review of the literature. *Canadian Journal of Psychiatry, 40*, 389–395.

Silverman, K., Evans, S. M., Strain, F. C., & Griffiths, R. R. (1992). Withdrawal syndrome after the double-blind cessation of caffeine consumption. *New England Journal of Medicine, 327*, 1109–1114.

Silverman, W. K., La Greca, A. M., & Wasserstein, S. (1995). What do children worry about? Worries & their relation to anxiety. *Child Development, 66*, 671–686.

Silverman, W. K., & Rabian, B. (1993). Simple phobias. *Child and Adolescent Psychiatric Clinics of North America, 2*, 603–622.

Silverstone, P. H., & Silverstone, T. (2004). A review of acute treatments for bipolar depression. *International Clinical Psychopharmacology, 19*, 113–124.

Silverstone, T. (1985). Dopamine in manic depressive illness: A pharmacological synthesis. *Journal of Affective Disorders, 8*(3), 225–231.

Simeon, D. (2009). Neurobiology of depersonalization disorder. In P. F. Dell & J. A. O'Neil (Eds.), *Dissociation and the dissociative disorders* (pp. 367–372). New York: Routledge.

Simeon, D., & Abugal, J. (2006). *Feeling unreal: Depersonalization disorder and the loss of the self*. Oxford, UK: Oxford University Press.

Simeon, D., Gross, S., Guralnik, O., Stein, M. B., Schmeidler, J., & Hollander F. (1997). Thirty cases of DSM III-R depersonalization disorder. *American Journal of Psychiatry, 154*, 1107–1113.

Simeon, D., Guralnik, O., Hazlett, E. A., Spiegel-Cohen, J., Hollander, E., & Buchsbaum, M. S. (2000). Feeling unreal: A PET study of depersonalization disorder. *American Journal of Psychiatry, 157*, 1782–1788.

Simeon, D., Guralnik, O., Knutelska, M., Hollander, E., & Schmeidler, J. (2001). Hypothalamic–pituitary–adrenal axis dysregulation in depersonalization disorder. *Neuropsychopharmacology, 25*, 793–795.

Simeon, D., Guralnik, O., Schmeidler, J., & Knutelska, M. (2004). Fluoxetine therapy in depersonalization disorder: Randomised controlled trial. *British Journal of Psychiatry, 185*, 31–36.

Simeon, J., Nixon, M. K., & Milin, R. (2005). Open-label pilot study of St. John's Wort in adolescent depression. *Journal of Child and Adolescent Psychopharmacology, 15*, 293–301.

Simon, F. J. (1997). Opiates: Neurobiology. In J. H. Lowinson, P. Ruiz, R. B. Millman, & J. G. Langrod (Eds.), *Substance abuse: A comprehensive textbook* (pp. 148–158). Baltimore: Williams & Wilkins.

Simon, R. I. (1999). The law and psychiatry. In R. F. Hales, S. C. Yudofsky, & J. A. Talbott (Eds.), *The American Psychiatric Press Textbook of Psychiatry* (3rd ed., pp. 1493–1534). Washington, DC: American Psychiatric Press.

Simon, R. I. (2003). The law and psychiatry. In R. F. Hales, S. C. Yudofsky, & J. A. Talbott (Eds.), *The American Psychiatric Press textbook of psychiatry* (4th ed., pp. 1585–1626). Washington, DC: American Psychiatric Press.

Simoneau, T. L., Miklowitz, D. J., Richards, J. A., Saleem, R., & George, F. L. (1999). Bipolar disorder and family communication: Effects of a psychoeducational treatment program. *Journal of Abnormal Psychology, 108*, 588–597.

Simonoff, E., Bolton, P., & Rutter, M. (1996). Mental retardation: Genetic findings, clinical implications and research agenda. *Journal of Child Psychology and Psychiatry, 37*, 259–280.

Simons, A. D., Murphy, G. F., Levine, J. L., & Wetzel, R. D. (1986). Cognitive therapy and pharmacotherapy for depression: Sustained improvement over one year. *Archives of General Psychiatry, 43*(1), 43–48.

Single, F., Robson, L., Rehm, J., & Xie, X. (1996). *The costs of substance abuse in Canada*. Ottawa, ON: Canadian Centre on Substance Abuse.

Sinha, B. K., & Watson, D. C. (2004). Personality disorder clusters and the defence style questionnaire. *Psychology and Psychotherapy: Theory, Research and Practice, 77*, 55–66.

Slutske, W. S., Heath, A. C., Dinwiddie, S. H., Madden, P. A. F., Bucholz, K. K., Dunne, M. P., … Martin, N. G. (1998). Common genetic risk factors for conduct disorder and alcohol dependence. *Journal of Abnormal Psychology, 107*(3), 363–374.

Siris, S. G. (1993). The treatment of schizoaffective disorder. In D. L. Dunner (Ed.), *Current psychiatric therapy* (pp. 160–165). Philadelphia: W. B. Saunders.

Skhiri, D., Annabi, S., Bi, S., & Allani, D. (1982). Enfants d'immigrés: Facteurs de liens ou de rupture? *Annales Medico-Psychologiques, 140*, 597–602.

Skilling, T. A., Harris, G. T., Rice, M. F., & Quinsey, V. L. (2002). Identifying persistently antisocial offenders using the Hare Psychopathy Checklist and DSM antisocial personality disorder criteria. *Psychological Assessment, 14*, 27–38.

Skinner, B. F. (1938). *The behavior of organisms*. New York: Appleton-Century-Crofts.

Skinner, B. F. (1948). *Walden two*. New York: Macmillan.

Skinner, B. F. (1971). *Beyond freedom and dignity*. New York: Knopf.

Skodol, A. E. (2005). Manifestations, clinical diagnosis, and comorbidity. In J. M. Oldham, A. E. Skodol, & D. S. Bender (Eds.), *Textbook of personality disorders* (pp. 57–87). Washington, DC: American Psychiatric Publishing.

Skodol, A. E., & Gunderson, J. G. (2008). Personality disorders. In R. E. Hales, S. C. Yudofsky, & G. O. Gabbard (Eds.), *The American Psychiatric Publishing textbook of psychiatry* (5th ed., pp. 821–860). Arlington, VA: American Psychiatric Publishing.

Skodol, A. E., Oldham, J. M., Bender, D. S., Dyck, I. R., Stout, R. L., & Morey, L. C., … Gunderson, J. G. (2005). Dimensional representations of DSM-IV personality disorders: Relationships to functional impairment. *American Journal of Psychiatry, 162*, 1919–1925.

Skodol, A. F., Oldham, J. M., & Gallaher, P. F. (1999). Axis II comorbidity of substance use disorders among patients referred for treatment of personality disorders. *American Journal of Psychiatry, 156*, 733–738.

Slade, J. (1999). Nicotine. In B. S. McCrady & F. F. Epstein (Eds.), *Addictions: A comprehensive guidebook* (pp. 162–170). New York: Oxford University Press.

Slutske, W. S., Heath, A. C., Dinwiddie, S. H., Madden, P. A. F., Bucholz, K. K., Dunne, M. P., … Martin, N. G. (1997). Modeling genetic and environmental influences in the etiology of conduct disorder: A study of 2, 682 adult twin pairs. *Journal of Abnormal Psychology, 106*, 266–279., 363–374.

Small, G. W. (1991). Recognition and treatment of depression in the elderly. The clinician's challenge: Strategies for treatment of depression in the 1990's. *Journal of Clinical Psychiatry, 52*, 11–22.

Smart, R. G. (1985). Alcohol and alcohol problems research: IV. Canada. *British Journal of Addiction, 80*, 255–263.

Smeets, G., de Jong, P. J., & Mayer, B. (2000). If you suffer from a headache, then you have a brain tumour: Domain-specific reasoning "bias" and hypochondriasis. *Behaviour Research and Therapy, 38,* 763–776.

Smeets, I., Tan, E., Vossen, H., Leroy, P., Lousberg, R., van Os, J., & Schieveld, J. N. M. (2010). Prolonged stay at the paediatric intensive care unit associated with paediatric delirium. *European Child & Adolescent Psychiatry, 19*(4), 389–393.

Smith, D. F., Marcus, M. D., & Kaye, W. (1992). Cognitive-behavioral treatment of obese binge eaters. *International Journal of Eating Disorders, 12,* 257–262.

Smith, D. F., & Wesson, D. R. (1999). Benzodiazepines and other sedative-hypnotics. In M. Galanter & H. D. Kleber (Eds.), *Textbook of substance abuse treatment* (2nd ed., pp. 239–250). Washington, DC: American Psychiatric Press.

Smith, G., Malla, A., Williams, R., Kopala, L., Love, L., & Balshaw, R. (2006). The Canadian National Outcomes Measurement Study in schizophrenia: Overview of the patient sample and methodology. *Acta Psychiatrica Scandinavica, 113*(430), 4–11.

Smith, G. R., Monson, R. A., & Ray, D. B. (1986). Psychiatric consultation in somatization disorder. *New England Journal of Medicine, 314,* 1407–1413.

Smith, G. T., & Oltmanns, T. F. (2009). Scientific advances in the diagnosis of psychopathology: Introduction to the special section. *Psychological Assessment, 21*(3), 241–242.

Smith, J. F., & Krejci, J. (1991). Minorities join the majority: Eating disturbances among Hispanic and Native American youth. *International Journal of Eating Disorders, 10,* 179–186.

Smith, M., & Pazder, L. (1980). *Michelle remembers.* New York: Pocket.

Smith, M. D. (1992). Community integration and supported employment. In D. F. Berkell (Ed.), *Autism: Identification, education, and treatment* (pp. 253–271). Hillsdale, NJ: Erlbaum.

Smith, M. L., Klim, P., & Hanley, W. B. (2000). Executive function in school-aged children with phenylketonuria. *Journal of Developmental and Physical Disabilities, 12,* 317–332.

Smith, P. G., & Cousens, S. N. (1996). Is the new variant of Creutzfeldt-Jakob disease from mad cows? *Science, 273,* 748.

Smith, P. M., Kraemer, H. C., Miller, N. H., DeBusk, R. F., & Taylor, C. B. (1999). In-hospital smoking cessation programs: Who responds, who doesn't? *Journal of Consulting and Clinical Psychology, 67*(1), 19–27.

Smith, S. F. (1993). Cognitive deficits associated with fragile X syndrome. *Mental Retardation, 31,* 279–283.

Smith, S. S., & Newman, J. P. (1990). Alcohol and drug abuse-dependence disorders in psychopathic and nonpsychopathic criminal offenders. *Journal of Abnormal Psychology, 99,* 430–439.

Smith, T. F., Bellack, A. S., & Liberman, R. P. (1996). Social skills training for schizophrenia: Review and future directions. *Clinical Psychology Review, 16,* 599–617.

Smith, T. W. (1992). Hostility and health: Current status of a psychosomatic hypothesis. *Health Psychology, 11*(3), 139–150.

Smoller, J. W., Block, S. R., & Young, M. M. (2009). Genetics of anxiety disorders: The complex road from DSM to DNA. *Depression and Anxiety, 26*(11), 965–975.

Smoller, J. W., Rosenbaum, J. F., Biederman, J., Kennedy, J., Dai, D., Racette, S. R., …

Slaugenhaupt, S. A. (2003). Association of a genetic marker at the corticotropin-releasing hormone locus with behavioral inhibition. *Biological Psychiatry, 54,* 1376–1381.

Smoller, J. W., Yamaki, L. H., & Fagerness, J. A. (2005). The corticotropin-releasing hormone gene and behavioral inhibition in children at risk for panic disorder. *Biological Psychiatry, 57,* 1485–1492.

Snyder, F. Y., Taylor, R. M., & Wolfe, J. H. (1995). Neural progenitor cell engraftment corrects lysosomal storage throughout the MPS VII mouse brain. *Nature, 374,* 367–370.

Snyder, S. H. (1976). The dopamine hypothesis of schizophrenia: Focus on the dopamine receptor. *American Journal of Psychiatry, 133,* 197–202.

Snyder, S. H. (1981). Opiate and benzodiazepine receptors. *Psychosomatics, 22*(11), 986–989.

Snyder, S. H., Burt, D. R., & Creese, I. (1976). Dopamine receptor of mammalian brain: Direct demonstration of binding to agonist and antagonist states. *Neuroscience Symposia, 1,* 28–49.

Sobell, M. B., & Sobell, L. C. (1978). *Behavioral treatment of alcohol problems.* New York: Plenum Press.

Sobell, M. B., & Sobell, L. C. (1993). *Problem drinkers: Guided self-change treatment.* New York: Guilford Press.

Social Development Canada. (2004). *Canada pension plan: Disability benefits* [Brochure]. Gatineau, QC: Author.

Society for Research in Child Development. (2007). *Ethical Standards for Research with Children.* Retrieved from www.srcd.org/ethicalstandards.html

Society for Research in Child Development, Committee for Ethical Conduct in Child Development Research. (1990, Winter). SRCD ethical standards for research with children. *SRCD Newsletter,* Chicago.

Sohn, C. H., & Lam, R. W. (2005). Update on the biology of seasonal affective disorder. *CNS Spectrums, 10,* 635–646.

Sohn, M., & Bosinski, H. A. G. (2007). Gender identity disorders: Diagnostic and surgical aspects. *Journal of Sexual Medicine, 4,* 1193–1208.

Sokolov, S., & Kutcher, S. (2001). Adolescent depression: Neuroendocrine aspects. In I. M. Goodyer (Ed.), *Depressed child and adolescent* (2nd ed., pp. 233–266). New York: Cambridge University Press.

Solai, L. K. K. (2009). Delirium. In B. J. Sadock, V. A. Sadock, & P. Ruiz (Eds.), *Kaplan & Sadock's comprehensive textbook of psychiatry* (Vol. I, 9th ed., pp. 1153–1167). Philadelphia: Lippincott Williams & Wilkins.

Soloff, P. H., George, A., Nathan, R. S., Schulz, P. M., Cornelius, J. R., Herring, J., & Perel, J. M. (1989). Amitriptyline versus haloperidol in borderlines: Final outcomes and predictors of response. *Journal of Clinical Psychopharmacology, 9,* 238–246.

Soloff, P. H., Lynch, K. G., Kelly, T. M., Malone, K. M., & Mann, J. J. (2000). Characteristics of suicide attempts of patients with major depressive episode and borderline personality disorder: A comparative study. *American Journal of Psychiatry, 157*(4), 601–608.

Solomon, A., Haaga, D. A. F., & Arnow, B. A. (2001). Is clinical depression distinct from subthreshold depressive symptoms? A review of the continuity issue in depression research. *Journal of Nervous & Mental Disease, 189,* 498–506.

Solomon, D. A., Keller, M. B., Leon, A. C., Mueller, T. I., Lavori, P. W., Shea, T., … Endicott, J. (2000). Multiple recurrences of major depressive

disorder. *American Journal of Psychiatry, 157*(2), 229–233.

Solomon, D. A., Keller, M. B., Leon, A. C., Mueller, T. I., Shea, M. T., Warshaw, M., … Endicott, J. (1997). Recovery from major depression: A 10-year prospective follow-up across multiple episodes. *Archives of General Psychiatry, 54,* 1001–1006.

Solomon, D. A., Leon, A. C., Coryell, W. H., Endicott, J., Li, C., Fiedorowicz, J. G., … Keller, M. B. (2010). Longitudinal course of bipolar I disorder: Duration of mood episodes. *Archives of General Psychiatry, 67*(4), 339–347.

Solomon, R. L. (1980). The opponent-process theory of acquired motivation: The costs of pleasure and the benefits of pain. *American Psychologist, 35,* 691–712.

Solomon, R. L., & Corbit, J. D. (1974). An opponent process theory of motivation: I. Temporal dynamics of affect. *Psychological Review, 81,* 119–145.

Somber news from the AIDS front. (1993). *Science, 260,* 1712–1713.

Somers, J. M., Goldner, F. M., Waraich, P., & Hsu, L. (2004). Prevalence studies of substance-related disorders: A systematic review of the literature. *Canadian Journal of Psychiatry, 49*(6), 373–384.

Somers, J. M., Goldner, F. M., Waraich, P., & Hsu, L. (2006). Prevalence and incidence studies of anxiety disorders: A systematic review of the literature. *Canadian Journal of Psychiatry, 51,* 100–113.

Song, X., & Rusak, B. (2000). Acute effects of light on body temperature and activity in Syrian hamsters: Influence of circadian phase. *American Journal of Physiology: Regulatory, Integrative, and Comparative Physiology, 278,* 1369–1380.

Sonuga-Barke, F. J., Daley, D., Thompson, M., Laver-Bradbury, C., & Weeks, A. (2001). Parent-based therapies for preschool attention-deficit/ hyperactivity disorder: A randomized, controlled trial with a community sample. *Journal of the American Academy of Child & Adolescent Psychiatry, 40*(4), 402–408.

Sorkin, A., Weinshall, D., Modai, I., & Peled, A. (2006). Improving the accuracy of the diagnosis of schizophrenia by means of virtual reality. *American Journal of Psychiatry, 163,* 512–520.

South, S. C., Oltmanns, T. F., & Krueger, R. F. (in press). The spectrum of personality disorders. In D. H. Barlow (Ed.), *Oxford handbook of clinical psychology.* New York: Oxford University Press.

Southwick, S. M., Krystal, J. H., Johnson, D. R., & Charney, D. S. (1992). Neurobiology of posttraumatic stress disorder. In A. Tasman & M. B. Riba (Eds.), *Review of psychiatry* (Vol. 11, pp. 347–367). Washington, DC: American Psychiatric Press.

Spangler, D. L., Simons, A. D., Monroe, S. M., & Thase, M. F. (1996). Gender differences in cognitive diathesis-stress domain match: Implications for differential pathways to depression. *Journal of Abnormal Psychology, 105,* 653–657.

Spangler, D. L., Simons, A. D., Monroe, S. M., & Thase, M. F. (1997). Comparison of cognitive models of depression: Relationships between cognitive constructs and cognitive diathesis-stress match. *Journal of Abnormal Psychology, 106,* 395–403.

Spanos, N. P. (1994). Multiple identity enactments and multiple personality disorder: A sociogenic perspective. *Psychological Bulletin, 116,* 143–165.

Spanos, N. P. (1996). *Multiple identities and false memories: A sociocognitive prospective.* Washington, DC: American Psychological Association.

Spanos, N. P., Cross, P. A., Dickson, K., & DuBreuil, S. C. (1993). Close encounters: An examination of UFO experiences. *Journal of Abnormal Psychology, 102,* 624–632.

Spanos, N. P., Weeks, J. R., & Bertrand, L. D. (1985). Multiple personality: A social psychological perspective. *Journal of Abnormal Psychology, 92,* 362–376.

Spector, I., Pecknold, J. C., & Libman, F. (2003). Selective attentional bias related to the noticeability aspect of anxiety symptoms in generalized social phobia. *Journal of Anxiety Disorders, 17,* 517–531.

Spector, I. P., & Carey, M. P. (1990). Incidence and prevalence of the sexual dysfunctions: A critical review of the empirical literature. *Archives of Sexual Behavior, 19*(4), 389–408.

Speer, D. C. (1992). Clinically significant change: Jacobson and Truax (1991) revisited. *Journal of Consulting and Clinical Psychology, 60,* 402–408.

Spence, J. D., Barnett, P. A., Linden, W., Ramsden, V., & Taenzer, P. (1999). Recommendations on stress management. *Canadian Medical Association Journal, 160,* S46–S50.

Spiegel, D. (1995). Hypnosis and suggestion. In D. L. Schacter (Ed.), *Memory distortion: How minds, brains, and societies reconstruct the past.* Cambridge, MA: Harvard University Press.

Spiegel, D. (in press). Dissociation in DSM5. *Journal of Trauma and Dissociation.*

Spiegel, D., Bloom, J. R., Kramer, H. C., & Gotheil, E. (1989). Effect of psychosocial treatment on survival of patients with metastatic breast cancer. *Lancet, 14,* 888–891.

Spiegel, D., & Cardena, E. (1991). Disintegrated experience: The dissociative disorders revisited. *Journal of Abnormal Psychology, 100*(3), 366–378.

Spiegel, D., Morrow, G. R., Classen, C., Riggs, G., Stott, P. B., Mudaliar, N., ... Heard, L. (1996). Effects of group therapy on women with primary breast cancer. *The Breast Journal, 2*(1), 104–106.

Spiegel, D. A., Wiegel, M., Baker, S. L., & Greene, K. A. I. (2000). Pharmacological management of anxiety disorders. In D. I. Mostofsky & D. H. Barlow (Eds.), *The management of stress and anxiety in medical disorders* (pp. 36–65). Needham Heights, MA: Allyn & Bacon.

Spielberger, C. D., & Frank, R. G. (1992). Injury control: A promising field for psychologists. *American Psychologist, 47*(8), 1029–1030.

Spielman, A. J., & Glovinsky, P. (1991). The varied nature of insomnia. In P. J. Hauri (Ed.), *Case studies in insomnia* (pp. 1–15). New York: Plenum Press.

Spiker, D., & Ricks, M. (1984). Visual self-recognition in autistic children: Developmental relationships. *Child Development, 55,* 214–225

Spinelli, S., Chefer, S., Suomi, S. J., Higley, J. D., Barr, C. S., & Stein, E. (2009). Early-life stress induces long-term morphologic changes in primate brain. *Archives of General Psychiatry, 66*(6), 658–665.

Spitzer, R. L. (1991). An outsider-insider's views about revising the DSMs. *Journal of Abnormal Psychology, 100*(3), 294–296.

Spitzer, R. L. (1999). Harmful dysfunction and the DSM definition of mental disorder. *Journal of Abnormal Psychology, 108,* 430–432.

Spitzer, R. L., Devlin, M. J., Walsh, B. T., Hasin, D., Wing, R., Marcus, M. D., ... Nonas, C. (1991). Binge eating disorder: To be or not to be in DSM-IV. *International Journal of Eating Disorders, 10,* 627–629.

Spitzer, R. L., Forman, J. B. W., & Nee, J. (1979). DSM-III field trials: 1. Initial interrater diagnostic reliability. *American Journal of Psychiatry, 136,* 815–817.

Spitzer, R. L., Williams, J. B. W., & Gibbon, M. (1994). *Structured Clinical Interview for DSM-IV.* New York: New York State Psychiatric Institute, Biometrics Research Department.

Spitzer, R. L., Yanovski, S. Z., Wadden, T., Wing, R., Marcus, M., Stunkard, A., ... Horne, R. L. (1993). Binge eating disorder: Its further validation in a multi-site study. *International Journal of Eating Disorders, 13,* 137–153.

Spoont, M. R. (1992). Modulatory role of serotonin in neural information processing: Implications for human psychopathology. *Psychological Bulletin, 112*(2), 330–350.

Spreen, O. (1988). Prognosis of learning disability. *Journal of Consulting and Clinical Psychology, 56,* 836–842.

Sprich, S., Biederman, J., & Crawford, M. H. (2000). Adoptive and biological families of children and adolescents with ADHD. *Journal of the American Academy of Child and Adolescent Psychiatry, 39,* 1432–1437.

Sprock, J. (2000). Gender-typed behavioral examples of histrionic personality disorder. *Journal of Psychopathology and Behavioral Assessment, 22,* 107–122.

Spurrell, F. B., Wilfley, D. F., Tanofsky, M. B., & Brownell, K. D. (1997). Age of onset for binge eating: Are there different pathways to binge eating? *International Journal of Eating Disorders, 21,* 55–65.

Srivastava, A., & Kahan, M. (2006). Buprenorphine: A potential new treatment option for opioid dependence. *Canadian Medical Association Journal, 174*(13), 1835–1836.

St. John, J., Krichev, A., & Bauman, F. (1976). Northwestern Ontario Indian children and the WISC. *Psychology in the Schools, 13,* 407–411.

Staal, W. G., Pol, H. F. H., Schnack, H. G., Hoogendoorn, M. L. C., Jellema, K., & Kahn, R. S. (2000). Structural brain abnormalities in patients with schizophrenia and their healthy siblings. *American Journal of Psychiatry, 157,* 416–421.

Stacy, A. W. (1995). Memory association and ambiguous cues in models of alcohol and marijuana use. *Experimental and Clinical Psychopharmacology, 3,* 183–194.

Stacy, A. W. (1997). Memory activation and expectancy as prospective predictors of alcohol and marihuana use. *Journal of Abnormal Psychology, 106,* 61–73.

Stahl, S. M. (2008). *Stahl's essential psychopharmacology* (3rd ed.). New York: Cambridge University Press.

Stam, H., & Steggles, S. (1987). Predicting the onset or progression of cancer from psychological characteristics: Psychometric and theoretical issues. *Journal of Psychosocial Oncology, 5*(2), 35–46.

Stanley, M. A., Beck, J. G., & Glassco, J. D. (1997). Generalized anxiety in older adults: Treatment with cognitive-behavioral and supportive approaches. *Behavior Therapy, 27,* 565–581.

Starkman, M. N., Giordani, B., Gebarski, S. S., Berent, S., Schork, M. A., & Schteingart, D. E. (1999). Decrease in cortisol reverses human hippocampal atrophy following treatment of Cushing's disease. *Biological Psychiatry, 46,* 1595–1602.

Starr, F., Szatmari, P., Bryson, S., & Zwaigenbaum, L. (2003). Stability and change among high-functioning children with pervasive developmental disorders: A 2-year outcome study. *Journal of Autism and Developmental Disorders, 33,* 15–22.

Statistics Canada. (1975). *Mental health statistics, volume III: Institutional facilities, services and finances, 1975.* Ottawa, ON: Minister of Industry, Trade and Commerce.

Statistics Canada. (1995). *Mental health statistics, 1992–93.* Ottawa, ON: Minister Responsible for Statistics Canada.

Statistics Canada. (1996). *National longitudinal survey of children and youth: User's handbook and microdata guide* (Microdata documentation: 89M0015GPF). Ottawa, ON: Statistics Canada.

Statistics Canada. (1997). *Initial results from the school component* (NLSC. Education Quarterly Review, Catalogue no. 81–003-XPB, 4(2)). Retrieved August 17, 2004, from http://www.ldac-taac.ca/english/indepth/bkground/stats01.htm

Statistics Canada. (2000). *The changing face of heart disease and stroke in Canada.* Ottawa, ON: Statistics Canada.

Statistics Canada. (2001a). *Census of population.* Ottawa, ON: Statistics Canada.

Statistics Canada. (2001b). *A profile of disability in Canada.* Ottawa, ON: Statistics Canada.

Statistics Canada. (2002a). *Canadian community health survey: Mental health and well-being.* Ottawa, ON: Statistics Canada.

Statistics Canada. (2002b). *Historical statistics of Canada, Section B. Vital statistics and health* (B35–50). Ottawa, ON: Statistics Canada.

Statistics Canada. (2003). *Alcohol consumption, by sex, age group and level of education.* Ottawa, ON: Statistics Canada.

Statistics Canada. (2004). *Family violence in Canada: A statistical profile.* Ottawa, ON: Statistics Canada.

Statistics Canada. (2006). *Canada's population, third quarter 2006.* Ottawa, ON: Statistics Canada.

Statistics Canada. (2007, March 6). Seniors as victims of crime. *The Daily.* Retrieved October 3, 2007, from http://www.statcan.ca/Daily/English/070306/d070306b.htm

Steadman, H. J., & Ribner, S. A. (1980). Changing perceptions of the mental health needs of inmates in local jails. *American Journal of Psychiatry, 137,* 1115–1116.

Steele, C. M., & Josephs, R. A. (1990). Alcohol myopia: Its prized and dangerous effects. *American Psychologist, 45*(8), 921–933.

Steffy, R. A., Hart, J., Craw M., Torney, D., & Marlett, N. (1969). Operant behaviour modification techniques applied to a ward of severely regressed and aggressive patients. *Canadian Psychiatric Association Journal, 14,* 59–67.

Steiger, H., Bruce, K. R., & Israel, M. (2003). Eating disorders. In G. Stricker & T. A. Widiger (Eds.), *Handbook of psychology: Clinical psychology* (Vol. 8, pp. 173–194). New York: John Wiley & Sons.

Steiger, H., Stotland, S., Trottier, J., & Ghadirian, A. M. (1996). Familial eating concerns and psychopathological traits: Casual implications of transgenerational effects. *International Journal of Eating Disorders, 19,* 147–157.

Stein, M. B., Forde, D. R., Anderson, G., & Walker, J. R. (1997). Obsessive-compulsive disorder in the community: An epidemiologic survey with clinical reappraisal. *American Journal of Psychiatry, 154,* 1120–1126.

Stein, M. B., Goldin, P. R., Sareen, J., Zorrilla, L. T. F., & Brown, G. G. (2002). Increased amygdala activation to angry and contemptuous faces in generalized social phobia. *Archives of General Psychiatry, 59,* 1027–1034.

Stein, M. B., Jang, K. L., & Livesley, W. J. (1999). Heritability of anxiety sensitivity: A twin study. *American Journal of Psychiatry, 156,* 246–251.

Stein, M. B., Jang, K. L., & Livesley, W. J. (2002). Heritability of social anxiety-related concerns and personality characteristics: A twin study. *Journal of Nervous and Mental Disease, 190,* 219–224.

Stein, M. B., Jang, K. L., Taylor, S., Vernon, P. A., & Livesley, W. J. (2002). Genetic and environmental influences on trauma exposure and posttraumatic stress disorder symptoms: A twin study. *American Journal of Psychiatry, 159,* 1675–1681.

Stein, M. B., & Kean, Y. M. (2000). Disability and quality of life in social phobia: Epidemiologic findings. *American Journal of Psychiatry, 157,* 1606–1613.

Stein, M. B., Liebowitz, M. R., Lydiard, R. B., Pitts, C. D., Bushnell, W., & Gergel, I. (1998). Paroxetine treatment of generalized social phobia (social anxiety disorder). A randomized clinical trial. *JAMA, 280,* 708–713.

Stein, M. B., Schork, N. J., & Gelernter, J. (2007). Gene-by-environment (serotonin transporter and childhood maltreatment) interaction for anxiety sensitivity, an intermediate phenotype for anxiety disorders. *Neuropsychopharmacology, 33*(2), 312–319.

Stein, M. B., Torgrud, L. J., & Walker, J. R. (2000). Social phobia symptoms, subtypes, and severity: Findings from a community survey. *Archives of General Psychiatry, 57,* 1046–1052.

Stein, M. B., Walker, J. R., & Forde, D. R. (1996). Public speaking fears in a community sample: Prevalence, impact on functioning and diagnostic classification. *Archives of General Psychiatry, 53,* 169–174.

Stein, M. I. (1978). Thematic apperception test and related methods. In B. B. Wolman (Ed.), *Clinical diagnosis of mental disorders: A handbook* (pp. 179–235). New York: Plenum Press.

Stein, M. T., Zucker, K. J., & Dixon, S. D. (2001). Sammy: Gender identity concerns in a 6-year-old boy. *Journal of Development and Behavioral Pediatrics, 22*(Suppl. 2), 43–47.

Stein, R. M., & Ellinwood, F. H. (1993). Stimulant use: Cocaine and amphetamine. In D. L. Dunner (Ed.), *Current psychiatric therapy* (pp. 98–105). Philadelphia: W. B. Saunders.

Steinberg, A. B., & Phares, V. (2001). Family functioning, body image, and eating disturbances. In J. K. Thompson & L. Smolak (Eds.), *Body image, eating disorders, and obesity in youth: Assessment, prevention and treatment* (pp. 127–147). Washington, DC: American Psychological Association.

Steinberg, M. (1991). The spectrum of depersonalization: Assessment and treatment. *Annual Review of Psychiatry, 10,* 223–247.

Steiner, M. (2002). Postnatal depression: A few simple questions. *Family Practice, 19,* 469–470.

Steinglass, J. E., Sysko, R., Glasofer, D., Albano, A. M., Simpson, H. B., & Walsh, B. T. (2010). Rationale for the application of Exposure and Response Prevention to the treatment of anorexia nervosa. *International Journal of Eating Disorders.* Advance online publication. doi:10.1002./eat.20784.

Steinglass, P., Weisstub, F., & Kaplan De-Nour, A. K. (1988). Perceived personal networks as mediators of stress reactions. *American Journal of Psychiatry, 145,* 1259–1264.

Steketee, G., & Barlow, D. H. (2002). Obsessive-compulsive disorder. In D. H. Barlow (Ed.), *Anxiety and its disorders: The nature and treatment of anxiety and panic* (2nd ed.). New York: Guilford Press.

Steketee, G., & Frost, R. O. (2007a). *Compulsive hoarding and acquiring: Client workbook.* New York: Oxford University Press.

Steketee, G., & Frost, R. O. (2007b). *Compulsive hoarding and acquiring: Therapist guide.* New York: Oxford University Press.

Steketee, G., Quay, S., & White, K. (1991). Religion and guilt in OCD patients. *Journal of Anxiety Disorders, 5,* 359–367.

Stellos, K., Panagiota, V., Sachsenmaier, S., Trunk, T., Straten, G., Leyhe, T., … Laske, C. (2010). Increased circulating progenitor cells in Alzheimer's disease patients with moderate to severe dementia: Evidence for vascular repair and tissue regeneration? *Journal of Alzheimer's Disease, 19*(2), 591–600.

Stephens, R. S., Roffman, R. A., & Simpson, F. F. (1994). Treating adult marijuana dependence: A test of the relapse prevention model. *Journal of Consulting and Clinical Psychology, 62,* 92–99.

Stephenson, J. (2003). Global AIDS epidemic worsens. *JAMA, 291,* 31–32.

Stermac, L., Reist, D., Addison, M., & Millar, G. M. (2002). Childhood risk factors for women's sexual victimization. *Journal of Interpersonal Violence, Journal of Interpersonal Violence, 17,* 647–670.

Stern, C. F., Owen, A. M., Look, R. B., Tracey, I., Rosen, B. R., & Petrides, M. (2000). Activity in ventrolateral and middorsolateral prefrontal cortex during non-spatial visual working memory processing: Evidence from functional magnetic resonance imaging. *Neuroimage, 11*(5), 392–399.

Stern, Y. (2009). Cognitive reserve. Neuropsychologia, 47(10), 2015–2028.

Stern, Y., Gurland, B., Tatemichi, T. K., Tang, M. X., Wilder, D., & Mayeux, R. (1994). Influence of education and occupation on the incidence of Alzheimer's disease. *JAMA, 271,* 1004–1010.

Sternberg, R. J. (1988). Intellectual development: Psychometric and information-processing approaches. In M. H. Bornstein & M. F. Lamb (Eds.), *Developmental psychology: An advanced textbook* (2nd ed.). Hillsdale, NJ: Erlbaum.

Stevens, J. (1987). *Storming heaven: LSD and the American dream.* New York: Atlantic Monthly Press.

Stewart, S. E., Jenike, E., & Jenike, M. A. (2009). Biological treatment for obsessive-compulsive disorder. In M. M. Antony & M. B. Stein (Eds.), *Oxford handbook of anxiety and related disorders* (pp. 375–390). New York: Oxford University Press.

Stewart, S. H., (1996). Alcohol abuse in individuals exposed to trauma: A critical review. *Psychological Bulletin, 120,* 85–112.

Stewart, S. H. (2002). The history, current prevalence and consequences of drinking problems. Transactions of the Royal Society of Canada, Seventh Series, Volume II, ISSN: 1710–2839.

Stewart, S. H., & Asmundson, G. J. G. (2006). Anxiety sensitivity and its impact on pain experiences and conditions: A state of the art. *Cognitive Behaviour Therapy, 35,* 185–188.

Stewart, S. H., & Brown, C. G. (2007). The relationship between disordered eating and substance use problems among women: A critical review. In L. Greaves, N. Poole, & J. Greenbaum (Eds.), *Highs and lows: Canadian perspectives on women and substance use* (pp. 157–163).

Toronto, ON: Centre for Addiction and Mental Health.

Stewart, S. H., Brown, C. G., Theakston, J. A., Devoulyte, K., & Larsen, S. (2003). *Why do women with alcohol use disorder binge eat? Exploring connections between binge eating and heavy drinking in Nova Scotia women.* Poster presented at the Dalhousie University Annual Psychiatry Research Day, Halifax.

Stewart, S. H., Buffett-Jerrott, S. F., & Finley, G. A. (2006). Effects of midazolam on explicit vs. implicit memory in a pediatric surgery setting. *Psychopharmacology, 188,* 489–497.

Stewart, S. H., Buffett-Jerrott, S. F., Finley, G. A., Wright, K. D., & Gomez, T. V. (2006). Effects of midazolam on explicit vs. implicit memory in a pediatric surgery setting. *Psychopharmacology, 188*(4), 489–497.

Stewart, S. H., Collins, P., Blackburn, J. R., Ellery, M., & Klein, R. M. (2005). Heart rate increase to alcohol administration and video lottery terminal (VLT) play. *Psychology of Addictive Behaviors, 19*(1), 94–98.

Stewart, S. H., & Conrod, P. J. (2008). Anxiety disorder and substance use disorder comorbidity: Common themes and future directions. In S. H. Stewart & P. J. Conrod (Eds.), *Anxiety and substance use disorders: The vicious cycle of comorbidity* (pp. 239–257). New York: Springer.

Stewart, S. H., Conrod, P. J., Gignac, M. L., & Pihl, R. O. (1998). Selective processing biases in anxiety-sensitive men and women. *Cognition & Emotion, 12,* 105–133.

Stewart, S. H., & Devine, H. (2000). Relations between personality and drinking motives in young people. *Personality & Individual Differences, 29,* 495–511.

Stewart, S. H., Finn, P. R., & Pihl, R. O. (1992). The effects of alcohol on the cardiovascular stress response in men at high risk for alcoholism: A dose response study. *Journal of Studies on Alcohol, 53,* 499–506.

Stewart, S. H., & Jefferson, S. (2007). Experimental methodologies in gambling studies. In G. Smith, D. C. Hodgins, & R. J. Williams (Eds.), *Research and measurement issues in gambling studies* (pp. 87–110). New York: Elsevier.

Stewart, S. H., Knize, K., & Pihl, R. O. (1992). Anxiety sensitivity and dependency in clinical and non-clinical panickers and controls. *Journal of Anxiety Disorders, 6,* 119–131.

Stewart, S. H., & Kushner, M. G. (2003). Recent research on the comorbidity of alcoholism and pathological gambling. *Alcoholism: Clinical & Experimental Research, 27,* 285–291.

Stewart, S. H., Loba, P., Blackburn, J. R., Ellery, M., & Klein, R. M. (2005). Heart rate increase to alcohol administration and video lottery terminal (VLT) play. *Psychology of Addictive Behaviours, 19* (1), 94–98.

Stewart, S. H., Morris, F., Mellings, T., & Komar, J. (2006). Relations of social anxiety variables to drinking motives, drinking quantity and frequency, and alcohol-related problems in undergraduates. *Journal of Mental Health, 15*(6), 671–682.

Stewart, S. H., Pihl, R. O., Conrod, P. J., & Dongier, M. (1998). Functional associations among trauma, PTSD and substance-related disorders. *Addictive Behaviors, 23,* 797–812.

Stewart, S. H., & Samoluk, S. B. (1997). Effects of short-term food deprivation and chronic dietary restraint on the selective processing of appetitive-related cues. *International Journal of Eating Disorders, 21,* 129–135.

Stewart, S. H., Samoluk, S. B., & MacDonald, A. B. (1999). Anxiety sensitivity and substance use and abuse. In S. Taylor (Ed.), *Anxiety sensitivity: Theory, research and treatment of the fear of anxiety* (pp. 287–319). Mahwah, NJ: Lawrence Erlbaum.

Stewart, S. H., Taylor, S., & Baker, J. M. (1997). Gender differences in dimensions of anxiety sensitivity. *Journal of Anxiety Disorders, 11,* 179–200.

Stewart, S. H., Taylor, S., Jang, K. L., Cox, B. J., Watt, M. C., Fedoroff, I. C., & Borger, S. C. (2001). Causal modeling of relations among learning history, anxiety sensitivity, and panic attacks. *Behaviour Research and Therapy, 39,* 443–456.

Stewart, S. H., & Watt, M. C. (2000). Illness Attitude Scale dimensions and their association with anxiety-related constructs in a non-clinical sample. *Behaviour Research and Therapy, 38,* 83–99.

Stewart, S. H., & Watt, M. C. (2001). Assessment of health anxiety. In G. J. G. Asmundson, S. Taylor, & B. J. Cox (Eds.), *Health anxiety: Clinical and research perspectives on hypochondriasis and related conditions* (pp. 95–131). New York: Wiley.

Stewart, S. H., & Westra, H. A. (2002). Introduction to the special issue on: Benzodiazepine side-effects: From the bench to the clinic. *Current Pharmaceutical Design, 8,* 1–3.

Stewart, W. F., Kawas, C., Corrada, M., & Metter, F. J. (1997). Risk of Alzheimer's disease and duration of NSAID use. *Neurology, 48,* 626–632.

Stice, E., Agras, W. S., Telch, C. F., Halmi, K. A., Mitchell, J. E., & Wilson, G. T. (2001). Subtyping binge eating disordered women along dieting and negative affect dimension. *International Journal of Eating Disorders, 30,* 11–27.

Stice, E., Shaw, H., & Marti, C. N. (2007). A meta-analytic review of eating disorder prevention programs: Encouraging findings. *Annual Review of Clinical Psychology, 3,* 207–231.

Stice, E., Akutagawa, D., Gaggar, A., & Agras, W. S. (2000). Negative affect moderates the relation between dieting and binge eating. *International Journal of Eating Disorders, 27,* 218–229.

Stice, E., Cameron, R. P., Killen, J. D., Hayward, C., & Taylor, C. B. (1999). Naturalistic weight-reduction efforts prospectively predict growth in relative weight and onset of obesity among female adolescents. *Journal of Consulting and Clinical Psychology, 67,* 967–974.

Stice, E., Schupak-Neuberg, E., Shaw, H. E., & Stein, R. I. (1994). Relation of media exposure to eating disorder symptomatology: An examination of mediating mechanisms. *Journal of Abnormal Psychology, 103,* 836–840.

Stip, E., Caron, J., & Lane, C. J. (2001). Schizophrenia: People's perceptions in Quebec. *Canadian Medical Association Journal, 164,* 1299–1300.

Stip, E., Fahim, C., Mancini-Marïe, A., Bentaleb, L. A., Mensour, B., Mendrek, A., & Beauregard, M. (2005). Restoration of frontal activation during a treatment with quetiapine: An fMRI study of blunted affect in schizophrenia. *Progress in Neuro-Psychopharmacology & Biological Psychiatry, 29*(1), 21–26.

Stock, W. (1993). Inhibited female orgasm. In W. O'Donohue & J. H. Geer (Eds.), *Handbook of sexual dysfunctions: Assessment and treatment* (pp. 253–277). Boston: Allyn & Bacon.

Stoller, R. J. (1976). Two feminized male American Indians. *Archives of Sexual Behavior, 5,* 529–538.

Stoller, R. J. (1982). Transvestism in women. *Archives of Sexual Behavior, 11,* 99–115.

Stone, A. B., Pearlstein, T. B., & Brown, W. A. (1991). Fluoxetine in the treatment of late luteal phase dysphoric disorder. *Journal of Clinical Psychiatry, 52*(7), 290–293

Stone, G. C. (1987). The scope of health psychology. In G. C. Stone, S. M. Weiss, J. D. Matarazzo, N. F. Miller, et al. (Eds.), *Health psychology: A discipline and a profession.* Chicago: University of Chicago Press.

Stone, J., Carson, A., Aditya, H., Prescott, R., Zaubi, M., Warlow, C., & Sharpe, M. (2009a). The role of physical injury in motor and sensory conversion symptoms: A systematic and narrative review. *Journal of Psychosomatic Research, 66*(5), 383–390.

Stone, J., Carson, A., Duncan, R., Coleman, R., Roberts, R., Warlow, C., … Sharpe, M. (2009b). Symptoms 'unexplained by organic disease' in 1144 new neurology out-patients: How often does the diagnosis change at follow-up? *Brain, 132*(Pt 10), 2878–2888.

Stone, J., Jeidler, M., & Sharpe, M. (2003). Misdiagnosis of conversion disorder. *American Journal of Psychiatry, 160,* 391.

Stone, J., LaFrance, W. C., Levenson, J. L., & Sharpe, M. (2010). Issues for DSM-5: Conversion disorder. *American Journal of Psychiatry, 167,* 626–627.

Stone, M. (1983). Psychotherapy with schizotypal borderline patients. *Journal of the American Academy of Psychoanalysis, 11,* 87–111.

Stone, M. H. (1986). Borderline personality disorder. In A. M. Cooper, A. J. Frances, & M. H. Sacks (Eds.), *The personality disorders and neuroses* (pp. 203–217). New York: Basic Books.

Stone, M. H. (1989). The course of borderline personality disorder. In A. Tasman, R. E. Hales, & A. J. Frances (Eds.), *Annual review of psychiatry* (Vol. 8, pp. 103–122). Washington, DC: American Psychiatric Press.

Stone, M. H. (1993). Cluster C personality disorders. In D. L. Dunner (Ed.), *Current psychiatric therapy* (pp. 411–417). Philadelphia: W. B. Saunders.

Stone, M. H. (2001). Schizoid and schizotypical personality disorders. In G. O. Gabbard (Ed.), *Treatment of psychiatric disorders* (Vol. 2, 3rd ed., pp. 2237–2250). Washington, DC: American Psychiatric Press.

Stone, R. (2000). Stress: The invisible hand in eastern Europe's death rates. *Science, 288,* 1732–1733.

Stoppard, J. M. (1989). An evaluation of the adequacy of cognitive/behavioural theories for understanding depression in women. *Canadian Psychology, 30,* 39–47.

Stoppard, J. M. (1999). Why new perspectives are needed for understanding depression in women. *Canadian Psychology, 40,* 79–90.

Stoppard, J. M. (2000). *Understanding depression: Feminist social constructionist approaches.* Florence, KY: Taylor & Frances/Routledge.

Stoppard, J. M., & McMullen, L. M. (Eds.). (2003). *Situating sadness: Women and depression in social context.* New York: University Press.

Strahl, C., Kleinknecht, R. A., & Dinnel, D. L. (2000). The role of pain anxiety, coping, and pain self-efficacy in rheumatoid arthritis patient functioning. *Behaviour Research and Therapy, 38,* 863–873.

Strain, E. C. (2009). Substance-related disorders. In B. J. Sadock, V. A. Sadock, & P. Ruiz (Eds.), *Kaplan & Sadock's comprehensive textbook of psychiatry* (Vol. I, 9th ed., pp. 1237–1268). Philadelphia: Lippincott Williams & Wilkins.

Strain, F. C., Mumford, G. K., Silverman, K., & Griffiths, R. R. (1994). Caffeine dependence syndrome: Evidence from case histories and experimental evaluations. *JAMA, 272,* 1043–1048.

Strassberg, D. S., Kelly, M. P., Carroll, C., & Kircher, J. C. (1987). The psychophysiological nature of premature ejaculation. *Archives of Sexual Behavior, 16,* 327–336.

Strathdee, S. A., Patrick, D. M., Currie, S. L., Cornelisse, P. G. A., Rekart, M. L., Montaner, J. S. G., … O'Shaughnessy, M. V. (1997). Needle exchange is not enough: Lessons from the Vancouver injecting drug use study. *AIDS, 11*(8), 59–65.

Straus, S. F. (1988). The chronic mononucleosis syndrome. *Journal of Infectious Disease, 157,* 405–412.

Straus, S. F., Tosato, G., Armstrong, G., Lawley, T., Preble, O. T., Henle, W., … Blaese, R. M. (1985). Persisting illness and fatigue in adults with evidence of Epstein Barr virus infection. *Annals of Internal Medicine, 102,* 7–16.

Strauss, J. S., Carpenter, W. T., & Bartko, J. J. (1974). An approach to the diagnosis and understanding of schizophrenia: Speculations on the processes that underlie schizophrenic symptoms and signs. *Schizophrenia Bulletin, 1,* 61–69.

Stravynski, A., Elie, R., & Franche, R. L. (1989). Perception of early parenting by patients diagnosed avoidant personality disorder: A test of the overprotection hypothesis. *Acta Psychiatrica Scandinavica, 80,* 415–420.

Stravynski, A., Lesage, A., Marcouiller, M., & Elie, R. (1989). A test of the therapeutic mechanism in social skills training with avoidant personality disorder. *Journal of Nervous and Mental Disease, 177,* 739–744.

Striegal-Moore, R. H., Cachelin, F. M., Dohm, F. A., Pike, M., Wifley, D. E., & Fairburn, C. G. (2001). Comparison of binge eating disorder and bulimia nervosa in a community sample. *International Journal of Eating Disorders, 29,* 157–165.

Striegel-Moore, R. H., & Franko, D. L. (2008). Should binge eating disorder be included in the DSM-V? A critical review of the state of the evidence. *Annual Review of Clinical Psychology, 4,* 305–324.

Striegal-Moore, R. H., Silberstein, L. R., & Rodin, J. (1986). Toward an understanding of risk factors for bulimia. *American Psychologist, 3,* 246–263.

Striegal-Moore, R. H., Silberstein, L. R., & Rodin, J. (1993). The social self in bulimia nervosa: Public self-consciousness, social anxiety, and perceived fraudulence. *Journal of Abnormal Psychology, 102*(2), 297–303.

Striegel-Moore, R. H., Wilson, G. T., DeBar, L., Perrin, N., Lynch, F., Rosselli, F., & Kraemer, H. C. (2010). Cognitive behavioral guided self-help for the treatment of recurrent binge eating. *Journal of Consulting and Clinical Psychology, 78*(3), 312–321.

Stringer, R., & Stanovich, K. F. (2000). The connection between reaction time and variation in reading ability: Unravelling covariance relationships with cognitive ability and phonological sensitivity. *Scientific Studies of Reading, 4,* 41–53.

Strobel, M. (2002, February 6). Sheena'd be proud. *Toronto Sun.* Retrieved June 24, 2004, from http://www.canoe.ca/Health0202/06_sheena-sun.html

Strober, M. (2002). Family–genetic perspectives on anorexia nervosa and bulimia nervosa. In K. D. Brownell & C. G. Fairburn (Eds.), *Eating disorders and obesity: A comprehensive handbook* (2nd ed., pp. 212–218). New York: Guilford Press.

Strober, M., Freeman, R., Lampert, C., Diamond, J., & Kaye, W. (2000). Controlled family study of anorexia nervosa and bulimia nervosa: Evidence of shared liability and transmission of partial syndromes. *American Journal of Psychiatry, 157,* 393–401.

Stroebe, M., Stroebe, W., & Abakoumkin, G. (2005). The broken heart: Suicidal ideation in bereavement. *American Journal of Psychiatry, 162,* 2178–2180.

Strohschein, L. (2005). Parental divorce and child mental health trajectories. *Journal of Marriage and Family, 67*(5), 1286–1300.

Stuart, H. L., & Arboleda-Florez, J. (2000). Homeless shelter users in the postdeinstitutionalization era. *Canadian Journal of Psychiatry, 45,* 55–62.

Stunkard, A. J., Sorensen, T., & Schulsinger, F. (1983). Use of the Danish adoption register for the study of obesity and thinness. In S. S. Kety, L. P. Rowland, R. L. Sidman, & S. W. Mathysse (Eds.), *The genetics of neurological and psychiatric disorders.* New York: Raven Press.

Stuss, D. T., & Cummings, J. L. (1990). Subcortical vascular dementias. In J. L. Cummings (Ed.), *Subcortical dementia* (pp. 145–163). New York: Oxford University Press.

Stuss, D. T., & Levine, B. (2002). Adult clinical neuropsychology: Lessons from studies of the frontal lobes. *Annual Review of Psychology, 53*(1), 401–433.

Suarez, F. C., Lewis, J. G., & Kuhn, C. (2002). The relation of aggression, hostility, and anger to lipopolysaccharide-stimulated tumor necrosis factor (TNF)-alpha by blood monocytes from normal men. *Brain, Behavior & Immunity, 16,* 675–684.

Suárez, L., Bennett, S., Goldstein, C., & Barlow, D. H. (2009). Understanding anxiety disorders from a "triple vulnerabilities" framework. In M. M. Antony & M. B. Stein (Eds.), *Oxford handbook of anxiety and related disorders* (pp. 153–172). New York: Oxford University Press.

Subramanian, S., Bandopadhyay, D., Mishra, P. K., Mathew, M., & John, M. (2010). Design and development of non-fibrillar amyloid β as a potential Alzheimer vaccine. Biochemical and Biophysical Research Communications, 394(2), 393–397.

Substance Abuse and Mental Health Services Administration, Office of Applied Studies (2003). *Emergency department trends from the Drug Abuse Warning Network, Final estimates 1995–2002.* DAWN Series D-24, DHHS Publication No. (SMA) 03-3780, Rockville, MD.

Sugiyama, T., & Abe, T. (1989). The prevalence of autism in Nagoya, Japan: A total population study. *Journal of Autism and Developmental Disorders, 19,* 87–96.

Sullivan, G. M., Kent, J. M., & Coplan, J. D. (2000). The neurobiology of stress and anxiety. In D. I. Mostofsky & D. H. Barlow (Eds.), *The management of stress and anxiety in medical disorders* (pp. 15–35). Needham Heights, MA: Allyn & Bacon.

Sullivan, G. M., & LeDoux, J. E. (2004). Synaptic self: Conditioned fear, developed adversity, and the anxious individual. In J. M. Gorman (Ed.), *Fear and anxiety: The benefits of translational research* (pp. 1–22). Washington, DC: American Psychiatric Publishing.

Sullivan, K. A. (2001). The clinical features of binge eating disorder and bulimia nervosa: What are the differences? *Canadian Journal of Counselling, 35,* 315–328.

Sullivan, M. J. (2003). Introduction: Emerging trends in secondary prevention of back pain disability. *The Clinical Journal of Pain, 19,* 77–79.

Sullivan, M. J. L., Bishop, S. R., & Pivik, J. (1995). The Pain Catastrophizing Scale: Development and validation. *Psychological Assessment, 7,* 524–532.

Sullivan, M. J. L., Lynch, M. F., & Clark, A. J. (2005). Dimensions of catastrophic thinking associated with pain experience and disability in patients with neuropathic pain conditions. *Pain, 113*(3), 310–315.

Sullivan, M. J. L., & Stanish, W. D. (2003). Psychologically based occupational rehabilitation: The Pain-Disability Prevention Program. *Clinical Journal of Pain, 19,* 97–104.

Sullivan, M. J. L., Thorn, B., Haythornthwaite, J. A., Keefe, F., Martin, M., Bradley, L. A., & Lefebvre, J. C. (2001). Theoretical perspectives on the relation between catastrophizing and pain. *Clinical Journal of Pain, 17,* 52–64.

Sullivan, M. J. L., Tripp, D. A., Rodgers, W. M., & Stanish, W. (2000). Catastrophizing and pain perception in sport participants. *Journal of Applied Sport Psychology, 12,* 151–167.

Sullivan, P. F. (1995). Mortality in anorexia nervosa. *American Journal of Psychiatry, 152,* 1073–1074.

Sullivan, S. S., & Guilleminault, C. (2009). Emerging drugs for insomnia: New frontiers for old and novel targets. *Expert Opinion on Emerging Drugs, 14*(3), 411–422.

Suls, J., & Bunde, J. (2005). Anger, anxiety, and depression as risk factors for cardiovascular disease: The problems and implications of overlapping affective dispositions. *Psychological Bulletin, 131,* 260–300.

Summerfeldt, L. J., Kloosterman, P. H., Antony, M. M., Richter, M. A., & Swinson, R. P. (2004). The relationship between miscellaneous symptoms and major symptom factors in obsessive-compulsive disorder. *Behaviour Research and Therapy, 42,* 1453–1467.

Summerfeldt, L. J., Richter, M. A., Antony, M. M., & Swinson, R. P. (1999). Symptom structure in obsessive-compulsive disorder: A confirmatory factor-analytic study. *Behaviour Research and Therapy, 37,* 297–311.

Suomi, S. J. (1999). Attachment in rhesus monkeys. In J. Cassidy & P. Shaver (Eds.), *Handbook of attachment: Theory, research, and clinical applications* (pp. 181–197). New York: Guilford Press.

Suomi, S. J. (2000). A biobehavioral perspective on developmental psychopathology. In A. J. Sameroff, J. Lewis, & S. M. Miller (Eds.), *Handbook of developmental psychopathology* (pp. 237–256). New York: Kluwer Academic/ Plenum.

Suppes, T., Baldessarini, R. J., Faedda, G. L., & Tohen, M. (1991). Risk of recurrence following discontinuation of lithium treatment in bipolar disorder. *Archives of General Psychiatry, 48*(12), 1082–1088.

Sussman, S. (1998). The first asylums in Canada: A response to neglectful community care and current trends. *Canadian Journal of Psychiatry, 43,* 260–264.

Sutherland, G. R., & Richards, R. l. (1994). Dynamic mutations. *American Scientist, 82,* 157–163.

Sutker, P. B., Bugg, F., & West, J. A. (1993). Antisocial personality disorder. In P. B. Sutker & H. F. Adams (Eds.), *Comprehensive handbook of psychopathology* (2nd ed., pp. 337–369). New York: Plenum Press.

Sutton, D. A., Moldofsky, H., & Badley, F. M. (2001). Insomnia and health problems in Canadians. *Sleep & Hypnosis, 24,* 665–670.

Suvisaari, J., Perälä, J., Saarni, S., Juvonen, H., Tuulio-Henriksson, A., & Lönnqvist, J. (2009). The epidemiology and descriptive and predictive validity of DSM-IV delusional disorder and subtypes of schizophrenia. *Clinical Schizophrenia & Related Psychoses, 2*(4), 289–297.

Swanson, M. C., Bland, R. C., & Newman, S. C. (1994). Antisocial personality disorders. *Acta Psychiatrica Scandinavica, 376*(Suppl.), 63–70.

Swartz, M., Blazer, D., Woodbury, M., George, L., & Landerman, R. (1986). Somatization disorder in a U.S. southern community: Use of a new procedure for analysis of medical classification. *Psychological Medicine, 16,* 595–609.

Swartz, M. S., Lauriello, J., & Drake, R. E. (2006). Psychosocial therapies. In J. A. Lieberman, T. S. Stroup, & D. O. Perkins (Eds.), *The American Psychiatric Publishing textbook of schizophrenia* (pp. 327–340). Washington, DC: American Psychiatric Publishing.

Swedo, S., Thorsen, P., & Pine, D. (2008, February 3-5). *Autism and Other Pervasive Developmental Disorders Conference.* Paper presented at the The Future of Psychiatric Diagnosis: Refining the Research Agenda, Sacramento, CA.

Swedo, S. E., (2002). Pediatric autoimmune neuropsychiatric disorders associated with streptococcal infections (PANDAS). *Molecular Psychiatry, 7,* S24–S35.

Swedo, S. F., Pleeter, J. D., Richter, D. M., Hoffman, C. L., Allen, A. J., Hamburger, S. D., ... Rosenthal, N. E. (1995). Rates of seasonal affective disorder in children and adolescents. *American Journal of Psychiatry, 152,* 1016–1019.

Sweet, R. A. (2009). Cognitive disorders: Introduction. In B. J. Sadock, V. A. Sadock, & P. Ruiz (Eds.), *Kaplan & Sadock's comprehensive textbook of psychiatry* (Vol. I, 9th ed., pp. 1152–1153). Philadelphia: Lippincott Williams & Wilkins.

Swift, R. M. (1999). Medications and alcohol craving. *Alcohol Research & Health, 23*(3), 207–213.

Swinson, R. P., Fergus, K. D., Cox, B. J., & Wickwire, K. (1995). Efficacy of telephone-administered behavioral therapy for panic disorder with agoraphobia. *Behaviour Research and Therapy, 33,* 465–469.

Szasz, T. (1961). *The myth of mental illness: Foundations of a theory of personal conduct.* New York: Hoeber-Harper.

Szasz, T. S. (1960). The myth of mental illness. *American Psychologist, 15,* 113–118.

Szatmari, P. (2000). The classification of autism, Asperger's syndrome, and pervasive developmental disorder. *Canadian Journal of Psychiatry, 45,* 731–738.

Szatmari, P. (2003). The causes of autism spectrum disorders. *BMJ, 326*(7382), 173–174.

Szatmari, P., Bryson, S. F., Streiner, D. L., Wilson, F., Archer, L., & Ryerse, C. (2000). Two-year outcome of preschool children with autism or Asperger's syndrome. *American Journal of Psychiatry, 157,* 1980–1987.

Szatmari, P., Georgiades, S., Bryson, S., Zwaigenbaum, L., Roberts, W., Mahoney, W., ... Tuff, L. (2006). Investigating the structure of the restricted, repetitive behaviours and interests domain of autism. *Journal of Child Psychology and Psychiatry, 47,* 582–590.

Szatmari, P., Offord, D. R., Siegel, L. S., Finlayson, M. A. J., & Tuff, L. (1990). The clinical significance of neurocognitive impairments among children with psychiatric disorders: Diagnosis and situational specificity. *Journal of Child Psychology & Psychiatry & Allied Disciplines, 31,* 287–299.

Szmukler, G. I., Fisler, I., Gillis, C., & Haywood, M. F. (1985). The implications of anorexia nervosa in a ballet school. *Journal of Psychiatric Research, 19,* 177–181.

Szyf, M., Weaver, I. C. G., Champagne, F. A., Diorio, J., & Meaney, M. J. (2005). Maternal programming of steroid receptor expression and phenotype through DNA methylation in the rat. *Frontiers in Neuroendocrinology, 26*(3/4), 139–162.

Tafti, M. (2009). Genetic aspects of normal and disturbed sleep. *Sleep Medicine, 10*(Suppl. 1), S17–S21.

Tager-Flusberg, H., Rogers, S., Cooper, J., Landa, R., Lord, C., Paul, R., … Yoder, P. (2009). Defining spoken language benchmarks and selecting measures of expressive language development for young children with autism spectrum disorders. *Journal of Speech, Language, and Hearing Research, 52*(3), 643–652.

Takahasi, T. (1989). Social phobia syndrome in Japan. *Comprehensive Psychiatry, 30,* 45–52.

Takei, N., Lewis, S., Jones, P., Harvey, I., & Murray, R. M. (1996). Prenatal exposure to influenza and increased cerebrospinal fluid spaces in schizophrenia. *Schizophrenia Bulletin, 22,* 521–534.

Talbott, J. A. (1990). Current perspectives in the United States on the chronically mentally ill. In A. Kales, C. N. Stefanis, & J. A. Talbott (Eds.), *Recent advances in schizophrenia* (pp. 279–295). New York: Springer-Verlag.

Tan, F. S. (1980). Transcultural aspects of anxiety. In G. D. Burrows & B. Davies (Eds.), *Handbook of studies on anxiety.* Amsterdam: Elsevier/North-Holland.

Tang, M. X., Jacobs, D., Stern, Y., Marder, K., Schofield, P., Gurland, B., … Mayeux, R. (1996). Effects of oestrogen during menopause on risk and age at onset of Alzheimer's disease. *Lancet, 348,* 429–432.

Tannock, R. (2009). Reading Disorder. In B. J. Sadock, V. A. Sadock, & P. Ruiz (Eds.), *Kaplan & Sadock's comprehensive textbook of psychiatry* (Vol. II, 9th ed., pp. 3475–3485). Philadelphia: Lippincott Williams & Wilkins.

Tanzi, R. F., & Parson, A. B. (2000). *Decoding darkness: The search for the genetic causes of Alzheimer's disease.* Cambridge, MA: Perseus Publishing.

Tarasoff v. Regents of University of California ("Tarasoff I"), 529 P. 2d 553 (Cal. Sup. Ct. 1974); ("Tarasoff II"), 551 P. 2d 334 (Cal. Sup. Ct. 1976).

Tarrier, N., Kinney, C., McCarthy, F., Humphreys, L., Wittkowski, A., & Morris, J. (2000). Two-year follow-up of cognitive behavioural therapy and supportive counseling in the treatment of persistent symptoms in chronic schizophrenia. *Journal of Consulting and Clinical Psychology, 68*(5), 912–922.

Tarrier, N., Wittkowski, A., Kinney, C. McCarthy, F., Morris, J., & Humphreys, L., (1999). Durability of the effects of cognitive-behavioural therapy in the treatment of chronic schizophrenia: 12-month follow-up. *British Journal of Psychiatry, 174,* 500–504.

Tattan, T., & Tarrier, N. (2000). The expressed emotion of case managers of the seriously mentally ill: The influence of expressed emotion on clinical outcomes. *Psychological Medicine, 30,* 195–204.

Tau, G. Z., & Peterson, B. S. (2010). Normal development of brain circuits. *Neuropsychopharmacology, 35*(1), 147–168.

Taubes, T. (1998). "Healthy avenues of the mind": Psychological theory building and the influence of religion during the era of moral treatment. *American Journal of Psychiatry, 155*(8), 1001–1007.

Tauscher, J., Hussain, T., Agid, O., Verhoeff, N. P. L. G., Wilson, A. A., Houle, S., … Kapur, S. (2004). Equivalent occupancy of dopamine D1 and D2 receptors with clozapine: Differentiation from other atypical antipsychotics. *American Journal of Psychiatry, 161*(9), 1620–1625.

Tauscher, J., Kapur, S., Verhoeff, P. L. G., Hussey, D. F., Daskalakis, Z. J., Tauscher-Wisniewski, S., … Zipursky, R. B. (2002). Brain serotonin 5–HT-sub(1A) receptor binding in schizophrenia measured by positron emission tomography and [-super(11)C]WAY-100635. *Archives of General Psychiatry, 59,* 514–520.

Tavares, H., Zilberman, M. I.., Hodgins, D. C., & el-Guebaly, N. (2005). Comparison of craving between pathological gamblers and alcoholics. *Alcoholism: Clinical and Experimental Research, 29*(8), 1427–1431.

Taylor, C. B., Sheikh, J., Agras, W. S., Roth, W. T., Margraf, J., Ehlers, A., … Gossard, D. (1986). Self-report of panic attacks: Agreement with heart rate changes. *American Journal of Psychiatry, 143,* 478–482.

Taylor, C. T., & Alden, L. F. (2005). Social interpretation bias and generalized social phobia: The influence of developmental experiences. *Behaviour Research and Therapy, 43,* 759–777.

Taylor, G. M., & Ste-Marie, D. M. (2001). Eating disorders symptoms in Canadian female pair and dance figure skaters. *International Journal of Sport Psychology, 32,* 21–28.

Taylor, J., & Lang, A. R. (2006). Psychopathy and substance use disorders. In C. J. Patrick (Ed.), *Handbook of psychopathy* (pp. 495–511). New York: Guilford Press.

Taylor, L., & Ingram, R. F. (1999). Cognitive reactivity and depressotypic information processing in children of depressed mothers. *Journal of Abnormal Psychology, 108,* 202–210.

Taylor, M. A., & Abrams, R. (1981). Early and late-onset bipolar illness. *Archives of General Psychiatry, 38*(1), 58–61.

Taylor, S. (1994). Comment on Otto et al. (1992): Hypochondriacal concerns, anxiety sensitivity, and panic disorder. *Journal of Anxiety Disorders, 8,* 97–99.

Taylor, S. (1995). Panic disorder and hypochondriacal concerns: Reply to Otto and Pollack (1994). *Journal of Anxiety Disorders, 9,* 87–88.

Taylor, S. (1996). Meta-analysis of cognitive behavioral treatment for social phobia. *Journal of Behavior Therapy and Experimental Psychiatry, 27,* 1–9.

Taylor, S. (Ed.). (1999). *Anxiety sensitivity: Theory, research, and treatment of the fear of anxiety.* Mahwah, NJ: Lawrence Erlbaum.

Taylor, S. (2001). Breathing retraining in the treatment of panic disorder: Efficacy, caveats and indications. *Scandinavian Journal of Behaviour Therapy, 30,* 49–56.

Taylor, S. (2003). *Health psychology* (5th ed.). San Francisco: McGraw-Hill.

Taylor, S., & Asmundson, G. J. (2009). Hypochondriasis and health anxiety. In M. M. Antony & M. B. Stein (Eds.), *Oxford handbook of anxiety and related disorders* (pp. 525–540). Oxford: Oxford University Press.

Taylor, S., & Asmundson, G. J. G. (2004). *Treating health anxiety: A cognitive-behavioral approach.* New York: Guilford Press.

Taylor, S., Asmundson, G. J. G., & Coons, M. J. (2003). Current directions in the treatment of hypochondriasi-s. Manuscript submitted for publication.

Taylor, S., & Cox, B. J. (1998). An expanded Anxiety Sensitivity Index: Evidence for a hierarchic structure in a clinical sample. *Journal of Anxiety Disorders, 12,* 463–483.

Taylor, S., & Koch, W. J. (1995). Anxiety disorders due to motor vehicle accidents: Nature and treatment. *Clinical Psychology Review, 15,* 721–738.

Taylor, S., Koch, W. J., & McNally, R. J. (1992). How does anxiety sensitivity vary across the anxiety disorders? *Journal of Anxiety Disorders, 6,* 249–259.

Taylor, S., Thordarson, D. S., Jang, K. L., & Asmundson, G. J. (2006). Genetic and environmental origins of health anxiety: A twin study. *World Psychiatry, 5*(1), 47–50.

Taylor, S., Thordarson, D. S., Maxfield, L., Fedoroff, I. C., Lovell, K., & Ogrdniczuk, J. (2003). Comparative efficacy, speed, and adverse effects of three PTSD treatments: Exposure therapy, FMDR, and relaxation training. *Journal of Consulting and Clinical Psychology, 71,* 330–338.

Taylor, S. E. (2002). *The tending instinct: How nurturing is essential to who we are and how we live.* New York: Henry Holt and Company.

Taylor, S. E. (2006). Tend and befriend: Biobehavioral bases of affiliation under stress. *Current Directions in Psychological Science, 15*(6), 273–277.

Taylor, S. E. (2009). *Health psychology* (7th ed.). New York: McGraw-Hill.

Taylor, S. F. (1999). *Health psychology* (4th ed.). Boston: McGraw-Hill.

Taylor, S. F., Klein, L. C., Lewis, B. P., Gruenewald, T. L., Gurung, R. A. R., & Updegraff, J. A. (2000). Biobehavioral responses to stress in females: Tend-and-befriend, not fight-or-flight. *Psychological Review, 107,* 411–429.

Taylor, S. F., Repetti, R. L., & Seeman, T. (1997). Health psychology: What is an unhealthy environment and how does it get under the skin? *Annual Review of Psychology, 48,* 411–447.

Teachman, B. A., & Woody, S. R. (2004). Staying tuned to research in implicit cognition: Relevance for clinical practice with anxiety disorders. *Cognition and Behavioral Practice, 11*(2), 149–159.

Teasdale, J. D. (1993). Emotion and two kinds of meaning: Cognitive therapy and applied cognitive science. *Behaviour Research and Therapy, 31*(4), 339–354.

Teasdale, J. D., Moore, R. G., Hayhurst, H., Pope, M., Williams, S., & Segal, Z. V. (2002). Metacognitive awareness and the prevention of relapse in depression: Empirical evidence. *Journal of Consulting and Clinical Psychology, 70,* 275–287.

Teasdale, J. D., Segal, Z. V., Williams, J. M., Ridgeway, V. A., Soulsby, J. M., & Lau, M. A. (2000). Prevention of relapse/recurrence in major depression by mindfulness-based cognitive therapy. *Journal of Consulting and Clinical Psychology, 68,* 615–623.

Teicher, M. H., Glod, C., & Cole, J. O. (1990). Emergence of intense suicidal preoccupation during fluoxetine treatment. *American Journal of Psychiatry, 147*(1), 207–210.

Telch, C. F., & Agras, W. S. (1993). The effects of a very low calorie diet on binge eating. *Behavior Therapy, 24,* 177–193.

Telch, C. F., Agras, W. S., & Rossiter, F. M. (1988). Binge eating increases with increasing adiposity. *International Journal of Eating Disorders, 7,* 115–119.

Telch, M. J. (1988). Combined pharmacologic and psychological treatments for panic sufferers. In S. Rachman & J. D. Maser (Eds.), *Panic: Psychological perspectives.* Hillsdale, NJ: Erlbaum.

Telch, M. J., Lucas, J. A., & Nelson, P. (1989). Non-clinical panic in college students: An investigation of prevalence and symptomatology. *Journal of Abnormal Psychology, 98,* 300–306.

Telch, M. J., Tearnan, B. H., & Taylor, C. B. (1983). Antidepressant medication in the treatment of agoraphobia. A critical review. *Behaviour Research and Therapy, 21,* 505–527.

Tellegen, A. (1978). *Manual for the Multidimensional Personality Questionnaire.* Unpublished manuscript, University of Minnesota, Minneapolis.

Tellegen, A. (1985). Structures of mood and personality and their relevance to assessing anxiety, with an emphasis on self-report. In A. H. Tuma & J. D. Maser (Eds.), *Anxiety and the anxiety disorders* (pp. 681–706). Hillsdale, NJ: Erlbaum.

Temoshok, L. R., Wald, R. L., Synowski, S., & Garzino-Demo, A. (2008). Coping as a multi-system construct associated with pathways mediating HIV-relevant immune function and disease progression. *Psychosomatic Medicine, 70,* 555–561.

Tenhula, W. N., Bellack, A. S., & Drake, R. E. (2009). Schizophrenia: Psychosocial approaches. In B. J. Sadock, V. A. Sadock, & P. Ruiz (Eds.), *Kaplan & Sadock's comprehensive textbook of psychiatry* (Vol. I, 9th ed., pp. 1557–1572). Philadelphia: Lippincott Williams & Wilkins.

Teplin, L. A. (1985). The criminality of the mentally ill: A dangerous misconception. *American Journal of Psychiatry, 142,* 593–599.

ter Bogt, T., Schmid, H., Gabhainn, S. N., Fotiou, A., & Vollebergh, W. (2006). Economic and cultural correlates of cannabis use among mid-adolescents in 31 countries. *Addiction, 101*(2), 241–251.

Teri, L., Gibbons, L. F., McCurry, S. M., Logsdon, R. G., Buchner, D. M., Barlow, W. E., ... Larson, E. B. (2003). Exercise plus behavioral management in patients with Alzheimer's disease: A randomized controlled trial. *JAMA, 290,* 2015–2022.

Terman, J. S., Terman, M., Lo, F., & Cooper, T. B. (2001). Circadian time of morning light administration and therapeutic response in winter depression. *Archives of General Psychiatry, 58,* 69–75.

Terman, M., & Terman, J. S. (2000). Light therapy. In M. H. Kryger, T. Roth, & W. C. Dement (Eds.), *Principles and practice of sleep medicine* (3rd ed., pp. 1258–1274). Philadelphia: W. B. Saunders.

Terman, M., Terman, J. S., & Ross, D. C. (1998). A controlled trial of timed bright light and negative air ionization of treatment of winter depression. *Archives of General Psychiatry, 55,* 875–882.

Testad, I., Ballard, C., Brønnick, K., & Aarsland, D. (2010). The effect of staff training on agitation and use of restraint in nursing home residents with dementia: A single-blind, randomized controlled trial. *The Journal of Clinical Psychiatry, 71*(1), 80.

Thaker, G. K., & Avila, M. (2003). Schizophrenia, V: Risk marks. *American Journal of Psychiatry, 160,* 1578.

Thapar, A., & McGuffin, P. (2009). Quantitative genetics. In M. G. Gelder, N. C. Andreasen, J. J. Lopez-Ibor Jr., & J. R. Geddes (Eds.), *New Oxford textbook of psychiatry* (Vol. 1, 2nd ed., pp. 212–221). Oxford: Oxford University Press.

Thase, M. E. (1990). Relapse and recurrence in unipolar major depression: Short-term and long-term approaches. *Journal of Clinical Psychiatry, 51*(Suppl. 6), 51–57.

Thase, M. E. (2009). Neurobiological aspects of depression. In I. H. Gotlib & C. L. Hammen (Eds.), *Handbook of depression* (2nd ed., pp. 187–217). New York: Guilford Press.

Thase, M. E., & Denko, T. (2008). Pharmacotherapy of mood disorders. *Annual Review of Clinical Psychology, 4,* 53–91.

Thase, M. E., & Kupfer, D. J. (1996). Recent developments in the pharmacotherapy of mood disorders. *Journal of Consulting and Clinical Psychology, 64,* 646–659.

Thies-Flechtner, K., Muller-Oerlinghausen, B. Seibert, W., Walther, A., & Greil, W. (1996). Effect of prophylactic treatment on suicide risk in patients with major affective disorders: Data from a randomized prospective trial. *Pharmacopsychiatry, 29,* 103–107.

Thirthalli, J., & Rajkumar, R. P. (2009). Statistical versus clinical significance in psychiatric research–an overview for beginners. *Asian Journal of Psychiatry, 2*(2), 74–79.

Thompson, B. (1999). Improving research clarity and usefulness with effect size indices as supplements to statistical significance tests. *Exceptional Children, 65,* 329–337.

Thompson, J. K., & Kinder, B. (2003). Eating disorders. In M. Hersen & S. Turner (Eds.), *Handbook of adult psychopathology* (4th ed., pp. 555–582). New York: Plenum.

Thompson, J. K., & Stice, E. (2001). Thin-idea internalization: Mounting evidence for a new risk factor for body-image disturbance and eating pathology. *Current Directions in Psychological Science, 11,* 181–183.

Thompson, J. R., Bradley, V. J., Buntinx, W. H. E., Schalock, R. L., Shogren, K. A., Snell, M. E., ... Yeager, M. H. (2009). Conceptualizing supports and the support needs of people with intellectual disability. *Intellectual and Developmental Disabilities, 47*(2), 135–146.

Thompson, M. A., Aberg, J. A., Cahn, P., Montaner, J. S. G., Rizzardini, G., Telenti, A., ... Schooley, R. T. (2010). Antiretroviral treatment of adult HIV infection. *JAMA, 304,* 321–333.

Thoresen, C. F., & Powell, L. H. (1992). Type A behavior pattern: New perspectives on theory, assessment and intervention. [Special issue: Behavioral medicine: An update for the 1990s]. *Journal of Consulting and Clinical Psychology, 60*(4), 595–604.

Thorndike, R. L., Hagen, F. P., & Sattler, J. M. (1986). *The Stanford-Binet Intelligence Scale: Fourth edition. Guide for administering and scoring.* Chicago: Riverside.

Thorne, S. (2000, February 17). Military will treat stress as a disability: Post-traumatic stress disorder eligible for compensation. *The Toronto Star,* A7.

Thorpe, G. L., & Burns, L. F. (1983). *The agoraphobic syndrome.* New York: John Wiley & Sons.

Thorpy, M., & Glovinsky, P. (1987). Parasomnias. *Psychiatric Clinics of North America, 10,* 623–639.

Thurston, R. C., & Kubzansky, L. D. (2009). Women, loneliness, and incident coronary heart disease. *Psychosomatic Medicine, 71*(8), 836–842.

Thyer, B. A. (1993). Childhood separation anxiety disorder and adult-onset agoraphobia: Review of evidence. In C. Last (Ed.), *Anxiety across the lifespan: A developmental perspective* (pp. 128–145). New York: Springer.

Tienari, P. (1991). Interaction between genetic vulnerability and family environment: The Finnish adoptive family study of schizophrenia. *Acta Psychiatrica Scandinavica, 84,* 460–465.

Tienari, P., Wynne, L. C., Laksy, K., Moring, J., Nieminen, P., Sorri, A., ... Wahlberg, K.-E. (2003). Genetic boundaries of the schizophrenia spectrum: Evidence from the Finnish adoptive family study of schizophrenia. *American Journal of Psychiatry, 160,* 1587–1594.

Tienari, P., Wynne, L. C., Moring, J., Lahti, I., Naarala, M., Sorri, A., ... Kaleva, M. (1994). The Finnish adoptive family study of schizophrenia: Implications for family research. *British Journal of Psychiatry, 23*(Suppl. 164), 20–26.

Tierney, M. C., Snow, W. G., Szalai, J. P., Fisher, R. H., & Zorzitto, M. L. (1996). A brief neuropsychological battery for the differential diagnosis of probable Alzheimer's disease. *Clinical Neuropsychologist, 10,* 96–103.

Tierney, M. C., Yao, C., Kiss, A., & McDowell, I. (2005). Neuropsychological tests accurately predict incident Alzheimer disease after 5 and 10 years. *Neurology, 64*(11), 1853–1859.

Tiffany, S. T. (1999). Cognitive concepts of craving. *Alcohol Research & Health, 23*(3), 215–224.

Tiffany, S. T., Cox, L. S., & Flash, C. A. (2000). Effects of transdermal nicotine patches on abstinence-induced and cue elicited craving in cigarette smokers. *Journal of Consulting and Clinical Psychology, 68*(2), 233–240.

Tiggemann, M. (2002). Media influences on body image development. In T. F. Cash & T. Pruzinsky (Eds.), *Body image: A handbook of theory, research and clinical practice* (pp. 91–98). New York: Guilford Press.

Tinbergen, F. A., & Tinbergen, N. (1972). *Early childhood autism: An ethological approach.* Berlin: Paul Parey.

Tingelstad, J. B. (1991). The cardiotoxicity of the tricyclics. *Journal of the American Academy of Child and Adolescent Psychiatry, 30,* 845–846.

Tjepkema, M. (2005). Insomnia. *Health Reports, 17,* 9–25.

Tjio, J. H., & Levan, A. (1956). The chromosome number of man. *Hereditas, 42,* 1–6.

Tollefson, G. D. (1993). Major depression. In D. L. Dunner (Ed.), *Current psychiatric therapy.* Philadelphia: W. B. Saunders.

Tomac, A., Lindqvist, F., Lin, L. F. H., Ögren, S. O., Young, D., Hoffer, B. J., & Olson, L. (1995). Protection and repair of the nigrostriatal dopaminergic system by GDNF in vivo. *Nature, 373,* 335–339.

Tondo, L., Jamison, K. R., & Baldessarini, R. J. (1997). Effect of lithium maintenance on suicidal behavior in major mood disorders. In D. M. Stoff & J. J. Mann (Eds.), *The neurobiology of suicide: From the bench to the clinic* (Vol. 836, pp. 339–351). New York: Academy of Sciences.

Toomey, R., Faraone, S. V., Simpson, J. C., & Tsuang, M. T. (1998). Negative, positive, and disorganized symptom dimensions in schizophrenia, major depression, and bipolar disorder. *Journal of Nervous and Mental Disorders, 186,* 470–476.

Torgersen, S. (1986). Genetics of somatoform disorder. *Archives of General Psychiatry, 43,* 502–505.

Torgersen, S., Onstad, S., Skre, I., Edvardsen, J., & Kringlen, F. (1993). "True" schizotypal personality disorder: A study of co-twins and relatives of schizophrenic probands. *American Journal of Psychiatry, 150,* 1661–1667.

Torrey, F. F. (1988a). *Nowhere to go: The tragic odyssey of the homeless mentally ill.* New York: Harper & Row.

Torrey, F. F. (1988b). Stalking the schizovirus. *Schizophrenia Bulletin, 14,* 223–229.

Torrey, F. F., Bowler, A. F., Taylor, F. H., & Gottesman, I. I. (1994). *Schizophrenia and manic-depressive disorder: The biological roots of mental illness as revealed by the landmark study of identical twins.* New York: Basic Books.

Torrey, F. F., Rawlings, R., & Waldman, I. (1988). Schizophrenic births and viral diseases in two states. *Schizophrenia Research, 1,* 73–77.

Toth, K., & King, B. H. (2010). Intellectual disability (mental retardation). In M. K. Dulcan (Ed.), *Dulcan's textbook of child and adolescent psychiatry* (5th ed., pp. 151–172). Arlington, VA: American Psychiatric Publishing.

Tracey, S. A., Chorpita, B. F., Douban, J., & Barlow, D. H. (1997). Empirical evaluation of DSM-IV generalized anxiety disorder criteria in children and adolescents. *Journal of Clinical Child Psychology, 26,* 404–414.

Trebbe, A. (1979, September 15). Ideal is body beautiful and clean cut. *USA Today,* 1–2.

Trimbell, M. R. (1981). *Neuropsychiatry.* Chichester, UK: John Wiley & Sons.

Trottier, K., Polivy, J., & Herman, C. P. (2005). Effects of exposure to unrealistic promises about dieting: Are unrealistic expectations about dieting inspirational? *International Journal of Eating Disorders, 37,* 142–149.

Trudel, G., Marchand, A., Ravart, M., Aubin, S., Turgeon, L., & Fortier, P. (2001). The effect of a cognitive-behavioral group treatment program on hypoactive sexual desire in women. *Sexual & Relationship Therapy, 16,* 145–164.

True, W. R., Rice, J., Fisen, S. A., Heath, A. C., Goldberg, J., Lyons, M. J., & Nowak, J. (1993). A twin study of genetic and environmental contributions to liability for posttraumatic stress symptoms. *Archives of General Psychiatry, 50,* 257–264.

Truscott, D., & Crook, K. H. (2004). *Ethics for the practice of psychology in Canada.* Edmonton, AB: University of Alberta Press.

Tsai, G. F., Condie, D., Wu, M. T., & Chang, I. W. (1999). Functional magnetic resonance imaging of personality switches in a woman with dissociative identity disorder. *Harvard Review of Psychiatry, 7*(2), 119–122.

Tsai, L. Y., & Ghaziuddin, M. (1992). Biomedical research in autism. In D. F. Berkell (Ed.), *Autism: Identification, education, and treatment* (pp. 53–74). Hillsdale, NJ: Erlbaum.

Tsao, J. C. I., Mystkowski, J. L., Zucker, B. G., & Craske, M. G. (2002). Effects of cognitive-behavioral therapy for panic disorder on comorbid conditions: Replication and extension. *Behavior Therapy, 33,* 493–509.

Tuchman, B. (1978). *A distant mirror.* New York: Ballantine Books.

Tucker, G. J., Ferrell, R. B., & Price, T. R. P. (1984). The hospital treatment of schizophrenia. In A. S. Bellack (Ed.), *Schizophrenia: Treatment, management, and rehabilitation* (pp. 175–191). New York: Grune & Stratton.

Tulsky, D. S., Zhu, J., & Prifitera, A. (2000). Assessment of adult intelligence with the WAIS-III. In G. Goldstein & M. Hersen (Eds.), *Handbook of psychological assessment* (pp. 97–129). New York: Pergamon Press.

Tuokko, H., Hadjistavropoulos, T., Miller, J. A., & Beattie, B. L. (1992). The Clock Test: A sensitive measure to differentiate normal elderly from those with Alzheimer Disease. *Journal of the American Geriatrics Society, 40,* 579–584.

Tuokko, H., Hadjistavropoulos, T., Rae, S., & O'Rourke, N. (2000). A comparison of alternative approaches to the scoring of clock drawing. *Archives of Clinical Neuropsychology, 15,* 137–148.

Tuokko, H., Kristjansson, F., & Miller, J. (1995). Neuropsychological detection of dementia: An overview of the neuropsychological component of the Canadian Study of Health and Aging. *Journal of Clinical & Experimental Neuropsychology, 17,* 352–373.

Turgeon, L., Marchand, A., & Dupuis, G. (1998). Clinical features in panic disorder with agoraphobia: A comparison of men and women. *Journal of Anxiety Disorders, 12,* 539–553.

Turk, C. L., Heimberg, R. G., & Hope, D. A. (2001). Social phobia and social anxiety. In D. H. Barlow (Ed.), *Clinical handbook of psychological disorders: A step-by-step treatment manual* (3rd ed., pp. 99–136). New York: Guilford Press.

Turk, C. L., Heimberg, R. G., & Magee, L. (2008). Social anxiety disorder. In D. H. Barlow (Ed.), Clinical handbook of psychological disorders: *A step-by-step treatment manual* (4th ed., pp. 123–163). New York: Guilford Press.

Turk, D. C. (1996). Biopsychosocial perspective on chronic pain. In R. J. Gatchel & D. C. Turk (Eds.), *Psychological approaches to pain management: A practitioner's handbook* (pp. 3–32). New York: Guilford Press.

Turk, D. C., & Gatchel, R. J. (2002). *Psychological approaches to pain management: A practitioner's handbook* (2nd ed.). New York: Guilford Press.

Turk, D. C., & Monarch, F. S. (2002). Biopsychosocial perspective on chronic pain. In D. C. Turk & R. J. Gatchel (Eds.), *Psychological approaches to pain management: A practitioner's handbook* (2nd ed.). New York: Guilford Press.

Turk, D. C., Meichenbaum, D., & Genest, M. (1983). *Pain and behavioral medicine: A cognitive-behavioral perspective.* New York: Guilford Press.

Turkat, I. D., & Maisto, S. A. (1985). Personality disorders: Applications of the experimental method to the formulation and modification of personality disorders. In D. H. Barlow (Ed.), *Clinical handbook of psychological disorders.* New York: Guilford Press.

Turkel, S. B., & Tavaré, C. J. (2003). Delirium in children and adolescents. *Journal of Neuropsychiatry and Clinical Neuroscience, 15,* 431–435.

Turkheimer, E., Haley, A., Waldron, M., D'Onofrio, B., & Gottesman, I. I. (2003). Socioeconomic status modifies heritability of IQ in young children. *Psychological Science, 14,* 623–628.

Turkheimer, F. (1998). Heritability and biological explanation. *Psychological Review, 105,* 782–791.

Turkheimer, F., & Parry, C. D. H. (1992). Why the gap? Practice and policy in civil commitment hearings. *American Psychologist, 47,* 646–655.

Turkheimer, F., & Waldron, M. C. (2000). Nonshared environment: A theoretical, methodological, and quantitative review. *Psychological Bulletin, 126,* 78–108.

Turkington, C. (1994, January). Wexler wins Lasker award for her work on Huntington's. *APA Monitor,* pp. 20–21.

Turner, S. M., Beidel, D. C., & Jacob, R. G. (1994). Social phobia: A comparison of behavior therapy and atenolol. *Journal of Consulting Psychology, 62,* 350–358.

Turovsky, J., & Barlow, D. H. (1996). Generalized anxiety disorder. In J. Margraf (Ed.), *Textbook of behavior therapy* (pp. 87–106). Berlin: Springer-Verlag.

Tweed, R. G., & Dutton, D. G. (1998). A comparison of impulsive and instrumental subgroups of batterers. *Violence & Victims, 13,* 217–230.

Tyas, S. L., Salazar, J. C., Snowdon, D. A., Desrosiers, M. F., Riley, K. P., Mendiondo, M. S., & Kryscio, R. J. (2007). Transitions to mild cognitive impairments, dementia, and death: Findings from the nun study. *American Journal of Epidemiology, 165*(11), 1231–1238.

Tynes, L. L., White, K., & Steketee, G. S. (1990). Toward a new nosology of obsessive-compulsive disorder. *Comprehensive Psychiatry, 31,* 465–480.

Tyrer, P., & Davidson, K. (2000). Cognitive therapy for personality disorders. In J. G. Gunderson & G. O. Gabbard (Eds.), *Psychotherapy for personality disorders* (pp. 131–149). Washington, DC: American Psychiatric Press.

U.S. Department of Energy Office of Science. (2009). *Human Genome Project Information.* Retrieved from http://www.ornl.gov/sci/techresources/Human_Genome/home.shtml

U.S. Department of Health and Human Services. (1990). *Seventh annual report to the U.S. Congress on alcohol and health from the secretary of health and human services.* Rockville, MD: National Institute on Alcohol Abuse and Alcoholism.

Uchino, B. N. (2009). Understanding the link between social support and physical health: A life-span perspective with emphasis on the separability of perceived and received support. *Perspectives on Psychological Science, 4,* 236–255.

Uchino, B. N., Cacioppo, J. T., & Kiecolt-Glaser, J. K. (1996). The relationship between social support and physiological processes: A review with emphasis on underlying mechanisms and implications for health. *Psychological Bulletin, 119*(3), 488–531.

Uchino, B. N., Uno, D., & Holt-Lunstad, J. (1999). Social support, physiological processes, and health. *Current Directions in Psychological Science, 8,* 145–148.

Uddo, M., Malow, R., & Sutker, P. B. (1993). Opioid and cocaine abuse and dependence disorders. In P. B. Sutker & H. F. Adams (Eds.), *Comprehensive handbook of psychopathology* (pp. 477–503). New York: Plenum Press.

Uditsky, B. (1994). Family, friends and community: Together a project to support deinstitutionalization. *Developmental Disabilities Bulletin* [Online]. Retrieved from http://.ualberta.ca/jpdasddc/bulletin/articles/aacl-deinstitutionalize.html

Uebelacker, L., & Whisman, M. (2006). Moderators of the association between relationship discord and major depression in a national population-based sample. *Journal of Family Psychology, 20,* 40–46.

Uhde, T. (1994). The anxiety disorder: Phenomenology and treatment of core symptoms and associated sleep disturbance. In M. Kryger, T. Roth, & W. Dement (Eds.), *Principles and practice of sleep medicine* (pp. 871–898). Philadelphia: W. B. Saunders.

Uhde, T., Cortese, B., & Vedeniapin, A. (2009). Anxiety and sleep problems: Emerging concepts and theoretical treatment implications. *Current Psychiatry Reports, 11*(4), 269–276.

Umbricht, D., & Kane, J. M. (1996). Medical complications of new antipsychotic drugs. *Schizophrenia Bulletin, 22,* 475–483.

UNAIDS. (2009). *AIDS epidemic update 2009.* Geneva: Joint United Nations Programme on HIV/AIDS (UNAIDS). Retrieved from http://www.who.int/hiv/pub/epidemiology/epidemic/en/index.html

Ungvari, G. S., Goggins, W., Leung, S.-K., & Gerevich, J. (2007). Schizophrenia with prominent catatonic features ('catatonic schizophrenia'). II. Factor analysis of the catatonic syndrome. *Progress in Neuro-Psychopharmacology and Biological Psychiatry, 31,* 462–468.

Urbszat, C., Herman, C. P., & Polivy, J. (2002). Eat, drink, and be merry, for tomorrow we diet: Effects of anticipated deprivation on food intake in restrained and unrestrained eaters. *Journal of Abnormal Psychology, 11,* 396–401.

Vaerum, V. N., & McCabe, S. B. (2001). Rejection of dysphoric actors and implications of depressive symptom display. *Journal of Social & Clinical Psychology, 20,* 431–451.

Vahia, I. V., & Cohen, C. I. (2009). Schizophrenia and delusional disorders. In B. J. Sadock, V. A. Sadock, & P. Ruiz (Eds.), *Kaplan & Sadock's comprehensive textbook of psychiatry* (Vol. II, 9th ed., pp. 4073–4081). Philadelphia: Lippincott Williams & Wilkins.

Vaillant, G. F. (1976). Natural history of male psychological health, V: The relation of choice of ego mechanisms of defense to adult adjustment. *Archives of General Psychiatry, 33,* 535–545.

Vaillant, G. F. (1979). Natural history of male psychological health. *New England Journal of Medicine, 301,* 1249–1254.

Vaillant, G. F. (1983). *The natural history of alcoholism.* Cambridge, MA: Harvard University Press.

Vaillant, G. F., Bond, M., & Vaillant, C. D. (1986). An empirically validated hierarchy of defense mechanisms. *Archives of General Psychiatry, 43,* 786–794.

Vaillant, G. F., & Hiller-Sturmhöfel, S. (1997). The natural history of alcoholism. *Alcohol Health & Research, 20,* 152–161.

Vallee, B. (1986). *Life with Billy.* Toronto, ON: McClelland and Stewart.

Vallee, B. L. (1998). Alcohol in the western world. *Scientific American, 278*(6), 80–85.

Valliant, P. M., Gristev, C., Pottier, D., & Kosmyna, R. (1999). Risk factors in violent and nonviolent offenders. *Psychological Reports, 85,* 675–680.

Vallis, M., Ruggiero, L., Greene, G., Jones, H., Zinman, B., Rossi, S., ... Prochaska, J. O. (2003). Stages of change for healthy eating in diabetes: Relation to demographic, eating-related, health care utilization, and psychosocial factors. *Diabetes Care, 26,* 1468–1474.

Vallis, T. M., Howes, J. L., & Standage, K. (2000). Is cognitive therapy suitable for treating individuals with personality dysfunction? *Cognitive Therapy & Research, 24,* 595–606.

Van Acker, R. (1991). Rett syndrome: A review of current knowledge. *Journal of Autism and Developmental Disorders, 21,* 381–406.

Van Ameringen, M., Mancini, C., Patterson, B., & Simpson, W. (2009). Pharmacotherapy for social anxiety disorder: An update. *The Israel Journal of Psychiatry and Related Sciences, 46*(1), 53–61.

Van Anders, S. M., Chernick, A. B., Chernick, B. A., Hampson, F., & Fischer, W. A. (2005). Preliminary clinical experience with androgen administration for pre- and postmenopausal women with hypoactive sexual desire. *Journal of Sex and Marital Therapy, 31,* 173–185.

van Beijsterveldt, C., Hudziak, J., & Boomsma, D. (2006). Genetic and environmental influences on cross-gender behavior and relation to behavior problems: A study of Dutch twins at ages 7 and 10 years. *Archives of Sexual Behavior, 35,* 647–658.

van der Does, A. J. W., Antony, M. M., Ehlers, A., & Barsky, A. J. (2000). Heartbeat perception in panic disorder: A reanalysis. *Behaviour Research and Therapy, 38,* 47–62.

van der Molen, G. M., van den Hout, M. A., van Dieren, A. C., & Griez, E. (1989). Childhood separation anxiety and adult-onset panic disorders. *Journal of Anxiety Disorders, 3,* 97–106.

van Hoeken, D., Veling, W., Sinke, S., Mitchell, J. E., & Hoek, H. W. (2009). The validity and utility of subtyping bulimia nervosa. *International Journal of Eating Disorders, 42*(7), 595–602.

van Kammen, D. P., Docherty, J. P., & Bunney, W. F. (1982). Prediction of early relapse after pimozide discontinuation by response to d-amphetamine during pimozide treatment. *Biological Psychiatry, 17,* 223–242.

van Laar, M., Volkerts, E., & Verbaten, M. (2001). Subchronic effects of the GABA-agonist lorazepam and the 5-HT2A/2C antagonist ritanserin on driving performance, slow wave sleep and daytime sleepiness in healthy volunteers. *Psychopharmacology (Berlin), 154,* 189–197.

Van Praag, H. M., & Korf, J. (1975). Central monamine deficiency in depressions: Causative of secondary phenomenon? *Pharmakopsychiatr Neuropsychopharmakol, 8,* 322–326.

Vandenberg, S. G., Singer, S. M., & Pauls, D. L. (1986). *The heredity of behavior disorders in adults and children.* New York: Plenum Press.

Vander Plate, C., Aral, S. O., & Magder, L. (1988). The relationship among genital herpes simplex virus, stress, and social support. *Health Psychology, 7,* 159–168.

Vanderwal, J. S., & Thelen, M. H. (2000). Predictors of body image dissatisfaction in elementary-age school girls. *Eating Behaviors, 1,* 105–122.

VanKammen, W. B., Loeber, R., & Stouthamer-Loeber, M. (1991). Substance use and its relationship to conduct problems and delinquency in young boys. *Journal of Youth and Adolescence, 20,* 399–413.

Vasterling, J. J., Brailey, K., Constans, J. I., & Sotker, P. B. (1998). Attention and memory dysfunction in posttraumatic stress disorders. *Neuropsychology, 12*(1), 125–133.

Veale, D. (2000). Outcome of cosmetic surgery and "DIY" surgery inpatients with body dysmorphic disorder. *Psychiatric Bulletin, 24*(6), 218–221.

Veale, D., Boocock, A., Gournay, K., Dryden, W., Shah, F., Willson, R., & Walburn, J. (1996). Body dysmorphic disorder: A survey of 50 cases. *British Journal of Psychiatry, 169,* 196–201.

Veale, D., Gournay, K., Dryden, W., Boocock, A., Shah, F., Willson, R., & Walburn, J. (1996). Body dysmorphic disorder: A cognitive behavioral model and pilot randomized control trial. *Behaviour Research and Therapy, 34,* 717–729.

Veale, D., & Riley, S. (2001). Mirror, mirror on the wall, who is the ugliest of them all? The psychopathology of mirror gazing in body dysmorphic disorder. *Behaviour Research and Therapy, 39,* 1381–1393.

Venables, P. H. (1996). Schizotypy and maternal exposure to influenza and to cold temperature: The Mauritius study. *Journal of Abnormal Psychology, 105,* 53–60.

Ventura, J., Nuechterlein, K. H., Hardesty, J. P., & Gitlin, M. (1992). Life events and schizophrenic relapse after withdrawal of medication: A prospective study. *British Journal of Psychiatry, 161,* 615–620.

Ventura, J., Nuechterlein, K. H., Lukoff, D., & Hardesty, J. P. (1989). A prospective study of stressful life events and schizophrenia relapse. *Journal of Abnormal Psychology, 98,* 407–411.

Ventura, J., Nuechterlein, K. H., Subotnik, K. L., Hardesty, J. P., & Mintz, J. (2000). Life events can trigger depressive exacerbation in the early course of schizophrenia. *Journal of Abnormal Psychology, 109*(1), 139–144.

Ventura, S. J., Peters, K. D., Martin, J. A., & Maurer, J. D. (1997). Births and deaths: United States, 1996. *Monthly Vital Statistics Report, 46*(Suppl. 2), 1–41.

Verma, K. K., Khaitan, B. K., & Singh, O. P. (1998). The frequency of sexual dysfunction in patients attending a sex therapy clinic in North India. *Archives of Sexual Behavior, 27,* 309–314.

Vermani, M., Milosevic, I., Smith, F., & Katzman, M. A. (2005). Herbs for mental illness: Effectiveness and interaction with conventional medicines. *Journal of Family Practice, 54,* 789–800.

Vernberg, F. M., LaGreca, A. M., Silverman, W. K., & Prinstein, M. J. (1996). Prediction of post-traumatic stress symptoms in children after Hurricane Andrew. *Journal of Abnormal Psychology, 105,* 237–248.

Verrier, R. L., Harper, R. M., & Hobson, J. A. (2000). Cardiovascular physiology: Central and autonomic regulation. In M. H. Kryger, T. Roth, & W. C. Dement (Eds.), *Principles and practice of sleep medicine* (3rd ed., pp. 179–191). Philadelphia: W. B. Saunders.

Vida, S., Monks, R. C., & Des Rosiers, P. (2002). Prevalence and correlates of elder abuse and neglect in a geriatric psychiatry service. *Canadian Journal of Psychiatry, 47,* 459–467.

Viens, M., De Koninck, J., Mercier, P., St-Onge, M., & Lorrain, D. (2003). Trait anxiety and sleep-onset insomnia: Evaluation of treatment using anxiety management training. *Journal of Psychosomatic Research, 54,* 31–37.

Viljoen, J. L., Roesch, R., & Zapf, P. A. (2002). Interrater reliability of the fitness interview test across 4 professional groups. *Canadian Journal of Psychiatry, 47,* 945–952.

Villeneuve, F., & Lemelin, S. (2005). Open-label study of atypical neuroleptic quetiapine for treatment of borderline personality disorder: Impulsivity as main target. *Journal of Clinical Psychiatry, 66,* 1298–1303.

Vinken, P. J., & Bruyn, G. W. (1972). The phakomatoses. In P. J. Vinken & G. W. Bruyn (Eds.), *Handbook of clinical neurology* (Vol. 14). New York: Elsevier.

Virag, R. (1999). Indications and early results of sildenafil (Viagra) in erectile dysfunction. *Urology, 54,* 1073–1077.

Visser, F. F., Aldenkamp, A. P., van Huffelen, A. C., Kuilman, M., Overweg, J., & van Wijk, J. (1997). Prospective study of the prevalence of Alzheimer-type dementia in institutionalized individuals with Down syndrome. *American Journal on Mental Retardation, 101,* 400–412.

Vitiello, B., & Lederhendler, I. (2000). Research on eating disorders: Current status and future prospects. *Biological Psychiatry, 47,* 777–786.

Vitousek, K., Watson, S., & Wilson, G. T. (1998). Enhancing motivation for change in treatment-resistant eating disorders. *Clinical Psychological Review, 18,* 391–420.

Voglmaier, M. M., Seidman, L. J., Niznikiewicz, M. A., Dickey, C. C., Shenton, M. E., & McCarley, R. W. (2000). Verbal and nonverbal neuropsychological test performance in subjects with schizotypal personality disorder. *American Journal of Psychiatry, 157,* 787–793.

Vohs, K. D., Bardone, A. M., Joiner, T. F., Jr., Abramson, L. Y., & Heatherton, T. F. (1999). Perfectionism, perceived weight status, and self-esteem interact to predict bulimic symptoms: A model of bulimic symptom development. *Journal of Abnormal Psychology, 108,* 695–700.

Vohs, K. D., Voelz, Z. R., Pettit, J. W., Bardone, A. M., Katz, J., Abramson, L. Y., ... Joiner, T. E., Jr. (2001). Perfectionism, body dissatisfaction, and self-esteem: An interactive model of bulimic symptom development. *Journal of Social and Clinical Psychology, 20,* 476–497.

Volkmar, F. R., & Cohen, D. J. (1991). Nonautistic pervasive developmental disorders. In R. Michels (Ed.), *Psychiatry* (pp. 201–210). Philadelphia: J. B. Lippincott.

Volkmar, F. R., & Klin, A. (2000). Diagnostic issues in Asperger syndrome. In A. Klin, F. R. Volkmar, & S. S. Sparrow (Eds.), *Asperger syndrome* (pp. 25–71). New York: Guilford Press.

Volkmar, F. R., Klin, A., & Schultz, R. T. (2005). Pervasive developmental disorders. In B. J. Sadock & V. A. Sadock (Eds.), *Kaplan & Sadock's comprehensive textbook of psychiatry* (pp. 3164–3182). Philadelphia: Lippincott Williams & Wilkins.

Volkmar, F. R., Klin, A., Siegel, B., Szatmari, P., Lord, C., Campbell, M., ... Towbin, K. (1994). Field trial for autistic disorder in DSM-IV. *American Journal of Psychiatry, 151,* 1361–1367.

Volkmar, F. R., Szatmari, P., & Sparrow, S. S. (1993). Sex differences in pervasive developmental disorders. *Journal of Autism and Developmental Disorders, 23,* 579–591.

Volkow, N. D., & Swanson, J. M. (2003). Variables that affect the clinical use and abuse of methylphenidate in the treatment of ADHD. *American Journal of Psychiatry, 160,* 1909–1918.

Volkow, N. D., Wang, G. J., Kollins, S. H., Wigal, T. L., Newcorn, J. H., Telang, F., ... Swanson, J. M. (2009). Evaluating dopamine reward pathway in ADHD: Clinical implications. *JAMA, 302*(10), 1084–1091.

Von Knorring, A. L., Cloninger, C. R., Bohman, M., & Sigvardsson, S. (1983). An adoption study of depressive disorders and substance abuse. *Archives of General Psychiatry, 40,* 943–950.

von Ranson, K. M., Iacono, W. G., & McGue, M. (2002). Disordered eating and substance use in an epidemiological sample: I. Associations within individuals. *International Journal of Eating Disorders, 31,* 389–403.

Voyer, P., McCusker, J., Cole, M. G., St-Jacques, S., & Khomenko, L. (2007). Factors associated with delirium severity among older patients. *Journal of Clinical Nursing, 16,* 819–831.

Voyer P., Verreault R., Mengue P., & Morin, M. C. (2006). Prevalence of insomnia and its associated factors in older long-term care residents. *Archives in Gerontology and Geriatrics,* 42, 1–20.

Vuchinich, S., Bank, L., & Patterson, G. R. (1992). Parenting, peers, and the stability of antisocial behavior in preadolescent boys. *Developmental Psychology, 28,* 510–521.

Waddell, J., Morris, R. W., & Bouton, M. E. (2006). Effects of bed nucleus of the stria terminalis lesions on conditioned anxiety: Aversive conditioning with long-duration conditional stimuli and reinstatement of extinguished fear. *Behavioral Neuroscience, 120,* 324–336.

Wadsworth, S. J., DeFries, J. C., Stevenson, J., Gilger, J. W., & Pennington, B. F. (1992). Gender ratios among reading-disabled children and their siblings as a function of parent impairment. *Journal of Child Psychology and Psychiatry, 33,* 1229–1239.

Wagner, A. W., & Linehan, M. M. (1994). Relationship between childhood sexual abuse and topography of parasuicide among women with borderline personality disorder. *Journal of Personality Disorders, 8,* 1–9.

Wagner, B. M. (1997). Family risk factors for child and adolescent suicidal behavior. *Psychological Bulletin, 121,* 246–298.

Wagner, M. (1990, April). *The school programs and school performance of secondary students classified as learning disabled: Findings from the National Longitudinal Transition Study of special education students.* Paper presented at Division G, American Educational Research Association Annual Meeting, Boston.

Wahlbeck, K., Cheine, M., Essali, A., & Adams, C. (1999). Evidence of clozapine's effectiveness in schizophrenia: a systematic review and metaanalysis of randomized trials. *American Journal of Psychiatry, 156,* 990–999.

Wakefield, J. C. (1992). The concept of mental disorder: On the boundary between biological facts and social values. *American Psychologist, 47,* 373–388.

Wakefield, J. C. (1999). Evolutionary versus prototype analyses of the concept of disorder. *Journal of Abnormal Psychology, 108, 3,* 374–399.

Wald, J. (2002). *The efficacy of virtual reality exposure therapy to treat driving phobia.* Unpublished doctoral dissertation, Department of Counseling Psychology, University of British Columbia.

Wald, J. (2004). Efficacy of virtual reality exposure therapy for driving phobia: A multiple baseline across subjects design. *Behavior Therapy, 35,* 621–635.

Wald, J., & Taylor, S. (2000). Efficacy of virtual reality exposure therapy to treat driving phobia: A case report. *Journal of Behavior Therapy & Experimental Psychiatry, 31,* 249–257.

Wald, J., Taylor, S., & Scamvougeras, A. (2004). Cognitive-behavioural and neuropsychiatric treatment of post-traumatic conversion disorder: A case study. *Cognitive Behaviour Therapy, 33*(1), 12–20.

Waldman, I. D., & Gizer, I. R. (2006). The genetics of attention deficit hyperactivity disorder. *Clinical Psychology Review, 26*(4), 396–432.

Waliszewski, B., & Smithouser, B. (1997). *Plugged in music review—Sarah McLachlan* [Review of the album Surfacing]. Retrieved June 25, 2004, from http://www.pluggedinonline.com/music/music/a0001196.cfm

Walker, D., Thompson, A., Zwaigenbaum, L., Goldberg, J., Bryson, S., Mahoney, W. J., ... Szatmari, P. (2004). Specifying PDD-NOS: A comparison of PDD-NOS, Asperger syndrome, and autism. *Journal of the American Academy of Child and Adolescent Psychiatry, 43,* 172–180.

Walker, F. (1991). Research on life-span development in schizophrenia. In F. F. Walker (Ed.), *Schizophrenia: A life-course developmental perspective* (pp. 1–6). New York: Academic Press.

Walker, F. F., Grimes, K. E., Davis, D. M., & Smith, A. J. (1993). Childhood precursors of schizophrenia: Facial expressions of emotion. *American Journal of Psychiatry, 150,* 1654–1660.

Walker, J. R., & Furer, P. (2006). Treatment of hypochondriasis and psychogenic movement

disorders: Focus on cognitive-behavior therapy. In M. Hallett, S. Fahn, J. Jankovic, A. F. Lang, et al. (Eds.), *Psychogenic movement disorders: Neurology and neuropsychiatry* (pp. 163–179). Philadelphia: Lippincott Williams & Wilkins Publishers.

Walker, L. (1979). *The battered woman.* New York: Harper & Row.

Wallace, C. S., Kilman, V. L., Withers, G. S., & Greenough, W. T. (1992). Increases in dendritic length in occipital cortex after 4 days of differential housing in weanling rats. *Behavioral and Neural Biology, 58,* 64–68.

Wallace, J., & O'Hara, M. W. (1992). Increases in depressive symptomatology in the rural elderly: Results from a cross-sectional and longitudinal study. *Journal of Abnormal Psychology, 101,* 398–404.

Waller, N. G., Putnam, F. W., & Carlson, F. B. (1996). Types of dissociation and dissociative types: A taxometric analysis of dissociative experiences. *Psychological Methods, 1,* 300–321.

Waller, N. G., & Ross, C. A. (1997). The prevalence and biometric structure of pathological dissociation in the general population: Taxometric and behavior genetic findings. *Journal of Abnormal Psychology, 106,* 499–510.

Walsh, B. T. (1991). Fluoxetine treatment of bulimia nervosa. *Journal of Psychosomatic Research, 35,* 471–475.

Walsh, B. T. (1995). Pharmacotherapy of eating disorders. In K. D. Brownell & C. G. Fairburn (Eds.), *Eating disorders and obesity: A comprehensive handbook* (pp. 313–317). New York: Guilford Press.

Walsh, B. T., Agras, W. S., Devlin, M. J., Fairburn, C. G., Wilson, G. T., Kahn, C., & Chally, M. K. (2000). Fluoxetine for bulimia nervosa following poor response to psychotherapy. *American Journal of Psychiatry, 157,* 1332–1334.

Walsh, B. T., Hadigan, C. M., Devlin, M. J., Gladis, M., & Roose, S. P. (1991). Long-term outcome of antidepressant treatment of bulimia nervosa. *Archives of General Psychiatry, 148,* 1206–1212.

Walsh, B. T., Wilson G. T., Loeb, K. L., Devlin, M. J., Pike, K. M., Roose, S. P., ... Waternaux, C. (1997). Medication and psychotherapy in the treatment of bulimia nervosa. *American Journal of Psychiatry, 154,* 523–531.

Walsh, J. K., Mayleben, D., Guico-Pabia, C., Vandormael, K., Martinez, R., & Deacon, S. (2008). Efficacy of the selective extrasynaptic GABA A agonist, gaboxadol, in a model of transient insomnia: A randomized, controlled clinical trial. *Sleep Medicine, 9*(4), 393–402.

Walsh, J. K., & Ustun, T. B. (1999). Prevalence and health consequences of insomnia. *Sleep, 22*(Suppl. 3), S427–S436.

Walsh, N. P. (2001, October 14). I never discuss my mistresses or my tailors. *The Observer.* Retrieved October 25, 2003, from http://observer.guardian.co.uk/life/story/0,6903,573496,00.html

Walsh, T. M., Stewart, S. H., McLaughlin, F., & Comeau, N. (2004). Gender differences in Childhood Anxiety Sensitivity Index (CASI) dimensions. *Journal of Anxiety Disorders, 18,* 695–706.

Walters, F. F., & Kendler, K. S. (1995). Anorexia nervosa and anorexia-like syndromes in a population based female twin sample. *American Journal of Psychiatry, 152,* 64–71.

Wampold, B. E., Minami, T., Tierney, S. C., Baskin, T. W., & Bhati, K. S. (2005). The placebo is powerful: Estimating placebo effects in medicine and psychotherapy from randomized clinical trials. *Journal of Clinical Psychology, 61*(7), 835–854.

Wang, J., & Patten, S. B. (2001). Perceived work stress and major depression in the Canadian employed population, 20–49 years old. *Journal of Occupational Health Psychology, 6,* 283–289.

Wang, J., & Patten, S. B. (2002). Prospective study of frequent heavy alcohol use and the risk of major depression in the Canadian general population. *Depression & Anxiety, 15,* 42–45.

Wang, P. S., Bohn, R. L., Glynn, R. J., Mogun, H., & Avorn, J. (2001). Hazardous benzodiazepine regimens in the elderly: Effects of half-life, dosage, and duration on risk of hip fracture. *American Journal of Psychiatry, 158,* 892–898.

Wang, Z., Neylan, T. C., Mueller, S. G., Lenoci, M., Truran, D., Marmar, C. R., ... Schuff, N. (2010). Magnetic resonance imaging of hippocampal subfields in posttraumatic stress disorder. *Archives of General Psychiatry, 67(3),* 296–303.

Wanklin, J. (1998). *Let me make it good: A chronicle of my life with borderline personality disorder* (chap. 15). Retrieved November 1, 2007, from http://www.geocities.com/anorexiannie/chapterfifteen.html

Ward, M. M., Swan, G. F., & Chesney, M. A. (1987). Arousal-reduction treatments for mild hypertension: A meta-analysis of recent studies. *Handbook of Hypertension, 9,* 285–302.

Ward, T., & Beech, A. R. (2008). An integrated theory of sexual offending. In D. R. Laws & W. T. O'Donohue (Eds.), *Sexual deviance: Theory, assessment, and treatment* (2nd ed., pp. 21–36). New York: Guilford Press.

Wardman, D., el-Guebaly, N., & Hodgins, D. (2001). Problem and pathological gambling in North American Aboriginal populations: A review of the empirical literature. *Journal of Gambling Studies, 17,* 81–100.

Warneke, L. B. (1991). Benzodiazepines: Abuse and new use. *Canadian Journal of Psychiatry, 36,* 194–205.

Warren, S. F., & Reichle, J. (1992). *Causes and effects in communication and language intervention.* Baltimore: Paul H. Brookes.

Warwick, H. M., & Salkovskis, P. M. (1990). Hypochondriasis. *Behaviour Research & Therapy, 28,* 105–117.

Warwick, H. M. C., Clark, D. M., Cobb, A. M., & Salkovskis, P. M. (1996). A controlled trail of cognitive-behavioural treatment of hypochondriasis. *British Journal of Psychiatry, 169,* 189–195.

Waschbusch, D. A. (2002). A meta-analytic examination of comorbid hyperactive-impulsive-attention problems and conduct problems. *Psychological Bulletin, 128,* 118–150.

Waschbusch, D. A., & Hill, G. P. (2001). Alternative treatments for children with attention-deficit/hyperactivity disorder: What does the research say? *Behavior Therapist, 24*(8), 161–171

Waschbusch, D. A., & Hill, G. P. (2003). Empirically supported, promising, and unsupported treatments for children with attention deficit/hyperactivity disorder. In S. O. Lilienfeld & S. J. Lynn (Eds.), *Science and pseudoscience in clinical psychology* (pp. 333–362). New York: Guilford Press.

Waschbusch, D. A., Kipp, H. L., & Pelham, W. F. Jr. (1998). Generalization of behavioral and psychostimulant treatment of attention-deficit/hyperactivity disorder (ADHD): Discussion and examples. *Behaviour Research & Therapy, 36,* 675–694.

Waschbusch, D. A., Pelham, W. F., Jr., & Massetti, G. (2005). The behavior education support and treatment (BFST) school intervention program: Pilot project data examining school wide, targeted-school, and targeted-home approaches. *Journal of Attention Disorders, 9,* 313–322.

Waterhouse, L., Wing, L., & Fein, D. (1989). Re-evaluating the syndrome of autism in light of empirical research. In G. Dawson (Ed.), *Autism: Nature, diagnosis and treatment* (pp. 263–281). New York: Guilford Press.

Waterhouse, L., Wing, L., Spitzer, R., & Siegel, B. (1992). Pervasive developmental disorders: From DSM-III to DSM-III-R. *Journal of Autism and Developmental Disorders, 22,* 525–549.

Waters, B. G. H. (1979). Early symptoms of bipolar affective psychosis: Research and clinical implications. *Canadian Psychiatric Association Journal, 2,* 55–60.

Watson, D. (2005). Rethinking the mood and anxiety disorders: A quantitative hierarchical model for DSM-V. *Journal of Abnormal Psychology, 114*[Special issue], 522–536.

Watson, D., Clark, L. A., & Harkness, A. R. (1994). Structures of personality and their relevance to psychopathology. *Journal of Abnormal Psychology, 103,* 18–31.

Watson, J. B. (1913). Psychology as a behaviorist views it. *Psychology Review, 20,* 158–177.

Watt, M. C., & Stewart, S. H. (2000). Anxiety sensitivity mediates the relationships between childhood learning experiences and elevated hypochondriacal concerns in young adulthood. *Journal of Psychosomatic Research, 49,* 107–118.

Watt, M. C., & Stewart, S. H. (2003). The role of anxiety sensitivity components in mediating the relationship between childhood exposure to parental dyscontrol and adult anxiety symptoms. *Journal of Psychopathology and Behavioral Assessment, 25,* 167–176.

Watt, M. C., Stewart, S. H., Birch, C. D., & Bernier, D. (2006). Brief CBT for high anxiety sensitivity decreases drinking problems, relief alcohol outcome expectancies, and conformity drinking motives: Evidence from a randomized controlled trial. *Journal of Mental Health, 15,* 683–695.

Watt, M. C., Stewart, S. H., & Cox, B. J. (1998). A retrospective study of the learning history origins of anxiety sensitivity. *Behaviour Research & Therapy, 36,* 505–525.

Way, B. M., & Taylor, S. E. (2010). Social influences on health: Is serotonin a critical mediator? *Psychosomatic Medicine, 72,* 107–112.

Weaver, I. C. G., Cervoni, N., Champagne, F. A., D'Alessio, A. C., Sharma, S., Seckl, J. R., ... Meaney, M. J. (2004). Epigenetic programming by maternal behavior. *Nature Neuroscience, 7*(8), 847–854.

Webster, C. D., Douglas, K. S., Faves, D., & Hart, S. D. (1997a). *HCR-20: Assessing risk for violence* (version 2). Vancouver, BC: Simon Fraser University.

Webster, C. D., Douglas, K. S., Faves, D., & Hart, S. D. (1997b). Assessing risk of violence to others. In C. D. Webster & M. A. Jackson (Eds.), *Impulsivity: Theory, assessment, and treatment* (pp. 251–277). New York: Guilford Press.

Webster-Stratton, C., & Hammond, M. (1997). Treating children with early-onset conduct problems: A comparison of child and parent training interventions. *Journal of Consulting and Clinical Psychology, 65,* 93–109.

Wechsler, D. (1997). *Wechsler Adult Intelligence Scale—Third Edition: Technical manual.* San Antonio, TX: The Psychological Corporation

Weems, C. F., Hayward, C., Killen, J., & Taylor, C. B. (2002). A longitudinal investigation of anxiety sensitivity in adolescence. *Journal of Abnormal Psychology, 111*(3), 471–477.

Weems, C. F., Silverman, W. K., & La Greca, A. M. (2000). What do youths referred for anxiety problems worry about? Worry and its relation to anxiety and anxiety disorders in children and adolescents. *Journal of Abnormal Child Psychology, 28,* 63–72.

Wegner, D. M. (1989). *White bear and other unwanted thoughts: Suppression, obsession, and the psychology of mental control.* New York: Guilford Press.

Wehr, T., Sack, D., Rosenthal, N. F., & Cowdry, R. W. (1988). Rapid cycling affective disorder: Contributing factors and treatment response on 51 patients. *American Journal of Psychiatry, 145,* 179–184.

Wehr, T. A., Goodwin, F. K., Wirz-Justice, A., Breitmeier, J., & Craig, C. (1982). Forty-eight-hour sleep-wake cycles in manic-depressive illness: Naturalistic observations and sleep-deprivation experiments. *Archives of General Psychiatry, 39,* 559–565.

Wehr, T. A., & Sack, D. A. (1988). The relevance of sleep research to affective illness. In W. P. Koella, F. Obal, H. Schulz, & P. Visser (Eds.), *Sleep '86* (pp. 207–211). New York: Gustav Fischer Verlag.

Weiden, P. J., Dixon, L., Frances, A., Appelbaum, P., Haas, G., & Rapkin, B. (1991). In C. A. Tamminga & S. C. Schulz (Eds.), *Advances in neuropsychiatry and psychopharmacology. 1: Schizophrenia research* (pp. 285–296). New York: Raven Press.

Weinberg, M. S., Lottes, I. L., & Shaver, F. M. (1995). Swedish or American youth: Who is more permissive? *Archives of Sexual Behavior, 24,* 409–437.

Weinberg, R. A. (1989). Intelligence and IQ: Landmark issues and great debates. *American Psychologist, 44,* 98–104.

Weinberger, D. R. (1995). Schizophrenia as a neurodevelopmental disorder. In S. R. Hirsch & D. R. Weinberger (Eds.), *Schizophrenia* (pp. 293–323). Oxford: Blackwell.

Weiner, D. B. (1979). The apprenticeship of Philippe Pinel: A new document, "Observations of Citizen Pussin on the insane." *American Journal of Psychiatry, 136,* 1128–1134.

Weiner, D. N. (1996). *Premature ejaculation: An evaluation of sensitivity to erotica.* Unpublished doctoral dissertation, State University of New York, Albany.

Weiner, J. M. (2000). Integration of nature and nurture: A new paradigm for psychiatry. *American Journal of Psychiatry, 157,* 1193–1194.

Weiner, M. F. (2003). Clinical diagnosis of cognitive dysfunction and dementing illness. In M. F. Wiener & A. M. Lipton (Eds.), *The dementias: Diagnosis, treatment and research* (3rd ed., pp. 219–283). Washington, DC: American Psychiatric Press.

Weiner, M. F., Hynan, L. S., Beekly, D., Koepsell, T. D., & Kukull, W. A. (2007). Comparison of Alzheimer's disease in American Indians, whites, and African Americans. *Alzheimer's & Dementia, 3*(3), 211–216.

Weiner, M. F., & Schneider, L. S. (2003). Drugs for behavioral, psychological, and cognitive symptoms. In M. F. Wiener & A. M. Lipton (Eds.), *The dementias: Diagnosis, treatment and research* (3rd ed., pp. 219–283). Washington, DC: American Psychiatric Press.

Weiner, M. W., Aisen, P. S., Jack, Jr., C. R., Jagust, W. J., Trojanowski, J. Q., Shaw, L., ...

Schmidt, M. (2010). The Alzheimer's Disease Neuroimaging Initiative: Progress report and future plans. *Alzheimer's and Dementia, 6*(3), 202–211, e207.

Weinshilboum, R. (2003). Inheritance and drug response. *New England Journal of Medicine, 348,* 529–537.

Weinstock, H., Berman, S., & Cates, W. (2004). Sexually transmitted diseases in American youth: Incidence and prevalence estimates. *Perspectives on Sexual and Reproductive Health, 36,* 6–10.

Weisburg, R. B., Brown, T. A., Wincze, J. P., & Barlow, D. H. (2001). Causal attributions and male sexual arousal: The impact of attributions for a bogus erectile difficulty on sexual arousal, cognitions, and affect. *Journal of Abnormal Psychology, 110,* 324–334.

Weiskrantz, L. (1980). Varieties of residual experience. *Quarterly Journal of Experimental Psychology, 32,* 365–386.

Weiskrantz, L. (1992, September/October). Unconscious vision: The strange phenomenon of blindsight. *The Sciences,* pp. 23–28.

Weisman, A. G. (1997). Understanding cross-cultural prognostic variability for schizophrenia. *Cultural Diversity and Mental Health, 3*(1), 23–35.

Weisman, A. G., & Lopez, S. R. (1997). An attributional analysis of emotional reactions to schizophrenia in Mexican and Anglo-Americans. *Journal of Applied Social Psychology, 27*(3), 223–244.

Weiss, M. D., Wasdell, M. B., Bomben, M. M., Rea, K. J., & Freeman, R. D. (2006). Sleep hygiene and melatonin treatment for children and adolescents with ADHD and initial insomnia. *Journal of the American Academy of Child and Adolescent Psychiatry, 45,* 512–519.

Weiss, R. D., & Iannucci, R. A. (2009). Cocaine-related disorders. In B. J. Sadock, V. A. Sadock, & P. Ruiz (Eds.), *Kaplan & Sadock's comprehensive textbook of psychiatry* (Vol. I, 9th ed., pp. 1318–1331). Philadelphia: Lippincott Williams & Wilkins.

Weisse, C. S. (1992). Depression and immune-competence: A review of the literature. *Psychological Bulletin, 111*(3), 475–489.

Weisse, C. S., Pato, C. W., McAllister, C. G., Littman, R., & Breier, A. (1990). Differential effects of controllable and uncontrollable acute stress on lymphocyte proliferation and leukocyte percentages in humans. *Brain, Behavior, and Immunity, 4,* 339–351.

Weissman, M. (1985). The epidemiology of anxiety disorders: Rates, risks, and familial patterns. In A. H. Tuma & J. D. Maser (Eds.), *Anxiety and the anxiety disorders.* Hillsdale, NJ: Erlbaum.

Weissman, M. (1995). *Mastering depression: A patient's guide to interpersonal psychotherapy.* Albany, NY: Graywind.

Weissman, M. M. (1993). The epidemiology of personality disorders: A 1990 update. *Journal of Personality Disorders, Supplement,* Spring, 44–62.

Weissman, M. M., Bland, R. C., Canino, G. J., Faravelli, C., Greenwald, S., Hwu, H.-G., … Yeh, E.-K. (1994). The cross national epidemiology of obsessive compulsive disorder. *Journal of Clinical Psychiatry, 55,* 5–10.

Weissman, M. M., Bland, R. C., Canino, G. J., Faravelli, C., Greenwald, S., Hwu, H.-G., … Yeh, E.-K. (1997). The cross-national epidemiology of panic disorder. *Archives of General Psychiatry, 54,* 305–312.

Weissman, M. M., Bland, R. C., Canino, G. J., Faravelli, C., Greenwald, S., Hwu, H.-G., …

Yeh, E.-K. (1996). Cross-national epidemiology of major depression and bipolar disorder. *JAMA, 276,* 293–299.

Weissman, M. M., Bland, R. C., Canino, G. J., Greenwald, S., Lee, C.-K., Newman, S. C., … Wickramaratne, P. J. (1996). The cross-national epidemiology of social phobia: A preliminary report. *International Clinical Psychopharmacology, 11,* 9–14.

Weissman, M. M., Bruce, M. L., Leaf, P. J., Florio, L. P., & Holzer, C. (1991). Affective disorders. In L. N. Robins & D. A. Regier (Eds.), *Psychiatric disorders of America: The epidemiologic catchment area study* (pp. 53–80). New York: Free Press.

Weissman, M. M., & Klerman, G. L. (1977). Sex differences and the epidemiology of depression. *Archives of General Psychiatry, 34,* 98–111.

Weissman, M. M., Klerman, G. L., Markowitz, J. S., & Ouellette, R. (1989). Suicidal ideation and suicide attempts in panic disorder and attacks. *New England Journal of Medicine, 321,* 1209–1214.

Weissman, M. M., & Markowitz, J. C. (1994). Interpersonal psychotherapy: Current status. *Archives of General Psychiatry, 51,* 599–606.

Weissman, M. M., & Olfson, M. (1995). Depression in women: Implications for health care research. *Science, 269,* 799–801.

Weitze, C., & Osburg, S. (1996). Transsexualism in Germany: Empirical data on epidemiology and application of the German transsexuals' act during its first ten years. *Archives of Sexual Behavior, 25,* 409–465.

Wekerle, C., & Wall, A.-M. (Eds.). (2002). *The violence and addiction equation: Theoretical and clinical issues in substance abuse and relationship violence.* New York: Brunner-Routledge.

Weller, F. B., & Weller, R. A. (1988). Neuroendocrine changes in affectively ill children and adolescents. *Endocrinology and Metabolism Clinics of North America, 17,* 41–53.

Wells, K. B., Stewart, A., Hays, R. D., Burnam, M. A., Rogers, W., Daniels, M., … Ware, J. (1989). The functioning and well-being of depressed patients: Results from the medical outcomes study. *JAMA, 262*(7), 914–919.

Wenden v. Trikha (1991), 116 A. R. 81 (Q. B.).

Wender, P. H., Kety, S. S., Rosenthal, D., Schlusinger, F., Ortmann, J., & Lunde, I. (1986). Psychiatric disorders in the biological and adoptive families of adopted individuals with affective disorders. *Archives of General Psychiatry, 43,* 923–929.

Wermter, A.-K., Kamp-Becker, I., Hesse, P., Schulte-Körne, G., Strauch, K., & Remschmidt, H. (2010). Evidence for the involvement of genetic variation in the oxytocin receptor gene (OXTR) in the etiology of autistic disorders on high-functioning level. *American Journal of Medical Genetics Part B: Neuropsychiatric Genetics, 153B*(2), 629–639.

Westen, D. (1997). Divergence between clinical and research methods for assessing personality disorders: Implications for research and the evolution of Axis II. *American Journal of Psychiatry, 154,* 895–903.

Westen, D. (2000). The efficacy of dialectical behavior therapy for borderline personality disorder. *Clinical Psychology: Science and Practice, 7,* 92–94.

Westermeyer, J. (1989). *Mental health for refugees and other migrants: Social and preventive approach.* Springfield, IL: C. C. Thomas.

Westphal, C. (1871). Die Agoraphobia: Fine neuropathische Fischeinung. *Archives für Psychiatrie und Nervenkrankheiten, 3,* 384–412.

Westra, H. A., & Stewart, S. H. (1998). Cognitive behavioural therapy and pharmacotherapy: Complementary or contradictory approaches to the treatment of anxiety? *Clinical Psychology Review, 18,* 307–340.

Westra, H. A., & Stewart, S. H. (2002). As-needed use of benzodiazepines in managing clinical anxiety: Incidence and implications. *Current Pharmaceutical Design, 8,* 59–74.

Westra, H. A., Stewart, S. H., Teehan, M., Johl K., Dozois D. J. A., & Hill, T. (2004). Benzodiazepine use associated with decreased memory for psychoeducation material in cognitive behavioral therapy for panic disorder. *Cognitive Therapy and Research, 28,* 193–208.

Wetherell, J. L., Thorp, S. R., Patterson, T. L., Golshan, S., Jeste, D. V., & Gatz, M. (2004). Quality of life in geriatric generalized anxiety disorder: A preliminary investigation. *Journal of Psychiatric Research, 38,* 305–312.

Wetter, D. W., Smith, S. S., Kenford, S. L., Jorenby, D. F., Fiore, M. C., Hurt, R. D., … Baker, T. B. (1994). Smoking outcome expectancies: Factor structure, predictive validity, and discriminant validity. *Journal of Abnormal Psychology, 103,* 801–811.

Wexler, N. S., Lorimer, J., Porter, J., Gomez, F., Moskowitz, C., Shackell, F., … Landwehrmeyer, B. (2004). Venezuelan kindreds reveal that genetic and environmental factors modulate Huntington's disease age of onset. *Proceedings of the National Academy of Science, 101,* 3498–3503.

Wexler, N. S., & Rawlins, M. D. (2005). Prejudice in a portrayal of Huntington's disease. *Lancet, 366*(9491), 1069–1070.

Whiffen, V. F. (1992). Is postpartum depression a distinct diagnosis? *Clinical Psychology Review, 12*(5), 485–508.

Whiffen, V. F. (2003). Looking outward together: Adult attachment and childbearing depression. In S. M. Johnson & V. F. Whiffen (Eds.), *Attachment processes in couple and family therapy* (pp. 321–341). New York: Guilford Press.

Whiffen, V. F. (2004). Myths and mates in childbearing depression. *Women & Therapy, 27,* 151–164.

Whiffen, V. F., & Clark, S. F. (1997). Does victimization account for sex differences in depressive symptoms? *British Journal of Clinical Psychology, 36,* 185–193.

Whiffen, V. F., & Demidenko, N. (2006). Mood disturbance across the life span. In J. Worell & C. D. Goodheart (Fds), *Handbook of girls' and women's psychological health: Gender and well-being across the lifespan* (pp. 51–59). New York: Oxford University Press, 2006.

Whiffen, V. F., & Gotlib, I. H. (1989a). Infants of postpartum depressed mothers: Temperament and cognitive status. *Journal of Abnormal Psychology, 98,* 274–279.

Whiffen, V. F., & Gotlib, I. H. (1989b). Stress and coping in maritally distressed and nondistressed couples. *Journal of Social and Personal Relationships, 6*(3), 327–344.

Whiffen, V. F., & Gotlib, I. H. (1993). Comparison of postpartum and nonpostpartum depression: Clinical presentation, psychiatric history, and psychosocial functioning. *Journal of Consulting and Clinical Psychology, 61*(3), 485–494.

Whisman, M., Weinstock, L., & Tolejko, N. (2006). Marriage and depression. In L. M. Corey & S. Goodman (Eds.), *A handbook for the social, behavioral, and biomedical sciences* (pp. 219–240). Boulder, CO: Cambridge University Press.

White, D. P. (2000). Central sleep apnea. In M. H. Kryger, T. Roth, & W. C. Dement (Eds.), *Principles and practice of sleep medicine* (3rd ed., pp. 827–839). Philadelphia: W. B. Saunders.

White, J. L., Moffitt, T. F., & Silva, P. A. (1989). A prospective replication of the protective effects of IQ in subjects at high risk for juvenile delinquency. *Journal of Consulting and Clinical Psychology, 57,* 719–724.

White, K., Lehman, D. R., Hemphill, K. J., Mandel, D. R., & Lehman, A. M. (2006). Causal attributions, perceived control, and psychological adjustment: A study of chronic fatigue syndrome. *Journal of Applied Social Psychology, 36*(1), 75–99.

White, K. S., & Barlow, D. H. (2002). Panic disorder with agoraphobia. In D. H. Barlow (Ed.), *Anxiety and its disorders: The nature and treatment of anxiety and panic* (2nd ed.). New York: Guilford Press.

White, W., & Kurtz, E. (2008). Twelve defining moments in the history of Alcoholics Anonymous. In M. Galanter & L. A. Kaskutas (Eds.), *Research on Alcoholics Anonymous and spirituality in addiction recovery: The twelve-step program model, spiritually oriented recovery, twelve-step membership, effectiveness and outcome research* (pp. 37–57). New York: Springer-Verlag.

Whitehurst, G. J., Fischel, J. F., Lonigan, C. J., Valdez-Menchaca, M. C., DeBaryshe, B. D., & Caulfield, M. B. (1988). Verbal interaction in families of normal and expressive-language-delayed children. *Developmental Psychology, 24,* 690–699.

Whitley, R., Kirmayer, L., & Groleau, D. (2006). Understanding immigrants' reluctance to use mental health services: A qualitative study from Montreal. *Canadian Journal of Psychiatry, 51*(4), 205–209.

Whitnam, F. L., Diamond, M., & Martin, J. (1993). Homosexual orientation in twins: A report on 61 pairs and three triplet sets. *Archives of Sexual Behavior, 22*(3), 187–206.

Whitney, C. W., Enright, P. L., Newman, A. B., Bonekat, W., Foley, D., & Quan, S. F. (1998). Correlates of daytime sleepiness in 4578 elderly persons: The cardiovascular health study. *Sleep, 21,* 27–36.

Whittal, M. L., Agras, W. S., & Gould, R. A. (1999). *Behavior Therapy, 30,* 117–135.

Whittal, M. L., Thordarson, D. S., & McLean, P. D. (2005). Treatment of obsessive-compulsive disorder: Cognitive behavior therapy vs. exposure and response prevention. *Behaviour Research and Therapy, 43,* 1559–1576.

Wichmann, C., Serin, R., & Motiuk, L. (2000). *Predicting suicide attempts among male offenders in federal penitentiaries.* Ottawa, ON: Correctional Service of Canada.

Wickramaratne, P. J., Weissman, M. M., Leaf, D. J., & Holford, T. R. (1989). Age, period and cohort effects on the risk of major depression: Results from five United States communities. *Journal of Clinical Epidemiology, 42,* 333–343.

Widaman, K. F. (2009). Phenylketonuria in children and mothers: Genes, environments, behavior. *Current Directions in Psychological Science, 18*(1), 48c52.

Widiger, T. A. (1991). Personality disorder dimensional models proposed for the DSM-IV. *Journal of Personality Disorders, 5,* 386–398.

Widiger, T. A. (1993). The DSM-III-R categorical personality disorder diagnoses: A critique and an alternative. *Psychological Inquiry, 4,* 75–90.

Widiger, T. A. (1997). Mental disorders as discrete clinical conditions: Dimensional versus categorical classification. In S. M. Turner & M. Hersen (Eds.), *Adult psychopathology and diagnosis* (3rd ed., pp. 3–23). New York: John Wiley & Sons.

Widiger, T. A., & Coker, L. A. (2003). Mental disorders as discrete clinical conditions: Dimensional versus categorical classification. In M. Hersen & S. M. Turner (Eds.), *Adult psychopathology and diagnosis* (4th ed., pp. 3–35). New York: John Wiley & Sons.

Widiger, T. A., & Corbitt, F. M. (1995). Antisocial personality disorder. In W. J. Livesley (Ed.), *The DSM-IV personality disorders* (pp. 103–126). New York: Guilford Press.

Widiger, T. A., & Edmundson, M. (in press). Diagnoses, dimensions, and DSM V. In D. H. Barlow (Ed.), *Handbook of clinical psychology.* New York: Oxford University Press.

Widiger, T. A., Frances, A. J., Pincus, H. A., Ross, R., First, M. B., & Davis, W. W. (Eds.). (1996). *DSM-IV sourcebook* (Vol. 2). Washington, DC: American Psychiatric Association.

Widiger, T. A., Frances, A. J., Pincus, H. A., Ross, R., First, M. B., Davis, W. W., et al. (Eds.). (1998). *DSM-IV sourcebook* (Vol. 4). Washington, DC: American Psychiatric Association.

Widiger, T. A., Livesley, W. J., & Clark, L. A. (2009). An integrative dimensional classification of personality disorder. *Psychological Assessment, 21*(3), 243–255.

Widiger, T. A., & Rogers, J. H. (1989). Prevalence and comorbidity of personality disorders. *Psychiatry Annual, 19,* 132.

Widiger, T. A., & Samuel, D. B. (2005). Diagnostic categories or dimensions? A question for the diagnostic and statistical manual of mental disorders (5th ed.). *Journal of Abnormal Psychology, 114,* 494–504.

Widiger, T. A., & Sankis, L. M. (2000). Adult psycho-pathology: Issues and controversies. *Annual Review of Psychology, 51,* 377–404.

Widiger, T. A., & Spitzer, R. L. (1991). Sex bias in the diagnosis of personality disorders: Conceptual and methodological issues. *Clinical Psychology Review, 11,* 1–22.

Widiger, T. A., & Trull, T. J. (1993). Borderline and narcissistic personality disorders. In P. B. Sutker & H. F. Adams (Eds.), *Comprehensive handbook of psychopathology* (2nd ed., pp. 371–394). New York: Plenum Press.

Widiger, T. A., & Trull, T. J. (2007). Plate tectonics in the classification of personality disorder: Shifting to a dimensional model. *American Psychologist, 62*(2), 71.

Widiger, T. A., Trull, T. J., Clarkin, J. F., Sanderson, C., & Costa, P. T., Jr. (1994). A description of the DSM-III-R and DSM-IV personality disorders with the five-factor model of personality. In P. T. Costa, Jr. & T. A. Widiger (Eds.), *Personality disorders and the five-factor model of personality* (pp. 41–56). Washington, DC: American Psychological Association.

Widiger, T. A., & Weissman, M. M. (1991). Epidemiology of borderline personality disorder. *Hospital and Community Psychiatry, 42,* 1015–1021.

Widom, C. S. (1977). A methodology for studying noninstitutionalized psychopaths. *Journal of Consulting and Clinical Psychology, 45,* 674–683.

Widom, C. S. (Ed.) (1984). Sex roles, criminality, and psychopathology. In *Sex roles and psychopathology* (pp. 183–217). New York: Plenum Press.

Wiebe, R. F., & McCabe, S. B. (2002). Relationship perfectionism, dysphoria, and hostile interpersonal behaviors. *Journal of Social & Clinical Psychology, 21,* 67–91.

Wiegel, M., Wincze, J. P., & Barlow, D. H. (2001). Assessment, treatment planning, and outcome evaluation for sexual dysfunction. In M. M. Anthony & D. H. Barlow (Eds.), *Handbook of assessment, treatment planning, and outcome evaluation: Empirically supported strategies for psychological disorders.* New York: Guilford Press.

Wiegel, M., Wincze, J. P., & Barlow, D. H. (2002). Sexual dysfunction. In M. M. Antony & D. H. Barlow (Eds.), *Handbook of assessment and treatment planning for psychological disorders* (pp. 481–522). New York: Guilford Press.

Wilamowska, Z. A., Thompson-Hollands, J., Fairholme, C. P., Ellard, K. K., Farchione, T. J., & Barlow, D. H. (2010). Conceptual background, development, and preliminary data from the Unified Protocol for the Transdiagnostic Treatment of Emotional Disorders. *Depression and Anxiety, 27*(10), 882–890.

Wilcox, H. C., Storr, C. L., & Breslau, N. (2009). Posttraumatic stress disorder and suicide attempts in a community sample of urban American young adults. *Archives of General Psychiatry, 66*(3), 305–311.

Wilfley, D. F., Schwartz, J. N. B., Spurrell, B., & Fairburn, C. G. (2000). Using the Eating Disorder Examination to identify the specific psychopathology of binge eating disorder. *International Journal of Eating Disorders, 27,* 259–269.

Wilfley, D. F., & Rodin, J. (1995). Cultural influences on eating disorders. In K. D. Brownell & C. G. Fairburn (Eds.), *Eating disorders and obesity: A comprehensive handbook* (pp. 78–82). New York: Guildford Press.

Wilfley, D. F., Welch, R., Stein, R. I., Spurrell, F. B., Cohen, L. R., Saelens, B. F., … Matt, G. E. (2002). A randomized comparison of group cognitive-behavioral and group interpersonal psychotherapy for treatment of overweight individuals with binge-eating disorder. *Archives of General Psychiatry, 59,* 713–721.

Wilgosh, L., Mulcahy, R., & Watters, B. (1986). Assessing intellectual performance of culturally different, Inuit children with the WISC-R. *Canadian Journal of Behavioural Science, 18,* 270–277.

Wilhelm, S., Otto, M. W., Lohr, B., & Deckersbach, T. (1999). Cognitive behavior group therapy for body dysmorphic disorder: A case series. *Behaviour Research and Therapy, 37,* 71–75.

Wilkie, C., Macdonald, S., & Hildahl, K. (1998). Community case study: Suicide cluster in a small Manitoba community. *Canadian Journal of Psychiatry, 43,* 823–828.

Wilkins, K. L., McGrath, P. J., Finley, G. A., & Katz, J. (2004). Prospective diary study of nonpainful and painful phantom sensations in a preselected sample of child and adolescent amputees reporting phantom limbs. *Clinical Journal of Pain, 20*(5), 293–301.

Wilkins, R. (1985). A comparison of elective mutism and emotional disorders in children. *British Journal of Psychiatry, 146,* 198–203.

Wilkinson-Ryan, T., & Westen, D. (2000). Identity disturbance in borderline personality disorder: An empirical investigation. *American Journal of Psychiatry, 157,* 528–541.

Willi, J., & Grossman, S. (1983). Epidemiology of anorexia nervosa in a defined region of

Switzerland. *American Journal of Psychiatry, 140,* 564–567.

Williams, D. (1992). *Nobody nowhere: The extraordinary autobiography of an autistic.* New York: Times Books.

Williams, J., Hadjistavropoulos, T., & Sharpe, D. (2006). A meta-analysis of psychological and pharmacological treatments for body dysmorphic disorder. *Behaviour Research and Therapy, 44,* 99–111.

Williams, L. (1994). Recall of childhood trauma: A prospective study of women's memories of child sexual abuse. *Journal of Consulting and Clinical Psychology, 62,* 1167–1176.

Williams, R. B., Barefoot, J. C., & Schneiderman, N. (2003). Psychosocial risk factors for cardiovascular disease; More than one culprit at work. *JAMA, 290,* 2190–2192.

Williams, R. B., & Schneiderman, N. (2002). Resolved: Psychosocial interventions can improve clinical outcomes in organic disease (Pro). *Psychosomatic Medicine, 64,* 552–557.

Williams, R. B., Marchuk, D. A., Gadde, K. M., Barefoot, J. C., Grichnik, K., Helms, M. J., ... Siegler, I. C. (2001). Central nervous system serotonin function and cardiovascular responses to stress. *Psychosomatic Medicine, 63,* 300–305.

Williams, R. B., Jr., Haney, T. L., Lee, K. L., Kong, V., & Blumenthal, J. A. (1980). Type A behavior, hostility, and coronary atherosclerosis. *Psychosomatic Medicine, 42,* 529–538.

Williams, R. J., & Schmidt, G. G. (1993). Frequency of seasonal affective disorder among individuals seeking treatment at a northern Canadian mental health center. *Psychiatry Research, 46,* 41–45.

Williams, S., Connolly, J., & Segal, Z. V. (2001). Intimacy in relationships and cognitive vulnerability to depression in adolescent girls. *Cognitive Therapy & Research, 25,* 477–496.

Williams, W. L. (1986). *The spirit and the flesh: Sexual diversity in American Indian culture.* Boston: Beacon Press. (Reprint 1991, with a new preface).

Wills, T. A., Vaccaro, D., McNamara, G., & Hirky, A. F. (1996). Escalated substance use: A longitudinal grouping analysis from early to middle adolescence. *Journal of Abnormal Psychology, 105,* 166–180.

Wilson, G. T. (1977). Alcohol and human sexual behavior. *Behaviour Research and Therapy, 15,* 239–252.

Wilson, G. T. (1987). Cognitive studies in alcoholism. *Journal of Consulting and Clinical Psychology, 55,* 325–331.

Wilson, G. T. (1993). Psychological and pharmacological treatments of bulimia nervosa: A research update. *Applied and Preventive Psychology, 2,* 35–42.

Wilson, G. T., & Fairburn, C. G. (2002). Treatments for eating disorders. In P. F. Nathan & J. M. Gorma (Eds.), *A guide to treatments that work* (2nd ed., pp. 559–592). New York: Oxford University Press.

Wilson, G. T., Loeb, K. L., Walsh, B. T., Labouvie, F., Petkova, F., Liu, S., & Waternaux, C. (1999). Psychological versus pharmacological treatments of bulimia nervosa: Predictors and processes of change. *Journal of Consulting and Clinical Psychology, 67,* 451–459.

Wilson, G. T., & Pike, K. M. (2001). Eating disorders. In D. H. Barlow (Ed.), *Clinical handbook of psychological disorders* (3rd ed.). New York: Guilford Press.

Wilson, K. G., Sandler, L. S., Asmundson, G. J. G., Larsen, D. K., & Ediger, J. M. (1991). Effects

of instructional set on self-reports of panic attacks. *Journal of Anxiety Disorders, 5,* 43–63.

Wilson, R. S., Aggarwal, N. T., Barnes, L. L., Mendes de Leon, C. F., Hebert, L. E., & Evans, D. A. (2010). Cognitive decline in incident Alzheimer disease in a community population. *Neurology, 74*(12), 951–955.

Winchel, R. M., Stanley, B., & Stanley, M. (1990). Biochemical aspects of suicide. In S. J. Blumenthal & D. J. Kupfer (Eds.), *Suicide over the life cycle: Risk factors, assessment and treatment of suicidal patterns* (pp. 97–126). Washington, DC American Psychiatric Press.

Wincze, J. P. (2009). Enhancing sexuality: *A problem-solving approach to treating dysfunction: Therapist Guide* (2nd ed). New York: Oxford University Press.

Wincze, J. P., Bach, A., & Barlow, D. H. (2008). Sexual dysfunction. In D. H. Barlow (Ed.), *Clinical handbook of psychological disorders: A step-by-step treatment manual* (4th ed., pp. 615–661). New York: Guilford Press.

Wincze, J. P., & Barlow, D. H. (1997). *Enhancing sexuality: A problem-solving approach client workbook.* San Antonio, TX: Graywind Publications/The Psychological Corporation.

Wincze, J. P., & Carey, M. P. (1991). *Sexual dysfunction: A guide for assessment and treatment.* New York: Guilford Press.

Wincze, J. P., & Carey, M. P. (2001). *Sexual dysfunction: A guide for assessment and treatment.* New York: Guilford Press.

Windgassen, K. (1992). Treatment with neuroleptics: The patient's perspective. *Acta Psychiatrica Scandinavica, 86,* 405–410.

Winick, B. J. (1997). *The right to refuse mental health treatment.* Washington, DC: American Psychological Association.

Winkelman, J. W. (2006). Efficacy and tolerability of open-label topiramate in the treatment of sleep-related eating disorder: A retrospective case series. *Journal of Clinical Psychiatry, 67,* 1729–1734.

Winker, M. A. (1994). Tacrine for Alzheimer's disease: Which patient, what dose? *JAMA, 271,* 1023–1024.

Winokur, G. (1985). Familial psychopathology in delusional disorder. *Comprehensive Psychiatry, 26,* 241–248.

Winokur, G., Coryell, W., Endicott, J., & Akiskal, H. (1993). Further distinctions between manic-depressive illness (bipolar disorder) and primary depressive disorder (unipolar depression). *American Journal of Psychiatry, 150,* 1176–1181.

Winokur, G., Pfohl, B., & Tsuang, M. (1987). A 40-year follow-up of hebephrenic-catatonic schizophrenia. In N. Miller & G. Cohen (Eds.), *Schizophrenia and aging* (pp. 52–60). New York: Guilford Press.

Winter, A. (1998). *Mesmerized powers of mind in Victorian Britain.* Chicago, IL: University of Chicago Press.

Winters, R. W., & Schneiderman, N. (2000). Anxiety and coronary heart disease. In D. I. Mostofsky & D. H. Barlow (Eds.), *The management of stress and anxiety in medical disorders* (pp. 206–219). Needham Heights, MA: Allyn & Bacon.

Wirz-Justice, A. (1998). Beginning to see the light. *Archives of General Psychiatry, 55,* 861–862.

Wise, M. G., Gray, K. F., & Seltzer, B. (1999). Delirium, dementia, and amnestic disorders. In R. F. Hales, S. C. Judofsky, & J. A. Talbott, (Eds.), *Textbook of psychiatry* (3rd ed., pp. 317–362). Washington, DC: American Psychiatric Press.

Wise, M. G., Hilty, D. M., & Cerda, G. M. (2001). Delirium due to a general medical condition, delirium due to multiple etiologies, and delirium not otherwise specified. In G. O. Gabbard (Ed.), *Treatment of psychiatric disorders* (Vol. 1, 3rd ed., pp. 387–412). Washington, DC: American Psychiatric Press.

Wise, R. A. (1988). The neurobiology of craving: Implications for the understanding and treatment of addiction. *Journal of Abnormal Psychology, 97,* 118–132.

Wiseman, C. V., Gray, J. J., Mosimann, J. F., & Ahrens, A. H. (1992). Cultural expectations of thinness in women: An update. *International Journal of Eating Disorders, 11,* 85–89.

Wiseman, F. K., Alford, K. A., Tybulewicz, V. L. J., & Fisher, E. M. C. (2009). Down syndrome—recent progress and future prospects. *Human Molecular Genetics, 18*(R1), R75–R83.

Witherington, R. (1988). Suction device therapy in the management of erectile impotence. *Urologic Clinics of North America, 15,* 123–128.

Wittchen, H. -U., Becker, E., Lieb, R., & Krause, P. (2002). Prevalence, incidence and stability of premenstrual dysphoric disorder in the community. *Psychological Medicine, 32,* 119–132.

Wittchen, H. -U., Knauper, B., & Kessler, R. C. (1994). Lifetime risk of depression. *British Journal of Psychiatry, 165*(Suppl. 26), 116–122.

Wittchen, H. -U., Zhao, S., Kessler, R. C., & Eaton, W. W. (1994). DSM-III-R generalized anxiety disorder in the national comorbidity survey. *Archives of General Psychiatry, 51,* 355–364.

Wittenberg, C. K. (1979, February 16). Kinsey report on homosexuality. *Psychiatric News, 1.*

Wolf, M. M. (1978). Social validity: The case for subjective measurement or how applied behavior analysis is finding its heart. *Journal of Applied Behavior Analysis, 11,* 203–214.

Wolf, S. S., Jones, D. W., Knable, M. B., Gorey, J. G., Lee, K. S., Hyde, T. M., ... Weinberger, D. R. (1996). Tourette syndrome: Prediction of phenotypic variation in monozygotic twins by caudate nucleus D2 receptor binding. *Science, 273,* 1225–1227.

Wolfe, D. A. (1991). *Preventing physical and emotional abuse of children.* New York: Guilford Press.

Wolff, S. (2000). Schizoid personality in childhood and Asperger syndrome. In A. Klin, F. R. Volkmar, & S. S. Sparrow (Eds.), *Asperger syndrome* (pp. 278–305). New York: Guilford Press.

Wolff, S., Townshed, R., McGuire, R. J., & Weeks, D. J. (1991). "Schizoid" personality in childhood and adult life. II: Adult adjustment and continuity with schizotypal personality disorder. *British Journal of Psychiatry, 159,* 615–620.

Wolf-Maier, K., Cooper, R. S., Banegas, J. R., Giampaoli, S., Hense, H., Joffres, M., ... Vescio, F. (2003). Hypertension prevalence and blood pressure levels in 6 European countries, Canada, and the United States. *JAMA, 289,* 2362–2369.

Wolfson, C., Wolfson, D. B., Asgharian, M., M'Lan, C. F., Ostbye, T., Rockwood, K., & Hogan, D. B. (2001). Clinical Progression of Dementia Study Group. A reevaluation of the duration of survival after the onset of dementia. *New England Journal of Medicine, 344,* 1111–1116.

Wolitzky-Taylor, K. B., Castriotta, N., Lenze, E. J., Stanley, M. A., & Craske, M. G. (2010). Anxiety disorders in older adults: A comprehensive review. *Depression and Anxiety, 27*(2), 190–211.

Wolpe, J. (1958). *Psychotherapy by reciprocal inhibition.* Stanford, CA: Stanford University Press.

Wonderlich, S. A., Gordon, K. H., Mitchell, J. E., Crosby, R. D., & Engel, S. G. (2009). The validity and clinical utility of binge eating disorder. *International Journal of Eating Disorders, 42*(8), 687–705.

Wood, F., & Kerr, T. (2006). What do you do when you hit rock bottom? Responding to drugs in the city of Vancouver. *International Journal of Drug Policy, 17*(2), 55–60.

Wood, F., Kerr, T., Small, W., Li, K., Marsh, D. C., Montaner, J. S. G., & Tyndall, M. W. (2004). Changes in public order after the opening of a medically supervised safer-injecting facility for illicit injection drug users. *Canadian Medical Association Journal, 171*(7), 731–734.

Wood, F., Tyndall, M. W., Qui, Z., Zhang, R., Montaner, J. S. G., & Kerr, T. (2006). Service uptake and characteristics of injection drug users utilizing North America's first medically supervised safer injecting facility. *American Journal of Public Health, 96*(5), 770–773.

Wood, J. M., Nezworski, M. T., & Stejskal, W. J. (1996). The comprehensive system for the Rorschach: A critical examination. *Psychological Science, 7,* 3–17.

Woodman, C. L., Noyes, R., Black, D. W., Schlosser, S., & Yagla, S. J. (1999). A 5-year follow-up study of generalized anxiety disorder and panic disorder. *Journal of Nervous and Mental Disease, 187,* 3–9.

Woods, F. R., Lin, Y. G., Middleman, A., Beckford, P., Chase, L., & DuRant, R. H. (1997). The associations of suicide attempts in adolescents. *Pediatrics, 99,* 791–796.

Woodside, D. B., Bulik, C. M., Halmi, K. A., Fichter, M. M., Kaplan, A., Berrettini, W. H., . . . Kaye, W. H. (2002). Personality, perfectionism, and attitudes towards eating in parents of individuals with eating disorders. *International Journal of Eating Disorders, 31,* 290–299.

Woodside, D. B., Bulik, C. M., Thornton, L., Klump, K. L., Tozzi, F., Fichter, M. M., . . . Kaye, W. H. (2004). Personality in men with eating disorders. *Journal of Psychosomatic Research, 57,* 273–278.

Woodside, D. B., Garfinkel, P. F., Lin, F., Goering, P., & Kaplan, A. S. (2001). Comparisons of men with full or partial eating disorders, men without eating disorders, and women with eating disorders in the community. *American Journal of Psychiatry, 158,* 570–574.

Woodworth, M., Peace, K. A., O'Donnell, C., & Porter, S. (2003). Forensic community programs: Recommendations for the management of NCRMD patients in the community. *Journal of Forensic Psychology Practice, 3,* 1–22.

Woodworth, M., & Porter, S. (2002). In cold blood: Characteristics of criminal homicides as a function of psychopathy. *Journal of Abnormal Psychology, 111,* 436–445.

Woody, G. F., & Cacciola, J. (1997). Diagnosis and classification: DSM-IV and ICD-10. In J. H. Lowinson, P. Ruiz, R. B. Millman, & J. G. Langrod (Eds.), *Substance abuse: A comprehensive textbook* (pp. 361–363). Baltimore: Williams & Wilkins.

Woolfolk, R. L., & Allen, L. A. (in press). Somatoform and physical disorders. In D. H. Barlow (Ed.), *Handbook of Clinical Psychology.* New York: Oxford University Press.

Wootton, J. M., Frick, P. J., Shelton, K. K., & Silverthorn, P. (1997). Ineffective parenting and childhood conduct problems: The moderating role of callous-unemotional traits. *Journal*

of *Consulting and Clinical Psychology, 65,* 301–308.

Worell, J., & Remer, P. (1992). *Feminist perspectives in therapy: An empowerment model for women.* New York: John Wiley & Sons.

World Health Organization (1992). *The ICD-10 classification of mental and behavioural disorders: Clinical descriptions and diagnostic guidelines.* Geneva, Switzerland.

World Health Organization. (2000). *Multisite intervention study on suicidal behaviours—SUPREMISS: Components and instruments.* Geneva, Switzerland: World Health Organization, Department of Mental Health and Substance Dependence.

Wulfert, F., Greenway, D. F., & Dougher, M. J. (1996). A logical functional analysis of reinforcement-based disorders: Alcoholism and pedophilia. *Journal of Consulting and Clinical Psychology, 64*(6), 1140–1151.

Wyatt v. Stickney, 344 F. Supp. 373 (Ala. 1972).

Wyllie, F., Glazer, J. P., Benbaids, S., Kotagal, P., & Wolgamuth, B. (1999). Psychiatric features of children and adolescents with pseudoseizures. *Archives of Pediatric and Adolescent Medicine, 153*(3), 244–248.

Wynne, L. C., Tienari, P., Nieminen, P., Sorri, A., Lahti, I. O., Moring, J., . . . Miettunen, J. (2006). I. Genotype-environment interaction in the schizophrenia spectrum: Genetic liability and global family ratings in the Finnish Adoption Study. *Family Process, 45*(4), 419–434.

Xing, G., Zhang, L., Russell, S., & Post, R. (2006). Reduction of dopamine-related transcription factors Nurr1 and NGFI-B in the prefrontal cortex in schizophrenia and bipolar disorders. *Schizophrenia Research, 84,* 36–56.

Yairi, F., & Ambrose, N. (1992). Onset of stuttering in preschool children: Selected factors. *Journal of Speech and Hearing Research, 35,* 782–788.

Yan, L. L., Liu, K., Matthews, K. A., Daviglus, M. L., Ferguson, T. F., & Kiefe, C. I. (2003). Psychosocial risk factors and risk of hypertension: The coronary artery risk development in young adults (CARDIA) study. *JAMA, 290,* 2138–2148.

Yang, J., Bagby, M., Costa, P. T. Jr., Ryder, A. G., & Herbst, J. H. (2002). Assessing the DSM-IV structure of personality disorder with a sample of Chinese psychiatric patients. *Journal of Personality Disorders, 16,* 317–331.

Yatham, L., Liddle, P. F., Shiah, I.-S., Lam, R. W., Ngan, F., Scarrow, G., . . . Ruth, T. J. (2002). PET study of [^{18}F]6–fluoro-L-dopa uptake in neuroleptic- and mood-stabilizer-naive first-episode nonpsychotic mania: Effects of treatment with divalproex sodium. *American Journal of Psychiatry, 159,* 768–774.

Yatham, L. N., Kennedy, S. H., O'Donovan, C., Parikh, S. V., MacQueen, G., McIntyre, R. S., . . . Beaulieu, S., CANMAT guidelines group (2006). Canadian Network for Mood and Anxiety Treatments (CANMAT) guidelines for the management of patients with bipolar disorder: Update 2007. *Bipolar Disorders, 8,* 721–739.

Ye, X., Mitchell, M., Newman, K., & Batshaw, M. L. (2001). Prospects for prenatal gene therapy in disorders causing mental retardation. *Mental Retardation and Developmental Disabilities Research Review, 7,* 65–72.

Yeaton, W. H., & Bailey, J. S. (1978). Teaching pedestrian safety skills to young children: An analysis and one-year follow-up. *Journal of Applied Behavior Analysis, 11,* 315–329.

Yeh, A. H., Taylor, S., Thordarson, D. S., & Corcoran, K. M. (2003). Efficacy of telephone-administered CBT for obsessive-compulsive spectrum disorders: Case studies. *Cognitive Behaviour Therapy, 32*(2), 75–81.

Yerkes, R. M., & Dodson, J. D. (1908). The relation of strength of stimulus to rapidity of habit-formation. *Journal of Comprehensive Neurologic and Psychology, 18,* 459–482.

Yeung, A., Yong X., & Chang, D. F. (2005). Prevalence and illness beliefs of sleep paralysis among Chinese psychiatric patients in China and the United States. *Transcultural Psychiatry, 42,* 135–145.

Yonkers, K. A., Warshaw, M., Massion, A. O., & Keller, M. B. (1996). Phenomenology and course of generalized anxiety disorder. *British Journal of Psychiatry, 168,* 308–313.

Young, A. M., & Herling, S. (1986). Drugs as reinforcers: Studies in laboratory animals. In S. R. Goldberg & I. P. Stolerman (Eds.), *Behavioral analysis of drug dependence* (pp. 9–67). Orlando, FL: Academic Press.

Young, A. R., & Beitchman, J. H. (2001). Learning disorders. In G. O. Gabbard (Ed.), *Treatment of psychiatric disorders* (Vol. 1, 3rd ed., pp. 109–124). Washington, DC: American Psychiatric Press.

Young, A. R., Beitchman, J. H., Johnson, C., Douglas, L., Atkinson, L., Escobar, M., & Wilson, B. (2002). Young adult academic outcomes in a longitudinal sample of early identified language impaired and control children. *Journal of Child Psychology and Psychiatry, 43,* 635–645.

Young, J., Rygh, J., Weinberger, A., & Beck, A.T. (2008). Cognitive therapy for depression. In Barlow, D. H. (Ed.), *Clinical handbook of psychological disorders* (4th ed., pp. 250–305). New York: Guilford Press.

Young, J. F., Weinberger, A. D., & Beck, A. T. (2001). Cognitive therapy for depression. In D. H. Barlow (Ed.), *Clinical handbook of psychological disorders* (3rd ed., pp. 264–308). New York: Guilford Press.

Young, R. (2007, August 8). Store owners to fight tobacco power-wall ban. *Transcontinental Media.* Retrieved September 1, 2007, from http:// novascotiabusinessjournal.com/index .cfm?sid50720&sc107

Yutzy, S. H., Cloninger, C. R., Guze, S. B., Pribor, F. F., Martin, R. L., Kathol, R. G., . . . Strain, J. J. (1995). DSM-IV field trial: Testing a new proposal for somatization disorder. *American Journal of Psychiatry, 152,* 97–101.

Zacharias, C. A., Goldberg, J., & Chapman, R. (1997, April). *Inspirational effects of a consumer-delivered cognitive therapy lecture.* Poster presented at McMaster University Department of Psychiatry, Annual Research Day, Hamilton, ON.

Zack, M., Toneatto, T., & MacLeod, C. M. (1999). Implicit activation of alcohol concepts by negative affective cues distinguishes between problem drinkers with high and low psychiatric distress. *Journal of Abnormal Psychology, 108,* 518–531.

Zadra, A., & Donderi, D. C. (2000). Nightmares and bad dreams: Their prevalence and relationship to well-being. *Journal of Abnormal Psychology, 109,* 273–281.

Zajonc, R. B. (1984). On the primacy of affect. *American Psychologist, 39*(2), 117–123.

Zajonc, R. B. (1998). Emotions. In D. Gilbert, S. T. Fiske, & G. Lindzey (Eds.), *Handbook of social psychology* (Vol. 1, 4th ed., pp. 591–632). New York: McGraw-Hill.

Zakowski, S. G., McAllister, C. G., Deal, M., & Baum, A. (1992). Stress, reactivity, and immune function in healthy men. *Health Psychology, 11,* 223–232.

Zakzanis, K. K., Troyer, A. K., Rich, J. B., & Heinrichs, W. (2000). Component analysis of verbal fluency in patients with schizophrenia. *Neuropsychiatry, Neuropsychology, & Behavioral Neurology, 13,* 239–245.

Zanarini, M. C., & Frankenberg, F. R. (1997). Pathways to the development of borderline personality disorder. *Journal of Personality Disorders, 11,* 93–104.

Zanarini, M. C., Frankenburg, F. R., Dubo, F. F., Sickel, A. F., Trikha, A., Levin, A., & Reynolds, V. (1998). Axis l comorbidity of borderline personality disorder. *American Journal of Psychiatry, 155,* 1733–1739.

Zanarini, M. C., Frankenburg, F. R., Hennen, J., Reich, D. B., & Silk, K. R. (2006). Prediction of the 10-year course of borderline personality disorder. *American Journal of Psychiatry, 163,* 827–832.

Zanarini, M. C., Gunderson, J., Marino, M., Schwartz, F., & Frankenburg, F. (1988). DSM-III disorders in the families of borderline outpatients. *Journal of Personality Disorders, 2,* 292–302.

Zanarini, M. C., Reichman, C. A., Frankenburg, F. R., Reich, D. B., & Fitzmaurice, G. (2010). The course of eating disorders in patients with borderline personality disorder: A 10-year follow-up study. *International Journal of Eating Disorders, 43*(3), 226–232.

Zanarini, M. C., Williams, A. A., Lewis, R. F., Reich, R. B., Vera, S. C., Marino, M. F., ... Frankenburg, F. R. (1997). Reported pathological childhood experiences associated with the development of borderline personality disorder. *American Journal of Psychiatry, 154,* 1101–1106.

Zapf, P. A. (2001). Assessing fitness to stand trial: the utility of the fitness interview test (revised edition). *Canadian Journal of Psychiatry, 26,* 426–432.

Zapf, P. A., & Roesch, R. (1997). Assessing fitness to stand trial: A comparison of institution-based evaluations and a brief screening interview. *Canadian Journal of Community Mental Health, 16,* 53–66.

Zaza, C., Sellick, S. M., Willan, A., Reyno, L., & Browman, G. P. (1999). Health care professionals' familiarity with non-pharmacological strategies for managing cancer pain. *Psycho-oncology, 8,* 99–111.

Zelazo, P. D., Burack, J. A., Boseovski, J. J., Jacques, S., & Frye, D. (2001). A cognitive complexity and control framework for the study of autism. In J. A. Burack & T. Charman (Eds.), *Development of autism: Perspectives from theory and research* (pp. 195–217). Mahwah, NJ: Lawrence Erlbaum.

Zelazo, P. D., Jacques, S., Burack, J. A., & Frye, D. (2002). The relation between theory of mind and rule use: Evidence from persons with autism-spectrum disorders. *Infant & Child Development, 11,* 171–195.

Zelkowitz, P., & Milet, T. H. (2001). The course of postpartum psychiatric disorders in women and their partners. *Journal of Nervous & Mental Disease, 189,* 575–582.

Zhou, J. N., Hofman, M. A., Gooren, L. J., & Swaab, D. F. (1995). A sex difference in the human brain and its relation to transsexuality. *Nature, 378,* 68–70.

Zigler, F., & Balla, D. (1982). *Mental retardation: The developmental-difference controversy.* Hillsdale, NJ: Erlbaum.

Zigler, F., & Cascione, R. (1984). Mental retardation: An overview. In F. S. Gollin (Ed.), *Malformations of development: Biological and psychological sources and consequences* (pp. 69–90). New York: Academic Press.

Zigler, F., & Hodapp, R. M. (1986). *Understanding mental retardation.* Cambridge: Cambridge University Press.

Zigler, F., Taussig, C., & Black, K. (1992). Farly childhood intervention: A promising preventative for juvenile delinquency. *American Psychologist, 47,* 997–1006.

Zigler, F. F., & Stevenson, M. F. (1993). *Children in a changing world: Development and social issues* (2nd ed.). Pacific Grove, CA: Brooks/Cole.

Zilbergeld, B. (1992). *The new male sexuality.* New York: Bantam Books.

Zilboorg, G., & Henry, G. (1941). *A history of medical psychology.* New York: W. W. Norton.

Zimmerman, M., & Coryell, W. (1989). DSM-III personality disorder diagnoses in a nonpatient sample. *Archives of General Psychiatry, 46,* 682–689.

Zimmerman, M., & Coryell, W. (1990). Diagnosing personality disorders in the community: A comparison of self-report and interview measures. *Archives of General Psychiatry, 47,* 527–531.

Zimmerman, M., & Mattia, J. I. (1998). Body Dysmorphic disorder in psychiatric outpatients: Recognition, prevalence, comorbidity, demographic, and clinical correlates. *Comprehensive Psychiatry, 39*(5), 265–270.

Zinbarg, R. F., & Barlow, D. H. (1996). Structure of anxiety and the anxiety disorders: A hierarchical model. *Journal of Abnormal Psychology, 105,* 181–193.

Zinbarg, R. F., Barlow, D. H., Liebowitz, M., Street, L., Broadhead, F., Katon, W., ... Kraemer, H. (1994). The DSM-IV field trial for mixed anxiety depression. *American Journal of Psychiatry, 151,* 1153–1162.

Zinbarg, R. F., Barlow, D. H., Liebowitz, M. R., Street, L., Broadhead, F., Katon, W., ... Kraemer, H. (1998). The DSM-IV field trial for mixed anxiety-depression. In T. A. Widiger, A. J. Frances, H. A. Pincus, R. Ross, M. B. First, W. Davis, et al. (Eds.), *DSM-IV sourcebook* (Vol. 4, pp. 735–799). Washington, DC: American Psychiatric Association.

Zipfel, S., Lowe, B., Deter, H. C., & Herzog, W. (2000). Long-term prognosis in anorexia nervosa: Lessons from a 21-year follow-up study. *Lancet, 355,* 721–722.

Zohar, J., Judge, R., & The OCD Paroxetine Study Investigators. (1996). Paroxetine vs. clomipramine in the treatment of obsessive-compulsive disorder. *British Journal of Psychiatry, 169,* 468–474.

Zuccato, C., & Cattaneo, E. (2009). Brain-derived neurotrophic factor in neurodegenerative diseases. *Nature Reviews Neurology, 5*(6), 311–322.

Zuchner, S., Cuccaro, M. L., Tran-Viet, K. N., Cope, H., Krishnan, R. R., Pericak-Vance, M. A., ... Ashley-Koch, A. (2006). SLITRK1 mutations in trichotillomania. *Molecular Psychiatry, 11,* 887–889.

Zucker, K. J. (2005a). Gender identity disorder in children and adolescents. *Annual Review of Clinical Psychology, 1,* 467–492.

Zucker, K. J. (2005b). Gender identity disorder in girls. In D. J. Bell, S. L. Foster, & F. J. Mash (Eds.), *Handbook of behavioral and emotional problems in girls.* New York, NY: Kluwer Academic/Plenum Publishers.

Zucker, K. J. (2010). The DSM diagnostic criteria for gender identity disorder in children. *Archives of Sexual Behavior, 39,* 477–498.

Zucker, K. J., & Bradley, S. J. (1995). *Gender identity disorder and psychosexual problems in children and adolescents.* New York: Guilford Press.

Zucker, K. J., & Bradley, S. J. (2004). Gender identity and psychosexual disorders. In Wiener, J. M., & Dulcan, M. K. (Eds.), *The American Psychiatric Publishing textbook of child and adolescent psychiatry* (3rd ed., pp. 813–835). Washington, DC: American Psychiatric Publishing.

Zucker, K. J., Bradley, S. J., & Ipp, M. (1993). Delayed naming of a newborn boy: Relationship to the mother's wish for a girl and subsequent cross-gender identity in the child by the age of two. *Journal of Psychology & Human Sexuality, 6,* 57–68.

Zucker, K. J., Green, R., Garofano, C., Bradley, S. J., Williams, K., Rebach, H. M., & Lowry Sullivan, C. B. (1994). Prenatal gender preference of mothers of feminine and masculine boys: Relation to sibling sex composition and birth order. *Journal of Abnormal Child Psychology, 22,* 1–13.

Zuroff, D. C., Blatt, S. J., Sanislow, C. A., III, Bondi, C. M., & Pilkonis, P. A. (1999). Vulnerability to depression: Reexamining state dependence and relative stability. *Journal of Abnormal Psychology, 108,* 76–89.

Zvolensky, M. J., Schmidt, N. B., & Stewart, S. H. (2003). Panic disorder and smoking. *Clinical Psychology: Science & Practice, 10,* 29–51.

Zwahlen, M., & Egger, M. (2006). *Progression and mortality of untreated HIV-positive individuals living in resource-limited settings: Update of literature review and evidence synthesis (UNAIDS Obligation HQ/05/42204).* Retrieved from http://data.unaids.org/pub/periodical/2006/zwahlen_unaids_hq_05_422204_2007_en.pdf

Zwaigenbaum, L., Bryson, S., Rogers, T., Roberts, W., Brian, J., & Szatmari, P. (2005). Behavioral manifestations of autism in the first year of life. *International Journal of Developmental Neuroscience, 23,* 143–152.

Zwaigenbaum, L., Szatmari, P., Jones, M., Bryson, S., MacLean, J. F., Mahoney, W., ... Tuff, L. (2002). Pregnancy and birth complications in autism and liability to the broader autism phenotype. *Journal of the American Academy of Child and Adolescent Psychiatry, 41,* 572–579.

Zwaigenbaum, L., Szatmari, P., Mahoney, W., Bryson, S., Bartolucci, G., & MacLean, J. (2000). High-functioning autism and childhood disintegrative disorder in half brothers. *Journal of Autism and Developmental Disorders, 30,* 121–126.

Name Index

A

Aarestad, S. L., 350
Aarsland, D., 564
Abbey, S. E., 331, 332
Abbott, D. W., 276
Abdolell, M., 278
Abel, G. G., 288, 358, 378, 380
Abela, J. R. Z., 236, 242
Abi-Darham, A., 495
Abrahamson, D. J., 368
Abrams, K., 143
Abrams, R., 228
Abramson, L. Y., 56, 228, 240, 241, 284
Abse, D. W., 464
Acampora, A., 425
Adair, R., 294, 295
Adams, C., 495
Adams, H. E., 364, 379
Adams, L. P., 257
Addington, D., 484
Addington, J., 484
Addison, M., 382
Adelson, N., 234
Ader, R., 319
Adlaf, E. M., 404, 407, 521
Adler, C. M., 184
Adler, P. S., 35
Adler, R. H., 196
Adrian, C., 238
Agid, O., 495
Agras, W. S., 153, 269, 274–276, 278, 279, 281, 285, 286–288, 358, 367
Agrawal, P., 406
Agyei, Y., 352
Ahles, T. A., 334
Aigner, M., 195
Akiskal, H. S., 221, 224, 228, 230, 238, 443
Akutagawa, D., 276
Albano, A. M., 154, 157, 160, 168, 171
Albert, M. L., 495
Albertini, R. S., 196, 197
Albright, C. A., 325
Alden, L. E., 120, 159, 160, 467
Aldous, J., 503
Aldrich, M., 296
Alexander, F. G., 10, 13, 14, 314
Alford, B. A., 252
Alger, S. A., 273
Allan, J. S., 301
Allani, D., 461
Allen, D., 211
Allen, J., 530
Allen, J. M., 230
Allen, K., 64
Allen, L. S., 352
Allen, N. B., 240
Allen-Hauser, W., 192
Allerdings, M. D., 329
Allmon, D., 462
Alloy, L. B., 241, 242, 246
Alpers, G. W., 184
Alpert, M., 483

A (cont.)

Altay, B., 370
Althof, S., 362, 363, 364, 368, 373–374, 376
Ambrose, N., 523
Amering, M., 144
Amir, N., 173
Anand, S. S., 327
Anastasi, A., 82–83
Ancoli-Israel, S., 111
Andersen, B. L., 350
Anderson, B., 323
Anderson, C., 361
Anderson, E. R., 457
Anderson, G., 171, 207
Anderson, M., 189
Anderson, R., 322
Andrade, C., 490
Andrade, L., 63, 234, 236, 244
Andrasik, F., 315, 334, 336
Andreasen, N. C., 479, 480, 484, 486, 500
Andreski, P., 410
Andrews, G., 20, 136, 523
Andrykowski, M. A., 24
Aneshensel, C. S., 564
Angleitner, A., 440
Anglin, M. D., 412
Angst, J., 221–222, 224, 228, 230
Anguilo, M. J., 209
Angus, L., 23
Anisman, H., 40
Annabi, S., 461
Annable, L., 500
Annas, P., 57
Anthony, D., 490
Anthony, W. A., 504
Antia, S. X., 467
Antle, M. C., 298
Antley, A., 502
Anton, R. F., 400, 429
Antoni, M. H., 321, 322
Antony, M. M., 150–156, 200
Anzengruber, D., 273
Apfelbaum, B., 364
Appelbaum, K. A., 336
Applegate, B., 516
Arato, M., 239
Arbisi, P., 48
Arboleda-Florez, J., 503, 583
Arenas, E., 562
Arenovich, T., 495
Armstrong, H. E., 462
Arnow, B., 285
Arnow, B. A., 236
Asarnow, J. R., 489
Asberg, M., 259
Aschoff, J., 298
Ashbaugh, A. R., 160
Asmundson, G. J. G., 60, 74, 105–106, 111, 142, 152, 160, 329
Asnis, L., 460
Assanand, S., 284
Atha, C., 261
Attia, E., 286
Attie, I., 275

A (cont.)

Attwood, A., 532
Aubin, S., 419
Aubry, T., 66
Auerbach, R. P., 242
Austin, G. W., 584
Ausubel, D., 91
Avila, M., 493
Avison, W. R., 245
Awad, A. G., 477
Axelsson, J., 230
Aydin, C., 242
Azmitia, E. C., 49
Azrin, N. H., 302

B

Bacchiochi, J. R., 585
Bach, A. K., 360, 368, 372, 373
Bach, M., 195
Bachicha, D. L., 27
Bachrach, L. L., 503
Badley, E. M., 291
Baer, D. M., 80
Baer, J. S., 426, 428
Bagby, M., 442
Bagby, R. M., 249, 441, 442, 585
Bailey, J. M., 352, 353, 357
Bailey, J. S., 338
Baillargeon, R. H., 519
Bakalar, J. B., 413
Baker, A., 355
Baker, B., 327, 328, 498
Baker, J. M., 142
Baker, L., 283
Bakker, A., 146
Bakkevig, J. F., 464
Baldessarini, R. J., 248, 250
Baldwin, J. D., 383
Baldwin, J. I., 383
Balfour, L., 321
Ball, J. C., 423
Balla, D., 539
Ballantine, H. T., 54
Ballard, C., 564
Balter, M. B., 294
Ban, T. A., 499
Bancroft, J., 352, 358, 366, 368, 371, 373, 377, 383
Bandopadhyay, D., 565
Bandura, A., 24, 27, 57, 133, 317
Bank, L., 458
Banon, E., 439
Barban, L., 205
Barbaree, H. E., 367, 380, 453
Barchas, J. D., 417
Bardone, A. M. J., 284
Bardone-Cone, A. M., 284
Barefoot, J. C., 314
Bargh, J. A., 58
Barinaga, M., 88
Barker, E. D., 454
Barkley, R. A., 514, 516–518
Barksdale, C., 20
Barlow, D. H., 6, 7, 24, 55, 57, 58, 61, 62, 63, 73, 74, 75, 77, 89, 96,

B (cont.)

98, 100, 113, 115, 129–134, 136, 137, 138, 139, 141–160, 164, 165, 167, 168, 169, 171–172, 173, 175, 184, 235, 236, 241, 244, 245, 246, 252, 263, 273, 288, 315, 317, 328, 335, 336, 358, 360, 367–368, 370, 376–377, 380, 383–385
Barnard, A., 199
Barnes, G. E., 503
Barnes, J., 366, 371
Barnett, P. A., 244, 326
Barnhardt, T. M., 58
Baron, M., 460
Barr, C. E., 496
Barr, H. M., 402
Barr, R. G., 518
Barraclough, B., 269
Barrera, M., 419
Barrett, D. H., 457
Barrett, S. P., 407, 410, 418
Barrios, L. C., 258
Barrowclough, C., 504
Barry, T., 302
Barsky, A. J., 181, 183, 184, 187
Bartak, L., 530
Barth, J. T., 86
Bartlett, N. H., 359
Bartlik, B., 362
Basoglu, M., 166
Bass, D., 458
Bassett, A. S., 493
Bassetti, C., 296
Basson, R., 362, 363, 368, 374
Bastien, C. H., 295
Bata, I., 328
Bateson, G., 498
Batshaw, M. L., 541
Bauchner, H., 294
Bauer, J., 287
Bauer, M. S., 230
Baum, A., 322
Baumal, Z., 230
Bauman, E., 85
Baumeister, R. F., 284
Baumgart, D., 532
Bawden, H. N., 514
Baxter, L. R., 52
Bazana, G., 66
Beach, S. R. H., 244
Bear, D., 209
Beard, J. H., 506
Beattie, B. L., 553
Beattie, T., 514
Beauregard, M., 482
Bebbington, P., 39, 497
Bebbington, P. E., 498
Beck, A. T., 235, 242, 252–254, 257, 259, 447, 436, 464, 465, 468, 504, 505
Beck, C. A., 250
Beck, J. G., 137, 140, 142, 358, 366, 367, 374
Beck, N. C., 232
Becker, D., 461

Subject Index

correlation
  comparative treatment, 112–113
  defined, 109
  epidemiological, 110–111
  experimental, 111–112
  hypothetical graph, 110*f*
  types of, 109
correlation coefficient, 109
Corson, Shayne, 142
cortical arousal, 455
cortical immaturity hypothesis, 455
corticotropin releasing factor (CRF)
    system, 132
cortisol, 239, 315
Cotard's syndrome, 480
counselling psychologists, 6
countertransference, 22
course, defined, 8
covert desensitization, 385*f*
covert sensitization, 427
crack cocaine, 409
creating images, 138
creativity, 234–235
Creutzfeldt-Jakob disease, 555,
    558, 561
criminal commitment
  case study, 582
  defined, 580
  summary, 589
criminality
  ASPD overlap, 452*f*
  characterization, 452–454
  fitness to stand trial, 583–584
  insanity defense, 580–585
  lifetime course, 458*f*
criterion gender bias, 444
cross-generational effect, 121
cross-sectional designs, 119–120
cross-tolerance, 423
Culture of Narcissism, The
    (Lasch), 466
cultural-familial intellectual
    disability, 538
cultural influences
  alcohol use, 421–422
  BDD, 198
  behavioural research, 122–123
  conversion disorders, 192, 193
  dementia, 561
  dietary restraints, 278
  dissociative fugue disorder, 203
  dissociative trance disorder, 204
  DSM-IV and, 95
  eating disorders, 270
  emotions, 63
  expressed emotions, 498*f*
  hypochondriasis, 183–184
  insomnia, 295
  major depressive disorder, 244–246
  mental disorder incidence and, 63
  mental retardation, 539–540
  mood disorders, 233–234, 244
  OCD, 171–172
  panic disorder, 143–144
  paranoid personality disorder, 446
  psychological disorders, 4–6
  PTSD and, 166–167
  schizophrenia, 489–490,
    497–498, 498*f*
  sexual behaviour, 350–352
  sexual dysfunction and, 370–371
  social phobias, 155–156
  specific phobias, 154
  stigmas, 63
  substance use disorders, 421–422
cyclothymic disorder
  antecedent, 230

characterization, 227
DSM-IV-TR criteria, 227*t*
cyproterone acetate, 386

D

d-lysergic acid diethylamide. *See* LSD
    (d-lysergic acid diethylamide)
Dallaire, Andre, 581
Dallaire, Roméo, 65, 166
dangerousness, 577
Darwin, Charles, 60
daytime sequelae, 292
defective genes, 36
defence mechanisms, 19
deinstitutionalization, 14, 577–579
delayed sleep phase–type disorders, 299
delirium
  case study, 548
  characterization, 548–549
  defined, 548
  DSM-IV-TR criteria, 549*t*
  DSM-5, 547
  environmental factors, 549
  exploring, 568
  prevention, 549–550
  statistics, 548–549
  summary, 568
  treatment, 549
delirium tremens (DTs), 401
delusional disorder, 487
delusions, 479–481
dementia, 550
dementia of Alzheimer's
  biological factors, 558–561
  causes, 558
  clinical description, 552–554
  drug therapy, 562–563
  DSM-IV-TR criteria, 553
  explanations for, 552–555
  exploring, 567
  head trauma and, 560–561
  occurrence, 550
  symptoms, 554–555
  tests for, 553*f*, 554*f*
dementia praecox, 477
dementia pugilistica, 560
dementias
  age-based prevalence, 551*f*
  alcohol use and, 401
  assertive responses, 564*t*
  biological therapy, 562–563
  caregiver issues, 561–562
  case study, 550–551
  causes, 550
  characterization, 550, 556*t*
  defined, 547
  diagnosing history, 92
  Down syndrome and, 537
  prevention, 565
  psychosocial factors, 561
  psychosocial therapy, 563–564
  statistics, 551–552
  subcortical, 557
  substance-induced persisting, 558
  symptoms, 550
  treatments, 561–564
  types of, 568
  vascular, 555
demons, 9–10
dendrites, 43
denial, 20, 337
dependence. *See* substance
    dependence
dependent personality disorder
  case study, 468
  causes, 468–469

characterization, 467
clinical description, 468
DSM-IV-TR criteria, 468*t*
treatment, 468–469
dependent variables, 105–106
depersonalization, 200
depersonalization disorder, 201–202
depressants. *See also specific drugs*
  alcohol, 400–405
  anxiolytic substances, 405–406
  characterization, 400
  hypnotic substances, 405–406
  sedative substances, 405–406
depression
  anxiety and, 231, 235–236
  cognitive vulnerability, 243–244
  comorbidity, 236
  cortisol levels and, 239
  dysthymic disorder with, 222–223
  elderly with, 233
  gender differences, 244–245
  grief and, 225
  joint heritability, 238
  learned helplessness theory of,
    241–242
  marital relations and, 244
  mix, 97–98
  personal account, 262, 263
  personality disorders and, 443
  postpartum, 228–229
  self-care and, 318
  symptoms specific to, 236*t*
  women with, 244–245
depressive cognitive triad,
    242, 242*f*
depressive disorders. *See also* dys-
    thymic disorder; major depressive
    disorder; unipolar mood disorders
  case study, 223
  characterization, 38–39
  defined, 38
  ECT for, 250–251
  historical view, 9
  length of, 228
  REM sleep and, 291
  single episode, 229*f*
  summary, 264
  types of, 224
depressive personality disorder, 471
derealization, 200
descriptive validity, 75
designer drugs, 415
desipramine, 425
deterministic genes, 560
development
  ASPD, 457
  equifinality principle, 67
  life-span, 66–67
  phobias and, 35
  psychosexual stages, 20–21
developmental disorders
  ADHD, 514–520
  characterization, 514
  DSM-5, 541, 547
  exploring, 542
  learning, 520–524
  mental retardation, 533–540
  perspectives, 547–548
  pervasive, 524–533
  prevention, 540–541
developmental psychopathology, 542
developmental view, 539
dexamethasone suppression test
    (DST), 239
dhat, 183
diagnosis
  classification, 89–92

defined, 73
history, 92–93
*Diagnostic and Statistical Manual
    (DSM-III)*, 93
*Diagnostic and Statistical Manual
    (DSM-III-R)*, 93
*Diagnostic and Statistical Manual
    (DSM-IV-R)*, 93–98
*Diagnostic and Statistical Manual
    (DSM-IV-TR)*, 93–98
  ADHD criteria, 515*t*
  alcohol intoxication criteria, 406*t*
  Alzheimer's criteria, 553*t*
  amnestic disorder criteria, 566*t*
  amphetamine use disorder
    criteria, 408
  anorexia nervosa criteria, 274*t*
  ASPD criteria, 451*t*
  anxiety-depression mix in, 96–97
  autistic disorder criteria, 526*t*
  avoidant personality disorder
    criteria, 467*t*
  BDD criteria, 197*t*
  BED criteria, 276
  bipolar II disorder criteria, 226*t*
  borderline personality disorder
    criteria, 460*t*
  breathing-related sleep disorders
    criteria, 298*t*
  bulimia nervosa criteria, 272*t*
  caffeine intoxication criteria, 411*t*
  cannabis intoxication criteria, 413*t*
  catatonic type schizophrenia
    criteria, 480*t*
  circadian rhythm sleep disorders
    criteria, 299*t*
  classification system, 73, 90–91
  cocaine intoxication criteria, 408*t*
  creation, 93–94
  criticisms of, 95–96
  cyclothymic disorder criteria, 227*t*
  defence mechanism, 20
  delirium criteria, 549*t*
  dependent personality disorder
    criteria, 468*t*
  depersonalization disorder
    criteria, 201*t*
  diagnostic categories, 98–100
  DID criteria, 205*t*
  disorganized type schizophrenia cri-
    teria, 485*t*
  dissociative amnesia criteria, 202*t*
  dissociative fugue criteria, 203*t*
  dissociative trance criteria, 204*t*
  dysthymic disorder criteria, 223*t*
  exhibitionism criteria, 378*t*
  factitious disorders criteria, 191*t*
  fetishism criteria, 377*t*
  GAD criteria, 136*t*
  gender identity disorder criteria, 354*t*
  hallucinogen intoxication criteria, 415
  histrionic personality disorder
    criteria, 463*t*
  hypoactive sexual desire disorder
    criteria, 360*t*
  hypochondriasis criteria, 182*t*
  learning disorders criteria, 521*t*
  major depressive disorder, single
    episode criteria, 220*t*
  major depressive episode criteria,
    91–92, 220*t*
  manic episodes criteria, 221*t*
  mental retardation criteria, 534*t*
  multiaxial system, 93–94
  narcissistic personality disorder
    criteria, 465*t*
  narcolepsy criteria, 297*t*

Somatoform Disorders

Somatization Disorder

Conversion Disorder

Hypochondriasis

Body Dysmorphic Disorder

Pain Disorder

Somatoform Disorder Not Otherwise Specified

Undifferentiated Somatoform Disorder

Factitious Disorders

Factitious Disorder

Factitious Disorder Not Otherwise Specified

Dissociative Disorders

Dissociative Amnesia

Dissociative Fugue

Dissociative Identity Disorder (Multiple Personality Disorder)

Depersonalization Disorder

Dissociative Disorder Not Otherwise Specified

Sexual and Gender Identity Disorders

Sexual Dysfunctions

Sexual Desire Disorders: Hypoactive Sexual Desire Disorder; Sexual Aversion Disorder/Sexual Arousal Disorders: Female Sexual Arousal Disorder; Male Erectile Disorder/Orgasm Disorders: Female Orgasmic Disorder (Inhibited Female Orgasm); Male Orgasmic Disorder (Inhibited Male Orgasm); Premature Ejaculation/Sexual Pain Disorders: Dyspareunia; Vaginismus/Sexual Dysfunctions Due to a General Medical Condition/Substance-Induced Sexual Dysfunction

Paraphilias

Exhibitionism/Fetishism/Frotteurism/Pedophilia/Sexual Masochism/Sexual Sadism/Voyeurism/Transvestic Fetishism

Gender Identity Disorders

Gender Identity Disorder: in Children/in Adolescents and Adults (Transsexualism)

Eating Disorders

Anorexia Nervosa

Bulimia Nervosa

Eating Disorder Not Otherwise Specified

Sleep Disorders

Primary Sleep Disorders

Dyssomnias: Primary Insomnia; Primary Hypersomnia; Narcolepsy; Breathing-Related Sleep Disorder; Circadian Rhythm Sleep Disorder (formerly Sleep-Wake Schedule Disorder)/Parasomnias; Nightmare Disorder (Dream Anxiety Disorder); Sleep Terror Disorder; Sleepwalking Disorder/Sleep Disorders Related to Another Mental Disorder

Sleep Disorder Due to a General Medical Condition

Substance-Induced Sleep Disorder

Dyssomnia Not Otherwise Specified

Parasomnia Not Otherwise Specified

Impulse Control Disorders Not Elsewhere Classified

Intermittent Explosive Disorder

Kleptomania

Pyromania

Pathological Gambling

Trichotillomania

Impulse-Control Disorder Not Otherwise Specified

Adjustment Disorder

Adjustment Disorder

With Anxiety

With Depressed Mood

With Disturbance of Conduct

With Mixed Disturbance of Emotions and Conduct

With Mixed Anxiety and Depressed Mood

Unspecified

Other Conditions That May Be a Focus of Clinical Attention

Pyschological Factors Affecting Medical Condition

Medication-Induced Movement Disorders

Relational Problems

Relational Problem Related to a Mental Disorder or General Medical Condition/Parent–Child Relational Problem/Partner Relational Problem/Sibling Relational Problem

Problems Related to Abuse or Neglect

Physical Abuse of Child/Sexual Abuse of Child/Neglect of Child/Physical Abuse of Adult/Sexual Abuse of Adult

Additional Conditions That May Be a Focus of Clinical Attention

Bereavement/Borderline Intellectual Functioning/Academic Problem/Occupational Problem/Childhood or Adolescent Antisocial Behavior/Adult Antisocial Behavior/Malingering Phase of Life

Problem/Noncompliance with Treatment for a Mental Disorder/Identity Problem/Religious or Spiritual Problem/Acculturation Problem/Age-Associated Memory Decline

AXIS II

Personality Disorders

Paranoid Personality Disorder

Schizoid Personality Disorder

Schizotypal Personality Disorder

Antisocial Personality Disorder

Borderline Personality Disorder

Histrionic Personality Disorder

Narcissistic Personality Disorder

Avoidant Personality Disorder

Dependent Personality Disorder

Obsessive-Compulsive Personality Disorder

Mental Retardation

Mild Mental Retardation/Moderate Mental Retardation/Severe Mental Retardation/Profound Mental Retardation